P9-DGW-578

PRINTED SOURCES

PRINTED SOURCES

A Guide to Published Genealogical Records

Edited by Kory L. Meyerink

Ancestry®

Library of Congress Cataloging-in-Publication data:

Printed sources : a guide to published genealogical records / edited by Kory L. Meyerink.
p. cm.
Includes bibliographical references and index.
ISBN 0-916489-70-1
1. Genealogy—Bibliography. 2. United States—Genealogy—Bibliography. I. Meyerink, Kory L. (Kory Leland), 1954- .
Z5311.P75 1998
[CS9]
016.929'373—dc21 98-10852

Ancestry Incorporated
P.O. Box 476
Salt Lake City, Utah 84110-0476
www.ancestry.com

First printing 1998
10 9 8

Printed in the United States of America

This book is dedicated to my wife, Claudine, who was one of the first to fan the ember of my interest in genealogy. And also to the excellent staff of the Family History Library, who have been my friends and occasional coworkers.

CONTENTS

FOREWORD

Here at the oldest institution in American genealogy, we have all been aware for more than two decades of the explosion of interest in our field. Genealogists are now much more numerous and genealogy much more popular than at any time in our national history. As this interest has proceeded, many authors and compilers have added immensely to the fast-growing multitude of printed sources for every kind of genealogy—compiled family or local histories, multi-ancestor works, new periodicals, guidebooks, printed source records, bibliographies, indexes, and reference works. Ancestry's *Printed Sources: A Guide to Published Genealogical Records* is the first overall guide to both the older literature and this rich new corpus. In effect, *Printed Sources* summarizes the work, especially of the last generation, and includes the entrance of genealogy into the electronic age. The variety of types of records now available in print, and the wide variety of actual records now transcribed, are all amply treated in this splendid new book. With a very useful division of categories of genealogical information (see page 6) and such distinctions as those among abstracts, extracts, transcripts, and translations, or among footnotes, endnotes, and source notes, the "Introduction and Foundation for Research" proceeds to, among other tasks, categorize the types of printed sources, tell readers how to acquire them, and describe libraries and library services.

Printed sources are often thought to be largely genealogies and local histories; these are treated in two of twenty chapters. The wide variety of other useful printed sources are the subjects of the other eighteen. Each chapter is proceeded by an overview outline. The "Ethnic Sources Overview," for example, begins with definitions, mentions the growth of interest, and discusses types of sources and where they are found. The "Ethnic Sources" chapter follows chapters on reference materials, instructional volumes, and maps, atlases, and gazetteers. Following all of these are chapters on bibliographies and indexes and then all of the kinds of printed source materials--vital, cemetery, church, census, tax, probate, land, court, military, and immigration records. Chapters on genealogies, local history, biographies, periodicals, and medieval and nobility sources compose the section on compiled records. Appendixes identify CD-ROM sources and major libraries, publishers, and booksellers.

Hundreds of individual research "tips" are provided and thousands of books are listed, and hundreds evaluated. The breadth of this volume can scarcely be imagined—nor its detail or carefully crafted distinctions. Kory Meyerink's introduction treats the difference between primary and secondary information in an original record, printed or not, and Kip Sperry's chapter on indexes mentions the difference in letter-by-letter or word-by-word alphabetization. Each chapter takes the reader by the hand and proceeds to whatever categories, book evaluations, and analyses the subject requires. Thus each chapter offers much more than its title might indicate. What libraries can do for researchers is kept constantly in mind.

Speaking more philosophically, most genealogical books are the products of 150 years of American genealogical scholarship. They certainly contain many errors; for half of that period, revisionist periodicals have attempted corrections. We are now embracing the world of CD-ROMs and the Internet, which will not so much replace the older literature as place it in a new format. Until and even after this conversion occurs, libraries will be at the center of genealogical research, and this seemingly all-inclusive new book will be able to guide researchers to many types of records they never suspected could help.

The authors of this new volume are all distinguished genealogists. With *The Source* (1984 and 1997) and *Ancestry's Red Book* (1992), *Printed Sources* forms a trilogy of essential large guidebooks that should be consulted by every genealogist and genealogical librarian in the United States. Both a guidebook and, in effect, a bibliography to the best printed material in the field, this volume evokes both the achievement of the past generation and the electronic formats to come. From a popular but comparatively quiet period in the 1950s and 1960s, genealogy has become one of the major intellectual pursuits of our age. Rooted in scholarship, it nonetheless extends to every family and individual in the United States. Indeed, family history research has become almost a cultural expectation. More than a leisure activity, it is now a humanistic science with thousands of practitioners whom this book will mightily help.

Ralph J. Crandall
Executive Director
New England Historic
Genealogical Society

PREFACE

> Most people dive into genealogical research with the notion that tracing their ancestors is a snap. It is not. One of the biggest roadblocks in reconstructing a family tree is not the lack of books, periodicals, and public records but their sheer numbers. Prospective researchers don't usually know what exists or how to find it.
>
> Lois Horowitz
> *Knowing Where to Look* (1988)

The whole purpose of published genealogical books is to make research easier and to make the sources more accessible. But as more and more books are published, it becomes, paradoxically, more difficult to use them. Which book is the best? How does one find a book, or even learn if one exists?

The purpose of *Printed Sources* is to make research easier by identifying, defining, and explaining the vast and growing number of published genealogical sources.

All research is based, at least in part, on the findings of previous researchers. This is as true of family history research as any kind of research, whether in the natural sciences or the social sciences (of which history is a part). Because researchers constantly use printed sources as reservoirs of previous research and as avenues of faster access to original records (either as abstracts or as reference aids), we should all be interested in using them more effectively.

Making the Best Use of *Printed Sources*

Printed Sources is a reference book. Most readers will not sit down and read it from cover to cover. It is better, rather, to become familiar with its content, browse a few topics of interest, and then, when preparing to use a particular record type, learn what the author of the chapter on that topic has to say. The chapters define each type of record and identify the key tools, such as indexes or bibliographies, needed to use the records.

There is, however, a key for making the best use of this book. Every user should read the "Introduction and Foundations for Research" early in his or her acquaintance with this book. Indeed, one reviewer was concerned that many of the concepts there would be overlooked, as readers tend to skip introductions. Reading the introduction to *Printed Sources* is vital because it provides a backdrop for the discussions in the rest of the book. Take the time to read and regularly review the introduction. Doing so will make *Printed Sources* (both the book and the sources it discusses) much more effective.

Don't forget to use the chapter bibliographies. Much effort has gone into providing reasonably complete listings, at least to the state level. While no bibliography is comprehensive, the various chapter bibliographies generally identify key bibliographies and instructional books for their subjects, as well as major indexes.

There is, of course, no better way to learn about printed sources than to actually read books and periodicals. The authors of *Printed Sources* have attempted to convey the richness of these sources, but, until they are experienced, a researcher will have only a vague notion of the thousands of genealogical questions that are fully or partially answered by the printed word.

Comments and Caveats

While no book can be ideal for all readers, especially one as large as this one that covers so complex a subject, we have attempted to bring to pass the best, most authoritative discussion of published genealogical sources ever attempted.

The editor and the authors recognize that mistakes may have crept in, despite our best efforts, and apologize for them. While everyone understands that it is impossible for any one genealogist to know all things about all topics, we have all been surprised to learn what we did not know about our topics as we began the writing process. It is indeed true that the writer/teacher learns more than the reader/student. Errors of fact are deeply regretted, and we hope to correct any that come to our attention in future printings and editions. Errors of omission are usually matters of opinion, exposure, and audience, and may not be errors so much as an intentional decisions based on these and other factors. We will be happy, however, to consider reviewers' comments for the future.

There is some duplication in the discussion of various printed sources. This has been, in part, intentional. The authors recognize that *Printed Sources,* as a reference book, will be used in an occasional manner to learn important facts about the sources it covers. Therefore, we have chosen to duplicate some material, providing cross-references where possible. However, some sources simply need to be discussed, at least in part, in more than one chapter. It is more important to provide a discussion at the point of need rather than referring the reader to another portion of the book. While this makes for some redundancy, we are not concerned; after all, teachers know that repetition is the key to learning. As authors, we would prefer that the information be found easily than risk its being overlooked altogether. In addition, each author has a slightly different perspective on a given source; in discussing major sources, it would be irresponsible to present only one opinion.

Librarians recognize that there is seldom only one source for the answer to a reference question. Genealogists recognize that any of a number of original or compiled records may answer a research question. In the same way, the editor and authors recognize that there is more than one way to use many sources, and more than one opinion about such sources.

As editor, I have approached some of the most knowledgeable people in their fields for contributions to this volume. I am very pleased with the contributing authors. I approached this task knowing that many of the best were too busy to contribute. It was disheartening, however, to find a small number of professional genealogists who would not make the sacrifice to participate in some way and to share their knowledge with the greater community. We are all poorer when such attitudes prevail.

I am therefore doubly grateful for those who did share their time and talents with this project. It was a sacrifice for all, for genealogical writing does not pay a living wage. The genealogical community is indebted to those who contributed to this and the thousands of other genealogical books published each year.

May your family history research be easier because of what you learn from this volume.

Kory L. Meyerink, AG
February 1998

ACKNOWLEDGMENTS

This volume is the product of dozens of people who have helped it along during a lengthy gestation period. Three of the many leading ladies in current American genealogy head the list. I must start with Arlene Eakle, whose invitation to contribute to the first edition of *The Source* began this journey. Also, her dedication to learning as much as possible about the records in order to squeeze as much information as possible out of them has inspired me to do the same with published sources. Johni Cerny invited me to participate with her when *Printed Sources* was initially conceived and kept expanding my writing assignments, eventually to the point of recommending me to complete the volume. And Loretto Szucs, then Ancestry's acquisition editor (and now vice-president of Print Publications), guided me through the maze that is text publishing and helped find excellent peer reviewers and new authors as the need arose.

I must also recognize John Sittner, former owner of Ancestry, whose vision has created some of the major textbooks of genealogy. He saw the value and viability of this project and took a chance on a then less-tested writer/editor to bring the project to fruition. Thanks also to Ancestry's current owners, Paul Allen and Dan Taggart, and others who believe in Ancestry, hold its banner high, and provided some of the support necessary to complete this massive project.

My deep gratitude must also go to Matt Grove, Ancestry's top-notch text editor, who has managed to make sense of inconsistent citations, lengthy sentences, and other *faux pas* of the grammatical and editorial sort, and to rectify them, all in an effort to make the text more readable.

The contributing authors, of course, deserve the lion's share of the recognition for whatever good the researcher finds here. Each of them extended him- or herself to learn more about their topic; they were invited to contribute to this project because of their ability and desire to do so.

Earlier authors were also critical in moving this project ahead. Many of them were not available to continue as the book changed from primarily a bibliography to an explanatory text. Nonetheless, much of the information they gathered (generally as bibliography) and some of the text they wrote found its way into the finished product. For their assistance, I thank Sherry Slaughter, Johni Cerny, Gareth Mark, Anita Milner, Alice Eichholz, and the late William Arbuckle and Milton Rubincam.

Ancestry and I extend a special thanks to the peer reviewers of the various chapters. They have helped us to ensure that our discussion of sources was as complete and correct as feasible. Each of them provided valuable comments; the editor and individual authors chose which comments to incorporate into the text and which ones did not fit the scope of the particular chapter. For their help, assistance, encouragement, and positive feedback, we all express our gratitude to:

James Hansen (Introduction and Foundations for Research)

Bonnie Stepenoff and Judith Reid (General Reference)

Paula Warren (Instructional Materials)

Jayare Roberts (Geographic Tools, Ethnic Sources, Immigration Sources)

Ray Wright (Bibliographies and Catalogs)

Pat Hatcher (Published Indexes)

Ted Naanes (Vital and Cemetery Records)

Frederick Weiser and David Koss (Church Sources)

Brad Steuart and Richard Saldana (Censuses and Tax Lists)

Gordon Remington (Published Probate Records)

Desmond Allen (Printed Land Records)

Helen Leary and George Ott (Court and Legal Records)

Ken Nelson (Military Sources)

Jake Gehring (Documentary Collections)

Carl Boyer (Family Histories and Genealogies)

P. William Filby (County and Local Histories)

J. Carlyle Parker (Biographies)

Michael Clegg and Kip Sperry (Genealogical Periodicals)

William R. Ward (Medieval Genealogy)

I also offer heartfelt thanks to Dr. Ralph Crandall of the New England Historic Genealogical Society, who believed enough in this project to take time from his busy schedule to review the finished manuscript and to write the foreword. And, of course, to all my friends and past students who kept asking when it would be done and encouraging me, through their words and actions, to keep working on it: Thanks! This is for all of you. May you find ever more success in the growing world of printed sources.

INTRODUCTION OVERVIEW

Key Concepts in the Introduction

- Printed genealogical sources are growing quickly and provide solutions to many research problems.
- Most guidebooks do not discuss published records in detail, but most researchers begin with published records.
- This introduction provides a critical foundation for effective use of this guide.
- Printed sources can contain primary, secondary, and tertiary information.
- Four categories of research sources include:
  - Background information
  - Finding aids
  - Original records
  - Compiled records
- Printed sources include records from all four categories.
- Records must be evaluated in at least seven respects:
  - Relevance
  - Origin of the information
  - Nature of the record
  - Format of the record
  - Directness of the evidence
  - Consistency and clarity of the facts
  - Likelihood of the event(s)
- A book's content can be evaluated on several levels.
- Understanding documentation is crucial for successful research.
- Copyright protects both the author and the researcher.
- Several sources can help the researcher learn what printed sources exist.
- Printed sources are available at a wide variety of repositories.
- Effective use of libraries includes understanding their services and catalogs.

INTRODUCTION AND FOUNDATIONS FOR RESEARCH

Kory L. Meyerink

The book. It has existed for thousands of years (and it will be around for thousands more, computers notwithstanding).

Printing. More than five hundred years ago, Gutenberg invented the movable press and started a revolution in printing and book publishing.

American genealogy. It is effectively 150 years old (dating from the founding of the New England Historic Genealogical Society in 1846) and has been married to printing and book publishing virtually from the start (the society's *Register* was first published in 1847).

Photo duplication. This process has provided inexpensive, short-run "printing" for thirty years.

Personal computers. They have been used to automate authors' and printers' tasks for more than twenty years.

The result of the above sequence has been an explosion of printed genealogical sources. Every day several new books are published by and for genealogists; some major genealogical publishers release three or more new books and reprints *every week*. It is time that genealogists (pardon—*family historians*) had a better understanding of the breadth and scope of this growing collection of resources. It is, after all, books from which most new family historians gather much of their information. And experienced researchers turn to books time and again for new leads to old (or new) problems.

THE NEED FOR THIS WORK

The first task of an introduction is to define the need for the work at hand. In family history, with so many books discussing the "how-to's" and the sources to be used, defining the need for the work at hand is even more important. In the last few years there has been a flood of new books with instructions for the researcher. Most of these books, however, suffer from a certain sameness; each one seems to reiterate much of the same material discussed before (Meyerink 1995, 12–23), and their treatment of specific records and record types is often superficial. It was the depth of its content that made the first edition of *The Source: A Guidebook ofAmerican Genealogy,* edited by Arlene Eakle and Johni Cerny (Salt Lake City: Ancestry, 1984), such a widely acclaimed success.

But even *The Source* could not discuss every aspect of every record; hence, it focused mostly on original records, which are often called primary sources. However, there is a large and growing body of printed material that is of great importance to the success of most genealogical searches. In fact, the number of printed sources has been growing at a phenomenal rate in the last few years, while very few "original" or "primary" records have become newly available. Thus, much of the limited discussion of printed sources found in older books has become outdated. As new printed sources become available, the careful researcher must learn about them, including their strengths, weaknesses, content, and usage.

A visible sign of this explosion is the growth of genealogy's chief bibliography of printed works, P. William Filby's *American and British Genealogy and Heraldry: A Select List of Books*. The second edition (which had a broader scope than the first edition), published in 1975 (before most of us were involved in genealogy), cited 5,125 printed sources. Within eight years, when the third edition was published in 1983, 9,773 printed sources were cited—an increase of 90 percent. The 1987 supplement to the third edition lists another 2,805 printed sources, an increase of 30 percent in just three years, yet it covers only the period 1982 to 1985.

Another measure of the increasing number of printed sources in genealogy is the growth of Netti Schreiner-Yantis's *Genealogical and Local History Books in Print*. In 1975, this valuable "buyer's guide" listed just over five thousand sources available from approximately one thousand vendors in its first edition. By the publication of the fourth edition in 1985, more than thirty thousand printed sources were listed for sale by 3,600 vendors. The 1990 supplement added approximately three thousand more printed sources, including 815 family histories, while the 1992 supplement added another 3,100 (of which 1,432 were family histories). The first volume of the fifth edition, edited by Marian Hoffman and issued in 1996, identified more than 4,600 family history titles. While many of the titles listed in this series are reprints, the fact that these volumes are being reprinted speaks of the growing interest in printed sources.

This increase in printed sources is the result of the growth of genealogy as an activity. Since the mid-1970s, membership in genealogical societies has skyrocketed, as has the actual number of societies and their publications. More and more Americans are interested in tracing their "roots" and are using new methods and technologies to do it, including personal computers. Yet, most researchers rely on books published five, ten, or even twenty years ago to teach them how to find their ancestors.

Although research methodology does not change rapidly, and original records are much the same as they were twenty or more years ago, there have been many changes in printed sources. In 1975 there were very few census indexes. The limited number of transcribed records meant limited access for the researcher. There were no computer programs or databases for family historians. Bibliographies and other research tools were fewer and much older than they are today. It is now time to treat these printed sources in as much depth as original sources received in *The Source*. That has been the goal of *Printed Sources:* it seeks to be a guide to published genealogical sources from which both the novice and experienced researcher can benefit. Use it as a reference book; turn to it for detailed information about a kind of source, with the hope of understanding the sources, and their related reference tools, better.

Most printed sources have had wider distribution than have original records; hence, printed sources are used more frequently by genealogists. They also vary considerably in quality and content, requiring better evaluation by the researcher. Original records contain information as it was first recorded, but the same is not true of most printed sources. The researcher must understand what the writer/compiler/editor intended and how the source was created. Therefore, this introduction will discuss how to locate, evaluate, and use printed sources.

A Foundation for Research

The second task of an introduction is to lay the foundation for the rest of the book. For *Printed Sources,* this means a discussion of the nature of printed sources. There are several important concepts that a researcher must understand when using any printed source. While each chapter that follows will discuss specific aspects of particular sources, there are significant general concepts to keep in mind whenever working with printed sources, whether they are for genealogical or other research. (Within this introduction, definitions of key terms appear in SMALL CAPS.)

The following sections of this introduction will provide a firm foundation for research:

- Origin of information
- Categories of research sources and tools
- Evaluation of printed sources
- Documentation and copyright
- Learning what printed sources exist
- Publishers and distributors
- Repositories of printed sources
- Effective use of libraries and archives

ORIGIN OF INFORMATION

For years, genealogists have tended to regard records as either primary or secondary in nature. Upon reflection, however, these terms are insufficient. Indeed, they have the potential of misleading the less experienced researcher.

Every genealogical record is a report of some event or situation. The report might have been made by someone who knew the facts firsthand, or by someone who learned it from other sources. The report itself might be the first recording of the information on an original form designed to report such facts (or even on blank paper), or it might have been compiled into another record. The information in the report may come from a variety of sources, each with limitations. For these reasons, as well as for evaluating what is found, it is important to clearly define both the origin of information and the kinds (categories) of records used in research.

It is important to understand the difference between the information and the record that reports the information. Too often, sources are considered by researchers to be simply either primary or secondary. Furthermore, many also equate "primary" with original (that is, handwritten) records and "secondary" with printed or typed sources. This association is much too simple and can lead to inaccurate research.

The popular notion that all printed material is secondary in nature is too simple to be accurate. The real concern: Was the information recorded in close proximity to the event being reported? Today, computers are often used for the initial recording of events, and documents are "printed" from a database of events. Does the fact that documents are printed from the database mean they are secondary? True, most printed sources provide secondary information, but with some, such as newspapers and city directories, there is no other original.

At the risk of dismaying many colleagues in genealogy, this author is suggesting some new, clearer, definitions for the materials genealogists use: Sources are best considered as either original or compiled records (see the discussion of "Categories of Research Sources and Tools," below); it is the *information* in the sources that is either primary or secondary. Of added concern is the concept of tertiary information, a division overlooked by others. The importance of these distinctions will become apparent in the discussion of "Evaluation of Printed Sources" later in this introduction.

Primary Information Versus Original Records

Historians have long considered that published sources can be primary or secondary in nature (Stephens 1991, 16). Most historians consider it sufficient to label sources as primary (created at the time of the event) and secondary (a synthesis of information based on other sources) because they deal mostly with sources as they attempt to obtain a broad picture of the happenings in a particular place at a certain time in the past. Genealogists cannot afford to be as vague when describing the quality of their sources because they need to examine their sources at a more minute level than historians often do. For the genealogist, it is the information within the source that is of utmost interest. Most original genealogical sources contain information that was current at the time the record was created *as well as* information that predates the record, often by years or full generations. Therefore, it is essential that genealogists refrain from calling the source as a whole either primary or secondary; it is the *information within that source* that must receive such distinction (Greenwood 1990, 63).

Primary and Secondary Information Found in Original Records

Original Record	*Primary Information*	*Secondary Information*
Death certificate	Date of death, name of decedent, residence at time of death, cause of death	Birth date of decedent, birthplace, parents' names and birthplaces
Birth record	Name of child, date and place of birth, parents' names, residence at birth	Parents' ages and birthplaces
Census record	Name of person, relationships, residence, occupation at the time	Birthplaces of adults, parents' birthplaces, year of immigration
Obituary	Name of person, current residence, survivors at the time, burial information	Parents, birth date and place, migration information, early occupations
Passenger list	Name of person, date of arrival, previous residence, destination	Birthplace

The traditional definition of a "primary source" has been that it is a record created at the time of the event by someone associated with the event. For example, a death record is usually considered to be a primary source because it is created at the time of the event by someone associated with the event, such as the attending physician or a close relative. However, only *some* of the information in a death record is primary in nature. Primary information must relate directly to the event being recorded. Thus, on a death certificate, the death date and cause of death are primary information, but the dead person's birth date or parents' names are *not* primary information. Such information, which significantly predates the event being recorded, is secondary information and is discussed further below. PRIMARY INFORMATION IS THE FACTS DIRECTLY RELATED TO AN EVENT, RECORDED BY SOMEONE WITH FIRSTHAND KNOWLEDGE OF THE FACTS.

Almost every major original record used in genealogical research includes some information that is not primary. The table above illustrates this fact for several common sources that have often been called "primary."

As the examples show, sources should not be described by the quality of the information they include (any record will include information of varying quality). It is better to describe sources based on their provenance (origin)—that is, how they were acquired or what (or where) they came from. Hence, sources either are *original* (the first recording of an event) or *compiled*. The varied information in each source should be considered apart from the source itself. Therefore, as stated earlier, it is the information within a source that is best described as primary or secondary.

Secondary Information

It is tempting to assume that any information that is not primary is secondary, but it is wrong to make such an assumption. It is also incorrect to claim that anything existing in printed form is secondary. These currently are broadly applied generalizations, but the researcher must remember that they are not always correct.

SECONDARY INFORMATION IS THAT WHICH IS RECORDED SOME TIME AFTER THE EVENT, USUALLY BY SOMEONE NOT DIRECTLY ASSOCIATED WITH THE EVENT. Often it is based on original records (or reports) and/or primary information. Most of the information in a compiled source, such as a family history, is secondary information, or what lawyers call hearsay information. However, it is possible to find primary information in a compiled source. For example, the preface to a census index may describe how the index was created; this is primary information, although it is not strictly genealogical in nature. A more practical example is a compiled source that quotes verbatim from an original record, such as a will or birth certificate, that includes primary information.

Tertiary Information

Some printed sources also contain tertiary information, which is a step further removed from primary information. TERTIARY INFORMATION REFERS RESEARCHERS TO OTHER RECORDS. Tertiary information has limited direct genealogical application, but not limited usage. Bibliographies are the first such sources that come to mind. Many directories (except city directories), finding aids, indexes, guides, and inventories are also tertiary in nature. Tertiary information is usually found in reference tools, which are described below.

Tertiary information almost always appears in printed form, although some such sources exist in manuscript form. Sources of tertiary information are the most widely available of all genealogical sources. They are found in most libraries (including those whose staffs are not aware that they have any genealogical material at all; much tertiary information is found in common reference books that all libraries have). Sources such as the *American Library Directory*, the *Guide to Reference Books,* and the *Encyclopedia of Associations*, although compiled directly from the sources they discuss, contain tertiary information because they refer users to other sources.

CATEGORIES OF RESEARCH SOURCES AND TOOLS

A researcher in any field can divide the books and records he uses into two classes: research sources and reference tools.[1] *Research sources* are those books and records which actually provide data that a researcher needs to solve a problem at hand. For family historians, these are the genealogical records which provide family data for charts and family group records. *Reference tools* provide auxiliary information to help researchers find the right research sources. Reference tools include bibliographies, indexes, instructional material, and other reference aids.

These two classes can be divided into four categories, and these categories form the basic structure of this book. Reference tools consist of (1) background information and (2) finding aids. Research sources, or, for genealogists' purposes, *genealogical sources,* include (1) original records (in this book the focus is restricted to *copied* original records) and (2) compiled records. (See "Categories of Genealogical Information" on the following page.)

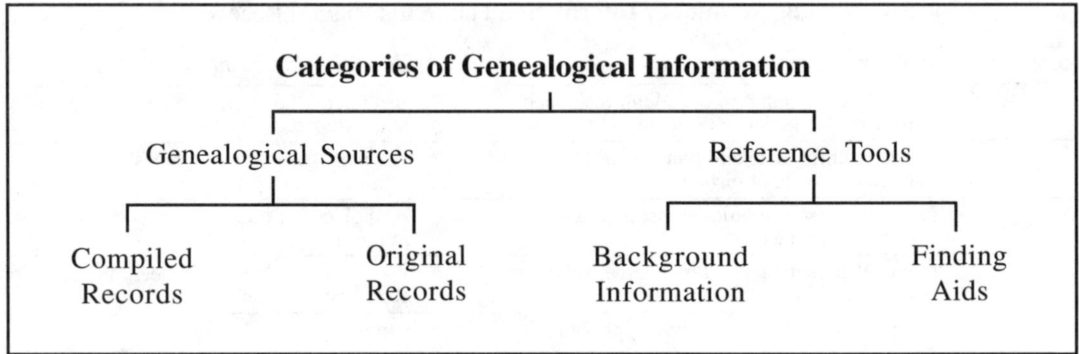

Background Information

BACKGROUND INFORMATION HELPS RESEARCHERS UNDERSTAND THE SETTINGS IN WHICH RECORDS WERE CREATED and the places, groups, or subjects of the records. Background information also includes descriptions of the circumstances of life in particular times or places. Generally, researchers use background information to help them select or use the best genealogical sources. Because sources containing background information can treat any subject, they are described here. Part 1 of *Printed Sources* provides specific discussion by format.

Dictionaries and Encyclopedias. Dictionaries and encyclopedias present related information with brief narrative entries, usually alphabetically. The most common kind of dictionary is the word dictionary, which lists words with their meanings. Almost any field of knowledge can be represented in a dictionary or encyclopedia format. *The Dictionary of American History*, for example, lists major events in American history and then defines them in a few brief paragraphs. These reference tools provide the background information genealogists need as they approach problems to be solved. Many helpful general dictionaries and encyclopedias are discussed in chapter 1, "General Reference."

In genealogical research, dictionaries often focus on the families of an area. Brief genealogical information about those families follows each surname. Biographical encyclopedias often work in the same way. In them, individuals are usually listed alphabetically by their names, followed by a biographical sketch (sometimes brief, sometimes lengthy). In such works the entries are not alphabetized; they rely on an index to provide access to specific entries. Various types of dictionaries and encyclopedias are discussed in chapter 16, "Family Histories and Genealogies," and chapter 18, "Biographies."

Gazetteers are dictionaries that focus on geographical terms for specific areas. They are often grouped with maps and atlases, which provide geographic background information in a pictorial format. In *Printed Sources* these are discussed in chapter 3, "Geographic Tools."

Instructions. Instructions are (or should be) the beginning point for any researcher. These come in the form of handbooks, manuals, guidebooks, or "how-to" books. Generally, they are narrative in style and represent their authors' suggestions regarding methodology and sources for research in a country, state, or county. *Printed Sources*, like *The Source*, is an example of such a book.

Instructional books that focus on research in specific states have emerged in the last few years. Many of these are really more like inventories or bibliographies and offer little in the way of suggestions for research. Both types are important and useful, but it is important to understand the book and its perspective before relying on it too heavily. For a fuller treatment of this type of printed source, see chapter 2, "Instructional Material."

Other Reference Tools. Every library contains other reference tools that provide background information for astute researchers. It is important to be aware of them, although they are generally less applicable to genealogical research than the sources described above. These include almanacs, chronologies, collected works, maps, picture books, statistics, and yearbooks. Some specific sources that appear in these formats are discussed in chapter 1, "General Reference." Almost unique to North American research are a host of sources that discuss the ethnic backgrounds of Americans' ancestors. These deserve separate treatment and are covered in chapter 4, "Ethnic Sources."

Finding Aids

FINDING AIDS INDICATE WHERE SPECIFIC INFORMATION CAN BE FOUND, either in a record (as with indexes) or in a repository (such as library catalogs). Generally, finding aids contain no genealogical information; rather, they serve as pointers so that researchers can find information faster. Throughout the various chapters of *Printed Sources*, much of the discussion of sources includes the key finding aids for the topic. Therefore, the concepts in part 2 are mostly theoretical—that is, they define the nature of the tools discussed, but identification of specific finding aids is left to the chapters dealing with genealogical sources.

Bibliographies and Catalogs. A BIBLIOGRAPHY IS A LIST OF SOURCES THAT HAVE A COMMON THEME—for example, *Local Histories in the Library of Congress*. Bibliographies alert researchers to sources that may be helpful in their research. Some bibliographies exist alone as books, but they are often found as parts of other books or references, such as lists of sources consulted in the creation of a book. Very few are truly comprehensive in listing every source in a field; rather, they are usually selective based on certain criteria determined by their editors. Many genealogical bibliographies attempt to list every source pertaining to the topic because they seek to be comprehensive finding aids for researchers looking for obscure references. Library catalogs, union lists, and books-in-print lists are also bibliographies.

Each entry in a bibliography should include complete publishing information about the book—specifically author, title, place of publication, publisher, and year published. In addition, the edition, number of volumes, and, occasionally, number of pages, is indicated. Some bibliographies (called union lists) include references naming at least one library where the book is located. Others are annotated—they include a brief statement about the book's value, content, arrangement, and so on.

CATALOGS ARE SIMILAR TO BIBLIOGRAPHIES IN THAT THEY ARE LISTS OF SOURCES. HOWEVER, THEY FOCUS ON THE COLLECTIONS (or parts of collections) OF SPECIFIC LIBRARIES. While most bibliographies and catalogs focus on published books and/or articles, manuscripts are often described in an *inventory*. INVENTORIES ARE LISTINGS OF THE HOLDINGS OF ARCHIVES AND OTHER MANUSCRIPT REPOSITORIES. By their nature, they are often more explanatory in nature than library catalogs. For a fuller discussion, see chapter 5, "Bibliographies and Catalogs."

Directories. DIRECTORIES ARE LISTS OF ADDRESSES THAT USUALLY FOCUS ON COMMON THEMES. Simple directories, such as telephone books, list only names, addresses, and telephone numbers. Most directories used for reference usually give more information. The entries may be of individuals, such as a directory of research interests which lists persons and the surnames, families, or individuals they are interested in researching.

Other directories list societies, organizations, or institutions with specific interests. Their value generally lies in the descriptions or annotations given with the addresses. It does little good to learn that a society exists if the researcher can learn nothing about the interests and activities of the society. Such directories of interest to genealogists include the *American Library Directory* and Mary K. Meyer's *Meyer's Directory of Genealogical Societies in the U.S.A. and Canada*. These and several other important directories are discussed in chapter 1, "General Reference."

City directories, like telephone books, are directories of names; they are also very valuable in genealogical research. However, they are not finding aids. They provide genealogical information and can be considered as original records (created at the time of the event by a house-to-house canvas) even though they were reproduced as printed books. City directories have been very well discussed in *The Source* and therefore are not included in this book.

Indexes. INDEXES ARE ALPHABETICALLY ARRANGED LISTS OF INFORMATION FOUND IN ANOTHER RECORD (or another location in the same record). They may refer to names in a census, topics or persons in a history, or words in a text. They serve the important purpose of helping the researcher find information within a source. Because indexes are created from other sources, they are always secondary or tertiary in nature. Generally, they do not make the difference between success and failure for a researcher, as other printed sources do, but they do allow researchers to pursue their goals much faster. There are many considerations in the use of indexes, such as the completeness of the index. These and other aspects of indexes are discussed in chapter 6, "Published Indexes."

Original Records

ORIGINAL RECORDS ARE THOSE SOURCES THAT CONTAIN THE FIRST RECORDING OF AN EVENT (birth, marriage, death, probate, land purchase, census enumeration, pension, etc.); THEY ARE GENERALLY RECORDED NEAR THE TIME OF THE EVENT BY SOMEONE WHO WAS PRESENT AND ASSOCIATED WITH THE EVENT. Because the record was made in proximity to the event, it should include primary information; as noted earlier, however, some of the information in an original record will be secondary in nature.

Original records can be wrong—a fact that *must* be recognized. Secondary and even primary information in an original source may have been recorded incorrectly. The church blessing record of this author's daughter calls her the "son of Kory Meyerink." The church clerk simply crossed out the wrong word on a pre-printed form which offered the choice between son and daughter. Likewise, a great-uncle's birth was recorded incorrectly in the Massachusetts town where he was born. Births were recorded on registration days in the 1880s; the town clerk inadvertently copied the birth date of the child recorded just prior to the great uncle's. Family records, and even the 1900 census, include the correct date, but the official town record, an original record, is in error.

The problems are compounded when researchers try to read too much into a source, even if it is an original record. What novice researcher has not been guilty of assuming that all the children listed in the 1850 census were born to the older man and woman of the same surname in the same household? This is a common assumption, yet the children could be nieces, nephews, stepchildren, cousins, siblings, adopted children, or perhaps not related to the "parents" at all. The same caution that a good researcher uses in evaluating compiled records and secondary information must be used with original records and primary information (see "Evaluation of Printed Sources," below).

Printed Original Records. Original records can exist in printed form and still contain primary information. Consider current methods of recording events. Much of what is written today is entered into computers that produce printed copies. No one would argue that a journal entry recorded near the time of an event is not an original record that also contains primary information. However, more and more journal entries today are being made and stored using home computers.

Some more-applicable examples for the genealogist are newspapers and city directories. Both of these sources have to be considered original records by the definition in use here, yet both are printed and contain primary information. The key consideration is their creation, not their format. Both newspapers and city directories contain the first recordings of one or more events by people close to the events. Often, newspaper reporters are more qualified and objective (even those in earlier days) than the eyewitnesses to an event; in fact, many reporters are eyewitnesses themselves to the events they write about. Again, it is the provenance, or origin, of the record that defines the kind of record it is. Certainly newspapers, like other original records, include secondary information, such as the birth information in an obituary. But they are original records and much of their information is primary.

W. B. Stephens writes about three sorts of "published primary sources": first, original materials later reproduced in published form, such as the *Territorial Papers of the United States;* second, microform editions of original material; and third, publications of governments and private concerns, such as "newspapers, pamphlets, directories, gazetteers, and the like" (1991, 19).

Copied Original Records

COPIED RECORDS ARE THOSE WHICH REPRODUCE, IN WHOLE OR IN PART, THE CONTENTS OF ORIGINAL RECORDS. Copies of original records, such as abstracts, extracts, transcripts, and translations, whether printed or made by hand, can also be considered versions of original records because they preserve the information, much of it primary, and the text (or key portions) found in the record.[2] The point here is that the copying is rather mechanical; the copyist did not evaluate the information or combine it with data from other sources (which would make it a compiled record).

There are, however, important concerns about copied original records, as expressed by Dr. Craig W. Horle, the chairman of the Publications Committee for the Genealogical Society of Pennsylvania:

> . . . despite the burgeoning appreciation for a professional approach to genealogy, there persists a gulf between the growing professionalism of many genealogists and the continuing amateurishness of too many genealogical publishers and publishing houses. Over the last decade there has been an incredible outpouring of publications of original records aimed at genealogists and also aimed at making a nice, quick, profit for small publishers, a development assisted by the rapid advances in computerized desktop publishing technology. While some of these publications reflect high standards, most do not, a disturbing trend that rankles historians, archivists, and professional genealogists alike (1992, 217–18).

How, then, should a distinction be made between a copied original record and the uncopied, "first-generation" record? Such a distinction does make a difference when it comes to evaluating research findings (see "Evaluation of Printed Sources," below). *Printed Sources* uses the term *actual document* when discussing first-generation records. These are precisely the kinds of records that are treated in *The Source;* its discussion includes, for instance, both newspapers and city directories. For this reason they are not included in *Printed Sources.*

Records and sources are copied in many different ways, especially with the growing use of computers. Some records have been entered into computer databases, and many others have been microfilmed. Some hand-copied records remain in manuscript form. This discussion, however, will focus on records that have been abstracted, extracted, transcribed, or translated and then printed. All of these methods of copying sources are used to make the sources more accessible to researchers. Therefore, the researcher must understand the essential differences in these types of copied sources.

Abstracts. ABSTRACTS ARE COPIES OF SOURCES THAT INCLUDE ONLY THE GENEALOGICALLY SIGNIFICANT MATERIAL FROM THE ORIGINAL. The issue here is this: what did the abstractor consider to be genealogically significant? All of the essential information from the document should be included, such as the date of the event, names of persons and places, relationships, and a brief description of the event. A good abstract will include the names of neighbors, witnesses, bondsmen, and others; however, many do not. An abstract does not have to comprise a word-for-word copy of the information, nor does it have to be in the exact order of the source document. Often, the abstracted information is presented in a brief tabular format, such as this fictitious example:

Name: Henry Wilcox
Date of will: Jan. 23, 1867
Bequests to: wife Mary, sons John, William, Henry Jr., daughters Sarah Goldsworthy, Susan Jenkins, Mary
Executor: Mary
Witnesses: Joseph Miles, Frank Williams
Residence: Henrico County

Note that the above example leaves much to be desired. It does not indicate the size of the estate, when the will was proved, who received what items under what conditions, or if daughter Mary was married. While this may not be a good example, it is typical of many abstracts. In most cases, the most important information is abstracted, but the greatest value of such abstracts may be as finding tools. Through them the researcher can learn if a will or probate exists, but she should then seek the original. Also, many abstracts have every-name indexes, so the researcher can learn if an ancestor was mentioned in records relating to someone else. Usually the original records are only indexed, if at all, under the names of the principal parties, such as the testator of a will or the grantor and grantee of a deed.

Extracts. Extracts are quite similar to abstracts; many researchers confuse them. Like abstracts, EXTRACTS INCLUDE ONLY THE ESSENTIAL INFORMATION. HOWEVER, THE ARRANGEMENT OF THE INFORMATION FOLLOWS THE ORIGINAL EXACTLY. The genealogical information is copied word for word from the original, but the entire original is not copied. Omissions from the original are indicated by ellipses—for example, "to John, Mary, and Henry. . . three acres of land each." Obviously, an extract may present the same concern as an abstract: What did the extractor consider important? Also, the meaning of a record is sometimes lost or obscured when some information is left out. On the other hand, the omission of legal terminology may make records easier to understand for the typical user.

Transcripts. TRANSCRIPTS ARE COMPLETE, WORD-FOR-WORD COPIES OF ENTIRE DOCUMENTS. Generally they exist to help researchers use and understand records originally recorded in old handwriting. In colonial America (and in pre-1800 England), most records were written by clerks who had been trained in any of a variety of handwriting styles; some of the styles bear little resemblance to modern cursive script. Sometimes the only way to clearly understand a document is to consider the complete text. If the reader's understanding is impeded by writing that is difficult to read, meaning in the record may be lost.

Probate records, especially wills, are frequent subjects of transcripts. Rarely are entire volumes of wills transcribed; all of the wills for a certain surname in a specific locality might be subjects for a particular transcription. Such transcriptions are most often found in family or surname periodicals. Census records and cemetery tombstones are also common candidates for transcription. Here, however, the entire record, such as a county census or all of the tombstones in a cemetery, is usually transcribed.

The limitations of transcriptions are different from those of abstracts or extracts. A transcript does not require the compiler to decide what information to include or exclude. However, as with other copied sources, the user must take into account the transcriber's ability to decipher the original document. Letters such as *L* and *S* look the same in some records. If only initials were used in a census, there are no complete names (such as Lucy or Susan) to provide clues to the transcriber as to what was actually written. Whole words may look similar. The names Daniel and David can be hard to distinguish because *v* and *n* are difficult to tell apart, as are *el* and *d*. A careful transcriber will outline in the work's preface how the work was done—how discrepancies or unclear entries were copied, for example. She should also indicate her qualifications for the work and the conditions under which she worked. It is useful to determine if the original source was actually transcribed from microfilm (a common method) or from the original document (a microfilm copy is usually not as legible as the original document; a transcription based on microfilm suggests an increased possibility of transcription errors). The physical conditions encountered by the transcriber may also have affected the work; were the lighting and temperature adequate? (A transcriber is not as careful if she is uncomfortable with the working conditions, such as in dark, cold, musty courthouse basements.)

A true transcript reproduces the record letter for letter as it appears in the original, including misspellings, abbreviations, corrections, etc. However, many transcribers cannot resist editing. They may make corrections in the record, expand abbreviations, omit words that were crossed out on the original, and perform other surgery on the text of the record. If these actions are explained and annotated throughout the transcription, they may be permissible. However, when a transcriber takes it upon himself to edit the original, he does a great disservice to the eventual user. If the original text is very difficult to understand without editing, it should be transcribed exactly as found and be accompanied by a modified text to help the reader understand the original. In such a case the original is still available (as a transcript) for comparison.

Translations. A TRANSLATION IS SIMILAR TO A TRANSCRIPT; THE DIFFERENCE IS THAT THE TRANSCRIPT'S ORIGINAL IS IN A FOREIGN LANGUAGE. Generally, the translator provides the entire record, although in some cases only an extracted translation is given. In U.S. research, of course, translations of original sources are rare, because most records were made in English originally. However, some important colonial records have been translated from the German (in Pennsylvania) and Dutch (in New York). The series New York Historical Manuscripts, Dutch, 1638–1662 (Holland Society of New York, 1974–78), is an example.

While any foreign-language record is a candidate for translation, court, probate, and (especially) church records are most commonly found as translations. Concerns to be aware of in using translations are much the same as for transcriptions. Try to determine how accurately the translation was done and what qualifying experience the translator had. For many New York and Pennsylvania church records, more than one translation/transcription may exist. The researcher will want to check each one. Read the prefatory material in such publications to learn how certain aspects of the work, such as abbreviations or odd spellings of names, were treated. Was all the information translated or were witnesses to a birth ignored? Often the original is no longer available, so be sure to evaluate the translation carefully.

Copied (published) original records are the most common printed genealogy sources. The nine chapters in part 3 discuss the nature of such sources, including their limitations, as well as the key reference tools and finding aids needed to make maximum use of these sources.

Compiled Records

Many printed sources are *compiled records*. A compiled record is the product of an editor or author who composed the arrangement or text of the work. Compiled records contain new information or new interpretations of existing information. Being derived from other sources or records, they generally provide secondary and tertiary information. They contain the results of research in books and documents, or the results of original experiments (in the pure sciences). A compiled record may be in the form of an essay, novel, report, or any other created work. The distinguishing characteristic of a compiled record is that the information contained in it is new in some way and not simply copied from another source. Indeed, the reference tools described above could also be considered compiled works. However, *Printed Sources*, as do many genealogical circles, uses a more limited definition: COMPILED RECORDS ARE THOSE RECORDS THAT PROVIDE ACTUAL GENEALOGICAL INFORMATION WHOSE CONTENT IS DERIVED FROM THE RESEARCH AND EVALUATION OF ORIGINAL RECORDS AND/OR OTHER PERSONS' RESEARCH. Thus, the use and evaluation of other sources (original and compiled) is the chief characteristic of compiled records.

A compiled source has its basis in other records. It may have been compiled from one or more original records, other compiled records, or some combination of both. The author may quote from some other sources, but the source's content is the responsibility of its creator. A good compiled source will contain an explanation of the methods of its creation and the sources it was based upon (see below under "Evaluation of Printed Sources"). A knowledgeable researcher can usually also determine the sources from which a compiled record was derived.

Researchers should not assume that a record is original simply because it is in handwritten form, or compiled because it is in printed form. Compiled sources are usually—*but not always*—printed. The most common forms of handwritten secondary sources are genealogical research notes and findings of other researchers.

Various forms of these sources are described in detail in part 4 of this book. Here it is sufficient to briefly define the major types of compiled records.

Histories. Histories provide important information to researchers about the areas where ancestors lived. They may also include information about particular ancestors or their immediate family or relatives. It is essential for researchers to have some background knowledge about the areas they are researching—when the county was created, what churches existed there at what times, where other settlers came from, and similar information. Usually the researcher relies on county and local histories, but national histories can also provide important information.

Histories come in a wide variety of formats and have varied contents; they can include biographies and family genealogies. Generally they are narrative in style (as opposed to the list style of many copied original records) and are very much the product of an author (or several authors), rather than an editor or compiler. Further discussion of numerous types of histories is found in chapter 17, "County and Local Histories," and chapter 18, "Biographies."

Family histories, or genealogies, are among the printed sources most commonly used by genealogists. They present the history of a family and appear in numerous formats. They may list all or some of a person's descendants or ancestors. They may provide only basic genealogical information or a longer narrative history about each person or family. A further discussion is in chapter 16, "Family Histories and Genealogies."

A special kind of compiled genealogy is that which discusses noble lineages. Although obviously not American sources, these represent a unique collection of printed sources that are frequently used by American researchers. In fact, some such sources are not compiled records; rather, they are copied (printed) original records. Because of the great interest in such noble lineages among American researchers, and because some Americans' ancestry can actually be traced to noble families, a discussion of these sources, including how to use them properly, is contained in chapter 20, "Medieval and Nobility Sources."

Periodicals. Periodicals are a unique form of printed source. A periodical can contain all of the above-described types of sources in a single issue. Periodicals are usually issued at regular intervals (such as quarterly) by a society or institution, or sometimes by an individual. Genealogical periodicals generally focus on a specific theme, such as the records of a particular locality or time period. Not only do they contain a variety of sources; the quality of their content can be very uneven because of the variety of authors who contribute to them. The lack of regular indexes can also make them difficult to use. Chapter 19, "Genealogical Periodicals," discusses this type of printed source in greater detail.

EVALUATION OF PRINTED SOURCES

Whatever sources are used in research, it is important to evaluate them to determine if they are accurate, complete, correct, logical, and reasonable. While all sources need to be evaluated carefully, the various printed sources have much in common, and there are several general principles to keep in mind when using them. After an overview of general evaluation concepts, this section will discuss the key ways of evaluating the books themselves and their contents.

General Evaluation Concepts

In the process of genealogical research, nothing is more important than the accurate evaluation of the evidence found during the research process. EVIDENCE IS ONE OR MORE STATEMENTS OF FACT OR PIECES OF INFORMATION THAT APPEAR TO PERTAIN TO THE SUBJECT OF RESEARCH. Genealogists often use dozens of sources, each with many "pieces" of information, as they seek to solve research problems and establish proof of relationships. However, not every source or piece of evidence carries the same weight. Some information found during research is simply more likely to be true than other information. The problem many researchers face, especially beginners, is identifying and understanding the many aspects of each record that must be evaluated.

Unfortunately, the terminology often used to describe a record's reliability is so general that many of these aspects are overlooked, greatly affecting the way a record can be judged and the information it supplies. A more careful description of the different aspects of evaluation allows for better teaching of the principles of evaluation; this, in turn, will lead to better proof of genealogical relationships.

Many researchers find it difficult to comprehend the differences between primary and secondary sources. Some have thus suggested that artificial descriptions of records that serve no real purpose in evaluating genealogical facts or conclusions should be discarded (Drake 1992, 12). The real solution, however, as noted in the previous sections, is to use clear and meaningful definitions. To divide the world of genealogical sources into categories and use descriptive terms for those categories is worthwhile because it allows discussion of the various aspects of evaluation. Furthermore, such descriptions enable teachers and writers to better instruct new genealogists about how they should weigh their findings.

As mentioned in the section on the "Origin of Information," there are two key issues: the nature of the records themselves (how they were created) and the origin of the information in the record. Simply categorizing a record as primary or secondary avoids the question of how good the information in that record is. Again, a death certificate is an excellent example—much of the information in such a record pertains to events that happened years before the event of death.

But it is not enough even to determine if the book is original or compiled, or if the information is primary or secondary. There are at least seven separate aspects of each source to consider when evaluating research findings: the relevance of the record; the origin of the information in it; the nature of the record itself; the record's format; and the evidence, facts, and events given in the record.

Relevance of the Record. It is first necessary to determine, if possible, if the record pertains at all to the family of interest. For example, a marriage record from the right place at the right time is not necessarily that of the husband and wife being sought. Be especially careful when researching common names in densely populated areas. Very seldom are all of the people with the same surname related to each other, and it is very common for persons of a similar age with the same names to be living in the same vicinity. It can be helpful to review other records of the locality to learn just how common the names are in that area. The assumption of "right place, right time, right name" has probably led to more erroneous connections than any other aspect of record evaluation.

Sometimes the decision about how relevant a record is must be delayed until further evidence is available. It may be possible to make that decision only after *all* of the potentially applicable records have been evaluated.

Origin of Information. As discussed earlier, the *information* in a record should be considered as primary or secondary. Most records contain both primary and secondary information. For example, the 1880 census identifies relationships at the time of the census; that can be considered primary information. However, the age of the adults in the same census is only secondary information, as is the birthplace. Be sure to identify what information was recorded at or near the time of the event (primary) and what was recorded much later than the event described (secondary).

Nature of Records. The nature of the record (that is, how it was created) is a consideration separate from the information in the record. A compilation of marriages taken from original county records still presents primary information; however, the nature of that record (a compilation) allows additional errors to occur. Here is where a consideration of the categories and formats of records is useful in the evaluation process.

As mentioned earlier, genealogical records (those which provide information about individuals, such as names, dates, or relationships) comprise two categories. *Original records* are those created to record certain events. They are generally created at or near the time of the event they record, and are usually the earliest record of that event. Thus, a baptismal record is an original record, as are obituaries, military pension papers, business account books, and even city directories and most newspaper articles. Every original record contains information written directly into the record by someone who was in a position to have accurate (often firsthand) knowledge of the information being recorded.

Compiled records (sometimes called records of previous research) represent gatherings of information from one or more additional sources (original records, other compiled records, or both). An important characteristic of a compiled record is that its author or compiler interpreted information found in other sources. Examples include family histories, biographies, and local histories. Many, but not all, compiled records are in the form of published books.

These two categories must be evaluated differently. Original records require that the researcher attempt to determine if the information in them was recorded correctly in the first place. When working with compiled records, the researcher must determine if the compiler found all applicable source records, analyzed them correctly, and came to valid conclusions.

Kinds of Formats. The format of a record(actual records versus various kinds of reproductions) is also significant when evaluating the evidence found therein. Recording errors can appear in any source, but the nature of errors changes with the format. The *actual document* (either an original or a compiled record) is often available to the researcher. Virtually as good as the actual document is a *photographic copy;* these include microfilm, microfiche, and photocopies. Either form represents the record as it was first made; any errors are the fault of the person who made the record. Copy errors can be introduced if the document is transcribed, extracted, or abstracted, an important consideration in evaluation. If such a copy is a *printed copy,* the genealogist must account for possible copyist and typographical errors. A *manuscript copy* can contain copyist errors, but there is also the possibility of misreading the handwriting in it. In brief, the further removed the copy is from the actual document, the more errors are likely to have been introduced.

Directness of Evidence. Evidence is the statement(s) of fact made in a record, or the interpretation of the facts in a record. A *direct* statement specifically states a fact, such as the date of death. An *indirect* statement (often called circumstantial evidence) reasonably implies a fact (Stevenson 1979, 181, 186). For example, a marriage record is direct evidence that a person was born but only indirect evidence of the time of birth, as the person may have been born sixteen or sixty years before the marriage. Genealogists usually prefer direct evidence because indirect evidence may be interpreted differently by others.

These first five aspects of evaluation include judgements that can be made by examining the single record (or source) alone. The last two aspects include the necessity of judging the information within the record (1) against itself (internal evaluation) and (2) against information from other sources (external evaluation).

Consistency and Clarity of Facts. Every record includes several facts (or alleged facts). The researcher must judge these facts in conjunction with other facts that may be in the same record or in other records.

First, the facts must be consistent with other known facts. For example, if a child's birth record shows that she was born a year after the known death of the father listed on the birth record, there is a serious disagreement that must be resolved before that record can be accepted as proof of the child's paternity. If the facts in a record conflict with other facts, determine which information, if any, is primary and, if so, if it was recorded correctly.

Second, are the facts clearly stated and easy to interpret? A record may contain difficult-to-read handwriting. In addition, many words were spelled differently in earlier years, and those varied spellings may obscure the meaning. Some records use obscure language, and the meanings of some words may have changed; legal terminology and the formal language used in some records, such as wills and deeds, are examples. Foreign-language records can also be difficult to comprehend. There are four elements to observe when evaluating the clarity of the stated facts:

- *Names.* Be sure to read them correctly and that any spelling variations are acceptable. Determine if they follow appropriate naming patterns, if any.

- *Dates.* Interpret the style of dates correctly. If all-numeric dates are used, determine if the month or day is listed first. Learn which calendar (Gregorian or Julian) was in use at the time.

- *Places.* Among the most difficult parts of a record to read are place names. Often they are unfamiliar, and they may be spelled incorrectly. There may be more than one place with the same name, and a city and county may share the same name.

- *Relationships.* A record may state relationships directly or may only imply them. Previous relationship terms, such as cousin and in-law, had different meanings at one time then they do today.

Likelihood of Events. Evaluation requires that the researcher consider whether the events, as shown in the record(s), really could have happened. Some events are less likely than others, such as an ancestor joining the military at the age of ten or twelve, being born on the father's birthday, or a probate inventory showing a considerably larger estate for a person than tax lists or census records indicate. For most situations there is a continuum of probability ranging from very likely to highly unlikely to impossible. This continuum will change with different cultures and time periods.

Evaluation and Proof. Every record can be evaluated individually based on the seven aspects described above, but PROOF IS THE ACCUMULATION OF ACCEPTABLE EVIDENCE. The judge (that is, the researcher) is responsible for determining if the accumulated evidence represents "clear and convincing" proof of a genealogical fact (Drake 1991, 153 and Devine 1992, 131).

When evaluating evidence, it is important to realize that original records are not inherently better (or worse) than compiled records. However, they do need to be evaluated differently. The same is true of the information contained in a record. Primary information is not necessarily more correct than secondary information. Every genealogist knows of cases where clerks made mistakes in recording events in original records. Such errors are sometimes corrected when a compiled record is created, making a better record of events and relationships than the originals they are based on.

The Book As a Product

While the above evaluation guidelines are useful for any genealogical source, printed sources provide additional elements to evaluate. One often-overlooked element is the book itself. Examine the book as a product. How good is the binding? Was the text composed professionally (typeset) or is it a typescript of uneven quality? Is there a preface, and how long is it? Is there a foreword and/or introduction? How large is the index in relation to the text? (Many people feel that the ratio should be relatively high for genealogical books. Many printed genealogies [family histories] have one index page for every ten [sometimes fewer] pages of text.) Is the publisher's name known in genealogical or research fields—or does the book appear to have been "self published?" What year was it published? Theories may have changed or been disproved in the years since it was published, and new sources that the book does not discuss or the compiler did not have access to when preparing the material may be available.

Look for other items, such as consistency in the style and formatting of the text and of bibliographic citations throughout the book. Are there misspellings? (It is difficult to have much confidence in a book that spells the name of the avocation as "geneology," yet that mistake is not unknown in published books.) These elements suggest the presence or absence of a careful, competent editor. Although no editor is perfect, and there will be mistakes, try to determine the amount and nature of the mistakes in judging a book.

A negative answer to any of these questions does not necessarily mean that the content of the book is useless. However, any concerns raised by them should make the researcher stop and ponder the nature of the book. Good material has been produced "on a shoestring," especially in genealogy, but bad material almost always is. On the other hand, a well-produced book by a well-known publisher may not live up to expectations. For example, when the American Library Association published Lois Gilmer's *Genealogical Research and Resources: A Guide for Library Use* (Chicago, 1988), the book was well received by many libraries and even received good reviews because of its publisher's reputation. However, the information in it was poorly arranged, outdated, and often of questionable value.

Don't place *too much* credence on the quality of a book's production. Gold edging and leather bindings do not mean the content is without error. Rather, they suggest that the person financing the publication had substantial financial resources. Generally speaking, however, poor production quality often means poor quality of content.

Content

The content of a book can be even harder to judge than the book itself, especially for the person who is not very experienced in genealogy. There are, however, some aspects to pay attention to. Often the researcher will be greatly rewarded for taking the extra time to learn about the author and the subject in order to evaluate a printed source.

The researcher should begin with his own knowledge of the subject. Seldom will there be a complete lack of familiar information in a new source. Regardless of how new a researcher may be to the subject, she brings some knowledge that can be compared with she reads in a printed source. This author often forms part of his judgment about a dictionary or encyclopedia by its treatment of his state or occupation—both of which he is very familiar with. If the work is careful and balanced on those topics, he feels more comfortable that it has treated other topics carefully. Maps and atlases can be easily evaluated by the detail and clarity with which they treat the location where the user lives or grew up.

Family histories are often taken at face value because they are used to extend ancestral lines, even if their users don't know anything about the families that had not been on their pedigrees before finding the book. Look carefully at the information for a family or generation that *is* familiar. Is it complete and correct? Use compiled records like family histories only to guide research. Take the time to trace a few families in original sources, such as census or probate records, and note whether the published book gives information that matches period documents.

Evaluate the Author. Evaluating an author may be difficult if he is unfamiliar to the researcher or if a publication is his first. Often the book itself will indicate something about the author, such as his educational level, profession, prior publications, or other achievements. Obviously the book will paint a very favorable picture of the author, so read past the glowing comments. Does it really matter that she is the mother of six children or descends from the kings of England? Do his awards and achievements have anything to do with the subject of the book? While achievements may indicate a certain amount of mental ability or research acumen, does being an army colonel have much bearing on his ability to link families together?

Learning an author's qualifications from outside sources can be difficult. Lists of genealogists who have met certain standards are available from several organizations, such as the Association of Professional Genealogists, The Board for Certification of Genealogists, and the Family History Library of The Church of Jesus Christ of Latter-day Saints (LDS church). *Who's Who in Genealogy and Heraldry* provides some information about the training, credentials, and background of the persons listed in it. Ask other researchers what they know about an author, and check library catalogs for other books written by her.

Deceased authors can be more difficult to evaluate. Notable authors are often eulogized in the periodicals of the societies they were most closely associated with. Such items are seldom very critical; however, they will attest to the author's activities, and generally only the most competent authors are eulogized.

A deceased author might also be easier to evaluate. The greater the distance between the user of a source and the writer, the easier it is to be constructively critical. (Death certainly places some distance between the reader and the author.) Many authors will have published several works and have a reputation in the field. Therefore, ask colleagues for their opinions. Briefly study an author's other works. Were they carefully compiled? Are sources cited? Are the works generally thorough?

Read Book Reviews. Seek reviews of the book being evaluated. Unfortunately, most book "reviews" are actually just notices and do not evaluate the book or author in any depth. Some periodicals that do include critical book reviews are noted in chapter 19, "Genealogical Periodicals." Even critical reviewers tend to be charitable; their intentions often seem to be to avoid discouraging genealogical publications, because their authors are rarely compensated very well. It is wise not to base an opinion solely on book reviews.

Evaluate Sources. Determine what the author's sources were. There should be a bibliography or source list, usually at the end of the book or at the end of each chapter. Determine if the author used a variety of sources. Did she use original records extensively, or do compiled records dominate? It may be impossible to compile a family history using only original records, but one that uses only compiled material cannot be relied upon as being as accurate as possible. Did the author use more than one source to support each statement made? Reliance on only one source for any point of fact shows an ignorance of research methodology.

Did the author find any contradictory information? If so, how did he deal with it? It is most unlikely that a compiler will not find some facts that conflict with others. Be sure that the author presented evidence that is clear and convincing. Find out how the author collected her data. Did she travel to the place where the events took place, and, if so, were the records she needed still "on location"? With the possible exception of using the Family History Library in Salt Lake City, it is very difficult to prepare a family history, or any of several other types of printed genealogical sources, by researching in only one location or institution. If the author corresponded for information, how good were his correspondents? Did he use the original sources, or abstracts, extracts, and transcripts? Often the writer of a history will use whole sections from an earlier history, frequently without acknowledgment. Today this practice is called plagiarism, but in earlier years it was the norm. One way to evaluate sources is to compare the information with that in other printed sources that deal with the same subject, such as a county's history or a family genealogy.

Read the Preface. The author's preface is the key to evaluating any printed source. There she usually reveals why and how she created the book. Thus, the preface may be the most important part of a book (but it is also the most overlooked section). Sometimes the user has to read between the lines, especially if the author is not very willing to reveal his process. The lack of a preface, or a very brief one, suggests that the book was put together in haste, or at least without due consideration of the reader, which may well imply carelessness.

It is important, for example, when reading a book of cemetery inscriptions, to know when the transcriptions were done and by whom. What kind of experience did the person have? What were the weather conditions? Did she carefully clean the hard-to-read stones or just guess at the inscription? Are there other, earlier transcriptions? Are sextons' records available? Were the complete inscriptions copied, or only the "genealogically significant material"? (This irritating phrase begs the question, Who determines what is "genealogically significant"?) Why are the names arranged the way they are in the book? Are they arranged alphabetically (ideally not), or by cemetery row and plot? Is there an index and, if not, why? Answers to such questions should be found in a preface.

Read Other Introductory Sections. The preface is usually written by the author(s). However, there are other parts of a book that will help in evaluating the content. The foreword is usually written by another person, often knowledgeable in the field, who the author hopes will lend credibility to the book. The comments will, of course, be positive, but a careful reading will nonetheless reveal more about the book and the author(s).

The introduction may provide information that the preface did not. Like the preface, it is usually written by the author(s) and seeks to explain the book. Even the acknowledgments can be helpful. They help the reader learn who else was involved with the book. Often a teacher, leader, or other mentor may be mentioned, from which something about the author may be inferred. What about assistants? What roles did they play? How much guidance did the editor or publisher give?

Check Publication Information. In evaluating the content of a book, look for other clues. How often has it been reprinted? How many copies were produced? (The publisher may be able to provide this information.) These facts give some clue as to the book's popularity and thus the opinions of other users. Although poor books have been reprinted, such situations are relatively rare. How recent is the edition? Try to use the most recent one. Although a first edition is valuable to book collectors, recent editions suggest changes in the text; they might only be updates, but they may also be corrections. A writer rarely revises a book unless she thinks that she can improve it thereby. Revisions often reflect new thinking, new theories, or even additional proof that the author has found.

Judge the Length. How long is the book? How does it compare in length to other books that cover the same subject? A book's ideal length may be hard to judge, but a brief discussion of genealogical "how-to" books will illustrate this point.

This author would be very uncomfortable with a one hundred-page booklet on research methodology that claimed to be "all the beginner needs to know." (It may be all the beginner wants to read, but he certainly needs to know more.) Many of the topics discussed in *Printed Sources* were chosen because relatively little has been written about them. How can this so when hundreds of different "how-to" books have been written on genealogy? A survey of the literature revealed that many books say the same things, only with different wording and arrangements. Certainly some new sources have come to light and many new indexes are now available, but research principles stay the same, and major record sources have not changed.

Interestingly enough, four of the most widely used and accepted introductory books were first published between sixty-seven and twenty-four years ago (*Genealogy as Pastime and Profession*, 1930; *Searching for your Ancestors*, 1937; *Genealogical Research: Methods and Sources*, 1960; and *The Researcher's Guide to American Genealogy*, 1973). They have endured, usually in several revised editions, while others have come and gone. Each takes a slightly different perspective and serves a different audience, but they do their jobs well. Yet, at least one hundred other such books have been published. All of them devote a similar amount of content to the major sources, such as census and probate records, and less on other sources (such as tax records). Not until *The Source* was first published in 1984 were original sources treated in greater depth than they had been in dozens of earlier books. Therefore, the size of *The Source* (846 pages in the current edition) becomes a measure of its usefulness. Its size equates to greater discussion than ever before of many common sources, and a focus on other sources (such as institutional and business records and city directories) that had seldom been treated in similar works.

In considering some of the topics for *Printed Sources*, potential users were surveyed, as were previously printed books. Most of the compiled sources treated in part 4 have previously received only brief mention in most books (including *The Source*). Compiled biographies, for example (see chapter 18), received no more than two or three pages of explanatory text in any of a dozen books reviewed. Often only a few paragraphs were used to describe this diverse and sometimes difficult type of source. The same was true for local histories and genealogical periodicals (see chapters 17 and 19).

This discussion serves to illustrate that length can be a method of evaluating a book. If a book is brief, does it add to the field? Evaluating a book based on its length requires that the researcher become familiar with the topic of the book she is evaluating, or at least that it be evaluated with other books in hand. A bibliography with fifty entries has to be judged against a similar bibliography covering the same topics with five hundred entries. There may be a purpose for the shorter bibliography (longer annotations, narrow selection criteria), but it should be justified.

Unfortunately, it can be difficult to find much of the information needed for evaluation within the book itself. Dr. Horle expresses his concerns about genealogical publications:

> Far too often, the reader is not told the qualifications of the transcriber, the repository of the original record, or the methodology used in the edition. Rarely do transcribers provide tips about dating of documents where appropriate, that is, whether the Julian or Gregorian calender was in use, nor do they indicate whether the transcription was made from microfilm or from the original manuscript. Similarly, with reprints of older works, a new introduction should be added that discusses the work itself . . . (1992, 218).

It is important, when evaluating a printed work, to take the time to carefully examine the book before accepting its assertions. Then, check other sources (reviews, other researchers) to learn about limitations of the book. The dozens of "how-to" books mentioned above are surprisingly brief on evaluation (hence this discussion). For further ideas about evaluation, two books stand out: *Family History for Fun and Profit* (formerly *Genealogical Research: A Jurisdictional Approach*), by Vincent L. Jones, Arlene H. Eakle, and Mildred H. Christensen (Salt Lake City: Genealogical Institute, 1972), and *Genealogical Evidence,* by Noel Stevenson (Laguna Hills, Calif.: Aegaen Park Press, 1979).

DOCUMENTATION AND COPYRIGHT

A printed source represents the creative work of a person, whether in correctly reproducing actual documents in the form of a printed book or compiling a biography, history, or family history from dozens or hundreds of different sources. It also represents the publisher's efforts (editing, layout, printing, and promotion) and money expended to help share the author's creative work with the public. The hallmark of a good researcher is knowing how to properly use the printed creative work; this includes knowing how to (1) understand the source(s) it was based upon (documentation) and (2) respecting the creator's ownership (copyright).

Documentation

Understanding the documentation in a printed source is crucial to the appropriate use of the source. The first question a researcher must ask about a printed source is, What is the source (or sources) for this information? The answer to this question is a measure of the quality of the book's content; knowing how to answer the question is a measure of the quality of the researcher. Virtually every printed source gives some indication as to the origin of its content. If it is a copy (abstract, extract, transcript) of an original record, then, by its nature, it will cite the original source. Many printed sources, however, are compiled sources, which generally means that their information came from more than one, and usually from several different, sources. The following discussion should help the researcher better evaluate sources that use these documentation systems.

Proper documentation is the hallmark of intellectual honesty. If the content is from the writer's own experience and analysis, there is no need to document a statement. But where facts, ideas, examples, illustrations, etc., are from another source and are not common knowledge, the honest writer must give credit to that source.

A well-documented book gives the reader a statement of origin for every fact that is not self-evident or generally accepted. Some "generally accepted" facts should also be documented (because they may not be generally known to the audience). Certainly, any material directly quoted from another source needs to be documented. Also, any information taken in whole or in part (whether quoted or not) from any other source, original or compiled, should be cited. Conclusions of the author, generally drawn from the material under discussion in the text, are not documented.

Too often authors cite only quotations but do not bother to state where specific facts came from. Such oversight can be a sign of laziness on the part of the author and, if it concerns genealogical information, it indicates that the author may have been as careless in his research as in citing his sources. Citing sources can be cumbersome; genealogical compilations, such as family histories, can potentially require a source statement for nearly every sentence. Fortunately, some conventions that allow a bit of latitude in these situations have developed in genealogy.

Documentary notes are usually of two types. THE SOURCE CITATION, with which this discussion is most concerned, TELLS THE READER SPECIFICALLY WHERE THE FACT(S) CITED CAME FROM. EXPLANATORY OR SUBSTANTIVE NOTES EXPLAIN A FACT RELATED TO, BUT NOT DIRECTLY PART OF, THE DISCUSSION IN THE TEXT. These two types may be separated or combined, depending on the author's and publisher's preference. Often a source citation includes some explanatory information. Generally there are far fewer explanatory notes than source citations in most texts.

Regardless of the nature of the documentation, several important elements should appear in any documentary statement. These include the author, title, and publication information (edition, place, publisher's name, and year) for the source cited. In addition, page references should indicate where in the source information was found. In short, the source should be so clearly described that anyone could locate it in a bibliography or library catalog. It should not take a special knowledge of the particular field to understand a reference. Subsequent references to the same work can be abbreviated if the abbreviations are clear, consistent, and conventional.

At least five different styles of documentation are used in genealogical books: *footnotes, endnotes, source notes, parenthetical references,* and *unnumbered notes*. Even if the sources of information are not clearly documented in a book, it is possible to learn something about the origin of the information. Such works are often called "undocumented sources," and they pose the biggest challenge to the researcher.

Footnotes. Footnotes are the most common method of documenting information; consequently, they are the method most people are most familiar with. WITH FOOTNOTES, NUMBERS ARE GENERALLY ASSIGNED CONSECUTIVELY THROUGHOUT THE TEXT TO THE ITEMS NEEDING DOCUMENTATION. CORRESPONDINGLY NUMBERED NOTES FOR EACH PAGE ARE PRINTED AT THE BOTTOM (FOOT) OF THE PAGE IN THE FORM OF A CITATION AND/OR EXPLANATION. Numbers may run consecutively through the whole book or only through a chapter, beginning again at number one in each new chapter. The current preference seems to be to begin each chapter or section with number one. In some older books, notes are numbered beginning with number one on each page. This form may be related to an even older style of footnote, which genealogists need to understand because researchers still use many books produced three or more generations ago.

In earlier years, symbols (instead of numbers) were used to mark items in the text requiring notes. The reader had only to glance at the bottom of the page and find the note with the corresponding symbol. These symbols are still used occasionally, usually in combination with other documentation methods, to allow for explanatory notes. The asterisk (*) and dagger (†) are familiar to most readers. They are the first two symbols in a proscribed series of symbols used by publishers. The series was usually repeated on each page, beginning with the asterisk (*). The following were generally used after the dagger: ‡ (double dagger), § (section mark), || (parallels), and # (number sign). In addition, these could be doubled and tripled in the same sequence if more were needed or some were not available (such as the parallels and number sign, which were not used as often): **, ††, ‡‡, §§, ||||, ##, ***, †††. . .

The popularity of footnotes has diminished because of the difficulty of publishing text using them; each page had to be planned to allow space for the footnotes at the bottom. The other systems described below were simply more convenient. However, computer word processing systems have made the use of footnotes much easier, so they are regaining popularity. Indeed, *The Chicago Manual of Style* describes footnotes as "still beloved by traditionalists, especially those in the humanities" (which includes the field of genealogy) (1993, 400).

Endnotes. Endnotes are simply footnotes that are not placed at the bottom of the page; rather, ENDNOTES ARE LISTED AT THE END OF THE TEXT OF A CHAPTER OR SECTION OR AT THE END OF THE BOOK. Like footnotes, they are assigned consecutive numbers and usually begin again with number one in each chapter or section. In genealogical works (notably family histories), endnotes are often placed at the end of the discussion of each family group. Endnotes are convenient for the reader because she is not distracted by information at the bottom of the page and because the notes are grouped for comparison, which is especially helpful for "op. cit." and "ibid." references. Often, however, the reader prefers that explanatory information be more readily available and closer to the text; the endnote system allows for the occasional presence of explanatory notes at the foot of a page using the symbols described above.

Source Notes. The source note is the least common form of citation. THE SOURCE NOTE SYSTEM CONSISTS OF A NUMBERED LIST OF SOURCES, OFTEN PLACED IN THE ORDER THEY ARE USED IN THE TEXT. The items in the text requiring citation are then numbered much as footnotes are, but the numbers refer to the numbers in the source list. Readers who are not accustomed to this style may be confused by the fact that the numbers are not consecutive throughout the text and are repeated when a source is cited a second time; however, such a system eliminates repeated citations of the same source. The major drawback of this system, besides its unfamiliarity, is that separate page numbers in the same source cannot be easily cited unless added to the source list as new citations—and that would eliminate the major utility of this system. However, in a genealogical application, where documents are generally only one or two pages in length (such as censuses, deeds, and wills), this system can work well.

Source notes also solve a problem encountered with consecutive footnotes or endnotes: the need to renumber the sequence when a source reference is added. Because it is the sources themselves that are numbered, the author needs only to add the new source to the source list and use the new number wherever necessary in the text. Source notes are placed much like endnotes—at the end of a chapter or section or at the end of the book. Some family histories use source notes as simple lists of sources at the end of each family discussion and do not mark each fact in the text with a source number. This practice does not place the citation with each fact, but it does lessen the confusion with superscripted numbers of generations, such as "John^{3}."

Parenthetical References. The parenthetical reference (or author-date) system, while less known to the average reader, is growing in popularity. It has been used in the natural sciences for several decades and is now finding favor in the social sciences and (on occasion) in the humanities. It is particularly popular where most of the citations refer to published sources. IN THE PARENTHETICAL REFERENCE SYSTEM, A SHORT REFERENCE TO THE SOURCE IS PLACED IN PARENTHESES WITHIN THE TEXT AFTER THE FACT CITED FROM THAT SOURCE. The complete citation is then given in a "reference list" at the end of the chapter, section, or book (similar to a source notes list but without the numbers). Generally, the reference includes the last name of the author (or a partial title if there is no acknowledged author), the year of publication, and the relevant page number of the work referred to. Thus, a reference could appear as "(Lackey 1980, 5)." If the author's name is mentioned in the text, only the year and page number are given in parentheses. The reference list is arranged alphabetically by author and then by date of the author's works to enable the reader to easily find the complete citation.

The advantage of this system is its ease of use for authors, publishers, and readers. *The Chicago Manual of Style* calls it "the system of documentation generally most economical in space, in time (for author, editor, and typesetter), and in cost (to publisher and public)—in short, the most practical (1993, 640)." The source citations in *Printed Sources* use the parenthetical reference system. For example, consider the several quotes from

Dr. Craig Horle used in this introduction. Each is cited briefly in the text, and each citation refers to the same entry in the "Reference List" at the end of this chapter—thus eliminating repetitive footnotes or endnotes.

While the parenthetical reference system is not yet the most accepted form in the genealogical world, it is growing in popularity in the social sciences and humanities, to which genealogy relates. It is used in *Printed Sources* because it has been adjudged by the editor and publisher to be the easiest to use for both the author and the reader. Parenthetical references provide more information to the reader at the point of use then does a simple number, and, once the reader knows which work is being cited, this note style recalls it to mind much easier. It also eliminates the cumbersome process of adding footnotes or endnotes to a prepared text, as well as the use of Latin abbreviations, with which many readers are unfamiliar today. The lack of standard approaches for brief citations of original records (censuses, deeds, marriage banns, etc.) means that the parenthetical reference system will not likely find widespread use in compiled genealogies. It does, however, work well in textual material, such as instructional books and other reference tools (of which *Printed Sources* is an example).

Until recently, one of the most popular and scholarly genealogical periodicals in the United states, *The American Genealogist,* used a form of the parenthetical reference system. However, the *American Genealogist*'s citation style was less structured. Many works were referred to using full citations in the text (in parentheses), including the complete author's name, book title, and publishing information. In other cases the *American Genealogist* used well-known abbreviations or initial letters to cite common genealogical sources. The full reference can be confusing to the reader seeking to find the end of the reference, and the brief references may not give the novice researcher enough information. On the other hand, longer citations meant that a bibliography was not needed with the article. It also solved the problem of citing genealogical sources when there was no author's name to use in the parenthetical reference.

Unnumbered Notes. Some publications include a list of sources used or a bibliography of books consulted, but do not use any kind of reference system to alert the reader about what information in the text came from which source. This is a much weaker system of documentation than those described above; it is acceptable only when a very few sources were used and it is clear what information came from which source, or when the majority of the information came from one source which is cited immediately afterwards. In such cases, the author may be bordering on plagiarism or even copyright infringement (see below) unless the information was used with permission.

Unfortunately, genealogists have been among the greatest offenders in producing such a citation system. Many books include a list of sources in the preface, acknowledgments, or bibliography, but sometimes this appears to have been done only to add an air of authenticity to the book. The Springer genealogy is an excellent example of this.

This 1881 family history purported to give the genealogy of the Springer family of America through Germany back to Charlemagne, in direct male descent "through the most renowned royalty of 1200 years." The volume included no documentation except a list of "references" on one of the beginning pages; this suggested, to the casual reader, that scholarly research had gone into the book. Sources cited included "Histories of France and Germany," "Collins' Peerage," "Life of Martin Luther," "History of the Reformation," and "History of the Thirty Years' War." In a nine-page critical review in the *American Genealogist,* Milton Rubincam fully disproved the claims of the book, focusing on the lack of genealogical scholarship throughout the text. Regarding this, at first glance, impressive list of sources (for 1881), he rightly comments:

> The inclusion in the Springer bibliography of general histories of France, Germany, Martin Luther, the Reformation, the Thirty Years' War, etc., makes the work practically worthless. It is uncertain how English 'peerages' were employed in tracing the genealogy of the [German] Springer family (1941, 99).

In short, while not all unnumbered source lists lack credibility, the researcher should exercise extreme caution whenever confronted with such lists in printed sources.

Undocumented Sources. Undocumented sources present the greatest challenge for the researcher, for it is much more difficult to judge a work without knowing where the information in it came from. Fortunately, it is possible to learn something about the sources for most printed books. Many of the concepts discussed earlier regarding the evaluation of printed sources are helpful when using books without source citations. The first step is to read the preface. It is the best source for information regarding the author's purpose for the book and the methods used in compiling it, and in it the author will often give some indication of where her information came from.

In the preface of a published genealogy the author will often indicate if he wrote to every person he could find with the surname being researched, or if he searched the town records in New England of every town where the family was known to have resided, or if he traveled extensively and visited families with the surname in ancestral towns. All of those methods and others have been used, often in combination with others, to produce family genealogies.

Sometimes the compiler will indicate that her father, uncle, great-aunt, or other relative had collected the information and left it to her to organize and publish. Whatever the methods the author used, the researcher who understands them has some perspective on the sources the book was drawn from and how much faith to place in its statements.

Seek reviews of the book in question and other books and articles dealing with the same topic. Periodicals often publish articles that refute, or enhance, statements made in published books. The Springer article, cited above, is an excellent example of such information See chapter 19 for more information on the use of periodicals for book reviews and updates to published genealogies.

Guides to Documentation. Whether the genealogist is writing a book or evaluating one that someone else has written, an understanding of documentation is critical; however, the standard style guides on writers' bookshelves do not deal with many considerations unique to genealogical writing. Fortunately, several helpful books are available to introduce genealogists to the complexities of documenting genealogical references.

A recent publication that addresses genealogists' needs very well is Elizabeth Shown Mills's *Evidence! Citation and*

Analysis for the Family Historian (Baltimore: Genealogical Publishing Co., 1997), which explains how to cite and analyze sources in an excellent and very readable manner. The first half of Mills's work provides clear guidelines regarding the fundamentals of how, when, where, and even why to document sources, followed by similarly clear guidelines relating to analyzing evidence. The second half of the book provides detailed, yet not overwhelming, instruction on citing sources. The many sample citations illustrate the formats for primary and subsequent citations, as well as bibliographic entries, for virtually every kind of source a family historian might use; these include the standard book and periodical formats as well as original and microform versions of many records. Of significance for today's writers, Mills even includes suggested formats for electronic sources (such as CD-ROMs and Internet sites). It provides documentation guidelines not covered by any other guide, as well as instruction on how to analyze information. The book's bibliography identifies the standard publishers' style guides as well; in them writers will find more extensive discussions of many related topics. Mills's book, however, may be the only guide that most genealogists need as the learn, and practice, documentation in their research.

An earlier work by Richard S. Lackey, while slightly outdated now, is still on the shelves in many libraries and will also aid the researcher who is learning about documentation from the perspective of evaluating other printed sources. *Cite Your Sources* (New Orleans: Polyanthos, 1980) discusses the nature of genealogical documentation and serves as a style guide for the citation of almost any genealogical document (except electronic sources). Lackey's section on the importance of documentation, common abbreviations, and how to make acknowledgments will always be valuable. His examples and the book's layout, while generally accurate, are not as clear as those in Mills's *Evidence!*

Lackey also produced *Write it Right* (with Donald R. Barnes) (Ocala, Fla.: Lyon Press, 1983), a companion volume that explains how to write a family history. In addition, it contains a description (only slightly flawed) of the standard systems in use today for arranging genealogical information. An understanding of the Register System, the Henry System, and the Sosa-Stradonitz System is critical to the use of printed family histories.

An even more clear and accurate description of these numbering systems is found in Joan Ferris Curran's *Numbering Your Genealogy: Sound and Simple Systems* (Arlington, Va.: National Genealogical Society, 1992). This booklet also describes the value and limitations of the most widely used and easily understood systems.

In addition to these sources, writers should obtain and use Patricia Law Hatcher's *Producing a Quality Family History* (Salt Lake City: Ancestry, 1996). In addition to an extensive discussion of writing and publishing one's own family history, Hatcher includes an excellent section on documentation that should be required reading for every researcher (not just those preparing to publish a book).

Researchers will also benefit from a review of *The Chicago Manual of Style* or other style guides. Despite their limitations for genealogists, they show writers how to present information in clear, logical, and structured ways. Their discussions of the numerous considerations involved in writing will help the researcher evaluate the writing of others better. (Sometimes an understanding eye is necessary to temper critical evaluations.) Understanding how a writer presented his information promotes a better understanding and appreciation of the information, even if it has drawbacks or errors. For an excellent discourse on the necessity of clearly documenting genealogical origins, see Elizabeth Shown Mills's "Documentation for Journal Articles," *APG Quarterly* 4 (2): 32 to 36 (Summer 1989).

Copyright

Any discussion of printed sources would be incomplete without consideration of copyright law. Copyright is very important to the author, for it gives her four exclusive rights in regard to her creation (see Section 106 of the 1976 law). These include the rights to reproduce it in copies, to produce works derived from it, to distribute the copies, and to perform and display the work in public.

The convenience of photocopying has benefitted genealogists greatly, but photocopying creates the possibility of copyright infringement. Many books, including *The Source* (see pages 28 and 29 of the revised edition), discuss copyright, so a lengthy treatment is not needed here. However, a few comments on the 1978 revision of the copyright law are of value. This law was passed in 1976 and went into effect on 1 January 1978. Genealogists seem most interested in three aspects of this law: what can be copyrighted, the provision for "fair use," and the duration of copyright.

What Can Be Copyrighted. Copyright protection extends the rights noted above to the author of an "original" work, provided that it is set down in a tangible form permanent enough for it to be communicated over a period of time. Thus, an audio recording or written words can be copyrighted, but an unrecorded speech is not protected. The form of the expression (written, magnetic disc, audio- or videotape, etc.) can be copyrighted, but not the underlying idea, concept, or process.

Derivative works, such as a translation of a copyrighted work, can only be copyrighted if the owner of the original copyright permits such a work to be derived from his material. Private manuscripts in the possession of a repository belong to that repository (or to the donor, depending on the conditions of deposit). A transcription of such a document can only be copyrighted if the owner gives permission. Most archives and repositories will give permission if asked.

A compilation (a selection or arrangement) of preexisting materials can be copyrighted if it conveys new information and thereby becomes an original work of authorship. If the preexisting materials are themselves copyrighted, permission must be obtained if the new work is substantially based on an earlier work. It would be considered a "derivative work."

Public records, including U.S. and states government publications, cannot be copyrighted. Many of the original sources that genealogists use, such as census records, civil records, county land and probate records, and tax lists are public records. Many government publications are reprinted by private publishers; the familiar pamphlet *Where to Write for Vital Records* is an example. If such a reprint carries a copyright notice, it does not pertain to material copied from government publications. Rather, it can only apply to information added by the publisher, such as a preface or instructions.

Certain other printed works cannot be copyrighted. These include words and short phrases, variations of lettering or coloring, mere listings of contents or ingredients, ideas, plans, and methods. Genealogists should note that blank forms, such as order forms, research calendars, family group records, pedigree charts, and other "organizers," are also considered as not eligible for copyright (Johnston 1982, 205). That is because they are designed for recording information and do not, in themselves, convey information. Instructions and other information on a form may be copyrighted, however, so the best course is the cautious one: ask permission before copying substantial portions of another person's creation.

Another category of works that cannot be copyrighted include those consisting entirely of information that is common property, such as calendars, weight charts, and tables taken from public documents. Such works include no original authorship, even if the information is arranged in a different manner when they are recreated. Recently the Registrar of Copyrights has interpreted this rule to disallow copyright protection for transcriptions and even indexes to public records (such as censuses, wills, cemeteries, and similar material). This determination is of grave concern to genealogists, for if such works cannot be protected, publishers and compilers will be reluctant to continue publishing such material.

Fair Use of Copyright. The previously noted exclusive rights of copyright owners do not exclude the "fair use" of the work by others. Before the 1976 law, "fair use" was left up to the courts to determine on a case-by-case basis. Over the years, several precedents developed and Congress wrote the concept of "fair use" into the new law. In any discussion of fair use, it is helpful to have the text of the new law at hand. Following is the entire text of Section 107:

> **§107. Limitations on exclusive rights: Fair use**
>
> Notwithstanding the provisions of section 106 [which deals with the exclusive rights noted above], *the fair use of a copyrighted work*, including such use by reproduction in copies or phono records or by any other means specified by that section, *for purposes such as criticism, comment*, news reporting, teaching (including multiple copies for classroom use), *scholarship, or research, is not an infringement of copyright.* In determining whether the use made of a work in any particular case is a fair use the factors to be considered shall include—
>
> (1) the purpose and character of the use, including whether such use is of a commercial nature or is for nonprofit educational purposes;
>
> (2) the nature of the copyrighted work;
>
> (3) the amount and substantiality of the portion used in relation to the copyrighted work as a whole; and
>
> (4) the effect of the use upon the potential market for or value of the copyrighted work. (Emphasis added.)

Copies made by libraries and archives are addressed in Section 108 of the law. Most individuals have interpreted the above section to mean that researchers, including genealogists, may make copies of pertinent pages of a copyrighted book for their own scholarship or research, especially as it falls under provisions 1 and 3: it is for nonprofit educational use and comprises a non-substantial portion of the work. The law does not specify, in terms of percentages, how much is considered "substantial," but many commentators have suggested that 10 percent is usually not a substantial portion of a copyrighted work.

The important considerations are the four factors listed in the fair use section. Consider how the copied portion is going to be used—whether for commercial or nonprofit purposes. Determine the nature of the work being copied; some works, such as reference works or public speeches, invite a degree of fair use, while other items, such as unpublished letters, would seem to require a narrow interpretation of fair use. Therefore, one should give careful consideration to the amount of material being copied; do not copy excessive amounts from a copyrighted work.

The effect of the copy on the market for the original work may be the easiest to judge. If a book is out of print, copying a few pages should not have a detrimental effect on the market for the book. However, copying the entire book without permission, even if it is out of print, would probably affect the potential sales of a reprint. The market effect of copying a family history and or any of many other books related to genealogy could be even more substantial because relatively few such books are printed. (See "Publishers and Distributors," below, for suggestions about how to purchase copies of genealogical books.)

Opinions vary regarding the nature of copies made by professional researchers for their clients. On the one hand, their research is for commercial gain, which falls under the purpose or character of use guidelines. On the other hand, if the researcher does not benefit financially from the copies (by passing the costs on, without profit, to the client), one could argue that the copies do not represent a commercial gain. The prevailing attitude seems to be that if a professional genealogist copies a few pages from a work in the process of researching and reporting findings from many works, she has not copied a "substantial portion" of any one work, nor has any work become a substantial portion of the new creation. In addition, the "scholarship or research" clause could be invoked. In any event, copying an entire work, or substantial portions, seems much more likely to be a violation of the copyright law than copying a few pages to support research conclusions.

Duration of Copyright. The 1976 law provides copyright for any new work upon its creation, not just upon its publication. Formal registration of copyright is not required but is encouraged, however, for it is the easiest way to ensure protection. Any artistic work, including a written work, created since 1 January 1978 is under copyright from its creation until fifty years after the death of the author. Works made for hire (including corporate authorship) and anonymous works are protected for one hundred years after creation or seventy-five years from publication, whichever period is shorter.

Most printed sources that genealogists deal with (especially those they want to copy) were printed before 1978. The old law, as modified by the new law, still applies to the expiration date of those copyrights. A simplified explanation: Historically, works could be copyrighted for a term of twenty-eight years from publication and then renewed (if renewal was requested during the final year of the first term) for another term of twenty-eight years. The 1976 law extends any work in its renewal term to forty-seven years past the initial expiration date, *if the work was under copyright when the new law went into effect (1 January 1978)* (that is, was renewed in 1950 or later). The 1992 Copyright Renewal Law provided automatic renewal (for forty-seven years) of copyright for any books copyrighted in 1964 or later. Thus, these laws provide seventy-five years of protection from the first copyright date if renewals were made correctly. Anything over seventy-five years old is not under copyright and is considered in the "public domain," as are works whose copyright was not renewed when the first term expired.

Thus, any work published from 1964 through 1977 is protected by copyright *if* it carries the copyright symbol (©) or the word *copyright.* All works created since 1977 are protected (even without the symbol). If it is published, the work should be registered within five years of publication to be protected. A change in the 1976 law provides that works published after March 1989 do not need to carry the copyright symbol or statement to be protected, but its presence is highly desirable for the author's greatest protection against infringement.

Copyrighted works published before 1964 may still be protected if the copyright was renewed. Copyrights for most books of genealogical interest were not renewed (except for books published by larger publishing companies), but the researcher must still check to be sure. Most public and academic libraries have copyright renewal books that are arranged by year; search the year the first term expired (twenty-eight years after the publication) and the previous year, just to be thorough. If copyright was not renewed, the book is in the public domain.

The following table may be helpful for applying the previous rules to current conditions.

Date Book Published	*Copyright Status*
1978 and later	Still under copyright (should be registered within five years of publication)
1964 through 1977, with copyright statement	Still under copyright (automatically renewed)
Seventy-five years ago through 1963, with copyright statement	May have been renewed; add twenty-eight years to date and check
More than seventy-five years ago	Book in public domain, not under copyright

It must be emphasized that this discussion is not a lawyer's interpretation of copyright law. Rather, it seeks to give a general understanding of how the law protects both the copyright holder and the user in the exercise of their rights. For further information about copyright law, several books are available at public libraries, including Donald F. Johnson's *Copyright Handbook* (New York: R. R. Bowker Co., 1978); New York Law School Review, *The Complete Guide to the New Copyright Law* (Dayton, Ohio: Lorenz Press, 1977); William F. Patry's *The Fair Use Privilege in Copyright Law* (Washington, D.C.: Bureau of National Affairs, 1985); and *The New Copyright Law: Questions Teachers and Librarians Ask* (Washington, D.C.: National Education Association, 1977). Further information is available from The Copyright Clearance Center (CCC), 21 Congress Street, Salem, MA 01970. For a genealogical interpretation of the copyright law, see Daniel J. Hay's *The Copyright Reference Guide for Genealogists* (Bountiful, Utah: Advance Resources, 1993.)

LEARNING WHAT PRINTED SOURCES EXIST

This section discusses how to find out what printed sources exist. (Information on finding a source in a library is discussed below under "Effective Use of Libraries and Archives.") There are two basic types of tools that will indicate if a printed source pertaining to a topic exists: bibliographies and indexes. Each of these types of tools is treated in great depth throughout *Printed Sources*, and they are topics of separate chapters. However, it is useful to provide an overview here and to indicate what topics are covered and in which chapters. Also, the specific bibliographies and indexes associated with particular types of printed sources are thoroughly discussed in each chapter. See chapter 2 of *The Source*, "Databases, Indexes and other Finding Aids," for additional information. Here it is sufficient to review the different types of bibliographies and indexes. The relationships of these tools to other genealogical sources are discussed above in the section on "Categories of Research Sources and Tools."

Bibliographies

Simply put, A BIBLIOGRAPHY IS A LIST OF BOOKS OR SOURCES. Usually, the books in such a list have some common element. The list may include all the works of a particular author or, more commonly, a selection of books (and/or articles, dissertations, programs, or other works) having a common subject. The list can be a *comprehensive* bibliography, meaning that every source applicable to the subject is included in it. Bibliographies may include original or published sources, or both. A bibliography may exist as a list of sources cited in a book or as a separately published book. For a full discussion of bibliographies, see chapter 5, "Bibliographies and Catalogs." The foremost genealogical bibliography is P. William Filby's *American and British Genealogy and Heraldry: A Select List of Books.* A few specific types of bibliographies having genealogical applications are described below.

Library Catalogs. Many libraries have published catalogs of their books and other holdings. These are usually book publications, but the largest catalog of genealogical sources is the annual *Family History Library Catalog*™, the current edition of which is available for sale on more than 2,700 microfiche. Other library catalogs of genealogical value that have been published include *Genealogies in the Library of Congress, Local Histories in the Library of Congress,* the *DAR Library Catalog,* the *Dictionary Catalog of the Local History and Genealogy Division of the New York Public Library,* and *The Catalog of the American Antiquarian Society.* Each of these bibliographies lists some of the sources available at the particular library, according to the cataloging rules of the library. Generally, sources are listed in them by the author and/or title and the subject. In genealogical bibliographies, the subject of a book may be a personal or family name, thus creating a surname catalog.

Union Lists. A UNION LIST OR CATALOG IS A SPECIAL BIBLIOGRAPHY THAT ATTEMPTS TO INDICATE ALL OF THE LIBRARIES THAT HAVE COPIES OF THE SOURCES LISTED. Most union lists are cooperative ventures among libraries with common interests. Some union lists are subject specific, while some seek to be comprehensive or universal. The best-known union list is the Library of Congress's *National Union Catalog;* it includes most books published in the United States and many published in other countries. It is available in most libraries and is updated regularly on microfiche. The problem with comprehensive union lists is that their very nature makes them large, and it can be difficult to find information in them. Also, sources are only listed once, usually by the author, or, if no author is given, by the title; there is no subject access in most union lists.

Books in Print. To find books that are currently available for sale, turn to any of several sources that list books in print. Although they list only new (or still available) books, lists of books in print help resolve the problem of where to find certain books. Most are arranged by subject, author, and title, and some are arranged by publisher. The most common is *Books in Print*, which can be found in every library and book store. Genealogists should also refer to *Genealogical and Local History Books in Print* (issued irregularly; the fifth edition was published in 1996 and 1997).

Serials. A serial is issued on a regular basis by an institution or organization, without a predetermined final issue. Usually called periodicals (or magazines), serials often receive separate treatment in bibliographies. A comprehensive bibliography is *Union List of Serials*, followed (since 1961) by *New Serial Titles*. For a list of currently published serials see *Ulrich's Standard Periodical Directory*. For genealogical periodicals, see chapter 19, "Genealogical Periodicals."

Series. Usually a series is a group of related books issued by a publisher over a relatively short time (often one or two years), with a specific number of books planned for the series from the beginning. Series allow the publisher to market the books as a set, as they generally appeal to the same market. Sometimes several older, out-of-print books are reprinted as a series. Thus there is some subject orientation to a series issued by a single publisher.

Many bibliographies and catalogs fail to identify series. The best source is *Books in Series*. It includes, for example, entire series devoted to the history of one religious denomination, such as the Dutch Reformed Church, with lists of pastors and histories of congregations, or of one ethnic group, such as Italians. The books in such series can provide needed background information for successful research.

Statewide Bibliographies. Many statewide bibliographies have been published. Often they are intended to include everything that has been written about a state. They are especially good sources for lists of all the local histories written for a state or town of interest. The chapter bibliography in chapter 17, "County and Local Histories," lists many such bibliographies.

Computer Networks. Many libraries participate in computer library networks for the purpose of sharing the cataloging of their books. One library may enter the information about a book and assign it a call number. Any other library on the network can copy that information and add it to its catalog, thus saving the time and expense of cataloging the book itself. These networks are a boon to researchers; if a library does not have the book sought, the network can be queried to learn which libraries anywhere in the United States have it. Thus, such a network is a kind of universal union catalog. The two largest networks are OCLC (Online Computer Library Center), which serves several thousand (mostly public) libraries, and RLIN (Research Library Network), which serves several hundred (mostly academic) libraries. Consult a local librarian about using one of these networks.

Indexes

Indexes are another tool for learning that a source that may be of interest exists. Some indexes are associated with bibliographies (or lists of sources which they index), such as Munsell's *Index to American Genealogies*, while others, such as the *Genealogical Index of the Newberry Library*, simply cite the book in each reference in the index. Throughout *Printed Sources*, the authors describe the indexes that are available for the sources being discussed. In addition, refer to chapter 6, "Published Indexes," for a fuller discussion. Some of the major indexes for general genealogy topics are listed. They are discussed in the applicable chapters.

Many indexes will help the researcher find previously compiled genealogies—notably the *American Genealogical-Biographical Index*, *The Greenlaw Index of the New England Historic Genealogical Society*, and the *Genealogical Index of the Newberry Library* (see chapters 16 and 17). For biographical information, search Gale Research Company's *Genealogy and Biography Master Index* (see chapter 18). To find articles of interest in genealogical periodicals, check Jacobus's *Index to Genealogical Periodicals*, *Genealogical Periodical Annual Index (GPAI)*, or *Periodical Source Index (PERSI)* (chapter 19). An excellent index to published immigration and naturalization indexes is Filby's *Passenger and Immigration Lists Index* (chapter 14). County and local histories are often indexed at the state level, but do not overlook the *Library of Congress Index to Biographies in State and Local Histories* (chapter 17). Each of these sources, and many other indexes, is described in the appropriate chapters of *Printed Sources*.

Bibliographies and indexes are vital, but researchers can learn about helpful sources in many other ways. Members of genealogical societies receive information through society periodicals and their members. A local library may have a "new book review shelf" where recent acquisitions are displayed, and publishers will send copies of their catalogs upon request.

Finally, many researchers have found that they cannot possibly know about every book of interest. Therefore, begin research by assuming that a book exists. Then try to find out, through the sources listed above and throughout *Printed Sources*, if one really does exist. This is a reversal of the usual process of determining what sources exist, but it forces the researcher to think about what has been found elsewhere, and to apply that thinking to new situations. If a book about silversmiths in Ohio exists, it is just as likely that one may exist for silversmiths in Virginia. And the fact that a local library does not list it in its catalog or that it is not in a bibliography is no reason to give up. Further searches will prove that one does exist.

PUBLISHERS AND DISTRIBUTORS

Any discussion of printed sources must include information about those to whom we are indebted for these sources. Without publishers and distributors there would be no such sources, and genealogical research would be much more difficult. In addition to providing the sources, publishers and distributors are a solution to the question discussed above: Where can that book be found?

Publishers

According to the 1996-97 edition of *Publishers, Distributors, and Wholesalers of the United States,* approximately eighty-six thousand companies are actively involved in publishing and distributing books in the United States. The number of them that are heavily involved in genealogical publishing is hard to determine, for the publisher of the above directory (Bowker) does not provide such specifics. However, a sister publication, the 1997 edition of *Literary Market Place*, the bible of booksellers, lists only forty-nine publishers under "Genealogy." In January 1983, the *APG Newsletter* included a list of approximately 180 genealogical publishers. (It was reprinted in the first edition of *The Source.*) The majority of these were what the publishing industry calls "small presses," and many of them were small companies that produced only a very few titles. Although many of them will not have survived through the intervening years, it is safe to assume that many more will have appeared. The best current list of publishers that have a significant focus on the genealogy market is the seventy-one companies in the third edition (1995) of Elizabeth Bentley's *The Genealogist's Address Book.* However, this list, as well as the list in appendix C, does not include most societies, libraries, and other groups whose primary focus is not in publishing.

Even some of these publishers do not rely solely on the genealogical market, which has proved to be small. Some have connections to a university or a historical society; some are community presses that are used by genealogists and others publishing on a small scale. In fact, there are only around twenty-five publishers that have any prominence in genealogical circles. Unfortunately, even many of them do not meet the standards set by publishers in other fields:

> Most genealogical publishing companies . . . appear to operate with little capital, and rather than seek subsidies to publish quality works, have decided on small press runs of hundreds of titles of indifferent quality for quick sale. Ideally, genealogists, librarians, archivists, and local historians should check such publications against the original records before purchasing or recommending such books and should demand greater reliability from the transcribers and a sound review process by the publishers (Horle 1992, 291).

Genealogical publishers tend to focus their efforts on one or two types of publications, such as reprints, family histories, reference books, and others. Knowing which publishers specialize in what kinds of books helps determine where to turn when seeking a specific book. Some of these different types of publications, and some publishers associated with them, are mentioned below (complete addresses are given in appendix C).

Reprints. Genealogy has grown tremendously in popularity over the last two decades. Many sources that were published a generation or two ago are still useful but were published in limited quantities and soon became unavailable. As more and more libraries have developed collections, and as the number of practicing genealogists (amateur and professional) has grown, the need for reprints of older works has become apparent. Many publishers focus on this important aspect of printed sources. Among them are the Genealogical Publishing Company, Heritage Books, The Reprint Company, Southwest Pennsylvania Genealogical Services, and University Microfilms International (UMI).

Family Histories. While most family histories today are "kitchen table" productions, some authors have sought publishers to help them put their histories into print. Usually they turn to vanity or subsidy presses (publishers that require the author to pay all of the costs and generally take care of the distribution). However, a few publishers, among them Higginson Books, Gateway Press, Family History Publishers, and Penobscot Press, have chosen to pursue the family history market.

Instructional Reference Books. The growing popularity of genealogy has also led to the increased publication of books that treat research methodology. These range from the standard "how-to" books to books that describe specific record types or repositories. Since 1984, Ancestry has become the leader in the field with this type of publication. Other publishers of instructional material include The Everton Publishers and Genealogical Publishing Company.

Source Books. The largest category of books being published in genealogy in recent years is composed of those which are source oriented. Source books provide information from actual records, such as names, dates, and relationships. The very existence of this book, *Printed Sources*, attests to the growth of source books and their importance in genealogy. Indexes to sources are included in this category. Many publishers are active in publishing source books, including Closson Press, Family Line Publications, Genealogical Publishing Company, Heritage Books, Kinship, Southern Historical Press, and TLC Genealogy.

County Histories. As noted in chapter 17, "County and Local Histories," there has been increased interest in county histories since 1960. In addition, many county histories from the nineteenth century have been reprinted. Some publishers focus their efforts on such publications, although local presses get the lion's share of such business. Among genealogical publishers, the following are active in this area: Anundsen Publishing Company, Curtis Media Corporation, Taylor Publishing Company, and Whipoorwill.

Library Reference Books. Many of the major references genealogists use are not produced specifically for genealogists; these include major directories and indexes and virtually all of the sources described in chapter 1, "General Reference." Many important reference books are produced for general library use by some of the United States' most prominent reference publishers. Some of these major publishers include Gale Research Company, G. K. Hall, Libraries Unlimited, ABC Clio Information Services, Scarecrow Press, Greenwood, Oryx Press, and Scholarly Resources.

How to Purchase Printed Sources

While most researchers simply find the books they want at libraries and research centers, others want to buy certain books for permanent home use. Unfortunately, neighborhood bookstores generally carry very few genealogical books, and they cannot easily order most such books because they are not published by trade publishers (the source of most bookstore books) or are out of print. However, there are many sources to turn to before asking a local bookstore to order a book.

Most printed sources that might be of interest are no longer in print—the books printed have been sold and no supplier has copies for sale. Out-of-print books are hard to find, and most books more than five to ten years old are out of print. (This is especially true of genealogical sources. An 1895 county history is certain to be out of print). Many books are reprinted at some point, including some county histories, but most family histories remain out of print. The best sources for such books are antiquarian dealers (discussed below) and "micro-reprinters," such as UMI.

The first step in locating any genealogical book is to find a genealogical book dealer or distributor—sometimes known as a vendor. The number of genealogical vendors is even more difficult to determine than the number of publishers. Many are very small and are not reported in the book trade literature. The forty-first edition of *American Book Trade Directory* (New York: Bowker, 1995–96) lists only ten genealogy dealers. This situation seems due to the fact that most genealogical distributors handle genealogy only as a side item and thus are listed under other topics. Of course, every publisher is a dealer, but many carry only their own books. However, there are thousands of persons and societies that deal with genealogical books. The 1985 edition of *Genealogical and Local History Books in Print* listed more than 3,600 vendors, most of which were self-publishers.

In fact, *Genealogical and Local History Books in Print* is the source to consult first. It attempts to list all books and microforms available for purchase that pertain to genealogy (except National Archives publications). However, because vendors must pay to list their book(s), some choose not to be included. The fourth edition, issued in 1985, lists more than thirty thousand genealogical sources for sale. This book lists items by topic, locality, and surname and gives a complete description of the book and its price. Each vendor is assigned a number, and each book description includes the vendor number. A list of vendors (ordered only by number, not by name or state) is in the front of the book. It is not possible to look up a specific vendor unless a book it sells is known; the vendor number can then be obtained from the book listing. Supplements issued in 1990 and 1992 each list approximately three thousand additional titles.

In 1995, the Genealogical Publishing Company acquired the rights to *Genealogical and Local History Books in Print*. In 1996 and 1997 it issued the four volumes of the fifth edition. The family history volume alone lists more than 4,600 titles. Earlier editions of this work are also important to researchers, for only around half of the listings in any edition are repeated in the next edition. The first edition was published in 1975, followed by others in 1977, 1981, and 1985.

A study of the vendors listed in this book and some of those on the records of the Family History Library suggests that there are roughly six different types of genealogical distributors. It is important to understand each kind, for seldom will the researcher find every book of interest through any one dealer. (Major vendors are listed in appendix C.)

Publishers. As mentioned above, virtually all publishers are distributors. Most sell only their own books, but some large ones, notably Ancestry, also sell a fairly large number of books by other publishers, including major genealogical publishers and small self-publishers. The publishers are usually the best sources for the major new publications that are noted so frequently in the periodical literature. Publishers that specialize in reprints can be good sources to inquire about the availability of older books that have the potential to be reprinted.

Genealogical Bookstores. These include more than the twenty or so bookstores listed in the trade literature. Practically every major population center has one or two bookstores that include genealogy as a specialty. Such bookstores may not advertise the fact in the yellow pages, but a search can begin there. The more sure way to learn about these stores is to talk to local genealogists, participate in genealogical societies, and attend local genealogical conferences and seminars. After purchasing a book or two, or even just expressing an interest, a customer will generally be added to the stores' mailing lists and will be regularly updated on available titles. Some stores have even begun including their catalogs on their own Internet sites.

Antiquarian Dealers. Antiquarian book dealers are the best sources for out-of-print books because they specialize in finding such books—generally those of a historical nature. Antiquarian book dealers are not simply sellers of used books that recycle best sellers from the past decade or two; rather, they are professional "book hounds" who buy old collections from estates, private individuals, libraries, and other sources. They produce catalogs every few months listing the titles available and generally maintain a "want list" for clients who are seeking specific books. There is no charge to be placed on an antiquarian dealer's list, but the law of supply and demand takes effect. If a dealer finds the desired title, it may not be cheap. Their prices reflect higher-than-normal overhead costs and the maintenance of a specialized, uncommon inventory. Most antiquarian dealers will look for a specific title upon request, but certain ones, such as Tuttle Antiquarian Books, specialize in genealogical books.

Societies. Genealogists can usually find books of interest through historical, patriotic (hereditary), and genealogical societies. Societies are noteworthy as book dealers because they often publish books. Generally they sell only the books that they publish, but some act as distributors for other titles related to their interests as a means of raising money. Often books published by a society remain available for many years because they are of limited interest outside the society and most of the demand is met through pre-publication orders. Because societies almost always print more copies than were ordered, there may still be copies of a bicentennial town history, for example, in a closet at the local historical society. Always inquire of local societies for any books published by them or related to their interests. Addresses change frequently, but many directories are available at public libraries. Seek societies in the *Encyclopedia of Associations*, *Directory of Historical Societies and Agencies*, and *Meyer's Directory of Genealogical Societies*. (See chapter 1, "General Reference," for more information on these and other directories.)

Individuals. Most genealogical vendors are individuals. Many authors, discouraged by the relatively low royalties offered by genealogical publishing companies, decide to publish and market their books themselves. While it is difficult to weigh the value of an aggressive publisher/distributor, many authors produce books that no publisher can use; their quality may not be good enough or the audience may be too limited. In such cases, the author is often forced to publish the book himself if he wants to see his efforts in print.

Individuals sometimes publish under their own names, or they may publish under another name, such as "Old West Publishing Company." Generally it is easier to locate a publisher who uses her own name; even if she moves, telephone directories can be used to find her. If it is suspected that a publisher's name is no more than an individual's business name, check the directories of publishers at a library and the yellow pages in the city where the book was published. If the publisher's name does not appear in those sources, it is likely the business name of a sole proprietor. In such cases, assume the author to be the publisher and look for her in telephone books and other sources. Because many such authors are avid genealogists, more recent addresses for them might be found in the numerous research exchange lists available today, such as Everton Publishers' "Root Cellar" (published in *Everton's Genealogical Helper*—see chapter 19, "Periodicals") or the Family History Library's Ancestral File™ (see chapter 16 for more information). Also, contact national and local genealogical societies which the author may belong to.

Micro-Publishers. Advances in microform technology have been of great benefit to researchers in the last few years. Today many sources are available on microfilm or microfiche that were inaccessible just five or ten years ago. Generically called microform, this type of reprinting allows low cost, on-demand reprints to be purchased by an institution or individual. While many institutions that microfilm their records (like the Family History Library) do not make their microform available for sale, some commercial companies are doing just that.

One of the major micro-publishers of printed genealogical sources is UMI in Ann Arbor, Michigan. Ranging from works that have recently gone out of print to books of many years past, the titles listed in UMI's catalogs are selections from approximately 200,000 out-of-print rare books stored as masters. Titles of family histories and genealogies are listed alphabetically by family name; state, local, and military records are listed alphabetically by states. UMI can reprint and deliver books within thirty days with soft- or hardcover bindings. For those in need of out-of-print reference books, UMI is a good source. Many sources are listed in the *UMI Guide to Family and Local Histories,* 3 vols. (Ann Arbor, Mich.: UMI, 1990, 1993, 1995). UMI also administers the Genealogy and Local History Program, formerly run by Microfilming Corporation of America. It is similar to the above service except that the books offered are on microfiche only; no paper copies are available. Acquiring micro-published copies is an especially useful way for libraries to increase their collections of genealogies and family histories.

REPOSITORIES OF PRINTED SOURCES

A tremendous advantage of printed sources is that, because they exist in printed form, they are available in many places. While genealogical books do not make the *New York Times* bestseller list (Alex Haley's *Roots* was a novel—mostly fiction—and not a true genealogical book; see Elizabeth Shown Mills and Gary B. Mills's "The Genealogist's Assessment of Alex Haley's *Roots,*" *NGS Quarterly* 72 [March 1984]: 35–39), and they are not printed in the hundreds of thousands, they are generally easier to find than are original sources (even on microfilm). The number of copies of a genealogical work that a publisher prints will vary greatly depending on the scope and coverage of the book and the perceived demand for the information. If the first printing sells out quickly, the publisher will order additional printings. First printings of genealogical books generally run between five hundred and three thousand copies, although individuals publishing their own books may print only two hundred to three hundred copies. Sales of a genealogical "best seller" seldom total more than twenty thousand to thirty thousand copies. However, consider a smaller book of only regional interest that may sell only five hundred copies. Perhaps half will be sold to private individuals and half to various repositories (libraries, archives, and others). Most of those 250 copies in repositories will probably be in a ten-state area, with an average of twenty-five copies per state. The researcher's task is to learn which library has a copy of the desired book.

A genealogical repository is simply a place in which genealogical sources are kept and used. There are many different repositories for printed sources; it is essential to understand and use each type of repository. They include public libraries, archives, special and private libraries, academic libraries, societies, rental libraries, law libraries, and LDS family history centers. ("Finding Genealogical Repositories," below, discusses how to find out about these libraries and their collections.) While many libraries fit into two or more of these categories, they are generally created to fill certain needs, and the purpose, or mission, of each determines what kind of library it is. Within each category is a wide variety of libraries. Each category contains major research libraries, as well as minor ones of regional value to the genealogist. Virtually every state has at least one library that is a major repository for printed genealogical sources—if not for the entire United States then at least for that state and likely the surrounding region. Major genealogical libraries are listed in appendix B.

Public Libraries

For most researchers, the closest library is the local public library, an often-overlooked place for genealogical research. Public libraries are supported by local tax dollars; one may serve a city, or county, or several cities and counties. Their collections reflects the needs and requests of local populations (and the budgets they get from governing agencies). Almost all public libraries have some of the major reference books discussed throughout *Printed Sources*, especially directories, bibliographies, and indexes. Public libraries are also the most involved in interlibrary loan programs and are the most likely sources to obtain obscure books on loan from other libraries.

In addition, most public libraries collect extensive information about their communities. Many have local history collections that include books found in few other places. Public libraries may also be closely tied to local historical and/or genealogical societies and may even house the collections of those societies. Some of the largest and most important genealogical research libraries are public libraries that have developed major genealogical collections. These include the New York Public Library, the Allen County (Indiana) Public Library, the Odom Library (Moultrie, Georgia), and the public libraries in Detroit, Dallas, Los Angeles, and Independence, Missouri.

Special and Private Libraries

Special libraries exist to serve specific clienteles. Their collections are very narrow in scope but deep in coverage within that scope. Usually they are affiliated with private institutions or companies. (Most major companies have small special libraries that focus on topics of interest to the company, such as chemical sources or financial information.)

Private libraries are much like special libraries; in fact, most special libraries are privately owned, and most private libraries usually function as special libraries by focusing their collections on a few topics.

Several excellent special and private libraries exist to serve genealogists and historical researchers. Some of the major special libraries of interest to genealogists include that of the American Antiquarian Society in Massachusetts, the Newberry Library in Chicago, and the Family History Library in Salt Lake City.

Societies

Societies are organizations of people who have similar interests. They exist to serve numerous purposes, including social, educational, research, fraternal, and financial. Genealogists are most often involved with historical and/or genealogical societies. Many societies sponsor libraries to serve their members, and in a very real sense these are special or private libraries because they belong to the organization. At the same time, most such organizations are public societies with national or state charters, and many of them receive some form of public funding through state or local budgets or national grants. In this sense their libraries can be considered public libraries, except that their collections are focused on specific items. Many local societies work jointly with local public libraries to reduce duplication of services and titles and so do not have separate libraries. Others cooperate with local public libraries but keep separate collections that are housed in the same buildings as the public libraries. In such cases the special collection only includes specialized sources in the field of the society's interest, while the general sources, such as directories and bibliographies, are part of the public library collection.

Three types of societies sponsor libraries having genealogical and historical emphases: historical, genealogical, and hereditary. Most states have both state historical societies and state genealogical societies. In some states the two are combined, but most often the state historical society is the larger organization; it usually houses the library and may receive some funding from the state. These libraries, sometimes combined with state libraries and/or archives, are major research centers in each state.

In addition, most of the more than three thousand counties in the United States and Canada, and most of the major cities, have county historical and/or genealogical societies. They, too, often sponsor libraries, although they are more likely to be associated with local public libraries; their collections help to make local public libraries important centers for genealogical research. The major societies with genealogical interests are listed in appendixes C and E of *The Source* (revised edition). Some of the societies that sponsor major libraries include the New England Historic Genealogical Society in Boston, the National Genealogical Society, the Daughters of the American Revolution (DAR) in Washington, D.C., the Case Western Reserve Historical Society in Cleveland, Ohio, the state historical societies of Minnesota, Montana, Pennsylvania, and Wisconsin, and the Sons of the American Revolution in Louisville.

State Libraries

Virtually every state sponsors a state library. These are wholly funded by the states and are in that sense public libraries. The scope and nature of these libraries varies greatly from one state to another, depending to a large extent on other resources in the state, such as the state archive and/or historical society. A state archive or historical society may operate the library or assume the major functions of a library, such as the housing and maintenance of a major book collection. However, where the state library actually functions as a library, it is a major resource for genealogists. Typically the library will seek to collect virtually anything published by or about the state, making it a good place to find obscure local histories and published copies of local records. Thus, such a library's catalog will be a virtually exhaustive bibliography of sources for the state. State libraries have also often sponsored the creation of major indexes and other research tools. In addition, many state libraries, such as the Connecticut State Library, have collected the published family histories of families who lived in that state. Several state libraries have genealogy sections with well-trained librarians. Examples include the New York and New Jersey state libraries, as well as the Sutro branch of the California State Library in San Francisco. The Library of Congress in Washington, D.C., is a kind of state (Federal) library; it houses one of the largest genealogical collections in the world.

Academic Libraries

Academic libraries are affiliated with colleges and universities and are perhaps the most underutilized repositories for genealogical research. While they exist to serve the college and university population and generally do not collect purely genealogical information, many of the sources discussed in *Printed Sources* can be found in academic libraries. Because the mission of an academic library is to support the curriculum of a college or university, it will obtain publications in the fields where the college or university offers degrees; history is almost always one of those areas.

Generally, academic libraries have few local histories for places outside their geographic areas. However, sources for their states, areas, or regions are often well represented in their collections. In addition, they have many of the finding aids that genealogists are interested in, such as bibliographies, indexes, periodical abstracting services, directories, and encyclopedias. In fact, their collections usually have greater reference value than local public libraries, especially if the academic library is in a relatively small "college" town. Some of the academic libraries with especially helpful collections for genealogists include the Lee Library at Brigham Young University in Provo, Utah, the Eugene Barker Texas History Center at the University of Texas at Austin, and Columbia University in New York.

The Federal government designates libraries (usually academic libraries) in each state to receive copies of published Federal records. These libraries are known as Federal Depository Libraries or Government Document Libraries. In most states there are several such libraries in private as well as public universities. Most of them are selective depositories and only receive certain documents. In each state one or two libraries are designated as regional depositories; they receive a much more extensive collection of government documents. Government publications include a wide variety of information, such as pension lists, private land claims, veterans burial lists, and individuals' petitions to Congress. The government documents librarian at a local university library can help researchers learn more about its important collections. However, because these libraries do not routinely support genealogical research, they may provide only limited assistance in using their large collections.

Also not to be overlooked at academic libraries are the law libraries that support the curriculums of university law schools. As discussed in chapter 12, "Court and Legal Records," these libraries house significant sources that the average family historian typically overlooks. Not only do they have printed court reports for their states and regions, but they may have national reports as well. In addition, they have copies of the state laws that affected our ancestors, as well as private relief laws passed by the states on behalf of individuals.

Rental Libraries

The growing number of rental libraries that serve genealogists represent another kind of private library. They have developed in response to the fact that many genealogists do their research at home and are not able to travel to major repositories. Rental libraries are also a response to the fact that, as important as local public, academic, and state libraries are, they lack many sources of interest to genealogists, and they seldom have sources for places outside their geographic areas. Rental libraries are run by individuals for profit (though the profit may amount to little). These individuals collect genealogical books (including local histories) and lend them via mail for a fee. Generally they publish catalogs or lists of available books which include bibliographic descriptions of the books, a brief annotation for each, and the rental fees. In many cases the fee also serves as a security deposit for the book. Thus, a rental library might charge twenty dollars for a county history, refunding 75 percent of the fee after the book is returned in good condition. The actual rental fee would be five dollars, which would go toward overhead, new additions to the collection, and a small profit.

These libraries provide a great service to genealogists by providing hard-to-find books at reasonable prices. However, the books they offer may be available elsewhere at lower cost, such as a nearby library, through interlibrary loan, or at a family history center (see below). One of the preeminent rental libraries is the Hoenstine Library (Hollidaysburg, Pennsylvania). Its catalog, with more than 2,700 sources for Pennsylvania research, includes an index to the surnames in most of the books. Other rental libraries are run by the National Genealogical Society, New England Historic Genealogical Society, American Genealogical Lending Library, and the Genealogical Center Library in Atlanta. These and many others advertise regularly in *Everton's Genealogical Helper* (published by The Everton Publishers, P.O. Box 368, Logan, Utah 84323).

Family History Centers

The more than 2,500 LDS family history centers throughout the world are unique repositories of genealogical sources. Microfilm and microfiche copies of the records held by the Family History Library can be borrowed through family history centers for a small handling fee, allowing LDS church members and the public to use the resources of the Family History Library without having to travel to Salt Lake City.

Family history centers have been established in almost every LDS stake (a group of six to twelve "wards," or congregations) throughout the United States and in dozens of foreign countries. Generally in or near large population centers, they are branches of the Family History Library in Salt Lake City and are therefore like special or private libraries, but they also operate somewhat like rental libraries (although they are not for profit). Areas of greater LDS population, such as the western United States, have more family history centers.

Each is equipped with microfilm and microfiche reading machines, a copy of the *Family History Library Catalog,* and other major indexes, such as the International Genealogy Index, Accelerated Indexing System's census indexes, and the *Periodical Source Index* (*PERSI*). Through these centers patrons can use the library's resources and request copies of sources not immediately available. In addition, each center has a small collection of reference books. Many printed sources are under copyright; in most such cases, the Family History Library cannot microfilm them. However, because of the size of the collection and the fact that many of the most difficult-to-find printed sources are older books in the public domain, such as county histories, most books that the researcher is seeking will be available on microfilm or microfiche.

Proselyting is not allowed in family history centers; approximately half of those who use them are not members of the LDS church. For more information on family history centers and the Family History Library, see appendix D in *The Source* (revised edition). A list of family history centers can be obtained from the Family History Library, 35 North West Temple, Salt Lake City, Utah, 84150. Some of the older, larger family history centers have collected several thousand books and hundreds of rolls of microfilm. Some of these "regional" libraries are found in or near the cities of San Diego, Los Angeles, Oakland, and Sacramento, California; Phoenix, Arizona; Provo and Logan, Utah; Las Vegas, Nevada; Calgary (Alberta), Canada; and Pocatello and Rexburg, Idaho.

Archives

Most genealogists think of archives as repositories of original (or microfilmed) records; this is true, but many archives also have reasonably good collections of printed sources. Many printed sources are necessary for the efficient use of original records—census indexes, for example. Archives generally have such secondary and tertiary information as is needed for using their collections. In the United States, archives are generally found at the national or state level. County courthouses are types of local archives, but their collections of printed sources are usually very limited.

The Library of Congress in Washington, D.C., can be considered an archive and library. One of its functions is to collect copies of most books published in America and others that deal with the United States. It also serves as the research library for the U.S. Congress and the Federal government, which necessitates a large collection of books and other printed sources. The United States National Archives, in Washington, D.C., has some printed sources of interest. In addition, consider the thirteen regional archives of the National Archives. They are located in or near Anchorage, Alaska; Atlanta, Georgia; Boston; Chicago; Denver; Fort Worth, Texas; Kansas City, Missouri; Los Angeles; New York; Philadelphia; Pittsfield, Massachusetts; San Francisco; and Seattle.

EFFECTIVE USE OF LIBRARIES AND ARCHIVES

In addition to learning about printed sources, including how to find and evaluate them, it is important to know how to use libraries. Libraries are the best places to find printed sources, and a researcher who does not understand a library's collection or services will not find the information sought as easily as possible. Researchers need to be aware of a library's general services, its catalog, any inventories, guides, or handbooks, and interlibrary loan service.

Finding Genealogical Repositories

There are almost as many sources to help locate libraries and archives as there are types of repositories. Several directories are available that list specific types of libraries or organizations, generally geographically. These directories can direct researchers to libraries in nearby towns and cities. In addition, repositories in the areas where an ancestor lived often have collections of value. Many researchers plan all or part of a family or personal vacation to visit the areas and repositories where ancestors lived. Always begin with the local public library. It can assist in locating these and other archives and libraries and may have a surprisingly useful collection itself.

The genealogical collections and services of more than 1,500 public, university, and private libraries, state archives, historical societies, and other libraries are described in P. William Filby's *Directory of American Libraries with Genealogy or Local History Collections* (Wilmington, Del.: Scholarly Resources, 1988). Through a survey, Filby queried each library about its major reference books and collections, thus learning the nature and scope of the genealogical collections of most major libraries in America. Thus, this directory can help determine if a specific library has a significant genealogical collection. Additional indexes in Filby's directory pinpoint libraries that have major collections of out-of-state material. The information given for each library includes the hours of operation and the genealogical expertise of its staff, in addition to the address and telephone number. Once the user understands how to use the information from the survey, it is a valuable tool for finding repositories of printed sources.

Another useful source designed for the genealogist is Bentley's *The Genealogist's Address Book*. It lists most societies, libraries, archives, and periodicals that genealogists might be interested in. Its library entries are not as detailed as those in Filby's directory and many of the addresses are out of date, but it is an inexpensive reference that most genealogists can afford to have in their personal collections.

The following directories should be available at local libraries. The most comprehensive source for libraries is the annual *American Library Directory*, compiled by the R. R. Bowker Company. This directory lists more than thirty-five thousand public, academic, government, and special libraries in the United States and Canada. Within each state or province, cities are listed alphabetically; each library is listed under the city where it is located. Information given includes the name, address, telephone number, and a brief description of the library, such as the size of its collection, any special collections it has, and its publications and other interests. A directory of many archives and manuscript collections is the National Historical Publications and Records Commission's *Directory of Archives and Manuscript Repositories in the United States*, 2nd ed. (1988). In addition to giving a brief description of approximately 4,500 archives, it notes the major manuscript collections of many of the archives.

Addresses of local historical societies are listed in Betty P. Smith's *Directory, Historical Societies and Agencies in the United States and Canada*, 13th ed. (1986). Arranged by state and thereunder by city, this gives the name, address, telephone number, staff size, and collection information for more than six thousand local historical societies, including every state and most county historical societies. Libraries run by each society and periodicals published by them are also given. Another directory of societies of particular interest to genealogists is Mary K. Meyer's biannual *Meyer's Directory of Genealogical Societies in the U.S.A and Canada*, 11th ed. (Mt. Airy, Md., 1996). This edition lists approximately 1,600 societies. Within each state, societies are listed by their names rather than by location. (Many societies did not return the registration information and are listed with only their addresses, but complete information is provided for four hundred societies.) In addition to their names and addresses there is information on the societies' memberships, publications, projects, and library facilities (if any).

Library Services

Libraries exist to serve their patrons. Usually, they are supported by tax dollars and therefore have to give equal treatment to the entire public. Every library, however, has rules regarding the treatment of its materials and can deny service to persons who do not treat the materials with care. Do not deface, tear, cut, write on, or in any other way damage library materials. Above all, never remove materials from a library in violation of any library policy. It is a sad fact that some patrons damage or steal library books. Unfortunately, many librarians believe (perhaps not without cause) that genealogists are more guilty of such sins than many other patrons. After all, genealogists often refer to books as having "my ancestors" in them. For some, it is a small step from this thought to the belief that they have some "right" to a book because "nobody else is interested in my family" or "I'm the only one who has all the correct information" or "it's out of print and the library has a microfilm copy of it anyway."

Some of the best research libraries are not public libraries; they do not have to allow the public to use their collections. The fact that they do allow public use should be met with gratitude. After all, such libraries are rendering all genealogists a great service. If a library one uses regularly is operated by a private society or foundation, it may be beneficial, in more than one sense, to join the society. Often, membership allows access to the collection at reduced rates (such as the DAR or National Genealogical Society libraries). Further, membership in a library's governing society provides more operating funds for the library and may allow members some voice in library matters. Many public libraries have a "Friends of the Library" society that can provide tremendous support politically and socially, as well as economically. Participation is a great way to "give something back" for all that we receive from libraries and archives.

Libraries offer many services to their patrons, which may include copying facilities, computer terminals, classes on research sources and methodology, reference consultation, brief correspondence replies, lists of professional researchers, and library publications. Most libraries have brief guides to their services that are available on request. A researcher who is planning to visit a library that she is not familiar with should contact its staff in advance to learn about the library's services and hours. It is frustrating to travel to a distant library only to learn that it is closed for a state holiday, remodeling, or some other reason. In addition, the researcher might learn when the library is less crowded (for instance, in the evenings or in the winter months when fewer persons travel) or if there is special information he should take to make his research most efficient.

In addition to rules about the treatment of their collections, libraries have other rules that make research more pleasant for all. The following rules apply to virtually all libraries:

- Do not smoke in any library, even in the restroom.
- Food is generally restricted in libraries. It may be allowed in a snack room, but do not take it into the research areas.
- Do not "hog" materials, such as books, microfilm, or microfilm readers.
- Allow others to use photocopy machines.
- Protect personal belongings. Libraries cannot be responsible for lost or stolen materials, and we know how precious our genealogical findings are.
- Maintain a quiet research atmosphere for all. Do not allow young children to distract others with their noise or activity.
- Limit talking in research areas.

In addition, many research libraries:

- Limit the amount of material that can be copied at one time or in one day.
- Offer locker rentals.
- Limit how long one person can use a microfilm reader or computer. (One might need to request the use of such resources in advance.)
- Allow only paper and pencils (no pens, briefcases, and so forth) in research areas.
- Have age restrictions for children.

Finally, be ready to leave when closing time approaches. Respect these and all other rules; observing them helps to protect the valuable records that are our collective heritage, and may change the attitudes of some librarians (a minority) who hold a certain disdain for genealogists.

Library Catalogs

The key to any library is its catalog, so it is essential to understand how catalogs work. In most libraries, every book or other item (microfilm, manuscript, periodical, etc.) in the collection is listed in the catalog. It may be a card catalog, a computer catalog, or some other variety. Materials are almost always arranged in the catalog by the author; usually the titles and subjects of the books are also listed. Some genealogical library catalogs also list materials according to the geographic emphasis of their contents (a type of subject listing). Most library catalogs are surprisingly similar in structure and usage. Do not hesitate to use libraries' catalogs; researchers cannot be successful without them. Also, never hesitate to ask librarians for assistance. Librarians realize that catalogs can be overwhelming to many users and are trained to assist them. In addition, many libraries have printed instructions to aid patrons in using their catalogs.

While a library's catalog usually includes all the items in the library's collection, it will not list or index every name in each publication. Most books are listed only by author, title, and two or three subjects. Family histories (genealogies) are listed under the surname of the main family discussed in the book and possibly two or three other major surnames in the book. Only in very rare cases are genealogies listed under more than six surnames, yet these books may include hundreds of surnames and thousands of persons. Other tools are available to help find information in these books; they are described in chapter 16, "Family Histories and Genealogies."

Most libraries use the Dewey Decimal Classification System or the Library of Congress (LC) Classification System to assign the call numbers and hence shelf placement for their books. Learn how these systems work; a brief overview is in chapter 1, "General Reference." If dealing with a library that uses a different system, be sure to ask the librarian for an explanation. Some libraries, such as the Family History Library, have modified one of the major systems to better fit their collections. Subject headings used in catalogs generally come from one of two similar systems: most libraries use either the Library of Congress Subject Headings or Sears Subject Headings to determine if a book is listed under "Automobiles" or "Cars." Fortunately, most catalogs have "see" and "see also" cross-references which direct the user to the proper (see) heading or alternate/related (see also) headings.

Some major libraries have published the genealogical and/or local history portions of their catalogs. Such publications allow much greater access to the material in the library and also act as excellent genealogical bibliographies. These are discussed in greater detail in chapter 1, "General Reference," and chapter 16, "Family Histories and Genealogies." Of course, as soon as a catalog is published it is slightly out of date because the library continues to receive new books. However, such catalogs (sometimes called "shelf lists") are a great help because they allow researchers to determine which libraries have certain books.

Some of the major organizations which have published catalogs of parts of their genealogy and local history collections include the New York Public Library, American Antiquarian Society, New England Historic Genealogical Society, DAR Library, Newberry Library, Library of Congress, Sutro Library, Swarthmore College Friends Historical Library, and Long Island Historical Society (see appendix B for addresses). A local library may have some of these published catalogs. The Family History Library publishes its entire catalog on microfiche each year, thus avoiding the datedness associated with printed catalogs. The *Family History Library Catalog* can be purchased in whole or in part by individuals and institutions. It is also available in CD-ROM format as part of the *FamilySearch*® system at 2,500 family history centers and at many other genealogical libraries.

Inventories, Guides, Handbooks

A library's catalog may be the key to its collection, but other tools are available to help the user learn about specific parts of a library and its holdings. Most archives have inventories, guides, handbooks, or periodicals that describe their records and how to use them. If possible, study these guides before visiting an archive in order to make the most effective use of the time available. Many of these are available at public or academic libraries or through interlibrary loan. These sources differ from catalogs in that they do not list every item in a collection; rather, they describe entire groups of materials within a library's collections.

There are similarities between inventories, guides, and handbooks, so many authors use the terms interchangeably. However, there are subtle differences. Inventories (or calendars) typically list or briefly describe all or most of the individual items in a specific collection, such as Papers of the Draper Collection of Manuscripts. Guides generally attempt to give an overview of all the holdings, or a substantial portion (such as all the manuscripts), in a particular institution. They may act as inventories but usually also provide some general information about the materials and how to access them. A handbook is a kind of "how-to" book that focuses on a specific institution. It may include instruction on the library's cataloging system, other services, and the general scope of the library's holdings.

A helpful guide to the major repositories in the Washington, D.C., area is Christina K. Schaefer's *The Center: A Guide to Genealogical Research in the National Capital Area* (Baltimore: Genealogical Publishing Co., 1996). It describes the records and services of the National Archives, Library of Congress, DAR Library, the Bureau of Land Management, the Library of the National Genealogical Society, and the three LDS family history centers in the area. A similar guide describing the genealogical collections of more than one hundred New York City-area repositories is Estelle M. Guzik, ed., *Genealogical Resources in the New York Metropolitan Area* (New York: Jewish Genealogical Society, 1989). It describes the records and services of the New York Public Library, the New York Genealogical and Biographical Society, several archives and university libraries in the New York City area, New York City record offices and archives, county offices of ten local counties, major state offices for New York and New Jersey, and approximately a dozen Jewish archives and libraries.

Guides to several other research libraries have also been published. The following is a list of guides or handbooks for other major repositories.

- Cavanaugh, Karen B. *A Genealogist's Guide to the Ft. Wayne, Indiana, Public Library*. 4th ed. Fort Wayne, Ind.: Watermill Publications, 1988.
- Cerny, Johni, and Wendy Elliott. *The Library: A Guide to the LDS Family History Library*. Salt Lake City: Ancestry, 1988.
- *Guide to Genealogical Research in the National Archives*. Rev. ed. Washington, D.C.: National Archives Trust Fund Board, 1985.
- Oldenburg, Joseph F. *Genealogical Guide to the Burton Historical Collection, Detroit Public Library*. Salt Lake City: Ancestry, 1989.
- Parker, J. Carlyle. *Going to Salt Lake City to do Family History Research*. 2nd ed. Turlock, Calif.: Marietta Publishing Co., 1993.
- Sinko, Peggy Tuck. *Guide to Local and Family History at the Newberry Library*. Salt Lake City: Ancestry, 1987.
- Szucs, Loretto Dennis, and Sandra Hargreaves Luebking. *The Archives: A Guide to the National Archives Field Branches*. Salt Lake City: Ancestry, 1988.

Interlibrary Loan

Many books that a genealogist will find useful can be obtained via interlibrary loan. This service is one of the most important and overlooked services provided by most public and academic libraries. It allows a local library to borrow a book that is not in its collection from another library. Because many libraries do not have large genealogical collections, interlibrary loan can be a good means for researchers to gain access to materials not in a local collection. Generally, the local librarian will need a complete bibliographic citation (author, title, publisher, and city and date of publication) for each item requested. (Bibliographies are the tools that provide this information; see chapter 5.) A local library will generally try to obtain a copy of almost any reference asked for. However, many are hard to locate, so if a library that has the record sought is known, include that information in the request.

Family histories can be difficult to obtain through interlibrary loan because the American Library Association's policy suggests that such books not be available for interlibrary loan. This policy is justified on the grounds that family histories form a special collection in many libraries and because patrons travel great distances to use such collections; many libraries do not want these books to be out of their collections when a patron arrives in person. However, some libraries do not follow this policy and will lend their family genealogies via interlibrary loan.

Notable libraries which do lend their genealogies include the Sutro Branch of the California State Library in San Francisco (generally only within California), the Mid-Continent Public Library, which houses the American Family Records Association (AFRA) Collection of genealogical and local history books, and the Alexander Mitchell Public Library, which houses the AFRA Collection of genealogical and local history periodicals, tapes, and films. A catalog of the AFRA Genealogical Circulating Collection is available for a small fee from AFRA.

Although many libraries restrict interlibrary loan usage of family histories, many do not restrict local histories or other genealogical books, such as transcripts of records. In addition, many microfilmed records are available through interlibrary loan. Newspapers are perhaps the most noteworthy. Many early newspapers have been microfilmed. Often they are housed at a state library or a public library in the town where the newspaper was published. Interlibrary loan makes it possible for researchers to search for an ancestor's obituary themselves, instead of asking a person in the ancestor's town to look for them. (When one searches for it herself, there is no question of how well the search was done.) Census microfilm is often available through interlibrary loan as well, and other research sources are also accessible in this way. For example, very few people realize that the vast collection of early Virginia records on microfilm at the Virginia State Library is available to local researchers at their public libraries.

CONCLUSION

The explosive growth and increasing value of printed sources cannot be overestimated. Today, more than ever before, time is at a premium; and printed sources provide exceptional assistance in finding more information about our ancestors faster then ever before possible. However, the best shortcut is useless if the researcher does not know how to use it correctly. The mission of *Printed Sources* is to help its readers learn about the printed genealogical sources that will best aid them in their research.

It is a mission, however, that cannot be accomplished by this book alone; it requires the partnership of the reader. Even for a volume as inclusive as *Printed Sources*, it is impossible to cite and describe every genealogical source or reference book a researcher might need to use. The chapter authors have used their best judgement in describing sources that will be of the most help to most researchers, but there is always room to differ. Be aware that the discussions in these chapters are, in a real sense, only an introduction to the breadth and scope of printed sources. For every directory, bibliography, dictionary, or index cited, dozens of others exist. *Printed Sources'* focus is on those with national or state importance, but not even all of them could be noted. It remains for the dedicated researcher to do the necessary work, beginning with the sources described here, to find other references that may be required to resolve a particular research problem.

The words of Donald Lines Jacobus, the dean of American genealogy, are fitting to end this introduction. Although Jacobus was writing mostly about family histories and other compiled records, and the quality of published works has generally improved in the intervening sixty plus years, his counsel is still useful:

> When I began, as a novice, to trace my own ancestry, I too trusted the printed word. And even today, after more than twenty years, mistakes which I copied long ago from genealogical books crop up to plague me. Several proficient amateurs who have long since graduated from the class of novices have told me of similar experiences.
>
> It is to aid the uninformed lovers of genealogy that I have issued so strong a warning against genealogical books. Always be critical of printed statements and do not accept them too readily; and always make a note of the volume and page from which you copy data. This is even more essential when copying from books than when copying from documentary sources. For the percentage of error in original records is very slight; but in books it is high, and if you later grow suspicious of statements you have copied, it will be important to be able to check them back to their source (1930, 130).

NOTES

1. In scientific fields, this kind of ordered classification is called a *taxonomy*. The best-known taxonomy is the Linnaean system (after Carolus Linnaeus, 1707–78), which is used in biology to class all life forms into the proper kingdom, phylum, class, order, family, genus, species, and variety levels. The levels used in this genealogical classification include class, category, group, and record type. The four parts of *Printed Sources* represent the four categories, while the chapters represent the major record types.
2. The idea that copies of original records can be considered the same as the originals is standard among historians, as noted by Jacques Barzun and Henry F. Graff (1977, 94): "In historiography, a primary source is distinguished from a secondary by the fact that the former gives the words of the witnesses or first recorders of an event. . . . The historian, using a number of such primary sources, produces a secondary source."

REFERENCE LIST

Barzun, Jacques, and Henry F. Graff. 1977. *The Modern Researcher*. 3rd ed. New York: Harcourt Brace Jovanovich Publishers.

The Chicago Manual of Style. 1993. 14th ed. Chicago: University of Chicago Press.

Devine, Donn. 1992. "Do We Really Decide Relationships by a Preponderance of the Evidence?" *NGS Newsletter* 18 (5).

Drake, Paul. 1991. "Some Thoughts Concerning Genealogical Evidence and Proof, Part 2: Establishing Proof." *NGS Newsletter* no. 6.

_____. 1992. "Evidence in Genealogy." *Heritage Quest* no. 40.

Horle, Craig W. 1992. "Commentary: The Current State of Genealogical Publishing." *The Pennsylvania Genealogical Magazine* 37.

Greenwood, Val. 1990. *The Researcher's Guide to American Genealogy*. 2nd ed. Baltimore: Genealogical Publishing Co.

Jacobus, Donald Lines. 1930. *Genealogy as Pastime and Profession*. New Haven, Conn.: Tuttle, Morehouse & Taylor Co.

Johnston, Donald F. 1982. *Copyright Handbook*, 2nd ed. New York: Bowker.

Meyerink, Kory L. 1995. "Getting Started in Genealogy: A Bibliographic Essay of Introductory Genealogical Books" *Genealogical Journal* 23.

Rubincam, Milton. 1941. "The Springer Genealogy: A Critical Review." *The American Genealogist* 18.

Stephens, W. B. 1991. *Sources for U.S. History*. New York: Cambridge University Press.

Stevenson, Noel. 1979. *Genealogical Evidence*. Laguna Hills, Calif.: Aegean Park Press.

Part 1
BACKGROUND INFORMATION

GENERAL REFERENCE OVERVIEW

Key Concepts in This Chapter

- Public libraries have many *unique reference sources.*
- *Directories* guide family historians to helpful information.
- *Encyclopedias* offer a starting point for genealogists.
- *Historical sources* help to recreate our ancestors' lives.
- *Dictionaries* offer aid in deciphering old documents.
- *Chronologies* and *timetables* create a window to the past.

Key Sources in This Chapter

- *Knowing Where to Look: The Ultimate Guide to Research*
- *American Library Directory* (lists more than thirty-seven thousand libraries nationwide)
- *Dictionary of American History* (an encyclopedic look at U.S. history)
- *Directories in Print* (a guide to more than fifteen thousand directories published nationwide)
- *Genealogist's Address Book* (an essential home reference source)
- *A to Zax: A Comprehensive Dictionary for Genealogists and Historians*
- *United States Government Manual*

1

GENERAL REFERENCE

Martha L. Henderson

THE UNIQUE RESOURCES IN PUBLIC LIBRARIES

Library sources are essential in the ever-expanding field of genealogy. For beginners who are just starting to research their family history and for more advanced researchers who believe they have exhausted potential sources of information, local libraries offer many sources that await discovery, and much information is hidden in basic reference sources. This chapter will introduce these sources and offer suggestions on how best to use them.

Genealogists often struggle with research problems that could be solved quickly by using library reference sources. Many researchers will have used these sources during their high school or college years. It is time to became reacquainted with them and to discover how standard reference works can help one learn more about her family's past. This chapter focuses on the basic reference books found in most public libraries; these include encyclopedias, historical indexes, dictionaries, almanacs, directories, and many others.

How To Use a Library

Libraries can be mysterious labyrinths. Many adult library patrons feel lost and uncomfortable in a place which they haven't used for many years. Such feelings are understandable—but not insurmountable. With a little knowledge and instruction, anyone can learn to use and appreciate libraries. Reading this chapter is the first step.

The best way to learn how to use a library is to ask a librarian or library clerk. Some researchers believe that it is better not to "bother" a librarian with questions. They often wander around a library, reluctant to ask questions and thus wasting valuable research time. Remember that librarians are there to help with questions, no matter how basic or unusual. Reference librarians are trained to help researchers. They and their assistants hold the keys to unlocking the many information sources that await researchers.

In a large library, it may be difficult to know which library worker approach. The reference department is the best place to begin. Once there, go to the information desk and ask for assistance. Better yet, when entering a library for the first time, ask for a tour of the library. While on tour, ask about any unique holdings or collections. Librarians are proud of their collections and their patrons' interest.

Often, only by asking a librarian about his library's unique holdings can one learn about them. For example, this author's local library has a card index to the marriages and obituaries found in the *Independence* [Missouri] *Examiner,* a local newspaper. Currently, the index covers the years 1919 to 1939. It is located in a back corner of the library and is often overlooked by researchers. Unless a patron asks the librarian, "What unique indexes or sources will I find in your library?," she may not be aware of the index and will thus miss a potentially valuable source.

Library Organization. Most libraries are organized into sections or areas. Smaller libraries usually have an area for adults and another for children. Larger libraries maintain separate departments for specific subject areas, such as the periodical department for magazines and the reference department for reference books. A reference department can occupy an entire floor of a large public library or a corner in a small library.

Within a library the books are labeled as circulating or reference. Circulating books can be borrowed by library patrons and taken home to read. These books include fiction books, such as romance novels, westerns, and mysteries; they also include nonfiction books, such as car repair manuals, cookbooks, and travel books. Circulating books are usually read in their entirety for information or enjoyment.

In contrast, reference books do not circulate and are shelved in an area designated for library use only. These books provide answers to specific questions and therefore must remain in the library for use by everyone. Whether one wants to know the specific dates of the American Revolution or needs a detailed description of Quaker beliefs and practices, answers can be found in reference sources. Reference books are usually not read from cover to cover and are often published in multivolume sets.

Reference areas contain a variety of books, microform (microfilm or microfiche) materials, and online sources (sources available through electronic databases and the Internet) selected by librarians as useful for answering questions. Reference materials are labeled with *Ref* or *R* above the catalog number to distinguish them from circulating nonfiction materials.

Cataloging Fundamentals. All library books are cataloged or classified in a particular order so that they can be easily found. Most libraries use one of two systems of classification: the

Dewey Decimal Classification System

Class	Number	Subject
000		Generalities
	001.9	Controversial and spurious knowledge
	011	General bibliographies
	030	Encyclopedias
	070	Journalism
100		Philosophy
	150	Psychology
	170	Ethics
	180	Philosophy
	190	Modern Western philosophy
200		Religion
	220	Bible
	231–239	Christianity
300		Social sciences
	320	Political science
	330	Economics
	340	Law
	360	Social services
	370	Education
	380	Commerce and communication
	390	Customs and folklore
	398.2	Folklore and fairy tales
400		Language
	420	English
	430	German
	440	French
	450	Italian
	460	Spanish, Portuguese
	470	Latin
	480	Greek
500		Pure sciences
	510	Mathematics
	520	Astronomy
	530	Physics
	540	Chemistry
	550	Earth sciences
	570	Life sciences
	580	Botany
	590	Zoology
600		Technology
	610	Medicine
	620	Engineering
	630	Agriculture
	640	Home economics
	650	Managerial services
	670	Manufacturing
	690	Buildings
700		The arts
	712	Landscape design
	720	Architecture
	730	Sculpture
	745.1	Antiques
	750	Painting
	760	Graphic arts
	770	Photography
	780	Music
	790	Recreation and performing arts
800		Literature
900		Geography and history
	920	Biography
	929	Genealogy
	930	Ancient world history
	940	European history
	950	Asiatic history
	970	North American history
	980	South American history

Dewey Decimal System or the Library of Congress Classification System. Both systems are based on the principle of assigning a unique number and/or letter combination to each library item for shelf placement and easy retrieval. The researcher who has mastered the basic principles of the Dewey and Library of Congress systems will feel comfortable using the holdings of any library.

Dewey Decimal System. Most public libraries use the Dewey Decimal Classification System, which was developed in 1873 by Melvin Dewey for the Amherst College Library in Amherst, Massachusetts. This system classifies books within ten basic groups or classes of knowledge, as shown above. Within these major classes, many subject divisions are possible. For example, the number 900 is reserved for all materials dealing with history and geography. Within the 900 class, the following divisions exist: numbers 910 through 919 are reserved for atlases and books on geography, 929.2 for family histories, and 974 through 979 for materials relating to individual states within the United States (see the facing page).

As each new book arrives in a library, a cataloger assigns a unique call number to it. That number is recorded on a three- by five-inch catalog card or in a computerized catalog database. The call number consists of the Dewey classification number and, beneath it, the Cutter number or symbol that represents the author. Charles Ammi Cutter, librarian of the Boston Anthenaeum Library, invented the Cutter number system in 1893. A Cutter number is composed of the first one or two letters of an author's surname followed by a number assigned to that individual author. Often a lowercase letter follows the Cutter number. That letter shows that the author has written several books by referring to the first word of each book title. Below is an example of a complete call number.

296.78 (classification number)
H15n (Cutter number)

Books are arranged on library shelves in numerical order according to the Dewey number. Library shelves are arranged in vertical sections that are individual numbering sections. Thus, when looking for a book by its call number, one is searching from left to right and from top to bottom within each shelf section (see figure 1-1). The following hypothetical books are in proper shelf order, reading from left to right:

929.2	929.2	929.2	929.201
C12a	C123	C25	B32a

In these examples, the 929.2 classification number places the numbers in the correct area of the library: within the 929.2 section. The bottom number assures proper shelf placement within the 929.2 section by using an alphabetic sequence and then a numeric sequence. Numbers that follow the decimal point and those that follow the letters in the Cutter number are decimals. Thus, 929.12 comes before 929.2; similarly, C123 comes before C25. Remember that call numbers are read in sequence from a lower number to a higher number.

Some libraries add variations to the Dewey system to fit their particular needs. The Family History Library of The Church of Jesus Christ of Latter-day Saints (LDS church) in Salt Lake City, Utah, has modified the Cutter number to refer to record categories rather than authors' names. For example, atlases of all regions carry the Cutter number E3, military service records M22, and cemetery records V22. The book *Men of Boston and New England* (Boston: Boston American, 1913) has the call number 974/D3m. The number *974* designates the U.S. region (northeast), *D3* stands for biography, and *m* indicates the first letter of the title. For a complete analysis of the Family History Library's record category designations, see chapter 5 in Norman E. Wright and David H. Pratt's *Genealogical Research Essentials* (Salt Lake City: Bookcraft, 1976).

Library of Congress Classification System. University libraries generally use the Library of Congress Classification System. That system differs from the Dewey system in its use of letters instead of numbers. The Library of Congress (LC) System contains twenty classes. Each of the twenty classes can be divided into a subclass when a second letter is added. As with the Dewey system, the LC system uses a Cutter number that usually identifies the author's name and book's title. Below, for example, is the LC call number for Forest W. McNair's *Forest McNair of Texas.*

CT275	(classification for biography, individual American)
.M444	(Cutter for McNair as subject of biography)
A3	(second Cutter, meaning autobiography)

Reference works of interest to genealogists are found in the following LC categories: AE (encyclopedias), BX (religious encyclopedias), CR (heraldry), CS (genealogy), CT (biographical dictionaries), E (American gazetteers, chronologies, and biographical encyclopedias), F (American history), and G (atlases). LC-cataloged books are arranged alphabetically on the library shelf by the LC letter or letters.

As one begins to understand library methods and terminology, libraries become easier to use. The researcher will feel more comfortable in his own local library and in libraries that he might visit on a genealogical research trip. Remember that

Dewey Decimal System Numbers for Regions and States within the United States

United States	973

Within the Dewey system, states are grouped by region:

Northeastern states	974
Southeastern states	975
South central states	976
North central states	977
Western states	978
Pacific states	979

States:

Alabama	976.1	Montana	978.6
Alaska	979.8	Nebraska	978.2
Arizona	979.1	Nevada	979.3
Arkansas	976.7	New Hampshire	974.2
California	979.4	New Jersey	974.9
Colorado	978.8	New Mexico	978.9
Connecticut	974.6	New York	974.7
Delaware	975.1	North Carolina	975.6
District of Columbia	975.3	North Dakota	978.4
Florida	975.9	Ohio	977.1
Georgia	975.8	Oklahoma	976.6
Hawaii	996.9	Oregon	979.5
Idaho	979.6	Pennsylvania	974.8
Illinois	977.3	Rhode Island	974.5
Indiana	977.2	South Carolina	975.7
Iowa	977.7	South Dakota	975.7
Kansas	978.1	Tennessee	976.8
Kentucky	976.9	Texas	976.4
Louisiana	976.3	Utah	979.2
Maine	974.1	Vermont	974.3
Maryland	975.2	Virginia	975.5
Massachusetts	974.4	Washington	979.7
Michigan	977.4	West Virginia	975.4
Minnesota	977.6	Wisconsin	977.5
Mississippi	976.2	Wyoming	978.7
Missouri	977.8		

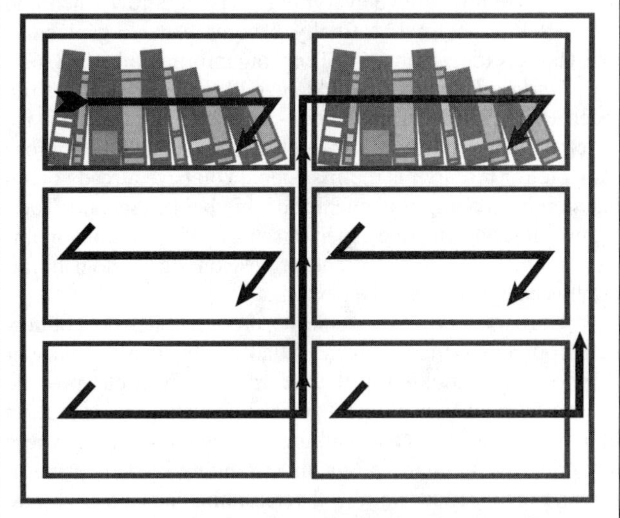

Figure 1-1. Arrangement of books on library shelves.

librarians and library assistants working in libraries or similar institutions are essential to helping unlock the many sources under their care. This chapter emphasizes sources that one should look for in the local library or in libraries that might be visited while on research trips. Reading a basic guide on library research will add to a researcher's knowledge of libraries and their resources; the researcher will also be a step ahead the next time she enters a library.

Guidebooks to Library Research

Researchers interested in learning more about libraries and their resources can consult several excellent guides. One is *Knowing Where to Look: The Ultimate Guide to Research* (Cincinnati: Writer's Digest Books, 1984), by Lois Horowitz, a reference librarian who is familiar with the needs of genealogical researchers. In the introduction to her book (page 4), Horowitz notes:

> If you're a genealogist, historian, or scholar, you're probably familiar with ships' passenger lists and little-known manuscript collections. But think of the time you've spent in roundabout searches for a middle name. Genealogy requires some of the most sophisticated forms of research; yet, because it is known as a hobby, most people underestimate the research know-how required to reconstruct a family tree. Professional genealogists tell me that many family histories are riddled with errors, omissions, and inaccuracies. Armed with a basic knowledge of research techniques, yours needn't be thus flawed.

Horowitz offers several important strategies for insuring research success. She suggests that researchers not judge a book by its cover because books often contain much more information than is indicated by their titles. For example, a book of deed abstracts might also contain wills that were found among the deeds.

Horowitz also believes that it is important to understand the arrangement of each reference book consulted. For example, surname indexes sometimes divide sections of a book. If one has not studied a book carefully and only checks in the back for an index, a valuable source of information could be overlooked. Horowitz offers additional suggestions for researchers, including these: do not believe everything in print; know when and how to ask for help; and, finally, become better organized in note-taking, citing sources, and copying information (1988, 62).

Finding Facts Fast by Alden Todd (Berkeley, Calif.: Ten Speed Press, 1992) offers a four-step plan for successful research. Reading about the subject to be studied and the sources available for research is the first step. (You have already taken that step by reading this chapter of this book.) Second, Todd suggests interviewing the expert or source person. Family members, neighbors, librarians, and professional genealogists fall into this category as source persons.

Third, observing for ourselves provides answers not normally found in written sources. Actually going to a cemetery or courthouse and looking at the records in person can provide answers to many genealogical puzzles. Traveling the migration routes of our ancestors and walking in the neighborhoods where they once lived enhances our understanding of their place in history. Finally, Todd suggests that reasoning in research should follow the known-to-the-unknown principle. This principle, preached by genealogy instructors for years, insures a steady progression of logical research (Todd 1972, 8–10).

Other books offer helpful tips on library research. *A Guide to Library Research Methods* (New York: Oxford University Press, 1990), by Thomas Mann, a reference librarian at the Library of Congress, presents a detailed discussion of library subject headings. Subject headings are the access points used to find books on particular subjects. To find books on heraldry, for example, look in a card catalog or an online catalog under the term *heraldry*. Sometimes the heading assigned to a particular subject is not familiar to a researcher or does not seem to make sense. As in all disciplines, certain rules guide the assignment of subject headings to books. Mann's guide assists in understanding these rules and offers suggestions for better utilizing library subject headings.

To find similar books on a subject, Mann suggests that a researcher locate a familiar book in a library's online or card catalog; then note the subject headings used by the library to describe the book and consult those particular subject headings within the catalog for additional book titles. For example, suppose one has just finished reading the book *Albion's Seed: Four British Folkways in America,* by David Hackett Fischer (New York: Oxford University Press, 1989), and wants to find the titles of similar books. Using a library's online catalog, one can look alphabetically under the title *Albion's Seed* and find the catalog entry for that book. The subject headings that describe *Albion's Seed* are "United States—Civilization—To 1783" and "United States—Civilization—English Influences." By then looking in the catalog under these two subject headings one finds that the library has 198 other books under the subject "United States—Civilization."

A valuable source for finding a wide assortment of subject headings used by libraries is *Library of Congress Subject Headings* (Washington, D.C.: Library of Congress, 1993–). This four-volume set contains subject headings created by catalogers and used by the Library of Congress to catalog books since 1898. From five thousand to seven thousand new and replaced headings and subheadings are added each year. The *see also* references found in this set offer researchers additional terms to consider when searching for subject headings. The use of these references is important when determining the subject heading used for family surnames (figure 1-2). "Crider family" is the subject heading "used for" (UF) the twelve variant spellings of that name. Note that a "related topic" (RT) to this surname is the surname Grider.

Learning to use library catalogs and numbering systems may seem confusing at first. However, with time and practice, most researchers find themselves at home in libraries and begin to discover the many new reference sources available to them.

Evaluating Reference Books

Before exploring the different types of printed reference sources available for use by genealogists, it is important to know how to evaluate reference books. Only regular, "hands-on" use of a reference book will make a researcher thoroughly familiar with its quality and content. Following are several suggestions to help in a preliminary examination of a book. (Also see the "Evaluation of Printed Sources" section in the introduction of this book.)

First, examine the title page for information about the author, such as a degrees, positions, and titles of earlier works. A book's cover (dust jacket) will often provide information about

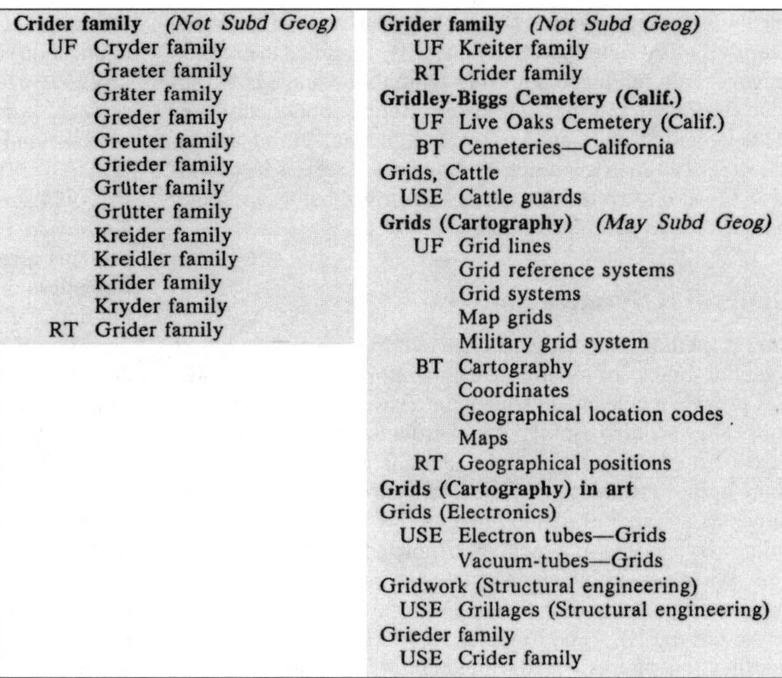

Crider family *(Not Subd Geog)*
UF Cryder family
Graeter family
Gräter family
Greder family
Greuter family
Grieder family
Grüter family
Grütter family
Kreider family
Kreidler family
Krider family
Kryder family
RT Grider family

Grider family *(Not Subd Geog)*
UF Kreiter family
RT Crider family
Gridley-Biggs Cemetery (Calif.)
UF Live Oaks Cemetery (Calif.)
BT Cemeteries—California
Grids, Cattle
USE Cattle guards
Grids (Cartography) *(May Subd Geog)*
UF Grid lines
Grid reference systems
Grid systems
Map grids
Military grid system
BT Cartography
Coordinates
Geographical location codes
Maps
RT Geographical positions
Grids (Cartography) in art
Grids (Electronics)
USE Electron tubes—Grids
Vacuum-tubes—Grids
Gridwork (Structural engineering)
USE Grillages (Structural engineering)
Grieder family
USE Crider family

Figure 1-2. From *Library of Congress Subject Headings.* "Crider family" is the subject heading "used for" (UF) the twelve variant spellings of that name. A "related topic" (RT) to this surname is the surname Grider.

the author as well. Look further for information about the author in the introduction or in a special note. Also note the name of the publisher and date of publication.

Take a few minutes to browse through the book. Flip through the pages and note whether there is an index, bibliography, or appendix. Look at the photographs or illustrations and become familiar with the layout of the book. Next, read the preface and introduction to understand the purpose and scope of the book. Also notice any special features claimed and any limitations as well. Compare the book with other books on the same subject by consulting *Books in Print* and other bibliographic references mentioned later in this chapter and in chapter 5.

Finally, examine the content of the book. Information should be quickly and easily extractable, meaning that the book should be well arranged, indexed, and cross-referenced. Is information found readily under logical subject, author, or title headings? Analyze the quality and kind of articles, noting whether they are popular or scientific, signed or unsigned, impartial or biased. Notice whether the article or book under study contains satisfactory bibliographical references. If the work purports to be a new edition, note carefully the extent of revision claimed for it and check by comparison with earlier editions. An important rule to remember when evaluating reference books is this one: don't trust any one source completely. Become aware of recently published sources by reading book reviews. Additionally, confirm information from one source by verifying it in another.

Learning to evaluate reference sources helps researchers overcome the tendency to rely too heavily only on the sources available within the local library. No one library can possibly acquire all materials needed to research a family history. Researchers must learn to broaden their scope and look to other sources for information.

If the Library Doesn't Have What One Needs

Librarians can suggest other libraries, institutions, associations, or governmental bodies that may offer additional or different types of sources. Several reference sources mentioned later in this chapter will lead the researcher to further sources of information. Interlibrary loan is an option to consider if one's local library does not own a reference source one would like to consult.

Many reference resources are now available through the Internet, and most libraries now have access to the Internet and other forms of electronic searching. Ask a librarian for help accessing them via home computer or through the Internet connection at a local or university library. Be sure to ask if you have not found what you are seeking. Library technology is changing rapidly, and new sources appear daily, offering unique options for searching.

REFERENCE SOURCES

Librarians define a reference source as anything used to answer a question. Such a broad definition means that there is a variety of sources available in a reference department. Encyclopedias, almanacs, yearbooks, directories, maps, newspaper clippings, pamphlets, and magazine articles serve as recognized examples of printed reference sources. Some printed sources are reproduced in microform format, either as microfilm or microfiche. These formats save valuable library space and often provide access to materials no longer available in printed form. Many reference sources are now available in computerized formats, such as CD-ROM, online databases, and the Internet. Examples of these sources include Elizabeth Petty Bentley's *Genealogist's All-in-One Address Book* (Baltimore: Genealogical Publishing Co., 1996) and *FamilySearch®* (Salt Lake City: Family History Department, annual), both on CD-ROM. Appendix A contains more information on these sources.

Librarians usually keep the most current editions of reference books. The currency of reference sources is especially important where population figures, addresses, and telephone numbers are concerned. Some reference books are published yearly because the information they contain changes that frequently. For example, the *American Library Directory* (discussed below) is published annually, reflecting the changes in library staffs, budgets, and holdings nationwide. Researchers can use this source to learn what libraries are in the geographical area of their family research.

Not all reference books have to be the most current editions to be of value. Some older reference books are valuable because they contain information no longer available in more current sources; this is true of gazetteers for earlier time periods and high school and college yearbooks. Such reference sources actually become more valuable with age.

A standard book that librarians use to locate reference sources is the *Guide to Reference Books,* 11th ed., edited by Robert Balay (Chicago: American Library Association, 1996). This edition lists more than fifteen thousand reference books in thirty-eight subject areas. David Heighton, a librarian at the Family History Library in Salt Lake City, compiled the section on genealogy reference books. Heighton's coverage is worldwide and includes the best genealogy reference books published in the United States, Canada, Europe, and Asia. A brief annotation describes each reference book and characterizes its usefulness. Most of the reference sources described below are found in the *Guide to Reference Books*.

General Reference Sources

Encyclopedias. Genealogists often overlook encyclopedias as potential sources of reliable, accurate information. Encyclopedias provide a convenient source for answers to specific questions. They are also useful for background information on new areas of study. That they can be found in every library and in many homes ensures their accessibility to researchers. Encyclopedias are also available in CD-ROM format and through online services, making them even more accessible.

When consulting an encyclopedia, pay close attention to the scope or purpose of the work. Does the introduction clearly define the emphasis and to whom the work is directed? These qualifications are especially important when using a subject encyclopedia. Is the encyclopedia authoritative? Is it up to date, accurate, and relatively objective? Are the contributors scholars in their fields and are their qualifications clearly stated? Are the articles objective and fair? Have both sides of an issue been presented or have controversial issues been ignored?

Many encyclopedias are published in multi-volume sets. There are two basic types: general encyclopedias and subject encyclopedias. The more familiar type is the general encyclopedia published for a specific age group or audience. This type includes, for example, the *Encyclopedia Americana* for adults and the *World Book Encyclopedia* for children and young adults. These sets contain information on almost every conceivable subject. Subject encyclopedias, on the other hand, provide in-depth information on one subject. The *Encyclopedia of Religion* (New York: Macmillan, 1993) is a subject encyclopedia.

General Encyclopedias. For genealogists, the general encyclopedia can provide a quick way to find information about countries and states pertinent to a family's migrational history, for example. Excellent maps and historical information offer the researcher sufficient background information to provide an overview and serve as a springboard for additional research. Most encyclopedic articles end with bibliographic references to other articles within the encyclopedia or to other books on the subject.

Three firms produce 75 percent of all general print encyclopedias published in North America. They are Encyclopædia Britannica, Inc., which produces the *Encyclopædia Britannica*, the largest and most prestigious encyclopedia in the English language, *Children's Britannica,* and others; Grolier Inc. publishes *Encyclopedia Americana,* the first multi-volume encyclopedia of any significance published in North America (1829), *The New Book of Knowledge, Academic American Encyclopedia,* and others; and World Book Inc., which publishes *World Book Encyclopedia*, the best-selling encyclopedia in North America, and *Childcraft: The How and Why Library* (Kister 1994, 10–11).

The largest, best known, and most prestigious general encyclopedia in the English language is the *Encyclopædia Britannica* (Chicago: Encyclopædia Britannica, 1768–1973). In publication since 1768, the *Britannica* is best known for its scholarly coverage, its well-balanced articles, and excellent bibliographies. It serves the serious student and educated adult researcher and is found in most libraries.

The fifteenth edition of the *Encyclopædia Britannica* was first published in 1974 under the name *The New Encyclopædia Britannica* (Chicago: Encyclopedia Britannica). This edition presents a radical change in arrangement from previous editions. It is divided into three interrelated parts: the Propædia, Outline of Knowledge, which serves as a topical guide to the contents of the encyclopedia; the Micropædia, Ready Reference, twelve volumes of short articles on specific persons, places, things, and ideas arranged in alphabetical order; and the Macropædia, Knowledge in Depth, seventeen volumes of longer, more-substantial articles. Both the Micropædia and Macropædia sections contain many illustrations and maps. A comparison can be drawn between the treatment of the subject "heraldry" in the Micropædia and Macropædia texts. The Macropædia article on heraldry is seventeen pages in length and includes an extensive bibliography. In contrast, the Micropædia article is only two columns long with a reference to the more extensive discussion in the Macropædia. A two-volume comprehensive index to the complete, thirty-volume *New Encyclopedia Britannica* guides the user to much information that would otherwise be difficult to find.

The thirty-volume *Encyclopedia Americana* (Danbury, Conn.: Grolier, 1829–) is a nationally recognized encyclopedia published since the early part of the nineteenth century. It is written for adults and older students with good reading skills. Its articles are strong in all aspects of North American life, including history, geography, and biography. It unquestionably has a greater emphasis on North America than any of the other general encyclopedias. The *Americana* is particularly useful for hard-to-find, little-known information about the United States. For example, a reference to the city of Ada identifies it as being located in southeastern Oklahoma, eighty-five miles southeast of Oklahoma City. According to the *Encyclopedia Americana*, Ada was settled in 1889 and named for Ada Reed, the daughter of its first postmaster.

Other good general encyclopedias exist. They include the twenty-four-volume *Collier's Encyclopedia* (New York: Macmillan Educational Co., 1949–); the twenty-one-volume *Academic American Encyclopedia* (Princeton, N.J.: Grolier, 1980–); and the twenty-two-volume *World Book Encyclopedia* (Chicago: World Book, annual). All three present accurate, readable, up-to-date articles easily read by students and adult researchers.

Yearbooks are published annually by most publishers of encyclopedias. Sometimes called annuals, these yearbooks present summaries of the previous year's major events. Their alphabetical arrangement and scope offer easy access to current biographies, obituaries, chronologies of events, and current statistics for answers to specific questions.

Other Types of Encyclopedias. One-volume encyclopedias answer the need for quick, accurate data. Usually, these encyclopedias are not found with the multi-volume sets on the library shelves, but are kept near the reference desk for quick referral. Well-known examples of one-volume encyclopedias are the *Columbia Encyclopedia*, 5th ed. (New York: Columbia University Press, 1993) and the *Concise Columbia Encyclopedia,* 2nd ed. (New York: Columbia University Press, 1989).

The Columbia Encyclopedia contains approximately 6.6 million words and fifty thousand brief articles. Its articles are arranged alphabetically and compare favorably with many multi-volume encyclopedias. As a ready reference, the *Columbia* is a valuable guide. Almost 70 percent of the entries are biographical or geographical in nature. The articles are written in a scholarly yet easily comprehensible style. More than sixty-five thousand cross-references provide quick access to over fifty thousand articles. The *Concise Columbia* is an abridged version of the *Columbia Encyclopedia;* it is available in large print and electronic formats.

For additional examples of one-volume encyclopedias and for an in-depth look at general encyclopedias, consult *Kister's Best Encyclopedias: A Comparative Guide to General and Specialized Encyclopedias* by Kenneth F. Kister (Phoenix: Oryx Press, 1994). This book examines more than one thousand print and electronic encyclopedias. For each encyclopedia profiled, Kister provides information on cost, number of articles, and editors and contributors, and comments on the scope and arrangement of each. Kister also surveys specialized encyclopedias, foreign-language encyclopedias, publishers, and distributors.

Subject Encyclopedias. Subject encyclopedias are directed toward specialized audiences; they feature thorough scholarship and depth of coverage. They are best suited for an exhaustive study of a topic but can also fill the need for an overview of a subject. *First Stop: The Master Index to Subject Encyclopedias* by Joe Ryan (Phoenix: Oryx Press, 1989) is an excellent guide to subject encyclopedias.

Subject encyclopedias are published in both multi-volume sets and in single-volume editions. They are not revised as often as general encyclopedias because the currency of their subject matter is not as critical as in general encyclopedias. Several subject encyclopedias should become standard sources of information for the serious family researcher. They include the *Encyclopedia of Religion* (cited earlier) and the older *Encyclopedia of Religion and Ethics* (New York: Scribner, 1908–27); *Encyclopedia of American History* (New York: HarperCollins, 1996) and *The Dictionary of American History,* rev. ed. (New York: Charles Scribner's Sons, 1976–78; supplement, 1996); and *Encyclopedia of World History,* 5th ed. (Boston: Houghton Mifflin, 1972). Each of these titles gives accurate, reliable information for genealogists seeking an understanding of the era in which an ancestor lived. They will provide data on an ancestor's religious beliefs, for example, and explain the world events taking place during that ancestor's lifetime.

The *Encyclopedia of Religion* introduces more than three thousand articles on religious beliefs and symbols from ancient times to the present. Traditional Western and Eastern religions are examined and discussed in it. Nontraditional cults, primitive religions, and esoteric religious themes and traditions are also included. Were your ancestors Quakers? For those who have Quaker ancestors, the *Encyclopedia of Religion* offers an excellent article on the Religious Society of Friends, as the Quaker religion is more formally known. The article gives a history of Quakerism, including its founding in England by George Fox and its spread to New England and especially to Pennsylvania. Coverage of this subject encompasses almost four pages of text and includes a four-paragraph bibliography. In contrast, the same subject is covered in four paragraphs with three bibliographic references in the more general *Academic American Encyclopedia* (Princeton, N.J.: Grolier, 1980–).

Encyclopedia of Religion and Ethics, published between 1908 and 1926, presents a less objective view of nontraditional, non-Western people and religions. The *Encyclopedia of Religion and Ethics* is the product of an era in the English-speaking world when scholars viewed the world with a definite Western bias. Keeping this bias in mind, the researcher can find in it excellent, comprehensive coverage of religious subjects. For example, the Quaker religion is covered in six pages with an extensive bibliography. A statistical table notes that as of 31 December 1910, there were 94,852 orthodox Quakers in the United States and 22,401 members of splinter branches (the Hicksites and Wilburites) (Hastings 1908–27, 147). Family historians looking for a detailed examination of an ancestor's religion will want to locate a copy of this reference source.

The history and beliefs of most major denominations are presented in encyclopedias of varying sizes. Researchers will find the *New Catholic Encyclopedia* (New York: McGraw-Hill, 1967–95) and *Encyclopedia Judaica* (New York: Macmillan, 1971–72) in most large public and university libraries. For additional religious sources, see chapter 8, "Church Records."

General History Sources. Locating sources that develop a historical background for one's family history is vital to genealogical research and eventual publication of that research. It is important to know the social, political, and economic history of an ancestor's homeland, for example. Such knowledge promotes a better understanding of the historical period in which an ancestor was born, lived, and died. Understanding why a family or group of families left ancestral homes for the raw frontier will greatly improve one's knowledge of them as real people rather than just names on a family chart. Knowing the many hardships and occasional joys they experienced on the frontier, or in immigrant ships, will aid in understanding the sacrifices these ancestors made.

Most of the sources mentioned below will be found in the reference sections of large public libraries. They offer quick access to historical information.

Several sources cover the history of the United States. The *Dictionary of American History* (cited earlier) is an excellent resource for finding quick answers to most questions on U.S. history. Although the word *dictionary* is used in its title, this multi-volume set is generally considered an encyclopedia because of its depth and scope. Although this set does not contain biographical entries, the analytical, or descriptive, index provides access to prominent names mentioned in each article.

Originally published in 1936, the *Dictionary of American History* was completely revised in 1976 during America's bicentennial. Articles on American prehistory, Native Americans, and African Americans were added to broaden its scope. A two-volume supplement published in 1996 brings the study of American history to the year 1995.

The *Dictionary of American History* offers genealogists concise, informative articles on nearly every aspect of American history. For example, the entry for the Black Hawk War gives the date of conflict (1832), the principle combatants (United States and a faction of Sauk, or Sac, and Fox Indians) and the location of the event (mainly Illinois and Wisconsin). This information appears at the beginning of the article on the Black Hawk War, followed by a discussion of the causes and consequences of the war. Suggestions for other books to read on the subject complete the article.

Another source, the *Encyclopedia of American History,* by Richard B. and Jeffrey B. Morris (New York: HarperCollins, 1996), offers a unique presentation of American history. It is arranged in four parts: the first part is chronological by year and covers major political and military events in U.S. history; the second part presents historical topics, such as national expansion, immigration, and economic trends; the third part consists of biographies of 450 notable Americans; part 4 presents the structure of the Federal government. An extensive index provides access to the material in all four sections. This arrangement allows the genealogist to pinpoint events that occurred during the time when an ancestor lived. Such information is especially useful for determining why a family moved from one area to another. Did a war, drought, or other force contribute to a family's migration? A researcher compiling a family genealogy will find this type of information useful when describing the time in which her ancestors lived and died. The *Encyclopedia of American History* is usually found on library reference shelves.

The *Encyclopedia of World History* (cited earlier) provides similar chronological data on an international level. Why ancestors moved from their homelands, crossed vast oceans, and adapted to a new life in a strange land are important questions. Were there forces at work in their homelands that caused such migrations? This encyclopedia will help to answer these questions by pinpointing major historical events and by providing a broad outline of world events and their chronological periods. Equipped with this information, the genealogist can search for more detailed explanations of historical events in an encyclopedia or a history book.

General histories of the United States can be found in libraries, bookstores, and even in our own homes. A child's school history textbook will often fill the need for a quick reference to a historical event. However, as one becomes more involved in genealogical research, it soon becomes apparent that more detailed, comprehensive studies of American history are needed.

The *Oxford History of the American People,* by Samuel Eliot Morison (New York: Oxford University Press, 1965), is an excellent example of a comprehensive study of American history written for the general reader. This history spans the time from prehistoric man to the assassination of President John F. Kennedy. It integrates the social history of the United States with the political history and complements the text with fine black and white illustrations.

Researchers sometimes need more than a basic history of the country or area settled in by an ancestor; they often require information about the cultural, political, or social customs of a particular time to better understand the actions taken by an ancestor. Several reference sources that are found in most libraries will direct the researcher to more detailed historical sources. The two-volume *Harvard Guide to American History,* edited by Frank B. Freidel, rev. ed. (Cambridge, Mass.: Belknap Press of Harvard University Press, 1974), provides an important first step in locating published works on American history. Vol. 1 is arranged by topics that include religion, education, marriage and the family, fur trade, pioneer life, and military frontier. Within each topic are references to books and periodical articles about that particular subject. Of further value is a short course on historical research that offers excellent suggestions on note-taking and aids to historical research and a good discussion on writing for publication. Vol. 2 is arranged chronologically and then by topic within each historical period. This arrangement is useful when searching for information on a particular time period, such as the Revolutionary War.

A serious drawback to this otherwise excellent resource is the fact that it was published in 1974. Researchers should be cautious when using vol. 1 because the sections on research centers and printed state and local histories are dated.

Another excellent guide for finding information on the lives and customs of our ancestors is the four-volume series titled *Index to America: Life and Customs,* edited by Norma O. Ireland (Westwood, Mass.: F. W. Faxon Co., 1976–84). This is an index to popular rather than scholarly works. *Index to America* was designed primarily for public and school library use. Its editors sought to index magazine articles and books that could be easily found in most libraries. It explores the customs and everyday life in particular time periods rather than historical or political events. Vol. 1 covers the seventeenth century; vol. 2 the eighteenth; vol. 3 the nineteenth; and vol. 4 the twentieth century to 1986. Each volume is arranged by subject with many cross-references to aid the user. Family historians will find references to specific place names, such as Jamestown and Dodge City; to specific subjects of interest, such as "homesteaders and homesteading"; and to unusual terms, such as *pauper's badges.*

Another index to American cultural history is *America: History and Life, a Guide to Periodical Literature* (Santa Barbara, Calif.: ABC-Clio, 1964–). This ongoing indexing project provides abstracts, or detailed descriptions, for each article mentioned. Coverage includes both U.S. and Canadian history with special emphasis on ethnic studies, family history, folklore, Indian-white relations, and military history. This index is also available online through DIALOG (see "Electronic Sources," below).

These sources are usually found in library reference areas and are therefore not available for borrowing. For a "popular" history book to take home and read at leisure, search the library's circulating section. Libraries using the Dewey Decimal System will offer a wide variety of American history books in the 973 section. These books can also be found in local bookstores and sometimes even in garage sales.

Researchers looking for individual county and state histories will find many suggestions in chapter 17, "County and Local Histories." Also see chapter 3, "Geographic Tools," for a discussion of atlases and maps and their importance in genealogical research.

Social History Sources. American social history is best studied on a regional basis because settlement of the United States occurred by regions. A standard study of the colonial experience is Daniel J. Boorstin's *The Americans,* vol. 1, *The Colonial Experience* (New York: Random House, 1958). Although written almost forty years ago, historian Boorstin's study provides invaluable historical insight into everyday life in colonial America. It is considered a standard source for colonial research.

Alice M. Earle's classic works on everyday life in colonial America provide an understanding of an age vastly different from our current one. These works include *Child Life in Colonial Days* (1899; reprint; Williamstown, Mass.: Corner Hse., 1975), *Colonial Dames and Goodwives* (reprint; Bowie, Md.: Heritage Books, 1988), and *Home Life in Colonial Days* (1898; reprint; Williamstown, Mass.: Corner Hse., 1975). Additional titles by Earle describe economic life in colonial America, the curious punishments used by our colonial ancestors, and the costume and religious observances of Puritan New England. Most libraries have copies of Earle's books; they are sometimes found in the circulating section.

Dale Van Every's historical volume *Forth to the Wilderness: The First American Frontier, 1754–1774* (New York: Morrow, 1961) examines the forces behind migration in America. It is the story of a small group of settlers who withstood the opposition of England and France, of every Indian nation, and of their fellow citizens to push westward across the Appalachian Mountains. This well-written history describes the political, economic, and social forces in pre-revolutionary America.

Everett N. Dick, historian and author of many historical works, is best known for his ability to capture the essence of frontier living in interesting and historically accurate accounts. Two of his most notable books are *The Sod-House Frontier, 1854–1890: A Social History of the Northern Plains from the Creation of Kansas and Nebraska to the Admission of the Dakotas* (New York: D. Appleton-Century Co., 1937) and *Vanguards of the Frontier: A Social History of the Northern Plains and Rocky Mountains from the Fur Traders to the Sod Busters* (Lincoln: University of Nebraska Press, 1941, 1965).

Dick's *The Dixie Frontier: A Social History of the Southern Frontier from the First Transmontane Beginnings to the Civil War* (reprint; Norman: University of Oklahoma Press, 1993) is an excellent example of regional social history. It is based on actual accounts of pioneers who settled in the Transmontane, a region encompassing southern Ohio, Indiana, and Illinois, Kentucky, Tennessee, and portions of Alabama, Mississippi, Louisiana, Arkansas, and Missouri. The author views this "Dixie" frontier in a much broader perspective than that of today. He views any pioneer with roots in Virginia, the Carolinas, or Georgia as a Southerner, relating daily life on the frontier with accuracy and compassion. The book's extensive bibliography provides references to period documents, diaries, reminiscences, and travel accounts.

The Reshaping of Everyday Life, 1790–1840 (New York: Harper & Row, 1988), by Jack Larkin, describes daily life during a time of great change in America. During this time a new government took shape, the movement westward accelerated with the development of a national road system, and the nation's economy expanded. Larkin describes in detail how Americans dealt with these changes and how these changes affected their daily lives. He describes their housing, clothing, food, and methods of hygiene. Although some Americans experienced new wealth and status, Larkin notes that the gap between rich and poor grew wider during this time. His descriptions of everyday life are taken from diaries, journals, and early chronicles. Larkin is chief historian at Old Sturbridge Village in Sturbridge, Massachusetts. His book is part of the Everyday Life in America Series, edited by Richard Balkin and published by Harper Collins Publishers. Other titles in the series include *The Expansion of Everyday Life: 1860–1876; Victorian America: Transformations in Everyday Life, 1876–1915;* and *The Uncertainty of Everyday Life, 1915–1945.*

Almanacs, Chronologies, and Statistical Sources. *Almanacs.* Almanacs are among the oldest types of reference sources used in the United States. Our ancestors used them to predict the weather, find home remedies, learn their multiplication tables, and even to consult stagecoach schedules (Horowitz 1988, 115). Today, almanacs provide quick, easy access to facts and statistics relating to countries, personalities, events, and subjects. Almanacs are composed of lists and tables of information gleaned from other sources and packaged compactly and inexpensively as books. Researchers and librarians use almanacs to quickly find facts, such as population figures, weights and measures, sports records, and similar types of information.

The United States' best-selling almanac, an authority since 1868, is the *World Almanac and Book of Facts* (New York: World Almanac, 1868–). Its many features include a perpetual calendar (a chart showing the day of the week corresponding to any given date over a period of many years) (figure 1-3). Addresses of genealogical societies are listed in the Associations and Societies section; the National Genealogical Society's address is in this almanac. A year-by-year history of the United States from 1492 to the present is also a feature of this useful reference source. Other reliable almanacs include *Information Please Almanac* (publisher varies, 1947–) and *Reader's Digest Almanac and Yearbook* (Pleasantville, N.Y.: Reader's Digest Association, 1966–). All three almanacs cover subjects of interest to American readers and are considered reliable sources of information.

Whitaker's Almanac (London: J. Whitaker & Sons, 1869–), a standard reference source in large libraries, focuses on Great Britain and the European continent. Its topics include royalty, "the Irish question," current exhibitions, and activities of the Commonwealth nations. Of special interest to those with British ancestry, *Whitaker's* provides a list of baronets and knights and an excellent list of common British abbreviations.

Chronologies. A chronology lists historical events in the order in which they occurred. Chronologies are useful to genealogists because they outline the important events of a given year. Genealogists preparing family histories can add life to their ancestors' stories by mentioning events that occurred in the political, cultural, and historical framework of their ancestors' times. For example, in 1845 the following events occurred: Texas joined the Union as the twenty-eighth state; the Methodist Episcopal Church in America split into northern and southern conferences; *The Raven and Other Poems,* by Edgar Allan Poe, was published; and potato crops failed throughout Europe, Britain, and Ireland, resulting in famines that killed 2.5 million people and led to a large migration to the United States from those areas (Trager 1992, 439–40).

The People's Chronology: A Year-by-Year Record of Human Events from Prehistory to the Present, by James Trager, 1st rev. ed. (New York: Henry Holt, 1992), groups yearly events by category rather than by nation or geographical area. Symbols to the left of each entry refer to a specific category of human endeavor and are explained in the "Key to Symbols." The recording of world events and human accomplishments is definitive and comprehensive in this chronology.

In contrast, *Timetables of History: A Horizontal Linkage of People and Events,* by Bernard Grun, 3rd rev. ed. (New York: Simon & Schuster, 1991), presents yearly events in a tabular format, as illustrated in figure 1-4. The tabular format is easy to read and aids in locating topics of interest quickly. *Timetables of History* is based on Werner Stein's *Kulturfahrplan* (*The Cultural Timetables*), which was produced in Germany in 1946. The third edition links events from 4500 B.C. to the year 1990. Both chronologies focus on Western civilization and contain few references to events in Asia or Africa.

Two additional reference books stand out as excellent sources of background material for authors compiling family

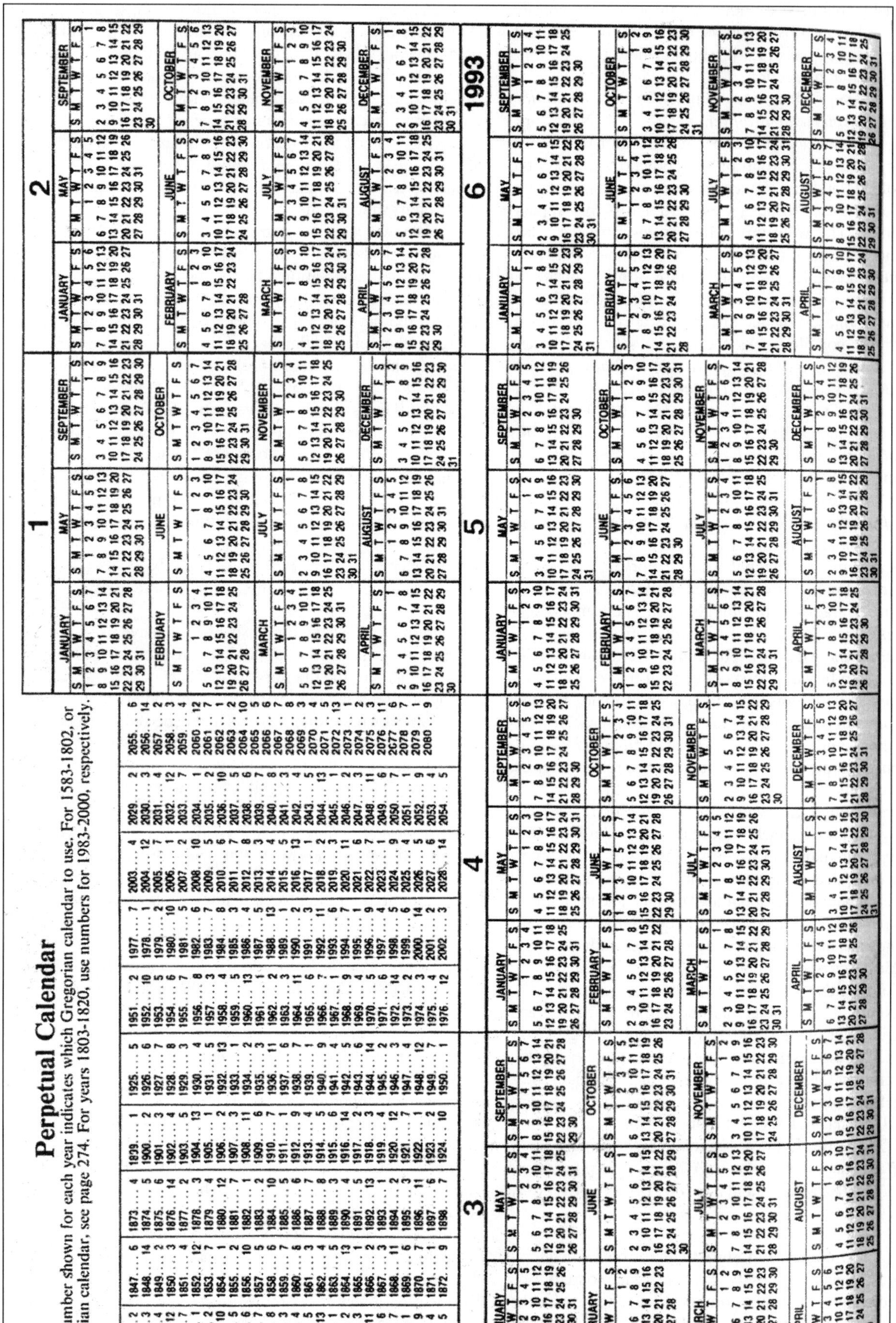

Perpetual Calendar

The number shown for each year indicates which Gregorian calendar to use. For 1583-1802, or for Julian calendar, see page 274. For years 1803-1820, use numbers for 1983-2000, respectively.

1821....2	1847....6	1873....4	1899....1	1925....5	1951....2	1977....7	2003....4	2029....2	2055....6
1822....3	1848...14	1874....5	1900....2	1926....6	1952...10	1978....1	2004...12	2030....3	2056...14
1823....4	1849....2	1875....6	1901....3	1927....7	1953....5	1979....2	2005....7	2031....4	2057....2
1824...12	1850....3	1876...14	1902....4	1928....8	1954....6	1980...10	2006....1	2032...12	2058....3
1825....7	1851....4	1877....2	1903....5	1929....3	1955....7	1981....5	2007....2	2033....7	2059....4
1826....1	1852...12	1878....3	1904...13	1930....4	1956....8	1982....6	2008...10	2034....1	2060..12
1827....2	1853....7	1879....4	1905....1	1931....5	1957....3	1983....7	2009....5	2035....2	2061..7
1828...10	1854....1	1880...12	1906....2	1932...13	1958....4	1984....8	2010....6	2036...10	2062..1
1829....5	1855....2	1881....7	1907....3	1933....1	1959....5	1985....3	2011....7	2037....5	2063..2
1830....6	1856...10	1882....1	1908...11	1934....2	1960...13	1986....4	2012....8	2038....6	2064..10
1831....7	1857....5	1883....2	1909....6	1935....3	1961....1	1987....5	2013....3	2039....7	2065..5
1832....8	1858....6	1884...10	1910....7	1936...11	1962....2	1988...13	2014....4	2040....8	2066..6
1833....3	1859....7	1885....5	1911....1	1937....6	1963....3	1989....1	2015....5	2041....3	2067..7
1834....4	1860....6	1886....6	1912....9	1938....7	1964...11	1990....2	2016...13	2042....4	2068..8
1835....5	1861....3	1887....7	1913....4	1939....1	1965....6	1991....3	2017....1	2043....5	2069..3
1836...13	1862....4	1888....8	1914....5	1940....9	1966....7	1992...11	2018....2	2044...13	2070..4
1837....1	1863....5	1889....3	1915....6	1941....4	1967....1	1993....6	2019....3	2045....1	2071..5
1838....2	1864...13	1890....4	1916...14	1942....5	1968....9	1994....7	2020...11	2046....2	2072..13
1839....3	1865....1	1891....5	1917....2	1943....6	1969....4	1995....1	2021....6	2047....3	2073..1
1840...11	1866....2	1892...13	1918....3	1944...14	1970....5	1996....9	2022....7	2048...11	2074..2
1841....6	1867....3	1893....1	1919....4	1945....2	1971....6	1997....4	2023....1	2049....6	2075..3
1842....7	1868...11	1894....2	1920...12	1946....3	1972...14	1998....5	2024....9	2050....7	2076..11
1843....1	1869....6	1895....3	1921....7	1947....4	1973....2	1999....6	2025....4	2051....1	2077..6
1844....9	1870....7	1896...11	1922....1	1948...12	1974....3	2000...14	2026....5	2052....9	2078..7
1845....4	1871....1	1897....6	1923....2	1949....7	1975....4	2001....2	2027....6	2053....4	2079..1
1846....5	1872....9	1898....7	1924...10	1950....1	1976...12	2002....3	2028...14	2054....5	2080..9

1

JANUARY
S M T W T F S
1 2 3 4 5 6 7
8 9 10 11 12 13 14
15 16 17 18 19 20 21
22 23 24 25 26 27 28
29 30 31

FEBRUARY
S M T W T F S
1 2 3 4
5 6 7 8 9 10 11
12 13 14 15 16 17 18
19 20 21 22 23 24 25
26 27 28

MARCH
S M T W T F S
1 2 3 4
5 6 7 8 9 10 11
12 13 14 15 16 17 18
19 20 21 22 23 24 25
26 27 28 29 30 31

APRIL
S M T W T F S
1
2 3 4 5 6 7 8
9 10 11 12 13 14 15
16 17 18 19 20 21 22
23 24 25 26 27 28 29
30

MAY
S M T W T F S
1 2 3 4 5 6
7 8 9 10 11 12 13
14 15 16 17 18 19 20
21 22 23 24 25 26 27
28 29 30 31

JUNE
S M T W T F S
1 2 3
4 5 6 7 8 9 10
11 12 13 14 15 16 17
18 19 20 21 22 23 24
25 26 27 28 29 30

JULY
S M T W T F S
1
2 3 4 5 6 7 8
9 10 11 12 13 14 15
16 17 18 19 20 21 22
23 24 25 26 27 28 29
30 31

AUGUST
S M T W T F S
1 2 3 4 5
6 7 8 9 10 11 12
13 14 15 16 17 18 19
20 21 22 23 24 25 26
27 28 29 30 31

SEPTEMBER
S M T W T F S
1 2
3 4 5 6 7 8 9
10 11 12 13 14 15 16
17 18 19 20 21 22 23
24 25 26 27 28 29 30

OCTOBER
S M T W T F S
1 2 3 4 5 6 7
8 9 10 11 12 13 14
15 16 17 18 19 20 21
22 23 24 25 26 27 28
29 30 31

NOVEMBER
S M T W T F S
1 2 3 4
5 6 7 8 9 10 11
12 13 14 15 16 17 18
19 20 21 22 23 24 25
26 27 28 29 30

DECEMBER
S M T W T F S
1 2
3 4 5 6 7 8 9
10 11 12 13 14 15 16
17 18 19 20 21 22 23
24 25 26 27 28 29 30
31

2

JANUARY
S M T W T F S
1 2 3 4 5 6
7 8 9 10 11 12 13
14 15 16 17 18 19 20
21 22 23 24 25 26 27
28 29 30 31

FEBRUARY
S M T W T F S
1 2 3
4 5 6 7 8 9 10
11 12 13 14 15 16 17
18 19 20 21 22 23 24
25 26 27 28

MARCH
S M T W T F S
1 2 3
4 5 6 7 8 9 10
11 12 13 14 15 16 17
18 19 20 21 22 23 24
25 26 27 28 29 30 31

APRIL
S M T W T F S
1 2 3 4 5 6 7
8 9 10 11 12 13 14
15 16 17 18 19 20 21
22 23 24 25 26 27 28
29 30

MAY
S M T W T F S
1 2 3 4 5
6 7 8 9 10 11 12
13 14 15 16 17 18 19
20 21 22 23 24 25 26
27 28 29 30 31

JUNE
S M T W T F S
1 2
3 4 5 6 7 8 9
10 11 12 13 14 15 16
17 18 19 20 21 22 23
24 25 26 27 28 29 30

JULY
S M T W T F S
1 2 3 4 5 6 7
8 9 10 11 12 13 14
15 16 17 18 19 20 21
22 23 24 25 26 27 28
29 30 31

AUGUST
S M T W T F S
1 2 3 4
5 6 7 8 9 10 11
12 13 14 15 16 17 18
19 20 21 22 23 24 25
26 27 28 29 30 31

SEPTEMBER
S M T W T F S
1
2 3 4 5 6 7 8
9 10 11 12 13 14 15
16 17 18 19 20 21 22
23 24 25 26 27 28 29
30

OCTOBER
S M T W T F S
1 2 3 4 5 6
7 8 9 10 11 12 13
14 15 16 17 18 19 20
21 22 23 24 25 26 27
28 29 30 31

NOVEMBER
S M T W T F S
1 2 3
4 5 6 7 8 9 10
11 12 13 14 15 16 17
18 19 20 21 22 23 24
25 26 27 28 29 30

DECEMBER
S M T W T F S
1
2 3 4 5 6 7 8
9 10 11 12 13 14 15
16 17 18 19 20 21 22
23 24 25 26 27 28 29
30 31

3

JANUARY
S M T W T F S
1 2 3 4 5
6 7 8 9 10 11 12
13 14 15 16 17 18 19
20 21 22 23 24 25 26
27 28 29 30 31

FEBRUARY
S M T W T F S
1 2
3 4 5 6 7 8 9
10 11 12 13 14 15 16
17 18 19 20 21 22 23
24 25 26 27 28

MARCH
S M T W T F S
1 2
3 4 5 6 7 8 9
10 11 12 13 14 15 16
17 18 19 20 21 22 23
24 25 26 27 28 29 30
31

APRIL
S M T W T F S
1 2 3 4 5 6
7 8 9 10 11 12 13
14 15 16 17 18 19 20
21 22 23 24 25 26 27
28 29 30

MAY
S M T W T F S
1 2 3 4
5 6 7 8 9 10 11
12 13 14 15 16 17 18
19 20 21 22 23 24 25
26 27 28 29 30 31

JUNE
S M T W T F S
1
2 3 4 5 6 7 8
9 10 11 12 13 14 15
16 17 18 19 20 21 22
23 24 25 26 27 28 29
30

JULY
S M T W T F S
1 2 3 4 5 6
7 8 9 10 11 12 13
14 15 16 17 18 19 20
21 22 23 24 25 26 27
28 29 30 31

AUGUST
S M T W T F S
1 2 3
4 5 6 7 8 9 10
11 12 13 14 15 16 17
18 19 20 21 22 23 24
25 26 27 28 29 30 31

SEPTEMBER
S M T W T F S
1 2 3 4 5 6 7
8 9 10 11 12 13 14
15 16 17 18 19 20 21
22 23 24 25 26 27 28
29 30

OCTOBER
S M T W T F S
1 2 3 4 5
6 7 8 9 10 11 12
13 14 15 16 17 18 19
20 21 22 23 24 25 26
27 28 29 30 31

NOVEMBER
S M T W T F S
1 2
3 4 5 6 7 8 9
10 11 12 13 14 15 16
17 18 19 20 21 22 23
24 25 26 27 28 29 30

DECEMBER
S M T W T F S
1 2 3 4 5 6 7
8 9 10 11 12 13 14
15 16 17 18 19 20 21
22 23 24 25 26 27 28
29 30 31

4

JANUARY
S M T W T F S
1 2 3 4
5 6 7 8 9 10 11
12 13 14 15 16 17 18
19 20 21 22 23 24 25
26 27 28 29 30 31

FEBRUARY
S M T W T F S
1
2 3 4 5 6 7 8
9 10 11 12 13 14 15
16 17 18 19 20 21 22
23 24 25 26 27 28

MARCH
S M T W T F S
1
2 3 4 5 6 7 8
9 10 11 12 13 14 15
16 17 18 19 20 21 22
23 24 25 26 27 28 29
30 31

APRIL
S M T W T F S
1 2 3 4 5
6 7 8 9 10 11 12
13 14 15 16 17 18 19
20 21 22 23 24 25 26
27 28 29 30

MAY
S M T W T F S
1 2 3
4 5 6 7 8 9 10
11 12 13 14 15 16 17
18 19 20 21 22 23 24
25 26 27 28 29 30 31

JUNE
S M T W T F S
1 2 3 4 5 6 7
8 9 10 11 12 13 14
15 16 17 18 19 20 21
22 23 24 25 26 27 28
29 30

JULY
S M T W T F S
1 2 3 4 5
6 7 8 9 10 11 12
13 14 15 16 17 18 19
20 21 22 23 24 25 26
27 28 29 30 31

AUGUST
S M T W T F S
1 2
3 4 5 6 7 8 9
10 11 12 13 14 15 16
17 18 19 20 21 22 23
24 25 26 27 28 29 30
31

SEPTEMBER
S M T W T F S
1 2 3 4 5 6
7 8 9 10 11 12 13
14 15 16 17 18 19 20
21 22 23 24 25 26 27
28 29 30

OCTOBER
S M T W T F S
1 2 3 4
5 6 7 8 9 10 11
12 13 14 15 16 17 18
19 20 21 22 23 24 25
26 27 28 29 30 31

NOVEMBER
S M T W T F S
1
2 3 4 5 6 7 8
9 10 11 12 13 14 15
16 17 18 19 20 21 22
23 24 25 26 27 28 29
30

DECEMBER
S M T W T F S
1 2 3 4 5 6
7 8 9 10 11 12 13
14 15 16 17 18 19 20
21 22 23 24 25 26 27
28 29 30 31

5

JANUARY
S M T W T F S
1 2 3
4 5 6 7 8 9 10
11 12 13 14 15 16 17
18 19 20 21 22 23 24
25 26 27 28 29 30 31

FEBRUARY
S M T W T F S
1 2 3 4 5 6 7
8 9 10 11 12 13 14
15 16 17 18 19 20 21
22 23 24 25 26 27 28

MARCH
S M T W T F S
1 2 3 4 5 6 7
8 9 10 11 12 13 14
15 16 17 18 19 20 21
22 23 24 25 26 27 28
29 30 31

APRIL
S M T W T F S
1 2 3 4
5 6 7 8 9 10 11
12 13 14 15 16 17 18
19 20 21 22 23 24 25
26 27 28 29 30

MAY
S M T W T F S
1 2
3 4 5 6 7 8 9
10 11 12 13 14 15 16
17 18 19 20 21 22 23
24 25 26 27 28 29 30
31

JUNE
S M T W T F S
1 2 3 4 5 6
7 8 9 10 11 12 13
14 15 16 17 18 19 20
21 22 23 24 25 26 27
28 29 30

JULY
S M T W T F S
1 2 3 4
5 6 7 8 9 10 11
12 13 14 15 16 17 18
19 20 21 22 23 24 25
26 27 28 29 30 31

AUGUST
S M T W T F S
1
2 3 4 5 6 7 8
9 10 11 12 13 14 15
16 17 18 19 20 21 22
23 24 25 26 27 28 29
30 31

SEPTEMBER
S M T W T F S
1 2 3 4 5
6 7 8 9 10 11 12
13 14 15 16 17 18 19
20 21 22 23 24 25 26
27 28 29 30

OCTOBER
S M T W T F S
1 2 3
4 5 6 7 8 9 10
11 12 13 14 15 16 17
18 19 20 21 22 23 24
25 26 27 28 29 30 31

NOVEMBER
S M T W T F S
1 2 3 4 5 6 7
8 9 10 11 12 13 14
15 16 17 18 19 20 21
22 23 24 25 26 27 28
29 30

DECEMBER
S M T W T F S
1 2 3 4 5
6 7 8 9 10 11 12
13 14 15 16 17 18 19
20 21 22 23 24 25 26
27 28 29 30 31

6 — 1993

JANUARY
S M T W T F S
1 2
3 4 5 6 7 8 9
10 11 12 13 14 15 16
17 18 19 20 21 22 23
24 25 26 27 28 29 30
31

FEBRUARY
S M T W T F S
1 2 3 4 5 6
7 8 9 10 11 12 13
14 15 16 17 18 19 20
21 22 23 24 25 26 27
28

MARCH
S M T W T F S
1 2 3 4 5 6
7 8 9 10 11 12 13
14 15 16 17 18 19 20
21 22 23 24 25 26 27
28 29 30 31

APRIL
S M T W T F S
1 2 3
4 5 6 7 8 9 10
11 12 13 14 15 16 17
18 19 20 21 22 23 24
25 26 27 28 29 30

MAY
S M T W T F S
1
2 3 4 5 6 7 8
9 10 11 12 13 14 15
16 17 18 19 20 21 22
23 24 25 26 27 28 29
30 31

JUNE
S M T W T F S
1 2 3 4 5
6 7 8 9 10 11 12
13 14 15 16 17 18 19
20 21 22 23 24 25 26
27 28 29 30

JULY
S M T W T F S
1 2 3
4 5 6 7 8 9 10
11 12 13 14 15 16 17
18 19 20 21 22 23 24
25 26 27 28 29 30 31

AUGUST
S M T W T F S
1 2 3 4 5 6 7
8 9 10 11 12 13 14
15 16 17 18 19 20 21
22 23 24 25 26 27 28
29 30 31

SEPTEMBER
S M T W T F S
1 2 3 4
5 6 7 8 9 10 11
12 13 14 15 16 17 18
19 20 21 22 23 24 25
26 27 28 29 30

OCTOBER
S M T W T F S
1 2
3 4 5 6 7 8 9
10 11 12 13 14 15 16
17 18 19 20 21 22 23
24 25 26 27 28 29 30
31

NOVEMBER
S M T W T F S
1 2 3 4 5 6
7 8 9 10 11 12 13
14 15 16 17 18 19 20
21 22 23 24 25 26 27
28 29 30

DECEMBER
S M T W T F S
1 2 3 4
5 6 7 8 9 10 11
12 13 14 15 16 17 18
19 20 21 22 23 24 25
26 27 28 29 30 31

Figure 1-3. Perpetual calendar from the *World Almanac and Book of Facts.*

histories: *Time Lines on File* (New York: Facts on File, 1988) and *Timetables of American History,* edited by Laurence Urdang (New York: Simon & Schuster, 1996). *Time Lines on File* is designed for use in history courses and offers genealogists more than three hundred illustrated charts that record history in a linear format. It is bound in a three-ring binder so that the pages can be removed and copied. Figure 1-5 is an example of a chart from *Time Lines;* it shows the dates when each state joined the union. Another excellent example is shown in figure 1-6.

Timetables of American History relates the history of America within the context of world events. Each year from 1000 to 1994 is divided into four broad topics: History and Politics, The Arts, Science and Technology, and Miscellaneous. Thus, one learns that in 1804 Thomas Jefferson was reelected president, Napoleon crowned himself emperor before the pope, bananas were imported for the first time from Cuba to the United States, and "Coonskin libraries" came into being when settlers along the Ohio River bartered coonskins for books from Boston merchants. Placing an ancestor's life in relation to such events in a family history lends life to the ancestor's story and makes a narrative more interesting to read.

Statistical Sources. Historical Statistics of the United States: Colonial Times to 1970 (Washington, D.C.: U.S. Department of Commerce, Bureau of Commerce, 1975) is not a chronology or timetable. It is a collection of American statistics from colonial times to 1970. Researchers will find this reference book useful for adding statistical information to reports, papers, and family histories. For example, figure 1-7 shows the number of U.S. immigrants by country of origin from 1820 to 1870. If an ancestor was an Irish immigrant who journeyed to the United States in 1847, she could be categorized as one of 105,536 other immigrants. Also, an ancestor could be further described as one of a mass of immigrants whose migration between 1846 and 1847 doubled the number of Irish coming to U.S. shores. These statistics show the effect the Irish Potato Famine had on immigration to the United States. Additional statistics from this standard reference source include "Foreign-Born Population by Country of Birth: 1850 to 1870" and "Immigrants by Major Occupation Group: 1820 to 1970." These examples are from the "International Migration and Naturalization" section. Other sections of interest to family historians include a government section that offers a table of "Military Personnel on Active Duty: 1789 to 1970" and a section on colonial and pre-Federal statistics.

Directories. Directories are alphabetical lists of people, organizations, associations, and institutions. They guide researchers to current information on many topics. Researchers can often restart stalled research by investigating and using the many directories available.

Directories are among the easiest reference tools to use. A directory's scope is often revealed in the title, such as *Directory of Archives and Manuscript Repositories in the United States* (Phoenix: Oryx Press, 1988). The information presented in a directory is usually limited to one topic. Directories range in scope from the common telephone book to more narrowly focused works, such as the *Directory of Family "One-Name" Periodicals* (Indianapolis: Ye Olde Genealogie Shoppe, 1994). Directories contain addresses, telephone numbers, and descriptive information for individuals, firms, and associations. Additionally, they provide information on an institution's holdings, hours of operation, and, sometimes, historical data about the institution.

Directories in Print (Detroit: Gale Research, 1989–) is actually a directory of directories. Published annually, *Directories in Print* describes more than fifteen thousand printed and non-printed directories, rosters, buyers' guides, and address lists published in the United States and worldwide. Almost two hundred entries appear in the "Biography and Genealogy" section of the fourteenth edition (1997) of *Directories in Print.* Figure 1-8 shows the broad coverage of this very useful reference book. Researchers interested in locating reference sources and facilities for southern New Jersey, for example, might be interested in purchasing the directory titled *Genealogical Resources in Southern New Jersey,* edited by Edith Hoelle, as shown in figure 1-8. Browsing through *Directories in Print* can reveal many new research clues for the family historian who thinks he has searched everywhere.

Categorizing directories into five broadly defined groups helps to outline the potential research capabilities that directories offer to genealogists. The five groups are: (1) local, (2) professional, (3) institutional, (4) groups and associations, and (5) source guides.

Local Directories. Telephone directories fall into this category. A telephone book is perhaps the first directory a person learns to use and is the one directory people often use daily. *Phonefiche* (Ann Arbor, Mich.: United Microfilms International) is a unique telephone directory found in large libraries. It offers a collection of more than 2,600 U.S. telephone directories on microfiche. Updated monthly, *Phonefiche* provides instant access to both yellow and white pages, primarily of Bell telephone systems in the United States.

Telephone directories are now available online through the Internet and in CD-ROM format. Pro CD (Danvers, Maryland), Digital Directory Assistance (Bethesda, Maryland), American Business Information (Omaha, Nebraska), and DeLorme Mapping (Freeport, Maine) all produce telephone directories on CD-ROM. A search for a surname within these databases may be limited by first name, state, city, ZIP code, area code, or any combination thereof. A search of the surname of this author's maternal ancestor showed that there are 310 and 180 Bremner listings in the western and eastern United States, respectively.

These electronic telephone listings provide genealogists with nationwide access to names and addresses of possible relatives. However, do not assume that the compilers of these listings have used all of the telephone company-produced directories from throughout the United States. Each publisher draws its information from different sources that may include city directories, drivers' licenses, utility listings, and other, similar lists. Duplicate entries may appear for some people, and some names may be absent altogether. These listings are not all-inclusive, but they can be especially useful to researchers who are searching for unusual names or specific names in certain places.

City directories, another type of local directory, offer genealogists an excellent source for family information. City directories provide alphabetical listings for persons by last name, by street address, and sometimes numerically by telephone number. They are usually published yearly and are available from early in American history. For a comprehensive look at city directories and their use in genealogical research, consult "Research in Directories," by Gordon Lewis Remington, chapter

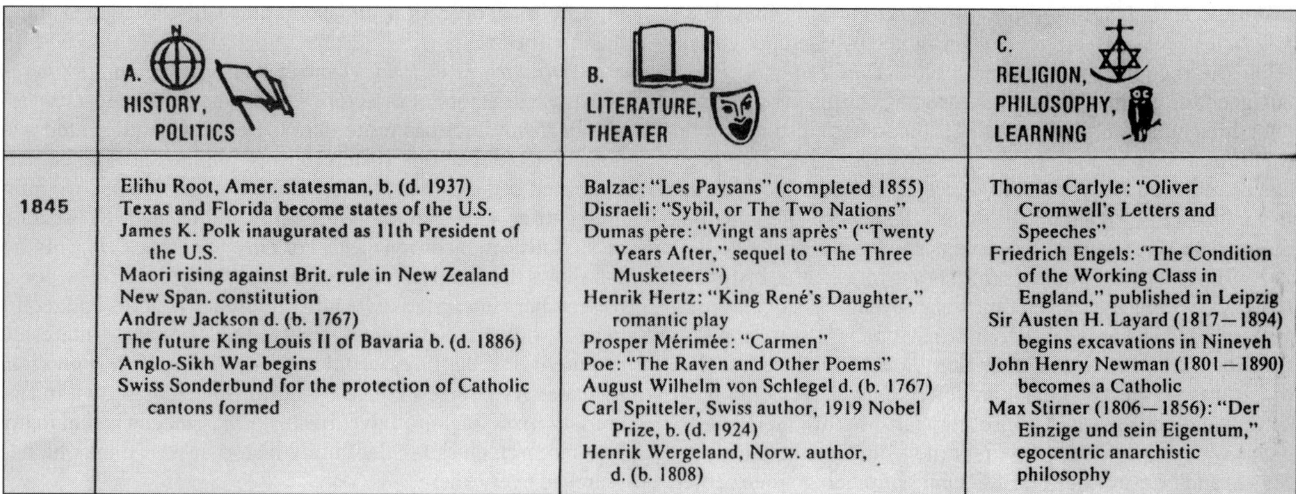

	A. HISTORY, POLITICS	B. LITERATURE, THEATER	C. RELIGION, PHILOSOPHY, LEARNING
1845	Elihu Root, Amer. statesman, b. (d. 1937) Texas and Florida become states of the U.S. James K. Polk inaugurated as 11th President of the U.S. Maori rising against Brit. rule in New Zealand New Span. constitution Andrew Jackson d. (b. 1767) The future King Louis II of Bavaria b. (d. 1886) Anglo-Sikh War begins Swiss Sonderbund for the protection of Catholic cantons formed	Balzac: "Les Paysans" (completed 1855) Disraeli: "Sybil, or The Two Nations" Dumas père: "Vingt ans après" ("Twenty Years After," sequel to "The Three Musketeers") Henrik Hertz: "King René's Daughter," romantic play Prosper Mérimée: "Carmen" Poe: "The Raven and Other Poems" August Wilhelm von Schlegel d. (b. 1767) Carl Spitteler, Swiss author, 1919 Nobel Prize, b. (d. 1924) Henrik Wergeland, Norw. author, d. (b. 1808)	Thomas Carlyle: "Oliver Cromwell's Letters and Speeches" Friedrich Engels: "The Condition of the Working Class in England," published in Leipzig Sir Austen H. Layard (1817–1894) begins excavations in Nineveh John Henry Newman (1801–1890) becomes a Catholic Max Stirner (1806–1856): "Der Einzige und sein Eigentum," egocentric anarchistic philosophy

Figure 1-4. *Timetables of History: A Horizontal Linkage of People and Events* presents yearly events in a tabular format.

11 in *The Source: A Guidebook of American Genealogy,* edited by Loretto Dennis Szucs and Sandra Hargreaves Luebking, rev. ed. (Salt Lake City: Ancestry, 1997).

Local community directories offer data not found in nationally focused directories. Yearly church directories, hospital directories, and local governmental directories are examples. Publications of local organizations such as chambers of commerce, Rotary clubs, and patriotic organizations usually list members' names, addresses, and other historical data. These directories can often be found in local libraries and historical societies. Community directories can also be found in reference or archive departments of state universities and state libraries and archives. Consult the following subject categories in a library catalog for possible references to local directories: Subject—State—County—Directories; for example: Churches—Illinois—Du Page County—Directories; or simply Physicians—Directories or Junior Colleges—Directories.

Professional Directories. Professional directories cover a wide range of professions and occupations at national, state, and local levels. Most national professional directories are listed in the previously mentioned *Directories in Print.* State and local professional directories can be found in libraries that have genealogy collections or in large public libraries.

The *APG Directory of Professional Genealogists* (Denver, Colo.: Association of Professional Genealogists; usually issued every two years) lists more than one thousand professional genealogists. Published as a guide for those who need assistance with their genealogical research, the *Directory* also fills the needs of lawyers, court officials, and geneticists. The 1997 edition is arranged alphabetically by country; the United States is listed first. Within each country the listing is by state and provides the following information for each entry: name, address, and telephone number, research specialty, related services, and geographic specialty. A short biography offers additional information for most entries. Three easy-to-use indexes provide access to entries by geographic specialties, U.S. ZIP code, and an alphabetical index to members of the Association of Professional Genealogists.

The Board for Certification of Genealogists publishes a biennial list of certified genealogists. *Certification Roster: Researchers, Editors, Instructors, Librarians, and Writers, 1997–98* (Washington, D.C.: Board for Certification of Genealogists) lists researchers, editors, instructors, lecturers, librarians, and writers. Arrangement is alphabetical by state. Each entry provides information concerning the type of research conducted, the geographic areas of speciality, and the research facilities consulted.

Who's Who in Genealogy and Heraldry, edited and published by Mary Keysor Meyer and P. William Filby (Savage, Md.: Who's Who in Genealogy & Heraldry, 1990), lists individuals prominent in the fields of genealogy and heraldry. Criteria used by the editors for inclusion in this directory were (1) contribution to the field, (2) significant achievement in the field, and (3) public interest in the person considered. Those chosen included authors and editors of significant genealogical/heraldic publications, selected accredited and non-accredited professionals, genealogical reference librarians, and publishers of genealogical/heraldic works. Useful when biographical information is needed about a genealogist, lecturer, librarian, or author in the field of genealogy, this reference source is used primarily by other professionals in the field.

Other types of professional directories can be of assistance when searching for ancestors who lived in large cities in the twentieth century. Directories of doctors, lawyers, labor leaders, and other professionals can be useful to family historians. The *Family History Library Catalog*™ of the Family History Library is an excellent place to search for these directories (see chapter 5, Bibliographies and Catalogs); look in it under the country, state, county, and city of interest.

Institutional Directories. Institutional directories lead researchers to libraries, archives, historical societies, and

D. VISUAL ARTS	E. MUSIC	F. SCIENCE, TECHNOLOGY, GROWTH	G. DAILY LIFE	
Wilhelm von Bode, Ger. art historian, b. (d. 1929) First artistic photo portraits by David Octavius Hill (1802—1870) J. T. Huvé completes Madeleine Church, Paris Ingres: portrait of the Countess Haussonville Adolf Oberländer, Ger. caricaturist, b. (d. 1923) The Portland Vase, a famous Grecian urn maliciously destroyed, completely restored	Gabriel Fauré, Fr. composer, b. (d. 1924) "Leonora," Amer. opera by W. H. Fry (1813—1864) produced at Philadelphia Lortzing: "Undine," opera, Magdeburg Wagner: "Tannhäuser," Dresden Charles Marie Widor, Fr. composer and organist, b. (d. 1937)	Sir William G. Armstrong (1810—1900) patents hydraulic crane Amer. inventor E. B. Bigelow (1814—1879) constructs power loom for manufacturing carpets Arthur Cayley (1821—1895): "Theory of Linear Transformations" First submarine cable laid across English Channel Fr. inventor Joshua Heilman (1796—1848) patents machine for combing cotton and wool Humboldt: "Cosmos" (—1862 five vols.) Ger. chemist Adolf Kolbe (1818—1884) synthesizes acetic acid Charles Laveran, Fr. physician, 1907 Nobel Prize for Medicine. b. (d. 1922) Brit. engineer William M'Naught develops compound steam engine Ilya Ilich Mechnikov, Russ. physiologist, 1908 Nobel Prize for Medicine, b. (d. 1916)	Knickerbocker Baseball Club codifies rules of baseball U.S. Naval Academy, Annapolis, Md., opened Oxford-Cambridge boat race transferred from Henley-on-Thames to Putney	1845

Figure 1-4 (continued).

similar research facilities. This type of reference source opens new avenues of research and can be found in most libraries nationwide.

The *American Library Directory* (New Providence, N.J.: R. R. Bowker, annual) lists more than thirty-seven thousand public, academic, government, and special libraries in the United States, Mexico, and Canada. Each listing includes the library's address, telephone number, number of volumes, and special collections held. This last point is important for genealogists because library special collections are often identified as "local history" or "genealogy." Figure 1-9 illustrates the special collections held by the Shelbina Carnegie Public Library in Shelbina, Missouri. The staff of this library is sufficiently proud of its special collections to include them in the library's entry in this directory. Resources found in smaller, local libraries are unique and should not be overlooked as local records found in them are often not available in larger libraries. The *American Library Directory* will help one find them.

This directory should be consulted when planning a research trip; it will direct one to small-town libraries to visit in the area where ancestors lived. The *American Library Directory* is also helpful when searching for the name of a library to contact for information about local sources and the names of local researchers.

Another important directory is the biennial *Directory of Special Libraries and Information Centers: A Guide to More Than 20,800 Special Libraries, Research Libraries, Information Centers, Archives, and Data Centers Maintained by Government Agencies, Business, Industry, Newspapers, Educational Institutions, Nonprofit Organizations, and Societies in the Field of Science and Engineering, Medicine, Law, Art, Religion, the Social Sciences, and Humanities*, 16th ed. (Detroit: Gale Research Co., 1993). This directory's subtitle aptly describes its scope and content. Use this source to locate research collections on specific topics. For example, to learn if there are special library collections on Polish Americans in the United States, consult the directory's index under Polish Americans. References show three collections: one in New Britain, Connecticut, at the Central Connecticut State University in the Elihu Burritt Library, Special Collections; one in Buffalo, New York, at the State University of New York at Buffalo in the Lockwood Memorial Library—Polish Collection; and one in Chicago at the Polish Museum of America in the Archives and Library. All three entries give addresses and telephone numbers and indicate that each is open to the public.

The *Directory of Archives and Manuscript Repositories in the United States* (cited earlier), published by the National Historical Publications and Records Commission, directs researchers to institutions that hold historical records. Descriptive information concerning each repository includes address, telephone number, and hours of operation. Additionally, information on copying facilities, materials solicited by the repository, holdings by total volumes, inclusive dates of those holdings, and a brief description of the holdings are included. Also noted is the existence of any guides published by the institution. A detailed subject index cites personal names, subjects, and geographical terms used in the descriptive narrative of each repository's holdings. An updated version of this source is now available on CD-ROM in *ArchivesUSA* (Alexandria, Va.: Chadwyck-Healey, 1996).

Locating archives and research institutions on the international level is best accomplished by using the annual *World of Learning* (London: Allen & Unwin, 1947–). Arranged alphabetically by name of country, this classic reference work lists libraries, archives, learned societies, research institutes, museums, and other institutions of higher education in nearly two hundred countries. Each listing provides an institution's address, telephone number, fields of interest, number of volumes held, catalogs published, and director's name.

Genealogists should be aware of two directories compiled specifically for family historians. The *Directory of American Libraries with Genealogy or Local History Collections,* by P.

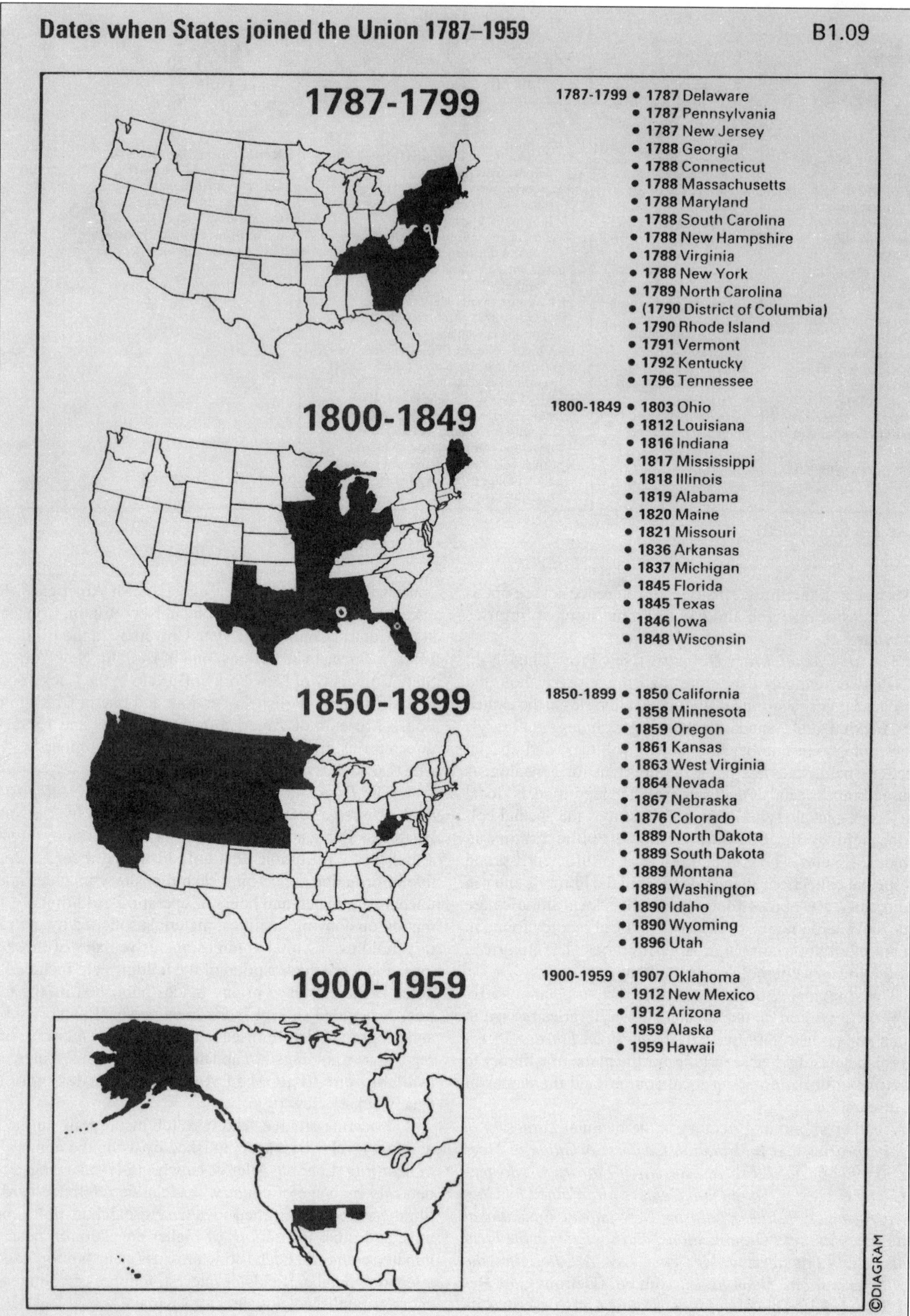

Dates when States joined the Union 1787–1959
B1.09
1787-1799
1787-1799 • 1787 Delaware
• 1787 Pennsylvania
• 1787 New Jersey
• 1788 Georgia
• 1788 Connecticut
• 1788 Massachusetts
• 1788 Maryland
• 1788 South Carolina
• 1788 New Hampshire
• 1788 Virginia
• 1788 New York
• 1789 North Carolina
• (1790 District of Columbia)
• 1790 Rhode Island
• 1791 Vermont
• 1792 Kentucky
• 1796 Tennessee
1800-1849
1800-1849 • 1803 Ohio
• 1812 Louisiana
• 1816 Indiana
• 1817 Mississippi
• 1818 Illinois
• 1819 Alabama
• 1820 Maine
• 1821 Missouri
• 1836 Arkansas
• 1837 Michigan
• 1845 Florida
• 1845 Texas
• 1846 Iowa
• 1848 Wisconsin
1850-1899
1850-1899 • 1850 California
• 1858 Minnesota
• 1859 Oregon
• 1861 Kansas
• 1863 West Virginia
• 1864 Nevada
• 1867 Nebraska
• 1876 Colorado
• 1889 North Dakota
• 1889 South Dakota
• 1889 Montana
• 1889 Washington
• 1890 Idaho
• 1890 Wyoming
• 1896 Utah
1900-1959
1900-1959 • 1907 Oklahoma
• 1912 New Mexico
• 1912 Arizona
• 1959 Alaska
• 1959 Hawaii
©DIAGRAM

Figure 1-5. From *Time Lines on File*—"Dates when States joined the Union 1787–1959."

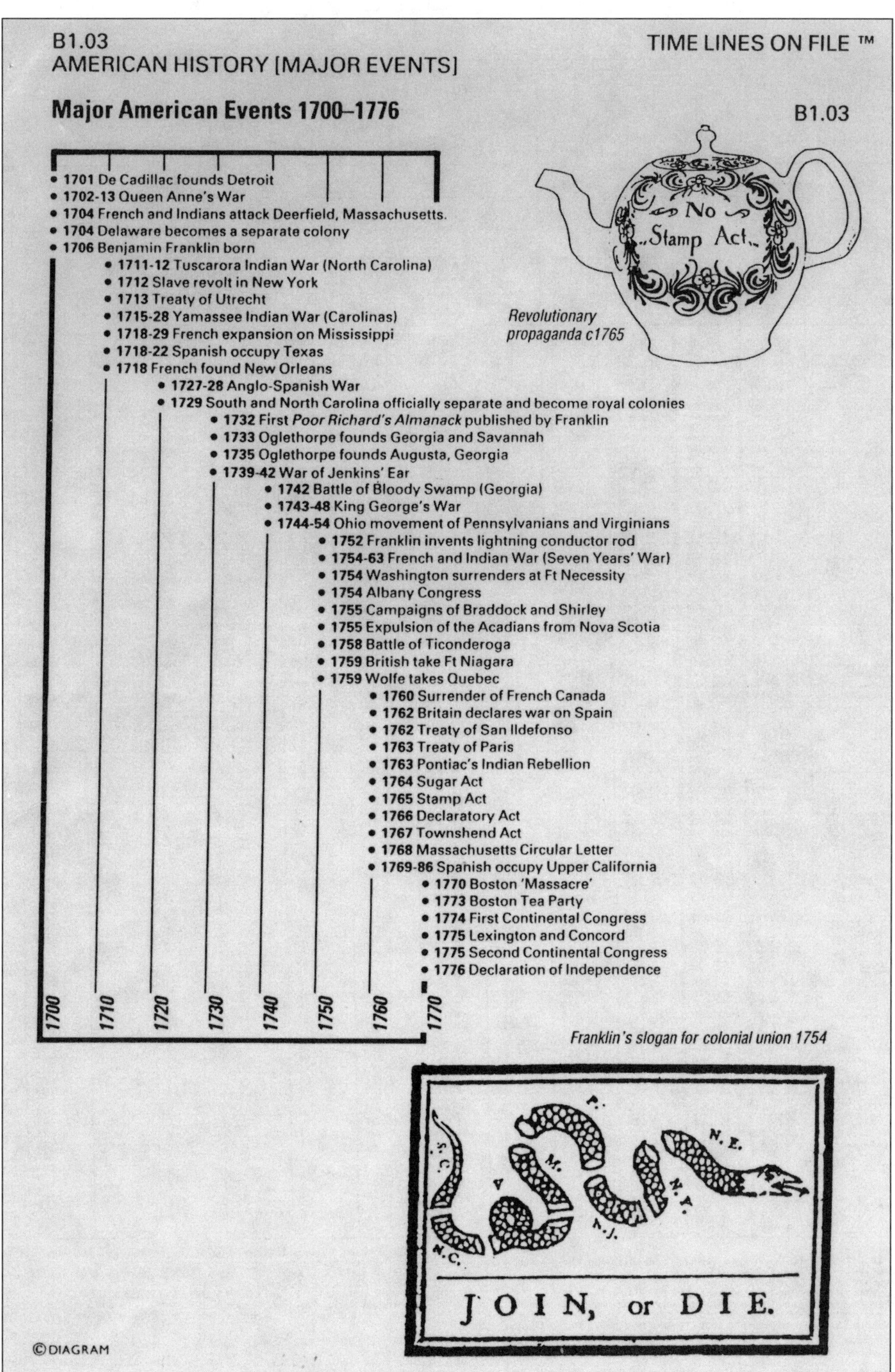

Figure 1-6. From *Time Lines on File*—"Major American Events 1700–1776."

Series C 89–119. Immigrants, by Country: 1820 to 1970—Con.

[For years ending June 30, except: 1820–1831 and 1844–1849, years ending Sept. 30; 1833–1842 and 1851–1867, years ending Dec. 31; 1832 covers 15 months ending Dec. 31; 1843, 9 months ending Sept. 30; 1850, 15 months ending Dec. 31; 1868, 6 months ending June 30]

Year	All countries[1]	Total	Europe										
			Northwestern Europe				Central Europe			Eastern Europe		Southern Europe	
			Great Britain	Ireland[2]	Scandinavia[3]	Other Northwestern[4]	Germany[5]	Poland	Other Central[6]	U.S.S.R. and Baltic States[7]	Other Eastern[8]	Italy	Other Southern[9]
	89	90	91	92	93	94	95	96	97	98	99	100	101
1890	455,302	445,680	69,730	53,024	50,368	20,575	92,427	11,073	56,199	35,598	723	52,003	3,960
1889	444,427	434,790	87,992	65,557	57,504	22,010	99,538	4,922	34,174	33,916	1,145	25,307	2,725
1888	546,889	538,131	108,692	73,513	81,924	23,251	109,717	5,826	45,811	33,487	1,393	51,558	2,959
1887	490,109	482,829	93,378	68,370	67,629	17,307	106,865	6,128	40,265	30,766	2,251	47,622	2,248
1886	334,203	329,529	62,929	49,619	46,735	11,737	84,403	3,939	28,680	17,800	670	21,315	1,702
1885	395,346	353,083	57,713	51,795	40,704	13,732	124,443	3,085	27,309	17,158	941	13,642	2,561
1884	518,592	453,686	65,950	63,344	52,728	18,768	179,676	4,536	36,571	12,689	388	16,510	2,526
1883	603,322	522,587	76,606	81,486	71,994	24,271	194,786	2,011	27,625	9,909	163	31,792	1,944
1882	788,992	648,186	102,991	76,432	105,326	27,796	250,630	4,672	29,150	16,918	134	32,159	1,978
1881	669,431	528,545	81,376	72,342	81,582	26,883	210,485	5,614	27,935	5,041	102	15,401	1,784
1880	457,257	348,691	73,273	71,603	65,657	15,042	84,638	2,177	17,267	5,014	35	12,354	1,631
1879	177,826	134,259	29,955	20,013	21,820	9,081	34,602	489	5,963	4,453	29	5,791	2,063
1878	138,469	101,612	22,150	15,932	12,254	6,929	29,313	547	5,150	3,048	29	4,344	1,916
1877	141,857	106,195	23,581	14,569	11,274	8,621	29,298	533	5,396	6,599	32	3,195	3,097
1876	169,986	120,920	29,291	19,575	12,323	10,923	31,937	925	6,276	4,775	38	3,015	1,842
1875	227,498	182,961	47,905	37,957	14,322	11,987	47,769	984	7,658	7,997	27	3,631	2,724
1874	313,339	262,783	62,021	53,707	19,178	15,998	87,291	1,795	8,850	4,073	62	7,666	2,142
1873	459,803	397,541	89,500	77,344	35,481	22,892	149,671	3,338	7,112	1,634	53	8,757	1,759
1872	404,806	352,155	84,912	68,732	28,575	15,614	141,109	1,647	4,410	1,018	20	4,190	1,928
1871	321,350	265,145	85,455	57,439	22,132	7,174	82,554	535	4,887	673	23	2,816	1,457
1870	387,203	328,626	103,677	56,996	30,742	9,152	118,225	223	4,425	907	6	2,891	1,382
1869	352,768	315,963	84,438	40,786	43,941	10,585	131,042	184	1,499	343	18	1,489	1,638
1868	138,840	130,090	24,127	32,068	11,985	4,293	55,831	–	192	141	4	891	558
1867	315,722	283,751	52,641	72,879	8,491	12,417	133,426	310	692	205	26	1,624	1,040
1866	318,568	278,916	94,924	36,690	14,495	13,648	115,892	412	93	287	18	1,382	1,075
1865	248,120	214,048	82,465	29,772	7,258	7,992	83,424	528	422	183	14	924	1,066
1864	193,418	185,233	53,428	63,523	2,961	5,621	57,276	165	230	256	11	600	1,162
1863	176,282	163,733	66,882	55,916	3,119	3,245	33,162	94	85	77	16	547	590
1862	91,985	83,710	24,639	23,351	2,550	4,386	27,529	63	111	79	11	566	425
1861	91,918	81,200	19,675	23,797	850	3,769	31,661	48	51	34	5	811	499
1860	153,640	141,209	29,737	48,637	840	5,278	54,491	82	----------	65	4	1,019	1,056
1859	121,282	110,949	26,163	35,216	1,590	3,727	41,784	106	----------	91	10	932	1,330
1858	123,126	111,354	28,956	26,873	2,662	4,580	45,310	9	----------	246	17	1,240	1,461
1857	251,306	216,224	58,479	54,361	2,747	6,879	91,781	124	----------	25	11	1,007	810
1856	200,436	186,083	44,658	54,349	1,330	12,403	71,028	20	----------	9	5	1,365	916
1855	200,877	187,729	47,572	49,627	1,349	14,571	71,918	462	----------	13	9	1,052	1,156
1854	427,833	405,542	58,647	101,606	4,222	23,070	215,009	208	----------	2	7	1,263	1,508
1853	368,645	361,576	37,576	162,649	3,396	14,205	141,946	33	----------	3	15	555	1,198
1852	371,603	362,484	40,699	159,548	4,106	11,278	145,918	110	----------	2	3	351	469
1851	379,466	369,510	51,487	221,253	2,438	20,905	72,482	10	----------	1	2	447	485
1850	369,980	308,323	51,085	164,004	1,589	11,470	78,896	5	----------	31	15	431	797
1849	297,024	286,501	55,132	159,398	3,481	7,634	60,235	4	----------	44	9	209	355
1848	226,527	218,025	35,159	112,934	1,113	9,877	58,465	–	----------	1	3	241	232
1847	234,968	229,117	23,302	105,536	1,320	24,336	74,281	8	----------	5	2	164	163
1846	154,416	146,315	22,180	51,752	2,030	12,303	57,561	4	----------	248	4	151	82
1845	114,371	109,301	19,210	44,821	982	9,466	34,355	6	----------	1	3	137	320
1844	78,615	74,745	14,353	33,490	1,336	4,343	20,731	36	----------	13	10	141	292
1843	52,496	49,013	8,430	19,670	1,777	4,364	14,441	17	----------	6	5	117	186
1842	104,565	99,945	22,005	51,342	588	5,361	20,370	10	----------	28	2	100	139
1841	80,289	76,216	16,188	37,772	226	6,077	15,291	15	----------	174	6	179	288
1840	84,066	80,126	2,613	39,430	207	7,978	29,704	5	----------	–	1	37	151
1839	68,069	64,148	10,271	23,963	380	7,891	21,028	46	----------	7	1	84	477
1838	38,914	34,070	5,420	12,645	112	3,839	11,683	41	----------	13	–	86	231
1837	79,340	71,039	12,218	28,508	399	5,769	23,740	81	----------	19	–	36	269
1836	76,242	70,465	13,106	30,578	473	5,189	20,707	53	----------	2	3	115	239
1835	45,374	41,987	8,970	20,927	68	3,369	8,311	54	----------	9	–	60	219
1834	65,365	57,510	10,490	24,474	66	4,468	17,686	54	----------	15	1	105	151
1833	58,640	29,111	4,916	8,648	189	5,355	6,988	1	----------	159	1	1,699	1,155
1832	60,482	34,193	5,331	12,436	334	5,695	10,194	34	----------	52	–	3	114
1831	22,633	13,039	2,475	5,772	36	2,277	2,413	–	----------	1	–	28	37
1830	23,322	7,217	1,153	2,721	19	1,305	1,976	2	----------	3	2	9	27
1829	22,520	12,523	3,179	7,415	30	1,065	597	–	----------	1	1	23	212
1828	27,382	24,729	5,352	12,488	60	4,700	1,851	1	----------	7	6	34	230
1827	18,875	16,719	4,186	9,766	28	1,829	432	1	----------	19	1	35	422
1826	10,837	9,751	2,319	5,408	26	968	511	–	----------	4	2	57	456
1825	10,199	8,543	2,095	4,888	18	719	450	1	----------	10	–	75	287
1824	7,912	4,965	1,264	2,345	20	671	230	4	----------	7	2	45	377
1823	6,354	4,016	1,100	1,908	7	528	183	3	----------	7	2	33	245
1822	6,911	4,418	1,221	2,267	28	522	148	3	----------	10	4	35	180
1821	9,127	5,936	3,210	1,518	24	521	383	1	----------	7	–	63	209
1820	8,385	7,691	2,410	3,614	23	452	968	5	----------	14	1	30	174

– Represents zero.
[1] For 1820–1867 excludes returning citizens; therefore, for those years, does not agree with series C 120 and C 138.
[2] Comprises Eire and Northern Ireland.
[3] Comprises Norway, Sweden, Denmark, and Iceland.
[4] Comprises Netherlands, Belgium, Luxembourg, Switzerland, and France.
[5] Includes Austria, 1938 to 1945.
[6] Comprises Czechoslovakia (since 1920), Yugoslavia (since 1920), Hungary (since 1861), and Austria (since 1861, except for the years 1938–1945, when Austria was included with Germany).
[7] Comprises U.S.S.R. (excluding Asian U.S.S.R. between 1931 and 1963, Latvia, Estonia, Lithuania, and Finland).
[8] Comprises Romania, Bulgaria, and Turkey in Europe.
[9] Comprises Spain, Portugal, Greece, and other Europe, not elsewhere classified.
[10] Between 1899 and 1919, included with Austria-Hungary, Germany, and Russia.

Figure 1-7. From *Historical Statistics of the United States: Colonial Times to 1970,* part 1. This table shows the number of U.S. immigrants by country of origin from 1820 to 1870.

William Filby (Wilmington, Del.: Scholarly Resources, 1988), provides information on genealogical holdings within certain libraries in the United States and Canada. This useful directory provides information on each library's operating hours, approximate number of books and microfilm in genealogy departments, whether the library lends its collection, and whether it answers telephone and mailed inquiries. Filby, a former librarian with the Maryland Historical Society and compiler of several major genealogical reference works, saw the great need for a directory of genealogical collections and sent a two-part questionnaire to more than four thousand libraries in the United States and Canada. The first part of the questionnaire was designed to provide information about each library's genealogical collections and their use and accessibility. The second part asked librarians if their collections contained certain genealogical books and periodicals. An example of the questionnaires used by Filby and the entry for Terrebone Parish Library in Houma, Louisiana, appear in figure 1-10. There are plans to publish a supplement to Filby's unique directory.[1]

The *Genealogist's Address Book,* by Elizabeth Petty Bentley, 3rd ed. (Baltimore: Genealogical Publishing Co., 1995), provides information on a variety of genealogical libraries and societies and ethnic, patriotic, and religious organizations. Also listed are major research centers, lineage and hereditary societies, computer interest groups, and genealogical lending libraries. Bentley's work also includes an index to genealogical periodicals and newsletters by title. Of special interest to family historians is the section on ethnic and religious organizations. The Polish section includes references to twenty organizations and research centers nationwide, with addresses, telephone numbers, society publications, and hours of operation. These Polish references do not duplicate those found in the *Directory of Special Libraries and Information Centers*, mentioned previously.

Another important directory compiled by Bentley is the *County Courthouse Book* (Baltimore: Genealogical Publishing Co., 1996). Based on information received in response to questionnaires sent to 4,700 courthouses throughout the United States, this directory provides the address, telephone number, and record holdings of each courthouse. It also gives dates of each county's organization, names of parent counties, and the types of record searches available. Costs for searches and photocopies are also given (although, as Bentley states in her introduction, all such charges are subject to change). Arranged alphabetically by state and county, this excellent guide furnishes the family historian with information needed to conduct an armchair search of county courthouse records.

Both of the above directories are now available in CD-ROM format under the title *The Genealogist's All-in-One Address Book* (cited earlier). This CD combines Bentley's *Address Book*, the *County Courthouse Book,* and another of Bentley's address directories, the *Directory of Family Associations*. Genealogists can now search all three titles quickly and easily on one CD-ROM. Keyword searching provides access to names and words that might not appear in indexes in the printed editions of

★12729★ Genealogical Periodical Annual Index
Heritage Books, Inc. (301)390-7708
1540 E. Pointer Ridge Pl. Free: 800-398-7709
Bowie, MD 20716 Fax: (301)390-7153

Publication Includes: List of about 260 periodicals published by genealogical societies and genealogists and used in indexing surnames, place names, and related topics for this book. **Entries Include:** Name of publication, name of publisher, address, issues indexed, title abbreviation used in book. Publication mainly consists of a list of 14,000 genealogical citations (surnames, place names, etc.). **Arrangement:** Alphabetical by title abbreviation. **Pages:** 285. **Frequency:** Annual, August. **Editor(s):** Laird C. Towle; Leslie K. Towle. **Price:** $25.

★12730★ Genealogical Records in Texas
Genealogical Publishing (301)837-8271
1001 N. Calvert St. Free: 800-296-6687
Baltimore, MD 21202 Fax: (410)752-8492

Frequency: Irregular, latest edition 1992; previous edition 1987. **Editor(s):** Imogene Kennedy; Leon Kennedy. **Price:** $38.50, postpaid.

★12731★ Genealogical Research Directory: Regional and International
Genealogical Research Directory
Box 795
North Sydney, NSW 2060, Australia

Covers: About 7,000 genealogists and genealogical societies; genealogical researchers of 150,000 family names; research libraries and archives in the United States, United Kingdom, Canada, France, Germany, Australia, New Zealand, South Africa, Scandinavia, and Ireland. **Entries Include:** For genealogists—Name, address. For societies—Name, address, library and newsletter details, membership information, key officials, meeting days. For libraries—Name, address. Introduction and explanatory notes in English, French, and German. Family names are not transferred from one edition to the next. **Arrangement:** Genealogists are by number assigned to name researched; societies are geographical. **Indexes:** Family name being researched. **Pages:** 1,248. **Frequency:** Annual, May. **Editor(s):** Keith A. Johnson; Malcolm R. Sainty. **Accepts advertising. Circulation:** 10,000. **Price:** $26, softbound; $33.80, hardbound. **U.S. distributor:** 3324 Crail Way, Glendale, CA 91206-1107, (818)790-2642, Fax: (818)952-3462.

★12732★ Genealogical Research and Resources: A Guide for Library Use
American Library Association (ALA) (312)944-6780
50 E. Huron St. Free: 800-545-2433
Chicago, IL 60611 Fax: (312)440-9374

Publication Includes: List of genealogical organizations and societies. Principal content of publication is information on genealogical research publications. **Arrangement:** Alphabetical. **Frequency:** Latest edition 1988. **Editor(s):** Lois C. Gilmer. **Price:** $18; $16.20 for ALA members.

★12733★ Genealogical Resources in Southern New Jersey
Gloucester County Historical Society
17 Hunter St.
Woodbury, NJ 08096 (609)845-4771

Covers: Historical societies, public libraries, colleges, and other sources of records and information for genealogical research. **Entries Include:** Name, address, phone, description of collection/records available, contact name, hours and days open, whether fee is charged, whether copier is available. **Arrangement:** Geographical by county. **Pages:** 35. **Frequency:** Irregular, previous edition 1989; latest edition 1994 edition. **Editor(s):** Edith Hoelle. **Price:** $6, postpaid.

★12734★ Genealogical Societies and Historical Societies in the United States
Ye Olde Genealogie Shoppe (317)862-3330
PO Box 39128 Free: 800-419-0200
Indianapolis, IN 46239 Fax: (317)862-2599

Covers: About 3,000 groups in the United States. **Entries Include:** Society name, address. **Arrangement:** Geographical. **Pages:** 80. **Frequency:** Annual. **Editor(s):** John Konrad. **Price:** $10, plus $4.00 shipping. **Formerly published by:** Summit Publications.

Figure 1-8. Entries from the "Biography and Genealogy" section of the fourteenth edition (1997) of *Directories in Print.*

SHELBINA — 2172

SHELBINA CARNEGIE PUBLIC LIBRARY, 102 N Center, 63468. SAN 309-2267. Tel 573-588-2271. FAX 573-588-2271. *Dir* Linda K Kropf; *Asst Dir* Bonnie Wood & Lillian Smith; Staff 3 (prof 1, cler 2)
Founded 1917. Pop served 2175; Circ 40,500
Library Holdings: Bk titles 31,761; Per sub 73; CD ROM titles 6; AV — Rec 150, Maps. VF 28
Special Collections: Genealogy (Burial Records of Shelby County, History of Schools, Churches & Families in Area); Centennial Farms Records of Shelby County Early Census Records of Shelby County; Shelby County Newspapers

Figure 1-9. An entry from the *American Library Directory* showing the special collections held by the Shelbina Carnegie Public Library in Shelbina, Missouri.

these books; thus, researchers using the CD-ROM format can access information that might not have been found when using the printed format.

Another well-known and respected source for locating courthouse records is *The Handy Book for Genealogists: United States of America,* 8th ed. (Logan, Utah: Everton Publishers, 1991). Arranged alphabetically by state, the *Handy Book* features excellent state maps, data on county origins, and holdings of county courthouses. This source is often called the bible of genealogists because it provides basic information on counties, their origins, and the census information available for each county. The *Handy Book* belongs in every genealogist's personal library because it offers worthwhile information in an easy-to-use format.

Directories of Groups and Associations. Directories in this section include a variety of works compiled at national, state, and local levels. Nationally, the most comprehensive directory is the annual *Encyclopedia of Associations: National Organizations of the U.S.* (Detroit: Gale Research Co., 1961–). Although titled as an encyclopedia, this work is actually a directory of more than twenty-three thousand national nonprofit organizations. Genealogical and related organizations are listed in two sections: section 10, "Fraternal, Nationality and Ethnic," and section 12, "Veterans, Hereditary and Patriotic" organizations. Figure 1-11 is the entry for the St. David's Society of the State of New York. Its founding date, 1801, is of special interest because one would expect the society to maintain membership information dating from that time. Also note that the society maintains a five hundred-volume library.

Also published by Gale Research is the *Encyclopedia of Associations: Regional, State and Local Organizations,* 5 vols. (Detroit: Gale Research Co., biennial). This five-volume set lists more than eighty thousand U.S. nonprofit membership organizations. The coverage is regional, state, and local. The set is divided into geographic regions and provides information on more local groups than the nationally oriented *Encyclopedia of*

Sample Questionnaire for the Directory of American Libraries with Genealogy or Local History Collections

Part 1

1. Days and hours open to the public.
2. Name of the head of your genealogy or local history section.
3. Approximate number of books by language in your genealogy or local history section.
4. Approximate number of manuscript collections concerning genealogy or local history in your library.
5. Approximate number of reels concerning genealogy or local history in your microfilm collection.
6. What geographical areas does your collection cover?
7. Do you answer questions by telephone or letter concerning genealogy or local history?
8. Is there a qualified genealogist on your staff?
9. Is there a charge for the use of your library?
10. Do you lend books from your genealogy or local history collection?
11. Do you lend microforms from your genealogy or local history collection?
12. Is there a published guide to your holdings?
13. List any unpublished indexes or other guides to your collection.
14. Have you a list of professionals who will research for a fee?
15. Is your collection on OCLC? Is your collection on RLIN?

HOUMA

Terrebonne Parish Library
424 Roussell St, 70360
Tel: 504-876-5861

1. M-Th, 9-8; F,Sa, 9-5
2. Dorotha Horvath, Genealogical Assistant
3. English, 2,700; French, 50
4. N/AN
5. 385
6. Lafourche Interior (Lafourche, Terrebonne, and Ascension Parishes); LA, southern states
7. Tel: yes, NC for limited requests; letter: yes, NC
8. Dorotha Horvath
9. No
10. Yes, duplicate copies
11. No
12. *Genealogical Resources Catalog*, $15. Available from Bayouland Library System, 301 W Congress St, Lafayette, LA, 70501
13. Index of the *Houma Courier* for births and deaths, computer index of cemeteries of Terrebonne Parish
14. No
15. No

Books & Sets: 1,3,10–12,24,25
Periodicals: 4

Figure 1-10. The questionnaire (left) sent to more than four thousand libraries in the United States and Canada for the *Directory of American Libraries with Genealogy or Local History Collections* and the printed response (right) from the Terrebonne Parish Library in Houma, Louisiana.

Associations. In it researchers will find addresses and names of local contact persons for many state and local genealogical groups.

Encyclopedia of Associations: International Organizations, 2 vols. (Detroit: Gale Research Co., 1993) expands the geographic scope of the Encyclopedia of Associations series by providing a guide to more than twelve thousand international nonprofit membership organizations. International genealogical organizations and associations are well represented in the "veterans, hereditary, and patriotic organizations" section of this directory.

The Encyclopedia of Associations series is available online and in CD-ROM format, providing global access to national and international associations. Many public and university libraries offer access to these electronic databases.

For those researchers seeking information on state and local historical and genealogical societies, there are two key sources to consult. *Meyer's Directory of Genealogical Societies in the U.S.A. and Canada,* by Mary K. Meyer, 11th ed. (Mt. Airy, Md.: the author, 1996) is published every two years. *Meyer's Directory*, as it is more commonly known, lists more than 2,200 genealogical societies in the United States and Canada. Listed alphabetically within a state or province, each entry gives the society's address, telephone number, date founded, membership, publications, and special projects.

Researchers should keep in mind the ever-changing nature of nonprofit organizations. In the introduction to the 1992 edition, Meyer notes that more than three hundred societies had changed addresses since the 1990 edition of the *Directory*. Meyer's *Directory* includes a separate listing of independently published genealogical periodicals and a listing of special interest organizations.

Researchers seeking information on historical societies should turn to the *Directory of Historical Organizations in the United States and Canada*, edited by Mary Bray Wheeler, 14th ed. (Nashville: American Association for State and Local History, 1990). First published in 1936, this directory has grown from 583 entries to its present listing of approximately thirteen thousand historical organizations. In compiling the directory, the staff of the American Association for State and Local History made every effort to provide ". . . an organized guide to the ongoing work of history groups everywhere (Wheeler 1990, ix)." *The Directory of Historical Organizations in the United States and Canada* can help genealogists locate historical societies in the county or region where an ancestor lived. Locating them is especially important when a search of the previously mentioned genealogical directories does not produce the name of a genealogical society in a certain area. Many historical societies sponsor genealogy committees that will answer mailed inquiries. See figure 1-12 for the Owyhee County Historical Complex in Murphy, Idaho.

Besides these national directories, many directories are published at the state and local levels. For example, the *Directory of Kentucky Historical Organizations* (Frankfort: Kentucky Historical Society, 1992) is a joint project of the Kentucky Historical Society and the Historical Confederation of Kentucky. In 1991 the Kentucky Historical Society conducted a survey of more than 250 historical organizations in the state. This direc-

Welsh

★17336★ ST. DAVID'S SOCIETY OF THE STATE OF NEW YORK (SDS)
71 W. 23rd St.
New York, NY 10010
James Thomas, Hon.Sec.
PH: (212)924-8415 FX: (212)989-1583
Founded: 1801. **Members:** 311. **Membership Dues:** individual, $20 (annual). **Staff:** 1. **Multinational.** Welsh persons, their descendants, and those connected with them. Collects and preserves information about Wales, its people, and their descendants in the U.S. cultivates knowledge of the history of Wales and of the Welsh language and literature. Aids distressed Welsh persons and their descendants. Supports Welsh language study program and summer schools. **Libraries:** Type: reference. Holdings: 500. **Awards:** St. David's Society Scholarship. Type: scholarship. Recipient: for students who attend Welsh colleges and to students of Welsh descent. **Committees:** Music and Literature. **Formerly:** Station David's Benevolent Society of the Cities of New York and Brooklyn; (1835) Station David's Benevolent Society; (1841) Station David's Benefit and Benevolent Society of the City of New York.
Conventions/Meetings: annual meeting - always Mar. 1, St. David's Day, the anniversary of the patron saint of Wales, New York City.

Figure 1-11. The entry for the St. David's Society of the State of New York in *Encyclopedia of Associations: National Organizations of the U.S.*

MURPHY

Owyhee County Historical Complex
[P.O. Box 67, 83650]; (208) 495-2319.

Owyhee

County agency/ 1961/ Owyhee County Historical Society/ staff:1(f); 3(p); 10(v)/ members:300/ publication: *Owyhee Outpost.*

MUSEUM: The Owyhee County Historical Complex is dedicated to the preservation of historical records, documents, sites, buildings,articles and artifacts pertaining to Owyhee County.

PROGRAMS: Collections; conservation; educational services; exhibits; historic preservation; oral history; publications; tours/ pilgrimages.

COLLECTIONS: [1865–1988] The Owyhee County Museum contains approximately 3000 artifacts pertaining to county history. The library and archives contain over 3,500 books, photographs, records, tapes and videos.

DALE M. GRAY, director (M.A., history of American West; Montana State Univ.).

Figure 1-12. The entry for the Owyhee County Historical Complex in Murphy, Idaho, in *The Directory of Historical Organizations in the United States and Canada.*

HISTORICAL SOCIETY OF HOPKINS COUNTY (Hopkins 1974)	
Address:	107 South Union Street, Madisonville, KY 42431
Phone/Contact:	502-821-3986 J. Harold Utley, President
Hours & Admission:	M-F 1-5pm; no fee
Staff:	3 paid genealogical and historical researchers
Membership:	Annual-$18, Life-$200, Endowment-$500
Function:	Preservation and dissemination of Hopkins County history through the operation of the Ruby Laffoon Birthplace Log Cabin Museum and a genealogical and local history library; genealogical research
Collection:	Library: census records, local histories, local newspapers, and other genealogical material Museum: Hopkins County artifacts
Special Programs:	Free limited Hopkins County genealogical research (charge for photocopies—send SASE); Historical Sites Survey; Heritage of Hopkins County (Family Histories); school group tours (call for appointment)
Publications:	Annual Yearbook—a collection of local history and photographs

Figure 1-13. An entry from the *Directory of Kentucky Historical Organizations.*

tory is the direct result of that survey. Figure 1-13 is an entry from the directory.

When consulting directories, do not overlook Elizabeth Bentley's *Directory of Family Associations* (Baltimore: Genealogical Publishing Co., 1996). As with the two previously mentioned directories compiled by her, this compilation provides information from more than five thousand questionnaires sent to family associations, reunion committees, and one-name (or surname) societies. Sometimes the information is from one individual who serves as a so-called clearinghouse and is actively interested in collecting information on a single surname. These individuals often offer to search their surname databases in exchange for additional surname information or for a specified fee.

Each entry in the *Directory of Family Associations* provides the association's name, address, contact person, and information on the association's publication. Some family associations gather information on several different surnames. For example, the Jacoby/Goble/Gibson/Tiller Family Association, based in O'Fallon, Missouri, collects data on several surnames. As illustrated in figure 1-14, the user is referred from the surname Goble to the entries for the surnames Jacoby, McIlraith, and Powell, where additional Goble information will be found. Also, note the Goff/Gough Family Association. Further on in the alphabetical listing of family associations, a *see* reference directs the reader from the surname Gough to the surname Goff. Researchers who are just starting in genealogy can use this directory to discover variant spellings of surnames and to consult with others who are researching similar surnames. As mentioned previously, this directory is available in CD-ROM format.

Genealogists often discover that an ancestor was a member of an organization that no longer exists. In such an instance, *Fraternal Organizations,* by Alvin J. Schmidt (Westport, Conn.: Greenwood Press, 1980), can be a useful reference source. This book describes different types of voluntary associations, some dating back to the beginning of the United States. These groups played a vital role in our ancestors' lives, often providing fellowship and vital personal services (Schmidt 1980, xxix). *Fraternal Organizations* describes each organization and gives references for further reading. Sometimes little is known about an organization, as with the Arctic Brotherhood, which was founded as a secret society in 1899 on the steamship *Seattle.* It seems that gold prospectors formed this society on their way to the fields of Alaska. The compiler notes that he was not able to determine whether this order still exists and conjectures that it is most likely does not (Schmidt 1980, 44).

William R. Ward's *A Guide to Hereditary and Lineage Societies* (Salt Lake City: Tradition Publications, 1993) is one of the best directories for locating information about currently active and defunct hereditary and lineage societies. The *Guide* provides the following information for each society: other names by which the society has been known, year founded, address and telephone number, eligibility requirements and whether membership is open or restrictive, publications, society library information, location, and accessibility of member records. Additionally, this guide includes a section on "Wearing Society Medals and Insignia." There is an extensive bibliography, a chronological list of hereditary and lineage societies, and a section on preparing lineage papers.

Additional organizational directories of interest include *Farmer's Organizations,* by Lowell K. Dyson (Westport, Conn.: Greenwood, 1986; *Labor Unions,* edited by Gary M. Fink (Westport, Conn.: Greenwood, 1977); *Cyclopedia of Fraternities,* by Albert Clark Stevens (New York: E. B. Treat and Co., 1907); and *Dictionary of Secret and Other Societies,* by Arthur Preuss (St. Louis: Herder Book Co., 1924).

Source Guides. Many useful directories apply specifically to one type of genealogical source (although most such directories were not compiled with genealogists in mind). Many such directories have been published by associations affiliated with specific industries or were published to identify certain types of businesses. Genealogists are often most interested in specific source guides for newspapers, funeral guides, and cemeteries.

When searching for living relatives in an area known to have been the home of an ancestor, it is often advantageous to place an advertisement in a local newspaper. Such an advertisement might simply say "Looking for the descendants of David Hall, known to have lived in Pottersville in 1890." Often, such an advertisement appears as a letter to the editor or as a personal advertisement. *Gale Directory of Publications and Broadcast Media* (Detroit: Gale Research Co., annual) can be useful in finding the name of a local newspaper, its address, frequency of publication, circulation numbers, and advertising rates. Found in most libraries, the *Gale Directory of Publications and Broadcast Media* was formerly known as *Ayer Directory of Publications*. Published annually since 1869, this directory contains entries for more than thirty-six thousand newspapers, magazines, journals, radio stations, television stations, and cable systems. It is another example of a standard library reference resource that holds research potential for genealogists and family historians.

The *Newspaper Genealogical Column Directory* (Bowie, Md.: Heritage Books, 1996) is an example of a printed source written specifically for genealogists. Compiled by Anita Cheek Milner, this directory lists more than 150 genealogy columns appearing in newspapers nationwide. Entries are arranged alphabetically by state and then by county. Each entry includes the name of the newspaper column, research area covered, newspapers in which the column appears, frequency, and requirements and charges for submitting a query to the column.

Anita Milner comments in the introduction to this directory that many columns appearing in early editions of the *Newspaper Genealogical Column Directory* no longer exist. Often, columnists have not received enough queries from readers to justify the existence of a column. Because publication of queries is free in most columns, genealogists should take advantage of the opportunity to publicize their research needs. The illustration in figure 1-15 shows the column "Family Trees," by Nancy Parks. Note that her column runs in three Mississippi newspapers. Queries are free, and there are no restrictions on length or area of interest in each query.

Funeral and cemetery directories offer useful information for genealogists and can be found in the reference departments of large public libraries and university libraries. The *American Blue Book of Funeral Directors* (New York: Kates-Boylston Publications, 1932–) is published approximately every two years and lists twenty-two thousand funeral homes, primarily in the United States and Canada. Listed geographically by state and then by city, entries provide the name of each funeral home, address, population served, and county in which located. The *American Cemetery Association Membership Directory and Buyers Guide* (Falls Church, Va.: American Cemetery Association, annual) lists three thousand cemeteries of all types (except governmental) that belong to the association. Entries are listed geographically and give cemetery name, address, telephone, facilities provided, and names and titles of key officials.

Cemeteries of the U.S.: A Guide to Contact Information for U.S. Cemeteries and their Records, edited by Deborah M. Burke (Detroit: Gale Research Co., 1994), lists more than 22,600 operating cemeteries arranged alphabetically by state and then by county. Information provided for each cemetery includes name, address, telephone and fax number, founding and closing

Goble (see Jacoby, McIlraith, Powell)

Goble
*Goble Surname Organization
2310 Juniper Court
Golden, CO 80401-8087
Phone (303) 526-1319
Terence T. Quirke, Jr., Ph.D., C.G., Proprietor

Goff
*Goff/Gough Family Association
8624 Wimbledon Drive
Knoxville, TN 37923
Phone (423) 690-2432
Bob B. Goff, Editor
Pub. *Goffs/Goughs, Their Ancestors and Descendants*, quarterly
$10.00 per calendar year membership

Jacoby
*Jacoby/Goble/Gibson/Tiller Family Association
114 Mariae Lane
O'Fallon, MO 63366
Phone (314) 240-3335
Betty Maude Gibson

McIlraith
*McIlraith Surname Organization
2310 Juniper Court
Golden, CO 80401-8087
Phone (303) 526-1319
Terence T. Quirke, Jr., Ph.D., C.G., Proprietor
(includes Grace, pre-1900, Sussex, England, and Goble pre-1900, Kent and Sussex, England)

Powell
*The Powell Memorial Society
7050 S.E. Morrison
Portland, OR 97215
April Ober
(includes descendants of three brothers and a sister: John Alkire Powell (and wife Savilla Smith), Noah Powell (and wife Mary Smith), Alfred Powell (and wives Sarah Bracken, Hannah Goble Shirrell, Abigal Lane, and Mary Cooper Churchill), and Lucinda Powell (husband Anthony Propst), who came to Oregon in 1851 and 1852 from Menard County, Illinois)
Annual reunion on the fourth Sunday of June in Oregon

Figure 1-14. Entries from the *Directory of Family Associations. The initial entry* refers the reader from the surname Goble to the entries for the surnames Jacoby, McIlraith, and Powell, where additional Goble information will be found.

WINSTON COUNTY

+ (1) FAMILY TREES by Nancy Parkes, POB 387, Louisville, MS 39339. (2) All of Mississippi counties, and anywhere else in America. (3) *Clarion Ledger/Jackson Daily News* (state-wide circulation). *The Macon Beacon* (weekly Noxubee County paper). Northeast Mississippi *Daily Journal* (Tupelo, MS). (4) Weekly. Sunday in *Clarion Ledger* and *Daily News*, and Thursday in *Macon Beacon*. (5) Spring of 1963. (6) No restrictions on queries, but better when brief. No limitations as to area; not just for Mississippi connections. (7) Free. (8) Columns not compiled and indexed. (11) Member of CGC.

Figure 1-15. An entry from the *Newspaper Genealogical Column Directory.*

dates, facilities, special services, location of records, religious affiliations, and name of owner. A unique feature of this directory is the inclusion of approximately seven thousand closed cemeteries. Also, the directory contains bibliographic citations to publications about individual, county, and state cemeteries. This information will lead researchers to published tombstone inscriptions.

As mentioned in the first part of this chapter, researchers should not rely on one source when seeking answers. This tenet is especially true when searching for cemetery information. An additional source for cemetery names and addresses is the *United States Cemetery Address Book, 1994–95,* by Elizabeth G. and James D. Kot (Vallejo, Calif.: Indices Publishing, 1994). Some of the cemeteries listed in this book do not appear in Burke's book, noted above. Similarly, some cemeteries listed in Burke's book do not appear in the Kots' book. This example demonstrates the need for researchers to continually be on the lookout for similar printed sources. Consulting just one source on a particular subject limits a researcher's scope. (Also see the discussion of these sources in chapter 7, "Vital and Cemetery Records").

Once a death date has been determined for an ancestor, the next logical step is to locate a copy of that ancestor's obituary. One can begin by consulting *Obituaries: A Guide to Sources,* by Betty M. Jarboe, rev. ed. (Boston: G. K. Hall, 1992). This useful guide provides access to obituaries and death notices listed in books, newspapers, and periodicals. Entries are arranged geographically by state with a section devoted to foreign sources. Included in the Appendix is an annotated list of Obituary Card Files located in major genealogical and historical libraries. For more information on other vital records sources, consult chapter 7, "Vital and Cemetery Records."

Dictionaries. A dictionary's primary function is to define the meaning of words. Dictionaries also provide the pronunciation and syllabification and sometimes the etymology, or origin, of words. Additionally, they define major place names; major personal names from history, mythology, and the Bible; foreign terms; phrases; synonyms and antonyms; abbreviations; and general slang terms. Most dictionaries are illustrated, and some are almost encyclopedic in nature.

As language evolves, the meanings of words change. An important function of the dictionary is to show that evolution. Some dictionaries help the reader with grammar and word definition by using a defined word in a sentence. Other types of dictionaries are specialized and refer to one specific topic. The average library has many different kinds of dictionaries. While a good general language dictionary will usually fit the needs of genealogists, there are occasions when a specialized dictionary is needed.

General Language Dictionaries. There are two types of general language dictionaries. One type, the unabridged dictionary, generally contains more than 250,000 entries. The second type is smaller, with from 130,000 to 180,000 entries; these include college and desk dictionaries.

The standard unabridged dictionary found in most libraries is *Webster's New International Dictionary of the English Language* (Springfield, Mass.: G. & C. Merriam), 2nd ed. (1934 and various publication dates thereafter) and 3rd ed. (1961 and various publication dates thereafter). It is common to find both the second and third editions in a library because the two differ so radically. The second edition contains 600,000 entries, while some 250,000 obsolete words were omitted from the third edition and 100,000 new words added for a total of 450,000 entries.

The second edition of *Webster's New International Dictionary of the English Language* is often kept by libraries for historical purposes. It contains a "reference history of the world," which served, in its time, as a basic handbook on world history; a pronouncing gazetteer; and a biographical dictionary, all of which were omitted from the third edition. The second edition is also useful because older, archaic words of the kind often found in wills and deeds are defined and used in sentences.

Additionally, unfamiliar and outmoded occupational terms can be found in unabridged dictionaries. *Webster's* second edition indicates that a *domer* is "one who attaches domes to gloves." A *dome* is defined as "a clip fastener, as for gloves" (*Webster's* 1957, 768).

Webster's Third New International Dictionary of the English Language, Unabridged (the third edition of the work mentioned above) was considered unconventional and controversial when it first appeared in 1961. It presented the language as currently used and therefore included many words regarded as colloquial or slang and thus incorrect. This edition contains 100,000 quotes taken from contemporary sources, while the 1934 edition contains classical and standard quotations. Both the second and third editions are useful dictionaries and are found in large public, university, and college libraries.

Using the example of the word *domer,* one will find in *Webster's Third New International Dictionary* the following definition: "an operator or a machine that shapes box tops" (1986, 671). The older definition of the word has been dropped and a more modern definition substituted.

Additional examples of unabridged dictionaries are *Funk and Wagnall's New International Dictionary of the English Language* (Chicago: J. G. Ferguson Publishing Co., 1987) and *Random House Dictionary of the English Language,* 2nd ed. (New York: Random House, 1987). Both are considered standard and reliable reference sources.

Historical/Etymological Dictionaries. Historical, or etymological, dictionaries are unique and offer a source for finding meanings of words that have changed or are no longer in use. Etymologies show the history of words from their first usage. They trace changes in word interpretation and meaning, using quotations to illustrate word usage. *The Oxford English Dictionary,* 2nd ed., 20 vols. (New York: Oxford University Press, 1989), is by far the best-known etymological dictionary. The *OED*, as it is commonly called, offers a lengthy historical discussion for each word. Usage of the word is arranged chronologically and is illustrated with quotations. Figure 1-16 illustrates the etymology of the word *genealogy.*

The *OED* is not a ready reference source. Rather, it is a definitive work to be used when conducting a serious study of words. Many libraries own an earlier edition of the *OED* published in 1933. The *OED* is also available on CD-ROM.

Two American works modeled after the *OED* are *Dictionary of American English on Historical Principles,* by Sir William Craigie and James R. Hulbert, 4 vols. (Chicago: University of Chicago Press, 1936–44); and *A Dictionary of Americanisms on Historical Principles,* by Mitford McLeod Mathews, 2 vols. (Chicago: University of Chicago Press, 1951).

Craigie's work shows changes in English words that took place in the American colonies up to the end of the nineteenth century. Also featured are words related to the development of the United States and the history of its people, such as *alligator, abolition, Bay State, and bourbon whisky.* Definitions appear chronologically with many quotations to illustrate usage.

A Dictionary of Americanisms on Historical Principles offers definitions of words peculiar to the United States—that is, words that originated in America. These Americanisms include *appendicitis* and *hydrant,* which are outright coinages. The words *adobe, campus,* and *gorilla* first became part of English usage in the United States (Mathews 1951, v). Also included are foreign words that are now part of everyday English—for example, the French words *cafe, buffet,* and *restaurant.*

Slang Dictionaries. Slang dictionaries offer definitions for unconventional words. Two well-known examples are *Dictionary of American Slang,* by Harold Wentworth and Stuart Berg Flexner (New York: Crowell, 1975), and *A Dictionary of Slang and Unconventional English,* by Eric Partridge (New York: Macmillan, 1984). Both dictionaries present definitions of slang and special terms from various vocations, geographical regions, and ethnic groups.

Partridge's *Dictionary of Slang and Unconventional English* includes colloquialisms and catch phrases, "fossilized" jokes and puns, general nicknames, and vulgarisms. An appendix of "items too unwieldy to fit comfortably into the main text" includes occupational names, Cockney English catch-phrases, and "Railwaymen's Slang and Nicknames." The latter is illustrated in figure 1-17.

The *Dictionary of American Slang* is one of the best American slang dictionaries. It features a ten-page overview of American slang and its evolution. Also included is an interesting discussion of groups within American culture responsible for the proliferation of slang in everyday English. Flexner notes that the vocabulary of the average American is estimated at ten thousand to twenty thousand words. Of this amount, Flexner estimates that two thousand are slang words and that they are among the most frequently used (Wentworth and Flexner 1975, viii).

Slang dictionaries often list words that have a specific or cultural emphasis, such as *Words of the Vietnam War,* by Gregory R. Clark (Jefferson, N.C.: McFarland, 1990), and *Dictionary of Afro-American Slang,* by Clarence Major (New York: International Publ., 1970). There are also dialect and regional

Genealogy (dʒenɪˌæ·lŏdʒi, dʒī-). Forms: 3 **genialogi, geneologi, -elogi,** 4 **-ologi,** (5 **genolagye,** 6 **-loȝe, -logy,** *Sc.* **genol(l)igie**), 4–6 **genelogie,** (5 **-gy**), 6 **genalogey,** 4–7 **genealogie,** (5–6 **-gye**), 4– **genealogy.** [a. OF. *gene(a)logie* (F. *généalogie*), ad. late L. *genealogia*, a. Gr. γενεᾱλογία tracing of descent, f. γενεᾱλόγος (whence L. *genealogus*) genealogist, f. γενεά race, generation + -λόγος that treats of: see -LOGY.]

1. An account of one's descent from an ancestor or ancestors, by enumeration of the intermediate persons; a pedigree.

a 1300 *Cursor M.* 7846 Tuix abraham and king daui, Yee herken nov þe geneologi. 1382 WYCLIF 1 *Tim.* i. 4 Nethir ȝyue tent to fablis and genologies withouten endes. *c* 1440 *York Myst.* xxv. 242 Of Juda come owre kyng so gent..þe Genolagye beres witnesse on. 1494 FABYAN *Chron.* VI. clxxiv. 170 And for the genelogy of Charlys the Conquerour ..maye the clerelyer appere..I shal [etc.]. 1589 PUTTENHAM *Eng. Poesie* I. xii. (Arb.) 43 The Poets first commended them [the gods] by their genealogies or pedegrees. 1683 *Brit. Spec.* Pref. 6 King James..whose genealogy from Cadwalladar I have here set down. *a* 1750 MIDDLETON *Reflections* Wks. 1752 II. 24 The two different genealogies of our Saviour's family. 1867 PEARSON *Hist. Eng.* I. 12 The early mention of genealogies in the Welsh laws is proof of the importance attached to noble birth. 1882 CUSSANS *Her.* xxi. (ed. 3) 281 A copious record .. is commonly called a Genealogy; but when the names only are inserted .. it is usually styled a Pedigree. Both words, however, are frequently used in the same signification.

fig. 1577 tr. *Bullinger's Decades* (1592) 486 Hee doth ..shew vs the genealogie, that is, the beginning and proceeding of sinne. 1793 BEDDOES *Math. Evid.* 170 They have reversed the progress of language, both in the formation of words and the genealogy of significations.

b. *Biol.* The line of development of an animal or plant from older forms.

1880 HAUGHTON *Phys. Geog.* vi. 284 The true Horse appears in the Upper Pliocene, and completes the genealogy of the horse.

†**2.** Lineage, pedigree, family stock. *Obs.*

a 1300 *Cursor M.* 5602 A man was of his genelogi Fro him bot to þe toþer kne. *c* 1440 *York Myst.* xxx. 29 Was nevir juge in þis Jurie of so jocounde generacion Nor of so joifull genolgie to gentrys enjoyned. 1447 BOKENHAM *Seyntys* (Roxb.) 29 Me thynkyth it best for me Ageyn to returne in to Italye..For ther is the issu of my genealogy. *a* 1533 LD. BERNERS *Huon* xiv. 38 With Amaury was is next frendes, all issuyd of yᵉ genalogey of Gannelon. 1549 *Compl. Scot.* Ep. 2 Illustir princes, engendrit of magnanime genoligie, & discendit of Royal progenituris.

†**3.** Progeny, offspring. *Obs.*

1513 DOUGLAS *Æneis* v. xii. 131 Thair sall thow lern all thi genealogy, And what cetie is to the destany. 1768 STERNE *Sent. Journ.* (1778) II. 187 (*Supper*), Five or six sons and sons-in-law and their several wives, and a joyous genealogy out of them.

4. The investigation of family pedigrees, viewed as a department of study or knowledge.

1768–74 TUCKER *Lt. Nat.* (1852) II. 466 Genealogy and chronology can scarcely be called sciences.

Hence †**Genea·logied** *pa. pple.*, traced back in line of descent. *rare*⁻¹.

1611 BROUGHTON *Require of Agreem.* Ep. Ded. 9 Iesus, Mary, Ely are Luc. 3. genealogied, not Ioseph.

Figure 1-16. Etymology of the word *genealogy* as it appears in the *Oxford English Dictionary.*

dictionaries for most areas within the United States. Figure 1-18 shows an entry found in the regional dictionary *Western Words: A Dictionary of the American West,* by Ramon Frederick Adams (Norman: University of Oklahoma Press, 1968).

Desk Dictionaries. There are many good desk dictionaries; every researcher probably has his or her own favorite. The following dictionaries are authoritative, give clear and concise definitions, and offer etymologies.

The *American Heritage Dictionary of the English Language,* 3rd ed. (Boston: Houghton Mifflin, 1992) contains approximately 200,000 entries and is larger than the usual desk dictionary. Created by the publishers of *American Heritage* magazine, it is attractive and well illustrated.

Merriam-Webster's Collegiate Dictionary (Springfield, Mass.: Merriam-Webster, 1993) is based on *Webster's Third New International Dictionary of the English Language.* It emphasizes standard language and contains very few slang or collo-

RAILWAYMEN'S SLANG AND NICKNAMES

Many items of railwaymen's s. are to be found scattered through the main text. Most are taken from Harvey Sheppard's *Dictionary of Railway Slang*, 1964, and later edd., or from Frank McKenna's *Glossary of Railwaymen's Talk*, 1970. The latter was the basis of his admirably informative book *The Railway Workers, 1840–1970*, pub'd 1980 by Messrs Faber & Faber Ltd, and I am most grateful to Mr McKenna and to the publishers for permission to draw on the book both to support entries in the main text, and for the lists, which I append here without additional comment, from pp. 239–41:

Signalling Terms	
back 'un	Distance signal
big dipper	High semaphore
biscuit	Signal line token
blackboard	Oblong ground signal
bullseye	Signal light
Christmas tree	Multiple aspect signal
clear pop	Clear signal
dolly, dodd, dummy	Ground signals
double yolk	Two yellows
fairy land	Multiple aspect signals
feathers	Lunar lights
Forever Amber	Fixed distant signals
gun	Radar speed trap
harbour lights	Lunar lights
Hitler salute	Upraised semaphore
iron man	IBS post
on the block	In the loop
orange peel	Plate-layers' orange jackets
peg, stick, board	Semaphore signals
persecuted minority	Employed, over-65s
pounded	Inside clear
spider	Signal apparatus in four foot
stairway to the stars	Ladder to signal's arm
triple crown	Three headlamps

Places of Interest	
Back Pan, the	Washwood Heath
Big Stacks, the	Brickfield Chimneys, Bedford
Block all Junction	Watford
Cupboard, the	Coppermill Junction, Eastern Region
Drain, the	Waterloo
Fernando's Hideaway	Plate-layers' cabin
Goal Post, the	Cricklewood
Hostile Territory	Another region
Indian Country	Eastern region
Land of Plenty	Overtime
Maze, the	Clapham Junction
Orchard, the	Cricklewood sidings
Plywood Sidings	Barking, Essex
Ponderosa, the	Kentish Town to Barking
Rat Hole, the	Euston Tunnel
Shanty, the; also Library	Messroom
Tea Gardens, the	Somers Town Sidings, St Pancras

Nicknames	
Abadan	Excessive oil user
College of Knowledge	The depot union representative
Dead-end kid	Person not taking promotion
Desk jockey	Clerk
Florence Nightingale	Shunter with lamp
Genial Menial	Shed labourer
Gruesome twosome	Joint chairmen
Gutta percha	Bird on shed roof
Jumping Jack	Lively chargehand
Mistletoe Men, Out Riders	Non-union men
Pail hands	Office cleaner
Set of grinders	Sheffield men
Siamese twins	Branch and LDC secretaries
Syndicate, the	Full meeting, management—unions
Talkies, the	Local negotiating meeting
Talking machine	Branch secretary
Traps	Guard's equipment
Whispering Baritone	Noisy person
Wigan blind	A grey puddeny mass. Dross, a mixture of dust found in coal wagons emanating from briquettes, cobbles, slack and nuts.

Figure 1-17. From Partridge's *Dictionary of Slang and Unconventional English.*

quial terms. In publication since 1893, this dictionary is frequently reprinted. Word etymologies are explicit and definitions appear in chronological order, with the most modern meaning given last. Appendixes offer biographical and geographical names, signs and symbols, and a style handbook.

Subject Dictionaries. Subject dictionaries explain terms associated with specialized subject fields, occupations, or professions. They define unique terms and words not usually found in general dictionaries. There are law dictionaries, mathematics dictionaries, music dictionaries, and genealogical dictionaries. Specialized dictionaries can be found in most library reference collections and should not be overlooked by family historians.

Colonial American English, by Richard M. Lederer, Jr. (Essex, Conn.: Verbatim Book, 1985), defines words and phrases used in colonial America from 1608 to 1783. The meanings of some words used during this period are now obscure and difficult to find in modern dictionaries. The author does not suggest that his dictionary replace *The Oxford English Dictionary* or similar unabridged works. Instead, he directs his readers to use his work for a better understanding of colonial writing (Lederer 1985, 7). Each word is defined according to figure of speech and is used in a sentence written in colonial America. Thus, the word *address* is described as a noun, and its first meaning is given as "skillful management." In 1775 General Heath, describing soldiers, wrote: ". . . great address and gallantry were exhibited." The word is also defined as: "A petition; in 1719 William Burd 'moved an address to the Governor'" (Lederer 1985, 10–11).

The Dictionary of Genealogy, by Terrick V. H. Fitzhugh (London: A. & C. Black, 1991), describes the meaning of English terms and phrases that have disappeared from common use in Great Britain. For example, Fitzhugh describes the term *half-baptized* as a "colloquial term meaning 'christened privately', i.e., not in church" (Fitzhugh 1991, 131). (Often, if a newborn was not expected to live, it was baptized at home. If the child did survive, the parents were required to bring the child to the church for a regular church ceremony. Occasionally both ceremonies were entered into the register as baptisms.) This dictionary also contains a "Guide to Ancestry Research"; this is a short instructional manual on English genealogy and a list of useful addresses. A revised edition of this work was published in 1994.

Several dictionaries provide definitions of American genealogical terms and foreign and archaic words. *A to Zax: A Comprehensive Dictionary for Genealogists and Historians,* by Barbara Jean Evans, 3rd ed. (Alexandria, Va.: Hearthside Press, 1995), resulted from the author's thirty years of collecting words and phrases she did not understand while conducting her own research and assisting others. Evans' focus is on words used in history and genealogy, including archaic and Norman words often found in old manuscripts. Foreign words appearing in the first edition of Evans' dictionary were eliminated from the later editions, although Latin phrase entries have been kept and expanded. The appendixes feature a list of nicknames and a list of Dutch-to-English and English-to-Dutch given names.

Ancestry's Concise Genealogical Dictionary (Salt Lake City: Ancestry, 1989), compiled by Maurine and Glen Harris, is, as the title implies, shorter and less definitive than *A to Zax.* It is compact and portable and usually provides only one definition per term. A bibliography lists the sources consulted. The authors suggest that the serious researcher consult these works for additional or more detailed definitions. A list of commonly found abbreviations appears at the end of the book.

Genealogical Dictionary, by Michael L. Cook (Evansville, Ind.: Cook Publications, 1979), is comparable in coverage to the *A to Zax* dictionary. Cook's dictionary gives the definitions of more than 2,500 words, including legal, medical, French, German, Spanish, and Latin terms. The definitions are informative and easily understandable, and they often include several different meanings for each term. Cook's dictionary also includes an alphabetical county index showing the state in which each county is found.

When searching for definitions of words found in documents, it is wise to consult all three genealogical dictionaries; some words appear in one or two of the dictionaries and not in the other. For example, the term *cousin* is used often in court documents, especially probate records, and is frequently misinterpreted by researchers. The example in figure 1-19 shows that this term can be used to mean the son or daughter of an uncle or aunt. It can also refer to a close friend or even to someone whose exact relationship is not known.

Black's Law Dictionary, by Henry Campbell Black (St. Paul, Minn.: West Publishing Co., 1990), is the standard dictionary for legal terms. For example, suppose one finds the term *penal sum* when reading a court record concerning an ancestor. It might be assumed that the words referred to some sort of prison obligation. *Black's Law Dictionary* provides the following definition for *penal sum:* "a sum agreed upon in a bond, to be forfeited if the condition of the bond is not fulfilled" (Black 1990, 1133). Although this dictionary primarily gives modern interpretations of words, references are often provided for the historical meanings of legal terms.

RING IN A COLD DECK

ring in a cold deck
In gambling, to substitute a marked deck of cards.

ring toter
An early-day name for a man who, with two green sticks and a cinch ring, branded mavericks on the range, trying to build a herd of calves that did not rightly belong to him; another name for a rustler.

ring up
In logging, to tally the number of pieces of lumber of a particular size, length, and grade and then enter the total beside the item on a record sheet and draw a ring around it.

riñón
A species of conifer.

RIVER-BOAT CREWS
See brigade, flatter, gas skinner, keelboatman, patron.

river donkey
A logger's name for a logging engine on a raft.

river drive
In logging, the action of floating or guiding logs down a river.

river driver
A logger who drives logs down the river in the spring; also called *river hog.*

RIVER HAZARDS
See bob sawyer, buoy, crossboard, floating island, hull inspector, planter, sawyer, towhead, wooden island.

river hog
See *river driver.*

river horn
In river boating, an early-day wooden trumpet used as a signaling device by navigators of western-river keelboats and flatboats.

RIVER LANDINGS
See boat landing, choke the stump, landing, levee, port, wharf, wooding station.

riverman's Bible
The Waterways Journal, the weekly trade paper founded in St. Louis in 1887 and devoted to steamboating affairs.

river mining
An early-day method of mining by diverting a stream temporarily and securing the gold from the dry, exposed bed. Such a project, undertaken only in the summer during the low-water season, allowed a maximum working period of five months.

RIVERS
See Big Muddy, big swimmin', break up, crooked river, crossings, drift, easy water, Father of Waters, over the willows, pop rise, reach, slough, snaggy, swimming water.

river sluicing
Hydraulic mining along a river.

river sniper
In mining, a gold panner.

river talk
In river boating, the colorful speech of the professional flatboat man. Like other frontiersmen, he spoke in an incessant series of metaphors, similes, and comparisons. He described everything, whether an inanimate object or some human action, by likening it to something else. And, like frontier people, he colored his discourse with references to his own occupation.

roach
To trim the hair of the mane or tail of a horse.

road agent
A robber, usually a robber of stagecoaches.

road agent's spin
A gun spin, the reverse of the *single roll, q.v.*; also called *Curly Bill spin, q.v.*

road brand
A special brand of any design for trail herds as a sign of ownership en route. Such a brand helped the herders keep from mingling their herd with outside cattle and spiriting off their home range those animals of disinterested ownership. (Philip A. Rol-

252

Figure 1-18. An entry from the regional dictionary *Western Words: A Dictionary of the American West.*

An interesting dictionary for both the casual reader and the family historian is *Morbus: Why and How Our Ancestors Died: A Genealogist's Dictionary of Terms Found in Vital Records with Descriptions of the Diseases as They Relate to the Health of Our Ancestors,* by Rosemary A Chorzempa (Chicago: Polish Genealogical Society of America, 1991). This dictionary lists the most common death terms and their meanings as used in eighteenth- and nineteenth-century Europe and America. *Morbus* is a Latin term for disease. It was used in early records

court week: at one time judges traveled a circuit much like that of a preacher. When court was in session a general relaxation of routine occurred and an almost party-like mood existed.
cous.: cousin.
cousin: 1) child of a sibling; 2) sometimes used to indicate a relationship by marriage rather than blood; 3) in early New England it can mean a niece or nephew; 4) sometimes used to refer to a close friend; 5) used to refer to someone who is kin, but the exact relationship is unknown.
cousin german: first cousin.
cousinhood: an association of cousins or kinfolk. A group of cousins is called a cousinry.
cousin red: the relationship of cousins.
cove: 1) the meadow or low land next to an inlet, sometimes quite swampy; 2) the inlet itself; 3) a strip of grassland penetrating the edge of a forest; 4) a small inner or bedroom; 5) a bay, inlet or creek along a coast where boats can seek shelter; 6) a sheltered spot in woods or hills; 7) a peddler; 8) an arch.
covenant: 1) a valid agreement or pact; 2) conditional promises of God to man; 3) a reason for a court action to recover monetary damages.
covenantor: the person who fulfills the promise contained in a covenant.
coventure: a cooperative venture which is ended when the project is finished.
covered bridge: a bridge with a roof and sides to protect the flooring from the weather. Many were toll bridges which was a fair practice considering the amount of money involved in the building of the bridge and toll gate.
coverlid: a woven bedspread, sometimes called a coverlet.

Figure 1-19. From *A to Zax: A Comprehensive Dictionary for Genealogists and Historians.* The entry for *cousin* shows that this term can refer to ason or daughter of an uncle or aunt. It can also refer to a close friend or even to someone whose exact relationship is not known.

as a shortened term for "cause of death." Thus, *morbus apoplexy* means "cause of death due to apoplexy" (stroke). Chorzempa's dictionary ends with a list, compiled by the Polish Genealogical Society, of common terms found as causes of death in German, Latin, Polish, and Russian.

Surname Dictionaries. A frequent question asked of librarians by inexperienced researchers is "What does my family surname mean?" The answer can be found in surname dictionaries commonly found on library reference shelves. One such dictionary is Eldson C. Smith's *New Dictionary ofAmerican Family Names* (New York: Harper & Row, 1973), previously published under the title *Dictionary of American Family Names.* Smith's book is the standard source for finding the meaning of American surnames. It's introduction contains an interesting discussion of the history and derivation of family names. Smith's extensive treatise on the four ways names have come into being—residence, occupation, father's name, and descriptive nickname—is an excellent introduction to the study of family names. More than 10,000 surnames are described in the *New Dictionary of American Family Names.* Each entry provides the country of origin followed by a brief description giving the meaning of the surname. Etymological origins of surnames are not given, nor are variant spellings.

In contrast, *A Dictionary of Surnames,* by Patrick Hanks and Flavia Hodges (New York: Oxford University Press, 1989), provides the origins of nearly 100,000 European surnames. The authors give references to variant surname spellings and compare similar names in other countries. The following is a comparison of entries from these two surname dictionaries for the surname Bowman. From Smith's *New Dictionary of American Family Surnames* (page 54):

> **Bowman** (Eng., Scot.) A fighting man armed with a bow; one who made bows; the servant in charge of the cattle.

Compare it with the entry for Bowman in Hanks's *A Dictionary of Surnames* (page 69):

> **Bowman** English: 1. occupational name for an archer, from OE *boga* bow + *mann* man. This name seems to be generally distinguished from BOWYER, which denoted a maker or seller of the articles. It is possible that in some cases the surname referred originally to someone who untangled wool with a bow. This process seems to have originated in Italy, but became quite common in England in the 13th cent. The vibrating string of a bow was worked into a pile of tangled wool, where its rapid vibrations separated the fibres, while still leaving them sufficiently entwined to produce a fine, soft yarn when spun.
> 2. in America, sometimes an Anglicized form of Ger. and Du. *Baumann* (see BAUER).
> Vars. (of 1):**Boman; Beauman** (see also BEAUMONT).
> COGN. (OF 1): FLEM., DU.:**BOOGMAN.**

A more recent entry, *The Encyclopedia ofAmerican Surnames,* by Amanda H. Robb (New York: Harper-Collins, 1995), treats only the five thousand most common U.S. surnames but provides much more depth than standard surname dictionaries. Of particular interest to the genealogist, this volume cites published family histories for many of the surnames described. It also identifies eminent people who share the surname.

Specialized surname dictionaries also exist for individual European countries, such as *Spanish Surnames in the Southwestern United States: A Dictionary,* by Richard D. Woods (Boston: G. K. Hall, 1978), and *German-American Names,* by George F. Jones (Baltimore: Genealogical Publishing Co., 1990). Search a library's card or online catalog under the subject heading Names—Personal—[country] for additional examples.

Language Dictionaries. Genealogists often come across documents written in languages foreign to them; this is especially true for Americans of German descent. Researchers can read German documents by using Ernest Thode's excellent *German-English Genealogical Dictionary* (Baltimore: Genealogical Publishing Co., 1992). Thode's book is the first genealogical dictionary devoted entirely to German words and their definitions. German words defined in this dictionary are from many German genealogical sources, including church records, civil registration records, and family correspondence. The words listed are not generally found in language dictionaries. This dictionary is well presented and easy to use; word definitions are short and there are no etymologies or pronunciation guides. The German alphabet with script variations is included to help the reader.

Thode suggests that genealogists using his dictionary should also consult a German-English dictionary and suggests *New Cassell's German-English, English-German Dictionary* (New York: Macmillan, 1978) or *Langenscheidt's New College German Dictionary* (Berlin: Langenscheidt, 1988). Each dictionary is divided into two parts: one German to English and the other English to German.

Central European Genealogical Terminology, by Jared M. Suess (Logan, Utah: Everton Publishers, 1978), includes definitions of Latin, French, Hungarian, and Italian words as well as German terms.

Biographical and Geographical Sources

Libraries offer a wide range of biographical and geographical sources. Biographical sources help the reader locate information about a person, while geographical sources help to locate places on maps or gazetteers. Biographical sources and indexes feature a wealth of information for the family historian; they are discussed in great detail in chapter 18, "Biographies." Maps, atlases, gazetteers, place name dictionaries, and guidebooks are discussed in chapter 3, "Geographic Tools."

Indexes

There are many indexes available within a library. Most pertain to a specific subject area, such as *Index to Plays* and *Index to Legal Medicine.* Within the genealogical field there are many well-known indexes, such as the *Newberry Index, Periodical Source Index (PERSI),* and *Index to American Genealogies.* These and other useful indexes are fully discussed in various chapters throughout *Printed Sources.* For a discussion of the use and value of indexes in family history research, see chapter 6.

Manuscripts

Manuscripts can play a major role in one's genealogical research strategy; their importance should not be overlooked. The annual *National Union Catalog of Manuscript Collections (NUCMC)* (Washington, D.C.: Library of Congress, 1959–) is an important finding aid for manuscripts held in repositories nationwide. Learn more about this valuable printed resource in chapter 5, "Bibliographies and Catalogs."

Government Documents

Government documents are the official publications of Federal, state, and local governmental bodies. They are published in a wide variety of formats, including book, pamphlet, magazine, report monograph, microform, and electronic database.

Most Federal government agencies publish documents about the agency and its function. The National Archives and Records Service is no exception. An important reference source published by that agency is the *Guide to Genealogical Research in the National Archives,* rev. ed. (Washington, D.C.: National Archives Trust Fund Board, 1985). This work describes the many types of records held by the National Archives and their use in genealogical research. It is well illustrated with samples of records. The National Archives also publishes numerous catalogs, describing reel by reel holdings of census, military, and other genealogical records held by the National Archives.

The National Archives has also published a three-volume set called *Guide to Federal Records in the National Archives of the United States* (Washington, D.C.: National Archives Trust Fund Board, 1996). This important reference book introduces users to archival records of the executive, legislative, and judicial branches of the Federal government. It covers all types of records—printed, electronic, and audiovisual. Vols. 1 and 2 describe the nearly 1.7 million cubic feet of Federal records transferred to the National Archives as of 1 October 1994. This information is organized into more than four hundred chapters that describe the records of many agencies. The third volume contains an extensive index.

Most Federal government documents are printed by the Government Printing Office and distributed by the U.S. Superintendent of Documents. The best guide to Federal government documents is *Introduction to United States Government Information Sources,* by Joe Morehead and Mary Fetzer, 5th ed. (Littleton, Colo.: Libraries Unlimited, 1996). This book gives a clear, concise explanation of how the Federal government publishes documents. It is arranged in an easy-to-read textbook format, and its many illustrations provide examples of governmental publications.

The U.S. Superintendent of Documents issues many catalogs that serve as bibliographies of government documents. The *Monthly Catalog of United States Government Publications* (Washington, D.C.: Government Printing Office, 1895–) is available in most large public libraries. Libraries rely on the *Monthly Catalog* for current information on government publications and use it as a finding aid for locating obscure government documents. Issued monthly in paperback format, the *Monthly Catalog* is also available on microfiche and through several online databases (BRS, DIALOG and ORBIT). Entries in the printed *Monthly Catalog* are arranged alphanumerically by Superintendent of Documents classification notation. The main entry section is followed by separate indexes for author, title, subject, series/reports, stock number, and title key word.

An examination of the June 1993 issue of the *Monthly Catalog* produced the following items of interest in the subject index: under "United States—History—Revolution, 1775–1783—Sources" is found "The Life of a Revolutionary War soldier: Simon Fobes goes to war. (AE 1.102:R32), 93-12884)"; and under "United States—History—Study and teaching" is found "The Behind-the-scenes tour of the National Archives. (AE 1.102:T 64/2), 93-12885." Figure 1-20 shows the *Monthly Catalog* citations for these two publications.

Knowing the location of government documents is as important as knowing that a government document might be useful in a family search. Almost 1,400 public, academic, state, and law libraries serve as "information links" with the Federal

93-12884

AE 1.102:R 32

The Life of a Revolutionary War soldier : Simon Fobes goes to war. — [Washington, DC : Produced by the staff of the National Archives Tour Office, Office of Public Programs, 1993?]
[4] p. : ill. ; 44 x 28 cm. folded to 22 x 28 cm. Caption title. Shipping list no.: 93-0097-P. ●Item 0569-B-02
1. United States — History — Revolution, 1775-1783 — Sources. 2. United States — Archival resources. 3. Teaching — Aids and devices. I. United States. National Archives and Records Administration. Volunteer and Tour Office. II. Title: Simon Fobes goes to war. OCLC 27688494

93-12885

AE 1.102:T 64/2

The Behind-the-scenes tour of the National Archives. — [Washington, DC : Produced by the staff of the National Archives Tour Office, Office of Public Programs, 1993?]
[4] p. : ill. ; 44 x 28 cm. folded to 22 x 28 cm. Caption title. Shipping list no.: 93-0097-P. ●Item 0569-B-02
1. United States — History — Study and teaching. 2. United States — Archival resources. 3. Teaching — Aids and devices. I. United States. National Archives and Records Administration. Volunteer and Tour Office. II. Title: Behind the scenes tour of the National Archives. OCLC 27665890

Figure 1-20. Citations from the *Monthly Catalog of United States Government Publications.*

government by maintaining collections of government publications. These collections are open to the public and are tailored to fit the needs of the local area. For a list of these depository libraries, write to:

Federal Depository Library Program
U.S. Government Printing Office
Stop: SM
Washington, DC 20402

Additionally, there are more than fifty regional depository libraries; each receives at least one copy of every Federal document printed. A list of these regional libraries is published in the *Monthly Catalog* and the *United States Government Manual* (described below).

Government documents are usually housed in separate collections within a depository library and are arranged and cataloged by document number. Repository libraries usually have trained government documents librarians who can assist researchers. One series of documents useful to genealogists is the annual *U.S. Serial Set* (Washington, D.C.: Government Printing Office, 1817–) (sometimes known as the Congressional Serial Set), an ongoing publication with more than fourteen thousand volumes. Begun in 1817, the *U.S. Serial Set* consists of congressional publications, such as House reports, Senate reports, House documents, Senate documents, Senate executive reports, and Senate treaty documents.

Many documents published in the *U.S. Serial Set* have great genealogical value. In them are the names of people who received pensions, patents, postal contracts, and many other types of government recognition. The set also includes the names of persons who made claims against the government for land and private relief. These volumes can generally be found in U.S. government depository libraries and in large public and university libraries.

Legislative and executive government documents dating from 1789 to 1823 were privately printed in a set of thirty-eight volumes known as the *American State Papers: Documents, Legislative and Executive, of the Congress of the United States*(Washington, D.C.: Gales & Seaton, 1832–61). The documents in these volumes are arranged in the following ten classes: (1) Foreign Relations, (2) Indian Affairs, (3) Finance, (4) Commerce and Navigation, (5) Military Affairs, (6) Naval Affairs, (7) Post-Office Department, (8) Public Lands, and (9) Claims.

Southern Historical Press published a nine-volume reprint set with the same title (Greenville, S.C.: Southern Historical Press, 1994). This set contains information from section 8, Public Lands, and section 9, Claims, of the official *American State Papers.*

A twelve-part index to the *U.S. Serial Set* covering 1789 through 1969 has been published by Congressional Information Services; it is called the *CIS U.S. Serial Set Index* (Washington, D.C.: Congressional Information Service, 1975–79). One section of this index includes the name of each individual requesting private relief or related actions from the government. For additional information on using the *American State Papers* and the *CIS U.S. Serial Set Index,* see "Genealogy Research in the *U.S. Serial Set,*" by Jacquelyn Glavinick, *Heritage Quest* (33) (March-April 1991): 14–16, and "The U.S. Serial Set: Your Ancestors Could Be Lurking Among the Pages of These Volumes," *Journal of Genealogy* (January 1988): 14–21.

Publications Reference File (Washington, D.C.: Government Printing Office, 1977–) is a bimonthly microfiche list of all publications available through the Superintendent of Documents. It lists between twenty-five thousand and thirty thousand titles available from Federal agencies. Most of these documents have been issued within the last five years. The *Publications Reference File* provides author, title, and subject access to government publications and availability, prices, and stock numbers. Many public libraries subscribe to this publication in microfiche format (*GPO Sales Publications Reference File*) or online through DIALOG (*GPO Publications Reference File*).

Genealogists can also locate government documents through twenty-four U.S. Government Bookstores that offer government documents for sale. They are open to the public and are located in the following cities: Birmingham, Alabama; Los Angeles; San Francisco; Denver; Pueblo, Colorado; Washington, D.C.; Jacksonville, Florida; Atlanta; Chicago; Laurel, Maryland; Boston; Detroit; Kansas City, Missouri; New York; Cleveland; Columbus, Ohio; Portland, Oregon; Philadelphia; Pittsburgh; Dallas; Houston; Seattle; and Milwaukee. Complete lists of bookstores with addresses and telephone and fax numbers can be found in the *Monthly Catalog of United States Government Publications* (described earlier), *The United States Government Manual,* and the *National Five Digit ZIP Code and Post Office Directory* (described below).

Many public libraries that are not depository libraries purchase selected government reference documents that offer opportunities for genealogical research. These include *The United State Government Manual, National Five Digit ZIP Code and Post Office Directory,* and *Where to Write for Vital Records.*

The United States Government Manual (Lanham, Md.: Bernan Press, annual) is the official handbook of the Federal government. Published annually, it provides information on agencies of the legislative, judicial, and executive branches. A typical agency description includes a list of principle officials, a statement of the agency's purpose and role in the Federal government, a brief history, a description of programs and activities, and a "Sources of Information" section. The section on the National Archives and Records Administration gives the address and telephone number for the National Archives in Washington, D.C., and for each of the National Archives' thirteen regional archives. This manual also provides information about educational courses offered by the National Archives. The popular "Introduction to Genealogy," a four-day course offered annually to introduce researchers to records stored in the National Archives, is mentioned.

The *National Five Digit ZIP Code and Post Office Directory* (Washington, D.C.: U.S. Postal Service, annual) can be found in every post office nationwide and in most libraries. It not only assists in finding ZIP codes for addressing letters, but it also can provide the addresses for county courthouses and other public buildings. Also included is a list of discontinued post offices; order blanks for purchasing Government Printing Office publications; ZIP codes for installations of the U.S. Army, U.S. Air Force, Marine Corps, U.S. Navy, and Coast Guard in the continental United States; and a U.S. naval fleet listing.

Another useful government publication is *Where to Write for Vital Records: Births, Deaths, Marriages, and Divorces*, DHHS Publication no. (PHS) 87-1142 (Hyattsville, Md.: U.S. Department of Health and Human Services, 1993). This thirty-page booklet is available at all government bookstores. It is an inexpensive source for accessing the vital records of all states and U.S. territories. It provides addresses for state vital records offices, remarks about their holdings, and suggestions about where to write for additional records and information. The cost for copies of birth, death, marriage, and divorce certificates is included. (The user should realize that such charges change often, however.) The booklet is updated every three years.

Sometimes state vital records offices require that requests for certificates be submitted on special forms. Blank application forms are published in the *International Vital Records Handbook,* 3rd ed., by Thomas J. Kemp (Baltimore: Genealogical Publishing Co., 1994). This source is further discussed in chapter 7.

State and local government agencies also publish documents of use to genealogists. These include official state manuals, state adjutant generals' reports, and state library and archive holdings catalogs. Information about these types of documents is available from individual state libraries and archives. Their addresses can be found in several of the directories mentioned previously—most notably in Bentley's *Genealogist's Address Book.*

Bibliographies

A bibliography is a list of books on a particular topic or subject. Additionally, a bibliography can verify the exact title of a book and provide publishing information. The standard information given in a bibliography is similar to that found on most library catalog cards: author, title, edition (if other than a first edition), place of publication, publisher, date of publication, a collation (i.e., number of pages, illustrations, size), and price.

Books in Print (New York: R. R. Bowker, annual) is the standard bibliography used by librarians nationwide. Genealogists find *Books in Print* a good source to search for titles currently in print and published by major genealogical and historical publishers. *Books in Print* is available in several formats: print, CD-ROM, and online. The more familiar format, and the one usually available in libraries, is the printed multi-volume set, which lists more than 1 million titles produced by forty-six thousand publishers. Access to these titles is provided by author and title in alphabetical listings. Each entry lists the title, author, edition, price, publisher, year of publication, number of volumes, Library of Congress catalog card number, and the International Standard Book Number (ISBN). This information is essential when purchasing a book through a bookstore or directly from the publisher. A separate volume provides name, address, and telephone number for all publishers listed. *Subject Guide to Books in Print* (New York: R. R. Bowker, annual) offers subject access to all nonfiction titles in *Books in Print.*

To locate genealogical books published at state and local levels, consult Netti Schreiner-Yantis's *Genealogical and Local History Books in Print* (Springfield, Va.: Genealogical Books in Print, 1985–90). This five-volume source lists thirty thousand books and microforms published by local and state genealogical societies and independent publishers. It is arranged alphabetically by state and therein by county. To learn what has been published for Shelby County, Missouri, for example, look in the section under that state and county.

The Genealogical Publishing Company (Baltimore) published the fifth edition of *Genealogical and Local History Books in Print* in four volumes compiled and edited by Marian Hoffman. The *Family History Volume* (Baltimore: Genealogical Publishing Co., 1996) contains more than four thousand recently published genealogies. The *General Reference and World Resources Volume* (1997) lists reference books currently available for a variety of genealogical topics, including adoption, computers, heraldry, and immigration. This volume also contains genealogy and local history books currently available for countries other than the United States. The *U.S. Sources and Resources Volume* (1997) is actually two volumes divided alphabetically by state. The first volume covers Alabama through New York. For additional information on this bibliography and on other useful bibliographies, consult chapter 5, "Bibliographies and Catalogs."

Electronic Sources

As we enter the twenty-first century, our world vision has been greatly expanded by the many advances made in the electronics and telecommunications fields. These advances are especially visible in libraries as computerized catalogs and electronic reference databases become more readily available. Libraries are subscribing to online databases and electronic bulletin boards to provide the most current information sources for their patrons; genealogists can profit from these new sources of information. Access to many of these databases is not free of charge; researchers should expect to pay some online charges.

DIALOG Information Retrieval Service, from Dialog Information Services, Inc., is one of the best-known online systems worldwide. In operation since 1972, DIALOG offers more than 450 databases covering a broad scope of disciplines, including science, business, technology, chemistry, and social sciences.

Many reference sources reviewed in this chapter are available on DIALOG, including *American Library Directory, Books in Print, Encyclopedia of Associations,* and the *Monthly Catalog of United States Government Publications* (described earlier). Other DIALOG databases of interest to genealogists include *America: History and Life; Biography Master Index;* and *Historical Abstracts*. The last indexes the world's periodical literature in history, social sciences, and the humanities from 1450 to the present (excluding U.S. and Canadian sources).

Several genealogical databases are available nationwide through the many family history centers of the Family History Library. They are Ancestral File™, the Social Security Death Index, and the International Genealogical Index®. Also available nationwide in major genealogical libraries is FamilySearch, the popular genealogical database developed by the LDS church. Another major genealogical database is Brøderbund Software's World Family Tree (see chapter 16, "Family Histories"). (For a complete list, see appendix A). Each of these databases offers a unique file of information and may be available in many formats, including online, microfiche, bulletin board, and CD-ROM. Because this technology is changing rapidly, it is important to consult current issues of journals devoted to computer applications, such as *Genealogical Computing,* published by Ancestry (P.O. Box 476, Salt Lake City, UT 84110-1476), and *NGS/CIG Digest*, a newsletter of the National Genealogical Society Computer Interest Group (National Genealogical Society, 4527 17th Street North, Arlington, VA 22207-2399).

Many libraries across the United States provide access to their electronic catalogs via computer modem. From their homes researchers can search local, state, and national library catalogs for holdings information. Some library online services include community calendars and even such data as local cemetery listings. Some public and university libraries offer document retrieval services via home computer. The Library of Congress recently announced that LOCIS (Library of Congress Information System) is available to the public through the Internet, a collection of computer networks that link tens of millions of computer users in more than one hundred countries. These advances in computerized research allow greater access to reference materials for the family historian.

Computer technology is changing and expanding so rapidly that what is written today will be out of date by the time it is published. The best way to keep up with developments is to read pertinent journals and to attend local, state, and national genealogy conferences.

CONCLUSION

Although access to records has changed and is becoming easier and faster, a researcher must still possess a knowledge of basic reference sources to ensure that her research is as complete as possible. This chapter has highlighted basic reference sources and has shown how these printed sources can greatly enhance genealogical research.

Encyclopedias offer an excellent starting point for information on an ancestor's birthplace and help to make research easier and faster. Additional information on the political, social, and cultural events that occurred during an ancestor's lifetime can be found in chronologies and timetables. Social history sources provide valuable cultural background information and should not be overlooked by serious researchers.

Dictionaries help to decipher old documents relating to our ancestors. Besides offering many different types of dictionaries, public library reference departments also offer sources that can direct the researcher to new and exciting research possibilities. All one has to do is ask.

The general reference sources described in this chapter expand research possibilities for both the beginning and advanced genealogist. Enhanced opportunities await the genealogist who puts these printed sources to good use.

NOTES

1. Telephone conversation with publisher's representative, 23 December 1996.

REFERENCE LIST

Black, Henry Campbell. 1990. *Black's Law Dictionary.* St. Paul, Minn.: West Publishing Co.

Fitzhugh, Terrick V. H. 1991. *Dictionary of Genealogy.* London: A. & C. Black.

Hastings, James. 1908–27. *Encyclopedia of Religion and Ethnics.* Vol. 6. New York: Scribner.

Horowitz, Lois. 1988. *Knowing Where to Look: The Ultimate Guide to Research.* Cincinnati: Writer's Digest Books.

Kister, Kenneth F. 1994. *Kister's Best Encyclopedias: A Comparative Guide to General and Specialized Encyclopedias.* Phoenix: Oryx Press.

Lederer, Richard M., Jr. 1985. *Colonial American English.* Essex, Conn.: Verbatim Book.

Mathews, Mitford McLeod. 1951. *Dictionary of Americanisms on Historical Principles.* Vol. 1. Chicago: University of Chicago Press.

Schmidt, Alvin J. 1980. *Fraternal Organizations.* Westport, Conn.: Greenwood.

Todd, Alden. 1972. *Finding Facts Fast: How to Find Out What You Want to Know Immediately.* New York: William Morrow & Co.

Trager, James. 1992. *The People's Chronology: A Year-by-Year Record of Human Events from Prehistory to the Present.* New York: Henry Holt.

Webster's New International Dictionary of the English Language. 1957. 2nd unabridged ed. Springfield, Mass.: G. & C. Merriam.

Webster's Third New International Dictionary of the English Language, Unabridged. 1986. Springfield, Mass.: Merriam.

Wentworth, Harold, and Stuart Berg Flexner. 1975. *Dictionary of American Slang.* New York: Crowell.

Wheeler, Mary Bray, ed. 1990. *Directory of Historical Organizations in the United States and Canada.* Nashville: American Association of State and Local History.

BIBLIOGRAPHY

Research Guides

Balay, Robert, ed. *Guide to Reference Books.* 11th ed. Chicago: American Library Association, 1996.

Brooks, Philip Coolidge. *Research in Archives: The Use of Unpublished Primary Sources.* Chicago: University of Chicago Press, 1969.

Cerny, Johni, and Wendy Elliott. *The Library: A Guide to the LDS Family History Library.* Salt Lake City: Ancestry, 1988.

Greenwood, Val D. *Researcher's Guide to American Genealogy*. 2nd ed. Baltimore: Genealogical Publishing Co., 1990.

Guide to Genealogical Research in the National Archives. Rev. ed. Washington, D.C.: National Archives Trust Fund Board, 1985.

Horowitz, Lois. *Knowing Where to Look: The Ultimate Guide to Research*. Cincinnati: Writer's Digest Books, 1988.

Library of Congress. Cataloging Policy and Support Office. *Library of Congress Subject Headings*. Washington, D.C.: Library of Congress, Cataloging Distribution Service, 1993–.

Mann, Thomas. *A Guide to Library Research Methods*. New York: Oxford University Press, 1990.

Parker, J. Carlyle. *Library Service for Genealogists*. Detroit: Gale Research Co., 1981.

Szucs, Loretto Dennis, and Sandra Hargreaves Luebking. *The Archives: A Guide to the National Archives Field Branches*. Salt Lake City: Ancestry, 1988.

_____, eds. *The Source: A Guidebook of American Genealogy*. Rev. ed. Salt Lake City: Ancestry, 1997.

Todd, Alden. *Finding Facts Fast*. 1992. Reprint. Berkeley, Calif.: Ten Speed Press, 1992.

Wright, Norman E., and David H. Pratt. *Genealogical Research Essentials*. Salt Lake City: Bookcraft, 1976.

Wright, Raymond S. *The Genealogists's Handbook, Modern Methods for Researching Family History*. Chicago: American Library Association, 1995.

Encyclopedias

Academic American Encyclopedia. Danbury, Conn.: Grolier, 1980–.

Childcraft: The How and Why Library. Chicago: World Book, 1993.

Children's Britannica. Chicago: Encyclopædia Britannica, 1993.

Collier's Encyclopedia. New York: Collier, 1949–.

Concise Columbia Encyclopedia. 2nd ed. New York: Columbia University Press, 1989.

The Dictionary of American History. Rev. ed. New York: Charles Scribner's & Son, 1976–78. Supplement, 1996.

Encyclopedia Americana. Danbury, Conn.: Grolier, 1829–.

Encyclopædia Britannica. Chicago: Encyclopædia Britannica, 1768–1973.

Encyclopedia Judaica. New York: Macmillan, 1971–72.

Encyclopedia of Religion. New York: Macmillan, 1993.

Hastings, James., ed. *Encyclopedia of Religion and Ethics*. 12 vols. New York: Scribner, 1908–27.

Kister, Kenneth F. *Kister's Best Encyclopedias: A Comparative Guide to General and Specialized Encyclopedias*. Phoenix: Oryx Press, 1994.

Langer, William Leonard. *Encyclopedia of World History*. 5th ed. Boston: Houghton Mifflin, 1972.

Morris, Richard B., and Jeffrey B. Morris. *Encyclopedia of American History*. New York: HarperCollins, 1996.

New Book of Knowledge: The Children's Encyclopedia. New York: Grolier, 1966–.

New Catholic Encyclopedia. New York: McGraw-Hill, 1967–95.

Columbia Encyclopedia. 5th ed. New York: Columbia University Press, 1993.

New Encyclopædia Britannica. 15th ed. Chicago: Encyclopædia Britannica, 1990.

Ryan, Joe. *First Stop: The Master Index to Subject Encyclopedias*. Phoenix: Oryx Press, 1989.

World Book Encyclopedia. Chicago: World Book, annual.

General History and Social History Sources

Atherton, Lewis E. *The Frontier Merchant in Mid-America*. Columbia: University of Missouri Press, 1971.

_____. *Main Street on the Middle Border*. Bloomington: Indiana University Press, 1954.

America: History and Life, a Guide to Periodical Literature. Santa Barbara, Calif.: ABC-Clio, 1964–. With supplements.

Billington, Ray Allen. *The Far Frontier, 1830–1860*. New York: Harper, 1956.

_____. *Westward Expansion: A History of the American Frontier*. New York: Macmillan, 1982.

Boorstin, Daniel J. *The Americans*, 3 vols. inclusive. New York: Random House. Vol. 1, *The Colonial Experience*, 1958; vol. 2, *The Democratic Experience*, 1973; vol. 3, *The National Experience*, 1965.

Dick, Everett N. *The Dixie Frontier: A Social History of the Southern Frontier from the First Transmontane to the Civil War*. New York: A. A. Knopf, 1948. Reprint. Norman: University of Oklahoma Press, 1993.

_____. *Lure of the Land: A Social History of the Public Lands from the Articles of Confederation to the New Deal*. Lincoln: University of Nebraska Press, 1970.

_____. *The Sod-House Frontier, 1854–1890: A Social History of the Northern Plains from the Creation of Kansas and Nebraska to the Admission of the Dakotas*. New York: D. Appleton-Century Co., 1937.

_____. *Vanguards of the Frontier: A Social History of the Northern Plains and Rocky Mountains from the Fur Traders to the Sod Busters*. Lincoln: University of Nebraska Press, 1941, 1965.

Dictionary of American History. New York: Charles Scribner's & Son, 1976–78. Supplement, 1996.

Earle, Alice M. *Child Life in Colonial Days*. 1899. Reprint. Williamstown, Mass.: Corner Hse., 1975.

_____. *Colonial Dames and Goodwives*. Reprint. Bowie, Md.: Heritage Books, 1988.

_____. *Home Life in Colonial Days*. 1898. Reprint. Williamstown, Mass.: Corner Hse., 1975.

Encyclopedia of American Social History. Edited by Mary Kupiec Cayton, Elliott J. Gorn, and Peter W. Williams. 3 vols. New York: Charles Scribner's Sons, 1993.

Fischer, David Hackett. *Albion's Seed: Four British Folkways in America*. New York: Oxford University Press, 1989.

Freidel, Frank Burt. *Harvard Guide to American History*. Rev. ed. Cambridge, Mass.: Belknap Press of Harvard University Press, 1974.

Fritze, Ronald H., et al. *Reference Sources in History: An Introductory Guide*. Santa Barbara, Calif.: ABC-Clio, 1990.

Ireland, Norma Olin. *Index to America: Life and Customs*. 4 vols. Westwood, Mass.: F. W. Faxon Co., 1976–84.

Langer, William Leonard. *Encyclopedia of World History*. 5th ed. Boston: Houghton Mifflin, 1973.

Larkin, Jack. *Reshaping of Everyday Life 1790–1840*. New York: Harper & Row, 1988.

McCutcheon, Marc. *The Writer's Guide to Everyday Life in the 1800's*. Cincinnati: Writer's Digest Books, 1993.

Men of Boston and New England. Boston: Boston American, 1913.

Mitterling, Philip I. *U.S. Cultural History: A Guide to Information Sources*. Detroit: Gale Research Co., 1980.

Morgan, Ted. *Wilderness at Dawn: The Settling of the North American Continent*. New York: Simon & Schuster, 1993.

Morison, Samuel Eliot. *Oxford History of the American People*. New York: Oxford University Press, 1965.

Morris, Richard B., and Jeffrey B. Morris. *Encyclopedia of American History*. New York: HarperCollins, 1996.

Unruh, John David. *The Plains Across: The Overland Emigrants and the Trans-Mississippi West, 1840–1860*. Urbana: University of Illinois Press, 1979.

Van Every, Dale. *Ark of Empire: The American Frontier, 1784–1803*. New York: Morrow, 1963.

_____. *Forth to the Wilderness: The First American Frontier, 1754–1774*. New York: Morrow, 1961.

Almanacs, Chronologies, and Statistical Sources

Grun, Bernard. *Timetables of History: A Horizontal Linkage of People and Events*. New York: Simon & Schuster, 1982. 3rd rev. ed. 1991.

Historical Statistics of the United States, Colonial Times to 1970. Washington, D.C.: U.S. Department of Commerce, Bureau of Commerce, 1975.

Information Please Almanac: Atlas and Yearbook. Publisher varies, 1947–. Annual.

Reader's Digest Almanac and Yearbook. Pleasantville, N.Y.: Reader's Digest Association, 1966–. Annual.

Time Lines on File. New York: Facts on File, 1988.

Trager, James. *The People's Chronology: A Year-by-Year Record of Human Events from Prehistory to the Present*. 1st rev. ed. New York: Henry Holt, 1992.

Urdang, Laurence, ed. *Timetables of American History*. New York: Simon and Schuster, 1996.

Whitaker's Almanac. London: J. Whitaker & Sons, 1869–. Annual.

World Almanac and Book of Facts. New York: World Almanac, 1868–. Annual.

Directories

American Blue Book of Funeral Directors. New York: Kates-Boylston Publications, 1932–.

American Cemetery Association Membership Directory and Buyers Guide. Falls Church, Va.: American Cemetery Association, annual.

American Library Directory. New Providence, N.J.: R. R. Bowker, annual.

APG Directory of Professional Genealogists. Washington, D.C.: Association of Professional Genealogists, biennial. Title varies.

Bentley, Elizabeth Petty. *County Courthouse Book*. Baltimore: Genealogical Publishing Co., 1996.

_____. *Directory of Family Associations*. Baltimore: Genealogical Publishing Co., 1996.

_____. *Genealogist's Address Book*. 3rd ed. Baltimore: Genealogical Publishing Co., 1995.

_____. *Genealogist's All-in-One Address Book* (database). Baltimore: Genealogical Publishing Co., 1996.

Burke, Deborah M., ed. *Cemeteries of the U.S.: A Guide to Contact Information for U.S. Cemeteries and Their Records*. Detroit: Gale Research Co., 1994.

Davenport, Robert R. *The Hereditary Society Blue Book*. Baltimore: Genealogical Publishing Co., 1994.

Directories in Print. Detroit: Gale Research Co., 1989–. Annual.

Directory of Historical Organizations in the United States and Canada. 14th ed. Nashville: American Association for State and Local History, 1990.

Directory of Kentucky Historical Organizations. Frankfort: Kentucky Historical Society, 1992.

Directory of Special Libraries and Information Centers: A Guide to More Than 20,800 Special Libraries, Research Libraries, Information Centers, Archives, and Data Centers Maintained by Government Agencies, Business, Industry, Newspapers, Educational Institutions, Nonprofit Organizations, and Societies in the Field of Science and Engineering, Medicine, Law, Art, Religion, the Social Sciences, and Humanities. 16th ed. Detroit: Gale Research Co., 1993. Biennial.

Dyson, Lowell K. *Farmer's Organizations*. Westport, Conn.: Greenwood, 1986.

Encyclopedia of Associations: National Organizations of the U.S. Detroit: Gale Research Co., 1961–. Annual.

Encyclopedia of Associations: International Organizations. 2 vols. Detroit: Gale Research Co., 1993.

Encyclopedia of Associations: Regional, State and Local Organizations. 5 vols. Detroit: Gale Research Co., biennial.

Filby, P. William. *Directory of American Libraries with Genealogy or Local History Collections*. Wilmington, Del.: Scholarly Resources, 1988.

Fink, Gary M. *Labor Unions*. Westport, Conn.: Greenwood, 1977.

Gale Directory of Publications and Broadcast Media. Detroit: Gale Research Co., annual.

Handy Book for Genealogists: United States of America. 8th ed. Logan, Utah: Everton Publishers, 1991.

Jarboe, Betty M. *Obituaries: A Guide to Sources*. Rev. ed. Boston: G. K. Hall, 1992.

Kemp, Thomas J. *International Vital Records Handbook*. 3rd ed. Baltimore: Genealogical Publishing Co., 1994.

Konrad, J., ed. *Directory of Family "One-Name" Periodicals*. 1993–94 ed. Indianapolis: Ye Olde Genealogie Shoppe, 1994.

Kot, Elizabeth G., and James D. Kot. *United States Cemetery Address Book, 1994–1995*. Vallejo, Calif.: Indices Publishing, 1994.

Meyer, Mary K. *Meyer's Directory of Genealogical Societies in the U.S.A. and Canada*. 11th ed. Mt. Airy, Md.: the author, 1996.

_____, and P. William Filby. *Who's Who in Genealogy and Heraldry*. Savage, Md.: Who's Who in Genealogy & Heraldry, 1990.

Milner, Anita Cheek. *Newspaper Genealogical Column Directory*. Bowie, Md.: Heritage Books, 1996.

National Historical Publications and Records Commission. *Directory of Archives and Manuscript Repositories in the United States*. Phoenix: Oryx Press, 1988.

National Trade and Professional Associations of the United States. Washington, D.C.: Columbia Books, annual.

Phonefiche. Ann Arbor, Mich.: United Microfilms International, monthly.

Preuss, Arthur. *Dictionary of Secret and Other Societies*. St. Louis: Herder Book Co., 1924.

Roster of Genealogists Certified. Falmouth, Va.: Board for Certification of Genealogists, annual.

Schmidt, Alvin J. *Fraternal Organizations*. Westport, Conn.: Greenwood Press, 1980.

Smith, Juliana Szucs. *The Ancestry Family Historian's Address Book: A Comprehensive List of Local, State, and Federal Agencies and Institutions and Ethnic and Genealogical Organizations*. Salt Lake City: Ancestry, 1998.

Stevens, Albert Clark. *Cyclopedia of Fraternities*. New York: E. B. Treat and Co., 1907.

Thode, Ernest. *Address Book for Germanic Genealogy*. 5th ed. Baltimore: Genealogical Publishing Co., 1995.

Ward, William R. *A Guide to Hereditary and Lineage Societies*. Salt Lake City: Tradition Publications, 1993.

World of Learning. London: Allen & Unwin, 1947–. Annual.

Yellow Book of Funeral Directors and Services. Youngstown, Ohio: Nomis Publications, annual.

Dictionaries

Adams, Ramon Frederick. *Western Words: A Dictionary of the American West*. Norman: University of Oklahoma Press, 1968.

American Heritage Dictionary of the English Language. 3rd ed. Boston: Houghton Mifflin, 1992.

Black, Henry Campbell. *Black's Law Dictionary*. St. Paul, Minn.: West Publishing Co., 1990.

Clark, Gregory R. *Words of the Vietnam War*. Jefferson, N.C.: McFarland, 1990.

Cook, Michael L. *Genealogical Dictionary*. Evansville, Ind.: Cook Publications, 1979.

Chorzempa, Rosemary A. *Morbus: Why and How Our Ancestors Died: A Genealogist's Dictionary of Terms Found in Vital Records with Descriptions of the Diseases as They Relate to the Health of Our Ancestors*. Chicago: Polish Genealogical Society of America, 1991.

Craigie, Sir William, and James R. Hulbert. *Dictionary of American English on Historical Principles*. 4 vols. Chicago: University of Chicago Press, 1936–44.

Drake, Paul. *What Did They Mean by That? A Dictionary of Historical Terms for Genealogists*. Bowie, Md.: Heritage Books, 1994.

Evans, Barbara Jean. *A to Zax: A Comprehensive Dictionary for Genealogists and Historians*. 3rd ed. Alexandria, Va.: Hearthside Press, 1995.

Fitzhugh, Terrick V. H. *Dictionary of Genealogy*. London: A. & C. Black, 1991.

Foreign Versions of English Names and Foreign Equivalents of United States Military and Civilian Titles. Detroit: Grand River Books, 1973.

Funk and Wagnall's New Standard Dictionary of the English Language. Chicago: J. G. Ferguson Publishing Co., 1987.

Gorr, Rabbi Shmuel. *Jewish Personal Names, Their Origin, Derivation and Diminutive Forms*. Teaneck, N.J.: Avotaynu, 1992.

Hanks, Patrick, and Flavia Hodges. *A Concise Dictionary of First Names*. New York: Oxford University Press, 1993.

_____. *A Dictionary of Surnames*. New York: Oxford University Press, 1989.

Harris, Maurine, and Glen Harris. *Ancestry's Concise Genealogical Dictionary*. Salt Lake City: Ancestry, 1989.

Jones, George F. *German-American Names*. Baltimore: Genealogical Publishing Co., 1990.

Langenscheidt's New College German Dictionary. Berlin: Langenscheidt, 1988.

Lederer, Richard M. *Colonial American English*. Essex, Conn.: Verbatim Book, 1985.

Major, Clarence. *Dictionary of Afro-American Slang*. New York: International Publ., 1970.

Mathews, Mitford M. *Dictionary of Americanisms on Historical Principles*. 2 vols. Chicago: University of Chicago Press, 1951.

Merriam-Webster's Collegiate Dictionary. Springfield, Mass.: Merriam-Webster, 1993.

New Cassell's German-English, English-German Dictionary. New York: Macmillan, 1978.

The Oxford English Dictionary. 2nd ed. 20 vols. New York: Oxford University Press, 1989.

Partridge, Eric. *A Dictionary of Slang and Unconventional English*. New York: Macmillan, 1984.

Pladsen, Phyllis. *Swedish Genealogical Dictionary*. St. Paul, Minn.: Swedish Genealogy Group, Minnesota Genealogical Society, 1991.

Random House Dictionary of the English Language. 2nd ed. New York: Random House, 1987.

Robb, Amanda H. *The Encyclopedia of American Surnames*. New York: Harper-Collins, 1995.

Suess, Jared M. *Central European Genealogical Terminology*. Logan, Utah: Everton Publishers, 1978.

Smith, Eldson C. *New Dictionary of American Family Names*. New York: Harper & Row, 1973.

Thode, Ernest. *German-English Genealogical Dictionary*. Baltimore: Genealogical Publishing Co., 1992.

Webster's New Collegiate Dictionary. Springfield, Mass.: Merriam, 1973.

Webster's New International Dictionary of the English Language. 2nd ed. Springfield, Mass.: G. & C. Merriam, 1934.

Webster's Third New International Dictionary of the English Language, Unabridged. 3rd ed. Springfield, Mass.: Merriam, 1961.

Wentworth, Harold, and Stuart Berg Flexner. *Dictionary of American Slang*. New York: Crowell, 1975.

Woods, Richard D. *Spanish Surnames in the Southwestern United States: A Dictionary*. Boston: G. K. Hall, 1978.

Government Documents

American State Papers: Documents, Legislative and Executive, of the Congress of the United States. 38 vols. Washington, D.C.: Gales & Seaton, 1832–61.

American State Papers: Documents, Legislative and Executive, of the Congress of the United States. 9 vols. Greenville, S.C.: Southern Historical Press, 1994. Contains information from section 8, Public Lands, and section 9, Claims, of the original *American State Papers* (above).

Bailey, William G. *Guide to Popular U.S. Government Publications*. 3rd ed. Englewood, Colo.: Libraries Unlimited.

Congressional Information Service. *C.I.S. U.S. Serial Set Index*. Washington, D.C.: Congressional Information Service, 1975–79.

Glavinick, Jacquelyn. "Genealogy Research in the U.S. Serial Set." *Heritage Quest* no. 33 (March-April 1991): 14-16.

Guide to Federal Records in the National Archives of the United States. Washington, D.C.: National Archives Trust Fund Board, 1996.

Guide to Genealogical Research in the National Archives. Rev. ed. Washington, D.C. : National Archives Trust Fund Board, 1985.

McMullin, Phillip W. *Grassroots of America: A Computerized Index to the American State Papers*. Conway, Ark.: Arkansas Research, 1990.

Morehead, Joe, and Mary Fetzer. *Introduction to United States Government Information Sources*. 5th ed. Littleton, Col.: Libraries Unlimited, 1996.

National Five Digit ZIP Code and Post Office Directory. Washington, D.C.: U.S. Postal Service, annual.

Publications Reference File. Washington, D.C.: Government Printing Office, 1977–. Bimonthly.

United States Government Manual. Lanham, Md.: Bernan Press, annual.

"The U.S. Serial Set: Your Ancestors Could be Lurking Among the Pages of These Volumes." *Journal of Genealogy* (January 1988) 14–21.

United States. Superintendent of Documents. *Monthly Catalog of United States Government Publications*. Washington, D.C.: U.S. Government Printing Office, 1895–.

U.S. Serial Set. Washington, D.C.: Government Printing Office, 1817–. Annual.

Where to Write for Vital Records: Births, Deaths, Marriages, and Divorces. Hyattsville, Md.: U.S. Department of Health & Human Services, 1993.

Bibliographies

Books in Print. 10 vols. New York: R. R. Bowker, annual.

Hoffman, Marian. *Genealogical and Local History Books in Print*. 4 vols. in 3. Baltimore: Genealogical Publishing Co., 1996–97. *Family History Volume* (1996). *General Reference and World Resources Volume* (1997). *U.S. Sources and Resources Volume* (1997).

National Union Catalog of Manuscript Collections (*NUCMC*). Washington, D.C.: Library of Congress, 1959–.

Schreiner-Yantis, Netti. *Genealogical and Local History Books in Print*. 5 vols. Springfield, Va.: Genealogical Books in Print, 1985–90.

Subject Guide to Books in Print. 5 vols. New York: R. R. Bowker, annual.

Electronic Sources

ArchivesUSA. CD-ROM. Alexandria, Va.: Chadwyck-Healey, 1996–.

Bentley, Elizabeth Petty. *The Genealogist's All-in-One Address Book*. CD-ROM. Baltimore: Genealogical Publishing Co., 1996.

FamilySearch®. CD-ROM. Salt Lake City: Family History Department, annual.

INSTRUCTIONAL MATERIALS OVERVIEW

Key Concepts in This Chapter

- The complexity of genealogical research requires a variety of instructional material.
- Most research guides focus on describing records.
- Twentieth-century research, including adoption, is often covered in separate publications.
- Most beginner's guides cover similar topics but in varying depth.
- Excellent manuals for young people are available.
- Many books focus on specific, related research skills.
- Instructional material should be carefully evaluated before classroom use.
- Periodical articles are excellent sources of instructional material.

Key Sources in This Chapter

- *Researcher's Guide to American Genealogy*
- Family History Library's Research Outline series
- *North Carolina Research: Genealogy and Local History*, 2nd ed.
- *Index to NGS and FGS Conferences and Syllabi*
- *The Source: A Guidebook of American Genealogy*
- *Roots for Kids*

2

INSTRUCTIONAL MATERIALS

Sandra Hargreaves Luebking

> Two things are required from every specialized treatise; it should clarify its subject and, in the second place, but actually more important, it should tell us how and by what methods we can attain it and make it ours.
>
> Longinus (ca. 213–373), *On the Sublime*

It is unlikely that Longinus had genealogy in mind when he stated the requirements of a functional essay. Yet the application is evident: his words provide a measure by which instructional material may be evaluated and offer guidance to any would-be author.

The complexity of genealogical research, the skills and knowledge it demands, and the need for critical evaluation of evidence require a family historian to become familiar with instructional materials. This instructional material must provide, according to Longinus's premise, techniques to understand and perform genealogical research.

Many types of instructional material meet this criterion. They include general guides or how-to manuals, textbooks, course work designed for home study, and curricula and lesson plans for use by teachers of genealogy. They may also include filmstrips, cassettes, games, and instructional visual aids.

The publication of such materials has proliferated over the past two decades. Gilbert Doane, in the 1960 edition of his *Searching for Your Ancestors*, noted that in 1937 there was "scarcely a handbook of genealogical research in print or available even in the second-hand book stores" (93). In 1960, he was able to list a dozen. Two decades later, in the 1980 edition, Doane selected twenty-eight titles of "handbooks and guides" (1980, 225–27) for his bibliography, only six of which were published before 1970.

Doane's co-author, James B. Bell, in completing the 1992 edition, may have needed weeks to evaluate the available handbooks before selecting eighty for his bibliography (with only twenty-one from the 1970s and three from the 1960s). The majority have been published since 1980 (eight were published in 1990 or later). An examination of *American and British Genealogy and Heraldry,* edited by P. William Filby, 3rd ed. (Boston: New England Historic Genealogical Society, 1983; 1982–85 supplement, 1987); *Genealogical and Local History Books in Print: General References and World Resources Volume,* edited by Marian Hoffman (Baltimore: Genealogical Publishing Co., 1997); and *Books in Print, Subject Guide* (New York: Bowker, annual), suggests the number of professionally produced handbooks and nonprint aids has surpassed three hundred. Privately published works bring the count to more than four hundred. Not all of these titles appear in this chapter or the chapter bibliography. However, most that do appear carry an annotation, and all are fully cited.

TYPES OF MATERIALS

With the increase in the amount of instructional material has come specialization in content and audience. Instructional material may be categorized as follows: how-to guides and manuals suitable for adult readers; guides for young people; skills and technologies associated with genealogy; and materials designed for formal instructional settings (that is, classroom or home-study guides). In addition, a multitude of articles in periodicals may be classified as tutorial. An analysis of each category follows, along with suggestions for locating instructional materials and articles and evaluating them for personal use or as enrichment aids in classrooms.

How-To Guides and Manuals for Adults

How-to guides and manuals for adults generally are a blend of methodology and record category description. Most are published for adult hobbyists who are just beginning genealogical research. However, lecturers, instructors of genealogy, and professional researchers may find these materials useful as quick refreshers or for detailed accounts of particular topics.

While writing styles vary in tone and quality, five themes, or approaches, predominate: records description, research as a process, twentieth-century family history, special groups (ethnic research), and regional and state guides.

Record Descriptions. The most widely used approach, record description, gives source material precedence over methodology or process. Chapters may stand independently of each other, and readers can understand one chapter without reading all preceding chapters. Self-contained sections are usually organized by type of source.

Text that is organized according to the agency or official who maintains a particular collection of records has a jurisdictional arrangement. Works organized this way generally categorize records in one of the following five levels of jurisdictions: private caretakers (perhaps the records have been stored in a private residence); local (such as newspapers); county; state; and Federal. Jurisdictional subheadings are the commonly accepted record group names. Within the Federal jurisdiction, for example, are census, military, U.S. district court, and ship passenger lists.

In *Printed Sources,* titles that deal with a single jurisdiction, such as *The Archives: A Guide to the National Archives Field Branches,* by Loretto D. Szucs and Sandra H. Luebking (Salt Lake City: Ancestry, 1988), or titles that focus on a single record group, such as *U.S. Military Records: A Guide to Federal and State Sources,* by James C. Neagles (Salt Lake City: Ancestry, 1994), appear in the chapters that correspond to the record category. Such titles will not be treated here.

One very successful handbook that covers a multitude of sources arranged by record descriptions is *The Source: A Guidebook of American Genealogy,* edited by Loretto D. Szucs and Sandra H. Luebking, rev. ed. (Salt Lake City: Ancestry, 1997). *The Source* includes sections on major U.S. record sources, immigration and ethnic groups, and twentieth-century research. Each section contains in-depth discussions of source categories or special fields, ranging from records of marriage and divorce to urban area research.

The Source has been labeled the single most comprehensive guide available in terms of its selection of resources and the detail with which they are explained. One of the book's greatest attributes is its use of many contributing authors, who collectively have attained a level of expertise that few single authors possess.

An excellent textbook is Val D. Greenwood's *The Researcher's Guide to American Genealogy,* rev. ed. (1990; reprint; Baltimore: Genealogical Publishing Co., 1997). Written by an instructor of genealogy who was frustrated by the lack of an adequate textbook, *The Researcher's Guide* admirably fills the gap. Using a records description approach, Greenwood divides his work into two major parts: "Background to Research" and "Records and Their Use."

"Background to Research" examines basic principles of genealogical research including the need for historical background, the concept of jurisdictions, use of libraries, and the use of primary sources versus secondary sources. "Records and Their Use" identifies and explains the most frequently consulted sources. The chapter titled "Abstracting Wills and Deeds" deviates from other guides in a significant way: detailed instructions are followed by actual deeds and wills in both full and abstracted forms.

The Researcher's Guide discusses not only the historical background of the record categories, but also the legal implications of these records. This innovative approach, plus a highly readable style, have made Greenwood's text a popular choice among genealogy teachers.

Other examples of records description are the research outlines published by the Family History Library of The Church of Jesus-Christ of Latter-day Saints (LDS church) in Salt Lake City, Utah. The outline for the United States introduces basic research strategies and twenty-six major record categories with concise but detailed information about general U.S. sources. State outlines are patterned after this general source booklet and are listed in this chapter's bibliography under "Regional and State Guides."

Research as a Process. *Process* is the highway along which research progresses. In instructional materials that use a process, or methodology, organization, sections and chapters are arranged sequentially to parallel the actual research procedure. The information in each chapter builds upon preceding chapters, so readers should study sequentially. The focus is on the process or methodology of research. Materials with this style of organization may need to be supplemented by works that deal with specific record categories.

A guide that exemplifies the process approach is *Voices in Your Blood: Discovering Identity through Family History,* by G. G. Vandagriff (Kansas City, Mo.: Andrews and McMeel, 1993) In this work, the message builds as the chapters progress. The approach is emphasized in chapter titles: "Asking Questions"; "Constructing a Bridge"; "Starting to Build"; "Using the Census as a Building Tool"; and "Building with Twentieth-Century Technology." One early chapter focuses on "Using the Largest Family History Library in the World." A later chapter discusses "The Finer Touches and Putting Your Work in Perspective."

Although it lacks a suitable number of references for supplementary reading and is not always adequate or accurate in citation of sources, titles, or terminology, *Voices in Your Blood* is highly motivating and presents some good advice about false leads and persons of the same name.

One value of the process approach is that, if the text is well written and comprehensive in scope, its life span and usefulness extend beyond that of most guides. Consider the enduring quality of *Searching for Your Ancestors,* by Gilbert H. Doane, originally published in 1937. Now in its sixth edition (Minneapolis: University of Minnesota Press, 1992), with updates and revisions by James B. Bell, this book has become a classic because of its gentle good humor, encouragement of sound collection procedures and analysis, and no-nonsense approach to verification.

Twentieth-Century Family History. Works in this category focus on finding living persons and contemporary information. Often, these works are produced for the general reading public by professional writers who do not claim to be family historians. Materials in this category include helps for planning reunions, establishing single-surname societies, producing family newsletters, writing autobiographies, and conducting oral interviews. They seldom can be classified as how-to guides, for they contain only superficial treatment of research methodology and sources. However, several recent works rooted in contemporary discovery offer practical advice on research practices and can effectively guide researchers concerned with finding living relatives, learning about adoptions, or preserving the stories of living family members. Included in this category are books on adoption research, such as *Search: A Handbook for Adoptees and Birthparents*, rev. ed. (Phoenix: Oryx Press, 1992), by Jayne Askin with Molly Davis.

In *Search,* Askin shares successful methods she used in seeking the facts of her birth. The authors list search and support groups, as well as both state and private reunion registries. *Search* identifies contact points not often used for family histories, such as state departments of motor vehicles, current voter lists, hospitals, and foundling homes and adoption agencies. The book's discussion of methodology and public records is useful for researchers who lack personal knowledge of living family members. The sound methodology, emphasis on fact over fiction, and outlining of process over "hit-and-miss" research provide a stepping stone for research into past generations.

Another significant contribution of works that focus on the assembly of current data is their ability to link family history to other disciplines. David E. Kyvig and Myron A. Marty, authors of *Your Family History: A Handbook for Research and Writing* (Arlington Heights, Ill.: Harlan Davidson, 1978), introduce issues of sociological and historical perspective. They note how clues, such as the script-type on a tombstone, might indicate a family's financial status and how the retention of certain cultural traditions suggests ways that immigrants adjusted to life in a new country.

Special Groups. Research on Native Americans, Hispanics, African Americans, Asian Americans, Jewish Americans, and many other groups requires special approaches. The sources and search methods appropriate for such groups must be presented within the context of their specific historical heritage. The unique features of this interweave of history, tactics, and sources may require researchers to read texts that pertain exclusively to the research and resources of special groups. Helpful books in this category include Cecelia Carpenter's *How to Research American Indian Blood Lines: A Manual on Indian Genealogical Research* (Bountiful, Utah: American Genealogical Lending Library, 1994); Arthur Kurzweil's *From Generation to Generation: How to Trace Your Jewish Genealogy and Personal History* (New York: HarperCollins, 1994); and Norma Flores and Patsy Ludwig's *A Beginner's Guide to Hispanic Genealogy* (San Mateo, Calif.: Western Book/Journal Press, 1993).

A few general how-to books provide quality advice about special groups. For example, a helpful chapter on Native Americans appears in Norman Wright's *Preserving Your American Heritage: A Guide to Family and Local History* (Provo, Utah: Brigham Young University Press, 1981). Chapters on Native Americans, Hispanics, African Americans, and Jewish Americans are contained in *The Source: A Guidebook of American Genealogy* (cited earlier). Ethnic research is a rapidly expanding area of family history study. Many more instructional and background sources for these groups are identified in chapter 4, "Ethnic Sources."

Regional and State Guides. Various guides have been written to describe the specific records and sources in particular regions or states. These are not how-to guides, and the quality and extent of their coverage varies considerably. Most begin with a narrative or chronology of state history, followed by a county-by-county listing of record groups, including their content, location, and beginning dates. These works tend to be descriptive rather than instructive, so they must be supplemented by more extensive works on methods and sources.

State or regional guides are seldom designed to present a comprehensive treatment of methodology. A notable exception, however, is the detailed and well-written *North Carolina Research: Genealogy and Local History,* 2nd ed., edited by Helen F. M. Leary (Raleigh: North Carolina Genealogical Society, 1996). Part 1 of *North Carolina Research,* "Research Techniques," includes a fine discussion of research strategies. Various sources are explained in general terms, followed by suggestions for analyzing findings within that record group. The book contains extensive information on the use of primary and secondary records and provides instructions for evaluating and ranking these sources. Each chapter is self-contained, making the book valuable as a reference manual. Charts, illustrations, and maps are plentiful, appropriate, and legible. The editor's attention to detail and consideration of readers' needs make this book an excellent resource.

Part 2, "County Records," and part 3, "State Records," include some discussion that is unique to North Carolina. However, the treatments are so comprehensive that the usefulness of these record explanations transcends state boundaries. The sections on Federal, private, and nonwritten records (parts 4, 5, and 6) also have universal appeal, are well constructed, and reflect a consultation of authoritative sources rather than the singular view of the editor. Selected references follow each chapter.

State guide outlines published by the Family History Library may be particularly useful for states for which no comprehensive material is available. The series consists of fifty state guides that range from eight to twenty-two pages. Each outline includes succinct commentaries on alphabetically arranged topics, from Archives and Libraries, to Cemeteries and Land, to Vital Records.

An ongoing effort by the National Genealogical Society is the production of the Research in the States series. Currently, the series contains informative and accurate guides for the District of Columbia, Indiana, Minnesota, Oregon, South Carolina, Texas, and Tennessee. These booklets are outgrowths of articles from the *National Genealogical Society Quarterly;* their content has been expanded and updated to include the most current information available at the time of publication. The series eventually will include guides for additional states: authoritative articles on Georgia, North Carolina, and Mississippi are being adapted for future booklets.

Several chapters in Alice Eichholz, ed., *Ancestry's Red Book,* rev. ed. (Salt Lake City: Ancestry, 1992), present current information on sources, repositories, and locations of records critical to successful searching. While the quality of the chapters varies, those written by authors who conduct research in the subject state tend to be well done. The American Society of Genealogists' *Genealogical Research: Methods and Sources,* edited by Milton Rubincam and Jean Stephenson, rev. ed., 2 vols. (New Orleans: Polyanthos, 1980–83), somewhat dated but carefully prepared, also provides background material to aid researchers.

Beginners' Guides. The titles in table 2-1 were selected from those that appear under the heading "How-To Guides and Manuals for Adults. This table is informational in nature and not evaluative, and the topics (subject matter) listed do not constitute recommendations. For example, half of the titles in the table discuss the change from the Old Style to the New Style calendar, yet one might question a beginner's need to know this.

The table is not intended to be critical of omissions in a text. An author's decision to include or exclude a topic may be explained in the works's introduction, preface, or title, and this fact should be considered. Marlin's *My Sixteen: A Self-Help Guide to Finding Your 16 Great-Great-Grandparents* might not be expected to provide a kinship chart.

Indication of a topic's inclusion does not mean that the discussion is in-depth or appropriately placed. For example, Croom's *Unpuzzling Your Past* discusses citing sources but is not explicit in linking family group sheet entries to the source (via a footnote or other attribution); Raymond Wright's *The*

Table 2-1. Topics Found in Beginners' Guides

Topics Covered	*Allen*	*Balhuizen*	*Wright, Norman*	*Croom*	*Leary*	*Greenwood*	*Wright, Raymond*	*Marlin*
Why do genealogy?	•	•	•	•			•	•
Cost factor	•							
"Begin with yourself"	•	•	•	•			•	
Family documents and photos	•	•	•	•	•	•	•	
Heirlooms	•				•			
Oral history, interview techniques	•	•	•	•	•	•	•	•
Finding previous research (already done by hereditary societies or published in family histories)	•	•	•			•	•	
Surnames—meanings and naming patterns	•	•		•		•		
Filing systems	•	•	•	•	•	•	•	
Family group sheets	•	•	•	•	•	•	•	
Pedigree charts	•	•	•	•	•	•	•	•
Pedigree numbering systems					•			
Research notes	•	•	•	•	•	•	•	
Use of photography to copy documents	•		•					
Sample family group sheets and pedigree charts for examples	•	•	•	•	•	•		•
Charting instructions	•	•		•	•	•		
Chart to determine kinship or relationship			•	•		•	•	
Primary and secondary sources	•	•	•	•	•	•	•	•
Citation of sources	•	•	•	•	•	•	•	
Institutions								
Libraries and finding aids	•	•	•	•	•	•	•	•
Family History Library, microfilming, or International Genealogical Index	•	•	•			•	•	•
Other major collections or institutes	•	•	•		•	•	•	•
Using indexes (census or others)	•	•	•		•	•	•	•
Manuscript collections (*National Union Catalog of Manuscript Collections,* etc.)	•	•			•	•	•	
Research Assistance								
Pitfalls: interpreting spelling/handwriting	•	•		•	•	•	•	•
Dating (change from the Old Style calendar)		•		•	•	•	•	
Research process/methodology	•	•		•	•	•		•
Allied/associated families	•				•		•	•
Problems associated with persons having the same name	•	•			•			
Correspondence	•	•	•	•	•	•	•	•
Abstracting (how to)					•	•		
Queries	•						•	
Maps	•	•			•	•	•	
Migration		•		•	•	•	•	
Research Etiquette (on site)	•	•		•	•			•
Sources								
Censuses, Federal	•	•	•	•	•	•	•	•

Topics Covered	*Allen*	*Balhuizen*	*Wright, Norman*	*Croom*	*Leary*	*Green-wood*	*Wright, Raymond*	*Marlin*
Censuses, state and territorial	•	•	•	•	•	•	•	•
Finding aids (for Federal censuses)	•	•	•	•	•	•	•	•
Examples of using censuses	•		•	•	•	•	•	•
Soundex key			•	•	•	•	•	•
Military records	•	•	•	•	•	•	•	•
World War I draft registrations	•			•	•	•	•	
Civil War pension records	•		•	•	•	•	•	
Civil War service records	•		•	•	•	•	•	
Records from other nineteenth- and twentieth-century wars	•		•	•	•	•	•	
Revolutionary war records			•	•	•	•	•	
Bounty-land records	•	•	•	•	•	•	•	
Homestead records	•		•	•	•	•	•	
Vital records	•	•	•	•	•	•	•	•
Cemeteries	•	•	•	•	•	•	•	•
Church records		•	•	•	•	•	•	
Court records								
Probate	•	•	•	•	•	•	•	
Civil/criminal court			•		•	•	•	
Divorce	•		•		•	•	•	•
Deeds	•	•	•	•	•	•	•	
Land records (state and public land systems described)	•		•		•	•	•	
Newspapers	•	•		•	•	•	•	•
Business and/or institutional records			•		•		•	
School records			•		•		•	
Medical records			•					
Coroners' records			•		•			
Social Security Death Index	•					•	•	•
City directories/telephone directories	•					•	•	•
Immigration records (general)	•	•	•	•		•	•	
Ship passenger lists	•		•	•	•	•	•	•
Naturalization records	•		•	•	•	•	•	•
Contemporary Interests								
Sharing information	•	•						•
Family reunions	•							
Family history publishing	•			•	•	•	•	
Locating twentieth-century families	•			•				•
Genealogical societies	•	•				•	•	
Adoption	•		•		•	•	•	
Archival supplies and preservation techniques	•	•						
Historic buildings	•				•			
Professional services	•					•		
Precautions for consumers	•							
Education: courses and conferences	•	•			•	•		
Computers and genealogy	•	•		•	•	•	•	•

Topics Covered	*Allen*	*Balhuizen*	*Wright, Norman*	*Croom*	*Leary*	*Green-wood*	*Wright, Raymond*	*Marlin*
Ethnic (General)	•	•			•		•	
American Indians	•		•	•	•	•	•	
African Americans	•			•	•	•	•	
Others (Jewish, Hispanic, etc.)					•	•		•
Book Contains								
Resources: addresses	•		•	•	•	•	•	•
Resources: titles (bibliography)	•	•	•	•	•	•	•	•
Glossary	•			•	•	•		
Index	•		•	•	•	•	•	•
Sample forms for reader to fill in		•		•			•	
Illustrations, diagrams, charts			•	•	•	•		
Sample documents			•		•	•	•	•

Genealogist's Handbook refers to source citation only in the chapter on writing a family history.

Works obviously will not refer to topics or sources that were not available at the time of publication. For example, the World War I draft (Selective Service) registrations were not accessible when Norman Wright's *Preserving Your American Heritage* was published. Below are the full citations for the works shown in the table.

- Allen, Desmond Walls, and Carolyn Earle Billingsley. *Beginner's Guide to Family History Research.* 3rd ed. Research Associates (P.O. Box 122, Bryant, AR 72089-0122), 1997.
- Balhuizen, Anne Ross. *Getting Started: How to Begin Researching Your Family History.* 1994. Reprint. Indianapolis: Ye Olde Genealogie Shoppe, 1997.
- Wright, Norman Edgar. *Preserving Your American Heritage: A Guide to Family and Local History.* Provo, Utah: Brigham Young University Press, 1981.
- Croom, Emily Anne. *Unpuzzling Your Past: A Basic Guide to Genealogy.* 3rd ed. White Hall, Va.: Betterway Publications, 1995.
- Leary, Helen F. M., ed. *North Carolina Research: Genealogy and Local History.* 2nd ed. Raleigh: North Carolina Genealogical Society, 1996.
- Greenwood, Val D. *The Researcher's Guide to American Genealogy.* Rev. ed. 1990. Reprint. Baltimore: Genealogical Publishing Co., 1997.
- Wright, Raymond S., 3rd. *The Genealogist's Handbook: Modern Methods for Researching Family History.* Chicago: American Library Association, 1995.
- Marlin, Robert W. *My Sixteen: A Self-Help Guide to Finding Your Sixteen Great-Grandparents.* Nashville, Tenn.: Land Yacht Press, 1996.

How-To Guides and Manuals for Young People

An audience that has received much recent attention is young people who are searching for knowledge of the past. Guides aimed at this age level generally emphasize tracing family history through interviewing relatives, exploring sources found in the home, and using published works at libraries. Archival and public record searches assume secondary importance or are completely disregarded. Another feature of guides for young people is descriptions of creative ways to display or report findings.

A popular children's manual is *My Backyard History Book,* by David Weitzman (Boston: Little, Brown & Co., 1975). Chapters titled "Wow, Have You Got Ancestors!" "Out on a Limb of the Family Tree," and "Families Come in All Shapes and Sizes" make research fun and manageable.

A few books are directed at youth groups, such as 4-H or scouting organizations. Elizabeth L. Nichols's *Genealogy* (Irving, Tex.: Boy Scouts of America, 1988) is used by the Boy Scouts of America for scouts seeking a merit badge in genealogy. Both *Genealogy* and *My Backyard History Book* can be used as teacher and classroom aids for integrating genealogy into the curricula of geography, social studies, math, and science courses.

Another excellent children's book is *Roots for Kids,* by Susan Provost Beller (1989; reprint; Baltimore: Genealogical Publishing Co., 1997). Intended for students as young as fourth grade, Beller's guide is the result of more than a decade of teaching genealogy in Vermont. *Roots for Kids* can be used as a textbook in a twelve-week enrichment class, as a guide for a mini-course, or as a self-teaching reader for students in sixth grade and above. (The text uses Vermont record-keeping systems, so allowances must be made for area terminology if the book is used outside of Vermont.) Beller presents the basics of genealogy in words and tone suitable for her intended audience. Her inclusion of sample request letters and abstract forms and examples is a welcome and essential addition to the text.

Early in *Roots for Kids,* Beller discusses good note-keeping and citing of sources. Her list of rules for handling courthouse and other records—beginning with "clean hands, please!"—is practical and appropriate. Chapter 8, "A Visit to the Town or County Clerk's Office," includes some universal cautions about visits to public records offices; for instance, "The most important plan for you as a student doing research is to have an adult go with you." The text is enjoyable to read and is not burdened with details that may interest adults but bore children. For example, Beller wisely advises readers to ask someone how to use the Soundex because it can be "tricky" (Beller 1997, 71).

Beller's treatment of sources is adequate for her audience. While a reviewer may take issue with statements such as, "If the person you are looking for died without a will, you usually will not get very much information from these [probate] records" (Beller 1997, 55), on the whole, *Roots for Kids* is a solid presentation of genealogy for young learners.

Genealogy Technologies and Refinement of Skills

Certain instructional publications focus on the mechanics or technologies of genealogy, or the refinement of skills of practicing researchers. This category includes discussions of manual and computerized record-keeping systems, the use of computers to meet the database or word processing demands of genealogy, and the enhancing of skills, such as recording oral or video histories or writing and publishing. Some materials in this category are devoted to helping researchers become professional genealogists.

Record-Keeping. One popular self-contained instructional unit is *Managing a Genealogical Project: A Complete Manual for the Management and Organization of Genealogical Materials,* by William Dollarhide, rev. ed. (Baltimore: Genealogical Publishing Co., 1996). A practical discussion and illustrations of forms for guiding research is supplemented by techniques for presenting research to non-genealogists. One useful feature of this book is a comparison of some of the numbering systems used in genealogy, namely, the Register System, the Record System, and the Henry Numbering System. Explanations of each system are followed by an analysis of its strengths and weaknesses. This work is well organized (as befits a manual on organization) and easy to read.

Computer Applications. A work that emphasizes technology but also does a credible job of defining research processes and sources is *Turbo Genealogy: An Introduction to Family History Research in the Information Age,* by John and Carolyn Cosgriff (Salt Lake City: Ancestry, 1997). *Turbo Genealogy* leads readers from a traditional organizational scheme (forms, documentation, family interviewing, and note-keeping and filing) to the benefits and selection of computer hardware and software.

Throughout this book, the authors encourage readers to formulate a research plan and to evaluate and resolve conflicts of evidence. This is a good how-to guide with an appendix and glossary of selected technical terms. Each chapter is supplemented by a strong bibliography. This book may change the future of how-to guides because texts that lack detailed information on computer-genealogy technology will be incomplete.

Oral and Video History. Guides to oral and video history are important for a generation of youthful newcomers to genealogical research whose parents, grandparents, and perhaps great-grandparents are still living. Once the province of highly trained interviewers preserving the words of the famous or infamous, oral history has overflowed these narrow confines and flooded the grasslands of local and personal history.

In the early 1980s, works from related fields were being adapted for use by family historians. Among these was *An Oral History Primer* (Salt Lake City: Primer Publications, 1973; tenth printing 1983), edited by Gary L. Shumway and W. G. Hartley. This book provides suggestions for choosing a tape recorder; interview questions and evaluations; and archival procedures for copying, handling, and storing the resulting documents. Within a few years, tape recorders were being supplemented with motion pictures in Derek Reimer's *Voices: A Guide to Oral History* (British Columbia, Canada: Provincial Archives of British Columbia, Sound and Moving Image Division, 1984). However, the most current edition (3rd ed., revised) of Willa Baum's *Oral History for the Local Historical Society* (Walnut Creek, Calif.: Alta Mira Press, 1995) focuses on the use of tape recorders rather than film or video. Video has received attention through such works as Mary Lou Peterman's *Gift of Heritage* (Minneapolis, Minn.: Mary Lou Productions, 1992), a 60-minute videocassette on how to create a family history on videotape.

Writing and Publishing. A recent trend of certain instructional manuals is the encouragement of a tangible outcome. Obtaining and recording the information become preliminaries to the creation of a permanent record, whether it is a complete family history or vignettes of incidents in the lives of individuals.

Family historians can now learn how to write, publish, and market their family histories. Seldom does this type of work offer methodology or source instruction. Nor do these books, such as Joan Neubauer's *From Memories to Manuscript: The Five-Step Method of Writing Your Life Story* (Salt Lake City: Ancestry, 1994), purport to be genealogy texts or encourage even contemporary family history. But their encouragement of self-knowledge and their emphasis on viewing personal experiences and decisions in a broader context certainly lay the groundwork for their readers' eventual pursuit of ancestors.

One publishing guide that does stress genealogy is Patricia Hatcher's *Producing a Quality Family History* (Salt Lake City: Ancestry, 1996). Hatcher's background as a genealogist enables her to authoritatively stress that quality production begins with quality material. Her instructions for accuracy, completeness, and proper citation of researched information makes this book a must for family historians planning to compose a publishable, quality history.

Advanced Skills and Professional Development. Basic how-to guides lose their charm for researchers whose interest and fascination with family history becomes a compulsion. At this point, researchers need advanced training through works that focus on a particular skill or function.

How researchers refine evaluation skills is one predictor of the level at which they will function. *Evidence! Citation and Analysis for the Family Historian,* by Elizabeth Shown Mills (Baltimore: Genealogical Publishing Co., 1997), is destined to become the definitive work on primary sources versus secondary sources and preponderance of evidence.

Three works that share the vast experience of prominent genealogists are Donald Lines Jacobus's *Genealogy as Pastime and Profession,* 2nd rev. ed. (1991; reprint; Baltimore: Genealogical Publishing Co., 1996), Milton Rubincam's *Pitfalls in Genealogical Research* (Salt Lake City: Ancestry, 1987), and Willard Heiss's *Working in the Vineyards of Genealogy* (Indianapolis: Indiana Historical Society, 1993), a collection of essays edited by Ruth Dorel.

Researchers considering a career in genealogy, meaning those who wish to establish an independent practice with the associated legal and financial responsibilities, have few sources to consult. Although little has been published on this topic, *How to Become a Professional Genealogist,* by Carolyn Billingsley and Desmond Walls Allen, 3rd ed. (Bryant, Ark.: Research Associates, 1997), provides a fine beginning. *How to Become a Professional Genealogist* answers questions that plague most candidates: Am I capable of becoming a professional genealogist? If so, how do I start and what can I expect from the occupation? Readers learn, for example, that grammar and spelling skills are critical for report writing; that attending national conferences and institutes are musts for skill-building and networking; and that "trial clients" provide a training period for prospective genealogists to evaluate the merits and shortcomings of genealogy as employment.

Courses and Programs of Study

The fourth category of instructional materials provides a somewhat structured and formal study opportunity by actively involving the student in the learning process. This is achieved through the use of audio or visual products, or through participants' written responses. Within this category are classroom aids for teachers, home-study courses, and self-improvement manuals for professionals.

Teacher Development and Classroom Aids. Tapes and syllabi from national conferences can be helpful for teachers who seek to improve their presentation skills. Topics include selecting curricula for beginning and advanced courses, understanding adult learning processes, planning and preparing lessons, and marketing a program of genealogy.

Appropriate tapes and syllabi can be found through *Index to NGS and FGS Conferences and Syllabi,* compiled by Joy Reisinger (Salt Lake City: National Genealogical Society and Federation of Genealogical Societies, 1993). The topic "Education" lists dozens of lectures presented between 1978 and 1993 pertaining to the development of teaching skills. Presentations on specific topics, such as record sources or methodology, enable instructors to gain deeper understanding and thus enrich their own lesson plans. The taped presentations are *not* for group use, however, because the copyright for the content rests with the presenters; public presentation would violate this copyright.

Classroom aids are not plentiful, but they are becoming more widely available than they were in the 1980s; then, teachers were forced to create their own lesson plans, visual aids, and handouts. Commercially and privately produced aids now range from originals suitable for handout or visual aid reproduction, to detailed lesson plans, such as Elizabeth L. Nichols's *Teaching Family History in Four Weeks: A Course Outline* (Salt Lake City: Family History Educators, 1990).

Self-Contained Instructional Material. An innovation in genealogical education has been the development of instructional materials for home study. The earliest of these are the programmed instructional works by Elizabeth L. Nichols, *The Genesis of Your Genealogy,* 3rd ed. (Salt Lake City: Family History Educators, 1992) and *Help Is Available,* 2nd ed. (Logan, Utah: Everton Publishers, 1980). Programmed instruction requires students to respond in spaces provided. By checking responses against an answer sheet, students can determine how much they have learned.

American Genealogy: A Basic Course, a very successful home-study program produced by the National Genealogical Society and implemented by staff members at society headquarters, was introduced in 1982 and is now in its fourth edition (Washington, D.C.: National Genealogical Society, 1996). With this award-winning course, students complete projects, then receive tests through the mail. Rather than being totally self-contained (as are Nichols's programmed instructional booklets), the *American Genealogy* course requires outside reading and exercises to enhance the basic course information. Students gain practical experience by visiting public record offices and libraries. In 1996 this home study course received accreditation from the Accrediting Commission of the Distance Education and Training Council for a five-year period.

Commercially produced audio- and videotapes are also useful for home study. With these tapes, researchers can bring the expertise of nationally acclaimed speakers right into their living rooms or cars. Those lectures delivered at national or state conferences that have been reproduced on audiotape can be identified by using *Index to NGS and FGS Conferences and Syllabi* (see "Teacher Development and Classroom Aids," above). This helpful publication indexes lectures by topic and by speaker. Ordering instructions explain where to write for the tape and how to get the handout or the entire syllabus.

A series of instructional tapes titled Fast Lane Learning Kits is available from Family History Unlimited, 3507 North University Avenue, Suite 350B, Provo, UT 84604. Fast Lane offers four hours of audiotaped instruction with an accompanying workbook.

During 1997–98, the Federation of Genealogical Societies and the Ohio Genealogical Society videotaped five teleconference sessions: Military Records; Immigration and Ship Passenger Records; American Land Records; American Court Records; and Modern Vital Records. Each 180-minute presentation includes a syllabus. They can be ordered from the Ohio Genealogical Society, P.O. Box 2625, Mansfield, OH 44906-0625 or from the Federation of Genealogical Societies, 1-888-FGS-1500 or (fax) 1-888-380-0500.

Periodical Articles

Educational courses and study programs can be supplemented by journal articles that present case studies, tips for instructors, and analyses of successful problem solving. Nationally circulated periodicals, such as *Association of Professional Genealogists' Quarterly*; the FGS *Forum* (published by the Federation of Genealogical Societies); the *National Genealogical Society Quarterly*; the *Genealogical Journal* (published by the Utah Genealogical Association); and the *New England Historical and Genealogical Register* (published by the New England Historic Genealogical Society), often contain valuable and sophisticated how-to articles. In almost every issue of these periodicals, readers can find articles on methodology or on particular sources or record-keeping agencies.

To find articles in these and other periodicals, researchers can consult the *Periodical Source Index* (*PERSI*), published by the Allen County Public Library Foundation in Fort Wayne, Indiana (Fort Wayne, Ind., 1987–). *PERSI* indexes more than two thousand genealogical and local history periodicals. Genealogy students may be interested in the listings under Research Methodology. Articles in *PERSI* include "Research Tips for Revolutionary Ancestors," "Secret Society Records," "Using Maps in Research," and "Path of Orphan Train Children." *PERSI* became available on CD-ROM from Ancestry in 1997.

Another index, *Genealogical Periodical Annual Index* (*GPAI*), compiled by Karen Ackermann and edited by Laird C. Towle (Bowie, Md.: Heritage Books, 1974–), lists instructional articles under the general heading "Methodology" and under specific headings according to technical subject. Kip Sperry's *Index to Genealogical Periodical Literature, 1960–1977* (Detroit: Gale Research, 1979), also focuses on methodology articles. Periodical indexes are described more fully in chapter 19, "Genealogical Periodicals."

IDENTIFYING AND EVALUATING INSTRUCTIONAL MATERIALS

Identifying and locating instructional materials is not always easy. Evaluating these materials is even more difficult, especially for newcomers to the field. Which guide was written for a quick sell and which will withstand the test of time, aging as gracefully as a well-researched and properly prepared family history? Annotated bibliographies can help researchers assess the value of instructional works.

Identifying and Obtaining Instructional Materials

Annotated bibliographies for genealogy are in short supply. Of these, a handful of contemporary works can help identify instructional materials. One modestly sized, slightly outdated, but authoritative and annotated work is *Genealogy: A Selected Bibliography,* 5th ed. (Birmingham, Ala.: Banner Press, 1983), by Milton Rubincam, editor emeritus of the *National Genealogical Society Quarterly*.

A more comprehensive listing appears in *American and British Genealogy and Heraldry,* by P. William Filby (Boston: New England Historic Genealogical Society, 1983), in the section titled "United States, General Reference, Records, Guides, Indexes." This section contains annotated titles of works known through its date of publication (1983).

Marian Hoffman has compiled and edited *Genealogical and Local History Books in Print: General References and World Resources Volume* (cited earlier). This volume is perhaps the most current source of instructional materials because new editions or supplements are to be issued on a regular basis. Many titles are submitted by authors or publishers; editors' comments, if any, should be noted. Two important features of this work are its complete list of vendors and special ordering information. There is an index of authors, titles, and advertisers.

Book reviews and advertisements in genealogical journals and magazines provide an excellent means of learning about new instructional publications. Most publishers advertise in *Everton's Genealogical Helper* (published by The Everton Publishers, Logan, Utah) and submit their books for review to several journals. Some journals critique each book; others merely describe the content of each book without evaluating its substance.

People can obtain how-to books easily through publishers or bookstores that specialize in genealogical publications and supplies. In addition, national, state, and local conferences have created opportunities for book vendors to display their merchandise, making customer examination and purchase very convenient. (See the introduction to *Printed Sources* for more information on purchasing genealogical books.)

Evaluating Instructional Materials

Gone are the days when researchers could learn their craft solely by practical application. Acquiring knowledge by trial and error is inefficient and unnecessary, and can jeopardize the research opportunities of those who follow.

Instructional material helps researchers progress from the personal to the universal. No longer can a family historian, a professional genealogist, or a teacher function autonomously. As members of the larger genealogical community, researchers must operate under a code of ethics and proper standards of conduct. This code includes not only adequately documenting and describing sources of information, but also developing an awareness of local and national concerns about records preservation and access. The best method of developing an appreciation of issues and a policy of responsible action is receiving quality instruction.

The introduction of online computer bulletin boards, the high attendance at national conferences, and the potential for networking among researchers certainly offer many instructional opportunities. But they do not alter a basic fact: the printed word reaches more researchers than any other medium and thus is most influential in transmitting skills, information, and attitudes. Genealogical society leaders, book reviewers, teachers, and professional genealogists are likely to be asked, "How do I begin?" These experienced researchers must be prepared to recommend the best instructional materials in the field. The following criteria should aid the selection process.

An important consideration in evaluating instructional material is the experience and expertise the author brings to the work.

- Is the author a practicing genealogist who has gained recognition among peers through writing or lecturing? Or is the author a professional writer who has chosen genealogy as the subject for a marketable book?
- Is the author familiar with the concepts, research principles, records, and regions that are described in the book?
- What training has the author received for this type of work?
- What other works have been prepared by this author and how well were they received by the genealogical community and reviewers?

This is not to imply that only a professional researcher can write a research guide or that only a practicing teacher can prepare instructional materials. Instead, it suggests that an author's credentials and reputation are a prime evaluative factor.

Another consideration in evaluation of instructional material is the reader's purpose. Is the reader seeking personal development? If so, on what skill level? Will the publication be used be as a classroom text or as reference material from which lessons or lectures will be prepared? With the purpose clearly in mind, book selectors first should examine the preface and the foreword. If readers need an authoritative reference on record categories, for instance, books that claim in the preface to focus upon methodology would be inappropriate. If a book's purpose, stated in the introduction, is to interest children in family history, adults may not find the guide compelling or helpful.

Book selectors should examine a work's table of contents closely.

- Do the topics parallel the author's stated intent?
- Does the selection of material seem comprehensive?
- Is the division of sources or methods reasonable?
- Is there adequate emphasis on the time periods and regions that readers are interested in?
- Are the topics appropriate to the skill level of readers? (An introductory how-to guide that purports to help readers take the first steps in writing a family history need not detail the deciphering of colonial handwriting or discuss the change to the Gregorian calendar. On the other hand, such discussions would be necessary in a how-to book intended for intermediate or advanced researchers.)

Next, book selectors should read a dozen or more pages of the publication.

- Is the writing clear and concise and the style pleasing?
- Are the examples drawn from a wide spectrum of experience rather than only the author's personal research?
- Are descriptions adequate or do they provide only a superficial account of topics for the sake of selling the book?
- Does the text contain typographical and grammatical errors? (Carefully edited books do not.)
- Did the editing process include a reading of the manuscript by an authority in the subject matter?
- Is the text free from technical errors?

Accuracy of information can be tested by checking some portion of the text against credible sources. For example, a typical error in material that discusses census records would be a statement like the following: "The 1880 Soundex indexes heads of households having children *under ten*"; actually, the 1880 Soundex indexes heads of households having children *aged ten or under*. This and other inaccuracies should be noted and weighed in the evaluation. Technical errors indicate that the author consulted mediocre sources in preparing the text.

Those who select books should also consider the currency and life span of the text.

- Does the publication address twentieth-century sources adequately?
- Is the information timeless, or does the book's focus limit its life?

Research methods do not change drastically over the years, but "shortcuts" may, as may prices, addresses, and locations of collections. Instructional materials that devote a great amount of space to these subjects are severely limited in their life span unless they also provide a worthwhile account of methodology or sources.

Next, book selectors should examine the bibliography.

- Does it contain an adequate number of titles for supplemental reading?
- Are these titles quality publications?
- Are the references divided into categories or annotated so that readers can identify works that will be helpful?
- Are the citations properly noted so that the reader can obtain them easily?

Book selectors should appraise maps, illustrations, charts, and tables. Are they relevant and legible? Poorly reproduced records and maps frustrate readers. Not all reproductions need to be in color nor of such high quality that the publication's cost soars beyond reason; however, illustrations and other graphics must be decipherable and appropriate to the text.

The index should be comprehensive enough to permit readers to locate specialized topics within larger categories. Broad index entries such as "Census" or "Military" are inadequate. Secondary entries, such as "Cross Index to Selected City Streets and Enumeration Districts, 1910 Census," or "War of 1812 Bounty Land Records," enable readers to access desired information quickly.

Finally, do book reviewers in respected genealogical journals and newsletters recommend the publication? If several reviewers recommend the book with a caution on its treatment of the Social Security Death Index, for example, readers can judge the usefulness of the book with confidence. While book selectors should use caution in making decisions on the basis of promotional material or paid advertisements, a publisher's notice that includes endorsements from recognized professionals serves as one measure of quality.

Selecting Textbooks for Classroom Use

The selection of textbooks in many ways relies upon the guidelines already discussed. The book must be pleasing to read, substantive, and current.

A textbook should also present a logically arranged balance of methodology and sources. The total research process should be a central theme throughout the book, with no single factor (note-keeping, location of records, etc.) dominating the text.

The book's availability and cost, along with the skill level of the intended users, should also be considered. Availability of a proposed text is often a crucial factor. If class is conducted in an area with limited access to certain texts, choices are obviously limited.

Price must be weighed, particularly if students are on fixed or limited incomes. Instructors should also consider the commitment of the students in general. For a five-week course, an inexpensive text may be more practical than a high-priced one; a semester's course might justify students' investing in a more expensive publication.

The skill level of students is a critical factor. Beginning genealogy classes may not benefit from textbooks used in advanced classes. Indeed, a comprehensive compendium such as *The Source* may overwhelm beginning students. One means of selecting appropriate textbooks may be to evaluate the texts selected by faculty at national institutes or other recognized programs of study.

The Institute of Genealogy and Historical Research at Samford University in Birmingham, Alabama, has been held annually for three decades. The institute, co-sponsored by the Board for Certification of Genealogists, offers five course levels and areas of coursework in U.S. genealogy. The following works were selected as texts in the 1994 sessions on U.S. research: Greenwood's *The Researcher's Guide to American Genealogy* (cited earlier) for course I, Fundamentals of Genealogy and Historical Research; *The Researcher's Guide to American Genealogy* for course II, Intermediate Studies in Genealogy and Historical Research; and the American Society of Genealogists' *Genealogical Research: Methods and Sources,* vol. 1 (cited earlier) for course III, Southern Colonies and States: Pennsylvania through Florida. (Course IV, Advanced Genealogy: Methodology and Research Techniques, and course V, Professional Genealogy, did not use textbooks in 1994.)

Students who subscribe to the home-study course of the National Genealogical Society, *American Genealogy: A Basic Course,* are assigned readings from *The Researcher's Guide to American Genealogy.* Other popular texts include Emily Croom's *Unpuzzling Your Past: A Basic Guide to Genealogy,* 3rd ed. (White Hall, Va.: Betterway Publications, 1995), Wright's *Preserving Your American Heritage* (cited earlier), Wilbur Helmbold's *Tracing Your Ancestry: A Step-by-Step Guide to Researching Your Family History* (Birmingham [Ala.]: Oxmoor House, 1976), and both *The Source* (cited earlier) and Johni Cerny and Arlene Eakle's *Ancestry's Guide to Research: Case Studies in American Genealogy* (Salt Lake City: Ancestry, 1985).

THE FUTURE OF INSTRUCTIONAL MATERIALS

No single instructional text is comprehensive enough to serve students from the beginning of their genealogical pursuits through the perfection of their skills. Beginners need practical and reliable information concerning basic sources available for genealogical research. They also need an introduction to fundamental research techniques. As students' skills, interest, and commitment grow, so does the need for more sophisticated analyses of methodology and sources. Serious students need detailed explanations of record categories, research techniques, and advanced strategies (for example, piecing together neighborhoods using early maps, censuses and land records, or researching kin or other associates when records for the person sought are sparse).

To achieve Longinus's goals of clarifying the subject and providing methods for mastering the subject, future instructional material must address the changing composition of its audience. In 1960, when Doane was revising his successful *Searching for Your Ancestors,* his readership consisted largely of retired people with the time, energy, and desire to investigate their heritage. Most of these people were born before 1900 and generally could begin by finding records for their parents in the 1880 Federal population census.

This situation no longer exists. Since that 1960 revision, the genealogical community has become younger; conference attendees, classroom participants, and library researchers are not exclusively retirees. Instructional material must reflect this demographic shift in at least two important ways: first, it needs to take advantage of video and computer multimedia technology; second, it must discuss the time period that beginning students will research. Instructional material must explain research techniques appropriate for both the time period being researched and the skill level of students.

A significant and rapidly growing number of genealogy students are under forty years of age. Of course, these people will not find themselves in the 1920 census or in the records of World War II. The Social Security Death Index may list parents, grandparents, and even great-grandparents of younger researchers. How-to guides published in the 1990s and beyond must accommodate this audience; therefore, manuals for beginners should focus their approach only on the past 120 years, with some "teaser" material extending back to 1850.

Basic guides need to discuss the use of national bibliographic and public documents databases, CD-ROM technology and sources, and the Internet. The problem of finding sources will likely be replaced by the challenge of successfully managing an abundance of sources.

The Julian calendar, the pre-1850 Federal population census schedules, colonial handwriting, Federal and colonial land grants, and even revolutionary war records (an almost obligatory topic of past generations of how-to authors) are no longer valid subjects for beginners who have been admonished to "work from yourself back, one generation at a time." Twentieth- and nineteenth-century records of adoption and divorce are much more relevant; one or both of these events have occurred in the recent history of many families. Prospective researchers need to be steered to good resource material and organizations (in the case of adoption) to assist in the searching of these subjects.

Focusing on contemporary time periods also changes the regions from which authors should draw examples and case studies. New England is no longer the point of origin for most researchers. The East remains important to those who have traced more than four generations of family members, but states such as Ohio, Pennsylvania, Tennessee, Virginia, Georgia, Indiana, and Illinois have become major areas for interim research. A beginner's handbook that does not acknowledge this shift in geography will shortchange many in its intended audience. The successful union of advanced technology and younger readers will depend on the responsiveness of instructional material to new form, function, and focus. Changes need not be made in the fundamentals: using proper etiquette, analyzing evidence, citing sources, and avoiding pitfalls. These skills have become even more critical as information has become easier to find. As the field of genealogy is flooded with information from an ever-increasing pool of well-intentioned but inadequately trained contributors, the need to effectively sort, sift, and scan information becomes paramount. Such basics as the orderly processing of a research plan in a logical, systematic manner will never be outdated.

Two other components that should always be part of instructional materials are inspiration and ethics. Instructional material should inspire, motivate, stimulate, encourage, and build confidence in students. It should also fill students with a sense of adventure and mystery that will help them persist through difficult, shadowed, and slippery research trails.

Inspiration, however, must be tempered with strict adherence to ethics and high research standards. Every genealogical author would do well to follow Leary's counsel from the first edition of *North Carolina Research:*

> As the research boom places greater and greater demands on their time, funds, and patience, directors of depositories are limiting service to the patrons for whom the facilities were established. The responsibility for an individual researcher's work rests with that individual researcher, not with the staff of the repository in which the records are kept. The responsi-

> bility for keeping those repositories open and their records available also rests with the individual researcher; foolish questions, arrogant behavior, and unreasonable demands by one researcher place additional obstacles in the path of the researcher who follows (1980, 56).

Instructional material should promote positive and professional conduct. The authors of such works have an obligation to do so. The discussion of standards and expectations clarifies the role of the genealogical researcher. Ultimately, the quality of instructional material will determine how well students master the art and skill of genealogy.

REFERENCE LIST

Beller, Susan Provost. 1997. *Roots for Kids*. Baltimore: Genealogical Publishing Co.

Doane, Gilbert H. 1960. *Searching for Your Ancestors: The How and Why of Genealogy*. 3rd ed. Minneapolis: University of Minnesota.

_____. 1980. *Searching for Your Ancestors: The How and Why of Genealogy*. 5th ed. Minneapolis: University of Minnesota.

Leary, Helen F. M., ed. *North Carolina Research: Genealogy and Local History.* Raleigh: North Carolina Genealogical Society, 1980.

BIBLIOGRAPHY

It would be impossible and impractical to identify every published work, article, or aid that could be defined as instructional material. Instead, the criteria are as follows:

1. Selections are limited to guides that provide instruction and not just a listing of sources, addresses, or published works.

2. The work must not be limited to a specific type of record or research facility.

3. The work must be reasonably easy to obtain.

4. The work must be professional in appearance, content, and selection of material.

Essentially, works that focus on U.S. sources and methodology, on states and ethnic group research within the United States, and on the acquisition of skills and knowledge that will aid the American researcher are included.

This bibliography seeks to identify most published works and instructional aids of quality that have been produced since 1980. In addition, a few pre-1980 works that are recognized as "classics" in the field are included. For titles of other works published before 1980, consult P. William Filby's *American and British Genealogy and Heraldry,* 3rd ed. (Boston: New England Historic Genealogical Society, 1983; 1982–85 supplement, 1987) and Marian Hoffman's *Genealogical and Local History Books in Print: General References and World Resources Volume* (cited earlier). Some of the classic older sources are in *Genealogy: A Selected Bibliography* (cited earlier). For recent publications see *Books in Print, Subject Guide* (New York: Bowker, annual), available at many libraries and bookstores. Articles appearing in journals and newsletters, sources of much how-to information, are not listed but may be located by the use of periodical indexes (as discussed previously under "Periodical Articles").

Most privately published titles are excluded due to concerns regarding availability or a general inconsistency in the quality of the content and appearance of these works. For the same reasons, only a limited number of titles produced by local historical or genealogical societies are listed in this bibliography. Most of the titles that do appear address a specific subject, such as research in a particular state. Often, privately produced works that focus on methodology or sources tend to be limited to local examples and case studies; thus, their effectiveness is reduced. A notable exception, *North Carolina Research: Genealogy and Local History,* was discussed earlier in this chapter. For the few publications from small presses, the publisher's address is also provided. Other publishers are generally listed in appendix C.

Titles using the words *index, checklist, inventory, catalog, collection, calendar,* or *compendium* are excluded even though they may contain practical suggestions for using the material they describe. It is assumed that the primary intent of these publications is to make a collection known and accessible and that the instructional aspects of the text are of only secondary importance. These, along with several guides to research in major repositories, are noted in the introduction to *Printed Sources.*

Discontinued or very outdated series could not be included in this bibliography because they are difficult to obtain. Pamphlets, such as *Genealogical Records in the National Archives*, General Information Leaflet no. 5, and *Is That Lineage Right?,* by the National Society, Daughters of the American Revolution, are generally excluded because their size makes them easily, though often irregularly, updated or revised. Two notable exceptions to the size policy are the two sets of state guides. These are the Research Outline series published by the Family History Library and the National Genealogical Society's Research in the States Series, edited by Gary B. Mills and Elizabeth Shown Mills. State guides that are chiefly bibliographies of printed sources are generally excluded from this list. Most of them appear in the bibliographies in chapter 16, "Family Histories and Genealogies," chapter 17, "County and Local Histories," and chapter 18, "Biographies."

This bibliography is arranged to reflect the divisions identified within the preceding discussion.

How-To Guides and Manuals for Adults

Record Descriptions

Baxter, Angus. *Do's and Don'ts for Ancestor Hunters.* Baltimore: Genealogical Publishing Co., 1988. A brief, easy-reading introduction for the beginner. Contains no real research methodology. Introduces record types for several major countries—just a few paragraphs each. The "If I can, you can" approach provides a very encouraging tone.

Beard, Timothy Field, and Denise Demong. *How to Find Your Family Roots.* New York: McGraw-Hill, 1977. Although the instructional material is limited, this work is often consulted for addresses that are difficult to locate elsewhere. Every state and almost every country is covered, along with the most often researched ethnic groups.

Crandall, Ralph. *Shaking Your Family Tree: A Basic Guide to Tracing Your Family's Genealogy.* Dublin, N.H.: Yankee Publishing, 1986. Now published in Emmaus, Pennsylvania, by

Yankee Books. Distributed by St. Martin's Press. Has an easy-to-read format, good selection of illustrations, and appropriate examples. Suitable for use as a beginner's text, although most examples are from New England families. A companion work is Maureen Elizabeth McHugh's *Shaking Your Family Tree Workbook: A Basic Guide to Tracing Your Family's Genealogy,* with a foreword by Dr. Ralph Crandall (Camden, Maine: Yankee Books, 1990). It provides a multitude of forms and step-by-step directions for their use.

Croom, Emily Anne. *Unpuzzling Your Past: A Basic Guide to Genealogy.* 3rd ed. White Hall, Va.: Betterway Publications, 1995. A fine choice for the classroom that explores family sources, interviewing, and background information. Appendixes include forms, addresses, a glossary, and abbreviations. Croom's *The Unpuzzling Your Past Workbook* (Cincinnati: Betterway Publications, 1996) contains blank forms for census work, extraction, and generation charts and sample letters for use in collecting information.

Draznin, Yaffa. *The Family Historian's Handbook.* New York: Jove Publications, 1978. Includes a section on special search problems of some "hyphenated Americans": Jewish, African, and Chinese Americans and Spanish Americans of Mexican descent.

Greenwood, Val D. *The Researcher's Guide to American Genealogy.* Rev. ed. 1990. Reprint. Baltimore: Genealogical Publishing Co., 1997. A breakthrough in guides when first published in 1973 because of its emphasis on the historical and legal background of records. The revised version is thorough and accurate without being overwhelming. Easily the most popular textbook choice of genealogy teachers.

Helmbold, F. Wilbur. *Tracing Your Ancestry: A Step-by-Step Guide to Researching Your Family History.* Birmingham, [Ala.]: Oxmoor House, 1976. 5th printing 1979. Very readable, well illustrated, with simple explanations. Although dated, still useful as a text for beginners when supplemented by lectures. The companion *Logbook,* edited by Karen Phillips (Birmingham: Oxmoor House, 1976), provides tear-off forms for record-keeping.

Latham, William. *How to Find Your Family Roots.* Rev. ed. Santa Monica, Calif.: Santa Monica Press, 1994. Not a revision of the exhaustive *How to Find Your Family Roots* by Timothy Beard and Denise Demong; rather, a first-step approach to research in libraries, churches, cemeteries, courthouses, and Federal repositories.

Leary, Helen F. M. *North Carolina Research: Genealogy and Local History.* 2nd ed. Raleigh: North Carolina Genealogical Society, 1996. Included in this section *and* the state section because of its excellent chapters on abstracting, strategies, methodology, note-taking, and other discussions of universal value.

Marlin, Robert W. *My Sixteen: A Self-Help Guide to Finding Your Sixteen Great-Great-Grandparents.* Nashville: Land Yacht Press, 1996. Unusual in that it discusses twentieth-century records and methods aimed mostly at identifying the immigrant ancestors within the four recent generations. While the work would have benefited from an editor knowledgeable about genealogy, Marlin's story is a good one and his instructions are clear.

Szucs, Loretto Dennis, and Sandra Hargreaves Luebking, eds. *The Source: A Guidebook of American Genealogy.* Rev. ed. Salt Lake City: Ancestry, 1997. Consulted for more than a decade, this definitive guide to record categories is marked by the use of well-qualified contributing authors. Highly detailed treatments of source materials might be too ambitious for beginners, but chapter 1, "The Foundations of Family History Research," will prove appealing and helpful. This work is indispensable for professional genealogists, teachers, writers, and lecturers.

United States Research Outline. Rev. ed. Salt Lake City: Family History Library, 1997. Descriptive paragraphs on sources for the beginner or advanced researcher. Fifty individual state outlines are also available (see "Regional and State Research Guides," below).

Westin, Jeane Eddy. *Finding Your Roots: How Every American Can Trace His Ancestors, at Home and Abroad.* New York: St. Martin's Press, 1977. Arrangement is by jurisdiction. Includes foreign research and heraldry. Easy to read but dated. Tends to present group stereotypes and oversimplifies through the omission of detail.

Wright, Norman Edgar. *Preserving Your American Heritage: A Guide to Family and Local History.* Provo, Utah: Brigham Young University Press, 1981. This extensive revision of *Building an American Pedigree* has rearranged and updated text, including a good section on Native American research. It lacks many of the illustrations found in the previous work but is well written and focuses on original sources.

Research As a Process

Allen, Desmond Walls, and Carolyn Earle Billingsley. *Beginner's Guide to Family History Research.* 3rd ed. Bryant, Ark.: Research Associates, 1997. Available from Research Associates, P.O. Box 122, Bryant, AR 72089-0122. An insightful yet inexpensive introduction to family history for adults. One hundred and nine well-organized pages with brief, concise information and emphasis on source citation.

American Society of Genealogists. *Genealogical Research: Methods and Sources.* Rev. ed. 2 vols. Edited by Milton Rubincam and Jean Stephenson. New Orleans: Polyanthos, 1980–83. Vol. 1 includes chapters on contributions to genealogy, traditions, interpretation, evidence, and publishing by authorities on these subjects. Other chapters and vol. 2 are research guides to selected states. Not designed for beginners.

Balhuizen, Ann Ross. *Getting Started: How to Begin Researching Your Family History.* 1994. Reprint. Indianapolis: Ye Olde Genealogie Shoppe, 1997. A practical and friendly guide filled with tips that reflect the author's years as an instructor. Defines the sources and research methods in a hands-on format. Covers details that other texts overlook—for example, how to examine a reference book (using the introduction, table of contents, etc.). A fine text for the beginner, though an index and glossary would have been helpful.

Carmack, Sharon DeBartolo. *The Genealogy Sourcebook.* Los Angeles: Lowell House, 1997. This text is enjoyable and easy to read. The author, a certified genealogical record searcher, encourages attention to detail, promotes the need for a solid and practical research plan, and encourages the careful recording and evaluation of uncovered information.

Cerny, Johni, and Arlene Eakle. *Ancestry's Guide to Research: Case Studies in American Genealogy.* Salt Lake City: Ancestry, 1985. Although not well organized, the case studies provide a different and refreshing approach to research. The use of specific examples of genealogy in action demonstrates some skills and thought processes necessary to conduct a search project. This work was intended as a companion volume to the first edition of *The Source: A Guidebook of American Genealogy.*

Croom, Emily Anne. *The Genealogist's Companion and Sourcebook: A Beyond-the-Basics, Hands-on Guide to Unpuzzling Your Past.* Cincinnati: Betterway Books, 1994. An appropriate guide for the intermediate researcher who will benefit from the case studies and inclusion of some not-so-common American research sources.

Doane, Gilbert H. *Searching for Your Ancestors: The How and Why of Genealogy.* 6th ed. Completely updated and revised by James B. Bell. Minneapolis: University of Minnesota Press, 1992. A most durable (in use since 1937) and readable introduction to genealogy, though with a New England focus. Not a textbook for beginners but required supplemental reading. A companion volume by Bell, *Family History Record Book*, was published by the University of Minnesota Press in 1980.

Drake, Paul. *In Search of Family History: A Starting Place.* Bowie, Md.: Heritage Books, 1992. An eclectic arrangement (four chapters) and unorthodox topic selection (indentured servants, redemptioners, and criminals are found in the chapter titled "Libraries") are disappointing in a work that adopts an otherwise no-nonsense manner. Readers are advised to take a course and are told, "this handbook will not teach you how to do good family research. Only practice will do that." Contains excellent illustrations that are well chosen and reproduced. Includes remarks on evidence, proof, citing sources, and good manners.

Jones, Vincent L., Arlene H. Eakle, and Mildred H. Christensen. *Family History for Fun and Profit* (formerly *Genealogical Research: A Jurisdictional Approach*). Salt Lake City: Genealogical Institute, 1972. 5th printing 1978. The principles and concepts are valuable for experienced researchers, as is the focus on process. Contains many illustrations and, despite its age, is not too outdated.

Kirkham, E. Kay. *Simplified Genealogy for Americans.* 3rd ed. Salt Lake City: Deseret, 1977. A good discussion of materials that are of special concern to beginners: the family Bible, how to copy records, using libraries, correspondence, research analysis. Contains a decent glossary but only a basic subject index.

Rose, Christine, and Kay Germain Ingalls. *The Complete Idiot's Guide to Genealogy.* New York: Alpha Books, 1997. Despite the title's implications, this book was not written for idiots. It promotes sound research methods and the need for cautious evaluation of evidence. The clever illustrations and cheerful tone make the text, written by two certified genealogists, fun to read.

Stryker-Rodda, Harriet. *How to Climb Your Family Tree: Genealogy for Beginners.* 1977. 1992. Reprint. Baltimore: Genealogical Publishing Co., 1997. A step-by-step approach that begins with theory, then moves to public records. The strongest feature is a discussion of the "why" of genealogy and using home sources. Lacks an index and some basic information.

Vandagriff, G. G. *Voices in Your Blood: Discovering Identity through Family History.* Kansas City, Mo.: Andrews and McMeel, 1993. Aimed at a non-genealogical readership that is comfortable with computers and possesses the education, time, and money to devote to self-discovery. Commercially marketed, this book has the potential to captivate a previously untapped audience. The text is easy to read and highly motivating, although the author fails to recommend the need for skill training or the availability of conferences, seminars, and institutes.

Williams, Ethel W. *Know Your Ancestors: A Guide to Genealogical Research.* 19th ed., reissued. Rutland, Vt.: Tuttle, 1976. Covers basic information but heavily oriented to New England and upper Midwest states. Terms and abbreviations are well explained. Easy and enjoyable reading; deserving of revision.

Willard, Jim, and Terry Willard with Jane Wilson. *Ancestors: A Beginner's Guide to Family History and Genealogy.* Boston: Houghton Mifflin, 1997. Produced as a companion to the PBS television series "Ancestors." Each chapter represents one of the ten programs in "Ancestors." Lavishly illustrated and clearly written, a highlight of this work is a unique chapter titled "Your Medical Heritage." Includes directions for African American research and "leaving a legacy."

Wright, Norman E. *Adventures in Genealogy: Case Studies in the Unusual.* Baltimore: Clearfield Co., 1994. Three interesting genealogy puzzles and a step-by-step explanation of how they were solved. The first involves an adoption and a family secret, the second confusing surnames, and the third an apparent "dead end."

Wright, Raymond S., 3rd. *The Genealogist's Handbook: Modern Methods for Researching Family History.* Chicago: American Library Association, 1995. An interdisciplinary approach to methods and sources divided by family and neighborhood, town, county and state, national, and ethnic resources. Includes a section on writing family history and discusses computers and genealogy.

Twentieth-Century (Adoption, Heirs, Missing Persons, Reunions)

Askin, Jayne, with Molly Davis. *Search: A Handbook for Adoptees and Birthparents.* Rev. ed. Phoenix: Oryx Press, 1992 (1st ed., Jayne Askin with Bob Oskam, 1982). A good revision of a popular manual by an adoptee who refused to be halted by frustration, discrimination, and closed doors. Her efforts uncovered her medical history and other details of her birth family, although she chose not to meet with her birth parents.

Brown, Barbara, and Tom Ninkovich. *Family Reunion Handbook: A Guide for Reunion Planners.* San Francisco: Reunion Research, 1992. Fourteen chapters on how to plan, develop, and implement a successful family gathering. Includes finances and record-keeping, food and activities, design of announcements, and more.

Culligan, Joseph J. *You, Too, Can Find Anybody: A Reference Manual.* Miami, Fla.: Hallmark Press, 1996. Chapters on car licensing divisions, Social Security, workers' compensation, corporation filings, and abandoned property.

_____. *Adoption Searches Made Easier.* Miami, Fla.: FJA, 1996. A licensed private investigator defines the legalities involved in adoption searches and two main sources of information: birth indexes and court records. Almost half of the book comprises directories listing the county for many cities within each state, county seats, and addresses for state governors and state police.

Heiderer, Michele. *Before the Search: An Adoption Searcher's Primer.* Indianapolis: Ye Olde Genealogie Shoppe, 1997. Guidelines for each state and the District of Columbia concerning what records are open to searches. Detailed information on the legal aspects of searches and what basic steps to take before searching. The author has been a confidential intermediary in Washington state since 1992.

Johnson, Lt. Col. Richard S. *How to Locate Anyone Who Is or Has Been in the Military: Armed Forces Locator Directory.* 6th ed. Burlington, N.C.: MIE Publishing Co., 1995. Information on how to find current and former members of the U.S. Army, U.S. Navy, Marine Corps, U.S. Air Force, U.S. Coast Guard, their reserve components, and the National Guard. Can help in finding records of deceased veterans and their relatives.

Klunder, Virgil L. *Lifeline: The Action Guide to Adoption Search.* Cape Coral, Fla.: Caradium Publishing, 1991.

Rillera, Mary Jo. *The Adoption Searchbook.* 2nd ed. Westminster, Calif.: Triadoption Publications, 1985. Written for adoptees, adoptive parents, and birth parents who are considering a search. The author defines the difference between wanting to *know* and wanting to *search.* For those who decide to search, there are many helpful suggestions within these pages.

Instructional Materials Pertaining to Special Groups (U.S. Research)

Also see "How-To Guides and Manuals for Young People," below (especially *A Student's Guide to . . . Genealogy Series*).

General

Smith, Jessie Carney, ed. *Ethnic Genealogy: A Research Guide.* Westport, Conn.: Greenwood Press, 1983. Part 1 consists of general information on sources, procedures, and research. Part 2 offers suggestions for researching in major repositories. Part 3 deals with the sources and research techniques pertaining to specific ethnic groups: Native Americans, Asian Americans, African Americans, and Hispanic Americans.

Acadians

Hebert, Timothy. *Acadian-Cajun Genealogy: Step by Step.* Lafayette: Center for Louisiana Studies, University of Southwestern Louisiana, 1993. Merges the basics of genealogical research with the quirks and sources specific to the ethnic group.

African Americans

Blockson, Charles L. *Black Genealogy.* 1977. Reprint. New York: Prentice-Hall, 1991. Where to begin and what sources to use in researching the heritage of African Americans.

Byers, Paula K., ed. *African American Genealogical Sourcebook.* Detroit: Gale Research, 1995.

Rose, James M., and Alice Eichholz. *Black Genesis.* Gale Genealogy and Local History Series, vol. 1. Detroit: Gale Research, 1978.

Streets, David H. *Slave Genealogy: A Research Guide with Case Studies.* Bowie, Md.: Heritage Books, 1986. Three case studies demonstrate methods used in analyzing slave records.

Thackery, David T., and Deloris Woodtor. *Case Studies in Afro-American Genealogy.* Chicago: Newberry Library, 1989.

Walker, James D. *Black Genealogy: How to Begin.* Athens: University of Georgia Center for Continuing Education, 1977.

Asian Americans

Byers, Paula K., ed. *Asian American Genealogical Sourcebook.* Detroit: Gale Research, 1995.

Palmer, Spencer J., ed. *Studies in Asian Genealogy.* Provo, Utah: Brigham Young University Press, 1972.

Hispanic Americans

Byers, Paula K., ed. *Hispanic American Genealogical Sourcebook.* Detroit: Gale Research, 1995.

Carr, Peter E. *Guide to Cuban Genealogical Research: Records and Sources.* The Cuban Index (P.O. Box 11251, San Bernardino, CA 92423), 1991. Explains how to locate and access lesser-known Cuban resources in the United States. Includes an explanation of the usage of Spanish surnames.

Flores, Norma, and Patsy Ludwig. *A Beginner's Guide to Hispanic Genealogy.* San Mateo, Calif.: Western Book/Journal Press, 1993.

Ryscamp, George R. *Finding Your Hispanic Roots.* Baltimore: Genealogical Publishing Co., 1997.

Irish Americans

Betit, Kyle J., and Dwight A. Radford. *Ireland: A Genealogical Guide for North Americans.* Salt Lake City: Irish at Home and Abroad, 1995. Describes how to conduct research from North America on Irish ancestors. Includes research strategies; good coverage of topics.

Italian Americans

Carmack, Sharon DeBartolo. *Italian-American Family History: A Guide to Researching and Writing about Your Heritage.* Baltimore: Genealogical Publishing Co., 1997.

Colletta, John Philip. *Finding Italian Roots: The Guide for Americans.* Baltimore: Genealogical Publishing Co., 1995.

Jewish Americans

Kurzweil, Arthur. *From Generation to Generation: How to Trace Your Jewish Genealogy and Personal History.* New York: HarperCollins, 1994. The first edition (1984) was long considered the authoritative work on Jewish genealogy. Topics in the new edition include Holocaust research, twentieth-century immigration-naturalization records, and Jewish cemetery research.

_____, and Miriam Weiner, eds. *The Encyclopedia of Jewish Genealogy.* Vol. 1, *Sources in the United States and Canada.* Northvale, N.J.: Jason Aronson, 1991. Limited in scope but, as new volumes are released, its effectiveness will increase.

Rottenberg, Dan. *Finding Our Fathers: A Guidebook to Jewish Genealogy.* New York: Random House, 1977. A pioneering work; now outdated.

Native Americans

Byers, Paula K., ed. *Native American Genealogical Sourcebook.* Detroit: Gale Research, 1995.

Carpenter, Cecelia Suinth. *How to Research American Indian Blood Lines: A Manual on Indian Genealogical Research.* Bountiful, Utah: American Genealogical Lending Library, 1994. A good discussion of northwestern Indians.

Kirkham, E. Kay. *Our Native Americans and Their Records of Genealogical Value.* 2 vols. Logan, Utah: Everton Publishers, 1980–83.

McClure, Tony Mack. *A Guide for Tracing and Honoring Your Cherokee Ancestors: Cherokee Proud.* Somerville, Tenn.: Chunannee Books, 1997.

Mooney, Thomas G. *Exploring Your Cherokee Ancestry: A Basic Genealogical Research Guide.* Tahlequah, Okla.: Cherokee National Historical Society, 1987. Provides basic information about Cherokee research source material.

Polish

Chorzempa, Rosemary. *Polish Roots.* 1993. Reprint. Baltimore: Genealogical Publishing Co., 1996. Part 1 offers basic information and advises which records in the United States are likely to produce the best results for Polish-American researchers. Part 2 moves the researcher across the ocean.

Regional and State Research Guides

General

American Society of Genealogists. *Genealogical Research: Methods and Sources.* Rev. ed. 2 vols. Edited by Milton Rubincam and Jean Stephenson. New Orleans: Polyanthos, 1980–83. Vol. 1 includes chapters on contributions to genealogy, traditions, interpretation, evidence, and publishing by authorities on these subjects. Other chapters and vol. 2 are research guides to selected states. Not designed for beginners.

Eichholz, Alice G., ed. *Ancestry's Red Book: American State, County and Town Sources.* Rev. ed. Salt Lake City: Ancestry, 1992. Provides overviews of the differences in regional research, then a state-by-state account of historical events and settlement, special groups, repositories, significant research collections, periodicals, and specific record sources.

New England

Crandall, Ralph J., ed. *Genealogical Research in New England.* Baltimore: Genealogical Publishing Co., 1984.

Lindberg, Marcia Wiswall, ed. *Genealogist's Handbook for New England Research.* 3rd ed. Boston: New England Historic Genealogical Society, 1993. Before publication, this third edition was reviewed by consultants, including professional genealogists, librarians, and a manuscripts curator. Covers each of the six New England states.

Sperry, Kip. *New England Genealogical Research: A Guide to Sources.* Bowie, Md: Heritage Books, 1988.

Alabama

Alabama Research Outline. Series US-States, no. 1. Salt Lake City: Family History Library, 1988.

Alaska

Alaska Research Outline. Series US-States, no. 2. Salt Lake City: Family History Library, 1988.

Arizona

Arizona Research Outline. Series US-States, no. 3. Salt Lake City: Family History Library, 1988.

Spiros, Joyce V. Hawley. *Genealogical Guide to Arizona and Nevada.* Gallup, N.M.: Verlene Publishing, 1983.

Arkansas

Arkansas Research Outline. Series US-States, no. 4. Salt Lake City: Family History Library, 1988.

Norris, Rhonda S. *A Genealogist's Guide to Arkansas Research.* Russelville, Ark.: Arkansas Genealogical Research, 1994.

California

California Research Outline. Series US-States, no. 5. Salt Lake City: Family History Library, 1988.

Colorado

Colorado Research Outline. Series US-States, no. 6. Salt Lake City: Family History Library, 1988.

Connecticut

Connecticut Research Outline. Series US-States, no. 7. Salt Lake City: Family History Library, 1988.

Morrison, Betty Jean. *Connecting to Connecticut.* Glastonbury: Connecticut Society of Genealogists, 1995.

Delaware

Delaware Genealogical Research Guide. Delaware Genealogical Society, 1989.

A forty-two-page summary of towns, churches, sources, and repositories in Delaware. *Delaware Research Outline.* Series US-States, no. 8. Salt Lake City: Family History Library, 1988.

Giles, Barbara S., comp. *Selected Delaware Bibliography and Resources.* The compiler, 1990. A collection of handouts, maps, lists, etc.

District of Columbia

Angevine, Erma Miller. *Research in the District of Columbia.* Arlington, Va.: National Genealogical Society, 1992. A Special Publication Paper from the NGS Research in the States Series, this is an updated expansion of an article from the *National Genealogical Society Quarterly.*

Babble, June Andrew. *Lest We Forget: A Guide to Genealogical Research in the Nation's Capitol.* 8th ed. Annandale, Va.: Annandale Stake of The Church of Jesus Christ of Latter-day Saints, 1992. A practical guide to the District of Columbia's facilities that also contains much helpful information on land records. See *The Center* by Schaefer (below).

District of Columbia Research Outline. Series US-States, no. 9. Salt Lake City: Family History Library, 1988.

Schaefer, Christina K. *The Center: A Guide to Genealogical Research in the National Capital Area.* Baltimore: Genealogical Publishing Co., 1996. An expansion of Babble's *Lest We Forget* (above), this work includes a recitation of types of data and a "Where do I start" introduction.

Florida

Florida Research Outline. Series US-States, no. 10. Salt Lake City: Family History Library, 1988.

Georgia

Davis, Robert Scott, Jr. *Research in Georgia: With a Special Emphasis Upon the Georgia Department of Archives and History.* Easley, S.C.: Southern Historical Press, 1981. Reprint. 1984, 1991.

Dorsey, James E., comp. *Georgia Genealogy and Local History.* Spartanburg, S.C.: Reprint Co., 1983.

Georgia Research Outline. Series US-States, no. 11. Salt Lake City: Family History Library, 1988.

Robertson, David H. *Georgia Genealogical Research: A Practical Guide.* Stone Mountain, Ga.: the author, 1989. Insubstantial but with a good, warm introduction.

Schweitzer, George K. *Georgia Genealogical Research.* Knoxville, Tenn.: the author, 1987.

Hawaii

Hawaii Research Outline. Series US-States, no. 12. Salt Lake City: Family History Library, 1988.

Kaina, Maria. *Target Your Hawaiian Genealogy and Others As Well: A Family guide Provided By the Hawaii State Public Library System.* Honolulu: Hawaii State Public Library System, 1991.

Idaho

Idaho Research Outline. Series US-States, no. 13. Salt Lake City: Family History Library, 1988.

Illinois

Illinois Research Outline. Series US-States, no. 14. Salt Lake City: Family History Library, 1988.

Szucs, Loretto D. *Chicago and Cook County: A Guide to Research.* Salt Lake City: Ancestry, 1996.

Volkel, Lowell M., and Marjorie Smith. *How to Research a Family with Illinois Roots.* Indianapolis: Ye Olde Genealogie Shoppe, 1977.

Indiana

Beatty, John D. *Research in Indiana.* Arlington, Va.: National Genealogical Society, 1992. A Special Publication Paper from the NGS Research in the States Series, this is an updated expansion of an article from the *National Genealogical Society Quarterly.*

Gooldy, Pat, and Ray Gooldy. *Manual for Indiana Genealogical Research.* Indianapolis: Ye Olde Genealogie Shoppe, 1991.

Indiana Research Outline. Series US-States, no. 15. Salt Lake City: Family History Library, 1988.

Miller, Carolynne L. *Indiana Sources for Genealogical Research in the Indiana State Library.* Indianapolis: Family History Section, Indiana Historical Society, 1984.

Robinson, Mona. *Who's Your Hoosier Ancestor? Genealogy for Beginners.* Bloomington: Indiana University Press, 1992.

Schweitzer, George K. *Indiana Genealogical Research.* Knoxville, Tenn.: the author, 1996.

Iowa

Iowa Research Outline. Series US-States, no. 16. Salt Lake City: Family History Library, 1988.

Kansas

Kansas Research Outline. Series US-States, no. 17. Salt Lake City: Family History Library, 1988.

Kentucky

Hogan, Roseann Reinemuth. *Kentucky Ancestry: A Guide to Genealogical and Historical Research.* Salt Lake City: Ancestry, 1992.

Kentucky Research Outline. Series US-States, no. 18. Salt Lake City: Family History Library, 1988.

Schweitzer, George K. *Kentucky Genealogical Research.* Knoxville: the author, 1983.

Louisiana

Boling, Yvette G. *A Guide to Printed Sources for Genealogical and Historical Research in the Louisiana Parishes.* Jefferson, La.: the author, 1985.

Louisiana Research Outline. Series US-States, no. 19. Salt Lake City: Family History Library, 1988.

Maine

Frost, John Eldridge. *Maine Genealogy: A Bibliographical Guide.* 1977. Rev. ed. Portland: Maine Historical Society, 1985.

Maine Research Outline. Series US-States, no. 20. Salt Lake City: Family History Library, 1988.

Maryland

Heisey, John W. *Maryland Research Guide.* Indianapolis: Heritage House, 1986.

Maryland Research Outline. Series US-States, no. 21. Salt Lake City: Family History Library, 1988.

Meyer, Mary Keysor. *Genealogical Research in Maryland: A Guide.* 4th ed. Baltimore: Maryland Historical Society, 1992.

Schweitzer, George K. *Maryland Genealogical Research.* Knoxville, Tenn.: the author, 1991.

Massachusetts

Massachusetts Research Outline. Series US-States, no. 22. Salt Lake City: Family History Library, 1988.

Schweitzer, George K. *Massachusetts Genealogical Research.* Knoxville: the author, 1990.

Michigan

McGinnis, Carol. *Michigan Genealogy Sources and Resources.* Baltimore: Genealogical Publishing Co., 1987.

Michigan Research Outline. Series US-States, no. 23. Salt Lake City: Family History Library, 1988.

Minnesota

Minnesota Research Outline. Series US-States, no. 24. Salt Lake City: Family History Library, 1988.

Porter, Robert B. *How to Trace Your Minnesota Ancestors.* Center City, Minn.: Porter Publishing Co., 1985.

Warren, Paula Stuart. *Minnesota Genealogical Reference Guide.* Warren Research & Publishing (1869 Laurel Avenue, St. Paul, MN 55104-5938), 1994.

Warren, Paula Stuart. *Research in Minnesota.* Arlington, Va.: National Genealogical Society, 1992. A Special Publication Paper from the NGS Research in the States Series, this is an updated expansion of an article from the *National Genealogical Society Quarterly.*

Mississippi

Lipscomb, Anne S., and Kathleen S. Hutchison. *Tracing Your Mississippi Ancestors.* Jackson: University Press of Mississippi, 1994. Combines how-to instruction with introduction to basic sources, bibliographies, discussion of repositories, and methodology for African American and Native American research.

Mississippi Research Outline. Series US-States, no. 25. Salt Lake City: Family History Library, 1988.

Missouri

Missouri Research Outline. Series US-States, no. 26. Salt Lake City: Family History Library, 1988.

Steele, Edward E. *A Guide to Genealogical Research in St. Louis.* St. Louis: St. Louis Genealogical Society, 1992.

Montana

Montana Research Outline. Series US-States, No. 27. Salt Lake City: Family History Library, 1988.

Richards, Dennis Lee. *Montana's Genealogical and Local History Records.* Detroit: Gale Research, 1981.

Nebraska

Nebraska Research Outline. Series US-States, No. 28. Salt Lake City: Family History Library, 1988.

Nebraska, a Guide to Genealogical Research. Lincoln: Nebraska State Genealogical Society, 1984.

Nimmo, Sylvia, and Mary Cutler. *Nebraska Local History and Genealogical Reference Guide.* Papillion, Nebr.: S. Nimmo, 1987.

Nevada

Nevada Research Outline. Series US-States, no. 29. Salt Lake City: Family History Library, 1988.

Spiros, Joyce V. Hawley. *Genealogical Guide to Arizona and Nevada.* Gallup, N.M.: Verlene Publishing, 1983.

New Hampshire

New Hampshire Research Outline. Series US-States, no. 30. Salt Lake City: Family History Library, 1988.

Towle, Laird C., and Ann N. Brown. *New Hampshire Genealogical Research Guide.* 2nd ed. Bowie, Md.: Heritage Books, 1983.

New Jersey

New Jersey Research Outline. Series US-States, no. 31. Salt Lake City: Family History Library, 1991.

Stryker-Rodda, Kenn. *New Jersey: Digging for Ancestors in the Garden State.* Detroit: Detroit Society for Genealogical Research, 1970.

New Mexico

New Mexico Research Outline. Series US-States, no. 32. Salt Lake City: Family History Library, 1988.

Spiros, Joyce V. H. *Handy Genealogical Guide to New Mexico.* Gallup, N.M.: Verlene Publishing, 1981.

New York

Clint, Florence. *New York Area Key: A Guide to the Genealogical Records of the State of New York. . . .* Elizabeth, Colo.: Keyline Publishers, 1979.

Epperson, Gwenn F. *New Netherland Roots.* Baltimore: Genealogical Publishing Co., 1994. A meticulous explanation of the author's process in tracking her own seventeenth-century ancestors from New Netherland back to their origins in the Netherlands, Germany, Belgium, and France.

Guzik, Estelle M., ed. *Genealogical Resources in the New York Metropolitan Area.* New York: Jewish Genealogical Society, 1989.

New York Research Outline. Series US-States, no. 33. Salt Lake City: Family History Library, 1988.

Schweitzer, George K. *New York Genealogical Research.* Knoxville: the author, 1988.

North Carolina

Hofman, Margaret M. *The Short, Short Course in the Use of North Carolina's Early County-Level Records in Genealogical Research.* The author (P.O. Box 446, Roanoke Rapids, NC 27870), 1992. Describes records, identifies locations, and explains the uses of each record in genealogy and local history. Three-hole punched for notebook use.

_____. *An Intermediate Short, Short Course in the Use of Some North Carolina Records in Genealogical Research.* The author (P.O. Box 446, Roanoke Rapids, NC 27870), 1992. Topics include cartographic and land records, newspapers, cemetery and church records, and oral history. Three-hole punched for notebook use.

Leary, Helen F. M., ed. *North Carolina Research: Genealogy and Local History.* 2nd ed. Raleigh: North Carolina Genealogical Society, 1996.

Schweitzer, George K. *North Carolina Genealogical Research.* Knoxville: the author, 1991.

North Dakota

North Dakota Research Outline. Series US-States, no. 35. Salt Lake City: Family History Library, 1988.

Ohio

Bell, Carol Willsey. *Ohio Genealogical Guide.* 6th ed. Youngstown, Ohio: Bell Books, 1995.

_____. *Ohio Guide to Genealogical Sources.* Baltimore: Genealogical Publishing Co., 1988.

Ohio Research Outline. Series US-States, no. 36. Salt Lake City: Family History Library, 1988.

Schweitzer, George K. *Ohio Genealogical Research.* Knoxville, Tenn.: the author, 1994.

Sperry, Kip. *Genealogical Research in Ohio.* Baltimore: Genealogical Publishing Co., 1997. Features a chronology of history, maps, and addresses of libraries, societies, and book publishers and dealers. Closes with a comprehensive bibliography of more than one hundred pages.

Oklahoma

Blessing, Patrick J. *Oklahoma: Records and Archives.* Tulsa, Okla.: University of Tulsa Publications, 1978.

Oklahoma Research Outline. Series US-States, no. 37. Salt Lake City: Family History Library, 1988.

Sperry, Kip. *Genealogical Research in Ohio.* Baltimore: Genealogical Publishing Co., 1997.

Oregon

Lenzen, Connie Miller. *Research in Oregon.* Arlington, Va.: National Genealogical Society, 1992. A Special Publication Paper from the NGS Research in the States Series, this is an updated expansion of an article from the *National Genealogical Society Quarterly.*

Oregon Research Outline. Series US-States, no. 38. Salt Lake City: Family History Library, 1988.

Pennsylvania

Heisey, John W. *Handbook for Genealogical Research in Pennsylvania.* Indianapolis: Heritage House, 1985.

Pennsylvania Research Outline. Series US-States, no. 39. Salt Lake City: Family History Library, 1988.

Pennsylvania Line: A Research Guide to Pennsylvania Genealogy and Local History. 4th ed. Laughlintown, Pa.: Southwest Pennsylvania Genealogical Services, 1990.

Schweitzer, George K. *Pennsylvania Genealogical Research.* Knoxville: the author, 1986.

Rhode Island

Rhode Island Research Outline. Series US-States, no. 40. Salt Lake City: Family History Library, 1988.

Sperry, Kip. *Rhode Island Sources for Family Historians and Genealogists.* Logan, Utah: Everton Publishers, 1986.

South Carolina

Hendrix, Ge Lee Corley. *Research in South Carolina.* Arlington, Va.: National Genealogical Society, 1992. A Special Publication Paper from the NGS Research in the States Series, this is an updated expansion of an article in the *National Genealogical Society Quarterly.*

Hicks, Theresa. *South Carolina: A Guide for Genealogists.* Rev. ed. Columbian Chapter, South Carolina Genealogical Society (P.O. Box 11353, Columbia, SC, 29211), 1996.

Holcomb, Brent Howard. *A Guide to South Carolina Genealogical Research and Records.* Rev. ed. Columbia, S.C.: the author, 1991.

Schweitzer, George K. *South Carolina Genealogical Research.* Knoxville: the author, 1985.

South Carolina Research Outline. Series US-States, no. 41. Salt Lake City: Family History Library, 1988.

South Dakota

South Dakota Research Outline. Series US-States, no. 41. Salt Lake City: Family History Library, 1988.

Tennessee

Bamman, Gale Williams. *Research in Tennessee.* Arlington, Va.: National Genealogical Society, 1993. A Special Publication Paper from the NGS Research in the States Series, this originally appeared in the *National Genealogical Society Quarterly.*

Fulcher, Richard Carlton. *Guide to County Records and Genealogical Resources in Tennessee.* Baltimore: Genealogical Publishing Co., 1987.

Schweitzer, George K. *Tennessee Genealogical Research.* Knoxville: the author, 1986.

Tennessee Research Outline. Series US-States, no. 42. Salt Lake City: Family History Library, 1988.

Texas

Bockstruck, Lloyd DeWitt. *Research in Texas.* Arlington, Va.: National Genealogical Society, 1992. A Special Publication Paper from the NGS Research in the States Series, this is an updated expansion of an article from the *National Genealogical Society Quarterly.*

Kennedy, Imogene K., and J. Leon Kennedy. *Genealogical Records in Texas.* Baltimore: Genealogical Publishing Co., 1987. Reprint. 1992. Discusses critical laws, boundary changes, land district records, and how to access the records of various repositories.

Texas Research Outline. Series US-States, no. 43. Salt Lake City: Family History Library, 1988.

Utah

Jaussi, Laureen, and Gloria Chaston. *Genealogical Records of Utah.* Salt Lake City: Deseret Book Co., 1974.

Utah Research Outline. Series US-States, no. 44. Salt Lake City: Family History Library, 1988.

Vermont

Eichholz, Alice. *Collecting Vermont Ancestors.* Montpelier, Vt.: New Trails, 1986.

Vermont Research Outline. Series US-States, no. 45. Salt Lake City: Family History Library, 1988.

Virginia

McGinnis, Carol. *Virginia Genealogy: Sources and Resources.* Baltimore: Genealogical Publishing Co., 1993. An overview of topics relating to the entire Commonwealth is followed by a focus on localities, records, organizations, and research centers.

Schweitzer, George K. *Virginia Genealogical Research.* Knoxville: the author, 1982.

Virginia Research Outline. Series US-States, no. 46. Salt Lake City: Family History Library, 1988.

Washington

Genealogical Resources in Washington State: A Guide to Genealogical Records Held at Repositories, Government Agencies, and Archives. Olympia, Wash.: Office of the Secretary of State, Division of Archives and Records Management, 1983.

Washington Research Outline. Series US-States, no. 47. Salt Lake City: Family History Library, 1988.

West Virginia

McGinnis, Carol. *West Virginia Genealogy: Sources and Resources.* Baltimore: Genealogical Publishing Co., 1988.

Stinson, Helen S. *A Handbook for Genealogical Research in West Virginia.* Rev. and exp. South Charleston, W. Va.: Kanawha Valley Genealogical Society, 1991.

West Virginia Research Outline. Series US-States, no. 48. Salt Lake City: Family History Library, 1988.

Wisconsin

Danky, James P. *Genealogical Research: An Introduction to the Resources of the State Historical Society of Wisconsin.* Rev. ed. Madison: State Historical Society of Wisconsin, 1986.

Herrick, Linda M. *Wisconsin Genealogical Research.* Janesville, Wis.: Origins, 1996.

Ryan, Carol Ward. *Searching for Your Wisconsin Ancestors in the Wisconsin Libraries.* 2nd ed. Green Bay, Wis.: the author, 1988.

Wisconsin Research Outline. Series US-States, no. 49. Salt Lake City: Family History Library, 1988.

Wyoming

Spiros, Joyce V. H. *Genealogical Guide to Wyoming.* Gallup, N.M.: Verlene Publishers, 1982.

Wyoming Research Outline. Series US-States, no. 50. Salt Lake City: Family History Library, 1988.

How-To Guides and Manuals for Young People

Also see "Courses and Programs of Study," below.

Beller, Susan Provost. *Roots for Kids.* 1989. Reprint. Baltimore: Genealogical Publishing Co., 1997. The twelve chapters can be used together as a textbook or as forty-five-minute presentations (recommended age group fourth grade and higher). Each segment has text and an assignment. Forms are included. The author is a fourth-grade teacher.

Chorzempa, Rosemary A. *My Family Tree Workbook: Genealogy for Beginners.* New York: Dover, 1982.

Climb Your Family Tree: A Genealogy Detective's Kit. Produced by becker&meyer!, Ltd. Text by Anne Depue. Illustrated by Doug Keith. Hyperion Paperbacks for Children (114 Fifth Avenue, New York, NY 10011-5690), 1996. A four-piece activity kit aimed at ages eight and up: cartoon-illustrated booklet with "let's get started" guidelines; a notepad for interviews; a pedigree chart for the wall; and a decorated box to hold documents.

Cooper, Kay. *Where Did You Get Those Eyes?* New York: Walker and Co., 1988.

Hilton, Suzanne. *Who Do You Think You Are? Digging for Your Family Roots.* Philadelphia: Westminster Press, 1976.

Kurzweil, Arthur. *My Generations: A Course in Jewish Family History.* West Orange, N.J.: Behrman House, 1983.

Nichols, Elizabeth L. *Genealogy.* Boy Scouts of America Merit Badge Series. Irving, Tex.: Boy Scouts of America, 1988.

Perl, Lila. *The Great Ancestor Hunt.* New York: Clarion Books, 1989. Fourth grade and up.

A Student's Guide to . . . Genealogy Series. Oryx Family Tree Series. Phoenix: Oryx Press, 1996–97. The twelve titles in the series are: African American, British American, Chinese American, German American, Irish American, Italian American, Japanese American, Jewish American, Mexican American, Native American, Polish American, and Scandinavian American. The series shows young people how to trace their ancestral roots and learn about their ethnic origins. Each book gives a simplified view of immigration and culture in the United States, first steps in gaining information, and twenty to forty pages of resource listings.

Weitzman, David. *My Backyard History Book.* Boston: Little, Brown & Co., 1975. Nicely done. Combines text and assignments in family and local history with captivating illustrations.

Wolfman, Ira. *My Family "Tis of Thee: The Kid's Book of Genealogy. An Official Ellis Island Book.* New York: Workman Publishing Co., 1990. As the official Ellis Island handbook, this provides a basic introduction to researching immigrants. Well illustrated with many sidebars.

_____. *Do People Grow on Family Trees? Genealogy for Kids and Other Beginners.* New York: Workman Press, 1991.

Skills and Technologies of Genealogy

Record-Keeping Systems

Dollarhide, William. *Managing a Genealogical Project: A Complete Manual for the Management and Organization of Genealogical Materials.* Rev. ed. Baltimore: Genealogical Publishing Co., 1996. Discussion of organization includes forms that may be photocopied without copyright restrictions. A Genealogy Starter Kit is available (1996), as is a twenty-six-page pamphlet on how to begin research: *Seven Steps to a Family Tree* (Bountiful, Utah: American Genealogical Lending Library, 1995).

Whitaker, Beverly DeLong. *Beyond Pedigrees: Organizing and Enhancing Your Work.* Salt Lake City: Ancestry, 1993. Includes research project management suggestions and useful charts and forms. The latter may be copied and adapted for individual use. Limited bibliography.

Computer Applications

Bonner, Laurie, and Steve Bonner. *Searching for Cyber-Roots: A Step-by-Step Guide to Genealogy on the World Wide Web.* Salt Lake City: Ancestry, 1997. Explains the Internet's history and possible future, terminology, and navigational tools: browsers, search engines, e-mail, newsreaders, FTP, and Telnet. Helps the reader locate online source data, other researchers, surname collections, and society home pages. Website addresses and troubleshooting help are provided as well.

Clifford, Karen. *Genealogy and Computers for the Complete Beginner.* Rev. ed. Baltimore: Clearfield Co., 1995. A textbook and home study course devised by a teacher (and accredited genealogist) who intended it for use in her classroom. Encourages good research habits and presents the fundamentals of computer use as well as beginning genealogy. Includes optional self-testing for the reader.

_____. *Genealogy and Computers for the Determined Researcher.* Baltimore: Clearfield Co., 1995. A more advanced version of the *Complete Beginner,* this work assumes the reader has used computers and has progressed beyond the beginning stage in research. Features pre-1850 census tips and instructions for accessing other records to expand one's research. A tutorial floppy disk (3 ½ or 5 ¼ inches) is provided with the publication for hands-on exercises.

_____. *Genealogy and Computers for the Advanced Researcher.* Baltimore: Clearfield Co., 1995. Advanced methodology and advice on designing and publishing one's genealogical research.

Cosgriff, John, and Carolyn Cosgriff. *Turbo Genealogy: An Introduction to Family History Research in the Information Age.* Salt Lake City: Ancestry, 1997. A well-organized manual offering a practical and systematic approach to research and the use of computers in genealogy. Documentation and evaluation are stressed. Could overwhelm the beginner but useful to the intermediate searcher.

Crowe, Elizabeth Powell. *Genealogy Online: Researching Your Roots.* New York: Windcrest/McGraw-Hill, 1995. Explains how to access and utilize computer databases, electronic bulletin boards, online library catalogs, and other online services. Appendixes list genealogy bulletin boards and online catalogs of most major genealogical libraries.

Howells, Cyndi. *Netting Your Ancestors: Genealogical Research on the Internet.* Baltimore: Genealogical Publishing Co., 1997. Aims at bringing researchers online quickly and effectively. Large print and plain language allow for easy reference. Treats e-mail, mailing lists and newsgroups, and the World Wide Web. Gives software requirements, examples of products, Websites, and instructions for downloading software, utilities, and demos.

Nichols, Elizabeth. *Genealogy in the Computer Age: Understanding FamilySearch.* 2 vols. Family History Educators (P.O. Box 510606, Salt Lake City, UT 84151-0606), 1994, 1997. Vol. 1 explains in detail the Family History Library's Ancestral File™, International Genealogical Index®, and the Social Security Death Index. Vol. 2 deals with Personal Ancestral File® and the *Family History Library Catalog.*

Oldfield, Jim, Jr. *Your Family Tree: Using Your PC.* Grand Rapids, Mich.: Abacus Press, 1997. One chapter reviews traditional sources for research, but more than two-thirds of the book details online searching. The three programs discussed are PC-based *Brother's Keeper, Family Origins,* and *Family Tree Maker.* Discussions of Microsoft Word and Microsoft Publisher are included.

Pence, Richard A. *Computer Genealogy: A Guide to Research through High Technology.* Rev. ed. Salt Lake City: Ancestry, 1991.

Renick, Barbara, and Richard S. Wilson. *The Internet for Genealogists: A Beginner's Guide.* La Habra, Calif.: Compuology, 1997. A practical guide for understanding the Internet, going online, and utilizing resources. Includes a glossary of Internet terms.

Oral and Video History Methodology

Akeret, Robert U., with Daniel Klein. *Family Tales, Family Wisdom: How to Gather the Stories of a Lifetime and Share Them with Your Family.* New York: Henry Holt & Co., 1991.

The author shares a ten-step Elder Tale Program he developed to encourage parents, grandparents, and others to tell their life stories. Does not give questions to ask in an interview; rather, teaches how to draw out the real stories from elders.

Arthur, Stephen, and Julia Arthur. *Your Life and Times: How to Put a Life Story on Tape.* Baltimore: Genealogical Publishing Co., 1987. Revised 1994. Includes a step-by-step approach based on periods of life for answering questions and preserving answers on tape.

Bannister, Shala Mills. *Family Treasures: Videotaping Your Family Treasures.* Baltimore: Clearfield Co., 1994. Questions for an oral interview comprise the main body of the book. The incomplete instructions for the use of video equipment are condensed to just five pages. No index or bibliography.

Baum, Willa K. *Oral History for the Local Historical Society.* 3rd ed. Walnut Creek, Calif.: Alta Mira Press, 1995. First published and kept in print by the American Association of State and Local History, this work is in constant use by professional oral historians.

Fletcher, William. *Recording Your Family History.* Berkeley: Ten Speed Press, 1989. An excellent set of questions to use when recording an oral history. "Life history interview" inquiries are arranged chronologically, then by topic. Includes special questions for Jewish Americans, African Americans, and Hispanic Americans.

Greene, Bob, and D. G. Fulford. *To Our Children's Children: Preserving Family Histories for Generations to Come.* New York: Doubleday, 1993. Poses questions to turn recollections into a personal legacy for future generations. The thirty themes range from childhood to parenthood, college to romance, food to habits, and "Moods, Attitudes, and Philosophies." The authors, a nationally syndicated columnist and his journalist sister, offer no research suggestions; yet, their reputations and an engagingly simple style could propel many a reader into the next crossroads of "memory lane": family history research.

Peterson, Mary Lou. *Gift of Heritage.* Videotape (VHS format). 60 minutes. 1992. Instructions on creating a family history on videotape. Received a national recognition award in 1992 from The Creative Thinking Association. Available from Mary Lou Productions, P.O. Box 17233, Minneapolis, MN 55417.

Reimer, Derek, ed. *Voices: A Guide to Oral History.* British Columbia, Canada: Provincial Archives of British Columbia, Sound and Moving Image Division, 1984. Highly regarded as a practical and straightforward introduction to interviewing.

Shull, Wilma Sadler. *Photographing Your Heritage.* Salt Lake City: Ancestry, 1988.

Shumway, Gary L., and William G. Hartley. *An Oral History Primer.* Salt Lake City: Primer Publications, 1973. Tenth printing 1983. Lecturers on oral history discuss process (preparation, techniques, and transcription) and provide samples and suggested topics for interviewing with a tape recorder.

Stillman, Peter. *Families Writing.* Cincinnati: Writer's Digest Books, 1992.

Writing and Publishing

Ames, Stanley Richard, Ph.D. *How to Write and Publish Your Family History Using WordPerfect, DOS Versions 5.1 and 6.0.* Interlaken, N.Y.: Heart of the Lakes Publishing, 1994. Instructions include exact keystrokes necessary at each stage of the preparation of a family history using WordPerfect. Takes the reader from preparing text to creating a mailing list to advertising the finished product.

Banks, Keith E. *How to Write Your Personal and Family History.* 2nd ed. Bowie, Md: Heritage Books, 1989.

Barnes, Donald R., and Richard S. Lackey. *Write it Right: A Manual for Writing Family Histories and Genealogies.* 2nd ed. N.p., 1988. Especially valuable because it provides examples of proper citation of sources. Available from the Board for Certification of Genealogists, P.O. Box 14291, Washington, DC 20044.

Boyer, Carl, 3rd. *How to Publish and Market Your Own Family History.* 4th ed. Santa Clarita, Calif.: the author, 1993. Although less than half of the book deals with publishing and marketing, these sections are well done and reflect the author's experience in these fields. The balance of the book is on writing a family history.

Carson, Dina C. *Easy and Affordable Video Production for Genealogical and Historical Societies and Their Members: A Step-by-Step Guide to Planning, Equipment Preparation, and Video Production.* Niwot, Colo.: Iron Gate Publishing, 1992.

_____. *The Genealogy and Local History Researcher's Self-Publishing Guide: How to Organize, Write, Print and Sell Your Family or Local History Book.* 2nd ed. Niwot, Colo.: Iron Gate Publishing, 1992. Includes such details as publishing and printing terminology, copyrights, and ISBN numbers.

Costello, Margaret F., and Jane Fletcher Fiske. *Guidelines for Genealogical Writing: Style Guide for "The New England Historical and Genealogical Register" with Suggestions for Genealogical Books.* Boston: New England Historic Genealogical Society, 1990. Provides general rules for format and presentation of material but emphasizes that these rules apply only after thorough research has been conducted.

Curran, Joan Ferris. *Numbering Your Genealogy: Sound and Simple Systems.* Washington, D.C.: National Genealogical Society, 1993. Explains the four widely accepted genealogical numbering systems: the *NGS Quarterly* System, the Register, the Sosa-Stradonitz (Ahnentafel), and the Multi-Surname. The use of one of the systems is considered necessary in a published family history.

Gouldrup, Lawrence P. *Writing the Family History Narrative.* Salt Lake City: Ancestry, 1989. A brief, well-designed guide with clear discussion about plot development through examples. Useful bibliography of books to use as samples. A companion publication, Gouldrup's *Writing the Family History Narrative Workbook* (Salt Lake City: Ancestry, 1993), provides forms for collecting data, "brainstorming," and attempting new writing techniques.

Hatcher, Patricia Law. *Producing a Quality Family History.* Salt Lake City: Ancestry, 1996. Defines the standards for good research and excellence in publishing research results. Includes chapters on giving "life" to ancestors through writing, style, book design, page layout and formatting, organizing and documenting, and formatting. Each chapter includes a checklist on the process described.

_____, and John V. Wylie. *Indexing Family Histories.* Arlington, Va.: National Genealogical Society, 1993. A systematic approach, in twenty-two pages, to planning and producing an index.

How to Write and Publish Your Family History. Genealogy Publishing Service (448 Ruby Mine Road, Franklin, NC 29734), 1992. Designed by a publishing firm to help potential customers organize data, prepare a draft manuscript, and ready photos or drawings for publication.

Ives, Edward D. *The Tape Recorded Interview: A Manual for Field Workers in Folklore and Oral History.* 2nd ed. Knoxville: University of Tennessee Press, 1995.

Kyvig, David E., and Myron A. Marty. *Your Family History: A Handbook for Research and Writing.* Arlington Heights, Ill.: Harlan Davidson, 1978. Contains many examples of turning oral history into the written word.

Neubauer, Joan R. *From Memories to Manuscript: The Five-Step Method of Writing Your Life Story.* Salt Lake City: Ancestry, 1994.

Polking, Kirk. *Writing Family Histories and Memoirs.* Cincinnati: Betterway Books, 1995. An emphasis on how and what to write is supplemented by a brief discussion of some genealogical sources. A chapter on editing and one on publishing include "twenty rules for good writing" and "proofreading checklist."

Reeder, Josh. *Indexing Genealogy Publications.* Damascus, Md.: Russell D. Earnest Associates, 1994. Depicts in five chapters the topics of indexing names, cross referencing, general indexing, compiling the index, and formatting the index. The index in the book illustrates the author's suggested layout.

Skalka, Lois M. *Tracing, Charting, and Writing Your Family History.* Rev. ed. New York: Pilot Books, 1990.

Advanced Skills and Professional Development

Billingsley, Carolyn Earle, and Desmond Walls Allen. *How to Become a Professional Genealogist.* 3rd ed. Bryant, Ark.: Research Associates, 1997. A twenty-six page, no-nonsense discussion of what it takes to become a professional and to practice as one. Covers everything from training to business cards to report writing to specialization. Answers the questions most often asked by those considering employment as a genealogist. Available from Research Associates, P.O. Box 122, Bryant, AR 72089-0122.

Clifford, Karen. *Becoming an Accredited Genealogist: Plus 100 Tips to Ensure Your Success.* Salt Lake City: Ancestry, 1998.

Heiss, Willard. *Working in the Vineyards of Genealogy.* Edited by Ruth Dorel. Indianapolis: Indiana Historical Society, 1993. These selected writings by a renowned Quaker and Indiana specialist are instructional in both content and presentation. The articles range from source descriptions (not just Indiana) to reflections on expectations and conclusions. Essential reading for discriminating researchers.

Jacobus, Donald Lines. *Genealogy as Pastime and Profession.* 2nd rev. ed. 1991. Reprint. Baltimore: Genealogical Publishing Co., 1996. An illuminating discussion of the reasons for genealogy and how one becomes a professional. Does not discuss record categories but focuses on principles and methodology with a New England emphasis. Although not a textbook, it is considered a classic in the field and should be read at some stage of a researcher's development.

Lackey, Richard S. *Cite Your Sources.* Jackson: University Press of Mississippi, 1986. Considered essential for anyone writing a family history or preparing an article for publication.

Mills, Elizabeth Shown. *Evidence! Citation and Analysis for the Family Historian.* Baltimore: Genealogical Publishing Co., 1997. The two main topics are (1) rules of evidence and standards of proof as they pertain to family historians and (2) the proper citation of sources of information, including microfilm and electronic references. Includes many sample citations used in endnotes, footnotes, and bibliographies.

The Professional Genealogist. Hosted by Stephen Conte. Videotape (VHS format). 1990. An interview with Melda B. Shippey, C.G., on the subject of certification, becoming a professional genealogist, and hiring a professional. Does not mention the Association for Professional Genealogists nor give the address of the Board for Certification of Genealogists. Available from Stephen Conte, P.O. Box 962, West Caldwell, NJ 07007.

Rubincam, Milton. *Pitfalls in Genealogical Research.* Salt Lake City: Ancestry, 1987. Mistaken identity, implausible family traditions, date discrepancy, and the yearning for royal ancestry are some of the common traps for the unwary researcher. These and more are described in this informative and entertaining work.

Stevenson, Noel C. *Genealogical Evidence: A Guide to the Standard of Proof Relating to Pedigrees, Ancestry, Heirship and Family History.* Laguna Hills, Calif.: Aegean Park Press, 1989. Written by an attorney. Explains what to do when the sources don't agree, when the sources are wrong, or when there doesn't seem to be a source. Relates the subject of genealogy proof to courtroom evidence and its acceptance or dismissal. Directed to the intermediate and more-advanced researcher.

Stratton, Eugene A. *Applied Genealogy.* Salt Lake City: Ancestry, 1988. More a collection of essays than a textbook. Highly focused on early New England genealogy. The three chapters on evidence, a fourth titled Standards and Documentation, and chapter 1, "Background and Purposes of Genealogy," may be of interest to intermediate and advanced researchers. *Not* a how-to for beginners.

Miscellaneous Topics

Arnold, Jackie Smith. *Kinship: It's All Relative.* 2nd ed. 1994. Reprint. Genealogical Publishing Co., 1996.

Balhuizen, Anne Ross. *Searching on Location: Planning a Research Trip.* Salt Lake City: Ancestry, 1993.

Earnest, Russell D. *Grandma's Attic: Making Heirlooms Part of Your Family History.* Russell D. Earnest Associates (P.O. Box 490, Damascus, MD 20872-0490), 1991. Contains forms and examples to help identify, interpret, and catalog family heirlooms. Preservation of artifacts and paper documents is discussed.

Frisch-Ripley, Karen. *Unlocking the Secrets in Old Photographs.* Salt Lake City: Ancestry, 1991. Identifying, dating, restoring, and caring for family photographs is the focus, although a chapter titled "Public Sources of Information" aims at linking a pictured event, such as a wedding, to the corresponding document (a marriage license or certificate).

Krause, Carol. *How Healthy Is Your Family Tree? A Complete Guide to Tracing Your Family's Medical and Behavioral History.* New York: Fireside, 1995. The author, a journalist who writes about health and medical issues, credits her medical family tree with allowing four women in her generation to survive cancer through early detection. Looks briefly at how genes work, inherited heart disease, depression , homosexuality, and alcoholism. Includes eight sample letters for querying civil, ecclesiastical, and personal sources.

Parker, J. Carlyle. *Going to Salt Lake City to Do Family History Research.* 2nd ed. Marietta Publishing Co. (2115 North Denair Avenue, Turlock, CA 95380), 1993. Discusses how to conduct research if one has already used an LDS family history center, has not used a center but has a local library, or has no center or local library. Offers a floor-by-floor review of the Family History Library with instructions on how to best use available time. Includes specific microfilm numbers and maps of Salt Lake City.

Sagraves, Barbara. *A Preservation Guide: Saving the Past and the Present for the Future.* Salt Lake City: Ancestry, 1997. Instructions for organizing, maintaining, storing, and preserving family documents, photographs, motion picture film, sound recordings, and textiles. Includes tips for restoring materials after fire or flooding.

Tuttle, Craig A. *An Ounce of Preservation: A Guide to the Care of Papers and Photographs.* Highland City, Fla.: Rainbow Books, 1995. Written by an archivist for the lay person, this book discusses the production, storage, cleaning, and repairing of paper, inks, and photographs. Includes tips to organize papers and photographs and recommends archival supplies and suppliers.

Warren, James W., and Paula Stuart Warren. *Getting the Most Mileage From Genealogical Research Trips.* 2nd ed. Warren Research & Marketing (1869 Laurel Avenue, St. Paul, MN 55104-5938, 1993. Contains checklists and step-by-step suggestions on preparing for travel to conduct searches.

_____. *Making the Most of Your Research Trip to Salt Lake City.* 5th ed (Warren Research & Publishing, 1869 Laurel Avenue, St. Paul, MN 55104-5938, 1996. The authors, who are professional researchers and leaders of tour groups, give a reference list for pre-trip preparations and practical hints for on-site research.

Courses and Programs of Study

Teacher Development and Classroom Aids

Davis, John Rivard. *Not Merely Ancestors: A Guide for Teaching Genealogy in the Schools.* Baltimore: Clearfield Co., 1993. Suggestions for presenting a genealogy project in middle school or high school classes. Offers advice for dealing with difficult or sensitive questions on adoption and illegitimacy.

Dollarhide, William. *Genealogy Starter Kit.* Baltimore: Genealogical Publishing Co., 1994. Brings together many addresses that a beginner will find useful and provides basic instruction on first steps. Samples of record-keeping forms are included.

Jaussi, Laureen R. *Genealogy Fundamentals.* Orem, Utah: Jaussi Publications, 1994. Intended for classroom use, this text offers twelve lessons supplemented by thirty-nine chapters of study material. Basic skills, such as note-keeping, correspondence, and computer applications precede discussions of repositories, sources, and evaluation of material. Directed at LDS researchers but of benefit to any beginner who has access to an LDS family history center. Also see Jaussi's *Genealogy Fundamentals in Twelve Lessons* under "Self-Contained Instructional Materials and Home Study Courses", below.

Krauch, Velma. *This is Your Life Story: How to Write It, How to Teach It.* Vacaville, Calif.: Encore Publishing, 1988. Part 1 offers optional methods for planning, writing, and organizing life stories. References are provided for additional reading. Part 2 provides seventy topic guide assignments and suggestions for breaking them into smaller segments. Part 3 provides an eight-week class plan for teachers.

Netherly, Mary, et al. *The Cultural Exchange: A Cross-Cultural and Interdisciplinary Multicultural Education Curriculum for Grades 4-8. Trace Your Own Roots.* Eureka, Calif.: Humboldt County Office of Education, 1980.

Nichols, Elizabeth L. *Teaching Family History in Four Weeks: A Course Outline.* Salt Lake City: Family History Educators, 1990. Available from Family History Educators, P.O. Box 510606, Salt Lake City, UT 84151-0606.

Perry, Annette Lutnesky. *Branch to Branch: A Manual for Teachers of Genealogy.* San Jose: Genealogical Consultants, 1992.

Reichert, Sharon J. *Journey Through Genealogy.* Videotape. The author (3065 West Avenue, Lancaster, CA 93536, 1991. Videotape and research outline (by the same title) of the first part of the video. Created from a lecture on how to begin genealogy. Many books are displayed (with permission), but only those available as of 1991.

Reisinger, Joy, comp. *Index to NGS and FGS Conferences and Syllabi.* Salt Lake City: National Genealogical Society and Federation of Genealogical Societies, 1993. This work indexes almost three thousand lectures presented at national conferences between 1981 and 1993. Arranged by topics, it provides titles, names of presenters, and directions for locating tapes and/or syllabi material. Also provides the addresses of all audiotaping companies which provided audio services at national conferences during these years.

Soghikian, Juanita Will. *My Origins: Discovering and Recording Family History.* Boston: Armenian Relief Society, 1976. Booklet designed to "help upper level elementary school students research and write their family history." Includes assignment sheets for teachers and students and lesson guides for teachers and parents.

Wynne, Frances H., and Cj Stevens. *Teaching Genealogy to Enrich the Curricula of the Intermediate, Middle, or Jr. High School.* Baton Rouge: Oracle Press, 1982.

Self-Contained Instructional Materials and Home Study Courses

Alex Haley—The Search for Roots. 16mm film or videotape. 18 minutes. Produced by WNET-TV, New York. 1977. Author Alex Haley explains how and why he came to write the book *Roots.* Suitable for ages ten to adult. Distributed by Films for the Humanities and Sciences, P.O. Box 2053, Princeton, NJ 08540.

Beginning Black Genealogy. Black Studies Series, part 4. 3/4- or 1/2-inch videotape. 60 minutes. Produced and distributed by University of Arizona Microcampus, Tucson, Arizona, n.d. How to use the census and other sources to learn about African American family ancestry.

Black Genealogy. Series of Genealogy Instruction. Produced by WGTV, University of Georgia, Athens, Georgia. Distributed by Maryland Center for Public Broadcasting, Owings Mill, MD 21117. Also see *Genealogy in Sign* (below). James D. Walker, then of the National Archives, discusses the specific problems that African Americans encounter when seeking their roots.

Circles. 16mm film. 20 minutes. 1979. Produced and distributed by Christie Allan-Piper, 1948 Hopewood Drive, Falls Church, VA 22043. Shows a dancer tracing her links with the past and future through six generations of family photographs. Suitable for children.

Dieterle, Diane. *Successful Genealogy.* Bountiful, Utah: AGLL Genealogical Services, 1995. A study guide for beginners. Includes a pack of one hundred forms (including pedigree and family group sheet).

Fast Lane Learning Kits. *Searching U.S. Census Records: An Invaluable Aid for Locating and Tracking Families*, presented by Jimmy B. Parker, 1993; *Using U.S. Military Records: A Rich Source of Information for Genealogists and Family Historians*, presented by Jimmy B. Parker, 1993; and *Doing Genealogy: Foundations for Successful Research*, presented by Kory L. Meyerink, 1993. Family History Unlimited, 3507 North University Avenue, Suite 350B, Provo, UT 84604. These learning kits include professionally recorded audiotapes and workbooks with text, exercises, and up to eighty-nine full-page photo illustrations.

Federation of Genealogical Societies and the Ohio Genealogical Society Teleconferencing Series Videotapes (Athens, Ohio: FGS/OGS, 1998). Order from the Ohio Genealogical Society, P.O. Box 2625, Mansfield, OH 44906-0625 or the Federation of Genealogical Societies, 1-888-FGS-1500 or (fax) 1-888-380-0500. Professionally produced videotapes of the FGS/OGS teleconferencing sessions held during 1997 and 1998. Each of the five tapes is 180 minutes long and includes a syllabus. Titles may be purchased separately: Military Records; Immigration and Ship Passenger Records; American Land Records; American Court Records; and Modern Vital Records.

The Genealogist's Video Research Guide. Video Knowledge, 32 North 200 East, Suite 1, Spanish Fork, UT 84660-9909. 1994. A three-hour, three-part video series on genealogy fundamentals. Tape 1 explains home sources, published histories, record-keeping, and some *FamilySearch*® options; tape 2 covers census and probate records; and tape 3 addresses land, military, and vital records. Gordon and Carolyn Casper are the instructors.

Genealogy in Sign. Series of Genealogy Instruction. Produced by WGTV, University of Georgia, Athens, Georgia. Distributed by Maryland Center for Public Broadcasting, Owings Mill, MD 21117. Also see *Black Genealogy* (above). Offers information on tracing family roots. Features a narrator who speaks and signs while key words are superimposed on the screen.

Hankey, Joan Rhodes. *NGS Genealogical Puzzles.* Reprint. Arlington, Va.: National Genealogical Society, 1992. Entertaining and challenging crosswords, acrostics, and logic problems for all skill levels that may be adapted to the classroom.

National Genealogical Society. *American Genealogy: A Basic Course.* 4th ed. Washington, D.C.: National Genealogical Society, 1996. A successful, award-winning home study course which requires completed assignments to be submitted on a regular basis. Available from the National Genealogical Society, Education Division, Dept. NL, 4527 Seventeenth Street North, Arlington, VA 22207-2363.

_____. *Beginner's Kit.* Includes *Instructions for Beginners in Genealogy* (3rd ed., rev. 1993), a booklet on how to start research and use of charts and basic sources. Includes enough pedigree charts and family group sheets to begin record-keeping.

Jaussi, Laureen R. *Genealogy Fundamentals in Twelve Lessons.* Orem, Utah: Jaussi Publications, 1994. A twenty-one-page self-study guide for stand-alone instruction or to accompany Jaussi's *Genealogy Fundamentals* (see above under "Teacher Development and Classroom Aids").

Nichols, Elizabeth L. *The Genesis of Your Genealogy.* 3rd ed. Salt Lake City, Utah: Family History Educators, 1992. Originally first in the series titled Simplified Step-by-Step Instruction Books for the Beginner in Genealogy, this programmed instruction book enables the reader to proceed at his or her own pace and to verify what he or she has learned through a series of simple tests. Completely revised and updated to include the use of computers.

_____. *Help is Available.* 2nd ed. Logan, Utah: Everton Publishers, 1980. Second in the series Simplified Step-by-Step Instruction Books for the Beginner in Genealogy.

Out of Your Tree! Crazy About Genealogy. Narrated by Robert A. Burns. Videotape. 38 minutes. Produced by Rondo Films. 1993. Includes a starter kit. Order from Cinetex, Inc., P.O. Box 549, Austin TX 78767. An on-site introduction to genealogy that takes viewers into a cemetery, a library, and a courthouse. Ideal for libraries or organizations wishing to acquaint newcomers with the basics of genealogy.

Prepare to Publish. Videotape. 28 minutes. Produced by Gateway Press. 1989. Order from Genealogical Publishing Co., 1001 Calvert Street, Baltimore, MD 21202-3879. Outlines the steps necessary to produce a publication from a manuscript.

Using Maps in Genealogical Research. Presentation by Ronald E. Grim. 2 videocassettes. 240 minutes. Produced by Family History Society of Arizona, 1997. Order from FHSA, P.O. Box 63094, Phoenix, AZ 85082-3094. Four lectures and handout material (Map Collections of the National Archives vs. the Library of Congress Using Nineteenth-Century U.S. Land Ownership Maps and Atlases, Sanborn Fire Insurance Maps, German Emigration to America As Documented By German and American Maps) from a presentation in 1997. Dr. Grim is the Specialist in Cartographic History, Library of Congress.

Publishers of Conference Recordings

Infomedix, 12800 Garden Grove Boulevard, Suite E, Garden Grove, CA 92643. Infomedix distributes tapes of lectures presented at the 1982 and 1983 national conferences of the Federation of Genealogical Societies.

Repeat Performance, 2911 Crabapple Lane, Hobart, IN 46342. Repeat Performance distributes taped lectures presented at national conferences between 1981 and 1991. Write for a catalog.

Triad, P.O. Box 120, Toulon, IL 61483. Triad distributes taped lectures presented at several national conferences since 1981. Write for a catalogue.

GEOGRAPHIC TOOLS OVERVIEW

Key Concepts in This Chapter

- Maps use symbols to represent physical features.
- The United States Geological Survey (USGS) is the Federal government's mapmaker.
- City maps can help researchers find people in census records.
- Topographic maps from the USGS provide excellent detail for almost any U.S. location.
- Gazetteers, or geographic dictionaries, can locate towns and features not found on maps.
- The Geographic Names Information System (GNIS) database identifies 2 million features and places.
- State gazetteers are important research tools.
- Postal and shipping guides may substitute for gazetteers.
- Many geographic tools are available for computers; some are on the Internet.

Key Sources in This Chapter

- *American Expansion: A Book of Maps*
- *Westward Expansion: A History of the American Frontier*
- *AniMap Plus County Boundary Historical Atlas*
- *Atlas of Historical County Boundaries*
- *Atlas of American History,* 2nd rev. ed.
- *A New and Complete Gazetteer of the United States*
- *Omni Gazetteer of the United States of America*
- *The Digital Gazetteer of the U.S.*

3

GEOGRAPHIC TOOLS: MAPS, ATLASES, AND GAZETTEERS

Carol Mehr Schiffman

What is a geographic tool? By definition, it is a tool related to geography, a science that deals with the earth and its life. Commonly used geographic tools are maps, atlases, gazetteers (geographical dictionaries), and postal guides.

A town is a specific place somewhere on planet earth. It might be in a valley, on a plain surrounded by lush farmland, in mountains in the midst of evergreens, or in a desert far from other habitation. Its surroundings will affect the lives of the people who live there and also its economy. There can be many towns with the same name, but only one of them can occupy a specific portion of land; thus, each town is uniquely identified by its location.

A *map* is a graphic representation (usually flat)—by means of signs and symbols and at an established scale—of the physical features (natural, artificial, or both) of a portion of the earth's surface. A topographic map will show the terrain of the land; the proximity of other communities; physical barriers, such as large rivers and mountains; roads and trails; and the approximate size of the town.

An *atlas,* another useful geographic tool, is a bound collection of maps; descriptive text usually is included as well. There is an atlas for nearly every place, and the types of maps and the information provided in each atlas can vary considerably. Historical atlases, atlases showing political boundaries and boundary changes, state and county road atlases, and commercial atlases can be particularly useful to family researchers.

If the location of a place name is unknown and it cannot be found on a map or in an atlas, a *gazetteer* is the tool to consult. Gazetteers list place names in countries, states, or geographical regions alphabetically for particular time periods. If a town is not listed in a gazetteer, it might be found in a *postal guide;* postal guides list post offices alphabetically by state.

The tool which the genealogist or family historian should use first depends on the nature of the problem.

- If the location of a place name is known, obtain a map of the location.
- If the location of a place name is known but there is a discrepancy with the jurisdiction (perhaps the record shows a different county name than the one indicated on the map), the answer might be found in an atlas showing county boundary changes.
- If the place name cannot be found on a map, the name might have changed, or the place might no longer exist. The name and additional information might be found in a gazetteer or a postal guide.

MAPS

The uses of maps are as varied as the types of maps available. A map can be a chart to plan a course of action, such as an ancestor chart that is used by a family researcher to plot the names of ancestors and the places where they lived. A simple, hand-drawn map can show directions to a friend's house, while a highly detailed topographic map will show natural and man-made features. Maps range from those that show soil conditions to others that display images from outer space, and they are used for many purposes by multitudes of organizations.

History of Cartography

The science of making maps, from surveying to drawing, is called *cartography*. The name probably derived from the term *chart* (chartography) (Greenhood 1964, xi).

More than four thousand years ago, the Babylonians mapped individual land holdings on clay tablets. These tablets represent one of man's earliest forms of graphic expression (Stephenson 1967, viii). Richard W. Stephenson stated that "it has been reported that Ramses II began a cadastral survey of Egypt in the thirteenth century B.C., and it is reasonable to assume that the surveys were recorded on maps. The Egyptians drew their maps on papyrus and, unfortunately, few have survived the ravages of time (1967, viii)." These early cadastral surveys, which were for describing and recording land ownership and apportioning taxes, served as the basis for map-making in Europe during the Middle Ages.

A cartographic revolution began in western Europe in the thirteenth century. The magnetic compass (for surveying the land) and the mariner's compass (for charting the seas) brought about radical changes in the methods of map-making. Rather than relying upon literary and mythological sources, cartographers (individuals who make maps) began to draw maps based on actual measurements and observations. These maps, which were intended for travelers, accurately portrayed an area as it was known at the time. Cadastral (depicting boundaries) surveys of small parcels of land in Europe in the Middle Ages were usually recorded in descriptive text rather than on maps. Not until the Renaissance were surveys of individual European estates frequently depicted cartographically.

Every technological advance brought with it an increase in the accuracy of maps. The telescope in 1609, the pendulum clock in 1657, the first modern marine sextant in 1730, and the marine chronometer in 1735 permitted accurate astronomical observations and the measurement of arcs on the earth's surface. Advances in printing techniques allowed map-makers to enhance their works with color detail. All of these advances led to the creation of more accurate, detailed maps and atlases. An early cartographic masterpiece was Jacques Cassini's *Déscription géometrique de la France*. Published in 1783, it contained 182 engraved maps showing France in great detail—everything from canyons to channels to churches (Makower 1992, 10).

All of the important items of the modern surveyor's equipment were in use by the end of the eighteenth century. The instruments were refined during the nineteenth century, and new survey methods were developed as national surveying commenced. Topographic mapping, with map scales ranging from 1:25,000 to 1:100,000 (see "Map Scale," below), began in all civilized countries during the nineteenth century. In the majority of countries, these maps were prepared by the national army. Two notable exceptions were the United States, where topographic mapping became the responsibility of the U.S. Geological Survey in 1879, and England, where maps were prepared by the British Ordnance Survey.

The key to finding the best maps available is knowing the types of maps that were made during particular time periods, where they might be found, and the scales to which they were drawn. To understand map scale, it is helpful to know how the world is measured.

Measuring the World

The world is round and has poles; midway between the poles is the equator, a circle that divides the globe into north and south halves. Additional lines circle the globe north and south of the equator at intervals of ten degrees. These circles are parallel to each other, so they are called parallels, or lines of latitude. Another set of lines runs from pole to pole at intervals of ten degrees. They are called meridians, or lines of longitude. The name for the zero meridian, or the longitude 0° line, is the prime meridian; and distance is measured as being east or west of it. The prime meridian can be anywhere a world power decides to put it, but the prime meridian used by the United States is the one that passes through Greenwich, England.

The earth takes twenty-four hours to complete a full circle of 360 degrees. There are twenty-four meridians, and they are spaced to represent one hour's turning of the earth toward or away from the sun (east or west of the prime meridian). In one hour the earth turns fifteen degrees, the distance between each meridian.

Measurement of the globe is referred to in terms of degrees and miles (or degrees and kilometers where the metric system is used). In order to determine how many miles there are in a degree, it is necessary to know where the measuring is being done. Distance around the world at the equator is 24,902 miles. At the equator each meridian is an equal distance of approximately 1,040 miles, but in the latitude of New York the meridians are only 784 miles apart (Greenhood 1964, 50).

In four minutes' time, the earth turns one degree, or 69.172 miles at the equator. Degrees are divided into minutes, and there are sixty minutes in one degree. A 15-minute map (one-fourth of a degree) represents the distance the earth turns in one minute of time. From 1894 until the 1950s, the 15-minute map was the map most commonly produced by the U.S. Geological Survey (Thompson 1987).

Map Scale

Map scale expresses the size relationship between the features shown on the map and the same features on the earth's surface; it is normally expressed as a ratio (for example, 1:24,000). The numerator, usually 1, represents map distance; the denominator, the larger number, represents ground distance.

The amount of detail shown on a map is proportionate to the scale of the map: the larger the map scale (the larger the fraction), the more detail is shown. For example, individual houses can be shown on 1:24,000-scale maps, but only landmark buildings are shown on 1:100,000-scale maps. The table below and figure 3-1 show some map scales commonly used in the United States.

Scale	*One Inch Represents*
1:3,168,000	50 miles
1:2,500,000	40 miles (approximate)
1:1,000,000	16 miles (approximate)
1:500,000	8 miles (approximate)
1:250,000	4 miles (approximate)
1:125,000	2 miles (approximate)
1:63,360	1 mile
1:62,500	1 mile (approximate)
1:31,680	0.5 mile
1:30,000	2,500 feet
1:24,000	2,000 feet

Maps printed in the United States and other countries using the inch/pound system usually express scale as a ratio of inches to feet or inches to miles. A common scale for a nineteenth-century English ordnance survey map is 1:63,360, meaning that one inch equals one mile (63,360 inches). Countries using the metric system normally express scale as a ratio of centimeters to kilometers. For example, if the scale is 1:100,000, one centimeter equals one kilometer (100,000 centimeters). When converted to the inch/pound system, one kilometer equals 0.62137 miles.

The scale to which a map is drawn is printed on it, usually as part of the map *legend*. The legend shows the different types of symbols used on the map and states what each symbol represents. Symbols are the graphic language of maps. Their shape, size, location, and color all have special significance (figure 3-2).

Mapping of a New Nation

Military Mapping. The United States' need for military maps dates from the American Revolution, when George Washington realized that accurate maps were of prime importance in planning his campaigns. The Military Cartographic Headquarters was established in 1777 to provide maps for planning campaigns. In 1807, under President Thomas Jefferson, the Survey of the Coast was created. Its responsibility was the development and dissemination of maps and charts to promote the safety and welfare of the people. Unfortunately, military mapping languished due to lack of funds, and the War of 1812 again demonstrated the need for accurate aids to navigation. Morris M. Thompson discusses the development of maps by the Federal government in *Maps for America: Cartographic Products of the U.S. Geological Survey and Others,* 3rd ed. (Washington, D.C.: U.S. Geological Survey, 1987).

Before the Civil War, the Federal government conducted limited surveys in the vast region extending to the western coast. The earliest surveys, usually made under the sponsorship of the U.S. Army, were exploratory in nature, partly to extend geographic knowledge and partly to gather information for military purposes. Early survey projects included the explorations of Lewis and Clark in the Northwest (1804 to 1806) and the Zebulon Pike expedition to the Rocky Mountains (1805 to 1807). The Corps of Topographical Engineers was established in 1838 to map the West. In the 1840s and 1850s, the corps' Office of Explorations and Surveys carried out surveys for wagon roads, railroad routes to the Pacific, and international boundaries (Thompson 1987, 4).

During the Civil War there was a great demand for maps and charts by the Coast Survey, and annual chart production grew from a pre-war count of fewer than ten thousand copies to sixty-six thousand copies by 1863 (Thompson 1987, 4). Topographers, cartographers, and hydrographers (individuals who chart bodies of water) on both sides of the conflict made important contributions to the military effort. The planning of every major campaign of the war depended on the availability of reliable maps and charts.

In 1866 the U.S. Navy's Hydrographic Office began to compile charts of the oceans, and negotiations began for the international exchange of data. In 1907 the Aeronautical Division of the Army Signal Corps was established. Extensive mapping of foreign areas by U.S. Federal agencies began with World War I, and during World War II there was a vast production of maps for the war effort. In 1972 the Department of Defense combined the various organizations engaged in map production and distribution under the command of the Defense Mapping Agency.

Surveying and Mapping of Public Lands. When the revolutionary war ended in 1783, the states ceded their disputed western lands to the new government, thereby creating the *public domain* (land owned by the Federal government). Thomas Jefferson, while chairing the congressional Committee on Public Land in 1784, proposed a large-scale surveying and mapping program of the new lands. His proposal resulted in the Land Ordinance of 1785, which established how land in the public domain would be surveyed and sold. No land in the public domain could be sold legally until the survey had been completed and accepted by the Federal government.

All government-owned land would be divided into *townships* (a survey unit approximately six miles square). This was done by establishing a *principal meridian* (line of longitude running north and south) and a *base line*

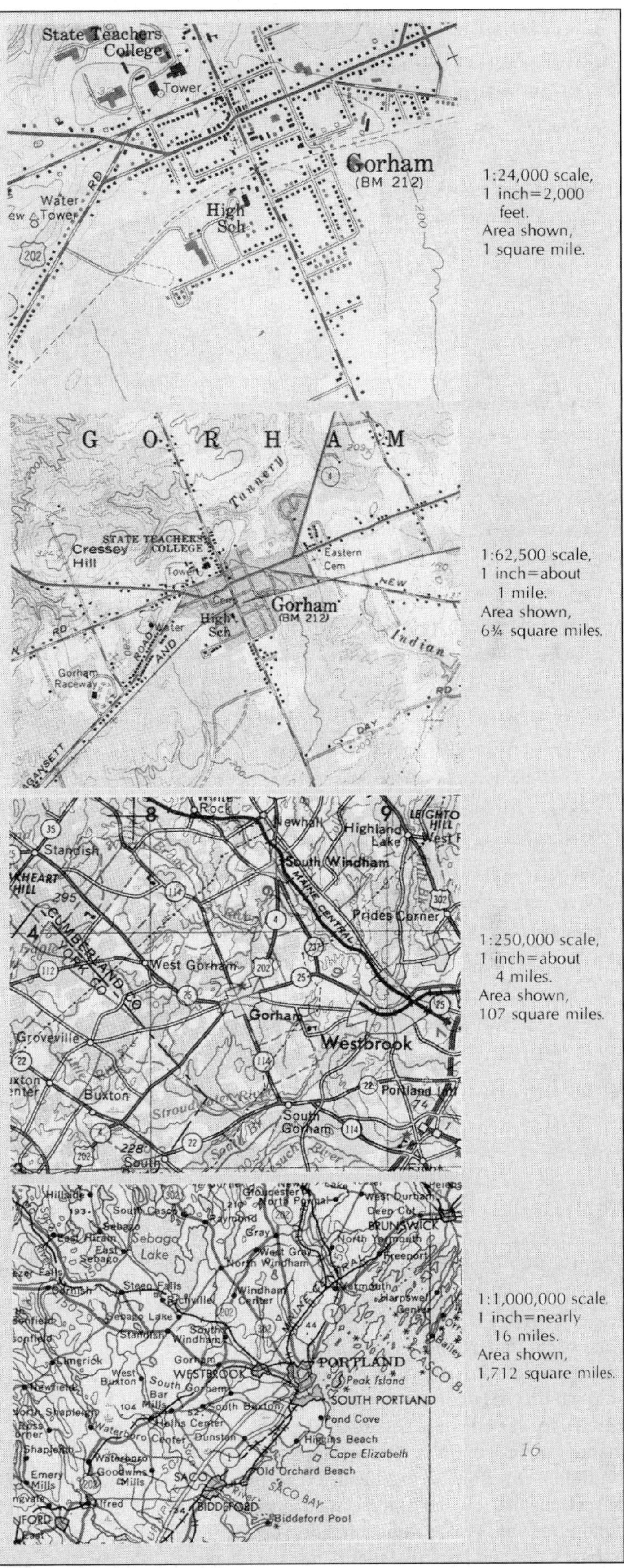

Figure 3-1. Comparison of maps covering the Gorham, Maine, area at various scales. From Morris M. Thompson's *Maps for America,* 2nd ed. (U.S. Geological Survey, 1981).

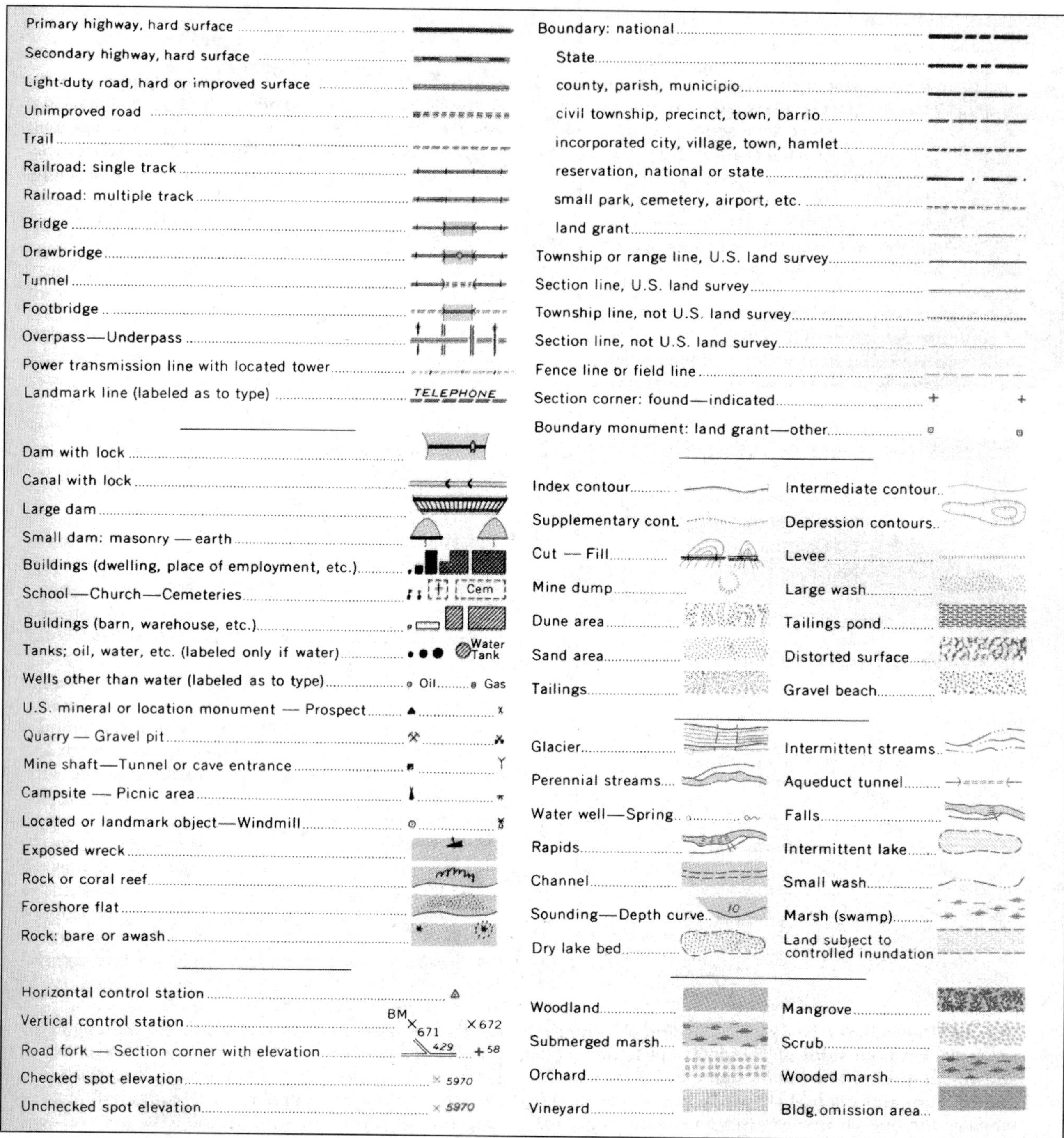

Figure 3-2. Topographic map symbols used by the U.S. Geological Survey.

(line of latitude running east and west) from which surveying would commence (see "Measuring the World," above). A township would contain thirty-six sections, each of which was numbered and was one mile square (640 acres). In order to properly identify each section in a township, townships were numbered south to north from an established base line, and *ranges* (rows of sections in a township) were numbered east or west of a principal meridian. For more information about the establishment of base lines and principal meridians, see chapter 8, "Research in Land and Tax Records," in *The Source: A Guidebook of American Genealogy*, edited by Loretto Dennis Szucs and Sandra Hargreaves Leubking, rev. ed. (Salt Lake City: Ancestry, 1997), pages 251 and 252 (figure 3-3).

Initial surveying began in September 1785 in eastern Ohio in an area referred to as the Seven Ranges. As soon as four ranges of townships had been surveyed, sale of land by the government commenced in September 1787. The floodgates opened, and a wave of pioneers flowed into Ohio.

In 1812 the General Land Office (GLO) was created. Its surveyors measured and subdivided the relatively well-known public lands of the United States into townships. The surveys consisted of *field notes* and *land plats*. The field notes provided

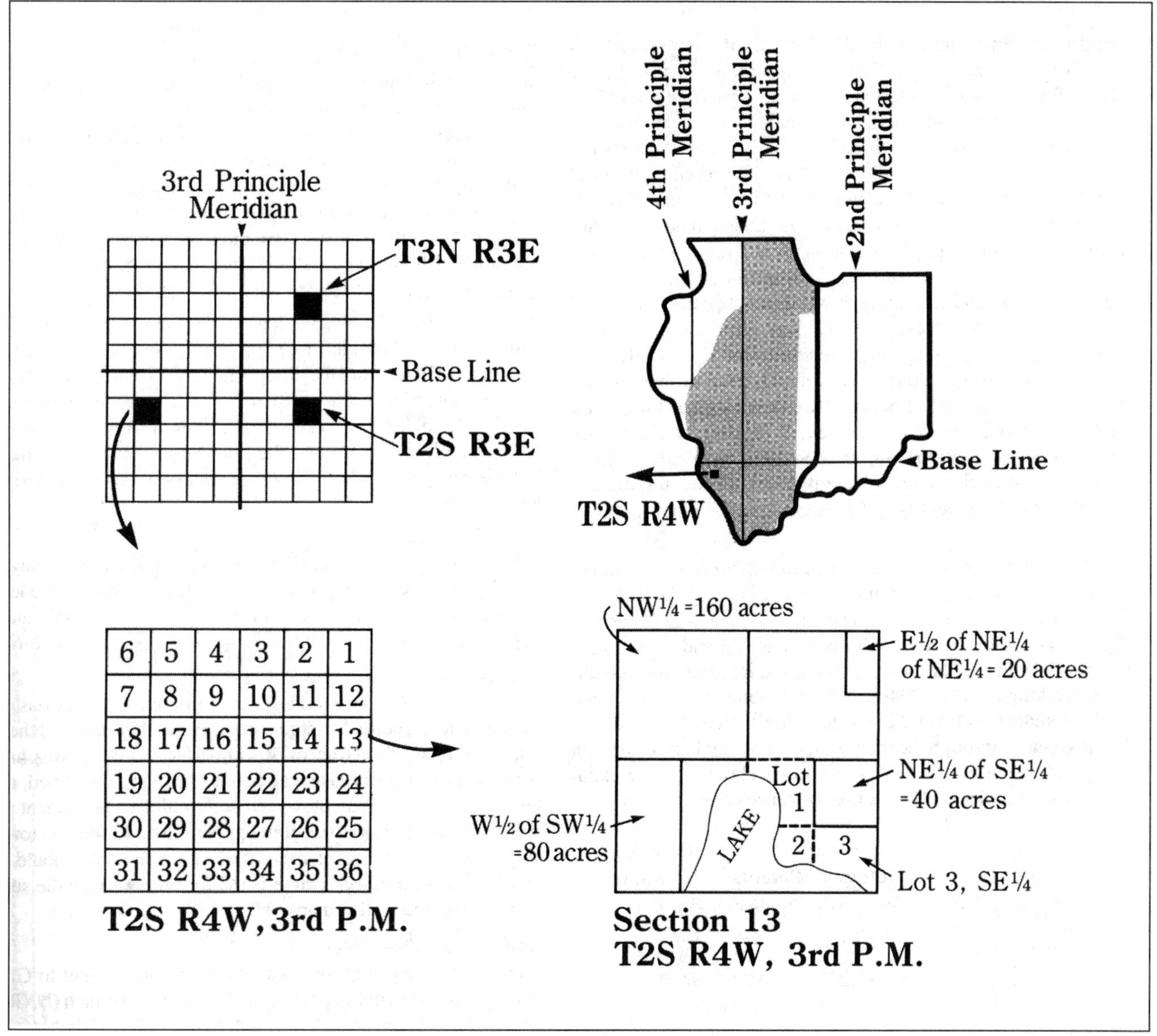

Figure 3-3. Legal descriptions in the Federal township and range system.

information on the character of the land, soil, and timber, the topographic features, and the relation of the rectangular surveys to other surveys. Land plats were diagrams drawn to scale that showed boundaries, subdivisions, and other details of tracts of land (for example, townships, private land claims, and mineral claims). The records date from around 1790 to 1946, and the majority were transferred from the GLO to the National Archives between 1941 and 1952. Most of the manuscript plats and survey field notes of the remaining public domain states were retained by the GLO, which became the Bureau of Land Management (BLM) after 1946.

Following the Civil War, there was an urgent need among people migrating westward for detailed information about the resources and natural features of the western portion of the United States. Congress authorized four Federal surveys to explore various parts of the West. They became known as the King, Hayden, Powell, and Whealer surveys (Thompson 1987, 4).

Key Sources—Surveying and Mapping of Public Lands

- Burke, Thomas Aquinas. *Ohio Lands: A Short History.* 3rd ed. Columbus, Ohio: auditor of state, 1991. This fine, free booklet discusses Ohio's major land surveys and the sale of public lands.

- *Field Notes from Selected General Land Office Township Surveys.* Washington, D.C.: National Archives and Records Service, 1979. The National Archives has microfilmed the volumes of field notes from original surveys of six states that were in its custody in 1979. The states are Illinois, Indiana, Iowa, Kansas, Missouri, and Ohio. The microfilms (281 reels) are available for searching at the National Archives, the Family History Library of The Church of Jesus Christ of Latter-day Saints (LDS church) in Salt Lake City, and local family history centers. See "United States—Land and Property, General Land Office" in the *Family History Library Catalog*™ (see chapter 5) for a list of maps and microfilm numbers.

- Karrow, Robert W., Jr., ed. *Checklist of Printed Maps of the Middle West to 1900*. 14 vols. in 12. Boston: G. K. Hall, 1981–83. The list describes 25,478 entries found in 127 different collections that include maps of cities and towns, panorama maps, fire insurance maps, and maps in government documents. The list includes all known landownership books for Illinois, Indiana, Iowa, Kansas, Michigan, Missouri, Nebraska, North Dakota, Ohio, South Dakota, and Wisconsin.

- Kelsay, Laura E., comp. *List of Cartographic Records of the General Land Office*. Special List no. 19. Washington, D.C.: National Archives and Records Service, 1964. In addition to listing the cartographic records that are available, this publication contains a brief history of the surveying of public lands.

- *Township Plats of Selected States*. Washington, D.C.: National Archives and Records Service, 1979. The National Archives microfilmed the original manuscript plats of townships that were in its custody in 1979. The states were Alabama, Illinois, Indiana, Iowa, Kansas, Mississippi, Missouri, Oklahoma, Wisconsin, and parts of Ohio, Oregon, and Washington. The microfilms (sixty-seven reels) are available for searching at the National Archives and the Family History Library and its family history centers. See "United States—Land and Property, Bureau of Land Management" in the *Family History Library Catalog* for a list of maps and microfilm numbers.

Routes to the West

Trails and Early Roads. During the seventeenth century, most European immigrants settled in the coastal lowlands on the eastern coast. Commerce between seaport towns and England thrived, but road building into the interior lagged, and the majority of inland towns were connected by Indian trails, most of which followed earlier animal trails. Later the trails were widened enough to accommodate packhorses and, ultimately, wagons. In 1673 an overland postal system was established, but early post roads were narrow trails or bridle paths that often followed Indian trails.

As the population swelled and the land east of the Appalachian Mountains, which extended from New Hampshire to Georgia, was colonized, there was a desire among many settlers to move farther west, where there was free land and opportunity to improve their economic situation. The mountains were a natural barrier to westward movement, and the land to the west was inhabited by hostile Indian tribes that were allied with French trappers, traders, and Jesuit missionaries. The French and Indian Wars ended in 1763, but the king of England issued a proclamation on 7 October 1763 that established the Appalachian highlands as the western boundary for white settlers. Despite this and later proclamations, the westward movement began. Before the revolutionary war ended, hardy pioneers had settled in the Ohio River Valley of Kentucky and Tennessee. Travel, however, was hampered by wretched roads.

Many early settlers crossed the Appalachian barrier by three crude overland routes. Braddock's Road, which was built in 1755 by British soldiers under Gen. Edward Braddock, connected Maryland and Fort Pitt (in Pittsburgh) at the forks of the Ohio River. Forbes Road, built in 1758 by British soldiers under Gen. John Forbes, connected eastern Pennsylvania and Fort Pitt.

Land speculators hired woodsmen like Daniel Boone to blaze trails over which settlers could travel. An example is the Wilderness Road, which was blazed by Boone in 1775 through the Cumberland Gap into Kentucky. This road connected with the Great Valley Road in Virginia so that settlers could travel from the Potomac River through the Shenandoah Valley, across the mountains, and into Kentucky (figure 3-4). Other early road systems included the Mohawk Turnpike, the Catskill Turnpike, the Great Genessee Road, Zane's Trace, and the Knoxville Road.

In 1806 Congress selected the route for the Cumberland Road, which also was known as the National Road. By 1819 this broad, paved road had reached Wheeling, Virginia (later West Virginia), on the Ohio River, and by 1833 it had been extended to Columbus, Ohio. It ultimately continued westward through Ohio, Indiana, and Illinois, reaching Vandalia in 1852.

In 1833 James Walker, a mountain man, was sent by Maj. Benjamin L. E. Bonneville to explore the great basin, desert, and range country to the west. Walker ultimately reached Monterey, California, before retracing his steps. Later known as the California Trail, his route became the main route used by settlers and people seeking gold in California. In 1834 Nathaniel Wyeth organized an expedition to establish a trading company in the Oregon country. He followed the south side of the North Platte and Sweetwater rivers, through South Pass (now in Wyoming), then northwest to the Snake River, which flowed into the Columbia River. This route became known as the Oregon Trail. In 1846 the Latter-day Saints (members of the LDS church) left Nauvoo, Illinois, and crossed southern Iowa. They generally followed the north side of the North Platte and Sweetwater rivers, and at South Pass they traveled southwest toward the valley of the Great Salt Lake, arriving in 1847. Their route became known as the Mormon Trail.

Improvement of roads languished until the end of the century. The development of the bicycle in 1877, the automobile in 1893, and the demands of farmers motivated local governments to improve their dismal roads.

Key Sources—Trail and Road Maps

- Billington, Ray Allen, and Martin Ridge. *Westward Expansion: A History of the American Frontier*. 5th ed. New York: Macmillan Publishing Co., 1982. The authors discuss in detail the western migration, problems associated with the frontier, and the settling of western lands. The book includes numerous maps of early trails and roads used by pioneers.

- Dollarhide, William. *Map Guide to American Migration Routes, 1735–1815*. Bountiful, Utah: American Genealogical Lending Library, 1997. This overview was written specifically for genealogists and includes thirteen maps showing various early roads (including the illustration in figure 3-4).

- *The Handy Book for Genealogists: United States of America*. 8th ed. Logan, Utah: Everton Publishers, 1991. This book contains eight maps showing early migration trails and roads in color.

- Ladd, Richard S., comp. *Maps Showing Explorers' Routes, Trails and Early Roads in the United States: An Anno-*

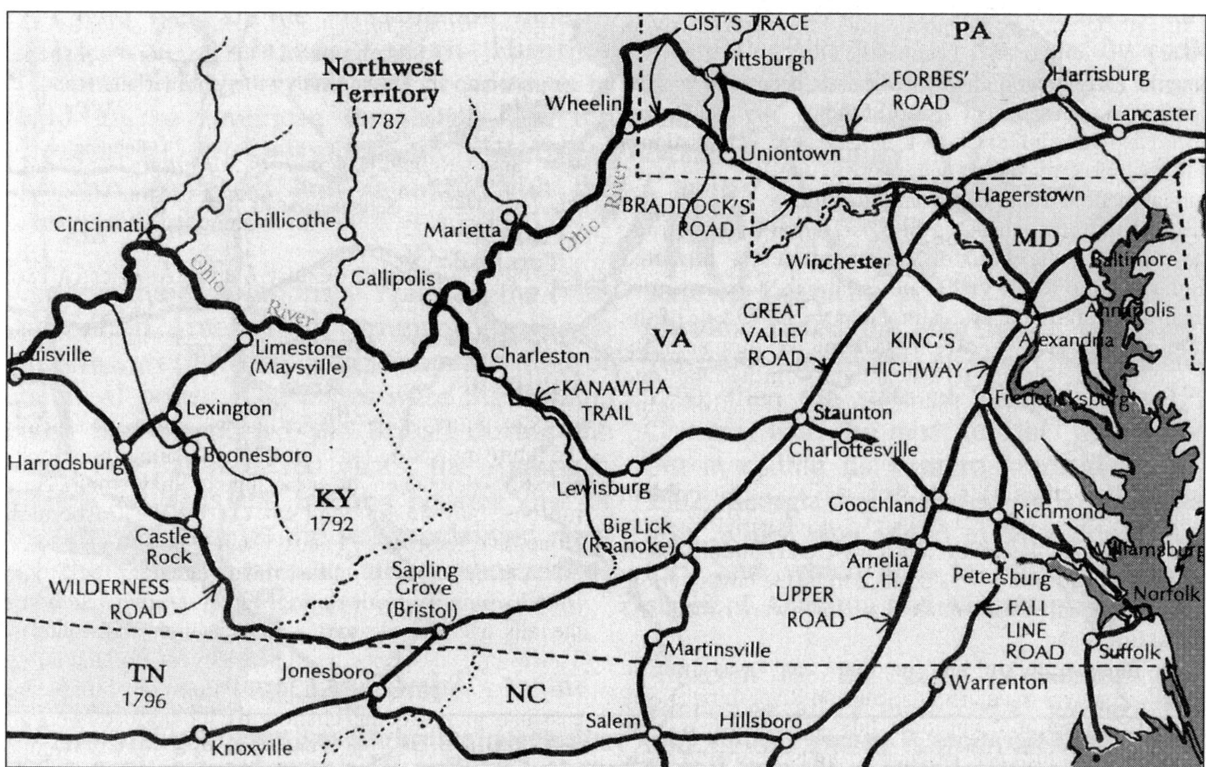

Figure 3-4. "The Way West, 1775–1795," from William Dollarhide's *Map Guide to American Migration Routes, 1735-1815* (Bountiful, Utah: American Genealogical Lending Library, 1997).

tated List. Washington, D.C.: Library of Congress, 1962. The annotated bibliography lists three hundred selected maps from the holdings of the Library of Congress.

- Lewis, Marcus W. *The Development of Early Emigrant Trails in the United States East of the Mississippi River.* Washington, D.C.: National Genealogical Society, 1972. An included map shows fifty-four trails.

- *Map of the Conterminous United States Showing Routes of the Principal Explorers from 1501 to 1844 Whose Work Had an Important Bearing on the Settlement of the Country and the Fixing of Its Successive Boundaries;* also known as the "U.S. Explorer's Map—USA." This map, which was produced by the U.S. Geological Survey, is based on a map prepared in 1907 by Frank Bond of the General Land Office.

- Mason, Philip P. *A History of American Roads*. Chicago: Rand McNally & Co., 1967. This publication describes the condition of colonial roads and the development of roads during the nineteenth and early twentieth centuries. Maps of Indian trails east of the Mississippi and colonial and early American roads are included.

- Sale, Randall D., and Edwin D. Karn. *American Expansion: A Book of Maps*. Lincoln: University of Nebraska Press, Bison Book, 1979. This book contains a fine set of maps showing the development of the United States from 1790 through 1900. There is a map for each decade, and each map is accompanied by a discussion of the important events that occurred during that time period.

- Waldman, Carl. *Atlas of the North American Indian*. New York: Facts on File, 1985. A section titled "Indian Trails and White Inroads" describes twenty trails and roads.

- See "Nineteenth-Century Maps—American History Atlases," below.

Canals and Waterways

The construction of modern canals began in Europe after the lock was developed in the fifteenth century. The lock was a chamber in which the water level could be raised or lowered as needed to transfer boats and barges between connecting waterways (*Encyclopedia Americana* 1956, 483). Before the American Revolution, canals were nonexistent in the American colonies. Towns and cities located on the coast or on navigable rivers were flourishing, but colonial trade to inland towns and villages suffered because of the lack of good roads to transport goods inexpensively.

Because of the miserable condition of the roads and trails, some of which passed through hostile Indian country, many early pioneers turned to the waterways to travel westward. Philip P. Mason states that

> during most of the eighteenth century it was cheaper, by at least half, to ship goods across the Atlantic from Philadelphia to Europe than to transport the same products 75 miles by land. Pittsburgh merchants found it less costly to transport goods several thousand miles by ship—via the Ohio and Mississippi rivers to New Orleans and then to Philadelphia—than to move the same products overland for 60 miles. It is not surprising that the water routes were preferred (1967, 15).

In Pittsburgh, the Allegheny and Monongahela rivers united at their confluence to become the Ohio River. This river became the early great highway to the west because it was the only major river in the eastern part of the country that flowed westward and downhill to Cairo, Illinois, where it emptied into the Mississippi River. Travel was one way until 1811, when a steamboat made a round trip from Pittsburgh to New Orleans and back. With the opening of the Mississippi River to trade and the lands to the west for settlement, people migrated through the Ohio River Valley and established many settlements in Ohio, Indiana, and Illinois on the north side of the river, and in Kentucky and Tennessee on the south side. By 1825 there were seventy-five steamboats on the Ohio and Mississippi rivers, and by 1840 there were 187 (Billington and Ridge 1982, 330).

A few canals were constructed in the 1790s, but most were only two or three miles in length. There was a need for a system to transport trade goods and people from the eastern seaport regions to and from the undeveloped west, and building canals that connected waterways was deemed to be the best solution. Charters for the building of numerous canals were issued, and the Canal Era began.

The most successful and important canal was the Erie Canal. The goal was to connect the Hudson River to Lake Erie by water. Construction began on 4 July 1817 at Rome, New York, and by 1823 the canal extended from Rochester to Little Falls, a distance of 180 miles. When completed and opened to transportation on 26 October 1825, the canal was 363 miles in length, forty feet wide, and four feet deep. There were seventy-seven locks, each ninety feet by fifteen feet.[1] Old communities along the canal's path flourished and new settlements were established. Building the canal provided employment for an estimated five thousand men, most of whom were immigrants from Ireland and Germany.

Harry Sinclair Drago stated, "by the late 1820s nine hundred people were arriving daily at Buffalo bound for the West" (1972, 210). From there they could travel on lake steamers to the country around Lake Erie and Lake Michigan. The Erie Canal immediately became the most important route to the west, and it was one of the few canals that were profitable. When the Erie Canal was completed, there were no railroads in the United States.

Upon completion of the Erie Canal in 1825, the opening of the Chicago Road in 1832, and the Territorial Road to St. Joseph, Michigan, in 1834, thousands of pioneers from New England and the middle states moved into southern Michigan, northern Indiana, and northern and central Illinois. By 1840 most Indian tribes had been removed to lands west of the Missouri River, making it possible for newcomers to move into Wisconsin and Iowa territories in their quest for cheap land. In the 1840s streams of emigrants from Europe, particularly Germans, settled in Illinois and Wisconsin. By 1850, 640,000 foreign-born immigrants lived in the Lake Plains area (Billington and Ridge 1982, 306). Between 1790 and 1850, 4,400 miles of hand-dug artificial waterways were built (Drago 1972, 7).

Key Sources—Canal Maps

- Billington, Ray Allen, and Martin Ridge. *Westward Expansion: A History of the American Frontier*. 5th ed. New York: Macmillan Publishing Co., 1982. Small maps show early western transportation routes, including canals.
- *The Handy Book for Genealogists: United States of America*. 8th ed. Logan, Utah: Everton Publishers, 1991. A map shows canals and the Cumberland Road, 1785 to 1850.
- Shaw, Ronald E. *Canals for a Nation: The Canal Era in the United States, 1790–1860*. Lexington: University Press of Kentucky, 1990. A map shows canals built by 1860.
- See "Nineteenth-Century Maps—American History Atlases," below.

Railroads

In 1829, a little-noticed event that would soon drastically alter the future transportation of people and commodities took place. Horatio Allen, an engineer, arranged to have four steam locomotives built in England for use by the Carbondale and Honesdale Railroad in Pennsylvania. On 8 August 1829, with Allen at the controls and a crowd watching, the Stourbridge Lion locomotive made its trial run at ten miles an hour down the rails, over a trestle one hundred feet high, and around a curve. This event is described by Rupert Sargent Holland in his book *Historic Railroads* (1927, 134-35). From this humble but successful beginning, other charters to build railroads were granted, and construction began. In 1830 there were only twenty-three miles of railroad in operation. On 15 January 1831, the first passenger train in the United States that was pulled by a locomotive made a run between Charleston and Hamburg, South Carolina. By 1836 there were 1,098 miles of railroad, most of which were in the seacoast states. Mileage was 9,021 in 1850, 30,055 by 1860, 52,922 by 1870, and 74,096 by 1875 (*Encyclopedia Americana* 1956, 410). The extensive railroad system in the North played an important part in the Union's winning the Civil War because it aided greatly in the transport of troops and equipment to and from the battlefields.

Most early railroads were individual segments that were not joined. They connected waterways, the seacoast, and the interior river system. By the late 1830s new technology had improved the steam engine and lowered the cost of building railroads. Because railroads could be built over rough terrain, they joined different market areas that were not dependent on waterways. By 1841 a railroad ran between Boston and Albany. High priority was given to building railroads from east to west, and by 1842 Albany was connected by rail to Buffalo. A line running through southern New York connected Pierpont on the Hudson to Lake Erie in 1851. Also in 1851, Albany and New York were connected by rail, making it possible to travel from New York by way of Albany to Lake Erie. Other lines ran between Philadelphia and Pittsburgh (1852) and Baltimore and Wheeling (1853) (Billington and Ridge 1982, 341). Transportation by rail was cheaper and more efficient than by canal barges or steamboats. Because canals could not compete economically with the flourishing railroads, the canal era came to a close.

As railroads extended farther west, pioneers traveled by trains to the newly opened lands. In 1856 a line was opened between Chicago and the Mississippi River. In the same year the Illinois Central completed a line from Galena down through the center of the state to Cairo and a branch line from Centralia to Chicago. The total distance was 705 miles; it was the longest railroad in the United States at the time. An average of seven thousand and sometimes as many as ten thousand Irish and

German immigrants were employed in its construction (Holbrook 1947, 103).

Railroads preceded the settlement of the country in the west. They linked isolated cities and towns and brought about the establishment of new towns. Industries appeared along the routes and pioneers settled on neighboring lands. On 10 May 1869 the Central Pacific and Union Pacific railroads joined at Promontory Summit, Utah, forming the first transcontinental railroad.

Key Sources—Railroad Maps

- Billington, Ray Allen, and Martin Ridge. *Westward Expansion: A History of the American Frontier*. 5th ed. New York: Macmillan Publishing Co., 1982. Small maps show early western transportation routes, including railroads.

- *Cram's Standard American Railway System Atlas of the World: Accompanied by a Complete and Simple Index of the United States Showing the True Location of All Railroads, Towns, Villages and Post Offices. . . .* Chicago: George F. Cram, 1895 (FHL microfilm no. 1421836, item 2).

- *The Handy Book for Genealogists: United States of America*. 8th ed. Logan, Utah: Everton Publishers, 1991. A map shows railroads built by 1860.

- McLaughlin, Patrick D., comp. *Transportation in Nineteenth-Century America: A Survey of the Cartographic Records in the National Archives of the United States.* Reference Information Paper no. 65. Washington, D.C.: National Archives and Records Service, 1973. The development of the transportation network in nineteenth-century America is documented in this survey of nine series of maps.

- Modelski, Andrew M., comp. *Railroad Maps of North America: The First Hundred Years*. Washington, D.C.: Library of Congress, 1984. This book traces the history of railroad mapping and includes ninety-two maps.

- ______. *Railroad Maps of the United States: A Selective Annotated Bibliography of Original 19th-Century Maps in the Geography and Map Division of the Library of Congress*. Washington, D.C.: Library of Congress, 1975 (FHL microfilm no. 1036024, item 6). This book includes thorough descriptions of 622 railroad maps chosen from the several thousand in the library's collection. It includes maps of five major geographical regions, maps of states (at least one for each state), and maps of individual railroads.

- See "Nineteenth-Century Maps—American History Atlases," below.

Political Maps

Political maps portray subdivisions imposed on areas by people (for example, territorial, state, county, township, city, and ward maps). The original territory of the United States was bounded on the north by Canada, on the south by the Spanish colonies of East and West Florida, and on the west by the Mississippi River. It included the thirteen original colonies and the areas claimed by them. The contested areas were ceded to the Federal government between 1781 and 1802; the Federal government held title to the new unappropriated lands and was responsible for administering the laws and ordinances relating to them. Later additions to the public domain included the Louisiana purchase in 1803, the Floridas in 1819, Oregon Territory in 1846, the Mexican cession in 1848, and the Gadsden Purchase from Mexico in 1853. Texas was allowed to hold title to its vacant unappropriated lands when it was annexed to the Union in 1845.

The objective of this chapter is to discuss maps and atlases that have been published since the founding of the Federal government. There are, however, some important maps and atlases in the National Archives that depict the colonial period and the revolutionary war. They are described in a list compiled by Patrick D. McLaughlin titled *Pre-Federal Maps in the National Archives: An Annotated List,* Special List no. 26 (Washington, D.C.: National Archives and Records Service, 1971).

Territorial Maps. On 13 July 1787 an important piece of legislation, the Ordinance of 1787 (the Northwest Ordinance), was enacted. It created the "Territory North West of the Ohio," or the Northwest Territory. Among provisions of the ordinance, it assured settlers of the right of self-government in the new frontier, and it established the procedures under which a new territory could obtain statehood.

In 1800 the Northwest Territory was divided into two parts: Indiana and Ohio territories. More than 250,000 people had settled in Ohio by 1812, so newcomers pressed westward into Indiana Territory. The Northwest Territory was divided further to create Michigan Territory in 1805 and Illinois Territory in 1809. Other early territories were Mississippi (1798) and Missouri (1812). As settlers moved west, there was a great need for maps of territories, states, and counties.

Key Sources—Territorial Maps

- *AniMap Plus County Boundary Historical Atlas*. The Gold Bug (Alamo, California). This CD-ROM not only shows the changing county boundaries for each of the forty-eight adjacent United States for all years since colonial times; it also includes maps showing state and territorial boundaries from the thirteen colonies to the present state boundaries.

- Hargett, Janet L., comp. *List of Selected Maps of States and Territories*. Special List no. 29. Washington, D.C.: National Archives and Records Service, 1971. This list describes approximately nine hundred maps in the archives of the following states and territories: Alaska, Arizona, Colorado, Hawaii, Idaho, Illinois, Indiana, Iowa, Kansas, Michigan, Minnesota, Mississippi, Missouri, Montana, Nebraska, Nevada, New Mexico, Oklahoma (including Indian Territory in the states of Oklahoma, Kansas, Nebraska, and Iowa), Oregon, Utah, Washington, Wisconsin, and Wyoming.

- *United States of America Showing the Extent of Public Land Surveys, Remaining Public Land, Historical Boundaries, National Forests, Indian Reservations, Wildlife Refuges, National Parks and Monuments.* Washington, D.C., U.S. Geological Survey, 1978. Referred to as the "Territories Map," it shows not only the acquisitions of the territories and historical boundaries, but also modern state boundaries.

- Van Zandt, Franklin K. *Boundaries of the United States and the Several States.* Washington, D.C.: U.S. Geological Survey, 1976. This book discusses the development of the public domain, land disputes between states, and changes in the national boundaries as a result of treaties. There are numerous maps showing boundary lines in various time periods (figure 3-5).

State and Regional Maps. With the foundation of the Federal government, accurate maps of states and regions were needed. The early colonies had ceded lands to the government, and disputed boundaries between states were ultimately settled. Newly formed states were carved out of territories as settlers petitioned for statehood. Commercial firms were involved early in the surveying and preparing of maps at the state and county levels, but they could not meet the demand. As a result, many states passed legislation for preparing maps based on county surveys. As early as 1816, Pennsylvania and Virginia encouraged county map preparation.

A typical state road map shows the locations of hundreds of towns and cities, although small town names are sometimes omitted from densely populated areas. The state capitol, county seats, and towns are represented by various symbols that also indicate population range (for example, five thousand to fifty thousand); county boundaries are defined as well. Additionally, the map will show the routes from one place to another, the distances between those places, and the relative conditions of roads. Physical features portrayed on such maps include hills, flatlands, and prominent mountain peaks; rivers, streams, canals, lakes, and reservoirs; and national forests, parks, and monuments.

Many state and regional maps have been designed for businesses to use in sales and marketing. These commercial atlases are collections of maps portraying the locations and commercial statistics of towns, cities, and metropolitan areas. The best known and most readily available commercial atlas is the annual *Rand McNally Commercial Atlas and Marketing Guide* (Chicago: Rand McNally & Co., 1936–). This atlas, which is the oldest continuously published atlas in the United States, provides a wealth of detailed economic and demographic information for approximately 128,000 populated places in the United States. Listings are by state. It is the most detailed, current resource for single-volume coverage of populated places nationwide.

Key Sources—State and Regional Maps

- Cobb, David A., and Peter B. Ives. *State Atlases: An Annotated Bibliography.* Chicago: CPL Bibliographies, 1983.

- Gerlach, Arch C., ed. *National Atlas of the United States of America.* Washington, D.C.: U.S. Geological Survey, 1970. This atlas contains 765 maps and charts on 335 pages.

- *Hardesty's Historical and Geographical Encyclopedia....* New York: H. H. Hardesty, 1884 (FHL microfilm no. 0928565, item 1; FHL microfiche nos. 6015282–6015287). This atlas contains maps of the United States and of the provinces of Canada, as well as Bible geography. There is a history of the United States and of each state and territory. Included is a history of the Declaration of Independence with biographical sketches of the signers. There is also biographical information about the presidents of the United States.

- Hargett, Janet L., comp. *List of Selected Maps of States and Territories.* Special List no. 29. Washington, D.C.: National Archives and Records Service, 1971. This describes approximately nine hundred state maps dating from the late eighteenth century to 1920 that are in the National Archives.

- Karrow, Robert W., Jr., ed. *Checklist of Printed Maps of the Middle West to 1900.* 14 vols. in 12. Boston: G. K. Hall, 1981–83. The list describes 25,478 entries found in 127 different collections that include maps of cities and towns, panorama maps, fire insurance maps, and maps in government documents. The list includes all known landownership books for Illinois, Indiana, Iowa, Kansas, Michigan, Missouri, Nebraska, North Dakota, Ohio, South Dakota, and Wisconsin.

- LeGear, Clara Egli, comp. *A List of Geographical Atlases in the Library of Congress.* Vols. 5–9. Washington, D.C.: Library of Congress, 1958–92. Philip Lee Phillips compiled vols. 1 through 4.

- ______. *United States Atlases: A List of National, State, County, City, and Regional Atlases in the Library of Congress.* Washington, D.C.: Library of Congress, 1950. Reprint. New York: Arno Press, 1971 (FHL microfilm no. 0980547). There are more than 3,500 bibliographical entries covering the period from 1776 to 1950. Many of the county atlases and plat books show land ownership. The pre-1920 atlases in Philip Lee Phillips's list are not included.

- *Maps of an Emerging Nation: The United States of America 1775–1987.* Washington, D.C.: U.S. Geological Survey, 1987. On the front is a map showing the United States in 1783. On the reverse are fourteen maps showing the growth of the nation.

- *The National Atlas.* Philadelphia, 1885. This atlas contains elaborate topographic maps of the United States and the Dominion of Canada with plans of cities and general maps of the world (FHL microfilm no. 0940936, item 1).

- Phillips, Philip Lee, comp. *A List of Geographical Atlases in the Library of Congress.* Vols. 1–4. Washington, D.C.: Library of Congress, 1909–20. Clara Egli LeGear compiled vols. 5 through 9.

- *Rand McNally Commercial Atlas and Marketing Guide.* Chicago: Rand McNally & Co., 1936–. Annual.

- *Rand McNally's Pioneer Atlas of the American West.* Chicago, Rand McNally & Co., 1969. This atlas contains facsimile reproductions of maps and indexes from the 1876 first edition of *Rand, McNally and Company's Business Atlas of the Great Mississippi Valley and Pacific Slope* (Chicago: Rand McNally & Co., 1876). It includes contemporary railroad maps and travel literature.

- Wheat, Carl I. *Mapping the Transmississippi West, 1540–1861.* 5 vols. San Francisco: Institute of Historical Cartography, 1957–63. The repository for each map mentioned in the text is listed.
- See the state-by-state listings in the chapter bibliography.

County Maps. County maps vary from one state to another, but usually they include city and town boundaries and all roads (from paved to primitive types). They usually include locations of cemeteries and physical features similar to those shown on state road maps. Depending on the size of the county, there may be more than one sheet per county.

The beginning family researcher quickly discovers that many important records were recorded at county courthouses. County boundaries changed throughout the nineteenth century as large parent counties were subdivided into smaller counties, and the boundaries of new counties sometimes changed again. It is necessary to study the history of a county in order to determine where a particular record might be found today. Fortunately, several excellent atlases that show the evolving boundary changes have been published.

A project titled *Atlas of Historical County Boundaries* (New York: Charles Scribner's Sons, 1993–), edited by John H. Long of the Newberry Library in Chicago, will be of great value to the family researcher when it is completed. It will simplify research at the county level by detailing the historical evolution of more than three thousand U.S. counties (figure 3-6). Every state that has a county boundary system will be included. The atlases that have been published are listed by state in the chapter bibliography.

Key Sources—County Maps

- *AniMap Plus County Boundary Historical Atlas.* The Gold Bug (Alamo, California). More than two thousand color maps on this CD-ROM show the changing county boundaries for each of the forty-eight adjacent United States for all years since colonial times. It also includes maps showing state and territorial boundaries from the thirteen colonies to the present state boundaries.

INDIANA

By the act approved May 7, 1800, to take effect on and after July 4 of that year, the "Territory northwest of the River Ohio" was divided into two parts, the eastern part to retain the old name, the western part to become the Territory of Indiana. (See fig. 26.) The description of the boundary line between these two Territories is given in the act (2 Stat. L. 58) as follows:

That from and after the fourth day of July next, all that part of the territory of the United States northwest of the Ohio River, which lies to the westward of a line beginning at the Ohio, opposite to the mouth of Kentucky river, and running thence to Fort Recovery, and thence

FIGURE 26.—Historical diagram of Indiana.

Figure 3-5. From a source containing territorial maps, Van Zandt's *Boundaries of the United States and the Several States.*

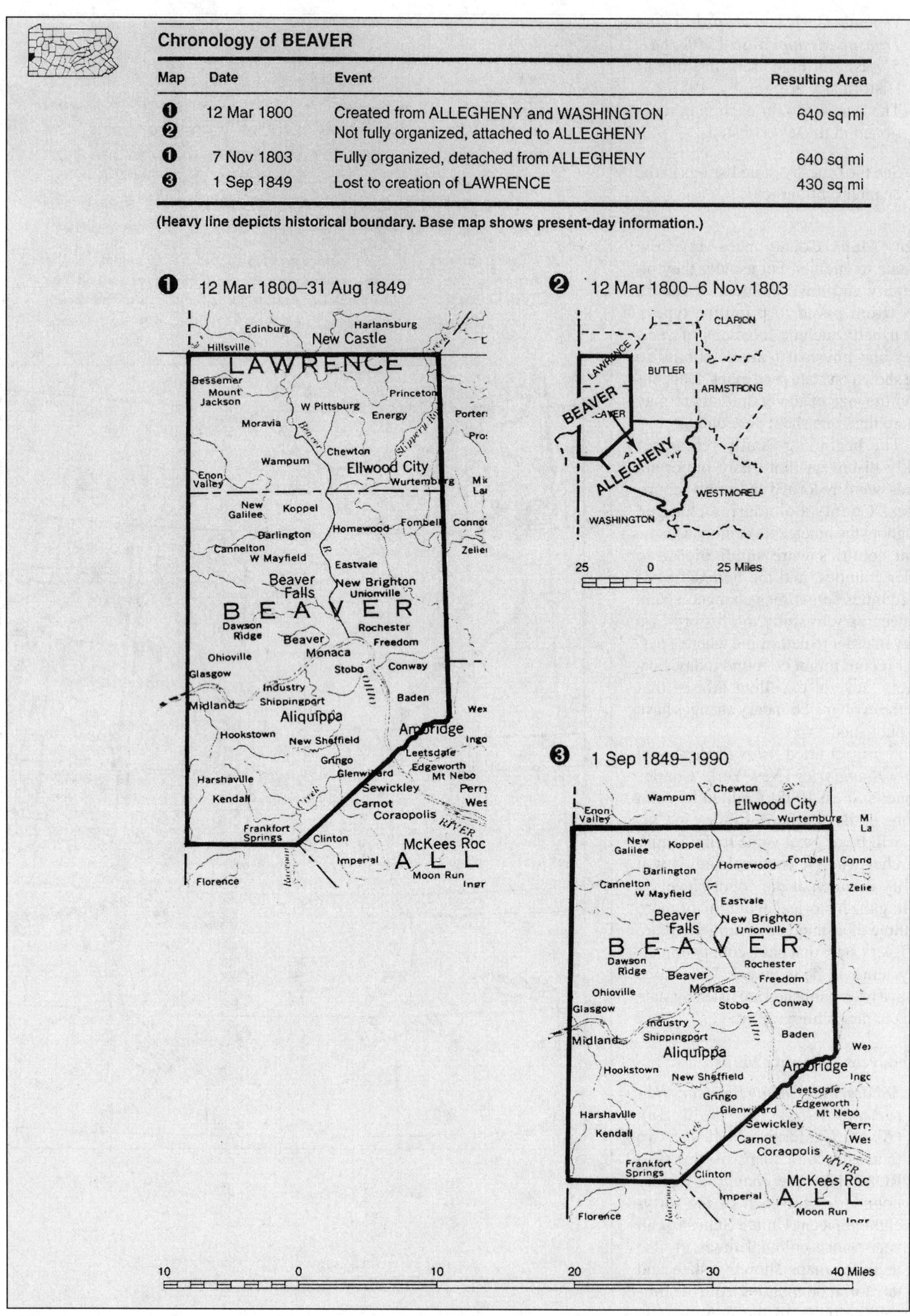

Chronology of BEAVER

Map	Date	Event	Resulting Area
❶	12 Mar 1800	Created from ALLEGHENY and WASHINGTON	640 sq mi
❷		Not fully organized, attached to ALLEGHENY	
❶	7 Nov 1803	Fully organized, detached from ALLEGHENY	640 sq mi
❸	1 Sep 1849	Lost to creation of LAWRENCE	430 sq mi

(Heavy line depicts historical boundary. Base map shows present-day information.)

Figure 3-6. Long's *Atlas of Historical County Boundaries* is a source of county maps. It will be of great value to the family researcher when it is completed, simplifying research at the county level by detailing the historical evolution of more than three thousand U.S. counties. The above is from *Pennsylvania* (page 23).

- Eichholz, Alice, ed. *Ancestry's Red Book: American State, County and Town Sources*. Rev. ed. Salt Lake City, Utah: Ancestry, 1992. For each state the book includes county outline maps, a list of counties, the date each county was created, and the parent county or territory from which it was organized. The book includes a brief history and a guide to record sources for each state.

- *Encyclopedia of U.S. Counties*. GenRef (Orem, Utah). This CD-ROM contains the organization date, progeny, and parent county information for each U.S. county.

- *The Handy Book for Genealogists: United States of America*. 8th ed. Logan, Utah: Everton Publishers, 1991. For each state this book includes county outline maps, a list of counties, the date each county was created, and the parent county or territory from which it was organized. The book includes a guide to record sources for each state.

- Kane, Joseph Nathan. *The American Counties: Origins of County Names, Dates of Creation and Organization, Area, Population Including 1980 Census Figures, Historical Data, and Published Sources*. 4th ed. Metuchen, N.J.: Scarecrow Press, 1983.

- Long, John H., ed. *Historical Atlas and Chronology of County Boundaries, 1788–1980*. 5 vols. Boston: G. K. Hall, 1984 (FHL microfiche no. 6051426, vol. 1 [3 microfiche]; 6051427, vol. 2 [6 microfiche]; 6051428, vol. 3 [1 microfiche]; 6051429, vol. 4 [5 microfiche]; 6051430, vol. 5 [6 microfiche]). This is an earlier and less comprehensive edition of the *Atlas of Historical County Boundaries* (described above).

- Rabenhorst, Thomas D., ed. *Historical U.S. County Outline Map Collection 1840–1980*. Baltimore: Department of Geography, University of Maryland, 1984.

- Thorndale, William, and William Dollarhide. *Map Guide to the U.S. Federal Censuses, 1790–1920*. Baltimore: Genealogical Publishing Company, 1987. This guide is devoted entirely to political maps portraying the status of county formation in the states at the time of each of the decennial U.S. censuses. On each of the nearly four hundred maps, the old county lines are superimposed over the modern ones to highlight the boundary changes at ten-year intervals. The index lists modern and defunct counties, along with a locality code for finding each county on state maps. Other information includes notes about the census, a state-by-state bibliography of sources, and a discussion of census accuracy.

- See state-by-state listings in the chapter bibliography.

Township Maps. New England counties are divided into minor political subdivisions called *towns;* derived from the word *township,* town refers to a subsection of a county rather than to a specific village, hamlet, or city. In the public domain states, a township is a survey unit approximately six miles square.

Key Source—Township Maps

- Andriot, Jay, comp. *Township Atlas of the United States*. McLean, Va.: Documents Index, 1991. This atlas contains maps of and indexes to the minor county subdivisions of the forty-eight conterminous states (the states enclosed within one common boundary). Maps of public domain states show the individual townships resulting from the Public Land Survey. County maps show the census county divisions and/or the minor civil divisions. A complete index identifies all subdivisions, followed by the county and state in which each subdivision is located.

  Earlier editions of the above atlas were published in 1977, 1979 (FHL microfilm no. 1597808, item 2), and 1987 (FHL microfiche no. 6049121).

City and Ward Maps. City maps usually show street names (with a street-name index), cemeteries, country clubs, golf courses, colleges and universities, and much more. Street and site names have changed over the years and new roads have been built, so it may be necessary to study an old city map to reconcile the differences. In the nineteenth century, the most detailed city maps were produced by the Sanborn Map Company (see "Fire Insurance Maps," below).

Most large cities are divided into wards, which are political units for representative, electoral, or administrative purposes. Ward boundaries changed frequently over the years as cities grew. Because census-taking in larger cities usually was organized by ward, the family researcher can identify the ward in which a particular street address was located for a specific census year by consulting a ward map (figure 3-7).

Key Sources—City and Ward Maps

- *Early Maps of Some of the Cities of the United States, ca. 1850–1877*. Two rolls of microfilms are available for searching at the Family History Library or family history centers. See "United States—Maps" in the *Family History Library Catalog* for a list of cities and the years for which maps are available and to obtain the microfilm numbers.

- Kirkham, E. Kay. *A Handy Guide to Record Searching in the Larger Cities of the United States: Including a Guide to Their Vital Records and Some Maps with Street Indexes with Other Information of Genealogical Value*. Logan, Utah: Everton Publishers, 1974. The book contains thirty-eight maps with ward boundaries and street indexes.

- Rhoads, James B., and Charlotte M. Ashby. *Preliminary Inventory of the Cartographic Records of the Bureau of the Census*. Preliminary Inventory no. 103. Washington, D.C.: National Archives and Records Service, 1958. These records include census enumeration district maps (1880 to 1940) and descriptions (1850 to 1940).

- Shelley, Michael H., comp. *Ward Maps of United States Cities: A Selective Checklist of Pre-1900 Maps in the Library of Congress*. Washington, D.C.: Library of Congress, 1975. These maps show the development of city wards in thirty-five cities between 1790 and 1899. Based on the 1880 Federal census, twenty-five of the cities had the largest populations, and the other ten cities were included because they also are frequently studied by researchers and family historians. Reproductions of the 232 maps described in this publication are available on 320 microfiche at the

Albany, New York 1866

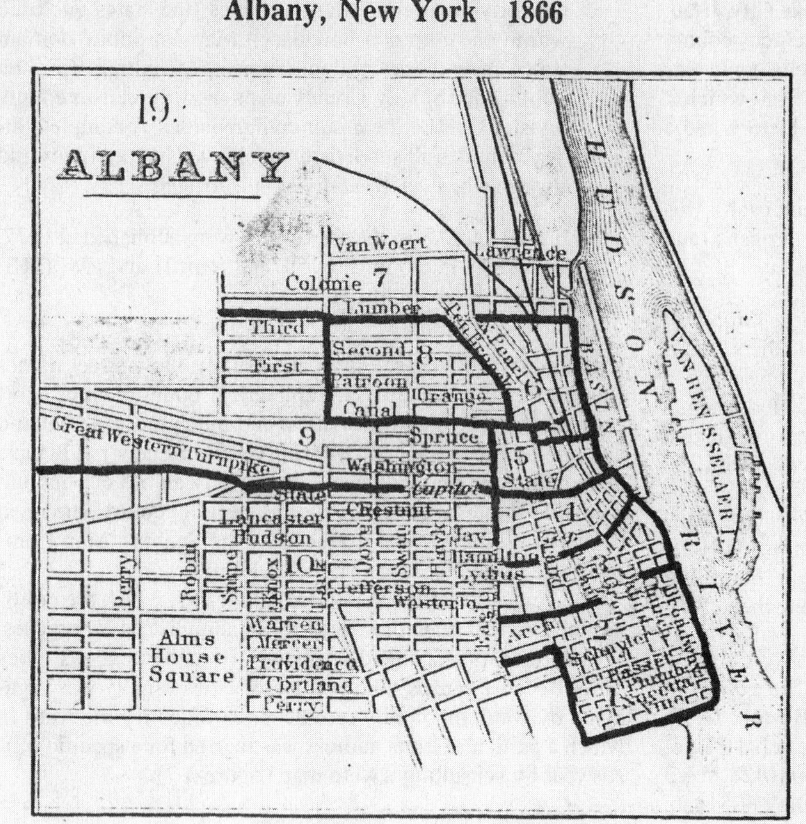

Albany, New York 1878

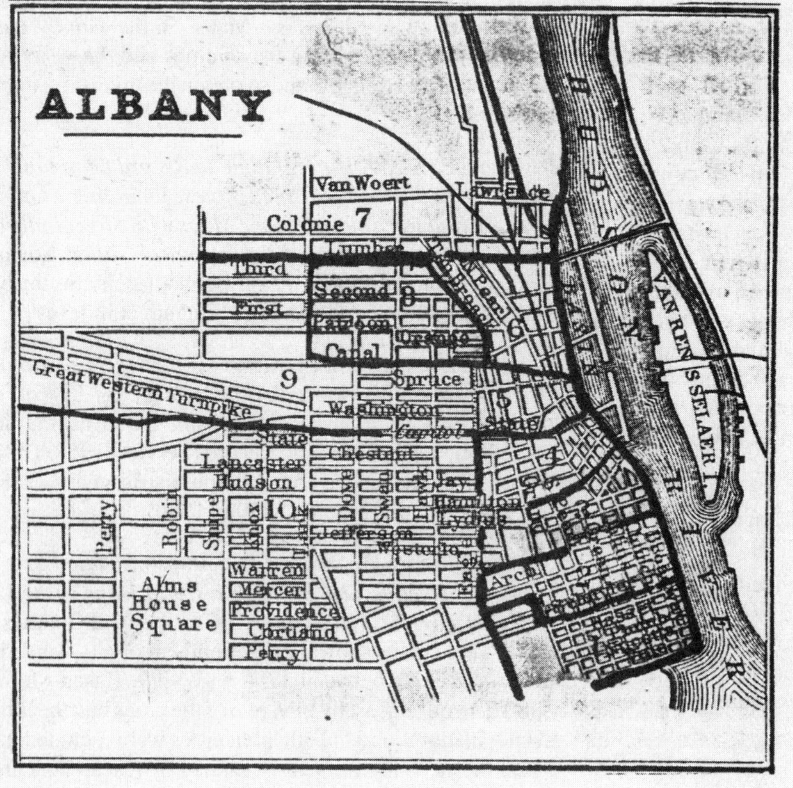

Figure 3-7. City maps from Kirkham's *A Handy Guide to Record Searching in the Larger Cities of the United States.*

Family History Library; unfortunately, the microfiche cannot be circulated to family history centers. For further information, see "United States—Maps" in the *Family History Library Catalog.*

Nineteenth-Century Maps

American History Atlases. These atlases usually contain maps and text that cover topics like exploration, the colonial era, the forming of the new nation, early transportation routes (trails, early roads, canals, and railroads), acquisitions of western lands, wars, and economic growth (figure 3-8).

Key Sources—American History Atlases

- Adams, James Truslow, ed. *Atlas of American History.* New York: Charles Scribner's Sons, 1943 (FHL microfilm no. 1415259, item 9). 2nd rev. ed. Edited by Kenneth T. Jackson. New York: Charles Scribner's Sons, 1984. This atlas contains maps portraying the changing face of the North American continent over the past four hundred years. A revised edition is listed below under Kenneth Jackson.

- *American Heritage Pictorial Atlas of United States History.* New York: American Heritage Publishing Co., 1966.

- *American History Atlas.* Parsons Technology (Hiawatha, Iowa). This 3 1/2-inch diskette contains more than 1,200 articles that describe the historical significance of each person, place, and event that shaped American history from 1492 to 1870. There are more than eighty detailed, full-color maps; longitude and latitude are displayed at the bottom of the screen. The atlas also includes the text of dozens of historical documents.

- *American History Explorer.* Parsons Technology (Hiawatha, Iowa). This CD-ROM contains an interactive sight-and sound guide to American history from A.D. 1000 through Reconstruction following the Civil War. In addition to timelines, there are ninety-three interactive maps that show where historical events happened.

- *Atlas of Early American History: The Revolutionary Era.* Princeton, N.J.: Princeton University Press, 1976.

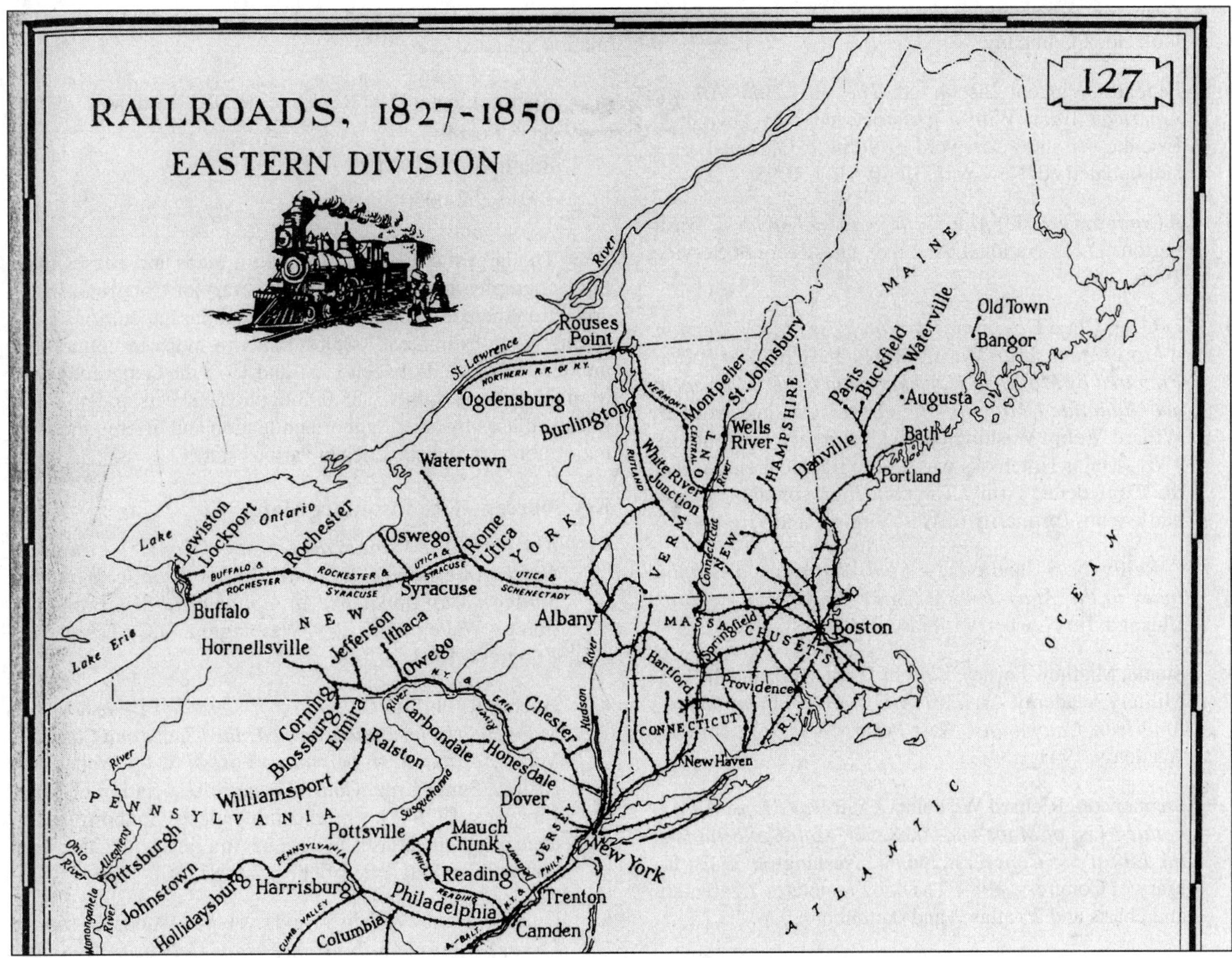

Figure 3-8. Portion of a map showing railroad routes from Jackson's *Atlas of American History.*

- Ferrell, Robert H., and Richard Natkiel. *Atlas of American History*. New York: Facts on File Publications, 1987.

- Gilbert, Martin. *The Dent Atlas of American History*. 3rd ed. London: JM Dent Ltd., 1993.

- Jackson, Kenneth. *Atlas of American History.* 2nd rev. ed. New York: Charles Scribner's Sons, 1984. A revision if the publisher's 1943 atlas.

- Jackson, Richard H., ed. *Historical and Genealogical Atlas of the United States*. Vol. 1. Provo, Utah: Gentech Press, 1974 (FHL microfilm no. 0908951, item 2). Vol. 1 covers the area east of the Mississippi.

- Kirkham, E. Kay. *A Genealogical and Historical Atlas of the U.S.A.* Logan, Utah: Everton Publishers, 1976. This atlas contains brief histories of the states and territories and is illustrated with contemporary maps.

- Morse, Sidney Edwards. *An Atlas of the United States on an Improved Plan Consisting of Ten Maps with a Complete Index to Each and a General Map of the Whole Country.* New Haven: W. & S. S. Jocelyn, 1823 (FHL microfilm no. 0002083, item 5).

- Schwartz, Seymour I., and Ralph E. Ehrenberg. *The Mapping of America*. New York: Harry N. Abrams, 1980. This book contains 223 map reproductions that document the history of American cartography. Part 1, by Seymour I. Schwartz, covers the years 1500 to 1800. Part 2, by Ralph E. Ehrenberg, covers the years 1800 to 1975.

- Woodard, Nell Sachse. *A Birdseye Atlas of American History*. Oceanside, Calif.: the author, 1982. This atlas illustrates the growth of the United States from 1612 to 1860.

Civil War Maps. The Civil War was fought between 12 April 1861 and 26 May 1865. It involved approximately 1,500,000 Union soldiers and 1,000,000 Confederate soldiers—approximately 7 percent of the population (one of every fourteen persons) (Schweitzer 1996, 3). Maps of the war show the locations of fortifications, major transportation routes, and sometimes the positions of the troops. Major collections of maps are in the Library of Congress and the National Archives.

Key Sources—Civil War Maps

- Cowles, Calvin D. *The Official Military Atlas of the Civil War.* Washington, D.C.: Government Printing Office, 1891. Reprint, with an Introduction by Richard Sommers.

Gramercy Books: Avenel, N.J., 1983. Distributed by Outlook Book Company.

- Esposito, Vincent Joseph, ed. *The West Point Atlas of American Wars*. With a prefatory letter by Dwight D. Eisenhower and a foreword by John R. Galvin. 1st rev. and updated ed. New York: Henry Holt, 1995.
- *A Guide to Civil War Maps in the National Archives*. Washington, D.C.: National Archives and Records Service, 1986.
- LeGear, Clara E., comp. *The Hotchkiss Map Collection: A List of Manuscript Maps, Many of the Civil War Period, Prepared by Maj. Jed. Hotchkiss, and Other Manuscript and Annotated Maps in His Possession*. Foreword by Willard Webb. Washington, D.C.: Library of Congress, 1951. Major Hotchkiss was a topographical engineer in the Confederate Army. The collection contains detailed battle maps (primarily of West Virginia and Virginia).
- O'Reilly, N. S., and others. *Civil War Maps, a Graphic Index to the Atlas to Accompany the Official Records*. Chicago, Ill: Newberry Library, 1987.
- Steele, Matthew Forney, Vincent J. Esposito, and the U.S. Military Academy. *Civil War Atlas to Accompany Steele's American Campaigns*. West Point, N.Y.: U.S. Military Academy, 1941.
- Stephenson, Richard W., comp. *Civil War Maps: An Annotated List of Maps and Atlases in Map Collections of the Library of Congress*. 2nd ed. Washington, D.C.: Library of Congress, 1989. The book annotates 2,240 maps and charts and 76 atlases and sketchbooks.

Fire Insurance Maps. Fire insurance maps and plans originated in London toward the end of the eighteenth century in response to the need of large fire insurance companies and underwriters for accurate and detailed information about the buildings they were insuring. In the United States only a limited number of these maps were produced in the early nineteenth century, but the industry began to boom following the Civil War. Although several surveyors and map publishers prepared fire insurance maps and atlases, most went out of business or were absorbed by the Sanborn Map Co., which was established in 1867.

By the mid-1950s Sanborn had mapped most of the communities in the United States with a population of 2,500 or more. Sanborn's archives contain almost 1 million highly detailed maps of thirteen thousand cities and towns in the United States, Canada, and Mexico; they cover the period from 1867 to the present. The maps show businesses, street names, addresses, water mains, fire hydrants, and other details. Every structure is colored to indicate construction materials. The older maps and atlases provide a historical record of urban growth for more than a century, and family historians will find the detailed data useful in documenting urban ancestors. The company continues to update its maps and atlases.

Sanborn will search its archives for a specific map for a fee (specific site information, such as a street address and the approximate time period desired, must be furnished.) The price of a map depends on its scale and sheet format. For more information, contact:

Environmental Data Resources (EDR)—Sanborn
3530 Post Road
Southport, CT 06490
1-800-352-0050

The largest collection of Sanborn maps and atlases is in the Geography and Map Division, Library of Congress. In its collection there are approximately fifty thousand editions consisting of an estimated 700,000 Sanborn maps in bound and unbound editions. Between 1955 and 1978 the Geography and Map Division withdrew 288,093 duplicate sheets and 432 duplicate atlases from its Sanborn collection and offered them to major libraries and societies in various states.

Key Sources—Fire Insurance Maps

- *Fire Insurance Maps in the Library of Congress: Plans of North American Cities and Towns Produced by the Sanborn Map Company: An Alphabetical List*. Introduction by Walter W. Ristow. Washington, D.C.: Library of Congress, 1981.
- Hoehn, R. Phillip. *Union List of Sanborn Fire Insurance Maps Held by Institutions in the United States and Canada*. Vol. 1, *Alabama to Missouri*. Foreword by Walter W. Ristow. Santa Cruz, Calif.: Western Association of Map Libraries, 1976. This publication indexes Sanborn insurance maps and atlases in various American and Canadian institutions (FHL microfiche no. 6081586).
- Peterson-Hunt, William S., and Evelyn L. Woodruff. *Union List of Sanborn Fire Insurance Maps Held by Institutions in the United States and Canada*. Vol. 2, *Montana to Wyoming; Canada and Mexico, with a Supplement and Corrigenda to Volume 1*. Santa Cruz, Calif.: Western Association of Map Libraries, 1977.

Indian Maps. The westward movement of settlers and the removal of Indians to western lands are interrelated. Before settlers could move into the newly created territories, the Indians had to cede their lands and be relocated on lands farther west. The Continental Congress created a committee to deal with the Indians in 1775. The responsibility for Indian relations was transferred to the secretary of war in 1789. A Bureau of Indian Affairs was created within the War Department in 1825, and the bureau was transferred to the civilian administration of the Department of the Interior in 1849. In 1938 most of the cartographic records (approximately 294 cubic feet) were transferred to the National Archives.

Key Sources—Indian Maps

- Kelsay, Laura E., comp. *Cartographic Records in the National Archives of the United States Relating to American Indians*. Reference Information Paper 71. Washington, D.C.: National Archives and Records Service, 1974. The maps are from the records of seven Federal agencies dealing with Indian activities and affairs. They relate to the exploration of Indian country, Indian land cessions, establishment of reservations, and population, transportation, and industry on the reservations.

- _____. *Cartographic Records of the Bureau of Indian Affairs*. Special List no. 13. Rev. ed. Washington, D.C.: National Archives and Records Service, 1977. The maps date from the early 1800s to the 1960s.

- Prucha, Francis Paul. *Atlas of American Indian Affairs*. Lincoln: University of Nebraska Press, 1990. The atlas covers Indian land cessions from 1784 through 1890 and selected tribal cessions from 1785 through 1889. It includes maps showing Indian reservations at different time periods and much other information relating to Indian culture and records.

- Waldman, Carl. *Atlas of the North American Indian*. New York: Facts on File, 1985. This atlas contains ninety-six maps relating to early Indian civilizations, migration of tribes, dominant language families, Indian wars, the growth of the United States, Indian land cessions (by region, date, and tribe), Indian land claims, and Indian culture.

Land Ownership Maps. Land ownership maps are portrayals of land purchased, granted, or inherited. They range in complexity from rough outlines of the boundaries of one tract of land to detailed county atlases showing every landowner at the time of compilation. Figure 3-9 is from a reprinted 1875 county atlas. These maps are especially important because they predate the topographic maps.

Key Sources—Land Ownership Maps

- Eichholz, Alice, ed. *Ancestry's Red Book: American State, County and Town Sources*. Rev. ed. Salt Lake City: Ancestry, 1992. For suggestions on locating early land ownership maps, land plats, plat books, and atlases, see the heading "Maps" within the section for each state.

- Stephenson, Richard W., comp. *Land Ownership Maps: A Checklist of Nineteenth Century United States County Maps in the Library of Congress*. Washington, D.C.: Library of Congress, 1967. The book contains a brief, but informative, history of early county mapping. It describes 1,449 county maps relating to 1,041 counties, most of which are in the northeast and north central states, Virginia, California, and Texas. Approximately one-third of all counties are represented in the collection, although there are few maps of counties in the western United States. The majority of the maps were prepared between 1840 and 1900.

  A microfiche set of the above maps consisting of 2,010 microfiche was prepared by the Library of Congress Photoduplication Services in 1983. The microfiche are available for searching at the National Archives, the Family History Library, and family history centers. See "United States—Land and Property, Library of Congress, Geography and Map Division" in the *Family History Library Catalog* for a list of maps and microfiche numbers.

Map Facsimiles. Old maps, map facsimiles, and historic maps are not to be confused. An *old map* is an antique map. Old maps are often prohibitively expensive; they are usually fragile and require careful handling. They represent geographical locations as they were known at the time of publication. Many original maps are found in the Library of Congress, the National Archives, and in libraries with major map collections.

Map facsimiles are reproductions of old maps and atlases. Modern printing methods enable map facsimiles to be produced fairly inexpensively.

Historic maps usually are recently published maps prepared by commercial firms to show such features as battlefields, military routes, early pioneer trails, or the paths taken by famous explorers. They usually are for sale to tourists at historical sites or events. While these maps are quite helpful, they should not be confused with old maps.

Commercial Sources—Map Facsimiles.

- A publication compiled by Barbara R. Noe titled *Facsimiles of Maps and Atlases: A List of Reproductions for Sale by Various Publishers and Distributors,* 4th ed. (Washington, D.C.: Library of Congress, 1980) lists 145 dealers that (in 1980) sold reproductions of approximately five hundred maps and atlases in the Library of Congress's collection.

The active and widespread interest in old maps has stimulated commercial firms to reprint old maps and atlases. The following firms specialize in publishing map facsimiles at economical prices. Each firm provides a catalog that describes the maps that are available for purchase. Some of the reproductions have been enlarged to improve detail, and others have been reduced to fit a particular page size.

The Gold Bug
P.O. Box 588
Alamo, CA 94507-0588

Historic Urban Plans, Inc.
Box 276
Ithaca, New York 14851

Jonathan Sheppard Books
Box 2020, Plaza Station
Albany, NY 12220

Panoramic Maps. From the 1860s to 1920, the panoramic map was a popular way of depicting American cities, towns, farms, and rural estates. Sometimes referred to as "bird's-eye view" maps, they depict cities and towns as if seen from above at an oblique angle. Although usually not drawn to scale, the views show street patterns, houses, and individual buildings. Many of these maps are beautifully illustrated and colored. Chambers of commerce, other civic organizations, businesses, and real estate agents endorsed the preparation of such maps, which were used to promote commercial growth, to advertise businesses, and to sell homes and properties. The maps also made attractive decorations for homes. Panoramic mapping was particularly popular in urban areas in the midwestern and eastern United States.

Key Sources—Panoramic Maps

- Hébert, John R., comp. *Panoramic Maps of Cities in the United States and Canada: A Checklist of Maps in the*

Figure 3-9. A land ownership map from L. H. Everts's *1875 History of Licking County, Ohio* (1875; reprint; Knightstown, Ind.: Bookmark, 1975).

Collections of the Library of Congress, Geography and Map Division. Revised by Patrick E. Dempsey. 2nd ed. Washington, D.C.: Library of Congress, 1984. This publication lists 1,726 panoramic maps in the collections of the Library of Congress. It is illustrated with a representative sample of twenty-seven panoramic maps.

- _____. "A History of Panoramic Maps." Edited by William L. Iscrupe. *Pennsylvania Genealogist and Historian* 20 (February 1993): 24–34.

Commercial Sources—Panoramic Maps

- Historic Urban Plans, Inc., sells map facsimiles of panoramic maps of cities not only in the United States but throughout the world.

  Historic Urban Plans, Inc.
  Box 276
  Ithaca, New York 14851

Post-Route Maps. A post-route map shows post offices, distances between them, frequency of service, and mail-carrying railroads by name of railroad. The maps include county boundaries and principal drainage features. A pamphlet titled *Records and Policies of the Post Office Department Relating to Place-names*, compiled by Arthur Hecht and William J. Heynen (see "Key Sources," below), describes two series of post-route maps that are among the records of the Post Office Department filed in the National Archives. The first series covers from 1867 to 1894 and consists of around forty-five items. A chronological list of maps is included in appendix 2 of the pamphlet. The second series covers the period from 1901 to 1960 and consists of approximately 450 items. Usually from two to six states, territories, or parts of states and territories are included on the maps. Some post-route maps are in the National Archives among records of agencies other than the Post Office Department; these are listed in appendix 3.

Key Sources—Post-Route Maps

- Burr, David H. *The American Atlas Exhibiting the Post Offices, Railroads, Canals, and the Physical and Political Divisions of the United States of America Constructed . . . Under the Direction of the Post Master General. . . .* Washington, D.C., 1839. The earliest known atlas of post offices and post-routes.

- Hecht, Arthur, and William J. Heynen, comps. *Records and Policies of the Post Office Department Relating to Place-Names.* Reference Information Paper no. 72. Washington, D.C.: National Archives and Records Service, 1975.

- _____, Frank J. Nivert, Fred W. Warriner, Jr., and Charlotte M. Ashby, comps. *Records of the Post Office Department.* Preliminary Inventory 168. Washington, D.C.: National Archives and Records Service, 1967.

- _____, Fred W. Warriner, Jr., and Charlotte M. Ashby, comps. *Records of the Bureaus of the Third and Fourth Assistant Postmasters General. . . .* Preliminary Inventory 114. Washington, D.C.: National Archives and Records Service, 1955. This publication includes post-route maps for the period 1901 to 1957 that are not included in the publication by Hecht, Nivert, Warriner, and Ashby (above).

- McLaughlin, Patrick D., comp. *Transportation in Nineteenth-Century America: A Survey of the Cartographic Records in the National Archives of the United States.* Reference Information Paper no. 65. Washington, D.C.: National Archives and Records Service, 1973. The development of the transportation network in the nineteenth century is documented in this survey of nine series of maps.

USGS Topographic Maps

The United States Geological Survey (USGS). The USGS was established in 1879 with Clarence King as its director. The duties of the new organization were not clearly defined, so King concluded that the intention of Congress

> was to begin a rigid scientific classification of the lands of the national domain for the general information of the people of the country and to produce a series of land maps which would show all those features upon which the intelligent agriculturists, mining engineers, and timbermen might hereafter base their operations and which obviously would be of the highest value to all students of the political economy and resources of the United States (Thompson 1987, 5).

Under the leadership of John Wesley Powell, the second director of the USGS, who was appointed in 1881 and served until 1894, official topographic mapping of the United States commenced. A topographic map accurately represents both natural and man-made features. The shape and elevation of the terrain are portrayed by contour lines, which are imaginary lines that follow the land surface or the ocean bottom at a constant elevation above or below sea level. Specific features (for example, water areas, vegetation, trails, roads, towns, and buildings) are portrayed by map symbols, lines, and colors. For a century the USGS has produced numerous types of accurate, detailed topographic maps.

The earliest maps produced by the USGS were in a map scale of 1:250,000 for one-degree maps and 1:125,000 for 30-minute maps. Gradually the scale was increased to meet demands for more detailed maps. In 1894, 66 percent of the maps produced were 15-minute maps (1:62,500), 31 percent were 30-minute maps (1:125,000), and 3 percent were one-degree maps (1:250,000). The scale of 1:62,500 prevailed until the 1950s, when the standard scale became 1:24,000 (Thompson 1987, 6) (see "Map Scale," above).

Although publication scales have changed, the system of subdividing areas for mapping purposes is the same as originally devised in 1882. The universal coordinate lines of latitude (parallels) and longitude (meridians) form the boundaries of four-sided figures called *quadrangles,* the units of area adopted for topographic mapping.

Earth Science Information Centers (ESIC). Part of the USGS National Mapping Division, Earth Science Information Centers (ESIC) are the primary sources of public information about the cartographic activities of the division and the earth science products of the USGS's Geologic and Water Resources divisions. The USGS operates a network of ESICs that provides information and sales service for USGS map products and earth science publications. There are Federal and state ESICs. Federal ESICs are located in the cities listed below. They can provide addresses of ESIC state offices and information about authorized map dealers. For additional information about ESICs, call 1-800-USA-MAPS.

Anchorage, Alaska

Anchorage-ESIC
U.S. Geological Survey
4230 University Drive, Room 101
Anchorage, AK 99508-4664
Telephone: 1-907-786-7011
Fax: 1-907-786-7050

Denver, Colorado

Lakewood-ESIC
U.S. Geological Survey
Box 25046, Building 810
Denver Federal Center, MS 504
Denver, CO 80225-0046
Telephone: 1-303-202-4200
Fax: 1-303-202-4188

Menlo Park, California

Menlo Park-ESIC
U.S. Geological Survey
Building 3, MS 532, Room 3128
345 Middlefield Road
Menlo Park, CA 94025-3591
Telephone: 1-415-329-4309
Fax: 1-415-329-5130

Reston, Virginia

Reston-ESIC
U.S. Geological Survey
507 National Center
Reston, VA 20192
Telephone: 1-703-648-6045
Fax: 1-703-648-5548
TDD (telecommunications device for the deaf): 1-703-648-4119

Rolla, Missouri

Rolla-ESIC
U.S. Geological Survey
1400 Independence Road, MS 231
Rolla, MO 65401-2602
Telephone: 1-573-308-3500
Fax: 1-573-308-3615

Salt Lake City, Utah

Salt Lake City-ESIC
U.S. Geological Survey
222 West 2300 South, 2nd Floor
Salt Lake City, UT 84119
Telephone: 1-801-975-3742
Fax: 1-801-975-3740
TDD: 1-801-975-3744

Sioux Falls, South Carolina

Sioux Falls-ESIC
U.S. Geological Survey
EROS Data Center
Sioux Falls, SD 57198-0001
Telephone: 1-605-594-6151
Fax: 1-605-594-6589
TDD: 1-605-594-6933

Spokane, Washington

Spokane-ESIC
U.S. Post Office Building, Room 135
904 West Riverside Avenue
Spokane, WA 99201
Telephone: 1-509-353-2524
Fax: 1-509-353-2872
TDD: 1-509-353-3235

Washington, D.C.

Washington, DC-ESIC
U.S. Geological Survey
U.S. Department of the Interior
1849 C Street, NW, Room 2650
Washington, DC 20240
Telephone: 1-202-208-4047

Topographic Quadrangle Maps. The USGS produces a variety of topographic maps covering different-size quadrangles. Each map sheet covers a specific quadrangle. Generally, the larger quadrangles are bounded by the degree lines of latitude and longitude, and smaller ones are delineated by subdividing the larger quadrangles, as shown in figure 3-10. Thus, a 1-degree quadrangle comprises four 30-minute quadrangles; a 30-minute quadrangle, four 15-minute quadrangles; and a 15-minute quadrangle, four 7.5-minute quadrangles (see "Measuring the World," above).

These excellent maps include contour lines, differentiation between land types (for example, forest and grassland), waterways, railroads and roads, townships and ranges, political boundaries, and man-made structures, such as cemeteries, schools, and buildings. The names on the maps are usually those in local usage. The maps are readily available and relatively inexpensive.

7.5-Minute Series. The scale of the 7.5-minute series generally is 1:24,000, although it is 1:25,000 in some states. One inch on the map represents two thousand feet on the ground, and each quadrangle covers from forty-nine to seventy square miles. There are 53,838 separate 7.5-minute quadrangle maps covering the conterminous United States, Hawaii, and the territories (Thompson 1987, 108). For Alaska, complete coverage is at 1:63,360 scale (see the 15-minute series below), with 1:25,000-scale coverage provided for population centers.

This popular map series is used for a variety of purposes. For example, a family researcher can precisely pinpoint the location of property in rural areas based on a legal land description. The maps also are popular among hikers, mountain bikers, fishermen, hunters, campers, and others.

7.5 x 15-Minute Series. The scale of this series is 1:25,000. One inch on the map represents approximately 2,083 feet on the ground, and each quadrangle covers from 98 to 140 square miles.

15-Minute Series. The scale of this series is 1:62,500 (1:63,360 for Alaska). One inch on the map represents approximately one mile on the ground at scale 1:62,500 and exactly one mile on the ground at scale 1:63,360. Each quadrangle covers from 197 to 282 square miles. The 1:62,500 series was discontinued with the completion of the 7.5-minute series.

30 x 60-Minute Series. The scale of this series is 1:100,000. One inch on the map represents approximately 1.6 miles on the ground, and each quadrangle covers from 1,568 to 2,240 square miles.

1 x 2-Degree Series. The scale of this series is 1:250,000. Each quadrangle covers an area one degree by two degrees. One inch on the map is approximately four miles on the ground, and each quadrangle covers from 4,580 to 8,669 square miles. This series consists of 474 sheets covering the conterminous United States (including Hawaii) and 153 sheets covering Alaska.

Topographic County Format Maps. Map scale is either 1:50,000 or 1:100,000, and complete county coverage often requires more than one map sheet. Few other published county maps equal these excellent maps in scale, in detail, and in the natural and man-made features shown.

Obtaining Topographic Map Names and Numbers

State-by-State Catalogs and Map Indexes. For each state, the USGS has prepared and distributes an *Index to Topographic and Other Map Coverage* and a *Catalog of Topographic and Other Published Maps*. The *Index* lists the types of maps available for the state and identifies quadrangle areas by reference code, map name, and scale. Each map series described above is included in the *Index*. The *Catalog* contains ordering instructions and the price of each map in the various map series; an order form is included.

Free indexes, catalogs, and literature can be obtained by writing to or visiting the nearest Federal ESIC or by contacting the main Denver address listed below under "Ordering Topographic Maps—Government Sources." When requesting an index or catalog, be sure to identify the state so that the proper material will be sent.

Gazetteers Listing Topographic Map Names and Numbers. The name and number of the 7.5-minute map is given for each geographical feature or place name listed in the *Omni Gazetteer of the United States of America Providing Name, Location, and Identification for Nearly 1,500,000 Populated Places, Structures, Facilities, Locales, Historic Places, and Geographic Features in the Fifty States, the District of Columbia, Puerto Rico, and U.S. Territories*, edited by Frank R. Abate, 11 vols. (Detroit: Omnigraphics, 1991).

The USGS, in cooperation with the U.S. Board on Geographic Names, has compiled a database titled the Geographic Names Information System (GNIS). The GNIS contains information about more than 2 million geographic features in the United States; the name and number of the 7.5-minute map is listed for each feature. This database is available on a CD-ROM; it can be accessed through the Internet as well. For more information about the *Omni Gazetteer* and the GNIS database, see "Gazetteers, Postal Guides, and Shipping Guides—Gazetteers," below.

Ordering Topographic Maps

Government Sources. The main distribution center for mail orders is:

USGS Map Distribution
Box 25286
Denver, CO 80225

This distribution center does not take telephone orders, and delivery time is slow. For information or ordering assistance, write to the distribution center or call 1-800-USA-MAPS. Federal ESICs sell topographic maps for the states in which they are located and also for nearby states.

Commercial Sources. There are more than three thousand authorized map dealers nationwide. The *Catalog of Topographic and Other Published Maps* for each state lists dealers that sell topographic maps in the state; it also lists the libraries that have been designated as depositories for many of the maps published by the USGS (see "Obtaining Topographic Map Names and Numbers," above).

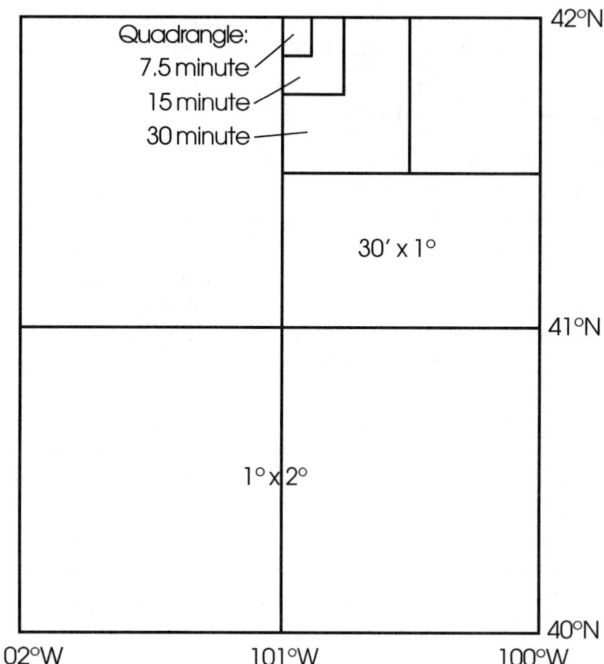

Figure 3-10. The quadrangle system of map layout.

The following companies provide quick service in supplying topographic maps and other USGS products (for example, National Park maps and National Atlas maps).

Map Link
30 South LaPatera Lane, Unit no. 5
Santa Barbara, CA 93117
1-805-692-6777
USGS Topo Fax: 1-800-627-1839
(This company also sells city maps and maps of most countries of the world.)

Map Express
P.O. Box 280445
Lakewood, CO 80228
1-800-627-0039

Powers Elevation
P.O. Box 440889
Aurora, CO 80044
1-800-824-2550

Digital Topographic Maps

The USGS is placing images of the topographic maps ranging in scale from 1:24,000 to 1:250,000 on CD-ROMs. The images are called digital raster graphics. Each CD-ROM includes the USGS topographic maps for a one-degree cell. The cells usually contain sixty-four 1:24,000-scale files, two 1:100,000-scale files, and one 1:250,000-scale file. A fact sheet titled Digital

Raster Graphics gives specific data about the program (see "Fact Sheets and General Interest Publications," below).

Out-of-Print Topographic Maps

In 1977 the USGS developed a computerized database called the Map and Chart Information System (MCIS). It indexed all topographic quadrangle maps ever produced by the agency. In 1978 the USGS microfilmed all topographic quadrangle maps in its archival collection, which consisted of approximately 120,000 sheets. A fine source for determining which out-of-print map to order is a guide prepared by Riley M. Moffat titled *Map Index to Topographical Quadrangles of the United States, 1882–1940: A Graphic Bibliography of Out-Of-Print Topographic Maps Published from 1882 to 1940 in the 15-, 30-, and 60-Minute Series for all States Except Alaska.* Foreword by Mary Larsgaard (Santa Cruz, Calif.: Western Association of Map Libraries, 1985) .

Topographic Maps from a Federal ESIC. A black-and-white reproduction of an out-of-print map may be ordered from the USGS. The prints are reasonably legible, although they are seldom as clear and sharp as the original maps. They are printed on light-sensitive paper, so the print will eventually fade. Official topographic mapping commenced in 1879, when the USGS was established. The old maps, which ranged in map scale from 1:62,500 to 1:250,00, are not as detailed as the modern 7.5-minute scale maps.

Any Federal ESIC can help in determining what map to order. It can also accept payment for the map and send the order to the Reston, Virginia, ESIC to be filled. For further information about this service, request a free guide titled Looking for an Old Map (see "Fact Sheets, Guides, and Pamphlets," below).

Topographic Maps at the Family History Library. The Family History Library has 291 rolls of microfilm of original quadrangle maps published by the USGS from around 1884 to 1979. See "United States—Maps, United States, Geological Survey" in the *Family History Library Catalog* for a list of maps and microfilm numbers. The library also has a collection of 473 national topographic maps in the 1:250,000 scale series that were published between 1943 and 1972. However, the set is incomplete, and these maps are not available on microfilm or microfiche.

Fact Sheets and General Interest Publications

The USGS has prepared useful fact sheets (papers that describe specific programs) and general interest publications that may be obtained from Federal ESICs. Titles frequently go out of print, and new ones are frequently published. The USGS maintains a current list of titles at the following World Wide Web site: <http://rmmcweb.cr.usgs.gov/public/gip.html>. A few useful titles are listed below.

- **Cartographic Data on CD-ROM**. This fact sheet describes the type of information available on specific CD-ROMs.
- **Digital Raster Graphics**. A digital raster graphic is a scanned image of a USGS topographic map. This fact sheet discusses the digitalization of the USGS topographic maps (see "Digital Topographic Maps," above).
- **Finding Your Way with Map and Compass**. This guide describes topographic maps, the importance of map scale, and how to use a compass.
- **Geographic Names Information System**. This fact sheet describes the GNIS, a database that contains more than 2 million geographic names relating to all fifty states. The database is available for searching on the Internet. See "Gazetteers," below.
- **How to Obtain Aerial Photographs**. This fact sheet shows samples of aerial photographs. An order form is included.
- **Looking for an Old Map**. This guide describes some checklists that are helpful for locating old maps in the National Archives, the Library of Congress, and the USGS.
- **National Atlas Maps**. The *National Atlas of the United States of America,* edited by Arch C. Gerlach, was published by the U.S. Geological Survey in 1970. Although it is out of print, many of the maps still are available for purchase. This guide provides ordering information (see "Ordering Topographic Maps—Commercial Sources," above).
- **Out-of-Print Maps**. This guide describes how to obtain copies of out-of-print topographic maps that have been microfilmed. (Most of these maps are on microfilm at the Family History Library. See "Out-of-Print Topographic Maps," above.)
- **Topographic Map Symbols**. This guide shows the symbols that are used on topographic maps to represent boundaries, contours, and features like trails, woods, rivers and lakes, canals, railroads, and buildings.
- **USGS Maps**. This excellent booklet gives a brief overview of each type of map that the USGS sells and distributes through ESICs and its map distribution facilities. It includes a color sample of each type of map.
- **Using Maps in Genealogy**. This fine, helpful pamphlet gives suggestions for locating and using maps, atlases, and gazetteers. It briefly describes maps published by the USGS, the cartographic collections of the National Archives and the Map and Geography Division of the Library of Congress.
- **World Wide Web Information**. This fact sheet provides specific USGS World Wide Web data and information sites.

Other Types of USGS Maps

All of the map series listed below are described and illustrated in the general interest publication titled *USGS Maps* (described above).

State Maps. There are three main editions: (1) base maps (no contours), (2) highway and contour maps (topographic features), and (3) shaded-relief maps (maps that appear to be three dimensional through the use of graded shadows and contour lines). The USGS has prepared a fine base map titled *United States Base Map*. It shows the conterminous United States, each state and county, and their names. The major waterways are printed in blue. Its size is forty-one by twenty-eight inches, and the scale is 1:5,000,000. It is available from an ESIC or the Denver distribution center.

National Park Maps. These topographic maps feature national parks, national monuments, or other National Park System units. Recreational features are highlighted.

Topographic-Bathymetric Maps. These maps are available for coastal zones. Contour lines show elevations of the land areas above sea level, and isobaths (bathymetric contours) show the form of the land below the water's surface.

Antarctic Maps. These maps range in scale from 1:50,000 to 1:5,000,000. The series includes satellite image maps.

Photoimage Maps. These maps are produced from aerial photographs. There are four main editions: (1) orthophotomaps (multicolored, distortion-free photographic image maps), (2) orthophotoquads (black-and-white, distortion-free, photographic image maps), (3) border maps (covering the U.S.-Mexico border and the international boundary from the Pacific Ocean to the Gulf of Mexico), and (4) satellite image maps (multicolored or black-and-white maps made from data collected from satellites).

Geologic Maps. These maps show the composition and structure of earth materials and their distribution across and beneath the earth's surface. They are used to identify geologic hazards, locate natural resources, and facilitate land-use planning.

Hydrologic Maps. These maps show a wide range of water-related information (for example, ground water, aquifers, flood plains).

Place and Feature Names

The names shown on quadrangle maps are those in local usage, as nearly as can be ascertained from officials and residents of the areas and from other sources, such as previously published maps, historical records, and reference publications.

In selecting names that are to be published, map-makers ensure that the most important ones are included and that the overall density of names and descriptive labels is appropriate for the scale of the map. Names that disagree with other government publications or are controversial in local usage are referred to the U.S. Board on Geographic Names. The quadrangle name itself is usually that of the most prominent city, town, or other feature appearing within the mapped area.

GAZETTEERS

Some family researchers believe it is necessary to find an old map to locate an old town. But due to the rapid growth and occasional demise of settlements in the United States, a map might have been printed before some places came into existence or after other places had disappeared. Compounding the problem, some states had several localities with the same name at the same or different time periods. Thus, a place name found on an old map might not be the place where the ancestor lived. An old map will not necessarily show all towns in existence when the map was printed because small towns might have been omitted.

A useful tool for locating towns is a *gazetteer,* which is a geographical dictionary that lists place names (for example, those of states, territories, counties, cities, towns, and townships) alphabetically for a geographical region. The type of information given in various gazetteers differs, but usually the state and county (and sometimes township) are listed. This information will help to locate a place name on a map and to determine the town or county in which the major records (for example, vital, land, probate) are located.

Nineteenth-Century National Gazetteers

The boundaries of the United States expanded rapidly following the revolutionary war. Numerous gazetteers for the nation and individual states were published at different time periods, and they reflected the growth of the new nation. A nineteenth-century gazetteer usually describes the character of a town, its industry, and physical surroundings. It also gives the town's location, frequently stating its distance and direction from Washington, D.C.

When one of the first U.S. gazetteers, *The United States Gazetteer* (cited below under "Key Sources"), was published by Joseph Scott in 1795 (figure 3-11), the United States consisted of the territory of the original thirteen states; the Mississippi River was the western boundary. As a result of the Louisiana Purchase in 1803 and the Florida purchase in 1819, the United States doubled in size. People began moving westward beyond the Mississippi River into the territories of Missouri, Arkansas, and Iowa. Daniel Haskel and J. Calvin Smith's *A Complete Descriptive and Statistical Gazetteer of the United States of America* (also cited below), which was published in 1843, reflected this growth. It described each town in great detail, often listing types of local businesses, the condition of the soil, the kinds and sometimes numbers of livestock, the number of schools and scholars, some historical highlights, population figures based on the census of 1840, and much more. Much of the information was obtained by correspondence.

Between 1845 and 1853, the United States again increased substantially in size, the result of Texas being admitted to the Union in 1845, title to the Oregon Territory being established in 1846, the Mexican cession in 1848, and the Gadsden Purchase in 1853. In only eight years, the western boundary of the United States was extended to the Pacific Ocean. By 1853 five new states had been admitted to the Union, and five new territories were organized.

In 1854 *A New and Complete Gazetteer of the United States* (cited below) was published by Thomas Baldwin and J. Thomas. The information given in it is similar to that in Haskel and Smith's work, but it has nearly double the number of pages because of new listings. It was the largest (in number of pages) and probably the most comprehensive nationwide gazetteer published until the twentieth century. It includes more than 34,400 entries identifying virtually every known place in the mid-1800s. There is great detail in the entries; often, even moderate-size and small towns are fully described, including number and denomination of churches, local industry, and 1850 population figures (figure 3-12). Nearby geographic features, such as rivers and mountains, are often included as well. At least 3,500 townships are identified throughout this gazetteer; many of them no longer carry the same name, making them difficult

RED, a ſmall river of Kentucky, riſing in the mountainous parts of Clarke-county, and thence running a W. direction, falls into Kentucky river, about 9 miles above Boonſborough. It is about 60 yards wide at its mouth.

REDHOOK, a ſmall poſt-town of the ſtate of New-York; ſituated on the E. ſide of Hudſon river, in Dutcheſs county. It is 116 miles N. of New-York, and 206 from Philadelphia

REDSTONE. See BROWNSVILLE.

REELFOOT, a ſmall navigable river of the Tennaſſee government, which riſes on the confines of Kentucky; thence running a W. by S. courſe, falls into the Miſſiſſippi, about 34 miles S. of the Ohio.

RENSSELLAER, a county of the ſtate of New-York, 33 miles in length from N. to S. and 22 in breadth from E. to W. It is bounded N. by Waſhington county, E. by part of the ſtates of Maſſachuſetts and Vermont, S. by Columbia county, and W. by the Hudſon, which ſeparates it from Albany and Saratoga counties. It is divided into the following townſhips, viz. Renſſellaerwyck, Hoſick, Pittſtown, Schatkoke, Troy, Stephentown, and Peterſborough. In the townſhip of Renſſellaerwyck are ſprings much celebrated for their medicinal quality. The number of inhabitants in this county, according to the cenſus of 1790, is 22,428, of whom 998 are ſlaves. Chief town, Lanſinburg

RUINEBECK, a ſmall poſt-town of the ſtate of New-York; ſituated in Dutcheſs county, two miles E. of Hudſon river, 100 N. of New-York city, and 190 from Philadelphia.

Figure 3-11. From the first U.S. gazetteer, Scott's *The United States Gazetteer* (1795).

for modern researchers to identify. Among the one hundred entries identifying places in New Mexico Territory, for example, are certain to be many ghost towns and other places lost to history. An appendix contains significant information for researchers; tables identify colleges, medical schools, and military posts, usually with founding dates. In 1996, Infobases of Orem, Utah, published this gazetteer as part of its CD-ROM *Geographic Reference Library.* It is now available from Ancestry Incorporated.

The demand for updated gazetteers continued. Political boundaries changed rapidly as states were carved out of territories, new counties were created, town names were changed, and boom towns became ghost towns. Alaska was purchased from Russia in 1867, and Hawaii was annexed in 1898. The need to learn about the new places and changes was as great in the nineteenth century as the need now to locate and learn about places of the past.

Key Sources—Nineteenth Century National Gazetteers

- Baldwin, Thomas, and J. Thomas. *A New and Complete Gazetteer of the United States; Giving a Full and Comprehensive Review of the Present Condition, Industry, and Resources of the American Confederacy: Embracing, also, Important Topographical, Statistical, and Historical Information from Recent and Original Sources; Together with the Results of the Census of 1850, and Population and Statistics in Many Cases to 1853.* Philadelphia: Lippincott, Grumbo & Co., 1854 (FHL microfilm no. 1036939, item 1).

- Brown, Samuel R. *The Western Gazetteer, or, Emigrant's Directory Containing a Geographical Description of the Western States and Territories, viz. the States of Kentucky, Indiana, Louisiana, Ohio, Tennessee and Mississippi; and the Territories of Illinois, Missouri, Alabama, Michigan, and North-Western with an Appendix, Containing Sketches of Some of the Western Counties of New-York, Pennsylvania and Virginia; a Description of the Great Northern Lakes; Indian Annuities, and Directions to Emigrants.* Auburn, N.Y.: H. C. Southwick, 1817. Reprint. Early American Imprints, Second Series, no. 40334, microfiche. New York: Arno Press and The New York Times, 1971 (FHL microfilm no. 0928110, item 12).

- Colange, Leo de. *The National Gazetteer: A Geographical Dictionary of the United States; Compiled from the Latest Official Authorities and Original Sources; Embracing a Comprehensive Account of Every State, Territory, County, City, Town and Village Throughout the Union, with Populations, from the Latest National Census.* London: Hamilton, Adams & Co., 1884. Reprint. Ann Arbor, Mich.: University Microfilms, 1973 (FHL microfilm no. 0845264, item 1; microfiche no. 6046725; also microfiche nos. 6010003–6010014).

- Conclin, George. *Conclins' New River Guide, or, A Gazetteer of All the Towns of the Western Waters; Containing Sketches of the Cities, Towns, and Countries Bordering on the Ohio and Mississippi Rivers, and Their Principal Tributaries; Together with Their Population, Products, Commerce, &c., &c., in 1848; and Many Interesting Events of History Connected with Them, Compiled from the Latest and Best Authority.* Cincinnati: H. S. & J. Applegate,

CHA CHE

CHAZY RIVER, of Clinton county, New York, falls into Lake Champlain, near its N. extremity.

CHEAPSIDE, a small village of Essex county, New Jersey, 10 miles W. from Newark.

CHEAP VALLEY, a post-office of Henry county, Tennessee.

CHEAT BRIDGE, a post-office of Preston county, Virginia.

CHEAT RIVER, of Virginia, the largest affluent of the Monongahela, is formed by the junction of the Laurel, Glade, Shavers, and Dry forks, which rise among the Alleghany mountains, near the northern border of Pocahontas county, and unite in the N. central part of Randolph county. Flowing thence N. and N. W. through Preston and Monongalia counties, it enters the Monongahela at the S. W. extremity of Fayette county, Pennsylvania. It traverses a hilly country, abounding in stone coal and iron, and well adapted to grazing. It is navigable 40 miles above Rowlesburg, (on the Baltimore and Ohio railroad,) though not in the lower part of its course, and furnishes fine water-power at several places.

CHEBOYGAN, an unorganized county of Michigan, forms the northern extremity of the lower Peninsula, bordering on the Straits of Mackinaw and Lake Huron. The area is estimated at 500 square miles. The census of 1850 furnishes no information respecting this county, which has but few white inhabitants.

CHEBOYGAN RIVER of Michigan. See SHEBOYGAN.

CHEHAW, a small river of South Carolina, flowing into St. Helena sound.

CHEEKSVILLE, a post-office of Marion county, Tennessee, 122 miles S. E. from Nashville.

CHEEKTOWAGA, a post-office of Erie county, New York.

CHEESEQUAKES, a post-office of Middlesex county, New Jersey.

CHELSEA, a post-village of Will county, Illinois, 177 miles N. E. from Springfield.

CHELTENHAM, a township in the S. E. part of Montgomery county, Pennsylvania, 10 miles N. from Philadelphia; drained by Tacony creek. Population, 1292.

CHEMUNG, a county in the S. W. central part of New York, bordering on Pennsylvania, has an area of about 518 square miles. It is intersected by Chemung river and Cayuta creek, and also drained by Catharine's and Wynkoop's creeks, which afford valuable water-power. Seneca lake touches its N. border. The surface is broken and hilly, with some considerable elevations. The alluvial flats along the rivers are in some parts very extensive and rich, and on the uplands the soil is generally fertile. Wheat, Indian corn, oats, and grass are the staples. In 1850 this county produced 223,340 bushels of wheat; 166,804 of corn; 368,450 of oats; 40,106 tons of hay, and 829,422 pounds of butter. There were 23 flour and grist mills, 154 saw mills, 14 tanneries, 5 iron foundries, 8 woollen factories, and 1 edge-tool manufactory. It contained 30 churches, and 9 newspaper offices. There were 9195 pupils attending public schools, and 181 attending academies or other schools. The Chemung river is navigable through this county. The New York and Erie railroad traverses the county, which is also partly intersected by the canal connecting Elmira with Seneca lake, and by the railroad extending from Junction to Geneva. Organized in 1836, having previously formed part of Tioga county, and named from the Chemung river. Capital, Elmira. Population, 28,821.

CHEMUNG, a post-township, forming the S. E. extremity of Chemung county, New York. Population, 2678.

CHEMUNG, a post-village in the above township, on the New York and Erie railroad, 270 miles from New York city.

Figure 3-12. From Baldwin and Thomas's *A New and Complete Gazetteer of the United States,* the largest (in number of pages) and probably the most comprehensive nationwide gazetteer published until the twentieth century.

1850. Reprint. Microfilm. Lexington: University of Kentucky, 1952 (FHL microfilm no. 0156896, item 20).

- Darby, William, and Theodore Dwight, Jr. *A New Gazetteer of the United States America; Containing a Copius Description of the States, Territories, Counties, Parishes, Districts, Cities and Towns—Mountains, Lakes, Rivers and Canals—Commerce, Manufacturers, Agriculture, and the Arts Generally of the United States . . . with the Population of 1830.* Hartford: Edward Hopkins, 1833.
- Davenport, Bishop. *A History and New Gazetteer, or Geographical Dictionary, of North America and the West Indies. . . .* Philadelphia: the author, 1838. Rev. ed. New York: S. W. Benedict & Co., 1843 (FHL microfilm no. 0924666, item 1, 1838 ed.).
- *Early American Gazetteer: 1833; 1853.* GenRef (Orem, Utah). This CD-ROM contains electronic versions of Darby's *A New Gazetteer of the United States of America* (above) and Hayward's *A Gazetteer of the United States of America* (cited below).
- *Fanning's Illustrated Gazetteer of the United States; Giving the Location, Physical Aspect, Mountains, Rivers, Lakes, Climate, Productive and Manufacturing Resources, Commerce, Government, Education, General History, Etc. of the States, Territories, Counties, Cities, Towns, and Post-*

Offices in the American Union, with the Population and Other Statistics from the Census of 1850. New York: Ensign, Bridgman, & Fanning, 1855. Reprint. Bowie, Md.: Heritage Books, 1990 (FHL microfilm no. 0599773, item 2; microfiche nos. 6010028–6010032).

- Gannett, Henry. *The Origin of Certain Place Names in the United States*. 2nd ed. Washington, D.C.: U.S. Geological Survey, 1905. Reprint. Baltimore: Genealogical Publishing Co., 1977.

- Haskel, Daniel, and J. Calvin Smith. *A Complete Descriptive and Statistical Gazetteer of the United States of America; Containing a Particular Description of the States, Territories, Counties, Districts, Parishes, Cities, Towns, and Villages—Mountains, Rivers, Lakes, Canals, and Railroads; with an Abstract of the Census and Statistics for 1840, Exhibiting a Complete View of the Agricultural, Commercial, Manufacturing, and Literary Condition and Resources of the Country*. New York: Sherman & Smith, 1843.

- Hayward, John. *A Gazetteer of the United States of America; Comprising a Concise General View of the United States, and Particular Descriptions of the Several States, Territories, Counties, Districts, Cities, Towns, Villages, Their Mountains, Valleys, Islands, Capes, Bays, Harbors, Lakes, Rivers, Canals, Railroads, &c.; with the Governments and Literary and Other Public Institutions of the Country; also, Its Mineral Springs, Waterfalls, Caves, Beaches, and Other Fashionable Resorts; to Which Are Added Valuable Statistical Tables, and a Map of the United States*. Hartford, Conn.: Case, Tiffany, and Co., 1853. Reprint. Ann Arbor, Mich.: University Microfilms, 1972. Reprint. Knightstown, Ind.: Bookmark, 1977 (FHL microfilm no. 0599735, item 1; microfilm no. 0896902, item 1; microfilm no. 0896901; microfiche no. 6046770).

- Mitchell, S. Augustus. *An Accompaniment to Mitchell's Reference and Distance Map of the United States: Containing an Index of all the Counties, Districts, Townships, Towns, &c., in the Union; Together with an Index of the Rivers; by Which any County, District, Township, &c., or River, May be Found on the Map, without Difficulty; also, a General View of the United States, and the Several States and Territories. . . .* Philadelphia: Mitchell and Hinman, 1834. Reprint. Ann Arbor, Mich.: University Microfilms, 1972 (FHL microfilm no. 0845264, item 2; microfiche nos. 6010021–6010024).

- Morse, Jedidiah. *The American Gazetteer, Exhibiting, in Alphabetical Order, Much More Full and Accurate Account, Than Has Been Given of the States, Provinces, Counties, Cities, Towns, Villages, Rivers, Bays, Harbours, Gulfs, Sounds, Capes, Mountains, Forts, Indian Tribes, and New Discoveries, on the American Continent, also of the West India Islands . . . with a Particular Description of the Georgia Western Territory. . . .* Boston: S. Hall, and Thomas & Andrews, 1797. Reprint. New York: Arno Press and The New York Times, 1971 (FHL microfilm no. 0924678, item 1; microfiche nos. 6010048–6010054).

- _____. *The Traveller's Guide, or, Pocket Gazetteer of the United States: Extracted from the Latest Edition of Morse's Universal Gazetteer, with an Appendix, Containing a Description of Some of the Principal Places in Canada*. 2nd ed. Enl., rev., and corr. New Haven, Conn.: S. Wadsworth, 1826 (FHL microfilm no. 0496936, item 9).

- Scott, Joseph. *The United States Gazetteer; Containing an Authentic Description of the Several States, Their Situation, Extent, Boundaries, Soil, Produce, Climate, Population, Trade and Manufactures. Together with the Extent, Boundaries and Population of their Respective Counties. Also, an Exact Account of the Cities, Towns, Harbours, Rivers, Bars, Lakes, Mountains, &c*. Philadelphia: Bailey, 1795 (FHL 0570810, item 3). Contains nineteen maps.

- Smith, John Calvin. *Harper's Statistical Gazetteer of the World: Particularly Describing the United States of America, Canada, New Brunswick, and Nova Scotia*. New York: Harper, 1855 (FHL microfilm no. 0856116).

Twentieth-Century National Gazetteers

Geographic Names Information System (GNIS). The Geographic Names Information System (GNIS) was developed by the USGS in cooperation with the U.S. Board on Geographic Names (see "Place and Feature Names," above). The GNIS is the United States' official repository of geographic names information. The GNIS Feature Names Data Base includes information on more than 2 million names of places, features, and areas in the United States that are identified by proper names. The data for each state or territory is compiled in two phases. The first phase, which is complete, includes most feature names printed on the large-scale topographic maps published by the USGS and the U.S. Forest Service, as well as the charts of the National Ocean Service. Other feature names were obtained from Federal Aviation Administration files, Federal Communications Commission files, and files of the Army Corps of Engineers. The second phase is a long-term project to gather additional name information from state and local materials. These include privately published current maps, historical maps, charts, and documents.

The GNIS database can be searched online at the following World Wide Web address: <http://www-nmd.usgs.gov/www/gnis/>. The query results include the following information:

- The name recognized by the Federal government for the feature.

- Feature type (for example, populated place, canal, or cemetery).

- State and county in which the feature is located.

- The name of the USGS 7.5-minute topographic map on which the feature appears.

- Latitude and longitude of the feature location.

- Former name and variant spellings of the official name.

In addition, the location of the feature name is linked with the Tiger Map Server. TIGER® is an acronym for Topographically Integrated Geographic Encoding and References, which is the name for the system and digital database developed by the Census Bureau to support its mapping needs. The link to the

Tiger Map Server produces a digital map which shows the location of the feature.

The entire GNIS Feature Names Data Base is available on a CD-ROM titled *The Digital Gazetteer of the U.S.* The CD-ROM contains considerably more feature names than the online database. For ordering information, contact any ESIC, or call 1-800-USA-MAPS.

National Gazetteer of the United States. The GNIS is the basis for the *National Gazetteer of the United States*, which is published by the USGS. Feature names are obtained from USGS topographic maps, other Federal and state materials, and from all available historical maps. Variant spellings of names are included. A gazetteer is published for each state after completion of the second phase of the GNIS project. Currently, published gazetteers are available for the states of Arizona, Delaware, Florida, Indiana, Kansas, New Jersey, North Dakota, and South Dakota. Interim gazetteers for the remaining states and territories are available in the form of bound computer listings and on magnetic tapes.

U.S. Gazetteer. The U.S. Gazetteer is a searchable database maintained by the U.S. Census Bureau. Called the 1990 Census Data Lookup Server, it includes the names of counties and places, but it does not contain unincorporated town names. For each town name it includes population statistics, location (longitude and latitude), and ZIP code(s), and the entry is linked to the Tiger Map Server. The map shows the location of the town and the surrounding area, and there are several options for customizing information (for example, adding highway numbers, parks, railroads, streets, ZIP codes, and census statistical information). These maps can be modified to show more information than the maps available through the GNIS database. The World Wide Web address for the U.S. Gazetteer is: <http://www.census.gov/cgi-bin/gazetteer>.

Omni Gazetteer. In 1991 the *Omni Gazetteer of the United States of America* (cited below under "Key Sources") was published. This comprehensive gazetteer provides information for approximately 1,500,000 places and features. Principal sources include:

- GNIS (approximately 1 million place and feature names).
- Federal Information Processing Standards: National Institute of Standards and Technology, Department of Commerce (approximately 190,000 places).
- *National Register of Historic Places*, National Park Service (approximately fifty-two thousand places).
- *1988 Population Estimates for Counties and Incorporated Places*, Bureau of the Census (population figures for approximately 39,800 places).

Vol. 10 of the *Omni Gazetteer* is an alphabetical index that lists all entries that appear in the other volumes. It gives the name of the state, island, or territory in which each entry is located as well. Because this volume includes thousands of entries that will not be found in other gazetteers, old or new, it is the best published source to consult.

The following information appears in columns for each entry listed in the first nine volumes: name with ZIP code, if known, and variant name; type of feature or population (for example, populated place, woods, school, cemetery); county; USGS map name and 7.5-minute series (if known); latitude/longitude coordinates; source(s); and other data (figure 3-13). If the USGS map name is listed, a 7.5-minute topographic map can be ordered, eliminating the need to obtain a catalog and map index from the USGS.

Key Sources—Twentieth-Century Gazetteers

- Abate, Frank R., ed. *American Places Dictionary: A Guide to 45,000 Populated Places, Natural Features, and Other Places in the United States.* 4 vols. Detroit: Omnigraphics, 1994.
- _____, ed. *Omni Gazetteer of the United States of America Providing Name, Location, and Identification for Nearly 1,500,000 Populated Places, Structures, Facilities, Locales, Historic Places, and Geographic Features in the Fifty States, the District of Columbia, Puerto Rico, and U.S. Territories.* 11 vols. Detroit: Omnigraphics, 1991.
- Heilprin, Angelo, and Louis Heilprin, eds. *Lippincott's New Gazetteer: A Complete Pronouncing Gazetteer or Geographical Dictionary of the World, Containing the Most Recent and Authentic Information Respecting the Countries, Cities, Towns, Resorts, Islands, Rivers, Mountains, Seas, Lakes, Etc., in Every Portion of the Globe.* Philadelphia: J. B. Lippincott Co., 1922.
- Orth, Donald J., comp. *Geographic Names and the Federal Government: A Bibliography.* Washington, D.C.: Library of Congress, 1990.
- Sealock, Richard B., Margaret M. Sealock, and Margaret S. Powell. *Bibliography of Place-Name Literature: United States and Canada.* 3rd ed. Chicago: American Library Association, 1982.
- Seltzer, Leon E., ed. *The Columbia Lippincott Gazetteer of the World.* With 1961 supplement. Morningside Heights, N.Y.: Columbia University Press, 1962.
- Stewart, George R. *American Place-Names: A Concise and Selective Dictionary for the Continental United States of America.* New York: Oxford University Press, 1970.
- ______. *Names on the Land: A Historical Account of Placenaming in the United States.* 4th ed. San Francisco: Lexikos, 1982.
- *The United States Dictionary of Places.* New York: Somerset Publishers, 1988.
- *Webster's New Geographical Dictionary.* Springfield, Mass.: Merriam-Webster, 1988.

Regional and State Gazetteers

Many fine gazetteers have been published that list place names in geographic regions (for example, New England) and in individual states. An exceptional example is the *Gazetteer of the State of New York Embracing a Comprehensive View of the Geography, Geology, and General History of the State, and a Complete History and Description of Every County, City, Town, Village, and Locality, with Full Tables of Statistics,* by J. H. French (Syracuse, N.Y.: R. Pearsall Smith, 1860). The information contained in this well-documented gazetteer includes: when a county was created, from what area, and subsequent changes; topography and soil conditions; internal improvements; county seats, including names of first county officers; brief historical sketch of each county; names and descriptions of villages, hamlets, and localities; and incidents of general and local interest (figure 3-14). Names of first settlers (including first birth, marriage, and death) and the first church, school, mill, and factory in a town may be listed.

Two indexes have been prepared that list the names of approximately sixteen thousand early settlers mentioned in the text: *Index of Names in J. H. French's Gazetteer of the State of New York (1860)*, compiled by Frank Place (Cortland, N.Y.: Cortland County Historical Society, 1983), and *All-Name Index to the 1860 Historical and Statistical Gazetteer of New York State, 1860, by J. H. French, and a Listing of Geographic Names Missing in the Original Index* (Interlaken, N.Y.: Heart of the Lakes Publishing, 1993).

Brown's Lake—Burkhart Creek

Name (ZIP) or Variant Name	**Type or Pop.**	**County**	**USGS Map (7.5′ series)**	**Lat/Long Coordinates**	**Source(s) & Other Data**
Brown's Lake—*See* Otter Lake					
Browns Lake (Cedar Park)	CDP	Racine			F
Brownstone Falls	falls	Ashland	High Bridge	46 22 35N-090 38 27W	G
Brown Street Sch	school	Milwaukee	Milwaukee	43 03 26N-087 56 16W	G
Brown Street Sch	school	Waukesha	Stonebank	43 08 35N-088 27 41W	G; el 891
Browns Valley	valley	La Crosse	North Bend	44 00 40N-091 02 54W	G
Browns Valley Sch	school	La Crosse	Four Corners	44 01 16N-090 59 18W	G; el 906
Brownsville 53006	450	Dodge	Lomira	43 36 59N-088 29 26W	G F C
Browntown 53522	320	Green	Browntown	42 34 40N-089 47 39W	G F C
Brownville	locale	Chippewa	Huron	45 01 53N-090 56 01W	G F; el 1151
Bruce 54819	930	Rusk	Bruce	45 27 25N-091 16 23W	G F C; el 1106
Bruce Creek	stream	Waushara	Spring Lake	44 03 13N-089 08 31W	G; BGN 1961
Bruce Creek—*See* Bruce Valley Creek					
Bruce Lake	lake	Lincoln	Harrison	45 24 41N-089 31 25W	G
Bruce Lake	lake	Rusk	Bruce	45 26 49N-091 17 08W	G; el 1081
Bruce Mound	summit	Clark	Merrillan	44 26 38N-090 47 32W	G; el 1355
Bruce Valley Ch	church	Trempealeau	Pleasantville	44 28 32N-091 21 39W	G
Bruce Valley Creek	stream	Trempealeau	Pleasantville	44 26 04N-091 21 45W	G; BGN 1970
Brueckerville Sch	school	Marathon	Corinth	45 00 12N-090 14 16W	G
Bruemmer County Park	park	Kewaunee	Kewaunee	44 27 38N-087 33 04W	G
Bruemmer Creek	stream	Kewaunee	Brussels	44 37 50N-087 31 30W	G
Bruemmerville	pop. pl.	Kewaunee	Algoma	44 36 24N-087 28 12W	G F
Brule 54820	pop. pl.	Douglas	Brule	46 33 11N-091 34 35W	G F
Brule (Town of)	550	Douglas			F C
Brule Creek	stream	Forest	Hagerman Lake	46 00 57N-088 51 31W	G
Brule Creek—*See* Kentuck Creek					
Brule Island Dam	dam	Florence	Florence East	45 56 52N-088 13 10W	G; el 1205
Brule Lookout Tower	locale	Douglas	Island Lake	46 27 56N-091 34 03W	G

Figure 3-13. From *Omni Gazetteer of the United States of America,* vol. 6,

Another fine example of a state gazetteer is "A List of Illinois Place Names," compiled by James N. Adams, *Illinois Libraries* 50 (4)–50 (6) (April-June 1968) (reprint; Springfield: Illinois State Library, 1989). The author searched records of the Post Office Department, and much of the information relates to post office names and changes. In 1958 the original list contained 8,908 names. The list was expanded to include place names mentioned in county histories, atlases, and newspapers. When the project was completed in 1961, the list contained 13,948 entries. The researcher looking for Franklin, Illinois, would find that there were twelve places named Franklin. In addition, there were seven other Franklins with the additional names of Corner, Courthouse, Crossing, Grove, Park, and Place (two entries); another place was named Franklin's Prairie.

For gazetteers of specific regions or states, see listings in the chapter bibliography.

POSTAL GUIDES AND SHIPPING GUIDES

Postal Guides

During the rapid growth of the nineteenth century, new settlements were established frequently and others disappeared. Before mail could be delivered, it was necessary for local residents to choose a town name and then send a petition to the Post Office Department in Washington, D.C., for a local post office. Upon approval, a postmaster was selected and delivery of mail commenced. Postal employees needed to learn of new settlements and the counties in which they were located in order to deliver the mail, so *postal guides* containing this information were published by the Post Office Department. Postal guides consisted of state-by-state listings of post offices and the counties in which they were located. Some guides listed post offices that had recently been closed, and often the names of postmasters were included. A postal guide is helpful in locating a town that was in existence for only a short period of time or that underwent a name change. Figure 3-15 is an example from the 1862 *List of Post Offices in the United States.*

Records of post offices were maintained by the Post Office Department, but many of the records have been transferred to the National Archives. These records are described in preliminary inventories 114 and 168, prepared by Hecht and others (1955 and 1967); they are listed below.

Postmasters are employees of the U.S. government, and appointment registers (170 volumes) dating from 1789 through 30 September 1971 are in the National Archives. For more information about records of postmasters, see chapter 14 in *Guide to Genealogical Research in the National Archives*, rev. ed. (Washington, D.C.: National Archives Trust Fund Board, 1985).

A readily available and relatively inexpensive postal guide is the *National Five-Digit ZIP Code and Post Office Directory* (cited below), which can be purchased at any post office. The five-digit ZIP (Zone Improvement Plan) code, which was introduced in 1963, was instituted to improve the delivery of mail; and in 1983 the ZIP + 4 code was added. The 1996 edition of the *Directory* lists the names of forty thousand post offices, stations, and branches that serve approximately 117 million homes, farms, and businesses across the United States.

The *Directory* has several sections. Section 3 lists town names alphabetically by state; the county name follows the town name. Section 4 lists the post offices, including the ZIP codes, under the appropriate counties within the respective states; the county seat is indicated. Section 5 is an alphabetical list that includes post offices, branch post offices, community post offices, named stations, and place names. Following the name of the town, the state in which it is located is listed; for example, there are twenty-seven towns named Franklin, each of which is in a different state, and there are nineteen towns with names ranging from Franklin Center to Franklinville. Section 6 is a numerical list of post offices by ZIP code and three-digit ser-

Wisconsin • 662 • *OMNI GAZETTEER OF THE UNITED STATES*

Name (ZIP) or Variant Name	Type or Pop.	County	USGS Map (7.5′ series)	Lat/Long Coordinates	Source(s) & Other Data
Budd (Bud)	pop. pl.	Vernon			F
Budsberg Lake	lake	Portage	Iola	44 32 48N-089 14 36W	G
Budsin	pop. pl.	Marquette	Germania	43 55 10N-089 18 43W	G F; el 822
Buehler Valley	valley	Buffalo	Dodge	44 09 42N-091 36 46W	G
Buell Valley	valley	Buffalo	Waumandee	44 20 52N-091 39 49W	G
Buena Lake	lake	Racine	Waterford	42 47 18N-088 13 09W	G
Buena Park	pop. pl.	Racine	Waterford	42 47 34N-088 13 15W	G F
Buena Vista	pop. pl.	Waukesha	Hartland	43 03 56N-088 21 06W	G F
Buena Vista (Town of)	1,100	Portage			F C
Buena Vista (Town of)	1,450	Richland			F C
Buena Vista Cem	cemetery	Portage	Blaine	44 20 08N-089 22 13W	G
Buena Vista Ch	church	Portage	Arnott	44 24 05N-089 26 49W	G; el 1134
Buena Vista Creek	stream	Portage	Kellner	44 22 08N-089 43 09W	G; BGN 1968
Buena Vista Creek—*See* Fourmile Creek					
Buena Vista House	hist. pl.	Walworth			H
Buena Vista Park	park	Buffalo	Alma	44 19 26N-091 54 40W	G
Buffalo	930	Buffalo			F C
Buffalo (Town of)	810	Buffalo			F C
Buffalo (Town of)	860	Marquette			F C
Buffalo—*See* Buffalo City					
Buffalo Bay	bay	Bayfield	Bayfield	46 50 56N-090 47 06W	G
Buffalo Ch	church	Marquette	Observatory Hill	43 43 24N-089 21 56W	G
Buffalo City	pop. pl.	Buffalo	Cochrane	44 13 50N-091 51 51W	G
Buffalo (County)	14,500	Buffalo			F C
Buffalo Island	island	Buffalo	Ella	44 35 07N-092 01 25W	G
Buffalo Lake	lake	Bayfield	Clam Lake	46 09 54N-090 57 12W	G; el 1456
Buffalo Lake	lake	Burnett	Yellow Lake	45 56 46N-092 23 33W	G; el 933
Buffalo Lake	lake	Douglas	Gordon	46 10 02N-091 50 20W	G

Great Lakes States.

vice areas (multicoded cities). A significant limitation of the *Directory* is that it lists only towns in which there is a post office, branch post office, community post office, or named station.

Many maps have been published showing the locations of post offices, the distances between them, frequency of service, and mail-carrying railroads by name of railroad (see "Nineteenth-Century Maps—Post-Route Maps," above).

Sometimes mail was addressed improperly. If the street name was listed but the name of the city or the state (or both) was omitted, for example, the mail was forwarded to the Division of Dead Letters. To aid in the delivery of the mail, a directory entitled *Street Directory of the Principal Cities of the United States Embracing Letter-Carrier Offices Established to April 30, 1908*, 5th ed. (Washington, D.C.: published by order of the postmaster general, 1908) was published. It lists the names of the streets, avenues, courts, places, lanes, roads, and wharves, and the states in which they were found. For example, for the street name Bouvee, the directory lists each town that had a street with that name. Amsterdam, New York, is the only town listed as having a street named Bouvee, so mail would have been forwarded to that city for delivery.

Key Sources—Postal Guides

- *Abridged United States Official Postal Guide*. Washington, D.C.: U.S. Government Printing Office, 1934.

- Bowen, Eli. *The United States Post-Office Guide*. New York: D. Appleton, 1851. Reprint. New York: Arno Press, 1976 (FHL microfilm no. 1036719, item 3).

- *Cram's Standard American Railway System Atlas of the World: Accompanied by a Complete and Simple Index of the United States Showing the True Location of All Railroads, Towns, Villages and Post Offices. . . .* Chicago: George F. Cram, 1895 (FHL microfilm no. 1421836, item 2).

- Hecht, Arthur, and William J. Heynen, comps. *Records and Policies of the Post Office Department Relating to Place-Names*. Reference Information Paper no. 72. Washington, D.C.: National Archives and Records Service, 1975.

- ________, Frank J. Nivert, Fred W. Warriner, Jr., and Charlotte M. Ashby, comps. Revised by Forrest R. Holdcamper. *Records of the Post Office Department*. Preliminary Inventory 168. Washington, D.C.: National Archives and Records Service, 1967.

- _____, Fred W. Warriner, Jr., and Charlotte M. Ashby, comps. *Records of the Bureaus of the Third and Fourth Assistant Postmasters General. . . .* Preliminary Inventory 114. Washington, D.C.: National Archives and Records Service, 1955.

- *List of Post Offices in the United States. . . .* These lists were published at the direction of the Post Office Department, and their titles vary slightly. Hecht and Heynen (above) listed the years and various publishers. The following editions have been reprinted or are available on microfilm or microfiche.

  1804. Early American Imprints, Second Series, no. 7538, microfiche.

  1807. Early American Imprints, Second Series, no. 16456, microfiche.

  1857 (FHL microfilm no. 0928192, item 4).

  1860–61. Marietta, Ohio: C. E. Clines, 1860. Reprint. Marietta, Ohio: Lemon Tree Press, ca. 1993.

- *National Five-Digit ZIP Code and Post Office Directory*. 2 vols. Washington, D.C.: U.S. Postal Service, 1974–. Annual.

- *Pratt's United States Post Office Directory, 1850*. New York: E. Loriston Pratt, 1849. Reprint. Holland, Mich.: T. Wierenga, ca. 1981. This directory was current to September 1849.

- Rapp, William F. "A Bibliography of State and Territorial Books and Articles on Postal History." *Postal History—U.S.A.* 3 (December 1974): 67–68.

- _____. "A Bibliography of State and Territorial Books and Articles on Postal History, Supplement 1." *Postal History—U.S.A.* 4 (March 1975): 7–8.

- Simmons, Don. *Post Offices in the United States*. Melber, Ky.: Simmons Historical Publications, 1991. The introduction to this book states that it is a complete listing of all post offices in the U.S. as of 12 December 1893.

OTSEGO COUNTY.

PLAINFIELD—was formed from Richfield, March 25, 1799. It is the N. W. corner town of the co. Its surface is a broken and hilly upland. Unadilla River, forming the W. boundary, is bordered by steep bluffs rising to the height of 400 to 600 ft. The soil is a clay and sandy loam. **Unadilla Forks,** (p. v.,) at the junction of the E. and W. branches of Unadilla River, contains 2 churches, a hoe factory, flouring mill, sawmill, and machine shop. Pop. 253. **Plainfield Center** contains a church and 15 houses; **Spooners Corners** is a p. o.; **Leonardsville,** (p.v.,) on the Unadilla, in the S. part, is mostly in Madison co. The first settlement was made at and near Plainfield Center, in 1793, by Ruggles Spooner, Elias Wright, and John Kilbourne.[1] The first church (Bap.) was formed and the church erected in 1800; Rev. John Wait the first preacher.[2]

RICHFIELD—was formed from Otsego, April 10, 1792. Exeter and Plainfield were taken off in 1799. It is the extreme northern town of the co. Its surface is rolling and moderately hilly, with a mean elevation of 150 to 200 ft. above Schuyler Lake,—Pray and Nine Hills, on either side of the head of the lake, rising about 200 ft. higher. Schuyler Lake, in the S. E. corner, occupies a deep valley; and into it flow several small streams from the N. and W. The soil is of a diversified character, consisting of gravel, slate, clay, and sandy loam, well cultivated and productive. About 500,000 pounds of cheese are made in the town annually,—being more than double that made in any other town in the co. **Richfield Springs,** (p. v.,) near the head of Schuyler Lake, in the N. E. corner of the town, contains 3 churches, a flouring mill, and 368 inhabitants.[3] **Monticello,** (Richfield p. o.,) near the center, contains a church and 139 inhabitants. **Mayflower** is a p. o; **Brighton** contains about 15 houses. Settlements were made prior to the Revolution; but they were broken up during the war. The first settlers after the war were John Kimball, Richard and Wm. Pray, John Beardsley, Joseph Coats, and Seth Allen, in 1787.[4] The first church (Prot. E.) was formed at Monticello, May 20, 1799; Rev. Daniel Nash was the first pastor.[5]

ROSEBOOM[6]—was formed from Cherry Valley, Nov. 23, 1854. It lies on the E. border of the co., N. of the center. The surface is a hilly upland, broken by the valleys of several streams. The hills are generally rounded, and their summits elevated 300 to 350 ft. above Schoharie Kil. The soil is a gravelly loam. **Roseboom,** (p. v.,) in the N. W. part, on the line of Middlefield, contains a church and 111 inhabitants; and **South Valley,** (p. v.,) in the S. E. part, 2 churches and 175 inhabitants. **Pleasant Brook** (p. o.) is a hamlet.[7] The settlements in this town were commenced about 1800. There are 5 churches in town.[8]

Figure 3-14. Information for each county described in French's *Gazetteer of the State of New York* includes when the county was created, from what area, and subsequent changes; topography and soil conditions; internal improvements; county seats, including names of first county officers; brief historical sketch of the county; names and descriptions of villages, hamlets, and localities; and incidents of general and local interest.

- *Table of Post Offices in the United States. . . .* These tables were published at the direction of the Post Office Department. Their titles vary slightly. Hecht and Heynen (above) listed the various publishers. The following editions have been reprinted or are available on microfilm or microfiche.

  1796. Early American Imprints, First Series, no. 47980, microfiche.

  1811. Early American Imprints, Second Series, no. 24322, microfiche.

  1813. Early American Imprints, Second Series, no. 30380, microfiche.

  1817. Early American Imprints, Second Series, no. 42748, microfiche.

  1819. Early American Imprints, Second Series, no. 49955, microfiche.

  1831 (FHL microfilm no. 0989449, item 1).

  1836 (FHL microfilm no. 1673339, item 2).

  1837. Washington, D.C.: Langtree and O'Sullivan. Reprint. Kokomo, Ind.: Selby Publishing, 1985.

  1846 (FHL microfilm no. 0599566, item 3; microfiche nos. 6016375–6016377).

  1851 (FHL microfilm no. 0928168, item 1; microfiche nos. 6016378–6016380).

  1857 (FHL microfilm no. 0928192, item 4).

LIST OF POST OFFICES IN THE UNITED STATES.

List of post offices in the United States, arranged alphabetically—Continued.

Office.	County and State.	Postmaster.	Office.	County and State.	Postmaster.
Newville	Cumberland ... Pa.	C. T. McLaughlin	Niven	Susquehannah . Pa.	Joseph W. Fisk
Newville	Sussex ... Va.		Niverville	Columbia ... N. Y.	Edward Carr
Newville	Vernon ... Wis.	Barnet S. Moore	Nixburgh	Coosa ... Ala.	
New Vineyard	Franklin ... Me.	Luther T. Voter	Noah	Shelby ... Ind.	Leander Kennedy
New Virgil	Kane ... Ill.	Wm. H. Robinson	Noank	New London .. Conn.	William Latham
New Virginia	Warren ... Iowa	John W. Harsh	*Noble* (*c. h.*)	Noble ... Ind.	Ira B. White
New Wakefield	Washington ... Ala.		Noble	Richland ... Ill.	Sam'l Hutchinson
New Washington	Clark ... Ind.	M. J. Tilford	Noble Centre	Branch ... Mich.	Sam'l S. Bushnell
New Washington	Clearfield ... Pa.	James Gallaher	Noblesborough	Lincoln ... Me.	Edmund Nugent
New Washington	Crawford ... Ohio	Ernst A. Hesse	Noblestown	Alleghany ... Pa.	Wesley Kerr
New Waterford	Columbiana ... Ohio	John Baker	*Noblesville* (*c. h.*)	Hamilton ... Ind.	Thos. W. Oliphant
New Waverly	Cass ... Ind.	John A. Forgy	Nobleton	Newton ... Mo.	Jas. L. Van Lear
New Way	Licking ... Ohio	David C. Brooks	Nobleville	Noble ... Ohio	Joseph Archer
New Westfield	Wood ... Ohio	Levi Taylor	Nobob	Barren ... Ky.	James E. Wilson
New Westville	Preble ... Ohio	Alex. P. Campbell	Nochway	Randolph ... Ga.	
New Wilmington	Lawrence ... Pa.	N. P. Chambers	Nockenut	Guadaloupe ... Texas	
New Winchester	Hendricks ... Ind.	Wm. M. Sanders	Noell	Iron ... Mo.	Samuel Tullock
New Windsor	Carroll ... Md.	Joseph Ecker	Nogallis Prairie	Trinity ... Texas	
New Woodburn	Warren ... Ky.	J. M. Wilkerson	Nohart	Richardson ... Neb.	Jos. H. Burbank
New Woodstock	Madison ... N. Y.	S. M. House	Nokomis	Montgomery .. Ill.	Horace F. Rood
New York (*c. h.*)°	New York ... N. Y.	Abram Wakeman	Noland's River	Johnson ... Texas	
New York	Montgomery .. Tenn.		Nolensville	Williamson ... Tenn.	
New York	Wayne ... Iowa	Albert De Golier	Nolin	Hardin ... Ky.	Joshua G. Dorsey
New York Mills	Oneida ... N. Y.	N. H. Hoag	Nominy Grove	Westmoreland, Va.	
New Zion	Clarendon ... S. C.		Non Intervention	Lunenburg ... Va.	
Ney	De Kalb ... Ill.	Daniel Corson	Nonpareil	Knox ... Ohio	Isaac D. Hyatt
Ney	Defiance ... Ohio	Wm. F. Kintigh	Noonday	Cobb ... Ga.	
Niagara Falls*	Niagara ... N. Y.	Wm. F. Evans	Nooseneck Hill	Kent ... R. I.	Daniel Hall

Figure 3-15. From *List of Post Offices in the United States, Including Various Postal Laws and Instructions of 1861, 1863, 1864 and 1865* (1862; reprint; Holland, Mich.: Theron Wierenga, 1981), page 122.

- *United States Official Postal Guide....* These guides were published yearly from 1874 through 1954 at the direction of the Post Office Department. Hecht and Heynen (above) listed the various publishers. The following editions have been reprinted or are available on microfilm or microfiche.

  1874. Reprint. Shelbyville, Mo.: K. Wilham Genealogical Research & Publishing, 1990.

  1903 (FHL microfilm no. 0928262, item 5).

  1905 (FHL microfilm no. 0928246, item 1; microfiche no. 6051281; also microfiche nos. 6016381–6016388).

  1923 (FHL microfilm no. 1320852, item 4).

  1925 (FHL microfilm no. 1036183, item 6).

For postal guides of a specific state, see listings in the chapter bibliography.

Shipping Guides

A shipping guide differs from a postal guide in that it is privately printed, and it lists the railroad station nearest every post office. It facilitates the shipment and delivery of freight. *Bullinger's Postal and Shippers Guide for the United States and Canada* (cited below under "Key Sources—Shipping Guides") has been published annually since 1871 (figure 3-16). The 1989 edition consists of two books. Book 1 lists the town name (alphabetically), county, state, post office, nearest railroad terminal point, ZIP code, and area code for more than 200,000 communities in the United States. Book 2 contains all information regarding post offices and railroad stations in Canada. The editions published after 1989 list cities where changes have occurred.

Key Sources—Shipping Guides

- *ABC Pathfinder Shipping and Mailing Guide*. Boston: New England Railway Pub. Co., ca. 1893 (FHL microfilm no. 1036075, item 2; also, FHL microfilm no. 0907834).

- Bullinger, Edwin W., comp. *The Monitor Post Office, Banking and Shipper's Guide: Containing Every Post Office in the United States*. New York: Bullinger, 1872 (FHL microfilm no. 1002373, item 1).

- *Bullinger's Postal and Shippers Guide for the United States and Canada: Containing Post Offices and Railroad Freight Stations with the Nearest Post Offices and Railroads on which Every Place or the Nearest Communicating Point is Located and the List of Railroads and Their Terminal Points*. Westwood, N.J.: Bullinger's Guides, 1871–. Annual. The FHL has one or more copies of the following editions (the titles and imprints vary): 1871, 1895(?), 1951, 1961, 1971, 1972, 1985, 1986, 1987, 1988, 1989, 1990, 1991, and 1992. The following editions are available on microfilm: 1878 (FHL microfilm no. 1002373, item 2),

Figure 3-16. *Bullinger's Postal and Shippers Guide for the United States and Canada* is a shipping guide. This example is from vol. 123, *1994–96.*

3-550 CLY **U.S. PLACES**

Clymer, NY *County:* Chautauqua
Mail: CLYMER, NY 14724
Ph:(716) *Airports:* BUF,JHW,8G2
Rail Loc: Columbus, PA (CR)
Clymer, PA *County:* Indiana
Mail: CLYMER, PA 15728
/PENN RUN, PA 15765
Ph:(412) *Airports:* PIT,LBE,IDI
Rail Loc: Clymer 1 Mine, PA (CR)
Clymer, PA *County:* Tioga
Mail: SABINSVILLE, PA 16943
Ph:(717) *Airports:* ROC,ELM,N38
Rail Loc: Wellsboro Junction, PA (CR) (WCOR)
Clymer 1 Mine ⊗, PA
County: Indiana
Mail: CLYMER, PA 15728
Ph:(412) *Airports:* PIT,LBE,IDI
RR: CR
Clymer Center, NY
County: Chautauqua
Mail: CLYMER, NY 14724
Ph:(716) *Airports:* BUF,JHW,D88
Rail Loc: Columbus, PA (CR)
Clymer Hill, NY
County: Chautauqua
Mail: CLYMER, NY 14724
Ph:(716) *Airports:* BUF,JHW,D88
Rail Loc: Columbus, PA (CR)
Clymers, IN *County:* Cass
Mail: LOGANSPORT, IN 46947
Ph:(219) *Airports:* FWA,LAF,GGP
Rail Loc: Clymers, IN (CR) (NS) (TPW) (WSRY)
Clymers ⊗, IN *County:* Cass
Mail: LOGANSPORT, IN 46947
Ph:(219) *Airports:* FWA,LAF,GGP
RR: CR, NS, NS(Clymers (WSRY)), TPW, WSRY

C M Pardey Ranch, WA
County: Okanogan
Mail: WAUCONDA, WA 98859
Ph:(509)
Airports: GEG,YKM,WA48
Rail Loc: Torboy, WA (BN)
C M Quarter Circle Ranch, MT
County: Flathead
Mail: LAKESIDE, MT 59922
Ph:(406) *Airports:* GEG,FCA,S27
Rail Loc: Kalispell, MT (BN)
Cm Ranch, WY *County:* Fremont
Mail: DUBOIS, WY 82513
Ph:(307) *Airports:* BIL,JAC,U25
Rail Loc: Riverton, WY (BDW)
C Munson Ranch, NE
County: McPherson
Mail: TRYON, NE 69167
Ph:(308) *Airports:* LNK,GLD,5V3
Rail Loc: Thedford, NE (BN)
C Newton, TX *County:* La Salle
Mail: COTULLA, TX 78014
Ph:(512) *Airports:* SAT,LRD,COT
Rail Loc: Artesia Wells, TX (MP)
C Nicholas Ranch, SD
County: Lawrence
Mail: SPEARFISH, SD 57783
Ph:(605) *Airports:* BIL,RAP,SPF
Rail Loc: Belle Fourche, SD (CNW)
C N Ranch, AZ *County:* Graham
Mail: WILLCOX, AZ 85643
Ph:(602) *Airports:* TUS,SVC,E37
Rail Loc: Safford, AZ (AZER)
Coabey, PR *County:* Jayuya
Mail: (N/A)
Ph:(809) *Airports:* SJU,BQN,PSE
Rail Loc: San Juan, PR (TMT)

Coahoma, MS *County:* Coahoma
Mail: COAHOMA, MS 38617
Ph:(601)
Airports: MEM,GLH,CKM
Rail Loc: Coahoma, MS (MSDR)
Coahoma ⊗, MS
County: Coahoma
Mail: COAHOMA, MS 38617
Ph:(601)
Airports: MEM,GLH,CKM
RR: MSDR
Coahoma, TX *County:* Howard
Mail: COAHOMA, TX 79511
Ph:(915) *Airports:* MAF,SJT,21XS
Rail Loc: Coahoma, TX (MP)
Coahoma ⊗, TX *County:* Howard
Mail: COAHOMA, TX 79511
Ph:(915) *Airports:* MAF,SJT,21XS
RR: MP
Coahoma Junior College, MS
County: Coahoma
Mail: CLARKSDALE, MS 38614
Ph:(601)
Airports: MEM,GLH,CKM
Rail Loc: Clover Hill, MS (MSDR)
Coahulla Ranch, TN
County: Bradley
Mail: MC DONALD, TN 37353
Ph:(615) *Airports:* CHA,AVL,3M3
Rail Loc: Chestuee, TN (CSXT)
Coakley, KY *County:* Green
Mail: GREENSBURG, KY 42743
Ph:(502) *Airports:* SDF,BWG,AAS
Rail Loc: Bonnieville, KY (CSXT)
Coakley, NC *County:* Edgecombe
Mail: HOBGOOD, NC 27843
Ph:(919) *Airports:* RDU,RWI,W55
Rail Loc: Tarboro, NC (CSXT)

1895 (FHL microfilm no. 1033518), 1951 (FHL microfilm no. 0483709), and 1961 (FHL microfilm no. 1320793, item 7).

MAPS, GAZETTEERS, AND THE COMPUTER

In this high-technology age, computer technology has revolutionized map-making with new cartographic tools and techniques. Maps can be easily modified and enlarged, segments can be isolated, and map scales can be changed. The information can be easily stored and retrieved, either in graphic form as digital maps or in numerical form as a body of data. It can be shared readily with cartographers and other individuals around the world via World Wide Web sites on the Internet or on CD-ROMs.

USGS Cartographic Databases

The USGS has compiled numerous cartographic databases, many of which are accessible on the Internet or on CD-ROMs. The databases listed below are particularly useful to family researchers. They have been discussed previously in this chapter; reference is made to the appropriate sections.

USGS Cartographic Databases on the Internet. See "Gazetteers—Twentieth-Century National Gazetteers—Geographic Names Information System (GNIS)," above, for information about the GNIS database, which contains more than 2 million place and feature names.

See "Gazetteers—Twentieth-Century National Gazetteers—Geographic Names Information System (GNIS)," above, for information about the Tiger Map Server, which is linked to the GNIS database and generates high-quality digital maps showing the locations of place and feature names.

See "Maps—Fact Sheets and General Interest Publications," above, for a list of USGS World Wide Web data and information sites.

USGS Cartographic Databases on CD-ROMs. See "Maps—Digital Topographic Maps" for information about topographic maps that have been digitally scanned and are available on CD-ROMs.

See "Gazetteers—Twentieth-Century National Gazetteers—Geographic Names Information System (GNIS)," above, for information about the GNIS database that is on a CD-ROM titled *The Digital Gazetteer of the U.S.* (There are considerably more place and feature names on the CD-ROM than in the online database version.)

Census Database on the Internet

See "Gazetteers—Twentieth-Century National Gazetteers—U.S. Gazetteer," above, for information about the database that is maintained by the U.S. Census Bureau and is linked to the Tiger Map Server.

Map Servers on the Internet

Tiger Map Server. This server was discussed above in connection with the USGS and Census databases. The World Wide Web address is <http://tiger.census.gov/>. From this database, a digital map can be customized for each town to show major and local highways, parks, railroads, streets, counties, and many other features.

Yahoo! Maps. The World Wide Web address is <http://www.proximus.com/yahoo/>. By giving two addresses (for example, the starting location and the destination), point-to-point driving directions via the shortest route are provided. Maps show major and local highways, streets, and the specific locations of the starting and destination addresses.

MapQuest. The World Wide Web address is <http://www.mapquest.com/>. Three programs are available: (1) TripQuest, which gives driving directions for the U.S.; (2) Personalized Maps; and (3) an Interactive Atlas for finding places using worldwide maps. The information and maps provided in TripQuest are similar to those available through Yahoo! Maps.

Mapping Software

Joel Makower, ed., *The Map Catalog: Every Kind of Map and Chart on Earth and Even Some Above It*, 3rd ed., newly rev. (New York: Vintage Books, a Division of Random House, 1992), describes numerous commercial mapping software programs. A few popular programs are listed below.

AAA Map'n'Go. Rel. 2. DeLorme Mapping, Freeport, Maine. This CD-ROM encompasses many of the features of *Street Atlas USA* (below). It also includes information about lodging, restaurants, and attractions.

Automap RoadAtlas. Rel. 4. Microsoft Corp., Redmond, Washington. This CD-ROM includes 150,000 places and more than 418,000 miles of roads. It includes interesting places to see and calculates distance from departure point to destination.

Automap Streets Plus. Microsoft Corp., Redmond, Washington. Virtually any street address in the United States can be located on this CD-ROM.

Rand McNally StreetFinder. 1997 ed. Rand McNally & Co., Chicago. Streets and addresses can be found easily on this CD-ROM. The program includes 1 million business listings.

Rand McNally TripMaker. 1997 ed. Rand McNally & Co., Chicago. This CD-ROM program simplifies travel planning. It includes thousands of attractions.

Street Atlas USA. Rel. 4. DeLorme Mapping, Freeport, Maine. This CD-ROM program includes virtually every street in the United States and more than 1 million lakes, rivers, railroads, airports, and other landmarks.

Tripmate* with *Street Atlas USA. Rel. 4. DeLorme Mapping, Freeport, Maine. Tripmate is a global positioning system receiver. When used with *Street Atlas USA* 4.0 and a portable (laptop) computer, this program shows the user's position on the map and moves on the screen as the user travels.

See "Maps—Territorial Maps" and "Maps—County Maps" for information regarding the *AniMap Plus County Boundary Historical Atlas*.

See "Maps—County Maps" for information regarding the *Encyclopedia of U.S. Counties*.

See "Maps—Nineteenth-Century Maps—American History Atlases" for information regarding the *American History Atlas*.

See "Maps—Nineteenth-Century Maps—American History Atlases" for information regarding the *American History Explorer*.

FINDING GEOGRAPHIC TOOLS

Geographic tools are produced by Federal and state governments, state and local tourism offices, historical and genealogical societies, and numerous commercial map companies.

Modern road maps for each state are available free of charge from each state's department of transportation, which usually is located in the state's capital city. Many such departments publish free catalogs that list the maps available for the state, counties, and cities and the agencies from which the maps may be obtained (if other than the department of transportation). Tourism or travel bureaus usually send state road maps free of charge upon request.

Local map stores may be listed in telephone directories. The International Map Dealers Association publishes a membership directory with a cross-reference by geographic location and type of products sold. For further information, contact:

International Map Dealers Association
P.O. Box 1789
Kankakee, IL 60901
1-815-939-4627

Since 1944, Rockford Map Publishers has published county plat maps, county atlases, state atlases, and sportsmen's guides, including atlases for more than six hundred counties. The county atlases contain one township to a page, and the names of landowners are listed. The main coverage is Illinois, Michigan, Minnesota, and Wisconsin, although some county atlases are available for other states. The company will make copies of out-of-print atlases. For further information, contact:

Rockford Map Publishers, Inc.
P.O. Box 6126
Rockford, IL 61125
1-800-321-1627

Numerous municipalities, counties, historical societies, libraries, and universities have reproduced early maps and atlases of their respective areas. For example, in 1979 the University of Kentucky published a set of ten maps that reflected the growth of the Commonwealth of Kentucky. A book by Thomas D. Clark titled *Historic Maps of Kentucky* (Lexington: University Press of Kentucky, 1979) described the maps, giving the background of each, and identified the map-makers and publishers.

Gazetteers, postal guides, and shipping guides will be found in the Geography and Map Division of the Library of Congress, in map libraries usually associated with major universities, in large public libraries, and in private libraries, such as the Family History Library. Some have been reprinted, and others are available on microfilm or microfiche.

Major Geographic Collections

Major libraries in the United States with geographic collections are described in David K. Carrington and Richard W. Stephenson, eds., *Map Collections in the United States and Canada: A Directory,* 4th ed. (New York: Special Libraries Association, 1985). David A. Cobb and Brent Allison's *Guide to U.S. Map Resources,* 2nd ed. (Chicago: American Library Association, 1990) provides detailed listings of the holdings of hundreds of public and private libraries; figure 3-17 is an example from that work's first edition. Makower's *The Map Catalog* (cited above under "Mapping Software") describes the numerous kinds of maps available today and lists many government and commercial sources for obtaining maps. Some libraries have prepared guides to their geographic collections.

Four notable map collections are described below. World Wide Web addresses are listed for libraries that have sites on the Internet.

Library of Congress. The Geography and Map Division of the Library of Congress has one of the world's great cartographic collections. The collection consists of more than 4 million maps, fifty-three thousand atlases, and thousands of other items. Among the library's vast holdings are excellent collections of nineteenth-century land ownership maps, fire insurance maps, ward maps, panoramic maps of cities, maps of explorers' trails, railroad maps, and Civil War maps. These maps are discussed in James C. Neagles and Mark C. Neagles's *The Library of Congress: A Guide to Genealogical and Historical Research* (Salt Lake City: Ancestry, 1990).

There is no single comprehensive catalog of the library's cartographic collection, but two free pamphlets are available upon request: *The Geography and Map Division* and *The Geography and Map Division List of Publications.* For further information, contact:

Library of Congress
Geography and Map Division
Washington, DC 20540-4650
<http:lcweb.loc.gov/>

Reproductions of individual maps and plates from atlases in the Library of Congress may be ordered through the library's Photoduplication Service for a fee (except where prohibited by copyright). Ordering information and prices may be obtained from the Geography and Map Division if a map citation (obtained from one of the division's publications) is supplied, or if specific information, such as site location and time period, is provided. The library's Photoduplication Service can sometimes provide ordering information and prices, but the Geography and Map Division is the better source. For further information, contact:

Library of Congress
Photoduplication Service
Washington, DC 20540-4650

National Archives. The National Archives has custody of almost 2 million maps produced by the Federal government since 1774. The *Guide to Cartographic Records in the National Archives* (Washington, D.C.: National Archives and Records Service, 1971) describes the collections.

The *Guide to Genealogical Research in the National Archives* (cited below under "Finding Aids—Geographic Collections") describes several cartographic series and checklists that are particularly useful to family researchers. These include census enumeration district maps from 1880 to 1960 (approximately 130,000), civil division outline maps (approximately five hundred), township survey plats (approximately forty-two thousand), U.S. land district maps, military maps from around 1770 to 1925, and post-route maps.

Virtually the entire cartographic collection at the National Archives is available for reproduction. Inexpensive black-and-white copies can be made, or photographic prints and negatives may be requested. Ordering information and prices can be obtained from the Cartographic and Architectural Branch if a map citation or specific information, such as site location and time period, is provided. For further information, contact:

The National Archives I (for most records of genealogical value)
Seventh and Pennsylvania Avenues NW
Washington, DC 20408
1-202-501-5400
<http://gopher.nara.gov/>

The National Archives II (for most cartographic material)
8601 Adelphi Road
College Park, MD 20470-6001
1-301-713-7040
Fax: 1-301-713-7488

American Geographical Society Collection (AGSC). This fine map collection includes approximately 448,350 maps, 7,916 atlases, 207,320 Landsat satellite images, 159,000 photographs, 130,000 volumes of geographic periodicals, an extensive book collection, and seventy-one rare and special globes. Some basic reference services are provided by mail and by telephone. For further information, contact:

The American Geographical Society Collection
The University of Wisconsin — Milwaukee
P.O. Box 399
Milwaukee, WI 53201
1-414-229-6282
1-800-558-8993
<http://leardo.lib.uwm.edu/>

68 **Massachusetts**

Massachusetts

400
Amherst College Library
Amherst, MA 01002
Tel. (413) 542-2319
Hours: 8:30–4:30, 6–9, M–F
Responsible Person: Merritt, Floyd S.
Special Strengths: United States
Employees: Full Time Part Time
Prof. 0 1
Non-Prof. 0 1
Holdings:
60000 Printed Maps
485 Atlases
4 Globes
175 Wall Maps
6 Raised Relief Maps
25 Microforms
155 Books
65 Gazetteers
3 Serial Titles
Chronological Coverage: 5% pre 1900; 95% post 1900
Map collection is cataloged 5%
Classification: LC Utility: OCLC
Formats: Cards, Online
Available to: Public, Students, Faculty
Average monthly use: 25
Copying Facilities: Copying machine, Microform
Equipment:
33 5-drawer cabinets
12 4-drawer cabinets
Square Footage: 784
Map Depositories: USGS (topo); USGS (geol); DMA (topo); GPO

402
Boston Athenaeum
10½ Beacon St.
Boston, MA 02117
Tel. (617) 227-0270
Hours: 9–5:30, M–F; 9–4, Sa (October–May)
Special Strengths: Boston (1870–1930), New England (pre-1900)
Employees: Full Time Part Time
Prof. 0 4
Holdings:
4000 Printed Maps
1000 Atlases
5 Globes
100 Books
50 Gazetteers
1 Serial Title
Chronological Coverage: 75% pre 1900; 25% post 1900
Map collection is cataloged 95%
Classification: LC Utility: OCLC
Formats: Cards
Preservation methods: Encapsulation, Deacidification, Japanese paper
Average monthly use: 20
Copying Facilities: Copying machine, Photographic reproduction
Equipment:
9 5-drawer cabinets
Deep shelving for large flat books
Square Footage: 350
Map Depositories: USGS (topo)

Figure 3-17. Cobb's *Map Collections in the United States and Canada: A Directory* provides detailed listings of the holdings of hundreds of public and private libraries.

The Family History Library and Local Family History Centers. The Family History Library, located in Salt Lake City, Utah, has hundreds of branches called family history centers that are located in or near major cities throughout the United States and in many foreign countries. The Family History Library has microfilm or microfiche copies of many geographic collections found at the National Archives and at other major archives and libraries. Most items that are on microfilm or microfiche may be ordered for searching at local family history centers.

United States Research Outline (Salt Lake City: Family History Library, 1988) gives specific instructions on how to locate geographic material in the *Family History Library Catalog.*

Finding Aids—Geographic Collections

- Allen, Desmond Walls. *Where to Write for County Maps.* Bryant, Ark.: Research Associates, ca. 1991 (FHL microfiche no. 6104917). This book lists the addresses of the departments of transportation in the various states.

- Bentley, Elizabeth Petty. *County Courthouse Book.* 2nd ed. Baltimore: Genealogical Publishing Co., 1996. This book lists the current addresses and telephone numbers of 3,351 county courthouses in the United States. Knowing their addresses and telephone numbers is helpful because plat maps are located in courthouses.

- _____. *The Genealogist's Address Book 1995–97.* 3rd ed. Baltimore: Genealogical Publishing Co., 1995. This book includes names and addresses of government agencies, societies, libraries, archives, professional organizations, periodicals, newspaper columns, publishers, booksellers, databases, and bulletin boards.

- Carrington, David K., and Richard W. Stephenson, eds. *Map Collections in the United States and Canada: A Directory.* 4th ed. New York: Special Libraries Association, 1985. This guide lists the major universities, public libraries, and historical societies that have geographic collections. For each institution, the information includes its address, the size of the collection, area of specialization (region or state), subject of specialization (for example, history, exploration, mining, Indians), and special cartographic collections. The institutions are arranged alphabetically by city within a state or province (in Canada).

- Clark, David Sanders. *Index to Maps of the American Revolution in Books and Periodicals Illustrating the Revo-*

lutionary War and Other Events of the Period 1763–1789. Westport, Conn.: Greenwood Press, 1974.

- Cobb, David A., and Brent Allison, comps. *Guide to U.S. Map Resources*. 2nd ed. Chicago: American Library Association, 1990.

- *Directory of Historical Organizations in the United States and Canada*. Nashville: AASLH Press, 1990.

- Grim, Ronald E. *Historical Geography of the United States: A Guide to Information Sources*. Geography and Travel Information Guide Series, vol. 5. Detroit: Gale Research, 1982. This guide covers cartographic sources and guides to map repositories, historical sources for geographers, directories and collective finding aids in archival and other historical institutions, and literature in historical geography. Each bibliographic listing is annotated.

- *Guide to Cartographic Records in the National Archives*. Washington, D.C.: National Archives and Records Service, 1971. This guide describes maps that were acquired through 1966. It contains comprehensive descriptions of the National Archives map collections, including record group numbers.

- *Guide to Genealogical Research in the National Archives*. Rev. ed. Washington, D.C.: National Archives Trust Fund Board, 1985. This guide explains the records preserved in the National Archives and what specific information is included in each type of record.

- Karrow, Robert W., Jr., ed. *Checklist of Printed Maps of the Middle West to 1900*. 14 vols. in 12. Boston: G. K. Hall, 1981–83. The list describes 25,478 entries found in 127 different collections, which include maps of cities and towns, panorama maps, fire insurance maps, and maps in government documents. The list includes all known landownership books for Illinois, Indiana, Iowa, Kansas, Michigan, Missouri, Nebraska, North Dakota, Ohio, South Dakota, and Wisconsin.

- Makower, Joel, ed. *The Map Catalog: Every Kind of Map and Chart on Earth and Even Some Above It*. 3rd ed. Newly rev. New York: Vintage Books, a Division of Random House, 1992. This fine book contains information about numerous types of maps, atlases, globes, map accessories, and computer software. The names and addresses of publishers are included.

- McLaughlin, Patrick D. *Pre-Federal Maps in the National Archives: An Annotated List*. Special List no. 26. Washington, D.C.: National Archives and Records Service, 1971.

- Morrow, Dale W., and Deborah Jensen Morrow, comps. *Where to Buy County Maps in the United States*. Center, Mo.: Traces, ca. 1984. This book contains the name, address, and phone number of the agency in each state that sells county maps.

- Neagles, James C., and Mark C. Neagles. *The Library of Congress: A Guide to Genealogical and Historical Research*. Salt Lake City: Ancestry, 1990. This fine guide describes the map collections in the Geography and Map Division of the Library of Congress.

- Schaefer, Christina K. *The Center: A Guide to Genealogical Research in the National Capital Area*. Baltimore: Genealogical Publishing Co., 1996. This guide discusses how to locate family history and geographic material in the National Archives, the Library of Congress, the National Society of the Daughters of the American Revolution, and the National Genealogical Society. It includes agencies with Federal land records and military records, and government and public facilities in nearby Maryland and Virginia that have genealogical records.

- *United States Research Outline*. Salt Lake City: Family History Library, 1988. This outline briefly discusses the major genealogical record sources in the United States. It explains how to find information in the *Family History Library Catalog* by locality, subject, surname, author, or title. For many of the record sources, it lists important books and guides and cites some library call numbers and microfilm/microfiche numbers.

USING GEOGRAPHIC TOOLS

Geographic tools can provide information about the lives of ancestors that is not readily available from other sources. Once found on a map, a town is no longer a name only; it is placed in a setting that shows the surrounding area and its proximity to other communities. It might not be possible to visit the ancestral home or the place where a joyful or tragic event occurred; however, the town and its surroundings can be mentally visualized by studying a detailed topographic map.

Many states were carved out of early territories. The house of a pioneer family located in the Territory of Missouri in 1820 may have been in what became the state of Missouri; however, the researcher must be aware that the Territory of Missouri encompassed the future states of Colorado (part), Iowa, Kansas, Minnesota (part), Montana, Nebraska, North Dakota, South Dakota, and Wyoming (part). Territorial maps show changing boundaries and help to illustrate the development of the United States.

One of the compelling reasons for moving westward was the opportunity to obtain free or inexpensive land. Many pioneer families settled in remote areas, traveling by way of rugged trails, crude roads, rivers, canals, and trains. They studied maps prepared by early explorers, and they talked with mountain men and others living in the frontier, seeking information about the trails ahead. Children were sometimes born in different settlements along the way, and searching public and private records in the various counties can yield clues to the past. Maps showing early trails, roads, canals, and railroads will be found in many historical atlases.

The westward expansion of the railroad affected migration patterns. European emigrants heading for destinations in the western states and newly created territories often sailed on ships to the port of New Orleans. With the completion of railroad lines to the Mississippi and Missouri rivers in the mid-1850s, many immigrants arrived at ports in New York, Philadelphia, and Boston. From there they traveled overland by train and then trekked westward.

The 7.5-minute topographic map is the basic tool for locating property in rural areas of public-domain states. With the map and the legal land description, the exact location of the property can be determined. The name of an early landowner also might appear on a land ownership map. There may be a panorama map showing the farm or the city in which the family lived. By using census entries and land and tax records, the rural neighborhood may be reconstructed.

Most vital records dating from before statewide registration were recorded in county courthouses (or towns in the New England states). County boundaries changed often throughout the nineteenth and early twentieth centuries; a family might have lived in the same house for many years but in different counties at different time periods. Records remain in the courthouses where they were originally recorded, so sometimes it is necessary to search courthouses in several counties to find the desired information. Several atlases and books have been published that show the genealogy of counties and their changing boundaries.

An old fire insurance map may show an outline of an ancestor's house. Fire insurance maps, city directories, and census entries are the basic tools for reconstructing urban neighborhoods. While the process takes time, the results can provide a clear picture of the ancestral family and their friends and neighbors.

The makeup of U.S. neighborhoods reflects economic status, social standing, and, often, ethnic and/or religious heritage. Chicago is a city of neighborhoods, many of which are more than a century old and still relatively intact. A fine book, *Historic City: The Settlement of Chicago* (Chicago: Department of Development and Planning, 1976), includes six maps that reflect the growth of the city from 1840 to 1950. The maps are color-coded to reflect the various ethnic settlements in the city at different time periods.

People who had ancestors living in the United States in 1861 may be descended from one or more Civil War veterans. Maps showing important battle sites and troop movements can add interest to a history.

A family history can be enriched by incorporating a description of the ancestral town as found in a gazetteer, which may include information about commerce and living conditions. For example, Baldwin and Thomas's 1854 *New and Complete Gazetteer of the United States* describes Kanesville, Iowa, as a flourishing Mormon town pleasantly situated on a prairie four or five miles east of the Missouri River and about 240 miles west by south from Iowa City; as the largest town in the western part of the state and a place of active business, with thirty or forty stores. There was a tabernacle, and many emigrants to Utah were outfitted there. Its population in 1853 was three thousand. It also was called Council Bluffs. (Some of the preceding information was extracted from the Council Bluffs entry.)

Early geographic tools helped ancestors travel to new areas, and now they are useful to family history researchers who seek to learn about those ancestors. Modern geographical tools are useful in planning trips because they provide information about highways, waterways, national parks, historic sites, places to visit, and other attractions.

NOTES

1. Erie Canal Chronology. URL: <http://www.history.rochester.edu/canal/chron.htm>.

REFERENCE LIST

Billington, Ray Allen, and Martin Ridge. 1982. *Westward Expansion: A History of the American Frontier*. 5th ed. New York: Macmillan Publishing Co.

Drago, Harry Sinclair. 1972. *Canal Days in America: The History and Romance of Old Towpaths and Waters*. New York: Clarkson N. Potter. Distributed by Crown Publishers.

The Encyclopedia Americana. "United States — Domestic Trade and Commerce." New York: Americana Corp., 1956.

Greenhood, David. 1964. *Mapping*. Chicago: University of Chicago Press, 1964.

Holbrook, Stewart H. 1947. *The Story of American Railroads*. New York: Crown Publishers.

Makower, Joel, ed. 1992. *The Map Catalog: Every Kind of Map and Chart on Earth and Even Some Above It*. 3rd ed. Newly rev. New York: Vintage Books, a Division of Random House.

Mason, Philip P. 1967. *A History of American Roads*. Chicago: Rand McNally & Co.

Schweitzer, George K. 1996. *Civil War Genealogy*. Knoxville, Tenn.: the author.

Stephenson, Richard W., comp. 1967. *Land Ownership Maps: A Checklist of Nineteenth Century United States County Maps in the Library of Congress*. Washington, D.C.: Library of Congress.

Thompson, Morris M. 1987. *Maps for America: Cartographic Products of the U.S. Geological Survey and Others*. 3rd ed. Washington, D.C.: U.S. Geological Survey.

BIBLIOGRAPHY

The following list of maps, atlases, and gazetteers only begins to cover the vast resources available to the genealogist. Researchers looking for sources not listed here should check with the Library of Congress and the National Archives (which have more than 6 million maps, atlases, and gazetteers between them), state libraries, historical societies, university map libraries, and local public libraries.

It would be difficult to list all gazetteers of the United States that have been published; the titles seem to be endless. Each bibliography section lists some titles not found in other publications.

Regional United States

Each of the regional sources listed below contains descriptions of maps, atlases, gazetteers, or postal guides that are available for three or more states.

Maps and Atlases

Ensign and Thayer's Travellers' Guide through the States of Ohio, Michigan, Indiana, Illinois, Missouri, Iowa and Wisconsin: with Railroad, Canal, Stage, and Steamboat Routes, Accompanied with a New Map of the Above States. New York: Ensign, Bridgman & Fanning, 1855.

Karrow, Robert W., Jr., ed. *Checklist of Printed Maps of the Middle West to 1900*. 14 vols. in 12. Boston: G. K. Hall, 1981–83. Includes maps of the north central states region, Illinois, Indiana, Iowa, Kansas, Michigan, Minnesota, Missouri, Nebraska, North Dakota and South Dakota, Ohio, and Wisconsin.

Long, John H., ed. *Atlas of Historical County Boundaries: Delaware, Maryland, and District of Columbia*. New York: Simon & Schuster, 1996.

____, and Gordon DenBoer, comp. *Atlas of Historical County Boundaries: Maine, Massachusetts, Connecticut, and Rhode Island*. New York: Simon & Schuster, 1994.

Rand, McNally and Company's Business Atlas of the Great Mississippi Valley and Pacific Slope. Chicago: Rand McNally & Co., 1876. Reprinted as *Rand McNally's Pioneer Atlas of the American West*. Historical text by Dale L. Morgan. Chicago: Rand McNally & Co., 1969. Includes maps of the states of Alaska, Arizona, California-Nevada, Colorado, Dakota, Idaho, Kansas, Montana, Nebraska, New Mexico, Oregon, Texas-Indian Territory, Utah, Washington, and Wyoming.

Gazetteers and Postal Guides

Hayward, John. *The New England Gazetteer: Containing Descriptions of All the States, Counties and Towns in New England; Also Descriptions of the Principal Mountains, Rivers, Lakes, Capes, Bays, Harbors, Islands, and Fashionable Resorts within That Territory.* Concord, N.H.: Israel S. Boyd and William White, and Boston: John Hayward, 1839. Reprint. Bowie, Md.: Heritage Books, 1997.

Landis, Robert L. *Post Offices of Oregon, Washington, and Idaho*. Portland, Oreg.: Patrick Press, 1969.

Northwestern Gazetteer: Minnesota, North and South Dakota and Montana Gazetteer and Business Directory. St. Paul, Minn.: R. L. Polk and Co., 1914.

Alabama

Maps and Atlases

Dodd, Donald B., and Borden D. Dent. *Historical Atlas of Alabama*. University, Ala.: University of Alabama Press, 1974.

Lineback, Neal G., and Charles T. Traylor. *Atlas of Alabama*. University, Ala.: University of Alabama Press, 1973.

Long, John H., ed. *Atlas of Historical County Boundaries: Alabama*. New York: Simon & Schuster, 1996.

Mason, Sara Elizabeth. *A List of Nineteenth Century Maps of the State of Alabama*. Birmingham, Ala.: Birmingham Public Library, 1973.

Yesterday's Faces of Alabama: A Collection of Maps, 1822–1909. Montgomery, Ala.: Society of Pioneers of Montgomery, 1978.

Gazetteers and Postal Guides

Harris, W. Stuart. *Dead Towns of Alabama*. University, Ala.: University of Alabama Press, 1977.

Read, William A. *Indian Place-Names in Alabama*. Baton Rouge: Louisiana State University Press, 1937.

Scruggs, J. H., Jr. *Alabama Postal History*. Birmingham, Ala.: the author, 1950–59.

Alaska

Maps and Atlases

Alaska Atlas and Gazetteer. 4th ed. Freeport, Maine: DeLorme Mapping Co., 1995.

Falk, Marvin W. *Alaskan Maps: A Cartobibliography of Alaska to 1900*. New York: Garland Pub., 1983.

Gazetteers and Postal Guides

Orth, Donald J. *Dictionary of Alaska Place Names*. Washington, D.C.: U.S. Government Printing Office, 1967.

Polk, R. L. & Co. *Alaska-Yukon Gazetteer and Business Directory*. 1902, 1903, 1905–06, 1907–08, 1909–10, 1911–12, 1915–16, 1917–18, 1923–24, 1932–35. Microfilm. The 1902 and 1907–08 gazetteers are available from Public Archives of Canada in Ottawa. The others are available from the Alaska State Library in Juneau.

Schorr, Alan E. *Alaska Place Names*. 4th ed. Juneau: Denali Press, 1991.

Arizona

Maps and Atlases

Arizona Atlas and Gazetteer. 2nd ed. Freeport, Maine: DeLorme Mapping Co., 1996.

Dreyfuss, John J. *A History of Arizona's Counties and Courthouses*. Tuscon: National Society of the Colonial Dames of America in the State of Arizona, 1972.

Walker, Henry P., and Don Bufkin. *Historical Atlas of Arizona*. 2nd ed. Norman: University of Oklahoma Press, 1986.

Gazetteers and Postal Guides

Barnes, Will C. *Arizona Place Names*. Tucson: University of Arizona Press, 1935. Rev. and enl. by Byrd H. Granger. Tucson: University of Arizona Press, 1960.

Granger, Byrd H. *Arizona's Names: X Marks the Place*. With a forward by Sen. Barry Goldwater. Tucson, Ariz.: Falconer Pub. Co., 1983. Distributed by Treasure Chest Publications.

Theobold, John, and Lillian Theobold. *Arizona Territory: Post Offices and Postmasters*. Phoenix: Arizona Historical Foundation, 1961.

Arkansas

Maps and Atlases

Arkansas Atlas and Gazetteer. Freeport, Maine: DeLorme Mapping Co., 1997.

Baker, Russell P. *Township Atlas of Arkansas*. Hot Springs: Arkansas Genealogical Society, 1984.

Puetz, C. J., comp. *Arkansas County Maps*. Lyndon Station, Wis.: Thomas Publishing Co., 1986.

Smith, Richard M., ed. *The Atlas of Arkansas: Official Atlas of the State of Arkansas*. Fayetteville: University of Arkansas Press, 1989.

Gazetteers and Postal Guides

Allsopp, Frederick W. "Arkansas Place Names." *Folklore of Romantic Arkansas* 1 (1931): 59–107.

Baker, Russell P. *From Memdag to Norsk: A Historical Directory of Arkansas Post Offices, 1832–1971*. Hot Springs: Arkansas Genealogical Society, 1988.

Work Projects Administration, Historical Records Survey. *List of Post Offices in Arkansas as Shown in Early Newspaper Files 1817–1874*. Little Rock: Arkansas History Commission, n.d.

California

Maps and Atlases

Beck, Warren A., and Ynez D. Haase. *Historical Atlas of California*. Norman: University of Oklahoma Press, 1974.

California Maps 1853–1943: Land Ownership, Special Information, Quadrangles. Berkeley, Calif.: J. P. Coll, 1969.

California Road Atlas and Driver's Guide. 3rd ed., rev. Irvine, Calif.: Thomas Brothers Maps, 1985.

Coy, Owen C. *California County Boundaries: A Study of the Division of the States into Counties and the Subsequent Changes in their Boundaries, with Maps*. Berkeley: California Historical Survey Commission, 1923. Reprint. Rev. ed. Fresno, Calif.: Valley Publishers, 1973.

Donley, Michael W. *Atlas of California*. Culver City, Calif.: Pacific Book Center, 1979.

Durrenberger, Robert W. *Patterns on the Land: Geographical, Historical, and Political Maps of California*. Palo Alto, Calif.: National Press Books, 1965.

Northern California Atlas and Gazetteer. 3rd ed. Freeport, Maine: DeLorme Mapping Co., 1996.

Preston, Ralph N. *Early California: Early Forts, Old Mines, Old Town Sites*. Northern ed. Corvallis, Oreg.: Western Guide Publishers, 1974. Reprinted as *Early California Atlas: Northern Edition*. 2nd ed. Portland, Oreg.: Binford & Mort Publishers, 1983.

______. *Early California: Early Forts, Old Mines, Old Town Sites*. Southern ed. Corvallis, Oreg.: Western Guide Publishers, 1974. Reprinted as *Early California Atlas: Southern Edition*. 2nd ed. Portland, Oreg.: Binford & Mort Publishers, 1974.

Southern and Central California Atlas and Gazetteer. 3rd ed. Freeport, Maine: DeLorme Mapping Co., 1994.

Gazetteers and Postal Guides

California City and Unincorporated Place Names. Sacramento: California Division of Highways, 1971.

Gudde, Erwin G. *California Place Names: The Origin and Etymology of Current Geographical Names*. 3rd ed. Rev. and enl. Berkeley: University of California Press, 1969.

Hanna, Phil T., comp. *The Dictionary of California Land Names*. Los Angeles: Automobile Club of Southern California, 1946.

Salley, Harold E. *History of California Post Offices, 1849–1976: Includes Branches and Stations, Navy Numbered Branches, Highway and Railway Post Offices*. La Mesa, Calif.: Postal History Associates, 1977.

Sanchez, Nellie Van de Grift. *Spanish and Indian Place Names of California—Their Meaning and Their Romance*. San Francisco: A. M. Robertson, 1930.

Colorado

Maps and Atlases

Colorado Atlas and Gazetteer. 2nd ed. Freeport, Maine: DeLorme Mapping Co., 1995.

Erickson, Kenneth A., and Albert W. Smith. *Atlas of Colorado*. Boulder: Colorado Associated University Press, 1985.

Gazetteers and Postal Guides

Bauer, William H., James L. Ozment, and John H. Willard. *Colorado Postal History: The Post Offices*. Crete, Nebr.: J-B Publishing Co., 1971.

Crofutt, George A. *Crofutt's Grip-Sack Guide of Colorado: A Complete Encyclopedia of the State, Resources and Condensed Authentic Descriptions of Every City, Town, Village, Station, Post Office and Important Mining Camp in the State*. 2nd ed. Omaha, Nebr.: Overland Publishing Co., 1885. Reprint. Golden, Colo.: Cubar Associates, 1966. Reprint. Boulder, Colo.: Johnson Books, 1981.

Dawson, J. Frank. *Place Names in Colorado*. Denver, Colo.: J. F. Dawson Publishing Co., 1954.

Eichler, George R. *Colorado Place Names: Communities, Counties, Peaks, Passes: With Historical Lore and Facts, Plus a Pronunciation Guide*. Boulder, Colo.: Johnson Publishing Co., 1980.

Gannett, Henry. *A Gazetteer of Colorado*. Washington, D.C.: Government Printing Office, 1906.

Connecticut

Maps and Atlases

Lunt, Dudley. *The Bounds of Delaware*. Wilmington, Del.: Historical Society of Delaware, 1952.

Thompson, Edmund B. *Maps of Connecticut Before the Year 1800*. Windham, Conn.: Hawthorn House, 1940. Reprinted as *Thompson's Maps of Connecticut*. 2 vols. in 1. Norwich, Vt.: G. B. Manasek, 1995.

_____. *Maps of Connecticut for the Years of Industrial Revolution, 1801–1860*. Windham, Conn.: Hawthorn House, 1942. Reprinted as *Thompson's Maps of Connecticut*. 2 vols. in 1. Norwich, Vt.: G. B. Manasek, 1995.

Town and City Atlas of the State of Connecticut. Boston: D. H. Hurd and Co., 1893.

Gazetteers and Postal Guides

Gannett, Henry. *A Geographic Dictionary of Connecticut*. Washington, D.C.: Government Printing Office, 1894. Reprinted as *A Geographic Dictionary of Connecticut and Rhode Island*. Baltimore: Genealogical Publishing Co., 1978.

Hughes, Arthur H., and Morse S. Allen. *Connecticut Place Names*. Hartford, Conn.: Connecticut Historical Society, 1976.

Patera, Alan H. *The Post Offices of Connecticut*. Burtonsville, Md.: The Depot, 1977.

Pease, John C., and John M. Niles. *A Gazetteer of the States of Connecticut and Rhode Island*. Hartford, Conn.: W. S. Marsh, 1819. Reprint. Bowie, Md.: Heritage Books, 1991.

Delaware

Maps and Atlases

Beers, Daniel G. *Atlas of the State of Delaware*. Philadelphia: Pomeroy & Beers, 1868. Reprint. Georgetown, Del.: Sussex Prints, 1978.

Maryland/Delaware Atlas and Gazetteer. 2nd ed. Freeport, Maine: DeLorme Mapping Co., 1996.

Gazetteers and Postal Guides

Bounds, Harvey C. *A Postal History of Delaware*. Newark, Del.: Press of Kells, 1938.

Gannett, Henry. *A Gazetteer of Delaware*. Washington, D.C.: U.S. Government Printing Office, 1904. Reprinted as *A Gaz-*

etteer of Maryland and Delaware. Baltimore: Genealogical Publishing Co., 1979.

Heck, L. W., and others. *Delaware Place Names*. Washington, D.C.: U.S. Government Printing Office, 1966.

District of Columbia

Maps and Atlases

Brown, Mary Ross. *An Illustrated Genealogy of the Counties of Maryland and the District of Columbia as a Guide to Locating Records*. Baltimore: French Bray Printing, 1967.

Gazetteers and Postal Guides

Martin, Joseph. *A New and Comprehensive Gazetteer of Virginia and the District of Columbia*. Charlottesville, Va.: the author, 1836.

Florida

Maps and Atlases

Fernald, Edward A., and Elizabeth D. Purdum, eds. *Atlas of Florida*. Gainesville: University Press of Florida, 1992.

Florida Atlas and Gazetteer. 3rd ed. Freeport, Maine: DeLorme Mapping Co., 1995.

Florida Road Atlas and Visitor's Guide. Comfort, Tex: Gousha, 1994.

Long, John H., ed. *Atlas of Historical County Boundaries: Florida*. New York: Simon & Schuster, 1996.

Puetz, C. J., comp. *Florida County Maps*. Lyndon Station, Wis.: Thomas Publishing Co., 1988.

Trakker Maps Florida State Road Atlas. Miami, Fla.: Trakker Maps, 1989. Annual.

Gazetteers and Postal Guides

Bradbury, Alford G., and Story Hallcock. *A Chronology of Florida Post Offices*. Florida Federation of Stamp Clubs. Handbook no. 2. Vero Beach, Fla., 1962.

Cline, Howard F. *Provisional Historical Gazeteer* [*sic*] *with Locational Notes on Florida Colonial Communities*. New York: Garland Pub., 1974.

Hawks, John M., ed. *The Florida Gazetteer*. New Orleans: Printed at the Bronze Pen Stfam [*sic*] Book and Job Office, 1871. Reprint. Microfiche. Louisville, Ky.: Lost Cause Press.

Morris, Allen C. *Florida Place Names*. Coral Gables, Fla.: University of Miami Press, 1974.

Georgia

Maps and Atlases

Bonner, James C. *Atlas for Georgia History*. Milledgeville: Georgia College, 1969. Reprinted from *Georgia Historical Quarterly* (September 1967).

Bryant, Pat, and Ingrid Shields. *Georgia Counties: Their Changing Boundaries*. Atlanta: Georgia Surveyor General Department, 1983.

Hall. *Original County Map of Georgia: Showing Present and Original Counties and Land Districts*. Atlanta: Hall Brothers, 1895.

Hemperley, Marion R. *Map of Colonial Georgia, 1773–1777*. Atlanta: Georgia Surveyor General Department, 1979.

______. *Georgia Early Roads and Trails Circa 1730–1850*. Atlanta: Georgia Surveyor General Department, 1979.

Hodler, Thomas W., and Howard A. Schretter. *The Atlas of Georgia*. Athens: Institute of Community and Area Development, University of Georgia, 1986.

Gazetteers and Postal Guides

Hemperley, Marion R. *Cities, Towns and Communities of Georgia between 1847–1962, 8,500 Places and the County in which Located*. Easley, S.C.: Southern Historical Press, 1980.

Krakow, Kenneth K. *Georgia Place-Names*. Macon, Ga.: Winship Press, 1975.

Sherwood, Adiel. *A Gazetteer of Georgia, Containing a Particular Description of the State, Its Resources, Counties, Towns, Villages, and Whatever Is Usual in Statistical Works*. 4th ed. Rev. and corrected. Atlanta: J. Richards, 1860. Reprint. Atlanta: Cherokee Publishing Co., 1970. Microfiche. Chicago: Library Resources, 1971.

Hawaii

Maps and Atlases

Armstrong, R. Warwick, and James A. Bier. *Atlas of Hawaii*. Honolulu: University Press of Hawaii, 1983.

Fitzpatrick, Gary L., comp. *Hawaii: A List of Early Maps in the Library of Congress and a Summary of Services of Current Maps and Cartographic Information*. Washington, D.C.: Library of Congress, 1980.

Gazetteers and Postal Guides

Alexander, W. D., comp. *Hawaiian Geographic Names*. Washington, D.C.: United States Coast and Geodetic Survey, 1902.

Coulter, John W., comp. *A Gazetteer of the Territory of Hawaii*. Research Publications, no. 11. Honolulu: University of Hawaii, 1935. Reprint. Ann Arbor, Mich.: University Microfilms.

Pukui, Mary W., Samuel H. Elbert, and Esther T. Mookini. *Place Names of Hawaii*. Rev. and enl. Honolulu: University Press of Hawaii, 1974.

Idaho

Maps and Atlases

Idaho Atlas and Gazetteer. Freeport, Maine: DeLorme Mapping Co., 1992.

Preston, Ralph N. *Maps of Early Idaho: Old Gold Mines, Indian Battle Grounds, Old Military Roads, Old Forts, Overland Stage Routes, Early Towns*. Corvallis, Oreg.: Western Guide Publishers, 1972. Reprinted as *Early Idaho Atlas*. 2nd ed. Portland, Oreg.: Binford & Mort Publishers, 1978.

Wells, Meryl W., comp. *An Atlas of Idaho Territory*. Boise: Idaho State Historical Society, 1978.

Gazetteers and Postal Guides

Gazetteer of Cities, Villages, Unincorporated Communities and Landmark Sites in the State of Idaho. 3rd ed. Boise: Idaho State-Wide Highway Planning Survey, 1966.

Kramer, Fritz L. "Idaho Town Names." *State Historical Department Biennial Report* 23 (1951–52): 14–114.

Schell, Frank R. *Ghost Towns and Live Ones: A Chronology of the Postoffice Dept. in Idaho, 1861–1973*. Twin Falls, Idaho, 1973.

Illinois

Maps and Atlases

Atlas of Illinois. Madison, Wis.: American Publishing Co., 1976.

Illinois Atlas and Gazetteer. Freeport, Maine: DeLorme Mapping Co., 1994.

Powell, Paul, comp. *Counties of Illinois: Their Origin and Evolution, with Twenty-Three Maps Showing the Original and the Present Boundary Line of Each County of the State*. Springfield, Ill.: secretary of state, 1972.

Warner and Beers. *Maps of Illinois Counties in 1876, Together with the Plan of Chicago and Other Cities and a Sampling of Illustrations*. Chicago: Union Atlas Co., 1876. Reprinted as *Atlas of the State of Illinois to Which Are Added Various General Maps and Illustrations*. Knightstown, Ind.: Mayhill Publications, 1972.

Gazetteers and Postal Guides

Adams, James N., comp. "A List of Illinois Place Names." *Illinois Libraries* 50 (4)–50 (6) (April-June 1968). Reprint. Springfield: Illinois State Library, 1989.

Beck, Lewis C. *A Gazetteer of the States of Illinois and Missouri. . . .* Albany: Charles R. and George Webster, 1823. Reprint. New York: Arno Press, 1975.

Illinois: Guide and Gazetteer. Chicago: Rand McNally & Co., 1969.

Peck, John M. *A Gazetteer of Illinois in Three Parts: Containing a General View of the State, a General View of Each County, and a Particular Description of Each Town, Settlement, Stream, Prairie, Bottom, Bluff, Etc. Alphabetically Arranged*. 2nd ed. Entirely rev., corrected, and enl. Philadelphia: Grigg & Elliott, 1837. Reprint. Microfiche. Louisville, Ky.: Lost Cause Press, 1977. Microfilm. New Haven, Conn.: Research Publications. Reprint with new place-name index. Bowie, Md.: Heritage Books, 1993.

Indiana

Maps and Atlases

Andreas, Alfred T. *Illustrated Historical Atlas of the State of Indiana*. Chicago: Baskin, Forster, & Co., 1876. Reprinted as *Maps of Indiana Counties in 1876: Together with the Plat of Indianapolis and a Sampling of Illustrations*. Indianapolis: Indiana Historical Society, 1968.

Kingsbury, Robert C. *An Atlas of Indiana*. With contributions from John M. Hollingsworth and others. Bloomington: Dept. of Geography, Indiana University, 1970.

Long, John H., ed. *Atlas of Historical County Boundaries: Indiana*. New York: Simon & Schuster, 1996.

New Topographical Atlas and Gazetteer of Indiana 1871. New York: George H. Adams and Co., 1871. Reprint. Evansville, Ind.: Unigraphic, 1975.

Puetz, C. J., comp. *Indiana County Maps*. Lyndon Station, Wis.: Thomas Publishing Co., 1991.

Gazetteers and Postal Guides

Baker, J. David. *The Postal History of Indiana*. 2 vols. Louisville, Ky.: Leonard H. Hartman, 1976.

Baker, Ronald L., and Marvin Carmony. *Indiana Place Names*. Bloomington: Indiana University Press, 1975.

Chamberlain, E., comp. *The Indiana Gazetteer or Topographical Dictionary of the State of Indiana*. 3rd ed. Indianapolis: the author, 1850. Reprint. Knightstown, Ind.: Bookmark, 1977.

Pence, George, and Nellie C. Armstrong. *Indiana Boundaries: Territory, State and County*. Indianapolis: Indiana Historical Bureau, 1933. Reprint. Indianapolis: Indiana Historical Bureau, 1967.

Scott, John. *The Indiana Gazetteer or Topographical Dictionary: Containing a Description of the Several Counties, Towns, Villages, Settlements, Roads, Lakes, Rivers, Creeks, and Springs, in the State of Indiana*. Centreville, Ind.: the author, 1826. 2nd ed. Carefully rev., corrected, and enl. Indianapolis: Douglas and Maquire, 1833. Reprint of 1826 ed. Indianapolis: Indiana Historical Society, 1954.

Iowa

Maps and Atlases

Andreas, Alfred T. *Illustrated Historical Atlas of the State of Iowa*. Chicago: Lakeside Press, 1875. Reprint. Iowa City, Iowa: State Historical Society, 1970.

Atlas of Iowa. Madison, Wis.: American Publishing Co., 1974.

Curtis, Peter H., comp. *Fire Insurance Maps of Iowa Cities and Towns: A List of Holdings*. Iowa City: Iowa State History Department, 1983.

Kelsey, Laura E., and Frederick W. Pernell, comp. *Cartographic Record Relating to the Territory of Iowa, 1938–1846*. Special List no. 27. Washington, D.C.: National Archives and Records Service, 1971.

Gazetteers and Postal Guides

Hair, James T., comp. *Iowa State Gazetteer*. Chicago: Bailey and Hair, 1865. Reprint. Microfiche. Louisville, Ky.: Lost Cause Press, 1978.

Hills, Leon C. *History and Legends of Place Names in Iowa: The Meaning of Our Map*. 2nd ed. Omaha, Nebr.: Omaha School Supply Co., 1938.

Mott, David C. "Abandoned Towns, Villages and Post Offices of Iowa." *Annals of Iowa* 17–18 (1930–32). Reprint. Council Bluffs, Iowa: J. W. Hoffman and S. L. Purington, 1973.

Patera, Alan H., and John S. Gallagher. *Iowa Post Offices, 1833–1986*. Lake Oswego, Oreg.: The Depot, 1986.

Kansas

Maps and Atlases

Baughman, Robert W. *Kansas in Maps*. Topeka: Kansas Historical Society, 1961. Reprint. St. Louis: Patrice Press, 1988.

Gill, Helen G. *The Establishment of Counties in Kansas, 1855–1903*. Kansas Historical Society Collections 8. N.p., 1904.

Kansas Atlas and Gazetteer. Freeport, Maine: DeLorme Mapping Co., 1997.

Official State Atlas of Kansas: Compiled from Government Surveys, County Records, and Personal Investigations. Philadelphia: L. H. Everts & Co., 1887. Reprint. Topeka: Kansas Council of Genealogical Societies, 1982.

Socolofsky, Homer E., and Huber Self. *Historical Atlas of Kansas*. Norman: University of Oklahoma Press, 1988.

Gazetteers and Postal Guides

Baughman, Robert W. *Kansas Post Offices, May 29, 1828–August 3, 1961*. Topeka: Kansas Postal History Society, 1961.

Gannett, Henry. *A Gazetteer of Kansas*. Washington, D.C.: U.S. Government Printing Office, 1898.

Rydjord, John. *Kansas Place Names*. Norman: University of Oklahoma Press, 1972.

Kentucky

Maps and Atlases

Clark, Thomas D. *Historic Maps of Kentucky*. Lexington: University Press of Kentucky, 1979.

Colton, Joseph H. *Colton's Kentucky and Tennessee*. New York: the author, 1864.

Downes, Randolph C. "Evolution of Ohio Kentucky Boundaries." *Ohio Archaeological and Historical Publications* 36 (July 1927): 340–477. Reprint. Columbus: Ohio Historical Society, 1970.

Jillson, Willard R. *Pioneer Kentucky: An Outline of its Exploration and Settlement, Its Early Cartography and Primitive Geography, Coupled with a Brief Presentation of the Principal Trails, Traces, Forts, Stations, Springs, Licks, Fords and Ferries Used Prior to the Year 1800*. Frankfort, Ky.: State Journal Company, 1934.

Karan, Pradyumna P., and Cotton Mather, eds. *Atlas of Kentucky*. Lexington: University Press of Kentucky, 1977.

Kentucky Atlas and Gazetteer. Freeport, Maine: DeLorme Mapping Co., 1997.

Puetz, C. J., comp. *Kentucky County Maps*. Lyndon Station, Wis.: Thomas Publishing Co., 1992.

Rone, Wendell R., Sr. *An Historical Atlas of Kentucky and Her Counties*. Owensboro, Ky.: the author, 1965.

Sames, James W., 3rd, comp. *Index of Kentucky and Virginia Maps 1562 to 1900*. Frankfort: Kentucky Historical Society, 1976.

Speed, Thomas. *The Wilderness Road: A Description of the Routes of Travel by Which the Pioneers and Early Settlers First Came to Kentucky*. Louisville, Ky.: Filson Club, 1886. Reprint. New York: Lenox Hill Pub. & Dist. Co., Burt Franklin, 1971.

Gazetteers and Postal Guides

Atkins, Alan T. *Postmarked Kentucky: A Postal History of the Commonwealth of Kentucky from 1792 to 1900*. Crete, Nebr.: J-B Publishing Co., 1975.

Field, Thomas P. *A Guide to Kentucky Place Names*. Lexington: College of Arts and Sciences, University of Kentucky, 1961.

Rennick, Robert M. *Kentucky Place Names*. Lexington: University Press of Kentucky, ca. 1984.

Louisiana

Maps and Atlases

Louisiana Historical Records Survey. *County-Parish Boundaries in Louisiana*. New Orleans: Department of Archives, Louisiana State University, 1939.

Newton, Milton B. *Atlas of Louisiana: A Guide for Students*. Baton Rouge: School of Geoscience, Louisiana State University, 1972.

Gazetteers and Postal Guides

Gibson, Dennis A., ed. *Index to Louisiana Place Names Mentioned in the War of the Rebellion: A Compilation of the Official Records of the Union and Confederate Armies*. Lafayette: University of Southwestern Louisiana, 1975.

Maine

Maps and Atlases

Eckstrom, Fannie H. "Maine Maps of Historical Interest." *Maine Bulletin* 42 (August 1939): ix–xxxv.

Maine Atlas and Gazetteer. 19th ed. Freeport, Maine: DeLorme Mapping Co., 1996.

Morris, Gerald E., ed. *The Maine Bicentennial Atlas: An Historical Survey*. Portland: Maine Historical Society, 1976.

Gazetteers and Postal Guides

Attwood, Stanley B. *The Length and Breadth of Maine*. Augusta, Maine: Kennebec Journal Print Shop, 1946. Reprint. Includes 1949 and 1953 supplements. Orono: University of Maine, 1973.

Dennis, Michael J. *Maine Towns and Counties: What Was What, Where and When*. Oakland, Maine: Danbury House Books, 1981.

Dow, Sterling T. *Maine Postal History and Postmarks*. Lawrence, Mass.: Quarterman Publications, 1976.

Rutherford, Philip R. *The Dictionary of Maine Place–Names*. Freeport, Maine: Bond Wheelwright Co., 1970.

Varney, George J. *A Gazetteer of the State of Maine, with Numerous Illustrations*. Boston: B. B. Russell, 1881. Reprint. Bowie, Md.: Heritage Books, 1991.

Maryland

Maps and Atlases

Brown, Mary R. *An Illustrated Genealogy of the Counties of Maryland and the District of Columbia as a Guide to Locating Records*. Baltimore: French Bray Printing, 1967.

Maryland/Delaware Atlas and Gazetteer. 2nd ed. Freeport, Maine: DeLorme Mapping Co., 1996.

Maryland State Planning Department. *The Counties of Maryland and Baltimore City: Their Origin, Growth, and Development, 1634–1967*. Publication no. 146. Baltimore: Staff Planning Commission, 1968. Reprint. Microfiche. Greenwich, Conn.: Johnson Associates, 1976.

Papenfuse, Edward C., and Joseph M. Coale, 3rd. *The Hammond-Harwood House Atlas of Historical Maps of Maryland, 1608–1908*. Baltimore: Johns Hopkins University Press, 1982.

Thompson, Derek, ed. *Atlas of Maryland*. College Park: University of Maryland, 1977.

Gazetteers and Postal Guides

Fisher, Richard S. *Gazetteer of the State of Maryland*. New York: J. H. Colton, 1852.

Gannett, Henry. *A Gazetteer of Maryland*. Washington, D.C.: U.S. Government Printing Office, 1904. Reprinted as *A Gazetteer of Maryland and Delaware*. Baltimore: Genealogical Publishing Co., 1979.

Kaminkow, Marion K. *Maryland A to Z: A Topographical Dictionary*. Baltimore: Magna Carta Book Co., 1985.

Kenny, Hamill. *The Placenames of Maryland: Their Origin and Meaning*. Baltimore: Maryland Historical Society, 1984.

Massachusetts

Maps and Atlases

Massachusetts, Secretary of the Commonwealth. *Historical Data Relating to Counties, Cities and Towns in Massachusetts*. Boston: the commonwealth, 1975.

Walling, Henry F., and O. W. Gray, comp. *Official Topographical Atlas of Massachusetts: From Astronomical, Trigonometrical and Various Local Surveys*. Boston: Stedman, Brown and Lyon, 1871.

Wilkie, Richard W., and Jack Tager, eds. *Historical Atlas of Massachusetts*. Amherst: University of Massachusetts Press, 1991.

Wright and DeForest. *Early Maps of the Connecticut Valley in Massachusetts*. Springfield, Mass.: the authors, 1911.

Gazetteers and Postal Guides

Davis, Charlotte P. *Directory of Massachusetts Place Names, Current and Obsolete*. Lexington, Mass.: Bay State News, 1987.

Federal Writer's Program, Massachusetts. *The Origin of Massachusetts Place Names of the State, Counties, Cities, and Towns*. Sponsored by the state librarian of the commonwealth of Massachusetts. New York: Harian Publications, 1941.

Gannett, Henry. *A Geographic Dictionary of Massachusetts*. Washington, D.C.: U.S. Government Printing Office, 1894. Reprint. Baltimore: Genealogical Publishing Co., 1978.

Hayward, John. *A Gazetteer of Massachusetts: Containing Descriptions of All the Counties, Towns and Districts in the Commonwealth. . . .* Rev. ed. Boston: J. P. Jewett & Co., 1849.

Nason, Elias. *A Gazetteer of the State of Massachusetts: With Numerous Illustrations on Wood and Steel*. Boston: B. B. Russell, 1874. Rev. and enl. by George J. Varney. Boston: B. B. Russell, 1890.

Spofford, Jeremiah. *A Gazetteer of Massachusetts: Containing a General View of the State, with an Historical Sketch of the Principal Events from Its Settlement to the Present Time, and Notices of the Several Towns Alphabetically Arranged*. Newburyport, Mass.: C. Whipple, 1828.

Table of Post Offices and Rates of Postage of Single Letters for Post Offices in the State of Massachusetts. . . . Philadelphia: Post Office Department, 1800. Reprint. Microfiche. Early American Imprints, First Series, no. 38908.

Michigan

Maps and Atlases

Bowen, B. F. *Bowen's Michigan State Atlas: Containing a Separate Map of Each County, Showing Section, Township and Range Lines, Railroad and Interurban Lines. . . .* Indianapolis: the author, 1916.

Karpinski, Louis C., and William L. Jenks. *Bibliography of the Printed Maps of Michigan, 1804–1880: With a Series of Over One Hundred Reproductions of Maps, Constituting an Historical Atlas of the Great Lakes and Michigan*. Lansing: Michigan Historical Commission, 1931.

Mapbook of Michigan Counties. Rev. ed. Lansing, Mich.: Two Peninsula Press, 1984.

Michigan Atlas and Gazetteer. 5th ed. Freeport, Maine: DeLorme Mapping Co., 1996.

Miles, William. *Michigan Atlases and Plat Books: A Check List 1872–1973*. Lansing, Mich.: State Library Services, 1975.

Puetz, C. J., comp. *Michigan County Maps*. Lyndon Station, Wis.: Thomas Publishing Co., 1990.

Sommers, Lawrence M., ed. *Atlas of Michigan*. East Lansing: Michigan State University Press. Grand Rapids, Mich.: William B. Eerdmans Publishing Co., 1977.

Walling, H. F., comp. *Atlas of Michigan, . . . Gazetteer of Places, Railroad Stations, Post Offices, Landings, Lakes, Rivers, Islands, Cities, Towns, Villages, Individual Map of Every County. . . .* Detroit: R. M. & S. T. Tackabury, 1873. Reprinted as the *1873 Atlas of Michigan. . . .* Knightstown, Ind.: Bookmark, 1977.

Welch, Richard W. *County Evolution in Michigan, 1790–1897*. Occasional Paper no. 2. Lansing, Mich.: State Library Services, 1972.

Gazetteers and Postal Guides

Blois, John T. *Gazetteer of the State of Michigan*. Detroit: S. L. Rood & Co., 1838. Reprint. New York: Arno Press, 1975. Knightstown, Ind.: Bookmark, 1979. Reprint. Microfiche. Louisville, Ky.: Lost Cause Press, 1974. Chicago: Library Resources, 1971.

Romig, Walter. *Michigan Place Names: The History of the Founding and the Naming of More than Five Thousand Past and Present Michigan Communities*. Grosse Pointe, Mich.: the author, 1973.

Minnesota

Maps and Atlases

Andreas, Alfred T. *An Illustrated Historical Atlas of the State of Minnesota*. Chicago: the author, 1874. Reprint. Evansville, Ind.: Unigraphic, 1976.

Atlas of the State of Minnesota: Containing a Map of Each County, Minnesota and the U.S. . . . Fergus Falls, Minn.: Thomas O. Nelson Co., 1982.

Lewis, Mary Ellen. "The Establishment of County Boundaries in Minnesota." Master's thesis, University of Minnesota, 1946.

Minnesota Atlas and Gazetteer. 2nd ed. Freeport, Maine: DeLorme Mapping Co., 1995.

Ostendorf, Paul J. *Every Person's Name Index to An Illustrated Atlas of the State of Minnesota*. Winona, Minn.: St. Mary's College, 1979.

Treude, Mai. *Windows to the Past: A Bibliography of Minnesota County Atlases*. Minneapolis: Center for Urban and Regional Affairs, University of Minnesota, 1980.

Gazetteers and Postal Guides

Patera, Alan H., and John S. Gallagher. *The Post Offices of Minnesota*. Burtonville, Md.: The Depot, 1978.

Upham, Warren. "Minnesota Geographic Names: Their Origin and Historic Significance." *Minnesota Historical Society* 17 (1920). Reprint. St. Paul: Minnesota Historical Society. 1969.

Mississippi

Maps and Atlases

Cross, Ralph D., and Robert W. Wales, eds. *Atlas of Mississippi*. Jackson: University Press of Mississippi, 1974.

Long, John H., ed., and Peggy Tuck Sinko, comp. *Atlas of Historical County Boundaries: Mississippi*. New York: Simon & Schuster, 1993.

Mississippi Maps 1816–1873. Jackson: Mississippi Historical Society, 1974.

Gazetteers and Postal Guides

Oakley, Bruce C. *A Postal History of Mississippi Stampless Period, 1799–1860*. Baldwyn, Miss.: Magnolia Publishers, 1969.

Rowland, Dunbar. *Mississippi: Comprising Sketches of Counties, Towns, Events, Institutions, and Persons, Arranged in Cyclopedic Form*. 4 vols. Atlanta: Southern Historical Publishing Association, 1907. Reprint. Microfiche. Chicago: Library Resources, 1971. Reprint. Spartanburg, S.C.: Reprint Co., 1976.

Missouri

Maps and Atlases

Ohman, Marian M. "Missouri County Organization 1812–1876." *Missouri Historical Review* 76 (April 1981): 253–81.

Rafferty, Milton D., Russel L. Gerlach, and Dennis J. Hrebec. *Atlas of Missouri*. Springfield, Mo.: Aux-Arc Research Associates, 1970.

Selby, Paul O. *A Bibliography of Missouri County Histories and Atlases*. Kirksville, Mo.: Northeast Missouri State Teachers College, 1966.

Gazetteers and Postal Guides

Beck, Lewis C. *A Gazetteer of the States of Illinois and Missouri. . . .* Albany: Charles R. and George Webster, 1823. Reprint. New York: Arno Press, 1975.

Campbell, Robert A. *Campbell's Gazetteer of Missouri: From Articles Contributed by Prominent Gentlemen in Each County of the State, and Information Collected and Collated from Official and Other Authentic Sources, By a Corps of Experienced Canvassers*. St. Louis, Mo.: the author, 1874. Reprint. Ann Arbor, Mich.: University Microfilms.

Ramsay, Robert L. "Our Storehouse of Missouri Place Names." *University of Missouri Bulletin* 53 (34). Reprint. Arts and Sciences Series 7 (1952). Columbia: University of Missouri, 1952. Reprint. University of Missouri Press, 1973.

Wetmore, Alphonso, comp. *Gazetteer of the State of Missouri: with a Map of the state . . . to Which Is Added an Appendix, Containing Frontier Sketches, and Illustrations of Indian Character*. St. Louis, Mo.: C. Keemle, 1837. Reprint. New York: Arno Press, 1975.

Montana

Maps and Atlases

County Maps, Montana. Prepared by the state of Montana, Department of Highways, Planning and Research Bureau, in cooperation with the U.S. Department of Transportation. Helena, Mont.: the bureau, 1976.

Montana Atlas and Gazetteer. Freeport, Maine: DeLorme Mapping Co., 1995.

Gazetteers and Postal Guides

Cheney, Roberta C. *Names on the Face of Montana: The Story of Montana's Place Names*. Rev. ed. Missoula, Mont.: Mountain Press, 1987.

Koury, Michael J. *The Military Posts of Montana*. Bellevue, Nebr.: Old Army Press, 1970.

Lutz, Dennis, and Meryl Lutz. "Montana Post Offices: 1864–1974." *Montana Postal Cache: Research Journal of the Montana Postal History Society* part 1, A–C, 1 (February 1975): M1–M24; part 2, D–I, 1 (May 1975): M25–M49; part 3, J–P, 1 (August 1975): M50–M74; part 4, Q–Z, 1 (November 1975): M75–M103.

Nebraska

Maps and Atlases

Everts and Kirk. *The 1885 Official State Atlas of Nebraska*. Reprinted with ten thousand-name index by Margie Sobotka. Fremont: Eastern Nebraska Genealogical Society, 1976.

Nebraska Atlas and Gazetteer. Freeport, Maine: DeLorme Mapping Co., 1997.

Nimmo, Sylvia. *Maps Showing the County Boundaries of Nebraska 1854–1925*. Papillion, Nebr.: the author, 1978.

Searcy, N. D., and A. R. Longwell. *Nebraska Atlas*. Kearney, Nebr.: Nebraska Atlas Publishing Co., 1964.

Gazetteers and Postal Guides

Fitzpatrick, Lilian L. *Nebraska Place-Names*. Lincoln: University of Nebraska, 1925. Reprinted as *Nebraska Place-Names, Including Selections from the Origin of the Place-Names of Nebraska*. Edited by G. T. Fairclough. Lincoln: University of Nebraska Press, 1967. Reprint of 1925 edition. Microfilm. Washington, D.C.: Library of Congress Photoduplication Service, 1986.

Perkey, Elton A. *Perkey's Nebraska Place Names*. Lincoln: Nebraska State Historical Society, 1982. Rev. ed. Lincoln, Nebr.: J & L Lee Co., 1995.

Rapp, William F. *The Post Offices of Nebraska*. Vol. 1. *Territorial Post Offices*. Crete, Nebr.: J-B Publishing Co., 1971.

Nevada

Maps and Atlases

Land Ownership Maps: Nevada. Washington, D.C.: Library of Congress, 1967.

Nevada Atlas and Gazetteer. Freeport, Maine: DeLorme Mapping Co., 1996.

Nevada Maps, Cities and Towns, 1885–1943. New York: Sanborn Perris Map Co., 1886. Reprint. Microfilm. Washington, D.C.: Library of Congress, 1980.

Gazetteers and Postal Guides

Carlson, Helen S. *Nevada Place Names: A Geographical Dictionary*. Reno: University of Nevada Press, 1974.

Harris, Robert P. *Nevada Postal History, 1861–1972*. Santa Cruz, Calif.: Bonanza Press, 1973.

Leigh, Rufus W. *Nevada Place Names: Their Origin and Significance*. Salt Lake City: Deseret News Press, 1964.

New Hampshire

Maps and Atlases

Cobb, David A. *New Hampshire Maps to 1900: An Annotated Checklist*. Hanover, N.H.: New Hampshire Historical Society. Distributed by University Press of New England, 1981.

Long, John H., ed., and Gordon DenBoer, comp. *Atlas of Historical County Boundaries: New Hampshire and Vermont*. New York: Simon & Schuster, 1993.

New Hampshire Atlas and Gazetteer. 10th ed. Freeport, Maine: DeLorme Mapping Co., 1996.

Town and City Atlas of the State of New Hampshire. Boston: D. H. Hurd and Co., 1892.

Wallings, H. F., and Charles H. Hitchcock. *Atlas of the State of New Hampshire*. New York, 1877.

Gazetteers and Postal Guides

Charlton, Edwin A., comp. *New Hampshire As It Is*. Claremont, N.H.: Tracy and Sanford, 1855.

Communities, Settlements and Neighborhood Centers in the State of New Hampshire. Concord: New Hampshire State Planning and Development Commission, 1937. Reprint. 1954.

Farmer, John, and Jacob B. Moore. *A Gazetteer of the State of New Hampshire*. Concord, N.H.: J. B. Moore, 1823.

Fogg, Alonzo J., comp. *The Statistics and Gazetteer of New Hampshire: Containing Description of All the Counties, Towns and Villages; also, Boundaries and Area of the State. . . .* Concord, N.H.: D. L. Guernsey, 1874.

Hayward, John. *A Gazetteer of New Hampshire: Containinag Descriptions of All the Counties, Towns, and Districts in the State, Also of its Principal Mountains, Rivers, Waterfalls, Harbors, Islands*. Boston: John P. Jewett, 1849. Reprint. Microfiche. Louisville, Ky.: Lost Cause Press, 1974.

Hunt, Elmer M. *New Hampshire Town Names and Whence They Came*. Peterborough, N.H.: Noone House, 1970.

Merrill, Eliphalet, and Phinehas Merrill. *Gazetteer of the State of New Hampshire*. Exeter, N.H.: C. Norris & Co., 1817. Reprint. Microfiche. Early American Imprints, Second Series, no. 41414. Reprint with new index. Bowie, Md.: Heritage Books, 1987.

Simonds, L. W. *New Hampshire Post Offices, 1775–1978*. New London, N.H.: Simonds, 1978.

New Jersey

Maps and Atlases

New Jersey Road Maps of the Eighteenth Century. Princeton, N.J.: Princeton University Library, 1981.

Snyder, John P. *The Story of New Jersey's Civil Boundaries 1606–1968*. Bulletin 67. Trenton, N.J.: Bureau of Geology and Topography, 1969.

Gazetteers and Postal Guides

An Alphabetical Listing of Local Places and Incorporated Municipalities in the State of New Jersey. . . . New Jersey Dept. of Transportation, 1967.

Gannett, Henry. *A Geographic Dictionary of New Jersey*. Washington, D.C.: U.S. Government Printing Office, 1894. Reprint. Baltimore: Genealogical Publishing Co., 1978.

Gordon, Thomas F. *Gazetteer of the State of New Jersey. . . .* Trenton, N.J.: Daniel Fenton, 1834. Reprint. Cottonport, La.: Polyanthos, 1973. Reprint. Microfiche. Louisville, Ky.: Lost Cause Press, 1975.

Kay, John L., and Chester M. Smith, Jr. *New Jersey Postal History: The Post Offices and First Postmasters, 1776–1976*. Lawrence, Mass.: Quarterman Publications, 1977.

New Jersey Local Names, Municipalities and Counties. Trenton, N.J.: State Department of Transportation, 1982.

Origin of New Jersey Place Names. Trenton, N.J.: Public Library Commission, 1945.

New Mexico

Maps and Atlases

Beck, Warren A., and Ynez D. Haase. *Historical Atlas of New Mexico*. Norman: University of Oklahoma Press, 1969.

Coan, Charles F. "The County Boundaries of New Mexico." *Southwestern Political Science Quarterly* 3 (December 1922): 252–86. Reprint. Santa Fe, N.M.: Legislative Council Service, 1965.

New Mexico in Maps. Albuquerque: University of New Mexico Press, 1986.

Gazetteers and Postal Guides

Dike, Sheldon H. "The Territorial Post Offices of New Mexico." *New Mexico Historical Review* 33 (October 1958) 322–27; 34 (January-October 1959): 55–69; 145–52, 203–26, 308–09.

Pearce, Thomas M., ed. *New Mexico Place Names: A Geographical Dictionary*. Albuquerque: University of New Mexico Press, 1965.

Ritch, William G., and Edgar Caypless. *A Complete Business Directory of New Mexico, and Gazetteer of the Territory for 1882*. Santa Fe, N.M.: New Mexican Printing and Publishing Co., 1882.

New York

Maps and Atlases

Beers, Frederick W. *Atlas of New York and Vicinity*. New York: F. W. Beers, A. D. Ellis and G. G. Soule, 1867.

Bien, Joseph R. *Atlas of the State of New York*. New York: J. Bien & Co., 1895.

Burr, David H. *An Atlas of the State of New York*. New York: the author, 1829.

Catalogue of Maps and Surveys in the Offices of the Secretary of State, State Engineer and Surveyor and Comptroller and the New York State Library. Albany, N.Y.: Charles Van Benthuysen, 1859.

Long, John H., ed., and Kathryn F. Thorne, comp. *Atlas of Historical County Boundaries: New York*. New York: Simon & Schuster, 1993.

New York State Atlas. 3rd ed. Albany, N.Y.: New York State Dept. of Transportation, 1983.

New York State Atlas and Gazetteer. 4th ed. Freeport, Maine: DeLorme Mapping Co., 1994.

Rayback, Robert J., and Edward L. Towle. *Richards Atlas of New York State*. 2nd ed. Rev. and supplemented. Phoenix, N.Y.: F. E. Richards, 1965.

Wright, Albert H. *A Check List of New York State County Maps Published 1779–1945*. Ithaca, N.Y.: Cornell University, 1965.

Gazetteers and Postal Guides

All-Name Index to the Historical and Statistical Gazetteer of New York State 1860 by J. H. French, and a listing of Geographic Names missing in the original index. Interlaken, N.Y.: Heart of the Lakes Publishing, 1993.

Disturnell, John. *A Gazetteer of the State of New York. . . .* Albany, N.Y.: the author, 1842.

French, J. H. *Gazetteer of the State of New York: Embracing a Comprehensive View of the Geography, Geology, and General History of the State, and a Complete History and Description of Every County, City, Town, Village, and Locality. With Full Tables of Statistics*. Syracuse, N.Y.: R. Pearsall Smith, 1860. Reprinted as *Historical and Statistical Gazetteer of New York State*. Interlaken, N.Y.: Heart of the Lakes Publishing, 1980. Reprinted with an index of names compiled by Frank Place. Baltimore: Genealogical Publishing Co., 1995. An every-name index to French's *Gazetteer* is *Index of Names in J. H. French's Gazetteer of the State of New York (1860)*, compiled by Frank Place (Cortland, N.Y.: Cortland County Historical Society, 1983).

Gazetteer of the State of New York. Albany, N.Y.: New York State Dept. of Health, 1980.

Gordon, Thomas F. *Gazetteer of the State of New York: Comprehending Its Colonial History . . . a Minute Description of Its Several Counties, Towns, and Villages. . . .* Philadelphia: the author, 1836.

Place, Frank, comp. *Index of Names in J. H. French's "Gazetteer of the State of New York (1860)."* Cortland, N.Y.: Cortland County Historical Society, 1983. Originally compiled by Frank Place and published under the title *Index of Personal Names in J. H. French's Gazetteer of the State of New York (1860)*, 1962. Reprinted with supplementary additions and corrections by Dorothy Raymoure, 1969. Reprinted, incorporating a supplementary index of places compiled by the Monroe County (N.Y.) Historical Office, with modifications by the Cortland County Historical Society.

Spafford, Horatio G. *A Gazetteer of the State of New York: Embracing an Ample Survey and Description of Its Counties, Towns, Cities....* Albany, N.Y.: H. C. Southwick, 1813. Reprint. Albany, N.Y.: B. D. Packard, 1824. Reprint. Interlacken, N.Y.: Heart of the Lakes Publishing, 1981.

North Carolina

Maps and Atlases

Clark, David S. *Index to Maps of North Carolina in Books and Periodicals Illustrating the History of the State from the Voyage of Verrazzano in 1524 to 1975*. Fayetteville, N.C.: the author, 1976.

Clay, James W., Douglas M. Orr, Jr., and Alfred W. Stuart, eds. *North Carolina Atlas: Portrait of a Changing Southern State*. Chapel Hill: University of North Carolina Press, 1975.

Corbitt, David L. *The Formation of the North Carolina Counties, 1663–1943*. 1950. Reprint with supplementary data and corrections. Raleigh: North Carolina State Department of Archives and History, 1969.

Cummings, William P. *North Carolina in Maps*. Raleigh: State Department of Archives and History, 1966.

North Carolina Atlas and Gazetteer. 2nd ed. Freeport, Maine: DeLorme Mapping Co., 1995.

Puetz, C. J., comp. *North Carolina County Maps*. Lyndon Station, Wis.: Thomas Publishing Co., 1991.

Stout, Garland P. *Historical Research Maps: North Carolina Counties*. 5 vols. Greensboro, N.C.: G. P. Stout, 1973.

Gazetteers and Postal Guides

Edwards, Richard, ed. *Statistical Gazetteer of the States of Virginia and North Carolina*. Richmond, Va.: published for the proprietor, 1856.

Powell, William S. *The North Carolina Gazetteer: A Dictionary of Tar Heel Places*. Chapel Hill: University of North Carolina Press, 1968.

North Dakota

Maps and Atlases

Goodman, Lowell R., and R. J. Eidem. *The Atlas of North Dakota*. Fargo: North Dakota Studies, 1976.

North Dakota CountyAtlas. Bismarck: North Dakota State Highway Dept., Planning Division, 1985.

Gazetteers and Postal Guides

Alphabetical Index to "Origins of North Dakota Place Names" by Mary Ann Barnes Williams. Bismarck: North Dakota State Highway Dept., 1977.

Phillips, George H. *Postoffices and Postmarks of Dakota Territory*. Crete, Nebr.: J-B Publishing Co., 1973.

Wick, Douglas A. *North Dakota Place Names*. Bismarck, N.D.: Hedemarken Collectibles, 1988.

Williams, Mary Ann B. *Origins of North Dakota Place Names*. Washburn, N.D.: the author, 1966.

Ohio

Maps and Atlases

Atlas of Ohio. Madison, Wisc.: American Publishing Co., 1975.

Burke, Thomas A. *Ohio Lands: A Short History*. 3rd ed. Columbus, Ohio: auditor of state, 1991.

Downes, Randolph C. "Evolution of Ohio Kentucky Boundaries." *Ohio Archaeological and Historical Publications* 36 (July 1927): 340–477. Reprint. Columbus: Ohio Historical Society, 1970.

Ohio Atlas and Gazetteer. 4th ed. Freeport, Maine: DeLorme Mapping Co., 1996.

Puetz, C. J., comp. *Ohio County Maps*. Lyndon Station, Wis.: Thomas Publishing Co., 1992.

Smith, Thomas H. *The Mapping of Ohio*. Kent, Ohio: Kent State University Press, 1977.

Walling, Henry F. *Atlas of the State of Ohio*. 1867. Reprint. Knightstown, Ind.: Bookmark, 1983.

Gazetteers and Postal Guides

Gallagher, John S., and Alan H. Patera. *The Post Offices of Ohio*. Burtonsville, Md.: The Depot, 1979.

Hawes, George W. *Geo. W. Hawes' Ohio State Gazetteer and Business Directory for 1860–'61*. Indianapolis, Ind.: the author, 1860.

Jenkins, Warren. *Ohio Gazetteer, and Traveler's Guide. . . .* Columbus, Ohio: Isaac N. Whiting, 1837. Jenkins' gazetteer is a continuation of Kilbourn's Gazetteers, discontinued in 1834, but is almost entirely rewritten and contains many additions and corrections.

Kilbourn, John, comp. *The Ohio Gazetteer, or, Topographical Dictionary: Being a Continuation of the Work Originally Compiled By the Late John Kilbourn*. 11th ed. Rev. and enl. Columbus, Ohio: Scott and Wright, 1833. Reprint. Knightstown, Ind.: Bookmark, 1978.

Overman, William D. *Ohio Town Names*. Akron, Ohio: Atlantic Press, 1958.

Oklahoma

Maps and Atlases

Morris, John W., ed. *Boundaries of Oklahoma*. Oklahoma City: Oklahoma Historical Society, 1980.

_____, Charles R. Goins, and Edwin C. McReynolds. *The Historical Atlas of Oklahoma*. 2nd ed. Rev. and enl. Norman: University of Oklahoma Press, 1985.

Oklahoma in Maps: An Interim Report. Stillwater: Cartography Service, Dept. of Geography, Oklahoma State University, 1979.

Gazetteers and Postal Guides

Gannett, Henry. *A Gazetteer of Indian Territory*. Washington, D.C.: U.S. Government Printing Office, 1905. Reprint. Tulsa, Okla.: Oklahoma Yesterday Pub., 1980.

Shirk, George H. *Oklahoma Place Names*. 2nd ed. Rev. and enl. Norman: University of Oklahoma Press, 1974.

Town and Place Locations. Oklahoma City: Oklahoma Department of Highways, 1975.

Oregon

Maps and Atlases

Brown, Erma S. *Oregon, County Boundary Change Maps, 1843–1916*. Lebanon, Oreg.: End of Trail Researchers, 1970.

Loy, William G. *A Preliminary Atlas of Oregon*. Eugene: Geography Dept., University of Oregon, 1972.

Oregon Atlas and Gazetteer. 2nd ed. Freeport, Maine: DeLorme Mapping Co., 1995.

Preston, Ralph N. *Historical Oregon: Old Forts, Old Military Roads, Indian Battle Grounds, Overland Stage Routes*. Corvallis, Oreg.: Treasure Chest Maps, 1969. Reprinted as *Early Oregon Atlas*. 2nd ed. Portland, Oreg.: Binford & Mort Publishers, 1978.

Gazetteers and Postal Guides

McArthur, Lewis A. *Oregon Geographic Names*. 5th ed. Portland: Oregon Historical Society, 1982.

Payne, Edwin R. *Oregon Post Offices*. 2nd ed. Rev. to January 1955. Salem, Oreg., 1955.

Pennsylvania

Maps and Atlases

Bien, Joseph R. *Atlas of the State of Pennsylvania: From Original Surveys and Various Local Surveys Revised and Corrected. . . .* New York: Julius Bien & Co., 1900.

Cuff, David J., and others, eds. *The Atlas of Pennsylvania: A Cooperative Project of the Three Commonwealth Research Universities: Temple University, University of Pittsburgh, and The Pennsylvania State University*. Philadelphia: Temple University Press, 1989.

Long, John H., ed. *Atlas of Historical County Boundaries: Pennsylvania*. New York: Simon & Schuster, 1996.

Pennsylvania Atlas and Gazetteer. 4th ed. Freeport, Maine: DeLorme Mapping Co., 1996.

Puetz, C. J., comp. *Pennsylvania County Maps*. Lyndon Station, Wis.: Thomas Publishing Co., 1987.

Russ, William A., Jr. *How Pennsylvania Acquired Its Present Boundaries*. University Park: Pennsylvania Historical Association, 1966.

Simonetti, Martha L., comp. *Descriptive List of the Map Collection in the Pennsylvania State Archives*. Edited by Donald H. Kent and Harry E. Whipkey. Harrisburg: Pennsylvania Historical and Museum Commission, 1976.

Walling, Henry F., and Ormando W. Gray. *New Topographical Atlas of the State of Pennsylvania. . . .* Philadelphia: Stedman, Brown & Lyon, 1872. Reprinted as the *1872 Historical Topographical Atlas of the State of Pennsylvania. . . .* Knightstown, Ind.: Bookmark, 1977.

Gazetteers and Postal Guides

Espenshade, Abraham H. *Pennsylvania Place Names*. Pennsylvania State College Studies in History and Political Science, no. 1. State College: Pennsylvania State College, 1925. Reprint. Baltimore: Clearfield Publishing Co., 1991.

Gordon, Thomas F. *A Gazetteer of the State of Pennsylvania. . . .* Philadelphia: T. Belknap, 1832. Reprint. New Orleans: Polyanthos, 1975. Reprint. Microfilm. New Haven, Conn.: Research Publications. Reprint. Microfiche. Louisville, Ky.: Lost Cause Press, 1976.

Kay, John L., and Chester M. Smith, Jr. *Pennsylvania Postal History*. Lawrence, Mass.: Quarterman Publications, 1976.

Scott, Joseph. *A Geographical Description of Pennsylvania: Also of the Counties Respectively, in the Order in Which They Were Established by the Legislature: With an Alphabetical List of the Townships in Each County; and Their Population in 1800*. Philadelphia: Robert Cochran, 1806. Reprint. Microfiche. Early American Imprints, Second Series, no. 11331.

Rhode Island

Maps and Atlases

Beers, Daniel G. *Atlas of the State of Rhode Island and Providence Plantations*. Philadelphia: Pomeroy & Beers, 1870.

Cady, John H. *Rhode Island Boundaries, 1636–1936*. Providence: State of Rhode Island and Providence Plantations, 1936.

"Chronological Checklist of Maps in Rhode Island in the Rhode Island Historical Society Library." *Rhode Island Historical*

Collections 11 (1918): 47–55. Continues serially through the next several volumes.

Wright, Marion I., and Robert J. Sullivan. *Rhode Island Atlas*. Providence: Rhode Island Publications Society, 1982.

Gazetteers and Postal Guides

Gannett, Henry. *A Geographic Dictionary of Rhode Island*. Washington, D.C.: U.S. Government Printing Office, 1894. Reprinted as *A Geographic Dictionary of Connecticut and Rhode Island*. Baltimore: Genealogical Publishing Co., 1978.

Merolla, Lawrence M., Arthur B. Jackson, and Frank M. Crowther. *Rhode Island Postal History: The Post Offices*. Providence: Rhode Island Postal History Society, 1977.

Pease, John Chauncey, and John M. Niles. *A Gazetteer of the States of Connecticut and Rhode Island*. Hartford, Conn.: William S. Marsh, 1819. Reprint. Bowie, Md.: Heritage Books, 1991.

South Carolina

Maps and Atlases

Black, James M. "The Counties and Districts of South Carolina." *Genealogical Journal* 5 (3) (September 1976): 100–13. Salt Lake City: Utah Genealogical Association, 1976.

Mills, Robert. *Atlas of the State of South Carolina*. Reprinted as *Atlas of the State of South Carolina, 1825*. Easley, S.C.: Southern Historical Press, 1980.

Puetz, C. J., comp. *South Carolina County Maps*. Lyndon Station, Wis.: Thomas Publishing Co., 1989.

Gazetteers and Postal Guides

Neuffer, Claude H., ed. *Names in South Carolina*. Vols. 1–12, 1954–1965. Columbia: Department of English, University of South Carolina, 1967. Reprint. Spartanburg, S.C.: Reprint Co., 1976.

South Dakota

Gazetteers and Postal Guides

Federal Writer's Project. *South Dakota Place Names*. Vermillion: University of South Dakota, 1940.

Phillips, George H. *Postoffices and Postmarks of Dakota Territory*. Crete, Nebr.: J-B Publishing Co., 1973.

______. *The Postoffices of South Dakota, 1861–1930*. Crete, Nebr.: J-B Publishing Co., 1975.

Sneve, Virginia D. H. *South Dakota Geographic Names*. Vermillion: University of South Dakota, 1941. Reprint. Sioux Falls, S.D.: Brevet Press, 1973.

Tennessee

Maps and Atlases

Foster, Austin P. *Counties of Tennessee*. Nashville: Department of Education, Division of History, state of Tennessee, 1923.

Puetz, C. J., comp. *Tennessee County Maps*. Lyndon Station, Wis.: Thomas Publishing Co., 1992.

Rhea, Matthew. *Map of the State of Tennessee*. 1832. Reprinted as *Eastin Morris' Tennessee Gazetteer, 1834, and Matthew Rhea's Map of the State of Tennessee, 1832*. Edited by Robert M. McBride and Owen Meredith. Nashville, Tenn.: Gazetteer Press, 1971.

Tennessee Atlas and Gazetteer. 3rd ed. Freeport, Maine: DeLorme Mapping Co., 1995.

Gazetteers and Postal Guides

Fullerton, Ralph O. *Place Names of Tennessee*. Tennessee, Division of Geology. Bulletin no. 73. Nashville: Department of Conservation, Division of Geology, State of Tennessee, 1974.

Morris, Eastin. *The Tennessee Gazetteer, or Topographical Dictionary. . . .* Nashville, Tenn.: W. H. Hunt & Co., 1834. Reprinted as *Eastin Morris' Tennessee Gazetteer, 1834, and Matthew Rhea's Map of the State of Tennessee, 1832*. Edited by Robert M. McBride and Owen Meredith. Nashville: Gazetteer Press, 1971. Reprint. Microfiche. Louisville, Ky.: Lost Cause Press.

Texas

Maps and Atlases

Atlas of Texas. Austin: Bureau of Business, University of Texas, 1979.

Day, James M., comp. *Maps of Texas 1527–1900: The Map Collection of the Texas State Archives*. Austin, Tex.: Pemberton Press, 1974.

Martin, James C., and Robert S. Martin. *Maps of Texas and the Southwest, 1513–1900*. Albuquerque: University of New Mexico Press, 1984.

Pool, William C. *A Historical Atlas of Texas*. Austin, Tex.: Encino Press, 1975.

Texas Atlas and Gazetteer. Freeport, Maine: DeLorme Mapping Co., 1995.

Gazetteers and Postal Guides

Gannett, Henry. *A Gazetteer of Texas*. 2nd ed. Washington, D.C.: U.S. Government Printing Office, 1904.

Massengill, Fred I. *Texas Towns: Origin of Name and Location of Each of the 2,148 Post Offices in Texas*. Terrell, Tex., 1936.

Tarpley, Fred. *1001 Texas Place Names*. Austin: University of Texas Press, 1980.

Texas State Gazetteer and Business Directory. St. Paul, Minn.: R. L. Polk and Co., 1882–83, 1884–85, 1890–91.

Wheat, James L. *Postmasters and Post Offices of Texas, 1846–1930*. Garland, Tex.: Lost and Found, 1974.

Utah

Maps and Atlases

Greer, Deon C., and others. *Atlas of Utah*. Ogden, Utah: Weber State College, 1981.

Miller, David E., comp. *Utah History Atlas*. 3rd ed. Salt Lake City: the author, 1977.

Moffat, Riley M. *Printed Maps of Utah to 1900*. Santa Cruz, Calif.: Western Association of Map Libraries, 1981.

Utah Atlas and Gazetteer. Freeport, Maine: DeLorme Mapping Co., 1995.

Gazetteers and Postal Guides

Gallagher, John S. *The Post Offices of Utah*. Burtonsville, Md.: The Depot, 1977.

Gannett, Henry. *A Gazetteer of Utah*. Washington, D.C.: U.S. Government Printing Office, 1900.

Gruber, Ted. *Postal History of Utah 1849–1976*. Crete, Nebr.: J-B Publishing Co., 1978.

Leigh, Rufus W. *Five Hundred Utah Place Names, Their Origin and Significance*. Salt Lake City: Deseret News Press, 1961.

Utah Writer's Project. *Origins of Utah Place Names*. Salt Lake City: State Department of Instruction, 1940.

VanCott, John W., comp. *Utah Place Names: A Comprehensive Guide to the Origins of Geographic Names*. Salt Lake City: University of Utah Press, 1990.

Vermont

Maps and Atlases

Long, John H., ed. *Atlas of Historical County Boundaries: New Hampshire and Vermont*. New York: Simon & Schuster, 1993.

Vermont Atlas and Gazetteer. 9th ed. Freeport, Maine: DeLorme Mapping Co., 1996.

The Vermont Road Atlas and Guide. Burlington, Vt.: Northern Cartographic, 1989.

Gazetteers and Postal Guides

Hayward, John. *A Gazetteer of Vermont: Containing Descriptions of All the Counties, Towns, and Districts in the State, and of Its Principal Mountains, Rivers, Waterfalls, Harbors, Islands, and Curious Places*. Boston: Tappan, Whittemore and Mason, 1849. Reprint. Microfiche. Louisville, Ky.: Lost Cause Press, 1975. Reprint with new index to people and places. Bowie, Md.: Heritage Books, 1990.

Slawson, George C., Arthur W. Bingham, and Sprague W. Drenan. *The Postal History of Vermont*. Collectors Club Handbook, no. 21. New York: Collectors Club, 1969.

Swift, Esther Monroe. *Vermont Place-Names: Footprints of History*. Brattleboro, Vt.: Stephen Greene Press, 1977.

Virginia

Maps and Atlases

County Road Map Atlas: Commonwealth of Virginia. Richmond, Va.: Department of Transportation, 1987.

Doran, Michael F. *Atlas of County Boundary Changes in Virginia, 1634–1895*. Athens, Ga.: Iberian Publishing Co., 1987.

Hale, John S. *A Historical Atlas of Colonial Virginia*. Staunton, Va.: Old Dominion Publication, 1978.

Hiden, Martha W. *How Justice Grew: Virginia Counties, an Abstract of Their Formation*. Charlottesville: University Press of Virginia, 1957. Reprint. Baltimore: Clearfield Co., 1992.

Sames, James W., 3rd, comp. *Index of Kentucky and Virginia Maps 1562 to 1900*. Frankfort: Kentucky Historical Society, 1976.

Sanchez-Saavedra, Eugene Michael. *A Description of the Country: Virginia's Cartographers and Their Maps 1607–1881*. Richmond: Virginia State Library, 1975.

Swem, Earl G., comp. *Maps Relating to Virginia in the Virginia State Library and other Departments of the Commonwealth: With the 17th and 18th Century Atlas-Maps in the Library of Congress*. Reprint. Richmond: Virginia State Library and Archives, 1989.

Virginia Atlas and Gazetteer. 2nd ed. Freeport, Maine: DeLorme Mapping Co., 1995.

Gazetteers and Postal Guides

Edwards, Richard, ed. *Statistical Gazetteer of the State of Virginia*. Richmond, Va.: the editor, 1855. Reprint. Microfiche. Louisville, Ky.: Lost Cause Press, 1975.

Gannett, Henry. *A Gazetteer of Virginia*. Washington, D.C.: U.S. Government Printing Office, 1904. Reprinted as *A Gazetteer of Virginia and West Virginia*. Baltimore: Genealogical Publishing Co., 1975.

Hanson, Raus M. *Virginia Place Names: Derivations, Historical Uses*. Verona, Va.: McClure Press, 1969.

Hummel, Ray O., Jr., ed. *A List of Places Included in 19th Century Virginia Directories*. Richmond, Va.: Virginia State Library, 1960. Reprint. 1981.

Martin, Joseph. *A New and Comprehensive Gazetteer of Virginia and the District of Columbia*. Charlottsville, Va.: the author, 1835.

Washington

Maps and Atlases

Abbott, Newton Carl, Fred E. Carver, and J. W. Helm, comp. *The Evolution of Washington Counties*. Yakima, Wash.: Yakima Valley Genealogical Society and Klickitat County Historical Society, 1978.

Preston, Ralph N. *Early Washington: Overland Stage Routes, Old Military Roads, Indian Battle Grounds, Old Forts, Old Gold Mines*. Corvallis, Oreg.: Western Guide Publishers, 1974. Reprinted as *Early Washington Atlas*. 2nd ed. Binford & Mort Publishers, 1974.

Scott, James R. *Washington: A Centennial Atlas*. Bellingham: Western Washington University, 1989.

Scott, James W., and Roland L. DeLorme. *Historical Atlas of Washington*. Norman: University of Oklahoma Press, 1988.

Washington Atlas and Gazetteer. 3rd ed. Freeport, Maine: DeLorme Mapping Co., 1996.

Gazetteers and Postal Guides

Landes, Henry. *A Geographic Dictionary of Washington*. Washington Geological Survey. Bulletin no. 17. Olympia, Wash.: F. M. Lamborn, 1917.

Meany, Edmond S. *Origin of Washington Geographic Names*. Seattle: University of Washington Press, 1923. Reprint. Detroit: Gale Research Co., 1968.

Phillips, James W. *Washington State Place Names*. Seattle: University of Washington Press, 1971.

West Virginia

Maps and Atlases

New Descriptive Atlas of West Virginia. Clarksburg, W.Va.: Clarksburg Publishing Co., 1933.

Puetz, C. J., comp. *West Virginia County Maps*. Lyndon Station, Wis.: Thomas Publishing Co., 1990.

Sims, Edgar B. *Making a State: Formation of West Virginia. . . .* Charleston, W.Va.: the author, 1956.

West Virginia Historical Records Survey. *West Virginia County Formations and Boundary Changes*. Charleston, W.Va.: Hist. Survey, 1938.

Gazetteers and Postal Guides

Gannett, Henry. *The Gazetteer of West Virginia*. Washington, D.C.: U.S. Government Printing Office, 1904. Reprinted as *A Gazetteer of Virginia and West Virginia*. Baltimore: Genealogical Publishing Co., 1975.

Kenny, Hamill. *West Virginia Place Names, Their Origin and Meaning, Including the Nomenclature of the Streams and Mountains*. Piedmont, W.Va.: Place Name Press, 1945.

Wisconsin

Maps and Atlases

Atlas of Wisconsin. Madison: University of Wisconsin Press, 1974.

Collins, Charles W. *An Atlas of Wisconsin*. 2nd ed. Madison, Wisc.: American Printing & Pub., 1972.

Fox, Michael J., comp. *Maps and Atlases Showing Land Ownership in Wisconsin*. Madison: State Historical Society of Wisconsin, 1978.

Galneder, Mary H., Elizabeth S. Maule, and Nancy Jo Pickett, comp. *A Union List of Topographic Maps of Wisconsin (1:24,000 to 1:1,000,000)*. Madison: Cartographic Laboratory, University of Wisconsin, 1975.

Kelsey, Laura E., and Charlotte M. Ashby, comp. *Cartographic Records Relating to the Territory of Wisconsin, 1836–1848*. Washington, D.C.: National Archives and Records Service, 1970.

Maule, Elizabeth. *Bird's Eye View of Wisconsin Communities*. Madison, Wisc., 1977.

Puetz, C. J., comp. *Wisconsin County Maps*. Lyndon Station, Wis.: Thomas Publishing Co., 1992.

Robinson, Arthur H. *The Atlas of Wisconsin: General Maps and Gazetteer*. Madison: University of Wisconsin Press, 1974.

Ziegler, Art, Christine Reinhard, and Jane Rouder. *Cartographic Catalog*. Madison: State Cartographer's Office, University of Wisconsin, 1979–91. This multi-volume work currently covers the cartographic records of sixty-one Wisconsin counties.

Wisconsin Atlas and Gazetteer. 4th ed. Freeport, Maine: DeLorme Mapping Co., 1996.

Wisconsin: Its Counties, Townships and Villages. Janesville, Wis.: Origins, 1994.

Gazetteers and Postal Guides

Gard, Robert E., and L. G. Sorden. *The Romance of Wisconsin Place Names*. New York: October House, 1968. Reprint. Minocqua, Wis.: Heartland Press, 1988.

Hale, James B., comp. *Wisconsin Post Office Handbook, 1921–1971*. Wisconsin Postal History Society. Bulletin no. 10. Madison: Wisconsin Postal History Society, 1971.

Hunt, John W. *Wisconsin Gazetteer. . . .* Madison, Wis.: P. Brown, 1853. Reprint. Microfiche. Louisville, Ky.: Lost Cause Press, 1974. Ann Arbor, Mich.: University Microfilms.

Maule, Elizabeth. *Bird's Eye View of Wisconsin Communities*. Madison, Wis., 1977.

Peck, George W., ed. *Wisconsin; Comprising Sketches of Counties, Towns, Events, Institutions and Persons Arranged in Cyclopedic Form*. Madison, Wis.: Western Historical Association, 1906.

Wyoming

Maps and Atlases

Wyoming Atlas and Gazetteer. Freeport, Maine: DeLorme Mapping Co., 1993.

Gazetteers and Postal Guides

Gallagher, John S., and Alan H. Patera. *Wyoming Post Offices: 1850–1980*. Burtonsville, Md.: The Depot, 1980.

Urbanek, Mae B. *Wyoming Place Names*. 1967. Reprint. Missoula, Mont.: Mountain Press Publishing Co., 1988.

ETHNIC SOURCES OVERVIEW

Key Concepts in This Chapter

- *Ethnic* refers to any group with a common history or heritage.
- All family history is, to some degree, ethnic.
- There has been a growing interest in the ethnic aspects of family history.
- Assimilation of the first generation or two may limit clues to ethnic origins.
- Clues to ethnic origins exist in a wide variety of home and other sources.
- General reference books provide overviews for more than one hundred ethnic groups.
- Many sources are found in ethnic research collections.
- A wide and growing number of sources are available for each ethnic group.
- Historical and genealogical societies can provide excellent help and resources.

Key Sources in This Chapter

- *Harvard Encyclopedia of American Ethnic Groups*
- *Ethnic Information Sources of the United States*
- *A Comprehensive Bibliography for the Study of American Minorities*
- *Immigration and Ethnicity*
- *Encyclopedic Directory of Ethnic Organizations in the United States*
- Ethnic Group series by Oceana Publications

4

ETHNIC SOURCES

Loretto Dennis Szucs

It is a common misconception to think of the word *ethnic* as applying to someone or something foreign; yet *Webster's Ninth New Collegiate Dictionary* (Merriam-Webster, 1986) defines *ethnic* as "of or relating to large groups of people classed according to common racial, national, tribal, religious, linguistic or cultural origin or background." By this definition, it would seem that all family history studies are ethnic.

North America has always been a land of ethnic diversity. Even Native Americans have varying traditions regarding their origins, pointing to ethnic diversity among America's earliest inhabitants. In the years since records have been kept, a massive stream of humanity—more than 50 million people—has crossed land and water to find a home in the United States (*Immigrant Nation* 1991, 34). "Ethnics" arrived speaking every language and representing every nationality, race, and religion.

Each of us has been touched in some way by the experiences, choices, attitudes, and even the genetic makeup of our ethnic ancestors. Those who have gone before us have had a profound influence in shaping our world. A knowledge of an ancestor's ethnic group, its history, and its laws and customs can lead us to specific and often unique record sources. Such background knowledge puts us in a better position to interpret whatever we may find in the records we use.

More importantly, ethnic sources can help us to understand our ancestors as real people. Unless family members have left detailed diaries or oral histories with their thoughts and activities, we can never get to know them to the degree that we might like. Without cultural background information, we can be at a loss to understand their actions. But with some comprehension of the whole group of which they were a part, and the time in which they lived, we can begin to understand them more clearly. More than lifeless names on family charts, we begin to see our ancestors as human beings with distinct personalities.

Each year more and more people, intrigued by such thoughts, are drawn to the search for their personal past. This search is not new. As early as the sixth century B.C., the words "know yourself" were inscribed in the temple of Apollo at Delphi. Almost every culture agrees that one of the best approaches to self-knowledge is in understanding the experiences of past generations.

ETHNIC APPROACH TO FAMILY HISTORY

Few of those whose ancestors arrived on the *Mayflower* would think of their families as "ethnic." However, if we adhere to the definition of the word, we have to concede that the English pioneers were as ethnic as the Native Americans who were their predecessors in North America. There are distinct skills and bodies of ethnic records that a *Mayflower* descendant needs in order to be fully effective in conducting her research.

The purpose of this chapter is to discuss the importance of the ethnic dimension in all family history research, and to suggest some specific ethnic research strategies, collections, and printed sources. It would require several volumes of encyclopedic dimensions to cite every ethnic source. While this chapter makes no claim to being all-inclusive, it should serve as a key for unlocking the door to a vast array of important and fascinating materials that will facilitate and enhance family research. Fortunately, the potential for success for Americans of all ethnic backgrounds has been transformed dramatically over the past two decades for several reasons.

Growing Interest in Ethnic Ancestry

Despite the desires of many to know more about their heritage, until the 1970s, the field of American genealogy was dominated by an elite few who could trace their ancestry back to European upper classes or to the Colonial and Revolutionary War periods in the United States. Except for the standard histories of various nations, there was little in print to facilitate what was then perceived as ethnic research. One of the most difficult aspects in this area of study is the fact that ethnic materials are decentralized and uncoordinated. Locating all the important ethnic collections and printed sources has been a matter of great skill—or pure luck, in some cases.

The Roots Phenomenon. Alex Haley set off an explosion of interest in the subject with his moving portrayal of his own ethnic family history. Whatever one may think of his work, no one can deny that the phenomenal success of Haley's *Roots* (Garden City, N.J.: Doubleday, 1976) and its subsequent television dramatization significantly advanced general awareness and acceptance of ancestral studies. When questioned about the excitement aroused by *Roots,* Haley responded: "In all of us there is a hunger, marrow deep to know our heritage—to know who we are and where we have come from. Without this enriching knowledge there is a hollow yearning" (Haley 1977). Inspired by Haley's epic, millions of Americans from all backgrounds set out to discover the lost histories of their own families. Because of this new interest, new resources opened up and continue to expand.

A Broader Approach to History. The newly aroused consciousness of personal history coincided with shifts in the way American history was being interpreted and rewritten in the 1960s and 1970s. Previously, academic historians had focused on questions and individuals of national importance while local history, the history of individual communities and common people, remained in the hands of "amateurs" or was ignored (Higham 1965, 15).

U.S. bicentennial celebrations brought an upsurge in popular historical awareness. The 1976 celebration encouraged an outpouring of publications focusing on states, counties, cities, towns, neighborhoods, institutions, and communities. The United States celebrated its ethnic diversity as never before, and the results included more being written about women, children, and immigrants.

Cultural Sensitivity. The civil rights movement also promoted ethnic culture sensitivity and appreciation. The positive results achieved by black nationalism encouraged other groups to insist that their history be included in school and college texts and that their nationalities be referenced with respect. Congress answered demands with passage of the Ethnic Heritage Studies Act of 1972. The act formally acknowledged "official recognition to ethnicity as a positive constructive force in our society today." Additionally, $15 million was appropriated to subsidize ethnic studies courses in schools and colleges in the United States (Divine 1984, 898).

Return to the Homeland. Tourism, too, has played a powerful role in promoting ethnic awareness. Economic advancement of sons and daughters of American immigrants has given many the means to revisit ancestral homes. In *The Americans: The Democratic Experience*, Daniel J. Boorstin says

> one of the beautiful ironies of modern American history was that the children of refugees from the Old World had the wealth, the leisure, and the technical means to return for a holiday to the scenes of their parents' poverty and oppression. The man whose ancestor had fled penniless and in desperation from Sicily or Ireland or Germany returned in air-conditioned comfort to rediscover the "romance" of the Old World (1973, 514).

Sociologists, demographers, social historians, and family historians alike have benefitted tremendously from the combination of factors that have heightened interest and facilitated research in ethnic studies.

Ethnic: An Ever-Changing Definition

Because scholars cannot agree on a completely acceptable definition of "ethnic," setting the parameters of this chapter presented a challenge. By some definitions, an ethnic group should have a sense of identity based on a visibly distinctive cultural pattern. National groups, such as Swedish or Polish immigrants, are clearly ethnic groups. So are many religious groups, such as Jews, Old Order Amish, and Mormons (members of The Church of Jesus Christ of Latter-day Saints). Similarly, some racial groups have retained clear ethnic identities, while others have not. Irish Catholics in the U.S. have been considered a religious ethnic group, whereas Italian Americans have been seen mainly as a national group. Immigrants from East Asia have been perceived chiefly as racial groups rather than as national or religious groups (Marden and Meyer 1973, 194).

Ethnic Identity and Assimilation. Many ethnic groups are not clearly delineated. Moreover, the status of every ethnic group is in a continual state of change. As new groups arrive in North America, they typically settle in communities with their kind, climb the social and economic class ladder, improve their living conditions, and are then replaced by a new low-status ethnic group. In almost all cases, newcomers have encountered some degree of hostility from the already established ethnic groups.

In times of war, the need to stress national unity has encouraged Americans to forget their diverse ethnic origins and to overlook cultural differences. Second- and third-generation Americans mix in a way that their parents would not have considered possible, thus making it difficult for recent generations to retain any ethnic identity. Over the years, with educational advancements and economic success, immigrant groups began to move into the American mainstream. In the assimilation process, some groups merged with others, diluting or completely losing their separate ethnic identities.

In many cases, first-generation Americans saw assimilation as a means of being accepted in an established society that was increasingly hostile toward foreigners. The era between the 1840s and the 1930s was an especially traumatic time for ethnic Americans. During this time, Irish, then German, then Asian, then Italians and Jewish Americans bore the brunt of anti-foreign sentiment. Throughout American history, there has been a deliberate attempt on the part of many foreign-born individuals to renounce their birth nationality. Persecution in the old country and rejection of foreigners in the new country made it desirable to erase painful traditions. For many, there was no feeling of nostalgia for the "good old days"; they simply wanted to forget the past and to begin anew as Americans. As a result of this "deliberate amnesia," surveys conducted on college campuses have shown that nearly half of the students polled could not identify their ethnic origins.

Criteria for Inclusion. While every ethnic group is important, space limitations do not allow for a full discussion of the less-populous groups in this chapter. Criteria for an ethnic group's inclusion in this chapter were based on U.S. census population figures (see table 4-1), as well as the interest level that has been documented at genealogical conferences and by ethnic genealogical societies across the United States.

The following concepts will help you make the best use of this chapter:

- It is not the purpose of this chapter to discuss the history of various ethnic groups; rather, it will identify (1) general reference sources and (2) ethnic research collections, followed by (3) a general discussion of sources for specific ethnic groups. The heart of the chapter follows with a list of individual ethnic group sources.

- The multi-ethnic general reference sources cited and described in this chapter will provide important background material for *every* ethnic group.

- Because many individuals do not know the origins of their family names, the general sources and strategies outlined in this chapter will aid in identifying surname origins.

- Religious sources (except for some special Jewish materials) are not covered here but may be found in the chapter on printed church records.

- The documented level of interest in genealogical research within the ethnic groups determined the size of the entry for each group in the section on "Sources for Specific Ethnic Groups" (below).

Sources for Determining Ethnic Origins

While some families have lost most of their ethnic identity, surprising clues survive in many sources, such as family traditions, letters, diaries, civil and religious records, ethnic literature, and studies of migration patterns. One researcher, for example, was able to discover the area in Germany from which her family had emigrated because of a photograph in which her grandmother appeared in a lace cap. As she learned from her studies, the lace was a distinctive part of the costume worn in a specific region of Germany. An African-American was able to determine the tribe from which his family had come through oral tradition and the distinctive pattern in cloth that had been handed down in the family. Yet another family learned its origins in France because of a silver medallion passed down through the generations. A watchmaker's descendant learned the precise town of the family's origin when she investigated the origin of a timepiece she had inherited.

Songs, dances, favorite foods, recipes, costumes, memorabilia, and a host of other things can provide important clues for finding ethnic origins. In addition, many of the standard genealogical sources, such as vital records, obituaries, and military, employment, and naturalization records, will provide important clues about ethnic origins. Should those sources fail, there are some other techniques, such as analyzing the surname, that, while not foolproof, may shed some light. Yet the clues will mean nothing unless one has an understanding of the customs, geography, and history of an ethnic group. Here the wealth of information in printed ethnic sources can truly be helpful in one's research.

Some of the key sources for determining ethnic origins are discussed below.

Home Sources. As in any other genealogical project, it is important for the researcher to begin a family study with himself and to work backward in time as each event is documented fully. With luck, a family member will remember where immigrant ancestors were born. In addition to family traditions, letters, or journals, seek postcards, photographs, scrapbooks, and mementoes that have been saved over the years.

The Census. The decennial U.S. population census schedules rarely reveal the exact birthplace of an individual, but the censuses from 1850 through 1920 show every person's country or state of birth; from 1880, the parents' birthplace usually appears. Because the census schedules for most states are indexed for almost all years, the census is a logical starting point for determining family origins. The 1900, 1910, and 1920 censuses solicited important immigration information. The 1920 census (the most recently available U.S. census) asked for the specific birthplace of anyone who had been born in a country whose boundaries had been changed by World War I (Austria, Germany, and Russia). Other clues in the 1920 census, such as mother tongue, may provide additional insights.

Table 4-1. Top Fifteen Ethnic Groups in the United States (1990 U.S. Census)

Ancestry Group	*Percent*
German	23.3
Irish	15.6
English	13.1
African American	9.6
Hispanic	7.0
Italian	5.9
Franco-American	5.3
Polish	3.8
Native American	3.5
Dutch	2.5
Scotch-Irish	2.3
Scottish	2.2
Swedish	1.9
Norwegian	1.6
Russian	1.2

Even if one is unable to find a particular ancestor's country of origin in census records, the discovery of another relative's origins or those of others of the same surname may prove helpful. Because there are many alphabetical and phonetic census indexes available, it may prove useful to survey the occurrence of a given surname in a statewide index. Frequently, individuals of the same family settled in close proximity, so pockets or concentrations of a surname provide a starting place to search for additional information. (Obviously, this approach will not work well with very common surnames.)

State censuses can also be useful for tracking family origins. In addition to the standard questions asked by the Federal census, the 1925 Iowa State Census, for example, asked for names of parents, mother's maiden name, nativity of parents, place of parents' marriage, military service, occupation, and religion. See chapter 9, "Censuses and Tax Lists," for more information.

Naturalization Records. Again, for uncommon surnames, it can be worthwhile to scan both printed and card or manuscript naturalization indexes for the possible origins of family names. Naturalization documents created after 1906 (and in some cases before that date) usually include individuals' specific birthplaces. As with a census index search, even though a relative may not show up in the index, someone of the same surname may point to the geographical area where an ancestor lived, thus enabling the researcher to focus on potential origins.

Passenger Lists. Most ship passenger lists reveal each passenger's country of origin, but only in later years (usually beginning in the 1890s) do they include the exact town of origin. See chapter 14, "Immigration Sources," for further information on naturalization records and passenger lists.

Printed Biographies, Genealogies, and Family Histories. The potential for finding ethnic origins in printed family histories and genealogies, compiled biographies, county and local histories, periodicals, and medieval and nobility sources cannot be overstated. Part 4 of this volume illuminates those important sources in five chapters.

Surname Sources. Because some families have been "American" for so many generations, the first problem a researcher may encounter is determining the origin of an ancestral surname.

Eldson Coles Smith's *American Surnames* (1969; reprint; Baltimore: Genealogical Publishing Co., 1986) is one of the standard references for identifying surnames. It includes the two thousand most common surnames in the United States today in the order of their frequency and with an estimated number of persons bearing each name. Smith's book is in six parts: "Classifications of Surnames," "Surnames from the Father's Name (Patronymics)," "Surnames from Occupation or Office," "Surnames from Description or Action (Nicknames)," "Surnames from Places," and "Surnames Not Properly Included Elsewhere." Some of the topics covered include abbreviated names, immigrant alterations, changing of names by immigrants, landscape names, town names, soldiers' names, Jewish surnames, surnames from periods of times, and hyphenated names.

Family names as they are recognized today developed from the eleventh to the fifteenth centuries in Europe. Today, many of those names, or ones derived from them, are in common use in the United States. According to Smith, the fifty surnames borne by the *Mayflower* pilgrims and the most common names in the United States at the enumeration of the first Federal census in 1790 remain among the most common names in the United States today (1969, 2).

A newer and more extensive study of names, Patrick Hanks and Flavia Hodges's *A Dictionary of Surnames* (New York: Oxford University Press, 1988), provides the origins of surnames, their world distribution, typology (types), and inclusion within national and cultural groups. The three-volume *New Century Cyclopedia of Names* (New York: Appleton-Century-Crofts, 1954) provides greater detail on many names than is found in other sources. The most comprehensive study may be Amanda H. Robb and Andrew Chelser's *Encyclopedia of American Family Names* (New York: Harper-Collins, 1995), which identifies the five thousand most common surnames in America and the derivations from these root names (bringing the total to more than ten thousand names) and provides information about each name's national origin. Most entries describe prominent Americans with the surname and, unique among surname books, identify some of the compiled genealogies that focus on families sharing the name.

GENERAL REFERENCE BOOKS FOR ETHNIC STUDIES

Once the ethnic origin of an ancestor has been discovered, there is a great and ever-increasing assortment of background materials that are worth pursuing. A public library is a good place to begin research; even the smallest will probably have some of the ethnic sources cited in this chapter. Most collections will also include a basic history for any given ethnic group. Through computer networking, libraries can track down even the most obscure materials that will facilitate the search and add to the enjoyment of any research project. Larger public libraries and university and college libraries generally have better and more finely detailed ethnic sources.

Harvard Encyclopedia of American Ethnic Groups

One of the most definitive and useful background sources for almost every ethnic group is Stephan Thernstrom's *Harvard Encyclopedia of American Ethnic Groups* (Cambridge, Mass.: Belknap Press of Harvard University Press, 1980). It assembles the basic information about the multitude of people who make up the population of the United States. It is a succinct, authoritative synthesis of the origins and histories of 106 ethnic groups, with twenty-nine thematic essays, eighty-seven maps, and a critical bibliography for each section (figure 4-1).

The editor of this encyclopedia admitted certain difficulties in making decisions about including several groups that are "made in America." The editor also concluded that

> . . . to equate 'ethnic' with 'foreign' is a mistake. The Mormons, for example, originated entirely within the United States, yet the fascinating account of their history in these pages explains why they belong in this volume. The Amish, the Hutterites and the Zoroastrians also have distinctiveness and cohesiveness that justifies such a judgment. The American regional groups included in the Encyclopedia—Appalachians, Southerners, and Yankees—were also 'Made in America.' They are not the same in character as immigrant or racial groups but possess a historical identity of their own (page vi).

As work began on the encyclopedia, each contributing author was given a checklist of seventeen suggested points to cover in each section (table 4-2). Among the categories of questions suggested to the section authors, there are many that we should ask ourselves as we develop the ethnic histories of our own families.

Ethnic Information Sources of the United States

Paul Wasserman and Alice E. Kennington, eds., *Ethnic Information Sources of the United States,* 2nd ed., 2 vols. (Detroit: Gale Research Co., 1983), assembles in one source information about the various ethnic groups that comprise the U.S. populace. The work's subtitle defines it as

> . . . a Guide to organizations, agencies, foundations, institutions, media, commercial and trade bodies, government programs, research institutes, libraries and museums, religious organizations, banking firms, festivals and fairs, travel and tourist offices, airlines and ship lines, bookdealers and publishers' representatives, and books, pamphlets, and audiovisuals on specific ethnic groups

This work is intended for use by individuals whose ancestors or relatives belong to particular ethnic groups and by students, educators, librarians, and others interested in learning about distinctive ethnic lines and the countries from which they

ABKHAZIANS: *see* North Caucasians

ACADIANS

More than 200 years after the British expelled the French Catholic Acadians from their farms in what are now the maritime provinces of Canada, Acadians still live in tightly knit communities in Louisiana and northern Maine. There are about 800,000 Acadians, popularly called Cajuns, in south central and south Louisiana, and another 20,000 living on the south side of Maine's St. John's River Valley, territory annexed by the United States following the 1842 Webster-Ashburton Treaty. In both areas the Acadians have clung tenaciously to their religion, language, and customs. Their original exile and suffering were immortalized by Henry Wadsworth Longfellow in the well-known poem *Evangeline* (1847).

Acadia and Diaspora

When France attempted to establish a North American colony in the early 17th century, families from northwest and central France, especially Normandy and Brittany, were recruited to settle the land called Acadie or Acadia, a region that then included Nova Scotia, New Brunswick, Prince Edward Island, and part of the state of Maine but that was generally restricted after 1713 to the present peninsula of Nova Scotia. They lived there as industrious colonials, producing most of their own necessities, farming, fishing, lumbering, and raising stock. Large families were common, and in isolation they held on to the traditions, speech, and customs of the French provinces from which they had come. Over time, just as English settlers and pioneers came to think of themselves as Americans, the Acadians began to consider themselves as a people distinct and apart from their fellow Frenchmen. They were not only a long way from Quebec but had come under English rule in 1713 as a result of the Treaty of Utrecht that ended one of several French-English wars. At the time they were directed to withdraw into French territory or to swear unconditional loyalty to the English monarch, but apparently they did neither and continued to prosper as before. The issue was raised again in 1730 when the Acadians finally agreed to an oath which they understood would exempt them from bearing arms against their own countrymen and their Indian allies. They were known as the "French Neutrals" and enjoyed another period of steady development until 1755 when the English authorities, for reasons still obscure, forced 6,000 to 8,000 Acadians at bayonet point to abandon their homes and flee for their lives. This mass displacement became known as *Le Grand Dérangement.* The exiles underwent great hardships as they were scattered by sea to other parts of British America, where they lived in extreme poverty and were persecuted because of their Roman Catholicism. It was only after the Treaty of Paris was signed in 1763, ending the last Anglo-French war in North America, that the refugees and exiles began to return to Canada or to relocate in France, Louisiana, and other French dominions. (*See also* French Canadians.)

The Acadians in Louisiana

As early as 1756 some Acadians probably reached the French colony of Louisiana from Maryland, the Carolinas, and Georgia. Louisiana was widely viewed as a hospitable place to begin life anew, and despite the fact that by secret treaty in 1762 (not made public for two years) it had become a Spanish possession, Acadians continued to migrate to the area. Many followed the rivers and streams that flow westward into the Mississippi and then traveled south to New Orleans.

Among the first Acadians to be noted in official government records were 193 refugees who had taken temporary refuge in Santo Domingo; they arrived in Louisiana in February 1765. Hundreds more came in 1765 and 1766 from the West Indies and the British colonies; they settled chiefly on the wide, fertile, and undeveloped plains of southwest and south central Louisiana. The Spanish officials who had arrived in New Orleans in 1766 were eager to aid the French exiles; they donated small parcels of land and provided food, seed, tools, and other necessities to the industrious Acadians, who chose to settle in the Attakapas and Opelousas regions. Areas settled later included Bayous Teche and Lafourche, the land bordering the Mississippi River south of New Orleans, and what eventually came to be known as the Acadian districts—St. James and Ascension.

The early Acadian migrants were joined, in the next twenty years, by others who had tried unsuccessfully to settle in France or the West Indies. Three thousand Acadian exiles left France between 1777 and 1788. They fanned out over southern Louisiana and established the villages of St. Martinville, Delcambre, Lafayette, Broussard, St. Landry, and Abbeville, the heart of Acadian Louisiana. Others continued to settle along the Mississippi River so that by 1788 St. James numbered 1,559 persons and Ascension 1,164. In the late 1780s Acadians moved into the lower Bayou Lafourche area; other groups migrated westward and settled around Lake Charles near the Texas border.

The Acadian settlers of the Louisiana frontier set to work raising livestock; they also planted sweet potatoes and sugar cane. The more prosperous bought slaves and expanded their land holdings. The inventory of Pierre Arceneaux's estate in St. Martinville taken in 1793 indicates the wealth accumulated by the more successful. At the time of his death, his estate was valued at $5,530, a sizable amount in the currency of that time. He owned several large buildings, 400 head of cattle, 15 horses, and numerous slaves.

Although Napoleon repossessed Louisiana in 1800 and then negotiated its sale to the United States in the famous Louisiana Purchase of 1803, the growth of the Acadian settlements was undisturbed. By 1810 St. James parish reported a population of 3,995 and Ascension more than 2,219. A second generation made its appearance, and the makeshift cabins of the exiles were

Figure 4-1. From the *Harvard Encyclopedia of American Ethnic Groups*.

Table 4-2. Topics Addressed for Ethnic Groups in *Harvard Encyclopedia of Ethnic Groups*

Origins	*Behavior and Personal or Individual Characteristics*
From where does the group originate?	Are there data on literacy, level of education, mental and physical health, etc.?
What language has the group spoken?	*Culture*
What is the racial composition of the group?	Has the group maintained its language?
What religious affiliations dominate in the group?	Folk customs?
Migration	Music?
Who migrated, why, how many, when?	Dance?
Arrival	Costume?
When did the group first arrive?	Does folk tradition survive?
How did they arrive?	*Religion*
Did they come in several groups?	What is the religious identity of the group?
Has the group been continually or sporadically refreshed by new arrivals?	What are the characteristic patterns of belief or unbelief?
Settlement	What features of religious practice have been important?
Where did the group settle? Rural/urban?	*Education*
What was the pattern of geographic mobility?	How has the group been educated?
Economic Life	*Politics*
What was entry employment?	When did the group enter local and national political life?
Was there specialization in economic activity?	What political organizations are characteristic?
What is the characteristic pattern of enterprise?	*Intergroup Relations*
Social Structure	What contacts has the group had with the Anglo-Americans and other ethnic groups?
Relation between class and ethnic group?	What conflicts/consensus marks interaction between the specific group and American society?
Stratification within ethnic group?	*Group Maintenance*
Social Organization	What resources have been utilized to maintain the boundaries of community?
What have been patterns of association?	What role is played by kinship and marriage patterns?
Voluntary associations?	What role is played by educational and religious institutions?
Parochial schools?	*Individual Ethnic Commitment*
Religious activities and institutions?	What are the individual roots of commitment?
Who are the group leaders?	Has there been a change over time?
Family and Kinship	*Bibliography*
What is the characteristic family form?	Important works that will be available to the reader
What is the importance of kinship ties?	
What are marriage patterns?	

are drawn. It is also for those who require information about the details of history, culture, customs, values, politics, and problems of ethnic groups in the United States. Topics and resources include standard ethnic sources and research institutions, as well as more obscure information (such as embassies, ethnic fraternal organizations, ethnic newspaper collections, dealers of ethnic books, and ethnic museums) that may be especially useful for genealogists. *Ethnic Information Sources* indicates, for example, that the American Irish Historical Society (991 Fifth Avenue, New York, NY 10028) maintains a library of more than twenty-five thousand volumes on Irish history and genealogy and the Irish in America.

A Comprehensive Bibliography for the Study of American Minorities

Wayne Charles Miller's *Comprehensive Bibliography for the Study of American Minorities*, 2 vols. (New York University Press, 1976), is a valuable ethnic source with an exhaustive, though dated, bibliography. It is divided into sections on the geographic areas from which ethnic people came: Africa, Europe, Eastern Europe and the Balkans, Asia, the islands (Puerto Rico and Cuba), Mexico, and Native American. Each section follows more or less the same format. Under "The Arab-American Experience," for example, is a brief history of Arabs in the United States, followed by:

Bibliographies of Bibliographies

Periodicals

Essays and Indexes Dealing with Periodicals

Periodicals in English

Periodicals in Arabic

History and Sociology

Education and Language

Religion

Biography and Autobiography

Literature

Literary Criticism

Folklore

Arts

The researcher who does not consider European ancestors as "minorities" might overlook this source, thereby missing some rather obscure yet important ethnic sources listed under the section "From Europe," which has subsections on the French, German, Spanish, Portuguese, Irish, Jewish, Greek, Swedish, Norwegian, Danish, Icelandic, Finnish, and Scandinavians as groups.

In the subsection titled "German Americans: A Guide to the German American Experience," the *Comprehensive Bibliography for the Study of Minorities* provides a historical sketch that ranges in time from the first permanent German settlement (1683) in Germantown, Pennsylvania, to World War I and what is probably the most extensive German-American bibliography published as of 1976.

The Ethnic Almanac

Stephanie Bernardo's *Ethnic Almanac* (Garden City, N.Y.: Dolphin Books, Doubleday & Co., 1981) takes a lighter yet interesting and useful look at twenty-five of the largest ethnic groups in the United States. The first chapter of the book is devoted to the "First Immigrants," providing a Brief Chronology of American Indians After Columbus; First and Facts about American Indians; Statistically Speaking—Indians in the United States Today; and Eighteen Famous Americans with Indian Ancestors.

The *Almanac* also provides a Brief Chronology of American Immigration and focuses on the "Ethnic Top Ten"—Italians, Germans, Canadians, British, Poles, Mexicans, Russians, Irish, Austrians, and Swedes. Another chapter is dedicated to the "Unwilling Immigrants—The Black Experience in America."

Other chapters in the *Ethnic Almanac* elaborate on ethnic contributions to America, including Language and Literature; Customs and Traditions; Fun and Games; Food and Drink; Mind and Body; and Pride, Prejudice and Stereotypes.

The third section of the book is essentially an ethnic who's who, covering notable people of ethnic background who made it to the top in such categories as Science and Invention; Business and Invention; Music, Art and Entertainment; and Power and Politics. A chapter on "Tracing Your Ancestry" provides some basics, but the great number of major developments in the field since the 1981 publication date drastically limit the usefulness of this chapter.

Immigration and Ethnicity

John D. Buenker, Nicholas C. Burckel, and Rudolph J. Vecoli's *Immigration and Ethnicity: A Guide to Information Sources* (Detroit: Gale Research Co., 1977) contains more than 1,500 annotated bibliographic entries. African Americans and Native Americans are not included; foreign language materials, which at least equal in volume those in English, are seldom cited; and only a sampling of thousands of doctoral dissertations devoted to immigration and ethnic topics appear in the guide. As the compilers note, to have included those categories of materials would have made it a multi-volume work, and to "attempt a bibliography of immigration and ethnicity literature is like taking a snapshot of an avalanche." However, the compilers' selection of material is excellent. It identifies most of the major published works available through the mid-1970s (figure 4-2). The sources it cites will provide a useful overview of an ethnic group for the family researcher.

Encyclopedic Directory of Ethnic Organizations in the United States

Lubomyr Wynar's *Encyclopedic Directory of Ethnic Organizations in the United States* (Littleton, Colo.: Libraries Unlimited, 1975), as its title suggests, is a guide to major ethnic organizations, such as cultural, historical, and financial societies. As Wynar states in the preface (page ix),

> the historian, sociologist, political scientist, or any other researcher studying American ethnicity must closely scrutinize the phenomenon of ethnic organized life as it is reflected in the objectives of various ethnic organizations. For the researcher, ethnic organizations serve as 'primary sources' since they reflect the social structure of the ethnic group.

The *Encyclopedic Directory* provides addresses for some 1,475 major ethnic organizations representing seventy-three ethnic groups and briefly describes the nature of their holdings, including, in most cases, references to printed ethnic sources held by each organization. For the researcher of Italian heritage, for example, the Italo American National Union cited in the *Directory* would provide some unique sources. A caution is in order regarding the date of the *Directory*. Since it was published in 1975, new organizations have been formed, some dissolved, and some have changed addresses and telephone numbers. The *Directory* nevertheless serves as an overview of some potentially useful ethnic sources.

Encyclopedic Directory of Ethnic Newspapers and Periodicals in the United States

Lubomyr and Anna T. Wynar's *Encyclopedic Directory of Ethnic Newspapers and Periodicals in the United States* (Littleton, Colo.: Libraries Unlimited, 1976) is another dated but valuable source of information on printed ethnic materials. As the Wynars state in the introduction, "the role of ethnic newspapers and periodicals as educational tools cannot be underestimated." There are hundreds of entries that will be of incalculable value to the family historian in this volume. Under Czech Press, for example, one learns that *Bratrsky Vestnik* (*Fraternal Herald*) in Cedar Rapids, Iowa, publishes material centering on the accomplishments of members of the sponsoring association. Biographies of deceased members are also included, especially when pertaining to Czech or Slovak history.

Ethnic Genealogy: A Research Guide

Jessie Carney Smith's *Ethnic Genealogy: A Research Guide* (Westport, Conn.: Greenwood, 1983) is essentially a beginner's guide to genealogical research. Section 1 of the volume discusses Librarians and Genealogical Research, Basic Sources for Genealogical Research, Library Records and Research, and Researching Family History. Section 2 covers two major repositories for genealogical research: the National Archives and

Old Immigration

177 ______. "English Migration to the American West, 1865-1900." HUNTINGTON LIBRARY QUARTERLY 27 (1964): 159-73.

Identifies some 140,000 English immigrants to the trans-Mississippi West between 1965 and 1900 and attributes their motivation to the economic change in England, coupled with the promotional activities of U.S. railroads and other industries.

FRENCH, FRENCH CANADIAN, DUTCH, SWISS

178 Avery, Elizabeth Huntington. "Influence of French Immigration on the Political History of the United States." Ph.D. dissertation, University of Minnesota, 1895. 157 p.

Discusses the impact of French political thought, as carried by both Huguenot and Catholic immigrants to the United States, upon American political thought and institutions. Contrasts the influence and experience of the two, attributing differences to religious character, opportunity, and pace of assimilation.

179 Baird, Charles W. HISTORY OF THE HUGUENOT EMIGRATION. New York: Dodd, Mead & Co., 1885. 328 p. Appendix.

Chronicles the history of Huguenot persecutions in France which prompted migration to America and settlement throughout the English colonies.

180 Beers, Henry Putney. THE FRENCH IN NORTH AMERICA: A BIBLIOGRAPHICAL GUIDE TO FRENCH ARCHIVES, REPRODUCTIONS AND RESEARCH MISSIONS. Baton Rouge: Louisiana State University Press, 1957. 413 p. Appendices, notes, bibliography, index.

Chapters deal with the range of archives in France, the use of French archives by American historians, the relevant holdings on North America in French archives, and collections in America of reproductions of some of this archival data.

181 Bissell, Clifford H. "The French Language Press in California." CALIFORNIA HISTORICAL SOCIETY QUARTERLY 39 (1960): 219-62.

Chronicles, in three parts, the history of the French language press in the Golden State from 1850 to post-1927. Discusses the activities of their founders, editorial policies, reasons for decline, and the bitter feuds among them for circulation.

182 Blick, Boris, and Grant, Roger H. "French Icarians in St. Louis." MISSOURI HISTORICAL SOCIETY BULLETIN 30 (1973): 3-28.

Based largely upon two 1859 issues of REVUE ICARIENNE, examines everyday life in the Utopian Socialist community

34

Figure 4-2. From *Immigration and Ethnicity: A Guide to Information Sources.*

Records Service and the Genealogical Society of Utah Library (now known as the National Archives and Records Administration and the Family History Library, respectively). Section 3 is the best reason for using *Ethnic Genealogy;* it covers four significant groups: American Indians, Asian Americans, African Americans, and Hispanics. Each ethnic section provides the fundamental principles for starting research, some case studies, document samples, and dated but useful bibliographies for each group.

Ancestry's Red Book

Alice Eichholz, ed., *Ancestry's Red Book: American State, County and Town Sources,* rev. ed. (Salt Lake City: Ancestry, 1992), is an expansive guide to the most useful resources in each of the fifty states and the District of Columbia. Every state's chapter includes a brief historical background discussion, including settlement patterns, that will provide helpful background information for ethnic research. Each state chapter concludes with a section titled "Special Focus Category" in which ethnic sources specific to the particular state are described.

The Oklahoma chapter in the *Red Book,* for example, provides a lengthy narrative on Native American collections in the state and a surprisingly large bibliography of Oklahoma Native American source materials. A separate bibliography cites volumes that analyze the role and impact of other major ethnic groups in the state. For example, the Oklahoma chapter identifies a series of books about blacks, British and Irish, Czechs, Italians, Germans, Germans from Russia, Mexicans, Jews, and Poles in Oklahoma.

Under the *Red Book*'s section on Pennsylvania are such references as John E. Bodnar's *Ethnic History in Pennsylvania: A Selected Bibliography* (Harrisburg: Pennsylvania Historical and Museum Commission, 1974). Also useful is David E. Washburn, comp. and ed., *The Peoples of Pennsylvania: An Annotated Bibliography of Resource Materials* (Pittsburg: University for International Studies, University of Pittsburgh, 1981). Individual ethnic groups included in the Pennsylvania ethnic bibliography section are the Quakers, Germans, Amish, Scotch-Irish, Swiss, and Welsh.

Its relatively recent publication date gives *Red Book* a distinct advantage over many of the sources mentioned above. It cites a great number of works not yet published when other major ethnic reference sources were released.

Local Sources

Some books cover several ethnic groups within one locality. An example is the Wayne State University Department of Sociology and Anthropology's *Ethnic Groups in Detroit* (Detroit: Wayne State University, 1951). Compiled for Detroit's 250th anniversary, it covers forty-three ethnic groups from Albanians to Ukrainians. The work lists the basic history of the group and when the peak periods of immigration occurred. More recent compilations on ethnic groups may be found in large libraries as well as within separate ethnic collections. Some are very obscure sources; it is wise to check library catalogs under any possible category (see "How to Find Ethnic Works in a Library Catalog," below).

ETHNIC RESEARCH COLLECTIONS

There are a number of surprisingly substantial ethnic collections in public and private libraries in the United States. Some focus on just one ethnic group, while others build their collections around several groups. These institutions collect a wide variety of original and published material dealing with ethnic groups and their experiences in America. This material—newspapers, books, periodicals, the records of churches, cultural societies, political and fraternal organizations, and the personal papers of immigrants—provides vivid evidence of the historical events and the physical and social conditions that shaped immigrant life.

Special Libraries with National Collections

The following institutions have the most significant collections for family historians researching their ethnic roots.

Balch Institute for Ethnic Studies. The Balch Institute for Ethnic Studies in Philadelphia was founded in 1971 with support from trusts established by the Balch family. The facility, however, did not open until 1976. The stated mission of the institute is to "document and interpret America's multi-cultural heritage." The institute is unique in its concern for all books, documents, and artifacts relating to America's more than one hundred ethnic groups.

The Balch Research Library's collections consist of fifty thousand books; five thousand reels of microfilm of newspapers; and 2,400 linear feet of manuscripts, photographs, posters, tape and phonograph recordings, and sheet music. These collections document and describe the reasons for immigration and the succession of adaptations that the immigrants and their children made in the new land.

The Balch Institute for Ethnic Studies is at 18 South Seventh Street, Philadelphia, PA 19106. For those who cannot visit personally, the institute has compiled reading lists for twenty-three ethnic groups. These reading lists provide short stories about a representative family from each group and an extensive bibliography related to different reading and research levels. A twenty-two-page overview reading list is titled "Immigration and Ethnicity."

Immigration History Research Center. The Immigration History Research Center was founded at the University of Minnesota (826 Berry Street, St. Paul, MN 55224) in 1965 with a dual purpose—(1) to encourage study of the role of immigration and ethnicity in shaping society and culture of the United States, and (2) to collect the records of twenty-four American ethnic groups originating from eastern, central, and southern Europe and the Near East. Working closely with these ethnic communities, the Immigration History Research Center has located, preserved, and made available for research priceless documents of immigrant America. Suzanna Moody and Joel Wurl's *The Immigration History Research Center: A Guide to Collections* (Westport, Conn.: Greenwood Press, 1991) describes the manuscript, periodical, newspaper, and book holdings for each of the ethnic groups represented at the center.

Family History Library. No library in the United States has a multi-ethnic collection surpassing that of the Family History Library of The Church of Jesus Christ of Latter-day Saints (LDS church) in Salt Lake City, Utah. The key to finding records in the library is the *Family History Library Catalog*™. It describes the library's records and provides the call numbers. Microfiche copies of the catalog are available at the Family History Library and the 2,500 family history centers that are located all over the United States and Canada. Additionally, the catalog is available at some large public and private libraries in various parts of the United States. The library publication *Tracing Immigrant Origins Research Outline* (Salt Lake City: Family History Library, 1992), available for sale from the library, is of special help to researchers of ethnic families.

Center for Migration Studies in New York. This private institution (209 Flagg Place, Staten Island, NY 10304) has an educational, cultural, and religious focus as it promotes the study of all aspects of human migration movements and ethnic group relations. It maintains a large library with several thousand volumes, as well as an archival collection of newspapers, manuscripts, and correspondence. The center publishes a quarterly titled *International Migration Review*.

Other Libraries with Ethnic Collections. The Detroit Public Library, as an example, has a wealth of material on a number of ethnic groups. Joseph Oldenburg, in *A Genealogical Guide to the Burton Historical Collection, Detroit Public Library* (Salt Lake City: Ancestry, 1988) explains that the library's collection focuses on ethnic groups in Michigan and specifically Detroit (page 45). A review of the Burton catalogs reveals information on more than fifty separate ethnic groups in the city. The entries include books, magazine articles, newspaper clippings, maps, photographs, and manuscripts.

The Newberry Library in Chicago has long been recognized as one of the United States' leading institutions for the study of local and family history. In addition to having one of the largest genealogy collections in the United States, the library collects local and ethnic histories. A very specialized booklet, David Thackery's *Afro-American Family History at the Newberry Library: A Research Guide and Bibliography* (Chicago: Newberry Library, 1988), is an example of publications that have been produced by many libraries to aid researchers in the use of specific ethnic collections. The Newberry is also known for its particularly strong British Isles Collection of printed materials. Chapter 5 in Peggy Tuck Sinko's *Guide to Local and Family History at The Newberry Library* (Salt Lake City: Ancestry, 1987) focuses on ethnic and Native American sources at that institution.

The Allen County Public Library in Fort Wayne, Indiana, also has nationwide collections. It has published bibliographies for some ethnic groups. Two of note are Curt B. Witcher's *A Bibliography of Sources for Native American Family History in the Allen County Public Library Genealogy Department,* rev. ed. (Fort Wayne, Ind.: Allen County Public Library, 1988), and Witcher's *A Bibliography of Sources for Black Family History in the Allen County Public Library Public Library Genealogy Department,* rev. ed. (Fort Wayne, Ind.: Allen County Public Library, 1989).

Though less known, important multi-ethnic and specific group collections exist in university libraries. Georgia V. Fleming-Haigh's *Ireland: The Albert E. Casey Collection and Other Irish Materials in the Samford University Library* (Birmingham, Ala.: Samford University Library, 1976) is an example of a guide to printed sources, many of which are rare titles that would be difficult, if not impossible, to find in any other collection. This guide was specifically designed to aid genealogists, historians, and other readers interested in Ireland.

Archives and Historical Societies

Every state has an archive, historical society, or other agency dedicated to preserving and making available the historical record of its people. Prominent ethnic groups are usually well represented in the literature of each state collection. Some states offer guides or descriptive pamphlets that describe their holdings. An outstanding example is *Genealogical Resources of the Minnesota Historical Society: A Guide,* by the Minnesota Historical Society Library and Archives Division (St. Paul: Minnesota Historical Society Press, 1989). An appendix to this guide advises researchers seeking information about ethnic groups in Minnesota to first consult *They Chose Minnesota: A Survey of the State's Ethnic Groups*, edited by June Drenning Holmquist (St. Paul: Minnesota Historical Society Press, 1981), a volume containing detailed information about more than sixty ethnic groups that have lived in Minnesota. The same bibliography calls attention to *Guide to Swedish-American Archival and Manuscript Sources in the United States* (Chicago: Swedish-American Historical Society, 1983); *Guide to the Minnesota Finnish American Family History Collection* (St. Paul: Immigration History Research Center, 1985); Ramedo Saucedo's *Mexican Americans in Minnesota: An Introduction to Historical Sources* (St. Paul: Minnesota Historical Society, 1977); and David V. Taylor's *Blacks in Minnesota: A Preliminary Guide to Historical Sources* (St. Paul: Minnesota Historical Society, 1976).

The Directory of Historical Organizations in the United States and Canada, edited by Mary Bray Wheeler, 14th ed. (Nashville: American Association for State and Local History, 1990), lists addresses, telephone numbers, and other important information for state historical societies and agencies as well as those for local and specialized collections. It also includes an index to "Ethnic/Religious/Cultural" societies. This directory is just one of the many volumes that list special ethnic collections, and it is readily available in most libraries. For those, for example, who want to broaden their knowledge of Dutch Colonial records and printed sources, a reference in the *Directory* will lead them to The Holland Society of New York (122 East 58th Street, New York, NY 10022) and to its publications, library, and period collections.

Genealogical Societies and Activities

After exhausting home and library sources in the search for ethnic information, consider also genealogical societies. A researcher might not have to leave home to benefit from the great body of printed material that has been created by these predominantly volunteer organizations. Local genealogical and historical societies tend to focus on the ethnic groups prominent in their respective areas, and this fact is reflected in their publications. Newsletters and quarterlies put out by societies can be especially rich sources of information on ethnic groups.

"Single-ethnic" genealogical societies, such as Palatines to America, have been organized to promote the study and preservation of specific cultures. Organizations devoted exclusively to one ethnic group are able to provide a more in-depth focus on materials and methodology that is of specific interest to their audiences. *The Ancestry Family Historian's Address Book: A Comprehensive List of Local, State, and Federal Agencies and Institutions and Ethnic and Genealogical Organizations* (Salt Lake City: Ancestry, 1997) lists addresses, telephone numbers, and Internet addresses for hundreds of ethnic genealogical societies, as well as historical societies, museums, and other agencies that house ethnic collections.

Specific ethnic genealogical society publications can be critical to the success of a research project. For instance, those with Jewish roots in the Ukraine would certainly benefit to know that "there are hundreds of Rabbinic books containing birth, death, marriage and divorce records from Ukrainian towns dating from 1849–1916 in the State Historical Archive of Ukraine." *Mispacha*, the quarterly publication of the Jewish Genealogy Society of Greater Washington, alerted its readers to that collection in addition to providing a number of other important and timely articles in its Summer 1993 issue.

Researchers who fail to keep up with the literature of the societies dedicated to aiding and informing specific ethnic group researchers are apt to miss a wealth of information and the rapid advances being made in those areas.

Genealogical Conferences

Ethnic presentations are popular options at national, state, and local genealogical conferences. The majority of conferences presented by the National Genealogical Society (NGS) and the Federation of Genealogical Societies (FGS), as well as some local presentations, have been tape recorded. These recordings (on cassette), together with presenters' lecture handouts, comprise yet another invaluable source of information.

The Index to NGS and FGS Conferences and Syllabi, compiled by Joy Reisinger (Arlington, Va., and Salt Lake City: National Genealogical Society and Federation of Genealogical Societies, 1993), is a guide to lectures, lecturers, and audiotapes. It is both a barometer of the demand for ethnic presentations and a tool for locating 632 ethnic presentations in conference syllabi, many recorded on audiotapes, as well as hundreds of other presentations on genealogy-related topics. Publications cited in conference handouts and bibliographies are especially useful because they are often the only published compilations of genealogical sources and techniques on particular ethnic groups.

The National Genealogical Society and Federation of Genealogical Societies syllabi are on the shelves of many libraries, and *The Index to NGS and FGS Conferences and Syllabi* makes their important contents easier to find. It is interesting to note that English, German, Canadian, Irish, Native American, Scottish, Jewish, Welsh, French, and Hispanic (in that order) made the "ethnic top ten" in terms of frequency of presentations.

Genealogical Periodical Indexes

Genealogical societies have been churning out publications for many years. Many of them regularly publish ethnic materials. One of the quickest and most efficient ways to locate articles that relate to an ethnic group of interest is to consult the *Periodical Source Index* (*PERSI*) (Fort Wayne, Ind.: Allen County Public Library Foundation, 1987–), a comprehensive place, subject, and surname index to current genealogical and local history periodicals. A section of *PERSI* on "Foreign Places," for example, can be particularly helpful in ethnic research because it is arranged first by country, then by record type. *PERSI* is now available on CD-ROM through Ancestry (Salt Lake City, 1997). Another source for finding periodical articles is *Genealogical Periodical Annual Index* (*GPAI*) (Bowie, Md.: Heritage Books, 1962–). Both of these indexes are discussed in depth in chapter 19, "Periodicals."

KINDS OF SOURCES FOR SPECIFIC ETHNIC GROUPS

While the sources discussed previously provide a basic overview of most ethnic groups, most people want to focus on the specific groups found in their own ancestry. Many printed sources provide the kind of detail necessary to fully understand the records and culture of a specific group.

National Sources for Specific Ethnic Information

As evidenced by the sources cited in the chapter bibliography under "Sources for Specific Ethnic Groups," there is a large selection of sources focusing on specific ethnic groups at the national level. From the lively popular histories, such as those published by Oceana Publications, to the very scholarly and statistically oriented ethnic studies coming from university presses, essentially every group has been described.

Vera Laska's *The Czechs in America, 1633–1977* (Dobbs Ferry, N.J.: Oceana Publications, 1978), Pamela Smit's *The Dutch in America, 1609–1970* (Dobbs Ferry, N.J.: Oceana Publications, 1972), James S. Pula's *The French in America 1488–1974* (Dobbs Ferry, N.J.: Oceana Publications, 1975), and Vladimir Wertsman's *The Ukrainians in America, 1608–1975* (Dobbs Ferry, N.J.: Oceana Publications, 1976), are brief histories that provide overviews of the respective cultures. Each book in the series has a section describing the group's contributions and contributors to the greatness of the United States. For the beginning family historian, these and other ethnically oriented titles published by Oceana Publications make for informative and enjoyable reading.

State and Local Ethnic Histories

While many individuals go unrecognized in printed sources focused on the national level, millions of individuals have gained recognition and prominence in printed sources focusing on state and local ethnic communities. These ethnic publications are among the most genealogically rich sources available for research today. Answers to questions regarding an ancestor's exact birthplace and other exciting and detailed biographical information can frequently be found in these local ethnic printed sources and nowhere else.

Books such as Duane Gilbert Meyer's *The Highland Scots of North Carolina 1732–1776* (Chapel Hill: University of North Carolina Press, 1961), *History of Welsh Settlements in Jackson and Gallia Counties Ohio,* translated by Phillip G. Davies (Ames: University of Iowa, 1988), and Lester C. Lamon's *Blacks in Tennessee 1791–1970* (Knoxville: University of Tennessee Press, 1980) can be extremely helpful in understanding an ancestor's background and lifestyle, but may be among the more difficult to locate unless catalogs and ethnic bibliographic sources are combed carefully. Two examples of the wide variety of these local, ethnic-specific sources are shown in figures 4-3 and 4-4.

University presses usually publish the most detailed ethnically oriented histories and bibliographies. Pauline R. Kibbe's *Latin Americans in Texas* (Albuquerque: University of New Mexico Press, 1946), David Kittleson's *The Hawaiians: An Annotated Bibliography* (Honolulu: University of Hawaii, 1985), and Richard D. Scheuerman and Clifford E. Trafzer's *The Volga Germans: Pioneers of the Northwest* (Moscow: University of Idaho Press, 1980) are significant examples.

Research volumes that focus on specific cities and states may also be helpful in finding ethnic sources in a particular geographical area. Robert Barnes's *Guide to Research in Baltimore City and County* (Westminster, Md.: Family Line Publications, 1989), for example, cites Ralph Clayton's *Black Baltimore, 1820–1870* (Bowie, Md.: Heritage Books, 1987). This source for the study of African Americans is but one of the many ethnic sources mentioned in Barnes's guide. Loretto D. Szucs's *Chicago and Cook County: A Guide to Research* (Salt Lake City: Ancestry, 1996) lists 215 ethnic sources and has a special section on German research in the Chicago area. Roseann Reinemuth Hogan's *Kentucky Ancestry: A Guide to Genealogical and Historical Research* (Salt Lake City: Ancestry, 1992) includes a special "African-American Bibliography for Kentucky."

Social Histories

After one has become generally acquainted with an ethnic group, social histories should not be overlooked. In ever-increasing numbers, social historians have been closely scrutinizing the communities of our ethnic ancestors. Hundreds of well-known (and some more obscure) ethnic studies have been published, many by university presses. One example is James G. Leyburn's *The Scotch-Irish: A Social History* (Chapel Hill: University of North Carolina Press, 1962). As is the usual format in this kind of work, the author presents a description of events leading up to emigration from the home country. Leyburn first draws a picture of the life, the mind, and the character of the typical Lowland Scot of 1600. Chapters in the first section of the book describe domestic life, poverty and insecurity, and religion before and after the Reformation, as well as the institutions that were a part of Scottish life in that time period. Part 2 of the book is a look at the causes for Scottish migration and the hardships endured by the Scots of the Ulster Plantation in Ireland. Part 3 is a study of the Scotch-Irish migration to America and their settlements in Pennsylvania, Virginia, the Carolinas, New England, the Middle Colonies, and the Tidewater South. In addition to providing an indispensable view of Scotch-Irish history, the notes and bibliography section suggest hundreds of sources used by the author to study his subject. The same sources used by Leyburn are potentially rich sources for the family historian as well.

Doctoral Dissertations

On a related theme, *Dissertation Abstracts International* (Ann Arbor, Mich.: University Microfilms International) is a compilation of abstracts of doctoral dissertations submitted to Uni-

Capron and Jefferson Prairie

Surrounding the little town of Capron, Boone county, not far from the Wisconsin boundary line, is to be found a large settlement of prosperous Norwegian farmers. The first immigrants to settle there were Thor Knutson Traim and Olson Kaasa, with their families. They came from Telemarken and arrived in 1843.

The following year a number came from Sogn and settled there. The most prominent of those were Lars Johnson Haave, Ole Aavri, Iver Ingebreitson Haave, Anfin Seim, Ole Orvedahl, Ole Tistel, Ingebreit and Ole Vange, all with families except Ole Vange. In 1845 a third party came, among whom were Elim Ellingson, three brothers Andres, Ole and Endre Hermundson (Numedal), of whom Andres and Ole were married; Johannes Olson Dale and Hans Simpson Halron, both with families, and finally Endre Olson Stadem and Johan Olson Føle with families. From Telemarken arrived in 1844 Bjørn Bakketoe, Johannes Kleiva and Ole Thorson Kaasa, all with families.

The first congregation in Capron was started in 1844 by Rev. J. W. C. Dietrichson, who was born at Fredriksstad, Norway, April 4, 1815, and died at Copenhagen, Denmark, from a stroke of paralysis, Nov. 14, 1883. His remains were taken to Norway and buried at Porsgrund, 1883. He was educated and ordained for the ministry in Norway. A dyer by the name of P. Sørensen in Christiania induced Mr. Dietrichson to come to America and preach the gospel for his countrymen. It is said that he was encouraged not only by words but also with a snug sum of money for the mission. He finally concluded to accept, and with this in view he was ordained in the Oslo Church by the bishop of Christiania stift, 1844. He arrived in Milwaukee, Aug. 5, 1844, and from there went first to Muskego, and in the last days of August, 1844, he arrived in Koshkonong prairie, where he held service in a barn.

The church in the neighborhood of Capron, Ill., was the second house of worship to be started by Dietrichson, but was completed first, and was dedicated Dec. 19, 1844. The other one was in Wisconsin in the town of Christiana. Elling Eielsen had, however, built a "meeting house" in the Fox River Settlement in 1842.

Rev. Dietrichson was an ardent Christian missionary, full of energy and pluck, but was lacking in that most important Christian virtue, forbearance. He often lost his mental equipoise. It must, however, be taken into consideration that he was brought up and educated, as were most of his confrères in the old country, to look down on the farmers as an inferior race that could be and was disciplined to obey without asking questions. That kind of despotism is still partly prevailing in the country parishes of Europe. When the farmers have breathed the exhilarating air of this free country they must be treated differently, as Dietrichson soon found out.

We will cite some instances illustrating the case in question. In one of his flocks he had a farmer by the name of Funkelien, who was one of those foolish and irritating individuals that consider it great fun to embarrass their pastors by asking them to solve scriptural conundrums or explain apparent contradictions. He was well read in the Scriptures and in constant controversy with Dietrichson, who finally became so impatient with him that he told him he was excom-

Figure 4-3. From A. E. Strand, comp. and ed., *A History of the Norwegians of Illinois* (Chicago: John Anderson Publishing Co., 1905).

versity Microfilms International (UMI) by more than four hundred cooperating institutions in the United States and Canada. Because some institutions do not send in all dissertations, it is not an all-inclusive source, but the tremendous number of ethnically oriented dissertations to be found in this source make it worthy of investigation.

Dissertation Abstracts International can usually be found in large public libraries and university and college libraries. Once an ancestor's ties to an ethnic group have been established, this "index" can lead to some amazingly detailed and rare sources of information. Doctoral dissertations such as "Chicago's Italians Prior to World War I" (Rudolph Vecoli, University of Wisconsin, 1970), "Religion, Family, and Community among Hungarians Migrating to American Cities, 1880–1930" (Paula Kaye Benkart, Johns Hopkins University, 1975), and "Mexican Immigration to the Urban Midwest During the 1920s" (Francisco A. Rosales, Indiana University, 1978) provide unique closeups of the lives and times of individuals involved with those communities. These are but a few of the subjects examined by those seeking doctoral degrees. The frequent updates of doctoral abstracts make *Dissertation Abstracts International* a source that should be continually checked for new material.

A very helpful listing of dissertations that deal specifically with ethnic groups is Francesco Cordasco's *American Ethnic Groups: The European Heritage, a Bibliography of Doctoral Dissertations Completed at American Universities* (Metuchen, N.J.: Scarecrow, 1981).

Immigrants' Letters

It is easy to understand why letters from people who had emigrated to America were treasured by those who remained in their homelands. In days before any means of rapid communication, those left behind were particularly eager to read firsthand accounts of life in the New World. Often, letters were the last remaining link with family and friends who would never be seen again.

A surprising number of letters have been saved in one form or another. Some have been printed in magazines and newspapers, some have been collected in books, and many more letters that were saved by families and friends are finding their way into print on a regular basis. While a researcher may have no luck in finding a letter or collection of letters written by anyone in her own family, a letter written by someone of the same ethnic group or the same locality, religion, or time period can often tell more about what an ancestor saw and felt than any other source. Not all printed immigrant letters will be easily found, for a great number are hidden among the titles of thousands of books and periodicals. See "Immigrant Letters" in the chapter bibliography for some published letters.

Ethnic Presses

Perhaps some of the best sources of information on groups or individuals come from the ethnic communities themselves. Immigrant groups clung together to keep alive their memories, culture, and communication with the old country. Every ethnic organization in the United States has played a role in preserving and perpetuating group identity and national pride. Hundreds of ethnic organizations flourished and published periodicals, newspapers, and historical and biographical albums—frequently in the native tongue.

Histories produced by ethnic presses may focus on the national, state, or local level. Typically, a volume will review the history of the group from its earliest involvement in American history, extol the group's contributions to the development of the United States, and pay tribute to members of the group who became prominent in the United States for one reason or another. Biographical sketches in these volumes tend to describe group members in only the most glowing terms, but frequently the degree of detail tends to be very useful. Many a genealogical breakthrough can be attributed to an ethnic biographical sketch. *Chicago und sein Deutschthum* (Cleveland: German Press Club, 1902 is one such example. Among the volume's biographical sketches are many that give a specific birth date and birthplace for the subject as well as date of immigration, former places of residence, arrival date in the country and the city, educational and occupational history, and names of parents, spouse, and children. It is necessary for the reader to be proficient in the language (or to hire someone who is) because this Chicago source was printed in German.

BIOGRAPHICAL SKETCHES. 353

DEVNEY, PATRICK F., public cabs, born in Galway, Ireland, Feb. 1, 1850. He was educated in the public schools of Boston. He is now engaged in this city in the public-cab business. In 1884 he represented Ward 19 in the Massachusetts House of Representatives.

DILLON, FRANK H., born in Charlestown, Mass., Sept. 22, 1861. He graduated at the Winthrop School in 1875; worked as painter for F. M. Holmes Furniture Company, and as superintendent for Eagle Metallic Brush Company. Later he established a saloon business. He was trustee of the Young Men's Catholic Lyceum of Charlestown, vice-president Quarterly Club, one of the organizers of the Moulton Associates, a member of Royal Order of Good Fellows; elected to the Common Council of 1887, '88, '89, and served on Committees on Fire Department, City Engineers, and Fourth of July. In 1881 was sergeant of Company D, Ninth Regiment.

DOHERTY, CORNELIUS F., service clerk, born in Boston, Jan. 15, 1852. He attended the Lyman School and St. Mary's Institute. He went to sea for three years, and upon his return served at the coppersmith trade, working at the business about eight years. In 1887 he engaged in the cigar and tobacco business in East Boston and also at Natick. He represented Ward 2 in the Common Council of 1879, '80, '81, and during six months of 1883, when he resigned on July 1 to accept his present position as service clerk in the Water Department of the city of Boston. He is a member of the Royal Order of Good Fellows, Fitton Literary Institute, Young Men's Catholic Lyceum of East Boston, Columbian Rowing Association, and secretary of the Fourth District Congressional Club.

DOHERTY, DANIEL, born in Ballyliffin, County Donegal, Ireland, in 1838. He was educated in the Irish national schools of his native place, and came to this country on June 15, 1863. He settled in Boston, and became employed by the Boston Gas-Light Company, with whom he remained almost twelve years. He engaged in the saloon business in 1874, and in 1876 formed a partnership with his brother, John Doherty, under the present firm name of D. & J. Doherty. He represented Ward 7 in the Common Council of 1876 and the Legislature of 1877–78. He has been a member of the Democratic Ward and City Committee for three years, and is a member of the Irish Charitable Society.

DOHERTY, JAMES D. Elected to the Common Council for the year 1889.

DOHERTY, JAMES J., restaurateur, born in County Donegal, Ireland, Aug. 15, 1848. When five years of age his parents immigrated to this country, and settled in Boston, where he received his education at the public schools. At the age of sixteen he enlisted in an unattached company of volunteer militia on duty in Boston Harbor. In 1877, '78, '79 he was a member of the Common Council, and in the latter year he was one of the Board of Directors of East Boston Ferries. He has been a member of the Democratic Ward and City Committee for several years, and in 1880 represented Ward 2 in the General Court.

DOHERTY, JOHN, born in Ballyliffin, County Donegal, Ireland, about 1846. He was educated in the Irish National schools, and came to this country in 1865. Shortly after his arrival in Boston he was employed in the freight department of the Boston & Maine Railroad, and later went to San Francisco, Cal., for five years. Upon his return to this city he entered the employ of the Boston Gas-Light Company, where he remained about four years. In 1876 he engaged in the saloon business with his brother, Daniel Doherty, under the present firm name of D. & J. Doherty. He represented Ward 7 in the Common Council of 1884–85 and in the Legislature of 1887–88. He is a member of the Charitable Irish Society.

Figure 4-4. From James Bernard Cullen, comp. and ed., *The Story of the Irish in Boston together with Biographical Sketches of Representative Men and Noted Women* (Boston: James B. Cullen & Co., 1889).

Special City Directories

The English-speaking publishers of city directories frequently omitted individuals who were recent immigrants or perceived to be immigrants, or who lived within distinctly ethnic neighborhoods. However, some national groups corrected such omissions by publishing city and town directories of their own. These special directories usually included only the members of the

Moneta, Augustynowicz & Prusiński, 730 Milwaukee Ave.
Niklas & Co., 589 Milwaukee Ave.
Suchy, Jan, 5000 S. Ashland Ave.
Urbanowicz, Zacharyasz K., 4833 S. Ashland Ave.

*

Mens' Clothes

Amuzamskis, Stan., 4556 S. Paulina St.
Slepski & Jagłowski, 249 W. Webster Ave.
Stemwedel & Schultz, 868 Milwaukee Ave.
The Bell (a Polish Company), 985-989 Milwaukee Ave.

*

Commission Merchants

J. C. Palt and Co., 181 W. Randolph St.
Waszko, H. R., 213 S. Water St.

*

Blacksmiths

Godniarek, Józ., 3210 S. Morgan St.
Gołembiewski, Józ., 7 Tell Place
Kierna, And., 109 W. Division St.
Malcak, Ant., 724 Throop St.
Mynarik, Józ., 605 W. 22nd St.
Tylkowski, Józ., 35 Elston Ave.

*

Booksellers

Dyniewicz, W., 532 Noble St.
Smulski, J. F., 565 Noble St.
Spółka Wydawnica Polskiego (Polish Publishing Co.), 141-143 W. Division St.
Zwierzyńska, Marya, 715 W. 17th St.

*

Doctors

Borncki, Felix, 8715 Commercial Ave.
Borzyncz, M. F., 519 Milwaukee Ave.
Butkiewicz, Kaz., 1038 Kimball Ave.
Dowiatt, Marya, 723 W. 18th St.

22

Figure 4-5. From *Polish Directory for the City of Chicago, 1903* (Milwaukee, Wis.: Polish Genealogical Society, 1981).

particular national group and were published in the native language. Figure 4-5 is an example from a directory of the *Polish in Chicago*.

HOW TO FIND ETHNIC WORKS IN A LIBRARY CATALOG

As mentioned earlier, a surprising number of ethnic histories can be found in public and university libraries as well as within separate ethnic collections. Some are very obscure sources, so it is wise to check card or computer catalogs under any possible category. Use the ethnic group as the subject heading—for example:

Country:	United States—Germans
State:	Michigan—Dutch
County:	Pierce county, Washington—Scandinavians
City or town:	Detroit, Michigan—Poles

Some catalogs list the ethnic group first, followed by the locality, such as Quakers in Pennsylvania or Italians in New York City. Also look for Library of Congress subject headings, such as "Colorado—Minorities" or "Virginia—Societies" or "New York City—Emigration and Immigration."

REFERENCE LIST

Boorstin, Daniel J. 1973. *The Americans.* Vol. 2, *The Democratic Experience.* New York: Random House.

Haley, Alex. 1977. "What *Roots* Means to Me." *Reader's Digest*, May 1977.

Higham, John, et al. 1965. *History.* Englewood Cliffs, N.J.

Marden, Charles F., and Gladys Meyer. 1973. *Minorities in American Society.* 4th ed. New York: D. Van Nostrand.

BIBLIOGRAPHY

Surname Studies

Adamic, Louis. *What's Your Name?* New York, 1942.

Ashley, Leonard R. N. *What's in a Name? Everything You Wanted to know.* Baltimore: Genealogical Publishing Co., 1989.

Bardsley, Charles Wareing. *A Dictionary of English and Welsh Surnames with Special American Instances.* 1901. Reprint. Baltimore: Genealogical Publishing Co., 1967.

Bardsley, Charles Wareing. *English Surnames, Their Sources and Significations.* Ninth impression. London, 1915.

Baring-Gould, Sabine. *Family Names and Their Story.* Baltimore: Genealogical Publishing Co., 1968.

Black, George Fraser. *The Surnames of Scotland.* New York: New York Public Library, 1946.

Brown, Samuel L. *Surnames Are the Fossils of Speech.* Minneapolis: North Central Publishing Co., 1967.

Carnoy, Albert. *Origin des Noms de Familles en Belgique.* Louvain, Belgium, 1953.

Chapuy, Paul. *Origin des Noms Patronymiques Francais.* Paris, 1934.

Chuks-orji, Ogonna. *Names from Africa: Their Origin, Meaning, and Pronunciation.* Chicago: Johnson Publishing Co., 1972.

Constantinescu, N. A. *Dictionar Onomastic Rominescu.* Bucharest, Romania, 1963.

Cottle, Basil. *The Penguin Dictionary of Surnames.* Harmondsworth, England: Penguin Books, 1967.

Dauzat, Albert. *Dictionnaire Etymologique des Noms de Famille et Prenoms de France.* 3rd ed. Rev. and augmented by Marie Therese Morlet. Paris: Larousse, 1967.

Ekwall, Eilert. *The Concise Oxford Dictionary of English Place-Names.* 4th ed. Oxford, England, 1960.

Ewen, Cecil Henry L'Estrange. *A Guide to the Origin of British Surnames.* London, 1938.

_____. *A History of Surnames of the British Isles.* London, 1931.

Fransson, Gustav. *Middle English Surnames of Occupation 1100–1350 With an Excursus on Toponymical Surnames.* Lund, 1935.

Fucilla, Joseph Guerin. *Our Italian Surnames.* Evanston, 1949.

Gottschald, Max. *Deutsche Namenkunde.* Dritte, Vermehrte Auflage. Berlin, 1954.

Hanks, Patrick, and Flavia Hodges. *A Dictionary of Surnames.* New York: Oxford University Press, 1988.

Hoffman, William F. *Polish Surnames: Origins and Meanings.* Chicago: Polish Genealogical Society of America, 1993.

Huizinga, A. *Encyclopedie Van Namen.* Amsterdam, 1955.

Jones, George F. *German American Names.* 2nd ed. Baltimore: Genealogical Publishing Co., 1995.

Kneen, John Joseph. *The Personal Names of the Isle of Man.* London, 1937.

Kaganoff, Benzion C. *Dictionary of Jewish Names and Their History.* New York: Schocken Books, 1977.

Levy, Paul. *Les Noms des Israelites en France.* Paris, 1960.

Linnartz, Kaspar. *Unsere Famililiennamen.* Bonn, Germany, 1958.

MacLysaght, Edward. *A Guide to Irish Surnames.* Dublin, 1964.

_____. *Irish Families: Their Names, Arms and Origins.* Dublin, 1957.

_____. *More Irish Families.* Galway and Dublin, 1960.

_____. *Supplement to Irish Families.* Dublin, 1964.

Matthews, Constance Mary. *English Surnames.* London, 1966.

Puckett, Newbell Niles. *Black Names in America: Origins and Usage.* Boston: G. K. Hall, 1975.

Reaney, Percy Hide. *A Dictionary of British Surnames.* 2nd ed. London: Routledge, 1976.

_____. *The Origin of English Surnames.* New York: Barnes and Noble, 1967.

Robb, H. Amanda, and Andrew Chelser. *Encyclopedia of American Family Names: The Definitive Guide to the 5,000 Most Common Surnames in the United States.* New York: HarperCollins, 1995.

Rosenthal, Eric. *South African Surnames.* Cape Town, South Africa, 1965.

Smith, Eldson Coles. *New Dictionary of American Family Names.* New York, 1973.

_____. *American Surnames.* 1969. Reprint. Baltimore: Genealogical Publishing Co., 1986.

Tibon, Gutierre. *Onomastica Hispano Americana.* Mexico: 1961.

Weekley, Ernest. *Surnames.* 3rd ed. New York, 1937.

Woulfe, Patrick. *Sloinnte Gaedheal is Gall: Irish Names and Surnames.* Dublin, 1923.

Immigrant Letters (English Language)

Barkai, Avraham. *Branching Out: German Jewish Immigration to the United States, 1820–1914.* New York: Holmes and Meier, 1984.

Barton, H. Arnold. *Letters from the Promised Land: Swedes in America, 1840–1914.* Minneapolis: University of Minnesota Press, 1975.

Blegen, Theodore C. *Land of Their Choice: The Immigrants Write Home.* St. Paul, Minn., 1955.

Conway, Alan, ed. *The Welsh in America: Letters from the Immigrants.* St. Paul, Minn., 1961.

Emerson, Everett, ed. *Letters from New England: The Massachusetts Bay Colony, 1629–1638.* Amherst, Mass., 1976.

Erickson, Charlotte. *Invisible Immigrants: The Adaptation of English and Scottish Immigrants in Nineteenth-Century America.* Coral Gables: University of Miami Press, 1972.

Hale, Frederick, ed. *Danes in North America.* Seattle, 1984.

Kamphoefner, Walter D., et al. *News from the Land of Freedom: German Immigrants Write Home.* Ithaca, N.Y.: Cornell University Press, 1991.

Newman, George Frederick. *Letters from Our Palatine Ancestors, 1644–1689.* Hershey, Pa.: Gary T. Hawbaker, 1984.

Peyser, Joseph L. *Letters from New France: The Upper Country.* Urbana: University of Illinois Press, 1992.

Smith, Clifford Neal. *Letters Home: Genealogical and Family Historical Data on Nineteenth-Century German Settlers in Australia, Bermuda, Brazil, Canada, and the United States.* McNeal, Ariz.: Westland Publishing, 1988.

Zempel, S. *In Their Own Words: Letters From Norwegian Immigrants.* St. Paul: University of Minnesota Press, 1991.

Multi-Ethnic Sources

Listed below are some of the most accessible and useful discussions of America's ethnic diversity. For additional sources dealing with immigration, see the bibliography in chapter 14, "Immigration Sources."

Allen, James Paul, and Eugene James Turner. *We the People: An Atlas of America's Ethnic Diversity.* New York: Macmillan Publishing Co., 1988.

Auel, Lisa B. *Ties That Bind: Communities in American History.* Washington, D.C.: National Archives, 1993.

Archdeacon, Thomas J. *Becoming American: An Ethnic History.* New York: Free Press, 1983.

Bahr, Howard M., and Bruce A. Chadwick, eds. *American Ethnicity.* Lexington, Mass.: Heath, 1979.

Bernardo, Stephanie. *The Ethnic Almanac.* Garden City, N.Y.: Dolphin Books, Doubleday & Co., 1981.

Bodnar, John. *The Transplanted: A History of Immigrants in Urban America.* Bloomington: Indiana University Press, 1985.

Bogue, Donald J. *The Population of the United States: Historical Trends and Future Projections.* New York: Macmillan, 1985.

Bolino, August C. *The Ellis Island Source Book.* Washington, D.C.: Kensington Historical Press, 1985.

Boorstin, Daniel J. *The Americans: The Democratic Experience.* New York: Random House, 1973.

Brye, David L. *European Immigration and Ethnicity in the United States and Canada: A Historical Bibliography.* Santa Barbara, Calif.: ABC-Clio Information Services, 1982.

Buenker, John D., Nicholas C. Burckel, and Rudolph J. Vecoli. *Immigration and Ethnicity: A Guide to Information Sources.* Detroit: Gale Research Co., 1977.

Cordasco, Francesco, ed. *Dictionary of American Immigration History.* Metuchen, N.J.: Scarecrow, 1990.

_____, and David N. Alloway, eds. *American Ethnic Groups: The European Heritage, a Bibliography of Doctoral Dissertations Completed at American Universities.* Metuchen, N.J.: Scarecrow, 1981.

Daniels, Roger. *Coming to America: A History of Immigration and Ethnicity in American Life.* New York: Harper Collins, 1990.

Dashefsky, Arnold, ed. *Ethnic Identity in Society.* Chicago: Rand McNally, 1976.

Dinnerstein, Leonard, and David M. Reimers. *Ethnic Americans: A History of Immigration.* New York: Harper and Row, 1987.

Dinnerstein, Leonard. *Natives and Strangers: Blacks, Indians and Immigrants in America.* 2nd ed. New York: Oxford University Press, 1990.

Joramo, Marjorie K. *Directory of Ethnic Publishers and Resource Organizations.* 2nd ed. Chicago: American Library Association, 1979.

The Directory of Historical Organizations in the United States and Canada. Edited by Mary Bray Wheeler. 14th ed. Nashville, Tenn.: American Association for State and Local History, 1990.

Dissertation Abstracts International. Ann Arbor, Mich.: University Microfilms International, annual.

Divine, Robert A., T. H. Breen, George M. Fredrickson, and R. Hal Williams. *America Past and Present.* Glenview, Ill.: Scott Foresman and Co., 1984.

Eichholz, Alice. *Ancestry's Red Book.* Rev. ed. Salt Lake City: Ancestry, 1992.

Ethnographic Bibliography of North America. 4th ed. 5 vols. Behavior Science Bibliographies. New Haven, Conn.: Human Relations Area Files, 1975. Supplement, 1990. 3 vols. A nearly complete listing of serious published accounts of North American cultures.

Family History Library Catalog. Salt Lake City: Church of Jesus Christ of Latter-day Saints, annual.

Filby, P. William. *Directory of American Libraries with Genealogy or Local History Collections.* Wilmington, Del.: Scholarly Resources, 1988.

Glazer, Nathan, and Daniel P. Moynihan, eds. *Ethnicity: Theory and Experience.* Cambridge, Mass.: Harvard University Press, 1975.

Greeley, Andrew M., and Gregory Baum, eds. *Ethnicity.* New York: Seabury Press, 1977.

Handlin, Oscar. *The American People in the Twentieth Century.* Cambridge, Mass.: Harvard University Press, 1954.

Handlin, Oscar. *The Uprooted: The Epic Story of the Great Migrations that Made the American People.* New York: Grosset and Dunlap, 1951.

Immigration and Naturalization Service. *Foreign Versions, Variations, and Diminutives of English Names, Foreign Equivalents of United States Military and Civilian Titles.* Washington, D.C.: Government Printing Office, 1970. This oversize publication is divided into two parts: the first has tables of twenty-three foreign versions of common English given names; the second defines equivalents for military and civilian titles. It is very useful for translating given names.

Jones, Maldwyn. *Destination America.* New York: Holt, Rinehart and Winston, 1976.

Lieberson, Stanley. *Ethnic Patterns in American Cities.* New York: Free Press, 1963.

Lind, Marilyn. *Immigration, Migration and Settlement in the United States: A Genealogical Guidebook.* Cloquet, Minn.: Linden Tree, 1985.

Makers of America. Edited by Wayne Moquin. 10 vols. Encyclopædia Britannica Corp., 1971.

Marden, Charles F., and Gladys Meyer. *Minorities in American Society.* 4th ed. New York: D. Van Nostrand, 1973.

Meyer, Mary K. *Meyer's Directory of Genealogical Societies in the U.S.A. and Canada.* 11th ed. Mt. Airy, Md., 1996.

Meyerink, Kory, and Loretto D. Szucs. "Immigration: Finding Immigrant Origins." Chapter 13 in *The Source: A Guidebook of American Genealogy.* Rev. ed. Edited by Loretto D. Szucs and Sandra H. Luebking. Salt Lake City: Ancestry, 1997.

Miller, Wayne Charles, et al. *A Comprehensive Bibliography for the Study of American Minorities.* 2 vols. New York: New York University Press, 1976. More than twenty-nine thousand entries—essays on ethnic groups with extensive bibliographies for each.

_____. *A Handbook of American Minorities.* New York: New York University Press, 1976.

Moody, Suzanna, and Joel Wurl. *The Immigration History Research Center: A Guide to Collections.* Westport, Conn.: Greenwood Press, 1991.

Oldenburg, Joseph. *A Genealogical Guide to The Burton Historical Collection, Detroit Public Library.* Salt Lake City: Ancestry, 1988.

Periodical Source Index (PERSI). Fort Wayne, Ind.: Allen County Public Library Foundation, 1987–.

Reimers, David M. *Still the Golden Door: The Third World Comes to America.* New York: Columbia University Press, 1985.

Records of Ethnic Fraternal Benefit Associations in the United States. St. Paul, Minn.: Immigration History Research Center, 1981.

Reisinger, Joy, comp. *Index to NGS and FGS Conferences and Syllabi.* Arlington, Va., and Salt Lake City: National Genealogical Society and Federation of Genealogical Societies, 1993.

Rosen, Philip. *The Neglected Dimension: Ethnicity in American Life.* South Bend, Ind.: Notre Dame Press, 1980.

Smith, Jessie Carney. *Ethnic Genealogy: A Research Guide.* Westport, Conn.: Greenwood, 1983.

Sollors, Werner, ed. *The Invention of Ethnicity.* Cambridge, Mass.: Harvard University Press, 1989.

Sowell, Thomas. *Ethnic America: A History.* New York: Basic Books, 1981. Chapters include "The American Mosaic," "The Irish," "The Germans," "The Jews," "The Italians," "The Chinese," "The Japanese," "The Blacks," "The Puerto Ricans," and "The Mexicans."

Thernstrom, Stephan. *Harvard Encyclopedia of American Ethnic Groups.* Cambridge, Mass.: Belknap Press of Harvard University Press, 1980.

Upton, Dell. *America's Architectural Roots: Ethnic Groups That Built America.* Washington, D.C.: National Trust for Historic Preservation, 1986.

Vecoli, Rudolph J., and Suzanne M. Sinke, eds. *A Century of European Migrations, 1830–1930.* Urbana, Ill.: University of Chicago Press, 1991.

Wasserman, Paul, and Alice E. Kennington, eds. *Ethnic Information Sources of the United States.* 2nd ed. 2 vols. Detroit: Gale Research Co., 1983.

_____, and Anna T. Wynar. *The Encyclopedic Directory of Ethnic Newspapers and Periodicals in the United States.* Littleton, Colo.: Libraries Unlimited, 1976.

Sources for Specific Ethnic Groups

The following citations identify some of the best ethnic research sources for family historians researching any of the fifty groups identified. Groups for which the greatest interest has been evidenced have the most sources listed. Occasional annotations have been added to clarify entries. The titles include histories of the ethnic groups and their immigration to North America and, where possible, key biographical references, genealogical instruction, and source books. For published lists of immigrants, see the bibliography in chapter 14, "Immigration Sources."

Ethnic histories, like local histories, tend to describe individuals and groups only in the most favorable terms. While this tendency is not necessarily bad, be aware that authors of ethnic literature are generous with praise—recounting only the achievements of the group and seldom mentioning any of the negative aspects that affect every human community. As with any other facet of research, it helps to keep the following in mind: Who wrote the book, and for what purpose?

African

Abajian, James de T. *Blacks in Selected Newspapers, Censuses, and Other Sources: An Index to Names and Subjects.* 3 vols. Detroit: Gale Research, 1977.

Amos, Preston E. *One Hundred Years of Freedom: A Selected Bibliography of Books About the American Negro.* Washington, D.C.: Association for Study of Negro Life and History, 1963.

Aptheker, H., ed. *A Documentary History of the Negro People in the United States.* New York: Citadel, 1971. Reprint. N.p., 1973.

Bennett, Lerone, Jr. *Before the Mayflower.* Chicago: Johnson, 1969. A history of African Americans, 1619 to 1968.

Black Studies: A Select Catalog of National Archives Microfilm Publications. Washington, D.C.: National Archives, 1984.

Blockson, Charles L., and Ron Fry. *Black Genealogy.* Englewood Cliffs, N.J.: Prentice-Hall, 1977.

Byers, Paula K. *African American Genealogical Sourcebook.* Detroit: Gale Research, 1995.

Curtis, James C., and Lewis L. Gould, eds. *The Black Experience in America.* Austin: University of Texas Press, 1970.

Davis, John P., ed. *The American Negro Reference Book.* Englewood Cliffs, N.J.: Prentice-Hall, 1966.

Davis, Lenwood G. *The Black Family in the United States: A Selected Bibliography of Annotated Books, Articles and Dissertations on Black Families in America.* Westport, Conn.: Greenwood Press, 1978.

Dennis, R. *The Black People of America: Illustrated History.* New York: McGraw-Hill, 1970.

Dorman, J. H., and R. R. Jones. *The Afro-American Experience: A Cultural History Through Emancipation.* New York: Wiley, 1974.

Drotning, Phillip I. *A Guide to Negro History in America.* Garden City, N.Y.: Doubleday, 1968.

Franklin, John Hope. *From Slavery to Freedom: A History of Negro Americans.* 4th ed. New York: Knopf, 1974. A comprehensive general survey.

Gutman, H. G. *The Black Family in Slavery and Freedom 1750–1925.* New York: Pantheon, 1976.

Jackson, F. *The Black Man in America 1619–1790.* New York: Franklin Watts, 1970.

Law, Nova. *African-American Genealogy Workbook for Beginners.* 2nd ed. Birmingham, Ala.: Legacy Publishing, 1993.

Lawson, Sandra M. *Generations Past: A Selected List of Sources for Afro-American Genealogical Research.* Washington, D.C.: Library of Congress, 1988.

Levine, Lawrence W. *Black Culture and Black Consciousness.* New York. Oxford University Press, 1977.

Logan, Rayford W., and Michael R. Winston. *Dictionary of American Negro Biography.* New York: W. W. Norton, 1982.

Low, Augustus W., and Virgil A. Clift. *The Encyclopedia of Black America.* New York: McGraw-Hill, 1981.

Madubuike, Ihechukwu. *A Handbook of African Names.* Washington, D.C.: Three Continents Press, 1976.

Meltzer, M. *In Their Own Words, A History of the American Negro 1619–1865.* New York: Crowell, 1964.

Newman, Debra L. *List of Free Black Heads of Families in the First Census of the United States.* Washington, D.C.: National Archives, 1973.

Newman, Debra L. *Black History: A Guide to Civilian Records in the National Archives.* Washington, D.C.: National Archives and Records Administration, 1984.

Rawick, George P., ed. *The American Slave: A Composite Autobiography.* Westport, Conn.: Greenwood, 1979.

Rose, James, and Alice Eichholz. *Black Genesis.* Detroit: Gale Research Co., 1978.

Sloan, Irving J. *Blacks in America, 1492–1977.* Dobbs Ferry, N.J.: Oceana Publications, 1977.

Streets, David H. *Slave Genealogy: A Research Guide with Case Studies.* Bowie, Md.: Heritage Books, 1986.

Taylor, David V. *Blacks in Minnesota: A Preliminary Guide to Historical Sources*. St. Paul, Minn.: Minnesota Historical Society, 1976.

Thackery, David T. *Afro-American Family History at The Newberry Library: A Research Guide and Bibliography*. Chicago: Newberry Library, 1988.

Walker, James D. *Black Genealogy: How to Begin.* Athens: University of Georgia Center for Continuing Education, 1977.

Weisbrod, Robert G. *Ebony Kinship: Africa, Africans and the Afro-Americans*. Westport, Conn.: Greenwood Press, 1973.

Windley, Lathan A. *Runaway Slave Advertisements: A Documentary History from the 1730s to 1790.* Westport, Conn.: Greenwood, 1983.

Witcher, Curt Bryan. *Bibliography of Sources for Black Family History in the Allen County Public Library Genealogy Department.* Rev. ed. Fort Wayne, Ind.: Allen County Public Library, 1989.

Woodson, Carter Goodwin. *Free Negro Heads of Families in the United States in 1830.* Washington, D.C.: Association for the Study of Negro Life and History, 1925.

Albanian

The Albanian in America: The First Arrivals. Boston: Society Fatbardnesia of Katundi, 1960.

Armenian

Armenian American Almanac: A Guide to Organizations, Churches, Newspapers. Glendale, Calif.: Armenian Reference Books Co., 1990.

Avakian, Arra. *The Armenians in America.* Minneapolis: Lerner Publications Co., 1977.

Der Nersessian, Sirarpie. *The Armenians.* New York: Praeger, 1970.

Kulhanjian, Gary A. *An Abstract of the Historical and Sociological Aspects of Armenian Immigration to the United States, 1890–1930.* San Francisco: R & E Research Associates, 1975.

Tashjian, James H. *The Armenians of the U.S. and Canada.* Boston: Armenian Youth Federation, 1947.

Waldstreicher, David. *The Armenians in America.* New York: Chelsea House, 1989.

Wertsman, Vladimir. *The Armenians in America, 1618–1976.* Dobbs Ferry, N.J.: Oceana Publications, 1978.

Asian (also see Chinese, Japanese)

Byers, Paula K. *Asian American Genealogical Sourcebook.* Detroit: Gale Research, 1995.

Daniels, Roger. *Asian America: Chinese and Japanese in the United States Since 1850.* Seattle: University of Washington Press, 1988.

Hoyt, Edwin Palmer. *Asians in the West.* Nashville: T. Nelson, 1974.

Kim, Hyung-Chan, ed. *The Dictionary of Asian-American History.* Westport, Conn.: Greenwood Press, 1986. Includes entries on the various groups from Asia and the Pacific Isles: individuals, events, places, terms, and other data applicable to Asian Americans.

Melendy, Howard Brett. *Chinese and Japanese Americans.* New York: Hippocrene Books, 1984.

Perrin, Linda. *Coming to America: Immigrants from the Far East.* New York: Delacorte Press, 1980.

Takaki, Ronald T. *Strangers From a Different Shore: A History of Asian Americans.* Boston: Brown, 1989.

Tong, Te-kong. *The Third Americans: A Select Bibliography on Asians in America.* Oak Park, Ill.: CHCUS, 1980.

Wong, James I. *A Selected Bibliography on the Asians in America.* Palo Alto, Calif.: R & E Research Associates, 1981.

Austrian

Senekovic, Dagmar. *Handy Guide to Austrian Genealogical Records.* Logan, Utah: Everton Publishers, 1979.

British

Eerthoff, Rowland Tappan. *British Immigrants in Industrial America, 1790–1950.* Cambridge, Mass.: Harvard University Press, 1953.

Erickson, Charlotte. *Invisible Immigrants: The Adaptation of English and Scottish Immigrants in Nineteenth-Century America.* Coral Gables: University of Miami Press, 1972.

Furer, Howard B. *The British in America, 1578–1970.* Dobbs Ferry, N.J.: Oceana Publications, 1972.

Irvine, Sherry. *Your English Ancestry: A Guide for North Americans.* Salt Lake City: Ancestry, 1993.

Lines, Kenneth. *British and Canadian Immigration to the United States Since 1920.* San Francisco: R & E Research Associates, 1981.

Moulton, Joy Wade. *Genealogical Resources in English Repositories.* Columbus, Ohio: Hampton House, 1988. Information on the principal repositories of England and their holdings.

Norton, Mary Beth. *The British Americans: The Loyalist Exiles in England, 1774–1789.* Boston: Little, Brown, 1972.

Rogers, Colin Darlington. *Tracing Your English Ancestors: A Manual for Analysing and Solving Genealogical Problems, 1538 to the Present.* New York: Manchester University Press, 1989.

Saul, Pauline A., and F. C. Markwell. *The A–Z Guide to Tracing Ancestors in Britain.* 4th ed. Baltimore: Genealogical Publishing Co., 1991.

Canadian

Baxter, Angus. *In Search of Your Canadian Roots: Tracing Your Family Tree in Canada.* Baltimore: Genealogical Publishing Co., 1989.

Jonasson, Eric. *The Canadian Genealogical Handbook: A Comprehensive Guide to Finding Your Ancestors in Canada.* 2nd ed. Winnipeg, Manitoba: Wheatfield Press, 1978. Although out of print and somewhat dated, this remains a useful handbook for determining what resources are available in each of the provinces and the territories. Addresses should be double-checked, as many have changed since its publication.

Kennedy, Patricia, and Janine Roy. *Tracing Your Ancestors in Canada.* Ottawa: Public Archives of Canada, 1987. Write to the Public Archives of Canada, 395 Wellington Street, Ottawa, Ontario K1A ON3, for this free pamphlet outlining repository addresses and an overview of holdings.

Merriman, Brenda Dougall. *Genealogy in Ontario: Searching the Record.* 2nd ed. Toronto: Ontario Genealogical Society, 1988.

Punch, Terrence M., ed. *Genealogist's Handbook for Atlantic Canada Research.* Boston: New England Historical Society, 1989. Covers the history and resources available for Prince Edward Island, Newfoundland, New Brunswick, Labrador, "Acadia," and Nova Scotia.

Woodcock, George. *The Century That Made Us: Canada 1814–1914.* Toronto: Oxford University Press, 1989.

Chinese

Tung, William L. *The Chinese in America, 1820–1973.* Dobbs Ferry, N.J.: Oceana Press, 1974.

Archer, Jules. *The Chinese and the Americans.* New York: Hawthorn Books, 1976.

Barth, Gunther. *Bitter Strength: A History of the Chinese in the United States, 1850–70.* Cambridge: Harvard University Press, 1964.

Chen, Jack. *The Chinese of America: From the Beginnings to the Present.* New York: Harper and Row, 1981.

Hsu, Francis L. *Americans and Chinese: Passage to Differences.* 3rd ed. Honolulu: University Press of Hawaii, 1981.

Lee, Rose Hum. *The Chinese in the United States of America.* Hong Kong: Hong Kong University Press, 1960.

Lyman, S. M. *Chinese Americans.* New York: Random House, 1974.

Miller, Stuart C. *Unwelcome Immigrant: The Image of the Chinese, 1785–1882.* Berkeley: University of California, 1969.

Cornish

Rowe, John. *The Hand-Rock Men: Cornish Immigrants and the North American Mining Frontier.* New York: Barnes and Noble, 1974.

Rowse, Alfred Leslie. *Cousin Jacks: The Cornish in America.* New York: Scribner, 1966.

Croatian (also see Yugoslav)

Eterovich, Adam S. *Croatian Pioneers in America, 1685–1900.* San Carlos, Calif.: Raguson Press, 1979.

Kraljic, Frances. *Croatian Migration to and from the United States Between 1900 and 1914.* Palo Alto, Calif.: Raguson Press 1978.

Preveden, Francis R. *A History of the Croatian People.* 2 vols. New York: Philosophical Library, 1956 (vol. 1), 1962 (vol. 2).

Prpic, George J. *The Croatian Immigrants in America.* New York: Philosophical Library, 1971.

Czech (also see Slovakian)

Capek, Thomas. *Czechoslovak Immigration.* New York: Service Bureau for Intercultural Education, 1938.

Capek, Thomas. *The Czechs (Bohemians) in America: A Study of Their National, Cultural, Political, Social, Economic, and Religious Life.* 1920. Reprint. New York: Arno Press.

Dvornik, E. *Czech Contributions to the Growth of the United States.* Chicago: Benedictine Abbey Press, 1962.

Laska, Vera. *The Czechs in America, 1633–1977.* Dobbs Ferry, N.J.: Oceana Publications, 1978.

Miller, K. D. *The Czecho-Slovaks in America.* New York: Doran, 1922.

Miller, Olga K. *Genealogical Research for Czech and Slovak Americans.* Detroit: Gale Research Co., 1978.

Psencik, L. F. *Czech Contributions to American Culture.* Austin: Texas Education Agency, 1970.

Roucek, Joseph S. *The Czechs and Slovaks in America.* Minneapolis: Lerner Publications, 1967.

Schlyter, Daniel M. *A Handbook of Czechoslovak Genealogical Research.* Buffalo Grove, Ill.: Genun Publishers, 1985.

Wellauer, Maralyn. *Tracing Your Czech and Slovak Roots.* Milwaukee: the author, 1980.

Danish (also see Scandinavian)

Bille, J. H. *A History of the Danes in America.* 1896. Reprint. San Francisco: R & E Research Associates, 1971.

Danus, E. *Danish American Journey.* Franklin, Mass.: Gauntlet, 1971.

Hale, Frederick, ed. *Danes in North America.* Seattle: University of Washington Press, 1984.

Hvidt, Kristian. *Flight to America: The Social Background of 300,000 Danish Emigrants.* New York: Academic Press, 1975.

Mortensen, Enok. *Danish American Life.* New York: Arno Press, 1978.

Nielsen, Alfred. *Life in American Denmark.* New York: Arno Press, 1978.

Dutch

Bertus, Harry Wabeke. *Dutch Emigration to America, 1624–1860.* New York: Arno Press, 1944.

De Jong, G. F. *The Dutch in America, 1609–1974.* Boston: Twayne, 1975.

Doezma, Linda Pegman. *Dutch-Americans: A Guide to Manuscript Sources.* Detroit: Gale Publications, 1979.

Fiske, John. *The Dutch and Quaker Colonies in America.* New York: Houghton Mifflin Co., 1899.

Lucas, Henry S. *Netherlands in America: Dutch Immigration to the United States and Canada, 1789–1950.* Ann Arbor: University of Michigan Press, 1955.

Lucas, Henry S., ed. *Dutch Immigrant Memoirs and Related Writings.* Assen, Netherlands: Van Gorcum & Co., 1955.

Smit, Pamela. *The Dutch in America, 1609–1970.* Dobbs Ferry, N.J.: Oceana Publications, 1972.

Swierenga, Robert P. *Dutch Households in U.S. Population Censuses, 1850, 1860, 1870: An Alphabetical Listing by Family Heads.* 3 vols. Wilmington, Del.: Scholarly Resources, 1987.

_____, ed. *The Dutch in America: Immigration, Settlement and Cultural Change.* New Brunswick, N.J.: Rutgers University Press, 1985.

Estonian

Pennar, Jaan. *The Estonians in America, 1627–1975.* Dobbs Ferry, N.J.: Oceana Publications, 1975.

Filipino

Kim, Hyung-Chan. *The Filipinos in America, 1898–1974.* Dobbs Ferry, N.J.: Oceana Publications, 1976.

Munoz, Alfredo. *The Filipinos in America.* Los Angeles: Mountainview Publishers, 1971.

Finnish

Guide to the Minnesota Finnish American Family History Collection. St. Paul, Minn.: Immigration History Research Center, 1985.

Hoglund, William. *Finnish Immigrants in America, 1880–1920.* Madison: University of Wisconsin Press, 1960.

Jalkanen, Ralph J. *The Finns in North America.* Hancock: Michigan University Press, 1969.

Karni, Michael, ed. *Finnish Diaspora II: United States*. Toronto: Multicultural History Society of Ontario, 1981.

Kolehmainen, John Ilmari. *The Finns in America: A Bibliographical Guide to Their History.* Hancock, Mich.: Teachers College, 1968.

Louhi, E. A. *The Delaware Finns: or The First Permanent Settlements in Pennsylvania, Delaware, West New Jersey, and Eastern Part of Maryland.* New York: Humanity Press, 1925.

Vincent, Timothy Laitila, and Rick Tapio. *Finnish Genealogical Research*. New Brighton, Minn.: Finnish Americana, 1994.

Wargelin, John *The Americanization of the Finns.* Hancock, Mich.: Finnish Lutheran Book Concern, 1924.

Wuorinen, J. H. *The Finns on the Delaware, 1638–1655.* 1938. Reprint. New York: Arno Press, 1966.

French

Franco-American Overview. Cambridge, Mass.: National Assessment and Dissemination Center, 1979.

Boudreau, Rev. Dennis M. *Beginning Franco American Genealogy.* Pawtucket, R.I.: American French Genealogical Society, 1986.

Butler, Jon. *Huguenots in America: A Refugee People in New World Society*. Cambridge, Mass.: Harvard Press, 1983.

Eccles, William J. *France in America.* New York: Harper & Row, 1972.

Fecteau, Edward. *French Contributions to America.* Soucy Press, 1945.

Hirsch, Arthur H. *The Huguenots of Colonial South Carolina.* Hamden, Conn.: Shoe String, 1973.

Kunz, Virginia B. *The French in America.* Minneapolis: Lerner Publications, 1966.

Lareau, Paul J., and Elmer Courteau. *French-Canadian Families of the North Central States: A Genealogical Dictionary.* 8 vols. St. Paul, Minn.: Northwest Territory French and Canadian Heritage Institute, 1980.

Lart, Charles E. *Huguenot Pedigrees.* 1924–28. Reprint. Baltimore: Genealogical Publishing Co., 1973.

Morgan, T. *On Becoming American.* Boston: Houghton Mifflin, 1978. A former French count, Sanche de Gramont, became an American citizen in 1977, shedding his title and his old name.

Pula, James S. *The French in America 1488–1974.* Dobbs Ferry, N.J.: Oceana Publications, 1975.

Thwaites, Reuben G. *France in America, 1497–1763.* New York: Cooper Square, 1968.

Zoltvany, Yves F. *The French in America.* Columbia: University of South Carolina Press, 1969.

German (also see Swiss)

Baxter, Angus. *In Search of Your German Roots: A Complete Guide to Tracing Your Ancestors in the Germanic Areas of Europe.* 3rd ed. Baltimore: Genealogical Publishing Co., 1994.

Bentz, Edna M. *If I Can, You Can Decipher Germanic Records.* Revised and corrected. San Diego: the author, 1987. Words and terms written in Old German script translated into German and English.

Billigmeier, Robert Henry. *Americans from Germany: A Study in Cultural Diversity.* Belmont, Calif.: Wadsworth Publishing, 1974.

Bittinger, Lucy F. *The Germans in Colonial Times.* New York: Russell & Russell, 1901. Reprint. N.p., 1968.

Boyers, Robert, ed. *The Legacy of the German Refugee Intellectuals.* New York: Schocken, 1972.

Brandt, Edward R., et al. *Germanic Genealogy: A Guide to Worldwide Sources and Migration Patterns*. St. Paul, Minn.: Germanic Genealogy Society, 1995.

Cobb, Sanford Hoadley. *The Story of the Palatines: An Episode in Colonial History*. 1897. Reprint. Bowie, Md.: Heritage Books, 1988.

Dearden, Fay, and Douglas Dearden. *The German Researcher: How to Get the Most Out of an L.D.S. Family History Cente*r. 4th ed. Minneapolis: Family Tree Press, 1990.

Faust, Albert. *The German Element in the United States with Special Reference to Its Political, Moral, Social, and Educational Influence*. 2 vols. 1927. Reprint. New York: Arno Press and the *New York Times,* 1969.

Fredericks, Heinz F. *How to Find My German Ancestors and Relatives.* Neustadt, West Germany: Verlag Degener & Co., 1985.

Furer, Howard. *The Germans in America, 1607–1970.* Dobbs Ferry, N.J.: Oceana Publications, 1973.

Gingerich, Hugh F., and Rachel W. Kreider. *Amish and Amish Mennonite Genealogies*. Gordonville, Penn.: Pequea Publishers, 1986.

Jensen, Larry O. *Genealogical Handbook of German Research.* Rev. ed. Pleasant Grove, Utah: Jensen Publications, 1978.

Keresztesi, Michael, and Gary R. Cocozzoli. *German-American History and Life: A Guide to Information Sources,* 1980.

Kloss, Heinz. *Atlas of German American Settlements.* Marburg, West Germany: N. G. Elwert, 1974.

Lehmann, Heinz. *The German Canadians, 1750–1937: Immigration, Settlement and Culture*. Translated by Gerhard P. Bassler. St. Johns, Newfoundland: Jesperson Press, 1986.

O'Connor, Richard. *The German Americans: An Informal History.* New York: Little, Brown & Co., 1946.

Pochmann, Henry August. *Bibliography of German Culture in America to 1940.* Revised and corrected by Arthur Schultz. Millwood, N.Y.: Kraus International Publications, 1982. Contains 18,500 entries.

Rippley, La Vern J. *The German Americans.* Boston: Twayne Publishers, 1976.

_____, and Robert J. Paulson *The German-Bohemians: The Quiet Immigrants*. New Ulm, Minn.: German-Bohemian Society, 1995.

Rothan, Emmet. *The German Catholic Immigrant in the United States, 1830–1860.* Washington, D.C.: Catholic University Press, 1946.

Sallet, Richard. *The Russian German Settlements in the United States.* Translated by J. Rippley and Armand Bauer. Frago: Institute of Regional Studies, 1974.

Schweitzer, George K. *German Genealogical Research.* Knoxville, Tenn.: the author, 1992.

Smith, Clifford Neal, and Anna Piszezan-Czaja Smith. *American Genealogical Resources in German Archives.* Munich, West Germany: Verlag Dokumentation, 1977.

_____. *Encyclopedia of German-American Genealogical Research.* New York : R. R. Bowker Co., 1976.

Smith, Kenneth Lee. *German Church Books: Beyond the Basics.* Camden, Maine: Picton Press, 1989.

Thode, Ernest. *Address Book for Germanic Genealogy.* 6th ed. Baltimore: Genealogical Publishing Co., 1997.

Thode, Ernest. *German-English Genealogical Dictionary.* Baltimore: Genealogical Publishing Co., 1992.

Tolzmann, Don Heinrich. *German Americana: A Bibliography.* Metuchen: Scarecrow Press, 1975.

Wagner, Ernst, et al. *The Transylvanian Saxons: Historical Highlights.* Cleveland: Alliance of Transylvanian Saxons, 1982.

Walker, Mack. *Germany and the Emigration, 1816–1885.* Cambridge, Mass.: Harvard University Press, 1964.

Wellauer, Maralyn A. *German Immigration to America in the Nineteenth Century: A Genealogist's Guide.* Milwaukee: Roots International, 1985.

Wood, Ralph, ed. *The Pennsylvania Germans.* Princeton, N.J.: Princeton University Press, 1942.

Wust, Klaus. *The Virginia Germans.* Charlottesville: University of Virginia Press, 1969.

_____, and Heinz Moos, eds. *Three Hundred Year History of German Immigrants in North America, 1683–1983.* 2nd rev. ed. Munich, Germany: 300 Jahre Deutsch in Amerika Verlag, 1983.

Germans from Russia

Miller, Michael M., comp. *Researching the Germans from Russia: Annotated Bibliography of the Germans from Russia Heritage Collection.* Fargo: North Dakota Institute for Regional Studies, North Dakota State University, 1987.

Sallet, Richard. *Russian-German Settlements in the United States.* Translated by La Vern J. Ripley and Armand Bauer. Fargo: North Dakota Institute for Regional Studies, 1974.

Scheuerman, Richard D., and Clifford E. Trafzer. *The Volga Germans: Pioneers of the Northwest* Moscow: University of Idaho Press, 1980.

Stumpp, Karl. *The Emigration from Germany to Russia in the Years 1763 to 1862.* Translated by Prof. Joseph S. Height and others. Lincoln, Nebr.: American Historical Society of Germans from Russia, 1982.

Greek

Burgess, T. *Greeks in America.* 1913. Reprint. New York: Arno Press, 1975.

Bywater, Lica Catsakis, and Daniel M. Schlyter. *Greek Genealogical Research.* Salt Lake City: Family History Library, 1988.

Cutsumbis, Michael. *A Bibliographic Guide to Materials on Greeks in the United States, 1890–1968.* New York: Center for Migration Studies, 1970.

Fenton, Heike, and Melvin Heckler. *The Greeks in America, 1528–1977.* Dobbs Ferry, N.J.: Oceana Publications, 1978.

Holden, David. *Greece Without Columns: The Making of Modern Greece.* Philadelphia: J. B. Lippincott Co., 1972.

Saloutos, Theodore. *The Greeks in the United States.* Cambridge, Mass.: Harvard University Press, 1964.

_____. *They Remember America: The Story of the Repatriated Greek-Americans.* Berkeley: University of California Press, 1956.

Woodhouse, C. M. *A Short History of Modern Greece.* New York: Praeger Publishers, 1968.

Xenides, J. P. *The Greeks in America.* New York: George H. Doran Co., 1922.

Zotos, Stephanos. *Hellenic Presence in America.* Wheaton, Ill.: Pilgrimage, 1976.

Hispanic (also see Mexican and Spanish)

Beers, Henry Putney. *Spanish and Mexican Records of the American Southwest.* Tucson: University of Arizona Press, 1979.

Byers, Paula K. *Hispanic American Genealogical Sourcebook.* Detroit: Gale Research, 1995.

Kibbe, Pauline R. *Latin Americans in Texas.* Albuquerque: University of New Mexico Press, 1946.

Ryskamp, George. *Tracing Your Hispanic Heritage.* Riverside, Calif.: Hispanic Family History Research, 1984.

Huguenot (see French)

Hungarian

Babo, Elemer. *Guide to Hungarian Studies: A Bibliography.* 2 vols. Hoover Institute Press, 1973.

Benkart, Paula Kaye. "Religion, Family, and Community among Hungarians Migrating to American Cities, 1880–1930." Doctoral dissertation, Johns Hopkins University, 1975.

Brandt, Edward R. *Contents and Addresses of Hungarian Archives: With Supplementary Material for Research on German Ancestors from Hungary.* 2nd, annotated ed. Minneapolis: the compiler, 1993.

Gracza, Rezsoe, and Margaret Gracza. *The Hungarians in America.* Minneapolis: Lerner Publications Co., 1969.

Hanzell, Victor E. *The Hungarians.* New Haven, Conn.: Human Relations Area Files, Yale University, 1955.

Hungarians in the U.S.A.: An Immigration Study. St. Louis: American Hungarian Review, 1967.

Korosfoy, John. *Hungarians in America.* Cleveland: Szabadsag, 1941.

Lengyel, Emil. *Americans from Hungary.* Westport, Conn.: Greenwood Press, 1975.

Puskas, Julianna. *From Hungary to the United States 1880–1914.* Budapest: Akademiai Kiado, 1982.

Suess, Jared H. *Handy Guide to Hungarian Genealogical Records.* Logan, Utah: Everton Publishers, 1980.

Szeplaki, Joseph. *The Hungarians in America, 1583–1974.* Dobbs Ferry, N.J.: Oceana Publications, 1975.

Vardy, Steven Bela. *The Hungarian Americans.* New York: Chelsea House Publishing, 1990.

Icelandic

Stefansson, Vilhjalmur. *Iceland: The First American Republic.* 1939. Reprint. Westport, Conn.: Greenwood Press, 1971.

Simundsson, Elva. *Icelandic Settlers in America.* Queenston House Publishing, 1981.

Irish

Adams, W. F. *Ireland and Irish Emigration to the New World: From 1815 to the Famine.* New Haven, Conn., 1932.

Begley, D. F. *Irish Genealogy: A Record Finder.* Dublin: Heraldic Artists, 1981.

Blessing, Patrick J. *The Irish in America: A Guide to the Literature and Manuscript Collections.* Washington, D.C.: Catholic University of America Press, 1992.

Byrne, Stephen. *Irish Emigration to the United States.* 1873. Reprint. New York: Arno Press, 1969.

Clark, Dennis. *Hibernia America: The Irish and Regional Cultures.* Westport, Conn.: Greenwood Press, 1986.

Cooper, Brian E., ed. *The Irish American Almanac and Green Pages.* Rev. and exp. New York: Harper and Row, 1990.

Crawford, E. Margaret. *Famine: The Irish Experience 900–1900.* Edinburgh: John Donald Publishers, 1989.

Curtis, Edmund. *A History of Ireland.* London: Methuen, 1968.

Diner, Hasia R. *Erin's Daughters in America.* Baltimore: Johns Hopkins University Press, 1983.

Doyle, David Noel. *Irish Americans, Native Rights, and National Empires.* New York: Arno Press, 1976.

Drudy, P. J., ed. *The Irish in America: Emigration, Assimilation and Impact.* London: Cambridge University Press, 1985.

Fallows, Marjorie. *Irish Americans: Identity and Assimilation.* Englewood Cliffs, N.J.: Prentice-Hall, 1977.

Falley, Margaret Dickson. *Irish and Scotch-Irish Ancestral Research.* 2 vols. Reprint. Evanston, Ill., 1962. Reprint. Baltimore: Genealogical Publishing Co., 1984.

Fleming-Haigh, Georgia V. *Ireland: The Albert E. Casey Collection and Other Irish Materials in the Samford University Library.* Birmingham, Ala.: Samford University Library, 1976.

Fitzgerald, Margaret E., and Joseph A. King. *The Uncounted Irish in Canada and the United States.* Toronto: P. D. Meany Publishers, 1990.

Greeley, Andrew M. *The Irish Americans: The Rise to Money and Power.* New York: Harper and Row, 1981.

_____. *That Most Distressful Nation: The Taming of the American Irish.* Chicago: Quadrangle Books, 1972.

Grenham, John. *Tracing Your Irish Ancestors: The Complete Guide.* Dublin: Gill and Macmillan, 1992.

Griffin, William D., comp. *The Irish in America.* Dobbs Ferry, N.J.: Oceana Publications, 1973.

_____. *A Portrait of the Irish in America.* New York: Charles Scribner's Sons, 1981.

Kennedy, Robert E. *The Irish: Emigration, Marriage and Fertility.* Berkeley: University of California Press, 1973.

Lees, Lynn Hollen. *Exiles of Erin: Irish Migrants in Victorian London.* Ithaca, N.Y.: Cornell University Press, 1979.

Maclysaght, Edward. *Irish Families: Their Names, Arms, and Origins.* New York: Crown, 1972.

Maguire, John Francis. *The Irish in America.* New York: Arno Press, 1969.

McCaffrey, Lawrence. *The Irish Diaspora in America.* Bloomington: Indiana University, 1978.

McCarthy, Tony. *The Irish Roots Guide.* Dublin: Lilliput, 1991.

Miller, Kerby. *Emigrants and Exiles: Ireland and the Irish Exodus in North America.* New York and London: Oxford University Press, 1985.

Mitchell, Brian. *Pocket Guide to Irish Genealogy.* Baltimore: Clearfield Co., 1991.

O'Grady, Joseph P. *How the Irish Became Americans.* New York: Twayne, 1973.

Ryan, James G. *A Guide to Tracing Your Dublin Ancestors.* Dublin: Flyleaf Press, 1988.

_____. *Irish Records: Sources for Family and Local History.* Rev. ed. Salt Lake City: Ancestry, 1997.

Schrier, Arnold. *Ireland and the American Immigration, 1850–1900.* 1958. Reprint. New York: Russell and Russell, 1970.

Shannon, William V. *The American Irish: A Political and Social Portrait.* Rev. ed. 1967. Reprint. New York, 1974.

Yurdan, Marilyn. *Irish Family History.* Baltimore: Genealogical Publishing Co., 1990.

Italian

Barzini, Luigi. *The Italians.* New York: Atheneum, 1964.

Briggs, John W. *An Italian Passage: Immigrants to Three American Cities, 1890–1930.* New Haven, Conn.: Yale University Press, 1978.

Cole, Trafford R. *Italian Genealogical Records: How to Use Italian Civil, Ecclesiastical, and Other Records in Family History Research.* Salt Lake City: Ancestry, 1995.

Colletta, John Philip. *Finding Italian Roots: The Complete Guide for Americans.* Baltimore: Genealogical Publishing Co., 1993.

Cordasco, Francesco. *The Italian Emigration to the United States, 1880–1930: A Bibliographic Register of Italian Views.* Fairview, N.J.: Junius-Vaught Press, 1990.

_____, ed. *Studies in Italian American Social History.* Totowa, N.J.: Rowman and Littlefield, 1975.

_____, ed. *Italian Immigrants Abroad: A Bibliography.* Detroit: Blaine Ethridge, 1979.

_____. *Italian Americans: A Guide to Information Sources.* Detroit: Gale Research, 1978.

_____, and Eugene Bucchioni, eds. *The Italians: Social Backgrounds of an American Group.* Clifton, N.J.: Augustus Kelley Publishers, 1974.

DeConde, Alexander. *Half Bitter, Half Sweet: An Excursion into Italian-American History.* New York: Charles Scribner's Sons, 1971.

Foerster, Robert F. *The Italian Emigration of Our Times.* 1924. Reprint. New York: Arno Press, 1969.

Gallo, Patrick J. *Ethnic Alienation: The Italian Americans.* Fairleigh-Dickinson University Press, 1978.

_____. *Old Bread, New Wine: A Portrait of the Italian Americans.* Chicago: Nelson-Hall, 1982.

Lo Gatto, A. F. *The Italians in America, 1492–1972.* Dobbs Ferry, N.J.: Oceana Publications, 1972.

Moquin, W., and D. Van Doren. *A Documentary History of the Italian-Americans.* New York: Praeger, 1974.

Null, G., and C. Stone. *The Italian Americans.* Harrisburg, Pa.: Stackpole Books, 1976.

Pisani, L. F. *The Italian in America.* New York: Exposition Press, 1957.

Rolle, Andrew F. *The American Italians: Their History and Culture.* Belmont, Calif.: Wadsworth Publishing Co., 1972.

Schiavo, Giovanni Ermenegildo. *Four Centuries of Italian American History.* New York: Vigo, 1958.

_____. *Italian-American History.* 2 vols. 1947–49. Reprint. New York: Arno Press, 1975.

Smith, Denis Mack. *Italy: A Modern History.* Ann Arbor: University of Michigan Press, 1969.

Tomasi, Silvano, and Madeline Engel, eds. *The Italian Experience in the United States.* New York: Center for Migration Studies, 1970.

Japanese

Ichihashi, Yamato. *Japanese in the United States.* New York: Arno Press, 1969.

Kitano, Harry. *Japanese-Americans: The Evolution of a Subculture.* Englewood Cliffs: Prentice-Hall, 1969.

Masako, H. *The Japanese in America, 1843–1973.* Dobbs Ferry, N.J.: Oceana Publications, 1974.

Peterson, William. *Japanese Americans: Oppression and Success.* New York: Random House, 1971.

Wakatsuki, Yasuo. "The Japanese Emigration to the United States, 1866–1924: A Monograph." *Perspectives in American History* 12 (1979), 389–516.

Jewish

Schleifer, Jay. *A Student's Guide to Jewish American Genealogy.* Phoenix, Ariz.: Oryx Press, 1997.

Angel, Rabbi Marc D. *La America.* Philadelphia: Jewish Publication Society, 1982.

Baron, Salo W., and Joseph L. Blau, eds. *A Documentary History of the Jews of the United States, 1790–1840.* 3 vols. Philadelphia: Jewish Publication Society, and New York: Columbia University Press, 1964.

Baum, C., and P. Hyman. *The Jewish Woman in America.* New York: Dial Press, 1976.

Birmingham, Stephen. *The Grandees: America's Sephardic Elite.* New York: Harper & Row, 1971.

Ehrenburg, Ilya, and Vasily Grossman. *The Black Book.* New York: Holocaust Library, 1980.

Handlin, Oscar. *Adventure in Freedom: 300 Years of Jewish Life in America.* New York: McGraw-Hill, 1954.

Higham, John. *Send These Unto Me: Jews and Other Immigrants in Urban America.* New York: Atheneum, 1975.

Howe, Irving. *The World of Our Fathers.* New York: Harcourt Brace Jovanovich, 1976.

The Jewish Encyclopedia. 12 vols. New York and London: Funk & Wagnalls, 1924.

Kaganoff, Benzion C. *A Dictionary of Jewish Names and Their History.* New York: Schocken Books, 1977.

Karp, Abraham J. *Golden Door to America: The Jewish Immigrant Experience.* New York: Viking Press, 1976.

Kurzweil, Arthur. *From Generation to Generation: How to Trace Your Jewish Genealogy and Personal History.* New York: Schocken Books, 1981.

_____, and Miriam Weiner. *The Encyclopedia of Jewish Genealogy. Volume I: Sources in the United States and Canada.* Northvale, N.J.: Jason Aronson, 1991.

Sanders, Ronald. *Shores of Refuge: A Hundred Years of Jewish Emigration.* New York: Henry Holt and Co., 1988.

Stern, Malcolm H. *First American Jewish Families.* Waltham, Mass.: American Jewish Archives, Cincinnati, and American Jewish Historical Society, 1978.

Zubatsky, David S., and Irwin M. Berent. *Sourcebook for Jewish Genealogy and Family Histories.* Teaneck, N.J.: Avotaynu, 1996.

Latvian

Akmentins, O. *Latvians in Bicentennial America.* Latvju Gramata, 1976.

Karklis, M., et al. *The Latvians in America, 1640–1973.* Dobbs Ferry, N.J.: Oceana Publications, 1974.

Lebanese and Syrian

Hitti, Philip K. *Syrians in America.* New York: George H. Doran Co., 1924.

Kayal, Joseph. *The Syrian Lebanese in America.* Boston: Twayne, 1975.

Wakin, Edward. *The Lebanese and Syrians in America.* Chicago: Claretian, 1971.

Lithuanian

Balys, J. *Lithuania and Lithuanians: A Selected Bibliography.* New York: Praeger, 1961.

Budreckis, A. M. *The Lithuanians in America, 1651–1975.* Dobbs Ferry, N.J.: Oceana Publications, 1976.

Kucas, A. *Lithuanians in America.* San Francisco: R & E Research Associates, n.d.

Roucek, J. S. *American Lithuanians.* New York: Lithuanian Alliance of America, 1940.

Mexican

Cardosa, Lawrence. *Mexican Emigration to the United States, 1897–1931.* Tucson: University of Arizona Press, 1980.

Cortes, Carlos, ed. *The Mexican American: Mexican American Bibliographies.* New York: Arno Press, 1974.

Garcia, Richard A. *The Chicanos in America, 1540–1974.* Dobbs Ferry, N.J.: Oceana Publications, 1977.

Martinez, J. *Mexican Emigration to the U.S.* San Francisco: R & E Research Associates, 1971.

McWilliams, Carey. *North from Mexico: The Spanish Speaking People of the United States.* New York: Greenwood Press, 1968.

Meier, Matt S. *The Chicanos: A History of Mexican-Americans.* New York: Hill and Wang, 1972.

_____. *Mexican American Biographies: A Historical Dictionary*. New York: Greenwood Press, 1988.

_____, and Feliciano Rivera. *The Dictionary of Mexican-American History.* Westport, Conn.: Greenwood Press, 1981.

Saucedo, Ramedo. *Mexican Americans in Minnesota: An Introduction to Historical Sources.* St. Paul: Minnesota Historical Society, 1977.

Pinchot, J. *The Mexicans in America.* Minneapolis: Lerner Publications, 1973.

Prago, Albert. *Strangers in Their Own Land: A History of Mexican-Americans.* New York: Four Winds Press, 1973.

Steiner, Stan. *La Raza: The Mexican Americans.* New York: Harper & Row, 1968.

Native American

Barr, Charles Butler. *Guide to Sources of Indian Genealogy*. Independence, Mo.: the author, 1989.

Brandon, William. *Indians.* Boston: Houghton Mifflin Co., 1989.

Byers, Paula K., ed. *Native American Genealogical Sourcebook.* Detroit: Gale Research, 1995.

Carpenter, Cecelia Swinth. *How to Research American Indian Blood Lines.* South Prairie, Wash.: Meico Associates, 1984.

Dictionary of Indian Tribes of the Americas. 4 vols. Newport Beach, Calif.: American Indian Publishing, 1980.

Galluso, John, ed. *Native America: Insight.* Singapore: APA, 1989.

Gannett, Henry. *A Gazetteer of Indian Territory.* Washington, D.C.: Government Printing Office, 1905.

Gideon, D. C. *Indian Territory—Descriptive, Biographical and Genealogical, Including the Landed Estates, County Seats, With General History of the Territory.* Chicago: Lewis Publishing Co., 1901.

Hill, Edward E. *Guide to Records in the National Archives of the United States Relating to American Indians*. Washington, D.C.: National Archives and Records Administration, 1981.

Index to the Final Rolls of Citizens and Freedmen of the Five Civilized Tribes in Indian Territory. Washington, D.C.: Government Printing Office, n.d.

Kirkham, E. Kay. *Our Native Americans and Their Records of Genealogical Value.* 2 vols. Logan, Utah: Everton Publishers, 1980, 1984.

Klein, Barry T. *Reference Encyclopedia of the American Indian.* 5th ed. West Nyack, N.Y.: Todd Publications, 1990.

Leitch, Barbara. *A Concise Dictionary of Indian Tribes of North America.* Algonac, Mich.: Reference Publications, 1979.

Lipps, Oscar Hiram. *Laws and Regulations Relating to Indians and Their Lands.* Lewiston Printing and Binding Co., n.d.

Native American Periodicals and Newspapers, 1828–1982: Bibliography, Publishing Record, and Holdings. Westport, Conn.: Greenwood Press, 1984.

Wissler, Clark. *Indians of the United States.* New York: Anchor Books, 1989.

Witcher, Curt Bryan. *A Bibliography of Sources for Native American Family History.* Fort Wayne, Ind.: Allen County Public Library, 1988.

Yenne, Bill. *The Encyclopedia of North American Indian Tribes.* Greenwich, Conn.: Brompton Books, 1986.

Norwegian (also see Scandinavian)

Anderson, Arlow William. *The Norwegian-Americans.* Boston: Twayne, 1975.

Bergmann, Leola N. *Americans from Norway.* Philadelphia: J. B. Lippincott Co., 1950.

Blegen, Theodore Christian. *The Norwegian Migration to America, 1825–1860.* 2 vols. 1931. Reprint. New York: Arno Press, 1969.

Flom, George T. *History of Norwegian Immigration to the United States from the Earliest Beginnings Down to the Year 1848.* 1909. Reprint. Bowie, Md.: Heritage Books, 1992.

Gesme, Ann Urness. *Between Rocks and Hard Places: Traditions, Customs and Conditions in Norway During the 1800s, Emigration from Norway, the Immigrant Community in America*. Cedar Rapids, Iowa: Gesme Enterprises, 1993.

Qualey, Carlton Chester. *Norwegian Settlement in the United States*. 1938. Reprint. New York: Arno Press, 1970.

Smith, Frank, and Finn A. Thomsen. *Genealogical Guidebook and Atlas of Norway.* Logan, Utah: Everton Publishers, 1979.

Wellauer, Maralyn A. *Tracing Your Norwegian Roots.* Milwaukee: the author, 1979.

Polish

Baker, T. Lindsay. *The First Polish Americans.* College Station, Tex.: A & M University Press, 1979.

Bolek, F., and L. J. Siekaniec. *Polish American Encyclopedia.* Buffalo, [N.Y.]: Polish American Encyclopedia Committee, 1954.

Bolek, F. *Who's Who in Polish America.* 1943. Reprint. New York: Arno Press, 1970.

Brozek, Andrzej. *Polonia Amerykaska: The American Polonia.* Warsaw, Poland: Interpress Publications, 1980.

Bukowczyk, John J. *And My Children Did Not Know Me: A History of the Polish-Americans.* Indianapolis: Indiana University, 1987.

Chorzempa, Rosemary A. *Polish roots = Korzenie polskie*. Baltimore: Genealogical Publishing Co., 1993.

Hoskins, Janina W. *Polish Genealogy and Heraldry: An Introduction to Research.* New York: Hippocrene Books, 1990.

Lopata, H. Z. *Polish Americans.* Englewood Cliffs, N.J.: Prentice-Hall, 1976.

_____. *Poland and the Poles in America.* Chicago: Polish American Congress, 1971.

Murdzek, Benjamin P. *Emigration in Polish Social-Political Thought, 1870–1914.* New York: Columbia University Press, 1977.

Obal, Thaddeus J. *A Bibliography for Genealogical Research Involving Polish Ancestry.* Hillsdale, N.J.: the compiler, 1978.

Ortell, Gerald A. *Polish Parish Records of the Roman Catholic Church: Their Use and Understanding in Genealogical Research.* 3rd rev. ed. Buffalo Grove, Ill.: Genun Publishers, 1989.

Renkiewicz, Frank A. *The Poles in America, 1608–1972.* Dobbs Ferry, N.J.: Oceana Publications, 1973.

Shea, Jonathan D. *Russian Language Documents from Russian Poland: A Translation Manual for Genealogists.* 2nd ed. Buffalo Grove, Ill.: Genun Publishers, 1989.

Thomas, William I., and Florian Znaniecki. *The Polish Peasant in Europe and America.* New York: Dover Publications, 1958.

Toor, Rachel. *The Polish Americans.* New York: Chelsea House, 1988.

Wandycz, D. S. *Register of Polish American Scholars, Scientists, Writers, and Artists.* New York: Polish Institute of Arts and Sciences in America, 1969.

Wytrwal, Joseph Anthony. *Behold! The Polish-Americans.* Detroit: Endurance Press, 1977.

Zurawski, Joseph W. *Polish American History and Culture: A Classified Bibliography.* Chicago: Polish Museum of America, 1975.

Portuguese

Baganha, Maria. *Portuguese Emigration to the United States, 1820–1930.* New York: Garland Publishing, 1990.

Cardozo, Manoel DaSilveira Soares. *The Portuguese in America, 590 B.C.–1974.* Dobbs Ferry, N.J.: Oceana Publications, 1976.

DosPassos, John. *The Portugal Story: Three Centuries of Exploration and Discovery.* New York: Doubleday & Co., 1969.

Livermore, H. V. *A Short History of Portugal.* Chicago: Aldine Publishing Co., 1973.

Pap, Leo. *The Portuguese-Americans.* Boston: Twayne Publishers, 1981.

Tuohy, Frank, and Graham Finlayson. *Portugal.* New York: Viking Press, 1970.

Williams, Jerry R. *And Yet They Came: Portuguese Immigration from the Azores to the United States.* Staten Island, N.Y.: Center for Migration Studies, 1983.

Puerto Rican

Cordasco, Francesco. *The Puerto Ricans, 1493–1973.* Dobbs Ferry, N.J.: Oceana Publications, 1973.

Larsen, Ronald J. *The Puerto Ricans in America.* Minneapolis: Lerner, 1973.

The Puerto Ricans: Migration and General Bibliography. New York: Arno Press, 1969

Romanian

Galitzi, Christine Avghi. *A Study of Assimilation Among the Roumanians of the United States.* Columbia Press, 1929.

Wertsman, Vladimir. *Guide to Romanian Sources. . . .* Detroit: Gale Research, 1980.

_____. *The Romanians in America, 1748–1974.* Dobbs Ferry, N.J.: Oceana Publications, 1975.

Russian

David, J. *The Russian Immigrant.* 1922. Reprint. New York: Macmillan, 1969.

Eubank, N. *The Russians in America.* Minneapolis: Lerner Publications, 1973.

Hutchinson, E. P. *Immigrants and Their Children: 1850–1950.* New York: John Wiley and Sons, 1956.

Wertsman, Vladimir. *The Russians in America.* Dobbs Ferry, N.J.: Oceana Publications, 1977.

Scandinavian

Fonkalsrud, Alfred O. *The Scandinavian-American.* San Francisco: R & E Research Associates, n.d.

Furer, Howard B. *The Scandinavian in America, 986–1970.* Dobbs Ferry, N.J.: Oceana Publications, 1972.

Malmberg, Carl. *American is Also Scandinavian.* New York: Putnam, 1970.

Nelson, O. N. *History of the Scandinavians and Successful Scandinavians in the U.S.A.* 1904. Reprint. New York: Haskell House, 1969.

Scotch-Irish

Bolton, Charles Knowles. *Scotch Irish Pioneers in Ulster and America.* Reprint. 1910. Baltimore: Genealogical Publishing Co., 1967.

Dinsmore, John W. *The Scotch-Irish in America: Their History, Traits, Institutions and Influence.* Chicago: Winona Publishing Co., 1906.

Durning, William P., Mary Durning, and Margaret Harris. *The Scotch-Irish.* La Mesa, Calif.: Irish Family Names Society, 1991.

Ford, Henry Jones. *The Scotch Irish in America.* 1915. Reprint. New York: Arno Press, 1969.

Hanna, Charles A. *The Scotch-Irish; or, the Scot in North Britain, North Ireland, and North America.* 1902. Reprint. Baltimore: Genealogical Publishing Co., 1968.

Johnson, James E. *Scots and Scotch Irish in America.* Minneapolis: Lerner, 1966.

Leyburn, James G. *The Scotch-Irish: A Social History.* Chapel Hill: University of North Carolina Press, 1962.

Meyer, Duane Gilbert. *The Highland Scots of North Carolina 1732–1776.* Chapel Hill: University of North Carolina Press, 1961.

Scottish

Black, G. F. *Scotland's Mark on America.* 1921. Reprint. San Francisco: R & E Research Associates, 1972.

Cory, Kathleen B. *Tracing Your Scottish Ancestry.* Edinburgh, Scotland: 1990.

Erickson, Charlotte. *Invisible Immigrants: The Adaptation of English and Scottish Immigrants in Nineteenth-Century America.* Coral Gables: University of Miami Press, 1972.

Ferguson, Joan P. S. *Scottish Family Histories.* 2nd ed. Edinburgh: National Library of Scotland, 1986.

Irvine, Sherry. *Your Scottish Ancestry: A Guide for North Americans.* Salt Lake City: Ancestry, 1997.

James, Alwyn. *Scottish Roots: A Step-by-Step Guide for Ancestor-hunters.* Gretna, La.: Pelican Publishing Co., 1981.

Moody, David. *Scottish Family History.* Baltimore: Genealogical Publishing Co., 1990.

Sinclair, Cecil. *Tracing Your Scottish Ancestors: A Guide to Ancestry Research in the Scottish Record Office.* Edinburgh, Scotland: HMSO, 1990.

Slavic

Balch, Emily G. *Our Slavic Fellow Citizens.* 1910. Reprint. New York: Arno Press, 1969.

Edwards, Charles E. *The Coming of the Slav.* 1921. Reprint. San Francisco: R & E Research Associates, 1972.

Gimbutas, Marija. *The Slavs.* New York: Praeger, 1971.

Portal, Roger. *The Slavs.* New York: Harper & Row, 1969.

Roucek, Joseph S. *Slavonic Encyclopedia.* 1949. Reprint. Port Washington, New York: Kennikat Press, 1969.

Roucek, Joseph S. *American Slavs: A Bibliography.* New York: Bureau of Intercultural Education, 1944. Reprint. The author, 1970.

Stipanovich, Joseph. *Slavic Americans: A Study Guide and Source Book.* San Francisco: R & E Research Associates, 1977.

Slovakian (also see Czech)

Bogatyrev, Petr. *The Functions of Folk Costume in Moravian Slovakia.* The Hague, The Netherlands: Mouton, 1971.

Stasko, J. *Slovaks in the United States of America.* Cambridge, [Mass.]: Dobra Kniha, 1974.

Stolarik, Marian Mark. *Immigration and Urbanization: The Slovak Experience 1870–1918.* New York: AMS Press, 1989.

Stolarik, Marian Mark. *The Slovak Americans.* New York: Chelsea House, 1988.

Slovenian

Prisland, Marie. *From Slovenia in America.* Chicago: Slovenian Women's Union of America, 1968.

Prpic, George P. *On South Slav Immigrants in America and Their Historical Background.* Cleveland: John Carroll University, 1972.

Dwyer, Joseph D. *Slovenes in the U.S. and Canada: A Bibliography.* St. Paul, Minn.: Immigration History Research Center, 1981.

Spanish (also see Hispanic)

Alford, Harold J. *The Proud Peoples: The Heritage and Culture of Spanish Speaking Peoples in the United States.* New York: David McKay Co., 1972.

Natella, Arthur A., Jr., comp. and ed. *The Spanish in America, 1513–1974.* Dobbs Ferry, N.J.: Oceana Publications, 1975.

Pike, Frederick B. *Spanish America, 1900–1970: Tradition and Social Innovation.* New York: Norton, 1973.

Swedish (also see Scandinavian)

Benson, Adolph B., and Naboth Hedin. *Americans from Sweden.* Philadelphia: Lippincott, 1950.

Guide to Swedish-American Archival and Manuscript Sources in the United States. Chicago: Swedish-American Historical Society, 1983.

Hasselmo, Nils. *Swedish America: An Introduction.* New York: Swedish Information Service, 1976.

Janson, Florence E. *The Background of Swedish Immigration, 1840–1930.* Chicago: University of Chicago Press, 1931.

Johansson, Carl-Erik. *Cradled in Sweden.* Logan, Utah: Everton Publishers, 1972.

Kastrup, Allan. *The Swedish Heritage in America.* Minneapolis: Swedish Council of America, 1975.

Lindberg, John S. *The Background of Swedish Emigration to the United States.* Minneapolis: University of Minnesota Press, 1930.

Nelson, Helge. *The Swedes and the Swedish Settlements in North America.* 2 vols. 1943. Reprint. New York: Arno Press, 1979.

Olsson, Nils William. *Tracing Your Swedish Ancestry.* Sweden: Swedish Institute, 1982.

Runblom, Harold, and Hans Norman. *From Sweden to America: A History of the Migration.* Minneapolis: University of Minnesota Press, and Uppsala, Sweden: Acta Universitatis Upsaliensis, 1976.

Westman, Erik. *The Swedish Element in America.* Chicago: Swedish-American Biographical Society, 1931.

Swiss

Haller, Charles R. *Across the Atlantic and Beyond: The Migration of German and Swiss Immigrants to America.* Bowie, Md.: Heritage Books, 1993.

Kuhns, Levi O. *German and Swiss Settlements of Colonial Pennsylvania.* 1901. Reprint. Detroit: Gale Research, 1979.

Nielson, Paul Anthon. *Swiss Genealogical Research : An Introductory Guide.* Virginia Beach, Va.: Donning, 1979.

Schelberd, Lev. *Swiss Migration to America.* New York: Arno Press, 1981.

Suess, Jared H. *Handy Guide to Swiss Genealogical Records.* Logan, Utah: Everton Publishers, 1978.

Gruenigen, John P. *Swiss in the United States.* Madison, Wis.: Swiss Historical Society, 1940.

Von Moos, Mario. *Bibliography of Swiss Genealogies.* Camden, Maine: Picton Press, 1993.

Wellauer, Maralyn A. *Tracing Your Swiss Roots.* Milwaukee: Wellauer, 1979.

Ukrainian

Chyz, Yaroslaw J. *The Ukrainian Immigrants in the United States.* Scranton, Pa.: Ukrainian Workingmen's Association, 1940.

Halich, Wasyl. *Ukrainians in the United States.* 1939. Reprint. New York: Arno Press, 1970.

Kubijovic, Volodymyr. *Ukraine: A Concise Encyclopedia.* Toronto: University of Toronto Press, 1963.

Kuropas, Myron B. *The Ukrainian Americans: Roots and Aspirations.* Toronto: University of Toronto Press, 1991.

Myroniuk, Halynn. *Ukrainians in North America: A Select Bibliography* Toronto: Multicultural History Society of Ontario, 1981.

Shtohryn, D. M. *Ukrainians in North America: A Biographical Directory of Noteworthy Men and Women of Ukrainian Origin in the United States and Canada.* Champaign, Ill.: Association for the Advancement of Ukrainian Studies, 1975.

Subtelny, Orest. *Ukrainians in North America.* Toronto: University of Toronto Press, 1991.

Wertsman, Vladimir. *The Ukrainians in America, 1608–1975.* Dobbs Ferry, N.J.: Oceana Publications, 1976.

Welsh

Hartmann, Edward G. *Americans from Wales.* Boston: Christopher Publishing House, 1967.

History of Welsh Settlements in Jackson and Gallia Counties Ohio. Translated by Phillip G. Davies. Ames: University of Iowa, 1988.

Rowlands, John. *Welsh Family History: A Guide to Research.* Aberystwyth, Wales: Association of Family History Societies of Wales in conjunction with the Federation of Family History Societies, 1993.

Greenslade, David. *Welsh Fever: Welsh Activities in the United States and Canada Today.* Cambridge, Wales: D. Brown, 1986.

Yugoslav

Colakovic, Branko Mita. *Yugoslav Migrations to America.* San Francisco: R & E Research, 1973.

Govorchin, Gerald G. *Americans from Yugoslavia.* Gainesville: University of Florida Press, 1961.

Eterovich, Adam S. *A Guide and Bibliography to Research on Yugoslavs in the United States and Canada.* Palo Alto, Calif.: Raguson Press, 1978.

Part 2
FINDING AIDS

BIBLIOGRAPHIES AND CATALOGS OVERVIEW

Key Concepts in This Chapter

- A *bibliography* is a list of books and other sources for a specific topic.
- To identify a bibliography, look for a *bibliography of bibliographies.*
- *Library catalogs* are the key to using and understanding library collections.
- *Key word* and *Boolean searches* make computer catalogs more useful.
- *Catalog networks* identify sources at distant libraries.
- *Commercial catalogs* identify sources available for purchase.

Key Sources in This Chapter

- *Guide to Reference Books*
- *Books in Print* (*BIP*)
- *Subject Headings in the Library of Congress*
- *National Union Catalog* (*NUC*)
- *National Union Catalog of Manuscript Collections* (*NUCMC*)
- *National Inventory of Documentary Sources* (*NIDS*)

5

BIBLIOGRAPHIES AND CATALOGS

David T. Thackery

Bibliographies and catalogs will not contain the answers to a genealogical search, but they can guide researchers to materials that do hold the answers. Knowledge of bibliographies and catalogs is critical to the development of good research skills in genealogy—or in any other field. This chapter will help the researcher become familiar with the organization, purposes, availability, and use of bibliographies and catalogs so that he can, to some degree, become his own reference librarian.

The field of genealogy and local history is a rapidly growing one. More and more materials are becoming available in a variety of formats; new books are being published and old ones are being reprinted or microfilmed or even stored in CD-ROM format; more and more manuscript collections are being cataloged and often microfilmed. Libraries and archives are making their holdings known in a variety of ways as thousands of institutions computerize their catalogs and join interlibrary cataloging networks. This chapter describes the basic avenues that a genealogist might follow to discover useful research materials. It also demonstrates that, once these materials are identified, there are many ways in which they can be accessed.

This chapter does not attempt to describe the many bibliographies and catalogs the genealogist can use during a search unless they are of a very general nature. Rather, it defines the nature and use of such important reference tools. Most bibliographies and many catalogs are subject-specific (for example, immigration sources, genealogical periodicals, and military unit histories) and, as such, most are well described in other chapters of *Printed Sources*. Such reference tools are mentioned in this chapter only as examples. However, where a bibliography or catalog is of a very broad or general nature (touching on many aspects of genealogy), it is described here.

BIBLIOGRAPHIES

A bibliography is a list of books—and often other research sources, such as periodical articles—that focus on a given subject or genre. Regardless of the size or scope of the bibliography, its purpose is always the same: to alert the researcher to the existence of sources which may be helpful in the study of a particular subject. Having obtained author and title information from a bibliography, the researcher is then in a position to locate or request the work at a library (either directly or through interlibrary loan) or from a bookstore or publisher. A bibliography may comprise an entire book; however, a bibliography may also be found at the close of a book chapter or, more commonly, as an appendix to a particular work. Bibliographies can also be found at the end of a journal or encyclopedia article. Doctoral dissertations always include a bibliography of related sources after the main text. A book which may only have a tenuous connection to the subject at hand may nevertheless contain a bibliography which will be very helpful because it leads the researcher to books which are more pertinent.

A bibliography may be limited to the holdings of a particular institution. Such a bibliography is an obvious aid for using the holdings of that institution, but it can also claim additional significance if the collection itself has exceptional depth. For example, Marion J. Kaminkow's *Genealogies in the Library of Congress: A Bibliography* (Baltimore: Magna Carta, 1972) and its supplemental volumes constitute a bibliography whose importance is not limited by its institutional scope, as the genealogies listed in its pages may be found in other libraries as well.

But bibliographies are not necessarily limited to broad subject areas. Indeed, almost any subject a genealogist may want information about is probably addressed by a specialized bibliography. While books are often the most commonly cited materials, bibliographies can also include journal and magazine articles. For example, a genealogist with Basque ancestry should find useful the bibliography *Basque Americans: A Guide to Information Sources* (Detroit: Gale Research Co., 1981), compiled by William A. Douglas and Richard W. Etulain. The listings are annotated; that is, they are followed by brief discussions of the titles being cited. This work contains more than twenty pages of citations covering the history of Basques in the United States. For example, it includes a reference to an article by Eleanor Davis, "The Basques of Malheur County [Oregon]," in the periodical *Commonwealth Review* (April 1927), with the annotation that it is the "first semi-scholarly article on the Basques of the Pacific Northwest." Published bibliographies are easy to find in a library catalog: look for the subject in question followed by the subheading Bibliography. Douglas and Etulain's book, for example, might be found under the subject heading "Basque Americans—Bibliography." A bibliography on Connecticut genealogical research would be found under the subject heading "Connecticut—Genealogy—Bibliography."

The researcher should also be aware of bibliographies of a more general nature, for, at the very least, they may guide her to sources which will provide historical context for a genealogical research project. Of these, Robert Balay's *Guide to Reference Books,* 11th ed. (Chicago: American Library Association, 1996), is a particularly important bibliography for researchers in any field because it identifies the important bibliographies, indexes, and other reference works for many subjects and genres. (Earlier editions were compiled under the direction of Eugene Sheehy, so "Sheehy" and this title were thought of as virtually synonymous.) Of course, this guide will not contain specific genealogical or historical information, but it will point toward reference works which, in turn, may guide one to helpful books or articles. For example, the genealogist interested in what newspapers exist for a particular town during a specified period will find reference in the section on American newspapers to Winifred Gregory's union list, *American Newspapers 1821–1936.* Subjects such as general American history, as well as particular topics or periods in American history, are covered as well. Subject encyclopedias, discussed in chapter 1, "General Reference," can also be easily found in Balay's *Guide*.

Another important bibliographical reference work is *Books in Print*. R. R. Bowker (New York) publishes this set annually, dividing it into listings by author, subject, and title of books currently available from a great range of publishers (figure 5-1). It is readily available at most libraries and bookstores. Because most genealogies, local histories, and record transcriptions are not produced by commercial publishers or academic presses, do not expect to find a comprehensive listing of all the currently available titles pertaining to a particular research project; nevertheless, do not ignore this bibliography.

Usually, the subject volumes of *Books in Print* are the most helpful. By consulting them, one can at the very least discover the titles of books that provide important historical context for genealogical research. For U.S. research, search for these titles by looking up subject headings for particular states or locales of interest; this can alert one to the existence of many titles before they may have been acquired by many libraries or found their way into published subject bibliographies. Note that *Books in Print* covers reprints as well as first-published works. Consequently, books originally published in the nineteenth century or earlier in the twentieth century might very well be found in *Books in Print* as reprints.

Another important bibliographical reference work is Wilson's *Cumulative Book Index* (New York: H. W. Wilson, 1898–), issued and cumulated periodically. It aims to be a comprehensive listing of all books published in the United States and Canada—*excluding* government documents, maps, sheet music, and paperbound books. Although the titles of some genealogical publishers are included in it, many genealogy and local history publications are not, if for no other reason than that so many are issued in paperbound format. Author, title, and subject entries are interfiled.

Genealogical Bibliographies

Many bibliographies that directly pertain to genealogical research are mentioned in other chapters of this book and need not be referred to here; however, two especially important bibliographies should be noted. The first is P. William Filby's *American and British Genealogy and Heraldry: A Selected List of Books*, 3rd ed. (Boston: New England Historic Genealogical Society, 1983), together with its supplemental volume (1987). Generally speaking, the items listed in this bibliography have a national or state focus, as distinguished from a more local one (see figure 5-2). These state-by-state listings constitute its greatest strength. This is a good reference work to consult if, for example, one wishes to find out if colonial will abstracts have been published for a particular state or if land grants have been published for another. The index is very thorough and is a major aid in searching through the sometimes extensive listings. However, it does not list genealogies or family histories, with the exception of some state or regional genealogical compendia.

Also significant, and more current, is Kory L. Meyerink's *Genealogical Publications: A List of 50,000 Sources from the Library of Congress* (Salt Lake City: Ancestry, 1997). As the title indicates, this CD-ROM publication draws from the Library of Congress catalog (described below under "Library Catalogs") and includes virtually any book directly related to genealogy, family history, and local history. It uses *FolioVIEWS®* software to provide complete "every word" searching and allows Boolean searches (described below) as well. While very easy to use, it is limited to those titles cataloged by the Library of Congress from 1969 until October 1995. While that library has an excellent collection of genealogical materials, it lacks some titles, especially self-published titles printed in small quantities. However, Meyerink's bibliography serves as an excellent update to the almost thirteen thousand entries in Filby's older, and more selective, source.

Bibliographies of Bibliographies

A unique and important special bibliography is one that lists only (or almost only) other bibliographies. Such tools can help one locate specific subject bibliographies that may not appear in other literature. Often, such bibliographies of bibliographies are short lists in larger reference works. For example, Balay's *Guide to Reference Books* (cited earlier) includes a section of bibliographies within many of its subdivisions, as does *Books in Print* (refer again to figure 5-1).

Of course, as mentioned above, a bibliography does not necessarily have to appear in book form. It can also be found as an appendix to a book or article, listing all the reference sources or a selection of the more important ones consulted in the course of researching the book or article. Many bibliographies that are only part of a larger work are listed in various issues of H. W. Wilson's *Bibliographic Index* (New York, 1937–). Issued periodically, *Bibliographic Index* contains citations not only for separately published bibliographies, but also for bibliographies found in periodicals and monographs. Among the many periodicals surveyed for the *Index* are many (but by no means all) of the important state historical journals.

Another important bibliography of bibliographies is Theodore Besterman's *World Bibliography of Bibliographies,* 4th ed. (Lausanne, Switzerland: Societas Bibliographica, 1965–66). In addition, there is a supplement: *A World Bibliography of Bibliographies, 1964–1974,* compiled by Alice F. Toomey (Totowa, N.J.: Rowman and Littlefield, 1977). Genealogists may find this title especially helpful for its listings of bibliographies from outside of the United States, although Filby's bibliography may be more useful for British sources.

LIBRARY CATALOGS

Catalogs are as old as libraries themselves, although their format has been and still is subject to change. Variations exist be-

BOOKS IN PRINT

Jola Publications Staff, ed. Wisconsin Medical Directory: October, 1991. rev. ed. 136p. 1991. pap. 12.00 (*1-878373-01-3*) Jola Pubns.

Lange, Marie A. & Mandt, Jinger, eds. Classified Directory of Wisconsin Manufacturers, 1994. 53th ed. 1100p. 1993. 120.00 (*0-942198-20-4*) WMC Serv.

—Wisconsin Services Directory, 1994. 6th ed. 1000p. 1994. 120.00 (*0-942198-19-0*) WMC Serv.

Marsh, Carole. The Wisconsin Bookstore Book: A Surprising Guide to Our State's Bookstores & Their Specialties for Students, Teachers, Writers & Publishers. (Wisconsin Bks.). (Illus.). 1994. lib. bdg. 24.95 (*0-7933-3002-5*); pap. 14.95 (*0-7933-3003-3*); disk 29.95 (*0-7933-3004-1*) Gallopade Pub Group.

—The Wisconsin Library Book: A Surprising Guide to the Unusual Special Collections in Libraries Across Our State for Students, Teachers, Writers & Publishers. (Wisconsin Bks.). (Illus.). 1994. lib. bdg. 24.95 (*0-7933-3152-8*); pap. 14.95 (*0-7933-3153-6*); disk 29.95 (*0-7933-3154-4*) Gallopade Pub Group.

—The Wisconsin Media Book: A Surprising Guide to the Amazing Print, Broadcast & Online Media of Our State for Students, Teachers, Writers & Publishers - Includes Reproducible Mailing Labels Plus Activities for Young People! (Wisconsin Bks.). (Illus.). 1994. lib. bdg. 24.95 (*0-7933-3308-3*); pap. 14.95 (*0-7933-3309-1*); disk 29.95 (*0-7933-3310-5*) Gallopade Pub Group.

Montgomery, Susan J., et al. Healthy Living in Wisconsin. (Orig.). 1988. pap. 12.95 (*0-929807-00-6*) Montgomery Media.

Niesen, Karen L. & Onaga, Christine Y. Wisconsin Directory of International Institutions. 261p. 1993. pap. 25.00 (*0-299-97079-5*) U of Wis Pr.

WISCONSIN–ECONOMIC CONDITIONS

Danziger, Sheldon & Witte, John, eds. State Policy Choices: The Wisconsin Experience. LC 88-40232. (C). 1989. text ed. 45.00 (*0-299-11710-3*) U of Wis Pr.

Directory of Wisconsin Owned & Managed Mutual Funds. 1988. pap. 5.00 (*0-318-23654-0*) UWIM CCA.

Fox, Micheal & McDonough, Kathleen. Wisconsin Municipal Records Manual. 102p. pap. 5.00 (*0-87020-208-1*) State Hist Soc Wis.

Hanna, Frank A., et al. Analysis of Wisconsin Income. (Studies in Income & Wealth: No. 9). 284p. 1948. reprint ed. 73.90 (*0-87014-164-3*) Natl Bur Econ Res.

Hurst, J. Willard. Law & Economic Growth: The Legal History of the Lumber Industry in Wisconsin, 1836-1915. LC 64-100116. (Illus.). 992p. 1984. text ed. 35.00 (*0-299-09780-3*) U of Wis Pr.

Merk, Frederick. Economic History of Wisconsin During the Civil War Decade. LC 72-180453. 414p. 1971. reprint ed. 10.00 (*0-87020-117-4*) State Hist Soc Wis.

Strang, William A., et al. The University of Wisconsin-Madison & the Local & State Economies: A Second Look. 1985. pap. 10.00 (*0-86603-019-0*) Bur Busn Wis.

Walsh, Margaret. The Manufacturing Frontier: Pioneer Industry in Antebellum Wisconsin 1830-1860. LC 72-619513. 263p. 1972. 12.50 (*0-87020-119-0*) State Hist Soc Wis.

WISCONSIN–GENEALOGY

•Anderson, Harry H., ed. The German-American Pioneers in Wisconsin & Michigan: The Frank-Kerler Letters, 1849-1864. LC 70-134341. (Illus.). 600p. 1989. 19.00 (*0-938076-00-0*) Milwaukee Cty Hist Soc.

Clinton Topper Staff. History of Clinton Wisconsin. (Illus.). 357p. 1987. 65.00 (*0-88107-091-2*) Curtis Media.

Irvin, John M. Cemetery Inscriptions from Green County, Wisconsin, Vol. 1&2. 2nd rev. ed. (Illus.). 72p. 1986. pap. 8.00 (*0-910255-47-4*) Wisconsin Gen.

—Index to Names in Commemorative Biographical Record of the Counties of Rock, Green, Grant, Iowa & Lafayette, Wisconsin, 1901. 107p. 1983. pap. 10.00 (*0-910255-42-3*) Wisconsin Gen.

Langkau, David A. Civil War Veterans of Winnebago Co, WI, Vol. I: A-H. 378p. (Orig.). 1994. pap. text ed. 27.50 (*1-55613-911-X*) Heritage Bk.

—Civil War Veterans of Winnebago County, Wisconsin Vol. 2, I-T. 384p. (Orig.). 1994. pap. text ed. 27.50 (*0-7884-0035-5*) Heritage Bk.

Lewis, Kathy A. The Norwegian Roots of the Sonsteby Family. LC 94-75407. (Illus.). 76p. 1994. lib. bdg. write for info. (*0-9620135-3-6*) K A Lewis.

Munnell, Michael D., ed. American Indian Marriage Record

WISCONSIN–HISTORY

Anderson-Sannes, Barbara. Alma on the Mississippi, 1848-1932. Doyle, Michael et al, eds. LC 80-68241. (Illus.). 198p. (Orig.). 1980. pap. 11.95 (*0-9604684-0-4*) Alma Hist Soc.

Anuta, Michael J. History of Rotary Clubs in Wisconsin & Michigan in District 6220. (Illus.). 500p. (Orig.). 1993. pap. text ed. 22.50 (*0-9637757-2-3*) M J Anuta.

Apps, Jerold W. Barns of Wisconsin. LC 77-5472. (Illus.). 1977. pap. 10.00 (*0-915024-14-4*) WI Trails.

Bailey, Marilyn. Index to Southwestern Wisconsin: A History of Old Crawford County, 1932. 59p. 1983. pap. 8.00 (*0-910255-41-5*) Wisconsin Gen.

Bailey, Marilyn J. Index to "History of Southeastern Wisconsin-Old Milwaukee Country" 1932. 67p. 1984. pap. 8.50 (*0-910255-43-1*) Wisconsin Gen.

Bailey, Sturges W. Index to a Standard History of Sauk County Wisconsin, 1918. (Illus.). 55p. (Orig.). 1983. pap. text ed. 8.00 (*0-910255-39-3*) Wisconsin Gen.

Behrnd-Klodt, Menzi L. & Mattern, Carolyn. Social Action Collections at the State Historical Society of Wisconsin: A Guide. LC 85-5007. 158p. 1983. pap. 12.00 (*0-87020-220-0*) State Hist Soc Wis.

Blegen, Theodore C. The Land Lies Open. LC 74-27727. 246p. 1975. reprint ed. text ed. 35.00 (*0-8371-7912-2*, BLLO, Greenwood Pr) Greenwood.

Boatman, John. At the Crossroads: Memories from a Rural Ethnic Community: The Saukville, Wisconsin Area. Schefft, Angela M., ed. 628p. (Orig.). (C). 1993. pap. text ed. 18.45 (*0-685-72296-1*) U Pr of Amer.

—Wisconsin American Indian History & Culture: A Survey of Selected Aspects. Dorgay, Carla, ed. 222p. (Orig.). (C). 1993. pap. text ed. 18.45 (*0-685-72295-3*) U Pr of Amer.

Boehlke, LeRoy & Silldorff, Donald. Freistadt & the Lutheran Imigration. Trinity of Freistadt Historical Society Staff, ed. Suelflow, Harry & Ruedt, Lucy W., trs. (Illus.). 141p. 1989. pap. 8.00 (*0-9622699-0-5*) TECOF.

Carlson, Bruce. Wisconsin's Vanishing Outhouse: A Collection of Illustrations & Stories about a Rapidly Vanishing Insitution in Wisconsin, the Little Outhouse Out Back. (Illus.). 168p. (Orig.). 1990. pap. 9.95 (*1-878488-27-9*) Quixote Pr IA.

•Connors, Dean M. Going for the Iron. 80p. 1994. 40.00 (*0-938627-23-6*) New Past Pr.

Current, Richard N. History of Wisconsin Vol. II: The Civil War Era, 1848-1873. LC 72-12941. (History of Wisconsin Ser.). (Illus.). 659p. 1976. 25.00 (*0-87020-160-3*) State Hist Soc Wis.

Davies, Phillips G. Welsh in Wisconsin. LC 82-10283. (Illus.). 39p. 1982. pap. 3.00 (*0-87020-214-6*) State Hist Soc Wis.

Eifert, Virginia S. Journeys in Green Places: The Shores & Woods of Wisconsin's Door Peninsula. rev. ed. LC 89-17428. (Illus.). xvi, 222p. 1989. reprint ed. 20.00 (*0-940473-13-5*); reprint ed. pap. 9.95 (*0-940473-12-7*) Wm Caxton.

Engels, Theresa R., ed. A Wisconsin Christmas Anthology. 2nd ed. (State Anthologies Ser.: No. 2). (Illus.). 1990. pap. 10.95 (*0-9621085-1-0*) Partridge Pr.

Fapso, Richard. Norwegians in Wisconsin. (Illus.). 40p. 1977. pap. 3.00 (*0-87020-171-9*) State Hist Soc Wis.

Fogle, Phil. Grassroots - Lake Geneva. (Illus.). 133p. (C). 1986. text ed. write for info. (*0-9611982-2-2*) Big Foot Pub.

—My Lake - Your Lake. (Illus.). 135p. (C). 1983. text ed. write for info. (*0-9611982-1-4*) Big Foot Pub.

Folsom, W. H. Fifty Years in the Northwest. (Illus.). 763p. 1994. reprint ed. lib. bdg. 77.50 (*0-8328-4025-4*) Higginson Bk Co.

Frederick, George G. Names from the Past: Supplement to When Iron Was King in Dodge County, Wisconsin. LC 93-86026. 152p. (Orig.). 1993. pap. 11.95 (*0-9638443-1-8*) G G Frederick.

—When Iron Was King in Dodge County, Wisconsin: 1845-1928. LC 93-86025. (Illus.). 750p. 1993. 39.95 (*0-9638443-0-X*) G G Frederick.

Friedman, Ruth L. Riverside Paper Corporation 1893-1993. 1994. write for info. (*0-9638996-0-0*); pap. write for info. (*0-9638996-1-9*) Riverside Paper.

Fries, Robert F. Empire in Pine: The Story of Lumbering in Wisconsin, 1830-1900. LC 89-15724. (Illus.). xii, 285p. 1989. reprint ed. 25.00 (*0-940473-10-0*); reprint ed. pap.

—Wiltonians: A Centennial History of the Wilton Area. (Illus.). 152p. (Orig.). 1990. pap. 21.95 (*0-938627-09-0*) New Past Pr.

Haeger, John D. Men & Money: The Urban Frontier at Green Bay, 1815-1840. (Illus.). 29p. 1971. pap. 2.00 (*0-916699-04-8*) CMU Clarke Hist Lib.

Hafstad, Margaret, ed. Guide to the McCormick Collection of the State Historical Society of Wisconsin. LC 73-1216. (Illus.). 94p. 1973. 10.00 (*0-87020-124-7*) State Hist Soc Wis.

Hale, Frederick. Swedes in Wisconsin. LC 82-23272. (Illus.). 32p. 1983. pap. 3.00 (*0-87020-217-0*) State Hist Soc Wis.

Ham, F. Gerald & Hedstrom, Margaret, eds. Guide to Labor Papers in the State Historical Society of Wisconsin. LC 78-23820. (Illus.). 140p. 1978. pap. 5.00 (*0-87020-177-8*) State Hist Soc Wis.

Harper, Josephine L., ed. Draper Manuscripts Guide. 464p. 1983. 70.00 (*0-87020-215-4*) Chadwyck-Healey.

Hass, Paul H. The Suppression of John F. Deitz: An Episode of the Progressive Era in Wisconsin. (Wisconsin Stories Ser.). 55p. 1979. pap. 1.75 (*0-87020-184-0*) State Hist Soc Wis.

Hayes, Jeffery A., ed. Tesla's Engine: A New Dimension for Power. LC 94-60502. (Illus.). 220p. (Orig.). 1994. pap. text ed. 19.95 (*1-884917-33-X*) Tesla Engine.

Haygood, William C. Red Child, White Child: The Strange Disappearance of Casper Partridge. (Wisconsin Stories Ser.). (Illus.). 146p. 1979. pap. 1.75 (*0-87020-185-9*) State Hist Soc Wis.

The History of Fon Du Lac County, WI. (Illus.). 1064p. 1994. reprint ed. lib. bdg. 107.50 (*0-8328-4268-0*) Higginson Bk Co.

History of Northern Wisconsin, 2 vols. LC 87-30160. 1218p. 1988. reprint ed. 35.00 (*0-933249-28-4*) Mid-Peninsula Lib.

Holand, Hjalmar R. History of Door County, Wisconsin: The County Beautiful, 2 vols., Set. (Illus.). 1100p. 1993. reprint ed. 100.00 (*0-940473-23-2*) Wm Caxton.

—Old Peninsula Days. 1990. pap. 9.95 (*1-55971-057-8*) NorthWord.

Holmes, Fred L. Old World Wisconsin. 1990. pap. 9.95 (*1-55971-056-X*) NorthWord.

Holzhueter, John O. Madeline Island & the Chequamegon Region. LC 74-20919. (Illus.). 64p. 1974. pap. 3.95 (*0-87020-146-8*) State Hist Soc Wis.

•Hubbell, Homer B. Dodge County, Wis., Past & Present, 2 vols., Set. (Illus.). 926p. 1995. reprint ed. lib. bdg. 89.50 (*0-8328-4484-5*) Higginson Bk Co.

Huffman, Thomas R. Protectors of the Land & Water: Environmentalism in Wisconsin, 1961-1968. LC 93-32479. (Illus.). xii, 252p. (C). 1994. text ed. 39.95 (*0-8078-2138-1*); pap. text ed. 14.95 (*0-8078-4445-4*) U of NC Pr.

Jackson, Ronald V. Wisconsin Census Index 1836. LC 77-86057. (Illus.). 1976. lib. bdg. 49.00 (*0-89593-152-4*) Accelerated Index.

—Wisconsin Federal Census Index, 1840. LC 77-86058. (Illus.). 1978. lib. bdg. 58.00 (*0-89593-153-2*) Accelerated Index.

—Wisconsin Federal Census Index, 1850. LC 77-86059. (Illus.). 1978. lib. bdg. 88.00 (*0-89593-154-0*) Accelerated Index.

—Wisconsin Historical & Biographical Index, Vol. 1. LC 78-53723. (Illus.). 1984. lib. bdg. 30.00 (*0-89593-205-9*) Accelerated Index.

•Kanne, Eunice. Were They Really the Good Old Days? (Illus.). 160p. (Orig.). 1994. pap. 10.00 (*0-938627-25-2*) New Past Pr.

Karis, Eleanor. A Journey Through Norwalk, 1894-1994. (Illus.). 63p. 1994. pap. 15.00 (*0-938627-20-1*) New Past Pr.

Kellogg, Louise P. The French Regime in Wisconsin & the Northwest. (BCL1 - United States Local History Ser.). 474p. 1991. reprint ed. lib. bdg. 99.00 (*0-7812-6321-2*) Rprt Serv.

Kellogg, Louise T. British Regime in Wisconsin & the Northwest. LC 74-124927. (American Scene Ser.). (Illus.). 1971. reprint ed. lib. bdg. 45.00 (*0-306-71047-1*) Da Capo.

Kort, Ellen. The Fox Heritage: A History of Wisconsin's Fox Cities. (Illus.). 256p. 1988. 26.95 (*0-89781-083-X*) Preferred Mktg.

Figure 5-1. From *Books in Print,* which is divided into listings by author, subject, and title of books currently available from a great range of publishers.

4687 *United States*

genealogical research. v.1- , 1957- . Aurora, N.Y. (Box 52, 13026).
Censuses, heads of Palatine families, New York settlements. Out-of-print years obtainable from Xerox Univ. Microfilms, Ann Arbor, Mich.

4687 **Yoshpe, Harry B.** Disposition of Loyalist estates in the southern district of the State of New York. New York, 1939.

4688 **Zimm, Louise S.**, and others. Southeastern New York, a history of the counties of Ulster, Dutchess, Orange, Rockland and Putnam. 3v. New York, 1946.
v.3 has biographies. Lewis pub.

NORTH CAROLINA

Settled ca. 1650; original state

Many works in this book concern both South and North Carolina. Since these will be entered in one or the other state, it is suggested that both Carolinas be consulted.

4689 **Arthur, John P.** Western North Carolina; a history, 1730-1913. 1914. Repr. Spartanburg, S.C.: Reprint Co., 1973.
Includes biographical sketches.

4690 **Ashe, Samuel A'Court (and others).** Biographical history of North Carolina from colonial times to the present. 8v. 1905-17. Repr. Spartanburg, S.C.: Reprint Co., 1971.

4691 **Bentley, Elizabeth P.** Index to the 1800 census of North Carolina. Baltimore: G.P.C., 1977.
61,000 main entries. Excellently transcribed and edited. Superior to Jackson, no.4746.

4692 ——— 1810. Baltimore: G.P.C., 1978.
64,000 heads of households. With useful introduction. Superior to Jackson, no.4747.

4693 **Bernheim, Gotthardt D.** History of the German settlements and of the Lutheran Church in North and South Carolina from the earliest period of the colonization of the Dutch, German, and Swiss settlers to the close of the first half of the present century. 1872. Repr. Spartanburg, S.C.: Reprint Co., 1972; Baltimore: G.P.C., 1975.

4694 **Broughton, Carrie L.** Marriage and death notices from *Raleigh register* and *North Carolina state gazette, Daily sentinel, Raleigh observer*...1799-1893. 6v. Raleigh, N.C.: State Lib., 1944-52.
The notices for 1799-1845 were included in the library's biennial report, 1942-47. and were repr. by G.P.C., Baltimore, 1962-68. 1799-1825 repr. Baltimore: G.P.C., 1975. 1846-67 repr. Baltimore: G.P.C., 1976. Supplanted by Neal: *Abstracts of vital records from Raleigh, N.C. Newspapers*, see no.4771.

4695 **Burns, Annie (Walker).** Abstract of pensions of North Carolina soldiers of the Revolution, War of 1812, and Indian Wars. 15v.? Washington, D.C., 1960-64?
Not easy to use. Projected ser., of which 15v. were pub.

4696 ——— North Carolina genealogical records. 1v.? Washington, D.C., 1943.
Abstracts of pension records. Difficult to use.

4697 **Cain, Barbara T., McGrew, E. Z.,** and **Morris, C. E.** Guide to private manuscript collections in the North Carolina Archives. 3rd rev. ed. Raleigh: Dept. of Cultural Resources, 1981.
1,640 collections of private papers; through June 1979.

4698 **Cartwright, Betty G. C.,** and **Gardiner, L. T.** North Carolina land grants in Tennessee, 1778-91. 1958. Repr. Memphis, Tenn.: The Authors, 1973.
This list of landowners and settlers constitutes the only substitute for a 1790 census of the part of North Carolina which became Tennessee in 1796.

4699 ——— Surname index. 5,000 grants. Searcy, Ark.: Presley Research, 1977.

4700 **Chreitzberg, Abel McKee.** Early Methodism in the Carolinas. 1897. Repr. Spartanburg, S.C.: Reprint Co., 1972.
Extensive information on Methodist preachers but of marginal interest to genealogists.

4701 **Clark, David S.** Index to maps of North Carolina in books and periodicals illustrating the history of the State from

272

Figure 5-2. From Filby's *American and British Genealogy and Heraldry: A Selected List of Books*. Generally speaking, the items listed in this bibliography have a national or state focus.

tween libraries; in fact, within many institutions there is a variety of catalogs. A catalog can be seen as a form of bibliography in that it is a listing of books and other library items. The major difference between a library catalog and a bibliography is that a catalog encompasses all of an institution's holdings (or at least attempts to) and is not limited by subject.

In medieval Europe the monastic libraries were established before the advent of the printing press—a time when books, being a rare commodity, were sometimes literally chained in place. These libraries were, of course, small by today's standards. A library's catalog would likely be maintained in a ledger with new acquisitions added to an ongoing list, perhaps categorized by subject or even size. These catalogs were little more than inventories.

With the rise of mass publishing and the increase in the size of libraries, an alternative to the book catalog had to be found. Thus arose the library card catalog, which, in the United States, enabled the library user to answer three questions about a collection:

- Is a particular book part of the collection?
- What books does the library hold by a given author?
- What materials are held by the library on a particular subject?

The first two aspects are determined by author and title headings, the last by subject headings. Author and title headings are fairly straightforward, and indeed are less used by genealogists than subject headings. For that matter, from the genealogist's perspective, subject headings are often a relatively simple affair, representing either a surname or place name (for example, "Perry family" or "Berks County, Pennsylvania—History"), although in other areas, such as immigration or military records, the subject headings may not be quite so straightforward and uniform. For this reason, it is important to discuss subject headings in some depth.

Subject Headings

Although the genealogist—or any other library user—does not need the cataloger's knowledge of subject headings to use a library effectively, some understanding of subject heading practices will enable one to become better versed in consulting catalogs. Most libraries use subject headings which have been devised and standardized by the Library of Congress, so a subject heading which proves helpful in one library is likely to be helpful in most others. To determine or confirm the exact wording of a subject heading, consult the most recent edition of *Subject Headings in the Library of Congress* (Washington, D.C.: Library of Congress), which is kept in the reference area at most medium- to large-size libraries.

Subject headings are not completely uniform among libraries; in fact, they are not always completely uniform within a library either. The number of subject headings assigned for the same title may vary among catalogers and among libraries. For example, in the case of a family history covering a dozen allied families, most libraries will only provide a subject heading for the first two or three surnames appearing in a title, while a library specializing in genealogy, such as the Family History Library of The Church of Jesus Christ of Latter-day Saints (LDS church) in Salt Lake City, may provide a subject heading for each or many of the surnames. Inevitably there will be variations in subject headings for titles concerning the same topic. In such instances, a single subject heading may not be as representative of a library's holdings on a particular topic as might be desired. For example, the researcher searching for Civil War regimental histories may find three or four relevant subject heading variations, all of them valid (for example, subject headings beginning "United States—History—Civil War, 1861–1865" versus "[name of state]—History—Civil War, 1861–1865").

Such problems with subject headings serve to point out the usefulness of bibliographies. For example, the library researcher who has identified a particular title in Charles E. Dornbusch's *Military Bibliography of the Civil War,* 3 vols. (New York: New York Public Library, 1961–1972; supplement 1987) (see chapter 13, "Military Sources") will have an author and title to seek and will not be misled by the different subject heading patterns which may be present in a library's catalog.

The arrangement of a library card catalog (or as reproduced in a book or in microform) can vary among institutions. One approach is to combine all the author, subject, and title entries in one alphabetical arrangement known as a dictionary catalog. When using such a catalog it is always important to bear in mind the order of card placement: author cards come before subject cards for the same surname. For example, *all* of the authors surnamed Putnam are listed together, being arranged alphabetically by first and middle names. Only after the final author card, say, for Zephaniah Putnam, will one find the subject heading cards for a Putnam County, in turn followed by subject heading cards for Putnam family. One should not, for example, look for the subject heading "Putnam family" before the author card for "Putnam, Frederick."

Another approach to card catalog organization is to separate the subject, author, and title entries into their own segregated sequences. Libraries with unique missions can adopt even more specialized methods of organization to better fit the needs of their patrons.

Family History Library Catalog

For genealogists, an important catalog with its own specialized organization is that of the Family History Library in Salt Lake City. Available in the library's branch family history centers as well as in unaffiliated genealogical collections around the world, the *Family History Library Catalog*™ is found on microfiche and is updated annually in that format. Its approach to subject headings is unique in that subject entries for genealogies (family histories) and for local histories and local source materials are segregated in their respective surname and locality catalogs. The locality catalog is organized alphabetically by country, with the exception of the United States and Canada, for which the state or province is the primary category (figure 5-3). For example, to discover the Family History Library's holdings on Champaign County, Ohio, look first under "Ohio" and thereunder for "Champaign County"; for a Prussian locality look first for the microfiche containing entries for Germany, then proceed to the subheading of Prussia, and thereunder to the province and locality within Prussia. This subject heading practice is not used in most other libraries, where the standard subject heading procedure is to begin with the *smallest* geographical unit. Those who do most of their work in the Family History Library and its centers should keep this difference in mind when working with the card catalogs of other libraries.

```
PATRON CATALOG-LOCALITY DIVISION                          11-MAR-97   G.S.
                                                          Page    91  Indx
--------------------------------------------------------------------  Code

**************************************************************************
TENNESSEE, MADISON - GENEALOGY
                                                          +-------------+
Smith, Jonathan Kennon Thompson.                          |US/CAN       |
    Several genealogical vignettes of Madison County, Tennessee /  |BOOK AREA    |
      by Jonathan K.T. Smith. -- [S.l. : s.n.], c1993. -- 47 leaves |976.827      |
      : ill., facsims., maps.                             |D2s          |
                                                          +-------------+
    Includes surname index.
    Contains a potpourri of records: bible, cemetery, taxation, school,
      military, vital, and so forth.

    Also on microfiche.  Salt Lake City : Filmed by        US/CAN
      the Genealogical Society of Utah, 1995.  2          FICHE AREA
      microfiche ; 11 x 15 cm.                            6110603

**************************************************************************
TENNESSEE, MADISON - GUARDIANSHIP
                                                          +-------------+
Guardian books, 1868-1879, Madison County, Tennessee / prepared by  |US/CAN       |
     the Historical Records Project. -- Salt Lake City : Filmed by  |FILM AREA    |
     the Genealogical Society of Utah, 1940. -- on 1 microfilm      |0024758      |
     reel ; 35 mm.                                        | item 3      |
                                                          +-------------+
    Microfilm of typescript at the Tennessee State Library in Nashville,
      Tennessee.
    Includes index.

**************************************************************************
TENNESSEE, MADISON - HISTORY
                                                          +-------------+
                                                          |US/CAN       |
                                                          |BOOK AREA    |
                                                          |976.8        |
The Goodspeed histories of Madison County, Tennessee. -- Columbia,  |H2h          |
     Tenn. : Woodward & Stinson Printing Co., 1972. -- p. 797-917   |v.   10      |
     -- (Goodspeed's history of Tennessee)                |1972         |
                                                          +-------------+
    Reprint.  Originally published:  Nashville, Tenn. : Goodspeed Pub. Co.,
      1887.

    Also on microfilm.  Salt Lake City : Filmed by the     US/CAN
      Genealogical Society of Utah, 1972. -- on 1         FILM AREA
      microfilm reel ; 35 mm.                             0896973
                                                           item 4.

**************************************************************************
TENNESSEE, MADISON - HISTORY
                                                          +-------------+
Smith, Jonathan Kennon Thompson.                          |US/CAN       |
    Campbell's Levee Turnpike and its successors in Madison County, |BOOK AREA    |
     Tennessee / by Jonathan K. T. Smith. -- Jackson, Tenn. :      |976.827      |
     J.K.T. Smith, c1993. -- 17 leaves : ill., maps, ports.         |H2sj         |
                                                          +-------------+

    Also on microfilm.  Salt Lake City : Filmed by the     US/CAN
      Genealogical Society of Utah, 1993.  on 1           FILM AREA
      microfilm reel ; 16 mm.                             1750734
                                                           item 51
```

Figure 5-3. From the locality section of the *Family History Library Catalog.* It is organized alphabetically by country, with the exception of the United States and Canada, for which the state or province is the primary category. (Reprinted by permission. Copyright 1987, 1997 by The Church of Jesus Christ of Latter-day Saints.)

The *Family History Library Catalog* also includes a section for subject headings which are not concerned with particular locales or families. It also contains an author/title catalog, which, of course, contains listings for works found in the other catalog sections. For example, Howland Delano Perrine's *The Wright Family of Oyster Bay, Long Island* will be found under "Perrine" in the author/title catalog and under "Wright family" in the surname catalog. Catalog information from the Family History Library is also found in the CD-ROM package *FamilySearch*®, although there are some limitations in using it in this format. (For example, the current CD-ROM version does not allow an author search.) For further discussion of the surname section of the *Family History Library Catalog*, see chapter 16, "Family Histories and Genealogies."

SPECIAL BOOK CATALOGS

The card catalog has not entirely displaced the book catalog. For the past thirty to forty years book catalogs have been published for various noteworthy collections. A few of these book catalogs have gone beyond a particular subject focus, a notable example being the book catalogs for the research collections of the New York Public Library; however, in most instances book catalogs have been published for the holdings of subject-specific collections, such as the Newberry Library's Edward Ayer collection on native peoples and the exploration and settlement of the Americas. The library of the National Society of the Daughters of the American Revolution (DAR) in Washington, D.C., has also published a catalog of its holdings. The holdings of this library are particularly important for the many transcriptions of local records, cemetery inscriptions, etc., produced in typescript by local DAR chapters over several decades. The vast majority of these materials are not commercially available, and they are often difficult to locate. Such published catalogs are helpful both in alerting researchers to what is in a particular library and for the contributions they make to general bibliographic knowledge.

More than four hundred published library catalogs are fully described, with a helpful subject index, in Bonnie R. Nelson's *Guide to Published Library Catalogs* (Metuchen, N.J.: Scarecrow, 1992). Several published catalogs listing family histories are described in detail in chapter 16, "Family Histories and Genealogies."

The most important book catalog is the *National Union Catalog* (*NUC*). As a union catalog, it combines entries for the holdings of the Library of Congress with those of more than one thousand other North American libraries. Published by the Library of Congress, it consists of catalog card reproductions arranged by author (or by title when author headings are not possible) (see figure 5-4). The largest installment, that for pre-1956 imprints, consists of 754 volumes, with supplementary series for 1956 to 1967, 1968 to 1972, and 1973 to 1977. Later dates are available on microfiche and CD-ROM. The *NUC* is an invaluable bibliographic source as well as a location aid. Often, older works of genealogy and local history are included in the *NUC*, which includes the holdings of many state libraries and historical societies. Sets of the *NUC* can usually be found in the reference sections of medium-size and larger university and research libraries, as well as in some larger public libraries. Of course, the author arrangement necessitates that the researcher know the name of the book's author and its approximate publication date. Entries processed after the Library of Congress's automation in 1969 are published on CD-ROM as *CD-MARC Bibliographic* (Washington, D.C.: Catalog Duplication Service, updated quarterly). Various editions include differing amounts of the Library of Congress catalog, but every edition can be searched by author, title, subject, key word, and several other categories. This CD-ROM publication ceased after the edition for the fourth quarter of 1996. The last edition will be available for sale for some time, however, and the entire database is also available via the Internet.

An important corollary reference tool is the *National Union Catalog of Manuscript Collections* (*NUCMC*), also published by the Library of Congress. Containing descriptions of manuscript collections found in the Library of Congress, state historical societies, major research libraries, and even county historical societies and local public libraries, *NUCMC* is an invaluable resource for the genealogist in search of manuscript source material. These manuscript sources can include the letters or diaries of ancestors or other family members, as well as business, school, and other institutional records (figure 5-5). *NUCMC* first appeared in 1962; it covered holdings reported received from 1959 through 1961. It has continued to be released in installments, the 1991 volume appearing in 1993. Through the 1991 volume, *NUCMC* has reported on more than sixty-five thousand collections in 1,369 different repositories. The twenty-seven volumes include almost 750,000 references to subjects and personal, family, and corporate names.

Indexes covering the *NUCMC* volumes for certain years have been published periodically; however, as more and more *NUCMC* volumes were printed, thus requiring more indexes, consulting the many indexes became an increasingly cumbersome and time-consuming undertaking. Two works have largely eliminated this problem: *Index to Personal Names in the National Union Catalog of Manuscript Collections 1959–1984* (Alexandria, Va.: Chadwyck-Healey, 1988), and *Index to Subjects and Corporate Names in the National Union Catalog of Manuscript Collections 1959–1984* (Alexandria, Va.: Chadwyck-Healey, 1994). In the former, one can look under relevant surnames to see if papers covering any person or family of interest have been reported to *NUCMC* over a twenty-five-year period. For example, looking under the subject heading "Watson family," reveals that a collection of papers concerning the Watson family of Marion County, West Virginia, was reported by the West Virginia University Library in 1960. In the second index to subjects the same listing would be found under the subject heading "Marion County, West Virginia." In addition to subject headings for locations, headings for organizations ("corporate names"), such as companies, churches, schools, clubs, etc., would also be found. Data on manuscript collections from around the United States continues to be submitted to the Library of Congress. After the information is translated into cataloging format, the catalog entries are entered into the two major online catalogs, OCLC and RLIN (covered later in this chapter).

KEY WORD AND BOOLEAN SEARCHES IN COMPUTER CATALOGS

The subject heading is a necessary addition to the author and title headings of a catalog. Without the subject heading, the library researcher would have to know the authors or titles of particular books in order to access them.

210 *The National Union Catalog Pre-1956 Imprints*

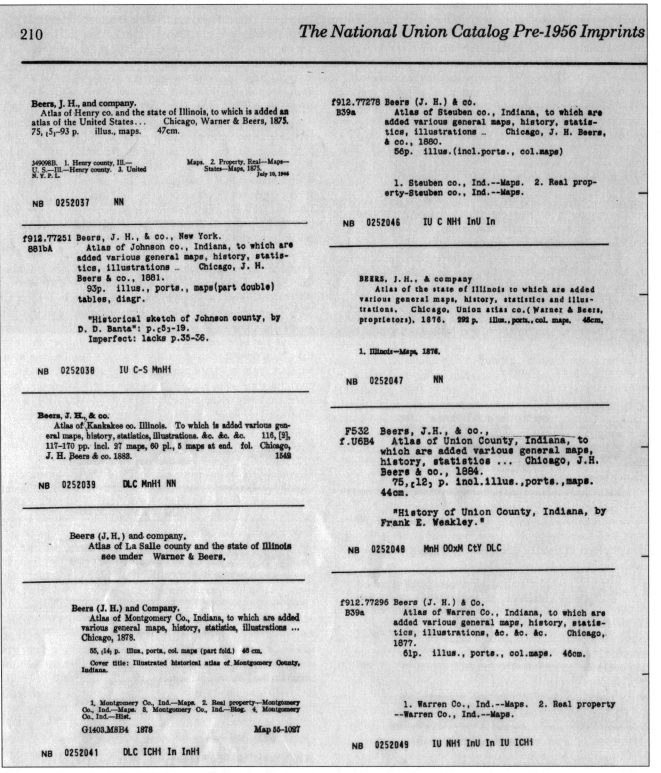

Beers, J. H., and company.
Atlas of Henry co. and the state of Illinois, to which is added an atlas of the United States... Chicago, Warner & Beers, 1875. 75, ₍5₎–93 p. illus., maps. 47cm.

349098B. 1. Henry county, Ill.—Maps. 2. Property, Real—Maps—U. S.—Ill.—Henry county. 3. United States—Maps, 1875.
N. Y. P. L. July 10, 1944

NB 0252037 NN

---

f912.77251 Beers, J. H., & co., New York.
881bA Atlas of Johnson co., Indiana, to which are added various general maps, history, statistics, illustrations ... Chicago, J. H. Beers & co., 1881.
93p. illus., ports., maps(part double) tables, diagr.

"Historical sketch of Johnson county, by D. D. Banta": p.₍5₎-19.
Imperfect: lacks p.35-36.

NB 0252038 IU C-S MnHi

Beers, J. H., & co.
Atlas of Kankakee co. Illinois. To which is added various general maps, history, statistics, illustrations. &c. &c. &c. 116, [2], 117–170 pp. incl. 27 maps, 60 pl., 5 maps at end. fol. Chicago, J. H. Beers & co. 1883. 1542

NB 0252039 DLC MnHi NN

Beers (J. H.) and company.
Atlas of La Salle county and the state of Illinois
see under Warner & Beers.

Beers (J. H.) and Company.
Atlas of Montgomery Co., Indiana, to which are added various general maps, history, statistics, illustrations ... Chicago, 1878.
55, ₍14₎ p. illus., ports., col. maps (part fold.) 46 cm.
Cover title: Illustrated historical atlas of Montgomery County, Indiana.

1. Montgomery Co., Ind.—Maps. 2. Real property—Montgomery Co., Ind.—Maps. 3. Montgomery Co., Ind.—Biog. 4. Montgomery Co., Ind.—Hist.

G1403.M8B4 1878 Map 55–1027

NB 0252041 DLC ICHi In InHi

---

f912.77278 Beers (J. H.) & co.
B39a Atlas of Steuben co., Indiana, to which are added various general maps, history, statistics, illustrations ... Chicago, J. H. Beers, & co., 1880.
56p. illus.(incl.ports., col.maps)

1. Steuben co., Ind.--Maps. 2. Real property-Steuben co., Ind.--Maps.

NB 0252046 IU C NHi InU In

BEERS, J. H., & company
Atlas of the state of Illinois to which are added various general maps, history, statistics and illustrations. Chicago, Union atlas co.(Warner & Beers, proprietors), 1876. 292 p. illus., ports., col. maps. 46cm.

1. Illinois—Maps, 1876.

NB 0252047 NN

F532 Beers, J.H., & co.,
f.U6B4 Atlas of Union County, Indiana, to which are added various general maps, history, statistics ... Chicago, J.H. Beers & co., 1884.
75,₍12₎ p. incl.illus.,ports.,maps. 44cm.

"History of Union County, Indiana, by Frank E. Weakley."

NB 0252048 MnH OOxM CtY DLC

---

f912.77296 Beers (J. H.) & Co.
B39a Atlas of Warren Co., Indiana, to which are added various general maps, history, statistics, illustrations, &c. &c. &c. Chicago, 1877.
61p. illus., ports., col.maps. 46cm.

1. Warren Co., Ind.--Maps. 2. Real property --Warren Co., Ind.--Maps.

NB 0252049 IU NHi InU In IU ICHi

Figure 5-4. Entries from the *National Union Catalog.*

However, subject headings are not always the perfect means to learn about titles on a particular topic. Sometimes, especially for genealogical titles, a library will not include every possible subject heading for a given work. In other instances a particular subject heading may, of necessity, be so broad that it encompasses an extremely large—and therefore cumbersome—number of titles. There may also be more than one acceptable subject heading for a particular topic, so works on the same subject may not share the same subject heading. Nor should one necessarily expect to find the same level of cataloging or the same subject heading practices and conventions within the same institution. Despite the standardization of Library of Congress subject headings, and the fact that the same cataloging rules are followed throughout most of the Anglo-American library world, there is still room for a fair amount of discretion on the part of the individual cataloger.

With the computerization of library catalogs, new possibilities have arisen which can improve subject access beyond the subject heading, helping to overcome some of the problems encountered in subject heading use. Although the particulars vary from one system to another, a computerized catalog generally enables the user to isolate and view all of the catalog records in a given system which contain a particular word, whether that word appears in a cataloging note or within the subject heading, author, or title. It is also possible (usually) to narrow such a search to a particular word that appears only in a particular part of the catalog record, such as the title.

A few examples will illustrate how such a word search, also referred to as a *key word search*, can be helpful to the genealogist. Although the majority of compiled genealogies focus on one particular family surname (often all the descents from a particular ancestral couple), many also cover "allied" families. Thus are found works such as the following, written by Alfred Stokes Andrews: *The Andrews, Clapp, Stokes, Wright, Van Cleve Genealogies: Compiled with Ainsworth, Black, Crowe, Dickey, Elston, Garibaldi, Heller, Patterson, Ross, Scott, Sanford, Urbine and Wilson Family Connections* (1985). In most libraries it would be unusual to find a subject heading assigned for each of the surnames in this title. Subject headings for each of the first three or four surnames might be the best one could hope for. However, in an online computer catalog, a word search within title for "Urbine," for example, would call up this title for the researcher interested in Urbines; a subject heading search would probably not have alerted the catalog user to the work. Of course, a search for "Black" (the genealogy also treats the Black surname) would not have as useful a result, because, in addition to this particular genealogy, any other book with the word *black* in the title would also be called up.

An important outgrowth of the key word search capacity is the *Boolean* search. Along with the key word search, the Boolean search capacity is also available in many online catalogs. Boolean logic, the logic of sets, is often encountered in high school algebra classes and is perhaps best recalled by memories of intersecting circles known as Venn diagrams. For those who have wondered whether these lessons would ever have any practical ap-

MS 67–1730

Tyson family.

Papers, 1803–1950. ca. 50 items and 28 v.

In Maryland Historical Society Library (981)

In part, transcripts.

Letter books (1803–62) of Matthew Smith; diary (1888), journals, account book, and exercise book of Anthony Morris Tyson (1866–1956), lawyer, of Baltimore; diary (1817–18) of Elisha Tyson's tour of Europe with advice of Evan Thomas, Jr., on the tour; diary (1869–70) of Catherine W. Smith; scrapbooks; genealogical data on the Tyson family; notes on the Baltimore fire of 1904; and business and personal papers of Matthew Smith and members of the Smith and Tyson families.

Gift of the estate of Anthony Morris Tyson, 1956.

MS 67–2118

Hodges, Bob Alex, 1869–1938.

Papers, 1906–38. ca. 3 ft.

In Trinity University Library (San Antonio, Tex.)

Correspondence and other papers collected by Hodges as chairman of the Historical Society of the Synod of Texas, Presbyterian Church in the U. S. A. Includes correspondence relating to the Cumberland Presbyterian Church in Texas prior to 1906.

Open to investigators under restrictions accepted by the library.

Deposited by the Hodges family.

MS 67–2119

Presbyterian Church in the U. S. A.

Texas records, 1842–1964. ca. 31 ft.

In Trinity University Library (San Antonio, Tex.)

Correspondence, reports, minutes, property records, and financial records of the Dallas, Paris, Trinity, and Texas Presbyteries, and minutes, account books, membership lists, and baptism and death records of local Presbyterian churches in Texas. Includes material relating to the Cumberland Presbyterian Church in Texas before its merger in 1906 with the Presbyterian Church in the U. S. A.

Deposited by the Stated Clerk of Trinity Presbytery and other local presbyteries and churches.

Open to investigators under restrictions accepted by the library.

MS 67–2122

Pease, Charles Elliot, 1833–1886.

Papers, 1854–82. ca. 100 items.

In Union College Library (Schenectady, N. Y.)

Union Army soldier. Correspondence and military papers relating to Pease's service in the Civil War, bills and reports (1855–56) as a student of Union College, and other personal papers. Includes an index (1863) of the States' regiments and commanding officers in the Army of the Potomac, and Pease's account of preliminaries to General Lee's surrender.

Figure 5-5. Entries from the *National Union Catalog of Manuscript Collections.*

plication, the time has now come! Boolean searches bestow a greater precision to key word searching on the computer catalog by allowing one to call up catalog entries containing not just one but two or more specified words. A few illustrations may help the reader to understand the Boolean search function and to appreciate the advantages it offers.

Return to the genealogy title just considered. While a key word search for "Urbine" would easily have isolated this particular work as one which contained genealogical information on Urbines, a key word search for "Black" would have pulled up this title along with probably many tens or even hundreds of other titles that did not pertain to genealogy but which did contain the word *black*. To refine this search using a Boolean function, one would want to call up all of the titles which contain the word *black* but which also contain another word that would probably be found in the catalog record for a genealogy. The most obvious word that comes to mind is *family;* any genealogy will contain that word in at least some—if not all—of its subject headings. In an online system, one would place a command asking the computer to call up all of the catalog records which contained both the word *black* and the word *family,* thereby weeding out most of the titles not concerned with genealogy. When this search was made on the computer catalog of a major research library, the key word search for "black" in all fields of the cataloging records came up with a total of 557 records, but a Boolean search of *black* and *family* came up with only nineteen titles which matched the revised search requirements—one of the titles being the genealogy cited above. This Boolean search could be expressed as follows: "black and family"; it is illustrated in figure 5-6.

Another example may be useful. Church records are often important sources for genealogical information. Assume that a researcher is interested in Chicago Lutheran church records and that a library in which she is conducting research holds the microfilmed sacramental registers of several Chicago Lutheran churches but has assigned various subject headings to them; no one subject heading is common to them all. Possibilities are: "Chicago—Church history," "Church records and registers—Illinois—Chicago," and even the more basic "Chicago—Genealogy." If only one of these subject headings was consulted, the researcher would miss the records of one or more of the churches. A Boolean search command of "Chicago and Lutheran" might be the only command that would call up cataloging records for all the sacramental records of interest. Of course, the results of the search would also include any histories of Chicago Lutheran churches, but their inclusion would probably be more an advantage than not.

The Boolean search also can improve on an unclear memory. Perhaps a researcher has a vague recollection of an index to early Ohio wills compiled by someone named Bell. He consults the computer catalog at a major research library and finds that there are almost one hundred author entries for people named Bell. The alternative, searching under the subject heading "Ohio—Genealogy," yields forty titles to check—not a great many, but still time consuming. Possessing a proper respect for his time, the researcher then decides to undertake the following Boolean search: "bell and wills." If anyone named Bell has written a book about wills, this search will pinpoint it, thus saving the time of going through all the entries for "Ohio—genealogy" or checking the works of the hundred Bell authors. Not surprisingly, only one work qualifies under the parameters of this search command: *Ohio Wills and Estates to 1850: An Index,* by Carol Willsey Bell.

Rather than narrowing the search field, the Boolean search is sometimes used to expand it. This is the other side of the Boolean search technique, although it is probably not used as frequently. In such a search one would want to see all catalog entries containing either one word or another word, and not limited to containing both, as was the case in the previous illustrations.

Again, one of the more obvious applications for this function would arise in a search for genealogies treating allied families. Assume that a researcher is looking for genealogies concerned with a Kerns family, in which the spelling "Kearns" sometimes predominates. A subject heading search for "Kerns family" or a key word search for "Kerns" in the title would pick up most of the genealogies that might be useful. But what if there is a genealogy which mentions twenty allied families in the title—one of them being Kearns? Because it is one of twenty allied families, the Kearns family in this title is not likely to earn a subject heading. Further, because it is not spelled in the more common fashion, it will not be picked up in a key word search for "Kerns." However, the Boolean search within title of "Kerns or Kearns" would work in this instance, because the researcher would be asking for titles that contain *either* Kerns or Kearns. Note the use of the word *or* instead of *and.* If the word *and* was used, the only titles that would qualify would have to contain *both* spelling variations.

Another form of Boolean searching allows the researcher to exclude some of the "hits" retrieved from one key word. Suppose a researcher working on the Winslow family in the southern states wanted to look for Winslow family histories, but wanted to exclude any that dealt with the large Massachusetts family. A search request for "Winslow not Massachusetts" would be the proper way to seek a more limited return.

The three words, *and, or,* and *not* used to connect the search terms are called Boolean *operators* and are used in a variety of computerized search programs for catalogs, bibliographies, and other databases. Additional operators are sometimes used for highly sophisticated searches, but 90 percent or more of the searches most researchers need can be easily made with just those three operators. Figure 5-6 uses Venn diagrams to illustrate how these words retrieve different sets of titles in a catalog with Boolean search capability.

Many computer catalog systems have key word search capacities as well as Boolean search options. Researchers who discover their availability in a system they are using should acquaint themselves with the ways in which such searches are executed within that particular system and how the search techniques may work in the collection they are using. As with most skills, researchers get better at key word searching and Boolean searching with practice; however, utilizing these powerful functions can very soon pay research dividends in the form of more comprehensive searches and much saved time.

CATALOG NETWORKS

Computer catalogs are not limited to those that reflect a single library's holdings. Catalog networks also exist which combine the computerized catalogs of hundreds of libraries into what amounts to a computerized union catalog. In effect, they are to the computer catalog what the printed *National Union Catalog* was to the card catalog. As was the case with the *NUC*, the catalog network is an important bibliographic aid as well as a tool for determining the locations of particular titles. Once the location is determined, the researcher can visit the library hold-

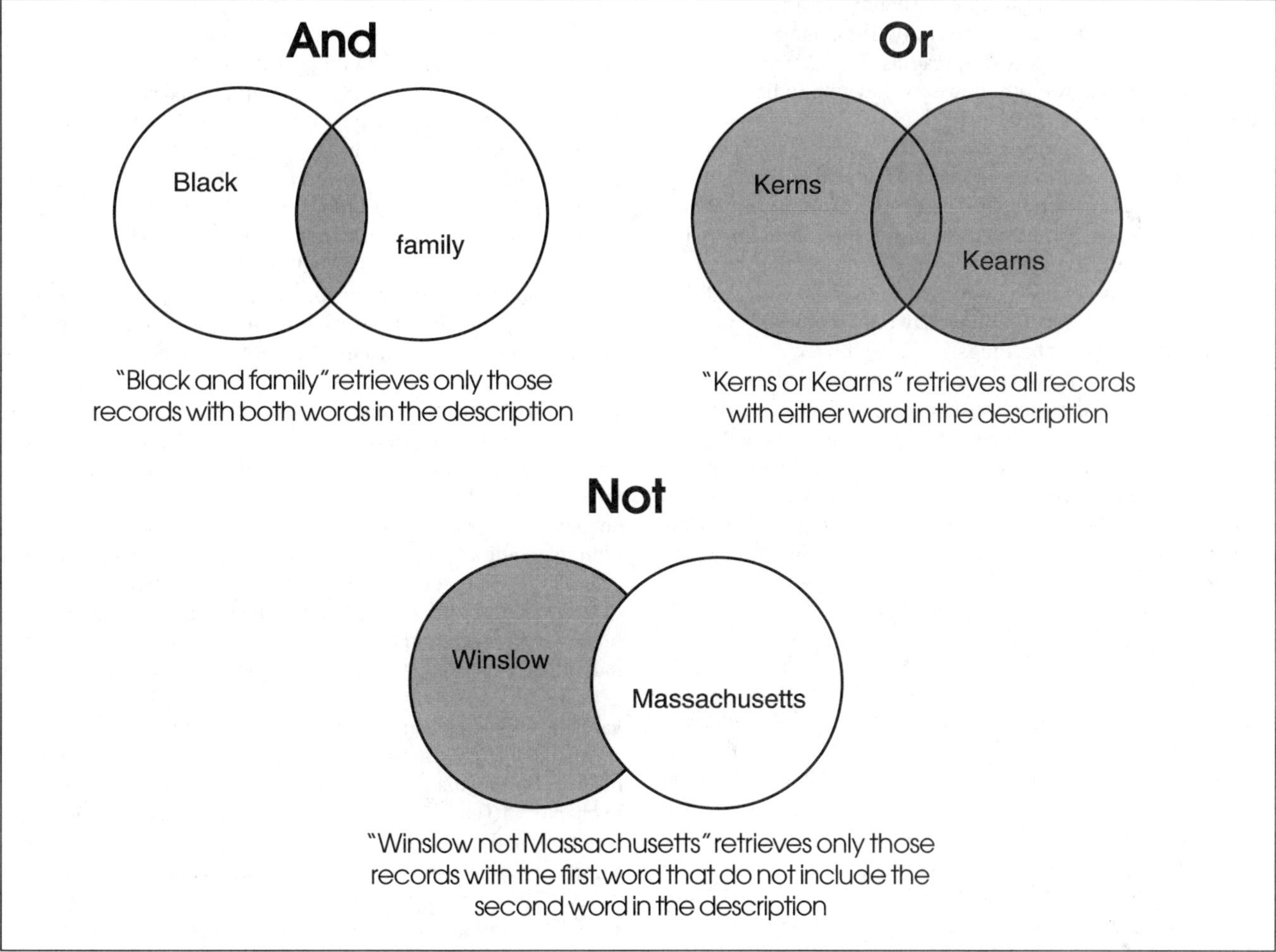
And
Black
family
"Black and family" retrieves only those records with both words in the description
Or
Kerns
Kearns
"Kerns or Kearns" retrieves all records with either word in the description
Not
Winslow
Massachusetts
"Winslow not Massachusetts" retrieves only those records with the first word that do not include the second word in the description

Figure 5-6. How Boolean searches work.

ing a desired item and request photocopies or, in some cases, borrow the book through interlibrary loan. Although many of the books in which genealogists are interested are non-circulating, meaning they must be used on the holding library's premises, there are important exceptions. For example, local histories contained in college and university libraries are often available through interlibrary loan. Despite the considerable advantages of computerized catalog networks, one limitation must be kept in mind: Not all of the participating institutions' holdings will be reflected in a given network because portions of their collections may still be cataloged in card format only.

One public library in particular has displayed an unusual dedication to making genealogical materials available through interlibrary loan. The MidContinent Public Library in Independence, Missouri, has issued a catalog (free as of this writing) of genealogy and local history titles available from it through interlibrary loan.

Online Networks

Most catalog networks are available "online"; that is, the computer catalog information is current as of the moment the request is typed into the computer terminal. This is generally accomplished by having all of the participating libraries connected to a central computer. Whenever one library changes a catalog entry or identifies itself as possessing a particular title, that information is available to all users.

The largest online network is known as the Online Computer Library Center—or, more commonly, as OCLC. When it was established in 1967 as the Ohio College Library Center it was limited to the academic libraries of that state. But it eventually became a far more extensive enterprise and grew to include both academic and non-academic libraries outside of Ohio. Today the network includes more than sixteen thousand participating libraries, including many public libraries.

Until recently, OCLC allowed only author and title searches; however, it is now possible to undertake key word searches as well as Boolean searches. Even so, this capability may not be of immediate relevance to library patrons because, in most libraries, OCLC terminals are not accessible to the public. (They are generally used by catalog or reference librarians.) In addition, OCLC search procedures are somewhat complex from the general public's point of view and are not easily undertaken by non-librarians. However, OCLC recently unveiled new search software called *FirstSearch*, a user-friendly reference service designed to link library patrons with OCLC and other databases; key word and Boolean searches are within its repertoire as well. It is intended for use by library patrons and so may be increasingly available in the public areas of libraries around the United States.

Libraries may belong to other networks as well. There are many state and regional networks which often include smaller libraries that would not normally be part of OCLC. On the other end of the spectrum is RLIN, the Research Libraries Network. Many of the more important university libraries belong to this network, which is not as widespread as OCLC. Some university libraries belong to both; however, few public libraries are affiliated with RLIN.

The world of library networks is a complex one and it is likely to become even more so. In addition, the online catalogs of a number of repositories are becoming available on World Wide Web sites constructed by those institutions, including many overseas libraries. Remember, though, that the catalogs of many libraries have not yet been converted to digital form, and that what the Internet user sees online may only represent a portion of a particular library's holdings.

Several online networks are also available that are not true library catalogs; rather, they are bibliographic and informational databases that can be searched with a personal computer and a modem. Services such as Dialog and BRS offer extensive menus of sources, some of which may prove very valuable for the experienced researcher. While not true "printed sources," they often lead to printed sources, and some of them function in the same role as bibliographies.

CD-ROM Networks

One distinct problem with online catalog networks covering large geographic areas is the cost of telecommunications; it is expensive to keep a computer modem hooked up via telephone lines or other forms of data transmission. One resolution being used by many states is the creation of a catalog network on CD-ROM. CD-ROMs are relatively inexpensive to create and can be updated frequently. In several states, the new cataloging information is collected regularly, then merged with information from other participating libraries and "published" on CD-ROM. In some states, this network is coordinated by a government agency, such as the state library; in other states a private or public institution, such as a university library, leads the effort. In either case, each participating library shares in the costs and benefits of creating a statewide union list of materials.

Many states make these CD-ROMs available to the public for a minimal price—often less than twenty-five dollars. Such network catalogs are a boon to the researcher who is focusing on records for one or two states, as virtually every local history and published genealogical source (for example, marriage abstracts) will find its way onto such a disc. The states known to have such CD-ROM catalogs include Iowa, Kansas, Louisiana, Maine, Mississippi, Missouri, Pennsylvania, Virginia, and Wisconsin. In addition, the Washington Library Network (WLN) produces a CD-ROM covering the collections of many libraries in the northwest (mostly Washington and Oregon). Contact the appropriate state library (listed in the *American Library Directory* [New Providence, N.J.: R. R. Bowker, annual]) for more information about specific catalogs.

COMMERCIAL AND OTHER INSTITUTIONAL CATALOGS

The fields of genealogy and local history constitute a growth industry for many publishers. Microform publishers not only make many manuscript and published sources available on microfiche and microfilm, but their catalogs also provide another means of alerting researchers to the existence of useful materials which may be accessible in a variety of ways and formats. At this writing two micropublishers especially stand out: the American Genealogical Lending Library (AGLL) (Bountiful, Utah) and University Microfilms International (UMI) (Ann Arbor, Michigan). The former produces an impressively hefty looseleaf catalog to which new pages are frequently added. Recently AGLL has also issued its catalog on microfiche and floppy diskette and, beginning in 1997, on CD-ROM. Titles usually constitute manuscript record groups from Federal, state, and local government entities, although the catalog has a growing component of published sources in microform as well (see figure 5-7). It boasts an especially impressive number of National Archives record groups. Most titles are available for purchase or borrowing.

UMI's Genealogy and Local History Series consists primarily of microfiche reproductions of published local history and genealogy titles microfilmed at a number of major repositories throughout the United States. Catalogs for new units in the series are published regularly. At this writing, there are thirty-seven units with matching catalogs. In addition, UMI offers three cumulated catalogs for units one through ten, eleven through twenty, and twenty-one through thirty, although the cataloging and indexing in the second and third cumulations are not as complete as in the individual unit catalogs. In addition to including many well-known genealogies and county and town histories, the UMI series is also valuable for its inclusion of many rare church and other local institutional histories, as well as for the many typescripts of original records. Further discussion of the scope of this collection is found in chapters 16 and 17. UMI also has the largest collection of dissertations and theses covering almost any subject, as well as other significant collections of books available as part of its "books on demand" program.

The National Archives is, of course, another important microform publisher. Its sales are now largely handled by Scholarly Resources (104 Greenhill Avenue, Wilmington, DE 19805-1897). The National Archives has published *Microfilm Resources for Research: A Comprehensive Catalog* (Washington, D.C.: National Archives, 1996), which lists all of its record groups available on microfilm. In addition, descriptive National Archives microfilm catalogs covering record groups on particular subjects are also available. Of particular interest are the catalogs covering African American sources, Native American sources, passenger and immigration lists, genealogical and biographical research, and military sources.

A catalog of a slightly different nature is the lending library catalog of the New England Historic Genealogical Society (NEHGS) in Boston, Massachusetts. As the first genealogical organization to be established in the United States, NEHGS boasts one of the top libraries in the field. One of the advantages of membership is the lending program, whereby books can be borrowed through the mail. The catalog covers both local history and genealogy titles, although it does not represent all of the titles in the library itself. Naturally, a special strength is in New England locales and families. The National Genealogical Society also offers a lending program with an extensive catalog of available books. Both of these collections are briefly described in chapter 16, "Family Histories and Genealogies."

Bookseller Catalogs

Many dealers of antiquarian (out of print) books offer genealogy and local history titles; however, it would be impossible to

Pennsylvania

PENNSYLVANIA –DAUPHIN– CHURCH HISTORY

V172-179, item 2 or **F-5402**, 1 fiche. Historical Sketch of Old Hanover Church, by Thomas H. Robinson. Contains Notes Relating to the Church at Conewago, and the New-Side Graveyard in Lower Paxtang Township, by A. Boyd Hamilton. Publ. 1878. 59p.

PENNSYLVANIA –DAUPHIN– CHURCH RECORDS

Reformed Church Records in Eastern Pennsylvania, comp. by William John Hinke.

V237-119, item 3. 1740-1864, Church Record of the Salem Reformed Church, Vol. 1, Harrisburg, Dauphin County, 1788-1842. Publ. 1940.

V237-119, item 7. 1740-1864, Church Record of the Lykens Valley Lower Church or David's Reformed Church, Killinger, Upper Paxtang Township, Dauphin County, 1774-1844. Publ. 1944.

V237-15, item 8. 1745-1879, Church Record of the Hoffman Reformed Church, Lykens Valley, Dauphin County, 1781-1855.

PENNSYLVANIA –DAUPHIN– HISTORY

V172-172, item 3 or **F-5388**, 6 fiche. Centenary Memorial of the Erection of the County of Dauphin [Pennsylvania], and the Founding of the City of Harrisburg, 1785-1885, ed. by William Henry Egle. Publ. 1886. Index. 397p.

V172-172, item 4 or **F-5389**, 4 fiche. Centennial: The Settlement, Formation and Progress of Dauphin County, Pennsylvania, from 1785 to 1876, by George H. Morgan. Publ. 1877. Index. 239p.

V172-274, item 2 or **F-5804**, 4 fiche. Historic Paxton, Her Days and Her Ways, 1722-1913, by Helen Bruce Wallace. Publ. 1913. 235p.

V172-179, item 3 or **F-5403**, 20 fiche. History of the Counties of Dauphin and Lebanon in the Commonwealth of Pennsylvania: Biographical and Genealogical, by William Henry Egle. Publ. 1883. Index. 300p.

V172-173, item 2 or **F-5391**, 8 fiche. The History and Topography of Dauphin, Cumberland, Franklin, Bedford, Adams, and Perry Counties: Containing a Brief History of the First Settlers, Notices of the Leading Events, Incidents, and Interesting Facts, comp. by I. Daniel Rupp. Publ. 1846. Index. 606p.

V172-179, item 1 or **F-6066**, 3 fiche. Welcome Home Celebration to World War II Veterans of East Hanover, West Hanover and Lower Paxtown Townships, Saturday, August 3, 1946, by the Robert H. Hoke Post 272 American Legion. Publ. 1946. Unpaged.

History of Dauphin County, Pennsylvania, with Genealogical Memoirs, by Luther Reily Kelker. Publ. 1907.

V172-178, item 1 or **F-5399**, 8 fiche. Vol. 1, Index in Vol. 2, 488p.

V172-178, item 2 or **F-5400**, 10 fiche. Vol. 2, Index. 490-1136p.

V172-178, item 3 or **F-5401**, 13 fiche. Vol. 3, Genealogical volume. Index. 727p.

PENNSYLVANIA –DAUPHIN– MAPS

V172-172, item 5 or **F-6071**, 2 fiche. Index to Combination Atlas Map of Dauphin County, Pennsylvania, comp. from personal examinations and surveys by Everts and Stewart, by Beulah Mohart Scott. Map orig. publ. in 1875. Publ. 1972. 65p.

PENNSYLVANIA –DELAWARE– CENSUS

M32-38 1800 Census: Crawford, Cumberland, Delaware, Fayette, and Franklin Counties

M252-47 1810 Census: Chester, Clearfield, Crawford, and Delaware Counties

M33-103 1820 Census: Delaware and Fayette Counties

M19-150 1830 Census: Cumberland and Delaware Counties

M704-457 1840 Census: Delaware County

M432-776 1850 Census: Delaware and Elk Counties

M653-1105 1860 Census: Delaware County

M593-1336 1870 Census: Delaware County (part)

M593-1337 1870 Census: Delaware County (part)

T9-1125 1880 Census: Dauphin (cont 119/15 - end), Elk, and Delaware (begin - 12/6) Counties

T9-1126 1880 Census: Delaware (cont 12/7 - end) County

M123-81 1890 Veteran's Census: Chester, Delaware, Lancaster, and York Counties

T623-1404 1900 Census: Dauphin (EDs 105-end) and Delaware (EDs 137-155) Counties

T623-1405 1900 Census: Delaware County (EDs 156-178, and ED 179 [part], sheets 1-17)

T623-1406 1900 Census: Delaware (ED 179 [part], sheet 18-end) and Elk (EDs 29-40 [part], sheet 2) Counties

T624-1338 1910 Census: Dauphin (EDs 115-130, 132-134) and Delaware (EDs 91-103, 106-108) Counties

T624-1339 1910 Census: Delaware County (EDs 104, 105, 109-138, 140-142)

T624-1340 1910 Census: Delaware County (EDs 139, 143-168, 170, 171)

T625-1560 1920 Census: Dauphin (EDs 131-141, 145, 146, 149-153) and Delaware (EDs 111-115, 151-154, 217, 155-161, 165) Counties

T625-1561 1920 Census: Delaware County (EDs 116-149)

T625-1562 1920 Census: Delaware County (EDs 162-164, 166-171, 218, 173-196, 199)

T625-1563 1920 Census: Delaware (EDs 197, 198, 200-205, 172, 206-215) and Elk (EDs 1-17) Counties

PENNSYLVANIA –DELAWARE– CHURCH HISTORY

V172-289, item 1 or **F-5658**, 6 fiche. The History of Old St David's Church, Radnor, Delaware County, Pennsylvania, by Henry Pleasants. Publ. 1915. 363p.

V172-264, item 8 or **F-5818**, 1 fiche. Proceedings, Friends' Meeting House, Darby, Pennsylvania, Centennial Anniversary, 1805-1905. 42p.

PENNSYLVANIA –DELAWARE– HISTORY

V172-177, item 3 or **F-5398**, 11 fiche. Biographical and Historical Cyclopedia of Delaware County, Pennsylvania, Comprising a Historical Sketch of the County, Together with Nearly Four Hundred Biographical Sketches of the Prominent Men and Families of the County, by Samuel T. Wiley. Rev. and ed. by Winfield Scott Garner. Publ. 1894. Index. 500p.

V172-265, item 1 or **F-5819**, 10 fiche. Chester and Its Vicinity, Delaware County, Pennsylvania with Genealogical Sketches of Some Old Families, by John Hill Martin. Publ. 1877. Index. 530p.

V172-174, item 1 or **F-5392**, 19 fiche. History of Delaware County, Pennsylvania, by Henry Graham Ashmead. Contains biographical sketches. Publ. 1884. Index. 767p.

V172-177, item 4 or **F-6069**, 2 fiche. Index to History of Delaware County, Pennsylvania, [Ashmead, 1884], as reprinted by the Concord Township Historical Society, 1768, by Hilda Chance. Publ. 1970. 179p.

SW16-91, item W. Village Record, or Chester and Delaware Federalist, comp. by Elizabeth A. Floyd. Westchester, Pennsylvania. 30p. of xeroxed copies of newspaper clippings, loaned by Elizabeth A. Floyd. Publ. 1818-24. Index.

67

Figure 5-7. Page from the catalog of the American Genealogical Lending Library.

list all of the dealers whose catalogs have at one time or another dealt with these subject areas. Even so, one dealer deserves mention because of a well-established specialization in the field: Tuttle Antiquarian Books of Rutland, Vermont, regularly issues a substantial genealogy and local history catalog.

There are also many U.S. firms that publish both original works and reprints in genealogy and local history. They are not enumerated here; most of the major ones are listed in appendix C. They issue complete catalogs of their offerings annually or even on a semiannual or quarterly basis.

Much important material is also published by individuals and by local genealogical and historical societies; it is often more difficult to learn about these less commercially ambitious offerings. One serial work in particular that will help keep track of new publications, whether issued by genealogical societies or some of the publishing firms, is *Genealogical and Local History Books in Print*, 5th ed., 4 vols. (Baltimore: Genealogical Publishing Co., 1996–97), currently compiled by Marian Hoffman. (Earlier editions were compiled by Netti Schreiner-Yantis.) Its fourth edition was published in 1985; supplements appeared in 1990 and 1992. The first volume of the fifth edition appeared in 1996. Important as this work is, it cannot be comprehensive because inclusion depends on the submissions of publishers. Even so, given the fact that the vast majority of genealogy and local history publications do not appear in *Books in Print*, this reference work meets a clear need.

Inventories and Descriptions of Manuscript Collections

Much important research material remains in manuscript form. It is therefore important for the genealogist to be familiar with the ways in which manuscript collections are organized and described. Archivists create inventories for manuscript holdings, organizing them by the individual or organization that created them and perhaps according to record type. Critical to the inventory is the size of the manuscript collection, which may be measured in terms of cubic feet or enumerated by individual sheets or ledgers. The level of description and the strategies for organization can vary considerably, depending on the manuscript collection and the inclination of the archivist. One significant inventory of manuscript collections is the *National Union Catalog of Manuscript Collections* (described earlier).

Many important inventories and manuscript collection descriptions have been published, although the documents they describe have not found their way into print. The Work Projects Administration, through the Historical Records Survey, sponsored the inventorying of many local records between 1935 and 1943. The inventories which resulted were published in limited editions, and they are often difficult to locate. Although the existence and location of a record group from forty to fifty years ago is not a sure predictor of its survival and location today, the Work Projects Administration inventories can nevertheless alert researchers to records of interest and perhaps assist in finding them. The *Checklist of Historical Records Survey Publications* (1943; reprint; Baltimore: Genealogical Publishing Co., 1969), by Sargent B. Child and Dorothy P. Holmes, will be helpful to the researcher who has an interest in these inventories. Of particular interest to the genealogist are the lists of inventories of county, municipal, and town records.

Aside from the Historical Records Survey publications, there are other published inventories and descriptions of manuscript collections. A particularly noteworthy example is found in connection with the Lyman C. Draper papers, which are held at the State Historical Society of Wisconsin and are also available on microfilm. An extensive collection of original documents, transcribed reminiscences, and other materials important to the historical and genealogical study of the trans-Appalachian frontier, the papers of Lyman Draper (1815–1891) provide information available nowhere else. Critical to the effective use of this collection is the *Guide to the Draper Manuscripts* (Madison: State Historical Society of Wisconsin, 1983), by Josephine Harper. The usefulness of this aid is considerably enhanced by its indexing.

Many inventories exist only as typescripts at the institution with the collection. The *National Inventory of Documentary Sources in the United States* (*NIDS*) (Teaneck, N.J.: Chadwyck-Healey, 1983–) is a collection of published and unpublished finding aids from hundreds of institutions throughout the United States. *NIDS* consists of microfiche copies of the actual inventories, finding aids, and/or indexes to the manuscript collections. With the copy of an inventory readily available at dozens of research libraries, researchers can learn enough about a collection to determine if it would be useful to consult in order to solve a given problem. *NIDS* is divided into four parts: (1) Federal records, including the National Archives, presidential libraries, and the Smithsonian Institution; (2) Manuscript Division of the Library of Congress; (3) state archives, libraries, and historical societies; and (4) academic and research libraries. The first two parts have printed indexes (or catalogs) to the inventories. Indexes for the other parts are on microfiche. Indexes for all four parts are also available on CD-ROM, along with a similar collection for British collections. A typical entry is the following:

> 631
> Roosevelt, Anna Eleanor, 1884–1962
> Papers, 1884–1964
> Extent: 1,095 ft.
> NUCMC: MS 74-317
> Microfiche: 1.3.134

This entry gives an indication of the type of material in the collection (papers) and the size of the collection. It also provides the entry for *NUCMC*, if available, and the microfiche number in the *NIDS* collection. The microfiche number refers the researcher to the inventory (microfiche 134 of the third repository in part 1).

Descriptions of Institutional Holdings

Although not catalogs or bibliographies *per se,* descriptions of the holdings of particular institutions fulfill to some degree the same functions as catalogs and bibliographies. The researcher who plans to visit an archive or library should always try to determine whether or not such a description is available. Such a description may be available from the institution itself or through a commercial publisher, although in some instances the only copy may be on site at the research facility. Such works can also alert one to the existence of particular titles or collections of interest at a given institution and thus actually prompt a visit or inquiry.

As already noted, the National Archives is critical to genealogical research in the United States. A general overview of its resources is found in Frank B. Evans's *Guide to the National Archives of the United States* (Washington, D.C.: National Archives, 1987), although the genealogist will especially benefit from the subject-oriented *Guide to Genealogical Research in the National Archives,* rev. ed. (Washington, D.C.: National Archives Trust Fund Board, 1985). In addition, the holdings of the National Archives' regional archives are thoroughly covered in *The Archives: A Guide to the National Archives Field Branches* (Salt Lake City: Ancestry, 1988), by Loretto Dennis Szucs and Sandra Hargreaves Luebking.

Ancestry Incorporated has also published important contributions in this genre, among them *The Library of Congress: A Guide to Genealogical and Historical Research* (Salt Lake City: Ancestry, 1990), by James C. Neagles; *The Library: A Guide to the LDS Family History Library* (Salt Lake City: Ancestry, 1988), by Johni Cerny and Wendy Elliott; and *Guide to Local and Family History at the Newberry Library* (Salt Lake City: Ancestry, 1987), by Peggy Tuck Sinko.

CONCLUSION

A good researcher is recognizable not only by the way in which she uses and interprets sources, but also by her ability to locate and access those sources in the first place. Genealogy and local history researchers face a growing array of forums and media in which to discover research sources and their locations. In this environment, bibliographies and catalogs, although always critical to research, become even more important as the gateways to information contained in a proliferation of printed, microform, manuscript, and even electronic formats. There will never be a time when every document or publication which could conceivably assist in a research project can be accessed in a single location; however, the means to learn about research sources has increased greatly over the last two decades, and to take adequate advantage of these opportunities the genealogist needs to be familiar with the organization, purpose, and terminology of bibliographies and catalogs. Remember that research is not only the analysis of source materials; it also includes the process of discovering them. A particular library may not contain the answers to every research question, but through the use of bibliographies and catalogs the researcher may be able to discover where to obtain the answers.

BIBLIOGRAPHY

Reference Works

Major bibliographies, catalogs, and reference works not discussed elsewhere in *Printed Sources*:

American Library Directory. New Providence, N.J.: R. R. Bowker, annual.

Balay, Robert, ed. *Guide to Reference Books.* 11th ed. Chicago: American Library Association, 1996.

Besterman, Theodore. *World Bibliography of Bibliographies.* 4th ed. Lausanne, Switzerland: Societas Bibliographica, 1965–66.

Bibliographic Index. New York: H. W. Wilson, 1937–. Issued periodically.

Books in Print. New York: R. R. Bowker, annual.

Catalogue of the Manuscript Collections of the American Antiquarian Society. 4 vols. Boston: G. K. Hall, 1979.

Child, Sargent B., and Dorothy P. Holmes. *Checklist of Historical Records Survey Publications.* 1943. Reprint. Baltimore: Genealogical Publishing Co., 1969.

Cumulative Book Index. New York: H. W. Wilson, 1898–.

Family History Library Catalog. Salt Lake City: Church of Jesus Christ of Latter-day Saints, annual.

Filby, P. William. *American and British Genealogy and Heraldry: A Selected List of Books.* 3rd ed. Boston: New England Historic Genealogical Society, 1983. Supplement, 1987.

Hoffman, Marian. *Genealogical and Local History Books in Print.* 5th ed. 4 vols. Baltimore: Genealogical Publishing Co., 1996–97.

Library of Congress. *Library of Congress Subject Headings.* 19th ed. 2 vols. Washington, D.C.: Library of Congress, 1996.

Meyerink, Kory L. *Genealogical Publications: A List of 50,000 Sources from the Library of Congress.* CD-ROM. Salt Lake City: Ancestry, 1997.

National Archives and Records Administration. *Microfilm Resources for Research: A Comprehensive Catalog.* Washington, D.C.: National Archives, 1996.

National Inventory of Documentary Sources in the United States (NIDS). Teaneck, N.J.: Chadwyk-Healey, 1983–.

National Union Catalog. 754 vols. London: Mansell, 1968–81. Pre-1956 imprints, with supplementary series for 1956–67, 1968–72, and 1973–77.

National Union Catalog of Manuscript Collections. Washington, D.C.: Library of Congress, 1962–. Annual. Partial index in *Index to Personal Names in the National Union Catalog of Manuscript Collections 1959–1984.* Alexandria, Va.: Chadwyck-Healey, 1988.

Index to Subjects and Corporate Names in the National Union Catalog of Manuscript Collections 1959–1984. Alexandria, Va.: Chadwyck-Healey, 1994.

Nelson, Bonnie R. *Guide to Published Library Catalogs.* Metuchen, N.J: Scarecrow, 1992.

Schreiner-Yantis, Netti. *Genealogical and Local History Books in Print.* 4th ed. Springfield, Va.: Genealogical Books in Print, 1985–90. Supplements 1990, 1992.

Toomey, Alice F. *A World Bibliography of Bibliographies, 1964–1974.* Totowa, N.J.: Rowman and Littlefield, 1977.

Guides to Repositories

Cerny, Johni, and Wendy Elliott. *The Library: A Guide to the LDS Family History Library.* Salt Lake City: Ancestry, 1988.

Evans, Frank B. *Guide to the National Archives of the United States.* Washington, D.C.: National Archives Trust Fund Board, 1985.

Guide to Genealogical Research in the National Archives. Rev. ed. Washington, D.C.: National Archives, 1985.

Harper, Josephine. *Guide to the Draper Manuscripts.* Madison: State Historical Society of Wisconsin, 1983.

Neagles, James C. *The Library of Congress: A Guide to Genealogical and Historical Research.* Salt Lake City: Ancestry, 1990.

Sinko, Peggy Tuck. *Guide to Local and Family History at the Newberry Library.* Salt Lake City: Ancestry, 1987.

Szucs, Loretto, and Sandra Luebking. *The Archives: A Guide to the National Archives Field Branches.* Salt Lake City: Ancestry, 1988.

PUBLISHED INDEXES OVERVIEW

Key Concepts in This Chapter

- *Indexes* are designed to provide additional access to information in the source itself.
- *Single-source indexes* are the most common. They are often "back-of-the-book" indexes.
- *Collective (multiple source) indexes* provide access to many similar sources, but they are seldom "every-name" indexes.
- A *master index* is a collective index that attempts to provide comprehensive coverage for its topic.
- *Nontraditional indexe*s include abstracts and library catalogs.
- Alphabetical arrangement is not as simple as it seems.
- Each indexer has a bias that determines the scope and depth of the index.
- No index is completely comprehensive or absolutely correct.
- The accuracy of an index is determined by both the source itself and the ability of the indexer(s).
- A key strategy for using an index is to understand the purpose of both the source and the index itself.
- A computer database can also serve as a type of index.
- Specific indexes are discussed thoroughly in other chapters of *Printed Sources.*

Key Sources in This Chapter

- *FamilySearch*™
- *An Index to Some of the Family Records of the Southern States*
- *An Index to some of the Bibles and Family Records of the United States*
- Vital record indexes
- Land record indexes
- Periodical indexes

6

PUBLISHED INDEXES

Kip Sperry

The labour and patience, the judgement and penetration which are required to make a good index, is only known to those who have gone through this most painful, but least praised part of a publication.

William Oldys (1696–1761)

Access to information. That is why indexes exist: to help researchers find information faster and easier. And they work; but they work much better when the researcher knows how to use them effectively. Today there are thousands of indexes available for American genealogists; they are housed in various libraries throughout the United States and elsewhere. These tools can indeed help researchers, but they are not as simple as they at first appear.

Some genealogical researchers view an index as merely an expanded table of contents. To others, the ideal index is a complete personal name index with every reference to names cited and appropriate page numbers and references if the name appears more than once on a page. Researchers quickly learn that some indexes are more reliable than others. Indexing is a multifaceted process, and understanding how indexes are created and the indexing process will enhance understanding of the effort involved in creating indexes and how to properly use them.

Genealogical indexes cover many different localities, subjects, and time periods. Knowing what genealogical indexes are available and how to effectively use them, as well as their strengths and limitations, will make research more productive. This chapter provides an overview of published genealogical indexes, describing key concepts and principles that will help all users understand indexes, and it suggests some strategies for using indexes effectively. This chapter is not intended to identify all of the major genealogical indexes one might want to use, for these indexes are described throughout *Printed Sources;* it does, however, identify some of the major indexes as it describes how to effectively use the wide variety of genealogical indexes.

There are different kinds of indexes and different arrangements within this variety. Indexes also vary according to what they were designed to include—and, of course, in their accuracy. Once these concepts are understood, the researcher needs to learn various strategies for effective use of indexes as well as how and where to locate indexes. Each of these topics is covered in this chapter, as is an overview of computer databases as indexes and a brief discussion of how these concepts apply to indexes for original and compiled sources. Lastly, this chapter identifies some current references to indexing methodology.

KINDS OF INDEXES

There are two kinds of genealogical indexes: (1) those which index only a single source, such as a county history or the 1850 census for a state, and (2) those which cite references from a large number of (usually) similar sources, such as family histories or passenger lists. In addition, genealogists use a number of "non-traditional" indexes—sources that were not designed as indexes but still point the researcher toward other references. Furthermore, any of these kinds of indexes may appear in one or more of several different formats.

Single-Source Indexes

By far the most common index used by family historians is the kind designed to provide a page number, or some other citation, for a specific piece of information in a single source. Ideally these are "every-name" indexes (meaning they include every personal name mentioned in the source), but often they are not (see the discussion below under "Inclusion").

Generally, single-source indexes are "back-of-the-book" indexes, or they are published separately, often by a different publisher than that of the indexed source. Finding a back-of-the-book index is not difficult (if there *is* an index at the back of the book); more effort is required to determine if a *separate* personal name index is available. Start by searching library catalogs and bibliographies. Examples of separately published indexes that can be found in library catalogs are Lake County (Ohio) Genealogical Society's *Every-Name Index to the History of the Western Reserve* (Painesville, Ohio: Lake County Genealogical Society, 1988) and *Index to the Microfilm Edition of Genealogical Data Relating to Women in the Western Reserve before 1840 (1850)* (Cleveland: Genealogical Committee, Western Reserve Historical Society, 1976). Interestingly, the latter title indexes frame numbers located at the bottom of each microfilmed page (not page numbers).

Sometimes the source itself is quite lengthy, such as the 1870 census of Pennsylvania, or the forty-volume *Genealogical Magazine of New Jersey.* In such cases, a single-source in-

Lawrence. Warfield's Hist. of Anne Arundel and Howard Cos., Md. The Thomas Book, by L. B. Thomas. Va. Co. Records, VI, VII.

Lawson. Va. Hist. Mag., IV, V. Lower Norfolk Co., Va., Antiquary. Middlesex, Va., Par. Reg. Wm. and Mary Quar., VI, XVIII. Va. Co. Records, II, V, VI, VII. Hanson's Old Kent, Md. MSS. Ped. of the Genealogical Assn.

Laydon. Va. Hist. Mag., V.

Ledbetter. Chamberlayne's Bristol Par. Reg.

Leake. Va. Hist. Mag., XI. Wood's Hist. of Albemarle. Wm. and Mary Quar., VI.

Lear. Wm. and Mary Quar., VII, IX. Va. Hist. Mag., XVII.

Leath. Chamberlayne's Bristol Par. Reg.

Lee. Campbell's Spotswood Gen. Campbell's Hist. of Va. Oliver's Carter Family Tree. Hayden's Va. Gen. Meade's Old Fam. and Churches. Richmond Critic, 30th July, 1888. Richmond Standard, I, III, IV. Slaughter's Bristol Par. Southern Bivouac, 1886. Wm. and Mary Quar., I, II, III, IX, X, XI. Va. Hist. Mag., V, VI. Va. Co. Records, I, II, V, VI, VII. Middlesex, Va., Par. Reg. Chamberlayne's Bristol Par. Reg. Of Sceptred Race, by Annah R. Watson. Lee Fam. of Va. and Md., by E. C. Mead, 1868. New Eng. Genl. and Hist. Reg., XXVI. Lee of Va., by Cassius F. Lee and J. Packard, 1872. Lee of Va., by J. Henry Lea, 1892. Lee of Eng. and Va., by the Rev. Frederick G. Lee, London, 1884. Some Notable Families of America, by Annah W. Watson, 1898. Lee of Va., by Edmund J. Lee, 1895.

Leftwich. Meade's Old Fam. and Churches. Va. Co. Records, V. Leftwich Gen. Chart, drawn by W. H. Abbott, 1903.

Legare. Richmond Standard, II. Legare Fam., by Mrs. E. C. K. Fludd, 1886.

Le Grand. Wm. and Mary Quar., IX.

Leigh. Richmond Standard, II, III, IV. Habersham Hist. Coll. of Ga., I.

Leiper. Campbell's Spotswood Gen. Richmond Standard, V. Founder of Anne Arundel Co., by J. D. Warfield. Thomas Fam. of Md., by L. B. Thomas.

Lemon. The Lemon Family of Va. and Illinois, by F. B. Lemon, 1898.

Figure 6-1. From *A Key to Southern Pedigrees,* edited by William Armstrong Crozier, 2nd ed. (Baltimore: Southern Book Co., 1953), page 44. This is an example of an early surname index.

dex may comprise several volumes. When an index spans several volumes, there must be a "break" between volumes. Usually the break is accomplished by splitting the alphabet, so the three volumes of a three-volume index might include *A* through *H, I* through *O,* and *P* through *Z,* respectively. A geographic split may be used, as in a state census index that splits the state into east, central, and west regions. When the source itself, such as a genealogical periodical, has several volumes, the cumulative index might be divided according to the volumes it covers, such as volumes 1 through 10, 11 through 20, 21 through 30, and so forth.

Some multi-volume sources lack a single, comprehensive index. Rather, the various volumes are indexed separately, usually at the end of the volume. Such is often the case when the source was created over a number of years, as with genealogical periodicals (where an annual index is common) or a series, such as the forty-two-volume *Documents Relating to the Colonial History of the State of New Jersey,* first series (Newark, N.J.: Daily Journal Establishment, 1880–).

Multiple Indexes in a Single Source. Personal names are certainly not the only topic of indexes (see below under "Inclusion"). Indexers often include several different indexes for a single source. Genealogical reference guides often contain personal name, geographic place names, author, title, and other indexes that can be very valuable in identifying reference sources. An excellent example of this type is the three-volume *UMI Guide to Family and Local Histories* (described in chapter 16, "Family Histories and Genealogies"). This major reference source is found in many large libraries; the titles identified in it are available on microfiche at major libraries throughout the United States. This multi-volume collection lists thousands of genealogies, local histories, primary source materials (printed vital records), and genealogical and local history serials (periodicals). Vol. 1, for example, includes author (arranged by surname), title, subject (for example, Baptists—Maryland), geographic, and personal name (surname and family name) indexes. Entries in the name index include the principal work (for example, Loomis family), variant spellings for a principal work (surname spelling differences), surnames of families related to the principal family in the work, and complete names of individuals cited on the book's title page (not complete name indexes for each work).

Many family histories also include multiple indexes at the back of the book. Often, they are all name indexes, such as those of all persons descended from the common ancestor, females who married men with the family surname, males who married women with the family surname, and others of the surname not related to the common ancestor.

Collective or Multiple-Source Indexes

As popular as single-source indexes are, another type of index is equally important but often overlooked by family historians: the growing collection of indexes that provide access to multiple sources. Generally, such indexes focus on a common theme or source, such as passenger lists or biographical sketches within a state. In the past, such indexes were composed of card entries (now preserved on microfiche or microfilm) from a library or institution that created the index over a number of years—for example, *The Greenlaw Index of the New England Historic Genealogical Society,* 2 vols. (Boston: G. K. Hall, 1979) (discussed in chapter 16, "Family Histories and Genealogies"). Computer technology has allowed many more such indexes to be created and published, often in multi-volume works.

Few such collective indexes are every-name indexes; the number of entries from what sometimes amounts to hundreds or thousands of sources would make that prohibitively expensive and time consuming. Rather, they seek to index the "subjects" of articles, paragraphs, books, chapters, or other subdivisions in the sources indexed. These subjects are almost always individuals or families. Thus, they are name indexes, but do not expect to find in them the name of every person mentioned in every work indexed. Indeed, earlier works often included only surname entries, not distinguishing between different individuals bearing the same family name (figure 6-1).

Nonetheless, collective indexes provide access to information that may be available in no other guise. In many cases, the sources included are not themselves individually indexed. An excellent example is "Combined Alphabetical Index," an important statewide finding aid to thirty early records series held by the South Carolina Department of Archives and History (Columbia, South Carolina) (available on microfilm from Scholarly Resources, Inc., 104 Greenhill Avenue, Wilmington, DE 19805-1897). This index is arranged alphabetically by personal names and localities. The types of records indexed in it are colonial land records, court records, property sales, fiscal records, revolutionary war records, and others.

The most significant, and most popular, source for North American research is the *International Genealogical Index* (see below under "FamilySearch"). It is, in reality, a collective index. It identifies entries in original and compiled sources from around the world and is the result of thousands of contributors' (indexers') efforts since the 1960s.

Most collective indexes give a reference number or a source abbreviation, along with a page number, after the index entry (figure 6-2). These reference numbers or abbreviations are then listed numerically or alphabetically in a "sources indexed" section at the beginning of the work; this is where the complete bibliographic citation of each title indexed, such as author, title, and publishing information, will usually be found. If the citation is not complete, a library's computer or card catalog may have a full citation. Sometimes librarians or volunteers have written the library call numbers of books in such bibliographic lists—helpful for a particular library; however, the call number for one library's copy of a source is usually not the same as another library's.

Master Indexes. A multiple-source index that attempts to identify and provide comprehensive coverage for all (or the most significant) sources of a particular type is called a *master index* (see again figure 6-2). These have become increasingly popular in recent years. In a master index the number of sources indexed is usually in the thousands, or is at least one hundred or more; thorough coverage of the topic is the intent. Joseph J. Felcone's *Trenton* [New Jersey] *Index* (Princeton, N.J.: Sheffield Press, 1976) indexes only three works, but that gives it fairly complete coverage of the topic. The many statewide indexes to biographical material in local histories discussed in chapter 17 are examples of master indexes; many of them include several hundred sources.

The following comprehensive master indexes are major sources for North American research. They are discussed in the chapters indicated:

- Accelerated Indexing Systems census indexes, 1790 to 1850, on microfiche (chapter 9)
- *Passenger and Immigration Lists Index* (chapter 14)
- Munsell's *Index to American Genealogies* (for pre-1900 publications) (chapter 16)
- *Biography and Genealogy Master Index* (chapter 18)
- *Periodical Source Index* (chapter 19)

```
HANLEY
  William Joseph, b.1891 (cont.)
    Sca 4:238; VanW 2:38
HANLON, Frank E., b.1907. Man 65:323//
    67:318
  James A., b.1867. Sco 2:123-124
  John, 1836-1875. MetN 75:49-50
  John, b.1870. Who 362
  Mrs. John, see Hanlon, Mary Amelia
    (Bonsall) 1837-1915
  John Francis, b.1883. Nk 11:198//14:
    232; Urq 3:337-338
  John Thomas, b.1859. LeeN 6:232
  Joseph J., fl.1899-1900. Harv 550-551
  Mary Amelia (Bonsall) 1837-1915. MetN
    15:109-110
HANLY, Frank J., fl.1867-1889. Els 135
  John J., fl.1897. Vai 131-132 (*123)
HANN, Augustus P., 1856-1887. Mem 3:59-
    61
  Mrs. Carol, fl.1979. MetS *79:9
  Edwin Forrest, 1876-1970. MetS 70:157*
  Mrs. Edwin Forrest, see Hann, Elsie
    (Driesbach) 1880-1976
  Edwin N., fl.1973. MetS *73:5
  Elsie (Driesbach) 1880-1976. MetS 77:
    141-142
  Enos, b.c1835. Hain 118-119
  Izetta (Reeve) 1856-1918. MetS 18:
    341-342
  Jacob, 1782-1867. Mem 3:60
  Peter S., 1857-1929. MedJ 26:416
  Philip H., 1819-1900. Bio 224; Mem 3:
    60; NJL 23:190; Snel 576-577*
  Samuel H., 1854-1918. MetS 19:511*
  Mrs. Samuel H., see Hann, Izetta
    (Reeve) 1856-1918
  Warren D., b.1870. Hes 4:439-440*
  William D., 1823-1905. NJH 77:205-206
HANNA, Charles Augustus, 1863-1950. NJH
    68:273-274; Soc 55:201-202; Who 362-
    363
  John, 1731-1801. Alex 36; Bla 81-82;
    Jer 3:17-18*; McL 141-143
  Mrs. John, see Hanna, Mary (McCrea)
    fl.1762-1789
  John A., d.1805. Alex 211
  John Smedes, b.1834. Spa 53-54
  Mary (McCrea) fl.1762-1789. Str 11
  Sarah B., see Thorn, Sarah B. (Hanna)
    d.1930
  William James, fl.1901-1945. Man 38:
    300-301//42:256-257; Mye 5:872
HANNAH, Charles, 1782-1857. Cus 355;
    MedJ *13:330
```

Figure 6-2. From *A New Jersey Biographical Index,* compiled by Donald Arleigh Sinclair (Baltimore: Genealogical Publishing Co., n.d.). It is both a collective and master index.

Non-Traditional Indexes

In addition to indexes specifically created as such, genealogists often use other sources to serve as indexes. Any source that refers the user to another source is often thought of as an index; the discussions later in this chapter under "Arrangement," "Inclusion," and "Accuracy" pertain to these indexes as well. Also,

Abstracts of Rev. War Pension Files

AARON, William, Rebecca (Rudd), W10287, BLW #67675-160-55, VA, 9 Oct 1832 Franklin Cty GA aged 79 or 80, srv VA Line, m 3 Nov 1829 Franklin Cty GA, wid filed 14 Apr 1857 Whitfield Cty GA, sol died 3rd Nov 1841
AARONS, Abraham, S30813, VA, 29 Nov 1832 Adair Cty KY aged 73, b 17 Mar 1759 Lancaster Cty PA, family moved to Pittsylvania Cty VA in 1771 moved to Greene Cty TN in 1816 thence to Adair Cty KY in 1824
ABBE, Eleazur or Eleazur Abby, BLW #267-100, CT, 13 Mar 1788 Hartford Cty CT filed Quit Claim
Jeduthan or Jeduthan Abbey or Abby, Lucretia Roberts former wid, W22125, CT, srv CT Line, sol filed 28 Mar 1818 Hampton Cty CT, aged 63 in 1820, wid filed 18 Mar 1837, m 36 Mar 1779, sol died 9 Feb 1821 & wid m 2nd a George Roberts of East Hartford CT 19 Mar 1822 who died 2 Oct 1824, a son Edmund Abbey was resident of East Hartford CT in 1837, wid was 81 in 1837
Mason, S32628, CT, srv CT Line, 16 Apr 1818 Hampshire Cty MA, aged 61 in 1820 with wife & 7 children
Nathaniel, Nancy (Moon) Little former wid, W26215, CT, wid filed 6 Jan 1843 Windham Cty CT aged 77, m 20 Sep 1784, sol died 11 Nov 1798 in NY & wid m 2nd Phlemon Little 29 Jun 1799 & he died 13 Jan 1840 sol's sis Anne Fisk wid of Chaplin Fisk aged 87 in 1843 states sol had 4 children
Reuben or Reuben Albe, Joanna, W10346, BLW #40906-160-55, MA, see Reuben Albe
Richard, Lydia, W17197, CT, 1 Oct 1838 Hartford Cty CT aged 74 a son of Richard Abbe a Capt in CT Mil sol m Lydia Stevenson 16 Jan 1783 Chatham CT, sol died 9 Aug 1831 Enfield CT, a son Joshua mentioned
Thomas, S38105, Cont Line & CT Line, 26 Oct 1818 Middleton CT aged 64, enl in Chatham CT, aged 69 ? in 1820 & living with his brother not named, sol died 24 Mar 1826
William or William Abbee, Lydia, W20556, CT & Cont Line, filed 16 Apr 1818 Onondaga Cty NY aged 60, in 1838 wid Lydia was 80, m Lydia Hall daughter of Thos Hall 5 Jun 1777, sol died 6 Aug 1930, family in 1820 wife Lydia, children; Nathan 33, Isabel 22, Lydia 20 & grandchild Eunice Abbee, enl Windham Cty CT
ABBEY, Edward, S34621, Cont & VA Line, 25 May 1829 Simpson Cty MS aged 79, wife Rebecca aged 60 in 1829, sol had removed to MS only a short time before 1829 from GA
Eliphalet, BLW #5391-100-9 Feb 1797 to heirs Jeduthen Abbey, Martha Vibbert, Rebecca Abbey & Sally Bunce, srv Sheldon's Cont Dragoons in CT Line as Pvt
George, S11931, CT, srv in CT Line, 25 May 1838 Hartford Cty CT aged 77, b 15 Jan 1763 Chatham CT
Hezekiah, S21034, CT, srv CT Sea Srv, 25 Jul 1832 Windham Cty CT aged 70 score yrs, b Windham Cty CT Jan 1755, his oldest child b in 1778 name not stated
James or Joseph James Abbey, R-#1, CT, see Joseph James Abbey

Figure 6-3. From White's *Genealogical Abstracts of Revolutionary War Pension Files,* vol. 1 (page 1). Typically, an abstract can be considered a single-source index.

many of the cautions noted below under "Strategies for Using Indexes" should be kept in mind when using such *non-traditional indexes.* One example of such an index is Clarence A. Torrey's *New England Marriages Prior to 1700* (further discussed below under "Indexes for Original Records"). The book version of Torrey's work is not intended to be an index; it simply provides the name of the couple who married and the date and place, if known. The hundreds of sources from which Torrey collected the data are not identified in the book. Torrey's manuscript (on microfilm) must be consulted to learn the source of an entry.

Computer databases are seldom thought of as indexes. However, a database often refers the user to more information in the original (or compiled) records and in such cases functions as an index. Several major examples are discussed below under "Computer Databases as Indexes."

Abstracts. Abstracts of genealogical records serve as indexes and summaries of contents of original documents. Typically, an abstract can be considered a single-source index; of course, abstracts include much more information than just a reference to the original records. Indeed, where the original records are already in a predictable order (such as alphabetical or chronological) or have their own index, the abstractor may not even include the specific page or entry number from the original record. Two excellent examples are Virgil D. White's *Genealogical Abstracts of Revolutionary War Pension Files,* 4 vols. (Waynesboro, Tenn.: National Historical Publishing Co., 1990–92) (see figure 6-3) and *Index to War of 1812 Pension Files,* rev. ed., 2 vols. (Waynesboro, Tenn.: National Historical Publishing Co., 1990–92). Vol. 4 of the revolutionary war set is a complete personal name index to this set. White's military abstracts are monumental genealogical reference tools.

Library Catalogs. Another popular source that often serves as an index is the library catalog. While library catalogs cannot be considered every-name indexes, they often provide a surprisingly large scope. Catalogers are well-trained and often quite thorough in their description of their libraries' holdings; thus, their published catalogs are excellent multiple-source topical (or subject) indexes. Library catalogs usually refer to books, but occasionally (especially in older catalogs) there are entries for chapters or sections within individual books. An excellent example is the *Genealogical Index of the Newberry Library,* 4 vols. (Boston: G. K. Hall, 1960), which provides detailed catalog entries for works published before 1918 (figure 6-4) and is further described in chapter 17, "County and Local Histories."

Published family histories are the subjects of numerous published library catalogs. The major published library catalogs are described in chapter 16, "Family Histories and Genealogies." They include:

- *Family History Library Catalog*
- *Genealogies in the Library of Congress: A Bibliography*
- *Dictionary Catalog of the Local History and Genealogy Division, New York Public Library*
- *DAR Library Catalog*

Index Formats

Indexes are available to genealogists in various formats: in electronic form (as computer indexes or on CD-ROM), as card indexes, book indexes, manuscript (unpublished) indexes, and so

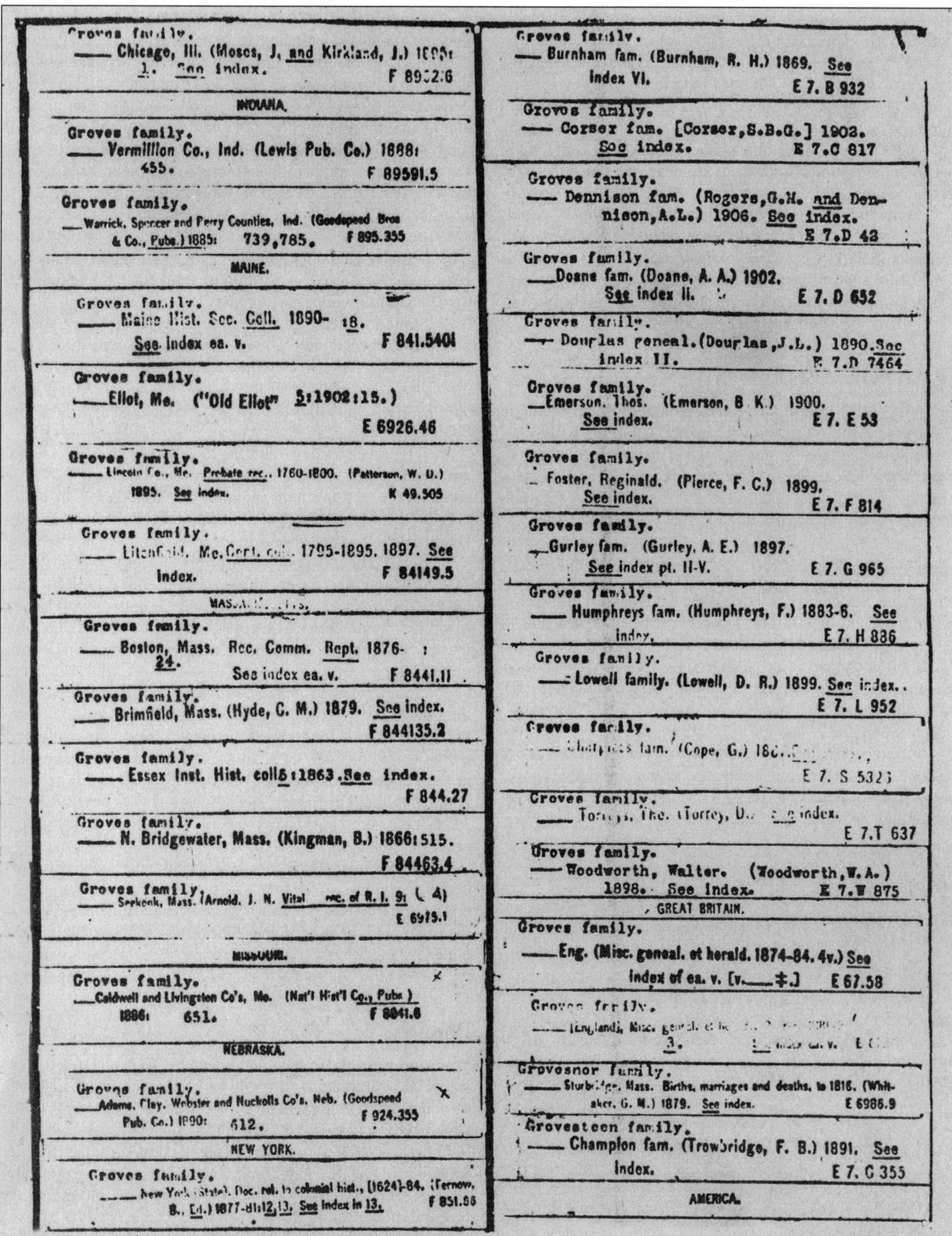

Groves family.
— Chicago, Ill. (Moses, J. and Kirkland, J.) 1895: 1. See index. F 8932.6

INDIANA.

Groves family.
— Vermillion Co., Ind. (Lewis Pub. Co.) 1888: 455. F 89591.5

Groves family.
— Warrick, Spencer and Perry Counties, Ind. (Goodspeed Bros & Co., Pubs.) 1885: 739,785. F 895.355

MAINE.

Groves family.
— Maine Hist. Soc. Coll. 1890- :8. See index ea. v. F 841.5401

Groves family.
— Eliot, Me. ("Old Eliot" 5:1902:15.) E 6926.46

Groves family.
— Lincoln Co., Me. Probate rec., 1760-1800. (Patterson, W. D.) 1895. See index. K 49.505

Groves family.
— Litchfield, Me. Cent. [illegible] 1795-1895. 1897. See index. F 84149.5

MASS[illegible]

Groves family.
— Boston, Mass. Rec. Comm. Rept. 1876- : 24. See index ea. v. F 8441.11

Groves family.
— Brimfield, Mass. (Hyde, C. M.) 1879. See index. F 844135.2

Groves family.
— Essex Inst. Hist. colls 1863. See index. F 844.27

Groves family.
— N. Bridgewater, Mass. (Kingman, B.) 1866: 515. F 84463.4

Groves family.
— Seekonk, Mass. (Arnold, J. N. Vital rec. of R. I. 9: [illegible] 4) E 6975.1

MISSOURI.

Groves family.
— Caldwell and Livingston Co's, Mo. (Nat'l Hist'l Co., Pubs.) 1886: 651. F 8941.6

NEBRASKA.

Groves family.
— Adams, Clay, Webster and Nuckolls Co's, Neb. (Goodspeed Pub. Co.) 1890: 612. F 924.355

NEW YORK.

Groves family.
— New York (State). Doc. rel. to colonial hist., [1624]-84. (Fernow, B., Ed.) 1877-81: 12, 13. See index in 13. F 851.66

Groves family.
— Burnham fam. (Burnham, R. H.) 1869. See index VI. E 7. B 932

Groves family.
— Corser fam. [Corser, S.B.G.] 1902. See index. E 7.C 817

Groves family.
— Dennison fam. (Rogers, G.H. and Dennison, A.L.) 1906. See index. E 7.D 43

Groves family.
— Doane fam. (Doane, A. A.) 1902. See index II. E 7. D 632

Groves family.
— Douglas geneal. (Douglas, J.L.) 1890. See index II. E 7.D 7464

Groves family.
— Emerson, Thos. (Emerson, B. K.) 1900. See index. E 7. E 53

Groves family.
— Foster, Reginald. (Pierce, F. C.) 1899. See index. E 7. F 814

Groves family.
— Gurley fam. (Gurley, A. E.) 1897. See index pt. II-V. E 7. G 965

Groves family.
— Humphreys fam. (Humphreys, F.) 1883-6. See index. E 7. H 886

Groves family.
— Lowell family. (Lowell, D. R.) 1899. See index. E 7. L 952

Groves family.
— [illegible] fam. (Cope, G.) 18[illegible] E 7. S 532[illegible]

Groves family.
— Torrey, Thc. (Torrey, D.) [illegible] index. E 7.T 637

Groves family.
— Woodworth, Walter. (Woodworth, W. A.) 1898. See index. E 7.W 875

GREAT BRITAIN.

Groves family.
— Eng. (Misc. geneal. et herald. 1874-84. 4v.) See index of ea. v. [v.— ‡.] E 67.58

Groves family.
— [illegible] 3. [illegible] ea. v. E [illegible]

Grovesnor family.
— Sturbridge, Mass. Births, marriages and deaths, to 1816. (Whitaker, G. M.) 1879. See index. E 6986.9

Grovesteen family.
— Champion fam. (Trowbridge, F. B.) 1891. See index. E 7. C 355

AMERICA.

Figure 6-4. From the *Genealogical Index of the Newberry Library.* It provides detailed catalog entries for works published before 1918.

forth. Many manuscript and printed indexes are available in microform (microfiche or microfilm) format.

Many genealogical indexes have been microfilmed by the Genealogical Society of Utah (of the Family History Department of The Church of Jesus Christ of Latter-day Saints [LDS church] in Salt Lake City). Sometimes the microfilmed index appears at the beginning of the volume, but usually it appears at the end of the volume. In some cases indexes are found throughout the volume.

Many indexes are available in typescript format, such as those compiled by the National Society, Daughters of the American Revolution (DAR).[1] Many of these indexes are listed in the DAR's published library catalog. Typescript indexes to local records compiled by the DAR and other organizations are available at many local libraries and genealogical societies.

ARRANGEMENT

The arrangement of terms in an index often is given little thought by the user. After all, many users expect an index will be arranged alphabetically; genealogical indexes, however, are not always alphabetical. Even when an index is arranged alphabetically, the indexer must make several decisions about where to file terms.

Alphabetization

From an indexer's perspective, the alphabet is not just the twenty-six letters *A* through *Z*. The indexer must decide whether to place capital letters before lowercase letters, how to handle spaces, numbers, punctuation (hyphens, apostrophes, periods, parentheses), foreign characters, and special characters (such as the ampersand, &). There is no single "correct" way to alphabetize an index.

Indexers usually ignore case and special characters when they alphabetize. However, there are two common ways to handle spaces: letter by letter or word by word. In the former, spaces are ignored and the indexer uses only the letters to arrange the list:

Neville
Newark
Newton
Newville
New Town
New York

With word-by-word filing, each word is treated as an entity; a complete word is filed before the same letter combination that is only part of a word:

Neville
New Town
New York
Newark
Newton
Newville

Most modern computer systems that alphabetize lists treat a space as a letter that files before the letter *A*, giving computer-generated indexes a de facto word-by-word arrangement.

Grammatical articles (a, an, the) are usually ignored when they appear at the beginning of an index entry (such as the title of a book), but they are not ignored when they appear elsewhere in the entry. Foreign language articles (for example, *le* in French or *der* in German) should also be ignored at the beginning of an entry, but if the indexer does not know the language, he or she is likely to include them. Some inexperienced indexers also apply the article rule to prepositions (of, in, by) and ignore them when they start an entry, although this is not the accepted practice.

Names also demand special treatment. How does the indexer treat names beginning with de, Mc, Mac, St., or van? Often they are placed at the beginning of the letter group (Mc before Manning); Mc and Mac are often filed together. Some indexers disregard certain prefixes (de, van).

Some indexers list abbreviations as if they were spelled out, while others do not. Some insist on spelling them out, thus referring to a word that is not really in the source; after all, "Jno" can stand for John or Jonathan. Nicknames can represent another problem: Bill is not always William. "St." can stand for Saint or Street.

Foreign characters (and the diacritical marks with them) are usually ignored by English-language indexers. However, some do present problems, notably the German *ß* (*ss*) (which may be misread as a *B* by an inexperienced indexer) and the Dutch *ÿ*, which sometimes is indexed as *ij* and just as often as *y*.

Some indexers ignore characters or names that are illegible, reasoning that the entry has no value if it cannot be read. Others use blanks (____) to represent the letters they cannot read, hoping the user will recognize the entry from the legible letters. Such entries are usually filed at the beginning of the index (figure 6-5).

Numbers can also create difficulty for the indexer and for the user. Library cataloging rules generally suggest that numbers be filed as if the number were spelled out; thus, 8 (eight) comes before 5 (five). Often, however, indexers place numbers at the beginning of the list, before words beginning with *A*. Numbers should be filed in ascending numerical order (8, 9, 10, 11, 12), but computers sometimes file numbers in digit-by-digit order (1, 10, 11, 2, 20, 21, 3).

Indexers usually do not correct misspellings in the work being indexed, so, if a name is misspelled or spelled more than one way in the source, it may appear in exactly the same way in the index. On the other hand, indexers sometimes file a name under a standardized spelling (Braun as Brown), believing that the user would not know of the variant (or incorrect) spelling.

Phonetic

Many indexers realize that names can be spelled in a variety of ways. To overcome the difficulty of locating variant spellings of names, some indexers arrange the entries according to the sound of the name. The most common such system is called the Soundex coding system. In a Soundex index, surnames that are pronounced the same but are spelled differently are grouped by a code (such as S-160 for Sperry, Spary, Sperri, etc.). Usually this system is used in manuscript indexes, such as the indexes to the 1880, 1900, 1910, and 1920 Federal census schedules, and the Index to New England Naturalization Petitions, 1791–1906. These indexes are available on microfilm at the Family History Library of the LDS church in Salt Lake City and at many other libraries. The Soundex code for any particular surname can be determined by a Soundex coding guide, such as that found in *Personal Ancestral File®* (*PAF*), versions 2.31 and earlier, and on the National Archives' World Wide Web site (http://www.nara.gov/genealogy/soundex/soundex.html).

Some published sources, especially computerized indexes, use the Soundex system to group similar names with different spellings. The *International Genealogical Index* (described below under "FamilySearch") uses a different phonetic system: surnames are arranged according to a standardized spelling while maintaining the spelling of the original in the index entry. Cross-references under the actual spelling refer the user to the standard spelling.

Other Arrangements

A few older indexes that were compiled before computers were available to alphabetize the entries have unique arrangements. Fortunately, most non-standard arrangements are found in manuscript indexes to original records (such as county probate indexes) and seldom appear in published indexes. In a family history, for example, the index might be subdivided into descent groups, listing all the descendants of the first son before the second. An index dealing with Scandinavian or Welsh names might be arranged by the first (given) name rather than the surname. Some indexes only arrange entries by the first letter, the entries beginning with a given letter being listed in the order they appear in the record. Other indexes use a system of key letters, names being filed according to the key letters only and any other letters in the name being ignored. Some indexes ignore vowels, arranging words by their consonants only. One index to New Hampshire vital records has the card entries arranged by the first and third letters; thus, Sm*i*th comes before Sa*n*derson.

Cross-References

Indexers realize that users will not always know how the indexer chose to refer to a subject (for example, *passenger lists* versus *immigration records*) or a name (Thompson versus Thomson), so they sometimes include *see* references as cross-references. A *see* reference indicates that a term is not used in the index and that the user should look under the term referred to instead. For example, personal names with variant spellings and changes in localities or jurisdictions might be referenced with *see* references. A *see also* cross-reference refers the user to another, related index heading that may be of interest.

Citations

Virtually every index includes some citation or reference to the information in the source it indexes. Usually this is a page number, but the indexer may choose to use a different system of references. If the source being indexed includes entry numbers (such as marriages in a county marriage license book), the indexer may choose to refer to the entry and not to the page number. Most family histories use a numbering system that assigns one number to each nuclear family (see chapter 16). Thus, some back-of-the-book indexes to family histories refer to the family number, not the page number. Collective indexes sometimes refer (via a source abbreviation) only to the source where the entry was found. The user must then rely on the index or alphabetical arrangement within the specific source to find the entry of interest.

NAME	CODE	PAGE
---,---	CY18	361A
---,---	CYW1	037C
---,---	CYW6	001B
---,---	FRPL	001A
---,---	JFCC	286A
---,---	MSSL	244C
---,---	MSSL	247A
---,---	MSSL	247B
---,---	MSSL	248C
---,---	SUW6	137D
---,ADAH	BEGO	040A
---,ANTONY	MDFA	347B
---,BARBARA	HM18	141C
---,BARBARA*	CYW4	269B
---,BURT W.*	CYW4	249B
---,CHARLES	CMBA	017A
---,CHRISTINE	HMW2	179A
---,DAVID E.	MDMS	330B
---,DORA	HMW2	178D
---,EDWARD	CMBA	017A
---,ELENOR	MRW1	196C
---,ERHERM	HMW3	234B
---,EVANGELAN	FRMF	334A
---,FRANCIS	CMBA	017A
---,FRANK	TRWR	388C
---,FRANK*	CMBA	031D
---,FRANK*	CYW9	005B
---,GEORGE HOMER*	CYW4	249B
---,HENRY*	CYW9	005B
---,HUBERT	CRHO	426D
---,JOHANA*	CYW5	417A
---,JOHN	BRPK	188A
---,JOHN	CRHO	416D
---,JOHN	CRHO	426D
---,JOHN	MHW3	404B
---,JOHN	MSSL	244D
---,JOHN	SCW6	294B
---,JOHN N.	CMBA	031C
---,JOHN V.	HMW5	071A
---,JOHN*	CYCL	336C
---,JOSEPH	CBSM	581C
---,JOSEPH	MDCN	381D
---,L. U.	SATO	136C
---,LEANDER	ADFR	014B
---,LEWIS	CYW1	004C
---,LIBBIE	CY12	301B
---,LIZZIE	FYMR	556C
---,LIZZIE	HM18	144A
---,LORA	MDPL	320B
---,MARGARET	CHGO	215A
---,MARTIN*	CYW9	005B
---,MARY	HDCE	050B
---,MARY	HM18	063B
---,MARY	MHW3	412A
---,MAX	MDLD	252C
---,MOTT	LUWA	131C
---,N. W.	FRPL	001A
---,OREN	MDCN	381D
---,PERRY T.	BRPK	188A
---,ROBERT A.	BRPK	188A
---,RUTHERD B.*	CMWA	354C
---,SETH C.	FYMD	569B
---,SUSAN*	CYW5	402D
---,TABITHA	CMBA	017A
---,THOMAS	LWPE	274A
---,WILBER	CMBA	017A
---,WILLIAM	PUSU	521D
---CK,LINCEN A.	MDSO	198D
---IHN,L. C.	MDDA	394D
??????ES,JACOB	CY15	132B
???DAK,MARY*	CY18	361A
???TMAN,LOGAN	MDFA	338D
??ARTMAN,CONRAD	HM21	470C
??ERGMAN,ANTON	HM21	472C
??GSTEN,CHAS. E.	SATO	135B

Figure 6-5. From *Ohio 1880 Census Index,* vol. 1 (Precision Indexing, 1991), page 1. It shows how some indexers use blanks (____) to represent the letters they cannot read, hoping the user will recognize the entry from the legible letters. Such entries are usually filed at the beginning of the index.

Another concern regards multiple references on the same page. Most indexes give no indication when a name appears two or more times on one page; yet, the second reference may be more important than the first. A user who doesn't know there is a second instance of the name may not look for it. Sometimes, however, a mark by the index entry (such as an asterisk) indicates that there are multiple occurrences.

Other notations may be included with the citation, such as indication that a portrait of the subject is on a particular page (often indicated by a symbol explained at the beginning of the index). If the citation refers to a footnote and not the regular text, the index may indicate so by an *n* with the page number, signifying *note.*

INCLUSION

"Indexers are always admonished—and rightly so—to keep in mind the prospective users of their work. Will the user look for the terms that have been chosen?" (Wellish 1991, 406) It is the indexer's challenge to provide index terms that the user will find useful. Careful indexers attempt to provide entries that are helpful and can be easily found by the user.

Index users range from beginners to experienced research professionals; some are experienced in using indexes properly, while others tend to overlook key words and terms. Among the greatest challenges for the genealogist is using those works that are poorly or only partially indexed. Indeed, according to Lois Horowitz,

> indexes vary in quality. Some are too detailed and refer you to scores of terms for which there is little information in the text; others are too cursory and cover only the major points of the book. Indeed, a book's index can determine the book's worth for you. If the book has the information you need, but the index doesn't reflect it, the book is only marginally useful to you (1984, 53).

Genealogical indexers are often paid very modestly for their work or receive no income at all; and many indexers of genealogical titles have little or no experience in indexing. Regardless of the circumstances, all indexers make decisions (some conscious, some unconscious) about what and how they index. These decisions determine what the indexer will include and exclude.

Typically, indexes are either complete name indexes (every-name indexes) or they only index the major names (subjects) in a chapter or article, such as the key person (the principal) discussed. Examples of subject indexes are the early indexes to county and local histories and biographies. For example, the index for *Biographical History of Northeastern Ohio Embracing the Counties ofAshtabula, Geauga and Lake* (Chicago: Lewis Publishing Co., 1893) refers only to the principal person featured in each of its biographical sketches. In the last twenty years or so, many local histories and biographical works have been re-indexed with complete name indexes compiled by genealogical and historical societies (many as a result of the U.S. bicentennial in 1976).

Key person or *principal* indexes are common among the collective indexes discussed earlier; they are typically associated with probate and land records. Usually only the testator or the grantor and grantee are indexed in them; seldom do they include others mentioned in wills or deeds, or the witnesses to those actions.

Where the source material warrants, good indexes contain subject (or topical) headings, such as references to methodology, or how-to, articles. Some indexes contain cross-references, such as names of brides and grooms, and some contain author and/or title entries that are indexed separately or are included in the name index. Indexes which contain more than just personal names are especially valuable to researchers; they are even more valuable if they include place names (localities).

Every indexer has a "bias"—a purpose for creating the index—and it determines what she chooses to index. Most census indexes for 1850 and later are termed *head of household* indexes because the indexers did not take the time to index every name in the census—only the names of persons judged to be heads of households. They did, however, usually include those sometimes termed *strays*—other adults in the household with different surnames (those who had "strayed" from their own homes or families). Some census indexes go further and index any male over a certain age (perhaps twenty years), regardless of whether he shares the surname of the head of the house. Even with fairly common parameters for census indexes, two independently created indexes for the same census often reveal names that one or the other did not include, as shown in figure 6-6.

An index's purpose usually causes some sources or perhaps certain terms or names within a source to be excluded. If the indexer is only interested in the subjects of biographical sketches in county histories, then town histories will not be part of the indexing project. If any biographical sketches in any published sources are of interest, the indexer still will usually exclude extensive information about an early pioneer if it was not part of the biographical section in one of the indexed books. On the other hand, J. Carlyle Parker's purpose, when indexing Rhode Island biographical material, also included locating genealogical lineages in the sketches. Therefore, he included "the earliest ancestor or earliest emigrant . . . from genealogical or family sketches or genealogies (Parker 1991, ix)." As another example, the *Greenlaw Index* (mentioned previously) only indexes material that provides at least three generations of information.

Even some every-name indexes are not as comprehensive as they appear. Some recently published every-name indexes to earlier historical books do not cover portions of the text that are composed of alphabetical lists (such as a directory of farmers or a list of Civil War soldiers).

An indexer who chooses to make only a surname index excludes a significant portion of the work (the individuals' given names) and makes researchers' work more difficult. Some indexers choose to index only the few names they are interested in, such as all the Coopers in the 1850 Federal census or all the Dutch households in the 1860 census.

ACCURACY

When using an index, one should keep in mind that no reference source is perfect and that it may have been affected by indexing, computer, or printing errors. Errors can occur when the original record is transcribed, when the index is being processed with a computer program, or in the editing or printing stages. Indexing errors and omissions can be found in some of the published statewide indexes to Federal census schedules covering the period 1800 through 1850.

CLINEFELDER, HENRY	SENE	095	THOMPSON
CLINEFELLER, JOHN	HURO	115	SHERMAN
CLINEFELLER, MARTHA	STAR	344	OSNABURG
CLINEFELTER, ADAM	SUMM	004	GREEN TW
CLINEFELTER, ELIZA	STAR	525	CANTON T
CLINEFELTER, JACOB	MARI	140	PLEASANT
CLINEFELTER, MARIA	STAR	344	OSNABURG
CLINEHEN, RHINEHART	HAMI	114	SPRINGFI
CLINEN, JOHN*	LICK	469	HOPEWELL
CLINENDON, JAMES*	WASH	877	WATERFOR
CLINER, ANDREW	HOLM	312	RIPLEY T
CLINER, HENRY	HAMI	295	CINCINNA
CLINER, MICHAEL	SCIO	234	WHEELERS
CLINES, JACOB	WILL	005	BRADY
CLINES, TENNY	MONT	415	MADISON
CLINES, THOMAS	MUSK	395	SALT CRE
CLINESCHMIDT, JOHN	DARK	310	WAYNE TW
CLINESMITH, A.	VAN	370	TULLY TW
CLINESMITH, BOLTIS	RICH	258	BUTLER T
CLINESMITH, BOLTIS	RICH	258	BUTLER T
CLINESMITH, CLARISSA	KNOX	282	GAMBIA
CLINESMITH, COONROD	GUER	292	CAMBRIDG
CLINESMITH, GEORGE	ROSS	338	TWIN TWP
CLINESMITH, HENRY	RICH	259	BUTLER T
CLINESMITH, HENRY	RICH	259	BUTLER T
CLINESMITH, WILLIAM	RICH	256	BUTLER T
CLINESMITH, WILLIAM	RICH	256	BUTLER T
CLINESON, JOHN	HAMI	252	CINCINNA
CLINETINK, ADAM	MONR	344	ENOCH TW
CLINEY, MICHAEL	FRAN	072	CLINTON
CLINEY, WILLIAM	HAMI	330	CINCINA
CLING, EDWARD	LUCA	090	OREGON T
CLING, GEORGE	HAMI	248	CINCINNA
CLING, HENRY	SHEL	273	WASHINGT
CLING, ISABELLA J.	RICH	208	CASS TWP
CLING, ISABELLA J.	RICH	208	CASS TWP
CLING, JAMES L.	PREB	245	EATON
CLING, JOHN	RICH	100	MADISON
CLING, LEWIS	WARR	841	CLEAR CR
CLING, LOUIS	HAMI	254	CINCINNA
CLING, LOUISA	RICH	309	FRANKLIN
CLING, MARY A.	ASHL	155	MIFFLIN
CLING, ROSANNE	LUCA	090	OREGON T
CLING, SARAH E.	WAYN	375	GREENE T
CLINGALL, CRISENA	ERIE	405	HURON TW
CLINGAMAN, CATHARINE	MAHO	501	JACKSON
CLINGAMAN, DANIEL	STAR	364	WASHINGT
CLINGAMAN, FERDINAND	STAR	480	NIMISHIL
CLINGAN, EDWARD	WARR	756	WAYNE TW
CLINGAN, EDWARD*	MAHO	579	COITSVIL
CLINGAN, JAMES	CRAW	050	TODD TWP
CLINGAN, JEHIAIL	TRUM	326	HUBBARD
CLINGAN, JESSE	MIAM	003	ELIZABET
CLINGAN, JOHN	MONR	461	CENTER T
CLINGAN, JOHN JR.	MONR	461	CENTRE T
CLINGAN, JOSEPH	MIAM	002	ELIZABET
CLINGAN, JOSEPH	WAYN	749	PLAIN TW
CLINGAN, MARY	RICH	274	WELLER T

CLINEFEEBRING, C	ADFR	28
CLINEFELDE, HENRY	SNTH	188
CLINEFELTER, ADAM	SUGR	6
CLINEFELTER, ELIZA	STCA	524
CLINEFELTER, HENRY	MWNO	406
CLINEFELTER, JOCOB L	MWNO	411
CLINEFELTER, JOHN	HUSH	228
CLINEFELTER, JOHN	MWCN	369
CLINEFELTER, JOSEPH	MWCO	465
CLINEFELTER, MARIA	STOS	344
CLINEFELTER, MARTHA	STOS	344
CLINEFELTER, MICHAEL	MWPE	425
CLINEHART, CASPER	KNJF	453
CLINEHEN, RHINEHART	HMSP	113
CLINENDON, JAMES	WSWF	877
CLINER, ADAM	HMLL	363
CLINER, ANDREW	HLRY	311
CLINER, HENRY	HMLL	294
CLINES, ISAAC	MUBR	97
CLINES, JACOB	WLBR	5
CLINES, THOMAS	MUSC	394
CLINES, WM C	MUBR	97
CLINESCHMIDT, JOHN A	DKWN	310
CLINESMITH, A	VWTU	190
CLINESMITH, BOLTIS	RIBU	515
CLINESMITH, COONROD	GUCA	292
CLINESMITH, GEORGE	RSTW	675
CLINESMITH, JOHN	MMPQ	376
CLINESMITH, WILLIAM	RIBU	510
CLINETUCK, ADAM	MNEN	343
*CLINEY, MICHL	FRCL	143
CLING, EDWARD	LUOR	9
CLING, GEORGE	HMW3	248
CLING, HENRY	SHWS	545
CLING, ISABELLA J	RICA	414
CLING, JOHN	RIMD	199
CLING, LEWIS	WRCL	421
CLING, LOUIS	HMWE	253
CLING, LOUISA	RIFR	617
CLING, MARY A	ASMF	309
CLING, SARAH C	WNGR	188
CLINGALL, CRISENA	ERHU	404
CLINGAMAN, CATHARINE	MHJK	501
CLINGAMAN, FERDINAND	STNI	479
CLINGAMAN, WILLIAM	SAJK	97
CLINGAN, EDWARD	MHCO	578
CLINGAN, EDWARD	WRWN	378
CLINGAN, JAMES	CRTO	98
CLINGAN, JEHIEL	TRHU	163
CLINGAN, JESSE	MMEL	2
CLINGAN, JOHN	MNCE	461
CLINGAN, JOHN JR	MNCE	461
CLINGAN, JOSEPH	MMEL	1
CLINGAN, JOSEPH	WNPN	375
CLINGAN, MARY	RIBU	547

Figure 6-6. Comparison of two 1850 census indexes for Ohio (Ronald Vern Jackson, editor, left, and Lida Flint Harshman, editor, right). The underlined names in each are those which do not appear in the other index.

Many factors influence the accuracy of an index. For a detailed examination of accuracy in published census indexes, including the causes of errors, see chapter 9, "Census and Tax Lists." The following is only a brief discussion.

Indexes do contain mistakes, but, when a researcher cannot find information in an index, it is just as likely because of problems with the record being indexed. There are many potential reasons why an indexer could have made a valid entry that nevertheless cannot be found by the user.

Spelling

Names (and other terms) have not always been spelled as they are today. The surname Thompson, for example, was often spelled without the *p*. The name Pierce is also commonly found as Peirce and sometimes as Pearce.

Source Errors

Original sources also include errors and omissions. Sometimes names that might be expected to be in a record simply were not recorded; an indexer cannot index what is not there. Conversely, the indexer has to index what is there, including any mistakes in a record.

The *Social Security Death Index* (published by several companies) is an excellent example of this problem. Many users believe it to be an index to all deaths in the United States or to all deaths of people who had Social Security numbers. In reality it is neither. It is a list of deceased persons *who received Social Security benefits*. Some others are listed, but only those whose deaths were reported to the Social Security Administration. The list also includes a few living persons who were wrongly placed in the file by the Social Security Administration (usually because the person's benefit check was handled by a third party, such as a long-term care facility).

Scope

Often the person sought is noted in the record, but he or she is not within the index's scope. Such is the case with subject indexes to local histories (that are not every-name indexes) or head-of-household census indexes. Refer to the discussion of "Inclusion," above.

Arrangement

Become familiar with how the indexer arranged the information, as discussed earlier. Note especially the treatment of surname prefixes (Mc, de).

Potential Problems

Indexers, especially inexperienced ones, make mistakes as well. Some mistakes to watch for include the following.

Handwriting. Consider the original source that was indexed. If it was a handwritten text (such as a census schedule, ship passenger list, or probate record), the indexer may have had difficulty reading the handwriting (figure 6-7). An inexperienced indexer may misread the old long *s* as an *f* or the double, long-short *s* as a *p*. Indeed, illegible handwriting is probably the cause of more indexing mistakes than any other source (Thorndale 1984, 18).

Inconsistency. The process of creating an index is a long and often tedious one, sometimes taking months or even years. Even when the same indexer works on a project throughout, he may forget or revise indexing guidelines. In the significant *American Genealogical-Biographical Index* (discussed below under "Family Histories and Genealogies"), sources were added after several early volumes had been published. An appendix to the source list identifies the additional sources, but it does not explain where to find the entries from the new sources that would have been in the volumes already published.

Multiple Indexers. A large indexing project may employ many researchers. The entries in the International Genealogical Index® were created by thousands of volunteer members of the LDS church. In such circumstances, not every indexer will understand the scope of the index or be equally trained in reading the records.

Omissions. Indexers sometimes inadvertently overlook terms that, even by their guidelines, should be included. Such an omission can result from skipping a page in the original record, for example, or from simple fatigue.

Careless Process. Even today, indexing is often a two-step process. In earlier days, it may have involved several steps. For example, an indexer would write (or type) each entry for the index on a small slip of paper or on a sheet that was then cut into small pieces. These *index slips* were then arranged in the order needed for the index; then they were re-typed in that order, but a slip could easily be lost or placed out of order. Even today, with the use of computers for indexing, the first stage often involves writing the entry on an indexing form, which is then given to an input typist.

Some such mistakes are difficult or impossible for the user to overcome. If the record should have an entry that the index does not include, search the record itself, ignoring the index if necessary. For a useful perspective on the problems that make census indexes less accurate and how to overcome some of these problems, see Richard H. Saldana's *A Guide to "Misteaks" in Census Indexes* (Bountiful, Utah: R. H. Saldana & Co., 1987). Although this work is designed to explain census indexes, many of the author's comments are valid for other indexes.

THE PROCESS OF USING INDEXES

Indexes should be used for genealogical research in a systematic and logical manner. After analyzing the pedigree and selecting one or more research objectives, identify indexes available in the area of research that will help reach those objectives. After identifying which repositories house the indexes of interest and finding them there, analyze and then search the indexes. Record the entries from the index; the actual sources of interest can then be used.

Most genealogical indexes are listings of personal names and place names arranged alphabetically, followed by page numbers or other references. At first glance it may appear easy to use a genealogical index. Yet, with experience, users are often able to locate items of interest in an index that others may overlook.

Identify Indexes to Use

As part of the research process, perform a survey to determine what research has been performed on the pedigree line of inter-

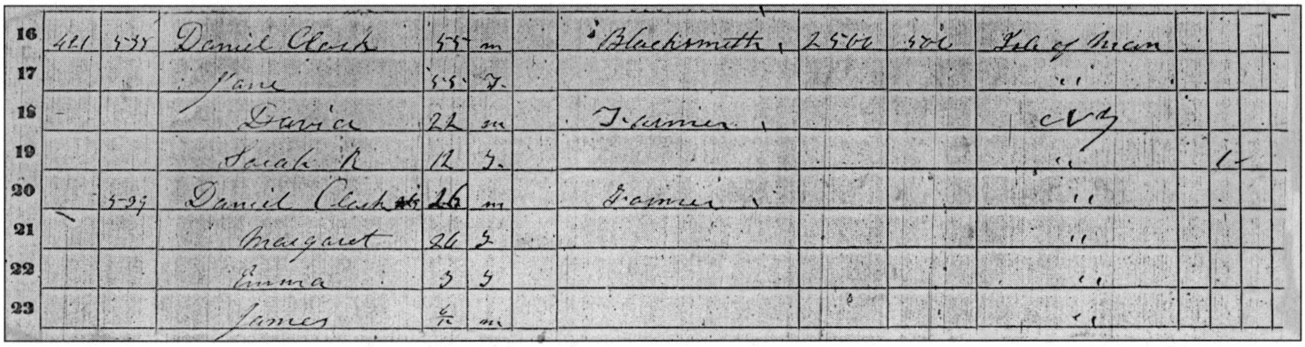

16	421	537	Daniel Clark	55	m	Blacksmith	2500	500	Isle of Man	
17			Jane	55	F				"	
18			David	22	m	Farmer			N Y	
19			Sarah R	12	F				"	1
20		537	Daniel Clark	26	m	Farmer			"	
21			Margaret	26	F				"	
22			Emma	3	F				"	
23			James	6/12	m				"	

Figure 6-7. An example of a difficult-to-read record. In this 1850 New York census record, the given name on lines sixteen and twenty could be read as Daniel or David.

est. Begin by searching indexes and compiled sources for clues, such as family histories, compiled genealogies, biographies, local histories, or computer databases. The chapters in part 4 of *Printed Sources* identify key indexes and other finding aids vital in this phase of research.

Plan to search all available indexes to a work or collection. For example, some Federal census schedules have been indexed by one or more commercial firms, and the same census year may also have been indexed by a genealogical or historical society. It is wise to check duplicate indexes published by organizations—for example, a census index published by a commercial firm and a census index for the same schedule published by a genealogical society.

Locate the Index

Genealogical indexes are available at major research libraries, such as the Family History Library, public and university libraries, genealogical libraries, historical societies, and others. More and more genealogical indexes and databases are becoming available on the Internet as well.

Most indexes are used by researchers in the libraries where they are housed. Although indexes and reference sources are generally not available through interlibrary loan, numerous indexes and genealogical sources have been microfilmed; the microfilms may be borrowed from lending libraries or other institutions, or through local LDS family history centers (branch libraries of the Family History Library). Many libraries will make a brief search of their indexes in response to a written request, making it possible to access the information in an index even when one cannot visit the repository that has it.

Within a library, many multiple-source indexes are located in the reference section (particularly major indexes and those that cover a large geographic area). Smaller indexes, especially indexes to single works, are usually kept on the shelves with the sources they index. For more information, see "Using Libraries to Locate Indexes," below.

Analyze the Index

Before looking up information in an index, read the introduction (if there is one). Next, observe the organization of the index. It can be helpful to select a few personal names from the work to learn how they are indexed. Determine whether multiple references to the same personal name on the same page are cited as multiple references in the index. (Some indexes show how many times a citation appears on a page. Such inclusiveness can be helpful in searching for an ancestor.)

Attempt to determine what the purpose of the index was when it was compiled. Was it a commercial venture, a project of a genealogical or historical society, or a "labor of love" by a dedicated genealogist? A preface or introduction will usually provide such information.

Next, evaluate the index before using it to determine the method or style of indexing. If an index is confusing, select a few random entries from the body of the work being indexed and then check the index to determine how the indexer entered them.

Note any abbreviations used in the index that correspond to a bibliographic key for the index. Was a duplicate index (in which each item is indexed twice and compared or audited before the index is published) or other verification used by the indexers to ensure accuracy? Indexing methodology may be described in the introduction to the index.

Understand the scope and arrangement of the index before actually using it. For example, a surname index in which entries appear throughout the volume is the reprint edition of *Early Connecticut Marriages as Found on Ancient Church Records Prior to 1800*, edited by Frederick W. Bailey, with additions and corrections by Donald Lines Jacobus (1896–1906; reprint; Baltimore: Genealogical Publishing Co., 1968). Not only can the names be hard to find (because of the multiple indexes throughout the book), but Bailey relied on others to copy Connecticut church registers; hence, this volume contains some errors and has omissions. It is always wise to check the original source (in this case the original church registers) when using indexes and compiled sources. Bailey's work is a good example of the need to do so.

Search the Index

Because the original source may have been difficult for the indexer to read, consider all possible spelling variations when using an index—especially census indexes. The capital letter *S* may have been transcribed as an *L* (or vice versa); *U* and *V* (or *I* and *J*) may have appeared the same to the indexer; *M* may be filed under *N* in the index—etc. An old-style (long) *S* misunderstood by an indexer who was unfamiliar with paleography (the reading of old handwriting) and early handwriting could result in *Mass* appearing as *Maps*. Substitute various vowels (*a* for *e*, *o* for *u*, etc.) when using an index to account for possible misinterpretations. In short, keep in mind various possibilities when looking for personal names in an alphabetically arranged index.

When using an index, it is important to look for names of close family members, such as the maiden surname of the wife, mother's surname, and the surnames of people who married each child in the family. These names can be very helpful when searching indexes to family histories and compiled genealogies, especially for common surnames, such as Smith, Brown, Jones, Johnson, etc. For example, rather than searching for a common name like John Smith in an index, first look for Smith's wife, perhaps an Effie Loomis, for there are likely to be fewer index entries for her name.

If there is more than one entry for each of two related persons in an index (such as a married couple), a useful approach is to compare page numbers where those two names appear in the index; this can help narrow the search to the most likely page(s).

Record Pertinent References

After locating a reference item or personal name of interest in an index, make note of the complete entry—name, page or folio number, volume number, date, locality, age of the person, type of document, bibliographic reference number, or other references or remarks shown in the index.

Genealogists often browse through indexes (such as indexes to census schedules) searching for personal names of interest. Whether or not an index contains personal names or other terms, it is important to record all pertinent references. Even if an ancestor of interest is not located, such a "negative" search might also prove valuable during future research for that family. As new names are found, it is wise to recheck the indexes and reference sources that may pertain to the pedigree at hand and begin the research process anew.

When There Is No Index

If there is no index to the work of interest, look carefully at each page, chapter, or place name. To search an unindexed census population schedule, determine the township or minor civil division where an ancestor lived and search those pages first. Use a map of the county to keep track of which localities have been searched. If using an unindexed local history, read the pages for the township or city where the ancestors resided.

USING LIBRARIES TO LOCATE INDEXES

While many libraries are converting their card catalogs into machine (computer)-readable form, some smaller libraries have not yet accomplished this. Some libraries, such as the Family History Library, have converted all of their bibliographical references into electronic form and do not have card catalogs. Other major research libraries, such as the Library of Congress; the Newberry Library in Chicago; and the Harvard, Yale, and many other university libraries, use both a card catalog and a computer catalog. Typically, older cataloged entries appear in the card catalog but are being converted into machine-readable form as the computer catalog replaces the card catalog. Many automated library catalogs, such as that of the Library of Congress, may be searched via the Internet.

The cards in a library card catalog are usually filed alphabetically by author, title, and subject. Special filing rules are often in effect, so check with a librarian or subject specialist to learn what they are. Examples of filing rules sometimes used in card catalogs:

- Articles (a, an, the) are disregarded.
- Surnames beginning with M and Mc are filed as though they are spelled Mac.
- Common abbreviations are arranged as though they are spelled out (U.S. is filed as United States).
- Word-by-word filing (New York before Newark) is usually used instead of letter-by-letter filing (see "Arrangement," above).

Libraries sometimes have leaflets or brochures which explain their filing rules; contact the library of interest for such research aids. Many of these catalog filing rules are used by indexers.

Try all possibilities of names and subjects when using a library's card catalog and searching for indexes. Carefully note the call number and whether it is a book or microform. If the work is on microfilm, note any item number (which indicates where the item is located on the microfilm). Many titles are available through interlibrary loan (especially microfilms), so check with the interlibrary loan office at the library of interest. Reference sources and genealogical indexes are frequently not available through interlibrary loan, however.

Indexes Unique to Particular Libraries

Many libraries, such as the Library of Congress (Local History and Genealogy Room) and the Newberry Library in Chicago, have name indexes to genealogies, local histories, and other published sources that are unique to them. Be sure to ask a reference librarian about any special genealogical indexes or guides available at a library. Some such indexes are printed, and some are available on microfilm or microfiche.

Locating Indexes in a Library

Identifying an index of interest in a card or computer catalog usually requires two steps: (1) look at the catalog entry for the source for a reference to an index for that source; (2) look in the title section of the catalog for the word "Index" followed by the title of the actual source. Examples of catalog entries for titles beginning with the word "index" might include:

- Index, Atlas of Ashtabula County, Ohio
- Index for Obituaries Appearing in Eagle Democrat, 1930–1939
- Index to 1860 Federal Census of South Carolina

These title references are usually found under "Index . . . ," "Index of . . . ," or "Index to . . . " Most library card and computer catalogs are alphabetically arranged by author, title, subject, and locality. See especially the subject headings "indexing" and "abstracting" in the library catalog of interest.

Local Archive Indexes

Many libraries and archives maintain indexes to records among their holdings. Examples include the card files in the Local History and Genealogy Room at the Library of Congress in Washington, D.C. These card files, known as Family Name Index, Analyzed Surname Index, Coats of Arms Index, and U.S. Biographical Index, are unique to the Library of Congress; they are valuable personal name indexes. Also very valuable as a finding aid is the analytical card index at the DAR Library in Washington, D.C. (which has not been microfilmed).

Other major libraries have special card files and genealogical indexes as well. The Ohio Historical Society (Columbus, Ohio) houses the *Ohio Surname Index*, a statewide index to names in many Ohio local histories. This index has been microfilmed and is available at the Family History Library.

Many genealogical organizations index members' records and have local indexing projects. Examples include the many indexes and published works produced by chapters of the Ohio Genealogical Society (Mansfield, Ohio). The society has a statewide *Ancestor Card File* containing more than 200,000 names of its members' ancestors. Arranged alphabetically by surname, this index has been microfilmed and is available from the Family History Library.

COMPUTER DATABASES AS INDEXES

The two major bibliographic databases of printed and manuscript sources are the Online Computer Library Center (OCLC), based in Ohio, and the Research Libraries Information Network (RLIN), based in California. Both are useful for locating genealogical indexes. OCLC is a computerized database available at many libraries, especially public libraries (often under the name FirstSearch). It is the largest collective database listing the holdings of multiple libraries in the United States. RLIN is a national research library consortium catalog which identifies the holdings of more than eighty U.S. research libraries, among them Yale University, Stanford University, Brigham Young University (titles cataloged since 1978), and many other major libraries. These databases are available through online access in libraries throughout the United States (except very small public libraries or private research libraries).

Titles found in OCLC and RLIN have descriptive entries that indicate what libraries have copies of them. Records may be searched in either database by author, title, subject, call number, location, and other "access points." University Microfilms International's (Ann Arbor, Michigan) Genealogy and Local History Series titles on microfiche, described later in this chapter, are identified in OCLC and RLIN. Hundreds of newspaper and manuscript titles are also available in these two databases. Both of these databases are further described in chapter 5, "Bibliographies and Catalogs."

Most major research libraries have computer stations which access various indexes, indexing services, and databases. Usually the researcher logs onto a system of interest and selects from a menu shown on the computer screen. In addition to databases of special interest to genealogists, researchers may also search religion, history, humanities, and other subject area indexes and databases and local area networks. Contact reference librarians for assistance in using computer databases and local area networks.

Of special interest to genealogists are *ProPhone* (Pro-CD, Inc., Danvers, Massachusetts) and *PhoneDisc* (Digital Directory Assistance, Bethesda, Maryland) CD-ROM telephone directories. Information from them may be printed or copied to a computer diskette. PhoneBooks and *PhoneDisc* are computerized telephone directories that show names and U.S. residential telephone numbers and addresses. The names in them are arranged alphabetically by geographic region. PhoneBooks can be searched by telephone number and by address; it is the most extensive of the two sources. Telephone directories are also available on microfiche.

The Internet

Major academic and other libraries (and many individuals) have access to the Internet, a worldwide communications network and link to thousands of computer networks. Major uses of the Internet include accessing library catalogs and the growing number of indexes (as well as copied records and copies of original records) posted at various World Wide Web sites. One of the major genealogical indexes available on the Internet is Family Tree Maker's FamilyFinder Index, an index to more than 123 million names (as of this writing). It is available at http://www.familytreemaker.com/index.html.

Names in the FamilyFinder Index have been taken from census and vital records, Social Security death records, genealogies, and other sources. This index will indicate if a personal name of interest is included on a CD-ROM set from Family Tree Maker (Novato, California) and other distributors. If a name of interest is located, this site will show which CD the name is found on. Family Tree Maker is one of the most popular Windows genealogy programs available.

Search the Internet for surnames and localities of interest. William R. Cutter's 4,600-personal-name index *New England Families*, vol. 1 (1916), is available on the Internet at the compiler's home page (The Roots Source, Pearland, Texas): http://www.ghgcorp.com/rootsource.

Ancestry, Inc. (Orem, Utah) has posted the entire *Social Security Death Index* on its World Wide Web site (http://www.ancestry.com) and is continually adding numerous other indexes and sources. Other Internet sites are potentially useful as well.

CD-ROM Databases

Many major databases that were previously available only through expensive online subscriptions or in annual printed volumes (with no cumulative indexes) have appeared on CD-ROM in recent years. Generally they are aimed at academic audiences, and few individuals choose to purchase these often expensive sets. They are available at major academic and some large public libraries.

America: History and Life (Santa Barbara, Calif.: ABC-Clio, annual) identifies thousands of scholarly U.S. and Canadian historical journal articles, book reviews, and dissertations. Indexes are available in printed form, online via computer, or on CD-ROM, where searches are available by author, subject, or key word. Similar searches are available in *Dissertation Abstracts International* (Ann Arbor, Mich.: University Microfilms International, annual), which gives citations and abstracts of published dissertations and many masters theses accepted by U.S. colleges and universities since 1985. Many of these titles are of interest to genealogists; they include local history and other subjects of interest.

Other useful computer-indexed databases, available on CD-ROM at most academic libraries, include *Index to Legal Periodicals*, *Humanities Index*, and University Microfilms

International's *Newspaper Abstracts* (which may be searched by author, title, key word, date, or by name of newspaper for specific articles). The *American Memory Project* database identifies thousands of photographs and slides available at the Library of Congress in Washington, D.C. Of particular interest to genealogists in this collection are the hundreds of Civil War photographs.

The *National Union Catalog of Manuscript Collections* (Washington, D.C.: Library of Congress, 1962–), often known as *NUCMC,* is a valuable source that describes many manuscript collections housed in libraries and archives (see chapter 5, "Bibliographies and Catalogs"). *NUCMC* is a cooperative cataloging program in which repositories in the United States report their manuscript holdings to the Library of Congress for publication in this work.

Until recently, researchers had to rely on annual and cumulative indexes within the *NUCMC* series (which have ceased in favor of online publication). Although much of the collection is now available on CD-ROM, there is an additional tool of interest for locating genealogical and historical manuscript collections. Major libraries will have *Index to Personal Names in the National Union Catalog of Manuscript Collections, 1959–1984,* 3 vols. (Alexandria, Va.: Chadwyck-Healey, 1988). This work is a cumulated alphabetical index to personal names appearing in the descriptions of the manuscript collections described in *NUCMC.* Two other significant sources of interest in locating manuscript material are the OCLC and RLIN computer databases described above.

Electronic Text As an Indexing System

The growing number of electronic, full-text sources being published on CD-ROM represent a relatively new kind of source for genealogists that has indexing potential. The full text of dozens and even hundreds of previously published sources can be published on one CD-ROM. Software usually included on the CD can then search the entire collection for *any* word, including personal names, places, events, or other terms. In addition to finding any word, the search software can usually perform Boolean searches (using connecting terms such as *and, or, not,* and similar words; see the discussion in chapter 5, "Bibliographies and Catalogs") and proximity searches (words appearing near other key words).

Any kind of published source may be found on CD-ROM, including biographies, periodicals, vital records, gazetteers, genealogical dictionaries, bibliographies, indexes, and other reference sources. Because of their ease of use and relatively low production costs, researchers can expect to find an increasing number of such sources in the future.

If the information was not in the original source to begin with, it will not appear in the electronic text either, no matter how good or sophisticated the search software is. Researchers need to learn how to make meaningful searches using the various kinds of software that publishers choose for their products. Standard search routines have not yet evolved for CD-ROM sources, unlike the print indexing field, where professional indexers follow long-established standards.

As of 1997, publishers providing full-text CD-ROMs include Ancestry, Search and Research, H-Bar Enterprises, and others. Several full-text CD-ROMs and their publishers are included in appendix A, "CD-ROMs for Family Historians."

FamilySearch

FamilySearch® is a system of search-and-retrieval programs that can help genealogists identify their ancestors and offer clues for further research. It is a collection of genealogical databases available on CD-ROM at major libraries, such as the Library of Congress, the New England Historic Genealogical Society (Boston), the Family History Library and its family history centers, and at public and other libraries. *FamilySearch* is among the sources that should be checked first by genealogists beginning their research. It contains computer databases of special interest to genealogists, regardless of the geographical area or time period of interest. As with every index, each file in *FamilySearch* has advantages and disadvantages.

FamilySearch consists of the following computer files (as of early 1998):

- *Ancestral File*™ is a computer database collection of linked genealogies and pedigrees containing more than 29 million names. The majority of the lines extend back three, four, or more generations. Although documentation (such as source references) is not included, names and addresses of submitters and interested persons are included, along with other information. Users are able to make corrections, if necessary. Ancestral File is continuing to expand as more people and family organizations contribute their genealogies to it. This database assists in coordinating the research efforts of individuals. Researchers are encouraged to submit their documented compiled genealogies to Ancestral File on computer diskette using a computer software program with GEDCOM (Genealogical Data Communications).

- The *International Genealogical Index*® (*IGI*) is one of the most valuable research tools available to genealogists. It is an index to more than 240 million names of deceased people found in birth (or baptism/christening) records and marriage records; it is international in scope. Names for those people listed in the United States and Canada are filed in one alphabetical grouping in the computer version; names are listed alphabetically for other regions of the world as well. Family groupings may be established by searching a Parent Index, although multi-generational linkages, family group records, and pedigrees are not included. The *IGI* does not index death records. Regular updated supplements are available beginning with the 1994 *IGI Addendum.*

  The entries in the *IGI* are from a wide variety of sources; they have been contributed by thousands of persons since the 1970s, so each entry has to be evaluated separately. Fortunately, the origin of almost every entry can be determined. As with most databases, never accept the facts in the *IGI* without checking the source; it will often reveal more information and will show how accurate the index entry is. Also note that, as with many databases used as indexes, the *IGI* was not created as an index to genealogical records. Rather, it is a list of persons for whom LDS temple ordinances have been performed posthumously. In this index, the accuracy of genealogical data and of the sources used is secondary—as it may be in other databases or indexes that were created for other purposes.

- The *Social Security Death Index* contains more than 53 million names of people with Social Security numbers who died between ca. 1962 through 1995 (although the database contains some names from as early as 1937) and whose deaths were reported to the Social Security Administration. A list of vital records offices with fees and addresses is included in this database. The *Social Security Death Index* is also available on CD-ROM from commercial firms and on the Internet from Ancestry (http://www.ancestry.com).

- The *U.S. Military Index* is an index to individuals in the U.S. military who died or were declared dead in the Korean and Vietnam conflicts. It covers the 1950 to 1975 and has more than 100,000 names. In addition to the person's name, it gives dates of birth and death, service number, and other information.

- *Scottish Church Records* lists names of 10 million deceased persons listed in Scottish church records (most dating from the 1500s to 1854). It is available as part of the *FamilySearch* versions found at LDS facilities, such as family history centers. Scottish Church Records is also available on microfiche at family history centers under the title "Old Parochial Records."

- The *Family History Library Catalog*™ provides bibliographic information on the records housed at the Family History Library in Salt Lake City. It also identifies titles available at some family history centers and therefore serves as a union catalog of Family History Library holdings. The CD-ROM version of the *Family History Library Catalog* is an automated edition of the catalog. While not an index as such, the CD-ROM version is valuable in linking one surname with another surname (or a surname with a locality, etc.) to determine if the Family History Library has sources of interest, such as compiled genealogies or original records. For example, the *Family History Library Catalog* has more than 550 references to the Roberts surname (number of records found), but only one reference to that surname when linked (key word added) with the town of Simsbury (Connecticut), and twenty-seven records for "Roberts" and "Connecticut."

In addition to the computer files described above, the *International Genealogical Index* and the *Family History Library Catalog* are available in a microfiche edition which may be purchased by libraries or individuals. This edition provides a useful way for genealogists to do research in their own homes (of course, a microfiche reader is required to use them). The microfiche version of the *Family History Library Catalog* provides full bibliographic information on titles (books, microfilm, microfiche, maps, etc.), including author, title, description, notes, and Family History Library call numbers. Researchers may search by locality, surname, or subject headings using the microfiche version.

The CD-ROM version of *FamilySearch* is available at all family history centers and at many public and private research libraries and other institutions. *FamilySearch* is available through network access at the Family History Library in Salt Lake City, at the Joseph Smith Memorial Building in Salt Lake City, and at Brigham Young University in Provo, Utah. *FamilySearch* is not available on the Internet. Researchers can make paper printouts or download (copy) genealogical information from the *Ancestral File, IGI, Social Security Death Index,* or the *U.S. Military Index* and can copy the data onto diskette via GEDCOM or as standard ASCII files.

Other genealogical databases are expected to be added to *FamilySearch* as they become available, such as the 1880 U.S. census index, 1881 English census index, indexes to U.S. Civil War military records, U.S. death records, U.S. immigration records (Ellis Island), and others. For more information about *FamilySearch,* including possible future files, see Kory Meyerink's "Databases, Indexes, and Other Finding Aids," chapter 2 in *The Source: A Guidebook of American Genealogy,* edited by Loretto Dennis Szucs and Sandra Hargreaves Luebking, rev. ed. (Salt Lake City: Ancestry, 1997).

INDEXES FOR ORIGINAL RECORDS

The following is a brief discussion of various indexes for original records. For a more detailed treatment, see the appropriate chapters of *Printed Sources.*

Census Indexes

The first Federal census was taken in 1790. Census population and other schedules are available on microfilm at many libraries; they represent a basic source for American genealogists. Indexes to decennial U.S. Federal census population schedules exist for various census years from 1790 through 1920.

Soundex indexes (arranged by Soundex code for surnames—see "Arrangement—Phonetic," above) are extant for the 1880, 1900, 1910, and 1920 U.S. censuses. (Although the 1910 census is not indexed for all states, it does include a Soundex index and a Miracode index for some states.) A published index to many (but certainly not all) surnames with Soundex codes is *The Soundex Reference Guide,* edited by Bradley W. Steuart (Bountiful, Utah: Precision Indexing, 1990).

Published census indexes are generally available for the census years from 1790 through 1860. More are currently being produced for the 1870 and 1880 U.S. census schedules, and more recently the 1910 census. The 1880 Ohio census index, as an example, is available in book form and on CD-ROM. Many census indexes and indexes to other records are available on CD-ROM, notably in the Family Archives series produced by Banner Blue, a division of Brøderbund Software (Novato, California). Other publishers are also beginning to produce titles and indexes on CD-ROM.

A microfiche index, Ronald Vern Jackson's *AIS Microfiche Indexes of U.S. Census and Other Records* (Bountiful, Utah: Accelerated Indexing Systems International, 1984), is available at many libraries and most family history centers. It indexes the Federal census for the years 1790 through 1850 and some records for later years. A nationwide version of the popular book census indexes from Accelerated Indexing Systems (Bountiful, Utah), the microfiche AIS indexes may be helpful in locating the names of heads of households in the U.S. census when a specific state is not known. For a full discussion of this index, see chapter 9, "Censuses and Tax Lists."

Some tax records have been published and indexed as substitutes for the 1790 census. Two excellent examples are Netti Schreiner-Yantis, comp., *The 1787 Census of Virginia,* 3 vols. (Springfield, Va.: Genealogical Books in Print, 1987), and Charles B. Heinemann's *First Census of Kentucky, 1790* (Baltimore: Southern Book Co., 1956). Most original tax lists recorded in books are alphabetically arranged by the first letter of the surname. Tax records often begin with the origin of a city or county and can prove very helpful to genealogists.

Vital Records Indexes

For each state, vital records indexes covering births, marriages, and deaths are available on a statewide basis dating from the beginning of state vital registration (and from before that date on a county and local basis). For the six New England states, statewide indexes (and indexes to town vital records for many towns) dating from the seventeenth century are available.

One of the best-known indexes in this category is the Barbour Collection, a statewide index to many births, marriages, and deaths in Connecticut before around 1850. The Barbour Collection is housed at the Connecticut State Library in Hartford; it is also available on microfilm at the Family History Library and many other libraries. Also available at the Connecticut State Library are microfilmed slip indexes to Bible and church records, census records, newspapers, and probate records.

Clarence A. Torrey, one of New England's prominent genealogists, compiled *New England Marriages Prior to 1700* (Baltimore: Genealogical Publishing Co., 1985), an index to approximately thirty-seven thousand couples who were married and later migrated to New England or were married in New England. Entries are alphabetically arranged by groom, and there is an index. The original manuscript is housed at the New England Historic Genealogical Society in Boston and is available on microfilm from the society or through the Family History Library system. Torrey's work is actually an index to marriage references. Two additional volumes, *Supplement to Torrey's New England Marriages Prior to 1700,* have been compiled by Melinde Lutz Sanborn (Baltimore: Genealogical Publishing Co., 1991, 1995). This source is an excellent example of the value of using an index even if an ancestor is not expected to be found.

Anyone researching colonial New England families should check these indexes, even if persons married by 1700 have not yet been identified. If a likely couple appears, or if significant references to the surname appear, access the original manuscript (or the microfilm copy) to learn in which sources Torrey found the family.

Other specialized indexes to vital records include a statewide index to marriage bonds for North Carolina (arranged by brides and grooms) titled *Index to Marriage Bonds Filed in the North Carolina State Archives*. It is available on microfiche at the Family History Library and other libraries.

Land Records Indexes

Indexes to deeds, land grants, and other land records are valuable for locating references to people listed in land records. Land record indexes have historically existed in manuscript (unpublished) form only, but this situation is changing. Typically, manuscript grantee (buyer) and grantor (seller) land indexes are available for counties and other localities. The original manuscript indexes are available at county courthouses and other repositories. Many of these indexes and land records in the United States have been microfilmed by the Genealogical Society of Utah (and are therefore available through the Family History Library system); most of them date from before 1900.

Grantee and grantor indexes were usually compiled contemporaneously with the land records, so the indexers were usually familiar with the personal names being indexed. In recent years, local societies and private individuals have been publishing local land indexes, sometimes as transcripts of the original manuscript indexes. In other cases, the index has been newly created from the transcribed deed books. In either case, these indexes usually only identify the grantor and grantee. Check with local libraries to learn if published indexes exist for the records being searched.

The Bureau of Land Management (BLM) is automating many of the pre-1908 Federal land records in its possession. This project is known as the General Land Office Automated Records Project (U.S. Department of the Interior, Bureau of Land Management, Eastern States Office, 7450 Boston Boulevard, Springfield, VA 22153). Automation creates an easily searchable database for which most of the fields are indexed; thus, the database can be searched by the name of the owner or by the description of the property—an example of the enhanced search capability available when using databases as indexes.

Land records are available on CD-ROM for the following states as of this writing: Alabama, Arkansas, Florida, Louisiana, Michigan, Minnesota, Mississippi, Ohio, and Wisconsin; other states will soon be available. The BLM CD-ROMs are available from the superintendent of documents—not through the BLM (Superintendent of Documents, P.O. Box 371954, Pittsburgh, PA 15250-7954). Researchers may contact the BLM and request a search of its indexes to Federal land records. Other Federal land records, such as homestead and bounty-land records, are available at the National Archives in Washington, D.C., although they are not as thoroughly indexed.

Probate Indexes

Few indexes to probate records are available in published form. Typically, these records are indexed at the county level, such indexes existing only in manuscript form (often in bound books) at the offices where the original records reside. Many of these records and related indexes have been microfilmed. Probate packets (estate files or case files) have generally not been microfilmed and are usually not as well indexed as other probate records, but they are extremely valuable for genealogical research.

Immigration and Naturalization Indexes

Indexes to naturalization records, passport applications, and other immigration records are also helpful in locating ancestors. One excellent example is the *Index to New England Naturalization Petitions*, arranged by Soundex index and covering the time period 1791 to 1906. It is housed at the National Archives—New England Region in Waltham, Massachusetts; it has been microfilmed. Another example is the index to New York City naturalization petitions, available at the National Archives—Northeast Region in New York City and also available on microfilm at the Family History Library.

Indexes for original ship passenger lists date generally from 1820 and continue into the twentieth century (except for New York City, for which ship passenger lists are not indexed for the period between 1847 and 1897; published passenger lists, such as those for Germans and Irish, and subsequent volume indexes help to fill this gap). Passenger list volumes are indexed by names of immigrants.

Earlier published immigration records are indexed in P. William Filby, et al., eds., *Passenger and Immigration Lists In-*

dex (Detroit: Gale Research Co., 1981–; includes supplements), the major index for locating colonial immigrants. Most titles indexed are for the seventeenth and eighteenth centuries, but many index entries are also included for the nineteenth century. Filby's index is valuable for locating immigrants to America for the period generally from the 1600s to the early 1800s.

Military Indexes

Indexes for military records (pension, service, and other military records) are important as genealogical finding aids. A general index to Civil War Union soldiers who applied for pensions, often known as the *Pension Index File,* is arranged by surname. It is available on microfilm through the Family History Library and other major libraries. General indexes to the service records of Confederate soldiers are also available on microfilm and are arranged by surname. Indexes for other wars are also available; many of them are housed at the National Archives in Washington, D.C., and most have been microfilmed and are available at the Family History Library and Brigham Young University. Military records created since World War I are generally restricted, with the exception of World War I draft records, which have been microfilmed and are available at the Family History Library.

Many states have indexes to pension, service, grave registration, and other, related military records. A fine example is *Grave Registrations of Soldiers Buried in Ohio*, a card index available at the Ohio Historical Society in Columbus and on microfilm at the Family History Library. Of special interest to researchers are the published indexes to military records compiled by Virgil D. White. They index records for the revolutionary war, War of 1812, Mexican War, and others.

Newspaper Indexes

Newspapers are useful because they contain original source material written at the time events occurred. Of special interest to genealogists are marriage and death notices and obituaries (and sometimes birth notices, especially during the twentieth century). Many libraries maintain indexes of newspaper obituaries and other news items from newspapers published in their localities.

Indexes for national and local newspapers are readily available. Some of the better-known indexes in this category are personal name and subject indexes to the *New York Times,* the *Chicago Tribune,* the *Wall Street Journal,* the *Los Angeles Times,* the *Washington Post,* the *Christian Science Monitor,* and the *London Times.* Newspaper indexes and microfilm copies of newspapers are available in major libraries throughout the United States (academic and public libraries especially).

Specialized newspaper indexes cite obituaries, news articles, and other items of interest to genealogists. A major index in this category is *The New York Times Obituaries Index,* 2 vols. (New York: New York Times, 1970–80). Libraries in many cities and towns maintain card indexes to newspapers published in their localities. An example is the Indianapolis Newspaper Index, which is housed at the Indiana State Library in Indianapolis.

Increasing numbers of indexes and references to newspapers can be found on the Internet. An example is the index to the *Star* (Kansas City, Missouri), which is available at http://www.kcstar.com. It can be searched for newspaper obituaries and other news items. Searching can be done by personal name, place name, or other key word. Searching for an article requires entering a word, several words, or a phrase in double quotes. Newspaper articles may also be found on the Internet with links to local, national, and international news; religion; classified advertisements; and feature articles.

Some newspapers include genealogy columns. An example is Joy Wade Moulton's column in the *Columbus Dispatch* (Columbus, Ohio), titled "Find Your Ancestors." It has been published since February 1975.

For more information on newspapers and their use in genealogy, see James Hansen's "Research in Newspapers," chapter 12 in *The Source: A Guidebook of American Genealogy* (cited earlier).

Other Indexes

Indexes to cemetery records and gravestone inscriptions are also very useful sources. Most such indexes are back-of-the-book indexes. On occasion all (or many) of the cemetery inscriptions for a county are included in one master index. A large card file that identifies published cemetery inscriptions at the Family History Library is the *Index to United States Cemeteries.* Although the actual inscriptions are not in this index, it does identify inscription sources for tens of thousands of cemeteries. The index is available on microfilm through the Family History Library system.

Indexes to hereditary and lineage society records, such as those of the DAR and the Sons of the American Revolution (SAR), are very useful. DAR Genealogical Record Committee typescripts (transcriptions of family Bible, vital, church, probate, military, land, town, and many other records) are usually indexed in each volume. These typescripts are housed at the DAR Library in Washington, D.C., and in state repositories; many have been microfilmed. A statewide index to Bible records, gravestones, vital records, obituaries, and wills for South Carolina (transcribed by the DAR) is available on microfiche through the Family History Library and some other libraries.

The DAR Library has also produced a massive, three-volume index to Revolutionary War soldiers titled *DAR Patriot Index, Centennial Edition* (Washington, D.C.: the society, 1994), in which names of patriot ancestors are arranged alphabetically. It is one of the most valuable indexes for the revolutionary war period and illustrates how an index often needs to have identifying information for the persons listed in order to distinguish between different persons of the same name. In this case, the index gives the birth and death dates and states, as well as the spouse, in addition to the patriot (see figure 6-8).

There are many indexes that can lead researchers to others who are researching the same family lines. The Iowa Genealogical Society has published the multi-volume *Iowa Genealogical Society Surname Index* (Des Moines: Iowa Genealogical Society, 1973–75; irregularly thereafter), which is the published version of the society's Family Surname File project. It provides genealogical information about ancestors of the society's members. This index serves as a finding aid to help researchers locate others who are working on the same family lines. In it, all personal names are cross-indexed alphabetically.

INDEXES FOR COMPILED SOURCES

A compiled source is a collection of information, such as a family history or a genealogy, gathered from other sources. Many, if

Figure 6-8. From the *DAR Patriot Index, Centennial Edition* (part 1, page 1), in which names of patriot ancestors are arranged alphabetically. It is one of the most valuable indexes for the American Revolution period and illustrates how an index often needs to have identifying information for the persons listed in order to distinguish between different persons of the same name.

```
ABBOTT: ABBETT, ABBIT, ABBOT, ABOTT
  Aaron: b 11-3-1758 CT d 12-9-1854 CT m Betsey --- Pvt Tms CT
    PNSR
  Aaron: b 4-2-1746 MA d 1-15-1821 NY m Mary Ayers Cpl MA
  Abel: b --- CT d p 1790 NY m Hannah Dibble Pvt CT
  Abiel: b 8-23-1749 MA d 12-5-1832 MA m Sarah Mann Pvt MA
  Abiel: b 4-19-1741 MA d 8-19-1809 NH m Dorcas Abbott Maj MA
  Abijah: b 7-11-1756 MA d 4-10-1810 MA m Rachel Jennings Pvt
    MA
  Amos Jr: b 7-15-1754 NH d 10-11-1834 NH m Judith Morse Cpl
    NH PNSR
  Asa: b 5-25-1756 CT d 7-29-1822 NY m Elizabeth Pratt Pvt CT
    WPNS
  Asa: b 10-28-1721 MA d 12-23-1796 MA m Elizabeth (Abbot)
    MM PS MA
  Bancroft: b 6-4-1757 NH d 10-29-1829 VT m Lydia White Pvt NH
  Barachias: b 5-14-1707 MA d 10-2-1784 NH m Hannah Holt PS MA
  Benjamin: b 1-26-1738 MA d 11-5-1778 m Joanna Barker Pvt MA
  Benjamin Sr: b 4-6-1730 MA d 1-5-1776 NH m Elizabeth Abbott
    Pvt MM NH
  Benjamin Jr: b 2-10-1750 NH d 12-11-1815 NH m Sarah Brown
    Sgt NH
```

not most, compiled sources include an index when they are published. Although the included index may not be an every-name index, it will still serve to provide some access to the information in the source. However, as discussed in chapters 16 through 19, many compiled sources can also be accessed through master indexes. Examples of such indexes are described below.

Family Histories and Genealogies

Many compiled genealogies (family histories) are well indexed, but some are only partially indexed or are not indexed at all. The most comprehensive index to family histories and to some other sources—such as the published 1790 U.S. census, *Pennsylvania Archives*, *Boston Transcript* (a newspaper genealogy column), and other sources—is *The American Genealogical-Biographical Index*, new series (Middletown, Conn.: Godfrey Memorial Library, 1952–). Formerly known as *Rider's Index,* the first series, edited by Fremont Rider, was published from 1942 to 1952. Known as *AGBI,* the new series is more comprehensive (although several volumes covering the end of the alphabet have not yet been published; they are being published annually by Godfrey Memorial Library). This reference work is a unique, every-name collective index alphabetically arranged by surname and given name to the titles included. Although only selected family history titles are indexed in it, *AGBI* should be consulted as a finding aid by all American genealogists, especially those doing pre-1900 research and those doing New England research. Joel Munsell's *Index to American Genealogies,* 5th ed. (1900; reprint; Baltimore: Genealogical Publishing Co., 1967) is a surname index to major American genealogical periodical titles, genealogies, and selected local histories. The reprint edition includes the *Supplement, 1900 to 1908.*

E. Kay Kirkham compiled *An Index to Some of the Family Records of the Southern States* (Logan, Utah: Everton Publishers, 1979), a surname index to DAR Bible records and family records. Many of these typescripts were microfilmed at the DAR Library in Washington, D.C. Index entries give surname, Family History Library microfilm number, and microfilm item number. This index is a useful finding aid for southern states genealogists, although many typescripts have been added to the DAR Library since Kirkham compiled this index. A companion volume by Kirkham, *An Index to Some of the Bibles and Family Records of the United States, Volume 2* (Logan, Utah: Everton Publishers, 1984), is arranged by New England states, North Central states, Mid-Central states, South Central states, and western states. As with other surname indexes, the multiple references to common surnames, such as Adams and Allen, can make these volumes more difficult to use for common names.

It is important to note when an index was compiled. Kirkham's volumes were compiled in the late 1970s and early 1980s and are based on records microfilmed in the 1970s and earlier. Because both the DAR Library and the Family History Library have continued to acquire more records of the kind indexed in these volumes, this index should not be considered comprehensive.

Biographical Sources

The major index to biographical sketches in national and vocational printed works is *Biography and Genealogy Master Index* (*BGMI*) (Detroit: Gale Research Co., 1975–). The series includes cumulations for various years and annual update volumes. *BGMI* is available in printed, microfiche, and electronic (CD-ROM or online) formats. This work indexes more than 8 million names of both living and deceased persons in current and retrospective biographical dictionaries and "who's whos," such as *Who's Who in America, Who's Who in Canada, Who's Who in the World,* and *The Dictionary of National Biography* (Great Britain), although the majority of the sources indexed cover individuals in the United States. Other works indexed include subject encyclopedias with biographical entries. *BGMI* does not index periodicals or books of biography about one individual only. *BGMI* and the biographical dictionaries it indexes are available at major research libraries.

Also significant for American biographical and historical titles are *American Biographical Index*, edited by Laureen Baillie (New York: K. G. Saur, 1993), and, for current biographies, *Index to Who's Who Books* (New Providence, N.J.: Marquis Who's Who, 1978–94). Other valuable indexes to biographies and local histories include a two-volume index compiled by William Prescott Greenlaw, *The Greenlaw Index of the New England Historic Genealogical Society*, 2 vols. (Boston: G. K. Hall,

1979). It indexes many early New England families and other localities as well. Also useful in locating names of ancestors, especially those in the Midwestern states, is a four-volume surname index compiled by the Newberry Library titled *The Genealogical Index of the Newberry Library, Chicago*, 4 vols. (Boston: G. K. Hall, 1960).

Many statewide master indexes to biographical sources are readily available to researchers. A fine example is *Indiana Biographical Index*, compiled by Jimmy B. Parker and Lyman De Platt (West Bountiful, Utah: Genealogical Indexing Associates, 1983; microfiche). It is a very useful index to many local history and biographical titles for Indiana. A published book index to biographical sketches in local histories is Charles Morford's *Biographical Index to the County Histories of Iowa* (Baltimore: Gateway Press, 1979). Statewide indexes to biographical works are available for most other states; they are noted in chapter 18.

Periodical Indexes

Genealogical periodicals contain compiled genealogies; methodology articles; abstracts from records, such as Bible records, vital records, church records, census records, etc.; book reviews; queries; and many other items of interest to genealogists. The first major attempt to index American genealogical periodicals on a large scale was Donald Lines Jacobus's *Index to Genealogical Periodicals*, 3 vols. in 1 (1932–53; reprint; Baltimore: Genealogical Publishing Co., 1978). Jacobus was a prolific compiler of American genealogies. The information in these three volumes was combined by Carl Boyer, 3rd, in *Donald Lines Jacobus's Index to Genealogical Periodicals*, rev. ed. (Newhall, Calif.: Boyer Publications, 1983). The latter is easier to use because its entries are arranged in one alphabetical grouping.

Also significant is *Genealogical Periodical Annual Index* (Bowie, Md.: Heritage Books, 1976–),[2] known as *GPAI*. Earlier *GPAI* volumes were compiled by Ellen Stanley Rogers and George Ely Russell; *GPAI* has been continued by Laird C. Towle and others. Vol. 1 was published in 1963; it covers titles published in 1962. Not all genealogical periodical titles have been indexed, and *GPAI* is not a complete name index to all names published therein. Nevertheless, *GPAI* is a useful index to personal names and records of localities.

The *Periodical Source Index* (Fort Wayne, Ind.: Allen County Public Library Foundation, 1986–), also known as *PERSI*, is a name and subject index to thousands of articles in genealogical and local historical periodicals (although it is not an every-name index to all personal names, nor does it provide page numbers for articles). A sixteen-volume retrospective index covering the years 1847 to 1985 is still being published, and annual indexes have been published since 1986. A microfiche version is available at LDS family history centers and at some other libraries, and Ancestry released a CD-ROM version in 1997. *PERSI* is the major index for genealogical periodicals and should be carefully searched by all American genealogists. *PERSI* is useful for locating references to personal names and locality records, such as gravestones and vital records, published in periodical articles.

A good example of a subject index for a genealogical periodical is *APG Article Index, 1979–1996* (supplement to *APG Quarterly*, December 1996). Arranged by topic, this index includes volume number, year, date, page number, and author's name. Examples of the topics indexed include marketing, professionals and professionalism, and publishing. Authors' names are not indexed separately. The Allen County Public Library in Fort Wayne, Indiana, will make copies of articles for a fee.[3]

Earl Gregg Swem's *Virginia Historical Index* (often known as Swem's Index), 2 vols. in 4 (1934–36; reprint; Gloucester, Mass.: Peter Smith, 1965), is a useful index for Virginia researchers. It indexes selected Virginia titles. Another valuable index is *The New England Historical and Genealogical Register Index of Persons, Volumes 1–50*, 2 vols. (1906–11; reprint; Camden, Maine: Picton Press, 1989). It is a significant index for American genealogists.[4] The *New England Historical and Genealogical Register* is also indexed by *The New England Historical and Genealogical Register Index of Persons, Volumes 51–148*, edited by Jane Fletcher Fiske, 4 vols. (Boston: New England Historic Genealogical Society, 1995). The *New England Historical and Genealogical Register* and cumulative indexes are available on CD-ROM from the New England Historic Genealogical Society. These indexes to the *Register* are monumental reference sources for American genealogists.

CURRENT INDEXING METHODS AND REFERENCES

Indexes to books or genealogical collections have been compiled by professional indexers and by persons who have little or no indexing experience. With the advent of computer-assisted indexing, the days of indexing with three- by five-inch index cards are gone. Two popular commercial indexing programs for genealogists include *SKY Index*[5] and *Picton Index*.[6] An excellent article by Patricia Law Hatcher and John V. Wylie, "Indexing Family Histories," *National Genealogical Society Quarterly* 81 (June 1993): 85–98, describes how to index family histories.

Indexing methodology and techniques, along with examples and illustrations, are found in Virginia Thatcher's *Indexes: Writing, Editing, Production* (Lanham, Md.: Scarecrow Press, 1995).[7] Thatcher discusses index format, alphabetization, style, and production. Indexing techniques and methods, including a chapter on personal names, are covered in Hans H. Wellisch's *Indexing from A to Z* (New York: H. W. Wilson Co., 1991).[8] Wellisch's alphabetically arranged reference book is written for people with little or no experience in indexing, as well as for professional indexers. (As comprehensive as Wellisch's work is, however, it does not cover genealogical indexing.) F. W. Lancaster's *Indexing and Abstracting in Theory and Practice* (Champaign, Ill.: University of Illinois Graduate School of Library and Information Science, 1991) discusses indexing principles, consistency of indexing, and quality of indexing.

Larry S. Bonura's *The Art of Indexing* (New York: John Wiley & Sons, 1994) is a practical book written for technical writers responsible for indexing and indexers who want to learn more about indexing techniques and methods. Harold Borko and Charles L. Bernier's *Indexing Concepts and Methods* (New York: Academic Press, 1978) covers the structure of indexes, indexing and editing procedures, computer-aided indexing, and other, related indexing subjects.

Additional indexing reference sources are Timothy C. Craven's *String Indexing* (Orlando, Fla.: Academic Press, 1986); Gerald Jahoda's well-illustrated *Information Storage and Retrieval Systems for Individual Researchers* (New York: John Wiley & Sons, 1970) (describes conventional and coordinate indexes, key-word-from-title indexes, citation indexes, and other indexes); Robert L. Collison's very popular *Indexes and Indexing* (London: Ernest Benn Ltd., 1972);[9] G. Norman Knight's *The Art of Indexing: A Guide to the Indexing of Books and Periodicals* (London: George Allen & Unwin, 1979) (a basic text that discusses the mechanics of indexing);[10] Jennifer E. Rowley's *Abstracting and Indexing,* 2nd ed. (London: Clive Bingley, 1988); and Leonard Montague Harrod, ed., *Indexers on Indexing* (New York: R. R. Bowker Co., 1978) (a selection of some of the best indexing articles published in *The Indexer*). Other indexing reference works can be found by searching in card or computer catalogs under "indexes and indexing" and in the bibliographies included in the works cited in this chapter.

Those interested in compiling a genealogical index should study Josh Reeder's *Indexing Genealogy Publications,* edited by Corinne Earnest (Damascus, Md.: Russell D. Earnest Associates, 1994). Reeder discusses general indexing principles, cross referencing, and tips for creating quality indexes. Michael Lewis Cook briefly outlines indexing procedures in his *Speed Indexing: How to Prepare Your Genealogical Book Index Rapidly and Accurately* (Evansville, Ind.: Cook Publications, 1978).

CONCLUSION

Access to genealogical material is best accomplished by effectively using indexes, reference guides, and library finding aids. An article that further discusses using indexes is John L. Thornton's "The Uses of Indexes," reprinted in Leonard Montague Harrod, ed., *Indexers on Indexing* (New York: R. R. Bowker, 1978), 39–41.

While many sources—such as local histories, church records, state census schedules, newspapers, etc.—are only partially indexed, these and many other sources, such as probate records and original records filed in estate files (probate packets), land records, military records, etc., need complete personal name indexes. While many hundreds of genealogical periodical articles have been partially indexed, a complete personal name index to all genealogical periodicals is not available. Genealogists need greater access to geographical and place-name databases.

Among genealogists' greatest needs is for more personal name indexes. A genealogical record without a personal name index is like a locality that is not included on a map or a gazetteer. It is frustrating for researchers to pick up an unindexed book, such as a county or other local history, and begin searching for ancestral names without the availability of an every-name index.

There is much to be done by the eager researcher who wishes to index records and help contribute to the genealogical literature. Genealogists with an interest in indexing should be willing to properly and thoroughly index records that will assist them and other researchers for years to come. With the aid of computers and computer indexing programs, many more indexes are expected in the years ahead. The growth of indexes and other sources on CD-ROM and the Internet has been phenomenal.

Researchers who wish to compile an index should first read chapter 17, "Indexes," in *The Chicago Manual of Style*, 14th ed. (Chicago: University of Chicago Press, 1993). This style manual is one of the standard reference sources for writers and editors. Publications by the American Society of Indexers, especially its professional journal, *The Indexer*, are also valuable for those who wish to compile indexes.

This chapter does not presume to define or describe every index, finding aid, or catalog available for American genealogists. Indeed, only selected indexes have been discussed. Most of the sources described here are available at the Family History Library in Salt Lake City. Many are also available at the Library of Congress in Washington, D.C., and at other major research centers throughout the United States.

In addition to the discussions in the other chapters of *Printed Sources*, indexes and related genealogical titles are discussed in Kory Meyerink's "Databases, Indexes, and Other Finding Aids," chapter 2 in *The Source: A Guidebook of American Genealogy* (cited earlier). *The Source* is available on CD-ROM from Ancestry as part of the *Ancestry Reference Library.* Another valuable reference is Raymond S. Wright, 3rd, *The Genealogist's Handbook: Modern Methods for Researching Family History* (Chicago: American Library Association, 1995).

NOTES

1. National Society, Daughters of the American Revolution, 1776 D Street NW, Washington, DC 20006-5392. Many of the typescripts and indexes in the DAR Library have been microfilmed by the Genealogical Society of Utah and are available at the Family History Library in Salt Lake City. Recently received records have not been microfilmed, however.
2. Heritage Books, 1540-E Pointer Ridge Place, Bowie, MD 20716.
3. Allen County Public Library, Historical Genealogy Research Center, P.O. Box 2270, Fort Wayne, IN 46801-2270.
4. Picton Press, P.O. Box 250, Rockport, ME 04856-0250.
5. SKY Software, P.O. Box 394, Maine, NY 13802-0394.
6. Picton Press, Rockport, Maine. *Picton Index* can import data from other programs. It is an easy-to-use, *Windows*-based computer program.
7. Also see M. D. Anderson's *Book Indexing* (Cambridge, England: Cambridge University Press, 1971); Gordon V. Carey's *Making an Index*, 3rd ed. (Cambridge, England: Cambridge University Press, 1963); Donald B. and Ana D. Cleveland's *Introduction to Indexing and Abstracting*, 2nd ed. (Littleton, Colo.: Libraries Unlimited, 1990); Anne G. Cutler's *Indexing Methods and Theory* (Baltimore: Williams and Wilkins, 1970); Nancy C. Mulvany's *Indexing Books* (Chicago: University of Chicago Press, 1993); Sina Spiker's *Indexing Your Book*, 2nd ed. (Madison: University of Wisconsin Press, 1952); and Martha Thorne Wheeler's *Indexing*, 5th ed. (Albany: State University of New York, 1957).
8. The author is a former president of the American Society of Indexers. Also see Hans W. Wellisch, *Indexing and Abstracting: An International Bibliography* (Santa Barbara, Calif.: ABC-Clio, 1980).
9. Collison has written several additional guides to abstracting and indexing. Although dated, his work covers many general principles of indexing still useful today.
10. Other indexing references of interest are American National Standards Institute, *Basic Criteria for Indexes* (New York: American National Standards Institute, 1984); Norma Olin Ireland's "So, You're Going to 'Make an Index'!," *Colonial Genealogist* 7 (1974–75): 694–97, 921–23, 1001–3; Bertha E. Josephson's "Indexing," *American Archivist* 10 (April 1947): 133–50; and G. Norman Knight, ed., *Training in In-*

dexing: A Course of the Society of Indexers (Cambridge, Mass.: M.I.T. Press, 1969). References to this subject can be found in card and computer catalogs.

REFERENCE LIST

Horowitz, Lois. 1984. *Knowing Where to Look: The Ultimate Guide to Research.* Cincinnati: Writer's Digest Books.

Parker, J. Carlyle. 1991. *Rhode Island Biographical and Genealogical Sketch Index.* Turlock, Calif.: Marietta Publishing Co.

Thorndale, William. 1984. "Census Indexes and Spelling Variants." In *The Source: A Guidebook of American Genealogy.* Edited by Arlene Eakle and Johni Cerny. Salt Lake City: Ancestry.

BIBLIOGRAPHY

American National Standards Institute. *Basic Criteria for Indexes.* New York: American National Standards Institute, 1984.

American Standard Basic Criteria for Indexes. New York: American Standards Association, 1969.

Anderson, M. D. *Book Indexing.* Cambridge, Mass.: Cambridge University Press, 1971.

Bonura, Larry S. *The Art of Indexing.* New York: John Wiley & Sons, 1994.

Borko, Harold, and Charles L. Bernier. *Indexing Concepts and Methods.* New York: Academic Press, 1978.

Brewer, Annie M., and Amy F. Lucas, eds. *Indexes, Abstracts, and Digests.* Detroit: Gale Research Co., 1982.

Carey, Gordon V. *Making an Index*, 3rd ed. Cambridge, Mass.: Cambridge University Press, 1963.

The Chicago Manual of Style. 14th ed. Chicago: University of Chicago Press, 1993.

Cleveland, Donald B., and Ana D. Cleveland. *Introduction to Indexing and Abstracting.* 2nd ed. Englewood, Colo.: Libraries Unlimited, 1990.

Collison, Robert L. *Indexes and Indexing.* 4th rev. ed. London: Ernest Benn Ltd., 1972.

Cook, Michael Lewis. *Speed Indexing: How to Prepare Your Genealogical Book Index Rapidly and Accurately.* Evansville, Ind.: Cook Publications, 1978.

Craven, Timothy C. *String Indexing.* Orlando, Fla.: Academic Press, 1986.

Curran, Joan Ferris. "Numbering Your Genealogy: Sound and Simple Systems." *National Genealogical Society Quarterly* 79 (September 1991): 183–93. Published separately as NGS Special Publication no. 59 (Arlington, Va.: National Genealogical Society, 1992).

Cutler, Anne G. *Indexing Methods and Theory.* Baltimore: Williams and Wilkins, 1970.

Dallas Public Library. *Indexes and Bibliographies for Use in Genealogical Research.* Dallas, Tex.: Texas History and Genealogy Department, Dallas Public Library, 1965.

Feinberg, Hilda, ed. *Indexing Specialized Formats and Subjects.* Metuchen, N.J.: Scarecrow Press, 1983.

Fetters, Linda K. *A Guide to Indexing Software.* 4th ed. American Society of Indexers, 1992.

Gouldesbrough, P. "Surnames in Indexing." *Archives* 10 (1972): 158–59.

Gray, J. C. "The Perplexing Personal Name." *Special Libraries* 11 (1920): 93–94.

Harrod, Leonard Montague, ed. *Indexers on Indexing: A Selection of Articles Published in The Indexer.* New York: R. R. Bowker Co., 1978.

Hatcher, Patricia Law, and John V. Wylie. "Indexing Family Histories." *National Genealogical Society Quarterly* 81 (June 1993): 85–98.

The Indexer. American Society of Indexers, serial.

Ireland, Norma Olin. "So, You're Going to 'Make an Index'!" *Colonial Genealogist* 7 (1974–75): 694–97, 921–23, 1001–3.

Jacobus, Donald Lines. "Hints on Indexing." *American Genealogist* 34 (1958): 89–94.

Jahoda, Gerald. *Information Storage and Retrieval Systems for Individual Researchers.* New York: John Wiley & Sons, 1970.

Josephson, Bertha E. "Indexing." *American Archivist* 10 (April 1947): 133–50.

Knight, G. Norman. *The Art of Indexing: A Guide to the Indexing of Books and Periodicals.* London: George Allen & Unwin, 1979.

_____, ed. *Training in Indexing: A Course of the Society of Indexers.* Cambridge, Mass.: M.I.T. Press, 1969.

Lancaster, F. W. *Indexing and Abstracting in Theory and Practice.* Champaign, Ill.: University of Illinois Graduate School of Library and Information Science, 1991.

Meyerink, Kory. "Databases, Indexes, and Other Finding Aids." In *The Source: A Guidebook of American Genealogy.* Edited by Loretto Dennis Szucs and Sandra Hargreaves Luebking. Rev. ed. Salt Lake City: Ancestry, 1997.

Mulvany, Nancy C. *Indexing Books.* Chicago: University of Chicago Press, 1993.

Reeder, Josh. *Indexing Genealogy Publications.* Edited by Corinne Earnest. Damascus, Md.: Russell D. Earnest Associates, 1994.

Rowley, Jennifer E. *Abstracting and Indexing.* 2nd ed. London: Clive Bingley Ltd., 1988.

Saldana, Richard. *A Guide to "Misteaks" in Census Indexes.* Bountiful, Utah: R. H. Saldana & Co., 1987.

Scheffler, E. M. "Name Index." *Illinois Libraries* 43 (June 1961): 449–61.

Sperry, Kip. "The Index: A Tool for the Genealogist." *Everton's Genealogical Helper* 30 (January 1976): 10–12.

_____. *A Survey of American Genealogical Periodicals and Periodical Indexes.* Gale Genealogy and Local History Series, vol. 3. Detroit: Gale Research Co., 1978.

Spiker, Sina. *Indexing Your Book.* 2nd ed. Madison: University of Wisconsin Press, 1952.

Thatcher, Virginia. *Indexes: Writing, Editing, Production.* Lanham, Md.: Scarecrow Press, 1995.

Thorndale, William. "Census Indexes and Spelling Variants." In *The Source: A Guidebook of American Genealogy,* edited by Arlene Eakle and Johni Cerny, 17–20. Salt Lake City: Ancestry, 1984).

Thornton, John L. "The Uses of Indexes." In *Indexers on Indexing: A Selection of Articles Published in The Indexer,* edited by Leonard Montague Harrod, 39–41. New York: R. R. Bowker, 1978.

Wellisch, Hans H. *Indexing and Abstracting: An International Bibliography*. Santa Barbara, Calif.: ABC-Clio, 1980.

_____. *Indexing from A to Z.* New York: H. W. Wilson Co., 1991.

Wheeler, Martha Thorne. *Indexing*. 5th ed. Albany: State University of New York, 1957.

Part 3

PRINTED ORIGINAL RECORDS

VITAL AND CEMETERY RECORDS OVERVIEW

Key Concepts in This Chapter

- Published vital records are drawn from government and non-government records.
- Marriage records are the most-published vital records.
- A growing number of statewide publications make research easier.
- "Evidences" of vital records can compensate for the lack of official records.
- There is a wide variety of printed vital records.
- Records are published in a variety of formats.
- Periodicals publish many vital records.
- Most published records of births and deaths are for the New England states.
- Bibliographies and library catalogs are the best finding aids.
- Evaluating how comprehensive the published records are is important.
- Printed vital records can greatly speed research.

Key Sources in This Chapter

- *An Index to Some of the Bibles and Family Records of the United States*
- Liahona Research early marriage collections
- "Hunting for Bears" marriage collections
- *Genealogical Publications: A List of 50,000 Sources from the Library of Congress*
- *Obituaries: A Guide to Sources*
- *International Genealogy Index* (*IGI*)
- *Parish and Vital Records List*
- *Vital Record Compendium*
- Massachusetts town records
- *Index to United States Cemeteries*
- *Cemeteries of the U.S.*
- *United States Cemetery Address Book*

7

VITAL AND CEMETERY RECORDS

Karen Clifford[1]

Vital records are those documents which attest to major life events, such as birth, marriage, and death. Although most records of this nature are maintained by civil authorities, Bible and cemetery records have been created and preserved by individuals and by private organizations. Additionally, many churches have recorded births, marriages, and deaths, as well as christenings and burials. Newspapers and many other records also document these vital events. While some British and European countries began keeping birth and death records nationally in the nineteenth century, the United States left government registration up to the individual states. The majority of states did not begin birth and death registration until the first quarter of the twentieth century; however, every state required marriage registration in some form at the time the state was created, except for New York, Pennsylvania, and South Carolina, where laws went into effect in the 1880s.

Towns and counties compiled early marriage records in most states, the first records dating from the time each town or county was created. The types of marriage records created differed from one place to another. Marriage records consist of applications, bonds, certificates, consents, contracts, intentions, licenses, registers, and returns, to name those used most widely.

Enforcement of early registration was haphazard, particularly in rural and frontier areas, and not everyone who was born or died during the initial registration periods was included in the records. Early records offer much less information than modern birth and death records, but they are usually considered the best evidence for those events nonetheless.

The purpose of this chapter is to explore the broad variety of published vital records. After some general discussion covering the nature of printed vital records, statewide indexes, and general finding aids, this chapter will cover the different sources of these records. They include local government vital records, "evidences" of vital records drawn from other sources, newspaper sources, Bible records, cemetery inscriptions, and several other sources that are often used as vital record substitutes. A bibliography of additional references and a compilation of printed vital sources arranged by state concludes this chapter.

The Source: A Guidebook of American Genealogy, edited by Loretto Dennis Szucs and Sandra Hargreaves Luebking, rev. ed. (Salt Lake City: Ancestry, 1997) and other genealogical texts cover the definition, roles, and characteristics of *original* vital records; it is the purpose of this chapter to discuss the unique value of *printed* vital records. The background and history of these records will be restricted to that information required to use the printed versions of these records. For an in-depth discussion of original vital records, where to find them, and how to use them, consult chapter 3, "Research in Birth, Death and Cemetery Records," and chapter 4, "Research in Marriage and Divorce Records," in *The Source.*

THE NATURE OF PUBLISHED VITAL RECORDS

The responsibility for creating and preserving vital records has been taken at various times by churches, state boards of health, military and naval personnel, local justices of the peace, colonial and state governors, and others. This situation has resulted in a great diversity of printed vital records, as will be demonstrated in the following pages.

Any printed record of birth, marriage, or death can be placed in the category of "vital record." Church records, which also document births, marriages, and deaths, are covered in chapter 8 of this book and so are mentioned only briefly in this chapter. Many local governments did not begin to keep records of birth and death until the first quarter of the twentieth century. This lack often causes uninformed genealogists to despair until they learn of the variety of equivalent records that can be used when civil registrations are not available.

Because the majority of government vital records created in the United States are modern documents, very few of them have been published (in part due to rights of privacy and because of limited interest in such recent records). Compilers and abstracters have focused on the earlier vital records, especially those of the colonial period in New England, which date from the seventeenth century in some towns. Only fourteen states initiated registration before 1880, and it stands to reason that printed vital records deal mostly with those states.

Rarely do published vital records include complete transcriptions (verbatim reproductions) of original records; rather, published records typically summarize, index, extract, or abstract original records from particular jurisdictions that were created when the events took place. The result is that only part of the original record is reproduced, meaning that researchers are drawing conclusions based on limited information, rather than a complete record of an event. Because every printed source contains errors and omissions, they should be used with cau-

MARRIAGE RECORDS OF ROWAN COUNTY, NORTH CAROLINA

GROOM	BRIDE	DATE
EVANS, Solomon	HUTZON, Honaur	02/05/1828
EVANS, Thomas	GREEN, Sarah C.	12/11/1845
EVANS, Waine	CRIDER, Polly	01/18/1813
EVANS, William	GRAHAM, Nicey	06/28/1804
EVANS, William	GRANGER, Elizabeth B.	06/12/1819
EVATT, James	JONES, Susan	06/21/1785
EVENS, John	LAURANCE, Betty	01/21/1782
EVERHART, Michael	LIVENGOOD, Mary	02/12/1822
EVERHEART, John	SOPHIA, Mary	08/24/1788
EVERITT, Alexander	CARRIGAN, Harriet A.	06/04/1844
EVNS, Hendrick	-----, Mary	09/10/1813
EXUM, David	RARY, Eliza A.	01/31/1832
EYTCHESON, Ely	DEAVER, Polly	12/02/1815
EZELL, Frederick	COX, Mary	03/28/1780
FAGENWINTER, Christopher	FAW, Barba	10/01/1785
FAGG, Joel	PEOLPES, Amey	06/04/1817
FAGGENWENTER, Henry	RANY, Catharine	04/15/1813
FALCKER, Samuel	KERN, Betsey	08/14/1817
FALKER, A.W.	GARVER, Catherine N.E.	12/11/1861
FALKERSON, Frederick	GIBSON, Sarah	07/02/1766

Figure 7-1. From Ingmire's *Rowan County, North Carolina Marriage Records, 1754–1866.*

tion. As a rule, researchers should examine documents in their original form whenever possible, especially if the printed version appears to have been poorly done. See the introduction to *Printed Sources* for guidelines on evaluating all types of printed sources.

The majority of published vital records are from the New England states, where births, marriages, and deaths were entered in town records as early as the seventeenth century. A large percentage of records from New England towns, especially those created before 1850, have been published. Typically, printed New England vital records offer births, marriages, and deaths arranged alphabetically in different sections, with some variations. These are discussed in more detail below.

More marriage records are in print than any other early record source. Recorded at the county level outside of New England, they are usually published as records from particular counties. Figure 7-1, from *Rowan County, North Carolina Marriage Records, 1754–1866,* compiled by Frances T. Ingmire (St. Louis, Mo.: Ingmire Publications, 1984), is typical of most published marriage records; an original marriage record might contain additional information.

Information contained in death records can span a lifetime if it includes the deceased's parents, birth date, birthplace, spouse, residence, death date, place of death, occupation, place of interment, etc.; the most useful printed death records include all of this information. Generally, printed death records serve more as indexes to original records because they are, at best, brief abstracts. Figure 7-2 is from Harold Torrey's *Death Records of Tekonsha Township, Calhoun County, Michigan, 1897–1907* (Tekonsha, Mich.: the author, 1981), an excellent death record publication.

While the records kept by civil authorities are generally the best sources for records of vital events, there are many other sources which offer direct evidence of births, marriages, and deaths. Newspapers, for example, are a rich source of vital records. Family Bibles often include the vital events of several generations. Military pension files, especially those that include applications from widows and orphans, often have birth, marriage, and death information. Indeed, the list of sources for vital events records is virtually endless, and all of these are used to compile published vital records.

Value of Published Vital Records

While all published records have limitations, they also have significant value. For example, using published vital record abstracts is often the easiest and quickest way to determine whether vital records were originally created and, if so, where they can be found. These published records provide quick access to pertinent genealogical information and can serve as finding tools for original documents.

Easier to Read. Transcribed renditions of the earliest vital records are generally much easier to read than the originals. In fact, all original registers of vital records contain handwritten data which can be difficult to decipher. Microfilmed copies of original records are sometimes rendered partially or completely indecipherable by dark smudges or faded ink, torn or folded edges, or tight bindings on the original, or simply by poor microfilming. A printed version taken from the original can solve the problem of deciphering the difficult passages.

Translation from a foreign language is another way in which a published record can be made easier to read, as the following example from Jeannie F. J. Robison and Henrietta C. Bartlett, eds., *The Colonial Dames of the State of New York—Genealogical Records—Manuscript Entries of Births, Deaths and Marriages, Taken From Family Bibles 1581–1917* (New York, 1917; reprint; Baltimore: Genealogical Publishing Co., 1972) (pages 250 and 252) shows. Both the actual Dutch transcript and English translations are given in it:

KILIAEN VAN RENSSELAER.

(Born 1663.)

Holy Bible in Dutch; dordrecht, Hendrick, Jacob en Pieter Keur, 1702.
contains the records of Kiliaen Van Rensselaer and Maria Van Cortlandt, his wife, with their children; also some earlier entries have been written in. It has descended to the present owner, Eugene Van Rensselaier, Esq., of Washington, D.C., who is the great-great-great-grandson of the original owner. The records are in Dutch and have been translated by Dr. L. Bendikson.
1645: 24 julij Donderdagh quartier voor eene is gebooren onse Dochter Maria van cortlandt N.S.
1674: 12 OCTr: op sondagh is mijn vader jaeremias van Rensselaer in Den Heer ontslaepen en op Den 15 dito begraven N.S.
1688/9: 24 janua is mijn Moeder Maria van Renssalaer in den Heer ontslaepen. O.S.
1663: 24 Augu op frijdagh en ochgent te achten is

gebooren Kiliaen van Rensselaer en op sondagh daer aen gedoept N.S. . . .

[TRANSLATION]

[1645: July 20th, Thursday, born at a quarter to one our daughter Maria van Cortlandt. (New Style).]
[1674: Oct. 12th, Sunday, died in the Lord, my father Jeremias van Rensselaer, and he is interred on the 15th of the same month (New Style).]
[1688/9: Jan. 24th, died in the Lord, my mother Maria van Rensselaer (Old Style).]
[1663: Aug. 24th, Friday, born at eight o'clock in the morning, Kiliaen van Rensselaer and baptized on the following Sunday (New Style).]

Faster to Locate. Published sources enable many more documents to be reviewed in the same amount of time, often because they are combined in one publication. The information in them is generally more concise, they are more likely to be accessible locally, and every-name indexes and finding aids in the published sources generally supersede such tools in the original records.

```
f.n. William H. Gordon
d.d: Oct. 22, 1897
Sex: Male; Color: White; Ae: 58yrs; 0mos.; 24das.
Married bp: Michigan; Occ: Farmer
f.n.: Wm. Gordon bp; Vermont
m.n.: Sarah Shapard bp: New York
pob: Windfall Cem.

          ##################################
d.d.: Nov. 8, 1897
f.n. Mrs Mary Ann Allen
Sex: Female; Color: White; Ae: 64yrs., 4mos., 5das.
Married; bp: Germany ; Occ: Farmer
f.n.: M. Stell bp: Germany
m.n: Unknown bp: Unknown
pob: Lyon Lake Cem.

          ##################################
d.d.: Jan. 7, 1898
f.n.: Chas. Witherill
Sex: Male; Color: White; Ae: 7yrs.
 Widower; bp: Unknown Occ: Farmer
f.n. & m.n..: Unknown bp: Unknown
pob: Burlington Cem.

          ##################################
d.d: Feb. 9, 1898
f.n.: Calvin Rich
Sex: Male; Color: White; Ae: 78yrs.;4mos.;27das.
Married bp: Unknown Occ.: Farmer
f.n.: ? Rich bp: Unknown
m.n.: Unknown bp: Unknown
pob: BurlingtonCem.
```

Figure 7-2. From Torrey's *Death Records of Tekonsha Township, Calhoun County, Michigan, 1897–1907.*

As Finding Tools. Printed vital records serve genealogists as finding tools for other records because so many families may be considered in one source; however, the researcher should not become overly dependent on any index, including those used for vital records (phonetic spellings were often used, with regional variations being picked up in the records). Besides indexes, spelling aids, and other helps, there may be guides to other aspects of research, such as the following guide to "Free Negro Surnames" in Jean M. Mihalyka's *Marriages Northampton County, Virginia 1660–1854 Recorded in Bonds, Licenses, Minister Returns, and Other Sources* (Bowie, Md.: Heritage Books, 1991), page 139:

FREE NEGRO SURNAMES

To facilitate research in African-American studies. Free Nigro, Mulatto or Slave has been indicated on the marriage entry when it could be ascertained. Many clerks and ministers were especially diligent in recording the race of the individuals to be married. If not so recorded, race can often be determined, especially for witnesses, since in the case of slaves and free blacks, they "had first to be charged as the law directs". (See Raleigh Thompson entry-1835). The record of free blacks who married slaves frequently gives interesting details supplied by the slaves' owners. (See Arther Becket and Edward Wickes entries, both 1839).

A very helpful indicator, of course, is the knowledge of family surnames. Most of the names listed below are predominantly those of free black families. Those marked by an asterisk in many instances are shared by both races. The list, of course has been drawn only from the marriage entries and is by no means inclusive of all the African-American families living on the Eastern Shore in the period covered.

*Ames	Drighouse	Mingo	Scisco
Anthony	Drigus	Morris	*Simkins
Becket	Francis	Moses	Stephens
Bevans	*Giddens	Nedab	Thompson
Bingham	*Harmon	Pool	Toyer
*Brickhouse	Jeffery	Press	Webb
*Carter	Jubilee	*Read	Weeks
Church	Lang	Rozelle	Wiecks
*Collins	Liverpool	Sample	
Cottrell	*Major	Satchell	

Background Information. The introduction of a printed vital records volume may provide information directing the researcher to the original records, give detailed methodology for searching the original records, or provide information on using the printed abstracts. For example, *Vital Records from Chicago Newspapers 1833–1839,* 7 vols. in 4 (Chicago: Chicago Genealogical Society, Newspaper Research Committee, 1971) (page v) provides excellent background information:

All the court records for Chicago and Cook County were destroyed in the fire of 1871. These lost records will be partially replaced by this first volume of genealogical data extracted from the Chicago newspapers.

Long obituaries have been abstracted to include only the vital data. Some death notices contained a

WAKE COUNTY MARRIAGES, 1770-1868

Hayes, Theophilus & Rebeckah Tabourn, 16 Nov 1808; John Chaves, bm.

Hayes, Thomas H. & Sally Barham, 4 Jan 1813; John Moore, bm.

Hayes, William M. & Emeline Farar, colored, 2 July 1856; Broadey Hayes, bm.

Hayes, Dr. Wm. P. & Sallie E. Wiggins, 28 April 1855; Jos. D. Hayes, bm; m 29 April 1855 by J. W. Tinnin, minister.

Hayles, James & Nancy Shaw, 11 Feb 1811; Osborn Lockart, bm.

Hays, Absalom & Rachel King, 14 Oct 1816; Anderson Page, bm.

Hays, Henry & Mary Barham, 7 Aug 1813; Absalom Hays, bm.

Hays, Richard & Eliza Curtis, 14 Nov 1866; George Hunter, bm; m 14 Nov 1866 by Robert Lucas.

Hays, William & Dolly Hardcastle, 23 April 1824; Willis Glenn, bm.

Haywood, Alexander & Huldia Auston, colored, 11 Oct 1865; Isaac Young, bm; m 11 Oct 1865 by John R. McCoy, Chaplain 120th.

Haywood, E. B. & Lucy Ann Williams, 12 Nov 1850; R. H. Haywood, bm.

Haywood, F. J. & Martha Whitaker, 8 Dec 1831; Alfred Williams, bm.

Haywood, Frank & Barbara Sturdavant, colored, 6 Oct 1866; Gaston Broughton, bm; m 10 Oct 1866 by W. M. Hayes.

Haywood, Henry & Frances Watkins, colored, 28 Jan 1868; m 2 Feb 1868 by T. C. Smith, J. P.

Haywood, John Lee & Hannah H. Lockhart, 14 May 1832; Fabius J. Haywood, bm.

Haywood, Joseph A., son of F. J. & Martha H. Haywood, & Mary A. Boylan, dau of W. M. & Mary Boylan, 9 May 1868; m 11 May 1868 by R. S. Mason, rector Christ Church, Raleigh.

Figure 7-3. From *Wake County, North Carolina Marriage Records, 1781–1867* by Brent H. Holcomb.

> request for an eastern newspaper to please copy. We have included these instructions since it might be a clue to the nativity of the deceased.
>
> We have included administrator's notices because in some cases the administrator appears to be a relative or spouse of the deceased. And the death notices were not always published.
>
> These newspaper extracts are prone to errors made by the reporter, the newspaper editor, and the typesetter. The Newspaper Research Committee has done its utmost to record the data exactly as printed in the newspapers, though some of the fine print was difficult to read. The spelling of names and places is as found in the original newspaper. The preserved Chicago newspapers are not complete. These too were lost in the Chicago Fire. Microfilm copies of the existing newspapers can be found at the Chicago Public Library, Chicago Historical Society, University of Chicago, and the Illinois State Historical Library in Springfield.

Some volumes indicate how to order copies of the original records. Explanatory material can also help the researcher to recognize relevant historical conditions associated with an area or its vital records.

Multiple Copies of a Record. Sometimes more than one published version of a set of records exists, and it is not unusual to find that such publications differ. For example, *Wake County, North Carolina Marriage Records, 1781–1867,* by Brent H. Holcomb (Baltimore: Genealogical Publishing Co., 1983) (figure 7-3) and *Marriages of Wake County, North Carolina, 1770–1868* by Frances T. Ingmire (St. Louis, Mo.: Ingmire Publications, 1985) (figure 7-4) contain transcripts of many of the same marriage records. For the marriage of Joseph A. Haywood and Mary A. Boylan, only Ingmire's work gives the date of marriage, while Holcomb's version gives more information overall. Check every available printed source, especially if the original document is not available.

Introductory Information. Some printed sources for vital records provide introductory material which may be applicable to research in many areas. Holcomb's *South Carolina Marriages: 1688–1799,* 3 vols. (Baltimore: Genealogical Publishing Co., 1980–81, 1984) is a good example of a printed vital record source that includes valuable additional information about the vital records covered in it. Holcomb's description of the scarcity of marriage records for South Carolina (vol. 1, page v) is applicable to research in many areas.

> The current marriage license law did not go into effect until 1911. Marriage records prior to that year are difficult to locate. . . . we must rely on the seven extant parish registers. . . . there were twenty-one parishes in South Carolina in the colonial period. Marriage bonds were also issued, but only two volumes of these have been found. One solitary record of marriage licenses issued is extant.

Holcomb then goes on to clearly identify the sources of the vital records covered in that particular volume. His source list (page vii) includes:

Hist Oburg	Giessendanner records, published in *The History of Orangeburg County, South Carolina,* by A. S. Salley.
St Hel PRs	St. Helenas Parish Register, Published in *South Carolina Historical and Genealogical Magazine (SCH&G)*
St John Luth Ch	Records of St. John's Lutheran Church, Charleston, S. C. Microfilm at S.C. Archives.
St Phil PR	St. Philip's Parish Register. Published separately (two volumes).

The actual records (pages v–vi, 1) appear as:

Abbott, William & Catherine Hope, P Licence by the Revd. Mr. Alexr. Garden, 16 October 1747. St. Phil PR

Abecklin, Kilian & Maria Schwartz, 12 Jan. 1741; Hans Freydigs, Christian Schwartz, wit. Hist Oburg

Abercrombie, John & Sarah Mitchell, widow, 4 Jan. 1777. St. Phil PR

Abraham, James & Sally Allgent, 14 Feb. 1773. St. John Luth Ch

Ackarman, Albert & Sarah Walker, 30 Apr. 1752. St. Hel PR

Published vital records can prove valuable if they are compiled in a systematic and complete manner. Those that are compiled accurately and preserve the spelling of the originals provide the researcher with several advantages: (1) they are fairly reliable indexes for performing a particular searches; (2) they aid in deciphering difficult-to-read or obliterated entries; and (3) they provide invaluable data when the originals from which they were compiled are no longer in existence.

Limitations of Published Vital Records

Relying solely upon printed vital records can complicate genealogical research when assumptions are made based on transcriptions only. Published vital records frequently omit entries from the original records, and they often do not contain all of the information given in each original entry. There are also other limitations in the use of published vital records, including:

- Limited jurisdictional coverage
- Lack of every-name indexes in early publications
- Most are finding aids only—not complete compilations
- Frequent transcription, typographical, or interpretation errors
- Dating inaccuracies resulting from different calendar systems
- Omissions in the abstractions
- Misleading titles which may imply a broader area or length of study than is actually covered

Presentation. Printed sources are sometimes arranged by surname, without an every-name index; hence, neighbors, family members, or others who might be associated with the person of interest through their proximity in an original list of names can go unrecognized.

Deletion or Addition of Material. To allow standard formats, most publications omit many of the details and descriptions included in the original documents. Such omitted information could be crucial to distinguishing between two families in an area with the same name. For example, these comments, found in the introduction to Hannah Benner Roach's "Seventeenth Century Birth Records in the Delaware Valley," *Pennsylvania Genealogical Magazine* 27: 83–91 (1971), should make us think about similar deficiencies in other sources (pages 83–84):

> Although the publication of William Wade Hinshaw's *Encyclopedia of American Quaker Genealogy* has been of inestimable value to genealogists, it should be used with caution, especially when searching for early records.
>
> Examples of such errors were found in the printed birth records listed in Hinshaw, when compared with the original entries in the Burlington Monthly Meeting Book of Births, Deaths, Marriages, 1677–1777. These records, now deposited in Friends Archives at 302 Arch Street, Philadelphia, belong to the Burlington Monthly Meeting of Friends in New Jersey. A comparison of the entries with the printed Hinshaw record disclosed thirty-four errors or omissions, evidence of the need to consult original records. In addition, the entries are of a special interest for they included names, in most cases, of the officiating midwives and the women who witnessed the births, all of which were omitted in Hinshaw.
>
> Elizabeth Powell Daughter of Robert & Prudence Powell in Burlington was Borne the 7th Seaventh of the 7th month 1677 Latte of London Chandler. witnesses then present: Ellin Harding, Mary Cripps, Ann Peachee.

MARRIAGE RECORDS OF WAKE COUNTY, NORTH CAROLINA

GROOM	BRIDE	DATE
HATCHET, William	WARREN, Eliza	07/25/1854
HATFIELD, Edwin	SIMMS, Ailey	12/19/1812
HATHCOCK, Francis M.	TURNER, Lucy Ann	09/18/1856
HATLER, Hasten	NICHOLS, Elizabeth	01/02/1802
HAVENS, T. J.	ANDERSON, Fannie	09/05/1857
HAWKINS, Harry	BARBREY, Mary	09/21/1866
HAWKINS, James	JEFFRIES, Matilda	12/22/1866
HAWKINS, Phillip H.	FULLER, Nancy H.	02/20/1838
HAWKINS, Samuel	WEST, Julia	02/18/1867
HAYES, Absalom	WATTS, Caty	11/16/1812
HAYES, E. D.	KIRKHAM, Mary E.	12/11/1859
HAYES, E. D.	BUCK, Elizabeth L.	04/11/1850
HAYES, George D.	LYNN, Martha A.	11/18/1855
HAYES, Hugh S.	COOKE, L. Frances	04/01/1857
HAYES, Isaah	BROWN, Harriett	01/30/1867
HAYES, J. C.	MORRIS, A. R.	04/01/1858
HAYES, John	BRASFIELD, Mahaley	07/29/1823
HAYES, Marvel	LUMBLEY, Elisabeth	11/29/1803
HAYES, Theolipus	TABOURN, Rebeckah	11/16/1808
HAYES, Thomas H.	BARHAM, Sally	01/04/1813
HAYES, William M.	FARAR, Emeline	07/02/1856
HAYES, Wm. P. Dr.	WIGGINS, Sallie E.	04/29/1855
HAYLES, James	SHAW, Nancy	02/11/1811
HAYS, Absolam	KING, Rachel	10/14/1816
HAYS, Henry	BARHAM, Mary	08/07/1813
HAYS, Richard	CURTIS, Eliza	11/14/1866
HAYS, William	HARDCASTLE, Dolly	04/23/1824
HAYWOOD, Alexander	AUSTON, Huldia	10/11/1865
HAYWOOD, E. B.	WILLIAMS, Lucy Ann	11/12/1850

Figure 7-4. From *Marriages of Wake County, North Carolina, 1770–1868,* by Frances T. Ingmire.

> Ann Wills ye daughter of Daniell & Marly Wills in Burlington was borne ye 1st of ye 10th month 1677. Witnesses then present: Jone Clift, Judy Olive, Prudence Cleyton, Mary Cripps, Mary Casly.
>
> William Blacke son of Wm. & Allis Blacke in Burlington was born ye 23rd of ye 3rd month 1678. Late of London Haberdaisher. Witnesses thereunto then present: Jone Clift mid: Jude Olive, Mary Wills, Prudence Cleyton, Mary Cripps, Ellin Harding.

Non-Uniform Presentation. Each compiler, author, or editor selects those details which he considers important, thereby possibly omitting facts that may have significance to some researchers. For example, an abstracted marriage entry might contain only the names of the people being married and not those of the bondsmen and parents. Other information present in the original records might be omitted as well. Reading such an abstracted entry might cause a researcher to come to an erroneous conclusion.

Typographical Errors. As in all published sources, errors in data entering and transcription can camouflage original names. For example, if the name Smith were typed as "Mith," it would be alphabetized under *M* (not *S*), resulting in an erroneous search.

Incorrect Interpretation. An abstractor's inability to decipher handwritten records can cause errors in a transcription. Some errors may be due to the abstractor's or editor's lack of knowledge of abbreviations used by the original recording clerk.

Misspelling and Phonetic Spellings. The misspelling of a name when it was originally recorded can cause problems in locating proper entries. Search for all possible variant spellings and be thoughtful in determining variations in spelling and pronunciation which may account for unexpected or "creative" entries.

Publication Variables. Different abstractors use different methods and abbreviations. Some volumes lack an every-name index and may fail to state so in the introductory remarks. If the user fails to make this determination, the inadequacies of the publication may go unnoticed and the researcher may fail to find valuable data that is in the original records.

Determine if the volume is truly what it seems to be. For example, it might include only selected records from counties important to the author rather than from the entire state. Many a beginning genealogist has given up looking for an individual in a particular area only to find later that the index being used covered only part of that area.

Incomplete Information. Most published sources omit some of the information contained in the original records. Consider the following entry from *McLean County* [Illinois] *Birth Records,* vol. 3, 1883–85 (Normal, Ill.: Bloomington-Normal Genealogical Society, 1982) (page 27):

> 1884
> Kershner, Grover Cleveland
> January 28 Bk. 3 pg. 145

The entry provides a reference to the exact book and page number in the original volume (which, of course, should direct the researcher to the original). However, it omits key information contained in the original. Grover Kershner's parents were born when neither New York nor Pennsylvania kept birth or marriage records; however, Grover's original birth record gives his mother's maiden name, the township, county, and state of his father's birth, and the city and state of his mother's birth—none of which is in the abstract. It would probably take dozens of research hours to establish that information. This is a good example of why original records must be searched.

A similar problem appears in *Marriage Records of Effingham County, Georgia, 1780–1875,* compiled by Mrs. Julian C. Lane (Statesboro, Ga.: the compiler, 1940), in which Thomas Marion Hodges and Julia Jane Colson are listed as having married on 7 August 1856. However, in the original, it is the marriage *license* that names the bride and groom and gives the date the license was issued as 7 August 1856. The printed volume lacks the minister's return certifying that the two actually were married and therefore does not give the date of the ceremony. The lack of the return does not mean the marriage did not take place (although that may have been the case); more often, it means that the minister or justice of the peace did not file the return. Clearly, the researcher must examine other records, such as deeds, census returns, and probates, to determine whether the marriage actually took place.

Accuracy of the Copy. Another problem with published sources concerns how accurately or completely they reflect information in original records. Often (and, of course, inadvertently), compilers omit entries that are in the original records. If an ancestor is known to have lived her entire life in one place, in all probability she married there and was enumerated in every census taken in that place during her lifetime. If her name is not listed in an index or a printed volume of records, it is a mistake to conclude that she did not marry there or was missed by the census taker. Instead of relying exclusively on published sources, search the original record line by line before reaching a negative conclusion.

Printed sources are only as valuable as their compilers are competent. Many well-intentioned compilers start a project without a design; what appears at first to be a straightforward process becomes complicated when unexpected information appears, changes in handwriting become a challenge, and documents are faded or damaged beyond readability. Compilers appear to make the most mistakes in reading handwriting styles. For example, one researcher searched Elizabeth P. Ellsberry's *Early Marriage Records of Randolph County, Missouri, 1829–1859* (n.p., n.d.) for the marriage of Jeremial Reynolds Taylor. The published book did not show Jeremial, but it did include an entry for the marriage of Harry R. Taylor to Elle E. McClean, 23 August 1839, which the researcher took interest in. Turning to the original entry, the researcher found that it clearly showed Jerry R. Taylor as the groom.

Unclear Titles. Another pitfall in using published vital and other records is not knowing the exact nature of the original source. Does the title "Marriage Records" refer to entries from a marriage register, or marriage bonds, or marriages inferred from deeds? Are the listings in a book of "Cemetery Records" from the sexton's records or are they tombstone inscriptions? When compilers omit such information it takes more time to find the original source. As in family histories and genealogies, every entry in a published record should lead back to the original.

Inadequate Indexes. In *Marriages from Early Tennessee Newspapers, 1794–1851* (Easley, S.C.: Southern Historical Press, 1978), edited by the Rev. Silas Emmett Lucas, Jr., Lucas indicates in the introduction that ". . . this book has not been indexed and . . . is arranged alphabetically by groom" (page 1). Thus, in the entries below, no index would lead the user to Reverend Hume, or to the people whose names appear incidentally in the abstract, such as those of parents or persons at whose homes marriages took place. However, because every entry was cross-referenced by bride, Marry Ann Compton would appear (page 2):

> Abbay, Mr. Richard married in Davidson county on the 24th inst., by the Rev. M. Hume to Miss Marry Ann Compton. National Banner Nashville Whig (Monday, March 28, 1831)
> Abbe, Miss Asenath A. married to Rutland, James B.
> Abbey, Mr. Anthony S. married in Davidson county on the 31st January by the Rev. Wm. Hume to Miss Susan L. Compton. National Banner Nashville Daily Advertiser. (Friday, Feb. 1. 1833)
> Abbott, Miss Elisabeth married to Dr. Pierce.
> Abbott, Mr. James T. married in Gibson County to Miss Rebecca C. Barton.
> Nashville Whig (Tuesday, April 21, 1846)

Formats of Published Vital Records

Printed vital records may be presented in full text, in an abbreviated form of a full text, with introductory information, or in summary form using tables, charts, lists, and abstracted lists. They also range from single-subject books to multi-volume periodical series. They can be found in compiled publications, such as printed town records or newspapers, or in abstracts done on a statewide, county, or regional basis. They may be abstracts, extracts, transcriptions, or simply indexes. Samples of various formats covering the three basic vital record categories are provided below:

Full Text. The following obituary for a revolutionary war veteran from Anna R. Rupley's "Obits of Revolutionary Veterans from the Franklin Repository and the Franklin Telegraph and Democratic Advisor," *Pennsylvania Genealogical Magazine* 11: 196–97 (1931), page 196, is a full transcription of the source.

> April 20, 1824: Died on the 14th ultimo at the residence of his son in Letterkenny township, in the 89th yr. of his age, Mr. William Kirkpatrick, having lived near eighty-six years in said township. His father was killed by Indians the year after Braddock's defeat, the son being at the same time enlisted as a soldier for the protection of the settlement of Pennsylvania against the Indians. He took an active part in the Revolutionary War; was in a camp under Washington at Princeton, Trenton, and New Brunswick. – *The Franklin Repository.*

Abbreviated Format. Military records sometimes include family Bible records submitted to support pension applications. Such information might be formatted in a standard, abbreviated manner in a publication, such as the example below from Chan Edmondson's *Revolutionary War Period Bible, Family, and Marriage Records Gleaned from Pension Applications, Volume 14* (Dallas, Tex.: Edmondson, 1993), page 3. As the example shows, not only is the death place of the soldier given, but also the maiden name of his wife and the date and place of their marriage:

> NH/NH BENJAMIN GEORGE m. ABIGALE NEWMAN, maiden name, 15 March 1780, at Derryfield, now Manchester, NH; Litchfield, Hillsborough Co., NH, town record. He was born July 1755, Derryfield; died 24 Sept 1838, leaving a widow, ABIGAIL GEORGE, who also died at Strafford, Orange Co., VT, 31 May 1839. EBENEZER GEORGE, HANNAH NORTHROP, HULDAH PRESTON, ISAAC GEORGE, ABEGAIL BEEDY, ELIZABETH DOTY, RACHEL FULLER, and BENJAMIN GEORGE her only surviving children. Probate in Bradford Dist, VT, JAMES FULLER, admr.

Another example from the first volume of the same series, by Helen M. Lu (Dallas, Tex.: Lu and Neuman, 1980), page 21, lists several marriages and deaths in one record:

> W-16805:
> JOHN ADDOMS (or ADDAMS) m. MARY TOWNSEND, 8 JUNE 1778, NY/NY City of Hopewell, Dutchess Co., NY. MARY of Wapping Creek.
> FAMILY RECORD:
> MARRIAGES:
>
> JOHN ADDOMS and CHARITY SMITH married 7 Nov. 1763.
> JOHN ADDOMS and MARY TOWNSEND married 8 June 1778.
> WILLIAM COE and MARTHA ADDOMS married 17 Jan. 1787.
> ROBERT REEVE and MARY ADDOMS married 12 Nov. 1797.
> JONAS SMITH ADDOMS and REBECCA ROGERS married 17 March 1804.
> BENJAMIN MOOERS and ELIZABETH ADDOMS married 24 May 1810.
> JONATHON BARLOW and PHEBE ADDOMS married 17 Nov. 1812.
> LUTHAR HAGAR and SARAH ADDOMS married 25 Aug. 1813.
> JOHN T. ADDOMS and HARRIET YOUNG married 1 April 1814.
> LEMUEL BARLOW and CHARITY ADDOMS married 17 Aug. 1814.
> HORRACE BOARDMAN and HARRIET ADDOMS married 21 March 1821.
> DEATHS:
> RICHARD ADDOMS died 3 Oct. 1767.
> RICHARD ADDOMS died 15 April 1769.
> CHARITY (wife of JOHN ADDOMS) died 17 Oct. 1775.
> JOHN ADDOMS, JR., died 31 Oct. 1776.
> PHEBE ADDOMS died 9 July 1784.
> JONAS SMITH ADDOMS died 6 May 1804.
> REBECCA ADDOMS his wife died 1804.

SANITARY RECORD OF SICK, INJURED, BIRTHS, DEATH, ETC. AT ROUND VALLEY INDIAN AGENCY									
Month and Year	Name	Sex	Tribe	Date of Death	Age	Date of Birth	Sex	Blood	Father
Apr 1890	Mrs. Jim Brown	F	C.C.			Apr 11, 1890	F	1	Jim Brown
	Geo. Garfiel	M	Ukie	Apr 6, 1890	under 5				
	Jennie Brown	F	C.C.	28 - (?)	over 5				
	Nellie Perinton	F	C.C.	Apr 6, 1890	over 5				
	Luther Webster	M	C.C.	Apr 7, 1890	under 5				
	Jim Whipple's Babe	F	L.L.	Apr 6, 1890	under 5				
	Masen Richardson	M	L.L.	Apr 14, 1890	under 5				
	Old Sally Mullen	F	C.C.	14 - (?)	over 5				

RECORD OF BIRTHS AMONG INDIANS OF ROUND VALLEY AGENCY							
Child's Number on This Record	Parents' Number on Family Register	Name	Date of Child's Birth	Sex of Child	Ages of Parents	Blood or Nationality of Parents	Tribe of Allegiance by Citizenship of Parents
10	530	Father: Edwin Smith Mother: Belle Smith Child:	Jan. 9, 1902	F	45 36	One-half Blood One-half Blood	Little Lake Little Lake
11	546 625	Father: Frank Whipple Mother: Annie Card Child:	Jan. 25, 1902	M	26 26	One-half Blood Full Blood	Little Lake Concow

Figure 7-5. From *Vital Records (Births and Deaths) of Indians of Round Valley Agency California 1890–99, 1906–15, 1924,* compiled by Jimmy B. Parker, pages 1–3.

ELISABETH MOOERS died 26 Jan. 1818.
LEMUEL BARLOW died March 1822.
CHARITY BARLOW died Sept. 1822.
JOHN ADDOMS, SR., died 8 June 1823.
ROBERT REEVE died 1830.

Not only are the soldiers' marriages included; if their widows had second marriages and collateral relatives were involved, they, too, are listed. Such information greatly expedites research and can lead to other records.

Table Format. *Vital Records (Births and Deaths) of Indians of Round Valley Agency California 1890–99, 1906–15, 1924* (Salt Lake City: Genealogical Society, 1972), compiled by Jimmy B. Parker, includes the births and deaths of the Indians of Round Valley Agency in Covelo, California. The information was taken from the records of the agency, which are presently housed in the San Francisco Federal Records Center; it was presented in tables as shown in figure 7-5.

List Format. Silas E. Lucas and Ella L. Sheffield, eds., *35,000 Tennessee Marriage Records and Bonds, 1783–1870* (Easley, S.C.: Southern Historical Press, 1981) is a three-volume set of marriage bonds and marriage records found in the index card file at the Tennessee State Library and Archives (Nashville). It is arranged alphabetically in list format and covers the period from 1783 to around 1870 (page 1):

ABANATHY, William to Cynthia Human-issued August 17, 1872, m. by: D. S. Long, J. P., August 18, 1872, FRANKLIN Co.
ABBEY, Richard to Mary Ann Compton-March 24, 1831, m. by: V. D. M., DAVIDSON Co.
ABBOTT, George to Frances Watson-issues July 25, 1827, m. by: P. C. Mills, J. P., July 25, 1827, SUMNER Co.
ABBOTT, George W. to Hariet Caroline Lane-issued March 12, 1846, Bondsman: Thomas Lyons, m. by: L. Priestley, J. P., March 14, 1846, MONTGOMERY Co.
ABBOTT, James to Sarah Crimes-issued April 9, 1812, DAVIDSON Co.
ABBOTT, James to Mariah Stone-issued June 20, 1836, Bondsman: George Love, m. by: L. B. Laurence June 20, 1836, SUMNER Co.
ABBOTT, Martin to Mary Reynolds-issued October 3, 1844, m. by: Thomas Farmer, J. P., ROBERTSON CO.

Abstracted Lists. Published vital record sources consist of transcripts of births, marriages, and deaths as well as a variety of parallel records, such as consent affidavits, declarations of intention, banns, bonds, contracts, and affidavits accompanying marriage records. Abstracts comprise the majority of printed vital records. Most of the examples above, as well of those which follow, are abstracts. Some include the word *abstract* in their titles, as illustrated in *Marriages Northampton County, Virginia*

RECORD OF DEATHS AMONG INDIANS OF ROUND VALLEY AGENCY										
No. on This Record	No. on Record of Births	No. on Family Register	Name	Age	Sex	Date of Death	Married, Single, Widow, Widower or Divorced	Name of a Living Relative	Relation	No. of Relatives on Family Register
1		164	Jennie Anderson	60	F	Jul 5, 1901		Albert Anderson	Nephew	158
2			Jim Wesley		M	Jul 17, 1901	Married			
3		118	Nancy Willies	32	F	Aug 10, 1901	Married	Carrie Perry	Daughter	120
4		113	Susie Perry	58	F	Dec 17, 1901	Married			
5			Alice Mullen		F	Dec 24, 1901	Married			
6			Peggy Brown		F	Dec 22, 1901	Married	Eva Brown	Daughter	450
7			Annie Sew	31	F	Aug 13, 1901	Married	Martha Sew	Daughter	335
8	6	327	Fannie Cooney	49	F	Oct 31, 1901	Married	Cooney	Husband	197
9			Baby Fulwider	3 days	F	Nov 22, 1901	Single	Emma Updergraff	Mother	128
10			Grace Leggett	19	F	July 4, 1901		Ralph Leggett	Brother	326

REGISTER OF VITAL STATISTICS FOR ROUND VALLEY DEATHS						
Date	Name	Age	Sex	Degree of Blood	Tribe	Residence
July 28, 1912	Mrs. Chas. Heath	65?	F	F	Calito	Round Valley Res.
Jan 20, 1913	Tall Jack	?	M		Wailaki	Round Valley Res.
Mar 21, 1913	Edith Woods	9	F		Little Lake	Round Valley Res.
May 1, 1913	Emma Smith	47	F		Little Lake	Round Valley Res.
Mar 19, 1913	Bonnie Hardin		F		Wailaki	Round Valley Res.

Figure 7-5 (continued).

1660–1854 Recorded in Bonds, Licenses, Minister Returns, and Other Sources, Abstracted and Compiled by Jean M. Mihalyka, 1990 (cited earlier). To be truly valuable, abstracts require at least some explanation, such as historical background, notes, abbreviation lists, and symbol keys. Samples of Mihalyka's abstracts demonstrate a need for such a key and the extensive keys she provided (page 1):

> ABDALE, ABDEEL, ABDELL, ABDIL, ABDILL
> ABDEEL Abel to Nancy Dixon 17 Jun 1779; d/o Tilney Dixon dec'd; Luke Heath sec.
> ABDELL Abel to Rachell Johnson 14 Sep 1807; Wm D James sec.
> ABDELL Ezekial to Sarah Dalby 16 Sep 1779; d/o Waterfield Dalby dec'd; Ezekiel s/o Abel Abdell con; Wm Abdeel sec.
> ABDILL George to Peggy Roberts 20 Apr 1802; d/o Moses Roberts who gives her age as 22y on 24 Jun (18010; John Harrison sec; Solomon Richardson wit; m (1802) by I Bratten.
> ABDELL George D to Miss Mary F Hallett 1 Feb 1853; (George of Acc Co); con/o Wm T Fitchett gdn/o Mary; Jas G Floyd wit; m 2 Feb 1853 by P Warren.
> ABDEEL Hancock to Keziah Dalby 7 Mar 1780; Henry Warren sec.
> ABDEEL Henry to Sarah Tankard 26 Apr 1781; wid/o John Tankard; Wm Belote sec.
> ABDIL Henry to Hetty Stott 1 Oct 1796; Thos Dowty sec; m (1796) by J Elliot.

Mihalyka provided substantial background information, as illustrated by the following quotes from her introduction (pages vii, viii, x).

> Reference background:
> In compiling his book, Nottingham abstracted some marriages, for which he found no bonds from the collection of ministers' returns (1791–1854) also in the Clerk's Office. But there are minister returns for nearly two thirds of the marriage bonds which Nottingham omitted from his compilation. They are a valuable resource. Each gives the exact marriage date, the minister's name, an indication of the possible religious persuasion of the couple and often some details not shown on the bond. Unfortunately the manuscript returns have been used only rarely by the average researcher. While the bond shows that a marriage was seriously intended, the minister's return is proof that the marriage did take place.
>
> Historical background:
> A brief overview of the marriage laws in Virginia may be helpful to clarify the relationship between banns, bonds and licenses. An act of the Grand Assembly in James City in September, 1632, was a "revisal and cleerer explanation of former acts" and stipulated that "noe mynister shall celebrate matrymony betweene any persons without a facultie or lycense graented by

> the Governor except the banes of matrymony have beene first published three severall Sondayes or holidayes in the tyme of divine service in the parish churches where the sayd persons dwell accordinge to the Booke of Common Prayer . . ." Later in the century, the clerk of court instead of the Governor was authorized to issue the licenses.
>
> Research techniques:
> When doing research it is often helpful to know the name of the person who served as security for the bond of 50 pounds in current money, as well as the names of witnesses. In most instances these individuals were parents, other relatives or close friends. These have been routinely recorded.

Terminology

Genealogical records frequently contain unique terms not commonly found elsewhere, or words with slightly different meanings than we normally associate with them; this is the case with many vital records. The following brief discussions should help clarify some of the terminology used in published sources.

Birth Terminology. Terminology used in printed birth records is usually quite self-explanatory, but some entries may seem strange to researchers. For instance, if no original birth certificate was created, the term *delayed birth certificate* may appear in the published source. Such a certificate is a legal document of a person's birth based on supportive primary and secondary evidence filed after the actual birth: a delayed registration of an earlier birth.

A petition made to the court stating the name, birth date, birthplace, residence; father's name, race, and birthplace; and other items required by the legal jurisdiction, along with evidence to support the facts given, was used to justify issuance of such a certificate. A delayed certificate was considered to be the legal equivalent of a regular birth certificate. Although more reliable than most secondary sources, delayed certificates are only as accurate as the sources from which the information in them was drawn.

When a religious ceremony was performed shortly after the birth of an infant, such as a baptism, christening, or church blessing, the date of that event was sometimes recorded in lieu of a birth date.

Marriage Terminology. Marriage data can be found under a variety of labels:

1. *Consent affidavits* gave permission, usually from a parent or guardian, for an individual (often underage) to be married. The affidavits are permission slips given to a licensing authority at the time the couple intended to be married, or when bonds were posted, banns published, or licenses issued. They are valuable for identifying parents, proving whether the parents were deceased or living, determining relationships of guardians to marriage partners, and the age of the couple, among other things.

2. A *declaration of intent* to marry was often a prerequisite to the marriage ceremony. It could only be waived by obtaining a special license from the state or colonial governor, the county court, or another designated authority.

3. A *bann* was a written public declaration of an intended marriage. This posting gave the people in an area an opportunity to step forward and submit any reason why the marriage should not take place. The bann was an ecclesiastical custom which occurred in almost every state during the seventeenth and eighteenth centuries.

4. *Intentions to marry* were recorded with county or town clerks.

5. A *bond* was a payment, usually made by the father or a brother of the bride, required before a license could be issued. If some cause existed, or was discovered, that would make the proposed marriage null, the person who posted the bond would forfeit the money, offsetting the cost of any litigation.

6. *Marriage contracts* often were enacted between well-to-do individuals in order to protect their individual interests in the property which each possessed at the time of the marriage. A marriage contract could protect the property of a widow if she remarried. Many relationships have been determined using these records, but they often contain no proof that the marriage actually took place. It is necessary to use probate records with such a contract because the original contracts were not filed until the time of death, the originals were destroyed in a courthouse disaster (such as a fire), or the original was filed in a different courthouse than the probate records.

7. A *marriage license* was issued by a proper authority as a legal means of avoiding the posting of banns and intentions.

8. The marriage license *application* has existed since the mid-1800s. Modern applications indicate that the couple is free from disease and not closely related. Earlier applications listed family relationships, ages, residence, etc.

9. The *marriage certificate* itself, or a duplicate copy, was given to the couple when they presented their license and were married.

10. *Marriage returns, ministers' returns,* and *registration of marriages* were all ways of notifying the court that the marriage actually took place.

When looking for marriage information, search for records using any or all of the above terms.

Death Terminology. Death records typically contain more than just the death date and name of the deceased. A volume of printed death records might include causes of death (such as those listed in a mortality index), next of kin, place of residence, place of death, spouse, age of deceased, occupation of deceased, military service, birth date and place, parents' names and birthplaces, funeral home, cemetery, etc.

Abbreviations

Although the list of terms associated with birth, marriage, and death records is not lengthy, abbreviations used in printed sources vary widely. When searching a new printed source, look in the front of the book for a list of abbreviations. They might include:

1. Ecclesiastical division abbreviations (which identify the church the marriage was performed in, for example):

Cumberland Presbyterian Church	CPC
Missionary Baptist Church	MBC
Methodist Episcopal Church South	MECS
Protestant Methodist Church	PMC
Primitive Baptist Church	PBC
Episcopal Protestant Church	EPC

2. Abbreviations for specific compiled sources:

BHM	*Bangor Historical Magazine*
DAC	*Daughters of American Colonists*
DAR	*Daughters of the American Revolution*
DFPA	*Daughters of Founders and Patriots*
GRC	*Gravestone Records Committee*
MHGR	*Maine Historical and Genealogical Recorder*
MHS	*Maine Historical Society*
NEHGR	*New England Historical and Genealogical Register*
NGSQ	*National Genealogical Society Quarterly*

3. Abbreviations for the types of records used as sources:

Cem	Cemetery
Gen	Genealogical
Hist	Historical
Misc	Miscellaneous
Pres	Presented
Rec	Records

4. Abbreviations for coding conventions commonly used in printed sources:

[ ] Large brackets are used for (1) the abstracter's insertion of words into the text, and for (2) inserting the more frequent spelling of the surname into the alphabetizing order of the abstracts.

D indicates the type of abstract (death).

M indicates the type of abstract (marriage).

B indicates the type of abstract (birth).

/ The slash (1) appears after the last legible letter of a line of type on a torn page and (2) separates the paper citations when needed.

. . . Ellipses are (1) used conventionally to indicate omissions of text matter, and (2) used unconventionally when phrases are lifted out of context for insertion in composite abstracts.

- One dash indicates one missing letter or numeral.

-- Two dashes show that several letters or a series of words are missing from the original text (--illeg--).

5. Sometimes the abbreviations and citations are listed in the back of the book rather than in the front. They may include references to other documents, such as this example, which reveals the use of several sources:

REF LET	DOCUMENTS
A	Chart A of researcher #11
B	Chart B of researcher #11
C, I	(Not assigned)
Cen	Census
D	*Kentucky Cemetery Records* VI, pp976-9
E	*The East Kentuckian*, Dec '65, pp3
F	Family Group Sheets of #11
G	*Kentucky Society*—DAR, V1, pp269
GH	*Genealogical Helper*
H	*Kentucky Ancestors*—'84 Summer, pp28
J	*The Kitchen Family'* by L M Carter Lib of Cong #89-80463
K	Ragland's *History of Logan County*
L	*Kentucky War of 1812 Pensioners*
LAT	*Los Angeles Times*
M	*Historical Register of Virginians In The Revolution*—John Gwathway
N	*Virginia Records*—Brumbaugh
Vl	*The Kentucky Land Grants*—Jillson 976.9 J563-1

6. Abbreviations for relationships and terms often used in publications:

Ac	acres	LN	Last name
B b	born	Lawr	Lawrence
Brd	buried	M m	Married, married
C	circa	M/o	Mother of
Cen	census	M1	Marriage #1
Cem	cemetery	M2	Marriage #2
c/o	Child of	MIL	Mother in Law
Co	County	MN	Middle name
D/o	Daughter	PI	Place interred
DST	District	REF	Reference
FN	First Name	S/o	Son of
F/o	Father of	Sd/o	Stepdaughter of
GF/o	Grandfather of	Ss/o	Stepson of
Gd/o	Grandaughter of	ST	State
Gs/o	Grandson of	w	with
H/o	Husband of	w wid	widow(er)
Hb/o	Half brother of	W/o	wife of
Hs/o	Half sister of	X	Was not married

Following are some additional abbreviations which often appear in published vital records (portions of this list are from Mihalyka's *Marriages, Northhampton County, Virginia 1660–1854* [cited earlier]):

&	and	lic	license
app't	appointed	m	married
b	born	Mbk	minute book
bet	between	MinRet	minister's return
br/o	brother of	m/o	mother of
Brec	Bible record	Obk	order book
Co	county	orp	orphan
Col	colonel	orp/o	orphan of

con	consent	perm	permission
con/o	consent of	sec	security
cou/o	cousin of	s/o	son of
CtRec	court record	secs	securities
d	died	sis/o	sister of
dau	daughter	sl/o	slave of
d/o	daughter of	Sr	senior
dec'd	deceased	test	testified
Esq	esquire	Wbk	will book
FN	free Negro(s)	wid	widow of
f/o	father of	widr	widower
gdn	guardian	wit	witness
gdn/o	guardian of	wits	witnesses
Gent	gentleman	w/o	wife of
grd/o	granddaughter of	wrd/o	ward of
inv	inventory	y	year(s)
Jr	junior		

STATEWIDE SOURCES

Some of the most useful published vital records are statewide indexes and abstracts, which are being produced in increasing numbers. They can serve as excellent finding aids when the state in which a vital event took place is not known. They are usually published by state governments or by private individuals or groups.

State Government Publications

State governments have been recording births and deaths for decades, some for more than one hundred years. In the course of this activity, most states have created indexes of to improve access to the records. Many of these indexes are annual (or multi-year) listings or card files. Today all states use computers to track births, deaths, and marriages, and some states have used computers to create indexes to records made long before computers were available. Usually these indexes are available for public use, although distribution may be restricted to major libraries and/or state vital records offices. Some states have recognized the value of these finding aids to aid individuals seeking certificates and have made their indexes available for sale. (If the researcher has already searched an index and has the correct reference number for a certificate before requesting a copy of a certificate, the state can do its task much more quickly and efficiently, and the patron is served faster.) Because of the size of these indexes, they are typically available on microfiche (if the index was done with the aid of computers) or microfilm (if done as cards or book volumes).

Usually these indexes contain just enough information to identify the individual, such as a name, date, place, and parents' names. Of course, the certificate number, as well as the volume and page (included in many cases), allows the researcher to request a copy of the actual record. In some cases microfilm copies of the actual records are available for research as well. Figure 7-6 is an example from the Kentucky Office of Vital Statistics' *Kentucky Death Index, 1911–1986* (Frankfurt: Kentucky Office of Vital Statistics, 1988), available on microfiche.

Typically, these indexes date from the early twentieth century for births and deaths. Most states did not centralize marriage records until later in the century, so state marriage indexes, if available at all, may date from the 1950s or later. Some states have published only their death indexes, choosing to provide some privacy to living persons represented in the birth indexes.

Private Publications

Over the years, many researchers and research societies have recognized the need to provide statewide indexes to vital records as finding aids. Typically, these efforts have focused on marriage records for the early years of particular states or colonies. This focus is due in part to the lack of birth and death records for the early years and the availability of early marriage records for many states. Early years have also proved popular because there are fewer sources (such as censuses) for those years to help find people in specific localities. And, because the population was smaller in earlier years, there are fewer records to compile.

Most of these records are compiled directly or indirectly from county and town records. However, in contrast to state government-published indexes, their compilers often fail to provide any reference to the original sources; the researcher must still learn what original records were kept and how to locate them in order to verify the information. As more and more of these collections become available on CD-ROM and on the Internet (forms in which people with less research training use them), failure to identify sources will become a growing problem. The chief difficulty stems from the fact that such compilations are virtually never comprehensive. Even if the compiler was diligent in locating and transcribing every known marriage record, many marriages (and births and deaths) went unrecorded originally and so will not be included. The discussion below under "Vital Record Evidences" indicates how many such records might be missed.

Two private publications serve as examples. Susan Ormesher's *Missouri Marriages Before 1840* (Baltimore: Genealogical Publishing Co., 1982) is based on existing marriage records in the various counties. Joseph T. Maddox published four volumes of early Georgia marriages; his statements about his sources are vague, but at least the first volume relied on the entries Maddox found in Georgia periodicals. These volumes are arranged by county, but there is no way to determine which counties are in which volumes. (These and many other such statewide publications are listed in the chapter bibliography. However, such a listing cannot be complete because more are published continually, often with little fanfare, so bibliographers do not know that they exist.)

Early Marriage Publications. Near the beginning of the twentieth century, compilers located and published early marriage records for many northeastern states. Frederic Bailey, for example, relied on church records for his collections for Connecticut and Massachusetts. Publications for New York, New Jersey, and Pennsylvania, however, relied on state licenses, which represent only a small portion of the actual marriages.

Liahona Marriages. This series of books, based on years of research by Jordan R. Dodd and the staff at Liahona Research, was first published by Precision Indexing, a division of American Genealogical Lending Library of Bountiful, Utah. It was an attempt to gather all of the early marriages (generally those preceding 1850) for each of nineteen states in one alphabetical list.

All of the marriages in this collection were found by Liahona Research in the myriad of published books and microfilmed copies of original records at the Family History Library of The Church of Jesus Christ of Latter-day Saints (LDS church) in Salt Lake City. Every effort was made to retain the spellings in the original

ABURY	GEO	1	U/1	ESTIL		09	18	27	041	20074	/27
ABURY	MARY		U/1	MNTGY		04	30	28	064	31917	/28
ABUSCHLAKE	CHAS	P	U/1	KENTN		04	28	26	022	10588	/26
ABVANS	THELMA		U/1	JCKSN		03	31	32	023	11439	/32
ABVAWS	CEPHAS		053	JCKSN	JACKSON	11	01	50	056	27537	/50
ACAKE	JAMES		072	KENTN		03	10	16	017	08224	/16
ACCARDO	THOMAS		047	JEFFN	JEFFERSON	08	07	48	034	16568	/48
ACCARDO	TONY		051	JEFFN	JEFFERSON	04	20	80	023	11374	/80
ACCIARDO	JILL	A	002	HARDN	HARDIN	12	18	58	057	28252	/58
ACCRE	DOUGLAS		031	CRSTN	CHRISTIAN	09	24	47	039	19343	/47
ACCREE	GEORGE	S	029	BATH	OHIO	12	24	42	052	25661	/42
ACECLEAR	PATRIE	V	040	DAVES		09	04	27	041	20042	/27
ACERKMAN	MARY	E	065	CLDWL		04	07	16	020	09838	/16
ACEY	CHARLIE		076	PLSKI	PULASKI	02	10	82	014	06717	/82
ACEY	CLARA	F	009	FYETE	FAYETTE	08	15	51	036	17823	/51
ACEY	DAN		040	HARLN	HARLAN	12	25	22	055	27026	/22
ACEY	DELLA	H	052	GARRD		08	07	23	042	20576	/23
ACEY	ELMER		053	PLSKI	PULASKI	08	13	62	039	19099	/62
ACEY	ETHEL		079	CMPBL	CAMPBELL	08	12	77	038	18658	/77
ACEY	JOHN	G	075	PLSKI	PULASKI	10	28	67	050	24999	/67
ACEY	JOSEPH	C	U/1	PLSKI		09	20	12	059	23445	/12
ACEY	LOUISA			PLSKI		07	22	12	046	18318	/12
ACEY	MANIZA	E	091	PLSKI	PULASKI	05	07	64	024	11682	/64
ACEY	MARY	E	082	PLSKI	PULASKI	08	08	56	039	19344	/56
ACEY	MATILDA	E	069	PLSKI	PULASKI	12	08	63	060	29896	/63
ACEY	ROBERT	F	081	PLSKI	PULASKI	02	16	54	017	08030	/54
ACEY	STELLA		071	PLSKI	PULASKI	08	13	85	044	21606	/85
ACEY	WILLIAM	W	078	PLSKI	PULASKI	09	18	69	047	23145	/69
ACH	RUBY		005	FULTN		01	15	25	002	00763	/25
ACH	WOLFGANG	M	058	BRECK	BRECKINRIDGE	01	17	84	005	02197	/84
ACHATZ	MARY		082	KENTN	INDIANA	09	25	65	042	20897	/65
ACHATZ	RAYMOND	V	080	KENTN	INDIANA	12	12	65	058	28629	/65
ACHBERGER	MINNIE	H	095	CLARK	CLARK	01	15	85	001	00293	/85
ACHERS	WALTER		025	PERRY		07	22	25	036	17822	/25
ACHERSON	ABRAHAM		072	CMPBL		08	19	16	041	20088	/16
ACHESON	DONALD	E	053	WARRN	WARREN	01	11	84	004	01909	/84
ACHESON	MARY	V	087	JEFFN	JEFFERSON	10	06	60	045	22467	/60
ACHHAMMER	JOSEPH		059	JEFFN		12	13	27	057	28167	/27

Figure 7-6. From the *Kentucky Death Index, 1911–1986,* available on microfiche.

texts and to find all possible records for the time period covered. However, as comprehensive as the Liahona volumes attempt to be, there are records that may have been overlooked or misspelled or that were not available to the researchers (many original county records have been destroyed by fire, floods, neglect, and carelessness). If a marriage is suspected to have occurred but is not found in the appropriate volume, further research in additional sources may locate the evidence.

The purpose in creating this collection was to indicate the time and place of as many marriages as possible. It is up to the researcher to examine the original records (usually available on microfilm) and gather whatever additional genealogical information is desired. Unfortunately, Liahona Research did not indicate which sources were used in this process, nor did it provide citations for the origin of each entry. However, careful researchers who wish to examine the original sources will find sufficient information (the date and county) to lead them to the sources.

In addition to the book volumes mentioned above, the Liahona marriages are available on microfiche and in electronic formats as well. American Genealogical Lending Library has published the data on microfiche, floppy diskette, and a single CD-ROM. In addition, there are two other CD-ROM versions: Brøderbund Software's (Novato, California) Family Tree Maker's Family Archives series and Ancestry, Inc.'s (Orem, Utah) Ancestry Genealogy Library. Table 7-1 identifies these various publications.

Hunting for Bears. Another useful collection, with 1.7 million marriage records covering several states, is the "Hunting for Bears" (a play on the term *hunting forebears*) marriages published on six CD-ROMs by Brøderbund as part of its Family Tree Maker's Family Archives series. The records were gathered by a small team of amateur genealogists during the 1970s and 1980s, both at courthouses within the states covered and from microfilm records at the Family History Library. The collection provides spotty coverage over a broad time period.

Sixteen states in the South and Midwest are represented in this collection. Content for most states includes marriages from the early years into the middle and late twentieth century. However, the coverage is incomplete; on average, only half of the counties in any state are included, and within those counties coverage varies significantly. Marriages for some counties number more than ten thousand and cover more than one hundred years. For other counties in the same state, the collection might have fewer than fifty marriages covering a decade or less.

This collection serves as a useful finding aid, and a copy of the actual marriage record can be found for almost all entries. However, because only a small percentage of the marriages that took place during the years given are actually in the collection, it does not obviate the need to search the county records if a marriage is thought to have taken place. Table 7-2 provides an overview of the coverage in this collection.

GENERAL FINDING AIDS

Finding published vital records is not difficult. Most local, county, state, and regional libraries and state archives, in addition to the major family history libraries nationwide, have printed

Table 7-1. Coverage and Availability of Liahona Research's Early Marriage Records

State	*Coverage*		*Book and Microfiche Titles (AGLL)*	*Floppy Diskette Titles*	*Family Tree Maker CD-ROM Number*	*Ancestry's Early American Marriages Region*
	Years	*Marriages*				
Alabama	To 1825	6,104	Early to 1825	Early to 1825	NA	Gulf South
Arkansas	To 1850	9,063	Early to 1850	Early to 1850	227	Gulf South
California	To 1850	75	NA	Early to 1850	227	NA
District of Columbia	To 1825	4,807	Early to 1825	Early to 1825	NA	Atlantic South
Georgia	To 1850	83,753	Early to 1800 1801–1825	Early to 1800 1801–1825 1826–1850	226	Atlantic South
Illinios	To 1850	79,093	Early to 1825	Early to 1825 1826–1850	228	Midwest
Indiana	To 1850	99,949	Early to 1825	Early to 1825 1826–1850	228	Midwest
Iowa	To 1850	10,618	Early to 1850	Early to 1850	227	Midwest
Kentucky	To 1850	72,593	Early to 1800	Early to 1800 1801–1825	229	Atlantic South
Louisiana	To 1850	14,823	NA	Early to 1850	227	Gulf South
Michigan	To 1850	6,917	NA	Early to 1850	NA	Midwest
Minnesota	To 1850	86	NA	Early to 1850	227	Midwest
Mississippi	To 1825	4,491	Early to 1825	Early to 1825	NA	Gulf South
Missouri	To 1850	63,057	Early to 1825 1826–1850	Early to 1825 1826–1850	227	Midwest
North Carolina	To 1825	51,879	Early to 1800 1801–1825	Early to 1800 1801–1825	229	Atlantic South
Oregon	To 1850	2,200	NA	Early to 1850	227	NA
Tennessee	To 1850	24,310	Early to 1800 1801–1825	Early to 1800 1801–1825	229	Atlantic South
Texas	To 1850	8,791	Early to 1850	Early to 1850	227	Gulf South
Virginia	To 1800	44,110	Early to 1800	Early to 1800	229	Atlantic South

vital records in their collections. The smaller and more local in focus the library, the more limited its collection is likely to be. Because printed vital records are less expensive than many other genealogy-related books, more libraries are able to include them in their budgets.

Be sure to take constantly changing county and regional jurisdictions into account; printed records are most easily found in repositories whose collections focus on the jurisdiction of interest. Marriage records are the most numerous of vital records; thousands of volumes of printed marriage records are available in libraries, record depositories, bookstores, and in historical and genealogical periodicals.

Bibliographies

Several bibliographies and lists of sources provide the starting point for finding published vital records. Some are general genealogical sources; others focus specifically on identifying vital sources.

American and British Genealogy and Heraldry. The standard genealogical bibliography is P. William Filby's *American and British Genealogy and Heraldry: A Selected List of Books,* 3rd ed. (Boston: New England Historic Genealogical Society, 1983). Together with its supplemental volume (1987), this source identifies 12,817 major genealogical books, several hundred of which are published vital records. Arranged by state, then alphabetically by author or title, this index is useful for locating specific kinds of vital records for states or areas of interest. For example, in the index under Pennsylvania are titles dealing with "early births," "German marriages," "southeastern early Lutheran baptisms and marriages," "vital records," and other references. The index refers to an entry number (not the page on which the entry is found). Generally speaking, the sources in *American and British Genealogy and Heraldry* have a national or state focus rather than a more local one.

Genealogical Publications. Because the supplement to Filby's *American and British Genealogy and Heraldry* has a closing date of Summer 1985, an alternative source is needed to identify vital records published after that date. The most comprehensive listing of recent published vital records (and thousands of other sources) was compiled by Kory L. Meyerink as *Genealogical Publications: A List of 50,000 Sources from the Library of Congress* (Salt Lake City: Ancestry, 1997). This electronic CD-ROM bibliography reproduces the complete Library of Congress catalog entries for selected books acquired by the library since 1969. Selection criteria for this bibliography included all English-language family histories, all books dealing with "genealogy," and several other genealogically significant topics. These include more than 7,800 titles with the subject heading "Registers of births, etc.," another 1,300 identified as "Marriage records," and approximately four hundred newspaper indexes and abstracts. The latest books in this listing are those

Table 7-2. Coverage of "Hunting for Bears" Marriage Records

State	*Coverage*		*Counties:*	*Family Tree Maker CD-ROM*
	Years	*Marriages*	*Included/Total*	*Number*
Alabama	1807–1902	45,000	32/67	3
Arkansas	1779–1992	154,000	19/75	6
Arkansas	1820–1949	27,000	16/75	5
Georgia	1699–1943	105,000	82/159	3
Illinois	1806–79	36,000	19/102	2
Indiana	1800–1901	44,000	52/91	2
Kentucky	1768–1900	136,000	67/120	2
Louisiana	1718–1925	285,000	58/64	1
Maryland	1655–1886	23,000	23/24	4
Mississippi	1776–1935	343,000	82/82	5
Missouri	1766–1983	59,000	62/114	5
North Carolina	1745–1903	130,000	98/100	4
Ohio	1789–1875	52,000	39/88	2
South Carolina	1641–1944	34,000	Not given	3
Tennessee	1720–1922	95,000	45/95	2
Texas	1814–1909	95,000	84/254	5
Virginia	1624–1915	94,000	59/96	4

cataloged by the Library of Congress up to October 1995. Because of the broad selection criteria, this source likely includes most book-length published vital records from 1970 to early 1995. Some titles, published in small quantities and not received by the library (or not yet cataloged by mid-1995), will not appear in the list (these include many self-published books).

Genealogical Publications uses FolioVIEWS® search and retrieval software, which allows users to search for any word or combination of words in an entry. The publisher also provided the capability to search the title, author, and subject fields, making it easy to find any recent publication of interest. Additional features include the capability to personalize the database with bookmarks, highlighters, and personal notes.

Genealogical and Local History Books in Print. Another source for recent publications is Marian Hoffman's *Genealogical and Local History Books in Print,* 5th ed., 4 vols. (Baltimore: Genealogical Publishing Co., 1996–97). The first four editions were compiled by Netti Schreiner-Yantis (Springfield, Va.: Genealogical and Local History Books in Print, 1975, 1976, 1981, 1985; supplement 1990, 1992); they provided, at the time of publication, the most comprehensive list of genealogy and local history books in print. As with the two previously listed sources, only some of the titles listed are for printed vital records, but the state and county arrangement of this work makes it easy to learn what has been recently published. Publishers had to pay a nominal listing fee, so some titles do not appear, but a significant number of vendors, including self-publishers, chose to list their publications.

Vital Record Compendium. An earlier effort to identify published vital records is John "D" Stemmons and E. Diane Stemmons's *The Vital Record Compendium: Comprising a Directory of Vital Records and Where They May Be Located* (Logan, Utah: Everton Publishers, 1979). This book lists, by state and county, upwards of twenty thousand church and government vital records collections. Although many of the sources are not published, this compendium identifies thousands of published lists. Its entries were drawn from approximately two hundred sources, many of them periodicals and society and state repositories. Other entries refer to microfilms at the Family History Library.

Each entry is followed by a code referring to one of the sources in the bibliography. If the reference is to a microfilm or book at the Family History Library, it is followed by the microfilm or book number. Periodical references are followed by the volume and page number. Although dated, this compendium is still a valuable source, in part because it includes periodical articles and collections at repositories other than the Family History Library.

Obituaries: A Guide to Sources. While newspaper obituaries are excellent sources of biographical and vital records, this guide by Betty M. Jarboe is more than just a list of the newspapers that have obituary indexes. *Obituaries: A Guide to Sources,* 2nd ed. (Boston: G. K. Hall, 1989), defines "obituary" very broadly to mean any record of death. Therefore, Jarboe's guide is a list, by state, of 3,547 articles and books that list death dates. While these include published obituary indexes, Jarboe also lists cemetery inscriptions, published Bible records, transcribed death records, and many similar sources (figure 7-7). While it may not be comprehensive, *Obituaries: A Guide to Sources* is a compact and useful starting point for seeking published death lists.

Another reference that deserves mention is Thomas J. Kemp's *International Vital Records Handbook,* 3rd ed. (Baltimore: Genealogical Publishing Co., 1994). Although not a guide to published vital records, as a published source itself this guide cannot be overlooked. Kemp surveyed each Australian and U.S.

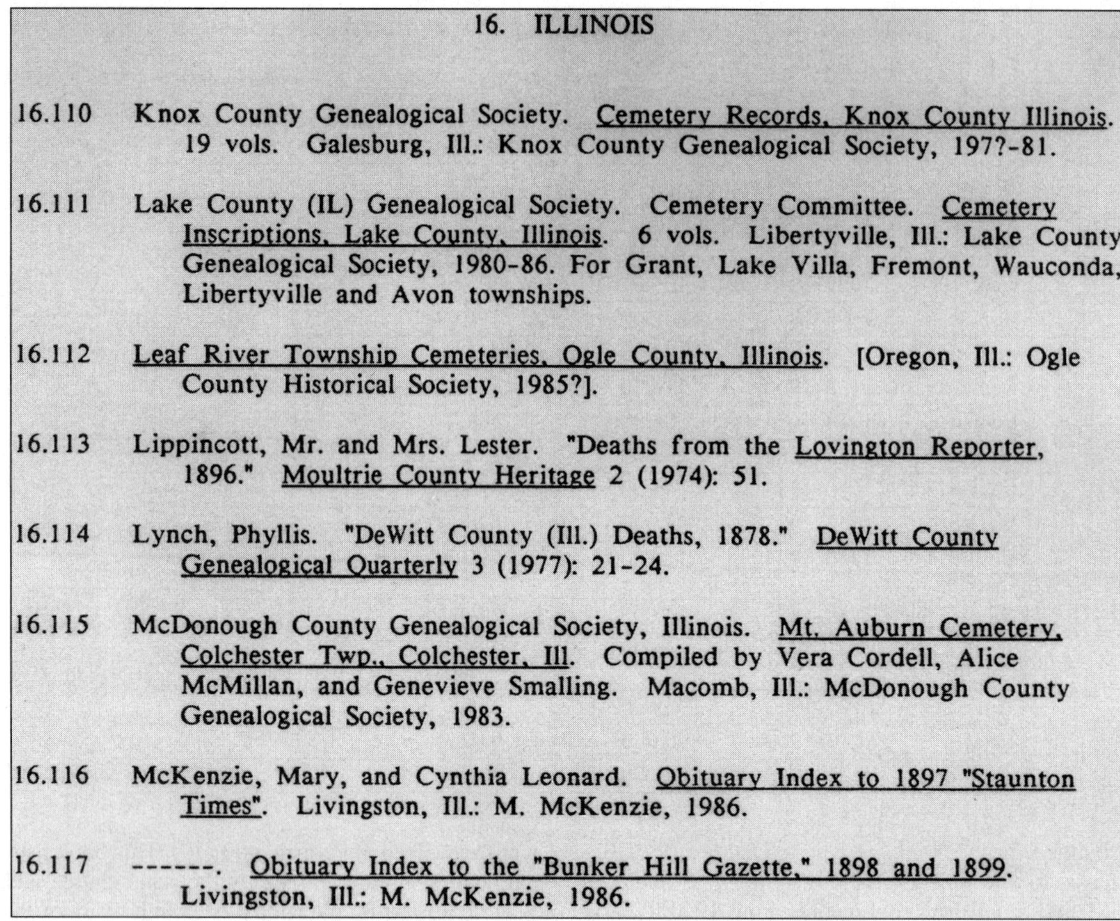

16. ILLINOIS

16.110 Knox County Genealogical Society. Cemetery Records, Knox County Illinois. 19 vols. Galesburg, Ill.: Knox County Genealogical Society, 197?-81.

16.111 Lake County (IL) Genealogical Society. Cemetery Committee. Cemetery Inscriptions, Lake County, Illinois. 6 vols. Libertyville, Ill.: Lake County Genealogical Society, 1980-86. For Grant, Lake Villa, Fremont, Wauconda, Libertyville and Avon townships.

16.112 Leaf River Township Cemeteries, Ogle County, Illinois. [Oregon, Ill.: Ogle County Historical Society, 1985?].

16.113 Lippincott, Mr. and Mrs. Lester. "Deaths from the Lovington Reporter, 1896." Moultrie County Heritage 2 (1974): 51.

16.114 Lynch, Phyllis. "DeWitt County (Ill.) Deaths, 1878." DeWitt County Genealogical Quarterly 3 (1977): 21-24.

16.115 McDonough County Genealogical Society, Illinois. Mt. Auburn Cemetery, Colchester Twp., Colchester, Ill. Compiled by Vera Cordell, Alice McMillan, and Genevieve Smalling. Macomb, Ill.: McDonough County Genealogical Society, 1983.

16.116 McKenzie, Mary, and Cynthia Leonard. Obituary Index to 1897 "Staunton Times". Livingston, Ill.: M. McKenzie, 1986.

16.117 ------. Obituary Index to the "Bunker Hill Gazette," 1898 and 1899. Livingston, Ill.: M. McKenzie, 1986.

Figure 7-7. From Betty M. Jarboe's *Obituaries: A Guide to Sources*. The second part of Jarboe's guide is a list, by state, of several hundred books that list death dates. While Jarboe's list does include published obituary indexes (manuscript indexes are the subject of the first section), she also includes cemetery inscriptions, published Bible records, transcribed death records, and many similar sources.

state and Canadian province and most foreign countries to learn about accessing their government vital records. He also learned the scope of the state or national collections, including the content and beginning dates and the fees for obtaining copies. For the United States and Canada, the book also includes reproductions of the various forms most often required to request records. As an aid to the researcher, Kemp included information (for the United States and some other countries) about how to obtain records faster (for example, by paying for faster searches) and about which of the records are available through the Family History Library.

Library Catalogs

Among the best places to find published vital records is the same source used for other published records: the catalog of a local research library. Genealogy libraries collect published vital records for the geographic areas they cover; usually they are filed under the names of the jurisdictions they cover (the specific town, county, or state) and under the subject heading "Vital Records." See chapter 1, "General Reference," and chapter 5, "Bibliographies and Catalogs," for more information on using libraries and their catalogs.

The Family History Library has the largest collection of printed vital records by virtue of having the largest collection of genealogical material anywhere. The National Society, Daughters of the American Revolution (DAR) has a large collection of printed vital records (especially Bible records) in its Washington, D.C., library; most of them have been microfilmed and are available at the Family History Library as well.

OCLC (On-line Computer Library Catalog), the largest worldwide bibliographic catalog electronic database, is another source for locating published vital records in libraries (see chapter 5). It can be searched at libraries that participate. The Internet is also a source for online catalogs, such as those of the Library of Congress and the Allen County Public Library in Fort Wayne, Indiana.

PERIODICALS

It is likely that more vital records have been printed in periodicals than in any other format, yet genealogical periodicals are perhaps the most overlooked sources for published vital records. Indeed, vital records are among the standard content items of most genealogical periodicals. Editors know they can seldom go wrong by publishing local Bible, cemetery, and other vital records. While many individual periodicals have every-name indexes, there is no comprehensive every-name index to all periodicals; thus, careful research is required to locate records of interest. Search for periodicals that cover the geographic area of interest; they are among the most likely sources for relevant published vital records. Then learn about the indexes to those periodicals.

General indexes to genealogical periodicals are also of great value to research. Because they are subject indexes, they do not index every name that appears in the periodicals. However, looking under the locality of interest will reveal the kinds of vital records published by particular periodicals for various time periods. The most important of these indexes is the *Periodical Source Index* (*PERSI*) (Fort Wayne, Ind.: Allen County Public Library Foundation, 1987–). *PERSI* is a comprehensive subject index to virtually all English-language genealogical periodicals; it covers both past and current issues. Within each locality (country, state, or county), the articles are listed under the appropriate record type. Records of births, marriages, and deaths are listed under "Vital Records," and tombstone inscriptions are listed under "Cemeteries." Records of church baptisms, weddings, and burials are listed under "Church." Family and Bible records are best found in the surname section of *PERSI*.

In addition to the book format found at many libraries, *PERSI* is available on CD-ROM from Ancestry (1997). For more information on *PERSI* and the other periodical indexes, see 19, "Periodicals."

Several books contain vital records extracted from periodicals. One example is *Ohio Marriages: Extracted from The Old Northwest Genealogical Quarterly* (Baltimore: Genealogical Publishing Co., 1977). Periodical reprints are convenient because they gather wide ranges of records, generally from particular areas, and make them more accessible to researchers. The table of contents of *Pennsylvania Vital Records: From the Pennsylvania Genealogical Magazine and the Pennsylvania Magazine of History and Biography,* 3 vols. (Baltimore: Genealogical Publishing Co., 1983), illustrates the variety of sources used for this collection of vital records, which is typical of other such works:

Source	*Samples*
Newspaper	Obituaries of Revolutionary Veterans
Board of Health	Earliest Records of Burials in Philadelphia from the Board of Health
Personal Papers	Marriage Docket of James Walton, Esq., East Fallowfield, Chester County, 1809–1832
Midwife	Midwife's Records, 1816–1828
Diary	The Diaries of Isaac Levan, Easton, Pennsylvania, 1823–1828 & 1842–1846

These "periodical reprint" volumes are discussed further in chapter 19. Table 19-2 (chapter 19) lists most of the reprint series compiled by Genealogical Publishing Co. (Baltimore). That company's efforts include at least a dozen volumes that focus specifically on vital records.

INTERNATIONAL GENEALOGY INDEX (IGI)

Most family historians soon learn about the *International Genealogical Index®* (*IGI*) because it is broadly available (in each of more than 2,500 LDS family history centers—see the introduction) and includes more than 240 million names. It is described more fully in chapter 2, "Databases, Indexes, and Other Finding Aids," of *The Source: A Guidebook of American Genealogy,* (cited earlier), as well as in chapter 6, "Published Indexes," of *Printed Sources*.

The *IGI* is the premier and largest example of a printed vital records source. Published on microfiche and CD-ROM (it is too large for printing in book format), it is a collection of birth and marriage entries from around the world; more than 50 million entries cover the United States and Canada. Because the entries are from thousands of submitters, each of whom could have used his sources differently, all of the cautions relating to compiled records must be exercised in the use of the *IGI*. A submitter or an extraction volunteer could have used any genealogical source for a particular entry, but by far the largest number of entries are from church and government records of births and marriages. While deaths are not generally listed in the *IGI,* a death record proves that a person was born, so death records are occasionally used as sources for birth entries.

Parish and Vital Records List (PVRL)

An important, and usually overlooked, part of the *IGI* is the *Parish and Vital Records List* (*PVRL*). It is the official list of the sources that were extracted by volunteers for the *IGI*. About half of the entries in the *IGI* are from extracted sources, so the *PVRL* is the key finding aid to learn what records have been extracted. Published only on microfiche, the *PVRL* is available wherever the microfiche version of the *IGI* is found. It is arranged by country, then county, and then town or church parish. Within the locality, the sources of the extracted entries are given by title (for example, "St. Anne's Parish").

Various columns identify the types of records extracted, the years included, the Family History Library call number, and a coded number for the source (figure 7-8); this number is the batch number as found in the *IGI*. In the early years of the extraction program, many published vital records were used as extraction sources for the northeastern states. These included published books, as well as articles in periodicals and yearbooks. Thus, *PVRL* can be used in at least two ways: (1) it will identify the sources for a locality that have been extracted and should appear in the *IGI* (however, the listing includes many sources in the process of being extracted that are not yet in the *IGI*); (2) it can be used to learn about published (and unpublished) vital record sources for any locality of interest. Note that, while *PVRL* does include the Family History Library call number, that number is often truncated for books, so additional research may be needed to completely identify a published source of interest.

LOCAL GOVERNMENT VITAL RECORDS

Most of the vital records in print are transcripts or abstracts of the records kept by local governments. The state-produced indexes to such records were noted earlier. However, most states did not begin to keep vital records until the early part of the twentieth century. Because most family historians seek vital records dating from before state registration, they are left with the records of towns and counties. In response to this need, individuals, genealogical societies, and publishing companies have published government-created vital records in increasing numbers. These publications generally fall into two groups: town vital records and county marriage records.

UNITED STATES — PARISH AND VITAL RECORDS LIST — SEP 1997
NEW YORK — PAGE 4,740

1. COUNTY	2. TOWN AND/OR PARISH	3. PERIOD FROM - TO	4. RECD TYPE	5. PRINTOUT CALL NO.	NUM FCH	6. PROJECT	7. SOURCE CALL NO.
GENESE	GENESEE COUNTY, 1880 CENSUS E.D. 06-8	-1880	CEN	NONE		C56031-3	## 1254835
GENESE	GENESEE COUNTY, 1880 CENSUS E.D. 09-11	-1880	CEN	NONE		C56031-4	## 1254835
GENESE	GENESEE COUNTY, 1880 CENSUS E.D. 12-14	-1880	CEN	NONE		C56031-5	## 1254835
GENESE	GENESEE COUNTY, 1880 CENSUS E.D. 15-17	-1880	CEN	NONE		C56031-6	## 1254835
GREENE	ATHENS, ZION LUTHERAN CHURCH	SEE: LOONENBURG, ZION LUTHERAN CHURCH					
GREENE	CATSKILL, DUTCH REFORMED CHURCH	1732-1800	CHR	# 1002777		C51054-1	0533479 IT 1-2
GREENE	CATSKILL, DUTCH REFORMED CHURCH	-1754	MAR	# 1002751		M51054-1	0533479 IT 1-2
		1732-1735	MAR				974.7 B2N V. 92
		1798-1833	MAR				974.7 B2N V. 92
GREENE	CATSKILL, KISKATOM REFORMED DUTCH PROTESTANT CHURCH	1842-1850	CHR	# 1002781		C51110-1	
GREENE	CATSKILL, KISKATOM REFORMED DUTCH PROTESTANT CHURCH	1842-1850	MAR	# 1205005		M51110-1	0533480
GREENE	CATSKILL, PROTESTANT REFORMED DUTCH CHURCH OF LEEDS	1833-1875	CHR	# 0882992		C51087-1	0533480
GREENE	CATSKILL, PROTESTANT REFORMED DUTCH CHURCH OF LEEDS	1833-1885	MAR	# 1205004		M51087-1	0533480
GREENE	COXSACKIE, DUTCH REFORMED CHURCH	1738-1800	CHR	# 1002750		C51055-1	974.7 B2N V. 88-91
GREENE	COXSACKIE, DUTCH REFORMED CHURCH	1797-1875	MAR	# 1002776		M51055-1	974.7 B2N V. 92-93
GREENE	DURHAM, FIRST PRESBYTERIAN CHURCH OF DURHAM	1798-1853	CHR	# 0882992		C51088-1	0533479
GREENE	DURHAM, REFORMED DUTCH CHURCH IN OAK HILL	1794-1832	CHR	# 0882992		C51089-1	0533480
GREENE	DURHAM, REFORMED DUTCH CHURCH IN OAK HILL	1798-1830	MAR	# 0882995		M51089-1	0533480
GREENE	DURHAM, SECOND PRESBYTERIAN CHURCH OF WEST DURHAM	1816-1872	CHR	# 0882992		C51090-1	0533479
GREENE	GREENE COUNTY, 1880 CENSUS E.D. 66-69	-1880	CEN	NONE		C56032-1	## 1254836
GREENE	GREENE COUNTY, 1880 CENSUS E.D. 70-73	-1880	CEN	NONE		C56032-2	## 1254836
GREENE	GREENE COUNTY, 1880 CENSUS E.D. 74-76	-1880	CEN	NONE		C56032-3	## 1254836
GREENE	GREENE COUNTY, 1880 CENSUS E.D. 77-80	-1880	CEN	NONE		C56032-4	## 1254836
GREENE	GREENE COUNTY, 1880 CENSUS E.D. 81-84	-1880	CEN	NONE		C56032-5	## 1254836
GREENE	GREENE COUNTY, 1880 CENSUS E.D. 85-88	-1880	CEN	NONE		C56032-6	## 1254836
GREENE	GREENE COUNTY, 1880 CENSUS E.D. 89-91	-1880	CEN	NONE		C56032-7	## 1254836, 1254837
GREENE	GREENVILLE, PRESBYTERIAN CHURCH	1789-1824	CHR	# 1002782		C51091-1	0533479
GREENE	GREENVILLE, PRESBYTERIAN CHURCH	1789-1824	MAR	# 1205002		M51091-1	0533479
GREENE	HUNTER, PRESBYTERIAN CHURCH	1822-1824	CHR	NONE		C53859-1	## 1310912
		1837-1870	CHR	NONE			## 1310912
GREENE	HUNTER, PRESBYTERIAN CHURCH	1837-1857	MAR	NONE		M53859-1	## 1310912
		-1870	MAR	NONE			## 1310912
		1883-1885	MAR	NONE			## 1310912
GREENE	KISKATOM, REFORMED PROTESTANT DUTCH CHURCH	SEE: CATSKILL, KISKATOM REFORMED DUTCH PROTESTANT CHURCH					
GREENE	LEEDS, PROTESTANT REFORMED DUTCH CHURCH	SEE: CATSKILL, PROTESTANT REFORMED DUTCH CHURCH OF LEEDS					
GREENE	LOONENBURG, ZION LUTHERAN CHURCH	1725-1800	CHR	# 1002781		C51056-1	974.7 B2N V. 82-85
GREENE	LOONENBURG, ZION LUTHERAN CHURCH	1705-1783	MAR	# 1002777		M51056-1	974.7 B2N V. 73
GREENE	NEW BALTIMORE, NEW BALTIMORE REFORMED CHURCH	1833-1875	CHR	# 1002782		C51113-1	0533480
GREENE	NEW BALTIMORE, NEW BALTIMORE REFORMED CHURCH	1833-1884	MAR	# 1205007		M51113-1	0533480
GREENE	OAK HILL, REFORMED DUTCH CHURCH	SEE: DURHAM, REFORMED DUTCH CHURCH IN OAK HILL					
GREENE	WEST DURHAM, SECOND PRESBYTERIAN CHURCH	SEE: DURHAM, SECOND PRESBYTERIAN CHURCH OF WEST DURHAM					
HAMLTN	HAMILTON COUNTY, 1880 CENSUS	-1880	CEN	NONE		C56033-1	## 1254837
HERKMR	COLUMBIA, DUTCH REFORMED CHURCH	1802-1836	CHR	# 1002592		C50707-1	0962643 IT 13
HERKMR	COLUMBIA, DUTCH REFORMED CHURCH	1825-1836	MAR	# 1002595		M50707-1	0962643 IT 13
HERKMR	FORT HERKIMER, REFORMED PROTESTANT DUTCH CHURCH OF GERMAN FLATS	SEE: GERMAN FLATS, REFORMED PROTESTANT DUTCH CHURCH					
HERKMR	FRANKFURT	-1888	MAR	NONE		M39324-3	## 0017127 IT.1
HERKMR	GERMAN FLATS, REFORMED PROTESTANT DUTCH CHURCH	1763-1795	CHR	NONE		C51508-1	0534219
		1811-1845	CHR				

Figure 7-8. A portion of the *Parish and Vital Records List.* Columns identify the type of records extracted, the years included, the Family History Library call number, and a coded number for the source.

Published Town Vital Records

Because vital records were not kept consistently outside of New England until the 1850s, published town birth and death records are rare for other locations. Many other published records (from church, cemetery, newspaper, and other sources) are available for most eastern states, however. While the following discussion focuses on New England publications, it is representative of what to consider as similar records from other localities are used.

Massachusetts Town Records. The largest collection of printed town vital records for any state belongs to Massachusetts, where a variety of formats and arrangements provide coverage for all but around twenty of the 364 towns and cities in the state. Generally they fall into three groups: periodical articles, typescript transcripts in library collections, and published books. The two major periodicals that have published Massachusetts town records are the *Mayflower Descendant* (published by the General Society of Mayflower Descendants, P.O. Box 3297, Plymouth, MA 02361) and the *New England Historical and Genealogical Register* (published by the New England Historic Genealogical Society, 101 Newbury Street, Boston, MA 02116) (see chapter 19, "Genealogical Periodicals"). Vital records in these journals are generally published serially over several issues, usually as verbatim transcripts from town clerks' records. While these sources are useful, finding them can be difficult. Very few sources indicate which towns' records are published in which volumes, and many libraries lack a complete set of one or both of these journals. The recent appearance of both of these journals on CD-ROM, however, certainly lessens the problem and provides, at the same time, an every-name index to help find references to specific families. A few of these articles have been reprinted as separate volumes.

Many other town records are available in typed transcripts made by earlier researchers and deposited at various libraries. Chief among these are the Rollin H. Cooke Collection at the Berkshire Athenaeum (Pittsfield, Massachusetts) and the Corbin Collection at the New England Historic Genealogical Society. Transcripts for a few towns are in the DAR Library. Fortunately, all of these collections are available on microfilm through the Family History Library and its centers. The vast majority of Massachusetts town records are available as separately published volumes, approximately two hundred of which were published between 1902 and the 1920s as part of an "Official Series" underwritten by the state. Records for around thirty-two other towns have been published separately from the official series (most at later dates).

It is instructive to examine the Official Series as a model of how *not* to compile vital records and what to be aware of as similar arrangements are encountered in other volumes. In 1902, the Massachusetts legislature provided for the purchase, by the state, of five hundred copies of any printed books with the records of births, marriages, and deaths of any town in the state, upon acceptance by the commissioner of public records and the board of free public library commissioners. These copies were to be distributed free of charge to libraries, public offices, and societies. Spurred by the promise of sales to the state, several societies, notably the New England Historic Genealogical Society, began publishing town records. However, the acceptable format was determined by the commission: the records are arranged alphabetically by surname (under the common spellings) and then given name within three sections: births, deaths, and marriages (figure 7-9). This arrangement eliminated evidence resulting from the chronological and family arrangement of names that was often part of the original records.

Eben Putnam analyzed the first forty-one volumes of the Official Series and identified another concern in *The Genealogical Magazine* 1 (1): 1–10 (April 1905), page 5: that "this form does not provide for all the information which the records contain." He illustrated this concern with several examples, comparing the information in the original records with that in the published volume. One of his examples from the Bellingham records is shown in figure 7-10.

Putnam continued his commentary (pages 7-8):

> The style of printing these records especially approved by the Commission is to place all the births in one section, by groups of same names (but different spellings of one family name are not brought together), and the given names follow alphabetically according to date. Thus families are divided and in such a way as to lose whatever value there is in the location of the original entry. The eldest children of a man may appear under the Z's and his youngest children under the A's; they may be even under different spellings of the surname. Any record additional to the record of birth . . . is taken away and placed in another section of the book. . . . The deaths are arranged in the same arbitrary manner. In the case of the marriages the entry appears in fuller extent under the husband but is practically repeated under the woman's name, where a simple cross reference would do. It is needless to state that an ordinary index to family names appended to a literal printed transcript of the records is quite as serviceable and less costly.

Another of the very great omissions in the Official Series is the omission of references to the pages of the original records where the entries may be found. Fortunately, these records are generally available on microfilm and microfiche, so recourse to the original is easy (and, as this discussion shows, necessary). Note that most of the volumes published separately from the Official Series reproduce the town records in the arrangement and format of the originals, with every-name indexes included; thus, they correct the most significant of these problems.

PERU BIRTHS. 31

KINGSLEY, Hannah, ch. Jedediah and Mary, Feb. 19, 1796.
Horace, ch. Jedediah and Mary, Oct. 3, 1786, in Becket.
Ira, ch. Jedediah and Mary, Apr. 15, 1788, in Becket.
Jedediah Jr., ch. Jedediah and Mary, Mar. 30, 1781, in Becket.
Mary, ch. Jedediah and Mary, Nov. 10, 1782, in Becket.
Sarah, ch. Jedediah and Mary, Feb. 26, 1792.

KINNE, Levi, s. Daniel and Hannah, Sept. 14, 1799.

KNIGHT, Charles Backus, ch. Rev. Caleb and w., Mar. 15, 1804.
Walter Tracy, ch. Rev. Caleb and w., July 31, 1802.

LALAND (see Leland), Polly, ch. Rev. John (Leland) and Hephzibah, June 5, 1785.

LAMB, Georgianna Albertson, d. Rufus A. and Susan R., Mar. —, 1845.

LATHROP, Minerva Preston, d. John S. and Sarah, Feb. 19, 1846.

LEGG, Aaron, ch. Nathan and Hannah, Mar. 11, 1789.
Betsey, ch. Nathan and Hannah, July 5, 1791.
Elijah, ch. Gershom and Mary, Mar. 27, 1779.
Experience, ch. Nathan and Hannah, Feb. 14, 1787.
Joshua S., s. Joshua and Sarah, Oct. 16, 1798.
Otis, ch. Gershom and Mary, Feb. 25, 1781.
Seth, ch. Nathan and Hannah, Dec. 9, 1784.

LELAND (see Laland), Aaron, ch. Rev. John and Hephzibah, Oct. 1, 1787.
Alta Maria, ch. John Jr. and Lydia, Apr. 4, 1807.
Anna Louisa, d. John and Lydia, June 24, 1809.
Claricy, d. Moses and Betsey, May 15, 1805.
Eda, ch. Moses and Betsey, July 23, 1799.
Emaline, d. Moses and Betsey, Jan. 26, 1807.
Ezra, ch. Moses and Betsey, May 29, 1801.
John 3d, [twin] ch. John Jr. and Lydia, Feb. 26, 1803.
John Lewis, ch. John Jr. and w., Apr. 8, 1816.
Lydia, [twin] ch. John Jr. and Lydia, Feb. 26, 1803.
Manerva Hepsabah, d. John Jr. and Lydia, Apr. 5, 1813.
Mary, ch. Moses and Betsey, Nov. 30, 1803.
Moses Jr., s. Moses and Betsey, Mar. 6, 1809.

LITTLE, Anna, ch. Moses and Hannah, Dec. 16, 1774.
Anna, ch. Capt. Ezekiel and Eunice, Oct. 13, 1780.
Asa, ch. Moses and Hannah, Feb. 10, 1782.

Figure 7-9. From a Massachusetts town vital records book for Peru, Massachusetts. The records are arranged alphabetically by surname (under the common spellings), destroying chronological and family arrangement evidence often part of the original records.

Barbour Collection. The Barbour Collection is a set of transcripts of town vital records for 137 Connecticut towns kept at the Connecticut State Library (Hartford). Well known to New England genealogists through the microfilm copy, the records are now being published in book form by Lorraine Cook White in *The Barbour Collection of Connecticut Town Vital Records* (Baltimore: Genealogical Publishing Co., 1994–). Thirty-seven towns are covered in the ten volumes that appeared through 1997. The series could approach forty volumes.

An examination of this collection and White's new series does much to reveal how many published transcripts have been produced and what to look for in evaluating such sources. Between 1911 and 1934, Lucius Barnes Barbour was the Connecticut examiner of public records. He undertook a project to copy vital record information from the original town clerk books throughout the state. Over the years, his assistants copied the

Transcript from the Original Records of Bellingham

Date of Registration	*Names of Groom and Bride*	*Condition*	*Age*	*Occupation*	*Date of Marriage*	*Residence & Official Station of Person by Whom Married*
May 6, 1846	Silas F. Thayer	single	24	Baker	May 4, 1846	Rev. N. G. Lovell
	Elizabeth Rockwood	single	24			Clergyman, Bellingham

Place of Birth	*Residence at Marriage*	*Names of Parents*	*Residence of Fathers*	*Informant*
Bellingham	Dedham	Ellery & Abigail Thayer	Bellingham	N.G. Lovell
Bellingham	Bellingham	Martin & Abigail Rockwood	Bellingham	

Published *Vital Records of Bellingham*

(Page 139).

ROCKWOOD
Eliazbeth, 24, d. Martin and Abigail, and Silas F. Thayer. May 4, 1846

(Page 151).

THAYER
Silas F.. 24, of Dedham, s. Ellery and Abigail, and Elizabeth Rockwood. May 4, 1846

Figure 7-10. Comparison of original records of Bellingham, Massachusetts, and the published *Vital Records of Bellingham.* From Eben Putnam's article in the *Genealogical Magazine* (page 5).

town books and then typed the information onto small slips of paper that served as index cards. Once the index slips for each town were completed, they were alphabetized and then retyped (in the sorted order) onto pages that were bound in books. The slips of paper were then integrated into one statewide index.

The new volumes by White are very faithful transcripts of the second typing of the town records (as is evident from reading the microfilm); thus, they retain the abbreviations and notations of Barbour's staff. However, for most towns, these volumes are (1) transcripts of (2) typescripts from (3) typed index slips that are based on (4) handwritten transcripts of the original clerks' records. Any record that is four generations removed from the actual document it represents must be carefully used because mistakes will have crept in.

White has followed Barbour's transcript carefully. There is only one deviation: she has given all surnames in bold, uppercase letters. This treatment includes spouses' names in marriage records, not just the surnames under which they are filed. White maintains Barbour's grouping of different spellings for the same apparent name, such as Curtis, Curtiss, Curtees, and Curtice. She does incorporate the handwritten corrections to Barbour's manuscript that were added by unknown users at later dates. However, in some cases White has noted that her work is "changed from original" without indicating what the original transcript included; other times she has not even made such a notation while incorporating the changed text.

As with Barbour's transcripts, White lists the marriage records under both the bride and the groom, alphabetically by surname, which appears to be the reason the books have no index. She also includes the volume and page numbers included by Barbour that reference the actual town books. Disappointingly, however, she has not included the brief preface given before the transcript for each town in the Barbour collection. These prefaces explain when and how Barbour's staff made each town book, and they differ in each instance. The prefaces also usually point out that Barbour's copy "has not been compared with the original . . . *doubtless errors exist"* (emphasis added).

These differences for each town are significant. For example, the typescript for Andover, Connecticut, was made from cards that are based on a 1924 photostatic copy of the town records. The town records had no page numbers, so the page numbers of the photostatic copy are used. The Ashford, Connecticut, volume is based on a 1911 copy (presumably made by hand) of the town records, with the notation that "the badly worn condition of these four books resulted in the loss of many names and dates." The Avon preface explains that the records were dispersed throughout the town land record volumes, thus explaining the notation "LR" in the volume column of the transcript. In Barkhamsted, the death entries came from a different manuscript and were typed in red in the Barbour collection to distinguish them, but this distinction does not appear in White's version. In each of these cases, important information which the researcher needs to interpret these dates and to find the originals is lost because the preface is not included in White's version.

Researchers should also note that Barbour did not transcribe records for every town; there were approximately 175 towns in Connecticut by 1890. Also, as with all New England town vital records, very few clerks recorded each and every birth, marriage, or death that occurred in the town. Indeed, events were often recorded many years after they had happened; and sometimes a clerk recorded an event that had happened in another town because the family had since moved and was living in the clerk's town.

Microfilms of the Barbour typescripts (index cards and town books) and the actual town clerks' books for most towns are available from the Family History Library and its centers. Thus, the researcher can examine the true original records if there is any doubt about the correctness of Barbour's transcripts or White's copies of them. Note also that the births from the Barbour collection were extracted and are included in the *IGI,* which serves as a useful statewide index if the microfilms are not available.

County Marriages

While many statewide marriage sources exist, as described earlier, most published marriage records are transcripts or abstracts of county marriage records. In the United States, most states required local jurisdictions to licence and/or record marriages within their borders virtually as soon as local governments were established. In the early 1600s, churches were sometimes charged with this responsibility (for example, in Massachusetts and Virginia). Eventually, the towns in New England and the counties in almost all other states kept these records. Notable exceptions were New York and Pennsylvania, which did not require the keeping of marriage records until late in the nineteenth century.

For the states outside of New England, marriage records are usually the only government-mandated vital records extant for periods before the late nineteenth or early twentieth centuries. Therefore, marriage records have attracted the attention of many transcribers and publishers. Some of these collections have grown so large that they have evolved into the statewide sources discussed above. Usually, however, the publication of county marriage records is random; any individual or society may choose to publish a county's marriages. Often only the earliest marriages are published—perhaps those from before 1850 or 1900—for, as the population has grown, the number of marriages has also, their number eventually outstripping the means of compilers to print and distribute them as books.

In contrast to the statewide databases described above, countywide publications can generally be expected to be fairly comprehensive (at least regarding the marriages that were recorded). Certainly some marriages were never recorded and the records of some lost, and couples sometimes chose to be married in other counties, but compilers and publishers have generally attempted to locate all known marriages. Sometimes two or more publishers have published the marriages for the same county; such duplication serves to check the accuracy of each publication. Most often in such cases, one duplication is an index only, while the other is a more complete abstract; or, one may contain the marriage bonds while another has the actual marriage returns. Perhaps one names ministers while another names the witnesses. Compare again figures 7-3 and 7-4, which show two different published versions of Wake County, North Carolina, marriage records.

Of great importance when using published marriage records is to clearly understand what records were used for a particular publication. Some states required a marriage bond—a legal contract ensuring that the persons to be married were legally free and able to do so; however, a bond is not proof that the marriage actually took place. Figure 7-11, from *Prince Edward County, Virginia Marriage Bonds, 1754–1866* (Salt Lake City: Genealogical Society of Utah, 1936), is from a printed volume of marriage bonds. Unlike many others, this publication lists each bondsman's relationship to the bride or groom (if it was given in the original record).

Sometimes bonds are used for marriage publications because the ministers' returns were not kept or have been lost. In other cases, bonds are published only for those marriages for which a return was not found. (The absence of a return does not mean the marriage did not take place; it means only that the compiler did not find the proof. In such situations, the researcher must search other genealogical records, such as land, probate, or census records, to be certain a couple who posted bonds actually did get married.)

Similar caveats apply to published marriage licences. If the publication does not indicate that there was also a marriage return, be sure to learn if the couple actually married. Sometimes, what appears to be a book of county marriage records is actually a set of abstracts from newspapers. For example, *Marriages in Whiteside Co., Illinois, 1856–1881,* by Jayne Kennedy Sweger (Nowata, Okla., 1973), is more clearly defined by its subtitle: "3000 marriage notices extracted from early county newspapers: the *Whiteside Sentinel* and the *Sterling Gazette,* and others." While these same marriages may be documented in the county marriage records, not all county marriages would have been reported in the newspapers of the time. Careless use of such a source could lead a researcher to believe that a marriage did not take place when, indeed, it may have (without appearing in a newspaper).

Lastly, be sure to note what information is included in the published marriage records. Some are merely indexes to marriages, but, because they name the bride and groom and provide the date of marriage, a researcher might stop without examining the actual marriage records. Admittedly, many county marriage records include precious little additional information; however, that additional information might include the name of the minister who performed the ceremony, giving a clue as to which church one or both of the persons attended. An index will not provide the names of witnesses, but they are often relatives of the bride or groom and should be sought in the actual record.

Many examples of county marriage publications have been given throughout this chapter and are not repeated here. Review them for a clearer understanding of what may or may not be found in these valuable publications.

Finding Aids

Many of the general finding aids discussed earlier identify local town or county vital records. However, check also the numerous state research guides (see chapter 2, "Instructional Material"), which often identify vital record publications. For example, Marcia Wiswall Lindberg's *Genealogist's Handbook for New England Research,* 3rd ed. (Boston: New England Historic Genealogical Society, 1993) discusses the published vital records for each state and, for some states, identifies towns whose records have been published.

State source guides are excellent sources for identifying published vital records. Most of these sources seek to identify all published books of value for genealogical research. For example, James E. Dorsey's *Georgia Genealogy and Local History: A Bibliography* (Spartanburg, S.C.: Reprint Company, 1983) is a list of approximately five thousand books and articles dealing with Georgia genealogy. In it, statewide sources are listed first by topic, followed by county sources listed alphabetically by title. Each county list includes several periodical articles, as well as some books, with county marriage records. The list also includes other sources of vital records, such as

PRINCE EDWARD COUNTY, VIRGINIA — Page 82

GROOM	BRIDE	DATE	BONDSMAN
Phillips, Peter T.	Ann Skip Harris	6 Oct. 1791	John Skip Harris Nottoway Co. - father
Phillips, Richard	Martha Smith	24 Dec. 1811	Owen Smith father
Phillips, Vincent	Harriet H. Hawkins	6 Nov. 1811	Benjamin Hawkins father
Pigg, James	Patsy Pennill	1 Dec. 1796	Pearce B. Pennill father
Pigg, John	Sally Brown	26 Sept.1804	George Brown - father Henry Pigg
Pilkington, Henry S.	Elizabeth Tucker	28 Nov. 1827	Joseph Tucker father
Piller, Benjamin F.	Mary A. Waddill	9 Apr. 1827	Walker Waddill father
Piller, John	Ann Berry	13 Nov. 1792	Joseph Berry father
Piller, John	Sally Vaughan	27 Dec. 1797	Thomas Vaughan father
Pinnell, John	Lucy B. Lilly	20 Dec. 1815	William A. Lilly father
Plant, James	Patty Womack	12 Dec. 1801	Massanello Womack father
Poe, Hasten	Silia Briant	6 Dec. 1813	Jesse Briant father
Poindexter, J. M.	Mary Ann Horton	15 May 1841	Samuel Horton father
Pollard, Ambrose	Mary Ann Waddle	22 Dec. 1789	Jacob Waddle - father Amelia Co.

Figure 7-11. From *Prince Edward County, Virginia Marriage Bonds, 1754–1866,* a printed volume of marriage bonds.

cemetery and church records. Another example is Connie Lenzen's *Oregon Guide to Genealogical Sources,* rev. ed. (Portland: Genealogical Forum of Oregon, 1994). In it, each county listing includes the topic "Vital Records," which identifies both microfilmed and published records. Typically only book sources, not periodical articles, are listed under published records.

Separate guides to vital records exist for some states. There are many volumes from the Historical Records Survey division of the Work Projects Administration (WPA) covering many states, but these do not identify published transcripts or abstracts. However, the following example from John Frost's *Guide to Maine Vital Records in Transcript* (n.p., 1963), pages i and ii, shows what might be found:

> Histories of the towns have been included only when they contain vital records other than collected genealogies. Historical material which does not contain vital records has been eliminated. This list does not supersede the Maine listings by Donald Lines Jacobus in his Index to Genealogical Periodicals; historical entries, valuable to the genealogist, comprise a large proportion of the Jacobus index. Many vital records of Maine towns are missing, and then often records which are not vital records per se must be used. Fire has been the worst hazard to Maine's vital records, a fact of which Portland residents are particularly aware.
>
> This volume does not record all of the vital records of Maine that have been transcribed. An effort has been made to note all, however, of which copies are in the Maine Historical Society's library. Only two exceptions have been noted here, the cemetery records of Exeter and Dexter. . . . The vital records of only twelve towns to 1892 have been published, in toto, by the Maine Historical Society, and no volumes have appeared for a number of years.

The following entries from Frost's guide (page 1) illustrate his brief approach:

> ALBANY
>
> Albany, Main. DAC. Records of Marriages. [24p.] Births and Deaths [27p.] Early Births and Deaths [45p.] Cemeteries. [21p.] Typscr.
>
> ALBION. See also SIDNEY.
>
> Albion, Maine Marriages Solemnized by Thomas Burrill. Included in his Diary. DAC. Maine Records, 3:10-13. Typscr.
>
> Albion, Main Town Records. DAC. Maine Records, 2: 84-88, 103-118. Typscr.
>
> Inscriptions, Crosby Cemetery, Albion, Me. [3p.] Typscr.
>
> Metcalf, Cemetery in Albion, Maine. DAR (1958), p.1.
>
> Records Taken from Tombstones in Old Burying Ground on Lovejoy Road... Albion, Me. Maine DAR Genealogical Records, v. 24 (1952), pt. 1, pp. 1-2. Typscr.

VITAL RECORD EVIDENCES

Almost any genealogical source can be used to provide some evidence of a person's birth, marriage, or death. Because these events are central to genealogical research, some compilers have created substitute vital record collections based on evidence found in other records. Evidences are records that were not originally designed to provide specific vital record information but that give indirect evidence of such events. Probate records, for example, are clear evidence of a person's death and suggest an approximate date of death. Wills also evidence the marriage (of the deceased) and birth (of the children) of some individuals. Because compilers want to associate a specific place and date with a birth, marriage, or death, other records, such as censuses, that do not provide such information are seldom used as evidences.

Although they do not provide the exact birth, marriage, or death dates in every instance, there are many printed sources that provide evidences which often can establish the date of a vital event to within a few months. One compiler, Alden G. Beaman, illustrated the value of these "evidences" by calculating how many marriages were *not* recorded in the official records. Using the marriages transcribed in James N. Arnold's *Vital Records of Rhode Island, 1636–1850: A Family Register for the People,* 20 vols. (Providence, R.I.: Narragansett Historical Publishing Co., 1891–1912), vol. 3, *Washington County,* and the Federal census figures, Beaman calculated that the marriage rate in part of the county would be 1.1 marriages per one thousand people per year during the early 1800s. In sharp contrast, the rate for the same area after the institution of more complete record-keeping in 1853 was 7.8 marriages per one thousand people per year.

> This change indicates not a sudden 7 fold jump in the true marriage rate, but rather that a much greater percentage of the marriages were recorded. Thus one may conclude that only one marriage in 7 which took place in the early 1800's in that area appeared in Arnold's Vol. 5. . . . The user of these volumes should bear in mind that if only one marriage in 7 is recorded in Arnold's Vol. 5, and if the author has about doubled this number, still less than one third of the marriages which actually took place can be found in Arnold's Vol. 5 and the author's present books combined. Thus much work remains to be done to extend the published birth and marriage records (Beaman 1977, i).

The following examples show how Beaman (1977, 1–2) used cemetery inscriptions as evidence of marriages and births:

> Adams, Abby, AND John Brown, cnb SK 1822-1830.
> Ann M., of Ebenezer & Mercy (Rose), b 9 Jan 1802, d 26 Oct 1900, AND William Shaerman, of Beriah & Giffie, b 14 Feb 1804, d 17 Apr 1871, bur SK.
> Fanning, of Major Ebenezer, b 1781, d 1848, AND Ann Atwell, of John C. & Mary, b 12 Apr 1793, d 10 Dec 1871, cnb 1822-1826, bur SK.
> John Fanning, of Nathan & Susan R., b 15 Sep 1829 d 5 Dec 1882, AND Ann E. Oatley, of William & Patty, b 25 Dec 1830, d 20 Feb 1873,bur SK. (SK5)
> Joseph, b 25 Apr 1779, d 9 Sep 1849, AND Lydia Tefft, b 29 May 1779, d Mar 1873, cb 1803, bur SK.
> Nathan, b 1784, d 8 Mar 1850, AND Susan R. Cottrell, of Samuel & Susan, b 1805, d 18 Jan 1861, cnb 1837-1840 bur SK.
> Allen, Andrew, b England 1816, d 4 Oct 1882, AND Jane Coulter, b 22 June 1820, d 17 Dec 1890, bur Ho.
> Ann, of Ray & Susannah, b 1810, d 1 May 1853, AND Nicholas N. Holland, bur SK (SK 5)
> Anne, AND Charles T. Hunt, cnb NK 1837-1841.

As Beaman indicated, these collections of evidences add new birth and marriage data to those contained in Arnold's earlier *Vital Records of Rhode Island.* Beaman explained that his purpose was to use the facts given in the gravestone inscriptions to compile birth and marriage records, rather than to simply re-copy the inscriptions verbatim. Frequently, the maiden name of the wife was given, and often the name of her father or both parents. Often several children were buried with their parents; the range of dates of birth of these children provided a good idea of the date of marriage for their parents (Beaman 1977, iii).

Only approximately 10 percent of the marriage entries duplicate those recorded in Arnold's *Vital Records of Rhode Island,* vol. 5, *Washington County.* Those were indicated by giving the reference to the same marriage in Arnold's vol. 5 in parentheses after the entry. The duplicates were not removed from this volume because they often include data on the parents of the bride and groom not given by Arnold (Beaman 1977, vii).

Beaman used four sources in assembling his compilation: (1) 1880–1882, George J. Harris's *Cemeteries of Ancient Kingstowne* (n.p., 1882), covering North Kingstown, South Kingstown, and Exeter; (2) the records of James N. Arnold; (3) a countywide Charles P. and Martha A. Benns compilation of the 1930s, *Rhode Island Cemetery Records, 1931–1941* (n.p., n.d.); and (4) the author's own collection of cemeteries in Westerly and Charlestown. A sample entry from Beaman's work (1977, viii) is interpreted below:

> Entry:
>
> Hall, Slocum, of Slocum & Almy (Fry), b 1794, d 5 Sep 1873, AND Charlotte Gardiner, of Ephraim & Hannah, b 17 Mar 1801, d 11 Dec 1892, cnb 1821-1839, bur NK.
>
> Interpretation:
>
> The above entry means that the gravestone inscriptions indicate that Slocum Hall, son of Slocum and Almy (maiden name Fry) Hall, who was born in 1794 and died 5 Sep 1873, AND Charlotte Gardiner, daughter of Ephraim and Hannah Gardiner, who was born 17 Mar 1801 and died 11 Dec 1892 were married and had children born between the years 1821 and 1839, and are buried in North Kingstown, Rhode Island. The range of dates of births of the children of the couple is of course that of the known children; the couple may have had additional children both before and/or after the dates given. The word AND in capital letters is used to separate the names of the bride and groom, while the ampersand sign (&) is used to separate the names of the parents of the bride and

groom. Cities and towns in RI not in Washington, Kent, and Newport counties are not abbreviated and the name of the state is not included (Beaman 1977, viii).

Another example of vital records evidences is the twenty-three volumes of *Maryland Marriage Records* by Annie W. B. Bell (Annapolis, Md.: the author, 1938–39), which were drawn from information found in pre-1800 wills, deeds, and court records. The entire collection is arranged alphabetically (rather then by source or locality). The dates in the books are those of the court records where the evidence was found.

A unique collection of marriage evidences drawn from compiled, rather than original, records is Clarence A. Torrey's *New England Marriages Prior to 1700* (Baltimore: Genealogical Publishing Co., 1985). This collection of seventeenth-century marriages was drawn from Torrey's examination of published family histories, genealogical dictionaries, town histories, periodical articles, and similar sources. The book is arranged alphabetically by groom, with an index to brides and others. It provides the marriage date and residence if given in the source, but to learn the source(s) of the information, the manuscript must be searched on microfilm (figure 7-12). Torrey's work is described more fully in chapter 16, "Family Histories and Genealogies."

NEWSPAPER SOURCES

The newspaper abstract is another type of vital record publication. Abstracts of vital records from newspapers can serve as excellent substitutes where government-sponsored vital records were not kept, have been destroyed, or are incomplete in their coverage. Even before vital records were recorded at the county or state levels, local newspapers often carried such information. An excellent example is a series of books by Fred Q. Bowman covering much of upstate New York before 1850, an area known for its lack of vital records. Whereas most newspaper vital record books cover the newspapers for specific towns, Bowman recognized that, in the area and time period he was covering, people moved often, and news was reported in distant newspapers. Therefore, in *10,000 Vital Records of Western New York, 1809–1850* (Baltimore: Genealogical Publishing Co., 1985), Bowman brought together records which ". . . covered an area more than twice that of Connecticut and Rhode Island combined" (page 1).

These records were drawn from the marriage and death columns of five western New York newspapers published before 1850. Birth announcements were not published in these early newspapers, but many of the marriage and death notices mentioned birth years, birthplaces, and parents' names. The books also list all the persons in each reference (not just the principal individuals listed).

Towns of residence are by no means confined to western New York; communities in the rest of the state as well as New England and the Midwest are frequently identified. Bowman explains that "except for surv by (survived by) and inf s (infant son) the abbreviations used here are those commonly found in genealogical writings (1985, v)," and, regarding locations, he comments that "unless otherwise noted all cities, towns, villages, and hamlets referred to are in New York (1985, v)."

Bowman's volumes are examples of the many published collections of newspaper vital records that combine the information from several newspapers serving an area. Such works will have introductory information explaining which newspapers were used, what dates they cover, and what code is used to refer to them in the abstracts. In *10,000 Vital Records of Western New York,* Bowman provides the table of sources shown in figure 7-13.

Bowman further explains that, because Geneva was on the border between central and western New York, the early records are more significant for western New York. Vital records covering 1828 through 1850 from the *Geneva Gazette* appear in Bowman's *10,000 Vital Records of Central New York, 1813–1850* (Baltimore: Genealogical Publishing Co., 1986).

Below is a sample listing from the *Western New York* volume (page 3).

> Abeel, John N. (Rev. Dr.), 42, one of the pastors of the Reformed Protestant Dutch Ch. of NYC, d 1/19/12 in NYC (3-2/5)
> Abel, Jacob C. m Mary Chase in Milo (3-6/6/27)
> Avel, William H. m 12/12/50 Sarah F. Van Amburg, both of Savonia, in S.; Rev. J. C. Mallory (2-12/25)
> Abell, James (Rev.) of Oswego m Laura G. Bogue in Clinton (3-4/22/29)
> Aber, Aaron m 3/26/50 Elizabeth Ann Cornwell, both of Bath, in B.; Rev. J. C. Mallory (2-4/6)
> Aber, Anna, 53, wf of Nathaniel, d 2/13/50 in Bath (2-2/20)
> Aber, T. J. m 5/1/ 50 Samantha B. Bramble in Bath; Rev.L. Merrill Miller. All of B. (2-5/8)
> Abery, Benjamin of Brutus, Cay. Co., m 8/21 22 Cynthia Hastings of Canadaigua in C. (3-9/18)
> Acher?, Chester m 6/25/44 Elizabeth Coon; Rev. William M. Ferguson. all of Palmyra. (5-7/3)
> Acker, Joseph, mo., s of David, d 9/17/26 in Seneca (3-9/20)
> Ackley, Charles, "about 28, colored man", d 2/8/ 36 in Jamestown (4-2/10)

Other volumes in Bowman's series include *10,000 Vital Records of Eastern New York, 1777–1834* (Baltimore: Genealogical Publishing Co., 1987) and *8,000 More Vital Records of Eastern New York State, 1804–1850* (Rhinebeck, N.Y.: Kinship, 1991).

Vital record abstracts from newspapers are generally published in one of two ways. Either the abstracts cover a single newspaper, usually chronologically with an every-name index, or information from several local newspapers is amalgamated into one source (as in the Bowman series just described). These compiled abstracts may be arranged chronologically or alphabetically.

As an example of a set of abstracts from a single newspaper, see the example from *Obituaries and Marriage Notices from the Tennessee Baptist: 1844–1862,* compiled by Russell Pierce Baker (Easley, S.C.: Southern Historical Press, 1979) (figure 7-14).

In publications based on multiple newspapers from the same locality, the abstracted vital records are usually arranged alphabetically, with a code to identify which newspaper printed the record (much like the Bowman example above). However, some publications provide a chronological arrangement, either mixing the entries from different newspapers or listing each

356 **NEW ENGLAND MARRIAGES PRIOR TO 1700**

HAWKINS, William & Dorothy _?_; b 1668; Boston
HAWKINS, William (-1723) & Lydia (**BALLOU**) [**GARDINER/GARDNER**?], w George; 14 Jun 1678; Providence
HAWKINS, William & [Hannah/Anna **BIRCHAM**], dau Edward; b 1684; ?Reading
HAWKINS, Zechariah/Zachary (?1639-1698) & Mary [**BIGGS**] (-1696+); b 1664?; Brookhaven, LI
HAWKINS, [?Thomas] & Agnes _?_; ca 1673, 5 ch bpt 1685; Marblehead
HOXWORTH/HAWKSWORTH, Peter & Elizabeth (**WEBSTER**) **STEPHENS**, w David; 27 Feb 1699, 1699/1700?; Boston
HAUXWORTH, Thomas & Mary _?_; b 1641; Salisbury
HAWLEY, Ebenezer (1654-1681) & Esther/Hester **WARD**, dau Wm., m/2 Ephraim **NICHOLS** 1682, m/3 Eliphalet **HILL** 1691, m/4 Robert **LORD** by 1696; m cont 19 Apr 1678; ?Fairfield, CT/Stratford, CT
HAWLEY, Ephraim (1659-1690) & Sarah **WELLS** (1664-1694), m/2 Ayer **TOMLINSON** 1692; 4 Dec 1683; ?Stratford, CT
HAWLEY, John (1661-1729) & Deborah **PIERSON** (1666-1739) & 23 Apr 1686; Stratford, CT
HAWLEY, Joseph (?1603-1690) & Catherine [**BOOTH/BIRDSEY**?] (-1692); ca 1646; Wethersfield, CT/Hartford, CT
HAWLEY, Joseph (1654-1711) & Lydia **MARSHALL** (?1655, 1657-1732), Windsor; 24 Sep 1676; ?Northampton
HAWLEY, Joseph (1675-) & Elizabeth **WILCOXSON** (1673-); 7 Jun 1697; Stratford, CT/Farmington, CT?
HAWLEY, [Richard] (-1698, ae 63) & Johanna _?_; ca 1670, 6 ch bpt 1684; Marblehead
HAWLEY, Samuel (ca 1647/8-1734) & 1/wf Mary **THOMPSON** (bpt 1653-1691, 1690?), Farmington; 20 May 1673; Stratford, CT
HAWLEY, Samuel (-1734) & 2/wf Patience (**NICHOLS**) [**HUBBELL**] (1660-1734), w John; 1691?; Stratford, CT
HAWLEY, Thomas (-1676) & 1/wf Emm/Emma/Amy _?_ (-Nov 1651); Roxbury
HAWLEY, Thomas (-1676) & 2/wf Dorothy (**HARBOTTLE**) **LAMB** (-1698), w Thomas; 2 Feb 1651, 1651/2; Roxbury
HAYE, Patrick/Peter (1658-1748, in 91st y) & 1/wf Mary **KIBBEE** (-1694); 26 Mar 1685; Reading/Charlestown/Lynn
HAY, Patrick/Peter (-1748) & Sarah _?_ (-1729, in 69th y); b 1696; Charlestown/Shoreham
HAY, Samuel & _?_; b 1683(4?); Ipswich
HAY/HAYES?, Thomas & Bridget _?_; b 1687; Boston
HAYDEN, Daniel (1640-1713) & Hannah **WILCOXSON** (-1722); 17 Mar 1664, 1694/5; Windsor, CT
HAYDEN, Ebenezer (1645-1718, ae 73) & Ann?/Hannah _?_; b 1673(4?); Milton/Braintree
HAYDEN, Edward & Hannah _?_; b 5 Feb 1696; Westchester, NY
HAYDEN, Ferman & [Elizabeth] _?_, m/2 Thomas **WATTS**; 5 May 1657; Boston
HAYDEN, James (1609-1675) & Elizabeth _?_ (-1680, ae 76); b 1638; Charlestown
HAYDEN, John (-1682) & Susan/Susanna _?_ (-1695+); ca 1634; Braintree
HAYDEN, John (1635-1718) & Hannah **AMES** (1641-1689); 6 Apr 1660; Braintree
HAYDEN, John (1639-1675) & Hannah **MAYNARD** (1653-1675); 14 Oct 1669; Charlestown
HADEN, John & Elizabeth/(Abigail in 1694(5?)) _?_; b 1680?; Westchester, NY
HAYDEN, John & [Mary] **WATERHOUSE**, w John; aft 1687; Saybrook, CT
HAYDEN, John & Elizabeth _?_ (-1694); Braintree
HAYDEN, Jonathan (1640-) & Elizabeth **LADD/LEE**; 20 Apr 1669; Braintree
HAYDEN, Jonathan & Hannah/Sarah? [**HOBART**] (1668-), dau Caleb; 1692; Bridgewater
HAYDEN, Joseph & Elizabeth _?_; b 1697; Braintree
HAYDEN, Josiah (1669-), Braintree & Elizabeth **GOODENOW** (1672-); 6 Mar 1691; Sudbury
HAYDEN, Nathaniel (1644-1706) & Sarah (**FRENCH**) **PARMELEE** (-1717), Guilford, w Nathaniel; 17 Jan 1667/8, 1677; Killingworth, CT
HOIDEN, Nehemiah (1648-1718) & Hannah **NEALE** (1663-1720); Mar 1678; Braintree
HAYDEN, Samuel (-1676) & Hannah **THAYER**, m/2 Jonathan **PADDLEFORD** 1679?; 28 Oct 1664; Braintree
HAYDEN, William (-1669, Killingworth, CT) & 1/wf _?_ (-1655) (sister of Sarah, wf. of Francis **STILES**); b 1640; Dorchester/Hartford/Windsor, CT/etc.
HAYDEN, William (-1669) & 2/wf Margaret [**WILCOXSON**] (-1668+, 1676), w William; aft 1655; Windsor, CT

Figure 7-12. From Torrey's *New England Marriages Prior to 1700.*

Citation Code #	*Publication Town*	*Newspaper Title*	*Date Span of Review*	*Number of Vital Records Secured*
1	Batavia	*Republican Advocate*	3/19/22–12/31/50	729
2	Bath	*Steuben Farmers Advocate*	1/5/31–12/31/50	1221
3	Geneva	*Geneva Gazette*	6/21/09–12/31/27	4975
4	Jamestown	*Jamestown Journal*	7/21/26–12/31/50	1117
5	Palmyra	*Wayne Sentinel* (*Palmyra Register*, 1817–21)	3/16/17–9/25/44	2014

Figure 7-13. Table of sources from Bowman's *10,000 Vital Records of Western New York,* page 1.

WOOD, A. BERTRAND d. June 11, 1845 in Wilson Co., Tenn. age 22	June 28, 1845
WOOD, ALEXANDER d. May 17, 1858 in Tipton Co. (?) age 78	June 12, 1858
WOOD, ELIZABETH d. 1845 near Nashville, Tenn. wife of "Major" Wood, age 17,	Jan. 18, 1845
WOOD, ELIZABETH d. Nov. 13, 1849 in Gibson Co., Tenn. wife of James S. Wood, age 19	April 4, 1850
WOOD, ELIZABETH d. June 18, 1854 in Spartanburg Dist., S.C. wife of John Wood, age 97	Aug. 5, 1854
WOOD, JAMES B. d. c. 1856 in Springfield, Tex.	March 15, 1856
WOOD, MARY d. Feb. 23, 1854 in White Co., Ark. wife of Joshua Wood, age 29	April 22, 1854
WOOD, NANCY d. April 24, 1851 at Jackson, Tenn. wife of Eld. Barnett Wood, age 76	June 14, 1851
WOOD, NANCY d. c. 1856 in Jefferson Co., Ala.	Feb. 9, 1856
WOOD, PATIENCE d. Aug. 20, 1854 in Smith Co., Tenn. wife of Josiah Wood, age 84	Sep.30, 1854
WOODARD, FELIX married to Anna Schluter Dec. 25, 1856 in Tennessee	Jan. 3, 1857
WOODERED, SARAH WILLIAMS d. Feb. 26, 1851 at Pulaski, Tenn.	March 15, 1851
WOODFIN, HANNAH d. __ 8, 1845 in Bedford Co., Tenn. wife of NOCHOLAS WOODFIN, age 80	Sept. 6, 1845
WOODRUF, A. W. d. April 9, 1854 in Greersborough, Miss.	

Figure 7-14. Obituary abstracts from Baker's *Obituaries and Marriage Notices from the Tennessee Baptist: 1844–1862,* page 125.

newspaper's entries separately by year, as the following table of contents for *Vital Records from Chicago Newspapers 1833–1839* (cited earlier), page vii, shows. Therefore, the researcher should copy the table of contents as well as the entry in order to cite the appropriate newspaper.

CONTENTS

The actual entries (page 11) are more like abstracts than the more common line-by-line entry:

1835
October 7, Died
Lately, at his residence in Cook County, near Juliet, of bilious fever, Mr. Virgil B. Barber, late of Simsbury, Conn.
October 21, died
At his residence in this town on Thursday evening, 15th inst. Col. Thomas J.V. Owen, aged about thirty years. Col. Owen was born in the State of Kentucky.
In this town, at the residence of J. Curtiss, Esq. of the bilious fever, on the 16th inst. Augustus Hubbard, aged 24 years, formerly of Champion, Jefferson county, N.Y.
On Indian Creek, Oct. 8th, Seth C. Johnson, formerly of Boston, aged 49 years.

Often, significant background information can be found in newspaper abstracts. In their introduction to *Vital Records from Maine Newspapers 1785–1820,* 2 vols. (Bowie, Md.: Heritage Books, 1993), David C. Young and Elizabeth Keene Young explain that

> at the time this data was first printed, Portland was the largest town in Maine, with a population of 7,169 in 1810. The harbor there was said to be deep, safe, capacious, and seldom frozen over. Bath, Hallowell and Augusta on the "Kennebeck" River were flourishing towns (1993, vii).
>
> Only essential genealogical information was abstracted. A citation is given with each abstract which identifies the publication and issue date. Thus researchers with access to the papers in the original or microfilm form may want to use this volume more as

> an index and refer to the newspapers for additional data.
>
> Many libraries will not permit the photocopying of their old newspaper collections. After we finished compiling data from the Maine Historical Society's collection in 1989, they closed their files to the membership as well as to the public. The MGS has been inventorying and microfilming their collection for the past three years while we have been putting the vital records into the data base. Some of the libraries we visited had microfilming services.
>
> We have built on the works of the late Miss Sybil Noyes; the late Dr. Cassie Turner of Portland, Maine; Ms Helen McPhee of Bath, Maine; Grace Blake Maxwell & Georgiana Lilly of the Daughters of the American Revolution; and we have expanded their project with the help of the following: Robert L. Taylor of Danville, Maine . . . (Young 1993, ix).

Sample entries from *Vital Records from Maine Newspapers 1785–1820* (page 400):

> MERRILL Charlotte m John HAGGETT in this town N4 9 Dec 1817
>
> MERRILL Clarrissa m Capt Aaron WEBBER in Falmouth N4 15 Feb 1813
>
> MERRILL Daniel 76y AmRev at Arundel N4 12 Sep 1808 & Capt N1 15 Sep 1808 & Capt 76y at Arundel d in bed N3 17 Sep 1808
>
> MERRILL Daniel mDorcas MERRRILL in Falmouth N1 28 Nov 1820 & H1 9 Dec 1820
>
> MERRILL Dolly 24y d/o Joshua d at New Gloucester N4 16 May 1803 & N2 16 May 1803
>
> MERRILL Dorcas m Daniel Merrill in Falmouth N1 28 Nov 1820
>
> MERRILL Dorothy m Robert MORRILL in Salisbury 01 30 Oct 185 & N1 1 Nov 1805
>
> MERRILL Edmond 90y d in NEw Casco E1 4 Dec 1806 & N1 4 Dec 1806 & N4 1 Dec 1806
>
> MERRILL Edwaryd 7y s/o Beniah d in Falmouth N4 24 Nov 1818 & N1 1 Dec 1818
>
> MERRILL Edward m by George PARCHER in Saco Elizabeth GOOGINS both of Saco N1 22 Dec 1818 & N4 22 Dec 1818

There are three significant limitations to the use of published abstracts of newspaper vital records: (1) Coverage of vital events in newspapers was very spotty. Not every newspaper printed vital events, and those which they printed amount to only a small percentage of the births, marriages, and deaths that actually occurred within the area of their readership. Indeed, births were seldom reported in newspapers before the twentieth century. (2) The published abstracts are often incomplete themselves, because many newspapers have not survived and because compilers cannot (or choose not to) access all possible copies. In addition, for some areas where abstracts have already been published, there are likely to have been other newspapers with additional vital records that have not been compiled. (3) Not all newspaper vital records have been abstracted into books that are easy to locate and use. Many more early newspapers remain to be abstracted then have already been done.

Newspapers are also excellent sources for obituaries. Many societies have re-published newspaper obituaries in recent years, but even more common are indexes to newspaper obituaries. Often these include the date of death, as well as the issue and page number where the obituary appears. Indexes do not reprint the entire obituary, so do not be content with the index entry alone, even if it provides significant death information. Contact the newspaper, local library, or local historical society and inquire about an obituary clipping file. The best source for learning about obituary indexes, as well as collected files, is Jarboe's *Obituaries: A Guide to Sources* (discussed under "General Finding Aids—Bibliographies," above).

BIBLE RECORDS

Bible records are familiar sources of vital statistics. Unlike government vital records, which remain in their original locations, the location of a bible record is unlikely to have any relationship to the location of the ancestors noted in it. Bibles have been handed down from generation to generation, and traveled with families wherever they moved. Frequently, an old family Bible is taken by the family member most interested in family history. Just as frequently, that person's children have no interest in the family's history and the Bible ends up in an estate sale. With luck, a family genealogist comes across the Bible, buys it, and places it in a collection.

As with other sources of vital records, Bible records are wherever the researcher finds them. Pages from family Bibles were sometimes included in revolutionary war pension and bounty land applications. Photostatic copies of Bible records can be found in the collections of many professional genealogists. The DAR Library is a major repository of Bible records contributed by Americans nationwide and complemented by the work of the various local chapters of the DAR to preserve the genealogy and history of their local areas.

Bible records are published primarily in the quarterlies and journals of genealogical societies, but there is no single finding aid to all published Bible records. Using published Bible records requires an important caution: if the published record does not identify the publisher and date of publication of the Bible in which the record was found, there is no way to determine whether the record was created at the time of the event or by later generations who recorded their family's history from memory.

No matter how careful the compilers of Bible records are, there is one aspect of original Bible records that is not obvious in print: original Bible records often show changes in handwriting, indicating when a new person began recording information. Most published Bible records do not indicate these changes; even those that do merely state that a change occurred.

Locating Published Bible Records

Many Bible records have been published in genealogical periodicals. In *PERSI,* most Bible records are listed in the surname section. The locality where the family lived is another category to search; Bible records noted there are listed under the topic "Vital Records." (For more information on *PERSI,* see chapter 19, "Genealogical Periodicals.") The relatively few book-length sources which contain Bible records are noted in the locality section of the *Family History Library Catalog*™ under the head-

MASSACHUSETTS 268

08875
Vital records of Sutton, Massachusetts, to the end of the year 1849/ Systematic History Fund. — Worcester, Mass.: Franklin P. Rice, 1907. — 478 p.; 23 cm. — Poor condition; Kept in office. MASS/COUNTIES/WORCESTER/SUTTON/VIT

08876
Vital records of Taunton, Massachusetts to the year 1850/ New England Historic Genealogical Society. — Boston, Mass.: The Society, 1928, 1929. — 3 v.; 23 cm. — CONTENTS: v.1. Births-- v.2. Marriages-- v.3. Deaths MASS/COUNTIES/BRISTOL/TAUNTON/VIT

08877
Vital records of Templeton, Massachusetts to the end of the year 1849/ Systematic History Fund. — Worcester, Mass.: The Fund, 1907. — 212 p.; 23 cm. MASS/COUNTIES/WORCESTER/TEMPLETON/VIT

08878
Vital records of Tewksbury, Massachusetts to the end of the year 1849/ The Essex Institute. — Salem, Mass.: The Institute, 1912. — 246 p.; 23 cm. MASS/COUNTIES/MIDDLESEX/TEWKSBURY/VIT

08879
Vital records of the town of Brewster, Massachusetts to the end of the year 1849/ literally transcribed under the direction of George Ernes Bowman. — Boston, Mass.: Massachusetts Society of Mayflower Descendants, 1904. — 281 p.; 23 cm. — Index.

08887
Vital records of Upton, Massachusetts to the end of the year 1849/ Systematic History Fund. — 190 p.; 23 cm. MASS/COUNTIES/WORCESTER/UPTON/VIT

08888
Vital records of Waltham, Massachusetts to the year 1850/ New England Historic Genealogical Society. — Boston, Mass.: The Society, 1904. — 298 p.; 23 cm. MASS/COUNTIES/MIDDLESEX/WALTHAM/VIT

08889
Vital records of Warren (formerly Western), Massachusets to the end of the year 1849/ Systematic History Fund. — Worcester, Mass.: The Fund, 1910. — 196 p.; 23 cm. MASS/COUNTIES/WORCESTER/WARREN/VIT

08890
Vital records of Washington, Massachusetts, to the year 1850/ New England Historic Genealogical Society. — Boston, Mass.: The Society, 1904. — 57 p.; 23 cm. MASS/COUNTIES/BERKSHIRE/WASHING-/TON

08891
Vital records of Wayland, Massachusetts to the year 1850/ New England Historic Genealogical Society. — Boston, Mass.: The Society, 1910. — 160 p.; 23 cm. MASS/COUNTIES/MIDDLESEX/WAYLAND/VIT

08892
Vital records of Wenham, Massachusetts to the

08900
Vital records of Westminster, Massachusetts to the end of the year 1849/ Systmatic History Fund. — Worcester, Mass.: The Fund, 1908. — 258 p.; 23 cm. MASS/COUNTIES/WORCESTER/WESTMINSTER

08901
Vital records of Westport, Massachusetts to the year 1850/ New England Historic Genealogical Society. — Boston, Mass.: The Society, 1918. — 296 p.; 23 cm. MASS/COUNTIES/BRISTOL/WESTPORT/VIT

08902
Vital records of Weymouth, Massachusetts: to the year 1850. — Boston, Mass.: New England Historic Genealogical Society, 1910. — 2 v.; 23 cm. — Poor condition; kept in office. — CONTENTS: v.1. Births-- v.2. Marriages and deaths. MASS/COUNTIES/NORFOLK/WEYMOUTH

08903
Vital records of Williamstown, Massachusetts to the year 1850/ New England Historic Genealogical Society. — Boston, Mass.: The Society, 1907. — 173 p.; 23 cm. — Poor condition; kept in office. MASS/COUNTIES/BERKSHIRE/WILLIAMS-/TOWN

08904
Vital records of Winchendon, Massachusetts to the end of the year 1849/ The Systematic History Fund. — Worcester, Mass.: The Fund, 1909. — 223 p.; Ac23 cm. MASS/COUNTIES/WORCESTER/WINCHENDON

08905

Figure 7-15. Part of the Massachusetts section of the second volume of the *DAR Library Catalog,* illustrating some of the vital record sources contained in the collection of the DAR.

ing "Bible Records." Most of the typescript DAR volumes are available on microfilm through the Family History Library.

Kirkham Indexes. Partial surname indexes to many of the DAR and other Bible record collections at the Family History Library were compiled by E. Kay Kirkham in two volumes. The first volume focuses on records from many of the southern states: *An Index to Some of the Family Records of the Southern States: 35,000 Microfilm References from the NSDAR Files and Elsewhere* (Logan, Utah: Everton Publishers, 1979). A later volume covers records throughout much of the United States, including additional records from some of the southern states covered earlier: *An Index to Some of the Bibles and Family Records of the United States: 45,500 References as Taken from the Microfilm at the Genealogical Society of Utah* (Logan, Utah: Everton Publishers, 1984).

DAR Library Catalog. The DAR published its library catalog in three volumes. Vol. 2 of the *DAR Library Catalog* references state and local histories and records, including the published vital records that are the subject of this chapter. The volume is arranged alphabetically by state in bibliographical form. Figure 7-15 shows a page from the Massachusetts section of the catalog; it illustrates some of the vital record sources contained in the collection of the DAR.

CEMETERY INSCRIPTIONS

Kory L. Meyerink[2]

The inscriptions on monuments and gravestones can provide important clues or validate facts in question, but it is not possible for most people to locate and visit every cemetery where ancestors may lie buried. For most researchers, cemetery inscriptions and their cousins—morticians', sextons', and burial records—are most often accessed through printed sources.

The value of published cemetery inscriptions cannot be overstated; however, they must be used more carefully than almost any other kind of published original record. It is very likely that more nineteenth-century ancestors, and their families, can be identified in cemetery records than in virtually any other source—except, perhaps, the Federal censuses (and cemetery inscriptions provide birth and death dates not given in census records). As noted earlier, vital records were not kept by most states or provinces until the end of the nineteenth century or later; marriage records can be fairly thorough, but not everyone married; land, probate, court, and other records generally focus on adult males; obituaries did not become popular until later in the nineteenth century; church records are inadequate for several of the major denominations; and immigration, naturalization, and military records, by their nature, record only a small percentage of the population.

But everyone dies, and in North America virtually everyone has been buried (especially before the mid-twentieth century) in a dedicated cemetery (except in the southern states, where individuals were commonly buried on home property). However, not everyone is listed in cemetery inscription books; not every burial received a permanent (stone) marker; and published inscriptions are not available for every cemetery.

Often, old cemeteries are moved or destroyed in the wave of progress. Old headstones are broken, stolen, or just weather away. Therefore, the time taken by someone to record information on headstones can create a timeless document for future research efforts. In figure 7-16 is just such a record. The Rogers Cemetery was located on Alexander Rogers's farm near the site of the old Welcome Church, about two miles south of Folsom,

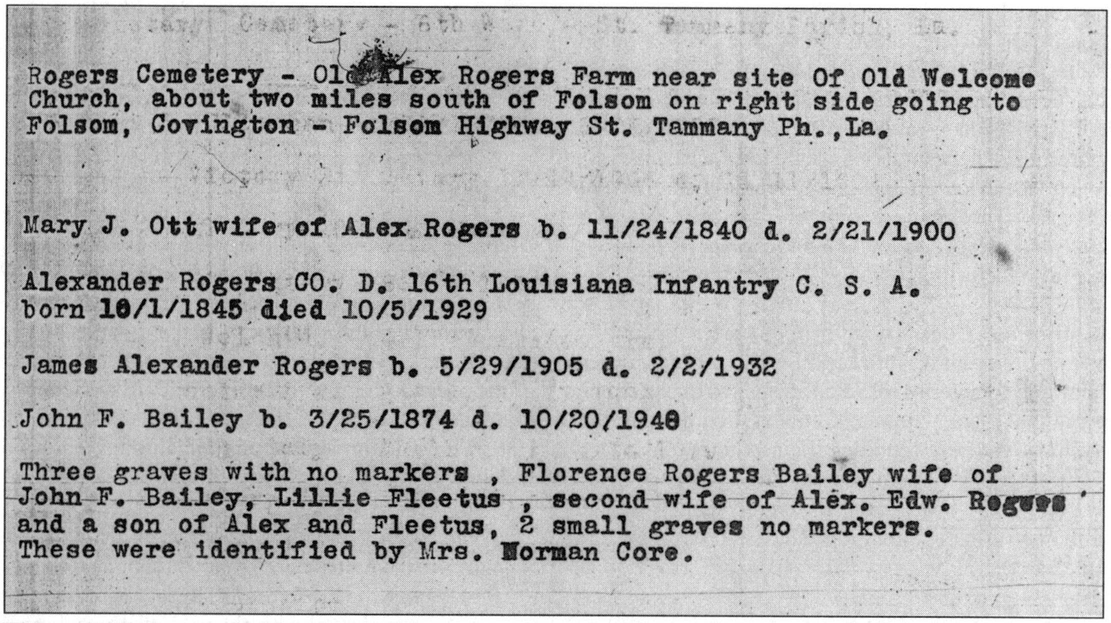

Rogers Cemetery - Old Alex Rogers Farm near site Of Old Welcome Church, about two miles south of Folsom on right side going to Folsom, Covington - Folsom Highway St. Tammany Ph.,La.

Mary J. Ott wife of Alex Rogers b. 11/24/1840 d. 2/21/1900

Alexander Rogers CO. D. 16th Louisiana Infantry C. S. A. born 10/1/1845 died 10/5/1929

James Alexander Rogers b. 5/29/1905 d. 2/2/1932

John F. Bailey b. 3/25/1874 d. 10/20/1948

Three graves with no markers , Florence Rogers Bailey wife of John F. Bailey, Lillie Fleetus , second wife of Alex. Edw. Rogers and a son of Alex and Fleetus, 2 small graves no markers. These were identified by Mrs. Norman Core.

Figure 7-16. A record of headstone inscriptions from the Rogers Cemetery near Folsom, Louisiana. From Dolores Powe Butler and Doris Martin Holden, comps., *Saint Tammany Parish, Louisiana, Cemetery Records,* vol. 2 (n.p., 1979).

Louisiana. The information recorded here may well have disappeared from the original resting place, but a bit of information about Alexander Rogers, who proudly served in the Confederate Army, his wife, Mary, and at least a bit about the next generation of the family has been preserved.

The Nature of Copied Cemetery Inscriptions

The vast majority of published cemetery records are the copied inscriptions in volumes on the shelves of genealogical libraries and in the pages of genealogical periodicals. But it is important to note that the best published cemetery inscriptions share one fault with the worst: sometimes the tombstone inscriptions themselves are wrong. Consider the Mark family, buried in a cemetery in Morehead, Kentucky. One grandfather's tombstone lists his birth date correctly, but has the wrong year of death. His wife's tombstone correctly records her date of death, but has the wrong year of birth. Another family tombstone has the wrong name. When the actual records are incorrect, published inscriptions cannot be better.

The helpful compiler who carefully alphabetizes the inscriptions also does the researcher a disservice. While alphabetizing makes the records somewhat easier to use, it destroys the associations that become apparent through physical proximity. For example, in the Mark family cemetery in Morehead, a man's tombstone is flanked by the tombstones of his two wives. His first wife is on the left; her tombstone has her maiden name on it rather than her married name. An alphabetical arrangement of the inscriptions removes her from the vicinity of her husband, making the relationship less obvious. Another couple is buried under a single headstone with the surname Mark, but no dates. Under some bushes nearby are two small stones of children with no surnames; their parents are identified by initials but, again, no surnames. They would be lost in an alphabetical listing. The Mark tombstones are surrounded by those of P'Simers and Wages, families that intermarried with the Mark family, and other tombstones in the cemetery are separated from this grouping. All of the obvious associations are lost in an alphabetical listing.

Several other aspects of published inscriptions require caution. They include:

Multiple Cemeteries Included in a Single Volume. The inscriptions for an entire cemetery can often be transcribed onto just a few pages; such a collection is hardly worth the effort of publication by itself. Therefore, many compilers/publishers include several cemeteries in a single volume. In such a volume, all of the cemeteries are usually from the same geographic location, such as a town, township, or county (or part thereof). This focus makes it easier to search for people whose last residence is known but the cemetery where they were buried is not. However, two problems may surface with such "multiple cemetery" publications. (1) Many such volumes lack a comprehensive index covering all cemeteries in the book. Often, each cemetery is indexed separately, usually right after the inscriptions, so a researcher must page through the entire volume, sometimes seeking dozens of indexes. Alphabetized lists are not indexed at all, and some inscriptions that only occupy a few pages are not indexed, requiring a line-by-line search for all the families of interest. (2) A volume many not include all of the cemeteries in the geographic area it covers. A large cemetery may have been excluded because there were too many inscriptions in it to transcribe; other cemeteries whose transcriptions were published previously may have been ignored (and sometimes the fact not noted in the newer volume); private cemeteries may not have permitted the transcriber to copy the inscriptions; and the transcriber may have skipped, overlooked, or been unaware of some obscure cemeteries.

Recent Burials Not Included. Some transcripts were created many years ago—some as early as the 1890s. Many transcripts date from the first half of the twentieth century and therefore may omit fifty or more years of burials. Always check the date of the transcript and seek more recent transcripts where necessary. (Do not rely on the date of publication; some recent publications are simply reprints, or first printings, of inscriptions that were copied decades ago.) On occasion, transcribers focus only on the "older" burials on the assumption that they are of greater interest or are in greater danger of weathering away. A transcriber may choose a "cutoff" date, not including any persons born after a certain date, or, more commonly, who died after the cutoff. Usually such details are noted in the preface, so always review those introductory sections.

Inadequate Indexes. Cemetery inscriptions are often poorly indexed. As mentioned above, brief listings may not be indexed at all, and multiple cemeteries are seldom indexed in one alphabet, or even in one place within a volume. Often the only indexes are surname indexes, requiring the user to check several pages. In such situations, be sure to search the entire page given in the index; often, two or more entries on the same page will have the surname of interest, but the index will not point out such multiple entries.

Incomplete Transcriptions. The recorded inscription is often incomplete. Most transcribers include any annotations that provide genealogical information, but, on occasion, only the dates are listed. Where only years are given, review the rest of the list. If none of the entries includes the day or month of death (or birth), it is likely that the transcriptions are incomplete. While some stones only include birth and death years, it is very uncommon for this practice to pertain to an entire cemetery.

More likely to be omitted are the wonderful epitaphs that speak of the life and character of the deceased or reveal the perceptions of his or her survivors. Ebenezer Peirce's tombstone in Peru, Massachusetts, includes his alleged last words, uttered three months after the Civil War ended: "I thank God that I have lived to see this rebellion closed and slavery abolished." Published transcripts do not include this insight into his beliefs and concerns of the day. Epitaphs may also give clues to occupations, military service, and even other relationships not stated elsewhere.

Incorrect Transcriptions. Tombstones are not always easy to read. Weathered stones, poor illumination, lichen and other growth on the stone, and a variety of other difficulties can cause transcribers to record information incorrectly. Errors also creep in during the publication process. Although many transcribers now take laptop computers into cemeteries, formerly the information was transcribed by hand, usually on pads of paper. Later, the transcriber (or some other volunteer who never visited the cemetery) typed these notes. If the list was to be arranged alphabetically, a second round of typing was needed after the first set was sorted; this was usually done by cutting apart the first set and rearranging the pieces of paper. Each step brought the possibility of errors.

Enhanced Inscriptions. On occasion, transcribers add information from other, sometimes unspecified, sources. While the intent is to make a publication more useful, it may actually compromise the evidence, especially if the added information is not labeled as such. In such situations, the researcher may be unable to determine what was actually on the stone and what was not. In the worst cases, the added information could be in error because the source was wrong or the compiler made a faulty connection. This last situation was the case with the following entry in the published inscriptions from the Tyringham, Massachusetts, cemetery (Hoogs 1985, 26):

> STEDMAN: Huldah Herrick, wife of Tristrim Stedman, died 13 March 1862, aged 65 years. (Tyr. VR: daughter of Francis and Huldah Herrick, born 16 January 1797.)

Here the source, the published Tyringham vital records, is cited, but the connection is wrong because of several problems. The first problem was the compiler's deciding that Huldah was born in Tyringham (the stone does not state where she was born) and that her birth was recorded in the town record books. Second, Huldah was not sixty-five years old. That is a misreading of the stone, which actually indicates sixty-seven years—but even that is incorrect. Huldah's granddaughter, Arcelli Spencer Hall, who was thirteen when Huldah died, later wrote in her family record book:

> Personally, I had a small monument placed at the graves of Tristrum Stedman Jr. and Huldah Herrick Stedman to replace the broken stone, in the Tyringham Cemetery. I was not pleased with the work that was done by George Warren. . . . Huldah's age should be 76, which is given 67. She died when visiting in our home (Hall 1932, 56).

Arcelli's comments are verified by the 1860 census and by the original town record of deaths, which correctly gave Huldah's age at death as seventy-six and indicated her father to be Hezekiah Herrick. Huldah was indeed born in Tyringham, but to a Baptist family, so there were no Congregational Church records (from which many of the entries in the published vital records book came) for this family.

Multiple Transcripts. Individuals and organizations have been transcribing cemetery inscriptions for more than a century. During that time, many cemeteries' inscriptions have been transcribed two, three, or even four times. Sometimes the later transcribers did not know of the earlier work; more often, however, they were attempting to update the older work. Often the earlier work was known to have been incomplete, and more people would have been interred since. Duplicated transcripts are actually very valuable to researchers because the different versions can be compared. Earlier publications may include inscriptions that no longer exist or that are now unreadable. However, later publications have often been based on the earlier ones, the same stones not being re-transcribed. Carefully read the preface to determine what use was made of older transcriptions.

Even with these drawbacks, cemetery records are rich and valuable sources of vital statistics. The information often includes data from a whole lifetime, and cemetery records can offer information that no other source yields. Tombstone epitaphs in particular can reveal the character of an ancestor. Figure 7-17 includes some interesting epitaphs published by Katherine A. Prichard in *Ancient Burying Grounds of the Town of Waterbury, Connecticut* (Waterbury, Conn.: Mattatuck Historical Society, 1917).

Organizations That Transcribe Inscriptions

Always take note of the organization or individual(s) who prepared the transcript; accuracy may depend to some extent on the individual and why she copied the inscriptions. Most have been done by volunteers, but a few have been transcribed by paid individuals. Some of the key groups are described below.

Local and State Genealogical and Historical Societies. Local societies are concerned with preserving local records. By far the greatest number of cemetery transcriptions are prepared and published by local genealogical and historical societies. Many cemeteries, especially those which have been abandoned, lack caretakers to help preserve them and the information they contain, so societies adopt such projects frequently. Such work may be done haphazardly as volunteers come forward, or the society may have a master strategy to identify all cemeteries and existing publications and then systematically transcribe and publish the inscriptions. Typically these transcripts are published as articles in the society's periodical or as a small series of booklets, each including the inscriptions of from one to dozens of cemeteries. Sometimes periodical articles are later collected and published together as booklets.

State societies also get involved in such activities. A state society may support or even coordinate the projects of local societies, or may simply produce a list of known cemeteries so that others can transcribe the inscriptions. Many of the statewide guidebooks described below are the result of state society projects. Other societies maintain card or computer files, such as the Kentucky Historical Society's long-term project to computerize the state's existing cemetery records.

Many of these projects are listed in the *FGS Membership Directory.* The Federation of Genealogical Societies encourages its five hundred member societies to list their publications in the published directory and on its World Wide Web site (http://www.fgs.org/~fgs/fgs-dir.htm).

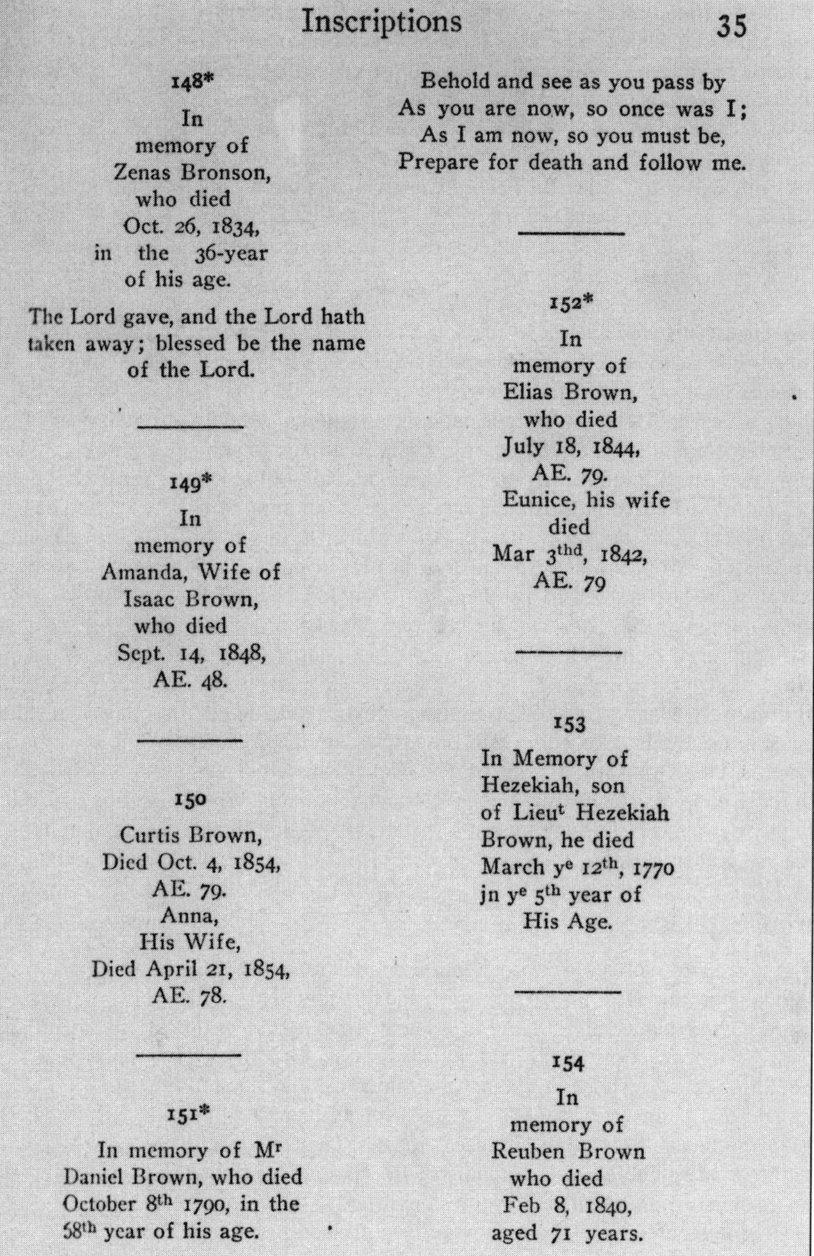

Inscriptions 35

148*

In
memory of
Zenas Bronson,
who died
Oct. 26, 1834,
in the 36-year
of his age.

The Lord gave, and the Lord hath taken away; blessed be the name of the Lord.

149*

In
memory of
Amanda, Wife of
Isaac Brown,
who died
Sept. 14, 1848,
AE. 48.

150

Curtis Brown,
Died Oct. 4, 1854,
AE. 79.
Anna,
His Wife,
Died April 21, 1854,
AE. 78.

151*

In memory of Mr
Daniel Brown, who died
October 8th 1790, in the
58th year of his age.

Behold and see as you pass by
As you are now, so once was I;
As I am now, so you must be,
Prepare for death and follow me.

152*

In
memory of
Elias Brown,
who died
July 18, 1844,
AE. 79.
Eunice, his wife
died
Mar 3thd, 1842,
AE. 79

153

In Memory of
Hezekiah, son
of Lieut Hezekiah
Brown, he died
March ye 12th, 1770
jn ye 5th year of
His Age.

154

In
memory of
Reuben Brown
who died
Feb 8, 1840,
aged 71 years.

Figure 7-17. Epitaphs published by Katherine A. Prichard in *Ancient Burying Grounds of the Town of Waterbury, Connecticut.*

Daughters of the American Revolution. Perhaps the most significant organization involved in preserving cemetery information is the DAR. For many years, volunteers from the DAR have identified and preserved the inscriptions in local cemeteries. Typically, these have been typed and "published" in books of which only a few copies were made, often through the use of carbon paper while typing. The carbon paper copies were then donated to the DAR's national library in Washington, D.C., and to local or state libraries or historical societies. Many are described in the *DAR Library Catalog* (mentioned above under "Bible Records—Locating Bible Records"). Fortunately, many have been microfilmed and are available through the Family History Library. Many of the microfilmed DAR volumes are described in the *Family History Library Catalog* under the name of the state (not the name of the county), as a volume may include many counties. In either case, they are listed under the heading "Cemetery Records" under the appropriate locality.

Genealogical Society of Utah. Another organization that was active in transcribing cemetery inscriptions, especially from the 1940s to the 1960s, was the Genealogical Society of Utah. This organization within the LDS church is responsible for the Family History Library and its excellent collection of records. Many members of the LDS church, and others, volunteered to locate cemeteries in the areas where they lived and to transcribe the inscriptions. The volunteers were conscientious, but they had little training for the task and may not have been as familiar with the names in these cemeteries as modern researchers who descend from those buried there. The transcripts were typed and sent to the society's library (now the Family History Library) in Salt Lake City, where they were bound in volumes and microfilmed. Volumes were compiled for almost every state, with multiple volumes for most (twenty-three for New York, twelve for Idaho, nine for Pennsylvania, etc.). The volumes may cover areas across each state, and each volume may contain cemeteries from distant localities, thus giving the giving the impression that all of the cemeteries were covered, though that is not the case. These and many other volumes are best accessed through *Cemeteries of the U.S.* (described below under "Finding Aids").

Government Programs. On occasion, local and state governments have sponsored cemetery transcripts, either directly through grants or indirectly through the activities of a government office. In 1997, the state legislature of Utah allocated a sizeable amount for the creation of a statewide index to cemetery records. Earlier, during the "make-work" days of the Depression, the Federal government funded the creation of cemetery listings and indexes by the Historical Records Survey division of the Work Projects Administration. Many of these transcripts were later published by others, including local societies. Other results of this effort remain as card indexes deposited at state and local archives and libraries.

Individuals. Many published inscriptions are the work of dedicated individuals who believe in preserving these precious records. These transcribers sometimes self-publish their efforts or receive the assistance of societies or commercial publishers. In any case, their efforts represent a significant portion of the records researcher use.

Finding Aids

The local nature of cemetery inscription publications (they are typically produced in limited quantities and distributed in small circles) can make it very difficult to locate a cemetery or a published set of inscriptions. In addition, researchers usually do not know exactly where ancestors were buried, so they need to know what cemeteries exist (or existed) for a given locality. Many finding aids provide assistance in locating cemeteries and, in many cases, published inscriptions. Three nationwide directories or lists (none of which identifies published transcriptions) are supplemented by two nationwide lists of inscriptions and many statewide guides, most of which do identify inscriptions.

Cemeteries of the U.S. More than 22,600 cemeteries are listed or described in *Cemeteries of the U.S.: A Guide to Contact Information for U.S. Cemeteries and Their Records,* edited by Deborah M. Burek (Detroit: Gale Research, 1994). This volume is arranged by state and subdivided by county. Cemeteries are listed alphabetically within each county with their addresses and, where possible, telephone numbers. For active cemeteries (the vast majority of the listings), the entry also provides the contact person, years of operation, ownership and affiliations (such as churches), facilities, services (hours of operation), and access to cemetery (sexton or burial) records. Additional information in some listings includes the fax number, former cemetery name(s), physical location, historical and architectural notes, and known publications about the cemetery (not necessarily publications of inscriptions). The volume also includes indexes to religious denominations and other affiliations, as well as a master index by cemetery name. While *Cemeteries of the U.S.* is not the most comprehensive listing of active cemeteries, it does provide the most information for those cemeteries it lists; unfortunately, it does not list those buried in the cemeteries. It is sometimes possible to locate a transcribed copy by writing to the cemetery.

United States Cemetery Address Book. A more comprehensive, if briefer, listing of active cemeteries is Elizabeth G. Kot and James D. Kot's *United States Cemetery Address Book: 1994–1995* (Vallejo, Calif.: Indices Publishing, 1994). While the title page indicates that this list has "more than 25,000 cemeteries," the number, by calculation, is closer to 28,500—at least 25 percent more than *Cemeteries of the U.S.* This directory is arranged by state and then by city, with cemeteries listed alphabetically under each city. The county is given after each city's name, so counties are scattered throughout a state's listing; this makes it somewhat more difficult to locate all the cemeteries in a single county. The listings are brief—usually containing just the name of the cemetery, address, and ZIP code. For many smaller cemeteries, no street address is provided—only the ZIP code, which can be used with the town and cemetery name to create an address. The *Cemetery Address Book* provides no information about when the cemetery was established, nor whom to contact. The method of compilation (various lists of inconsistent quality) results in a few cemeteries being listed twice. For example, some appear under different names (but the same address) or are listed under neighboring towns, one being the location, the other the mailing address. (Occasionally two separate, neighboring cemeteries do share the same address if they are administered by the same agency.)

While the researcher will benefit from using both directories, a comparison of listings for the same county indicates that the Kots's *Cemetery Address Book* is more inclusive. For Berrien County, Michigan, *Cemeteries of the U.S.* has only nine listings, while Kot's *Cemetery Address Book* has twenty-two entries for twenty different cemeteries, which were listed under separate towns. Only six of the entries appear in both directories.

American Genealogical Gazetteer. The most comprehensive single list of U.S. cemeteries is in Douglas B. McKay and Kory L. Meyerink's *American Genealogical Gazetteer* (Orem, Utah: Ancestry, 1996) CD-ROM. This geographic tool, based on the listings of the U.S. Geological Survey, identifies every cemetery listed on the USGS 7.5-minute map series (see chapter 3, "Geographic Tools"). The *American Genealogical Gazetteer* includes 105,966 cemeteries. While some cemeteries that had not been mapped are not listed in it, many now-inactive cemeteries and family burial grounds are included.

The listings are very brief, providing only the name, county, and state of each cemetery. (For more detailed information, refer to the original database by the U.S. Geological Survey, which also includes latitude and longitude coordinates to help pinpoint each cemetery.) The *American Geographical Gazetteer* lists thirty-nine cemeteries in Berrien county, Michigan—almost twice as many as the Kots's *Cemetery Address Book.* The total number of cemeteries in this list is approximately four times the number in either of the two directories described above. However, this listing includes inactive as well as active cemeteries and does not include the city or address of the cemetery.

Index to United States Cemeteries. The best, most comprehensive nationwide list that identifies published cemetery inscriptions is *Index to United States Cemeteries* (Salt Lake City: Family History Library, 1988). Although it is called an index, it does not index names; rather, it indexes cemeteries and identifies published transcripts that exist for them. This list, on twenty-five rolls of microfilm, includes hundreds of thousands of index cards, most of which indicate where a set of cemetery inscriptions can be found. Created by the staff of the Family History Library to provide better access to thousands of obscure cemetery collections, this file is arranged by state and county. Each card provides the name and town (or township) of a cemetery with the microfilm or book number of a volume, periodical, or section of a book where the inscriptions may be found, or a fuller description of the cemetery (see figure 7-18). The cards are typed or handwritten; for some cemeteries, the first three inscriptions are included on the card. In a few cases there are two or more cards for the same cemetery because the inscriptions were located in several sources. While most microfilm numbers have not changed, book numbers may have changed, and some books may no longer be available, having been replaced with microfilm copies.

The Family History Library's cemetery card file was closed in 1985, so recent acquisitions are not included in the *Index to United States Cemeteries*. While it is always advisable to use the *Family History Library Catalog* when accessing sources at the Family History Library, this index provides access which the catalog does not because *every* listing is filed under the specific location and name of the cemetery. For an average county there are between one hundred and two hundred cards, providing dozens of sources for the researcher to investigate. For example, there are 122 cards for Berrien County, Michigan, identifying upwards of one hundred different cemeteries for that county. There are thousands of published cemetery lists that are not in *Index to United States Cemeteries*, both within and outside the Family History Library, but no other reference comes close to identifying as many sources.

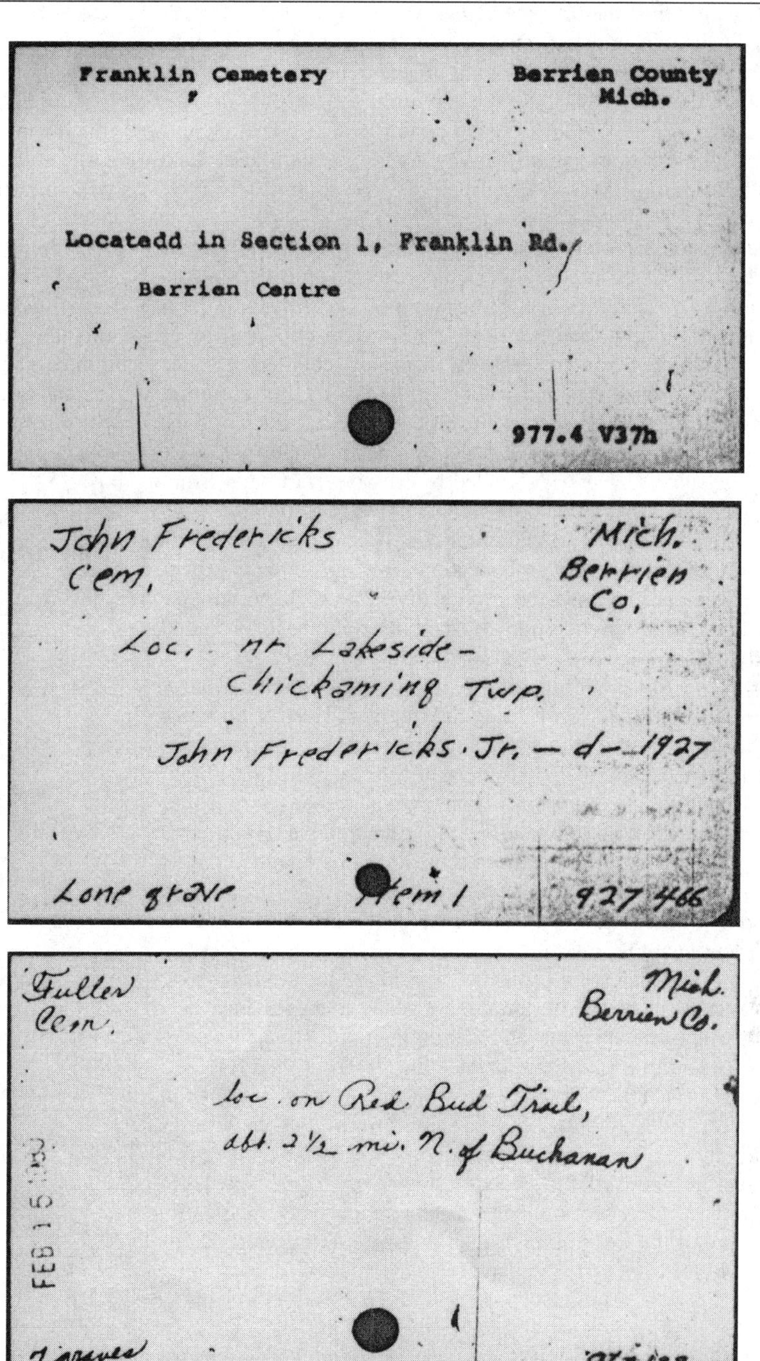

Franklin Cemetery Berrien County Mich.

Locatedd in Section 1, Franklin Rd.
Berrien Centre

977.4 V37h

John Fredericks Cem. Mich. Berrien Co.

Loc. nr Lakeside-Chickaming Twp.
John Fredericks. Jr. — d — 1927

Lone grave Item 1 927 466

Fuller Cem. Mich. Berrien Co.

loc. on Red Bud Trail,
abt. 2 1/2 mi. N. of Buchanan

7 graves 962138

Figure 7-18. Index cards from *Index to United States Cemeteries.* Each card provides the name and town (or township) of a cemetery with the microfilm or book number of a volume, periodical, or section of a book where the inscriptions may be found (or a fuller description of the cemetery).

Cemetery Record Compendium. An earlier effort to identify published cemetery inscriptions is *The Cemetery Record Compendium: Comprising a Directory of Cemetery Records and Where They May Be Located,* compiled by John "D" Stemmons and E. Diane Stemmons (Logan, Utah: Everton Publishers, 1978). This work lists, by state and county, upwards of ten thousand or more cemeteries and refers to published inscriptions. It was drawn from around 125 sources, mostly periodicals and microfilms at the Family History Library; several cemeteries are listed for each of approximately 2,100 counties. Where known, the cemeteries are listed by township within each county. Each cemetery name is followed by a code referring to one of the sources in the bibliography. If the reference is to a microfilm or book at the Family History Library, it is followed by the microfilm or book number; periodical references are followed by the volume and page number. Although *Cemetery Record Compendium* has far fewer references than the *Index to United States Cemeteries*, it is still a valuable, if somewhat dated, source, in part because it includes periodical articles and collections in other repositories. It is now available on CD-ROM, combined with the same authors' *Vital Record Compendium* (discussed earlier under "General Finding Aids—Bibliographies"), as *Vital Records Locator* (Salt Lake City: Ancestry, 1997).

Statewide Guidebooks. Cemetery research is local by its nature, so the best sources for cemetery research are local sources; therefore, researchers need to be aware of a growing number of statewide guides to cemeteries and published inscription sources. Currently, such sources exist for at least twenty-seven states. Most are published books, while some are card or computer files residing in libraries and historical societies. Each of these sources is unique and provides different information. For example, *Ohio Cemeteries,* edited by Maxine Hartmann Smith (Mansfield: Ohio Genealogical Society, 1978), and *Addendum* (1990) are primarily listings by county and township of the known cemeteries, with the location given by surveyor's township designations and a description of roads which the cemeteries are near. References to published inscriptions are provided, but only for a few periodicals and county source books.

The State Library of Michigan's *Michigan Cemetery Source Book* (Lansing: Library of Michigan, 1994) is primarily a listing of inscription sources at the state library (including periodicals) accompanied by a list of cemetery locations. Statewide sources are almost always more comprehensive (for their areas) than the nationwide lists described above. For Berrien County, Michigan, the nationwide sources listed nine, twenty, and thirty-nine cemeteries, while the *Michigan Cemetery Source Book* identifies eighty-three; inscriptions for seventy-two of them are on file at the state library.

Some statewide projects go as far as to provide master indexes to cemetery inscriptions. For years, volunteers have been indexing cemetery inscriptions throughout the Canadian province of Ontario. They have created the *Ontario Cemetery Finding Aid* (*OCFA*), now published on CD-ROM (Orem, Utah: GenRef, 1996), with 1.2 million names from 2,400 cemeteries. Although the complete entries are not provided, the index provides the name of the deceased, cemetery name, township, county, a reference number, and the supporting organization (source of the inscriptions). As a finding aid, this work is outstanding; by not providing all of the information for each entry, it requires the researcher to refer to the published inscriptions so that important clues will not be overlooked.

Table 7-3 identifies known statewide guides to cemeteries. The depth and timeliness of these guides varies greatly. Some only give the locations of the cemeteries, while many indicate if published inscriptions are available. Few, if any, of these projects can be considered comprehensive; nevertheless, they usually provide the best listings and are excellent starting places for cemetery research. (The books noted in table 7-3 are cited fully in the chapter bibliography.)

Other Sources. There are many other ways to locate published cemetery inscriptions. Always check the catalogs of libraries with significant genealogical collections for the areas where ancestors died (including the Family History Library), but also check local public libraries and state libraries and historical societies. Contact local genealogical societies as well; their members are usually aware of publications that cover local cemeteries. Some states have cemetery preservation societies which might also be able to advise about the existence of published inscriptions. Lastly, contact local funeral directors; they can identify currently active cemeteries, although they may not know much about older, inactive cemeteries. After locating some active cemeteries in the area of interest, contact them; their staffs will know of published inscriptions and may also know of publications covering older, inactive cemeteries.

Many sextons' and morticians' records are now being published. These records can be informative; they often include exact ages, places of birth, surviving spouses' names, parents' names, and other important information. (Unfortunately, such information can be unreliable. People who give the information to the sextons and morticians may not know the correct answers; even when people know the correct information, the emotional stress of a family death can cause them to forget and to make mistakes.)

Checklist for Evaluating Published Cemetery Inscriptions

- When was the transcript made? Could an ancestor have died since that date?
- Are there multiple transcripts?
- Is all of the information included, or only the dates?
- Who transcribed the inscriptions? Was the person experienced in reading headstones?
- Who published the inscriptions—a private individual or a society?
- Is the data from the tombstones, from sextons' records, or both?
- Was any information added from additional sources?
- Is the list alphabetized or is it in plot order?
- How comprehensive is the list of cemeteries?

CHURCH RECORDS AS VITAL RECORDS

North American church records can be excellent sources of vital event information. Churches were often concerned with recording the same kinds of information that governments recorded: births (or baptisms), marriages, and deaths (as burials). Indeed, many churches were recording some or all of these events long before local or state governments began to do so.

The following discussion serves to illustrate the importance of these records as published vital records. For a more detailed discussion, see chapter 8, "Published Church Sources."

As apparent by its title, Frederic Bailey's *Early Connecticut Marriages, as Found on Ancient Church Records Prior to 1800* (1896–1906; reprinted with integrated errata; 7 books in 1 vol.; Baltimore: Genealogical Publishing Co., 1982) is based on the records of various churches, although it appears as a statewide list of marriages. Bailey's introduction explains the scope of this publication (pages iv and v):

> The first settlers of Connecticut came from Massachusetts Bay and Plymouth Colonies and located at

Table 7-3. Statewide Cemetery Guides

State	*Format*	*Title*	*Author or Location*
Arkansas	Book*	*Index to Sources for Arkansas Cemetery Inscriptions*	DAR
California	Book*	*California Cemetery Inscription Sources*	Kot and Thomson
Colorado	Book*	*Colorado Cemetery Directory*	Merrill
Connecticut	Microfilm†	*Charles R. Hale Collection*	Hale
Georgia	Book*	*Georgia Cemetery Directory and Bibliography*	Brooke
Illinois	Cards	Illinois Cemetery Project	Illinios State Historical Society
Indiana	Cards*	Cemetery Locator File	Indiana State Library
Iowa	Film†	*Iowa Cemetery and Grave Records*	WPA Project
Kansas	Books†	*Abandoned and Semi-active Cemeteries of Kansas*	Ford
Kentucky	File†	Contact the Kentucky Historical Society	
Maine	File*	MOCA Inscription Project	Maine Old Cemetery Association
Maryland	Book*	*Directory of Maryland Cemeteries*	Genealogical Council of Maryland
Michigan	Book*	*Michigan Cemetery Source Book*	Library of Michigan
Minnesota	Book*	*Minnesota Cemeteries in Print*	Pope
Missouri	Book*	*Missouri Cemetery Inscription Sources*	Kot and Thomson
Montana	Book*	*Montana's Genealogical and Local History Records*	Richards
Nebraska	Book*	*Nebraska Cemeteries and Burial Sites*	Nebraska State Genealogical Society
Nevada	Book†	*Nevada Tombstone Record Book*	Taylor
New Hampshire	File	Contact the New Hampshire Old Graveyard Association	
North Carolina	Film	*Cemetery Inscription Card Index*	WPA card file
Ohio	Book*	*Ohio Cemeteries* and *Supplement*	Smith
Oklahoma	Book	*Union List of Oklahoma Cemeteries*	Oklahoma Geneal. Society
Oregon	Book	*Oregon Cemetery Directory*	Oregon Heritage Council
Rhode Island	Microfilm†	*James Arnold Tombstone Records Collection*	
South Dakota	Book	*South Dakota Cemeteries*	Krueger
Texas	Book*	*A Reference to Texas Cemetery Records*	Parsons
Utah	Book	*Cemetery Listing (Utah)*	Utah State Archives and Records Service
Vermont	Book*	*Index to known cemetery listings in Vermont*	Nichols
Virginia	Book	*Virginia Cemeteries: A Guide to Resources*	Hogg
Washington	Book	*A Directory of Cemeteries and Funeral Homes in Washington State*	
West Virginia	Cards	Cemetery Card File	Archives and History Library
Wisconsin	File	Surname index and newsletter	Wisconsin State Old Cemetery Society

* Identifies published inscriptions
† Source includes inscriptions

Windsor, Hartford and Wethersfield. All alike being devoted disciples of Christ, Gospel ministers came also, and at once Christian worship was established and parishes formed. . . .

Prior to the year 1659 there were in Connecticut eleven parish organizations. Before 1700 the eleven had increased to thirty-three. And by 1750 to 137, which number by the year 1800 had reached 200.

It is to this large but limited number that our attention has been directed. From among these copies of baptisms and marriages have been secured, out of which the following complete records of marriages have been taken.

We cannot speak in too high praise of that faithfulness to duty which seems as a rule to have possessed the early pastors who, amidst their studious cares, gave close attention to their parish records carefully to note both the marriages and baptisms among their own. Every parish seems to have possessed at some time these inherited treasures. At the same time have we reason to regret that lack of appreciation and careless indifference on the part of some responsible church official, whose possible neglect had been the cause of the total or partial loss of the interesting and valuable manuscripts alone telling the church's story of the first families' spiritual life. Over and over again has come to us the sad [p.v] report that the early church records had been lost or

> burned or somehow destroyed, possibly carried away and never returned, no one seemingly enough interested to trace and restore them to their proper place.

Bailey's lamentation in the last paragraph serves to remind us that these (and all published church records) should be considered incomplete. Many records have been lost or destroyed and, despite Bailey's optimism, many were never created at all. Of course, many couples choose not to marry in a church or to have their children baptized. Note also that Bailey refers to baptisms but that his book contains only marriages; never assume that a publication has included all possible records. Carefully read the introductory sections to understand the scope of the work.

Bailey printed the marriages just as they appeared in the church registers, as the following illustration from book 7, page 77, of the 1982 edition shows:

> **Barkhamsted.**
> LITCHFIELD COUNTY.
> The town of Barkhamsted was incorporated Oct. 1779. The Congregational Church was organized April 20, 1781. Rev. Ozias Eells was pastor from 1787 to 1813.
> Mr. _______ Marsh of Harwinton & Delight Wilson daughter of John Wilson & wife, March 19, 1787
> John Humphry & Widow Mary Olmstead, Aug. 28, 1787
> John Hopkins, Jr,. & Phebe Harrinton, Nov. 15, 1787
> Levi Tiffany of Hartland & Unice Wetmore, Dec. 25, 1787
> John Wetmore & Cinthia King, July 13, 1787
> Jeremiah Crane & Elisabeth Johnson, ___, 1787
> Abijah Hall & Anna Hutson of Cheshire, July 13, 1788
> Allyn Risley(?) of New Hartford & Lucy Spencer of Hartland, Feb. 21, 1789
> Stephen Parker & Unice Parker, March 11, 1789
> Seelye Crofut of Danbury & Hannah C. Holcomb, April 12, 1790
> William Lloyd & Jane Harvey of Granville, June 24, 1790
> Jesse Gates of Hartland & Rhoda Reed, Feb. 22, 1791
> Clement B. Willy of Barkhamsted & Sarah Hart of Farmington, March 29, 1791

Some church record publications include information from several churches in an area. An excellent example is *Vital Historical Records of Jackson County, Missouri 1826–1876* (Kansas City, Mo.: Kansas City Chapter, Daughters of the American Revolution, 1933–34). The prefatory note (page ix) explains the nature of the records, including the fact that many records were lost:

> The records of early churches furnish important history of a community; consequently, many of those of Jackson County were obtained and valuable information secured. Unfortunately, much data of this nature had been destroyed and some of the membership rolls lost. . . . The Committee makes no claim that these records are complete; they realize that they are not. Every effort has been made to have them as nearly complete as possible with the information obtainable.

Even with these limitations, the collection provides much information. In some cases it indicates where immigrants were born in their native countries, as examples from the book show (figure 7-19).

Even in the New England states, despite the many published town vital records, researchers sometimes need to rely on other sources of vital events. Church records are often excellent substitutes. The following sample is from Priscilla Hammond's *Vital Records from the Parish Register of Queen's Chapel Portsmouth, New Hampshire* (Concord, N.H., 1939), page 4.

> BAPTISMS
> 1739
> Portsmouth Decbr 16th 1739 Samuel Willey (adult).
> " Decbr 23 1739 (Zilla) Twins - children of John (Bathsheba) & ----------Mills.
> " Janry 20th 1739 George son of Daniel & Elizabeth Wentworth
> 1740
> Portsmouth Aprill 6th 1740 Sa--- (mutilated).
> " Aprill 13th 1740 Robert son of -----Robins

OTHER SOURCES FOR PUBLISHED VITAL RECORDS

Records of vital events can be found in numerous sources other than those discussed above, and many of them have been used to create printed sources. In each case, attempt to clearly understand what source was abstracted and how completely the work was done. The following are just a few examples of what diligent researchers will find.

Funeral Home Records

The value of early funeral home records has been recognized in recent years, and they have been published by many local genealogical societies. Many funeral homes have been owned by one or two families for more than one hundred years, their records predating government-mandated death records. While not everyone has been interred with the assistance of a mortician, and many localities had more than one mortuary, these records are generally fairly complete. In small localities (especially those served by only one mortuary), a large proportion of the local deaths are likely to have been recorded by mortuaries. The published versions of these records have usually been printed in small quantities, so they are usually found only at local libraries and societies (and in the few nationwide genealogical libraries that strive to obtain every published source).

Personal Diaries and Journals

Many people have kept diaries and journals, but a few writers, such as doctors, midwives, and circuit preachers, made a practice of identifying births, marriages, and deaths among the persons they knew or served. An example of such a published vital record source is this diary from *Pennsylvania Vital Records:*

BAPTISMS AND BIRTH RECORDS OF THE CATHOLIC CONGREGATION OF KANSAS RIVER RECORDED BY THE MISSIONARY PRIESTS IN 1834 AND THE SUCCEEDING YEARS.
(Copied from the original records kept in the vault of the Cathederal of the Immaculate Conception in Kansas City, Missouri, through the courtesy of Monsignor James J. McCaffrey, by Miss Dorothy E. Buzby.)
Mary Lessert, b. July 11, 1830; parents, Clement Lessert, Julia Roy; bap. Feb. 23, 1834;
sponsors, Andrew Roy, Cecelia R.C.Roy.
Martin Prudhomme, b. April 10, 1827; parent, Susan Prudhomme; bap. Feb. 23, 1834;
sponsors, Martin, Margaret Vallet.
Peter Napoleon Prudhomme, b. Sep. 21, 1929; parent, Susan Prudhomme; bap. Feb. 23, 1834;
sponsors, Francis Trimley, Mary Vallet Trimley
Francis Sassonessassinary, b. March 10, 1829; parents, Francis Sassonessassinary, Kakane; bap. Feb. 23, 1834;
sponsors, John Francis Trimbley, Eleanor Chalifoux Laliberte.
Benedict Chavamon Chouteau, B. Feb. 22, 1833; parents, Francis Chouteau, Teresa Menard; bap. Feb. 27, 1834;
sponsors, B. Roux, Elizabeth Roy.
Eleanor Lessert, b. B. Feb. 3, 1834; parents, Clement Lessert, Julia Roy; bap. March 15, 1834;
sponsors, Cyprian Chouteau, Theresa Chouteau Menard.

RECORD OF THE DEATHS IN THE CHURCH OF THE HOLY CROSS INDEPENDENCE, MISSOURI
Francis Hauqnsy, died July 9, 1850. Age 35 years.
Francis Jacob Kelly, died July 22, 1850. Age, 2 years. Son of William Kelly and Theresa Aud.
Thomas Moran, died May 27, 1851. Age, 5 months. Son of Martin Moran.

FIRST LUTHERAN CHURCH KANSAS CITY, MISSOURI (Contributed by Rev. A. W. Lindquist, Pastor; Copied by Miss Ethel M. Merwin; Organized January, 1870, by Dr. A. W. Dahlsten).
Hannson, Jons, b. Oct. 20, 1843, in Blentorps. Came to America in 1870 from Blentorps, Malmo [Sweden].
Johnson, John Henry, b. dec. 14, 1841, in Enontekis. Came to Kansas City from Linsberg, Kansas, in 1875.
Johnson, Karin Lind, wife of John Henry Johnson, b. May 18, 1848, in Nordsjon. Came to Kansas City from Linsberg, Kansas, in 1875.
Johnson, William Oscar, son of John Henry and Karin Johnson, b. Nov. 6, 1873, in Kansas City.
Ekelund, Carl Johan, b. Oct. 14, 1853, in Skara Parish. Came to America in 1875 from Skara, Jonkoping [Sweden].

Figure 7-19. *Vital Historical Records of Jackson County, Missouri 1826–1876,* sometimes indicates where immigrants were born in their native countries (pages 90–91, 116, 183).

From The Pennsylvania Genealogical Magazine and the Pennsylvania Magazine of History and Biography (cited earlier), vol. 1, page 8: "Memoranda From The Diary of John Dyer of Plumstead, Bucks County, PA."

November the 16th 1763 Father's family moved to Maryland-
March 1st 1764 Butler's moved to Father's place-
9th Mary Shaw Departed this Life the ninth Day of June 1764 and was buryed the tenth in the afternoon-
23 in the afternoon Set Wm. Preston Departed this life-
7 this morning Isaac Fell hanged him Self in his own Barn-
14 about Six of the Clock this Evening Wm. Reders house was struck with Lightning and several people were very much hurt - Joseph Watson and Robert Kirkbridge being not able to move home.
17 Kirkbridge moved home - Watson being gone a Day or two-
19 Elizabeth Elicott Departed this Life About one of the Clock this morning of the smallpox
23 Arthur Allen Dyed of a Consump
6-18 Edward Good was married to Eleanor Harris at Joh Browns-
2 Wm John Grifeth from England was at Plumstead-
12-31 Frances Dawes married to Mary-

Court and Legal Records

Vital events—particularly marriage dates—can be found in a multitude of legal records. An example is *Georgia Marriages 1811 Through 1820 Prepared from Extant Legal Records, and Published Sources,* edited by Mary Bondurant Warren (Danielsville, Ga.: Heritage Papers, 1988).

Naturalizations

Abstracted originals of naturalization records (see chapter 14, "Immigration Sources") also provide vital record evidence. *Naturalization Records, Canadian Extracts,* compiled by Allen E. and Joyce S. Jewitt (Hamburg, N.Y.: A. E. Jewitt, Sr., n.d.) from Erie County Hall, Buffalo, N.Y., is an example. The only names extracted were of those who listed Canada as their place of birth or country of allegiance. An example from page 12 is below.

Beech, George
Canada, 704-Vol. 4-Pg.54, Supreme Court
5-4-1910
Born 4-30-1876
Arrived in U.S.-4-1-1903, Buffalo, N.Y.
Wife-Helen Mary Beech, Born-Canada
Children-Marjorie Beatrice Beech-Born-3-30-1905, Buffalo, N.Y.
Earl George Beech- " 11-1-1906, " "

All reside 594 Masten St., Bflo., N.Y.
Beitz, Wendel William
Canada (Gt. Britain), 7119-60-69, Supreme Court
4-2-1919
Born 3-17-1866
Arrived in U.S.-6-14-1911, Niag. Falls, N.Y.
Wife-Caroline, Born-Canada

Children-Roy H.	Born-1-16-1893, Canada	
Frederick	" 6-25-1894 "	
Stanley	" 3-6-1898 Bflo., N.Y.	
Amelia	" 3-23-1901 Canada	
Magdalena	" 3-25-1902 "	
Joseph	" 3-19-1903 "	
Evelyn	" 2-8-1905 "	
Margaret	" 3-20-1909 "	
Genevieve	" 12-17-1910 "	New York

Names Being Researched By Others

Many state organizations have taken on large vital record projects, such as *Oklahoma Genealogical Society Surname, Special Publication No. 1,* edited by Jo Ann Garrison (Oklahoma City: Projects Committee of the Oklahoma Genealogical Society, 1969). It began as Project No. 1 of the OGS Projects Committee on 25 April 1968. Some of the information contributed for this project by Oklahoma Genealogical Society members had been proved; some of it had not. Any inquiries concerning surnames were directed to the society members who contributed the data. The finding aid for this project is the *OGS Surname Index.* It was designed to include miscellaneous information and queries as well as the following facts (when the data was known): the surname and given name(s) of a person, dates of birth and death, the surname and given name(s) of the person's spouse, their marriage date, and the state or country of birth and burial.

This information was tabulated in separate columns *unless* the society member included information in addition to the specified items, such as the name of the town or the cemetery where a person was buried. In such cases, the information was not tabulated but reads continuously across the page, the major items of information being separated by semicolons. Headings of the *OGS Surname Index* columns appear on the first page only; surnames appear in uppercase letters throughout the work. An example from page 10 is below.

T- 5 BOWEN, Anna 1818-1903 SKINNER, William 1844 KY IA
T- 5 BOWEN, Anna need info about her parents
E-20 BOWEN, Nancy c1801 c1846 BLASSINGAME, Robert c1820 -
O-5 Bowen, Susan b c1848 in KY; d in Tulsa OK; m ______ FESSINGER
G-23 HELMS, Rev. Aaron Sylvester b 1816 NC?; d 1883 AL;

Military Records

Where there is military action, there are likely to be deaths. Family historians are often interested in those who died during particular wars, and there are many lists that provide this information. For the larger and more recent wars (the Civil War and the two world wars), these lists have not been consolidated into easy-to-use publications. Lists for some of the smaller, earlier wars, however, have been compiled—many by Clarence Stewart Peterson. It is difficult to identify every person who died in the early wars because records were kept sporadically. Indeed, as Peterson says, the number of dead in these wars is not generally agreed upon. In his introduction to *Known Military Dead During the War of 1812* (Baltimore: the author, 1955), Peterson states:

> Volume 5, *Dictionary of American History* states that United States deaths in the War of 1812 totaled 1877. This number is questionable. For instance, the Battle of Plattsburgh, unique because it was an engagement waged on land and sea, deserved to rank as one of the decisive battles of the world. Exactly what the losses of the land battle at Plattsburgh were is not known. Prevost's dead, wounded and deserted have been placed as low as 235 and as high as 2500, while Macomb's casualties have been estimated to be under 100. In the naval battle Macdonough reported 52 killed and 58 wounded. The British reported 57 killed and 72 wounded.
>
> 'At the time of the burning of Washington by the British on August 24, 1814, the historically valuable records were destroyed,' from Preface of *General Entry Book of American Prisoners of War at Quebec,* by Mrs. Henry James Carr.

Peterson identifies approximately 3,500 known dead based on a variety of sources which he cited in his bibliography. An example of some of his entries is shown in figure 7-20.

CONCLUSION

Records of vital events have occupied a central place in genealogical research, and there has been a great effort to publish such records, thereby making them much easier to access. Records of vital events come not just from government-sponsored sources but from a variety of other sources as well, including newspapers, Bible records, and cemetery inscriptions. The interest in vital events is so great that researchers have even compiled evidences of births, marriages, and deaths based on numerous other records.

Careful use of published vital records is necessary because virtually none of them provides complete coverage. Even recently published statewide sources are usually just collections of various records from several counties; they are seldom all-inclusive. Whenever finding a reference to a vital event in a published source, try to obtain a copy of the original document

Smith, William W.	Lieut.	Lt. Art.	Killed	11-11-13	
Snell, Theodore		R.I.	Died	3-16-15	Dartmoor Prison
Snead, Jacob	Private	1 Rfls.Va.Mil.	"	11-22-14	
Snediger, Moses	Private	U.S. Inf.	"	3-25-14	
Sneed, Zeakle	Private		"	2- 4-13	Quebec Prison
Snow, Mark	Seaman	Constitution	Killed	12-29-12	

Figure 7-20. Entries from Peterson's *Known Military Dead During the War of 1812,* page 62.

to check for transcription errors and overlooked information. When a person sought does not appear in published records, turn to the original records, because many published collections are incomplete, and many original records have not yet been published. The evaluation checklist in table 17-4 will serve as a reminder of the cautions to exercise as these useful records are searched.

NOTES

1. Clifford acknowledges the assistance of Gareth Mark, whose earlier draft provided some significant elements of this chapter.
2. Meyerink compiled this section on cemetery records with the assistance of Gareth Mark, Ted Naanes, and Karen Clifford.

REFERENCE LIST

Beaman, Alden G. 1977. *Vital Records of Rhode Island, New Series. Volume III: Washington County, Rhode Island Births and Marriages from Gravestone Inscriptions, 1688–1850: Comprising the Towns of North Kingstown, South Kingstown, Exeter, Westerly, Charlestown, Richmond, Hopkinton.* Princeton, Mass.: the compiler.

Bowman, Fred Q. 1985. *10,000 Vital Records of Western New York, 1809–1850.* Baltimore: Genealogical Publishing Co.

Hall, Arcelli Spencer. 1932. Spencer and Stedman Family Record Book. Manuscript copy in possession of Kory L. Meyerink.

Hoogs, Cynthia Tryon. 1985. *Cemetery Inscriptions Tyringham, Massachusetts.* Great Barrington, Mass.: the author.

Lucas, Silas E., and Ella L. Sheffield, eds. 1981. *35,000 Tennessee Marriage Records and Bonds, 1783–1870.* 3 vols. Easley, S.C.: Southern Historical Press.

Young, David C., and Elizabeth Keene Young. 1993. *Vital Records from Maine Newspapers 1785–1820.* 2 vols. Bowie, Md.: Heritage Books.

BIBLIOGRAPHY OF SELECTED PRINTED VITAL RECORD SOURCES

The following bibliographical section emphasizes major collections of printed vital records which encompass large areas. Thousands of published vital records are available for the towns, cities, and counties of the United States. Many can be found in one of the five editions of *Genealogical [and Local History] Books in Print* (see below under Nettie Schreiner-Yantis and Marian Hoffmann) or the other finding aids listed. In addition

Table 17-4. Evaluation Checklist

If	*Then*
The published source is an abstract . . .	Are all the essential facts included?
The published source is an extract . . .	Was the entire document extracted, or were only "relevant" portions of it extracted?
Random selections of the transcribed copy compared with original documents . . .	Are there errors and/or omissions in the copy? Are all names in the original are shown in the transcription, including residences, ages, places, parents, and witnesses within the text?
The published source's editor or compiler is new to you, what is his or her reputation?	Is the work the editor's first publication? If not, is the editor known for accurate work, or does he or she concede exactness to save time or space? Is the editor familiar with the names and places of the area, the paleography of the time period, and the general use of probate records?
The title appears to cover a large time period . . .	Is the compilation complete? Based on other publications or on experience, are there sufficient entries for the approximate population in the jurisdiction during the period covered?
The work was published before the advent of computers . . .	Is it completely indexed? (See the next item.)
The work contains an index . . .	Check a number of entries to determine if every name appears in the index. Check names contained in long lists to see if these names are indexed. If not, does the introduction, foreword, or preface specify those records or portions of the volume that are not listed in the index?
The area or time period under consideration is unfamiliar . . .	Consider the scholarship put into the work. Does it contain adequate explanation of terms, abbreviations used, citation of original sources, and location of original records?

to general and statewide sources, this work also lists sources cited in the text as examples of printed vital records.

General Indexes, Bibliographies, and Guides

Cemeteries of the U.S.: A Guide to Contact Information for U.S. Cemeteries and Their Records. Edited by Deborah M. Burek. Detroit: Gale Research, 1994.

Daughters of the American Revolution. *Library Catalog, Vol. 2, 3.* Washington, D.C.: National Society, Daughters of the American Revolution, 1986, 1992.

Directory of United States Cemeteries. San Jose, Calif.: Cemetery Research, 1974.

Filby, P. William. *American and British Genealogy and Heraldry: A Selected List of Books*. 3rd ed. Boston: New England Historic Genealogical Society, 1983. Supplement, 1987.

Hoffman, Marian. *Genealogical and Local History Books in Print.* 5th ed. Baltimore: Genealogical Publishing Co., 1996–97.

Jarboe, Betty M. *Obituaries: A Guide to Sources*. 2nd ed. Boston: G. K. Hall, 1989.

Kemp, Thomas J. *International Vital Records Handbook.* 3rd ed. Baltimore: Genealogical Publishing Co., 1994.

Kot, Elizabeth G., and James D. Kot. *United States Cemetery Address Book: 1994–95.* Vallejo, Calif.: Indices Publishing, 1994.

Kirkham, E. Kay. *An Index to Some of the Bibles and Family Records of the United States: 45,500 References as Taken from the Microfilm at the Genealogical Society of Utah.* Logan, Utah: Everton Publishers, 1984. Kirkham's indexes are compiled from records of the DAR.

_____. *An Index to Some of the Family Records of the Southern States: 35,000 Microfilm References from the NSDAR Files and Elsewhere.* Logan, Utah: Everton Publishers, 1979.

Index to United States Cemeteries. Compiled by the staff and volunteers of the U.S. Reference Unit. Salt Lake City: Family History Library, 1988.

McKay, Douglas B., and Kory L. Meyerink. *American Genealogical Gazetteer*. CD-ROM. Orem, Utah: Ancestry, 1996.

Meyerink, Kory. *Genealogical Publications: A List of 50,000 Sources from the Library of Congress*. CD-ROM. Salt Lake City: Ancestry, 1997.

Ontario Cemetery Finding Aid (*OCFA*). Orem, Utah: GenRef, 1996.

Periodical Source Index (*PERSI*). Fort Wayne, Ind.: Allen County Public Library Foundation, 1987–.

Peterson, Clarence S. *Known Military Dead During the War of 1812*. Baltimore: the author, 1955.

Schreiner-Yantis, Netti. *Genealogical and Local History Books in Print.* Springfield, Va.: Genealogical Books in Print, 1985–90. First through fourth editions.

Stemmons, John "D," and E. Diane Stemmons, comps. *The Cemetery Record Compendium: Comprising a Directory of Cemetery Records and Where They May Be Located.* Logan, Utah: Everton Publishers, 1978.

_____. *The Vital Record Compendium: Comprising a Directory of Vital Records and Where They May Be Located.* Logan, Utah: Everton Publishers, 1979.

_____. *Vital Records Locator*. Salt Lake City: Ancestry, 1997. An CD-ROM version of the two Stemmons volumes above.

United States—General

Bolton, Charles Knowles. *Marriage Notices, 1788–1794, for the Whole United States: Copied From the Massachusetts Centinel and The Columbian Centinel*. Baltimore: Genealogical Publishing Co., 1980.

Clemens, William M. *American Marriage Records Before 1699.* Pompton Lakes, N.J.: Bibliography Co., 1926. Contains records primarily from New England and the Atlantic states.

Dodd, Jordan R., ed. *[State] Marriages, Early to [year]* and *[state] Marriages [year] to [year]: A Research Tool.* Compiled by Liahona Research. Bountiful, Utah: Precision Indexing, 1990–94. A series of dozens of volumes covering most southern and midwestern states.

Hayward, Elizabeth. *American Vital Records from the Baptist Register: Volumes 1–10, 1824–1834.* Rochester, N.Y.: American Baptist Historical Society, 1956–62.

Lu, Helen M. *Revolutionary War Period: Bible, Family, and Marriage Records Gleaned From Pension Applications.* Vols. 11–17 compiled and issued by Chan Edmondson. 17 vols. Dallas, Tex.: the author, 1980–95. Extracts of selected records from revolutionary war pensions and bounty land warrant application files, 1800 to 1900, in microfilm publication M-805, Record Group 15, of the National Archives.

St-Pierre, Rosaire. *Mariages americains de personnes nees dans Bellechasse, 1845–1955.* Beaumont, Quebec: the author, 1983. Contains American marriages of persons born in the Quebecois county of Bellechasse. Information often includes parents and birthplaces. Most of the immigrants settled in New England and the Great Lakes region.

Watkins, Raymond W. *Cemetery Records Including Many Confederate Burial Records.* The author, 1978.

Atlantic States

Ackerman, Herbert S., and Arthur J. Goff. *New York and New Jersey Cemeteries.* Microfilm. Salt Lake City: Genealogical Society of Utah, 1948.

Stillwell, John E. *Historical and Genealogical Miscellany: Data Relating to the Settlement and Settlers of New York and New Jersey.* 5 vols. New York City: the author, 1903–32.

Turner, Joseph B. *Genealogical Collection: Of Miscellaneous Church, Cemetery, and Vital Records of Delaware, Maryland, and New Jersey.* Microfilm. Salt Lake City: Genealogical Society of Utah, 1948.

New England

Lindberg, Marcia Wiswall. *Genealogist's Handbook for New England Research.* 3rd ed. Boston: New England Historic Genealogical Society, 1993.

Torrey, Clarence A. *New England Marriages Prior to 1700.* Baltimore: Genealogical Publishing Co., 1985.

Southern States

Biggerstaff, Inez B. *Some Tombstone Inscriptions From Oklahoma, Arizona, Louisiana, Mississippi, and Texas.* The author, 1955.

Cheek, John Carl. *Selected Tombstone Inscriptions From Alabama, South Carolina, and Other States.* N.p., 1970.

Francis, Elizabeth Wheeler. *Lost Links: New Recordings of Old Data from Many States.* Baltimore: Genealogical Publishing Co., 1975.

Gray, Ralph D. *Gray's Cemetery Records.* Fort Worth, Tex.: American Reference Publishing, 1968. Cemetery records from Texas, Arkansas, Colorado, Oklahoma, and Missouri.

Holcomb, Brent H. *Marriage and Death Notices from the Southern Christian Advocate.* Easley, S.C.: Southern Historical Press, 1979. Two volumes cover the years 1837 to 1867. They concern mainly the states of South Carolina and Georgia.

Lauderdale County Library (Florence, Alabama). *Vertical Files, Cemetery Records.* Microfilm. 2 reels. Salt Lake City, Utah: Genealogical Society of Utah, 1978. The vertical files contain cemetery records—primarily from the states of Alabama and Tennessee.

Lester, Memory Aldridge. *Old Southern Bible Records.* Baltimore: Genealogical Publishing Co., 1974.

Mid-South Bible Records. 18 vols. Memphis, Tenn.: Daughters of the American Revolution, 1973.

Includes primarily nineteenth-century Bible records from Virginia, Tennessee, North Carolina, Mississippi, and other southern states.

Alabama

Alabama Cemetery Records. Typescript. Salt Lake City: Genealogical Society of Utah, 1942–45.

Alabama Genealogical Records. Alabama Genealogical Records Commission, DAR, 1964–65. Reprint. Microfilm. Salt Lake City: Genealogical Society of Utah, 1970.

Austin, Jeannette H. *Alabama Bible Records.* Riverdale, Ga.: the author, 1987.

Bible and Cemetery Records. Birmingham, Ala.: Birmingham Genealogical Society, 1963.

Cemetery Records of Alabama. 6 vols. LDS Church in Alabama, 1946–64.

England, Flora Dainwood. *Alabama Notes.* 4 vols. Baltimore: Genealogical Publishing Co., 1977. Contains vital records, deeds, wills, and cemetery records from various counties.

Foley, Helen S. *Marriage and Death Notices from Alabama Newspapers and Family Records, 1819–1890.* Easley, S.C.: Southern Historical Press, 1981. Primarily covers southern Alabama.

Gandrud, Pauline M., and Kathleen P. Jones. *Alabama Records.* Easley, S.C.: Southern Historical Press, 1981. This collection of 244 volumes of Alabama records is arranged by county; each volume is individually indexed. Selected abstracts include vital records, cemetery records, probate records, land records, censuses, military records, court records, and newspapers.

_____. *Marriage, Death, and Legal Notices From Early Alabama Newspapers, 1819–1893.* Easley, S.C.: Southern Historical Press, 1981.

Alaska

Alaska's Kenai Peninsula Death Records and Cemetery Inscriptions. Kenai, Alaska: Kenai Totem Tracers, 1983.

Cemetery Records of Alaska. Typescript. Salt Lake City: Genealogical Society of Utah, 1962. Cemetery records pertaining mainly to Anchorage, Fairbanks, and Fort Richards.

Cemetery Records, Anchorage, etc., Alaska. Typescript. Salt Lake City: Genealogical Society of Utah, 1963.

Cemetery records from Anchorage, Fort Richards, Nome, and Palmer are included in this selection.

Arizona

Arizona Cemetery Records. Salt Lake City: Genealogical Society of Utah, 1959.

Arizona Death Records: An Index Compiled From Mortuary, Cemetery, Church Records. Tucson: Arizona State Genealogical Society, n.d. Includes cemetery records from all fourteen counties of Arizona.

Arkansas

Cemetery Records of Arkansas. 11 vols. Typescript. Salt Lake City: Genealogical Society of Utah, 1957–66.

Index to Sources for Arkansas Cemetery Inscriptions. North Little Rock, Ark.: Daughters of the American Revolution, 1976.

Morgan, James Logan. *Marriages and Divorces of Arkansas.* Newport: Arkansas Records Association, 1973.

Threet, Joan Garey. *Little Rock Birth Records.* 2 vols. Alexander: Arkansas Family Research, 1991.

Watkins, Raymond W. *Confederate Burials in Arkansas Cemeteries.* Typescript. N.p., 1981.

California

Bruner, Helen Maria. *California's Old Burying Grounds: Prepared for the National Society of Colonial Dames Resident in the State of California.* Tucson, Ariz.: W. C. Cox Co., 1974.

California State Library (Sacramento). *List of Deaths Copied from Records in the California State Library.* Sacramento: California State Library, n.d.

Death records extracted from censuses, death and internment records, cemeteries, and other sources.

California State Register. *California Vital Records Indexes.* Microfiche. Sacramento, Calif.: Office of the State Registrar, 1983. The California vital records indexes include indexes to marriage records from 1960 through 1981 and death records from 1940 through 1983.

Cemetery Records of California. 11 vols. Typescript. Salt Lake City: Genealogical Society of Utah, 1954–63.

Crabtree, Kathryn Rae. "Cemeteries in California and Nevada: A Western Thanatopsis." Masters thesis, Sonoma State University, n.d.

Graves and Sites on the Oregon and California Trails : A Chapter in OCTA's Efforts to Preserve the Trails. [Independence, Mo.]: Oregon-California Trails Association, 1991.

Kot, Elizabeth Gorrell, and Shirley Pugh Thomson. *California Cemetery Inscription Sources: Print and Microform.* Vallejo, Calif. : Indices Publishing, 1994.

Parker, Jimmy B. *Vital Records (Births and Deaths) of Indians of Round Valley Agency California 1890–99, 1906–15, 1924.* Salt Lake City: Genealogical Society, 1972.

Pompey, Sherman L. *Genealogical Records of California.* Fresno, Calif.: the author, 1968.

_____. *A List of Mexican War Veterans Buried in California.* Fresno, Calif.: the author, 1968.

_____. *Some Early California Deaths, 1851–1905.* Fresno, Calif.: the author, 1968.

Colorado

Burdick, Liz, and Kay Merrill. *Colorado Collections.* Microfilm. Salt Lake City: Genealogical Society of Utah, 1983. Includes Bible records and other vital records from the Golden DAR Pioneer Museum.

Marriages of Arapahoe County, Colorado, 1859–1901: Including Territory That Became Adams, Denver, and Other Counties. Denver: Colorado Genealogical Society, 1986.

McQueary, Lela O. *Colorado Cemetery Inscriptions.* Englewood, Colo.: K. R. Merrill, 1987.

Merrill, Kay R. *Colorado Cemetery Directory.* Denver: Colorado Council of Genealogical Societies, 1985.

Pompey, Sherman L. *Confederate Soldiers Buried in Colorado.* Independence, Calif.: Historical and Genealogical Publishing Co., 1965. Each soldier is listed alphabetically under the state from which he served.

Connecticut

Bailey, Frederic. *Early Connecticut Marriages, as Found on Ancient Church Records Prior to 1800.* 1896–1906. Reprinted with integrated errata. 7 books in 1 vol. Baltimore: Genealogical Publishing Co., 1982.

Barbour, Lucius C. *Barbour Collection: Connecticut Vital Records Prior to 1850.* Microfilm. Salt Lake City: Genealogical Society of Utah, 1949.

The Barbour Collection includes many town vital records of Connecticut, including an alphabetical surname index. Included in the index are the place and date of event, related persons, and the specific source used.

Bible Records from Connecticut, Index Cards. Microfilm. Salt Lake City: Genealogical Society of Utah, 1949. Lists vital statistics and family relationships as found in family Bible records at the Connecticut State Library in Hartford.

Cemetery Inscriptions, Records of Veterans, and Other Miscellaneous Records from the Connecticut State Library. Microfilm. Salt Lake City: Genealogical Society of Utah, 1979.

Hale, Charles R. *Hale Collection.* Microfilm. Salt Lake City: Genealogical Society of Utah, 1949–50. The Hale Collection (360 reels) includes cemetery records and newspaper notices from Connecticut. Among the vital record items of importance are the index to death notices by newspaper, the surname index to marriage notices, the index to marriage notices by newspaper, and the newspapers with death and marriage notices.

Hearn, Daniel. *Connecticut Gravestones, Early to 1800.* Microfilm. Salt Lake City: Genealogical Society of Utah, 1989. Records are arranged by town, and within each town by cemetery. Cemeteries are individually indexed.

Prichard, Katherine A. *Ancient Burying Grounds of the Town of Waterbury, Connecticut.* Waterbury, Conn.: Mattatuck Historical Society, 1917.

White, Lorraine Cook, comp. *The Barbour Collection of Connecticut Town Vital Records.* 10 vols. through 1997. Baltimore: Genealogical Publishing Co., 1994–.

Delaware

Delaware, Bureau of Vital Statistics. *Index Cards to Delaware Marriages, Baptisms, Births, and Deaths, 1680–1913.* Microfilm. 18 reels. Salt Lake City: Genealogical Society of Utah, 1949. Marriages 1680 to 1850, baptisms 1759 to 1890, births 1759 to 1890, and deaths before 1888. These indexes should be used with the vital records of the Delaware Bureau of Vital Statistics.

District of Columbia (also see Maryland)

Register of Burials in District of Columbia Cemeteries, 1847–1938. Microfilm. Salt Lake City: Genealogical Society of Utah, 1971.

Sluby, Paul E. *Civil War Cemeteries of the District of Columbia Metropolitan Area.* Washington, D.C.: Columbian Harmony Society, 1982.

Florida

Cemetery Records of Florida and Georgia (Compiled by Members of the Florida Stake). Microfilm. 6 reels. Salt Lake City: Genealogical Society of Utah, 1960.

Hayes, E. H. *Cemetery Records of Florida.* 9 vols. Typescript. Salt Lake City: Genealogical Society of Utah, 1946.

Jacksonville Branch Genealogical Library (Florida). *Vital Records Card File for Northern Florida and Southern Georgia, 1895–1945.* Microfilm. Salt Lake City: Genealogical Society of Utah, 1977.

Veterans Graves Registration Project. *Register of Deceased Veterans, Florida.* Salt Lake City: Genealogical Society of Utah, 1953. This collection is arranged by cemetery; an index to names is included. Most counties participated in this project, which was coordinated by the Work Projects Administration.

Georgia

Austin, Jeannette H. *Georgia Bible Records.* Baltimore: Genealogical Publishing Co., 1985.

Baker, Pearl R. *'Neath Georgia Sod: Cemetery Inscriptions. . . .* Albany: Georgia Pioneers Publications, 1970.

Brooke, Ted O. *Georgia Cemetery Directory and Bibliography of Georgia Cemetery Reference Sources.* Marietta, Ga.: the author, 1985.

Cemetery Records of Georgia. 16 vols. Typescript. Salt Lake City: Genealogical Society of Utah, 1946–52.

Dorsey, James E. *Georgia Genealogy and Local History: A Bibliography.* Spartanburg, S.C.: Reprint Company, 1983.

Georgia Society of the Colonial Dames of America. *Some Early Epitaphs in Georgia*. Foreword and sketches by Mrs. Peter W. Meldrim. Durham, N.C. : Sceman Printery, 1924.

Ingmire, Frances T. *Colonial Georgia Marriage Records from 1760–1810*. St. Louis: the author, 1895.

Lane, Mrs. Julian C., comp. *Marriage Records of Effingham County, Georgia, 1780–1875*. Statesboro, Ga.: the compiler, 1940.

Maddox, Joseph T. *Early Georgia Marriages*. Irwinton, Ga.: the author, 1980.

_____. *Early Georgia Marriage Round-up*. Irwinton, Ga.: the author, 1975.

_____. *37,000 Early Georgia Marriages*. Irwinton, Ga.: the author, 1976.

_____, and Mary Carter. *40,000 Early Georgia Marriages*. Irwinton, Ga.: the authors, 1977. These four volumes of early Georgia marriage records are arranged by county. Each volume includes the marriage records of different localities.

Warren, Mary B. *Marriages and Deaths 1763–1820 Abstracted from Extant Georgia Newspapers*. 2 vols. Danielsville, Ga.: Heritage Papers, 1968.

_____, ed. *Georgia Marriages 1811 Through 1820 Prepared from Extant Legal Records, and Published Sources*. Abstracted by Frances H. Beckermeyer, Susan Jenkins, Jack M. Jones, Robert S. Lowery, Amy W. Sanders and Mary B. Warren. Danielsville, Ga.: Heritage Papers, 1988.

Hawaii

Hawaii Cemetery Records. 2 vols. Typescript. Salt Lake City: Mrs. Jessie H. Lindsey and the Genealogical Society of Utah, 1942–54.

Index to Archives of Hawaii Collection of Marriage Records, 1826–1910. Honolulu, Hawaii: Bishop Museum, n.d.

Index to Births, Marriages, and Deaths in Hawaii Newspapers Prior to 1950. Microfilm. 6 reels. Salt Lake City: Genealogical Society of Utah, 1977.

Zabriskie, George Olin. *Tombstone Inscriptions from the Royal Mausoleum*. The author, 1969.

Idaho

Cemetery Records of Idaho. 12 vols. Typescript. Salt Lake City: Genealogical Society of Utah, 1952–68.

Illinois

Cemetery Records of Illinois. 13 vols. Typescript. Salt Lake City: Genealogical Society of Utah, 1960–66.

Illinois Veterans Commission (Springfield, Illinois). *Soldier's Burial Places in the State of Illinois for Wars, 1774–1898*. Microfilm. 31 reels. Springfield: Illinois Veterans Commission, 1975.

Records of soldiers are divided into soldiers whose military service is documented, soldiers whose military service is unknown, and soldiers who died in peacetime.

McLean County [Illinois] *Birth Records*. Vol. 3, 1883–85. Normal, Ill.: Bloomington-Normal Genealogical Society, 1982.

Sanders, Walter. *Marriages from Illinois Counties*. 6 vols. Litchfield, Ill.: the author, 1976.

Sweger, Jayne Kennedy. *Marriages in Whiteside Co., Illinois, 1856–1881*. Nowata, Okla., 1973.

Vital Records from Chicago Newspapers, Volume 1–7, 1833–1848. Chicago: Chicago Genealogical Society, Newspaper Research Committee, 1971.

Walker, Harriet J. *Soldiers of the American Revolution Buried in Illinois: From the Journal of the Illinois State Historical Society*. Baltimore: Genealogical Publishing Co., 1967.

Indiana

Cox, Carroll O. *Cemetery Records (Illinois and Indiana)*. Microfilm. Salt Lake City: Genealogical Society of Utah, 1983.

Indiana State Library, Genealogical Division. *Cemetery Locator File*. Indianapolis: Indiana State Library, n.d. The file includes the name of the township and county in which each cemetery is located.

Iowa

Burgess, JoAnn, and Rita Goranson. *Bible Records from Iowa Libraries and Museums*. 4 vols. N.p., 1977. The four volumes are separately indexed.

Fretwell, Sheila S. *Iowa Marriages Before Statehood, 1835–1846*. Waterloo, Iowa: the author, 1985.

Arranged alphabetically. Includes the names of the bride and groom, the marriage date, and the county from which the record was extracted.

Iowa Cemetery and Grave Records by the Grave Registration Project of the Works Progress Administration and the Daughters of the American Revolution. Microfilm. 21 reels. Salt Lake City: Genealogical Society of Utah, 1978. Arranged by county.

Kansas

Cemetery Records of Kansas (Compiled by Members of the Kansas Mission). 18 vols. Typescript. Salt Lake City: Genealogical Society of Utah, 1956–. Arranged by county. A separate index to the records was published by James D. Moore.

Cemetery Records in Southeastern Kansas and Southwestern Missouri. Microfilm. Salt Lake City: Genealogical Society of Utah, 1984.

Ford, Don L. *Abandoned and Semi-Active Cemeteries of Kansas*. 3 vols. Decorah, Iowa: Anundsen Publishing, 1983–85.

Kentucky

Ardery, Julia H. *Kentucky Records: Early Wills and Marriages Copied from Court House Records by Regents, Historians and the State Historian, Old Bible Records and Tombstone Inscriptions, Records from Barren, Bath, Bourbon, Clark, Daviess, Fayette, Harrison, Jessamine, Lincoln, Madison, Mason, Montgomery, Nelson, Nicholas, Ohio, Scott, and Shelby Counties*. 2 vols. Baltimore: Southern Book Co., 1958. Includes "early wills and marriages copied from court house records . . . old Bible records and tombstone inscriptions" from various counties of Kentucky.

Clift, Garrett Glenn. *Kentucky Marriages, 1797–1865.* Baltimore: Genealogical Publishing Co., 1966. Primarily extracts from Lexington, Kentucky, newspapers.

Daughters of the American Revolution and Captain John Waller Chapter (Lexington, Kentucky). *Kentucky Inscriptions, Bible and Family Records.* Microfilm. Salt Lake City: Genealogical Society of Utah, 1971.

Daughters of the American Revolution. Fincastle Chapter (Louisville, Kentucky). *Kentucky Wills, Inscriptions, Marriages, and Miscellaneous Records.* Microfilm. Salt Lake City: Genealogical Society of Utah, 1971. Microreproduction of an original typescript (ninety-two pages) written in 1949.

Johnson, Robert Foster. *Wilderness Road Cemeteries in Kentucky, Tennessee and Virginia.* Owensboro, Ky.: McDowell Publications, 1981.

Kentucky Office of Vital Statistics. *Births and Deaths Index, 1911–1954.* Microfilm. Salt Lake City: Genealogical Society of Utah, 1960.

_____. *Kentucky Death Index, 1911–1986.* 183 microfiche. Frankfurt: Kentucky Office of Vital Statistics, 1988.

Kentucky Marriage Records from the Register of the Kentucky Historical Society. Baltimore: Genealogical Publishing Co., 1983.

McAdams, Ednah W. *Kentucky Pioneer and Court Records.* Baltimore: Genealogical Publishing Co., 1975.

McAdams's collection of early Kentucky records includes miscellaneous wills, marriage records, Bible records, cemetery records, and genealogies.

Walker, Emma Jane, et al. *Kentucky Bible Records.* 6 vols. Lexington: Kentucky Society, Daughters of the American Revolution, 1962–81.

Louisiana

Be It Known and Remembered: Bible Records. 4 vols. Baton Rouge: Louisiana Genealogical and Historical Society, 1960.

Bourguard, Shirley Chaisson. *Marriage Dispensations in the Diocese of Louisiana and the Floridas: 1786–1803.* New Orleans: Polyanthos, 1980.

Daughters of the American Revolution. Louisiana (New Orleans). *Louisiana Tombstone Inscriptions.* 22 vols. Microfilm. Salt Lake City: Genealogical Society of Utah, 1970.

DeVille, Winston. *The New Orleans French, 1720–1733.* Baltimore: Genealogical Publishing Co., 1973. Marriage records of early New Orleans French settlers.

Frazier, John Purnell. *Tombstone Inscriptions of Northwest Louisiana Cemeteries.* Pittsburg, Tex.: the author, 1986.

Hebert, Donald J. *South Louisiana Records.* 12 vols. Cecilia, La.: the author, 1978. This set includes civil and church records and is arranged alphabetically within each volume. Each volume pertains to a specific territory.

_____. *Southwest Louisiana Records: Church and Civil Records.* 33 vols. Eunice, La.: the author, 1974–85.

Louisiana Tombstone Inscriptions. 11 vols. Louisiana Society, Daughters of the American Revolution, 1957. Indexed.

Maine

Cemetery Inscriptions and Odd Information of Various Towns in the State of Maine: In the Counties of Lincoln, Oxford, Penobscot, Somerset, Waldo. Compiled by unknown individuals for various years. Edited by Charles D. Townsend. Sarasota, Fla.: Aceto Bookmen, 1995.

Daughters of the American Revolution. Frances Scott Chapter (District of Columbia). *Maine Records.* Microfilm. Salt Lake City: Genealogical Society of Utah, 1958.

Daughters of the American Revolution (Maine). *Genealogical and Miscellaneous Records Collected 1925–1972.* Microfilm. Salt Lake City: Genealogical Society of Utah, 1971–72.

Frost, John. *Guide to Maine Vital Records in Transcript.* N.p., 1963.

Maine Old Cemetery Association Cemetery Inscription Project: Series One, Two and Three. Edited by Katherine W. Trickey. Bangor, Maine: Northeast Reprographics, 198(?), 1982, 1987(?).

Maine Division of Vital Statistics. *Index to Vital Records, 1892–1907.* Microfilm. 184 reels. Salt Lake City: Genealogical Society of Utah, 1954.

_____. *Index to Vital Records, 1908–1922.* Microfilm. 148 reels. Salt Lake City: Genealogical Society of Utah, 1954.

_____. *Index to Vital Records: Bride Index to Marriages, 1895–1953.* Microfilm. 111 reels. Salt Lake City: Genealogical Society of Utah, 1954.

_____. *Index to Vital Records Prior to 1892 of . . . Eighty Towns.* Microfilm. 141 reels. Salt Lake City: Genealogical Society of Utah, 1953. An index of birth and delayed birth registrations.

_____. *Delayed Return for Births, Deaths, and Marriages, ca. 1670–1891.* Microfilm. 109 reels. Salt Lake City: Genealogical Society of Utah, 1954.

The Maine Historical and Genealogical Recorder. 9 vols. Portland, Oreg.: S. M. Watson, 1884–98.

Maine Marriages 1892–1966: A Complete List. Edited by Lewis Bunker Rohrbach. CD-ROM. Rockport, Maine: Picton Press, 1996.

Maine State Archives. *Cemetery Index of Veterans.* Microfilm. 11 reels. Photographic Science Corporation, 1975. Arranged by county, town, and cemetery. There is also an "out-of-state" arrangement.

_____. *Veterans Cemetery Records.* Microfilm. 15 reels. Photographic Science Corporation, 1975. Arranged by war from King Philip's War through World War I (not including the Civil War).

Noyes, Benjamin L. *Vital Records Copied from Town, Church, and Cemetery Records in Various Towns and Counties of Maine Along the Atlantic Coast.* Microfilm. 2 reels. Salt Lake City: Genealogical Society of Utah, 1971.

Young, David C., and Elizabeth Keene Young. *Vital Records from Maine Newspapers 1785–1820.* 2 vols. Bowie, Md.: Heritage Books, 1993.

Maryland

Barnes, Robert. *Marriages and Deaths from the Maryland Gazette, 1727–1839.* Baltimore: Genealogical Publishing Co., 1973.

_____. *Maryland Marriages, 1634–1777.* Baltimore: Genealogical Publishing Co., 1975.

_____. *Maryland Marriages, 1778–1800.* Baltimore: Genealogical Publishing Co., 1978.

Bell, Annie W. B. *Maryland Marriage Records.* 23 vols. Annapolis, Md.: the author, 1938–39. Arranged alphabetically. Includes "proofs of marriages taken from court records such as wills, deeds, etc." The date given is that of the court record.

_____. *Maryland Records of Deaths, 1718–1777.* Annapolis, Md.: the author, 1936. Indexed.

Brumbaugh, Gaius Marcus. *Maryland Records: Colonial, Revolutionary, County and Church from Original Sources.* 2 vols. Baltimore: Genealogical Publishing Co., 1967.

Illustrated; includes marriage, birth, cemetery, census, and naturalization records.

Chance, Hilda. *Western Maryland Pioneers: Alphabetical Lists of Marriages, Births, and Deaths of 8000 Early Settlers.* 2 vols. Microfilm. Salt Lake City: Genealogical Society of Utah, 1968.

Directory of Maryland Cemeteries. Baltimore: Genealogical Council of Maryland, irregular.

Ridgely, Helen West, ed. *Historic Graves of Maryland and the District of Columbia: With the Inscriptions Appearing on the Tombstones in Most of the Counties of the State and in Washington and Georgetown.* Edited under the auspices of the Maryland Society of the Colonial Dames of America. Baltimore: Genealogical Pub., 1967.

Wright, F. Edward. *Maryland Eastern Shore Vital Records: 1648–1825.* 5 vols. Silver Spring, Md.: Family Line Publications, 1986.

Massachusetts

Bailey, Frederick W. *Early Massachusetts Marriages Prior to 1800: With the Addition of Plymouth Colony Marriages, 1692–1746.* 3 vols. in 1. Baltimore: Genealogical Publishing Co., 1968.

Massachusetts, Secretary of the Commonwealth. *Indexes to Births, Marriages, and Deaths, 1841–1971.* Microfilm. Salt Lake City: Genealogical Society of Utah, 1974–85.

Divided into periods of five to ten years and arranged alphabetically within each period.

_____. *Index to Delayed and Corrected Births, Recorded 1893–1970.* Microfilm. Salt Lake City: Genealogical Society of Utah, 1974–85.

Mayflower Source Records: Primary Data Concerning Southeastern Massachusetts, Cape Cod, and the Islands of Nantucket and Martha's Vineyard. Selected and introduced by Gary Boyd Roberts. Baltimore: Genealogical Publishing Co., 1986.

Vital Records of [town], *Massachusetts, to the Year 1850.* Boston: New England Historic Genealogical Society, 1902–ca. 1920. The Official Series of published vital records, for approximately two hundred towns, was published by this and some other societies with a subsidy from the state.

Michigan

Grand Army of the Republic (Michigan). Microfilm. 3 reels. *Cemetery Index, 1800s–1900s.* Microfilm. Salt Lake City: Genealogical Society of Utah, 1976.

Mohnecke, Edward H. *Cemetery Inscriptions, Michigan.* 3 vols. Grand Rapids, Mich.: the author, 1938–44.

State Library of Michigan. *Michigan Cemetery Source Book.* Lansing: State Library of Michigan, 1994.

Torrey, Harold. *Death Records of Tekonsha Township, Calhoun County, Michigan, 1897–1907.* Tekonsha, Mich.: the author, 1981.

Minnesota

Daughters of the American Revolution (Minnesota). *Genealogical Collection.* Microfilm. Salt Lake City: Genealogical Society of Utah, 1971.

Pope, Wiley R. *Minnesota Cemeteries in Print: A Bibliography of Minnesota Published Cemetery Inscriptions, and Burials, Etc.* 1st ed. St. Paul: Minnesota Family Trees, 1986.

Mississippi

Mississippi Cemetery and Bible Records. 3 vols. Jackson: Mississippi Genealogical Society, 1954.

Missouri

196 Cemeteries of Missouri. 3 vols. N.p., 1948–68.

Brooks, Linda B. *Missouri Marriages to 1850.* 3 vols. St. Louis: Distributed by Ingmire Publishing, 1983.

Campbell, Kathryn H. *Early Bible and Graveyard Records.* 2 vols. Dallas, Tex.: the author, 1972–74.

Contains primarily records of northeastern counties.

Carter, Mrs. J. R. *Early Missouri Marriages to 1840.* 3 vols. Sedalia, Mo.: the author, n.d.

Cemetery Records of Missouri. 15 vols. Microfilm. Salt Lake City: Genealogical Society of Utah, 1973.

East Central Missouri Cemetery and Bible Records. 3 vols. Afton, Mo.: John Sappington Chapter, Daughters of the American Revolution, 1974.

Ellsberry, Elizabeth P. *Bible Records of Missouri.* 8 vols. in 3. Chillicothe, Mo.: the author, 1963.

_____. *Cemetery Records of Missouri.* 3 vols. Chillicothe, Mo.: the author, 1965.

_____. *Early Marriage Records of Randolph County, Missouri, 1829–1859.* N.p., n.d.

Hodges, Nadine, Mrs. John Vineyard, and Mrs. Howard W. Woodruff. *Missouri Pioneers, County and Genealogical Records.* 30 vols. Independence, Mo.: the authors, 1967–. Various records from many counties.

Kot, Elizabeth Gorrell, and Shirley Pugh Thomson. *California Cemetery Inscription Sources: Print and Microform.* Vallejo, Calif.: Indices Publishing, 1995.

Langley, Elizabeth B. *Bible Records of Missouri.* 3 vols. Billings, Mo.: the author, 1968.

Ormesher, Susan. *Missouri Marriages Before 1840.* Indexed by Robert Barnes and Catherine Barnes. Baltimore: Genealogical Publishing Co., 1982.

Pompey, Sherman L. *Master List of Missouri Civil War Veteran Burials.* Microfilm. Salt Lake City: Genealogical Society of Utah, 1967.

Vital Historical Records of Jackson County, Missouri 1826–1876. Kansas City, Mo.: Kansas City Chapter, Daughters of the American Revolution, 1933–34.

Montana

Cemetery Records of Montana. 3 vols. Typescript. Salt Lake City: Genealogical Society of Utah, 1947–61. Cemetery records from selected counties in Montana.

Moog, Una. *Cemetery Inscriptions and Church Records from Hingham, Rudyard, Inverness, Whitlash, Lothair, Joplin and Chester, Montana*. Chester, Mont.: Broken Mountains Genealogical Society, 1986.

Richards, Dennis L. *Montana's Genealogical and Local History Records: A Selected List of Books, Manuscripts, and Periodicals*. Detroit: Gale Research Co., 1981.

Nebraska

Nebraska Cemeteries and Burial Sites. 2 parts. Lincoln: Nebraska Genealogical Society, 1996.

Nevada

Ostrander, Edna E. *Index to Marriage Licenses and Marriage Notices in Miscellaneous Nevada Newspapers, 1906–1968.* A project of the Las Vegas Branch Genealogical Library. Microfilm. Salt Lake City: Genealogical Society of Utah, 1968.

Paterson, Verna S. *Nevada Cemeteries: Tombstone Inscriptions of Nevada Cemeteries Collected by Local DAR Chapters Throughout Nevada*. Salt Lake City: Genealogical Society of Utah, 1995.

Taylor, Richard B. *The Nevada Tombstone Record Book*. Las Vegas: Nevada Families Project, 1986.

New Hampshire

Daughters of the American Revolution (New Hampshire). *Genealogical Collection.* Microfilm. Salt Lake City: Genealogical Society of Utah, 1971.

Driscoll, Marion Lang. *Marriage Records from Early New Hampshire Newspapers, 1801–1840.* Microfilm. Salt Lake City: Genealogical Society of Utah, 1951.

Folsom, Mrs. Wendell B. (Wendell Burt). *New Hampshire Gravestone Inscriptions of Early Date*. New Hampshire Chapter, Daughters of the Founders and Patriots of America, 1938.

Goss, Winifred L. *Colonial Gravestone Inscriptions in the State of New Hampshire.* Dover, N.H.: National Society of the Colonial Dames of America, 1942.

Hammond, Priscilla. *Vital Records from the Parish Register of Queen's Chapel Portsmouth, New Hampshire.* Concord, N.H., 1939.

New Hampshire Historical Society. *Card Index to Bible Records.* Microfilm. 1 reel. Salt Lake City: Genealogical Society of Utah, 1975.

New Hampshire Registrar of Vital Statistics. *Index of Marriages, Early to 1900.* Microfilm. 102 reels. Salt Lake City: Genealogical Society of Utah, 1975–76. Arranged alphabetically according to the first and third letters of the groom's surname. The bride's index (below) refers to this source.

_____. *Brides's Index, 1640–1900.* Microfilm. 17 reels. Salt Lake City: Genealogical Society of Utah, 1975–76.

_____. *Index of Births, Early to 1900.* Microfilm. 60 reels. Salt Lake City: Genealogical Society of Utah, 1974.

_____. *Index to Deaths, Early to 1900.* Microfilm. 60 reels. Salt Lake City: Genealogical Society of Utah, 1974.

_____. *Index to Divorces and Annulments Prior to 1938.* Microfilm. 8 reels. Salt Lake City: Genealogical Society of Utah, 1975.

_____. *Index to Early Town Records of New Hampshire, 1639–1910.* Microfilm. 111 reels. Salt Lake City: Genealogical Society of Utah, 1950–54.

New Jersey

Nelson, William. *New Jersey Marriage Records, 1665–1800.* Baltimore: Genealogical Publishing Co., 1967.

New Jersey Cemetery Inscriptions. Salt Lake City: Genealogical Society of Utah, 1976.

New Jersey Tombstone Inscriptions. Microfilm. 7 reels. Salt Lake City: Genealogical Society of Utah, 1969.

New Mexico

Myers, Lee. *Cemetery Records from Southern New Mexico*. The author, 1982.

Some Marriages of the State of New Mexico, ca. 1880–1920. 2 vols. New Mexico Chapter, Daughters of the American Revolution, 1971–73.

New York

Bowman, Fred Q. *10,000 Vital Records of Central New York, 1813–1850.* Baltimore: Genealogical Publishing Co., 1986.

_____. *10,000 Vital Records of Eastern New York, 1777–1834.* Baltimore: Genealogical Publishing Co., 1987.

_____. *10,000 Vital Records of Western New York, 1809–1850.* Baltimore: Genealogical Publishing Co., 1985.

_____. *8,000 More Vital Records of Eastern New York State, 1804–1850.* Rhinebeck, N.Y.: Kinship, 1991.

Cormack, Marie Noll. *New York State Cemetery Inscriptions: Albany County, Herkimer County, Montgomery County, Saratoga County, Schenectady County.* Federal Writers Project of Works Progress Administration of State of New York. Microfilm. Salt Lake City: Genealogical Society of Utah, 1967.

Jewitt, Allen E., and Joyce S. Jewitt. *Naturalization Records, Canadian Extracts.* Hamburg, N.Y.: A. E. Jewitt, Sr., n.d.

New York, Secretary of State. *Names of Persons for Whom Marriage Licenses Were Issued by the Secretary of the Province of New York, Prior to 1784.* Albany, N.Y.: Weed, Parsons, and Co., 1860.

New York State Library. *Vital Records Card File.* Microfiche. Albany, N.Y.: New York State Library, Photoduplication Department, 1979.

New York State Cemeteries (copied by missionaries and members of the East State Mission). 23 vols. Typescript. Salt Lake City: Genealogical Society of Utah, 1940–69. Arranged by cemetery. An index to cemeteries, but not to names, is included.

The New York Times Obituaries Index. 2 vols. New York: the Times, 1970.

Robison, Jeannie F. J., and Henrietta C. Bartlett, eds. *The Colonial Dames of the State of New York—Genealogical Records—Manuscript Entries of Births, Deaths and Marriages, Taken From Family Bibles 1581–1917.* New York, 1917. Reprint. Baltimore: Genealogical Publishing Co., 1972.

Scott, Kenneth. *Joseph Gavit's American Deaths and Marriages, 1784–1829: Index to Non-Principals.* New Orleans: Polyanthos, 1976.

Scott, Kenneth. *New York Marriage Bonds, 1753–1783.* New York: St. Nicholas Society of the City of New York, 1972.

Welch, Richard F. *Memento Mori: The Gravestones of Early Long Island, 1680–1810.* Syosset, N.Y.: Friends for Long Island's Heritage, ca. 1983.

North Carolina

Cemetery Records of North Carolina. 8 vols. Typescript. Salt Lake City: Genealogical Society of Utah, 1947–61.

Clemens, William M. *North and South Carolina Marriage Records: From the Earliest Colonial Days to the Civil War.* New York: E. P. Dutton and Co., 1927.

Holcomb, Brent H. *Wake County, North Carolina Marriage Records, 1781–1867.* Baltimore: Genealogical Publishing Co., 1983.

Ingmire, Frances T. *Marriages of Wake County, North Carolina, 1770–1868.* St. Louis, Mo.: Ingmire Publications, 1985.

_____. *Rowan County, North Carolina Marriage Records, 1754–1866.* St. Louis, Mo.: Ingmire Publications, 1984.

King, Henry. *Tar Heel Tombstones and the Tales They Tell.* Asheboro, N.C.: Down Home Press, 1990.

McEachern, Leora H. *North Carolina Gravestone Records.* 10 vols. Wilmington, N.C.: the author, 1971–81.

North Carolina Division of Archives and History. *An Index to Marriage Bonds Filed in the North Carolina State Archives.* 88 microfiche. Raleigh, N.C.: North Carolina Department of Cultural Resources, 1977.

Spence, Wilma C. *North Carolina Bible Records. . . .* Logan, Utah: Unique Printing Service, 1973.

Wellborn, Mrs. John Scott. *North Carolina Tombstone Records.* Microfilm. 3 vols. in 2 reels. Salt Lake City: Genealogical Society of Utah, 1941. Indexed.

Works Progress Administration, Historical Records Survey Services Division. *Pre-1914 Cemetery Inscription Card Index.* 26 vols. Raleigh: North Carolina Department of Archives and History, 1972. A post-1914 index exists as well.

North Dakota

Fargo Genealogical Society. *North Dakota Cemeteries.* 16 vols. Fargo, N.D.: Fargo Genealogical Society, 1972–77.

Ohio

Baldwin, Henry R. *The Henry R. Baldwin Genealogy Records.* 67 vols. Fort Wayne, Ind.: Allen County Public Library, 1983. Includes vital, court, church, cemetery, and other genealogical records in eastern Ohio and western Pennsylvania for the period 1867 to 1913. A complete index is included.

Daughters of the American Revolution (Ohio). *Early Vital Records of Ohio, 1750–1970.* Microfilm. Salt Lake City: Genealogical Society of Utah, 1972.

Index to Grave Records of Servicemen in the War of 1812, State of Ohio. Lancaster, Ohio: Society of the United States Daughters of 1812, 1969.

Middle Western Section Records. Colonial and Genealogical Records Committee, Daughters of the American Revolution, Ohio. Fort Wayne, Ind.: Allen County Public Library, 1983.

Ohio Cemetery Records: Extracted from the "Old Northwest Genealogical Quarterly." Baltimore: Genealogical Publishing Co., 1984.

Smith, Marjorie, ed. *Ohio Marriages: Extracted from the Old Northwest Genealogical Quarterly.* Baltimore: Genealogical Publishing Co., 1980.

Smith, Maxine Hartmann, ed. *Ohio Cemeteries.* Mansfield: Ohio Genealogical Society, 1978. *Addendum.* 1990.

Short, Mrs. Don R., and Mrs. Denver Eller. *Ohio Bible Records.* 2 vols. N.p., 1971.

Oklahoma

Bode, Frances M. *Oklahoma Territory Weddings.* Geary, Okla.: Pioneer Book Committee, 1983.

Bogle, Dixie. *Cherokee Nation Births and Deaths, 1884–1901.* Utica, Ky.: Cook and McDowell Publishers, 1980.

A compilation of birth and marriage records from the Cherokee Nation. Contains interesting historical genealogical information, as well as dates of birth and death; the sources, however, are not always clear.

_____. *Cherokee Nation Marriages, 1884–1901.* Utica, Ky.: Cook and McDowell Publishers, 1980.

Carselowey, James Manford. *Cherokee Notes.* Tulsa: Oklahoma Yesterdays Publications, [1980].

Cemetery Records of Oklahoma. 9 vols. Typescript. Salt Lake City: Genealogical Society of Utah, 1959–62.

Cook, Mrs. John P. *Collection of Oklahoma Bible and Family Records.* N.p., 1954.

Oklahoma Genealogical Society Surname, Special Publication No. 1. Edited by Jo Ann Garrison. Oklahoma City: Projects Committee of the Oklahoma Genealogical Society, 1969.

Tiffee, Ellen, and Gloryann Hankins Young. *Oklahoma Marriage Records, Choctaw Nation, Indian Territory.* 10 vols. Howe, Okla.: the author, n.d.

Tyner, James W. *Our People and Where They Rest.* 10 vols. Norman: University of Oklahoma, 1969–78.

Union List of Oklahoma Cemeteries. Oklahoma City: Oklahoma Geneal. Society, 1969.

Oregon

Lenzen, Connie. *Oregon Guide to Genealogical Sources.* Rev. ed. Portland: Genealogical Forum of Oregon, 1994.

Oregon Cemetery Directory. Salem: Oregon Heritage Council, 1976.

Oregon Cemetery Records. 2 vols. Typescript. Salt Lake City: Genealogical Society of Utah, 1956–61.

Oregon Death Records Index, 1903–1970. Microfilm. 12 reels. Salem: Oregon State Archives and Records Center, n.d. Arranged alphabetically within any given year.

Pennsylvania

Barba, Preston A. *Pennsylvania German Tombstones: A Study in Folk Art.* Pennsylvania German Folklore Society, 1954.

Cemetery Records of Pennsylvania. 9 vols. Typescript. Salt Lake City: Genealogical Society of Utah, 1946.

Fisher, Charles A. *Central Pennsylvania Marriages, 1700–1895.* Baltimore: Genealogical Publishing Co., 1974.

_____. *Early Pennsylvania Births, 1675–1875.* Baltimore: Genealogical Publishing Co., 1975.

Gearhart, Heber G. *Pennsylvania Gravestone Inscriptions Collection.* Microfilm. Salt Lake City: Genealogical Society of Utah, 1967.

Humphrey, John T. *Pennsylvania Births,* [name] *County,* [year]–[year]. Washington, D.C. : Humphrey Publications, 1992–. A series of vital records books consolidating various church and other records for a given county. As of 1997, the following counties and years had been published:

Bucks, 1682–1800

Chester, 1682–1800

Delaware, 1682–1800

Lancaster, 1723–77

Lancaster, 1778–1800

Lebanon, 1714–1800

Lehigh, 1734–1800

Montgomery, 1682–1800

Northampton, 1733–1800

Philadelphia, 1644–1765

Philadelphia, 1766–80

Names of Persons for Whom Marriage Licenses Were Issued in the Province of Pennsylvania Prior to 1790. Baltimore: Genealogical Publishing Co., 1963.

Pennsylvania Vital Records: From the Pennsylvania Genealogical Magazine and the Pennsylvania Magazine of History and Biography. 3 vols. Baltimore: Genealogical Publishing Co., 1983. The records include marriages between Americans and foreigners, with long lists of witnesses.

Record of Pennsylvania Marriages Prior to 1810. 2 vols. Baltimore: Genealogical Publishing Co, 1987.

Sundry Tombstone Inscriptions and Church Data. Microfilm. Salt Lake City: Genealogical Society of Utah, 1973.

Rhode Island

Arnold, James N. *Vital Records of Rhode Island, 1636–1850: A Family Register for the People.* 20 vols. Providence, R.I.: Narragansett Historical Publishing Co., 1891–1912. *Index to Arnold's Rhode Island Vital Records: Rhode Island Cemetery Records.* Microfilm. 11 reels. Salt Lake City: Genealogical Society of Utah, 1950.

Separated into counties by volume, and then alphabetically within each locality. The collection includes county, church, periodical, military, newspaper, and other records.

Beaman, Alden G. *Vital Records of Rhode Island, New Series.* 13 vols. Princeton, Mass.: the compiler, 1975–87. This series contains abstracts of probate, cemetery, marriage, death, and other records that give evidence of vital information for Kent, Newport, and Washington counties.

Benns, Charles P., and Martha A. Benns. *Rhode Island Cemetery Records, 1931–1941.* 6 vols. N.p., n.d. Microfilm. Salt Lake City: Genealogical Society of Utah, 1960.

Briggs, Anthony T. *Briggs Collection of Cemetery Records, Wills, Record Books of Genealogy and Scrapbooks of Vital Records and Historical Events.* Microfilm. Salt Lake City: Genealogical Society of Utah, 1950. Also includes a surname index.

Brown, Clarence I. *Rhode Island Cemetery and Genealogical Records.* Microfilm. 2 reels. Salt Lake City: Genealogical Society of Utah, 1950.

Snow, Edwin M., Charles V. Chapin, Dennett L. Richardson, and Michael J. Nestor. *Alphabetical Index of the Births, Marriages and Deaths Recorded in Providence.* 32 vols. Providence, R.I., 1879–[1946].

South Carolina (also see North Carolina)

Cemetery Records of Confederate Soldiers Buried in South Carolina. Typescript. Salt Lake City: Genealogical Society of Utah, 1947. Forty-six pages.

Holcomb, Brent H. *South Carolina Marriages: 1688–1799.* 3 vols. Baltimore: Genealogical Publishing Co., 1980–81, 1984. Primarily records of 1688 to 1820; indexed.

Huey, Olga Crosland. *South Carolina Cemetery Epitaphs.* Microfilm. Salt Lake City: Genealogical Society of Utah, 1974.

Works Progress Administration, South Carolina Historical Records Survey. *Index to Tombstone Inscriptions, 1930s.* Spartanburg, N.C.: Historical Records Survey, n.d. Each entry in this handwritten compilation includes name of the decedent, information on the tombstone, cemetery and county of burial, and printed source, if any, from which the information was extracted.

South Dakota

Some Black Hills Area Cemeteries, South Dakota. Rapid City, S.D.: Rapid City Society for Genealogical Research, 1973.

Krueger, Maurice, and Florence Krueger. *South Dakota Cemeteries, 1990.* Mina, S.D.: the authors, 1990.

Tennessee

Acklen, Jeannette T. *Tennessee Records: Bible Records and Marriage Bonds.* Baltimore: Genealogical Publishing Co., 1967.

_____. *Tennessee Records: Tombstone Inscriptions and Manuscripts, Historical and Biographical.* Nashville, Tenn.: Cullom and Ghertner, 1976.

Baker, Russell Pierce. *Obituaries and Marriage Notices From the Tennessee Baptist: 1844–1862.* Easley, S.C.: Southern Historical Press, 1979.

Bible Records of Families in East Tennessee and Their Connections in Other Areas. 3 vols. Genealogical Record Committee, Daughters of the American Revolution, 1959–60. Indexed.

Hays, Tony. *West Tennessee Death Records.* Kitchen Table Press, 1987.

Lucas, Silas E., and Ella L. Sheffield, eds. *35,000 Tennessee Marriage Records and Bonds, 1783–1870.* 3 vols. Easley, S.C.: Southern Historical Press, 1981. Indexed.

_____. *Marriages From Early Tennessee Newspapers, 1794–1851.* Easley, S.C.: Southern Historical Press, 1978.

Sistler, Byron, and Barbara Sistler. *Early East Tennessee Marriages.* 2 vols. Nashville, Tenn.: Byron Sistler and Associates, 1987.

_____. *Early Middle Tennessee Marriages.* 2 vols. Nashville, Tenn.: Byron Sistler and Associates, n.d.

_____. *Early West Tennessee Marriages.* 2 vols. Nashville, Tenn.: Byron Sistler and Associates, n.d. Each set includes separate volumes for brides and grooms.

Sneed, Adele Weiss. *Bible Records of Families of East Tennessee and Their Connections From Other Areas.* 3 vols. Knoxville Chapter of the Daughters of the American Colonists and James White Chapter of the Daughters of the American Revolution, 1959–60.

Tennessee State Board of Health. *Index to Births, Enumerator Record Series, 1908–1912.* Microfilm. Nashville, Tenn.: Tennessee State Library and Archives, 1980.

_____. *Index to Deaths, 1914–1925.* Nashville, Tenn.: Microfilm. Tennessee State Library and Archives, 1981.

_____. *Index to Deaths, Enumerator Series, 1908–1912.* Microfilm. Nashville, Tenn.: Tennessee State Library and Archives, 1980.

Tennessee State Library and Archives, Manuscript Section. *Bible Records Collection, ca. 1700–1970.* Microfilm. 5 reels. Nashville, Tenn.: State Library and Archives, 1974. Arranged alphabetically by surname.

Texas

Biggerstaff, Mrs. Malcolm B. *4000 Tombstone Inscriptions from Texas, 1745–1870: Along the Old San Antonio Road and the Trail of Austin's Colonists.* Oklahoma Historical Society, 1952.

Cemetery Records of Texas. 6 vols. Typescript. Salt Lake City: Genealogical Society of Utah, 1956–63.

Daughters of the American Revolution. Alamo Chapter (San Antonio, Texas). *Texas Cemetery Records, Miscellaneous Bible Records, 1782–1955.* San Antonio, Tex.: Microfilm Center, 1973.

Frazier, John P. *Northeast Texas Cemeteries.* Shreveport, Calif.: S. and W. Enterprises, 1984.

Gracy, Alice D., Emma G. S. Gentry, and Jane Sumner. *Early Texas Birth Records, 1838–1878.* 2 vols. Austin, Tex.: the authors, 1969, 1971. Arranged alphabetically by the name of the parents. The child's name, the county of birth, and the date of birth are included.

Grammer, Norma R. *Marriage Records of Early Texas, 1826–1846.* Fort Worth, Tex.: Fort Worth Genealogical Society, 1971.

Parsons, Kim. *A Reference to Texas Cemetery Records.* Humble, Tex.: the author, 1988.

Reynolds, Bess. *Records of Southern Families: From Bibles, Tombstones, Sketches, Newspapers, 1740–1957.* Microfilm. Dallas, Tex.: Microfilm Sales & Service, 1961.

Swenson, Helen S. *8,800 Texas Marriages, 1824–1850.* 2 vols. Round Rock, Tex.: the author, 1981. Indexed.

Utah

Cemetery Listing (Utah). Salt Lake City: Utah State Archives and Records Service, 1986.

Cemetery Records of Utah. 13 vols. Salt Lake City: Genealogical Society of Utah, 1953. Indexed. Includes transcripts of sextons' records.

McClay, Irvin C. *Cemeteries in Utah.* Salt Lake City: Utah State Archives and Records Service, 1980.

Miscellaneous Marriage Records Index: Compiled From Civil Records. Microfilm. 19 reels. Salt Lake City: Genealogical Society of Utah, 1972.

Utah Death Index: 1891–1905 (Excluding Salt Lake County). Edited by Judith W. Hansen. Monograph Series, no. 2. Salt Lake City: Professional Chapter, Utah Genealogical Association, 1995.

Vermont

Daughters of the American Revolution (Vermont). *Genealogical Collection.* Microfilm. Washington, D.C. : Reproduction Systems for the Genealogical Society of Utah, 1971.

Nichols, Joann H. *Index to Known Cemetery Listings in Vermont.* Brattleboro, Vt.: the author, 1976.

Vermont, Secretary of State. *General Index to Vital Records of Vermont, 1871–1908.* Microfilm. 120 reels. Salt Lake City: Genealogical Society of Utah, 1967.

_____. *General Index to Vital Records of Vermont, to 1870.* Microfilm. 287 reels. Salt Lake City: Genealogical Society of Utah, 1951.

Virginia

Bible Records From Virginia. Microfilm. 4 reels. Salt Lake City: Genealogical Society of Utah, 1947.

Borden, Duane L. *Tombstone Inscriptions (Virginia).* 9 vols. Ozark, Mo.: Yates Pub. Co., ca. 1981–ca. 1986.

Crozier, William A. *Early Virginia Marriages.* Baltimore: Genealogical Publishing Co., 1982.

Daughters of the American Revolution. Virginia. Genealogical Records Committee. *Miscellaneous Bible, Tombstone and Court Records Submitted by Various Virginia Chapters of the Daughters of the American Revolution.* Microfilm. Salt Lake City: Genealogical Society of Utah, 1970.

Hart, Lyndon H., 3rd. *Guide to Bible Records in the Archives Branch, Virginia State Library.* Richmond: Virginia State Library and Archives, 1985.

Hogg, Anne M., and Dennis A. Tosh. *Virginia Cemeteries: A Guide to Resources.* Charlottesville: University of Virginia, 1986.

McDonald, Cecil D. *Some Virginia Marriages, 1700–1799.* 25 vols. in 2. Seattle: the author, 1972.

_____. *Some Virginia Marriages, 1800–1825.* 12 vols. in 1. Seattle: the author, 1973.

_____. *Some Virginia Marriages, 1826–1850.* 2 vols. in 1. Seattle: Cecil D. McDonald, 1975.

Some Marriages in the Burned Record Counties of Virginia. Richmond: Virginia Genealogical Society, 1979.

Mihalyka, Jean M. *Marriages Northampton County, Virginia 1660–1854 Recorded in Bonds, Licenses, Minister Returns, and Other Sources*. Bowie, Md.: Heritage Books, 1991.

Prince Edward County, Virginia Marriage Bonds, 1754–1866. Typescript. Salt Lake City: Genealogical Society of Utah, 1936.

Virginia Marriage Records: From the Virginia Magazine of History and Biography, the William and Mary's College Quarterly, and the Tyler's Quarterly. Baltimore: Genealogical Publishing Co., 1982.

Virginia Vital Records: From the Virginia Magazine of History and Biography, the William and Mary's College Quarterly, and the Tyler's Quarterly. Baltimore: Genealogical Publishing Co., 1982.

Vogt, John, and T. William Kethley. *Marriage Records in the Virginia State Library: A Researcher's Guide*. Athens, Ga: Iberian Press, 1984.

Wulfeck, Dorothy F. *Marriages of Some Virginia Residents, 1607–1800.* 2 vols. Baltimore: Genealogical Publishing Co., 1986.

Washington

Carter, John D., ed. *Washington's First Marriages of the Thirty-Nine Counties.* Spokane: Eastern Washington Genealogical Society, 1986.

Cemetery Records of Washington. 6 vols. Salt Lake City: Genealogical Society of Utah, 1957–60.

Clubb, Mrs. Robert Earl. *Family Records of Washington Pioneers Prior to 1891*. Daughters of the American Revolution of the State of Washington. Microfilm. Salt Lake City: Genealogical Society of Utah, 1960.

A Directory of Cemeteries and Funeral Homes in Washington State. Washington Interment Association and the Washington State Funeral Directors Association. Orting, Wash.: Heritage Quest, 1990.

Washington Bureau of Vital Statistics. *Index to Birth Certificates, 1907–1959.* Olympia, Wash.: Bureau of Vital Statistics, 1960. Divided by sets of several years and subsequently in alphabetical order. The certificate numbers and place codes can be used to locate the original records.

_____. *Index to Death Certificates, 1907–1959, 1960–1979.* Olympia, Wash.: Bureau of Vital Statistics, 1954–60.

West Virginia

Daughters of the American Revolution (West Virginia). *Genealogical Collection.* Microfilm. Salt Lake City: Genealogical Society of Utah, 1970.

Watkins, Raymond W. *Confederate Burials in West Virginia Cemeteries.* Typescript. Salt Lake City: Genealogical Society of Utah, 1978.

Wisconsin

Daughters of the American Revolution. Wisconsin. Genealogical Records Committee. *Bible and Cemetery Inscriptions from Wisconsin.* Microfilm. Salt Lake City: Genealogical Society of Utah, 1970.

Daughters of the American Revolution. Wisconsin. Genealogical Records Committee. *Bible and Cemetery Records, 1700–1940.* Microfilm. Salt Lake City: Genealogical Society of Utah, 1970.

Daughters of the American Revolution. Wisconsin. Genealogical Records Committee. *Bible and Cemetery Records, 1800–1940.* Microfilm. Salt Lake City: Genealogical Society of Utah, 1970.

Inscriptions 1 (1) (March 1972). *Inscriptions* is published by the Wisconsin State Old Cemetery Society.

Wisconsin, Bureau of Health Statistics. *Index to Registration of Births, 1852–1907.* 41 microfiche. Madison: Wisconsin State Historical Society, 1979. Arranged in chronological order. See below for the alphabetical index to birth registration. Use with the original birth records of Wisconsin counties; the county and the volume are noted in the index.

_____. *Unedited Index to Registration of Births, 1852–1907.* 38 microfiche. Madison: Wisconsin State Historical Society, 1979.

_____. *Index to Registration of Marriages, 1852–1907.* 77 microfiche. Madison: Wisconsin State Historical Society, ca. 1980. Each marriage record is indexed alphabetically by the name of both bride and groom. The index gives the county and a marriage book page number.

_____. *Pre-1907 Death Index By Name.* 29 microfiche. Madison: Wisconsin State Historical Society, 1981.

Wyoming

Lovell, Evelyn, and Marlys Allbert Bias. *Davis Funeral Home records for 1918–1951, Riverton, Wyoming: Master Index.* Riverton, Wyo.: Fremont County Genealogical Society, 1987.

Martin, Phyllis J. *Uinta County, Wyoming Cemetery Records.* Evanston, Wyo. : the author, 1982.

Natrona County, Wyoming, Cemetery Records. 3 vols. Natrona County Genealogical Society. Casper, Wyo.: Natrona County Genealogical Society, 1986–90.

PUBLISHED CHURCH RECORDS OVERVIEW

Key Concepts in This Chapter

- Published parish registers, while popular, require caution when used.
- Many church records are published in genealogical periodicals.
- Church newspapers represent an excellent, untapped source.
- Denominational histories provide excellent background, as well as some biographical material.
- Congregational histories often identify every former or early member.
- Denominational encyclopedias provide detailed information, including information on church leaders.
- Denominational directories locate specific congregations.
- General religious reference sources provide brief, but helpful, overviews.

Key Sources in This Chapter

- *A Survey of American Church Records,* 4th ed.
- *Obituaries: A Guide to Sources,* 2nd ed.
- *Periodical Source Index* (*PERSI*)
- *Handbook of Denominations in the United States*
- *Encyclopedia of American Religions,* 4th ed.
- *Yearbook of American and Canadian Churches*
- *The Directory of Religious Organizations in the United States*, 3rd ed.
- *National Directory of Churches, Synagogues, and Other Houses of Worship*

8

PUBLISHED CHURCH RECORDS

Richard W. Dougherty

The records of local religious congregations rank among the best of all records in terms of genealogical value. And every year, more such records are made available in published form. Many congregations, in preparing histories commemorating major anniversaries of their churches, publish transcriptions of their baptismal, marriage, and burial records.

Most published church records are confined to what Roman Catholics call parish registers: baptismal, marriage, death, and sometimes confirmation and communicant records. But many American churches have not kept records of this sort. Some are opposed to infant baptism on principle and usually have not recorded the ages and parentages of people who were baptized. Some of those that do not regard marriage as a sacrament have not recorded marriages. However, even churches of this general persuasion (for example, the Baptists) usually keep lists of members. These, especially the admissions and dismissals of members, can be extremely useful to genealogists. (Unfortunately, few of these lists have been published.)

The social circumstances of frontier America led to the creation of a new type of church record: the denominational newspaper. These came to play a significant role in the life of the churches they served. As one church historian put it, "There has been a saying among Disciples of Christ [Christian Churches and Churches of Christ] that our brotherhood does not have bishops, but that it has editors" (Spencer 1962, introduction). For the genealogist these denominational periodicals can be valuable because they often printed obituaries and sometimes marriages. To be sure, some church newspapers featured obituaries chiefly of ministers, ministers' wives, and teachers. But certain newspapers of the smaller denominations contained obituaries of lay members who were not prominent in civic or denominational affairs.

Some of these denominational newspapers lie crumbling in church archives, having never been microfilmed. Others have been microfilmed but are not yet indexed. And many have been indexed for certain time periods but not for the complete life of the journal. Hence, the sum of the titles named in this chapter should be regarded as a preliminary survey. As genealogy groups show interest, more denominational newspapers will no doubt be rediscovered and indexed.

A chapter-length discussion of published church records cannot be exhaustive; space forbids listing every local church record that has been published in the United States over the past 150 years. Hence, this chapter specifically identifies only the published records that are of more than local interest, and it provides only a brief overview of local records, such as parish registers and congregational histories. For a detailed discussion of the types of American church records and how to locate and use the original records of various denominations, see chapter 6, "Research in Church Records," in *The Source: A Guidebook of American Genealogy,* edited by Loretto Dennis Szucs and Sandra Hargreaves Luebking, rev. ed. (Salt Lake City: Ancestry, 1997).

This chapter does cite bibliographical sources that can lead the reader to sources not discussed below. The chapter bibliography, while listing the specific sources discussed here, also includes more than one hundred additional sources of state and nationwide value for various denominations.

TYPES OF PUBLISHED CHURCH SOURCES

There is a wide variety of published church sources. For most family historians, published *parish registers* are the most familiar. Generally, these provide dates of baptisms, marriages, and burials and sometimes other "pastoral acts," such as confirmations. However, other published sources often are overlooked. Genealogical periodicals often publish parish registers, and *denominational newspapers* publish obituaries and other news about a church's members. In addition, *church histories,* an often overlooked source, can provide excellent information, both on a local and state or nationwide basis. Furthermore, some general reference sources, including *church encyclopedias,* require explanation as convenient sources for background (as well as some biographical and geographical) information about particular religions. Lastly, *directories* help researchers locate ancestral churches and usually their records as well.

Published Parish Registers

Most researchers need no introduction to church parish registers (although the term may differ from one denomination to another). Parish registers are churches' records of vital events in their members' lives. They are seldom as complete as government vital records, and many denominations have not kept such records. In other cases, records were kept by ministers and did not remain with the local congregations as pastors moved on to other churches—primarily because the ministers saw the

The Pennsylvania-German Society.

1761.

Anna Catharina Geiger, d. Joh. Georg and Elisabeth; b. Dec. 21, 1760; bap. Jan. 1.
Johann Gottfried Klug, s. Carl and Susannah.
Margaret Bernhardt, d. Thomas and Margaret; b. Jan. 8; bap. Jan. 11.
Johannes Schreiber, s. Johannes and Anna Eva; b. Dec. 26, 1760; bap. Jan. 18.
Conrad Wüst, s. Georg Adam and Elisabeth; b. Nov. 22, 1760; bap. Jan. 18.
Catharina Jeyser, d. Joh. Friedrich and Catharina; b. Jan. 22; bap. Jan. 25.
Johann Benedict Betz, s. Johannes and Maria; b. May 10, 1760; bap. Feb. 12.
Gottlieb Gottschall, s. Peter and Catharina; b. Jan. 19; bap. Feb. 15.
Margaret Elisabeth Kayser, d. Michael and Johannetta Maria; b. Feb. 10; bap. Feb. 15.
Maria Catharina Wild, d. Jacob and Catharina; b. Jan. 25; bap. Feb. 15.
Eva Susannah Schweizer, d. Stephan and Magdalena; b. Jan. 28; bap. Feb. 22.
Margaret Gruys, d. Christoph and Catharina; b. Jan. 13; bap. Feb. 22.
Anna Catharina Hornberger, d. Stephan and Magdalena; b. Feb. 17; bap. Feb. 22.
Elisabeth Crafford, d. Philipp and Elisabeth; bap. Feb. 27.
Johann Heinrich Berntheusel, s. Martin and Eva Maria; b. Feb. 26; bap. March 1.
Anna Maria Schott, d. Ludwig and Maria Barbara; b. Nov. 16; bap. March 1.
Maria Magdalena Braun, d. Johannes and Margaret Elis.; b. Dec. 1, 1760; bap. March 1.
Jacob Sprecher, s. Jacob Andreas and Margaret; b. March 3; bap. March 5.
Maria Zehmar, d. Anton and Sophia; b. Feb. 23; bap. March 8.
Maria Barbara Guntaker, d. Michael and Margaret; b. March 12; bap. March 18.
Elisabeth Barbara Umborn, d. Philipp and Dorothea; b. Jan. 29; bap. March 15.
Anna Elisabeth Heinkel, d. Johannes and Anna Elisabeth; b. Feb. 7; bap. March 22.
Susanna Catharina Keppele, d. Christoph and Eva; b. Dec. 21, 1760; bap. March 20.
Anna Margareta Burg, d. Christian and Margareta; b. March 7; bap. March 22.

Figure 8-1. Translated entries from the baptismal register of the Trinity Lutheran Church in Lancaster, Pennsylvania, originally published by the Pennsylvania German Society and reprinted by the Genealogical Publishing Company in *Pennsylvania German Church Records of Births, Baptisms, Marriage, Burials, Etc.*, vol. 1 (page 48).

records as belonging to them, not to the church. Of course, many ministers served several congregations as circuit preachers.

At least two factors affect the information contained in the published versions of parish registers: the quality of the original records and the quality of the transcription or translation. Some baptismal records merely record the name of the child and its parents and the date of the baptism. Others include additional data, such as date of birth, the father's occupation, names and occupations of the witnesses, and, occasionally, the parents' birthplaces.

The same is true for marriage records. Some clergymen merely recorded the names of the bride and groom and the date of the marriage; others included the names of the witnesses and the names of the nuptial pair's parents. Occasionally the pastor listed the birthplaces of the bride and groom, which can be of enormous assistance in determining an immigrant's place of origin.

Death or burial registers can also vary widely in content—from mere lists of funerals (burial dates) to brief "biographies" that list the birth date and place of the deceased, names of his or her parents, surviving spouse and children, cause of death, and funeral text.

Depending upon the denomination, parish registers may also include confirmation and communicant registers, membership rolls, pew rental fees, disciplinary records, family registers, etc. Such records can be of enormous genealogical value.

Problems with Published Parish Registers. Certain problems tend to appear in published versions of handwritten church records. Sometimes they are incomplete. A translation of the baptismal register of the Trinity Lutheran Church in Lancaster, Pennsylvania, originally published by the Pennsylvania German Society and reprinted by the Genealogical Publishing Company of Baltimore as *Pennsylvania German Church Records of Births, Baptisms, Marriage, Burials, Etc.*, 3 vols. (1983) (figure 8-1), is an example. As Don Yoder notes in the introduction, "the translator purposefully omitted the godparents' names (1983, xi)." This omission is unfortunate, for, as any experienced genealogist knows, godparents' names often yield priceless clues to familial relationships. To compensate for this failing, Debra D. Smith and Frederick S. Weiser have issued two of a projected five volumes of the records of this church (through Closson Press). These translations include godparents, marginal notations, and even pew rentals.

A second problem concerns incorrect transcriptions and translations. Such an error is illustrated in a typewritten transcription of the baptismal register of Dunkel's Church in Greenwich township, Berks County, Pennsylvania, from around 1758–1760, titled Church Record for the Dunkel's Reformed Congregation in Greenwich Towhship, Berks Co. 1746–1832 (figure 8-2). A family had previously identified a daughter of George Bräuner, baptized on 6 April 1760, as a possible child of their ancestor George Michael Breiner, in part because the child's godfather, Michael Ley, was George Michael Breiner's brother-in-law. When a researcher searched the register for other children of George Michael, he noted an entry for Catharina, daughter of George Bromer [*sic*] and Catharina, baptized 26 March 1758—interesting because the wife of George Michael Breiner was Catharina Ley. A check of the original, handwritten, record confirmed the researcher's suspicion. The original record lists the child's father as Jörg Broiner. The dot of the *i*, however, was so faint that it could easily have been overlooked, making the name appear to be

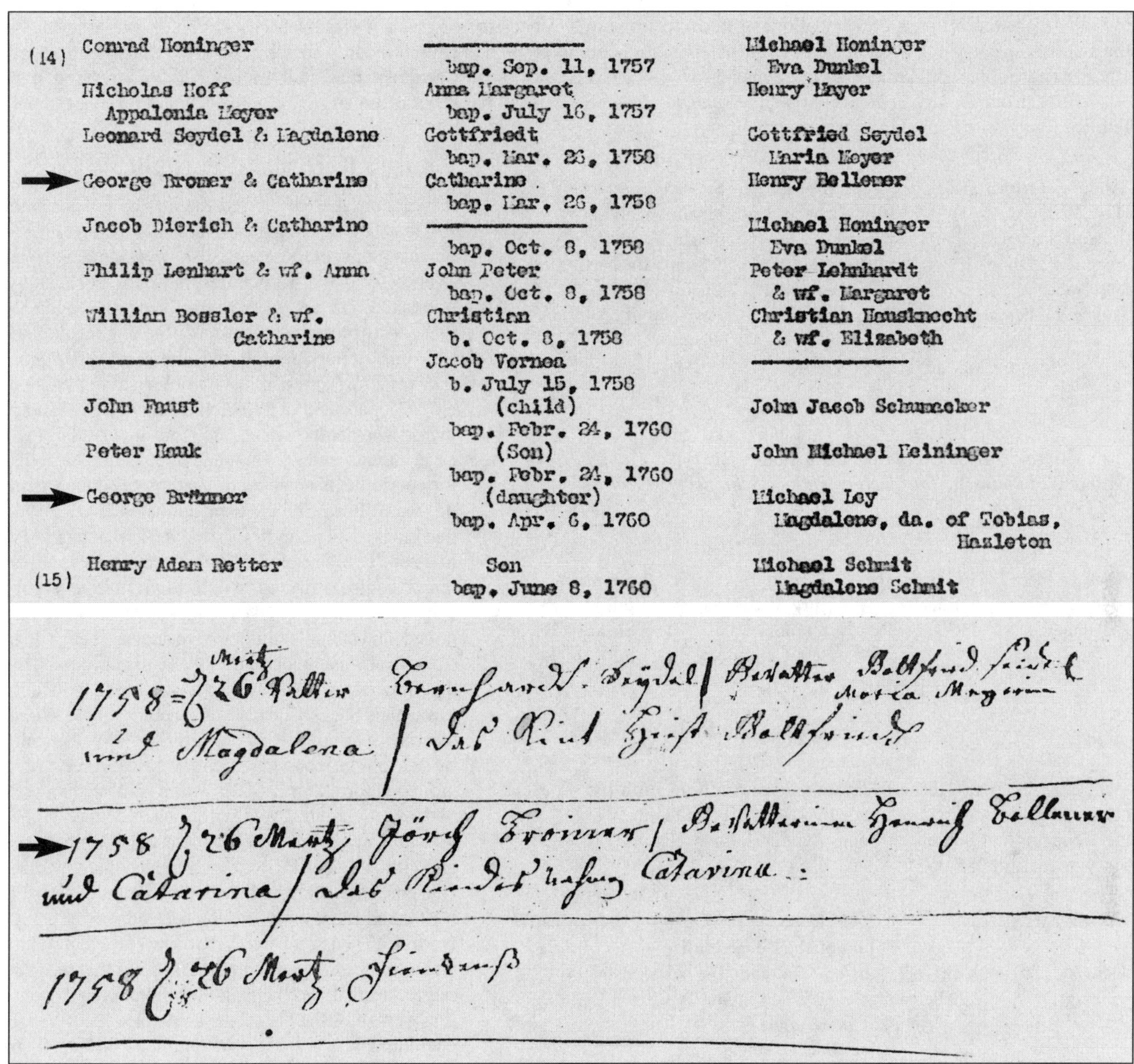

(14)	Conrad Honinger	——— bap. Sep. 11, 1757	Michael Honinger Eva Dunkel
	Nicholas Hoff Appalonia Meyer	Anna Margaret bap. July 16, 1757	Henry Mayer
	Leonard Seydel & Magdalene	Gottfriedt bap. Mar. 26, 1758	Gottfried Seydel Maria Meyer
	George Bromer & Catharine	Catharine bap. Mar. 26, 1758	Henry Belleuer
	Jacob Dierich & Catharine	——— bap. Oct. 8, 1758	Michael Honinger Eva Dunkel
	Philip Lenhart & wf. Anna	John Peter bap. Oct. 8, 1758	Peter Lehnhardt & wf. Margaret
	William Bossler & wf. Catharine	Christian b. Oct. 8, 1758	Christian Hausknecht & wf. Elizabeth
	———	Jacob Vernea b. July 15, 1758	———
	John Faust	(child) bap. Febr. 24, 1760	John Jacob Schumacher
	Peter Hauk	(Son) bap. Febr. 24, 1760	John Michael Heininger
	George Bräuner	(daughter) bap. Apr. 6, 1760	Michael Ley Magdalene, da. of Tobias, Hasleton
(15)	Henry Adam Retter	Son bap. June 8, 1760	Michael Schmit Magdalene Schmit

Figure 8-2. Incorrectly transcribed entries from the baptismal register of Dunkel's Church in Greenwich township, Berks County, Pennsylvania, from around 1758–1760 (top). A family had previously identified a daughter of George Bräuner, baptized on 6 April 1760, as a possible child of their ancestor George Michael Breiner, in part because the child's godfather, Michael Ley, was George Michael Breiner's brother-in-law. When a researcher searched the register for other children of George Michael, he noted an entry for Catharina, daughter of George Bromer [*sic*] and Catharina, baptized 26 March 1758—interesting because the wife of George Michael Breiner was Catharina Ley. A check of the original, handwritten, record (bottom) confirmed the researcher's suspicion. The original record lists the child's father as Jörg Broiner. The dot of the *i,* however, was so faint that it could easily have been overlooked, making the name appear to be Bromer.

Bromer. This example is vindication of Yoder's advice that "with any translated church record it is good policy for the genealogist to check the originals as a matter of course" (1983, xi).

Indeed, because the error was one of transcription rather than of translation, one could take Yoder's advice a step further and state that, with any transcribed church record, it is good policy to check the original record. Of course, it is not always possible to do so. For example, most original Lutheran records in archives are not available for research, but most have been microfilmed. Where they are not available, it is wise to examine all available transcriptions or translations. The baptismal registers of Lutheran pastor Daniel Schumacher constitute a very important genealogical source for the German settlers of Berks County, Pennsylvania, around 1760 to 1780. Three translations are available in the Family History Library of The Church of Jesus Christ of Latter-day Saints (LDS church) in Salt Lake City: one by Pastor Frederick S. Weiser, originally published under the auspices of the Pennsylvania German Society, and the others on microfilm. Note the following three versions of the baptismal entry for Johann Jacob, son of Jurg Michaell Breiner and Catharina, baptized 26 December 1767.

First, from *Daniel Schumacher's Baptismal Register* in Publications of the Pennsylvania German Society:

Child, Baptismal Day	*Father, Mother*	*Sponsors*
The 26th	Jurg Michaell	Johann Jacob Leÿbÿ
Johann Jacob	Breiner	Single
born the 11th of	Catharina	Susanna Bachern
November	a brother of old	single
baptized Allemangel	Leÿ's son-in-law	

(Weiser 1968, 334)

Compare the above with the translation and typescript by Arthur G. Schuman, *Taufbuch of Daniel Schmacher, 1754 to 1774*:

Date & Place	Child & Age	Parents	Sponsors
Dec 26	Joh Jac	Jurg Mich Breiner	Joh Jac Lyby
Allemaengel	Nov 11	a tailor	Susanna Bacher
		wfe Catharina	both single

(1957, 87)

Now, compare these translations/transcriptions with the handwritten copy of a copy made by J. W. Early and housed at the Genealogical Society of Pennsylvania (Family History Library microfilm 385,062):

DATE OF BAPTISM	BAPTISMS	DATE OF BIRTH
	Jurg Michell B. & Cath.	
Dec. 26, 1767	Breiner, Joh. Jac. ^ (a tailor, the old Allemaengel. Leÿen son in law ?) Sp. Joh. Jac. Lÿbÿ, single & Sus. Bacher, single	Nov 11

(Early n.d., 192)

Unfortunately, the original has never been microfilmed for public use. But by comparing the three translations, one can often determine the genealogical relationships, even when some startling differences exist among the translations of a particular entry.

The pitfalls illustrated by these examples drawn from Pennsylvania German church records occur elsewhere. One author laments, "It is regrettable that when church records are included in published vital records, the admissions and dismissals are generally omitted" (Dodge 1980, 146). This statement alludes to another important fact about published church records, especially those of New England. Many published vital records of towns incorporated data from church records when they were compiled (see chapter 7, "Vital and Cemetery Records"). Sometimes the church records bridge gaps in the town records, and they often predate the town records by many decades. But, as noted above, the published versions do not always include all information of genealogical value; therefore, one should always check the originals if possible. Still, for all of their drawbacks, published church records are tremendously valuable to the genealogist. Carefully translated, transcribed, and indexed, published parish records can save countless hours for researchers.

Church Records in Periodicals

A great number of church records have been published as articles in genealogical and historical periodicals. Some of these have also been published later in book form, but many others have not. Fortunately, published indexes make the information contained in an array of periodicals accessible to genealogists. The most important of these is the *Periodical Source Index* (*PERSI*), prepared and published by the Genealogy Department of the Allen County Public Library in Fort Wayne, Indiana. *PERSI* first appeared in 1987 as an annual review of all genealogical and local history periodicals received in 1986 by the department; this was followed by a second annual volume in 1988 that indexed all periodicals received in that year. Also in 1988, a three-volume retrospective index covering periodicals from 1847 through 1985 was published. Eventually, twelve retrospective volumes were issued, and annual volumes have appeared each year.

PERSI is divided into five distinct sections, the first three of which are arranged according to locality (the United States, Canada, and other localities). Within the U.S. section, entries are arranged alphabetically by state postal abbreviation (thus, Massachusetts, MA, is filed before Maine, ME); within each state, alphabetically by county; and within each county, alphabetically by record type. To determine whether the church records of First Church in Needham, Massachusetts, have been published, for example, use an atlas to find the county in which Needham lies (it is Norfolk). Then check the *PERSI* entries for that county under the record type "church." It shows that the marriages, deaths, and baptisms for the church in question were published in subsequent volumes of *NEHG* beginning with vol. 55, issue number 3, in July 1901. The four-letter journal code list in *PERSI*'s appendix A shows that *NEHG* stands for *New England Historical and Genealogical Register.* The appendix also shows which states the journal covers—in this instance, the six New England states. For more information on *PERSI,* see chapter 19, "Genealogical Periodicals."

PERSI is a very effective tool for determining whether the church records of a given locality have been published in a periodical. It is also useful for determining whether obituaries for a given locality have appeared in a periodical. For example, under the category "Illinois, Cook, Obituaries, Chicago," the researcher learns that obituaries originally appearing in *Der Christliche Botschafter,* 1844 to 1871, were published in vol. 11, number 4 (Summer 1979), of the *Chicago Genealogist.*

PERSI's geographical arrangement has its limitations. It does not work as well for journals that feature obituaries drawn from a wide geographical area. For instance, *Der Christliche Botschafter* was the German-language newspaper of the Evangelical Association, which later merged with the United Brethren to form the Evangelical United Brethren (EUB). Still later, the EUB, as it was generally called, merged with the Methodist

Church to form the United Methodist Church. Dr. David H. Koss, associate professor of religion at Illinois College, has been extracting obituaries from this paper and others published by the churches of German Methodist orientation in his journal, *The Bush Meeting Dutch* (published in Jacksonville, Illinois, by the Department of Religion, Illinois College).

PERSI lists *The Bush Meeting Dutch* in the Research Methodology portion of its 1987 annual under the code AMBM, meaning it is "general American" in scope. Under "title of article," *PERSI* indicates "Evangelical and/or United Brethren." But it does not state that every issue of the journal features obituaries abstracted from the various periodicals of the denomination. Flaws of this sort will undoubtedly be eliminated as the index is perfected.

PERSI has some other limitations. First, it only includes periodicals received by the Genealogy Department of the Allen County Public Library in Fort Wayne, Indiana. However, this is not a serious limitation; the library attempts to identify and acquire all genealogical periodicals. The second limitation is that yearbooks, annuals, and irregular "publications of" and "proceedings of" titles are not presently considered periodicals for the purpose of indexing them in *PERSI*. Indeed, by strict definition they are not periodicals. Many early church records have been published in such sources, though, and it is unfortunate that they cannot currently be accessed through *PERSI*.

A second periodical index available in many public libraries is *Genealogical Periodical Annual Index* (*GPAI*) (Bowie, Md.: Heritage Books). This index has appeared every year since 1962 (except 1973). It is not cumulative, so every year must be searched individually. Nor is it all-inclusive; the only periodicals indexed are those that provide free copies to the compiler. Most major genealogical periodicals are covered in this index, however.

No discussion of periodical indexes would be complete without mentioning Carl Boyer, 3rd, *Donald Lines Jacobus's Index to Genealogical Periodicals,* rev. ed. (Newhall, Calif.: Boyer Publications, 1983). This index covers eighty-five genealogical periodicals through 1952. Jacobus did not include journals for which indexes had already been prepared (for example, the first fifty volumes of the *New England Historical and Genealogical Register* and the first thirty-nine volumes of *The Virginia Magazine of History and Biography*). The 1983 revised edition contains a list of the periodicals included and those deliberately excluded.

For a thorough survey of genealogical periodicals and their indexes, see chapter 19, "Genealogical Periodicals." For a list of religious periodicals currently being published, see the *Yearbook of American and Canadian Churches*, described under "General References," below.

Newspaper Sources

A very important complement to the various genealogical periodical indexes is Betty M. Jarboe's *Obituaries: A Guide to Sources,* 2nd ed. (Boston: G. K. Hall, 1989). The first edition of this book, published in 1982, contains many references to articles in serials that indexed or abstracted obituaries. Because of the publication of *PERSI,* Jarboe added very few entries of this type in the second edition; thus, her book is primarily an index of published obituaries in book form. In the second edition, she also included published compilations of cemetery records, a list of obituary card files that have been compiled by major libraries, and a list of online databases that contain obituaries. (The last two items are in separate appendixes at the back of the book.)

Apart from the two appendixes, the book is arranged geographically: the United States, followed by individual states and a few foreign countries (among them the United Kingdom and Ireland, France, Germany, and Canada). Published lists in the United States of more than local interest are listed under United States (for example, Brent H. Holcomb's *Marriage and Death Notices from the Lutheran Observer, 1831–1861, and the Southern Lutheran, 1861–1865* [Easley, S.C.: Southern Historical Press, 1979]). Obituaries from more-locally oriented newspapers are listed under the states in which they were published.

This geographical arrangement works reasonably well, though there are a few lapses. For instance, a 1967 book privately published by Mrs. A. R. Seder in Naperville, Illinois, titled *Index to the Subjects of Obituaries (Sterbfälle, Todesanzeigen): Abstracted from Der Christliche Botschafter of the Evangelical Church, 1836–1866* (Naperville, Ill.: the author, 1967) is not listed under United States or Illinois but under Ohio. *Der Christliche Botschafter* was published in Cleveland, but it contained obituaries of active members from many states. Hence, if a given item is not listed in the appropriate geographical category, one should check the overall index at the back of the book, which alphabetically lists authors, titles, subjects, and the number of the page featuring the pertinent entry. A work of somewhat broader nature is Anita Cheek Milner's *Newspaper Indexes: A Location and Subject Guide for Researchers,* 3 vols. (Metuchen, N.J., and London: Scarecrow Press, 1977–82).

A substantial number of church newspapers have been microfilmed in the series *American Periodicals, 1741–1900* (Ann Arbor, Mich.: University Microfilms, 1956). Jarboe's *Obituaries: A Guide to Sources* cites a number of obituary indexes prepared from newspapers that appear in this series. For a more complete index see Jean Hoornstra and Trudy Heath's *American Periodicals 1741–1900; an index to the microfilm collections, American Periodicals, Eighteenth Century; American Periodicals, 1800–1950; American Periodicals, 1850–1900; and Civil War Second Reconstruction* (Ann Arbor, Mich.: University Microfilms International, 1979).

Some Catholic diocesan newspapers published obituaries of active members and even those of non-Catholic spouses of active members. Few of these have been indexed, and many have not been microfilmed. The most concise guide to these newspapers is Virginia Humling's *U.S. Catholic Sources: A Diocesan Research Guide* (Salt Lake City: Ancestry, 1995). Also useful is *The Official Catholic Directory* (Wilmette, Ill.: P. J. Kenedy, annual). This directory lists the name and address of the current editor of each diocesan newspaper as well as the current diocesan archivist. See the supplemental biography for a more complete guide to Catholic periodicals.

An very useful guide to published sources of German churches of colonial North America is Emil Meynen, comp. and ed., *Bibliography on the Colonial Germans of North America* (Baltimore: Genealogical Publishing Co., 1982). Originally published in 1937 under a slightly different title, this work remains valuable. For instance, it lists the various smaller denominations and whatever material had been published about them up to the time of its compilation, which was around 1932.

Meynen's landmark book has been supplemented and enhanced by Henry A. Pochmann, ed., *Bibliography of German Culture in America to 1940* (Millwood, N.Y.: Kraus International, 1982), and by Arthur R. Schultz's *German-American Relations and German Culture in America: A Subject Bibliography, 1941–1980* (Millwood, N.Y.: Kraus International, 1984). For an exhaustive list of German-language newspapers, including many denominational papers, consult Karl J. R. Arndt and May E. Olson's *The German-Language Press of the Americas 1732–1968, History and Bibliography,* 3 vols. (Pullach/München: Verlag Dokumentation, 1967–80).

The above discussion largely concerns church records published in periodicals and newspapers; of course, Jarboe's work does list church periodicals that have been indexed and published in book format. For a guide to currently available published church records in book or microform, the best source is Marian Hoffmann's *Genealogical and Local History Books in Print,* 5th ed. (Baltimore: Genealogical Publishing Co., 1996–97.

Church Histories

Printed church source often overlooked by researchers are the increasingly numerous histories of various churches. Generally, there are two different kinds of histories. *Denominational histories* detail the history and growth of an entire denomination within some geographic area, typically throughout the United States or within a state; occasionally the emphasis is on a region within a state. *Congregational histories* focus on a specific congregation. In a sense, these can be compared to state and local histories (see chapter 17, "County and Local Histories") in their value for family historians; however, they are less understood, less used, and less available then the more popular geographically oriented histories.

Denominational Histories. While histories of entire denominations provide excellent background information, they also contain surprisingly large amounts of biographical information on various members. Histories of smaller religious groups, such as Disciples of Christ or the Brethren, cover a larger percentage of their members than those of larger churches. However, there are also significant clues in histories of larger churches. This example from a statewide Methodist history, William Blake's *Cross and Flame in Wisconsin: The Story of United Methodism in the Badger State* (Sun Prairie, Wisc.: United Methodist Church, Wisconsin Conference, 1973), page 40, tells about an early settler:

> The first German-speaking settler in Wisconsin, who was at the same time a devoted member of the Evangelical Association, appears to have been James Martin. With his wife, Mary, he came from Montgomery County, Pennsylvania, in 1838. On a tract of 160 acres in the town of Granville, 12 miles northwest of Milwaukee, he built a long house, followed a little later by a barn. In 1839 his father-in-law, Abraham Leister, Sr., bereft of his wife, came with his motherless family (two other daughters and four sons) to live near them, and James Martin's brother George joined them the same year. These settlers came from that same areas of Pennsylvania in which Jacob Albright had lived, preached, and organized his converts into religious societies.

The activities of members chronicled in such histories can provide clues about their residence and movements, and such histories can identify the locations of various congregations of a particular church. For example, in Thomas H. Campbell, et al., *Arkansas Cumberland Presbyterians, 1812–1984: A People of Faith* (Memphis, Tenn.: Arkansas Synod Cumberland Presbyterian Church, 1985), page 233, a lay member of the church is mentioned as a major influence on the growth of the religion in the area:

> In April, 1919, the newly organized Foster's Chapel congregation, North of Searcy, was received. F.E. Chumbler, an elder in the Searcy congregation, who a few years earlier had been instrumental in organizing a church at Blytheville, was instrumental in organizing Foster's Chapel.

For virtually every denomination there are available several histories that discuss the general history of that church—sometimes throughout the world but at least within the United States. For states where a particular denomination had (or has) many adherents, one will find statewide histories similar to the two previous examples. A representative sample of such histories, as well as general church histories, makes up the majority of the entries in the chapter bibliography. To locate additional titles, check the denomination of interest in the various major religious repositories (see the discussion of the *Yearbook of American and Canadian Churches* under "General Reference Sources," below.

Congregational Histories. Of even greater value than denominational histories, and seldom used, are the thousands of histories written about particular congregations. These seem to be popular with almost every denomination, but they are most common in the eastern states, where some churches have existed for hundreds of years. Such histories are often published on significant anniversaries of local congregations, such as their jubilee (seventy-five year) or centennial (one hundred year) celebrations. Many such histories, which document the earliest years of a congregation, were published in the latter half of the nineteenth century and early in the twentieth century. In addition to discussing the original organization of the church, they mention the ministers and lay leaders, sometimes even naming the Sunday School teachers who have served over the years. Some of these histories include a list of members (sometimes called communicants), such as that shown in figure 8-3, from the *Centennial of the Congregational Church of Hinsdale, Massachusetts* (Pittsfield, Mass.: Sun Printing Co., 1896).

Locating congregational histories can be difficult. The first place to turn is the church itself (if it is still active); the minister or one of the staff is likely to have a copy, and local libraries are also likely to have copies. However, there is no master bibliography of congregational histories. In fact, even the denominational repositories are unlikely to have comprehensive lists, although they will have collected many such histories and are another source of inquiry. Most genealogical research libraries have not collected these histories with any degree of comprehensiveness, and this includes the Family History Library; its collection consists mostly of those titles that were included as records were microfilmed at local or state libraries. A helpful source for many older congregational histories is the Genealogy and Local History (GLH) collection of microfiche produced by University Microfilms International (Ann Arbor, Michigan). This collection of genealogies and local histories is fully explained in chapters 16 and 17.

General Reference Sources

On occasion during church record research, significant detail about a denomination is not required. It may suffice to learn a few quick facts about the founding of a church, or to learn in what region of the United States it was most prominent. For such purposes, general religious reference books are often sufficient. The volumes mentioned below are available at most public and academic libraries.

A useful and popular single-volume overview of religious denominations is Frank S. Mead's *Handbook of Denominations in the United States*, now in its eighth edition and edited by Samuel S. Hill (Nashville, Tenn.: Abingdon Press, 1985). It provides brief sketches on 225 religious bodies. Arranged by religious "families" (for example, all Baptist groups are discussed in the same general section, with smaller sections for different Baptist groups), it provides a brief historical background, religious doctrines, and church organization. The *Handbook* includes statistics about church members and number of churches as well as related church institutions (schools, universities, seminaries, etc.).

For greater detail or a broader scope that includes more religious groups, consult John Gordon Melton's *Encyclopedia of American Religions,* 4th ed. (Detroit: Gale Research, 1993). This book describes 1,730 religious bodies within the United States and Canada. It begins with introductory essays about the development of religion in the United States and Canada, followed by historical essays defining the growth and development of each of the twenty families into which the religious groups are categorized. The "directory section," organized by the same twenty sections plus two miscellaneous sections, is the largest, providing detailed information on each religious group. For each group, the *Encyclopedia* provides its name, address, size of membership, educational facilities sponsored, periodicals published, and sources for further information about each religion (figure 8-4). The editor's effort to be inclusive ensures coverage of virtually every church and religious group in North America. Groups qualified if they seek their members' primary religious loyalty and if they had more than two thousand members or multiple congregations, or if their membership was drawn from more than one state and beyond a single metropolitan area. The sources cited with most entries identify books one can turn to for more information.

Another helpful source for the one hundred most prominent religions is *An Encyclopedia of Religions in the United States: One Hundred Religious Groups Speak for Themselves*, edited by William B. Williamson (New York: Crossroad Publishing Co., 1992). As the subtitle indicates, the information in this work was written by prominent members of each group. Each multi-page description includes general information, history, beliefs and doctrine, forms of worship, organization, significant terms, and a bibliography.

The Centennial List of Members.

WITH YEAR OF ADMISSION, DISMISSION, DEATH AND AGE.

NOTE.—The Clerk of the Church desires information that will assist in completing the record of dismissions, death and age of former members.

"A," denotes that the member was dropped from the roll by his or her request, or for other reasons; "L," admitted by letter from another church; "W," withdrew to some other denomination without taking a letter. Numbers out of the regular succession refer to admission a second time, and also to married name. Cases of discipline are on the church records only.

	No.	1795.	Dismissed.	Approximate Date of Death and Age.	
L	1.	Rev. Theodore Hinsdale,		Dec. 1818.	80
L	2.	Richard Starr,		Feb. 1805.	87
L	3.	Ephraim Hubbard,		May 1810.	63
L	4.	Elizur Burnham,		Mch. 1811.	78
L	5.	Nathan Hibbard,		1825.	88
	6.	Joseph Skinner,			
	7.	Jonathan Skinner,			
	8.	Giddeon Peck,			
L	9.	Seth Wing,		Feb. 1812.	67
L	10.	Asa Goodrich,			
L	11.	Nehemiah Frost,	Feb. 1806.	June 1850.	83
	12.	Benjamin Sawyer.			
	13.	Asa Parks.			
	14.	Mrs. Anne Hinsdale–Theodore.		Mch. 1817.	69
	15.	Sarah Sawyer.			
	16.	Elizabeth Babcock.			
L	17.	Mrs. Anne Goodrich–Asa.			
	18.	Mrs. Rebecca Frost–Amasa,	Feb. 1806.	Oct. 1823.	55
	19.	Priscilla Parks.			
	20.	Jerusha Skinner.			
	21.	Hulda Wing–Seth,		Oct. 1824.	78
L	22.	Mrs. Hannah Hubbard–Ephraim,		Jan. 1843.	89
L	23.	Mrs. Elizabeth Frost–Nehemiah.	Feb. 1806.	Sept. 1840.	72
		1796.			
	24.	Mrs. Pheobe Hibbard–Nathan.			
L	25.	Mrs. —— Peck–Giddeon.			
	26.	Widow Lucy Loomer,		July 1820.	60
	27.	Nancy Hinsdale,	Aug. 1834.	May 1851.	82
		1797.			
	28.	William Burnham,		Sept. 1850.	83
	29.	Moses Yeomans,		1814.	
	30.	Mrs. Eunice Babcock–John.			
	31.	Mrs. Lucy Pease–James.			

Figure 8-3. *Centennial of the Congregational Church of Hinsdale, Massachusetts,* a congregational history, includes this list of members.

Increasingly dated but particularly useful for finding church records is E. Kay Kirkham's *A Survey of American Church Records: Major Denominations Before 1880,* 4th ed. (Logan, Utah: Everton Publishers, 1978). This guide is arranged by state and town, listing what records are available for the various denominations and where to find them. It is by no means complete, but it does identify some of the collections at the Family History Library, as well as major church repositories.

For current addresses and statistical information on virtually every North American church, consult the *Yearbook of American and Canadian Churches,* currently edited by Kenneth B. Bedell (Nashville, Tenn.: Abingdon Press, 1916–; annual) for the National Council of the Churches of Christ in the U.S.A. The two most important sections are "Directories" and the "Statistical Section." The directory section includes lists of cooperative organizations, seminaries and Bible schools, religious periodicals, and, most importantly for genealogists, "Depositories of Church History Materials" and "Religious Bodies in the United States Arranged by Families" (Canada is in a similar section). The last-named section provides a summary de-

★179★
EVANGELICAL FREE CHURCH OF AMERICA
1551 E. 66th St.
Minneapolis, MN 55423

The Evangelical Free Church of America was formed in 1950 by the merger of two Scandinavian independent Pietistic churches which had grown out of nineteenth-century revivals: the Swedish Evangelical Free Church and the Norwegian-Danish Evangelical Free Church Association. The Swedish Evangelical Free Church came into existence in 1884. It was composed of congregations that did not want to enter the merger of Swedish synods that took place the following year, the merger forming the Swedish Evangelical Mission Covenant Church of America. These congregations had strong feelings about maintaining their own autonomy, and at the same time desired to sponsor missionary ministry overseas through an association of churches rather than the typical synodical structure. This association was established at a meeting in Boone, Iowa in 1884. An independent religious periodical, *Chicago-Bladet*, established by John Martenson, was a catalyst that brought together the 27 representatives at Boone.

The Norwegian-Danish Evangelical Free Church Association was formed by immigrants from Denmark and Norway who had been influenced by the pietistic revivals in their homeland. The ministry of Rev. Fredrick Franson of Bethlehem Church in Oslo led to the formation of the Mission Covenant Church of Norway, to which some of the immigrants had belonged. In 1889 a periodical *Evangelisten*, was launched in Chicago; and in 1891 the Western Evangelical Free Church Association was organized. Later that same year an Eastern Association of Churches was formed. A merger of the Eastern and Western groups was made in 1909, with the church taking the name of the Norwegian-Danish Evangelical Free Church Association.

The church formed in 1950, the Evangelical Free Church of America, adopted a Confession of Faith which stresses the essentials of the Reformation tradition, though the definite influence of evangelicalism is evident. The Bible is declared to be "the inspired Word of God, without error in the original writings." The second coming is seen as personal (meaning Jesus will come in person), premillennial (he will come before the millennium to bind Satan, and he will reign for a thousand years with his saints on earth), and imminent. Polity is congregational. There is an annual conference to oversee the cooperative endeavors of the church, including the credentialing ministers and a ministerial fellowship.

Mission work is carried on in Japan, Singapore, the Philippines, Malaysia, Zaire, Hong Kong, Peru, Venezuela, Belgium, Austria, and Germany. The church has two children's homes in the United States, and six nursing home facilities. Overseas there are two hospitals, a children's home, a seminary, a Bible institute, and other related institutions.

Membership: In 1984 the Church reported 900 churches with a membership of 106,000 (constituency 146,000).

Educational facilities: Trinity Evangelical Divinity School, Deerfield, Illinois; Trinity College, Deerfield, Illinois; Trinity Western College, Langley, British Columbia, Canada.

Periodicals: *The Evangelical Beacon*, 1515 E. 66th Street, Minneapolis, MN 55423.

Sources: Arnold Theodore Olson, *Believers Only*. Minneapolis: Free Church Publications, 1964; W. Wilbert Norton, et al, *The Diamond Jubilee Story*. Minneapolis: Free Church Publications, 1959; Arnold Theodore Olson, *This We Believe*. Minneapolis: Free Church Press, 1961.

★180★
MORAVIAN CHURCH IN AMERICA
Northern Province
69 W. Church St.
Box 1245
Bethlehem, PA 18018

The Moravian Church in America dates to the arrival of Bishop August Gottlieb Spangenberg in Georgia. After the Georgia work was established, he traveled to Pennsylvania and began work there, setting the stage for the arrival of Bishop David Nitschamann and the settlements of Nazareth, Bethlehem, and Lilitz. From these three centers a concentrated effort was made to bring into the Moravian Church the many groups which William Penn had brought to Pennsylvania: Quakers, Mennonites, and Brethren. The church spread as other Moravian settlements were established.

In 1752 Spangenberg began work in North Carolina, in a town first called Bethania, later called Salem, now called Winston-Salem. The town is in what is now Forsyth County. Salem became the headquarters for the Southern Province. In the 1850s work was begun in Wisconsin among the German and Scandinavian immigrants, and just before the turn of the century in California.

No discussion of the Moravians would be complete without mentioning their missionary zeal. They were among the first of the modern churches to realize that the world would remain essentially un-Christian and that Christians would therefore always have to be missionaries. Before the Moravians, Christians believed Christianity eventually would become the dominant religion of the whole world. The Moravians saw that belief as unrealistic and, recognizing Christians as a minority, saw the implications for ministering to the non-Christians. They began work in the West Indies in 1732 and a main motive in coming to America was to preach to the Indians. The Moravians began the first missions to the slaves and stand

266

Figure 8-4. *Encyclopedia of American Religions* provides name, address, size of membership, educational facilities sponsored, periodicals published, and sources for further information about each religion.

scription of each organization, along with key addresses and telephone numbers, and a list of officers or executive committee members (figure 8-5).

Denominational Encyclopedias. For more detailed information about a specific denomination, turn to one of the many church-specific encyclopedias. These single- or multiple-volume publications are available for virtually all of the major denominations and many of the smaller ones. They provide easy access to key concepts, history, congregations, and people associated with particular churches. Each denominational encyclopedia differs significantly from the others, some having a stronger history focus and others devoting most of their pages to theological issues. The chapter bibliography identifies the existing church encyclopedias; here it is sufficient to profile two widely differing examples.

The New Catholic Encyclopedia, produced by The Catholic University of America (New York: McGraw-Hill Book Co., 1967, 1974, 1979), is a 14-volume set with two supplements. Its broad scope is indicated by its 778-page index and 200-page biographical listing of consultants and contributors. The five hundred contributors represent a diverse authorship writing from the experiences of their own involvement in and reflection on the life of the Roman Catholic Church. Many of the articles are theological in nature, while others delve into the early (pre-American) history of the church. Still, the *Encyclopedia* devotes more than one page to the Catholic Calvert family of Maryland, identifying five generations of this significant family, with birth, death, and marriage information for the key members. Two pages deal with various members of the Carroll family, providing family connections as well as their contributions to Maryland history. The articles also include brief bibliographies that point to additional information.

On the other side of the spectrum is the one-volume *Lutheran Cyclopedia,* edited by Erwin Louis Lueker (St. Louis: Concordia Publishing House, 1954), whose 1,160 pages supply brief information on more than 7,500 subjects of religious significance, past and present, by 112 major contributors from the U.S. and abroad. Entries include hundreds of historic personages, such as the following (page 364):

> **Falckner, Daniel** (1666–ca. 1741). B. at Langen-Reinsdorf, Saxony, where his father Daniel, was pastor; studied theology in Germany; member of the pietistic circle of A. H. Francke; came to America (1694) and associated with German pietists in Pa.; visited Germany (1698) and returned with his brother Justus and others to Germantown (1700); attorney for Frankfort Land Company; lost all through the intrigues of his partners; in later years he served congregations along the Raritan River in N.J.; 1724–25 he officiated at congregations on the Hudson previously served by Kocherthal; in 1731 he was succeeded by Wolff.

In addition to identifying historical persons and places, including congregations, districts, synods and other church jurisdictions, encyclopedias define organizations within and related to churches, such as fraternal or social groups that ancestors may have associated with. Encyclopedias can therefore be sources of explanation for obscure organizations mentioned in other records.

Wisconsin Evangelical Lutheran Synod

Organized in 1850 at Milwaukee, Wisc. by three pastors sent to America by a German mission society, the Wisconsin Evangelical Lutheran Synod still reflects its origins, although it has now has congregations in 50 states and three Canadian provinces.

The Wisconsin Synod federated with the Michigan and Minnesota Synods in 1892 in order to more effectively carry on education and mission enterprises. A merger of these three Synods followed in 1917 to give the Wisconsin Evangelical Lutheran Synod its present form.

Although at its organization in 1850 the Synod turned away from conservative Lutheran theology, today it is ranked as one of the most conservative Lutheran bodies in the United States. The Synod confesses that the Bible is the verbally inspired, infallible Word of God and subscribes without reservation to the confessional writings of the Lutheran Church. Its interchurch relations are determined by a firm commitment to the principle that unity of doctrine and practice are the prerequisites of pulpit and altar fellowship and ecclesial cooperation. It does not hold membership in ecumenical organizations.

HEADQUARTERS

2929 N. Mayfair Rd., Milwaukee, WI 53222 Tel. (414)771-9357 Fax (414)771-3708

Publ. Rel. Dir., Rev. James P. Schaefer, 2929 N. Mayfair Rd., Milwaukee, WI 53222 Tel. (414)771-9357 Fax (414)771-3708

OFFICERS

Pres., Rev. Carl H. Mischke

1st Vice-Pres., Rev. Richard E. Lauersdorf, 105 Aztalan Ct., Jefferson, WI 53549

2nd Vice-Pres., Rev. Robert J. Zink, S68 W14329 Gaulke Ct., Muskego, WI 53150

Sec., Rev. David Worgull, 1201 W. Tulsa, Chandler, AZ 85224

OTHER ORGANIZATIONS

Bd. of Trustees, Admn., Mr. Clair V. Ochs

Bd. for Worker Trng., Admn., Rev. Wayne Borgwardt

Bd. for Parish Services, Admn., Rev. Wayne Mueller

Bd. for Home Missions, Admn., Rev. Harold J. Hagedorn

Bd. for World Missions, Admn., Rev. Duane K. Tomhave

PERIODICALS

Wisconsin Lutheran Quarterly; Northwestern Lutheran; Lutheran Educator, The

Figure 8-5. From *Yearbook of American and Canadian Churches.* It contains current addresses and statistical information for virtually every North American church.

Directories

Because more significant church records remain unpublished than have been printed, researchers sometimes need to contact churches and other religious organizations and repositories to locate original records. Two sources mentioned above, the *Yearbook of American and Canadian Churches* and the *Encyclopedia of American Religions,* can provide some of the addresses needed, but they cover only the major repositories and the headquarters of the churches themselves. Other directories are available; there are denominational directories for most major religions. Two national directories are first worthy of note.

The Directory of Religious Organizations in the United States, edited by J. Gordon Melton, 3rd ed. (Detroit: Gale Research Co., 1993) is a kind of companion volume to Melton's *Encyclopedia of American Religions* (cited earlier) in that this 728-page directory provides access to religious organizations that support the work of various churches. It describes some 2,500 Christian and non-Christian organizations engaged in religious activities. These include evangelical (missionary) organizations, academic institutions, media, religious social groups, and a variety of special ministries. Each group's listing includes address, telephone number, religious affiliation, year founded, a description of the group, and publications supported by the group.

In an effort to identify all of the local congregations of all churches throughout the United States, Gale Research of Detroit first issued the *National Directory of Churches, Synagogues, and Other Houses of Worship* in 1994. This four-volume set is arranged by regions of the United States. Within each volume, churches are presented by state, then alphabetically by town/city; within each town/city the religious groups are presented alphabetically. The houses of worship for twenty-four major religious organizations are represented in this directory. Unfortunately, it is far from complete. Many local churches and similar facilities are not listed, and those that are include only the address, with no information on the nature of the records that may be available and usually not even the name of a person or officer to contact. While this work is an admirable start, most serious researchers will be better served by using a denomination-specific directory (if one exists).

Denominational Directories. The best, most reliable way to determine the address of a local congregation is to turn to a directory that is focused on the denomination of interest. While such directories are not available for every religious group, they are available for many of the larger denominations. Perhaps the best example is *The Official Catholic Directory* (cited earlier), which is issued annually and identifies virtually every office and parish in each diocese. For parishes, it indicates what year each was established and the name(s) of the current parish ministers.

Other directories are not much more than telephone books. For example, the *1986 Update Directory of Southern Baptist Churches* (Nashville, Tenn.: Sunday School Board of the Southern Baptist Convention, 1986) is a simple computer listing, in columns, that provides the post office, state, ZIP code, church name, mailing address, and telephone number.

Other directories fall somewhere between these extremes. The directory for the Evangelical Lutheran Church in America (ELCA) actually comprises the largest portion (75 percent) of the church's annual yearbook. Titled "Roster of Congregations," it is arranged by state. Under each town it lists the name of the congregation, its location or mailing address, and ZIP code. However, it also identifies which regional synod the congregation belongs to, its internal identification number, telephone number, and the pastor's name, as well as membership and budget statistics.

The greatest challenge in using these directories is, first, finding them. Often it is best to contact a currently active congregation of the denomination of interest in one's own town; the local office is likely to have a current directory. Second, be sure that the directory pertains to the denomination that the congregation of interest currently belongs to (often, the church attended by an ancestor— where his records may still be housed— will have changed its affiliation since the ancestor went to church there). As explained below, many groups have merged and/or split over the last two centuries in North America. For example, do not expect to find the address of a Wisconsin Synod Lutheran parish in the ELCA yearbook, because that synod did not join the ELCA.

DENOMINATIONAL RECORDS

Given the complexity of U.S. religious life, the bewildering array of denominations, and space limitations, the arrangement of this chapter inevitably posed some difficulties. Because it was written for a genealogically oriented audience, those churches organized after 1900, which include most of the Pentecostal churches, are not discussed. *PERSI,* Jarboe's *Obituaries: A Guide to Sources,* and Hoffman's *Genealogical and Local History Books in Print* are arranged primarily according to locality, as are most library catalogs, so this chapter is organized by denominational groupings. This arrangement should prove complementary to the works cited.

Space permits this chapter to address only the major denominations in America through the nineteenth century. For smaller, or more recent, denominations, one will, of course, find fewer materials in print; however, they are worth pursuing nonetheless. Bibliographies for virtually all denominations are available at major research libraries. The "Research in Church Records" chapter in *The Source: A Guidebook of American Genealogy* (cited earlier) provides the addresses of major repositories for many denominations.

Adventists

Relatively little published material exists for those churches in the Adventist family. The associate secretary of the General Conference of the Seventh-Day Adventists advised E. Kay Kirkham that the Adventists' general church periodical, the *Review and Herald,* carries obituaries of leading individuals. The title of this journal is now *Adventist Review* (6856 Eastern Avenue NW, Washington, DC 20012).

Baptists

One of the leading experts on Baptist genealogy has stated, "Baptist church records are neglected for genealogical and biographical research because they are almost totally lacking in family group information" (Helmbold 1973, 168). However, Baptist denominational newspapers often contain valuable genealogical data. For instance, some of the Primitive Baptist newspapers published an obituary for every person in their fellowships, not just those of ministers and prominent laymen.

Two major repositories that collect Baptist records, including long-defunct newspapers, are the American Baptist Historical Society (Rochester, New York) and the Southern Baptist

Historical Commission (Nashville, Tennessee). The curator of the Rochester collection, Dr. Edward C. Starr, has worked for more than twenty-five years to compile a biographical card index and *A Baptist Bibliography, Being a Register of Printed Material by and about Baptists,* 25 vols. (Rochester, N.Y.: American Baptist Historical Society, 1947–; in progress).

The Dargan-Carver Library, associated with the Southern Baptist Historical Commission, has collected and microfilmed a great deal of material, including many state Baptist newspapers. Many feature obituaries of ministers and prominent lay members. Jarboe's *Obituaries: A Guide to Sources* lists indexes to those that have been published. Check both the U.S. section and the various state sections in Jarboe's work.

A book not listed in Jarboe's work is *Portraits: Primitive Baptist Ministers,* compiled by Walter Cash (Marceline, Mo.: the compiler, 1896). This book features portraits and biographies of 130 Primitive Baptist ministers, some of whom were deceased by the time of publication. The biographical data is quite reliable concerning place and date of birth.

Primitive Baptist newspapers are difficult to obtain because very few of them have been microfilmed. The best source for defunct Baptist periodicals is *Union List of Baptist Serials* (Fort Worth, Tex., 1960). One of the older Primitive Baptist periodicals still extant is the *Primitive Baptist,* currently published by Elder W. H. Cayce (South Second Street, Thornton, Arkansas 71766). For information on other Primitive Baptist periodicals, contact the Primitive Baptist Archives, Elon College, Elon, NC 27244. The library at Samford University (Birmingham, Alabama) also acts as a clearinghouse for information regarding the location of Baptist records in other repositories. The Baptist Information Retrieval System (BIRS), located in Nashville, Tennessee, is a computer-managed system for indexing periodicals, newspapers, and holdings of archives (both current and retrospective).

The Primitive Baptists represent a fascinating aspect of the Second Great Awakening, one that ran "against the current" in that it stressed what might be called the Calvinistic side of the Protestant tradition. Ethnically, the Primitive Baptists were usually of English and Scotch-Irish heritage. Indeed, today most Americans tend to think of the Baptists in their various denominations as predominantly English or Scotch-Irish in ethnicity. Yet, a century ago, no one would have assumed this; the Baptists conducted an aggressive and successful missionary campaign among the thousands of Swedish and German immigrants who flocked to the United States during the nineteenth century. One of the giants of the Social Gospel movement in the United States around 1900, Walter Rauschenbusch, was of German-Baptist stock.

Over time, German and Swedish Baptists were assimilated into the U.S. mainstream, and there are now few references to them on the genealogical lecture circuit. Yet the German Baptists published a newspaper, *Der Sendbote,* that featured obituaries of active members as well as the clergy. *Der Sendbote*, which began publication in 1852 and finally ceased in 1954, is difficult to locate today. According to the standard bibliographic work on German-American newspapers, partial sets are available at the Southern Baptist Seminary Library (Louisville, Kentucky) and at the American Baptist Historical Society Library (Rochester, New York) (Arndt and Olson 1967, 467). It is available on microfilm. Dr. David H. Koss of Illinois College has compiled indexed abstracts of the obituaries in *Der Sendbote* for the years 1854 to 1882, but they have not been published.

For information concerning Swedish Baptist newspapers, see Lilly Setterdahl's *Swedish American Newspapers* (Rock Island, Ill.: Swenson Swedish Immigration Research Center, 1981). A publication concerning New England Baptists is David Young and Robert L. Taylor's *Death Notices from Freewill Baptist Publications 1811–1851* (Bowie, Md.: Heritage Books, 1985). The introduction to this work briefly discusses the origins of the denomination and the newspapers indexed.

A survey of this length cannot possibly cover all of the publications of the various churches in the Baptist family. For information about the publications of the various black Baptist churches and those groups that have dissented from the mainstream of Baptist thought and practice, contact the library at Samford University (Birmingham, Alabama).

Brethren

The term Brethren is used by various churches, some of which are closely related theologically and historically, others quite distant. For instance, the Church of the Brethren originated in Germany in 1708. The Brethren churches of German origin were popularly known as the Dunkers, from the German word *tunken,* "to dip or immerse." On the other hand, the Plymouth Brethren developed in nineteenth-century Britain. The largest single meeting was held at Plymouth, England—hence the name, which has never been officially used by any of the various groups.

Neither group is close to the United Brethren, which originated in Pennsylvania and flourished among German-Americans on the frontier in the early nineteenth-century United States. Because it is essentially Methodist in theology and policy and has now merged with the Methodists, the United Brethren denomination is discussed under "Methodists," below.

As with other denominations, disagreements concerning doctrine and practice have produced various divisions over the decades—hence, such groups as the Church of the Brethren (Conservative Dunkers), the Brethren Church (Progressive Dunkers), and the Old German Baptist Brethren (Old Order Dunkers). Still another group stemming from German pietism is the River Brethren, officially the Brethren in Christ, and the various groups that have split from it. The historical background of these churches is discussed in Mead and Hill's *Handbook of Denominations in the United States* (cited earlier).

The earliest adherents of the largest of these churches, the Church of the Brethren, settled in Pennsylvania in 1719. They printed the first German Bible in America at Germantown, and in 1743 they circulated the first American religious periodical. The Church of the Brethren did not stress record-keeping to the extent that the Lutherans did; very few of their churches kept records before 1880. However, they published various newspapers, beginning in 1851, that contained obituaries of deceased members. These include the *Vindicator,* the *Gospel Visitor,* and the *Christian Family Companion Weekly.* The Brethren Historical Library and Archives, Elgin, Illinois, has prepared a card file to these obituaries for the years 1851 to 1875. This index has not been published, but the library will search it for individual entries.

As a result of a doctrinal dispute in 1881, the German Baptist Brethren, as the Church of the Brethren was then called, suffered a schism. Those who withdrew from the main body called themselves the Old German Baptist Brethren; they are now popularly known as the Old Order Brethren. This group retained control of the denominational newspaper, the *Vindica-*

tor. Recently, the Old Order Brethren published a complete index to the obituaries listed in this periodical from 1 January 1870 to November 1989. It is available from Alva C. Riffey, Rt. 2, Box 59, Westphalia, KS 66903. Ms. Riffey has a complete set of the *Vindicator* and can locate any obituary listed in the index.

In addition to its periodicals, in the first two decades of the twentieth century, the Church of the Brethren encouraged the publication of histories of its local churches and regional districts. An excellent example is *History of the Church of the Brethren of the Southern District of Ohio,* edited by Elder Jesse O. Garst (Dayton, Ohio: Otterbein Press, 1920). This six hundred-page work contains detailed histories of individual congregations, including considerable information about individual members and their families. The second half of the book provides biographies of ministers and prominent lay leaders. Recently, Carolyn Teach Denlinger compiled an every-name index to this book: *Index to the History of the Church of the Brethren of the Southern District of Ohio* that was published by the Southern Ohio District, Church of the Brethren Historical Committee, Old Happy Corner Meeting House, Clayton, OH 45315. For a fairly complete list of district histories and other works published by or about the Church of the Brethren before 1932, see Maynen's *Bibliography on the Colonial Germans of North America* (cited earlier).

Christian Church (Disciples of Christ)

Unlike the Church of the Brethren, which can trace its roots to continental Europe, the Disciples of Christ originated on the American frontier during the Second Great Awakening of the early nineteenth century. Their founding father was Thomas Campbell, a dissident Presbyterian minister from Ulster who settled in western Pennsylvania in 1807; for this reason, the Disciples were sometimes called the Campbellites (especially by their detractors). Many Disciples preferred the term Christian Church, and in many communities it is known by that name. The denomination is officially known as The Christian Church (Disciples of Christ). A related group of churches that split from the Disciples are the Churches of Christ. The Disciples have no central organization, but they publish more than one hundred periodicals.

This emphasis on publications continues a legacy that has long been a part of the Disciples' tradition. Shunning any form of hierarchial organization, they created a situation in which church newspapers played a key role in denominational affairs. Fortunately for the genealogist, few churches have made a greater effort to make the contents of their leading periodicals accessible to the general public. The result of this effort was *The Christian-Evangelist Index 1863–1958,* published jointly in 1962 by the Christian Board of Publication (St. Louis, Missouri) and the Disciples of Christ Historical Society (Nashville, Tennessee). The following periodicals are indexed:

The Gospel Echo, 1863–72

The Gospel Echo and Christian, 1872–73

The Evangelist, 1865–82

The Christian, 1874–82

The Christian-Evangelist, 1882–1958

The three-volume index is all-inclusive, covering a variety of topics. Of greatest interest to genealogists are the obituaries. While not every member of this fairly large denomination rated an obituary, prominent lay members as well as the clergy did. This index is a major source for anyone researching families of The Christian Church.

Church of God

According to Mead and Hill's *Handbook of Denominations* (cited earlier), at least two hundred religious groups in the United States bear the name Church of God in one form or another. Many of these date from the late nineteenth century. For a brief historical discussion of the larger groups bearing this name, see the *Handbook of Denominations.* Current information concerning names and addresses of officials and periodicals can be found in the *Yearbook of American and Canadian Churches* (cited earlier).

A denomination called Churches of God in North America (General Eldership) grew out of a revival among the Pennsylvania Germans in 1825, led by John Winebrenner; hence its popular name, Churches of God-Winebrenner. Beginning in 1846, the denomination published a newspaper, *Church Advocate,* that is rich in obituaries of members in good standing. A complete set is on file at Winebrenner Theological Seminary, 701 East Melrose Avenue, Findlay, OH 45840.

The Church of Jesus Christ of Latter-day Saints (LDS Church)

No church in the world has devoted more effort to the collection and preservation of church records than The Church of Jesus Christ of Latter-day Saints. Paradoxically, very few published versions of LDS records exist. The Family History Library staff and volunteers have prepared several indexes for various types of membership records, such as the Utah Immigration Card Index (more commonly known as the Crossing the Plains Card Index) and the European Emigration Card Index (more commonly known as the Crossing the Ocean Index). These and many other indexes have been combined in the *Early Church Information File,* a card index now available on microfilm through the Family History Library and its family history centers (see the introduction to *Printed Sources*).

There has always been a great interest in LDS church history, both within and outside the church; hundreds of volumes have been published on various aspects over the years. Many of the significant ones were republished electronically on the *LDS Collector's Library* (Provo, Utah: Infobases, 1997) CD-ROM and on the *LDS Family History Suite* (Provo, Utah: Infobases, 1996) CD-ROM. Both of these CD-ROMs include copies of the most significant early LDS newspapers, including the *Evening and Morning Star* (Independence, Missouri, 1832–34); the *LDS Messenger and Advocate* (Kirtland, Ohio, 1834–37); the *Elder's Journal* (Kirtland, Ohio, 1837–38); and the *Times and Seasons* (Nauvoo, Illinois, 1839–1846).

Of greatest interest to descendants of the early members of the LDS church is a fifty-volume set by Susan Easton Black, *Membership of The Church of Jesus Christ of Latter-day Saints: 1830–1848* (Provo, Utah: Brigham Young University Religious Studies Center, 1989). This published database seeks to identify vital records and LDS ordinances for all members of the LDS church through 1847. It provides a brief biographical listing for each, with references identifying which of the more than seventy published and one hundred unpublished sources include information about the early member. This series is available on the two CD-ROMs noted above and on microfiche at every North American LDS family history center.

Histories of individual LDS wards (congregations) and stakes (groups of congregations) are much less plentiful than congregational or district histories of other denominations, perhaps because of the relative youth of many LDS wards. Copies of those histories that have been published are generally deposited at the LDS Church History Library (rather than the Family History Library) in Salt Lake City.

Episcopal (Protestant Episcopal or Anglican)

Referred to historically as the Protestant Episcopal Church, this denomination enjoyed a privileged status as the established church in many of the American colonies before the American Revolution. Even though it lost that status as a result of the revolution, it has continued to play an important role in U.S. religious history to the present day.

Given the Episcopal Church's role as the established church and its sacramental theology, it is not surprising that Episcopal records rank high in terms of genealogical value. Many records of individual Episcopal churches have been published in book and periodical article form. Search in *PERSI* for those that have appeared in the various genealogical periodicals. The various editions of the *Genealogical Periodical Annual Index* (cited earlier) are useful for compilations that have appeared in book format and are still in print. For older books, again see Kirkham's *Survey of American Church Records* (cited earlier).

In regard to Episcopalian newspapers, the only sources that Jarboe's *Obituaries: A Guide to Sources* lists for obituaries are the *Clerical Directory of the Protestant Episcopal Church in the United States of America* (New York: Church Hymnal Corporation, 1898–68) and the *Episcopal Church Annual* (formerly the *Living Church Annual*) (New York: Morehouse-Gorham, 1830–). Each has a necrology section that lists clergymen who died the previous year. Also of interest is a journal called the *Churchman*.

Finally, no discussion of Protestant Episcopal records in America would be complete without mentioning the work of William Stevens Perry, especially his five-volume *magnum opus*, *Historical Collections Relating to the American Colonial Church* (Hartford, Conn., 1870–78; reprint; New York: AMS Press, 1969). While parish registers are not included in these volumes, Perry has transcribed scores of early documents concerning the Episcopal Church in Virginia, Pennsylvania, Massachusetts, and Delaware. Particularly fascinating are the letters sent by the presiding bishops to the various parishes regarding conditions and the replies of the ministers.

Evangelical Congregational Church

This denomination, generally Methodist in doctrine and policy (although it has retained a separate identity), is discussed under "Methodists—German Methodists," below.

Greek Orthodox

Contact Archives of the Greek Orthodox Diocese of North America, 10th East 79th Street, New York, NY 10021, for information regarding periodicals and published records. For information about other Eastern Orthodox church archives, see the current *Yearbook of American and Canadian Churches* (cited earlier).

Huguenot (French Protestants of the Reformed Church)

The best discussion of published Huguenot records appears in Cameron Allen's "Huguenot Migrations," in Kenn Stryker-Rodda, ed., *Genealogical Research: Methods and Sources,* vol. 2, rev. ed. (Washington, D.C.: American Society of Genealogists, 1983).

Jewish

The most current general discussion of Jewish research is Gary Mokotoff's "Tracking Jewish-American Family History," chapter 17 in *The Source: A Guidebook of American Genealogy* (cited earlier); additional discussion here would be redundant. Another useful discussion of published sources is Malcolm H. Stern's "Jewish Migrations" in Stryker-Rodda's *Genealogical Research* (cited earlier), vol. 2.

Lutheran

Lutheran records rank among the best available in terms of genealogical content. Most published Lutheran records are from the eastern states (for example, Pennsylvania), which experienced significant German immigration during the eighteenth century. German Lutheran records of Pennsylvania and other states are listed in the bibliographic works of Meynen, Pochmann, and Schultz, discussed earlier. Also worth checking are the various editions of Hoffman's *Genealogical and Local History Books in Print* (cited earlier).

Worthy of special mention are the various compilations of early Pennsylvania church records published by the Genealogical Publishing Co. (Baltimore) with introductions by Don Yoder, such as *Pennsylvania German Church Records,* Pennsylvania German Society Proceedings and Addresses (Baltimore: Genealogical Publishing Co., 1983), and *Pennsylvania Vital Records: From the Pennsylvania Genealogical Magazine and the Pennsylvania Magazine of History and Biography,* 3 vols. (Baltimore: Genealogical Publishing Co., 1983). While not all of the church records listed are Lutheran, a good percentage of them are. A few Lutheran marriage records appear in Donna R. Irish, comp., *Pennsylvania German Marriages* (Baltimore: Genealogical Publishing Co., 1982).

Finally, no discussion of Pennsylvania Lutheran records would be complete without mentioning the efforts of Pastor Frederick S. Weiser. Space does not permit a listing of all the German church records in Pennsylvania and Maryland that he has translated and transcribed. Many of these exist only as typescripts at the A. R. Wentz Library in Gettysburg, Pennsylvania, and on microfilm. In recent years the Pennsylvania German Society has inaugurated a series titled Sources and Documents of the Pennsylvania Germans. Among its publications are translations and transcriptions of church records by Pastor Weiser. For information concerning this series and other publications of the society, write to the Pennsylvania German Society, P.O. Box 397, Birdboro, PA 19508.

Weiser and Peggy Joyner have issued lists of eighteenth-century German church records in Maryland and Virginia—see *The Report*, vol. 38 (1982), of the Society for the History of the Germans in Maryland. Klaus Wust issued twelve volumes of

Virginia German church records in English (published by Shenandoah History, Edinburg, Virginia). Charles H. Glatfelter's *Pastors and People,* vol. 1, *Pastors and Congregations,* Publications of the Pennsylvania German Society, vol. 12 (Breinigsville: Pennsylvania German Society, 1980), lists most colonial Lutheran and Reformed congregations in Pennsylvania and states in which years the records were begun. Pastor Weiser is preparing for publication a chronological listing of the records of John Casper Stover; they cover 1728 to 1779.

Pastor Weiser has also published a series titled Guides to Central Pennsylvania Lutheran Church Records, organized by county. These can be obtained from the author at Parrehof (New Oxford, Pennsylvania). Weiser has not confined his efforts to Pennsylvania. In 1986, Pastor Weiser began a new series titled *Maryland German Church Records,* published by the Noodle-Doosey Press (Manchester, Maryland). Thus far, eleven separate volumes (of a projected twenty) have appeared; they are roughly equally divided between German Reformed and Lutheran congregations.

As did many American churches, the various Lutheran synods published newspapers and other periodicals. But, as a general rule, these did not include obituaries to the extent that the newspapers of some other denominations did. Of course, there are exceptions to the above generalization; a good example is Holcomb's *Marriage and Death Notices from the Lutheran Observer, 1831–1861, and the Southern Lutheran, 1861–1865* (cited earlier). Another source of obituaries is the annual *Lutheran Church Missouri Synod StatisticalYearbook* (St. Louis: Concordia Publishing House, 1984–). This yearbook, which was published in German until 1917, contained a necrology section that listed deceased pastors and teachers. Contact the Concordia Historical Insititute, 801 De Mun Avenue, St. Louis, MO 63105.

For the American Lutheran Church, which recently merged with the Lutheran Church in America, various publications listed obituaries, mostly of clergymen. The American Lutheran Church Archives at Wartburg Seminary (Dubuque, Iowa) has a master list of deceased clergymen that indicates locations of their obituaries.

For the Norwegian Lutherans, various sources exist, including the *Lutheran Herald,* the denominational newspaper of the old Norwegian Lutheran Church in America, which later took the name Evangelical Lutheran Church before merging with the American Lutheran Church in 1960. The *Lutheran Herald* featured obituaries and is indexed. For information contact the Archivist, Luther-Northwestern Theological Seminary, 2375 Como Avenue West, St. Paul, MN 55108.

For the Danish Lutherans who merged with the American Lutheran Church in 1960 (the United Evangelical Lutheran Church, headquartered in Blair, Nebraska), an important source is the *Dansk Almanak* (Danish Almanac). This yearbook contained a considerable amount of biographical data on clergy and lay members. In 1954 the name was changed to *Dansk Nytaar* (Danish News) and the format changed as well, but the yearbook continued to contain a great deal of biographical data. For specific inquiries, contact the College Library, Dana College (Blair, Nebraska).

Mennonites and Related Churches

Few U.S. religious groups have pursued genealogy and family history with greater zeal than the Mennonites. Of those groups originating in central Europe, only the Jews approach the Mennonites in their level of organization. Undoubtedly some of this emphasis stems from their being "a people apart." In the sixteenth and seventeenth centuries the Mennonites were persecuted, all too often dependent upon the Christian compassion of local lords for their very survival. Given their "underground" status, it is hardly surprising that finding recorded evidence of the Mennonites in seventeenth- and eighteenth-century German and Swiss records is very difficult. Indeed, tracing Mennonite and other Anabaptist immigrants from Pennsylvania back to their places of origin ranks among the most challenging tasks facing German-American genealogists.

To further complicate matters, Mennonite records in Pennsylvania tend to be rather fragmentary (compared with those of Lutheran and Reformed congregations), reflecting the Mennonites' history of persecution and, to some extent, their theology. On the other hand, the Mennonites have published an impressive series of scholarly works concerning their history for the past sixty years. This series, titled Studies in Anabaptist and Mennonite History, is published by Herald Press (Scottdale, Pennsylvania) in cooperation with the Mennonite Historical Society, Goshen College (Goshen, Indiana). The series leans toward biographical studies of early church leaders and analytical studies of such topics as the role which the pacifist Mennonites played in the U.S. Civil War.

A journal more specifically genealogical in its emphasis is the *Pennsylvania Mennonite Heritage,* originally called the *Mennonite Research Journal* (1960–77), published by the Lancaster Mennonite Historical Society, 2215 Millstream Road, Lancaster, PA 17602. A second journal devoted to genealogy and family history is *Mennonite Family History,* published by Mennonite Family History, P.O. Box 171, Elverson, PA 19520-0171. As its subtitle, "Devoted to Mennonite, Amish, and Brethren Genealogy and Family History," indicates, this journal covers more topics than strictly Mennonite family history. The Brethren referred to are the Church of the Brethren and those churches that split from it as a result of doctrinal disputes. Both journals are highly recommended for anyone interested in tracing families of Anabaptist persuasion.

For Mennonite publications, *Zionsbote Index,* 4 vols. (Fresno, Calif.: Center for Mennonite Brethren Studies, Board of Christian Literature of the General Conference of Mennonite Brethren Churches, 1984) features marriage, anniversary, and death notices of members in good standing from 1884 to 1984.

An excellent bibliography of published Mennonite family histories is Hugh F. Gingerich and Rachel W. Kreider's *Amish and Amish Mennonite Genealogies* (Gordonville, Pa.: Pequea Publishers, 1986). For pre-1932 published records concerning the Mennonites, see Meynen's *Bibliography on the Colonial Germans of North America* (cited earlier).

Methodists

The present-day United Methodist Church was formed in 1968 by the union of the Methodist Church and the Evangelical United Brethren Church, which shared a common historical and spiritual heritage. The Methodist churches generally served people of Anglo-Saxon heritage, but the Methodists conducted an active and successful missionary effort among Swedish and German immigrants in the second half of the nineteenth century. The overwhelming majority of those who called themselves Methodists spoke English.

The Evangelical United Brethren Church was itself a merger of the Evangelical and United Brethren churches in 1946.

These churches were Methodist in theology and organization, but their ethnic heritage was German. They grew out of the frontier camp meetings that characterized the Second Great Awakening of the early 1800s. For this reason they have been called the Bush Meeting Dutch.[1] As with other frontier American churches, the Methodists and their German-speaking brethren published newspapers as a means of keeping their scattered flock in contact with one another. However, the geographical scope of these denominational periodicals differed between the English- and German-speaking groups.

The English-speaking Methodists (historically often referred to as "Methodist-Episcopal") generally organized themselves into state conferences similar to those of the Baptists. Typically, several of these state conferences would join to publish a regional newspaper often called the *Christian Advocate*. Some of these are still in existence (such as the *Methodist Christian Advocate*, published in Birmingham, Alabama). These newspapers often carried obituaries of clergymen, their wives, and prominent laymen of the particular conferences. They are generally stored in regional repositories.

Fortunately, the United Methodist Church is making a concerted effort to collect microfilm copies of these newspapers at its central archive at Drew University in Madison, New Jersey. For a fee, the staff will search the holdings (if provided with a place and date of death). Contact the General Commission on Archives and History, United Methodist Church, P.O. Box 127, Madison, NJ 07940. Also, a number of published compilations of obituaries from various regional conference editions of the *Christian Advocate* have appeared in recent years; see Jarboe's *Obituaries: A Guide to Sources* (cited earlier) for a fairly complete list. For a complete listing of Methodist periodicals, see the work by Batsel and Batsel in the chapter bibliography.

German Methodists. Unlike their English-speaking brethren, the German Methodists (in the broad sense of the term) published newspapers that covered news of the entire denomination rather than just a regional conference. These newspapers are among the lesser-known sources of German-American genealogy. The late Dorothea Seder and Dr. David H. Koss have devoted considerable effort to making the genealogically valuable contents of these journals available to the public.

These periodicals are of great interest to genealogists because they typically feature obituaries of all active members, not just those of ministers and prominent laymen. The only compilation of obituaries from these newspapers that has appeared in book form is *Index to the Subjects of Obituaries (Sterbfälle, Todesanzeigen): Abstracted from Der Christliche Botschafter of the Evangelical Church, 1836–1866* (cited earlier). *Der Christliche Botschafter* was the publication of a German-American Protestant church called Der Evangelische Gemeinschaft (Evangelical Association). Methodist in theology and organization, the church was organized in the early 1800s by Jacob Albright and his associates. Indeed, its members were often called Albrecht's Leute (Albrecht's people) in the nineteenth century.

The Evangelical Association suffered a schism in the early 1890s that could not be resolved. The result was the formation of the United Evangelical Church in 1894. The church published its own newspaper, the *Evangelical,* until 1922; it featured obituaries of active members. An attempt to heal the schisms in the 1920s was only partly successful; the United Evangelical Church took the name Evangelical Congregational Church in 1928. It remains separate and publishes its own newspaper, the *United Evangelical* (Myerstown, Pennsylvania).

The Evangelical Association and the majority of the United Evangelical church rejoined in 1922, taking the name Evangelical Church. In 1946 the church merged with the United Brethren, another church that was basically Methodist but German-American in terms of ethnic background.

Most of the newspapers of the Evangelical United Brethren Church have been microfilmed and are available at various seminary libraries of the United Methodist Church. With the exception of the General Commission on Archives and History in Madison, New Jersey (mentioned previously), none of these libraries has sufficient staff to search for obituaries. Dr. David Koss of Illinois College, Jacksonville, Illinois, will search for obituaries (as time permits) in the church newspapers of the former Evangelical United Brethren Church, its predecessors, and its sister churches—among them the *Evangelical Messenger* (begun 1848) and *Der Christliche Botschafter* (begun 1836) of the Evangelical Association; the *Evangelical* (1889–1922) for United Evangelicals; and the *Religious Telescope,* the *Fröhliche Botschafter,* and *Die Geschaeftige Martha* of the United Brethren. In addition, Koss will search issues of *Der Christliche Apologete,* published by the German Conference of the Methodist Church (available from the late 1880s at Garrett Evangelical Theological Seminary, Evanston, Illinois), for a nominal fee per search and a self-addressed, stamped envelope.

In addition to the *Index to the Subjects of Obituaries (Sterbfälle, Todesanzeigen): Abstracted from Der Christliche Botschafter of the Evangelical Church, 1836–1866,* Dorothea Seder compiled a card index to obituaries published in that journal for the years 1866 to 1879. Dr. Koss is in possession of this index and plans to publish it.

Of the journals cited above, all are available through interlibrary loan except *Der Christliche Apologete* (1839–1941) of the German Methodist Conference. Its lack of availability is unfortunate because the genealogical value of its obituaries is very high; they often indicate the exact place of birth of the deceased. A translation of a typical obituary from *Der Christliche Apologete,* 11 April 1895, page 238, appears below (the original obituary notice appears in figure 8-6):

> Koch - sister Sophie Koch nee Moor died 24 March 1895 of a stroke. She was born in Grosseneixen, Mecklenburg-Schwerin, the 1st of June 1831. She came to this country in 1857 and married Christoph Koch the same year. Christmas Eve of the same year they converted to God with the help of Brother Fischback and joined the church. In 1864 they came from Jackson County to here and joined the parish of Zion. Sister K was a faithful member to the end. In addition to her grieving husband, she leaves 7 adult children and 2 grandchildren.
>
> Zion, Ohio J.G. Grimmer,
> Assistant pastor in the Ironton District

Garrett Evangelical Seminary has a fairly complete set from the late 1880s to 1941, when the journal ceased publication. For the earlier years, the most complete set is at the central Methodist Archive (Madison, New Jersey).

The United Brethren Church also experienced a schism in the late 1880s. The minority group, popularly known as the "Old

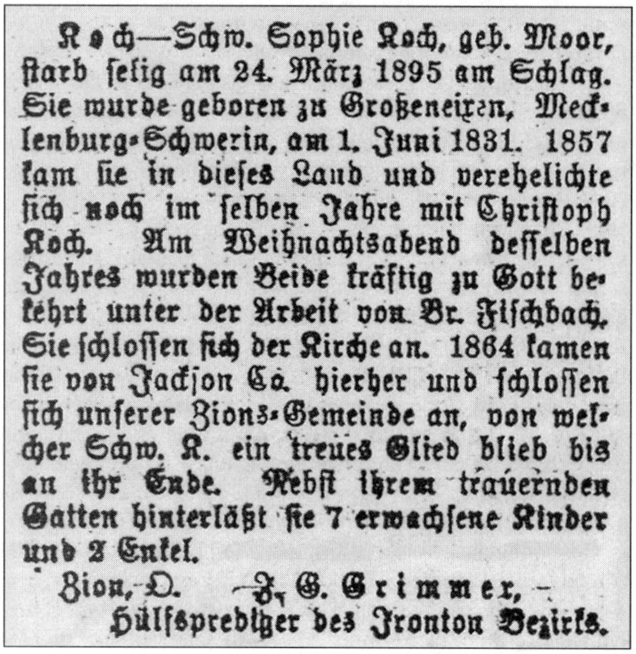

Koch—Schw. Sophie Koch, geb. Moor, starb selig am 24. März 1895 am Schlag. Sie wurde geboren zu Großeneixen, Mecklenburg-Schwerin, am 1. Juni 1831. 1857 kam sie in dieses Land und verehelichte sich noch im selben Jahre mit Christoph Koch. Am Weihnachtsabend desselben Jahres wurden Beide kräftig zu Gott bekehrt unter der Arbeit von Br. Fischbach. Sie schlossen sich der Kirche an. 1864 kamen sie von Jackson Co. hierher und schlossen sich unserer Zions-Gemeinde an, von welcher Schw. K. ein treues Glied blieb bis an ihr Ende. Nebst ihrem trauernden Gatten hinterläßt sie 7 erwachsene Kinder und 2 Enkel.

Zion, O. —J. G. Grimmer, —
Hülfsprediger des Ironton Bezirks.

Figure 8-6. Obituary notice from *Der Christliche Apologete,* 11 April 1895, page 238.

Constitution" United Brethren, is officially known as the United Brethren in Christ. It published a newspaper called the *Christian Conservator* from 1885 to 1954 which listed obituaries and weddings of active members; it has been indexed. Contact United Brethren Historical Center, Huntington College, (Huntington, Indiana).

A useful bibliography to published works concerning Methodism is Kenneth E. Rowe, ed., *Methodist Union Catalog Pre-1976 Imprints,* vols. 1–6 (Metuchen, N.J., and London: Scarecrow Press, 1976).

Moravian Church (Unitas Fratrum, "Unity of Brethren")

Although the Moravian Church in America has never been numerically large, its records are of considerable genealogical interest for at least two reasons. First, the Moravians established themselves in Pennsylvania around 1740 and in North Carolina around 1752. In addition, their records are of unusually good quality.

The name Moravian Church is somewhat misleading, for most of the church's adherents were German-speaking—even those who came from Bohemia and Moravia. The name arose from the fact that the church originated in Moravia, which is now part of the Czech Republic, in 1457. The official name of the church is Unitas Fratrum (Unity of Brethren). Inevitably, it has been confused with the Church of the Brethren or the Evangelical United Brethren, but, apart from both being Protestant and having German-speaking origins, these groups have no direct connection.

Fortunately for the genealogist, some of the Moravian records have been translated into English and published in book form. Among the most interesting is a short book by Georg Neisser titled *A History of the Beginnings of Moravian Work in America,* translated by William N. Schwarze and Samuel H. Gapp (Bethlehem, Pa.: Archives of the Moravian Church, 1955). Neisser was an early leader of the Moravian church in Pennsylvania; the book is a translation of his manuscripts covering the years 1732 to 1742. It is rich in genealogical data, including places of origin of many early Moravian immigrants.

No discussion of published Moravian records would be complete without mention of the truly monumental compilation by Adelaide L. Fries, ed., *Records of the Moravians in North Carolina 1752–1879,* 11 vols. (Raleigh, N.C.: Edwards and Broughton Printing Co., 1922–69). Another interesting compilation of eighteenth-century Moravian records is William M. Beaucharus, ed., *Moravian Journals Relating to Central New York, 1745–1766* (Syracuse, N.Y.: Dehter Press, 1916). While not as massive as Fries's *magnum opus,* Beaucharus's work offers a fascinating glimpse of conditions in upstate New York when it was mostly wilderness.

While these two compilations are very valuable contributions to an understanding of eighteenth-century life on the American frontier, a note of caution seems warranted. Neither purports to be a complete translation of all the extant records in question. Both compilations consist of extracts chosen and translated by their editors. Furthermore, neither was prepared primarily for genealogical purposes, although the North Carolina volumes contain a great deal of valuable genealogical data. These books should be regarded as guides to the archival material from which they were derived, rather than as the final authority on genealogical questions concerning ancestors of the Moravian persuasion.

Presbyterian

Presbyterian Church records, generally speaking, rank just below those of the so-called "sacramental churches" (for example, Roman Catholic, Lutheran, and Episcopalian) in terms of genealogical value. Many individual Presbyterian churches, such as the famous Old Tennant Church in Monmouth County, New Jersey, have published their records; and many state genealogical societies, such as the New York Genealogical and Biographical Society, have published records of Presbyterian churches in their periodicals.

As did other nineteenth-century Protestant denominations, Presbyterians published newspapers that listed obituaries and marriages, but relatively few of these have been abstracted and published. Jarboe's *Obituaries: A Guide to Sources* (cited earlier) lists several, some of which are found under the heading "United States," while others are listed under the states in which they were originally published. Perhaps the best approach is to check the general index under the heading "Presbyterian."

The Presbyterians also conducted a missionary program among German immigrants in the nineteenth century. One result of this effort was a newspaper called *Der Presbyterianer,* which contained marriages and obituaries. A fairly complete run of this journal is housed at the University of Dubuque, Dubuque, Iowa.

A nineteenth-century publication of outstanding value for Presbyterian genealogy is Alfred Neven, ed., *Encyclopedia of the Presbyterian Church in the United States of America: Including the Northern and Southern Assemblies* (Philadelphia: Presbyterian Encyclopedia Publishing Co., 1884). This 1,248-page volume, which covers both the northern and southern assemblies of the church, consists primarily of short biographies of prominent Presbyterian clergymen and laymen. It also features capsule histories of important Presbyterian churches, presbyteries, and colleges.

For more recent biographical data concerning Presbyterian clergymen, contact the Presbyterian Historical Society and Department of History, United Presbyterian Church in the United States, 425 Lombard Street, Philadelphia, PA 19147. It maintains a centralized biographical index to all past and present Presbyterian clergymen in the United States.

A work of more than local interest is Howard McKnight Wilson's *The Lexington Presbytery Heritage* (Verona, Va.: McClure Press, 1971). This prize-winning study contains a great deal of genealogical information. It lists ministers, deacons, and elders in the churches of the Presbytery dating back to the mid-eighteenth century. The Lexington Presbytery once covered a huge area extending from the Blue Ridge Mountains in western Virginia to the Ohio River.

Howard McKnight Wilson has played a role in writing and compiling the history of the Presbyterian Church in Virginia which parallels that of Pastor Frederick S. Weiser in Pennsylvania German records. Among Wilson's other publications is *Records of the Synod of Virginia on Microfilm* (Richmond, Va.: Synod of Virginia, 1970). This is an index to the 510 reels of microfilm that constitute the official records of the Presbyterian Church in Virginia.

Kirkham's *Survey of American Church Records* (cited earlier) lists a number of histories concerning the Presbyterian Church in the United States, both on the national and state levels. Because many of these have long been out of print, this list forms a useful supplement to those listed in Hoffman's *Genealogical and Local History Books in Print* (cited earlier). For a discussion of Presbyterian journals published before 1830, see the articles by Gordon Albaugh listed in the chapter bibliography.

Protestant Episcopal

See Episcopal

Quakers (Society of Friends)

Quaker records enjoy great notoriety among genealogists, in large part because of the sheer excellence of the records themselves. The Friends did not have an ordained clergy to baptize their children, celebrate their marriages, or bury their dead. Consequently, they had to record their own vital statistics to protect themselves in questions concerning the validity of their marriages, the legal status of their children, and inheritance of property.

Adding to their records' intrinsic value is their accessibility, thanks to the existence of William Wade Hinshaw's *Encyclopedia of American Quaker Genealogy,* 6 vols. (Ann Arbor, Mich.: Edwards Brothers, 1936–50; reprint; Baltimore: Genealogical Publishing Co., 1969). Vol. 1 contains meeting records for North Carolina, South Carolina, Georgia, and Tennessee; vol. 2, New Jersey and Pennsylvania; and vol. 3, New York City and Long Island. Vols. 4 and 5 include meetings in southwestern Pennsylvania, all of Ohio, and one meeting in Michigan. Vol. 6 covers records for Virginia.

These published records include all of the older meeting records for North Carolina, South Carolina, Virginia, and Ohio. Compiled, but unpublished, material that Hinshaw had collected was deposited after his death in the Friends Historical Library at Swarthmore College. This collection is called the William Wade Hinshaw Index to Quaker Meeting Records; it includes more Pennsylvania and New Jersey meeting records, as well as records from meetings in California, Iowa, Kansas, and Indiana. This index has been microfilmed by the LDS Family History Library and is available at the main library in Salt Lake City. A list of all the meeting records in this index can be found in an article by Frederick B. Tolles, "A New Tool for Genealogical Research: The William Wade Hinshaw Index to Quaker Meeting Records," *NGS Quarterly* 38 (2) (June 1950), reprinted in *General Aids to Genealogical Research* (Washington, D.C.: National Genealogical Society, 1962). Also see Ruth Priest Dixon's "The Origins of Hinshaw's Encyclopedia of Quaker Genealogy," *Pennsylvania Genealogical Magazine* 39 (Spring-Summer 1995): 58–64.

Under the editorial leadership of Willard Heiss, the Indiana Historical Society has published the Indiana records copied by William Hinshaw with additional material found since Hinshaw's death. It is called *Abstracts of the Records of the Society of Friends in Indiana, Part One through Six (1962–1975) with Index,* vol. 7 of *Encyclopedia of American Genealogy* (Indianapolis: Indiana Historical Society, 1977).

In addition, the Family History Library made a typescript of the Iowa Quaker meeting records copied by Hinshaw titled The William Wade Hinshaw Index to Iowa Quaker Meeting Records. This typescript has been reproduced on microfiche and is available at many LDS family history centers.

A more complete listing of published Quaker records can be found in the published version of a lecture Willard Heiss gave at the World Conference on Records in Salt Lake City in 1980, "American Quaker Records and Family History," World Conference on Records, vol. 4, *North American Family and Local History,* part 2, series 358 (Salt Lake City: Church of Jesus Christ of Latter-day Saints, 1980).

A type of Quaker record not discussed in the Heiss article is obituaries in Quaker periodicals. A major contribution in this regard is *Quaker Necrology* from the Haverford College Library (Haverford, Pennsylvania) (Boston: G. K. Hall and Co., 1961). This two-volume work lists fifty-nine thousand entries in the necrology file index of the Quaker collection in Haverford College Library. Each card in the index gives not the date of death but the volume, year, and page number of each death notice in one of the following major Quaker journals: the *Friend,* published by orthodox Quakers in Philadelphia beginning in 1828; the *Friend's Weekly Intelligence,* published by the Hicksite Friends beginning in 1844; and the *Friends Review,* published by the more evangelically oriented orthodox in Philadelphia in 1848. (In 1894, the last journal merged with the *Christian Worker* to create the *American Friend,* published first in Philadelphia and later in Richmond, Indiana.) In 1955 the Philadelphia Yearly Meetings reunited. As a result, they merged the *Friend* and the *Friend's Weekly Intelligence* to form the current *Friends Journal.* Thus, the index contains entries from the years 1828 to 1959.

Reformed (Dutch Reformed)

In New Netherland, the predecessor to New York, the Dutch Reformed Church was the established church. In New York City, fairly complete records for the Dutch Reformed Church exist from December 1639 to the present except for a few gaps during the American Revolution. The New York Genealogical and Biographical Society published the baptisms and marriages to 1800 in three volumes, ca. 1890 to 1902: *Collections of the New York Genealogical and Biographical Society, Records of the Reformed Dutch Church in New Amsterdam and New York,* edited by Samuel S. Purple, Thomas Grier Evans, and Tobias Alexander Wright (New York, 1902; reprint; Upper Saddle River, N.J.: Gregg Press, 1968).

The New York City records are only the most notable of many Dutch Reformed and other church records of New York and adjacent states that have appeared in the *New York Genealogical and Biographical Record,* the official journal of the society since 1870. Fortunately, a master index has been compiled covering the years 1870 to 1982: Jean Worden, comp., *The New York Genealogical and Biographical Master Index, 1870–1982* (Franklin, Ohio: T. D. Worden, 1983).

The publications of the Holland Society of New York (122 East 58th Street, New York, NY 10022) are a second major source of published records of the Dutch Reformed Church. Indeed, the Genealogical Publishing Co. reprinted published transcriptions of the Dutch Reformed churches in Brooklyn, Albany, and New Paltz, New York, that were originally published by the Holland Society.

Space considerations do not permit listing all of the church records that the Holland Society has transcribed and published; see the master index, *The Holland Society of New York Index to Publications 1885,* edited by Louis Duermyer (New York: Holland Society, 1977). Photocopies of the society's yearbooks (1897 to 1929) are available from the society at the above address. The *Yearbook* and other publications of the Holland Society are not yet in *PERSI.*

Another major source of published Dutch Reformed Church records is *Proceedings of the New Jersey Historical Society,* which took the name *New Jersey History* in 1967. A subject index exists for the years 1845 to 1919, and each volume published since then includes an index. This journal is included in *PERSI.*

A useful and inexpensive guide to Dutch Reformed Church records is Melody Takken Meeter's *Guide to Local Church Records in the Archives of the Reformed Church in America and to Genealogical Resources in the Gardner Sage Library* (New Brunswick, N.J.: New Brunswick Theological Seminary, 1979). This book not only lists the holdings of the library but also contains an appendix showing which of these records have been published and in which journal.

In regard to vital statistics published in periodicals, the Dutch Reformed Church published a newspaper in New York City called the *Christian Intelligencer.* It was begun in 1830 and regularly published obituaries and marriage notices without charge through December 1871. In January 1872 it began charging for the notices, so very few were published after that. Roy Cowen Sawyer extracted seven volumes of obituaries from *The Christian Intelligencer* covering the years 1830 to 1871, according to Jarboe's *Obituaries: A Guide to Sources* (1989, 161), but these extracts have never been published. Those obituary extracts from the journal concerning deaths in Pennsylvania are available on microfilm at the Family History Library in Salt Lake City (microfilm no. 860,290). Obituaries extracted for New Jersey deaths from this periodical are on microfilm at the DAR Library in Washington, D.C.

The Family History Library also has two microfilm reels of a typescript of marriage notices Sawyer extracted and abstracted from the *Christian Intelligencer* covering the years 1830 to 1871. The original typescript is in the Queens Borough Public Library in New York City, where the seven volumes of the obituary extracts are housed.

Arthur C. M. Kelly has transcribed and published numerous Dutch Reformed Church records of the Hudson River Valley. For a complete list of his publications, contact Arthur C. M. Kelly, 60 Cedar Heights Road, Rhinebeck, NY 12572.

Reformed—German

See United Church of Christ.

Roman Catholic

Roman Catholic parish registers, or sacramental registers as they are officially called, rank among the best available in terms of genealogical value. Unfortunately, relatively few have been published. Particularly noteworthy among those that have are the works of the Rev. Fr. Donald J. Hebert in southern Louisiana. He has translated, transcribed, and published some forty printed volumes of Louisiana Catholic parish registers: *Southwest Louisiana Records to 1897* and *Southern Louisiana Records to 1895* (Hebert Publications, Box 31, Eunice, LA 70535).

A work of comparable merit is the multi-volume translation and transcription of Catholic parish registers in the Pacific Northwest by Harriet Duncan Munnick in collaboration with Mikell Delores Warner, *Catholic Church records of the Pacific Northwest* (St. Paul, Oreg.: French Prairie Press, 1972–89). There are seven volumes in this series to date.

While not technically a transcription or translation of church records, the two-volume *Genealogy of the French Families of the Detroit River Region* by the Rev. Fr. Christian Denissen, rev. ed. (Detroit: Detroit Society for Genealogical Research, 1987) merits mention with the works of the Father Hebert and Harriet Duncan Munnick. It is based largely on the Catholic parish registers of the Detroit area dating back to 1704. In its latest revision, it includes families from 1704 to 1936.

In the early years of the twentieth century, the American Catholic Historical Society of Philadelphia occasionally published transcriptions of Catholic records in its journal, *American Catholic Historical Researches,* vols. 1 through 29 (now available from University Microfilms International, Ann Arbor, Michigan); this journal merged into *Records of the American Catholic Historical Society of Pennsylvania* (Philadelphia) in 1912. A typical example is "Father Peter Helbron's Baptismal Register at Sportsman's Hall, Penna.," which was reprinted with an index under the title *Catholic Baptisms in Western Pennsylvania, 1799–1828* (Baltimore: Genealogical Publishing Co., 1985). The American Catholic Historical Society also has published two indexes to its journal, one in 1920 for vols. 1 through 31 (covering 1886 to 1920), the second in 1956 for vols. 32 through 41 (covering 1921 to 1930).

The American Catholic Historical Society is not to be confused with the United States Catholic Historical Society based in New York City. The latter's journal, *Historical Records and Studies,* features obituaries of prominent Catholics, both clergy and laymen. The index for vols. 1 through 10 (covering 1899 to 1917) appears in vol. 11, while the index for vols. 15 through 23 appears in vol. 24.

In regard to Catholic newspapers, see Humling's *U.S. Catholic Sources: A Diocesan Research Guide* (cited earlier) and *The Official Catholic Directory* (cited earlier). A more complete treatment of Catholic serials is the series compiled by Eugene P. Willging and Herta Hatzfeld, *Catholic Serials of the Nineteenth Century in the United States: A Descriptive Bibliography and Union List* (Washington, D.C., 1966–).

Unitarian-Universalist

This denomination, as its name implies, resulted from a merger of two churches, the Unitarian and the Universalist. See Kirkham's *Survey of American Church Records* (cited earlier) for brief statements of their record-keeping policies.

Regarding Unitarian records, see the discussion of published Congregational records under "United Church of Christ," below. Unitarianism developed out of congregationalism in the late eighteenth century. Many Unitarian churches in Massachusetts were originally Congregational churches; hence, their records reflect Congregational record-keeping practice.

In terms of obituaries, Jarboe (cited earlier) lists an article by Marion Lang Driscoll, "New England Records" (copied from *Universalist Watchman,* published in Montpelier, Vermont, issue of 11 February 1837), in *NGS Quarterly* 24 (1936): 105.

United Church of Christ

More vital records (christening, marriage, and death records) of the United Church of Christ have been published than of any other in the United States. The denomination stems from a 1957 merger between the former Congregational Christian Church and the Evangelical and Reformed Church.

The Congregational Church grew out of the Puritan churches of New England, while the Christian churches originated as a restorationist movement in the late eighteenth century. The two churches merged to form the Congregational Christian Church in 1931. The Evangelical and Reformed Church stemmed from a 1934 merger between the German Evangelical Synod of North America and the Reformed Church in the United States (formerly called the German Reformed Church).

Given the striking difference in the ethnic backgrounds of the churches forming the United Church of Christ, it seems best to treat them separately. A second reason for this approach is geographical. The Congregational Church dominated colonial New England, while the German Reformed Church was strong in the mid-Atlantic colonies, especially Pennsylvania.

Congregational Church Records. The best single source of published records of Congregational churches is the *New England Historical and Genealogical Register,* published by the New England Historic Genealogical Society in Boston (101 Newbury Street, Boston, MA 02116). Indeed, it is the best single source for published church records of all denominations of colonial New England. An every-name index to vols. 1 through 50 of the *Register* covering persons, subjects, and places, originally printed from 1907 to 1911, was reprinted by the Genealogical Publishing Company in 1972 and by Picton Press (Camden, Maine) in 1989. For subsequent volumes of the *Register,* see the new index to vols. 51 through 148, edited by Jane Fletcher Fiske, *Index of Persons in the New England Historical and Genealogical Register, Volumes 51 through 148,* 4 vols. (Boston: New England Historic Genealogical Society, 1995).

Another source of published New England church records, especially of Essex County, Massachusetts, is *Historical Collections of the Essex Institute* (Salem, Mass.: Essex Institute, 1859–). It includes a cumulative index and is also indexed in *PERSI.* Also worthy of mention in this regard is the periodical *American Genealogist* (published by David L. Green, P.O. Box 398, Demorest, GA 30535). But perhaps the easiest way to determine whether the records of a given church have been published in a periodical is to check the locality section of the *PERSI* index.

Listing all of the Congregational Church records of New England that have appeared in book format is beyond the purview of this chapter. One example with an unusually broad scope is Frederic W. Bailey, ed., *Early Connecticut Marriages as Found on Ancient Church Records Prior to 1800,* 7 vols. in 1 (reprint; Baltimore: Genealogical Publishing Co., 1968). Many Congregational Church records were used in the compilation of published town vital records for New England, especially Massachusetts. These records are discussed more thoroughly in chapter 7, "Vital and Cemetery Records."

E. Kay Kirkham's *Survey of American Church Records* (cited earlier), which lists New England church records arranged by state, is still useful. To be sure, it includes churches other than the Congregational and is by no means complete.

Some of the best published Congregational Church records for Massachusetts are found in Publications of the Colonial Society of Massachusetts. This series appears as an annual yearbook and is therefore not indexed in *PERSI.* For an excellent discussion of Congregational and other church records in New England, see Ralph J. Crandall, ed., *Genealogical Research in New England* (Baltimore: Genealogical Publishing Co., 1984).

German Reformed Records. As noted above, one of the churches forming part of the United Church of Christ is the Reformed Church in the United States, formerly known as the German Reformed Church. This denomination was particularly strong in the mid-Atlantic states, especially Pennsylvania.

The bibliographical works by Meynen, Pochmann, and Schultz, mentioned earlier, are useful guides to published works concerning the German Reformed Church. It is necessary to consult all three because Meynen's bibliography does not cover works published after 1932 and Schultz bibliography does not repeat works listed in the volume originally compiled by Pochmann, which extended to 1940.

For German Reformed records that have appeared in book form, see the three-volume *Pennsylvania German Church Records,* cited earlier under "Denominational Records—Lutheran." It contains records from German Reformed churches as well. The same holds true for the three-volume set *Pennsylvania Vital Records* and *Pennsylvania German Marriages.*

Pennsylvania German Church Records is actually a reprint of records originally printed in Pennsylvania German Society Proceedings and Addresses, vols. 1 through 63 (1890 to 1966). This series has been continued under a new title, Publications of the Pennsylvania German Society (1968–), which also serves as a continuation of Yearbooks of the Pennsylvania German Society. These publications are not indexed in *PERSI* because they are not periodicals in the strict sense of the term, but they are indexed in the works of Meynen, Pochmann, and Schultz.

An overall guide to German Reformed Church records is Florence M. Bricker's *Church and Pastoral Records in the Archives of the United Church and the Evangelical and Reformed Historical Society* (Lancaster, Pa., n.d.). The Evangelical and Reformed Historical Society (555 West James Street, Lancaster, PA 17603) holds the transcripts made by William J. Hinke and others of many of the colonial and early national German Reformed church records. It also houses many original registers and newspapers of the denomination, which featured obituaries of clergy and prominent lay members.

Another denomination included in the United Church of Christ is the German Evangelical Synod of North America. This church developed as a result of the extensive German immigration to the Mississippi Valley during the nineteenth century. Theologically, it reflected the enforced merger in 1817 of the Lutheran and Reformed churches in Prussia. Relatively few of the German Evangelical Synod's records have been published. The synod published a journal, *Der Friedensbote,* from 1850 to 1958; the issues for 1850 to 1935 are available on microfilm. This journal featured obituaries of pastors, pastors' wives, and teachers in the synod's schools. Dr. David H. Koss is indexing these obituaries, but they have not yet been published.

CONCLUSION

Published church sources vary from one denomination to another, but there is a fair degree of commonality among them. Some churches, notably the German Lutheran and Reformed, as well as the Dutch Reformed, have seen many of their parish registers printed. Friends (Quaker) records have also been extensively published. A growing number of Roman Catholic records are also appearing in print. While printed parish registers of other denominations are generally less common, many other sources are available. Church newspapers are increasingly easy to access, with more and more abstracts and indexes now in print; they provide access to information from denominations that did not keep thorough parish registers. In addition, church histories, both at the denominational and congregational levels, provide much information often overlooked by the casual researcher. Lastly, one should not overlook the abundance of reference sources and directories to provide additional information not included in this chapter.

NOTES

1. The term was coined by Don Yoder and adopted by David Koss as the title of his journal.

REFERENCE LIST

Arndt, Karl, and May Olson. 1967. *The German Language Press of the Americas.* Vol. 1. München: Verlag Dokumentation.

Dodge, Winifred Lovering Holman. 1980. "Massachusetts," in *Genealogical Research: Methods and Sources.* Edited by Milton Rubincam. Rev. ed. Washington, D.C.: American Society of Genealogists.

Early, J. W. N.d. Typescript. Genealogical Society of Pennsylvania. Family History Library microfilm 385,062.

Helmbold, F. Wilbur. 1973. "Baptist Records for Genealogy and History." *NGS Quarterly* 61 (September 1973).

Jarboe, Betty M. 1989. *Obituaries: A Guide to Sources.* 2nd ed. Boston: G. K. Hall.

Schuman, Arthur G. 1957. *Taufbuch of Daniel Schmacher, 1754 to 1774.* Typescript. Lancaster, Pa.: Evangelical and Reformed Archives. Family History Library microfilm 940,443.

Spencer, Claude E. 1962. *The Christian Evangelist Index.* St. Louis: Christian Board of Education. Nashville, Tenn.: Disciples of Christ Historical Society.

Weiser, Frederick Sheely. 1968. *Daniel Schumacher's Baptismal Register.* Publications of the Pennsylvania German Society, vol. 1. Allentown: Pennsylvania German Society, 1968. Reprinted with corrections by the same author as *The Record Book of Daniel Schumacher, 1754–1773.* Rockport, Maine: Picton Press, 1994.

Yoder, Don. 1983. *Pennsylvania German Church Records of Births, Baptisms, Marriages, Burials, Etc.* Pennsylvania German Society Proceedings and Addresses. 3 vols. Baltimore: Genealogical Publishing Co.

BIBLIOGRAPHY

Compiled by Kory L. Meyerink and Ted Naanes

This is a bibliography of selected sources intended only to represent the vast amount of published material on American churches of value to family historians. It includes the sources discussed in the chapter, as well as many other national and statewide sources for major denominations. There are thousands of congregational histories that cannot be listed here, as well as many district, conference, and synod histories. The newspapers discussed throughout the chapter are not repeated here. After a list of general sources, the bibliography is arranged by the denominations used in the chapter. Selected statewide sources are listed under their respective denominations, generally only for the most prevalent religions in a given state. Selections were in part chosen for their availability. Older titles are available on microfilm through the Family History Library.

General Reference

Arndt, Karl J. R., and May E. Olson. *The German-Language Press of the Americas 1732–1968, History and Bibliography.* 3 vols. Pullach/München: Verlag Dokumentation, 1967–80.

Bradley, James E. , and Richard A. Muller. *Church History: An Introduction to Research, Reference Works, and Methods.* Grand Rapids, Mich.: William B. Eerdmans Pub. Co., 1995.

The Directory of Religious Organizations in the United States. Edited by J. Gordon Melton. 3rd. ed. Detroit: Gale Research Co., 1993.

An Encyclopedia of Religions in the United States: One Hundred Religious Groups Speak for Themselves. Edited by William B. Williamson. New York: Crossroad Publishing Co., 1992.

Ganstadt, Edwin Scott. *Historical Atlas of Religions in America.* New York: Harper & Row, 1962.

Glatfelter, Charles H. *Pastors and People.* Vol. 1, *Congregations and Pastors.* Publications of the Pennsylvania German Society, vol. 13. Breinigsville: Pennsylvania German Society, 1980.

Hoornstra, Jean, and Trudy Heath. *American Periodicals 1741–1900, an Index to the Microfilm Collections, American Periodicals, Eighteenth Century; American Periodicals, 1800–1950; American Periodicals, 1850–1900; and Civil War Second Reconstruction.* Ann Arbor, Mich.: University Microfilms International, 1979.

Irish, Donna R., comp. *Pennsylvania German Marriages.* Baltimore: Genealogical Publishing Co., 1982.

Jarboe, Betty M. *Obituaries: A Guide to Sources.* 2nd ed. Boston: G. K. Hall, 1989.

Mead, Frank S., and Samuel S. Hill, eds. *Handbook of Denominations.* 8th ed. Nashville, Tenn.: Abingdon Press, 1985.

Melton, John Gordon. *The Encyclopedia of American Religions.* 4th ed. Detroit: Gale Research, 1993.

Mode, Peter George. *Source Book and Bibliographical Guide for American Church History.* Boston: J. S. Canner, 1964.

Meynen, Emil, comp. and ed. *Bibliography on the Colonial Germans of North America.* Baltimore: Genealogical Publishing Co., 1982.

National Directory of Churches, Synagogues, and Other Houses of Worship. 4 vols. Detroit: Gale Research, 1994.

Kirkham, E. Kay. *A Survey of American Church Records: Major Denominations Before 1880.* 4th ed. Logan, Utah: Everton Publishers, 1978.

Melton, J. Gordon. *Religious Bodies in the United States: A Directory.* [2nd ed.] New York: Garland Publishing, 1992. This book is a revised edition of *A Directory of Religious Bodies in the United States* (1977).

Milner, Anita Cheek. *Newspaper Indexes: A Location and Subject Guide for Researchers.* 3 vols. Metuchen, N.J., and London: Scarecrow Press, 1977–82.

National Directory of Churches, Synagogues, and Other Houses of Worship. 1st ed. Detroit: Gale Research, 1994.

Norton, Wesley, Religious Newspapers in the Old Northwest to 1861: A History, Bibliography and Record of Opinion. Athens: Ohio University Press, 1977. This book, while not written for a genealogical audience, is an excellent discussion of the social, political, and religious currents reflected in the denominational press of the states concerned. Of particular interest to genealogists is the bibliography of religious newspapers with library holdings.

Pennsylvania Vital Records: From the Pennsylvania Genealogical Magazine and the Pennsylvania Magazine of History and Biography. 3 vols. Baltimore: Genealogical Publishing Co., 1983.

Pochmann, Henry A., ed. *Bibliography of German Culture in America to 1940.* Millwood, N.Y.: Kraus International, 1982.

Schultz, Arthur R. *German-American Relations and German Culture in America: A Subject Bibliography, 1941–1980.* Millwood, N.Y.: Kraus International, 1984.

Setterdahl, Lilly. *Swedish American Newspapers.* Rock Island, Ill.: Swenson Swedish Immigration Research Center, 1981.

Suelflow, August Robert. *A Preliminary Guide to Church Records Repositories.* St. Louis: Society of American Archivists, Church Archives Committee, 1969.

Union List of Serials in Libraries of the United States and Canada. 3rd ed. 5 vols. New York: H. W. Wilson, 1965.

Yearbook of American and Canadian Churches. Nashville, Tenn.: Abingdon Press, 1916–. Annual

Yoder, Don. *Pennsylvania German Church Records.* Pennsylvania German Society Proceedings and Addresses. Baltimore: Genealogical Publishing Co., 1983.

General Religious Biography

Barker, William P. *Who's Who in Church History.* Grand Rapids, Mich.: Baker House, 1977.

Bowden, Henry Warner. *Dictionary of American Religious Biography.* Westport, Conn.: Greenwood Press, 1977. 2nd ed. 1993

Kessell, John L. *Friars, Soldiers, and Reformers: Hispanic Arizona and the Sonora Mission Frontier, 1767–1856.* Tucson: University of Arizona Press, 1976.

Moyer, Elgin. *Wycliffe Biographical Dictionary of the Church.* Chicago: Moody Press, 1982.

Sprague, William Buell. *Annals of the American Pulpit: Or Commemorative Notices of Distinguished American Clergymen of Various Denominations, from the Early Settlement of the Country to the Close of the Year Eighteen Hundred and Fifty-Five with Historical Introductions.* 9 vols. New York: Robert Carter & Brothers, 1859.

Who's Who in Religion. Chicago: Marquis Who's Who, 1975–76.

Adventists

Seventh-day Adventists Encyclopedia. Edited by Dan F. Neufeld. Rev. ed. Washington, D.C.: Review and Herald Publishing Association, 1976.

Spaulding, Arthur W. *Origin and History of Seventh-day Adventists.* 4 vols. Washington, D.C.: Review and Herald Publishing Association, 1961.

Baptists

1986 Update Directory of Southern Baptist Churches. Nashville, Tenn.: Sunday School Board of the Southern Baptist Convention, 1986.

Ahlstrom, L. J. *Eighty Years of Swedish Baptist Work in Iowa, 1853–1933.* Des Moines: Swedish Baptist Conference of Iowa, 1933.

Alley, Reuben Edward. *A History of Baptists in Virginia.* 1st ed. Richmond: Virginia Baptist General Board, [1969].

American Baptist Register. Philadelphia: American Baptist Publication Society, 1853–.

Asplund, John. *The Universal Register of the Baptist Denomination in North America, for the Years 1790, 1791, 1792, 1793, and Part of 1794.* New York: Arno Press, 1980. The 1980 edition is a reprint of the 1794 edition, originally printed in Boston by J. W. Folsom, 1794.

Baptist Clergy Census Directory 1840–1849, 1850–1852. North Salt Lake, Utah: Accelerated Indexing Systems International, 1988. The only names indexed are those of persons who appear as ministers. Includes the following information: county from which the record comes or the location where the minister had his congregation; name of the state; page number as listed in the *American Baptist Register;* and the year the census was taken.

Benedict, David. *A General History of the Baptist Denomination in America, and Other Parts of the World.* 2 vols. in 1. Boston: Lincoln & Edmunds, 1813.

Biographical History of Primitive or Old School Baptist Ministers of the United States, including a Brief Treatise on the Subject of Deacons. . . . Anderson, Ind.: Herald Publishing Co., 1909.

Campbell, J. H. *Georgia Baptists: Historical and Biographical.* Macon, Ga.: J. W. Burke & Co., 1874.

Cash, Walter, comp. *Portraits: Primitive Baptist Ministers.* Marceline, Mo.: the compiler, 1896.

Coffey, Achilles. *A Brief History of the Regular Baptists, Principally of Southern Illinois*. With an appendix by Thomas J. Carr. Elizabethtown, Ill.: Nelson Publishing, 1984. Originally published Paducah, Ky.: Martin & Co. Steam Printers and Binders, 1877.

Colonial Baptists and Southern Revivals. New York: Arno Press, 1980. Reprint of *Baptist Foundations in the South: Tracing Through the Separates the Influence of the Great Awakening, 1754–1787*, by William L. Lumpkin (Nashville, Tenn.: Broadman Press, 1961) and of *Elder John Leland, Jeffersonian Itinerant*, by L. H. Butterfield, Proceedings of the American Antiquarian Society, vol. 62 (Worcester, Mass., 1952).

Colonial Baptists: Massachusetts and Rhode Island. New York: Arno, 1980. Reprint of two works: the first printed in 1652 by H. Hills, London; the other edited by W. G. McLoughlin and M. W. Davidson and reprinted from Massachusetts Historical Society Proceedings, 1964.

Cook, Richard B. *The Early and Later Delaware Baptists*. Philadelphia: American Baptist Publication Society, 1880.

Cotton, Gordon A. *Of Primitive Faith and Order: A History of the Mississippi Primitive Baptist Church, 1780–1974*. Raymond, Miss.: Keith Press, 1974.

Craigmiles, Joe E., 3rd. *Primitive Baptist Association Minutes of the United States.* Edited by Mrs. Donald W. Griffin. Thomasville, Ga.: Craigmiles & Associates, 1993.

Crocker, Henry. *History of the Baptists in Vermont.* Bellows Falls, Vt.: P. H. Gobie, 1913.

Douglass, Robert Sidney. *History of Missouri Baptists*. Kansas City, Mo.: Western Baptist, 1934.

Encyclopedia of Southern Baptists. 4 vols, including 2 supplements. Edited by Norman W. Cox. Nashville, Tenn.: Boardman, 1958, 1971, 1982.

Griffiths, Thomas Sharp. *A History of Baptists in New Jersey*. Hightstown, N.J.: Barr Press Publishing Co., 1904.

Hamby, Robert P. *Brief Baptist Biographies, 1707–1982*. Greenville, S.C.: A Press, 1982.

History of Baptist Churches in Maryland Connected with the Maryland Baptist Union Association. Baltimore: J. F. Weishampel, Jr., 1885.

History of the Baptist Denomination in Georgia: With Biographical Compendium and Portrait Gallery of Baptist Ministers and Other Georgia Baptists. Atlanta, Ga.: J. P. Harrison & Co., 1881.

Hurlin, William. *The Baptists of New Hampshire*. Manchester: New Hampshire Baptist Convention, 1902.

Masters, Frank M. *A History of Baptists in Kentucky*. Publications of the Kentucky Baptist Historical Society, no. 5. Louisville: Kentucky Baptist Historical Society, 1953.

Mattoon, Charles Hiram. *Baptist Annals of Oregon, 1844–1900*. 2 vols. McMinnville, Oreg.: Telephone Register Publishing Co., 1913.

McLaughlin, William G. *New England Dissent, 1630–1833: The Baptists and Separation of Church and State*. 2 vols. Cambridge: Harvard University Press, 1971.

Mitchell, S. H. *Historical Sketches of Iowa Baptists*. Burlington, Iowa: Burdette Co., 1886.

Pair, C. L. *A History of the Arizona Southern Baptist Convention, 1928–1984*. Commissioned by the Executive Board of the Arizona Southern Baptist Convention. Arizona Southern Baptist Convention, 1989.

Randolph, Corliss Fitz. *A History of the Seventh Day Baptists in West Virginia: Including the Woodridgetown and Salemville Churches in Pennsylvania and the Shrewsbury Church in New Jersey.* Plainfield, N.J.: American Sabbath Tract Society, 1905.

Rogers, J. S. *History of Arkansas Baptists*. Little Rock, Ark.: Executive Board of Arkansas Baptist State Convention, 1948. Includes a section of brief biographies of preachers and others.

Ryland, Garnett. *The Baptists of Virginia, 1699–1926*. Richmond: Virginia Baptist Board of Missions and Education, 1955.

Schroeder, Gustavus W. *History of the Swedish Baptists in Sweden and America: Being an Account of the Origin, Progress, and Results of That Missionary Work During the Last Century.* New York: the author, 1898.

Semple, Robert Baylor. *History of the Baptists in Virginia*. Revised and extended by G. W. Beale with a preface by Joe M. King. Cottonport, La.: Polyanthos, 1972. Originally published 1810.

Spencer, John H. *A History of Kentucky Baptists from 1769 to 1885, Including More Than 800 Biographical Sketches*. Cincinnati: J. R. Baumes, [1886].

Starr, Edward C. *A Baptist Bibliography, Being a Register of Printed Material by and about Baptists.* 25 vols. Rochester, N.Y.: American Baptist Historical Society, 1947–.

Townsend, Leah. *South Carolina Baptists, 1670–1805*. Florence, S.C.: Florence Printing Co., 1935.

Trowbridge, Mary Elizabeth Day. *History of Baptists in Michigan*. Philadelphia: Michigan Baptist State Convention, 1909.

Union List of Baptist Serials. Fort Worth, Tex., 1960.

Young, David, and Robert L. Taylor. *Death Notices from Freewill Baptist Publications 1811–1851*. Bowie, Md.: Heritage Books, 1985.

Yonts, Wesley. *History of Old Time Baptists in America.* Utica, Ky.: McDowell Publications, 1988.

Brethren

Blough, Jerome E. *History of the Church of Brethren of the Western District of Pennsylvania*. Elgin, Ill.: Brethren Publishing House, 1916.

Brechbill, Laban T. *History of the Old Order River Bretheren*. Brechbill & Strickler, 1972.

Church of the Brethren. Western District of Pennsylvania. *Two Centuries of the Church of the Brethren in Western Pennsylvania, 1751–1950*. Elgin, Ill.: Brethren Publishing House, 1953.

The Brethren Encyclopedia. 3 vols. Philadelphia: Brethren Encyclopedia, 1983–84.

Brumbaugh, Martin Grove. *A History of the German Baptist Brethren in Europe and America.* New York: AMS Press, 1971. Reprint of a previous edition (Mount Morris, Ill.: Brethren Publishing House, 1899).

Climenhaga, Asa W. *History of the Brethren in Christ Church.* Nappanee, Ind.: E. V. Publishing House, 1942.

Craik, Elmer LeRoy. *A History of the Church of the Brethern in Kansas*. McPherson, Kans.: the author, 1972.

Durnbaugh, Donald F. *The Brethren in Colonial America: A Source Book on the Transplantation and Development of the Church of the Brethern in the Eighteenth Century.* Elgin, Ill.: Brethren Press, 1967.

Hamer, Maryanna. *History of the Church of the Brethren on the Northern Plains*. N.p., 1977.

Heckman, John. *Brethren in Northern Illinois and Wisconsin*. Elgin, Ill.: Brethren Publishing House, 1941.

Henry, J. Maurice. *History of the Church of the Brethren in Maryland.* Elgin, Ill.: Brethren Publishing, 1936.

A History of the Church of the Brethren. Los Angeles: the church, 1917.

History of the Church of the Brethren in Indiana. By historical committees of the districts. Winona Lake, Ind.: Light and Life Press, 1952.

History of the Church of the Brethren of the Southern District of Ohio. Edited by Elder Jesse O. Garst. Dayton, Ohio: Otterbein Press, 1920.

Miller, D. L. *Some Who Led, or, Fathers in the Church of Brethren Who Have Passed Over*. Elgin, Ill.: Brethren Publishing House, 1912.

Rodabaugh, Willis P. *A History of the Church of the Brethren in Southern Iowa*. Elgin, Ill.: Brethren Publishing House, 1924.

Sappington, Roger Edwin. *The Brethren Along the Snake River: A History of the Church of the Brethren in Idaho and Western Montana.* Elgin, Ill.: Brethren Press, 1966.

Sappington, Roger Edwin. *The Brethren in Virginia: The History of the Church of the Brethren in Virginia.* Harrisonburg, Va.: Committee for Brethren History in Virginia, 1973.

Shuman, Herman. *Highlights and Heartaches of Brethren Pioneers, North Dakota, Minnesota, Wisconsin.* Pendleton, Ind.: the author, 1981.

Wilmore, Augustus Cleland. *History of the White River Conference of the Church of the United Brethren in Christ, Containing an Account of the Antecedent Annual Conferences*. Dayton, Ohio: United Brethren Publishing House, 1925.

Christian Church (Disciples of Christ)

Cauble, Commodore Wesley. *Disciples of Christ in Indiana: Achievements of a Century*. Indianapolis: Meigs Publishing, 1930. Also includes biographies.

The Christian-Evangelist Index 1863–1958. Nashville, Tenn.: Christian Board of Publication, St. Louis, Missouri, and the Disciples of Christ Historical Society, 1962.

Garrison, Winfred Ernest. *The Disciples of Christ: A History.* St. Louis: Bethany Press, 1958.

Hayden, A. S. *Early history of the Disciples in the Western Reserve, Ohio: With Biographical Sketches of the Principal Agents in Their Religious Movement*. Cincinnati: Chase & Hall, 1875.

Haynes, Nathaniel Smith. *History of the Disciples of Christ in Illinois, 1819–1914*. Cincinnati: Standard Publishing Co., 1915.

McAllister, Lester G. *Arkansas Disciples: A History of the Christian Church (Disciples of Christ) in Arkansas*. The author, 1984.

Shaw, Henry K. *Buckeye Disciples: A History of the Disciples of Christ in Ohio*. St. Louis: Christian Board of Publication, 1952.

Spencer, Claude E. *The Christian Evangelist Index.* St. Louis, Mo.: Christian Board of Education; Nashville, Tenn.: Disciples of Christ Historical Society, 1962.

The Church of Jesus Christ of Latter-day Saints (LDS Church)

Black, Susan Easton. *Membership ofThe Church of Jesus Christ of Latter-day Saints: 1830–1848*. 50 vols. Provo, Utah: Brigham Young University Religious Studies Center, 1989.

Encyclopedia of Mormonism: The History, Scripture, Doctrine, and Procedure of The Church of Jesus Christ of Latter-day Saints. 4 vols. New York: Macmillan, 1992.

Jenson, Andrew. *Encyclopedic History of The Church of Jesus Christ of Latter-day Saints*. Salt Lake City: Corp. of the Pres. of The Church of Jesus Christ of Latter-day Saints, 1941.

LDS Collector's Library. CD-ROM. Provo, Utah: Infobases, 1997.

LDS Family History Suite. CD-ROM. Provo, Utah: Infobases, 1996.

Episcopal (Protestant Episcopal)

Bentley, George R. *The Episcopal Diocese of Florida, 1892–1975.* With a foreword by Frank S. Cerveny. Gainesville: University of Florida Press, 1989.

Berrian, William. *An Historical Sketch of Trinity Church, New York*. Stanford and Swords, 1847. Contains a list of church officers associated with Trinity Church, founded in 1664.

Bolton, S. Charles. *Southern Anglicanism: The Church of England in Colonial South Carolina*. Westport, Conn.: Greenwood Press, 1982.

Breck, Allen duPont. *The Episcopal Church in Colorado, 1860–1963*. Denver: Big Mountain Press, 1963.

Beardsley, E. Edwards. *The History of the Episcopal Church in Connecticut*. New York: Hurd and Houghton, 1865.

The Church of England in Pre-Revolutionary Connecticut: New Documents and Letters Concerning the Loyalist Clergy and the Plight of Their Surviving Church. Edited by Kenneth Walter Cameron. Hartford, Conn.: Transcendental Books, 1976.

Clerical Directory of the Protestant Episcopal Church in the United States of America. New York: Church Hymnal Corporation, 1898–68.

Dalcho, Frederick. *An Historical Account of the Protestant Episcopal Church in South Carolina: From the First Settlement of the Province, to the War of the Revolution; with Notices of the Present State of the Church in Each Parish and Some Account of the Early Civil History of Carolina, Never Before Published.* Charleston, S.C.: E. Thayer, 1820.

Episcopal Church. Diocese of Maine. *One Hundredth Anniversary of the Diocese of Maine, 1820–1920: Christ Church, Gardiner, Maine, May Thirtieth to June Third*. Gardiner, Me.: the church, 1920.

Episcopal Church Annual (formerly the *Living Church Annual*). New York: Morehouse-Gorham, 1830–.

The Episcopal Church in North Carolina, 1701–1959. Edited by Lawrence Foushee London and Sarah McCulloh Lemmon. Raleigh, N.C.: Episcopal Diocese of North Carolina, 1987.

The Episcopal Diocese of Massachusetts, 1784–1984: A Mission to Remember, Proclaim, and Fulfill. Edited by Mark J. Duffy. [Boston]: Episcopal Diocese of Massachusetts, 1984.

Gray, Marcus Lemon. *1806–1906, the Centennial Volume of Missouri Methodism, Methodist Episcopal Church, South*. Kansas City, Mo.: Press of Burd & Fletcher, ca. 1907.

Hodges, George. *The Episcopal Church: Its Doctrine, Its Ministry, Its Discipline, Its Worship and Its Sacraments*. New York: Thomas Whittaker, 1892.

History of the American Episcopal Church from the Planting of the Colonies to the End of the Civil War. New York: Thomas Whittaker, 1890.

Jarvis, Lucy Cushing. *Sketches of Church Life in Colonial Connecticut: Being the Story of the Transplanting of the Church of England into Forty-Two Parishes of Connecticut, with the Assistance of the Society for the Propagation of the Gospel*. Written by members of the parishes in celebration of the two hundredth anniversary of the society. New Haven, Conn.: Tuttle, Morehouse & Taylor, 1902.

Malone, Henry Thompson. *The Episcopal Church in Georgia, 1733–1957*. Atlanta, Ga.: Protestant Episcopal Church in the Diocese of Atlanta, 1960.

McDonald, Margaret Simms. *White Already to Harvest: The Episcopal Church in Arkansas, 1838–1971*. Sewanee, Tenn.: Episcopal Diocese of Arkansas, 1975.

McDonnold, Benjamin Wilburn. *History of the Cumberland Presbyterian Church*. 2nd ed. Nashville, Tenn.: Board of Publication of Cumberland Presbyterian Church, 1888.

Painter, Bordon W. *The Anglican Vestry in Colonial America*. New Haven, Conn.: Yale University Press, 1965. The vestry exercised local government functions as well as church administrations. Vestry minutes for most of the Episcopal parishes in Virginia have been printed by the Virginia Historical Society.

Perry, William Stevens. *The Bishops of the American Church, Past and Present: Sketches, Biographical and Bibliographical, of the Bishops of the American Church, with a Preliminary Essay on the Historic Episcopate and Documentary Annals of the Introduction of the Anglican Line of Succession into America*. New York: Christian Literature Co., 1897.

Perry, William Stevens. *The History of the American Episcopal Church, 1587–1883*. 2 vols. Boston: James R. Osgood, 1885.

_____, ed. *Historical Collections Relating to the American Colonial Church* [Episcopal]. 5 vols. Hartford, Conn., 1870–78. Reprint. New York: AMS Press, 1969. Vol. 1, Virginia; vol. 2, Pennsylvania; vol. 3, Massachusetts; vol. 4, Maryland; vol. 5, Delaware.

Peterkin, George William. *A History and Record of the Protestant Episcopal Church in the Diocese of West Virginia: and Before the Formation of the Diocese in 1878, in the Territory Now Known as the State of West Virginia*. Charleston, W.Va.: Tribune Co., 1902.

Silliman, Charles A. *The Episcopal Church in Delaware, 1785–1954*. Wilmington: Diocese of Delaware, 1982.

Taylor, Blanche Mercer. *Plenteous Harvest: The Episcopal Church in Kansas, 1837–1972*. Prepared for the Diocese of Kansas by Blanche Mercer Taylor. The diocese, 1973.

Thomas, Albert Sidney. *A Historical Account of the Protestant Episcopal Church in South Carolina, 1820–1957: Being a Continuation of Dalcho's Account, 1670–1820*. Columbia, S.C., 1957.

Wilson, James Grant. *The Centennial History of the Protestant Episcopal Church in the Diocese of New York, 1785–1885*. New York: D. Appleton & Co., 1886.

Huguenot

Baird, Charles Washington. *History of the Huguenot Emigration to America*. Baltimore: Genealogical Publishing Co., 1973. Reprint of an 1885 edition published by Dodd, Mead of New York.

Brock, R. A. *Documents, Chiefly Unpublished, Relating to the Huguenot Emigration to Virginia and to the Settlement at Manakin-Town, with an Appendix of Genealogies, Presenting Data of the Fontaine, Maury, Dupuy, Trabue, Marye, Chastain, Cocke, and Other Families*. Reprint. Baltimore: Genealogical Publishing Co., 1962.

Cobb, Georgia Nellie Chandler. *Register of Huguenot Ancestors*. Washington, D.C.: National Huguenot Society, 1975.

Currer-Briggs, Noel. *Huguenot Ancestry*. Chichester, Sussex, England: Phillimore, 1985.

Gannon, Peter Steven. *Huguenot Refugees in the Settling of Colonial America*. New York: Huguenot Society of America, 1985.

Goree, Langston James. *Master Index to The Huguenot: The Biennial Publications of the Huguenot Society, Founders of Manakin in the Colony of Virginia, and, Index to Vestry Book of King William Parish, Virginia, 1707–1750*. Bryan, Tex.: Family History Foundation, 1986.

Harris, Nancy E. *National Directory and Ancestor Index*. 2 vols. Bloomington, Minn.: National Huguenot Society Headquarters, 1995.

Hill, Glenna See. *Huguenot Ancestors Documented by the Huguenot Society of New Jersey, Inc*. Bloomfield, N.J.: Huguenot Society of New Jersey, 1975.

Lee, Hannah Farnham Sawyer. *The Huguenots in France and America*. 2 vols. Cambridge: J. Owen, 1843.

Reeve, Vera. *Register of Qualified Huguenot Ancestors of the National Huguenot Society*. Reprint with corrections of the 1983 third edition compiled by Vera Reeve. Bloomington, Minn.: National Huguenot Society, 1993.

Lutheran

American Lutheran Church. *American Lutheran Church Shelf List Index to Their Church Records Microfilmed as of 1987*. N.p., 1988.

Bernheim, G. D. *History of the German Settlements and of the Lutheran Church in North and South Carolina: From the Earliest Period of the Colonization of the Dutch, German and Swiss Settlers to the Close of the First Half of the Present Century*. Philadelphia: Lutheran Book Store, 1872.

Bodensieck, Julius, ed. *The Encyclopedia of the Lutheran Church*. 3 vols. Minneapolis: Augsburg Publishing House, 1965.

Cassell, C. W. *History of the Lutheran Church in Virginia and East Tennessee*. Published by the authority of the Lutheran Synod of Virginia. Strasburg, Va.: Shenandoah Publishing House, 1930.

Confessional Lutheran Migrations to America, 150th Anniversary. [Buffalo, N.Y.]: Eastern District of the Lutheran Church, Missouri Synod, 1988.

Craig, Peter Stebbins. *The 1693 Census of the Swedes on the Delaware: Family Histories of the Swedish Lutheran Church Members Residing in Pennsylvania, Delaware, West New Jersey and Cecil County, Md., 1638–1693*. Winter Park, Fla.: SAG Publications, 1993.

Finck, William J. *Lutheran Landmarks and Pioneers in America: A Series of Sketches of Colonial Times*. 3rd ed. Philadelphia: United Lutheran Publication House, 1913.

Holcomb, Brent. *Marriage and Death Notices from the Lutheran Observer, 1831–1861, and the Southern Lutheran, 1861–1865.* Easley, S.C.: Southern Historical Press, 1979.

Kreider, Harry Julius. *History of the United Lutheran Synod of New York and New England.* Philadelphia: Muhlenberg Press, 1954.

Lueker, Erwin L., ed. *Lutheran Cyclopedia.* St. Louis: Concordia, 1975.

The Lutheran Yearbook of the Evangelical Lutheran Church. Minneapolis, Minn.: Augsburg Publishing House, 1949–.

Evangelical Lutheran Church in America. *Biographical Directory of Clergy.* Minneapolis: Augsburg Publishing House/ Fortress Press, 1988.

History of the Evangelical Lutheran Synod of South Carolina, 1824–1924. Edited by S. T. Hallman. Columbia, S.C.: Evangelical Lutheran Synod of South Carolina, [1924].

Lutheran Church Missouri Synod Statistical Yearbook. St. Louis, Mo.: Concordia Publishing House, 1984–. Annual.

Matteson, Jean M. *Blossoms of the Prairie: The History of the Danish Lutheran Churches in Nebraska.* Lincoln, Nebr.: Blossoms of the Prairie, 1988.

Schmauk, Theodore E. *A History of the Lutheran Church in Pennsylvania, 1638–1820, from Original Sources.* Lancaster: Pennsylvania German Society, 1903.

United Evangelical Lutheran Synod of North Carolina. *History of the Lutheran Church in North Carolina.* United Evangelical Lutheran Synod of North Carolina, 1953.

Weiser, Frederick Sheely. *Maryland German Church Records.* 11 vols. to date. Manchester, Md.: Noodle-Doosey Press, 1986–.

_____. *Daniel Schumacher's Baptismal Register.* Publications of the Pennsylvania German Society, vol. 1. Allentown: Pennsylvania German Society, 1968. Reprinted with corrections by the same author as *The Record Book of Daniel Schumacher, 1754–1773.* Rockport, Maine: Picton Press, 1994.

Wentz, Abdel Ross. *History of the Evangelical Lutheran Synod of Maryland of the United Lutheran Church in America, 1820–1920: Together with a Brief Sketch of Each Congregation of the Synod and Biographies of the Living Sons of the Synod in the Ministry.* Evangelical Lutheran Synod of Maryland, 1920.

Mennonites (including Anabaptist, Amish, and Hutterite)

Clark, Allen B. *This is Good Country: A History of the Amish of Delaware, 1915–1988.* Gordonville, Pa.: Gordonville Print Shop, 1989. Revised edition of *History of the Amish of Delaware,* 1963.

Giesbrecht, Herbert. *Mennonite Brethren Church: Bibliographical Guide.* 2nd ed. Fresno, Calif.: Board of Christian Literature, General Conference of Mennonite Brethren Churches, 1983.

Gingerich, Hugh F., and Rachel W. Kreider. *Amish and Amish Mennonite Genealogies.* Gordonville, Pa.: Pequea Publishers, 1986.

Gingerich, Melvin. *The Mennonites in Iowa: Marking the One Hundredth Anniversary of the Coming of the Mennonites to Iowa.* Iowa City: State Historical Society of Iowa, 1939.

Graber, Arthur. *Swiss Mennonite Ancestors and Their Relationship from 1775.* Freeman, S.D.: Pine Hill Press, 1980.

Gratz, Delbert L. *Bernese Anabaptists and Their American Descendants.* Studies in Anabaptist and Mennonite history, no. 8. Scottdale, Pa.: Herald Press, 1953.

Guth, Hermann. *Palatine Mennonite Census Lists, 1664–1793.* Elverson, Pa.: Mennonite Family History, 1987.

Haury, David A. *Index to Mennonite Immigrants on United States Passenger Lists, 1872–1904.* North Newton, Kans.: Mennonite Library and Archives, 1986.

Hostetler, John Andrew. *Amish Society.* Rev. ed. Baltimore: Johns Hopkins University Press, 1968.

_____. *Hutterite Society.* Baltimore: John Hopkins University Press, 1974.

Hutterite Centennial Steering Committee. *Hutterite Roots.* Freeman, S.D.: Pine Hill Press, n.d.

Lind, Hope Kauffman. *Apart and Together: Mennonites in Oregon and Neighboring States, 1876–1976.* Studies in Anabaptist and Mennonite History, no. 30. Scottdale, Pa.: Herald Press, 1990.

McKee, Wilma. *Growing Faith: General Conference Mennonites in Oklahoma.* Mennonite Historical Series. Newton, Kans.: Faith and Life Press, 1988.

The Mennonite Encyclopedia: A Comprehensive Reference Work on the Anabaptist-Mennonite Movement. 4 vols. Hillsboro, Kan.: Mennonite Brethren Publishing House, 1955–59.

Mennonite Yearbook and Directory. Vol. 1 [1911]. Scottdale, Pa.: Mennonite Publishing House, 1990.

Plett, Delbert F. *Pioneers and Pilgrims: The Mennonite Kleine Gemeinde in Manitoba, Nebraska, and Kansas, 1874 to 1882.* Steinbach, Manitoba: D. F. P. Publications, 1990.

Stucky, Harley J. *The Swiss (Volhynian) Mennonite ship list, 1874, of the Immigrants Who Came from Russia.* North Newton, Kans.: Swiss Mennonite Cultural and Historical Association, 1974.

Toews, John A. *A History of the Mennonite Brethren Church: Pilgrims and Pioneers.* Fresno, Calif.: Board of Christian Literature, General Conference of Mennonite Brethren, 1975.

Unrau, Ruth. *Index to Obituaries in the Mennonite Weekly Review, 1924–1955* and *1924–1990.* 2 vols. North Newton, Kans.: Bethel College, 1989, 1991.

Who's Who Among the Mennonites. North Newton, Kans.: Bethel College Press, 1943.

Zionsbote Index. 4 vols. Fresno, Calif.: Center for Mennonite Brethren Studies, Board of Christian Literature of the General Conference of Mennonite Brethren Churches, 1984.

Methodists (including German Methodists)

Allen, Stephen. *History of Methodism in Maine, 1793–1886.* 2 vols. in 1. Augusta, Maine: Charles E. Nash, 1887.

Atkinson, John. *Memorials of Methodism in New Jersey: From the Foundation of the First Society in the State in 1770, to the Completion of the First Twenty Years of its History Containing Sketches of Ministerial Laborers, Distinguished Laymen and Prominent Societies of That Period.* 2nd ed. Philadelphia: Perkinpine & Higgins, 1860.

Batsel, John D., and Lyda K. Batsel. *Union List of United Methodist Serials, 1773–1973.* Evanston, Ill., 1974. The most complete compilation available of the journals published by the various denominations which merged to form the United Methodist Church in 1968.

Bumgarner, George W. *Methodist Episcopal Church in North Carolina, 1865–1939.* Winston-Salem, N.C.: Hunter Publishing, 1990.

Chreitzberg, A. M. *Early Methodism in the Carolinas.* Nashville, Tenn.: Publishing House of the Methodist Episcopal Church, South, 1897. Reprint. The Reprint Co., 1972.

Conable, Francis W. *History of the Genesee Annual Conference of the Methodist Episcopal Church: from Its Organization by Bishops Asbury and M'Kendree in 1810, to the Year 1872.* New York: Nelson & Phillips, 1876. Includes an alphabetical list of conference members.

Finley, James Bradley. *Sketches of Western Methodism: Biographical, Historical and Miscellaneous, Illustrative of Pioneer Life.* Cincinnatti: Methodist Book Concern, 1856.

Fox, Henry J. *Fox and Hoyt's Quadrennial Register of the Methodist Episcopal Church and Universal Church Gazetteer.* Hartford, Conn.: Case, Tiffany & Co., 1852.

Harmon, Nolan B., ed. *The Encyclopedia of World Methodism.* 2 vols. Prepared and edited under the supervision of the World Methodist Council and the Commission on Archives and History. Nashville, Tenn.: United Methodist Publishing House, 1974.

_____. *Understanding the Methodist Church.* Rev. ed. Nashville, Tenn.: Methodist Publishing House, 1961.

Heller, Herbert L. *Indiana Conference of the Methodist Church, 1832–1956.* Indiana, 1956.

Hobart, Chauncey. *History of Methodism in Minnesota.* Minnesota Annual Conference, 1887. Reprint. Brooklyn Park, Minn.: Park Genealogical Books, 1992.

Holliday, F. C. *Indiana Methodism, Being an Account of the Introduction, Progress, and Present Position of Methodism in the State: And Also a History of the Literary Institutions Under the Care of the Church with Sketches of the Principal Methodist Educators in the State, Down to 1872.* Cincinnati: Hitchcock and Walden, 1873.

Kern, Charles W. *God, Grace, and Granite: The history of Methodism in New Hampshire, 1768–1988.* Canaan, N.H.: Published for the New Hampshire United Methodist Conference by Phoenix Publishing, 1988.

Little, Brooks R. *Methodist Union Catalog of History, Biography, Disciplines, and Hymnals.* Lake Junalaska, N.C.: Association of Methodist Historical Societies, 1967.

Loofbourow, Leonidas Latimer. *Cross in the Sunset: The Development of Methodism in the California-Nevada Annual Conference of the Methodist Church, and of Its Predecessors with Roster of All Members of the Conference.* San Francisco: Historical Society of the California-Nevada Annual Conference of the Methodist Church, 1966.

Macmillan, Margaret Burnham. *The Methodist Church in Michigan: The Nineteenth Century.* Grand Rapids, Mich.: W. B. Eerdmans Publishing Co., 1967.

Melton, J. Gordon. *Log Cabins to Steeples: The Complete Story of the United Methodist Way in Illinois Including All Constituent Elements of The United Methodist Church.* Commissions on Archives and History, Northern, Central and Southern Illinois Conferences, 1974.

Mills, Edward Laird. *Plains, Peaks and Pioneers: Eighty Years of Methodism in Montana.* Portland, Oreg.: Binfords & Mort, 1947.

Moore, M. H. (Matthew H.). *Sketches of the Pioneers of Methodism in North Carolina and Virginia.* Nashville, Tenn.: Southern Methodist Publishing House, 1884.

Norwood, Frederick A. *The Story of American Methodism.* Nashville: Abingdon Press, 1975.

Redford, A. H. *The History of Methodism in Kentucky.* 3 vols. Nashville, Tenn.: Southern Methodist Publishing, 1868–70.

Rowe, Kenneth E., ed. *Methodist Union Catalog Pre-1976 Imprints.* Vols. 1–6. Metuchen, N.J., and London: Scarecrow Press, 1976.

Seder, Mrs. A. R. *Index to the Subjects of Obituaries (Sterbfälle, Todesanzeigen): Abstracted from Der Christliche Botschafter, 1836–1866.* Naperville, Ill.: the author, 1967.

Simpson, Matthew. *Cyclopaedia of Methodism: Embracing Sketches of its Rise, Progress, and Present Condition, with Biographical Notices and Numerous Illustrations.* Rev. ed. Philadelphia: Louis H. Everts, 1880.

Smith, George G. *The History of Methodism in Georgia and Florida: From 1785 to 1865.* Macon, Ga.: John W. Burke & Co., 1877.

Smith, John L. *Indiana Methodism: A Series of Sketches and Incidents, Grave and Humorous Concerning Preachers and People of the West; with an Appendix Containing Personal Recollections, Public Addresses and Other Miscellany.* Valparaiso, Ind.: J. L. Smith, 1892.

Todd, Robert W. *Methodism of the Peninsula, or, Sketches of Notable Characters and Events in the History of Methodism in the Maryland and Delaware Peninsula.* Introduction by Bishop John F. Hurst. Philadelphia: Methodist Episcopal Book Rooms, 1886.

Tucker, Frank C. *The Methodist Church in Missouri: 1798–1939, a Brief History.* The author, 1966.

Waring, Edmund H. *History of the Iowa Annual Conference of the Methodist Episcopal Church: Including the Planting and Progress of the Church Within Its Limits, from 1833 to 1909.* N.p., n.d.

Moravian Church

Beaucharus, William M., ed. *Moravian Journals Relating to Central New York, 1745–1766.* Syracuse, N.Y.: Dehter Press, 1916.

Hutton, J. E. *A History of the Moravian Church.* 2nd ed., rev. and enl. London: Moravian Publication Office, 1909.

Fries, Adelaide L., ed. *Records of the Moravians in North Carolina 1752–1879.* 11 vols. Raleigh, N.C.: Edwards and Broughton Printing Co., 1922–69.

Moravian Journals Relating to Central New York, 1745–66. Syracuse, N.Y.: Dehler Press, 1916.

Neisser, Georg. *A History of the Beginnings of Moravian Work in America.* Translated by William N. Schwarze and Samuel H. Gapp. Bethlehem, Pa.: Archives of the Moravian Church, 1955.

Reichel, Levin Theodore. *The Early History of the Church of the United Brethren (Unitas Fratrum) Commonly Called Moravians, in North America, A.D. 1734–1748.* Transactions of the Moravian Historical Society, vol. 3. Nazareth, Pa.: Moravian Historical Society, 1888.

Russell, George Ely. *Moravian Families of Carroll's Manor, Frederick County, Maryland.* Middletown, Md.: Catoctin Press, 1989.

Presbyterian

Albaugh, Gordon. "American Presbyterian Periodicals and Newspapers, 1752–1830, with Library Locations." *Journal of Presbyterian History* 41–42 (September 1963–June 1964).

Campbell, Thomas H., et al. *Arkansas Cumberland Presbyterians, 1812–1984: A People of Faith.* Memphis, Tenn.: Arkansas Synod Cumberland Presbyterian Church, 1985.

Associate Reformed Synod of the South. *The Centennial History of the Associate Reformed Presbyterian Church, 1803–1903.* Charleston, S.C.: Presses of Walker, Evans and Cogswell, 1905.

Barrus, Ben M. *A people Called Cumberland Presbyterians.* Memphis, Tenn.: Cumberland Presbyterian Church, 1972.

Beecher, Willis J. *Index of Presbyterian Ministers, Containing the Names of All the Ministers of the Presbyterian Church in the United States of America: With References to the Pages on Which Those Names are Found in its Records and Minutes, from A.D. 1706 to A.D. 1881.* Philadelphia: Presbyterian Board of Publication, 1883, 1888.

Edgington, Frank E. *A History of the New York Avenue Presbyterian Church: One Hundred Fifty-Seven Years, 1803–1961.* Washington, D.C.: New York Avenue Presbyterian Church, 1961.

Edson, Hanford A. *Contributions to the Early History of the Presbyterian Church in Indiana: Together with Biographical Notices of the Pioneer Ministers.* Cincinnati: Winona Publishing Co., 1898.

Edwards, Maurice Dwight. *History of the Synod of Minnesota, Presbyterian Church U.S.A.* St. Paul, Minn.: Webb Printing, 1912.

Howe, George. *History of the Presbyterian Church in South Carolina.* 2 vols. Columbia, S.C.: Duffie & Chapman, 1870, 1883

Glasgow, William Melancthan. *Cyclopedic Manual of the United Presbyterian Church of North America: Comprising a Brief History of Her Ancestral Branches, Ministry, Congregations, Institutions, Courts, Boards, Missions, Periodicals. . . .* Pittsburgh: United Presbyterian Board of Publication, 1903.

______. *History of the Reformed Presbyterian Church of America.* Baltimore: Hill and Harvey, 1888.

Kelsey, Hugh Alexander. *The United Presbyterian Directory, a Half-Century Survey, 1903–1958.* Pittsburgh: Pickwick Press, [1958].

Klett, Guy Soulliard. *Presbyterians in Colonial Pennsylvania.* Philadelphia: University of Pennsylvania Press, 1937.

Kurtz, Grace W. *The Story of the Fourth Presbyterian Church of Washington D.C., Bethesda, Maryland: A Past to Remember—a Future to Mold.* South Hackensack, N.J.: Custombook, 1978.

Logan, J. B. *History of the Cumberland Presbyterian Church in Illinois, Containing Sketches of the First Ministers, Churches, Presbyteries and Synods; also a History of Missions, Publication and Education.* Alton, Ill.: Perrin & Smith, 1878. The sketches are biographical and historical in nature.

Nevin, Alfred. *Encyclopaedia of the Presbyterian Church in the United States of America: Including the Northern and Southern Assemblies.* Philadelphia: Presbyterian Encyclopaedia Publishing Co., 1884.

One Hundred Years of the Iowa Presbyterian Church. Cedar Rapids, Iowa: Laurance Press Co., n.d.

Rudolph, L. C. *Hoosier Zion: The Presbyterians in Early Indiana.* New Haven: Yale University Press, 1963.

Stacy, James. *A History of the Presbyterian Church in Georgia.* Completed and edited by C. I. Stacy. Elverton, Ga.: Press of the Star, 1912.

Thompson, Ernest Trice. *Presybterians in the South.* 3 vols. Richmond: John Knox Press, 1963–73.

Union Catalog of Presbyterian Manuscripts. Presbyterian Library Association, 1964. Lists Presbyterian and Reformed records.

Webster, Richard. *A History of the Presbyterian Church in America: From Its Origin Until the Year 1760. With Biographical Sketches of Its Early Ministers.* Philadelphia: Joseph M. Wilson, 1857.

White, Henry Alexander. *Southern Presbyterian Leaders.* New York: Neale Publishing Co., 1911.

Wicher, Edward Arthur. *The Presbyterian Church in California, 1849–1927.* New York: F. H. Hitchcock, 1927.

Wilson, Howard McKnight. *The Lexington Presbytery Heritage.* Verona, Va.: McClure Press, 1971.

______. *Records of the Synod of Virginia on Microfilm.* Richmond: Synod of Virginia, 1970.

Quakers (Society of Friends)

Anscombe, Francis Charles. *I Have Called You Friends: The Story of Quakerism in North Carolina.* Boston: Christopher Publishing House, 1959.

Berry, Ellen Thomas. *Our Quaker Ancestors: Finding Them in Quaker Records.* Baltimore: Genealogical Publishing Co., 1987.

Burton, Ann Mullin. *Michigan Quakers: Abstracts of Fifteen Meetings of the Society of Friends, 1831–1960.* Decatur, Mich.: Glyndwr Resources, 1989.

Finding Friends Around the World: Handbook of the Religious Society of Friends (Quakers). London: Friends World Committee for Consultation, 1988.

Hamm, Thomas D. *The Transformation of American Quakerism: Orthodox Friends, 1800–1907.* Religion in North America. Bloomington: Indiana University Press, 1988, 1992.

Heiss, Willard. *Abstracts of the Records of the Society of Friends in Indiana, Part One through Six (1962–1975) with Index.* 6 vols. Indianapolis: Indiana Historical Society, 1962–77. Published as vol. 7 of William Wade Hinshaw and Thomas Worth Marshall's *Encyclopedia of American Quaker Genealogy* by the Indiana Historical Society under the above title.

_____. "American Quaker Records and Family History." Vol. 4 of *North American Family and Local History,* part 2, series 358. Salt Lake City: Church of Jesus Christ of Latter-day Saints, 1980.

_____. *Quakers in the South Carolina Back Country, Wateree and Bush River.* Indianapolis: Indiana Quaker Records, 1969.

Hinshaw, William Wade. *Encyclopedia of American Quaker Genealogy.* Edited and compiled by Thomas Worth Marshall. Ann Arbor, Mich.: Edwards Brothers, 1936–50. Reprint. Baltimore: Genealogical Publishing Co., 1969. Vol. 1, North Carolina Yearly Meeting of Friends; vol. 2, Philadelphia Yearly Meeting of Friends; vol. 3, New York City and on Long Island; vol. 4, Ohio Yearly Meetings: Wilbur and Gurney Branches; vol. 5, Wilmington Yearly Meeting, Clinton Co., Ohio, and Indiana Yearly Meeting, Richmond, Indiana; vol. 6, Virginia Yearly Meeting and Baltimore Yearly Meeting.

_____. *The William Wade Hinshaw New Jersey Quaker Meeting Records.* 4 vols. Kokomo, Ind.: Selby Publishing and Printing, 1990.

Ingle, H. Larry. *Quakers in Conflict: The Hicksite Reformation.* Knoxville: University of Tennessee Press, 1986.

Janney, Samuel M. *History of the Religious Society of Friends, from Its Rise to the Year 1828.* 4 vols. Philadelphia: T. Ellwood Zell, 1861.

Jones, Louis Thomas. *The Quakers of Iowa.* Iowa City: State Historical Society, 1914.

Quaker Necrology. Haverford College Library, Haverford, Pennsylvania. 2 vols. Boston: G. K. Hall and Co., 1961.

Rhode Island Quakers in the American Revolution, 1775–1790. Providence, R.I.: Published for Providence Monthly Meeting of Friends, 1977.

Thomas, Allen Clapp. *A History of the Friends in America.* Pennsbury Series of Modern Quaker Books. 5th ed., rev. and enl. Philadelphia: John C. Winston Co., 1919.

Wetherill, Charles. *History of the Religious Society of Friends Called by Some Free Quakers, Living in the City of Philadelphia.* Philadelphia, 1894. Includes a list of members who are known or believed to be deceased and a list of present (as of 1894) members (mainly from Pennsylvania, but also from Louisiana, Maryland, Missouri, New Jersey, and New York).

Reformed (Dutch Reformed)

Bready, Guy P. *History of Maryland Classis of the Reformed Church in the United States: Or, the History of the Reformed Church in Maryland since 1820.* Taneytown, Md.: Carroll Record Print, 1983.

Brown, W. D. *History of the Reformed Church in America.* New York: Board of Publication of the Reformed Church in America, 1928.

Collections of the New York Genealogical and Biographical Society, Records of the Reformed Dutch Church in New Amsterdam and New York. Edited by Samuel S. Purple, Thomas Grier Evans, and Tobias Alexander Wright. New York, 1902. Reprint. Upper Saddle River, N.J.: Gregg Press, 1968.

Corwin, Edward Tanjore. *A Manual of the Reformed Church in America (Formerly Ref. Prot. Dutch Church), 1628–1902.* 4th ed. Rev. and enl. New York: Board of Publication of the Reformed Church in America, 1902.

De Jong, Gerald F. *The Dutch Reformed Church in the American Colonies.* Historical Series of the Reformed Church in America, no. 5. Grand Rapids, Mich.: Wm. B. Eerdmans Publishing Co., 1978.

Gasero, Russell L. *Historical Directory of the Reformed Church in America, 1628–1992.* Historical Series of the Reformed Church in America, no. 23. Grand Rapids, Mich.: Wm. B. Eerdmans Publishing Co., 1992.

Good, James Isaac. *History of the Reformed Church in the United States, 1725–1792.* Reading, Pa.: Daniel Miller, 1899.

Harmelink, Herman, 3rd. *The Reformed Church in New Jersey.* Woodcliff-on-Hudson, N.J.: Synod of New Jersey, 1969.

The Holland Society of New York Index to Publications 1885. Edited by Louis Duermyer. New York: Holland Society, 1977.

Meeter, Melody Takken. *Guide to Local Church Records in the Archives of the Reformed Church in America and to Genealogical Resources in the Gardner Sage Library.* New Brunswick, N.J.: New Brunswick Theological Seminary, 1979.

Reformed Church in America. Commission on History. *Historical Directory of the Reformed Church in America, 1628–1965.* New Brunswick, N.J.: Reformed Church in America, Commission on History, 1966. Successor to C. E. Corwin's *A manual of the Reformed Church in America 1628–1922,* 5th ed. (1922).

Tilton, Edgar. *The Reformed Low Dutch Church of Harlem, Organized 1660: Historical Sketch.* New York: Consistory, 1910.

Roman Catholic

The American Catholic Who's Who. St. Louis: B. Herder, 1911–81.

Baudier, Roger, 1893. *The Catholic Church in Louisiana.* New Orleans: Louisiana Library Association, Public Library Section, 1972.

Blanchard, Charles. *History of the Catholic Church in Indiana.* Logansport, Ind.: A. W. Bowen & Co., 1898.

Casper, Henry Weber. *History of the Catholic Church in Nebraska.* Milwaukee: Catholic Life Publications, 1960–66.

Catholic Baptisms in Western Pennsylvania, 1799–1828. Baltimore: Genealogical Publishing Co., 1985.

The Catholic Church in America: An Historical Bibliography. New Brunswick, N.J.: Scarecrow Press, 1956.

Cross, Crozier and Crucible: A Volume Celebrating the Bicentennial of a Catholic Diocese in Louisiana. New Orleans: Archdiocese of New Orleans, 1993.

Cullen, Thomas Francis. *The Catholic Church in Rhode Island.* North Providence, R.I.: Franciscan Missionaries of Mary, 1936.

Curran, Francis X., S.J. *Catholics in Colonial Law*. Chicago: Loyola University Press, 1965.

Delaney, John J. *Dictionary of American Catholic Biography*. Garden City, N.Y.: Doubleday, 1984.

Denissen, Rev. Fr. Christian. *Genealogy of the French Families of the Detroit River Region.* 2 vols. Rev. ed. Detroit: Detroit Society for Genealogical Research, 1987.

Elder, Benedict, et al. *American Catholic Who's Who*. Washington, D.C.: National Catholic News Service. Irregular.

Ellis, John Tracy. *Catholics in Colonial America*. Baltimore: Helicon Press, 1963.

Hayman, Robert W. *Catholicism in Rhode Island, and the Diocese of Providence, 1780–1886*. Diocese of Providence, 1982.

Humling, Virginia. *U.S. Catholic Sources: A Diocesan Research Guide*. Salt Lake City: Ancestry, 1995.

The New Catholic Encyclopedia. 14 vols. 2 supplements. New York: McGraw Hill Book Co., 1967, 1974, 1979.

Noel, Thomas J. *Colorado Catholicism and the Archdiocese of Denver, 1857–1989.* Introduction by J. Francis Stafford. University Press of Colorado, 1989.

O'Connell, Jeremiah J. *Catholicity in the Carolinas and Georgia: Leaves of Its History*. New York: D. & J. Sadlier, 1879. Reprint. Spartanburg, S.C.: Reprint Co., 1972.

The Official Catholic Directory. Chicago: Hoffman Bros., [1886–]. Annual. Title and publisher vary. Currently published by P. J. Kenedy (Wilmette, Illinois). Earlier issues are worldwide in coverage; current issues primarily cover the United States.

O'Hara, Edwin V. *Pioneer Catholic History of Oregon*. Centennial ed. Paterson, N.J.: St. Anthony Guild Press, 1939.

Vollman, Edward R., S.J. *The Catholic Church in America: An Historical Bibliography*. New York: Scarecrow Press, 1972.

Warner, Mikell De Lores Wormell, and Harriet Duncan Munnick. *Catholic Church Records of the Pacific Northwest*. 7 vols. St. Paul, Oreg.: French Prairie Press, 1972–89.

Willging, Eugene P., and Herta Hatzfeld. *Catholic Serials of the Nineteenth Century in the United States: A Descriptive Bibliography and Union List.* Washington, D.C., 1966–. This series consists of individual volumes for the various states—Wisconsin (1960), Illinois (1961), Ohio and Kentucky (1966), and others. It supersedes all previous bibliographies concerning Catholic journalism.

Unitarian Universalist

Bull, Elias B. *Founders and pew renters of the Unitarian Church in Charleston, S.C., 1817–1874*. Charleston: Unitarian Church in Charleston, S.C., Press, 1970.

MacDonald, Edith Fox. *Rebellion in the Mountains: The story of Universalism and Unitarianism in Vermont.* Concord, N.H.: New Hampshire Vermont District of the Unitarian Universalist Association, 1976.

Wright, Conrad. *The Beginnings of Unitarianism in America*. Boston: Beacon Press, 1955.

United Church of Christ (Congregational and German Reformed)

Atkins, G. G. *History of American Congregationalism*. Boston: Pilgrim Press, 1942.

Bailey, Frederic W., ed. *Early Connecticut Marriages as Found on Ancient Church Records Prior to 1800*. 7 vols. in 1. Reprint. Baltimore: Genealogical Publishing Co., 1968.

Bricker, Florence M. *Church and Pastoral Records in the Archives of the United Church and the Evangelical and Reformed Historical Society.* Lancaster, Pa., n.d.

Bullock, Motier Acklin. *Congregational Nebraska*. N.p., 1905.

The Congregational Year-Book. Boston: Congregational Publishing Society, 1879–1928. Published from 1923 to 1928 in New York by the National Council of Congregational Churches.

Dunn, David. *A History of the Evangelical and Reformed Church*. Philadelphia: Christian Education Press, 1961. Reprint with new introduction. New York: Pilgrim Press, 1990.

Congregational Work of Minnesota 1832–1920. Edited and partly written by Warren Upham. Minneapolis: Congregational Conference of Minnesota, 1921.

Correll, Charles M. *A Century of Congregationalism in Kansas, 1854–1954*. 1st ed. Topeka.: Kansas Congregational and Christian Conference, 1953.

Dexter, Frank N. *A Hundred Years of Congregational History in Wisconsin*. Fond Du Lac: Wisconsin Congregation Conference, 1933.

Dunning, Albert Elijah. *Congregationalists in America: A Popular History of Their Origin, Belief, Policy, Growth and Work.* Boston: Pilgrim Press, 1894.

Eisenach, George J. *A History of the German Congregational Churches in the United States*. Yankton, S.D.: Pioneer Press, 1938.

Evangelical and Reformed Historical Society. *Church and Pastoral Records in the Archives of the United Church of Christ and the Evangelical and Reformed Historical Society, Lancaster, Pa.*. Lancaster, Pa.: Evangelical and Reformed Historical Society, 1982.

Fiske, Jane Fletcher, ed. *Index of Persons in the New England Historical and Genealogical Register, Volumes 51 through 148*. 4 vols. Boston: New England Historic Genealogical Society, 1995.

Historical Collections of the Essex Institute. Salem, Mass.: Essex Institute, 1859–.

Johnson, P. Adelstein. *The First Century of Congregationalism in Iowa, 1840–1940*. Congregational Christian Conference of Iowa, 1945.

Manning, Barbara. *Genealogical Abstracts from Newspapers of the German Reformed Church 1830–1839 and 1840–1843.* Bowie, Md.: Heritage Books, 1992, 1995.

Miller, Daniel. *Early History of the Reformed Church in Pennsylvania*. Introduction by W. J. Hinke. Reading, Pa.: the author, 1906.

Taylor, Richard H. *The Congregational Churches of the West.* Benton Harbor, Mich.: the author, 1992.

Walker, Williston. *A History of the Congregational Churches in the United States*. New York: Scribner's, 1894, 1916.

Yearbook (United Church of Christ). New York: United Church of Christ, 1962–. Continued as the *Year Book of the Congregational Christian Church* and the *Year Book of the Evangelical and Reformed Church*.

CENSUSES AND TAX LISTS OVERVIEW

Key Concepts in This Chapter

- Census indexes help locate ancestors about whom very little is known.
- Types of census indexes include heads-of-households indexes and every-name indexes.
- Census indexes are available for national, state, region, county, and local levels.
- Ninety-nine percent of existing Federal censuses from 1790 to 1900 are at least partially indexed.
- Nationwide and regional indexes assist in finding persons even when their home states are unknown.
- CD-ROM census indexes offer some advantages over book indexes.
- Countywide census and tax list indexes are important but are often overlooked.
- Catalogs and periodical indexes can identify countywide indexes.
- Colonial, territorial, state, and special census indexes help fill gaps between Federal censuses.
- Tax records can substitute for censuses.
- Both census takers and census indexers made errors that cause researchers to overlook some names.
- With effort, researchers can find up to 97 percent of the names which should be in an index.
- Approximately 44 percent of state indexes are duplicated by competing indexes; duplicate indexes can be used to overcome index omissions.

Key Census Indexes

- *AIS Microfiche Indexes of U.S. Census and Other Records*
- *Master Name Index to Automated Archives, Inc. CD-ROMs* on CD-ROM for MS-DOS
- Family Tree Maker's Family Archives *Census Index: U.S. Selected States/Counties* series on CD-ROM
- Family Tree Maker's *Family Finder Index and Viewer* on CD-ROM for Windows

Key Census Index and Tax List Finding Tools

- *Family History Library Catalog*™
- Family History Library state research outlines
- *Periodical Source Index* (*PERSI*)
- *Map Guide to the U.S. Federal Censuses, 1790–1920*

Major Census Index Publishers

- Accelerated Indexing Systems
- Brøderbund Software, Banner Blue division (formerly Automated Archives)
- Genealogical Publishing Company
- Precision Indexing and Index Publishing

9

CENSUSES AND TAX LISTS

G. David Dilts

The proliferation of statewide census indexes has been an important development in the history of American genealogy. While their existence is almost taken for granted today, the availability of census indexes for most states has revolutionized genealogy. There is a wide assortment of published census and tax records, and published census transcripts are available for town and county censuses; the Federal government has printed statewide census transcripts for 1790. Census indexes vary in their coverage from towns to counties to states, all the way up to the nationwide level, and they are available for censuses dating from colonial times to the twentieth century. Nationwide combinations of state census indexes are now available as well. Census indexes are significant locator tools and make pinpointing individuals easy; few sources require so little prerequisite information to use, and few are as comprehensive or as easy to use.

Most American genealogists begin their research with census indexes. Census and tax list indexes save time and can lead to much additional information. Census indexes serve as the gateways to original and compiled records by identifying where people lived; tax lists can serve as substitutes for missing census records. Researchers and indexers also use other lists, such as those of people attending town meetings or of petition signers, as substitutes for censuses. Most published tax lists are for local jurisdictions, such as towns or counties. Currently, these published census records, tax records, and related indexes appear mainly as books, microforms, and compact discs (CD-ROMs). Regardless of whether a researcher uses a book, microfiche, CD-ROM, or Internet site to search a census index, it is crucial to understand the limits of such indexes. Just as valuable is learning how to overcome those limits.

This chapter is not a comprehensive discussion of censuses; rather, the goal of this chapter is to explain the use of published censuses, tax lists, and their related indexes and the reference tools needed to use them effectively.

For a full discussion of the use of original census records and Soundex and Miracode indexes, see chapter 5, "Research in Census Records," in Loretto Dennis Szucs and Sandra Hargreaves Luebking's *The Source: A Guidebook of American Genealogy,* rev. ed. (Salt Lake City: Ancestry, 1997).

This chapter covers the following major topics:

- Types of Census Indexes
- Published Tax Lists and Indexes
- Other Census Substitutes
- Strengths of Census Indexes and Similar Publications
- Weaknesses and How to Overcome Them
- Accuracy of Census Indexes
- Major Census Index Publishers
- Instructional Literature and Reference Tools

TYPES OF CENSUS INDEXES

Researchers use a variety of census indexes. This section explains their characteristics, value, availability, and limitations, and possible ways to overcome those limitations.

Statewide Federal Census Indexes

Statewide indexes are usually alphabetical lists of names accompanied by the associated localities and page numbers in an original Federal census of a state. Many indexes also include additional census data, such as age, birthplace, occupation, or value of real estate and of personal estate. A few are census *transcripts*—verbatim reproductions of all the data in the original census. Most are in book form, but some exist only on microfilm. Statewide indexes are so convenient and easy to use that they are among the first sources which American genealogists consult. Researchers primarily use indexes to locate where families lived and to find census information to help fill out family groups.

Some indexes have been created by individual researchers and local genealogical societies, but most are commercial publications. Accelerated Indexing Systems (AIS) (Bountiful, Utah) is the oldest indexing company; it offers the most titles. AIS has also merged many statewide indexes into regional and nationwide indexes, or databases.

Who Is Indexed? Publishers have indexed every name (except for accidental omissions) in the available Federal decennial censuses made from 1790 to 1840—but those censuses list heads of households only. The 1850 Federal census and every subsequent Federal census list everyone in each household. Nevertheless, for 1850 and later years, publishers have usually

Table 9-1. Percent of Census Names in Selected AIS Head-of-Household Indexes

State and Year	*Population*	*Index Entries*	*Percent of Population Listed in Index*
Alabama 1870	996,992	145,181	14.6
Florida 1850	87,445	14,544	16.6
Maryland 1850	583,034	172,786	29.6
New Hampshire 1860	326,073	114,137	35.0
North Carolina 1850	869,039	141,292	16.3
Ohio 1850	1,980,329	584,747	29.5
Oregon 1850	13,294	5,040	37.9
Texas 1850	212,592	44,471	20.9
Vermont 1850	314,120	104,119	33.1
Wyoming 1870	9,118	4,324	47.4

limited their indexes to heads of households and strays (people in a household having a different surname).

Heads-of-Households Indexes. The most common type of statewide census index lists only heads of households and strays; thus, these indexes do not include every resident of a state. Most women and young family members are omitted; only an estimated fifteen to 25 percent of names in these indexes are recognizably female names. The heads of households and strays that AIS has indexed from 1850 to 1880 include between 15 and 47 percent of the total census names for a state (see table 9-1). For example, Vermont had a population of 314,120 in 1850, but Ronald Vern Jackson's heads-of-households *Vermont 1850 Census Index* (Bountiful, Utah: Accelerated Indexing Systems, 1978) has 104,119 entries—33.1 percent of the total.

Every-Name Indexes. A second, less-common type of statewide index is the *every-name index.* The intent of an every-name index is to list every name that appears in the original census, but in actuality this is not always so. For example, Jackson's *New Mexico 1860 Census Index* (Bountiful, Utah: Accelerated Indexing Systems, 1981) has 83,980 entries for the 93,516 names in the census—approximately 89.8 percent of the population. Conversely, Bryan L. Dilts's *1860 South Carolina Census Index,* 2 vols. (Salt Lake City: Index Publishing, 1985), has 335,854 entries for a population of 301,302. This index represents 111.5 percent of the population because hard-to-read names were entered under alternate spellings.

Of course, indexes cannot include names omitted from the original records; nor can censuses include people who moved out of a state before the next census.

Reconstructed Censuses. Some statewide census indexes are actually reconstructed lists of inhabitants drawn from one or more sources (seldom from censuses). Indexers sometimes turn to substitutes to replace destroyed or lost censuses or censuses that were never created. They use tax lists, land records, state and local censuses, vital records, rent rolls, and other records because these indicate or imply residence. Researchers sometimes refer to these alphabetized lists as *reconstructed censuses*. They usually have as much locality information as regular census indexes and are as useful for locating ancestors. An example of this kind of index is *Virginia in 1740: A Reconstructed Census* (Miami Beach, Fla.: T.L.C. Genealogy, 1992). This index cites 131 sources, mostly deeds, wills, tax lists, and order books (figure 9-1). AIS's Early American Series (for example, Jackson's *Early Alabama* [Bountiful, Utah: Accelerated Indexing Systems, 1981]) and the AIS "decennary" indexes (for example, Jackson's *Alabama 1811–1819 Decennary Census Index* [Bountiful, Utah: Accelerated Indexing Systems, 1983]) are also reconstructed censuses, but their sources are not specifically cited. For further details about AIS reconstructed census indexes, see "Other Census Substitutes" later in this section.

Transcribed Censuses. Occasionally, the compilers of census indexes transcribe or extract nearly all of the information on a census. The transcriber may arrange the names in alphabetical order, but usually retains the order of the original census and provides an index to the names. *Transcribed censuses* are useful because the full text of a census sometimes provides additional clues that a researcher can use to identify an ancestor; regular census indexes sometimes leave out these clues. While transcribed indexes eliminate the need to read the old handwriting of original censuses, there is always a slight chance that information was misread or incorrectly entered during transcription.

For early censuses in particular, many indexers transcribe the actual census data. The 1790 census indexes shown in figure 9-2 are transcriptions. The page numbers given in the indexes of most transcriptions (including those of the 1790 census) usually refer to the *transcript* pages, not the pages of the original censuses (which are available on microfilm).

Census Tallies or Towns. For the census years 1790 to 1820, the largest index publisher, AIS, has published indexes that list *either* the actual census tallies for each household (like an abstract) or the town where the family lived, but not both. Beginning with the 1830 census, all AIS Federal census indexes show towns only and no census tallies. For 1790, AIS reprinted the Federal government's book transcripts, which show the towns and census tallies for all states. However, on AIS microfiche indexes, Massachusetts and Pennsylvania show only the towns for 1790, while the other states show the census tallies. For the 1800 census, all AIS indexes include actual census tallies (except the Vermont index and the index for the one surviving county census for Ohio). In each successive census year, fewer AIS state indexes include the actual census tallies. Table 9-2 summarizes this situation.

What the Tallies Show. Where census data is given, it appears in columns. For example:

Year(s)	*Pattern*	*Example*
1790 microfiche	aa bb cc dd ee	04 02 03 00 00
1800–10	abcde-fghij-kl	32101-01101-24
1820	abcdef-ghijk-lm	640001-10010-02

```
VA in 1740                                               190

Meadows                                  Mary. Richmond, North Farnham,
  Joel. Amelia, 004                        095
Mealy                                    Richard. Prince William, 130
  Ann. Northumberland, 081, 082          Richard. Richmond, 097, 099
  Daniel. Northumberland, 081,           Richard. Richmond, North
    082                                    Farnham, 095
  Patrick. Northumberland, 081         Megginson
Meanly                                   W. Goochland, 038
  John. Henrico, 044                     William. Goochland, 037, 038,
Mears                                      039, 040
  John Jr. Accomack, 001                 William. Goochland, St James',
  William. Accomack, 003                   040
Meaux                                  Meggs
  Miss. Gloucester, 035                  Barsheba. Essex, 022, 023
Mecoy                                    John. Essex, 022, 023
  Mark. Hanover, St Paul's, 042        Meginnes
Medarst                                  William. Goochland, 126
  Charles. Middlesex, Christ           Meginnis
```

```
VA in 1740                                          IV

References are as follows:
Book Num.          Reference
--------   -------------------------------------
001        Accomack Co Wills 1737-1743
002        Accomack Co Deeds, Etc, 1737-1746
003        Accomack Co Orders, 1737-1744
004        Amelia Co Order Book 1, 1735-1746
005        Amelia Co Deed Book 1, 1734-1743
006        Amelia Co Will Book 1 1734-1761
007        Amelia Co Tithables, 1736-1771
008        List of Baptisms, 1740-1749, by Rev. John Craig,
             First Pastor of Old Stone Church in Augusta Co
009        Brunswick Co Deeds & Wills, Etc, no 1, 1732-1740
010        Brunswick Co Deed Book 2, 1740-1745
011        Marriage Records of Brunswick Co, By A.B.
             Fothergill
012        Brunswick Co Orphans Book #1, 1740-1781
013        Brunswick Co Wills 2, 1739-1750
```

Figure 9-1. *From Virginia in 1740: A Reconstructed Census.* A portion of the index (page 190, top) and part of the list of references (page iv, bottom). This index cites 131 sources—mostly deeds, wills, tax lists, and order books.

The columns have the following meanings:

1790

a. free white males age sixteen and older
b. free white males under age sixteen
c. free white females
d. all other free persons
e. slaves

1800–10

a. free white males to age ten (under age ten)
b. free white males to age sixteen (of ten and under sixteen)
c. free white males to age twenty-six (of sixteen and under twenty-six)
d. free white males to age forty-five (of twenty-six and under forty-five)
e. free white males over age forty-five
f. free white females to age ten (under age ten)
g. free white females to age sixteen (of ten and under sixteen)
h. free white females to age twenty-six (of sixteen and under twenty-six)
i. free white females to age forty-five (of twenty-six and under forty-five)
j. free white females over age forty-five
k. other free persons (except Indians not taxed)
l. slaves

1820

a. free white males to age ten (under age ten)
b. free white males to age sixteen (of ten and under sixteen)
c. free white males between ages *sixteen* and eighteen

42 FIRST CENSUS OF THE UNITED STATES

BERKS COUNTY—Continued.

NAME OF HEAD OF FAMILY.	Free white males of 16 years and upward, including heads of families.	Free white males under 16 years.	Free white females, including heads of families.	All other free persons.	Slaves.
ROCKLAND TOWNSHIP—continued.					
Slonecker, Jno	1		5		
Michael, Philip	1	1	2		
Long, Jno	1	1	3		
Sheyrer, Chas	2	2	3		
Keim, Jacob	1	1	3		
Overdorff, Herman	2	1	5		
Mathias, Jno	1		4		
Levy, Jno	1		1		
Try, Geo	5	2	4		
Spring, Adam	1	1	5		
Ritz, Peter	1	3	1		
Bender, Ludwig	1		2		
Hilbert, Jno	2		1		
Hilbert, Jno. Geo	1		1		
Hilbert, Jno., Jur	1		5		
Mertz, Cond	2	2	2		
Delp, Valen*	1		2		
Groscup, Paul	1	4	4		
Hilbert, Jno	1	3	1		
Hilbert, Geo	1	2	1		
Hilbert, Jno, Jur (of Geo.)	1	1	4		
Hoffman, Henry	2	1	4		
Pick (Widow)		1	1		
Pick, Geo	1		1		
Sheffer, Henry	2	2	4		
Keller, Chrisr	1	3	2		
Kercher, Geo	1	2	4		
Sands, Thos	1	2	3		
Groh, Jacob	1	3	2		
Minges, Cond	2	3	5		
Zimmerman, Herman	1	3	2		
Keim, Chrisn	1	2	2		
Ruppert, Adam	2	1	2		
Ruppert, Casper	1	3	2		
Becher, Jacob	1		1		
Geiger, Jno	2	4	6		
Becher, Jacob, Jur	1	1	2		

NAME OF HEAD OF FAMILY.	Free white males of 16 years and upward, including heads of families.	Free white males under 16 years.	Free white females, including heads of families.	All other free persons.	Slaves.
RUSCOMB TOWNSHIP—continued.					
Smehl, Adam, Jur	1	2	1		
Keely, Peter	1	1	3		
Katzenmyer, Rosina			4		
Miller, Jacob	2	1	4		
Fuchs, Theodore	1	1	3		
Fuchs, Margt			4		
Miller, Anthony	1		2		
Shead, Chrisr, Jnr	1	3	2		
Shead, Chrisr, Senr	1		1		
Wagner, Elias	1	3	5		
Brombash, Emanuel	1	7	2		
Huffnagel, John	1		2		
Bingeman, Fredk	2	2	3	1	
Reeffs, Wm	2	1	1		
Slotman, Alexr	1	1	2	2	
Mourer, Danl	1	6	2		
Old, Geo., Senr	1		1		
Old, Jno, Junr	1	2	6		
Specht. Jno	1	1	4		
Reisdorff, Peter	1	1	1		
Barto, John	1	2	3		
Barlet, Paul	1	2	3		
Reder, Conrad	1	4	2		
Bernhart, Frances			1		
Moyer, Leonard	1	4	2		
Betz, Adam	1		4		
Burkhart, Chrisn	1	2	4		
Lautensleger, Jacob	1		4		
Snell, Jacob	1				
Dribitz, Jacob	1	1	2		
Wagner, Joseph	3	1	5		
Wagner, Abm	1		2		
Wagner, Jacob	1		1		
Swartz, Henry (Labr)	1	1	1		
Price, Conrad, Senr	1		4		
Price, Isaac	1		1		
Price, Abm	1	1	1		

NAME OF HEAD OF FAMILY.	Free white males of 16 years and upward, including heads of families.	Free white males under 16 years.	Free white females, including heads of families.	All other free persons.	Slaves.
TULPEHOCKEN TOWNSHIP—continued.					
Holsman, Jacob	2	3	1		
Heckman, Peter	1		2		
Klein, Philip	2	2	7		
Klein, Davd	2	4	6		
Kleh, Jeremiah	3	4	3		
Kiener, Chrisn	4	3	4		
Noll, Jno	2	1	5		
Moyer, Geo	1		1		
Miller, Jno, Senr	2	1	3		
Miller, Davd	4	1	3		
Nine, Sylvester	4	1	6		
Roan, Jno	2	3	4		
Roan, Geo	1	1	3		
Riehm, Nichs	2	1	4		
Moyer, Michl	1	1	3		
Rigle, John (Miller)	1	3	5	1	
Smith, Peter	1	4	3		
Sheffer, Jacob	1				
Shead, Saml	1	2	2		
Shead, Michl	2		2		
Speicher, Peter	2	1	4		
Sharp, John	1	2	2		
Spankugen, Bastian	1	2	3		
Ulrich, Geo	1		5		
Winter, Chrisr	1		3		
Wenrich, Jno	2		2		
Wagoner, Geo	1	1	3		
Zerbe, Cath*	1	3	2		
Steiner, Jno	1	3	2		
Zerbe, Leond	2	2	3		
Riegel, Jno, Senr	2		1		
Wenrich, Paul	1		1		
Gilbert, Cond	2		4		
Hahn, Michl	1	1	2		
Berger, Philip	1	1	2		
Winter, Chrisr, Jur	2		1		
Howman, Valentine	1	2	3		

Figure 9-2. From *Heads of Families at the First Census of the United States Taken in the Year 1790, Pennsylvania,* page 42. (Washington, D.C.: Government Printing Office, 1908; reprint; Bountiful, Utah: Accelerated Indexing Systems, 1978).

d. free white males to age twenty-six (of *sixteen* and under twenty-six)
e. free white males to age forty-five (of twenty-six and under forty-five)
f. free white males over age forty-five
g. free white females to age ten (under age ten)
h. free white females to age sixteen (of ten and under sixteen)
i. free white females to age twenty-six (of sixteen and under twenty-six)
j. free white females to age forty-five (of twenty-six and under forty-five)
k. free white females over age forty-five
l. slaves
m. free colored persons

Early Published Census Indexes. The Federal government was a pioneer publisher of statewide indexes to Federal censuses. In 1907 and 1908 the government published a series of state indexes to the 1790 Federal census (figure 9-2). These early publications have proved so popular that many publishers have reprinted them under their own imprints. Moreover, the Work Projects Administration (WPA) helped create countywide census transcripts for some counties. In the early 1960s, with the growing popularity of genealogy and the release of more census microfilms, individuals and societies began to index some censuses. (These indexes usually cover only one county.)

Computerized Census Indexing. The development of computers made possible the rapid indexing of censuses for profit by commercial publishers. Accelerated Indexing Systems was the first major census index publisher to use computers. Beginning in 1967, AIS published more than six hundred statewide census indexes. Several other companies have entered the market in recent years, and individual researchers and genealogical societies also have put personal computers to work alphabetizing census data. AIS frequently published competing indexes to match the statewide indexes of other publishers. The availability of so many easy-to-use indexes has changed the way American genealogists do research. The combined efforts of all these publishers make indexes easy sources for American genealogists to use in locating their ancestors. Once the time and place where an ancestor lived are known, further documentation can usually be found in the form of vital records, church records, land records, and other sources that are associated with specific times and places.

Index Coverage. Publishers have printed statewide census indexes for every available Federal census from 1790 to 1860. There are also 1870 indexes for forty-seven states (or parts of states) and the District of Columbia. Seventeen (mostly western) states have 1880 indexes other than the Soundex. The 6,160 names on the surviving fragments of the 1890 census (the majority of the schedules for this census were destroyed by fire) are indexed. Indexers have published indexes for all of the surviving veterans schedules from Kentucky to Wyoming (except

Ohio and Pennsylvania). There are even some 1900 and 1910 indexes for some smaller western states. AIS has published indexes for all of the available mortality schedules for 1850, 1860, 1870, and 1880. The Federal government created a set of statewide phonetic Soundex indexes for the households having children age ten and under in the 1880 census. There is statewide Soundex coverage for all households in the 1900 and 1920 censuses, and for the 1910 census there is Soundex (or the similar Miracode) coverage for all households for twenty-one states.

Tables 9-3 and 9-4 show the indexes published for each state or territory for each Federal census year. Although the tables identify the major publishers, the index format is not indicated because many book indexes are becoming available on CD-ROM. In addition, some indexes are available on microfiche or microfilm. The tables also indicate which are every-name indexes (e) or reconstructions (R) from substitutes for lost Federal census records; they further show (*) if the Federal census lacks more than 25 percent of a state's counties and which states have only partial indexes (‡) (even though the census is complete). The tables also show most competing indexes.

Competing Indexes for the Same State and Year. A glance at tables 9-3 and 9-4 shows many *competing indexes*—indexes of the same state and census year by different publishers. One hundred and fifty of the 340 indexes for census taken from 1790 to 1890 have one or more competing indexes (44 percent); every state has at least one set of competing indexes. The existence of competing indexes can make it easier to find persons and to overcome index omissions. However, competing census indexes can differ from each other: one might index every name, while another might index only heads of households (see 1860 for South Carolina); one might provide ages, while another might not (see 1870 for Virginia). Sometimes their coverage will also differ. For example, two companies released book indexes labeled "1870 Long Island, New York." The index by Precision Indexing (Bountiful, Utah) included the traditional three counties on Long Island: Kings (Brooklyn), Queens, and Suffolk. The AIS index labeled "Long Island" omitted Kings County (where the majority of the island's population lived) but included Dutchess County (on the mainland) and Richmond County (the physically separated Staten Island). Even when competing indexes have the same scope, there is often a difference in the names indexed. Figure 9-3 shows sections from the same part of the alphabet for two different 1850 indexes for the same state; each index includes entries not shown in the other index.

Existing Coverage. As the tables indicate, index coverage is extensive. Ninety-nine percent of the possible census indexes through 1900 exist at least in part. For 1790 to 1900, every *available* state is at least partially indexed (except three for 1870 and two—Ohio and Pennsylvania—for 1890 veterans). However, several states with large populations have only partial indexes for 1870, as noted in table 9-5, and 1910 census indexes are still lacking for twenty-six states. The 1880 Soundex only shows families with children age ten and under. Note that in the major eastern states for 1870, most indexing has focused on counties with major cities. These indexes are particularly useful because finding a family in census records is most difficult in large cities. For some of these states, additional county indexes have been published by local societies and private individuals. (See the discussion of "Countywide Federal Census Indexes" later in this chapter.)

Table 9-2. AIS Federal Census Indexes: Census Tallies or Towns

State	*1790 Microfiche*	*1800*	*1810*	*1820*
Alabama	—	—	Towns	Towns
Connecticut	Tallies	Tallies	Towns	Towns
Delaware	—	Tallies	Towns	Towns
District of Columbia	—	Tallies	—	Towns
Florida	—	—	—	Towns
Georgia	—	—	—	Towns
Illinois	—	—	—	Towns
Indiana	—	—	—	Towns
Kentucky	—	—	Tallies	Towns
Louisiana	—	—	Tallies	Towns
Maine	Tallies	Tallies	Towns	Towns
Maryland	Tallies	Tallies	Towns	Towns
Massachusetts	Towns	Tallies	Towns	Towns
Michigan	—	—	—	Towns
Mississippi	—	—	Towns	Tallies
New Hampshire	Tallies	Tallies	Towns	Towns
New York	Tallies	Tallies	Tallies	Towns
North Carolina	Tallies	Tallies	Towns	Towns
Ohio	—	Towns	Towns	Towns
Pennsylvania	Towns	Tallies	Towns	Towns
Rhode Island	Tallies	Tallies	Towns	Towns
South Carolina	Tallies	Tallies	Towns	Tallies
Tennessee	—	—	Towns	Tallies
Vermont	Tallies	Towns	Towns	Towns
Virginia	—	—	Tallies	Towns

Index Styles. Indexes for the years 1790 to 1840 often include the actual census tallies for the ages of male and female household members in rows like this:

010302-10000-00

The introduction to the index usually helps to interpret what each tally means. (Also see the previous discussion about census data under "What the Data Shows"). As noted earlier, most indexes for post-1850 censuses list only the name of the head of household, town, county, state, and census page number. In addition, the indexes published by Precision Indexing list the age, gender, race, birthplace, and census microfilm reel for each name.

Prerequisite Knowledge. The only information required to use an index is the name of the person being sought. However, statewide indexes are most useful if the state where a person or his family lived during a census year is known or can be surmised.

Statewide indexes are subject to the same limitations as all census indexes. For example, transcription errors occasionally make names hard to find, and many statewide indexes use short county abbreviations that can be difficult to decipher. AIS's statewide indexes rarely cite the census records indexed. Therefore, it is often necessary to consult a second reference book or

Table 9-3. Indexes to Pre-1850 Federal Censuses

State	*1790*	*1800*	*1810*	*1820*	*1830*	*1840*
Alabama	—	—	R*	R* R	A	A
Arkansas	—	—	R	R	A	A
Connecticut†	C	A	A	A	A	A
Delaware	R R	A	A	A	A	A
District of Columbia	See Maryland	A*	Lost	A	A	A
Florida	—	—	—	R	A B	A B
Georgia	RG	R*	R*	A G R	A B B	A B B
Illinois†	—	R	A*	A B B	A B	A B
Indiana	—	lost	R*	A B	A	A B
Iowa	—	—	—	—	—	A B
Kentucky	R	R	A G	A G	A B‡	A
Louisiana	—	—	A B	A B‡	A	A
Maine	C	A	A	A	A	A
Maryland	C	A B	A	A G	A*	A
Massachusetts	C	A G	A	A	A	A
Michigan	—	Lost	A* B*	A	A	A B
Minnesota	—	—	—	—	—	A
Mississippi	R	—	R*	A B B	A B	A B B
Missouri	—	—	R*	Lost	A B	A B
New Hampshire	C	A* B*	A	A*	A	A
New Jersey	R	A*	Lost	Lost	A	A
New York	C	A G B	A	A	A	A
North Carolina	C	A G	A G B	A B	G A	A
Ohio	—	A* B*	A*	A B	A B	A B
Pennsylvania	C	A G B	A B	A	A	A
Rhode Island	C	A	A	A	A	A
South Carolina	C	A G B	A	A B	A B	A
Tennessee	R	R	A*	A* G	A B	A B
Texas	—	—	—	—	R	R
Vermont	C	A G	A	A	A	A
Virginia	RR	A*	A*G*R*	A G	A	A
Wisconsin	—	Lost	Lost	See Michigan	A B	A B

A = AIS index (book, microfiche, CD-ROM)
G = Genealogical Publishing Co. Index
B = book index, neither AIS nor GPC (many are also on microfilm)
C = Census Bureau-published transcript (1908) (also indexed by AIS)
R = reconstructed substitute based on state censuses, tax lists, etc.
— = no census records exist/were made for this area
* = limited coverage—25 percent or more of the counties are missing from the census
‡ = indexes only part of the existing census for the state
† = collective index for multiple years available on microfilm at the state library and Family History Library

catalog to find the microfilm of the original census. If the state where a family lived is not known, it can be advantageous to use nationwide or regional indexes (described later).

Formats. Publishers print statewide indexes in a variety of formats. Some are typescripts on onion-skin paper. A few others are card indexes available on microfilm only, but most of the microfilm indexes are the Federal Soundex indexes. In recent years some publishers have started selling statewide indexes on computer diskettes and CD-ROMs. Historically, most statewide census indexes have been commercially published books.

Multi-Volume Book Indexes. When the size of an index exceeds seven hundred or eight hundred pages, it usually is bound in two or more volumes. There are essentially four ways to divide multiple index volumes:

- Alphabetically by surname
- Alphabetically by county
- Geographically by county
- Randomly by county

Indexes that are divided alphabetically by surname are easy to use and create little confusion. For example, Index Publishing divided Dilts's *1860 South Carolina Census Index* (cited earlier) with *A* to *L* surnames in vol. 1 and *K* to *Z* surnames in vol. 2.

Multi-volume divisions based on counties require the researcher to know which county to search or to search several volumes. A researcher who is unaware of the geographic division of an index might mistakenly think a search of one volume covers the entire state. Consider Jackson's *Tennessee 1860 Census Index* (Salt Lake City: Accelerated Indexing Systems, 1981). It indexes the forty-two counties from Anderson through Knox like this: vol. 1, surnames *A* to *D;* vol. 2, *E* to *K;* vol. 3, *L* to *R;* vol. 4, *S* to *Z.* When the remaining forty-two counties from Lauderdale County to Wilson County are indexed, there will be four more volumes to search.

Some publishers divide multi-volume indexes geographically. Frequently, the large cities are separate from the rest of the state. For example, for the 1860 census, Jackson indexed St. Louis separately from the rest of Missouri. Some publishers divide states into geographic regions. AIS split Jackson's *Pennsylvania 1860* census index (North Salt Lake, Utah: Accelerated Indexing Systems International, 1986–87) into (1) Philadelphia, (2) Pittsburgh, (3) Pennsylvania East, (4) Pennsylvania Central, and (5) Pennsylvania West.

Sometimes publishers use counties to divide an index into several volumes, but they do not divide them based on alphabetical county names, nor on geographic regions. The result is a random pattern of counties covered in each volume. Two ex-

Table 9-4. Indexes to 1850 and Later Federal Censuses

State	*1850*	*1860*	*1870*	*1880*	*1890 Veterans*	*1900*	*1910*	*1920*
Alabama	A	A	A B‡	S	B*	S	S	S
Alaska	—	—	—	R	Lost	A S	None	S
Arizona	—	See New Mexico	A	S A B	Lost	S	None	S
Arkansas	ABeB‡	A B	A	S	Lost	S	S	S
California	A B	A P	A	S	—	S	S	S
Colorado	—	Ae	Ae B	S Ae	—	S		S
Connecticut	A B	A P	**None**	S	—	S		S
Delaware	A B	A P	A P	S	—	S		S
District of Columbia	A	A P	A P	S	A B*	S		S
Florida	A	A P	A Pe	S	—	S	S	S
Georgia	A	A B	A P	S	B*	S	S	S
Hawaii	—	—	—	—	—	A S	A	S
Idaho	—	See Utah	Ae Be	Ae Be	—	S	C B	S
Illinois	A B	A	**A‡P‡**	S A	B*	S	S	S
Indiana	ABB	ABBe	**A‡**	S B‡	—	S		S
Iowa	A	A	A	S	—	S		S
Kansas	—	A	A	S	—	S	S	S
Kentucky	A B‡	A	A	S	A* P*	S	S	S
Louisiana	A	A	A	S	A P	S	S/S	S
Maine	A B‡	A B‡	**B‡**	S	A P	S		S
Maryland	A	A	**A‡P‡**	S	P	S		S
Massachusetts	A	A	**A‡**	S	P	S		S
Michigan	A B	A B‡	**A‡B‡**	S	P	S	S	S
Minnesota	A B	A B	Ae	S A	P B	S		S
Mississippi	A B	A B	A	S	A P	S	S	S
Missouri	A B‡	A B‡	A P‡	S	P	S	S	S
Montana	—	Ae	Ae	S A B	A	B‡ S		S
Nebraska	—	A B	B	S	A	S		S
Nevada	—	See Utah	Ae B	S A	A	A	A P	S
New Hampshire	A	A	**None**	S	A	S		S
New Jersey	A	A	**A‡**	S	A B*	S		S
New Mexico	A B	A	Ae	S	A	S		S
New York	A	A	**A‡P‡**	S	P B*	S		S
North Carolina	A B‡	A	A P	S	AB B*	S	S	S
North Dakota	A	Ae	Ae	SAe	A B	S		S
Ohio	A B	A‡ B	**A‡**	S P	None	S	S	S
Oklahoma	—	A	—	S	A B	S	S	S
Oregon	A B	A P	A P	S A	A B	S		S
Pennsylvania	A	A	P	S	None	S	S/S	S
Rhode Island	A	A P	A P	S	A	S		S
South Carolina	A	APeB	A P	S	A	S	S	S
South Dakota	—	Ae	Ae	SAe	A B*	S		S
Tennessee	A B	Ae‡ B	B	SB‡	A	S	S‡	S
Texas	A B	A	A	S A	CP B*	S	S	S
Utah	A B B	AeB	A B	SA B	A	S		S
Vermont	A	A	**None**	S	A	S		S
Virginia	A	A	A P	S	A P	S	S	S

State	1850	1860	1870	1880	1890 Veterans	1900	1910	1920
Washington	A	Ae	Ae	S Ae	A	S		S
West Virginia	See Virginia	A	A P	S B	A P	S	S	S
Wisconsin	A Be	A‡ Be	Be	S	A	S		S
Wyoming	See Utah	A	A	SAe	A	S	A P	S

A = AIS index (book, microfiche for 1850 and some for 1860 to 1880, CD-ROM for most)
B = other index—neither AIS nor Precision Indexing (most are books; some are only on microfilm)
P = Precision Indexing/Index Publishing book and diskette indexes
R = reconstructed substitute based on a non-Federal census, tax lists, etc.
S = Soundex or Miracode (1880 only for families with children age ten and under)
e = every-name index
* = limited coverage—25 percent or more of the counties are missing from the census
‡ = indexes only part of the existing census for the state
— = no census records exist/were made for this area
Blank = census exists but not yet indexed
Bold = complete statewide index not yet available
Note: North and South Dakota published as Dakota for 1850 to 1880

Name	Code	Page
MIERS, T	SCBL	319
MIERS, WILLIAM	FABE	462
MIERS, WILLIAM	RSHU	661
MIESE, MATILDA	PCDA	176
MIESER, CATHARINE	CABR	189
MIESNER, JOHN	CLGE	128
MIESSE, JOHNATHAN	RSSC	177
MIESSIE, DAVID	CKGR	249
MIESSIE, DAVID	FACL	485
MIESSIE, GABIREL	CKGR	249
*MIESY, CORNELUIS	FAGF	381
*MIESY, JONATHAN R	FAGF	381
MIFFENDISH, SARAH	TUSU	209
MIFFIN, JOHN	ABWI	485
*MIFFORD, ASH	LGRL	110
MIFFORD, ED	LGRL	110
MIFFORD, JOHN	BULE	469
MIFFORD, WM	BULE	460
MIFLIN, WILLIAM	FYJA	157
MIGEEL, BERNARD	HMW8	632
MIGEL, FREDERICK	WSAD	519
MIGEN, ROBT H	TUOX	349
MIGENT, JAMES	ERPO	50
MIGHAN, HUGH	CUSN	363
MIGHAN, MARGARET	HMW6	28
MIGHEL, J W	HMW2	150
MIGHEL, RACHEL	HMSR	383
MIGHEL, WM	HMSM	428
MIGHEN, AMOS	WRDE	65
MIGHEN, PATRICK	WRDE	65
MIGHILL, JOHN	WRDE	64
MIGHT, SAMUEL	MSSM	2
MIGHTON, CHAS	LRCL	874

Name	County	Page	Township
MIERS, SYLVESTER	LICK	482	HOPEWELL
MIERS, WILLIAN	ROSS	331	HUNTINGT
MIESE, MATHILCA	PICK	089	DARBY TW
MIESNER, DANIEL S.	DELA	174	DELAWARE
MIESNER, JOHN	DELA	129	GENCA TW
MIESSE, JONATHAN	ROSS	089	SCIOTO T
MIESSE, JONATHAN	ROSS	089	SCIOTO T
MIESSE, MORRIS*	ATHE	027	ATHENS T
MIESSEE, GABRIEL	DARK	250	GREENVIL
MIESSER, JOSEPH	RICH	106	MADISON
MIESSIE, DANIEL**	FAIR	485	OAKLAND
MIET, JOHN	FRAN	226	COLUMBUS
MIETHENER, CHARLES H.	TUSC	459	NEW PHIL
MIFFENDISH, SARAH*	TUSC	418	SUGAR CR
MIFFIN, JOHN	ASHT	485	WINDSOR
MIFFORD, A. H.	LOGA	110	RICHLAND
MIFFORD, WILLIAM	BUTL	460	LEMON TW
MIFLIN, WILLIAM	FAYE	157	JASPER T
MIGAN, OWEN	ERIE	396	KELLYS I
MIGER, CORNLIUS	CUYA	152	CLEVELAN
MIGER, GEORGE	CUYA	287	CLEVELAN
MIGGER, SILVESTER	STAR	479	NIMISHIL
MIGH, WILLIAM	MIAM	365	WASHINGT
MIGHAN, HUGH	GUER	364	MT EPHRA
MIGHAN, MARGARET	HAMI	028	CINCINAT
MIGHEL, RACHEL	HAMI	383	SYCAMORE
MIGHEL, WILLIAM	HAMI	429	SYMMES T
MIGHELS, J. M.	HAMI	151	CINCINNA
MIGHEN, AMOS	WARR	130	DEERFIEL
MIGHEN, PATRICK	WARR	130	DEERFIEL
MIGHEN, THOMAS	WARR	132	DEERFIEL
MIGHILL, JOHN	WARR	127	DEERFIEL
MIGHTMAN, MARIA	GEAU	175	MUNSON T
MIGHTON, CHARLES	LORA	438	CARLISLE

Figure 9-3. Comparison of two 1850 indexes for Ohio. At left is a portion of Ohio Family Historians and Their Friends, *Index to the 1850 Federal Population Census of Ohio* (Mineral Ridge, Ohio: Lida Flint Harshman, 1972), page 666; at right is part of Ronald Vern Jackson's *Ohio 1850 Census Index,* vol. 2 (South Bountiful, Utah: Accelerated Indexing Systems, 1978), page 857. Each index includes entries not shown in the other index.

Table 9-5. Partially Completed 1870 Census Indexes (Most from AIS and Precision Indexing)

State	*Completed Counties (Major Cities)*
Connecticut	None
Illinois	Cook County (Chicago area)
Indiana	Marion County (Indianapolis)
Maryland	Baltimore (city and county)
Massachusetts	Hampden County (Springfield area)
Michigan	Kent, Saginaw, Wayne (Detroit) counties. Also five regional indexes covering all but the southern tiers of counties
New Jersey	Essex, Hudson, Mercer, Passaic counties
New Hampshire	None
New York	Dutchess, Kings, Queens, New York, Richmond, Suffolk, Westchester counties
Ohio	Cuyahoga, Franklin, Hamilton, Montgomery counties
Vermont	None

amples of this less useful pattern are Jackson's *Missouri 1860* census index (North Salt Lake, Utah: Accelerated Indexing Systems International, 1986–87) and the *Indiana 1860 Census Index with Alternative Names, Ages and Birth Places* (Salt Lake City: Kratz Indexing, 1986–87).

County-by-County Statewide Indexes. Some "statewide" indexes are actually county-by-county indexes—surnames are alphabetized within each county, requiring the user to search alphabetical listings of surnames in county after county until the surname of interest is found (unless there is some knowledge of where the person resided). An example of this kind of index is William A. Marsh's *1880 Census of West Virginia,* 13 vols. (Parsons, W.Va.: McClain Print, 1979–92).

Finding Aids. The state research outlines published by the Family History Library of The Church of Jesus Christ of Latter-day Saints (LDS church) and Alice Eichholz, ed., *Ancestry's Red Book: American State, County and Town Sources,* rev. ed. (Salt Lake City: Ancestry, 1992), are good sources to begin learning more about specific statewide censuses and their indexes. The *Family History Library Catalog*™ (Salt Lake City: Genealogical Society of Utah, annual) of the Family History Library is also a good place to look for census indexes—especially ones that are too new to be mentioned in other sources. They can be found in the catalog's locality section under the name of the territory or state followed by the subject "Census" or "Census—Indexes."

Availability. The Family History Library has copies of nearly all statewide census indexes, as do most of the National Archives regional archives and major genealogical libraries. Most of the smaller family history centers of the LDS church (see the introduction to *Printed Sources*) lack individual statewide indexes (except those for their own states). Many genealogical and historical societies collect individual statewide census indexes, and public libraries with good genealogical collections and academic libraries often have good collections of statewide census indexes. Most statewide census indexes are still in print and available from their publishers. As more and more are released on CD-ROM, smaller libraries, family history centers, and individuals purchase them, making access even easier.

Soundex and Miracode Statewide Indexes

The Federal government created a phonetic Soundex indexing system for the 1880, 1900, 1910, and 1920 statewide Federal censuses. Although these are significant indexes for the later censuses, they are not "printed sources" and are not discussed in this chapter. See chapter 5, "Research in Census Records," in *The Source: A Guidebook of American Genealogy* (cited earlier) for more details. Researchers can rent Soundex microfilms from commercial companies, such as American Genealogical Lending Library (Bountiful, Utah) (see appendix C).

Nationwide AIS Microfiche Indexes

Jackson's *AIS Microfiche Indexes of U.S. Census and Other Records* (Bountiful, Utah: Accelerated Indexing Systems International, 1984) is a composite of AIS census indexes for the 1790 to 1850 census indexes and some from the 1860 to 1880 censuses. (Parts of the indexes refer to other sources, such as mortality schedules, state censuses, tax lists, land records, vital statistics, and other records from 1607 to 1906.) The nine microfiche indexes (called *searches*) on 1,344 microfiche are alphabetical lists of some of the people who lived in the United States from 1607 to 1906. Each search covers a selected time period and group of states. A few of the names omitted from AIS's microfiche indexes might be found in the AIS book indexes or in MicroQuix's *U.S. Census Index Series* (Orem, Utah: Automated Archives, 1991–94) on CD-ROM—or vice versa.

Value. The *AIS Microfiche Indexes of U.S. Census and Other Records* is among the largest sets of census indexes. The broad time period and large number of states covered make these indexes very important locator tools. Researchers frequently use the *AIS Microfiche Indexes* to find ancestors whose places of residence are not known. Using them, a relative can sometimes be located using no more starting information than a name. These indexes often are helpful in tracing the movements of a family from state to state over many years as well. They are easy-to-use sources for locating specific places where ancestors lived and when they lived there. The broad nature of the *AIS Microfiche Indexes* also makes them valuable for identifying previously unknown places to search for relatives. They might reveal new areas to search for further or larger clusters of family members.

Availability. The *AIS Microfiche Indexes of U.S. Census and Other Records* is available at the Family History Library and the approximately one thousand family history centers in the United States. Some of the larger and better funded genealogical libraries also have microfiche copies. As the CD-ROM versions of AIS indexes become available, they can be used as substitutes for the microfiche indexes. The CD-ROM indexes are less expensive and are more widely available at genealogical and historical societies.

How AIS Microfiche Indexes Was Created. AIS was a commercial publisher that indexed censuses and other genealogical sources. *AIS Microfiche Indexes* was formed by merging the individual statewide census indexes that AIS published before 1984. AIS created this larger composite index to help researchers who do not know which state their ancestors lived in.

Table 9-6. AIS Microfiche Index Searches Summary

Search	*Time Period*	*Localities*
1	1607–1819	Entire United States
2	1820–29	Entire United States
3	1830–39	Entire United States
4	1840–49	Entire United States
5	1850 (and half of 1860)	Southern states: Ala., Ark., D.C., Fla., Ga., Ky., La., Md., Miss., N.C., S.C., Tenn., Va., (Tenn. 1860, Anderson through Knox counties only)
6	1850	Northern states: Conn., Del., Mass., Maine, N.H., N.J., N.Y., Ohio, Pa., R.I., Vt.
7	1850 and some 1860, 1870, 1880; miscellaneous to 1906	Midwestern and western states: Alaska, Ariz., Calif., Colo., Iowa, Idaho, Ill., Ind., Kans., Minn., Mich., Mo., Mont., Nebr., Nev., N.M., N.D., Ohio, Okla., Oreg., S.D., Tex., Utah, Wash., Wis., Wyo.
7a	1850–1906	Entire United States (searches 5, 6, 7 combined)
8	1850–80 and one 1885	All U.S. mortality schedules and 1885 S.D. mortality schedule

Table 9-7. Post-1850 Indexes in Searches 7 and 7a of *AIS Microfiche Indexes of U.S. Census and Other Records*

State	*1860*	*1870*	*1880*
Arizona	•	•	•
Colorado	•	•	•
Idaho		•	•
Kansas	•		
Minnesota	•	•	
Montana	•	•	
Nebraska	•		
Nevada	•	•	•
New Mexico	•	•	
North Dakota	•	•	•
South Dakota	•	•	•
Utah	•		
Washington	•	•	•
Wyoming		•	•

Arrangement. The searches are organized as shown in table 9-6. Table 9-7 shows the regular Federal censuses from 1860 to 1880 included in searches 7 and 7a.

Non-Census Records in the Index. Some miscellaneous records are also indexed in search 7 for Alaska, Arizona, Iowa, Kansas, Nebraska, and Utah. Similarly, miscellaneous sources like tax lists, state censuses, land records, and vital statistics were indexed for searches 1, 2, 3, and 4. Researchers sometimes have difficulty identifying these miscellaneous sources; colonial sources indexed in search 1 are especially difficult to identify.

Subsequent Indexes. AIS continued to index Federal census records after it published the *AIS Microfiche Indexes of U.S. Census and Other Records* in 1984. AIS has since indexed many 1860, 1870, and 1880 censuses which are not in the 1984 edition of the microfiche indexes. With the advent of CD-ROM editions of these indexes (described below) updates to the 1984 microfiche are not expected.

Which Data is Listed. The *AIS Microfiche Indexes* includes virtually the same information as the individual statewide indexes that were merged to create the microfiche. However, the space for counties is wider in the microfiche, so county names are usually spelled out; the same is true for cities and towns. If the ward number for a city is cut short in the book indexes, the microfiche indexes are likely to show the full ward number. The AIS microfiche indexes also list the state, census page number, locality, and census year. The mortality schedule, search 8, lists name, county, state, age at death, gender, month of death, place of birth, cause of death, an occupation code, and census year.

Accuracy. The *AIS Microfiche Indexes* is a merger of statewide indexes and is no more accurate than the book editions of those indexes. It is subject to all the transcription errors of the statewide indexes. AIS may have corrected a few transcription errors found in the book indexes, but this is hard to verify. None of the AIS book index problems (see table 9-14) had been corrected in the 1984 *AIS Microfiche Indexes.*

1790 Entries. The 1790 book census indexes published by AIS were actually reprints of 1908 government indexes. To publish the 1790 microfiche census index, AIS was forced to input the census data in electronic form for the first time; thus, the indexes at the back of the AIS 1790 book indexes do not perfectly match the AIS 1790 microfiche index. The page numbers are the most evident difference.

Repeated Names. Some index entries appear more than once on a microfiche search, and all of the searches appear to have at least a few duplicate entries. Some searches seem to have an inordinate number of duplicates, as shown in figure 9-4. Searches 1, 4, 7, 7a, and 8 seem to have a 10- to 40-percent duplication rate, meaning that 10 to 40 percent of the entries appear to match exactly or very closely with another entry in the index. It is time-consuming (and mildly annoying) to search for individual names among all the duplicates. (However, if the name sought is one that is duplicated, the chances of noticing it are increased.)

Overwhelming Number of Names. The *AIS Microfiche Indexes* contain so many names that they can sometimes be overwhelming. Merely finding all of the entries from a particular state can take a long time among entries from all fifty states. A common name like David Jones may appear so often in the microfiche index that it is difficult to find or identify the correct David Jones. If little is known about the person and where he or she lived, it becomes even more difficult to determine which entry is the correct one to pursue. When the process of elimination is used to find a relative, these large indexes may produce long lists that take much time to search; sometimes it is easier to use the statewide book index.

Instructional Literature. Because *AIS Microfiche Indexes* is available at most U.S. LDS family history centers, the Family

BECTNER, JACOB *	[illegible]HIGH CO.	PA	245	LOW HILL TWP	1840
BECTOL, AARON	MORGAN CO.	VA	196	NO TWP LISTED	1840
BECTON, ANN*	BURKE CO.	GA	143	64TH DISTRICT	1840
BECTON, ANN*	BURKE CO.	GA	143	64TH DISTRICT	1840
BECTON, FREDERICK	JONES CO.	NC	285	NO TWP LISTED	1840
BECTON, GEORGE W.	RUTHERFORD CO.	TN	080	NO TWP LISTED	1840
BECTON, GEORGE W.	RUTHERFORD CO.	TN	080	[illegible] TWP LISTED	1840
BECTON, HARVEY	DES MOINES CO.IOWA	106	2300001	-002001	1840
BECTON, HARVEY	DES MOINES CO.IOWA	106	2300001	-002001	1840
BECTON, J M.	RUSK	CO.TX	NPN	NO TWP LISTED	TX1846
BECTON, JOHN	VICTORIA	CO.TX	NPN	NO TWP LISTED	TX1846
BECTON, JOHN E.	WAYNE CO.	NC	225	BUCK SWAMP DISTRICT	1840
BECTON, JOHN H.	SHELBY CO.	TN	233	NO TWP LISTED	1840
BECTON, JOHN H.	SHELBY CO.	TN	233	NO TWP LISTED	1840
BECTON, LEWIS*	BURKE CO.	GA	143	64TH DISTRICT	1840
BECTON, LEWIS*	BURKE CO.	GA	143	64TH DISTRICT	1840
BECTON, SIMON	JONES CO.	NC	286	NO TWP LISTED	1840
BECTOR, LEWIS*	BURKE CO.	GA	143	64TH DISTRICT	1840
BECTOR, LEWIS*	BURKE CO.	GA	143	64TH DISTRICT	1840
BECTORTHA, ELI	HAMPDEN CO.	MA	156	W SPRINGFIELD	1840
BECTY, ERASTUS *	SENECA CO.	NY	213	SENECA FALLS VILLAGE	1840
BECUI, A.*	SENECA CO.	NY	286	OVID	1840
BECUM, S.	ESSEX CO.	MA	259	SALEM	1840
BEDAGEW, ALEXANDER	ATHENS CO.	OH	349	ALEXANDER TWP	1840
BEDAIS, DENNIS	ST. LOUIS CO.	MO	145	4TH WARD	1840
BEDALL, ILLIAM	QUEENS CO.	NY	170	HEMPSTEAD	1840
BEDALL, SAMUEL	KNOX CO.	IN	055	NO TWP LISTED	1840
BEDALL, SEAMAN	QUEENS CO.	NY	170	HEMPSTEAD	1840
BEDAN, PETER	ALBANY CO.	NY	022	W TROY 1ST WARD	1840
BEDAN, ZEBEDEE*	FAIRFIELD CO.	CT	177	NEW CANAAN	1840
BEDAND, JOHN P.	PHILADELPHIA CO.	PA	088	LOCUST WARD	1840
BEDANGAN, A. *	ST LAWRENCE CO.	NY	036	OGDENSBURG	1840
BEDANKOFF, JOHN	MONTGOMERY CO.	NY	374	CHARLESTON	1840
BEDANT, JESSE	NEW LONDON CO.	CT	116	LEDYARD	1840
BEDARD, ANTHONY	BERKSHIRE CO.	MA	195	PITTSFIELD	1840
BEDAT, [illegible]ANCIS*	W BATON ROUGE P.	LA	060	NO TWP LISTED	1840
BEDAU, [illegible]AVIER	CRAWFORD CO.	PA	438	MEAD TWP	1840
BEDBOUT, [illegible]DAN	WASHINGTON CO.	PA	223	ANNVILLE TWP	1840

Figure 9-4. Duplicate entries in AIS microfiche. Searches 1, 4, 7, 7a, and 8 seem to have approximately a 10- to 40-percent duplication rate.

History Library publishes the four-page *Accelerated Indexing Systems U.S. Census Indexes (on Microfiche) Resource Guide* (Salt Lake City: Family History Library, 1992) to explain the indexes and abbreviations used. Older family history centers may also have copies of the *Accelerated Indexing Systems, Inc. Microfiche Indexes Branch Genealogical Libraries Instructional Materials* (Salt Lake City: Genealogical Society of Utah, 1984). This thirty-eight-page booklet gives more details about when and how to use the indexes, showing how to interpret statistical information and providing a key to occupational codes. It also includes many examples and practice exercise questions. The appendices show which states and years are in each search. AIS also sells Jackson's *AISI Microfiche Data-Base List Manual* (1984; reprint; Bountiful, Utah: Accelerated Indexing Systems, 1988). This eighty-nine-page book explains what the index is, how it works, and how specific information in it can be ordered.

Some older family history centers have a 772-page publication called *Records Indexed by AIS,* Genealogical Library Reference Aids Series B, no. 11 (Salt Lake City: Genealogical Society of Utah, 1984). It should be used with caution, because not all of the call numbers cited are Family History Library call numbers, nor is every AIS index source cited. If this publication does not help find the index's source, or if the source is unavailable, search John D. Stemmons's *The United States Census Compendium: A Directory of Census Records, Tax Lists, Poll Lists, Petitions, Directories, etc. Which Can Be Used as a Census* (Logan, Utah: Everton Publishers, 1973). It indicates census substitutes for the state and year that are similar to the sources cited in the AIS microfiche indexes. The *Family History Library Catalog* is another source to search for elusive AIS microfiche index sources.

Nationwide and Regional Indexes on CD-ROM

CD-ROM technology enables researchers to use very large databases on personal computers. CD-ROMs store vast amounts of information in convenient, small, inexpensive packages. Banner Blue, a division of Brøderbund Software (Novato, California), sells almost all of the AIS census index titles as well as most Precision Indexing titles on CD-ROM. Two related and similar sets of nationwide and regional CD-ROM census indexes are available to researchers, each with its own master index:

- For MS-DOS computers: *U.S. Census Index Series* (1991–94) by MicroQuix (published by Automated Archives). Indexed by *Master Name Index to Automated Archives, Inc. CD-ROMs* (Orem, Utah: Automated Archives, 1994).

- For Windows computers: Family Tree Maker's Family Archives *Census Index: U.S. Selected States/Counties* (1995) series by Brøderbund Software. Indexed by *Family Finder Index and Viewer* (Novato, Calif.: Brøderbund Software, 1995).

Census indexes were first marketed in CD-ROM format as MicroQuix's MS-DOS-based *U.S. Census Index Series*. Pro-

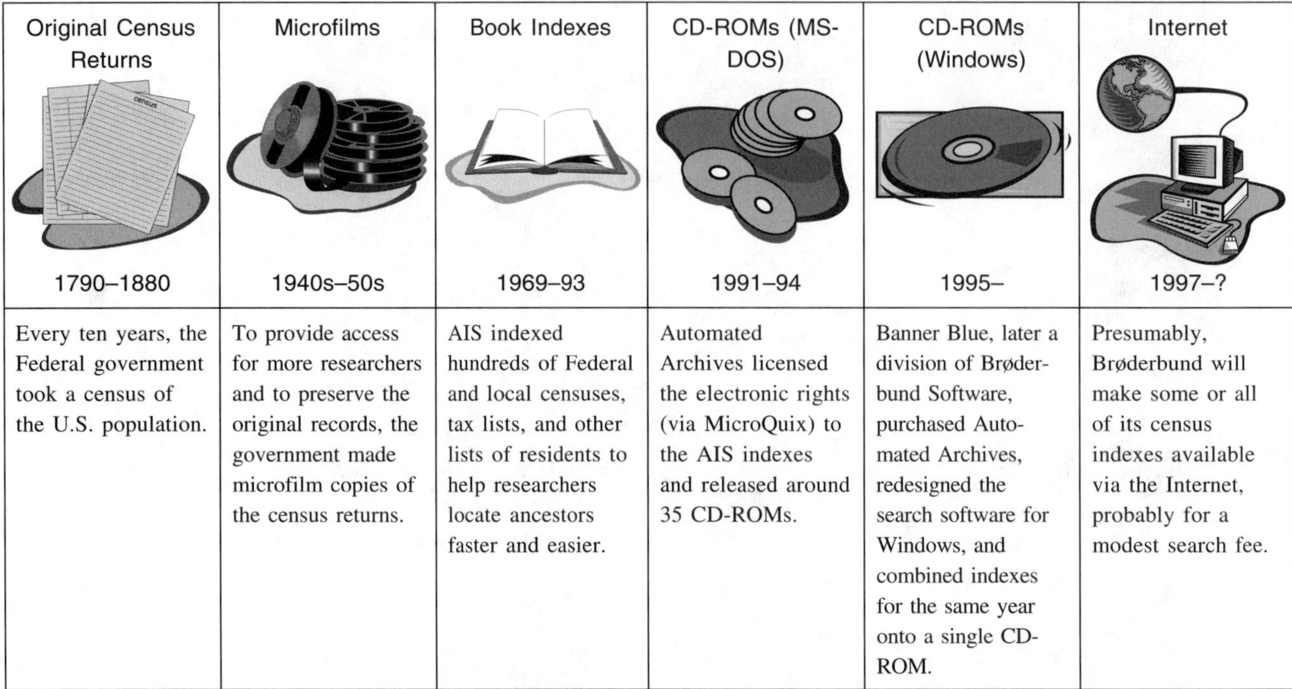

Original Census Returns	Microfilms	Book Indexes	CD-ROMs (MS-DOS)	CD-ROMs (Windows)	Internet
1790–1880	1940s–50s	1969–93	1991–94	1995–	1997–?
Every ten years, the Federal government took a census of the U.S. population.	To provide access for more researchers and to preserve the original records, the government made microfilm copies of the census returns.	AIS indexed hundreds of Federal and local censuses, tax lists, and other lists of residents to help researchers locate ancestors faster and easier.	Automated Archives licensed the electronic rights (via MicroQuix) to the AIS indexes and released around 35 CD-ROMs.	Banner Blue, later a division of Brøderbund Software, purchased Automated Archives, redesigned the search software for Windows, and combined indexes for the same year onto a single CD-ROM.	Presumably, Brøderbund will make some or all of its census indexes available via the Internet, probably for a modest search fee.

Figure 9-5. Evolution of Brøderbund Software's Family Archive Census Indexes on CD-ROM.

prietary computer software created by Automated Archives (Orem, Utah) makes these CD-ROM indexes easy to use. It allows quick access to long lists of selected census index names and thorough searches on name fragments or variant spellings. The user can search any part of the census data using "free text" searches.

After releasing these MS-DOS products, Automated Archives was acquired in 1994 by Banner Blue Software, which became a division of Brøderbund Software in 1995. Brøderbund Software then released the same census and family history material for Windows in a software and CD-ROM collection called Family Tree Maker's Family Archives *Census Index: U.S. Selected States/Counties* (Novato, Calif.: Brøderbund Software, 1995) series. Much of the index data from the older series is combined on fewer discs in the new series (figure 9-5). In addition, Brøderbund has continued to release some new material not previously available on the MS-DOS editions.

Availability. The *U.S. Census Index Series* and *Census Index: U.S. Selected States/Counties* series are available at more than one hundred genealogical societies and large public libraries known for their genealogical collections. The Family History Library and some of its family history centers also have the CD-ROM census indexes. Many individual researchers have purchased the system from its publisher for their private use. The number of sites with the Windows-based system is expanding steadily. (The MS-DOS version is no longer available for sale.) Over time, most libraries will probably replace their older, MS-DOS-based *U.S. Census Index Series* with the new Windows editions, especially as additional indexes are offered.

Master Indexes. The master index for the MS-DOS-based *U.S. Census Index Series* (1991 to 1994) is called *Master Name Index to Automated Archives, Inc. CD-ROMs* (1994). It gathers in one alphabetical list all of the names from the separate census index and many other genealogical CD-ROMs sold by Automated Archives (such as marriage records and family pedigrees). The master index for *Census Index: U.S. Selected States/Counties* series CD-ROMs is called the *Family Finder Index and Viewer*. This master index for Windows allows researchers to search for any name among all census years and all states available in the Family Tree Maker's Family Archives CD-ROM collection; thus, it is possible to find the same person listed for several separate census years (mostly among the 1790 to 1870 censuses). As a person moved from place to place, he or she may appear in several states. The accuracy of this master index is directly related to the accuracy of the original book indexes. In addition to census indexes, many other items, such as pedigrees, vital records, and histories, are indexed in the *Family Finder Index and Viewer*.

No more than a name is required to search the *Family Finder Index and Viewer*. Less-common names are easier to search for because they result in fewer "hits." To start a search, click on the "Search Expert." (Some configurations require clicking on "Search for Someone NOT from your Family File.") Then enter the name, either in spoken order or with the surname first followed by a comma and given names.

If the index has the name searched for, it will display the name on a results list. The sought-for person may be distinguished from other persons of the same name if the years and states where the person would most likely appear are known. The search-results screen displays twelve lines of names. They appear in alphabetical order starting with the ones that match the search name. If none match, they start with the first name in the alphabet following the search name. The born, married, died, or resided date appears in the estimated date range field following the name. The location field shows a state or country. The final field is the archive type. Archive types include census index, Social Security, mortality index, World Family Tree (compiled pedigrees), and family pedigrees. The *Family Finder Index and Viewer* does not show the county, locale, page, or enumeration district of the original census. Researchers must obtain and search the appropriate separate CD-ROM, book, or microfiche census index to find that information.

The *Family Finder Index and Viewer* is also available on the Internet at http://www.familytreemaker.com (at no charge). However, researchers must obtain copies of the separate CD-ROM, book, or microfiche census indexes to learn the details needed to quickly find the names in the original census schedules; indeed, Brøderbund hopes that researchers will purchase the indexes to learn details.

Regions. All of the U.S. 1790 census indexes are on one CD-ROM in MicroQuix's old MS-DOS-based *U.S. Census Index Series*. For later years, Automated Archives usually merged several states in the same region onto one CD-ROM. For example, the disc for 1850 New England includes Maine, New Hampshire, Vermont, Massachusetts, Rhode Island, and Connecticut. A few of the larger indexes, such as New York 1850, New York 1860, and Ohio 1880, have only one index per CD-ROM. All AIS indexes from 1790 to 1850 were issued on CD-ROM for MS-DOS except 1830 Missouri and North Carolina and 1850 California, New Mexico, North Dakota, Oregon, Utah, and Washington. All of these regional indexes are also indexed in *Master Name Index to Automated Archives, Inc. CD-ROMs*.

Brøderbund Software has re-published all of the MS-DOS indexes and will publish more state indexes on its Windows-based CD-ROMs. Eventually, nearly all AIS indexes will be available on CD-ROM. In the newer *Census Index: U.S. Selected States/Counties*, most state indexes for a particular census year have been published together as a nationwide index. There is a Colonial America index from 1607 to 1798, and nationwide indexes for each of the census years 1790, 1800, 1810, 1820, 1830, 1840, 1850, 1860, 1870 (partial), and 1880 (partial). There are also regional CD-ROM indexes for 1870 North and South Carolina and for 1870 Virginia and West Virginia. All of these census indexes are also indexed in the master *Family Finder Index and Viewer*. Table 9-8 summarizes the differences between these two editions.

Accuracy. Automated Archives and Brøderbund Software have eliminated many duplicate names that existed in AIS microfiche indexes and have corrected some other index problems. For example, Automated Archives corrected the New Jersey problem described in table 9-9. The CD-ROM census indexes are nearly as accurate as the AIS book indexes. Where corrections were made, the discs are more accurate (see table 9-9).

CD-ROM Omissions. When Automated Archives used AIS computer tapes to create the *U.S. Census Index Series* CD-ROMs, some of the tapes were apparently unreadable or overlooked, as some sections of census indexes are missing from the CD-ROMs. This omitted material may represent a substantial portion of the names from selected states. For example, five counties having 8.9 percent of Pennsylvania's population in 1850 were completely omitted from the CD-ROM census indexes. In another example, Jackson's *Mississippi 1850 Census Index* (Bountiful, Utah: Accelerated Indexing Systems, 1977) has a supplement of twelve pages at the beginning for census names in Pike, Pontotoc, and Rankin counties. The names from this supplement are not on the CD-ROM index. The missing counties accounted for 5.2 percent of the 1850 Mississippi population.

Each *U.S. Census Index Series* CD-ROM index has a list of all the counties included in the index. It is easy to compare this list with all of the census counties in the reference books by Leonard H. Smith, Jr., and J. Carlyle Parker, and in Jackson's *United States Federal Census Place Enrollment Schedules,* 2 vols. (North Salt Lake, Utah: Accelerated Indexing Systems International, 1991). Several counties which have 1850 census records have been omitted or mislabeled in the CD-ROM indexes. Table 9-10 lists sections that are missing from or mislabeled in the CD-ROM indexes but which are correct in the AIS book indexes.

Counties were omitted from seven out of eight (MS-DOS) *U.S. Census Index Series* CD-ROM indexes available for 1850 censuses. (The omitted county on one disc was also omitted in the book index.) In other words, 75 percent of the 1850 CD-ROMs lack some of the names found in the book indexes. Most of the missing counties do appear on the newer, Windows-based *Census Index: U.S. Selected States/Counties* series discs.

This comparison does not include mislabeled or missing counties in the 1790 to 1840 and 1860 CD-ROM indexes. Missing counties are not as likely in 1860 CD-ROM indexes because the 1860 indexes were published more recently; the computer tapes are not as old. Most of the 1790-to-1840 book indexes are older than most of the 1850 indexes; therefore, the chances are high that counties are missing from 1790 to 1840 CD-ROM indexes because of unreadable computer tapes.

It is important to put the problem in perspective. In a random sample (described later under "How Accurate are Census Indexes?") of 101 names from 1790 to 1850 census indexes, only two of the eighty-nine names found in the AIS book indexes were missing from the CD-ROM indexes. One of those two had also been omitted from the AIS microfiche indexes. To put it another way: approximately 98 percent of the names in AIS book indexes and 99 percent of the names in the AIS microfiche indexes are found in the Automated Archives (MS-DOS) CD-ROM indexes.

Value. CD-ROM census indexes have several advantages over book and microfiche indexes:

- The computer search software is
    - Easy to use
    - Fast (it can locate and list thousands of names in seconds)
- The DOS version is flexible; it can search for
    - Variable spellings
    - Name fragments in the beginning, middle, or end of a name
    - Intermittent spelling
- The CD-ROM indexes include most 1860 indexes, including those for states east of the Mississippi River which are not in the AIS microfiche indexes
- Some of the CD-ROM indexes have corrections which are not available in books or microfiche
- The CD-ROM indexes allow regional or nationwide searches
- The CD-ROM indexes cost much less per name

Table 9-8. Availability of Census Indexes on CD-ROM (Brøderbund Software)

Year	*States (and D.C.) Fully Covered Compared to Number with Existing Federal Census Records*	*CD-ROM Series Number(s)* MS-DOS	*CD-ROM Series Number(s)* Windows	*Comments (added means additional states from alternate sources* ** = as part of other states or territories* *† = incomplete coverage [1–5 counties] in original source* *partial = partial of existing census records)*
1607–1789	No Federal schedules	136	310	Includes various name lists from parts of 23 future states: Ala.†, Conn., Del.†, Ill.†, La.†, Mass., Md., Maine, Mich.†, Mo.†, Miss.†, N.C., N.H., N.J., N.Y.†, Ohio†, Pa., R.I., S.C., Va., Vt.
1790	11 of 11	137	311	16 added: Ala.†, Calif., D.C., Del., Ga., Ill., Ky., La.†, Mich.†, Mo.†, Miss.†, N.J., N.M., Ohio†, Tenn.†, Va.†
1800	13 of 13	138, 151	312	12 added: Alaska†, Ga.†, Ind.†, Ky., La.†, Mich.†, Mo.†, Miss., N.J., Ohio, Tenn., Va.
1810	16 of 16	149, 151	313	11 added: Ala., Ark.†, D.C.†, Ga.†, Ill., Ind.†, Mich.†, Mo.†, Miss.†, N.J., Ohio
1820	23 of 23	139, 154	314	7 added: Ala., Ark., Fla., N.J., N.M., Tex., Wis.*
1830	28 of 28	140, 148	315	6 added: Ariz., Calif., Iowa*, Minn.*, Tex., Wis.*
1840	30 of 30	141, 142, 152, 153	316	4 added: Hawaii, Minn.,* N.M., Tex.
1850	36 of 36	40–47 (32 states)	317	2 added: Kans.*, Nebr.*
1860	33 Of 40	21, 22, 24, 26, 27, 34 (22 states)	318	7 added: Ariz.*, Colo.*, Mont.*, Nev.*, Okla.*, W.Va.* 7 not included: Md., Mich., Mo., Ohio, Oreg., R.I., and Dakota
1870	34 of 46	None	319, 285–291	Added: Alaska Partial: Ill., Md., Mont., N.Y., Pa., Wis. 12 not included: most Eastern and Midwestern states
1880	14 of 46	20 Ohio only	320, 20	Added: Alaska Partial: Ill., N.Y.

Source: AIS via Micro-Quix (MS-DOS), AIS, AGLL (Windows)

CD-ROM indexes can be used to find ancestors if it is not known where they lived, and sometimes relatives can be identified without knowing any more than a name. The broad scope of the states indexed in them and their ease of use make CD-ROM indexes valuable for identifying previously unknown places to search for relatives. They can lead researchers to discover that they have been searching the "wrong" counties or states and to find new areas where missing family members are clustered.

Unfortunately, the *Census Index: U.S. Selected States/Counties* series does not permit the flexible searches of the older MS-DOS versions. Neither the individual discs nor the master *Family Finder Index and Viewer* offer the ability to search for anything except a name and its Soundex equivalents.

Information Displayed. The results of MS-DOS-based *U.S. Census Index Series* CD-ROM searches are displayed on a computer monitor in two sections. A heading displays the county, state, year, and CD-ROM year/state. Below the heading are entries from the county in alphabetical order. The parts of the index that match the search request are highlighted. The following information is displayed (if it is available): Soundex code, name, township, page, type, and notes. The CD-ROM "fields" contain more space than is present in the book indexes, so county names are usually written out more fully. Sometimes entire fields found on the CD-ROMs are omitted in the books.

The results of *Census Index: U.S. Selected States/Counties* series searches are displayed twelve lines at a time. Each line shows the name, state, county, locale, census page, and year of the census.

Limitations. There are a few limitations to the MS-DOS-based *U.S. Census Index Series* CD-ROM indexes.

- The search software may be difficult for some to use. For example, the program displays the first item that matches any part of the search request, rather than the item that most fully matches the search request. The user may have to scroll the screen several times before reaching the closest match.

Table 9-9. Examples of Problems Found in AIS Census Indexes

State	*Year*	*Family History Library Microfilm*	*Problem*
Alabama	1870	545500 to 545544	Index page 662 ends with McMillian, Levi. Page 663 starts with McNeal, Isaac; many names between are missing. The 1850 census showed 141 names between these two names, and the 1860 showed 160 names between them.
California	1860	803069	An entire microfilm (Siskiyou, Solano, and Sonoma counties) omitted.
Georgia	1850	442894	All of Upson County incorrectly listed as Richmond County. Any name listed for Richmond County, 86th Dis., is actually for Upson County, 86th Dis.
Louisiana	1850	009696	Assumption Parish (pages 85–104) is listed as "ASCE"—Ascension Parish.
		443482	St. Bernard Parish is listed as "W BE" Parish.
Mississippi	1850	443592	Pike, Pototoc, and Rankin counties indexed in a twelve-page supplement before the other counties.
New Jersey	1860	803711	Warren County from census pages 1–58 indexed as Mercer County. Hope Township and part of Oxford Township should be listed as Mercer County.
New York	1850	444331	An entire microfilm for half of Westchester County omitted in the index.
North Carolina	1850	444642	Duplin County, page 18, to Edgecombe County, page 188, omitted from the index.
Ohio	1850	444707	Montgomery County census pages 455–467 omitted from the index.
		444708	Morgan County census pages 1–60 omitted from the index.
		444709	Morrow County (the entire film) pages 349–532 and 1–68 omitted.
		444710	Muskingum County census pages 68–113 omitted from the index.
Pennsylvania	1860	805111	Franklin County census pages 246–390 (1,898 names) alphabetized separately and appear at the front of the published book index.
Vermont	1850	444926	Rutland County census pages 348–416 omitted from the index.
		444927	Washington County census pages 62–132 omitted from the index.
		444928	Windham County census pages 1–51 omitted from the index.
Vermont	1860	805315	Addison County (the entire film) census pages 1–616 omitted.
Virginia	1830	029680	All of Fairfax County (census pages 230–263) incorrectly listed as Northumberland County; however, page numbers are correctly indexed. Both counties are on the same microfilm.
	1850	029710	Bath County listed as nonexistent Back County.

- Some AIS book indexes were never placed on CD-ROM.
- Only two nationwide searches (1790 and pre-1790) are available (each on one CD-ROM). The remaining discs are limited to regions or individual states. The *Master Name Index to Automated Archives, Inc. CD-ROMs* enables a nationwide search of all the discs at once.
- Some AIS book data may not have been completely transferred to CD-ROM, and some names in the books may be missing from the CD-ROMs.
- So much data is available so quickly from CD-ROM indexes that it is easy to become overwhelmed. Researchers might have to adjust their research methods to fit the volume of information they can find on CD-ROM indexes.

Most *Census Index: U.S. Selected States/Counties* (Windows) CD-ROMs do not have these limitations. Series discs cover the entire United States, and some of the missing data has been restored on these discs. The software and display screens are relatively easy to understand. The major limitation that most affects both the old and new series is the overwhelming number of names in them, which can make it difficult to identify which of the names refers to the ancestor being sought.

Countywide Federal Census Indexes

The most under-used type of Federal census index is the countywide index. These are similar to statewide indexes except that their coverage is limited to a single county or a few counties. Most of them are typewritten abstracts. Some were created before computers made indexing entire states a more

Table 9-10. Counties Omitted or Mislabeled on 1850 CD-ROM Indexes

State	*County*	U.S. Census Index Series *(MS-DOS)*	Census Index: U.S. Selected States/Counties *(Windows)*
Alabama	DeKalb	Omitted	Included
Georgia	Irwin	Omitted	Omitted
Kentucky	Davies	Omitted	Omitted
	Owsley	Omitted	Included
Mississippi	Pike	Omitted	Omitted
	Pontotoc	Omitted	Omitted
	Rankin	Omitted	Omitted
New Jersey	Mercer	Omitted	Included
New York	Broome	Mislabeled Rockland	Listed under both counties
	Cayuga	Omitted	Included
	Parts of New York City	Listed as Pa., only on Pa. disc	Corrected
	Seneca	Mislabeled St. Lawrence	Listed under both counties
Pennsylvania	Armstrong	Omitted	Included
	Carbon	Mislabeled Cambria	Listed under both counties
	Columbia	Omitted	Included
	Erie	Omitted	Included
	Lancaster	Omitted	Included
	Lawrence	Omitted	Included
Tennessee	Part of Cocke	Listed as Cooke	Corrected
	Hardeman	Mislabeled Hardin	Listed under both counties
	Obion	Mislabeled Robertson	Listed under both counties
Vermont	Windham	Omitted	Included
Virginia	Bath	Mislabeled Princess Anne	Listed under both counties
	Brooke	Mislabeled Rockingham	Listed under both counties
	Caroline	Mislabeled Carroll	Listed under both counties
	Floyd	Mislabeled Fayette	Omitted
	Gloucester	Mislabeled Logan	Listed under both counties
	Richmond	Omitted	Included
	Tazewell	Mislabeled Stafford	Listed under both counties
	Future W.Va. counties		Listed under Va. and W.Va.

manageable task, and some have been created as part of local genealogical society projects.

Countywide indexes are sometimes created as part of a marketing strategy. Steve Kratz informed this author that he sold more copies of his index divided into counties than he sold of his statewide *Indiana 1860 Census Index With Alternative Names, Ages, and Birth Places* (cited earlier).

Varieties. Examples of the variety of county census indexes are provided by the states of Kentucky and Michigan. Some of the abstracts are in alphabetical order or are indexed. For example, Anna Hubble's *Madison County, Kentucky, 1840 Census* (Whitefish, Mont.: the author, 1979) is an alphabetical abstract. Mrs. Verle Hamilton Parrish's *1850 Census of Floyd County, Kentucky* (Stamping Ground, Ky., n.d.) is an abstract with a surname index. A full name index is provided in Faye Sea Sanders's *1860 Federal Census Washington County, Kentucky* (Louisville, Ky.: the author, 1982). Randolph N. Smith's *Cumberland County, Kentucky Census Index and Abstracts, 1800–1850* (Burkesville, Ky.: R. N. Smith and L. L. Butler, 1975) abstracts six sources for one county and includes a unified index for all of them. Thirteen counties are indexed in Mrs. M. T. Parrish's *1850 Census Index of Eastern Kentucky* (Stamping Ground, Ky.: the author, 1973).

Local genealogical societies often publish transcripts of the censuses for their areas in their society periodicals. "1830 Census, Morgan County, KY," *East Kentuckian* 2 (1): 13–14 and 2 (2): 13–15, is an abstract with no apparent index. However, the index to a society's periodical can serve as an indirect index to the census. James R. Glacking's "Index Federal Census, Grant County, Kentucky 1820," *Kentucky Ancestors* 10 (3): 121–24, is indexed at the end of the periodical. The cumulative index to vols. 11 to 15 serves as an index to Mrs. E. B. Kresge's "Federal Census of Wayne Co., Mich. 1820," *Detroit Society for Genealogical Research Magazine* 12: 101–05, 129–32.

The two largest census indexing companies, AIS and Precision Indexing, often created county or large city indexes for the later censuses (notably 1870) as part of an overall plan to index entire states; however, in many cases the high cost of indexing has not allowed the rest of the state to be completed. These indexes for large cities and populated counties do provide important assistance, as families are much harder to locate in large metropolitan areas than in smaller rural communities. Table 9-5 identifies most of these "metropolitan" census indexes for 1870.

The number of countywide census indexes varies widely from state to state. As of 1996, there were at least 123 countywide census indexes or alphabetical abstracts for Kentucky, but only three for Massachusetts. Maryland had twenty-five countywide census indexes, and Michigan had at least eighty.

Value. Because countywide indexes are most often created by residents of the subject counties, their creators are more likely to be familiar with the names of the counties' residents; thus, their census indexes may be more accurate than many statewide indexes. Sometimes local compilers annotate their transcripts and indexes with supplemental information not found in the original censuses. For example, Ruth T. Dryden's *Somerset County, Maryland, 1850* ([Silver Spring, Md.: Family Line Publications, 198(?)]) is a good example of an alphabetical census abstract with biographical and marriage annotations (figure 9-6). Countywide indexes can sometimes be used to find names which are omitted from statewide indexes, or for censuses which are not yet indexed statewide.

Searching a census index is usually thought of as part of a quick preliminary survey of available records, but easy access to statewide census indexes causes many researchers to think of census indexes as primarily being statewide sources. Therefore, researchers often overlook the numerous census indexes that exist at the county or local level.

Pompey's Indexes. Countywide census "indexes" by Sherman Lee Pompey are not always as useful as their titles imply. In the mid-1960s, Pompey published a series of brief countywide census abstracts, usually arranged in alphabetical order, like the two-page *1850 Census Records of Mendocino County, California* (Independence, Calif.: Historical & Genealogical Pub., 1965). This alphabetical abstract shows names, ages, sexes, occupations, and birthplaces, but some of Pompey's publications have limited value as indexes and should be considered more as simple typed abstracts. His *Indexes to American and Western Canada Census and Tax Records, 1800–1900* (Salt Lake City: Genealogical Society of Utah, 1967; microfilmed typescript, [196(?)]) list names from selected small counties in sixteen states and British Columbia. The names are listed by state and by county within each state and census year; the names within each county are arranged alphabetically. Census page numbers are not cited, nor are towns. No information except the alphabetical list of names, the county, the state, and the census year is given, and there is no cumulative index. It is difficult to determine a use for a series of short abstracts that give no information beyond what the researcher must know in order to find a name in them.

Finding Aids. There is no comprehensive list of county indexes. One of the best sources is the *Family History Library Catalog*. If the county where an ancestor lived is known, search the *Family History Library Catalog* for census indexes for that county. If there is an Index Publishing census index for the state being searched, the bibliography in its introduction will include a comprehensive list of statewide and countywide census indexes for the state. *The United State Census Compendium* (cited earlier) and Ronald Vern Jackson and Lee Smeal's *Encyclopedia of Local History and Genealogy: Census Encyclopedia* (Bountiful, Utah: Accelerated Indexing Systems, 1979) also help to identify some countywide indexes, although the lists are dated.

The countywide census indexes published in local genealogical periodicals sometimes require extensive searching to find. Search for the place (state, county, or town) where an ancestor lived in periodical indexes, such as *Periodical Source Index* (*PERSI*) (Fort Wayne, Ind.: Allen County Public Library Foundation, 1987–) or *Genealogical Periodical Annual Index* (*GPAI*), compiled by Karen Ackermann and edited by Laird C. Towle (Bowie, Md.: Heritage Books, 1981–). When the place is found, look for census transcripts published in local genealogical periodicals. If a census transcript for the right year is found, determine if the periodical has its own index or if there is an annual or cumulated surname index to help find the ancestor's name in the transcript. Periodicals frequently have an annual index in the final issue for the year. If the periodicals cited are not at a local library, they may be obtainable through interlibrary loan. See chapter 19, "Genealogical Periodicals," for more information about periodical indexes.

Availability. Countywide Federal census indexes are usually harder to access than statewide indexes; their availability at genealogical libraries is usually less certain. The Family History Library has a good collection of countywide indexes, but it is by no means complete. Because only a few of these indexes exist on microfilm, the Family History Library's family history centers can order only a limited number of them. The Library of Congress has a good collection of these indexes, and libraries known for their good genealogical collections should be able to provide access to the genealogical periodicals that include many countywide Federal census indexes. Local genealogical and historical societies in the counties where ancestors lived are likely to have copies of countywide indexes for their counties as well.

Colonial, Territorial, and State Census Indexes

Individual states sometimes took censuses, often in years between the Federal censuses. For example, the state of New York took censuses in 1845, 1855, 1865, 1875, 1892, 1905, 1915, and 1925. There are territorial and state censuses for Illinois for the years 1810, 1818, 1820, 1825, 1830, 1835, 1840, 1845, 1855, and 1865. Some of these are indexed, such as the Illinois censuses from 1810 to 1855. Many colonial, territorial, and state censuses are available in published form.

Some censuses were made during the colonial period. Carol M. Meyers's *Early New York State Census Records, 1663–1772* (Gardena, Calif.: RAM Publishers, 1965), Bettie Stirling Carothers's *1776 Census of Maryland* (Lutherville, Md.: the author, 1972), and Virginia Langham Olmsted's *Spanish and Mexican Colonial Censuses of New Mexico: 1790, 1823, 1845* (Albuquerque: New Mexico Genealogical Society, 1975) are examples of printed colonial census indexes. Territories often took special censuses when they were first acquired by the United States, or to prove that their populations were large enough to apply for statehood. For example, Utah Territory took a census in 1856 to accompany an application for statehood.

Bobbie Jones McLane's *An Index to the Three Volumes, Arkansas 1911 Census of Confederate Veterans* (Hot Springs, Ark.: Arkansas Ancestors, 1988) is an interesting example of a state census index because it is for a more recent, less-well-known census (see figure 9-7).

Substitutes for Federal Censuses. Territorial and state censuses which have been used as substitutes for missing Federal census records include:

- 1782–85 Virginia state
- 1810 Mississippi territorial (including part of Alabama)
- 1820 Alabama state
- 1880 Cherokee Indian territorial (Oklahoma)

QU#652
Isaac H. GILES 24 coach smith
in HH. Beacham Hull

BC#353
John P. GILES 52 farmer
Martha " 47
John " 26 farmer
Sarah C. " 24
Elizabeth " 21
Sarah A. " 15
Ardelia " 12
Rachael " 9
Clarisa " 6

BC#448
Thomas GILES 12
in HH. Eben. Waller

John GILES m. Kiturah Phillips
23 Oct 1821

QU#648
Lyphlet??GILES 33 farmer
Susan " 28
William F." 6
Samuel Thos." 4
Charlotte C." 10/12

QU#621
Sydney GILES 30 farmer
Ann " 30
Clarianer" 6 fem.
Mary E. " 4
Alonzo " 1

QU#633
William GILES 56 farmer
Kitura " 55(1794-1862)
Thomas " 22(1827-1900)
Ann Mariah" 16
Martha E. " 5

Thomas GILES m. Betsy Leatherbury 18 Dec 1798
William GILES m. Catharine DORMAN 17 Dec 1816

Thomas GILLIS and wife Mary were transported into Somerset from Northampton Co. Va. in 1665 by Mark Manlove. His son John patented 300 acres of land called "Barren Creek" a name still used for that area, which in 1724 was part of Nanticoke Hundred. In early records the name was spelled Gilis,Gilliss & Gilley.

BC#567
Beaucham GILLIS 25 school tea-
Martha " 19 cher
infant " 2/12
(Beaucham b.Del.1821-1880)

QU#699
Clement GILLIS 29 farmer
Sally " 26
James N. " 2
Phillis " 60

BC#533
Joseph GILLIS 35 sailor
Nancy " 54
John " 21 sailor
ElihuBRADLEY 20

QU#674
Napoleon GILLIS 20
in HH. Geo. Twilly

BC#529
Samuel GILLIS 45 laborer
George W. " 10
Sally A. " 8
Samuel J. " 3

BC#594
Clement GILLIS 29 laborer
Bridget A." 29
Mary T. " 3
Marcellus J." 2
John C. " 10/12

BC#575
James GILLIS 38 carpenter
Leah E." 30(1819-1890)
Josiph A." 10
Columbus Jas." 8
George B. " 6
Mary E. " 4
Margaret H. " 1
(James 1812-1898)

BC#528
Sarah A. GILLES 35
Columbus " 24 carpenter
(a Sallie Holbrook Gillis
b.1815 d.1878 Princess Anne Md.)

BC#344
William GILLY 22
in HH.Betsy Robertson

Ezekiel McClemmy GILLISS m. Sally Dennis Holbrook 23 Feb 1802
Joseph GILLISS m. Esther Dashiell 6 May 1800 (d/o Robert)
Josiah GILLISS m. Betsy Gray 19 Jan 1813
Josiah GILLISS m. Nancy Gray 4 Feb 1817
Peter Gilliss m. Elizabeth Nelson 17 Nov 1827

Figure 9-6. From Dryden's *Somerset County, Maryland, 1850,* page 86. It is a good illustration of an alphabetical census abstract with biographical and marriage annotations.

Page 40 | **An Index to the Three Volumes Arkansas 1911 Census of Confederate Veterans**

Name	Vol.	Page
Castleberry, Caldona	I	94
Castleberry, Hariet M. P	I	94
Castleberry, Laura E.	I	94
Castleberry, Rena	I	94
Castleberry, Samuel L.	I	94
Castleberry, Wm.	I	94
Castleberry, Wm. Jackson	I	94
Castleberry, Wm. T.	I	94
Caswell, L. & Jean H.	I	107
Catching, Allie	I	157
Catching, Lela	I	157
Cates, Pratt & Carrie E.	II	10
Cates, Sarah	III	98
Ceasil, Minnie	III	51
Ceasil, Virginia	III	51
Cecil, Allen & Betsey	I	95
Cecil, Eddie W. & Ola	I	95
Cecil, Eliz. M.	I	95
Cecil, Ennis & Lucy M.	II	165
Cecil, Euele	I	95
Cecil, Henry Hararison	I	95
Cecil, James R. & Mary	I	95
Cecil, John	II	134
Cecil, John	III	149
Cecil, John & Eliz.	I	153
Cecil, Lillie May	I	95

CASS, Wm., of Prairie Grove, Ark. was born on 4/1/1844 in Polk Co., Tenn. the son of John Cass, who was the son of John Cass of McMinn Co., Tenn. and Va. and Nancy White, dau. of John White (moved from SC to Tenn.) John White was a Revolutinary Soldier. Subject was a Democrat and a Miss. Baptist. Served in Co. E, 5th Tenn. Cavalry, full time service in ranks and in prison. Married Hariett Cohea, dau. of Amos and Mary Cohea of Washington Co. Ark. in 1873. Children:

1. Ed Cass, Prairie Grove, Ark.
2. Chas. Cass - Briggsdale, Calif.
3. Wm. Cass "
4. Clifford "
5. Maynard Prairie Grove, Ark.

No Certification

CASSIDY, Patrick, of Emerson, Ark. was born Jan. 25, 1842 at Belfast, Ireland the son of Tom Cassidy of Belfast, Ireland and Mary McKay. Subject was a farmer, a Republican and a Catholic. He served in Co. B, 38th Ohio Regt., 3rd Brigade, 3rd Div. under Col. Phelps, served 3 years. Married Roxy Burton, 1896 at Lewisville, Ark. Children:

1. Bertha Cassidy, Emerson, Ark.
2. Barnie Cassidy, "
3. Minor Cassidy "

Certified by Auby Rowe, Assessor of Columbia Co., Ark. Aug. 1, 1912

CASTLEBERRY, William Jackson, of Greenbrire, Ark. was born Sept. 24, 1847 at Grub Springs, Monroe Co., Miss. the son of William Castleberry of Walker Co., Ala. who lived at Calhoun Co., Miss. He was a Sargeant in the Civil War, entered the war in July 1862 and died in the Army in Sept. Maiden name of subject's mother was Hariet Malinda Pierce, dau. of Thos. J. and his wife Mary A. Pierce of Cleveland, Ark. Subject was a constable, Democrat, Missionary Baptist and an Odd Fellow. Was a private in Forest's command from Dec 1860 to 1865. Wife not listed, but children were:

1. Alice Ardella Castleberry
2. Laura Emaline Castleberry
3. William Thos. Castleberry
4. Caldona Castleberry
5. Samuel Leroy Castleberry

Figure 9-7. From *An Index to the Three Volumes, Arkansas 1911 Census of Confederate Veterans* (top), page 40. It is an example of a state census index for a more recent, less-well-known census. It indexes (bottom) Bobbie J. McLane and Capitola Glazner's *Arkansas 1911 Census of Confederate Veterans* (n.p., 1977) (page 94).

- 1890 Oklahoma territorial and Cherokee Indian territorial (Oklahoma)

Quality. The reliability, amount of the population covered, and information in these censuses and their indexes varies widely. Some colonial censuses list only a fraction of the population. Some territorial censuses are padded with names of people who had died, moved on, or never existed. Some state censuses are more complete and contain more and better information than Federal census records.

Value. The main reason for using these censuses and their indexes is to locate people, especially for periods before or between Federal censuses. They can help fill gaps between Federal censuses, and sometimes they contain considerable information about a family.

Finding Aids. Jackson's *AIS Microfiche Indexes of U.S. Census and Other Records* (cited earlier) includes some of these kinds of censuses. Most are listed in Ann S. Lainhart's *State Census Records* (Baltimore: Genealogical Publishing Co., 1992). The *Family History Library Catalog* is another good source to search for colonial, territorial, and state census records. They can be found in the catalog under the name of the territory or state followed by the subject "Census" or "Census—Indexes." Each Family History Library state research outline, as well as Eichholz's *Ancestry's Red Book* (cited earlier), briefly discusses colonial, territorial, and state census records in the respective states.

Availability. A limitation of these kinds of printed indexes is their availability. The Family History Library has an excellent collection of colonial, territorial, and state censuses, but only those that exist on microfilm are available through its family history centers. Other major genealogical libraries will have many of them. Genealogical societies are likely to have copies for their areas only. Many original census records are found at the appropriate state archives, while an individual state's index is usually also available at the state's academic libraries, large public libraries, some of its local genealogical libraries, the state historical society, and the state library or archive.

Special Federal Censuses and Schedules

The Federal government sometimes paid for or took special statewide and territorial censuses. During the regular census years, special separate schedules were made at the same time as the regular population schedules. *Mortality schedules* for people who had died in the twelve months preceding the census were made for the Federal censuses from 1850 to 1885. In 1840 and 1890, special schedules of military pensioners and war veterans were made. The 1850 and 1860 censuses include *slave schedules* listing slaveowners and the number of slaves they owned. From 1840 to 1910 the government also kept agricultural and industrial census schedules with information about farms, businesses, and industries. Native Americans were frequently listed in a variety of special censuses or on Indian schedules from 1840 to 1942. Some of these records are indexed.

Data Listed Depend on the Census. These special censuses were taken to obtain information about specific segments of the population. The 1885 censuses should list all of the residents of the seven states and territories covered. Mortality schedules list only deceased persons, who do not appear on the regular census schedules. The 1890 veterans schedules comprise the largest remaining part of the 1890 census, most of which was destroyed by fire in 1921. The 1910 Indian schedules include detailed questions about tribes and families. Although these special censuses and schedules list only a small part of the overall population, they are very helpful to researchers who are fortunate enough to find relatives listed in them.

Off-Year Censuses. The Federal government made the following special Federal censuses of states and territories:

- 1857 Minnesota
- 1864 Arizona
- 1885 Alaska, Colorado, Florida, Nebraska, New Mexico, North Dakota, and South Dakota
- 1907 Oklahoma (records for Seminole County only remain)

An excellent example of a published index for a special Federal census is William T. and Patricia Martin's *1885 Florida State Census Index* (Miami: the authors, 1991) (figure 9-8).

Most of these special state and territorial Federal censuses are available from the states' archives and the National Archives. Because they are less well known than regular censuses, only a few have been indexed. The printed indexes are available at the states' libraries or archives and at larger genealogical libraries. The Family History Library research outline for each state and Eichholz's *Ancestry's Red Book* briefly discuss the special Federal census records and indexes that exist for each state.

Slave Schedule Indexes. Accelerated Indexing Systems has published some slave schedule indexes. For example, Jackson's *Delaware 1850/1860 Slave Schedules* (Salt Lake City: Accelerated Indexing Systems International, 1986) lists the slaveowner's name, county, state, census schedule page, town, and census year (S1850 or S1860). The CD-ROM indexes already include some slave schedules. Names of slaves are not normally listed on slave schedules—only their numbers, age, sex, color, and whether fugitive or manumitted.

Slave schedules can be used to fill in gaps in the population schedules and for historical or biographical purposes, but for only a small part of the population. Approximately 2.4 percent of the 1850 Delaware population were slaves; only 1.6 percent were in 1860. The names of 1,422 slaveowners, approximately 0.7 percent of the combined 1850 and 1860 populations, are listed in *Delaware 1850/1860 Slave Schedules*. Jackson's *Texas 1850 Slave Schedules* (North Salt Lake, Utah: Accelerated Indexing Systems International, 1988) lists 8,516 slave holders—5.5 percent of the white population.

For the 1850 and 1860 censuses, the slave schedules are on microfilm but are separate from the population schedules for the slave states. The slave schedule indexes are available from Accelerated Indexing Systems. The Family History Library has only a few slave schedule indexes. Larger genealogical societies and public libraries with large genealogical collections may have acquired these indexes.

Black Census Indexes. As the Civil War approached, some city leaders, especially in the North, felt it necessary to learn

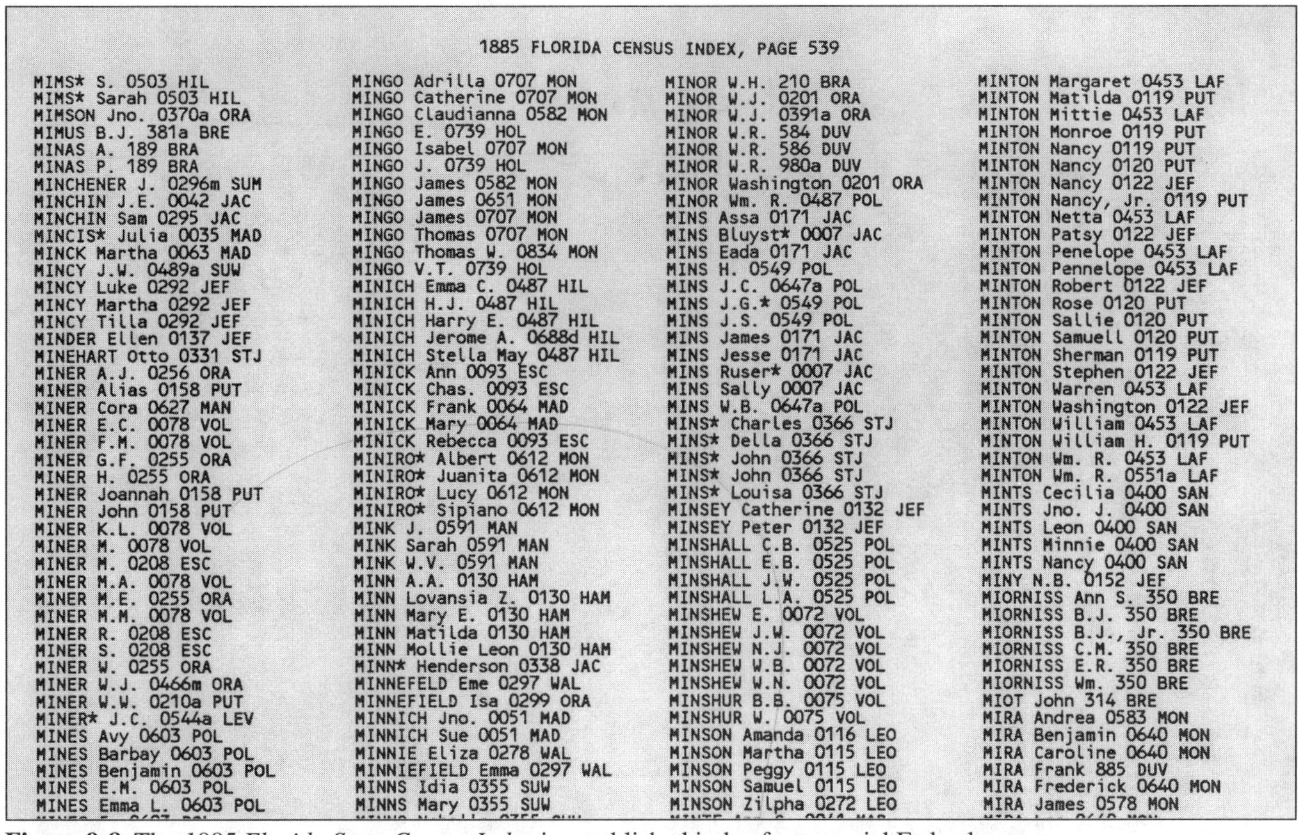

1885 FLORIDA CENSUS INDEX, PAGE 539

MIMS* S. 0503 HIL
MIMS* Sarah 0503 HIL
MIMSON Jno. 0370a ORA
MIMUS B.J. 381a BRE
MINAS A. 189 BRA
MINAS P. 189 BRA
MINCHENER J. 0296m SUM
MINCHIN J.E. 0042 JAC
MINCHIN Sam 0295 JAC
MINCIS* Julia 0035 MAD
MINCK Martha 0063 MAD
MINCY J.W. 0489a SUW
MINCY Luke 0292 JEF
MINCY Martha 0292 JEF
MINCY Tilla 0292 JEF
MINDER Ellen 0137 JEF
MINEHART Otto 0331 STJ
MINER A.J. 0256 ORA
MINER Alias 0158 PUT
MINER Cora 0627 MAN
MINER E.C. 0078 VOL
MINER F.M. 0078 VOL
MINER G.F. 0255 ORA
MINER H. 0255 ORA
MINER Joannah 0158 PUT
MINER John 0158 PUT
MINER K.L. 0078 VOL
MINER M. 0078 VOL
MINER M. 0208 ESC
MINER M.A. 0078 VOL
MINER M.E. 0255 ORA
MINER M.M. 0078 VOL
MINER R. 0208 ESC
MINER S. 0208 ESC
MINER W. 0255 ORA
MINER W.J. 0466m ORA
MINER W.W. 0210a PUT
MINER* J.C. 0544a LEV
MINES Avy 0603 POL
MINES Barbay 0603 POL
MINES Benjamin 0603 POL
MINES E.M. 0603 POL
MINES Emma L. 0603 POL

MINGO Adrilla 0707 MON
MINGO Catherine 0707 MON
MINGO Claudianna 0582 MON
MINGO E. 0739 HOL
MINGO Isabel 0707 MON
MINGO J. 0739 HOL
MINGO James 0582 MON
MINGO James 0651 MON
MINGO James 0707 MON
MINGO Thomas 0707 MON
MINGO Thomas W. 0834 MON
MINGO V.T. 0739 HOL
MINICH Emma C. 0487 HIL
MINICH H.J. 0487 HIL
MINICH Harry E. 0487 HIL
MINICH Jerome A. 0688d HIL
MINICH Stella May 0487 HIL
MINICK Ann 0093 ESC
MINICK Chas. 0093 ESC
MINICK Frank 0064 MAD
MINICK Mary 0064 MAD
MINICK Rebecca 0093 ESC
MINIRO* Albert 0612 MON
MINIRO* Juanita 0612 MON
MINIRO* Lucy 0612 MON
MINIRO* Sipiano 0612 MON
MINK J. 0591 MAN
MINK Sarah 0591 MAN
MINK W.V. 0591 MAN
MINN A.A. 0130 HAM
MINN Lovansia Z. 0130 HAM
MINN Mary E. 0130 HAM
MINN Matilda 0130 HAM
MINN Mollie Leon 0130 HAM
MINN* Henderson 0338 JAC
MINNEFELD Eme 0297 WAL
MINNEFIELD Isa 0299 ORA
MINNICH Jno. 0051 MAD
MINNICH Sue 0051 MAD
MINNIE Eliza 0278 WAL
MINNIEFIELD Emma 0297 WAL
MINNS Idia 0355 SUW
MINNS Mary 0355 SUW

MINOR W.H. 210 BRA
MINOR W.J. 0201 ORA
MINOR W.J. 0391a ORA
MINOR W.R. 584 DUV
MINOR W.R. 586 DUV
MINOR W.R. 980a DUV
MINOR Washington 0201 ORA
MINOR Wm. R. 0487 POL
MINS Assa 0171 JAC
MINS Bluyst* 0007 JAC
MINS Eada 0171 JAC
MINS H. 0549 POL
MINS J.C. 0647a POL
MINS J.G.* 0549 POL
MINS J.S. 0549 POL
MINS James 0171 JAC
MINS Jesse 0171 JAC
MINS Ruser* 0007 JAC
MINS Sally 0007 JAC
MINS W.B. 0647a POL
MINS* Charles 0366 STJ
MINS* Della 0366 STJ
MINS* John 0366 STJ
MINS* John 0366 STJ
MINS* Louisa 0366 STJ
MINSEY Catherine 0132 JEF
MINSEY Peter 0132 JEF
MINSHALL C.B. 0525 POL
MINSHALL E.B. 0525 POL
MINSHALL J.W. 0525 POL
MINSHALL L.A. 0525 POL
MINSHEW E. 0072 VOL
MINSHEW J.W. 0072 VOL
MINSHEW N.J. 0072 VOL
MINSHEW W.B. 0072 VOL
MINSHEW W.N. 0072 VOL
MINSHUR B.B. 0075 VOL
MINSHUR W. 0075 VOL
MINSON Amanda 0116 LEO
MINSON Martha 0115 LEO
MINSON Peggy 0115 LEO
MINSON Samuel 0115 LEO
MINSON Zilpha 0272 LEO

MINTON Margaret 0453 LAF
MINTON Matilda 0119 PUT
MINTON Mittie 0453 LAF
MINTON Monroe 0119 PUT
MINTON Nancy 0119 PUT
MINTON Nancy 0120 PUT
MINTON Nancy 0122 JEF
MINTON Nancy, Jr. 0119 PUT
MINTON Netta 0453 LAF
MINTON Patsy 0122 JEF
MINTON Penelope 0453 LAF
MINTON Pennelope 0453 LAF
MINTON Robert 0122 JEF
MINTON Rose 0120 PUT
MINTON Sallie 0120 PUT
MINTON Samuell 0120 PUT
MINTON Sherman 0119 PUT
MINTON Stephen 0122 JEF
MINTON Warren 0453 LAF
MINTON Washington 0122 JEF
MINTON William 0453 LAF
MINTON William H. 0119 PUT
MINTON Wm. R. 0453 LAF
MINTON Wm. R. 0551a LAF
MINTS Cecilia 0400 SAN
MINTS Jno. J. 0400 SAN
MINTS Leon 0400 SAN
MINTS Minnie 0400 SAN
MINTS Nancy 0400 SAN
MINY N.B. 0152 JEF
MIORNISS Ann S. 350 BRE
MIORNISS B.J. 350 BRE
MIORNISS B.J., Jr. 350 BRE
MIORNISS C.M. 350 BRE
MIORNISS E.R. 350 BRE
MIORNISS Wm. 350 BRE
MIOT John 314 BRE
MIRA Andrea 0583 MON
MIRA Benjamin 0640 MON
MIRA Caroline 0640 MON
MIRA Frank 885 DUV
MIRA Frederick 0640 MON
MIRA James 0578 MON

Figure 9-8. The *1885 Florida State Census Index* is a published index for a special Federal census.

about the free blacks who were moving into their cities by taking a census of them. Some of the censuses are indexed; for example, Lewis J. Bellardo, Jr., "Frankfort, Kentucky, Census of Free Blacks, 1842," *National Genealogical Society Quarterly* 63 (4): 272–75, is an alphabetical list that includes short biographical entries. There are also publications like Alice Eichholz and James M. Rose's *Free Black Heads of Households in the New York State Federal Census, 1790–1830* (Detroit: Gale Research, 1981). In this tradition, Brøderbund Software released (in 1996) an index to blacks in the 1870 census for several major states and cities: *African Americans in the 1870 Census,* Family Tree Maker's Family Archives, no. 165 ([Novato, Calif.]: Brøderbund, 1996). It includes entries from the states of Georgia, North Carolina, Pennsylvania, South Carolina, Virginia, and West Virginia, as well as Baltimore, Chicago, New York City (including Long Island), and St. Louis.

Agricultural Schedule Indexes. Indexed agricultural schedules are rare and hard to locate. Jackson's *Louisiana Sugar Censuses 1850–1860* (North Salt Lake, Utah: Accelerated Indexing Systems, 1987) indexes an unusual type of agricultural census that is not part of the normal Federal agricultural schedules. This index lists each sugar farmer's name, parish (county), state (Louisiana), census schedule page, locale (which bank of which water course), and census year.

Manufacturers Schedule Indexes. Manufacturers schedules were made at the same time as population schedules. They can partially fill gaps in the population schedules, but only for the small part of the population who were business owners. They provide interesting information about American businesses. An example of a publication about this type of census is *Indexes to Manufacturers Census of 1820* (Knightstown, Ind.: Bookmark, 1977). It lists the census marshals, counties and their page numbers, industries, and each manufacturer's name (and business) alphabetically for each state (figure 9-9). The biggest limitation of this kind of index is the very small fraction of the population included in manufacturers schedules—far less than 1 percent. *Indexes to Manufacturers Census of 1820* appears to be the only such nationwide index, but local indexes to manufacturers schedules are available for some localities. Manufacturers schedules are available through the National Archives.

Mortality Schedule Indexes. All of the available mortality schedules from 1850 to 1880 and South Dakota's for 1885 are indexed in search 8 of Jackson's *AIS Microfiche Indexes of U.S. Census and Other Records,* and in *Census Index: U.S. Selected States/Counties,* CD-ROM no. 164 of the Family Tree Maker's Family Archives. AIS also published book indexes for each individual state. AIS indexes list the following data: name of the deceased, county, state, age, sex, month of death, place of birth, cause of death, and a code for the deceased person's occupation. Other publishers have also indexed some of these records—for example, *Index, Louisiana Mortality Records for the Years Ending June 1, 1850, 1860, 1870* (typescript, n.d.). These schedules and indexes list only the small part of the population that died in the twelve months before the census was taken, and some names may have been overlooked.

1840 Pensioner Indexes. The 1840 Federal census included a special list of revolutionary war pensioners. The printed list, *A Census of Pensioners for Revolutionary or Military Services:*

28 1820 CENSUS OF MANUFACTURES INDEX

INDIANA

121 documents reproduced on microfilm roll 20

A photocopy of any original document listed in this index may be obtained from The Bookmark, the publishers, for $2.00 taxpaid and postpaid, regardless of number of pages in the document, or from the National Archives' Photocopy Department. [*Inquire as to cost*]. As the ink is faded, the quality may be poor.

Although documents 11, 84, 103, 105, and 120 contain statements that the information on them was omitted from the abstract and the word "omitted" was written on many schedules in other documents, no abstract has been found.

Document 105 is a schedule showing the production of numerous types of manufactures for a society that had settled five years earlier in the town of Harmonie, Harmonie Township, Posey County. No wages were paid, but wages would have amounted to $20,000 if paid. This schedule may refer to the Harmony Community whose members had emigrated from Pennsylvania in 1814.

For the taking of the manufacturing census returns, many Indiana assistant marshals "demanded" or "claimed", in some cases, specific sums of money varying from $2.00 (see document 60) to $15.00 (see document 48), and, in other cases, the "highest compensation" (see document 17), "as much as the law allows" (see document 68), or "as much as the Secretary of State thinks reasonable" (see document 116).

Indexes have not been prepared for the domestic manufactures in Dearborn County listed on document 26. While Perry County had no manufacturers' schedule, the assistant marshal wrote the occupation of each manufacturer alongside each name of a manufacturer shown on the population schedule.

Marshals

MARSHAL —*JOHN VAWTER*

ASSISTANT MARSHALS

Beggs, James
Espey, Hugh Jr.
Huston, Alexander
Johnson, B.
Nelson, William
Tucker, Martin H.

Indiana County References

The schedules and related records have been filmed in the following order. *To locate county, refer to these numbers in using the index.*

County	Documents	County	Documents
Clark	1-10	Martin	95-97
Crawford	15-26	Orange	98-104
Dearborn	11-14	Perry	see notes
		Posey	105
Fayette	27-59	Scott	106-108
Franklin	60	Sullivan	109
Jefferson	61	Vigo	110-113
Knox	62-92	Washington	114-181
Lawrence	93-94	Randolph	182

1820 CENSUS OF MANUFACTURES INDEX 29

Indiana Index to Industries

Numbers shown in the *Index to Types of Industry* and to the *Name Index* are the beginning document page. By comparing these numbers with those under the *County References*, above, one can determine the county of origin for any document.

Baker 9
Blacksmith's work 9, 27, 41, 50, 51, 54, 88, 90, 94, 99, 105, 118, 119, 120
Books 9
Bricks 9, 40, 43, 112, 119
Butter 105
Cabinet ware 9, 32, 42, 52, 53, 56, 57, 58, 77, 81, 93, 94, 101, 115, 119, 120
Chairs 9, 70, 87, 94, 115
Clocks 9
Coaches, carts, and chaises 105, 114
Cooper's work 9, 27, 40, 50, 78, 91, 94, 110, 112, 117
Copperware 9
Cordage, rope, cables, and twine 105
Earthenware and pottery 9, 21, 30, 31, 43, 48, 68, 71, 94, 105, 107
Firearms 9, 12, 47, 54
Flour and Meal 9, 13, 14, 15, 18, 19, 23, 24, 29, 33, 45, 46, 59, 72, 94, 97, 105, 110, 111, 112, 113, 117
Gold, silver, and plated ware 9
Gunpowder 9
Hats and bonnets 22, 27, 31, 33, 43, 49, 51, 58, 60, 75, 100, 102, 105, 106, 109, 110, 112, 115, 119, 120
Houses 81, 93
Iron 9
Jewelry 9
Leather 9, 11, 12, 15, 16, 20, 35, 49, 52, 58, 64, 93, 104, 108, 109, 110, 111, 116, 117, 118
Lumber 9, 24, 26, 29, 33, 45, 46, 48, 59, 96, 111, 112, 113, 117
Machinery 53, 76
Meat 112
Saddles, bridles, and harnesses 9, 74, 79, 80, 92, 94, 98, 103, 105, 116, 118
Shoes and boots 9, 48, 73, 86, 94, 105, 109, 110, 114
Skins 12, 15, 16, 20, 28, 35, 49, 58, 64, 104
Textiles 9, 11, 17, 25, 29, 34, 39, 52, 60, 84, 105, 111, 117, 118, 119
Tinware 61, 105
Tobacco 16
Tools 67, 89, 105
Wagons 9, 53, 67, 89, 105, 114
Wheelwright's work 9, 29, 32, 66, 70, 87, 94
Whiskey and other spirits 2, 3, 4, 5, 6, 7, 8, 9, 13, 14, 18, 23, 24, 25, 32, 33, 35, 36, 37, 38, 44, 46, 50, 51, 54, 55, 56, 57, 59, 62, 63, 65, 69, 82, 83, 85, 105, 110, 111

Indiana Name Index

ALDRIDGE, William 131
ALLEN, Claiborne 15
ALLEN, Isaac, heirs of 15
ALSOP, Joseph 109
ARMFIELD, Jonathan 116
ARRAWOOD, Jacob 25
ATKINSON, Elijah 120
ATKINSON, Stephen 120
BAILEY, Judah 60
BAKER, Michael 118
BALDWIN, Amos 94
BALL, Stephen 43
BARD, William 119
BATES, Hervey 39
BAUTON, Henry 40
BAUTON, Stephen 40
BAXTER, Thomas 49
BEEBE, Samuel 25
BELL, Hugh 55
BELL, Samuel 55
BERNARD, Reuel 117
BLASDOL, Jacob 24
BONNER, James 64
BOYD, James 50
BROOKS, James 109
BROWN, Manasseh 86
BRUCE, William 84
CAIN, Dennis 34
CATT, Thomas 66
CHRISTLER, Allen 59
CHURCH, Uzziel 32
CLARK, George 62
CLARK, James 104
CLARKE, John E 119
COCHRAN, James 61
COFFIN, Stephen 118
COFFIN, Thomas 103
COLEMAN, Isaac 73
CONNER, John 37, 46
CONWAY, William 94
COON & DECKER 65
COOPER, John 114
COX, Ashen 39
CROUCH, Nathan 31
CULBERSON, Joseph 93
CURRY, John 115
CUTTER, James 101
DALE, Sydnor 42
DAVISON, John 57
DEHAVEN, Jacob 54
DEHAVEN, Samuel 54

Figure 9-9. From *Indexes to Manufacturers Census of 1820.*

With Their Names, Ages, and Places of Residence, as Returned by the Marshals of the Several Judicial Districts, under the Act for Taking the Sixth Census (Washington, D.C.: Blair and Rives, 1841), is indexed in *A General Index to a Census of Pensioners for Revolutionary Service, 1840* (Baltimore: Genealogical Publishing Co., 1965). The latter shows the pensioner's name and page in the list; it does not show the place of residence as found in the book. It includes approximately twenty-one thousand names. The AIS index, Jackson's *United States Census of Pensioners of 1840: Index of Names with Ages to the Original 1841 Government Publication* (Bountiful, Utah: Accelerated Indexing Systems International, 1984), does show the residence.

1890 Population Schedule Index. Most of the 1890 census was destroyed by the government after an accidental fire. Ken Nelson indexed the 6,160 names on the surviving population schedule fragments in *1890 U.S. Census Index to Surviving Population Schedules and Register of Film Numbers to the Special Census of Union Veterans,* rev. ed. (Salt Lake City: Family History Library, 1991). Helen Swenson also indexed them in an earlier, competing index. Nelson's index gives the name of the individual, state, county, township, and census page number. He indexed fragments from these states:

- Alabama
- District of Columbia
- Georgia
- Illinois
- Minnesota
- New Jersey
- New York
- North Carolina
- Ohio
- South Dakota
- Texas

The names from the population schedule fragments for Minnesota, New York, and Texas are also included in the veterans schedule indexes published by Index Publishing.

On rare occasions, state or local copies of censuses believed to have been destroyed appear. This was the case with the 1890 census for Asencion Parish, Louisiana. When the original notes of the census enumerator were found, Rita Butler published them as *Ascension Parish, Louisiana, 1890 U.S. Census* ([Baton Rouge, La.]: Oracle Press, 1983).

1890 Veterans Schedule Indexes. All of the thirty-four surviving statewide 1890 Civil War veterans schedules (alphabetically from Kentucky to Wyoming) have been indexed (except Ohio and Pennsylvania). The schedules for sixteen states (Alabama to Kansas) were destroyed with the rest of the 1890 census. Although the veterans schedules represent only a fraction of the population, they contain a significant number of names. For example, Dilts's *1890 New York Census Index of Civil War Veterans or Their Widows* (Salt Lake City: Index Publishing, 1984) includes 134,633 entries—approximately 2.2 percent of the New York population. The Missouri veterans index lists 91,090 names—approximately 3.3 percent of the population. Maine's veterans index holds 29,549 names—4.5 percent of Maine's 1890 population. (Some of the entries are for extra, alternate spellings.) Jackson's *South Carolina 1890 Census Index of Civil War Veterans* (1984) has the fewest—only 2,510 names, as there were relatively few Union veterans in South Carolina. The veterans schedules were intended to enumerate Union veterans only, but some Confederate veterans were listed as well. Unfortunately, the census takers apparently missed many veterans who should have been listed. The published indexes list the veteran's or his widow's name, census supervisor's district, county, locale, and veterans schedule page number or enumeration district.

On the Confederate side there are some veterans indexes as well. For example, Houston C. Jenks's *An Index to the [Louisiana] Census of 1911 of Confederate Veterans or Their Widows* ([Baton Rouge, La.: Jenks], 1989) shows the name of the veteran or widow, parish (county), age, state where he enlisted, regiment, company, the value of his property, occupation, any infirmities of the former soldier or widow, marriage date, and veterans schedule microfilm number. This index lists 5,600 names—0.3 percent of Louisiana's 1910 population. McLane's *An Index to the Three Volumes, Arkansas 1911 Census of Confederate Veterans* (cited earlier) is another example of a Confederate veterans index—by coincidence, for the same year.

Most 1890 veterans schedule indexes are still in print and available from their publishers. They are also available at the Family History Library and larger genealogical libraries. Individual states' 1890 veterans indexes are usually also available at each state's academic libraries, large public libraries, some genealogical libraries, state historical society, and the state library or archive.

Indian Schedule Indexes. The government sometimes took special Indian censuses, or had special schedules for Indians during regular censuses. For example, in the 1910 Nevada Federal census, Indian schedules are microfilmed as part of the population schedules. As a result, the printed index includes the names on these Indian schedules. But most Indian census records are found in catalogs and other finding aids under the various tribes, and only a few have been indexed. Two records which serve as substitute censuses and which have been indexed are the Dawes Commission Records and the Guion Miller Rolls.

In 1893 the Commission to the Five Civilized Tribes (Dawes Commission) was established to exchange tribal lands of the Cherokee, Choctaw, Chickasaw, Creek, and Seminole tribes for individual allotments in Indian territory. Applications were taken between 1899 and 1907. A few names were added as late as 1914 (Family History Library 1992).

In 1905 the Eastern Cherokee were awarded a settlement for a claim against the United States. Guion Miller, a special agent of the Interior Department, was given the task of compiling a roll of eligible persons. Applications submitted include English and Indian name, residence, age, birthplace, spouse, tribe, and children of the applicant. Similar information was given about parents, grandparents, brothers, sisters, aunts, and uncles. Strict qualifying requirements may have excluded many individuals from the list (Family History Library 1992).

The National Archives and the Family History Library have copies of these Indian records and indexes on microfilm. Look for other Indian censuses in the *Family History Library Catalog* and in National Archives finding aids.

Dutch-Americans. There is an unusual selective index for three Federal censuses in Robert P. Swierenga's *Dutch Households in U.S. Population Censuses 1850, 1860, 1870* (Wilmington,

Del.: Scholarly Resources, 1987). This large, three-volume set includes only names from counties with clusters of more than fifty people born in the Netherlands. The editor indexed 91.4 percent of the Dutch-born people in the 1850 census, 80.6 percent for 1860, and 76.3 percent for 1870. His work is essentially an alphabetical transcript of selected names from the three censuses.

Census Indexes for International Areas

Indexes for U.S. censuses are more useful and more widely available than for any other country. However, a few census indexes are available for censuses taken outside the United States. Census records outside the United States vary widely in their content. Many are chiefly statistical, but a few provide more information than U.S. censuses.

Canada. Bryan Lee Dilts's *1848 and 1850 Canada West (Ontario) Census Index* (Salt Lake City: Index Publishing, 1984) is an example of a Canadian provincial census index. It lists only a portion of Ontario's residents because only a portion of the census was available to the indexer. Other Canadian census indexes include:

- 1770–77 Nova Scotia
- 1800–42 Canada
- 1851 Nova Scotia
- 1851 New Brunswick
- 1871 Ontario
- 1881 Manitoba
- 1881 Northwest Territories
- 1881 British Columbia

Search the *Family History Library Catalog* for Canadian provincial census records and indexes. They can be found in the locality section under the name of the territory or province followed by the subject "Census" or "Census—Indexes." Canadian indexes are available from their publishers and at the Family History Library. Few of them are on microfiche or microfilm and therefore they are not available through family history centers. Some, such as the indexes for Ontario for 1871, are on CD-ROM.

Great Britain. The Federation of Family History Societies and the Family History Library are compiling an index for the nationwide 1881 census of Britain and Wales. The Family History Library published the index for each county on microfiche as it was completed and has completed all of England and Scotland. The indexes include the following information: surname, given name, age, sex, relationship to head of household, marital status, census place, occupation, name of head of household, birthplace, Public Records Office reference number, and Family History Library microfilm number. Several separate indexes are created from this data, as illustrated in figure 9-10:

- Surname index
- Birthplace index
- Census place index
- Census as enumerated

The microfiche is available at the Family History Library and at its family history centers.

The 1851 Census of England and Wales (Salt Lake City: Genealogical Society of Utah, 1997) is exactly the same kind of index but is limited to three counties: Devon, Norfolk, and Warwick. It is available in both microfiche and CD-ROM formats. No plans exist to index any other counties for 1851.

Ireland. Some census fragments exist for Ireland. Two of these have been indexed in *Ireland Census Index: Londonderry County, 1831 [and] Cavan County, 1841*. Automated Archives, no 197. ([Orem, Utah]: Automated Archives, 1994), which includes entries for Londonderry for 1831 and Cavan for 1841.

PUBLISHED TAX LISTS AND INDEXES

Governments keep careful records of taxpayers and tax delinquents. Researchers can find records of taxes on individuals, various kinds of property, imports, services, and income. Local, county, state, and Federal governments all collect taxes and keep tax records. However, county governments were especially likely to tax property (either commodities or real estate). Tax records usually concern resident heads of families and property owners; married women, children, paupers, indentured servants, and slaves are not usually recorded in tax records. Taxes were most often collected annually, and annual tax records extending over periods of many years are often available. Researchers usually find tax records at the archive of the government which collected the taxes; for example, county courthouses are most often the places to search for property tax records. See "Taxes" in chapter 8, "Research in Land and Tax Records," in *The Source: A Guidebook ofAmerican Genealogy* (cited earlier) and Arlene H. Eakle's *Tax Records: A Common Source with an Uncommon Value* ([Salt Lake City: Family History World], 1978) for detailed discussions of the nature, value, and limitations of tax records.

Tax Lists as Census Substitutes

Tax lists are valuable both as substitutes for census records and in their own right. Tax records imply residence, and finding where someone lived is one of the main reasons for using census records and indexes; therefore, indexers often use tax lists as substitutes for reconstructing "census" records. Often, tax records show most of the same persons that a heads-of-households census would show. (But every-name censuses contain a much larger part of the population than do most tax records.) Another reason tax lists are used as census substitutes is that tax records are usually available for years prior to the first census records and for years between censuses. When using tax lists, note whether the years of the indexed tax lists actually correspond with the years of the censuses they are intended to replace.

Value and Limitations

Printed tax lists and indexes are subject to the same weaknesses and strengths discussed regarding census indexes. A hard-of-hearing clerk might have spelled a non-English-speaking immigrant's name incorrectly; the indexer might have been unable to read old handwriting or faded microfilm; the records may be missing some years; alphabetized lists may obscure kinships implied by people's proximity in neighborhoods; the indexer might have omitted a name or made transcription and typographical errors; the abstract might have left out important identifying details; or the book manufacturer may have shuffled pages. But alphabetized, printed tax lists are easier and faster to use than microfilms of originals, and sometimes printed lists are more easily available from libraries. In addition, statewide tax list indexes are valuable locator tools when the place of residence is unknown.

"Censuses" Reconstructed from Tax Lists

Virginia has some classic examples of tax lists used to reconstruct census records. The 1790 Virginia census was destroyed in the War of 1812, so the Federal government created a substitute census from the annual state censuses for 1782 to 1785 and the Greenbriar County 1783 and 1786 tax lists. It is called *Heads of Families at the First Census of the United States Taken in the Year 1790, Virginia: Records of the State Enumerations, 1782 to 1785* (1908; reprint; Baltimore: Genealogical Publishing Co., 1986). This index includes 37,900 names from thirty-nine counties. However, forty-one Virginia counties were not included in this substitute for the 1790 census. To make up the difference, Augusta Brigland Fothergill and John Mark Naugle published another index, *Virginia Tax Payers, 1782–1787, Other Than Those Published by the United States Census Bureau* (1940; reprint; Baltimore: Genealogical Publishing Co., 1974), based on tax lists from the remaining forty-one counties. This index lists approximately 33,150 names.

Netti Schreiner-Yantis and Florene Speakman Love compiled another substitute census, *The 1787 Census of Virginia* (Springfield, Va.: Genealogical Books in Print, 1987), mostly from 1787 tax lists and a few 1786 and 1788 tax lists (for counties where none survived for 1787). The compilers used land tax lists, petition signatures, and a list of insolvents (poor people) for one county and 1789 tax lists for two counties that are in present-day Kentucky. By their estimate, 95 to 98 percent of white taxable males over age twenty-one are included in the index. It includes approximately eighty-four thousand entries and is the most carefully compiled of the Virginia census substitutes mentioned.

The 1810 census schedules for eighteen Virginia counties were also burned in the War of 1812. Elizabeth P. Bentley indexed the census for the surviving counties in *Index to the 1810 Census of Virginia* (Baltimore: Genealogical Publishing Co., 1980), which includes approximately 83,500 names. Netti Schreiner-Yantis published *A Supplement to the 1810 Census of Virginia: Tax Lists of the Counties for Which the Census Is Missing* (Springfield, Va.: Genealogical Books in Print, 1971) to fill in information for the eighteen missing counties. It lists approximately nineteen thousand names.

Value of Tax Records. Tax records are also valuable in their own right. The great majority of American heads of households have owned enough property to be liable for taxes. Tax lists usually contain historical and biographical details missing from most census records, often describing individuals more uniquely than do census records. Because governments usually collect taxes annually, tax records are often available for years when census records do not exist. Researchers often can use tax records, especially at the time of transfer from one generation to the next, to identify kinship.

Indexes that are based on tax records compiled over several years are more complete and reliable because one tax list may omit some people, but a series of tax lists is likely to show most of the residents in an area. This coverage is the value of Jackson's *New Jersey Tax Lists, 1772–1822* (Salt Lake City: Accelerated Indexing Systems, 1981), which lists multiple tax years in a single index. The names are arranged alphabetically followed by the county, state, tax list page, town, and tax date. The same person's name may appear repeatedly for each separate tax year listed, as in figure 9-11. However, there are possible disadvantages to the use of lists compiled over several years. Compilers may not be able to present material uniformly if the information recorded in separate tax years or counties is variable. Nor does indexing multiple tax years assure that all available tax records will be indexed. In *New Jersey Tax Lists, 1772–1822*, Hunterdon County appears to be missing entirely from the index. The compiler does not explain what his sources were or why Hunterdon County is missing.

Comparing tax lists to census records and other local records is useful. Tax records sometimes list the names of older (adult male) children decades before census records list their names. But later census records sometimes show members of households who are not listed in tax records. A researcher is likely to find more implied clues about a family by using multiple records that show changes over time.

Formats. Tax lists are published in many forms. Thomas E. Partlow's *Tax Lists of Wilson County, Tennessee, 1803–1807, With Names in Court Records, 1802–1822* (Baltimore: Clearfield, 1981) is an example of a countywide tax list. Some county histories include early tax lists, especially from the county's first years; however, indexes to such county histories do not always include the names in the tax lists. For example, William A. Foster and Thomas Allan Scott's *Paulding County [Georgia]: Its People and Places* (Roswell, Ga.: W. H. Wolfe Associates, 1983) includes portions of an 1871 tax digest that is not included in the index.

Some tax lists are published in genealogical and historical society periodicals. For example, the Pennsylvania Archives series includes various tax lists. The 1780 lists for all the counties except Northampton and Westmoreland were extracted and indexed separately in John D. and E. Diane Stemmons's *Pennsylvania in 1780: A Statewide Index of circa 1780 Pennsylvania Taxlists* (Laughlintown, Pa.: Southwest Pennsylvania Genealogical Services, 1978). "New Jersey Rateables, 1773–1774" is published in *Genealogical Magazine of New Jersey* (vols. 36–37). The same names were later published separately as part of Kenn Stryker-Rodda's *Revolutionary Census of New Jersey: An Index, Based on Rateables, of the Inhabitants of New Jersey During the Period of the American Revolution*, rev. ed. (Lambertville, N.J.: Hunterdon House, 1972; reprint; 1986), which also includes the years 1778 to 1780 and 1784 to 1786.

As mentioned previously, tax lists have been used as partial substitutes for missing Federal censuses in Delaware, Georgia, Kentucky, New Jersey, Tennessee, Virginia, and other places. Published tax lists and indexes are found at larger genealogical libraries.

Finding Aids. Jackson's *AIS Microfiche Indexes of U.S. Census and Other Records* includes some tax records. The *Family History Library Catalog* is another good source to search for tax records and indexes. They can be found in the *Catalog*'s locality section under the name of the territory or state followed by the subject "Taxation." Each Family History Library state research outline, as well as Eichholz's *Ancestry's Red Book,* briefly discusses state tax records and indexes in the respective states.

1881 CENSUS-SCOTLAND NATIONAL SURNAME INDEX

REID , Clement PAGE: 56172

DATA FROM THE 1881 CENSUS OF SCOTLAND © BRITISH CROWN COPYRIGHT 1982.
MICROFICHE EDITION OF THE 1881 CENSUS OF SCOTLAND © COPYRIGHT 1996, BY CORPORATION OF THE PRESIDENT OF THE CHURCH OF JESUS CHRIST OF LATTER-DAY SAINTS.

SURNAME	FORENAME	AGE	SEX	RELATIONSHIP TO HEAD	MARITAL CONDITION	CENSUS		OCCUPATION	NAME OF HEAD	WHERE BORN		NOTE	REFERENCES			
													GRO FOR SCOTLAND			G.S.U. FILM NUMBER
						CO	PARISH			CO	PARISH		VOLUME NUMBER	ENUM. DIST.	PAGE NO	
REID	Clement	94	M	Head	W	RFW	West Green+	Formerly Gard+	Self	AYR	---		564-3	12	14	0203574
REID	Clementina	64	F	Wife	M	FOR	Dunnichen	Butchers Wife	REID, William	FOR	Forfar		283	1	10	0203491
REID	Clementina	61	F	Head	U	STI	Larbert	Letter Carrier	Self	STI	Kilsyth		485	4	18	0203543
REID	Clementina	60	F	Head	W	ZET	Sandsting +	Crofter	Self	ZET	Sandsting		009	4	8	0203395
REID	Clementina	52	F	Head	U	EDN	Inveresk	House Proprie+	Self	EDN	Inveresk		689	8	8	0224013
REID	Clementina	50	F	(Head)	U	BAN	Aberlour	Dressmaker	Self	BAN	Keith		145	2	4	0203436
REID	Clementina	38	F	Wife	M	FOR	Dundee	---	REID, John	BAN	Keith		282-4	33	35	0203488
REID	Clementina	28	F	Wife	M	FOR	Monifieth	---	REID, Thomas	KNC	Glenbervie		310	4	5	0203496
REID	Clementina	12	F	Daur	-	KNC	Fordoun	Scholar	REID, John	KNC	Fordoun		259	5	2	0203470
REID	Clementina E.	1m	F	Daur	-	KNC	Banchory D+	---	REID, James	KNC	Banchory Devenick	*	251-2	5	8	0203468
REID	Clemintina	3	F	Daur	-	ABD	Fyvie	---	REID, Arthur	ABD	Culsalmond		197	10	17	0203456
REID	Colin	70	M	Head	M	ROC	Cromarty	House Factor	Self	ROC	Cromarty		061	1	1	0203407

1881 Scotland National Surname Index

1881 CENSUS-SCOTLAND NATIONAL BIRTHPLACE INDEX

AYR Killmarnock , HAY PAGE: 10897

DATA FROM THE 1881 CENSUS OF SCOTLAND © BRITISH CROWN COPYRIGHT 1982.
MICROFICHE EDITION OF THE 1881 CENSUS OF SCOTLAND © COPYRIGHT 1996, BY CORPORATION OF THE PRESIDENT OF THE CHURCH OF JESUS CHRIST OF LATTER-DAY SAINTS.

WHERE BORN		SURNAME	FORENAME	AGE	SEX	RELATIONSHIP TO HEAD	MARITAL CONDITION		CENSUS		NOTE	REFERENCES			
												GRO FOR SCOTLAND			G.S.U. FILM NUMBER
CO	PARISH							NAME OF HEAD	CO	PARISH		VOLUME NUMBER	ENUM. DIST.	PAGE NO	
AYR	Killmarnock	HAY	Janet	38	F	Wife	M	HAY, James	LAK	East Kilbride		643	6	25	0203628
AYR	Killmarnock	PURDIE	Robert	29	M	Head	M	Self	LAK	New Monkland		651-1	4	1	0203696
AYR	Killmarnock	SCOTT	Archibald	33	M	Head	M	Self	RFW	Paisley High Church		573	13	26	0203581
AYR	Killmarnock	WELSH	Agness	4	F	Daur	-	WELSH, William	KRK	Kirkpatrick Durham		874	1	15	0224058
AYR	Killmarnock	WILLOCH	George	54	M	Head	M	Self	RFW	Paisley Low Church		573	71	6	0203584
AYR	Killmars	LAIRD	Elizabeth	34	F	Wife	M	LAIRD, Hugh	RFW	West Greenock		564-3	6	9	0203573
AYR	Killmars	WYELIE	Michael	69	M	Head	M	Self	LNL	Bo'ness		663	5	11	0203707
AYR	Killmichael	MC PHAIL	Elizabeth	63	F	Head	U	Self	RFW	Eastwood		562	8	29	0203568
AYR	Killmichael	MC PHAIL	Mary	60	F	Sis	U	MC PHAIL, Eli+	RFW	Eastwood		562	8	29	0203568
AYR	Killnamil	RITCHIE	J.	30	M	Crpl	U	I-"EDINBURGH +	EDN	Edinburgh Canongate		685-4	96	11	0224007
AYR	Killw	MC CULLOCH	Annie	7	F	Daur	-	MC CULLOCH, W+	AYR	Dundonald		595	8A	10	0203599
AYR	Killw	MC CULLOCH	Catherine	7	F	Daur	-	MC CULLOCH, W+	AYR	Dundonald		595	8A	10	0203599

1881 Scotland National Birthplace Index

1881 CENSUS-SURNAME INDEX, COUNTY: DERBYSHIRE

BAND , Louisa PAGE: 00400

CENSUS DATA © BRITISH CROWN COPYRIGHT 1982.
MICROFICHE EDITION OF THE INDEXES © COPYRIGHT 1990, BY CORPORATION OF THE PRESIDENT OF THE CHURCH OF JESUS CHRIST OF LATTER-DAY SAINTS.

SURNAME	FORENAME	AGE	SEX	RELATIONSHIP TO HEAD	MARITAL CONDITION		OCCUPATION	NAME OF HEAD	WHERE BORN		NOTE	REFERENCES			
												PUBLIC RECORD OFFICE			G.S.U. FILM NUMBER
						CENSUS PLACE			CO	PARISH		PIECE ROll/	FOLIO NO	PAGE NO	
BAND	Louisa	19	F	GDau	U	Belper	---	PEEL, Isaac	DBY	Derby		3412	122	1	1341816
BAND	Margaret E.	9	F	Daur	-	Derby St Werbu+	Scholar	BAND, Charles	---	St Werburghs Parish +		3396	107	10	1341812
BAND	Martha	29	F	Sis	U	Glossop Dale	Housekeeper	BAND, John S.	DBY	Wooley Bridge Glossop		3460	78	14	1341828
BAND	Martha	5	F	Daur	-	Glossop Dale	Scholar	BAND, Joseph	DBY	Woolley Bridge Gloss+		3460	84	25	1341828
BAND	Mary	6	F	Daur	-	Derby St Alkmu+	Scholar	BAND, John	DBY	---		3406	93	14	1341815
BAND	Mary A.	1	F	Daur	-	Glossop Dale	---	BAND, Charles D.	DBY	Glossop		3458	40	26	1341827
BAND	Mary Ann	44	F	Sis	U	Glossop Dale	Cotton Weaver	BAND, John S.	CHS	Hollingworth		3460	78	14	1341828
BAND	Mary E.	26	F	Daur	U	Derby St Werbu+	Milliner & Dr+	BAND, Charles	---	St Peters Parish Der+		3396	107	10	1341812
BAND	Robert C.	20	M	Son	U	Hayfield	Engraver Lbr	BAND, Joseph	---	Manchester		3462	8	10	1341829
BAND	Samuel E.	12	M	Son	-	Derby St Werbu+	Scholar	BAND, Charles	---	St Werburghs Parish +		3396	107	10	1341812
BAND	Sarah	36	F	Wife	M	Glossop Dale	Masons Wife	BAND, Charles D.	DBY	Hayfield		3458	40	26	1341827
BAND	Sarah	9	F	Daur	-	Glossop Dale	Scholar	BAND, Joseph	DBY	Woolley Bridge Gloss+		3460	84	25	1341828

1881 Surname Index, Derby

Figure 9-10. From the Scotland and England 1881census indexes compiled by the Federation of Family History Societies and the Family History Library.

Availability. Tax record indexes are available at larger genealogical libraries. Usually, an individual state's index is also available at that state's academic libraries, large public libraries, some of the state's local genealogical libraries, the state historical society, and the state library or archive.

OTHER CENSUS SUBSTITUTES

AIS Census Substitutes

AIS has indexed a variety of records which identify or imply residence, among them tax lists, wills, petitions, land records, local censuses, sheriffs' censuses, voter lists, and vital records. AIS created two groups of indexes from these sources. The Early American Series includes titles like Jackson's *Early Alabama* (cited earlier), *Early California* (Bountiful, Utah: Accelerated Indexing Systems, 1980), and *Early Connecticut* (Bountiful, Utah: Accelerated Indexing Systems, 1980). About fifty-two titles for twenty-seven states in the AIS catalog carry the "early" description. All of the states with indexes in the Early American Series lie east of the Mississippi River except Missouri, Louisiana, Utah, and California. Early American Series indexes almost always index more than one source—sometimes a dozen sources spread over several decades. AIS included most of the Early American Series published through 1983 in its microfiche indexes. Many published since 1983 also appear on MicroQuix's

1881 CENSUS-BIRTHPLACE INDEX, COUNTY: DERBYSHIRE

BRODIE , DBY Staveley PAGE: 01214

SURNAME	WHERE BORN		FORENAME	AGE	SEX	RELATION-SHIP TO HEAD	MARITAL CONDITION		CENSUS PLACE	NOTE	REFERENCES: PUBLIC RECORD OFFICE			G.S.U. FILM NUMBER
	CO	PARISH						NAME OF HEAD			PIECE RG11/	FOLIO NO	PAGE NO	
BRODIE	DBY	Staveley	Sarah Ann	3	F	Daur	U	BRODIE, Mark	Staveley		3442	134	20	1341823
BRODIE	DBY	Staveley	Thomas	17	M	Son	U	BRODIE, Mark	Staveley		3442	134	20	1341823
BRODIE	DUR	Warrington Hill	Mark	45	M	Head	M	Self	Staveley		3442	134	20	1341823
BRODIE	SUS	Eastbourne	Ninian	16	M	Bord	U	JOHNSON, David	Fairfield		3454	46	31	1341826
BRODIE	SUS	Eastbourne	Stuart Moor	12	M	Bord	U	JOHNSON, David	Fairfield		3454	46	31	1341826
BRODIE	SUS	Howards Heath	Mary	40	F	Wife	M	BRODIE, Mark	Staveley		3442	134	20	1341823
BRODLY	CHS	Marple	George	32	M	Head	M	Self	Glossop Dale		3461	29	4	1341828
BRODLY	CHS	Marple	Herbert	12	M	Son	U	BRODLY, George	Glossop Dale		3461	29	4	1341828
BRODLY	DBY	Glcssop	Jane	3	F	Daur	U	BRODLY, George	Glossop Dale		3461	29	4	1341828
BRODLY	DBY	Glossop	Sarah A.	30	F	Wife	M	BRODLY, George	Glossop Dale		3461	29	4	1341828
BRODLY	DBY	Glossop	Sarah A.	7	F	Daur	U	BRODLY, George	Glossop Dale		3461	29	4	1341828
BRODLY	DBY	Glossop	Thomas	5	M	Son	U	BRODLY, George	Glossop Dale		3461	29	4	1341828

1881 Birthplace Index, Derby

1881 CENSUS-CENSUS PLACE INDEX, COUNTY: DERBYSHIRE

BABBS , Pilsley In Ches PAGE: 00282

SURNAME	CENSUS PLACE	FORENAME	AGE	SEX	RELATION-SHIP TO HEAD	MARITAL CONDITION		WHERE BORN		NOTE	REFERENCES: PUBLIC RECORD OFFICE			G.S.U. FILM NUMBER
							NAME OF HEAD	CO	PARISH		PIECE RG11/	FOLIO NO	PAGE NO	
BABBS	Pilsley In Chesterfield	Stephen	2	M	Son	-	BABBS, Thomas	DBY	Stonebroom		3428	133	6	1341820
BABBS	Pilsley In Chesterfield	Thomas	42	M	Head	M	Self	DBY	Stavely		3428	133	6	1341820
BABBS	Staveley	Sarah	57	F	Wife	M	BABBS, William	STF	Kingsinford		3443	131	29	1341824
BABBS	Staveley	William	56	M	Head	M	Self	WOR	Bilbrington		3443	131	29	1341824
BABBS	Whittington	Ann Barker	8	F	GDau	-	BARKER, Charles	DBY	Whittington		3437	80	26	1341822
BABBS	Whittington	Fanny B.	10	F	Niec	-	DANN, William	DBY	Whittington		3437	78	21	1341822
BABBS	Whittington	Sarah B.	12	F	Niec	-	DANN, William	DBY	Whittington		3437	78	21	1341822
BABBS	Whittington	William	68	M	Head	W	Self	DBY	Staveley		3437	82	29	1341822
BABER	Tansley	Alice A.	53	F	Wife	M	BABER, John	DBY	Ashover		3451	58	2	1341826
BABER	Tansley	Alice A.	21	F	Daur	U	BABER, John	DBY	Tansley		3451	58	2	1341826
BABER	Tansley	Eleanor	15	F	Daur	U	BABER, John	DBY	Tansley		3451	58	2	1341826
BABER	Tansley	Ernest	12	M	Son	-	BABER, John	DBY	Tansley		3451	58	2	1341826

1881 Census Place Index, Derby

1881 CENSUS-AS ENUMERATED, COUNTY: DERBYSHIRE

Shipley , 3325 45 30 PAGE: 01464

CENSUS PLACE	HOUSEHOLD		SURNAME	RELATIONSHIP TO HEAD		MARITAL CONDITION				WHERE BORN		NOTE	REFERENCES: PUBLIC RECORD OFFICE			G.S.U. FILM NUMBER
	ADDRESS			FORENAME			AGE	SEX	OCCUPATION	CO	PARISH		PIECE RG11/	FOLIO NO	PAGE NO	
Shipley	Nutbrook Canal		POLKEY	John	---	M	60	M	Boatman Barge+	LEC	Lough Borough		3325	45	30	1341793
Shipley	Nutbrook Canal		ORSE	John	(Hea	M	52	M	Master Bargem+	BUK	---		3325	45	30	1341793
Shipley	Nutbrook Canal		ORSE	Jane	---	M	49	F	Master Bargem+	HAM	Gosport		3325	45	30	1341793
Shipley	Nutbrook Canal		HOLLIS	Joseph	---	U	20	M	Boatman Barge+	BUK	---		3325	45	30	1341793
Shipley	Nutbrook Canal		COOPER	John	---	M	49	M	Master Bargem+	NTH	Bucbrook		3325	45	30	1341793
Shipley	Nutbrook Canal		GOODMAN	John	---	M	53	M	Boatman Barge+	LEC	Thurmaton		3325	45	30	1341793
Shipley	Nutbrook Canal	//	WINKLESS	John	(Hea	M	50	M	Master Bargem+	WAR	Nalsh		3325	45	30	1341793
Shipley	Nutbrook Canal		WINKLESS	Eliza	---	M	47	F	Master Wife	WAR	Nalsh		3325	45	30	1341793
Shipley	Nutbrook Canal		WINKLESS	Eliza	---	U	18	F	Masters Daugh+	LEC	---		3325	45	30	1341793
Shipley	Nutbrook Canal		WINKLESS	John	---	-	9	M	Masters Son	LEC	Bramston		3325	45	30	1341793
Shipley	Nutbrook Canal		WINKLESS	Stephen	---	-	5	M	Masters Son	LEC	Bramston		3325	45	30	1341793
Ilkeston	Heanor Road	//	BRADLEY	Henry	Head	W	83	M	Inn Keeper	DBY	Ilkeston		3325	49	1	1341793

1881 As Enumerated, Derby

Figure 9-10 (continued).

U.S. Census Index Series CD-ROM indexes. However, the names from one Early American Series book index covering more than one decade may be divided into separate microfiche searches or separate CD-ROMs.

A second, smaller group of AIS substitute census indexes includes decennary and tax indexes. These are compiled from territorial, state, county, and city censuses and from sheriffs' censuses, military censuses, and tithables and tax records. Titles from this group include Jackson's *Alabama 1811–1819 Decennary Census Index* (Bountiful, Utah: Accelerated Indexing Systems, 1983) and his *Texas Census Records 1841–1849* (also known as *Texas 1840–49*) (North Salt Lake, Utah: Accelerated Indexing Systems International, 1981). They index more than one source, but not as many sources as a typical Early American Series index. The range of years covered is always ten or less and is usually not the full range of years listed in the title. Names from the decennary indexes sometimes appear in indexes of the Early American Series (and vice versa) but apparently are from different records. AIS included most, but not all, of the decennary indexes in the *AIS Microfiche Indexes* and on the *U.S. Census Index Series* CD-ROM indexes. Some names on the CD-ROM indexes are missing from the microfiche (and vice versa).

Unfortunately, AIS indexes rarely include details or citations for their sources, so it is sometimes a challenge to determine what was indexed in the Early American Series or the decennary indexes. For detailed instructions on how to find obscure AIS index sources, see "Instructional Literature" (page 310).

GRANDINE, WILLIAM	MONMOUTH CO.	NJ 005	FREEHOLD TWP	JUN.AUTX1790
GRANDINE, WILLIAM	MONMOUTH CO.	NJ 009	FREEHOLD TWP	JULTX1784
GRANDINE, WILLIAM	MONMOUTH CO.	NJ 005	FREEHOLD TWP	JUN.AUTX1792
GRANDINE, WILLIAM	MONMOUTH CO.	NJ 004	DOVER TWP	JULTX1779
GRANDINE, WILLIAM	MONMOUTH CO.	NJ 016	MIDDLETOWN TWP	AUGTX1790
GRANDINESY, DANIEL	SOMERSET CO.	NJ 003	BEDMINSTER TWP	AUGTX1796
GRANDING, SAMUEL	MONMOUTH CO.	NJ 001	DOVER TWP	AUGTX1796
GRANDING, WILLIAM*	MONMOUTH CO.	NJ 001	DOVER TWP	AUGTX1796
GRANDLEVIER, PETER*	SUSSEX CO.	NJ 002	NEWTON	SEPTX1774
GRANE, FRANCES	GLOUCESTER CO.	NJ 003	WOOLWICH TWP	MAYTX1780
GRANE, ISRAEL*	BERGEN CO.	NJ 020	SADDLE RIVER	JUNTX1822
GRANS, D. *	SOMERSET CO.	NJ 002	BERNARDS TWP	DECTX1787
GRANT, ABRAHAM	SOMERSET CO.	NJ 004	BERNARDS TWP	AUGTX1789
GRANT, CHARLES	ESSEX CO.	NJ 019	NEWARK TWP	TX1821
GRANT, CHARLES	ESSEX CO.	NJ 018	NEWARK TWP	TX1820
GRANT, DAVID	SOMERSET CO.	NJ 004	BERNARDS TWP	AUGTX1789
GRANT, DAVID	SOMERSET CO.	NJ 005	BERNARDS TWP	AUGTX1792
GRANT, DAVID	SOMERSET CO.	NJ 006	BERNARDS TWP	AUGTX1790
GRANT, DAVID	SOMERSET CO.	NJ 006	BERNARDS TWP	AUGTX1791
GRANT, EDWARD	MONMOUTH CO.	NJ 003	SHEWSBURY TWP	TX1808
GRANT, G. *	SOMERSET CO.	NJ 004	BERNARDS TWP	AUGTX1785
GRANT, GABRIEL	ESSEX CO.	NJ 016	NEWARK TWP	TX1793
GRANT, GEORGE	SOMERSET CO.	NJ 006	BERNARDS TWP	AUGTX1791
GRANT, GEORGE	SOMERSET CO.	NJ 006	BERNARDS TWP	AUGTX1790
GRANT, GEORGE	SOMERSET CO.	NJ 004	BERNARDS TWP	AUGTX1788
GRANT, GORGO	SOMERSET CO.	NJ 004	BERNARDS TWP	AUGTX1789
GRANT, HUGH	ESSEX CO.	NJ 007	SPRINGFIELD	TX1812
GRANT, ISRAEL	MONMOUTH CO.	NJ 002	DOVER TWP	TX1779
GRANT, IWLLIAM	ESSEX CO.	NJ 018	NEWARK TWP	TX1796
GRANT, JACOB	ESSEX CO.	NJ 013	NEWARK TWP	TX1810
GRANT, JACOB	GLOUCESTER CO.	NJ 011	WOOLWICH TWP	JU-AUTX1796
GRANT, JACOB	GLOUCESTER CO.	NJ 010	WOOLWICH TWP	JU-AUTX1796

Figure 9-11. From *New Jersey Tax Lists, 1772–1822*. It indexes multiple tax years; the same person's name may appear repeatedly for each separate tax year listed, as shown here.

Many individuals and organizations have published indexes that imply residence and serve as substitute census indexes. But no matter who publishes them, census substitutes usually share certain characteristics.

Census Substitute Limitations

Census substitutes are seldom as comprehensive as actual censuses. Tax lists are probably the best substitutes because tax collectors attempted to be thorough, as census takers did. But most of the other records used as sources for reconstructed censuses were never intended as comprehensive lists of all the residents of an area. Petition signers, jurors, and names in newspapers represent only a fraction of the people in a county or state.

Nor are the substitute records always from the years they represent. It is possible to find published substitute records that were originally created eight or nine years prior to or later than the census they are intended to substitute for. In areas where there has been extensive migration, such a discrepancy can mean that a significant portion of the population is not represented in a reconstructed census.

Coverage

Most reconstructed censuses are for the older (eastern) states. The larger populations of eastern states make the need for substitute censuses greater when Federal censuses are missing. Western states usually have fewer records to index, and Federal censuses are adequate for most western areas.

Two examples of reconstructed censuses demonstrate the variety of records sometimes substituted for censuses. *Virginia in 1740: A Reconstructed Census* (cited earlier) was compiled from 131 sources, including wills, deeds, order books, tithables (taxpayers), baptisms, marriages, guardians, land trials, vestry books, surveys, county histories, road order books, court records, cemeteries, town council minutes, criminal trials, land patents, Huguenot immigration, newspapers, Quaker genealogy, and land grants. In Marie De Lamar and Elisabeth Rothstein's *Reconstructed 1790 Census of Georgia: Substitutes for Georgia's Lost 1790 Census* (Baltimore: Genealogical Publishing Co., 1985), the authors used headright grants, tax defaulters, jurors, newspapers, militia lists, land court journals, witnesses on deeds, voters lists, and estate sale advertisements, mostly for the years before 1820.

Sources

Other records that are sometimes used as census substitutes include early poll lists, rent rolls, accounts, passenger arrival lists, naturalizations, and denizations. City and county directories often include more names than censuses, so they are sometimes used as substitutes as well. Some states, such as Rhode Island and Louisiana, took military censuses to determine who could serve in their militias. The "great registers" (voting lists) of California and Arizona show residence and can also be used as census substitutes. Chicago 1890 voting registers can be used as replacements for the missing 1890 census.

STRENGTHS OF CENSUS INDEXES AND SIMILAR PUBLICATIONS

Little Foreknowledge Required

An important strength of census indexes is that they are easy to use with little prerequisite knowledge. Sometimes individuals can be identified in census indexes with no more information to begin with than a name; however, it is worthwhile to know more. Approximately when and where a person lived is information that makes census indexes easier to use. Such information is usually easy for family historians to determine, but it is not necessary to have precise information to use census indexes. For example, if a researcher can surmise that a head of household lived in the United States between 1790 and 1920, there is an excellent chance the researcher could quickly find that person in Federal census indexes.

Help to Locate People and Their Records

Many researchers use census indexes to turn imprecise guesses into definite information so they can find more original records. Once a person is found in a census index, it is easy to confirm the information and find more by turning to the original census records (or a transcript). When the person's identity is confirmed, exactly where the person lived and when she lived there will be revealed by the census records. These two pieces of information are usually crucial in locating more original records about vaguely identified people.

Comprehensiveness

Censuses and tax lists must be as comprehensive as possible, and census takers and tax collectors were motivated to identify everyone they could. Most censuses and tax lists are "snapshots" of entire target populations at a place and time, while most other original records result from ongoing efforts; they are compiled over many years. Most original records include only a few members of a population at any one moment; census records are designed to show all, and they often succeed very well.

Help to Avoid Tedious Searches

Census indexes and alphabetical census transcripts can save researchers hours by preventing the uncertainty of searching through page after page of unrelated names on faded, handwritten censuses. (When forced into unsuccessful page-by-page searches, researchers often wonder if they might accidentally have passed over an ancestor in a moment of haste or dulled alertness due to boredom.)

Ease of Use

Another strength of printed censuses is their ease of use (compared with microfilm copies). Their book format is usually more convenient than microform and the attendant machinery needed to read it. More important, typeset (or typewritten) text is usually easier to read than the handwritten script of the original records or microfilm copies. Microfilm copies sometimes appear blurred or faded or show poor contrast. The compilers of printed censuses often arrange the text to help users find individuals more easily than in the originals, and census indexes on computer diskettes and CD-ROMs usually include easy-to-use search software.

Additional Information

A final advantage of published censuses and indexes is that compilers occasionally enhance them with information from other sources. Such enhanced indexes are most likely to be found in local or county census transcripts published in local genealogical periodicals.

WEAKNESSES AND HOW TO OVERCOME THEM

Published censuses, census indexes, and tax lists usually serve their purposes well and save researchers much time, but they are subject to several notable weaknesses. Occasionally such a weakness hinders a researcher's efforts to find an ancestor's name.

There are ways to cope with, mitigate, or overcome these problems; they usually involve some extra effort or vigilance by the researcher. Two general rules help to reduce most problems. First, use all available sources; this will reduce the chances of an error due to over-reliance on a single record or kind of record. Second, be flexible and try to determine what could have gone wrong if a record that is expected to exist cannot be found.

Census and Tax List Problems

First, there can be errors in the census or tax list itself. Printed copies or indexes usually perpetuate such errors.

Overcounts. Census takers sometimes had motives for "padding" their counts. For example, one objection to statehood for Utah Territory was its insufficient population. To overcome this objection, Utah officials submitted an 1856 census showing nearly seventy-seven thousand residents. (It is interesting to note that four years later the Federal census showed only 40,273 residents for the territory.) Some names on the 1856 census are fictitious, repeated, or are those of nonresidents of Utah Territory. The names of several identical persons appear in different census districts. Some names listed are of people who died while crossing the plains to Utah. Some persons are listed under three variations of their names. Further evidence of padding is that virtually every page and most columns begin with a surname that is different from that which ends the previous one, the last family in each column having exactly enough members to reach the last available line (Dilts 1983, iii).

In 1910, census takers in Tacoma, Washington, were convicted of fraudulently padding their schedules by 38 percent (Thorndale and Dollarhide 1987, xxi). In another example, seven counties in southwest Minnesota's special 1857 Federal census held no white inhabitants. Nevertheless, to support ballot fraud, politicians fabricated census schedules (Thorndale and Dollarhide 1987, 172).

Undercounts. Undercounts are more common than overcounts. As comprehensive as censuses are intended to be, they do tend to miss some people. For example, the 1860 census of Boston shows 8 percent fewer names than the 1860 city directories (Thorndale and Dollarhide 1987, xxi); census takers inadvertently overlooked some people, and some residents avoided government officials. Some people avoid census takers because they fear persecution or being identified as illegal aliens. Some people even avoid census takers or intentionally mislead them for religous reasons: according to the Bible, a great pestilence resulted when King David sinned by numbering the people (2 Samuel 24).

Researchers can cope with the problem of overcounts and undercounts by comparing census schedules and tax lists to other records for the same time and place. Consulting more records makes it more likely that census problems will be discovered and overcome.

Misspellings. Even when people cooperated fully with census takers and tax collectors, as most did, censuses and tax lists are still subject to data errors. Language differences sometimes caused names and other information to be altered. Even when census takers and census informants spoke the same language, misunderstanding sometimes resulted; researchers find misspelled names on almost all census and tax records. (The prescribed spelling of words is a new phenomenon; word spellings, even of names, were inconsistent two hundred years ago. A census taker late for dinner on a long, hot, dusty, summer day might not have cared whether a name was spelled Stuart or Stewart.)

Cope with this common problem by being flexible. When a name with the correct spelling cannot be found, search for alternate spellings. If the census taker recorded the name incorrectly, the most likely error is an incorrect vowel. Table 9-11 shows alternative ways that names may be spelled in original records.

Name Changes. Some family names have changed over time—for example, from Hartpence to Hart. A Native American might have changed her name several times—White Pine Sally might have become Julie Dishwater overnight. Family traditions sometimes (often incorrectly) tell of name changes; otherwise, searching all available records for a family is the best way to detect unexpected name changes.

Misunderstandings. Even among English-speaking people, a softly spoken name or the poor hearing of a census taker could cause names to entered incorrectly in census schedules. Jewish, Greek, Russian, or Japanese immigrants may have spelled their names with letters of an alphabet an English-speaking person had never seen before. Sometimes census takers and local residents were incapable of or unwilling to communicate at all; one befuddled census taker in the 1860 California census listed pages of Chinese laborers under the same "Lee" surname. Being flexible while searching for spellings of names helps to overcome such problems. Again, table 9-11 can assist with these kinds of problems.

False Information. Some people may have been reluctant to divulge their true ages, and polygamous families may have had reason to hide their relationships. A census taker may even have forgotten to note the change in a street name when turning a corner. There are almost as many potential causes for mistakes on census or tax lists as there are entries on them, and indexes are likely to perpetuate many of them. Using a variety of sources will help the researcher to recognize misleading information.

Missing Years and Records. The "snapshot" of the population that makes a census or tax list so comprehensive can also be a weakness because much can happen in the ten years between Federal censuses. For example, the birth of an infant can go unnoticed if it died before the next census.

Census records of some towns, counties, and states are missing. As mentioned earlier, almost all of the 1890 population schedules were destroyed. Schedules for twenty-two counties in east Tennessee are missing from the 1820 census, and there are dozens of records missing from most census years. These missing records make the gap between some Federal censuses at least twenty years—nearly long enough for a generation to have grown up and left home.

William Thorndale and William Dollarhide's *Map Guide to the U.S. Federal Censuses, 1790–1920* (Baltimore: Genealogical Publishing Co., 1987) can identify gaps and missing Federal census records. State or local censuses can sometimes fill gaps in the Federal censuses, and tax lists are often useful substitutes for missing census years. Use all of the available genealogical sources to make a more complete picture of a family for periods when Federal census years are missing, or for the years between censuses.

Boundary (Jurisdiction) Confusion. National, state, county, and local borders have changed frequently as localities were annexed or ceded territory to each other, sometimes resulting in confusion about the area a census index covers. For example, the 1830 Miller County, Arkansas, census includes eleven present-day Texas counties (Hodge 1963, 68). Jackson's *Alabama 1811–1819 Decennary Census Index* lists "MISSISSIPPI TERR.CENSUS" 1816 as a source (1983, 1). The *1856 Utah Census Index* lists Malad, Idaho, and Green River, Wyoming (Dilts 1983, xvii). Here is a list of some additional boundary change examples (Dowling 1990, 70):

- 1790 Washington, D.C., is with Montgomery and Prince George's counties, Maryland
- 1800 to 1860 West Virginia is with Virginia (1860 index is separate)
- 1820 and 1830 Wisconsin is with Michigan (1830 index is separate)
- 1840 Montana is with Clayton County, Iowa
- 1836 Minnesota is with Iowa
- 1860 Arizona is with New Mexico
- 1860 Colorado is divided between Kansas, Nebraska, and New Mexico (index is separate)
- 1860 Montana, Wyoming, and northeast Colorado are with Nebraska (indexes are separate)
- 1860 Nevada is with Utah
- 1860 Oklahoma is with Arkansas (1860 index is separate)

Consult the notes and maps in *Map Guide to the U.S. Federal Censuses, 1790–1920,* to become familiar with such situations; they usually illuminate possible census oddities, such as missing years and boundary changes. The better index publishers explain census and tax list anomalies in the introductions to their works. Being aware of unusual situations will help the researcher better understand the census being used.

Index Shortcomings

Refer to chapter 6, "Published Indexes," for a discussion of some generic shortcomings of indexes (including several difficulties mentioned below) and how to overcome them. This section focuses on those problems which are most prominent in census and tax list indexes.

Transcription Errors. Census and tax indexes are more prone to transcription errors than indexes to family histories, whose authors are likely to know each name well. A census input typist might spend long hours hunched over difficult-to-read, faded microfilms. The result can be typing mistakes, omitted names, misread information, overlooked page changes, or inconsistent copying of locality data; further, the typist might not always

Table 9-11. Phonetic Substitutes Table

Original	*Letters Which Might Have Been Substituted for the Original*	*Original*	*Letters Which Might Have Been Substituted for the Original*
a	e, i, o, u, y, ey, eh	mb (as in *comb*)	mm, lm, mn
au	ow, ou	n	nn, ng, gn (as in *gnat*), kn, m
b	p, v, bb, pp	ng	n, nk, ch, k, q
bb	b, p, pp	nk	ng, ch, k, q
c (as in *catch*)	k, g, gh, q, cc, ck	nn	n
c (as in *chin*)	ch, cz, s, sh, tch, tsh, z, dg	o	a, e, i, u, aw, ow, eau (as in *beau*)
ch	c, k, g, gh, sh, h (as in *Chanukah*), ju (as in San *Juan*)	oey	oy, oe, oi
chr	kr, gr, cr	oi	oy, oe, oey
ck	k, c, g, q	oo	u, ow, ew
cr	kr, chr, gr	ou	u, au, ow, ew, oo
cz	c, ch, ts, tz, s, sh, tch, tsh	ow	au, ou, eau (as in *beau*)
d	dd, t, dt	oy	oi, oe, oey
dd	d, t, tt	p	b, pp, ph, bb
dg (as in *dodge*)	g, j, ch, gg, tj	pf	f, p, ph, gh, v, lf
ds (as in *bends*)	z, ts	ph	f, gh (as in *laugh*), pf, lf, p
dt	d, t, tt	ps (as in *psalm*)	s
e	a, ee, i, o, u, y, ie, ea	q	c, ch, g, k, gh, cc, ck, ng, nk
ea	e, i, y, ie, ei	r	rr, wr, rh
eau (as in *beau*)	o, aw, ow, au, ou	rh	r, rr, wr
ee	ie, e, i, y, ea, ei	rr	r, rh, wr
ew	u, oo, ou	s	c, sh, tch, z, cz, ss, x
f	v, ph, pf, gh, lf (as in *calf*), ff	sch (as in *school*)	sh, s, sc, sk, sq
ff	f, ph, gh, v, lf (as in *calf*)	sch (as in *Schwarz*)	s, sh
g	c, ch, gg, gh, j, k, q, dg, h (as in *Gila* Monster)	sch (as in *Tisch*)	sh, tsh, tch, ch, cz, ti (as in *nation*), ss
gg	g, ch, k, q, j	sh	s, c, ch, cz, sch, ti (as in *nation*), ss
gh (as in *ghost*)	c, ch, g, gg, ch, k, q	sk	sch, sh, s, sc, sq
gh (as in *laugh*)	f, ph, pf, v, lf	sq	sc, sk, sch, sh
gn (as in *gnat*)	n, kn	ss	s, c, ch, ci, sh, sc, z
gr	chr, kr	t	d, dd, tt, th
h	(h is sometimes omitted) ch, wh, w, g (as in *Gila* Monster), ju (as in San *Juan*)	tch	s, sh, c, ch, cz, s, tsh
i	a, e, o, u, y, ei, uy, aye	th	t, tt, d
ie	e, i, y, ee, ea, ei	ti (as in *nation*)	sh, si, tsh, tch, ch
ij	y, i, ei, ii	tj	j, g, ch, dj, dg, tch, tsch, s
j	ch, g, dg, gg	tt	d, dd, t, th, dt
ju (as in San *Juan*)	h, wh, ch	ts	tz, cz, z
k	c, ch, g, gh, q, nk, cc, ck	tz	ts, cz, z
kn (as in *knot*)	n, gn	u	a, e, i, o, ou, ew, oo
kr	chr, cr, gr	v	b, f, lf, w
ks	x	w	wh, v, au, oa, h, ju (as in San *Juan*)
l	ll	wh	w, h, ju (as in San *Juan*),oa
lf (as in *calf*)	f, v, ph, pf, gh	wr	r, rh, rr
Ll	l, th	x	s, z, ks, chs
lm (as in *calm*)	m, mm, mb, mn	y	i, e, ij
m	mm, lm, mb, mn, n	z	s, c, sh, sch, x, ds

have followed the indexer's rules for transcribing unusual names. Federal censuses since 1850 list every person by name, but most indexers include only the head of household's name and "stray" names which do not match with the head of household's surname; however, indexers are especially apt to inadvertently omit stray names. These are probably the most common kinds of census and tax index shortcomings.

Census indexes are infamous for their inaccuracies. Some authors are quick to point out and emphasize these limitations, usually with personal anecdotes (see Adams 1983, 108; Heiss 1976, 4; Johnson 1974, 2960; Martin 1978, 54; McMillon 1977, 206). A researcher who travels a hundred miles to read a census record has good reason for being frustrated by misleading census indexes, but, while indexes may not be perfect, it is better to have them than nothing at all. (Indeed, a researcher should not assume that a census index is totally accurate; such an assumption might lead to important information being missed.) The answer to imperfect indexes is simple but often overlooked by researchers: If a name is missing from an index, search the original record; it may be there. "Good effective research can begin with a published [census] index, BUT MUST NOT END THERE" (McMillon 1977, 206). Think of an index as a useful shortcut, not as the only path to finding a name in a census or tax record.

Consider William Thorndale's point of view in the first edition of *The Source: A Guidebook of American Genealogy,* in which he points out how accurate indexes are. For example, in a 90-percent-accurate index a researcher will easily find a name an average of nine out of ten times; the name sought will be found an average of forty-nine out of fifty times if the index is 98 percent accurate, so researchers ought to be grateful to indexers for saving them from many tedious searches rather than condemning indexers for missing or mangling some names. Only the rarest index is completely reliable. A good researcher simply learns how to compensate when they are not (Eakle 1984, 18).

Census index accuracy varies widely. It is possible to find census indexes that are only 70 percent accurate; the average is more likely to be between 90 and 98 percent accurate. Good indexers can usually produce indexes that are more than 95 percent accurate. The section titled "How Accurate are Census Indexes?" (below) explores census index accuracy further. Table 9-14 shows some index errors found in a random sample of census names and their indexes; they illustrate the nature of census index errors.

How Some Indexers Prevent Transcription Errors

To help prevent transcription errors, some of the better indexers have two different typists input the same names. If the second typist's entry of a name differs from the first typist's entry, a computer program halts input until a correct version is agreed upon. This method helps to significantly reduce the number of transcription errors because at least two people must agree on what should be typed.

Another approach used by some indexers also requires two or more input typists. In it, a typist is encouraged to make more than one entry for any name whose spelling is uncertain. A computer program compares all entries and discards extra duplicates, but no attempt is made to decide whether one potential spelling is more correct than another. All variations and interpretations are put in the index. This "the more, the merrier" approach assumes that at least one of the typists' versions is likely to be found by researchers. One indexer put it this way:

> If a census name can be read more than one way, we have tried to index each possible spelling. Of course, some of the alternate spellings we list are wrong. But our method also means we put significantly more correct names in our indexes (Dilts 1986, iv).

How Researchers Can Overcome Transcription Errors

Index inaccuracies and the mistakes of census takers often result in researchers failing to find names that are in census or tax lists. Unusual names are especially prone to be misspelled or mistranscribed. In addition to the discussion below, further discussion of census index errors and techniques for overcoming them is found in William Thorndale's "Census Indexes and Spelling Variants," *Association of Professional Genealogists Newsletter* 4 (5) (May 1982): 6–9 (reprinted in the first edition of *The Source: A Guidebook of American Genealogy* [Salt Lake City: Ancestry, 1984, 17–20]) and David Paul Davenport's "Census Indexes: A Primer," *Illinois State Genealogical Society Quarterly* 23 (Fall 1991): 130–39.

Name transcription errors can be overcome by searching for alternative spellings of a name. For example, the old handwritten uppercase *S* is often mistaken for an uppercase *L,* resulting in "Lemuel" rather than "Samuel" or vice versa. Typists can easily mistake the handwritten "David" for "Daniel." Both Index Publishing and Precision Indexing census index introductions include tables and instructions explaining common transcription errors and how to overcome them.

If an index omits a name, a patient researcher can search for the name in the original census record (if the place of residence can be determined). Many researchers have been rewarded by finding a name in the census when it was omitted or significantly altered in the index.

Census indexes can also give incorrect page or locality data. Federal census pages usually have one or more handwritten page numbers and one or more stamped ("crash") numbers on them. Researchers must be prepared to use any of these numbers on the census because indexers may have used any of them. If the index gives the incorrect page number, the county and town information in the index can be used to find the name in the census without using the page number.

Omissions. Sometimes indexers inadvertently overlook names in the records they are indexing, but not all apparent omissions are true omissions. Sometimes a name is so badly misread or badly mistyped that it is lost in the index (for practical research purposes, it is as good as omitted). Nor is it safe to judge an index by its thickness. Thinner indexes with more lines per page often have more names than thicker indexes with fewer names per page: Byron Sistler's 599-page *1840 Census Tennessee* (Nashville: Byron Sistler & Associates, 1986) has eighteen fewer names than Jackson's 260-page *Tennessee 1840 Census Index* (Bountiful, Utah: Accelerated Indexing Systems, 1976). Thickness is not a measure of accuracy or number of "findable" names either. Most true omissions occur one at a time when typists simply overlook one of the names on a page. Occasionally, a typist may have unusual difficulty reading a name and decide that it is easiest to skip it.

Stray Name Omissions. Beginning with the 1850 Federal census, every person in every family is named in the U.S. Federal censuses—but very few census indexes for this and later censuses are every-name indexes. The majority of indexes list only the head of household and strays—people with surnames different from the head of household's; family members are not supposed to be indexed and are not considered to have been omitted. The most common individual omissions in indexes for censuses since 1850 are overlooked stray names. Strays should be indexed, but often appear to be part of a family. An index typist who fails to notice a different surname will assume the stray's name is that of another family member and routinely overlook it.

Omitted Census Pages. Occasionally, one or more pages of an census are skipped—for example, when the indexer turns a page, he may inadvertently turn two pages, easily resulting in one or two pages of names being omitted. Sometimes more drastic problems occur and many pages of indexing are lost at once: the indexer might get the impression that she is at the end of a roll of microfilm and stop, when, in reality, the film continues; or a full day's typing may be accidentally deleted from the computer. Jackson's *North Carolina 1850 Census Index* (North Salt Lake, Utah: Accelerated Indexing Systems, 1976) skips 170 out of 198 pages on census microfilm 444642 (M432 no. 629): the first seventeen pages for Duplin County, North Carolina, are indexed, then the index skips all names from census page 18 to page 188; the index picks up again at page 189 in Edgecombe County and continues on to the end of the microfilm. Eighty percent of the available census pages for Duplin County and 92 percent of the pages for Edgecombe County are omitted from the index; nor can the omitted names be found in search 5 of Jackson's *AIS Microfiche Indexes of U.S. Census and Other Records* (cited earlier).

Omitted Census Microfilms Groups. Occasionally an entire census microfilm is mistakenly omitted. One of the eighteen microfilms for Jackson's *California 1860 Census Index* (North Salt Lake, Utah: Accelerated Indexing Systems International, 1984) was completely overlooked. The film included Siskiyou, Solano, and Sonoma counties—4.8 percent of California's population.

Omitted Census Microfilm Groups. Even a whole set of microfilms can be inadvertently neglected. Index Publishing was ready to print Dilts's *1848 and 1850 Canada West (Ontario) Census Index* (cited earlier) when it was realized that several additional microfilms of this census were accessible in Canada; seven of the eleven available microfilms had nearly been skipped. For the same censuses, Accelerated Indexing Systems printed a supplement to Jackson's *Ontario Census 1848/1850 (Upper Canada-Heron* [*sic*]*) District* (Bountiful, Utah: Accelerated Indexing Systems, 1984) when it was discovered what had been overlooked: *Upper Canada 1848/1850 Ontario* (North Salt Lake: Accelerated Indexing Systems International, 1986).

Overcoming Omissions. Omissions are among the most difficult census index problems to overcome. Researchers often are not aware of the omissions, mistakenly thinking the ancestor lived somewhere outside the scope of the index. If a researcher realizes an omission may have occurred, the options for finding the omitted name are usually time consuming. The easiest option is to look for a competing index from another company for the same state and year. Refer again to figure 9-3, which shows the differences in two indexes' coverage of the same state. The *Family History Library Catalog* is the best source to search for competing indexes.

If an omission is suspected, periodical indexes like *PERSI* or *GPAI* can be consulted. Do not search for a surname from the census in such indexes, however; search for the *place* where an ancestor lived in *PERSI* and *GPAI*—usually the state, county, or town. Both indexes have many volumes to search, so searching all of them might require significant time. Once the appropriate locality in *PERSI* or *GPAI* has been found, look for citations of census index book reviews (only in *GPAI*) or citations of census transcripts in local genealogical periodicals; book reviews can point to less-well-known indexes.

State and local genealogical societies often print transcripts of censuses or tax lists in their periodicals; these transcripts are sometimes arranged alphabetically by surname. Often, names from the transcripts are indexed in the periodicals' annual indexes. This strategy is most likely to uncover a county or town transcript of a Federal census; therefore, success is more likely if the county or town where an ancestor lived is already known. In counties with small populations, it might be faster to search the original census than to search for a citation to a census transcript in one of the many volumes of *PERSI* or *GPAI*.

Finally, if a census index omission is suspected, the original census can be searched name by name; this is more practical if the area to be searched, such as a rural county, had a small population. For large cities, try to find a street address for the person in a city directory before attempting to find the unindexed person or family in the Federal census records.

Examples of Large Omissions. Table 9-9 shows some of the mistakes found in several AIS census indexes. None of these problems was corrected in the AIS microfiche indexes, and only the New Jersey problem was corrected on the MS-DOS CD-ROM edition.

Locality Errors. Index typists sometimes enter the wrong place in the index; this happens occasionally when the census locality changes but the typist fails to notice. Sometimes such a mistake is serious—sometimes not. For example, in Jackson's *Virginia 1830 Census Index* (Bountiful, Utah: Accelerated Indexing Systems, 1976), every entry for Fairfax County is listed as Northumberland County. Because the page numbers are correct and both counties are on the same microfilm, the researcher can easily find the original census entry by ignoring the county information and following the page number.

Unfortunately, if the incorrectly listed county is on a different microfilm, the researcher can be led to order the wrong microfilm. Jackson's *New Jersey 1860 South* census index (North Salt Lake, Utah: Accelerated Indexing Systems, 1986) incorrectly lists fifty-eight pages of names from Hope township and part of Oxford township as part of Mercer County; they are actually in Warren County. A researcher finding one of these names in the index would naturally search the census microfilm for Mercer County but would not find the indexed name. When the incorrect county is listed, neither the town data nor the page number data will match what the researcher sees on the census microfilm for the incorrect county—the clue that either the locality or the page number information in the index is incorrect. For example, Hope township goes from page one to page forty-five and Oxford township from page forty-seven to page sixty-two. Mercer County, outside of Trenton, begins with page 155. Such discrepancies should alert the researcher that some kind of mismatch has occurred.

Abbreviated Localities. In some indexes the names of counties are abbreviated, and sometimes the abbreviations are so short that two or more counties could share the same abbreviation. For example, Jackson's *New York 1850 Census Index* (Bountiful, Utah: Accelerated Indexing Systems, 1977) uses the abbreviation ST., which could be for either Steuben or St. Lawrence. The abbreviation SCH could be for Schenectady, Schoharie, or Schuyler counties. In Jackson's *Tennessee 1850 Census Index* (Bountiful, Utah: Accelerated Indexing Systems, 1977), the abbreviation HARD could be for either Hardeman or Hardin counties.

AIS indexes usually lack tables of abbreviations. To overcome this deficiency, look in the AIS microfiche indexes, which allow more space for county names, or find the town (provided in the index) in a gazetteer to determine the county.

Some book indexes also truncate town and city names. For example, the *New York 1840 Census Index* (Salt Lake City: Accelerated Indexing Systems, 1978) in book form only shows "NEWYORK" as the city, but the New York City census schedules for 1840 are divided among five microfilms and seventeen wards. To make the search easier, turn to either the AIS microfiche index or to Family Tree Maker's Family Archives *Census Index: U.S. Selected States/Counties* series, where a more complete entry would appear as "NEW YORK CITY 13TH WARD."

Other indexers also abbreviate localities but usually include tables of abbreviations to indicate their meaning. Lida Flint Harshman's *Index to the 1860 Federal Population Census of Ohio* (Mineral Ridge, Ohio: the author, 1979) uses four-letter abbreviations. The first two letters indicate the county, the last two the town; for example, WDBL is for Wood County, Bloom township, as shown in the abbreviation table in the introduction.

Overcoming Locality Problems. If a name is in an index, it should be somewhere in the corresponding census. If the name does not appear on the census page cited in the index, check to see that the county and town for the census page number correspond to those listed in the index. If the page, county, and town data do not all match with the census, the locality data is probably incorrect, or the page number cited in the index is incorrect. Use a gazetteer to verify which county the town should be in. J. Carlyle Parker's *City, County, Town and Township Index to the 1850 Federal Census Schedules* (Detroit: Gale Research, 1979) can also help identify counties and which page numbers belong to the localities in the 1850 census. It lists every small locality, associated county, state, microfilm number, and page numbers for that locality in the 1850 census. However, the page numbers used by Parker may not be the same page numbers which indexers used. Accelerated Indexing Systems published a similar reference work: Jackson's *United States Federal Census Place Enrollment Schedules* (cited earlier); vol. 1 is for 1790 to 1830 and vol. 2 covers 1840 and 1850. Leonard H. Smith's *United States Census Key 1850, 1860, 1870* (Bountiful, Utah: American Genealogical Lending Library, 1987) can also help identify which microfilm should cover a selected locality, but it lacks page number citations.

Sometimes the county and page number are shown correctly in the index, but the incorrect town is indicated. Because the town name is not normally needed to find the original census entry, this is usually not a serious problem.

Page Number Errors. Sometimes index typists enter incorrect census page numbers in an index; this happens occasionally when the census page changes but the typist forgets to note the change. Sometimes such a discrepancy presents serious difficulties; sometimes it does not. Such an error will almost always confuse the researcher, however. If a name does not appear on the census page cited in the index, search three or four pages preceding and following the cited page; this usually helps to locate a name for which the wrong page number was indicated. If the name still can't be found, check the locality and county information at the top of the census page to see if they match with the index.

Sometimes typists use one of several page numbers on a census which the researcher might not expect to be used. If the name does not appear on the page cited in the index, check for an alternate page numbering system on the census to see if one of those was used for the index.

Occasionally a computer program used by an indexer truncates a page number (especially the four-digit page numbers found in AIS indexes). For example, page 1042 might appear in the index as 104. Checking page 104 of the census, the researcher will not find the name but will probably notice that the locality does not match that indicated in the index. This clue should alert the researcher to a page number or locality error problem in the index citation. If a truncated page number is suspected, search the ten census pages that begin with the three digits given (pages 1040 to 1049 for the example above). If that does not work, use a gazetteer to verify which county the town is in; then use census reference tools like the ones mentioned above under "Overcoming Locality Problems" to determine which microfilm should have a particular county and locality. Use the locality data in the index to find the part of the census to search for the name, disregarding the incorrect page number.

Sometimes the page number cited in an index is not a page number in the original record; instead, it may be a page number in a transcript. For example, in Jackson's *Heads of Families at the First Census of the United States Taken in the Year 1790, Pennsylvania* (Bountiful, Utah: Accelerated Indexing Systems, 1978), the index refers to the transcript at the front of the book rather than the original census page number; there is no citation of the original census record page number.

Arrangement Errors. Computers are wonderful tools and have made possible the census index revolution in genealogy. But they are also subject to programming errors that result in incorrectly alphabetized names. For example, in the first few copies of Bryan Lee Dilts's *1860 California Census Index* (Salt Lake City: Index Publishing, 1984), all of the surnames from Placer County which started with *A* appeared at the end of the *A* section for all the other counties. In other words, some of the names on pages thirty to thirty-one were out of proper alphabetical sequence and should have been on pages one to thirty. The error was discovered and corrected in later copies. In Jackson's *Pennsylvania 1860 Central* (North Salt Lake, Utah: Accelerated Indexing Systems International, 1986-87) census index, all of the names in Franklin County from census pages 246 to 390 were initially omitted. AIS corrected the problem by inserting pages with the missing Franklin County names at the beginning, so the page numbers run 1 to 23, then 1 to 661.

Jackson's *Alabama 1870 Federal Census Index* (Salt Lake City: Accelerated Indexing Systems, 1989) apparently has more than 160 names missing between the name McMillian, Levy, at the bottom of page 662 and McNeal, Isaac, at the top of page 663. The page numbers were typed manually using a typewriter, while the index data itself is in the form of a computer printout. It appears that, when the page numbers were being manually typed, a page (or more) of index data was lost. Ideally, the omitted names will appear in a future CD-ROM edition of the index.

Occasionally books are bound with pages missing or out of order. One of the two Family History Library copies of Jackson's *District of Columbia 1870* census index (North Salt Lake, Utah: Accelerated Indexing Systems International, 1986) has its pages bound as follows: 1 to 456, 473 to 494, 457 to 472, 495 to 614; the other copy is in proper page number order. The Family History Library's copy of Jackson's *Michigan 1860 Federal Census Index* (North Salt Lake, Utah: Accelerated Indexing Systems International, 1988) is missing pages 822, 889, 891, 893, 895, 897, 899, 901, 903, 905, and 907. In Jackson's *New York 1820 Census Index* (Bountiful, Utah: Accelerated Indexing Systems, 1977) the names appear in correct alphabetical order but the page numbers are erratic, going from 1 to 59, 50 to 59, and 70 to 537.

Occasionally names from two different counties or two different states are incorrectly combined in an index, but this rarely causes a researcher to miss finding a name in the index. It can, however, lead to confusion about where to find the original entry. For example, names from Lincoln County, Maine, appear in both Jackson's *Maine 1830 Census Index* (Bountiful, Utah: Accelerated Indexing Systems, 1977) and his *New Hampshire 1830 Index Census* [*sic*] (Bountiful, Utah: Accelerated Indexing Systems, 1977).

The best way for researchers to cope with arrangement errors is to be alert for separately printed supplements, inserted pages, or errata information in the introduction that warns of the errors. A quick scan through the pages may reveal incorrectly ordered pages. If an arrangement problem goes unnoticed, the researcher will probably miss an incorrectly placed name, thinking that it was simply omitted.

Physical Quality. Some indexes are poorly printed. For example, the left margins are defective on pages 370 to 371 and 375 to 380 of Jackson's *Brooklyn, New York 1870 Federal Census Index* (North Salt Lake, Utah: Accelerated Indexing Systems International, 1988). This defect makes the surnames that should have appeared near that margin fade illegibly. Some indexes are printed on poor quality paper. Other kinds of physical quality weaknesses are less common. As mentioned above, collating mistakes sometimes cause misplacement of index pages, while some indexes are bound so tightly that data near the inside margins is difficult to read. Occasionally, part of an index entry is trimmed off at the page edge. Try to find a duplicate index, a different edition, or a competing index to overcome this kind of problem. The Family History Library has two copies of most census indexes—one on its shelves and one on the census index tables. Note that most indexes published by AIS are also available on *AIS Microfiche Indexes of U.S. Census and Other Records* (cited earlier); these are not subject to the physical quality problems that can occur with book indexes, nor are the CD-ROM editions of the book indexes. Also, if asked, the indexer or publisher is normally willing to consult a master copy to supply information missing from a poorly manufactured index.

Proximity. Families and neighbors tend to move to the same new neighborhoods together. Census indexes sometimes help and sometimes hinder the researcher's ability to recognize related neighbors. For example, an unknown adult brother might be discovered in an index in a case where he was separated from the family by many pages in the original census—but married sisters who lived just next door to one another might not be obvious at all in a census or tax list index. Always view the original census records to determine who the neighbors were.

Vague Source References. The sources used to compile an index are not always obvious. The largest index publisher, AIS, rarely cites the sources of its indexes. For example, in Jackson's *Oklahoma 1860 Census Index* (Salt Lake City: Accelerated Indexing Systems, 1984), no effort is made to explain to the user that the microfilm census source of this index (FHL microfilm 803052) is part of the Arkansas census. Researchers can turn to reference books to learn which microfilms hold Federal census records, but the sources of substitute indexes for unavailable Federal, state, and county census records are usually harder to identify. Vaguely identified source references in off-year "census indexes" often turn out to be tax lists; but other, sometimes obscure, records are sometimes used as sources for such indexes as well. For example, the sources for an Alaska index are U.S. Senate and House of Representatives executive documents which list whalers, seal hunters, petitioners, and several small, local censuses.

Occasionally, indexers refuse to cite their sources even when asked. In the introductions to some of the indexes in its Early American Series—*Early American Series Mississippi, Volume 2,* for example—AIS states, "Do not write for documentation for we have said this *is* the original source" (Jackson 1984, [iv]). Apparently the compiler wants researchers to use the work as a locator tool to determine an ancestor's place of residence, but not to use it to identify the source of that information. By researching all the original records (especially name lists) for the locality indexed, the researcher is likely to stumble on the source of such an index anyway.

Vague or unlisted sources are more vexation than roadblock. Because they do show where people lived, indexes without source citations can still help the researcher.

If the indexer refuses to divulge his source(s), the researcher must search for clues. Make note of the years and localities listed; these are the clues needed to identify the sources. For AIS indexes, look for sources in *Records Indexed by AIS* (cited earlier), which is available at many family history centers. Researchers can also use the *Family History Library Catalog* to find sources which match the record types and localities cited in indexes. Finally, local archivists can be of help in identifying the sources of undocumented indexes. For example, some of the localities and years listed in the *Alabama 1811–1819 Decennary Census Index* (cited earlier), page 1, are:

1. Alabama Mobile Co.	Mississippi Terr. Census 1816
2. Alabama Clarke Co.	Search Vital Records 1819

Table 9-12. Frequently Misread Letters

Intended	*Sometimes Mistakenly Indexed as . . .*	*Intended*	*Sometimes Mistakenly Indexed as . . .*
A	**H**, C, O	N	**H**, W, V, St, Ne
a	**o**, u, ei, ie, n, w	n	**u**, a, o, ee, ie, ei, w, m
B	**R**, P, S	O	C, U, V, D
b	li, le, t, h, l	o	**a**, u, n, ee, ll, ie, ei, tt
C	G, E, O, Ce	P	R, B, I, J, S, L
c	e, i, o, u	p	ss, g, js, k, f, fs, fa, fi, fr
D	G, S, I, J, T, Ir	Q	**Z**, D, I, J, G, C
d	**u**, a, n, ie, ei, ee, ct, o	q	**g**, y, z, f, ej, ij, j
E	**C**, G, Ee	R	**Pi**, B, S, Pe, Pr, Re
e	**i**, **c**	r	**e**, **s**, i, ei, a
ee	**u**, **n**, ll, a o, ie, ei, w	S	**L**, I, J, St, Se, F, G, R, T
F	**T**, S, G, Ti, L	s	**r**, i, e, c
f	s, j, g, q, t	sc	x
G	S, Q, Z, Ci, L, Se, ls	ss	**fs**, **p**, rr, w, m, n
g	y, z, q, f	T	**F**, S, L, D, Q
H	**N**, W, He, Sl, St, A, F	t	**l**, f, lr, i
h	**K**, li, lc, le	te	k
I	**J**, L, S, Q, F, T	tt	**ll**
i	e, c, l	U	V, A, O, N, H
ie	ei, u, ee, n, a, o, w, il	u	**ee**, a, o, n, ie, ei, ll, w
J	**I**, L S, Q, F, T, P	V	N, W, Ir, Jr, B
j	y, g, f, q, z	v	u, n, b, rr, s, r, o, ee, ei, ei
Jno	Mr, Mo	W	**M**, N, U, H, St
K	**H**, R, B, tr, te	w	m, rr, ur, nr, ui, ni, eu, en
k	h, le, lr, te, R, B, H	X	**H**, Z, N, J
L	**S**, T, F	x	**sc**, c, r
l	e, i, t	Y	**T**, F, Z, Q
ll	**tt**, ee, u, a, o, ie, ei	y	g, q, j, z, p, ej, ij, if
M	**W**, H, N, A, Al, Me	Z	G, Q, Y
m	w, rr, ni, in, iv, ev, ai, ui, iu	z	g, q, y, j, p

3. Alabama Madison Co. Tax List 1815

4. Alabama Madison Co. Indian Creek 1811

5. Alabama Madison Co. Flint River Lands 1811

None of these localities and dates matches sources listed in *Records Indexed by AIS*. The *Family History Library Catalog*, however, shows two state "census" records of Mississippi for 1816 that may be the source of the first citation. The catalog also shows several sets of marriage records for Clarke County in 1819, one of which is probably the source of the second citation. Lines four and five are probably from Madison County land records of 1811, also described in the catalog. Only the 1815 "Tax List" is not easy to find in the *Family History Library Catalog*. Stemmons's *United States Census Compendium* (cited earlier) lists 1811 and 1812 tax lists but none for Madison County in 1815. Nor does Jackson and Smeal's *Encyclopedia of Local History and Genealogy: Census Encyclopedia* (cited earlier) shed any light on this source. The Alabama Department of Archives and History could be of help in finding possible sources of that citation.

Spelling Substitution Tables. Two kinds of spelling errors are found in census indexes. One kind of error is the result of the census enumerator's misspelling the name in the original record. The other kind of error is the result of the indexer's misreading the original or mistyping the index entry.

Table 9-12 shows how indexers sometimes misread handwriting. The column on the left shows the actual spelling. The column on the right shows how the indexer might have interpreted the letter. (The letters in bold type are especially likely substitutes.)

Occasionally the spelling in the index is correct but the spelling in the original record is slightly off. Sometimes census takers made phonetic spelling substitutions. Table 9-12 is a list of letters that a census enumerator or tax collector might have inadvertently substituted for the correct spelling. First, search for an apparently missing name with substitute vowels. For example, if the sought-for name is not found under FRAZIER, the table suggests FREZER or FREYZIR as possible alternative spellings with vowel substitutes. If the name is still not found, use the table to substitute consonants, consonant combinations, or consonant-vowel combinations. For example, the table shows that *s* can substitute for *z*, so FRASIER is a possible substitute.

Problems and Misunderstandings on the Part of Researchers

Researchers sometimes fail to understand or use published censuses, tax lists, and their indexes properly.

Scope. Sometimes researchers fail to realize what is included in or excluded from a publication. Better indexers explain in the introductions to their works exactly what they did and did not index. Read the introductions of indexes to learn what was indexed.

Researchers sometimes expect more from an index than its creator intended to deliver. For example, some researchers expect nearly every name found in an original census to appear in the index; in fact, this is fairly unusual. From 1790 to 1840, Federal censuses listed only heads of households by name; most women and youths were intentionally excluded. Therefore, 1790 census indexes show only the names of heads of households. The same holds true for census indexes from 1800 to 1840; only a few women, and virtually no children, are listed in them.

Starting with the 1850 Federal census, every person was listed by name, but very few statewide indexes for 1850 and

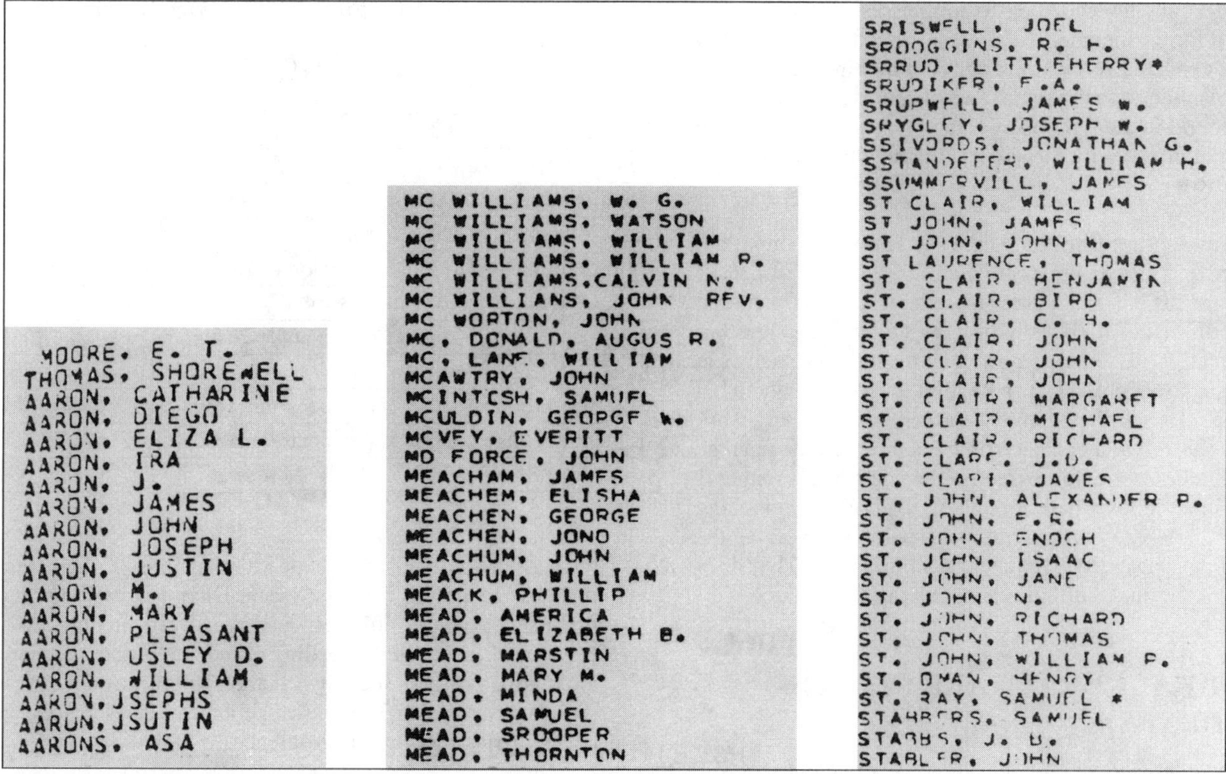

MOORE, E. T.
THOMAS, SHOREWELL
AARON, CATHARINE
AARON, DIEGO
AARON, ELIZA L.
AARON, IRA
AARON, J.
AARON, JAMES
AARON, JOHN
AARON, JOSEPH
AARON, JUSTIN
AARON, M.
AARON, MARY
AARON, PLEASANT
AARON, USLEY D.
AARON, WILLIAM
AARON,JSEPHS
AARON,JSUTIN
AARONS, ASA

MC WILLIAMS, W. G.
MC WILLIAMS, WATSON
MC WILLIAMS, WILLIAM
MC WILLIAMS, WILLIAM R.
MC WILLIAMS,CALVIN N.
MC WILLIANS, JOHN REV.
MC WORTON, JOHN
MC, DONALD, AUGUS R.
MC, LANE, WILLIAM
MCAWTRY, JOHN
MCINTOSH, SAMUEL
MCULDIN, GEORGE W.
MCVEY, EVERITT
MD FORCE, JOHN
MEACHAM, JAMES
MEACHEM, ELISHA
MEACHEN, GEORGE
MEACHEN, JONO
MEACHUM, JOHN
MEACHUM, WILLIAM
MEACK, PHILLIP
MEAD, AMERICA
MEAD, ELIZABETH B.
MEAD, MARSTIN
MEAD, MARY M.
MEAD, MINDA
MEAD, SAMUEL
MEAD, SROOPER
MEAD, THORNTON

SRISWELL, JOEL
SROOGGINS, R. H.
SRRUD, LITTLEHERRY*
SRUDIKER, F.A.
SRUPWELL, JAMES W.
SRYGLEY, JOSEPH W.
SSIVORDS, JONATHAN G.
SSTANDEFER, WILLIAM H.
SSUMMERVILL, JAMES
ST CLAIR, WILLIAM
ST JOHN, JAMES
ST JOHN, JOHN W.
ST LAURENCE, THOMAS
ST. CLAIR, BENJAMIN
ST. CLAIR, BIRD
ST. CLAIR, C. H.
ST. CLAIR, JOHN
ST. CLAIR, JOHN
ST. CLAIR, JOHN
ST. CLAIR, MARGARET
ST. CLAIR, MICHAEL
ST. CLAIR, RICHARD
ST. CLARE, J.D.
ST. CLARI, JAMES
ST. JOHN, ALEXANDER P.
ST. JOHN, E.R.
ST. JOHN, ENOCH
ST. JOHN, ISAAC
ST. JOHN, JANE
ST. JOHN, N.
ST. JOHN, RICHARD
ST. JOHN, THOMAS
ST. JOHN, WILLIAM P.
ST. RYAN, HENRY
ST. RAY, SAMUEL *
STAHBERS, SAMUEL
STABBS, J. B.
STABLER, JOHN

Figure 9-12. Mis-filed entries due to computer alphabetization. Names misplaced by inconsistent use of spaces sometimes are found at the beginning of an index; a blank space (space bar on the keyboard) files before the letter *A*—compare the filing of the names [space] MOORE, E. T. and AARON,JSEPHS (left example, from Jackson's *Alabama 1860* [North Salt Lake, Utah: Accelerated Indexing Systems, 1985], page 1). A name like MC WILLIAMS would file before MC, DONALD or MCAWTRY (middle example, from Jackson's *Alabama 1850 Census Index* [Bountiful, Utah: Accelerated Indexing Systems, 1976], page 146). The surname ST. JOHN could fall under either the ST's or ST. (right example, from Jackson's *Alabama 1850 Census Index,* page 204).

later are every-name indexes. Most indexes list only heads of households and "stray" names—those which differ from heads of households' names (such as those of servants or boarders). Finding someone in this kind of list might require guessing who the head of the household was.

Some census indexers are more careful than others to define stray names and to explain whose names were indexed other than those of the heads of households. Each head of household is easy to distinguish in the census schedules, but the stray names can be relatively difficult to distinguish. Therefore, indexers are more likely to inadvertently overlook strays. Some census indexers have been more consistent than others in including strays.

Another common misunderstanding regarding the scope of indexes is related to boundary changes. Historical boundary changes sometimes affect the scope of original censuses and, consequently, related census indexes. For example, what is now Nevada was originally part of Utah Territory, and at least one Utah census index includes names of people who lived in what is now Nevada. Researchers can find out about boundary changes from Thorndale and Dollarhide's *Map Guide to the U.S. Federal Censuses, 1790–1920* (cited earlier).

Alphabetical Arrangement. Researchers are sometimes unaware of how most computer-alphabetized lists are arranged. Most punctuation marks and numbers file before the letter *A*. A blank space (space bar on the keyboard) also files before the letter *A*. Therefore, names misplaced because of the inconsistent use of spaces sometimes are found at the beginning of an index. A name like "Mc Donald, Zerabubel" would file before "McDonald, Aaron," and "O Toole" would file before "O'Neil," which itself files before "Oakley." An omitted space after a comma can also cause problems; for example, "Smith, Lee" files before "Smith, David." The surname "St. John" could fall under "St." or "Saint" (see figure 9-12).

Census Page Numbers. Most census schedules have several "page" numbers on each page. At least one set of stamped numbers and at least one set of handwritten numbers can usually be found—frequently even more. Stamped page numbers in census books are usually on every other page (that is, on right-hand pages only). Therefore, the page numbers in an index often refer to the pages *before* or *after* the stamped numbers. While *most* indexes refer to the stamped page numbers, be prepared to use any of the several numbering systems to find the page cited in the index. If one doesn't work, try the next. If none of them works, try again, searching two or three pages before or after the cited number in case the typist forgot to enter a new page number. If all else fails, use the locality data in the index to find the location of the name in the original census.

Overlooking Clues. Sometimes researchers fail to take advantage of clues in printed census lists, tax lists, and their indexes.

Almost all statewide census indexes list the county and town for each name. If the name sought is not where it was expected to be, look for people with the same or similar names in the same town or county; they may even be found in a neighboring town or county. Also, watch for neighbors with the same surname; they may well be relatives.

Misunderstanding the Accuracy Rate. It is important to have a proper perspective on the accuracy of census and tax list indexes. Some researchers express frustration and disgust over errors in indexes. Other researchers behave as if indexes were flawless—the ultimate sources in census research. The correct attitude lies somewhere between. For all their faults, census indexes usually work and save researchers much time and effort. Remember the rule: indexes are not perfect. If the name being sought is not in an index where it ought to be, don't stop looking for it. Try searching for alternate spellings, or search the original census. Indexes are a beginning point. They do not represent the final word in census and tax list research.

Table 9-13. Findability of Heads of House and

State	*Year*	*Author or Publisher*	*Index Population*
California	1860	Index Publishing	298,607
California	1860	AIS	298,607
Maine Veterans	1890	Index Publishing	29,549
Maine Veterans	1890	AIS	29,549
North Carolina	1870	Precision Indexing	295,375
North Carolina	1870	AIS	295,375
Ohio	1850	Ohio Family Historians	131,700
Ohio	1850	AIS	131,700
All States, 1790 to 1850		AIS book indexes	63,710,000
All States, 1790 to 1850		AIS microfiche index	63,710,000
All States, 1790 to 1850		CD-ROM indexes	63,710,000

HOW ACCURATE ARE CENSUS INDEXES?

Anecdotal evidence in genealogical periodicals confirms that census indexes are not always accurate. Several articles cite names that were hard to locate. One article mentions that a statewide census index omits 56 of 799 entries for the 1800 Federal census of Clinton County, New York (Martin 1978, 54); thus, the index was 93 percent accurate for Clinton County. How accurate was it for the rest of the New York counties? Researchers have only a hazy picture of the problem. Are all census indexes equally accurate? If not, which indexes are more accurate? How is accuracy defined and measured? Are all errors equally serious? How careful and scientific are the methods used to research census index accuracy?

Each census index published by Index Publishing mentions a random sample taken by the company to find the index's accuracy. Are reliable figures cited?

The Need for Further Research

There is a need for comprehensive, in-depth, scientific studies into census index accuracy. It would help to know how accurate each of the available census indexes really is. Table 9-13 shows the accuracy of several census indexes, but larger samples are needed to produce more precise figures. It would be a great benefit for the family history community to expand and complete this table for all census indexes.

Incorrect Methodology

Some previous studies of census index accuracy are highly suspect. One investigator started by looking up a random entry in index "A." Then the investigator tried to find the name in the original census to determine its spelling. Finally, the investigator looked in a competing index, "B," to see if that index had an entry to match the entry in index A and the original census record.

This methodology is seriously flawed. By starting with any one index, the investigator guaranteed that he would never notice omissions in *that* index, if there were any. The investigator was also influenced to expect the spelling of the name in index A by starting with that index. If the handwriting on the original census was difficult to read, the investigator would have been prone to accept the spelling of index A without exploring alternative possible spellings. If the spelling in index A was different from the original census spelling, the investigator would be less likely to notice the difference.

Considerations for a Proper Methodology

Any authoritative study of index accuracy must begin with an examination of the original census record, not the census index, and must use valid random sampling techniques. For example, picking a name from every tenth census schedule page does not constitute random sampling. A random number table should be used to choose page numbers for the sample; this ensures that the investigator will draw a proper random sample from throughout the original census and spreads the sample randomly through the work of all index typists. Nor is it acceptable to choose the first line on a census page or the last line on a page because some index typists consistently input more accurately near the top of the page than at the bottom, or vice versa. Therefore, a second random number table should be used to select the line on the page to be sampled. Finally, researchers should carefully define how they measure errors and what they do in unusual situations.

The Methodology of This Study

To provide readers of *Printed Sources* with a useful understanding of census index accuracy, this author conducted a short study, analyzing more than one hundred census entries in several censuses and then locating them in the appropriate indexes. The goal of this study was to determine the accuracy of several sets of competing census indexes and the overall accuracy of Jackson's *AIS Microfiche Indexes of U.S. Census and Other Records* (cited earlier) and MicroQuix's *U.S. Census Index Series* (cited earlier) CD-ROM indexes from 1790 to 1850. The methodology for the study of the 1860 California census is described here; the methodology for each other state and year was nearly identical. The methodology is included in the hopes that others will conduct similar and even more precise studies.

The first step was to determine the total number of original census pages in the 1860 California census; there are 9,778

Stray Census Names in Selected Census Indexes

Sample Size	*Number of Omissions*	*Major Errors*	*Minor Errors*	*Findability (%)*	*Sampling Error (%)*
100	8	2	2	90.0	± 4.9
100	27	3	6	70.0	± 7.5
100	3	0	4	97.0	± 2.8
100	3	0	3	97.0	± 2.8
100	7	2	3	91.0	±4.7
100	2	2	12	96.0	±3.2
100	4	2	7	94.0	±3.9
100	15	1	12	84.0	±6.0
101	5	6	17	89.2	± 5.0
101	6	6	18	88.2	± 5.2
101	7	6	18	87.2	± 5.4

pages. The *U.S. Army Audit Agency Statistical Sampling Program* (Karen Santmyer, 1985), version 2.0, was then used to generate a list of one hundred random numbers between 1 and 9,778 to be used as page numbers for selecting the sample. (The precision of and confidence in this sampling technique could be significantly increased by using a larger sample.) Another random number table was used to select one of the forty lines per census page as the name to sample.

If the selected line on the index page showed a head of household, the name on that line was used in the sample. If it showed a different surname from that of the head of household (a stray), that name was used in the sample. If the line selected showed a family member, the head of household's name was used for the sample. Where the selected line was blank, blotted out, or unreadable, the next line above was checked for a usable sample, continuing up the page until a usable name was found. If necessary, the search was extended to the bottom of the previous page and continued up the page until a usable name was found.

Each sample microfilm number, page number, line number, and name was then written on a card. Next, the appropriate competing census indexes were searched for a match with the name on the original census. Each match was noted; each mismatch or apparent omission was also noted. If a sample name was not located in the index, the neighboring entries were searched for variant spellings of the name. Index variations in the page numbers and locality data were also noted. At the end the cards were reviewed and the results tallied.

Table 9-13 summarizes the findings. All statistics from this table are at the 90-percent confidence level. For example, based upon a sample of one hundred from the total population of 298,607, we are 90 percent confident that 70 percent of the heads of households and stray names in the California 1860 census are findable in AIS's *California 1860 Cen-*

Guidelines for Finding Misplaced Names in Census Indexes

1. **Competing Indexes.** Look for the elusive name in a competing index by another company, if one is available.
2. **Neighboring Entries.** Find the place in the index where the name should be, and search at least one page preceding and one page following that place for similar names. Look for slightly different spellings of the name.
3. **Initials or Abbreviations.** Look for the surname with the given or middle names as initials or abbreviations. For example, look for the name Green, James William, under such variations as Green, J.; Green, J. W.; Green, Jas. W.; Green, Jas. Wm.; or Green, James W.
4. **Middle Name.** Look for the middle instead of the given name. For example, instead of the name Walker, George Herbert, try Walker, Herbert.
5. **Vowels.** Look for the name spelled with different vowels. For example, look for GILLESPIE under GALLESPIE, GELLESPIE, GOLLESPIE, GULLESPIE, or GYLLESPIE.
6. **Double Letters.** Search the index for the name with double letters added or deleted. For example, for the name FULLER, try FULER. For the name BAKER, try BAKKER.
7. **Transposed Letters.** Look for the elusive name under spellings with each of the first four letters transposed. For example, look for WIGHTMAN under IWGHTMAN, WGIHTMAN, WIHGTMAN, and WIGTHMAN.
8. **Misread Letters.** Use table 9-12 to find possible substitute letters for the elusive name. Based on this table the name CARTER might be searched for under GARTER, EARTER, OARTER, CEARTER, CEIRTER, CAETER, CASTER, and so forth.
9. **Phonetic Substitutes.** Use table 9-12 to find possible phonetic substitutes for the name. Based on that table the name RADCLIFFE might be searched for under RHADCLIFFE, RATCLIFFE, RADDCLIFFE, RADKLIFFE, RADGLIFFE, RADCLIVE, or RADCLIPHE.
10. **Relatives.** Look for the names of parents, children, brothers, sisters, uncles, and aunts in the index. If relatives are found in the index, search the original census to see if the person sought lived nearby.
11. **First Letter.** Look at all the surnames that begin with the same letter as the name sought. For example, if the surname Kelly cannot be found, scan all the surnames that begin with *K* for incorrect or misplaced spellings of Kelly.
12. **Alternative Indexes.** Search for alternative census indexes for the place where an ancestor lived—especially the county. The *Family History Library Catalog*, Lainhart's *State Census Records* (cited earlier), and Stemmons's *United State Census Compendium* (cited earlier) are sources to search for alternative indexes. Also search for the place where an ancestor lived in periodical indexes, such as *PERSI*. After finding the place, look for census index book reviews or census transcripts published in local genealogical periodicals. If there is a census transcript for the right year, determine whether the periodical has its own surname index to assist in finding the ancestor's name in the transcript.
13. **Original Censuses.** Search the original census for the area where a person lived to find names that were omitted from an index.

sus Index (cited earlier). The sampling error is plus or minus 7.5 percent.

Definitions

Index population in table 9-13 and for statistical purposes is *not* the entire population of the state in a given year. The index population was found by counting the entries in the largest heads-of-households-and-strays index for the state and year. Heads of households and strays range from 15 to 50 percent of the total census population (depending on the state and year).

Number of omissions is the number of sampled census entries that were not found in the index where they should have been; nor were they found by a quick search in the neighboring index entries. (A more thorough search would probably reveal that some of the "omissions" are actually in the index but seriously misspelled.)

Errors are names which were found in the census and then in the index but which did not match the spelling of the sample on the original record. *Major errors* shows the number of index entries in which at least one of the first two consonants (or initial vowel and first consonant) was wrong or transposed in either the surname or given name. It was not considered an error if an abbreviation in the original was spelled out in the index. Examples of major errors are:

Original	*Index Major Errors*
ANDREWS, Laban	[Omitted]
BROWN, Robert	BROWN, Rogert
DARBY, Oliver	DAILEY, Oliver
EHOLTS, Frederick	CHOLTS, Frederick
EUVIARD, Peter	EURRARD, Peter
HAWK, N.	HAWK, W.
JACKABOY, Lonis	JACKABOY, Sonis
SKAGGS, Joseph	SKAGGS, James

Minor errors are mistranscribed index entries which do not seriously affect the order of the index. Middle or ending vowels may be wrong or transposed; the third or other remaining consonants may be wrong or transposed; middle names or initials may be wrong; census page numbers may be wrong; locality data may be incorrect. These are considered minor because researchers can normally identify minor error entries in an index and find the name on the census page, as described earlier in this chapter. Examples of minor errors are:

Original	*Index Minor Errors*
BARTER, Henry A.	BARTER, Henry H.
BARTLETT, William	BARTLETT, Wiliam
COPP, Lewis	CAPP, Lewis
FAILES, Orris	FAILES, Orrin
GILLIS, J.	GILIS, J.
GRANADAS, Francisco	GRANADAL, Francisco
SCOTT, James	SCOTT, Jams
SPRECKELS, Diederich	SPRICKELS, Diederich
1042 (page it is on)	104 (page cited)

Findability is accuracy—the percentage of index entries which exactly match the original record samples or match with only minor errors (see above).

Sampling error is the percentage by which the sample may be off. For example, consider 90-percent findability with a sampling error of plus or minus 4.9 percent; this means the percentage of findable census names in the complete index should fall between 85.1 and 94.9 percent.

Analysis

California 1860. AIS overlooked or omitted all index entries for microfilm 803069 (M653 no. 69) for Siskiyou, Solano, and Sonoma counties. The aggregate population of these three counties in 1860 was 26,665 out of the total California population of 560,247 (*Ninth Census* 1872, 14–15). In other words, AIS completely skipped 4.8 percent of the 1860 California population. These three counties made up 8.0 percent of the random sample. In a larger sample these three counties would likely be represented by 4.8 rather than 8.0 percent of the sample. It seems likely that a larger sample would result in a slightly higher findability percentage for the AIS index—approximately 72- to 73-percent findability.

AIS did not handle Chinese names well. Chinese immigrants typically had names like Ah Chin or Ah Ling. "Ah" is not a name but a sort of polite title that approximately corresponds to "little." AIS must have had difficulty determining strays in households because of this naming custom; many of the omissions in the random sample were Chinese names which should have been in the index as strays but were overlooked. Eight percent of the random sample were Chinese names. There were 34,933 Chinese in the census—6.2 percent of the California population (*Ninth Census* 1872, 15). AIS omitted five out of eight Chinese who should have been entered in the random sample. If all Chinese names are disregarded in the random sample, the findability rate in the AIS index rises to 81.5 percent for the non-Chinese population.

In the introduction to Dilts's *1860 California Census Index*, Index Publishing claims a 95-percent accuracy rate (± 2.0 percent) based on a random sample of 438 census names (Dilts 1984, x). This random sample of one hundred showed that the Index Publishing findability rate is 90 percent (± 4.9 percent). The two figures overlap slightly. The findability of census names in the index may be in the area where the plus or minus ranges overlap—somewhere between 93.0 and 94.9 percent. It is also possible that slightly different definitions of findability (accuracy) were used.

Maine 1890 Veterans. Usually, the county and enumeration district numbers from the indexes are needed to find names in the veterans schedules. However, institutions like jails, hospitals, the almshouse, and the Eastern Branch of the National Home for Disabled Veteran Soldiers were not assigned enumeration district numbers. The introduction to Index Publishing's index explains where to find these institutions in the schedules. The AIS index gives no such information. A researcher using the AIS index alone might be compelled to search an entire county to find a name in an institution. Nor does the AIS introduction indicate which microfilm to use to find a given county. Even the map in the AIS index is for a different date and could be slightly misleading.

North Carolina 1870. The statistics from this study present a mixed finding. The AIS index is somewhat more accurate than the Precision Indexing index (at least as far as omissions and major errors). However, the AIS index has four times as many minor errors.

One of the difficulties with ethnic names that appeared in the California index was repeated in the North Carolina index. The AIS index turned the American Indian census name CANOT, Oo-too-da-J into the index name CANOT, Orton D. J.

Ohio 1850. The Ohio Family Associates index is clearly more accurate than the competing AIS index. Likewise, the Ohio Family Associates index has fewer minor errors. Not surprisingly, among the downfalls of both are "stray" names. Several of the omissions by each publisher are names that were not of the head of household but were different surnames that should have been indexed.

The AIS index omits all 20,280 names from Morrow County. Morrow County's population was almost exactly 1 percent of Ohio's 1850 population of 1,980,329. By chance, one random sample (1 percent of samples) was taken from Morrow County. This means that the omission of Morrow County names in the AIS index is reflected very accurately in the overall sample.

Overall. A random sample of 101 Federal census names from 1790 to 1850 showed that 89.2 percent of the names were findable in the AIS Federal census index books, 88.2 percent were findable in the AIS microfiche indexes, and 87.2 percent were findable in the CD-ROM editions of the indexes. Minor errors were found in 17.8 percent of the findable index entries. The minor errors ranged from missing page numbers or towns to incorrect middle initials and incorrect vowels in names.

The sample was scattered randomly among the population of the censuses of states with available AIS book, microfiche, and CD-ROM indexes as follows:

1790:	5 samples
1800:	7 samples
1810:	11 samples
1820:	10 samples
1830:	13 samples
1840:	24 samples
1850:	31 samples

Table 9-14 shows the census samples which had major errors and six examples of samples with minor errors.

The sample revealed some slight differences between the book, microfiche, and CD-ROM indexes. AIS reprinted the Government Printing Office 1790 census indexes. The reprint listed the name of Laban Andrews, but he was omitted from the AIS microfiche and CD-ROM indexes. In a similar situation, William Bartlett from the 1790 Vermont census is listed correctly in the reprint, but in the microfiche and CD-ROM indexes his first name is spelled with only one *l*. The AIS microfiche and CD-ROM indexes also cited page numbers in the reprints instead of page numbers in the 1790 census records.

All names for 1850 Erie County, Pennsylvania, were omitted from the CD-ROM. Since they are included in the book and microfiche indexes, it appears that the contents of a computer storage tape were not (or could not be) loaded onto the computer when the CD-ROMs were created. The computer tape may have been overlooked or lost, or it may have deteriorated from overuse.

In the overall sample, 30.7 percent of the names sampled were from the 1850 census, but 46.2 percent of the major errors or omissions were found in 1850 indexes (71.4 percent of the omissions in the sample). Why might the 1850 indexes have more than their fair share of omissions? For 1790 to 1840 indexes, the typists were instructed to type every name listed in the census. But in 1850 and later censuses, the typists usually typed only selected names—chiefly those of the heads of households. Apparently the selection process caused some names to be inadvertently overlooked.

Summary

Random samples of several competing census indexes show that the findability (accuracy) of names in them varies widely. The sample showed 97 percent of the names were findable in the most accurate indexes. In the least accurate index the findability was 70 percent. Although some AIS indexes are highly accurate, AIS's competitors sometimes publish more-accurate indexes (sometimes notably more so). Another important finding is that, when using AIS indexes from 1790 to 1850, the researcher will find the names where they should be in the index slightly fewer than nine out of ten times. Finally, the sample shows that indexes which list every name on the census (such as 1790 to 1840 indexes) are usually more accurate than heads-of-households-and-strays indexes (such as most 1850 and later indexes).

MAJOR CENSUS INDEX PUBLISHERS

A brief history and description of major census index publishers may give some insights into their products and services. In addition to the following publishers, state and local genealogical societies, such as the Ohio Genealogical Society and the Detroit Society for Genealogical Research, have published excellent indexes for their areas. Individual compilers have also produced some important statewide census indexes.

Federal Government

At the request of Congress, the Government Printing Office was the first to publish a major series of statewide Federal census indexes. In 1907 and 1908, transcripts with indexes of twelve surviving or reconstructed 1790 statewide Federal censuses were produced in an 8½- by 11-inch format. The type was very small but the production quality was excellent. Headings clearly indicate counties and towns. The actual census data is shown but the pages of the original census are not cited. Although not perfect, the accuracy of the transcription and index seems to be quite good. These indexes have been reprinted by Genealogical Publishing Company, Accelerated Indexing Systems, Precision Indexing, and others.

Accelerated Indexing Systems

In business from 1967 to 1995, Accelerated Indexing Systems (AIS) has been the most prolific census index publisher. The main editor at AIS was Ronald Vern Jackson. AIS's catalog contained more than 279 statewide U.S. Federal census population schedule index titles (not including the microfiche indexes). Jackson and his company indexed every available ten-year Federal statewide census from 1790 to 1860 (Ohio and Tennessee

Table 9-14. Errors Found in a Random Sample of 1790–1850 AIS Census Indexes

Year	*State*	*Microfilm No.*	*Name*	*County*	*Town*	*Page*	*Error*
			All Major Errors				
1790	New York	568146	ANDREWS, Laban	Ulster	Woodstock	159/2	Omitted from microfiche and CD-ROM
1810	New York	181381	DARBY, Oliver	Essex	Ticonderoga	60	DAILEY, Oliver (and town omitted)
1810	Pennsylvania	193670	EHOLTS, Frederick	Adams	Cumberland	101	CHOLTS, Frederick
1820	Massachusetts	193736	ELY, Alfred, Rev.	Hampden	Monson	359	ALFRED, Rev.
1830	Massachusetts	337917	HANDY, Walter	Bristol	New Bedford	317	Omitted
1840	New York	17192	HIBBERD, Joel	Madison	Brookfield	161	HILLARD, Jeol
1840	Pennsylvania	444642	CEIGER, John	Somerset	Southampton	141	GEIGER, John
1850	New York	444280	MUNSON, Seldon	Oneida	Camden	238	Omitted
1850	North Carolina	444642	WOODARD, Elizth	Edgecombe	—	153	Omitted
1850	Ohio	444687	EUVIARD, Peter	Highland	Clay	316/631	EURRARD, Peter
1850	Ohio	444714	COCHRON, John	Pike	Union	272/544	Omitted
1850	Ohio	444748	RAMSPIKER, Nicholas	Fayette	Springfill	934/469	Omitted
1850	Pennsylvania	444746	KEEDER, Ransom	Erie	Elk Creek	369/735	Omitted from CD-ROM
			Examples of Minor Errors				
1790	Vermont	568152	BARTLETT, William	Chittondon	Waitsfield	167	BARTLETT, Wiliam on microfiche and CD-ROM
1800	Vermont	218688	WOOSTER, Moses	Essex	Guildhall	402/397	Page number omitted
1810	New Hampshire	218686	ALLEN, David	Coos	Bartlett	4/1/295	ALLIN, David
1830	New Jersey	337935	PIERSON, Samuel	Morris	Morris	71	Town listed as HarrisTwp.
1830	Pennsylvania	20633	GILLIS, J.	Philadelphia	Middle Ward	197	GILIS, J.
1840	Rhode Island	22261	TOLMAN, Randall	Providence	Smithfield	196	TALMAN, Randlal

are only partially complete), most 1870, and many 1880 Federal censuses. They also have indexed all of the available 1850 to 1880 census mortality schedules and many of the available 1890 Civil War veterans schedules. There are twenty-seven AIS 1890 veterans schedule indexes and hundreds of mortality, reconstructed, and state census indexes.

The company name has evolved over the years. Accelerated Indexing Systems became Accelerated Indexing Systems International in 1985 when Jackson published *Ontario Census 1848/1850 (Upper Canada-Heron* [*sic*]*) District*. In the 1990s the company was known as Ancestral Genealogical Endexing Schedules (A.G.E.S.) and sometimes as Ancestral Genealogical Extended Schedules. (Both forms of the new name can be found in one book, on pages ii and 1 of the *Massachusetts 1860 South Federal Census Index* [Salt Lake City, Utah, 1992].) In 1995, Jackson sold all of his rights, data, and inventory of books and computer tapes to Genealogical Services, which has started re-issuing many index books.

Mr. Jackson has a noble vision of census indexing. He long held the dream of creating a single, comprehensive index of all Federal censuses. He partially attained his goal of a single index to Federal censuses by publishing *AIS Microfiche Indexes of U.S. Census and Other Records* and licensing his data (through MicroQuix) to Automated Archives and later to Banner Blue and Brøderbund Software for CD-ROM editions.

The broad scope of Jackson's goal is impressive, and the wide reach of his work is a major accomplishment. Jackson's vision and pioneering efforts in large-scale computerized indexing have opened many doors for thousands of American genealogists.

Style. Although there is a variety of statewide census index styles among the many titles AIS offers, there is a typical AIS style (see figure 9-13). Most AIS indexes are xerographic copies on 8½- by 11-inch paper. Most have 414 entries in small type on each page in three dense columns. The pages have no headings except for the page numbers, and there are no column titles. The index usually lists name, county, census page number, and locality; the county name is usually abbreviated to four letters. The census page number cited is usually three digits—even if some page numbers require four digits. The state and census year are often featured in more recent AIS publications. The quality of the printing is uneven. Most of the 1790 indexes are reprints of the 1907–08 Federal government publications with AIS title pages added.

Introductions. The introductions to AIS census indexes generally consist of the same general, rambling history of censuses and computing, with outdated library and government addresses for the fifty states. The introductory material often comprises forty or fifty pages. In recent years AIS introductions have included an article titled "The Principles of Understanding Census Bloopers and Census Indexing" and a certificate of authenticity. Often included as well is a list of U.S. Federal census

PAGE 61

RAMSDEN. THOMAS JR.	WASHINGTON CO.	MN	075	STILLWATER PRECINCT	1850
RAMSDEN. THOMAS	WASHINGTON CO.	MN	075	STILLWATER PRECINCT	1850
RAMSEY. ALEXANDER	RAMSEY CO.	MN	037	ST. PAUL	1850
RAMSEY. ANNA E.	RAMSEY CO.	MN	037	ST. PAUL	1850
RAMSEY. JUSTIS C.	RAMSEY CO.	MN	037	ST. PAUL	1850
RAMVILLE. ADALAIDE	PEMBINA CO.	MN	020	PEMBINA DISTRICT	1850
RAMVILLE. FRANCOIS	PEMBINA CO.	MN	020	PEMBINA DISTRICT	1850
RAMVILLE. FREGINE	PEMBINA CO.	MN	020	PEMBINA DISTRICT	1850
RAMVILLE. JOSEPH	PEMBINA CO.	MN	020	PEMBINA DISTRICT	1850
RAMVILLE. JOSEPH	PEMBINA CO.	MN	020	PEMBINA DISTRICT	1850
RAMVILLE. MADALINE	PEMBINA CO.	MN	020	PEMBINA DISTRICT	1850
RANDALL. WILLIAM	RAMSEY CO.	MN	037	ST. PAUL	1850
RANDALL. WILLIAM H.	RAMSEY CO.	MN	046	ST. PAUL	1850
RANDALL. WILLIAM H. JR.	RAMSEY CO.	MN	046	ST. PAUL	1850
RANDEL. BENJAMIN H.	DAKOTAH CO.	MN	010	FORT SNELLING	1850
RANDOLPH. RANSUN F.	WASHINGTON CO.	MN	076	STILLWATER PRECINCT	1850
RANKIN. SARAH	WABASHAW CO.	MN	062	DISTRICT 1	1850
RANKIN. SARAH	DAKOTAH CO.	MN	006	TRAVERSE DES SIOUX	1850
RASHNOKD. CHARLOTTE	PEMBINA CO.	MN	022	PEMBINA DISTRICT	1850
RASHNOLD. ALEXIS	PEMBINA CO.	MN	022	PEMBINA DISTRICT	1850
RASHNOLD. ANTOINE	PEMBINA CO.	MN	022	PEMBINA DISTRICT	1850
RASHNOLD. ANTOINE	PEMBINA CO.	MN	022	PEMBINA DISTRICT	1850

A portion of a typical AIS index. From Jackson's *Minnesota 1850 Census Index* (South Bountiful, Utah: Accelerated Indexing Systems, 1981), page 61.

28 NEVADA 1910

name	cnty	page	town
CLAYTON, LENA	WASH	151	RENO 5TH
CLAYTON, LUCILE	ESME	140	RAWHIDE
CLAYTON, MARGARET E	ELKO	167	SO FORK
CLAYTON, PATSY B	ESME	164	AURORA
CLAYTON, WILLIAM M	NYE	108	PHONOLIT
CLEARY, JAMES	LINC	312	BARCLAY
CLEARY, JAMES	NYE	159	TONOPAH
CLEARY, JAMES M	NYE	135	CLARK
CLEARY, JOHN	ESME	14	SILVER P
CLEARY, MICHAEL	ELKO	185	ELKO
CLEARY, THOMAS	WHIT	335	CHERRY C
CLEASY, WILLIAM	NYE	142	TONOPAH
CLEATFIELD, FRED W	WASH	124	RENO 4TH
CLEATOR, ROBERT	WASH	71	RENO 1ST
CLEAVELAND, JOHNIE	ESME	152	SCHURZ
CLEGG, FRANK	LAND	320	BATTLE M
CLEGG, GEORGE W	WASH	168	RENO 6TH
CLEGG, JAMES	WHIT	257	RIEPETOW
CLEGG, SAMUEL	WASH	125	RENO 4TH
CLEGG, SAMUEL L	WASH	141	RENO 4TH
CLEINE, JAMES M*	LINC	277	PIOCHE
CLEM, CLINTON*	ESME	113	GOLDFIEL
CLEME, JAMES M*	LINC	277	PIOCHE
CLEMENS, EARLE R	NYE	73	RHYOLITE

name	cnty	page	town
CLINTON, CHARLES	EURE	179	GARRISON
CLINTON, ERGEST	NYE	70	RHYOLITE
CLINTON, ERNEST	NYE	70	RHYOLITE
CLINTON, HARRY V	CHUR	11	NEW RIVE
CLINTON, HELEN	ORMS	226	CARSON
CLINTON, HENRY	WHIT	267	REIPETOW
CLINTON, HOBERT	ELKO	179	ELKO
CLINTON, JOHN	WASH	171	RENO 6TH
CLINTON, RAY W	NYE	107	LODI
CLINTON, WM F	WHIT	257	RIEPETOW
CLIPPNIGER, ALBERT B	ESME	66	LIDA PCT
CLISSO, JOHN*	ESME	53	COLUMBIA
CLOCE, ANTONI	ELKO	214	WELLS
CLOCK, FRANK E	WASH	189	RENO 7TH
CLOHASY, MARY	STOR	29	GOLD HIL
CLOHERY, MARY	STOR	29	GOLD HIL
CLOKE, JOHN A	NYE	144	TONOPAH
CLONAN, MARTIN	HUMB	216	IMLAY
CLOND, GEORGE WAST*	ESME	113	GOLDFIEL
CLOPATH, MATHIES	WASH	227	SPARKS
CLOPTON, GEORGE	NYE	104	BERLIN
CLORE, BEATRICE	WHIT	278	ELY
CLORO, WESLEY*	WASH	205	RENO
CLOSE, BYRON	ORMS	215	CARSON

name	cnty	page	town
COCHRAN, WILLIAM A	NYE	113	MANHATTA
COCHRAN, WILLIAM R	NYE	176	TONOPAH
COCHREN, WILLIAM G	STOR	25	VIRGINIA
COCHUN, JOHN	ORMS	201	CARSON
COCK EYE, JOHNNIE*	HUMB	298	WINNEMUC
COCKBURN, WILLIAM	ESME	113	GOLDFIEL
COCKE, HENRY	WHIT	284	ELY
COCKE, HENRY L	WHIT	238	MAGILL
COCKE, HENRY S	WHIT	238	MAGILL
COCKELL, JOHN	LYON	28	MASON VA
COCKERD, HYRAM A	STOR	5	VIRGINIA
COCKIGEN, ANA	NYE	93	SMOKY VA
COCKING, JOHN**	STOR	5	VIRGINIA
COCKING, THOMAS	STOR	32	GOLD HIL
COCKING, THOMAS	STOR	4	VIRGINIA
COCKINGS, THOS B	ESME	127	GOLDFIEL
COCKINY, THOMAS	STOR	32	GOLD HIL
COCKRAN, ELMER D	ESME	84	GOLDFIEL
COCKRAN, JAMES A	ESME	18	BLAIR
COCKRAN, JOHN L	CHUR	36	S CLAIR
COCKRELL, O E	ELKO	153	BRYAN
COCKS, JOHN A	STOR	24	VIRGINIA
COCKUPE, JOHN*	WASH	266	PYRAMID
COCROFT, LEMUEL	WHIT	304	LANE CIT

Part of a typical Index Publishing index. Each index page has a heading which gives the page number, census year and state. From Dilts's *1910 Nevada Census Index* (Salt Lake City: Index Publishing, 1984), page 28.

Pennsylvania [West] 1870

Census Index of Western Counties

LATTA - LAUGHERY

Series M593

Name	Age	S	R	B-PL	County	Locale	Roll	Pg
LATTA								
Elizabeth	87	f	w	PA	Westmoreland	Mt Pleasant Twp	1466	431
John	30	m	w	PA	Westmoreland	Mt Pleasant Twp	1466	406
John	34	m	w	PA	Westmoreland	Greensburg Boro	1465	327
John	80	m	w	PA	Westmoreland	Unity Twp	1466	723
Joseph	28	m	w	PA	Westmoreland	S Huntingdon Twp	1466	645
Lucinda	39	f	w	PA	Washington	California Boro	1463	62
Margaret	25	f	w	PA	Allegheny	Elizabeth Boro	1292	43
Margaret	75	f	w	PA	Westmoreland	Mt Pleasant Twp	1466	406
Moses	74	m	w	PA	Westmoreland	S Huntingdon Twp	1466	645
Nancy	57	f	w	PA	Westmoreland	Mt Pleasant Twp	1466	416
Richard	47	m	w	IREL	Erie	Waterford Twp	1341	508
Samuel	45	m	w	PA	Fayette	Bulskin Twp	1342	39
Sarah	74	f	w	IREL	Westmoreland	S Huntingdon Twp	1466	645
Thomas	50	m	w	PA	Allegheny	Findley Twp	1292	87
William	53	m	w	PA	Washington	Monongahela	1462	428
LATTEMORE								

Series M593

Name	Age	S	R	B-PL	County	Locale	Roll	Pg
LAUER								
Conrad	45	m	w	HCAS	Allegheny	8-Wd Allegheny	1291	667
George	44	m	w	BAVA	Erie	Union Boro	1341	427
Peter	37	m	w	PRUS	Allegheny	S Fayette Twp	1299	471
Peter	47	m	w	HCAS	Allegheny	7-Wd Allegheny	1291	618
Theodore	16	m	w	PA	Westmoreland	Unity Twp	1466	729
LAUF								
Thomas	70	m	w	IREL	Cambria	1-Wd Johnstown Bo	1317	194
LAUFENBERGER								
Albert	14	m	w	PA	Warren	Connewaugo Twp	1461	58
Jacob	42	m	w	FRAN	Warren	Pleasant Twp	1461	259
John	32	m	w	FRAN	Warren	Warren Boro	1461	81
Mary	7	f	w	PA	Warren	Warren Boro	1461	88
Philipp	38	m	w	FRAN	Warren	Warren Boro	1461	83
Sophia	78	f	w	FRAN	Warren	Warren Boro	1461	83
LAUFER								
George	15	m	w	PA	Beaver	Phillipsburgh Bo	1303	102
John	13	m	w	PA	Beaver	Phillipsburgh Bo	1303	102
John	51	m	w	FRAN	Warren	Warren Boro	1461	81
LAUFFER								

Part of a typical Precision Indexing index. Each page has a header showing the census state and year are also found at the top of each page. From Steuart's *Pennsylvania West 1870 Census Index,* vol. 2 (Bountiful, Utah: Precision Indexing, 1993), page 933.

Figure 9-13. Examples of typical indexes from Accelerated Indexing Systems, Index Publishing, and Precision Indexing.

records created from 1790 to 1910. There is usually a list of modern counties in the state and a modern county boundary map (instead of a map for the census year). The introductory pages sometimes finish with a one-page guide to the contents of each index column.

AIS introductions rarely pertain to the index at hand, rarely cite the sources indexed, and rarely provide much information about how to use the index. AIS frequently modified title pages as the name and address of the company changed; sometimes a recent logo and address can be found next to a years-old publication date with no indication of reprints or new editions. Occasionally the publication date on the copyright page predates by several years the date when AIS actually produced and shipped the index.

Findability. Overall, the findability, or accuracy, of AIS indexes seems to be lower than that of other indexers' products, although some individual AIS indexes are outstanding. In general, the earlier, smaller indexes seem to be more accurate. A random sample of 101 entries from 1790 to 1850 censuses showed AIS book index entry findability to be 89.2 percent, plus or minus 5.0 percent. The findability for the same sample in the AIS microfiche indexes was 88.2 percent, plus or minus 5.2 percent. In MicroQuix's *U.S. Census Index Series* CD-ROM editions, the same sample was 87.2 percent findable (plus or minus 5.4 percent).

Starting with the 1850 census, the names of strays tend to be omitted more often than heads of households. Chinese and American Indian names are not always indexed consistently, and names like McDonald and O'Kelly are sometimes indexed Mc Donald and O Kelly.

Availability. AIS products are available from:

Genealogical Services
P.O. Box 11584
West Jordan, UT 84084
Telephone: 801-280-1554

Automated Archives and Brøderbund

Automated Archives first licensed the AIS census indexes in 1991 and began marketing MS-DOS-based CD-ROMs as the *U.S. Census Index Series.* The name MicroQuix appears on the product because MicroQuix had licensed the indexes from AIS earlier. Automated Archives created the *Master Name Index to Automated Archives, Inc. CD-ROMs* CD-ROM to help identify which of many Automated Archives CD-ROMs have names of interest. CD-ROM technology has allowed Automated Archives and its successor companies to place dozens of book indexes on single CD-ROMs. Genealogical Research System (GRS) software by Automated Archives uses a personal computer to search CD-ROMs for names, places, dates, page numbers, or any other information in the database. A search can find hundreds of matching entries for display in less than a minute (usually in seconds).

In 1994, Automated Archives was purchased by Banner Blue, which later became a division of Brøderbund Software. Brøderbund has issued Windows-based CD-ROMs under the series name Family Tree Maker's Family Archives *Census Index: U.S. Selected States/Counties*. They are based on the same AIS census indexes as is the *U.S. Census Index Series.* This series is indexed by *Family Finder Index and Viewer*.

Value. The Genealogical Research System software and discs are fast and easy to use, and the MS-DOS version's search capabilities are broad and very flexible. Names with variable spellings, names cut off at either end or in the middle, and names with intermittent spellings can be found, and "wild card" searches can be made. The search capabilities of the Windows version are not as flexible. The CD-ROM format makes the cost per indexed name less and allows large indexes to be stored in less space.

Coverage. The newer *Census Index: U.S. Selected States/Counties* series for Windows includes all available AIS Federal census indexes from 1790 to 1850 (except for 1850 North Dakota and Washington). As of early 1997, the series included CD-ROMs covering thirty-nine states for the 1860 census indexes. Many reconstructed AIS census indexes from state censuses, tax lists, and other records are also included. Banner Blue/Brøderbund Software also distributes the Ohio Genealogical Society's *1880 Ohio Census Index* ([Orem, Utah]: Automated Archives, 1993), published in print by Precision Indexing, as well as several non-census products.

Accuracy. Automated Archives claimed to have corrected some of the transcription errors in the AIS book and microfiche indexes. However, a random sample of 101 census entries from 1790 to 1850 did not reveal any of these corrections. The findability of names from the censuses in the MS-DOS-based *U.S. Census Index Series* CD-ROM editions of AIS census indexes was 87.2 percent, plus or minus 5.4 percent; this is slightly less than that of the books (89.2 percent) and microfiche index (88.2 percent) for the same sample. Apparently some of the census index computer tapes deteriorated before all of the data could be transferred to CD-ROM. In the newer *Census Index: U.S. Selected States/Counties* series, a few of the omissions have been rectified. (However, these corrections would only raise the overall accuracy by a fraction of a percent.)

Availability. The older, MS-DOS-based CD-ROMs are no longer available. The new Windows-based discs are sold as the *Census Index: U.S. Selected States/Counties* series with the master index *Family Finder Index and Viewer* on CD-ROM. They are now available from:

Brøderbund Software
P.O. Box 6125
Novato, CA 94948-6125
Telephone: 415-382-4770
Fax: 415-382-4419
Internet: http://www.familytreemaker.com

Index Publishing

Between 1983 and 1986, Index Publishing produced thirty-two census indexes. Bryan Lee Dilts is listed as the compiler of each index. The goal of Index Publishing was to produce more, higher quality indexes to supplement what AIS had done. Index Publishing was the first to publish a series of 1890 veterans schedule indexes and also published an index for some of the counties in the 1848 and 1850 Canada West (Ontario) censuses. Index Publishing's products are generally of higher quality both in content and manufacture, and findability and accuracy in them is generally a bit better than that of AIS indexes; this is partly because Index Publishing intentionally entered a census name more than once if its spelling could be interpreted more than one way, increasing the chances that the correct spelling of a doubtful name was included in the index. The introductions to Index Publishing indexes are more pertinent to the particular index and thus useful than those of competing indexes.

Style. Index Publishing books manufactured before 1989 were made with xerographic printing on 8½- by 11-inch acid-free paper with buckram bindings. Each index page has a heading which includes the page number, census year, and state (figure 9-13). From 300 to 315 entries are printed on each page in three columns, and there are column headings at the top of each page. The information appears in the following order: surname, given name, county abbreviation, census page, and locale. Index Publishing also produced each of its indexes on computer-output microfiche.

Introductions. Each Index Publishing title page indicates whether the index is an every-name index or a heads-of-households index. Library of Congress cataloging-in-publication data is included as well. Each index includes a one-page set of "Fast Start Instructions" as well as a longer, formal introduction. The introduction to each index is thirty to fifty pages long (depending on the length of the bibliography; states with many counties usually have more extensive bibliographies). Each introduction includes the historical background of the particular state and the census year and indicates how many entries are found in the index compared to the population of the state. A section on sources indicates precisely what sources were indexed.

Index Publishing's indexing rules are also explained in each introduction. Index Publishing sampled original censuses and compared them to its indexes to determine how accurate most of its indexes were. A table of common transcription errors helps the researcher overcome some indexing mistakes. The introductions also include information about where the census microfilms can be accessed and a description of the census data. A unique feature of Index Publishing introductions is an exhaustive bibliography of census indexes for the state. This bibliography includes both statewide and countywide indexes. A list of abbreviations, county-by-county census microfilm numbers, and a census map produced by William Thorndale and William Dollarhide finish each Index Publishing introduction.

Availability. Index Publishing census indexes are now available through Precision Indexing.

Precision Indexing

Precision Indexing continues the practice of higher quality indexing. Brad Steuart is listed as Precision Indexing's editor. Precision Indexing is a division of the American Genealogical Lending Library (AGLL), which lends (rents out) genealogical microfilms, especially censuses. Precision Indexing's indexes help researchers know which microfilms to rent, thereby promoting orders for AGLL. Precision Indexing has created 1870 census indexes for at least ten states. Six of those states have been completely covered, and the indexes for the other four states are for major cities. Precision Indexing is known as an indexer of larger, more populous states and cities. It sells its indexes in book, microfiche, and computer floppy diskette formats. VISION/View Plus™ computer software (sold separately) helps to search and read the diskettes. Some of Precision Indexing's microfiche indexes are available in Soundex order, and many are available on a county-by-county basis. Its indexes are also available on CD-ROM from Brøderbund.

Style. The 1870 indexes come in multiple volumes because each index page has only one set of columns, which allows approximately one hundred entries on an 8½- by 11-inch page with no breaks between entries. Only one set of columns fits because Precision Indexing's philosophy is to include more census data to help researchers identify the correct names; this helps researchers to order the proper microfilm. Precision Indexing indexes list surname, given name(s), age, sex, color, birthplace, census locale, county, National Archives series microfilm number, microfilm roll number, and census page number. Each page also has a header showing the state and year of the census (figure 9-13). Column titles are also found at the top of each page; a copyright statement, address, and index page numbers are at the foot. At least one index has a slightly more elaborate format that includes larger, boldface surnames with given names in smaller type indented beneath. The print quality is usually excellent. A Soundex code search is available for many of the diskette indexes.

Introductions. Precision Indexing's introductions are around thirty-eight pages in length. Many of them have a foreword by a prominent genealogist that explains the history of the state and census year. An explanation of the index's format includes the order of data and how the entries are alphabetized. Indexing rules are also given. Precision Indexing always includes "A Short Guide to 'Mistakes' Made in the Census Indexes." A census map produced by William Thorndale and William Dollarhide map is included as well. Each introduction usually ends with a list of abbreviations.

Some Precision Indexing multi-volume indexes are split alphabetically (for example, *A* through *F, G* through *M,* and *N* through *Z*), but most are split geographically. For example, Philadelphia 1870 has a separate volume and alphabet from the West Pennsylvania 1870 index.

Availability. Researchers can obtain Precision Indexing catalogs and products from:

AGLL
P.O. Box 329
Bountiful, UT 84011-0329
Telephone: 800-657-9442
Fax: 801-298-5468

Genealogical Publishing Company

Over the years, Genealogical Publishing Company (GPC) has produced a series of reprints of government census indexes and original census indexes, primarily of eastern states and for census years from 1790 to 1820. In addition to reprinting the 1790 census transcripts, GPC has published around twenty pre-1850 census indexes. However, the bulk of GPC's business continues to be in publishing other kinds of genealogy, local history, and immigration sources.

Style. Most of the original indexes published by GPC are printed on six- by nine-inch paper. They list the surname, given name(s), county, and census page number. Sometimes given names are indented under the surname if there is more than one individual with the surname in the index.

The photo-reprints of government indexes are on 8½- by 11-inch paper of better quality than the original editions. They include transcripts of the censuses and indexes at the back.

Introductions. The government index reprints typically have one- or two-page introductions. Original indexes have five- or six-page introductions. Acknowledgments are prominent in most of these introductions; maps, sources, and indexing rules are not usually provided. However, the introductions in indexes compiled by Elizabeth P. Bentley indicate how to access the census microfilms and comment on their readability. Bentley discusses census spelling peculiarities and how she handled especially illegible census entries, describes the additional information on the censuses, and includes an abbreviation table. Bentley is unique in listing each microfilm roll number and the beginning and ending census page numbers of each county—especially helpful for those rare cases when census page numbers are mistyped in the index.

Availability. Although most GPC census indexes are out of print, a catalog and available census indexes are available from:

Genealogical Publishing Co.
1001 North Calvert Street
Baltimore, MD 21202-3897
Telephone: 800-296-6687
Fax: 410-752-8492

INSTRUCTIONAL LITERATURE AND REFERENCE TOOLS

The following sources make it easier to use printed censuses, tax lists, and their indexes.

General Guides

Among the best instructional guides is David Davenport's "Census Indexes: A Primer," *Illinois State Genealogical Society Quarterly* 23 (Fall 1991): 130–39. It discusses spelling errors made by census takers and census transcribers, profiles the three major indexing companies, and illustrates indexing errors and how to overcome them. Thorndale's "Census Indexes and Spelling Variants" (cited earlier) also discusses census index accuracy and how to overcome indexing errors. A longer discussion that includes illustrations of hard-to-index census entries is Richard H. Saldana's *A Practical Guide to the "Misteaks" Made in Census Indexes* (Salt Lake City: the author, 1989).

The focus of Jimmy Parker and Robert L. Hales's four-hour audiotape *Searching U.S. Census Records* (Provo, Utah: Family History Unlimited, 1992) is more on the nature of census records and interpreting them, but it does include some instruction about census indexes. Eakle's *Tax Records: A Common Source with an Uncommon Value* (cited earlier) discusses who is found in tax records, how taxes were levied, special tax processes, and how the resulting records can be used by family historians.

Census Index Finding Aids

The Family History Library publishes a series of "research outlines" for the United States in general and for each state. Each of these outlines briefly cites and discusses the censuses and tax records available for the area. They are good sources to begin learning about statewide censuses and indexes. Eichholz's *Ancestry's Red Book* (cited earlier) includes a brief census section and tax section for each state; it may be more current and slightly more detailed than some state research outlines. The *Family History Library Catalog* includes an outstanding list of censuses, census indexes, and substitute records which may be more current than either the research outlines or *Ancestry's Red Book*.

Thorndale and Dollarhide's *Map Guide to the U.S. Federal Censuses, 1790–1920* (cited earlier), is one of the most helpful reference tools for census researchers. It discusses the history of census growth and census accuracy, technical facts about each census, sources regarding each state's old county lines, and which counties have available census records. In addition to the regular maps for the decennial censuses, many "off-year" Federal census maps are included. The maps are arranged alphabetically by state and within each state by census year. It is an outstanding source for clear, concise explanations of census availability by state, county, and census year.

Lainhart's *State Census Records* (cited earlier) is an inventory and description of state (as opposed to Federal or colonial) census records and their indexes. The list includes several reconstructed censuses which use tax lists and other substitutes as sources. Most entries describe the data available in the census cited. The work also identifies the few state census indexes available as of the publication date. Lainhart occasionally defers to Henry J. Dubester's *State Censuses: An Annotated Bibliography of Censuses of Population Taken After the Year 1790* (Washington, D.C.: U.S. Government Printing Office, 1948), which is an older but still useful list. Evarts B. Greene and Virginia D. Harrington's *American Population Before the Federal Census of 1790* (1932; reprint; Baltimore: Genealogical Publishing Co., 1993) can be used as a supplement to Lainhart because it deals with years that Lainhart's work does not. Greene and Harrington include Illinois, Kentucky, and Tennessee as well as the thirteen colonies. Although it is primarily statistical, Greene and Harrington's work cites sources which are either colonial censuses or excellent census substitutes. In the sixty-six years since it was first published, some overlooked material has come to light. Stemmons's *United States Census Compendium* (cited earlier) is a good list of sources, but it gives no descriptions of the records other than year and record type. It contains many census substitute sources not noted by Lainhart or Greene and Harrington. It is arranged by state, county, town, and year. The bibliography is more a list of addresses of the sources' compiler-publishers. Many, but not all, sources for AIS's Early American Series and AIS's decennary census indexes can be identified in this compendium.

The bibliographies in the introductions to Index Publishing census indexes include exhaustive lists of Federal census indexes (both statewide and countywide within the state). They even include indexes in local genealogical society periodicals. However, only twenty-one states and the District of Columbia were indexed by Index Publishing. These bibliographies do not necessarily list off-year census indexes or reconstructed censuses from substitute records (nor, of course, do they identify indexes created in the almost ten years since they were published).

PERSI is an important reference tool for finding census and tax list transcripts and indexes in some two thousand genealogical and historical periodicals. The name indexes in *PERSI* do not normally include the names in census transcripts published in periodicals. On the other hand, for each set of years there is an alphabetical place index. To use it, first find the state and then the county or town for which there may be an index or transcript; then search for the subject headings "census" or "tax." Census and tax list transcripts in periodicals are sometimes indexed at the end of the periodical volume or in cumulated indexes for several volumes. *GPAI* can be used in the same way to find similar material.

G. Eileen Buckway and Fred Adams's *U.S. State and Special Census Register: A Listing of Family History Library Microfilm Numbers,* rev. ed., 2 vols. (Salt Lake City: Family History Library, 1992) lists Family History Library sources, including authors, titles, publishers, publication dates, and call numbers. The contents of the census, restrictions on access, original location, indexes, and whether available through interlibrary loan are sometimes indicated. The front side of a page cites the census, and the back side lists its contents. It is arranged by state and census year.

The *Encyclopedia of Local History and Genealogy: Census Encyclopedia* (cited earlier) can be useful for finding the more obscure sources used to compile AIS's Early American Series, the AIS decennary census indexes, the AIS microfiche indexes, and MicroQuix's *U.S. Census Index Series* CD-ROM editions of AIS indexes. It lists the years and availability of Federal population schedules, mortality schedules, non-population schedules (such as agricultural and manufacturers schedules), and colonial, territorial, state, and special Federal schedules. A county-by-county and year-by-year list of National Archives microfilm series numbers is also included. The encyclopedia also lists the 1880 and 1900 Soundex microfilm roll numbers. At the end of each state section is a list of county indexes and source codes. The source codes are repeated on pages 87 through 886 with addresses of the source publishers. This reference work should be used with caution, for it is older and may not be as accurate as other publications.

Microfilm Number Finding Aids

Several sources help researchers order the correct microfilms or make sense of confusing page numbers or enumeration districts. Smith's *United States Census Key 1850, 1860, 1870* (cited earlier) shows the county on each microfilm with both the National Archives roll number and the Family History Library number. If the county is divided on more than one microfilm, it also shows each town on the microfilm. It is arranged by year, state, and microfilm number, which is usually arranged alphabetically by county. *A Key to the United States 1880 Federal Census: Identifying Enumeration District Numbers and Microfilm Numbers of the National Archives and the Genealogical Library* (1986; reprint; Bountiful, Utah: American Genealogical Lending Library, 1988) is essentially the same with enumeration districts rather than towns or page numbers. G. Eileen Buckway's *U.S. 1910 Federal Census: Unindexed States: A Guide to Finding Census Enumeration Districts for Unindexed Cities, Towns, and Villages* (Salt Lake City: Family History Library, 1992) also helps identify enumeration districts and Family History Library census microfilm numbers. It includes twenty-two unindexed states, the District of Columbia, and Puerto Rico. Towns are listed alphabetically for each state, and the enumeration district is indicated in order to eliminate the need for a wider search of an entire county or state in the original census.

Parker has listed all of the localities in the 1850 census in alphabetical order in the *City, County, Town and Township Index to the 1850 Federal Census Schedules* (cited earlier). Next to each locality Parker indicates the microfilm number(s) where it is found and the beginning and ending census page numbers for that locality. The page numbers are extremely useful when census indexes have incorrect page citations. However, the census page numbers which Parker cites are not always from the same set of page numbers used by the indexers.

Accelerated Indexing Systems has created a similar tool in *United States Federal Census Place Enrollment Schedules* (cited earlier). The AIS version shows only the beginning page number of each locality. It includes the years 1790 to 1850 in the first two volumes and is arranged by year, state, county, and town/page number. The CD-ROM indexes also have lists of places but no page numbers. The National Archives catalogs of census microfilms can also be used in a similar way.

Big City Census Finding Aids

The large cities of America have too many residents to make searching census records practical without name indexes. If the researcher can discover the street address of the person sought, it is easier to find the person in the census records. The following records help researchers find streets in large city censuses:

- Guide to the Use of the United States, Census Office, 10th Census 1880 New York City. Typescript. 1963.
- United States. Census Office. 10th Census, 1880. *Census Descriptions of Geographic Subdivisions and Enumeration Districts, 1880.* National Archives Microfilm Publications, T1224. Washington, D.C.: National Archives and Records Service, 1978.
- United States. Bureau of the Census. *Census Descriptions of Geographic Subdivisions and Enumeration Districts, 1910.* National Archives Microfilm Publications, T1224. Washington, D.C.: National Archives and Records Service, 1978.
- Justensen, Elaine. *New York City 1915 State Census Street Address Index.* Salt Lake City: Family History Library, 1992.
- Kirkham, E. Kay. *A Handy Guide to Record-Searching in the Larger Cities of the United States: Including a Guide to Their Vital Records and Some Maps with Street Indexes with Other Information.* Logan, Utah: Everton, 1974.

Soundex Guide

An explanation of the Soundex coding system used for the 1880, 1900, 1910, and 1920 censuses and codes for 125,000 names are found in Bradley W. Steuart's *The Soundex Reference Guide: Soundex Coded to Over 125,000 Surnames* (Bountiful, Utah: Precision Indexing, 1990).

REFERENCE LIST

Accelerated Indexing Systems U.S. Census Indexes (on Microfiche) Resource Guide. 1992. Salt Lake City: Family History Library.

Adams, Enid Eleanor. 1983. "Who is 'XZLLY MZFGIN'?" *The American Genealogist* 59: 108.

Dilts, Bryan Lee. 1983. *1856 Utah Census Index.* Salt Lake City: Index Publishing.

_____. 1984. *1860 California Census Index.* Salt Lake City: Index Publishing.

_____. 1986. *1890 West Virginia Census Index of Civil War Veterans or Their Widows.* Salt Lake City: Index Publishing.

Dowling, Heidi. 1990. "Census Problems." *Whitman County Genealogical Society Newsletter* 6 (9) (July–August): 70.

Eakle, Arlene, and Johni Cerny. 1984. *The Source: A Guidebook of American Genealogy.* Salt Lake City: Ancestry.

Heiss, Willard. 1976. "It's a Bird, It's a Plane, It's a Speedy Census Index." *Genealogy* no. 24 (August): 1–4.

Hodge, Jack E. 1963. "The 'Texas' Census of 1830." *Stirpes* 3 (June): [68].

Jackson, Ronald Vern. 1984. *Early American Series Mississippi, Volume 2.* Bountiful, Utah: Accelerated Indexing Systems.

Johnson, William Perry. 1974. "1800 Census of North Carolina." *North Carolina Genealogy* 20 (1) (Spring-Summer): 2957–61.

McMillon, Lynn C. 1977. "An Index Can Be a Roadblock." *Virginia Genealogist* 21: 205–06.

Martin, David Kendall. 1978. "New York 1800 Census Index." *The American Genealogist* 54: 53–54.

Ninth Census of the United States: Statistics of Population, Tables I to VIII Inclusive. 1872. Washington, D.C.: Government Printing Office.

Thorndale, William, and William Dollarhide. 1987. *Map Guide to the U.S. Federal Censuses, 1790–1920.* Baltimore: Genealogical Publishing Co.

BIBLIOGRAPHY

Instructional and Reference Sources

Accelerated Indexing Systems, Inc. Microfiche Indexes Branch Genealogical Libraries Instructional Materials. Salt Lake City: Genealogical Society of Utah, 1984.

Accelerated Indexing Systems U.S. Census Indexes (on Microfiche) Resource Guide. Salt Lake City: Family History Library, 1992.

Adams, Enid Eleanor. "Who is 'XZLLY MZFGIN'?" *The American Genealogist* 59 (1983).

Branch Genealogical Libraries Accelerated Indexing Systems, Inc. Microfiche Indexes Instructional Materials. Salt Lake City: Genealogical Library, 1984.

Brewer, Mary M. *Index to Census Schedules in Printed Form.* Huntsville, Ala.: Century Enterprises, 1969. Supplement, 1970–71.

Buckway, G. Eileen, et al. *U.S. 1910 Federal Census: Unindexed States: A Guide to Finding Census Enumeration Districts for Unindexed Cities, Towns, and Villages.* Salt Lake City: Family History Library, 1992.

_____, and Fred Adams. *U.S. State and Special Census Register: A Listing of Family History Library Microfilm Numbers.* Rev. ed. 2 vols. Salt Lake City: Family History Library, 1992.

A Census of Pensioners for Revolutionary or Military Services: With Their Names, Ages, and Places of Residence, as Returned by the Marshals of the Several Judicial Districts, Under the Act for Taking the Sixth Census. Washington, D.C.: Blair and Rives, 1841.

Davenport, David Paul. "Census Indexes: A Primer." *Illinois State Genealogical Society Quarterly* 23 (Fall 1991): 130–39.

Directory of Census Information Sources. Munroe Falls, Ohio: Summitt Publ., 1980.

Dowling, Heidi. "Census Problems." *Whitman County Genealogical Society Newsletter* 6 (9) (July-August 1990): 70.

Dubester, Henry J. *State Censuses: An Annotated Bibliography of Censuses of Population Taken After the Year 1790.* Washington, D.C.: U.S. Government Printing Office, 1948.

Eakle, Arlene Haslam. "Census Records." In *The Source: A Guidebook of American Genealogy.* Salt Lake City: Ancestry, 1997.

_____. *Tax Records: A Common Source with an Uncommon Value.* [Salt Lake City: Family History World], 1978.

Eichholz, Alice, ed. *Ancestry's Red Book: American State, County and Town Sources.* Rev. ed. Salt Lake City: Ancestry, 1992.

[Family History Library]. "Dawes Commission Records/Guion Miller Rolls." [Salt Lake City: Family History Library, 1992].

Family History Library Catalog. [Salt Lake City: Genealogical Society of Utah], annual. Available on CD-ROM or on 2,884 microfiche.

AIS advertisement. *Genealogical Helper* 40 (2) (March-April 1986) : 207.

Greene, Evarts B., and Virginia D. Harrington. *American Population Before the Federal Census of 1790.* 1932. Reprint. Baltimore: Genealogical Publishing Co., 1993.

Guide to the Use of the United States, Census Office, 10th Census 1880 New York City. Typescript, 1963.

Heiss, Willard. "It's a Bird, It's a Plane, It's a Speedy Census Index." *Genealogy* no. 24 (August 1976): 1–4.

Hodge, Jack E. "The 'Texas' Census of 1830." *Stirpes* 3 (June 1963): [68].

Jackson, Ronald Vern. *AISI Microfiche Data-Base List Manual.* 1984. Reprint. Bountiful, Utah: Accelerated Indexing Systems, 1988.

_____. *United States Federal Census Place Enrollment Schedules.* Vol. 1, 1790–1830; vol. 2, 1840–1850. North Salt Lake, Utah: Accelerated Indexing Systems International, 1991.

_____, and Lee Smeal. *Encyclopedia of Local History and Genealogy: Census Encyclopedia.* Bountiful, Utah: Accelerated Indexing Systems, 1979.

Johnson, William Perry. "1800 Census of North Carolina." *North Carolina Genealogy* 20 (1) (Spring-Summer 1974): 2957–61.

Justesen, Elaine. *New York City 1915 State Census Street Address Index*. Salt Lake City: Family History Library, 1992.

Kirkham, E. Kay. *A Handy Guide to Record-Searching in the Larger Cities of the United States: Including a Guide to Their Vital Records and Some Maps with Street Indexes with Other Information.* Logan, Utah: Everton, 1974.

Lainhart, Ann S. *State Census Records.* Baltimore: Genealogical Publishing Co., 1992.

Luebking, Sandra Hargreaves. "Research in Land and Tax Records." In *The Source: A Guidebook of American Genealogy.* Edited by Loretto Dennis Szucs and Sandra Hargreaves Luebking. Rev. ed. Salt Lake City: Ancestry, 1997.

Martin, David Kendall. "New York 1800 Census Index." *The American Genealogist* 54 (1978): 53–54.

McMillon, Lynn C. "An Index Can Be A Roadblock." *Virginia Genealogist* 21 (1977): 205–06.

Ninth Census of the United States: Statistics of Population, Tables I to VIII Inclusive. Washington, D.C.: Government Printing Office, 1872.

Parker, J. Carlyle. *City, County, Town and Township Index to the 1850 Federal Census Schedules.* Detroit: Gale Research, 1979.

Parker, Jimmy, and Robert L. Hales. *Searching U.S. Census Records.* Provo, Utah: Family History Unlimited, 1992. Recorded lecture on four audiocassettes with an accompanying workbook.

Records Indexed by AIS. Genealogical Library Reference Aids Series B, no. 11. Salt Lake City: Genealogical Society of Utah, 1984.

Saldana, Richard H. *A Practical Guide to the "Misteaks" Made in Census Indexes.* Salt Lake City: the author, 1989.

Santmyer, Karen. *U.S. Army Audit Agency Statistical Sampling Program.* Version 2.0. N.p., 1985.

Smith, Leonard H., Jr. *United States Census Key 1850, 1860, 1870.* Bountiful, Utah: American Genealogical Lending Library, 1987.

The Source: A Guidebook of American Genealogy. Edited by Loretto Dennis Szucs and Sandra Hargraves Luebking. Rev. ed. Salt Lake City: Ancestry, 1997.

Stemmons, John D. *The United States Census Compendium: A Directory of Census Records, Tax Lists, Poll Lists, Petitions, Directories, etc. Which Can Be Used as a Census.* Logan, Utah: Everton Publishers, 1973.

Steuart, Bradley W. *The Soundex Reference Guide: Soundex Coded to Over 125,000 Surnames.* Bountiful, Utah: Precision Indexing, 1990.

Szucs, Loretto Dennis. "Research in Census Records." In *The Source: A Guidebook of American Genealogy.* Edited by Loretto Dennis Szucs and Sandra Hargraves Luebking. Rev. ed. Salt Lake City: Ancestry, 1997.

Tauber, Irene Barnes. *General Censuses and Vital Statistics in the Americas.* Washington, D.C.: U.S. Government Printing Office, 1943.

Thorndale, William. "Census Indexes and Spelling Variants." *Association of Professional Genealogists Newsletter* 4 (5) (May 1982): 6–9. Reprinted in *The Source: A Guidebook of American Genealogy.* Salt Lake City: Ancestry, 1984, 17–20.

_____, and William Dollarhide. *Map Guide to the U.S. Federal Censuses, 1790–1920.* Baltimore: Genealogical Publishing Co., 1987.

U.S./Canada Reference Staff and Volunteers of the Genealogical Library of The Church of Jesus Christ of Latter-day Saints. *A Key to the United States 1880 Federal Census: Identifying Enumeration District Numbers and Microfilm Numbers of the National Archives and the Genealogical Library.* 1986. Reprint. Bountiful, Utah: American Genealogical Lending Library, 1988.

Vallentine, John F. "Census Records and Indexes." *Genealogical Journal* 2 (1973): 133–39.

_____. "Effective Use of Census Indexes in Locating People." *Genealogical Journal* 4 (1975): 51–60.

Wynne, Frances Holloway. *North Carolina Extant Voter Registrations of 1867.* Bowie, Md.: Heritage Books, 1992.

Indexes Cited

(Arranged by state for authors with multiple titles.)

"1830 Census, Morgan County, KY." *East Kentuckian* 2 (1): [13–14], (2): [13–15].

1851 Census of England and Wales [Transcription and Indexes]: Devon (or Norfolk, or Warwick). Salt Lake City: Genealogical Society of Utah, 1996 (microfiche), 1997 (CD-ROM).

1881 Census of England and Wales [Transcription and Indexes]: Cambridgeshire. Salt Lake City: Genealogical Society of Utah, 1991.

1881 Census of England and Wales [Transcription and Indexes]: Derby. Salt Lake City: Genealogical Society of Utah, 1995.

1881 Census of Scotland [Transcription and Indexes]: National. Salt Lake City: Genealogical Society of Utah, 1996.

African Americans in the 1870 Census. Family Tree Maker's Family Archives, no. 165. 1 CD-ROM. [Novato, Calif.]: Brøderbund, 1996.

Automated Archives, Inc. *U.S. Census Index—1860: Delaware, New Jersey and Pennsylvania.* CD-ROM. [Orem, Utah]: Automated Archives, 1992.

Bellardo, Lewis J., Jr. "Frankfort, Kentucky, Census of Free Blacks, 1842." *National Genealogical Society Quarterly* 63 (4): 272–75.

Bentley, Elizabeth Petty. *Index to the 1810 Census of Virginia.* Baltimore: Genealogical Publishing Co., 1980.

Bohannan, Larry C. *Fourth Census of the United States 1820 Illinois Population Schedules.* Huntsville, Ark.: Century Enterprises, 1968.

Butler, Rita Babin. *Ascension Parish, Louisiana, 1890 U.S. Census.* [Baton Rouge, La.]: Oracle Press, 1983.

Carothers, Bettie Stirling. *1776 Census of Maryland.* Lutherville, Md.: the author, 1972.

Census Index: U.S. Selected States/Counties. Version 3.0. Family Tree Maker's Family Archives, 310–320. [Novato, Calif.]: Brøderbund Software, 1995.

De Lamar, Marie, and Elisabeth Rothstein. *The Reconstructed 1790 Census of Georgia: Substitutes for Georgia's Lost 1790 Census.* Baltimore: Genealogical Publishing Co., 1985.

Dilts, Bryan Lee. *1860 California Census Index.* Salt Lake City: Index Publishing, 1984.

_____. *1848 and 1850 Canada West (Ontario) Census Index.* Salt Lake City: Index Publishing, 1984.

_____. *1890 Maine Census Index of Civil War Veterans or Their Widows.* Salt Lake City: Index Publishing, 1984.

_____. *1910 Nevada Census Index.* Salt Lake City: Index Publishing, 1984.

_____. *1890 New York Census Index of Civil War Veterans or Their Widows.* Salt Lake City: Index Publishing, 1984.

_____. *1860 South Carolina Census Index.* 2 vols. Salt Lake City: Index Publishing, 1985.

_____. *1856 Utah Census Index.* Salt Lake City: Index Publishing, 1983.

_____. *1890 West Virginia Census Index of Civil War Veterans or Their Widows.* Salt Lake City: Index Publishing, 1986.

Dryden, Ruth T. *Somerset County, Maryland, 1850.* [Silver Spring, Md.: Family Line Publications, 198(?)].

Eichholz, Alice, and James M. Rose. *Free Black Heads of Households in the New York State Federal Census, 1790–1830.* Detroit: Gale Research, 1981.

Family Finder Index and Viewer. Version 3.0. Family Tree Maker's Family Archives, Index. [Novato, Calif.]: Brøderbund Software, 1995.

Family Tree Maker. *Census Index: Colonial America 1607–1789.* CD-ROM. [Novato, Calif.]: Brøderbund Software, 1995.

Foster, William A., and Thomas Allan Scott. *Paulding County: Its People and Places.* Roswell, Ga.: W. H. Wolfe Associates, 1983.

Fothergill, Augusta Brigland, and John Mark Naugle. *Virginia Tax Payers, 1782–1787, Other Than Those Published by the United States Census Bureau.* 1940. Reprint. Baltimore: Genealogical Publishing Co., 1974.

Genealogical Periodical Annual Index (GPAI). Compiled by Karen Ackermann and edited by Laird C. Towle. Bowie, Md.: Heritage Books, 1981–.

A General Index to a Census of Pensioners for Revolutionary or Military Service, 1840. Baltimore: Genealogical Publishing Co., 1965.

Glacking, James R. "Index Federal Census, Grant County, Kentucky 1820." *Kentucky Ancestors* 10 (3): 121–24.

Harshman, Lida Flint. *Index to the 1860 Federal Population Census of Ohio.* Mineral Ridge, Ohio: the author, 1979.

Heads of Families at the First Census of the United States Taken in the Year 1790, Virginia: Records of the State Enumerations, 1782 to 1785. 1908. Reprint. Baltimore: Genealogical Publishing Co., 1986.

Hubble, Anna Joy Munday. *Madison County, Kentucky, 1840 Census.* Whitefish, Mont.: the author, 1979.

"Index Federal Census, Grant County, Kentucky 1820." *Kentucky Ancestors* 10 (3): 121–24.

Index, Louisiana Mortality Records for the Years Ending June 1, 1850, 1860, 1870. Typescript, [19(?)].

Index to Heads of Families 1830 Census of Georgia. Albany, Ga.: Delwyn Associates, 1974.

Indexes to Manufacturers Census of 1820. Knightstown, Ind.: Bookmark, 1977.

Indiana 1860 Census Index with Alternative Names, Ages and Birth Places. Salt Lake City: Kratz Indexing, 1986–87.

Ireland Census Index: Londonderry County, 1831 [and] Cavan County, 1841. Automated Archives, no. 197. 1 CD-ROM. [Orem, Utah]: Automated Archives, 1994.

Jackson, Ronald Vern, ed. *AIS Microfiche Indexes of U.S. Census and Other Records.* Microfiche. Bountiful, Utah: Accelerated Indexing Systems International, 1984.

_____. *Early Alabama.* Bountiful, Utah: Accelerated Indexing Systems, 1981.

_____. *Alabama 1811–1819 Decennary Census Index.* Bountiful, Utah: Accelerated Indexing Systems, 1983.

_____. *Alabama 1850 Census Index.* Bountiful, Utah: Accelerated Indexing Systems, 1976.

_____. *Alabama 1860.* North Salt Lake, Utah: Accelerated Indexing Systems, 1985.

_____. *Alabama 1870 Federal Census Index.* Salt Lake City: Accelerated Indexing Systems, 1989.

_____. *Alaskan Census Records 1870–1907.* Bountiful, Utah: Accelerated Indexing Systems, 1976.

_____. *Early California.* Bountiful, Utah: Accelerated Indexing Systems, 1980.

_____. *California 1860 Census Index.* North Salt Lake, Utah: Accelerated Indexing Systems International, 1984.

_____. *Early Connecticut.* Bountiful, Utah: Accelerated Indexing Systems, 1980.

_____. *Delaware 1850/1860 Slave Schedules.* Salt Lake City: Accelerated Indexing Systems International, 1986.

_____. *District of Columbia 1870.* North Salt Lake, Utah: Accelerated Indexing Systems International, 1986.

_____. *Georgia 1830 Census Index.* North Salt Lake, Utah: Accelerated Indexing Systems, 1976.

_____. *Georgia 1850.* North Salt Lake, Utah: Accelerated Indexing Systems, 1979.

_____. *Illinois 1820 Census Index.* Bountiful, Utah: Accelerated Indexing Systems, 1977.

_____. *Chicago, Cook County, Illinois 1870 Federal Census Index.* Salt Lake City: Accelerated Indexing Systems International, 1988.

_____. *Louisiana Sugar Censuses 1850–1860.* North Salt Lake, Utah: Accelerated Indexing Systems, 1987.

_____. *Maine 1830 Census Index.* Bountiful, Utah: Accelerated Indexing Systems, 1977.

_____. *Maine 1890 Veterans.* North Salt Lake, Utah: Accelerated Indexing Systems International, 1990.

_____. *Massachusetts 1860 South Federal Census Index.* Salt Lake City, Utah: Ancestral Genealogical Extended Schedules, 1992.

_____. *Michigan 1860 Federal Census Index.* North Salt Lake, Utah: Accelerated Indexing Systems International, 1988.

_____. *Minnesota 1850 Census Index.* South Bountiful, Utah: Accelerated Indexing Systems, 1981.

_____. *Early American Series Mississippi, Volume 2.* Bountiful, Utah: Accelerated Indexing Systems, 1984.

_____. *Mississippi 1850 Census Index.* Bountiful, Utah: Accelerated Indexing Systems, 1977.

_____. *Missouri 1860.* North Salt Lake, Utah: Accelerated Indexing Systems International, 1986–87.

_____. *New Hampshire 1830 Index Census* [*sic*]. Bountiful, Utah: Accelerated Indexing Systems, 1977.

_____. *New Jersey Tax Lists, 1772–1822.* Salt Lake City: Accelerated Indexing Systems, 1981. Hunterdon County is entirely absent.

_____. *New Jersey 1860 South.* North Salt Lake, Utah: Accelerated Indexing Systems, 1986.

_____. *New Mexico 1860 Census Index.* Bountiful, Utah: Accelerated Indexing Systems, 1981.

_____. *New York 1820 Census Index.* Bountiful, Utah: Accelerated Indexing Systems, 1977.

_____. *New York 1840 Census Index.* Salt Lake City: Accelerated Indexing Systems, 1978.

_____. *New York 1850 Census Index.* Bountiful, Utah: Accelerated Indexing Systems, 1977.

_____. *Brooklyn, New York 1870 Federal Census Index.* North Salt Lake, Utah: Accelerated Indexing Systems International, 1988.

_____. *Long Island ([plus] Dutchess, Queens, Suffolk and Richmond) New York 1870 Federal Census Index.* 2 vols. North Salt Lake, Utah: Accelerated Indexing Systems International, 1989.

_____. *North Carolina 1850 Census Index.* North Salt Lake, Utah: Accelerated Indexing Systems, 1976.

_____. *North Carolina 1870 Census Index.* North Salt Lake, Utah: Accelerated Indexing Systems International, 1989.

_____. *Ohio 1850 Census Index.* North Salt Lake, Utah: Accelerated Indexing Systems, 1978.

_____. *Oklahoma 1860 Census Index.* Salt Lake City: Accelerated Indexing Systems, 1984.

_____. *Ontario Census 1848/1850 (Upper Canada-Heron* [*sic*]*) District.* Bountiful, Utah: Accelerated Indexing Systems, 1984. Also see Jackson's *Upper Canada 1848/1850 Ontario.*

_____. *Heads of Families at the First Census of the United States Taken in the Year 1790, Pennsylvania.* Bountiful, Utah: Accelerated Indexing Systems, 1978.

_____. *Pennsylvania 1860.* North Salt Lake, Utah: Accelerated Indexing Systems International, 1986–87.

_____. *South Carolina 1860 Census Index.* North Salt Lake, Utah: Accelerated Indexing Systems International, 1988.

_____. *South Carolina 1890 Census Index of Civil War Veterans.* Bountiful, Utah: Accelerated Indexing Systems, 1984.

_____. *Tennessee 1840 Census Index.* Bountiful, Utah: Accelerated Indexing Systems, 1976.

_____. *Tennessee 1850 Census Index.* Bountiful, Utah: Accelerated Indexing Systems, 1977.

_____. *Tennessee 1860 Census Index.* Salt Lake City: Accelerated Indexing Systems, 1981.

_____. *Texas Census Records 1841–1849.* North Salt Lake, Utah: Accelerated Indexing Systems International, 1981. Also titled *Texas 1840–49* on some copies.

_____. *Texas 1850 Slave Schedules.* North Salt Lake, Utah: Accelerated Indexing Systems International, 1988.

_____. *United States Census of Pensioners of 1840: Index of Names with Ages to the Original 1841 Government Publication.* Bountiful, Utah: Accelerated Indexing Systems International, 1984.

_____. *Upper Canada 1848/1850 Ontario.* North Salt Lake: Accelerated Indexing Systems International, 1986. Also see *Ontario Census 1848/1850 (Upper Canada-Heron* [*sic*]*) District.*

_____. *Vermont 1850 Census Index.* Bountiful, Utah: Accelerated Indexing Systems, 1978.

_____. *Virginia 1830 Census Index.* Bountiful, Utah: Accelerated Indexing Systems, 1976.

Jenks, Houston C. *An Index to the [Louisiana] Census of 1911 of Confederate Veterans or Their Widows.* [Baton Rouge, La.: Jenks], 1989.

Kresge, Mrs. E. B. "Federal Census of Wayne Co., Mich. 1820." *Detroit Society for Genealogical Research Magazine* 12: 101–05, 129–32.

Marsh, William A. *1880 Census of West Virginia: Compiled Alphabetically by Counties.* 13 vols. Parsons, W.Va.: McClain Print, 1979–92.

Martin, William T., and Patricia Martin. *1885 Florida State Census Index.* Miami: the authors, 1991.

Master Name Index to Automated Archives, Inc. CD-ROMs. CD/ Automated Archives, Index. Orem, Utah: Automated Archives, 1994.

McLane, Bobbie Jones. *An Index to the Three Volumes, Arkansas 1911 Census of Confederate Veterans.* Hot Springs, Ark.: Arkansas Ancestors, 1988.

_____, and Capitola Glazner. *Arkansas 1911 Census of Confederate Veterans.* N.p., 1977.

Meyers, Carol M. *Early New York State Census Records, 1663–1772.* Gardena, Calif.: RAM Publishers, 1965.

MicroQuix, Inc. *U.S. Census Index Series.* Orem, Utah: Automated Archives, 1991–94. Twenty-nine CD-ROMs for use with Automated Archives's proprietary *Genealogical Research System* (*GRS*) computer software.

Nelson, Ken. *1890 U.S. Census Index to Surviving Population Schedules and Register of Film Numbers to the Special Census of Union Veterans.* Rev. ed. Salt Lake City: Family History Library, 1991.

"New Jersey Rateables, 1773–1774." *Genealogical Magazine of New Jersey* 36, 37.

Norton, Margaret Cross. *Illinois Census Returns 1820.* 1934. Reprint. Baltimore: Genealogical Publishing Co., 1969.

Ohio Family Historians and Their Friends. *Index to the 1850 Federal Population Census of Ohio.* Mineral Ridge, Ohio: Lida Flint Harshman, 1972.

Ohio Genealogical Society. *Ohio 1880 Census Index.* 1 CD-ROM. [Orem, Utah]: Automated Archives, 1991.

Olmsted, Virginia Langham. *Spanish and Mexican Colonial Censuses of New Mexico: 1790, 1823, 1845.* Albuquerque: New Mexico Genealogical Society, 1975.

Parrish, Mrs. M. T. *1850 Census Index of Eastern Kentucky.* Stamping Ground, Ky.: the author, 1973.

Parrish, Mrs. Verle Hamilton. *1850 Census of Floyd County, Kentucky.* Stamping Ground, Ky., [19(?)].

Partlow, Thomas E. *Tax Lists of Wilson County, Tennessee, 1803–1807, With Names in Court Records, 1802–1822.* Baltimore: Clearfield, 1981.

Periodical Source Index (*PERSI*). Fort Wayne, Ind.: Allen County Public Library Foundation, 1987–.

Pompey, Sherman Lee. *The 1850 Census Records of Mendocino County, California.* Independence, Calif.: Historical & Genealogical Pub., 1965.

_____. *Indexes to American and Western Canada Census and Tax Records, 1800–1900.* Salt Lake City: Genealogical Society of Utah, 1967. Microfilmed typescript, [196(?)].

Precision Indexing Databases. *Pennsylvania West 1870.* CD-ROM. [Orem, Utah]: Automated Archives, 1994.

Register, Mrs. Alvaretta Kenan. *Index to the 1830 Census of Georgia.* Baltimore: Genealogical Publishing Co., 1982.

Sanders, Faye Sea. *1860 Federal Census Washington County, Kentucky.* Louisville, Ky.: the author, 1982.

Schreiner-Yantis, Nettie, and Florene Speakman Love. *The 1787 Census of Virginia.* Springfield, Va.: Genealogical Books in Print, 1987.

_____. *A Supplement to the 1810 Census of Virginia: Tax Lists of the Counties for Which the Census Is Missing.* Springfield, Va.: Genealogical Books in Print, 1971.

Sistler, Byron. *1840 Census Tennessee.* Nashville: Byron Sistler & Associates, 1986.

Smith, Randolph N. *Cumberland County, Kentucky Census Index and Abstracts, 1800–1850.* Burkesville, Ky.: R. N. Smith and L. L. Butler, 1975.

Stemmons, John D., and E. Diane Stemmons. *Pennsylvania in 1780: A Statewide Index of circa 1780 Pennsylvania Taxlists.* Laughlintown: Southwest Pennsylvania Genealogical Services, 1978.

Steuart, Bradley W., ed. *Chicago, IL (Including Cook Co.) 1870 Census Index.* Bountiful, Utah: Precision Indexing, 1990.

_____. *Long Island, NY 1870 Census Index.* 2 vols. Bountiful, Utah: Precision Indexing, 1989.

_____. *North Carolina 1870 Census Index.* 3 vols. Bountiful, Utah: Precision Indexing, 1988.

_____. *Pennsylvania West 1870 Census Index.* Bountiful, Utah: Precision Indexing, 1993.

Stryker-Rodda, Kenn. *Revolutionary Census of New Jersey: An Index, Based on Rateables, of the Inhabitants of New Jersey During the Period of the American Revolution.* Rev. ed. Lambertville, N.J.: Hunterdon House, 1972. Reprint. 1986.

Swenson, Helen Smothers, and Frances Terry Ingmire. *Index to 1890 Census of the United States.* St. Louis, Mo.: F. T. Ingmire, 1981.

Swierenga, Robert P. *Dutch Households in U.S. Population Censuses 1850, 1860, 1870.* 3 vols. Wilmington, Del.: Scholarly Resources, 1987.

Virginia in 1740: A Reconstructed Census. Miami Beach, Fla.: T.L.C. Genealogy, 1992.

PUBLISHED PROBATE RECORDS OVERVIEW

Key Concepts in This Chapter

- Understanding printed probate records requires a knowledge of the probate process and its terminology.
- Published probate records include abstracts, extracts, transcriptions, and indexes covering a state, county, or region.
- Some printed probate records include research methodology.
- Periodicals are a rich source of printed probate records.
- Locating published probate records can be challenging.
- Advantages of using printed probate record abstracts include:
  - Ease and speed of locating information
  - Conciseness of information provided
  - Instruction in the use of probate records for area or time period
  - Local accessibility
  - Every-name indexes and finding aids
  - Statewide indexes can help to determine the county of residence
- Limitations of using printed probate records include:
  - Limited jurisdictional coverage or scope
  - Lack of an every-name index in early publications
  - Most are finding aids only, not complete compilations
  - Frequent transcription, typographical, and interpretation errors
  - Dating inaccuracies resulting from different calendar systems
  - Omissions in the abstractions
  - Individual cases in printed probate collections may be incomplete
- The quality of printed probate materials must be carefully evaluated.

Key Sources in This Chapter:

- Statewide probate indexes
- County and regional publications
- Sources for locating printed probate records

10

PUBLISHED PROBATE RECORDS

Wendy B. Elliott[1]

Probate records include a variety of documents created to support court proceedings in the settlement of an individuals' estates. The number and type of probate records created may vary over time in different jurisdictions and due to the amount of real and personal property involved. The various documents generated in the probate process are rarely filed together.

Probate records may consist of one or more of the following court-generated documents: will and associated records, letters testamentary, orders, appointment(s) of administrator(s) or executor(s), letters of administration, bonds, inventory, estate sale(s), guardianship, claims, list of heirs, petitions, accounts, releases, claims, dower apportionments, widow's one-year support, commissioners' reports, receipts, judgments, and division of property. Probate records are among the most important of genealogical records because they can identify families and provide proof of relationships— information that is absent or only implied in most other original records. Published probate records frequently provide faster access. These printed materials can provide pertinent genealogical information and can serve as finding aids to original documents.

Records associated with probate proceedings and estate settlements frequently furnish the details needed to document a lineage, and they often name family members and state the testator's (person making the will) relationship to each. Therefore, wills and accompanying probate records, whether original or published, are valuable tools for the genealogist.

Probate records can contain an abundance of genealogical data or can be disappointing depending on a number of circumstances: whether the testator included many or few details about his property and relatives, whether the estate was contested by the heirs, whether there was a sizeable estate, whether a person who died without a will had debts requiring the sale of his property, and whether or not the records generated can be found.

This chapter provides a brief survey of the nature of printed probate records and defines records available in both testate and intestate cases at both the state and county levels. It includes a brief description of typical published statewide, county, or regional indexes, abstracts, transcriptions, and research methods. It also includes a discussion of the advantages and limitations of printed probate records and identifies sources for locating published probate records. Finally, it concludes with a bibliography of additional references as well as a compilation of printed probate sources arranged by state.

THE PROBATE PROCESS

The word *probate* refers to the "action or process of proving before a competent judicial officer or tribunal that a document offered for official recognition and registration as the last will and testament of a deceased person is genuine," but the commonly accepted form of the word includes "the right or jurisdiction of hearing and determining questions or issues arising in matters concerning the probate of wills or the administration of decedents' estates," according to *Webster's Third New International Dictionary*.

When there is a will, the case is termed *testate;* when there is no will or a will is not accepted by the court, the case is termed *intestate.* The person making a will is the *testator,* and those receiving any designated portion of the estate are the *legatees* or *devisees.* Generally, a *will* denotes the distribution of real estate, while a *testament* suggests the distribution of personal property. Because this discussion concerns the law, there are, of course, numerous other important terms unique to both testate and intestate procedures. A brief discussion of some key terms follows. For more information on original probate records and the probate process, see "Probate" on pages 201 through 211 of *The Source: A Guidebook of American Genealogy,* edited by Loretto Dennis Szucs and Sandra Hargreaves Luebking, rev. ed. (Salt Lake City: Ancestry, 1997).

Terms Used in Testate Procedures

While there are many terms unique to the probate process, the following have direct bearing on testate records.

Administrator. If the executor appointed in a will refuses to serve or dies before the probate action is complete, the court appoints an *administrator,* and the record of appointment is appended to the will. It is the administrator's duty to settle the estate and distribute the assets according to the laws governing inheritance in the state at the time.

Caveat. A *caveat* is a legal notice filed by another interested party with a proper legal authority, often when contesting a will, directing the court to stop action until the interested party is heard. Caveats may be included in any one of a number of printed probate records.

Codicil. *Codicils* are additions attached to a will that change the will's distribution of property. A codicil may be added after the birth, marriage, or death of a child and thus provide an approximate date for those events. However, some codicils reflect changes concerning the child or widow's allotment. The codicil normally has a different date than the will and also requires two or more witnesses.

Executor. The testator normally appoints, in the will, an individual (usually a family member or close friend) as an *executor* to act in his behalf.

Nuncupative. A *nuncupative* will is a verbal statement made by the testator and reported to the court by witnesses relating the deceased's wishes as to the disposition of real and/or personal property. If the nuncupative will is accepted by the court, it is processed in the same manner as a drawn or written will.

Will. The most commonly abstracted and published records are *wills.* These are documents written by the testator (or his agent) that direct how his estate will be distributed after his death. They are signed by the testator and witnesses. If the testator was illiterate or too ill to write his name, the signature may be a mark.

Witness. Two or more *witnesses* (the number varies according to the laws of the various states) are usually required to witness a will, whether written or nuncupative. These witnesses are required to verify the will by deposition and to aver to its validity and to the competence of the testator. Witnesses are often relatives or close friends of the family, and their names should always be noted.

Additional Terms Used in Intestate Procedures

Intestate cases follow much the same format as proceedings for testate actions. If a person did not leave a will (which was the case with the majority of our ancestors), intestate procedures took over. Many people mistakenly believe that, because their family was not wealthy, probate records were not produced. Although that is occasionally true, the death of an individual who owed money often resulted in even more paperwork, and thus greater genealogical clues, than some wills.

The evaluation of intestate probate items can reveal many genealogical clues, such as places of residence, and names of individuals, such as children, widows, siblings, friends, business associates, debtors, and other relatives who might qualify as (or who hoped to qualify as) heirs. Occasionally, items are mentioned which might link one family to another, such as a family heirloom or a slave. Clues involving the individual's profession or rank in the community might help to distinguish between two individuals of the same name who lived during the same period.

Administrator. The court appoints an administrator who may be required to post bond and submit letters of administration. The duties of an administrator and an executor are essentially the same: to settle the estate. A few administrations and related probate records have been published as separate collections; a good example is *Genealogical Data from Administration Papers from the New York State Court of Appeals in Albany,* abstracted by Dr. Kenneth Scott (New York: National Society of Colonial Dames in the State of New York, 1972) (figure 10-1). Sometimes administration records are published with court record abstracts. Frequently they are included in such published works when the publication is an index or finding aid to probate records for a particular jurisdiction.

Inventory. Normally, the deceased's estate had to be inventoried; real estate and personal assets and obligations were enumerated in an *inventory.* Estate inventories usually reveal clues and provide data for the genealogist. Original inventories and their published abstracts vary in length and particulars. Brief entries in published works may provide little more than a reference to the location and date of the original record, such as "p. 45 In the court of Ordinary 24th August 1805 On application David Burton allowed further time to deliver an inventory on the estate of D. A. Thomson &c" (Holcomb ca. 1983, 16).

Other publications provide additional data in entries for inventories. One which provides the wife's given name is Weynette Parks Haun's *Craven Precinct-County North Carolina Court Minutes 1730 thru 1741, Book II* (Durham, N.C.: the author, ca.1981). It provides an entry which reads: "Salome CALVERT widow & Exectrx. of Perter CALVERT Dec'd came into court & Exhibeted an Inventory of the Estate of the sd Peter CALVERT so far forth as hath come to her hands & prays it be Recorded. Granted" (page 121).

Another example of a publication which includes inventory details is Judy Henley Phillips and Betty Moore Majors's abstracts in "Coffee County, Tennessee County Court Loose Papers," *Coffee County Historical Quarterly* 22 (1993). The following example (page 4) gives names of individuals financially involved and another court case bearing on the deceased's estate:

> 29. 1866 Nov. 5 - A list of property & effects belonging to the estate of Pierce B. ANDERSON, dec'd. Notes on: Solomon WILSON, Samuel COMER drawn by Benjamin ALLEN, W.H. ANTHONY, Wm. CARROLL, John BAKER, Thomas BROWN, J. ANGELL, Alfred E. WINKLER, Dr. KINCAID drawn by Oliver CON, Wm. J. ROGERS payable to Wilie H. CUNNINGHAM, Geo. WORK, O.G. MURRELL, Joseph S. PAYNE. P.C. ISBELL special admr. of P.B. ANDERSON, dec'd. . . . mentions a suit in Circuit by the exor. of William CONWAY, dec'd. against James W. DEADRICK and P.C. HILL. S.C. CARNES, security.

Pre-1865 inventories for slave owners are particularly important to those tracing African American ancestry because these documents usually include names and some details about the slaves. A typical entry from Rosalie Edith Davis's abstracted and compiled *Hanover County, Virginia, Court Records, 1733–1735: Deeds, Wills, and Inventories* (Manchester, Mo.: Heritage Trails, 1979) includes an inventory of the estate of Reverend William Swift which provides names and relationship of slaves as, "Negro named Phillipy, 3 children Bob, Jane, Jenny" (page 48). Mary L. Jackson Fears's, *Slave Ancestral Research: It's Something Else* (Bowie, Md.: Heritage Books, 1995), page 32, provides a sample of an inventory which lists several slaves by name, age, and value. One thirty-six-year-old women is identified as the mother of children whose names are not stated:

SMITH, William, of Huntington, S Co., Esq. - Adm. (5 July 1784) Paschall Nelson Smith, son of dec'd - Bd.: Paschall Nelson Smith, Isaac Sears and Eliakim Raymond, all of NYC, merchants - Wit.: Thomas and Nathaniel H. Tredwell.

SMITHMAN, John, of NYC, painter - Pet. (5 Sept. 1796) of Catharine Smithman, adm., for relief.

SMYTHIES, William, of NYC, surgeon - Adm. (11 Feb. 1782) Robert Nicholls Auchmuty, of NYC, Esq., principal creditor.

SNEDEKER, Theodorus, of Haverstraw, O Co., farmer - Ren. (19 Apr. 1771) of Dericke Snedeker, w. of dec'd - Wit.: Joannis Snedeker, Abraham Thew.

SNEDEN, John, of Eastchester, W Co. - Pet. (4 Mar. 1790) of Robert Sneden, of Eastchester, adm., for leave to sell real estate - Account (1 Mar. 1790) of Robert Sneden for cash received of Rebeccah Sneden, w. of dec'd, for sundry articles sold at auction - Inventory (24 Feb. 1790) of goods of dec'd - Affid. (3 May 1790) of Jonas Farrington, of Eastchester, farmer, concerning bond - Affid. (6 May 1790) of John Vermyllia (exec. of Johannis Vermyllia) concerning bond (see inventory).

SNEDEN, Robert, of O Co., carpenter - Ren. (26 Sept. 1766) of Abraham Sneden, of NYC, boatman, in favor of his brother, Dennis Sneden, of O Co., farmer - Wit.: Francis Child, John Sneden.

SNELL, Jacob, of Palatine District, Montgomery Co., Esq. - Adm. (5 July 1784) John Snell, eldest son of dec'd - Bd.: John Snell, Gerhart Walrad and George Pletz, all of Canijohary, Montgomery Co., yeoman - Wit.: Christopher P. Yates.

Figure 10-1. From Scott's *Genealogical Data from Administration Papers from the New York State Court of Appeals in Albany.*

Inventory and Appraisement of the estate of James Duncan dec'd

1 Moses about 26 years old	1000.00
2 Emily " 34 " "	600.00
3 Matilda " 36 " " and children	1800.00
4 Little Penny " 16 " "	900.00
5 Big Penny " 53 " "	400.00
6 Hannah " 7 " "	600.00
7 Warren " 19 " "	1200.00
8 Green " 13 " "	900.00
9 Ben " 9 " "	800.00
1 Horse Mule	140.00
1 Horse Mule	130.00
1 Horse Mule	90.00
1 Horse Mule	100.00
35 Head Stock Hogs	100.00
1 Two Horse Wagon	50.00
1 Ox Cart	20.00
1 Buggy & Harness	100.00
500 acres of land	3000.00
1 Patent Watch	18.00
1 Bed stead, Covering	35.00
1 Do Do Do	40.00
1 Bureau	6.00
1 Bedstead & Mattress	18.00
1 Lot quits, counterpanes, coverlets	75.00
1 Lot Books	20.00
1 Bed Stead & coverings	35.00

Published inventory data taken from court records rarely includes the entire accounting of property. In those that do, a mention of notes and monies which the deceased owed to others may be included; for instance, the source above enumerates the inventory of goods of Philip Chipins, including the entries "to Cash by Robt. Melton 1.; to cash by Daniel Green .5" (page 60). These entries provide clues for the genealogist to follow.

Other tidbits can be gleaned from inventories. A man's occupation may be identified through a listing of sundry tools, such as those for a carpenter, blacksmith, or surveyor; the approximate birth date of a child may be surmised by an entry for a debt to a midwife; property in other locations may be enumerated. Certainly, inventories with extensive listings of household, real estate, and personal property indicate a family's or individual's financial circumstances.

Accounts, Petitions, Renunciations. *Accounts* were returned to the court by the administrator(s) or executor(s) at intervals. These depict the expenses incurred as the estate was being administered and settled. Accounts usually show all paid debts, credits collected, and services rendered during the period between reporting. Accounts may also record the names of heirs who died and female heirs who married. The final accounting normally lists receipts and disbursements and may include the last division of the estate with a list of heirs, their respective portions, and places of residence. *Petitions* to the court were made by individuals seeking action relating to the estate. *Let-*

ters of renunciation are those in which a person declined the responsibilities of administering the estate.

A brief article from a state publication, *Arkansas Family Historian* 26 (2) (June1988), pages 98–99, follows:

> Found in the loose probate records of Pulaski County, Arkansas: Notice published under date of August 25, 1872, paper not identified:
>
> NOTICE
>
> Notice is hereby given that the Executors, Administrators and Guardians of the following estates have filed their accounts-current, for the settlement and confirmation, to the October term, 1872, of the Pulaski county Probate Court. All persons interested in the settlement of said estates must come forward and file their exceptions thereto on or before the second day of the next January term, 1873, of said court, or they will be forever barred from excepting to such accounts, or any item thereof, to-wit: [followed by a list of administrators or executors with the respective names of the deceased].

Dower Rights. A very simple definition of *common law dower* is: a widow's right to a life interest in one-third of the real property belonging to her deceased husband. However, there were differences in dower in various areas of the United States during different time periods. Proceedings for dower rights normally include the widow's given name and that of her deceased husband; their relationship is stated in the record. The first entry for a dower apportionment enables the death date of the deceased to be estimated. Prenuptial agreements and marriage settlements are sometimes recorded in court minutes, providing worthwhile clues to family relationships. Dower allotments may be found printed along with miscellaneous court records or land and property record abstracts, as well as in periodical probate publications.

Inheritance laws were constantly changing. For example, in 1682, when one group of English colonists first arrived, the law provided for the widow to receive one-third of the estate, for the children to divide equally another third, and the final third to be taken care of by a will. If the wife was also deceased, two-thirds went to the children. This custom also existed in London. One year later (1683) a law giving the eldest son a double portion was passed (Shammas 1987, 30).

Even without a will, the relationships of people to the deceased can be determined if you are familiar with the inheritance laws of the time period when the death occurred. For example, in an estate settlement, the following amounts of the settlement were given: Hannah Smith ninety-nine pounds; Isaac, Samuel, and James Smith thirty-three pounds each; and nine other individuals eleven pounds. Hence, Hannah was the widow, and Isaac, Samuel, and James were sons. The other nine individuals were most likely relatives.

Some publications include petitions for dower along with associated probate records. An example is Thomas E. Partlow's *Wilson County, Tennessee: Genealogical Resource Material, 1827–1869* (Greenville, S.C.: Southern Historical Press, 1997), page 133:

> Sally Sanders, widow of John Sanders, petitions for her dower. John Sanders departed this life in 1828 intestate, seized and possessed of 800 acres. Heirs: Sally Sanders, the widow; Mary Sanders and husband James W. Sanders; Sally Sanders, Jr.; Joicy Sanders; George W. Sanders; George W. McPeak and wife Elizabeth; James Sanders, children of John Sanders and all of lawfull age; Richard Sanders, a minor child of John Sanders, Jr.; and Benjamin R. Sanders and Sarah J. Sanders, minor children of Richard Sanders. Jul 1839. (Pp. 492–495).

Carol Wells's *Abstracts of Giles County, Tennessee: County Court Minutes, 1813–1816 and Circuit Court Minutes, 1810–1816* (Bowie, Md.: Heritage Books, 1995), page 63, includes an entry showing court action to provide the widow with support: "Order William Henderson, Archibald Young & Brittain Yarborough allot to Martha Robertson widow of Jas Robertson decd sufficient portion of estate to maintain herself & family for one year from the time Jas Robertson departed this life."

Background Sources

Additional information concerning original probate and estate records is available in a number of sources.

In addition to the section of *The Source* mentioned earlier, see chapters 13 and 14 in Val D. Greenwood's *The Researcher's Guide to American Genealogy,* 2nd ed. (Baltimore: Genealogical Publishing Co., 1990). Also see chapter 7, "Probing Probate," in Ralph J. Crandall's *Shaking Your Family Tree* (Camden, Maine: Yankee Publishing, 1986) and chapter 6, "Court Records," in Norman Edgar Wright's *Preserving Your American Heritage* (Provo, Utah: Brigham Young University Press, 1981).

For a better understanding of American colonial law and court systems, see Roscoe Pound's *Organization of Courts* (Boston: Little, Brown, and Co., 1940); Bradley Chapin's *Criminal Justice in Colonial America, 1606–1660* (Athens: University of Georgia Press, 1983); and Carole Shammas, Marylynn Salmon, and Michel Dahlin's *Inheritance in America: From Colonial Times to the Present* (New Brunswick: Rutgers University Press, 1987).

For procedural explanations, see Clarence N. Callender's *American Courts: Their Organization and Procedures* (New York: McGraw-Hill Book Co., 1927) and Henry J. Abraham's *Courts and Judges: An Introduction to the Judicial Process* (New York: Oxford University Press, 1962).

Several other works may also assist in gaining a better understanding of the probate system: Donald Lines Jacobus's "Probate Law and Custom," *American Genealogist* 9 (1932): 4–9, Fannie J. Klein's *Federal and State Court Systems: A Guide* (Cambridge: Ballinger Publishers, 1977), and Joseph F. Zimmerman's *State and Local Government* (New York: Barnes and Noble, 1962).

Legal terminology used in court records is often frustrating to researchers. Two helpful references are Henry Campbell Black's *Black's Law Dictionary: Definitions of the Terms and Phrases of American and English Jurisprudence, Ancient and Modern,* 6th ed. (Centennial Edition, 1891–1991. St. Paul, Minn.: West Publishing Co., 1990) and William C. Burton's *Legal Thesaurus* (New York: Macmillan Co., 1981).

NATURE OF PRINTED PROBATE RECORDS

There is much diversity in the publication and content of published probate records. Some probate records appear in book form, some in periodicals, and others in collected works. Even within a single publication the content and focus varies considerably. Printed probate records may concentrate on a period, a location, or a specific kind of probate record. Some printed works deal only with wills; others include administrations, and still others incorporate guardianships, dower rights, inventories, and related records. Some cover ecclesiastical areas, such as parishes, rather than governmental jurisdictions, such as counties. Some deal with the colonial period only, while others bridge long time spans.

The details included also differ from one publication to another; some offer extensive detail, while others provide little more than a name and reference. One compilation may merely list surnames and dates while another provides extracts or detailed abstracts. One may list only a date for each court-related action, while another cites dates, volume, and pages for complete citations. Some show more than one set of pagination references, with or without explanation. Some contain every-name indexes, while others are arranged in alphabetical order. Some may be organized only by location within a greater region or state, while others are arranged chronologically. Many contain two or more aspects of these organizational schemes.

The majority of published probate records are abstracts or indexes of originals in a particular jurisdiction. Very few published volumes include complete transcriptions of estate documents. As would be expected, published indexes are helpful guides to locating appropriate records.

Types of Probate Records

Published probate records fall into three general categories: abstracts, extracts, and transcriptions. There are also printed probate indexes and research methodology sources.

Abstracts. *Abstracts* are abbreviated or abridged summaries of the original documents in which only data considered to be essential is copied. These usually contain brief synopses which may include all names, dates, places, and relationships identified within the record. Printed abstracts of original estate records may also name those persons who served as witnesses or acted in any capacity related to the proceedings. Many abstracts include some reference to the property location, and all denote the county in which the record was filed. Most, if not all, cite dates on which a will or probate proceeding was begun and/or registered.

Extracts. *Extracts* are verbatim transcriptions of portions of the original documents. Some published extracts are verbatim renderings of whole documents from the complete source.

Transcriptions. *Transcriptions* are complete printed copies of records, usually transcribed from original handwritten documents. Contemporary transcriptions may be (but are not always) verbatim copies.

Indexes. *Indexes* to wills and probate records are very beneficial because they can quickly lead the researcher to areas or individuals in question. *Index to Fayette County, Pennsylvania Wills, 1783–1900,* compiled by Bob and Mary Closson (Apollo, Pa.: Closson Press, 1980), is one such publication. This concise record lists the names of those individuals who left wills, the volume in which the will was found among the court records, the first page number of the will, and the date the will was probated (figure 10-2).

NAME	VOL. PAGE	PROB. DATE
THOMPSON, Mary	10-141	1896
THOMPSON, Mathew	1-132	1811
THOMPSON, Moses	1-128	1809
THOMPSON, Samuel	11-292	1899
THOMPSON, William	1-109	1813
THORNDELL, George H.	5-341	1881
THORNTON, Delilah M.	5-310	1881
THORNTON, Joseph	2-158	1839
THORNTON, Mary	2-253	1842
THORNTON, Sarah J.	4-464	1873
THORP, William	4-118	1865
THORPE, James	5-314	1881
THORPE, Ruben	2-408	1848
THRASHER, John	4-537	1875
TIARNEY, James	9-054	1893
TIERMAN, John	5-103	1877
TIERNAN, Thomas C.	4-006	1862
TILLARD, Thomas	2-399	1847
TIPPINS, Sarah	11-081	1899
TISHUE, Charles	10-203	1897
TISHUE, John K.	10-116	1896
TISUE, Sabastian	3-077	1853
TITUS, Eli	12-050	1896
TOBIN, Lydia	2-338	1845
TOBIN, Thomas	2-309	1844
TODD, Alexander	1-130	1810
TODD, Ewing	8-259	1891
TODD, Sarah Ann	7-080	1888
TODD, Thomas	3-183	1855
TOMKIN, Richard	1-092	1809
TOOD, Ostrander D.	7-381	1889
TOOMAN, Andrew Sr.	1-143	1814
TORRENCE, James	1-283	1826
TORRENCE, James	4-101	1865
TORRENCE, Joseph	1-324	1831
TORRENCE, Margaret	2-283	1843
TORRENCE, Margaret	5-060	1876
TORRENCE, Mary A.	5-293	1881
TOWNSEND, Aaron	11-417	1900

Figure 10-2. From *Index to Fayette County, Pennsylvania Wills, 1783–1900.*

Research Methodology. The publications' introductory remarks often include some details relating historical background, jurisdictional information, and pertinent laws for the relevant period. With the added advantage of computer-generated indexes, today's printed sources can be superior to many created even two decades ago. Computer-generated indexes can also be riddled with typographical and transcription errors; therefore, these must be used with care.

Table 10-1. Published U.S. Statewide (or Major Cities) Probate Indexes*

State	*Author(s)*	*Years*	*Scope*	*Names*	*Comments*
Alabama	Alabama DAR	1808–70	Wills	App. 9,000	—
Arkansas	Stevenson	1830s–1900	Wills and administrations	—	Arranged alphabetically within each county. No comprehensive index.
Colorado	MacDougall	—	Probates	—	Early Denver
Connecticut	Manwaring	1635–1750	Probates	—	Hartford; state card index on microfilm
Delaware		1680–1800	Probate	App. 10,000	By county; Kent to 1850 (wills only)
D.C.	Bell	1776–1815	Wills	400	Abstracts
Georgia	Austin Brooke	To mid-1800s 1733–1860	Wills and intestates Wills	App. 27,000 14,500	—
Indiana	Franklin	To 1880	Wills	33,000	—
Kentucky	Jackson	To 1851	Wills	21,700	—
Maine	Frost	1687–1800	Probate	8,700	Abstracts
Maryland	Magruder Cotton Wright	1634–1777 1635–1743 1743–79	Wills Wills Wills	16,000	 Abstracts Abstracts
Massachusetts		1600s–1800s	Probates	—	For 5 counties
Mississippi	Wiltshire	1800–1900	Wills	App. 10,000	
New Hampshire	State papers	1635–1771 1769–1800	Probates Probates	App. 4,200	Abstracts Indexes
New Jersey	Jackson Secretary of State	1689–1890 Pre-1901	Wills Probates	—	By county
New York	Fernow Pelletreau	1626–1836 1665–1801	Wills Probates	2,165 App. 25,000	Abstracts in Albany Abstracts (downstate)
North Carolina	Mitchell	1665–1900	Wills	App. 75,000	—
Ohio	Bell	To 1850	Wills and estates	App. 64,000	—
Oklahoma	Wever	1892–1908	Probates		Cherokee Nation
Pennsylvania	Williams	1682–1850	Wills and administrations		Philadelphia
Rhode Island	Beaman	1636–1850	Wills	12,900	—
South Carolina	Houston Moore Holcomb	1670–1850s 1670–1784 1746–1821	Wills Wills Probates	—	Not Charleston Abstracts Abstracts
Tennessee	Sistler	1779–1861	Wills	—	Also administrations for all but 13 counties
Virginia	Torrence	1632–1800	Wills and administrations	App. 50,000	—
West Virginia	Johnston	1753-1850	Estates	App. 12,000	Also see Virginia

*Complete citations are in the chapter bibliography.

Statewide Publications

Most statewide compilations relating to probate only serve as general guides to county records and provide minimal information, such as name, date, county, and record type. These guides may be indexed or alphabetically arranged.

Indexes and compilations of estate and/or probate records have been published for many states. Although these vary a great deal in the quantity of information they provide, collectively they are of inestimable value to the genealogical researcher because they serve as finding aids. In addition to identifying place and date of specific probate actions, statewide indexes also indicate in which counties various surnames can be located and a general time frame of those families' residence therein. Thus, these statewide compilations serve as quick references to locate clusters of family names in particular locations within a state.

Statewide publications are organized in numerous ways. Some are strictly indexes to wills alone, as is Jeannette Holland Austin's *Index to Georgia Wills*, 2nd ed. (Baltimore: Genealogical Publishing Co., 1985), or to wills and estates together, as in Thornton W. Mitchell's *North Carolina Wills: A Testator Index, 1665–1900,* corrected and rev. ed. in 1 vol. (Baltimore: Genealogical Publishing Co., 1992). Some contain abstracts, as found in Kenneth Scott and James A. Owre's *Genealogical Data from Inventories of New York Estates 1666–1825* (New York: New York Genealogical and Biographical Society, 1970).

Other statewide publications are arranged by counties within the state and lack comprehensive indexes, but these are still helpful in locating records, surnames, and residences within specific counties. An example of this format is Mrs. James Harold Westbrooke and Mrs. Edward Lynn Westbrooke, comps. and eds., *Index to Wills and Administrations of Arkansas from the Earliest to 1900* (Jonesboro, Ark.: Vowels Printing Co., 1986). All are limited in the years they cover, but most at least incorporate data through the colonial or territorial periods. For some states more than one compilation is available. A few of these may contain data that overlaps in either time or focus, but in every case all available sources should be reviewed and compared if possible. Table 10-1 identifies the major published statewide sources for probate records; these sources are detailed in the chapter bibliography.

A few statewide publications contain much detail; others furnish few particulars and may be restricted to entries that show only county, surname, and a document date (see, for example, figure 10-3). Statewide sources are especially helpful because they pinpoint exact counties or at least indicate where the surname is common; a search of the actual records could provide the information sought. Limitations to these records also exist. Some do not include entries for *all* counties in the state, for example. When using a published record, it is crucially important to determine two things: what the title *says* it covers and what it actually covers (true not only of printed materials but of the new electronic formats produced on CD-ROM as well). For example, Martha Lou Houston compiled *Indexes to the County Wills of South Carolina* (1939; reprint; Baltimore: Genealogical Publishing Co., 1964, 1970, 1975, 1982). However, the title page notes that

> this volume contains a separate index compiled from the W.P.A. copies of each of the County Will Books, except those of Charleston County Will Books, in the South Carolina Collection of the University of South Carolina Library.

This information immediately alerts the researcher that the work is *not* a complete statewide index. Further study of the foreword and table of contents shows that many more counties were omitted, and the index shows that wills for only twenty-one counties are included in this volume.

If two or more published sources are available, it is important to consult both. Comparison of the wills Houston lists for Spartanburg County with those cited in Brent H. Holcomb's *Spartanburg County, South Carolina Will Abstracts 1787–1840* (Columbia, S.C.: the author, ca. 1983), shows that Houston's index is incomplete. The "original wills" abstracted in Holcomb's volume do not appear in Houston's index (figure 10-4). However, wills that Holcomb lists from "Will Book B" match entries in the Houston volume (figure 10-5).

For North Carolina there are three separate published works for wills and estate records: Thornton W. Mitchell's *North Carolina Wills: A Testator Index, 1665–1900* (cited ealier); J. Bryan Grimes's *Abstract of North Carolina Wills: Compiled from Original and Recorded Wills in the Office of the Secretary of State* (1910; reprint; Baltimore: Genealogical Publishing Co., 1980),[2] and Fred A. Olds's *An Abstract of North Carolina Wills from about 1760 to about 1800: Supplementing Grimes' Ab-*

VIRGINIA WILLS AND ADMINISTRATIONS 87

Wm. 1783 w.
King George
Jno. 1799 w.
Pittsylvania
Thos. 1798 i.
Stafford
Jno. 1758 i.
CLIFTON
Fairfax
Wm. 1772 i.
Eliz. 1773 w.
Thos. 1794 a.
King George
Wm. 1781 w.
Prince George
Thos. 1724 i.
Southampton
Benj. 1772 w.
Thos. 1779 i.
Thos. 1781 w.
Cordey 1798 i.
Stafford
Burdit 1762 w.
Sussex
Wm. 1756 w.
York
Mary 1724 i.
Benj. 1728 w.
CLINCH
Brunswick
Christopher 1763 i.
Culpeper
Jacob 1777 w.
Surry
Christopher 1679 w.
Christopher 1737 w.
Hannah 1739 w.
Jas. 1747 i.
Jos. Jno. 1756 i.
Philip 1768 i.
Wm. 1786 w.
CLINKER
Middlesex
Thos. 1728 i.
CLINTON
Essex
Eliz. 1726 w.
Thos. 1734 i.
CLITHRELL
York
Jno. 1748 i.
CLONINGER
Augusta
Valentine 1784 w.
CLOPTON
Cumberland
Reubin 1796 i.
Robt. 1783 w.
Goochland
Benj. 1791 i.
Benj. C. 1797 w.
York
Mary 1678 w.
CLORE
Albemarle
Jacob 1759 w.
Culpeper
Geo. 1751 w.
Peter 1762 w.
Eliz. 1766 i.
Jno. 1785 w.
Jno. 1787 i.
CLOTTIER
Isle of Wight
Jno. 1727 i.
CLOTWORTHY
Henrico
Walter 1701 i.
CLOUD
Frederick
Mordecai 1789 w.
Shenandoah
Henry 1788 w.
CLOUDAS
Charlotte
George 1783 i.
Essex
Jno. 1791 w.
Abner 1794 i.
Goochland
Geo. 1789 w.
Middlesex
Wm. 1780 w.
CLOUGH
Powhatan
Molly 1779 w.
CLOUSER
Frederick
Henry 1772 a.
CLOVELL
Accomack
Peter 1692 w.
CLOWDAS
Essex
Jno. 1775 w.
Middlesex
Wm. 1770 i.
CLOWES
Princess Anne
Wm. 1700 i.
CLOWSER
Frederick
Henry 1764 i.
CLOYD
Augusta
Jno. 1761 i.
Jno. 1767 a.
Rockbridge
David 1789 w.
David 1792 w.
Eliz. 1797 w.
Andrew 1798 i.
CLUTTEN
Lancaster
Jesse 1792 i.
CLUTTON
Lancaster
Jno. 1784 w.
CLYBORN
Henrico
Jno. 1685 i.
Jno. 1689 i.
Frances 1712 i.
CLYBORNE
Chesterfield
Jonas 1798 i.
COALE
Lancaster
Jno. 1700 i.
COANE
Northumberland
Jno. 1761 w.
Martha 1768 w.
COARTNEY
Westmoreland
Jno. 1749 i.
COAT
Norfolk
Agnis 1783 i.
COATES
Essex
Saml. 1780 w.
Mary 1785 w.
Henrico
Jno. 1692 i.
Richmond
Saml. 1718 i.
Surry
Jno. 1744 w.
COATS
Halifax
Judith 1760 i.
Saml. 1797 i.
Lancaster
Thos. 1749 i.
Jno. 1765 i.
Geo. 1769 w.
Norfolk
Jno. 1714 w.
Princess Anne
Willis 1779 w.
Jesse 1788 i.
COBB
Accomack
Ingold 1708 w.
Amelia
Theodosha 1782 w.
Chesterfield
Jno. 17— i.
Matthew 1766 w.
Isle of Wight
Nicholas 1686 nw.
Pharoah 1701 i.

Figure 10-3. From Clayton Torrence, comp., *Virginia Wills and Administrations 1632–1800* (1931; reprint; Baltimore: Genealogical Publishing Co., 1985). Arranged alphabetically by surname, this work identifies more than fifty thousand probate actions.

ORIGINAL WILLS

ALLEN, JOSEPH File #292

Will of Joseph Allen of the County of Spartanburg...to wife Rachel, all the property I am entitled to both real and personal; after her decease the tract of 150 acres where I now live to my son William; to my wife, half of all my moveable property; the other half to my sons William and David; son William and Matthew Landers, exrs. 5 May 1792. Joseph Allen (Seal)
Wit: Wm Ford
Cassander (Ↄ) Ford
James Ford.
Proved by William Ford, 13 Jan 1795 (from court minutes).

ANDERSON, REBECCA File #286

Will of Rebecca Anderson of Spartingburg District...to my sister Sarah Breakin, whom I constitute extx., all the hole of my land whereon I now live, and all clothing, etc.... 10 March 1820
Wit: David Anderson
Henrietta Chamblin
Jas. Chamblin.
her
Rebecah X Anderson
mark
Proved 20 Nov 1820 by James Chamblin.

BRICE, SAML File #412

Will of Samuel Brice of Spartinburgh County, 8 Sept 1795....to wife Jean Brice, two cows and calves, one sorrel mare, pewter, etc, and the cear of my three little girls; to my son William Brice, two cows and calves, one horse & plow, etc; to my son James Brice, two cows & calves, etc; to my son Samuel Brice, one two year old mare, and half of the land; to my son John Brice, the other half of the land; friends Francis Dodds, Thomas Paden, exrs.
Wit: Thomas Peden
Francis Dodds
John Calwall
Jas. T. White.
his
Samuel X Brice
mark

BROWN, JOHN File #488

Will of John Brown...to my son Syms Brown, the Tract of land on which he now lives, and also a Tract of 200 acres at the mouth of Tygar River, and a negroe boy Nimrod; I also order that my said son Syms to collect the sum of £ 540 from Mr. Davis, and for his trouble he is to have £ 140 of said money; to my daughter Ann a negro girl named Lucy, a horse, bridle and saddle, and at her marriage she is to have the fourth part of what stock is remaining at the death of my wife, if it should please God that she survives me; to John Collins a negro boy Caesar, 150 acres of land on Warriors Creek, and the second best horse or man that is on the plantation; to my daughter Martha, negro girl Daphne, a horse, bridle and saddle, a bed and furniture, and also at her marriage the fourth part of what stock; to my beloved wife Sarah Brown, the liberty of living on any of my possessions during life, and to own a negroe man named Pompey, another negroe man Straphan, and another negroe man called Bill, and another named Charles, and a negro girl named Doll, and another named Mitty, and all her household furniture, plantation Tools, with the waggon and the tract of land on which I now live on the waters of Tygar River, and also a tract of land on Kings Creek, containing 200 acres to be appraised and equally divided between my two daughters Ann and Martha, and also at the decease of my said wife Syms Brown and John Collins are to get each a negroe of them which I leave to my wife; my wife, Syms Brown, and John Collins, exrs. 3 Nov 1789

86

Figure 10-4. Comparison of indexes by Holcomb *(Spartanburg County, South Carolina Will Abstracts 1787–1840)* and Houston (*Indexes to the County Wills of South Carolina)* for Spartanburg County, South Carolina, shows Houston's index to be incomplete. Of the first six names in Holcomb's volume (above), only two appear in Houston's index (right), and the dates shown do not match.

SPARTANBURG COUNTY

WILLS

Name	Vol.	Date	Section	Page
Abbott, Solomon	3	1840-1858	D	451
Alexander, Robert	3	1840-1858	D	416
Allen, Caleb	3	1840-1858	D	244
Allen, James	1	1821-1829	B	66
Allen, John	1	1821-1829	B	26
Allen, Willis	3	1840-1858	D	131
Anderson, David	1	1821-1829	B	99
Anderson, Denny. (Sr.)	2	1830-1835	C	40
Anderson, Rebeccah	2	1830-1835	C	16
Anderson, Samuel	2	1830-1835	C	8
Arndell, Reddick	2	1830-1835	C	43
Arnold, John	1	1787-1820	A	35
Austell, Joseph	1	1821-1829	B	33
Bagwell, Sarah	1	1840-1858	D	248
Ballenger, Edward	1	1821-1829	B	30
Ballenger, James (Sr.)	1	1787-1820	A	31
Barnett, Agnes	3	1840-1858	D	284
Barnett, Edward	1	1787-1820	A	130
Barnett, Micajah (Planter)	2	1830-1835	C	87
Barry, Andrew	1	1787-1820	A	16
Barry, Margaret	1	1821-1829	B	44
Barry, Richard	1	1787-1820	A	82
Bates, Anthony	3	1840-1858	D	37
Bates, George	2	1830-1835	C	77
Bearden, Isaac	2	1830-1835	C	45
Bearden, John	3	1840-1858	D	127
Bennett, James (Sr.)	1	1821-1829	B	62
Bennett, William	2	1830-1835	C	89
Benson, Robert	1	1787-1820	A	33
Bishop, Eli	3	1840-1858	D	484
Bishop, Isaac	1	1821-1829	B	13
Bishop, William	2	1830-1835	C	71
Blackstock, William	3	1840-1858	D	8
Bobo, Absalom	3	1840-1858	D	143
Bobo, Burrell	2	1830-1835	C	19
Bobo, Salley	1	1787-1820	A	69
Bobo, Spencer	1	1787-1820	A	77
Bomar, Edward	3	1840-1858	D	358
Bonner, Anny	3	1840-1858	D	220
Bonner, Benjamin (Plant.)	1	1787-1820	A	48
Brewton, George	1	1787-1820	A	60
Brewton, John	3	1840-1858	D	282
Brewton, Jonas (Sr.)	3	1840-1858	D	454
Brewton, see also - Bruton				
Brice, Samuel	3	1840-1858	D	200
Brockman, James	3	1840-1858	D	476
Brown, James	3	1840-1858	D	64
Brown, Jesse	3	1840-1858	D	190
Brown, John (Farmer)	3	1840-1858	D	424
Brown, Wylie S.	1	1821-1829	B	108
Bruton, David (Sr.)	1	1787-1820	A	71
Bruton, Susannah	2	1820-1835	C	114
Bruton, see also - Brewton				
Buise, Jonathan	3	1840-1858	D	111

206

Figure 10-4 (continued).

WILL BOOK A

Christopher Rhodes (LS). Wit: William Stewart, A. Casey, Martin Newman. Proven by Aaron Casey (no date). W. Lancaster, O. S. D.

Pp. 28-30: L. W. & T. of Thomas Williamson, of Spartanburgh Dist; rec. 12 July 1813 to wf Ann Williamson, one third of land & negroes; to son William Williamson & son in law John Means, remainder of negroes; remaining 2/3 of property to be sold & money divided between William Williamson, John Means, & my daughter Elizabeth Alexander, decd, my daughter Elizabeth part to be equally divided between her three children, viz., James, Thomas & Ann Alexander; son William & son in law John Means, Exrs; Thomas Williamson (SEAL). Wit: Danl McKie, James Otts, Thomas Drummond. Dated 2 Apr 1813. Proven by James Ott & Thomas Drummond, 14 July 1813. W. Lancaster, O. S. D.

Pp. 30-31: L. W. & T. of Edward Herring of Dist. of Spartanburgh; rec. 14 July 1813; made 26 July 1811; wife Marian Herrin have all property and at her death to divide amongst my children (not named); Edward Herring. Wit: Jesse Mathis, William Cantrell, Manning Barnes (X) Proven by Jesse Mathis 5 July 1813. W. Lancaster O. S. D.

Pp. 31-33: L. W. & T. of Peter Frie of Dist. of Spartanburgh; rec. 2 Sept 1813; allow my wife Mary Frie her bed & furniture, cow & calf I bought from Vinsent Bomar also pewter dish & plates; my four children William, Barbara, Gilbert & Tarleton; to son Gilbert, upper part of plantation I now live on; conditional line betwixt Mr. Abrahams & myself; to son Tarleton, lower part of plantation; friends John Ridings & William Kelso, Esqr. & Hugh Ewing, Exrs; 11 Jan 1813; Peter Frie (X) (SEAL). Wit: Geo. Welch, Daniel Morrow, William Jackson. Proven by George Welch & William Jackson 2 Aug 1812. W. Lancaster O. S. D.

Pp. 34-35: L. W. & T. of James Ballenger Senr. of Dist. of Spartanburgh; rec. 3 Sep 1813; plantation on which I now live, Negroes, cattle to my wife Dorcas Ballenger during her life; to my daughter Frances Ballenger, $300; unto my daughter Peggy Lewis a mare; to Richard Foster, $1; to my sons John Ballenger, Edward Ballenger, James Ballenger, William Ballenger, Elijah Ballenger, Peggy Lewis, Frances Ballenger, & Tabitha Foster, an equal share of my estate; sons Edward & James, Exrs; 19 July 1813; James Ballenger (Seal). Wit: W. Perrin, Edward Ballenger Senr., James Ballenger, son of John. Proven by James Ballenger & William Perrin 2 Aug 1813. W. Lancaster, O. S. D.

Pp. 35-38: L. W. & T. of Robert Benson, Esqr. of Spartanburgh Dist; rec. 8 Sept 1813; to my sister Nancy Walker a negro woman Rose; to my brother Elias Benson, one negro boy Osburn; to my brother Nimrod Benson, negro Stephen; to brother James Benson, tract on the glassy mountain which was allotted to me as part of my Fathers estate; to my brother Abner Benson, land purchased by him & myself of Edmond Bishop, 300 A; on Lawsons Fork, also my part of land purchased of George Hughe adj. the sd. tract, also tract purchased from James Templeton; also land purchased from the heirs of Rolley Faucet by him & myself; also sd. Abner, a tract lying near to the widow Seays, which was allotted to me as part of my Fathers estate; Abner, Elias, Nimrod Benson, Exrs; 15 May 1813; Robert Benson (LS). Wit: E. Roddy, E. B. Benson, Elijah Foster. Proven by Ephraim Roddy, & Elias B. Benson; 6 Sep 1813; W. Lancaster OSD.

Pp. 38-40: L. W. & T. of John Arnold of Spartanburgh Dist; rec. 23 Nov 1813; to wife Nancy, my house and land

110

Figure 10-5. From Holcomb's *Spartanburg County, South Carolina Will Abstracts 1787–1840.* Wills that Holcomb lists from "Will Book B" match entries in Houston's *Indexes to the County Wills of South Carolina.*

stract of North Carolina Wills 1663–1760, 2nd ed. (Southern Book Co., 1954; reprint; Baltimore: Genealogical Publishing Co., 1978). In this unusual case, all three sources should be consulted.

Mitchell's work is a standard for statewide indexes to wills, for, although it lists only the testator's name, county of registration, year, citation of book and page, and present location of the original documents, it provides a listing for the entire state with some seventy-five thousand wills in its present one-volume edition. Although Mitchell's work is an index and Grimes's and Olds's are abstracts, it is wise to use all three, comparing them to achieve a better perception of North Carolina wills and estate records.

While both Olds's and Grimes's works are abstracts, they differ in several ways. Olds's is limited to wills dated between 1760 and 1800, while Grimes's abstracts end in 1760. Olds's entries are alphabetically arranged by counties, and there is no index; to locate a particular name, it is necessary to review the listings for each county. In Grimes's abstracts, the testators' names are arranged in alphabetical order, and the respective county is shown across from the name. Additionally, Grimes's abstracts contain more information. For example, two of Olds's entries (page12) for Beaufort County read:

> 1759 ALLEN, TIMOTHY, Rebecca (wife), Ephraim, Martha, Prudence, Salathiel, Jeremiah and Elizabeth.
>
> 1797 ARCHBELL, SAMUEL, Elizabeth (wife); William, John, Martha.

Two entries from Grimes's work (page 67) contain this information:

> CAVENA, CHARLES Edgecombe County.
> April 8, 1756. February Court, 1757. *Sons*: David (one shilling), Needham (50 acres of land on Beech run), Aquilla (60 acres land on west side of Beech Run), Nicolas (one shilling), Arther [*sic*] (60 acres of land "joining to Needham land on the River"), Charles and Henry ("the remainder of my land"). *Daughter*: Mary Cavena (300 acres land "on the south side of Northuntee Mach"). *Witnesses*: John Fountaine, John Murphree, Abigal Pittman. *Clerk of the Court*: Jas. Montfort.
>
> CAWDREY, THOMAS Craven County.
> August 1, 1748. December, 1748. *Executor and sole devisee and legatee:* John Brown. *Witnesses:* Peter Glair, Patterson Gillett and John Harper. *Clerk of the Court:* – Smith.

Additionally, it should be noted that the index in Grimes's compilation does not include the names in the thirty-one-page appendix. Although Mitchell's work is an index, it contains valuable material for the genealogist and should be thoroughly reviewed by those with North Carolina ancestry (figure 10-6). Mitchell compiled the data from several sources; they are described in his comprehensive and useful introduction (figure 10-7).

Use As a Research Strategy. Using statewide printed will indexes as part of a basic research strategy can save time. For example, the surname Horn was being studied in Georgia because descendants were found in Arkansas on census records listing Georgia as their ancestral home; however, the county in Georgia was unknown. The individual in question left Georgia before the 1850 census and the given names were unknown for the parents in question.

Austin's *Index to Georgia Wills* (cited earlier) shows entries for Horn families in the counties of Stewart, Floyd, Harris, and Chattooga after 1850 and in Jones County before 1823. Even earlier Horn families were found in Austin's *Georgia Intestate Records* (Baltimore: Genealogical Publishing Co., 1986), pages 155–56; these were in Chatham, Columbia, Morgan, and Warren counties before 1850 and Houston and Webster counties after that date. Therefore, a search of probate and other records of those counties might lead to clues about the Horn family as part of a surname-locality approach to research. If the individual in question was not listed in the intestate records or wills but was identified in property records, inventory or estate papers may provide the necessary proof of relationship.

Because more people died without wills than with them, a major value of a statewide index is its ability to guide the researcher to areas where individuals of the same surname were common.

Published works can also be an asset to understanding a jurisdiction's estate records. An example is Jim Edgar's *Illinois Probate Act and Related Laws, Effective January 5, 1988,* rev. ed. (St. Paul, Minn.: West Publishing Co., 1988). Although this publication addresses current laws for the state, it provides helpful information.

County and Regional Publications

Many county and regional lists of wills and estate proceedings have been published in a variety of formats. Some are merely indexes; others are abstracts for a certain number of years; others abstract only a limited group of individuals; and others serve as guides for entire collections. Most cover an entire county.

A variety of people have been involved in the creation of published probate records, including amateur and professional genealogists, history enthusiasts, part-time government employees (such as those involved in the Work Projects Administration's Historical Records Survey programs), and full-time appointed or elected officials. It is not surprising, therefore, that such a large variety of records exists today among the regional and county probate collections.

County and regional boundaries change as people move into an area, providing some challenges for those searching for probate materials. In which county should you look first, and why? The solution to that challenge will be discussed after the various formats are demonstrated.

County and Regional Indexes. Indexes are created for various reasons. It is necessary to understand the scope of any work to determine if it will include the information being sought. Elijah George edited *Index to the Probate Records of the County of Suffolk, Massachusetts, from the Year 1636 to and including the Year 1893* (Boston: Rockwell and Churchill, 1895). It is contained in three volumes divided into *A–F, G–O,* and *P–Z.* Several people actually worked on the project together. The title and published data indicate this work's scope.

The *Genealogical Index to the Clackamas County, Oregon, Probate Records from 1845 to 1910 Inclusive,* by Lloyd and Wythle Brown (Oregon City, Oreg.: Mt. Hood Genealogical Forum of Clackamas Co., 1974), and *Genealogical Abstracts of the First 2500 Probate Records in Marion County, Oregon,* compiled by Daraleen Phillips Wade for the Willamette Valley Genealogical Society (Salem, Oreg., 1985), are other good examples of countywide indexes developed specifically for genealogists. These abstracts are cross-indexed and are grouped in three volumes: *A–G, H–Q,* and *R–Z.*

Other indexes were prepared by state or county employees and then made available to the public. For example, the *Index to the Probate Records of the County of Middlesex, Massachusetts: First Series, from 1648 to 1871* (Cambridge, Mass., 1914), prepared under the supervision of Samuel H. Folsom and William E. Rogers, indexes registers of probate and insolvency for the county of Middlesex. These probate abstracts are arranged alphabetically by case name and include cases up to around 1905 with some data for later years.

Name	Co.	Date	Recorded Copy	Original	Name	Co.	Date	Recorded Copy	Original
Jenkins, Thomas	046	1771	WB-A/193	AR	Jennings, Thomas	061	1845	WB-1/29	AR
Jenkins, Thomas D.	051	1853	WB-A/351		Jennings, William	104	1838	WB-4/227	
Jenkins, Thomas S.	044	1885	WB-23/526	CTY	Jennings, William	075	c1854	WB-M2/15	AR
Jenkins, Thomas W.N.	051	1883	WB-C/30	AR	Jennings, William	N	1687	Orig. Only	SS/AR
Jenkins, Timothy P.	089	c1864	WB-1/293		Jennings, William	030	1729	Orig. Only	SS/AR
Jenkins, W. A.	092	1897	WB-6/472	AR	Jennins, Mary	030	1729	Orig. Only	SS/AR
Jenkins, William	105	1870	WB-2/31		Jenoure, Joseph	N	1732	SS 876/265	SS/AR
Jenkins, William	063	1791	WB-1/176		Jenson, Anna M	013	1899	WB-D/332	AR
Jenkins, William	063	1894	WB-4/133	AR	Jerkins, Sarah	001	1874	WB-2/100	AR
Jenkins, William F.	047	1846	WB-4/252		Jerkins, Thomas	028	1856	WB-D/253	AR
Jenkins, William P.	051	1886	WB-C/344	AR	Jernagan, Godwin	010	1820	WB-G/76	AR
Jenkins, Winborn	071	1814	WB-3/113	AR	Jernagan, John	010	1733	Orig. Only	SS/AR
Jenkins, Winborn	071	1793	WB-2/40	AR	Jernigan, Ann	056	1793	WB-1/68	AR
Jenkins, Winborn	041	1815	WB-2/97	AR	Jernigan, Benjamin	010	1800	WB-E/112	AR
Jenkins, Wineford	010	1828	WB-G/176	AR	Jernigan, David	103	1793	WI-A/539	AR
Jenkins, Zady	073	1885	WB-H/369	CTY	Jernigan, David	103	1791	WI-A/215	AR
Jenneret, Elias	012	1765	DB-A/15		Jernigan, Ferney	087	1867	WB-2/120	AR
Jennel, Joseph	053	1795	RW-1/264		Jernigan, Furnifold	103	1853	RD-11/294	AR
Jennett, Elizabeth	053	1870	WB-11/22	AR	Jernigan, George	010	1874	WB-I/58	AR
Jennett, James	070	1815	WB-AB/228	AR	Jernigan, George	103	1792	Orig. Only	AR
Jennett, Jesse	030	1796	WB-2/78		Jernigan, Henry	056	c1781	WB-2/275	AR
Jennett, Jesse W.	070	1853	WB-C/562	AR	Jernigan, Isbel	103	1783	WI-A/25	AR
Jennett, John	053	1774	RW-1/58		Jernigan, Jasper	056	1787	WB-1/8	AR
Jennett, John	096	1749	Orig. Only	SS/AR	Jernigan, Jerusha	056	1868	WB-3/1	AR
Jennett, Jones S.	053	1894	WB-11/315	AR	Jernigan, Jesse	010	1785	WB-D/37	AR
Jennett, Joseph	053	1813	RW-1/484	AR	Jernigan, Joseph J.	056	1868	WB-2/113	AR
Jennett, Robert	053	1857	WB-8/249	AR	Jernigan, Kador	103	1844	RD-9/60	AR
Jennett, Thomas	053	1879	Orig. Only	AR	Jernigan, Lemuel R.	051	1867	WB-B/108	AR
Jennett, Thomas G.	053	1821	WB-4/212		Jernigan, Lydda	103	1798	Orig. Only	AR
Jennings, Ann	075	1720	SS 875/224		Jernigan, Miles H.	051	1843	WB-A/192	
Jennings, Ann P.	026	1888	WB-2/357	AR	Jernigan, Nathaniel	010	c1866	WB-I/10	AR
Jennings, Arthur	075	1791	WB-K/221	AR	Jernigan, Phereby	010	1804	WB-E/252	AR
Jennings, Benjamin	075	1774	WB-I/83	AR	Jernigan, Sally	051	1882	WB-C/285	AR
Jennings, Caleb	075	1761	WB-I/22	AR	Jernigan, Sarah	105	1858	WB-1/48	AR

Figure 10-6. From Mitchell's *North Carolina Wills: A Testator Index, 1665–1900* (page 267).

An example of a regional index that includes entries concerning estate settlements made under another nation's jurisdiction is *Index to the Archives of Spanish West Florida, 1782–1810,* with an introduction by Stanley Clisby Arthur (New Orleans: Polyanthos, 1975). This compilation of nineteen indexes to documents recorded under the Spanish government of West Florida, District of Baton Rouge, covers the region of Louisiana east of the Mississippi River, south of the Mississippi state line, north of lakes Pontchartrain and Maurepas, and extending to the Pearl River. This area today encompasses the parishes of East and West Feliciana, East Baton Rouge, St. Helena, Livingston, Tangipahoa, Washington, and St. Tammany. The collection contains references to an assortment of records, including those dealing with probate, such as in the section for "Volume II," the entry for Jean Baptiste Doiron, which lists "debts, 219; inventory, 218, 220; succession, 218" (page 13) and, in the portion under "Index to Volume IX," the reference to the will of John Moore on page 305 (page 129).

Some titles do not adequately describe a publication's regional focus. For instance, editor Joseph W. Porter's nine volumes (bound in four) of the *Maine Historical Magazine,* formerly the *Bangor Historical Magazine,* Special Publication no. 14 (Bangor: Maine Genealogical Society, 1993) encompasses data for Penobscot, Hancock, Washington, and Lincoln counties. This invaluable publication includes transcriptions of a plethora of primary sources.

County or Regional Abstracts. Abridged summaries of the original documents may be found in abstracts, such as *Abstracts of Bristol County, Massachusetts, Probate Records* compiled by H. L. Peter Rounds (Baltimore: Genealogical Publishing Co., 1987). This collection of abstracts is divided into two volumes covering the periods 1687 to 1745 and 1745 to 1762, respectively. It has the following explanation in its introduction:

> The probate records for Bristol County, Massachusetts are located in the Registry of Probate in Taunton, Massachusetts. . . . In addition to the regular bound volumes, the Registry of Probate in Taunton also has most of the original probate documents themselves, from which these volumes were prepared.

This explanation indicates to the researcher the work's limitations, lists where the original records are housed, and includes information concerning other available records. Although the title may not indicate so, some works include abstracts of wills and probate proceedings. An example is Lewis Preston Summers's *Annals of Southwest Virginia, 1769–1800* (1929; reprint 1970, 1976; third printing, one volume in two parts; Baltimore: Genealogical Publishing Co., 1996). This work covers the counties of Botetourt, Fincastle, Montgomery, Washington, and Wythe as well as forts in that section of the state. A history of Tazewell County appears in an appendix.

The publication's introduction furnishes an overview of the region's early history and an explanation for the work's publication. This section also gives background of included records and informs of missing records for this region and time. It explains that some lists are not indexed but are listed alphabetically within the pertinent county; this informs the user that sepa-

INTRODUCTION

In 1963 the late William Perry Johnson began publication of a series which he titled Index to North Carolina Wills, 1663-1900. The research that led to that work was begun at least as early as 1955, and by 1973 lists of recorded wills in twenty-three counties had been published. Johnson's work was not really an index, because he listed only recorded wills, with either the probate or preparation date, in the order in which they were entered in the will books or registers for each county. To locate a specific will from the four volumes that Johnson published, the searcher had to know the county and approximate date of probate.

Johnson began work on his will lists several years before the local records program of the North Carolina Division of Archives and History started in 1959. Because of that program essential county records were microfilmed for security purposes, and valuable records no longer needed in daily operations were removed to the State Archives. It was not until 1971 that local records archivists and microfilm camera operators had visited all counties in the state at least one time, and microfilm copies of recorded wills for all counties were readily available in Raleigh. Neither copies of the county will books nor files of original wills were accessible at a central point at the time Johnson did most of his work. It was necessary, therefore, for him to visit county courthouses to make lists of wills from the will books, and his research was delayed accordingly.

After publishing the fourth volume of his index, which carried the project through Columbus County but did not include Bute County, Johnson discontinued the project, in part, because of poor health. In 1977, after I expressed an interest in continuing and completing the will index, Johnson loaned me his notes which I had microfilmed. Those notes, which are now the property of the Friends Historical Collection, Guilford College, Greensboro, North Carolina, have been useful in preparing the present testator index, and they have been used with the permission of the curator of the collection. It is significant that beginning with Craven County, the next county alphabetically following Columbus, few of the county listings were complete; in some instances the notes were based on the devisor indexes in the county concerned. Although Johnson included some alphabetical listings of the original wills that were in the State Archives, both in his published will indexes and in his notes, he did not compare the recorded and original versions of the same will.

vii

Figure 10-7. The introduction to Mitchell's *North Carolina Wills: A Testator Index, 1665–1900.*

rate lists as well as the index must be carefully checked. Additionally, the author notes that the "records of the courts are copied *ver batim,* both as to spelling and punctuation for the period mentioned until 1784. . . ." Under the will section for each county an abstract of early wills is provided, but some entries denote other records related to probate, such as the following entry: "Page 14. Appraisement of the estate of Thomas Robinette. Thomas Dunn. administrator" (page 586).

A sample of a county publication is Joseph Crook Anderson, 2nd, *York County, Maine Will Abstracts 1801–1858,* Maine Genealogical Society Special Publication no. 27, 2 vols. (Rockport, Maine: Picton Press, 1997). This work includes complete abstracts of all York County wills, supplementing Frost's earlier work, which referenced wills only up to 1800.

Some county sources furnish valuable genealogical information. In William Ronald Cocke, 3rd, *Hanover County Chancery Wills and Notes: A Compendium of Genealogical, Biographical and Historical Material as Contained in Cases of the Chancery Suits of Hanover County, Virginia* (1940; reprint; Baltimore: Genealogical Publishing Co., 1978), the title notes that this work contains data collected from wills and various sources. The following extracts (pages 50–52) depict how such entries provide sufficient detail to document relationships and provide exact or approximate dates:

> CLOUGH, JOHN Sr., and Sarah his wife, on 2 November 1819 executed a Deed of Trust to Leonard J. Clough and John T. Clough. On 12 Sept. John Clough, Sr. alone, executed a Deed of Trust to George N. Clough. John Calvin Dickinson also had executed a Deed to George N. Clough who was his brother in law, covering loans made from time to time to Dickinson by Clough said to have amounted to over $10,000.00. No copy of such deed is exhibited. Dickinson was insolvent. George Nelson Clough caused a number of depositions to be taken in his effort to prove that he was financially capable of making such a loan, which fact had been questioned in court:

Following this entry are extractions taken from twenty-two depositions which support George Nelson Clough's claim. It is noted by the author that sixteen additional depositions were included in the case file but had not been transcribed for this volume. The extracted depositions, taken between 1843 and 1846, include genealogical details, examples of which include:

> ALVIS, JOSHUA, in 1844 . . . had known George N. Clough for forty years . . . [Clough] married Miss Timberlake . . . his uncle Edward N. Clough. . . .

> GREEN, BERNARD W., in 1844 . . . had known Geo. N. Clough since 1819–20 . . . He married Miss Caroline Timberlake . . . and received [legacies] from Emily and Hardinia Timberlake, dec'd . . . Mrs. Martha Timberlake. . . . He likewise had the use and management of the money of Miss J. E. Timberlake, Harriet Timberlake, Mary Timberlake, and of Mrs. Martha Timberlake during her lifetime. . . . 'My mother was a Timberlake, sister of Clough's first wife. . . .'

> TILMAN, EDWARD, in 1843, deposed that . . . George N. Clough . . . received legacies from Benjamin Timberlake's Estate, William E. Harris' Estate, Edward N. Clough's Estate, and John Clough's Estate.

> HALL, ZACHARIA, in 1846 . . . had known George N. Clough all his life. '. . . I married his sister.'

> WHITE, COL. WILLIAM L., in 1846, deposed that he has known George N. Clough since he was a boy. Clough is about 40 years old. . . .

> GOODALL, CHARLES P. in 1844 deposed that Geo. N. Clough received 1/7th part of Benjamin Timberlake's Estate, his first marriage being to Timberlake's daughter. Benjamin Timberlake had a daughter Hardenia who died single, also a daughter Emily who died single. Clough received 1/5th of the Estate of Martha, widow of Benjamin Timberlake. 'Clough's second wife was a daughter of my neighbor William S. Harris.'

> LEDBETTER, ISAAC, in 1843, deposed that . . . Edward N. Clough left to George N. and Leonard J. Clough all his real estate.

> VAUGHAN, Lemuel, deposed that . . . George N. Clough . . . had received of Benjamin Timberlake's Estate, Martin Timberlake's Estate, Emily Timberlake's Estate, Hardenia Timberlake's Estate, Edward N. Clough's Estate and William E. Harris' Estate, legacies. . . .

> HARRIS, MOSES, in 1844 . . . deposed that he was Executor of his father, William Ely Harris' Estate. That George N. Clough had married his sister, Martha B. Harris . . . .

> TERRELL, JOSEPH T., in 1843 . . . deposed . . . that Clough had married Dickinson's sister.

> DUNN, JAMES, a shoe-maker, in 1844 . . . deposed that John C. Dickinson's sister married George N. Clough, whose father was John Clough, Dec'd.

Some publications cover a variety of records, such as the *Cowlitz County, Washington, Probate Court Records, 1861–1907,* 7 vols. (Longview, Wash.: the compiler, 1986), compiled and indexed by Charlotte Tadlock Hagle. Specific volumes cover such topics as wills, doctors and attorneys, supplemental death records, etc. Although each volume contains its own index, the work includes a comprehensive index.

Often, the abstracts are arranged according to the court listing (a docket or calendar) of wills. An example of a will calendar book is *Calendar of Wills on File and Recorded in the Offices of the Clerk of the Court of Appeals, of the County Clerk at Albany and of the Secretary of State, 1626–1836,* compiled and edited by Berthold Fernow (Baltimore: Genealogical Publishing Co., 1967).

Other examples of regional probate books are those covering specific ethnic groups, such as *Pennsylvania German Wills,* by Russell Wieder Gilbert (Allentown: Pennsylvania German Folklore Society, 1950), and those whose coverage extends across state boundaries, such as *Pennsylvania Wills Recorded in New Jersey: Researched and Reprinted from the New Jersey Archives* (Newtown, Pa.: Will-Britt Books, 1987), researched and reprinted from the New Jersey Archives.

Carefully read the introduction. This section usually indicates the location of the original sources and the limitations of the publication. Ralph V. Wood, Jr., transcribed *Plymouth County Massachusetts, Probate Index 1686–1881* (Camden, Maine: Picton Press, 1988). He notes on page three of the introduction that "These 'old series' probate records, covering 1686–1881 are organized on a docket system."

Research Methodology. Often, entire books are devoted to helping the genealogist find records of a particular subject group or locality. Ruth Wilder Sherman and Robert S. Wakefield wrote *Plymouth Colony Probate Guide: Where to Find Wills and Related Data for 800 People of Plymouth Colony, 1620–1691* (Warwick, R.I.: Plymouth Colony Research Group, 1983), which is a specific guide to the use of regional probate materials.

Periodical Publications

Special mention should be made of articles in genealogical periodicals that print abstracts or extracts of court and estate records. While there is no single or comprehensive index to all of the county, regional, state, and national publications available, the section titled "How to Locate Printed Probate Records," below, provides effective methods for finding the majority of records available.

Periodicals published by state, county, and regional genealogical and historical societies frequently include articles dealing with probate and estate records. The motives for the publication of such articles vary, but usually the purpose is to make the data available to subscribers and interested parties. Sometimes county records about to be discarded or destroyed are salvaged by individuals or groups and transcribed for publication in a periodical.

Length and Completeness. Periodical articles vary considerably in length and comprehensiveness. An article by Jacquelyn L. Ricker in *The Connecticut Nutmegger* 19 (2) (September1986), page 334, consisted of a single probate record:

Abstract Will of Joseph Scribner
Westchester Co. Wills
1664-1784

N.Y. 1898

Joseph Scribner, Pound Ridge
Wife Mary
Son Isaac
Sons Joseph, Elias, Samuel
Dtgs [*sic*] Mary Nash, Eunice Jons [*sic*], Sarah Seely, Joanah [*sic*] Mead
Son Isaac and Elazer Lockwood Exec. Jan. 13, 1700 Pro. June 23, 1779.

Note that one of the two dates in this abstract appears to be in error. If the 13 January 1700 date is correct, the 23 June 1779 date is questionable. The original record should be reviewed to obtain the complete and accurate data.

In other cases, an item or article in a periodical consists of only a few records. Examples include the single "Will of John Anglin of Carter County, Kentucky," *Bluegrass Roots* 15 (1): 6–7 (Spring 1988) (published by the Kentucky Genealogical Society) and a list of nine cases in "Obion County Court Records: Guardianship Inventories and Settlements, 1845 and 1846," *Obion Origins* 6 (2): 19 (May 1988) (published by The Obion County Genealogical Society). In contrast, there are lengthy articles that appear in serial format across several issues.

Finding Aids. Periodicals and statewide compilations provide guides to locating original and published sources. Some societies publish an annual index to their quarterlies; others compile an index which covers many years of publication. One typical of the latter is William Doub Bennett's *North Carolina Genealogical Society Journal 1975–1984: Consolidated Index* (Baltimore: Clearfield Co., 1997). This volume indexes the first ten volumes of the North Carolina Genealogical Society's quarterly journal. The "Introductory Notes" provide details about editors and descriptions of earlier indexes from which this compilation was created. This publication indexes article titles, individuals' full names, and record types.

Such a finding aid will denote articles pertaining to individuals, families, counties, or types of records. For instance, this alphabetically arranged work lists under the entry "Probate Records" twenty-one North Carolina counties, three individuals, and three other states (Georgia, South Carolina, and Virginia) for which probate records were published in the *Journal* (page 444).

The *Nutmegger Index: An Index to Non-Alphabetical Articles and a Subject Index to The Connecticut Nutmegger Volumes 1–28, 1968–1996,* by Helen S. Ullmann, was published by Picton Press and the Connecticut State Society of Genealogists. The compilation, which contains 105,353 entries of persons alone, provides a quick reference tool for both individuals and topics. County abstracts are frequently included in statewide periodicals; an example is "Lagrange County, Indiana Will Abstracts, 1842–49," by Ruth Dorell, in *Hoosier Genealogist* 32 (1): 28–33 (March 1992).

Statewide indexes to probate records or wills also serve as finding aids. Betty Couch Wiltshire's *Mississippi Index of Wills, 1800–1900* (Bowie, Md.: Heritage Books, 1989) is an attempt to index all wills available in the state for one hundred years. She not only includes wills found in probate books but those noted in marriage records, inventory books, and other unusual places. Her compilation lists more than ten thousand testators and provides surname, given name, county where the will was located, book and page, and date. Such a publication allows the user to locate counties in which particular names appear.

Some state guides also identify published as well as original probate sources. Marilyn Davis Barefield's *Researching in Alabama: A Genealogical Guide*, edited by Yvonne Shelton Crumpler (Easley, S.C.: Southern Historical Press, 1987), lists published sources for each county. Although not every county has printed probate records, such a compilation may prove helpful in identifying additional publications.

Less helpful for locating probate records, *The New York Genealogical and Biographical Record: 113 Years, Master Index, 1870–1982,* compiled by Mrs. Jean D. Worden (Franklin, Ohio: the compiler, ca. 1983), serves as a master index to individuals mentioned in the *New York Genealogical and Biographical Record* but does not define the type of record in which an individual name appears. Data included in each entry is surname, given name(s), year of the publication, volume, number, and pages.

If the county of origin is known, a published guide to county wills or probate records will enable the researcher to identify and order the proper record from the county repository. One such guide is Richard T. Williams and Mildred C. Williams's *Index of Wills and Administration Records, Berks County, Pennsylvania, 1752–1850* (Danboro, Penn.: the authors, 1973).

Education. Published state guides to records will provide the researcher with a solid understanding of the sources available. Perhaps the finest in this category are the court and probate record chapters by Raymond A. Winslow, Jr., in Helen F. M. Leary's *North Carolina Research: Genealogy and Local History,* 2nd ed. (Raleigh: North Carolina Genealogical Society, 1996).

Some publications include informative articles depicting various aspects of estate records. Articles such as Albert C. Bates's compilation "List of Connecticut Probate Districts," *Connecticut Nutmegger* 17 (4): 574–82 (March 1985), provide an alphabetical arrangement by probate district and by town within each district. Included in Bates's compilation are the date constituted and the area covered in the original jurisdiction. Where applicable, a list of other records contained in the compilation is noted with dates of these records. Below are some randomly selected examples.

BRIDGEPORT–Includes Bridgeport, Easton, Monroe, and Trumbull.
Constituted June 4, 1840, from STRATFORD.
Contains the records of STRATFORD from May session, 1782, to June 4, 1840; and the records of EASTON, which include the records of WESTON.

CORNWALL–Includes Cornwall.
Constituted June 15, 1847, from LITCHFIELD.

HARTFORD–Includes Bloomfield, Glastonbury, Hartford, Newington, Rocky Hill, West Hartford, Wethersfield, and Windsor Locks.
Constituted May session, 1666, as a County Court.

Articles about court or other records also have bearing on probate issues. For example, an article addressing indexing problems also relates valuable information about the published sets of Pennsylvania laws. Joan Appleton Jones, of the Legislative Reference Bureau in Harrisburg, Pennsylvania, authored "Access to Early Pennsylvania Law: An Indexer's Dream," *American Society of Indexers' Newsletter* 89: 1, 7 (November-December 1988). This article discusses the limitations and availability of various published works regarding Pennsylvania colonial and state statutes.

Twenty-five years of study went into an article written by Mrs. Philip W. (Martha Woodroof) Hiden: "Virginia County Court Records: Their Background and Scope," *Virginia Magazine of History and Biography* 54 (1): 3–17 (January 1946). It was the featured article for the 1946 publication and included several illustrations (figure 10-8).

Reprint volumes are available for many early periodicals; many of them are published by Genealogical Publishing Company (Baltimore, Maryland). Reprint volumes often include the published probate abstracts or indexes from these older periodicals. One example is *Mayflower Source Records: Primary Data Concerning Southeastern Massachusetts, Cape Cod, and the Islands of Nantucket and Martha's Vineyard* (Baltimore: Genealogical Publishing Company, 1986). The text was selected and introduced by Gary Boyd Roberts and covers records from the *New England Historical and Genealogical Register*. The reprint includes births, marriages, deaths, burials, cemetery inscriptions and epitaphs, probate records, diary, church records, baptisms, dismissals, impressments, abstracts from wills, and marriage intentions. For additional information about such reprints and the use of periodicals in general, see chapter 19, "Genealogical Periodicals."

HOW TO LOCATE PRINTED PROBATE RECORDS

Locating printed county and regional probate transcriptions or indexes is easier today than ever before due to electronic media. Major library catalogs are now available at local libraries on network computer systems, in CD-ROM format, through telephone communication systems, or as microfiche copies. See chapter 5, "Bibliographies and Catalogs," for further information on how these can be used.

Importance of Learning the Correct Locality

As indicated earlier, county boundaries have frequently changed, and these changes can prove challenging for those seeking probate materials. Which county should you look at first, and why? What if there is no comprehensive statewide index? Such a situation can best be illustrated in a research strategy case study.

Research Strategy. A family that lived in Virginia for many generations serves as an example. The last place they are known to have lived was the Henry County, Virginia, area. Finding aids, such as Alice Eichholz, ed., *Ancestry's Red Book: American State, County and Town Sources,* rev. ed. (Salt Lake City: Ancestry, 1992), provide the parent counties from which Henry County was formed. The parent county of Henry was Pittsylvania; Pittsylvania was formed from Halifax, and Halifax from Lunenberg, and so on back through a total of six counties in only fifty-six years. The *Red Book* provides a basic list of counties in the order in which their probate records should be searched.

Henry County was formed in 1776 from Pittsylvania. *Henry County, Virginia, Will Abstracts, Vol. I and II, 1777–1820,* was abstracted and compiled by Lela C. Adams (Easley, S.C.: Southern Historical Press, 1985). She also compiled *Abstracts of Pittsylvania County, Virginia Wills, 1767–1820* (Easley, S.C.: Southern Historical Press, 1986). Another set of abstracts, *Pittsylvania County, Virginia, Abstracts of Wills, 1768–1800,* was compiled and indexed by Thomas P. Hughes and Jewel B. Standefer (Memphis, Tenn.: T. P. Hughes, 1973). Both abstracts of Pittsylvania wills should be consulted.

Pittsylvania County was formed from Halifax County in 1766, and Halifax was formed from Lunenburg in 1752. Two works provide assistance: *Will Book O, 1752–1773, Halifax County, Virginia,* by Marian Dodson Chiarito (Nathalie, Va.: Clarkton Press, 1982), and another work by the same author, *Will Books, Halifax County, Virginia* (Nathalie, Va.: Clarkton Press, 1984), covering will book 1, 1773–83, in vol. 1, and will book 2, 1783–92, in vol. 2. Both include indexes.

Lunenburg County was formed from Brunswick in 1745–46, so the next books to consult include *Lunenburg County, Virginia Wills, 1746–1825,* by Landon C. Bell, indexed by Lorraine L. Fuller and Jean V. Sipe (Berryville, Va.: Virginia Book Co., 1972); and *Early Wills, 1746–1765, Lunenburg County, Virginia,* compiled by Katherine Blackwell Elliott (South Hill, Va.: the compiler, 1967). Another author, June Banks Evans, in *Lunenburg County, Virginia Will Books,* 3 vols. (New Orleans: Bryn Ffyliaid Publications, 1991), begins with page 307 of Lunenburg County will book 2, where Elliott's publication stopped. Vol. 1 covers will book 2, 1767–78; vol. 2 covers will book 3, 1778–91; and vol. 3 covers will book 4, 1791–99. These volumes also include maps that illustrate the evolution of the counties.

Brunswick County was formed in 1720 from Prince George County and, later, parts of the Isle of Wight and Surry counties, so the next abstracts or indexes to be checked include *Brunswick County, Virginia Wills* (Miami Beach, Fla.: T.L.C. Genealogy, 1991), which covers 1739 to 1750. Finally, Prince George County was formed in 1700–02 from Charles City County, and the Isle of Wight was formed from James City County in 1652, so if the family under study is thought to have been in the area at the time, a variety of sources apply, including:

- Weisiger, Benjamin B., comp. *Charles City County, Virginia Wills and Deeds*. Richmond, Va.: the compiler, 1984.
- Davis, Eliza Timberlake. *Wills and Administrations of Surry County, Virginia, 1671–1750.* Indexed by Thomas L. Hollowak. Baltimore: Genealogical Publishing Co., 1980.
- Hart, Lyndon H. *Surry County, Virginia, Wills, Estate Accounts and Inventories, 1730–1800.* Easley, S.C.: Southern Historical Press, 1983.
- Hopkins, William Lindsay. *Surry County, Virginia Deeds 1684–1733 and Other Court Papers*. 3 vols. Richmond, Va.: the compiler, 1991–92.

Hopkins's three-volume work has various titles, and all three volumes contain entries of wills, deeds, and estate accounts and sales. Hopkins's first volume contains abstracts from county deed book 3, which covers 1684 to 1687, and continues through county deed book 7 for 1715 to 1730. Vol. 2 of this collection, titled *Surry County, Virginia Deeds and Estate Accounts 1734–1755,* should also be consulted for those branches of the family that remained in the area. Some abstracted records list both landowners and non-propertied residents.

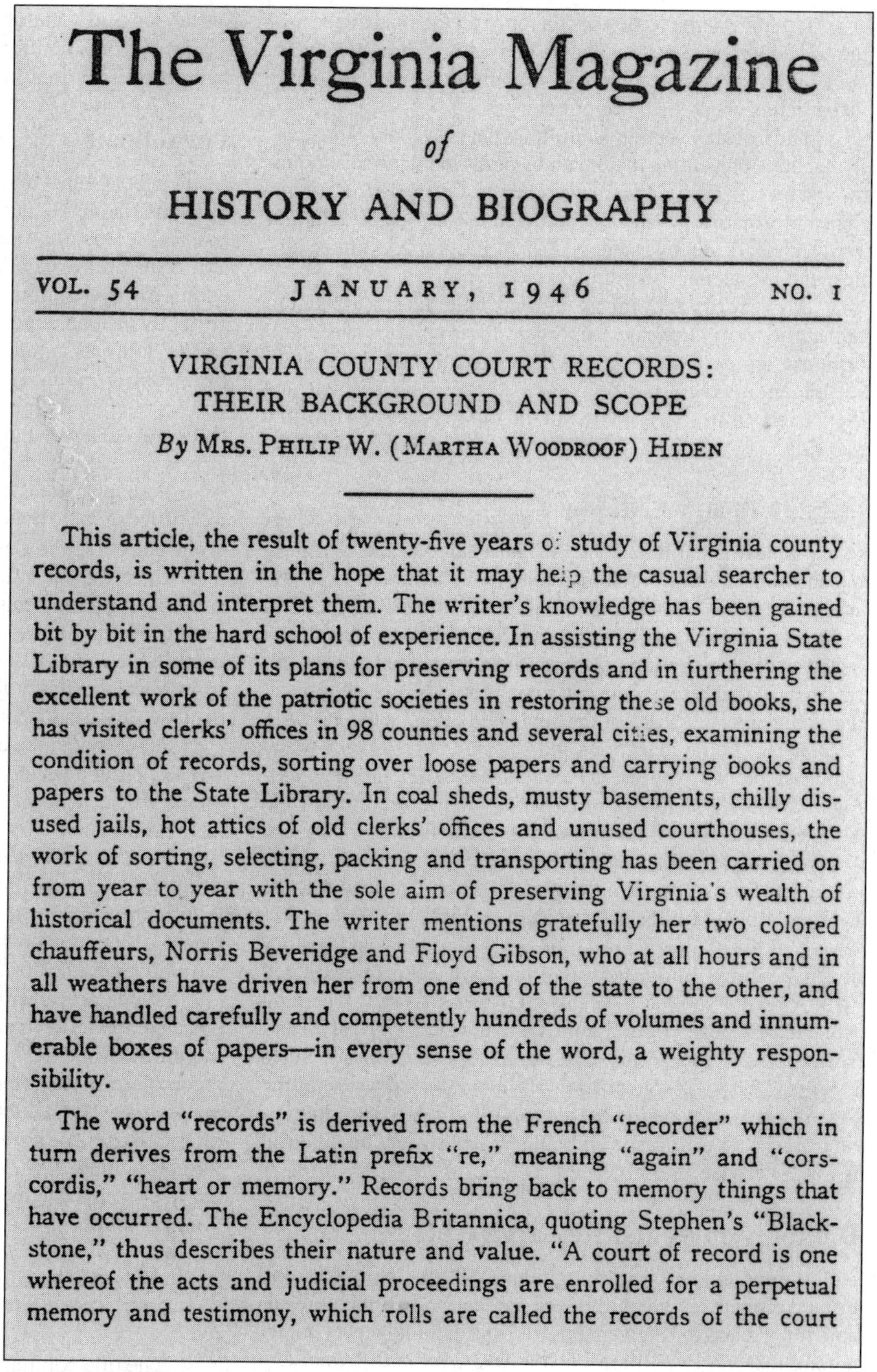

The Virginia Magazine

of

HISTORY AND BIOGRAPHY

VOL. 54 JANUARY, 1946 NO. 1

VIRGINIA COUNTY COURT RECORDS: THEIR BACKGROUND AND SCOPE

By Mrs. Philip W. (Martha Woodroof) Hiden

This article, the result of twenty-five years of study of Virginia county records, is written in the hope that it may help the casual searcher to understand and interpret them. The writer's knowledge has been gained bit by bit in the hard school of experience. In assisting the Virginia State Library in some of its plans for preserving records and in furthering the excellent work of the patriotic societies in restoring these old books, she has visited clerks' offices in 98 counties and several cities, examining the condition of records, sorting over loose papers and carrying books and papers to the State Library. In coal sheds, musty basements, chilly disused jails, hot attics of old clerks' offices and unused courthouses, the work of sorting, selecting, packing and transporting has been carried on from year to year with the sole aim of preserving Virginia's wealth of historical documents. The writer mentions gratefully her two colored chauffeurs, Norris Beveridge and Floyd Gibson, who at all hours and in all weathers have driven her from one end of the state to the other, and have handled carefully and competently hundreds of volumes and innumerable boxes of papers—in every sense of the word, a weighty responsibility.

The word "records" is derived from the French "recorder" which in turn derives from the Latin prefix "re," meaning "again" and "cors-cordis," "heart or memory." Records bring back to memory things that have occurred. The Encyclopedia Britannica, quoting Stephen's "Blackstone," thus describes their nature and value. "A court of record is one whereof the acts and judicial proceedings are enrolled for a perpetual memory and testimony, which rolls are called the records of the court

Figure 10-8. Example of a periodical article: Hiden's "Virginia County Court Records: Their Background and Scope."

Correspondence

As shown, knowledge of county formation can lead to a multitude of sources. Once these counties have been identified, other basic reference books, such as *The Handybook for Genealogists* or the *Genealogist's Address Book,* can provide the names and addresses of local county societies. Writing to local county history and genealogical societies is often rewarding for locating printed sources for probate records, as well as other records which may be associated with them. See chapter 1, "General Reference," for the basic reference books that would give the names and addresses of county societies. Also check libraries in the area, which are likely to have such books.

The Family History Library Catalog

Using the *Family History Library Catalog*™, or *FHLC*, which is available on microfiche and CD-ROM, is one of the fastest methods for locating probate materials for those who are close to the Family History Library of The Church of Jesus Christ of Latter-day Saints (LDS church) in Salt Lake City or one of its more than 2,500 branch facilities, which are known as family history centers. (See the introduction for more on family history centers.)

Both the microfiche and CD-ROM versions of the catalog make it is simple to find a record. First, select the state of interest; second, select the county of interest; third, select the category "Probate Records."

Use the Author/Title section (only on the microfiche edition) if you know the actual name of a book or are looking for books by a particular author—for example, any of the books listed in this chapter's bibliography.

The Locality section identifies what is available for a particular area, presenting major subdivisions of material by country and by states within the United States. On the *FHLC* microfiche, information is listed *according to the highest jurisdiction first*, alphabetically by category, then by categories within counties, and by categories within towns.

All records relating to any probate action are listed under the term "Probate Records"; this includes wills and orphans' court records as well as administrations, estate settlements, executor's bonds, etc. Figure 10-9 illustrates the variety of probate entries in the *Family History Library Catalog*.

Other Library Catalogs

Every genealogical library has a significant collection of published probate records for the areas its collection covers. Be sure to learn the terminology and process for finding probates in the catalog for each library used. Some libraries have published their catalogs in book form or in microform, or via the Internet, so that researchers can search for published records at their convenience. Some of the published catalogs described in chapter 16, "Family Histories and Genealogies," include many published probate records. In particular see the *Dictionary Catalog of the Local History and Genealogy Division* (of the New York Public Library), as well as the *Sutro Library State and Local History Catalog*.

The Sutro Library is a branch of the California State Library. Located in San Francisco, it publishes a quarterly listing of all its new acquisitions in American local history and genealogy. Early compilations have been microfiched also. A recent sample is Frank J. Glover's "New Arrivals in American Local History and Genealogy, Quarterly List, Spring 1997," 5th Series, List no. 13 (San Francisco: Sutro Library, 1997). A large portion of the published works at the Sutro Library are available through interlibrary loan to public libraries in California and other states where the material is not otherwise available.

Bibliographies and Research Guides

Bibliographies and research guides will also help you find printed probate records. Both seek to identify the sources available for research on a given topic or for a certain locality. Chief among these is P. William Filby's *American and British Genealogy and Heraldry: A Selected List of Books* (Boston: New England Historic Genealogical Society, 1983; supplement, 1987), which lists published books (except family and county histories and immigration materials) of value for family historians. The state-by-state listings include many books with wills and other probate records. Also note Kory L. Meyerink's CD-ROM publication *Genealogical Publications: A List of 50,000 Sources from the Library of Congress* (Salt Lake City: Ancestry, 1997), which includes more than seven hundred sources for the United States and Great Britain that include the words "wills," "probate," or "inventories" in their subject headings. More than one hundred other sources, usually under the subject "genealogy," include these words in their titles or descriptions. Both of these works are described in chapter 5, "Bibliographies and Catalogs." In addition, guides specific to research in a city, county, or state usually list the published probate records for that locality.

Periodicals

Local genealogical and historical society newsletters and publications frequently publish abstracts of or indexes to wills and probate records. State and regional quarterlies and monthly newsletters also may include articles pertaining to these topics. In addition, organizations announce or advertise forthcoming and currently available publications in local, regional, and state societies' journals and newsletters. For example, each month the *California State Genealogical Alliance Newsletter* publishes notices of compilations and publications in progress as well as those available for purchase. Most of these are local society efforts that are not widely advertised.

Perhaps the easiest means of locating articles pertaining to wills or probate materials in local, regional, state, and ethnic group periodicals is to use the *Periodical Source Index* (*PERSI*). *PERSI* is a topical index to the thousands of articles found in genealogical periodicals and journals. It is published by the Allen County Public Library Foundation in Fort Wayne, Indiana, and is available in book and microfiche formats and on CD-ROM from Ancestry (Salt Lake City, 1997). Because it indexes more than two thousand periodicals, it should not be overlooked. *PERSI* does not index every name or locality mentioned within articles, but it does index all names and places which appear in article titles. It also indexes articles which address research methodology.

PERSI is divided into three sections: locality, research methodologies, and family. The locality sections are particularly helpful for locating short abstracted or indexed probate records. First look up the locality of interest and then the record type, either "wills" or "probate."

States are arranged alphabetically by their two-letter postal abbreviations (not by the spelling of the full state name); therefore, Iowa [IA] comes before Idaho [ID]. Countywide records are listed after statewide entries under the locality's *present-day* county. Probate records and wills are listed separately; entries for both record types must be checked for each locality within *PERSI*. Thus, the wills of Guilford County, North Carolina, are listed apart from the other intestate records. For example:

NC	Guilford	Wills	Early Wills 1756–65
NC	Guilford	Probate	Estate Settlements 1774–78

The title column provides a descriptive entry (not the exact title of the article). Once items have been located, the appropriate journal citation can be found in the five columns to the right, where the title of the journal is given as a four-letter abbreviation (an abbreviation key is included in an appendix to *PERSI*). The journal title is followed by the periodical's volume number, issue number, month, and year. *PERSI* does not indicate the page numbers of the articles. A more complete discussion of *PERSI* and several other periodical indexes is in chapter 19, "Genealogical Periodicals."

Other Sources

Books which are privately published and are not advertised broadly are sometimes difficult to locate. Many publications

```
******************************************************************************
KENTUCKY, GARRARD - PROBATE RECORDS
                                                                +------------+
Bell, Annie W. B. (Annie Walker Burns), b. 1894.                |US/CAN      |
    Kentucky vital statistics, record of wills in Garrard County,|BOOK AREA   |
      Kentucky, for the period of years 1796 to 1851 inclusive / |976.9525    |
      compiled by Annie Walker Burns Bell. -- 1933. -- 107 leaves.|S2b        |
                                                                +------------+
    Typescript.
    Includes index.

    Also on microfiche.  Salt Lake City : Filmed by              US/CAN
      the Genealogical Society of Utah, 1991.  3                 FICHE AREA
      microfiche ; 11 x 15 cm.                                   6088005

******************************************************************************
KENTUCKY, GARRARD - PROBATE RECORDS
                                                                +------------+
Bell, Annie W. B. (Annie Walker Burns), b. 1894.                |US/CAN      |
    Record of wills in Garrard County, Kentucky for the period of|FILM AREA  |
      years 1796 to 1851 inclusive / compiled by Annie Walker Burns|0851650  |
      Bell. -- Salt Lake City : Filmed by the Genealogical Society| item 12. |
      of Utah, 1971. -- on 1 microfilm reel ; 35 mm.            +------------+

    Microreproduction of original typescript (107 p.) written in 1933.
    Includes index.

******************************************************************************
KENTUCKY, GARRARD - PROBATE RECORDS
                                                                +------------+
Franklin, Charles M.                                            |US/CAN      |
    Garrard County wills and estates / compiled by Charles M.   |BOOK AREA   |
      Franklin. -- Indiannapolis, Ind. : Heritage House,        |976.9525    |
      c1986-    . --     v.                                     |P28f        |
                                                                +------------+
    Title varies:  Garrard County, Kentucky, will abstracts.
    Includes surname index in each volume.
    Contents:  v. 1. 1796-1819 -- v. 2. 1819-1833

******************************************************************************
KENTUCKY, GARRARD - PROBATE RECORDS
                                                                +------------+
Garrard County (Kentucky).  Clerk of the County Court.          |US/CAN      |
    Estate settlements, 1910-1928. -- Lexington, Ky. : Ron Cooper|FILM AREA  |
      Co., 1988. -- 1 microfilm reel ; 16 mm.                   +------------+

    Microfilm of originals at the county courthouse, Lancaster.
    Includes index for each volume.

    Vols. 1-3         1910-1928 - v. 1 has no index -------------- 1689807

******************************************************************************
KENTUCKY, GARRARD - PROBATE RECORDS
                                                                +------------+
Garrard County (Kentucky).  Clerk of the County Court.          |US/CAN      |
    Inventory, appraisement and sale bills, 1815-1881. --       |FILM AREA   |
      Lexington, Ky. : Ron Cooper, 1988. -- 1 microfilm reel ; 16 +----------+
      mm.

    Microfilm of originals at the county courthouse, Lancaster
    Includes name index.

    Vol. 1            1815-1881 ---------------------------------- 1689808

******************************************************************************
KENTUCKY, GARRARD - PROBATE RECORDS
                                                                +------------+
Kentucky.  County Court (Garrard County).                       |US/CAN      |
    Probate records, 1797-1958. -- Salt Lake City : Filmed by the|FILM AREA  |
      Genealogical Society of Utah ; Lexington, Ky. : Ron Cooper +-----------+
      Co., 1959, 1988. -- 11 microfilm reels : maps ; 16 & 35 mm.

    Microfilm of original and typescript at the Garrard County
      courthouse in Lancaster, Kentucky.
    Includes general indext to testators (deceased) and indexes for each
      volume unless otherwise noted.
    Contains wills, inventories and appraisements, division of
      lands, and guardian accounts.

    Index    1906-1945 - This is apparently an index -------------- 1689809
      to loose papers.
    Index      1797-1958 ------------------------------------------ 0009019
    Vols. A-D         1787-1820 (By date volume B & --------------- 0183232

      C have been misnumbered but they are in the
      general index in this way)
    Vols. E-G         1819-1835 ---------------------------------- 0183233
    Vols. H-I         1834-1839 ---------------------------------- 0183234
    Vols. K-L         1839-1848 (Apparently there is ------------- 0183235
```

Figure 10-9. Examples of Probate entries in the *Family History Library Catalog.* (Reprinted by permission. Copyright 1987, 1997 by The Church of Jesus Christ of Latter-day Saints.)

are created through the efforts of individuals whose efforts are not widely known, but these works serve the genealogical community. For instance, compiler and editor Harold Oliver's quarterly *Virginia in the 1600's: An Index to Who Was There!—and Where!* is a series of indexes to individuals named in various Virginia sources during the 1600s. Oliver's sources included wills, court records, and deeds. Each issue is arranged alphabetically and provides names, age if known, event, date, source, and a list of sources used.

Some privately published or unpublicized works can be located by referring to the four volumes of *Genealogical and Local History Books in Print*, compiled and edited by Marian Hoffman, 5th ed. (Baltimore: Genealogical Publishing Co., 1996–97). This publication is divided into three subjects: "U.S. Sources and Resources" (in two volumes), "General Reference and World Resources," and "Family History."

For instance, if seeking published wills or probate records for Gentry County, Missouri, reference the first volume (Alabama-New York) of the U.S. Sources and Resources set. A quick perusal of the county-arranged entries shows that eight publications are listed, one of which is *Gentry County, Missouri Probate Index, 1885–1902.* A vendor code enables the user to identify the name and address of the society which published the work.

Another invaluable source is an index to publications for a state, regional, ethnic, or county organization. The *Indiana Source Book: Genealogical Material from The Hoosier Genealogist, 1979–1981* (Indianapolis: Indiana Historical Society, 1987) is one of a series which reprints useful genealogical materials from periodicals. The contents include "County Records," "Early Newspaper Extracts," "Miscellaneous Records," and "Family Records." The first section contains will abstracts and other court records.

Another example is *The Southside Virginian: A Journal of Genealogy and History, Table of Contents and Indexes to Volumes I through VIII (October 1982–December 1990)* (Richmond, Va.: Southside Virginian, ca.1992). This work is a compilation of the table of contents and every-name indexes of the *Southside Virginian: A Journal of Genealogy and History.* Entries arranged alphabetically by title and county complete the first section, which also includes the author's name and volume, number, and beginning page of the article. The next eight sections consist of a separate index for each volume. With a bit of effort on the researcher's part, cross-referencing of individual names, counties of interest, and type of information can be identified.

Records for one jurisdiction may be published while those for an adjoining area go unpublished, but do not despair if you do not quickly find records. Some records that would be expected to be found under a probate court's jurisdiction might instead be filed among land and property records. For example, if a probate record cannot be found, a partition of the deceased's property may be registered among the county deeds. Some power-of-attorney appointments and even trusteeships related to probate are listed in land records rather than probate court documents.

Sometimes the pertinent record is registered in another county or state. When the needed document cannot be located in the county of interest, undertake an expanded search for relevant records in adjacent counties and states. Such a survey can be much easier to accomplish in printed sources. It is useful to check published volumes or indexes to wills and administrations for surrounding counties using a statewide index, if available. For example, two abstracted wills of Virginians from Northumberland and Richmond counties which were recorded in North Carolina were the subject of a brief article by David B. Gammon. Entitled "Abstracts of Wills Probated in Edgecombe County, North Carolina Which Refer to Tidewater Virginia," it was recently published in *Tidewater Virginia Families: A Magazine of History and Genealogy* 1 (4): 210 (February-March 1993) (figure 10-10).

Because jurisdictional boundaries sometimes were contested, some probates were recorded outside of today's state boundaries. As an example, see Boyd Crumrine's *Virginia Court Records in Southwest Pennsylvania: Records of the District of West Augusta and Ohio and Yohogania Counties, Virginia, 1775–1780,* excerpted and reprinted from *Annals of the Carnegie Museum,* 3 vols. (Pittsburgh, Pa.: 1902–05). It includes many records from Augusta and surrounding counties in Virginia that were registered as far away as Pittsburgh, Pennsylvania. Crumrine's compilation is a helpful guide to these records.

Some probate-related documents are recorded in more than one source in the same county, such as both probate and land records. Some are recorded in two or more counties, particularly if the parties resided in separate counties or states. The following extract from Mrs. W. O. Absher's *Surry County, North Carolina Deeds: Books D, E and F, 1779–1797* (N.p., n.d.), page 100, refers to such a case.

> Page 163. 14 October 1794. Anne BAKER, James BAKER, David BAKER, Samuel JONES, Evan JONES, John BAKER, Peleg BAKER, Joseph BAKER, Jonathan BAKER, and Joshua BAKER (all of State of Kentucky and heirs and legatees Michael BAKER, deceased, of North Carolina), appointed our Brother Moses BAKER of North Carolina, our lawful attorney to sell, etc., tract of land Surry County, North Carolina, whereon Michael BAKER died. Signed: Anne BAKER, David BAKER, Evan JONES, Joseph BAKER . . . Town Lexington, Fayette County, Kentucky, above letter Attorney produced in Court and ordered recorded 17 October 1794 and 3rd year Commonwealth. Signed: Levi TODD, C.C., Surry County, North Carolina. February Term 1795, above letter Attorney produced in Court and ordered recorded. Signed: Jo WILLIAMS, C.C.

As another example, Richard Harrison, who lived in Pickering County, Mississippi Territory, at the time of his death in 1799, formerly lived in Jefferson County, Kentucky, where the most informative records were found. It seems he was entitled to a military land warrant for 2,666 2/3 acres in Kentucky. Richard entered three separate entries: two for 1,000 acres each and another for 666 2/3 acres. These parcels were located below the Tennessee River in Indian country (present-day Alabama) and had not been surveyed in 1807. He also possessed "a just claim to a preemption of 1,000 acres on the Kentucky River about three miles above Boonesborough, which was granted to him by the commissioners on the application of Col. Richard Henderson." Because Richard Harrison owned so much land in Kentucky and his heirs found it "inconvenient" to oversee the sale of it, an attorney was appointed to administer that portion of the estate, and a verbatim copy of Richard's will was recorded in the Kentucky court of appeals eight years after it was written (Cook 1985, 228–29).

ADVANTAGES OF PRINTED PROBATE RECORDS

Original probate records may be difficult to locate or read in either the original format or from microform copies.

- There may be no index, the index may be inadequate, or the entries may have an unusual arrangement.
- The estate record may be filed in a county other than where the deceased lived or owned property.
- The handwriting may be difficult to decipher, or the ink so faded that sections of the document are illegible.
- Legal terms or phrases and unfamiliar abbreviations may obscure the meaning for the present-day researcher.
- The researcher may not understand the probate process of the time.

Although there are always dangers in relying *solely* on printed material, the advantages of published probate and estate records greatly outweigh the disadvantages if you are thorough, careful, and consistently review the original documents as well. Overall, published statewide indexes to wills and estate records serve as valuable finding aids. Other benefits of printed volumes include fast retrieval, concisely recorded data, easy-to-read text, and broad availability.

Abstracts of Wills Probated in Edgecombe County,
North Carolina
Which Refer to Tidewater Virginia

Abstracted by David B. Gammon

WILLIAM GILL of Northumberland Co., VA 19 Sep 1794 Nov Ct 1794 "...being very sick and weak in body..." Sister MARY GILL - Negroes Sarah and Winne. Brother RICHARD GILL - Negro Isaac and my saling boat named "Betsee Vecommecoe". Brother WINDER GILL - Negro Jude. Ex. brothers GEORGE GILL and WINDER GILL.
Wit. John Willeford, Martin Pitman, Edward (X) Pitman.
Edgecombe County (NC) Will Book C, p.288.

WILLIAM NORTHEN 18 July 1790 Feb Ct 1793 Northen
Sons EDMUND NORTHEN, WILLIAM NORTHEN, MYNTA NORTHEN, JOHN NORTHEN, GEORGE NORTHEN - ten shillings each as their full part of my estate. Daughter SARAH NORTHEN - 100 silver dollars, and if she should die, this sum shall fall to her first child to arrive at the age of twenty-one, but if she leaves not issue this shall fall to my daughters CATEY, NELLY and LUCY NORTHEN. Daughters MARGARET NORTHEN, ANN NORTHEN, MARY NORTHEN, son RUBEN NORTHEN and daughter LUANER NORTHEN - ten shillings each as their full part of my estate. Son PETER NORTHEN - all my lands in Richmond County, Virginia, also all my stock, Negro Siner and her children;, Negro George, all my money. Sons MERIMON NORTHEN and KILBEY NORTHEN - ten shillings each as their full part of my estate. Daughters CATEY, NELLY and LUCY NORTHEN - all my land in Edgecombe county, as well as Negroes in Edgecombe and Negroes in Virginia, to be divided when CATEY is twenty-one. Daughter ELIZABETH NORTHEN - ten shillings as her full share of my estate.
Ex. friends Jacob Sessums, Thomas Hodges
Wit. Alexander Sessums, Alice Sessums, Rebekah Sessums, Polley Sessums.
Edgecombe County (NC) Will Book C, p.218.

David B. Gammon, 119 Brooks Avenue, Raleigh, NC 27607, contributed these wills found in the records of Edgecombe County, North Carolina (1732-1910). They will be included in the book he is publishing of Edgecombe County Wills.

210

Figure 10-10. Gammon's "Abstracts of Wills Probated in Edgecombe County, North Carolina Which Refer to Tidewater Virginia."

Indexes

The most valuable printed works include verbatim transcripts and every-name indexes. Most provide citations to identify the facility where the original records are stored. High-quality abstracts include volume and page numbers and/or case numbers from original records; these can serve as practical and reliable indexes to the original documents.

Earlier printed compilations of estate records may not have included an every-name index, but most publications issued within the past twenty years do. Often, *all* persons listed in the records are included in indexes to published probate records—not just the testators. Such every-name indexes identify individuals mentioned within a will or probate record whose names do not appear in most indexes to the actual court record; this is particularly beneficial when there are no *devisee* (one who receives any designated portion of the estate) indexes. Every-name indexes alone make printed probate sources invaluable to the researcher.

Of course, some published probate records are solely indexes, as described earlier. While their formats vary, all are valuable and serve as useful finding aids. Most statewide compilations are listed in the chapter bibliography. Some of the difficulties in using statewide indexes are discussed below under "Limitations of Printed Probate Records—Limitations of Scope."

Ease and Speed of Use

Another key advantage of using a published source is the ease and speed with which such records can be scanned. Reading unfamiliar handwritten documents can be difficult under the best of circumstances. When compounded by poor microfilming, faded ink, torn pages, ink that has bled through paper writ-

PREFACE

OHIO WILLS AND ESTATES TO 1850: AN INDEX is the culmination of a ten-year project to provide a comprehensive index to the probate records in Ohio. It was the brainchild of Anita Short, then editor of Gateway to the West: Ohio, who began collecting the records in 1971, while gathering material for her periodical. Volunteer help was solicited around the state, but volunteers did not beat a path to the door! By 1978, Anita had made the decision to discontinue her involvement in genealogy, and I agreed to see the project to completion. Sixty counties remained incomplete or untouched, and it became my duty to browbeat my friends and others into giving their time to help complete the project.

The stories of success (and failure) are many and varied...in one county (Lawrence), the volunteer was limited by courthouse personnel to two afternoons per week to examine genealogical records. In another county, when the volunteers arrived, the records had been removed for microfilming and were unavailable for some time. In a northeastern county, I was told by local genealogists that one person could never complete that county, due to its size. I completed it alone in six hours! In a few counties, volunteers could not be located. At this point, records on microfilm from Salt Lake City were examined by such kind folks as Helen L. Harriss, Certified Genealogist, of Pittsburgh, Pa; Robert J. Boroughf of Reno, Nevada; Frances Le Blanc of La Habra, Calif.; Merna McClenathan and Oneita Wilde, both of Goleta, Calif. To each one of them, I extend special thanks. Some counties, such as Geauga, Knox and Trumbull, have records which required a page-by-page search, since no general index is available. Other counties, notably Licking, Hamilton, Delaware and Adams, have had damaging courthouse fires, necessitating the use of substitute records such as deeds, newspapers, or surviving fragmented records, and the researcher must be aware that these counties may be incomplete in this index.

This project has generated the compilation of will and estate abstracts by many individuals and genealogical societies. These abstracts are listed under each county in the introduction. In some cases, notably Licking, Harrison, Franklin and Highland, the published abstract is cited in addition to the original court record. In a number of cases, articles published in Gateway to the West: Ohio, Ohio Records and Pioneer Families, and the O.G.S. Report were compared to the court records, and listed in this index as a secondary source, and may be more readily available to the researcher than the actual court records. It is advised that in all cases, when possible, the original record should be consulted to insure accuracy.

The user of this index should also be aware that there may be discrepancies in spelling and interpretation of a name. Corrections and additions would be welcomed by the compiler. The researcher should also be aware that there may be numerous other sources in additional court records, besides the reference listed here. Space limitations made it necessary to use only the primary entry, such as a will book or case file number, when in fact, there may have been additional listings reported. When a will book volume and page is given as the reference, there may also be a case file packet, containing the original will and all of the settlement papers. The mention of property in a will should suggest the possibility of deed records as an additional source to be checked. Ownership of land may also have generated a case in Chancery, offering still another source to be examined. In some cases, there may be nothing more to be found.

It should be mentioned that Probate Court was formed in 1852, taking over those functions of the Common Pleas Court which had previously been handled by that office. In most Ohio counties, the records were transferred to the new court, but in a few counties the original probate matters have remained in the Common Pleas Court records. In any case, the serious researcher will want to examine those records for possible additional information.

It is the sincere wish of the compiler that OHIO WILLS AND ESTATES TO 1850: AN INDEX will help to solve the genealogical puzzles which beset all of us, and will provide the needed clues in the pursuit of Buckeye ancestors.

Carol Willsey Bell, Certified Genealogist

Columbus, Ohio August 1981

Figure 10-11. Preface from Carol Willsey Bell's *Ohio Wills and Estates to 1850: An Index.*

ten on both sides, or tight bindings, the problems are greatly intensified.

Conciseness

Carefully edited abstracts also have the advantage of conciseness. Original probate records may be verbose, and many of the legal phrases used in them are irrelevant to genealogy research. Concisely recorded abstracts eliminate much of this verbiage while including significant facts.

Explanation

In the introduction, preface, and/or acknowledgment of a printed record, the editor may explain the location of the original records, identification of sources, abbreviations used in the text (figure 10-11), historical references, and special arrangements or formatting of the text. These sections may also include suggested reference material, specific instructions to the reader, a glossary of terms, and other necessary explanations relating to text or subject.

Some introductions explain legal terms and/or foreign words used in the text. A thorough reading of these pages will afford the genealogist a much better understanding of the volume and furnish a working knowledge necessary to attain success. The best published volumes also include a map or maps relating to the period and area referred to in the abstracts.

An explanation of the indexing and related pagination methods—for example, unindexed categories of names or items—should also appear in the introduction. Without this information, references noted in the index may not be found in the normal manner. Below, from Haun's *Craven Precinct-County North Carolina Court Minutes 1730 thru 1741, Book II* (cited earlier), page i, is an example of how an editor helps the reader with specific details:

> The original pages are numbered. For indexing purposes (and to conserve search time) EACH page has been assigned a page number. These assigned numbers appear at the left margin, have been underscored and are the page numbers referred to in the index. The numbers appearing to the right of the underscored numbers are the original page numbers.

The editor may also provide explanations for frequently included foreign words, dated phrases, misspelled names or locations, and references to names, places, or situations no longer identified in the same manner today. Such information will help you interpret the information provided.

When the compiler or editor is thoroughly familiar with the region, its records, its history, its families, the handwriting of various clerks, legal terms, and abbreviations employed in the records, the resulting publication is an excellent tool for researchers.

Availability

Another benefit of printed records is their accessibility. Published estate and court records are more plentiful than ever before; numerous county and state estate and court records are published every year. Originals are usually accessible only at county courthouses or state archives, but published records are available through libraries using organizations which provide interlibrary loan services, at lending libraries for members of genealogical societies, and through special-interest groups that provide similar services to members and patrons.

Substitutes for Missing Records

While it is normally best to trust only original documents for completeness and accuracy, exceptions to this general rule depend upon the condition and availability of the original records. From county to county and from record to record, the condition of original records varies significantly. Some may be unfaded, firmly bound, and easy to read, while others are faded, torn, and crumbling; some pages may even be missing. In some courthouses, disintegrating records have been preserved by laminating them, but in others, documents and books have been mutilated, destroyed, stolen, and lost. In some cases only printed transcripts of early records, many of them made during the late 1800s and during the 1930s, remain. When original sources are irrevocably lost, these transcripts are priceless, no matter their limitations.

Example. Hanover County, Virginia, suffered "the destruction of most of the records . . . on April 3, 1865" (Cocke, 1978, ii). Therefore, researchers dealing with county families are enormously grateful for those court records that have been compiled and published. An example of the types of records to be found in printed probate records is shown below (Cocke 1978, 9):

> I, Martin Baker of Gordonsville, Orange County, Va., possessing a sound mind and disposing memory do hereby make my last will and testament in manner and form following: 1st. I lend to my wife Mona [*sic*] during her life or so long as she remains my widow the following property and funds for her use hereafter mentioned and expressed, viz: I lend her my Gordonsville estate, lands, slaves, crops, stock, furniture, plantation furniture, utensils, &c &c. I wish my executors to lend out the amount of such bonds and money as may be in my possession at the time of my death to borrowers of good credit to be well secured to collect the interest thereon annually and pay it to my wife. I wish the tract of land I own in the County of Giles, a tract on Chickahominy Swamp in the County of Hanover, and a small lot adjoining Woodson Pleasants in Solomon Mark's plan in the County of Henrico sold by executors upon such credit as they may think desirable. The amount of such sales to be loaned out, the interest annually collected and paid over to my wife as heretofore directed. The amount of my interest or claims in the estate of my father I wish disposed of in the same manner. These funds, namely, the profits of my estate at Gordonsville, the interest arising from the amount of sales of my lands, and my claims in the estate of my father, I lend to my wife Maria [*sic*] for the purpose of supporting herself, boarding, clothing and educating our children which is to be done without charge against any of them. 2ndly. If any of my servants should prove unsuitable I wish them sold or hired out, and the amount of such sales or hires reinvested in same kind of property or disposed of as the funds named in the first clause of this my will. 3rdly. I give to my son John M. Baker my gold watch which I imported and now wear. I also give to each of the rest of my children one hundred and fifty dollars to make them equal to him in this bequest. 4th. After the death of my wife my executors may use their discretion in selling or renting out my Gordonsville landed property until my youngest child arrives to lawful age at which time it must be sold upon such credits as they may think advisable. 5thly. I wish my daughter Marion to have a likely negro girl over and above the part and portion of the rest of my children. 6thly. The balance of my estate I wish equally divided amongst all my children to them and their heirs forever, except my daughter Marion whose part in the equal division as well as the negro girl extra, I lend to her during her life only, and at her death to be equally divided among all my children or their heirs. But if my daughter Marion should recover from her lameness, then her part before named is given to her and her heirs forever. 7thly. If my wife should marry a second time she is to forfeit all claim to my estate whatsoever. 8thly. If any of my children should become of age or marry before the final division of my estate, I wish my executors to advance them six hundred dollars. I nominate constitute and appoint my nephew Wm. W. Baker and Thomas Swift, Jr., executors to this my last will and testament hereby revoking all wills heretofore made by me. In witness whereof I have hereunto set my hand and seal this 15th day of June 1835.
>
> Martin Baker (Seal)
>
> Teste: Leroy Chandler, George Parrott, James Quarles. Probated Orange County 23 May 1836 by Wm. W. Baker, one of the Executors, with Clevears Baker, John R. Quarles and Richard S. Boulware, his securities. Teste, Reynolds Chapman, Clk.

The above quote is an extract of the will of Martin Baker. It gives the names of witnesses, dates of will, date and place of probate, residence of the deceased, property in several locations, wife's name, some of his children's names, a suggestion that the children are under legal age, names of security for the witness, and court clerk's name. Even in such cases, transcriptions must be used wisely and somewhat cautiously. One error seems apparent in this transcription: the wife's name appears as both Mona and Maria. This mistake calls for a review of the original record to clarify the mistake—difficult to do if the original no longer exists. The only alternative in this case would be a painstaking and tedious search of other documents. However, as this example shows, such a will can lead a researcher to additional documents where records are extant. In addition, accounts, partitioning, and guardianship papers should provide names of the other children.

LIMITATIONS OF PRINTED PROBATE RECORDS

Some excellent compilations of estate records have been produced; however, others leave much to be desired. As useful as published probate information is, the researcher must still be aware of some significant limitations.

Limited Coverage or Information

Some printed sources serve only as finding aids; they indicate that a record pertaining to a certain surname exists in a specific county, without showing given names or any detail from the document. Others provide added details but still have such limited data that they merely serve as locating tools, such as those that give only the names of people specified as relatives while ignoring names of people who do not appear to be relatives, such as in-laws, neighbors, etc.—names that are very valuable to the research process.

Frequently, the range of dates covered in a publication is narrow. But sometimes an estate is finalized many years after the testator's death; this happens often when stipulations for distribution of property are determined by the beneficiaries' situations—for example, when property is not to be divided until after the widow's demise or the youngest child's marriage or death. In such cases, the probate appears many years after the subject's death. If the published probate record does not include the later years, the researcher working only in the death date period may not find the probate record.

A will may have been recorded more than once in original court records, particularly if a codicil was added, a caveat was filed against the property, the will was contested, or the executor died or ceased to act. In such a case, one of the records could be missing from a printed record because of jurisdictional changes (county boundary changes, territorial-to-state government changes, etc.). With only part of the proceeding at hand, the compiler might be unaware of all the related documents.

Finding a printed probate record is never a guarantee that the complete probate record has been published. Because the inheritance process can extend over several years, printed collections are often incomplete for individual cases. Also, most abstracted printed probate records are compilations that cover specific jurisdictions; they require knowledge of at least the county of residence to locate the record. Therefore, you might need to consult other records, such as census records, land and property records, and county histories, to find this information before you can begin a search of the printed probate records.

Errors in Transcription, Typing, or Interpretation

When any record is abstracted or extracted, problems can arise. Most, if not all, published transcripts contain errors; these include omissions, misread handwriting, typographical mistakes, and illegible sections due to faded ink or torn pages in the original. Additional problems with abstracts and extracts arise when those who perform the transcribing function are unfamiliar with the handwriting, legal terminology, clerks' notations and abbreviations, and/or proper names of people and places in the area during the pertinent period. If you believe a published record should show a probate, even though it is not included in the published version, review the original records.

Other cautions against using *only* published probate and estate records: valuable details may have been omitted from an abstract; the reference date or pagination may be incorrect in the published work; and the compiler may have misread the original handwriting. A case of misread handwriting was noted in *Southside Virginian: A Journal of Genealogy and History*, wherein it was noted that the surname Harrup had been misread in the original record and published in the journal as Harris (Hooper 1993, 37). The editor added,

> this should be a lesson to all of us. Search for ALL variations and spellings of any name which you are researching. Be familiar with other names in the area in which you are researching which may be similar in spelling or sound to those of interest.

Unfortunately, many compilers and editors miss or are unaware of technicalities with procedures or details that affect the process and record. A transcriber or abstractor may be unfamiliar with family names in a particular county or area, consequently interpreting them incorrectly. There may be difficulty in reading handwriting in the original documents, resulting in incorrectly transcribed data. At times, errors in names, dates, and references do appear in printed works and/or indexes.

The invaluable loose papers associated with probate cases are rarely published. Additionally, the availability of such records is seldom noted in a printed collection.

Inaccuracies in Dates. Dates in publications must be carefully reviewed. Typographical errors that affect dates occur easily and are difficult to find in editing. Incorrect recording of Gregorian calendar dates or incorrect conversion of dates from the Gregorian to Julian calendar may adversely affect the information. Watch for such mistakes in entries for 1752 and earlier. (Records that show January and February dates with a double year, such as 1726/7, reflect the transition between the two calendars.)

Numbers usually contain a higher percentage of typographical errors that go undetected by the editor than do text or names. Carefully check dates and book and page references. One way to check the accuracy of dates is to check sequential entries preceding and following the one in question. If all or most other entries are chronological or consecutive and one is not, the date or book and page numbers should be considered questionable, and the data should be verified using the original whenever possible.

Problems with Indexes

Every-name indexes are very valuable, but assuming that all indexes are of this type can be very misleading. Be wary if the indexer has not explained the principle of indexing used and which categories of names were included or omitted. The editor may have purposefully omitted certain classes of names from the index to reduce its size. While most probate indexes include the names of the testator or the decedent (if an index to intestate records), there may be many other names in the record that were not included in the index.

Common groups of names that may be omitted in published probate indexes include those of the witnesses, executor, and legatees to the will and other persons mentioned incidentally, such as legatees' spouses. Indexes to intestate records may fail to name the administrator, those who inventoried the estate, and the heirs.

In a few publications, the problem is the reverse: all of the associated persons are in the index, yet the testator or decedent is not listed because the compiler has arranged the abstracts in alphabetical order by decedent! It is the researcher's responsibility to examine the book thoroughly and determine the principles upon which the indexing was conducted and what degree of reliance may be placed upon it.

Some extracts or abstracts are so poorly indexed that the compilation would actually be better if left unindexed—then researchers would not be led into thinking that the work had a full index. As mentioned, names may be "lost" in the index because of typographical errors, misread handwriting, or unexpected differences in spelling in the original document. Typographical errors can affect one or two letters or whole names.

As with many types of records, published compilations of estate records created long ago often contain less detail and frequently lack the every-name indexes normally found in similar publications today. For example, they may give only the names of those specified as relatives.

Transposed letters frequently cause difficulties in locating proper entries in an index. For example, "Mtason" may be the name entered for Matson; the name John Swartz could be lost in the index as "Kpjm Destyx" if the typist's fingers shifted one key to the right.

Other problems with indexes may result from a misspelled original or indecipherable handwriting. Landers may be misread for Sanders. Surnames may be spelled incorrectly, such as "Hambleton" for Hamilton and "Umphries" for Humphries. Charles McRoddy could appear as "Charles M. Roddy." Quakenbush may be shown as "Zuakenbush." The names Edmund/Edmunds, Daniel/David, Lemuel/Samuel, and Edward/Edwards are exchanged frequently.

Given names can be wrongly transcribed in an index: Jehu may be misread as "John," and Daniel may be shown as "David." Extra letters may be typographically added; examples found in indexes include "Hklein" and "Kmartin." When possible, it is best to compare different publications for completeness and accuracy.

Omissions Within the Abstracts

Many details in an original are necessarily eliminated in an abstracted version. In addition to the published volume, the original document must always be reviewed to determine what data has been omitted (if the original still exists).

Due to size limitations, most compilations cannot include all information contained in the original record; thus, the abstract may be lacking pertinent details for the genealogist. These include names and relationships of individuals mentioned in the record, legal descriptions of real estate, itemized personal property, details of the property divisions, connections with other individuals, references to earlier records or transactions, and other details. Some abstracts or extracts are poorly indexed, yet they give the illusion of completeness when they are not inclusive at all; for example, some countywide titles include only limited years or only abstract certain surnames.

Limitations of Scope

Supposed statewide indexes to wills and probate records can prove beneficial but, as mentioned previously, some do not include entries for *all* counties in the state. In cases where more than one published record exists for a particular county, they may duplicate each other to a greater or lesser extent. Compare and evaluate transcripts and the original source.

In a review of one of Weynette Parks Haun's publications, *Surry County, Virginia, Court Records (Deed Book 1), 1664 thru 1671,* (Durham, N.C.: the author, 1988), Richard Slatten, editor of the *Virginia Genealogical Society Magazine* and co-editor of the society's newsletter, states:

> These volumes by Mrs. Haun . . . cover much the same material previously published by Elizabeth T. Davis in her *Surry County Records, 1652–1684,* a book which quickly became a much-quoted reference item. Inevitably, of course, a new reading would appear to supplement Davis'. No single transcription of records of this age and importance could ever be considered definitive, and a comparison of the two texts shows numerous differences. In critical passages, researchers should compare the two versions and where doubt remains, [compare] both with the original. Researchers should also be aware that the Haun version is the first verbatim copy of the Surry court minutes, thus the reading embodying all the assets that a full copy has over a partial one, regardless of how faithful in its details the partial copy might be (Slatten 1988, 5).

Finally, remember that, while there are more intestate cases than testate cases, their treatment in printed literature seems to be the reverse: there are many more wills in printed literature than intestate cases. Therefore, if the wills for a particular location have been published, do not assume that the intestate cases have been published also, or that there is no record of intestate cases. Contact the appropriate jurisdiction and determine the best way to search intestate files.

Misleading Titles

Sometimes the titles of publications are misleading. Who would imagine, for example, that parish registers could include references to wills? Yet, during the early colonial period, the parishes kept track of most records because they provided the greatest structure in the society of the time. Because so many early colonial records have been lost, it is of real value to have books such as that by William F. Boogher, Esq., *Overwharton Parish Register, 1720–1760* (n.p., n.d.). However, the work's title is misleading in two ways: (1) it includes records only for 1723 through 1758; (2) and many people would not consider such a title to contain published probate materials.

A later volume on the same topic, *The Register of Overwharton Parish, Stafford County, Virginia 1723–1758 and Sundry Historical and Genealogical Notes,* compiled and published in 1961 by George Harrison Sanford King (reprint; Easley, S.C.: Southern Historical Press, 1986), is not a strict abstraction of the parish register but includes annotations with reference to wills and court records. King notes in the preface to the reprint edition (page x),

> to make up for the sparseness of the early period of the Register, I have presented in Section III a transcription from a Stafford County Quit Rent Roll for 1723. The names of the Tenders of Tobacco in

> Overwharton Parish in 1724, presented in Section IV, also assist in filling the gap in the sparse recordings for the early years of the Register.
>
> . . . My purpose there has been to vest some of those mentioned in The Register of Overwharton Parish with more than their mere names and to supplement the information usually found in the now lost colonial vestry books. Much of this material has been found in primary sources, although I have drawn heavily upon some secondary sources which I consider reliable.

King goes on to explain the content, arrangement, location, and condition of the original records.

Certain statewide works may not include records for all counties because some county records are housed in separate locations. Thus, a title for a state collection may be somewhat misleading. For example, in Robert M. Dructor's *Guide to Genealogical Sources at the Pennsylvania State Archives* (Harrisburg: Pennsylvania Historical and Museum Commission, 1988), only forty-three of sixty-seven counties' probate records are discussed.

Many publications with varying titles contain references or citations from estate records. Examples include Marjorie Hood Fischer's *Tennessee Tidbits, 1778–1914,* vol. 1 (Easley, S.C.: Southern Historical Press, 1986), and Ruth Blake Burns, *Tennessee Tidbits, 1778–1914,* vol. 2 (Vista, Calif.: Ram Press, 1988). These contain abstracts of court records, including wills, probates, administrations, dower allotments, petitions, guardianships, and actions against estates.

Volumes titled "court records" usually include probate and estate records. One example is the following entry from Ruth Sparacio's *Deed Abstracts of Middlesex County, Virginia 1679–1688* (McLean, Va.: R & S Sparacio, 1989), page 65.

> p. 213 Att a Courte held the 5th of January 1685 Att ye house of Mr. RICHARD ROBINSON for Christ Church Parish Middx County
>
> Presente
>
> Major ROBERT BEVELY
> Coll: CUTH: POTTER
> Mr. Robert SMITH
> Mr. RICHARD ROBINSON
> Mr. ABRAHAM WEEKS
> Mr. WILLIAM DANIELL
> Mr. CHRISTOPHER ROBINSON
> Mr. JOHN WORTHAM
> Mr. MATHEW KEMPE
> Mr. WILLIAM CHURCHILL
> Mr. OSWALD CARREY
> Mr. ROBERTE PRICE
>
> It is ordered by this present Vestry yt: Mr. WILLIAM DANIELL present Church Warden for Middle Precinct for the ensueing yeare doe immediately take possesition of ye hundred acres of land lefte by the laste will & Testamente of Mr. WILLIAM GORDAN lately deceased for ye use & bennefitt of a FREE SCOOLE togather with twoe Cows & their Increase & the sd Church Warden doe prseed accordingly to ye Will of the Testator.
>
> Testa JOSEPH HARVY Clrk ye Parish
>
> January 30th 1685/6 then delivered to me WILLIAM DANIEL Church Warden within specified tooe Cows called Mary & Pye marked with a slitte & brider keeled on the righte eare & cropte on the lefte eare being the twoe Cows lefte by the last will & Testamente of William Gordan late of Midex. County for ye use of the afsd SCHOOLE Accordingly to be takene into the possion of ye peresh I say delivered by me. JNO. GORDAN

EVALUATION

The researcher must be careful not to accept a record just because it is in print. The research process must include an evaluation of the source and its information as well as that of the original. The process of publishing data allows errors to creep in, so published records should generally be used as reference or finding tools.

Virtually any transcribed record contains errors that may be typographical in nature or incorrect renderings. Some compilations appear to be statewide in coverage when they are not; one or more counties may be missing from an otherwise comprehensive compilation for the state.

Sometimes librarians realize the inadequacy of a published work. In one such case, a librarian did something about it. Apparently, years ago a person working for the Genealogical Society of Utah (GSU) entered a note in one of its many volumes. On the first page of Annie Walker Burns's *Virginia Genealogies and County Records* (Washington, D.C.: the compiler, 1941), vol. 1, is the following handwritten warning:

> Note: Numerous discrepancies have been found in this record as well as in J. Estelle Stewart King's compilation of the same material. Va./Alc and Va./R7b [old GSU call numbers]. The researcher should consult both records.

Evaluation Checklist

The researcher should learn the limitations of a transcript, extract, or abstract, and be aware of the possible pitfalls of relying solely upon transcribed records. Certain points need to be examined in order to determine the accuracy and completeness of a printed source. For example, are the facts thoroughly covered or are many blatant errors found when comparing a sample of the original with the transcription? Were the compiler and/or editor obviously familiar with the location, the handwriting, and the probate process? Before the advent of computers, indexing was a laborious process, and indexes were often incomplete. Does the index under consideration have a thorough or a partial index? Does the introduction or foreword give any indication of the limitations of the publication and an explanation of how the records can be used? The checklist in table 10-2 will provide some help in evaluating transcribed records.

CONCLUSION

Those who use printed probate record indexes for genealogical interests usually use them as finding aids to locate complete original records or to find localities where other genealogical records for a particular individual or surname cluster might be found. Hopefully, this chapter has enlightened you regarding

Table 10-2. Evaluation Checklist

If . . .	*Then*
It is an abstract . . .	Are all the essential facts included?
It is an extract . . .	Is the entire document extracted, or only "relevant" portions of it?
A comparison of random selections of the transcribed copy with original documents can be made . . .	Are there errors and/or omissions? Are all names in the original shown in the transcription, including those of witnesses, litigants, court clerks, places, and names within the text?
The editor is unfamiliar to you . . .	What is his or her reputation? Is it the editor's first publication? If not, is the editor known for accurate work or does he or she concede exactness to save time or space? Is the editor familiar with the names and places of the area, the paleography of the period, and the general use of probate records?
The title appears to cover a large time period . . .	Is the compilation complete? Based on other publications or your own experience, are the cases included sufficient for the approximate population in the jurisdiction during the period covered?
It was published before the advent of computers . . .	Is it completely indexed? (See below.)
It contains an index . . .	Check a number of entries in the text to determine if every name appears in the index. Check names contained in long lists to see if these names are indexed. If not, does the introduction, foreword, or preface specify those records or portions of the volume that are not listed in the index?
The area or time period under consideration is unfamiliar to you . . .	Consider the scholarship put into the work: does it contain an adequate explanation of legal terms, abbreviations used, citation of original sources, and location of original records?

the many other advantages of using printed probate collections—especially the use of the introductory materials, which can save the hours or days necessary to learn about the particular inheritance processes in effect during a particular period in a locality.

Published compilations of estate records offer many valuable features, including availability, finding aids, fast retrieval, concisely abstracted data, and an easy-to-read version of the original. In addition, although the original records rarely include every-name indexes, printed probate records as a group are better indexed than civil court records, and more have been published than general court records.

NOTES

1. The author wishes to express her gratitude to Karen Clifford, who assisted in the preparation of this chapter.
2. Grimes published a second work in 1912 with a similar title that was different in scope. Do not mistake his *North Carolina Wills and Inventories Copied from Original and Recorded Wills and Inventories in the Office of the Secretary of State* (Raleigh, N.C.: Edwards and Broughton, 1912) with his book of abstracts (1910). The 1912 volume is a selection of "representative" wills and inventories chosen to reflect "the varied phases of domestic life in the colony. . . ."

REFERENCE LIST

This list only includes those references cited (quoted) parenthetically in the chapter text. References to sources mentioned in passing are included in the bibliography that follows.

Cocke, William Ronald, 3rd, comp. 1978. *Hanover County Chancery Wills and Notes: A Compendium of Genealogical, Biographical, and Historical Material as Contained in Cases of the Chancery Suits of Hanover County, Virginia.* Baltimore: Genealogical Publishing Co.

Cook, Michael L., and Bettie A. Cook. 1985. *Kentucky Court of Appeals Deed Books H–N.* Vol. 2. Evansville, Ind.: Cook Publications.

Crumrine, Boyd. 1902–05. *Virginia Court Records in Southwestern Pennsylvania: Records of the District of West Augusta and Ohio and Yohogania Counties, Virginia, 1775–1780.* Excerpted and reprinted from *Annals of the Carnegie Museum.* 3 vols. Pittsburgh.

Holcomb, Brent H. Ca. 1983. *Spartanburg County, South Carolina Will Abstracts 1787–1840.* Columbia, S.C.: the author.

Hooper, Christopher M. 1993. "Harrup vs Harris—Reading Original Records." *Southside Virginia: A Journal of Genealogy and History* 11 (1) (January-March).

Houston, Martha Lou, comp. 1939. *Indexes to the County Wills of South Carolina.* Reprint. 1964, 1970, 1975, 1982. Baltimore: Genealogical Publishing Co.

Scott, Kenneth, and James A. Owre. 1970. *Genealogical Data from Inventories of New York Estates 1666–1825.* New York: New York Genealogical and Biographical Society.

Shammas, Carole, Marylynn Salmon, and Michel Dahlin. 1987. *Inheritance in America: From Colonial Times to the Present.* New Brunswick: Rutgers University Press.

Slatten, Richard, and Janice Abercrombie, eds. 1988. *The Virginia Genealogical Society Newsletter,* 14 (4) (July-August).

Webster's New World Dictionary of the English Language. 1972. New York: World Publishing Co.

BIBLIOGRAPHY

Instructional Material: Probate Records

Ditz, Toby L. *Property and Kinship: Inheritance in Early Connecticut, 1750–1820.* Princeton, N.J.: Princeton University Press, 1986.

Dorman, John Frederick. "Colonial Laws of Primogeniture." I-12. World Conference on Records. Salt Lake City: Genealogical Society of Utah, 1969.

Dructor, Robert M. *Guide to Genealogical Sources At the Pennsylvania State Archives.* Harrisburg: Pennsylvania Historical and Museum Commission, 1988.

Greenwood, Val D. *The Researcher's Guide to American Genealogy.* 2nd ed. Baltimore: Genealogical Publishing Co., 1990.

Jacobus, Donald Lines. "Probate Law and Custom." *American Genealogist* 9 (1932): 4–9.

Leary, Helen F. M. *North Carolina Research: Genealogy and Local History.* 2nd ed. Raleigh: North Carolina Genealogical Society, 1996.

Rubincam, Milton, ed. *Genealogical Research Methods and Sources.* Washington, D.C.: American Society of Genealogists, 1960.

Salmon, Marylynn. *Women and the Law of Property in Early America.* Chapel Hill: University of North Carolina Press, 1986.

Shammas, Carole, Marylynn Salmon, and Michel Dahlin. *Inheritance in America: From Colonial Times to the Present.* New Brunswick: Rutgers University Press, 1987.

Speth, Linda E. "More Than Her 'Thirds': Wives and Widows in Colonial Virginia." *Women, Family, and Community in Colonial America*, edited by Linda E. Speth and Alison Duncan Hirsch. New York: Institute for Research in History and the Haworth Press, 1983.

Stevenson, Noel C. *Search and Research: The Researcher's Handbook.* Rev. ed. N.p., 1959.

Szucs, Lorretto D., and Sandra H. Luebking, eds. *The Source: A Guidebook of American Genealogy.* Rev. ed. Salt Lake City: Ancestry, 1997.

Ward, Barbara McLean. "Women's Property and Family Continuity in Eighteenth Century Connecticut." In *Early American Probate Inventories*. The Dublin Seminar for New England Folklife Annual Proceedings 1987. Edited by Peter Benes. Boston University, 1989.

Wright, Norman Edgar. *Building an American Pedigree: A Study in Genealogy.* Provo, Utah: Brigham Young University Press, 1974.

Instructional Material: Court Records

Abraham, Henry J. *Courts and Judges: An Introduction to the Judicial Process.* New York: Oxford University Press, 1962.

Callender, Clarence N. *American Courts: Their Organization and Procedures.* New York: McGraw-Hill Book Co., 1927.

Chapin, Bradley. *Criminal Justice in Colonial America, 1606–1660.* Athens: University of Georgia Press, 1983.

Ford, Jeanette W. "Federal Law Comes to Indian Territory." *Chronicles of Oklahoma* 57 (4) (Winter 1980–81). Discusses the historical development of the court system in Oklahoma and describes records contained under the various court jurisdictions.

Klein, Fannie J. *Federal and State Court Systems: A Guide.* Cambridge: Ballinger Publishers, 1977.

Pound, Roscoe. *Organization of Courts.* Boston: Little, Brown, and Co., 1940.

Zimmerman, Joseph F. *State and Local Government.* New York: Barnes and Noble, 1962.

Reference Works

Black, Henry Campbell. *Black's Law Dictionary: Definitions of the Terms and Phrases of American and English Jurisprudence, Ancient and Modern.* 6th ed. Centennial Edition, 1891–1991. St. Paul, Minn.: West Publishing Co., 1990.

Burton, William C. *Legal Thesaurus.* New York: Macmillan Co., 1981.

Friedman, Lawrence M. *A History of American Law.* 2nd ed. New York: Touchstone Book, Simon & Schuster, 1985.

Gifis, Steven H. *Law Dictionary.* Woodbury, N.Y.: Barron's Educational Series, 1975.

Hall, Kermit L., William M. Wiecek, and Paul Finkelman. *American Legal History: Cases and Materials.* New York and Oxford, England: Oxford University Press, 1991.

Miller, Charles A. *Official and Political Manual of the State of Tennessee.* 1890. Reprint. Spartanburg, S.C.: Reprint Co., Publishers, 1974.

Winfree, Waverly K., comp. *The Laws of Virginia: Being a Supplement to Hening's The Statutes at Large 1700–1750.* With an editorial note by Randolph W. Church. Richmond: Virginia State Library, 1971.

Statewide and Regional Probate Records and Indexes

Included in this listing are statewide indexes as well as significant indexes and abstracts of probate records for parts of states, such as early counties covering larger regions or districts.

Alabama

Alabama Society, Daughters of the American Revolution. *Index to Alabama Wills 1808–1870.* Ann Arbor, Mich.: Edwards Brothers, 1955. Reprint. Baltimore: Genealogical Publishing Co., 1977. Includes all known wills—approximately nine thousand entries.

England, Flora Dainwood, comp. *Alabama Notes.* 4 vols in 2. Baltimore: Genealogical Publishing Co., 1977. Includes vital, genealogy, probate, and land and property records.

Arkansas

Stevenson, Mrs. James Harold, and Mrs. Edward Lynn Westbrooke, comps. and eds. *Index to Wills and Administrations of Arkansas from the Earliest to 1900.* Jonesboro, Ark.: Vowels Printing Co., 1986. Arranged by county without a comprehensive index. The researcher must review the list of wills and administrations for each county to identify all entries for the appropriate surname. Covers period of 1830s to 1900.

Colorado

Ella Ruland MacDougall. *Abstracts of Early Probate Records.* N.p., n.d. Lists early Denver probates.

Connecticut

Manwaring, Charles William, comp. *A Digest of the Early Connecticut Probate Records.* Hartford, Conn.: R. S. Peck & Co., 1904–06. Hartford District, 1635 to 1750, in three volumes.

The Public Records of the Colony of Connecticut (1636–1775). 15 vols. Vols. 1–3 edited by J. H. Trumbull; vols. 4–15 edited by C. J. Hoadly. Hartford, Conn.: Case, Lockwood & Brainard Co., 1850–90.

The Public Records of the State of Connecticut (1776–1792). 7 vols. Hartford, Conn.: Lockwood & Brainard, 1894–1948.

Ullman, Helen S. *Nutmegger Index: An Index to Non-Alphabetical Articles and a Subject Index to The Connecticut*

Nutmegger Volumes 1–28, 1968–1996. Rockport, Maine: Picton Press and Connecticut State Society of Genealogists, 1996.

Delaware

deValinger, Leon, Jr. *Calendar of Kent County, Delaware, Probate Records, 1680–1850.* Dover, Del.: Public Archives Commission, 1944. Contains approximately six thousand entries.

_____. *Calendar of Sussex County, Delaware, Probate Records, 1680–1800.* Dover, Del.: Public Archives Commission, 1964. Contains approximately 2,100 entries.

Historical Research Committee. Delaware Society of the Colonial Dames of America. *A Calendar of Wills, New Castle County, 1682–1800.* New York: 1911. Reprint. Baltimore: Genealogical Publishing Co., 1969. Contains approximately 1,700 entries.

Virdin, Donald O. *Colonial Delaware Wills and Estates to 1880: An Index.* Bowie, Md.: Heritage Books, 1994.

District of Columbia

Bell, Mrs. Alexander H. *Abstracts of Wills in the District of Columbia, 1776–1815.* 2 vols. Washington, D.C.: the author, 1946. Contains approximately four hundred abstracts.

Provine, Dorothy S. *Index to District of Columbia Wills.* Baltimore: Genealogical Publishing Co., 1992. Provides name, year, and box number.

Florida

General Index to Probate Related, Dade County, Florida. Photocopy. Salt Lake City: Genealogical Society of Utah, 1986. Comprises four volumes up to 1982.

Index to the Archives of Spanish West Florida, 1782–1810. With an introduction by Stanley Clisby Arthur. New Orleans: Polyanthos, 1975.

Georgia

Abstracts of Colonial Wills of the State of Georgia, 1733–1778. 1962. Reprint. Spartanburg, S.C.: Reprint Co., 1981. Contains approximately four hundred abstracts.

Austin, Jeannette Holland. *Index to Georgia Wills.* 2nd ed. Baltimore: Genealogical Publishing Co., 1985. Originally published in 1976 by Jeannette Holland McCall. Indexes approximately seventeen thousand wills to the mid-1800s, but only for those counties created before the 1832 land lottery.

Austin, Jeannette Holland. *Georgia Intestate Records.* Baltimore: Genealogical Publishing Co., 1986. Contains "abstracts of the intestate records of fifty-seven Georgia counties formed before the 1832 Land Lottery." Although the volume does not include wills and is not comprehensive for all Georgia counties, it is indispensable. Arranged alphabetically by surname, it includes ten thousand abstracts and has a helpful foreword, a table of sources arranged in alphabetical order by county name (more than one source was used for most counties), a key to abbreviations, and an every-name index.

Brooke, Ted O. *In the Name of God, Amen: Georgia Wills, 1733–1860: An Index.* Atlanta: Pilgrim Press, 1976. Complements Austin's work (see above). Includes only wills—approximately 14,500.

Early Georgia Wills. Salt Lake City: American Heritage Research, ca. 1976. Contains indexes to original will books in each county.

Index to Probate Records of Colonial Georgia, 1735–1778. Atlanta: R. J. Taylor, Jr. Foundation, ca. 1983. Indexes records available at the Georgia Department of Archives and History in original manuscript or microfilm copies. Other records cited are located in manuscript form at the University of Georgia libraries.

Index to Probate Records of Colonial Georgia, 1733–1778. Atlanta: R. J. Taylor, Jr., Foundation, 1983.

Holcomb, Brent H. *Spartanburg County, South Carolina Will Abstracts 1787–1840.* Columbia, S.C.: the compiler, ca. 1983.

Illinois

Edgar, Jim. *Illinois Probate Act and Related Laws, Effective January 5, 1988.* Rev. St. Paul, Minn.: West Publishing Co., 1988.

Illinois. Probate Court (St. Clair County). *Wills, 1772–1800.* Springfield, Ill.: Office of the Secretary of State, Micrographics Division, Source Documents Unit, 1982.

Randolph County, Illinois Probate Records, Bonds, Executors, Administrators, April 2, 1829–Aug. 5, 1835 and Abstracts of Administrations, 1844–1849 and Abstracts of Guardianships, April 2, 1833–Nov. 6, 1849. Springfield, Ill.: Wanda Warkins Allers and Eileen Lynch Gochanour, 1986.

Sapp, Peggy Lathrop. *Randolph County, Illinois, Probate Court Estate Inventories and Sales, Nov. 5, 1832–Aug. 7, 1835.* N.p., n.d.

Territory of Illinois. County Court. *Court Records, 1796–1818.* Springfield, Ill.: Office of the Secretary of State, Micrographics Division, Source Documents Unit, 1986. Includes an index and guardian- and probate-related records.

Indiana

Dorrel, Ruth. "Lagrange County, Indiana Will Abstracts, 1842–49." *Hoosier Genealogist* 32 (1): 28–33 (March 1992).

Franklin, Charles M. *Index to Indiana Wills: Phase 1, Through 1850* and *Phase 2, 1850 Through 1880.* 2 vols. Indianapolis: Heritage House, 1986–87. Indexes thirty-three thousand wills between the two volumes. Contains surname index to wills by county, year, book, and page.

Indiana Source Book: Genealogical Material from The Hoosier Genealogist, 1979–1981. Indianapolis: Indiana Historical Society, 1987.

Kentucky

Cook, Michael L. *Virginia Supreme Court District of Kentucky: Order Books, 1783–1792.* Evansville, Ind.: Cook Publications, 1988.

Davis, Virginia. "McLean County Administrators Bonds—1867–1800." *Bluegrass Roots* 18 (1): 13–20 (Spring 1991).

Jackson, Ronald Vern. *Index to Kentucky Wills to 1851, the Testators.* Bountiful, Utah: Accelerated Indexing Systems, 1977. Identifies approximately 21,800 wills.

King, Junie Estelle Stewart. *Abstract [sic] of Early Kentucky Wills and Inventories.* 1933. Reprint. Baltimore: Genealogical Publishing Co., 1969.

Louisiana

Daughters of the American Revolution. Louisiana. Genealogical Records Committee. *Early Court Records and Wills.* Typescript. 1967–68. Includes an index and incudes wills, marriages, land grants, etc.

Maine

Anderson, Joseph Crook, II. *York County, Maine Will Abstracts*

1801–1858. Maine Genealogical Society Special Publication no. 27. 2 vols. Rockport, Me.: Picton Press, 1997.

Frost, John Eldridge. *Maine Probate Abstracts.* Vol. 1, 1687–1775; vol. 2, 1775–1800. Rockport, Maine: Picton Press, 1991. Indexes names, subjects, places, and occupations.

Sargent, William M. *Maine Wills, 1640–1760.* 1887. Reprint. Baltimore: Genealogical Publishing Co., 1972.

Maryland

Cotton, Jane Baldwin. *Index to Wills of the Colonial Period, Books 1–41, 1634–1777.* Annapolis: Hall of Records Commission, 1947. Original typescript at Hall of Records, Annapolis, Maryland.

Cotton, Jane Baldwin. *The Maryland Calendar of Wills: From 1635 to 1743.* 8 vols. 1904–28. Reprint. Baltimore: Genealogical Publishing Co., 1968.

Magruder, James Mosby. *Magruder's Maryland Colonial Abstracts, Wills, Accounts and Inventories, 1772–1777.* 1934–39. Reprint. 5 vols. in 1. Baltimore: Genealogical Publishing Co., 1968. An index to colonial wills contained in the Prerogative Court records as wills, Libers 1041 in the Hall of Records in Annapolis.

Magruder, James M., Jr. *Index of Maryland Colonial Wills, 1634–1777.* 1933. Reprint. Baltimore: Genealogical Publishing Co., 1967. Indexes approximately sixteen thousand names.

Maryland. Provincial Court. *Judicial and Testamentary Business of the Provincial Court: 1637–1683.* Edited by William Hand Browne. Archives of Maryland. Court Series, vols. 1–4, 8, 10–15. Baltimore: Maryland Historical Society, 1887–1964. The title varies: vols. 49–70, *Proceedings of the Provincial Court of Maryland.*

Skinner, Vernon L. *Abstracts of the Inventories of the Prerogative Court of Maryland.* Westminster, Md.: Family Line Publications, 1988–91. Abstracts 1720 to 1777 in seventeen volumes.

_____. *Abstracts of the Inventories and Accounts of the Prerogative Court of Maryland.* Westminster, Md.: Family Line Publications, 1988–91. Abstracts 1674 to 1718 in twelve volumes.

Wright, F. Edward. *Maryland Calendar of Wills: From 1744 – 1779.* 8 vols. numbered 9 through 16. Westminster, Md.: Family Line Publications., 1988.

Massachusetts

Busiel, Alice. *Miscellaneous Index and Records (1659–1692) Prior to the Appointment of a Judge of Probate in 1692.* N.p, n.d.

Dolan, Arthur W. *Index to the Probate Records of the County of Suffolk, Massachusetts, from the Year 1894 to and including the Year 1909.* 2 vols. Boston: Printing Department, 1911–13.

Essex County, Massachusetts, Probate Index, 1638–1840. Transcribed by Melinde Lutz Sanborn from the original by W. P. Upham. 2 vols. Boston: Sanborn, 1987.

George, Elijah. *Index to the Probate Records of the County of Suffolk, Massachusetts, from the Year 1636 to and including the Year 1893.* 3 vols. Boston: Rockwell and Churchill, 1895.

Index to the probate records of the County of Worcester, Massachusetts, from July 12, 1731, to January 1, 1920: Series A and B. 5 vols. Worcester, Mass.: Oliver B. Wood, 1898.

Massachusetts. Probate Court (Middlesex County). *Index to the Probate Records of the County of Middlesex, Massachusetts: First Series, from 1648 to 1871.* Cambridge, Mass., 1914.

_____. *Index to the Probate Records of the County of Middlesex, Massachusetts: Second Series.* 8 vols. Cambridge, Mass., 1912–53. Covers 31 December 1870 to 31 December 1949.

Mayflower Source Records: Primary Data Concerning Southeastern Massachusetts, Cape Cod, and the Islands of Nantucket and Martha's Vineyard. Selected and introduced by Gary Boyd Roberts. Baltimore: Genealogical Publishing Co., 1986.

Pease, Janet K. (Janet Kathleen). *Worcester County, Massachusetts Probate Abstracts, 1748–1751.* N.p., 1979.

Probate Index, Norfolk County, Massachusetts, 1793–1900. 2 vols. Dedham, Mass.: Transcript Press, 1910.

Probate Records of Essex County, Massachusetts. 3 vols. Salem, Mass.: Essex Institute, 1916–20. Reprint. Newburyport, Mass.: Parker River Researchers, and Decorah, Iowa: Anundsen Pub., 1988. Covers 1635 to 1681.

Pulsifer, David. *Deeds, Wills, Inventories, etc. 1647–1714: Records of the County of Norfolk, in the Colony of Massachusetts.* Salem, Mass., n.d.

Roser, Susan E. *Mayflower Deeds and Probates: From the Files of George Ernest Bowman at the Massachusetts Society of Mayflower Descendants.* Baltimore: Genealogical Publishing Co., 1994.

Rounds, H. L. Peter. *Abstracts of Bristol County, Massachusetts, Probate Records.* 2 vols. Baltimore: Genealogical Publishing Co., 1987.

Sherman, Ruth Wilder, and Robert S. Wakefield. *Plymouth Colony Probate Guide: Where to Find Wills and Related Data for 800 People of Plymouth Colony, 1620–1691.* Warwick, R.I.: Plymouth Colony Research Group, 1983.

Simmons, C. H., Jr., ed. *Plymouth Colony Records.* Camden, Maine: Picton Press, 1996. Contains wills and inventories for 1633 to 1669.

Sullivan, Arthur W. *Index to the Probate Records of the County of Suffolk, Massachusetts, from the Year 1910 to and including the Year 1922.* 2 vols. Boston: Printing Dept., 1927.

Suffolk County Wills: Abstracts of the Earliest Wills Upon Record in the County of Suffolk, Massachusetts. Baltimore: Genealogical Publishing Co., 1984.

Wood, Ralph V., Jr.. *Plymouth County Massachusetts, Probate Index 1686–1881.* Camden, Maine: Picton Press, 1988.

Mississippi

Hendrix, Mary L. *Mississippi Court Records: From the Files of the High Court of Errors and Appeals, 1799–1859.* Jackson, Miss., n.d. Contains some probate records.

King, J. Estelle. *Mississippi Court Records.* 1936. Reprint. Baltimore: Genealogical Publishing Co., 1969. Covers five counties (Adams, Amite, Claiborne, Hinds, and Warren) for 1799 to 1835.

Wiltshire, Betty Couch, comp. *Mississippi Index of Wills, 1800–1900.* Bowie, Md.: Heritage Books, 1989. Lists more than ten thousand wills found in probate, marriage, and inventory books as well as other unusual places.

Missouri

Northwest Missouri Genealogical Society. *Gentry County, Mis-*

souri Probate Index, 1885–1902. St. Joseph, Mo.: the society, n.d.

New Hampshire

Index to Probate Records in New Hampshire, Counties of Rockingham, Cheshire, Strafford, Grafton (and) Hillsborough. N.p., n.d. Covers Rockingham County, 1753 to 1800, and all other counties, 1769 to 1800.

Probate Records of the Province of New Hampshire. Vols. 31–39 of *New Hampshire Provincial and State Papers.* Concord, N.H.: State Printer, 1867–1943. Reprint. 9 vols. in 12. Bowie, Md.: Heritage Books, 1989–90. Abstracts approximately 4,200 probate records from 1635 to 1771.

New Jersey

Index to Wills, Inventories, Etc. in the Office of the Secretary of State Prior to 1901. 3 vols. 1912. Reprinted as *New Jersey Index to Wills.* Baltimore: Genealogical Publishing Co., 1969. Indexes probates to 1901. Most county records begin with 1705 except Salem, for which records are included from 1679.

Index to Wills, Office of Secretary of State, State of New Jersey, 1804 to 1830. Trenton, N.J.: John L. Murphy Publishing Co., 1901.

Smeal, Lee, and Ronald Vern Jackson. *Index to New Jersey Wills, 1689–1890, The Testators.* Salt Lake City: Accelerated Indexing Systems, 1979. As a single alphabetical sequence this work is easy to use, but it often gives only partial source citations.

New York

Barber, Gertrude Audrey. *Index to Letters of Administration of New York County from 1743–1875.* 6 vols. New York: the compiler, 1950–51.

Cook, William Burt. *Abstracts of Albany Co., N.Y. Probate and Family Records.* Washington, D.C.: Library of the National Society of the Daughters of the American Revolution, 1930.

Fernow, Berthold, comp. *Calendar of Wills on File and Recorded in the Offices of the Clerk of the Court of Appeals, of the County Clerk at Albany, and the Secretary of State, 1626–1836.* New York: Colonial Dames of the State of New York, 1896. Reprint. Baltimore: Genealogical Publishing Co., 1967. Abstracts 2,165 wills.

Pelletreau, William Smith, ed., and Robert H. Kelby, indexer. *Abstracts of Wills on File in the Surrogate's Office, City of New York, 1665–1801.* Vols. 25–41 in the collection of the New York Historical Society. New York: New York Historical Society, 1892–1909. Abstracts approximately fifteen thousand wills and more than ten thousand intestate files.

Sawyer, Ray C., comp. and ed. *Index of Wills for New York County, 1662–1875.* 6 vols. New York: the compiler, 1930–51.

Scott, Kenneth, and James A. Owre, eds. *Genealogical Data from Inventories of New York Estates, 1666–1825.* New York: New York Genealogical and Biographical Society, 1970.

_____, ed. *Genealogical Data from New York Administration Bonds, 1753–1799.* Collections of the New York Genealogical and Biographical Society, vol. 10. New York, 1969.

_____. *Genealogical Data from Further New York Administration Bonds, 1791–1798.* New York Genealogical and Biographical Society Collections, vol. 11. New York, 1971.

Wiles, Harriett M. *Abstracts of Wills of Ontario County, New York: in the Courthouse, Canadaigus* [sic], *N.Y., 1794–1834.* N.p., 1971.

Worden, Mrs. Jean D., comp. *The New York Genealogical and Biographical Record: 113 Years Master Index, 1870–1982.* Franklin, Ohio: the author, ca. 1983.

North Carolina

Bennett, William Doub. *North Carolina Genealogical Society Journal 1975–1984: Consolidated Index.* Baltimore: Clearfield Co., 1997.

Grimes, J. Bryan. *Abstract of North Carolina Wills: Compiled from Original and Recorded Wills in the Office of the Secretary of State.* 1910. Reprint. Baltimore: Genealogical Publishing Co., 1981.

Haun, Weynette Parks. *Craven Precinct-County North Carolina Court Minutes, 1730 thru 1741, Book II,* Durham, N.C.: by author, ca. 1981.

Mitchell, Thornton W. *North Carolina Wills: A Testator Index, 1665–1900.* Baltimore: Genealogical Publishing Co., 1987. Reprint. Corrected, rev., and enl. in 1 vol. Baltimore: Genealogical Publishing Co., 1992. An index with approximately seventy-five thousand entries; includes data for all counties within the state; provides reference to location of original records.

Olds, Fred A. *An Abstract of North Carolina Wills from about 1760 to about 1800: Supplementing Grimes' Abstract of North Carolina Wills, 1663–1760.* 2nd ed. Southern Book Co., 1954. Reprint. Baltimore: Genealogical Publishing Co., 1978. Arranged by county without an index; the researcher must review the list of wills in each county to identify all entries for the appropriate surname. Limited to only forty years.

Ohio

Bell, Carol Willsey. *Ohio Wills and Estates to 1850: An Index.* Youngstown, Ohio: Bell Books, 1981. A statewide index that identifies approximately sixty-four thousand probates.

Loveless, Richard William. *Records of the District of West Augusta, Ohio County, and Yohogania County, Virginia: District of West Augusta, Minutes of the Court (1775–1776), Deeds (1775–1776); Ohio County, Minutes of the Court (1777–1780); Yohogania County, Minutes of the Court (1776–1780), Wills (1776–1780).* Columbus, Ohio: State University Printing Dept., 1970.

Oklahoma

Wever, Orpha Jewell. *Probate Records, 1892–1908, Northern District Cherokee Nation.* 2 vols. Vinita: Northeast Oklahoma Genealogical Society, 1982–83. Includes names of non-natives, freedmen, and natives who filed probate in the U.S. Federal Court.

Oregon

Brown, Lloyd, and Wythle Brown. *Genealogical Index to the Clackamas County, Oregon, Probate Records from 1845 to 1910 Inclusive.* Oregon City, Oreg.: Mt. Hood Genealogical Forum of Clackamas Co., 1974.

Reiner, Mary Hedges. *Early Oregon Wills, Multnomah County, 1884–1887.* Vol. 3. N.p., 1953.

_____. *Probated Intestate Estates: Early Oregon, Multnomah County, 1884–1887, with a Few as Early as 1852.* N.p., 1953.

Wade, Daraleen Phillips, comp. *Genealogical Abstracts of the First 2500 Probate Records in Marion County, Oregon.* Salem, Oreg. : Willamette Valley Genealogical Society, 1985.

Pennsylvania

Anderson, Bart, et al. *Index to Chester County, Pennsylvania, Wills and Intestate Records, 1713–1850.* Danboro, Pa.: Richard T. and Mildred C. Williams, 1970.

Closson, Bob, and Mary Closson, et al. The Clossons have produced a series of county volumes with titles: *Index to* [county name], *Pennsylvania Wills,* [dates]. Apollo, Pa.: Closson Press, 1979–93.

The series includes:

Armstrong County, Pennsylvania Wills, 1805–1900

Beaver County, Pennsylvania Wills, 1800–1900

Bedford County, Pennsylvania Wills, 1771–1900

Butler County, Pennsylvania Wills, 1800–1900

Cambria County, Pennsylvania Wills, 1804–1900

Fayette County, Pennsylvania Wills, 1783–1900

Fulton County, Pennsylvania Wills, 1850–1900

Greene County, Pennsylvania Wills, 1796–1900

Indiana County, Pennsylvania Wills, 1803–1900

Jefferson County, Pennsylvania Wills, 1852–1906

Mercer County, Pennsylvania Wills, 1804–1900

Northampton County, Pennsylvania Wills, 1752–1802

Somerset County, Pennsylvania Wills, 1795–1900

Washington County, Pennsylvania Wills, 1781–1900

Westmoreland County, Pennsylvania Wills, 1773–1896

York County, Pennsylvania Wills, 1749–1900

Gilbert, Russell Wieder. *Pennsylvania German Wills.* Vol. 15 in *Pennsylvania German Folklore Society.* Allentown, Pa.: Pennsylvania German Folklore Society, 1950.

Lapp, Dorothy B. *"Entries of the Orphans Court" of Chester County, Pennsylvania, 1716–1730, 1732–1734.* Danboro, Pa.: Richard T. and Mildred C. Williams, 1973.

_____, and Frances B. Dunlap. *Orphans Court Minutes, Chester County, Pennsylvania, 1734–1746/7.* Danboro, Pa.: Richard T. and Mildred C. Williams, 1974.

_____. *Records of the Orphans Court for Chester County, Pennsylvania, 1747–1761.* Danboro, Pa.: Richard T. and Mildred C. Williams, 1975.

Martin, Jacob. *Abstract of Wills of Chester County, Pennsylvania.* Indexed by Gilbert Cope. 4 vols. N.p., 1900–01. Covers 1714 to 1825.

Pennsylvania Wills Recorded in New Jersey: Researched and Reprinted from the New Jersey Archives. Newtown, Pa.: Will-Britt Books, 1987.

Smith, Frances Schive. *Abstracts from Benjamin Franklin's Pennsylvania Gazette, April 17, 1755 to December 27, 1764.* 3 vols. Magnolia, N.J.: A.W. Smith, 1990. Covers 17 April 1755 to 29 January 1767.

Williams, Richard T., and Mildred C. Williams. *Index of Bucks County, Pennsylvania Wills and Administration Records, 1684–1850.* Danboro, Pa.: Richard T. Williams, 1971.

_____. *Index of Wills and Administration Records, Berks County, Pennsylvania, 1752–1850.* Danboro, Pa.: the authors, 1973.

_____. *Index to Wills and Administration Records, Philadelphia, Pennsylvania, 1682–1850.* 4 vols. Danboro, Pa.: Richard T. Williams, 1971–72.

Rhode Island

Beaman, Nellie M. C. *Index of Wills, 1636–1850.* Vol. 16 in *Rhode Island Genealogical Register.* New Series. Princeton, Mass.: Rhode Island Families Association, 1992. Indexes all 12,900 Rhode Island wills for this period (abstracts for which appeared in earlier volumes of the *Register*).

Field, Edward, ed. *Index to the Probate Records of the Municipal Court of the City of Providence, Rhode Island: From 1646 to and including the Year 1899.* Providence, R.I.: Providence Press, 1902.

Wakefield, Robert S. *Index to Wills in Rhode Island Genealogical Register, Volumes 1 through 4.* Warwick, R.I.: Plymouth Colony Research Group, 1982.

South Carolina

Holcomb, Brent H. *Probate Records of South Carolina.* 3 vols. Easley, S.C.: Southern Historical Press, 1977. Fully indexed, this work contains records from 1746 to 1821.

Houston, Martha Lou, comp. *Indexes to the County Wills of South Carolina.* 1939. Reprint. Baltimore: Genealogical Publishing Co., 1964. Indexes most pre-1860 wills, but does not include Charleston County.

Moore, Carolina T., and Agatha Aimar Simmons. *Abstracts of the Wills of the State of South Carolina.* 3 vols. Columbia, S.C.: the compilers, 1960–69. Includes records for 1670 to 1784.

Young, Willie Pauline. *A Genealogical Collection of South Carolina Wills and Records.* 2 vols. 1955. Reprint. Easley, S.C.: Southern Historical Press, 1981.

Tennessee

Fischer, Marjorie Hood. *Tennessee Tidbits, 1778–1914.* Vol. 1. Easley, S.C.: Southern Historical Press, 1986. Contains abstracts of court records for fifteen counties for 1778 to 1914.

_____, and Ruth Blake Burns. *Tennessee Tidbits, 1778–1914.* Vol. 2. Vista, Calif.: Ram Press, 1988. Contains abstracted court records for Bedford, Claiborne, Dyer, Fentress, Jackson, Madison, McMinn, Obion, Roane, Robertson, Sevier, Stewart, Washington, and Wilson counties.

_____. *Tennessee Tidbits, 1778–1914.* Vol. 3. Vista, Calif.: RAM Press, 1989. Third volume in a series with genealogical information abstracted primarily from court minutes. Contains abstracts for the counties of Anderson, Bradley, Carroll, Decatur, Grainger, Johnson, Macon, Marion, Monroe, Rhea, Warren, and Tipton.

Partlow, Thomas E. *Wilson County, Tennessee: Genealogical Resource Material, 1827–1869.* Greenville, S.C.: Southern Historical Press, 1997.

Phillips, Judy Henley, and Betty Moore Majors. "Coffee County, Tennessee County Court Loose Papers." *Coffee County Historical Quarterly* 22 (1993).

Sistler, Byron, and Barbara Sistler. *Index to Tennessee Wills and Administrations, 1779–1861.* Nashville, Tenn.: Byron Sistler & Associates, 1990. Indexes wills from 1779 to 1861 statewide, but no administrations are listed for thirteen counties.

Wells, Carol. *Abstracts of Giles County, Tennessee: County Court Minutes, 1813–1816 and Circuit Court Minutes, 1810–1816.* Bowie, Md.: Heritage Books, 1995.

Whitley, Edythe Whitley. *Tennessee Genealogical Records: Records of Early Settlers from State and County Archives.* Baltimore: Genealogical Publishing Co., 1981. Includes indexes or abstracts of wills for Carter, Davidson, Henry, Jefferson, and Smith counties.

Texas

Index to Probate Cases of Texas. 1940. Reprint. San Antonio: Bureau of Research in the Social Sciences, University of Texas, 1980. Compiled by the Work Projects Administration for thirty-one counties.

Virginia

Adams, Lela C. *Abstracts of Pittsylvania County, Virginia Wills, 1767–1820.* Easley, S.C.: Southern Historical Press, 1986.

_____. *Henry County, Virginia, Will Abstracts, Vol. I and II, 1777–1820.* Easley, S.C.: Southern Historical Press, 1985.

Bell, Landon Covington. *Lunenburg County, Virginia Wills, 1746–1825.* Berryville, Va.: Virginia Book Co., 1972.

Boogher, William F., Esq. *Overwharton Parish Register, 1720–1760.* N.p., n.d.

Brunswick County, Virginia Wills. Miami Beach, Fla.: T.L.C. Genealogy, 1991.

Chiarito, Marian Dodson. *Will Book O, 1752–1773, Halifax County, Virginia.* Nathalie, Va.: Clarkton Press, 1982.

_____. *Will Books, Halifax County, Virginia.* 2 vols. Nathalie, Va.: Clarkton Press, 1984.

Clemens, William Montgomery, comp. *Virginia Wills Before 1799: A Complete Abstract Register of All Names Mentioned in Over Six Hundred Recorded Wills. . . .* Pompton Lakes, N.J.: Biblio Co., 1924.

Cocke, William Ronald, 3rd. *Hanover County Chancery Wills and Notes: A Compendium of Genealogical, Biographical and Historical Material as Contained in Cases of the Chancery Suits of Hanover County, Virginia.* 1940. Reprint. Baltimore: Genealogical Publishing Co., 1978.

Currier-Briggs, Noel. *Virginia Settlers and English Adventurers: Abstracts of Wills, 1484–1798, and Legal Proceedings, 1560–1700, Relating to Early Virginia Families.* 3 vols. Baltimore: Genealogical Publishing Co., 1970.

Davis, Eliza Timberlake. *Wills and Administrations of Surry County, Virginia, 1671–1750.* Baltimore: Genealogical Publishing Co., 1980.

Davis, Rosalie Edith, comp. *Hanover County, Virginia, Court Records, 1733–1735: Deeds, Wills, and Inventories.* Manchester, Mo.: Heritage Trails, 1979.

Elliott, Katherine Blackwell, comp. *Early Wills, 1746–1765, Lunenburg County, Virginia.* South Hill, Va.: the compiler, 1967.

Evans, June Banks. *Lunenburg County, Virginia Will Books.* 3 vols. New Orleans: Bryn Ffyliaid Publications, 1991.

Hart, Lyndon Hobbs. *Surry County, Virginia, Wills, Estate Accounts and Inventories, 1730–1800.* Easley, S.C.: Southern Historical Press, 1983.

Haun, Weynette Parks. *Surry County, Virginia Court Records (Deed Book 1), 1664 thru 1671.* Durham, N.C.: the compiler, 1988.

Hopkins, William Lindsay. *Surry County, Virginia Deeds 1684–1733 and Other Court Papers.* 3 vols. Richmond, Va.: the compiler, 1991–92.

Hughes, Thomas P., and Jewel B. Standefer. *Pittsylvania County, Virginia, Abstracts of Wills, 1768–1800.* Memphis, Tenn.: T. P. Hughes, 1973.

Oliver, Harold, comp. and ed. *Virginia in the 1600's: An Index to Who Was There!—and Where!* Riverside, Calif:: D & H Publishing Co., 1992.

The Register of Overwharton Parish, Stafford County, Virginia 1723–1758 and Sundry Historical and Genealogical Notes. Compiled by George Harrison Sanford King. 1961. Reprint. Easley, S.C.: Southern Historical Press, 1986.

Summers, Lewis Preston. *Annals of Southwest Virginia, 1769–1800.* 1929. Reprint. 1970, 1976. 1 vol. in two parts. Baltimore: Genealogical Publishing Co., 1996.

Torrence, Clayton, comp. *Virginia Wills and Administrations 1632–1800: An Index of Wills Recorded in Local Courts of Virginia, 1632–1800, and of Administrations on Estates Shown by Inventories of the Estates of Intestates Recorded in Will (and Other) Books of Local Courts, 1632–1800.* 1931. Reprint. Baltimore: Genealogical Publishing Co., 1985. Arranged alphabetically by surname. Identifies more than fifty thousand probate actions.

Vogt, John, and T. William Kethley, Jr. *Will and Estate Records in the Virginia State Library: A Researcher's Guide.* Athens, Ga.: Iberian Publishing Co., 1987.

Weisiger, Benjamin Boisseau, comp. *Charles City County, Virginia Wills and Deeds, 1725–1731.* Richmond, Va.: the compiler, 1984.

Washington

Hagle, Charlotte Tadlock. *Cowlitz County, Washington, Probate Court Records, 1861–1907.* 7 vols. Longview, Wash.: the compiler, 1986.

West Virginia

Johnston, Ross B. *West Virginia Estate Settlements, 1753–1850: An Index to Wills, Inventories, Appraisements, Land Grants and Surveys to 1850.* Excerpted from *West Virginia History,* vols. 17–24. 1955–63. Reprint. Baltimore: Genealogical Publishing Co., 1977. Arranged by county and indexed, this work includes approximately twelve thousand probate references for the thirteen counties formed by 1800. Also see publications for Virginia.

PRINTED LAND RECORDS OVERVIEW

Key Concepts in This Chapter

- Knowing the background and history of land records is helpful to understand their use.
- Land records document ownership.
- Land records may include relationships, death and marriage dates, and important clues to other sources.
- The advantages of using printed land extracts include ease of reading and broad availability.
- Printed land extracts are good finding tools for researching specific areas.
- Often, transcribers have added historical and jurisdictional information, as well as every-name indexes.
- Limitations of printed land extracts include:

  Masking of clues through rearrangement of information

  Inaccuracies resulting from typographical errors and incorrect transcriptions

  Omissions of names or dates
- Published abstracts and finding aids cover a variety of land transfers, including:

  Bounty-land applications
  Colonial grants
  Company grants
  Confiscated lands
  County land transfers
  Deed abstracts
  Early settler lists
  Headright and proprietary grants
  Individual grants
  Land entries
  Patents
  Plat book indexes
  Private land claims
  Public domain indexes
  Quitrents
  State land lotteries
  Statewide land grants
  Town lots
  Warrant lists
- Understanding the terminology and abbreviations is necessary for success.
- Printed land records can be found at five levels: national, regional, state, county, and town.

Key Sources in This Chapter:

- *Federal Land Series*
- *American State Papers: Public Lands*
- *Grassroots of America*
- *Digested Summary and Alphabetical List of Private Claims . . .*
- *Territorial Papers of the United States*
- Bureau of Land Management (BLM) Automated Retrieval System

11

PRINTED LAND RECORDS

Wendy B. Elliott and Karen Clifford

Documentation relating to the ownership of real estate and personal property in the United States began with the earliest colonists. As Priscilla Harriss Cabell states in the introduction to *Turff and Twigg: The French Lands* (Richmond, Va.: the author, 1988), a book about the French refugee settlements in Virginia in 1700,

> . . . [the] wills and deeds within tell a story that is two hundred and eighty-eight years old. The finest homes will eventually crumble; possessions consumed in flames or otherwise lost, but the land survives and so should our knowledge of it.

Land records are important to genealogists and historians alike. If, as Donald Lines Jacobus points out, "The most important town records [in Connecticut], genealogically, are the land records" (Jacobus 1960–71 vol. 1, 129), imagine their importance in areas where few town or vital records have ever existed, such as the southern or mid-Atlantic states. Their existence alone makes land records notable among genealogical sources, and the immense quantity of the records that have survived enables unparalleled views of local conditions and events.

Whereas *The Source: A Guidebook of American Genealogy,* edited by Loretto Dennis Szucs and Sandra Hargreaves Luebking, rev. ed. (Salt Lake City: Ancestry, 1997); Val D. Greenwood's *The Researcher's Guide to American Genealogy,* 2nd ed. (Baltimore: Genealogical Publishing Co., 1990); *Genealogical Research: Methods and Sources*, edited by Milton Rubincam and Kenn Stryker-Rodda, 2 vols. (Washington, D.C.: American Society of Genealogists, 1960–71); and other genealogical texts cover the definition, role, and characteristics of land records per se, the purpose of this chapter is to discuss the unique value of printed land records to the genealogist. The background and history of these records is restricted to information researchers require to understand the use of land records in genealogical research. This chapter explains the types of information contained in printed land records, as well as their advantages and limitations. The great variety of published land abstracts or finding aids is discussed, as are the terminology and abbreviations commonly used. This section also discusses the types of historical information and variety of publications housed at the national, regional, state, county, and town levels. Finally, this chapter includes descriptions of several sources that can help researchers locate the records.

BACKGROUND AND HISTORY

Surveying Systems

The process of identifying and describing land by means of fixed points is called surveying. Ownership of land in the United States has involved several different kinds of surveying systems. Some published land records include the surveyor's description of the land, so it is useful to briefly describe the major systems used.

Metes and Bounds. Most land grants in the colonial states were measured in metes and bounds. *Metes* refers to the measurements. *Bounds* are the limits or boundaries that mark a person's real property. In the metes and bounds system, watercourses, natural features, roads, or adjacent property boundaries were used to describe the boundaries of one's land. Metes and bounds were used by all the American colonies, as well as Tennessee, Vermont, Kentucky, West Virginia, Texas, Hawaii, and parts of Ohio.

Rectangular Survey. The Rectangular Survey (or Public Lands Survey) was inaugurated with the acquisition of the Northwest Territory and an act of Congress known as the Northwest Ordinance of 1785. In this system of land measurement, land in the public domain was described based on principal meridians and base lines (figure 11-1). Land was divided by north and south lines according to the principal meridian and by other lines crossing at right angles that divided the area into townships of thirty-six square miles each. The township was subdivided into sections that usually contained 640 acres or one square mile each (figure 11-2).

Other. As early as 1604, Spain, Portugal, and Latin America began using a system of land measurement based upon a unit of measurement called a *vara*. Spanish control of areas that would eventually become the southern and southwestern United States contributed to the recording of early land records in terms of *varas*. Just as the length of one foot originally varied from person to person, a *vara* varies in length from thirty-one to forty-three inches, depending upon the locality. For instance, in Texas the standard for a *vara* was equal to 33 inches.

From the first French settlements in the sixteenth century, a measurement called an *arpent* was used in areas under French jurisdiction in America. One *arpent* is approximately equal to 85 percent of an acre. An *arpent* was also a unit for linear mea-

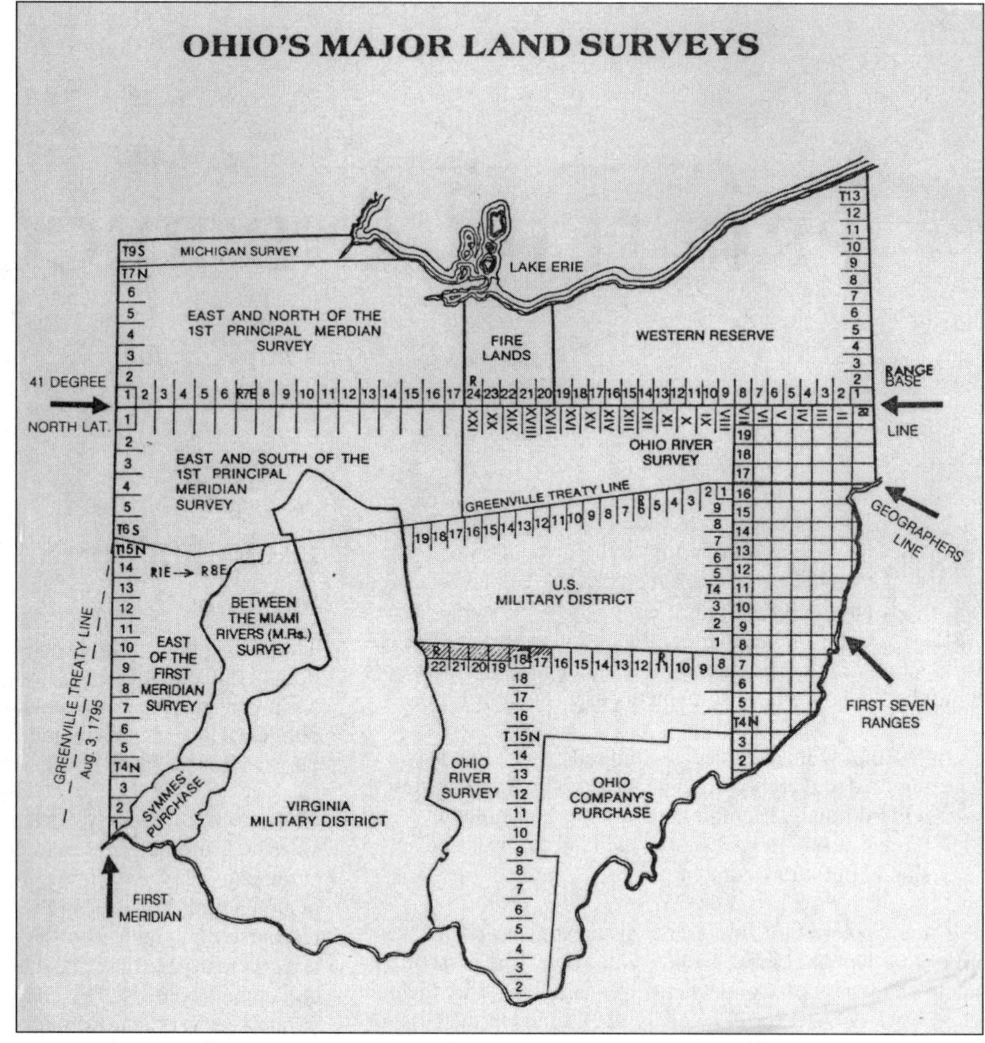

Figure 11-1. From *Ohio Lands: A Short History,* 6th ed. (Auditor's Office, State of Ohio, 1995). In the Rectangular Survey (or Public Lands Survey) system of land measurement, land in the public domain was described based on principal meridians and base lines.

surement that approximately equals 11 ½ rods or 66 ¼ yards. Regions originally under French jurisdiction did not follow customary English Common Law methods (as many other states did). For instance, French civil law was used in Louisiana records for land and property transfers. In Louisiana, land records are filed under "Conveyances," and early documents are recorded in either French or Spanish.

In Hawaii, early land rights were founded on a hierarchial basis. Rights for use were issued to individuals by the king through his local chiefs and subchiefs. When Europeans arrived and were given rights to use land, they misinterpreted these rights, assuming they had final and absolute ownership. *The Source: A Guidebook of American Genealogy* states, "in 1848, a Royal Land Commission sought to resolve the confusion and allocate permanent ownership by confirming royal patents or allocating land to the government, which then awarded grants" (Szucs and Luebking 1997, 270).

Public Domain Land

After the American Revolution, several of the former colonies claimed the same pieces of land west of the Allegheny Mountains. To resolve ownership problems and provide for orderly settlement of the frontier, the states ceded their land claims to the Federal government. This land became known as the public domain and was sold by the Federal government to individuals. The Northwest Ordinance of 1785 established the process. Land ceded by the states and purchased from Native Americans was surveyed and divided into townships and sections according to the Rectangular Survey system. Some land was reserved to be used for military bounty land, and section 16 of each township was set aside for public school lands. Remaining lands were presented for sale at auctions. The first public auction of land was held in 1787 in New York for land in western Pennsylvania. The price was one dollar per acre, and absolute title was given with all finalized land sales.

Also in 1787, Congress passed a second Northwest Ordinance. It established additional provisions and procedures regarding the distribution of public land. Among other conditions, this act stipulated that when a land owner died intestate (without a will), his widow was entitled to one-third of the land. The remaining land was divided equally among his children. Primogeniture (the right of the eldest son to inherit most or all of a parent's property) and entail (the limitation of inheritance of property to one's direct descendants; if there are none the property reverts to the estate) were abolished. This ordinance also required wills and deeds to be formally and legally recorded and proven within one year of the transaction date. Residents and nonresidents were to be taxed, but government land was not. No change in the price of land was instituted until 1796,

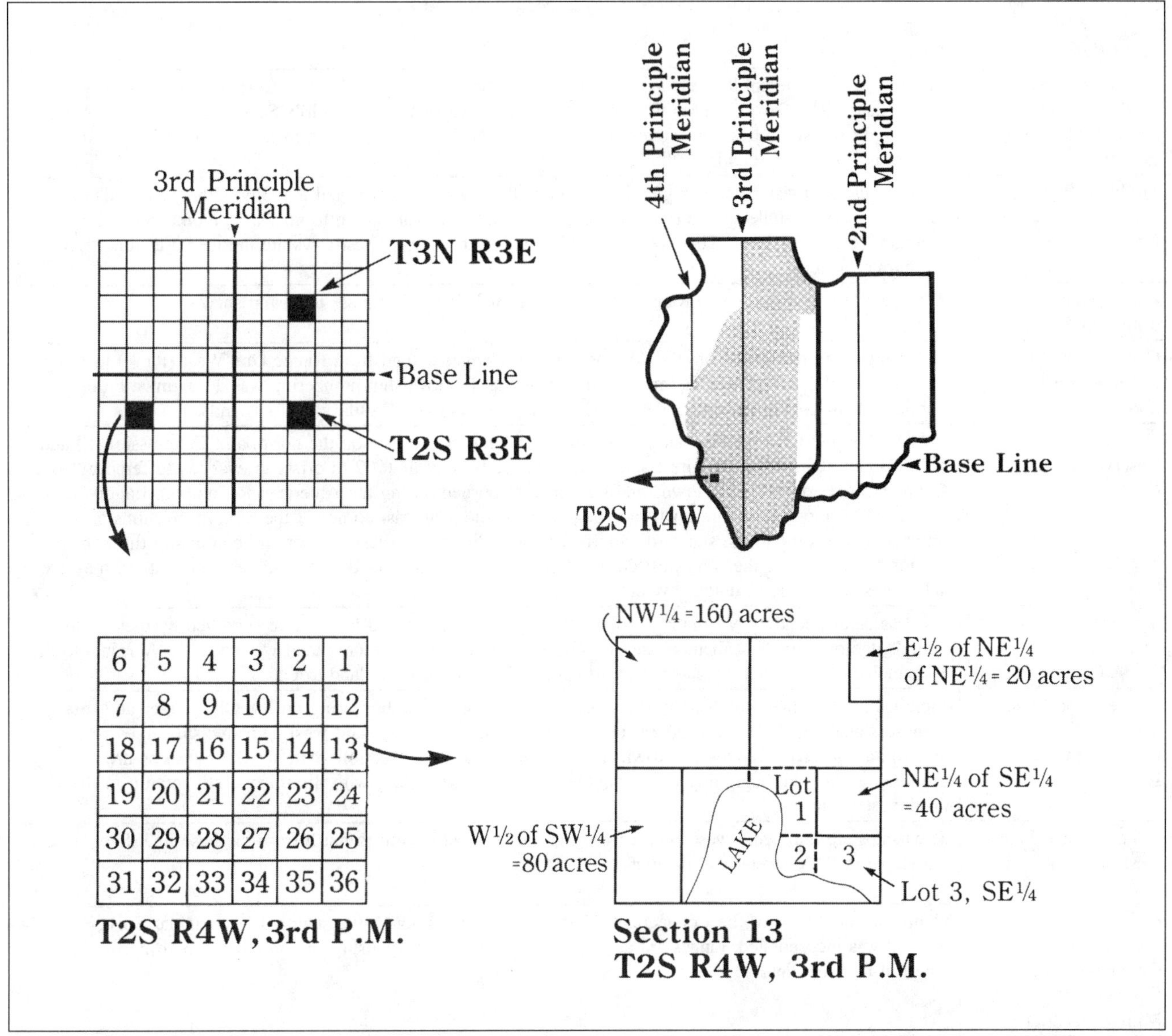

Figure 11-2. In the Rectangular Survey (or Public Lands Survey) system, land was divided by north and south lines according to the principal meridian and by other lines crossing at right angles that divided the area into townships of thirty-six square miles each. The township was subdivided into sections that usually contained 640 acres or one square mile each.

when the price of public domain land was raised to two dollars per acre.

Ohio served as the testing place for the Rectangular Survey system. Ten different measurement methods were tried, ranging from the metes and bounds used in the colonial states to the finalized Rectangular System used in public land states. Pertinent facts concerning land records in Ohio are discussed in the booklet *Ohio Lands: A Short History,* 6th ed. (Auditor's Office, State of Ohio, 1995), which was originally prepared under the direction of Thomas E. Ferguson, an early state auditor. This booklet contains maps and text that explain many issues concerning land records in Ohio (see figure 11-1). The booklet can help researchers understand the survey system(s) used in any location within the United States. A summary of these systems is provided in table 11-1. As this table shows, measurement methods vary even within states. To locate the appropriate land record repository and identify other records relating to specific properties, researchers must understand the system used in the area being studied.

Contents of Land Records

Land records serve as a major source of information for historians and genealogists alike because they often provide much more than names of the buyers and sellers and the location of the property. Land records may also list other places of residence, provide dates of the transaction and recording, and describe the parcel or lot, its price and consideration, and the circumstance of the transfer of ownership. Land records frequently include details such as relationships, approximate dates of marriage or death, previous land ownership, occupation, titles, military or community service, and other special circumstances or details. Table 11-2 summarizes the types of useful data in land records and suggests additional sources for continued research. For fur-

Table 11-1. Survey Systems of Ohio

Land Range	*Survey System*
Old Seven Ranges, southeast Ohio, south and east of Carroll County	The first area of the public domain to be surveyed. The area was divided into townships approximately six miles square. The Seven Ranges were numbered from east to west. In Ohio's Seven Ranges, townships are numbered from south to north. Township 1 North (T1N) in each range begins at the Ohio River ,which, despite its curves and bends, is the base line.
Modified Rectangular Survey, southeast Ohio	Includes the Refugee Tract, Congressional Lands, the Donation Tract, and the Ohio Company lands divided into customary six-mile-square townships that are numbered from south to north, beginning at the southern boundary, the Ohio River. Therefore, townships within the east-to-west rows are numbered differently from the current pattern.
U.S. Military District, central Ohio	The region west of the Seven Ranges. Used an unusual five-mile-square township survey.
Congressional Lands beginning in 1799 in northeast central Ohio	Townships are numbered from the Ohio River, and Ranges extend from Range One West (R1W) to Range Twenty-One West (R21W). The main difficulty is that the township numbering was a continuation of the public domain system from southeastern Ohio, skipping the U.S. Military District lands.
Connecticut's Western Reserve in northeast Ohio	Bordered by the Ohio/Pennsylvania state line on the east, Lake Erie on the north, and Congressional Land on the south, it included the Fire Lands that were established in 1792 to offset grievances suffered by some Connecticut residents whose towns and homes were burned during the American Revolution. Land was organized in five-mile-square townships beginning at the southeast corner of the reserve. Sections are numbered according to the standard pattern, beginning in the northeast corner and continuing through section twenty-five in the southwest corner. Some townships are not divided into sections; rather, they are subdivided according to unique systems.
Virginia's Military Tract	Used as bounty land by Virginia for Revolutionary War service. All tracts were surveyed by metes and bounds, the measurement method used in Virginia. Remaining ungranted land was ceded by Virginia to the U.S. in 1852; nineteen years later, the Federal government gave the land to Ohio.
Between the Miami and Little Miami rivers and the Ludlow Line	Includes the Symmes Purchase in the lower third of the region bordering on the Ohio River and the Congressional Lands in the northern portion. Range lines run east and west and township lines run north and south; therefore, ranges and townships are reversed. Also, sections within the townships are uniquely numbered, beginning in the southeast corner and ending with the thirty-sixth section in the northwest corner.
Congressional Lands west of the Miami River	Townships are numbered west to east from the meridian and south to north from the base line. Sections are numbered in the conventional manner.
Congressional Lands north of the Greenville Treaty Line and the Virginia Military District	Comprises land west of the Connecticut Western Reserve. Although the standard Rectangular Survey method was incorporated, ranges are arranged west to east and townships are numbered both north and south of the base line.
Michigan Survey region	An area five to eight miles wide between the Ohio/Michigan boundary and the Fulton Line, west of Lake Erie. It was surveyed from Michigan's principal meridian and base line.

ther insights into the use of land records in the United States, readers should examine chapter 8 of *The Source: A Guidebook of American Genealogy* (cited earlier), chapters 16 and 17 of Greenwood's *The Researcher's Guide to American Genealogy* (cited earlier), and pages 144 to 163 of *Genealogy and Computers for the Determined Researcher* (Monterey, Calif.: Genealogy Research Associates, 1992).

A typical work that provides the researcher with an overview of the distribution of land in a particular area is Thomas Lloyd Miller's *The Public Lands of Texas, 1519–1970* (Norman: University of Oklahoma Press, 1971). This volume describes the management and disposition of land in Texas.

Despite the survival of land records when other records have been lost or destroyed, the information contained in these records would be difficult to retrieve without the help of printed indexes, abstracts, and other finding aids. Before the existence of printed and electronic abstracts, indexes, cross-indexes, and a variety of other access tools, land records had several limitations: they were difficult to read; they were not fully indexed and were rarely cross-indexed; and they were so numerous and full of legal terms that they were difficult and time-consuming to use.

ADVANTAGES OF PRINTED LAND RECORDS

While the advantages of all printed records apply to published land records, some particular benefits are highlighted below.

Legibility

Transcribed versions of land records are easier to read than original land registers (original land registers contain handwritten data that is often difficult to decipher). Transactions recorded in the seventeenth and eighteenth centuries are even more difficult to read than those registered in the nineteenth and twentieth

Table 11-2. Information in Land Records

Information	*How To Use the Information*	*Check These Sources*
Place of residence	Can help researchers differentiate between two men of the same name in different localities at the same time. Many white men owned land before the Civil War, so, if no reference to ownership in a rural area can be found, the individual may not have lived in that area.	Census or tax records in same county or land records in surrounding counties.
Former residence or other residence	Potential place of birth, marriage, or other land purchases.	Vital, census, land, and tax records in new locality
Names	Ascertain a widow's or wife's given name.	Vital records
Religion	The word *jurat* following the name of a witness meant that the witness swore an oath. Witnesses who "affirmed the deed" were Quakers.	Church records
Dates of transaction and recording	Indicates a period of residence in an area and clues to individuals' arrival and departure dates. Could imply an approximate or actual death date of a landowner.	Probate, cemetery, or vital records
Description of the parcel or lot	If a property description given in the early 1700s still exists in the family in the late 1800s, it could prove line of descent even though no written deed was located.	Earlier land records found in statewide sources
Price or consideration or circumstances of the transfer	Could indicate a special relationship, such as "for love and affection" or "for the price of an orange blossom branch on [a specific date]."	Vital, probate, or other land records
Power of attorney	May lead to other places of residence.	Land, vital, probate in other place of residence
Relationships	Could identify groups of people with the same surname. In many areas, a female listed first in a deed indicates the woman is a widow and the male following is her son.	Census records, vital records, Bible records
Approximate dates	Could indicate the approximate or actual death date of a landowner. In some states, men could not sell land until a certain age; this can help establish approximate birth dates.	Vital records, other land records
Military service	Terms such as *Col., Cpt., Lieutenant, e*tc., might indicate membership in a local or state militia unit.	Military records
Social standing in the community, titles, occupation, or education	Terms such as *Mr., Esq., yeoman, farmer, merchant,* etc., and a signature (versus a mark, as X) may distinguish one individual of the same name from another.	Occupational records
Previous owners	May identify a wife's or widow's maiden name, father, or parents on dower or inherited property.	Other property records, census, tax, and vital records.
Neighbors	Land could pass through several generations with no recorded deed. Neighboring landowners of the individuals being researched might have recorded those individuals as neighbors, thus establishing their residence or ownership.	Other land records

Source: Malcolm J. Rohrbaugh's *The Land Office Business: The Settlement and Administration of American Public Lands, 1789–1837* (New York: Oxford University Press, 1968).

centuries. Reading records in Old English handwriting takes experience and practice, and an expert's transcription can be extremely helpful. By using published sources, researchers can review many more documents in the same amount of time.

Additionally, some microfilmed copies of original records contain dark smudges or faded ink, torn or folded edges, or tight bindings that prevent the entire page from being read. Printed versions generally are easier to decipher.

The genealogical clues mentioned in table 11-2 are often buried within the legal verbiage of property transactions. Legal language is usually excluded in good abstracts, so valuable data can be extracted with little effort.

Accessibility

Until recently, land records were rarely available except through in-person research or microfilmed copies of original land records obtained by interlibrary loan. Microfilmed copies are still available through some county courthouses and state archives, as well as through the Family History Library of The Church of Jesus-Christ of Latter-day Saints (LDS church) in Salt Lake City, Utah, and through local family history centers operated by the LDS church. However, an increasing number of county, state, and Federal land records are being published and becoming available throughout the United States in large libraries, research facilities, and even small public libraries with genealogical collections. Many published land records are accessible in university, genealogical, and public libraries. Other works are available through interlibrary loan.

Helpful as Finding Tools

Printed patent, grant, and land transactions often are helpful finding tools, especially for colonial times, periods prior to census availability, and periods for which other records have been lost or destroyed. Printed land records help researchers place individuals and groups in historical settings with neighbors, friends, and related families at a specific location and time so that other sources can be efficiently searched.

Unpublished county, state, and Federal land records rarely include an every-name index. However, published records usually contain an every-name index that provides an easy means of locating each entry for an individual, whether the person was a witness, neighbor, former owner, or participant in a transaction.

The best transcriptions include an every-name and -place index that may aid researchers in locating every mention of the subject in question, either by person or by place. However, researchers should not become overly dependent on these indexes because spelling in most early land transactions was inconsistent. Record-keepers spelled phonetically and carried the local accent directly into the handwriting. For example, an early English immigrant named Hardison might "swallow" the *H* as he spoke his name. It would be written as "Ardison" in the record and in the index. If the records show that a Mr. Ardison purchased land on Black River Run and later a Mr. Hardison sold the land, the two could be the same person.

Margaret M. Hofmann's *Colony of North Carolina, 1735–1764, 1765–1775: Abstracts of Land Patents,* 2 vols. (Weldon, N.C.: Roanoke News Co., 1982, 1984) and her *Granville District of North Carolina, 1748–1763: Abstracts of Land Grants,* 2 vols. (Weldon, N.C.: Roanoke News Co., 1986–87) (and other references in the chapter bibliography) are good examples of books that include an every-name and -place index that enables researchers to quickly identify records for specific communities, watercourses, or other geographical subdivisions in the area.

Valuable for Background Information

Volumes of abstracts often provide data that can help researchers understand the period and circumstances during which certain records were created. In their introductions, many printed sources contain information directing researchers to original records, detailing methodology required for searching the original records or explaining how to use the printed abstracts. For example, the 1861 *Records of the Colony of New Plymouth in New England,* edited by Nathaniel B. Shurtleff and David Pulsifer, 12 vols. in 10 (Boston: William White, 1855–61) devotes its entire introduction to a discussion of colonial handwriting and terminology. By reading the introduction, researchers can learn about the transcription process (figure 11-3).

The introduction to *Genealogical Abstracts, Revolutionary War Veterans, Scrip Act, 1852/Abstracted from the Bureau of Land Management, Record Group 49, National Archives Branch, Suitland, Maryland,* by Margie Brown (Oakton, Va.: the author, 1990), explains how to use the application number to order the court documents and depositions given by claimants. Revolutionary war veterans were given bounty land in lieu of cash payments for their military service (figure 11-4). In his introduction to Lowell M. Volkel's *War of 1812 Bounty Lands in Illinois* (Thomson, Ill.: Heritage House, 1977), James D. Walker of the National Archives drew upon his excellent background in the use of Federal records to write a step-by-step historical narrative of the bounty-land process and detailed instructions for ordering the bounty-land application files. The beginning of the text also discusses historical conditions relating to the area and its land records.

Shawneetown: Land District Records 1814–1820, also by Lowell M. Volkel (Indianapolis: Heritage House, 1978), presents a history of the early settlers, place name abbreviations, variant spellings, information on determining locations for land transfers, and maps of the area. It also explains the use and location of the Federal land records (figure 11-5).

Joan E. Brookes-Smith's *Master Index Virginia Surveys and Grants 1774–1791* (Frankfort: Kentucky Historical Society, 1976) contains a three-page glossary of land and property terms. The introduction to William Lindsay Hopkins's *Virginia Revolutionary War Land Grant Claims 1783–1850 (Rejected)* (Richmond, Va.: Gen-N-Dex, 1988) discusses the history of land grants and bounty warrants (page i):

> As a man completed his agreed upon service time, he was issued a warrant for a minimum of 100 acres or more of land. An enlisted man received the smallest amount of land and an officer was rewarded for his service with an amount of land dependent upon his rank and length of service in that particular rank.

Hopkins then provides clues to the importance of these records or how they could also be used (page i):

> During this period of almost seventy years (1783–1850), the applications often name children and grandchildren of the veteran and tell where they are then living. A number of veterans lived to be in their 80s and 90s and, although they may be living as far west as Missouri by that time, they usually tell who enlisted them, where in Virginia this happened, the year and the unit.

When Winston De Ville wrote *English Land Grants in West Florida: A Register for the States of Alabama, Mississippi, and Parts of Florida and Louisiana, 1766–1776* (Ville Platte, La.: the author, 1986), his understanding of history made his work all the more compelling (pages 1–5):

> . . . much too little has been written for the genealogies of the families that settled the two areas [eastern Florida and western Florida] and, as it turned out, permanently changed a Latin culture to a non-Latin one . . . true, during the American Revolution, these people were Loyalists, and many came south to remove themselves from pre-revolutionary agitations up East. But, we believe, they were more loyal to their own personal freedom than to political alliances. . . . English "Loyalists" in the deep South contributed to the success of the American Revolution in their own way. . . . But what of the present work? We believe that this is one of the most important finding aids in evidential genealogy for the first permanent non-Latin families of the Gulf South.

MARKS AND CONTRACTIONS.

A Dash ¯ (or straight line) over a letter indicates the omission of the letter following the one marked.

A Curved Line ˜ indicates the omission of one or more letters next to the one marked.

A Superior Letter indicates the omission of contiguous letters, either preceding or following it.

A Caret ‸ indicates an omission in the original record.

A Cross × indicates a lost or unintelligible word.

All doubtful words supplied by the editor are included between brackets, [ ].

Some redundancies in the original record are printed in Italics.

Some interlineations, that occur in the original record, are put between parallels, ‖ ‖.

Some words and paragraphs, which have been cancelled in the original record, are put between ‡ ‡.

Several characters have special significations, namely:—

@, — annum, anno.
ā, — an, am, — curiā, curiam.
ã, — mãtrate, magistrate.
ƀ, — ber, — numƀ, number; Roƀt, Robert.
c̃, — ci, ti, — ac̃on, action.
c̃õ, — tio, — jurisdicc̃õn, jurisdiction.
ꝯ, — cre, cer, — aꝯs, acres; cleriꝯ, clericus.
đ, — đđ, delivered.
ẽ, — Trẽr, Treasurer.
ē, — committē, committee.
g̃, — g̃ñal, general; Georg̃, George.
ħ, — cħr, charter.
ĩ, — begĩg, beginĩg, beginning.
ł, — łre, letter.
m̃, — mm, mn, — com̃ittee, committee.
m̃, — recom̃daс̃õn, recommendation.
m̃, — mer, — form̃ly, formerly.
m̃, — month.
n̄, — nn, — Pen̄, Penn; an̄o, anno.
ñ, — Dñi, Domini.
ñ, — ner, — mañ, manner.
ō, — on, — mentiō, mention.
õ, — mõ, month.
p̃, — par, por; p̃t, part; p̃tion, portion.
p̃, — pre, — p̃sent, present.
ꝑ, — per, par, pur, pear, — ꝑsuite, pursuite; appd, appeared; ꝑson, person; ꝑte, parte.
ꝓ, — pro, — ꝓporc̃õn, proportion.
ꝓ, — proper.
ꝗ, — ꝗstion, question.
ꝗ, — esꝗ, esquire.
r̃, — Apr̃, April.
s̄, — s̄, session; s̄d, said.
s̃, — ser, — s̃vants, servants.
t̃, — ter, — neut̃, neuter; secret̃, secretary.
t̃, — capt̃, captain.
ũ, — uer, — seũal, seueral; goũ, gouernor.
ū, — aboū, aboue, above.
ṽ, — ver, — seṽal, several.
ṽ, — ver, verse, verses.
w̃, — w̃n, when.
y[e], the; y[m], them; y[n], then; y[r], their; y[s], this; y[t], that.
ꝫ, — us, ue; vilibꝫ, vilibus; annoqꝫ, annoque.
ꝰ, — es, et, — statutꝰ, statutes.
ꝛc̃, &c̃, &c[a], — et cætera.
vizꝫ, — videlicet, namely.
·/ — full point.

Rꝰ, Regis; RRꝰ, Regni Regis.

Figure 11-3. This from the introduction to Shurtleff and Pulsifer's *Records of the Colony of New Plymouth in New England* informs the reader about the transcription process.

Figure 11-4. The introduction to *Genealogical Abstracts, Revolutionary War Veterans, Scrip Act, 1852* explains how to use the application number to order the court documents and depositions given by claimants.

HOW TO USE:

APPLICATION NUMBER is the key to access these files. Volume 43, "A list of Claims satisfied by the issuance of Scrip, Virginia Military Warrants Act of August 31, 1852". Bureau of Land Management, Record Group 49, contains a scattered index of these files, but often will list them by claim number. If more than one application number is listed, it will be necessary to read each file, to show the family as it is presented in this book.

COURT DOCUMENTS listed under the Veterans service, will tell you where the families resided, and time period of that residence. The documents vary, but often include copies of Wills and family letters between the claimants and their legal council. If the date of the documents does not continue into the 1850's, then it is likely that those warrants were owned by land speculators, and it will be the speculators family that is chronicled. Many purchasers of warrants have provable Revolutionary service. The last date listed in the Court documents, i.e. January 1870, is how the family descent stood as of that time. If an heir was living, his children will not be listed, only the deceased heirs will list further descent.

DEPOSITIONS are extremely important as the deponent frequently cites his own service and place of residence. He or she may also show family relationships.

NUMBERING SYSTEM is straight forward. The superscript indicates the generation, i.e. ^{4} will be a great grandchild of ^{1}. Indentation and the word (Issue) also show the line of descent.

List the following items when requesting copies:

Record Group # 49
Bureau of Land Management
Scrip Act of 1852
Veterans Name, Application Numbers, and Service

Send to: Suitland Reference Branch (NNRR)
National Archives and Records Administration
Washington, D.C. 20409

Charges will vary. Price information must be requested from the National Archives. Please look at all of the ORIGINAL PAPERS. There may be other information of importance that has not been included in these abstracts.

Finally, in Kenneth Scott and Rosanne Conway's *New York Alien Residents, 1825–1848* (Baltimore: Genealogical Publishing Co., 1978), the introduction explains alien depositions as a valuable source, what can be found in these records, where they can be found, and what years and events are covered, as well as how legislation affected the aliens' decisions.

The brief historical background of an area that is included in some books' introductory sections occasionally explains nuances pertaining to the records and is helpful when it enhances a researcher's understanding of the requirements, customs, and recording procedures of the abstracted records covered in the text. This type of information is rarely included in the original volume of land transcriptions. For instance, *Western New York Land Transactions, 1804–1824: Extracted from the Archives of the Holland Land Company,* by Karen E. Livsey, 2 vols. (Baltimore: Genealogical Publishing Co., 1991), is preceded by an invaluable introduction, which includes a discussion of the organization, location, and origination of the records. The introduction also lists published works that provide additional background. One part explains how to use the book, links counties with township descriptions, explains the abbreviations and symbols used within the text, lists villages, and provides references to the original sources by microfilm reel numbers, inventory numbers, and associated dates.

The following excerpt from the introduction to Jane Kizer Thomas's *Blount County, Tennessee, Deeds: Deed Book 1, 1795–1819* (Maryville, Tenn.: Blount County Genealogical and Historical Society, 1990), reveals the importance of reading the introductory material (page 1):

> On February 7, 1807, the Commissioners of Blount County ordered that the register's book of deeds be transcribed into a larger and more complete book. Over a period of years, ending August 31, 1878, other deed books were transcribed into the same book, which was then designated Book 1.
>
> As a convenience for the reader each deed is numbered. Numbers in parentheses indicate the page number of Book 1 on which the deed is found. The first date shown is the date the deed was written: second is the date of registration. Then follows the

The Shawneetown Land Office opened in 1812 with the first sales being recorded in 1814. There were two officials operating in each land office, the Register and the Receiver. The Register would accept applications for land purchases and make the appropriate journal entries. The Receiver kept a daily register of all receipts of land payments. It is the record of the latter office for the period from July 18, 1814, through June 30, 1820, which is reproduced on the following pages.

Land Acts of the U. S. Congress in 1796, 1800, and 1804, created a credit system for the sale of public lands. These acts provided for the purchase of quarter sections (160 acres) at $2.00 per acre, with one-twentieth payable at the time of purchase, and installment payments to be made over a period of four years. Each time an individual made a payment to the Receiver, an entry was recorded in the Register of Receipts Ledger. Thus, in the journal here reproduced, several entries for the same man and the same property are found, one for each time a payment was made. This day by day account will permit the researcher to reconstruct a more precise profile of a person's activities, as it was necessary for the purchaser to either make the payment in person or trust an associate or friend to make it for him.

After an individual had completed all of his payments on a particular piece of land, a patent would be issued from Washington. All patents within a land district were sent to the Register of that district. He was responsible for the delivery of the patents (the first deeds) to the land purchasers. These patents are sometimes mistakenly called grants. A grant was free land usually issued in return for military service. As all land transactions in this volume were for purchase lands, they cannot be considered grants.

Occasionally, evidence is found of settlers in the Shawneetown District before 1814. There was some land in the far eastern portion of the district which may have been sold in the Vincennes (Indiana) Land Office prior to 1814. That office was established in 1804. It is also known that there were some squatters (people living on the land without having paid for it) in the area. Mention of some pre-1814 residents in the region can be found in Clarence E. Carter's TERRITORIAL PAPERS OF THE UNITED STATES, Volumes II and III, THE NORTHWEST TERRITORY; Volumes VII and VIII, THE INDIANA TERRITORY; and Volumes XVI AND XVII, THE ILLINOIS TERRITORY (U. S. Government Printing Office, Washington D. C.), and in the AMERICAN STATE PAPERS, THE PUBLIC LAND SERIES by Gales and Seaton.

Figure 11-5. Volkel's *Shawneetown: Land District Records 1814–1820* presents a history of the early settlers, place name abbreviations, variant spellings, information on determining locations for land transfers, and maps of the area. It also explains the use and location of the Federal land records.

amount or type of consideration paid, description of the property, and signatures of the seller and witnesses. Signatures made by a "mark" are indicated "(X)." Date of acknowledgment before the court is not shown unless it was deemed to have some genealogical significance.

Note: The Holston River referred to in these deeds is today's Tennessee River. The Tennessee River referred to is now known as Little Tennessee River.

Quality abstracts include all names, dates, watercourses, neighbors, witnesses, property descriptions, and other pertinent background information. For instance, in *Abstracts: Deed Books I and II, Allegheny County, Pennsylvania* by Helen L. Harriss (the compiler, 1984), the introductory material includes several beneficial maps of the area. One shows the Donation Lands in Pennsylvania (figure 11-6) to assist in using the abstracts. The abstracts in this and similar works include the original location and date of recorded transactions, as well as the names, residences, and occupations (if noted) of the individuals involved. The abstracts also note the monetary sum that was exchanged

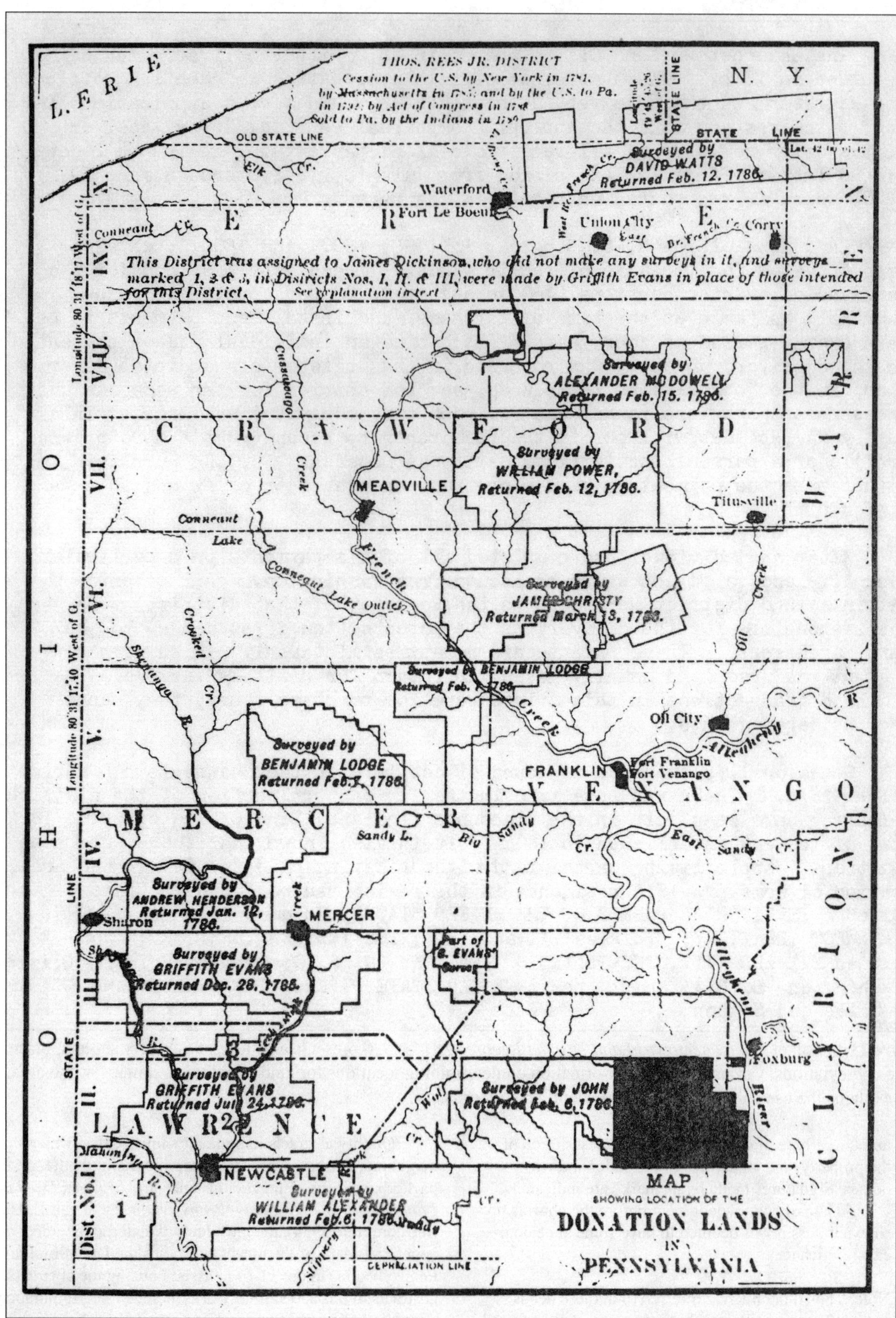

Figure 11-6. The introductory material in Harriss's *Abstracts: Deed Books I and II, Allegheny County, Pennsylvania* includes several beneficial maps of the area. This one shows the Donation Lands in Pennsylvania to assist in using the abstracts.

in the transaction, the grant number, and an incomplete description of the land, including the number of acres. The signer(s) and witness(es) are also listed. Special considerations and additional data sometimes are noted briefly in abstracts.

LIMITATIONS OF PRINTED LAND RECORDS

While land records themselves are very abundant, only a fraction have been published. Sole reliance upon printed land records can complicate genealogical research when assumptions are made based on transcriptions only. Below are other possible difficulties.

Poor Organization

If records are rearranged alphabetically by surname without an every-name index, associated names (such as those of neighbors or family members) may be lost. For example, successive deeds often were recorded on the same day on successive pages. If the compiler of the printed record rearranges the materials alphabetically by grantor or grantee, this clue is destroyed.

Deletion or Addition of Material

Only partial information is used in printed compilations. Most publications omit many details and descriptions included in the original documents. Some omissions are helpful, but valuable details may be deleted. For example, transcriptions that omit waterways hinder southern states research, for waterways are often helpful in determining family relationships.

In colonial North Carolina, records rarely were made that listed the full names of individuals with more than a given and last name. Therefore, when Jo White Linn, a noted North Carolina genealogist, noticed that John Williams Carpenter and John Henry Taylor were listed in a record, she cautioned readers that they might actually be John Williams, carpenter, and John Henry, tailor; some deeds may have been inadvertently indexed by occupation, therefore, and not by name. The original record should ultimately be researched (Rae 1991, 2).

Non-Uniform Presentation

Presentation of material may not be uniform. Compilers, authors, and editors select details they believe are important and may omit facts that are significant to other researchers. For example, names may be listed without family relationships even though these relationships are clearly stated in the record. After reading abstracted entries, researchers may assume, for example, that a certain individual is a spouse rather than a sister.

Typographical Errors

Published sources contain errors. Some mistakes are typographical; for instance, data entry and transcription errors can camouflage the original name. If the first *e* in the surname Sevier is mistyped as a *w* or *r*, the name becomes Swvier or Srvier. Typographical errors can so effectively confuse or misplace a reference that researchers may experience great difficulty locating the data or citation.

Poor Handwriting

An abstractor's inability to decipher handwritten records may cause errors in the transcription. Some errors may result from the author's or editor's lack of knowledge of abbreviations used by a recording clerk. Such a situation was the motivation behind an article by Weynette Parks Haun in the *Magazine of Virginia Genealogy* 24 (November 1986) titled "Watching Your 'P's and Crossing Them." The article begins with the following paragraph (page 44):

> Many researchers who have worked with early Virginia records are aware of the letter symbol "p" and its peculiar uses. . . . [The symbol] was most frequently utilized by parish clerks as a short-hand device to indicate "par" in *par*ish (*P*ish), "pre" in *pre*cinct, (*P*cinct), and in the Latin *per me* (by me). When the scribe was careful to give a back swoop of the pen to form the symbol, called by some "the crossed P," a researcher is alerted to the fact that it stands for something other than the usual orthographic symbol "p." But other clerks made little distinction between the letter as a consonant and the letter as a short-hand device. A quick dip of the pen with a bit of an arc on the ascending stroke served for letter and device alike.

In addition to clerks' abbreviations, handwriting itself in the original records frequently is difficult to decipher, so some names are obscured in the printed record. Sometimes the first letter of the surname is even misread, as in the case of the uppercase *L*, which may be difficult to distinguish from the uppercase *S*. Thus, the surname Landers may be entered as Sanders.

Some authors or compilers may be unfamiliar with the names in a particular county during a certain period; consequently, the handwriting may be read incorrectly and mistranscribed, and the names may be so misconstrued as to be lost to the researcher.

Case Study: Misread Records. Printed land records can solve difficult research problems. The following case study, from Nell Marion Nugent's *Cavaliers and Pioneers: Abstracts of Virginia Land Patents and Grants, 1695–1732,* vol. 3 of 5 (Richmond: Virginia State Library, 1979), demonstrates how these records can be used successfully (page 6):

> Research established that Thomas Boyte [variant spellings found in other records include "Boyt" and "Boyet"] was a resident of Nansemond County, Virginia, a county where the records had been destroyed. No land records for the late seventeenth and early eighteenth centuries are extant except for those grants and patents issued by the Commonwealth. A review of the published abstracts of Virginia land records established that Thomas Boyt owned property in the county as the following abstracted entry shows:
>
> HENRY JENKINS, 665 acs., Up. Par. of Nansemond Co; on NW side of the Back Swamp; 6 June 1699, p. 195. Beg. at a fork or point made by sd. swamp & the long branch: adj. Thomas Boyt. . . .

There was no other index entry for Thomas; consequently, the record of Thomas's original purchase was not found. After an examination of other sources, an in-depth review of the index provided a lead. An alert researcher found the following entry for "Boyle, Thomas" (page 15):

> THOMAS BOYLE, 129 acs. Up. Par. of Nansamond [*sic*] Co; S. side of the back Sw. of Sumerton; 28 Oct. 1697, p. 110. Adj. Thomas Jernakan [*sic*] & land of Samll. Watson. Trans. of 3 pers: John Wike, William Walker, Humphry Minson.

Although the surnames were different, the property description was similar, so a copy of the original record was ordered from the Land Office, Virginia State Library, in Richmond. At first glance, the original appeared to be for a Thomas Boyle, not a Thomas Boyt or Boyte, but a closer examination showed that the clerk crossed few *T*'s in the document. The words *south,* Somerton, *the,* and others appear as *soulh,* Somerlon, and *lhe.* The *t* in Samuel Watson's name was uncrossed. In contrast, the *l* in the abbreviation Sam'l appears to be crossed because a line above the word is used to indicate that letters are missing.

The mystery of the missing land record seemed to be solved, but additional proof was imperative. The only other extant record for Nansemond County for this period is the 1704 quitrents. This record was reviewed in published sources (des Cognet 1981, 201). The record shows that Thomas Boyt was assessed for four hundred acres, but the essential validation was the names Tho. Jernegan Junr and Samll Watson. These two names, listed near that of Thomas Boyt, provide tangible evidence that the grant as recorded in the published abstracts incorrectly shows Thomas Boyle instead of Thomas Boyte.

Additional searches were conducted to further substantiate this hypothesis. The researcher reviewed the entire 1704 quitrent list for any Boyle but found none. An early list of patentees for the colony shows three pertinent 1717 patents: a 292-acre patent to "Tho. Boyd, Jr.," a 150-acre patent to "Edw'd Boyt," and a 244-acre patent to "Tho. Boyt Jr." (des Cognet 1981, 201).

Researchers also examined later records. Wilmer L. Hall's *The Vestry Book of the Upper Parish, Nansemond County, Virginia 1743–1793* (Richmond: Virginia State Library, 1949), shows that no Boyles resided there, but the book includes several entries for the surnames Boyd, Boyet, Boyt, and Boyte. Later residents of Nansemond and Isle of Wight counties were listed on an 1784 petition. This document was evaluated; no Boyle was enumerated, but William Boyt, Thomas Bogit, and David Boyd were listed.

Review of original records, knowledge of the intricacies in deciphering handwritten records, awareness of related indexing problems, and precise documentation were essential. During subsequent research, similar techniques proved successful. Under a variety of misspellings, earlier entries for Thomas Boyte of Nansemond County, Virginia, were located and documented (Elliott 1987, 1–7).

In every case, researchers should examine the original record after locating an abbreviated printed version. Then they should compare the original to the abstract to fill in details. Original records usually furnish additional evidence or suggest research paths to follow. For instance, a word-by-word examination makes it possible to review and compare property descriptions.

Occasionally, a lack of records makes the substantiation of relationships difficult. When other sources are unavailable, one effective method of identifying family relationships is to delineate the property of the individuals, which is much easier to accomplish by using published land records. When property descriptions match exactly, residents of the same parcel of land can be determined. Researchers can surmise that two individuals are related if they owned the same property at different times, particularly if they share the same surname. When records are scarce, this type of connection may be the only evidence available.

Omissions

Omission of names or dates is a frequent problem in land record abstracts. Some abstracted works and many compilations that are indexes to land records do not include all names, dates, witnesses, full property descriptions, and other pertinent information.

Misspellings and Phonetic Spellings

Misspelling of names can make it difficult to locate proper entries. Although printed volumes are much easier to read than original records, researchers must be aware of the possibility of problems and consider the deficiencies common in published sources. Misspelling of a name frequently occurs in the original and therefore in the transcribed sources. Even the surname Jones is found in early records spelled Joanes or Joans; the given name Jonas may even be recorded as Jones. Smith can be spelled Smyth, Smithe, and Smythe. An incredible number of variations can be found for less common surnames and given names.

Genealogical researchers must use imagination in determining the variations in spelling and pronunciation that may account for unexpected or creative entries; for instance, the place name Albemarle appears in one original record as *arbel marbel.*

Publication Variables

Abstractors of land records use various methods and abbreviations. Some volumes are not every-name indexed but fail to state this fact in the introductory remarks. Researchers unaware of this fact may fail to find valuable data that is in the organized records. A few published land records do not show acreage or provide a full description of the property. Some show only names and number of acres.

Some volumes appear to contain comprehensive statewide information but actually do not. Some contain only selected land records from counties the author deemed important. Many beginning genealogists quit looking for an individual in a particular area, only to find later that the index they used contained only a partial listing for that area.

Some land record publications are only indexes to the original records, and many of those are not every-name indexes. Readers should review the book's introduction and text to determine the book's research value.

Place Name Changes

Original land grants and patents often contain Native American or foreign principality location names that no longer exist. Using a good gazetteer that parallels the time period of the records and the land transcriptions can save researchers considerable time and energy. For example, gazetteers of different periods illustrate that the Moratock/Muratuck/Morratuook River in North Carolina later became known as the Roanoke River.

Printed abstracts can be valuable but must be used with caution. Because land transactions must be abbreviated in a printed work, many of the details are omitted; this allows more deeds to be included in the publication and simplifies the material, but it also may lead to the exclusion of valuable information or clues for researchers. Whenever land transactions are printed in two or more sources for the same period and county, researchers should compare data from all sources, including original sources.

TYPES OF PRINTED LAND RECORDS

Although grants (the first titled deeds are also called *patents*) are the most frequently published type of land record, any part of the granting procedures may be the subject of a printed volume. One volume may have as its topic only *entries,* while another may focus on *warrants* or *surveys*. The process of obtaining a land grant was specified by law and involved several steps that produced valuable documentation, much of which remains in files and can be obtained for evaluation.

This section discusses documents that were created by land transfers. Most records deal with the transfer of ownership or related documents. The land might have been transferred by a foreign sovereign to an individual, a company, or the Federal government of the United States. It also might have been transferred from a collective company to an individual, from the Federal government to an individual, or from one individual to another.

Various authors disagree as to the meaning of the words *patent* and *grant*. These words have different meanings in different regions of the United States. For example, in *Turff and Twigg: The French Lands* (cited earlier), Priscilla Cabell states, "A land patent is an official document issued by a sovereign power conveying land **before** the American Revolution. After the Revolution these documents were called land *grants*" (page 1); this is true in Virginia, Cabell's area of study, but the term *patent* is used much later than the revolutionary period in other parts of the United States. The types of printed land transfers described below are discussed according to their approximate time period and class.

Land Grants from Colonies to Individuals (1607–1776)

Land Company Grants. As colonial, Federal, and state governments began distributing vast tracts of land to individuals, they chartered land companies or allowed them to exist (if unchartered). Land companies received large grants of land from the government, then subdivided the land for sale to individuals. Because these sales involved private companies and individuals, the Federal, state, or colonial government often made no record of these transactions. Often, no local government existed in the area because the land had just been opened for settlement. In such situations, documentation of land ownership may exist only in the files of the involved land company.

One example of land ownership documentation is the 1861 *Records of the Colony of New Plymouth in New England* (cited earlier). This collection covers the full range of records kept by the Plymouth Colony in New England. Volume 1 is divided into two parts that cover the allotments of land from 1620 to 1651. The first part was written by Governor Bradford, with the exception of fewer than ten pages, which were written by an unknown author. The second part was written by Edward Winslow, Nathaniel Sowther, Antony Thacher, Nathaniel Morton, William Paddy, Samuel Sprague, and William Bradford. It was published to satisfy an order from the legislature of the Commonwealth of Massachusetts in 1861 for a "Book of Indian Records for Their Land." The rest of the volumes cover court orders and proceedings of the General Court and the Court of Assistants from 1633 through 1691; judicial acts of the General Court and Court of Assistants from 1636 through 1692; miscellaneous records including births, marriages, deaths, and burials; treasury accounts; lists of freemen and others from 1633 through 1689; acts of the commissioners of the United Colonies of New England from 1643 through 1679; and laws of the colony from 1623 through 1682.

Records of some land companies have been published, in whole or in part. For example, the Susquehanna Company was chartered by Connecticut to distribute the Wyoming Valley claims in northeastern Pennsylvania (land to which Connecticut laid claim). Before the American Revolution, the Susquehanna Company issued land to more than five thousand settlers. Many claims were not settled until the early 1800s. During the 1960s, the records were published in eleven volumes as *Susquehannah Company Papers* by Julian P. Boyd and Robert J. Taylor (Ithaca, N.Y.: Cornell University Press, 1962–71).

Another example of records from land companies is Livsey's two-volume compilation of the Holland Company papers in *Western New York Land Transactions, 1804–1824: Extracted from the Archives of the Holland Land Company* (cited earlier). The publication's purpose is "to associate a name (person) with a location in a given time period. And it also functions as an index to the Land Tables in the archives of the Holland Land Company in Amsterdam" (vol. 1, page v).

Another publication that deals with this land company is *Reports of Joseph Ellicott as Chief of Survey (1797–1800): And as Agent (1800–1821) of the Holland Land Company's Purchases in Western New York* (Buffalo, N.Y.: Buffalo Historical Society, 1937–41), edited by Robert Warwick Bingham, director of the Buffalo Historical Society. This publication provides easy-to-read reports prepared by Ellicott. The names of purchasers are listed, along with the date of their contracts, the exact location of the land, the number of acres that were sold, and the selling price. Many smaller land companies operated in the midwestern states; their records may appear in published abstracts of the early land offices.

Originally, Massachusetts had two settlements known as Plymouth Colony and the Massachusetts Bay Company. A grant of land was made to a group of *commoners* or *proprietors* (these terms were used interchangeably) (Stoddard 1979, 556–64). The town could perform transactions with the proprietors, who then could make grants to the town. Proprietors' records were not kept for plantations on which everyone was a commoner. (Also see *Puritan Village: The Formation of a New England Town* by Sumner Chilton Powell [Middletown, Conn.: Wesleyan University Press, 1963].)

Some books simply identify the existence of these grants. *Publications of the Colonial Society of Massachusetts,* vol. 4, *Collections* (Boston: the society, 1910), includes "Papers relating to the Land Bank of 1740," from which figure 11-7 is taken.

CALENDAR OF LAND-BANK PAPERS. 11

Massachusetts Archives.

42. 102: 116. 30 December, 1740.

Letter of John Higginson enclosing on separate sheet list of Land-Bank Mortgages in Essex County.

43. 102: 117–119. 30 December, 1740.

Registry of Deeds, Essex County: A List of the names of those who have mortgaged any part of their estates in Essex County to the Manufactory Society, so called. 115 names.

44. 102: 120. 30 December, 1740.

Registry of Deeds, Barnstable County: List of names of all such persons as have mortgaged any part of their estates in Barnstable County to the Society which has put forth bills called Manufactory Bills. Drawn up in obedience to the Governor and Council. Ten names.

Figure 11-7. "Calendar of Land-Bank Papers" in *Publications of the Colonial Society of Massachusetts.*

Headright and Proprietary Grants. Headright grants are similar to regular land grants, except that in substitution for direct payment for land, paid passage from Europe to the colony was the commodity of exchange. Established to encourage the importation of colonists, a few colonial governments offered land in exchange for passage payment from Europe for individuals, families, or groups.

The best-known of the headright sources is *Cavaliers and Pioneers: Abstracts of Virginia Land Patents and Grants* (cited earlier). It consists of five volumes and a supplement. This resource lists the individuals who received the headright, the number of acres they received, the county in which the land was located, and a brief description of the grant, including the date and the number and names of the people for whom passage was provided. Two samples from vol. 3 follow (pages 3 and 15):

> JOHN SAXON, 460 acs., New Kent Co; W. side of the N. br. of Pamunkey River; adj. land, now or late, or Wm. Overton; 28 Oct 1697, p. 106. Trans of 9 pers: Frank, Moll, Sampson, Tom, Sue, Robin, Peter, Dead, Betty.
>
> ROBERT COLEMAN, 450 acs., Up. Par. of Nansamond Co., near Wickham Swamp, 28 Oct. 1697, p. 109. Adj. Thomas & John Milner; & Lawrance's land. Trans. of 9 pers: Jeremiah Brooks, Mary Chapman, Elinor Ford, John Knight, Thomas Buller, Eliza. Watts, Margt. Robinson, Cha. Maccartee, Tho. Pratt.

Beth Mitchell compiled *Beginning at a White Oak: Patents and Northern Neck Grants of Fairfax County, Virginia* (Fairfax, Va.: McGregor and Werner, 1979). In Virginia, the transaction rate was one paid passage for fifty acres. Thus, Hugh Campbell of Isle of Wight County, Virginia, received 1,200 acres for paying the transportation costs of twenty-four immigrants (Nugent 1979, 26). Colonel Philip Ludwell was entitled to two thousand acres for transporting forty persons from Europe (Dabney 1971, 51). In South Carolina, immigrant headright grants were instigated in 1669 with one hundred acres. They were lowered to seventy and then sixty acres in 1679, and eventually were lowered to fifty acres.

South Carolina is home to many records of proprietary grants and indentures. The first abstracts of these grants were written in 1766 and sent to England. Many of the originals were lost; some appear in scattered sources. Researchers who cannot locate colonial records of an individual purchasing land from an individual, county, or state generally can consult the proprietary or headright grants to determine whether it was the first grant to that land. For more information concerning headright grants, see "Warrants," below.

Patents. When issued and registered, a patent secured a person's title to a property. This term is also used for land transferred from a proprietary government. Generally, patents are the only land grant records that have been preserved. They are usually located in the respective state archive, foreign national repository, state land office, or in the National Archives.

The following represents a typical abstract of a North Carolina colonial government grant (Hofmann 1986–87, vol. 1, 15):

> 143 pg. 26 CAPT NEEDHAM BRYAN 7 February 1759 600 acres in Bertie County, joining the sd. BRYANS own corner, WIDOW BRYAN, and DAVID HARRELL OR: /s/ NEEDHAM BRYAN Wits: RUTH WOODAARD, BENJ WYNNS surveyed 27 March 1751 OC: LEONAARD HULL, WM SIMMONS BENJ WYNNS Survr

Some area-wide studies of colonial Virginia land patents are discussed in Louise Pledge Heath Foley's two-volume *Early Virginia Families Along the James River: Their Deep Roots and Tangled Branches* (Richmond, Va.: the author, 1974–78). Vol. 1 covers Henrico and Goochland counties, and vol. 2 covers Charles City County and Prince George County. By focusing on the information she gleaned from quitrent rolls, land patents, calendar changes, and maps, Foley has assembled a useful historical work intended to aid other researchers in untangling the intermarrying families of this location and time period.

Early Dutch land patents in New York were published in *New York Historical Manuscripts: Dutch Land Papers, Volumes GG, HHH, and II,* by Charles T. Gehring (Baltimore: Genealogical Publishing Co., 1980). The introduction to the book states that although most of the land papers are patents, "some contain 'Indian deeds' which record the purchase of land from the natives for the West India Company and several patroons." The first recorded patent is to Andries Hudden for one hundred morgens of land, dated 20 July 1638. Up to this time colonists were allowed to "choose and take possession of as much land as they [could] properly cultivate with the approval of the director and council of New Netherland"(page 1). An Indian deed for lands in New Jersey in 1630 is provided in vol. GG.

The government's desire to settle a largely unpopulated area of New York that afforded poor protection from Natives led New York's Governor Thomas Dongan to grant huge patents of 850,000 acres in 1665 and establish a manorial lifestyle in this area. The governor offered two types of grants—manors and patents. When a group of individuals belonging to different families wanted to own an area (a common occurrence among New England land owners), lordship title with feudal privileges could not exist. In such collectivized arrangements, grants became patents. The governor showed his favoritism toward the wealthy by charging trivial quitrents for these new patents. He gave such large grants to local men of wealth and prominence because, with a scattered populace, he found it convenient to govern through these men, who could help him remain in office.

Frederick Van Wyck wrote *Select Patents of New York Towns* (Boston: A. A. Beauchamp, 1938) using the records of the period. He provides some good historical background and distinguishes between boroughs, towns, and county towns.

Quitrents. In some colonies, grants were written with stipulations that new owners make some sort of payment, called a *quitrent,* to proprietors. Some of these grants required services or payment of revenues, a practice that endured from feudal Europe; some required military service; still others stipulated payment of another person's transportation from Europe to the colony.

The practice of quitrents was utilized mostly in the South, in colonies such as Virginia and North Carolina. The 1704 quitrents of Virginia are listed in Louis des Cognet, Jr., *English Duplicates of Lost Virginia Records* (Baltimore: Genealogical Publishing Co., 1981) and Annie Laurie Wright Smith's *The Quit Rents of Virginia, 1704* (Baltimore: Genealogical Publishing Co., 1980). Smith divides quitrents into two parts: the first comprises the fourteen counties that paid tribute to the King of England, and the second encompasses the five counties known as The Northern Neck that paid quitrents to the Lord's Proprietors, the Fairfax-Culpepper family. Each county maintained one copy of the rent rolls for the proprietary colonies.

Rent rolls similar to quitrents were maintained in the proprietary colonies of Delaware, Maryland, Pennsylvania, North and South Carolina, Maine, and New Hampshire. Payments required in these colonies were similar to today's property taxes.

Quitrents were not used in New England except in early New Hampshire and Maine, nor were they used in early Dutch New York (Greenwood 1990, 323). Later, however, they were used in New York. Figure 11-8 is an example of the information found in Elijah Ellsworth Brownell's *List of Patents of Lands, Etc. To Be Sold in January, 1822, for Arrears of Quit Rent* (Philadelphia, 1937).

Warrants. When a settler first appeared before the governor or council to ask for land (in some cases due to headright), the governor or council issued a warrant for the land. The warrant was recorded by the provincial secretary and delivered to the settler. This warrant ordered a survey to be taken. When the plat and return of survey were made, the secretary checked them against his record of the warrant and certified them. A copy of the plat was made for the secretary, who drew up the grant. The governor and council members signed the grant, and the registrar of the province recorded the action. Unless the settler obtained the grant within ninety days of receiving the plat, the settler's claim to the land lapsed.

In some areas, such as in South Carolina, proprietors used the grant procedure to create a lengthy indenture process in which the land was deeded in exchange for quitrents. Eventually, a less-complex system was instituted to waive quitrents for those who paid a purchase price. Most of the original plats and returns of survey were lost. Some settlers claimed title to land without a grant or warrant on the basis of the plat alone. Many tenants without formal papers were recognized as rightful owners and charged quitrents.

By themselves, the warrants are not effective for tracing actual land grant ownership because many settlers who applied for land died or left the area before the process was complete. However, warrants can be used to determine the number of

Whereas there are arrears of QUIT RENT due upon each of the Patents or Grants of Land, within this State, herein after mentioned and described, viz:

Patentees' names	Date of grant	Acres	County when granted	County now situated in	Description of property, popular names, etc.
Robert Walter, Peter Matthews, John Chollwell, Leigh Atwood, Cornelius De Peyster, Richard Slator, Barne Cosens, Lancaster Simes, Matthew Clarkson, Robert Lurting, and Caleb Heathcot	2 Mar 1701	6,200	Westchester	Westchester	Bounded NE by the oblong; SE by the state of Connecticut
Robert Grant	7 Aug 1764	3,000	Albany	Essex	This pat. is bounded N. by Allen Campbell, S. by Donald Campbell, and E. by Lake Champlain

Figure 11-8. An example of the information found in Brownell's *List of Patents of Lands, Etc. To Be Sold in January, 1822, for Arrears of Quit Rent* (pages 1, 24).

members in applicants' families; the number of indentured servants and slaves belonging to the families; the date of the applicant's arrival in the colonies; and occasionally the occupations, family relationships, and nationalities of applicants and their families (Salley 1973, i–xv). In 1910, A. S. Salley, Jr., who was secretary of the Historical Commission of South Carolina, published *Warrants for Lands in South Carolina 1672–1711*, rev. ed. (Columbia: University of South Carolina Press, 1973). The following are examples of records contained in Salley's book (page 3, 23):

> Carolina./
> By the Governo[r] by and with the)
> advice and consent of the Councill)
> You are forthw[th] to cause to be admeasured and layd out for M[r] John Coming Three hundred and twenty five acres of land being the proporcon allowed to him by the Lords Prop[rs]. Concessions for himselfe Affera his Wife and the halfe share of one Serv[t]. namely John Neale arriveing in the first ffleet, or soe much thereof as you shall find to be contained between the lines of the lands allotted to be layd out to M[r] Henry Hughes to the South and M[r] Richard Cole to the North without prejudicing either of the said lines And a Certificate specifying the scituacon bounds and quantity thereof you are to returne to us with all convenient speed And for yo[r] soe doeing this shall be yo[r] sufficient warr[t].
> Given under my hand at Charles Towne this xxvij[th] day of July 1672./
> John Yeamans
> To John Culpeper
> Surveyo[r] Generall./

> Carolina./
> By the Governo[r] by and with the)
> advice and consent of the Councill)
> You are forthw[th] to cause to be admeasured and layd out for Richard Cole foure hundred and fifty acres of land (being the full proporcon due to him by the lords prop[rs]. concessions for himselfe and two Serv[ts]. namely Dennis Mahoone and Richard Crossland arriveing in the first ffleet) or soe much thereof as is or shall be found to be conteyned between the lines of the lands allotted to be layd out M[r]. John Coming and Affera his Wife to the South and M[r]. Joseph Dalton to the North without prejudicing or removeing either of the said allotted lines (deducting soe much therefrom as his Towne lott and Tenn acre lott amounts to if any he hath) And a Certificate fully specifying the scituacon bounds and quantity thereof yo[u] are to returne to us wth all convenient speed and for yo[r] soe doeing this shall be yo[r] sufficient warr[t]. Given under my hand at Charles Towne this xxvij[th] day of July 1672./
> John Yeamans
> To John Culpeper
> Surveyo[r] Generall./

Special Grants. Special grants were made for political and social reasons. New England states granted land to veterans of colonial conflicts. Virginia granted land to Huguenot refugees for a time and denied applications from Quakers in another period. Special grants contain an abundance of relationship evidence. For example, Cabell's *Turff and Twigg: The French Lands* (cited earlier) explains that in 1700, King William III donated ten thousand acres in Virginia to the French refugees who settled at Manakintowne on the southern bank of the James River. This tract of land is believed to be in the counties of Powhatan and Chesterfield. Clearly, hundreds of transaction variations are possible, depending on the subdivisions of each patent.

Licenses. Some colonies issued licenses granting permission to individuals to take possession of certain tracts of land. Many of these records have been preserved and are housed in the appropriate state land offices.

Land Transfers from Foreign Powers and Colonies to the United States (1780–1867)

Confiscated Lands. Lands seized by colonial governments from individuals who opposed these governments in various wars were called confiscated lands. During the American Revolution, lands were taken from individuals loyal to the British government. Herbert Burleigh's *New York State—Confiscations of Loyalists* (Toronto, Ontario: United Empire Loyalists Association of Canada, 1970) lists these confiscations. Figure 11-9 contains a sample listing.

The Disposition of Loyalist Estates in the Southern District of the State of New York by Harry Yoshpe (New York: Columbia University Press, 1939) reports the reasons for confiscation and the disposal of these lands in the counties of New York, Kings, Queens, Suffolk, Westchester, and Richmond. Yoshpe discusses the speculation that resulted, the manner in which claims were liquidated, and the litigation that followed. These affairs resulted in many sources for the genealogist. One chapter in Yoshpe's book explains the disposing of the loyalist estates in New York County. The author provides very helpful case studies; for example, he explains the background of the DeLancey family, one of the wealthiest families in the colonies before the American Revolution. Yoshpe includes several maps and illustrations of the land confiscated from the DeLanceys and identifies more than twenty-three purchasers of the confiscated property. The bibliography lists other sources concerning the area that are valuable to genealogists.

Federal authorities confiscated land from Native Americans. Some of the claims that were made later have been published. In North Dakota, the records of the Sioux Indians have been partially compiled in *Sioux Personal Property Claims from the Original Ledger* by Ruth Brown (Medford, Oreg.: Rogue Valley Genealogical Society, 1987). The book mentions various land allotments and other records.

Treaties. When the New York Commissioners of Indian Affairs produced the *Proceedings of the Commissioners of Indian Affairs Appointed By Law for the Extinguishment of Indian Titles in the State of New York* (Albany, N.Y.: J. Munsell, 1861), Franklin B. Hough added very insightful comments. The book's more than 490 pages cover the period between 1784 and 1790. Since the publication of these early records of treaties, increasing numbers of genealogists have used them in research. Some publishers even specialize in reference materials concerning Native Americans. Histree Publishers (23011 Moulton Parkway D-12, Laguna Hills, CA 92653) has produced several volumes on American Indian treaties. The company's catalog states that

Name	Town	County	Addition	Indictment When Found	Judgment When signed
John Adams	Scaghticoke	Albany	Farmer	294 Indep	14–7–1783
John Adams	Hosick Dist	Albany	Yeoman	29.7.5 Indep	14–7–1783
Wm Allen son of Wm	Charlotte Pre	Dutch	Yeoman	18.5.5	14–7–1783

Figure 11-9. A sample listing from Burleigh's *New York State—Confiscations of Loyalists* (page 1).

> Indian treaties are the backbone for most records that have historical and genealogical significance. These publications are indexed. In some volumes materials are included that are not treaties, but are connected to treaties or caused records to be created that have historical and genealogical value. Some of the treaties required an enumeration of the tribe to be appended to the treaty.

From these treaties, land formerly occupied by many Native American tribes was parcelled out to white settlers.

Transfers from the Federal Government to Individuals

Land Entries. Land entry petitions or applications were usually made by the settler to the colonial governor for colonial land transfers or to the ruling body in New England colonies. Few of these early colonial land entries have been published; land entry papers exist at the Federal level. These applications contain testimonies, warrants, and supporting documents sent to the General Land Office (now known as the Bureau of Land Management, or BLM) to acquire land patents. In the past they were generally inaccessible, but now they have been scanned onto computer disks and made available via computer modem. Researchers can obtain the index to these applications by writing to the BLM, 7450 Boston Boulevard, Springfield, VA 22153, or calling 703-440-1600.

Bounty-Land Applicants. Bounty land was offered to military veterans to encourage men to enlist and to reward them for military service from the colonial period up to 1855. These applications can prove military service and help researchers locate individuals in an area so that other records might be searched.

A great variety of printed bounty land applicant lists have been published including *Arkansas Military Bounty Grants (War of 1812)* by Katheren Christensen (Hot Springs, Ark.: Arkansas Ancestors, 1971); *Index to the Headright and Bounty Grants of Georgia, 1756–1909,* rev. ed. (Greenville, S.C.: Southern Historical Press, 1992); *Bounty and Donation Land Grants of Texas 1835–1888* (Austin: University of Texas Press, 1967) by Thomas Lloyd Miller; Lowell M. Volkel's *War of 1812 Bounty Lands in Illinois* (cited earlier); *Catalogue of Revolutionary Soldiers and Sailors of the Commonwealth of Virginia: To Whom Land Bounty Warrants Were Granted by Virginia for Military Service in the War for Independence*, compiled by Samuel M. Wilson from official records in the Kentucky State Land Office at Frankfort, Kentucky (Baltimore: Genealogical Publishing Co., 1967); *Revolutionary War Records: Virginia Army and Navy Forces with Bounty Land Warrants for Virginia Military District of Ohio, and Virginia Military Script from Federal and State Archives* by Gaius Marcus Brumbaugh (Washington, D.C.: 1936; reprint; Baltimore: Genealogical Publishing Co., 1967); and *Index: The Balloting Book, and Other Documents Relating to Military Bounty Lands in the State of New York by M. Francis Ferris* (Syracuse, N.Y.: Onondaga Historical Association, 1954).

Military warrants that eventually may have led to grants have also been published. These warrants can help researchers determine an individual's previous place of residence. For example, in *Old Tuskaloosa Land Office Records and Military Warrants 1821–1855*, compiled by Marilyn Davis Hahn (Barefield) (Easley, S.C.: Southern Historical Press, 1984), the date of the warrant is stated, followed by the individual's name, residence, section, township, and range. By watching for others who registered on the same day, researchers may be able to identify individuals who might be related or moved together. Figure 11-10 is an example from Hahn's book.

Several military warrant books, such as *Old Cahaba Land Office Records and Military Warrants 1817–1853*, compiled by Marilyn Davis Hahn (Barefield), rev. ed. (Birmingham, Ala.: Southern University Press, 1986), contain excellent maps and illustrations to aid the researcher in locating a particular family (figure 11-11). Figure 11-12 is an excerpt from Hahn's text showing the types of data these records contain.

Figure 11-13 is from Volkel's index to the *War of 1812 Bounty Lands in Illinois* (cited earlier).

Even rejected claims can provide genealogical clues. William Lindsay Hopkins's *Virginia Revolutionary War Land Grant Claims 1783–1850 (Rejected)* (cited earlier) contains the following entries (the comments in brackets have been added to highlight the clues these entries provide) (pages 1, 240, and 241):

> Abbott, William, Sr. -Soldier-Army-Culpeper CO, VA William Abbott, Sr. and William Abbott, Jr. enlisted for two years. They served under Gen. George Rogers Clark in the Illinois Regt. and the Western army. [*The regimental histories and the personal history of Gen. George Rogers Clark could indicate the counties in Illinois from which enlisted these men. This is important in case other family members lived there as well.*] Benjamin Roberts, late Capt., on 12 Feb 1835 in Shelby CO., KY states that he enlisted William Abbott, Sr. of Culpeper CO in his company in the Fall of 1779 and that he served until 25 Dec 1780. Capt. Roberts commanded a company attached to Col. Joseph Crockett's Regt. and Col. George Slaughters' Corps. July Court 1835: Heirs of William Abbott, Sr. are Joseph Abbott, Charlotte Abbott, Phoebe Pritchard, Hannah Skillman widow of Joseph Skillman, William Abbott, Robert Abbott and French Abbott, Roxalana Boe wife of Joseph Boe, William Henry Abbott, Fanny Neale wife of Thompson neale and Lucian Abbott. (A majority of the heirs live in Scott CO and Bourbon CO, KY). [*The census entries for 1830/40 in Scott and Bourbon*

TUSKALOOSA LAND OFFICE REGISTER OF RECEIPTS 2 July 1821 through 25 February 1835					
DATE	NAMES	RESIDES IN	SEC	TWP	RANGE
7/3/1821	John McLaughlin, Jr.	Shelby Co.	1	17	1E
"	John McLaughlin, Sr.	Shelby Co.	21	17	1E
"	Alexander McLaughlin	Shelby Co.	21	171	1E
"	Will Rowen	St. Clair Co.	2	17	1E
"	James McLaughlin	Shelby Co.	10	17	1E
"	Thomas C. Bradford	St. Clair Co.	4	171	1E
"	William Gilbert	Shelby Co.	16	17	1E
"	Joseph Taylor	Shelby Co.	10	17	1E
"	Henry Coxe	Shelby Co.	10	17	1E
"	David Neal	Shelby Co.	11	17	1E
"	James A. Givens	Shelby Co.	29	17	1E
"	Joseph Ray	Shelby Co.	15	17	1E
"	Joseph K. Sparks	Shelby Co.	21	17	1E
"		Dallas Co.	20	17	1E

Figure 11-10. An example from Hahn's *Old Tuskaloosa Land Office Records and Military Warrants 1821–1855* (page 1).

counties, Kentucky, may provide more information for these individuals. Land and property records, probate records, and vital records may also be useful.] 6 Feb 1834: William Abbott, Jr., decd., heirs are Roxalana Abbott, William Abbott, Hannah Skillman, French Abbott and Polly Barbee, late Polly Abbott, who died leaving Joseph Barbee and other children. [*Probate records, land and property records, census entries, and other records may contain information on William Jr. With basic information provided by this rejected claim and other sources, researchers assembled entire family units.*]

Wood, Meade - Drummer - Warwick CO, VA
Warwick CO, VA Court on 9 Feb 1837 on the motion of Miles Wood certifies that William Wood of Warwick CO, VA enlisted in the Regt of Col. Marshall as a Fifer and Meade Wood enlisted as a Drummer. In York CO, VA on 3 Mar 1837, William Burcher, Sr., Miles L. Wood, Matthew Wood, John Hopkins, Rebecca Stacy, Edmund Powell and John Wood as Heirs of William Wood and Meade Wood state that William and Meade Wood were survived by a brother, John Wood. Heirs of John Wood, formerly of Warwick CO, VA and surviving brother of William and Meade Wood, on 20 Feb 1837 in York CO, VA state that John Wood died leaving children viz (1) Edward Wood who died leaving issue Elizabeth Wood who married Miles Wood; (2) Meade Wood who is dead leaving issue Ann Wood who married John Hopkins; (3) John Wood who is dead leaving issue Miles Wood; (4) William Wood who is dead leaving issue viz John Wood and Martha Wood who married Edmund Powell; (5) Elizabeth Wood who married William Burcher; (6) Rebecca Wood who married William Stacy and survives him and (7) Susan Wood who married William Lloyd. Henry Buchanan, aged 75, on 29 Aug 1836 in York CO, VA states that Meade Wood of Warwick CO, VA and William Wood of Warwick CO enlisted under Col. Marshall. [*Obviously, two Wood families intermarried. Marriage, probate, and land and property records of York County, Virginia, could contain more information and could lead to more sources that eventually may extend this line. Because Henry Buchanan was 75 years old in 1836, he was probably born in 1761; ages can be estimated for William and Mead Wood, who enlisted at the same time.*]

Woodrow, Andrew - Brigade Quarter Master - Army
On 13 Aug 1783, back pay to Andrew Woodrow, Brigade QM, paid to Capt. Pemberton. John Jack, aged 66, of Hampshire CO, VA on 8 Nov 1833 states that he knew Andrew Woodrow of Hampshire CO, VA from 1778 until his death in 1814. [*Andrew Woodrow's age could be estimated at around 56 at the time of his death, assuming he was 20 years old when he served in the military as Quarter Master. He lived in Hampshire County between 1778 and 1814, so his probate, tax, land, and property records should exist.*]

Andrew Woodrow left children viz Matilda Woodrow the wife of John McDowell, Emily Jean Woodrow the wife of Samuel Kercheval, Jr., Andrew Woodrow and

William C. Woodrow. Andrew Woodrow's grandchildren are Mary Ann Dailey, James Dailey, Edward Dailey, Andrew Woodrow Dailey, William W. Dailey and John Dailey, the children of Elizabeth Woodrow who married James Dailey and both of them are dead. Also, Mary Ann Dailey, James Dailey and Edward Dailey are dead without issue. Smith Thompson, aged 86, of August CO, VA on 22 Nov 1833 states that he was in the war and knew Capt. Andrew Woodrow. [*Andrew Woodrow's children were Matilda McDowell, Emily Kercheval, Andrew Woodrow, and William Woodrow. He also had grandchildren Mary Ann Dailey, Andrew Woodrow Dailey, William W. Dailey, John Dailey, and others not named. Family histories on the McDowell, Kercheval, and Dailey families could be searched, as well as the Woodrow histories of Virginia.*]

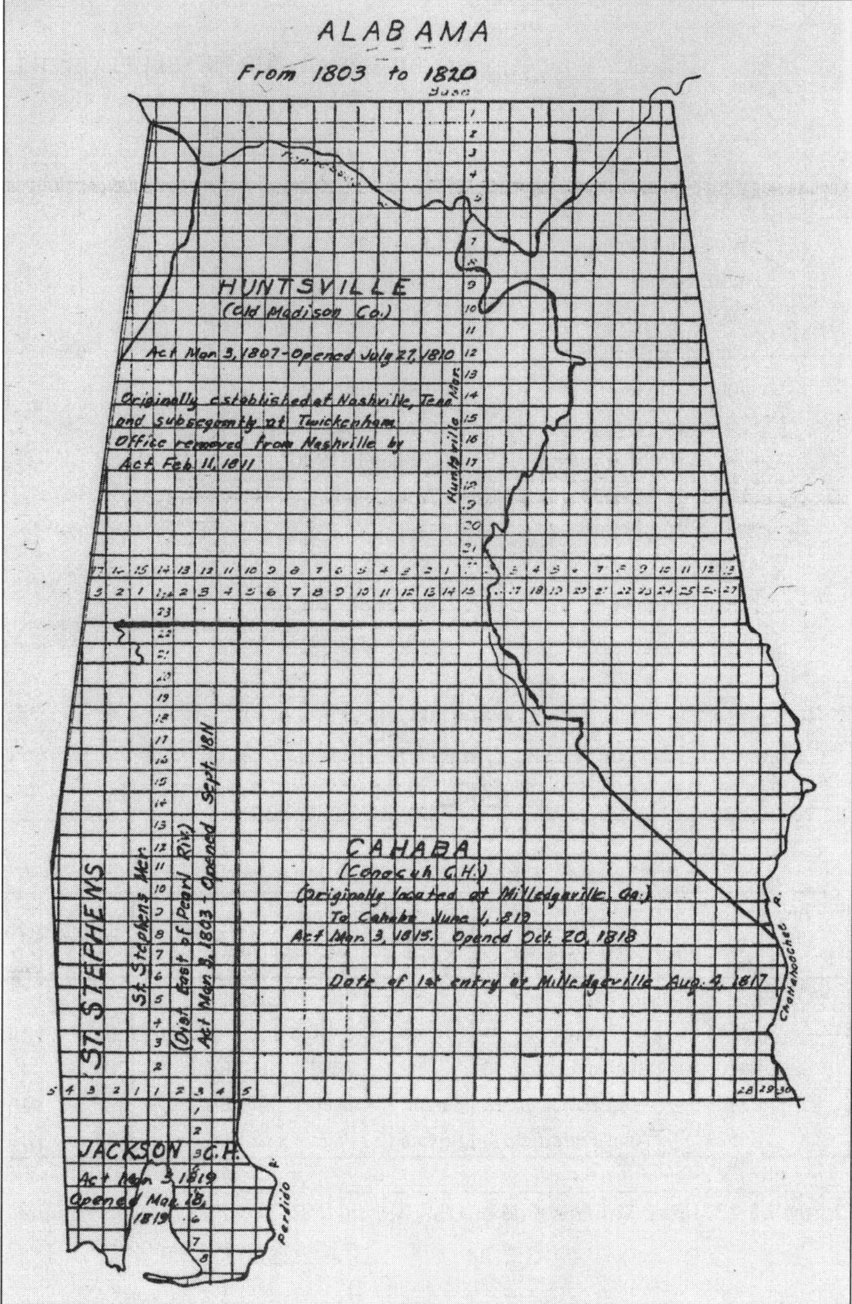

Figure 11-11. Hahn's *Old Cahaba Land Office Records and Military Warrants 1817–1853* contains excellent maps and illustrations.

In some cases, military bounty grants have been compiled as a substitute for other, missing records. For example, *Arkansas Military Bounty Grants (War of 1812)* was intended to replace the lost 1820 Arkansas census. However, researchers must be careful not to assume too much from grant records. In the Arkansas index, for instance, which lists more than six thousand grantees, fewer than 1 percent were listed in the same county in the 1830 census. Fifty-two percent were listed in the state, but in different counties. Many people received land grants, but they did not necessarily settle on the property and did not appear on later records (Christensen 1971, v).

Grants made before 1812 have proved the most helpful in placing individuals in a locality at a certain time so that other records, if they exist, can be searched. However, 1812 bounty-land grant applications contain much more genealogical information than some earlier grant records. Figure 11-14, from *Arkansas Military Bounty Grants (War of 1812),* illustrates this fact.

Territorial Lands. Many early settlers in the frontier regions of the United States are listed in published Federal and state territorial papers. Georgia, Illinois, Indiana, Kentucky, Louisiana, Maine, Massachusetts, Missouri, North Carolina, Ohio, Rhode Island, South Carolina, Vermont, Virginia, and West Virginia have published land records for at least part of the colonial or early settlement period. Three examples are *Early Settlers of Missouri As Taken from Land Claims in the Missouri Territory,* by Walter Lowrie (reprint; Easley, S.C.: Southern Historical Press, 1986); Charles R. Maduell's *Federal Land Grants in the Territory of New Orleans: The Delta Parishes* (New Orleans: Polyanthos, 1975), adapted from *American State Papers, Public Lands,* vol. 2; and *First Settlers of the Mississippi Territory* (Nacogdoches, Tex.: Ericson Books, n.d.). The latter is organized in three sections: nonresident British grants; claims presented (British patents, occupancy, pre-emption, Spanish warrant, etc.); and abstracts of certificates entered with the register of the land office west of the Pearl River during the month of July 1805 grounded on British and Spanish patents. Land records for even the western territorial states are listed in *An Inventory and Index to the Records of Carson County, Utah,*

RECEIVERS OFFICE IN MILLEDGEVILLE, GA.
August 1817–November 181
BOOK 300

PURCHASER	RESIDENCE	LOCATION PURCHASED TWP	RANGE	DATE
Absalom Carter	Jones Co., Ga.	11	13	8/4/1817
William Gary	Jones Co., Ga.	11	14	8/5/1817
William Ogle	Miss. Territory	11	13	8/5/1817
George Miller	Columbia Co., Ga.	9	15	8/5/1817
John K. Lyle	Eatonton, Ga.	9	16	8/5/1817
James Pingston	Hancock Co., Ga.	9	16	8/5/1817
Taliaferro Livingston	Abbeville, S. C.	10	16	8/6/1817
Uriah G. Mitchell	Washington Co., Ga.	10	16	8/6/1817
Toddy Robinson	Anson Co., N. C.	13	17	8/6/1817
William Peacock	Montgomery Co., N.C.	13	17	8/6/1817
George Wyche	Greenville Co., Va.	14	17	8/16/1817
Charles Williamson	Milledgeville, Ga.	16	17	8/16/1817

Figure 11-12. From Hahn's *Old Cahaba Land Office Records and Military Warrants 1817–1853* (page 1).

War of 1812 Bounty Lands in Illinois

Date of Patent	No. of Warrant	Name of Patentee	In what Capacity Served	Of what Corps or Reg't	1/4 sec	Twp	Range	To whom delivered	When delivered
1817									1817,
Oct 6	2446	William Pool	Private	D. Ketchum's 25th inf	SE5	4 n	8 w	Samuel Berrian, NY	Nov 18
"	6706	Shubel Lockwood	"	Read's 6th Infantry	SW 5	4 n	8 w.	Samuel Berrian, NY	Nov 18
"	3508	John H. Kimmel	Sargnt	Beeker's 6th Inf.	NE 3	4 n	6 w.	John H. Kimmel	Oct. 6
"	6823	John Porterfield	Private	Palmer's 2d Inf.	NW 3	4 n	6 w.	Samuel Berrian, NY	Nov. 18

Figure 11-13. From Volkel's index to the *War of 1812 Bounty Lands in Illinois* (page 21).

and Nevada Territories, 1855–1861 (Reno, Nev.: Grace Dangberg Foundation, 1984), compiled by Marion Ellison. Many other statewide records are listed in the bibliography at the end of this chapter.

After the acquisition of the Northwest Territory by the United States, a policy of territorial government was established for sparsely populated areas until statehood was achieved. The paperwork produced by the territories was edited by Clarence Edwin Carter and published in a twenty-six-volume set titled *Territorial Papers of the United States* (Washington, D.C.: Government Printing Office, 1934–62). These published abstracts include actions and correspondence relating to land and court proceedings. They may also include petitions made by the early residents and other early settler lists. They provide valuable information about the territorial residents. *Territorial Papers of the United States* covers the following areas of the midwestern and southern states:

Volume(s)	*Territory and Years*
1	General papers pertaining to two or more territories
2–3	Northwest of the River Ohio, 1787–1803
4	South of the River Ohio, 1790–1796
5–6	Mississippi, 1809–1817
7–8	Indiana, 1800–1816
9	Orleans, 1803–1812
10–12	Michigan, 1805–1837
13–15	Louisiana, 1803–1821
16–17	Illinois, 1809–1819
18	Alabama, 1817–1819
19–21	Arkansas, 1819–1836
22–26	Florida, 1821–1845
27–28	Wisconsin, 1836–1848

To Whom Patented	Warrant No.	Patent Date	Comments
Wyley Adams son & Hrs of Jno Adams	24,511	1821	
Catherine Bayzand daughter & the other hrs at law of Jas H. Anderson	26,837	1836	
Harriet Beddel daughter & the other hrs at law of John Bigelow	26,635	1835	

Figure 11-14. 1812 bounty-land grant applications contain much more genealogical information than some earlier grant records, as shown in this portion from *Arkansas Military Bounty Grants (War of 1812),* page 1. (The abbreviation *hrs* means *heirs.*)

While land evidences comprise only a small part of this collection, researchers investigating the territorial years in these states should not overlook them. For more information on this set, see chapter 15, "Documentary Collections."

Private Land Claims. After the American Revolution, the original colonies ceded rights and interests to land outside their borders to the Federal government. This land, essentially all west of the Appalachian Mountains, became part of the public domain. However, many of these colonies, especially Virginia, had already granted land (usually for military service) to settlers in those areas. Some of these lands were received directly from England, France, or Spain. (In 1803, the United States government bought even more land from France through the Louisiana Purchase.) These countries had also granted land to early settlers. Thus, the Federal government faced a difficult problem: It had just become the owner of vast expanses of land that it could either grant or sell to pay its debts. However, some tracts of land already had settlers, most of whom held what they believed to be legitimate grants from previous governments—either colonial or foreign.

In addition, frontier settlers (or "squatters") had simply settled, cultivated, and built structures on other tracts of land. To treat these early settlers fairly, the Federal government provided that individuals who believed they had legitimate claims to land in these new territories could make their claims to the U.S. Congress. Congress would then accept or deny each claim. Because settlers claimed that these lands were private property before the Federal government controlled the area, these claims are called *private claims to the public lands* (McMullin 1972, i).

Congress appointed commissioners to hear, evaluate, and act on these private claims. Their findings, petitions, depositions, and other claimant documents were sent to Congress. Using these records, Frances Ingmire compiled a three-volume work called *Citizens of Missouri* (St. Louis: the author, ca. 1984). These volumes contain records from 1787 through 1835. The following example is drawn from vol. 1 (page 31). It covers the years 1787 to 1810 in the area now known as St. Charles County, which is north of St. Louis (comments concerning ways these records might be used are italicized and enclosed in brackets):

> John FERRELL, assignee of William HARPER claiming 500 arpens of land situate waters of Hubbles Creek, District of Cape Giradeau, produces to the Board as a special permission to settle list B, on which William HARPER is No. 8 a deed of transfer from said HARPER to claimant dated 3rd August, 1805. [*To determine if a relationship existed between John Ferrell and David Ferrell, one would look for other records under both names.*]
>
> David FERRELL, duly sworn, says HARPER built a small cabin & cultivated a small spot of ground on this tract in the year 1803 and inhabited during all that year. Then sold his right to claimant no improvement since. HARPER had a wife and 7 children in the year 1803. Laid over for decision. [*To determine the names of Harper's wife and children, check later land, court, and tax records.*]
>
> . . .
>
> Joseph WORTHINGTON, sworn, says that some trifling improvement were made on this land in the year 1803, [land claimed by Joseph Thomson Sr.] but no inhabitation. The improvement was continued until the year 1805, when he removed, built two good houses and cultivated about 10 or 12 acres and continued to live there until his death. His widow and family still inhabits and cultivated. (Book 4, pg. 296). Laid over for decision. [*Joseph Thomson died between 1805 and 1835, when this statement was made. Other records in this book, as well as other county records, should be checked.*]

The following example is from vol. 2 (pages 6 and 7) of Ingmire's work, which contains grants made from 1787 to 1835 in the present states of Missouri, Arkansas, and Oklahoma:

> Charles FINDLEY, assignee of William PATTERSON claiming 450 arpens of land. See Book No. 1, pg. 493, Book No. 4, pg. 90. James FINDLEY assignee of William PATTERSON in Book No. 1, pg. 403 is a (cannot read) Charles FINDLEY, assignee of William PATTERSON (?) is also error in Book 4, pg. 90 in this, an (cannot read) survey to William PATTERSON from Henry (cannot read last name) dated 19th December, 1800 is produced and not list No. 1369 as stated. The Board confirm to William PATTERSON or his legal representatives four hundred arpens, within the bounds of a survey formerly made for said William PATTERSON recorded in Book B, pg. 393 of the Recorders Office and the same is ordered to be surveyed.
>
> Charles FINDLEY, assignee of Richard GREEN claiming 350 arpens of land. See Book No. 1, pg. 493 for James FINDLEY, assignee of Richard GREEN, which is a mistake. It ought to have been Charles FINDLEY, assignee of Richard GREEN.

The following testimony in the foregoing claim taken by Frederick BATES, Comm'r., at New Madrid June 15th, 1808 by authority from the Board.

William Smith, duly sworn, says that premises were cultivated and inhabited in the year 1802 at which time a house was built and a field of a few acres cleared, enclosed and cultivated. Constantly inhabited and cultivated to this time. GREEN had a wife and 3 or 4 children in 1803.

It is the opinion of the Board that this claim ought not to be granted.

Charles FINDLEY, assignee of Resa BOWIE claiming 300 arpens of land, produces to the Board an order of survey from Henry PEYROUX to Resa BOWIE dated 19th December, 1800. Recorded Book C, pg. 409 of the Recorders Office. See Book No. 4, pg. 91. See, also, Book No. 1, pg. 497 James FINDLEY, assignee of Resa BOWIE, which is a mistake. It ought to have been Charles FINDLEY, assignee of Resa BOWIE. The Board confirm to Charles FINDLEY three hundred arpens as described in a platt of survey found on record in Book B, pg. 394 of the Recorders Office and dated 19th June, 1801 on Joseph STORYs Surveyors Registry. (There is error in the decision of this claim; for further proceedings of the Board in this claim see pg. 21.)

. . .

In the decisions of the claims of Charles FINDLEY, assignee of William PATTERSON and Charles FINLEY, assignee of Resa [*sic*] BOWIE in this days minutes, there is error, in as much as the orders of survey bears date subsequent to the 1st of October 1800, which was overlooked by the Board when the decisions were made...therefore rescind the said decisions and are of opinion that said claims ought not to be confirmed and have caused it to be stated in the margin opposite said claims that the decision is error. Wednesday December 5th, 1810. [*These examples show that researchers need to consult all findings of the land commission before drawing conclusions. Other records referred to in these documents should also be checked.*]

Congress authorized the publishing of private land claims as part of the *American State Papers: Documents of the Congress of the United States in Relation to the Public Lands 1789–1837 and Claims.* This nine-volume set of government documents was printed by Gales and Seaton between 1832 and 1861. It details the work of Congress from 1789 to 1837. The documents are divided into ten classes, which include (among other items) the following topics: public lands, foreign relations, Indian affairs, finance, military affairs, and naval affairs.

Other publishers, such as Ingmire Publications, and authors, such as Marilyn Davis Hahn (Barefield), have also compiled information drawn from the government documents but in smaller publications directed toward specific geographical interests. One such title, Carolyn Ericson and Frances T. Ingmire's *First Settlers of the Missouri Territory,* 2 vols. (Nacogdoches, Tex.: Ericson Books, ca. 1983), contains land claims that were presented when Missouri became a territory in 1812. The examples below (vol. 2, page 23) are representative of the records in this book:

LEON N. ST. CYR, claiming four hundred and nine arpents of land, situate in the district of St. Louis; produces to the Board a concession from CHARLES D. DELASSUS, Lieutenant Governor, for the same, dated 1st January, 1800; a survey of the same, taken 3d January, and certified 2d March, 1802.

ANTOINE SOULARD'S testimony in the foregoing claim applies to this claim; also, same opinion and decision of former Board, as in preceding claim of HYACINTH ST. CYR, Jun.

Testimony taken. January 31, 1809. HYACINTH ST. CYR, sen. sworn, says that claimant is seventeen or eighteen years of age at this time; was born in the country, and has always resided in it.

July 16, 1810: Present, LUCAS, PENROSE, and BATES, commissioners. It is the opinion of the Board that this claim ought not to be granted.

ABSALOM KINNERSON, claiming six hundred and forty arpents of land, situate on Bois Bruile, district of St. Genevieve; produces to the Board a notice to the recorder, dated 29th June, 1808; produces, also, a certificate of permission to settle, sworn to by CAMILLE DELASSUS, as commandant ad interim; said permission on file.

Testimony taken. January 31, 1809. JOHN SMITH, sworn, says that claimant came to the country in 1800, and has resided in it ever since; in 1803 claimant had a wife and nine children; claimant never settled on the tract claimed until about eighteen months ago.

July 16, 1810: Present, LUCAS, PENROSE, and BATES, commissioners. It is the opinion of the Board that this claim ought not to be granted.

Hahn (Barefield) has published several collections of records dealing with early Federal land records: *Old Cahaba Land Office Records and Military Warrants, 1817–1853* (cited earlier); *Old Sparta and Elba Land Office Records and Military Warrants, 1822–1860* (Easley, S.C.: Southern Historical Press, 1983); *Old St. Stephen's Land Office Records and American State Papers, Public Lands* (Easley, S.C.: Southern Historical Press, 1983); *Old Huntsville Land Office Records and Military Warrants, 1810–1854* (Easley, S.C.: Southern Historical Press, 1985); and *Old Tuskaloosa Land Office Records and Military Warrants, 1821–1855* (cited earlier). The last book contains records that also appear in *American State Papers, Public Lands (discussed below).* In *Old St. Stephen's Land Office Records and American State Papers, Public Lands* (page iii), Hahn provides important information about these records:

> There are in the Mississippi Territory and in other parts of the United States, a number of speculators who are anxious to engross as much of the valuable land of the Territory as possible, while, on the other hand, there are a number of poor men who have settled themselves down on vacant land and made improvements, who are well worthy of protection. Some of the lands were granted by the British Government while it was a British province, and others again by the Spaniards, while under the Government of Spain. In consequence of many persons settling where it suited them, on vacant or

patented land, without regard either to British or Spanish grants, there has arisen a great variety of clashing claims to lands, which have been spun out by the memorialists to the number of thirty-two kinds or classes of claims; but all these may be comprised within a few principal heads. The following, it is presumed, will be found to embrace the whole of those which have been enumerated, viz:
1st. Lands granted by the British Government, and held in possession ever since by the first proprietors, or their assigns, to the present time
2nd. Lands granted by the British Governors by virtue of mandamus from the King, which have never been occupied by the grantees or their agents.
3d. Lands granted by British letters patent, containing certain conditions, to be performed in three years from the date of grant; otherwise to be forfeited, on failure of the improvements.
4th. Spanish grants on vacant lands.
5th. Spanish grants on lands formerly granted by the British.
6th. Lands sold by the Spanish Government, for the supposed rebellion of the proprietor, during the siege of Pensacola.
7th. Lands for which warrants of survey had been obtained before the Spanish treaty, but not presented till after the treaty.
8th. Warrants obtained since, and no patent.
9th. Settlements by occupancy.
10th. Companies claiming under Georgia.

Sometimes these smaller compilations are faster to use when an individual is known to have owned land in a particular area; however, if researchers need to search many areas, they may need to consult the largest collection, *Public Lands,* which comprises eight volumes of the *American State Papers* set. An earlier set of records relating to public lands, also titled *American State Papers,* was printed by Duff Green in five volumes in 1834. The first three volumes in this set are similar to the Gales and Seaton edition, but the last two volumes contain significantly less information than the Gales and Seaton edition. They also cover claims only through early 1834 (rather than 1837 for the Gales and Seaton edition). More than eighty thousand Americans are discussed in these pages, with documents providing more information on their families than is available in any other source. The eight *Public Lands* volumes of the Gales and Seaton set, along with a ninth volume, *Claims*, have recently been reprinted by Southern Historical Press as *American State Papers: Public Lands* (Greenville, S.C., 1994).

American State Papers: Public Lands includes records for thirteen states west of the original colonies in the areas that became known as the Old Southwest and Old Northwest. The Old Southwest included all or parts of Alabama, Arkansas, Florida, Louisiana, Mississippi, and Missouri. The Old Northwest included all or parts of Illinois, Indiana, Iowa, Michigan, Minnesota, Ohio, and Wisconsin.

The types of claims "are primarily the settlement of claims under previous sovereigns, pre-emption rights, homestead settlements, military bounty lands, and militia claims" (McMullin 1972, i). Anyone researching families who lived in these areas before statehood should search these documents for references. The new reprint will make it much easier to obtain copies of these volumes.

There are some unique aspects of using the *American State Papers*. First, because several documents were written for each claim or set of claims, names of interest may appear on the pages following the initial reference. Second, most names deal with immigrants, so there may be several versions of both given and last names: Peter may appear as Pedro, and John as Juan or Jean, depending on which sovereign granted the land. Surnames are spelled in various ways and sometimes even translated into English or truncated. Typesetting errors were common in the original edition; for example, Royette appears as Rolette. At the end of names, vowels, especially *e,* may have been dropped, and consonants may have been doubled (for example, *ll, rr, tt*). In each of these cases, the index described below will sort these names in different places. Most names are mentioned several times on a page, although the index only has one entry per page per name (McMullin 1972, vi).

Documents are arranged in chronological order, and each volume has an index. However, those indexes are fragmentary, spotty, and uneven. To improve access, Phillip McMullin published *Grassroots of America: A Computerized Index to the American State Papers: Land Grants and Claims (1789–1837)* (Salt Lake City: Gendex Corp., 1972; reprint; Greenville, S.C.: Southern Historical Press, 1994). This index identifies every individual named in the eight volumes of *Public Land* (Gales and Seaton edition), as well as the *Claims* volume (vol. 9 of the Southern Historical Press reprint). The reprint edition of this index should be available wherever the *American State Papers* reprint is found, and it is available in many smaller libraries that have purchased the index separately from the reported volumes.

Other Private Claims. From time to time, especially before the Civil War, individuals presented various claims to Congress seeking compensation for some real or perceived wrong. While many of these claims do not deal with land matters, they often refer to land matters. These claims or their abstracts were often printed at the request of Congress. Of particular value to the researcher interested in land records is the 1853 *Digested Summary and Alphabetical List of Private Claims Which Have Been Presented to the House of Representatives from the First to the Thirty-First Congress*. This list, reprinted in three volumes in 1970 by the Genealogical Publishing Company (Baltimore), indicates the action taken on each claim, with reference to the appropriate House journal entry or bill number. Many of the land claim entries refer to the same individuals as those addressed in *American State Papers;* however, the *Digested Summary* focuses on congressional action, not on the documents collected and acted upon by local land commissioners. Of the more than fifty thousand entries in these three volumes, at least 10 percent appear to pertain to land claims, many of which are for public lands and hence are not in the private land claims. Of course, not every individual whose claim appears in *American State Papers* will have pursued that claim to the House of Representatives.

In addition to the reprinted *Digested Summary*, alphabetical lists of various claims presented to Congress from 1789 to 1909 are in published summaries or digests (tables) at the National Archives and Federal repository libraries (at major university libraries). The Family History Library has the digests for the House of Representatives from 1789 to 1871.

Public Domain Indexes. After the Federal government took possession of the great tracts of lands described above, it began granting that new public land to individuals. This land was transferred in a variety of ways: by credit (from 1800 to 1820) or cash entry (from 1820 to 1908); through donation land claims, which granted 160 to 320 acres of free land in the territories of Oregon, Florida, and Washington (from 1840 to 1850) to individuals who proved U.S. citizenship; through warrant and script claims (see "Bounty Land Applicants," above); through homestead entries, which granted 160 acres but required application, cultivation, and improvement of the land and residence for a five-year period after 1862; and through specialty titles (from 1831 to 1891) such as railroad lands, timber and stone, desert lands, timber culture, and pre-emption claims (which gave squatters first choice and which could be later changed to homestead entries). Tens of thousands of documents now reside with the BLM (formerly known as the General Land Office).

In an attempt to identify many the earliest public land documents, Clifford Neal Smith created a detailed catalog (or calendar) of many of the original land patents. His calendar, along with thorough indexes to the names of all individuals mentioned in the documents, the topics addressed, and the tract descriptions, was published as *Federal Land Series: A Calendar of Archival Materials on the Land Patents Issued by the United States Government, with Subject, Tract and Name Indexes,* 4 vols. (Chicago: American Library Association, 1972–86). It catalogs and describes more than fourteen thousand documents created from 1788 to 1835. It also references more than thirty-five thousand individuals named in those records.

This collection provides a means of locating early settlers before Federal censuses were taken. The calendar lists the date of the record, the names mentioned in the papers, the subject of the manuscript, the names of the patentees, and the location (including microfilm roll) of the manuscript. Although the information covers primarily Ohio land tracts, patents are also included for settlers in Alabama, Illinois, Indiana, Louisiana, and Tennessee. Research in the original records is necessary to learn if the name noted is the person sought by the researcher and to learn about other genealogical or biographical information.

Computerized Sources. The BLM's Eastern States Office in Springfield, Virginia, holds more than 5 million documents relating to Federal land, including patents, plats, and field notes. These documents relate to the public land states east of the Mississippi River. The BLM has recently instituted the Automated Retrieval System, which stores optical images of these documents to expedite the research process. Currently, records are online for six states: Arkansas, Florida, Louisiana, Michigan, Minnesota, and Wisconsin. Federal land records for Mississippi, Ohio, and Alabama will soon be online; and records for Illinois, Indiana, Iowa, and Missouri will be added. Researchers who open an account with the BLM (which requires a major credit card and a password) can retrieve the actual scanned documents through a modem.

As the documents are entered, they are indexed so that search requests can be made using six different "descriptors": land description, patentee name, patent authority, land office, certificate number, and county. No longer will the complete legal description of the parcel be necessary to obtain the desired data. The records are indexed on CD-ROM and can be purchased for thirty-five dollars or less. CDs are available for Arkansas, Florida, Louisiana, Michigan, Minnesota, Mississippi, Ohio, and Wisconsin. For additional information, write to the BLM, Eastern States, General Land Office Automated Records Project (GLO), 7450 Boston Boulevard, Springfield, VA 22153, or call 703-440-1600.

Early Settler Lists

Some early abstracted records, such as the New Madrid Land Grants, have been published in Lowrie's *Early Settlers of Missouri As Taken from Land Claims in the Missouri Territory* (cited earlier). It does not contain detailed illustrations from the original records, but it does have a valuable index.

Transfers from States to Individuals

Caveat Proceedings. Nell Marion Nugent's *Caveat Proceedings* (n.p., 1970) provides another form of published land records. *Caveat* is a Latin legal term meaning "Let him beware." A *caveat* proceeding gives formal notice of a delay in the process of obtaining a grant to provide opportunity for an opposing view to be documented. The proceeding temporarily or permanently may prevent the carrying out of a patent. Two examples from Nugent's work (pages 1 and 75) follow:

> Davies vs Bruce. Entered 8 May 1786. Let no grant issue to Samuel Bruce on survey from Ohio Co. of 400 acs. by virtue of entry on part of Pre-emption Warrant #2499 granted to Silas Hedges, who assigned to said Bruce, situate on waters of Buffalo Cr., adj. John Tilton, because Azariah Davies had a prior settlement and obtained a Pennsylvania Warrant while it was in the state of Pennsylvania after the running of the Temporary Line and previous to the running the fixed Boundary of the said State of Pennsylvania and had the same surveyed and returned to the Land Office for Patenting.

> Walker vs DuVal. Entered 21 March 1809. Let no grant issue to Philip Duvall for 35 acs. in Buckingham County upon survey dated 3 April 1807 pursuant to entry made 7 June 1805, because John M. Walker & Susanna his wife, late Susanna Christian, only daughter & heiress at law of John Christian & Joice Christian, claim same by virtue of fair purchase made of the Executrix of James Hundley by virtue of the testament & last will of said Hundley for the payment of his debts when said John Christian became the purchaser, who devised it to his wife Joice, who died intestate &, therefore, the wife of said Walker being heiress to both John & Joice Christian is entitled to same; and because said James Hundley entered upon the same lands, cleared & cultivated the same and regularly paid taxes & quit rents therefor both before and since 1772 until his death; taxes have been regularly paid from that period to the present time by the Executrix of said Hundly & by said John Christian after his purchase to his death & by said Joice Christian till her death, which happened in the last year.

Alien Resident Lands. Aliens (non-citizens) who came to the English colonies could not possess or bequeath property. If an alien ever acquired property, it returned to the crown upon the person's death. Likewise, after the American Revolution, the real estate of a resident alien became the property of the state (instead of the crown) upon the alien's death. However, many states did provide ways for aliens to keep property. For example, in 1825, New York passed legislation to help resident aliens retain real estate. An alien with property was required to make a deposition stating that "he is a resident in, and intends always to reside in the United States and to become a citizen thereof as soon as he can be naturalized; and that he had taken such incipient measures as the law of the United States required, to enable him to obtain naturalization" (Scott and Conway 1978, iii). If, after six years, the alien had not been naturalized or become a resident of the United States, the land would return to the state of New York.

In *New York Alien Residents, 1825–1848* (cited earlier), Scott and Conway provide some valuable sources for genealogical research from aliens' depositions in the New York State Library in Albany. The book lists each alien's place of residence by village, town, city, or county. It also states the alien's country of birth and occasionally the name of the county or department. Some listings also include the individual's date of birth, age upon arrival in the United States, date of arrival in the United States, and deposition date. A few entries list female aliens' marital status (single, married, or widowed), and, if applicable, husband's name and trade or profession. Some entries also contain filings made by parents on behalf of children and the professional status of resident aliens. The following examples from Scott and Conway's book (pages 1 and 27) represent the types of information the entries provide:

AKHURST
James, of Schaghticoke, Rensselaer Co., baker - 17 Nov 1836
James Henry, of Brooklyn, Kings co., born in Kent Co., Eng., about 1817; came to U.S. in 1836 - 19 Aug. 1844

DAVIDSON
Agnes, of Albany, born in Paisley, Co. of Renfrew, Scotland, age now about 40 - 13 Jan. 1841
Charles, of Pavilion, Genesee Co. - 29 Jan. 1844
James, of NYC, slater - 23 July 1831
Jeannette (wife of John Davidson, of Albany), of Albany; her maiden name was McLaren; she was born in town of Callender, the parish of Callender, Co. of Perth; age now about 42 - 13 Feb. 1841

Warrant Lists. After an application had been approved, a warrant was issued. The warrant gave a person the right to select property and have it surveyed. Many of these records are filed in state land offices. The following example of a printed warrant abstract is from Margie Brown's *Genealogical Abstracts, Revolutionary War Veterans, Scrip Act, 1852 . . .* (cited earlier) (pages 76, 77):

Application: 301 THRU 309, 467
EBENEZER FINLEY
Captain, Virginia Continental Line

Henrico Co, VA. Court 1 Jun 1840

EBENEZER FINLEY joined the Continental Line at Somerset Co, MD. He later transferred to Harrison's Brigade in the Virginia Continental Line. EBENEZER[1] FINLEY died testate in 1784 without issue. His eldest brother SAMUEL[1] FINLEY was his heir at law. SAMUEL died unmarried in 1800 leaving two brothers, JOHN[1] and JAMES EDWARD[1] FINLEY, and a niece ELIZABETH ANN[2] MORSE as heirs.

JOHN H.[1] FINLEY (Bro) d 1800 New Brunswick, NJ.
Issue:
1. SAMUEL R.[2] FINLEY d bef 1840 liv Easton, PA.
Issue:
1. JOHN H.[3] FINLEY
2. SARAH[3] FINLEY m SAMUEL SHICK
3. JAMES[3] FINLEY liv N.Y. City 1842
4. SAMUEL[3] FINLEY
5. DANIEL[3] FINLEY liv N.Y. City 1842
6. ANDREW[3] FINLEY liv N.Y. City 1842
7. GEORGE[3] FINLEY Pittsfield, MA. 1840
8. CATHERINE[3] FINLEY
2. GEORGE[2] FINLEY
3. EVE[2] FINLEY m JOHN VAN HORNE Reading, PA. 1840

JAMES BURR[1] FINLEY (Bro) d ca 1820 m MARY
Issue:
1. WILLIAM[2] PERONNEAU FINLEY liv Charleston, SC.
2. MARY H.[2] FINLEY d w/o issue
3. JAMES EDWARD[2] BURR FINLEY d 1840 m MARIA ____ Charleston, SC.
Issue:
1. JAMES HAMILTON[3] FINLEY
2. WILLIAM WASHINGTON[3] FINLEY
3. WILLIAM CARSON[3] FINLEY
4. MARIA[3] FINLEY
REBECCA[1] FINLEY d bef 1834 m ____ BREASE (sis)
Issue:
1. ELIZABETH ANN[2] BREASE m ___ MORSE (niece) d bef 1840
Issue:
1. SAMUEL F. B.[3] MORSE
2. SIDNEY E.[3] MORSE
3. RICHARD C.[3] MORSE

Depositions: J. Pryor (RWS); Gabriel Long (RWS); Robert Wilmott (RWS); John Jordan (RWS)

Note: EBENEZER FINLEY'S father was President of what is now Princeton University. WILLIAM PERONNEAU FINLEY was President of Charleston S.C. College. SAMUEL F. B. MORSE was inventor of the Morse code.

State Land Lottery Indexes. For several years, the state of Georgia granted land by lottery. The following groups were eligible: white males over eighteen years of age who had been residents of the state for at least three years; veterans of the American Revolution; widows of revolutionary war soldiers; orphans; and others who had not drawn land in a previous lottery.

LAND LOTTERY REGISTER—NO. 1
NOTE: Sec 1 is Lee County 2 Muscogee 3 Troup 4 Coweta 5 Carrol
First and Second days Drawing—6th & 7th March

COLUMBIA

Fortunate Drawers	Capts Dist	No.	Dt.	Sec.
Susan Daniel, orphan	Adams	88	1	3
Sylvester Hoof, illegit.	Dranes	246	23	2
George Flinn	Adams	78	10	3
Joseph Lantern	Coles	211	19	2

LAND LOTTERY REGISTER—NO. 8
NOTE: Sec 1 is Lee County 2 Muscogee 3 Troup 4 Coweta 5 Carrol
117th DAY'S DRAWING—March 26

COLUMBIA

Fortunate Drawers	Capts Dist	No.	Dt.	Sec.
Nancy Welch's illegitimate	Carrolls	87	19	2
Seaborn P. Huchlingson's orphans	Bealls	171	8	1
Nancy Yarborough, wid.	Ramseys	280	6	5
John Parish	Dranes	109	5	5

GLYNN

Fortunate Drawers	Capts Dist	No.	Dt.	Sec.
John McLeod, soldier	McLeods	214	21	2
Samuel Burnett	Burnetts	53	6	3

Figure 11-15. From *Reprint of Official Register of Land Lottery of Georgia, 1827* (pages 1 and 49) .

In *Reprint of Official Register of Land Lottery of Georgia, 1827* (1928; reprint; Easley, S.C.: Southern Historical Press, 1986), Martha Lou Houston shows how this lottery list also acted as a census. The introduction to the reprint edition states that the book does not include the complete 1827 lottery: more than six hundred Revolutionary War soldiers are not listed. The introduction also points out that Native Americans vacated one area spanning the counties of Muscogee, Troup, Coweta, Lee, and Carroll so that the land would be available for the lottery. These counties were named to honor the Muscogee Indians from whom the land was acquired. The introduction also contains an 1829 map of the area.

Houston's book is divided into the various "draws" made on land and filed in the Office of the Secretary of the State of Georgia. The draws are subdivided by county and date of the drawing, beginning 6 March and ending 25 May. Examples from the 1986 edition of Houston's book appear in figure 11-15.

Deeds and Certificates of Purchase (Reconstruction Period). During the Reconstruction period after the Civil War, many former slaves settled upon land that had belonged to their white owners. By 1876, approximately fourteen thousand black families had settled in South Carolina with help from the South Carolina Land Commission. These records are explained in *The Promised Land: The History of the South Carolina Land Commission 1869–1890,* by Carol K. R. Bleser (Columbia: University of South Carolina Press, 1969). The thousands of papers produced by this commission are very helpful for South Carolina research.

Transfers from Individuals to Individuals

Deed Abstracts. Deeds are documents that transfer any property, from large acreage farms to small town lots, from one individual to another. An example of published sources covering deed abstracts is Silas Lucas Emmett, Jr., *An Index to Deeds of the Province and State of South Carolina, 1719–1785 and Charleston District, 1785–1800* (Easley, S.C.: Southern Historical Press, 1977). More published sources are listed in the bibliography at the end of this chapter. However, this bibliography is not an exhaustive list of available records. Many more indexes need to be compiled to make deed abstracts readily acceptable.

Mortgage Lists. Not everyone owned land once the frontier had been conquered or cities were established. A *mortgage* indicated that a pledge of property was given to a creditor as security for payment of a debt. Few mortgage records have been published, but some, such as E. Russ Williams, Jr., *Abstracts of Deeds: Marion County, Mississippi: Containing Deeds, Marks and Brands, Bond, Mortgages, and Deeds of Gift* (Bogalusa, La.: the author, 1962), are listed in the bibliography at the end of this chapter.

Deeds of Trust. A deed that conveys a fair right or interest in property distinct from legal ownership is called a *deed of trust*.

The title is held by someone else to secure payment. If the payment is not made, the property may be sold at public auction. Deeds of trust are usually included in the same printed sources as regular deeds.

County Land Transfer Abstracts. These books may cover an entire county's history of land transfers for designated time periods. Examples include *York Deeds* (Portland, Maine: John T. Hull, 1887; various publishers for next seventeen volumes, 1887–1910), which encompasses the period from 1642 to 1737 (before 1760, York County included all of the current state of Maine); *Land Deed Genealogy of Bedford County Tennessee 1807–1852* by Helen and Timothy Marsh Marsh (Easley, S.C.: Southern Historical Press, 1988); *Washington County, Tennessee: Deeds, 1775–1800* by Loraine Rae (Greenville, S.C.: Southern Historical Press, 1991); and *Blount County, Tennessee, Deeds: Deed Book 1, 1795–1819* by Jane Kizer Thomas (cited earlier).

Land Description Aids

Survey Abstracts. To allow ownership, land must be measured and charted in a graphic form. This plat or map of the property is drawn, described, and recorded. In Tennessee, a survey is frequently recorded as an "entry." Not all colonies or states maintained these surveys. Some are filed under county jurisdiction and can be found among early land and property records. Fortunately, several surveys have been abstracted.

ABSTRACT OF SURVEYS

Page 207

Christopher Wagoner, 400 acres, Head Branches of Long Meadows, a branch of the North Branch of Shenandoah. Adjoining Thomas Bryant, Reuben Harrison. July 14, 1772.

George Lewis, 106 acres, Middle River. Adjoining Robert Read, John Patterson, William Oldham, William Hamilton. December 9, 1772.

James Anderson, 137 acres, Head Spring of the Long Glade. Adjoining Samuel Curry. December 5, 1772.

Hugh Donohue, 1227 acres, Naked Creek. Adjoining Robert McCutchen, John King, John Seawright, William Blair. Mentioned James Leeper. June 18, 1773.

Page 208

John Poage, 650 acres, Middle River. Adjoining Robert Young, James Anderson, James Allison, William Hamilton, John Patterson. Mentioned Robert King, William Sharp, John King. January 7, 1773.

Thomas Connely, 250 acres, branch of Middle River. Adjoining John Campbell, Alexander Walker, John McMahan, Hugh Donahue, Hooks. March, 1773.

John Burnside. Adjoining The Stone Meeting Houseland, Samuel McKee and his own land. January 2, 1773.

Andrew McComb, 40 acres, branch of Naked Creek. December 24, 1772.

Page 209

David Gibson, 260 acres, Drafts of Naked Creek. Adjoining John Stepheson, John King, Andrew McComb. November 27, 1772.

Figure 11-16. From Kaylor's *Abstract of Land Grant Surveys, 1761–1791* (1938; reprint; Baltimore: Clearfield Co., 1976). The names of adjacent land holders are noted in the text, but they are not included in the index.

One example is Peter Cline Kaylor's *Abstract of Land Grant Surveys, 1761–1791* (1938; reprint; Baltimore: Clearfield Co., 1976). Abstracts in this book list the name of the landowner, number of acres, watercourse, adjacent property lines, and date of the survey. The book does not include an every-name index. As figure 11-16 shows, the names of adjacent land holders are noted in the text, but they are not included in the index.

In Dorothy Williams Potter's *Original Surveyor's Record Book, 1836–1887, Coffee County, Tennessee: With Additional Material on Early Tullahoma* (Tullahoma, Tenn.: the author, 1976), the surveyors' depictions of the property are included for reference. These records provide the exact written description and a line-drawing of each property. An example is provided in figure 11-17.

Plat Book Indexes. Plat books contain drawings that show boundaries, divisions, or other land features of property and often indicate the names of the property owners. A survey plat is a map on which land surveys are commonly recorded at a scale of two inches to the mile. Each plat usually shows one township. An example is R. Wayne Bratcher's *Index to Commissioner of Locations, Plat Books A and B, 1784–1788: In Addition to Families Naming Swamps, Branches, Creeks, Ponds, Rivers, Roads, and Counties of the Lower Ninety-Six District from the Coast of South Carolina as Far Inland as There Were Settlements* (Greenville, S.C.: A Press, 1986). The lower ninety-six district comprises the present-day towns of Abbeville, Aiken, Allendale, Anderson, Bamberg, Barnwell, Beaufort, Colleton, Dorchester, Edgefield, Greenwood, Hampton, Jasper, Lexington, McCormack, Oconee, Pickens, and Saluda (the area between the Savannah River and the Saluda River to the point where the Saluda connects to the Edisto River, then to the Atlantic Ocean). The maps in this book are photocopies of the original survey maps, and an index to the names on the maps is provided as displayed in figure 11-18.

The nicely produced plat map books of the midwestern and western states provide researchers with pictures of the neighborhoods occupied by their ancestors. With these maps, researchers can see easily that "grandpa married the girl next door." The maps provide clues to neighbors whose histories could be searched for verification of the families being researched. Plat map books often contain both the plat maps and an overall map of the county with each of its townships, riverways, canals, levees, and railroads. (For more information on maps, see chapter 3, "Geographic Tools.")

I surveyed for **David Simpson** forty acres of Land in Coffee County on the west fork of Hickory Creek Beginning at a Hickory in the west Boundary of sd. David Simpson's 163 acre tract Running west one hundred and twenty six polls to a Black oak & pointers thence North Eighty polls to a Black Jack in the south boundary of David Bank's Land on which he now lives then East twenty fore polls to a Chesnut, Bank's South East Corner thence North one hundred and twelve polls to a stake thence East twenty polls to a Mulberry, David Simpson's Corner of his Old tract thence south with Simpson's line in all one hundred and Eighty fore polls to a stake in the barrens thence East Eighty two polls to a stake thence south to the beginning.

Jesse Banks)
David Simpson S.C.C.) Surveyed Sept. 7 - 1838 [signed]
John O. Brixey) John O. Brixey

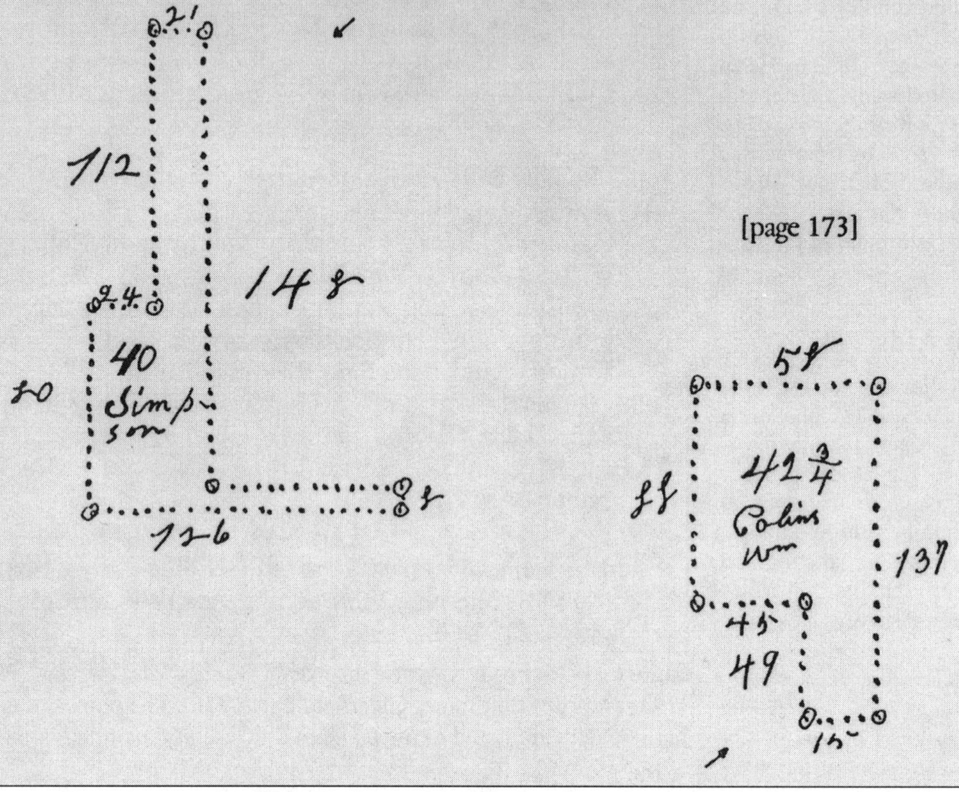

[page 173]

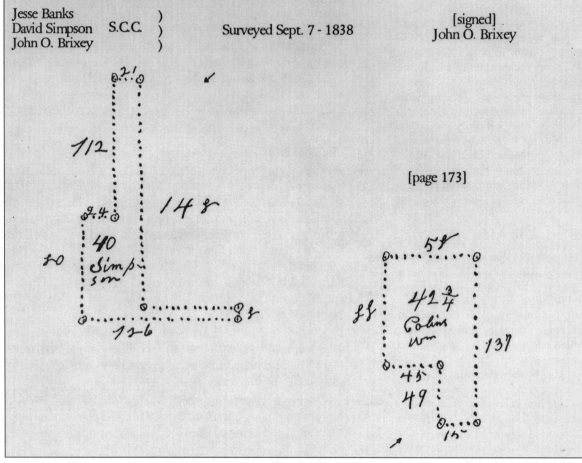

Figure 11-17. Potter's *Original Surveyor's Record Book, 1836–1887, Coffee County, Tennessee: With Additional Material on Early Tullahoma* (Tullahoma, Tenn.: the author, 1976) includes the surveyors' depictions of the property.

Other Types of Records

Records Reconstructed for Destroyed County Records. Sometimes other records are needed to prove land ownership in areas where land records have been destroyed. Fires appear to have been the most serious threat to public records. Benjamin B. Weisiger, 3rd, has compiled information from the Virginia contested election files in *Burned County Data 1809–1848: As Found in the Virginia Contested Election Files* (Richmond, Va.: the author, 1986). Contested elections specified whom everyone voted for; there was no secret ballot. In Virginia before 1818, only white male landowners could vote; but in 1818, the General Assembly of Virginia changed election laws to give the vote to every male citizen twenty-one years old or older (except free Negroes, mulattoes, or aliens) who possessed twenty-five or more acres of land with a house or a lot in town (with a long list of requirements). If the land was in several counties, the holder could vote only in the county with the greater parcel. If there was joint ownership of property, one vote could be cast jointly. *Burned County Data 1809–1848* contains information to 1850 on the "burned counties" of Hanover, Buckingham, Charles City, Gloucester, New Kent, James City, and Carolina. Below are two examples from the book (pages 74 and 24–25, respectively):

> Samuel Coleman of Caroline Co., possessed of 664 acres and slaves: Joe, Ned, Tener, Charlotte, Caesar, James, Eliza, Robert, Tom, Rose, Hannah, Washington, Moses, Mercer, George, Polly and her child George, Farsee, Richard, Esther, Tansey, John, Albert, Atera and Lucy and various items, vested in the tract, adjoining part I am in possession of expectant of life estate of my mother Susannah Coleman, 213 acres and 1/2 of a tract called "Crows Nest" 175 acres purchased by my father the late Samuel Coleman from John Sutton 3

Name	Book	Page	Acres	Location	Date Recorded
Abney, William	A	152	200	On Saludy River	6 Nov 1784
Abney, William	A	237	128	On Saludy River	22 Feb 1785
Abney, William	B	162	400	Upper Terpin Creek	23 Sep 1786
Acker, Peter	B	193	617	SW Side Saludy Riv	5 Mar 1787
Acre, Tobias	B	99	203	On Steven's Creek	13 Dec 1785
Acre, Tobias	B	99	276	On Big Horse Creek	13 Dec 1785

Figure 11-18. Bratcher's *Index to Commissioner of Locations, Plat Books A and B, 1784–1788,* includes an index to the names on the original survey maps.

March 1827. I as party of the 1st part, Edward Wethers of Stafford Co. as party of 2nd part, and Mary D. Coleman, now wife of said Samuel, and Samuel, Reuben S., Robert E. and James W. Coleman, children of said Samuel and Mary of 3rd part, for love and affection.

3 May 1827

Signed: Samuel Coleman and Mary D. Coleman.

BUCKINGHAM COUNTY

Depositions taken in contested 1809 election between David Patteson and John Pittman.

William Gibson, Sr. says he knows of only two other William Gibsons in the county; one is his son and the other is his brother's son. Neither is a freeholder.

William Tapscott says he voted on a right held by his father for 1300 acres. 500 acres were willed by his father to be sold and residue left to his wife to raise his children, and then to be sold and money divided among them. There are 7 legatees, and he has purchased the part of one of them and has lived there 3 years. His mother is living. (Abstract of clause from the father's will: I desire land adjoining Mr. John Winfrey to be sold as far as the branch below the clearing. Also to sell land adjoing [sic] Mr. Charles Cottrill. Rest to be divided among 7 children at death of wife). There is 553 acres adjoining Cottrill and 80 acres in other tract.

. . .

Michael Jones says he went with David Patteson to John Jennings's but he was not at home. Mrs. Jenings says they owned 957 acres from Waldron, her brother several years ago.

. . .

Nathan Ayres says he has a son in the county named Matthias Ayres who is not a freeholder. The 482 acres charged to Matthias Ayres is that of his deceased brother.

Regional Abstracts. Some regional compilations of abstracts divide the records into distinct jurisdictions such as counties, precincts, or districts. Others present records as a combined collection for the whole state or region. The volumes of North Carolina land grants prepared by Margaret M. Hofmann are organized according to county jurisdictions: vol. 1 of this series presents abstracts for seven counties; vol. 2 lists entries for eight counties. An entry for Dobbs county is shown below (Hofmann 1986–87, vol. 1, 50):

> 474 pg. 113 WILLIAM SPEIGHT 2 February 1762 72 acres in Dobbs County on the N. side of Great Contentnea Creek, joining Speights Farther's (sic) line and LEONARD LANGSTON OR: /s/ WM SPEIGHT JR Wits: DAVID GORDON, FRA MACKILWEAN, surveyed 24 June 1761 CB: JNO THOMSON, EDWD BOYT CHARLES YOUNG Survr.

Another example of regional abstracts is Edgar B. Sims's *Sims Index to Land Grants in West Virginia* (Charleston: Auditor's Office, 1952; supplement, 1963). This book is a good source for finding individuals whose county of residence is not known but who lived in the area that later became West Virginia. Figure 11-19 is an example from it.

A different approach is found in the *Master Index Virginia Surveys and Grants 1774–1791*, compiled by Joan E. Brookes-Smith (cited earlier). Most of the grants in this book are from Kentucky. The author has reconstructed maps of the original land grants that show the earliest settlements and describe the transactions, indicating the volume number of the original book, the original survey number, the name(s) of original grantees, acreage, county, watercourse, survey date, original book and page number, grantee, grant date, and the original book and page number for grantee.

USING PRINTED LAND RECORDS

After gaining a firm understanding of the information available in published land records, researchers should learn how to use them effectively. First one must learn the historical background of the records, then analyze how those records relate to the research question that needs to be solved. Having done this, the researcher can use the records in several ways, perhaps most importantly as a finding aid for locating names. For this purpose, the best collections of published land records are for regional areas, for an entire state, or for significant portions of a state.

Figure 11-19. Sims's *Sims Index to Land Grants in West Virginia* is a good source for finding individuals whose county of residence is not known but who lived in the area that later became West Virginia.

GILMER COUNTY

Name of Grantee	Acres	Local Description	Year	Bk	Page
Watson, James O.	400	Adj Wm Stalnaker	1847	1	421
Watson, James O.	400	Stinking Creek	1847	1	422
Watson, James O.	200	Stone Creek Run	1849	1	492
Watson, Wm A.					
et al	234	Pigeon Run	1858	3	4
West, John	79	Pike Run	1854	2	441
West, John	137	Pike Run	1860	3	70

Historical Background

Knowledge of an area's history can help researchers locate early land records. Documents for a particular county may be filed in another jurisdiction. For example, the boundary between Virginia and North Carolina was not settled until William Byrd's survey in 1726. As a result, several early colonial residents of the southern portion of Nansemond County, Virginia (particularly those whose property was south of the Somerton River), were actually residents of the territory of North Carolina. However, early land records and most county records for Nansemond County were destroyed; extant county records begin in 1866. Locating pertinent documentation could be impossible without the knowledge that Nansemond County merged with Suffolk City on 1 January 1974, and that land and other records are now housed in Suffolk under the Clerk of the Circuit Court. Early land transactions are filed in Virginia; later deeds for the same piece of property may be found in the records of adjacent North Carolina counties.

Colonial land grants and patents for Nansemond County are filed with the Virginia State Land Office in Richmond. In Virginia, *processioning* of land was required. Processioning was conducted every fourth year to verify the bounds of each person's land to determine land titles. Parish records include processioning date, name of the person whose land was processioned, and a physical description of the property, including adjoining neighbors' names. After three processionings, one's land boundaries were determined to be fixed. This procedure was ordered by the county court, then conducted and filed under the jurisdiction of the local parish. Therefore, some colonial land records for the county are available in church records. Figure 11-20 shows such an excerpt from Hall's *The Vestry Book of the Upper Parish, Nansemond County, Virginia 1743–1793* (cited earlier).

Other counties and states experienced similar jurisdictional changes. For instance, early land documents for Maine can be found in Massachusetts records. Kentucky and West Virginia were once part of Virginia; thus, these states' earliest records are filed in Richmond. Both New York and New Hampshire claimed jurisdiction over Vermont; Virginia and Connecticut claimed parts of the Ohio Territory; some Tennessee records prior to 1790 can be found in North Carolina archives; the region of present-day Alabama, Mississippi, and Florida was administered by the French and Spanish before American territorial government; and as late as 1860, Colorado records were filed in Arapahoe County, Kansas.

Knowledge of the historical background of an area may help researchers find clues to the nature of boundary disputes, such as those between New Hampshire and Massachusetts, North Carolina and Virginia, South and North Carolina, Tennessee and Kentucky, Virginia and Pennsylvania, and New York and Vermont. Interestingly, in regions of disputed boundaries, the cost of land under one jurisdiction may have been different than under the other. Thus, before definite boundary lines were established in areas of disputed borders, many settlers filed their claim under the jurisdiction that offered land at a lower price. For example, a large area in the southwestern corner of Pennsylvania was disputed with Virginia. Land in southwestern Pennsylvania sold for five pounds per one hundred acres, but in neighboring Virginia, land prices were considerably less expensive, at only ten shillings per one hundred acres. Thus, land of some residents of Fayette County, Pennsylvania, was purchased at Virginia prices and recorded in Augusta County, Virginia. This type of data is often included in introductory sections of printed land records.

Pioneers in an area often "squatted" on land without the benefits of ownership. For years battles raged in Congress over the legalities of pre-emption lands. As Billington reported, "in 1838, and again in 1840, bills allowing squatters already living on the public domain to pre-empt their lands were manipulated through House and Senate." In September 1841, a similar bill passed that "authorized all settlers on the public domain to build a cabin, make improvements, and purchase a quarter-section of land when it went on sale at $1.25 an acre" (Billington and Ridge 1982, 337).

Researchers with knowledge of an area's history are better able to understand the records and the recording process. Published land records often contain concise but detailed outlines of regions. These outlines can be invaluable research aids. For instance, Loraine Rae's *Washington County, Tennessee: Deeds, 1775–1800* (cited earlier) includes fifteen pages of historical information with accompanying maps to illustrate the organization of the county from its parent state, North Carolina.

Unfortunately, some publications provide little background information. In such cases, the researcher must do additional work to identify the laws and provisions that affect the records for the period and area under study.

Arrangement of the Work

Some published property transactions are organized alphabetically by surname, grouping all entries for a particular surname and lacking an index. Because records have been taken out of chronological order, names mentioned within the context of a document may not be discovered by even the most diligent researcher.

Published land records arranged chronologically usually incorporate an every-name index; some, however, do not. For example, hundreds of names of individuals appear in the many lists and appendices in Nancy Hope Sober's *The Intruders: The Illegal Residents of the Cherokee Nation, 1866–1907* (Ponca City, Okla.: Cherokee Books, 1991). This work is indexed, but the index does not include the names mentioned in the fifty-four pages of appendices.

Surveyors' Measures

Researchers should also become familiar with the relationships between common measurements used in the two major types of surveys:

Metes and Bounds System
625 square links = 1 square pole
16 square poles = 1 square chain
10 square chains = 1 acre

Rectangular Survey System
640 acres = 1 square mile
640 acres = 1 section
36 square miles = 1 township

N° 8

Ordered that James Winbourn and Wm Harriss Junr[34] [in][35] Presence of the Inhabitants Procession all the Bounds of Land from John Poorters to Sumn Road. thence the North Side Summn Road to the Bever dam Swamp by Capt Hunters, thence up the Swamp to South Key Road by Jno Butlers on the South side to the flat Swamp, thence Down the East Side the Sd swamp, to James Coupland's, thence to the first Station, Includeing all the Land in the Sd Bounds, you are to go Round Every Mans Land and Renew the Land Marks and Return to the Vestry an Accot of Every Mans Land you Procesn with the Names of the Persons Prest at the same, and what Land in your Prect you Shall fail to procesn you are to give an Accot with the Particur Reasons of Such failure, and if Any Refuse to have their Land Processd you are to Certify the Same to the Church Wardens within Tenn Days from Under your Hands &c

Figure 11-20. Some colonial land records for the county are available in church records. This is such an excerpt from Hall's *The Vestry Book of the Upper Parish, Nansemond County, Virginia 1743–1793.*

Abbreviations

In virtually every abstract, the compiler used abbreviations to fit more information into less space, work faster, and abstract more records. However, when using abstracts, researchers must be careful not to misread abbreviations. There is no system of universal abbreviations, so the user must learn those that the compiler used. Abbreviations should be listed at the front of abstract books for reference. Researchers should consider photocopying these lists and keeping them with any copies of accompanying abstracts.

Land Records as Finding Aids

Because published records often include an every-name index, printed land records are usually easier to use than original records. Index entries should be carefully reviewed for names of witnesses or adjacent property holders listed in the primary entry to determine whether they are indexed.

When a name is not in the index to a compilation for the location where the family is thought to have resided, researchers must conduct a thorough review of the contents. If a place-name index is included, the watercourse on which the family resided may be used to help identify records for those who owned property thereon. If the source contains no place-name or every-name index, a laborious record-by-record examination of the material may be necessary. When looking for common surnames in such a collection, researchers should try to locate names of associated, collateral, and extended family members.

Collections that contain an every-name index enable the researcher to look up the entries that appear under *both* the person's name and the county or other jurisdiction of residence. If the name of interest is listed in several counties, the researcher should consult other records for each jurisdiction to determine the correct jurisdiction.

Publications that contain land records for the majority of counties within a state can serve as general finding aids, especially for the colonial era and periods before census availability. If the county from which a family moved is unknown, the researcher may ascertain the state of prior residence from other records. If the state of prior residence is known, the researcher can review general published works, such as land records for a large region, territory, or state. Entries in these books may pinpoint the county or counties in which the family name is located. In this way, published land records for the state help identify the counties in which families of the same surname lived during the approximate period of concern. These records can also provide clues to the families' migration paths.

The date of the transaction and date of recording often differ in land and property records. In some cases, a deed was enacted many years before it was recorded. The Northwest Ordinance of 1787 included a section stating that, to be valid, wills and deeds had to be duly recorded and proved within one year. However, before 1787 many land and property transactions were officially recorded long after the documents were written and signed by the participants. In addition, many states were not included in that ordinance. Others simply did not comply with the ruling.

When county records were destroyed by fire or other natural causes, county officials often requested re-recording of documents. Additionally, land transactions filed after such destruction may include re-copied land records filed to establish a person's right to sell the property.

Although original land records may be difficult to access, and their wording is verbose and repetitive, these documents should be reviewed even after abstracts are located. The style in which deeds were worded changed over time, and researchers need to become familiar with the terminology used in documents pertaining to land and property. A comparison between an abstract in Nugent's *Cavaliers and Pioneers* (page15) and the original deed is provided below to show the material omitted from the abstract:

Definitions

Land records often have a vocabulary of their own. To be successful using printed land records, one must be able to define unique terms. Following are definitions for the terms most frequently used in land records. Additional definitions may be found in *Black's Law Dictionary: Definitions of the Terms and Phrases of American and English Jurisprudence, Ancient and Modern,* 6th ed. (Centennial Edition, 1891–1991; St. Paul, Minn.: West Publishing Co., 1990).

abstract: summary or abridgement of a record

abstract of title: history of the title to a piece of property

acquired land: Federal land that is not public and is usually obtained by the government through purchase, condemnation, gift, or exchange

acre: measure of land containing 10 square chains which is equal to 160 square rods, or 43,560 square feet

aliquot part: a portion equal to the other portions that together make the whole; a quarter section of land

allodial title: absolute ownership not subject to any feudal duties or burdens

appropriated land: public domain land that has been entered or patented, or has other type of disposal

arpent: an old French land measure of varying value, usually equal to .84 acres; also a linear measure equal to approximately 11.5 rods

assignee: a person to whom a claim, right, property, etc., is transferred; or a person appointed to act for another

base line: the east-west line used for surveying public domain lands

bounty land: public land awarded to soldiers for military service

bounty land warrant (BLW): script awarded for military service (only through 1855) that could be used to purchase land

cadastral maps: maps that identify boundaries, buildings, subdivision lines, and related details; a register of property with its value, tax, and ownership

cash certificate: final certificate issued in cash entry

chain: one hundred links of a surveyor's chain, or 66 feet; 10 square chains equal 1 acre; 16 square poles equal 1 square chain

chain bearers: often abbreviated C.B., indicates names of those who carried the measuring chains for initial survey of the land

charter: a written instrument or document from the sovereign power of a state or country, granting or guaranteeing rights

conveyance: a legal document by which title to property (real or personal) is transferred

credit entry: cash entry that allows installment payments

deed: a written document that conveys property

deed of gift: a formal document conveying a gift of real or personal property

deed of partition: a property deed by those holding joint title

deed of trust: a trust deed similar to a mortgage; a deed that conveys an equitable right or interest in property distinct from legal ownership thereof; title is held by one or more individuals to secure payment; also, a property interest held by one person for the benefit of another

deponent: one who gives evidence

devisee: the person who receives land or other real property through a will

devisor: one who, through the act of a will, grants land to another (also see *testator*)

district office: land office that handles transactions for applicants for land within its district

dower: that portion of, or interest in, real estate of a deceased husband that the law provides for a widow

dower right: the right of a widow to receive a portion of or interest in her deceased husband's property; usually only a life entitlement

eminent domain: the superior dominion of the sovereign power over property within the state, which authorizes it to appropriate all or any part thereof for necessary public use, reasonable compensation being made

entry: record of transaction; means of acquiring title; agreement to pay for and/or improve land for right to ownership

et al, et all, or *et alls:* Latin abbreviation meaning "and others"

et ux: Latin abbreviation meaning "and spouse"

fee simple: an absolute inheritance, an estate in fee made by one without condition or restriction

fee tail: an estate of inheritance limited to a class of heirs

field notes: written record of a cadastral survey that includes the boundaries, location, and description of the land

final proof: statement made by the applicant and witnesses of having met all prescribed requirements

freehold: a tenure of real property by which an estate of inheritance in fee simple or for life is held; also, an estate held by such tenure

furlong: (survey) measure of distance, equals 10 chains or 1/8 mile

General Land Office: Department of the U.S. government responsible for execution and administration of public land laws

grant: property bestowed formally, as a privilege; to make conveyance of property; to give possession or title of, especially a formally recorded transfer of title; a thing of property gifted, especially a tract of land from a governing body

grantee: a person or persons to whom a grant or deed is made; buyer

grantor: the person by whom a grant, conveyance, or lease is made

homestead act: law that provided for the issuance of property patents to those who settled on and improved certain public lands

indenture: a deed or agreement in writing; usually prepared in duplicate or triplicate, the parts were originally notched or cut so as to correspond to the copy number; also, a contract in which an apprentice is bound to a master

intestate: without having made a valid will; a person whose property was not disposed of by will

jurisdiction: authority of a sovereign power to legislate; authority, control; a sphere of authority

legacy: something left to an individual, as by will

legatee: one to whom a legacy is bequeathed

lien: claim of one or more parties upon property of another, used as security for payment of debt

lieu: place; stead; usually used as "in leu of"

link: (survey) smallest unit of survey measure, equal to 7.92 inches

master title plat: plat or survey of the new status record showing data to identify and describe land in the public domain and detailing any limitations or restrictions

meander: in surveying, a line traversing the margin of a permanent natural body of water

memorial: a statement of facts addressed to a government or some branch of it, often accompanied by a petition

mortgage: contract transferring title for specified monetary payments

original survey: cadastral survey that established boundaries for the first time

pace: (survey) a measure of distance, 2 ½ feet

partition: jointly held property that is divided by deed of partition

patent: an instrument in writing granting a conveyance of property in the public domain; also a deed

perfected patent: supplementary patent to provide the required official signatures

petition: a formal written request addressed to a sovereign or magistrate asking for relief or requesting certain rights thought to be due the requestor

plat of survey: a drawing showing boundaries, divisions or other land features; a drawing of property

pole: (survey) measure of distance, equal to 1 rod or 16 ½ feet; 1 square pole equals 625 square links; 16 square links equals 1 square chain

preemption entry: a squatters's right; based on laws enacted to protect title for those who had settled upon and improved land in the public domain

principle meridian: true north-south line running through an initial point

private entry: cash entry for public land sold; direct transfer with settler on property

public domain lands: lands that have remained under Federal ownership

public land: land owned by a government; that part of the U.S. public domain subject to sale or disposal; the public land states are Alabama, Arizona, Arkansas, California, Colorado, Florida, Idaho, Illinois, Indiana, Iowa, Kansas, Louisiana, Michigan, Minnesota, Mississippi, Missouri, Montana, Nebraska, Nevada, New Mexico, North Dakota, Ohio, Oklahoma, Oregon, South Dakota, Utah, Washington, Wisconsin, Wyoming

quitclaim: a deed conveying the interest of the grantor at the time; in many states, more than a release, used as a simple conveyance for making a transfer of land

quitrent: (law) a fixed rent payable in communication of certain feudal services; fixed rent due from a tenant

range: a tier of townships running vertical of north-south; often abbreviated as *R* in land descriptions

Rectangular Survey: measure based on principal meridian and base line used for public domain

registrar: official in charge of the recording of the land in some counties; also, official in the district land office

rod: see *pole*

scrip: certificate of entitlement that allowed the holder to select a specified number of acres from available designated public land

section: (survey) 640 acres or 1 square mile area; abbreviated as *Sec.* in some documents

supplementary patent: a patent issued to change or modify a previous patent

surrender: to release a lease before time of expiration, usually with consent of both parties

surface rights: right to land without rights to the minerals connected with the property

survey: the operation of finding and delineating the dimensions of a piece of land by applying the principles of geometry and trigonometry; a measured plan and description

survey plat: a map on which land surveys are recorded at a scale of 2 inches to the mile; each plat usually shows one township

township: (survey) 36 square miles in the public domain, usually abbreviated as *twp* or *T;* in New England states, a local unit of government; an area

tract book: a log that is an index to and digest of all essential actions that affect public lands

trust deed: usually a type of mortgage; title to property; see *deed of trust*

vara: a Spanish or Portuguese term of measure that varies in length from 32 to 43 inches in different localities; in Texas it is equal to 33.33 inches

warrant: a negotiable government certificate entitling the holder to be in possession of a designated amount of public land or other appropriation by the U.S. Congress; a statement that the seller has clear title and has the right to defend said title

warranty deed: a deed in which the seller warrants and defends title and possession of the estate which is being transferred

Abstract

> THOMAS BOYLE, 129 acs., Up. Par. of Nansamond Co; S. side of the back Sw of Sumerton; 28 Oct. 1697, p. 110. Adj. Thomas Jernakan & land of Samll Watson. Trans. of 3 pers: John Wike, William Walker, Humphry Minson.

Actual Grant

> To all as whereas as now know you that the Said -- Emdm Andros Lieut Gov'r with the advise and consent of the councill of State accordingly give and grant unto Thomas Boyle [*sic:* Boyte] of Nansamd County one hundred twenty nine acres of Land lying on the South Side of the back Swamp of Sumerton in ye upper parish of Nansamond County beginning at a marked pine a corner near Thomas Jornahans land standing on the Southward side ye back swamp and runs thence Southeasterly eight degrees one hundred eighty seven poles to a marked pine bounding on Jornahams thence Southwesterly Seventy nine Degrees eighty nine poles to a marked white oake in a branch thence north westerly to only five degrees eighty four poles to Sam'll Watsons Corner a white oake thence along watsons line trees northwesterly forty five degrees seventy four poles to a marked Cyprus in ye back Swamp thence up the back Swamp and bounded thereon to the first Station the Said Land being due unto Thomas Boyle [*sic:* Boyte] --- and for the transportacon of three persons into this Colony whose names are to be in ye records mentioned and this patent to have and to hold --- to b- h-der Voiding and paying as provided as dated the 28th day of October 1697. E. Andros.

In this example, the abstract omits the complete description of the land. Also, some surnames have been transcribed incorrectly in the abstract (see "Case Study: Misread Records," above). However, the abstract contains some information from another document that names the three people whose transportation to the colony was paid. The brevity and clarity of the abstract make it much easier to scan quickly, but the original provides more comprehensive information.

Some land records include notices of the granting of powers of attorney. Individuals who needed to conduct business in a county of former residence could give power of attorney to a person who remained in that county. The person accepting the power of attorney then acted in the interest of the other individual to obtain inherited property, sell land, or conduct necessary business. These transactions are usually filed in the records of both the new and former counties of residence. The document usually includes a statement indicating the individual's new domicile.

In some western states, such as Montana, very few printed land records have been compiled, even for individual counties. However, some interesting land "substitute" records have been published, such as *VanDersal and Conner's Stockgrowers Directory of Marks and Brands for the State of Montana, 1872–1900: Comprising an Alphabetical List of Names of All Livestock Companies and . . . Sheep and Wool Growers* (Glendive, Mont.: Review Printing Co., 1974). Such publications can help researchers find early homesteaders. Within the next few years, the BLM collection will probably spur the publication of more collections for the western states.

Formats of Published Records

Virtually no collection of printed land records contains complete transcriptions of each record. Rather, published land records present the information as an *abstract* (in which only the key information is recorded), or an *extract* (in which portions of the record are copied verbatim). Published works employ a variety of abbreviations and means of presenting data.

A variety of formats are also used. Even within a single book, the arrangement of the information may vary. For instance, *Old Kentucky Entries and Deeds: A Complete Index to All of the Earliest Land Entries, Military Warrants, Deeds and Wills of the Commonwealth of Kentucky* (Louisville: Standard Printing Co., 1926; reprint; Baltimore: Genealogical Publishing Co., 1987), by Willard Rouse Jillson, is arranged in several ways: the first group of entries is for general Kentucky records, and the following sections are divided by counties, military warrants, military entries, and appellate court records (figure 11-21).

Brief Abstracts. Abstracts of deeds can be as brief as the following examples:

> Page 11 Indenture: April 5, 1823, Josephas Simmons to Thomas Davis for $1,000 a tract of land Fractional Section No 1, 200 acres. Gilbert Stoval, C.C.C. (Williams 1962, 22).

> 64. (40) Alexander MALCOM to Alexander MALCOM, Jr.: 25 Feb 1803, 20 May 2804, $360, land lying on Nails Creek, adj Robert BOID, John McCALLEY, Bays Mountain. Wit: John PICKENS, John MALCOLM (Thomas 1990, 9).

> Jacob Mire, 50 acres, East side Shenandoah River. Adjoining his own land. September 30, 1762 (Kaylor 1991, 2).

> GABRIEL HUNOT, Jr., claiming a lot of one arpent, situate as aforesaid, and produces as aforesaid. December 2, 1811: Present, a full Board. It is the opinion of the Board that this claim ought not to be granted (Lowrie 1986, 530).

Figure 11-22 is from a typical published abstract of county deeds, in which only brief abstracts are provided.

Abstracts in an index to records are extremely brief because they are meant to serve as a guide to the voluminous original records. The following abstracts are taken from indexes to various compilations:

> 28 pg 6 HENRY COSSART 12 November 1754 3840 acres in Anson County on both sides of Yadkin River at the N. and S. fork (Hofmann 1986–87, vol. 1, 5).

> Samuel H. Morgan 23No16 63 000302 W 494-0107 (Livsey 1991–96, vol. 1, 174).

FAYETTE ENTRIES 129

Entree	Acres	Book	Page	Entry Date	Watercourse	Notes
Meredith, Samuel	400	1	14	11–30–1782	Licking	
Meredith, Samuel	2,000	1	15	12– 2–1782	Big Bone Lick	Surveyed
Meredith, Samuel	2,000	1	15	11–30–1782	Big Bone Lick	Surveyed
Meredith, Samuel	400	1	14	11–30–1782	Hingstons Fk	
Meredith, William	500	2	10	1– 9–1783	Ohio R	
Meredith & Breckenridge	72	4	342	9– 9–1816	None	
Meriweather, James	500	1	28	12– 3–1782	S Fk Elkhorn	Surveyed
Merham & Fishback	3,138	3	135	1– 2–1784	None	Surveyed
Metcalfe, Chas	950	3	25	10–31–1783	Ohio R	
Metcalfe, Jno	2,972	3	157	1–19–1784	Licking	Surveyed
Metcalfe, Jno	1,520	3	227	3–14–1784	Licking	Surveyed
Metcalfe, Jno	3,800	4	218	8–10–1785	Eagle Cr	
Michael, John Frederick	133	1	202	12–20–1782	Hingstons Fk	Surveyed

MILITARY WARRANTS 323

Name	Acres	Warrant	Service	Date
Chambers, James	200	4249	During war soldier Vriginia line	1– 6–1787
Chambers, Robert	200	3201	3 years sergeant Virginia line	6–24–1784
Chandler, Jesse	200	4482	During war soldier Virginia line	12– 2–1789
Chandler, Thomas	1,666⅔	3763	3 years lieutenant Virginia navy	2–28–1785
Chandler, Thomas	1,200	3764	3 years lieutenant Virginia navy	2–28–1785
Chaners, John	100	193	3 years soldier Virginia Cont. line	3–24–1783
Chapen, Benjamin	6,000	4565	During war surgeon Virginia navy	1–21–1792
Chapin, John	100	1302	3 years soldier Virginia line	6–30–1783
Chapin, Solomon	100	3852	3 years soldier Virginia line	5– 6–1785
Chaplin, Abraham	2,666⅔	2683	3 years lieutenant Virginia line	3– 3–1784
Chapman, John	4,000	789	3 years captain state line	6–12–1783
Chapman, John	200	2124	3 years sergeant Virginia line	12–15–1783
Chapman, Thomas	100	926	3 years soldier Virginia line	6–20–1783
Charity, Charles	200	2789	During war soldier Virginia line	3–18–1784
Charles, Samuel	200	1860	3 years sergeant Virginia line	11– 6–1783
Charles, William	100	1850	3 years soldier Virginia line	10–11–1783

MILITARY ENTRIES 375

Entree	Acres	Book	Page	Entry Date	Watercourse	Notes
Bradford, Samuel K	900	1	113	8–13–1784	Big Barren R	
Bradley, James	1,000	1	8	8– 3–1784	Cumberland R	
Bradley, Jas	1,000	1	20	8– 4–1784	Cane Cr	Surveyed
Bradley, Jas	1,000	1	31	8– 5–1784	Delaware Cr	
Bradley, Jas	1,000	1	72	8–10–1784	None	
Brashear, Richard	1,000	1	12	8– 3–1782	Mouth Obyan Cr	
Brashear, Richard	1,000	1	38	8– 6–1784	Virginia & Carolina Line	
Brashear, Richard	1,000	1	79	8–10–1784	Cumberland R	Surveyed
Brashear, Richard	1,000	1	102	8–12–1784	Mayfield Cr	
Brent, Wm	2,000	1	16	8– 4–1784	None	
Brent, Wm	2,666⅔	1	102	8–12–1784	Island Cr	
Brent, Wm	2,000	1	108	8–12–1784	None	
Broadus, Wm	1,000	1	65	8– 7–1784	N Fk W Fk Red R	Surveyed
Brodhed, Daniel Jr	1,000	1	151	12– 6–1785	Green R	Surveyed
Brodhed, Daniel Jr	1,000	1	151	12– 6–1785	Green R	Surveyed
Brodhed, Daniel Jr	1,000	1	152	12– 7–1785	None	Surveyed
Brodhed, Daniel Jr	1,000	1	152	12– 7–1785	None	Surveyed
Brodhead, Daniel Jr	750	1	154	12– 7–1785	Buck Cr	

COURT OF APPEALS DEEDS—GRANTEES 447

Grantee	Residence	Deed Date	Acres	Book	Page	Watercourse
Shrader, Jas W & Jno W	Oldham	12–21–1838	894	27	4	In Daviess Co
Shreader, Jacob	———	8– 8–1809	734	N	12	Rough Cr
Shreave, Leven L	———	8–28–1819	5,500	T	162	Rough & Panther Cr
Shyrock, Gideon	Fayette	12– 4–1832	75	Z	243	Shelbyville Pike
Shyrock, Gideon	Fayette	12– 6–1832	1,310	Z	244	Donelsons Fk
Shuff, Isaac	Scott	5–15–1830	———	Y	464	Silas & Cherry Run
Shyrin, Mrs Ann	Frankfort	11– 1–1801	Lot	H	598	Frankfort
Siesnan, Luke	Baltimore	11–12–1824	11,113	X	22	Ky R
Silvers, Jno	Nelson	6–23–1789	200	B-2	64	Skeggs Cr
Silvertooth, Geo	Mercer	9–22–1788	560	B-2	330	Chaplins Fk
Simms, Jesse	Alexandria	1– 3–1800	13,982	E	138	Rolling Fk & Little Ky
Simon, Joseph	Lancaster	6– 1–1786	2,000	A-2	406	Fox Run
Simond, Lewis	New York	7– 1–1812	1,793	P	536	None

Figure 11-21. Jillson's *Old Kentucky Entries and Deeds: A Complete Index to All of the Earliest Land Entries, Military Warrants, Deeds and Wills of the Commonwealth of Kentucky* is arranged in several ways: the first group of entries is for general Kentucky records, and the following sections are divided by counties, military warrants, military entries, and appellate court records.

TRANSCRIBED DEED BOOK 1

Page
1. 18 Mar.1802. Will of John ROSE, dec'd, of Westmoreland Co., Va.
3. 10 Sept.1814. Lawrence BERRY, Wm. ROBISON and Margaret ROSE, Exrs. and Trustees of Estate of John ROSE, dec'd, and Alex. F. ROSE, Exr. of Estate of Henry ROSE, dec'd, and Trustee appointed by the Court of King George Co., Va., to Richard HULITT, 1500A.
7. 26 Apr.1815. Margaret ROSE, Wm. ROBISON, Lawrence BERRY, Alex. F. ROSE, Exrs. of Estate of Henry ROSE, dec'd, Trustees of the legal representatives of Robert ROSE, dec'd, of Va., by their att'y James TAYLOR of Campbell Co., Ky., to Richard HULITT of Ross Co., Ohio, 1500 A. in Ross Co., Ohio.
9. 7 Sept.1814. Martin D. HARDIN and Elizabeth hw and Mark HARDIN of Frankfort, and Curtis FIELD and Rosanna hw, late HARDIN, of Richmond, all of Ky., to Dan'l BURGESS of Highland Co., 200A., which land was held by said Martin, Mark and Rosanna together with Davis HARDIN and Sara McHENRY, wife of Barnabas McHENRY, as children and heirs of John HARDIN, dec'd.
10. 25 May 1815. Wm. FULTON and Eliza hw of Ross Co., Ohio to George SPICKARD of Highland Co., 90A. (Bk. M, pg. 21: Grantor's name given as SPEKARD and SPEKNARD.)
11. __ Apr.1815. Isaac McPHERSON and Betsy hw to Jacob LADD, 100A. (Bk. M, pg. 22: Date is 4 Apr.)
11. 31 Jan.1815. Thomas DUNAGAN and Elizabeth hw to Thomas SMITH, land in Hillsboro.
12. 21 Feb.1815. Shadrach STAFFORD and Marion hw to James STAFFORD, 120A.
13. 20 Mar.1815. Joseph BELL and Sallie hw to Sarah McCORD, land in Greenfield.
14. 22 Apr.1815. Nath'l POPE and Martha hw and James JOHNSON and Sarah hw, to John UPP, 100A.
15. 6 May 1815. John BORDEN, Exr. of Estate of Nicholas BORDEN, dec'd, to Jacob BORDEN, $91\frac{1}{2}$A.

Figure 11-22. From David N. and Jane N. McBride, comps., *Records of the Recorder's Office of Highland County, Ohio (1805–1850)* (Ann Arbor, Mich.: Edwards Letter Shop,1969), page 1. It is a typical published abstract of county deeds, in which only brief abstracts are provided.

> Hamilton, John .... 1,000.... 2...322....7-14-1783...Leestown & Elkhorn.......Surveyed (Jillson 1987, 106).

> Page 11 Indenture: April 5, 1823, Josephas Simmons to Thomas Davis for $1,000 a tract of land Fractional Section No1, 200 acres. Gilbert Stoval, C.C.C. (Williams 1962, 22).

Detailed Abstracts. In contrast, some abstracts are considerably more detailed and informative, as the following examples illustrate:

> RHEA, John and COHGRAN 24-302
> A lot in the suburb of St. Mary containing 60 feet fronting Levee street, 61 feet to the rear and measuring 303 feet on one side and 313 on the other bounded on the N.E. by a lot belonging to Joseph McNEIL, on the N.W. by Magazine street, and on the S.W. by Gravier street. This land was part of that inherited by Bertram GRAVIER and inherited from his wife Mary DELOND who sold same to Joseph HERVIER on March 15, 179- who ultimately sold it to RHEA and COHGRAN (Maduell 1975, 10).

> ALLISON HOWARD #59,307
> Father & heir-at-law of William Howard, deceased, late a private in Capt. Hamilton's Co. Battalion, Ga. Mounted Vols. John G. Winter, assignee. NW 1/4 of Section 24 Township 24 Range 19 East in District of lands subject to sale at Montgomery, Ala., containing 160 acres. Mar. 1, 1851 (Gandrud 1951, 71).

For examples of more complete abstracts of county deed records, see figure 11-23, which contains abstracts drawn from Jane Kizer Thomas's *Blount County, Tennessee Deeds: Deed Book 1, 1795–1819* (page 9).

The majority of extracts include most significant details, including names of chair bearers, witnesses, surveyors, and examiners, and explain inconsistencies in the records. An example of such an extract for Johnston County, North Carolina, follows (Hofmann 1986–87, vol. 2, 207).

> 3266 pg. 233 JAMES MOORE 12 January 1761 598 acres in Johnston County in the Parish of St Patrick on the S side of Neuse river and on both sides of little creek - including Moores improvement OR: /s/ (mar) Wit: JAS CARY JR examined by: J. MONTFORT and JOHN JOHNSTON surveyed 10 June 1760 CB: CORNELIUS TERRELL, ELIAS CRAFORD CHARLES YOUNG Surveyor Plat reads "land on the S side of Neuse River"; grant reads "land on the N side of Neuse River."

Following is an example of a detailed abstract (Gandrud 1932, 33).

Clement, (*sic*) **Charles** assigns all right and title to this bill in right of wife Polly Oldham, otherwise Polly Clements, to Jonathon Bird for value received of him. 27 Nov. 1819. Witnesses: William Crider, Jolly Jones. Later called a deed of gift. Polly signs away her part also. Later Charles Clements states that he married Polly Oldham, daughter of Tapley Oldham, and that Tapley Oldham died in the state of South Carolina, Pendleton District. By bill of sale date 12 April 1808, he deeded to his three daughters, viz: Polly now my wife, Elizabeth and Lucinda Oldham, certain slaves. Lucinda was then a minor. Slaves were to be sold when Lucinda, the youngest, was married or of age. Lucinda is now married so I am entitled to Polly's one third. Bk. 1 p. 27.

BLOUNT COUNTY DEEDS

paid in and to a part of that tract of land of 100,000 ac by us and Josiah Danforth and Amos EDWARDS from Stockley DONALDSON for 7,000 ac and also as much more as may not exceed $1,000 at the rate of $25 per 100 ac; crosses west fork of Pistol Creek near Widow McDOWEL's, crossing east fork of said creek to Robert CULTON's. Wit: Robert CRAIG, John WILKINSON, David TAYLOR. John JOHNSTON releases for Amos EDWARDS who is not now present.

61. (38-39) Stockley DONALDSON of Roane Co. to "my trusty friend" Josiah DANFORTH: 5 May 1803, 16 May 1803, power of attorney for two years, to sell 33,000 ac west of Clinch and Tenn. Rivers; 10,000 ac on Clinch and Powell Rivers adj what is called Henderson's & Co. survey of 2,000 ac; 5,000 ac in Cloyd's Cove; 5,000 ac on Ellejoy Creek, 1,500 ac on French Broad River; two tracts of 5,000 ac each on Little Pigeon River. Wit: James SLOAN, Abram GHORMLEY, J. W. LACKEY, Andrew THOMPSON, Barclay McGHEE.

62. (39) Robert KING of Roane Co. to John McGHEE/McKEE: 20 Apr 1803, 10 May 1803, one-half undivided moiety of Grant #203 from N.C. for 1,000 ac on north side Tenn. River above mouth of Nine Mile Creek, including an island in the River, "whereas the said John McGHEE owned one-half of the warrant on which such grant was founded." Sig: Robert (X) KING, James TRIMBLE, Thomas McCURREY.

Figure 11-23. Abstracts from Thomas's *Blount County, Tennessee Deeds: Deed Book 1, 1795–1819* (page 9).

As indicated previously, land data may be recorded in a compilation of records extracted from other sources. Figure 11-24 shows how the town records of Manchester, Massachusetts, include land records.

LOCATING PUBLISHED LAND RECORDS

Published land records can be especially difficult to locate. They are often printed in small quantities and aren't listed in many library catalogs. Therefore, the first step in finding land records is determining whether the records of interest have been published. To determine whether the records have been published, the researcher should query large libraries and libraries in the area of interest. The researcher should check major library computer cataloging networks, such as the Online Computer Library Center (OCLC) (see chapter 5) and the Family History Library's collection (see below).

Bibliographies and Catalogs

Unlike many areas of genealogical publishing, no bibliographies or library catalogs attempt to identify published land records. Therefore, researchers must consult the general genealogical bibliographies discussed in the introduction of this book and in chapter 5, "Bibliographies and Catalogs." The older the bibliography, the greater the likelihood that it will not list the publication needed because many printed land records have been published only recently.

Many older abstracts and published sources are listed in Filby's *American and British Genealogy and Heraldry: A Selected List of Books,* 3rd ed. (Boston: New England Historic Genealogical Society, 1983) and its *1982–1985 Supplement* (Boston: New England Historic Genealogical Society, 1987). The *Family History Library Catalog*™ is the most comprehensive catalog for printed land records; it contains almost all known published land records. The *Family History Library Catalog* is available on microfiche or as part of *FamilySearch*®, a CD-ROM available at many larger libraries.

Researchers can find land records in the *Family History Library Catalog* quickly by entering the name of the place to be searched (by state and county, if possible), then entering the desired record type. For example, if a person was searching for land and property records in the county of Crittenden, Arkansas, the following entry would be correct: *Arkansas, Crittenden—land and property.*

Local Societies and Repositories

Among the best sources of information about printed land records are the local societies in the area of interest. Often, local genealogical societies sponsor or encourage the publication of land record abstracts. Officers in local societies and genealogical librarians at local libraries are usually aware of such publications.

Periodicals

Frequently, land records are included in state, county, and local genealogical and historical society publications, including journals, quarterlies, and books. In these projects, the people who compile the original land records are often familiar with the names that appear in the records. This familiarity can help or hinder the finished results: if the abstractor changes an entry from the original spelling to conform to the name as it is currently used or as the abstractor considers it should be spelled, the record is less valuable. If abstractors use their knowledge of local family names and locations to assist in deciphering old handwriting, the results are usually positive.

Some articles in periodicals focus on other issues but include some data concerning land records. For example,

TOWN OF MANCHESTER. 83

the sum of fifteen shillings and the over plush being eigh shillings and two penc to return to the sealect men for the use of the town

[79] At A town meeting leagually warned and met together upon the 4th day of november 1698 It is voted & fully agreed that Mr george norten shall have a small parsill of Land lying before the meting hous to wit, that parsil of land whare on his hous frame now standeth which was formerly granted to the aforesd mr George norten in the year 1695 upon conditions which land is bounded as foloweth, southerly with the river 5 pols wide esterly with the towns land 6 pole upward & northerly 2 pols wide with the towns land aforsd & westerly with ye landing place down to the river aforesd the aforsd mr George norton to have & to hold the above bounded parsil of land with all the privileges & apurtenances thereto belonging to him & his heirs forever At a town meting november the 4th richard walker is chosen to sarve on the gran Jury John cro & Daniel williams on the jury of tryals at the next superior cort to be holden at Salam on the 2^d Tuesday of november instant

[135] It Boston Desember the 2^d 1698 Reseived of m^r Abraham mastus constable of manchester eight pounds four shillings and nine pence in full Recd for m^r Jams taylor treasurer

[138] Boston Desember 2^d 1698 Received of m^r Isaack Whitteyer constable of manchester seaven pounds ten shillings in full of the within mentioned warrant recd for m^r James tayler Treasurer

Jer Allens

[134] At a meting of the select Reckned with Samuell Ley this 18th Day of march $169\frac{8}{9}$ for the rent of the parsonage Land for the year 97 and the yeare 98 and the afore sd Lee hath ballanced and cleared all accounts with us the sealect men namely Mr Georg norton m^r thomas West m^r Robberd Leach Sealectmen

Figure 11-24. Land data may be recorded in a compilation of records extracted from other sources. This example shows how the town records of Manchester, Massachusetts, include land records. From *Town Records of Manchester From the Earliest Grants of Land, 1636, When a Portion of Salem until 1736, as Contained in the Town Records of Salem, Second and Third Book of Records of the Town of Manchester,* vol. 1 (Salem, Mass.: Salem Press Publishing and Printing Co., 1889), page 83.

"Rush County Old Settlers Deaths," *Hoosier Genealogist* 33 (June 1993), by Ruth Dorrel, includes the following land data (page 91):

> . . . [of the] 902 [pioneers of Rush County] who had resided in the county 50 years and over, there were 58 eighty years old and over, that there were only 12 living on land entered by themselves, and 49 on land entered by their parents. . . .

Following this information is a list of those who had died in 1888.

Often, lists of early residents and land owners are published in historical and genealogical society periodicals under a variety of subjects. One such article, "History of Colesburg, Iowa," from the Fall 1968 issue of *Annals of Iowa*, describes the history of a town and includes names, dates of arrival, and former residence of the first settlers.

Journals and quarterlies often publish articles reporting newly located original records. "Bucks County Original Deeds Found at Antique Shop," an article in the issue of *Western Pennsylvania Genealogical Society Quarterly* 16 (4) (Spring 1990), reports the following (page 29):

> While buying books at a vendor display at South Hills Village, member Virginia Patton met Mrs. E. L. Miltenberger, owner of EMMA'S ANTIQUES, 436 S. Main St., Phg [Pittsburgh] . . . [who] stated that her family had picked up some original deeds which Bucks County Pa. had thrown out in the 1920s. Most are on parchment paper. Some go back to the 1700s. . . ."

The article then lists forty-two entries with names, dates, and townships for those deeds. The first reads, "STOUT, Peter & Jacob executors of John HEANY, June 2, 1807 Rockhill Twp" (page 29).

Winston De Ville's "A Quebedo Land Grant in Early Illinois," *Louisiana Genealogical Register* (March 1983): 49–50, explains in detail a brief grant and helps readers understand the time period and recording practices at the time the grant was written. At the end of the article is a helpful bibliography.

Some articles concerning land records are as brief as index abstracts; some provide an extensive list of land record abstracts. The *South Dakota Genealogical Society Quarterly* recently published a two-part series listing one county's homesteaders along with township names and numbers, section numbers, and land ranges. Figure 11-25 is an excerpt from the article.

Researchers should not overlook book reviews and book notices in the periodicals covering areas of interest. By browsing the most recent issues, researchers may find references to published land records. Bibliographic citations can help researchers find copies of records more easily. The *Periodical Source Index (PERSI)* (see chapter 6, "Published Indexes") may also be helpful for locating land records mentioned in periodicals.

Documentary Collections and Histories

Published town records in some New England states incorporate early land records. Many of New England's town records have been published as abstracts or transcripts. In Jean Burr's *Lyme Records 1667–1730: A Literal Transcription of the Minutes of the Town Meetings . . . to Which Hath Been Appended Land Grants and Ear Marks* (Stonington, Conn.: Pequot Press, 1968), records of land grants are included in the text, transcribed in their entirely from the originals.

Some general genealogical collections include references or citations of deeds. Edythe Rucker Whitley's *Overton County, Tennessee: Genealogical Records* (Baltimore: Genealogical

Volume 11 Number 2 **SOUTH DAKOTA GENEALOGICAL SOCIETY** October 1992

MARSHALL COUNTY HOMESTEAD MAP INDEX

In the last issue of the Quarterly I started the 1885 census index for Marshall County. As I continued to index it I was still having difficulty reading many of the names. Then I made copies of the Homestead maps out of the Centennial Atlas put out by the Centennial Atlas Company of P. O. Box 1452, Watertown, SD 57201, Phone 605\882-4725. They were of some help, but a few names were unreadable to them also. We aren't sure where they got the names for the homestead township maps, but Laura Glum thinks they came from the Tract Books which are all on microfilm and available from the State Archives on InterLibrary Loan. I wished I had checked them against the Tract Books, but I didn't have time. If anyone checks them and finds mistakes or clarifications, please let me know. - Judy Huber, October 1992.

Last and First Names	Township Name	Section #	Township #	Range
?eeson, John	White	6	128N	57W
?oren, James	White	2	128N	57W
?ormick, Martha	White	30	128N	57W
A??????, Leon	Pleasant Valley	33	127N	57W
Aadland, Olaus	Veblen	25	129N	53W
Aalmbo, Peter	Norland	15	127N	56W
Aalmbo, Peter	Norland	14	127N	56W
Aasen, Alf	Dumarce	4	127N	54W
Aasen, Severin	Dumarce		127N	55W
Aastrom, Charley	Buffalo	23	125N	53W
Aastrom, George	Buffalo	24	125N	53W
Aastrom, Hans	Buffalo	24	125N	53W
Aastrom, Hans	Buffalo	24	125N	53W
Aastrom, Thoams	Buffalo	24	125N	53W
Abel, Alice	McKinley	17	127N	53W
Abel, Alice	McKinley	32	127N	53W
Abel, Joseph	McKinley	20	127N	53W
Abel, Martha	McKinley	17	127N	53W
Abel, Mary	McKinley	17	127N	53W
Abel, Mary	McKinley	30	127N	53W

Figure 11-25. From "Marshall County Homestead Map Index," *South Dakota Genealogical Society Quarterly* 11 (October 1992-January 1993), page 61. This article lists one South Dakota county's homesteaders along with township names and numbers, section numbers, and land ranges.

Publishing Co., 1979) contains a section of deeds from various land record volumes for the county (figure 11-26). For more information on these types of sources, see chapter 15, "Documentary Collections."

Many published county histories include lists of early landowners, particularly those who acquired land during the early stages of the county's formation. Some volumes are indexed only partially, so the names listed may not be included in the index; therefore, researchers should search the text rather than merely scanning the index.

Additionally, many manuscript collections contain land records; guides or calendars to these collections frequently note land records. Figure 11-27 is an undated entry taken from the first calendar published for the Draper Manuscript Collection, *The Preston and Virginia Papers of the Draper Collection of Manuscripts* (Madison: State Historical Society of Wisconsin, 1915).

Computer Databases

Increasingly, computerized databases are being created that relate to land records in the United States. Many of these are local in coverage; some are regional, several are statewide, and a few are Federal. Many states are beginning to automate their early land records, and some counties have automated more recent deed filings. (See "Transfers from the Federal Government to Individuals—Computerized Sources," above, for more information concerning the automation project of the General Land Office.)

One example of a recent state project is the computerized database of land entries recorded at the Fort Wayne Land Office from 1823 through 1852. Public lands in the Fort Wayne district of Indiana were sold beginning in 1823. The district included the counties of Adams, Allen, Blackford, Cass, Clinton, DeKalb, Delaware, Grant, Howard, Huntington, Jay, Kosciusko,

Figure 11-26. Some general genealogical collections include references or citations of deeds. This excerpt from Whitley's *Overton County, Tennessee: Genealogical Records* (page 10) contains deeds from various land record volumes for the county.

Deeds B, Page 287. Tennessee Grant No.2154. 89 acres on waters of Lick Creek to James Davisson. District No.4. No.875 founded on warrant No.1358 issued by John Carter and John Foster, for 300 acres 1 May 1792. Entry dated 17 May 1811. for 100 acres issued to James Davisson the Enterer. 89 acres in District of Winchester, on waters of Lick Creek near Colonel Chisman's line.

Deeds M, Page 284. Blair R. Davidson from Doak H. Capps.

Deeds D, Page 309. James Davidson, Tennessee Grant.

Deeds D, Page 22. William Gibson of Overton County to Stephen Senter of Roane County, Tennessee. Indenture 24 June 1813, for 50 acres on Caney Fork and said Cumberland Road, the consideration being $780. including place said Gibson now lives.

Deeds D, Page 29. Thomas Cope of Overton County, conveys one negro 7 years old named Mariah to Molly Cope for love and affection for my daughter, 22 August 1815. Signed Thomas Q. Cope. Adam Huntsman. Joseph Harris.

Deeds D, Page 43. William Earp to Timothy Carpenter, 300 acres in Poplar Creek on waters of Obed's River. 1816.

Deeds B, Page 49. Jacob Anderson sells 160 acres to Moses Fisk Anderson of Jackson County. 1806.

Figure 11-27. Many manuscript collections contain land records; guides or calendars to these collections frequently note land records. This example is from *The Preston and Virginia Papers of the Draper Collection of Manuscripts* (page 300).

n. d. 12ZZ79	[Finley, John E.] Abstracts of title to land on branch of Fish Creek granted to Thomas Mason and Augustine Pillager, Oct. 25, 1784, and known as "South Cove" and "Walford" respectively. A. D. 1 p.
n. d. 12ZZ350	[Finley, John E.] Antidote for laudanum. A. N. 1 p.
n. d. 12ZZ346–348	[Finley, John E.] Excerpts from Gibbon's *Surveying*. 3 pp.

Lagrange, Madison, Miami, Noble, Randolph, Steuben, Tipton, Wabash, Wells, and Whitley. The records for these counties are organized into twelve fields for searching. Further information is available through the Indiana State Archives, Commission of Public Records, 140 North Senate Avenue, Indianapolis, IN 46204.

SUMMARY

Despite the problems researchers encounter when working with published land records, these records help genealogists in a variety of ways:

- Printed land records provide an easy-to-use method of locating records for individuals and families, particularly if every-name indexes are included.
- Land record publications frequently include valuable information about the region and about laws affecting the records.
- Published records in libraries are more readily available than the original records.
- Compilations frequently cover many years and condense a multitude of records into one indexed volume.
- Published land records help researchers link families and individuals who resided in the same area during the same period.
- Regional compilations of printed land records are valuable finding aids.
- Printed land records are easier to read than the original handwritten documents.
- Some county and local histories include lists of early settlers and provide clues that help researchers locate original records.
- Printed land records can guide researchers to pertinent entries in original sources.
- Land records often provide important genealogical details.

REFERENCE LIST

Billington, Ray Allen, and Martin Ridge, eds. 1982. *Westward Expansion: A History of the American Frontier.* 5th ed. New York: Macmillan Publishing Co.

Christensen, Katheren. 1971. *Arkansas Military Bounty Grants (War of 1812).* Hot Springs, Ark.: Arkansas Ancestors.

Dabney, Virginius. 1971. *Virginia: The New Dominion.* Charlottesville: University Press of Virginia.

des Cognet, Louis, Jr., comp. 1981. *English Duplicates of Lost Virginia Records.* Baltimore: Genealogical Publishing Co.

Elliott, Wendy L. 1987. "Fallibility of Indexes." *APG Quarterly: Official Publication of the Association of Professional Genealogists* 2 (2): 1–7 (Summer).

Gandrud, Pauline Jones, comp. 1932. *Alabama Records: Volume 3, Tuscaloosa County.* . . . The author.

_____, comp. 1951. *Alabama Records: Volume 121, Original Land Records in Alabama.* The author.

Greenwood, Val D. 1990. *The Researcher's Guide to American Genealogy.* 2nd ed. Baltimore: Genealogical Publishing Co.

Hofmann, Margaret M. 1986–87. *The Granville District of North Carolina, 1748–1763: Abstracts of Land Grants.* 2 vols. Weldon, N.C.: Roanoke News Co.

Jacobus, Donald Lines. "Connecticut." In *Genealogical Research: Methods and Sources.* Edited by Milton Rubincam and Kenn Stryker-Rodda. 2 vols. Washington, D.C.: American Society of Genealogists, 1960–71.

Jillson, Willard Rouse. 1987. *Old Kentucky Entries and Deeds: A Complete Index to All of the Earliest Land Entries, Military Warrants, Deeds and Wills of the Commonwealth of Kentucky.* Louisville: Standard Printing Co., 1926. Reprint. Baltimore: Genealogical Publishing Co., 1987.

Kaylor, Peter Cline. 1991. *Abstract of Land Grant Surveys, 1761–1791.* 1938. Baltimore: Clearfield Co., 1991.

Livsey, Karen E. 1991–96. *Western New York Land Transactions, 1804–1824: Extracted from the Archives of the Holland Land Company.* 2 vols. Baltimore: Genealogical Publishing Co.

Lowrie, Walter, ed. 1986. *Early Settlers of Missouri As Taken from Land Claims in the Missouri Territory.* Reprint. Easley, S.C.: Southern Historical Press, 1986.

Maduell, Charles R. 1975. *Federal Land Grants in the Territory of Orleans: The Delta Parishes.* New Orleans: Polyanthos. Adapted from *American State Papers, Public Lands,* vol. 2, and arranged by counties as they existed in 1812.

McMullin, Phillip W. 1972. *Grassroots of America: A Computerized Index to the American State Papers: Land Grants and Claims (1789–1837).* Salt Lake City: Gendex Corp. Reprint. Greenville, S.C.: Southern Historical Press, 1994.

Nugent, Nell Marion. 1979. *Cavaliers and Pioneers: Abstracts of Virginia Land Patents and Grants, 1695–1732.* Vol. 3 of 5. Richmond: Virginia State Library.

Rae, Loraine. 1991. *Washington County, Tennessee: Deeds, 1775–1800.* Greenville, S.C.: Southern Historical Press.

Scott, Kenneth, and Rosanne Conway. 1978. *New York Alien Residents, 1825–1848.* Baltimore: Genealogical Publishing Co.

Szucs, Loretto Dennis, and Sandra Hargreaves Luebking, eds. 1997. *The Source: A Guidebook of American Genealogy.* Salt Lake City: Ancestry.

Stoddard, David F. 1979. "Land System of the New England Colonial Colonies." *Connecticut Nutmegger* 11: 556–64.

Williams, E. Russ, Jr., comp. and ed. 1962. *Abstracts of Deeds: Marion County, Mississippi: Containing Deeds, Marks and Brands, Bond, Mortgages, and Deeds of Gift.* Bogalusa, La.: the author.

BIBLIOGRAPHY

Historical Background of Land Records

Billington, Ray Allen, and Martin Ridge, eds. *Westward Expansion: A History of the American Frontier.* 5th ed. New York: Macmillan Publishing Co., 1982.

Bogue, Margaret Beattie. *Patterns from the Sod: Land Use and Tenure in the Grand Prairie, 1850–1900.* Springfield: Illinois State Historical Library, 1959.

Bond, Beverley Waugh. *The Quit-Rent System in the American Colonies.* New Haven, Conn.: Yale University Press, 1919.

Brinker, Russell. *Elementary Surveying.* Scranton, Pa.: International Textbook Co., 1963.

Chazanof, William. *Joseph Ellicot and the Holland Land Company: The Opening of Western New York.* Syracuse, N.Y.: Syracuse University Press, 1970.

Conover, George Stillwell. *The Genesee Tract: Cessions between New York and Massachusetts—The Phelps and Gorham Purchase—Robert Morris—Captain Charles Willaimson and the Pulteney Estate.* Geneva, N.Y.: 1889.

Conover, Milton. *The General Land Office: Its History, Activities and Organization.* 1923 Reprint. New York: AMS Press, 1974.

Foss, Phillip O., ed. *Public Land Policy.* Boulder: Colorado Associated University Press, 1970.

Powell, Sumner Chilton. *Puritan Village: The Formation of a New England Town.* Middletown, Conn.: Wesleyan University Press, 1963.

Rohrbough, Malcolm J. *The Land Office Business: The Settlement and Administration of American Public Lands, 1789–1837.* New York: Oxford University Press, 1968.

White, C. Albert. *A History of the Rectangular Survey System.* Washington, D.C.: U.S. Department of the Interior, Bureau of Land Management, Government Printing Office, 198(?).

Instructional Material

Elliott, Wendy L. "Fallibility of Indexes." *APG Quarterly: Official Publication of the Association of Professional Genealogists* 2 (2) (Summer 1987).

_____. *Using Land Records to Solve Genealogical Research Problems.* Bountiful, Utah: American Genealogical Lending Library, 1989.

Genealogy and Computers for the Determined Researcher. Monterey, Calif.: Genealogy Research Associates, 1992.

Greenwood, Val D. *The Researcher's Guide to American Genealogy.* 2nd ed. Baltimore: Genealogical Publishing Co., 1990.

Haun, Weynette Parks. "Watching Your 'Ps' and Crossing Them." *Magazine of Virginia Genealogy* 24 (November 1986).

Szucs, Loretto Dennis, and Sandra Hargreaves Luebking, eds. *The Source: A Guidebook of American Genealogy.* Rev. ed. Salt Lake City: Ancestry, 1997.

United States

Ainsworth, Fern. *Private Land Claims: Illinois, Indiana, Michigan and Wisconsin.* Natchitoches, La.: the author, 1985.

Bockstruck, Lloyd DeWitt. *Revolutionary War Bounty Land Grants Awarded by State Governments.* Baltimore: Genealogical Publishing Co., 1996.

Brown, Margie. *Genealogical Abstracts, Revolutionary War Veterans, Scrip Act, 1852/Abstracted from the Bureau of Land Management, Record Group 49, National Archives Branch, Suitland, Maryland.* Oakton, Va.: the author, 1990.

Carter, Clarence Edwin, comp. and ed. *The Territorial Papers of the United States.* 26 vols. Washington, D.C.: Government Printing Office, 1934–62. These twenty-six volumes cover the midwestern and southern states.

Digested Summary and Alphabetical List of Private Claims Which Have Been Presented to the House of Representatives from the First to the Thirty-First Congress. 1853. Reprint. 3 vols. Baltimore: Genealogical Publishing Co., 1970.

House, Charles J., comp. *Names of Soldiers of the American Revolution Who Applied for State Bounty under Resolves of March 17, 1835, March 24, 1836, and March 20, 1837, as Appears of Record in the Land Office.* 1893. Reprint. Baltimore: Genealogical Publishing Co., 1963. This publication serves as a partial index to the twelve reels of microfilmed *Revolutionary War Veterans Land Records for Maine.*

McMullin, Phillip W. *Grassroots of America: A Computerized Index to the American State Papers: Land Grants and Claims (1789–1837).* Salt Lake City: Gendex, 1972. Reprint. Greenville, S.C.: Southern Historical Press, 1994.

Smith, Clifford Neal, comp. *Federal Land Series: A Calendar of Archival Materials on the Land Patents Issued by the United States Government, with Subject, Tract and Name Indexes.* 4 vols. Chicago: American Library Association, 1972–86.

United States Congress. *American State Papers: Documents of the Congress of the United States in Relation to the Public Lands 1789–1837 and Claims.* 9 vols. Washington, D.C.: Gates and Seaton, 1832–61. Reprinted as *American State Papers: Public Lands.* Greenville, S.C.: Southern Historical Press, 1994. Indexed by McMullin (see above).

United States. Court of Private Land Claims. *Certification of Deposit and List of Grants Rejected by the Court, and Oaths of Office.* Santa Fe: University of New Mexico, 1955–57.

United States. General Land Office. *Letters Sent By the General Land Office and the Treasury Department to Surveyors General, 1796–1816.* Washington, D.C.: National Archives, 1963. For an index use Smith's *Federal Land Series: A Calendar of Archival Materials on the Land Patents Issues by the United States Government* (see above).

State Sources

The following bibliography identifies published land records covering all or a major portion of forty states. Most such works are for land grants during the early settlement of the state. Later records, if published at all, are usually limited to local areas, such as counties. This list is not comprehensive, so further research is needed in the appropriate bibliographies and catalogs. Many states are also covered by nationwide sources, especially the *American State Papers* and *The Territorial Papers of the United States.* For five states (Iowa, Kansas, Nebraska, Utah, and Wyoming), the bibliography includes only books *about* the land records of that state.

Alabama

Ainsworth, Fern. *Private Land Claims: Alabama, Arkansas, Florida.* Natchitoches, La.: the author, 1978.

(Barefield), Marilyn Davis Hahn. *Old Cahaba Land Office Records and Military Warrants, 1817–1853.* Birmingham, Ala.: Southern University Press, 1986.

_____. *Old Huntsville Land Office Records and Military Warrants, 1810–1854.* Easley, S.C.: Southern Historical Press, 1985.

_____. *Old Sparta and Elba Land Office Records and Military Warrants, 1822–1860.* Easley, S.C.: Southern Historical Press, 1983.

_____. *Old St. Stephen's Land Office Records and American State Papers, Public Lands.* Easley, S.C.: Southern Historical Press, 1983.

_____. *Old Tuskaloosa Land Office Records and Military Warrants, 1821–1855.* Easley, S.C.: Southern Historical Press, 1984.

De Ville, Winston. *English Land Grants in West Florida: A Register for the States of Alabama, Mississippi, and Parts of Florida and Louisiana, 1766–1776.* Ville Platte, La.: the author, 1986.

Gandrud, Pauline Jones, comp. *Alabama Records: Volume 121, Original Land Records in Alabama.* The author, 1934.

Cowart, Margaret Matthews. *Old Land Records of* [county], *Alabama.* Huntsville, Ala.: the author, ca. 1980–86. (Land patent abstracts found under the name of the county.)

Alaska

Arnold, Robert D., and Janet Archibald, eds. *Alaska Native Land Claims.* Rev. ed. Anchorage: Books Alaska, 1978.

1991: Making It Work: A Guide to Public Law 100-241, 1987 Amendments to the Alaska Native Claims Settlement Act. Anchorage: Alaska Federation of Natives, 1989.

Also see the Juneau U.S. Geological Survey and U.S. Bureau of Mines reports between 1923 and 1960.

Arizona (Arizona Territory was part of New Mexico Territory from 1851 to 1863)

Van Ness, John R., and Christine Van Ness. *Spanish and Mexican Land Grants in New Mexico and Colorado.* Manhattan, Kans.: AG Press, 1981.

Arkansas

Ainsworth, Fern. *Private Land Claims: Alabama, Arkansas, Florida.* Natchitoches, La.: the author, 1978

Allen, Desmond Walls. *Arkansas Land Patents,* [counties], *Granted through 30 June 1908.* Conway, Ark.: Arkansas Research, ca. 1990–93. (Land patent abstracts found under the name of the county.)

Christensen, Katheren. *Arkansas Military Bounty Grants (War of 1812).* Hot Springs, Ark.: Arkansas Ancestors, 1971.

Ingmire, Frances Terry. *Containing Grants in Present States of Missouri, Arkansas and Oklahoma.* St. Louis: the author, 1984.

Original Purchasers of Land in Southwest Arkansas from 1826, Book 1. Hope, Ark.: Hempstead County Genealogical Society, 1990.

California

Avina, Rose Hollenbaugh. *Spanish and Mexican Land Grants in California.* New York: Arno Press, 1976.

Bowman, J. N. *Index to the Spanish-Mexican Private Land Grant Records and Cases of California.* Bancroft Library, University of California, 1970.

Cowan, Robert Granniss. *Ranchos of California: A List of Spanish Concessions, 1775–1822, and Mexican Grants, 1822–1846.* Fresno, Calif.: Academy Library Guild, 1956.

Colorado

Van Ness, John R., and Christine Van Ness. *Spanish and Mexican Land Grants in New Mexico and Colorado.* Manhattan, Kans.: AG Press, 1981.

Connecticut

Burr, Jean Chandler, comp. and ed. *Lyme Records 1667–1730: A Literal Transcription of the Minutes of the Town Meetings with Marginal Notations, to which hath been Appended Land Grants and Ear Marks.* Stonington, Conn.: Pequot Press, 1968.

Colonial Land Records of Connecticut, 1640–1846. 5 vols. Hartford: Connecticut State Library, n.d. Bound volumes of chronologically arranged original documents at the state library which include patents, deeds, and land surveys.

Delaware

Delaware's Fugitive Records: An Inventory of the Official Land Grant Records Relating to the Present State of Delaware. Dover: Department of State, Division of Historical and Cultural Affairs, 1980. Delaware land records found in New York and Pennsylvania archives.

Original Land Titles in the Delaware, Commonly Known as the Duke of York Records . . . 1646 to 1679. Wilmington, Del.: Sunday Star Print, [1899].

Weinberg, Allen, and Thomas E. Slattery. *Warrants and Surveys of the Province of Pennsylvania Including the Three Lower Counties, 1759.* 1965. Reprint. Knightstown, Ind.: Bookmark, 1975.

Florida

Ainsworth, Fern. *Private Land Claims: Alabama, Arkansas, Florida.* Natchitoches, La.: the author, 1978.

De Ville, Winston. *English Land Grants in West Florida: A Register for the States of Alabama, Mississippi, and Parts of Florida and Louisiana, 1766–1776.* Ville Platte, La.: the author, 1986.

Historical Records Survey, Division of Professional and Service Projects, Work Projects Administration. *Spanish Land Grants in Florida: Briefed Translations from the Archives of the Board of Commissioners for Ascertaining Claims and Titles to Land in the Territory of Florida.* 5 vols. Tallahassee, Fla.: State Library Board, 1940–41.

Georgia

Davis, Robert S., Jr., and Silas E. Lucas, comps. *The Georgia Land Lottery Papers, 1805–1914: Genealogical Data from the Loose Papers Filed in the Georgia Surveyor General Office Concerning the Lots Won in the State Land Lotteries and the People Who Won Them.* Easley, S.C.: Southern Historical Press, 1979.

Houston, Martha Lou. *Reprint of Official Register of Land Lottery of Georgia, 1827.* 1929. Reprint. Easley, S.C.: Southern Historical Press, 1986.

Index to the Headright and Bounty Grants of Georgia, 1756–1909. Rev. ed. Greenville, S.C.: Southern Historical Press, 1992.

Lucas, Silas Emmett, Jr. *The 1832 Gold Lottery of Georgia: Containing a List of the Fortunate Drawers in Said Lottery.* Easley, S.C.: Southern Historical Press, 1976.

_____, comp. *The Fourth or 1821 Land Lottery of Georgia.* Easley, S.C.: Southern Historical Press, 1986.

_____, comp. *The Second or 1807 Land Lottery of Georgia.* Easley, S.C.: Southern Historical Press, 1986.

_____, comp. *The Third or 1820 Land Lottery of Georgia.* Easley, S.C.: Southern Historical Press, 1986.

Wood, Ralph V., and Virginia S. Wood. *The 1805 Land Lottery of Georgia.* Cambridge, Mass.: Greenwood Press, 1964.

Hawaii

Chinen, Jon J. *Original Land Titles in Hawaii.* N.p., ca. 1961.

_____. *The Great Mahele: Hawaii's Land Division of 1848.* Honolulu: University Press of Hawaii, ca.1958.

Hawaii, Registrar of Bureau of Conveyances. *Deeds and Other Records, 1844–1900.* Honolulu: Department of Land and Natural Resources, ca. 1970.

Idaho

Thousands of Idaho Surnames: Abstracted From Rejected Federal Land Applications. 5 vols. Portland, Oreg.: Genealogical Forum of Portland, Oregon, 1980–87.

Illinois

See Ainsworth under "United States" sources, above.

Carlson, Theodore Leonard. *The Illinois Military Tract: A Study of Land Occupation, Utilization and Tenure.* Urbana: University of Illinois Press, 1951.

Volkel, Lowell M. *War of 1812 Bounty Lands in Illinois.* Thomson, Ill.: Heritage House, 1977.

_____. *Shawneetown: Land District Records, 1814–1820.* Indianapolis: Heritage House, 1978.

Indiana

See Ainsworth under "United States" sources, above.

Dorrel, Ruth. "Rush County Old Settlers Deaths." *Hoosier Genealogist* 33 (June 1993): 91.

Lux, Leonard. *The Vincennes Donation Lands.* Indianapolis: Indiana Historical Society, 1949.

Waters, Margaret R. *Indiana Land Entries.* 2 vols. Reprint. Knightstown, Ind.: Bookmark, 1977. Index of land entries for the Cincinnati Land District, 1801 to 1840, and Vincennes Land District, 1807 to 1877.

Iowa

Lokken, Roscoe L. *Iowa: Public Land Disposal.* Iowa City: State Historical Society of Iowa, 1942.

Kansas

Homestead Guide of Kansas and Nebraska. Waterville, Kans.: F. G. Adams, 1873.

Kentucky

Jillson, Willard Rouse. *Old Kentucky Entries and Deeds: A Complete Index to All of the Earliest Land Entries, Military*

Warrants, Deeds and Wills of the Commonwealth of Kentucky. Louisville: Standard Printing Co., 1926. Reprint. Baltimore: Genealogical Publishing Co., 1987.

_____. *The Kentucky Land Grants: A Systematic Index to All of the Land Grants Recorded in the State Land Office at Frankfort, Kentucky, 1782–1924.* 1 vol. in 2. Baltimore: Genealogical Publishing Co., 1971. Originally published as Filson Club Publication no. 33. (Louisville: Standard Printing Co., 1925).

Louisiana

De Ville, Winston. *English Land Grants in West Florida: A Register for the States of Alabama, Mississippi, and Parts of Florida and Louisiana, 1766–1776.* Ville Platte, La.: the author, 1986.

First Settlers of the Louisiana Territory: Orleans Territory Grants from American State Papers, Class viii, Public Lands. 2 vols. Nacogdoches, Tex.: Ericson Books, and St. Louis: Ingmire Publications, ca. 1983.

Historical Records Survey, Division of Professional and Service Projects, Work Projects Administration. *Survey of Federal Archives in Louisiana: Land Claims and Other Documents, ca. 1800–1860.* Baton Rouge: Archives and Records Service, n.d.

Maduell, Charles R. *Federal Land Grants in the Territory of Orleans: The Delta Parishes.* New Orleans: Polyanthos, 1975. Adapted from *American State Papers, Public Lands,* vol. 2, and arranged by counties as they existed in 1812.

Pintado, Vincente Sebastian. *Pintado Papers, 1795–1842.* Baton Rouge: Archives and Records Service, n.d.

Maine

York Deeds. 18 vols. First volume published in Portland, Maine: John T. Hull, 1887. Various publishers for next 17 vols., 1887–1910. Encompasses the 1642-to-1737 period. York County included all of what is now Maine before 1760.

Maryland

Skordas, Gust. *The Early Settlers of Maryland: An Index to Names of Immigrants Compiled From Records of Land Patents, 1633–1680.* 1968. Reprint. Baltimore: Genealogical Publishing Co., 1986.

Massachusetts

Pope, Charles Henry. *The Plymouth Scrap Book: The Oldest Original Documents Extant in Plymouth Archives Printed Verbatim.* Boston: C. E. Goodspeed, 1918.

Publications of the Colonial Society of Massachusetts, vol. 4, *Collections.* Boston: the society, 1910.

Shurtleff, Nathaniel B., and David Pulsifer, eds. *Records of the Colony of New Plymouth in New England.* 12 vols. in 10. Boston: William White, 1855–61. Vol. 12 includes colony deeds from 1620 to 1651.

Michigan

Ainsworth, Fern. *Private Land Claims, Illinois, Indiana, Michigan and Wisconsin.* Natchitoches, La.: the author, 1985.

See Ainsworth under "United States" sources, above.

Minnesota

Kinney, Gregory. *A Guide to the Records of Minnesota's Public Lands.* St. Paul: Minnesota Historical Society, 1985.

Orfield, Matthias N. *Federal Land Grants to the States with Special Reference to Minnesota.* University of Minnesota Studies in the Social Sciences. Minneapolis: the author, 1915.

Mississippi

Ainsworth, Fern. *Private Land Claims of Mississippi and Missouri.* Natchitoches, La.: the author, n.d.

De Ville, Winston. *English Land Grants in West Florida: A Register for the States of Alabama, Mississippi, and Parts of Florida and Louisiana, 1766–1776.* Ville Platte, La.: the author, 1986.

First Settlers of the Mississippi Territory. Nacogdoches, Tex.: Ericson Books, n.d.

Williams, E. Russ, Jr., comp. and ed. *Abstracts of Deeds: Marion County, Mississippi: Containing Deeds, Marks and Brands, Bond, Mortgages, and Deeds of Gift.* Bogalusa, La.: the author, 1962.

Missouri (also see Mississippi)

Dunaway, Maxine, comp. *Missouri Military Land Warrants, War of 1812.* Springfield, Mo.: the compiler, ca. 1985.

_____, comp. *Land Sales in Area of Polk County, Missouri: From Tract Books of the Bureau of Land Management, Washington, D.C.* Springfield, Mo.: the author, 1984.

Ericson, Carolyn, and Frances Ingmire. *First Settlers of the Missouri Territory.* 2 vols. Nacogdoches, Tex.: Ericson Books, ca. 1983.

Ingmire, Frances Terry. *Citizens of Missouri.* 3 vols. St. Louis: the author, ca. 1984. Vol. 1 covers 1787 to 1810. Vols. 2 and 3 contain grants in present states of Missouri, Arkansas, and Oklahoma, 1787 to 1835.

_____. *Containing Grants in Present States of Missouri, Arkansas and Oklahoma.* St. Louis: the author, 1984.

Lowrie, Walter, ed. *Early Settlers of Missouri As Taken from Land Claims in the Missouri Territory.* Reprint. Easley, S.C.: Southern Historical Press, 1986.

Missouri Land Claims. 1835. Reprint. New Orleans: Polyanthos, 1976.

Montana

VanDersal and Conner's Stockgrowers Directory of Marks and Brands for the State of Montana, 1872–1900: Comprising an Alphabetical List of Names of All Livestock Companies and . . . Sheep and Wool Growers. Glendive, Mont.: Review Printing Co., 1974.

Nebraska (also see Kansas)

Sheldon, Addison E. *Land Systems and Land Policies in Nebraska: A History of Nebraska Land, Public Domain and Private Property.* Lincoln: Nebraska State Historical Society, 1936.

Nevada

Ellison, Marion. *An Inventory and Index to the Records of Carson County, Utah and Nevada Territories, 1855–1861.* Reno, Nev.: Grace Dangberg Foundation, 1984. Chiefly land records.

New Hampshire

Provincial and State Papers. 40 vols. Concord, N.H.: state printer, 1867–43.

New Jersey

The Minutes of the Board of Proprietors of the Eastern Division of New Jersey from . . . 1685–1794. 3 vols. Perth Amboy, N.J.: General Board of Proprietors of the Eastern Division of New Jersey, 1949–60. Vol. 4. Newark, N.J.: New Jersey Historical Society, 1985. Include petitions for land grants, warrants for surveys, and quitrent payments.

Nelson, William. *Patents and Deeds and Other Early Records of New Jersey, 1664–1703.* Baltimore: Genealogical Publishing Co., 1976. Reprinted from vol. 26 of *Documents Relating to the Colonial History of the State of New Jersey.*

New Mexico

New Mexico (Territory). Surveyor-General's Office. *Press Copies of Grant Papers.* Santa Fe: University of New Mexico Library, 1955–57.

New York

Bingham, Robert Warwick, ed. *Reports of Joseph Ellicott as Chief of Survey (1797–1800): And as Agent (1800–1821) of the Holland Land Company's Purchases in Western New York.* Buffalo, N.Y.: Buffalo Historical Society, 1937–41.

Bowman, Fred Q. *Landholders of Northeastern New York, 1739–1802.* Baltimore: Genealogical Publishing Co., 1983.

Brownell, Elijah Ellsworth. *List of Patents of Lands, Etc. to be Sold in January, 1822, for Arrears of Quit Rent.* Philadelphia, 1937.

Burleigh, H. C. *New York State—Confiscations of Loyalists.* Toronto, Ontario: United Empire Loyalists Association of Canada, 1970.

Calendar of N.Y. Colonial Manuscripts, Indorsed (sic) Land *Papers in the Office of the Secretary of State of New York, 1643–1803.* Albany, N.Y.: Weed, Parsons and Co., 1864.

Duane, James. *State of the Evidence and Argument in Support of the Territorial Rights and Jurisdiction of New York Against the Government of New Hampshire and the Claimants Under It and Against the Commonwealth of Massachusetts.* New York: printed for the New York Historical Society, 1871.

Gehring, Charles T. *New York Historical Manuscripts: Dutch Land Papers, Volumes GG, HH, II.* Baltimore: Genealogical Publishing Co., 1980.

Kim, Sung Bok. *Landlord and Tenant in Colonial New York: Manorial Society, 1664–1775.* Chapel Hill: University of North Carolina Press, 1978.

Livsey, Karen E. *Western New York Land Transactions, 1804–1824: Extracted from the Archives of the Holland Land Company.* 2 vols. Baltimore: Genealogical Publishing Co., 1991, 1996.

New York. Commissioners of Indian Affairs. *Proceedings of the Commissioners of Indian Affairs Appointed by Law for the Extinguishment of Indian Titles in the State of New York.* Albany, N.Y.: J. Munsell, 1861.

Scott, Kenneth, and Rosanne Conway. *New York Alien Residents, 1825–1848.* Baltimore: Genealogical Publishing Co., 1978.

Yoshpe, Harry B. *The Disposition of Loyalist Estates in the Southern District of the State of New York.* New York: Columbia University Press, 1939.

North Carolina

Enochs, Richard A. *Rowan County, North Carolina: Vacant Land Entries, 1778–1789.* Indianapolis: the author, 1988.

Hofmann, Margaret M. *Colony of North Carolina, 1735–1764, 1765–1775: Abstracts of Land Patents.* 2 vols. Weldon, N.C.: Roanoke News Co., 1982, 1984.

_____. *The Granville District of North Carolina, 1748–1763: Abstracts of Land Grants.* 2 vols. Weldon, N.C.: Roanoke News Co., 1986, 1987.

_____. *Province of North Carolina, 1663–1729: Abstracts of Land Patents.* Weldon, N.C.: Roanoke News Co., 1979.

Holcomb, Brent. *Deed Abstracts of Tryon, Lincoln and Rutherford Counties, North Carolina, 1769–1786 and Tyron County Wills and Estates.* Easley, S.C.: Southern Historical Press, 1977.

Pruitt, Bruce, and Grace Turner. "Surry Co., NC, Land Entries Withdrawn in 1790." *North Carolina Genealogical Society Journal* 18 (November 1992): 209–12.

Van Wyck, Frederick. *Select Patents of New York Towns.* Boston: A. A. Beauchamp, 1938.

North Dakota

Brown, Ruth. *Sioux Personal Property Claims from the Original Ledger.* Medford, Oreg.: Rogue Valley Genealogical Society, 1987.

Ohio (also see Smith under "United States" sources, above)

Clark, Marie Taylor. *Ohio Lands—Chillicothe Land Office: Entries Encompassing the Lands of Congress Lands, Refuge Tract, United States Military District, and French Grants; Contains Maps and Histories of Land Areas, 1800–1829.* The author, 1984.

_____. *Ohio Lands South of the Indian Boundary Line.* Chillicothe, Ohio: the author, 1984.

Dyer, Albion Morris. *First Ownership of Ohio Lands.* Baltimore: Genealogical Publishing Co., 1982.

Ferguson, Thomas E. *Ohio Lands: A Short History.* 6th ed. Auditor's Office, State of Ohio, 1995.

McBride, David N., and Jane N. McBride, comps. *Records of the Recorder's Office of Highland County, Ohio (1805–1850).* Ann Arbor, Mich.: Edwards Letter Shop, 1969.

Peters, William Edwards. *Ohio Lands and Their Subdivision.* 2nd ed. Athens, Ohio: the author, 1918.

Sherman, C. E. *Original Ohio Land Subdivision Being Volume III: Final Report Ohio Cooperative Topographic Survey.* Columbus: State Reformatory Press, 1925.

Oklahoma

Ingmire, Frances Terry. *Containing Grants in Present States of Missouri, Arkansas and Oklahoma.* St. Louis: the author, 1984.

Sober, Nancy Hope. *The Intruders: The Illegal Residents of the Cherokee Nation, 1866–1907.* Ponca City, Okla.: Cherokee Books, 1991.

Oregon

Index of Oregon Donation Land Claims. 2nd ed. Portland: Genealogical Forum of Portland, 1987.

Pennsylvania

Boyd, Julian P., and Robert J. Taylor. *Susquehannah Company Papers.* 11 vols. Ithaca, N.Y.: Cornell University Press, 1962–71.

Harriss, Helen L., comp. *Abstracts: Deed Books I and II, Allegheny County, Pennsylvania.* The compiler, 1984.

Munger, Donna Bingham. *Pennsylvania Land Records: A History and Guide for Research.* Wilmington, Del.: Scholarly Resources, 1991.

Weinberg, Allen, and Thomas E. Slatterly. *Warrants and Surveys of the Province of Pennsylvania Including the Three*

Lower Counties, 1759. Philadelphia: City of Philadelphia, Department of Records, 1965.

Rhode Island

Arnold, James N. *The Records of the Proprietors of the Narragansett, Otherwise Called the Fones Record.* Providence, R.I.: Narragansett Historical Publishing, 1894.

Worthington, Dorothy, comp. *Rhode Island Land Evidences.* Vol. 1, 1648–96. Providence: Rhode Island Historical Society, 1921. Reprinted with a preface by Albert T. Klyberg. Baltimore: Genealogical Publishing Co., 1970.

South Carolina

Bleser, Carol K. Rothrock. *The Promised Land: The History of the South Carolina Land Commission 1869–1890.* Columbia: University of South Carolina Press, 1969.

Bratcher, R. Wayne. *Index to Commissioner of Locations, Plat Books A and B, 1784–1788: In Addition to Families Naming Swamps, Branches, Creeks, Ponds, Rivers, Roads, and Counties of the Lower Ninety-Six District from the Coast of South Carolina as Far Inland as There Were Settlements.* Greenville, S.C.: A Press, 1986.

Langley, Clara A. *South Carolina Deed Abstracts 1719–1772.* Easley, S.C.: Southern Historical Press, 1983.

Lucas, Silas Emmett, Jr. *An Index to Deeds of the Province and State of South Carolina 1719–1785 and Charleston District 1785–1800.* Easley, S.C.: Southern Historical Press, 1977.

Jackson, Ronald Vern. *Index to South Carolina Land Grants, 1784–1800.* Bountiful, Utah: Accelerated Indexing Systems, 1977.

Salley, A. S., Jr., and R. N. Olsberg, eds. *Warrants for Land in South Carolina 1672–1711.* Rev. ed. Columbia: University of South Carolina Press, 1973.

South Dakota

Green, Charles L. *The Administration of the Public Domain in South Dakota.* Pierre, S.D.: Hipple Printing, 1939.

Tennessee

Marsh, Helen C., and Timothy R. Marsh, comps. *Land Deed Genealogy of Bedford County Tennessee 1807–1852.* Easley, S.C.: Southern Historical Press, 1988.

Potter, Dorothy Williams, ed. *Original Surveyor's Record Book, 1836–1887, Coffee County, Tennessee: With Additional Material on Early Tullahoma.* Tullahoma, Tenn.: the editor, 1976.

Rae, Loraine. *Washington County, Tennessee: Deeds, 1775–1800.* Greenville, S.C.: Southern Historical Press, 1991.

Thomas, Jane Kizer. *Blount County, Tennessee, Deeds: Deed Book 1, 1795–1819.* Maryville, Tenn.: Blount County Genealogical and Historical Society, 1990.

Whitley, Edythe Rucker, comp. *Overton County, Tennessee: Genealogical Records.* Baltimore: Genealogical Publishing Co., 1979.

Texas

Miller, Thomas Lloyd. *Bounty and Donation Land Grants of Texas 1835–1888.* Austin: University of Texas Press, 1967.

_____. *The Public Lands of Texas, 1519–1970.* Norman: University of Oklahoma Press, 1971.

Utah

Ellison, Marion. *An Inventory and Index to the Records of Carson County, Utah and Nevada Territories, 1855–1861.* Reno, Nev.: Grace Dangberg Foundation, 1984. Chiefly land records.

Fox, Feramorz Young. *The Mormon Land System—A Study of the Settlement and Utilization of Land Under the Direction of the Mormon Church.* Logan: Utah State Agricultural College, n.d.

Vermont

Bogart, Walter Thompson. *The Vermont Lease Lands.* Montpelier: Vermont Historical Society, 1950.

Charters Granted by the State of Vermont, 1779–1846. 2 vols. Vermont Public Records Division, 1974.

Denio, Herbert Williams. *Massachusetts Land Grants in Vermont.* Cambridge, Mass.: John Wilson and Son, University Press, 1920. Reprinted from *Publications of the Colonial Society of Massachusetts* 24 (March 1920): 35–99.

Holbrook, Jay Mack. *Vermont's First Settlers.* Oxford, Mass.: Holbrook Research Institute, 1976. Alphabetically arranged land grants in Vermont, 1763 to 1803.

State Papers of Vermont. 17 vols. Montpelier: secretary of state, 1918–69. Volumes have separate subjects. Vol. 5 is entitled *Petitions for Land Grants, 1778-1881.* Vol. 7 covers *New York Land Patents, 1668-1768, Covering Land and Included in the State of Vermont.*

Virginia

Brookes-Smith, Joan E. *Master Index Virginia Surveys and Grants 1774–1791.* Frankfort: Kentucky Historical Society, 1976.

Cabell, Priscilla Harriss. *Turff and Twigg: The French Lands.* Richmond, Va.: the author, 1988.

Dabney, Virginius. *Virginia: The New Dominion.* Charlottesville: University Press of Virginia, 1971.

des Cognet, Louis, Jr., comp. *English Duplicates of Lost Virginia Records.* Baltimore: Genealogical Publishing Co., 1981.

Foley, Louise Pledge Heath. *Early Virginia Families Along the James River: Their Deep Roots and Tangled Branches.* Vol. 1, *Henrico County-Goochland County, Virginia.* Vol. 2, *Charles City County-Prince George County, Virginia.* Richmond, Va.: the author, 1974–78.

Hall, Wilmer L., ed. 1949. *The Vestry Book of the Upper Parish, Nansemond County, Virginia, 1743–1793.* Richmond: Virginia State Library.

Hopkins, William Lindsay. "Virginia Land Patent Books." *Magazine of Virginia Genealogy.* Richmond: Virginia Genealogical Society, 1984 to date. Serial publication of later patent books covering 1732 to 1742 as of February 1988, vol. 26, no. 1.

_____. *Virginia Revolutionary War Land Grant Claims 1783–1850 (Rejected).* Richmond: Gen-N-Dex, 1988.

Hudgins, Dennis, ed. *Cavaliers and Pioneers: Abstracts of Virginia Land Patents and Grants, 1732–1741.* Vol. 4 of 5. Richmond: Virginia Genealogical Society, 1994.

_____, ed. *Cavaliers and Pioneers: Abstracts of Virginia Land Patents and Grants, 1741–1749.* Vol. 5 of 5. Richmond: Virginia Genealogical Society, 1994.

Kaylor, Peter Cline. *Abstract of Land Grant Surveys, 1761–1791.* 1938. Baltimore: Clearfield Co., 1991.

Mitchell, Beth. *Beginning at a White Oak: Patents and Northern Neck Grants of Fairfax County, Virginia.* Fairfax, Va.: McGregor and Werner, 1979.

Nugent, Nell Marion. *Caveat Proceedings.* N.p., 1970.

_____. *Cavaliers and Pioneers: Abstracts of Virginia Land Patents and Grants, 1623–1666.* Vol. 1 of 5. Richmond, Va.: Dietz Printing Co., 1934. Reprint. Baltimore: Genealogical Publishing Co., 1983.

_____. *Cavaliers and Pioneers: Abstracts of Virginia Land Patents and Grants, 1666–1695.* Vol. 2 of 5. Richmond: Virginia State Library, 1977.

_____. *Cavaliers and Pioneers: Abstracts of Virginia Land Patents and Grants, 1695–1732.* Vol. 3 of 5. Richmond: Virginia State Library, 1979.

_____. *Cavaliers and Pioneers: Abstracts of Virginia Land Patents and Grants. Supplement, Northern Neck Grants No. 1, 1690–1692.* Richmond: Virginia State Library, 1980.

Parks, Gary. *Virginia Land Records: From the Virginia Magazine of History and Biography, the William and Mary College Quarterly, and Tyler's Quarterly.* Baltimore: Genealogical Publishing Co., 1982.

Smith, Annie Laurie Wright, comp. *The Quit Rents of Virginia, 1704.* Baltimore: Genealogical Publishing Co., 1980.

Schreiner-Yantis, Netti. *Montgomery County, Virginia—Circa 1790: A Comprehensive Study, including the 1789 Tax Lists, Abstracts of Over 800 Land Surveys and Data Concerning Migration.* Springfield, Va., 1972.

Weisiger, Benjamin B., 3rd. *Burned County Data 1809–1848: As Found in the Virginia Contested Election Files.* Richmond, Va.: the author, 1986.

Wilson, Samuel Mackay. *Catalogue of Revolutionary Soldiers and Sailors of the Commonwealth of Virginia: To Whom Land Bounty Warrants Were Granted By Virginia for Military Service in the War for Independence.* Baltimore: Genealogical Publishing Co., 1967.

Washington

Washington Territory Donation Land Claims: An Abstract of Information in the Land Claim Papers of Persons Who Settled in Washington Territory Before 1856. Seattle: Seattle Genealogical Society, 1980.

West Virginia

Sims, Edgar B. *Sims Index to Land Grants in West Virginia.* Charleston: Auditor's Office, 1952. Supplement, 1963. Includes Northern Neck grants in northern West Virginia and northern Virginia.

Wisconsin

See Ainsworth under "United States" sources, above.

Wisconsin Domesday Book: Town Studies. Publications of the State Historical Society of Wisconsin. Minasha, Wisc.: George Santa Publishing Co., 1924. First volume of a projected series to identify the 1860 landholders on township maps. Includes twenty towns.

Wyoming

Bolger, Eileen. *Preliminary Inventory of the Records of the BLM, Wyoming.* Denver: Federal Archives and Records Center, 1983.

COURT AND LEGAL RECORDS OVERVIEW

Key Concepts in This Chapter

- Millions of court cases appear in published sources.
- Abstracts of court minute books are common for local courts.
- The most commonly published court records are for colonial courts.
- *Reporters* are published decisions of higher courts.
- *Tables of cases* are indexes to individual reporters.
- *Digests* summarize cases from throughout the United States.
- Law libraries are helpful repositories for reporters and digests.
- Private laws enacted by state and Federal legislatures identify the individuals whom they benefit.

Key Sources in This Chapter

- State archive collections that publish court records
- *1906 Decennial Edition of the American Digest*
- *Federal Digest*
- Case reporters
- American Digests System
- *Martindale-Hubbell Directory*
- *Black's Law Dictionary*

12

COURT AND LEGAL RECORDS

Benjamin Barnett Spratling, 3rd[1]

In the course of research, many genealogists limit their searches to probate court records for wills, administrations, and guardianships, or turn to court records for naturaliza tions. However, there are other court records that should not be overlooked. Court records can establish family relationships and places of residence, and they often provide occupations, descriptions of individuals, and other excellent family history information.

Mention of ancestors can often be found in court records; they may appear as defendants, plaintiffs, witnesses, or jurors. Not only have our ancestors participated in cases involving probate or naturalization; they might also be noted in actions involving divorce, debt, adoption, guardianship, licenses, appointment to public offices, taxes, contract disputes, personal injuries, property disputes, crimes, or any of many other matters brought before a court.

Two main types of cases are found in court records:

- *Civil.* In civil cases, one or more individuals or legal entities, such as corporations, file suit against other individuals or entities to enforce private rights or to receive compensation for the violation of rights. Civil lawsuits can be filed for such matters as property damage, trespass, libel, divorce, personal injury, breach of contract, and wrongful death, whether real or imagined.

- *Criminal.* Criminal cases involve offenses alleged to have been committed against the state, in which the state prosecutes those persons who are accused of public wrongs. Society is or may be harmed by the violation of criminal laws, such as murder, theft, arson, and treason. Serious crimes are *felonies;* minor crimes are *misdemeanors.*

Most U.S. courts and their published records are discussed in this chapter. However, because of their great importance to family history research, court records related to probate (chapter 10) and naturalization (chapter 14) are discussed separately.

The United States has a dual court system that has existed since the effective date of the U.S. Constitution (1789). The various state courts that had functioned since the beginning of the colonial period were not abolished by the Constitution. Rather, provision was made for Federal (national) courts to handle cases that were deemed inappropriate for state courts (for example, cases involving the U.S. Constitution or Federal statutory laws). Even though Federal courts have been granted greater jurisdiction in recent years, most cases are still tried in state courts. Somewhat surprisingly, this complex dual system of Federal and state courts has, for the most part, worked smoothly.

State and Local Courts

Each state has two basic levels of courts. The higher level consists of the *appellate courts.* At this level is the state court of last resort, usually called the *state supreme court.* There are intermediate appellate courts in many states. The main function of these appellate courts is to review the decisions of the lower trial courts. The appellate courts and their decisions, most of which have been published, are discussed below under "Case Reporters: Published Court Decisions."

The lower level of courts is made up of *trial courts.* Trial courts are generally divided into two major types: (1) *courts of general jurisdiction,* which are general trial courts that usually handle felony criminal trials and major civil cases; and (2) *courts of limited or special jurisdiction,* which typically have jurisdiction to try misdemeanor cases, conduct preliminary hearings for felony offenses, try traffic cases, adjudicate civil matters involving small amounts of money, and handle wills and estates.

Each court has jurisdiction over designated geographical areas and specific types of legal matters. The names and responsibilities of the courts in each state have changed over the years. Some examples of the types of local and state courts are:

- Chancery courts
- Circuit courts
- Common pleas courts
- County courts
- Courts of ordinary
- Courts of oyer and terminer
- Courts of quarter sessions
- General session courts
- Hustings courts

- Prerogative courts
- Probate courts
- District courts
- Orphans' courts
- Superior courts
- Supreme courts
- Surrogate courts

State courts handle both criminal and civil cases involving a state's constitution, laws, and statutes. Because state courts derive their authority from the individual states, there are great differences in their number, names, and relationships to courts in the other states.

Every controversy is presumed to be within the jurisdiction of the trial court of general jurisdiction unless the law has placed it within the exclusive cognizance of some other court. A trial court of limited jurisdiction is a court whose authority is confined to certain types of controversies.

Unfortunately, the large number of state courts with ever-changing names and jurisdictions is often confusing. Every state, however, has one supreme tribunal or "court of last resort" by which all questions of law may be finally determined, and one or more trial courts in which all cases not within the exclusive jurisdiction of the Federal courts may be heard and decided. There is no provision for appeal from state courts to the Federal courts, except in certain limited cases specified in the U.S. Constitution.

Many U.S. courts have been divided, according to the form of their proceedings and the nature of the remedies they can apply, into the following classes: (1) *law courts*, which are descendants of the ancient common law courts of England; they have jurisdiction over actions to recover money damages for past injuries and over other matters which, by custom or statute, have been placed under their control; (2) *courts of chancery or equity*, which were introduced in England after the Norman Conquest; they administer "equity" in the sense of finding a solution that is just and fair by providing a remedy in cases in which the common law courts historically did not provide an adequate remedy; and (3) *probate courts*, which were created to supervise the settlement of the estates of deceased persons and insolvents, and sometimes for the appointment and direction of guardians of infants and "incapables."

The distinction between courts of law and courts of equity has varied greatly. Most of the original states continued their separate courts of chancery or equity, and they were imitated in this regard by a few of the newer states. Over the last two hundred years, chancery (equity) courts have been eliminated in all but a few states by the gradual fusion of law courts and equity courts. Now courts in most states routinely administer equity through the same judges who apply the common law. It should be noted, however, that many local courts, especially during the colonial and early post-revolutionary periods, handled probate matters in addition to criminal and civil actions.

Federal Courts

Federal courts derive their authority from the Constitution of the United States and the acts of Congress. These include (1) the *supreme court*, which has original jurisdiction over cases in which a state may be a party and appellate jurisdiction over certain classes of cases arising in the other Federal courts; (2) the *circuit courts of appeals*, which have appellate jurisdiction over all cases arising in the inferior Federal courts (except those which must be appealed to the supreme court); (3) the *district courts*, which have original jurisdiction over numerous civil and criminal cases arising under the laws of the United States, or to which citizens of different states are parties; and (4) the *court of claims*, which has jurisdiction of claims against the United States which are based on contracts or statutes. The jurisdiction of the Federal courts is sometimes exclusive of, and sometimes concurrent with, that of the state courts. When concurrent, if an action is first instituted in a state court, it is completed there unless removed by proper legal methods to the Federal courts.

CONTENTS OF COURT RECORDS

Generally, a court record is an official written account of what occurred in the court. It is, in a sense, a written history of the proceedings of a case. Although the words *record*, *docket*, and *minutes* are sometimes used interchangeably, record generally carries a broader meaning than docket and minutes.

Docket often refers to the list of cases heard by a court, which is sometimes called the *court calendar*. Dockets typically list the names of plaintiffs and defendants and case file numbers. Dockets also usually contain brief descriptions of important acts done in court in the conduct of a case, including the date a case was heard and a list of important documents related to the case. Dockets are usually kept in chronological (not alphabetical) order. Many courts have several different dockets, such as criminal, civil, and equity dockets. Dockets serve as tables of contents to court cases; a study of dockets is only genealogically significant in that it can give the researcher more details about a specific case.

The term *minutes* generally refers to notes made by the clerk of the court in the course of proceedings. Minutes are brief accounts kept by the clerk of all actions taken by the court. They usually include the names of the plaintiff and defendant and a brief description or summary of the action taken. They are usually kept in chronological order. When minutes are written out by the clerk in proper and final form, they become part of the court record. Commonly it is the minutes of local courts that appear in published form and are available for genealogical research.

A court *record* consists not only of minutes, but also of pleadings and other documents which are filed with the court, such as written evidence, bonds, correspondence, petitions, and depositions. The record also includes orders and rulings of the court, which may be called *judgments, decrees,* or *orders*. Orders sometimes include a brief description of the case. Some actions of a court reflected in court orders—such as orders granting citizenship, appointing guardians, and re-recording deeds to replace destroyed land records—are not found in other court records.

The form that a court record takes varies greatly from one court to another and from one time period to another. Often, court minutes are kept in *record books*. In some courts, there are separate docket books and separate order books. Documents which are part of the record but cannot physically be included in the record book are kept in *case files,* which consist of folders, packets, or bundles of all the loose documents relating to

Wednesday February the 18th. 1801. The Court met according to adjournment. Present The Worshipful John HOGG, Thomas JONES, Isaac MCCALLUM, John ROGERS, Tingnal JONES, Senr, Nathaniel JONES (WP), John Grant RENCHER, Esquires.

28. The State vs William ANDREWS: Upon a bill of Indictment for an Assault and Battery, to which the Deft. plead not Guilty the following Jury, to wit;
Henry BROWN, William CAMP, William DANIEL, Robert FLEMING, Reuben HUNTER, Joshua SUGG, Isaac HICKS, Thomas SPAIN, James JONES, John RHODES, Moses LASSITER and George COLE were impaneled and sworn the truth to say on the issues Joined, find the defendant not guilty. On motion of the deft. for the prosecutor to pay Costs, Ordered that the defendant take nothing by his motion.

Figure 12-1. From a typical book of court records, Haun's *Wake County, North Carolina, County Court Minutes (Court of Pleas and Quarter Sessions) 1801 thru 1803, Book V.*

the case. Case files and folders are usually put in storage and so are not readily available for research and are more difficult to abstract; this leaves the court minute books and the docket books as the most accessible and the record types most often found in printed form. While the clerk of the court prepares the court record, in doing so, he or she is supposed to be acting under the authority and control of the judge of that court.

Often, a court will be said to be a *court of record* or a *court not of record.* In a broad sense, a court of record is one which is required by law to keep a record of its proceedings. Whether or not a court is a court of record is primarily important to the researcher only in helping determine the likelihood that records of that court still exist. Naturally, courts of record, which are supposed to keep permanent records, are more likely to have records that have survived than courts not of record, which are not required to keep permanent records. There have been (and still are) many courts not of record in America. Because, generally, these courts were not required to keep permanent records of proceedings, the likelihood is that many, if not most, of the early records of such courts have not survived.

PUBLISHED COURT RECORDS

Some court records can be found on the shelves of most libraries with genealogical collections. These published court records, most in an abstracted format, should not be confused with the published appellate court decisions that are found in *case reporters*. Case reporters normally contain only decisions in cases appealed from trial courts and are printed by official court printers or major law book publishers when decisions are released by an appellate court. Case reporters, which are primarily found in law libraries, are discussed later in this chapter under "Case Reporters: Published Court Decisions."

Court records and decisions are not usually published at the time they are created or recorded. Rather, if they are published at all, it is usually by a genealogical publisher many years later. Abstracts or transcripts of minute books or docket books, often published by individual genealogists, local genealogical publishing companies, or local genealogical societies, are probably the most likely published court records to be found. Figure 12-1 is an excerpt from a typical book of court records, Weynette Parks Haun's *Wake County, North Carolina, County Court Minutes (Court of Pleas and Quarter Sessions) 1801 thru 1803, Book V* (Durham, N.C.: the author, n.d.).

Although entire case files, which may contain loose documents having a wealth of personal information concerning ancestors, are not usually printed, the trial court records that are published can be quite helpful to genealogists. Many, if not most, consist of abstracts of records (rather than verbatim, or word-for-word, transcripts).

Like abstracts of any records, abstracts of court records should be used only with knowledge of their limitations. Original court records are always more accurate than abstracts and should be used when possible. However, published court records can often help researchers find original records (including many documents in case files that have not been published). Because original court records do not contain every-name indexes, indexed published abstracts are of immense help in locating individuals within records.

Some court records are faded, crumbling, or torn or have missing pages (and many have been destroyed or lost). Experienced editors frequently are better at interpreting such material than untrained researchers (especially researchers who are not familiar with legal terms and abbreviations used by court clerks). Therefore, printed abstracts and transcripts can be extremely useful, especially those prepared by well-trained and reliable editors. Most libraries and archives with genealogical collections have some printed abstracts and transcripts of court records, and major genealogical libraries have numerous volumes for some states.

Many abstracts of, or excerpts from, early court records have been printed recently. It seems that court records for some states are being published so often that researchers must frequently check to see what has been published most recently. (Despite this apparent flurry of court record printing, however, most court records remain unpublished.)

If published court records for the right time and location can be found, the chances of finding ancestors in them should not be underestimated. Many relatively petty disputes were resolved in court, and even people who were not parties to litigation may have been called as jurors or otherwise participated in court proceedings.

COLONIAL COURTS AND THEIR RECORDS

Courts played prominent roles in the lives of our colonial ancestors. Because church and state were inseparable in many colonies, court proceedings involved controversies not encountered in modern court hearings. Civil and criminal actions concerning church attendance, proper sabbath observance, disputes with ministers and church officials, witchcraft, fornication, adultery, and other moral improprieties are commonplace in court minutes.

When the American colonies were first established, judicial power was exercised by colonial governors who were appointed by the king. During the earliest years, a few courts were established to serve in an advisory capacity to the governors. The judges of these courts served at the pleasure of the governor and had limited authority to resolve matters.

As time passed and the population of the colonies grew, it became necessary to establish some county and town courts to provide local authorities for settling conflicts. Similar county and town courts had been established earlier in England and were adopted by the colonies. In England, the office of justice of the peace, an appointed official, had developed to handle local judicial needs. Justices of the peace were usually landowners or merchants who had no formal legal training. This system of local justices who had authority to resolve petty civil disputes and minor criminal matters was transported essentially unchanged to the colonies. Decisions of these local and county courts could be appealed to the governor and the assembly and, ultimately, to the courts of England. However, such appeals were rare. The matters before these courts were such that the time and expense of appeals normally were not justified.

With the continued growth of the colonies, additional courts were established to respond to increased litigation. As commerce increased, so did the need for courts to resolve differences. Some colonies began to divide cases between courts and to create specialized jurisdictions. In addition, new courts were established to handle certain kinds of cases. Higher courts of appeals began to appear as well.

Many of the early court records of the original colonies and some later states have been published in various series called *archives,* such as the Pennsylvania Archives. Such series are often called *documentary collections;* they typically include early court records, along with many other sources (for more information, see chapter 15, "Documentary Collections"). Most of the published colonial court records are from the county court level. They are very helpful to genealogists because these records concern a larger percentage of the population of the time than do later court records. In many areas where vital and church records are lacking, a court record might be the only source containing a description of an ancestor. It was not uncommon for individuals' ages to be included as part of colonial court record proceeding; in many cases such records might be the only ones in existence from which an estimated birth year can be deduced. Figure 12-2 is from State Department of Archives and History, *North Carolina Higher-Court Records, 1670–1696,* edited by M. E. Parker (Raleigh, N.C., 1968).

The following, from Ruth and Sam Sparacio's *Virginia County Court Records: Order Book Abstracts of Lancaster County, Virginia, 1666–1669* (McLean, Va.: Antient Press, 1993), page 51, also illustrates the content of such records.

> – THOMAS CAPRELL. Servt. to Mr. RA TRAVERS, comeing into this Countrey wth:out Indenture & appeareing at this Cort., is adjudged thirteene yeres of age & is ordered to serve eleaven yeres from his arrivall
>
> – ADAM ARMESTRONG, Servannt to THOMAS WARWICKE, comeing into this Countrey wth:out Indenture & appeareing at this Cort., is adjudged thirteene yeres of age & is ordered to serve eleaven yeres from his arrivall
>
> – JONATHAN STANLEY, Servt. to HUMPHREY JONES, comeing into this Countrey wth:out Indenture & appeareing aat this Cort., is adjudged fifteene yeres of age & is ordered to serve nyne yeres from his arrivall

The following is a discussion, by colony, of various courts that existed before the American Revolution. The sources cited below are described in detail here and so are not repeated in the chapter bibliography.

Connecticut

Colonial Courts. The *general court* (*general assembly* after 1637) was the highest court in Connecticut throughout the colonial era. It handled many criminal and civil cases. Beginning in 1638, the *particular court* was the primary court of jurisdiction for all matters of law, including appeals from *town courts.* The particular court was succeeded by the *court of assistants* (1665–1711). In 1711, the *superior court* replaced the court of assistants. Beginning in the 1630s, *town* and *borough courts* had jurisdiction over some civil matters in towns. *Justice of the peace courts* were established in 1686 to handle similar matters in areas without town courts. Beginning in 1666, *county courts* had jurisdiction over civil disputes and minor criminal cases as well as chancery and divorce matters.

Published Works. Many of the general assembly records and records of the particular court/court of assistants were published in *The Public Records of The Colony of Connecticut (1636–1775)*, 15 vols. (Hartford, Conn.: Case, Lockwood & Brainard Co., 1850–90). Published records also include *Records of the Particular Court of Connecticut, 1637–1663,* Connecticut Historical Society Collections, vol. 22 (Hartford: Connecticut Historical Society and the Society of Colonial Wars in the State of Connecticut, 1928), which contains proceedings of the particular court; and Charles J. Hoadley, ed., *Records of the Colony or Jurisdiction of New Haven, from May 1653 to the Union, Together with the New Haven Code of 1656* (Hartford, Conn: Case, Lockwood, 1858).

Delaware

Colonial Courts. Early courts in Delaware included the *court of general quarter sessions*, the *oyer and terminer,* and the *justice of the peace*. The office of clerk of the peace, or prothonotary, dates from 1642. *Chancery courts* were established in 1684. Beginning in 1701, *courts of common pleas* were established in each county.

Published Works. Many of the early colonial court records of Delaware have been published, such as *Records of the Court of New Castle on Delaware 1676–1681*, with a second volume for the years 1681 to 1699 (Lancaster: Colonial Society of Pennsylvania, 1904, 1934). Another example is *Court Records of Kent County, Delaware 1680–1705*, edited by Leon de Valinger, Jr. (Washington, D.C.: American Historical Association, 1959).

Georgia

Colonial Courts. The earliest colonial court in Georgia was the *governor and council.* Later Georgia colonial courts were the *general court of pleas* and the *court of quarter sessions.*

Published Works. Some colonial court records were published in William H. Dumont's *Colonial Georgia Genealogical Data 1748–1783* (Arlington, Va.: National Genealogical Society, n.d.).

Maryland

Colonial Courts. Beginning in 1637, the *provincial court* (later *general court*) was a colonywide court in Maryland that ruled on capital crimes, land disputes, and other civil matters. Also, beginning in 1637, *county courts* had jurisdiction over some criminal and civil cases. Starting in 1668, the *chancery court* was a statewide court with jurisdiction over equity cases.

Published Works. The earliest surviving proprietary and royal papers for the period 1637 to 1785 were published in *Calendar of Maryland State Papers No. 1, The Black Books* (1934; reprint; Baltimore: Genealogical Publishing Co., 1967). An index to chancery depositions, 1668 to 1789, was published in the *Maryland Historical Magazine* 23 (1928): 101–54, 197–242, 293–343. Other early court and related records have been published and indexed, such as provincial and county records from 1637 to the 1780s in volumes of *The Archives of Maryland.* One interesting sample of information from county court records is Millard Millburn Ride, ed., *This Was the Life: Excerpts from the Judgment Records of Frederick County, Maryland 1748–1765* (1979; reprint; Baltimore: Genealogical Publishing Co., 1984). For the Eastern Shore, there are abstracts of court books in Edward F. Wright's *Citizens of the Eastern Shore of Maryland, 1659–1750* (Silver Spring, Md.: Family Line Pub., 1986).

The Deposition of Francis Jones aged fifty seven yeares or therabout testifyeth and saith that he very well knew Hazelelpony Willix Anna Willix Susanah Willix all three the reputed daughters of Belshashar Willix sometime of Exetor in New England and Anna his wife to whom the abovementioned three sisters were borne and owned to be the Children of the said Belshashar and Anna his wife the deponent further testifyeth that he very well knew Robert Riskoe who Maried Anna one of the three sisters above named which afterward went to Roanoke or North Carolina and as the deponent understood said Riskeo there died the said Anna became wife to one Blount and after his decease to one Sothell and last of all the wife of one Colonel Lear in Virginia and further saith not.

The mark of Francis Jones

Province of New Hampshire SS.

Francis Jones appeared before Nathanll. Fryer Esqr. President of said Province and made Oath to the abovewritten testimony the 15th day of Aprill 1696.

By me Nath. Fryer president

Francis Jones came and appeared before me William Redford Notary publick for the Province of New Hampshire being duely administred <43> sworne and acknowledged the above Instrument to be his act and deed and that he had taken the Oath thereto as above this was acknowledged at my office at Portsmouth in the said Province the 18th day of Aprill 1696 in the 8th year of his Majesties Reigne in witnes wherof I have sett to my hand and affixed the Seal of the office.

W. Redford Notary Public [*seal*]

Figure 12-2. From *North Carolina Higher-Court Records, 1670–1696.* It was not uncommon for individuals' ages to be included as part of colonial court record proceeding, as in this example.

Massachusetts

Colonial Courts. In Massachusetts, the *general court* was established around 1620. *County courts* or *quarter courts*, originally called *inferior quarter courts,* existed from 1636 to 1692. These courts were replaced in 1692 by the *superior courts of judicature*, *courts of common pleas* (which handled civil cases), and *courts of quarter sessions*. From around 1692, *general sessions courts* handled criminal cases in Massachusetts. *Justice of the peace courts* existed beginning in 1630. Other early courts included the *court of assistants* (1630 to 1692), the *stranger's* or *merchant's court* (1639 to 1684), and *vice-admiralty courts*.

Published Works. For more information on colonial courts, see *Law in Colonial Massachusetts, 1630–1800* (Boston: Colonial Society of Massachusetts, 1984). Some colonial court records are in print: Nathaniel B. Shurtlett and David Pulsifer, eds., *Records of the Colony of New Plymouth in New England,* 12 vols. in 10 (Boston: William White, 1855–61); *Records of the Court of Assistants of the Colony of the Massachusetts Bay, 1630–1692*, 3 vols. (Boston: Rockwell & Churchill Press, 1901–28); Nathaniel B. Shurtleff, ed., *Records of the Governor and Company of the Massachusetts Bay in New England,* 5 vols. in 6 (Boston: W. White, 1853–54); *Records and Files of the Quarterly Courts of Essex County, Massachusetts,* 9 vols. (Salem, Mass.: Essex Institute, 1911–75) (covers 1636 to 1686); *Catalogue of Records and Files in the Office of the Clerk of the Supreme Judicial Court for the County of Suffolk* (n.p., 1890); and Franklin P. Rice, comp., *Records of the Court of General Sessions of the Peace for the County of Worcester, Massachusetts from 1731–1737* (Worcester, Mass.: Worcester Society of Antiquity, 1882).

New Hampshire

Colonial Courts. New Hampshire was under Massachusetts' jurisdiction until 1679. Beginning around 1682, *justices of the peace* had jurisdiction over some minor civil and criminal matters. The *superior court of judicature* was established around 1699 and the *court of appeals* around 1714. *Superior courts*, which are trial courts of general jurisdiction today, were established in 1769, as were *courts of general quarter sessions*, which handled some civil and criminal matters, and *courts of common pleas*, which had jurisdiction over some civil matters.

Published Works. Some colonial court records are in vol. 40 of *State Papers of New Hampshire*, 40 vols. (Concord: State printer, 1867–1943).

New Jersey

Colonial Courts. Beginning in 1675, *courts of general quarter sessions of the peace* in New Jersey handled some minor criminal cases. They also handled some civil cases before the creation of the *courts of common pleas* in 1704. From 1693, *courts of oyer and terminer and general gaol delivery* had jurisdiction over crimes, except for certain capital offenses. *Justices' courts*, which were presided over by justices of the peace, existed beginning in 1675. From 1684 to 1696 and again beginning in 1705, the *court of chancery* had equity jurisdiction. *Circuit courts* had civil jurisdiction over many cases beginning in 1799. Starting in 1682, the then *supreme court* was a major trial court handling many civil and criminal cases. Early courts also included *orphans' courts*, which handled estates and guardianships, and *prerogative courts*, which handled estate disputes.

Published Works. Some court records for the proprietary period have been published in Preston W. Edsall, ed., *Journal of the Courts of Common Right and Chancery of East New Jersey, 1683–1702* (Philadelphia: American Legal Historical Society, 1937) and H. Clay Reed and George J. Miller, eds., *The Burlington [County] Court Book: A Record of Quaker Jurisprudence in West New Jersey 1680–1790* (Washington, D.C.: American Historical Association, 1944). The state archive has an index to *Supreme Court Cases Before and After the Revolution, 1709 to 1842*, and an *Early Index to Burlington Court Minutes, 1681–1709* (Trenton, N.J.: Historical Records Survey, 1938).

New York

Colonial Courts. Beginning in 1665, *courts of general quarter sessions of the peace* handled some criminal and civil cases in New York. These courts also handled probate matters from 1665 to around 1683. After 1691, they only handled criminal cases. Beginning in 1691, *courts of common pleas* were established to handle civil cases. Established in 1683, the *court of oyer and terminer and general gaol delivery* was a county court that had jurisdiction over capital crimes, such as treason and murder. From 1653 to 1674, *courts of schouts and schepens* were the Dutch courts having criminal and civil jurisdiction. They were replaced by the *mayor's court*. From 1665 to 1683, the *court of assizes* was the highest provincial court established in New York City; it heard both civil and criminal cases and, along with the *court of sessions*, had jurisdiction over probates. From 1674 to 1784, the *mayor's court* existed in New York City; it handled civil suits, apprenticeships, and naturalizations. From 1686 to 1778, *prerogative courts* were county courts which had jurisdiction over marriages and estates.

Published Works. Records of courts of schouts and schepens are found in Edmund Bailey O'Callaghan, trans., and Berthold Fernow, ed., *New Netherland Documents: The Records of New Amsterdam from 1653 to 1674 Anno Domini*, 7 vols. (1897; reprint; Baltimore: Genealogical Publishing Co., 1976). The records for courts of assizes for 1665 to 1682 have been published as Peter R. Christoph and Florence A. Christoph, eds., *New York Historical Manuscripts: English Records of the Court of Assizes for the Colony of New York, 1665–1682* (Baltimore: Genealogical Publishing Co., 1983). Abstracts of some colonial New York City court records have been published in Kenneth Scott's *New York City Court Records, 1684–1760* (Arlington, Va.: National Genealogical Society, 1982). Early mayor's court records are in Kenneth Scott, ed., *New York Historical Manuscripts: Minutes of the Mayor's Court of New York, 1674–1675* (Baltimore: Genealogical Publishing Co., 1983) and in Richard B. Morris, ed., *Select Cases of The Mayor's Court of New York City, 1674–1784* (Washington, D.C.: American Historical Association, 1935; reprint; Millwood, N.Y.: Kraus Reprint Co., 1975).

North Carolina

Colonial Courts. From 1670 to 1754, North Carolina's *general court*, sometimes called the *court of grand council*, the *grand court*, or the *court of Albemarle*, handled civil cases involving large sums of money, major criminal cases, and some probates. *District courts* replaced the general court in 1754. From 1663 to 1776, the *court of chancery*, comprising the governor and council, handled equity cases. Also, during the colonial period, *county courts of pleas and quarter sessions* handled many minor civil and criminal cases and probate matters. These courts were composed of justices appointed by the legislature.

Published Works. Court records pertaining to the Province of North Carolina (1670 to 1730) are contained in Robert J. Cain, ed., *The Colonial Records of North Carolina*, 2nd series, 7 vols. (Raleigh: state archives, 1984). Early court records may also be found in William L. Saunders, comp. and ed., *The Colonial Records of the State of North Carolina*, 30 vols. (n.p., 1886–1914). Published abstracts of court records for many counties have been completed by private publishers.

Pennsylvania

Colonial Courts. Beginning in 1664, *courts of quarter sessions of the peace* in Pennsylvania were countywide courts that handled criminal cases, roads, taverns, and peddlers. The *court of common pleas*, which existed at least as early as 1707, had jurisdiction over many civil and criminal cases. Colonial courts included *oyer and terminer, justice of the peace,* and *chancery courts*. From 1683 to 1707, the *provincial court* was the appellate court until replaced by the *supreme court*.

Published Works. Some provincial court records have been transcribed in *Minutes of the Provincial Council of Pennsylvania: From the Organization to the Termination of the Proprietary Government (1683–1775),* 10 vols. (Philadelphia: the state, 1851–52).

Rhode Island

Colonial Courts. Colonial courts in Rhode Island included the *quarter court of freeman,* the *court of election,* the *superior court of judicature, courts of common pleas, courts of general sessions, courts of arbitration, justice courts, courts of admiralty, court of vice-admiralty,* and the *court of equity*. From 1647 to 1729, the *general court* was a colonywide court with jurisdiction over civil and criminal matters; in 1671 it became the *general court of trials. Courts of common pleas* were established in each county in 1730; they had jurisdiction over most local criminal and civil matters. The *superior court of judicature* replaced the *general court of trials*. After 1747, several *superior courts of judicature* were established as countywide courts.

Published Works. Rhode Island court records for 1636 to 1670 were published with every-name indexes in John R. Bartlett's *Records of the Colony of Rhode Island and Providence Plantations in New England*, 10 vols. (Providence: A. C. Green, 1856–65). Also see *Rhode Island Court Records: Records of the Court of Trials of the Colony of Providence Plantations, 1647–1670*, 2 vols. (Providence: Rhode Island Historical Society, 1920–22), and Dorothy S. Towle, ed., *Records of the Vice-admiralty Court of Rhode Island, 1716–1752* (1936; reprint; Milwood, N.Y.: Kraus Reprint, 1975).

South Carolina

Colonial Courts. Before 1769, proprietary and crown courts were convened at Charleston. These were known as the *general court* and the *grand council*. From 1769 to 1772, a *circuit court* system was begun. Beginning in 1703, there was also a *court of common pleas*. The *court of general sessions* was a statewide court from 1769. Equity jurisdiction was exercised by the *court of chancery* beginning in 1671.

Published Works. For more information about colonial court records, see Anne King Gregorie's *Records of the Court of Chancery of South Carolina, 1671–1779* (Washington, D.C.: American Historical Association, 1950); Caroline T. Moore's *Records of the Secretary of the Province of South Carolina, 1692–1721* (Columbia, S.C.: R. L. Bryan Co, 1978); and Mary Bondurant Warren's *South Carolina Jury Lists* (Danielsville, Ga.: Heritage Papers, 1977) (1718 through 1783) .

Virginia

Colonial Courts. From 1607 until 1618, the colonial governor and his council heard and decided all civil and criminal cases in Virginia. Once county courts were established in 1618, the governor and council began to hear appeals of decisions made by those courts. County courts, which were called *monthly courts* from around 1618 to 1634 and were later called *courts of the shire*, heard minor civil and criminal cases as well as probate and guardianship matters. Starting in 1618, as well, *quarter courts* began to meet in March, June, September, and December to handle major civil cases, capital crimes, chancery, and appellate matters. The quarter court's name was changed to the *general court* in 1661, and it was assigned the responsibility of hearing county court appeals as well as major civil cases, capital crimes, and probate matters.

Published Works. Most of the early council and general court records have been lost or destroyed. A few surviving records have been published. One collection containing some colonial Virginia court records is Beverley Fleet's *Virginia Colonial Abstracts* (Baltimore: Genealogical Publishing Co., 1988). Published abstracts of court records for many counties have been completed by private publishers. A good example of an extensive work on a county basis is Lyman Chalkley's *Chronicles of the Scots-Irish Settlement in Virginia: Extracted from the Original Court Records of Augusta County, 1754–1800*, 3 vols. (1912; reprint; Baltimore: Genealogical Publishing Co., 1980).

STATE COURTS AND THEIR RECORDS

The basic structures of most state court systems are similar; however, the functions of state courts can vary widely. Among states the number of trial courts of limited or special jurisdiction also varies greatly. Most states have only one or two types of trial courts of general jurisdiction.

Each state is divided into judicial circuits or districts, with each circuit or district usually covering one or more counties, depending upon population. In each circuit or district, a general trial court exists. These courts are known by a number of different names (depending on the state).

County courts are also part of each state's court system. Most county courts are courts of limited jurisdiction. Courts on a county basis not only had judicial functions but had some administrative and legislative ones as well (especially in the eighteenth and nineteenth centuries). Such roles of the courts as licensing midwives and ministers; appointing militia officers; overseeing the building and upkeep of roads, bridges, and ferries; and organizing the collection of taxes resulted in a large number of county citizens being mentioned in county court books—making the county court record books very valuable for identifying ancestors.

Trial courts (and their records) are frequently identified by or with a particular county, regardless of whether the trial court is known as a state circuit court, a county court, a district court, or by some other name. For example, a state circuit court trying a case in Jefferson County might be known as the Circuit Court in and for Jefferson County. So, in a broad sense, many, if not most, printed trial court records are county court records. Consequently, in the genealogical collections of many libraries, researchers will find published state court records classified as county court records.

Many states also authorize courts of general jurisdiction to exercise some appellate jurisdiction over courts of limited jurisdiction. When there is such an appeal to a general court, there normally will be a completely new trial. This process is very different from an appeal to a regular appellate court, such as a state supreme court, where there is no new trial—only a review of the record of the previous trial to determine if any error was made by the trial court.

Many of the published records and indexes of state courts are found in genealogical libraries. Some libraries also have microfilm or microfiche copies of indexes, minutes, dockets, and orders from local courthouses.

Following is a state-by-state discussion of state courts.

Alabama

State Courts. The court of general jurisdiction in Alabama is the circuit court. Circuit courts were established by the 1819 Constitution of Alabama, the state's first constitution. Generally, circuit courts exercise jurisdiction in major civil and criminal cases. The geographical jurisdiction of a circuit court is a judicial circuit comprising one or more counties.

Courts of limited jurisdiction are district courts, municipal courts, and probate courts. District courts are countywide courts, created in 1975, which generally handle minor civil and criminal cases. Municipal courts have jurisdiction of cases arising under municipal ordinances. Probate courts, which have existed since the early 1800s, have probate jurisdiction, which includes such matters as the probate of wills, administration of estates, adoptions, and guardianships.

Other Early State Courts. Before 1977, Alabama did not have a uniform system of courts, so a number of courts existed at various times in different parts of the state. Among them were chancery courts (abolished in 1915), superior courts, intermediate courts, inferior courts, courts of common pleas, civil courts, criminal courts, law and equity courts, general sessions courts, and law and juvenile courts. Justice of the peace courts, which handled minor civil and criminal cases, existed from 1819 until they were abolished in 1972. In certain cities before 1977, commissioners' courts and mayors' courts handled minor civil and criminal cases occurring within a city.

Published Works. Some Alabama court records are included in Kathleen Paul Jones and Pauline Jones Gandrud's *Alabama Records* (n.p., 1934–69). The series is being reprinted by Southern Historical Press (Easley, S.C., 1981–); around one hundred volumes had been reprinted by 1997.

Alaska

State Courts. The court of general jurisdiction in Alaska is the superior court. Superior courts and magistrate courts have existed in Alaska only since 1959. Superior courts have statewide jurisdiction in all civil and criminal matters. They also have exclusive jurisdiction of probate, guardianship, adoption, juveniles, and titles to real estate.

Courts of limited jurisdiction are district courts and magistrate courts. District court jurisdiction is limited to minor civil and criminal matters, such as issuing marriage licenses and arrest warrants, hearing misdemeanor cases, and acting as the temporary custodian of the property of deceased persons.

Other Early State Courts. Before 1959, when Alaska became a state, the district court of the Territory of Alaska administered its judicial affairs. The U.S. commissioner's courts administered the justices of the peace. The pre-1959 district courts were districtwide courts that had jurisdiction over civil and criminal affairs. From 1884 to 1903 there was one district court located in Sitka. From 1903 to 1909 there were three district courts (Juneau, St. Michaels, and Eagle City). From 1909 to 1959 there were four district courts (Juneau, Nome, Valdez, and Fairbanks). The court in Valdez moved to Anchorage in 1943.

Published Works. An inventory of Alaskan Territorial Court Records is available through the state archive in a booklet titled *Record Group Inventory: District and Territorial Court System* (Juneau: Alaska State Archives, Department of Administration, 1987).

Arizona

State Courts. The court of general jurisdiction in Arizona is the superior court. The superior court superseded district and probate courts. There is only one superior court for the entire state; it is divided by county. It has jurisdiction in major criminal and civil cases, including all equity cases, cases at law which involve title to or possession of real property, all other cases at law where the amount in controversy is one thousand dollars or more, probate cases, divorce cases, and juvenile cases.

Courts of limited jurisdiction are justice of the peace courts. Justices of the peace hear minor civil and criminal cases, while municipal courts hear cases arising under town or city ordinances.

Other Early State Courts. From 1852 to 1863, New Mexico county had district courts and probate courts. From 1864 to 1912, district courts had countywide jurisdiction over records of chancery, criminal cases, and divorces. Naturalizations were also handled by these courts until 1906 when the U.S. district court was given exclusive jurisdiction.

Published Works. An inventory of some of Arizona's territorial court records was published in Norman E. Tutorow's *Preliminary Inventory of the Records of the Arizona Territorial Court in the Los Angeles Federal Records Center* (Los Angeles: Federal Records Center, 1970).

Arkansas

State Courts. The courts of general jurisdiction in Arkansas are circuit courts and chancery courts. Circuit courts have jurisdiction over criminal cases and major civil cases. Chancery courts have jurisdiction of all cases in equity, and of divorce, probate, and adoptions.

Courts of limited jurisdiction are courts of common pleas, county courts, municipal courts, and justice of the peace courts. The courts of common pleas are established only in certain counties, and their jurisdiction is limited to minor, non-real estate civil cases. County courts have jurisdiction in matters relating to county taxes, roads and bridges, "paupers," elections, and claims against the county. Justice of the peace courts have jurisdiction over minor contract and personal property disputes. Municipal courts have jurisdiction over violations of city ordinances and other minor criminal and civil cases.

Other Early State Courts. Probate courts used to be separate from chancery courts. For most purposes, probate courts were consolidated with chancery courts by State Constitutional Amendment 24.

Published Works. Information on circuit, county, and chancery court records in Arkansas is included in Jack Damon Ruple's *Genealogist's Guide to Arkansas Courthouse Research* (Arkansas, 1989).

California

State Courts. The general court in California is the superior court. Each county has a superior court, which is a countywide court that has jurisdiction in all cases except those given by statute to other trial courts. The jurisdiction of the superior court includes both civil and criminal cases, probate and juvenile matters, and appeals from justice and municipal courts.

Courts of limited jurisdiction are municipal courts and justice courts. Some counties have both municipal and justice courts; others have only one or the other (in addition to the superior court). The jurisdictions of municipal and justice courts are almost the same—both courts handle only minor civil and criminal cases.

Other Early State Courts. Early courts in California that no longer exist include district courts and county courts.

Published Works. A helpful publication is *Index to Transcripts of Court Cases in State Archives* (Sacramento: Attorney General, n.d.).

Colorado

State Courts. Courts of general jurisdiction in Colorado are the district courts, the Denver probate court, and the Denver juvenile court. The district court has jurisdiction in civil and criminal matters, including equity cases, divorce proceedings, coroners' inquests, civil cases, criminal cases, probate matters, adoptions, and paternity suits.

Courts of limited jurisdiction are county courts and municipal courts. County courts have countywide jurisdiction concurrent with district courts over misdemeanors, preliminary hearings, the issuance of some warrants, some bail matters, and minor civil matters. Every city has a municipal court which has jurisdiction of cases arising under ordinances of the city within which it is organized.

Other Early State Courts. The Denver superior court used to have jurisdiction over appeals from the Denver county court and concurrent jurisdiction with district courts over minor civil matters for the city and county of Denver. County courts used to have jurisdiction over probates. Justice of the peace courts existed in Colorado until 1965, when they were abolished. Generally, the jurisdiction of justice courts was transferred to the new county court system in 1965.

Published Works. An inventory of Colorado's territorial court records was published in *Inventory of Federal Archives in the States, Series 2, Federal Courts, No. 6, Colorado* (Denver: Colorado Historical Records Survey, 1939).

Connecticut

State Courts. The court of general jurisdiction in Connecticut is the superior court. First established in 1711, the superior court now has trial jurisdiction in all criminal matters and in all civil matters in law and equity, except matters over which probate courts have original jurisdiction.

The court of limited jurisdiction is the probate court. Probate courts have jurisdiction in all matters pertaining to probate of wills, trusts, estates, and adoptions.

Other Early State Courts. From the 1630s to 1961, town and borough courts had jurisdiction over civil matters in towns. Justice of the peace courts (1686 to 1961) handled similar matters in areas without a town court. These courts were succeeded by circuit courts. From 1666 to 1855, the county courts had jurisdiction over civil disputes and minor criminal cases as well as chancery and divorce matters. From 1855 to 1870 this court's duties were assumed by the town and justice courts and the superior court. From 1869 to 1975, courts of common pleas replaced county courts and were reorganized in 1975 to include the circuit court.

Published Works. For more information concerning Connecticut courts, see Dwight Loomis and Joseph Gilbert Calhoun's *Judicial and Civil History of Connecticut* (Boston: Boston History Co., 1895). Also see the *Guide to Archives in the Connecticut State Library*. A guide to the court record holdings of the Connecticut State Library is *Records of the Judicial Department (Part A): Court Records in the Connecticut State Library, 1636–1945*, rev. ed. (Hartford: Connecticut State Library, 1977).

Delaware

State Courts. Courts of general jurisdiction in Delaware are superior courts and courts of chancery. Superior courts, first established in 1831, are county courts with jurisdiction over major criminal and civil cases. Chancery courts, which were established in 1684, are countywide courts with jurisdiction over all cases in equity.

Courts of limited jurisdiction are courts of common pleas, family courts, justice of the peace courts, and the municipal court of Wilmington. Beginning in 1701, courts of common pleas were established in each county; today they hear minor civil suits, minor criminal cases, adoptions, and terminations of parental rights. Family courts have jurisdiction in civil and criminal cases involving children. Justices of the peace have jurisdiction over minor civil and criminal cases. The municipal court of Wilmington has jurisdiction over most misdemeanors committed in the city of Wilmington and violations of city ordinances.

Other Early State Courts. Orphans' courts were countywide courts in 1792; they continued to exist until recently. They had jurisdiction over property rights, estates of minors, guardianships, and adoptions. Early courts also included the court of general quarter sessions, the oyer and terminer, and the justice of the peace. The office of clerk of the peace, or prothonotary, dates from 1642. The clerk of the peace was clerk of the court of general quarter session, court of oyer and terminer, and court of common pleas.

Published Works. The Delaware Historical Records Survey prepared an *Inventory of the County Archives of Delaware; No. 1, New Castle County* (Dover, Del.: Public Archives Commission, 1941). Although published for only one county, this volume explains the various courts of Delaware from the time of its settlement and describes the types of court records found in Delaware counties. Some court records are included in Charles H. B. Turner's *Some Records of Sussex County, Delaware* (Philadelphia: Allen, Lane & Scott, 1909).

District of Columbia

District of Columbia Courts. The court of general jurisdiction in the District of Columbia is the superior court. The superior court was established in 1928 and has jurisdiction of all civil cases not within the exclusive jurisdiction of the Federal courts. It also has criminal jurisdiction over cases involving violations of laws applicable exclusively to the District of Columbia.

Other Early District of Columbia Courts. In 1801, the first court system was established in the District of Columbia with the creation of the circuit court, which heard both civil and criminal cases. In 1863, the circuit court was replaced by a newly created District of Columbia Supreme Court, which in turn relinquished jurisdiction to the newly created superior court in 1928. From 1801 to 1871, the levy court governed Washington County outside the city of Washington and assessed taxes.

Published Works. A helpful book is Homer A. Walker's *Historical Court Records of Washington, D.C.* (Washington, D.C., n.d.).

Florida

State Courts. The court of general jurisdiction in Florida is the circuit court. First established in 1821, circuit courts have jurisdiction over major civil and criminal cases, including all probate matters and all cases in equity.

The court of limited jurisdiction is the county court. County courts have jurisdiction over minor civil and criminal cases.

Other Early State Courts. The judicial system of Florida was reorganized in 1973. Before that reorganization, courts included justices of the peace, city courts, probate courts, and civil and criminal courts. Municipal courts were abolished in 1977. From 1822 to 1974, county judges kept probate, marriage, administration, and guardianship records. From 1887 to 1974, criminal courts kept records of criminal cases not punishable by capital punishment. Also, from 1915 to 1974, civil courts existed in counties with populations of more than 100,000. In these counties, the civil court took the place of the county court.

Published Works. Some early legal records were published in William A. and Janet B. Wolfe's *Names and Abstracts From the Acts of the Legislative Council of the Territory of Florida, 1822–1845*, rev. ed. (Tallahassee: Florida State Genealogical Society, 1991). Also, an inventory of Florida's territorial court records was published in *Inventory of Federal Archives in the States, Series 2, Federal Courts, No. 9, Florida* (Jacksonville, Fla.: Historical Records Survey, 1940).

Georgia

State Courts. The court of general jurisdiction in Georgia is the superior court. Other courts are state courts, juvenile courts, probate courts, magistrate courts, civil courts, county recorders' courts, and municipal courts. Superior courts have jurisdiction in most civil and criminal cases, except for certain probate proceedings that are heard by probate courts. In every county there are juvenile courts with jurisdiction over juvenile matters. Georgia does not have a uniform system of courts of limited jurisdiction; each county has its own system of inferior courts. These inferior courts include state courts created by the state general assembly for certain counties, which usually have jurisdiction in most civil and non-felony criminal cases concurrent with that of superior courts. Other inferior courts found in many counties are city, municipal, and county courts and magistrates' courts.

Other Early State Courts. In 1777, superior courts were established at the county level to hear civil and criminal cases, including cases dealing with divorce, naturalization, military discharges, homesteads, prisons, and slaves. Simultaneously, courts of ordinary were created to hear and record cases involving probate matters. These courts also dealt with indentures, paupers, licenses, voting, and marriage. From 1777 to the modern era, courts of ordinary were countywide courts with jurisdiction over probates (1777 to 1798 and after 1852), homesteads, land warrants, licenses, indentures, paupers' registers, voting registers, and marriage records. Also, from 1798 to the modern era, inferior courts were countywide courts with jurisdiction over probates (1798 to 1852), civil matters (except for divorce and equity cases), and minor criminal offenses.

Published Works. See Robert S. Davis, Jr., *Research in Georgia: With Special Emphasis on the Georgia Department of Archives and History* (Easley, S.C.: Southern Historical Press, 1981) for a breakdown of court records by county. Some early court records have been published, such as those found in Margaret Elliott Higgins, ed., *Georgia Genealogical Gems* (Arlington, Va.: National Genealogical Society, n.d.) and in Grace Gilliam Davidson's *Early Records of Georgia, Volumes 1 and 2* (1933; reprint; Easley, S.C.: Southern Historical Press, 1967).

Hawaii

State Courts. The general court in Hawaii is the circuit court. The land court and the tax appeal court are divisions of the circuit court. Circuit courts have jurisdiction of all criminal cases under state law and all civil cases, probate, and divorce cases.

Courts of limited jurisdiction are district courts and family courts. The jurisdiction of the district court is limited to minor criminal and civil cases. Juvenile cases are under the jurisdiction of the family court. Family court cases usually involve paternity, guardianship, adoption, misdemeanors, and felonies.

Other Early State Courts. Both the circuit court and the district court have existed since 1848.

Published Works. One helpful book is Hawaii Circuit Court, *Divorce Records, 1849–1915* (Salt Lake City: Genealogical Society of Utah, 1977).

Idaho

State Courts. The court of general jurisdiction in Idaho is the district court. A division of the district court which has lesser jurisdiction is the magistrate division of district court. District courts have jurisdiction in all cases, both at law and in equity. Magistrate divisions of district courts are assigned court cases by the various district courts; these cases generally include minor civil and criminal cases, including probate and juvenile matters. Thus, there are no courts that can be specifically noted as having limited jurisdiction.

Other Early State Courts. Probate courts (abolished in 1971) had jurisdiction over proceedings for the probate of wills, administration of estates, and adoptions. All former duties of probate courts were assumed by the magistrate divisions of the district courts in 1971. Justice of the peace courts (abolished in 1971) had jurisdiction over minor cases; their jurisdiction was assigned to the magistrate divisions of the district courts in 1971.

Illinois

State Courts. The court of general jurisdiction in Illinois is the circuit court. The state constitution of 1818 established Illinois circuit courts. Since 1970, circuit courts have had jurisdiction of virtually all cases, including civil and criminal cases, probate and estate matters, guardianships, and divorces.

In 1970, various courts of limited jurisdiction, such as the superior court of Cook County, probate courts, county courts, city courts, municipal courts, justices of the peace, and police magistrates, were abolished and their functions were consolidated in circuit courts.

Other Early State Courts. From 1779 until the beginning of the territorial period, the County Court for the County of Illinois of the State of Virginia functioned as a trial court in what would later become the state of Illinois. From 1788 to 1805 and from 1809 to 1811, courts of quarter sessions existed. From 1788 to 1809 and from 1811 to 1818 there were courts of common pleas. Orphans' courts existed from 1795 to 1805. Circuit courts existed from 1795 to 1812 and from 1814 to 1818. When Illinois became a state in 1818, circuit courts were accorded constitutional status in the first state constitution. Jurisdiction for circuit courts included criminal cases, civil suits for more than twenty dollars, appeals from the justices of the peace, and naturalization. Additional responsibilities were added through the years, including local, county, and state judicial elections.

In the 1840s, a county court system was created statewide. These county courts handled probate cases and misdemeanors. Some county courts handled small civil suits for ten years (beginning in 1853). Over the years, the jurisdiction of county courts increased frequently until all county court functions were assumed by the circuit court in 1970. Before their abolition, county courts generally had jurisdiction over minor civil and criminal cases and, in some counties, probate matters. Other early courts included municipal courts, which had jurisdiction with circuit courts over certain civil and criminal actions; justices of the peace, which had jurisdiction over misdemeanors and minor civil cases; and the Chicago court system, which included mayor, superior, criminal, and family courts.

Published Works. For information about state courts and their records, see John Clayton's *The Illinois Fact Book and Historical Almanac* (Carbondale: Southern Illinois University Press, 1970).

Indiana

State Courts. Courts of general jurisdiction in Indiana are superior courts and circuit courts. Circuit courts have jurisdiction over civil and criminal cases, except where exclusive jurisdiction is conferred upon some other court. Superior courts, which exist in most (but not all) counties, generally (with some exceptions) exercise concurrent jurisdiction with circuit courts.

Courts of limited jurisdiction are county courts, probate courts, city and town courts, and the small claims court of Marion County. County courts have jurisdiction over minor civil and criminal cases, as do city and town courts.

Other Early State Courts. From 1796 to 1813, the court of quarter sessions was a court with jurisdiction over both civil and criminal matters, including some probates. From 1790 to 1817 and again from 1853 to 1873, there was a court of common pleas which heard cases dealing with insanity, guardianship, probates, naturalizations, equity, criminal cases, and many civil actions. Justices of the peace, which were abolished in 1976 and replaced by county courts, used to have jurisdiction for petty crimes and minor civil cases. Circuit courts have existed since 1813, and superior courts have existed since 1909.

Published Works. A work with information about Indiana's early courts is Oliver Hampton Smith's *Early Indiana Trials and Sketches* (Cincinnati: Moore, Wilstock, Keys & Co., 1858).

Iowa

State Courts. The court of general jurisdiction in Iowa is the district court. The state is divided into judicial districts, which are composed of several counties. District courts have original jurisdiction in all cases, including civil, criminal, and probate matters.

The district court has certain divisions with limited jurisdiction. Thus, there are no specific courts under other titles to be considered for limited jurisdiction.

Other Early State Courts. District courts have existed since 1838, when the Iowa Territory was established. From the time of statehood in 1846 until 1907, there was considerable change in the structure and the divisions of the district court. Today the district court continues as the court of general jurisdiction in Iowa. Superior courts were early courts which had jurisdiction over minor civil and criminal cases. They were replaced in some areas by municipal courts, which, in turn, were replaced by district courts. Early courts also included circuit courts, which had jurisdiction over juvenile, criminal, and civil cases. At one time circuit courts also handled some probate cases. Justice of the peace courts were early courts that had jurisdiction over minor misdemeanors, search warrants, and town or city ordinance violations.

Published Works. John P. Dolan, Jr., and Lisa Lacher's *Guide to Public Records of Iowa Counties* (Des Moines, Iowa: Connie Wimer, 1986) includes information on court records.

Kansas

State Courts. The court of general jurisdiction in Kansas is the district court. There is a state district court in each county. The district court has jurisdiction in all matters civil, criminal, juvenile, and probate.

There are no courts to be specified with limited jurisdiction.

Other Early State Courts. Most early courts in Kansas were abolished in 1977. These included county courts, which had countywide jurisdiction over some criminal cases and minor civil cases, probate courts, and magistrate and city courts, which had citywide jurisdiction over minor criminal matters and traffic matters in some cities. Justices of the peace were also abolished in Kansas.

Published Works. Denis Berckefeldt's *Kansas County Records* (A Pathfinders Publication, n.d.) includes a list of court records by county.

Kentucky

State Courts. The court of general jurisdiction in Kentucky is the circuit court. The circuit court has jurisdiction of all criminal and civil cases, both in law and equity, except cases exclusively delegated to the district court.

The court of limited jurisdiction is the district court, which has a small claims division. The district court handles minor criminal and civil cases.

Other Early State Courts. Early courts and their jurisdictions were changed from time to time in Kentucky. From 1787 to

1802 courts of quarter sessions heard suits involving large amounts of money. Established in 1780, county courts initially had jurisdiction over civil and criminal cases. Later, these courts recorded deeds and bonds and handled probate and juvenile matters. Circuit courts were established in 1802 and quarterly courts in 1852. Beginning in 1852, quarterly courts and circuit courts began handling most criminal cases, with quarterly courts having jurisdiction over minor criminal cases. Circuit courts, which still exist today, handled major criminal and civil cases, including divorces. Other early courts included the justice's court, court of oyer and terminer, examining court, and general court.

Published Works. Some Kentucky trial court records have been transcribed and published. A helpful and well-organized guide to Kentucky courts as genealogical sources can be found in Roseann Reinemuth Hogan's *Kentucky Ancestry: A Guide to Genealogical and Historical Research* (Salt Lake City: Ancestry, 1992). For more information about Kentucky's early courts, including their jurisdiction, organization, and history, see Robert M. Ireland's *The County Courts in Antebellum Kentucky* (Lexington: University Press of Kentucky, 1972) and William C. Richardson's *An Administrative History of Kentucky Courts to 1850* (Frankfort: Kentucky Department for Libraries and Archives, 1983). Also see Michael L. Cook's *Virginia Supreme Court District of Kentucky: Order Books, 1783–1792* (Evansville, Ind.: Cook Publications, 1988) and Michael L. Cook and Bettie A. Cook's *Kentucky Court of Appeals Deed Books H–N*, vol. 2 (Evansville, Ind.: Cook Publications, 1985).

Louisiana

State Courts. The court of general jurisdiction in Louisiana is the district court. District courts have jurisdiction in all civil and criminal matters (except for matters specifically assigned to other courts). In New Orleans there is a civil district court, which handles civil cases, and a criminal district court, which has jurisdiction of crimes, misdemeanors, and offenses committed within the parish of Orleans.

Courts of limited jurisdiction are parish courts, justice of the peace courts, city courts, mayor's courts, the East Baton Rouge family court, juvenile courts, the municipal court of New Orleans, and the traffic court of New Orleans. Parish, city, and justice of the peace courts have jurisdiction over minor civil and criminal cases.

Other Early State Courts. From 1679 to 1769, the *conseil superieur*, or the French Superior Council, had jurisdiction over land and court matters. The Spanish *cabildo* was the Spanish government for the province of Louisiana from 1769 to 1803; it presided over court and land matters. The district court was established in the 1800s and continues today as the trial court of general jurisdiction. Parish courts were also established in the 1800s; they had jurisdiction over criminal and minor civil cases. Although a few parish courts still exist, most were abolished in 1846.

Published Works. For a discussion of Louisiana's court system and its laws of the nineteenth and twentieth centuries, see Albert Tate, Jr., "The Splendid Mystery of the Civil Code of Louisiana," *Louisiana Review* 2 (2) (1974), and Coleman Lindsey's *The Courts of Louisiana* (n.p., n.d.). Many French and Spanish court records are summarized in *English Language Summaries of the Records of the French Superior Council and the Judicial Records of the Spanish Cabildo, 1714–1800* (Work Projects Administration, n.d.).

Maine

State Courts. The court of general jurisdiction in Maine is the superior court. It has jurisdiction in major civil and criminal cases.

Courts of limited jurisdiction are district courts, probate courts, and administrative courts. State district courts handle minor civil and criminal cases. The jurisdiction of probate courts includes the administration of estates of deceased persons, wills, guardianships, adoptions, and changes of name.

Other Early State Courts. From 1699 to 1839, inferior courts of common pleas had jurisdiction over some civil matters. Inferior courts were replaced by early district courts, which had jurisdiction over minor civil and criminal cases. These early district courts existed only from 1839 to 1852. In 1852, the powers of the district courts were assumed by the supreme judicial court, which had been established in 1782. The supreme judicial court, which is the court of final appeal, also served as the trial court for most major cases until that function was taken over by superior courts. Beginning in 1868, superior courts were established by individual counties in various years. By 1929, the superior court had become the trial court of general jurisdiction in all counties. From 1699 until 1831, the court of general sessions had jurisdiction over minor civil and criminal cases; it became the county commissioners' court in 1831 and was replaced by the current district court in 1961. From 1821 until 1961, justices of the peace handled minor civil matters. Because Maine was under Massachusetts' jurisdiction until 1820, some court records for York, Cumberland, Lincoln, Hancock, and Washington counties are a part of Suffolk County, Massachusetts, court records.

Published Works. A guide to the historical development of Maine's courts is David Q. Whittier, Esq., *History of the Court System of the State of Maine*. Some early court records were published in Charles T. Libby, Robert E. Moody, and Neal W. Allen, eds., *Province and Court Records of Maine*, 6 vols. (Portland: Maine Historical Society, 1928–).

Maryland

State Courts. The court of general jurisdiction in Maryland is the circuit court. Circuit courts have existed since 1851; they exercise jurisdiction over major civil and criminal cases and appellate jurisdiction over district courts.

Courts of limited jurisdiction are district courts, orphans' courts, and tax courts. District courts, created in the 1800s and known by several different titles before 1971, have jurisdiction over lesser criminal and civil cases.

Other Early State Courts. From 1637 to 1805, the provincial court (later general court) was a statewide court that ruled on capital crimes, land disputes, and other civil matters. From 1637 to 1851, county courts were countywide courts that had jurisdiction over criminal and civil cases. County courts were replaced by circuit courts in 1851. From 1668 to 1851, the chancery court was a statewide court with jurisdiction over equity cases, including divorces, name changes, mortgage foreclosures, and guardianships.

Published Works. A good source on the court records available for each county and the dates they cover is Morris L. Radoff's *County Courthouses and Records of Maryland* (Annapolis: Hall of Records Commission, 1963). A useful index is Eleanor Phillips Passano's *An Index to the Source Records of Maryland: Genealogical, Biographical, Historical* (Baltimore: Genealogical Publishing Co., 1967).

Massachusetts

State Courts. The court of general jurisdiction is the superior court. The superior court has jurisdiction over all civil and criminal cases (except those expressly given by statute to other courts).

Courts of limited jurisdiction are the district court, the Boston municipal court, the land court, the housing court, the probate court, and the juvenile court. The district court and the Boston municipal court have jurisdiction (concurrent with the superior court) in civil actions seeking money damages. The district court and the Boston municipal court have limited criminal jurisdiction. The probate court has jurisdiction of the probate of wills, the administration of estates, and the appointment of guardians. In addition, the probate court has jurisdiction, concurrent with the superior court, in all equity cases.

Other Early State Courts. From 1692 to 1859, general sessions courts handled criminal cases in Massachusetts and courts of common pleas handled civil cases. Superior courts replaced general sessions courts in 1859. District courts and municipal courts have existed since around 1822. Justice of the peace courts also existed for many years in Massachusetts.

Published Works. For more information see Catherine S. Menand's *A Research Guide to the Massachusetts Courts and Their Records* (Boston: Massachusetts Supreme Judicial Court, Archives and Records Preservation, 1987) and Michael S. Hindus's *The Records of the Massachusetts Superior Court and Its Predecessors* (Boston: Archives Division, Office of the Secretary of the Commonwealth, 1977). Information about court procedures and records can be found in Carroll D. Wright's *Report on the Custody and Condition of the Public Records of Parishes, Towns, and Counties* (Boston: Wright and Potter, 1889). Abstracts of pre-1860 Plymouth court records are in David Thomas Konig, ed., *Plymouth Court Records 1686–1859: The Court of Common Pleas and General Sessions of the Peace*, 16 vols. (Wilmington, Del.: Michael Glazier, 1978–81).

Michigan

State Courts. The courts of general jurisdiction are circuit courts and the court of claims. Circuit courts have jurisdiction in all equity cases and all major cases in law. Circuit courts also have jurisdiction in all criminal cases, except those involving misdemeanors and ordinance violations. The court of claims has jurisdiction of most claims against the state.

Courts of limited jurisdiction are district courts, probate courts, and municipal courts. District courts have jurisdiction over misdemeanors, ordinance violations, and minor civil matters. Probate courts have jurisdiction of matters relating to estates of deceased persons, trust administration, and appointment of guardians. Municipal courts have citywide jurisdiction in minor criminal and civil cases.

Other Early State Courts. When the Michigan Territory was established in 1805, county courts handled many legal matters. County courts were abolished in 1833. After statehood (1837), Michigan courts included circuit courts, municipal courts, and justice courts. Justice courts were abolished in 1969.

Minnesota

State Courts. The court of general jurisdiction in Minnesota is the state district court. District courts, which have existed since 1849, have jurisdiction in most civil and criminal cases.

Courts of limited jurisdiction are county courts and municipal courts. Each county court has a probate division, a family court division, and a civil and criminal division. County courts have jurisdiction over administration of estates, guardianship proceedings, and minor criminal and civil cases. Most municipal courts have merged into the county court system.

Other Early State Courts. Beginning in the 1800s, municipal courts in local cities and towns had jurisdiction over misdemeanor cases. Now municipal courts have merged into the county court system, except in Hennepin and Ramsey counties. Justice courts also used to handle minor cases until they were abolished.

Mississippi

State Courts. Courts of general jurisdiction in Mississippi are circuit courts and chancery courts. Circuit courts have jurisdiction of major criminal cases and civil cases at law. Mississippi chancery courts have jurisdiction of all cases in equity and divorce cases. Chancery courts also exercise probate jurisdiction.

Courts of limited jurisdiction are county courts, municipal courts, justice courts, and family courts. County courts exist only in certain counties. In those counties where county courts exist, they have jurisdiction in minor civil and criminal cases. Justice courts handle small claims and some misdemeanors. Family courts exist only in certain large counties; in those counties, they deal with juvenile delinquency, neglect of children, and adult crime against juveniles.

Other Early State Courts. The orphans' court was established by the 1817 Constitution of Mississippi as an inferior court to handle probate matters and guardianships. Its name was changed to the probate court in 1832. In 1869, the probate court was abolished. Since 1869, probate jurisdiction has been exercised by the chancery court. During a relatively brief period between 1857 and 1869, the circuit court in Mississippi exercised chancery jurisdiction.

Published Works. For more information about state courts and their records, see *Survey of Records in Mississippi Court Houses* (Jackson: Mississippi Genealogical Society, 1967), Mary L. Hendrix's *Mississippi Court Records: From the Files of the High Court of Errors and Appeals, 1799–1859* (Jackson, Miss., 1950), and May Wilson McBee's *Natchez Court Records*, 1767–1805 (Greenwood, Miss.: the author, 1953).

Missouri

State Courts. The court of general jurisdiction in Missouri is the circuit court. It has original jurisdiction of all civil and criminal cases.

Courts of limited jurisdiction are associate circuit courts, county courts, and the probate division of the circuit court. Associate circuit courts have jurisdiction of minor civil and criminal cases. County courts handle all claims against counties. The probate division of the circuit court has jurisdiction over matters pertaining to probate.

Other Early State Courts. Courts of common pleas were countywide courts that existed in some counties before the 1880s. They had jurisdiction over minor civil and criminal matters. Magistrate courts had citywide jurisdiction over minor criminal offenses and some small claims.

Published Works. Lois Stanley, George F. Wilson, and Maryhelen Wilson's *Divorces and Separations in Missouri, 1808–1853* (n.p., n.d.), contains court records of early Missouri divorces and separations.

Montana

State Courts. The court of general jurisdiction in Montana is the district court. District courts have jurisdiction over most civil and criminal cases. Also, since 1889, district courts have exercised probate jurisdiction.

Courts of limited jurisdiction are justice courts, city courts, and municipal courts. Justice of the peace courts have jurisdiction over minor civil and criminal cases. City courts exists in all cities and towns which do not have municipal courts. Only cities with populations of more than four thousand may have municipal courts. City courts handle the enforcement of ordinances and some misdemeanor cases. In addition to jurisdiction similar to city courts, municipal courts have concurrent jurisdiction with justice courts.

Other Early State Courts. Probate courts had jurisdiction over probates, marriages, and minor civil and criminal matters. Probate courts were disbanded in 1889 when their functions and records were transferred to the district courts.

Published Works. I. W. Choate's *The Revised Codes of 1921 Containing the Permanent Laws of the State in Force at the Close of the Seventeenth Legislative Assembly of 1921* (San Francisco: Bancroft-Whitney Co., 1921) includes information about some early Montana legal records.

Nebraska

State Courts. The court of general jurisdiction in Nebraska is the district court. The district court has jurisdiction of most criminal cases and most civil cases (except for probate matters).

Courts of limited jurisdiction are county courts and juvenile courts. County courts have jurisdiction in all matters of probate and concurrent jurisdiction with district courts in minor civil and criminal cases. Juvenile courts may exist in any county with a population of seventy-five thousand or more.

Other Early State Courts. During the territorial period (1855 to 1867) there were justice courts (justices of the peace) and probate courts in addition to district courts. County courts have existed since statehood; they assumed the functions of probate courts when they were created. District courts were provided for by the state's first constitution and continue today as the state's trial courts of general jurisdiction. Justice courts continued to exist until 1970, when they were abolished. Early courts also included police magistrate courts, which were abolished in 1972.

Published Works. See *The Courts of Nebraska: A Report on Their Structure and Operation* (Lincoln: State Court Administrator, 1979) and *Collection Guide for Records of the Nebraska Territorial Court System* (Lincoln: Nebraska State Historical Society, n.d.).

Nevada

State Courts. The court of general jurisdiction in Nevada is the district court. The district court has jurisdiction in most criminal and civil cases, whether in equity or at law. Probate jurisdiction is also exercised by the district court sitting in probate. District courts also have appellate jurisdiction over cases originating in justices' courts or municipal courts.

Courts of limited jurisdiction are justices' courts and municipal courts. Justices' courts have jurisdiction in criminal misdemeanor cases and minor civil cases. Municipal courts have jurisdiction over violations of city ordinances and minor public offenses.

Published Works. Bill Greathouse's *Nevada Local Court Records Project Records Inventory Sheet at Carson City, Nevada, March-September, 1987* (Carson City, Nevada: Greathouse, 1987) includes Nevada's minimum records retention schedule for district courts.

New Hampshire

State Courts. The court of general jurisdiction in New Hampshire is the superior court. The superior court has jurisdiction in all major criminal and civil cases, including cases at law or in equity.

Courts of limited jurisdiction are district courts and probate courts. District courts, which were established in 1964, have jurisdiction in minor civil and criminal cases. Probate courts exercise probate jurisdiction.

Other Early State Courts. From 1769 to 1794 and again from 1820 to 1824, courts of general quarter sessions handled some civil and criminal matters. From 1769 to 1820 and then from 1824 to 1859, courts of common pleas had jurisdiction over some civil matters. From 1682 to the modern era, justices of the peace had jurisdiction over some minor civil and criminal matters. Municipal courts existed for many years until they were abolished in 1964 (except in those towns which elected to keep them until the sitting judge was no longer in office). Superior courts have existed since 1769 (except for the periods between 1813 and 1816 and between 1855 and 1901).

Published Works. Some of the earlier court records were published in the *Provincial and State Papers*, 40 vols. (Concord, N.H: State Printer, 1867–1943). For more information on the *Provincial and State Papers*, see R. Stout Wallace's "The State

Papers? A Descriptive Guide," *Historical New Hampshire* 31 (Fall 1976): 119–28.

New Jersey

State Courts. The court of general jurisdiction in New Jersey is the superior court, which has a law division and a chancery division. The superior court, which was created in 1947, superseded the former supreme court, court of chancery, prerogative court, and circuit court. The superior court has jurisdiction over almost all civil and criminal cases.

Courts of limited jurisdiction are surrogate courts, municipal courts, and tax courts. Surrogate courts handle probate matters. Municipal courts handle some civil cases involving small claims and some minor criminal cases.

Other Early State Courts. From 1675 to 1947, courts of general quarter sessions of the peace had jurisdiction over some minor criminal cases. They also had some civil jurisdiction before the creation of the courts of common pleas in 1704. From 1693 to 1947, courts of oyer and terminer and general gaol delivery had jurisdiction over crimes committed within the county (except for certain capital offenses). From 1704 to 1947, courts of common pleas handled many civil cases; they also handled appeals from justices of the peace. In 1947, county courts took over the functions of the courts of common pleas, oyer and terminer, general quarter sessions, special sessions, and orphans' courts. County courts were abolished in 1978, and their pending cases were transferred to the superior courts. Justices' courts, which were presided over by justices of the peace, existed from 1675 to the modern era. Justices of the peace performed marriages, issued summons for debts, and handled minor civil suits. They also had criminal jurisdiction over minor cases. Justices' courts were replaced in the twentieth century by district and superior courts. From 1877 until 1983, district courts also had jurisdiction over minor criminal offenses and civil suits. They replaced justices' courts in most places but were abolished in 1983. All cases pending in district courts in 1983 were transferred to superior courts. From 1684 to 1696 and from 1705 until 1947, the court of chancery had equity jurisdiction. Circuit courts had civil jurisdiction over many cases from 1799 to 1947. From 1682 to 1947, the former supreme court was a major trial court handling many civil and criminal cases. In 1947, the former supreme court, the circuit court, and the chancery court were replaced by the superior court. Early courts also included orphans' courts, which handled estates and guardianships, and prerogative courts, which handled estate disputes.

Published Works. For information about early New Jersey courts, see William M. Clevenger and Edward Q. Keasbey's *The Courts of New Jersey: Their Origin, Composition and Jurisdiction . . . Some Account of their Origin and Jurisdiction* (Plainfield, N.J.: New Jersey Law Journal Publishing Co., 1903).

New Mexico

State Courts. The court of general jurisdiction in New Mexico is the district court. The district court, which was first established in 1850, has jurisdiction of almost all cases, both criminal and civil. Probate courts handle informal probate proceedings. Other probate matters are handled by the district court.

Courts of limited jurisdiction are probate courts, magistrate courts, municipal courts, and the Bernallilo County metropolitan court. Magistrate courts, which were established in the 1800s, handle minor criminal and civil cases. Municipal courts hear municipal ordinance violations. The Bernallilo County metropolitan court handles minor civil and criminal cases.

Other Early State Courts. From 1598 to 1847, the *alcalde ordinario* (mayors' courts) and *audiencia* (courts of appeals) were statewide courts in Mexico that handled civil and criminal cases. During several periods New Mexico was under the jurisdiction of courts in Mexico City, Guadalajara, Durango, Chihuahua, and Parral. From 1846 to 1850, the prefect's court was a statewide court that handled civil and criminal cases. Circuit courts were also established during the period of the military government of New Mexico to handle civil and criminal cases from 1846 to 1850.

Published Works. Tom Wiltsey's *Preliminary Inventory of the Records of the United States District Court of New Mexico: Record Group 21* (Denver: Archives Branch, Federal Archives and Records Center, 1980) includes information on court records for New Mexico Territory and later for the state of New Mexico.

New York

State Courts. Courts of general jurisdiction in New York are supreme courts and county courts. The supreme court of New York, unlike the supreme courts of other states, is the state's major trial court instead of the state's appellate court of last resort. New York's supreme courts, which have existed since the colonial era, have jurisdiction over most civil and criminal cases. County courts, established in 1847, also have jurisdiction over most criminal cases, but their civil jurisdiction generally is limited to cases involving no more than twenty-five thousand dollars.

Courts of limited jurisdiction are family courts, surrogate courts, city courts, justice courts, court of claims, district courts, the civil court of the city of New York, and the criminal court of the city of New York. Surrogate courts were created in 1787 and continue today as the courts that exercise probate jurisdiction. Justice courts have existed from the colonial era to the present; they handle minor civil and criminal cases.

Other Early State Courts. From 1665 to 1895, courts of general quarter sessions of the peace handled some criminal and civil cases. These courts also handled probate matters from 1665 to around 1683. After 1691, they only handled criminal cases. The jurisdiction of these courts was transferred to county courts in 1896. Beginning in 1691, courts of common pleas were established to handle civil cases; they also handled appeals from justices of the peace. In most counties these courts were replaced by county courts in 1847. In New York City, the court of common pleas and the superior court were abolished in 1895 and their jurisdiction was assumed by the supreme court. From 1683 to 1895, the court of oyer and terminer and general gaol delivery was a county court that had jurisdiction over capital crimes (such as treason and murder). The court of probates handled all probates from 1778 to 1787 and some probate matters until 1823. From 1823 to 1847, the court of chancery had equity jurisdiction, including divorces, guardianships, and child custody. It also absorbed the court of probate and had appellate jurisdiction over surrogate courts. After 1847, equity jurisdiction was assigned to the supreme courts. From 1821 to the modern era, there were also circuit courts, which handled a number of different types of civil cases.

Published Works. For more information about New York courts, see Alden Chester's *Courts and Lawyers of New York, a History, 1609–1925* (New York: American Historical Society, 1925). Helpful works include New York (State) Archives, *List of Pre-1874 Court Records in the State Archives* (Albany: Office of Cultural Education, New York State Education Department, 1984), and Historical Records Survey, *Inventory of the County Archives of New York State*, 6 vols. (New York, 1937–40), which covers Albany, Broome, Cattaraugus, Chautauqua, Chemung, and Ulster counties only. Some early quarter sessions records have been published in Kenneth Scott, ed., *New York City Court Records, 1684–1804, Genealogical Data from the Court of Quarter Sessions,* 4 vols. (Arlington, Va.: National Genealogical Society, 1982–88).

North Carolina

State Courts. The court of general jurisdiction in North Carolina is the superior court. Superior courts, first established in 1806, have jurisdiction of most types of civil cases and of all criminal actions that constitute felonies. Superior courts also handle probate matters.

Courts of limited jurisdiction are district courts and magistrates' courts. The current district courts, created throughout the state between 1965 and 1971, should not be confused with the early district courts that were abolished in 1806; current district courts handle divorces and minor civil and criminal cases. Magistrate courts handle small claims not in excess of two thousand dollars and perform other functions formerly handled by the office of the justice of the peace, which was abolished by the Judicial Department Act of 1965.

Other Early State Courts. From the colonial period until 1868, courts of pleas and quarter sessions handled many minor civil and criminal cases and probate matters. These courts (sometimes called county courts or, after 1806, inferior courts) were composed of justices appointed by the legislature. The court of pleas and quarter sessions of each county was also the governing body of the county, so it constituted both the judicial and legislative branches of county government. From 1754 to 1806, district courts handled major civil and criminal cases.

Published Works. For more information about North Carolina courts, see Helen F. M. Leary's *North Carolina Research: Genealogy and Local History,* 2nd ed. (Raleigh: North Carolina Genealogical Society, 1996), and George Stevenson and Ruby D. Arnold's *North Carolina Courts of Law and Equity Prior to 1868* (North Carolina Division of Archives and History, 1977). Many North Carolina court records have been published. Examples are Weynette Parks Haun's *Wake County, North Carolina, County Court Minutes (Court of Pleas and Quarter Sessions) 1801 thru 1803, Book V* (cited earlier) and Haun's *Morgan District, North Carolina, Superior Court of Law and Equity* (Durham, N.C.: the author, 1987).

North Dakota

State Courts. The court of general jurisdiction in North Dakota is the district court. District courts have jurisdiction of most civil cases (both at law and equity), criminal cases, and juvenile matters.

Courts of limited jurisdiction are county courts and municipal courts. County courts have exclusive jurisdiction in probate and testamentary matters, and concurrent jurisdiction with district courts over minor civil cases and misdemeanors. Municipal courts have citywide jurisdiction over certain minor criminal cases.

Other Early State Courts. Early courts included justice courts, which had jurisdiction over misdemeanors and some small civil cases.

Ohio

State Courts. The court of general jurisdiction in Ohio is the court of common pleas; it was first established in 1787. There is a court of common pleas in each county which has jurisdiction in all civil cases in which the amount in dispute exceeds five hundred dollars and in all criminal cases (except those involving minor offenses). Probate jurisdiction is also exercised by the common pleas court through its probate division.

Courts of limited jurisdiction are municipal courts, county courts, and mayors' courts. Municipal courts handle minor civil and criminal cases. County courts also handle minor civil cases. Some cities have mayors' courts, which have jurisdiction over traffic violations and violations of ordinances.

Other Early State Courts. From 1851 to 1883, district courts had jurisdiction over many civil and criminal cases, including equity and divorce cases. Then, from 1883 to 1912, circuit courts handled civil and criminal cases, including equity and divorce cases. Probate courts existed from 1787 until 1802 and then again from 1852 until the modern era. Probate jurisdiction is now exercised by the probate division of the court of common pleas. Justice of the peace courts and police courts also existed in Ohio from the 1800s to the modern era.

Published Works. For more information about Ohio courts, see Carrington Tanner Marshall's *A History of the Courts and Lawyers of Ohio* (New York: American Historical Society, 1934). Carol Willsey Bell's *Ohio Guide to Genealogical Sources* (Baltimore: Genealogical Publishing Co., 1988) provides information about the location of some court records.

Oklahoma

State Courts. The court of general jurisdiction in Oklahoma is the district court. District courts have existed since around 1890, when they were established in the Oklahoma territory. Most judicial districts are composed of more than one county. The jurisdiction of Oklahoma district courts extends to all cases—civil, criminal and probate—except for those few types of cases which, by law, must be handled by other courts.

Courts of limited jurisdiction are the court of tax review, the workers' compensation court, and municipal courts. The court of tax review handles tax protest cases, and the workers' compensation court handles cases involving workers' bodily injuries sustained on the job. Municipal courts have jurisdiction of cases involving certain violations of city ordinances.

Other Early State Courts. From 1844 to 1889, the U.S. District Court for the Western District of Arkansas had jurisdiction over some criminal and civil cases in the Indian Territory. Beginning in 1889, the U.S. District Court for the Eastern District of Texas assumed this jurisdiction.

Published Works. Charles Butler Barr's *Records of the Choctaw-Chickasaw Citizenship Court Relative to Records of the Enrollment of the Five Civilized Tribes, 1898–1907* (Independence, Mo.: the author, 1990), contains court records of applications for citizenship.

Oregon

State Courts. The court of general jurisdiction in Oregon is the circuit court. Circuit courts have jurisdiction in major civil and criminal cases and, in some counties, in probate matters and juvenile cases.

Courts of limited jurisdiction are county courts, district courts, justice courts, and municipal courts. Probate jurisdiction and juvenile jurisdiction are exercised by county courts in other counties. Justice courts handle minor civil and criminal cases. In some counties, district courts have replaced, or exist along with, justice courts. In those counties where district courts exist, they also handle minor civil and criminal cases. Municipal courts have jurisdiction of cases involving violations of municipal ordinances.

Published Works. *Members of the Legislature of Oregon, 1843–1967* (Salem: Oregon State Library, 1968) includes information about some early Oregon legal records.

Pennsylvania

State Courts. The court of general jurisdiction in Pennsylvania is the court of common pleas. The court of common pleas, which has existed since at least 1707, has jurisdiction over most civil and criminal cases.

Courts of limited jurisdictions are district justice courts, Philadelphia municipal courts, and Pittsburgh city magistrates. District justice courts handle minor civil and criminal cases, as do Philadelphia municipal courts. Pittsburgh city magistrates have jurisdiction over certain minor criminal cases.

Other Early State Courts. From 1664 to the modern era, courts of quarter sessions of the peace were countywide courts that handled criminal cases, roads, taverns, and peddlers. Other early courts included chancery, mayors', justice of the peace, and admiralty courts.

Published Works. For more information about Pennsylvania courts, see Sylvester K. Stevens and Donald H. Kent's *County Government and Archives in Pennsylvania* (Harrisburg: Pennsylvania History and Museum Commission, 1947) and Boyd Crumrine's *Virginia Court Records in Southwestern Pennsylvania: Records of the District of West Augusta and Ohio and Yohogania Counties, Virginia, 1775–1780,* excerpted and reprinted from *Annals of the Carnegie Museum,* 3 vols. (Pittsburgh, 1902–05).

Rhode Island

State Courts. The court of general jurisdiction in Rhode Island is the superior court. Superior courts have existed in Rhode Island since around 1905 and district courts since before the 1890s. Superior courts have jurisdiction over major civil and criminal cases.

Courts of limited jurisdiction are district courts, family courts, municipal courts, and probate courts. District courts handle minor civil and criminal cases. Family courts handle divorces and juvenile matters. Municipal courts have jurisdiction over traffic violations and miscellaneous ordinances. Probate jurisdiction is exercised by probate courts.

Other Early State Courts. Courts of common pleas were established in each county in 1730. They had jurisdiction over most local criminal and civil matters until around 1898. The superior court of judicature replaced the general court of trials. After 1747, several superior courts of judicature were established as countywide courts. Other early courts included the court of election, which existed between approximately 1640 and 1854; the county courts of general sessions, which existed between approximately 1729 and 1838; justice courts, which existed between approximately 1729 and 1886; courts of magistrates, which existed between approximately 1845 and 1886; and the admiralty court, which existed between approximately 1767 and 1789 (known as the maritime court from 1776 to 1780).

South Carolina

State Courts. The court of general jurisdiction is the circuit court, which is known as the court of common pleas when handling civil cases and as the court of general sessions when handling criminal cases. Circuit courts, which have existed since around 1772, have jurisdiction over major civil and criminal cases. The court of common pleas was a statewide court from 1703 until 1790, when a common pleas court having jurisdiction over guardianships and civil matters was established for each district.

Courts of limited jurisdiction are family courts, magistrate courts, municipal courts, and probate courts. Family courts handle juvenile and domestic matters. Magistrates' courts handle minor civil and criminal cases, and municipal courts also handle minor criminal cases. Probate jurisdiction is exercised by probate courts.

Other Early State Courts. The court of general sessions was a statewide court from 1769 until 1790, when a general sessions court having jurisdiction over criminal cases was established for each district. These courts continued until around 1798. From 1785 to 1798, county courts heard minor civil and criminal cases. Equity jurisdiction was exercised by the court of chancery from 1671 to the 1790s and by courts of equity from 1791 to 1900.

Published Works. For more information about South Carolina's courts, see George K. Schweitzer's *South Carolina Genealogical Research* (Knoxville, Tenn.: the author, 1985) and Mary Bondurant's "A Guide to South Carolina Court Records," *Family Puzzlers* no. 791 (16 December 1982) (Danielsville, Ga: Heritage Papers). Many early court records have been published, such as Brent H. Holcomb's *Edgefield County, South Carolina, Minutes of the County Court, 1785–1795* (Easley, S.C.: Southern Historical Press, 1979).

South Dakota

State Courts. The court of general jurisdiction in South Dakota is the circuit court. Circuit courts have jurisdiction in all cases except those few over which limited jurisdiction has been granted to other courts by the legislature.

The court of limited jurisdiction is the magistrate court. Magistrate courts hear some minor civil and criminal cases.

Other Early State Courts. Justices of the peace used to have countywide jurisdiction over minor civil and criminal cases. Municipal courts had citywide jurisdiction over minor civil and criminal cases. District county courts had countywide jurisdiction over misdemeanors, minor civil cases, probates, guardianships, and juvenile matters.

Published Works. Ross H. Oviatt's *South Dakota Justice: The Judges and the System* (Watertown, S.D.: Interstate Publishing Co., 1989) includes information on South Dakota's judicial system.

Tennessee

State Courts. Courts of general jurisdiction in Tennessee are circuit courts and chancery courts. Circuit courts, which have existed since the early 1800s, have jurisdiction of all common law contract or tort cases where value exceeds fifty dollars. Chancery courts, which have also existed since the early 1800s, have general equity jurisdiction where value exceeds fifty dollars. Chancery courts also have concurrent jurisdiction with circuit courts over most other civil cases; they also now exercise probate jurisdiction (except in Shelby, Davidson, Gibson, and Dyer counties).

Courts of limited jurisdiction are law and equity courts, justice courts, general sessions courts, criminal courts, municipal courts, and probate courts. Law and equity courts exist only in Gibson, Dyer, Blount, and Montgomery counties, where they generally have both equity and law jurisdiction. Justice courts, which are presided over by justices of the peace, have jurisdiction in minor civil and criminal cases. Courts of general sessions have essentially the same jurisdiction as justice courts. Criminal courts, which exist in several parts of the state, are essentially branches of the circuit court that handle only criminal cases. Municipal courts handle cases involving violations of municipal ordinances. Probate courts exist only in Shelby and Davidson counties. In other counties, probate jurisdiction is exercised by the chancery court (except in Gibson and Dyer counties, where probate jurisdiction is exercised by the law and equity court).

Other Early State Courts. Tennessee has had various courts in the past. Some larger counties had superior courts of law and equity, which heard civil and equity cases until 1809. Probate cases normally were under the jurisdiction of the county court, which was made up of justices of the peace; however, contested probate cases could be handled by the chancery court. All probate jurisdiction, formerly vested in county courts, was in recent years transferred to chancery courts in most counties. Early courts also included courts of pleas and quarter sessions.

Published Works. For more information about Tennessee courts, see *Survey to Tennessee County Court Records, Prior to 1860, in the Second, Third and Fourth Districts* (Nashville: Historical Records Survey, 1943), and Henry R. Gibson's *Gibson's Suits in Chancery*, 3rd ed. (Cleveland: Baldwin Law Book Co., 1929). Some county, circuit, and chancery court records are abstracted in Majorie Hood Fischer, comp., *Tennessee Tidbits, 1778–1914*, 2 vols. (vol. 1, Easley, S.C.: Southern Historical Press, 1986; vol. 2, Vista, Calif.: RAM Press, 1988).

Texas

State Courts. The court of general jurisdiction in Texas is the district court. District courts, which have existed since the 1800s, generally have jurisdiction over all major civil and criminal cases.

Courts of limited jurisdiction are county courts, municipal courts, justice of the peace courts, and probate courts. County courts, which also have existed since the 1800s, have jurisdiction in minor civil and criminal cases, as well as probate jurisdiction in all counties (except a few larger counties where special probate courts have been created). In a few counties, the jurisdiction of county courts is limited to probate matters. Municipal courts have jurisdiction over minor criminal cases. Justice of the peace courts, established in 1845, handle minor civil and criminal cases.

Other Early State Courts. Court names and jurisdictions in Texas have changed over time. Commissioners' courts, which have existed since at least 1837, are now administrative bodies for Texas counties. The commissioners' courts used to have some judicial functions; their court records often include records of other courts, such as county courts.

Published Works. Hans Peter Nielson Gammel, ed., *Gammel's Laws of Texas* (Austin, Tex.: Austin Printing Co., 1905) includes information about some early county legal records. Helen M. Lu and Gwen B. Neumann's *First Half Dozen Years: Dallas County, Texas, As Seen Through the Commissioners' Court Minutes* (Dallas, Tex.: the authors, 1982) contains some early court records of the Commissioner's Court of Dallas County, Texas.

Utah

State Courts. The court of general jurisdiction in Utah is the district court. District courts have jurisdiction over most civil and criminal cases and probate matters.

Courts of limited jurisdiction are circuit courts and justices' courts. Circuit courts have jurisdiction over minor civil and criminal cases; however, some circuit courts have recently become district courts, and all of the remaining circuit courts will become district courts no later than 1998. Justices' courts handle small claims and violations of certain misdemeanors. State district courts have existed since Utah became a state in 1896. Justice of the peace courts have also existed since 1896. Circuit courts, which are in the process of becoming district courts, were first created in 1977.

Other Early State Courts. Although the ecclesiastical era officially ended in 1849, church courts of The Church of Jesus Christ of Latter-day Saints (LDS church) handled some civil and criminal cases from 1847 until around 1890 (until 1910 in some southern Utah communities). From 1851 to 1896, Federal district courts had jurisdiction over major criminal and civil cases. The responsibilities of the Federal district courts were transferred in 1896 to the state district courts. County probate courts were created in 1850 and abolished in 1896. From 1906 to 1977, city courts had jurisdiction in minor civil and criminal cases. They were replaced by circuit courts in 1977.

Published Works. For more information on Utah courts, see Douglas S. Beckstead's *The Judicial System in Utah: Organic Act to the Twentieth Century* (Salt Lake City: Utah State Archives, 1988).

Vermont

State Courts. The court of general jurisdiction in Vermont is the superior court. Superior courts, sometimes called county courts, have existed in Vermont since 1777. Superior courts have jurisdiction over major civil and criminal cases.

Courts of limited jurisdiction are district courts, family courts, and probate courts. District courts handle minor civil and criminal cases. Family courts handle divorces and juvenile and other domestic matters. Probate jurisdiction is exercised by probate courts.

Other Early State Courts. From 1786 until the modern era, justice courts had jurisdiction over civil and criminal cases. As other courts were created, the jurisdiction of justice courts was reduced. Other early courts included courts of common pleas, courts of quarter sessions, courts of chancery, and municipal courts.

Published Works. Some early court records were published in *The Upper Connecticut: Narratives of Its Settlement and Its Part in the American Revolution* (Montpelier: Vermont Historical Society, 1943).

Virginia

State Courts. The court of general jurisdiction in Virginia is the circuit court. Circuit courts, which have existed since the early 1800s, are the major trial courts in Virginia; they have jurisdiction over most civil and criminal cases.

Courts of limited jurisdiction are general district courts and juvenile and domestic relations district courts. General district courts, not to be confused with the early district courts that were abolished in the early 1800s, have jurisdiction over minor civil and criminal cases. Juvenile and domestic relations district courts handle juvenile matters and limited domestic relations matters.

Other Early State Courts. From the early colonial period until 1902, county courts (called monthly courts from around 1618 to 1634 and later called courts of the shire) handled minor civil and criminal cases, as well as probate matters. Their jurisdiction was assumed by the circuit superior courts of law and chancery in 1902. From the colonial period until 1851, the general court had jurisdiction over major civil and criminal cases and some probate matters. From 1788 until around 1809 there were district courts, which handled civil and criminal cases. These courts were replaced by circuit superior courts of law from 1809 to 1831. Superior courts of chancery, which exercised equity jurisdiction, existed from 1802 until 1831. Circuit superior courts of law and chancery replaced both superior courts of chancery and circuit superior courts of law; in 1902, they also assumed the duties of county courts.

Published Works. Many Virginia court records have been published. Examples are Lyman Chalkley's *Chronicles of the Scots-Irish Settlement in Virginia: Extracted from the Original Court Records of Augusta County, 1754–1800*, 3 vols. (1912; reprint; Baltimore: Genealogical Publishing Co., 1980), Weynette Parks Haun's *Surry County, Virginia, Court Records* (Durham, N.C.: the author, n.d.), and Eliza Timberlake Davis's *Surry County Records, Surry County, Virginia* (Baltimore: Genealogical Publishing Co., 1980).

Washington

State Courts. The court of general jurisdiction in the state of Washington is the superior court. Superior courts have jurisdiction over most civil and criminal cases, including probate matters.

Courts of limited jurisdiction are district courts and municipal courts. District courts have jurisdiction over some minor civil and criminal cases.

Other Early State Courts. In Washington Territory, the trial courts were district courts, probate courts, and justice courts. Probate courts were the primary courts for probate matters until 1891, when this responsibility was assumed by the superior courts. In some areas, the probate court had concurrent civil and criminal jurisdiction with the district courts.

Published Works. For more information on territorial court records, see *Frontier Justice: Abstracts and Indexes to the Records of the Territorial District Courts, 1853–1889* (Olympia, Wash.: Secretary of State, Division of Archives and Records Management, 1987).

West Virginia

State Courts. The court of general jurisdiction in West Virginia is the circuit court. Circuit courts, which have existed since 1852, have jurisdiction of most civil and criminal cases.

Courts of limited jurisdiction are county magistrates' courts, county commissions, and municipal courts; however, probate jurisdiction is exercised by county commissions (sometimes called county courts). County magistrates' courts handle minor civil and criminal cases, and municipal courts handle violations of misdemeanors.

Other Early State Courts. West Virginia was part of Virginia until 1863 and had the same courts until then. After 1863, statutory courts were created at various times by special acts of the state legislature. The jurisdictions of these courts varied but generally included limited jurisdiction of civil and criminal cases. They existed in various counties (usually the most populous) under different names, such as criminal courts, intermediate courts, or common pleas courts. Justice courts, which existed from 1863 to the modern era, had jurisdiction over minor criminal and civil cases.

Published Works. For court records involving settlers of West Virginia, see Lyman Chalkley's *Chronicles of the Scotch-Irish Settlement of Virginia* (1912; reprint; Baltimore: Genealogical Publishing Co., 1980). Early court records for the area which became West Virginia are printed in Richard Williams Loveless's *Records of the District of West Augusta, Ohio County, and Yohogania County, Virginia; District of West Augusta, Minutes of the Court (1775–1776); Deeds (1775–1776); Ohio County Minutes of the Court (1777–1780); Yohogania County, Minutes of the Court (1777–1780); Wills (1776–1780)* (Columbus, Ohio: State University Printing Department, 1970).

Wisconsin

State Courts. The court of general jurisdiction in Wisconsin is the circuit court. Circuit courts, which have existed since the 1800s, have jurisdiction in almost all civil and criminal cases (including all probate matters).

The court of limited jurisdiction is the municipal court. Municipal courts, which have existed since 1836, have citywide jurisdiction over misdemeanors and ordinance violations.

Other Early State Courts. Justices of the peace were first appointed in 1803. In 1818, the justices' courts dealt with minor civil cases of twenty dollars or less, and county courts covered civil cases not to exceed one thousand dollars and non-capital criminal cases. When Wisconsin Territory was created in 1836, the judicial system included district courts, probate courts, and justice of the peace courts, which were retained when statehood was attained in 1848. Justices of the peace were not abolished until the modern era. Federal and territorial courts handled many early court cases. From 1848 to the modern era, county courts had countywide jurisdiction concurrently with circuit courts for some criminal and civil cases, and exclusive jurisdiction for probate matters.

Published Works. David J. Delgado's *Guide to the Wisconsin State Archives* (Madison: State Historical Society of Wisconsin, 1966) includes information on court records. Some of the territorial court records have been published.

Wyoming

State Courts. The court of general jurisdiction in Wyoming is the district court. District courts have jurisdiction over most civil and criminal cases, including divorces and probate matters.

Courts of limited jurisdiction are county courts, justice courts, and municipal courts. Justice of the peace courts have jurisdiction over minor civil cases and misdemeanors. In some counties, county courts have replaced justice courts and exercise the jurisdictions previously exercised by justice of the peace courts. Municipal courts handle cases involving violations of municipal ordinances.

Other Early State Courts. At the time of statehood in 1890, district courts and justice of the peace courts became the state trial courts in Wyoming.

Table 12-1 contains a state-by-state summary of state trial courts.

FEDERAL COURTS AND THEIR RECORDS

The Federal court system began in 1789 when the U.S. Congress passed the Judiciary Act of 1789. At the Constitutional Convention in Philadelphia in 1787, the delegates had voted by a narrow margin to establish only a supreme court and to prohibit the establishment of any Federal trial courts. Then, in a move that would forever change the structure of the American judicial system, James Madison proposed a compromise that would leave to Congress the question of whether or not to establish Federal trial courts. Of course, Madison's compromise made it into the final version of the U.S. Constitution, which provided for a supreme court and such trial courts, if any, as Congress should establish.

When the first Congress met in 1789, it resolved the issue by creating a system of Federal trial courts that would function alongside the existing state trial courts. A Federal *district court* was established as a trial court in each state. The creation of national trial courts to operate simultaneously with existing state trial courts was, at the time, a new concept which had not been tried before.

As the population grew, some states were divided into two or more Federal court districts. There are presently eighty-nine districts in the fifty states. The district courts usually had jurisdiction over Federal civil and equity cases, with limited criminal jurisdiction until 1866. Their jurisdiction has included admiralty, trade, bankruptcy, land seizure, naturalization, and, after 1815, non-capital criminal cases.

Three Federal circuits were established to cover the whole country in 1789. The number gradually expanded to nine by 1866. Federal *circuit courts* had jurisdiction over all matters (especially criminal) covered by Federal law; they also had some appellate functions from the district courts. In 1891, *circuit courts of appeals* were created to hear appeals from the district courts; they had the same boundaries (or circuits) as the circuit courts. The original circuit courts retained limited powers that often overlapped those of the district courts. In 1911, the original circuit courts were abolished.

The records of most pre-1950 Federal district and circuit courts have been collected by the National Archives regional archives.

Many Federal court decisions are published in case reporters, which are discussed in detail under "Case Reporters: Published Court Decisions," below. Other than those decisions found in case reporters, only a few Federal court records have been printed. The following are representative publications for some states.

District of Columbia

The district court for the District of Columbia has functioned as a Federal court since 1813. See United States District Court (District of Columbia), *Record of the U.S. District Court for the District of Columbia as Relating to Slaves, 1851–1863* (Washington, D.C.: National Archives, 1963).

Florida

For information about Federal court records in Florida, see *Inventory of Federal Archives in the States: Series II. The Federal Courts No. 9, Florida* (Jacksonville, Fla.: Historical Records Survey, 1940).

Indiana

Federal court records in Indiana are described in Warren B. Griffin's *Preliminary Inventory: Records of the U.S. Courts for the District of Indiana* (Chicago: Federal Records Center, 1967).

Kentucky

For information on early Federal courts in Kentucky, see Mary K. Bonsteel Tachau's *Federal Courts in the Early Republic: Kentucky 1789–1816* (Princeton, N.J.: Princeton University Press, 1978.) Also see Warren B. Griffin's *Preliminary Inventory of the United States Courts from the District of Kentucky* (Chicago: Federal Records Center, 1968).

Table 12-1. State Trial Courts

State	*Trial Courts of General Jurisdiction*	*Trial Courts of Limited Jurisdiction*	*Probate Courts*	*Other Early State Trial Courts*
Alabama	Circuit court	District courts, municipal courts, probate courts	Probate courts	Chancery courts, superior courts, intermediate courts, inferior courts, courts of common pleas, civil courts, criminal courts, law and equity courts, general sessions courts, law and juvenile courts, justice of the peace courts, commissioners' courts, mayors' courts
Alaska	Superior court	District courts, magistrates' courts	Superior courts	U.S. District Court of theTerritory of Alaska, U.S. commissioners' courts
Arizona	Superior court	Justice of the peace courts, municipal courts	Superior court	District courts, probate courts
Arkansas	Circuit courts and chancery courts	Courts of common pleas, county courts, municipal courts, justice of the peace courts	Chancery courts	Probate courts
California	Superior court	Municipal courts, justice courts	Superior court	District courts, county courts
Colorado	District courts, Denver probate court, Denver juvenile court	County courts, municipal courts	District courts	Denver superior court, county courts, justice of the peace courts
Connecticut	Superior court	Probate court	Probate court	Town and borough courts, justice of the peace courts, circuit courts, courts of common pleas
Delaware	Superior courts, courts of chancery	Courts of common pleas, family courts, justice of the peace courts, municipal court of Wilmington	Courts of chancery	Orphans' courts, court of general quarter sessions, court of oyer and terminer, justice of the peace court
District of Columbia	Superior court		Superior court	Circuit court, District of Columbia Supreme Court, levy court
Florida	Circuit court	County court	Circuit court	Justices of the peace, city courts, probate courts, civil and criminal courts, municipal courts
Georgia	Superior court	State courts, juvenile courts, probate courts, magistrates' courts, civil courts, county recorders' courts, municipal courts	Probate courts	Superior courts, courts of ordinary, inferior courts
Hawaii	Circuit court, land court, tax appeal court	District courts, family courts	Circuit courts	
Idaho	District courts, magistrates' division of district court		Magistrates' division of district court	Probate courts, justice of the peace courts
Illinois	Circuit courts		Circuit courts	Superior Court of Cook County, probate courts, county courts, city courts, municipal courts, justices of the peace, police magistrates, County Court for the County of Illinois of the State of Virginia, courts of quarter sessions, courts of common pleas, orphans' courts, Chicago mayor, superior courts, criminal courts, family courts

State	*Trial Courts of General Jurisdiction*	*Trial Courts of Limited Jurisdiction*	*Probate Courts*	*Other Early State Trial Courts*
Indiana	Superior courts, circuit courts	County courts, probate courts, city and town courts, Small Claims Court of Marion County	Probate courts	Court of quarter sessions, court of common pleas, justices of the peace
Iowa	District court		District court	Superior courts, municipal courts, circuit courts, justice of the peace courts
Kansas	District court		District court	County courts, probate courts, magistrate and city courts, justices of the peace
Kentucky	Circuit court	District court	Circuit court	Courts of quarter sessions, county courts, quarterly courts, justices' court, court of oyer and terminer, examining court, general court
Louisiana	District court	Parish courts, justice of the peace courts, city courts, mayors' courts, East Baton Rouge family court, juvenile courts, municipal court of New Orleans, traffic court of New Orleans, civil district court of New Orleans	District court	Conseil superieur (French Superior Council), Spanish cabildo
Maine	Superior court	District courts, probate courts, administrative courts	Probate courts	Inferior courts of common pleas, supreme judicial court, superior courts, court of general sessions, county commissioner's court, justices of the peace
Maryland	Circuit court	District courts, orphans' courts, tax courts	Orphans' courts (circuit court in Montgomery and Harford counties)	Provincial court (later general court), county courts, chancery court
Massachu-setts	Superior court	District court, Boston municipal court, land court, housing court, probate court, juvenile court	Probate court	General sessions courts, courts of common pleas, justice of the peace courts
Michigan	Circuit courts, court of claims	District courts, probate courts, municipal courts	Probate courts	County courts, justice courts
Minnesota	District court	County courts, municipal courts	Probate division of county courts	Justice courts
Mississippi	Circuit courts, chancery courts	County courts, municipal courts, justice courts, family courts	Chancery courts	Orphans' court, probate court
Missouri	Circuit court	Associate circuit courts, county courts, probate division of the circuit court	Probate division of circuit court	Courts of common pleas, magistrate courts
Montana	District court	Justice courts, city courts, municipal courts	District court	Probate courts
Nebraska	District court	County courts, juvenile courts	County courts	Justice courts, probate courts, police magistrate courts

State	*Trial Courts of General Jurisdiction*	*Trial Courts of Limited Jurisdiction*	*Probate Courts*	*Other Early State Trial Courts*
Nevada	District court	Justices' courts, municipal courts	District court	
New Hampshire	Superior court	District courts, probate courts	Probate courts	Courts of general quarter sessions, courts of common pleas, justices of the peace, municipal courts
New Jersey	Superior court	Surrogate courts, municipal courts, tax courts	Surrogate courts	Courts of general quarter sessions, special sessions, orphans' court, prerogative courts, courts of common pleas, courts of oyer and terminer, general gaol delivery, county courts, justices' courts, district courts, court of chancery, circuit courts, supreme court
New Mexico	District court	Probate courts, magistrate courts, municipal courts, Bernallilo County Metropolitan Court	Probate courts, district court	Alcalde ordinario (mayors' courts), audiencia (courts of appeals), prefect's court, circuit courts
New York	Supreme courts, county courts	Family courts, surrogates' courts, city courts, justice courts, court of claims, district courts, civil court of the City of New York, criminal court of the City of New York	Surrogate courts	Courts of general quarter sessions of the peace, county courts, courts of common pleas, superior court, court of oyer and terminer and general gaol delivery, court of probates, court of chancery, circuit courts
North Carolina	Superior court	District courts, magistrates' courts	Superior courts	Courts of pleas and quarter sessions, county courts, inferior courts
North Dakota	District court	County courts, municipal courts	County courts	Justice courts
Ohio	Court of common pleas	Municipal courts, county courts, mayor's courts	Court of common pleas	District courts, circuit courts, probate courts, justice of the peace courts, police courts
Oklahoma	District court	Court of tax review, workers' compensation court, municipal courts	District court	U.S. District Court for the Western District of Arkansas, U.S. District Court for the Eastern District of Texas
Oregon	Circuit court	County courts, district courts, justice courts, municipal courts	Circuit courts or county courts	
Pennsylvania	Court of common pleas	District justice courts, Philadelphia municipal courts, Pittsburgh city magistrates	Orphans' court division of court of common pleas	Courts of quarter sessions of the peace, chancery, mayors', justice of the peace, admiralty courts
Rhode Island	Superior court	District courts, family courts, municipal courts, probate courts	Probate courts	Courts of common pleas, general court of trials, superior court of judicature, court of election, county courts of general sessions, justice courts, courts of magistrates, admiralty court (maritime court)
South Carolina	Circuit court (also known as court of common pleas or court of general sessions)	Family courts, magistrate courts, municipal courts, probate courts	Probate courts	Court of general sessions, county courts, court of chancery, courts of equity

State	*Trial Courts of General Jurisdiction*	*Trial Courts of Limited Jurisdiction*	*Probate Courts*	*Other Early State Trial Courts*
South Dakota	Circuit court	Magistrates' court	Circuit court	Justices of the peace, municipal courts, district county courts
Tennessee	Circuit courts, chancery courts	Law and equity courts, justice courts, general sessions courts, criminal courts, municipal courts, probate courts	Chancery court, probate court, or law and equity court	Superior courts of law and equity, county court, courts of pleas and quarter sessions
Texas	District courts	County courts, municipal courts, justice of the peace courts, probate courts	County courts or probate courts	Commissioners' courts
Utah	District court	Circuit courts, justices' courts	District court	Church courts of the LDS church, Federal district courts, probate courts, city courts
Vermont	Superior court (county court)	District courts, family courts, probate courts	Probate courts	Justice courts, courts of common pleas, courts of quarter sessions, courts of chancery, municipal courts
Virginia	Circuit court	General district courts, juvenile and domestic relations district courts	Circuit courts	County courts (monthly courts or courts of the shire), circuit superior courts of law and chancery, general court, district courts, circuit superior courts of law, superior courts of chancery, circuit superior courts of law and chancery
Washington	Superior court	District courts, municipal courts	Superior courts	District courts, probate courts, justice courts
West Virginia	Circuit court	County magistrates' courts, county commissions, municipal courts	County commissions	Statutory courts (criminal courts, intermediate courts, or common pleas courts), justice courts
Wisconsin	Circuit court	Municipal court	Circuit court	Justices of the peace, district courts, probate courts, county courts
Wyoming	District court	County courts, justice courts, municipal courts	District courts	District courts, justice of the peace courts

Missouri

For information about Federal court records in Missouri, see William D. White's *Preliminary Inventory of the Records of the United States Courts for the Western District of Missouri* (Kansas City, Mo.: Federal Archives Center, 1969).

Nebraska

Records of U.S. circuit and district courts from 1855 to 1961 are at the National Archives—Central Plains Region. For more information about these records, see Fred W. Hons and Delbert A. Bishop's *Preliminary Inventory: Records of the United States District Court for the District of Nebraska* (Kansas City, Mo.: Federal Records Center, 1967).

New Mexico

More information about New Mexico Federal court records is in E. Stuart Howard's *Preliminary Inventory: Records of the United States District Court for the District of New Mexico* (Denver: Federal Archives and Records Center, 1968).

CASE REPORTERS: PUBLISHED COURT DECISIONS

Case reporters contain published decisions of appellate courts arranged in chronological order; they do not contain word-for-word transcripts of trials or other court proceedings. Only a minority of states publish a few selected trial court decisions in case reporters, so the vast majority of cases in reporters are those appealed from trial courts. Not all appellate court decisions are published; however, most states now attempt to publish all of their highest courts' opinions.

The cases published in case reporters consist of the court's disposition of the case and the reasoning through which the court reached its decision. The format is fairly standard for each case: a few sentences or paragraphs lay out the facts, followed by the judge's application of the law as it bears upon the situation, and, ultimately (sometimes after a great deal of discussion and reasoning), the decision of the court.

The facts of the case are what the genealogist seeks; the rest of the court's opinion may be fairly uninteresting. However, a researcher who finds an ancestor mentioned in one of these opinions will want to read the entire decision because it may well contain clues that will lead to further research in other types of records.

While some mistakes undoubtedly have occurred, court decisions published in case reporters are generally considered accurate. There usually are few typographical errors, and names, dates, and locations are, if not correct, at least consistently given in the opinions. As to the spelling of surnames, a printed decision probably reflects exactly how the lawyers spelled their clients' names.

Case reporters are published for individual states, for regions, for Federal cases, and for more specialized areas within the law, such as bankruptcy. Virtually all law libraries have reporters for the state in which they are located and frequently for surrounding states. Major law libraries, such as those of universities, have reporters for all states (usually arranged in alphabetical order by state).

Under a particular state, reporters are arranged chronologically, with the volume number and, often, the years covered appearing on the binding. It is easy to check the books covering the years of an ancestor's known residence in a particular state by beginning at the earliest year of residence in the reporter for that state and checking each volume.

Tables of Cases

Each case reporter volume typically has an index, often at the front of the book—but it is not called an index. The term used is *table of cases*. Entire books titled "Table of Cases," containing surnames, can be found in other parts of a law library. These books provide reference to thousands of cases in several different reporters.

Modern tables of cases list, in alphabetical order, all plaintiffs and defendants mentioned in case reporters. Many earlier tables list only the first named plaintiff in each case and no defendants. It is not uncommon also to find a separate alphabetical listing of plaintiffs and one for defendants immediately after the list of plaintiffs. Unfortunately, no case reporters include alphabetical listings of other people named in the cases.

Many state reporters have ceased publication, giving way to a system of regional reporters which cover several states in the same geographic area. The state reporters are more convenient for genealogists to use and are found in most of the larger law libraries.

Court cases in which an ancestor was a plaintiff or a defendant should be analyzed carefully—not only for the information that can be gleaned from the case, but also for clues to other record sources. In the search for ancestors, the difference between a Federal and a state case is usually unimportant (except in determining where to search for the case). Neither is the difference between "official" (published by a state) and "unofficial" (published by a commercial company) reporters usually important.

For a complete list of reporters (official and unofficial—state, regional, and Federal), see Frederick C. Hicks's *Material and Methods of Legal Research,* 3rd rev. ed. (Rochester, N.Y.: Lawyers Co-operative Publishing Co., 1942). The extensive list of state case reporters in Hicks's guide is especially helpful because it tells what years cases were reported for each state.

A state-by-state list of state appellate courts appears in table 12-2.

AMERICAN DIGESTS

The American Digest System is a series of volumes that summarize cases from all over the United States. Every ten years the publishers issue a decennial index to the cases reported. Genealogists will take particular interest in the first one, *1906 Decennial Edition of the American Digest*, "A Complete Table of American Cases From 1658 to 1906," vols. 21–25.

While those five volumes do not actually comprise a complete index to all appellate court cases in the United States from 1658 to 1906, they do comprise an index to thousands of cases; they probably form the most notable genealogical tool in a law library.

Significant drawbacks should be noted: the *1906 Decennial Edition* is an index to plaintiffs only. If initials are used, the initials will be indexed, not the last name; for example, D. B. Walling Company would be found under *D* instead of *W.* Despite the *Decennial Edition*'s claim to being an index back to 1658, it covers very few cases in the period from 1658 to 1789, and most of those are from Maryland. (The year 1789 is a key one in American law: it was at around this time that the new republic ceased following new English law and cases and established a system based on old English and new American law and cases.)

The beauty of the *1906 Decennial Edition of the American Digest* is the great number of names found in it. No other research tool is likely to contain as many surnames in such a compact form. For the family historian looking for an elusive family name, there is a good chance it may appear in the *Decennial Edition;* for those collecting all instances of a surname or trying to locate an ancestor's home state, it is also a good place to look.

Here is a typical citation from the *Decennial Edition:*

Hobbs v. Griefenhagen 194 Ill. 73, 62 N.E. 303;

It is actually two citations: *194 Ill. 73* and *62 N.E. 303.* The legal system uses a system of citation called the *tripartite system.* With this system, the volume number is given first, then the name of the reporter, and then the page number. (Other citations following the semicolon can be ignored; only the information preceding the semicolon is of value to genealogists.) Thus, the case of *Hobbs v. Griefenhagen* is reported in vol. 194 of the Illinois reporter, starting on page 73. The case will also be found in vol. 62 of the Northeastern Reporter, beginning on page 303. The Illinois reporter is a state reporter, and the Northeastern Reporter is part of the regional reporter system mentioned earlier. All abbreviations, such as *Ill.* and *N.E.,* are easily translated by using the guide found in the front of each of the volumes of the *Decennial Edition.*

Once the citation has been "translated," it is a simple matter to go to the section of the library that houses the state reporters or the regional reporters and find the case. Although not every citation is a double one (as the above example is), the two citations increase the odds of finding the case because both citations will produce exactly the same report.

Because regional reporters publish exactly the same cases as do state reporters, some states have dropped their state reporting systems and have come to rely solely on regional reporters.

Sometimes the reporters cited will not be available in a law library. For instance, the Illinois reporter might have been

Table 12-2. State Appellate Courts

State	*Intermediate Appeals Court*	*Court of Last Resort*	*State*	*Intermediate Appeals Court*	*Court of Last Resort*
Alabama	Court of criminal appeals; court of civil appeals	Supreme court (established 1819)	Montana	None	Supreme court
Alaska	Court of appeals	Supreme court	Nebraska	Court of appeals	Supreme court
Arizona	Court of appeals	Supreme court	Nevada	None	Supreme court
Arkansas	Court of appeals	Supreme court	New Hampshire	None	Supreme court (established 1813)
California	Court of appeals	Supreme court	New Jersey	Appellate division of superior court	Supreme court
Colorado	Court of appeals	Supreme court	New Mexico	Court of appeals	Supreme court
Connecticut	Appellate court	Supreme court	New York	Appellate division of supreme court	Court of appeals
Delaware	None	Supreme court	North Carolina	Court of appeals	Supreme court
Florida	District court of appeals	Supreme court	North Dakota	None	Supreme court
Georgia	Court of appeals	Supreme court	Ohio	Court of appeals	Supreme court (established 1787)
Hawaii	Intermediate court of civil appeals	Supreme court	Oklahoma	Court of appeals	Supreme court; court of criminal appeals
Idaho	Court of appeals	Supreme court	Oregon	Court of appeals	Supreme court
Illinois	Appellate court	Supreme court	Pennsylvania	Superior court; commonwealth court	Supreme court (established 1707)
Indiana	Court of appeals	Supreme court	Rhode Island	None	Supreme court
Iowa	Court of appeals	Supreme court	South Carolina	Court of appeals	Supreme court
Kansas	Court of appeals	Supreme court	South Dakota	None	Supreme court
Kentucky	Court of appeals	Supreme court	Tennessee	Court of appeals; court of criminal appeals	Supreme court
Louisiana	Court of appeals	Supreme court (established 1804 as superior court)	Texas	Court of appeals	Supreme court; court of criminal appeals
Maine	None	Supreme judicial court (established 1782)	Utah	Court of appeals (established 1987)	Supreme court (established 1896)
Maryland	Court of special appeals	Court of appeals (established 1776)	Vermont	None	Supreme court
Massachusetts	Appeals court	Supreme judicial court (established 1782)	Virginia	Court of appeals	Supreme court
Michigan	Court of appeals	Supreme court	Washington	Court of appeals	Supreme court
Minnesota	Court of appeals	Supreme court	West Virginia	None	Supreme court
Mississippi	None	Supreme court	Wisconsin	Court of appeals	Supreme court (established 1836)
Missouri	Court of appeals	Supreme court	Wyoming	None	Supreme court

the only reference given, and it might not be in a particular library. All the researcher then has to do is make a note of the citation and write to the state law library in the appropriate state (in this case Illinois), enclosing a stamped, self-addressed envelope and requesting the price for a copy of the reported case. A local library can provide the address of the state law library.

Despite its drawbacks, the *1906 Decennial Edition of the American Digest* is a valuable tool for genealogists and should be used, if possible. The *American Digest* is still being issued, and the later volumes are more complete. Around fifty years ago, the *Digest* began indexing both plaintiffs and defendants, and the tripartite citation system is in universal use by the legal community.

The American Digest System is found in many law libraries and even in the law sections of large university libraries. State law library librarians may be willing to photocopy the page with the surname of interest from the *1906 Decennial Edition of the American Digest.*

FEDERAL DIGEST

Records of the Supreme Court of the United States are indexed in the *Supreme Court Digest*. Records of the Supreme Court of the United States, the U.S. circuit courts of appeals, and the district courts of the United States are all indexed in the *Federal Digest*. These publications are available at most law libraries and U.S. Document Depository libraries. Vols. 66, 67, and 68 of the *Federal Digest* (published by West Publishing Co. in 1941) contain an index (by name of plaintiff) of cases from 1754 to 1941. The following is an excerpt from vol. 66 of the *Federal Digest,* p. 5.

> **Alford v. Cornell**, NY, 56 SCt 500, 297 US 708, 80 LEd 995, reh den 56 SCt 589, 297 US 728, 80 LEd 1011.
> **Alford v. Crofford**, Miss, 54 US 447, 13 How 447, 14 LEd 217. See McAfee v. Crofford.
> **Alford v. McConnell,** DCOkl, 27 F Supp 176, aff Maryland Casualty Co v. Alford, 111 F2d 388, cert den 61 SCt 27, two cases, 311 US 668, 85 LEd __.

Each reference identifies the state of the action followed by several three-part citations, each one separated by commas. Each citation includes first the volume number, then an abbreviation for the reporter, followed by the page number; thus, "56 Sct 500" refers to vol. 56 of the *Supreme Court Reporter,* p. 500.

Cases Decided in the Court of Claims of the United States reports cases from 1863 to the present, and vol. 89 is an index to vols. 1 through 89, which cover cases from 1863 through 1939. *Reports of the Court of Claims Submitted to the House of Representatives* covers an earlier period, from 1855 to 1863, but may be found only in larger libraries.

Federal Cases (Circuit and District Courts), 1789–1880, is a thirty-one-volume set reporting Federal cases. Vol. 31 is the index to the first thirty volumes of reports. It is a plaintiff and defendant index, and there is an overlap of dates with the *1906 Decennial Edition of the American Digest,* which covers 1658 to 1906. The researcher should use both sets, if possible, because the *Decennial Edition* covers both state and Federal cases and also covers more years, even if not completely.

PUBLISHED LAWS

The most important collections in a law library are case reporters and statutes. That is because the two major components of "the law" are rulings by courts and statutes (including constitutions). *Statutes* are laws enacted by legislatures. Legislative acts usually address the general concerns of society, while court rulings typically address only the facts of a single dispute and issues raised by the parties involved in specific lawsuits. The statutes (laws) enacted by legislatures are published chronologically in what are called *session laws*. Most statutes are also arranged by subjects in *codes*.

Any law library will most likely have a set of the current statute laws for the state it is in, arranged in alphabetical order by subject; that is called a *state code*. A large law library may have other material. Early private laws, for example, would be a valuable find, and such volumes are often indexed.

Private laws are those passed by a legislature for the benefit or relief of private individuals. Early legislative divorces might be found among them, as well as such things as name changes, adoptions, and naturalizations. These laws did not become part of the state code, but were strictly individual matters. Figure 12-3 shows a typical private law.

Session laws, not codes, contain genealogical information. Unfortunately, session laws often must be checked volume by volume because there may be no index of names. Sometimes surnames can be found under "Reliefs" in the index.

The U.S. government also passed laws for the relief of private individuals, just as the states did. Two indexes with hundreds of names of such individuals are *U.S. Session Laws, 1789–1873,* and *U.S. Statutes at Large, 1789–1845.*

DIRECTORIES OF THE LEGAL PROFESSION

The *Martindale-Hubbell Directory* is a listing of lawyers. It is useful to the researcher if the city and state in which the lawyer practiced are known because it is sorted in that manner. Martindale-Hubbell directories dating back to the 1800s are sometimes found in major law libraries. Information regarding a lawyer may include the place and date of his or her birth, the college or university attended, the degrees attained there and the dates those degrees were attained, and the law firm with which he or she was associated.

Some cities and counties have published "bench and bar" books. These list the lawyers practicing in a particular city or county at the time of publication and often include lengthy biographical sketches.

OTHER SOURCES AT LAW LIBRARIES

The holdings of a law library fall into two main groups: statutes and case reporters; all the other holdings revolve around these two groups. Law libraries contain other resources that should not be overlooked by family researchers. Considering the thousands of volumes in a typical law library, it is likely that a million or more decisions have been printed in book form. Though no law library would have all of them, it is amazing to think of all the genealogical information that could be found in those works.

As with so many research tools used by genealogists, law libraries are not set up for family researchers; therefore, they must be approached in special ways. A big difference between

Figure 12-3. A typical private law. From *The State Records of North Carolina,* edited by Walter Clark (Goldsboro, N.C., 1906; reprint; Wilmington, N.C.: Broadfoot Publishing Co., 1994), page 101.

LAWS OF NORTH CAROLINA—1790. 101

CHAPTER XXXVI.

An Act for the Relief of Thomas Ridge.

Whereas, it is represented to this General Assembly that Thomas Ridge, of Surry county, hath been charged with house burning in the course of the late war; and as it appears that the said Thomas Ridge proceeded in the matter charged against him agreeable to the command of his officers.

I. Be it enacted by the General Assembly of the State of North Carolina, and it is hereby enacted by the authority of the same, That the said Thomas Ridge be pardoned and clearly exonerated from the charge aforesaid; any law to the contrary notwithstanding.

CHAPTER XXXVII.

An Act to Alter the Names of Certain Persons therein mentioned.

Whereas, Benjamin Wheatly, of the county of Martin, has by petition requested that the names of Henry, Mary, Lydia and Benjamin Nobles, children of Elizabeth Nobles should be altered, and that they should henceforward be known by the names of Henry, Mary, Lydia and Benjamin Wheatly: and whereas, it appears that the said Benjamin Wheatly is the reputed father of the said Henry, Mary, Lydia and Benjamin Nobles, and having no lawful issue is desirous of leaving to them the property he possesses:

I. Be it therefore enacted by the General Assembly of the State of North Carolina, and it is hereby enacted by the authority of the same, That for henceforward and forever hereafter, the said Henry, Mary, Lydia and Benjamin Nobles, shall be known and distinguished by the names of Henry Wheatly, Mary Wheatly, Lydia Wheatly and Benjamin Wheatly, and by those names shall have the right to inherit and claim any estate, either real or personal, which may be devised to them or either of them by the said petitioner, Benjamin Wheatly, in as full and ample a manner as if they the said Henry, Mary, Lydia and Benjamin had been born in wedlock, and had been from the time of their births considered as the legitimate children of the said Benjamin Wheatly and Elizabeth Nobles; and shall forever be placed in the same situation and be considered to all intents and purposes in the same point of view, as though they legally descended from the said Benjamin Wheatly and Elizabeth Nobles, and had been born in wedlock as aforesaid.

legal research and genealogical research is that the lawyer will be searching for new cases and new laws to support whatever legal theory is being explored, while the family researcher will be delving into the older cases and older laws in an attempt to locate an ancestor.

Other material for the state of interest may be on the shelves as well. State house and senate journals are in major law libraries. Many resolutions about individuals are passed by one or both houses of a legislature. These resolutions are not statutes and so will not be found in session laws or codes. Unfortunately, even when there are indexes to these journals, they are often incomplete.

Some law libraries have collections of early law books or rare books that will have valuable information; some books that are not so rare are put in storage because of lack of open shelf space. Card catalogs for holdings on a particular state may be of help. The law library of the state of interest should contain a great deal of material on that state (back to the date of statehood and perhaps before that).

Many other printed court records may be available in a law library, depending on how extensive the individual library's collection is. Here the researcher may want to browse through the stacks for other resource material.

American Decisions and Reports is yet another resource which might be found in the law library. These reports consist of selected decisions from courts of last resort in many states. The cases reported in this set can also be found in state reporters; they were selected for publication in this set by the editors because of their broad application; they are of more than local interest. Vol. 3 is a table of cases (that is, index) for 1760 to 1887. Later volumes covered succeeding years.

Computer technology, of course, has affected the legal world. LEXIS, a service of Mead Data Central, and WESTLAW, a service of West Publishing Company, are the two leading computer-assisted legal research systems. Computer technology allows indexing to be done in much more depth than in the past, and genealogists have expressed hope that the millions of names that appear in the reporters will eventually be indexed; however, this does not seem more than a remote possibility. LEXIS and WESTLAW are directed toward the legal field, and lawyers have little concern or need for cases from as far back as the eighteenth century; they are more concerned with the precedents set by a case in (for example) 1994.

It is nevertheless encouraging to realize that material in our legal system today will be more accessible in the future. In the meantime, today's genealogists can use their own techniques to find mention of ancestors on the shelves of a law library. Researchers should not discount research in law libraries on the grounds that their "ancestors weren't rich enough to afford a lawyer." Poor people went to court, too, and half of each case may well have involved a defendant who did not want to go to court in the first place.

LOCATING LAW LIBRARIES

Every county seat has a law library; many counties have large central libraries with branches in smaller judicial districts. It is impossible to predict what will be in any particular law library, but each will undoubtedly have a good collection for the state in which it resides, and it is not uncommon for even a small law library to have reporters for surrounding states. The library will be found somewhere near (or in) the courthouse. A telephone directory will have its number and address.

Because not all states offer public use of their law libraries, it is best to call first to find out if there are any restrictions and if they can be waived. Many law schools have huge law libraries that are generous with library privileges. Often, such libraries are separate from the regular university library. To locate one, see the *American Association of Law School Libraries (AAAL) Directory and Handbook* (New York: Commerce Clearing House, annual).

American Bar Association-accredited law schools draw students from other states who plan to return to their home states to take their bar exams, so they are more likely to have reporters from other states.

Law library staff members can be very helpful to genealogists (if they have time). They usually deal only with people who want recent statutes and recent court decisions, so some find it refreshing to delve among the older materials.

A large university library may also have a good legal collection (even if the university does not have a law school). It is not unusual to find the American Digest System (discussed above) in such a library, although the reporters cited in a digest may not be at that library. The reporters for the state where the university is located may very well be at the university's library, too, as may other law material covering that state.

Private law firms also have large libraries dealing with sources for the states in which they practice, but their libraries are usually closed to the public. However, law firms are familiar with publicly accessible law libraries in their areas and can direct researchers to the nearest one.

TERMINOLOGY

Court records and indexes to law books are filled with legal terms. A researcher who is unfamiliar with these terms may need to consult a law dictionary. One of the best-known dictionaries is Henry Campbell Black' *Black's Law Dictionary* (St. Paul, Minn.: West Publishing), the first edition of which was published in 1891. Revised editions were published in 1910, 1933, 1951, 1957, 1968, 1979, and 1990. A genealogist will usually want to use the earliest edition available; fortunately, many law libraries have early editions on their shelves. Other helpful law dictionaries, glossaries, and thesauri are *Ballentine's Law Dictionary,* by Jack Handler (Rochester, N.Y.: Lawyer's Cooperative Pub., 1993); William C. Burton's *Legal Thesaurus,* 2nd ed. (New York: Macmillan, 1992); and Kenneth Redden and E. Veron's *Modern Legal Glossary* (Charlottesville, Va.: Michie Co., 1980).

INSTRUCTIONAL MATERIAL

Some court records are difficult to use. Fortunately, printed court records are generally much easier to use than original court records. Still, court names and jurisdictions have changed from time to time, and their records may contain many legal terms and abbreviations. A very helpful guide prepared for non-lawyers is John Corbin's *Find the Law in the Library: A Guide to Legal Research* (Chicago: American Library Association, 1989).

NOTES

1. Mr. Spratling gratefully acknowledges the role of Anita Cheek Milner in preparing an initial draft of certain sections of this chapter regarding the use of law libraries and their collections. He also expresses appreciation to George Ott for his assistance in completing this chapter and reworking certain elements of the text. Some of the materials presented in this chapter were drawn in part from the Family History Library's *Research Outlines*, Series US-STATES. The author wishes to thank The Church of Jesus Christ of Latter-day Saints for its cooperation in consenting to the preparation of the portions of this chapter derived from the Family History Library's *Research Outlines*. The author also would like to express appreciation for the assistance of Mary E. Ambridge and Susan Foy Spratling in preparing this chapter.

BIBLIOGRAPHY OF REFERENCE SOURCES

This bibliography includes only references that discuss court procedures and records. It does not list published court records. Because there are relatively few such records at the state level, they are noted within this chapter's text. They many hundreds of sources at the local level, such as for counties, are listed in bibliographies and library catalogs.

Abraham, Henry J. *Courts and Judges: An Introduction to the Judicial Process.* New York: Oxford University Press, 1962.

American Judicature Society. *Intermediate Appellate Courts.* Report no. 20. Chicago: American Judicature Society, 1968.

Aumann, Francis R. *The Changing American Legal System.* Columbus: Ohio State University Press, 1940.

Ball, Walter V. "Family Records from County Court Order Books." *National Genealogical Society Quarterly* 58 (1970): 3.

Becker, Theodore L. *Political Behaviorism and Modern Jurisprudence.* Chicago: Rand McNally, 1961.

Black, Henry Campbell. *Black's Law Dictionary: Definitions of the Terms and Phrases of American and English Jurisprudence, Ancient and Modern,* 6th ed. St. Paul, Minn.: West Publishing Co., 1990.

Bramwell, B. S. "Frequency of Cousin Marriages." *Genealogists' Magazine* 8 (1939): 305–16.

Burton, William C. *Legal Thesaurus.* New York: Macmillan Publishing Co., 1980.

Callender, Clarence N. *American Courts: Their Organization and Procedures.* New York: McGraw-Hill Book Co., 1927.

Chapin, Bradley. *Criminal Justice in Colonial America, 1606–1660.* Athens: University of Georgia Press, 1983.

Cohen, Morris L. *Legal Research in a Nutshell.* 4th ed. St. Paul, Minn.: West Publishing Co., 1985.

Connor, Seymour V. "Legal Materials as Sources of History." *American Archivist* 23 (1960): 157–65.

Dorman, John Frederick. "Colonial Laws of Primogeniture." I-12. World Conference on Records. Salt Lake City: Genealogical Society of Utah, 1969.

Dumbauld, Edward. "Legal Records in English and American Courts." *American Archivist* 36 (1973): 15–32.

Farnham, Charles W. "Lower Court Cases: A Genealogist's Tool." *National Genealogical Society Quarterly* 49 (1961): 200.

Ford, Jeanette W. "Federal Law Comes to Indian Territory." *The Chronicles of Oklahoma* 57 (4) (Winter 1980–81).

Friedman, L. *A History of American Law.* N.p, 1975.

Green, Milton D. *Civil Procedure, Basic.* Mineola, N.Y.: Foundation Press, 1977.

Greenwood, Val D. "Court Records in the United States." *Genealogical Journal* 6 (1977): 159–68.

Haskins, George L. "Court Records and History." *William and Mary Quarterly*, 3rd series, 5 (1948): 547–52.

Jackson, R. *The Machinery of Justice in England.* 6th ed. N.p., 1972.

Jacobstein, J. Myron. "Some Reflections on the Selective Publication of Appellate Court Opinions." *Stanford Law Review* 27 (1975): 791.

Jahnige, Thomas P., and Sheldon Goldman. *The Federal Judicial System.* New York: Holt, 1968.

Johnson, Claudius O. *American State and Local Government.* 4th ed. New York: Thomas Y. Crowell Co., 1965.

Klein, Fannie J. *Federal and State Court Systems: A Guide.* Cambridge: Ballinger Publishers, 1977.

Kunz, Christina L., et al. *The Process of Legal Research.* Boston: Little, Brown, 1986.

Leary, Helen F. M. *North Carolina Research: Genealogy and Local History,* 2nd ed. Raleigh: North Carolina Genealogical Society, 1996.

Maduell, Charles R. "Genealogy from Law Books." *New Orleans Genesis* 9 (1972): 42–43.

Morris, Richard B. *Studies in the History of American Law with Special Reference to the Seventeenth and Eighteenth Centuries.* New York: Columbia University Press, 1930.

Patterson, Edwin W. *Jurisprudence: Men and Ideas of the Law.* Mineola, N.Y.: Foundation Press, 1953.

Pound, Roscoe. *Organization of Courts.* Boston: Little, Brown, and Co., 1940.

Stevenson, Noel. "Genealogical Research in the Law Library." *American Genealogist* 18 (1941): 100–03.

Vanderbilt, Arthur T. *The Challenge of Law Reform.* Princeton, N.J.: Princeton University Press, 1956.

Vanlandingham, T. "The Decline of the Justice of the Peace." *Kansas Law Review* 389 (1964): 380–97.

Zimmerman, Joseph F. *State and Local Government.* New York: Barnes and Noble, 1962.

MILITARY SOURCES OVERVIEW

Key Concepts in This Chapter

- Published military sources provide genealogical, biographical, and historical information.
- Printed original records include service lists and benefits records.
- Compiled records include biographical sources, unit histories, and hereditary society sources.
- Most records for colonial wars are rosters and payment lists.
- Published statewide lists of revolutionary war soldiers are usually incomplete.
- Many loyalist sources identify thousands who remained loyal to England.
- The Civil War continues to generate new and reprinted literature.
- For most states there are published, multi-volume rosters of their Civil War soldiers.
- Unit histories are available for many Civil War regiments.
- Many states have published rosters of their World War I veterans.

Key Sources in This Chapter

- *U.S. Military Records: A Guide to Federal and State Sources*
- *Bibliography of Military Name Lists from Pre-1675 to 1900: A Guide to Genealogical Research*
- *Genealogical Abstracts of Revolutionary War Pension Files*
- *Military Bibliography of the Civil War*
- *Official Records of the Union and Confederate Armies in the War of the Rebellion*
- *Compendium of the War of the Rebellion*
- *Compendium of the Confederate Armies*
- *Confederate Veteran*

13

MILITARY SOURCES

David T. Thackery

Most American genealogists—especially those whose roots in North America predate the twentieth century—have ancestors who participated in one or more of America's military conflicts. The further back one's ancestry goes in North America, the more likely it is that one's pedigree chart will include soldiers or sailors who took part in the Civil War, the War of 1812, the American Revolution, or even the colonial wars.

There is an abundance of printed material devoted to U.S. military history. This chapter concentrates, although not exclusively, on printed works which focus on individual military personnel—or else works which assist the researcher in identifying such titles and which are therefore most likely to be useful. However, researchers must not lose sight of the larger historical context if their research is to be effective and rewarding. To this end, it may be useful to consider the reasons for incorporating military research into family history before discussing the sources themselves. Broadly speaking, military sources can be considered as doing three things for the genealogist: (1) They can provide genealogical information or information that will be directly useful for genealogical research. (2) They can provide biographical information on an ancestor. (3) They provide historical context for the events which shaped our ancestors' lives.

Military Sources as Genealogical Source Material

Genealogical research revolves around the proof of familial relationships. In arriving at such proofs the genealogist usually needs to consider the timeline—or possible timeline—of an ancestor's life. Equally as critical is the identification of the place or places where that person was born, married, had children, and died. Printed military sources pertaining to pensions can prove family relationships; however, military sources are also useful to the genealogist as a means of establishing an ancestor's year of birth and places of residence, thus opening the way to further research in the appropriate local records.

Military Sources as Biographical Material

While the necessity (or perceived necessity) which has resulted in war from ancient times to the present may be deplorable, one cannot deny war's drama or the fact that generation after generation has felt itself defined by the conflicts of its time. Oliver Wendell Holmes declared his generation of Civil War veterans to be "touched with fire," and he was not the only American who would look to his wartime experience as profoundly formative. In this respect, the simple fact of an ancestor's participation in war should be of importance to the family historian who endeavors to reconstruct an ancestor's life in as full and detailed a manner as the sources permit. It is sometimes possible to learn a great deal about an ancestor's military experiences, and when such is the case the family historian will be able to add an important chapter to the biography of that ancestor's life. People of times past did not live on pedigree charts, and the genealogist who fully realizes this will embark on a more rewarding research experience than will the one who loses sight of this simple truth.

Military Sources as Historical Context

Although modern social historians have adopted a different approach, traditional historians addressed their subject matter in broad strokes, focusing on the great events and movements that encompassed the experiences of large groups of people; the only individuals treated tended to be those in leadership positions. The "ordinary person" was not part of the picture.

Family historians run the risk of being on the opposite extreme—trying to piece together ancestors' lives with little knowledge of the context in which those lives were played out. In terms of military sources, some knowledge of the history of an ancestor's regiment or ship and of the campaigns and engagements in which it played a part will help the family historian better to understand an ancestor's military experience. Of course, there are limits as to how far one might wish to go in the quest for historical context; for example, one could spend a lifetime (and some people do) reading about the Civil War. One must be governed by one's inclinations in this regard. Do not lose sight of the fact that there *is* historical context to the lives of our progenitors. One of the more stimulating aspects of family history is that the life of an ancestor can provide a gateway into the study of the broader historical experience. In brief, it is a way to personalize history.

Availability and Accessibility of Sources

Generally speaking, the sources which have broad coverage—especially those which have been published or reprinted in recent years by genealogical publishers—are more readily available in many repositories, while those with very specific coverage (that is, concerning the military history of a particular state, locality, or the experiences of a particular unit) may not be as widely distributed. Even so, increasing numbers of repositories are making their catalogs (in whole or in part) available through the Internet, even as they contribute their cataloging to online networks which can be accessed at many public libraries. By taking advantage of these resources, the researcher can determine what repositories hold titles of interest and can then make plans to visit them or perhaps obtain some titles through interlibrary loan. Of course, many researchers are unable to travel, and therefore write letters of inquiry to repositories; such letters should be concise (do not inquire about half a dozen ancestors from three different military conflicts) and questions should be focused on a particular work, preferably with a complete citation, including author and title. Include a self-addressed, stamped envelope for the response.

Although the great majority of works covered in this chapter are books, the periodical literature is also rich in published military sources. The *Periodical Source Index* (*PERSI*) (Fort Wayne, Ind.: Allen County Public Library Foundation, 1987–), for example (see chapter 19, "Genealogical Periodicals"), includes an index category for military records and narratives. Further, Horowitz's bibliography (discussed below) includes more listings of periodical articles than it does book-length treatments.

CATEGORIES OF PRINTED MILITARY SOURCES

Reference Tools

Reference works seldom answer a specific genealogical query. Rather, they are designed to lead the researcher to those materials which do contain the answers. Reference works are critical to the research process and are so frequently consulted by library patrons that libraries usually do not allow these books to circulate. Several types of reference works are available to the researcher of military genealogy.

Research Guides. Anyone reading this book is probably no stranger to the fact that there has been and will continue to be a great deal of guidance published for the benefit of genealogical researchers. Not surprisingly, some books are better than others, while those that are good are apt to become less useful if they are not updated as the years progress.

Guides to research in particular states or at particular institutions, such as the Library of Congress or the Family History Library of The Church of Jesus Christ of Latter-day Saints (LDS church) in Salt Lake City, usually devote some attention to military sources. A small number of publications are devoted to the research of ancestors in particular conflicts.

One of the more generally useful books to see print in recent years is *U.S. Military Records: A Guide to Federal and State Sources, Colonial America to the Present* (Salt Lake City: Ancestry, 1994), by James C. Neagles. After discussing the types of records available, Neagles guides the researcher through the holdings of the National Archives and other major Federal repositories. He then treats each of the states, first laying out the military holdings of major repositories, such as the state historical society or archive, and then concludes with a bibliography of printed sources pertinent to the state's military history.

For example, the researcher with an interest in Civil War Ohio would discover in Neagles's section on that state that the Ohio Adjutant General published the rosters of its Civil War military organizations in twelve volumes and that a Work Projects Administration index to the entire work was completed in 1938. The researcher would further discover that the original muster-in and muster-out rolls are available on microfilm at the Ohio Historical Society, together with a number of other potentially interesting state record groups.

At least one institutional research guide deserves particular mention: the *Guide to Genealogical Research in the National Archives,* rev. ed. (Washington, D.C.: National Archives Trust Fund Board, 1985). Its treatment of various Federal military record groups is especially important because it indicates which of them is available on microfilm in other repositories outside Washington, D.C. To this end, another National Archives publication, *Military Service Records: A Select Catalog of National Archives Microfilm Publications* (Washington, D.C.: National Archives and Records Service, 1985), may also be useful to the researcher.

Also, for those conducting research at the Family History Library in Salt Lake City or at its constituent family history centers (see the introduction to *Printed Sources*), the Family History Library's introductory booklet *U.S. Military Records Research Outline* (Salt Lake City: Family History Library, 1993) will be especially useful. As with many of the booklets in this series, one does not necessarily have to use the Family History Library network to find this guide helpful.

Another book geared more to "missing persons" research is Richard S. Johnson's *How to Locate Anyone Who Is or Has Been in the Military,* 7th ed. (Houston: Military Information Enterprises, 1996). Compiled primarily for veterans seeking lost comrades, this book may also be helpful if one is researching or seeking a veteran of the middle to late twentieth century.

Bibliographies. Bibliographies (lists of books and other published—sometimes unpublished—research materials concerning a particular subject) are important to historical research. A bibliography may take the form of a book devoted to the literature of a particular war, as with Charles Dornbusch's *Military Bibliography of the Civil War* (described under "Civil War," below), or it may take the form of an appendix to a book or a segment of a book, as with the bibliographic components in Neagles's *U.S. Military Records* (see above). As a researcher becomes more experienced in the research process, he will probably find himself turning ever more frequently to the bibliography which concludes the book or article he is consulting.

After identifying an article or book citation (that is, complete author, title, publisher, and year of publication), the researcher will have taken a significant step forward in research. Instead of making blind inquiries as to whether or not a library has a history of a particular regiment or a transcription of militia rosters from a certain colonial war, the researcher will be able to ask whether or not a repository holds a specific work. By providing a citation to an interlibrary loan librarian or to the reference librarian in an out-of-state library, one can make the answer to a question much easier. The researcher is also armed with the knowledge that such a work exists; all that remains is to find a copy.

An extensive—although by its own admission an uneven—bibliography covering all types of lists of military participants is Lois A. Horowitz's *Bibliography of Military Name Lists from*

Pre-1675 to 1900: A Guide to Genealogical Research (Metuchen, N.J.: Scarecrow Press, 1990). In more than one thousand pages Horowitz marshals 6,656 entries covering books and articles containing muster rolls, lists of military pensioners or prisoners of war, and bounty-land recipients—even, in one instance, a list of local Quakers exempted from military service during the American Revolution. Although it lists many books, the greatest strength of this bibliography is probably its numerous citations to articles culled from approximately 450 periodicals. In some instances the compiler also provides references to lists in the volumes of published state archive series.

The arrangement of Horowitz' work is especially conducive to local genealogical research; citations are arranged chronologically by war and then by state and locality. For example, for militia lists from Berks County, Pennsylvania, during the revolution, go first to the revolutionary war section. Then, after perusing the citations for lists covering Pennsylvania in general, proceed to those covering Berks County in particular.

Horowitz notes in her introduction that she was limited in the resources she could consult and thus makes no declaration of comprehensiveness; however, she does make the modest claim that her bibliography "represents a good beginning," an assertion that no researcher should wish to dispute.

Military "Lineage" Works. Genealogists normally associate the term "lineage" with human descent; however, the term is also applied to the history of military regiments and other organizations. During periods of national crisis, such as the Civil War, the government might raise volunteer regiments, which muster out at the close of hostilities; however, the United States also maintains a professional army, also referred to as the Regular Army, and has done so since the early days of the republic. The regiments and other units of the Regular Army have their own histories, which may include changes in unit designation and affiliation. State national guard units also have their own histories, which link them with the Regular Army in many cases. The lineages and histories of these military units may be of interest if one has an ancestor who served in them. James A. Sawacki's *Infantry Regiments of the U.S. Army* (Dumfries, Va.: Wyvern, 1981) covers the lineage and history of all U.S. infantry regiments which have existed since World War I, regardless of their status at the time of publication. Similar lineage books have been published by the army's Department of Military History; however, their coverage is limited to organizations that were active at the time of publication. Two other reference works covering U.S. army unit histories are John T. Controvich's *United States Army Unit Histories: A Reference and Bibliography* (Manhattan, Kans.: Kansas State University, 1983) and George S. Pappas's *United States Army Unit Histories* (Carlisle Barracks, Pa.: U.S. Army Military History Institute, 1971–78).

The serious researcher may also wish to consult Marvin A. Kreidberg and Morton G. Henry's *History of Military Mobilization in the United States Army, 1775–1945* (Washington, D.C.: Government Printing Office, 1955), for a treatment of military recruitment and organization.

Printed Original Records

Genealogists are interested in military records because they contain information about individual soldiers. We have already seen how research guides and bibliographies can guide you to sources containing such information. These printed materials can take one of three forms: transcriptions, abstracts, or indexes. A transcription is the publication of the complete record, while an abstract is the summary of what its compiler considers the most important information. Failing the availability of published transcriptions or abstracts, a published index is the next best thing; it will at least provide a citation for an original record when the time comes to view the original on microfilm or to request a copy from the appropriate archive.

Service Records and Lists. In the colonial era, when all able-bodied men from grandfathers to grandsons might be expected to serve in the militia to meet some local emergency, the sense of who might be of "military age" was far less exclusive than it is today. But with the development of large national armies that might be expected to serve in extended campaigns far away from home, the military establishment discouraged older recruits who might not be physically fit, while those who were "underage" (usually under eighteen) were also excluded, especially when the military threat to the community was not immediate. By the time of the Civil War, recruiters were instructed to ask the age of enlistees, although the question did not necessarily guarantee a truthful answer.

Military rosters showing the ages of recruits can therefore be important to the genealogist. Such a roster might be the only source for an ancestor's birth year. Conversely, the reported age of a soldier at enlistment might enable one to distinguish among several soldiers of the same name. For example, say a genealogist knows that an ancestor, Peter Black, served in the Union army during the Civil War from a particular state but does not know his unit; unfortunately, a dozen Peter Blacks served from that state in the Civil War. The genealogist wishes to send to the National Archives for copies of Peter Black's pension file, but does not know which Peter Black is the correct one. By consulting the published rosters for that state, the genealogist, who knows Peter Black's year of birth, may be able to narrow his search down to two or three (or maybe one) candidates.

Militia rosters from the colonial era can be useful for a different reason. Companies were organized locally, so the identification of an ancestor in a particular company will often establish his place of residence, thus guiding the researcher to the records for that area.

Many military lists and rosters have been published in printed form over the years. Horowitz' bibliography (discussed earlier) can provide an entry point into many published rosters, often in obscure sources; however, in the discussion of particular wars which forms the latter portion of this chapter, the focus is on the more important published lists and rosters. Many veterans from a given state who served in a particular war are listed in rosters published by state adjutant general's offices.

Veterans' Benefits Records. The most genealogically useful class of all military sources arises from the U.S. government's establishment of pensions—not only for veterans but for widows and other surviving family members. Pension records have great genealogical value insofar as they contain proofs of relationship arising from the application for benefits on the part of a veteran's widow, children, or even parents. While one should view these records in their manuscript format, published abstracts and indexes to pension files can assist the family historian in identifying and accessing the original records. Fortunately, there are a number of pension publications encompassing lists, abstracts, and indexes covering veterans' pension files.

Another class of records arises from the award of bounty lands to veterans. Although they are not generally as useful as the pension records, genealogists often discover uses for bounty-land records. Some lists and indexes are in print.

Grave Records. Listings of veterans' graves often see print. Hereditary societies that trace descent from ancestors in the American Revolution or perhaps the War of 1812 are often especially concerned with identifying the graves of veterans from "their" war which are found in their locality or state. Similar interests on the part of state historical or genealogical societies may produce the same results, while government agencies may also undertake surveys of all veterans' graves. In some states the Federal Work Projects Administration undertook such surveys. A similar example may also be found in Illinois, where the Veterans' Commission published a multi-volume *Honor Roll* in 1956 for all veterans buried in the state (unfortunately, not every county was included in the project).

A number of national cemeteries have been set aside as final resting places for veterans. If contemplating a visit to one of them, one may wish to consult Dean W. Holt's *American Military Cemeteries: A Comprehensive Illustrated Guide to the Hallowed Grounds of the United States, Including Cemeteries Overseas* (Jefferson, N.C.: McFarland, 1992).

Soldiers' Writings. Soldiers often wrote about their military experiences in a private capacity, and as a population's general literacy increased, servicemen were more likely to generate such writings. In years following the conflict their diaries or letters might be published in book form—at their own initiative, by their family or descendants, or by unrelated researchers who come upon their work in an archive or published in a local newspaper. Those veterans who were more consciously literate might even compose their memoirs for publication (although such works may not be as historically trustworthy as diaries and journals produced at the time of the events under consideration). For the genealogist whose ancestor produced such writings their value is obvious; however, such ancestors are rare. The value of such works for the family historian lies more often in the possibility that a comrade from an ancestor's unit or ship may have written such a work. In such instances the researcher may learn more about the experiences of his or her military ancestor and may even find some mention of him.

Compiled Records

Biographical Sources. One can often find in a research library biographical dictionaries covering prominent or semi-prominent military men of particular conflicts, or similar works listing Regular Army and navy men over much of U.S. history.

Most genealogists with ancestors in the military will not be researching regular officers in the standing military; however, those who are will find a starting point in Francis B. Heitman's *Historical Register and Dictionary of the United States Army, from its Organization, September 29, 1789 to March 2, 1903* (Washington, D.C.: Government Printing Office, 1903). Other related titles are listed in the bibliography at the end of this chapter.

Occasionally available are comprehensive biographical works dealing with the veterans from a locality who served in a particular conflict. As often as not, such works are concerned with revolutionary war veterans. For example, there are a number of such publications for New York counties, such as Isabel Bracy's *Records of Revolutionary War Veterans Who Lived in Madison County, New York* (Interlaken, N.Y.: Heart of the Lakes, 1988). Less common are biographical registers for soldiers of particular units, such as Frank N. Schubert's *On the Trail of the Buffalo Soldier* (see the discussion of "Indian Wars," below).

Unit Histories. As with published soldiers' writings, unit histories can be of great interest to the family historian. It is sometimes possible to find specific reference to an ancestor in a history written about his unit; but even if that is not the case, the account of his unit's service usually provides context to the details that might be garnered about an ancestor's military service from a government service record or pension file. Information about an ancestor's death in combat or from wounds or disease or of his bad health as a result of service will be more meaningful if one fully understands the circumstances surrounding his experiences. A unit history provides that context and may take the form of a three hundred-page book, a two- or three-page account in an adjutant general's report, or a short entry in a reference work. Regardless of length, the researcher who consults such a history is closer to integrating the life of an ancestor into the world which surrounded him.

Hereditary Societies. Hereditary, or lineage, societies abound. Membership in them is based on proven descent from an ancestor who meets certain criteria—participated in a particular military conflict, for example. Thus, there are societies for descendants of soldiers in the colonial wars, the American Revolution, the War of 1812, etc. The national or state organizations of such societies often publish lineage books—books that detail the descents of their members from appropriate ancestors. Such societies sometimes also publish lists of "approved" ancestors from whom present or potential members might descend.

A SELECTIVE SURVEY OF PUBLISHED SOURCES FOR THE MAJOR CONFLICTS

The more important published sources concerning particular wars and the veterans of those wars are discussed in this section. Bear in mind that this chapter can only provide an introduction to military research for genealogists. For more detail, consult Neagles' *U.S. Military Records* (cited earlier), as well as the various bibliographies and guides highlighted below.

Colonial Wars

The American colonies were frequently embroiled in wars with the Native Americans and with the French. Perhaps the best known is the last of these wars, the so-called French and Indian War (1754 to 1763), concerning which one might wish to consult James G. Lydon's *Struggle for Empire: A Bibliography of the French and Indian War* (New York: Garland, 1986). The "Military Organizations" chapter cites regimental histories and muster rolls, including those from periodicals. For historical background, Douglas E. Leach's *Arms for Empire: A Military History of the American Colonies in North America, 1607–1763* (New York: Macmillan, 1973) is useful.

Records from the French and Indian War and from the earlier colonial wars usually take the form of roster or pay lists and, occasionally, bounty lists. As previously noted, the genealogical research value of these lists lies primarily in their placing of a colonial soldier in a certain place at a certain time. Militia groups under a particular captain were probably made up of near neighbors.

Some such lists have been printed as parts of published state archive series (see chapter 15, "Documentary Collections." They may also have been published separately or as an appendix to a historical narrative. The earliest such instance is George M. Bodge's *Soldiers in King Philip's War: Being a Critical Account of That War, with a Concise History of the Indian Wars of New England from 1620–1677* (Leominster, Mass.: the author, 1896; reprint; Baltimore: Genealogical Publishing Co., 1967), which contains several soldier lists from Massachusetts and Connecticut. Since then, the Society of Colonial Wars in the Commonwealth of Massachusetts and the New England Historic Genealogical Society have published Massachusetts militia lists for these wars through the French and Indian War, which are listed in the bibliography at the close of this chapter. Virginia is also well covered in this regard by Lloyd DeWitt Bockstruck's *Virginia's Colonial Soldiers* (Baltimore: Genealogical Publishing Co., 1988); its compilation required the consultation of numerous archival and printed sources.

Like many other hereditary societies, the Society of Colonial Wars has published its lineage records. In 1922 it brought out its first index of ancestors and rolls of members, together with a section detailing the services of members during World War I. Since then the society has published two supplements (see this chapter's bibliography). Many state societies of the Society of Colonial Wars have also launched similar publications.

Revolutionary War

Bibliographies. For the serious researcher, the most comprehensive bibliography on the American Revolution is Ronald M. Gephart's two-volume *Revolutionary America 1763–1789: A Bibliography* (Washington, D.C.: Library of Congress, 1984). Although it will not, of course, reflect publications after 1984, there is no more thorough bibliographic treatment of what was published up until 1984, including citations from periodicals and series. Soldier lists and unit histories are listed in the section titled "The States and the Revolution."

General History and Personal Narratives. A perusal of Gephart's bibliography reveals the great scope of publishing on the revolution. For a general history, perhaps the most accessible scholarly introduction to the subject in a single volume is Robert Middlekauf's *The Glorious Cause: The American Revolution 1763–1789* (New York: Oxford University Press, 1982). It is the second volume in the *Oxford History of the United States* (hence the title's range of years, which predate and postdate the actual revolution). Military operations in particular are well covered in Page Smith's two-volume *A New Age Now Begins: A People's History of the American Revolution* (New York: McGraw-Hill, 1976). There are also innumerable books dealing with particular battles and campaigns, leaders, and the progress of the revolutionary movement in particular states. The social history of the war is covered in two works: Charles Patrick Neimeyer's *America Goes to War: A Social History of the Continental Army* (New York: New York University Press, 1996) and Holly A. Mayer's *Belonging to the Army: Camp Followers and Community During the American Revolution* (Los Angeles: University of Southern California Press, 1996).

Genealogists may also find special sympathy with John C. Dann's *The Revolution Remembered: Eyewitness Accounts of the War for Independence* (Chicago: University of Chicago Press, 1980), which consists of narratives found in revolutionary war pension files. Personal narratives of a different sort are found in the series Eyewitness Accounts of the American Revolution (New York: New York Times and Arno Press, 1968–71), which reprints material from a variety of published sources.

Unit Histories. There are not many published regimental histories for the American Revolution. Once again, Gephart's bibliography may be useful to genealogists in this regard, especially in identifying shorter histories which have appeared in periodicals. Even so, such histories continue to be published on occasion—works such as T. W. Egley's *History of the First New York Regiment 1775–1783* (Hampton, N.H.: Peter Randall, 1981) and the more genealogically oriented *The German Regiment of Maryland and Pennsylvania in the Continental Army 1776–1781* (Westminster, Md.: Family Line, 1991), by Henry J. Retzer. If an ancestor served in the Continental Army, as distinct from militia organizations, one might also wish to consult Fred A. Berg's *Encyclopedia of Continental Army Units, Battalions, Regiments, and Independent Corps* (Harrisburg, Pa.: Stackpole, 1972), which provides brief organizational sketches and identifies the commanding officers of Continental units. Also, Robert K. Wright's *The Continental Army* (Washington, D.C.: United States Army Center of Military History, 1983) features short histories of permanent units in the Continental Army. Wright's historical treatments are generally more detailed than Berg's, and the bibliographies are especially helpful.

Soldier Lists. There is no comprehensive listing for all who fought in the patriot cause; nor is there ever likely to be one. The only list in print that comes close is Virgil D. White's *Index to Revolutionary War Service Records* (Waynesboro, Tenn.: National Historical Publishing Co., 1996), which is a transcription of the National Archives record group (M860) that indexes the service records held there. This record group is far from comprehensive; for example, many soldiers from militia organizations are not included. In all of the original thirteen states there has been some attempt to publish lists of soldiers from each state who served in the revolution. Although they vary in terms of comprehensiveness, detail, and overall quality, these state lists should be consulted in addition to the index to compiled service records. A selected list of such state titles is included in the bibliography which concludes this chapter.

Interestingly enough, one genealogical index series, *The American Genealogical-Biographical Index to American Genealogical, Biographical and Local History Materials* (Middletown, Conn.: Godfrey Memorial Library, 1952–), indexes several of these state lists, and can effectively act as a master index to them. For example, it indexes the seventeen-volume *Massachusetts Soldiers and Sailors of the Revolutionary War* (Boston: Wright & Potter, 1896–1908), John H. Gwathmey's *Historical Register of Virginians in the Revolution: Soldiers, Sailors, Marines: 1775–1783* (Richmond, Va.: Dietz Press, 1938; reprint; Baltimore: Genealogical Publishing Co., 1973), and the North Carolina Daughters of the American Revolution's *Roster of Soldiers from North Carolina in the American Revolution: With an Appendix Containing a Collection of Miscellaneous Papers* (Durham, N.C.: Daughters of the

American Revolution, 1932; reprint; Baltimore: Genealogical Publishing Co., 1972).

Another source is *Pierce's Register* (reprint; Baltimore: Genealogical Publishing Co., 1973), which was originally published in 1915 as a government document. It indexes the final 1783 payment records of John Pierce, the paymaster general for the Continental Army. Though far from comprehensive, it is an important source which can confirm a revolutionary war ancestor's service.

Some other published service lists deserve mention. If there is a possibility that a revolutionary war ancestor died during the war, the book to consult is Clarence S. Peterson's *Known Military Dead During the American Revolutionary War 1775–1783* (reprint; Baltimore: Genealogical Publishing Co., 1967). Although many sailors of the revolution are covered in the various state publications, Marion J. and Jack Kaminkow's *Mariners of the American Revolution* (Baltimore: Magna Carta Book Co., 1967) should also be consulted in researching American seamen. Documentation for these men, especially for those sailing as privateers, is generally more sparse than for soldiers. Based largely on British prisoner records, the Kaminkows' work probably documents many sailors who are not represented in other published lists or indexes. Charles E. Claghorn's *Naval Officers of the American Revolution: A Concise Biographical Dictionary* (Metuchen, N.J.: Scarecrow Press, 1988) provides coverage on the other end of the spectrum.

Daughters of the American Revolution. The best known of the hereditary societies based on descent from a revolutionary war ancestor is the Daughters of the American Revolution (DAR). This society has also been an active publisher. Probably its most important contribution to Revolutionary War genealogy is the current "centennial edition" of the *Patriot Index* (Washington: DAR, 1994) in three volumes. It is a list of patriots compiled from approved membership applications and various published works. Again, it is not a comprehensive listing of all revolutionary war patriots. Also note that it is a revised edition; therefore, names have not only been added to the list but in some cases have been removed when it was determined that the documentation for a particular name was questionable, even though the research was once thought acceptable.

It is well that the organization is exercising more critical attention in this direction, because questionable genealogy is found in some of the earlier volumes of the DAR *Lineage Books* (1890–1921), which present a line of descent from revolutionary war patriots to society members over a period of a little more than three decades. The indexing is to the ancestor and not the member, which is unfortunate from the perspective of some researchers, who may know that a grandmother or great-grandmother belonged to the DAR without knowing the identity of the revolutionary war ancestor. If the indexing were to the member, the researcher's goal could be realized, but that is not the case, and he or she is left with 166 volumes to contemplate. Even so, the *Lineage Books* are yet another stop in the investigation of revolutionary war ancestry.

Another set derived from DAR publications is Patricia Law Hatcher's four-volume *Abstract of Graves of Revolutionary Patriots* (Dallas: Pioneer Heritage Press, 1987–88), which brings together data published in the DAR's annual reports and the *DAR Magazine.*

Many DAR state organizations have published their own lineage records and membership rolls; however, note that these publications concern DAR members residing in the state at the time of publication and do not necessarily reflect descent from patriots who were living in the state.

Other hereditary societies based on descent from revolutionary war soldiers include Sons of the American Revolution, Sons of the Revolution, and the Society of the Cincinnati. The national and state organizations of these societies have also generated publications which may be helpful to genealogists.

Pensions and Other Compensations. As a class, pension papers are probably the most genealogically useful of U.S. military records. Pension files can document an ancestor's family relationships as well as his military experience, in addition to his whereabouts and movements following military service.

Revolutionary pension records' coverage of individuals and families in the late eighteenth through early nineteenth centuries is especially fortunate from a genealogical perspective. In this period families were highly mobile, while local governmental record-keeping, especially on the frontier, was often not as thorough as it would be in later years. Genealogical difficulties are further compounded by the fact that the Federal census would not enumerate all members of free households by name until 1850.

A fire in the War Department destroyed most revolutionary war records in 1800, and many of the early revolutionary war pension files were lost when the British burned Washington, D.C., during the War of 1812. Consequently, the majority of the surviving pension records pertain to veterans who may not have qualified for a government pension until Congress passed the first comprehensive pension act for all revolutionary war veterans in 1832. The act required that to receive a pension veterans should have served a minimum of six months and that they should produce testimony and proof of service in a court of law. Because official documentation of the veteran's service may have been sparse or nonexistent, it was in the applicant's best interest to be as detailed as possible in his recollections. As one historian has noted, "the pension application process was one of the largest oral history projects ever undertaken" (Dann 1980, xvii). In addition to these sometimes detailed recollections, the documentation provided by family members having to prove their relationship to a veteran makes these files an especially promising resource for the family historian.

An index to these files by pensioner, *Index to Revolutionary War Pension Applications in the National Archives* (Arlington, Va.: National Genealogical Society, 1976), was published in celebration of the national bicentennial and is available in many libraries; however, it has been essentially superseded by Virgil D. White's four-volume *Genealogical Abstracts of Revolutionary War Pension Files* (Waynesboro, Tenn.: National Historical Publishing Co., 1990–92). Especially useful is an all-name index that enables one to locate individuals other than the pensioner who are mentioned in the files. Some entries in this work cross-reference records concerning Federal bounty lands, as well as various state pensions and claims.

One example illustrates the value of these records and of White's abstracts, in which there is a listing for a William Brooks, who served in the Virginia Line. The abstracts indicate that he lived in Culpeper County, Virginia, during the war and for about three years following it, after which he went to Rutherford County, North Carolina, where his wife died. He had four sons and one daughter, all of whom are named in the abstracts. Brooks died while visiting his son in Fairfield District, South Carolina.

Also mentioned are his daughter, Susannah Chedester, who was around eighty-seven years old and living in Greene County, Tennessee, in 1857—and her eldest son, James B. Chedester, who was forty-six in the same year (White 1990, 404). Here is genealogical information spanning three generations over four states. The value of the published abstracts in particular becomes clearer in view of the fact that there were ten William Brooks pension files, making the abstracts a major research aid and time saver.

The Federal government kept track of revolutionary war pensioners with periodic enumerations and lists that have been reprinted in recent years as Murtie June Clark's *Pension Lists of 1792–1795* (Baltimore: Genealogical Publishing Co., 1991), *Pension List of 1820* (Baltimore: Genealogical Publishing Co., 1991), and the four-volume *Pension Roll of 1835* (Baltimore: Genealogical Publishing Co., 1992). Pensioners were also specifically enumerated as part of the 1840 Federal census, and the resulting list was published as a government document in 1841; it shows name, age, pensioner's residence, and name of the head of the household in which the pensioner was living. It has since been reprinted as *A Census of Pensioners for Revolutionary or Military Service* (Baltimore: Genealogical Publishing Co., 1967).

Following the war, many civilians received compensation for contributions they made to the revolutionary military effort. These records have gradually been coming into print—for example, Dorothy A. Stratford and Thomas B. Wilson's *Certificates and Receipts of Revolutionary New Jersey* (Lambertville, N.J.: Hunterdon House, 1996) and Janice L. Abercrombie's three-volume *Virginia Publick Claims* (Athens, Ga.: Iberian Publishing Co., 1992). The listings in the latter set are also available in separate county volumes.

Bounty lands were also offered to revolutionary war veterans by Federal and state governments. As already mentioned, Virgil White's pension abstracts can offer an entry point into the Federal bounties, while the more recently published *Revolutionary War Bounty Land Grants Awarded by State Governments* (Baltimore: Genealogical Publishing Co., 1996), compiled by Lloyd DeWitt Bockstruck, provides coverage for all state bounty-land grants to revolutionary war veterans.

Loyalists. It has been estimated that one-third of the colonists remained loyal to the crown during the revolution. In some states the proportion was probably greater than a third and in others less. Many of these loyalists served alongside the British, fighting against their fellow colonists. Many fled—or were driven from—the United States after the war and settled in Canada, while others returned to Great Britain or made new homes in other British colonies. Others decided to make their peace with the new political reality and remained. Of those who left, some returned to the United States. Some of the descendants of those who remained in Canada eventually gravitated south and west in the pioneering movement which embraced both sides of the border. Given these facts, it should not be surprising that there are many in the United States with Loyalist ancestry.

The genealogist with a Loyalist background is fortunate in having a number of published works to draw upon. Gregory Palmer's *Bibliography of Loyalist Source Material in the United States, Canada and Great Britain* (Westport, Conn.: Meckler, 1982) is an important reference aid for anyone undertaking Loyalist research, while his *Biographical Sketches of Loyalists of the American Revolution* (Westport, Conn.: Meckler, 1984) consists of information extracted from Loyalist claim records and will excite the appreciation of any genealogist fortunate enough to find an ancestor included in its pages. Palmer's *Biographical Sketches* also functions as something of a successor volume to an older biographical dictionary, Lorenzo Sabine's *Biographical Sketches of the American Revolution* (reprint; Baltimore: Genealogical Publishing Co., 1979), although it should be emphasized that many individuals treated in Sabine's work are not included in Palmer's, and vice versa.

Among the Loyalist refugees were a significant number of slaves who responded to the British government's promise of emancipation in exchange for their loyalty. Many of them settled in Canada. The most comprehensive list of these Loyalists is Graham R. Hodges's *The Black Loyalist Directory: African Americans in Exile after the American Revolution* (New York: Garland, in association with the New England Historic Genealogical Society, 1996).

As for Loyalist soldier lists, the most extensive publication is Murtie Jane Clark's *Loyalists in the Southern Campaign of the Revolutionary War* (Baltimore: Genealogical Publishing Co., 1981). Genealogists with Loyalist ancestry in New England or the Mid-Atlantic states should not dismiss this work, because many Loyalist units from the Northeast were in fact deployed in the southern campaign. Philip R. Katcher's *Encyclopedia of British, Provincial and German Army Units 1775–1783* (Harrisburg, Pa.: Stackpole Books, 1973) provides brief historical sketches for Loyalist units.

Following the war, the British government was not unmindful of the Loyalist refugees' plight and implemented a program of partial compensation for losses suffered as a consequence of their adherence to the crown. A royal commission reviewed thousands of cases between 1783 and 1790, and payments were eventually made to successful claimants. These claims are documented in three published works based on three sets of records held in the Public Record Office and, surprisingly, the Library of Congress. Although there is some overlap among the three groups, all three should be consulted. The three published works are: *United Empire Loyalists: Enquiry into the Losses and Services in Consequence of Their Loyalty: Evidence in Canadian Claims* (Toronto, 1905), W. Bruce Antliff's *Loyalist Settlements 1783–1789: New Evidence of Canadian Loyalist Claims* (Toronto: Ministry of Citizenship and Culture, 1985), and Peter W. Coldham's *American Loyalist Claims* (Washington, D.C.: National Genealogical Society, 1980). In Coldham's work, for example, is the summary of the claim of John Miller of Fish Kill, Dutchess County, New York, who

> left home Aug. 1776 and joined Army at Newtown, Long Island. Was appointed Lt. in Royal American Regt. and was at storming of Fort Montgomery; served as Capt. in the defense of blockhouse at Fort Lee and bore arms until the peace. . . . (1980, 346)

His claim for the loss of five hundred acres, a house, cattle, etc., was rejected for unknown reasons.

In an effort to honor the Loyalists who had settled in Canada, the governor general ordered that a list of "United Empire Loyalists" be compiled. The list was closed in 1798 but was not published until 1885; it has since been reprinted as *The Old United Empire Loyalists' List* (Baltimore: Genealogical Publishing Co., 1969). It is a parallel to the DAR's *Patriot Index,* although, unlike the DAR list, it is frozen and cannot be revised or augmented. Hence, any errors contained in it will not be corrected.

For many Canadians, Loyalist descent is considered a mark of honor. Consequently, there is a published series of Loyalist lineages which has so far yielded but a few volumes, but which is worth noting: *Loyalist Lineages of Canada* (Toronto: Generation Press, 1984–). Finally, another title which acts as a master index to a number of Loyalist sources is Paul J. Bunnell's two-volume *The New Loyalist Index* (Bowie, Md.: Heritage, 1989, 1996).

German Soldiers. The British crown was allied with a number of German states and principalities, and consequently it deployed approximately twenty-five thousand German soldiers against the rebellious colonists. These soldiers were called "Hessians"; however, they were not all from the Hesse region. Their morale was often poor, and many deserted to make a new life in America. The Marburg Archives in Germany initiated a roster project for these soldiers and published *Hessische Truppen im Amerikanischen Unabhängigkeitskrieg* (Marburg, Germany: Institut für Archivwissenschaft, 1972), known as the HETRINA lists. Arthur C. M. Kelly has since published these lists in five volumes as *Hessian Troops in the American Revolution: Extracts from the HETRINA* (Rhinebeck, N.Y.: Kinship, 1991–95).

War of 1812

The only genealogist's guide to the War of 1812 is George K. Schweitzer's *War of 1812 Genealogy* (Knoxville, Tenn.: the author, 1983), which provides a basic introduction to the history of the conflict and its records. Probably the most comprehensive bibliography on the war is Dwight La Vern Smith's *War of 1812: An Annotated Bibliography* (New York: Garland, 1985), which includes citations from several Canadian publications.

Very little has been published on the history of the War of 1812 in recent years, although (not surprisingly) a great deal more was published in the nineteenth century, particularly concerning the naval war, which captured the imaginations of many Americans. Even so, a few historical treatments of campaigns and battles have been published recently. For a reasonably detailed overall treatment of the war see Donald A. Hickey's *The War of 1812: A Forgotten Conflict* (Chicago: University of Illinois, 1989), while an overview of the land war is found in George F. G. Stanley's *War of 1812 Land Operations* (Ottawa: National Museums of Canada, 1983). Reginald Horsman's *The War of 1812* (New York: Alfred A. Knopf, 1969) also provides a general introduction to the conflict.

There is no published index to the compiled service records of War of 1812 volunteers; however, there are a number of published lists which cover the servicemen of the war by state. One of the better such compilations of recent years is F. Edward Wright's eight-volume *Maryland Militia, War of 1812* (Silver Spring, Md.: Family Line, 1979–92). An especially helpful guide for Virginia researchers is Stuart Lee Butler's *Guide to Virginia Militia Units in the War of 1812* (Athens, Ga.: Iberian Publishing Co., 1988). Ideally, similar guides will be generated for other states. American dead are covered by Clarence S. Peterson in *Known Military Dead During the War of 1812* (Baltimore: the author, 1955).

Pensions were not quickly granted to War of 1812 veterans. Congress approved a pension benefit in 1871, but it was a very restricted benefit and few veterans or their widows could qualify. However, in 1878 Congress declared that any War of 1812 veteran who had seen at least fourteen days' service could qualify, as could his widow; by this time the number of veterans and widows had considerably diminished. The National Archives index to these records (M313) has been transcribed by Virgil D. White in his three-volume *Index to War of 1812 Pension Files*, rev. ed., 2 vols. (Waynesboro, Tenn.: National Historical Publishing Co., 1990–92). The index also encompasses bounty-land warrants for War of 1812 veterans, who were eligible for land grants in Illinois, Missouri, and Arkansas. Publications covering bounty-land grants in these three states are included in this chapter's bibliography.

Mexican War

For the reader seeking a general introduction to the Mexican War, John S. D. Eisenhower's *So Far from God: the U.S. War with Mexico 1846–1848* (New York: Random House, 1989) is a good choice. James M. McCaffrey's *Army of Manifest Destiny: The American Soldier in the Mexican War, 1846–1848* (New York: New York University Press, 1992) is a social history of the American military experience and features a very helpful bibliography, including references to many manuscript collections.

Norman E. Tutorow's *The Mexican-American War: An Annotated Bibliography* (Westport, Conn.: Greenwood, 1981) provides general coverage of books and periodicals. Elizabeth R. Snoke's *The Mexican War: A Bibliography of MHRC Holdings for the Period, 1835–1850* (Carlisle Barracks, Pa.: U.S. Army Military History Institute, 1973) may also provide some helpful citations, although it is based on the holdings of a single institution. Some states have published rosters of their servicemen who participated in the Mexican War, sometimes combined with the publication of roster lists for the Civil War (as was the case, for example, in Ohio) or with roster lists for wars that came before the Mexican War (as in Connecticut). Many Mexican War veterans served in the Civil War or were in the various Indian wars as Regular Army soldiers; if they received pensions, it was not for their Mexican War service but for serving in other conflicts. Even so, many Mexican War veterans received pensions for their service in the years 1846 to 1848. The index to the pension applications has been transcribed from National Archives microfilm (T317) and published as *An Index to Mexican War Pension Applications* (Indianapolis: Heritage House, 1985). Virgil D. White has also transcribed and published this index. American dead from this war are listed in Clarence S. Peterson's *Known Military Dead During the Mexican War, 1846–48* (Baltimore: the author, 1957).

Civil War

The American Civil War probably exerts more fascination over the general public than does any other conflict in American history. It was a well-documented conflict, with a high proportion of literate (though some of them barely so) combatants. Consequently, the war has generated a great deal of published works, and the demand is such that the flood of print shows no sign of abating. The researcher with access to a good genealogical library will find it increasingly easier to identify a Civil War ancestor and to learn about the experiences of his military unit (and perhaps, by extension, about the ancestor's experiences as well).

Research Guides. The revised edition of Bertram H. Groene's *Tracing Your Civil War Ancestor,* 4th ed. (Winston-Salem, N.C.: John F. Blair, 1995) is a personable and well-written introduction to Civil War research. He frequently employs examples of research problems he has encountered to good effect. Also potentially helpful is George K. Schweitzer's *Civil War Genealogy: A Basic Research Guide for Tracing Your Civil War Ancestors* (Knoxville, Tenn.: the author, 1980). For general coverage of repositories, James C. Neagles's *U.S. Military Records* (cited earlier) is still the best source, while the *Guide to Genealogical Research in the National Archives* (cited earlier) probably provides the best overview of basic Federal records pertaining to Civil War soldiers. But Federal records obviously do not tell the entire story when it comes to Confederate research; genealogists with Confederate ancestry will likely find useful Neagles's *Confederate Research Sources: A Guide to Archive Collections*, rev. ed. (Salt Lake City: Ancestry, 1997). Although some of the coverage in this guide may be duplicated in *U.S. Military Records,* researchers with a strong interest in Confederate research may find it more convenient to consult this more focused work. Another introduction to Confederate research is J. H. Segars's *In Search of Confederate Ancestors: The Guide,* vol. 9 in the Journal of Confederate History Series (Murfreesboro, Tenn.: Southern Heritage Press, 1993).

Bibliographies. The most frequently consulted Civil War bibliography is Charles E. Dornbusch's three-volume *Military Bibliography of the Civil War* (New York: New York Public Library, 1961–72). A supplemental volume was published in 1987. For the genealogist the most useful section is the one covering unit histories and personal narratives (published journals, memoirs, and letters). This component, which comprises the bulk of the bibliography, is organized by state. Each state listing begins with titles having statewide significance, such as state roster lists. They are followed by citations for regimental and other unit histories, as well as published personal narratives arranged first by arm of service (artillery, cavalry, infantry) and then by unit. For example, if one is interested in the Fifty-fourth Massachusetts Volunteer Infantry (the subject of the movie *Glory*), consulting Dornbusch reveals first of all that the Massachusetts adjutant general published roster lists for all state regiments, so a roster for the Fifty-fourth is available in that format. The regimental listings would then reveal a citation for Luis F. Emilio's *History of the Fifty-Fourth Regiment of the Massachusetts Volunteer Infantry 1863–1865* (Boston: Boston Book, 1891). In other instances, one might discover that Dornbusch does not list anything for a unit; however, bear in mind that, even since the publication of the supplemental volume in 1987, a great deal of Civil War regimental history and personal narrative has found its way into print. Therefore, the lack of a Dornbusch citation for a particular unit does not rule out the possibility that something has been published concerning it in recent years.

Dornbusch embarked upon his task to correct and update the *Bibliography of State Participation in the Civil War* (Washington, D.C.: Government Printing Office, 1913). This government publication cites local histories containing lists of Civil War soldiers, a bibliographic category ignored by Dornbusch. In addition, the serious researcher might appreciate the more detailed and comprehensive treatment accorded both state and Federal official publications in this earlier work.

Many genealogists become interested in the Civil War as a result of discovering a Civil War ancestor and begin to read more widely on the subject, in part to further contextualize a forebear's experience. However, when confronted with the vast array of Civil War literature, a beginning researcher might feel overwhelmed. What are the best books on a given battle? Is there a definitive biography for a particular Civil War general? These sorts of questions may be answered by consulting David J. Eicher's *The Civil War in Books: An Analytical Bibliography* (Champaign: University of Illinois, 1996), which covers 1,100 titles critical to the study of the Civil War.

Miscellaneous Reference. Not all researchers have ready access to published unit histories or state rosters; however, it is somewhat more likely that they will find in a library—or may be able to purchase—reference works which provide a brief overview of a regiment's service. On the Federal side is Frederick Dyer's classic *Compendium of the War of the Rebellion* (Des Moines, Iowa: the author, 1908), which is also available in reprint. For each Union regiment and battery the *Compendium* provides the basic facts: dates and places of organization and mustering out, a brief account of its career covering every day of service (in addition to battles and campaigns, dates and places of encampment and garrison duty, etc.), and total number of casualties, together with an account of brigade, division, and corps affiliation. For the beginning researcher, an entry in Dyer's work can be a good starting point.

Stewart Sifakis's *Compendium of the Confederate Armies* (New York: Facts on File, 1992–) provides coverage for Confederate units similar to Dyer's for the Federals.

Occasionally one may encounter unofficial names for military units. These might be half-humorous sobriquets; more often, they refer to a unit's commanding officer. Because research on an ancestor's military career depends upon the identification of his unit, it is important to be able to translate these local usages into an official military designation. The reference work which accomplishes this match for both Union and Confederate units is a two-volume set entitled (rather non-descriptively) *Personnel of the Civil War* (New York: Yoseloff, 1961). For example, consulting this work reveals that a Massachusetts unit called "Kent's Independent Fighting Company" was in fact Company G of the Sixtieth Militia Infantry, while a reference to a unit called the "Lincoln hunters" was to Company E of the Twenty-sixth Virginia Infantry.

The 128 volumes of the *Official Records of the Union and Confederate Armies in the War of the Rebellion* (Washington, D.C.: Government Printing Office, 1880–1900) (usually referred to simply as the *OR*), form the bedrock for Civil War research. The researcher can follow an engagement's progress—and of the part an ancestor's regiment may have played in it—through the reports of regimental, brigade, and division commanders.[1] Even so, do not expect to find an ancestor mentioned in the *OR* unless he was an officer, because it consists of official reports and correspondence. In any event, there is a master index to the entire set. The original edition was widely distributed and is found in many research libraries. In addition, the set has been reprinted by Broadfoot Publishing (Wilmington, North Carolina), an important Civil War publisher, substantially increasing its availability.

Making use of the *Official Records* can be a challenge; Alan C. and Barbara A. Aimone's *User's Guide to the Official Records of the American Civil War* (Shippensburg, Pa.: White Mane, 1993) may be helpful to some researchers. The entire *Official Records,* as well as subsets of the *Official Records* dealing with particular campaigns, have been released on CD-ROM. Broadfoot is also publishing a multi-volume *Supplement to the Official Records of the Union and Confederate Armies in the War of the Rebellion*(1994–) that includes reports and correspondence which escaped inclusion in the *OR,* in addition to the National Archives' *Compiled Records Showing Service of Military Units in Volunteer Union Organizations* (M594), together with a parallel record group for Confederate units (M861), both often referred to simply as the "record of events." Before leaving the realm of the *Official Records,* note the existence of its counterpart, the thirty-one volume *Official Records of the Union and Confederate Navies in the War of the Rebellion* (Washington, D.C.: Government Printing Office, 1894–1922).

Two other reference works deserve mention. The best single-volume reference work to the war is still Mark M. Boatner, 3rd, *Civil War Dictionary,* rev. ed. (New York: Vintage, 1987), which is made up of concise articles covering battles, campaigns, biography, and other subjects. A more recent publication, the four-volume *Encyclopedia of the Confederacy,* edited by Richard N. Current (New York: Simon and Schuster, 1993), provides lengthier articles covering the same range of subjects, although, of course, it is limited to the Confederacy. Neither work includes much unit history.

Histories. There is no lack of Civil War histories. Of the general histories, three in particular deserve attention. James M. McPherson's *Battle Cry of Freedom: The Civil War Era* (New York: Oxford University Press, 1988), an installment in the Oxford History of the United States series, is at once military, political, and social history. It is arguably the best single-volume treatment of the war. On the other end of the spectrum, both in terms of length and approach, is Shelby Foote, best known for his ubiquitous presence in Ken Burns' television series on the war. His appearance in the series flowed from his authorship of the three-volume *The Civil War: A Narrative* (New York: Vintage Books, 1958–74). A good, though lengthy, read, Foote's trilogy does not purport to be a scholarly history, which is both its strength and its weakness. Somewhere in between is Bruce Catton, a popular and prolific Civil War historian. His three-volume *Centennial History of the Civil War* (New York: Doubleday, 1961–65) reads well, but it is not as lengthy as Foote and is more scholarly.

The two classics authored by Bell Irving Wiley, *The Life of Billy Yank: The Common Soldier of the Union* (1951; reprint; Baton Rouge: Louisiana State University Press, 1995) and *The Life of Johnny Reb: The Common Soldier of the Confederacy* (1943; reprint; Baton Rouge: Louisiana State University Press, 1995), should be required reading for any genealogist with an interest in the Civil War. Built upon the examination of hundreds of diaries and letters, these two books make up a highly readable social history of military life in the Civil War. For the genealogist who is anxious to put the experiences of a Civil War ancestor in historical context, Wiley's books are an essential starting point. Three other scholarly works expand on similar themes: Gerald E. Linderman's *Embattled Courage: The Experience of Combat in the American Civil War* (New York: Free Press, 1987), Reid Mitchell's *Civil War Soldiers* (New York: Viking, 1988), and James I. Robertson, Jr., *Soldiers Blue and Gray* (Columbia: University of South Carolina Press, 1988).

Civil War military scholarship has advanced greatly in recent years, so the general reader with access to a good historical library will have little difficulty in accessing well-researched books on most major battles and campaigns. In addition, there is an extensive literature covering the biographies of Civil War leaders, both military and civilian. A number of biographical dictionaries are also in print; a few of them are cited in this chapter's bibliography. Remember, too, that there are numerous biographical articles in Boatner's *Dictionary* and in the *Encyclopedia of the Confederacy* (both cited above).

Soldier Lists. Many genealogists enter Civil War research knowing that a particular ancestor was in the war but not knowing the unit in which he served. Others may not know if an ancestor was in the war but want to find out. In either case the first step in research is to identify the ancestor as belonging to a particular military unit.

If the ancestor served in the Confederate forces, he is likely to be listed in *The Roster of Confederate Soldiers 1861–1865,* 16 vols. (Wilmington, N.C.: Broadfoot, 1995–96), edited by Janet B. Hewett. This is essentially the publication of the National Archives consolidated index to compiled Confederate service records, which is also available on microfilm (M253), and covers all states in a single listing. Wonderful as *The Roster* may be, neither it nor the National Archives record group from which it is taken is comprehensive; however, it is probably very close to being so and as close as any published list is ever likely to be.

The genealogist with Union ancestry has no single comprehensive listing to consult; however, at this writing Broadfoot has launched Hewett's *Roster of Union Soldiers, 1861–65* (1997–). As with the Confederate effort, it amounts to a transcription of the series of National Archives indexes to compiled service records; a major difference is its state-by-state arrangement (with additional sequences for the United States Colored Troops and the Regular Army) and the fact that this index does not include draftees and substitutes, a distinction not made in the Confederate listings.

Simply finding the name of an ancestor in either of these sets does not necessarily guarantee a correct identification, especially in cases of common or somewhat common names. Some sort of followup is usually called for. Before sending off to the National Archives for copies of pension or compiled service records or to state archives for copies of Confederate pension papers, the researcher might wish to consult some other sources.

The first step should be to seek out a published state roster. States which remained in the Union at some point published rosters of their Civil War soldiers, usually under the direction of the state adjutant general. In some cases, publication began during the war or shortly after the war's end, while in other cases these publication projects were not completed until several decades had passed. Indexes were not always published with these rosters, although in many cases indexes were compiled and published after the fact. The Confederate states were slower to publish lists of their military personnel; for some states, such as Mississippi and Alabama, there is still no authoritative and comprehensive listing of Confederate soldiers. On the other hand, more recently published rosters from the Confederate states, such as those for North Carolina and Florida, are exceptionally well done and have benefited from modern editorial standards.

Consulting state roster volumes can aid in making a definitive identification of a Civil War veteran ancestor whose name may have appeared in the indexes to compiled service records. Age and residence at the time of enlistment are often included in the state roster lists. In addition, the more basic facts of life and death which are reflected in the roster listings might confirm or rule out an identification. If a John Smith in a particular Virginia regiment was killed at Chancellorsville, he can be excluded from the circle of possible ancestors if great-great-grandfather John Smith was alive and well at the time of the 1870 census.

There are listings of Civil War dead which might assist the genealogical researcher, who, if nothing else, may be interested to discover the final resting place of an ancestor. Originally published in twenty-seven volumes by the U.S. Quartermaster's Department, the *Roll of Honor: Names of Soldiers Who Died in Defense of the American Union Interred in the National Cemeteries* was reprinted in ten volumes in 1994 by the Genealogical Publishing Company (Baltimore), which substantially increased the value of the set by adding an index. In a somewhat similar vein, *Confederate P.O.W.s: Soldiers and Sailors Who Died in Federal Prisons and Military Hospitals in the North,* published and distributed by Frances T. Ingmire and Carolyn Ericson (Nacogdoches, Tex.: Ericson Books, 1984), may be of interest to the Confederate researcher.

In addition, some states, for purposes of their own, enumerated Civil War veterans within their borders; some of these lists have been printed, examples being the *Alabama 1907 Census of Confederate Soldiers* (Cullman, Ala.: Gregath, 1982–83), the *List of Ex-Soldiers, Sailors and Marines Living in Iowa* (Des Moines, Iowa: Adjutant General, 1886), and *United States Civil War Soldiers Living in Michigan in 1894* (St. Johns, Mich.: Genealogists of Clinton County Historical Society, 1988). Such lists may confirm an ancestor's military unit (this information is provided in some of these surveys, although, for example, in the Michigan work cited it is not) or, at the very least, locate a veteran in a non-census year.

Pension Lists

There is no comprehensive published list of Union Civil War pensioners, although a pensioners list was published by the U.S. Pension Bureau before the eligibility requirements were liberalized in the 1890s. It is the *List of Pensioners on the Roll, January 1, 1883, Giving the Name of Each Pensioner, the Cause for Which Pensioned, the Post Office Address, the Rate of Pension per Month, and the Date of Original Allowance as Called for by Senate Resolution of December 8, 1882* (reprint; Baltimore: Genealogical Publishing Co., 1970). The title says its all. Note that the organization is not alphabetical but, rather, geographical. Of course, this list will also include veterans' survivors drawing a pension.

Confederate veterans did not receive Federal pensions, although the former Confederate states—and at least one of the border states which did not secede—established their own pension programs for Confederate veterans. There is no master list covering Confederate pensioners for all states, although some publications dealing with pensioners and pension applications in a given state have appeared. An example is Confederate Tennessee, for which one can consult both Samuel Sistler's *Index to Tennessee Confederate Pension Applications* (Nashville: Byron Sistler, 1995) and Edna Wiefering's *Tennessee Confederate Widows and Their Families: Abstracts of 11,190 Confederate Widows' Applications* (Cleveland, Tenn.: Cleveland Public Library, 1992). Several such publications are included in the state listings for the Civil War in the bibliography which concludes this chapter.

Unit Histories and Personal Narratives. Civil War regimental histories began to appear even before the war was over and the regiments mustered out. The same is true for published personal narratives—memoirs, diaries, and letters. Even so, the publication of such works slacked off with the end of hostilities; both veterans and civilians were tired of war and were not inclined to read about it. It would be around two decades before such publications began to appear again in substantial numbers. This renewal paralleled the rise of veteran organizations and, later, the mood of national reconciliation which hit its stride by the turn of the century.

Most unit histories are for regiments, although there are occasional company histories, as well as brigade and division histories. This first wave of postwar publishing arose from the ranks of the veterans themselves; many of the histories were sponsored by regimental reunion associations. Some were original works rich in humor and anecdote and penned by one or more veterans, often as much memoir as history; and some were fairly dry reproductions of the official reports submitted by the regiment's colonel to brigade command. As for the historical value of the histories published in this period, remember that, because many of the veterans were still alive at the time of publication, regimental controversies or questionable performance in the field may not have received close attention (although veiled or even explicit criticism of commanding generals may arise).

Many regimental histories also include a roster. For Federal regiments this might simply be a reproduction of the roster from the published adjutant general's report. On the other hand, some histories conclude with short biographical sketches giving some account of veterans' postwar activities. Not surprisingly, officers were often the subjects of moderately detailed biographical sketches.

It was more likely for a regimental history to be published for a given Federal regiment than for a Confederate regiment during this period. There are probably a number of reasons for this—among them a higher literacy rate in the North and a less prosperous economy in the South. In some cases, though, the absence of a history for a Confederate regiment is mitigated by the existence of a brigade history. Confederate brigades were usually made up of four to six regiments or other units, sometimes designated battalions. They were usually from the same state, lending a greater homogeneity to Confederate brigades than was usually the case with Federal brigades.

Currently there is a boom in Civil War books arising not only from the presses of "buff" publishers and other publishers specializing in military subjects, but also from academic presses and large commercial publishers. These include many regimental histories, as well as diaries and letters brought to light from attic trunks or transcribed from the pages of wartime newspapers. Happily, many of these pertain to units for which there had hitherto been little, if any, published history.

Even as new histories are written, older unit histories are becoming more widely available in microform (microfilm or microfiche). Two microform publishers have brought out unit histories and personal narratives published in the nineteenth and early twentieth centuries. The two sets are *Civil War Unit Histories: Regimental Histories and Personal Narratives,* published by University Publications of America (Frederick, Maryland), and *Regimental Histories of American Civil War,* published by University Microfilms International (Ann Arbor, Michigan). Both sets include the adjutant general roster publications, while the University Publications of America set also includes published histories pertaining to the contributions of universities, specific cities and counties, and other special groups. One or the other of these sets or parts of them can be found in many genealogical and historical research libraries. Keep in mind that a library may not have cataloged the books in these microfiche series as single titles. Instead, the entire set may have been cataloged as one item. If such is the case, seek the published contents guide that accompanies both microform publications.

Veterans' Publications. The paucity of published Confederate regimental histories has been to some extent mitigated by the *Confederate Veteran,* a veterans' magazine published from 1893 to 1932. Its pages are rich in memoir and biography, including obituaries for many veterans, such as George H. Nicholas, who is identified as the son of Lorenza and Martha J. Nicholas, born in Buckingham County, Virginia, on 21 March 1844. He served in the Twenty-fifth Virginia Battalion and then the Fifty-seventh Virginia Infantry, in whose ranks he surrendered at Appomattox. It is noted that it

> was his pleasure to attend all reunions and seemed as a boy of the sixties mingling with old comrades. . . . This good comrade, who never faltered in his duty as soldier or citizen, was reared amidst environments typical of the best traditions of the South (*Confederate Veteran* 1922, 269).

The complete run of the *Confederate Veteran* has been reprinted in forty volumes by Broadfoot (Wilmington, N.C., 1986), together with a new and comprehensive index that would, for example, guide one to the obituary of George H. Nicholas. Perhaps surprisingly, there is nothing comparable to the *Confederate Veteran* for Union veterans, although the state and local chapters of two Union veterans' organizations, the Grand Army of the Republic and (especially) the Military Order of the Loyal Legion of the United States, published personal war narratives and biographical works.

Local Publications. It was a rare county in the Midwest or Mid-Atlantic region which did not see at least one county history published within twenty or thirty years of the closing of the Civil War. The same may be said for New England town histories. The war was usually the pivotal point in local historical memory, and the roll of local men who served in the Civil War was frequently an important part of the military history section in the local history (see chapter 17). This section might take the form of a listing of those who had lost their lives, although it is not unusual to find a listing of all local men who served, because such lists had been kept by local governments in keeping with the conscription laws during the war.

Communities across the North erected Civil War monuments, and the dedication programs were sometimes published (especially in New England). These programs often included the names of local men who died in the conflict. Works of this nature are covered to a great extent in the *Bibliography of State Participation in the Civil War* (cited above). For a number of reasons local historical publishing was not as prolific in the South; however, to the extent that it did occur, the war and the roll of local servicemen were also important features.

Most Civil War regiments were volunteer units raised locally under state authority. A company (sometimes an entire regiment) was made up predominantly of men from the same locality. Thus, a county or town history may cover the history of a local regiment in great detail. As well, membership in a particular company or regiment may be a good indicator of where the serviceman was living at the time of enlistment.

Indian Wars

The U.S. government was at war with various Native American tribes and confederations for the better part of the nineteenth century. The soldiers who faced them were primarily regulars, both army and cavalry, although these forces were supplemented at times by militia and state volunteer regiments. The term "Indian Wars," though, is often applied only to those conflicts which occurred from roughly the period of the Civil War through the turn of the century. Conflict with the Indians that was contemporaneous with the Civil War is documented to some extent in the *Official Records* and in Broadfoot's *Supplement* (covering, for example, events in Colorado). Joseph P. Peters's *Indian Battles and Skirmishes on the American Frontier, 1790–1898. . . .* (New York: Argonaut Press, 1966) provides a summary and overview of the fighting between whites and American Indians. For an overview of earlier Indian conflicts see Francis Prucha's *The Sword of the Republic: The United States on the Frontier, 1783–1846* (New York: Macmillan, 1968).

In the course of researching the Indian Wars, one finds frequent references to forts and military posts. Two reference works can assist in fully identifying and locating them: Francis Paul Prucha's *Guide to the Military Posts of the United States 1789–1895* (Madison: State Historical Society of Wisconsin, 1964) and Robert B. Roberts's *Encyclopedia of Historic Forts: The Military, Pioneer, and Trading Posts of the United States* (New York: Macmillan, 1988). The latter largely supersedes the former and has a broader chronological scope. Both can be important reference tools for researching other conflicts as well.

The number of Regular Army units engaged in the Indian Wars was relatively limited. Their experiences often generated unit histories and published personal narratives. There is, for example, no shortage of books on William Armstrong Custer and the Seventh Cavalry. In many cases, though, a regular unit history would not be limited to the Indian Wars, but might also, for example, include experiences in the Spanish American War, such as Herschel Cashin's *Under Fire with the Tenth U.S. Cavalry* (Chicago: American Publishing House, 1902), a fairly scarce work which covers the African American "buffalo soldiers" of the Ninth and Tenth Cavalry and the Twenty-fourth and Twenty-fifth Infantry. In this regard, Frank N. Schubert's *On the Trail of the Buffalo Soldier: Biographies of African Americans in the U.S. Army, 1866–1917* (Wilmington, Del.: Scholarly Resources, 1995) is also worth noting. It is a unique publication, featuring sometimes surprisingly extensive collections of biographical data from pension files and other official records, as well as from unit histories, such as Cashin's. Although the focus of such a work can only be on one or a few units, ideally, more publications of a similar nature will appear in the future. Robert Utley provides a good social history of frontier military service in *Frontiersmen in Blue: The United States Army and the Indian, 1848–1865* (New York: Macmillan, 1967) and in *Frontier Regulars: The United States Army and the Indian, 1866–1891* (New York: Macmillan, 1974). Similarly, Don Rickey, Jr., *Forty Miles a Day on Beans and Hay: The Enlisted Soldier Fighting the Indian Wars* (Norman: University of Oklahoma Press, 1963) may also be of interest to the researcher.

The Indian Wars pension files are covered in print, once again by Virgil D. White, in his two-volume *Index to Indian Wars Pension Files 1892–1926* (Waynesboro, Tenn.: National Historical Publishing Co., 1987). As with his work on revolutionary war pensions, White has abstracted much of the more important information, which, as we have seen, substantially enhances the value of such a publication. In perusing these entries, for example, one is struck by the number of instances in which soldiers are listed as having aliases.

Spanish-American War

Histories. The Spanish-American War, waged on two continents during a span of just a few months in 1898, launched the United States as a world—and many would say imperial—power, even as it administered a final blow to a much weakened Spanish empire. Two books have appeared in recent years which could provide the general reader with an introduction to this conflict: David P. Trask's *The War with Spain in 1898* (New York: Macmillan, 1981) and George J. A. O'Toole's *The Spanish War, an American Epic* (New York: W. W. Norton, 1984).

Anne Cipriano Verzon's *The Spanish-American War: An Annotated Bibliography* (New York: Garland, 1990) provides good coverage for published rosters and unit histories together with some personal narratives. The bibliography's value is further enhanced by the inclusion of citations to periodical articles.

U.S. casualties were minimal in this war and in the lengthier conflict of the Philippine Insurrection, which followed the war with Spain. Known casualties are summarized, once again, by Clarence S. Peterson in his *Known Military Dead During the Spanish American and the Philippine Insurrection, 1898–1901* (Baltimore: the author, 1958).

Regimental histories for the Spanish-American War are relatively scarce, although, as previously noted, the histories of Regular Army regiments up to World War I often encompass service in both the Indian Wars and the war with Spain. As in the Civil War, the individual states raised volunteer regiments for service in this conflict, and in a number of instances state governments subsequently published roster lists. Consult Neagles's *U.S. Military Records* (cited earlier) to learn if such a published roster exists for the state of interest.

World War I

The United States entered the First World War in 1917 and would be a belligerent for the last nineteen months of the conflict, which had begun in 1914. Even so, more than 1 million American soldiers were in Europe by war's end. Additional servicemen had been mobilized but not shipped out.

Reference and Bibliography. The genealogist with a World War I ancestor who saw action in Europe should consult *The United States in the First World War: An Encyclopedia* (New York: Garland, 1995) for historical background. In addition to articles on battles and campaigns, this reference work includes articles of a respectable length on those U.S. divisions engaged in the fighting. Each article concludes with a concise but helpful bibliography, which, in the case of the division articles, includes references to unit histories and personal narratives.

The American Expeditionary Force was made up of forty-three divisions that fell into three categories: (1) Regular Army soldiers already in service before hostilities were declared, (2) National Guard soldiers, and (3) the soldiers of the so-called National Army divisions raised after hostilities were declared. With the exception of two African American divisions, the National Guard and National Army divisions were usually made up of regiments from the same state or region. For an organizational context for the unit to which an ancestor belonged, consult the *Order of Battle of the United States Land Forces in the World War* (Washington: Government Printing Office, 1937–49), which also provides a record of events for each of the divisions.

Two reference works cited earlier in this chapter cover unit histories for World War I: Controvitch's *United States Army Unit Histories: A Reference and Bibliography* and Pappas's *United States Army Unit Histories: A Bibliography*. In addition there is Charles E. Dornbusch's *Histories of American Army Units, World Wars I and II and Korean Conflict* (Washington, D.C.: Office of the Adjutant General, Special Services Division, 1956).

The researcher might also wish to consult David R. Woodward's *America and World War I: A Selected Annotated Bibliography of English Language Sources* (New York: Garland, 1985). Charles V. Genthe's *American War Narratives 1917–1918: A Study and Bibliography* (New York: David Lewis, 1969) may also be of limited interest (although the criterion for inclusion was simply that a work had been published in the United States, so it includes some European soldier narratives). In addition, the citations are not organized by unit, which will hamper the researcher attempting to identify sources pertaining to an ancestor's division or regiment.

General History. Americans seeking a historical introduction to World War I must remember that U.S. participation was limited to approximately the final third of the war, so a general history of the war will not put the Americans on center stage. With that fact in mind, James L. Stokesbury's *A Short History of World War I* (London: Hale, 1981) is good for a general overview, while at least one important American perspective on the war can be found in Gen. John J. Pershing's *My Experiences in the World War* (New York: Stokes, 1931). General treatments of the American role in the war are found in Laurence Stalling's *The Doughboys: The Story of the AEF, 1917–1918* (New York: Harper & Row, 1963) and in Frank Freidel's *Over There: The Story of America's First Great Overseas Crusade* (Philadelphia: Temple University Press, 1990).

Published Rosters. Many states—but far from the majority of them—published lists of service personnel who served in World War I. Some of these took the form of the standard state adjutant general rosters, while others had a different format. Ohio, for example, published a twenty-three-volume alphabetical listing of its servicemen with short entries that included nativity information in addition to an account of the veteran's military service.

As with the Civil War, local servicemen in World War I—or at least those who died in the conflict—were often listed in the county histories of the time (although by the 1920s the heyday of the old county histories was beginning to fade). Some localities generated publications chronicling the role their citizens played in the conflict. Such publications were not limited to large population centers, an example being Victor G. Lundeen's 288-page *Otter Tail County Minnesota in the World War: An Illustrated Historical Record of the People from Otter Tail County, Minnesota, Who Participated in the World War, Both at Home and Abroad. . . .* (Fergus Falls, Minn.: the author,

1919). Such works could be more celebratory, such as Madison County, New York's *Madison County's Welcome Home for Her Sons and Daughters Who Served in the World War 1917–1919* (Oneida, N.Y.: Oneida Dispatch Press, 1919). Also, if an ancestor was in college at the time of his enlistment, one might want to look through the school yearbooks for the period, as students who enlisted often received special notice. American servicemen who died during the war are listed in the three-volume set *Soldiers of the Great War* (Washington, D.C.: Soldiers Record Publishing Association, 1920), compiled by W. M. Haulsee, F. G. Howe, and A. C. Doyle; photographs of many servicemen are included.

CONCLUSION: FUTURE PROSPECTS

The last fifteen years have seen several publishing trends in the field of military genealogy. If the interest in military history and in genealogy continues to grow, we can certainly expect to see their continuation. We might also expect to see some parallel developments in the digital recording of information and its availability on CD-ROM and on the Internet.

An obvious trend has been the transcription and publication of indexes to National Archives record groups, such as pension files and compiled service records. Virgil White has been especially active in this regard, while Broadfoot has made and is making valuable contributions to Civil War research by publishing the indexes to compiled service records for both Confederates and Federals. Indeed, it often takes the commercial incentive of book publishing to bring such projects to conclusion, while volunteer and nonprofit efforts to make such information available online may lag. Many of the more important indexes have been published, and we should expect to see a continuation of the transcription and publication of National Archives record groups, particularly those which are indexes. With the increase in the price of National Archives microfilm, such projects are especially welcome for libraries which are better able to afford the acquisition of published transcriptions than large sets of microfilm. They also make it possible for researchers to make such indexes a component of their personal libraries.

The reprinting of scarce works is another pattern which has become especially pronounced in recent years. Older government publications, which in their original editions may be especially fragile, are now more generally available as a result of their reprinting by commercial genealogical publishers, such as the Genealogical Publishing Company. Usually such works concern records for conflicts prior to the Civil War, although Broadfoot Publishing has reprinted a few key state publications for the Civil War, such as Samuel P. Bates's *History of Pennsylvania Volunteers* (Harrisburg, Pa.: state printer, 1869–71; reprinted with an every-name index, 1993–94), to which a comprehensive index was added. Even so, there are still a great many such publications which could stand to be reprinted. For example, the Civil War adjutant general rosters for many states have been reproduced on microform, but the use of a good reprint is still preferable to most researchers. Whether commercial publishing interests will eventually tackle such projects or whether the initiative will come from states' historical and genealogical communities remains to be seen. We might also note that interest in the Civil War appears to have eclipsed an interest in subsequent conflicts to some extent. Published state rosters for the Spanish-American War and, more importantly, World War I often remain especially scarce and have not been reprinted or made commercially available on microform.

The microfilming of military publications has seen great advances in recent years. The microfilming of published Civil War unit histories, rosters, and personal narratives by University Publications of America and University Microfilms International has been an especially important development, while stray military titles also find their way into University Microfilm International's Genealogy and Local History microfiche series. Even so, as noted above, it would be especially gratifying if a similar focus could be achieved for scarce published rosters, unit histories, and personal narratives for conflicts after the Civil War—although, of course, copyright problems are more likely with more recently published works.

New compilations are still seeing print as well. Research covering the colonial era and the early republic has in recent years produced new works documenting local militia lists and bounty-land grants. There is also a need for published authoritative state rosters for the American Revolution, the War of 1812, and the Civil War in those cases when a previously published work is incomplete or otherwise inadequate, or when such a list was never published in the first place. Once again, assuming that the general interest in genealogy and military history is sustained, we are likely to see a continuation of the advances enjoyed over the last two decades. Civil War unit histories and personal narratives have also been appearing in great abundance, and it is likely that the trend will continue, which might lead one to wonder whether we could see more publishing of a similar nature for other conflicts. For example, is the paucity of book-length unit histories from the Revolutionary War justified by an ostensible lack of source material? Is it assumed there would only be very limited interest in such a work? It would be interesting if a sufficiently skilled and motivated genealogist or historian would push the limits of such assumptions.

Finally, the challenge of bibliographic coverage remains a constant. Research into all of the conflicts considered here is to some extent made easier by the publication of appropriate bibliographies. Yet, as the years advance and publishing escalates, the need for bibliographic updates becomes more urgent. In addition, bibliographers will always find themselves in the position of discovering older published works that were missed when a bibliography was initially compiled and published. The inclusion of periodical citations in bibliographies also becomes more important as the literature grows. The challenge can be great. For example, a comprehensive bibliography of the Civil War similar to Gephart's for the American Revolution would probably be an impossibility, while simply focusing on Civil War unit histories and personal narratives, as did Dornbusch, would be challenge enough today, especially if coverage of periodical articles from popular Civil War enthusiast magazines was included.

Genealogy continues to be a rapidly expanding publication field, as does military history. When the two are combined, there are a great many books, both out of print and current, to consider. There is also the prospect of a great many more to come.

NOTES

1. Although it provides excellent coverage for campaigns and battles, the *Official Records'* documentation of skirmishes has

been shown to be less thorough. See Dallas Irvine's "Rootstock of Error," *Prologue* 2 (1) (Spring 1970).

REFERENCE LIST

Coldham, Peter W. 1980. *American Loyalist Claims.* Washington, D.C.: National Genealogical Society.

Confederate Veteran. 1922. 30 (7) (July).

Dann, John C. 1980. *The Revolution Remembered: Eyewitness Accounts of the War for Independence.* Chicago: University of Chicago.

White, Virgil D. 1990. *Genealogical Abstracts of Revolutionary War Pension Files.* Vol. 1. Waynesboro, Tenn.: National Historical Publishing Co.

BIBLIOGRAPHY

With contributions by the late William Arbuckle

General Reference

Family History Library. *U.S. Military Records Research Outline.* Salt Lake City: Family History Library, 1993.

Guide to Genealogical Research in the National Archives. Rev. ed. Washington, D.C.: National Archives Trust Fund Board, 1985.

Holt, Dean W. *American Military Cemeteries: A Comprehensive Illustrated Guide to the Hallowed Grounds of the United States, Including Cemeteries Overseas.* Jefferson, N.C.: McFarland, 1992.

Horowitz, Lois A. *Bibliography of Military Name Lists from Pre-1675 to 1900: A Guide to Genealogical Research.* Metuchen, N.J.: Scarecrow Press, 1990.

Johnson, Richard S. *How to Locate Anyone Who Is or Has Been in the Military.* 7th ed. Houston: Military Information Enterprises, 1996.

Kreidberg, Marvin A., and Morton G. Henry. *History of Military Mobilization in the United States Army, 1775–1945.* Washington, D.C.: Government Printing Office, 1955.

Military Service Records: A Select Catalog of National Archives Microfilm Publications. Washington, D.C.: National Archives and Records Service, 1985.

Neagles, James C. *U.S. Military Records: A Guide to Federal and State Sources, Colonial America to the Present.* Salt Lake City: Ancestry, 1994.

Regular Army and Navy

Controvich, John T. *United States Army Unit Histories: A Reference and Bibliography.* Manhattan, Kans.: Kansas State University, 1983.

Callahan, Edward W., ed. *List of Officers of the Navy of the United States and of the Marine Corps from 1775 to 1780.* Reprint. New York: Haskell House, 1969.

Cullum, George W. *Biographical Register of the Officers and Graduates of the U.S. Military Academy at West Point, N.Y.* Boston: Houghton-Mifflin, 1891–1950.

Heitman, Francis B. *Historical Register and Dictionary of the United States Army, from Its Organization, September 29, 1789, to March 2, 1903.* Washington, D.C.: Government Printing Office, 1903.

Mahon, John K. *Infantry.* Army Lineage Series. Washington, D.C.: Office of the Chief of Military History, U.S. Army, 1972.

Pappas, George S. *United States Army Unit Histories.* Carlisle Barracks, Pa.: U.S. Army Military History Institute, 1971–78.

Sawacki, James A. *Infantry Regiments of the U.S. Army.* Dumfries, Va.: Wyvern, 1981.

Spiller, Roger J., ed. *Dictionary of American Military Biography.* 3 vols. Westport, Conn.: Greenwood Press, 1984.

Stubbs, Mary Lee. *Armor-cavalry.* Army Lineage Series. Washington, D.C.: Office of the Chief of Military History, 1960.

Colonial Wars

Bibliography

Baker, Mary Ellen. *Bibliography of Lists of New England Soldiers.* Boston: New England Historic Genealogical Society, 1911. Reprinted from *New England Historical and Genealogical Register* 64–65 (1910–11).

Lydon, James G. *Struggle for Empire: A Bibliography of the French and Indian War.* New York: Garland, 1986.

General History

Coleman, Emma Lewis. *New England Captives Carried to Canada Between 1677 and 1760 During the French and Indian Wars.* 2 vols. Portland, Oreg.: Southworth Press, 1925.

Leach, Douglas E. *Arms for Empire: A Military History of the American Colonies in North America, 1607–1763.* New York: Macmillan, 1973.

Drake, Samuel G. *A Particular History of the Five Years French and Indian War 1744–1749.* 1870. Reprint. Bowie, Md.: Heritage Books, n.d.

Selected Published Lists

Bockstruck, Lloyd DeWitt. *Virginia's Colonial Soldiers.* Baltimore: Genealogical Publishing Co., 1988.

Bodge, George M. *Soldiers in King Philip's War: Being a Critical Account of That War, with a Concise History of the Indian Wars of New England from 1620–1677. Official Lists of the Soldiers of Massachusetts Colony Serving in Philip's War. . .* . Leominster, Mass.: the author, 1896. Reprint. Baltimore: Genealogical Publishing Co., 1967. First published periodically in the *New England Historical and Genealogical Register* (1883–91).

Clark, Murtie Jane. *Colonial Soldiers of the South 1732–1774.* Baltimore: Genealogical Publishing Co., 1983. Lists approximately fifty-five thousand soldiers who served in Maryland, Virginia, Georgia, and the Carolinas.

Donahue, Mary E. *Massachusetts Officers and Soldiers, 1702–1722: Queen Anne's War to Dummer's War.* Boston: Society of Colonial Wars in the Commonwealth of Massachusetts, 1980.

Doreski, Carole. *Massachusetts Officers and Soldiers in the Seventeenth-Century Conflicts.* Boston: Society of Colonial Wars in the Commonwealth of Massachusetts and The New England Historic Genealogical Society, 1982.

Drake, S. A. *The Border Wars of New England.* 1897. Reprint. Tucson, Ariz.: Americana Unlimited, n.d.

Goss, David, and David Zarowin. *Massachusetts Officers and Soldiers in the French and Indian Wars, 1755–1756.* Boston: Society of Colonial Wars in the Commonwealth of Massachusetts and the New England Historic Genealogical Society, 1985.

Peirce, Ebinezer W. *Peirce's Colonial List.* Baltimore: Genealogical Publishing Co., 1968. A list of persons who held civil, military, or professional positions in Plymouth and Rhode Island colonies from 1621 to 1700.

Rawlyk, G. A. *Yankees at Louisburg.* Orono, Maine: the author, 1967.

Society of Colonial Wars

An Index of Ancestors and Roll of Members of the Society of Colonial Wars. New York, 1922.

A First Supplement to the 1922 Index of Ancestors and Roll of Members of the General Society of Colonial Wars. Hartford, Conn., 1941.

A Second Supplement to the 1922 Index of Ancestors and Roll of Members, General Society of Colonial Wars. Baltimore, 1977.

Society of Colonial Wars, Illinois. *List of Officers and Members Together with a Record of the Service Performed by Their Ancestors in the Wars of the Colonies.* Chicago: Society of Colonial Wars, 1900.

Selected State Roster Lists and Related Publications

Connecticut

Andrews, Frank DeWitte, comp. *Connecticut Soldiers in the French and Indian War.* Vineland, N.J.: the compiler, 1923.

Buckingham, Thomas. *Roll and Journal of Connecticut Service in Queen Anne's War 1710–1711.* New Haven, Conn.: Acorn Club of Connecticut, 1916.

Connecticut Historical Society. *Rolls of Connecticut Men in the French and Indian War, 1755–1762.* 2 vols. Hartford, Conn.: the society, 1903–05.

Robinson, George Frederick, and Albert Harrison Hall. *Watertown Soldiers in the Colonial Wars and the American Revolution.* Watertown, Mass.: Historical Society of Watertown, 1939.

Shepard, James. *Connecticut Soldiers in the Pequot War of 1637.* Meriden, Conn.: Journal Publishing Co., 1913.

Society of Colonial Wars. *Register of Pedigrees and Services of Ancestors.* Hartford, Conn.: the society, 1941.

Delaware

Public Archives Commission. *Delaware Archives.* 5 vols. Wilmington, Del.: the commission, 1911–. These records include material from the colonial period through the Civil War. The records of the colonial period are indexed in vol. 2.

Maine (also see Massachusetts)

Society of Colonial Wars. *Register of the Officers and Members of the Society of Colonial Wars in the State of Maine; also History, Roster and Record of Colonel Jedidiah Preble's Regiment, Campaign of 1758; Together with Capt. Samuel Cobb's Journal.* Portland, Oreg.: Marks Printing House, 1905.

Massachusetts

Donahue, Mary E. *Massachusetts Officers and Soldiers 1702–1722: Queen Ann's War to Dummer's War.* Boston: Society of Colonial Wars, 1980 .

Doreski, Carole. *Massachusetts Officers and Soldiers of the Seventeenth Century Conflicts.* Boston: Society of Colonial Wars, 1982.

MacKay, Robert E. *Massachusetts Soldiers in the French and Indian Wars 1744–1755.* Boston: Society of Colonial Wars, 1978.

MacLean, John P. *A Historical Account of the Settlements of Scotch Highlanders in America Prior to the Peace of 1783.* Baltimore: Genealogical Publishing Co., 1968.

Stachiw, Myron O. *Massachusetts Officers and Soldiers, 1723–1743: Dummer's War to the War of Jenkin's Ear.* Boston: Society of Colonial Wars in the Commonwealth of Massachusetts and The New England Historic Genealogical Society, 1979.

Voye, Nancy S., ed. *Massachusetts Officers in the French and Indian Wars 1748–1763.* Boston Society of Colonial Wars, 1975. Includes information on officers from Maine compiled from the muster rolls of the French and Indian Wars in the Massachusetts archives, vols. 91–99.

New Hampshire

Potter, Chandler E. *The Military History of the State of New Hampshire 1623–1861.* 2 vols. in 1. Baltimore: Genealogical Publishing Co., 1972. Reprint of 1866 edition with added indexes. Includes rosters and muster rolls for the War of 1812 and Mexican War.

New Jersey

Ricord, Frederick W. *General Index to the Documents Relating to the Colonial History of the State of New Jersey.* Newark, N.J.: Daily Journal Establishment, 1880.

New York

New York Historical Society. *Muster Rolls of New York Provincial Troops 1755–1764.* New York: the society, 1892.

State Historian. *Second Annual Report 1896.* Albany, N.Y.: Wynkoop, Hallenbeck, Crawford Co., 1897. *Third Annual Report, 1897.* Together, these two reports provide lists and indexes to servicemen from 1664 to 1775.

North Carolina

Saunders, William L., ed. *The Colonial Records of North Carolina.* Raleigh, N.C.: the state, 1886–1914.

Pennsylvania

Provincial Council. *Colonial Records.* 16 vols. Philadelphia: the state, 1853.

Nolan, James B. *Officers and Soldiers in the Service of the Province of Pennsylvania, 1744–1764.* Philadelphia: University of Pennsylvania, 1936.

Rhode Island

Chapin, Howard Miller. *Rhode Island in the Colonial Wars: A list of Rhode Island Soldiers and Sailors in King George's War, 1740–1748.* Providence: Rhode Island Historical Society, 1920.

_____. *Rhode Island in the Colonial Wars: A List of Rhode Island Soldiers and Sailors in the Old French and Indian Wars, 1755–1762.* Providence: Rhode Island Historical Society, 1918.

_____. *Rhode Island Privateers in King George's War, 1739–1748.* Providence: Rhode Island Historical Society, 1926.

Smith, Joseph J. *Civil and Military List of Rhode Island 1647–1850.* 3 vols. Providence, R.I.: Preston and Rounds, 1900.

Society of Colonial Wars. *Nine Muster Rolls of Rhode Island Troops Enlisted During the Old French War.* Providence, R.I.: the society, 1915.

Virginia

Bockstruck, Lloyd DeWitt. *Virginia's Colonial Soldiers.* Baltimore: Genealogical Publishing Co., 1988.

Eckenrode, H. J. *List of the Colonial Soldiers of Virginia.* 1905. Reprint. Baltimore: Genealogical Publishing Co., 1974.

Crozier, William Armstrong. *Virginia Colonial Militia, 1651–1776.* 1905. Reprint. Baltimore: Genealogical Publishing Co., 1982.

Kentucky Land Office. *A Calendar of the Warrants for Land in Kentucky. Granted for Service in the French and Indian War.* Baltimore: Genealogical Publishing Co., 1967.

Lewis, Virgil A. *Soldiery of West Virginia in the French and Indian War: Lord Dunmore's War: The Revolution: The Later Indian Wars: The Whiskey Insurrection: The Second War with England: The War with Mexico, and Addenda Relating to West Virginians in the Civil War.* Baltimore: Genealogical Publishing Co., 1967.

Neville, John D. *Bacon's Rebellion.* Jamestown Foundation, n.d.

Taylor, Philip F. *A Calendar of the Warrants for Land in Kentucky, Granted for Service in the French and Indian War, Excerpted from the Year Book of the Society of Colonial Wars of Kentucky.* 1917. Reprint. Baltimore: Genealogical Publishing Co., 1967.

Revolutionary War

Bibliography

Blanco, Richard L. *The War of the American Revolution: A Selected Annotated Bibliography of Published Sources.* New York: Garland Publishing, 1984.

Gephart, Ronald M. *Revolutionary America 1763–1789: A Bibliography.* Washington, D.C.: Library of Congress, 1984.

General History

Dann, John C. *The Revolution Remembered: Eyewitness Accounts of the War for Independence.* Chicago: University of Chicago Press, 1980.

Eyewitness Accounts of the American Revolution. New York: New York Times and Arno Press, 1968–71.

Mayer, Holly A. *Belonging to the Army: Camp Followers and Community during the American Revolution.* Los Angeles: University of Southern California Press, 1996.

Middlekauf, Robert. *The Glorious Cause: The American Revolution 1763–1789.* New York: Oxford University Press, 1982.

Neimeyer, Charles Patrick. *America Goes to War: A Social History of the Continental Army.* New York: New York University Press, 1996.

Smith, Page. *A New Age Now Begins: A People's History of the American Revolution.* New York: McGraw-Hill, 1976.

Unit History Reference

Berg, Fred A. *Encyclopedia of Continental Army Units, Battalions, Regiments, and Independent Corps.* Harrisburg, Pa.: Stackpole, 1972.

Katcher, Philip R. *Encyclopedia of British, Provincial and German Army Units 1775–1783.* Harrisburg, Pa.: Stackpole Books, 1973.

Wright, Robert K. *The Continental Army.* Washington, D.C.: United States Army Center of Military History, 1983.

Selected Lists, Indexes, and Abstracts of National Scope

The American Genealogical-Biographical Index to American Genealogical, Biographical and Local History Materials. Middletown, Conn.: Godfrey Memorial Library, 1952–.

Bockstruck, Lloyd DeWitt. *Revolutionary War Bounty Land Grants Awarded by State Governments.* Baltimore: Genealogical Publishing Co., 1996.

Census of Pensioners for Revolutionary or Military Service. Baltimore: Genealogical Publishing Co., 1967.

Clark, Murtie June. *The Pension Lists of 1792–1795.* Baltimore: Genealogical Publishing Co., 1991.

Daughters of the American Revolution. *Lineage Books.* 166 vols. 1890–1921.

_____. *Patriot Index.* Centennial Edition. 3 vols. Washington: Daughters of the American Revolution, 1994.

Hatcher, Patricia H. *Abstract of Graves of Revolutionary Patriots.* 4 vols. Dallas, Tex.: Pioneer Heritage Press, 1987–88.

Kaminkow, Marion, and Jack Kaminkow. *Mariners of the American Revolution.* Baltimore: Magna Carta Book Co., 1967.

Peterson, Clarence S. *Known Military Dead During the American Revolutionary War 1775–1783.* Reprint. Baltimore: Genealogical Publishing Co., 1967.

Pierce's Register. Reprint. Baltimore: Genealogical Publishing Co., 1973.

U.S. Congress, 20th Congress, 1st Session, 1828. *List of the Names of Such Officers and Soldiers of the Revolutionary Army as Have Acquired a Right to Lands from the United States and Who Have Not Yet Applied Therefor.* Vol. 132. Senate Doc. 42.

U.S. Congress. *Digested Summary and Alphabetical List of Private Claims, Which Have Been Presented to the House of Representatives from the First to the Thirty-first Congress.* 3 vols. House Misc. Doc. Reprint. Baltimore: Genealogical Publishing Co., 1970.

U.S. Department of Interior. *Report of the Secretary of the Interior, with a Statement of Rejected or Suspended Applications for Revolutionary War Pensions, 1852.* Senate Exec. Doc. 37. Reprint. Baltimore: Genealogical Publishing Co., 1969. The reprint contains an index of the names.

U.S. War Department. *Letter From the Secretary of War, Communicating a Transcript of the Pension Lists of the United States, June 1, 1813.* Washington, D.C., 1813. Reprinted as *Revolutionary Pensioners; a Transcript of the Pension List of 1813.* Baltimore: Genealogical Publishing Co., 1959.

_____. *Letter From the Secretary of War, Transmitting a Report of the Names, Rank and Line of Every Person Placed on the Pension List, in Pursuance of the Act of 18th March, 1818.* Washington, D.C., 1820. Reprint. Baltimore: Genealogical Publishing Co., 1955.

_____. *Message From the President of the United States, Transmitting a Report of the Secretary of War in Compliance . . ."A list of the pensioners of the United States, the sum annually paid to each, and the state or territories in which the said pensioners reside.*" Washington, D.C.: 1818. Reprinted as *Revolutionary Pensioners of 1818,* with an index added. Baltimore: Southern Book Co., 1959.

_____. *Letter from the Secretary of War, Transmitting a List of the Names of Pensioners Under the Act of 18th of March 1818, Whose Names Were Struck Off the List by Act of 1st May 1820, and Subsequently Restored.* Washington, D.C., 1836. Reprinted as *Pensioners of Revolutionary War Struck off the Roll.* Baltimore: Genealogical Publishing Co., 1969.

_____. *Report from the Secretary of War . . . in Relation to the Pension Establishment of the United States.* Senate Doc. 514. 3 vols. Reprinted as *The Pension Roll of 1835,* 4 vols. (Baltimore: Genealogical Publishing Co., 1992).

White, Virgil D. *Genealogical Abstracts of Revolutionary War Pension Files.* 4 vols. Waynesboro, Tenn.: National Historical Publishing Co., 1990–92.

_____. *Index to Revolutionary War Service Records.* Waynesboro, Tenn.: National Historical Publishing Co., 1996.

Prisoners of War

Colburn, Jeremiah. "A List of Americans Committed to Old Mill Prison Since the American War." *New England Historical and Genealogical Register* 32 (1878): 42–44, 184–88, 305–08, 395–98.

Dandridge, Mrs. Danske. *American Prisoners of the Revolution.* Charlottesville, Va.: Michie Co., 1911. Reprint. Baltimore: Genealogical Publishing Co., 1967.

Society of Old Brooklynites. *A Christmas Reminder; Being the Names of About 8,000 Persons, a Small Portion of the Number Confined on Board the British Prison Ship During the War of the Revolution.* Brooklyn, N.Y.: the society, 1888.

Loyalists

Antliff, W. Bruce. *Loyalist Settlements 1783–1789: New Evidence of Canadian Loyalist Claims.* Toronto: Ministry of Citizenship and Culture, 1985.

Biographical Sketches of Loyalists of the American Revolution. Westport, Conn.: Meckler, 1984.

Bunnell, Paul J. *The New Loyalist Index.* 2 vols. Bowie, Md.: Heritage, 1989, 1996.

Clark, Murtie June. *Loyalists in the Southern Campaign of the Revolutionary War.* Baltimore: Genealogical Publishing Co., 1981.

Coldham, Peter Wilson. *American Loyalist Claims.* Washington, D.C.: National Genealogical Society, 1980.

Hodges, Graham R. *The Black Loyalist Directory: African Americans in Exile after the American Revolution.* New York: Garland, in association with the New England Historic Genealogical Society, 1996.

Katcher, Philip R. *Encyclopedia of British, Provincial and German Army Units 1775–1783.* Harrisburg, Pa.: Stackpole Books, 1973.

Loyalist Lineages of Canada. Toronto: Generation Press, 1984–.

The Old United Empire Loyalists' List. Reprint. Baltimore: Genealogical Publishing Co., 1969.

Palmer, Gregory. *A Bibliography of Loyalist Source Material in the United States, Canada and Great Britain.* Westport, Conn.: Meckler, 1982.

Sabine, Lorenzo. *Biographical Sketches of the American Revolution.* Reprint. Baltimore: Genealogical Publishing Co., 1979.

United Empire Loyalists: Enquiry into the Losses and Services in Consequence of Their Loyalty: Evidence in Canadian Claims. Toronto, 1905.

French and German (Hessian) Soldiers

DeMarce, Virginia Easley. *Mercenary Troops from Anhalt-Zerbst, Germany Who Served with the British Forces During the American Revolution.* German-American Research Monograph no. 19. McNeal, Ariz.: Westland Publications, 1984.

Dulfer, Kurt. *Hessische Truppen im Amerikanishen Unabhangigkeitskrieg.* Vol. 6. Marburg, Germany: Institut für Archivwissenschaft, 1972.

France, Ministere des affairs etrangeres. *Les Combattants Francais de la Guerre Americaine, 1778–83.* Paris: Ancienne Maison Quantin, 1903. Reprint. Baltimore: Genealogical Publishing Co., 1969.

Kelly, Arthur C. M. *Hessian Troops in the American Revolution: Extracts from the HETRINA.* Rhinebeck, N.Y.: Kinship, 1991–95.

Noailles, Amblard. *Marins et Soldats Francais en Amerique pendant la Guerre de L'Independence des Etats-Unis (1778–1783).* Paris: Perrin & Co., 1974. Lists of officers and vessels of the revolution.

Smith, Clifford Neal. *Mercenaries From Ansbach and Bayreuth, Germany, Who Remained in America After the Revolution.* German-American Research Monograph no. 2. Thomson, Ill.: Heritage House, 1974.

_____. *Muster Rolls and Prisoner-of-War Lists in American Archival Collections Pertaining to the German Mercenary Troops Who Served with the British Forces During the American Revolution.* DeKalb, Ill.: Westland Publications, 1976.

African Americans

Greene, Robert E. *Black Courage, 1775–1783.* Washington, D.C.: National Society of the Daughters of the American Revolution, 1984.

Nell, William G. *Services of Colored Americans in the Wars of 1776 and 1812.* Boston, Mass.: Prentiss & Sawyer, 1976.

Newman, Debra S. *List of Black Servicemen, Compiled from the War Department Collections of Revolutionary War Records.* National Archives Special List no. 36. Washington, D.C.: National Archives, 1974.

Officers and Other Topics

Barnes, John S. *The Logs of the Serapis, Alliance, Ariel, Under the Command of John Paul Jones, 1779–1880.* Naval Historical Society, 1911.

Claghorn, Charles E. *Naval Officers of the American Revolution: A Concise Biographical Dictionary.* Metuchen, N.J.: Scarecrow Press, 1988.

Duncan, Louis C. *Medical Men in the American Revolution, 1775–1783.* Army Medical Bulletin no. 25. Carlisle Barracks, Pa.: Medical Service School, 1931.

Ellet, Elizabeth F. *Women of the Revolution.* New York: Haskett House, 1969.

Heitman, Francis B. *Historical Register of Officers of the Continental Army During the War of the Revolution, April 1777 to December 1783.* Washington, D.C.: Rare Book Shop Publishing Co., 1914. Reprint. Baltimore: Genealogical Publishing Co., 1969.

Long, Richard S., comp. *Biographies of Continental Marine Officers.* History and Museum Division, Headquarters, U.S. Marine Corps, 1974.

Saffell, William T. R. *Records of the Revolutionary War Containing the Military and Financial Correspondence of Distinguished Officers.* Names of officers and privates, regiments, companies, and corps and a list of distinguished prisoners of war. Baltimore: C. C. Saffell, 1894. For a partial index to this work see McAllister under "Virginia," below.

Selected State Roster Lists and Related Publications

Alabama

Alabama, Department of Archives and History. *Revolutionary Soldiers in Alabama, Being a List of Names Compiled from Authentic Sources, of Soldiers of the American Revolution, Who Resided in the State of Alabama.* Montgomery, Ala.: Brown Printing Co., 1911. Reprint. Baltimore: Genealogical Publishing Co., 1967. Contains biographies of approximately five hundred men.

Fritot, Jesse R. *Pension Records of Soldiers of the Revolution Who Removed to Florida, with Record of Service.* Daughters of the American Revolution, Jacksonville chapter, 1946.

Owen, Thomas M. *Revolutionary Soldiers in Alabama.* Alabama State Archives Bulletin 5. 1911. Reprint. Baltimore: Genealogical Publishing Co., 1967.

Connecticut

Connecticut. Adjutant General. *Record of Service of Connecticut Men in the War of the Revolution, War of 1812, Mexican War.* Hartford, Conn.: Case, Lockwood & Brainard, 1889.

Connecticut Historical Society. *Rolls and Lists of Connecticut Men in the Revolution, 1775–1783.* Collections of the Connecticut Historical Society, vols. 8, 12. Hartford, Conn.: 1901–09.

Mather, Frederick Gregory. *The Refugees of 1776 from Long Island to Connecticut.* Baltimore: Genealogical Publishing Co., 1972.

U.S. Bureau of Pensions. *Pension Records of the Revolutionary Soldiers from Connecticut.* Washington, D.C.: Government Printing Office, 1919.

Delaware

Delaware, Public Archives Commission. *Delaware Archives,* vols. 1–3. Wilmington, Del.: James and Walls, Printers, 1875.

Peden, Henry C. *Revolutionary Patriots of Delaware, 1775–1783.* Westminster, Md.: Family Line, 1996.

Whitely, William G. *The Revolutionary Soldiers of Delaware.* Wilmington, Del.: James and Walls, Printers, 1875.

Georgia

Georgia, Department of Archives and History. *Revolutionary Soldiers' Receipts for Georgia Bounty Grants.* Atlanta, Ga.: Foote and Davies Co., 1928. Lists those who received certificates of land grants during 1781, 1782, and 1783. Gives names, dates, acreage, rank, and unit served in.

Georgia, Secretary of State. *Authentic List of All Land Lottery Grants Made to Veterans of the Revolutionary War by the State of Georgia, Taken from Official State Records in the Surveyor-General Department, Housed in the Georgia Department of Archives and History.* Atlanta, Ga.: 1955. Lists the names, county of residence, and the location of land granted in the Georgia 1820 and 1827 lotteries.

Houston, Martha Lou, comp. *Reprints of Official Register of Land Lottery of Georgia, 1827.* Columbus, Ga., 1929. Reprint. Baltimore: Genealogical Publishing Co., 1967. Lists names of those receiving lands in the 1827 lottery, designating those with revolutionary service as a qualification.

_____. *Six Hundred Revolutionary Soldiers Living in Georgia in 1827–28.* Washington, D.C.: 1932.

_____. *Six Hundred Revolutionary Soldiers and Widows of Revolutionary Soldiers Living in Georgia, 1827–1828.* Athens, Ga.: 1965. Available from Heritage Press, Danielsville, Georgia.

Knight, Lucian L. *Georgia's Roster of the Revolution.* Atlanta, Ga.: Index Printing Co., 1920. Reprint. Baltimore: Genealogical Publishing Co., 1967.

Richardson, Marian M., and Mize, Jessie J. *1832 Cherokee Land Lottery, Index to Revolutionary Soldiers, Their Widows and Orphans Who Were Fortunate Drawers.* Danielsville, Ga.: Heritage Press, 1969. Names of soldiers, widows, and orphans. Place of residence is given.

Illinois

Illinois State Genealogical Society. Devanny, Mrs. John S., comp. *Soldiers of the American Revolution Buried in Illinois.* Springfield, Ill., 1975.

Walker, Mrs. Harriet J. *Revolutionary Soldiers Buried in Illinois.* Los Angeles: Standard Printing Co., 1917. Reprint. Baltimore: Genealogical Publishing Co., 1967.

Indiana

English, William H. *Conquest of the Country Northwest of the River Ohio, 1778–1783, and Life of Gen. George Rogers Clark.* Indianapolis and Kansas City, Kans.: 1896. Lists the soldiers who served with Clark and who were granted land in Indiana.

O'Bryne, Mrs. Estella. *Roster of Soldiers and Patriots of the American Revolution Buried in Indiana.* 2 vols. Brockville: Indiana DAR, 1938, 1966.

Waters, Margaret R. *Revolutionary Soldiers Buried in Indiana. Three Hundred Names Not Listed in the Roster by Mrs. O'Bryne.* 2 vols. 1949, 1954. Reprinted in 1 vol. Baltimore: Genealogical Publishing Co., 1970.

_____. *Revolutionary Soldiers Buried in Indiana: A Supplement; 485 Names Not Listed in the "Roster of Soldiers and Patriots of the American Revolution Buried in Indiana" (1938); nor in "Revolutionary Soldiers Buried in Indiana" (1949).* Indianapolis, 1954. Reprint. Baltimore: Genealogical Publishing Co., 1970.

Kentucky

Jillson, Willard. *Old Kentucky Entries and Deeds.* Filson Club Publication no. 35. Louisville, Ky., 1926. Reprint. Baltimore: Genealogical Publishing Co., 1969.

Lindsay, Kenneth G. *Kentucky's Revolutionary War Pensioners, Under the Acts of 1816, 1832.* Evansville, Md.: Kenman Publishing Co., 1977.

Quisenberry, Anderson C. *Revolutionary Soldiers in Kentucky.* Excerpted from the Year Book, Kentucky Society, Sons of the American Revolution (1896). Baltimore: Genealogical Publishing Co., 1959.

Maine

Fisher, Carleton E. *Soldiers, Sailors, and Patriots of the Revolutionary War, Maine.* Louisville, Ky.: National Society of the Sons of the American Revolution, 1982.

Flagg, Charles A. *An Alphabetical Index of Revolutionary Pensioners Living in Maine.* Dover, Maine, 1920. Reprint. Baltimore: Genealogical Publishing Co., 1967. Lists approximately 3,500 men. Gives age at the time the pension was compiled and residence at that time.

House, Charles L., comp. *Names of Soldiers of the American Revolution Who Applied for State Bounty under Resolves of March 17, 1835, March 24, 1836, and March 20, 1838, as Appears of Record in Land Office.* Augusta, Maine, 1893. Reprint. Baltimore: Genealogical Publishing Co., 1967. The list contains both soldiers and widows. Gives date and place of death where appropriate.

Maryland

Brumbaugh, Gaius Marcus. *Revolutionary Records of Maryland.* Washington, D.C.: Rufus H. Darby, 1924.

Clements, S. Eugene. *The Maryland Militia in the Revolutionary War.* Westminster, Md.: Family Line, 1987.

Maryland Historical Society. *Muster Rolls and Other Records of Service of Maryland Troops in the American Revolution, 1775–1783.* Archives of Maryland, vol. 18. Baltimore, 1900. Reprint. Baltimore: Genealogical Publishing Co., 1972.

Maryland, Treasurer's Office. *A List of Invalid Pensioners.* Annapolis, Md.: J. Hughes, Printer, 1822.

McGhee, Lucy K. *Maryland Revolutionary War Pensions, Revolutionary, 1812, and Indian Wars.* Washington, D.C.: 1952.

Newman, Harry W. *Maryland Revolutionary Records: Data Obtained from 3,050 Pension Claims and Bounty Land Applications, Including 1,000 Marriages of Maryland Soldiers and a List of 1,200 Proved Services of Soldiers and Patriots of Other States.* Washington, D.C.: 1938. Reprint. Baltimore: Genealogical Publishing Co., 1967.

Massachusetts

Allen, Gardner W. *Massachusetts Privateers of the Revolution.* Collections of the Massachusetts Historical Society, vol. 77. Boston, 1927.

Massachusetts. Department of the State Secretary. *Massachusetts Soldiers and Sailors of the Revolutionary War.* Boston: Wright & Potter, 1896–1908.

New Hampshire

Batchellor, Albert S., ed. *Miscellaneous Revolutionary Documents of New Hampshire.* Provincial and State Papers of New Hampshire, vol. 30. Manchester, N.H., 1910.

Hammond, Isaac W., ed. *Rolls of the Soldiers in the Revolutionary War.* Provincial and State Papers of New Hampshire, vols. 14–17. Concord and Manchester, N.H., 1885–89. Reprint. New York: AMS Press, 1973.

"Rolls and Documents Relating to Soldiers in the Revolutionary War." New Hampshire Provincial and State Papers, vols. 14–17. Concord and Manchester, N.H., 1885–89.

Potter, Chandler E. *The Military History of the State of New Hampshire From its Settlement, in 1623, to the Rebellion in 1861.* 2 vols. New Hampshire Adjutant General's Report. Concord, N.H., 1866–68. Reprint. Baltimore: Genealogical Publishing Co., 1972. The reprint has several additional indexes.

Walterworth, Mrs. E. J. *Location of Graves of New Hampshire Revolutionary Soldiers.* N.p., n.d. Copied from the records of the Harold B. Twombly Graves Registration Office of the New Hampshire American Legion. Names are listed by town and county where the graves are located.

New Jersey

Jackson, Ronald V. *Index to Military Men of New Jersey, 1775–1815.* Bountiful, Utah: Accelerated Indexing Systems, 1977.

New Jersey. Adjutant General. *Official Register of the Officers and Men of New Jersey in the Revolutionary War.* Trenton, N.J.: W. T. Nicholson, 1872.

Stratford, Dorothy A., and Thomas B. Wilson. *Certificates and Receipts of Revolutionary New Jersey.* Lambertville, N.J.: Hunterdon House, 1996.

New York

Fernow, Berthold, ed., and New York State Archives. *New York in the Revolution.* Documents Relating to the Colonial History of the State of New York, vol. 15. Albany, N.Y., 1887. Reprint. Cottonport, La.: Polyanthus, 1972. Contains approximately thirty-four thousand men; comprises the "Roster of State Troops."

Green, Nelson, ed. *The History of the Mohawk Valley.* 4 vols. Chicago: S. J. Clarke Publishing Co., 1925. Vol. 2 has thousands of names of those who served in Tyron and Albany counties, both in the militia and the regular New York regiments.

New York, Comptroller's Office. *New York in the Revolution as Colony and State.* 2 vols. Albany, N.Y.: J. B. Lyon and Co., 1904.

New York, Secretary of State. *The Balloting Book and Other Documents Relating to Military Bounty Lands, in the State of New York.* Albany, N.Y., 1825.

New York, State Historian. *Third Annual Report of the State of New York, 1897; Transmitted to the Legislature, March 14, 1898.* New York City and Albany, N.Y.: Wynkoop Hahlenbeck Crawford Co., 1898. Contains muster rolls by county and military company. There is an index of names.

North Carolina

Burns, Annie W. *Abstracts of Pension Papers of North Carolina Soldiers of the Revolution, 1812, and Indian Wars.* 15 vols. Washington, D.C.: 1960–66. Summary-type abstracts of pension files at the National Archives. Much detail is given and the claim and certificate numbers are listed. Each volume has its own index.

Carter, Mary. *North Carolina Revolutionary Soldiers, Sailors, Patriots and Descendants.* 2 vols. Albany, Ga.: Pioneers Publications, 1978.

Cartwright, Betty G., and Lillian J. Gardiner. *North Carolina Land Grants in Tennessee, 1778–1791.* Memphis, Tenn.: Division of Archives, 1958.

Clark, Walter E., ed. *State Records of North Carolina.* Goldsboro, N.C.: Nash Brothers, 1899. Vol. 16, "List of 12 Months Recruits from Caswell County," p. 619; "Officers of the North Carolina Line, March 30, 1782," pp. 71–75, 575–77; "Roster of the Continental Line from North Carolina," pp. 1002–1197. Vol. 17, "Abstracts of Pension Applications of North Carolina Soldiers in the Revolutionary War," pp. 189–263; "List of Prisoners on Board Forbay Prison Ship," p. 1044; "Payrolls of the First North Carolina Regiment of Militia," pp. 1054–61.

Daughters of the American Revolution, North Carolina. *Roster of Soldiers from North Carolina in the American Revolution: With an Appendix Containing a Collection of Miscellaneous Papers.* Durham, N.C.: Daughters of the American Revolution, 1932. Reprint. Baltimore: Genealogical Publishing Co., 1972.

White, Katherine K. *The King's Mountain Men.* 1924. Reprint. Baltimore: Genealogical Publishing Co., 1977. Includes an alphabetical list of soldiers with biographies.

Ohio

Ohio, Adjutant General's Office. *The Official Roster of the Soldiers of the American Revolution Buried in the State of Ohio.* Columbus, Ohio: F. J. Heer Printing Co., 1929–59.

Pennsylvania

Linn, John Blair. *Pennsylvania in the War of the Revolution, Battalions and Line 1775–1783.* Harrisburg, Pa.: state printer, 1880.

Pennsylvania, State of. *Pennsylvania Archives.* 138 vols. Harrisburg, Pa.: Pennsylvania Historical and Museum Commission, 1852–1914. There are nine series of this publication. Revolutionary war soldiers are listed in series 2, 3, 5, and 6.

Rhode Island

Arnold, James N. *Cowell's Spirit of '76: An Analytical Explanatory Index.* 1901. Reprinted with *Vital Records of Rhode Island,* vol. 12. Baltimore: Genealogical Publishing Co., 1973. Indexed by Benjamin Cowell as follows.

Cowell, Benjamin. *Spirit of '76 in Rhode Island.* Boston: A. J. Wright, 1850.

Smith, Joseph J. *Civil and Military List of Rhode Island, 1647–1800.* 3 vols. Providence, R.I.: Preston and Rounds, 1901. Vol. 2 has military lists from 1776. An index to the first two volumes is in vol. 3.

Walker, Anthony. *So Few the Brave: Rhode Island Continentals, 1775–1783.* Newport, R.I.: Seafield, 1981.

South Carolina

Ervin, Sara Sullivan. *South Carolinians in the Revolution.* 1949. Reprint. Baltimore: Genealogical Publishing Co., 1965.

Ervin, Sara A., ed. *South Carolinians in the Revolution, with Service Records and Miscellaneous Data . . . 1775–1855.* Ypsilanti, Mich., 1959. Reprint. Baltimore: Genealogical Publishing Co., 1971. Contains data gathered from a variety of South Carolina sources, including pension rolls, DAR lists, wills, burial lists for other states, and many others. There is a general index of names and a separate index of women's names.

Revill, Janie. *Revolutionary Claims Filed in South Carolina.* Baltimore: Genealogical Publishing Co., 1969. These are the records kept by James McCall, auditor-general of the state.

Moss, Bobby Gilmer. *Roster of South Carolina Patriots in the American Revolution.* Baltimore: Genealogical Publishing Co., 1983.

Salley, Alexander S., comp. *Records of the Regiments of the South Carolina Line.* Baltimore: Genealogical Publishing Co., 1977. Contains muster rolls and returns of the Sixth South Carolina Regiment, which formed before 1776 and was detailed to the Continental Line.

South Carolina, Department of Archives and History. *Stub Entries to Indents Issues in Payment of Claims Against South Carolina Growing Out of the Revolution.* 12 vols. Columbia, S.C., 1919–57.

Tennessee

Allen, Penelope J. *Tennessee Soldiers in the Revolution.* Baltimore: Genealogical Publishing Co., 1975.

Armstrong, Zella, comp. *Some Tennessee Heroes of the Revolution Compiled from Pension Statements.* Chattanooga, Tenn.: Lookout Publishing Co., 1933. Reprint. Baltimore: Genealogical Publishing Co., 1975.

______. *Twenty-four Hundred Tennessee Pensioners of the Revolution, War of 1812.* Chattanooga, Tenn.: Lookout Publishing Co., 1937.

Haywood, John. "List of North Carolina Revolutionary Soldiers Given Land in Tennessee, by the Act of 1782–83." In *The History of Tennessee,* pp. 218–20. Knoxville, Tenn.: Keiskell & Brown, 1823. Reprint. New York: Arno Press, 1971.

Vermont

Crockett, Walter Hill. *Revolutionary Soldiers Buried in Vermont.* 1903–07. Reprint. Baltimore: Genealogical Publishing Co., 1959.

Fisher, Carleton E. *Soldiers, Sailors, and Patriots of the Revolutionary War, Vermont.* Camden, Maine: Picton Press, 1992.

Goodrich, John E., comp. and ed. The Vermont Legislature. *Rolls of Soldiers in the Revolutionary War, 1775–1783.* Rutland, Vt.: Tuttle Co., 1904.

Virginia

Abercrombie, Janice L. *Virginia Publick Claims.* 3 vols. Athens, Ga.: Iberian Publishing Co., 1992.

Burgess, Louis A., comp. and ed. *Virginia Soldiers of 1776, Compiled from Documents on File in the Virginia Land Office; Together with Material Found in the Archives Department of the Virginia State Library and Other Reliable Sources.* 3 vols. Richmond, Va.: Richmond Press, 1927–29. Reprint. Spartanburg, S.C.: Reprint Co., 1973. Abstracts from the Virginia Land Office bounty records. Names of the soldiers and some descendants.

Brumbaugh, Gaius M. *Revolutionary War Records: Virginia Army and Navy Forces with Bounty Land Warrants for Virginia Military District of Ohio and Virginia Scrip, From Federal and State Archives.* Washington, D.C.: 1936. Reprint. Baltimore: Genealogical Publishing Co., 1967. Has more than seven thousand names. Indexed.

Dorman, John F. *Virginia Revolutionary Pension Applications.* Washington, D.C.: the author, 1958–. A continuing series of transcripts.

Egle, William Henry. *Old Rights, Property Rights, Virginia Entries and Soldiers Entitled to Donation Lands.* Harrisburg, Va.: C. M. Busch, state printer, 1896.

Gwathmey, John H. *Historical Register of Virginians in the Revolution: Soldiers, Sailors, Marines: 1775–1783.* Richmond, Va.: Deitz Press, 1938. Reprint. Baltimore: Genealogical Publishing Co., 1973.

McCallister, Joseph T. *Index to Saffell's List of Virginia Soldiers in the Revolution.* Hot Springs, Va.: McAllister Publishing Co., 1913. This work indexes not only most of Saffell's book (see above under "Officers and Other Topics"), but also indexes Palmer's book (below).

Palmer, William P., ed. *Calendar of Virginia State Papers and Other Manuscripts . . . Preserved in the Capitol.* Vols. 1–3. Richmond, Va., 1875–83.

Ready, Anne W. *West Virginia Revolutionary Ancestors Whose Services Were Non-Military and Whose Names, Therefore, Do Not Appear in Revolutionary Indexes of Soldiers and Sailors.* 1930. Reprint. Baltimore: Genealogical Publishing Co., 1963.

Tazewell, Littleton, W. *A List of Claims for Bounty Land for Revolutionary Services Acted Upon by the Governor Since April, 1884.* Richmond, Va.: State Library, 1835.

U.S. Congress: Committee on Revolutionary Claims. *Virginia Revolutionary Claims, Bounty Lands and Commutation Pay.* Washington, D.C.: Blair and Rivers Printers, 1840.

Virginia State Library, Department of Archives and History, and H. J. Eckenrode, comp. *List of Revolutionary Soldiers of Virginia.* Richmond, Va.: D. Bottom, 1911, 1912, 1913. Until the publication of Gwathmey (above), which incorporated Eckenrode's work, this was a major publication for Virginia soldiers.

Wilson, Samuel M. *Catalogue of Revolutionary Soldiers and Sailors of the Commonwealth of Virginia to Whom Land Bounty Warrants Were Granted by Virginia for Military Services in the War for Independence.* Baltimore: Genealogical Publishing Co., 1967.

_____. *Virginia Revolutionary Land Bounty Warrants.* Baltimore: Southern Book Co., 1953. Gives name, rank, type of service, number of years served, date of warrant, and number of acres awarded.

Virginia Genealogical Society. *Virginia Revolutionary War State Pensions.* Richmond, Va.: the society, 1980.

West Virginia

Johnston, Ross B., comp. *West Virginians in the Revolution.* Baltimore: Genealogical Publishing Co., 1977.

Lewis, Virgil A. "The Soldiery of West Virginia in the French and Indian War, Lord Dunmore's War, The Revolution . . . the War with Mexico." In *Third Biennial Report of the State Department of Archives and History*, pp. 39–118. Charleston, W.Va.: News-Mail Co., 1910. Reprint. Baltimore: Genealogical Publishing Co., n.d.

War of 1812

General

Hickey, Donald A. *The War of 1812: A Forgotten Conflict.* Chicago: University of Illinois, 1989.

Horsman, Reginald. *The War of 1812.* New York: Alfred A. Knopf, 1969.

Schweitzer, George K. *War of 1812 Genealogy.* Knoxville, Tenn.: the author, 1983.

Smith, Dwight La Vern. *War of 1812: An Annotated Bibliography.* New York: Garland, 1985.

Stanley, George F. G. *The War of 1812 Land Operations.* Ottawa: National Museums of Canada, 1983.

Name lists (also see the listings under "Revolutionary War")

Carr, Mrs. Henry J. *Index to Certified Copy of List of American Prisoners of War, 1812–1815, General Entry Book, Ottawa, Canada.* Washington, D.C.: National Society, U.S. Daughters of 1812, 1924. Copies of these lists are at the Library of Congress and at the society's headquarters.

Galvin, Eleanor S. *Ancestor Index of the National Society U.S. Daughters of 1812, 1892–1970.* Washington, D.C.: the society, 1970. Gives service of each ancestor and some family data.

Christensen, Kathryn. *Arkansas Military Bounty Grants (War of 1812).* Hot Springs, Ark.: Arkansas Ancestors, 1971.

Dunaway, Maxine. *Missouri Military Land Warrants, War of 1812.* Springfield, Mo.: the author, 1985.

Ordway, Frederick I. *Register of the General Society of the War of 1812.* Washington, D.C.: the society, 1972. Contains an index to ancestors and members and gives lineages of members.

Peterson, Clarence S. *Known Military Dead During the War of 1812.* Baltimore: the author, 1955.

U.S. General Land Office. *War of 1812 Bounty Lands in Illinois.* Reprint. Thomson, Ill.: Heritage House, 1977.

U.S. Pension Bureau. *List of Pensioners on the Roll, 1883.* Baltimore: Genealogical Publishing Co., 1970.

White, Virgil D. *Index to War of 1812 Pension Files.* Rev. ed. 2 vols. Waynesboro, Tenn.: National Historical Publishing Co., 1990–92.

Georgia

Kratovil, Judy S. *Index to War of 1812 Service Records for Volunteer Soldiers from Georgia.* Atlanta, Ga.: the author, 1986.

Illinois

Volkel, L. *War of 1812 Bounty Land Patents in Illinois.* Thompson, Ill.: Heritage House, 1977.

_____. *War of 1812 Bounty Lands in Illinois.* Thompson, Ill.: Heritage House, 1977.

Indiana

Franklin, Charles W. *Indiana, War of 1812 Soldiers: Militia.* Indianapolis: Ye Olde Genealogie Shoppe, 1984.

U.S. Adjutant General's Office. *Muster Pay and Receipt Rolls of Indiana Territory Volunteers or Military of the Period of the War of 1812.* 4 vols. Washington, D.C.: Adjutant General, n.d.

Kentucky

Adjutant General's Office. *Kentucky Soldiers of the War of 1812.* Baltimore: Genealogical Publishing Co., 1969.

_____. *Index to Veterans of American Wars from Kentucky.* Frankfort: Kentucky Historical Society, 1966.

Kentucky Adjutant General's Office. *Report of the Adjutant General of Kentucky Soldiers of the War of 1812.* Frankfort, Ky., 1891.

Wilder, Minnie S. *Kentucky Soldiers of the War of 1812.* Baltimore: Genealogical Publishing Co., 1969.

Louisiana

Adjutant General's Office. *The Compiled Service Records of Louisianans in the War of 1812.* Baton Rouge: Adjutant General's Office, n.d.

Pierson, M. J. B. *Louisiana Soldiers in the War of 1812.* Baton Rouge: Louisiana Genealogical and Historical Society, 1963.

Maine and Massachusetts

Adjutant General's Office. *Records of the Massachusetts Volunteer Militia Called Out by the Governor of Massachusetts to Suppress a Threatened Invasion During the War of 1812–14. . . .* Boston: Wright & Potter, 1913.

Maryland

Marine, William M. *The British Invasion of Maryland: 1812–1815.* Baltimore, 1913. Reprint. Baltimore: Genealogical Publishing Co., 1977. Has an appendix containing eleven thousand names.

Wright, F. Edward. *Maryland Militia, War of 1812.* 8 vols. Silver Spring, Md.: Family Line Publications, 1979–92.

Michigan

Miller, Alice Turner. *Soldiers of the War of 1812, Who Died in Michigan.* Ithaca, Mich.: the author, 1962.

Mississippi

Department of Archives and History. *Roster of Mississippi Men Who Served in the War of 1812 and Mexican War.* Jackson, Miss.: Department of Archives and History, n.d.

Rowland, Mrs. Dunbar. *Mississippi Territory in the War of 1812.* Baltimore: Genealogical Publishing Co., 1968.

Nebraska

Nebraska Secretary of State. *Roster of Soldiers, Sailors, and Marines of the War of 1812, The Mexican War, and The War of the Rebellion Residing in Nebraska, June 1, 1891.* Lincoln, Nebr.: State Journal Co., 1892.

New Jersey

Adjutant General's Office. *Records of Officers and Men of New Jersey in Wars, 1791–1815.* 1909. Reprint. Baltimore: Genealogical Publishing Co., 1970.

New York

Adjutant General's Office. *Index of Awards on Claims of the Soldiers of the War of 1812.* Baltimore: Genealogical Publishing Co., 1963.

Hastings, Hugh. State Historian. *Military Minutes of the Council of Appointments of the State of New York.* Albany, N.Y.: state printer, 1901. Includes appointments of militia officers form 1783 to 1821 and an index.

North Carolina

North Carolina Adjutant General's Office. *Muster Rolls of the Soldiers of the War of 1812 Detached from the Militia of North Carolina in 1812 and 1814.* Winston-Salem, N.C.: Barber Publishing Co., 1969.

Ohio

Diefenbach, Mrs. H. B. *Index to the Grave Records of Soldiers in the War of 1812 Buried in Ohio.* The author, 1945.

Garner, Grace. *Index to Roster of Ohio Soldiers, War of 1812.* Spokane, Wash.: Eastern Washington Genealogical Society, 1974.

Ohio Adjutant General's Office. *Roster of Ohio Soldiers in the War of 1812.* Baltimore: Genealogical Publishing Co., 1968.

Ohio Society U.S. Daughters of 1812. *Index to the Grave Records of Servicemen of the War of 1812, State of Ohio.* The society, 1969.

Pennsylvania

Pennsylvania Historical and Museum Commission. *Pennsylvania Archives.* 138 vols. Harrisburg, Pa.: Pennsylvania Historical and Museum Commission, 1852–1914. Series 2, vol. 12, has lists of soldiers and index to officers only. Series 4, vol. 5, index in series 4, vol. 12. Series 6, vol. 7, 8, 9, index in series 7.

Tennessee

McCown, M. H., and I. E. Burns. *Soldiers of the War of 1812 Buried in Tennessee.* Johnson City, Tenn.: Society of U.S. Daughters of 1812, 1959.

Moore, Mrs. J. T. *Record of Commissions of Officers in the 1796–1815 Tennessee Militia.* Baltimore: Genealogical Publishing Co., 1977.

Texas

Fay, Mary Smith. *War of 1812 Veterans in Texas.* New Orleans: Polyanthos, 1979.

Vermont

Clark, Byron N. *A List of Pensioners of the War of 1812, Vermont Claimants.* Baltimore: Genealogical Publishing Co., 1969.

Vermont Adjutant General's Office. *Roster of Soldiers in the War of 1812–1814.* Montpelier, Vt.: Herbert T. Johnson, Adjutant General, 1933.

Virginia

Auditor's Office. *Muster Rolls of the Virginia Militia in the War of 1812.* Richmond, Va.: Auditor's Office, 1852.

_____. *Pay Rolls of Militia Entitled to Land Bounty Under Act of Congress of 1850.* Richmond, Va.: Auditor's Office, 1851.

Butler, Stuart Lee. *Guide to Virginia Militia Units in the War of 1812.* Athens, Ga.: Iberian Publishing Co., 1988.

_____. *Virginia Soldiers in the United States Army, 1800–1815.* Atlanta: Iberian Publishing Co., 1986.

Wardell, Patrick G. *War of 1812 Virginia Bounty Land and Pension Applicants.* Bowie, Md.: Heritage Books, 1987.

Mexican War

Eisenhower, John S. D. *So Far from God: The U.S. War with Mexico 1846–1848.* New York: Random House, 1989.

McCaffrey, James M. *Army of Manifest Destiny: The American Soldier in the Mexican War, 1846–1848.* New York: New York University Press, 1992.

Peterson, Clarence S. *Known Military Dead during the Mexican War, 1846–48.* Baltimore: the author, 1957.

Snoke, Elizabeth R. *The Mexican War. A Bibliography of MHRC Holdings for the Period, 1835–1850.* Carlisle Barracks, Pa.: U.S. Army Military History Institute, 1973.

Tutorow, Norman E. *The Mexican-American War: An Annotated Bibliography.* Westport, Conn.: Greenwood, 1981.

White, Virgil D. *Index to Mexican War Pension Files.* Waynesboro, Tenn.: National Historical Publishing Co., 1989.

Wolfe, Barbara S. *Index to Mexican War Pension Applications.* Indianapolis: Heritage House, 1985.

Name Lists

Arkansas

Payne, Dorothy. *Arkansas Pensioners 1818–1900.* Easley, S.C.: Southern Historical Press, 1985. Includes muster rolls of Arkansas regiments, 1836 to 1847.

Connecticut

Connecticut Adjutant General. *Record of Service of Connecticut Men, III, Mexican War.* Hartford, Conn.: Case, Lockwood, and Brainard, 1889.

Florida

Davis, T. Frederick. "Florida's Part in the War with Mexico." *Florida Historical Quarterly* 20 (January 1942): 235–39.

Illinois

Illinois Adjutant General's Office. *Record of the Service of Illinois Soldiers in the Black Hawk War, 1831–32, and the Mexican War, 1846–48.* Springfield, Ill.: H. W. Q. Rokker, 1882. This volume is indexed in vol. 9 of *Index to Report of the Adjutant General.*

Illinois Soldiers' and Sailors' Home at Quincy: Admissions of Mexican War and Civil War Veterans. Thompson, Ill.: Heritage House, 1975.

Kentucky

Kentucky Adjutant General. *Report of the Adjutant General of the State of Kentucky, Mexican War Veterans.* Frankfort, Ky.: Capitol Office, 1889.

Ohio

Roster Commission. *Official Roster of the Soldiers of the State of Ohio in the War of the Rebellion, 1861–1866.* Akron, Ohio: Werner Co., 1886–95. Vol. 12 includes soldiers of the Mexican War.

Pennsylvania

Pennsylvania Historical and Museum Commission. *Pennsylvania Archives.* 138 vols. Harrisburg, Pa.: Pennsylvania Historical and Museum Commission, 1852–1914. Series 6, vol. 10, index in series 7, vols. 1–5.

Tennessee

Brock, Reid. *Volunteers: Tennesseans in the War with Mexico.* 2 vols. Salt Lake City: Kitchen Table Press, 1986.

Texas (including the Republic of Texas)

Barton, Henry W. *Texas Volunteers in the Mexican War.* Wichita Falls, Tex.: Texan Press, 1970.

Spurlin, Charles D. *Texas Veterans in the Mexican War.* St. Louis: Ingmire Pub., 1984.

Barron, John C., et al. *Republic of Texas Pension Application Abstracts.* Austin, Tex.: Austin Genealogical Society, 1987.

Daughters of the Republic of Texas. *Muster Rolls of the Texas Revolution.* Austin, Tex.: Daughters of the Republic of Texas, 1986.

Rosenthal, Phil, and Bill Groneman. *Roll Call at the Alamo.* Fort Collins, Colo.: Old Army Press, 1985.

Utah

Larson, Carl V. *A Database of the Mormon Battalion.* Providence, Utah: K. W. Watkins, 1987.

Civil War

General History

Catton, Bruce. *The Centennial History of the Civil War.* New York: Doubleday, 1961–65.

Foote, Shelby. *The Civil War: A Narrative.* 3 vols. New York: Vintage Books, 1958–74.

Linderman, Gerald E. *Embattled Courage: The Experience of Combat in the American Civil War.* New York: Free Press, 1987.

McPherson, James M. *Battle Cry of Freedom: The Civil War Era.* Oxford History of the United States. New York: Oxford University Press, 1988.

Mitchell, Reid. *Civil War Soldiers.* New York: Viking, 1988.

Robertson, James I., Jr. *Soldiers Blue and Gray.* Columbia: University of South Carolina Press, 1988.

Wiley, Bell Irvin. *The Life of Billy Yank: The Common Soldier of the Union.* 1951. Reprint. Baton Rouge: Lousiana State University Press, 1995.

_____. *The Life of Johnny Reb: The Common Soldier of the Confederacy.* 1943. Reprint. Baton Rouge: Louisiana State University Press, 1995.

Research Guides

Aimone, Alan C., and Barbara Aimone. *User's Guide to the Official Records of the American Civil War.* Shippensburg, Pa.: White Mane, 1993.

Beers, Henry P. *Guide to the Archives of the Government of the Confederate States.* Washington, D.C.: National Archives, 1986.

Coulter, E. Merton. *Travels in the Confederate States.* Norman: University of Oklahoma Press, 1948.

Crute, Joseph, Jr.. *Units of the Confederate States Army.* Midlothian, Va.: Dewent Books, 1987.

Groene, Bertram H. *Tracing Your Civil War Ancestor.* 4th ed. Winston-Salem, N.C.: John F. Blair, 1995.

Lester, Robert E. *Civil War Unit Histories-Regimental Histories and Personal Narratives.* Bethesda, Md.: University Publications of America, 1992.

Munden, Kenneth White. *Guide to Federal Archives Relating to the Civil War.* Washington, D.C.: National Archives and Record Service, 1962.

Neagles, James. *Confederate Research Sources: A Guide to Archive Collections.* Rev. ed. Salt Lake City: Ancestry, 1997.

Schweitzer, George. *Civil War Genealogy: A Basic Research Guide for Tracing Your Civil War Ancestors.* Knoxville, Tenn.: the author, 1980.

Segars, J. H. *In Search of Confederate Ancestors: The Guide.* Journal of Confederate History Series, vol. 9. Murfreesboro, Tenn.: Southern Heritage Press, 1993.

Bibliographies

Bibliography of State Participation in the Civil War. Washington, D.C.: Government Printing Office, 1913.

Cooling, B. Franklin. *Bibliography of the Era of the Civil War, 1820–1876.* Carlisle Barracks, Pa.: U.S. Army Military History Research Collection, 1974.

Dornbusch, Charles E. *Military Bibliography of the Civil War.* 3 vols. New York: New York Public Library, 1961–72. Supplement, 1987.

Eicher, David J. *The Civil War in Books: An Analytical Bibliography.* Champaign: University of Illinois, 1996.

Miscellaneous Works

Amann, William, ed. *Personnel of the Civil War.* 2 vols. New York: Yoseloff, 1961.

Boatner, Mark M. 3rd. *The Civil War Dictionary.* Rev. ed. New York: Vintage, 1987.

Confederate Veteran. Veterans' magazine published from 1893–1932. Reprinted in 40 vols. by Broadfoot (Wilmington, North Carolina, 1986) with an added index.

Current, Richard N., ed. *Encyclopedia of the Confederacy.* 4 vols. New York: Simon & Schuster, 1993.

Dyer, Frederick. *Compendium of the War of the Rebellion.* Des Moines, Iowa: the author, 1908.

Official Records of the Union and Confederate Armies in the War of the Rebellion. 128 vols. Washington, D.C.: Government Printing Office, 1880–1900.

Official Records of the Union and Confederate Navies in the War of the Rebellion. Washington, D.C.: Government Printing Office, 1894–1922.

Sifakis, Stewart. *Compendium of the Confederate Armies.* New York: Facts on File, 1992–96.

Supplement to the Official Records of the Union and Confederate Armies in the War of the Rebellion. Wilmington, N.C.: Broadfoot, 1994–.

Selected Biographical Dictionaries

Allardice, Bruce S. *More Generals in Grey.* Baton Rouge: Louisiana State University Press, 1995.

Hunt, Roger D., and Jack R. Brown. *Brevet Brigadier Generals in Blue.* Gaithersburg, Md.: Olde Soldier Books, 1990.

Krick, Robert K. *Lee's Colonels: A Biographical Register of the Field Officers of the Army of Northern Virginia.* 3rd ed. Dayton, Ohio: Morningside, 1990.

Sifakis, Stewart. *Who Was Who in the Civil War.* New York: Facts on File, 1988.

U.S. Adjutant General. *Official Army Register of the Volunteer Force of the United States Army for the Years 1861, 1864, 1865.* 8 vols. Washington, D.C.: U.S. Adjutant General's Office, 1865–67. Reprint. Gaithersburg, Md.: Olde Soldier Books, 1987.

Wakelyn, Jon L. *Biographical Dictionary of the Confederacy.* Westpoint, Conn.: Greenwood Press, 1977.

Warner, Ezra J. *Generals in Blue: Lives of the Union Commanders.* Baton Rouge: Louisiana State University Press, 1959.

_____. *Generals in Grey: Lives of the Confederate Commanders.* Baton Rouge: Louisiana State University Press, 1959.

Name Lists of National or Regional Scope

Army Department of Northern Virginia. *The Appomattox Roster.* New York: Antiquarian Press, 1962.

Britzell, Edwin W. *Point Lookout Prison Camp for Confederates.* Available from Edwin W. Britzell, Box 107, Abell, MD 20606.

Confederate P.O.W.s: Soldiers and Sailors Who Died in Federal Prisons and Military Hospitals in the North. Nacogdoches, Tex.: Ericson Books, 1984.

Hewett, Janet, ed. *The Roster of Confederate Soldiers, 1861–1865.* 16 vols. Wilmington, N.C.: Broadfoot, 1995–96.

_____. *The Roster of Union Soldiers, 1861–65.* 33 vols. projected. Wilmington, N.C.: Broadfoot, 1997–.

House of Representatives. *Pardons by the President.* Reprint. Bowie, Md.: Heritage Books, 1986.

List of Pensioners on the Roll, January 1, 1883. . . . Reprint. Baltimore: Genealogical Publishing Co., 1970.

Mills, Gary B. *Civil War Claims in the South: An Index of Civil War Damage Claims Filed Before the Southern Claims Commission, 1871–1880.* Laguna Hills, Calif.: Aegean Park Press, 1980.

National Society of Andersonville. *Atwater Report: List of Prisoners Who Died in 1864–65 at Andersonville Prison.* Andersonville, Ga.: for the society, 1981.

Pompey, Sherman Lee. *Civil War Veteran Burials.* 2 vols. Independence, Calif.: Historical and Genealogical Publishing Co., 1965.

_____. *Civil War Veterans Burials from California, Nevada, Oregon and Washington Regiments Buried in Colorado.* Independence, Calif.: Historical and Genealogical Publishing Co., 1965.

_____. *Military Records. Alabama, Arizona, Arkansas, Indians of North America, Maryland, Missouri, Texas, Georgia, Mississippi, Tennessee.* Independence, Calif.: Historical and Genealogical Publishing Co., 1965.

_____. *Interment of Union Soldiers in United States Territories During the Civil War.* Independence, Calif.: Historical and Genealogical Publishing Co., 1965.

Roll of Honor: Names of Soldiers Who Died in Defense of the American Union Interred in the National Cemeteries. Reprint. 10 vols. and an added index. Baltimore: Genealogical Publishing Co., 1994. With an added index.

U.S. Christian Commission. *Record of the Federal Dead Buried from Libby, Bell Island, Danville and Camp Lawton.* Philadelphia: James B. Rodgers, 1865.

Selected State Roster Lists and Pension Publications, Etc.

Alabama

Alabama 1907 Census of Confederate Soldiers. Cullman, Ala.: Gregath, 1982–83.

Arkansas

Allen, Desmond Walls, comp. *Arkansas' Damned Yankees: An Index to Union Soldiers in Arkansas Regiments.* Conway, Ark.: the author, ca. 1987.

_____. *Index to Arkansas Confederate Soldiers.* Conway, Ark.: Arkansas Research, ca. 1990.

Arkansas. Adjutant General. *Report of the Adjutant General of Arkansas.* Washington, D.C.: Government Printing Office, 1867. Rosters of Federal units raised in Arkansas. Excludes blacks.

Ingmire, Frances T. *Arkansas Confederate Veterans and Widows Pension Applications.* St. Louis: the author, 1985.

Pompey, Sherman Lee. *Muster Lists of the Arkansas Confederate Troops.* 2 vols. Independence, Calif.: Historical and Genealogical Publishing Co., 1965.

California

California Adjutant General's Office. *Records of California Men in the War of the Rebellion, 1861 to 1867.* Sacramento, Calif.: State Office, 1890.

Parker, J. Carlyle. *A Personal Name Index to Orton's Records of California Men in the War of the Rebellion.* Detroit: Gale Research Co., 1978. Index to the above title.

Colorado

Pompey, Sherman Lee. *Confederate Soldiers Buried in Colorado.* Independence, Calif.: Historical and Genealogical Publishing Co., 1965.

Connecticut

Connecticut. Adjutant General. *Catalogue of Connecticut Volunteer Organizations.* Hartford, Conn.: adjutant general, 1869.

Connecticut Adjutant General's Office. *Record of Service of Connecticut Men in the Army and Navy in the War of the Rebellion.* Hartford, Conn.: Case, Lockwood and Brainard, 1889.

District of Columbia

Sluby, Paul E., Sr. *Civil War Cemeteries of the District of Columbia Metropolitan Area.* Washington, D.C.: Columbia Harmony Society, n.d. Includes listings of interments.

Florida

Hartman, David W., and David Coles. *Biographical Rosters of Florida's Confederate and Union Soldiers 1861–1865.* Wilmington, N.C.: Broadfoot, 1995.

White, Virgil D. *Register of Florida CSA Pension Applications.* Waynesboro, Tenn.: National Historical Publishing Co., 1989.

Georgia

Brightwell, Juanita S. *Index to the Confederate Records of Georgia.* Spartanburg, S.C.: Reprint Co., 1982.

Candler, Allen D. *The Confederate Records of the State of Georgia.* Atlanta, Ga.: C. P. Byrd, state printer, 1909–11.

Georgia. State Division of Confederate Pensions and Records. *Roster of the Confederate Soldiers of Georgia 1861–1865.* Reprint. Hapeville, Ga.: Longina & Porter, 1959–64.

Illinois

Illinois. Adjutant General. *Report of the Adjutant General of the State of Illinois.* Springfield, Ill.: Rokker, 1886.

Indiana

Indiana Adjutant General's Office. *Indiana in the War of the Rebellion.* 8 vols. Indianapolis: W. H. H. Terrell, 1869.

Indiana. Adjutant General. *Report.* Indianapolis: adjutant general, 1865–69.

Trapp, Glenda K. *Index to the Report of the Adjutant General of the State of Indiana.* Evansville, Ind.: the author, 1986. Indexes only vols. 1 and 4 of the *Report.*

Iowa

Iowa. Adjutant General. *List of Ex-Soldiers, Sailors and Marines Living in Iowa.* Des Moines, Iowa: adjutant general, 1886.

Roster and Record of Iowa Soldiers in the War of the Rebellion. Des Moines, Iowa: state printer, 1908–11.

Kansas

Decker, Eugene Donald. *A Selected, Annotated Bibliography of Sources in the Kansas State Historical Society Pertaining to Kansas in the Civil War.* Emporia, Kans.: State Teacher's College, 1961.

Kansas Adjutant General's Office. *Report of the Adjutant General, C. K. Holliday, December 31, 1864.* Leavenworth, Kans.: adjutant general, 1865.

_____. *Report of the Adjutant General, T. J. Anderson, of the State of Kansas in 1861–1865.* 2 vols. Topeka, Kans.: adjutant general, 1867–70.

Pompey, Sherman Lee. *An Honor Roll of Kansas Civil War Veterans.* Kingsburg, Calif.: Pacific Specialists, 1972.

Kentucky

Kentucky. Adjutant General. *Report of the Adjutant General of the State of Kentucky.* Frankfort, Ky.: Harney, state printer, 1867. Contains Federal rosters only.

Report of the Adjutant General of the State of Kentucky. *Confederate Kentucky Volunteers, War of 1861–65.* Frankfort, Ky.: state printer, 1915.

Simpson, Alicia. *Kentucky Confederate Veteran and Widows Pension Index.* Hartford, Ky.: Cook & McDowell, 1979.

Louisiana

Booth, Andrew B. *Records of Louisiana Confederate Soldiers and Louisiana Confederate Commands.* Reprint. Spartanburg, S.C.: Reprint Co., 1984.

Maine

Maine. Adjutant General. *Annual Report.* Augusta, Maine: state printer, 1862–67.

Maryland

Hartzler, Daniel D. *Marylanders in the Confederacy.* Silver Spring, Md.: Family Line, 1986.

Maryland Hall of Records Commission. *Index to the Maryland Line in the Confederate Army, 1861–1865.* Publication no. 3. Annapolis, Md.: adjutant general, n.d.

Pompey, Sherman Lee. *Muster Lists of the American Rifles of Maryland, Baltimore Artillery, Dias Maryland Artillery, Maryland Guerilla Zouaves, and Captain Walter's Company.* Bakersfield, Calif.: Historical and Genealogical Publishing Co., 1965.

Wilmer, L. Allison. *History and Roster of Maryland Volunteers, War of 1861–5.* Reprint. Silver Spring, Md.: Family Line, 1987.

Massachusetts

Massachusetts. Adjutant General. *Massachusetts Soldiers, Sailors and Marines in the Civil War.* Brookline, Mass.: adjutant general, 1931–35.

Massachusetts Adjutant General's Office. *Record of Massachusetts Volunteers, 1861–1865.* 2 vols. Boston, Mass.: Adjutant General's Office, 1868–70.

Michigan

Michigan. Adjutant General. *Record of Service of Michigan Volunteers in the Civil War. Indexed in Alphabetical General Index to Public Library Sets of 85,271 Names in the Civil War.* Lansing: Michigan secretary of state, 1915.

Michigan Adjutant General's Office. *Annual Report of the Adjutant General 1865–1866.* 3 vols. Lansing, Mich.: John A. Kerr & Co., 1866.

United States Civil War Soldiers Living in Michigan in 1894. St. Johns, Mich.: Genealogists of Clinton County Historical Society, 1988.

Minnesota

Minnesota in the Civil and Indian Wars, 1861–1865. St. Paul: Pioneer Press, 1890–93.

Mississippi

Rietti, John C. *Military Annals of Mississippi.* Reprint. Spartanburg, S.C.: Reprint Co., 1976. Includes incomplete listings of Civil War officers and enlisted men.

Wiltshire, Betty Crouch. *Mississippi Confederate Pension Applications.* Carrollton, Miss.: Pioneer Publishing Co., 1994.

Missouri

Langley, Elizabeth B. *Taney County, Missouri Soldiers Who Fought in the Civil War Including Soldiers of Southwest Missouri and Northwest Arkansas; Also the Cherokees Under Stand Watie.* Billings, Mo.: the author, 1963.

Missouri. Adjutant General. *Report.* Jefferson City, Mo., 1864–66.

Pompey, Sherman Lee. *Muster Lists of the Missouri Confederates.* 9 vols. Independence, Calif.: Historical and Genealogical Publishing Co., 1965.

Nebraska

Nebraska. Adjutant General. *Roster of Nebraska Volunteers 1861 to 1869.* Hastings, Nebr.: Wigton & Evans, 1888.

New Hampshire

New Hampshire. Adjutant General. *Revised Register of New Hampshire Soldiers and Sailors in the War of the Rebellion.* Concord, N.H.: adjutant general, 1895.

New Jersey

New Jersey. Adjutant General. *Records of Officers and Men of New Jersey in the Civil War, 1861–1865.* Trenton, N.J.: J. L. Murphy, 1876–78.

New York

New York Adjutant General's Office. *A Record of Commissioned Officers, Non-commissioned Officers and Privates.* Albany, N.Y.: Comstock & Cassidy, 1864–68.

New York. *Adjutant General. Registers in the War of the Rebellion.* Albany, N.Y.: J. B. Lyon, 1894–1906.

Phisterer, Frederick. *New York in the War of the Rebellion, 1861 to 1865.* Albany, N.Y.: J. B. Lyon, 1912.

North Carolina

Manarin, Louis H., and Weymouth T. Jordan, Jr. *North Carolina Troops 1861–1861: A Roster.* Raleigh, N.C.: State Department of Archives and History, 1966–.

Ohio

Ohio Roster Commission. *Official Roster of the Soldiers of the State of Ohio in the War of the Rebellion.* Various publishers, 1886–95.

Oklahoma

Pompey, Sherman Lee. *Muster Lists of the Cherokee Confederate Indians.* Independence, Calif.: Historical and Genealogical Publishing Co., 1965.

_____. *Muster Lists of the Creek and Other Confederate Indians.* Independence, Calif.: Historical and Genealogical Publishing Co., 1966.

Oregon

Myers, Jane. *Honor Roll of Oregon Grand Army of the Republic, 1881–1935.* Cottage Grove, Oreg.: Cottage Grove Genealogical Society, 1980.

Pekar, M. A. *Soldiers Who Served in the Oregon Volunteers: Civil War Period, Infantry and Cavalry.* Portland, Oreg.: Genealogical Forum of Portland, 1961.

Pennsylvania

Bates, Samuel P. *History of Pennsylvania Volunteers.* Harrisburg, Pa.: state printer, 1869–71. Also *Index to History of Pennsylvania Volunteers.* Wilmington, N.C.: Broadfoot, 1994.

Rhode Island

Rhode Island. Adjutant General. *Report.* Providence, R.I.: adjutant general, 1866.

South Carolina

Salley, A. S., Jr. *South Carolina Troops in Confederate Service.* Columbia, S.C.: R. L. Bryan, 1913–30.

Tennessee

Dyer, Gustavus. *The Tennessee Civil War Veterans Questionnaires.* 5 vols. Easley, S.C.: Southern Historical Press, 1985.

Sistler, Samuel. *Index to Tennessee Confederate Pension Applications.* Nashville: Byron Sistler, 1995.

Tennesseeans in the Civil War. Nashville: Civil War Commission, 1965. Covers both Federals and Confederates.

Wiefering, Edna. *Tennessee Confederate Widows and Their Families: Abstracts of 11,190 Confederate Widows' Applications.* Cleveland, Tenn.: Cleveland Public Library, 1992.

Texas

Kinney, John M. *Index to Applications for Texas Confederate Pensions.* Austin, Tex.: Archives Division, Texas State Library, 1977.

Pompey, Sherman L. *Muster Lists of the Texas Confederate Troops.* Independence, Calif.: Historical and Genealogical Publishing Co., 1966.

White, Virgil D. *Index to Texas CSA Pension Files.* Waynesboro, Tenn.: National Historical Publishing Co., 1989.

Vermont

Vermont. Adjutant General. *Revised Roster of Vermont Volunteers and Lists of Vermonters Who Served in the Army and Navy of the United States during the War of the Rebellion, 1861–66.* Montpelier, Vt.: Watchman, 1892.

Virginia

Howard, H. E. *The Virginia Battles and Leaders Series.* Lynchburg, Va.: the author, 1984–. This is a continuing series, having reached thirty-six volumes in 1992. The series describes battles and prominent persons.

_____. *Virginia Regimental History Series.* Lynchburg, Va.: H. E. Howard, 1982–.

West Virginia

Lang, Theodore F. *Loyal West Virginia from 1861 to 1865.* Baltimore: Deutsch, 1895.

West Virginia. Adjutant General. Annual Reports for 1864 and 1865.

Wisconsin

Grand Army of the Republic. *Soldiers' and Citizens' Album.* 2 vols. Chicago, Ill.: Grand Army Publishing Co., 1888, 1890.

Wisconsin Adjutant General's Office. *Annual Report of the Adjutant General, 1865.* Madison, Wis.: Democrat Printing, 1912.

Wisconsin. Adjutant General. *Roster of Wisconsin Volunteers, War of the Rebellion 1861–1865.* Madison: Democrat Print Co., 1886.

Indian Wars

Board of State Institutions. *Soldiers of Florida in the Seminole Indian, Civil and Spanish-American Wars.* Live Oak, Fla.: Democrat Book, 1903.

Grandrud, Pauline M. *Alabama Soldiers in the Revolutionary, War of 1812 and Indian Wars.* Hot Springs, Ark.: B. J. McLane, 1975.

Hammer, Kenneth. *Men with Custer.* 2 vols. Fort Collins, Colo.: Old Army Press, 1972.

The Black Hawk War, 1831–1832. Collections of the Illinois State Historical Society, vol. 35. Springfield, Ill.: State Historical Society, 1970.

Loftus, Carrie. *Indiana Militia in the Black Hawk War.* The author, n.d.

Peters, Joseph P. *Indian Battles and Skirmishes on the American Frontier, 1790–1898, Comprising a Record of Engagements with Hostile Indians within the Military Division of the Missouri from 1868 to 1882: Chronological List of Actions, etc. with Indians from January 1, 1866 to January 1891: and a Compilation of Indian Engagements from January 1837 to January 1866.* New York: Argonaut Press, 1966.

Prucha, Francis Paul. *Guide to the Military Posts of the United States 1789–1895.* Madison: State Historical Society of Wisconsin, 1964.

_____. *The Sword of the Republic: The United States on the Frontier, 1783–1846.* New York: Macmillan, 1968.

Rickey, Don, Jr. *Forty Miles a Day on Beans and Hay: The Enlisted Soldier Fighting the Indian Wars.* Norman: University of Oklahoma Press, 1963.

Roberts, Robert B. *Encyclopedia of Historic Forts: The Military, Pioneer, and Trading Posts of the United States.* New York: Macmillan, 1988.

Sattlerlee, John L. *The Black Hawk War and the Sangamo Journal.* The author, n.d.

Schubert, Frank N. *On the Trail of the Buffalo Soldier: Biographies of African Americans in the U.S. Army, 1866–1917.* Wilmington, Del.: Scholarly Resources, 1995.

Stephens, Robert W. *Texas Rangers Indian War Pensions.* Quanah, Tex.: the author, 1975.

U.S. Adjutant General. *Record of Service of Illinois Soldiers in the Black Hawk War and Mexican War.* Springfield, Ill.: Isaac H. Elliot, 1882.

U.S. War Department. *Officers and Soldiers Killed in Battle and Died in Service During the Florida War.* Washington, D.C.: Government Printing Office, 1882.

Utley, Robert. *Frontier Regulars: The United States Army and the Indian, 1866–1891.* New York: Macmillan, 1974.

_____. *Frontiersmen in Blue: The United States Army and the Indian, 1848–1865.* New York: Macmillan, 1967.

White, Virgil D. *Index to Indian Wars Pension Files 1892–1926.* Waynesboro, Tenn.: National Historical Publishing Co., 1987.

Spanish-American War

O'Toole, George J. A. *The Spanish War, an American Epic.* New York: W. W. Norton, 1984.

Peterson, Clarence S. *Known Military Dead during the Spanish American War and the Philippine Insurrection, 1898–1901.* Baltimore: the author, 1958.

Trask, David P. *The War with Spain in 1898.* New York: Macmillan, 1981.

Verzon, Anne Cipriano. *The Spanish-American War: An Annotated Bibliography.* New York: Garland, 1990.

Selected State Roster Lists

Connecticut

Connecticut Adjutant General's Office. *Record of Service of Connecticut Men in the Army, Navy and Marine Corps of the U.S. in the Spanish-American War.* Hartford, Conn.: Case, Lockwood, and Brainard, 1919.

Florida

Board of State Institutions. *Soldiers of Florida in the Seminole Indian, Civil and Spanish-American Wars.* Live Oak, Fla.: Democrat Book, 1903.

Georgia

Thaxton, Carlton J. *A Roster of Spanish-American War Soldiers from Georgia.* Americus, Ga.: the author, 1984.

Indiana

General Assembly of Indiana. *Record of Indiana Volunteers in the Spanish-American War 1898–1899.* Indianapolis: W. B. Burford, 1900.

Kentucky

Kentucky Adjutant General's Office. *Report of the Adjutant General of the State of Kentucky: Kentucky Volunteers, War with Spain 1898–1899.* Frankfort, Ky.: Globe Printing, 1908.

New York

Saldana, Richard H., ed. *Index to the New York Spanish-American War Veterans.* 2 vols. Albany, N.Y.: James B. Lyon, 1900.

North Carolina

North Carolina Adjutant General's Office. *Roster of the North Carolina Volunteers in the Spanish-American War, 1898–1899.* Raleigh, N.C.: Edwards and Broughton, 1900.

Ohio

Ohio Adjutant General's Office. *The Official Roster of Ohio Soldiers in the War with Spain 1898–1899.* Columbus, Ohio: Edward T. Miller Co., 1916.

Oregon

Gantebein, C. U., comp. *The Official Records of the Oregon Volunteers in the Spanish War and Philippine Insurrection.* Salem, Oreg.: J. R. Whitney, state printer, 1903.

Pennsylvania

Stewart, Thomas J. *Record of Pennsylvania Volunteers in the Spanish-American War.* Philadelphia: Adjutant General's Office, 1901.

Utah

Prentiss, A. *The History of the Utah Volunteers in the Spanish-American War and the Philippine Islands.* Salt Lake City: W. F. Ford, 1900.

Vermont

Johnson, Herbert T. *Vermont in the Spanish-American War.* Montpelier, Vt.: adjutant general, 1929.

World War I

Bureau of Navigation. *Officers and Enlisted Men of the United States Navy Who Lost Their Lives During the World War from April 6, 1917 to November 11, 1918.* Washington, D.C.: Government Printing Office, 1920.

Dornbusch, Charles E. *Histories of American Army Units, World Wars I and II and Korean Conflict.* Washington, D.C.: Office of the Adjutant General, Special Services Division, 1956.

Freidel, Frank. *Over There: The Story of America's First Great Overseas Crusade.* Philadelphia: Temple University Press, 1990.

Genthe, Charles V. *American War Narratives 1917–1918: A Study and Bibliography.* New York: David Lewis, 1969.

Haulsee, W. M., F. G. Howe, and A. C. Doyle. *Soldiers of the Great War.* 3 vols. Washington, D.C.: Soldier's Record Publishing Co., 1920.

Order of Battle of the United States Land Forces in the World War. Washington: Government Printing Office, 1937–49.

Pershing, John J., Gen. *My Experiences in the World War.* New York: Stokes, 1931.

Stalling, Laurence. *The Doughboys: The Story of the AEF, 1917–1918.* New York: Harper & Row, 1963.

Stokesbury, James L. *A Short History of World War I.* London: Hale, 1981.

Venzon, Anne Cipriano, ed. *The United States in the First World War: An Encyclopedia.* New York: Garland, 1995.

Woodward, David R. *America and World War I: A Selected Annotated Bibliography of English Language Sources.* New York: Garland, 1985.

IMMIGRATION SOURCES OVERVIEW

Key Concepts in This Chapter

- Understanding the history of immigration makes one a better researcher.
- More than three thousand published sources list immigrants.
- Approximately 30 percent of pre-1900 immigrants to North America appear in published sources.
- More than 6,500,000 names in published lists are easy to locate.
- Virtually all known pre-1820 immigrants appear in printed sources.
- Published transcripts are available for many ports of arrival and various ethnic groups.
- Ship indexes help locate others who arrived on an ancestor's ship.
- Many foreign departure lists supplement U.S. arrival records.
- Published naturalization abstracts and indexes usually cover the county level.
- Printed lists of settlers often are based on early land records.
- Compiled sources often provide excellent information about groups of immigrants.
- Genealogical dictionaries of early settlers provide excellent information about immigrants.
- Many important periodical articles naming immigrants have been reprinted.

Key Sources in This Chapter

- *They Came in Ships*
- *American Passenger Arrival Records*
- *Passenger and Immigration Lists Bibliography* (identifies 2,500 published sources)
- *Migration, Emigration, Immigration: Principally to the United States*
- *Passenger and Immigration Lists Index* (with 2.6 million entries)
- *The Famine Immigrants* (with more than half a million names)
- *Germans to America* (listing more than 3 million immigrants)
- *Italians to America*
- *Pennsylvania German Pioneers*
- *The Complete Book of Emigrants* (from 1607 through 1776)
- *The Great Migration Begins: Immigrants to New England 1620–1633*

14

IMMIGRATION SOURCES

Kory L. Meyerink

Immigration is one of the most popular topics in North American genealogy. Virtually everyone in North America (except full-blooded Native Americans) has immigrant ancestors. Some, whose American origins extend back to the 1600s, may descend from hundreds of immigrants. Indeed, the goal of many family historians is to determine who their immigrant ancestors were and to document where they came from. Fortunately, documentation exists for the vast majority of the more than 57 million people who have arrived on America's shores since 1607 (Szucs and Luebking 1997, 444). Even more fortunate is the fact that a growing number of those immigrants are documented in published literature; surprisingly, they include many immigrants often thought to be hard to find, such as colonial-era immigrants and the millions listed in unindexed passenger arrival lists.

The purpose of this chapter is to identify and discuss the major published sources of immigration information. These sources include lists of immigrants, but this chapter also covers the various reference tools and immigration histories that provide the necessary background information to understand American immigration and the records that document the ancestors who made the difficult journey (not always by choice) to a new land. This chapter can only serve to introduce the large and growing literature on this popular topic. The family historian will want to explore the many aspects of immigration through use of the sources discussed here. A good beginning place, where the genealogist can gain an understanding of the topic of immigration as it relates to genealogy as well as the use of the original records that document immigrants, is "Immigration: Finding Immigrant Origins," chapter 13 in *The Source: A Guidebook of American Genealogy,* rev. ed., edited by Loretto Dennis Szucs and Sandra Hargreaves Luebking (Salt Lake City: Ancestry, 1997).

There is a wide variety of published works dealing with the topic of immigration. Immigration information is found in all four categories of genealogical records (see the discussion of "Categories of Research Sources and Tools" in the introduction), so the arrangement of this chapter mirrors, to a degree, that of *Printed Sources* itself. The first part of the chapter covers the key background information sources that provide the foundation for understanding immigration and the records that document ancestors. The section on "Finding Aids" describes the key sources that help researchers access the sources that document immigrants. The largest portion of this chapter discusses the wide variety of published copies of original records, such as passenger lists and naturalization records, that contain information on specific immigrants. Lastly, the section on "Compiled Records" reminds us that, with so much previous research done on American immigrants, compiled records form a significant body of literature.

ORIGINS OF PUBLISHED IMMIGRATION SOURCES

Most published sources that list immigrants are based on original records—commonly the passenger lists and naturalization records kept by various government jurisdictions. Before 1820, very few passenger arrival lists were made. The notable exceptions are the lists kept by Pennsylvania colonial authorities of non-British persons (virtually all of whom were Germans at that time) who arrived in Philadelphia from 1727 to 1808. Beginning in 1820, the U.S. Customs Office was charged with obtaining and maintaining a list of all persons who arrived at U.S. ports. These original lists, often called the *customs passenger lists,* usually did not include much more information than the name, age, occupation, and country of origin for each immigrant. An increasing number of these lists are being published, some according to port of arrival, others by ethnic group; they are discussed below under "Copied Original Records." Beginning in 1883 for Philadelphia and 1891 for most other ports, responsibility for the lists was shifted to immigration officials. Under their direction, the lists became increasingly more detailed, eventually including town of birth or last residence, destination in the United States, and even the name of a relative in the native country. These lists are generally described as the *immigration passenger lists;* relatively few have been printed. All surviving passenger lists (both customs and immigration lists) have been reproduced on microfilm, and many have been indexed on Soundex or index cards (which are also on microfilm).

Original naturalization records created before the first Federal naturalization law of 1798 are rare. Beginning in 1798, U.S. law allowed almost any court, state or Federal, to naturalize foreigners. Individual states decided which of their courts could naturalize aliens. Beginning in 1906, the Federal government took a more active role, and eventually most naturalizations came to be done by the Federal courts. Original naturalization records reside in the various courts where they were created or in state and Federal archives. Most are available on microfilm, and many have been indexed within the jurisdictions that created them. An increasing number are being published (especially state court naturalizations from the nineteenth century).

For more information on original passenger lists and naturalization records, see the various instructional books discussed below under "Background Information."

There are more than three thousand published original and compiled records that document immigrants (Filby 1988, vii). Many are brief articles in periodicals or sections of books that may name only a handful of immigrants. This chapter (and its bibliography) can only profile the most significant sources, with examples of others to show what the researcher can find with a little searching. Therefore, the sources described here are generally those that directly discuss many immigrants (usually five hundred or more). The chapter bibliography attempts to identify all of the significant book-length sources that cover an entire state or multi-state region. Virtually all of the published lists of immigrants pertain to pre-1900 immigrants to the United States, of whom there were 19.1 million from 1820 (*Immigrant Nation* 1991, 34). Adding 2 million for pre-1820 immigration, as well as immigration to Barbados, Bermuda, and Canada, yields approximately 21 million arrivals to North America by 1900. More than 6 million names are now in published sources (table 14-1), meaning that 30 percent of pre-twentieth-century immigrants can easily be found in printed sources (and that number is growing by 100,000 or more each year).

Other sources described in this chapter are necessary to identify all of the possible printed sources of immigration. Family historians will also want to investigate the standard compiled genealogical records, such as biographies, genealogies, and local and family histories, because immigrants are often the focus of such works. See chapters 16, 17, and 18 for more information on these sources. For additional background information on immigrant groups, refer to the many sources discussed in chapter 4, "Ethnic Histories."

All aspects of immigration appear in published sources; however, the greatest interest, both regarding the history of immigration and the sources of information on individual immigrants, has historically focused on the colonial period (including the period up to around 1820). Since the 1970s, the focus has included the Ellis Island period (1892 to 1954). However, as a general rule, the further back in time one goes, the more immigration literature one is likely to find.

Although genealogists are mostly interested in lists of immigrants, American immigration is a vast topic with many very different facets. Therefore, it is important to know the major reference works in the field, not just the key indexes to names. There are actually three different aspects of immigration: (1) Some people want information on the experience of immigration from a particular immigrant's point of view. (2) Others, such as immigration historians, are interested in the demographic aspects of immigration (what groups came when, and in what numbers). (3) The average genealogist, amateur or experienced, most often seeks lists of passengers on which an ancestor may appear. The sources used to answer immigration questions vary with the nature of the question.

Researchers must also remember that many sources dealing with immigration are listed in indexes and bibliographies under "ethnic" headings. The study of minorities and ethnic groups in America almost always deals with immigration. Therefore, several of the reference tools in this chapter focus on ethnic minorities.

BACKGROUND INFORMATION

The effective researcher needs to learn about all aspects of immigration, including what caused members of a particular ethnic group to come to America, where they settled, and when they generally arrived. It is also useful to understand the factors that influenced immigration in North America and how the immigrants traveled there. All of this information, and much more, is found in the extensive background information available on American immigration and European emigration.

Handbooks and Encyclopedias

Studies in immigration have tended to focus on specific groups and not on immigration as a whole. Thus, few broad reference works have been published in the guise of handbooks or encyclopedias on this topic. Probably the largest single work is Encyclopædia Britannica's ten-volume Makers of America series, edited by Wayne Moquin (1971). It is a documentary look at immigration from *The Firstcomers* (vol. 1) in 1586 to the *Emergent Minorities* (vol. 10) of the 1960s. This series reproduces the major documents and period commentaries as they pertain to the immigration and growth of America. It is very helpful for the researcher seeking contemporary attitudes regarding immigration issues, such as the abolishment in 1965 of the 1924 quota system.

A concise, yet thorough, one-volume encyclopedia is the *Harvard Encyclopedia of American Ethnic Groups,* edited by Stephan Thernstrom (Cambridge, Mass.: Harvard University Press, 1980). It treats more than one hundred different ethnic groups (including "Yankees") in articles from one to six or more pages long. Each article includes information on the origins, migration, arrival, settlement, and other aspects of each group. Articles on larger groups, such as Germans, include tables and maps to enhance the text. Even for lesser-known groups, such as Russian Georgians, there are two informative pages devoted to each. The alphabetical arrangement and six-page introduction aid the reader in using and understanding this source.

Wayne Charles Miller's *A Handbook of American Minorities* (New York: New York University Press, 1976) treats similar topics differently. Each of its articles is a combination history, sociology, and bibliographic essay detailing the arrival and settlement of a particular ethnic group. It also discusses the fluctuations in immigration numbers and their causes.

Instructional Books and Literature Guides

The large number and broad scope of immigration sources make it easy for researchers to overlook possible sources. Other researchers seeking immigrant ancestors do not know how to proceed to effectively search the records—especially the thousands of passenger arrivals with their millions of names. Those sources that explain the literature or how to conduct effective research provide important background information. A number of useful sources are available.

They Came in Ships. One of the most significant guidebooks for the genealogist learning about immigration is John Colletta's *They Came in Ships: A Guide to Finding Your Immigrant*

Table 14-1. Major Published Immigration Sources

PILB No.*	*Title*	*Scope*	*No. of Immigrants*
2048	*Passenger and Immigration Lists Index,* 14+ vols.	2,500 lists, 1600 to 1900	2.6 million
2468+	*Germans to America,* 54+ vols.	U.S. port arrivals, 1850–87	3.1 million+
1921+	*Famine Immigrants,* 7 vols.	New York arrivals, 1846–51	545,000
	Italians to America, 7+ vols.	U.S. port arrivals, 1880–	390,000+
	Migration from the Russian Empire, 2+ vols.	New York arrivals, 1875–82	105,000
1219+	*Complete Book of Emigrants; Emigrants in Bondage,* 6 vols.	English departures, 1607–1776	153,000**
9983+	*German Immigrants . . . to New York,* 4 vols.	Bremen departures, with towns of origin, 1847–71	137,000**
205+	*Czech Immigration Passenger Lists*	New York arrivals, 1846–1880, Galveston and other ports	104,000**
8057+	*Wuerttemberg Emigration Index,* 6+ vols.	Permissions to leave, from 1815–1914	100,000**
9082	*Dutch Immigrants, Dutch Emigrants,* 3 vols. total	U.S. port arrivals, 1820–80 Dutch departures, 1835–80	81,000**
2041	*Philadelphia Naturalization Records*	Index covering 1789–1880	120,000**

*Filby's *Passenger and Immigration Lists Bibliography.*
**Included in Filby's *Passenger and Immigration Lists Index.*

Ancestor's Arrival Record, 2nd ed., rev. and enl. (Salt Lake City: Ancestry, 1993). The author, an eminent immigration researcher, explains exactly what a researcher needs to know when trying to find an ancestor in the various passenger lists. After discussing where to obtain the necessary biographical information on an immigrant, Colletta discusses the nature and availability of passenger lists, both prior to the Federal government lists of 1820 and the government lists created through the end of immigration through Ellis Island (1954). Of great interest is his extensive discussion of how to effectively and efficiently search the unindexed years; he includes a number of alternate sources and helpful finding aids.

American Passenger Arrival Records. The other significant guide to passenger lists is Michael H. Tepper's *American Passenger Arrival Records: A Guide to the Records of Immigrants Arriving at American Ports by Sail and Steam* (Baltimore: Genealogical Publishing Co., 1988). It is more an explanation of the lists than a discussion of how to use them. Such an explanation is necessary, however, because the official U.S. Customs lists and the Immigration and Naturalization lists have long been confusing for typical researchers to understand. This book sheds helpful light on this topic, addressing both content and location questions. It fully describes the use and usefulness of these important American documents, beginning with the scanty colonial lists and then exploring why the Federal government decided to keep passenger lists. The second half discusses the difference between the earlier U.S. Customs lists and the later Immigration and Naturalization passenger lists. It is recommended for every researcher, experienced or amateur, who deals with immigration lists.

American Naturalization Processes and Procedures. John J. Newman's *American Naturalization Processes and Procedures, 1790–1985* (Indianapolis: Indianapolis Historical Society, 1985) provides an excellent overview of naturalization laws, processes, and the accompanying documents. Newman briefly discusses the nature of naturalization and its historical development through the 1906 naturalization law and its later amendments. The text also covers derivative citizenship, as well as naturalization based on military service. Of reference value is a chronological summary of required procedures for naturalization, as well as sample documents showing how the records changed in different periods.

They Became Americans. *They Became Americans: Finding Naturalization Records and Ethnic Origins,* by Loretto Dennis Szucs (Salt Lake City: Ancestry, 1998), is the most extensive discussion in the genealogical literature about "how to discover your family or ancestors in naturalization records." This book explains the methods and techniques needed to use the naturalization records created by the various courts. Thoroughly illustrated, it explains the historical background of the naturalization process in the United States. It covers naturalization records in the colonial period, records from 1790 to 1906, and post-1906 records. It also discusses where to search for naturalization documents, including state and local courts as well as Federal courts and the National Archives. Additional information includes Work Projects Administration naturalization indexes and the use of naturalization records in conjunction with other sources. Recognizing the fact that many immigrants were never naturalized, Szucs has added alternative routes for finding ethnic origins. For example, in addition to an explanation of naturalization records in the custody of the Immigration and Naturalization Service, there is a lengthy discussion of alien records available from that agency. The chapter on "Naturalization Records and Ethnic Origins via the Internet" points to emerging sources and strategies for immigration research on the Internet. Appendixes include an immigration chronology, key addresses, a description of the Soundex index codes, and a bibliography.

A wide variety of other guidebooks are noted in the chapter bibliography. For example, many researchers will find August C. Bolino's *The Ellis Island Source Book* (Washington, D.C.: Kensington Historical Press, 1985) to be very helpful. Its 107-page bibliography lists many general and "ethnic specific" sources. It also includes a listing of *New York Times* articles dealing with Ellis Island. The body of the book has many helpful suggestions for research dealing with all aspects of immigration. Hugh T. Law's *How to Trace Your Ancestors to Europe* (Salt Lake City: Cottonwood Books, 1987) provides an eclectic mix of advice and sources, but its most valuable section is part 1, which has 117 success stories from a variety of researchers illustrating how they successfully found the origins of immigrant ancestors. For German immigration (one of the largest groups and one of the most difficult to track), consult Maralyn A. Wellauer's *German Immigration to America in the Nineteenth Century: A Genealogist's Guide* (Milwaukee: Roots International, 1985). While this book is somewhat uneven and repeats some unproven concepts, it does provide encouragement and direction for the German researcher. It also identifies a significant number of sources for the confusing array of German states.

Immigration History Books

In addition to general handbooks and instructional guides for immigration information, some specific narrative books on broad immigration topics from which the interested researcher can get additional background are useful. There are hundreds of such books, but the following are those that are generally still available or are easily found in most public libraries. Oscar Handlin's *The Uprooted: The Epic Story of the Great Migrations that Made the American People* (New York: Grosset and Dunlap, 1951), although aging, still paints a broad picture of the arrival and assimilation of immigrants to America.

Two books by Maldwyn A. Jones, *American Immigration* (Chicago: University of Chicago Press, 1960; the second edition of 1992 [Chicago: University of Chicago Press] contains a new chapter covering immigration from 1960 to 1991) and *Destination America* (New York: Holt, Rinehart and Winston, 1976) update Handlin's book somewhat and are easier to read, with their numerous illustrations and charts. Another excellent overview of immigration is Roger Daniels's *Coming to America: A History of Immigration and Ethnicity in American Life* (New York: Harper Collins, 1990).

For a discussion of the causes of immigration from Europe, see Philip A. Taylor's *The Distant Magnet: European Emigration to the U.S.A.* (London: Eyre and Spottiswoode, 1971). For the process of the immigrant's assimilation into American culture, including a useful discussion of naturalization, see Thomas J. Archdeacon, *Becoming American: An Ethnic History* (New York: Free Press, 1983).

Many immigration histories focus on a specific time period. Two exemplary studies, each covering one side of the Civil War, are Marcus Lee Hansen's *The Atlantic Migration, 1607–1860,* rev. ed. (Cambridge, Mass.: Harvard University Press, 1940; reprint; New York: Harper and Row, 1961), and Walter Nugent's *Crossings: The Great Transatlantic Migrations, 1870–1914* (Bloomington: Indiana University Press, 1992). A smaller yet significant period of time is covered in Bernard Bailyn's Pulitzer Prize-winning *Voyagers to the West: A Passage in the Peopling of America on the Eve of the Revolution* (New York: Alfred A. Knopf, 1986), which is based on a comprehensive analysis of an obscure but detailed source of British departure lists from 1773 to 1776.

Almost any aspect of immigration can be the subject of a specialized treatment. For example, early immigration to New England (of especial interest for genealogists) is well covered in David Cressy's *Coming Over: Migration and Communication Between England and New England in the Seventeenth Century* (New York: Cambridge University Press, 1987), while those interested in nineteenth-century emigration from England to America will find Terry Coleman's *Going to America* (New York, Pantheon Books, 1972) very informative and interesting. For books dealing with the immigration of specific ethnic groups, see the sources discussed in chapter 4, "Ethnic Sources."

Because not all immigrants came of their own free will, it may be useful to review books such as Peter W. Coldham's *Emigrants in Chains: A Social History of Forced Emigration to the Americas of Felons, Destitute Children, Political and Religious Non-conformists, Vagabonds, Beggars and other Undesirables, 1607–1776* (Baltimore: Genealogical Publishing Co., 1992), which provides a good explanation of a less-discussed aspect of immigration. For a perspective on immigrant settlement in American cities and how they affected the growth of the cities, see David Ward's *Cities and Immigrants: A Geography of Change in Nineteenth Century America* (New York: Oxford University Press, 1971). The scholar seeking information on the laws that encouraged (and later discouraged) immigration to the United States will find a detailed analysis in Edward P. Hutchinson's *Legislative History of American Immigration Policy 1798–1965* (Philadelphia: University of Philadelphia Press, 1981).

The great interest in immigration research has lead to the creation of some important research collections. One of the best collections of published materials is available from Research Publications (Woodbridge, Connecticut), which has reproduced some six thousand published books dealing with immigration from 1820 to 1929 on approximately four hundred rolls of microfilm. The collection includes books covering thirty-seven different ethnic groups.

Immigration Periodicals

The scholarly periodicals of the major immigration societies comprise a significant source of background information on immigration. The major journal dealing specifically with the topic of migration is the *International Migration Review* (1973–), published by the Center for Migration Studies (Staten Island, New York). This quarterly generally includes around five lengthy articles in each issue as well as a dozen or more critical book reviews on the current literature. In addition, a section reviews recent articles in other publications. It is indexed or abstracted in more than a dozen different academic research databases. The center also publishes *Migration World* (1973–), a magazine focusing on the newest immigrant and refugee groups, including government policy and legislation.

The organ of the U.S. Immigration and Naturalization Service is the quarterly *I and N Reporter* (1943–). It includes official government statistics, charts, illustrations, and other information detailing the activities and interests of the Immigration and Naturalization Service. There are many other organizations, including many private and public foundations, that deal with immigrants; many of them publish regular newsletters that help keep their members and interested scholars apprised of their activities, including publications, collections, and exhibits. Brief articles are also found in such periodicals.

Two exemplary newsletters from organizations that focus on the history of immigration are the semiannual *Immigration History Newsletter* (1969–), published by the Immigration History Society (St. Paul, Minnesota), and the semiannual *New Dimensions* (1979–), published by the Balch Institute for Ethnic Studies (Philadelphia). For the genealogical use of periodicals and periodical articles in immigration research, see "Compiled Records" later in this chapter.

Ships

Most immigrants came to the United States on ships. Interest in the ships of immigrants appears in every aspect of immigration research. From the historian interested in a particular ship or shipping line to the genealogist who wants information about the ship on which an ancestor arrived, ships hold a fascination for many. Immigrant ships were essentially of two types: sailing ships, generally used before the Civil War, and steamships, whose use increased after the war. For information on sailing ships, see Carl C. Cutler's *Queens of the Western Ocean: The Story of America's Mail and Passenger Sailing Lines* (Annapolis, Md.: United States Naval Institute, 1961).

Most available information concerns the big steamers of the late nineteenth century. Eugene W. Smith's *Passenger Ships of the World Past and Present* (Boston: George H. Dean Co., 1978) discusses steamships and the shipping companies that operated them. Arranged by ocean and shipping line, it gives a brief description of each ship, including who built it, its size, when and where its maiden voyage was, and what eventually became of it. An index to ship names helps locate specific ships. For pictures of most passenger steamships, refer to Michael J. Anuta's *Ships of Our Ancestors* (Menominee, Mich.: Ships of Our Ancestors, 1983).

A family historian may know about a specific ship or shipping line in which he or she is interested. Because many arrival lists are not indexed by passenger but are arranged by date of arrival, it is often beneficial to learn the date(s) on which ships arrived—especially if an ancestor came on a known ship at an unknown date. An excellent source is the *Morton Allan Directory of European Steamship Arrivals: For the Years 1890 to 1930 at the Port of New York and for the Years 1904 to 1926 at the Ports of New York, Philadelphia, Boston, and Baltimore* (1931; reprint; Genealogical Publishing Co., 1980, 1987). It lists the names of vessels and the dates of arrival by year and by steamship line.

A similar guide covering earlier years is Bradley W. Steuart's *Passenger Ships Arriving in New York Harbor,* vol. 1, *1820–1850* (Bountiful, Utah: Precision Indexing, 1991). Arranged both by date of arrival and by ship name, this reference also indicates the type of vesssel, the captain's name, port(s) of departure, the National Archives microfilm roll number (within series M237), and the manifest (list) number. Of particular interest for those using this list to determine which lists to search, the publisher also identified the three most prevalent nationalities shown on the passenger lists.

For a guide to ship arrivals in other ports, see Lawrence B. Bangerter's *The Compass: A Concise and Factual Compilation of All Vessels and Sources Listed, with Reference Made of All of Their Voyages and Some Dates of Registration,* 2 vols. (Logan, Utah: Everton Publishers, 1983–90). Vol. 1 identifies ships arriving in Baltimore from 1820 to 1891 and provides the name, port of departure, registration date of the manifest, and the Family History Library microfilm number of that manifest. Vol. 2 provides similar information for the port of Boston, 1820 to 1860.

Monograph Series

Thousands of books have been written over the years dealing with various aspects of immigration and the associated ethnic groups. Many of these were written fifty to one hundred years ago and are long out of print. The researcher should be aware, however, that some reprint series are available that include many helpful books for researchers of many levels. Arno Press (New York) has reprinted more than fifty early books in the American Immigration Collection (two series). These series include such titles as *Immigration: Select Documents and Case Records, Ukrainians in the United States, Two Portuguese Communities in New England*, and *Who's Who in Polish America*. Arno Press has also issued other reprint series, many of them for specific ethnic groups, such as the Italian American Experience—reprints of thirty-nine books dealing with Italians in America.

Twayne Publishers (Boston) collected and reprinted twenty-four books dealing with different ethnic groups' immigration experience in its Immigrant Heritage of America series. Titles included *German Culture in Texas, How the Irish Became Americans, Norwegian-Americans,* and *South Slavic Immigration in America*.

AMS Press (New York) has issued dozens of original (not reprint) scholarly studies in its Immigrant Communities and Ethnic Minorities in the United States and Canada series since the mid-1980s. With more than eighty titles, this outstanding collection provides detailed treatments of ethnic groups, often in specific communities. Representative titles include *Ethnicity and Ethnic Group Persistence in an Acadian Village in Maritime Canada* and *The German Community in Winnipeg, 1872–1919*. These sources provide crucial historical background and often suggest areas of the old country from where the immigrants may have originated.

Another series (also not a reprint series) is Oceana Publications' thirty-two-volume Ethnic Chronology Series. Each of these chronology and fact books focuses on one of thirty ethnic groups. The volumes average approximately 150 pages, half of which is a detailed chronology of the ethnic group in America from its first arrival to 1970. The second half of each reproduces the text (in typescript) of notable documents pertaining to the group. The last dozen pages contain a briefly annotated bibliography to guide the researcher to further sources. Two supplemental volumes carry the chronology and documents up to 1980 and include an index to the entire series. These volumes are identified in the bibliography of chapter 4, "Ethnic Sources."

FINDING AIDS

As discussed in the introduction to *Printed Sources*, finding aids—sources that identify where specific information can be found—provide the necessary service of locating the records researchers are seeking (bibliographies, directories, etc.) or actually identifying the names of persons in the records (indexes). Without them, genealogists and other researchers would find their efforts much more difficult and time consuming. Fortunately, there are some excellent finding aids for immigration sources, including a comprehensive bibliography of virtually all published lists of immigrants and a companion index with more than two and a half million names.

Bibliographies

Passenger and Immigration Lists Bibliography. Genealogists are primarily interested in names of immigrants. Over the years, thousands of lists of immigrants have appeared in print. The first place to search for a list of such sources is P. William Filby's *Passenger and Immigration Lists Bibliography, 1538–1900,* 2nd ed. (Detroit: Gale Research, 1988), whose subtitle defines it as "a guide to published lists of arrivals in the United States and Canada." Thoroughly comprehensive (at the time of its publication), this bibliography identifies approximately 2,600 published sources of immigration, emigration, naturalizations, and other evidence of foreign origin. Each source is described completely, with author, title, publication information, and number of pages indicated. The detailed annotations describe the source, where the immigrants came from or were going to, identify duplicate publications of the same list, and often give the number of immigrants in that source. The compiler's goal was to identify all published lists, regardless of the format they appeared in or the language of the publication. Names of immigrants are not in this bibliography but are in a companion work, Filby's *Passenger and Immigration Lists Index* (described below under "Indexes").

Begun from an earlier work by Harold Lancour, *A Bibliography of Ship Passenger Lists, 1538–1825, Being a Guide to Published Lists of Early Immigrants to North America,* 3rd ed., rev. and enl. by Richard J. Wolfe (New York: New York Public Library, 1963), Filby's bibliography completely supersedes that effort. It also covers a longer time period, identifying lists of passengers and immigrants to around 1900.

A careful analysis of the entries in the bibliography indicates the broad scope of this list. Relatively few (less than 10 percent) are books or pamphlets whose full text, or most of their text, includes information on immigrants. The majority of entries, approximately two-thirds, are articles from a wide variety of periodicals. Most of the remaining entries are citations to portions (chapters, sections, appendixes, etc.) of published books, wherein the book deals with some aspect of an immigrant group and includes a list of immigrants.

The definition of *immigrant* in Filby's bibliography is also quite broad. Adopting Lancour and Wolfe's criteria, Filby states that

> the standard for including a list . . . is *proof of overseas origin* [of the immigrants named]. I have reserved the right of judgement in this manner . . . *usefulness* being the deciding factor in borderline cases. And again, no claim is made for unerring judgement or for completeness, though I have made every effort to make the present edition as complete and comprehensive as possible (1988, vii).

There is no requirement that the immigrants' home town, or even country, be noted in the lists cited, although the country is usually given. And despite Filby's disclaimer, the bibliography is quite thorough for pre-1988 publications.

A wide variety of genealogical sources identify immigrants. The most common are passenger lists and naturalization records, but a surprising number of other sources also indicate the foreign origins of immigrants. These can include, but are not limited to, lists of early settlers, headrights and early land holders, voter lists (which indicate naturalization), compiled genealogies focusing on groups of immigrants, lists of freemen, histories indicating immigrant settlement, records of immigrant churches, newspaper lists and queries seeking immigrants, as well as census, vital records, tax, court, and military records.

Filby's bibliography can be confusing for the first-time user. It is arranged alphabetically by the author of each source listed. Where no author is given, the title of the book or article is used (figure 14-1). Each entry is preceded by an item number (usually of four digits); they are arranged sequentially. At times a decimal point and one or two additional digits are required (for example, 3703.27) to keep the item numbers sequential while maintaining the alphabetical arrangement of author or title. This item number is the key to using both the bibliography's subject index and the companion name index because it is the reference number for the source cited.

Be sure to distinguish between books and articles when using the bibliography, because articles will not be found by their authors' names when sought in a library card catalog (there they must be looked up by the name of the periodical). The consistent format of the entries helps in reading them. The author (or title, in absence of an author) is always given in bold uppercase letters (**SMITH, FRANK**), while titles of books and periodicals appear in italic type (*Immigration to the Americas*). The titles of articles in periodicals appear in quotation marks ("Swedish Immigration") followed by the word "In" and the title of the periodical in italics (refer again to figure 14-1). The rest of the publication information, including the page numbers for an article or portion of a book, follows the title in the same paragraph. Each entry is annotated with an indented sentence or paragraph after the entry (in a smaller typeface).

An excellent subject index is part of Filby's bibliography. It helps researchers find numerous lists to search—important because not all lists have been indexed. Also, researchers sometimes do not yet know the immigrant's name (or the spelling used in a list) but may know where the immigrant settled or the region where the immigrant lived in the old country. Index topics are drawn from the source citation and its annotation and include places of arrival, departure, settlement, and towns of origin, as well as ethnic groups and ship names (see figure 14-2). Thus, for example, a researcher trying to learn what published sources identify the Dutch settlers of Pella, Iowa, could turn to the index and look up "Iowa, Dutch to," and find a reference to source 0675, which is a 1922 history of Pella that includes the settlers who went there. Alternately, the researcher could look in the subject index under "Dutch to Iowa (Pella)" or "Pella, Iowa, Dutch, French to," and find the same reference to source 0675, as well as to sources 9385 and 9387, which are vols. 1 and 3 of an 1897 Dutch-language history of Pella that lists the Dutch persons living in Pella or arriving from Rotterdam between 1849 and 1860.

No library has all of the sources listed in this bibliography, but some, such as the Allen County Public Library in Fort Wayne, Indiana, the Family History Library of The Church of Jesus Christ of Latter-day Saints (LDS church) in Salt Lake City, and the Library of Congress, attempt to acquire as many as they can. However, some of the sources cited in Filby's bibliography are obscure articles in foreign-language periodicals that are difficult to find in North America. Using the full citation to completely identify the book or periodical will assist you in finding copies of the citations of interest.

Publication of this bibliography, with the accompanying indexing of the names in the various sources, has had a catalytic

2467.7 **Passenger and Immigration Lists Bibliography • 2nd Edition** **Page 66**

2467.7
"THE GERMAN SETTLERS WHO ARRIVED IN 1684." In *Krefeld Immigrants and Their Descendants*, vol. 1:1 (1984), p. 5.

Several immigrants from Mulheim, Krefeld and Mors. From various sources.

2468.4
GERMANS TO AMERICA: Lists of Passengers Arriving at U.S. Ports, 1850-1855. Ira A. Glazier, editor; P. William Filby, associate editor. Wilmington, Del.: Scholarly Resources, 1987, vol. 1. 725p.

Contains 70,000 names. Set to be issued in 10 volumes through 1988. It will list about 700,000 passengers from Germany to all American ports. Names, ages, occupations, dates of embarkation, ports and ships.

2474—2476
GEUE, CHESTER W., translator. "Verein Immigrants to Texas in 1845." In *Stirpes.*

2474
Vol. 7:3 (Sept. 1967), pp. 87-89.

2475
Vol. 9:2 (June 1969), p. 64.

2476
Vol. 10:3 (Sept. 1970), p. 110-111.

Indexed list of Verein immigrants to Texas taken from the German list in the Verein Collection in the University of Texas archives, Austin. Contains names of those who left the port of Bremen in 1845 but does not include those who left from the port of Antwerp. Place of residence in Germany and ship used are given. Geue intended to continue this work but died shortly after the last contribution.

2484
GEUE, CHESTER W., and ETHEL HANDER GEUE, compilers. *A New Land Beckoned: German Immigration to Texas 1844-1847.* 1966. New and enlarged ed. Waco [Texas]: Texian Press, 1972. 178p. Reprinted by Genealogical Publishing Co., Baltimore, 1982.

Names 7,000 immigrants, giving European home place, ship taken, and usually birth and death dates. See no. 2504, Geue, for the years 1847-1861.

2494
GEUE, CHESTER W., and MRS. CHESTER W. GEUE. "Passagierliste des Schiffes Nr. 109 *Sophie* aus Hamburg . . . 1852 nach Galveston und Indianola in Texas, USA." In *Footprints* (Fort Worth, Texas, Genealogical Society), vol. 12:3 (Aug. 1969), pp. 96-97.

Names and places of origin of passengers on the ship *Sophie* from Hamburg, 1852.

2504
GEUE, ETHEL HANDER, compiler. *New Homes in a New Land: German Immigration to Texas, 1847-1861.* Waco [Texas]: Texian Press, 1970. 166p. Reprinted by Genealogical Publishing Co., 1982.

From German newspapers in Texas, records on microfilm of passenger lists of those who arrived at the port of Galveston. Also names from Hamburg Archives. Includes about 6,000 immigrants, of whom 588 were Wends. Listed on pages 4 and 5 are names of early German settlers in Texas, before 1836. See also Wends in no. 0578, Blasig; no. 1067, Caldwell; and no. 1858, Engerrand. Another Geue title, no. 2484, covers the years 1844-1847.

2514
GEUE, ETHEL HANDER (Mrs. Chester W.). "Passagierliste des Schiffes, *Reform* (und *Magnet*), Galveston from Bremen, 1851." In *Footprints* (Fort Worth Genealogical Society), vol. 12:2 (May 1969), pp. 66-67.

Taken from the *Galveston Zeitung*, 1851. Names and places of origin. See also no. 8317, Seele.

2518
GEUE, ETHEL HANDER. "Ship *Canapus*, Departed Bremen; Arrived Galveston, December 19, 1848." In *The Roadrunner*, vol. 7:4 (Aug. 1981), p. 6.

Names 30 persons, with ages and places of origin and destination. Extracted from Geue, *New Homes in a New Land . . . 1847-1861* (item no. 2504) and previously taken from microfilm in state archives, Austin, Texas.

2524
GHIRELLI, MICHAEL. *A List of Emigrants from England to America, 1682-1692, Transcribed from the Original Records at the City of London Record Office.* Introductory notes by Marion J. Kaminkow. Baltimore: Magna Carta, 1968. 106p. Available from Tuttle Co., Rutland, Vt.

From the Lord Mayor's Waiting Books. Mostly involves bonded servants.

2525.15
GIBBS, ANN. "Earliest Ripley County [Indiana] Naturalizations, 1818-1843." In *The Hoosier Genealogist*, vol. 22:3 (Sept. 1982), pp. 63-67.

About 100 persons, each name with age, place of origin, date of immigration, and date of naturalization or of first papers.

2525.40
GIBBS, ANN. "Switzerland County [Indiana] Naturalizations, Oct. 1825-Apr. 1829." In *The Hoosier Genealogist*, vol. 22:2 (June 1982), pp. 42-44.

About 80 persons, mostly from Switzerland and the British Isles. Indicates date of intention to become a citizen; identifies name of court and country of origin.

2526.10
GIBSON, J.S.W. "Sponsored Emigration of Paupers from Banbury Union, 1834-1860." In *The Oxfordshire Family Historian*, vol. 2:7 (Spring 1982), pp. 211-215.

Many to Australia and Canada, 1830s-1850s. Ages, destinations, sometimes occupations and name of ship.

Figure 14-1. From Filby's *Passenger and Immigration Lists Bibliography, 1538–1900.*

INDEX **Passenger and Immigration Lists Bibliography • 2nd Edition** **Page 300**

Figure 14-2. From the subject index in Filby's *Passenger and Immigration Lists Bibliography, 1538–1900.*

effect on the publication of passenger and related lists. An increasing number of such lists are being published, both in book and periodical form. Unfortunately, the publisher of Filby's bibliography has announced that it does not plan to update this useful work; however, Filby continues to add to the list of published immigration sources and incorporates them into the companion *Passenger and Immigration Lists Index* (described below under "Indexes"). In fact, the extensive citations and annotations are now part of the "Sources Indexed" list in each annual volume of the *Passenger and Immigration Lists Index*. This chapter's bibliography, although focusing only on book-length publications, does include most of the major new publications, with an annotation noting that it is not listed in the 1988 edition of Filby's bibliography.

Migration, Emigration, Immigration. An earlier list that provides a topical and geographic arrangement (by state) is Olga K. Miller's two-volume *Migration, Emigration, Immigration: Principally to the United States and in the United States* (Logan, Utah: Everton Publishers, 1974, 1981). Drawn from the comprehensive collection of the Family History Library, this listing actually has a much broader scope than Filby's bibliography. In addition to published lists of immigrants, it includes a significant number of internal migration sources, many immigration histories, and background information, as well as unpublished (microfilm) list of immigrants (to the United States) and emigrants (departures from foreign countries) (figure 14-3). In fact, it appears that less than 10 percent of Miller's listings are included in Filby's bibliography. In most cases this is because Miller's entries do not provide "proof of overseas origin," but it appears that Filby may have overlooked some of the sources in Miller's work. It would seem that titles of articles such as "Polish Pioneers of Virginia and Kentucky" or "The Jewish Colony at Waterview" could not help but mention the names of some immigrants. For genealogists, Miller's work is also the most accessible listing of background information deal-

134 **Migration, Emigration, Immigration**

NORTH DAKOTA

1803 The Louisiana Purchase brought southwestern North Dakota under the jurisdiction of the United States.

1812 First permanent settlement was made by Scottish and Irish settlers at Pembina.

1818 Eastern North Dakota acquired by United States.

1861 Dakota Territory was organized. It included the present states of North and South Dakota, and much of Montana and Wyoming.

1863 Dakota territory opened for homesteading.

1864 The limits of the territory narrowed to only present day Dakotas.

1889 North Dakota was admitted to the Union.

STATE HISTORICAL SOCIETY OF NORTH DAKOTA:

Liberty Memorial Building, Bismarck, 58501. Founded in 1905. Publishes: *North Dakota History: Journal of the Northern Plains.*

SUGGESTED SOURCES:

Compendium of History and Biography of North Dakota; Containing a History of North Dakota, Early Explorations. Chicago, 1900. (**978.4 D3c).

History of Red River Valley, Past and Present, . . . From the Time of Their First Settlement. By various writers. Chicago, 1909. (**977 H2hr).

"Official Immigration Activities of Dakota Territory." In *North Dakota Historical Quarterly*, Vol. VII, No. 1, Oct. 1932, p. 5. (**978.4 B2ha, new series).

"Pioneers in North Dakota, Previous to 1862." In *Collections of the State Historical Society of North Dakota*, Vol. 1, p. 355.

CANADA:

Wade, Mark Sweeten: *The Overlanders of '62.* Archives of British Columbia, Memoir No. IX, Victoria, B. C., 1931, Vol. 7, Nos. 2-3, p. 179. (**978.4 B2ha, new series).

ICELAND:

Jackson, Thorstina S.: *History of Icelanders in North Dakota.* Winnipeg, 1926. (*5003).

Thorlakson, Rev. Pall: "The Founding of the Icelandic Settlement in Pembina County." In *North Dakota Historical Quarterly*, new series, Vol. 6, No. 2, p. 150.

NORWAY:

"Early Norwegian Immigration to Griggs County, Red River Valley." In *Collections of the State Historical Society*, Vols. 1, 3, 7.

RUSSIAN GERMANS:

Aberle, Rt. Rev. George P.: *From the Steppes to the Prairies: German Russians.* Bismarck, North Dakota, Bismarck Tribune Co., n.d.

Aberle, Rt. Rev. George P.: *Pioneers and Their Sons - German Russians.* 165 family histories. Bismarck, North Dakota, n.d. (**978.4 W2a).

Pfaller, Rev. Louis: "Bishop Vincent Wehrle and the German Immigrants in North Dakota." In the *North Dakota Quarterly*, Vol. 29, No. 3.

SWEDEN:

Bemis, Myrtle: "History of the Swedish Settlement in North Dakota." In *Collections of the State Historical Society of North Dakota*, Vol. 3, p. 247.

*Call numbers for microfilms at the Genealogical Society of the Church of Jesus Christ of Latter-day Saints.
**Call numbers for books at the Genealogical Society of the Church of Jesus Christ of Latter-day Saints.

Figure 14-3. Miller's two-volume *Migration, Emigration, Immigration: Principally to the United States and in the United States* provides a topical and geographic arrangement (by state).

ing with immigrants to various parts of North America, and many such sources mention immigrants incidentally. Miller's bibliography is older than Filby's, and most of its entries are not annotated. In fact, some entries are not complete; the authors of many articles are not listed.

Miller's list of sources is arranged in four parts. The "General" part includes references to colonial immigration, New England, indentured servants, convicts, foreigners in American wars, general passenger lists, migration sources, and citizenship (naturalization) titles. Part 2 covers "Religious and Refugee Groups" such as Acadians, United Empire Loyalists, Huguenots, Jews, Lutherans, Mennonites, Moravians, Quakers, and Roman Catholics. A brief part 3 identifies "Heraldry" sources, while part 4 covers the states of the United States alphabetically, each being subdivided as needed into ethnic groups or migration to or from other states.

Approximately 4,000 sources are noted in vol. 1 and approximately 1,500 in the vol. 2. The subject indexes reference authors, ships' names, nationalities, religious groups, and other immigration-related terms. A separate list identifies the various periodicals cited with complete addresses. While vol. 2 includes sources overlooked in vol. 1 (or published since 1974), it also covers topics not in the first volume (such as Gypsies). It also appears to have many more migration and ethnic history sources and more foreign titles. Although most of the sources with name lists are in Filby's bibliography, Miller's volumes still have value. Their topical arrangement makes some sources easier to identify, and the combination of migration, early settler histories, and immigration lists is helpful in many research situations.

Microfilmed Passenger Lists. Although microfilmed passenger lists are not published sources, they are listed in a published source that all researchers should be aware of. Virtually all surviving Federal government passenger lists created from 1820 through 1945 are available on microfilm. The National Archives' *Immigrant and Passenger Arrivals: A Select Catalog of National Archives Publications,* rev. ed. (Washington, D.C.: National Archives Trust Fund Board, 1991) is a bibliography of the comprehensive collection of microfilmed original records in the National Archives. With it the researcher can determine which original records to search after exhausting the printed literature (or which records to search to confirm the information found in a published source).

Background Sources. The nature of academic immigration studies has led to the creation of numerous bibliographies covering different aspects of this topic. A good place to begin research is Wayne Charles Miller's *A Comprehensive Bibliography for the Study of American Minorities* (New York: New York University Press, 1976), a companion volume to his *Handbook of American Minorities* (cited earlier). It includes more than twenty-nine thousand entries for thirty-seven American minorities and includes essays for each minority group. A briefer, more select reference work available in most collections is John D. Buenker's *Immigration and Ethnicity: A Guide to Information Sources* (Detroit: Gale Research Co., 1977). It cites more than 1,400 books, articles, and dissertations dealing with immigration after World War II. It is arranged topically with author and subject indexes and includes other information sources, such as government agencies.

Francesco Cordasco has published extensively in the field of immigration and ethnic groups. Many of his works can be very helpful for the researcher beginning a project. In 1978 he reprinted a 1956 George Washington University study, *A Report on World Population Migrations as Related to the United States of America,* under the title *A Bibliography of American Immigration History* (Fairfield, N.J.: Augustus M. Kelly) without the initial essays from the original. A few post-1956 sources are included in Cordasco's new introduction, but the bulk of the text comes from the earlier study. He added a name index, but not the needed annotations to the older citations (which often perpetuate old misconceptions). Two other important bibliographies by this author/editor focus on two important aspects of this topic: women and modern (post-1965) illegal immigrants. Both *The Immigrant Woman in North America: An Annotated Bibliography of Selected References* (Metuchen, N.J.: Scarecrow, 1985) and *The New American Immigration: Evolving Patterns of Legal and Illegal Emigration, a Bibliography of Selected References* (New York: Garland, 1987) treat their topics from a broad selection of sources, books, articles, dissertations, etc. They have a few shortcomings: the parameters for selection are not fully described, and the subject indexes are inadequate; however, they are, on balance, helpful bibliographies for researchers who take the time to study them carefully.

Dissertations are sources for reference material that are frequently untapped. Not only do they usually offer new approaches and treatments of immigration, but they also include lengthy bibliographies themselves. A. William Hoglund has provided excellent access to more than 3,500 doctoral dissertations dealing with immigrants in *Immigrants and Their Children in the United States: A Bibliography of Doctoral Dissertations, 1885–1982* (New York: Garland, 1986). Although it is based on *Dissertation Abstracts International,* a comprehensive listing of virtually all U.S. university dissertations published annually by University Microfilms International (Ann Arbor, Michigan), the author did use other sources to thoroughly comb the field. Arrangement is by author, and the annotations are brief. A short subject index is helpful but could be more comprehensive.

Many bibliographies cover only works published within a given time period. The United Nations Department of Economic and Social Affairs' *Analytical Bibliography of International Migration Statistics, Selected Countries, 1925–1950* (New York: United Nations, 1955) is helpful for accessing publications of the second quarter of the twentieth century containing statistical data, such as those sought by demographers. Articles, books, dissertations, and other sources published from 1955 to 1962 are found in J. J. Mangalam's *Human Migration: A Guide to Migration Literature in English, 1955–1962* (Lexington: University of Kentucky Press, 1968). Two of its three sections (books and articles from three specific journals) are not annotated. It includes a subject index. A brief, affordable bibliography for post-World War II immigration is available from the Smithsonian Institution as *Recent Immigration to the United States: The Literature of the Social Sciences* (Washington, D.C.: Smithsonian Institution Press, 1976). It is arranged by topic but has no indexes. A comprehensive listing of recent sources (1973 to 1979) is David L. Brye's *European Immigration and Ethnicity in the United States and Canada: A Historical Bibliography* (Santa Barbara, Calif.: ABC Clio, 1983). Its more than four thousand entries are from *America: History and Life,* a publication and database of periodical literature dealing with Canadian and U.S. history (including many genealogical journals), and they include the concise but clear abstracts that are the hallmark of *America: History and Life* (see chapter 17). Brye's work is arranged by ethnic groups within the two countries. Access is enhanced by the inclusion of thorough subject and author indexes.

Another source of value to genealogists interested in immigration is a brief guide by the Library of Congress, *Immigrant Arrivals: A Short Guide to Published Sources* (Washington, D.C.: Library of Congress, n.d.), which introduces major reference works.

Archive and Library Guides. Additional sources of information on published (and manuscript) immigration sources are the guides to the major archives and libraries that collect in this field. An excellent example is *The Immigration History Research Center: A Guide to Collections,* edited by Suzanna Moody and Joel Wurl (Westport, Conn.: Greenwood Press, 1991.) In addition to describing the manuscript, newspaper, and periodical collections of the Immigration History Research Center (University of Minnesota, St. Paul), the guide includes essays about the extensive monograph (book) holdings in its collection. Each essay highlights significant titles, providing an opportunity for researchers to evaluate those titles.

Indexes

Some of the most useful published immigration sources are those that index names of immigrants. All but the most recent such indexes are identified in Filby's *Passenger and Immigration Lists Index* (described below). In addition, more and more lists of arrivals are being published in book form, with indexes. This discussion focuses on printed indexes, so it does not include the card (Soundex) indexes to the microfilm copies of Federal passenger arrival lists.

Table 14-2. Coverage of *Passenger and Immigration Lists Index*

	Number of Sources Indexed	*Number of Index Entries*
Base Set (1981)	350	480,000
1982–85 cumulation	750	650,000
1986–90 cumulation	695	630,000
1991–95 cumulation	610	633,000 (=2,410,000)
1996 annual	110	131,000
1997 annual	150	128,000
Totals	2,665	2,652,000

Passenger and Immigration Lists Index (PILI). By far the most significant index for family historians (and others seeking to identify a specific immigrant) is P. William Filby's *Passenger and Immigration Lists Index* (*PILI*), 10+ vols. (Detroit: Gale Research, 1981–). This monumental, ongoing source indexes (or will eventually index) virtually all published lists that document immigration to the United States and Canada. As a companion publication to Filby's *Passenger and Immigration Lists Bibliography, 1538–1900* (cited earlier), *PILI* has the same broad scope in identifying sources to index. Indeed, Filby's bibliography was created to list the sources projected for this index. By 1997 there were more than 2.6 million entries in the index, with more than 2,600 sources having been indexed.

The index began with three volumes published in 1981 as a master index of approximately 500,000 immigrants in three hundred published sources. Each year an annual supplemental volume adds between 120,000 and 140,000 new index entries from approximately one hundred or more different sources. Because each annual volume is a separate index (*A* through *Z*), the publisher issues a cumulated supplement every five years so that researchers do not have to check each annual volume. Thus, there are cumulated supplements for 1982 to 1985, 1986 to 1990, and 1991 to 1995 (table 14-2). All major genealogical libraries subscribe to the index (but many of them do not have the cumulated supplements).

Because *PILI* indexes only published lists, it is best used for colonial American immigration (because all known extant colonial immigration sources have been published). However, only about 2 percent of North American immigrants arrived before 1820, so most of the names in Filby's index are from published sources that list post-1820 immigrants. Individual names from periodical articles and other sources are well indexed. *PILI* does not index official U.S. arrival lists, which are not published, except where individual lists have appeared in published books and articles. Even in these cases, the index cites the published source, not the original manuscript (or microfilm copy). A few of the very large publications of immigrants that list hundreds of thousands of names, such as *Germans to America* (discussed below under "Arrival Lists"), also are not indexed in *PILI*. (They are easier to access than many sources; by omitting them, *PILI* can focus on the more obscure sources.)

Because *PILI* is a master index (see chapter 6, "Published Indexes for American Genealogy") that references hundreds of different sources, not every entry is equally useful: some of the sources referenced are incomplete or inaccurate, and some of them may be obscure and hard to obtain. In some cases, the same name appears more than once in the index because the immigrant is noted in several sources. Another problem with master indexes is the sheer volume of names in them. *PILI* often includes several persons of the same name; it is the researcher's task to determine which, if any, is the immigrant he or she is seeking.

PILI is fairly easy to use. Names are listed strictly alphabetically according to the spelling in the source indexed. The surname and given name are followed by the passenger's age (if given in the source), place of arrival, year of arrival, a numeric source code (indicating the list where the immigrant was named), and the page number in that source. Thus, a sample entry appears as:

Richards, Tho 24; Bermuda, 1635 **8835** p354

If no age is given in the source, the abbreviation *n.a.* appears. Some sources (some naturalization lists, for example) do not include the immigration date. In such cases, the date given in *PILI* usually refers to the date of the record. The source code (always in bold typeface) refers to a list at the front of the index; a complete citation for the source where the immigrant appears is included there. (The source code corresponds to the item number for the same source in Filby's companion *Passenger and Immigration Lists Bibliography,* described above.) Figure 14-4 shows several entries.

As excellent as Filby's index is, it does not include every immigrant (even among those listed in published sources). With more than 2.6 million entries, it references only approximately 5 percent of the total immigrants to North America (and just 12 percent of pre-1900 immigrants). Here are some reasons why an ancestor might not be found in *PILI:*

- The immigrant might not be listed in any published source
- The person being sought might not have been an immigrant but rather the child of an immigrant
- Females and children usually were not listed in pre-1820 lists
- The published source containing the immigrant may not yet have been indexed
- Some published sources (master indexes) containing hundreds of thousands of names may never be referenced in *PILI*

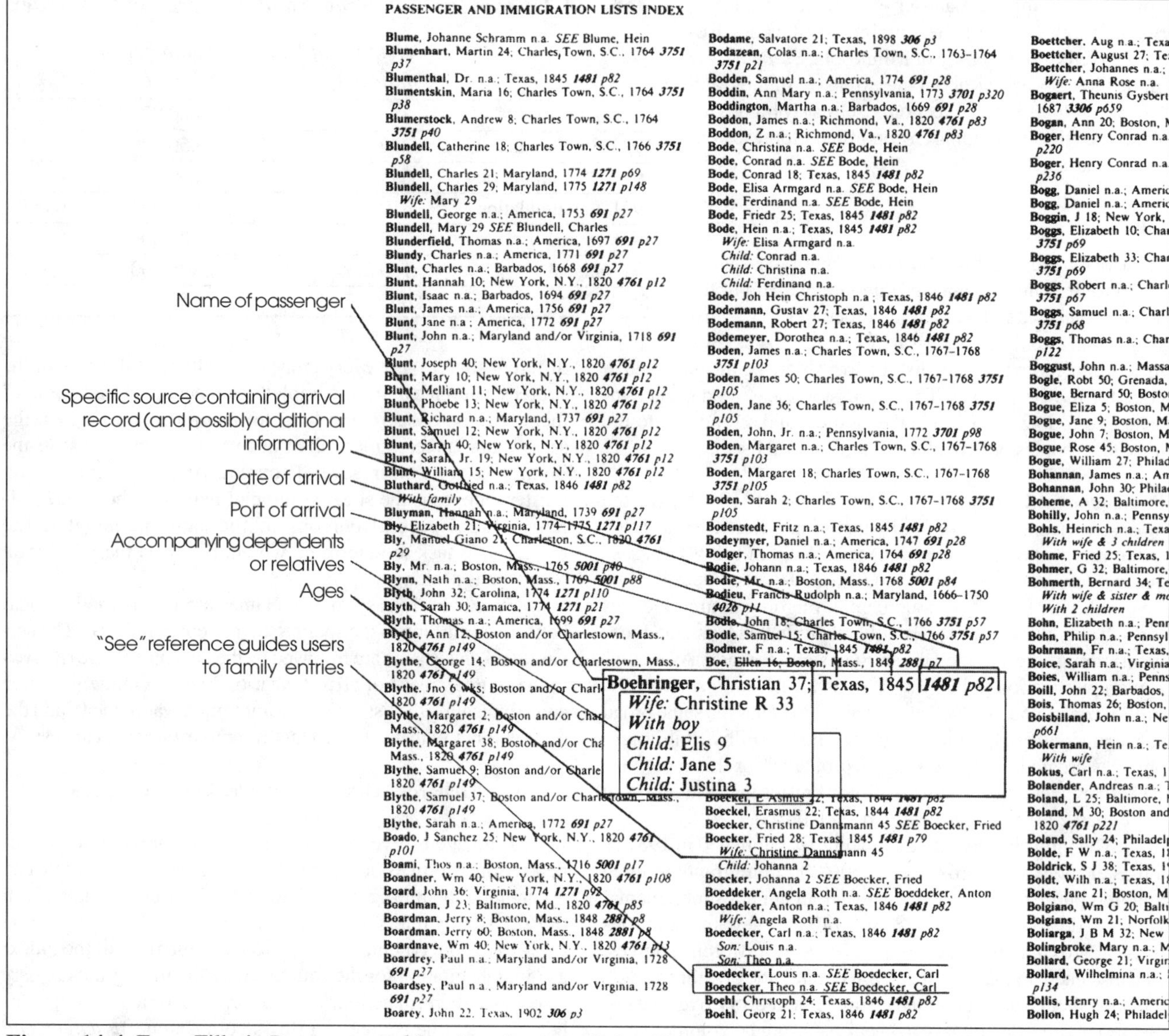

PASSENGER AND IMMIGRATION LISTS INDEX

Blume, Johanne Schramm n.a. *SEE* Blume, Hein
Blumenhart, Martin 24; Charles Town, S.C., 1764 ***3751*** *p37*
Blumenthal, Dr. n.a.; Texas, 1845 ***1481*** *p82*
Blumentskin, Maria 16; Charles Town, S.C., 1764 ***3751*** *p38*
Blumerstock, Andrew 8; Charles Town, S.C., 1764 ***3751*** *p40*
Blundell, Catherine 18; Charles Town, S.C., 1766 ***3751*** *p58*
Blundell, Charles 21; Maryland, 1774 ***1271*** *p69*
Blundell, Charles 29; Maryland, 1775 ***1271*** *p148*
Wife: Mary 29
Blundell, George n.a.; America, 1753 ***691*** *p27*
Blundell, Mary 29 *SEE* Blundell, Charles
Blunderfield, Thomas n.a.; America, 1697 ***691*** *p27*
Blundy, Charles n.a.; America, 1771 ***691*** *p27*
Blunt, Charles n.a.; Barbados, 1668 ***691*** *p27*
Blunt, Hannah 10; New York, N.Y., 1820 ***4761*** *p12*
Blunt, Isaac n.a.; Barbados, 1694 ***691*** *p27*
Blunt, James n.a.; America, 1756 ***691*** *p27*
Blunt, Jane n.a.; America, 1772 ***691*** *p27*
Blunt, John n.a.; Maryland and/or Virginia, 1718 ***691*** *p27*
Blunt, Joseph 40; New York, N.Y., 1820 ***4761*** *p12*
Blunt, Mary 10; New York, N.Y., 1820 ***4761*** *p12*
Blunt, Melliant 11; New York, N.Y., 1820 ***4761*** *p12*
Blunt, Phoebe 13; New York, N.Y., 1820 ***4761*** *p12*
Blunt, Richard n.a.; Maryland, 1737 ***691*** *p27*
Blunt, Samuel 12; New York, N.Y., 1820 ***4761*** *p12*
Blunt, Sarah 40; New York, N.Y., 1820 ***4761*** *p12*
Blunt, Sarah, Jr. 19; New York, N.Y., 1820 ***4761*** *p12*
Blunt, William 15; New York, N.Y., 1820 ***4761*** *p12*
Bluthard, Gottfried n.a.; Texas, 1846 ***1481*** *p82*
With family
Bluyman, Hannah n.a.; Maryland, 1739 ***691*** *p27*
Bly, Elizabeth 21; Virginia, 1774–1775 ***1271*** *p117*
Bly, Manuel Giano 21; Charleston, S.C., 1820 ***4761*** *p29*
Bly, Mr. n.a.; Boston, Mass., 1765 ***5001*** *p40*
Blynn, Nath n.a.; Boston, Mass., 1769 ***5001*** *p88*
Blyth, John 32; Carolina, 1774 ***1271*** *p110*
Blyth, Sarah 30; Jamaica, 1774 ***1271*** *p21*
Blyth, Thomas n.a.; America, 1699 ***691*** *p27*
Blythe, Ann 12; Boston and/or Charlestown, Mass., 1820 ***4761*** *p149*
Blythe, George 14; Boston and/or Charlestown, Mass., 1820 ***4761*** *p149*
Blythe, Jno 6 wks; Boston and/or Charl[...] 1820 ***4761*** *p149*
Blythe, Margaret 2; Boston and/or Cha[...] Mass., 1820 ***4761*** *p149*
Blythe, Margaret 38; Boston and/or Cha[...] Mass., 1820 ***4761*** *p149*
Blythe, Samuel 9; Boston and/or Charle[...] 1820 ***4761*** *p149*
Blythe, Samuel 37; Boston and/or Charlestown, Mass., 1820 ***4761*** *p149*
Blythe, Sarah n.a.; America, 1772 ***691*** *p27*
Boado, J Sanchez 25; New York, N.Y., 1820 ***4761*** *p101*
Boami, Thos n.a.; Boston, Mass., 1716 ***5001*** *p17*
Boandner, Wm 40; New York, N.Y., 1820 ***4761*** *p108*
Board, John 36; Virginia, 1774 ***1271*** *p92*
Boardman, J 23; Baltimore, Md., 1820 ***4761*** *p85*
Boardman, Jerry 8; Boston, Mass., 1848 ***2881*** *p8*
Boardman, Jerry 60; Boston, Mass., 1848 ***2881*** *p8*
Boardnave, Wm 40; New York, N.Y., 1820 ***4761*** *p13*
Boardrey, Paul n.a.; Maryland and/or Virginia, 1728 ***691*** *p27*
Boardsey, Paul n.a., Maryland and/or Virginia, 1728 ***691*** *p27*
Boarey, John 22; Texas, 1902 ***306*** *p3*

Bodame, Salvatore 21; Texas, 1898 ***306*** *p3*
Bodazean, Colas n.a.; Charles Town, S.C., 1763–1764 ***3751*** *p21*
Bodden, Samuel n.a.; America, 1774 ***691*** *p28*
Boddin, Ann Mary n.a.; Pennsylvania, 1773 ***3701*** *p320*
Boddington, Martha n.a.; Barbados, 1669 ***691*** *p28*
Boddon, James n.a.; Richmond, Va., 1820 ***4761*** *p83*
Boddon, Z n.a.; Richmond, Va., 1820 ***4761*** *p83*
Bode, Christina n.a. *SEE* Bode, Hein
Bode, Conrad n.a. *SEE* Bode, Hein
Bode, Conrad 18; Texas, 1845 ***1481*** *p82*
Bode, Elisa Armgard n.a. *SEE* Bode, Hein
Bode, Ferdinand n.a. *SEE* Bode, Hein
Bode, Friedr 25; Texas, 1845 ***1481*** *p82*
Bode, Hein n.a.; Texas, 1845 ***1481*** *p82*
Wife: Elisa Armgard n.a.
Child: Conrad n.a.
Child: Christina n.a.
Child: Ferdinand n.a.
Bode, Joh Hein Christoph n.a.; Texas, 1846 ***1481*** *p82*
Bodemann, Gustav 27; Texas, 1846 ***1481*** *p82*
Bodemann, Robert 27; Texas, 1846 ***1481*** *p82*
Bodemeyer, Dorothea n.a.; Texas, 1846 ***1481*** *p82*
Boden, James n.a.; Charles Town, S.C., 1767–1768 ***3751*** *p103*
Boden, James 50; Charles Town, S.C., 1767–1768 ***3751*** *p105*
Boden, Jane 36; Charles Town, S.C., 1767–1768 ***3751*** *p105*
Boden, John, Jr. n.a.; Pennsylvania, 1772 ***3701*** *p98*
Boden, Margaret n.a.; Charles Town, S.C., 1767–1768 ***3751*** *p103*
Boden, Margaret 18; Charles Town, S.C., 1767–1768 ***3751*** *p105*
Boden, Sarah 2; Charles Town, S.C., 1767–1768 ***3751*** *p105*
Bodenstedt, Fritz n.a.; Texas, 1845 ***1481*** *p82*
Bodeymyer, Daniel n.a.; America, 1747 ***691*** *p28*
Bodger, Thomas n.a.; America, 1764 ***691*** *p28*
Bodie, Johann n.a.; Texas, 1846 ***1481*** *p82*
Bodie, Mr. n.a.; Boston, Mass., 1768 ***5001*** *p84*
Bodieu, Francis Rudolph n.a.; Maryland, 1666–1750 ***4026*** *p11*
Bodle, John 18; Charles Town, S.C., 1766 ***3751*** *p57*
Bodle, Samuel 15; Charles Town, S.C., 1766 ***3751*** *p57*
Bodmer, F n.a.; Texas, 1845 ***1481*** *p82*
Boe, Ellen 16; Boston, Mass., 1849 ***2881*** *p7*
Boeckel, E Asmus 22; Texas, 1844 ***1481*** *p82*
Boeckel, Erasmus 22; Texas, 1844 ***1481*** *p82*
Boecker, Christine Dannsmann 45 *SEE* Boecker, Fried
Boecker, Fried 28; Texas, 1845 ***1481*** *p79*
Wife: Christine Dannsmann 45
Child: Johanna 2
Boecker, Johanna 2 *SEE* Boecker, Fried
Boeddeker, Angela Roth n.a. *SEE* Boeddeker, Anton
Boeddeker, Anton n.a.; Texas, 1846 ***1481*** *p82*
Wife: Angela Roth n.a.
Boedecker, Carl n.a.; Texas, 1846 ***1481*** *p82*
Son: Louis n.a.
Son: Theo n.a.
Boedecker, Louis n.a. *SEE* Boedecker, Carl
Boedecker, Theo n.a. *SEE* Boedecker, Carl
Boehl, Christoph 24; Texas, 1846 ***1481*** *p82*
Boehl, Georg 21; Texas, 1846 ***1481*** *p82*

Boettcher, Aug n.a.; Texa[...]
Boettcher, August 27; Te[...]
Boettcher, Johannes n.a.; [...]
Wife: Anna Rose n.a.
Bogaert, Theunis Gysbert[...] 1687 ***3306*** *p659*
Bogan, Ann 20; Boston, [...]
Boger, Henry Conrad n.a. [...] *p220*
Boger, Henry Conrad n.a. [...] *p236*
Bogg, Daniel n.a.; Americ[...]
Bogg, Daniel n.a.; Americ[...]
Boggin, J 18; New York, [...]
Boggs, Elizabeth 10; Char[...] ***3751*** *p69*
Boggs, Elizabeth 33; Char[...] ***3751*** *p69*
Boggs, Robert n.a.; Charl[...] ***3751*** *p67*
Boggs, Samuel n.a.; Charl[...] ***3751*** *p68*
Boggs, Thomas n.a.; Char[...] *p122*
Boggust, John n.a.; Massa[...]
Bogle, Robt 50; Grenada, [...]
Bogue, Bernard 50; Bosto[...]
Bogue, Eliza 5; Boston, M[...]
Bogue, Jane 9; Boston, M[...]
Bogue, John 7; Boston, M[...]
Bogue, Rose 45; Boston, [...]
Bogue, William 27; Philad[...]
Bohannan, James n.a.; Am[...]
Bohannan, John 30; Phila[...]
Boheme, A 32; Baltimore, [...]
Bohilly, John n.a.; Pennsy[...]
Bohls, Heinrich n.a.; Texa[...]
With wife & 3 children
Bohme, Fried 25; Texas, [...]
Bohmer, G 32; Baltimore, [...]
Bohmerth, Bernard 34; Te[...]
With wife & sister & m[...]
With 2 children
Bohn, Elizabeth n.a.; Penn[...]
Bohn, Philip n.a.; Pennsyl[...]
Bohrmann, Fr n.a.; Texas, [...]
Boice, Sarah n.a.; Virginia[...]
Boies, William n.a.; Penns[...]
Boill, John 22; Barbados, [...]
Bois, Thomas 26; Boston, [...]
Boisbilland, John n.a.; Ne[...] *p661*
Bokermann, Hein n.a.; Te[...]
With wife
Bokus, Carl n.a.; Texas, [...]
Bolaender, Andreas n.a.; [...]
Boland, L 25; Baltimore, [...]
Boland, M 30; Boston and[...] 1820 ***4761*** *p221*
Boland, Sally 24; Philadel[...]
Bolde, F W n.a.; Texas, [...]
Boldrick, S J 38; Texas, [...]
Boldt, Wilh n.a.; Texas, [...]
Boles, Jane 21; Boston, M[...]
Bolgiano, Wm G 20; Balti[...]
Bolgians, Wm 21; Norfolk[...]
Boliarga, J B M 32; New [...]
Bolingbroke, Mary n.a.; M[...]
Bollard, George 21; Virgin[...]
Bollard, Wilhelmina n.a.; [...] *p134*
Bollis, Henry n.a.; Americ[...]
Bollon, Hugh 24; Philadel[...]

Figure 14-4. From Filby's *Passenger and Immigration Lists Index.* Reproduced from a promotional brochure issued by Gale Research Co., 1982.

- The spelling of the immigrant's name being used by the researcher may be different in the published source and thus in *PILI*

Some smaller indexes to immigrants deserve mention because they are representative of a host of such projects. Most other published sources of immigrants are transcripts of lists; they are discussed below under "Copied Original Records." The following serve as indexes; the researcher must go to the sources indexed to find complete information.

Wuerttemburg Emigration Index. Emigrants from European countries are also appearing in growing numbers in the published literature. Many such published sources are among the lists described below under "Copied Original Records," but a few are simply indexes to original records. An excellent example is Trudy Schenk's continuing series, *The Wuerttemberg Emigration Index,* 7 vols. to date (Salt Lake City: Ancestry, 1986–). This series lists thousands of persons who applied for permission to leave the former German state of Wuerttemberg; it serves as an index to the official emigration records of various Wuerttemberg district administrative offices. Each of the projected seven volumes indexes the microfilmed records from several different districts. Because the original records are textual (not tabular), chronological, arranged by district, and written in the old Gothic German script, they are difficult for most American researchers to use successfully. The *Wuerttemburg Emigration Index* provides great assistance in identifying the emigrant, the date of his or her application to leave, town of origin, district, and file number, making it possible for any researcher to find the actual emigration documents on microfilm.

The finished index will have approximately 100,000 entries, but this number may account for only 20 to 25 percent of all the emigrants from Wuerttemberg. This fact exemplifies several factors that affect records of British and European emigration: in this case, not all of the emigration files survived (perhaps only half); some were not microfilmed (they were lost before filming); and up to half of the persons leaving Wuerttemberg were "clandestine" emigrants who did not seek permission to leave (Wollmershäuser 1990, 35).

Philadelphia Naturalization Records. Another example of an index to original records is P. William Filby's *Philadelphia Naturalization Records: An Index to Records of Aliens' Declarations of Intention and/or Oaths of Allegiance, 1789–1880* (Detroit: Gale Publishing Co., 1982). This is an index to declarations of intention and oaths of allegiance from 1789 through 1880 as found in various order books of ninety-two local courts in Philadelphia. As an index, it provides only the name of the alien, the court, the year of the record, and the country to which the alien owed allegiance. It is a very useful index but is confusing for the first-time user because it does not clearly explain how to access the original information (which is available on microfilm through the Family History Library) and because many users are not trained in understanding naturalization records. Many family historians who find a name in this index assume that it refers to the immigrant being sought simply because "he arrived in Philadelphia." However, naturalization required that an immigrant had been a resident of a state for a certain length of time, and the person usually was naturalized in the city where he or she lived—but only a small percentage of those who arrived in Philadelphia actually stayed in that city. This fact, combined with the factor of common names among some immigrants, means that most new citizens listed in this index are not who researchers believe they are. While such problems can occur with any record and any locality, *Philadelphia Naturalization Records* multiplies those problems because it deals with a port city, an extensive range of years, and includes a very large number of names (120,000).

Back-of-the-Book Indexes. Most of the passenger and immigration lists being published today in book form include indexes within their covers. These "back-of-the-book" indexes are helpful because many of those publications will not be indexed through Filby's *Passenger and Immigration Lists Index* for years to come. However, such indexes do not provide the same information as found in Filby's index. Usually the index citations do not provide the year of immigration or the immigrant's age, nor are families listed together as they sometimes are in Filby's index. A back-of-the-book index only indexes the accompanying source, so there is no source code indicating in which source the entry is found; there is only a page number. In multi-volume sets, each volume normally has its own index; if the immigrant's point of arrival is not known, it is necessary to search the indexes to several volumes. In such cases, more than one candidate might be found. Be sure to evaluate the information contained in the published source to confirm that the right immigrant has been found.

The major multi-volume published passenger lists which contain their own indexes are discussed below under "Copied Original Records"; they include the works of Peter Wilson Coldham, who focuses on colonial British lists in works such as *The Complete Book of Emigrants* (discussed below under "Copied Original Records—Foreign Records") and others, and Ira Glazier, who focuses on nineteenth-century ethnic groups, such as the Irish in *The Famine Immigrants* and Germans in *Germans to America* (both discussed below under "Copied Original Records—Arrival Lists."

Topical indexes. Genealogists seeking lists of names often stop after consulting the indexes described above. However, many researchers, including historians and demographers, will want to explore various immigration topics in the academic literature. Indexes can serve any researcher, regardless of his or her research objective; however, the choice of index to be used will depend on that objective. General researchers might want to begin an index search with INFOTRAC, a computer-assisted index available in many libraries. It covers many different magazines, many of which are general interest in nature, but it includes numerous topical magazines and journals as well. The user can enter any subject word and the system will find articles indexed under that subject. Related subjects are also listed.

For historical perspectives on immigration, the best indexes are the two parts of *America: History and Life* (see chapter 17): part B, "Book Reviews," and part D, "Annual Index with List of Periodicals." Part B leads the researcher to newly published books on any of several aspects of immigration, while part D indexes the other three parts (including part C, which is a bibliography). The comprehensive nature of this annual index (and its subject references) allows it to serve as an important access tool to the other three parts.

The other history index, *Writings on American History* (discussed in chapter 17), provides a subject arrangement to articles published each year. Separate sections in this annual publication cover immigration and immigrant minority groups, African American history, and Jewish history. Although it is actually a bibliography, its focus on periodical articles suggests its usage as an index.

Several indexes are helpful for the social scientist interested in immigration. *Social Sciences Index* from H. W. Wilson (New York, 1974–) provides the initial starting point for researchers. Besides the author references, this index includes several immigration subjects, among them migration, aliens, children of immigrants, refugees, deportation, and most ethnic groups. Many groups have subtopics, such as "Italians in the United States—Immigration and Emigration"; from them, the researcher can turn to specific indexes. Articles dealing with immigration as a current topic can be sought in *PAIS Bulletin* (New York: Public Affairs Information Services, 1915–). Demographic studies are best located using *Population Index* (Princeton, N.J.: Princeton University, Office of Population Research, 1935–), a quarterly index and bibliography of books and periodical literature on all phases of population problems, including immigration. It includes annual indexes to author and country and is, in turn, indexed in *Social Sciences Citation Index* (Philadelphia: Institute for Scientific Information, 1976–), *PAIS*, and others.

Articles about immigration in genealogical periodicals are not adequately indexed by any of the above indexes. There are some important genealogical periodical indexes that reference articles in hundreds of less common periodicals; however, they generally do not list individual immigrants' names that may have been included in lists published in genealogical journals.

For articles published before 1953, consult Carl Boyer, 3rd, *Donald Lines Jacobus's Index to Genealogical Periodicals*, rev. ed. (Newhall, Calif.: Boyer Publications, 1988). This work is a revision of Donald Lines Jacobus's *Index to Genealogical Periodicals*, published in three volumes from 1932 to 1953. Articles published since 1962 are found in *Genealogical Periodical Annual Index* (*GPAI*) (Bowie, Md.: Heritage Books, 1962–). This annual publication includes citations from approximately three hundred periodicals; they are indexed by topic and geographic location of the article's subject. The best and most comprehensive index to genealogical periodicals is the annual *Periodical Source Index* (*PERSI*) (Fort Wayne, Ind.: Allen County Public Library Foundation, 1987–), which is also available in a retrospective set that indexes genealogical periodicals from 1847 through 1985. Again, it does not index individual names; rather, the title of the article is indexed by geographic location and, in some cases, by a key word. All of these indexes are further described in chapter 19, "Genealogical Periodicals."

Ship Indexes. A useful approach to learning the home town of an immigrant is to learn about the origins of the persons the immigrant traveled with. This approach is especially useful for colonial research, for which other sources that indicate immigrants' origins are scarce. While standard immigration indexes often identify an immigrant and his or her ship, it is not so easy to identify others on that ship if a standard passenger list does not exist. Even if a list did survive, the lists seldom (virtually never in colonial times) identify the immigrant's home town. However, a wide range of other sources (discussed below under "Copied Original Records" and "Compiled Records"), especially records from Great Britain and Europe, do note emigrants' ships. To facilitate research into co-travelers, many publishers have provided ship indexes with their publications which identify the origins of immigrants. These indexes are virtually always at the back of the book, article, or collection of articles and are easy to use: the name of the ship is followed by the year of arrival and the page numbers on which passengers are identified; this allows the researcher to learn the origins of other passengers and, in turn, suggests where the immigrant may have originated. Many of the sources listed in this chapter's bibliography include ship indexes (notably those dealing with Pennsylvania immigration or German emigration), and they are so noted. An early ship index to several sources is in Charles M. Hall's *"Pal-Index": A Surname Index of Eighteenth-Century Immigrants* (Salt Lake City: Global Research Systems, 1979).

Directories

As noted earlier, immigration is a subset of ethnic studies, and it is to this broader field that researchers must turn to find the unpublished material they may be looking for. Many directories which lead to information on ethnic organizations and topics are available. For more detail (and more organizations) than the *Encyclopedia of Associations* (see chapter 1, "General Reference") provides, turn to Lubomyr Wynar's *Encyclopedic Directory of Ethnic Organizations in the United States* (Littleton, Colo.: Libraries Unlimited, 1975). Arranged by ethnic groups, this directory includes genealogical (such as the Holland Society of New York), cultural (Dutch Immigrant Society), and educational-historical (Netherlands-America Foundation) societies with a list of principal officers, size of staff, membership dues and requirements, and a brief description of the activities of each.

To go beyond societies and organizations, consult Paul Wasserman and Alice E. Kennington's *Ethnic Information Sources of the United States,* 2nd ed., 2 vols. (Detroit: Gale Research Co., 1983). Also arranged by ethnic group, it includes almost every conceivable source for information on any such group. In addition to fraternal, cultural, and historical organizations, it includes others, such as tourist offices, United Nations missions, embassies and consulates, professional groups, and charitable and religious organizations. It also lists research centers, museums, special libraries, newspapers, magazines, radio and television programs, banks, airline offices, shipping lines, book dealers, festivals, and audiovisual information pertaining to twenty-seven different groups. Some entries are annotated; others include only addresses or bibliographic citations. With its book list, *Ethnic Information Sources* is the first place to turn for ethnic information, and it can be found in virtually all public libraries. It is not the only source, however; some areas that it treats (such as organizations) are covered better elsewhere.

The American Library Association (ALA) has produced two ethnic reference aids that researchers should be aware of. Though becoming somewhat dated and not as inclusive as the directories noted above, they are still helpful. Both were compiled by Beth J. Shapiro. *Directory of Ethnic Publishers and Resource Organizations,* rev. ed. (Chicago: American Library Association, 1976), includes information on almost three hundred of the smaller publishers that deal with ethnic sources. Large publishers are excluded from it, as are the almost four hundred that did not respond to inquiries. Its alphabetical arrangement (by name of publisher) is aided by a subject index that is predominately ethnic in nature. Major published works, notably periodicals, are noted in the description of each publisher. *Directory of Ethnic Studies Librarians* (Chicago: American Library Association, 1976) identifies, by name, approximately 250 librarians who have a special interest in ethnic studies. They are indexed by residence, institution, subject, and type of library to help researchers locate librarians in their areas who have interests (and knowledge) that may fit their needs.

COPIED ORIGINAL RECORDS

While most of the reference tools discussed above are of interest primarily to immigration historians, the average genealogist generally seeks a specific immigrant among a list of names. The key indexes and bibliographies described above will assist in that task, but eventually genealogists find themselves dealing with a list of some type which indicates that a person with the name they are seeking came to North America from a foreign country. A growing number of those lists are simply printed versions of the original records of immigration which have been rescued from unknown (to the genealogist) archives and published in books or journal articles so that more researchers have access to the information. For a full discussion of the value of published original records, as well as their limitations, see the introduction to this work. Here it is sufficient to say that the original records which provide names of immigrants vary considerably in type and format, and that variation is only exacerbated by publication. Some compilers seek to publish entries that mirror the actual documents, while others abstract the information. Others alphabetize lists, thus destroying the clues that exist when the names appear in their original order.

Some compilers amalgamate information from two (or more) different sources, at which point, depending on how much editorial change is effected by the compiler or publisher, the source may be more of a compiled source than a published original record. In any event, the researcher should access the actual document (or a microfilm version of it), especially is there is any confusing or unclear information in the printed version. Accessing the actual document may not be easy for many researchers, however, especially when the information is from foreign sources that are not available on microfilm; therefore, always read the preface and introduction to the published source to learn as much as possible about the source, the compiler, and the published version being used. It may indicate, for example, that not every person in the actual document was listed in the published version, or that the annotations are from an alternate source or from additional records not directly related to the printed information.

The most common records of immigrants to appear as copied originals include passenger arrival lists, foreign departure lists, naturalization records, and lists of early settlers (often taken from early land grants made to immigrants). Sometimes immigrants are noted in other original records, such as newspapers, court records, church registers, military lists, and voter registrations. In addition to foreign departure lists, emigrants may appear in other foreign records, such as probate and court records. The great benefit of finding an emigrant in a translated and transcribed foreign record is that is will often provide a specific town of origin (or at least significant clues to assist that aspect of research). All known North American records dealing with groups of immigrants prior to 1820 have been published. Some such records may remain unpublished in foreign countries, but generally they too are published as they are discovered. Thus, the published literature is the best place to begin research on the origins of colonial and early American immigrants.

Arrival Lists

Until well into the twentieth century, every immigrant to North America arrived on a ship as a passenger (except ship crewmen who decided to stay). Most ships kept lists of the passengers they carried, and a surprisingly large number of those lists have survived. Passenger lists are usually the preferred form of documentation for immigrants; because of that preference, many ship passenger arrival lists are now available in print. Certainly, the majority of the passenger arrival lists for the 55 million documented arrivals in the United States from 1820 thorough 1989 have not been published (this is especially true for the later years); virtually no twentieth-century lists have been published. However, a growing number of nineteenth-century lists are now in print, and recently several hundred thousand names have been published each year.

Most arrival lists are published as transcripts of the significant material therein. This information includes the name of the ship, captain, ports of departure and arrival, and date of arrival. The transcript usually includes each passenger's name, age, sex, occupation, previous residence, and intended destination. Until the 1880s or 1890s, the actual lists included very little additional information, so published versions of them generally are full transcripts. However, each compiler/publisher applied different selection criteria to determine which immigrants to include in each publication.

Most published arrival lists are transcripts from the U.S. Customs lists; therefore, they cover part of the 1820-to-1900 period. Because these often include part of the great unindexed portion (New York arrivals from 1847 to 1896), they provide access to lists normally avoided by researchers. The largest collections are compiled according to ethnic group. The chapter bibliography lists published sources for the following groups:

- Armenians, 1891–1901
- Czechs, 1847–1906
- Irish, 1846–51
- Germans, 1850–87
- Greeks, 1885–1910
- Irish, 1846–51
- Italians, 1880–99
- Mennonites, 1872–1904
- Russian Empire (including Jews), 1875–86
- Swedes, 1820–50

Many of these are ongoing projects, so additional years will be published. A few of the groups are very significant and deserve separate mention. The four series discussed below are composed of transcripts produced from original U.S. Customs passenger lists that were deposited at the Balch Institute for Ethnic Studies' Center for Immigration Research (Philadelphia). Each was produced under the direction of Ira A. Glazier. The original lists are not always identical to the microfilm copies, for the National Archives microfilm copies of the original lists (series M237 for New York) include "a large number of [handwritten] copies for the period 1820–74 which were inserted in place of missing or illegible originals" (Tepper 1988, 71). Generally, the copies agree with the originals, except that initials occasionally appear on the copies instead of given names for some passengers. However, in cases where the copies were used to replace missing originals, it appears that the Balch Institute skipped those ships rather than turning to the microfilm copies for its transcripts.

Each of the volumes in these series contains between six hundred and seven hundred pages. A preface of several pages discusses the project and the immigration background of the particular ethnic group; the major part of each volume (approximately 70 percent) is a chronological set of transcripts of the ships' passenger lists (figure 14-5). The rest of the book is an every-name index; it provides the page number for each passenger listed. There is no comprehensive index covering all of the volumes for any of the four series, and, to date, none of the series seems to be included in Filby's *Passenger and Immigration Lists Index*. It is unlikely that they will be included in Filby's index for many years because they are readily available (and it appears that the publisher of Filby's index wants to provide access to lesser-known sources). Thus, researchers must search the volumes of the series as needed using the individual volume indexes.

The Famine Immigrants. The first set of passenger list transcripts from the Balch Institute was issued by Ira A. Glazier and Michael Tepper as *The Famine Immigrants: Lists of Irish Immigrants Arriving at the Port of New York, 1846–1851,* 7 vols. (Baltimore: Genealogical Publishing Co., 1983–86). The purpose of this series was to identify the immigrants arriving from Ireland during the great potato famine, but it is unclear how "Irish" was defined. Clearly, any passenger who gave his or her origin as Ireland should be listed (and usually is). However, often the lists indicate only that the passenger came from "Great Britain"; in such cases, inclusion is sporadic. Most ships leaving Irish ports were included, as were most from Liverpool, but some "ships from London, Greenock (Scotland), and Bristol that had passengers with clearly Irish names are sometimes excluded from the series" (Remington 1990, 136). Note also that

PASSENGER	AGE	SEX	OCCUPATION	PRV VIL DES
SHIP: TRINACRIA				
FROM: GLASGOW				
TO: NEW YORK				
ARRIVED: 27 JUNE 1872				
DANN, AUGUSTA-W.	19	F	UNKNOWN	GRZZZZUSA
WILLANIR, GOTTFRIED	40	M	LABR	GRZZZZUSA
VANDERVORST, H.	24	M	CL	GRZZZZUSA
LIEHE, CHRISTOPHER	26	M	CL	GRZZZZUSA
KINZER, HENRICH	21	M	LABR	GRZZZZUSA
LOGAV, ANNA-B.	20	F	UNKNOWN	GRZZZZUSA
SCHAANSON, MARGARET	20	F	UNKNOWN	GRZZZZUSA
GEORGE	18	M	UNKNOWN	GRZZZZUSA
RUGRAND, OTTO	19	M	UNKNOWN	GRZZZZUSA
WAIKI, CARL-J.	25	M	LABR	GRZZZZUSA
ZACHARIUS	18	M	LABR	GRZZZZUSA
JACOB	17	M	LABR	GRZZZZUSA
TERVAVANDA, JACOB	38	M	LABR	GRZZZZUSA
HALSTEN, GUSTAV	32	M	LABR	GRZZZZUSA
WIKKALA, MADS	40	M	LABR	GRZZZZUSA
HOFDAMAKI, ERICK-L.	22	M	FARMER	GRZZZZUSA
SALTHAMMERVAL, ANDREAS-	37	M	FARMER	GRZZZZUSA
MEINHART, GOTTFRED	70	M	FARMER	GRZZZZUSA
WEISS, HERMAN	25	M	UNKNOWN	GRZZZZUSA
BERTHA	22	F	UNKNOWN	GRZZZZUSA
SHIP: PAULINE DAVID				
FROM: HAMBURG				
TO: PHILADELPHIA				
ARRIVED: 28 JUNE 1872				
RUTTER, FERDINAND	20	M	PNTR	GRZZZZUSA
SHIP: ABYSSINIA				
FROM: LIVERPOOL AND QUEENSTOWN				
TO: NEW YORK				
ARRIVED: 29 JUNE 1872				
KRATOCHWILL, JOSEPH	50	M	MCHT	GRZZZZUSA
MRS.	48	F	W	GRZZZZUSA
MATTHIAS, FRANCISKA	23	F	NRS	GRZZZZUSA
HOFFMAN, RACHEL	7	F	CHILD	GRZZZZUSA
JANE	6	F	CHILD	GRZZZZUSA
ANNA	2	F	CHILD	GRZZZZUSA
ESTHER	.10	F	INFANT	GRZZZZUSA
CORBAS, LOUIS	34	M	CL	FRZZZZUSA
VOGTLING, HENRI	20	M	LABR	FRZZZZUSA
BELTZER, JACGUES	23	M	LABR	FRZZZZUSA
KERIEGAR, JACGUES	31	M	LABR	FRZZZZUSA
MARGARETT	36	F	W	FRZZZZUSA
MARGARETT	8	F	CHILD	FRZZZZUSA
MARIA	2	F	CHILD	FRZZZZUSA
CATHE.	.10	F	INFANT	FRZZZZUSA
HANRIN, LUDWIG	19	M	LABR	FRZZZZUSA
SCHNEIDER, EMIL	33	M	LABR	FRZZZZUSA
SEEGER, BERNHARD	25	M	LABR	FRZZZZUSA
DUTT, CAROLINE	21	F	SVNT	GRZZZZUSA
THOS, DANIEL	27	M	SHMK	GRZZZZUSA
EGGMANN, WILHELM	42	M	LKSH	FRZZZZUSA
BONRI, AUGUSTE	42	M	LABR	FRZZZZUSA
MALIN, VICTOR	24	M	LABR	FRZZZZUSA

PASSENGER	AGE	SEX	OCCUPATION	PRV VIL DES
KRAFT, HERMANN	24	M	TLR	GRZZZZUSA
BAIER, CAROLINE	26	M	TLR	GRZZZZUSA
GADIENT, JOSEPH	46	M	LABR	FRZZZZUSA
MARIA	38	F	W	FRZZZZUSA
MARIA	11	F	CH	FRZZZZUSA
MARGARETH	10	F	CH	FRZZZZUSA
BARTANA	6	F	CHILD	FRZZZZUSA
CHRISTINE	3	F	CHILD	FRZZZZUSA
CATHE.	2	F	CHILD	FRZZZZUSA
CAROLINE	.09	F	INFANT	FRZZZZUSA
KUPP, MARGT.	6	F	CHILD	FRZZZZUSA
MUTZLER, ANNA	29	F	SP	GRZZZZUSA
SCHROFER, CHRIST.	50	M	CPTR	GRZZZZUSA
CHRIST.	31	M	CPTR	GRZZZZUSA
URSELINE	27	F	W	GRZZZZUSA
EHRLER, ANTOINE	26	M	ENGR	GRZZZZUSA
GIESIN, EDOUARD	33	M	ENGR	GRZZZZUSA
DEBUS, MICHEL	20	M	BLKSMH	FRZZZZUSA
DEISER, JOHANN	20	M	TLR	GRZZZZUSA
WERNE, AUGUST	24	M	LABR	GRZZZZUSA
HERDI, FRIEDRICH	23	M	LABR	SRZZZZUSA
MAIER, MA--	23	M	LABR	FRZZZZUSA
BIEHLER, ULRICH	33	M	LABR	SRZZZZUSA
KOHLER, GUILLANNER	17	M	LABR	FRZZZZUSA
GUARICH, JN.BABT.	34	M	LABR	FRZZZZUSA
WEBER, GUILLANNER	39	M	CL	FRZZZZUSA
BIGOT, ANNA	38	F	W	FRZZZZUSA
WEBER, GUILLANNER	.11	M	INFANT	FRZZZZUSA
PRINCE, F.	31	M	CL	FRZZZZUSA
PEE, JEAN-J.	32	M	LABR	GRZZZZUSA
VICTOR, FRANCIS	40	M	CL	FRZZZZUSA
SCHANFERT, JACOB	18	M	FARMER	GRZZZZUSA
SCHNEIDER, JOHANN	22	M	BLKSMH	GRZZZZUSA
PFEIFFER, GEORG	24	M	LABR	GRZZZZUSA
WEYRIES, HILARUS	23	M	LABR	GRZZZZUSA
WOTH, STEPHAN	22	M	LABR	GRZZZZUSA
CORNET, PAUL	25	M	LABR	GRZZZZUSA
GILSON, JULES	27	M	LABR	GRZZZZUSA
RANCK, GOTTFRIED	22	M	LABR	GRZZZZUSA
CATH.	25	F	W	GRZZZZUSA
VONTE, PIERRE	52	M	LABR	FRZZZZUSA
HUFFEL, LEORAN	56	M	LABR	FRZZZZUSA
VICTORIA	53	F	W	FRZZZZUSA
SERAPHINE	24	F	SVNT	FRZZZZUSA
PRUDENCE	22	F	SVNT	FRZZZZUSA
HENRI	27	M	LABR	FRZZZZUSA
PITTS, CHAS.VANCE.	23	M	LABR	FRZZZZUSA
MELANIE	26	F	W	FRZZZZUSA
SOHRGUERE, AUGUST	22	M	LABR	FRZZZZUSA
BRANVERE, JEAN-D.	32	M	LABR	FRZZZZUSA
CLEMENZ	24	M	LABR	FRZZZZUSA
VANHUFFEL, PIERRE	25	M	LABR	FRZZZZUSA
CLEMENZ	23	M	LABR	FRZZZZUSA
LEVIN	2	M	CHILD	FRZZZZUSA
VANSCHWINK, AUGUST	35	M	TLR	GRZZZZUSA
BARBARA	40	F	W	GRZZZZUSA
KINSCHOFF, S.K.	20	M	MLR	GRZZZZUSA
KONIG, FRIED.	20	M	BKR	GRZZZZUSA
FELLER, JOHANN	20	M	CPTR	GRZZZZUSA
HOLTMAN, JACOB	24	M	JNR	GRZZZZUSA
NICLAUS	54	M	LABR	GRZZZZUSA
SCHRAM, LUDWIG	16	M	BRR	GRZZZZUSA
LANG, BARBARA	30	F	MA	GRZZZZUSA
KURD	1	M	CHILD	GRZZZZUSA
KOHLE, CATHA.	25	F	SVNT	GRZZZZUSA
ERNST, HEIN.	18	M	BCHR	GRZZZZUSA
JAGER, MICLAUS	24	M	BKR	GRZZZZUSA
RIDDER, JOHANN	32	M	BRR	GRZZZZUSA
KOENIGS, NICLAUS	22	M	BRR	GRZZZZUSA
CUSPARS, MATHIAS	19	M	BRR	GRZZZZUSA
STEFFES, MARG.	21	M	BRR	GRZZZZUSA
MULLER, ERNST	44	M	MSN	GRZZZZUSA
CATHE.	40	F	W	GRZZZZUSA
NICLAUS	11	M	CH	GRZZZZUSA
LUZIA	9	F	CHILD	GRZZZZUSA

Figure 14-5. From Glazier and Filby's *Germans to America: Lists of Passengers Arriving at U.S. Ports,* vol. 27, page 329.

persons with stated origins other than Ireland, or occasionally Great Britain, are not listed, even if they arrived on a ship with a large number of Irish immigrants. One other caveat should be mentioned: more than 1 million people left Ireland for the United States and Canada during the famine years, but this series totals only approximately 545,000 immigrants. Many of the remaining one-half million people landed at other ports (notably Boston) or arrived on ships to New York that are not included among these transcripts. Of course, emigration from Ireland did not stop at the end of 1851, although it did slow. An Irish immigrant who does not appear in this series may simply have arrived later.

Germans to America. Clearly, the most ambitious project undertaken by the Balch Institute center is the transcribing of German arrivals over the last half of the nineteenth century. Ira A. Glazier and P. William Filby are the editors of *Germans to America: Lists of Passengers Arriving at U.S. Ports,* 54+ vols. (Wilmington, Del.: Scholarly Resources, 1987–). This ongoing series covers arrivals at *all* U.S. ports, not just New York, and begins with the year 1850. Projected to include the 4 million Germans who immigrated through 1893, the series includes fifty-four volumes (as of early 1997) that list approximately 3 million Germans. Because of the broad scope of this series and interest in German immigration, these volumes have been the focus of careful study by well-trained genealogists. Two published studies include Gordon Remington's review essay "Feast or Famine: Problems in the Genealogical Use of *The Famine Immigrants* and *Germans to America*," *National Genealogical Society Quarterly* 78: 135–46 (June 1990), and Michael Palmer's even more detailed and documented discussion, "Published Passenger Lists: A Review of *German Immigrants* and *Germans to America*," *Bulletin of the German Genealogical Society of America* 4: 69–90 (May-August 1990). Both authors arrived at similar conclusions—that the series is very incomplete, due in part to inconsistent application of the editors' own list selection criteria and to the fact that lists missing from the Temple-Balch Institute center's collection (for which copies exist on the microfilm) were not transcribed.

In fairness to the series' publisher, these reviews were written during the initial phase of publication, when the selection criteria were much more lax than at present. The series was first intended to cover only those Germans who arrived between 1850 and 1855 and was designed to include only those passenger lists that contained a minimum of 80-percent German surnames. Those lists, however, were published in their entirety (whereas *The Famine Immigrants'* lists omitted passengers who were not from Ireland). Both studies show considerable omissions from the first five years' of passenger lists, even given the 80-percent minimum. Palmer compared the number of known German immigrants for 1850 to 1855 from the reports of the U.S. secretary of state to the number found in *Germans to America* and found only 86-percent total coverage in the latter. Even that group, he argues, contains a sizeable number of Swiss and Austrians (by his estimate, 10 percent); he concluded that only approximately 75 percent of the Germans coming to America from 1850 to 1855 are in the series (Palmer 1990, 74). Palmer goes on to find significant under-representation in the series of Germans sailing by way of British ports (1990, 83) and a gap of two months in 1851 which accounts for 130 ship lists (on the microfilm) not being included in the series (1990, 84).

Fortunately, the editors and publisher listened to the concerns of German-oriented researchers and, upon extending the series beyond the initial 1855 cutoff date, changed the inclusion criteria. Starting with the 1856 volumes, the transcripts contain

> . . . all ships with German passengers, regardless of the percentage. [However], only those calling themselves Germans are now listed; all other passenger names are deleted. [Furthermore,] these German immigrants include those coming not only from German states or territories, but also from countries such as France, Switzerland, or Luxembourg (Glazier and Filby 1997, vol. 54, ix).

Even with this change of focus, there are still at least three existing situations that will exclude hundreds of thousands of Germans from this series: (1) This series begins with 1850, omitting more than half a million Germans in the U.S. Customs lists from 1820 through 1849, 40 to 50 percent of whom fall into the unindexed (post-1846) portion of the New York lists; (2) no plans have been announced to return to the 1850-to-1855 lists to "pick up" the omitted immigrants; (3) the series still relies on the original records at the Balch Institute, so it will omit the many lists that exist only in copied form (yet are easy to find among the microfilm copies from the National Archives). These deficiencies should serve to remind the researcher that, as useful as published original records are (3 million German immigrants have been indexed and the number is increasing), they may not be sufficient for all research purposes. Access to the microfilm copies is easy, and they comprise a valuable alternate source if the immigrant does not appear in the published lists.

Italians to America. With the commercial success of *Germans to America*, the same editors embarked on a similar project treating Italians, but with a later chronological setting. Ira A. Glazier and P. William Filby have begun issuing *Italians to America: Lists of Passengers Arriving at U.S. Ports, 1880–1899,* 7+ vols. (Wilmington, Del.: Scholarly Resources, 1992–). As of early 1997, seven volumes covering the years 1880 through September 1893 had appeared; they document approximately 390,000 Italian immigrants—just over half of the Italians who came to America between 1880 and 1899. The publisher has announced plans to publish additional volumes for the 1900-to-1915 period.

The selection criterion for the transcriptions is much like that for *The Famine Immigrants* and the later volumes of *Germans to America* (post-1855): "Italian passengers on these lists who disembarked at New York are published in their entirety; the names of non-Italian passengers are deleted (Glazier and Filby 1992, vol. 1, ix)." Of course, this criterion leaves the same problems that plagued both the Irish and German lists discussed above: Just who was "Italian?" Ethnic Italians also lived in, and emigrated from, Ticino canton in Switzerland, as well as several coastal areas of the Austro-Hungarian Empire. If a list indicates that an immigrant is from Switzerland or Austria, do not expect to find his or her name in *Italians to America,* even if the name is Italian.

Two of the three caveats mentioned regarding the German lists also pertain here: many Italians arrived in America before the beginning of this series (1880); and these transcripts are based on the original records, therefore omitting any missing originals for which copies were available when the lists were microfilmed by the National Archives. In addition, a third caution is necessary: although the series is intended to cover arrivals at all ports (as does *Germans to America*), the first volumes will cover only New York arrivals; later volumes will list those who arrived at other U.S. ports. This coverage differs from the German series, which lists arrivals at all ports chronologically.

Migration from the Russian Empire. The newest series from the Balch Institute Center for Immigration Research lists immigrants from Russia. Ira Glazier, editor of *Migration from the Russian Empire: Lists of Passengers Arriving at the Port of New York* (Baltimore: Genealogical Publishing Co., 1995), has issued two volumes in a series that is projected to list the 2.3

million Russian immigrants who came to America between 1875 and 1910. Approximately 105,000 immigrants through September of 1886 are listed in them. The introduction to the volumes is vague, mentioning only that the passengers listed are of Russian nationality (which it seems to define as Poles, Finns, and Russians) and that non-Russian nationals are excluded. However, because the lists vary over the years regarding the information provided about the immigrants, it is difficult to know how "Russian" was defined. Apparently the transcribers relied upon the name of the country the passenger claimed to have been a citizen of (in the lists prior to 1882) and the native country (beginning with the 1882 lists). In any event, the ethnic group leaving the Russian Empire in the greatest numbers during the period covered by this series was the Jews, followed by Poles. A wide variety of other ethnic groups are also represented in these volumes.

In addition to these four major series, there is a host of other, smaller publications offering transcripts of U.S. passenger arrival records. They may not suffer from the same deficiencies as the major series, but they still must be used with the cautions mentioned above in mind.

Ethnic, or country of origin, lists are not the only form which publishers have used to make passenger arrival transcripts available; some publishers have issued transcripts of the arrival lists for specific ports during specific years. Such lists include all immigrants, regardless of ethnic group, for the specified time period. Generally, these published lists cover the smaller ports or earlier years, when fewer passengers were arriving. Some predate formal U.S. Customs lists, while others cover the early Customs lists period. The chapter bibliography lists published sources for the following ports and time periods:

- All ports: 1819–20, 1820–23
- Boston: 1715–16, 1762–69
- Rhode Island: Providence, 1798–1808, 1820–72; Bristol and Warren, 1820–71
- Philadelphia: non-British, 1727–1808; all (baggage lists), 1800–19
- Baltimore: 1820–34
- Charleston: 1820–29
- New Orleans: 1820–23
- Galveston: 1850–55, 1846–71
- San Francisco: 1850–52 (reconstructed)

A brief discussion of some of these lists will help the researcher to understand the nature of these and similar publications.

Pennsylvania German Pioneers. A significant, and classic, publication—actually, the largest single collection of colonial passenger arrival lists—is Ralph Beaver Strassburger and William John Hinke's transcription of *Pennsylvania German Pioneers: A Publication of the Original Lists of Arrivals in the Port of Philadelphia from 1727 to 1808,* 3 vols. (Norristown: Pennsylvania German Society, 1934). It has been reprinted several times (usually only the first and third volumes)—most often by the Genealogical Publishing Company (Baltimore). However, in 1992 Picton Press (Rockport, Maine) reprinted all three volumes, including the rare vol. 2, which includes the signatures of most of the German heads of families who arrived in Philadelphia. The 1992 edition also includes two lists that were not available for the 1934 printing.

So significant is *Pennsylvania German Pioneers* that virtually all Pennsylvania-German immigration research revolves around it. Both American and German publications dealing with Pennsylvania Germans refer to families within these volumes by page number. Other authors often use the numbered ship lists to compile ship indexes for their own works. The introduction (in vol. 1) is an excellent discussion of German immigration into Pennsylvania and the nature of the lists used for this collection. During the colonial years, up to three lists noting the heads of families were made for each ship disembarking in Philadelphia. One was the captain's list, made on the ship and based on the ship's manifest. The second list was an "Oath of Allegiance to the King of Great Britain"; it was signed by all males over sixteen years of age (who were taken, as a group, to a magistrate's office in the city of Philadelphia for signing). The third list, signed at the courthouse, again by males over sixteen years of age, was an oath of fidelity and abjuration. The published version includes copies of all three lists (those that have survived), allowing comparisons of spelling, handwriting, and sequences of names (friends and relatives were usually listed near each other). Because only males over sixteen are named in these lists, the editors estimate that the 29,800 names represent upwards of seventy thousand German immigrants—more than two-thirds of the total German arrivals before the Revolutionary War.

The lists include the name of each ship, its captain, ports of departure and arrival, and the date of arrival. The list of names then follows in exactly the order found on the original lists. Where the immigrant signed with a mark, a symbol accompanying the name indicates that the spelling is not in the handwriting of the immigrant (see figure 14-6). Earlier editions of some of these lists were published in Israel D. Rupp's *A Collection of Upwards of 30,000 Names of Germans, Swiss, French and Other Immigrants in Pennsylvania, 1727–1776* (1876; reprint; Baltimore: Genealogical Publishing Co., 1985), and William H. Egle, ed., *Names of Foreigners Who Took the Oath of Allegiance to the Province and State of Pennsylvania, 1727–1775* (Harrisbug, Pa.: E. K. Meyers, 1890; reprint; Baltimore: Genealogical Publishing Co., 1967). They include some additional material, but the transcripts by Strassburger and Hinke are considered much more accurate and complete.

Other Port Lists. Two of the larger ports of the early nineteenth century were Philadelphia and Baltimore. They are partially covered in two publications by Elizabeth P. Bentley and Michael H. Tepper. *Passenger Arrivals at the Port of Philadelphia, 1800–1819: The Philadelphia Baggage Lists* (Baltimore: Genealogical Publishing Co., 1986) represents the advent of Federal passenger lists. These are not the U.S. Customs lists (which did not begin until 1820); rather; they resulted from a 1799 act of Congress which exempted incoming passengers from paying duty on personal baggage (Tepper 1988, 49–50). Philadelphia appears to be the only port to have consistently maintained these lists; even so, the lists are incomplete. Some forty thousand names were taken from more than 4,700 ship lists; the average of fewer than nine names per list suggests that some passengers are not listed. (Some may not have possessed sufficient baggage to justify a listing in the minds of those making the lists.) An important fact, however, is that the vessels used in the early 1800s did not have the large passenger capacity of those used later in the nineteenth century. It also is apparent that not all passengers in these lists were immigrants; some certainly were U.S. citizens returning from abroad. If Hansen's annual estimates are correct, then approximately 160,000 emigrants came to America in the first two decades of the nineteenth century (1961, 68–106). Bromwell's study of immigration statistics for the 1820-to-1855 period shows that in the 1820s, Philadelphia received an average of approximately two thousand passengers per year. Further, Philadelphia was often matched in that decade by Boston, Baltimore, and New Orleans and surpassed by New York (1856, 21–169). If the 1820s pattern of immigration is representative of the first two decades of the century, the five major (and several minor) ports shared the immigrants with some degree of equality. Thus, the forty thousand arrivals listed in the pre-1820 baggage lists may account for many of the Philadelphia passengers.

The same editors also prepared *Passenger Arrivals at the Port of Baltimore, 1820–1834, from Customs Passenger Lists* (Baltimore: Genealogical Publishing Co., 1982), based on microfilms of the surviving originals and copies of the arrival lists for this significant port. Of the fifty thousand immigrants listed, approximately 75 percent are German; the rest are mostly British and Irish. This list provides the name, age, occupation, country of origin and destination, ship name, and date of arrival. The names are arranged alphabetically, so researchers should refer to the microfilm copies to learn who immigrated with the immigrant.

[List 192 C] At the Court House at Philadelphia, Thursday, the Second of November, 1752.

Present: Edward Shippen, Esqr.

The Foreigners whose Names are underwritten, imported in the Ship called the Phoenix, John Spurrier, Commander, from Rotterdam but last from Portsmouth in England, took the usual Qualifications to the Government.

Bastian (+) Kender	Johannes Stehlert
Johann Henrich Schleich	Johans Michel Bürger
Johan Jacob Wetzal	Hans Philip Dosch
Johann Baltzar Kleinschmit	Johann Conrad Wassum
Lorentz Michel	Johanes (+) Wassom
Hans Michel Fries	Leonhart (+) Wassom
Philipp Jacob Horn	Joh. George (×) Wassom
Hagen Horn	Adam (×) Heins
Johannes Riess	Christoff Kuhn
Matthias Wilhelm Henning	Hans Christoph Schlessmann
Johan Michael Wissler	Frantz Ihmme
Johan Wolf Wissler	Johann Ludwig Peiffer
Johan Casper Wissler	Siep Kurz
Peter Dahlmann	Abraham Bauman
Henrich Becker	Johanis Schmid
Jo. Hennrich Katzebach	Johanis Schmit
Conrad (×) Rooss	Johan Christian Heydt
Joachim Ströver	Johannes Götzelman
Thomas (××) Geisler	Hans Michel Ötzel
Phillip Herdel	Andereas (+) Bower
J. Jacob (IS) Shellbecher	Stephan (+) Bower
Jost Phillipp Schnelbacher	Michael (+) Bower
J. Henry (×) Sholtes	Hans Seubert
Jacobus Frütranck	J. Jacob (+) Götzelman
Johann Michael Bäcker	Johann Adam Binner
Johanes Borischt	Georg Hörner

Figure 14-6. From Strassburger and Hinke's *Pennsylvania German Pioneers: A Publication of the Original Lists of Arrivals in the Port of Philadelphia from 1727 to 1808* (page 501). Where the immigrant signed with a mark, a symbol accompanying the name indicates that the spelling is not in the handwriting of the immigrant.

Smaller ports are often overlooked by researchers. Publication of lists from smaller ports draws attention to the lists and makes them easier for family historians to search. Two examples are Brent H. Holcomb's *Passenger Arrivals at the Port of Charleston 1820–1829* (Baltimore: Genealogical Publishing Co., 1994), which contains 6,300 names taken directly from the Customs passenger lists and State Department transcripts that represent the only known lists for that port; and Maureen Taylor's *Rhode Island Passenger Lists: Port of Providence 1798–1808; 1820–1872 and Port of Bristol and Warren 1820–1871* (Baltimore: Genealogical Publishing Co., 1995), which contains four thousand names from original records at the Rhode Island Historical Society (supplemented by the National Archives microfilms). Taylor included the rare Alien Registration Lists for Providence (1798 to 1808) and found that many of the original 1820-to-1872 lists are missing from the National Archives microfilm copies. Each of these volumes presents transcripts of the lists and provides indexes to locate the names within those lists.

German Immigrants. A unique contribution to the literature of published arrival lists is the work of the late Gary J. Zimmerman and his co-author, Marion Wolfert, in *German Immigrants: Lists of Passengers Bound from Bremen to New York,* 4 vols. (Baltimore: Genealogical Publishing Co., 1985–93). These volumes serve as a partial reconstruction of the long-since-destroyed Bremen, Germany, departure lists. Zimmerman discovered that approximately 21 percent of the Bremen arrival lists for the port of New York included specific birthplaces for the immigrants. Recognizing the significance of this information for researchers, the pair issued three volumes before Zimmerman's death; they cover lists from 1847 through 1867. Wolfert completed the series with a fourth volume covering 1868 to 1871, after which the lists no longer indicate the town of origin. Together, the volumes identify 137,000 immigrants, many of whom are not in the *Germans to America* series due to the earlier start date and the selection criteria of that series; Palmer's essay notes that dozens of lists omitted from the larger series are included in Zimmerman and Wolfert's volumes (1990, 83). The transcripts were made from the National Archives microfilm copies of arrival lists. The immigrants are listed alphabetically within them, with family members grouped under the head of the family.

Among the greatest problems researchers have in using any of these major lists, each having tens of thousands of names, is properly identifying immigrants. Among 500,000 Irish or 3 million Germans, there are likely to be several immigrants having the same name arriving in the same time period. To clearly identify which is the correct immigrant, it is necessary to know as much as possible about the immigrant *before* seeking him or her in these lists. Knowing (from other research) who was in the family, their ages, residences, and as precise a date of immigration as possible makes it easier to determine which of several immigrants is the one being sought. For more information, see chapter 13, "Immigration: Finding Immigrant Origins," in *The Source: A Guidebook of American Genealogy* (cited earlier).

Foreign Departure Lists

While the largest collections of published immigration lists pertain to U.S. arrival lists, many other lists of immigrants have been published. Often overlooked by North American researchers are a growing number of publications that transcribe or index foreign records that document emigrants leaving their home countries.

In many European countries, permission was required to leave the country. While many emigrants (perhaps up to half in many localities) did not seek or obtain such permission, many others did, leaving behind a rich documentary heritage with details of their former lives not known to their American descendants. Often these records reveal the emigrant's home town, as well as other information. Other departure lists are available for ports where the emigrants embarked on their voyage to a new life. While foreign port departure lists are not as plentiful, nor as well preserved, as the North American arrival lists, some lists do exist and a few are available in print. Of the hundreds of such published lists, a few representative samples are discussed here.

Passengers leaving Great Britain or Ireland were rarely well documented after the colonial period because the government seldom kept any of the departure lists that may have been created. However, a few lists from the shipping lines themselves have surfaced; this is the case with Brian Mitchell's *Irish Passenger Lists, 1847–1871: Lists of Passengers Sailing from Londonderry to America on Ships of the J. & J. Cooke Line and the McCorkell Line* (Baltimore: Genealogical Publishing Co., 1988). These lists provide the emigrant's name, age, address, and the name of the ship, along with information about when the ship sailed. The address includes the actual place of residence, making these lists a boon for those descending from one of the 27,495 passengers listed.

During the 1700s, Swiss authorities in the canton of Zurich became concerned about the number of their citizens who were emigrating to the New World. They requested local authorities (chiefly the church ministers) to identify those who had left and were leaving their parishes. The cantons of Bern and Basel also kept regular records of people requesting permission to emigrate. Together, these three cantons account for much of the Swiss emigration of the time. Abstracts from the records, which are still in Swiss archives, were published by Albert Bernhardt Faust and Gaius Marcus Brumbaugh as *Lists of Swiss Emigrants in the Eighteenth Century to the American Colonies,* 2 vols. (Washington, D.C.: National Genealogical Society, 1920–25; reprint with additional notes; Baltimore: Genealogical Publishing Co., 1976). Together, the two volumes identify approximately five thousand individuals who left Switzerland, most bound for the American colonies.

Over the course of the nineteenth century, more emigrants left the various German states than any other country in the world, with millions of them coming to North America. The German states made a more frequent practice of requiring permission to emigrate did than other countries. *The Wuerttemberg Emigration Index*, described above under "Finding Aids—Indexes," is drawn from such surviving documents. Several German publications include abstracts from similar emigration records housed in state archives. One excellent example is Inge Auerbach's *Auswanderer aus Hessen-Kassel 1840–1850,* vol. 2 (Veroeffentlichungen der Archivschule Marburg, Institut fuer Archivwissenschaft, no. 12) (Marburg, Germany: Institut für Archivwissenschaft, 1988). Most of this volume is an alphabetical list of persons named in the emigration documents, but it serves to abstract those records because it provides the emigrant's name, age, town of residence, others traveling with him, destination, year of departure, and a reference to the document naming the individual (figure 14-7). Because a person might be named in several documents, the twenty-nine thousand entries represent approximately ten thousand names.

Other, similar sources are listed in the chapter bibliography for:

- Grand Duchy of Brunswick (Braunschweig)
- District of Trier
- Prussian Saarland
- Districts of Minden and Muenster (Westphalia)
- Duchy of Nassau
- Waldeck
- Principality of Lippe

Naturalization Records

Naturalization records are also favorite sources for documenting immigrants, but they seldom provide as much information as do passenger lists; however, they seem to be equally popular subjects for publishers. As noted above under "Finding Aids—Indexes," many published naturalization records are really indexes to the actual documents (or microfilm copies). However, because most naturalization records provide so little information about the immigrant—typically name, country of former allegiance, and dates of declaration and/or petition—an index which provides this information is practically an abstract of the record.

In North America, naturalization is mostly a post-revolutionary war phenomenon. Before the war, British subjects were permitted to settle anywhere in the British Empire, including North America, without the need to seek citizenship. There-

SCHWARZ	ZACHARIAS		SALZSCHLIRF/FD	T	113		A		46	FD384,148
SCHWATZER	GEORG	32	BREITENBACH/ROF	T	400	TI	AN	99	46AU	1B/11,442
SCHWATZER	KIND D.GEORG	1	BREITENBACH/ROF				AN	99	46JL	1B/11,442
SCHWATZER	KIND D.GEORG	4	BREITENBACH/ROF				AN	99	46JL	1B/11,442
SCHWEDES	HENRICH	23	BRUENDERSEN/WOH	T	75	SN	DP +		42AU	2E/16,339
SCHWEDES	HENRICH	23	BRUENDERSEN/WOH	T	75	SN	DP +		42JL	1B/11,345
SCHWEDES	HENRICH	23	BRUENDERSEN/WOH	T	75	SN	DP +		42AU	2A/32,108
SCHWEDLER	JAKOB RUDOLF	24	KASSEL			KF	DP +		41JA	2E/16,190
SCHWEDLER	JAKOB RUDOLF	26	KASSEL			KF	DP +		41JA	1B/11,201
SCHWEDLER	JAKOB RUDOLF	26	KASSEL			KF	DP +		41JA	2A/32,31
SCHWEER	HENRICH	37	ALGESDORF/RI				DSL+		41DE	1B/11,281
SCHWEER	HENRICH	37	ALGESDORF/RI				DSL+		41DE	2A/32,71
SCHWEER	HENRICH	37	ALGESDORF/RI				DLD+		41DE	2D/4,237
SCHWEINSBERG	FRAU D.GEORG		ROCKENSUESS/ROF				AN	99	46MR	2A/37,294
SCHWEINSBERG	GEORG	38	ROCKENSUESS/ROF	T	200	TG	AN	2	46MR	1A/4,294
SCHWEINSBERG	GEORG	38	ROCKENSUESS/ROF	T	200	TG	AN	99	46MR	1B/11,393
SCHWEINSBERG	GEORG	38	ROCKENSUESS/ROF	T	200	TG	AN	99	46MR	2A/37,293
SCHWEINSBERG	GEORG	38	ROCKENSUESS/ROF	T	200	TG	AN	2	46MR	2A/39,372
SCHWEINSBERG	GEORG	38	ROCKENSUESS/ROF	T	200	TG	AN	99	46MR	2A/36A,61
SCHWEINSBERG	HENRICH	44	ALLENDORF/WIZ			XH	OW		42JL	2E/1,176
SCHWEINSBERG	HENRICH	20	GOTTSBUEREN/HOG			WL	AN		49DE	HG130,35
SCHWEINSBERG	HENRICH	29	LICHTENAU/WIZ	T	130	SU	A		44MR	1A/4,155
SCHWEINSBERG	HENRICH	29	LICHTENAU/WIZ	T	150	SU	A		44MR	1B/11,138
SCHWEINSBERG	HENRICH	29	LICHTENAU/WIZ	T	130	SU	A		44MR	2A/33,3
SCHWEINSBERG	HENRICH	29	LICHTENAU/WIZ	T	130	SU	A		44MR	2A/35,171
SCHWEINSBERG	HENRICH	29	LICHTENAU/WIZ	T	150	SU	A		44MR	2A/32,204
SCHWEINSBERG	HENRICH CHRSTPH	45	HEISEBECK/HOG	T	78	SM	A	4	40MR	HG133,216
SCHWEINSBERG	HENRICH CHRSTPH		HEISEBECK/HOG				AN	1	40	1A/4,10
SCHWEINSBERG	KIND D.GEORG	13	ROCKENSUESS/ROF				AN	99	46MR	1B/11,393
SCHWEINSBERG	KIND D.GEORG	11	ROCKENSUESS/ROF				AN	99	46MR	1B/11,393

Figure 14-7. From Auerbach's *Auswanderer aus Hessen-Kassel 1840–1850,* vol. 2 (page 434).

fore, what few colonial naturalization lists exist focus on non-British foreigners. The colonial term was *denization,* meaning that a person was admitted to residence in a foreign country and was entitled to all or part of the rights of citizenship (*Webster's* 1928, 595). The actual records for the colonial time period, insofar as they have survived, seldom consist of more than a few pages with lists of the naturalized citizens and the countries to which they formerly belonged. During the revolutionary war, oaths of allegiance were sometimes required (or expected) of all adult males as a declaration of loyalty to the revolutionary government. Given these special circumstances, such oaths clearly do not always indicate that the person was of foreign birth.

Published nineteenth-century naturalization records (the procedures and requirements for naturalization in the new United States of America were not well codified until 1798) seldom cover a large number of immigrants or large geographic area in any one collection. The exception of the published Philadelphia naturalization index was described above under "Arrival lists—Other Port Lists." Most, rather, focus on the naturalization records of a county, often being published in periodical articles. Approximately 25 percent of the sources cited in Filby's *Passenger and Immigration Lists Bibliography* (cited earlier) are naturalization indexes or abstracts that are easily found through the subject index of that source.

There are some colonial collections to be aware of. The largest single collection apparently is Montague S. Giuseppi's *Naturalizations of Foreign Protestants in the American and West Indian Colonies . . .,* Publications of the Huguenot Society of London, vol. 24 (1921; reprint; Baltimore: Genealogical Publishing Co., 1964, 1979). The several thousand names are from two entry books of the Lords Commissioners for Trade and Plantations at the Public Record Office in London; they include persons living in the Carolinas, Virginia, Maryland, New York, and Pennsylvania. Approximately three thousand Pennsylvania names, most of them of Quakers, are listed in a more complete form in "Persons Naturalized in the Province of Pennsylvania [1740–1773]" in *Pennsylvania Archives,* series 2, vol. 2 (1876), pages 345 to 486. This section was excerpted and reprinted by the Genealogical Publishing Company in 1967.

Kenneth Scott has published several collections of New York naturalizations. With Kenn Stryker-Rodda, his *Denizations, Naturalizations, and Oaths of Allegiance in Colonial New York* (Baltimore: Genealogical Publishing Co., 1975) identifies several thousand denizations, licenses, and oaths of allegiance dating back as far as the seventeenth century. Scott's largest work, *Early New York Naturalizations: Abstracts of Naturalization Records from Federal, State, and Local Courts, 1790–1840* (Baltimore: Genealogical Publishing Co., 1981) identifies ten thousand persons with name, age, and place of residence and birth as well as the approximate date of arrival in America.

In addition to New York, two other states with a significant number of non-British foreigners were Pennsylvania and

Maryland. Key sources for these states include Egle's *Names of Foreigners Who Took the Oath of Allegiance to the Province and State of Pennsylvania, 1727–1775* (cited earlier), which is a version of the arrivals listed in the Strassburger volumes described above, and Jeffrey and Florence L. Wyand's *Colonial Maryland Naturalizations* (Baltimore: Genealogical Publishing Co., 1975; reprint; 1986), which documents 1,600 naturalization between 1660 and 1775.

Settler Lists

Other sources for identifying immigrants are lists of early settlers. While not every settler in a given location was an immigrant, many of them were during the colonial era. One of the major factors that drew immigrants to America was the availability of land; immigrants, therefore, often became the first settlers in many areas. Most lists of early settlers seem to be based on land grants of one kind or another. In some southern states these settler lists are from headrights—documentation of having transported a certain number persons to settle on, and improve, tracts of land. In New England, early settlers are sometimes determined from the lists of freemen—men granted full rights within a town to own land and hold office. While not every freeman was an immigrant, many were, especially in towns settled by recent immigrants. Thus, to be effective lists of immigrants, settler lists need to pertain to the first settlement of a locality known to have attracted immigrants during the early history of North America. For example, homesteads, while they attracted some immigrants and are certainly records of the first settlers on certain lands, do not serve well as lists of immigrants because many non-immigrants also applied for homesteads.

Land records are the basis for Gust Skordas's *Early Settlers of Maryland: An Index to the Names of Immigrants Compiled from Records of Land Patents, 1633–1680, in the Hall of Records, Annapolis, Maryland* (Baltimore: Genealogical Publishing Co., 1968; reprint; 1986). This alphabetical index of more than twenty-five thousand settlers identifies virtually all of the immigrants who remained in Maryland (as opposed to those who landed there and then moved on to other colonies). It provides each immigrant's full name, approximate date of immigration, residence, the basis for the claim for land, and a reference to the source of the information. This series has been continued by Peter Wilson Coldham in his five-volume series *Settlers of Maryland*, which covers the years from 1679 through 1783 (Baltimore: Genealogical Publishing Co., 1995–96). Coldham used the same Land Office books at the Maryland Hall of Records as did Skordas to identify approximately twenty-four thousand more settlers for the revolutionary war period. Each entry provides the name of the settler, county, name of tract granted or purchased, number of acres, date, and a reference to the original source.

Colonial immigration to Virginia is of great interest to the millions of descendants of the early settlers, but it can only really be documented in the early land records. As George Greer indicated,

> the records of the Land Office in Richmond remain the only source from which these names [of immigrants] can now be obtained. As the records stand, it is simply impossible, without the most extensive and expensive research, to obtain names of persons who came to Virginia, unless they themselves were patentees of land; and the great majority of immigrants to the colony do not appear as patentees (1912, 3).

However, Greer recognized, as have many others, that the names of thousands of immigrants lie buried in those patents because of the system of headrights. In order to qualify for their own land, the patentees listed the persons they had transported to the colony. Greer was the first to extract the names of immigrants from those lists. He issued them as *Early Virginia Immigrants, 1623–1666* (1912; reprint; Baltimore: Genealogical Publishing Co., 1982). However, this list of some twenty-five thousand immigrants does not even serve as an index to the patents, nor as a good indicator of where the immigrant settled. The list contains the name of the immigrant, year of the land patent, name of the patentee or person who transported the immigrant, and the county where the patent was located (figure 14-8).

Nell Marion Nugent abstracted the same patent books at the Virginia Land Office to provide a more useful list in *Cavaliers and Pioneers: Abstracts of Virginia Land Patents and Grants,* vol. 1 (Richmond: Dietz Printing Co., 1934); vols. 2 and 3 (Richmond, Va.: Virginia State Library, 1977, 1979). These three volumes cover records and immigrants from 1623 through 1732, being patent books 1 through 14. Dennis Hudgins, ed., continued the series with a fourth volume, *Cavaliers and Pioneers: 1732–1741* (Richmond: Virginia Genealogical Society, 1994). Together, these volumes document approximately fifty thousand or more immigrants transported to the colony for the sake of land.

A composite list for Georgia, drawn from early passenger lists and other records of first settlers, is E. Merton Coulter and Albert B. Saye's *A List of the Early Settlers of Georgia* (Athens: University of Georgia Press, 1949); 2nd ed. (Baltimore: Genealogical Publishing Co., 1967). Approximately three thousand settlers, most of them immigrants, are brought together in this list.

Foreign Records

Foreign lists of departures, as described above, are obvious sources of information and documentation of immigrants. However, there are a host of other records in the countries our immigrant ancestors came from that also document their status as emigrants. These include records of persons banished from their countries (exiles), political and religious refugees, servants, indentured people and apprentices sent overseas, court depositions and actions mentioning immigrants (including probates), adventurers, and land company proprietors (not all of whom came to North America).

One of the first to recognize the value of this variety of records in Great Britain was John Camden Hotten. He gathered many such lists together, transcribed them, and published them as *The Original Lists of Persons of Quality; Emigrants; Religious Exiles; Political Rebels; Serving Men Sold for a Term of Years; Apprentices; Children Stolen; Maidens Pressed; and Others Who Went from Great Britain to American Plantations 1600–1700* (1874; reprint; Baltimore: Genealogical Publishing Co., 1974). Although mostly superseded by later books (such as the following set), this volume, which lists an estimated ten thousand emigrants, is a standard in immigration literature and provides evidence of the variety of records in which researchers can seek emigrants from Great Britain.

The Complete Book of Emigrants. Peter Wilson Coldham borrowed Hotten's idea and extended it significantly as he collected evidence of approximately 100,000 people who emigrated from England to the colonies before the revolutionary war. Incorporating some of Hotten's lists and adding many more that both he and others had discovered, he produced *The Complete Book of Emigrants 1607–1660: A Comprehensive Listing Compiled from English Public Records of Those Who Took Ship to the Americas for Political, Religious, and Economic Reasons; of Those Who Were Deported for Vagrancy, Roguery, or Non-Conformity; and Those Who Were Sold to Labour in the New Colonies* (Baltimore: Genealogical Publishing Co., 1987) and three subsequent volumes covering later dates. Those volumes, also published by the Genealogical Publishing Company, are *The Complete Book of Emigrants, 1661–1699* (1990), *The Complete Book of Emigrants, 1700–1750* (1992), and *The Complete Book of Emigrants, 1751–1776* (1993).

74 EARLY VIRGINIA IMMIGRANTS

Collett, Margarett, 1640, by William Jones, Accomack Co.
Collect, John, 1642, by Georg Smith, Accomack Co.
Collett, Eliz., 1637, by James Warradine, Charles City Co.
Collier, Mary, 1653, by Mr. Richard Barnhouse, Jr., Gloucester Co.
Collier, Henry, 1648, by Tho. Ludwell, Gent., James City Co.
Coleman, John, 1649, by Capt. Ralph Wormley, ——— Co.
Collinge, Eliz., 1654, by Randall Chamblett, ——— Co.
Collier, Tho., 1655, by John Hinman, Northampton Co.
Collington, Georg., 1636, by William Roper, Accomack Co.
Collison, Miles, 1639, by Richard Preston, Upper New Norfolk Co.
Collison, Eliza, 1650, by George Taylor, ——— Co.
Colmer, Thomas, 1643, by Capt. Wm. Peirce, Esq., ——— Co.
Collin, Stephen, 1652, by Peter Knight, Gloucester Co.
Collins, Richard, 1653, by Major Abra. Wood, Charles City Co.
Collins, John, 1655, by George Frizell and Tho. Moore, Northampton Co.
Collins, Elizabeth, 1654, by John Cox, Lancaster, Co.
Collins, Elios, 1638, by Edward Hill, Charles City Co.
Collins, William, 1640, by John Geary, Upper Norfolk Co.
Collins, William, 1639, by Oliver Sprye, Upper New Norfolk Co.
Collins, Tho., 1635, by Wm. Garry, Accomack Co.
Collins, Elizabeth, 1636, by Wm. Clarke, Henrico Co.
Collins, Giers, 1635, by Capt. Thos. Willowbye ——— Co.
Collins, Hen., by Hugh Cox, Charles City Co.
Collins, Walter, 1635, by Thos. Baywell, ——— Co.
Collins, Walter, 1638, by Thomas Bogwell, Charles City Co.
Collins, Jon., 1638, by Stephen Charlton, Accomack Co.

Figure 14-8. Greer's *Early Virginia Immigrants, 1623–1666* contains the name of the immigrant, year of the land patent, name of the patentee or person who transported the immigrant, and the county where the patent was located.

Each volume is arranged chronologically. A one-paragraph abstract under each date provides a brief citation from an original record or a previously published transcript of records that identifies an emigrant in some way (figure 14-9). The abstract ends with a parenthetical abbreviation (called a reference) that identifies the source of the information. Because the sources are usually arranged chronologically, it is easy in theory to find the complete information in the actual documents. However, many of the sources cited are unpublished records in English archives, and most of them are not even available on microfilm.

Although these volumes contain abstracts of original records, they are compilations in that the abstracts were taken from several different sources; this illustrates both the strengths and weaknesses of the work. A wide variety of sources (both published and manuscript) were used in order to document as many emigrants as possible. Many of these sources have never been copied or transcribed in any other way, and most researchers would not have access to the information without this series. Also, because references from all possible sources are combined, the researcher is not left wondering if there are other records documenting a person's emigration that should be checked.

However, such a collection provides a false assurance to the family historian. Clearly, these volumes do not represent a *complete* list of all English emigrants; the compiler himself bemoans the fact (in the preface) that many records were not kept and that others have been destroyed. These volumes are complete only in the sense that every known record was used to compile them, and they are not always comprehensive for the records they do include. For example, in his discussion of the Port Books, from which Coldham extracted the names of persons who shipped goods to America (on the basis that some of them were also emigrants), he admits that not every record was abstracted:

> . . . at least *one* of the Port Books (usually the most extensive) for each year for which records have survived has been examined for each major port in order to abstract entries for publication. . . . It will be obvious, therefore, that there remains ample scope for further research in this class of record should additional detail be sought (Coldham 1990, iv).

Not only could persons shipping goods have been overlooked, but, admittedly, not all shippers were emigrants. Furthermore, Coldham reminds us that

> . . . the greater number of emigrants taking ship carried little more than their personal possessions which, being exempt from duty, figured not at all in the customs officer's returns (1990, iv).

Coldham mixed published and unpublished sources, so some of the references are a step further removed from the actual documents and are therefore more subject to transcription or copy errors. While not a serious problem, this fact reminds us that each entry has to be evaluated on its own merits; some are less accurate than others.

A companion volume, also by Peter Wilson Coldham, abstracts records of persons sent to the colonies by force. *The Complete Book of Emigrants in Bondage, 1614–1775* (Baltimore: Genealogical Publishing Co., 1988), and *Supplement*

Figure 14-9. From Coldham's *The Complete Book of Emigrants 1607–1660* (page 264). A one-paragraph abstract under each date provides a brief citation from an original record or a previously published transcript of records that identifies an emigrant in some way.

1653

January. Probate of will of Peter Ambrose of Toxteth, Lancs, who made bequests to Joshua and Daniel Henshawe in New England. *(EEAC).*

January. Probate of will of Robert Houghton of St. Olave, Southwark, Surrey, whose sister Mary was wife of Francis Norton of New England. *(EEAC).*

23 February. Deposition re the capture by the French of the *Welcome*, Mr. John Cutting, in June 1651 after she had loaded tobacco in James River, Virginia. *(EAE).*

11 March. Agreement made by Thomas Hobbs for his son Henry Hobbs to serve the Mayor of Dorchester for six years as his apprentice in New England. *(Dorchester Borough Records).*

12 March. Depositions re the capture by the Dutch of the *John and Sarah* on her homeward voyage from New England and Barbados. *(EAE).*

April. Probate of will of Joseph Torkington of Virginia. *(EEAC).*

1 April. Licence to Sir John Clotworthy to transport 500 natural Irishmen to America. *(CSPC).*

4 April. Depositions by Jane Hillyard of London, widow aged 76, and Katherine, wife of Stephen Pace of St. Mary Savoy, barber surgeon, made at the request of Anne Pace of the Savoy, spinster, that Lancelot Pace and Thomasine his wife, both lately deceased at Barbados, formerly lived in London and that the said Anne Pace is their daughter and sole heir. Miles Cason, Master of the *Seaflower*, has been appointed to receive goods in Barbados belonging to the said Lancelot Pace deceased. *(MCD 4).*

5 April. Deposition by James Heyden, planter in New England aged 44 but living at St. Dunstan in the East, London, and others re the voyage from Boston, New England, to London in 1652 of the *Adventure*, Mr. Thomas Graves. *(EAE).*

(1992) provides documentation for approximately fifty-three thousand unwilling emigrants. Most of these names were published earlier in the nine volumes of *Bonded Passengers to America* (Baltimore: Genealogical Publishing Co., 1983) and two volumes of *English Convicts in Colonial America* (New Orleans: Polyanthos, 1974), both also by Coldham, but the newer volumes include some new records. Altogether these records are from at least thirty-nine different courts and a variety of other collections. The information is highly condensed, but most entries contain the person's name, parish of origin, sentencing court, nature of the offense, date of the sentence, date and ship on which transported, and the place of landing in America.

Scottish Colonists. English records are not the only sources that document emigrants who came to North America. Taking an approach similar to Coldham's, David Dobson published *The Original Scots Colonists of Early America, 1612–1783* (Baltimore: Genealogical Publishing Co., 1989), based on a wide variety of Scottish records. They included family and estate papers, deed registers, sheriff's court records, customs registers, contemporary diaries, journals, newspapers, and magazines, Privy Council records, church records, and other sources. Some seven thousand people are listed with name, date of information, source, and, where possible, date of immigration, occupation, education, residence, parents' names, spouse, children, and other data. The same author also issued the *Directory of Scottish Settlers in North America, 1625–1825,* 7 vols. (Baltimore:

Genealogical Publishing Co., 1984–86, 1993). He used a variety of sources from both sides of the Atlantic, but mostly from Scotland, to identify Scottish immigrants in an approach akin to a dictionary. Between fifteen and twenty thousand Scots are identified in this collection. Each of the seven volumes draws from different sources, as identified here:

Volume	*Major Source(s) of Information*
1	British ship passenger lists
2	Government serials, newspapers, periodicals, and family histories
3	Scottish newspapers and magazines
4	Services of heirs; Register of Testaments of the Commissariat of Edinburgh
5	Records in the Public Archives of Ontario
6	Edinburgh Register of Deeds
7	Variety of printed books and public records

Probate Records. For years, genealogists have realized that, among the family members that immigrants left behind in their native lands, some mentioned in their wills relatives who had emigrated. Many researchers have pored over old British probate records seeking mention of sons, brothers, cousins, or other relatives "in new England" or described in some other way as being in the British colonies. The first major work to publish this kind of information was Henry F. Waters' *Genealogical Gleanings in England: Abstracts of Wills Relating to Early American Families, with Genealogical Notes and Pedigrees Constructed from the Wills and from Other Records*, 2 vols. (1901, 1907; reprint; Baltimore: Genealogical Publishing Co., 1969). Similar records were published by Sherwood (1932–33) and Withington (1903–29); they are noted in the chapter bibliography.

Peter Wilson Coldham has issued two titles that pick up where these earlier researchers left off. *American Wills and Administrations in the Prerogative Court of Canterbury, 1610–1857* (Baltimore: Genealogical Publishing Co., 1989), focuses on the records of a specific court. *American Wills Proved in London, 1611–1775* (Baltimore: Genealogical Publishing Co., 1992) attempts to identify and abstract all of the wills not already included in Waters's, Withington's, or Sherwood's works.

While most of the interest in foreign records as proof of emigration has centered around English records, David Dobson has used a similar approach in his ongoing efforts to document the origins of Scottish immigrants to North America. Three of his volumes, all published by Genealogical Publishing Company, are *Scottish-American Court Records, 1733–1783* (1991); *Scottish-American Heirs, 1683–1883* (1990); and *Scottish-American Wills, 1650–1900* (1991)

Other Foreign Records. Raymond D. Adams culled approximately 3,200 entries from a wide variety of Irish records for his *Alphabetical Index to Ulster Emigration to Philadelphia, 1803–1850* (Baltimore: Clearfield Co., 1992). Some of the records were an early townland index, passenger lists of Irish shipping lines, and emigration lists from civil parishes maintained at the Public Record Office of Northern Ireland. In addition to the names of the passengers, the index identifies the port and date of arrival, address and county of origin, and the name of the ship.

While the publication of these "alternate" foreign sources has been predominantly of British records, a few continental European sources are available. One of the most notable is *HETRINA*, the popular title of *Hessische Truppen im Amerikanischen Unabhängigkeitskreig* (Hessian troops in the American Revolution), Veroeffentlichungen der Archivschule Marburg, Institut für Archivwissenschaft, no. 10, 6 vols. (Marburg, Germany: Institut für Archivwissenschaft, 1972–87). This source is drawn from documents in Hessian archives which indicate what soldiers were sent to North America to fight for the British in the American Revolution. While the majority of these soldiers returned home to Hesse, many remained in the new world. This publication, while not specifically identifying which soldiers became "immigrants" by staying, does reference approximately ten thousand soldiers, allowing researchers to learn towns of origin for those who did indeed become Americans.

Other Printed Sources

A variety of other printed sources provide proof of immigration. They include newspapers, church records, military records, civil and court records, and voter registration records (great registers). The following is a brief discussion of the kinds of records to look for.

Newspapers. While newspapers are common genealogical sources for vital events, such as deaths, few people realize that advertisements and newspaper articles sometimes mention immigrants. The growth of published abstracts of newspaper items also includes volumes that abstract advertisements for friends and relatives who disappeared into the growing population of America. The most significant collection is Ruth-Ann Harris and Donald M. Jacobs (later B. Emer O'Keefe), eds., *The Search for Missing Friends: Irish Immigrant Advertizements Placed in the Boston Pilot* (Boston: New England Historic Genealogical Society, 1989–96). Its five volumes, covering 1831 to 1865, list approximately twenty-five thousand Irish people thought to have resided in the Boston area. A smaller collection for Pennsylvania Germans is Edward W. Hocker's *Genealogical Data Relating to the German Settlers of Pennsylvania and Adjacent Territory* (1935; reprint; Baltimore: Genealogical Publishing Co., 1981, although not all of the references in this source pertain to immigrants.

Other newspaper abstracts or indexes sometimes mention immigrants without specifically focusing on them as a group. For example, Jeffrey G. Herbert's *Index of Death and Other Notices Appearing in the Cincinnati Freie Presse 1874–1920* (Bowie, Md.: Heritage Books, 1993) was not designed to locate immigrants; because the *Cincinnati Freie Presse* was a German newspaper in a heavily German city, however, one would expect that many of the thirty-eight thousand entries pertain to German immigrants or their family members. Farley Grubb's *Runaway Servants, Convicts, and Apprentices Advertised in the Pennsylvania Gazette, 1728–1796* (Baltimore: Genealogical Publishing Co., 1992) does not focus on immigrants, but most of the servants and others mentioned in the advertisements were immigrants.

Church Records. For many immigrants, the local church was the center of the community. Where a church served a specific ethnic group, published church records might identify immigrants. Filby's *Passenger and Immigration Lists Bibliography* (cited earlier) lists a few parish register abstracts that mention immigrants, but another excellent example (for the records it includes) is Albert Cook Myers's "List of Certificates of Removal from Ireland Received at the Monthly Meetings of Friends in Pennsylvania, 1682–1750," first published in *Immigration of the Irish Quakers into Pennsylvania. 1682–1750* (1902) and reprinted as *Irish Quaker Arrivals to Pennsylvania: 1682–1750* (Baltimore: Genealogical Publishing Co., 1964).

Military Lists. Filby's *Bibliography* also lists a few military sources that identify immigrants (or imply immigration). Typically they pertain to the early wars up to the War of 1812, as in this example, compiled by Kenneth R. Scott: *British Aliens in the United States During the War of 1812* (Baltimore: Genealogical Publishing Co., 1979). It names approximately ten thousand persons known to be British aliens during this last war against England.

Civil Records. Local governments in North America have frequently maintained lists that identify immigrants. These include the lists of freemen mentioned earlier in the discussion of naturalization, but they also include any number of other sources. One example is *Record of Indentures of Individuals Bound Out as Apprentices, Servants, Etc. and of German and Other Redemptioners in the Office of the Mayor of the City of Philadelphia, October 3, 1771 to October 5, 1773,* Pennsylvania-German Society Proceedings and Addresses, vol. 16 (n.p., 1905; Lancaster, Pa., 1907; reprint; Baltimore: Genealogical Publishing Co., 1973).

Great Registers. In some far western states, voter registration lists were published toward the end of the nineteenth and beginning of the twentieth centuries. These are known as *great registers;* they are most common in California, although Arizona and Oregon published some. In California, great registers date from as early as 1866. After 1872, California law required each county to publish an alphabetical list of voters every two years, with supplements published before each election. Approximately 80 percent of the counties published these indexes to the great registers. Because eligibility to vote was a privilege of citizenship, these great registers indicated the county or country of birth as well as naturalization facts for every registered voter (figure 14-10); thus, they list the naturalized immigrants in each county. While not every voter was an immigrant, in some counties the percentage of immigrants reached 25 percent or more. Publication of great registers ceased after 1909 in California, and the published lists have not survived for every year or every county. However, they are quite common in California, and the various genealogical societies in that state are completing a project to compile the registers for 1890 into a composite statewide list (to partially replace the missing 1890 census). Lists for various years and counties continue to be published in many California genealogical periodicals, and others have been reprinted in whole. Many of them are listed in Filby's *Passenger and Immigration Lists Bibliography* (cited earlier).

COMPILED RECORDS

Although original records of immigration, and the printed versions of them, are the most popular, plentiful, and useful sources to document immigration, there are several compiled records that deserve mention as well. Because of the popularity of immigration research in North American family history, many individuals have focused their efforts and publications on discussions of immigrants. Where such sources have been compiled by knowledgeable and experienced researchers, they provide excellent, documented help to the family historian. Many compilations focus on groups of immigrants who settled in specific areas, while others proceed from the old countries, discussing groups that left foreign areas for the New World. In addition, a number of periodical reprint series provide better access to sometimes obscure articles that document immigrants. This section also briefly introduces local and group histories, sources for royal connections, and published family histories. Some of these sources are not always appreciated as immigration sources; hence, many are not in Filby's *Passenger and Immigration Lists Bibliography.*

Immigrant Groups

As nations of immigrants, the United States and Canada contain areas that were settled in large part by people from other countries. Many of these areas have been the subjects of genealogical dictionaries or compendia (see chapter 16) that explore the first two or three generations of these settlers. While many of these sources fail to identify the towns the immigrants left, they do discuss the lives of the immigrants in North America and provide some of the important clues necessary to identify them in foreign records.

Early Dictionaries. Some of the earliest genealogical publications have been *genealogical dictionaries.* These summarize the known information about individuals and are generally arranged alphabetically. One of the most familiar is James Savage's *A Genealogical Dictionary of the First Settlers of New England Showing Three Generations of Those Who Came Before May, 1692 . . . ,* 4 vols. (reprint; Baltimore: Genealogical Publishing Co., 1965) . Discussed more fully in chapter 16, this source provides information about hundreds of early New England immigrants, sometimes identifying relationships in England that help prove places of origin.

Similar dictionaries are available for nearly every New England state, such as Charles Henry Pope's *The Pioneers of Massachusetts, 1620–1650* (1900; reprint; Baltimore: Genealogical Publishing Co., 1965). Unlike Savage's dictionary, this source does not attempt to link several generations; rather, it provides brief paragraphs about those known to have settled in the Bay State (meaning both the Massachusetts Bay and Plymouth colonies) by 1650.

Because of the great interest in the earliest New England settlers, Charles Edward Banks attempted to reconstruct the lists of passengers of the most prominent early ships, with notes regarding their origins. His series of books draws from a variety of sources on both sides of the Atlantic and is an early attempt to provide sources for the entries. He published three books in 1929 and 1930 (see the chapter bibliography) which have been reprinted several times by Genealogical Publishing Company. He later summarized his findings, while adding the names of several more immigrants, in *Topographical Dictionary of 2885 English Emigrants to New England, 1620–1650,* edited and indexed by Elijah Ellsworth Brownell (1937; reprint; Baltimore: Southern Book Co., 1987) (figure 14-11).

38 Great Register of Humboldt County, California.

NO.	NAME.	VOTED.	AGE.	COUNTRY OF NATIVITY.	OCCUPATION.	LOCAL RESIDENCE.	NATURALIZED. DATE.	NATURALIZED. PLACE.	NATURALIZED. BY WHAT COURT.	Date of Registration.	Sworn.
2826	McIntosh, John		33	N Brunswick	Engineer	Eureka	Apr 9 1881	Humboldt co	Superior Ct.	May 19 1882	Sworn
2827	McClelland, Robert		27	Ireland	Millman	do	June 6 1882	do do do	do do do	June 6 1882	do
2828	McKenzie, Daniel Alex		40	P Edwards I	Carpenter	do	do 12 do	do do do	do do do	do 12 do	do
2829	McGeorge, William James		22	California	Clerk	do				do do do	do
2830	McMillan, Donald Randall		35	Scotland	Logger	Arcata	July 12 1882	Humboldt co	Superior cor't	do do do	do
2831	McFee, James Albert		29	N Brunswick	Lumberman	Eureka	do 13 do	do do do	do do do	do 13 do	do
2832	McLeod, Robert Lindsay		35	do	Millman	Table Bluff	do do do	do do do	do do do	do do do	do
2833	McMillan, Neil		35	Nova Scotia	Shoemaker	Eureka	June 27 1882	do do do	do do do	do 27 do	do
2834	McCoy, James		21	California	Millman	Arcata				do 29 do	do
2835	McCutchen, James		48	N. Brunswick	Blacksmith	do	Mar 24 1882	Humboldt co	Superior c'rt	do 31 do	do
2836	McDonough, John		36	Ireland	Farmer	Ferndale	June 22 1882	do do do	do do do	June 22 1882	do
2837	McCann, Charles Frederick		39	Maine	Laborer	Eureka				Aug 29 1882	do
2838	McLaughlin, Kirk Posy		43	Mass	do	do				Sep 13 1882	do
2839	McCormack, Hueston		29	Penn	Lumberman	Arcata				do do do	do
2840	McCann, Charles Edward		48	N Brunswick	do	Camp Grant	Mar 14 1882	Humboldt co	Superior co'rt	do 15 do	do
2841	McGhan, Martin		52	New York	Farmer	Arcata				do 18 do	do
2842	McLean, John Robert		25	Mass	Lumberman	do				do 20 do	do
2843	McCullens, David		40	Ireland	Laborer	Eureka	Feb 2 1882	Humboldt co	Superior Ct.	do 30 do	do
2844	McGrade, William		34	do	Cook	Arcata	By virtue of	the naturaliz'	tion of father	Oct 2 1882	do
2845	McLaughlin, Owen		35	do	Lumberman	do	Sep 1868	Phil'ia, Penn	Municipal Ct	do do do	do
2846	McFarren, Robert		56	do	Laborer	Ferndale	Sep 3 1855	Sacram'to co.	District court	do do do	do
2847	McGowan, Daniel Walter		21	W Territory	do	Arcata				do 7 do	do
2848	McCarthy, Eugene		39	Ireland	do	Table Bluff	By virtue of	naturalizat'n	of his father	do 23 do	do
2849	McDonald, James Henry		26	Canada	do	Rohnerville	do do do	do do do	do do do	Feb 12 1883	do
2850	McKinnon, James Corsini		24	California	Clerk	Eureka				Aug 10 1883	do
2851	McDermott, Henry		40	Ireland	Farmer	Rohnerville	July 11 1871	Klamath Co	District court	Oct 3 1883	do
2852	McLaughlin, William Stanley		37	N Brunswick	Laborer	Kneeland P'r	Sep 7 1882	Humboldt co	Superior co'rt	Feb 25 1884	do
2853	McGhan, Richard Porter		22	Michigan	Farmer	Dow's Pra'ie				April 28 1884	do
2854	McMonagle, Connell Charles		33	Ireland	Fireman	Eureka	Dec 13 1876	Humboldt co	8th Dist court	do 29 do	do
2855	McFarland, Samuel Wellington		44	N Brunswick	Lumberman	Arcata	May 9 1884	do do do	Superior co'rt	May 9 1884	do
2856	McFarlan, George Frederick		21	California	Teamster	Eureka				do 15 do	do
2857	McDonald, Simon Alexander		32	N Brunswick	Millman	do	By virtue of	naturalizati'n	of his father	do 23 do	do
2858	McQuaid, John A.		51	Ohio	Lawyer	do				do 24 do	do
2859	McIsaac, John		32	Nova Scotia	Woodsman	do	Feb 15 1883	Humboldt co	Superior c'rt	June 3 1884	do
2860	McGowan, Charles		43	New York	Hotel Keep'r	do				do 6 do	do
2861	McCullach, John		34	N Brunswick	Merchant	do	Oct 7 1882	Nevada	U S Circuit ct	do 9 do	do
2862	McKinley, Robert		26	Ireland	Lumberman	do	Jan 8 1884	Humboldt co	Superior cor't	do 10 do	do
2863	McSurely, William		44	Iowa	Laborer	do				do 16 do	do

Figure 14-10. Portion of a great register: *List of the Names and Registration of the Domiciled Inhabitants of the County of Humboldt: Copied from the Great Register of Humboldt County, October 7th, 1884* (Times-Telephone Office, 1884). Great registers indicated the county or country of birth as well as naturalization facts for every registered voter.

Other colonial areas besides New England have been the subjects of detailed discussion regarding immigrants. For example, Amandus Johnson includes a lengthy appendix in vol. 2 of his *Swedish Settlements on the Delaware, 1638–1664,* 2 vols. (1911; reprint; Baltimore: Genealogical Publishing Co., 1969). It identifies the officers, soldiers, servants, and settlers of the New Sweden colony from 1638 through 1656 and indicates the ships used, names of passengers, dates of arrival, and male inhabitants in 1643–44. It also includes a list of surviving settlers from 1648.

While most of the information on the families in these and dozens of other early sources has been superseded by more recent works, some collective, and many individual family histories, these sources still provide good overviews of early research about the families covered.

Recent Scholarship. In the past few decades, genealogical scholarship has improved, creating significant compiled research with the highest degree of reliability. An excellent example of a meticulously researched, accurate list of passengers is George E. McCracken's *The Welcome Claimants Proved, Disproved and Doubtful with an Account of Some of Their Descendants* (Baltimore: Genealogical Publishing Co., 1970). In this work, McCracken took some twenty or more versions of the passenger list for an early Pennsylvania-bound ship and carefully analyzed the names in contemporary sources to determine who really was among the first settlers.

Another excellent compiled source, praised for its documentation and careful compilation, is Henry Z Jones's *The Palatine Families of New York: A Study of the German Immigrants Who Arrived in Colonial New York in 1710,* 2 vols. (Universal City, Calif.: the author, 1985). Jones, working with original records in New York and Germany, identified all of the immigrants who arrived in this first of the major German groups to come to America. He then defined their families in New York and, for approximately 60 percent of them, identified the town and family relations in Germany which they had left behind.

Early Germans also settled in Virginia, and many authors have contributed toward an understanding of their origins in the old country. A useful example is a series of twelve brief monographs by Johni Cerny and Gary J. Zimmerman, *Before Germanna: The Origins and Ancestry of Those Affiliated with the Second Germanna Colony of Virginia* (Bountiful, Utah: American Genealogical Lending Library, 1990). This series discusses each of the major founding families of this colony, ex-

Figure 14-11. From Banks's *Topographical Dictionary of 2885 English Emigrants to New England, 1620–1650* (page 184).

WORCESTERSHIRE

NAME OF THE EMIGRANT	ENGLISH PARISH NAME	SHIPS NAME	NEW ENGLAND TOWN	VARIOUS REFERENCE
WINSLOW, Edward	Droitwich	May-flower	Plymouth, Massachusetts	Savage
Gilbert	Droitwich	May-flower	Plymouth, Massachusetts	Pope
John	Droitwich	Fortune	Plymouth, Mass.	Pope
Kenelm	Droitwich		Plymouth, Mass.	Savage
WASHBURNE, John	Evesham		Plymouth, Mass. Duxbury	E.A.B.B.
COLEMAN, Thomas	Evesham		Wethersfield, Connecticut	Savage
SOULE, George	Eckington	May-flower	Plymouth, Mass. Duxbury	Soule Genealogy
BROWN, Nicholas	Inkberrow		Lynn, Massachusetts	N.E.G.R. 44/281 66/99
Nicholas	Morton, Abbots		Reading, Massachusetts	Aspinwall
CHECKETT, Joseph	Peopleton		Scituate	Banks Mss.
NASH, Thomas	Ribbesford (Bewdley)		Guildford New Haven, Connecticut	Banks Mss.
WAKEMAN, John	Ribbesford	Fellow-ship	New Haven, Connecticut	College of Arms
HUBBALD, Richard	Ribbesford		Pequonnock, Connecticut	College of Arms
DOOLITTLE, Abraham	Ribbesford (Bewdley)		New Haven, Connecticut Wallingford	Banks Mss.
BLANTON, William	Upton on Severn		Boston, Massachusetts	Pope
JORDAN, Rev. Robert	Worcester		Scarboro, Maine	Pioneers of Maine
ROBERTS, Thomas	Wollaston		Dover	Banks Mss.

Total number of Emigrants from Worcestershire is 17 from 11 Parishes.

ploring their ancestry in Germany and their descendants in the colonies.

Clearly the most comprehensive collection for its scope, coverage, and thoroughness is Robert Charles Anderson's *The Great Migration Begins: Immigrants to New England 1620–1633* (Boston: New England Historic Genealogical Society, 1995). This three-volume genealogical dictionary fully discusses some nine hundred heads of household who settled in Plymouth and Massachusetts Bay colonies through 1633. Anderson has explored every available source, both compiled and original, in all of the early towns, as well as the colonial records. The discussion of each family occupies from two pages to ten or more and includes each immigrant's documented activities in the colonies, his estate, children, associates, and, of course, vital information, including (where proved) his origin in England. Most discussions also include a forthright discussion of the strengths and limitations of existing genealogical literature (family histories, periodical articles, and compendia) about that family.

Most users will see Anderson's work as merely a tremendous genealogical compendium, forgetting that the very people Anderson discusses were actually the first immigrants to New England. *The Great Migration Begins* is an excellent example of the variety of compiled sources that deal with various immigrant groups. While few sources attain the excellence and scope of Anderson's work, there are many other similar sources that will greatly assist research about an immigrant and shed light on his (rarely a female's) origin. As with all such compiled works, each book or article needs to be evaluated on its own merits and should not be lauded or scorned simply because of the type of source (that is, compiled) that it is.

As a partial guide to some of the genealogical literature about very early immigrants, consult Meredith B. Colket, Jr., *Founders of Early American Families: Emigrants from Europe, 1607–1657,* rev. ed. (Cleveland: General Court of the Order of Founders and Patriots of America, 1985). This is a recent and very useful compendium that names most of the significant early immigrants, while also identifying what published sources are available for further research. It was designed as a research tool for Founders and Patriots of America, a lineage society. Membership in the society requires descent, in the surname line, from an immigrant to one of the colonies that are now part of the United States who arrived in the first fifty years of settlement. However, because of *Founders of Early American Families'* coverage, any person researching early immigrants will find it valuable. The restrictions of the lineage society result in only those immigrants who have documented descent being included (through several generations in the surname line). A great many eligible families have not been documented and consequently are not covered in this work; however, it still includes upwards of four thousand early settlers. Each entry includes the surname and given name (with spelling variations, residence in the colonies (with dates), date and place of death, and a published source of further information on the immigrant and some of his descendants. Where known, Colket includes the birth date, origin in England or Europe, and immigration information.

Emigration Areas

The same excellent care and documentation evident in new compilations about immigrant groups has begun to appear in discussions of emigrants, particularly those Germans who settled Pennsylvania in the eighteenth century. Leading this effort has been Annette K. Burgert with several brief pamphlets regarding the origins of certain German emigrants, as well as four definitive volumes discussing, in great detail, the origins and families of several hundred emigrants. Her first two volumes, *Eighteenth Century Emigrants from German-Speaking Lands to North America,* Publications of the Pennsylvania German Society, vols. 16 and 19 (Breinigsville: Pennsylvania German Society, 1983, 1985) cover *The Northern Kraichgau* (vol. 1) and *The Western Palatinate* (vol. 2) and document at least 1,100 emigrants with detailed discussions of their families, both in Germany and in North America. While these volumes concern families from areas of extensive German emigration, a later volume of Burgert's covers a less popular area. *Eighteenth Century Emigrants from the Northern Alsace to America* (Camden, Maine: Picton Press, 1992) covers only a portion of modern France from which at least 628 persons emigrated, still providing the depth of information and documentation that all researchers seek. Burgert co-authored a similar volume with Henry Z Jones: *Westerwald to America: Some 18th Century German Immigrants* (Camden, Maine: Picton Press, 1989), which documents 265 emigrant families and individuals from one region in southern Germany who settled in Pennsylvania, New Jersey, New York, Maryland, and the Shenandoah Valley of Virginia.

Periodicals

As discussed in chapter 19, genealogical periodicals are major sources of compiled information. Immigration records are popular topics in periodical articles, often because the length of such records does not make book-length publication practical. In a periodical, an author can contribute a single ship list or write an article on the foreign origins of a single family. With the advent of Filby's *Passenger and Immigration Lists Index,* an increasing number of articles have appeared as authors and editors realized that the *Index* would eventually include their articles, making it easier for others to benefit from their efforts to locate, transcribe or abstract, and publish the information. The *Periodical Source Index,* also discussed in chapter 19, will help locate articles about immigration, either by subject or locality, and is especially useful for articles published since the 1988 publication of Filby's *Passenger and Immigration Lists Bibliography.* However, the *Periodical Source Index* is not an every-name index, so researchers will have to use Filby's *Index* to find specific immigrants in periodical articles.

Periodicals dealing specifically with the genealogical aspect of immigration are very few and are limited to specific groups. The bibliography in chapter 19 includes *The Second Boat, Mayflower Descendant,* and *Palatine Immigrant,* which focus specifically on immigrants. Many periodicals that focus on ethnic groups also publish material about immigrants. In fact, any local, state, or national periodical will, on occasion, include articles dealing with passenger lists, naturalizations, origins of immigrants, and similar information.

Worth noting here are several collections of periodical reprints that focus on immigration sources. For a fuller discussion of the various periodical reprint series, see chapter 19.

English Origins of American Colonists from the New York Genealogical and Biographical Record, compiled by Henry B. Hoff (Baltimore: Genealogical Publishing Co., 1991), reprints four lengthy articles that appeared in the *New York Genealogical and Biographical Record* (issued by the New York Genealogical and Biographical Society) between 1903 and 1916. These articles abstract English probate records and depositions, providing essential clues to the English homes of many early settlers.

Another collection of articles from one periodical are the 132 articles from Michael J. O'Brien in *Irish Settlers in America: A Consolidation of Articles from The Journal of the Irish American Historical Society,* 2 vols. (Baltimore: Genealogical Publishing Co., 1979). The articles vary widely, some being based on ship passenger lists; others are drawn from O'Brien's research in other sources. The volumes identify approximately twenty-five thousand Irish pioneers and settlers.

Boyer Reprints. During the late 1970s, Carl Boyer, 3rd, noted that many of the immigration periodical articles referenced in Lancour's *A Bibliography of Ship Passenger Lists* (cited earlier) were out of print and very difficult for researchers to find. He set out to reprint dozens of those articles in a series. Published by Boyer in Newhall, California, each volume reproduces between twenty-six and forty-four articles and lists, most of which were first published in various periodicals. Each volume also includes indexes to ship names, place names, and from 6,500 to 12,000 personal names, along with variant spellings of surnames. Reprinting has kept these obscure yet very useful lists available in print since the original compilation. Boyer's volumes include *Ship Passenger Lists, National and New England (1600–1825)* (Newhall, Calif., 1978); *Ship Passenger Lists, New York and New Jersey (1600–1825)* (Newhall, Calif., 1978); *Ship Passenger Lists, the South (1538–1825)* (Newhall, Calif., 1979); *Ship Passenger Lists, Pennsylvania and Delaware (1641–1825)* (Newhall, Calif., 1980).

Tepper Reprints. Michael H. Tepper, chief editor of Genealogical Publishing Company, also realized the value of reprinting many of the lists Lancour had identified. For these reprints the articles were photomechanically reproduced and consequently have the appearance of the articles as originally published. Each volume's table of contents identifies the original articles completely, and each volume's introduction discusses the selection criteria as well as the availability of other articles. Each volume also includes indexes to ships and to personal names as well. Some of the articles were also reprinted by Boyer, though many were not. The four titles (five volumes) that Tepper compiled and published through his company include:

- *New World Immigrants: A Consolidation of Ship Passenger Lists and Associated Data from Periodical Literature,* 2 vols. (Baltimore: Genealogical Publishing Co., 1979). Reprints of ninety-seven articles.
- *Immigrants to the Middle Colonies: A Consolidation of Ship Passenger Lists and Associated Data from the New York Genealogical and Biographical Record* (Baltimore: Genealogical Publishing Co., 1978). Reprints of fifteen articles.
- *Passengers to America: A Consolidation of Ship Passenger Lists from the "New England Historical and Genealogical Register" (1847–1961)* (Baltimore: Genealogical Publishing Co., 1977). Reprints of thirty-five articles.
- *Emigrants to Pennsylvania, 1641–1819: A Consolidation of Ship Passenger Lists from the "Pennsylvania Magazine of History and Biography" (1877–1934)* (Baltimore: Genealogical Publishing Co., 1975). Reprints of fourteen articles.

Yoder Reprints. Don Yoder focused on obscure articles dealing with Pennsylvania German immigrants in the two reprint volumes he prepared. Each of his volumes includes thousands of names in the index and includes a ship index as well. They were reissued by Genealogical Publishing Company:

- *Pennsylvania German Immigrants, 1709–1786: Lists Consolidated from Yearbooks of the Pennsylvania German Folklore Society* (Baltimore: Genealogical Publishing Co., 1980; reprint; 1984). Reprints of five lists originally published between 1936 and 1951.
- *Rhineland Emigrants: Lists of German Settlers in Colonial America* (Baltimore: Genealogical Publishing Co., 1981; reprint; 1985). Reprints of twenty-four articles from *Pennsylvania Folklife*.

Each of these volumes includes thousands of names, many of them not found in any other source. They represent significant contributions toward the accessibility of immigration literature, and together they reproduce most of the major articles in American periodicals through the first half of the twentieth century.

Local and Group Histories

Other compiled records that provide excellent assistance in documenting immigrants to North America are the hundreds of local and group histories published over the past 150 years. These sources are the topics of chapter 4, "Ethnic Sources," and chapter 17, "County and Local Histories," so they are not described in depth here. It is sufficient to identify a few examples from the many similar titles. Obviously, local and group histories that deal with immigrant groups will be most helpful; often they include biographical sketches of several immigrants. The sketches often identify the immigrant's home town and include standard biographical material, such as names of family members, occupations, and residences. The sources described in chapters 4 and 17 will help in locating such sources.

Rose Rosicky was the daughter of a Czech newspaper publisher. Drawing heavily on her father's files, as well as back issues of his newspaper, she wrote *A History of Czechs (Bohemians) in Nebraska* (Omaha: Czech Historical Society of Nebraska, 1929), which provides information on a large percentage of the Czech immigrant settlers of the late nineteenth and early twentieth centuries.

Representative of the "mug books" of the early twentieth century (see chapter 17, "County and Local Histories"), although oriented somewhat toward specific ethnic groups, is Frank Eshleman's *Swiss and German Pioneer Settlers of Southeastern Pennsylvania* (1917; reprint; Baltimore: Genealogical Publishing Co., 1991). As with other books of this sort, the information was largely contributed by the subjects themselves and may be skewed to represent them in a positive light. On the other hand, where immigrants are the subjects, the information they supplied about their origins usually has a high degree of accuracy.

Martin Ulvestad spent many years interviewing immigrants and their families to compile his *Nordmaenderne in Amerika deres historie og rekord* (Norwegians in America: their history and record) (Minneapolis: History Book Company's Forlag, 1907). This history identifies many of the Norwegians who arrived before 1850 and includes the home town in Norway of many (figure 14-12).

Swiss Colonists in 19th Century America (Rockport, Maine: Picton Press, 1995) is a new printing of Adelrich Steinach's original 1889 German text. This printing includes a new forward, introduction, and four complete indexes, all in English. The German text provides brief biographical sketches of some nine thousand Swiss individuals and families—a large portion of the entire Swiss immigration for that century. Most of the sketches identify the town or canton of origin in Switzerland, as well as the person's residence and occupation in America.

Immigrant Indexes for Local Histories. A new type of index that attempts to identify immigrants in local histories has begun appearing, and two examples represent this new approach. Don Heinrich Tolzman compiled an index to several local histories dealing with Germans in the Ohio Valley. Although not a history itself, his *Ohio Valley German Biographical Index* (Bowie, Md.: Heritage Books, 1992) identifies approximately 3,750 Germans living in that area, most of whom were immigrants or the sons of immigrants.

Bill and Martha Reamy examined eight local history and biography sources for Maryland and found approximately 1,600 immigrants. They abstracted that information as *Immigrant Ancestors of Marylanders as Found in Local Histories* (n.p., 1993).

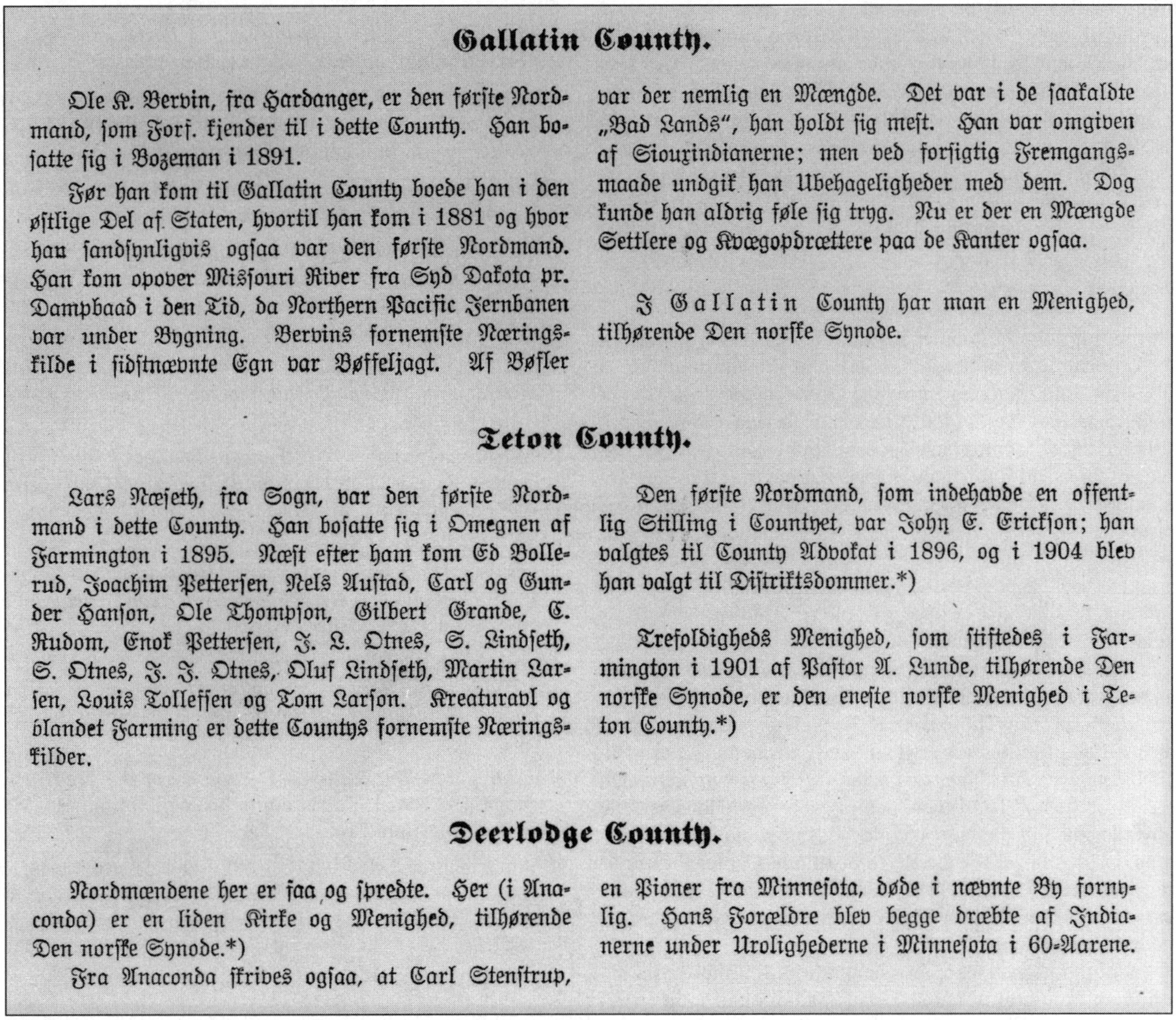

Gallatin County.

Ole K. Bervin, fra Hardanger, er den første Nordmand, som Forf. kjender til i dette County. Han bosatte sig i Bozeman i 1891.

Før han kom til Gallatin County boede han i den østlige Del af Staten, hvortil han kom i 1881 og hvor han sandsynligvis ogsaa var den første Nordmand. Han kom opover Missouri River fra Syd Dakota pr. Dampbaad i den Tid, da Northern Pacific Jernbanen var under Bygning. Bervins fornemste Næringskilde i sidstnævnte Egn var Bøffeljagt. Af Bøfler var der nemlig en Mængde. Det var i de saakaldte „Bad Lands", han holdt sig mest. Han var omgiven af Siouxindianerne; men ved forsigtig Fremgangsmaade undgik han Ubehageligheder med dem. Dog kunde han aldrig føle sig tryg. Nu er der en Mængde Settlere og Kvægopdrættere paa de Kanter ogsaa.

I Gallatin County har man en Menighed, tilhørende Den norske Synode.

Teton County.

Lars Næseth, fra Sogn, var den første Nordmand i dette County. Han bosatte sig i Omegnen af Farmington i 1895. Næst efter ham kom Ed Bollerud, Joachim Pettersen, Nels Austad, Carl og Gunder Hanson, Ole Thompson, Gilbert Grande, C. Rudom, Enok Pettersen, J. L. Otnes, S. Lindseth, S. Otnes, J. J. Otnes, Oluf Lindseth, Martin Larsen, Louis Tolleffen og Tom Larson. Kreaturavl og blandet Farming er dette Countys fornemste Næringskilder.

Den første Nordmand, som indehavde en offentlig Stilling i Countyet, var John E. Erickson; han valgtes til County Advokat i 1896, og i 1904 blev han valgt til Distriktsdommer.*)

Trefoldigheds Menighed, som stiftedes i Farmington i 1901 af Pastor A. Lunde, tilhørende Den norske Synode, er den eneste norske Menighed i Teton County.*)

Deerlodge County.

Nordmændene her er faa og spredte. Her (i Anaconda) er en liden Kirke og Menighed, tilhørende Den norske Synode.*)

Fra Anaconda skrives ogsaa, at Carl Stenstrup, en Pioner fra Minnesota, døde i nævnte By fornylig. Hans Forældre blev begge dræbte af Indianerne under Urolighederne i Minnesota i 60-Aarene.

Figure 14-12. From Ulvestad's *Nordmaenderne in Amerika deres historie og rekord* (Norwegians in America: their history and record). This history identifies many of the Norwegians who arrived before 1850 and includes the home town in Norway of many.

Royal Connections

North American genealogists have always had a fascination with potential connections to British and, to some degree, European nobility and royalty (chapter 20, "Medieval Genealogy," explores some of the key sources that relate to this aspect of family history research). It is useful to remember that every American connection to foreign nobility is through an immigrant; as pointed out in chapter 20, this connection is usually where errors in such lineages creep in. Because of the problems involved in proving such lineages and the popular appeal of noble ancestry, published sources that identify such connections are popular. Currently, most accepted lines are briefly sketched, with the immigrants noted, in three easily accessible sources:

- Weis, Frederick Lewis, Walter L. Sheppard, Jr., and David Faris. *Ancestral Roots of Certain American Colonists Who Came to America Before 1700*. 7th ed. Baltimore: Genealogical Publishing Co., 1992.
- Roberts, Gary Boyd. *The Royal Descents of 500 Immigrants to the American Colonies or the United States Who Were Themselves Notable or Left Descendants Notable in American History*. Baltimore: Genealogical Publishing Co., 1993.
- Faris, David. *Plantagenet Ancestry of Seventeenth-Century Colonists*. Baltimore: Genealogical Publishing Co., 1996.

For more information on these and many other sources for nobility connections, see chapter 20.

Family Histories

As should be evident at this point, almost any compiled record may contain information on immigrants. Many genealogical dictionaries focus on the first settlers of a locality and therefore discuss immigrants, and many family histories focus on the first person(s) of a specific surname to come to America. Local histories usually identify the first settlers in an area, who may have been immigrants. These sources are covered in-depth in chapters 16, 17, and 18; however, some compiled works focus specifically on immigrant ancestors of American families. Two representative titles were privately published by John Brooks Threlfall: *Fifty Great Migration Colonists to New England and Their Origins* (Madison, Wis.: the author, 1990) and *Twenty-six Great Migration Colonists to New England and Their Origins* (Madison, Wis.: the author, 1993).

CONCLUSION

With immigration a popular research topic, family historians are fortunate to have a wide variety and growing number of published sources documenting the arrival and assimilation of immigrants into the United States and Canada. More than 6 million names of immigrants appear in published sources; hundreds of thousands more names appear as emigrants in the published sources of many foreign countries. Most of these sources are transcripts or abstracts of the actual documents, so the information in them is usually reliable. However, researchers should always be prepared to verify the information by checking the actual records or photographic (microfilm) copies, especially where discrepancies occur.

The vast majority of these published immigration sources can be easily found through Filby's *Passenger and Immigration Lists Bibliography*. Those sources, as well as others published since Filby's bibliography was issued, are being indexed in Filby's ongoing *Passenger and Immigration Lists Index,* which adds more than 120,000 new names each year. However, the names in some of the largest collections, especially those prepared by Ira Glazier for the Balch Institute's Center for Immigration Research, are not likely to appear in the index for many years because they can be easily accessed through their separate publications.

Immigration researchers should not limit their research to finding immigrants' names. Many background sources exist that can provide a fuller understanding of the immigrant experience; they can help us determine settlement patterns, reasons for immigration, and the many factors that influenced all aspects of immigration, from the choice of ports to the decision about whether to become naturalized. This kind of information helps us appreciate our many immigrant ancestors and the struggles through which they established themselves in the New World.

REFERENCE LIST

An Immigrant Nation: United States Regulation of Immigration, 1798–1991. 1991. Washington, D.C.: U.S. Department of Justice.

Bromwell, William J. 1856. *History of Immigration to the United States, exhibiting the number, sex, age, occupation, and country of birth, of passengers arriving in the United States by sea from foreign countries, from September 30, 1819 to December 31, 1855.* New York: Redfield, 1856. Reprint. New York: Arno Press and A. M. Kelley, 1969.

Coldham, Peter Wilson. 1990. *The Complete Book of Emigrants, 1661–1699.* Baltimore: Genealogical Publishing Co.

Filby, P. William. 1988. *Passenger and Immigration Lists Bibliography, 1538–1900.* 2nd ed. Detroit: Gale Research.

Glazier, Ira A., and P. William Filby. 1992. *Italians to America: Lists of Passengers Arriving at U.S. Ports, 1880–1899.* 7+ vols. Wilmington, Del.: Scholarly Resources.

Glazier, Ira A. and P. William Filby. 1997. *Germans to America: Lists of Passengers Arriving at U.S. Ports.* 54+ vols. Wilmington, Del.: Scholarly Resources.

Greer, George C. 1912. *Early Virginia Immigrants, 1623–1666.* Reprint. Baltimore: Genealogical Publishing Co., 1982.

Hansen, Marcus Lee. 1961. *The Atlantic Migration, 1607–1860.* Rev. ed. Cambridge, Mass.: Harvard University Press, 1940. Reprint. New York: Harper and Row.

Palmer, Michael. 1990. "Published Passenger Lists: A Review of *German Immigrants* and *Germans to America*." *Bulletin of the German Genealogical Society of America* 4: 69–90 (May-August).

Remington, Gordon. 1990. "Feast or Famine: Problems in the Genealogical Use of *The Famine Immigrants* and *Germans to America*." *National Genealogical Society Quarterly* 78: 135–46 (June).

Szucs, Loretto Dennis, and Sandra Hargreaves Luebking, eds. 1997. *The Source: A Guidebook of American Genealogy.* Rev. ed. Salt Lake City: Ancestry.

Tepper, Michael. 1988. *American Passenger Arrival Records: A Guide to the Records of Immigrants Arriving at American Ports by Sail and Steam.* Baltimore: Genealogical Publishing Co.

Webster's New International Dictionary of the English Language. 1928. W. T. Harris, editor in chief. Springfield, Mass.: G. & C. Merriam Co.

Wollmershäuser, Friedrich R. 1990. "The Wuerttemberg Emigration Index: How Complete Is It?" *CGSA Bulletin* 4 (2) (March-April).

BIBLIOGRAPHY

This bibliography is divided into three parts: (1) works that contain lists of immigrants, (2) works that contain lists of emigrants, and (3) reference books (those that do not contain lists of names). The first two parts focus on published books that list many immigrants. Usually these lists identify at least one thousand immigrants, unless the source was highly significant for a group, locality, or time period, in which cases fewer immigrants might be named. Most of the books listed have statewide or greater coverage. Some of them have been reprinted, often several times. Where known, the most recent reprint date is given; regardless, reprints are identified as such. Few articles in journals and portions of books are cited here, but many have been consolidated in the works by Boyer, Tepper, and Yoder. In addition to regular bibliographic information, this list includes each book's reference number in Filby's *Passenger and Immigration Lists Bibliography* [in brackets] and, where known, the number of names {in braces}. Books not referenced in Filby are cited as [----]; reference numbers followed by an asterisk (*) indicate the source is not in Filby's 1988 bibliography but was assigned a number and indexed in a recent annual supplement to Filby's companion work, the *Passenger and Immigration Lists Index.*

Published Lists of Immigrants

Filby, P. William. *Passenger and Immigration Lists Index.* 10+ vols. Detroit: Gale Research, 1981–. An excellent index to

2,600,000 names found in more than 2,600 published sources. The first three volumes comprise a combined alphabetical index; they were published in 1981. Supplemental volumes have been issued annually. There are also cumulated supplements for 1982 to 1985, 1986 to 1990, and 1991 to 1995. This work does not index official U.S. arrival lists, but many of the names are from post-1820 published sources.

U.S. Port of Arrival Transcripts

Avakian, Linda L. *Armenian Immigrants: Boston 1891–1901, New York 1880–1897*. Rockport, Maine: Picton Press, 1996. [----] {7,300}

Baca, Leo. *Czech Immigration Passenger Lists*. 6 vols. Richardson, Tex.: Old Homestead Publishing Co., 1983–95. [0205, 0206*+] {104,000}

Bentley, Elizabeth P., and Michael H. Tepper. *Passenger Arrivals at the Port of Baltimore, 1820–1834, from Customs Passenger Lists*. Baltimore: Genealogical Publishing Co., 1982. [0253] {50,000}

_____. *Passenger Arrivals at the Port of Philadelphia, 1800–1819: The Philadelphia Baggage Lists*. Baltimore: Genealogical Publishing Co., 1986. [6466.4] {40,000}

Blaha, Albert J. *Passenger Lists for Galveston, 1850–1855*. Houston, Tex.: the author, 1985. [----]{5,949}

Cassady, Michael. *New York Passenger Arrivals, 1849–1868*. Edited by Sylvia Nimmo. Papillion, Nebr.: S. Nimmo, 1983. [6200] {10,200}

Glazier, Ira A., ed. *Migration from the Russian Empire: Lists of Passengers Arriving at the Port of New York*. 2 vols., 1875–82 and 1882–86. Baltimore: Genealogical Publishing Co., 1995.

_____, and Michael Tepper, associate ed. *The Famine Immigrants: Lists of Irish Immigrants Arriving at the Port of New York, 1846–1851*. 7 vols. Baltimore: Genealogical Publishing Co., 1983–86. [1921.1–1921.7] {545,000}

_____, and P. William Filby, eds. *Germans to America: Lists of Passengers Arriving at U.S. Ports*. 54+ vols. Wilmington, Del.: Scholarly Resources, 1987–. [2468.4 = vol. 1] {approximately 3,100,000 through fifty-four volumes} This ongoing series covers arrivals from 1850 on; fifty-four volumes as of early 1997.

_____, eds. *Italians to America: Lists of Passengers Arriving at U.S. Ports, 1880–1899*. 7+ vols. Wilmington, Del.: Scholarly Resources, 1992–. [----] {390,000 through seven volumes} Ongoing series; seven volumes as of early 1997.

Haury, David A. *Index to Mennonite Immigrants on United States Passenger Lists, 1872–1904*. North Newton, Kans.: Mennonite Library and Archives, 1986. [2930] {15,000}

Holcomb, Brent H. *Passenger Arrivals at the Port of Charleston 1820–1829*. Baltimore: Genealogical Publishing Co., 1994. [----] {6,300}

Olsson, Nils William. *Swedish Passenger Arrivals in New York, 1820–1850*. Chicago: Swedish Pioneer Historical Society, 1967. [611] {4,000}

_____. *Swedish Passenger Arrivals in U.S. Ports, 1820–1850 (Except New York)*. St. Paul, Minn.: North Central Publishing Co., 1979. [6412]

Prins, Edward. *Dutch and German Ships: Passenger Lists 1846–1856*. Holland, Mich.: the author, 1972. Focuses on those who settled the Holland colony in Michigan. [6890] {12,500}

Rasmussen, Louis J. *San Francisco Ship Passenger Lists*. 4 vols. Coloma, Calif.: the author, 1965–70. Vol. 1. Reprint. Baltimore: Genealogical Publishing Co., 1978. Rasmussen "reconstructed" the original lists by using other contemporary sources; mostly covers 1850 to 1852. [7156-7162]

Rieder, Milton P., and Norma Gaudet Rieder, eds. *New Orleans Ship Lists*. 2 vols. Metairie, La.: the editors, 1966–68. [7460-7461] Covers 1820 through 23 June 1823.

Rockett, Charles Whitlock. *Some Shipboard Passengers of Captain John Rockett (1828–1841)*. Mission Viejo, Calif.: the author, 1983. Ships from Le Havre to New York. [7460] {1,500}

Schlegel, Donald M. *Passengers from Ireland: Lists of Passengers Arriving at American Ports Between 1811 and 1817*. Baltimore: Genealogical Publishing Co., 1980. [8099] {7,380}

Ships Passenger Lists, Port of Galveston, Texas, 1846–1871. Easley, S.C.: Southern Historical Press, 1984. [8429.11] {7,500}

Swierenga, Robert P., comp. *Dutch Immigrants in U.S. Ship Passenger Manifests, 1820–1880*. 2 vols. Wilmington, Del.: Scholarly Resources, 1983. [9082] {approximately 60,000}

United States Department of State. *Passenger Arrivals, 1819–1820: A Transcript of the List of Passengers Who Arrived in the United States from the 1st October, 1819, to the 30th September, 1820*. 1821. Reprint. Baltimore: Genealogical Publishing Co., 1991. [9258] {10,247}

_____. *Passengers Who Arrived in the United States, September 1821–December 1823*. Baltimore: Magna Carta Book Co., 1969. [9268] {15,500}

Voultsos, Mary. *Greek Immigrant Passengers, 1885–1910*. 3 vols. Worcester, Mass.: the author, 1992. [----] {15,000} Lists only approximately 7 percent of total Greek immigrants in this time period.

Zimmerman, Gary J., and Marion Wolfert. *German Immigrants: Lists of Passengers Bound from Bremen to New York*. Vol. 1, 1847–54; vol. 2, 1855–62; vol. 3, 1863–67; vol. 4 (without Zimmerman), 1868–71. Baltimore: Genealogical Publishing Co., 1985, 1986, 1988, 1993. [vols. 1 and 2: 9983.10, 9983.11] {approximately 137,000 total}

Australia

An Index to Assisted Immigrants Arriving Queensland, 1860–1869. Rockhampton, Queensland, Australia: Central Queensland Genealogical Association, 1989.

Fidlon, Paul G., R. J. Ryan, and Joyce Cowell. *The First Fleeters: A Comprehensive Listing of Convicts, Marines, Seamen, Officers, Wives, Children, and Ships*. Sydney, Australia: Australian Documents Library, 1981.

McClelland, James. *Index to All Readable Names of Convicts and Free Persons Arriving Australia*. 4 vols. Silverdale, New South Wales, Australia: James McClelland Research, 1983.

Ryan, R. J. *The Second Fleet Convicts: A Comprehensive Listing of Convicts Who Sailed in HMS Guardian, Lady Juliana, Neptune, Scarborough and Surprise*. Sydney: Australian Documents Library, 1982.

_____. *The Third Fleet Convicts: An Alphabetical Listing of Names, Giving Place and Date of Conviction, Length of Sentence, and Ship of Transportation*. Cammeray, New South Wales, Australia: Horwitz Grahame, 1981.

Barbados

Brandow, James C., ed. *Omitted Chapters from Hotten's Original Lists of Persons of Quality . . . Census Returns, Parish Registers, and Militia Rolls from the Barbados Census of 1679/80.* Baltimore: Genealogical Publishing Co., 1982. [0776] {6,500}

Kent, David L., ed. *Barbados and America.* Arlington, Va.: the author, 1980. [3800.25] {13,000}

Bermuda

Mercer, Julia E. *Bermuda Settlers of the 17th Century: Genealogical Notes from Bermuda.* Baltimore: Genealogical Publishing Co., 1982. Reprint. 1992. [5400] {5,000}

Canada

Crowder, Norman K. *Early Ontario Settlers: A Source Book.* Baltimore: Genealogical Publishing Co., 1993. [----]

Elliott, Bruce S. *Irish Migrants in the Canada: A New Approach.* Montreal: McGill-Queen's University Press, 1988. [----] {775}

Holt, Ruth, and Margaret Williams. *Genealogical Extraction and Index of the Canada Company Remittance Books, 1843–1847.* 3 vols. Weston, Ontario, Canada: R. Holt, 1990. [----]

Passengers to New Brunswick: The Custom House Records, 1833, 1834, 1837, 1838. St. John, New Brunswick, Canada: New Brunswick Genealogical Society, 1987. [6637.17] {10,700}

Reisinger, Joy, and Elmer Courteau. *The King's Daughters.* Sparta, Wis.: Reisinger, 1988. [----]

Smith, Leonard H., Jr. *A Dictionary of Immigrants to Nova Scotia, Vol 1. Pre-Confederation Peninsular Immigrants.* Clearwater, Fla.: Owl Books, 1984. [8750.1] {7,350}

_____, and Norma H. Smith. *Nova Scotia Immigrants to 1867.* Baltimore: Genealogical Publishing Co., 1992. [----] {thousands}

_____. *Nova Scotia Immigrants to 1867: From Non-Nova Scotia Periodicals and from Published Diaries and Journals.* Baltimore: Genealogical Publishing Co., 1994. [----] {10,000}

Whyte, Donald. *A Dictionary of Scottish Emigrants to Canada before Confederation.* 2 vols. Toronto: Ontario Genealogical Society, 1986, 1995. Vol. 1 [9758], vol. 2 [----] {23,714 total}

United States—Multiple-State Sources (also see New England)

Bolton, Charles Knowles. *Scotch Irish Pioneers in Ulster and America.* 1910. Reprint. Baltimore: Genealogical Publishing Co., 1986. [----] {1,500}

Boyer, Carl, 3rd, ed. *Ship Passenger Lists, National and New England (1600–1825).* Newhall, Calif., 1978. [0702] {7000} Includes index to ship names. Some lists also reprinted by Tepper.

_____, ed. *Ship Passenger Lists, the South (1538–1825).* Newhall, Calif.: 1979. [0720] {12,000} Includes an index to ship names. Some lists also reprinted by Tepper.

Boyer, Carl, 3rd—also see under New York, Pennsylvania.

Colket, Meredith B., Jr. *Founders of Early American Families: Emigrants from Europe, 1607–1657.* Rev. ed. Cleveland: General Court of the Order of Founders and Patriots of America, 1985. [1262] {3,500}

English Origins of American Colonists from the New York Genealogical and Biographical Record. Compiled by Henry B. Hoff. Baltimore: Genealogical Publishing Co., 1991. [----] {10,000}

Faris, David. *Plantagenet Ancestry of Seventeenth-Century Colonists.* Baltimore: Genealogical Publishing Co., 1996. [----]{100}

Feldman, Lawrence. *Anglo-Americans in Spanish Archives: Lists of Anglo-American Settlers in the Spanish Colonies of America.* Genealogical Publishing Co., 1991. [----] {7,000}

Founders and Patriots of America Index. Genealogical Publishing Co., 1967. Reprint. 1993. [----] {4,000}

Giuseppi, Montague S. *Naturalizations of Foreign Protestants in the American and West Indian Colonies (Pursuant to Statute 13 George II, c.7).* Publications of the Huguenot Society of London, vol. 24. 1921. Reprint. Baltimore: Genealogical Publishing Co., 1964, 1979. [2,564]

Jones, Henry Z. *More Palatine Families: Some Immigrants to the Middle Colonies, 1717–1776, and Their European Origins, Plus New Discoveries on German Families Who Arrived in Colonial New York in 1710.* Universal City, Calif.: the author, 1991. [----]

O'Brien, Michael J. *Irish in America: Immigration, Land, Probate, Administrations, Birth, Marriage and Burial Records of the Irish in America in and about the Eighteenth Century.* Baltimore: Genealogical Publishing Co., 1990. [6276] {1500} Excerpted from *The Journal of the American Irish Historical Society.*

_____. *Irish Settlers in America: A Consolidation of Articles from The Journal of the American Irish Historical Society.* 2 vols. Baltimore: Genealogical Publishing Co., 1979. [6280] {25,000}

Reeve, Vera. *Register of Qualified Huguenot Ancestors.* 3rd ed. Washington, D.C.: National Huguenot Society, 1983. Supplement by Arthur Louis Finnell, 1993. [----] {c. 280+145}

Roberts, Gary Boyd. *The Royal Descents of 500 Immigrants to the American Colonies or the United States Who Were Themselves Notable or Left Descendants Notable in American History.* Baltimore: Genealogical Publishing Co., 1993. [----] {500}

Scott, Kenneth R., comp. *British Aliens in the United States During the War of 1812.* Baltimore: Genealogical Publishing Co., 1979. [8195] {10,000}

Sack, Sallyann Amdur, ed. *The Russian Consular Records Index and Catalog.* New York: Garland Publishing, 1987. [----]

Tepper, Michael, ed. *Immigrants to the Middle Colonies: A Consolidation of Ship Passenger Lists and Associated Data from the New York Genealogical and Biographical Record.* Baltimore: Genealogical Publishing Co., 1978. [9135] {5,500} Reprints fifteen articles; includes ship indexes.

_____, ed. *New World Immigrants: A Consolidation of Ship Passenger Lists and Associated Data from Periodical Literature.* 2 vols. Baltimore: Genealogical Publishing Co., 1979. [9143-44] {27,500} Reprints of ninety-seven articles—including twenty (mostly in vol. 2) about German emigrants. Includes ship indexes. Many lists are also in Boyer's four volumes.

_____. *Passengers to America: A Consolidation of Ship Passenger Lists from the "New England Historical and Genea-*

logical Register" (1847–1961). Baltimore: Genealogical Publishing Co., 1977. [9151] {18,000}

Tepper, Michael—also see under Pennsylvania.

Virkus, Frederick A. *Immigrant Ancestors: A List of 2,500 Immigrants to America Before 1750.* 1942. Reprint. Baltimore: Genealogical Publishing Co., 1986. [9448] {2,500}

Weis, Frederick L., Walter L. Sheppard, Jr., and David Faris. *Ancestral Roots of Certain American Colonists Who Came to America Before 1700.* 7th ed. Baltimore: Genealogical Publishing Co., 1992. [----] {100}

Whittemore, Henry B. *Genealogical Guide to the Early Settlers of America.* Baltimore: Genealogical Publishing Co., 1967. [----] {10,000} Reprinted from *The Spirit of '76,* 1898–1906. Covers surnames beginning with *A* through *Prior.*

United States—New England (also see individual states)

Anderson, Robert Charles. *The Great Migration Begins: Immigrants to New England 1620–1633.* 3 vols. Boston: New England Historic Genealogical Society, 1995. [----] {900}

Banks, Charles Edward. *Topographical Dictionary of 2885 English Emigrants to New England, 1620–1650.* Edited and indexed by Elijah Ellsworth Brownell. 1937. Reprint. Baltimore: Genealogical Publishing Co., 1992. [0275] {2,885}

Bolton, Ethel Stanwood. *Immigrants to New England 1700–1775.* Salem, Mass.: Essex Institute, 1931. Reprint. Baltimore: Genealogical Publishing Co., 1966. [0658]

English Origins of New England Families. 2 series. 6 vols. Baltimore: Genealogical Publishing Co., 1984–85. [----] Extracted from *The New England Historical and Genealogical Register.*

Davis, William Thomas. *Genealogical Register of Plymouth Families.* 1899. Reprint. Baltimore: Genealogical Publishing Co., 1975. [----]

Drake, Samuel G. *Result of Some Researches Among the British Archives for Information Relative to the Founders of New England.* 1860. Reprint. Baltimore: Genealogical Publishing Co., 1963. [1672] {10,000}

Holmes, Frank R. *Directory of the Ancestral Heads of New England Families, 1620–1700.* 1923. Reprint. Baltimore: Genealogical Publishing Co., 1989. [----] {15,000}

Savage, James. *A Genealogical Dictionary of the First Settlers of New England Showing Three Generations of Those Who Came Before May, 1692. . . .* 4 vols. 1860, 1862, 1873, 1884. Reprint. Baltimore: Genealogical Publishing Co., 1994. [----]

Stratton, Eugene Aubrey. *Plymouth Colony: Its History and People 1620–1691.* Salt Lake City: Ancestry, 1986. [----]

Threlfall, John Brooks. *Fifty Great Migration Colonists to New England and Their Origins.* Madison, Wis.: the author, 1990. [----]

_____. *Twenty-six Great Migration Colonists to New England and Their Origins.* Madison, Wis.: the author, 1993. [----]

Alabama

Connick, Lucille Mallon. *Lists of ships' passengers, Mobile, Alabama.* 2 vols. Mobile, Ala.: the author, 1988–89. Vol. 1, 1838–40; vol. 2, 1841–60. [----]

Mitchell, Mrs. Lois Dumas. *Mobile Ship News.* Mobile, Ala., 1964. [5715] {550}

Arkansas

Index to Naturalization Records in Arkansas, 1809–1906. Little Rock, Ark.: Immigration and Naturalization Records Indexing Project Service Division, United States Work Projects Administration, 1942. [9280]

Connecticut

Hinman, Royal R. *A Catalogue of the Names of the First Puritan Settlers of the Colony of Connecticut from 1635, with Time of the Arrival in the Colony.* Hartford, Conn.: Case, Tiffany & Co., 1852. [3197] Surnames *A* through *D* only.

Delaware (also see Pennsylvania)

Johnson, Amandus. *The Swedish Settlements on the Delaware, 1638–1664.* 2 vols. 1911. Reprint. Baltimore: Genealogical Publishing Co., 1969. [3560]

Georgia

Coulter, E. Merton, and Albert B. Saye. *A List of the Early Settlers of Georgia.* Athens: University of Georgia Press, 1949. 2nd ed. Baltimore: Genealogical Publishing Co., 1967. Reprint. 1983. [1322] {3,000}

Immigrants from Great Britain to the Georgia Colony. Morrow, Ga.: Genealogical Enterprises, 1970. [3388] {1,000}

Jones, George F. *The Germans of Colonial Georgia, 1733–1783.* Baltimore: Genealogical Publishing Co., 1986. [----] {2,800} Indexes twenty-nine different sources.

Indiana

An Index to Indiana Naturalization Records . . . Prior to 1907. Indianapolis: Family History Section, Indiana Historical Society, 1981. [3434] {42,000}

Iowa

Cassady, Michael. "Iowa Bound Arrivals at the Port of. . . ." Series of articles in *Hawkeye Heritage.* 1984–. [3437.22+] {5,300+}

Palen, Margaret Krug. *German Settlers of Iowa: Their Descendants and European Ancestors.* Bowie, Md.: Heritage Books, 1994. [----] {2,000 names in index}

Louisiana

Brasseaux, Carl A. *The "Foreign French": Nineteenth-Century French Immigration into Louisiana.* 3 vols. Lafayette: Center for Louisiana Studies, University of Southwestern Louisiana, 1990–93. Vol. 1, 1820–39; vol. 2, 1840–48; vol. 3, 1849–52. [778.5*]

Conrad, Glenn R. *The First Families of Louisiana.* 2 vols. Baton Rouge: Claitor's Pub. Division, 1970. [1290.1-2]

Rieder, Milton P., and Norma Gaudet Rieder, eds. *The Acadian Exiles in the American Colonies, 1755–1768.* Metairie, La: the editors, 1977. [7430] {3,000}

Riviere, Mary Ann. *From Palermo to New Orleans.* The author, 1987.

Villerâe, Sidney Louis. *The Canary Islands migration to Louisiana, 1778–1783: The History and Passenger Lists of the Islenos Volunteer Recruits and Their Families.* Baltimore: Genealogical Publishing Co., 1972.

Maine and New Hampshire

Pope, Charles Henry. *The Pioneers of Maine and New Hampshire, 1623–1660.* 1908. Reprint. Baltimore: Genealogical Publishing Co., 1965. [----]

Maryland

Coldham, Peter Wilson. *Settlers of Maryland.* 5 vols. Baltimore: Genealogical Publishing Co., 1995–96. Vol. 1, 1679–1700; vol. 2, 1701–30; vol. 3, 1731–50; vol. 4, 1751–65; vol. 5, 1766–83. [----] {24,600}

Dobson, David. *Scots on the Chesapeake, 1607–1830.* Baltimore: Genealogical Publishing Co., 1992. [----] {several thousand}

Newman, Harry Wright. *To Maryland from Overseas.* Baltimore: Genealogical Publishing Co., 1985. [----]{1,400}

Reamy, Bill, and Martha Reamy. *Immigrant Ancestors of Marylanders as Found in Local Histories.* N.p., 1993. [----] {1,600} Indexes and abstracts eight local history and biography sources.

Skordas, Gust. *The Early Settlers of Maryland: An Index to the Names of Immigrants Compiled from Records of Land Patents, 1633–1680, in the Hall of Records, Annapolis, Maryland.* Baltimore: Genealogical Publishing Co., 1968. Reprint. 1986. [8510] {25,000}

Wyand, Jeffrey A., and Florence L. Wyand. *Colonial Maryland Naturalizations.* Baltimore: Genealogical Publishing Co., 1975. Reprint. 1986. [9916] {1,600}

Also see Bentley under "U.S. Port of Arrival Transcripts," above.

Massachusetts

Banks, Charles Edward. *The English Ancestry and Homes of the Pilgrim Fathers Who Came to Plymouth on the 'Mayflower' in 1620, the 'Fortune' in 1621, and the 'Anne' and the 'Little James' in 1623.* 1929. Reprint. Baltimore: Genealogical Publishing Co., 1989. [0255]

Banks, Charles Edward. *The Planters of the Commonwealth: A Study of the Emigrants and Emigration in Colonial Times: To Which are Added Lists of Passengers to Boston and to the Bay Colony; the Ships Which Brought Them; Their English Homes, and the Places of Their Settlement in Massachusetts.* 1930. Reprint. Baltimore: Genealogical Publishing Co., 1991. [0263] {3,600}

Banks, Charles Edward. *The Winthrop Fleet of 1630: An Account of the Vessels, the Voyage, the Passengers. . . .* 1930. Reprint. Baltimore: Genealogical Publishing Co., 1994. [0281] {700}

Harris, Ruth-Ann, and Donald M. Jacobs (later B. Emer O'Keefe), eds. *The Search for Missing Friends: Irish Immigrant Advertizements Placed in the Boston Pilot.* 5 vols. Boston: New England Historic Genealogical Society, 1989, 1991, 1993, 1995, 1996. Vol. 1, 1831–50; vol. 2, 1851–53; vol. 3, 1854–56; vol. 4, 1857–60; vol. 5, 1861–65. [----] {25,000}

Munroe, J. B. *A List of Alien Passengers, Bonded from January 1, 1847 to January 1, 1851, for the Use of the Overseers of the Poor in the Commonwealth of Massachussetts.* 1851. Reprint. Baltimore: Genealogical Publishing Co., 1991. [5881.1*] {5,000}

Pope, Charles Henry. *The Pioneers of Massachusetts, 1620–1650.* 1900. Reprint. Baltimore: Genealogical Publishing Co., 1965. [----]

Whitmore, William H. *Port Arrivals and Immigrants to the City of Boston 1715–1716 and 1762–1769.* Reprint. 1900. Baltimore: Genealogical Publishing Co., 1989. [9750] {3,500}

Mississippi

Index to Naturalization Records, Mississippi Courts, 1798–1906. Jackson, Miss.: Old Law Naturalization Records Project, 1942. [6401]

Montana

Fuhrman, Diane. *Swedish Immigrants Living in Montana, 1900.* Bozeman, Mont.: the author, 1989.

Nebraska

Rosicky, Rose. *A History of Czechs (Bohemians) in Nebraska.* Omaha: Czech Historical Society of Nebraska, 1929. [7710]

Sobotka, Margie. *Nebraska, Kansas Czech Settlers, 1891–1895.* Omaha, Nebr.: the author, 1980. [8774.11]

New York

Bevier, Louis. *Genealogy of the First Settlers of New Paltz.* 1909. Reprint. Baltimore: Genealogical Publishing Co., 1965. [----]

Boyer, Carl, 3rd, ed. *Ship Passenger Lists, New York and New Jersey (1600–1825).* Newhall, Calif.: the editor, 1978. [0714] {8,500 names} Reprints of twenty-six articles, mostly identifying Dutch and Germany arrivals. Some also reprinted in Tepper, above (under "United States—Multiple-State Sources"). Includes ship index.

Camann, Eugene W. *Uprooted from Prussia—Transplanted in America.* Buffalo, N.Y.: Gilcraft Printing, 1991. [----] {800}

Evjen, John O. *Scandinavian Immigrants in New York, 1630–1674: With Appendices on Scandinavians in Mexico and South America . . . Canada. . . .* Minneapolis: K. C. Holter, 1916. Reprint. Baltimore: Genealogical Publishing Co., 1972, 1983. [1898] {375}

Jones, Henry Z. *The Palatine Families of New York: A Study of the German Immigrants Who Arrived in Colonial New York in 1710.* 2 vols. Universal City, Calif.: the author, 1985. [3620.1] {500}

MacWethy, Lou D. *The Book of Names, Especially Relating to the Early Palatines and the First Settlers of the Mowhawk Valley.* 1933. Reprint. Baltimore: Genealogical Publishing Co., 1985. [----] {thousands}

Scott, Kenneth, and Kenn Stryker-Rodda. *Denizations, Naturalizations, and Oaths of Allegiance in Colonial New York.* Baltimore: Genealogical Publishing Co., 1975. [8270]

Scott, Kenneth. *Early New York Naturalizations: Abstracts of Naturalization Records from Federal, State, and Local Courts, 1790–1840.* Baltimore: Genealogical Publishing Co., 1981. [8197] {10,000}

North and South Carolina

Dobson, David. *Directory of Scots in the Carolinas, 1680–1830.* Baltimore: Genealogical Publishing Co., 1986. [1639.2] {6,000}

Ohio

Herbert, Jeffrey G. *Index of Death and Other Notices Appearing in the Cincinnatti Freie Presse 1874–1920.* Bowie, Md.: Heritage Books, 1993. [----] {38,000}

Smith, Clifford Neal. *Early Nineteenth-Century German Settlers in Ohio (Mainly Cincinnati and Environs), Kentucky, and Other States.* McNeal, Ariz.: Westland Publications, 1984. [8582] {700}

Tolzman, Don Heinrich. *Ohio Valley German Biographical Index.* Bowie, Md.: Heritage Books, 1992. [----] {3,754}

Pennsylvania

Boyer, Carl, 3rd, ed. *Ship Passenger Lists, Pennsylvania and Delaware (1641–1825).* Newhall, Calif.: the editor, 1980. [0717] {6,500} Reprints of thirty-two articles—mostly lists of emigrants from Germany to Pennsylvania. Some also reprinted in Tepper (below). Includes ship index.

Braun, Fritz, and Frederick S. Weiser. *Marriages Performed at the Evangelical Lutheran Church of the Holy Trinity in Lancaster, Pennsylvania 1748–1767.* Publications of the Pennsylvania German Society, vol. 7 (1973) and in *Schriften zur Wanderungsgeschichte der Pfaelzer,* no. 34. Kaiserlautern, Germany: Heimatstelle Pfalz, 1973. [----] {approximately 340 immigrants identified} Includes ship index.

Egle, William H., ed. *Names of Foreigners Who Took the Oath of Allegiance to the Province and State of Pennsylvania, 1727–1775.* Harrisbug, Pa.: E. K. Meyers, 1890. Reprint. Baltimore: Genealogical Publishing Co., 1967. [1804] {42,000} Most of these names are also in the Strassburger volumes (below).

Eshleman, H. Frank. *Swiss and German Pioneer Settlers of Southeastern Pennsylvania.* 1917. Reprint. Baltimore: Genealogical Publishing Co., 1991.

Filby, P. William. *Philadelphia Naturalization Records: An Index to Records of Aliens' Declarations of Intention and/or Oaths of Allegiance, 1789–1880.* Detroit: Gale Publishing Co., 1982. [2041] {120,000}

Grubb, Farley. *German Immigrant Servant Contracts Registered at the Port of Philadelphia, 1817–1831.* Baltimore: Genealogical Publishing Co., 1994. [----] {1,035} Almost all in 1817 to 1819.

_____. *Runaway Servants, Convicts, and Apprentices Advertised in the Pennsylvania Gazette, 1728–1796.* Baltimore: Genealogical Publishing Co., 1992. [----] {5,754}

Hall, Charles M. *"Pal-Index": A Surname Index of Eighteenth-Century Immigrants.* Salt Lake City: Global Research Systems, 1979. [2883] {6,500} Indexes approximately fifty different sources.

Hocker, Edward W. *Genealogical Data Relating to the German Settlers of Pennsylvania and Adjacent Territory.* 1935. Reprint. Baltimore: Genealogical Publishing Co., 1981. [3211.7]

LeVan, Russel George. *Early Immigrants from Germany and Switzerland to Eastern Pennsylvania.* Baltimore: Gateway Press, 1990. [----]

McCracken, George E. *The Welcome Claimants Proved, Disproved and Doubtful with an Account of Some of Their Descendants.* Baltimore: Genealogical Publishing Co., 1970.

Myers, Albert Cook. "List of Certificates of Removal from Ireland Received at the Monthly Meetings of Friends in Pennsylvania, 1682–1750." In *Immigration of the Irish Quakers into Pennsylvania. 1682–1750,* 277–390. N.p., 1902. Reprinted as *Irish Quaker Arrivals to Pennsylvania: 1682–1750.* Baltimore: Genealogical Publishing Co., 1964. [5917]

Myers, Albert Cook. *Quaker Arrivals at Philadelphia 1682–1750.* 1902. Reprint. Baltimore: Genealogical Publishing Co., 1957, 1978. [5924] Companion volume to the above; very few duplicate entries.

Persons Naturalized in the Province of Pennsylvania, 1740–1773. Pennsylvania Archives, series 2, vol. 2 (1876), 345–486. Reprint. Baltimore: Genealogical Publishing Co., 1967. [6680] {3,000}

Record of Indentures of Individuals Bound Out as Apprentices, Servants, Etc. and of German and Other Redemptioners in the Office of the Mayor of the City of Philadelphia, October 3, 1771 to October 5, 1773. Pennsylvania-German Society Proceedings and Addresses, vol. 16. N.p., 1905. Lancaster, Pa., 1907. Reprint. Baltimore: Genealogical Publishing Co., 1973. [7207]

Rupp, Israel D. *A Collection of Upwards of 30,000 Names of Germans, Swiss, French and Other Immigrants in Pennsylvania, 1727–1776.* 1876. Reprint. Baltimore: Genealogical Publishing Co., 1985. [7820] {27,000} Most of these names are in the Strassburger volumes (below), which were more carefully prepared.

Sheppard, Walter Lee, Jr. *Passengers and Ships Prior to 1684.* Publications of the Welcome Society of Pennsylvania, vol. 1. Baltimore: Genealogical Publishing Co., 1970. [8370] {3,000}

Strassburger, Ralph Beaver, and William John Hinke. *Pennsylvania German Pioneers: A Publication of the Original Lists of Arrivals in the Port of Philadelphia from 1727 to 1808.* 3 vols. Norristown: Pennsylvania German Society, 1934. Reprint. Vols. 1 and 3. Baltimore: Genealogical Publishing Co., 1992. [9041, 9042] {29,800}

Tepper, Michael. *Emigrants to Pennsylvania, 1641–1819: A Consolidation of Ship Passenger Lists from the "Pennsylvania Magazine of History and Biography" (1877–1934).* Baltimore: Genealogical Publishing Co., 1975. [9120] {6,000}

Yoder, Don, ed. *Pennsylvania German Immigrants, 1709–1786: Lists Consolidated from Yearbooks of the Pennsylvania German Folklore Society.* Baltimore: Genealogical Publishing Co., 1980. Reprint. 1984. [9964] {1,528 families} Includes ship indexes.

_____. *Rhineland Emigrants: Lists of German Settlers in Colonial America.* Baltimore: Genealogical Publishing Co., 1981. Reprint. 1985. [9968] {4,000 names} Excerpted from *Pennsylvania Folklife.*

Rhode Island

Taylor, Maureen. *Rhode Island Passenger Lists: Port of Providence 1798–1808; 1820–1872 and Port of Bristol and Warren 1820–1871.* Baltimore: Genealogical Publishing Co., 1995. [----] {4,000}

South Carolina

Baldwin, Agnes Lelans. *First Settlers of South Carolina 1670–1700.* Easley, S.C.: Southern Historical Press, 1985. [----] {3,300}

Holcomb, Brent H. *South Carolina Naturalizations, 1783–1850.* Baltimore: Genealogical Publishing Co., 1985. [3250.7] {7,500}

Jones, Jack Moreland, and Mary Bondurant Warren. *South Carolina Immigrants, 1760 to 1770.* Danielsville, Ga.: Heritage Papers, 1988. [----]

Revill, Janie. *A Compilation of the Original Lists of Protestant Immigrants to South Carolina, 1763–1773.* 1939. Reprint. Baltimore: Genealogical Publishing Co., 1968. [7343]

Stephenson, Jean. *Scotch-Irish Migration to South Carolina, 1772.* Strasburg, Va.: Shenandoah Publishing House, 1971. [8980]

Warren, Mary Bondurant. *Citizens and Immigrants—South Carolina, 1768.* Danielsville, Ga.: Heritage Papers, ca. 1980. [9598]

Texas

Ericson, Carolyn Reeves. *Citizens and Foreigners of the Nacogdoches District, 1809–1836.* 2 vols. Nacogdoches, Tex.: the author, 1981–85. [1866.2-3] {hundreds}

_____. *First Settlers of the Republic of Texas: Headright Land Grants Which Were Reported as Genuine and Legal By the Traveling Commissioners, January 1840.* 2 vols. Reprint. 1841. Nacogdoches, Tex.: the author. 1982.

Fey, Everett Anthony. *New Braunfels: The First Founders.* 2 vols. N.p., 1995 [----] {240 families} "Family Trees for four generations of each of the First Founders." Eight thousand names.

McManus, J. *Comal County, Texas, and New Braunfels, Texas, German Immigrant Ships, 1845–1846.* St. Louis, Mo.: F. T. Ingmire, 1985. Passengers of forty-one ships are enumerated and indexed.

Virginia

Brock, Robert A. *Documents, Chiefly Unpublished, Relating to the Huguenot Emigration to Virginia and to the Settlement at Manakintown.* 1886. Reprint. Baltimore: Genealogical Publishing Co., 1979. [0953]

Cerny, Johni, and Gary J. Zimmerman. *Before Germanna: The Origins and Ancestry of Those Affiliated with the Second Germanna Colony of Virginia.* Monograph series, 1–12. Bountiful, Utah: American Genealogical Lending Library, 1990. [----]

Foley, Louise Pledge Heath. *Early Virginia Families Along the James River.* 2 vols. 1978. Reprint. Baltimore: Genealogical Publishing Co., 1990. [----]

Greer, George C. *Early Virginia Immigrants, 1623–1666.* 1912. Reprint. Baltimore: Genealogical Publishing Co., 1982. [2772] {25,000} Names from the Virginia State Land Office.

Hudgins, Dennis, ed. *Cavaliers and Pioneers: 1732–1741.* Richmond: Virginia Genealogical Society, 1994. [----]

Hume, Robert. *Early Child Immigrants to Virginia, 1618–1642.* Baltimore: Magna Carta Book Co., 1986. [3315] {468}

Nugent, Nell Marion. *Cavaliers and Pioneers: Abstracts of Virginia Land Patents and Grants.* 3 vols. Vol. 1. Richmond: Dietz Printing Co., 1934. Vols. 2 and 3. Richmond: Virginia State Library, 1977, 1979. Vol. 1 reprinted by Genealogical Publishing Co., 1991. Vol. 1, 1623–66; vol. 2, 1666–95; vol. 3, 1695–1732. [6220, 6221, 6223] {approximately 45,000}

Stanard, William Glover. *Some Emigrants to Virginia: Memoranda in Regard to Several Hundred Emigrants to Virginia During the Colonial Period Whose Parentage is Shown or Former Residence Indicated by Authentic Records.* 1911. Reprint. Baltimore: Genealogical Publishing Co., 1979. [8925]

Wisconsin

Johnson, Martin William. *Old Lutherans in Wisconsin and Minnesota Membership Lists, Cemeteries, Passenger Lists, etc.* 2 microfiche. Belvidere, Ill.: the author, 1990. Includes records from Lutheran churches and cemeteries in Wisconsin and Minnesota, passenger lists of Lutherans arriving in New York and emigrating to upper New York state and Wisconsin in 1843.

Podoll, Brian A. *Prussian Netzlanders and other German Immigrants in Green Lake, Marquette and Waushara Counties, Wisconsin.* Bowie, Md.: Heritage Books, 1994. [----] {est. 1,500}

Published Lists of Emigrants

This list is arranged by the country from which the emigrants left. In addition to regular bibliographic information, this list includes the reference number in Filby's *Passenger and Immigration Lists Bibliography* in brackets [ ]. Where possible, the number of names in the source is given in braces { }. (Books not in Filby's bibliography are cited as [----].)

Belgium

Hall, Charles M. *Antwerp Emigration Index.* Salt Lake City: Heritage International, 1986. [2885] {5,100} Only includes emigrants during 1855.

England

Coldham, Peter Wilson. *American Wills and Administrations in the Prerogative Court of Canterbury, 1610–1857.* Baltimore: Genealogical Publishing Co., 1989. [----] {6,300}

_____. *American Wills Proved in London, 1611–1775.* Baltimore: Genealogical Publishing Co., 1992. [----] All wills not included in Waters, Withington, or Sherwood.

_____. *The Bristol Registers of Servants Sent to Foreign Plantations, 1654–1686.* Baltimore: Genealogical Publishing Co., 1988. [----] {10,000} Apparently in *Complete Book of Emigrants. . . .*

_____. *Child Apprentices in America, From Christ's Hospital, London, 1617–1778.* Baltimore: Genealogical Publishing Co., 1990. [----] {1,000}

_____. *The Complete Book of Emigrants 1607–1660: A Comprehensive Listing Compiled from English Public Records of Those Who Took Ship to the Americas for Political, Religious, and Economic Reasons; of Those Who Were Deported for Vagrancy, Roguery, or Non-Conformity; and Those Who Were Sold to Labour in the New Colonies.* Baltimore: Genealogical Publishing Co., 1987. [1219.4] {30,000}

_____. *The Complete Book of Emigrants, 1661–1699.* Baltimore: Genealogical Publishing Co., 1990. [----] {30,000}

_____. *The Complete Book of Emigrants, 1700–1750.* Baltimore: Genealogical Publishing Co., 1992. [----] {25,000}

_____. *The Complete Book of Emigrants, 1751–1776.* Baltimore: Genealogical Publishing Co., 1993. [----] {15,000}

_____. *The Complete Book of Emigrants in Bondage, 1614–1775.* Baltimore: Genealogical Publishing Co., 1988. Supplement, 1992. [----] {53,000} Most of these names were published earlier in the nine volumes of *Bonded Passengers to America* and two volumes of *English Convicts in Colonial America*, but it does include some new records.

_____. *Emigrants From England to the American Colonies, 1773–1776.* Baltimore: Genealogical Publishing Co., 1988. [----] {6-7000} From Public Record Office. A better version of the records transcribed by Fothergill in 1913.

_____. *English Adventurers and Emigrants. Abstracts of Examinations in the High Court of Admiralty with Reference to Colonial America.* 2 vols. Baltimore: Genealogical Publishing Co., 1984–85. Vol. 1, 1609–60; vol. 2, 1661–1733. [1220.1-.2] {2,000}

_____. *English Estates of American Colonists: American Wills and Administrations in the Prerogative Court of Canterbury.* 3 vols. Baltimore: Genealogical Publishing Co., 1980–81. Vol. 1, 1610–99; vol. 2, 1700–99; vol. 3, 1800–58. [----] {3,000}

_____. *Supplement to the Complete Book of Emigrants in Bondage, 1614–1775.* Baltimore: Genealogical Publishing Co., 1992. [----] {3,000}

French, Elizabeth. *List of Emigrants to America from Liverpool, 1697–1707.* 1913. Reprint. Baltimore: Genealogical Publishing Co., 1962, 1983. [2212] {1,500}

Ghirelli, Michael. *A List of Emigrants from England to America 1682–1692: Transcribed from the Original Records at the City of London Record Office.* Baltimore: Magna Carta Book Co., 1968. [2524] {960}

Hotten, John Camden. *The Original Lists of Persons of Quality; Emigrants; Religious Exiles; Political Rebels; Serving Men Sold for a Term of Years; Apprentices; Children Stolen; Maidens Pressed; and Others Who Went from Great Britain to American Plantations 1600–1700.* 1874. Reprint. Baltimore: Genealogical Publishing Co., 1974. [3283] {10,000}

Jewson, Charles Boardman. *Transcript of Three Registers of Passengers from Great Yarmouth to Holland and New England, 1637–1639.* Norwich, England: Norfolk Record Society, 1954. Reprint. Baltimore: Genealogical Publishing Co., 1964, 1990. [3540] {1,000}

Kaminkow, Jack, and Marion J. Kaminkow. *A List of Emigrants from England to America, 1718–1759: A New Edition Containing 46 Recently Discovered Records.* Baltimore: Magna Charta Book Co., 1964. Reprint with additional records. Baltimore: Genealogical Publishing Co., 1981. [3690.1] {3,000}

_____. *Original Lists of Emigrants in Bondage from London to the American Colonies, 1719–1744.* Baltimore: Magna Carta Book Company, 1967. [3700] {6,300}

Sherwood, George Frederick Tudor. *American Colonists in English Records; a Guide to Direct References in Authentic Records, Passenger Lists Not in "Hotten."* 2 vols. Reprint. 1932–33. Baltimore: Genealogical Publishing Co., 1961, 1982. [8400]

Smith, Frank. *Immigrants to America Appearing in English Records.* Logan, Utah: Everton Publishers, 1976. [8715] {2,000+}

Wareing, John. *Emigrants to America: Indentured Servants Recruited in London 1718–1733.* Baltimore: Genealogical Publishing Co., 1985. [9579.10] {1,544}

Waters, Henry F. *Genealogical Gleanings in England: Abstracts of Wills Relating to Early American Families, with Genealogical Notes and Pedigrees Constructed from the Wills and from Other Records.* 2 vols. 1901, 1907. Reprint. Baltimore: Genealogical Publishing Co., 1969. [----]

Withington, Lothrop. *Virginia Gleanings in England: Abstracts of 17th and 18th Century English Wills and Administrations Relating to Virginia and Virginians.* Baltimore: Genealogical Publishing Co., 1980. Originally printed in *Virginia Magazine of History and Biography* (1903–29). [----] {15,000}.

France

Schrader-Muggenthaler, Cornelia. *The Alsace Emigration Book.* 2 vols. Apollo, Pa.: Closson Press, 1989, 1991. [----] {21,500}

Smith, Clifford Neal. *Immigrants to America from France (Haut-Rhin Departement) and Western Switzerland, 1859–1866.* French-American Genealogical Research Monograph no. 1. McNeal, Ariz.: Westland Publications, 1983. [8635.5] {1,000}

Toups, Neil J. *Mississippi Valley Pioneers.* Lafayette, La.: Neilson Publishing Co., 1970. [9190] French emigrants to Louisiana, 1718 to 1721.

Germany—Eighteenth Century (also see Pennsylvania, above)

Burgert, Annette K. *Eighteenth Century Emigrants from German-Speaking Lands to North America.* Publications of the Pennsylvania German Society, vols. 16 and 19. Breinigsville: Pennsylvania German Society, 1983, 1985. [1031.8-9] {1,100} Includes ship index.

_____. *Eighteenth Century Emigrants from the Northern Alsace to America.* Camden, Maine: Picton Press, 1992. [----] {628 emigrants} Includes ship index.

_____. *Emigrants from Eppingen to American in the Eighteenth and Nineteenth Centuries.* Myerstown, Pa.: AKB Publications, 1987. [1031.18] {400 emigrants} Includes ship index.

_____, and Henry Z Jones. *Westerwald to America: Some 18th Century German Immigrants.* Camden, Maine.: Picton Press, 1989. [----] {265 emigrants} Includes ship index.

Burkett, Brigitte. *Emigrants from Baden and Wuerttemberg in the 18th Century.* Vol. 1, Baden Durlach and vicinity. Rockport, Maine: Picton Press, 1996. [----] {435 families} Includes ship index.

Burgoyne, Burce E. *Waldeck Soldiers of the American Revolutionary War.* Bowie, Md.: Heritage Books, 1991. [----] {1,225, of whom 250 stayed in the United States}

Ehman, Karl. *Die Auswangerung in die Neuengland-Staaten aus Orten des Enzkreises im 18. Jahrhundert. Sudwestdeutsche Blaetter fuer Familien- und Wappenkunde.* Special supplement. Stuttgart, Germany: Verein für Familien and Wappenkunde in Wuerttemberg und Baden, 1977. [1815] {1,700 emigrants} Includes ship references.

Gieg, Ella. *Auswanderungen aus dem Odenwaldkreis.* Vol. 1. Michelstadt: the author, 1988. Vol 2–5. Lützelbach: the author, 1989–92. [----]

Hacker, Werner. *Auswanderungen aus Baden und dem Breisgau: Obere und mittlere rechtsseitige Oberrheinlande im 18. Jahrhundert archivalisch documentiert.* Stuttgart, Germany: Konrad Theiss, 1980. [2855.5] {11,666; 1,000+ to America}

_____. *Auswanderungen aus Rheinpfalz und Saarland im 18. Jahrhundert.* Stuttgart, Germany: Konrad Theiss, 1987. [2856.15] {16,802 entries; 5,000+ to America}

_____. *Eighteenth Century Register of Emigrants from Southwest Germany.* Apollo, Pa.: Closson Press, 1994. [----]

_____. *Kurpfaelzische Auswanderer vom Unteren Neckar: Rechtsrheinische Gebiete der Kurpfalz.* Sonderveroeffentlichung des Stadtarchivs Mannheim, 4. Stuttgart, Germany: Konrad Theiss, 1983 [2857] {2,300; 500 to America}

Hessische Truppen in Amerikanischen Unabhängigkeitskreig (HETRINA). 6 vols. Veroeffentlichungen der Archivschule Marburg, Institut für Archivwissenschaft, no. 10. Marburg, Germany: Institut für Archivwissenschaft, 1972–87. [——] {80,000 entries; approximately 10,000 names}

Knittle, Walter A. *Early Eighteenth Century Palatine Emigration.* Philadelphia: Dorrance & Co.,1937. Reprint. Baltimore: Genealogical Publishing Co., 1965, 1989. [3983-4010] {approximately 12,000} Includes several articles listed separately by Filby.

Krebbs, Friedrich. *Emigrants from the Palatinate to the American Colonies in the Eighteenth Century.* Norristown, Pa.: Pennsylvania German Society, 1953. [4329]

Schrader-Muggenthaler, Cornelia. *The Baden Emigration Book.* Apollo, Pa: Closson Press, 1992. [----] {7,000}

Simmendinger, Ulrich. *True and Authentic Register of Persons Who in 1709 Journeyed From Germany to America.* St. Johnsville, N.Y.: Enterprise and News, 1934. Reprint. Baltimore: Genealogical Publishing Co., 1991. [8480] {500} Included in Knittle (above).

Germany—Nineteenth Century (also see France)

Auerbach, Inge. *Auswanderer aus Hessen-Kassel 1840–1850.* Vol. 2. Veroeffentlichungen der Archivschule Marburg, Institut für Archivwissenschaft, no. 12. Marburg, Germany: Institut für Archivwissenschaft, 1988. [——] {29,000 entries; approximately 10,000 names}

Diener, Walter. "Die Auswanderung aus dem Amte Gemuenden (Hunsrueck) im 19. Jahrhundert. Nach den Buergermeistereiakten." *Rheinische Vierteljahrsblaetter,* Jahrgang 5 (1935): 190–222. [1612]

_____. "Die Auswanderung aus dem Kreise Simmern (Hunsrueck) im 19. Jahrhundert." *Rheinische Vierteljahrsblaetter,* Jahrgang 8 (1938): 91–148. [1616] {2,000}

Germanic Emigrants Register. 23 microfiche. Diepholz, Germany: Germanic Emigrants Register, 1992. [----] {240,000}

Gruhne, Fritz. *Auswanderlisten des Ehemaligen Herzogtums Braunschweig: ohne Stadt Braunschweig und Landkreis Holzminded 1846–1871.* Quellen und Forschungen zur Braunschweigischen Geschichte, vol. 20. Brunswick, Germany: Braunschweigischer Geschichtsverein, 1971. [2822] {7,305 names}

Guenther, Kurt. "Hessian Emigrants to America." *Germanic Genealogist* no. 14 (1978): 302–06 (part 1, 1832); no. 15 (1978): 374–77 (parts 2 and 3, 1833–34). [2828]

Iwan, Wilhelm. *Die altlutherische Auswanderung um die Mitte des 19. Jahrhunderts.* 2 vols. Ludwigsburg, Germany: Eichhorn Verlag Lothar Kallenburg, for the Johann Hess Institute, Breslau, 1943. [3474 and 8655] {5,000}

Kell, J. H., and Josef Werner. "Die Auswanderunger aus dem Kreise Merzig im 19. Jahrhundert." *Verein für Heimatkunde im Kreise Merzig* 3 Jahrbuch (1934): 9–54. [3788]

Let's go to America! The Path of Emigrants from Eastern Westphalia to the USA. Loehne: Hermann Brackmann KG, 1985. [4610.10]

Mergen, Josef, comp. *Amerika-Auswanderung aus dem Regierungsbezerk Trier im 19ten Jahrhundert.* 5 vols. Typescript. Salt Lake City: Genealogical Society, 1958. [5441-5] {11,952}

Mergen, Josef. *Die Auswanderung aus den ehemals preussischen Teilen des Saarlandes im 19ten Jahrhundert.* Veroeffentlichungen des Instituts für Landeskunde im Saarland, vol. 28. Saarbrücken, Germany: Instituts für Landeskunde im Saarland, 1987. [——] {4,800 families}

Moersdorf, Robert. *Die Auswanderung aus dem Birkenfelder Land.* Bonn, Germany: Ludwig Roehrscheid Verlag, 1939. [5728] {3,200}. Approximately two hundred emigrants came between 1697 and 1815.

Mueller, Friedrich. "Westfaelische Auswanderer im 19. Jahrhundert Auswanderung aus dem Regierungsbezirk Minden, Part 1: 1816–1900 (Erlaubte Auswanderung)." *Beitraege zur westfaelischen Familienforschung* 38–39 (1980–81): 3–711. [5860] {9,642}

_____. "Westfaelische Auswanderer im 19. Jahrhundert Auswanderung aus dem Regierungsbezirk Muenster, Part 1. 1803–1850." *Beitraege zur westfaelischen Familienforschung* 22–24 (1964–66): 7–484. [5861] {6,453}

Die Pommerschen Leute. 1982–. Edited and compiled by Myron and Norma Gruenwald, 1260 Westhaven Drive, Oshkosh, WI 54904. [6799] {thousands} A periodical devoted to Pommeranian immigration

Schenk, Trudy, and Ruth Froelke. *The Wuerttemberg Emigration Index.* 7 vols. Salt Lake City: Ancestry, 1986–. [8057.4+] {100,000 entries}

Smith, Clifford Neal. *Cumulative Surname Index and Soundex to Monographs 1 through 12 of the German-American Genealogical Research Series.* German-American Genealogical Research Monograph, 13. McNeal, Ariz.: Westland Publications, 1983. [8565] {approximately 8,000 surnames}

Smith, Clifford Neal. *Emigrants from France (Haut-Rhin Departement) to America, Part 1: 1837–1844.* McNeal, Ariz.: Westland Publications, 1986. [8588] {800}

_____. *German Revolutionists of 1848: Among Whom Many Immigrants to America.* German-American Genealogical Research Monograph, 21. 4 parts. McNeal, Ariz.: Westland Publications, 1985. [8625] {3,650}

_____. *From Bremen to America in 1850: Fourteen Rare Emigrant Ship Lists.* German-American Genealogical Research Monograph, 22. McNeal, Ariz.: Westland Publications, 1987. [8608.15] {2,450}

_____. *Nineteenth-Century Emigration from the Siegkreis, Nordrhein-Westfalen, Germany, Mainly to the United States.* German-American Genealogical Research Monograph, 10. McNeal, Ariz: Westland Publications, 1980. [8653] {800}

_____. *Nineteenth-Century Emigration of "Old Lutherans" from Eastern Germany (Mainly Pomerania and Lower Silesia) to Australia, Canada, and the United States.* German-American Genealogical Research Monograph, 7. McNeal, Ariz: Westland Publications, 1980. [8655] {5,000}

_____, and Anna Piszczan-Czaja Smith. *American Genealogical Resources in German Archives (AGRIGA): A Handbook.* Munich, Germany: Verlag Dokumentation, 1977. [8697] {3,000}

_____. *Reconstructed Passenger Lists for 1850: Hamburg to Australia, Brazil, Canada, Chile, and the United States.* 4 vols. McNeal, Ariz.: Westland Publications, 1980. Based on Hamburg emigration lists.

Stumpp, Karl. *The Emigration from Germany to Russia in the Years 1763 to 1862.* Lincoln, Nebr.: American Historical Society of Germans from Russia, 1978. [——] {22,000 families}

Struck, Wolf-Heino. *Die Auswanderung aus dem Herzogtum Nassau (1806–1866): Ein Kapitel der modernen politischen und sozialen Entwicklung.* Geschichtliche Landeskunde, Veroeffentlichungen des Instituts für Geschichtliche Landeskinde and der Universitaet Mainz, vol. 4. Weisbaden, Germany: Franz Steiner Verlag, 1966. [9061] {4,000 names}

Thomas, Karl. *Die waldeckische Auswanderung zwischen 1829 und 1872*. 2 vols. Koeln, Germany: M. Thomas, 1983. [9159.15] {7,609 names}

Van Kempen, Wilhelm. "Uebersee-Auswanderer aus dem Raume Goettingen 1847–1876." *Norddeutsche Familienkunde* 9–10. Jahrg. (1960–61): 274–88 [9356] {800}

Verdenhalven, Fritz. *Die Auswanderer aus dem Fuerstentum Lippe (bis 1877)*. Sonderveroeffentlichungen des Naturwissenschaftlichen und Historischen Vereins für das Land Lippe, vol. 30. Detmold, Germany: Naturwissenschaftlicher und Historischer Verein für das Land Lippe, 1980. [9417] {10,000 names}

Ireland

Adams, Raymond D. *An Alphabetical Index to Ulster Emigration to Philadelphia, 1803–1850*. Baltimore: Clearfield Co., 1992. [53.26*] {3,200}

Hackett, J. Dominick, and Charles M. Early. *Passenger Lists from Ireland*. Baltimore: Genealogical Publishing Co., 1981. [2859.11] {5,100} Excerpted from *The Journal of the American Irish Historical Society*.

McDonnell, Frances. *Emigrants from Ireland to America: 1735–1743*. Baltimore: Genealogical Publishing Co., 1992. [4971*] {2,000; index has approximately 1,500}

Mitchell, Brian. *Irish Emigration Lists, 1833–1839: Lists of Emigrants Extracted from the Ordnance Survey Memoirs for Counties Londonderry and Antrim*. Baltimore: Genealogical Publishing Co., 1989. [----] {3,000}

_____. *Irish Passenger Lists, 1803–1806: Lists of Passengers Sailing from Ireland to America, Extracted from the Hardwicke Papers*. Baltimore: Genealogical Publishing Co., 1995. [----] {4,500}

_____. *Irish Passenger Lists, 1847–1871: Lists of Passengers Sailing from Londonderry to America on Ships of the J. & J. Cooke Line and the McCorkell Line*. Baltimore: Genealogical Publishing Co., 1988. [----] {27,495}

Italy

Bolognani, Bonifacio. *A Courageous People from the Dolomites: The Immigrants from Trentino on U.S.A. Trails*. Trento, Italy: TEMI, 1981. [——] {3,800}

Lichtenstein

Jansen, Norbert. *Nach Amerika: Geschichte der liechtensteinischen Auswanderung nach den Vereinigten Staaten von Amerika*. Vaduz, Lichtenstein: Verlag des Historichen Vereins für das Fuerstentum Liechtenstein, 1976. [3495] {700}

Luxembourg

Gonner, Nicholas. *Luxembourgers in the New World*. 2 vols. Esch-sur-Alzette, Luxembourg: Editions-Reliures Schortgen, 1987. [2699.1-.2] {50,000} Translation of a German-language edition published in Dubuque, Iowa, 1889.

Owen, Robert Edward. "Lists of Luxembourgers." *Luxembourg Society of Wisconsin Newsletter*, 1982– (various issues). [6428]

Netherlands (Dutch)

Swierenga, Robert P. *Dutch Emigrants to the United States, South Africa, South America, and Southeast Asia, 1835–1880: An Alphabetical Listing by Household Heads and Independent Persons*. Wilmington, Del.: Scholarly Resources, 1983. [9081] {21,800 names}

Norway

Naeseth, Gerhard. *Norwegian Immigrants to the United States: A Biographical Directory, 1825–1850*. Madison, Wis., 1993. [----] {4,000}

Ulvestad, Martin. *Nordmaendeme in Amerika deres historie og rekord* (Norwegians in America: their history and record). Minneapolis: History Book Company's Forlag, 1907. [----]

Scotland

Cameron, Viola R. *Emigrants from Scotland to America, 1774–1775: Copied from a Loose Bundle of Treasury Papers in the Public Record Office, London, England*. 1930. Reprint. Baltimore: Genealogical Publishing Co., 1990. [1088] {2,000}

Dobson, David. *Directory of Scottish Settlers in North America, 1625–1825*. 7 vols. Baltimore: Genealogical Publishing Co., 1984–86, 1993. [1640.1-.6] {14,600+}

_____. *Directory of Scots Banished to the American Plantations, 1650–1775*. Baltimore: Genealogical Publishing Co., 1984. [1639] {3,000}

_____. *The Original Scots Colonists of Early America, 1612–1783*. Baltimore: Genealogical Publishing Co., 1989. [----] {7,000}

_____. *Scottish-American Court Records, 1733–1783*. Baltimore: Genealogical Publishing Co., 1991. [----]

_____. *Scottish-American Heirs, 1683–1883*. Baltimore: Genealogical Publishing Co., 1990. [----] {2,650}

_____. *Scottish-American Wills, 1650–1900*. Baltimore: Genealogical Publishing Co., 1991. [----] {2,000}

Lawson, Bill. *A Register of Emigrant Families from the Western Isles of Scotland to the Eastern Townships of Quebec, Canada*. Eaton Corner, Quebec, Canada: Compton County Historical Museum Society, 1988. [4537.3*]

Whyte, Donald. *A Dictionary of Scottish Emigrants to the USA*. 2 vols. Baltimore: Magna Carta Book Co., 1972, 1986. Reprint. Baltimore: Genealogical Publishing Co., 1992. [9760-9761] {7,470}

Sweden and Finland

Louhi, Evert Alexander. *The Delaware Finns or The First Permanent Settlements in Pennsylvania, Delaware, West New Jersey and Eastern Part of Maryland*. New York: Humanity Press, 1925. [4870]

Switzerland

Faust, Albert Bernhardt, and Gaius Marcus Brumbaugh. *Lists of Swiss Emigrants in the Eighteenth Century to the American Colonies*. 2 vols. Washington, D.C.: National Genealogical Society, 1920–25. Reprint. Baltimore: Genealogical Publishing Co., 1976. [1952, 1960] {5,000}

Macco, Hermann Friedrich, comp. *Swiss Emigrants to the Palatinate and to America 1650–1800, and Huguenots in the Palatinate and Germany*. 6 vols. Typescript. Salt Lake City: Genealogical Society of The Church of Jesus Christ of Latter-day Saints, 1954. [4916] {20,000}

Schrader-Muggenthaler, Cornelia. *The Swiss Emigration Book*. Vol. 1. Apollo, Pa.: Closson Press, 1993. [----] {7,000}

Steinach, Adelrich. *Swiss Colonists in 19th Century America*. 1889. Reprint with a new forward, introduction, and indexes. Rockport, Maine: Picton Press, 1995. [----] {9,000} Biographical sketches.

Wales

Glenn, Thomas Allen. *Welsh Founders of Pennsylvania.* 1911–13. Reprint. Baltimore: Genealogical Publishing Co., 1970. [----] {3,000}

U.S. Immigration Reference Books

(not including lists of passengers or immigrants)

Handbooks and Encyclopedias

Allen, James Paul, and Eugene James Turner. *We the People: An Atlas of America's Ethnic Diversity.* New York: Macmillan Publishing Co., 1988.

Makers of America. 10 vols. Edited by Wayne Moquin. Encyclopædia Britannica, 1971.

Miller, Wayne Charles. *A Handbook of American Minorities.* New York: New York University Press, 1976.

Smith, Clifford Neal, and Anna Piszczan-Czaja Smith. *Encyclopedia of German-American Genealogical Research.* New York: R. R. Bowker, 1976. Has a bibliography of published emigration lists (arranged by locality). Slightly out of date.

Thernstrom, Stephan, ed. *Harvard Encyclopedia of American Ethnic Groups.* Cambridge, Mass.: Harvard University Press, 1980.

Bibliographies

Brye, David L., ed. *European Immigration and Ethnicity in the United States and Canada: A Historical Bibliography.* Santa Barbara, Calif.: ABC Clio, 1983.

Buenker, John D., et al. *Immigration and Ethnicity: A Guide to Information Sources.* Detroit: Gale Research Co., 1977. A bibliography of 1,468 books and articles.

Cordasco, Francesco, ed. *A Bibliography of American Immigration History.* Fairfield, N.J.: Augustus M. Kelly Publishers, 1978.

_____, ed. *The Immigrant Woman in North America: An Annotated Bibliography of Selected References.* Metuchen, N.J.: Scarecrow, 1985.

_____, ed. *The New American Immigration: Evolving Patterns of Legal and Illegal Emigration, a Bibliography of Selected References.* New York: Garland, 1987.

_____, and David N. Alloway, eds. *American Ethnic Groups: The European Heritage, a Bibliography of Doctoral Dissertations Completed at American Universities.* Metuchen, N.J.: Scarecrow, 1981.

Filby, P. William. *Passenger and Immigration Lists Bibliography, 1538–1900.* 2nd ed. Detroit: Gale Research, 1988. Completely describes more than 2,500 published sources of immigration, emigration, and naturalization lists.

Hoglund, A. William. *Immigrants and Their Children in the United States: A Bibliography of Doctoral Dissertations, 1885–1982.* New York: Garland, 1986.

Immigrant Arrivals: A Short Guide to Published Sources. Reference Guides Series, no. 6. Washington, D.C.: Library of Congress, n.d.

Lancour, Harold, comp. *A Bibliography of Ship Passenger Lists, 1538–1825, Being a Guide to Published Lists of Early Immigrants to North America.* 3rd ed. Rev. and enl. by Richard J. Wolfe. New York: New York Public Library, 1963. This work has been incorporated into P. William Filby's *Passenger and Immigration Lists Bibliography, 1538–1900.*

Mangalam, J. J. *Human Migration: A Guide to Migration Literature in English, 1955–1962.* Lexington: University of Kentucky Press, 1968.

Miller, Olga K. *Migration, Emigration, Immigration: Principally to the United States and in the United States.* 2 vols. Logan, Utah: Everton Publishers, 1974, 1981. A bibliography of sources arranged by state and country; includes background information.

Miller, Wayne. *A Comprehensive Bibliography for the Study of American Minorities.* New York: New York University Press, 1976.

National Archives Trust Fund Board. *Immigrant and Passenger Arrivals: A Select Catalog of National Archives Publications.* Rev. ed. Washington, D.C.: National Archives Trust Fund Board, 1991.

Recent Immigration to the United States: The Literature of the Social Sciences. Washington, D.C.: Smithsonian Institution Press, 1976.

United Nations, Department of Economic and Social Affairs. *Analytical Bibliography of International Migration Statistics, Selected Countries, 1925–1950.* Population Studies no. 24. New York: United Nations, 1955.

Guides to Literature and Documents

Auerbach, Frank L. *Immigration Laws of the United States.* Indianapolis: Bobbs-Merrill, 1961.

Bolino, August C. *The Ellis Island Source Book.* Washington, D.C.: Kensington Historical Press, 1985. Has uneven coverage.

Colletta, John P. *They Came in Ships: A Guide to Finding Your Immigrant Ancestor's Arrival Record.* 2nd ed., rev. and enl. Salt Lake City: Ancestry, 1993.

Franklin, Frank G. *The Legislative History of Naturalization in the Untied States From the Revolutionary War to 1861.* Reprint. New York, 1969.

Guide to Genealogical Research in the National Archives. Rev. ed. Washington, D.C.: National Archives and Records Administration, 1985.

Jensen, Larry O. *A Genealogical Handbook of German Research.* Rev. ed. Pleasant Grove, Utah: the author, 1978.

Law, Hugh T. *How to Trace Your Ancestors to Europe.* Salt Lake City: Cottonwood Books, 1987.

Lawson, James. *The Emigrant Scots: An Inventory of Extant Ships' Manifests (Passenger Lists) in Canadian Archives for Ships Travelling from Scotland to Canada before 1900.* Aberdeen, Scotland: Aberdeen & North-East Scotland Family History Society, 1990.

Meyerink, Kory L., and Loretto Dennis Szucs. "Immigration: Finding Immigrant Origins." In *The Source: A Guidebook of American Genealogy.* Edited by Loretto Dennis Szucs and Sandra Hargreaves Luebking. Salt Lake City: Ancestry, 1997.

Miller, Michael M. *Researching the Germans from Russia: Annotated Bibliography of the Germans from Russia Heritage Collection.* N.p., 1987.

Moody, Suzanna, and Joel Wurl, eds. *The Immigration History Research Center: A Guide to Collections.* Westport, Conn.: Greenwood Press, 1991.

Neagles, James C., and Lila Lee Neagles. *Locating Your Immigrant Ancestor*. 2nd ed. Logan, Utah: Everton Publishers, 1986. An inventory of naturalization records at many county and Federal courts; lists the years that declarations and petitions are available.

Newman, John J. *American Naturalization Processes and Procedures, 1790–1985*. Indianapolis: Indianapolis Historical Society, 1985. An excellent overview.

Smith, Clifford Neal, and Anna Piszczan-Czaja Smith. *American Genealogical Resources in German Archives (AGRIGA): A Handbook*. München, Germany: Verlag Dokumentation, 1977.

Smith, Jessie C., ed. *Ethnic Genealogy: A Research Guide*. Westport, Conn.: Greenwood Press, 1983.

Szucs, Loretto Dennis. *They Became Americans: Finding Naturalization Records and Ethnic Origins*. Salt Lake City: Ancestry, 1998.

_____, and Sandra Hargreaves Luebking. *The Archives: A Guide to the National Archives Field Branches*. Salt Lake City: Ancestry, 1988.

Tepper, Michael. *American Passenger Arrival Records: A Guide to the Records of Immigrants Arriving at American Ports by Sail and Steam*. Baltimore: Genealogical Publishing Co., 1988. An in-depth discussion of colonial and Federal immigration lists.

Wasserman, Paul, and Alice E. Kennington, eds. *Ethnic Information Sources of the United States*. 2nd ed. 2 vols. Detroit: Gale Research Co., 1983.

Wellauer, Maralyn A. *German Immigration to America in the Nineteenth Century: A Genealogist's Guide*. Milwaukee: Roots International, 1985.

Wolfman, Ira. *Do People Grow on Family Trees?* New York: Workman Publishing, 1991.

Directories

Appel, John J. *Immigrant Historical Societies in the USA*. New York: Arno Press, 1980.

Wynar, Lubomyr R., and Anna T. Wynar. *Encyclopedic Directory of Ethnic Newspapers and Periodicals in the United States*. 2nd. ed. Littleton, Colo.: Libraries Unlimited, 1976.

Wynar, Lubomyr R. *Encyclopedic Directory of Ethnic Organizations in the United States*. Littleton, Colo.: Libraries Unlimited, 1975.

Shapiro, Beth J. *Directory of Ethnic Publishers and Resource Organizations*. Rev. ed. Chicago: American Library Association, 1976.

_____. *Directory of Ethnic Studies Librarians*. Chicago: American Library Association, 1976.

History and Background

Abbot, Edith. *Historical Aspects of the Immigration Problem: Select Documents*. Reprint. New York: Arno Press, 1969.

Adamic, Louis. *From Many Lands*. New York: Harper and Bros., 1940.

Agueros, Jack, et al., eds. *The Immigrant Experience*. New York: Dial Press, 1971.

Altman, Ida, and James Horn, eds. *To Make America: European Emigration in the Early Modern Period*. Berkeley: University of California Press, 1991.

Appel, John J. *The New Immigration*. New York: Pitman Pub., 1971.

Archdeacon, Thomas J. *Becoming American: An Ethnic History*. New York: Free Press, 1983.

Bailyn, Bernard. *Voyagers to the West: A Passage in the Peopling of America on the Eve of the Revolution*. New York: Alfred A. Knopf, 1986.

Baird, Charles W. *Huguenot Emigration to America*. 2 vols. 1885. Reprint (2 vols. in 1). Baltimore: Genealogical Publishing Co., 1991.

Barton, Josef J. *Peasants and Strangers*. Cambridge: Harvard University Press, 1975.

Benton, Barbara. *Ellis Island: A Pictorial History*. New York: Facts on File, 1985.

Bernard, Richard. *The Melting Pot and the Altar*. Minneapolis: University of Minnesota Press, 1980.

Bittinger, Lucy Forney. *The Germans in Colonial Times*. Reprint. 1901. Bowie, Md.: Heritage Books, 1990.

Bodnar, John. *The Transplanted: A History of Immigrants in Urban America*. Bloomington: Indiana University Press, 1985.

Bromwell, William J. *History of Immigration to the United States, exhibiting the number, sex, age, occupation, and country of birth, of passengers arriving in the United States by sea from foreign countries, from September 30, 1819 to December 31, 1855*. New York: Redfield, 1856. Reprint. New York: Arno Press and A. M. Kelley, 1969.

Cobb, Sanford H. *The Story of the Palatines*. Reprint. 1897. Bowie, Md.: Heritage Books, 1992.

Coldham, Peter W. *Emigrants in Chains: A Social History of Forced Emigration to the Americas of Felons, Destitute Children, Political and Religious Non-conformists, Vagabonds, Beggars and other Undesirables, 1607–1776*. Baltimore: Genealogical Publishing Co., 1992.

Coleman, Terry. *Going to America*. New York, Pantheon Books, 1972.

Commager, Henry Steele, ed. *Immigration and American History*. Minneapolis: University of Minnesota Press, 1961.

Cordasco, Francesco, ed. *Dictionary of American Immigration History*. Metuchen, N.J.: Scarecrow Press, 1990.

Cressy, David. *Coming Over: Migration and Communication Between England and New England in the Seventeenth Century*. New York: Cambridge University Press, 1987.

Daniels, Roger. *Coming to America: A History of Immigration and Ethnicity in American Life*. New York: Harper Collins, 1990. (FHL 973 W2ro)

Diffenderffer, Frank R. *The German Immigration Into Pennsylvania Through the Port of Philadelphia from 1700 to 1775, and the Redemptioners*. 1900. Reprint. Baltimore: Genealogical Publishing Co., 1988. Mostly background history; five pages have lists.

Douglas, David, and Charles Douglas. *North Atlantic Seaway*. Rev. ed. 4 vols. Vancouver, British Columbia, Canada, 1975. History of the passenger services between the Old World and the New.

Erickson, Charlotte, ed. *Emigration from Europe, 1815–1914: Select Documents*. London: Adam and Charles Black, 1976.

Fleming, Thomas J. *The Golden Door*. New York: W. W. Horton, 1970.

Ferenczi, Imre. *International Migrations, Vol. I: Statistics*. New York: National Bureau of Economic Statistics, 1929. Reprint. New York: Arno Press, 1970.

Glazer, Nathan, and Daniel Patrick Moynihan. *Beyond the Melting Pot*. Cambridge, Mass.: Harvard University Press, 1963.

Haller, Charles R. *Across the Atlantic and Beyond: The Migration of German and Swiss Immigrants to America*. Bowie, Md.: Heritage Books, 1993. (FHL 973 W2aa)

Handlin, Oscar, ed. *Immigration as a Factor in American History*. Englewood Cliffs, N.J.: Prentice-Hall, 1959. A collection of multi-author readings.

Handlin, Oscar. *The Uprooted: The Epic Story of the Great Migrations that Made the American People*. New York: Grosset and Dunlap, 1951.

Hansen, Marcus Lee. *The Atlantic Migration, 1607–1860*. Rev. ed. Cambridge, Mass.: Harvard University Press, 1940. Reprint. New York: Harper and Row, 1961.

Harkness, George E. *The Church and the Immigrant*. New York: Doran, 1921.

Heaps, Willard A. *The Story of Ellis Island*. New York: Seabury Press, 1967.

Heaton, Elizabeth Putnam. *Steerage*. New York: L. Heaton, 1919.

History of the Immigration and Naturalization Service. Washington, D.C.: Government Printing Office, 1980.

Holli, Melvin G., and Peter d' A. Jones, eds. *The Ethnic Frontier*. Grand Rapids, Mich.: Eerdmans Pub., 1977.

Hutchinson, Edward P. *Legislative History of American Immigration Policy 1798–1965*. Philadelphia: University of Philadelphia Press, 1981.

Immigration: Dimensions of Ethnicity. Selections from the Harvard Encyclopedia of Ethnic Groups. Cambridge, Mass.: Belknap Press of Harvard University Press, 1980.

Jones, Maldwyn Allen. *Destination America*. New York: Holt, Rinehart and Winston, 1976.

_____. *American Immigration*, 2nd ed. Chicago: University of Chicago Press, 1992.

Kettner, James H. *The Development of American Citizenship, 1607–1870*. Chapel Hill: University of North Carolina Press, 1978. (FHL 973 P4k)

Kraus, Michael. *Immigration: The American Mosaic*. Princeton, N.J.: D. Van Nostrand Co., 1966. (FHL 973 W2ks)

Kraut, Alan. *The Huddled Masses: The Immigrant in American Society, 1880–1921*. Arlington Heights, Ill.: Harlan Davidson, 1982. Discusses how immigrant groups adjusted to American society.

Meinig, D. W. *The Shaping of America: A Geographical Perspective on 500 Years of History, Vol. 1: Atlantic America, 1492–1800*. New Haven, Conn.: Yale University Press, 1986. (FHL 973 E3me)

Mims, Edwin. *American History and Immigration*. Bronxville, N.Y.: Sarah Lawrence College, 1950.

Novotny, Ann. *Strangers at the Door.* Riverside, Conn.: Chatham Press, 1971. Describes the immigration process at New York's Castle Garden and Ellis Island.

Nugent, Walter. *Crossings: The Great Transatlantic Migrations, 1870–1914*. Bloomington: Indiana University Press, 1992. (FHL 973 W2nu)

Pitkin, Thomas M. *Keepers of the Gate: A History of Ellis Island*. New York: New York University Press, 1975. (FHL 973 W2pt)

Reimers, David M. *The Immigrant Experience*. New York: Chelsea House Publishers, 1989.

Scott, Franklin D. *The Peopling of America: Perspectives on Immigration*. Washington, D.C.: American Historical Society Association, 1972.

Sowell, Thomas. *Ethnic America: A History*. New York: Basic Books, 1981.

Szucs, Loretto Dennis. *Ellis Island: Gateway to America*. Salt Lake City: Ancestry, 1986.

Taylor, Philip A. *The Distant Magnet: European Emigration to the U.S.A*. London: Eyre and Spottiswoode, 1971. (FHL 973 W2t)

Tift, Wilton. *Ellis Island*. Chicago: Contemporary Books, 1990.

Vecoli, Rudolph J., and Suzanne M. Sinke, eds. *A Century of European Migrations, 1830–1930*. Urbana, Ill.: University of Chicago Press, 1991.

Ward, David. *Cities and Immigrants: A Geography of Change in Nineteenth Century America*. New York: Oxford University Press, 1971.

Wittke, Carl F. *We Who Built America: The Saga of the Immigration*. Cleveland: Western Reserve University Press, 1964.

Ships

Anuta, Michael J. *Ships of Our Ancestors*. Menominee, Mich.: Ships of Our Ancestors, 1983. Contains pictures of most passenger steamships.

Bangerter, Lawrence B. *The Compass: A Concise and Factual Compilation of All Vessels and Sources Listed, with Reference Made of All of Their Voyages and Some Dates of Registration*. 2 vols. Logan, Utah: Everton Publishers, 1983–90.

Cutler, Carl C. *Queens of the Western Ocean: The Story of America's Mail and Passenger Sailing Lines*. Annapolis, Md.: United States Naval Institute, 1961.

Dunn, Laurence. *Famous Liners of the Past, Belfast Built*. London: A. Coles, 1964. Descriptions arranged by steamship line. Many of the ships included were built in the twentieth century.

Gibbs, Charles R. V. *British Passenger Lines of the Five Oceans, a Record of the British Passenger Lines and Their Liners from 1838 to the Present Day*. London: Putnam, 1963.

_____. *Passenger Liners of the Western Ocean, a Record of the North Atlantic Steam and Motor Passenger Vessels from 1838 to the Present Day*. 2nd ed., rev. London: Staples Press, 1957.

Greenhill, Basil. *The Great Migration: Crossing the Atlantic under Sail*. London: National Maritime Museum, H.M. Stationery Office, 1968. Includes sketches of shipboard life reproduced from the *Illustrated London News*.

Guillet, Edwin C. *The Great Migration: The Atlantic Crossing by Sailing Ship Since 1770*. Rev. ed. Toronto: University of Toronto Press, 1963. An account of what the voyage was like.

Kludas, Arnold. *Great Passenger Ships of the World*. 6 vols. Translated from a German edition by Charles Hodges. Cambridge, England: Patrick Stephens, 1975. Information about and photographs of all major passenger ships, 1858 to 1975.

Lubbock, Basil. *The Western Ocean Packets*. New York: Dover, 1988.

Maxtone-Graham, John. *The Only Way to Cross.* New York: Macmillan Co., 1972. Describes steamship construction.

Morton Allan Directory of European Steamship Arrivals: For the Years 1890 to 1930 at the Port of New York and for the Years 1904 to 1926 at the Ports of New York, Philadelphia, Boston, and Baltimore. 1931. Reprint. Genealogical Publishing Co., 1980, 1987. Lists the names of vessels and dates of arrival by year and by steamship line.

Smith, Eugene W. *Passenger Ships of the World Past and Present*. Boston: George H. Dean Co., 1978. Discusses steamships and the shipping companies which operated them.

Steuart, Bradley W., ed. *Passenger Ships Arriving in New York Harbor.* Vol. 1, *1820–1850.* Bountiful, Utah: Precision Indexing, 1991. Extracted from National Archives microfilm M1066, *Registers of Vessels Arriving at the Port of New York*. . . .

Tut, Warren. *Atlantic conquest; the ships and the men of the North Atlantic passenger services, 1816–1961*. London: Cassell, 1962.

Monograph Series

Ethnic Chronology Series. 32 vols. Dobbs Ferry, N.Y.: Oceana Publications, 1971–77, 1979, 1980.

The American Immigration Collection. Series 1. 42 vols. New York: Arno Press and the *New York Times,* 1969.

The American Immigration Collection. Series 2. 15 vols. New York: Arno Press and the *New York Times,* 1970.

Periodicals

I and N Reporter. 1943–. Published quarterly by the U.S. Immigration and Naturalization Service, Superintendent of Documents, Washington, DC 20402.

Immigration History Newsletter. 1969–. Published semiannually by the Immigration History Society, Minnesota Historical Society, 690 Cedar Street, St. Paul, MN 55101.

International Migration Review. 1973–. Published quarterly by the Center for Migration Studies, 209 Flagg Place, Staten Island, NY 10304.

Migration World. 1973–. Published bimonthly by the Center for Migration Studies, 209 Flagg Place, Staten Island, NY 10304.

New Dimensions. 1979–. Published semiannually by the Balch Institute for Ethnic Studies, 18 South Seventh Street, Philadelphia, PA 19106.

Population Index. 1935–. Princeton, N.J.: Princeton University, Office of Population Research.

DOCUMENTARY COLLECTIONS OVERVIEW

Key Concepts in This Chapter

- Documentary collections are various records with a common theme, published under a standard or common name.
- Documentary collections may focus on the records of a governmental unit, a group, or an individual.
- Virtually any kind of original record may appear in a published collection.
- Every-name indexes make these collections especially useful.
- Most collections are published in many volumes over many years.
- Collections exist for all of the thirteen original states and most other early states.
- *Documentary histories* often mix historical commentary with published records.
- *Annals* arrange history and documents in chronological order.
- *Personal papers* of notable Americans include hundreds of names of "common" persons.
- Academic and other research libraries are the best places to find documentary collections.

Key Sources in This Chapter

- *The Territorial Papers of the United States*
- *Papers of the Continental Congress*
- *American State Papers*
- *American Archives*
- *Pennsylvania Archives*
- *New Jersey Archives*
- *New York Historical Society Collections*
- *Colonial Records of the State of Georgia*
- *Detailed Reports on the Salzburger Emigrants Who Settled in America*
- *The Papers of Thomas Jefferson*

15

DOCUMENTARY COLLECTIONS

Kory L. Meyerink[1]

As family historians search records, we find ourselves drawn into courthouses, archives, and libraries, where we can examine original documents item by item and event by event. To find sales of property we look for deeds; to learn about inheritance and estates we delve into wills. Researchers tend to look for specific sources, in original form or published abstracts, such as the deeds of Baltimore County, Maryland, or Bath County, Virginia, marriage records. In most cases, this direct approach is proper and very productive. Often overlooked, however, are many records available to us in printed form that are not so easily identifiable but which are vital for historical and genealogical research. These are *documentary collections*—various records gathered together at central archives or libraries and published under a standard or common name. Documentary collections include such sources as the *Pennsylvania Archives,* Wisconsin Historical Society Publications, and *Papers of the Continental Congress.* These collections include diaries and journals, land grants, militia lists, correspondence, tax lists, marriages, pension files, and numerous other records.

DEFINITIONS

Documentary collections constitute those publications which pertain either to the original records of an archive or library, or to a collection of various sources under a single heading or title. Technically speaking, all collections of original records in published form can be considered documentary collections, but here the term *documentary collections* is restricted to groups of records which cannot be readily described by either their location or a specific record type. A publication titled *The Deeds of Franklin County, Georgia,* is well defined by its title, whereas one might not even think to search the *Collections of the Illinois State Historical Library* for information on Virginia soldiers in the American Revolution.

The concept of gathering significant documents and publishing them has existed for more than two hundred years. Ebenezer Hazard, a New York bookseller (and later U.S. postmaster), spent more than twenty years gathering and copying records relating to the early history of the United States. His two volumes, published in 1792 and 1794, began the process of providing the historian, in Thomas Jefferson's words, with "materials which he would otherwise acquire with great difficulty and perhaps not at all" (Publishing 1994, 1).

Documentary collections exist in every state where there is a major archive, historical society, or library which endeavors to publish a portion of its holdings to make information available for scholarly research, as well as to make people aware of its collections. Documentary collections, as printed sources, are those collections of records that have been deemed of sufficient value to edit and publish, as a whole, for historians and other scholarly researchers to study and evaluate in their ongoing research.

Most such publications are not prepared with genealogists in mind, but genealogists are instant beneficiaries of these publications. Every such collection has a common theme, but *not* in that it is comprised entirely of the same *type* of record; rather, each collection is comprised of records that somehow pertain to each other, usually because they were created by the same government, group, or individual. Defining this subject can be difficult. One could argue that all published forms of original records—court records, diaries and journals, letters, official papers, newspapers, etc.—are documentary collections. A better definition, and one that is more applicable to documentary collections as genealogical sources, is that published documentary collections pertain to collections of records that are best known by the name of their creator, rather than as record types, such as *The Papers of Booker T. Washington, The Records of the Moravians in North Carolina,* or the *Territorial Papers of the United States.*

The concept of the collection is important in understanding published documentary collections. Collections that have been edited and published based on the type of record they contain more often are categorized according to that particular topic (such as probate records or land deeds) rather than as documentary collections. A documentary collection, on the other hand, may contain several important record types. For instance, the three volumes of *Pennsylvania German Pioneers,* by Strassburger and Hinke, which is one of the standard sources for Pennsylvania German research, comprise vols. 42, 43, and 44 of the continuing series known as the Publications of the Pennsylvania German Society. This series is, in part, a documentary collection.

Documentary collections' value to genealogists should, upon reflection, be apparent. Because such collections bring together many records, often from an early time period in a frontier area, they make research in such areas much easier. The presence of every-name indexes in many volumes speeds research and allows users to find names and research clues they would never find if they were searching the actual documents upon which the collection is based. The very nature of printing and publishing these documents preserves the information in them and provides much greater access to the information in the records. Very often the records will not have even been microfilmed, meaning that the actual documents are available only in one archive, often at a great distance from the researcher. Some documentary collections were published more than a hundred years ago and, in some cases, the documents upon which they were based are no longer extant *or* on microfilm. In these cases, the published documentary collection represents the only access to the information. A 1992 study on the use of historical sources in America clearly defined the value of such publications:

> What is it that researchers gain from edited documents? According to the survey, the most valuable elements of the editorial contribution itself are the index, accurate transcriptions of text, the compilation of documents from numerous repositories, and identification of persons and events (Gordon, 83).

Despite the great value of these works, they are, by and large, overlooked or ignored by genealogists; in fact, most family researchers are not aware that works of this kind exist. Those who know anything about such collections are usually aware of prominent collections, such as the published *Pennsylvania Archives* (discussed below under "State and Colonial Collections), not realizing that similar collections exist for most eastern states and that other collections exist for other groups of documents. The purpose of this chapter, then, is to introduce the concept and existence of documentary collections to the family historian in hopes that family historians can then find the best collections for their own research. This chapter can only be an overview of such sources; there is no comprehensive bibliography of documentary collections (such as there is for published immigration sources or county histories, as noted in chapters 14 and 17), nor is there one or more published library catalogs that easily identify such collections (such as the various family history catalogs identified in chapter 16). Indeed, there is not yet even a clear consensus as to what a documentary collection is. Different terms are used by different researchers, and many include microfilm copies of the original documents in their lists of "documentary collections." This chapter will focus on collections, as described above, that have generally been published as series, although a few examples of single-volume collections will be noted. After the different kinds of documentary collections are described, with key examples and some illustrations, the section "Locating Documentary Collections" will offer suggestions and sources for learning about these valuable resources.

Document Editors

Those who prepare documentary collections for publication are known as *document editors.* They have evolved into a select group in the community of document publishers. A principle purpose of document editing is to evaluate sources for other researchers as the records are published and made available to the public. This process has both positive and negative aspects. Scholarly editing introduces new information to researchers in a way that informs and defines previously "buried" information. On the other hand, the bias and prejudice of a particular editor can "slant" a document. Another drawback of the process is that, whenever an original document is edited and printed, spelling and phrasing errors that can change the whole nature of a document may be introduced. A name like James may be misread as Francis, for example; dates can be misconstrued; or words omitted which could effect the meaning of a document. It is the goal of document editors to avoid such errors, but they inevitably occur. Today's document editors are carefully trained and generally do excellent work; however, genealogists often use documentary collections published a century or more ago, when careful attention was not given to the transcribing of original records into published format.

Content

Within any documentary collection, researchers are likely to find a wide variety of materials, including (but not limited to) correspondence, land claims, military documents, probate records, tax lists, speeches, court orders, executive decrees, legislative actions, and many more. In short, any kind of original document (and some compiled ones) may appear in a documentary collection. This chapter will define many of these collections in general, and some that contain significant genealogical material specifically. Probably the most common records found in documentary collections are, first, the papers of prominent persons and, second, the acts of colonial and early state legislatures. While these two sources are not high among the preferences of most family researchers, the presence of indexes to such publications, as well as the occasional "standard" genealogical sources (tax lists, wills, militia lists, etc.), should encourage all serious researchers to locate and use these collections.

Because documentary collections' contents vary, family historians will find that some collections have greater value for their research than others. Collections such as those for New York or New Jersey, which publish probate abstracts, among other items, or the *Pennsylvania Archives,* with its tax and assessment lists and muster rolls, should be on every genealogist's list of sources to search. Other collections that primarily publish the papers of early state or colonial leaders or the legislature will only be used by those doing detailed, in-depth research in those areas. Most researchers will be surprised, however, at the number of names of early citizens to be found in the less-used governmental records. Of course, an editor's purpose as he or she prepares a documentary collection is to help all researchers learn everything possible about the subject, including all of the fascinating people mentioned in the documents.

While documentary collections have been described here as sets of transcribed documents, such transcriptions are not necessarily the only materials in a published series, and some collections discussed in this chapter are not *strictly* documentary collections. Rather, some collections include compiled histories and other material not derived from transcribed documents. Generally such material is found in publications with titles such as Collections of the . . . Historical Society, in which some volumes are indeed collections of transcribed documents and others are historians' accounts of significant events in local history. Sometimes the number of true "documentary collection" volumes in such a series is minimal, but because of the difficulty of finding them, many of these "partial documentary collections" are noted in this discussion or in the chapter bibliography.

Indexes

The presence of indexes in printed collections enhances their value. As with other genealogical sources, there is little consistency in the indexing of documentary collections. Many collections provide every-name indexes to some or all of the collection, while others do not. Sometimes the index is at the end of each volume. Other times it is a separate publication, perhaps published many years later by a different editor and/or publisher. Many documentary collections include several volumes dedicated to one set of related records, such as the papers of an early governor, and then include other records, from other sources, in other volumes. In such cases, the index to the papers of the governor may be part of the final volume transcribing those documents and refer to the preceding three, four, five, or more volumes.

Of course, every-name indexes are not provided with every documentary collection. Some include only a subject index, while a few offer no index at all—simply a table of contents. When using an unindexed collection, review the table of contents closely. Many are quite detailed and, in their description of what records are included, will point the researcher to a specific document on just a few pages. For more guidelines about using indexes in general, see chapter 6, "Published Indexes."

Arrangement and Publication

As with indexes, the arrangements of documentary collections, especially those published many years ago, vary. Some collections consist of several series (usually numbered), each with many volumes. The content of one series may differ radically from another series in the collection. Other times the only difference is a new editor or resumption of a previously ceased (or interrupted) publication program. Sometimes, as was the case with *American Archives* (described below), several series may be planned, but fewer are actually published. In other collections, each volume is simply the next number in the collection and there are no separate series. The Collections of the Massachusetts Historical Society managed to do both in its publication history: the first seventy volumes comprised seven series of ten volumes each; beginning with vol. 71 the series numbering was discontinued. In this case the numbering had been continued consecutively from one series to the next. Usually that is not the case. If a collection was (or is) published in various series, each series is numbered from vol. 1 forward. On occasion, two or more series may be published at the same time, each reflecting a different set of documents in the collection, but usually one series ends before the next begins.

Virtually every documentary collection consists of several unrelated sets of documents. Often all they have in common is the archive that collected them or the organization that published them. In such cases, these different sets appear throughout the published collection and may include their own volume number that is separate and distinct from that of the overall collection or any series they may be part of. For example, the *Records of the Moravians in North Carolina* was published as a series of eleven volumes, each numbered consecutively, as part of the Collections of the North Carolina Historical Commission, yet the volumes were not issued consecutively within the collection; rather, they were issued over many years, from 1922 to 1969, and other volumes of the overall collection were issued in various intervening years.

Most collections include all the records of a similar agency, or of the same person, in consecutive volumes, but some do not. In the *Archives of Maryland,* different groups of records were published non-consecutively, apparently as the volumes were ready for the press. In this collection there are at least eight different sets of documents, with, for example, the *Proceedings of the Provincial Council* scattered through eleven volumes between vol. 3 and vol. 32 (see "State and Colonial Collections," below).

Publication information varies considerably over the many years during which a collection is published. Most collections take at least ten years or more to be published; some may continue for fifty or more years. Naturally the editors change over time, but often the printer, publisher, and even sponsoring society also change. Sometimes the change only reflects a new name for the same agency, as appears to be the case with the Collections of the North Carolina Historical Commission, which is now being published under the direction of the North Carolina Department of Archives and History because the name was changed in the 1950s. Sometimes the collection is known by more than one name. The Archives of the State of New Jersey is more formally called Documents Relating to the Colonial History of the State of New Jersey. Because of the eclectic nature of these collections, some volumes in a set may have more interest for researchers than others, and sometimes those are reprinted one or more times, sometimes by different publishers. In the reprinting they may lose their connection to the collection as a whole.

Volumes were (are) not necessarily issued on a predictable timetable. Documentary collections are time consuming to prepare for publication, and often several volumes are in preparation at the same time. On occasion, several volumes are issued at the same time; or there may be several years between consecutive volumes. Even a series which sounds like a periodical or journal title, such as Collections of the Historical Society of . . ., for which one would assume an annual volume is issued, are not always published regularly. Such is the nature of documentary collections, which should be considered much more as published *series,* not *serials.* (See the introduction to *Printed Sources* for more information on series publication.)

All of these aspects, and others, create difficulties for bibliographers, library catalogers, and, of course, historians trying to find, use, and cite references to documentary collections. Some catalogs treat the collection as one series and have one descriptive entry for the set in their catalog. Others describe and catalog each volume separately insofar as the content allows (for example, a three-volume set on the papers of a revolutionary war officer will receive only one catalog entry that mentions all three volumes).

Kinds of Documentary Collections

As discussed above, documentary collections are best defined by the creator of the collection. The creator is not always the publisher of the collection, however; rather, it is that organization or person who wrote the documents (or the majority of them) in the collection. For the purposes of this chapter, these creators can be divided into four groups. *Government collections* are those sets of documents that represent the records of various states or the Federal government. *Papers of groups* are collections created by (generally) nongovernmental organizations, such as a land company or a religious group. *Regional and local collections* contain records (governmental and private) that deal with a specific locality, and *writings of individuals* are collections that focus on one person, such as the various papers of the U.S. presidents that have been published.

GOVERNMENT COLLECTIONS

Many documentary collections are based on the records created, kept, and/or housed by governmental agencies. They are of particular interest to family historians because government records are the backbone of American genealogy. Most such collections were published at the state level, but some significant ones were published by the Federal government or include records pertaining to the entire United States (not just one state).

Federal Collections

Six genealogically significant documentary collections are based on Federal records. There are, of course, many thousands of volumes of government documents, many of which have genealogical value, such as the *Congressional Record,* which provides an account of all petitions, claims appeals, and proposals that have been made in Congress. These include claims for pensions, compensation for services, petitions for land, and many other records of interest. However, in this chapter we are covering those records of significant early historical importance. Some of the following collections include major portions of the early Federal government records.

Territorial Papers of the United States. Beginning in 1787 and lasting until 1912, the Federal government of the United States has dealt with territorial issues as, one by one, twenty-eight different territories were created and then became states. Numerous documents relating to the federal administration of the territories ended up in various collections in Washington, D.C. Over time, historical agencies proposed that the U.S. government make these records more readily available through publication. In 1925, Congress passed the Ralson Act, which authorized the secretary of state to collect, transcribe, arrange, edit, and publish the various papers relating to the territories. Early funding was sporadic, and its absence sometimes interrupted the selection, arrangement and preparation of the volumes. Eventually funding became more readily available and, beginning in 1934, the Government Printing Office began issuing volumes of *The Territorial Papers of the United States*. Compiled and edited by Clarence Edwin Carter, twenty-eight volumes were issued by 1976. They contain the significant administrative documents for twelve of the oldest territories.

The vast amounts of documents available for the territories necessitated that some selection be exercised in the preparation of the volumes. Since the focus was on Federal administration, papers pertaining to local jurisdictions seldom appear in the collection. Also, only those papers which had been deposited in Washington, D.C., repositories were candidates for publication. Matters relating to Indians were generally omitted as being broader than a single territory. Much of the material consists of correspondence, land applications, decrees, policies, and a variety of other records pertaining to the early settlement of these territories. Papers previously published, such as those in the *American State Papers* (see below), were usually omitted. While much of the material is correspondence between territorial executives and the appropriate Federal departments, Clarence Carter, the editor of the series, describes two classes of papers he believes to be of great value to genealogists: first, the petitions and memorials sent by the inhabitants to congress, and, second, records relating to the public lands. As Carter explains regarding the first class of papers, petitions were sent year after year

> . . . for redress of grievances, or for a change of government. Attached to these petitions are long lists of name of subscribers. . . . These would almost appear to constitute a veritable census (1949, 94).

Although he admits that these names are not an accurate or complete census, Carter believes that nearly every pioneer farmer and townsman signed a petition sometime during his life (figure 15-1). Comparing the names in vol. 16, an Illinois volume, with the names in the published 1810 Federal and 1818 and 1820 state censuses, Carter suggests "that the census takers missed a very great many of the settled inhabitants" (1949, 94).

While many of the public lands papers deal with plans and policies and contain relatively few names, many papers deal with the land claims of individuals. Also not to be overlooked are the many lists of appointments to county and local offices, as well as licenses granted for certain aspects of commerce, such as keeping a tavern or a ferry.

Each volume has a detailed preface describing the history of the territory at the time and the nature of the documents in the volume. The editor also identifies other sources for researchers interested in the time period. The comprehensive indexes at the back of each volume (after the introductory pages on the microfilm copy) provide easy access to the hidden names all family researchers seek.

Papers for each territory are divided into chronological parts, often representing the administrations of the various governors. Each territory is covered in one to five volumes, as shown below.

Vol. 1	General overview, preliminary printing (final edition never published)
Vols. 2–3	The Territory Northwest of the River Ohio, 1787–1803 (Ohio)
Vol. 4	The Territory South of the River Ohio, 1790–96 (Tennessee)
Vols. 5–6	The Territory of Mississippi, 1809–17
Vols. 7–8	The Territory of Indiana, 1800–16
Vol. 9	The Territory of Orleans, 1803–12 (Louisiana)
Vols. 10–12	The Territory of Michigan, 1805–37
Vols. 13–15	The Territory of Louisiana- Missouri, 1803–21 (Missouri)
Vols. 16–17	The Territory of Illinois, 1809–18
Vol. 18	The Territory of Alabama, 1817–19
Vols. 19–21	The Territory of Arkansas, 1819–36
Vols. 22–26	The Territory of Florida, 1821–45
Vols. 27–28	The Territory of Wisconsin, 1836–48

Papers of the Continental Congress. Although the collection known as the *Papers of the Continental Congress* (1774–89) is not a true documentary collection as we have defined them, it deserves mention for three reasons. First, it is a collection of documents providing significant detail of American life for a

remain, for the reasons which are herein expressed, in the situation and under the Government which we now live; and which we believe, to be the most suitable, to our present situation and Circumstances.

And Your Memorialists, as in duty bound will ever pray.—

DETROIT *November* 11th 1822.—

Luc Joliet
Jn Bte [MS. torn]
Jacques Campau
Thomas tranbles
Benoit Chapoton
Jean Baptiste [MS. faded]
Jophe Endres
Louis Allard
Pir rivard
Antoine Renault
Maurisce Morin
sa mar
franssois X tibo
que
Pascasle X Bodevan
Medar Goüin
Joseph Sosier
louis chapotons
Joseph Louis Tramblé
Francois Rivard
Antoine boiyer
Charles Rivard fils
Louis Denoyers
Léon Rivard
François St Aubin
Joseph Forton
J Btis Chandonnai
David Druillard
Noël prunier
Jno R. Williams
Jean Bt Chovin fils
Peter Van Every
Sa
Yacente X Dejardain
marque
Joseph F. Marsac
Rob. Marsac
Louis Desonier
Jacques Marsaque
Charles Chovin
Lambert Chovin
Simon Chovin
François Pitre
Leon Rivard
John Kirby Junr

Renéz Marsaque
Henrie Tramblé
Jean Bt St Aubin
Nicolas Rivard
Gaétan Tramblé
Loui Greffard père
Loui Greffard fils
Lauran Greffard
pierre Greffard père
pierre Greffard fils
ven Gile Champiengne
Pierre Rivard
Léon Pierre [74] Rivard
Louis Charles Rivard
Antoine Bt Rivard
Joseph Campau
Henri Chauton
Jacque Thibeau
Ambroise Tramblé
Léon Ladouseur
Jacque Alard Fils
François Alard
Joseph Robert Jane
Jacque Alard pere
Joseph, Dubé
Mayire Robert Jane
Charles Vernie dit Laduseur
Larant Ladouseur
James Grosbeck
Jean Tramblé
François Grefard
Michel Rivard pere
Jean Bt Rivard
Louis Morin
Dominique Grefard
Pierre Dequindre
J. Baptiste Yaxe
Bap[tis]te Peltier
Conrad Seek
Sa
Pieririe X Larivierere
marque
Peter Lemon
Charles N Delisle
Francis, E, Duret
Martin Dunning

[74] The middle name was inserted in a different hand. The same is true of the two following signatures.

Figure 15-1. A list of petitioners in Detroit, 1822, from vol. 11 of the *Territorial Papers of the United States*.

BROWNLEE, WILLIAM
Brownlee, William. To George Gray. Nov. 10, 1778. 1 p. *M247, r192, i173, v1, p187.*
Unknown. Return of officers in Gist's Regt. July 1780.* 2 p. *M247, r170, i152, v9, p57.*
BROWNLOW, RICHARD
Allegheny Mountains, inhabitants of the country west of the. To Cong. 1784.* 4 p. Copy. *M247, r62, i48, p281.*
BROWNMAN, NATHANIEL
Auditor General. Account of Georgia with the U.S. May 1779. 2 p. Signed by John Gibson. *M247, r146, i136, v3, p317.*
BROWNRIGG, J. S.
Brownrigg, J. S. Newport. To unknown. Nov. 27, 1778. 3 p. Extract. *M247, r72, i59, v2, p135.*
Sullivan, John. Providence. To Gen. Washington. Dec. 20, 1778. 2 p. *M247, r178, i160, p215.*
BROWNRIGS, ---
Sutherland, William. Account, 1772-1778. Undated. 4 p. *M247, r65, i51, v1, p317.*
Sutherland, William. Account with Joseph Cope. May 0-July 20, 1774. 3 p. *M247, r65, i51, v1, p321.*
Noblet, George. Receipt for stockings for Joseph Cope. May 11, 1774. 1 p. *M247, r65, i51, v1, p325.*
BROWNSON, ELI
Washington, George. Phila. To Gov. Chittenden. Jan. 1, 1782. 4 p. Copy attested by Richard Varick, Feb. 10, 1783. *M247, r47, i40, v2, p369.*
BROWNSON, GIDEON
New Hampshire Grants, inhabitants of. New England. To Gov. Wentworth. Oct. 18, 1769. 11 p. *M247, r47, i40, v1, p38.*
Marsh, William, and Samuel Rose. Manchester. To Peter V.B. Livingston. June 28, 1775. 2 p. Copy. *M247, r47, i40, v1, p407.*
New Hampshire Grants, North District Committee. Dorset. Proceedings. July 27, 1775. 2 p. Copy. *M247, r47, i40, v1, p425.*
Hopkins, Wait, and Gideon Brownson. Phila. To Cong. Sept. 10, 1776. 2 p. *M247, r56, i42, v8, p153.*
Warner, Seth. Albany. To J. Hancock. Oct. 4, 1776. 3 p. *M247, r104, i78, v23, p315.*

Figure 15-2. From *Index: The Papers of the Continental Congress 1774-1789.*

period for which research can be difficult. Second, although the collection consists mostly of original documents on microfilm, some of the collection has been printed, notably the *Journals of the Continental Congress*. Third, a comprehensive index to the collection has been published.

The actual papers of the Continental Congress consist of about 50,000 documents totaling almost 200,000 pages—mostly correspondence, committee reports, motions, Congressional journals, account books, and other miscellaneous official documents. Because they are governmental in nature, they deal with military, diplomatic, and economic activities. Many of the names mentioned are of military officers, both of the Continental line and state militias. (Enlisted men are seldom mentioned in these documents.) There are many names in the petitions to Congress which come from all areas of the new country. As the indexer of the papers noted,

> thousands of individuals or groups of individuals petitioned Congress for a wide variety of reasons. For example, there are petitions and memorials from urban residents wanting to locate the U.S. capitol in their town, from frontier settlers wanting protection from the Indians, from merchants interested in the passage of laws on trade and commerce, from government officials asking for salary increases, and from citizens complaining about postal service (Butler 1977, 6).

Petitions came from large groups and from smaller groups and individuals. Approximately fourteen thousand pages titled "Miscellaneous Letters Addressed to Congress" include mention of prisoners of war, foreign diplomats and officers, military officers, and many others. Other papers deal with Indians, Loyalists, and African Americans. The entire collection, including the thirty-four published volumes of the *Journals of the Continental Congress,* is available on 206 rolls of microfilm from the National Archives.

It is the comprehensive index that makes this collection worthwhile for the researcher. Approximately half a million entries in the index attest to the breadth and scope of the collection. Personal names account for about 80 percent of the index entries, the remainder being subjects and place names. Indeed, it is easy to use the index to locate all of the documents that deal with specific places, and from there to read all of the documents or cross-reference the personal names of interest to learn if a relative was noted in the index. Compiled by John P. Butler, *Index: The Papers of the Continental Congress 1774–1789* (Washington D.C.: National Archives and Records Service, 1978) is five large volumes; it provides a brief summary for each entry (figure 15-2). Researchers seeking to find the names mentioned in the *published* journals of Congress need to use *Index/Journals of the Continental Congress 1774–1789*, compiled by Kenneth E. Harris and Steven D. Tilley (Washington, D.C.: National Archives and Records Service, 1976), as individual names of persons in the published journals are not included in the 1978 index.

U.S. Serial Set. Petitions to Congress by individuals and groups did not end with the revolutionary war. As the United States grew in size and population, they increased. Individuals petitioned Congress to pass private relief acts, to substantiate claims for land in newly acquired U.S. territory, for government appointments, and numerous other causes. These records and many more are hidden in one of the most massive publications ever made, the *U.S. Serial Set.* This is an ongoing collection of federal documents published by the authority of Congress; it dates back to 1789. By 1969 it consisted of more than fourteen thousand volumes with at least 11 million pages. To be sure, most of the information in these pages has no genealogical value, especially that of the late nineteenth century and later, when Congress began to greatly limit its private relief acts. Despite its size, this collection does not include every act of Congress. Rather, Congress determines what will be included in the *Serial Set.* It usually includes Congressional journals and administrative reports, private legislation, reports of Congressional committees and investigations, reports of federal agencies, and other information. If an ancestor or relative had any dealings with Congress, such as holding an appointed position (for example, a postmaster), applying for a patent, requesting a pension, proving a land claim, or any of dozens of other reasons, reference will likely be made to him or her in the *Serial Set.*

The sheer size of the *Serial Set* may cause most researchers to pause and wonder how to access the information in it. Fortunately, the Congressional Information Service (CIS) published a comprehensive, twelve-part index covering the *Serial Set* from 1789 through 1969: *CIS U.S. Serial Set Index* (Bethesda, Md.: Congressional Information Service, 1975–79). Later years are published annually as an ongoing project. Available in book, microfiche, and CD-ROM format, the index is used mostly by scholars and historical researchers, but genealogists can benefit from it as well. Each "part" of the index includes several volumes and covers from three to ten Congresses (for example, the seventy-fourth through seventy-ninth Congresses), except the first part, which covers through the thirty-fourth Congress (1857). Much of the index is comprised of the "Index to Subjects and Keywords," but family historians will be more interested in the "Private Relief and Related Actions: Index of Names of Individuals and Organizations." This section refers to proper names cited in the titles of private legislation.

As a government publication, the *U.S. Serial Set* is usually found in Federal government depository libraries, which include many major university libraries. Where the *Serial Set* is available, the *CIS U.S. Serial Set Index* usually is as well. For more information on the *Serial Set* and the CIS index, see "The U.S. Serial Set," *Journal of Genealogy* 2 (January 1977): 15–21.

American State Papers. A special portion of the U.S. Serial Set that is of particular interest to family historians is the *American State Papers*, which essentially comprises the documents of the first twenty U.S. Congresses. Formally titled *American State Papers: Documents, Legislative and Executive, of the Congress of the United States* (Washington, D.C.: Gales & Seaton, 1832–61), it comprises thirty-eight volumes, with indexes at the end of each volume. Each of the Congressional documents is placed into one of nine "classes" and then arranged generally chronologically:

Class 1, 6 vols.:	Foreign relations, 1st–20th Congress (1789–1820)
Class 2, 2 vols.:	Indian affairs, 1st–19th Congress (1789–1827)
Class 3, 5 vols.:	Finance, 1st–20th Congress (1789–1828)
Class 4, 2 vols.:	Commerce and navigation, 1st–17th Congress (1789–1823)
Class 5, 7 vols.:	Military affairs, 1st–25th Congress (1789–1838)
Class 6, 4 vols.:	Naval affairs, 3rd–24th Congress (1794–1836)
Class 7, 1 vol.:	Post office department, 1st–22nd Congress (1790–1883)
Class 8, 8 vols.:	Public lands, 1st–24th Congress (1790–1837)
Class 9, 1 vol.:	Claims, 1st–17th Congress (1790–1823)
Class 10, 2 vols.:	Miscellaneous, 1st–17th Congress (1789–1823)

While name of relatives and ancestors may appear in any of the nine classes, most genealogical attention has been paid to Class 8, Public Lands. The eight volumes in that class reproduce thousands of claims to public land that arose after the federal government took control of land previously belonging to other countries. Some of that land was already settled, often having been granted to the settler by the previous government. To clarify title to the land, and to protect the claims of those already in possession of what they believed was their private land, Congress established a process for documenting those claims. Class 8 has been comprehensively indexed by Phillip McMullin as *Grassroots of America: A Computerized Index to the American State Papers* (Provo, Utah: Gendex, 1972. Reprint. Conway, Ark.: Arkansas Research, 1990) and has been reprinted, with the index, by Southern Historical Press. For more information about this significant part of the *American State Papers*, see chapter 11, "Printed Land Records."

American Archives. One of the earliest attempts to collect and publish documents of significance in American history was undertaken by Peter Force in his *American Archives*, which is reasonably described by its subtitle: *Consisting of a Collection of Authentick Records, State Papers, Debates, and Letters and Other Notices of Publick Affairs, the Whole Forming a Documentary History of the Origin and Progress of the North American Colonies; of the Causes and Accomplishment of the American Revolution; and of the Constitution of Government for the United States, to the Final Ratification Thereof* (Washington, D.C.: M. St. Clair Clarke and Peter Force, 1837–1853). Prepared and published under the authority of Congress and originally designed to comprise six series, from the discovery and settlement of the North American colonies through the ratification of the 1787 constitution of the United States, the collection was never completed. The only volumes to appear were the six volumes of the fourth series, "From the King's message of March 7th, 1774, to the Declaration of Independence, by the United States," and three volumes of the fifth series, "From the Declaration of Independence, in 1776, to the Definitive Treaty of Peace with Great Britain in 1783." (The fifth series actually ends with the year 1776.)

Each of the existing nine volumes reproduces significant documents from Federal and colonial governments, as well as some from the English Parliament. While numerous individuals are named throughout these volumes, some of the documents include lists of freeholders and other inhabitants of the colonies. For example, in vol. 3 (fourth series), the 1775 "General Association of Freeman, Freeholders, and Inhabitants of the City and County of New York" was signed by members of the Pro-

NEW-YORK ASSOCIATION.

General Association adopted by the Freemen, Freeholders, and Inhabitants of the City and County of NEW-YORK, *on* SATURDAY, *the 29th of* APRIL, 1775, *and transmitted for signing to all the Counties in the Province.*

Persuaded that the salvation of the rights and liberties of *America* depends, under *God*, on the firm union of its inhabitants in a vigorous prosecution of the measures necessary for its safety, and convinced of the necessity of preventing the anarchy and confusion which attend the dissolution of the powers of Government, we, the Freemen, Freeholders, and Inhabitants [*of the City and County of* NEW-YORK,] being greatly alarmed at the avowed design of the Ministry to raise a revenue in *America*, and shocked by the bloody scene now acting in the *Massachusetts-Bay*, do, in the most solemn manner, resolve never to become slaves; and do associate under all the ties of religion, honour, and love to our Country, to adopt and endeavour to carry into execution whatever measures may be recommended by the Continental Congress, or resolved upon by our Provincial Convention, for the purpose of preserving our Constitution, and opposing the execution of the several arbitrary and oppressive Acts of the *British* Parliament, until a reconciliation between *Great Britain* and *America*, on constitutional principles, (which we most ardently desire,) can be obtained; and that we will in all things follow the advice of our General Committee, respecting the purposes aforesaid, the preservation of peace and good order, and the safety of individuals and private property.

MEMBERS OF THE PROVINCIAL CONGRESS WHO SIGNED THE ASSOCIATION.

P. V. B. Livingston, *President.*	Nathaniel Tom,	Richard Yates,
	Abraham Brasher,	Jacob Blackwell,
Volkert P. Douw, *Vice-President.*	Richard Thorne,	Gouverneur Morris,
	Jonathan Lawrence,	Samuel Verplanck,
Walter Livingston,	Abraham Lent,	Benjamin Kissam,
Dirck Swart,	Melancton Smith,	Philip Cortlandt,
Robert Yates,	James Beekman,	John Morin Scott,
Abraham Yates, Jr.,	Gilbert Livingston,	James Van Cortlandt,
Nathaniel Woodhull,	Lewis Graham,	Gysbert Schenck,
Peter Clowes,	John Thomas, Jr.,	Ephraim Paine,
Henry Williams,	David Pye,	James Holmes,
James Clinton,	David Dayton,	J. Hardenbergh,
John V. Cortlandt,	William Williams,	Paul Micheau,
Chris. P. Yates,	John Hazeltine,	Michael Jackson,
John Marlatt,	Paul Spooner,	Joseph French.

SIGNERS OF THE ASSOCIATION IN THE TOWN AND NEIGHBOURHOOD OF NEW-PALTZ, IN ULSTER COUNTY.

Abraham Doian,	Isaac Freer,	Johannes Walron,
Nathaniel Dubois,	Jacob Bevier,	Henry Lits,
Gerret Freer, Jun.,	Solomon Loun,	Stephen Bedford,
Thomas Tomkins,	Christophal Doyo,	Jonas Bedford,
Jacob Hasbrouck, Jr.,	Benjamin Freer,	Cornelius Bedford,
Jedediah Dean,	Isaac Monyon,	Ebenezer Gilbert,
Zophar Perkins,	Christophel Dugain,	Nathaniel Wyatt,
Oliver Grey,	John Terwilger,	Justus Hubbell,
Leonard Lewis,	Israel Cole,	David Whitney,
John Stevens,	John Neely,	John Woolsey,
Daniel Fowler,	P. Z. Schoonmaker,	Eleazer Cole,
Daniel Woolsey	Abraham Hass,	Simon Dubois,
Alexander Lane,	Josaphat Hasbrouck,	Dirck D. Wynkoop,
Zacharias Hasbrouck,	Isaac Harris,	Jacob Carring,
Petrus Freer,	Johannes M. Loun,	John Lemyon,
Abrm. Doian, Jun.,	Jonathan Lefever,	Michael Palmeteer,
Petrus Hasbrouck,	Henry Herald,	Jacobus Hasbrouck,
Simon Freer,	Jacob Dubois,	David Hasbrouck,
Lewis T. Dubois,	Lewis Puntenear,	Abraham Donaldson,
Abrm. Vandermerken,	Hendricus Dubois,	John Lefever,
Michael Devoe,	William Hood,	Jonathan Presler,
Richard Tomkins,	Abraham Ein,	H. Wesemuller,
William Keeck,	Abraham Lefever,	Joseph Griffin,
Isaac Lefever,	Elias Hardenbergh,	John Griffin, Jun.,
Andries Lefever, Jun.,	Daniel Lefever,	Jacob Louw,
Abraham Eltinge,	Cornelius Dubois,	Simeon Louw,
Johannes Low,	Daniel Dubois,	Matthew Lefever,
Simon Doyo, Jun.,	Johannes W. Smith,	John York,
Petrus Van Wagenen,	Jacob T. Freer,	Solomon Bevier,
Cornelius Eltinge,	Philip Doian,	John B. Doyo,
John A. Hardenbergh,	Isaac Dubois,	Daniel Freer,
Joseph Hasbrouck,	Joseph Terwilger,	Zachariah Sickels,
Peleg Ransom,	Paulus Freer,	Frederick Hymes,
Ebenezer Perkins,	Jonas Freer,	Solomon Lefever,
Johannes Eckert,	Josaias Hasbrouck,	Thomas Shirky,
Daniel Freer, Jun.,	Jonathan Doian,	Thomas Dunn, Jun.,
Roelof J. Eltinge,	George Wirtz,	Nathaniel Lefever, Jr.,
Samuel Bevier,	Jonas Freer, Jun.,	James Dunn,
Andries Lefever,	Tennis Van Vliet,	Samuel Teerpenningh,
Hugo Freer, Jun.,	Cornelius Dubois, Jr.,	Thomas Dunn,
Benj. Hasbrouck, Jr.,	W. Schoonmaker,	Joseph Freer,
Nathaniel Potter,	Isaac Louw,	Johannes Freer,
Daniel Diver,	Henry Green,	Simeon Campbell,
Samuel Johnson,	Robert Phenix,	Jedodiah Thomson,
John McDaniel,	Jonathan Terwilger,	Peter Viely,
Ralph Trowbridge,	Jacob Weaver,	Hendricus Dubois, Jr.,
Benjamin Elsworth,	Joseph Elsworth,	Petrus Vandermerken,
Isaac Thomkins, Jr.,	Thomas Lemunyun,	Methusalem Dubois,

Figure 15-3. General Association of Freeman from *American Archives*.

vincial Council and sent to all counties in New York for inhabitants to sign. Twenty pages of text contain the lists of names of persons from thirty-five towns in six counties throughout New York who either signed, or refused to sign the "Association" (figure 15-3). Also included in the fourth series are many of the documents from the various colonial councils and committees of safety, which were the local and colonial revolutionary committees.

Most of the volumes in the series have individual indexes to the personal names, as well as place names and topics or subjects. Since the nine volumes are available on microfilm from the Family History Library, it is fairly easy for researchers to access these volumes. Many academic libraries will also have copies.

Official Record of the War of the Rebellion. Another documentary collection dealing with the entire United States reproduces the key record of the American Civil War. In 128 volumes, the *Official Records of the Union and Confederate Armies in the War of the Rebellion* (Washington, D.C.: Government Printing Office, 1880–1900) reproduces much of the correspondence and official reports from many of the military units engaged in this pivotal part of American history. The set has been reprinted and is now also available on CD-ROM with broad search capabilities. Because this collection deals only with military records, it is not discussed in depth here, but it is described further in chapter 13, "Military Sources." Alan C. and Barbara A. Aimone's *User's Guide to the Official Records of the American Civil War* (Shippensburg, Pa.: White Mane, 1993) explains how to make effective use of the *Official Records*.

State and Colonial Collections

Although Federal government collections are sometimes useful for the researcher, the United States is a large country, both in terms of size and population, so even a nationwide collection that contains up to half a million names can offer minimal chances of finding an ancestor or relative. Of greater use for most family historians are the many state and colonial collections that have been published over the years. In them researchers will find reference to the common man—the typical farmer or shopkeeper whose business with local government created a record that became part of a published collection.

Documentary collections are quite common at the state level; collections exist for all of the original states and for most states east of the Mississippi River, as well as for some others. Many of these collections are so large that virtually any adult male who lived during the time covered may well be noted at least once in a collection. These publications are so numerous that only a few representative collections can be profiled in this chapter. Others are listed in the chapter bibliography and still others await the researcher who diligently seeks them.

Generally, a state or colonial collection is one of two types. Published state *archives* are usually printed directly by the state and consist, almost exclusively, of transcripts of early documents. *Collections,* on the other hand, are typically published by a private or quasi-governmental organization, such as a state historical society. While published collections often include documents, frequently they also include other material, notably researched and compiled histories. Sometimes the title includes phrases such as "Publications of the [_______] Society" or "Yearbook of the [_______] Society."

In various states, particularly colonial states, the recording of some records, such as deeds or wills, was under the jurisdiction of the colonial governor. In such situations these records, which are so crucial to the family historian, were centralized virtually from the beginning of the colony. As more and more people became interested in history (particularly after the U.S. centennial in the 1870s), many of the older states began publishing those early records in their possession. In some states these collections consist primarily of governmental actions, such as state laws, journals of the state (or colonial) legislature, or documents from the executive branch. While these collections may have less genealogical value, their historical value is priceless, and they can offer hitherto unknown clues regarding the whereabouts or associates of family members.

The following is a brief discussion of some of the most significant statewide documentary collections.

Pennsylvania Archives. Probably the most popular of all documentary collections among genealogists is the massive, 136-volume set of *Pennsylvania Archives* (Philadelphia: J. Severns and Co., 1851–1935). Virtually every kind of original genealogical and historical record can be found in one or more of its ten different series: militia and muster rolls, church records, colonial land warrants, tax lists, and governors' papers. Included in these published records are minutes of the Provincial Council, 1683–1775; minutes of the Council of Safety, 1775–77; colonial tax lists for each county; marriage records; records pertaining to Virginia's claims to Western Pennsylvania; land warrantees and records of the donation land claims; oaths of allegiance; and many records pertaining to the military history of the state from provincial militia through the American Revolution and up to the Mexican War. The militia lists for the American Revolution are some of the most complete and thoroughly indexed records for any state (figure 15-4).

Genealogists will find that the second, fifth, and sixth series have the most names and the most documents concerning "regular" people, but locating a name anywhere in this collection can be challenging. Indexes are available, but seldom in a consistent location; for example, the Colonial Records series has a separate index first published in 1992—Mary Dunn's *Index to Pennsylvania's Colonial Records Series* (Baltimore: Genealogical Publishing Co.). The second series has no master index; rather, each volume has its own index. The index to the fifth series is actually vol. 16 of the sixth series, while that series (the sixth) is indexed by the five volumes of the seventh series. An excellent discussion of the background and publishing history of this significant research tool, as well as an expanded description of its contents, is Henry Howard Eddy's *Guide to the Published Archives of Pennsylvania . . .* (Harrisburg: Pennsylvania Historical and Museum Commission, 1976). *Pennsylvania Archives* is summarized below.

Vols.	*Series and Content*
	Colonial Records: Minutes of the . . .
1–10	Provincial council, 1683–1775
10–11	Council and Committee of Safety, 1775–77
11–16	Supreme Executive Council, 1777–9-
1–12	**First Series:** Papers from the Office of Secretary of the Commonwealth
	Second Series: Various records, indexes generally at the end of each volume
1	Minutes of the Board of War and the Navy Board
2	Marriage licenses prior to 1790; naturalizations, 1740–73
3	Oaths of allegiance, 1776–94; revolutionary war papers: minutes of the provincial deputies; conference and convention proceedings; officers of the state of Pennsylvania in the revolution
4	Whiskey Insurrection papers, 1794; journal of Col. Proctor; frontier defense papers, 1790–96
5	Papers relating to the colonies on the Delaware, 1614–82
6	French occupation of western Pennsylvania
7	Boundary disputes, selections from *Documents Relative to the Colonial History of the State of New York.*
8–9	Marriage records from church registers (prior to 1810)
10	Revolutionary war rosters, 1775–83
11	Orderly books, 1778–1780; pension payments
12	Muster rolls: Pennsylvania volunteers, War of 1812
13–14	Pennsylvania in the war of the revolution: associated battalions and militia, 1775–83 (lists of soldiers, muster rolls of associates and militia, by county)
15	Orderly books, 1778–80; pension payments
16	Pennsylvania-Maryland boundary disputes
17	Oaths of allegiance, 1727–75; foreigners arriving, 1786–1808
18	Connecticut claims; Wyoming Valley controversy
19	Minutes of the Board of Property
	Third Series: Various lists (many were redone with better accuracy in the fifth series)
1–4	Minutes of the Board of Property and other land papers (including Virginia claims in western Pennsylvania)

Figure 15-4. Militia Lists from *Pennsylvania Archives*.

188 ASSOCIATORS AND MILITIA.

A GENERAL RETURN OF THE THIRD BATTALION WHEN CALLED INTO ACTUALE SERVICE JULY 1777. (c.)

Third Battalion, ...Capt'n. George Esterly Comp'y.

Militia Men's Nam's.	Private Substi'tes.	Remarks.
	First Class.	
Charles Snyder, ...	....	Excused at apeal.
John Fox, ...	William Maulsby,....	Served his Tour.
George Pepper, ...	....	paid 16th Aug't, '77.
Friederich Jeremiah,..	....	Served his Tour.
Conrad Haase, ...	....	Served his Tour.
Nicholaus Hess, ...	Philip Hess, ...	Served his Tour.
William Chambers, ...	....	In Coll. Flowers Batt'n.
James Hatman, ...	....	Excused at apeal.
William Pay, ...	....	Excused at apeal.
John Hattey, ...	....	Excused at apeal.
William Chatten, ...	....	Can't be found.
Jacob Raffee, ...	....	Can't be found.
John Handy, ...	....	Served his Tour.
William Sorgenhouse, D'r.	....	Excused at apeal.
David Otte, School-master.	....	Excused at apeal.
James Watkins, ...	....	paid 11th Aug't, '77.
	Second Class.	
Leonard Kessler, ...	....	paid 11th Aug't, '77.
Joseph Marpole, ...	....	paid 15th Aug't, '77.
Charles Eyres, ...	....	Can't be found.
Godfry Kennar, ...	Thos. Rothe,..........	Served his Tour.
Isaac Stall, ...	John Westward, ...	Served his Tour.
Friederich Weckerly,..	....	Served his Tour.
Robert Stackhouse, ...	....	Excused at apeal.
Thomas Tilier, ...	....	paid 18th Aug't, '77.
John Stroop, ...	....	Served his Tour.
Anthony Sybert, (Schoolmaster).	....	Excused at apeal.
John Ward, ...	....	Excused at apeal.
James McCoy, ...	....	Excused at apeal.
John Tittemaer, ...	....	Served his Tour.
James McClotham,....	....	Can't be found.
John Cashman, ...	....	Served his Tour.
	Third Class.	
John Houke, ...	....	Can't be found.
Jacob Snyder, ...	....	Served his Tour.
Jacob Silsell, ...	....	Served his Tour.
Philip Hyde, ...	John Hyde, ...	Served his Tour.
John Stroop, ...	....	Served his Tour.
Valentine Warr, ...	....	Served his Tour.
Lazarus Levy, ...	....	paid the 23 Sept'r, 1779.
John Kehmly, ...	....	Excused at apeal.

5–7	Accounts from the Office of State Treasurer, 1777–1889 (especially military expenditures)
8–10	Commissions granted and proclamations issued in Pennsylvania, 1733–90
11–22	Assessment lists for proprietary and state taxes, 1765–91
23	Muster rolls of Pennsylvania navy, line, militia, and rangers, 1775–83; pensioners, 1818–32
24–26	Warrantees of land in the several counties of Pennsylvania, 1830–1898
27–30	Index to vols. 11–26 of the third series
Appendix: twenty-four maps from Spanish explorers to 1792	
	Fourth Series: Papers of the governors
1–12	Includes addresses, general messages, special messages, veto messages, proclamations, correspondence and biographies of the governors. Vol. 12 includes an index to this series.
	Fifth Series: Muster and militia rolls for the French and Indian and revolutionary wars
1	Officers and soldiers: providence of Pennsylvania, 1744–65; Pennsylvania navy muster rolls, 1776–79
2	Riflemen battalion and regiment returns, 1776–77; Pennsylvania Continental Line rosters
3–4	Pennsylvania Continental Line: rosters for revolutionary war, depreciation pay; pension applications; soldiers' pay; enlistments, 1783–85
5–8	Associators and militia muster rolls: Bedford through Northumberland counties
	Sixth Series: Militia rolls (post Revolution), vital records, estate sales, etc.
1–2	Associators and militia rolls through York County
3	Militia rolls, 1783–90: Bedford through York counties
4	Pennsylvania Line officers, 1775–83; militia officer returns, 1790–1817
5	Militia muster rolls, 1790–1800
6	Baptisms and marriages for Lehigh (1734–1824) and Lancaster (1752–1786) counties; marriage licenses, 1784–86
7–8	Pennsylvania volunteers: War of 1812 troop lists and muster rolls
9–10	War of 1812 expenditures (pay rolls), pensioners, war with Mexico
11	Election returns, generally 1756–89
12–13	Forfeited estates: inventories and sales, 1776–82
14	Early petitions (1680–1770); orderly books, 1778–80; Continental Line
15	Index to fifth series
1–5	**Seventh Series:** Indexes to vols. 1–14 of the sixth series
1–8	**Eighth Series:** Volumes and proceedings of the House of Representatives of the Province of Pennsylvania, 1682–1776
1–10	**Ninth Series:** Executive minutes (official actions of the governors), 1790–1883 (essentially an extension of the fourth series)

New Jersey Archives. Similar to the *Pennsylvania Archives*, although not as broad in scope nor as large in size, is the collection *Documents Relating to the Colonial History of the State of New Jersey,* edited by William A. Whitehead, William Nelson, A. V. Honeymun, Elmer Hutchinson, and others (Newark, N.J.: The Daily Journal Establishment and others, 1880–1949, 1974–1986). The archivists of New Jersey have been publishing selected portions of their large collection of records for many years. Of significance to family historians are the thirteen volumes of abstracts for all probate actions, 1680 through 1817, and sixteen volumes of newspaper abstracts, which begin in 1704. Before the revolutionary war, New Jersey did not have its own newspaper, so the editors of this series scoured Philadelphia and New York City newspapers for any mention of New Jersey news or people (figure 15-5). The result, when combined with the every-name index at the back of each volume, is a truly useful finding aid for obscure persons, while it provides more information than many typical genealogical sources.

Usually called the *New Jersey Archives*, this series was published in three series of forty-two, five, and five volumes, respectively. A summary of the content is as follows:

First Series
Letters, memorials, proclamations, proceedings, minutes, speeches, petitions, orders, reports, etc., by and to the early governors and executives of New Jersey, 1664–1776; vols. 1–10
Journal of the governor and council of New Jersey, 1682–1773; vols. 13–18
Extracts from American newspapers relating to New Jersey, 1704–75; vols. 11, 12, 19, 20, 24–29, 31
Calendar of New Jersey wills, administrations, etc., ca.1680–1817; vols. 23, 30, 32–42
Patents, deeds and other early records of New Jersey, 1664–1703; vol. 21
New Jersey marriages (bonds and licenses), 1665–1800; vol. 22.
Second Series
Extracts from American newspapers, 1776–82; vols. 1–5
Third Series
Minutes of Governor's Privy Council; vol. 1
Laws of the royal colony of New Jersey, 1703–1773; vols. 2–5

New York Historical Society Collections. This series, published from 1876 to 1927, includes the full text of the papers, letters, and journals of prominent New York leaders, especially of the revolutionary war, and abstracts of significant genealogical documents for the state of New York. Especially notable among these is the series of Abstracts of Wills on File in the Surrogates Office, City of New York, with Letters of Administration Granted, published in vols. 25 through 41. Each volume in the series is individually indexed unless it is part of a short series, when the index appears in the final volume of the short series. A summary of the contents, by volume, follows:

1	Chalmer's Political Annals and journal of the New York Council
2	Clarendon Papers, 1660s, miscellaneous documents
3	New Hampshire boundary dispute and miscellaneous documents
4–7	Papers of Gen. Charles Lee, 1754–1811
8	Letters of Gen. James Pattison, 1779–80 and to Gen. Lewis Morris, 1775–1782
9–10	Letters of Lieutenant Governor Colden, 1760–75
11–13	Revolutionary Papers (series)
14	Montresor family journals, 1757–78
15	Journal of Lieutenant von Krafft and letter book of Capt. Alexander McDonald

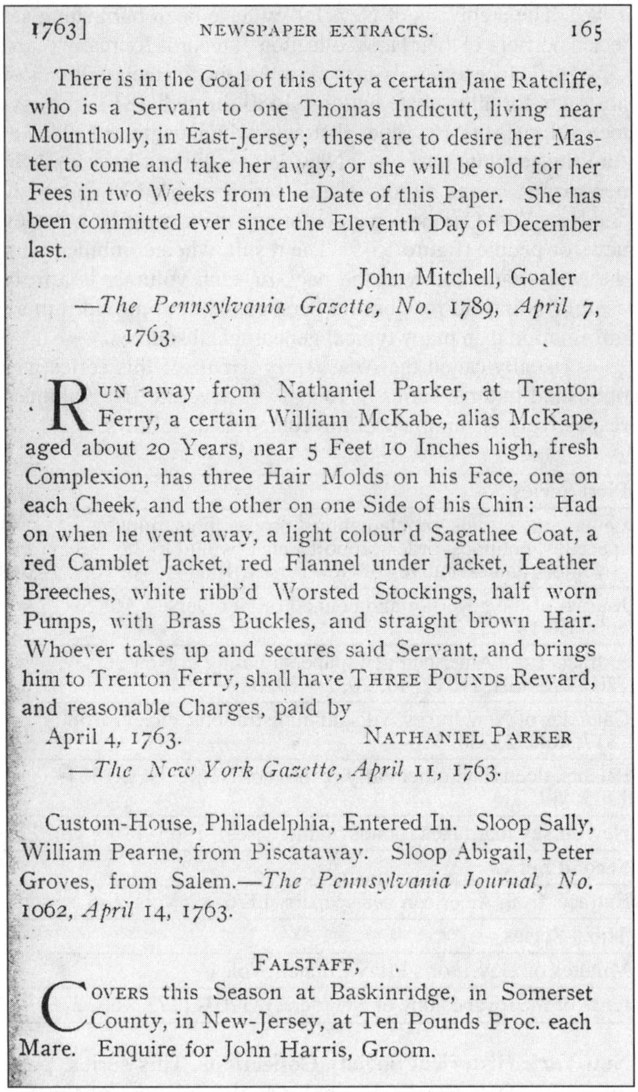

1763] NEWSPAPER EXTRACTS. 165

There is in the Goal of this City a certain Jane Ratcliffe, who is a Servant to one Thomas Indicutt, living near Mountholly, in East-Jersey; these are to desire her Master to come and take her away, or she will be sold for her Fees in two Weeks from the Date of this Paper. She has been committed ever since the Eleventh Day of December last.

John Mitchell, Goaler

—*The Pennsylvania Gazette, No.* 1789, *April* 7, 1763.

RUN away from Nathaniel Parker, at Trenton Ferry, a certain William McKabe, alias McKape, aged about 20 Years, near 5 Feet 10 Inches high, fresh Complexion, has three Hair Molds on his Face, one on each Cheek, and the other on one Side of his Chin: Had on when he went away, a light colour'd Sagathee Coat, a red Camblet Jacket, red Flannel under Jacket, Leather Breeches, white ribb'd Worsted Stockings, half worn Pumps, with Brass Buckles, and straight brown Hair. Whoever takes up and secures said Servant, and brings him to Trenton Ferry, shall have THREE POUNDS Reward, and reasonable Charges, paid by

April 4, 1763. NATHANIEL PARKER

—*The New York Gazette, April* 11, 1763.

Custom-House, Philadelphia, Entered In. Sloop Sally, William Pearne, from Piscataway. Sloop Abigail, Peter Groves, from Salem.—*The Pennsylvania Journal, No.* 1062, *April* 14, 1763.

FALSTAFF,

COVERS this Season at Baskinridge, in Somerset County, in New-Jersey, at Ten Pounds Proc. each Mare. Enquire for John Harris, Groom.

Figure 15-5. Newspaper abstracts from *New Jersey Archives*.

16–17	Journal of Stephen Kemble and British Army order books
18	Freemen of New York City, 1675–1866
19–23	Papers of Silas Deane, 1774–90
24	Muster rolls of New York troops, 1755–64
25–41	Abstracts of wills, 1665–1801
42	Ledger, New York City Chamberlain, 1691–99, and indentures of apprentices, 1718–27
43–44	Tax lists, New York City, 1695–99, 1791
45	Minutes, Supreme Court of Judicature, 1693–1701
46	Early deeds and papers, 1640–99
47–48	Muster and pay rolls, 1775–83
49	Proceedings of British Army of New York, 1781
50–51	Letters and papers Cadwallader Colden, 1711–42
57–58	Minutes, Committee for Detecting Conspiracies in New York, 1776–78
59–60	Lloyd family papers, 1654–1826

Archives of Maryland. This collection has fewer documents of direct interest to the average family historian, as it consists mostly of various proceedings and journals of government bodies; however, it illustrates the kind of information often found in statewide collections. It also illustrates how the different sets of documents can be published in several, non-sequential, volumes over the life of the collection. Researchers interested in the colonial era should be aware of such collections in whatever state they research. Each of the seventy-two volumes of *Archives of Maryland* (Baltimore: Maryland Historical Society, 1883–1972) is indexed and contains transcripts of original records from the colonial period through the revolutionary war. The records include:

Proceedings of the Provincial Council, 1636–1770; vols. 3, 5, 8, 15, 17, 20, 23, 25, 28, 31, 32
Proceedings of the Provincial Court, 1637–83; vols. 4, 10, 41, 49, 57, 65–70
Proceedings and acts of the General Assembly, 1637–1774; vols. 1, 2, 7, 13, 19, 22, 24, 26, 27, 29, 30, 33–40, 42, 44, 46, 50, 52, 55, 56, 58, 59, 61–64
Journals and correspondence of the Council of Safety, 1775–77; vols. 11, 12, 16
Journals and correspondence of the State Council, 1777–93; vols. 21, 43, 45, 47, 48, 71, 72
Muster rolls of Maryland troops in the Revolutionary War; vol. 18
Proceedings of the Court of Chancery and various county courts; vols. 51, 53, 54, 60
Correspondence of Gov. Horatio Sharpe, 1753–71; vols. 6, 9, 14

Colonial Records of the State of Georgia. Several collections have been printed for Georgia, but perhaps the most significant is Allen D. Candler, comp., *Colonial Records of the State of Georgia* (Atlanta: Franklin Printing and Publishing, and others, 1904–16, 1977–89). Again, the majority of documents in this collection are governmental correspondence and legislative journals, but among the records are some which name many of the inhabitants (figure 15-6). The following summary of contents illustrates the variety of sources awaiting the family historian.

1	Charter of the Colony, List of Trustees, 1732–48
2	Minutes of the Common Council of the Trustees, 1732–52
3	General Account of All Monies and Effects...for Establishing the Colony, 1732–52
4	Journal of Col. William Stephens, 1737–41
5	Journal of the Earl of Egmont, 1738–44
6	Proceeding of the President and Assistants, 1741–55
7–12	Proceedings and Minutes of the Governor and Council, 1754–82
13–15	Journal of the Commons House of Assembly, 1755–1782
16–17	Journal of the Upper House of Assembly, 1755–74
18	Statutes Enacted by the Royal Legislature of Georgia, 1754–68
19	Statutes, Colonial and Revolutionary
20–26	Correspondence to the Trustees, James Oglethorpe and Others, 1732–52
27–28	Original Papers of Gov. John Reynolds, 1754–63
29–31	Trustees' Letter Book, 1732–52
32–34	Entry Books of Commissions . . ., Leases, Grants of Land, etc. By the Trustees, 1732–45

These kinds of collections are repeated throughout the various states. For example, the *Colonial Records of South Carolina* include volumes pertaining to Indian affairs, such as petitions, correspondence, lists of residents, and treaties. *The Collections of the Illinois State Historical Library* include the 1810, 1818, and 1820 state census returns, while other volumes include records of the Black Hawk War (1831–32). The *Territorial Papers of Florida* include the Spanish Land Grants in Florida. *The State Papers of Vermont* include the Proceedings of the General Assembly; New York Land Patents, 1688–1786 (in western Vermont); Petitions for Grants of land, 1778–1811; Confiscation and Sale of Loyalist Estates; and various public papers of the governors.

PAPERS OF GROUPS

There are many documentary collections that do not focus on the records of a state or colony; rather, they usually relate to a group—often a nongovernmental group, such as a religious or social group, but sometimes a group chartered by a government for a specific purpose. Because their records pertain mostly to those who belonged to or had dealings with the group, the scope of the documents is not as broad as those of the collections already discussed. However, when an ancestor was part of such a group or lived in an area where the group was active, such collections can be major sources of previously untapped historical and biographical material. For the purposes of illustration, the collections of three such groups are briefly profiled here.

86 GOVERNOR AND COUNCIL.

Lots Granted to the Settlers of Wrightsborough. St Paul's Parish Viz^t^

Names of Persons.	No. of Lots	Names of Persons.	No. of Lots
Henry Ashfield	70	Alexander Oliver	60
Richard Austin	3	Samuel Oliver	91
George Beck	59	John Oliver	11
Cornelius Cochran	78	James Oliver	36
John Carson	95	Ephraim Owen	34
Joel Cloud	19	John Perkins	14
Stephen Day	61	John Stubbs	2
Benjamin Dunn	75	John Slater	67
Abraham Dennis	29	Jonathan Sall	23
Jacob Dennis	19	John Sidewell	59
John Dennis	16	Jonathan Sall	24
William Ellam	25	Richard Smith	33
James Emitt	26	Amos Vernon	18
Edward Eakles	96	Isaac Vernon	10
William Tanner	21	John Whitsett	73
James Hart	76	Samuel Wilson	13
John Howard	45	Thomas Watson	32
John Hodgin	85	John Welsh	62
William Hixxon	30	Thomas Ansley	28
Absolum Jackson	17	Peter Hart	1
Isaac Jackson	89	Samuel Hart	52
Thomas Jackson	31	John Hunter	15
Isaac Low	68	Benjamin Jackson	51
Robert Lockridge	20	William Miles	71
Joseph Maddock	66	Richard Moore	42
Edward Murphy	41	Peter Perkins	48
William Mitchell	43	Jacob Watson	63
Robert McClean	64	John Watson	87
Joseph Mooney	27	Robert Walden	12
John Moore	5	Samuel Winslete	94
Holland Middleton Junr.	38	Thomas Moore	72
James McFarlin	50	Richard Moore	46
Mordecai Moore	7	Henry Sall	8

Samuel Samson . . . Lot No. 83

Figure 15-6. From *Colonial Records of the State of Georgia.*

In the mid-1700s, Connecticut claimed land that is now in northeastern Pennsylvania. In order to sustain that claim, the colonial assembly chartered a land company to provide for the distribution and settlement of Connecticut citizens on that land. *The Susquehannah Company Papers,* Julian P. Boyd and Robert J. Taylor, eds. (Cornell, N.Y.: Cornell University Press, 1962–71) reproduces, in eleven volumes, the documents of that company. These volumes include letters, minutes of meetings, resolutions of the Connecticut Assembly, and other pertinent documents covering the years from 1750 to 1808. Because the company's specific purpose was to help settle this land, anyone researching families living in this area of Pennsylvania or seeking people who disappeared from Connecticut about this time should investigate this collection.

One of the significant early settlements of Georgia centered around a group of approximately 1,500 German Protestants from Salzburg, Austria, who settled in present-day Effingham County in 1734. Because this group existed and emigrated as an organized body, they created many documents that have been preserved better than those of many other early immigrants to America. Their pastors, John Martin Boltzius and Christian Israel Gronau, kept a daily register of emigrants and many related documents. As early as 1735, Samuel Urlsperger gathered and edited the various reports, letters, and travel diaries and published them in German as *Ausfürliche Nachricht von den Saltzburgischen Emigranten, Die Sich in America*

Table 15-1. Topical Documentary Editions

Book editions sponsored by the National Historical Publications and Records Commission (NHPRC)*

Title	Volumes Done/Projected
Black Abolitionist Papers	5
Circular Letters of Congressmen to their Constituents, 1789–1829	3
Documentary History of the Ratification of the Constitution	10 of 16
Letters of Delegates to Congress, 1774–1789	19 of 25
Documentary History of the First Federal Congress of US, 1789–1791	9 of 23
Documentary History of the First Federal Elections, 1788–1790	4
Freedom: Documentary History of Emancipation, 1861–1867	6 of 11
Documentary History of George Rapp's Harmony Society	7 of 10
J. Franklin Jameson and the Development of Huministic Scholarship in America	1 of 4
Mississippi Provincial Archives: French Dominion	5
Naval Documents of the American Revolution	9 of 18
The Naval War 1812: A Documentary History of . . .	2 of 3
Plymouth Court Records, 1686–1859	16
Documentary Relations of the Southwest—Civil-Military	2 of 7
Documentary History of the Supreme Court, 1789–1800	4 of 8
Susquehannah Company Papers	11
Territorial Papers of the United States	28
Yellowstone National Park: Its Exploration and Establishment	1

*For complete bibliographic information, see the sales catalog issued by the NHPRC.

Niedergelassen Haben. In the 1960s, George Fenwick Jones and others gathered these published records, had them translated, and published them as *Detailed Reports on the Salzburger Emigrants Who Settled in America,* Samuel Urlsperger, ed. (Athens: University of Georgia Press, 1968–197[?]). The eighteen volumes in this collection span just twelve years, from 1733 to 1745, and provide more details about this group of immigrants than can be found for virtually any other such group. Any historian interested in early Georgia or colonial immigration from Europe, and, of course, family historians tracing members of this group, will find much of interest in this collection.

Another religious group's records appear in a documentary collection that illustrates a different way of preparing and publishing these papers. The eleven volumes of *Records of the Moravians in North Carolina, 1752–1879* (Raleigh, N.C.: Edwards and Broughton Printing, 1922–69), were actually published intermittently over almost fifty years as part of a larger collection: the Collections of the North Carolina Historical Commission (later the North Carolina Department of Archives and History). While these documents were in preparation, the commission continued to publish other materials, including documents relating to public education in the state. Some of the other publications were histories (not documentary collections), as the interests of the commission were wide-ranging. The Moravian records, like the Salzburger ones mentioned above, constitute a significant collection that provides information from original records in a more accessible manner. This collection certainly covers a major part of early North Carolina history; all interested researchers should investigate it.

The records of many groups have been collected in published sets of documents. Those listed in table15-1 have been sponsored by the National Historical Publications and Records Commission (NHPRC). The commission is discussed below under "Locating Documentary Collections."

REGIONAL AND LOCAL COLLECTIONS

Documentary collections are not limited to statewide records or those of major groups. Perhaps of greatest value to family historians are those collections with a smaller geographic coverage. We all recognize that most of our ancestors were not closely involved in the nationwide or even statewide events recorded in the larger documentary collections. Rather, they lived their lives at the local level, and documents about them will generally be found at the county level. For some regions there are publications that do more than just abstract one specific record type, instead providing easy access to a wide variety printed of sources for that locality.

Sometimes these volumes are difficult to identify, especially because they do not have a broad geographic scope and usually comprise only one to three volumes. Indeed, most libraries classify them as histories, and, in part, they are. However, a significant percentage of their content is given over to reproducing period documents. As an introduction to this type of record, examples from the three major kinds of local collections are profiled below.

Historical Records Collections

Some local collections follow the pattern of statewide documentary collections—that is, they reproduce, with minimal editing or historical interpolation, a myriad of documents from a specific area. Typically these cover a county or a region that was once part of one county. Many of these publications are created specifically for genealogists rather than for the historical community at large. Usually they are developed by a local researcher who recognizes the value of the early documents and who desires to make them available for others to research. Some of the information may be in abstract form, such as for land or probate information, wherein the text of various documents is repetitive, but the essential fact is that the work is rooted in many original documents and is not easily classed as a specific record.

An excellent example is Lyman Chalkley, comp., *Chronicles of the Scotch-Irish Settlement in Virginia, Extracted from the Original Court Records of Augusta County 1745–1800,* 3 vols. (1912; reprint; Baltimore: Genealogical Publishing Co., 1965). As the title indicates, these three volumes were taken from the court records, which, in the period covered, included almost every kind of record created in that county. In addition to the expected record of litigation, the court records included here discuss probate, land, tax, and equity matters. A few marriages are recorded also, and the various depositions relating to the different cases provide a wealth of personal and biographical information for virtually every resident, and certainly the adult males, of the area.

Another example, used by genealogists for more than one hundred years, is Ebenezer W. Peirce's *Civil, Military and Professional Lists of Plymouth and Rhode Island Colonies, Comprising Colonial, County and Town Officers, Clergymen, Physicians and Lawyers, with Extracts from Colonial Laws Defining Their Duties, 1621–1700* (Boston, 1881; reprint; Baltimore: Genealogical Publishing Co., 1968). The civil lists for these two colonies include colonial officers: governors, deputy governors, secretaries, treasurers, governors' assistants, marshals, and coroners. County officers listed include magistrates, clerks of court, registers of deeds, treasurers, marshals and goal (jail) keepers. The following town officers are listed for twenty-nine different towns: selectmen, constables, representatives, grand jurymen, surveyors of highways, innkeepers, licensed retailers of spirituous liquors, collectors of the excise, and collectors of ministers' rates.

The military lists include militia companies by county, giving locations (towns), names of officers, dates of commissions, dates of discharge, and causes of discharge. Company rolls of towns contain "the names of all male persons residing in Plymouth Colony, between the ages of sixteen and sixty years, who were able to perform military duty, in August, 1643 . . ." (page 73). Rolls included noncommissioned officers and privates.

The professional lists for several towns identify clergymen, physicians, and lawyers. Generally they give date when settled, when dismissed, and cause of dismissal (clergy), term of service (lawyers), or term of practice (physicians). Unfortunately, there is no indication in the book regarding from where the original the information was taken to compile these lists or the locations of the original documents. This lack, however, is typical of such early (1881 in this case) attempts to provide greater access to the records. That much it does, and the surname index makes it possible to search a much broader collection of material much faster.

Chapter Seven

Yonkers 1820-1830

Yonkers During 1820

[The date given in the record book is April 4, 1820.] At a Town Meeting held at the house of Elisha Williams it being a day appointed by the law of the State of New York for the purpose of electing Town officers and making such regulations as they think proper viz [namely] the following officers were chosen:

Isaac Vermillya Supervisor		Sworn
Caleb Smith Town Clerk		"
Samuel Lyon	Assessor	"
Moses Shearwood	Assessor	"
Daniel Robert	Assessor	"
Moses Shearwood	Overseer of the Poor	"
Oliver Rhead	Overseer of the Poor	"
Lewis Rich	Constable & Collector	"
Peter Underhill	Commissioner of the Highways	"
Jacob Odell	Commissioner of the Highways	"
Jacob Shearwood	Commissioner of the Highways	"
Aaron Vark	Commissioner of Common Schools	"
Benjamin Fowler	Commissioner of Common Schools	"
Daniel Robert	Commissioner of Common Schools	"
Isaac Vermillya	Inspector of Common Schools	"
Israel Pinkney	Inspector of Common Schools	"
Horace S. Martin	Inspector of Common Schools	"
Henry M. Groshon	Inspector of Common Schools	"
Sampson Simpson	Inspector of Common Schools	"
Oliver Rhead	Overseer of Highways	"
James Post	Overseer of Highways	"
Lewis Rich	Overseer of Highways	"
Wilsey Austen	Overseer of Highways	"
Joseph Tompkins	Overseer of Highways	"
Benjamin Post	Overseer of Highways	"
Peter Underhill	Overseer of Highways	"
Jacob Lynt	Overseer of Highways	"
Stephen Oakley	Overseer of Highways	"

107

Figure 15-7. From *A Documentary History of Yonkers, New York* by Joseph P. Madden, 3 vols. (Bowie, Md.: Heritage Books, 1992-1994).

Documentary Histories

A popular approach by historians is to create a *documentary history* of an area wherein up to half or more of the history is presented in transcriptions of key documents from the area. Such a source provides access to published versions of important records, but the user must be aware of this limitation: the historian selects documents which prove the point that he or she wants to make; the historian does not set out to reproduce each and every record. Documentary histories are often drawn from narrative accounts, such as court records or letters, but another favorite of authors are lists of early inhabitants, such as voters at an election or a tax list. These histories are found at both the local and state level, such as the well-known *Documentary History of the State of New York,* 4 vols., arranged under the direction of Christopher Morgan, secretary of state, by E. B. O'Callaghan (Albany: Weed, Parson, Public Printers, 1849). The many lists published in this history have frequently been reprinted.

An example of a modern version of this kind of volume is *A Documentary History of Yonkers, New York,* by Joseph P. Mad-

1796.] *ANNALS OF BUFFALO VALLEY.* 299

January 18, George Clark, Lazarus Finney, and Roan McClure made a valuation of the real estate, &c., of White Deer township. Real estate, $37,445; personal, $4,438; buildings, $6,448.

March 18, Conrad Weiser moved from Tulpehocken to his place on the Isle of Que.—*Spyker's Journal.*

May 6, Bishop Christian Newcomer, of the United Brethren Church, visited the Valley, and held meetings on the 6th, 7th, 8th, and 9th. Many souls confessed their sins, among the rest a woman came forward leading her daughter. Blessed be God! she, with many others, found mercy.—*Newcomer's Journal.*

James Jenkins sold his slave, Tom, to Colonel John Patton, of Centre county. Tom was thirty years old when the emancipation act of 1780 was passed, but was registered defectively, and lived in the belief that he was still a slave. After living many years with Colonel Patton, he came back to Buffalo Valley, and became a charge. The overseers removed him to Ferguson, in Centre, and that township had to keep him.

List of Inhabitants of East Buffalo.

The occupation, where not mentioned, is that of farmer; improvements, when not added to the name, are log-house and barn; c, for cabin: Alsbach, Mathias; Anderson, William, c; Aurand, John; Aurand, Dietrich, c; Aurand, Peter, c; Bailey, John; Baker, Wendell; Baldy, Christopher; Barber, Martha, c; Barnhart, Henry; Barton, John, on Jasper Ewing's place; Baum, Charles; Baum, Samuel; Beatty, Alexander; Beatty, John; Betzer, William; Betz, Abram; Betz, Solomon; Bickel, Christopher; Bickel, Jacob; Billmyer, Andrew, tavern-keeper; Boveard, James, c; Bower, Casper; Bower, George; Bower, Jacob; Burd, David, c; Campbell, John, on William Gray's place; Carothers, Samuel; Cherry, Charles, on C. Baldy's place; Christ, Adam; Croninger, Joseph; Colpetzer, Adam, c; Conaly, John, distiller; Connell, William, c; Coryell, Abram, joiner; Coryell, George; Covert, Luke, c; Cox, Tunis; Dale, Samuel, Esquire; Davis, Robert; Derr, George; Dempsey, Widow, c; Dennis, John; Dersham, Christian; Donnell, Andrew, Esquire; Doughman, Stephen; Dreisbach, Henry; Dreisbach, Jacob; Dreisbach, Martin; Dunlap, William, c; Dunkle, Jacob;

Figure 15-8. From *Annals of Buffalo Valley, Pennsylvania, 1755–1855.*

den, 3 vols. (Bowie, Md.: Heritage Books, 1992–94). Madden made liberal use of many of the records of this suburb of New York City to create a readable, interesting, and usable history (see figure 15-7). Much of the text is his narrative of the events that transpired, but even there is seems apparent that he drew his information from period documents (as we would expect any historian to do). As with all such documentary histories, the reader must exercise caution and understand that not every statement has a document behind it. Nonetheless, such histories are generally more valuable for the family historian than fully narrative histories, which usually do not include as many references to common people.

Annals

The third format often chosen by historians is the *annals* approach, wherein the history of an area is presented in a chronological form, year by year. Each author applies this formula differently, but generally much of the content in a set of annals is taken directly from documents of the period covered. There will be historical interpolation, but often this is just to make transitions from document to document, or convey information found in the authors research not easily cited from a document (such as oral information). One typical shortcoming of this approach is that many of the documents used are not well described or defined. Usually the reader has to make inferences from the text to learn what sources were used. In these situations, carefully read the writer's preface or introduction for it often explains how the work was assembled, and from what sources.

A good example is *Annals of Buffalo Valley, Pennsylvania, 1755–1855,* by noted Pennsylvania historian John Blair Linn. Originally published in 1877 (Harrisburg, Pa.: L. S. Hart), it has been reprinted several times—twice in 1975 (New Orleans: Polyanthos, and Swengel, Pa.: Reiner Publications). Linn gathered his information from several sources, including "old timers" who remembered many of the events of the early years or recalled their parents' descriptions of early events. However, rather then relying only on the memories of the participants, Linn had recourse to many early documents. Often he identifies his sources, such as "Roan's Journal," or describes that he is indebted to someone, such as "O.N. Worden, late of the Lewisburg *Chronicle* for the following narrative he took down at the time" (page 377). In other areas, such as his annual lists of births and deaths, he leaves the modern researcher wondering if this data came from newspapers, county records, or a variety of sources collected during his research (such as family papers). The result, in this as well as many similar sources, is an interesting, often highly readable, collection of records and history (figure 15-8). Another example from this source that is more narrative in nature is illustrated in figure 17-12 (chapter 17).

The best way to find any of these kinds of local documentary collections is to carefully study the library catalogs for libraries that collect heavily in the area of interest. If possible, search for titles such as *Documentary History of*. . . or *Annals of*. . . . Also note the subject headings. When actual sources are used in a volume, library catalogers indicate this by adding the word *sources* after the subject, such as History—Sources or History—Colonial Period—Sources.

WRITINGS OF INDIVIDUALS

Another type of documentary collection pertains to published journals, diaries, and personal correspondence. Oral histories might also be categorized with these sources, as they pertain to very personal accounts of events. These are often published in verbatim form, maintaining the spelling and vocabulary of the writer. Because each focuses on the writings or papers of one person, they are not the diverse "collections" of many different documents discussed so far; therefore, they are often called *documentary editions* because each is a special edition of all (or selected) documents related to the person who is the subject of the volume.

Such collections are often found in connection with private collections or with historical societies, but many have been published by universities and other private schools. An increasing number of very large sets is becoming available. They have proved very popular with historians, who can now consult the voluminous papers of notable persons much more easily. In addition, the many editors' annotations, often in the form of footnotes (or endnotes), provide excellent insights into the events and persons of the time. Writings of individuals can be divided into three groups: the personal papers of individuals, collections of related letters, and diaries and journals (autobiographical).

Personal Papers

Among historians, the personal papers of U.S. presidents and other famous men and women are very popular. Of course, these are among the people who really made history, and they are the subject of study by many scholars. Family historians, however, rarely use such volumes in the belief that the people they are seeking were not associated with presidents, inventors, humanitarian workers, or other famous persons. This assumption, however, is not necessarily true. Many of the most notable persons interacted with a significant number of "common" people in the course of their careers. While these papers may not have significant genealogical information about an obscure ancestor, the mere mention of a relative's name in connection with a noted personality is of interest to the family and makes the family history more intriguing. The most useful aspect of the published personal papers of the noteworthy may well be the every-name indexes that nearly always accompany them. Thus, if a family tradition states, for example, that a relative "explored the west with Fremont," then quick recourse to the four published volumes of his expedition papers will quickly confirm (or disprove) this statement, and in the process perhaps lead to new clues.

Presidential papers are perhaps the best-known of this type of documentary collection, but, as table15-2 shows, the papers of many others are also available in print. An example of a personal papers collection is Julian P. Boyd's *The Papers of Thomas Jefferson* (Princeton, N.J.: Princeton University Press, 1950–), of which thirty volumes had appeared by 1993 from a collection of materials that is projected to require eighty-three volumes to complete. According to the preface of vol. 1, "the editors have aimed at the inclusion of everything legitimately Jeffersonian by reason of authorship or of relationship, and at the exclusion of great masses of materials that have only a technical claim to being regarded as Jefferson materials" (page xiv).

The Papers of Thomas Jefferson are being published in two series. The first series, with twenty-five current volumes, is organized chronologically and will comprise about four-fifths of the volumes. It consists primarily of letters written by or addressed to Jefferson, but it will also include messages, speeches, reports, legislative bills, state papers, memoranda, travel journals, resolutions, petitions, advertisements, minutes of proceedings, and other non-epistolary documents (figure 15-9). The second series is organized topically and will comprise approximately one-fifth of the total volumes. This series will include (1) autobiographical material, (2) legal papers, (3) architectural and other drawings, (4) maps, surveys, and land papers, (5) account books, miscellaneous accounts, and itineraries, (6) the Farm Book, the Garden Book, meteorological data, and recipes, (7) literary and linguistic papers and documents pertaining to the University of Virginia, and (8) unclassified and supplementary documents. Five volumes have appeared in the second series. As with any large series requiring more than forty years to publish, various editors have worked with the series editor, but currently the volumes appear at the rate of about one every three years. The work is painstakingly slow, as the editors work toward providing a comprehensive understanding of the material and conduct detailed research for their annotations.

The individual volumes of Jefferson's papers were not indexed. The original plan was to issue, periodically, temporary indexes to groups of the volumes. These temporary indexes were to be followed by a permanent index after each decimal volume of the papers. The first twenty volumes are indexed in the first permanent index by Charles T. Cullen, ed., *The Papers of Thomas Jefferson: Volume 21, Index to Volumes 1–20* (Princeton, N.J.: Princeton University Press, 1983), which explains (page viii) that

> this volume . . . is the first of the periodic 'permanent' indexes now expected to appear after each decimal volume of *Papers*. In addition, each single volume of the *Papers* will henceforth contain an index prepared by the Editors. . . . [This is] a comprehensive cumulative index for [the first] twenty volumes of Jefferson's papers. . . .

The index, with thousands of entries, includes events, foreign countries, personal names, place names, political bodies, publications, ships' names, topics or subjects, and numerous other categories. Clearly, any family historian researching Virginia families in the 1760-to-1791 era (the coverage dates for the first twenty volumes) may find interesting references in such a comprehensive index.

Perhaps more typical of the kinds of published personal papers is *The Letters of Franklin K. Lane, Personal and Political,* edited by Anne Wintermute Lane and Louise Herrick Wall (Boston and New York: Houghton Mifflin Co., 1924). Franklin Knight Lane (1864–1921) was born near Charlottetown, Prince Edward Island, Canada, and immigrated with his family to California in 1871, settling at Napa, then Oakland, in 1876. He was a newspaper man, a lawyer, and a politician. He served as interstate commerce commissioner under presidents Theodore Roosevelt and Taft and as secretary of the interior under President Wilson. The contents of this volume include politics and journalism, 1884–94; law practice and political activities; railroads and the nation's politics, 1906–12; secretary of the interior, 1913–15; European war and personal concerns, 1914–15; American and Mexican affairs, 1916; cabinet notes in wartime,

1918; letters to Elizabeth (his wife), 1919–20; and, of course, an index. While Lane was indeed a significant government official, few today have heard of him. It may be that there is a similar published collection for someone else whom an ancestor or relative was affiliated with and who has been forgotten today.

Another example of published personal papers from an even more obscure person is Geraldine Primrose Carson's *From the Desk of Henry Ralph* (Austin, Tex.: Eakin Press, 1990). Henry Ralph was born in Texas in 1838, the son of an Irish immigrant who left his family when Henry was just two years old; the family never really knew what happened to him. Henry Ralph married twice and was the father of fourteen children born from 1859 to 1892 in Jasper County, Texas. He served with the 13th Texas Cavalry during the Civil War. The contents of this three hundred-page book, taken strictly from Henry's letters, include the Texas Republic days and early statehood; family biographies; Old Zavalla, 1834–49; early days of statehood, 1850–60; the 13th Texas Cavalry; county militia to Pine Bluff, 1862; reconstruction and a new family, 1866–69; Sophia's last years, 1870–79; service as a state representative, 1880–89; relatives out West, 1890–99; and family genealogies. Imagine the abundance of family data in such a source, not to mention fulfillment of the objective of many family historians, the opportunity to go far beyond mere dates and places. It is especially in this aspect of family history that published personal papers truly excel.

The average pioneer is the subject of Margaret Smith Ross, ed., *Letters of Hiram Abiff Whittington: An Arkansas Pioneer from Massachusetts, 1827–1834,* Bulletin Series (Little Rock, Ark.: Pulaski County Historical Society, 1956). In just fifty-nine pages, these thirty-eight letters written by Hiram Whittington, a resident of Little Rock and Hot Springs, Arkansas, to his brother in Massachusetts, give an interesting view of these towns during the years covered by the letters. Also included are some discussions about Hiram's interactions with the Cherokee Nation. The parts of the letters presented in this publication deal more with events than with people, but there is mention of a number of people. Of interest are the eighty-six endnotes after the letters; some of them give much detail about the people involved. From a genealogical standpoint, these endnotes are probably more informative than the letters themselves. However, there are no sources given for the facts presented in the endnotes. The editor also comments that the original transcriber and compiler, Dallas T. Herndon, omitted "a great mass of purely personal family information," providing a suggestion to diligent family researchers that more specific family information may be available. In the meantime, anyone researching this early period in Arkansas will learn much from these firsthand accounts of life more than 170 years ago.

Table 15-2. Papers of Notable Americans

Book editions sponsored by the National Historical Publications and Records Commission (NHPRC)*

Individual/Family	*Series Title*	*Volumes Done/Projected*
PRESIDENTS		
Adams, John family	Adams Papers	32 of app.100
Eisenhower, Dwight	Papers of . . .	13 of 23
Grant, Ulysses	Papers of . . .	18 of 25
Jackson, Andrew	Papers of . . .	5 of 17
Jefferson, Thomas	Papers of . . .	30 of 83
Johnson, Andrew	Papers of . . .	10 of 12
Madison, James	Papers of . . .	17 of 60
Polk, James K.	Correspondence of . . .	7 of 11
Washington, George	Papers of . . .	17 of 75
Wilson, Woodrow	Papers of . . .	69
OTHER NOTABLE PERSONS		
Asbury, Francis	Journal and Letters of . . .	3
Backus, Isaac	Diary of-	3
Bartlett, Josiah	Papers of . . .	1
Bouquet, Henry	Papers of . . .	6
Brandeis, Louis D.	Papers of . . .	5
Bray, Dr. [Thomas]	Correspondence of the Associates of . . .	1
Bryant, William Cullen	Letters of . . .	6
Burr, Aaron	Political Corres. and Public Papers of . . .	2
Calhoun, John C.	Papers of . . .	20 of 25
Carroll, John	Papers	3
Cattell, James McKeen	Journal and Letters	1
Chestnut, Mary	Civil War [diary]	1
Child, Lydia Maria	Selected Letters, 1817-1880	1
Clay, Henry	Papers of . . .	11
Cooper, James Fenimore	Letters and Journals of . . .	6
Davis, Jefferson	Papers of . . .	7 of 14
Debs, Eugene V.	Letters of . . .	3
Douglass, Frederick	Papers	5 of 16
Drinker, Elizabeth	Diary of . . .	3
Edison, Thomas A.	Papers of . . .	2 of 15 to 20
Franklin, Benjamin	Papers of . . .	30 of 50
Frémont, Jessie Benton	Letters of . . .	1
Frémont, John Charles	Expeditions of . . .	3 + 1

*For complete bibliographic information, see the sales catalog issued by the NHPRC.

Letter Collections

Many documentary collections are simply collections of letters from various persons, each collection having a related theme. Chapter 4, "Ethnic Sources," mentions some of the many collections of published letters of immigrants that, while documenting specific families, also help descendants of virtually any immigrant better understand the life and times of their ancestors. Collections of letters exist for many groups of individuals,

Individual/Family	*Series Title*	*Volumes Done/Projected*
French, Benjamin Brown	A Yankee's Journal, 1828-1870	1
Garvey, Marcus	and Universal Negro Improvement Assn. Papers	8 of 10
Gompers, Samuel	Papers	4 of 12
Greene, General Nathanael	Papers of . . .	6 of 13
Gregg, David Lawrence	Diaries of . . . An American Diplomat in Hawaii	1
Hamilton, Alexander	Papers of . . .	27
Henry, Joseph	Papers of . . .	7 of 16
Iredell, James	Papers of . . .	2 of 5
Irving, Washington	Letters of . . .	4
Jay, John	Papers of . . .	2 of 3
Jones, Mother	Papers of . . .	2
King, Martin Luther Jr,	Papers of . . .	1 of 12
Latrobe, Benjamin Henry	Papers of . . .	8
Laurens, Henry	Papers of . . .	13 of 15
Lewis and Clark	Journals of . . .	8 of 11
Livingston, William	Papers of . . .	5
Long, Stephen H.	Journals of . . .	1
Marshall, George Catlett	Papers of . . .	4 of 6
Marshall, John	Papers of . . .	7 of 12
Mason, George	Papers of . . .	3
Mazzei, Philip	Selected Writings and Correspondence	3
Morris, Robert	Papers of . . .	7 of 9
Olmsted, Fredrick Law	Papers of . . .	6 of 12
Peale, Charles Willson and Family	Selected Papers of . . .	3 of 7
Penn, William	Papers of . . .	6
Pike, Zebulon Montgomery	Journals of, with Letters and Related Documents	2
Rogers, Will	Writings of . . .	22
Ross. Chief John	Papers of . . .	2
Schoolcraft, Henry R.	Papers of . . .	4 of 7
Skipwith Family	"Dear Master": Letters of slave family	1
Summer, Charles	Selected Letters of . . .	2
Szilard, Leo	Papers of . . .	3
Vance, Zebulon Baird	Papers of . . .	4
Vargas, Diego de	Journals of . . .	3 of 16
Washington, Booker T.	Papers of . . .	14
Webster, Daniel	Papers of . . .	15
Williams, Roger	Correspondence of . . .	2

including, for example, those who crossed the plains and settled the far West.

A different example is John W. Blassingame, ed., *Slave Testimony: Two Centuries of Letters, Speeches, Interviews, and Autobiographies* (Baton Rouge: Louisiana State University Press, 1977), a volume of almost eight hundred pages with name and subject index, including place names. This volume is divided into seven parts: part 1, "Letters, 1736–1864," consists of 111 letters written by fifty-five different correspondents, including letters written by slaves to black relatives and friends, letters from native-born Africans, letters from fugitive slaves, letters by former slaves in Liberia, and letters from slaves to their owners. Part 2 is composed of various speeches by slaves given from 1837 to 1862. Part 3, "Newspaper and Magazine Interviews, 1827–1863," includes interviews taken from seventeen newspapers and magazines and given by forty-one men and seventeen women. Twenty-one had been slaves in the upper South, thirty-three were from the lower South, and twenty-two were from Cuba and Puerto Rico. Part 4, "American Freedmen's Inquiry Commission Interviews, 1863," reproduces interviews of forty-eight slaves and former slaves from Kentucky, Louisiana, Maryland, North Carolina, South Carolina, Tennessee, and Virginia. Part 5, "Newspaper and Magazine Interviews, 1864–1938," comprises interviews with former slaves taken from twenty-six newspapers and magazines. Part 6 consists of interviews with twelve former slaves done by amateur and professional historians. The final part, 7, contains reprints of thirteen autobiographies published in periodicals and books from 1829 to 1878, most of them written in a school setting.

Although only relatively few slaves are reported in this collection, every family historian researching slave families will gain much by learning about the nature of life and the society these slaves experienced. This kind of background knowledge is often what makes the difference between a run-of-the-mill family historian and an excellent, successful researcher.

Published Diaries

Published diaries, journals, and autobiographies comprise a larger segment of the literature than many may be aware of. The sources used to locate published diaries are discussed in chapter 18, "Biographies." Here is noted just one example of what diligent researchers may find: "James Clyman: His Diaries and Reminiscences" in *California Historical Society Quarterly* 4: 104–44; 5: 44–84; and 6: 58–68 (1925–27) is a typical example. Clyman was born in Virginia in 1792 and moved with his family to Ohio at age fifteen, where he served in the War of 1812. He spent most of the next forty years wandering the western frontiers. He was a storekeeper and homesteader in Illinois and Wisconsin in the 1830s and joined the migration to Oregon in 1844. He settled in California in 1848 and married Hannah McComb at Napa, California, in 1849. They had five children; four died young. Their daughter, Lydia, married Beverly Lamar Tallman and was the mother of their only grandchildren. Clyman died in California in 1881. His writing describes the early years of the Rocky Mountain fur trade, overland journeys to Oregon and California, and life in early California. Even when we do not find first-hand accounts of our own relatives, these kinds of sources shed light on what it was like to live in a particular era.

From James Downie and William Thompson, with Jefferson's Instructions

SIR Hanover Court House 4th. May 1781.

As prisoners of War on parole at this place we beg leave to address the Executive, hoping no offence will be given.

We were Commanders of Privateers and taken some time past in Hampton Road, since which part of the time we have been in close Confinement. The request we have to make is that our paroles may be extended and permitted to go to New York where our families and Connections are, either by the way of Portsmouth or any other way as will be most agreable.

We are induced to make this Request as we are informed a greater part of the Officers taken by Generals Phillips and Arnold have received general Paroles to go where they pleased.

Our situation is still more disagreable, being detached from our friends, living at an amazing expence, and scarcely any Cloaths but those on our Backs.

Should your Excellency be pleased to indulge us, be assured we shall strictly Comply with the Tenor of our Paroles and return when called for.

We are Sir Your Mo. Obedt & very hble Servants,

JAMES DOWNIE
WILLM. THOMPSON

P.S. If this Request is denied us, paroles only to Portsmouth would be more agreable than our present situation.

To be paroled to Portsmouth TH: J

RC (Vi); addressed and endorsed. TJ's instructions are in his hand.

In pursuance of TJ's authorization, Davies wrote Downie and Thompson that the Governor had indulged their request and that "As the British have required from the American prisoners paroles similar to the inclosed, I have tho't it proper to require the same from you, to which I do not presume you will have any objection and you will accordingly proceed by the nearest and most direct rout to Portsmouth" (Davies to "Capts. Thomson & Downie," 8 May 1781, War Office Letter Book, Vi). See also Davies to TJ, 13 Apr. 1781.

Figure 15-9. From *Papers of Thomas Jefferson.*

LOCATING DOCUMENTARY COLLECTIONS

As mentioned earlier, there is no standard bibliography of printed documentary collections, nor is there a major library catalog that identifies most of them. Indeed, the manner in which they have been and are being published makes it difficult even to identify them in the standard historical bibliographies and catalogs. There are, however, some strategies that will help the researcher in the search for useful documentary collections.

Book Reviews and Periodicals

As new documentary collections are published (especially the papers of notable persons), they are usually reviewed in major historical quarterlies (such as *Reviews in American History*). Regularly browse these periodicals, especially those that publish in areas of interest. The index, *America: History and Life: A Guide to Periodical Literature* (Santa Barbara, Calif.: ABC-Clio, annual), is also worth checking for new book titles and book reviews. It, as well as some historical book review sources, is discussed further in chapter 17, "County and Local Histories."

The *Periodical Source Index* (*PERSI*), discussed in chapter 19, "Genealogical Periodicals," is beginning to index some of the older collections of historical societies. For example, the 1997 edition of *PERSI* on CD-ROM (Salt Lake City: Ancestry) included 681 entries for articles published in the Kansas State Historical Society Collections from 1881 to 1928—many of which, judging from their titles, appear to be published documents. Since *PERSI* is strictly an index to periodicals, it will never index the many documentary collections that were not published as part of a periodical. However, over time, it will provide increasingly better access to regularly issued (that is, periodically) "collections" of various societies.

Libraries

Major research and academic libraries collect many documentary collections. Be aware of the major libraries in areas of geographic interest, and search their catalogs for possible collections. Where catalogs have word-search capability, search for the phrases common to documentary collection titles, such as *Papers of . . .*, or search for several words in a title, such as *collections, historical,* and *society.*

Many collections of especial interest to family historians are available at the Family History Library of The Church of Jesus Christ of Latter-day Saints in Salt Lake City. That library's catalog will identify the collections, which the researcher can then obtain at many other libraries. Of course, the *Family History Library Catalog*™ is readily available at thousands of family history centers throughout the world.

Bibliographies and Guides

As one continues to research in a particular area, he or she will become familiar with the key bibliographies for that area. For example, chapter 17 identifies the key historical bibliographies for each state. Some of these are dated and will not include titles from the past ten or twenty years, but many documentary collections were published early in the twentieth century. There are also bibliographies for almost any subject of interest to researchers, including ethnic and religious groups. These sources will also identify the published collections of value to research in those groups.

Contact historians and historical societies dealing with the topic or area of interest. In the course of their scholarly study, they will likely have learned about bibliographies and even specific collections to assist research. Guides to research for specific topics or areas should also identify key sources and published collections. For example, it is inconceivable that a book on Pennsylvania research will not mention the wonderful *Pennsylvania Archives,* discussed earlier. What is surprising is that authors of such guides sometimes overlook some key sources. This only means that perhaps someone else should have written such a guide, not that such sources do not exist.

Historical Societies

Many prominent historical societies, museums, universities, and other private organizations have archival collections that have been placed there by prominent persons or their families, or by institutions seeking to make their early records available for scholarly research. Historical societies, such as the previously mentioned Pennsylvania German Society, produce "publications" series of records from their collections or of discourses given in their meetings, or of manuscripts relating to their collections. Some religious organizations, such as the Mennonites and the Moravians, publish church records, correspondence, journals, and ministerial records. The papers of presidents, historical figures, and other prominent individuals are often published by societies and universities.

A recent poll of sixty state historical societies and agencies found that thirty-six were currently involved in publishing documentary volumes and that others were seeking funds to do so (Gordon 1992, 75). For example, The Holland Society of New York published a series of volumes under the heading New York Historical Manuscripts. These volumes consist of collections of records from seventeenth-century New York and particularly during the Dutch occupation of New York. One such volume is *The Minutes of the Mayors Court of New York (City) 1674–1688.*

Major Organizations

Two major organizations are involved in the creation of current documentary collections. One is a government agency that sponsors and encourages the publication of documentary editions. The other is a professional association of persons involved in the creation of these sources.

National Historical Publications and Records Commission. This organization, usually referred to by its initials, NHPRC, is an office of the National Archives and since 1964 has received annual grants from Congress to assist editors and publishers with the publication, in book and microfilm, of documentary editions. Occasionally the NHPRC publishes a catalog, *Historical Documentary Editions,* which identifies all of the editions they have supported, providing a complete description, with price, ordering information and ISBNs. Indeed, this catalog is the only real list of documentary editions, but it identifies only a small number of the many documentary collections that have appeared over time.

Association for Documentary Editing. This association, comprised of many of the best documentary editors in the country, provides training, assistance, and publications of interest to editors. It is the hub of a significant network of document editors which, when tapped, will lead to previously unknown collections. The association even commissioned a book about its craft: *Editing Documents and Texts: An Annotated Bibliography,* by Beth Lucy (Madison, Wis.: Madison House Publishing, 1990). While this book does not directly identify documentary collections (rather, it identifies sources that discuss the craft and profession of document editing), it does mention many collections in the course of its annotations.

CONCLUSION

In using documentary collections, two aspects are very important. First, documentary collections may contain many different types of records and sources that are not available or published elsewhere. It is important to evaluate the content of these collections at the beginning of any research project to be aware of what records might be available. Second, documentary collections, being made up of a variety of original records, often including personal papers, diaries, correspondence, and other such records, often serve to provide information about an ancestor on a regular basis, as new family relationships and individuals are identified.

Although they may be difficult to find, documentary collections can be well worth the search, if only because their indexes allow the researcher to locate much more information much faster than almost any other kind of source. Since they often present verbatim transcripts of original records, documentary collections avoid the wrong conclusions sometimes drawn by authors of compiled material, allowing the researcher to draw his or her own conclusions.

NOTES

1. The writer wishes to thank James W. Petty, Jake Gehring, and especially Carol Ekdahl for their assistance in the research and writing of this chapter.

REFERENCE LIST

Butler, John P. 1977. "The Papers of the Continental Congress as an Unusual Source for Genealogical Research." *Tree Talks* 17: 3–8 (March).

Carter, Clarence E. 1949. "The Territorial Papers as a Source for the Genealogist." *National Genealogical Society Quarterly* 37: 93–94 (December).

Gordon, Ann D. 1992. *Using the Nation's Documentary Heritage: The Report of the Historical Documents Study.* Washington, D.C: National Historical Publications and Records Commission, National Archives.

"Publishing the Papers of the President." 1994. *The Record: News from the National Archives and Records Administration* 1: 1–2 (November).

SELECTED BIBLIOGRAPHY

The following bibliography represents many of the major documentary collections, as well as representative samples of other collections. In many cases it has not been possible to obtain complete publication information—especially the total number of volumes published and the publication dates. Many collections are published over many years as a series, so editors and publishers may vary. For some collections not fully described in the text of the chapter, this bibliography lists contents of various volumes (so far as is known).

About Documentary Collections/Guides to Collections

Aimone, Alan C., and Barbara A. Aimone. *A User's Guide to the Official Records of the American Civil War.* Shippensburg, Pa.: White Mane, 1993.

Burke, Frank G. "Family history resources; U.S. local and family histories in published documentary sources." *World Conference on Records: Preserving Our Heritage. Vol. 3, North American Family and Local History, Part I.* Session 332. Salt Lake City: Corporation of the President of The Church of Jesus Christ of Latter-day Saints, 1980. Pt. 28.

Gordon, Ann D. *Using the Nation's Documentary Heritage: The Report of the Historical Documents Study*. Washington, D.C: National Historical Publications and Records Commission, National Archives, 1992.

Historical Documentary Editions, 1993. Washington, D.C: National Historical Publications and Records Commission, National Archives, 1993.

Kline, Mary-Jo. *A Guide to Documentary Editing.* Baltimore: Johns Hopkins University Press, 1987.

Lucy, Beth. *Editing Documents and Texts: An Annotated Bibliography.* Madison, Wis.: Madison House Publishing, 1990.

General U.S. Collections

Force, Peter. *American Archives: Consisting of a Collection of Authentick Records, State Papers, Debates, and Letters and Other Notices of Publick Affairs, the Whole Forming a Documentary History of the Origin and Progress of the North American Colonies; of the Causes and Accomplishment of the American Revolution; and of the Constitution of Government for the United States, to the Final Ratification Thereof.* In 6 series. Washington, D.C.: M. St. Clair Clarke and Peter Force, 1837–53. Prepared and published under authority of an act of Congress. The only volumes published were the six volumes of the fourth series and three volumes of the fifth series.

Jesuit Relations and Allied Documents: Travels and Explorations of the French Jesuit Missionaries among the Indians of Canada and the Northern and North-Western States of the United States, 1610–1791, with Numerous Historical, Geographical and Ethnological Notes, Etc., and an Analytical Index. Edited by Reuben Gold Thwaites. 73 vols. Cleveland: Burrows Brothers Co., 1895–1901. A verbatim reprint of the very rare French, Latin, and Italian originals, both manuscript and printed, accompanied by a complete English translation. "The story of New France is also, in part, the story of much of New England, and of states whose shores are washed by the Great Lakes and the Mississippi River. . . . We owe our intimate knowledge of New France, particularly in the seventeenth century, chiefly to the wandering missionaries of the Society of Jesus. . . . It is the purpose of the editor to present this mass of selected material in chronological order, so far as proves practicable, and furnish such scholarly helps as will tend to render more available than hitherto for daily use by students of American history. To this end will be given an English translation, side by side with the original text" (from the "General Preface").

Slave Testimony: Two Centuries of Letters, Speeches, Interviews and Autobiographies. Edited by John W. Blassingame. Baton Rouge: Louisiana State University Press, 1977.

American State Papers: Documents, Legislative and Executive, of the Congress of the United States. 38 vols. Selected and edited under the authority of Congress. Washington, D.C.: Gales and Seaton, 1832–61.

American State Papers: Public Lands: Documents, Legislative and Executive, of the Congress of the United States. 5 vols. Selected and edited under the authority of the Senate by Walter Lowrie. Washington, D.C.: Duff Green, 1834. This is a different, and for later years less complete, version of the documents published by Gales and Seaton.

Contents:

Vol. 1.: 1st–10th Congress, 1789–1809, no. 1–157.

Vol. 2: 11th–13th Congress, 1809–15, no. 158–232.

Vol. 3: 14th–18th Congress, 1st session, 1815–24, no. 233–413.

Vol. 4: 18th Congress 2nd session to 20th Congress 1st session, 1824–28, no. 414–563.

Vol. 5: 20th Congress 1st session to 23rd Congress 1st session, 1828–34, no. 564–956.

Index/Journals of the Continental Congress 1774–1789. Compiled by Kenneth E. Harris and Steven D. Tilley. Washington, D.C.: National Archives and Records Service, General Services Administration, 1976.

Gibbes, Robert Wilson. *Documentary History of the American Revolution.* Eyewitness Accounts of the American Revolution, series 3. New York: New York Times and Arno Press, 1971.

Digested Summary and Alphabetical List of Private Claims: Presented to the House of Representatives from the Forty-Second to the Forty-Sixth Congress, Inclusive, Exhibiting the Action of Congress on Each Claim, with References to the Journals, Reports, Bills, Etc., Elucidating its Progress. Finished under the direction of Edward McPherson. Washington, D.C.: Government Printing Office, 1882.

Digested Summary and Alphabetical List of Private Claims: Which Have Been Presented to the House of Representatives from the First to the Thirty- First Congress, Exhibiting the Action of Congress on Each Claim, with References to the Journals, Reports, Bills, Etc., Elucidating its Progress. Compiled by order of the House of Representatives. 3 vols. Baltimore: Genealogical Publishing Co., 1970. Originally printed for the House of Representatives, 32nd Congress, 1st Session, as House, Miscellaneous documents, unnumbered, Series 653–655, Washington, D.C., 1853.

The Territorial Papers of the United States. Compiled and edited by Clarence Edwin Carter. 28 vols. Washington, D.C. : Government Printing Office, 1934–76.

Groups

Records of the Moravians in North Carolina, 1752–1879. 11 vols. Raleigh, N.C.: Edwards and Broughton, 1922–69.

Urlsperger, Samuel, ed. *Detailed Reports on the Salzburger Emigrants Who Settled in America*. Edited with an introduction by George Fenwick Jones. Translated by Hermann J. Lacher.

18 vols. Athens: University of Georgia Press, 1968–. Publications of the Wormsloe Foundation, nos. 9–14.

Localities

New England

Peirce, Ebenezer Weaver. *Civil, Military and Professional Lists of Plymouth and Rhode Island Colonies: Comprising Colonial, County and Town Officers, Clergymen, Physicians and Lawyers, with Extracts from Colonial Laws Defining Their Duties 1621–1700.* Boston, 1881. Reprint. Baltimore: Genealogical Publishing Co., 1968.

Alaska

Documents on the History of Russian-American Company. Translated by Marina Ramsey. Edited by Richard A. Pierce. Materials for the Study of Alaskan History, no. 7. Kingston, Ontario, Canada: Limestone, 1976. Translation of Kistorii Rossiisko-amerikanskoi kompanii.

Arkansas

Whittington, Hiram Abiff. *Letters of Hiram Abiff Whittington, an Arkansas pioneer from Massachusetts, 1827–1834.* Little Rock, Ark.: Pulaski County Historical Society, 1956.

Colorado

Willard, James Field, ed. *Experiments in Colorado Colonization, 1869–1872: Selected Contemporary Records Relating to the German Colonization Company and the Chicago-Colorado, St. Louis-Western and Southwestern Colonies.* Historical collections, University of Colorado, vol. 3. Colony Series, University of Colorado, vol. 2. Boulder: University of Colorado, 1926.

Connecticut

Collections of the Connecticut Historical Society. Collections of the Connecticut Historical Society. 3 vols. Hartford, Conn.: the society, 1860–95.

The Public Records of the Colony of Connecticut, 1636–1776. Transcribed and published in accordance with a resolution of the General Assembly. 15 vols. Hartford, Conn.: Case, Lockwood & Brainard Co., 1850–90. A continuation, published uniformly with the above, was titled *The Public Records of the State of Connecticut.*

Contents:

Vol. 1: Records of the General and particular courts, April 1636–May 1650.

Vol. 2: The Charter of Connecticut, records of the General Court, May 1665–October 1677. Journal and correspondence of the council, 1675–1677.

Vol. 3: Records of the colony of Connecticut, May 1678–June 1689.

Vol. 4: Aug. 1689–May 1706. Council journal, May 1696–May 1698.

Vol. 5: Oct. 1706–Oct 1716. Council journal, October 1710–February 1717.

Vol. 6: May 1717–Oct. 1725. Council journal, May 1717–April 1726.

Vol. 7: May 1726–May 1735. Council journal, May 1726–February 1727/8.

Vol. 8: October 1735–October 1743.

Vol. 9: May 1744–November 1750.

Vol. 10: May 1751– February 1757.

Vol. 11: May 1757–March 1762.

Vol. 12: May 1762–October 1767.

Vol. 13: May 1768–May 1772. Council journal, May 1770–May 1772.

Vol. 14: October 1772–April 1775. The Susquehannah case (1774).

Vol. 15: May 1775–June 1776. Journal of the Council of Safety, June 7, 1775–October 2, 1776.

Hoadly, Charles J. *Records of the Colony and Plantation of New Haven, from 1638 to 1649.* Transcribed and edited in accordance with a resolution of the General Assembly of Connecticut. Hartford, Conn.: Case, Tiffany and Co., 1857.

______. *Records of the Colony or Jurisdiction of New Haven, from May 1653, to the Union: Together with the New Haven Code of 1656.* Transcribed and edited in accordance with a resolution of the General Assembly of Connecticut by Charles J. Hoadly. Hartford, Conn.: Case, Lockwood and Co., 1858.

The Public Records of the State of Connecticut: With the Journal of the Council of Safety . . . and an Appendix. Published in accordance with a resolution of the General Assembly by Charles J. Hoadly. 7 vols. Hartford, Conn.: Case, Lockwood & Brainard Co., 1894–1948. A continuation of *The Public Records of the Colony of Connecticut, 1636–1776* (listed above).

Contents:

Vol.1: October, 1776–February 1778. Journal of the Council of Safety, Providence Convention, Springfield Convention, New Haven Convention.

Vol. 2: May 1778–April 1780. Journal of the Council of Safety, Depositions in regard to the invasion of New Haven, Fairfield, and Norwalk, Hartford Convention, Philadelphia Convention.

Vol. 3: May 1780–October 1781. Journal of the Council of Safety, Boston Convention, Hartford Convention, Abortive Providence Convention, Providence Convention.

Vol. 4: 1782. Journal of the Council of Safety.

Vol. 5: 1783 and 1784. Journal of the Council of Safety; index to vols. 4 and 5.

Vol. 6: May 1785 through January, 1789. Records of the Governor and Council, Constitutional Ratifying Convention.

Vol. 7: May 1789 through October 1792. Records of the Governor and Council.

Delaware

Delaware. Public Archives Commission.*Delaware Archives.* 5 vols. Wilmington, Del., 1911–.

Contents:

Vol. 1: Military.

Vol. 2: Military and naval records.

Vol. 3: Revolutionary war in three volumes and index.

Vol. 4–5: Military records.

Minutes of the Council of the Delaware State from 1776–1792. Wilmington: Historical Society of Delaware, 1887. Originally published in Papers of the Historical Society of Delaware, 6.

Governor's Register, State of Delaware: Appointments and Other Transactions by Executives of the State from 1674 to 1851. Wilmington: Public Archives Commission of Delaware, 1926.

Florida

Connor, Jeannette M. Thurber. *Colonial Records of Spanish Florida: Letters and Reports of Governors and Secular Persons*. Publications of the Florida State Historical Society, no. 5. 2 vols. Deland: Florida State Historical Society, 1925, 1930.

Georgia

Candler, Allen D. *The Revolutionary Records of the State of Georgia*. 3 vols. Atlanta: Franklin-Turner Co., 1908.

Colonial Records of the State of Georgia. Compiled by Allen D. Candler. 34 vols. Atlanta, Ga.: Franklin Printing and Publishing, and others, 1904–16, 1977–89.

Hawes, Lilla M. *Proceedings and Minutes of the Governor and Council of Georgia, October 4, 1774, through November 7, 1775: and September 6, 1779, through September 20, 1780.* Collections of the Georgia Historical Society, vol. 10. Savannah: Georgia Historical Society, 1952.

Wilson, Caroline Price. *Annals of Georgia, Important Early Records of the State.* 3 vols. New York: Grafton Press, 1928.

Contents:

Vol. 1: Liberty county records and a state revolutionary pay roll.

Vol. 2: Mortuary records in city hall at Savannah and burials in colonial cemetery and nearby localities.

Vol. 3: Effingham County records and connecting links in other counties.

Warren, Mary B. *Georgia Governor and Council Journals.* 2 vols. Danielsville, Ga.: Heritage Papers, 1991. Contents: Vol. 1, 1753–60; vol. 2, 1761–67.

Illinois

Greene, Evarts Boutell, ed. *Governors' Letter-Books, 1840–1853*. Collections of the Illinois State Historical Library, vol. 7. Collections of the Illinois State Historical Library, Executive Series, vol. 2. Springfield: Trustees of the Illinois State Historical Library, 1911.

Kansas

Collections of the Kansas State Historical Society. 17 vols. Topeka, Kans.: State Printing Office, 1881–1928. Continues *Collections of the Illinois State Historical Library.* Continued by *Kansas Historical Quarterly.* Volumes are individually indexed. Contains address at annual meetings, memorials, copies of early records, and miscellaneous papers.

Kentucky

Robertson, James Rood. *Petitions of the Early Inhabitants of Kentucky to the General Assembly of Virginia, 1769 to 1792.* Filson Club publications, no. 27. Louisville, Ky.: John P. Morton, 1914.

Louisiana

French, Benjamin Franklin. *Historical Collections of Louisiana: Embracing Many Rare and Valuable Documents Relating to the Natural, Civil and Political History of That State, Compiled with Historical and Biographical Notes, Part I. Historical Documents from 1678 to 1691*. New York: Wiley & Putnam, 1846.

Maine

Province and Court Records of Maine. 6 vols. Portland: Maine Historical Society, 1928–75.

Contents:

Vol. 1: Under Sir Ferdinando Gorges and his councillors, 1636–52; under Ferdinando Gorges the Younger, 1661–65; under the Commissioners of Charles II, 1665–68.

Vol. 2: York County court records, 1653–79.

Vol. 3: Province of Maine records 1680–92.

Vol. 4: The court record of York County, Maine, 1692–1710/11.

Vol. 5: The court records of York County, Maine, 1711–18.

Vol. 6: The court records of York County, Maine, 1718/19–1727.

Farnham, Mary Frances. *The Farnham Papers*. 2 vols. Portland: Maine Historical Society, 1901–02. "Documents relating to the territorial history of Maine."

Baxter, James Phinney, ed. *The Baxter Manuscripts*. Documentary History of the State of Maine, vols. 4–6, 9–24. 19 vols. Portland: Maine Historical Society, 1889–1916.

Maryland

Archives of Maryland. Published by authority of the State under the direction of the Maryland Historical Society. 72 vols. Baltimore: Maryland Historical Society, 1883–1972.

Archives of Maryland. New Series. Annapolis: Maryland State Archives, 1990–.

Brumbaugh, Gaius Marcus. *Maryland Records: Colonial, Revolutionary, County and Church, from Original Sources*. 2 vols. Baltimore: Williams & Wilkins, 1915, and Lancaster, Pa.: Lancaster Press, 1928. Reprint. Baltimore: Genealogical Publishing Co., 1967, 1975.

Massachusetts

Allen, Gardner Weld. *Papers of John Davis Long, 1897–1904*. Selected and edited by Gardner Weld Allen. Massachusetts Historical Society Collections, vol. 78. Boston: Massachusetts Historical Society, 1939.

Collections of the Massachusetts Historical Society. Boston: the society, 1792–.

Plymouth Court Records, 1686–1859. Edited by David Thomas Konig. With an introductory essay by William E. Nelson. 16 vols. Wilmington, Del.: Michael Glazier, Inc., in association with the Pilgrim Society, 1978–81.

Contents:

Vols. 1–4: General Sessions of the Peace, 1686–1827.

Vols. 5–16: The Court of Common Pleas, 1702–1859.

Allen, Gardner Weld. *Papers of John Davis Long, 1897–1904*. Historical Society. Collections, vol. 78. Boston: Massachusetts Historical Society, 1939.

Warren-Adams Letters: Being Chiefly a Correspondence among John Adams, Samuel Adams, and James Warren. Massachusetts Historical Society Collections, vols. 72–73. Boston: Massachusetts Historical Society, 1917–25. Contents: Vol. 1., 1743–77; vol. 2, 1778–1814.

Mississippi

Rowland, Dunbar, ed. *Mississippi Provincial Archives: French Domination.* 5 vols. Jackson: Press of the Mississippi Department of Archives and History, 1927–32, 1984. Contents: Vol. 1, 1729–40; vol. 2, 1701–29; vol. 3, 1704–43; vol. 4, 1729–48; vol. 5, 1749–63.

Mississippi Provincial Archives, 1763–1783; English Dominion: Transcripts of Archives in the Public Record Of-

fice, London, England. Collected by Dunbar Rowland. 10 vols. Jackson, Miss.: Department of Archives and History, 1969.

New Hampshire

New Hampshire Provincial and State Papers. 40 vols. Concord, N.H.: George E. Jenks, 1867–1943. Published by authority of the legislature of New Hampshire.

Contents:

Vols. 1–7: Provincial papers.

Vol. 8: State papers.

Vol. 9: Town papers.

Vol. 10: Provincial and state papers.

Vols. 11–13: Town papers.

Vols. 14–17: Rolls and documents relating to soldiers in the revolutionary war.

Vol. 18: Miscellaneous and state papers.

Vol. 19: Provincial papers.

Vols. 20–22: Early state papers.

Vol. 23: A list of documents in the Public Record Office in London . . . relating to New Hampshire.

Vols. 24–25: Town charters.

Vol. 26: New Hampshire grants.

Vol. 27–28: Township grants.

Vol. 29: Documents relating to the Masonian patent.

Vol. 30: Miscellaneous Revolutionary documents.

Vol. 31–39: Probate records of the province of New Hampshire.

Vol. 40: Court records, 1640–92.

New Jersey

Documents Relating to the Colonial History of the State of New Jersey. 42 vols. Newark, N.J.: The Daily Journal Establishment, 1880–1949.

New Jersey in the American Revolution, 1763–1783: A Documentary History. Edited by Larry R. Gerlach. Trenton: New Jersey Historical Commission, 1975.

Stevens, Henry. *An Analytical Index to the Colonial Documents of New Jersey, in the State Paper Offices of England*. Compiled by Henry Stevens. Edited with notes and references to printed works and manuscripts in other depositories by William A. Whitehead. Collections of the New Jersey Historical Society, vol. 5. New York : Published for the Society by D. Appleton and Co., 1858.

New York

Collections of the New York Historical Society. 60 vols. New York: New York Historical Society, 1876–1927.

Delaware Papers. Vol. 1 edited and vol. 2 translated and edited by Charles T. Gehring. New York Historical Manuscripts: Dutch. Published under the direction of the Holland Society of New York. Baltimore: Genealogical Publishing Co., 1977–81.

Contents:

Vol. 1: Delaware papers (English period); documents pertaining to the regulation of affairs on the Delaware, 1664–82.

Vol. 2: Delaware papers (Dutch period); documents pertaining the regulation of affairs on the South River of New Netherland, 1648–64.

The Documentary History of the State of New York. Arranged under the direction of Christopher Morgan, secretary of state, by E. B. O'Callaghan. 4 vols. Albany, N.Y.: Weed, Parson, Public Printers, 1849.

The Minute Book of the Committee of Safety of Tryon County: The Old New York Frontier. New York: Dodd, Mead and Co., 1905.

New York Historical Manuscripts, English. Edited by Peter R. Christoph. Published under the direction of the Holland Society of New York. 5 vols. Baltimore: Genealogical Publishing Co., 1980–.

Contents:

Vol. 1: Administrative papers of governors Richard Nicolls and Francis Lovelace, 1664–73.

Vol. 2: Books of general entries of the colony of New York, 1664–73.

Vol. 3: Books of general entries of the colony of New York, 1674–88.

Vol. 4: Records of the Court of Assizes for the colony of New York, 1665–82.

Vol. 5: Minutes of the Mayors Court of New York, 1674–75.

Andros Papers, 1674–1680: Files of the Provincial Secretary of New York During the Administration of Governor Sir Edmund Andros, 1674–1680. Edited by Peter R. Christoph and Florence A. Christoph. With translations from the Dutch by Charles T. Gehring. 3 vols. New York: Holland Society of New York, 1989, 1991.

New York. Secretary of State. *Calendar of N. Y. Colonial Manuscripts, Indorsed Land Papers; in the Office of the Secretary of State of New York, 1643–1803*. Albany, N.Y.: Weed, Parsons and Co., 1864.

North Carolina

Cain, Robert J., ed. *Records of the Executive Council, 1664–1734*. The Colonial records of North Carolina, Second Series, vols. 7–8. Raleigh, N.C.: Department of Cultural Resources, Division of Archives and History, 1984–.

The Colonial Records of North Carolina Published . . . By Order of the General Assembly. Compiled and edited by William L. Saunders. 30 vols. Raleigh, N.C.: Nash Brothers, 1886–1914. Vols. 1–10 are titled "The Colonial Records of North Carolina, 1662–1776." Vols. 11–26 are titled "The State Records of North Carolina, 1776–1790."

Index to the Colonial and State Records of North Carolina, Covering Volumes I–XXV: Published under the Supervision of the Trustees of the Public Libraries, by Order of the General Assembly. Collected and edited by William L. Saunders, Secretary of State. 2 vols. Raleigh, N.C.: P. M. Hale, 1886. Reprint. Wilmington, N.C.: Broadfoot Publishers, 1993.

Jones, H. G. *For History's Sake: The Preservation and Publication of North Carolina History, 1663–*. Chapel Hill: University of North Carolina, 1966.

Powell, William Stevens. *The Regulators in North Carolina: A Documentary History, 1759–1776*. Compiled and edited by William S. Powell, James K. Huhta, Thomas J. Franham. Raleigh, N.C.: State Dept of Archives and History, 1971.

Pennsylvania

Dunn, Mary. *Index to Pennsylvania's Colonial Records Series.* With a foreword by Jonathan R. Stayer of the Pennsylvania Historical and Museum Commission. Baltimore: Genealogical Publishing Co., 1992.

Pennsylvania Archives. 136 vols. Philadelphia: J. Severns and Co., 1851–1935.

William Penn and the Founding of Pennsylvania, 1680–1684: A Documentary History. Edited by Jean R. Soderlund. Philadelphia: University of Pennsylvania Press, 1983.

Rhode Island

Records of the Colony of Rhode Island and Providence Plantations in New England. Printed by order of the legislature. Transcribed and edited by John Russell Bartlett. 10 vols. Providence, R.I.: A. C. Green, 1856–65.

South Carolina

Carroll, Bartholomew Rivers. *Historical Collections of South Carolina: Embracing Many Rare and Valuable Pamphlets, and Other Documents Relating to the History of That State, from Its First Discovery to Its Independence, in the Year 1776.* Compiled, with various notes and an introduction, by B. R. Carroll. 2 vols. New York: Harper & Brothers, 1836.

Hemphill, William Edwin. *Extracts from the Journals of the Provincial Congresses of South Carolina, 1775–1776.* The State Records of South Carolina, vol. 2. Columbia: South Carolina Archives Dept., 1960.

The Colonial Records of South Carolina. Publisher varies. Published for the South Carolina Department of Archives and History.

Volumes include:

The Journal of the Commons House of Assembly. Edited by J. H. Easterby. Columbia: Historical Commission of South Carolina, 1951–.

Records in the British Public Record Office Relating to South Carolina, 1663–1684. Indexed by A. S. Salley, Jr. Atlanta: Foote & Davies Co., 1928.

The State Records of South Carolina. Publisher varies. Published for the South Carolina Department of Archives and History.

Volumes include:

Journals of the House of Representatives, 1783–1794. Edited by Theodora J. Thompson. Columbia: University of South Carolina Press, 1977–88.

Tennessee

Whitley, Edythe Johns Rucker. *Tennessee Genealogical Records: Records of Early Settlers from State and County Archives.* Baltimore: Genealogical Publishing Co., 1981.

Texas

Papers Concerning Robertson's Colony in Texas. 17 vols. Compiled and edited by Malcom M. McLean. Arlington, Tex.: The UTA Press, 1980–91.

Vermont

Slade, William. *Vermont State Papers: Being a Collection of Records and Documents, Connected with the Assumption and Establishment of Government by the People of Vermont, Together with the Journal of the Council of Safety, the First Constitution the Early Journals of the General Assembly.* Middlebury, Vt.: J. W. Copeland, Printer, 1823.

State Papers of Vermont. 17 vols. Montpelier, Vt.: secretary of state, 1918–69.

Selected volumes:

Vol. 3: *Journals and Proceedings of the General Assembly of the State of Vermont, 1778–1791.* 4 parts. 1924–28.

Vol. 8: *General petitions, 1778–1787.* 1952.

Vols. 12–16: *Laws of Vermont, 1777–1799.* 1964–68.

Vol. 17: *The Public Papers of Governor Thomas Chittenden.* 1969.

Virginia

The Committees of Safety of Westmoreland and Fincastle: Proceedings of the County Committees, 1774–1776. Edited by Richard Barksdale Harwell. Virginia State Library publications, no. 1. 1956. Reprint. Richmond: Virginia State Library, 1974.

Colonial Records of Virginia. Richmond: R. F. Walker, Superintendent Public Printing, 1874. Reprint. Baltimore: Genealogical Publishing Co., 1964.

McIlwaine, Henry Read, ed. *Legislative Journals of the Council of Colonial Virginia.* 3 vols. Richmond, Va.: The Colonial Press, Everett Waddey, 1918–19.

Shepherd, Samuel. *The Statutes at Large of Virginia: From October Session 1792, to December Session 1806 (I.e. 1807), Inclusive, in Three Volumes (New Series), Being a Continuation of Hening.* 3 vols. 1835. Reprint. New York: AMS Press, 1970.

Executive Journals of the Council of Colonial Virginia, 1680–1775. 6 vols. Richmond: Virginia State Library, 1925–45, 1978.

Journal of the Senate of Virginia. 8 vols. Richmond: Virginia State Library, 1949, 1951, 1972–77. Reprint of the original manuscripts of selected Virginia Senate journals, 1792–1803.

West Virginia

Biennial Report, West Virginia Department of Archives and History. Charleston: Dept. of Archives and History West Virginia, 1908–.

Representative Papers of Individuals

Burton, Elijah P. *Diary of E. P. Burton, Surgeon, 7th Reg. Ill., 3rd Brig., 2nd Div. 16 A. C.* Prepared by the Historical Records Survey, Division of Professional and Service Projects, Work Projects Administration. Des Moines, Iowa: Historical Records Survey, 1939. Dr. E. P. Burton served mainly in the states of Georgia and Tennessee.

"James Clyman: His Diaries and Reminiscences." *California Historical Society Quarterly* 4: 104–44; 5: 44–84; 6: 58–68 (1925–27).

The Official Records of Robert Dinwiddie, Lieutenant-Governor of the Colony of Virginia, 1751–1758, Now First Printed from the Manuscript in the Collections of the Virginia Historical Society. Introduction and notes by R. A. Brock. Collections of the Virginia Historical Society, New Series, vols. 3–4. Richmond: Virginia Historical Society, 1883.

Furman, Moore. *The Letters of Moore Furnman, Deputy Quarter-Master General of New Jersey in the Revolution.* Compiled and edited by the Historical Research Committee of the

New Jersey Society of the Colonial Dames of America. New York: F. H. Hitchcock, 1912.

The Papers of James Iredell, Sr., 1767–1783. Edited by Don Higginbotham. 2 vols. Raleigh: Division of Archives and History, North Carolina Department of Cultural Resources, 1976. James Iredell served on the U.S. Supreme Court. Three additional volumes are planned.

The Papers of James Jackson, 1781–1798. Edited by Lilla M. Hawes. Collections of the Georgia Historical Society, vol. 11. Savannah: Georgia Historical Society, 1955. James Jackson was a revolutionary soldier, governor, and U.S. senator.

The Papers of Thomas Jefferson. Edited by Julian P. Boyd. 30 vols. Princeton, N.J.: Princeton University Press, 1950–. Through 1993, thirty volumes of a projected eighty-three had been published.

The Letters of Franklin K. Lane, Personal and Political. Anne Wintermute Lane and Louise Herrick Wall, eds. Boston and New York: Houghton Mifflin Co., 1924.

Public Papers and Letters of Angus Wilton McLean: Governor of North Carolina, 1925–1929. Edited by David LeRoy Corbitt. Raleigh: North Carolina Council of State, 1931.

Carson, Geraldine Primrose, ed. *From the Desk of Henry Ralph.* Austin, Tex.: Eakin Press, 1990.

Part 4
COMPILED RECORDS

FAMILY HISTORIES AND GENEALOGIES OVERVIEW

Key Concepts in This Chapter

- *Family histories* preserve some genealogical information from sources that are no longer available.
- The approximately ninety thousand North American *published genealogies* include information about 100 million or more people.
- A family history includes more biographical and historical information than a genealogy.
- The *Register* and *National Genealogical Society Quarterly (NGSQ)* systems are the preferred methods of showing descent genealogy.
- *Pedigree charts* and *Ahnentafel* arrangements are common ways to show ascent genealogy.
- The number of book genealogies has grown rapidly since the 1970s.
- *Journal articles* are a common way to publish briefer information.
- *Compendia* and *dictionaries* provide concise information on many families in a geographic area.

Key Sources in This Chapter

- The Surname Section, *Family History Library Catalog* lists 129,000 titles
- *Genealogies in the Library of Congress*, with its supplements, lists forty-two thousand titles
- *A Complement to Genealogies in the Library of Congress* adds twenty-three thousand titles
- *American Genealogical-Biographical Index* indexes almost 6 million names in eight hundred sources
- *The Greenlaw Index* gives complete references for articles covering three generations or more
- *Index to American Genealogies* indexes surnames in almost all pre-1908 publications
- *Compendium of American Genealogy* covers fifty-four thousand lineages in seven volumes
- *Ancestral File* is a lineage-linked compilation on CD-ROM with 29 million individuals
- *World Family Tree* CD-ROMs include more than 20 million names, including duplicates

16

FAMILY HISTORIES AND GENEALOGIES

Kory L. Meyerink

Published family histories and genealogies contain more answers to genealogical problems than any other kind of source. A family history or genealogy is a compilation of information about several generations in one or more families. They are among the most important compiled sources that genealogists use and are among the most common and frequently sought sources. Family histories and genealogies also cause more problems than any other kind of source when researchers rely to an undue extent on the information in them.

Seeking published family histories and genealogies is proper research methodology—as long as the researcher does not rely too heavily on a genealogy compiled by someone else. Although no family history is without errors, they contain important clues for further research, as well as much correct factual information. There are more accurate statements than false statements in almost any family history, and the clues they provide can expedite the research process immensely. In short, there is no reason for a researcher to avoid using genealogies in the course of research. A wise researcher will go to great lengths to determine whether a genealogy already exists for the family of interest and will go to equal lengths to locate a copy of that genealogy.

The beginning stages of research on any line should include an investigation of available published family histories and genealogies. They can furnish information that extends a lineage one or more generations, particulars on the ancestral home or prior residence of an immigrant, dates or places previously unknown, details for extended and collateral family members, and supplementary evidence that can give new or added direction to later research efforts. Fortunately for most researchers, there is likely to be at least one family history or genealogy (in fact, there are likely to be several) that deals with a portion of his or her ancestry.

Most researchers can find parts of their families in a published genealogy simply because so many have been printed and so many names are included in them. Upwards of ninety thousand printed family history and genealogy books are available for families who lived in the United States and Canada. While the number of persons in any one of these genealogies can vary from a few dozen to more than ten thousand, the average number is more than 1,300 people.[1] These numbers suggest that approximately 115 million names appear in published genealogies. There is some duplication; certainly some individuals are listed in two, three, four, or even more genealogies. However, many of the names in these genealogies predate the 1920s. The population of the United States in 1920 was approximately 106 million, while the cumulative population of the country, from 1620 to 1920, was approximately 225 million.[2] Thus, printed genealogies could account for a significant portion of all people who have lived in the United States. Clearly, then, the genealogist must spend time learning about and using family histories.

This chapter discusses the nature of family histories and genealogies, defines their similarities, explains their formats, introduces several types of finding aids and shows how to use them, and discusses the evaluation of genealogies. In addition to family histories in book form, there are many well-documented genealogies in genealogical and historical periodicals. Additional sources include genealogical dictionaries, compendia, indexes, local histories, and biographies.

DEFINING FAMILY HISTORIES AND GENEALOGIES

The differences between genealogies and family histories are often in the eye (or mind) of the researcher. Certainly a genealogy will include genealogical information about individuals, usually over several generations. Many family histories also include genealogical information. However, there is more to each. For the purposes of this chapter, these works are defined below.

A *genealogy* is a collection of compiled information about the members of an extended family, usually linking three generations or more of the same family. It includes, at a minimum, birth, marriage, death, and/or relationship information about members of that family. A genealogy may be published or unpublished, documented or undocumented, and it may take any of several forms, including pedigree charts and family group sheets, ancestor tables, formatted descendancy lists, or narrative stories.

A *family history* is the history of a family. It includes genealogical, biographical, and historical information about many members of an extended family. Usually, but not necessarily, narrative in structure, it may treat the family as descendants or ancestors of a central person or couple. At a minimum, it should discuss the key historical events experienced by its subjects. According to one historian,

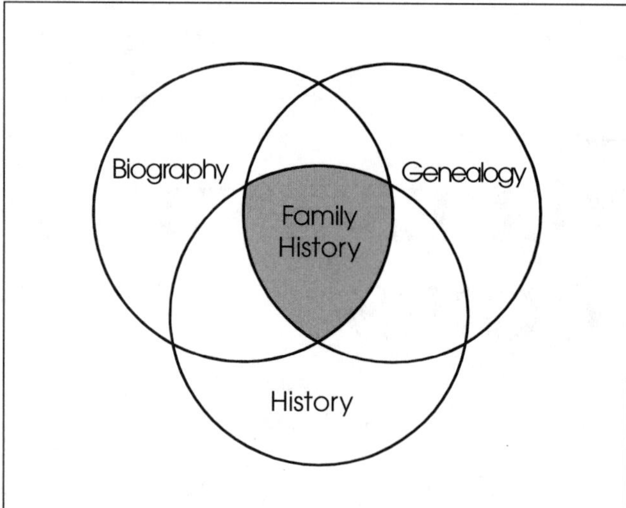

Figure 16-1. The interrelationships among the fields of biography, genealogy, and history.

> there is a difference . . . between a family history and a genealogy. A genealogy is concerned primarily with lineal descent. . . . A family history fleshes out the information found in genealogical charts by placing a family into a broader context and by telling more about family members (Kyvig and Marty 1978, 10).

John R. Totten, former editor of the *New York Genealogical and Biographical Record,* defined some key terms.

> Genealogy has to do solely with *who* one's various ancestors may have been. When one seeks to ascertain *what* these ancestors may have been, one enters the field of biography (1921, 297).

While a family history could be viewed as a subset of a genealogy, a family history actually goes much further than a simple genealogy. While a genealogy need only include the essential genealogical information (births, relationships, etc.), a family history should provide more "meat" to flesh out the ancestors and relatives it discusses. Indeed, according to Patricia Law Hatcher, one very positive shift in recent genealogical publications is

> . . . the move toward family history. Placing people in context both helps in our research and makes the published results more interesting to our audience. In other words, we are transitioning from publishing *genealogy* to publishing *family history* (1996, 14).

The line is a fine one. At what point does a genealogy include enough additional information about its subjects to become a family history? Perhaps the best description of a true family history comes from Milton Rubincam, who suggested that

> the history of a family is one continuous adventure. If properly investigated, it is not a mere record of births, marriages, and deaths. A published genealogy that contains only vital statistics makes dull reading indeed. But letters, diaries, memoirs, court records, etc., clothe the bones with flesh and blood, revivify them, and make our long-dead ancestors distinct personalities (1960, 10).

A family history therefore incorporates elements of history and biography, as well as genealogy. The illustration in figure 16-1 shows the interrelationships among these three fields.

Most researchers use these terms interchangeably. In fact, one scholar was so frustrated by the inconsistent use of *family history* that he coined his own term. In his view, *family biography* conveyed the meaning better (Roberts 1987, 13). Generally, in this chapter, the term *genealogy* is used because a family history is a special kind of genealogy.

Content and Arrangement

What will one find in a genealogy? The fundamentals were mentioned above: names of family members; their birth, marriage, and death information; and their relationships to others, typically their parents. Further information is minimal. As Hatcher explains,

> early genealogies tend to focus on names and dates. They may note other records created by the individual, such as deeds, but the overall reliance is on vital records, wills, and family-supplied information. Documentation, if it is included, is often a simplistic reference to a town vital record (1996, 14).

In addition to content, we must consider how that information is arranged. A genealogy usually begins with one individual (or one couple when both the husband and wife are included), known as the *subject.* It then proceeds to trace the subject's relatives, usually forward (descendants) or backward (ancestors) in time. Some genealogies extend in both directions. In actual usage, *genealogy* usually refers to a compilation of a couple's descendants for several generations. The terms *ancestry, lineage,* and *pedigree* are usually used when a person's ancestors are traced.

Further variations also appear in compiled genealogies. Some genealogies (and this is particularly true of many family histories) trace only a single line of descent (forward in time) or ascent (backward in time). Most such genealogies focus on the surname (or *patriarchal*) line of the subject, discussing the son and his father, grandfather, great-grandfather, and so forth. Of course, a genealogy may begin with the great-grandfather, followed by the grandfather, then the father, and, last, the son. A much rarer form of "single-line" genealogy traces only the mother-daughter connections; these are called *matriarchal* or *umbilical* genealogies. (In fact, matriarchal genealogies may be the most trustworthy genealogies, because it is much easier to prove the maternity of the child than the paternity [assuming the mother's name can be found in the records].)

Other versions of single-line genealogies do not trace only the father or mother; rather, they follow either parent in each generation until reaching a specific ancestor. Such a single-line genealogy is often called a *lineage,* a term popularized by lineage societies, such as the Daughters of the American Revolution (DAR); the object is to trace one's descent to a specific person who qualifies one for membership in the society. Thus, a woman's DAR lineage might extend from her through her father, his mother, her father, his mother, her father, his father, and, finally, to his father, the soldier. The lineages found in the records of the DAR and dozens of other lineage societies are also genealogies, yet they are overlooked by most researchers.

Of course, a genealogy can include any combination of these and other forms. Many genealogies of colonial New England immigrants focus on the immigrant, giving his or her complete known ancestry in the Old World (often only two to four generations) as a preface, while the body of the genealogy treats male descendants through four to eight (rarely more) generations. Often, female lines are not carried forward; rather, females' lives and marriages are summarized under their father's record and only their brothers' lines are continued. Such genealogies are sometimes called *agnate,* or male-line, genealogies. Many Mormon genealogies, for example, focus on the first male to join The Church of Jesus Christ of Latter-day Saints (LDS church). His paternal ancestry may be given (as a sort of preface) back to the first of his line to come to America. The body of the work might then trace all descendants, both male and female, of the "convert" ancestor.

With such a variety of forms, there is no set arrangement for the information in a genealogy. However, some arrangements have become more popular over the years. Short discussions of four popular arrangements are in Donald R. Barnes and Richard S. Lackey's *Write it Right: A Manual for Writing Family Histories and Genealogies* (Ocala, Fla.: Lyon Press, 1983) and Joan Ferris Curran's *Numbering Your Genealogy: Sound and Simple Systems* (Arlington, Va.: National Genealogical Society, 1992). The most common genealogies, historically, have been the agnate (male line) descendancy genealogies, for which three arrangements have been popular.

70 *Five Generations of Connecticut Harrisons* [Jan.

2. ENSIGN THOMAS^{2} HARRISON (*Richard*^{1}), ancestor of the Connecticut Harrisons, born in England about 1630, died at Branford towards the end of 1704. He married first, in Feb. 1655/6, DOROTHY (———) THOMPSON, widow of John, who was called "farmer;" and secondly, 29 Mar. 1666, ELIZABETH (———) STENT, widow, whose husband had died on the voyage to America. He took the oath of allegiance at New Haven 4 Apr. 1654, but settled at Branford. He was ensign in King Philip's War, and was elected deputy to the General Court 10 May 1677. In a land record dated 14 Nov. 1688 he calls himself 58 years of age.

Children by first wife, born at New Haven:

3. i. THOMAS,^{3} b. 1 Mar. 1656/7.
4. ii. NATHANIEL, b. 13 Dec. 1658.

Children by second wife:

iii. ELIZABETH, b. at New Haven in Jan. 1667/8; m. WILLIAM BARKER of Branford.
iv. MARY, b. at Branford 10 Feb. 1668/9; m. 6 June 1699 JOHN LINSLEY, 3D.
5. v. JOHN, b. at Branford 1 Mar. 1670/1.
6. vi. SAMUEL, b. at Branford 11 Aug. 1673.
7. vii. ISAAC, b. at Branford in 1678.

3. LIEUT. THOMAS^{3} HARRISON (*Thomas*,^{2} *Richard*^{1}), born at New Haven 1 Mar. 1656/7, died at Branford 1 Jan. 1725/6. He married, in 1689, MARGARET STENT, daughter of his stepmother; and administration on the estate of Margaret (Stent) Harrison was granted 7 Jan. 1730/1. He served in King Philip's War, was ensign in 1697, was a lieutenant in 1709, in Queen Anne's War, and was also in the expedition to Canada.

Children, born at Branford:

i. LYDIA,^{4} b. 24 Aug. 1690; m. 4 Mar. 1712/13 JOSEPH MORRIS.
ii. JEMIMA, b. 12 Mar. 1692/3; d. in 1730; m. in Jan. 1727/8, as his second wife, CALEB PARMELEE, who m. (1) Elizabeth Foote and m. (3) Mary Durham.
8. iii. THOMAS, b. 12 Oct. 1694.
iv. ABIGAIL, b. 17 Mar. 1696/7; m. 9 Dec. 1736 JOSIAH POND.
9. v. BENJAMIN, b. 7 Aug. 1698.
10. vi. JOSEPH, b. 25 May 1700.
11. vii. DAVID, b. 7 Feb. 1702/3.
viii. AARON, b. 4 Mar. 1704/5; d. 20 Nov. 1708.
ix. JACOB, b. 6 Oct. 1708; d. *s.p.*; estate administered 20 May 1737; m. 24 Jan. 1734/5 SARAH WARDELL, dau. of Uzal and Phoebe, who m. (2) 22 Oct. 1744 Jonathan Brown.

4. CAPT. NATHANIEL^{3} HARRISON (*Thomas*,^{2} *Richard*^{1}), born at New Haven 13 Dec. 1658, died at Branford 1 Jan. 1727/8. He married HANNAH FRISBIE, born in 1669, died 27 Sept. 1723, daughter of Edward and Hannah. He was deputy in the Assembly and justice of the peace, 1717–1725.

Children, born at Branford:

i. HANNAH,^{4} b. 28 July 1690; d. 5 Oct. 1753; m. JAMES TALMADGE of New Haven.
12. ii. NATHANIEL, b. 26 Jan. 1692/3.
13. iii. DANIEL, b. 12 Sept. 1694.
iv. MARY, b. 24 Apr. 1696; d. 28 Oct. 1747; m. (1) 7 Jan. 1718/19 WILLIAM HOADLEY; m. (2) 19 Feb. 1742/3 SAMUEL ROSE.

Figure 16-2. An example of the Register System of descent genealogies from *New England Historical and Genealogical Register* 70 (January 1916).

The Register System. The Register System of identifying the descendants of the earliest person (or couple) in the genealogy takes its name from the *New England Historical and Genealogical Register,* which has used this system for more than one hundred years (figure 16-2). In the Register System, the first (earliest) ancestor being discussed is assigned the number 1; this is usually the immigrant, pioneer, or earliest known ancestor of a surname. A brief discussion of his life is given, including the dates of his birth, marriage, and death (if known); his wife's name and similar dates for her life are given (if known). Additional historical information is often included, such as positions held in local societies, military service, or the location of land. The ancestor's children are then listed in order of birth; they are indented and numbered on the left with lowercase roman numerals (*i, ii, iii, iv, v, vi, vii . . .*). Each child who is continued in the genealogy (usually any male who married and had children) also is assigned an Arabic num-

1909.] *The Hoppe-Hoppen-Hopper Lineage.* 123

THE HOPPE-HOPPEN-HOPPER LINEAGE.

BY HOPPER STRIKER MOTT.

(Continued from Vol. XL., p. 15, of THE RECORD.)

IV. MATTHIJS ADOLPHUS[2] HOPPEN (Andries[1]), bap. in New Amsterdam, March 3, 1658; wits.: Lambert Huijbertszen Mol, Arie Corneliszen, Christena Harmens and Engeltje Wouters. He m. in the Dutch Church there, Anna, dau. of Júrck Paúlús, May 2, 1683; he being of N. Y. and she of New Albany, but living at the former place. According to the custom she was known as Antje Jorkse. They removed to Hackensack where they were accepted as members of the church 1687 by Domine Petrus Tassemaker. Hoppen bought a farm adjoining his brother's at Saddle River and was elected deacon of the church May 25, 1704. He returned to N. Y. and bought the farm in Bloomingdale with which his name has become identified, Aug. 13, 1714. Soon after his marriage he dropped his middle name and it was to Mathias Hoppe that the deed was drawn. Issue:

70 i. Andries,[3] Winfield states he was b. in Bergen, April 2, 1684, and that he was alive in 1725. He m. Elizabeth Bras, Aug. 12, 1710, who was b. at Hackensack, in which town they resided. On Jan. 28, 1711, Annetje, their first child was baptized. Mattias, their son, was baptized April 6, 1713, before Mattis Hoppe and Lea Hoppe, his grandfather and aunt. He m. Aaltje Kuypen (Cuyper), Nov. 9, 1741. *Vide* Rockland Co., N. Y., Records for descendants, where a child was bap. in 1742.

71 ii. Christijna, Hackensack records make her baptism July 25, 1686, in presence of Gerrit van Dien and Maijna Pouwels. Van Dien is the son of Geertje Hoppe and Dirck Gerritse van Duyn, heretofore mentioned. She joined the church of her native place upon confession, April 12, 1708, and the next year (May 21) she m. Johannes Huijsman, a young man who was born there and there the couple lived. For issue *vide*, Staten Island Mss. in Holland Society Library.

72 iii. Lea, b. in Hackensack and bap. there Sept. 13, 1695; wits.: Hendrick and Catharijn Hoppe.

73 iv. Rachel, bap. Feb. 20, 1703, in presence of Cornelús Breyandt and Hendrickje Houseman.

74 v. Johannes, was bap. in Hackensack, May 19, 1706; wits.: Roelof Bogert and Belitie de Groot.

72. LEA[3] HOPPE (Matthijs,[2] Andries[1]), m. Johannes van den Hoef, a young man b. in Albany, but living at Hackensack, May 15, 1714. The N. Y. Church records give issue:

Figure 16-3. An example of the NGSQ System (modified register) of descent genealogies from *New York Genealogical and Biographical Record* 40 (1909).

ber (*2, 3, 4 . . .*) in birth order; it is located to the left of the lowercase roman numeral. At this point in the genealogy, only the name, and perhaps the birth year, is given for each individual to be continued. After the discussion of the earliest ancestor (number 1) and his family is completed, a discussion of number 2 follows, with complete (as far as known) information about his birth, marriage, death, and other historical and biographical facts. His children are listed again, with lowercase roman numerals (beginning again with *i*). Those to be further continued receive the next available Arabic number (for example, 6, if numbers 2 through 5 were used for the children of number 1). This system makes it simple to follow the lineage forward or backward by following the Arabic numbers of the line of interest.

The NGSQ System. The simplicity of the Register System has one drawback. Once numbers are assigned, it is difficult to add new generations without disturbing the existing number scheme. A similar system, first used (inconsistently) by the *New York Genealogical and Biographical Record,* is now exemplified in the *National Genealogical Society Quarterly* (*NGSQ*). The NGSQ System (also called the Record or Modified Register system) assigns Arabic numbers to all descendants of the initial ancestor (figure 16-3) (roman numerals are still used to identify the children in each family unit); thus, the first person is number 1, and his six children would be numbered 2, 3, 4, 5, 6, and 7. Those who are continued in the genealogy (again, usually male children who had children themselves) usually have a "plus" sign (+) to the left of their identification number; it tells the reader that more information is available about that person further into the genealogy. In most other respects, the arrangement of the information is similar to the Register System. Note, however, that the ability to add names within the NGSQ System only extends one generation. After that point, the numbering system still breaks down. (See "The Henry System," below.)

The Register and NGSQ systems have been the most commonly used systems for agnate descent genealogies in book format, and they are especially popular with the scholarly genealogical journals that publish compiled genealogies. Today, virtually all major journals use the NGSQ System.

The Henry System. Although the NGSQ System makes it easier to add newly found generations, it is still cumbersome when several successive generations need to be added (especially during the research phase). Reginald Buchanan Henry devised a system that assigns a unique number to every descendant based on his or her relationship to the earliest ancestor discussed. With this system, each person receives a number based on the number of the parent being traced and his or her birth position in their family. Therefore, the first ancestor is number 1. His children are 11 (one-one, not eleven), 12 (one-two), 13, 14, and so on. The children of the fourth child are numbered 141 (one-four-one), 142, 143, 144, etc. Thus, a child numbered 15382 is understood as the second child of the eighth child of the third child of the fifth child of the earliest given ancestor. This system has not found as much favor in published genealogies as the Register or NGSQ systems, primarily for two reasons. First is the difficulty of handling families with more than nine children; second is the nature of the numbers, which increase by one digit for each generation. Today, computer programs make it much easier to use the widely accepted NGSQ System (often called the Modified Register style in computer programs) because the programs can easily renumber the descendants whenever new ones are entered.

Many other systems exist; often they are modifications of one of the three primary systems described above. Some are vain attempts by researchers to invent a "better mousetrap," but they are usually more unwieldy and, hence, less useful. The advent of computer technology, however, has encouraged the growth of another arrangement of genealogical descendancy.

The Outline System. Popular for years in British and European genealogies, the Outline System of descent has appeared in American genealogies more frequently in the last fifteen years because many genealogical computer programs use it as their chief (and, in early versions, the only) form for showing descent. In this system, each generation of children is indented from its parents and listed immediately after them, except for descendants of older siblings, who are listed under their parents and before the sibling of the parent. If this seems confusing in theory, it is not much easier to follow in practice. The earliest ancestor's name is given at the extreme left of the page; the ancestor's spouse is listed directly below. On the next line, indented, is the name of their oldest child. If that child married, the name of his or her spouse is, again, listed directly below. Their oldest child follows on the next line, indented an additional level. This process continues until the youngest generation descended from the first child of the original couple is reached, then all the children of that family are listed together (indented the maximum number of levels). They are followed by the next oldest sibling of their parent, followed by the children of that aunt or uncle.

Eventually the outline works back to the left, where the second child of the original couple is listed, and the process continues. In this system, all children of the same generation are indented an equal distance; to find siblings, one only needs to look up and down the chart at the same level of indentation until coming to a person indented farther to the left (who is the parent, aunt, or uncle of the siblings being traced). This system is complicated by the lack of the usual individual numbers (although sometimes Henry System numbers are used) and because all members of one family are not immediately next to one another; this makes it very difficult to study family groups. An example from this author's family (figure 16-4) illustrates the Outline System.

The amount of genealogical information for each person in such a system varies—from name and birth year only to a paragraph with complete genealogical facts. The problems of such a system seem apparent (including the great amount of wasted space). Unfortunately, one of the most popular genealogical software programs, *Personal Ancestral File*® (developed

```
Arthur Percy Chamberlain
sp-Ruth Alida Pierce
    Harriet
    sp-George
        Gale
        sp-Tony
            Kelly
            Todd
        Gretchen
        sp-Richard
            Ruth
            Esther
            Benjamin
        sp-Ray
            Samuel
        Peter
        sp-Betty
        Kory
        sp-Claudine
            Krystine
            Arthur
            Deborah
            Sarah
            Aaron
        Penny
        sp-Roy
            Diewuke
            Charles
            Ryan
        sp-Dave
            Stephanie
            Valerie
            Kimberly
            Pamela
            Thomas
            Bonnie
    Gordon
    sp-Betty
        Lynn
        Carol
    Eleanor
    sp-Norman
        Cliff
        sp-Gloria
            Shawn
        sp-Lyn
        Cathy
        sp-Paul
            Jonathan
            Andrew
    Dorothy
    sp-Dart
        Nancy
        sp-Skip
        Susan
        sp-Tim
            Lauren
            Quinn
            Olivia
        Tom
        sp-Becky
            Jesse
    Douglas
```

Figure 16-4. An example of the Outline System.

by the LDS church) and the largest computerized genealogical database (the same church's Ancestral File) presently use this system, so researchers will have to get used to interpreting information in this arrangement. Fortunately, many other genealogical software programs offer other versions of descendancy lists. Also, commercial and shareware add-on programs that produce other arrangements are available for *Personal Ancestral File.*

Descent Charts. A less common arrangement in which descent can be given is the use of individually designed charts. Because the number of descendants is unpredictable, preprinted *descent charts* are generally not available (as opposed to pedigree charts, described below). However, researchers often create descent charts, usually by listing the subject couple at the top of a page (sometimes at the left side) and then drawing downward lines, with each child's name at the end of one line. Lines then descend from each child, each listing a grandchild, and so forth. Descent charts can become large and unwieldy after just four generations; due to their size, they are seldom printed. Usually they are found in manuscript genealogies and sometimes as periodical articles or illustrations in genealogy books. Most genealogical software programs can create one or more styles of descent charts.

The previously described systems deal with genealogical information about descendants. But genealogies are often arranged to show the ascent (ancestors) of an individual as well. Three similar systems have consistently been the most popular.

Pedigree Charts. Also known as *lineage charts* or *ancestry charts,* these are the familiar preprinted forms that use lines to connect a person to his or her parents. The first person—the subject—appears on a line at the center of the left side of the chart, usually with birth, marriage, and death dates and places given under his or her name. The horizontal line with the subject's name is connected to a vertical line which, in turn, is connected to two horizontal lines, one farther up and one farther down the chart. The subject's parents appear on these lines, which, in turn, are connected to other lines farther to the right; there the parents of the subject's parents are listed. Using this basic arrangement (figure 16-5), anywhere from three to six generations can be shown on a sheet, which is usually letter size (but in the past was often legal size). Each chart in a pedigree is numbered, and continuations of the pedigree are referenced to another chart by its number. Several different numbering schemes exist.

Each pedigree chart may be accompanied by several *family group records,* which contain more information about the couples on the chart, including lists of all their children and, ideally, the sources of information for the statements on the charts. Although these forms, with various arrangements, have been used for more than fifty years, they were popularized by the LDS church in the 1950s and 1960s. Relatively few published genealogies of ascent use these charts (except for LDS Books of Remembrance), but they are now almost universally used as worksheets by genealogists. They are also the forms of choice for most genealogical software programs. Many manuscript genealogies include such forms as well.

An older form of the pedigree chart (which appeared in some genealogies up to the 1930s but is rare today) is the *fan chart* (figure 16-6). On such a chart, the subject person (or couple) appears in the center of a circle or at the bottom center of a semicircle, surrounded by several concentric rings representing generations of ancestors. The first ring (or semi-ring) is divided into two halves, with each parent's names in each half. The next ring has four sections, for the grandparents, then eight, and so forth to the outermost ring (seldom more than six or seven generations). As with pedigree charts, the amount of information given for the earlier generations is minimal (usually just a name). Fan charts are sometimes called *sunburst charts* because of their appearance.

Ancestor Tables. Also called *Ahnentafel* (from the German name for this arrangement) or the *Sosa-Stradonitz System,* the ancestor table is the preferred arrangement for publishing information of a direct ancestral nature. It is related to the pedigree chart because it uses a numbering system common to most pedigree charts. The subject of the ancestry is assigned the number 1. A line or paragraph of information about the subject follows the number and his or her name. The father follows as number 2, again with a line or paragraph of information; the mother is number 3. Each person's father then has a number equal to two times his or her own number, while the mother's number is twice his or her number plus one. The information can then be arranged in a table numbered down the left-hand side or as a series of numbered paragraphs on several pages, each line or paragraph describing an individual with as much detail as desired. The numbers used in an ancestor table are the same used on most pedigree charts, where the parents' numbers are twice (and twice plus one) that of the child (figure 16-7).

Ancestor List (Multi-Family Genealogies). Some genealogies simply present a list of ancestors with varying amounts of information (sometimes quite complete) for each person. Such a list is sometimes a variation of the ancestor table (described above), but often it has more information and less structure. A common way to present an *ancestor list* is to consider each surname of a person's ancestry, usually as a lineage (see below). Surnames may be presented alphabetically, with the most recent ancestor of that name described first, followed by his or her father, then each generation's father until the earliest known ancestor of that name is identified; because in most American families the surname is taken from the father, this creates a set of patriarchal lineages. In other variations, the ancestor list presents the lineages in order of appearance on a pedigree chart, discussing the father's surname first, followed by the mother's, the father's mother's name, the mother's mother's line, and so forth. Constructing a person's pedigree from such a list can be confusing, but usually all the persons of one surname are discussed together. Sometimes called the "all my ancestors" or *allied families* style, the preferred term is now *multi-family genealogy.* Mary Walton Ferris's *Dawes-Gates Ancestral Lines* (Milwaukee, 1931) is often cited as an excellent example of this approach. Several other excellent examples using variations on this arrangement are listed in the bibliography of Meredith B. Colket's *Founders of Early American Families: Emigrants from Europe, 1607–1657,* rev. ed. (Cleveland: General Court of the Order of Founders and Patriots of America, 1985), discussed below.

In addition to these arrangements of descent and ascent genealogies, some researchers choose to present information in other ways.

Two-Way (or Ancestors and Descendants) Genealogies. Many genealogists choose to present their information as a combina-

Pedigree Chart

Chart no. ____

No. 1 on this chart is the same as no. ____ on chart no. ____

1 Carlton Aaron PIERCE
Born: 7 Mar 1851
Place: Peru, Berkshire, MA
Marr: 29 Oct 1879
Place: Hinsdale, Berkshire, Mass
Died: 31 Oct 1934
Place: Hinsdale, Berkshire, MA

Fannie Abigail FRANCIS
Spouse

2 Aaron PEIRCE
Born: 6 Jun 1819
Place: Peru, Berkshire, Mass
Marr: bef Jun 1850
Place: Berkshire, Mass
Died: 7 Nov 1851
Place: Peru, Berkshire, Mass

3 Martha THOMSON
Born: 29 Dec 1820
Place: Peru, Berkshire, Mass
Died: 5 Feb 1907
Place: Hinsdale, Berkshire, Mass

4 Ebenezer PEIRCE
Born: 29 Nov 1788
Place: Peru, Berkshire, MA
Marr: 22 May 1816
Place: Peru, Berkshire, MA
Died: 15 Jul 1865
Place: Peru, Berkshire, MA

5 Electa PHILLIPS
Born: 16 Apr 1794
Place: Peru, Berkshire, MA
Died: 15 May 1872
Place: Worthingham, Hampshire, MA

6 Nathan THOMSON
Born: 27 Feb 1776
Place: Peru, Berkshire, MA
Marr: 6 Oct 1805
Place: Peru, Berkshire, Mass
Died: 4 May 1846
Place: Peru, Berkshire, MA

7 Polly LELAND
Born: 5 Jun 1785
Place: Peru, Berkshire, MA
Died:
Place:

8 Ebenezer PEIRCE cont. ___
Born: 9 Jun 1745
Place: Sutton, Worcester, MA
Marr: abt 1775
Place: Berkshire, Mass
Died: 1 Aug 1802
Place: Marietta, Washington, OH

9 Eunice LOOMIS cont. ___
Born: 2 Oct 1749/50
Place: Coventry, Tolland, CT
Died: 10 Feb 1826
Place: Peru, Berkshire, MA

10 Smith PHILLIPS cont. ___
Born: 11 Jul 1761
Place: Hopkinton, Middlesex, MA
Marr: abt 1790
Place: Mass
Died: 25 Jul 1843
Place: Peru, Berkshire, MA

11 Lydia LELAND cont. ___
Born: 8 Jan 1770
Place: Holliston, Middlesex, MA
Died: 25 Apr 1828
Place: Peru, Berkshire, MA

12 Nathan THOMSON cont. ___
Born: 8 Oct 1747
Place: Bellingham, Norfolk, MA
Marr: abt 1775
Place: of Peru, Berkshire, Mass
Died: 22 May 1815
Place: Granville, Washington, NY

13 Dorothy (Dolly) cont. ___
Born: 1752
Place:
Died: 31 Jan 1831
Place: Granville, Washington, NY

14 John LEALAND Rev, Capt cont. ___
Born: 12 Jan 1744
Place: Holliston, Middlesex, MA
Marr: abt 1768
Place: Mass
Died: 1826
Place: Amherst, Hampshire, MA

15 Hephzibah LEALAND cont. ___
Born: 12 Mar 1747
Place: Sherborn, Middlesex, MA
Died: 5 Jun 1808
Place: Peru, Berkshire, MA

Prepared 1 Jul 1996 by:

Figure 16-5. Example of a pedigree chart.

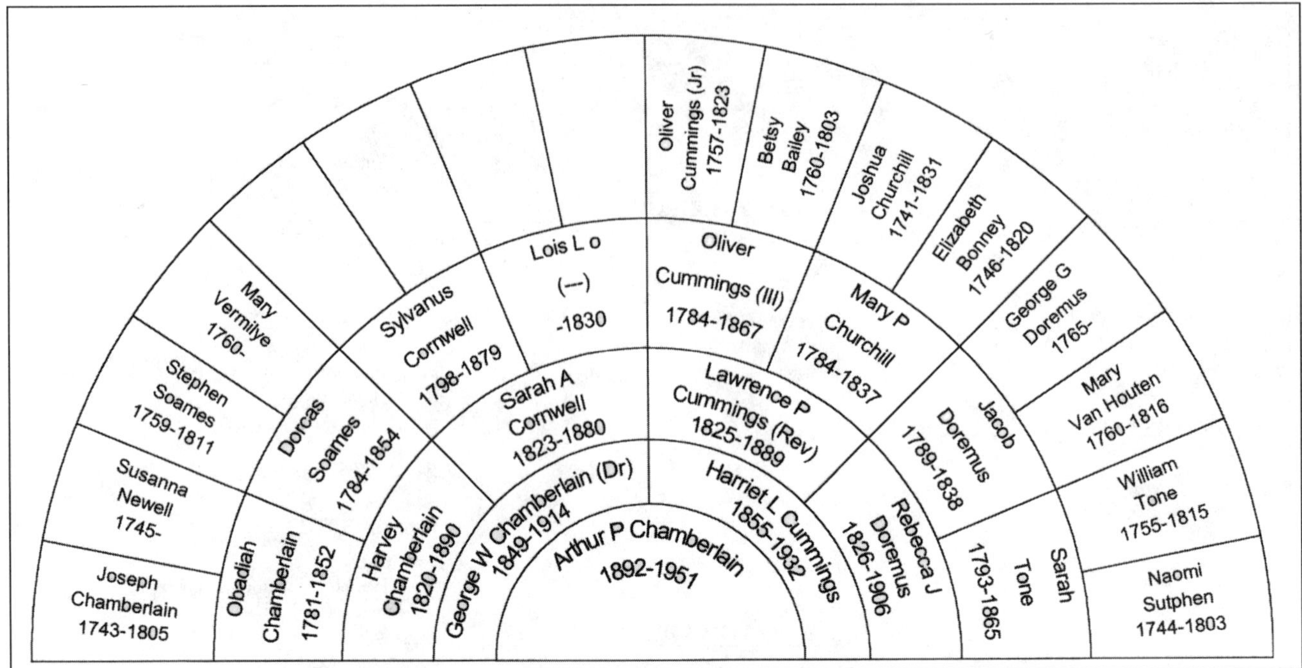

Figure 16-6. An example of a fan chart. (Prepared by Kory Meyerink using *PAF*Mate.*)

tion of descent and ascent information. In most such cases, the writer presents the ancestors and descendants of a chosen person or couple. This type of genealogy has become more and more popular in recent years, as true agnate descent genealogies have become more difficult to compile. Often one of the compiler's own ancestors—a great-great-grandfather, for example—is the subject, so the descendants are usually fairly well known to the genealogist; they are close cousins (first, second, and third degree), so there is heavy reliance upon family sources and correspondence with relatives for the descendancy information. The genealogist then researches the ancestry of the subject, often back to the immigrant ancestors or to the earliest ancestors that can easily be found. Sometimes ancestors in all lines are traced— sometimes only those of the subject's father's and mother's surnames.

A 1993 analysis of many such genealogies at the Family History Library of the LDS church in Salt Lake City showed that most of the subject ancestors were born in the late 1700s or early 1800s. Therefore, the coverage for any particular surname is not comprehensive because the subject ancestor usually lived during the nineteenth century. Indeed, some such books are actually updates to one or two branches of an earlier published agnate descent genealogy.

Lineage. A *lineage* can be thought of as either a descent or an ascent genealogy because it does not attempt to be comprehensive in either direction. Rather, a lineage simply presents one line of generational links connecting two individuals. It may be presented either as the lineage of a recently living person traced back to an earlier ancestor, such as an immigrant, or as the descent from an early ancestor to a later (usually living) person. In most cases, a lineage also identifies the spouse in each generation. Sometimes the children of each ancestor are identified, but only the one through whom the lineage is traced is continued.

Surname Dictionaries. On occasion, a researcher collects much information about several people with the same surname, but many are not related to one another; perhaps several different families with the same name are included, or there is not enough information to link families into generations. In such cases, the researcher may prepare a dictionary of the surname. An example is John H. Sherman's *Sherman Directory: An Alphabetical Listing of Over 25,000 Shermans with Known Vital Records and Relationships,* 4 vols. (Baltimore: Gateway Press, 1991). These compilations usually arrange individuals by their first names (because they share the same surname) and then present a biographical paragraph or more of information (whatever the researcher found) about the individuals. If children or parents are known, they are named in the brief biography and then must be found elsewhere in the directory for more information. Where many people share the same given name, an identification number or the year of birth may be used to distinguish among them.

Directories. Occasionally, a genealogy focuses on living individuals and their residences. When there are no generational links, such compilations can hardly be called genealogies, but a few have shown up in genealogical bibliographies and catalogs. They are most appropriate when they appear as part of a compiled genealogy, listing, for example, the current residences of persons of the surname considered in the genealogy. Such directories are best arranged alphabetically, although some may have geographic subdivisions (by state or country). Some are arranged by residence, usually sorted by the ZIP code. For a discussion of "Beatrice Bayley"-type books, see the discussion below of "Generic Surname Books."

As this discussion illustrates, there are many ways to arrange a genealogy, depending to a great extent on the nature of the contents. Of course, many individuals have found other ways to present their research findings, and in cases where the ar-

Ancestor Table for Harriet Lawrence CUMMINGS

First Generation
1. Harriet Lawrence CUMMINGS 1855–1932; Manhattan, NY & Greenwich, CT

Second Generation
2. Lawrence Pierson CUMMINGS 1825–1889; Salem, MA & Manhattan, NY
3. Rebecca Johnson DOREMUS 1826–1906; New York, NY

Third Generation
4. Oliver CUMMINGS III 1784–1867; Sumner, ME & New York, NY
5. Mary (Polly) CHURCHILL 1784/1786–1837; Plympton & Salem, MA
6. Jacob DOREMUS 1789–1838; Ponds, NJ & New Orleans, LA
7. Sarah TONE 1793–1865; South Amboy, NJ & Brooklyn, NY

Fourth Generation
8. Oliver CUMMINGS Jr. 1757–1823; Dunstable, MA & Sumner, ME
9. Betsy BAILEY 1760–1803; Nottingham West, NH & Sumner, ME
10. Joshua CHURCHILL 1741/1742–1831; Plympton, MA & Sumner, ME
11. Elizabeth BONNEY 1746–1820; Plympton, MA and Sumner, ME
12. George G DOREMUS 1765–1808; Ponds, NJ & New York, NY
13. Mary VAN HOUTEN about 1760–after 1819; Franklin, NJ
14. William TONE 1755–1815; South Amboy, NJ
15. Naomi SUTPHEN about 1744–1803; South Amboy, NJ

Fifth Generation
16. Oliver CUMMINGS 1728–1810; Dunstable, MA
17. Sybil WHITNEY 1733–1812; Killingly, CT & Dunstable, MA
18. Timothy BAILEY 1729–unknown; Bradford & Chelmsford, MA
19. Sarah FRENCH 1733–unknown; Dunstable, MA
20. Ebenezer CHURCHILL 1705–1751; Plympton, MA
21. Leah KEEN 1702–1781; Plympton, MA
22. Isaac BONNEY 1701–1772; Plympton, MA
23. Mary HORRELL 1706–unknown; Beverly & Plympton, MA
24. George (Joris) G. DOREMUS Jr. 1722–unknown; Hackensack, Bergen, NJ
25. Margaret TIETSOORT 1723–1767; Raritan & Lower Preakness, NJ
26. Jacob R. VAN HOUTEN 1721–unknown; Franklin & Hackensack, NJ
27. Neeltje STAGG 1728–unknown; Siconac & Acquackanonk, NJ
28. John TONE 1719–1791/1794; Dublin, Ire. & Freehold, NJ
29. Margaret HARVEY about 1712–unknown; Suffolk, Eng. & Freehold, NJ
30. Derick SUTPHEN 1712–1794; New Utrach, NY & Tennant, NJ
31. Mary about 1714–1794; Marlborough & Tennant, NJ

Figure 16-7. An ancestor table. This is the preferred arrangement for publishing information of a direct ancestral nature.

rangement is not familiar, the researcher must carefully read the preface of the genealogy to fully understand how the compiler arranged the information. Failure to do so will result in misunderstanding the genealogy and misinterpreting the information, which leads to erroneous research.

Family histories can also use any of these arrangements. The key difference, again, is the amount of historical and/or biographical information which is added to the genealogical facts about the individuals discussed.

Format

While a genealogy or family history may be presented in any of several arrangements, an equally large number of formats or media can be used to distribute a genealogy. Books are probably the most common format, with more than seventy thousand having been published in North America during the last two centuries. Other formats include articles in periodicals, compendia and dictionaries, lineage books, local histories, and, of course, manuscript collections. The finding aids used to locate genealogical material in these formats are discussed after the following descriptions.

Book Genealogies. The objective of many genealogists is to publish the results of their research in a book, to preserve the family heritage and to share it with relatives. This format has grown in popularity along with genealogy. Recent studies by the author and by the staff of the Family History Library have yielded a greater understanding of the nature and scope of book genealogies. A book about the Samuel Stebbins family, published in 1771, is generally credited as being the first published book genealogy (Wright 1974, 88). However, the growth of book genealogy publishing did not begin for another fifty years. Whitmore's 1875 bibliography of book genealogies is arranged

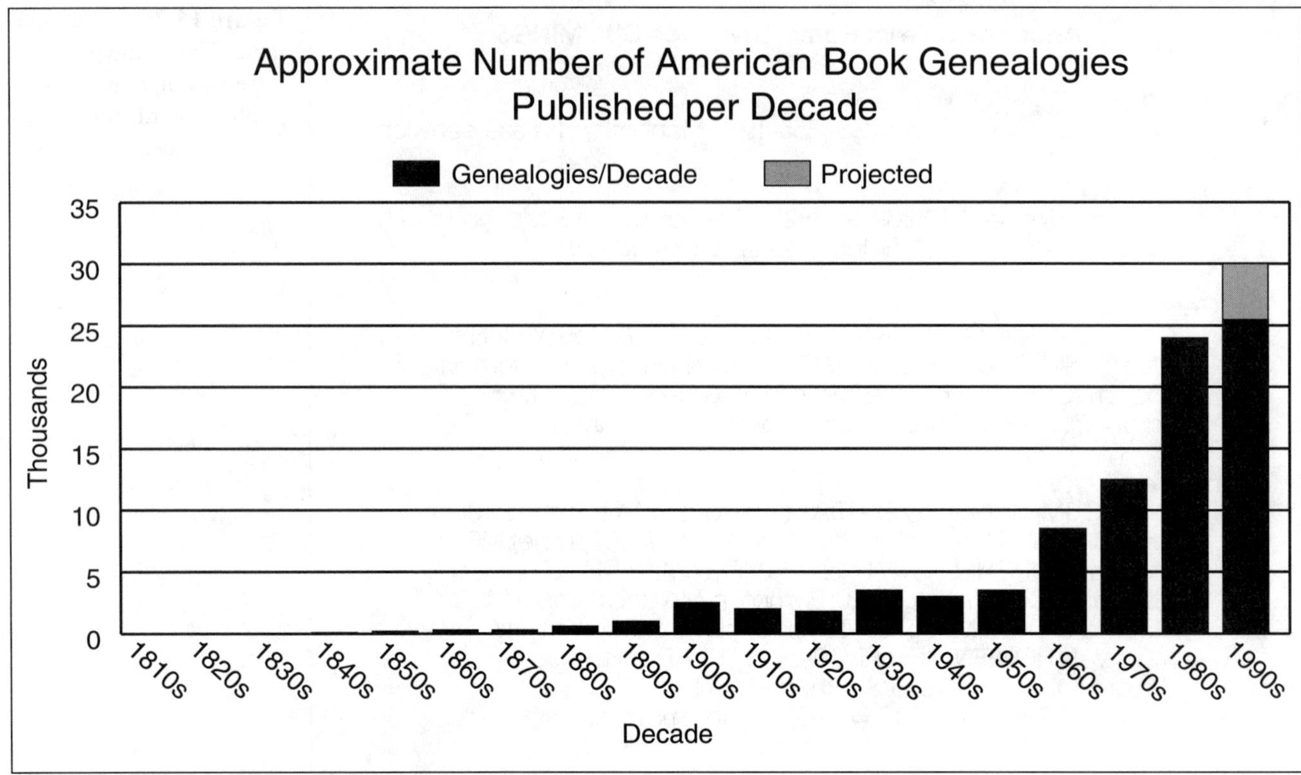

Figure 16-8. Approximate number of American book genealogies published per decade.

by year of publication and shows the Stebbins book in 1771, followed by books in 1787, 1806, 1813, 1816, 1819, and so forth, for a total of only twelve books published before 1832. Eight were published in the 1830s, 55 in the 1840s, 167 in the 1850s, and 237 in the 1860s. The next comprehensive bibliography, Munsell's *Index to American Genealogies . . . and Kindred Works (Known as Munsell's Index)* (discussed later under "Genealogical Indexes—Index to American Genealogies") was published in 1900; it identifies approximately 2,700 titles published to that date.

No comprehensive bibliography or library catalog has been published since 1900, but a careful study and analysis of the catalogs and bibliographies discussed later in this chapter permit some calculations to be made regarding the publishing history of book genealogies. Indeed, the 1997 edition of the *Family History Library Catalog*™ (discussed below under "Surname Section, Family History Library Catalog") includes approximately seventy-eight thousand American book genealogies. Because the *Family History Library Catalog* is not a comprehensive listing, it is clear that at least eighty-five thousand have been published since the 1830s. Figure 16-8 shows the approximate number of books published in each decade since 1810, while figure 16-9 shows the cumulative growth of total U.S. genealogy books. Clearly, the so-called "roots" craze that began in the mid-1970s has greatly fueled the production of these books, aided, no doubt, by the growing ease of first "kitchen-table" and now desktop publishing.

The nature of book genealogies varies widely. Indeed, it is difficult to define what a genealogy is and what it is not. Most current lists of genealogies are part of a library catalog (the major ones are discussed later), but the nature of published library catalogs means that other sources are included. Most library catalogs include genealogies along with other sources for which the catalogers have provided a surname entry; these include foreign genealogies, family newsletters, biographies, manuscript genealogical collections, genealogical charts, and abstracts of specific surnames from original records (such as censuses or vital records). For the purpose of this chapter, such books will not be considered book genealogies (which, however, does not diminish their value for research). Even after such sources are excluded, there remains a wide variety of book genealogies.

The first book genealogies were relatively brief accounts of a family, usually focusing on the descendants of an early immigrant to America. Most were fewer than 50 pages, and few exceeded 120 pages. Often titled "Family Record" or "Genealogical Memoir," there is no consistent organization among them; the Register System was not fully developed until 1883. Colket quotes the 1870 lament of the editor of the *New England Historical and Genealogical Register* (Col. Albert H. Hoyt) as "everyone who compiles a genealogy has his own plan for arranging his matter. Hence there are as many plans as there are volumes" (Colket 1968, 253).

Hoyt's efforts to establish the Register System did much to standardize the style in which descent genealogies were presented in North America (but, unfortunately, not in Britain or Europe). Even today's most common arrangement (the NGSQ System) is a modification of the Register System. Around this time (the 1880s) there was increasing interest in publishing genealogies, and their size began to grow as well. Many large books with several hundred pages identifying thousands of descendants appeared in the late nineteenth century, and the numbers have continued to grow since then. Typical of the turn-of-the-century book-length genealogies are the agnate genealogies of colonial immigrants to the New England states. Often these genealogies include eight or more generations of male-line descendants and contain upwards of ten thousand names. Such

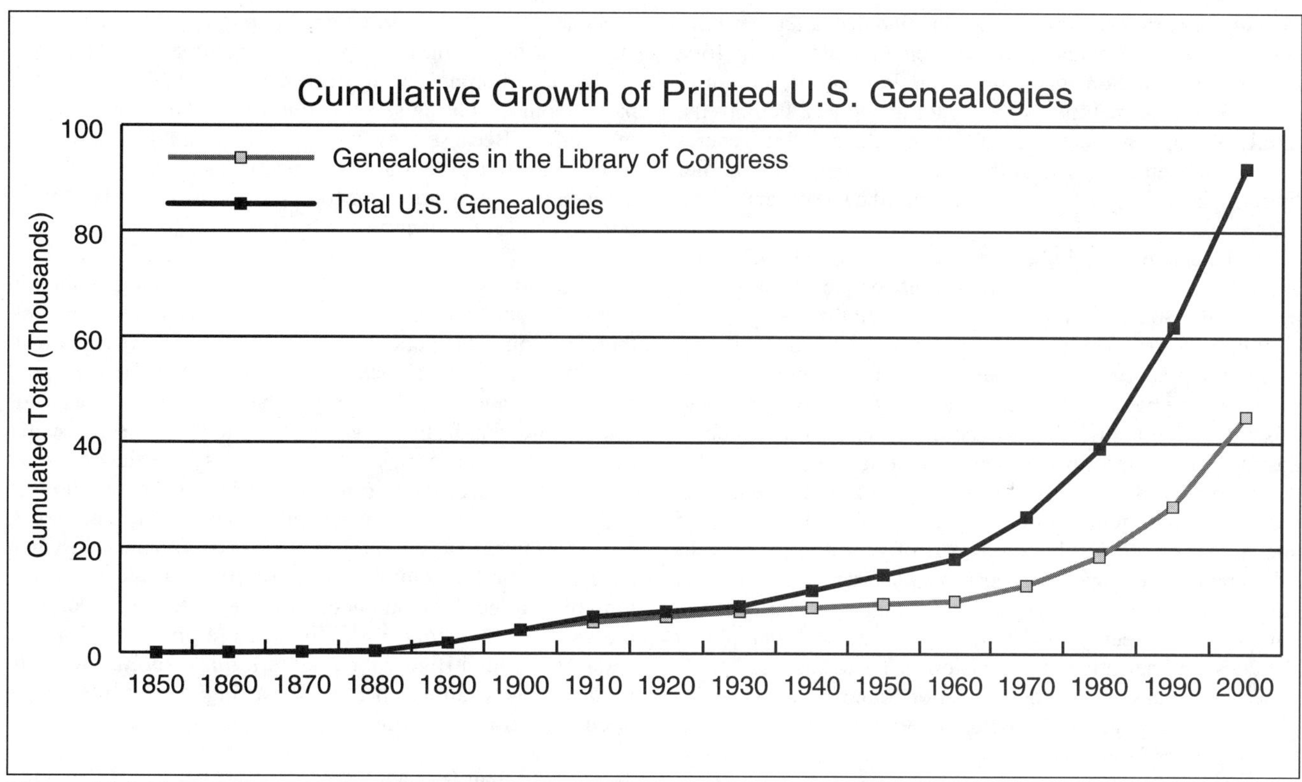

Figure 16-9. Cumulative growth of printed U.S. genealogies.

genealogies were very expensive to publish and, like most even today, were labors of love. The compiler seldom planned to make any money on the venture and was usually satisfied if production (printing, binding, and mailing) costs were met. The hundreds of hours involved in researching the families were virtually never compensated monetarily. Despite the tendency of compilers to include a lot of historical information about the first and second generations, these are really genealogies, even though some may call them family histories.

For an interesting perspective about writing family histories in the late nineteenth century, see W. P. W. Phillimore's *How to Write the History of a Family: A Guide for the Genealogist* (London: Elliot Stock, 1887). Written by a prominent British genealogist for English family histories, it is instructive in understanding both English and American genealogies of the late nineteenth century because many American writers followed the formats already popular in England.

Of the many arrangements discussed above, the Register (now NGSQ) and Record systems were by far the most popular well into the twentieth century. However, the nature and arrangement of book-length genealogies has broadened during the last fifty years. While lengthy, detailed agnate genealogies are still published by dedicated researchers, most modern genealogies have a narrower focus. By the last third of the twentieth century, Colket could say

> there has been a growing interest in compiling the genealogy of descendants of a member of an intermediate generation. . . . The larger task of compiling all the descendants in the male line of the first progenitor seems prohibitive, while the smaller task seems within the realm of possibility. Often the intermediate ancestor selected lived during the Revolutionary War. He broke away from the original area of settlement and became the forebear of persons of the name in the State or Territory to which he migrated (1968, 246).

In recent years, Colket's "intermediate generation" descendancy seems to have evolved into the two-way genealogies discussed earlier. A post-immigrant ancestor is still the subject ancestor, but as much attention is paid to his (or, if a couple, their) ancestry as to the descendants.

Another approach, which seems to have gained momentum in the 1920s and 1930s, focuses on all or some of the ancestors of the compiler. The acceptance of this arrangement was certainly enhanced by the works of Walter Goodwin Davis, Mary and Winifred Holman, and Herbert Seversmith, among others. It allows the researcher to focus on part of a person's ancestry (later volumes can include other ancestors), and promises a relatively finite and predictable number of persons to cover, rather than an unknown number of descendants. Such *ancestor books* also allow the researcher to include more personal and family history. They continue to prove popular, perhaps encouraged by the LDS church's focus on ancestors rather than descendants.

Today, in fact, virtually all of the arrangements described earlier have been used in the creation of book genealogies. A small sampling of book genealogies in the *Family History Library Catalog* showed that just under 60 percent focused on descendants, approximately 30 percent were two-way genealogies, roughly 5 percent were single lineages, and approximately 5 percent were multiple-ancestor books. In addition, many writers now attempt to include more history in their genealogies—to the point that possibly more family histories (albeit not scholarly histories) than pure genealogies are presently being written.

Periodical Articles. Many researchers find that, after they have completed their research, there is not enough information for a full-length book. Sometimes the researcher simply runs out of energy, enthusiasm, time, or money for the project. Perhaps the family is simply not large enough, or only three or four generations have been compiled. If the researcher wants to share her findings, an article in a genealogical periodical is often the best solution.

Genealogical periodicals have been published since 1847, and compiled genealogies were a chief feature of most early periodicals. Sometimes these articles treated the first few generations in America or the ancestry of a specific individual, still a common practice today. However, increasing numbers of periodicals have begun published in the last twenty-five years, and this has forced many editors to accept other material, such as abstracts and transcripts of source material (see chapter 19, "Genealogical Periodicals"). Genealogical articles are as varied in their arrangements as the genealogical books mentioned above. During the first hundred years of genealogical periodicals, agnate genealogies and ancestor tables were by far the most common arrangements. They still enjoy much popularity today, but they have been joined by pedigree charts, biographical sketches, and narrative family histories. There has also been a welcome increase in the documentation found in such genealogies. In fact, genealogical articles are often better documented than any other format used today.

Genealogical books and articles are treated separately in this discussion because the tools for locating an article about a family are usually different from those used to find genealogy books. These tools are discussed below under "Finding Family Histories and Genealogies." For more information on genealogical periodicals and their indexes, see chapter 19.

Compendia or Dictionaries. Many brief genealogies have been published in genealogical books called compendia or dictionaries. Unfortunately, most genealogists are unaware of many such publications and therefore miss important clues about their ancestors. Compendia and dictionaries include short genealogical accounts of several families that are often unrelated to one another. These accounts usually range from one paragraph to a few pages in length (seldom more). They are almost always strictly genealogical and include virtually no history or biography. The arrangement of the contents varies with almost every compendium or dictionary. The families are usually treated alphabetically, but within a family, either descendants or ancestors may be discussed (usually only one or the other in any given compendium). The information may be presented in a structured format, like the Register System, with a pedigree chart or ancestor table, or it may simply be a narrative, stating "John's children, Albert (1822), Sarah (1825), Susan (1827), and David (1830), were born in Springfield."

Genealogical compendia and dictionaries are two of the earliest forms of genealogical literature in America. One of the first American genealogical books was John Farmer's *A Genealogical Register of the First Settlers of New England* (1829). Every compendium has a focus that ties the included families together. Usually this focus is geographical, such as the families of a town, state, or region. Sometimes the focus is a specific ethnic or religious group. The compiler may try to include every family that fits certain qualifications, but usually the selection is somewhat more arbitrary, such as those families who sent in information about an ancestor or those about whom the compiler could find information. Although the information for any given family may be sparse, compendia are often quite lengthy and thorough. Many exceed five hundred or a thousand pages (some requiring several volumes) and discuss hundreds of families. Because they rely heavily on family information (often gathered by untrained genealogists), errors abound in compendia; the information found in them should be treated only as clues for further research.

Lineage Books. A lineage book is similar to a compendium in that it is a published collection of brief genealogies; however, there are some distinctions. A lineage book always deals with one line of a person's ancestry, although it may be presented either as the ancestry of the subject back to a "target" ancestor or as the descent from a target ancestor to the subject. Usually published by lineage societies, these books serve the important purpose of preserving, in print, the lineages of those who join the society. Therefore, a lineage book may present lineages of persons who have a revolutionary soldier or colonial clergyman as an ancestor, for example (figure 16-10). Lineage books often are arranged like an ancestor table, but, of course, only the specific ancestors in the lineage are given. Sometimes spouses are identified. Documentation is seldom offered in lineage books, although the sponsoring society may have documentation in its files.

Town and Local Histories. Compiled genealogies are also published in *town histories* and *local histories;* this has been a common practice since the first town histories were published for New England towns more than a century ago. Often the genealogies comprise half or more of the history. The early genealogies of this type were usually agnate descendancy genealogies. While they usually only covered the generations of the family that lived in the town, town histories often discussed every family in the town (insofar as the records allowed). Some local histories, especially those outside of New England, provided the information in an approach more akin to a "surname dictionary," especially where limited records made it difficult to determine exact relationships. While the actual histories seldom included sources, it was understood that the town records formed the backbone of the information. Family records and previously printed genealogies were often used to supplement inadequate records.

As the publishing of histories moved toward the Midwest, *county histories* were produced instead of town histories. Genealogical sections were replaced by biographical sketches of prominent men of the county. The biographies in these county histories sometimes provide important genealogical information (although it is usually limited to a few generations of the subject's surname line).

Since the 1960s, many local histories have been published; they are reminiscent of the early New England town histories. Their focus is often a small town or township, and much of the book consists of genealogical information provided by the present residents, especially those whose families resided in the locality for several generations. The series of County Heritage books published in North Carolina (see chapter 17) is a particularly good example of this kind of combined genealogy and history. As with their New England predecessors, sources are seldom given, except for the name of the resident submitting the information. It should be understood that the sources of such genealogies are usually family records, supplemented by whatever research the submitter did.

The arrangement of local histories is unlike the older town histories. The genealogies in these modern "scrapbook" histories often include much ancestral information, as well as some descendants. The subject of the genealogy typically is an older, living resident of the locality. The genealogy focuses on the subject's surname ancestors who settled that locality and the families of those ancestors. Nevertheless, these local histories can be quite comprehensive for some families, even including second and third cousins.

For a fuller discussion of local histories and their use and importance in research, see chapter 17, "County and Local Histories."

MARY CAROLINE WILLIS (MRS. EDWIN DYER HATHAWAY). 497

Born Boston, Mass.

Descendant of Isaac Cummings, of Massachusetts, through the Revolutionary ancestor, Ebenizer Cummings, as follows:

2. James Davis Knowles Willis (Sept. 24, 1829-April 24, 1902) and
Ellen Amanda Cummings (March 18, 1836-living Feb., 1910).
3. Robert Means Cummings (Feb. 22, 1802-Oct. 21, 1882) and
Mary Ann Osgood (Oct. 9, 1809-Feb. 8, 1880).
4. Moody Cummings (Oct. 10, 1777-April 3, 1826) and
Lucy Dennis (Dennes) (March 27, 1781-Feb. 28, 1826).
5. Ebenezer Cummings (Jan. 29, 1730-1804) and
Sarah Stevens (1726-Nov. 12, 1772).
6. William Cummings (April 24, 1702-Aug. 29, 1757) and
Sarah Harwood (June 26, 1706-1769).
7. John Cummings (1657-....) and
Elizabeth Kinsley (Nov. 22, 1657-July 3, 1706).
8. John Cummings (1630-Dec. 1, 1700) and
Sarah Howlet (....-Dec. 7, 1700).
9. Isaac Cummings (1601-May, 1677) and

Isaac Cummings was in Watertown prior to 1687.

Ebenezer Cummings (1730-....) born Nottingham, W. N. H., was a volunteer in Capt. Samuel Greely's Co. at the Lexington Alarm and was a member of the Committee of Inspection and Safety June 12, 1775-79.

Figure 16-10. From *Lineage Book of the National Society of Daughters of Founders and Patriots of America,* vol. 8 (1920). A lineage book may present lineages of persons who have a revolutionary war soldier as an ancestor, as in this example.

Lineage Databases. With the advent of computer technology in the genealogical world since the 1980s, a new format has begun to appear: the *lineage database.* Although presently there are only a few commercial lineage databases, this format holds much promise for the future. Lineage databases are collections of genealogically linked information. Although a database can be a manual collection, most often the term is used in connection with computerized files. Manual databases (such as the Family Group Records Archives at the Family History Library) are not published and hence are outside the scope of this book. Many computer databases exist only in the files of a single computer and in that sense are not published either. However, when such databases can be accessed via the Internet, they should be considered as published sources. The two major CD-ROM lineage databases, discussed later, are certainly published sources (that is, "electronic printed sources"), because they can be purchased.

Because lineage databases are still quite new, there are no straightforward guidelines for the use of such collections. Generally they are available as GEDCOM (Genealogical Data Communication—a standard file format that allows transfer of data between dissimilar computer programs) files, which allows them to be passed from one researcher to another. This transferability presents serious evaluation problems, for if a researcher gets part of a lineage database from another researcher, it can be difficult to determine who actually did the research. Also, sources are often not fully described, making it very difficult to evaluate the accuracy of the lineage statements.

In addition to providing the data in electronic format for adding to personal databases, published lineage databases can produce paper copies. Usually the ancestral information is printed in standard pedigree chart and family group record formats, while descendancy information, if available at all, may appear in any of the arrangements described earlier (although the outline style is currently the most popular). Two of the chief benefits of published lineage databases are (1) the fact that they can be updated with more lines or corrected information and (2) their tremendous size; they can contain hundreds of thousands, even millions, of names. They are also relatively inexpensive when considered on a cost-per-name basis because the high cost of paper publication is avoided.

Manuscripts. Many compiled genealogies have never been printed in any of the formats discussed above, but they are "printed (compiled) sources" and therefore deserve brief treatment. Manuscript genealogies appear in all of the arrangements discussed earlier and also in many unique, individual styles. Manuscripts dealing with descent may be arranged by one of the common systems; or they may be arranged as a descendancy chart. Those discussing the ancestry of a person often utilize pedigree charts and family group records to record the information found. There usually are any number of random notes on various pieces of paper and many letters from correspondents interested in the researcher's work. Often these papers are poorly arranged, if they are arranged at all. There is usually no index, so every page should be carefully checked. Because they usually include the researcher's notes, manuscripts often include some source citations; however, those notes may be cryptic abbreviations of obscure sources. Researchers who find manuscript genealogies can be well rewarded if they are prepared to take a lot of time to study the manuscript and ferret out the hidden information.

Generic Surname Books. A special kind of genealogy book requires discussion—partly because of the attention these books have received in the genealogical literature; these are the *generic surname books.* Although certainly not true genealogies or family histories, they are included here because of their focus on surnames and because they often appear on library shelves with traditional genealogies. Since the late 1970s, various publishers have offered to the public, usually via mail-order, books that appear to be family histories written uniquely for the particular family's surname. Often called Beatrice Bayley books for the name of one of the earliest publishers, these books are misunderstood by both the general public and many genealogists. They do serve a purpose, but their publishers tend to advertise them in unclear—indeed, often deceptive—ways.

Often regarded as having no genealogical value, generic surname books actually serve two important purposes in genealogy: they introduce the interested non-genealogist to the world of genealogical research, and they provide a directory of names and addresses of persons who share the same surname. Until the advent of recent "telephone directory" CD-ROMs, such national directories were very difficult and expensive to come by.

While generic surname books have been published by at least two (if not more) publishers, their contents are very similar and can be easily described. The books' titles vary, but they always include the surname of the family to whom they are advertised. A current title is "The World Book of [surname]." The books consist of general information about families, names, and genealogy, including the stories of ethnic groups, immigration to America, heraldry, the origins and meanings of names, some instruction about how to conduct research, addresses for obtaining vital records, blank charts and forms for recording information, and, of course, the surname directory (for only one spelling of one surname).

Although "Beatrice Bayley" has long been out of business (postal authorities forced closure of that company for its deceptive advertising), the same books were offered under the names of other authors, including Elizabeth Ross and Mary Whitney. These offers always came from towns in eastern Pennsylvania. Sharon Taylor, a name used by Halbert's (Bath, Ohio), seems to have had more success—at least in complying with postal regulations and providing slightly fuller disclosure in advertising. Still operating in 1998, Halbert's added major foreign countries to its name directory and began including a directory of immigrants having the surname (taken from Filby's *Passenger and Immigration Lists Index* [see chapter 14, "Immigration Sources"]).

While most experienced genealogists view them with disdain, generic surname books have been helpful in getting new people started in the world of genealogy. Realistically, the directory alone was often worth the price. These directories do not list everyone of the given surname, and some addresses may be five or more years out of date. However, a brief study by the author showed that such books have as many or more names in their directories as the currently popular CD-ROM telephone directories. The genealogical value of such books is limited—even more so now that there are more-current directories on CD-ROM—and the ongoing misleading advertising continues to annoy trained genealogists.

FINDING FAMILY HISTORIES AND GENEALOGIES

It is a poorly informed researcher who does not attempt to find a compiled genealogy for the family of interest. Genealogies and family histories (in one format or another) have been compiled for nearly every surname that has existed in the United States for more than a few generations. While a family history compiled for a certain surname may not include the specific family of interest, whether it does or not can only be discovered by searching that history. Compiled genealogies are most common for families that have been in the United States for several generations. The further back in time a researcher's ancestry goes, the more likely it is that someone who shares some of those ancestors has already compiled important information. Assume this author's parents have twenty-five descendants: only twenty-five people, plus their spouses, are potentially interested (genealogically speaking) in the author's parents. However, this author's grandmother has those twenty-five descendants plus another eighteen, and her mother has more than one hundred descendants. The number of descendants of any one ancestor increases geometrically for each generation back in time. It has been estimated that this author's wife's second great-grandfather, Reynolds Cahoon, born in 1790, has approximately ten thousand descendants in seven generations. Obviously, there is more potential genealogical interest in him than there is in a person only one generation back.

Most colonial American ancestors have tens of thousands of descendants today. Many have more than 100,000, and some of the earliest immigrants to America's shores have a million or more descendants. The small troupe of souls who stepped off the *Mayflower* in 1620 may have upwards of 20 million descendants today. Small wonder, then, that there is so much interest in *Mayflower* families. It only requires one or two dedicated and interested descendants among those thousands to compile a genealogy of many of the descendants.

While compiled genealogies seldom include every descendant, they usually include enough to be of interest to the researcher. Because the "traditional" family history or genealogy focuses on the immigrant ancestor and his male descendants for four to six (or more) generations, the further back researchers trace their ancestries, the more likely they are to find several genealogies that pertain to their pedigrees. This phenomenon is most common with New England families, especially those of the three southern New England states—Connecticut, Massachusetts, and Rhode Island. However, it is also common in the Mid-Atlantic and Southern states.

Several tools have been created to help genealogists find compiled genealogies. The choice of which tools to use depends on the type of genealogy being sought. Book genealogies are perhaps the easiest to locate because there are several tools, or finding aids, that can identify their existence. Genealogical articles are usually found in compendia or through periodical indexes. Genealogies in local histories can be found through selected indexes and catalogs. The various types of finding aids include library catalogs, booksellers' catalogs, bibliographies, genealogical indexes, compendia and dictionaries, major lineage books, periodical indexes, CD-ROMs, and other compiled sources.

Library Catalogs

Many libraries house genealogical collections, and many of the largest have published catalogs of their genealogies and family histories. Most catalogs can be purchased, but some are distributed to members of the sponsoring organization only. Most are also available for research in large libraries. Although library catalogs list only what the library owns, they are valuable to all researchers—not just to the ones who can go to that library and use its collection—because they indicate what printed genealogies exist. The researcher can then determine how to access a copy of the desired genealogy. Table 16-1 summarizes much of the information discussed below.

Surname Section, Family History Library Catalog. As of March 1997, the Family History Library collection included

Table 16-1. Major Catalogs and Bibliographies of Genealogies

Title or Repository	*Date*	*Titles*	*References*	*Scope*
Family History Library Catalog, Surname Section	1997	129,000	650,000	Worldwide
New York Public Library*	1974	26,000	75,000	United States
Library of Congress	1972	20,054	32,000	United States
Two *Supplements to Library of Congress*	1977, 1987	13,000	20,000	Recent U.S. titles
Genealogies Cataloged by the Library of Congress since 1986	1992	8,997	8,997	Recent genealogies
Meyerink's *Genealogical Publications*	1997	22,500		1969–95 genealogies
Complement to Genealogies in the Library of Congress	1981	21,500	30,000	United States
DAR *Library Catalog,* vols. 1, 3	1982–92	19,150	30,000	United States
Long Island Historical Society	1935	9,050	9,050	Eastern U.S., pre-1935
Los Angeles Public Library	1960, 1965	3,800	3,800	United States, post-1900
National Genealogical Society	1988	3,100	3,100	Lending list
New England Historic Genealogical Society	1992	7,000	7,000	Lending list
Genealogical and Local History *Books in Print,* 3rd–5th eds.	1981–96	12,356	36,000	Recent U.S. titles
UMI Guide to Family and Local Histories	1990–95	5,844	30,000	Older U.S. titles
American Genealogist	1900	2,700	see index	United States
Biographical Books 1876–1949	1983	16,500	40,300	With biographies
Genealogical Helper Index	1983	3,100	3,100	Books published 1971–83
NUCMC	1962–	10,000	200,000	Manuscripts

*Not including local history titles.

approximately 129,000 separate titles cataloged according to one or more surnames. Usually, between three hundred and four hundred new titles are added each month; however, many of the catalog entries are not for American genealogies or family histories. An informal study by this author and some of the library's staff in 1993 concluded that almost 18 percent of the titles were for foreign countries—predominantly British (approximately 7 percent) and Germanic (approximately 5 percent)—and that approximately 22 percent, while focusing on American families, were not truly book genealogies. This last percentage included manuscript collections, various genealogical charts, biographies, surname periodicals, family Bible records, and other surname-oriented books. Thus, approximately 60 percent of the titles in the Surname Section of the catalog pertain to U.S. families (figure 16-11); this amounts to approximately seventy-eight thousand American family histories, making the *Family History Library Catalog*™ the most important and comprehensive bibliography of genealogies available.

Because most genealogies deal with other families in addition to the subject family, the *Family History Library Catalog* includes references to some of these other families. Although the catalog does not note every surname in every volume in the collection, it lists the major surnames in each published genealogy, as well as other material pertaining to families. Each book is listed under an average of five to six surnames; some titles have as many as twelve or more such references. Hence, the Surname Section of the catalog includes at least 400,000 or more references for American families.

The catalog is produced on microfiche, and copies are sent to each of the more than 2,500 family history centers every year. The 1997 version of the Surname Section consisted of 393 microfiche. The microfiche catalog is updated annually. The library also produces a CD-ROM version with the two most popular sections of the catalog, the Surname and Locality sections. These are generally updated at least annually and are available at the library and family history centers.

Searching the Surname Section differs according to the catalog format. In the microfiche version, titles are arranged first by surname and then by the author of the book. The books within each surname listing are listed by author, or by title if no author is listed (figure 16-12). Books about a specific person are listed alphabetically by that person's name, after the listings for the same surname. Thus, books about Abraham Lincoln are listed after the books under the Lincoln surname. The catalog includes complete bibliographic information, as well as a brief contents note that is valuable in determining which of several books about a surname may have information about a specific ancestor. Content notes are usually one to three sentences in length and mention the subject ancestor (the first generation in descendancy genealogies or the most recent generation in ancestral genealogies). The notes usually also include the major geographic locations where the family lived and other surnames mentioned prominently in the genealogy.

The CD-ROM version allows additional search capabilities. It first searches for all genealogies with the same surname spelling entered in the search screen and reports the number of such titles found. It also supplies a list of alternate spellings for the surname and the number of titles listed under those spellings (some of which may be the same titles listed under the spelling requested, because some books are cataloged under

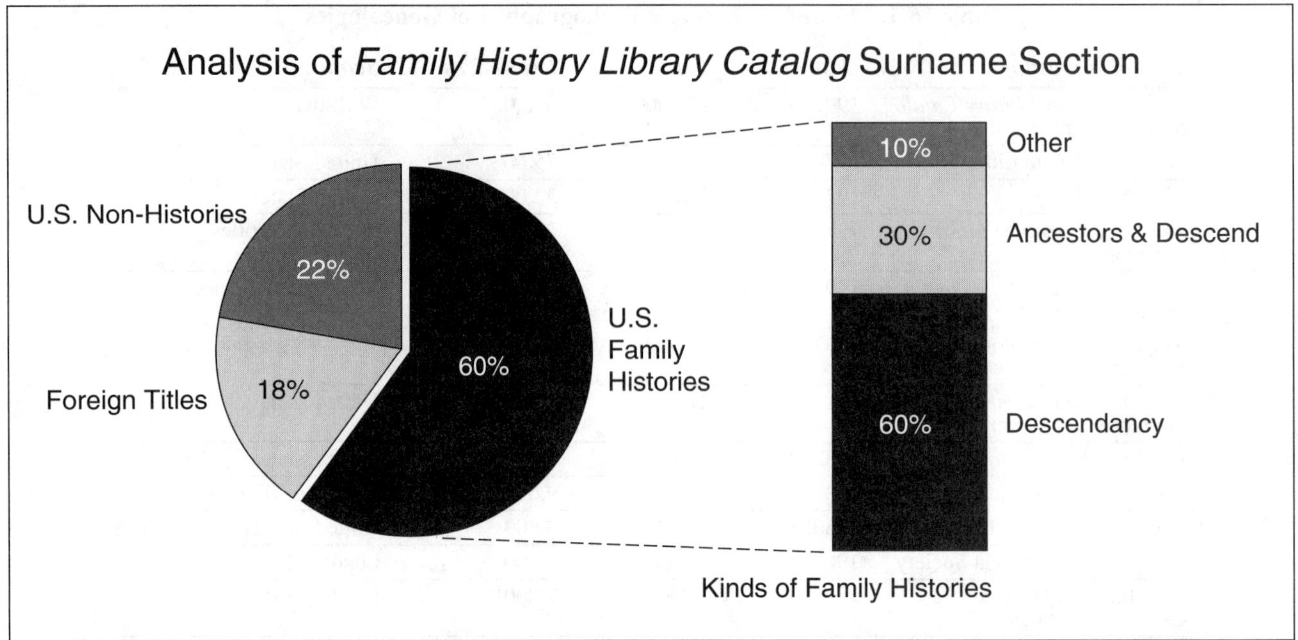

Figure 16-11. Analysis of the Surname Section of the *Family History Library Catalog* (based on a sample of 120 entries). Note that approximately 60 percent of the titles in the Surname Section pertain to U.S. families

similar spellings). Once the list of titles is selected, the computer can display just the title and content notes or the full entry, including the call number for the book or microfilm. The search may be further refined by searching for titles containing key words in the cataloging description; this is especially valuable for researchers seeking books about common surnames. For example, the search may report 204 books dealing with the surname Pierce. If the key words *New* and *Jersey* are added, the computer will show that eighty-five books include New in their descriptions and seventeen use Jersey. Only sixteen books have both words in the description. This method makes it much easier to limit a search to books that are most likely to be of interest.

The *Family History Library Catalog* is available at all family history centers; in addition, the microfiche version of the catalog can be purchased by individuals and institutions. Researchers may purchase the Surname Section as a whole or in smaller segments of the alphabet. At fifteen cents per microfiche, the entire Surname Section cost fifty-seven dollars in 1996. (As of early 1998, the CD-ROM version of the catalog was not available for sale to the public.)

Dictionary Catalog of the Local History and Genealogy Division. The New York Public Library (Fifth Avenue and Forty-second Street, New York, NY 10018) houses an excellent collection of genealogical research material. The large, eighteen-volume catalog for its genealogical collection, the *Dictionary Catalog of the Local History and Genealogy Division* (Boston: G. K. Hall, 1974), consists of photoduplications of the typed and handwritten, alphabetically arranged card catalog. Copies of these volumes are available at many major research libraries in the United States (figure 16-13). The catalog includes approximately 300,000 references to the 100,000 volumes that were in the collection before 1972. Although most of the books are local histories, approximately twenty-six thousand titles, and perhaps seventy-five thousand references, are for genealogies and family histories. Many of the titles are typescripts, manuscripts, or published books of which only a few copies were published; therefore, references in this catalog may not appear in many other libraries. The cards provide complete bibliographic citations, enabling a researcher to search for the titles at a local research library.

Like most published catalogs, the *Dictionary Catalog* has not been updated since publication. The library has added thousands of other, mostly new, family histories since the 1970s. Each year these additions are used to compile the *Bibliographic Guide to North American History* (Boston: G. K. Hall, annual). A few entries in the guide are for book genealogies (listed under the name of the family—for example, "Carter family"), but a better use for this source is to locate recently published local histories that may include genealogies. Because there is no accumulation for family histories published since the mid-1970s, researchers will want to use other sources to locate recent genealogies.

Genealogies in the Library of Congress: A Bibliography. The Library of Congress has perhaps the second-largest collection (after the Family History Library) of genealogies and family histories in the United States. An older, 1919 bibliography has been completely superseded by Marion J. Kaminkow's two-volume *Genealogies in the Library of Congress: A Bibliography* (Baltimore: Magna Charta Book Co., 1972) and its two supplements (1977, 1986), which cover 1972 to 1976 and 1976 to 1986. The initial catalog lists 20,054 books in the library's genealogy collection as of early 1972. Be sure to check the addenda in each volume; for example, the addenda for the 1972 catalog includes 736 titles of recent books. Like other libraries, the Library of Congress has added cross-references for surnames mentioned prominently in books about other families. These two volumes include approximately twelve thousand such references, yielding a total of approximately thirty-two thousand references.

Unfortunately, the Library of Congress collection and its catalogs suffer from the same shortcoming as the *Family History Library Catalog:* many books are listed that are not Ameri-

```
************************************************************************************
PIERCE.
                                                                 +-------------+
Pierce, H. L.                                                    |US/CAN       |
    The Pierce family of West Jersey / compiled by H. L. Pierce. -- |FILM AREA    |
      Salt Lake City : Filmed by the Genealogical Society of Utah,  |1005010      |
      1976. -- on 1 microfilm reel ; 35 mm.                      | item 3      |
                                                                 +-------------+
    Microreproduction of typescript.
    Richard Peirce died in 1749.

************************************************************************************
PIERCE.
                                                                 +-------------+
                                                                 |US/CAN       |
Pierce, Harold H., 1937-                                         |BOOK AREA    |
    Melton family history / by Harold H. Pierce and other Melton |929.273      |
      family members. -- Edmond, Okla. : H.H. Pierce, [1984?].   |M495p        |
                                                                 +-------------+
    Cover title.
    John Wesley Melton (1854-1934) married Louisa Ann Buffalo about 1877,
       and moved from Missouri to  Batson, Arkansas in 1896/1897. Descen-
       dants lived in Missouri, Arkansas, Oklahoma, Texas and elsewhere.
       Some descendants became Mormons, living in Arkansas and elsewhere.
    Includes Buffalo, Fuqua, Gilbreath, Homan, Pierce, Wann and related
       families.

************************************************************************************
PIERCE.
                                                                 +-------------+
Pierce, Harvey Cushman, b. 1859.                                 |US/CAN       |
    Seven Pierce families : a record of births, deaths and       |BOOK AREA    |
      marriages of the first seven generations of Pierces in     |929.273      |
      America, including a record of the descendants of Abial    |P611ph       |
      Peirce to the present / collected by Harvey Cushman Pierce. +-------------+
      -- Washington, D. C. : H.C. Pierce, c1936 (Strasburg, Va. :
      Shenandoah Publishing House). -- xlviii, 324 p., [2] leaves
      of plates : ports.

    This work contains the genealogical data about the first seven
       generations of seven families of the Pierce name, however spelled,
       who immigrated to New England.  The following are the names of the
       seven immigrant ancestors: Abraham Peirce (ca.1600-ca.1673), Daniel
       Peirce ((1611-1677); John Pers or Pierce (ca.1588-1661); Michael
       Pierce (ca.1615-1676); Richard Pearce (1590-1641); Robert Peirce
       (d.1665); and Thomas Pierce (1583/1584-1666).  Descendants and rela-
       tives lived in New England, New York, Pennsylvania, Michigan,
       Illinois and elsewhere.
    Includes indexes.
    Includes Chase, Hathaway, Hoskins, Mason, Parker, Rice and related
       families.

    Also on microfiche.  Salt Lake City : Filmed                 US/CAN
       by the Genealogical Society of Utah, 1984.                FICHE AREA
       5 microfiches ; 11 x 15 cm.                               6046859
```

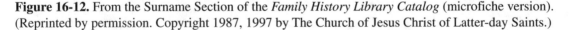

Figure 16-12. From the Surname Section of the *Family History Library Catalog* (microfiche version). (Reprinted by permission. Copyright 1987, 1997 by The Church of Jesus Christ of Latter-day Saints.)

can genealogies. A small sampling showed that only around two-thirds of the entries were for American genealogy books. Just over 10 percent were for foreign countries; 5 percent (each) were biographies and genealogical charts. Other entries were local histories with surname entries, compendia, surname periodicals, reports of family meetings, and other records. Therefore, the 1972 volumes include approximately 13,500 American genealogies, none of which are dated after 1970.

Figure 16-14 shows typical entries. Complete bibliographic references make it easy to search any research library for a title found in *Genealogies in the Library of Congress.* All major genealogy libraries have these two volumes, as well as the supplements. To update this catalog, three supplements have been published. The first covers 2,798 books added to the collection from 1972 through 1976 (although most were published from 1970 to 1974). The second supplement adds approximately 10,200 books cataloged between January 1976 and June 1986 (most were published between 1976 and 1985). A third supplement was published in 1992 under the name *Genealogies Cataloged by the Library of Congress Since 1986;* it includes 8,997 titles received and cataloged from 1 January 1986 to 31 July 1991. Together, the three supplements list approximately twenty-two thousand titles which, using the percentages found in the 1972 catalog, would identify approximately fifteen thousand recent American book genealogies. With cross-references, they include approximately forty thousand American references. Note that the second supplement lists only the cross-references (in the back of the book under "Index of Secondary Names"), so be sure to look at the separate "Index of Secondary Names" at the back of this volume. Figure 16-9 illustrates the growth of the Library of Congress collection compared to the overall growth of genealogies.

Dictionary Catalog of the Local History and Genealogy Division 449

Chamberlain, Daniel Henry, 1835-1907. IXZ p.v.173

Chamberlain, Leander Trowbridge, 1837-1913.
An address on the early history of old Brookfield, Mass., delivered at West Brookfield, Mass., his native town, by the Rev. L. T. Chamberlain ... at the invitation, and under the auspices, of the West Brookfield branch of the Quaboag historical society. And remarks by his brother, the Hon. D. H. Chamberlain, of New York, at the after-dinner exercises. [Brooklyn, N. Y., Press of Larkin & co., 1895?]
36 p. 22½cm.
1. Brookfield, Mass.—Hist. I. Chamberlain, Daniel Henry, 1835-1907.
11—6067
Library of Congress F74.B8C4
[a33b1]

APV (Glidden)

Chamberlain, George Walter.
The descendants of Charles Glidden of Portsmouth and Exeter, New Hampshire, compiled by George Walter Chamberlain, edited by Lucia Glidden Strong. Published as a memorial to her father and mother. Boston, Mass., 1925.
420 p. front., plates, ports., maps. 25cm.
Genealogy div.
1. Glidden family. ~~2. Glidden family (Charles Glidden, ca. 1632-1707?)~~ I. Strong, Mrs. Lucia Mabel (Glidden) 1857- ed.
26-9317
Library of Congress CS71.G559 1925

Chamberlain, George Walter, editor. APR (Lebanon)

Lebanon, Me.
Vital records of Lebanon, Maine, to the year 1892 ... editor, George Walter Chamberlain ...
[Boston] Under authority of the Maine historical society, 1922-23.
3 v. 23½cm.
Contents: v.1.Births. v.2.Marriages. v.3.Deaths.
1. Registers of births, etc.—Lebanon, Me. I. Chamberlain, George Walter, ed. II. Title.
22-17061
Library of Congress F29.L4L4 Genealogy div.
[5]

APV (Chamberlain)

CHAMBERLAIN, ERNEST LORENE, 1884-
Chamberlain genealogy. [Olivia, Minn., 1966]
110 l. ports. 28cm.
Title from label mounted on cover.
1. Chamberlain family.
NN 7.67 p/F OC(1b+) PC,1 SL G,1
(LC1,X1)

APV (Webber)

Chamberlain, George Walter.
Descendants of Michael Webber of Falmouth, Maine, and of Gloucester, Massachusetts, by George Walter Chamberlain, M. S.; with a preface by Winslow L. Webber. Wellesley Hills, Mass., Webber foundation [°1935]
5 p. l., [9]-78 p. 24½cm.
On cover: The Webber genealogy, 1630-1934.
1. Webber family ~~(Michael Webber, 1630-1729)~~
35-24683
Library of Congress CS71.W37 1935
——— Copy 2.
Copyright A 89327 GENEALOGY DIV.

Chamberlain, George Walter, editor. APV (Paine)

Paine, Nathaniel Emmons, 1853-
Thomas Payne of Salem and his descendants: the Salem branch of the Paine family, by Nathaniel Emmons Paine; an enlargement of The Southold branch of the Paine family, by Horace Marshfield Paine. [Haverhill, Mass.: Record Pub. Co.,] 1928.
178 p. facsims., front., plates, ports. 8°.
Some plates printed on both sides.
"The editorial work in preparing this volume for the press has been done by George Walter Chamberlain of Malden."
Genealogy Div.
417411A. 1. Paine family. 2. Paine, Horace Marshfield, 1827-1903. 3. Chamberlain, George Walter, editor.
N. Y. P. L. July 3, 1929

Chamberlain, Esther (Shelford), ed.

*Z1-114
Film Reproduction
DAUGHTERS OF THE AMERICAN REVOLUTION. California. San Diego chapter.
Collection of Genealogical records, containing copies of Bible records, birth certificates, death certificates, family records, marriage certificates, tombstone inscriptions, war service records [and] wills. Compiled by Mrs. Harry W. R. Chamberlain [and] Mrs. George W. Fisher (Genealogical records committee) [San Diego? Calif.] 1958. 1 v. geneal. tables.
(Continued)
NN R 2. 67 r/L (OC)I, Ib, II, IIb OS PC, 1, I, II SL G, 1, I, II
(UM1, LC1, X1)

A.P.V.

Chamberlain, George Walter.
One branch of the descendants of Thomas Chamberlain of Woburn, 1644 16 pp, 1 port
Weymouth, Mass.: W. B. Chamberlain,
1897, 4°
Chamberlain family
Genealogy div.
LENOX GENEAL.

Chamberlain, George Walter. APV

Wellman, Joshua Wyman, 1821-1915.
Descendants of Thomas Wellman of Lynn, Massachusetts, by Rev. Joshua Wyman Wellman, D. D. Boston, Mass., A. H. Wellman, 1918.
xv, 581 p. pl., ports. (incl. front.) fold. facsim., col. coat of arms. 25cm.
Edited by George Walter Chamberlain. *cf.* Pref.
Genealogy div.
1. Wellman family. 2. Wellman family (Thomas Wellman, d. 1672) I. Chamberlain, George Walter. II. Wellman, Arthur Holbrook, 1855- III. Title.
19-5763
Library of Congress CS71.W452 1918
[5]

Figure 16-13. From the *Dictionary Catalog of the Local History and Genealogy Division* of the New York Public Library. It consists of photoduplications of the typed and handwritten, alphabetically arranged card catalog.

1612 BIRCHARD. The Birchard-Burchard genealogy, with history and records of the kindred in North America, descendents (!) of Thomas Birchard (1635) Norwich, Connecticut. Mrs. Elizabeth Birchard, publisher; Mr. Casius Birchard, secretary. Philadelphia, 1927. 8 l., 207 numb. l. ports. 28½ cm. Text mimeographed; printed t.-p. "The founding of this genealogy of the Burchards is due to ... Nathan Burchard". Leaf 82. "This edition is published by a son of Mrs. Elizabeth Birchard ... Gordon F. Birchard". Leaf 1. 33-29115.
CS71.B6288 1927

BIRCHARD. See also SMITH, 1924

BIRCKHEIMER. See BERKHEIMER.

1613 BIRD. Genealogical sketch of the Bird family, having its origin in Hartford, Conn. (By Isaac Bird) Hartford, E. Geer, steam printer and stationer, 1855. 24 p. 22cm. Dedication signed: Isaac Bird. 33-34826.
CS71.B629 1855

1614 BIRD. The Bird family. A genealogy of Thomas Bird, of Dorchester, Massachusetts, and some of his descendants. Prepared for Matthew Bird, of New York, by William Blake Trask ... Boston, Printed by D. Clapp & son, 1871. 40 p. 26 cm. "Reprinted from the New-England historical and genealogical register for January, 1871." 17-19208.
CS71.B629 1871

1615 BIRD. Bird genealogy. By William Bird Wylie ... Saint Louis, Mo., 1903. 1 p. l., 13 p. 27 cm. 3-14254.
CS71.B629 1903

Figure 16-14. Typical entries from *Genealogies in the Library of Congress* (page 142).

The general catalog of the Library of Congress was used in 1997 as the source for an electronic bibliography that includes approximately 22,500 U.S. and British family histories. *Genealogical Publications: A List of 50,000 Sources from the Library of Congress,* compiled by Kory L. Meyerink (Salt Lake City: Ancestry, 1997), uses the October 1995 electronic catalog as the source of the entries on this "every-word" searchable CD-ROM database. The library's electronic catalog only includes titles cataloged since 1969, so this compilation effectively replaces the three supplements described above (and brings them to mid-1995), but does not replace the 1972 two-volume set.

A Complement to Genealogies in the Library of Congress. Contrary to popular opinion, the Library of Congress does not have a copy of every book ever printed in the United States. It especially lacks genealogies and family histories because they are often printed in small quantities and distributed through personal networks. Realizing this, Kaminkow, the editor of *Genealogies in the Library of Congress,* set out to locate genealogies *not* in the Library of Congress. The result was *A Complement to Genealogies in the Library of Congress: A Bibliography* (Baltimore: Magna Charta Book Co., 1981). This catalog, or bibliography, of genealogies covers twenty-four major research libraries, among them the public libraries in St. Louis, Denver, Los Angeles, New York City, and, particularly, the Allen County Public Library in Fort Wayne, Indiana (for the extensive collections of its Genealogy Department), as well as the historical societies of Cincinnati, Long Island, Philadelphia, and St. Paul. The twenty-three thousand titles include complete bibliographic citations and an abbreviation for the libraries that listed the title in their catalogs as of 1979. Only books published through 1976 were included, in order to compare the listings to those in the initial volumes and first supplement of the Library of Congress catalog.

As with other library catalogs, many of the entries are not for American book genealogies. Approximately 10 percent are for charts, biographies, and family reunion reports. Slightly more than 10 percent are for foreign countries, with the heaviest emphasis on German-language books. A few surname periodicals, compendia, and other sources are also listed, leaving approximately 75 percent, or approximately seventeen thousand American genealogies.

A Complement to Genealogies in the Library of Congress provides the researcher with some rather obscure titles and gives the location of at least one copy of each. However, it is not comprehensive; the editor/compiler allowed each library to determine the level of its involvement, and several libraries surveyed only part of their collections. For example, the Long Island Historical Society is represented only by its 1935 catalog (described below), and the State Library of Ohio surveyed only 10 percent of its holdings for comparison with the Library of Congress catalogs. The number of titles contributed by each participating library varies widely. Around two-thirds of the titles come from the Allen County, Indiana, and New York City public libraries. These two libraries, plus six other libraries (which amount to one-third of those surveyed), account for more than 80 percent of the entries.

In addition to the twenty-four libraries that participated, the collection at the Allen County Public Library (the largest contributor, with 40 percent of the total listings) includes copies of genealogies from twenty-three other public and private libraries that were not surveyed because of their inclusion in the Allen County collection. However, the *Complement to Genealogies in the Library of Congress* does not identify which of the Allen County titles came from these other libraries, so it cannot be used to determine their holdings.

Many libraries with major genealogical collections did not participate, and they may have titles not included in either the Library of Congress volumes or the *Complement.* Indeed, for the libraries that did participate, those for which figures are available show that between one-quarter and over one-third of their genealogy collections are not in the Library of Congress. These figures likely pertain to other research libraries as well. Note also that the titles in the *Complement* may be in many other libraries as well, so be sure to check the catalog of any local research library. For example, the staff of the Family History Library has been analyzing its holdings, comparing them with both *Genealogies in the Library of Congress* and the *Complement* in an attempt to acquire the titles it does not yet have. Other libraries may have done similarly. It is also noteworthy that the Family History Library is not one of the libraries included in the *Complement* because its catalog is widely available to the public.

Daughters of the American Revolution (DAR) Library Catalog. The *Daughters of the American Revolution (DAR) Library Catalog,* vols. 1 and 3 (Washington, D.C.: Daughters of the American Revolution, 1982, 1992), is another important tool for locating compiled genealogies. While the DAR Library includes most of the major published genealogies, its collection is unique in that it has many genealogies that were published in very small numbers (sometimes fewer than a dozen copies). Many of its typescript genealogies can be found in no other research library. For example, a brief comparison of the 1984 DAR supplement with the 1986 supplement to *Genealogies in the Library of Congress* suggests that approximately 45 percent of the DAR collection may not appear in the Library of Congress volumes.

Vol. 1 of the DAR catalog, published in 1982, lists only the "Family Histories and Genealogies" at the library. Along with a small supplement published in 1984, the catalog lists 15,031 titles. The catalog is arranged alphabetically by the name of the primary family treated. The entries include complete bibliographic citations, as well as the DAR library call number. In addition to an author index, the catalog has a surname index, with approximately twenty-six thousand entries indicating the books in which a surname is prominently mentioned, even if the name is not included in the title of the book. Vol. 3 of the DAR catalog includes locality sources (as did vol. 2), as well as 4,123 new genealogies acquired from 1984 through October 1991. Unlike the catalogs described above, the DAR catalogs appear to have a much higher percentage of American book genealogies—probably more than 90 percent.

The five catalogs discussed above probably identify more than 95 percent of the published genealogy and family history books of North American families. All, or most, of these catalogs are available in every major genealogical library; they should be the first sources consulted when one is beginning research on a new family or when one finds new information about an earlier generation. Of course, they can also help solve "dead-end" problems if one has not already searched them thoroughly.

Any library catalog is a source for family histories because most histories in a library are cataloged by the surname(s) covered. Union catalogs and cataloging networks (see chapter 5, "Bibliographies and Catalogs") for groups of libraries are also valuable sources (if they can be searched by subject). There are, however, several smaller library catalogs which researchers need to be aware of. These can be consulted if the researcher has access to the library described, or if the researcher simply wants to be more thorough.

A Catalog of American Genealogies in the Long Island Historical Society. Reprinted in 1969, *A Catalog of American Genealogies in the Long Island Historical Society,* edited by Emma Toedteberg (1935; reprint; Baltimore: Genealogical Publishing Co.) is very useful in identifying book-length genealogies published before 1935. The catalog is arranged alphabetically by the first surname of each book. No cross-references are provided; this works well for most of the books listed because they focus on only one surname, such as *Genealogy of the Fairbanks Family in America.* However, Oscar E. Schmidt's *Smaller New York and Family Reminiscences; DeRham, Schmidt, Bache, Barclay, Paul Richard* (1899) can only be found under the DeRham surname. Complete bibliographic information includes the number of pages and the size (octavo, quarto, etc.) of the book. Citations list 8,202 published books, virtually all of which are American genealogies, but around 250 of these are in a separate alphabetical appendix. There is also a separate list of 850 genealogical manuscripts. The 945 titles in this catalog that are not in the Library of Congress (as of 1976) were included in *A Complement to Genealogies in the Library of Congress.* However, it is still a fairly comprehensive listing of significant American genealogies published before the mid-1930s.

Catalogue of Printed and Manuscript Genealogies. Compiled by Ellen C. Barrett, *A Catalogue of Printed and Manuscript Genealogies Issued in Separate Form to be Found in the Genealogy and Local History Division of the Los Angeles Public Library* (Los Angeles: Los Angeles Public Library, 1960; supplement, 1965) of book genealogies has approximately 2,800 entries arranged by the major surname treated in each book. It gives the author, a short title of the book, the year published, and the number of pages. The minimal cross-references mean that books are listed only under the primary family. Published in 1960, the catalog refers mostly to books that date between 1900 and 1959, making it a good complement to older catalogs which cover the pre-1910 books more thoroughly. The catalog was reissued in 1965, with a supplement bound before the main body of the text.

National Genealogical Society Library Book List. Members of this society who belong to its library loan program receive the *National Genealogical Society Library Book List,* 5th ed. (Arlington, Va.: National Genealogical Society, 1988), and periodic supplements. Although not all books in the collection circulate, most are available through the mail for a small fee (plus shipping charges) to members who pay a one-time registration fee. Titles are listed by author, so the user must consult another catalog or bibliography to determine the author of a desired book. Most of the titles were published within the last thirty years, and most recent additions are newly published genealogies. Thus, the 3,100 titles in the fifth edition supplement the older catalogs that have not been updated.

Circulating Library Catalogs (for the New England Historic Genealogical Society). Members of the New England Historic Genealogical Society can participate in its book loan service for a small additional membership fee and a shipping fee for each book borrowed. The fifth edition of the popular *Circulating Library Catalogs* for the New England Historic Genealogical Society lists more than seven thousand genealogies, each arranged by the primary surname. Each entry includes the author, title, publication date, and library call number; there are no cross-references to other surnames treated in the books. The catalog's coverage is to 1992, so it includes many recent books. Also, many titles date from the nineteenth century, so the catalog provides excellent coverage of the last one hundred years of book-length New England genealogies.

Booksellers' Catalogs

Many recent books and some out-of-print genealogies can be obtained from genealogical booksellers. However, because book genealogies are often self-published in small quantities, do not expect to find every new (or old) genealogy in the following sources.

Genealogy and Local History Guides. Since 1979, this series, now produced by University Microfilms International (UMI) (Ann Arbor, Michigan), has provided a growing collection of genealogical materials on microfiche. Published genealogies comprise a major division in UMI's Genealogy and Local History Series. Several hundred titles are collected, microfiched, and cataloged as a set or "part" of the collection. These parts are then sold (as a unit) to libraries and archives. Each part is described by a guide which includes complete catalog information, with subject, title, and surname indexes. With every ten parts that are issued, the booklets are consolidated into a catalog. In 1995, vol. 3 of *UMI Guide to Family and Local Histories: A Microfiche Program* (Ann Arbor, Mich.: University Microfilms International, 1990, 1993, 1995) was issued. The three volumes identify 5,844 family histories that researchers may purchase, individually, on microfiche. However, many research libraries subscribe to this collection. Many of these are rare titles, usually published before 1920 and in limited numbers.

The same company also has a separate collection of more than 1,100 genealogies on microfilm which may be purchased through its Books on Demand department, either as microfilms or as books. These titles are usually different from those in the Genealogy and Local History Series. The titles available from Books on Demand are listed in UMI's *Genealogy* catalog and in the fourth edition of *Genealogical and Local History Books in Print* (see below). Books on demand can produce copies of thousands of other books, theses, and dissertations which have been preserved on microfilm. Catalogs and information are available from University Microfilms International, 300 North Zeeb Road, Ann Arbor, MI 48106 (1-800-521-0600).

Genealogical and Local History Books in Print. Many recent genealogies and family histories, including new publications and reprints of older genealogies, are listed in the various editions of *Genealogical and Local History Books in Print,* edited by Marian Hoffman (currently in its fifth edition) (Baltimore: Genealogical Publishing Co., 1996–97). Genealogical books from hundreds of vendors are listed in the "Family History" volume. In addition to family genealogies, this section includes family newsletters, biographies, and early diaries. The third edition (1981) includes 1,277 genealogies and family histories, especially books published or reprinted since the mid-1970s. The fourth edition (1985) was originally issued in two thick volumes, but when it was later reprinted it was divided into three volumes, with the 4,232 titles in the "Family Genealogy" section comprising the third volume. It includes 1,162 titles from UMI's Books on Demand and 1,820 reprints of early (mostly pre-1920) genealogies by Higginson Books (Salem, Massachusetts). The indexes to family histories in the third and fourth editions provide approximately 26,750 references to these titles, an average of almost four surnames in each book.

After the fourth edition was published, two supplements labeled as vols. 4 and 5 (of the fourth edition) were issued. The 1990 supplement (vol. 4) added 815 titles (391 from Higginson). The 1992 supplement (vol. 5) added 1,432 titles (with 1,230 reprints from Higginson). Publication of the fifth edition began in 1996 with a volume of family histories (genealogies) that identifies more than 4,600 titles, also with many reprints. The many reprints listed in the fourth and fifth editions make this book an excellent tool for locating copies of old, hard-to-find genealogies. There are also hundreds of recent titles, which make this catalog an excellent supplement to the major library catalogs described above. The first and second editions (both 1975) of this catalog are also valuable search tools, with only limited duplication of titles in the latest two editions. Most genealogy libraries have (or should have) these catalogs.

Other Booksellers' Catalogs. Several other booksellers include a significant number of family histories and genealogies in their catalogs. Most of them are discussed in the introduction to *Printed Sources,* including Higginson Books and Tuttle Antiquarian Books. Most such companies focus on "out-of-print" books and rarely have more than one or two copies of an original genealogy available. These companies provide inexpensive catalogs with thousands of titles. However, many of the titles may not be available for very long, especially once they appear in a catalog. Higginson Books has partially solved this problem. In addition to its stock of used books for resale, Higginson maintains a large library of early original genealogies, which it will photomechanically reprint upon request. For a small fee, one can receive a copy of Higginson's catalog, which contains more than 5,300 titles; more are added with each issue. The New England Historic Genealogical Society also has a catalog of approximately six hundred genealogies for sale (mostly photocopies, with some new titles). Tuttle's catalogs, with upward of six thousand genealogies, include some photocopied titles. These and other booksellers are listed in appendix C.

It is unusual to find titles of books in these bookseller catalogs which are not also in the catalogs described above. However, as explained in the introduction, these booksellers are good places to find a copy of a desired genealogy to purchase.

Bibliographies

Several bibliographies of genealogies have been published over the years, and the early ones usually attempted to list all works published to date. As the numbers of books, articles, and other sources grew, however, such coverage became impractical, and library catalogs (described earlier) generally replaced bibliographies of genealogies. However, some recent bibliographies with a specific focus are important to know. (For more information on the use of bibliographies in genealogical research, see chapter 5.)

The American Genealogist. *The American Genealogist, Being a Catalogue of Family Histories . . . Published in America, from 1771 to Date* (1900; reprint; Baltimore: Genealogical Publishing Co., 1971) is a comprehensive bibliography of "monographs of American families" published up to 1900. The approximately 2,700 citations are arranged by the primary surname of the genealogy; they include complete bibliographic information. Many of the titles include popular agnate descent genealogies of New England immigrants. This bibliography is the fifth edition; it completely supersedes three earlier editions by W. H. Whitmore. Thomas Glenn's 1897 bibliography *A List*

Table 16-2. Major Indexes to Printed Genealogies

Title	*Date*	*Number of Entries*	*Sources*	*Scope*
AGBI	1952–	5,750,000+	830+	Every-name index
Genealogical Index of the Newberry Library	1960	530,000	Unknown	Pre-1918, eastern U.S.
Greenlaw Index	1979	35,000	Unknown	New England to 1940
Old Surname Index File	1964	100,000	Unknown	English language
Index to American Genealogies . . . (Munsell's Index)	1908	55,000	8,000	Eastern states
Sutro Library Family History Subject Catalog, 3rd ed.	1990	119,000	8,000	Analytical catalog
Surname Index to Sixty-five Volumes of Colonial Pedigrees	1964	8,900	65 vols.	Compendia
Catalogue of the . . . Library of the Colonial Dames of the State of New York	1912	7,500	Unknown	Pre-1912, analytical
Key to Southern Pedigrees	1910	8,000	Unknown	Southern states
Founders of Early American Families	1985	4,400	Unknown	Pre-1657 immigrants
New England Marriages Prior to 1700	1985	174,000	2,000	New England
Index of the . . . Lineage Books of the DAR	1916–40	160,000	160 vols.	Revolutionary war
PERSI	1847+	1,000,000	2,000+	Periodicals
Donald Lines Jacobus' Index to Genealogical Periodicals	1983	20,000	85	Periodicals to 1953
Virginia Historical Index	1934–36	100,000	8 serials	Southeastern states

of Some American Genealogies Which Have Been Printed in Book Form (1897; reprint; Baltimore: Genealogical Publishing Co., 1969) includes some biographies, charts, compendia, and memorials not noted in *The American Genealogist.* However, *The American Genealogist* gives better coverage to book genealogies. The major surnames included in the books cited here are also included in the companion volume, *Index to American Genealogies* (described below).

Biographical Books, 1876–1949 and 1950–1980. Genealogy and biography go hand in hand. Most biographies include genealogical information, and most genealogies include biographies of some persons. *Biographical Books, 1876–1949 and 1950–1980,* 2 vols. (New York: Bowker, 1980, 1983), seeks to identify all book-length biographies published between 1876 and 1980; these include all books for which the Library of Congress assigned a personal name as a cross-reference. Many genealogies and family histories focus on the descendants (or ancestors) of a specific person and therefore receive a personal name cross-reference. For example, *The Cummings Memorial,* a genealogy of the descendants of Isaac Cummings, an early settler of Topsfield, Massachusetts, is listed under "Cummings family (Isaac Cummings, 1601–1677)" in this bibliography. *Biographical Books* is another excellent source for identifying early agnate descendancy genealogies. Because most of these were published before 1950, the 1876-to-1949 volume is most helpful, having 40,300 citations providing complete bibliographical references for 16,500 biographical and genealogical books. For more information about this source, see chapter 18, "Biographies."

"New on the Bookshelf" Section of Everton's Genealogical Helper. For years, *Everton's Genealogical Helper* (published by The Everton Publishers, P.O. Box 368, Logan, UT 84323) has published brief notices of new genealogical books. This ongoing annotated bibliography includes many genealogies and family histories. The annotations include the address where the book can be purchased, the price, and a brief summary of the book's contents. *The Genealogical Helper Index to "New on the Bookshelf" Section* references the book notices that have appeared in the *Genealogical Helper* from 1971 through 1983, including approximately 3,100 genealogies. The index provides the full name of the subject ancestor for each genealogy, the state or country where the family originated, and a reference to the issue of the *Genealogical Helper* in which the book notice was printed. Because most genealogical collections in research libraries include the *Genealogical Helper,* this index can help researchers find recent genealogies that may include their ancestries.

American and British Genealogy and Heraldry. *American and British Genealogy and Heraldry: A Selected List of Books,* 3rd ed. (Boston: New England Historic Genealogical Society, 1983; supplement, 1987) is a geographically arranged, annotated bibliography. It does not include single-name family histories and genealogies, but it does include titles of genealogical dictionaries, compendia, and periodicals under the appropriate headings and localities. It is described in the introduction to *Printed Sources* and in chapter 5, "Bibliographies and Catalogs."

Genealogical Indexes

The following indexes, including several analytical catalogs, can help researchers locate briefer sources of genealogical information not found in standard library catalogs and bibliographies. In an analytical catalog, the cataloger, in the process of

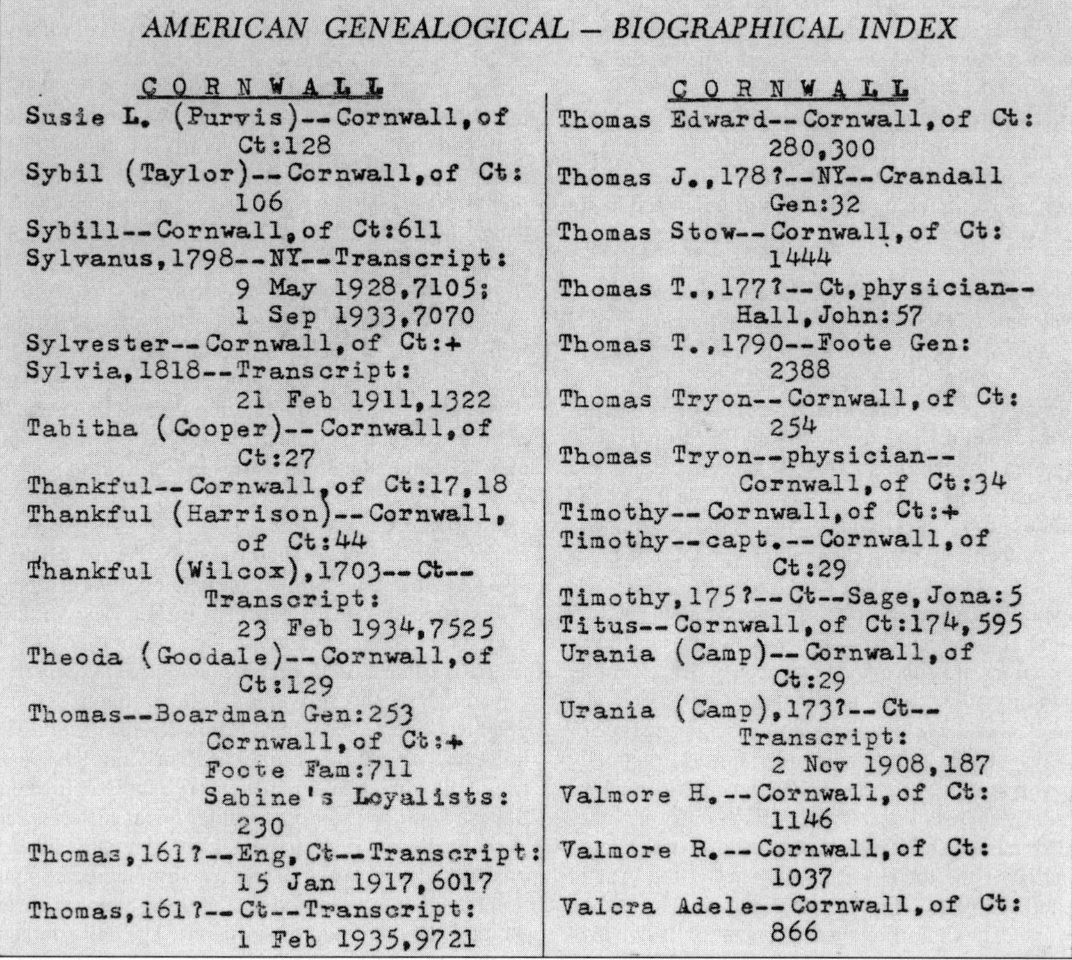

AMERICAN GENEALOGICAL – BIOGRAPHICAL INDEX

CORNWALL

Susie L. (Purvis)--Cornwall,of Ct:128
Sybil (Taylor)--Cornwall,of Ct: 106
Sybill--Cornwall,of Ct:611
Sylvanus,1798--NY--Transcript: 9 May 1928,7105; 1 Sep 1933,7070
Sylvester--Cornwall,of Ct:+
Sylvia,1818--Transcript: 21 Feb 1911,1322
Tabitha (Cooper)--Cornwall,of Ct:27
Thankful--Cornwall,of Ct:17,18
Thankful (Harrison)--Cornwall, of Ct:44
Thankful (Wilcox),1703--Ct--Transcript: 23 Feb 1934,7525
Theoda (Goodale)--Cornwall,of Ct:129
Thomas--Boardman Gen:253
Cornwall,of Ct:+
Foote Fam:711
Sabine's Loyalists: 230
Thomas,161?--Eng,Ct--Transcript: 15 Jan 1917,6017
Thomas,161?--Ct--Transcript: 1 Feb 1935,9721

CORNWALL

Thomas Edward--Cornwall,of Ct: 280,300
Thomas J.,178?--NY--Crandall Gen:32
Thomas Stow--Cornwall,of Ct: 1444
Thomas T.,177?--Ct,physician--Hall,John:57
Thomas T.,1790--Foote Gen: 2388
Thomas Tryon--Cornwall,of Ct: 254
Thomas Tryon--physician--Cornwall,of Ct:34
Timothy--Cornwall,of Ct:+
Timothy--capt.--Cornwall,of Ct:29
Timothy,175?--Ct--Sage,Jona:5
Titus--Cornwall,of Ct:174,595
Urania (Camp)--Cornwall,of Ct:29
Urania (Camp),173?--Ct--Transcript: 2 Nov 1908,187
Valmore H.--Cornwall,of Ct: 1146
Valmore R.--Cornwall,of Ct: 1037
Valora Adele--Cornwall,of Ct: 866

Figure 16-15. From *The American Genealogical-Biographical Index,* vol. 34.

analyzing a book or periodical, provides catalog entries for each chapter, article, family section, or similar subdivision in each book, thus creating a "key subject index." Although analytical catalogs are not true indexes, they provide much more coverage than a regular library catalog. Most of these sources are published books that can be found in many genealogical collections. Table 16-2 summarizes much of the following information.

American Genealogical-Biographical Index (AGBI). Also called "Rider's index," *The American Genealogical-Biographical Index to American Genealogical, Biographical and Local History Materials* (*AGBI*), 1–188+ vols. (Middletown, Conn.: Godfrey Memorial Library, 1952–), is an ambitious project that is intended to index *every* name in almost 750 book-length genealogies and family histories and around eighty other genealogical sources. Begun in 1952, the index will have upwards of 6.25 million entries when it is completed (projected for 1998 or 1999). By early 1997, approximately 5.75 million references were found in 188 volumes, covering surnames from *A* through *Warren.* Usually, four volumes are published each year. The importance of this index is its objective to include every name in each source, something that even the indexes in the sources themselves often fail to do. *AGBI* is easy to use and usually distinguishes very well among many people who have the same name. Each entry contains the subject's complete name, birth year and state (if known), occasional biographical data (such as military rank), an abbreviation for the source, and the page number. When the birth date is unknown, estimates are made based on other information in the book being indexed (figure 16-15). *AGBI* is strictly alphabetical. Because it has so many volumes, alternate spellings of an ancestor's name may appear in different volumes.

Each volume contains an explanation of the index. Full bibliographic citations for the sources indexed are found in vols. 1, 10, 34, and 54, with a supplement in vol. 70. Several of the sources indexed do not have separate indexes, or the indexes are incomplete. With the additional identifying information in *AGBI,* it is easier to find the right Thomas Pierce in this index than in the index to the Pierce genealogy, where there are dozens of Thomases without identifying information.

In addition to traditional genealogies, *AGBI* indexes the entire printed 1790 census for the United States, some local histories and vital record collections, several volumes of colonial military records, and the more than 2 million names in the genealogical query column of the *Boston Transcript,* which published detailed questions and answers about the ancestry of several thousand colonial families between 1906 and 1941. In fact, the amount of information and the scope of this column made it practically a "serial compendium" of northeastern genealogy.

AGBI is available in around 170 libraries throughout the United States, including most major research libraries. As of 1997, plans were under way to sell microfilm copies of the out-of-print volumes (1 through 105).

An earlier edition of *AGBI,* covering most of the same published genealogies but very few of the other sources, was published in forty-eight volumes as *The American Genealogical Index.* Each source in the first edition is also indexed in the new version.

Genealogical Index of the Newberry Library. Sometimes called the "Wall Index," the four-volume *Genealogical Index of the Newberry Library* (Boston: G. K. Hall, 1960) reproduces the old analytical catalog of the genealogical collection at the Newberry Library, a private, endowed research library in Chicago. Between 1896 and 1916, the library staff prepared index cards for references to families in the many genealogies and local histories then in the library's collection. While it is not an every-name index to the approximately three thousand books cited, it is comprehensive, often referencing even single paragraphs about an individual or the person's family.

The photocopies of cards comprise approximately 530,000 entries arranged alphabetically by surname and variant spellings. Most surnames are subdivided by locality; for example, the Griswald family has separate headings for Connecticut and Massachusetts. General, nationwide references precede state or local entries. The entries in the index may appear cryptically brief to the new researcher (figure 16-16), but careful study of the entries usually reveals the reference. Each entry includes only the author's name; a brief reference to the title of the book, such as the name of the town, county, or family; the year of publication; and the page reference (or a notation to see the index of the work). Thus, "Torrington, Ct. (Orcutt, S.) 1878:752" refers to page 752 of an 1878 history of Torrington, Connecticut, by Samuel Orcutt.

If an entry is difficult to understand, search the library catalog or an appropriate bibliography for the name of the author, town, or surname. Read the references in the catalog carefully for one that matches the brief information in the index. Be sure to match the publication year; many authors issued later editions of their works, which carry later dates and different information. In such a case, the page numbers cited in the *Genealogical Index of the Newberry Library* would not locate the reference. If the index entry still is difficult to interpret, ask a librarian for help.

Because the *Genealogical Index of the Newberry Library* is so comprehensive, it is an excellent source for information on obscure families. In addition, its relatively heavy coverage of midwestern sources counterbalances the many indexes and catalogs with an eastern emphasis. However, eastern sources are not ignored. Because the index was discontinued in 1917, no books published after that date are included. The Newberry Library has, of course, continued to add new books to its collection since that time, so this index in no way represents a complete list of the library's holdings. Although the four volumes are out of print, microfilm copies are available from the publisher.

The Greenlaw Index of the New England Historic Genealogical Society. *The Greenlaw Index of the New England Historic Genealogical Society* (Boston: G. K. Hall, 1979) is a reproduction of an analytical card catalog that covers part of the collection of the New England Historic Genealogical Society. This catalog complements the *Genealogical Index of the Newberry Library* very well, as it includes books published between around 1900 and 1940; however, it is easier to use and more selective in its contents. The two-volume index includes only genealogical data and records containing three or more generations. Typical sources for the thirty-five thousand entries include local histories, genealogical compendia, and genealogical periodicals. The book index fully reproduces each index card in the catalog, so the references are quite easy to understand (figure 16-17). The entries are arranged alphabetically by surname and given name. They include the subject ancestor of the family, the subject's residence, and the time period, as well as the full title, author, and publication date of the source cited. Also valuable is the annotation regarding the number of pages of information; this can help the researcher choose which sources may be the most helpful for his or her research.

Old Surname Index File. Before 1964, the Library of the Genealogical Society of Utah (now the Family History Library) also kept an analytical surname catalog, the *Old Surname Index File,* on twenty-one microfilm rolls (Salt Lake City: Genealogical Library, 1964). Although the selection criteria were more restrictive than those for the *Genealogical Index of the Newberry Library,* this index provides 100,000 references to family, biographical, and genealogical information from worldwide sources; however, most of the sources are from English-speaking countries, split almost evenly between Great Britain and the United States. Sources indexed included local histories, compendia, periodicals, and book genealogies. The cards are arranged alphabetically by surname and usually include complete bibliographic citations. Around half of the references pertain to individuals, the other half to surnames. The call numbers for most books have changed; if the search is being done at the Family History Library or one of its centers, look up the new call number in the *Family History Library Catalog.* The card index is available on twenty-one rolls of microfilm at the library and at some family history centers.

Index to American Genealogies. One of the first attempts to index every printed genealogical reference was by Joel Munsell's Sons, an Albany printing house, in the late nineteenth century. Despite its age, *Index to American Genealogies and to Genealogical Material Contained in all Works Such as Town Histories, County Histories, Local Histories . . . and Kindred Works (Known as Munsell's Index)* (Albany, N.Y.: Joel Munsell's Sons, 1900; reprint; Baltimore: Genealogical Publishing Co., 1967) has remained one of the most valuable tools for locating early genealogical information, including information printed in separate books or "in all works, such as town histories, county histories, local histories, historical society publications, biographies, historical periodicals, and kindred works (Munsell 1900, i)." With the 1908 supplement, this index provides more than fifty-five thousand references to surnames from an estimated eight thousand different sources. It is not comprehensive, but it does include the major occurrences of family information in the books cited.

Each surname is followed by a list of books in which genealogical information can be found. The citations are very brief but can be easily interpreted with practice (figure 16-18). Local histories, the backbone of the index, are usually cited with the author's surname and the name of the locality, such as

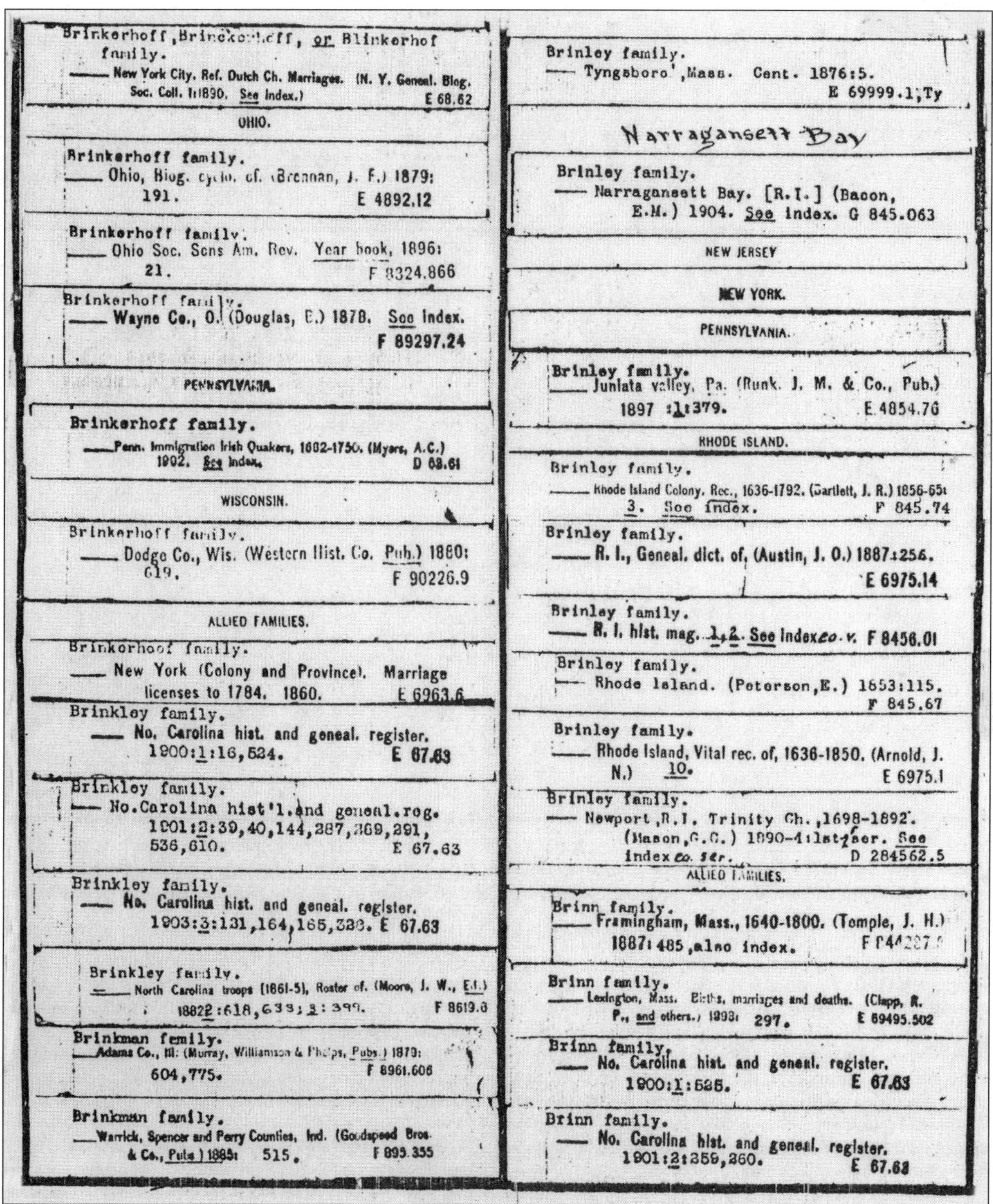

Brinkerhoff, Brinckerhoff, or Blinkerhof family.
—— New York City. Ref. Dutch Ch. Marriages. (N. Y. Geneal. Biog. Soc. Coll. 1:1890. See index.) E 68.62

OHIO.

Brinkerhoff family.
—— Ohio, Biog. cyclo. of. (Brennan, J. F.) 1879: 191. E 4892.12

Brinkerhoff family.
—— Ohio Soc. Sons Am. Rev. Year book, 1896: 21. F 8324.866

Brinkerhoff family.
—— Wayne Co., O. (Douglas, E.) 1878. See index. F 89297.24

PENNSYLVANIA.

Brinkerhoff family.
—— Penn. Immigration Irish Quakers, 1682-1750. (Myers, A.C.) 1902. See index. D 68.61

WISCONSIN.

Brinkerhoff family.
—— Dodge Co., Wis. (Western Hist. Co. Pub.) 1880: 619. F 90226.9

ALLIED FAMILIES.

Brinkerhoof family.
—— New York (Colony and Province). Marriage licenses to 1784. 1860. E 6963.6

Brinkley family.
—— No. Carolina hist. and geneal. register. 1900:1:16,524. E 67.63

Brinkley family.
—— No. Carolina hist'l. and geneal. reg. 1901:2:39,40,144,287,369,291, 536,610. E 67.63

Brinkley family.
—— No. Carolina hist. and geneal. register. 1903:3:131,164,165,338. E 67.63

Brinkley family.
—— North Carolina troops (1861-5), Roster of. (Moore, J. W., Ed.) 1882 2:618,633; 3:399. F 8619.8

Brinkman family.
—— Adams Co., Ill. (Murray, Williamson & Phelps, Pubs.) 1879: 604,775. F 8961.606

Brinkman family.
—— Warrick, Spencer and Perry Counties, Ind. (Goodspeed Bros. & Co., Pubs.) 1885: 515. F 895.355

Brinley family.
—— Tyngsboro', Mass. Cent. 1876:5. E 69999.1;Ty

Narragansett Bay

Brinley family.
—— Narragansett Bay. [R.I.] (Bacon, E.M.) 1904. See index. G 845.063

NEW JERSEY

NEW YORK.

PENNSYLVANIA.

Brinley family.
—— Juniata valley, Pa. (Runk, J. M. & Co., Pub.) 1897 :1:379. E 4854.76

RHODE ISLAND.

Brinley family.
—— Rhode Island Colony. Rec., 1636-1792. (Bartlett, J. R.) 1856-65: 3. See index. F 845.74

Brinley family.
—— R. I., Geneal. dict. of. (Austin, J. O.) 1887:256. E 6975.14

Brinley family.
—— R. I. hist. mag. 1,2. See index co. v. F 8456.01

Brinley family.
—— Rhode Island. (Peterson, E.) 1853:115. F 845.67

Brinley family.
—— Rhode Island, Vital rec. of, 1636-1850. (Arnold, J. N.) 10. E 6975.1

Brinley family.
—— Newport, R.I. Trinity Ch., 1698-1892. (Mason, G.C.) 1890-4:1st ser. See index co. ser. D 284562.5

ALLIED FAMILIES.

Brinn family.
—— Framingham, Mass., 1640-1800. (Temple, J. H.) 1887: 485, also index. F 844287.5

Brinn family.
—— Lexington, Mass. Births, marriages and deaths. (Clapp, R. P., and others.) 1898: 297. E 69495.502

Brinn family.
—— No. Carolina hist. and geneal. register. 1900:1:585. E 67.63

Brinn family.
—— No. Carolina hist. and geneal. register. 1901:2:359,360. E 67.63

Figure 16-16. From *Genealogical Index of the Newberry Library.* Each entry includes only the author's name; a brief reference to the title of the book, such as the name of the town, county, or family; the year of publication; and the page reference (or a notation to see the index of the work).

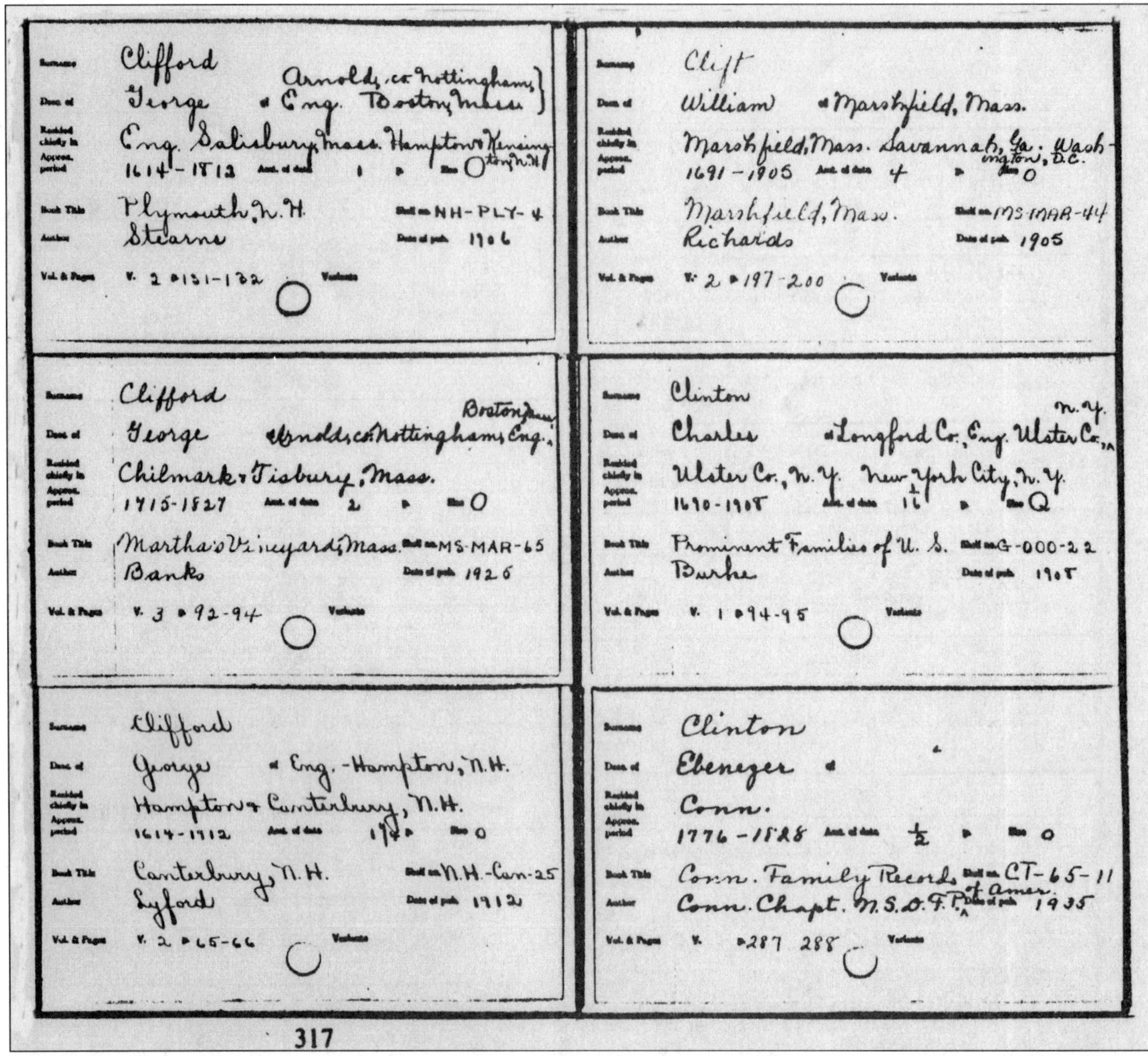
Clifford
George b. Arnold, co. Nottingham, Eng. Boston, Mass.
Eng. Salisbury, Mass. Hampton & Kensington, N.H.
1614-1812
Plymouth, N.H. NH-PLY-4
Stearns 1906
v. 2 p. 131-132

Clift
William b. Marshfield, Mass.
Marshfield, Mass. Savannah, Ga.; Washington, D.C.
1691-1905 4
Marshfield, Mass. 975 MAR-44
Richards 1905
v. 2 p. 197-200

Clifford
George b. Arnold, co. Nottingham, Eng. Boston, Mass.
Chilmark & Tisbury, Mass.
1715-1827 2
Martha's Vineyard, Mass. MS-MAR-65
Banks 1926
v. 3 p. 92-94

Clinton
Charles b. Longford Co., Eng. Ulster Co., N.Y.
Ulster Co., N.Y. New York City, N.Y.
1690-1908
Prominent Families of U.S. G-000-22
Burke 1908
v. 1 p. 94-95

Clifford
George b. Eng.-Hampton, N.H.
Hampton & Canterbury, N.H.
1614-1912
Canterbury, N.H. N.H.-Can-25
Lyford 1912
v. 2 p. 65-66

Clinton
Ebenezer b.
Conn.
1776-1828 ½
Conn. Family Records CT-65-11
Conn. Chapt. N.S.D.F.P. of Amer. 1935
p. 287 288

317

Figure 16-17. From *The Greenlaw Index of the New England Historic Genealogical Society.* The *Greenlaw Index* is a reproduction of an analytical card catalog that covers part of the collection of the New England Historic Genealogical Society.

"Cochrane's Hist. of Antrim N.H." Each citation includes the page number(s) where the family is discussed. Genealogies are usually cited by title, date of publication, and the number of pages, such as "Crozer Gen. (1866) 29 pages." Volume numbers of histories or periodicals are cited with lowercase roman numerals between the title and the page number. Full references of published genealogies cited in the index can be found in the companion volume, *The American Genealogist* (described above under "Bibliographies"). A similar bibliography, *List of Titles of Genealogical Articles in American Periodicals and Kindred Works* (Albany, N.Y.: Joel Munsell's Sons, 1899), provides full references for periodical articles.

The fifth edition of the index has been reprinted several times (most often by Genealogical Publishing Company of Baltimore, Maryland). It completely supersedes earlier editions (the first three were edited by Daniel S. Durrie), which should not be used. The 1908 supplement, which was issued separately, is reprinted as an appendix to the 1900 (fifth) edition and must be searched separately. The same publishers issued a partial 1933 edition covering genealogies published between 1900 and 1930, but the 1933 index only includes surnames beginning with *A* through *D*.

Sutro Library Family History Subject Catalog. The Sutro branch of the California State Library is another major repository for compiled genealogies. Located in San Francisco, the collection contains more than eight thousand volumes of genealogies and family histories, in addition to many other research sources. Most works in the collection are available through interlibrary loan to public libraries in California. Libraries in other states may also request the books if the works are not available in their own areas. The Sutro Library's surname card catalog is now available on 110 microfiche for research purposes. *The Sutro Library Family History Subject Catalog,* 3rd ed. (Sacramento: California State Library Foundation, 1990) includes 119,000 index cards. The analytical entries in the catalog provide separate cards for every significant article or subject in a book. For example, there is a reference for a three-page genealogy in a local history and a reference for an appendix in a genealogy dealing with a line not directly connected to the main topic of the book. This catalog is an important resource for genealogists. Its relatively low cost (around fifty dollars) allows many libraries and researchers to acquire it.

Surname Index to Sixty-five Volumes of Colonial and Revolutionary Pedigrees. Many genealogical compendia and lineage books were published in the early part of this century with inadequate or nonexistent indexes; this has made it difficult for researchers to locate information already compiled. Two major sets of lineage books have more than twenty volumes each, and neither set has a cumulative index. The surnames in these sets (described under "Compendia and Dictionaries," below) and those in several additional volumes are indexed in George Rodney Crowther, 3rd, *Surname Index to Sixty-five Volumes of Colonial and Revolutionary Pedigrees* (Washington, D.C.: National Genealogical Society, 1964). In addition to the surname, the index entry includes the country of the family's origin, the colony or state in which the family resided, and the volume and page number of the reference. The approximately 8,900 entries include several references to the same surnames and to noble lineages of dubious quality. The index is valuable, but the lineages referred to must be very carefully evaluated.

Catalogue of the Genealogical and Historical Library of the Colonial Dames of the State of New York. The *Catalogue of the Genealogical and Historical Library of the Colonial Dames of the State of New York* (1912; reprint; Ann Arbor, Mich.: Gryphon Books, 1971) is an analytical catalog that identifies most major genealogies and local histories published before 1912. The approximately 7,500 entries are arranged alphabetically and refer to localities, authors, titles, and approximately 4,500 families. Many entries have valuable annotations which list the families discussed in local histories or genealogical compendia.

Key to Southern Pedigrees. Although Munsell's index includes some southern genealogies, like many other indexes, it focuses on eastern (especially northeastern) families. William A. Crozier's *A Key to Southern Pedigrees* (Southern Book Co., 1953) is similar in arrangement to Munsell's index, but its focus is southern families. Most of its citations are from local histories, periodicals, and other published historical works, although it does include some book genealogies. Approximately eight thousand entries refer to works published before 1910. The brief source citations can be interpreted in a manner similar to those in Munsell's index.

Founders of Early American Families. Genealogists quickly learn that immigrant ancestors are a favorite focus of many printed genealogies and family histories. Of particular interest are those ancestors who arrived during the first fifty years of settlement in the colonies (between 1607 and 1657), a period that is often called the "Great Migration." This interest results because so many people descend from these immigrants and

Pickett — American Ancestry ii, 95
Green's Kentucky Families
Pickle — Chambers' N. J. Germans
Pickman — Heraldic Journal ii, 26
Smith's Founders of Mass. Bay 156–63
Vinton's Giles Genealogy 330
Pickrell — Power's Sangamon 566
Pickup — Calnek's Annapolis N. S. 562
Pickworth — Savage's Dict. iii, 425
Pidgin — Dow's Hampton N. H. 927
Pier — Olin Gen. by Nye (1892) 98–107
Young's Chautauqua 239, 368
Pierce — Adams Gen. (1895) 38–40
Am. Anc. i, 62; ii, 95; iii, 93; ix, 85; xi, 220
Austin's R. I. Genealogical Dictionary 153
Ballou Genealogy 344–6
Ballou's History of Milford Mass. 969–71
Blake Genealogy 46, 62–9
Blood's History of Temple's N. H. 239
Bond's Watertown Mass. 393–402, 869–71
Brewster's Portsmouth N. H. ii, 359–62
Butler's History of Groton Mass. 427, 476
Chandler's History of Shirley Mass. 969–71
Cleveland's History of Yates Co. N. Y. 591
Cochrane's History of Antrim N. H. 645
Cochrane's Hist. Francestown N. H. 883
Cothren's History of Woodbury Ct. 669–72
Cutter's History of Jaffrey N. H. 420–8
Daniels' History of Oxford Mass. 645
Davis' Landmarks of Plymouth 206–8
Deane's History of Scituate Mass. 325
Dow's History of Hampton N. H. 927
Draper's History of Spencer Mass. 246
Eaton's History of Thomaston Me. ii, 358
Gold's History of Cornwall Ct. 244
Hayward's Hist. of Hancock N. H. 807–9
Hemenway's Vermont Gaz. v, 101
Heywood's Hist. Westminster Mass. 825–8
Hubbard's History of Springfield Vt. 409–12
Hubbard's Stanstead Co. Canada 128–31
Hudson's Hist. of Lexington Mass. 181–5
Hyde's History of Brimfield Mass. 446
Judd's History of Hadley Mass. 552
Lapham's History of Norway Me. 576

Figure 16-18. From *Index to American Genealogies.* Each surname is followed by a list of books in which genealogical information can be found.

because relatively few immigrants came for the next several decades. There has been so much interest in these immigrants that the lineage society Founders and Patriots of America was organized in 1896 for persons who could trace their lineage through a revolutionary war ancestor on their mother's or father's surname line whose immigrant ancestor (of the same surname) arrived before 1657. The society's research efforts over the last century have identified many of those immigrants who have male descendants today. Meredith B. Colket's *Founders of Early American Families, Emigrants from Europe 1607–1657,* rev. ed. (Cleveland, Ohio: Order of Founders and Patriots of America, 1985) is a useful discussion and index of approximately 3,500 such immigrants. It includes references to published genealogies for each immigrant family. A researcher seeking an ancestor whose immigrant ancestor (of the same name) may have arrived by 1657 can use this index to identify acceptable agnate genealogies in which to continue the search. Compiled by a renowned genealogist,[3] this index also serves as a well-qualified checklist of recent genealogical scholarship on these early immigrant families. While the genealogies cited have been evaluated as trustworthy, they are seldom fully documented, so do not accept the titles cited in this index as the final word on the family; rather, use them as a starting point for further research.

New England Marriages Prior to 1700. Although appearing as an index to vital records, Clarence A. Torrey's *New England Marriages Prior to 1700* (Baltimore: Genealogical Publishing Co., 1985) serves to alert the researcher that a published genealogy exists for an ancestor. Torrey, an accomplished, scholarly genealogist, spent much of his lifetime searching virtually every published genealogy of New England families prior to the 1950s for evidence of marriages before 1700. The result is this list of seventy-four thousand New England adults of the seventeenth century, which probably cites more than ninety-five percent of the marriages in that area and period. It is, therefore, almost an "every-couple" index to more than two thousand New England genealogies; however, it must be used with care.

Finding an entry is a two-step process. The published book is arranged by the name of the groom; it gives the name of his wife, the marriage date (or birth of the first child), and the place. The index to the book includes the brides' names and other names appearing out of sequence. The source of the information is not given; rather, the researcher must search Torrey's handwritten notes, which are arranged on seven rolls of microfilm, alphabetically by the groom's name. Torrey's notes include cryptic, abbreviated references to the published genealogies. Usually the reference consists of the surname of the genealogy containing the marriage and perhaps the author's surname or a number Torrey assigned to that genealogy; references like "Smith 7" can be frustrating to the researcher. The microfilms, as well as the meaning of perplexing citations, are available from the New England Historic Genealogical Society. A list identifying most of the sources Torrey used was compiled by Alicia Williams and is also available from the New England Historic Genealogical Society.

Torrey made no attempt to evaluate the information in the genealogies; hence, the index, and his notes, contain conflicting information. The researcher must determine which, if any, of the sources is correct. *New England Marriages Prior to 1700* is a good example of a source being several steps away from the original information; it is a finding aid based on secondary sources. Supplements (by Melinda Lutz Sanborn) published in 1991 and 1995 add some 1,500 entries, including corrections (with source citations) taken from recently published genealogies and periodicals.

Index of the Rolls of Honor in the Lineage Books of the Daughters of the American Revolution (DAR). Between 1895 and 1939, the DAR published the lineages of its members. The results were 166 volumes containing 166,000 lineages, usually covering three to eight generations from the living DAR member back to her revolutionary ancestor. The lineage books (figure 16-19) provide only basic genealogical information and cite no sources. However, they cover the post-colonial period (in contrast to the many colonial sources available elsewhere), and the lineages provide an estimated one-half million names. Indexes for the first 160 volumes were published in four volumes, each covering forty volumes of lineage books; however, they are often bound as two books, meaning that each book has two separate indexes. The index only refers to the revolutionary ancestor, not to the DAR member or the intervening generations. Listed under each patriot's name are two numbers, the first one being the volume number and the second being the page in the lineage book. Most patriot ancestors are represented by several lineages and may appear in all four index volumes.

If a researcher has any ancestors who served in the American Revolution, there is an excellent chance that they are mentioned in this index. If one establishes that a DAR member descended from a common ancestor, the National Society (1776 D Street, Washington, DC 20006) may be able to provide the researcher with a copy of the lineage papers, which often provide some (but not many) sources for the lineage.

English Indexes. Most colonial ancestors were of British stock. For the genealogist who wants to pursue his or her ancestors in England, some important indexes are also available. Although they are generally outside the scope of this book, researchers should be aware of the four major indexes. George W. Marshall's *The Genealogist's Guide* (1903; reprint; Baltimore: Genealogical Publishing Co., 1980), often called "Marshall's guide," indexes pedigrees published in English books before 1903. John B. Whitmore's *Genealogical Guide: An Index to British Pedigrees in Continuation of Marshall's Genealogists Guide* ("Whitmore's guide") (London: Society of Genealogists, 1953) is a continuation (with corrections) of Marshall's guide; it indexes all genealogies in more than five hundred British publications from 1900 to 1950. For the period from 1950 to 1975, consult Geoffrey B. Barrow's *The Genealogist's Guide: An Index to Printed British Pedigrees and Family Histories, 1950–1975* (London: Research Publishing, 1977). It indexes genealogies in British periodicals and includes an addendum to Whitmore's guide. Consult Theodore Radford Thomson's *Catalogue of British Family Histories*, 2nd ed. (London: Edward O. Beck, 1935), for book-length family histories.

Compendia and Dictionaries

Hundreds of genealogical compendia and dictionaries have been published during the last 150 years. While many focus on a specific locality or group of persons, the following generally have nationwide or regional importance.

American Ancestry. The American Ancestry series (Albany, N.Y.: Joel Munsell's Sons), published between 1887 and 1899, gives the name and descent, in the male line, of Americans whose ancestors settled in America before 1776. The first of its twelve volumes contains families from Albany, New York, and the second volume focuses on Columbia County, New York. The last ten volumes include lineages from the entire United States. Most of the lineages occupy less than one page; they begin with a living person, usually a male of the upper class. His lineage is then set forth, tracing to his father, grandfather, and so forth, on his surname line, back as far as needed to reach the immigrant to America. Each volume has a surname index, and the entire set is indexed (by surname) in Munsell's *Index to American Genealogies* (described above under "Genealogical Indexes—Index to American Genealogies"), which was produced by the same publisher. Sources are not cited, and with only the direct ancestral line given, this compendium has limitations. However, it provides specific dates and places, and the identification of the immigrant can make this series useful for any researcher with colonial lines.

Burke's American Families with British Ancestry. Originally published in 1939 as a supplement to *Burke's Peerage, Burke's American Families with British Ancestry* (Baltimore: Genealogical Publishing Co., 1977) is a compendium that preserves the lineages of 1,600 "distinguished" families of British origin who lived in the United States. Although the editor does not define how the families are distinguished, it appears that most are of the upper class (or upper-middle class) in the United States and can trace their ancestry, in the surname line, to the immigrant (usually colonial). In addition, there may well have been a fee assessed to the families for inclusion in this work. The immigrant ancestors were not necessarily of the English gentry, although editorial comments would lead one to believe this was the case.

180 DAUGHTERS OF THE AMERICAN REVOLUTION.

MRS. FRANCES VIOLA SEYMOUR MCAFFEE. 11471

Born in Massachusetts.

Wife of William D. McAffee.

Descendant of Capt. Ezekiel Herrick, of Massachusetts.

Daughter of Philander Seymour and Laura M. Belding, his wife.

Granddaughter of Aaron Belding and Fanny Herrick, his wife.

Gr.-granddaughter of Amasa Herrick and Polly Robinson, his wife.

Gr.-gr.-granddaughter of Ezekiel Herrick and Abigail Wilson, his wife.

Ezekiel Herrick was a member of the General Court. He served in the Berkshire county militia, and, 1776, was appointed captain of the Ninth Company.

MRS. NANCY L. CONKLIN. 11472

Born in New Hampshire.

Wife of Dorsey T. Conklin.

Descendant of Maj. Robert Wilson, of New Hampshire.

Daughter of James Swan and Mary W. Grant, his wife.

Granddaughter of James W. Swan and Agnes Nancy Blair, his wife.

Gr.-granddaughter of Jeremiah Swan and Anna Wilson, his wife.

Gr.-gr.-granddaughter of Robert Wilson and Mary Hodge, his wife.

Robert Wilson, who was born in Ireland, and had fought under Wolfe, held many offices of trust during the Revolution. He responded to the Lexington Alarm, was major at Bennington, Saratoga, and detailed to escort six hundred Hessian prisoners to Boston. He died at Peterborough, 1790, aged fifty-three.

Also Nos. 1650, 10429.

Figure 16-19. From *Lineage Book of the National Society of the Daughters of the American Revolution,* vol. 12 (1896).

Each article begins with a brief biographical note about the subject, a living (or recently deceased) American of minor importance. This note usually provides the subject's town of residence, occupation, memberships, education, and birth and marriage dates. It is followed by a list of the person's children's names and birth dates. The surname lineage then follows, beginning with the earliest known ancestor in America. Each succeeding son in the direct lineage is listed by name with birth, marriage, and death information, when available. The lineage ends with the father of the subject and the subject's siblings. The children are numbered in British style, all sons (brothers of the subject) being listed first in order of birth (numbered 1, 2, 3 . . .). All daughters (sisters of the subject) follow, also numbered (again, 1, 2, 3 . . .) in order of birth; the assigning of duplicate numbers to boys and girls can be confusing to the researcher. The 1939 street address of the subject concludes the article. In some articles, additional children or descendants of the intervening generations are also given.

Each article uses between one-quarter page and a full page, allowing for some fifty thousand individual names in the 492 pages. There is no index (except for a one-page list of surnames that have been changed), but the articles are arranged alphabetically by surname. Sources are not provided, so the researcher does not know how the information was compiled. It can be surmised that the lineages are the result of the subjects' research efforts in the 1930s and, therefore, rely heavily on family records and printed genealogies. The family information in the most recent two or three generations is most likely to be correct, but it is best to record this information as clues to the identification of colonial immigrants and their early descendants. If a lineage traces to a colonial immigrant, it is likely that there is a published genealogy about that immigrant and some of his descendants. Use the indexes and catalogs described in this chapter to find such sources.

Colonial and Revolutionary Lineages of America. The twenty-five volume *Colonial and Revolutionary Lineages of America: A Collection of Genealogical Studies, Completely Documented, and Appropriately Illuminated, Bearing on Notable Early American Lines and Their Collateral Connections* (West Palm Beach, Fla.: American Historical Co., 1939–68) is described as "a collection of genealogical studies, completely documented, and appropriately illuminated, bearing on notable early American lines and their collateral connections." Published between 1939 and 1968, these "vanity volumes" preserve the results of research (usually by individuals on their own families) into the ancestry of "well-to-do" Americans. These lineages begin with the earliest known ancestor (usually the immigrant ancestor or an alleged noble ancestor) and provide detailed information about each direct ancestor on the lineage, down to the subject family. Usually several pages are devoted to each family, and abundant biographical information is presented for the subject and for many of the subject's ancestors.

For each generation, all known children of the ancestor are given. The child who is in direct line of descent to the subject is further described. Several different lineages are given on successive pages under one subject family. As the lineage descends to recent generations, the number of branches can be confusing. Furthermore, the immediate generations often include lengthy biographical information on several brothers, sisters, and cousins. Careful study of the lineages and use of the index is necessary to find all of the family history (not just genealogical) information buried in these volumes. The content and arrangement of the genealogies vary slightly according to what their authors contributed. For most family groups, some documentation is cited in the articles, making it possible for the researcher to verify the conclusions of the original author. However, in most cases, this documentation comes from secondary sources, such as published genealogies and local histories or records "in the possession of the family." Each volume has an index to the major families (ancestral couples) treated in the volume, but no every-name index is available. A cumulative surname index is included in Crowther's *Surname Index to Sixty-five Volumes of Colonial and Revolutionary Pedigrees* (described above under "Genealogical Indexes").

Many of the genealogies presented in *Colonial and Revolutionary Lineages of America* connect to noble or "glorious" families of the Middle Ages. Such connections must be suspect in the light of more modern research, however. In the early years of this century (and to a great degree today), many connections to notable ancestors were made without foundation. As such connections were published, they became more and more accepted, even as more and more of them were debunked in the scholarly literature. It has come to the point where now there are more disproved "royal and noble" lines that people *believe* are valid than there are truly proven ones. See chapter 20, "Medieval Genealogy," for more information. As with most genealogies of this nature, verify what is documented, consider the recent generations to be grounded in reasonably accurate family records, use the early American generations for clues to further research, and generally discard lineages in the old country, especially if they connect to nobility.

Colonial Families of America. Edited by Ruth Lawrence, *Colonial Families of America* (New York: National Americana Society) is a twenty-seven-volume compendium published between 1927 and 1948. It is similar to *Colonial and Revolutionary Lineages of America* (above) in its style, arrangement, and contents. It devotes less attention to noble lineages but has a greater emphasis on coats of arms; the production quality is significantly worse. Fewer families are treated in each volume, and they are treated with less depth. Most crucially, no documentation is included, although several sections seem to have been excerpted from published genealogies. The every-name index in each volume is perhaps the most useful aspect of this set. A typical volume provides around 2,800 references to specific individuals. The major surnames are also indexed in Crowther's *Surname Index to Sixty-five Volumes of Colonial and Revolutionary Pedigrees*. The same cautions noted above apply here as well (if not more so) because of the lack of source documentation. *Colonial and Revolutionary Lineages of America* and *Colonial Families of America* are difficult to find in their entirety. Individual volumes were typically purchased by family members, but few libraries purchased the complete sets. Neither set has been reprinted.

Colonial Families of the United States of America. George Norbury Mackenzie's *Colonial Families of the United States of America,* 7 vols. (1907–20; reprint; Baltimore: Genealogical Publishing Co., 1966) gives "the history, genealogy and armorial bearings of colonial families who settled in the American colonies from the time of the settlement of Jamestown . . . to the Battle of Lexington [1775]" (Mackenzie 1907, title page). Originally published from 1907 to 1920, this popular set provides surname lineages for at least six hundred families in more than five thousand pages. Each volume has an every-name index; if combined, these indexes would reference more than 125,000 names. The work's arrangement is similar to *Burke's American Families* (described above), but it provides much more detail, each lineage occupying around five or more pages. The subjects are upper-class Americans living in the early twentieth century. Their genealogical information, including children, is listed first, followed by a long paragraph of biographical information. The lineage then begins with the colonial ancestor and often includes biographical as well as genealogical information. All the children of the direct ancestor are listed in each generation, with the specific ancestor continued in the next paragraph. Biographical information is provided for direct ancestors when their prominence permits, while other entries have only brief genealogical facts. In many articles, similar information is provided for other lineages of the subject, sometimes including ancestor (or pedigree) charts. A coat of arms heads each article, with no disclaimer about its appropriateness to the family or any documentation showing that it actually pertains to the family being discussed.

Most of the genealogical information is limited to the surname receiving treatment, although each book's index lists every name in that volume. The surname articles are arranged alphabetically, but there is no table of contents to provide a ready list of the major surnames included. Although the editor claimed that these records were "obtained from original records of established authority" (preface), documentation is not provided for these lineages. It must be assumed, as noted before, that the lineages are the result of research by individual family members, mostly in compiled sources. Indeed, the editor comments that "material other than that derived from public or official documents must necessarily be contributed by the members of the various families who may be interested" (preface). The details in the biographical information of some early ancestors reveal a fair amount of research and provide excellent clues for documentary follow-up. Again, the connections to nobility should be discarded and not even used for clues. The recent generations provide access to information in family records not available in most public records. Information about the immigrant is probably accurate, but if it discusses the person's origins in Europe or Britain, be cautious. The actual lineage should only be a clue to further research.

The Compendium of American Genealogy. Probably the most commonly used compendium, Frederick A. Virkus's *The Compendium of American Genealogy,* 7 vols. (1925–42; reprint; Baltimore: Genealogical Publishing Co., 1987), has been the focus of more discussion than most other compiled genealogies. Reprinted with a new, explanatory foreword in 1987, these volumes were originally published between 1925 and 1942 in an effort to provide a collection of genealogical information about all Americans. The prefaces in the early volumes hint that the sweeping tide of WASP (White Anglo-Saxon Protestant) nationalism and the need for genealogical "background" information for potential government employees and military servicemen were the catalysts behind this collection. However, these considerations seem to have faded into the background as the project continued over the next fifteen years. Although many lineages trace back to New England, other areas are represented as well.

The genealogical information is presented in a greatly abbreviated form, allowing the seven volumes to contain approximately seventeen thousand genealogical "records" (subjects) consisting of more than fifty-four thousand distinct lineages and upwards of 425,000 individual names. The brevity of the information is probably why the first three volumes were published as *The Abridged Compendium of American Genealogy.* The user must be very careful when extracting information from the compendium to avoid erroneously connecting parts of two different lineages that both belong to the same subject.

Each record traces the known ancestry of one subject (typically a person living at the time the volume was compiled). The subject may have several lineages, each tracing a specific surname back to the first known American ancestor. A generational numbering system is used to trace the ancestors of each lineage. The subject is always number 1, his parents are 2, grandparents (in each line of descent) 3, and so forth. The earliest known ancestor in each lineage has the highest number in that lineage.

Each record typically occupies one-quarter to one-half of a page and is divided into sections, each ending with a period, as follows: first is the name of the subject (number 1) in bold print, with her date and place of birth. Second is the paternal lineage of the father's surname (called the *main stem*), from the earliest known American ancestor down to the subject's father (number 2). On this and subsequent lineages, the surname being traced is printed only once, in boldface, at the earliest generation; this alerts the user that the following generations (to the next boldface surname) carry the same surname. Third is any lineage that branches from the paternal line, starting with the earliest ancestor of that lineage and descending to the generation where it connects with the main stem. The next section is the lineage of the mother's surname, from the earliest ancestor to the mother (also number 2); this is followed by any branches from this maternal lineage. After the lineages comes the parents section, where both parents are described together under the number 2, including all of their children. The last two sections are the marriage information of the subject, including any children, and, finally, biographical information on the subject. Carefully examine figure 16-20 to understand how this system works. Often, the best way to extract information from the compendium is to carefully write the information on a pedigree chart, beginning with number 1 (at the end of the published record) and then the parents (number 2), and then tracing each surname lineage by following the generational numbers in ascending order. Remember that these are not pedigree or Ahnentafel numbers; rather, they represent generations from the subject.

Despite the different method of arrangement, it is worthwhile to examine this source because of the sheer number of names included. Each volume has an every-name index, but there is no cumulative index, so one ought to search each volume; however, there is an advantage in beginning with the index to vol. 7, because it partially cross-references the earlier indexes. An asterisk (*) by a surname in vol. 7 indicates that the surname occurs frequently in earlier volumes; however, thousands of surnames occurring only once or a few times are not referenced in vol. 7, so be sure to check all of the indexes. Each volume also has an alphabetical appendix of immigrant ancestors whose names appear so frequently "that repetition of the identical data would be burdensome and superfluous" (Virkus 1942, 965). The list in vol. 7 seems to be the most complete, having approximately 2,500 entries. It has been separately reprinted as *Immigrant Ancestors: A List of 2500 Immigrants to America Before 1750* (1942; reprint; Baltimore: Genealogical Publishing Co., 1986).

The biggest shortcoming of *The Compendium of American Genealogy* is its total lack of source citations. The information in these records was supplied by the subjects, who were obligated to purchase a copy of the book. Apparently the editor/publisher made some effort to verify the facts or genealogical links, but he could not possibly consider documenting every statement. Virkus was a competent (but not scholarly) biographer and genealogist, and his notes show that he omitted material that he judged to be extraneous or doubtful (Filby 1987, ii).

1-**WAITT, Laura Haynes (Mrs. Ernest Bailey),** *b* Greeneville, Tenn., Mar. 3, 1880.
4-George **Haynes** (*b* 1757), Am. Rev.; Winchester, Va., to Carter Co., Tenn.; *m* Margaret McInturf (John[5]);
3-Jonathan Gaines (1805-94), Washington Co., Va.; 1st lt. in War Bet. the States; *m* 1st, 1830, Sarah Williams (1815-60);
2-Benjamin Franklin (2 below).
7-Samuel **Duff** (will probated 1796), Washington Co., Va; *m* Margaret—;
6-William (*d* 1819), landowner, Washington Co.; *m* Agnes Thatcher;
5-Mary *m* 1790, William **Doran** (*d* 1835), Rutherford Co., Tenn. (son of James[6] [*d* 1799], from Ire., *m* Margaret Gordon of Scot.);
4-Nancy (1794-1865), *m* 1st, ca. 1810, Andrew Miller **Alexander** (*d* 1814), at Battle of New Orleans, War 1812; removed to Tenn. (John[5], of Md., *m* Mary Miller);
3-John Doran (1813-70), Rutherford Co., Tenn.; *m* 1837, Mary Rowena Baird;
2-Rebecca Tennessee (2 below).
7-William (Beard) **Baird,** of Franklin Co., Pa.;
6-John (*d* 1784), of Lincoln Co., N.C.; *m* Frances— (*d* 1787);
5-James (*d* 1808), Am. Rev.; *m* Meney—;
4-William Dinwiddie (1780-1843), to Rutherford Co., Tenn., 1803; *m* 1803, Abigail Martin (1784-1855; Josiah[5], wounded in battles of King's Mountain and Cowpens, *m* Mary, dau. of Robt. McClery, Am. Rev., *m* Abigail, dau. of John McDowell; John[6], of Mecklenburg Co., N.C., in French and Indian War);
3-Mary Rowena (1816-51), *m* John Doran **Alexander** (3 above);
2-Rebecca Tennessee (1841-1912), *m* 2d, 1878, Benjamin Franklin **Haynes** (*b* 1848), Washington and Greene cos., Tenn.; issue: 1-Frank Hartley (*b* 1879); 2-Laura (1 above); 3-Charles (1882-87).
1-*m* Aug. 6, 1902, Ernest Bailey Waitt, *b* Charlotte, N.C., Nov. 15, 1876; son of Malcolm Graham Waitt, of Atlanta, Ga.; issue (all *b* Atlanta, Ga.): 1-Laura Haynes, *b* May 29, 1903; *m* Aug. 27, 1932, Charles Edward Davis, Jr., of Paterson, N.J.; 2-Ernest Bailey, Jr., *b* May 5, 1905; *m* Feb. 22, 1934, Rose (Kohler) Coryell, of N.Y.; 3-Emma Rebecca, *b* Mar. 10, 1910; *m* Dec. 19, 1936, Shelton Bainbridge, son Legare Jones Lamarr, M.D., of Atlanta, and Milledgeville, Ga.; 4-Malcolm Graham, *b* May 5, 1912; *m* May 31, 1934, Gladys Rebecca, dau. of L. M. Landrum, of Oglethorpe Co., Ga. (issue: Rebecca Graham, *b* Apr. 14, 1937).
1-Mem. U.D.C. Presbyterian. Home: 1089 Blue Ridge Av., Atlanta, Ga.

Figure 16-20. From *The Compendium of American Genealogy,* probably the most commonly used compendium.

Given the avowed purpose of these volumes—to provide "background" information on individuals of interest to the government and others—some spurious lineages surely are included. Most errors, however, are likely be errors of faulty research, typical of the amateur approach to genealogy in the first part of the twentieth century.

A Genealogical Dictionary of the First Settlers of New England. James A. Savage's *A Genealogical Dictionary of the First Settlers of New England . . .*, 4 vols. (reprint; Baltimore: Genealogical Publishing Co., 1965), first published from 1860 to 1862, is one of the most important early New England sources for compiled genealogies. Savage spent twenty years compiling "three generations of those who came before May 1692" from numerous published and original sources. This compendium is arranged alphabetically by surname. The text for each name is narrative; one or two sentences describe each male (and some females) with that surname. The individuals are listed alphabetically by their first names within the narrative, which includes information about their residences, births, marriages, deaths, and parentages. When using "Savage," as this dictionary is often called, read the entire entry for the surname, taking care to note the various relationships given in the text; this helps to reconstruct the lineage links that are easily obscured by the format. The reprint includes some corrections and additions published later, as well as a cross-index to names appearing out of the alphabetical sequence. This dictionary is very old, and more complete genealogies are available for most families. However, many authorities agree that Savage has relatively few errors (although it is certainly not comprehensive) and is still a good source to begin research on colonial New England families.

Historical Southern Families. An excellent contribution to southern genealogies is John Bennet Boddie's set of twenty-three volumes published between 1957 and 1980: *Southern Historical Families* (Baltimore: Genealogical Publishing Co.). Each of the small volumes (around two hundred pages each) treats a dozen or so major families. Including related families, the lineages of approximately seven hundred families are presented. Usually the account starts with the first known ancestor of a particular family. Biographical and genealogical information, with sources, is provided for each person in the direct line of descent. All of the children, grandchildren, and many great-grandchildren are listed, in outline style, under each direct ancestor. The lineage then picks up with the next ancestor in the lineage, with his biographical information and three generations of descent. Thus, the siblings, cousins, nieces, and nephews of each direct-line ancestor are provided, making this series more valuable than many compendia that focus only on the specific ancestor (to the exclusion of his family). Sources are cited by author, title, and page number (in parentheses) for most statements of fact. Although most of the sources are from compiled records, they go beyond published genealogies to include transcripts of original records; at times the original record itself is cited. Each account ends with the name and address of the researcher/compiler/submitter. The every-name index in each volume makes this an easy-to-use source, but be aware that the index usually omits the middle names of individuals in the text. There is no cumulative index.

This discussion has focused on genealogical compendia and dictionaries that cover the entire United States, or at least several states. There are, however, dozens of other sources with limited geographic coverage. A county is often the subject of scope, as is an area within a state, such as the Mohawk Valley (New York), Long Island, or the Virginia tidewater area. Other sources focus on an ethnic group, such as the Germans in New Jersey. Representative state dictionaries are included in the chapter bibliography. One can learn about other such sources from various bibliographies and statewide instructional books.

Lineage Books

The more than one hundred past and present lineage societies in the United States have made a considerable contribution to printed genealogies. Because membership in a lineage society requires that a lineage be traced from a specific ancestor to the prospective member, these societies have a wealth of genealogical information in their files, and many lineage societies have published these lineages. Most societies are relatively small (in terms of membership), so their lineage books usually comprise only one or two volumes (though many of the older societies have published several volumes during their long histories).

The most notable collection of lineage books was published by the DAR. Often known as Rolls of Honor, 166 volumes were published by the DAR between 1895 and 1939. Each volume includes one thousand lineages, giving the name of the revolutionary war soldier, the "daughter(s)" (that is, descendants) who joined the society, and brief genealogical information about the intervening generations. Like most lineage books, they do not include sources, but the lineage covers the post-revolutionary period, which can be difficult for American research. An index to this series is described above under "Genealogical Indexes."

Other societies (either national or various state chapters) that have published significant lineage books include:

- National Society of the Sons of the American Revolution
- Society of the Descendants of the Colonial Clergy
- National Society, Daughters of the American Colonists
- National Society, Daughters of the Revolution of 1776
- Order of the Founders and Patriots of America
- National Society of the Daughters of Founders and Patriots of America (forty-five volumes)
- General Society of Colonial Wars
- General Society of Mayflower Descendants
- General Society of the War of 1812
- Hereditary Order of the Descendants of Colonial Governors
- National Society of Colonial Dames of America
- National Society of the Sons and Daughters of the Pilgrims
- National Society of the Colonial Daughters of the Seventeenth Century

- Order of the Crown of Charlemagne in the United States of America

Lineage societies have published other useful sources as well, including indexes of members and qualifying ancestors. For more information on these and other societies, see chapter 20, "Tracking Through Hereditary and Lineage Organizations," in Loretto Dennis Szucs and Sandra Hargreaves Luebking's *The Source: A Guidebook of American Genealogy,* rev. ed. (Salt Lake City: Ancestry, 1997).

Periodical Indexes

As discussed above, many genealogies are printed in genealogical periodicals. These can often be found through careful use of several periodical indexes. For a full discussion of genealogical periodicals and their contents, uses, and indexes, see chapter 19, "Genealogical Periodicals."

The serious researcher looking for compiled genealogies and family histories should be aware of the three major indexes to genealogical periodicals. *Donald Lines Jacobus's Index to Genealogical Periodicals* (Newhall, Calif.: Boyer Publications, 1983), revised by Carl Boyer 3rd, provides access to periodicals published through 1952. *Genealogical Periodical Annual Index* (Bowie, Md.: Heritage Books, 1962–) has been published each year since 1962 (except 1970 to 1973); it indexes articles by surname, subject, and locality. The Allen County (Indiana) Public Library's *Periodical Source Index* (*PERSI*) is an annual "comprehensive place, subject, and surname index to current genealogical and local history periodicals," beginning with 1986 issues. A retrospective index covers periodicals published from 1847 to 1985. For articles published before 1900, see the 1,400 citations in Munsell's *List of Titles of Genealogical Articles in American Periodicals and Kindred Works* (mentioned above under "Genealogical Indexes").

Compact Disc (CD-ROM) Sources

The advent of computer technology in genealogy recently has led to the availability of the first true electronic genealogies. Using the vast storage capacity of CD-ROMs, institutions and private companies are making *lineage-linked* genealogical information widely available. The difference between lineage-linked information and other collections of compiled research is that each piece of information in a lineage-linked database is linked to other information; the researcher can enter the name of a person and, if that person is in the database, learn the names of any ancestors and/or descendants also in the file. Two major systems currently dominate the field.

Ancestral File. The most significant genealogical database of the 1990s is Ancestral File™. Ancestral File is a lineage-linked database with significant genealogical information on approximately 29 million persons. In just a few years, it has become one of the most important compiled sources a genealogist can use when beginning research on any family.

First released in 1989 by the Family History Department of the LDS church, Ancestral File is a computerized database on CD-ROM which offers genealogists a way to share their findings about their ancestors with other researchers. The 1996 version was released on seven CD-ROMs in early 1997.

As a part of FamilySearch®, a set of related genealogy databases, Ancestral File was designed for the novice computer user. When the user selects Ancestral File, the computer prompts the user to enter the name of a person. A birth date may be added if the name is common. The computer then retrieves the alphabetical portion of the database index for that surname. The index gives the name, birth year, state or country, and a parent or spouse's name; usually this is enough to determine if any of the index entries pertain to the ancestor being sought. The researcher can then choose to view more detailed individual information, a pedigree, family groups, or a descendant list for the subject. Each of these options is displayed on the screen. They can also be printed by the computer's printer, or the researcher can download the information onto a floppy diskette for use on a personal computer. At any point, the researcher can learn who submitted the information in the file; this can help the user locate sources for the information.

The initial data for Ancestral File came from LDS church members. They were asked to verify each item on their family group sheets, resolve discrepancies found in versions submitted earlier, cite their sources, and resubmit the first four generations of their ancestry with a pedigree chart by July 1981. Nearly 200,000 family group sheets listing several million names were received. More than 16 percent listed all of the sources used in compiling the sheets, while almost all had some source citation. These sheets were microfilmed and the genealogical information was entered into Ancestral File. Although the source information is not included, the computer program does provide the microfilm numbers of the original submissions so that researchers can evaluate the sources.

Because the file began with the four-generation ancestry of many LDS families, it does have limitations for some researchers. However, as more and more researchers have contributed their ancestry, the file has become more useful for all people. Because of rights of privacy, information on living persons (less than ninety-five years old) is not displayed on Ancestral File. Linkages are preserved with the notation "Living" in place of the person's name. Names are given for living members of the LDS church (on the basis of implied consent), but no further information is given.

The file not only continues to grow, but improvements are being made that allow it to do more for the researcher. For example, it is possible to edit the information in the file. This allows users to correct information, such as incorrect dates and places, and to merge two entries for the same person. Future enhancements are being studied; they may include direct access to source information and searches on given as well as last names. Ancestral File is found at the Family History Library, virtually all American family history centers, and at major research libraries in North America.

World Family Tree. The largest commercial producer of genealogical information on CD-ROM is the Banner Blue division of Brøderbund Software (Novato, California). Pioneered by Automated Archives before its acquisition by Banner Blue, lineage-linked pedigree information has been available on CD-ROM since around 1992. Since 1995, these products have been released as part of the Family Archives series of CD-ROMs, designed to be used with Brøderbund's *Family Tree Maker,* a popular genealogy database software program. As part of its World Family Tree project, Brøderbund solicits and receives computer files from *Family Tree Maker* users and other genealogists providing the results of their research. Approximately six thousand separate files, often containing almost 3 million names altogether, are included on each World Family Tree CD-ROM. The CD-ROMs can then be read either by the *Family Tree Maker* software or the *Family Archive CD Viewer* (for those who do not own *Family Tree Maker* software). The entries usually contain standard genealogical information, including date and place of birth, marriage, and death, as well as relatives' names, but the amount of information and its accuracy depend on what the individual submitter provided. After evaluating the information, the user may print the appropriate information or download it to a floppy diskette for use on a personal computer with any genealogy program that supports the GEDCOM standard.

The various files on World Family Tree CD-ROMs are not merged with one another, as is the case with Ancestral File. Rather, each file, and the research it represents, stands on its own; thus, the same individual may appear several times on each disc, as well as on subsequent discs, sometimes with conflicting information (provided by other researchers). In a way, this is no different than finding the same ancestor in several of the printed compendia and book genealogies discussed above. However, it appears that the contributions to the World Family Tree discs come mostly from users of *Family Tree Maker,* who are generally understood to be novice family historians with little training in research and evaluation of evidence. Furthermore, much of the information they contribute includes their living relatives, which, in the interest of privacy, is excluded from World Family Tree discs (except for name, gender, and family links). Thus, for a substantial number of individuals, there is only limited information.

As of early 1997, seven discs had been released with a total of some 20 million names. Some of the files in the first two volumes seem to have been more carefully compiled, and many lineages extend to colonial times, thus providing a nice complement to the recent lineages in Ancestral File and the more recent World Family Tree discs.

Brøderbund also published some "Family Pedigree" collections separately from its World Family Tree project. These are typically older files inherited from Automated Archives. They are separate because they do not support the GEDCOM standard or because permission was lacking for inclusion in the World Family Tree. They may require different software, but that is included on the CD-ROMs.

Although Ancestral File and World Family Tree dominate the discussion of lineage-linked data on CD-ROM, others are beginning to publish such material. Kindred Konnections claims to have compiled 8 to 10 million names in pedigree and family group form and is releasing them on CD-ROM, as well as through its Internet site (http://www.kindredkonnections.com). Family Forest compiles "trees" of related groups of persons and then publishes them on CD-ROM using *Family Tree Maker*. Other companies will likely follow suit.

Electronic "Reprints." A growing number of other compiled genealogies and family histories are appearing on CD-ROM, in part because thousands of pages of text can be included on a single disc and reproduced inexpensively. These discs do not include GEDCOM files or provide lineage-linked pedigrees; rather, they are, in effect, reprints of previously published works.

Brøderbund's Family Archives CD-ROMs include the Family History Collection series, which includes the texts of genealogical books. The first disc in this series includes seventeen autobiographies, one hundred biographies, sixty-five family histories (that is, book genealogies), nine local histories, two compendia (including vol. 1 of Virkus's *Compendium of American Genealogy,* discussed above under "Compendia and Dictionaries"), and several miscellaneous sources. In partnership with Genealogical Publishing Company, Brøderbund has also released CD-ROMs containing many of the new and reprint compilations from that leader in genealogical publishing. Most of these are "image" discs, wherein the page image is stored on the disc and is viewed on a computer screen. Also on the disc is a searchable index to the volumes that identifies which image has the name(s) of interest. A few discs (where electronic files already existed) have every-word search capability.

Ancestry (Salt Lake City) has also begun to release information on CD-ROM and on the Internet. These products consist entirely of electronic text; they include the powerful *FolioVIEWS®* search software to find and retrieve any desired text string in the product. While Ancestry's earliest products did not contain compiled sources, such sources are part of current releases.

Any electronic "reprint" may contain books that were first printed many decades ago; the genealogical information may not be documented and may have been superseded by more recent research. However, such reprints do provide a fast way to search several important titles at once.

Other Compiled Sources

Many other compiled sources exist that provide access to genealogies and family histories, including manuscript collections. These collections represent the findings of prominent genealogists and dedicated family researchers, who often cited published genealogies in their notes. There are also two major catalogs to manuscript collections, discussed below.

National Union Catalog of Manuscript Collections (NUCMC). Many compiled genealogies have never been published. For any number of reasons, the work of many genealogists remains in manuscript form in dozens, perhaps hundreds, of different repositories. The Library of Congress has headed an effort to identify the thousands of manuscript collections around the United States. Published annually since 1962, the *National Union Catalog of Manuscript Collections* (*NUCMC*) (Washington, D.C.: Library of Congress) provides a brief description of approximately 65,325 different collections at 1,369 different repositories (through the 1991 catalog). While most of these collections are not genealogical in nature, many are biographical, and approximately ten thousand include genealogical information. The two-volume, cumulative *Index to Personal Names in the National Union Catalog of Manuscript Collections, 1959–1984* (Alexandria, Va.: Chadwyck-Healey, 1988), is an alphabetical arrangement of all the "personal and family names appearing in the descriptions of manuscript collections cataloged from 1959 to 1984." Many of the 200,000 names in the index are entries for family information, which is typically genealogical in nature. This index is an excellent source to begin a search for research notes that someone else may have compiled on a specific family.

National Inventory of Documentary Sources (NIDS). Many manuscript collections are too large to be fully described in the brief paragraphs in *NUCMC.* Most repositories create inventories or finding aids for their large manuscript collections, and researchers can often determine if a manuscript collection has information of value by consulting them. Unfortunately, most such finding aids have very limited distribution; often they exist only within the library or archive that houses the collection. Recognizing the value of these tools, Chadwyck-Healey has begun publishing the finding aids of many research libraries on microfiche. The microfiche are accompanied by an index to the key subjects and persons mentioned in the finding aid. The *National Inventory of Documentary Sources* (*NIDS*) allows the researcher to get one step closer to the manuscript collection and to learn whether its contents will be of value. While most of these collections have little to do with genealogy, many that do include genealogical information are also described. *NIDS* is available at many large research libraries, including government repository libraries. The index to the microfiche copies of the archive inventories is now available on CD-ROM, allowing every-name searches of the inventory descriptions (but not the inventories or the manuscript collections).

For more information on these two sources and related information, see chapter 5, "Bibliographies and Catalogs."

SEARCHING FAMILY HISTORIES AND GENEALOGIES

Finding a genealogy or family history is really only the first of three essential steps in using it properly. The second step is to carefully search the genealogy, and the last step is to evaluate the information in it. Actually, these last two steps are closely related, for some of the information learned in the search of the compiled genealogy will aid in its evaluation.

Most genealogists are not interested in a complete family history; rather, they are interested in only one line: the ancestry (or descendancy) of one individual (or couple). Therefore, the genealogist usually turns immediately to the index to seek the name of the ancestor, hoping that person is included in the family history. This is not always an efficient way to search a compiled genealogy, however, and it often results in missing important information about the family. Keep in mind that a negative search (not finding the desired information) can also be helpful. In addition, many family histories contain background information that can prove useful in further searches. Researchers must familiarize themselves with the scope, arrangement, and indexes of every genealogy they search.

Scope

Although all humans are, ultimately, related to one another, no single genealogy could possibly include all individuals who have ever lived. Therefore, each author/compiler must determine whom to include in his or her compilation. As described earlier, the author may try to trace all the descendants of a given person, or all of his or her ancestors; sometimes these tasks are combined. More often than not, the author will settle for some or most instead of all ancestors or descendants. It is therefore crucial that the user of a genealogy understand whom the author intended to include. Does a particular compendium claim to include all of the families who lived in a certain town, or only those who moved there before a specific date? Does an ancestor chart include all known ancestors, or only those who lived in North America? Are other immigrants of the same name discussed, or only the one whose descendants are traced?

The answers to these questions are usually found in the genealogy itself, so there is seldom any need to guess. The first step to make after obtaining a genealogy is to read the preface or the introduction (or whatever else the author termed the preliminary material). Almost every author is anxious to explain what the work is intended to do, yet the preface is often the least-read portion of any book. In a book-length genealogy, the preface may be several pages in length, and because it obviously will not answer any specific research problems, most researchers skip it. However, it is from the introduction that one learns the scope of a genealogy. If the preface indicates that the book deals with the descendants of a man who moved from Massachusetts to Virginia in 1660, an ancestor lost in Vermont in 1780 will not be mentioned. However, the same introduction may mention other books or articles that deal with other New England branches of the same family; these could point in the direction of other sources that will provide an answer.

Arrangement

Before interpreting the information found in any genealogy, one must be familiar with its arrangement. Several of the various arrangements commonly used in compiled genealogies were discussed at the beginning of this chapter. Familiarity with each of the common arrangements makes it easier to find and evaluate the information in a genealogy. However, as mentioned before, many authors develop their own systems to present their findings. In such cases it is essential for the user to understand the author's system. Some systems, for example, separate children from parents or spouses from each other. Not knowing how to read the information makes the genealogy essentially useless.

Fortunately, an explanation is usually included in the introduction. If the system used to present the information is unique, there may be a separate section which explains it. (Most authors who develop unique systems think they have done genealogy a great favor and are more than willing to explain it.) Ideally, the explanation will be clear in the first reading; if not, spend some time on the material to be sure that important information will not be missed.

Often, the explanation is given in the beginning of the main text. If the introduction does not explain the arrangement, read the first few pages of the first chapter. Even if it is not given there, the arrangement may become obvious through a reading of the first chapter. The contents of the first chapter may also answer questions about the scope of the genealogy, indicating whether it is an agnate descendancy genealogy, a lineage covering only one line, or a combination of arrangements.

A list of common abbreviations may also appear at the beginning of a genealogy; the user must know whether *b.* stands for birth, baptism, or burial. Sometimes an abbreviation has more than one meaning, or a nonstandard abbreviation is used. For example, one genealogy of a Pennsylvania German family used a *t* to stand for baptism, probably for the German word *Taufe,* which means "baptism."

After reading the preface or introduction and the first part of the text, turn to the end of the genealogy. See if any appendixes are included; usually they are just before the index(es). Appendixes can include important information which aids in understanding the genealogy. Often, authors provide information about other persons with the surname who do not belong to (or can't be placed in) the genealogy in an appendix. Some authors place information about immigrant origins in an appendix, while others include information received too late for the main part of the text. The Converse genealogy (descendants of Edward Converse) included speculative suggestions about the English origins in the preface, from which others had built a connection to nobility. However, the appendix included the results of recent research that clearly established the origin of the family in England and disproved the earlier suggestion that had led to an incorrect noble line (Converse 1905, 5, 590).

Indexes

Only after becoming familiar with the scope and arrangement of the genealogy should one look in the index for an ancestor. Actually, there is one other thing to do before looking for the name: read the introduction to the index. Indexes are amazingly complex. Not only are filing rules different from one indexer to another (Do Mc and Mac come before M, for instance?), but the contents of indexes also vary considerably. Each author/indexer selects terms to include in the index, but seldom is every key word there. In genealogies, names are the focus, but often not every name is indexed. For example, the publisher of the journal of Anson Call indicated in a conversation that Reynolds Cahoon was mentioned more than once in the journal, and his name did appear on three pages; however, Cahoon was not included in the index. Such discrepancies are not uncommon in genealogies. Names may be omitted by oversight or by design, so do not put the book back on the shelf just because an ancestor's name is not in the index.

The introduction to the index, if there is one, explains who should be included. For example, the husbands of the daughters in an agnate descendancy may not be indexed, or the women may have their married names included in the index in parentheses (however, sometimes the name in parentheses is the maiden name of a woman who married into the family). Learn what the numbers in the index stand for. They are not always page numbers; in fact, in genealogies, they often stand for the individual's number, or perhaps the number of the individual's father or family.

If there is no introduction to the index, test it by turning to a page in the main text of the book, finding a name, and then trying to find that name in the index. Do this several times to learn how complete the index is and to discover whether the index number refers to a page or a person's number.

Many a large genealogy has more than one index. The Loomis genealogy (1908) has fifteen indexes! Some are place-name indexes, but there are also indexes to descendants named Loomis, children of Loomis girls, persons who married into the family, military service, inventors, and authors named Loomis.

Once the index is understood, a search in it for an ancestor can begin. A caveat: it's not always best to search for the most obvious name. For example, if searching for Mary Loomis, looking under that name in the index to a Loomis genealogy might be *too* fruitful; while the surname Loomis is uncommon enough in most indexes, there are likely to be many Marys in the index to a Loomis genealogy. Instead, look for the name of her spouse (if he is included in the index)—even if it is a common name, such as John Jones. There will be fewer Jones entries in the Loomis family than there are Mary Loomises. For additional suggestions about using indexes, see chapter 6, "Published Indexes."

EVALUATING A GENEALOGY OR FAMILY HISTORY

What a thrill it is to locate a volume on a library shelf or an article in a publication and find that it includes an ancestor's name and identifying data! The excitement increases with each additional piece of information that is gleaned from the printed record, but the work has just begun. Once the details are obtained, evaluation of the genealogy and verification of the information is necessary, even if the book does not cite the evidence on which the facts are presented.

For a thorough review and critique, the researcher must review family histories and genealogies with an analytical eye. Published family histories and genealogies are, by their very nature, compiled sources with secondary information. The best are those that acknowledge this fact and include documentation for each name, event, date, and place. However, relatively few genealogies include documentation that would be considered complete, or even adequate, by today's standards, though this is no reason to dismiss a compiled genealogy without evaluation. Standards of proof were much more relaxed in past years, when many of the major genealogies were printed. Further, many family histories today are produced by well-meaning, dedicated family members who do not intend their work to be broadly disseminated or carefully scrutinized by critical professionals. While this is no excuse for a poorly prepared and undocumented genealogy, it is nonetheless a fact that they exist, and the serious researcher must deal with them. Even the most poorly prepared genealogy may be of value if understood and used properly.

Fact is fact, wherever it is found. An honest researcher does not ridicule the source of the facts; rather, the researcher is grateful for the preservation of true and valid information. Neither does the researcher form a premature judgment of the truth and then dismiss, without cause, conflicting information. The difficult task is to sift the truth from the traditions, errors, falsehoods, typographical errors, illogical conclusions, and simple mistakes.

Much of the discussion in the introduction of this book, under the heading "Evaluation of Printed Sources," applies to genealogies and is not repeated here. However, because so few genealogies are well documented, several elements of evaluation will help in considering the information in a compiled genealogy or family history; these include the purpose for the creation of the book, its publication and author, the contents, the researcher's knowledge of the family, and the sources that are credited. The process of evaluation involves asking several questions about each of these areas.[4]

Creation and Purpose

How was the genealogy created? The process of the genealogy's compilation is important to understand in order to fully evaluate the final product. Many agnate genealogies have been compiled largely by correspondence, their authors writing to all the persons of the surname that could be found and asking them for their family records and known lineages.

> These family members may have had personal memory of people and events of the nineteenth century. They may have heard family stories (in those pre-television days) that went back for several

additional generations. They may have seen family records that are no longer available to us and read tombstones that are now illegible (Hatcher 1996, 130).

The author then combined the various responses with the results of research in local records, such as town vital, probate, and land records. Knowing whether the author used such a process will suggest what sources may have provided the information given in the genealogy. Other genealogies are created by combining previously researched information, such as articles in periodicals, lineages in compendia, and local histories. The preface is the best place to find an answer to this question.

What is the author's purpose? Who is his intended audience? Does the author have a motive or special interest in the lineage? These questions seek to establish why the genealogy was written. If the author is preserving family tradition without having found documentary evidence of the truth of the tradition, the researcher can be more skeptical of the accuracy of the information. An author hired by a family to compile a genealogy may be a trained professional (see "Author," below). An author trying to prove descent from a specific ancestor may be inclined to examine or use only those sources that support this objective. If the book publishes lineages from a lineage society, remember that each lineage is only as good as the member who submitted it and the rules of documentation in effect at the society when it was submitted. Generally, lineages submitted before the mid-1970s are substantiated by little documentation.

Publication

When was the genealogy published? The date of publication says much about a genealogy. Fifty, seventy-five, or one hundred years ago, the standards of proof were much different from those of today, so be cautious when accepting information that may have not been well compiled. Knowing the publication date also allows for comparison with other genealogies printed around the same time. Compare to determine if the genealogy is generally better, worse, or the same in terms of quality of information. Obviously, the older a genealogy, the more likely it is that newer information has come to light. Many of the major genealogies of the late nineteenth century have been corrected or augmented by short articles appearing in genealogical journals. Also, many genealogies published in the last forty years were reviewed in journals at the time they were published. Find these reviews and get the opinions of other genealogists. For information on book reviews, see chapter 19, "Genealogical Periodicals."

Who was the publisher? What is the quality of the production? These questions address production values. Consider how well the publication was produced. Unfortunately, it is often true that poor form equals poor content. Determine whether the book was a "kitchen-table, cut-and-paste" job or the product of a major publishing company. While the author must bear the responsibility for the contents, the choice of publisher does say something about the quality of the author's work. This avenue of evaluation is more useful for recent genealogies than for those published over forty years ago. Earlier generations had essentially two choices: produce an inexpensive typescript/carbon paper/mimeograph genealogy, or pay a full-service printer to typeset the book, make printing plates, print the book, and bind it.

Today anyone can afford to have a few copies "printed" at the local copy shop. Given the affordability of "quick print" publications, the lack of quality in many of today's publications, while amazing and frightening, is not surprising. Several vanity presses specialize in genealogical printing, so the conscientious author who has worked hard to compile a worthwhile genealogy can have it printed with quality, even if the demand for it is not great enough to interest a commercial publisher. Publishers are in business to make money; while quality may sell a few more books, it also costs a lot more. However, most new genealogies and family histories published today are not published by the major genealogical publishers.

Reprints of older "classics" are very common today. The fact that any one is chosen to be reprinted is a partial measure of its quality. These reprints are valuable for researchers, because many older books were printed in limited quantities and are no longer on the market. In fact, many of the major compendia and dictionaries discussed in this chapter have been reprinted in recent years. However, popularity, while it sells books, does not always equal quality. Companies reprint books to make money, so they will reprint popular books that are of questionable usefulness. Generally, fraudulent genealogical books have not been reprinted, but some with questionable accuracy have reappeared. A new preface discussing the accuracy and usefulness of the book may accompany the reprint—a valuable tool for evaluation. Also, critical book reviews will appear for the reprint which may point out its shortcomings.

A reprint may be done by a descendant or by a family organization that shares the ancestry in the book. In some cases, the reprint is more like a new edition, including updates to the older edition, such as Edith Whitcraft Eberhart's *Doremus Family in America 1687–1987* (Baltimore: Gateway, 1990), which is called a "revised edition" while it is acknowledged that it is based on the 1897 book of the same name by William Nelson. Because the new author included source notes in the 1990 edition, it is easy to see that, for many families, the original 1897 edition is the only source of information. However, many branches are brought up to date, and some errors in the first edition that were brought to the new author's attention were corrected.

While production values should not be the deciding factor in judging a genealogy or family history, they should offer some insights into the overall quality of the contents and the carefulness of the author.

Where was the work published? Was it in a journal? If so, which journal? While much of this discussion of publication quality has focused on books, similar questions can be posed for articles. Each journal has different standards of acceptance. The scholarly journals demand documentation for every factual statement in an article, but this is a relatively recent requirement (generally within the last thirty years). Of course, good articles have appeared since the 1930s. The publication of a genealogy in a periodical of limited circulation or of only local interest may suggest that the author's reasoning or the sources used do not meet present standards. However, keep in mind the author's options; in the 1920s, for example, there were only a very few genealogical journals in which to publish a compiled genealogy. Even today, most periodicals publish local records rather than compiled genealogies.

Author

Is the author known for reputable work? The reputation of the author is one of the most important means available to evaluate a genealogy. The works of some authors, such as Donald Lines Jacobus and Walter Goodwin Davis, are almost above reproach. However, if they were here today, these authors would be among the first to encourage researchers to verify even what they wrote. The works of other authors, among them Gustav Anjou and Horatio Gates Somerby, should not be trusted at all. Most authors fall between these two ends of this "credibililty continuum." It may take some effort, but usually one can learn something of an author's reputation. Determine what she does (or did) for a profession. Find out what organizations she belongs to and what honors she has received. The small but worthy group of Fellows of the American Society of Genealogists are elected by their peers based specifically on the quality of their published genealogical work. Certified and accredited genealogists must pass a detailed examination and peer review. Contributing editors to the major genealogical periodicals are chosen because of the demonstrated quality of their research and writing.

Mary K. Meyer and P. William Filby's *Who's Who in Genealogy and Heraldry* (Savage, Md.: Who's Who in Genealogy & Heraldry, 1990) may describe an author's experience and major publications. With the publication of the second edition of this significant reference work, it should be asked of living authors, Are they listed? If not, why? The editors of these volumes had very broad inclusion criteria. The author who is not concerned enough about the field of genealogy (even if it is not his or her profession) to request a listing does a disservice to genealogy and calls his or her own abilities into question.

Does the author understand the terminology used during the period? Does the author cite authoritative sources for period terminology? Can the author correctly transcribe the old handwriting in original records? Closely related to the author's reputation are the author's training and abilities. Learn about the author's background. A genealogist learned in the complexities of colonial research may stumble over a foreign name in a twentieth-century passenger list. An author who can read Gothic script from the 1700s may not be able to read English court hand from the same time period. Don't stop at noting the initials AG (accredited genealogist), CG (certified genealogist), or FASG (fellow of the American Society of Genealogists) after the author's name. Learn what area(s) the author is accredited or certified in. Even though certified genealogist is a more stringent qualification than certified genealogical record specialist (CGRS), the certified genealogist's experience may not qualify him for the focus of the genealogy being evaluated.

Do not be unduly impressed by academic degrees which have nothing to do with genealogy, history, library science, or related subjects. A qualified engineer or retired army colonel is not necessarily a trained genealogist. While some of the sources mentioned above will help in this part of the evaluation, carefully read the preface of the genealogy and the acknowledgments, if there are any. Here one is likely to gain some understanding of the author's background for the work at hand.

Is the author's interpretation of the material logical and unbiased? Is it complete? Objectivity can be difficult to evaluate. The author's purpose (see above under "Creation and Purpose") may be revealing. This part of the evaluation, however, mostly requires careful contemplation of the author's material. Consider other possible interpretations. Determine whether additional sources may exist that could support or deny the author's hypotheses.

Note how the author states her conclusions. Sometimes a weak conclusion can be veiled with words of assurance which are not as meaningful as they appear. As Eugene Stratton commented,

> words such as 'most likely,' 'must have been,' 'obviously,' 'clearly,' and the like are too often used by genealogists, as by lawyers, to give their theories the aura of inescapable fact, especially if the facts are not cited upon which the characterization rests. . . . The wise reader, on being confronted by such leading expressions as 'most likely,' will search for another reasonable explanation of the observed facts (1985, 96).

Colket's description of a good author/compiler of a family genealogy applies equally well to the reader/researcher seeking clues from that published genealogy. It

> requires a good mind so that he can recognize and discard wishful thinking. He must acquire the skill of weaving together the data he has assembled from many sources. He must have the ability to analyze evidence and to determine with good judgement whether certain presumed relationships are actually correct (1968, 252).

Can the author be contacted for missing facts or documentation? This likelihood pertains to modern publications. If possible, contact the author for additional evidence or sources of information needed to verify the material. When a family history contains complete dates for births, deaths, and marriages, but no documentation is cited, it may be possible to contact the author and ask about the sources. If the author is deceased, it may be possible to determine where his research notes are deposited. Many genealogists deposit their research materials at one of their favorite archives or libraries, or their heirs do so. The *National Union Catalog of Manuscript Collections,* the *National Inventory of Documentary Sources* (both discussed earlier), or other reference or biographical sources may help to identify where the manuscripts have been deposited.

Contents

Are names, events, dates, and places supported with document citations? Do not be concerned at this point with the nature of the sources, but simply determine whether sources are cited at all. Lack of source citations reflects poorly on the author and his interest in a quality genealogy.

Are dates, places, and events logical? If not, is there an adequate explanation, including documentary evidence? If the first child of a couple was not born in or near the town where they married, there should be an explanation or a notice of the family's removal. If the wife was significantly older—five or more years—than her husband, the author should comment, if only to confirm the age difference. If children were born well past the mother's fortieth birthday, this, too, should be explained. If the surname(s) involved are fairly common, the author should make a special effort to explain how she distinguished among different persons of the same name. These comments may be made in footnotes or in the body of the text, but some comment should appear. Whenever researchers find information that stretches credulity, they should examine it carefully. Such occurrences can be the "tip-off" of a careless compiler.

Is the text well footnoted? Does it include source acknowledgments? Are scholarly standards met? These are the marks of a careful author, but their absence, especially in older genealogies, is not necessarily cause to reject a work.

Are there many errors, typographical or otherwise? Excessive errors make the quality of the entire work suspect. The author who was not concerned enough to proofread for mistakes in production was very possibly too careless to notice mistakes in logic or reasoning when assembling the genealogy.

Is the format easy to understand? If the book is not well organized or the material is presented poorly, the sources may be difficult to determine. A unique organization also suggests that the author is not very experienced in genealogy.

Does the author intentionally leave out negative events, such as bigamy, illegitimacies, children conceived before their parents' marriage date, divorces, murders, and criminal records? Most genealogies are labors of love, and their authors usually have a somewhat reverent attitude toward the family (after all, they are usually relatives). While an effort to present the best side of the family may stem from noble intentions, it also bespeaks a disregard for quality research. Acknowledging the failings of ancestors makes them more human and easier to understand. Keeping the skeletons in the closet (for long-deceased family members) helps no one and can obscure important genealogical information.

What is the scope of the work? Are only male lines continued? Have other interrelated families been left out or dropped? An extensive scope or lack of it does not make a genealogy good or bad, but being aware of the scope helps the user understand the purpose of the author and the possibility that a specific ancestor is included. If the plan of the genealogy is to present only the specific line of descent from an early ancestor to a recent ancestor, do not be dismayed if a specific ancestor is not recorded. The person may simply belong to a different branch of the family.

Comparison with Other Sources

How does it compare with what is known about the family? One of the best ways for a researcher to evaluate any book is to review what it says about a subject the researcher is knowledgeable of. If an author is accurate, complete, and fair in treating a subject the researcher is familiar with, the same will often be true of other topics. Genealogies are particularly easy to evaluate using this method. Whenever a researcher finds a genealogy about his or her family, it must connect to some information the researcher already knows. The researcher should examine how the author treats the generations that connect to her present knowledge of the family. Do the dates and places match, or are there conflicts? Are all the children included? Read the description of the family, their occupations, residences, and religion, and compare the information with what is known about the family. If there are discrepancies, note whether the author addresses these problems or cites sources for the information.

Do other genealogies of this family provide additional or conflicting information? This comparison is similar to the process mentioned above, but it does not require personal knowledge of the family. Many families are treated in more than one genealogy. The husband and wife may be linked with separate agnate descent genealogies, or a town history or genealogical compendium may treat some of the same generations as does a book-length family history. Compare the two versions. One of them generally will provide more information than the other, but some information will be unique to each. Look for discrepancies and missing information. *The Pratt Family: Or the Descendants of Lieut. William Pratt, One of the First Settlers of Hartford and Say-Brook, with Genealogical Notes of John Pratt, of Hartford; Peter Pratt, of Lyme; John Pratt (Taylor,) of Say-Brook* (Hartford, Conn.: Case, Lockwood and Co., 1864) and *The Buckingham Family; or the Descendants of Thomas Buckingham, One of the First Settlers of Milford, Conn.* (Hartford, Conn.: Case, Lockwood & Brainard, 1872) both discuss the Nathan Buckingham family, but with some surprising differences (figure 16-21). The information in the Pratt genealogy is very brief, naming six children but giving only one questionable birth date. The Buckingham genealogy gives more information, including complete birth dates, deaths for two children, marriages of the children, and the father's second marriage. However, the Buckingham genealogy omitted the eldest son, whose existence was proved in contemporary documents.

Be careful when doing this analysis to determine that one source was not simply copied from the other. In such cases, of course, the information will not contradict, but that is only because the earlier genealogy is the source for the later genealogy. Don't mistake such similarity for confirmation that the information is true. Rather, seek the source of the original information in the earlier genealogy.

Sources

The sources of a family history or genealogy are the most important aspect of evaluation. However, it is not enough to notice that sources are present; they also must be checked to determine if they were accurately cited and that proper conclusions were drawn from them. Take the time to look at the sources and determine whether the author used them correctly. While it may be too time-consuming to look up every source in a published genealogy, it is worthwhile to check some sources. After finding the parts of a published genealogy that are of most interest, "spot check" by selecting some of the sources cited and looking them up; it is helpful to select those that are easiest to access. If the following questions can be applied satisfactorily, the researcher generally can feel good assured using the genealogy. If not, it is necessary to evaluate more, and possibly all, of the sources cited.

Are the sources accurately and completely recorded? Again, this consideration reflects the care of the author. Check the documentation against the original records. Sources that are not fully cited may occupy less space on the page, but they waste the researcher's time, and time is eminently more important than paper.

Does the text include all the information that was recorded in the original sources? It is necessary to look up some of the sources to make this judgment. Wrong conclusions can be made when only part of a source is used. Researchers who are familiar with sources can often tell if the whole source was cited. For example, the 1900 Federal census includes information about naturalization, immigration, and number of years married. If that census is cited for an immigrant family, this information should be included in the genealogy, or an explanation should be given for its absence.

Were original documents used for verification of the data? If not, the accuracy of the published work must be evaluated. Many genealogists use transcripts or abstracts of the original

210 DESCENDANTS OF WILLIAM PRATT.

1765.

MARY ELVIRA PRATT, daughter of Wolcott and Mary Pratt, born July 31, 1800, was married to *Nathan Buckingham*, about the year 1820, and had by him, six children. They reside at Sandwich, De Kalb County, Illinois.

CHILDREN.

2056. Charles, (Buckingham,) born April 1, 1821.
2057. Francis Eugene, "
2058. Frederick, "
2059. Almus, "
2060. Mary Jane, "
2061. Joseph, "

1534.

NATHAN BUCKINGHAM, son of Nathan and Rhoda (*Tucker*) Buckingham, born July 3, 1798; was twice married. (1), to *Marg E. Pratt*, Jan. 26, 1829. Mrs. Mary E. Buckingham died Nov. 14, 1855. (2), to *Ann Stevens*, Oct. 22, 1856. Resides at Sandwich, DeKalb County, Illinois.

CHILDREN.

2029. William F., } Twins, born Oct. 19, 1830; killed in California, Jan. 17, 1857.
2030. Frederick, } Twins, born Oct. 19, 1830; died Sept. 1, 1864, in Nashville, Tenn.
2031. Almus W., " May 8, 1832; m. *Zelina Cheever*.
2032. Mary Jane, " Aug. 24, 1835; m. *Mr. Disbrow*.
2033. Joseph Miner, " June 2, 1842.

Figure 16-21. The Nathan Buckingham family as described in *The Pratt Family: Or the Descendants of Lieut. William Pratt, One of the First Settlers of Hartford and Say-Brook, with Genealogical Notes of John Pratt, of Hartford; Peter Pratt, of Lyme; John Pratt (Taylor,) of Say-Brook* (top) and *The Buckingham Family; or the Descendants of Thomas Buckingham, One of the First Settlers of Milford, Conn.* (bottom).

information. While these can be helpful because they are easier to search, reference to the original documents makes a better genealogy. Of course, if only the abstracts were consulted, the author should only cite the abstracts. Remember that most transcripts, abstracts, and extracts have errors. Even if the errors are few, how does the researcher know that the one mistake is not in the very abstract pertaining to the family he is researching? Even if the author used transcribed sources, the user should consult the originals when evaluating the lineage of interest.

Are there additional sources for the time and place that can be reviewed to confirm the lineage? Do these verify or disprove the assertions made in the text? Very few genealogists use every available source. When using a compiled genealogy or family history, take the time to look up some of the information in sources the author did not use. This method serves as an excellent double-check on the accuracy of the genealogy.

Does the author discuss all the records that were consulted, including those in which no information was found? The absence of information is itself information. If an ancestor does not appear in the land records at the time when he lived in the county, why not? If the author discusses such "negative searches," the researcher can be more comfortable knowing that a sufficient number of sources were used to compile the genealogy.

Are family traditions included? Family traditions are unreliable and must be well documented to be considered credible. Two nationally known authors offer the following comments: Norman E. Wright states that "the researcher must be careful in accepting family tradition at face value, for it can be deceptive" (1974, 5), and Val D. Greenwood writes, "family tradition also tells us much about family origins; however, such traditions, on the whole, are notoriously unreliable, and no tradition should ever be accepted at face value (1983, 51)."

A family tradition was repeated over the years in various branches of one family. It maintained that a third great-grandmother, Jane "Jennie" (Davis) Stewart, was a cousin of Jefferson Davis, president of the Confederacy. Because of the detailed and documented family histories and biographies available for Jefferson Davis, very little time was needed to prove that there was no connection whatsoever between the two Davis families, even though a biography of Jane's grandson in a published county history proudly claimed the relationship.

Family traditions cannot be accepted as truth without proof. Whether the tradition is that three brothers came to America or that the family is related to a notable person, most traditions have little to substantiate them. Family traditions have proved over and over again to be untrustworthy, but most of them do include some truth or, at least, clues upon which the genealogist can begin research.

> Tradition is a chronic deceiver, and those who put faith in it are self-deceivers. This is not to say that tradition is invariably false. Sometimes a modicum of fact lies almost hidden at its base. The probability of its falsehood increases in geometric ratio as the lineage claimed increases in grandeur. . . . Every experienced genealogist knows of erroneous and thoroughly disproved traditions which must have originated in some . . . way. Nor are . . . erroneous traditions restricted to claims of exalted lineage or connection. They may refer merely to the nationality of the immigrant ancestor, or to the original place of residence in this country, or to any other detail of the family history (Rubincam 1960, 14–15).

Most family histories, genealogies, and biographies include family traditions. While it is worthwhile for these traditions to be preserved, they are often published without verification of the details; indeed, they are often published as fact, with no indication of the flimsy origins on which they are based. Thus, a tradition is further propagated, providing novice genealogists with what they feel is valid evidence. Be wary of family histories that cite tradition, especially when there is little additional documentation. For many, it is difficult to accept that something Mother or Grandfather "knew" cannot be supported by fact. The fact is, family traditions cannot be accepted as truth without proof.

Summary

Even if some or all of the above criteria are not met, a genealogy may have some redeeming features. Do not ignore a source just because it doesn't meet established standards. Instead, use the material as clues. Verify the information to the extent possible. Sometimes such a genealogy is the only available record of a family. If it is, but the information can't be proved, play the devil's advocate—try to disprove it. Look at every record, even if they do not meet standard criteria; they may provide the only clues from which to work.

If the content is well footnoted and includes accurate and complete source acknowledgments, use that information to locate and investigate those sources. If names, events, dates, and places are referenced, the effort of locating evidence to confirm the published data decreases significantly. Always check the original sources. Additional research in other records may be required to fully verify and document a lineage because older books or articles were often published before other sources became available, and sometimes documented publications use only some of the available records. All sources, including newly released or newly available works, should be used to confirm and supplement the material in an older or incompletely researched publication.

EVALUATION EXAMPLES

by Wendy Elliott

It is often much easier to learn a principle if one can see it in action. To this end, the following evaluation examples should help researchers learn how to understand the information found in published genealogies, and how to use this information to find more facts.

Example 1

Always begin with the preface or introduction to a genealogy or family history. It will provide some background and give an overview of the author's purpose and the book's limitations. Consider the following preface:

> In presenting this small value to the members of the Burnett family most intimately concerned, we who are directly responsible for its conception and preparation want to make clear at the outset what the aims, scope, and limitations of the book are–in short, what it is and what it is not.
>
> The chief purpose has been to record, for our own satisfaction and especially for our children, grandchildren, and for generations yet to come, as much information as possible about the ancestry and descendants of a *single* line of the Burnett family. To have attempted more would have involved years (and fruitless years in the end, as became readily apparent) of searching for long-lost collateral relatives.
>
> Thomas Burnett (1755–1780), our American Revolutionary ancestor, provided the focal point for this history. From him the lineage was sought to more remote forebears. It has been carried down through Thomas's older son, Swan Pritchett Burnett, and in turn to some extent through the latter's thirteen children, but in greatest detail through his youngest son, Jesse Montreville Lafayette Burnett.
>
> Although it would have been gratifying to include in equal detail those less closely related Burnetts whom we do know and value as kinsmen, even that amount of clambering along the limbs and twigs of the family tree would have entailed more time, labor, and funds than could be allotted to this undertaking. However, in both the sections on history and on pure genealogy fairly full summaries of collateral families are given. This, it is hoped, will stimulate those related branches to gather data for their own complete genealogies.
>
> Because Jesse M. L. Burnett's wife, Henrietta Sarah Cody, was an exceptional person in her own right, had an incalculable influence on her descendants, and is held in vivid and loving memory by her grandchildren–those of us who now constitute the oldest living generation–special attention is given to her. It is as a Burnett, not as a Cody, that emphasis is placed on her. For more than sixty years after her marriage she was so completely identified with the Burnett family that they came to regard her as one of their own.
>
> As a supplement to this book, for the Burnett-Cody line only, there will later be issued a booklet devoted to a condensed history of the Cody family and a skeleton Cody genealogy–though we emphatically deny that there are any skeletons in the family closet!
>
> To shift to a more personal note of greater immediacy, I want to say that one of the greatest delights of working on this project was the letters which came to me along with completed data sheets. Almost all those to whom questionnaires were sent responded promptly and with interest and enthusiasm. In a few instances, however, enthusiasm was tempered by other reactions.
>
> . . . [I] consider this book a matter not merely of family history (though it is primarily so), but also of history in the broader sense. . . . The motivation has *not* been that of vainglorious pride of family although, fortunately, we can be justifiably and humbly grateful that ours is an honorable family. The pages that follow will show in some measure how the Burnetts played a part, sometimes significant, sometimes insignificant, in the history of nations, which is the history of civilized man.
>
> . . . Personal reminiscences and anecdotes, which abound in any family, added to mere names and dates will make a warm and living record for posterity of ancestors dead and gone whom they would otherwise know, if at all, only as names and shadowy creatures of the past.
>
> . . . To infuse with life, giving them the warmth, glow, and human traits they possessed as flesh-and-blood persons is precisely what I had hoped to do in the American section of this Burnett history. That I did not achieve this aim is a keen disappointment. The failure is due (in addition to my shortcomings as a writer)

> primarily to two factors: First, my memory and that of my contemporaries goes back only to our grandmother, Henrietta Cody Burnett, and to a quite vague recollection of Great-uncle Jefferson Burnett in our very early youth. He was the only one of his generation living at that period. The untimely death of Grandfather (Jesse M. L.) Burnett deprived all his grandchildren of ever knowing him. Second, to capture and recreate in writing the person and personality of Grandmother would require a volume in itself. . . .
>
> . . . the late Dr. Edmund Cody Burnett . . . worked assiduously to search out and preserve personal papers, family Bible records, legal documents and state records that might throw light on the obscure area of the earlier American Burnetts (and Codys). Death left his work incomplete but invaluable. . . . [He] brought the added contribution of a scholar's meticulous concern for accuracy and critical analysis of every detail. It was my good fortune to have access to his files of family papers and pertinent correspondence. . . . These papers were the starting point for additional research (Gass 1964, xi–xiv).

Several of the questions for evaluation above are answered or addressed in this preface. First, it states that the purpose is to record the history for personal satisfaction and for posterity; no scholarly endeavor is indicated. The genealogy is then defined as covering only the descendants of a *single* line, and is further explained as dealing with one line of one line of one line. Apparently, only the author's direct line of descent is given; this is not necessarily a negative, but it does limit the possibility of finding information on collateral lines. The author further explains that he had neither the time, money, nor interest to document families of nondirect ancestors, but "fairly full summaries of collateral families are given . . . to stimulate . . . [others] to gather data for their own complete genealogies."

Next the author explains that his grandmother deserves and receives special consideration, but that the emphasis is only on her life after she married. This means that little information is presented about her parents, siblings, or relatives. Readers are informed that a "booklet" on her family will be issued later.

Also stated is a straightforward denial of any "skeletons in the family closet." Therefore, it is unlikely that the history includes any negative aspects, even if they were discovered. The next paragraph mentions that at least some of the details in the history were gathered from questionnaires sent to living descendants. Historical content is included, if the content of the book follows what is outlined in the preface. The book includes names and dates and is enhanced with anecdotes, but the documentation of facts is not mentioned. In fact, the next paragraph indicates that the book is limited because memory was lacking; this suggests that much of the history is based on family tradition. The author also informs the reader that some of his objectives were not achieved.

Finally, on the fourth page of the preface, the reader is advised that scholarly work and criteria were used in the compilation of this family history. Furthermore, the "meticulous" work compiled by Dr. Burnett was "the starting point for additional research." Records used in this compilation are mentioned and described. The reader is told that a "professionally careful, detailed, and wide-ranging search" was conducted of "all pertinent records of Virginia Burnetts in the immediate pre-Revolutionary period." Copies of original land grants and photocopies of land records were obtained, and research was conducted in the Library of Congress, the National Archives, and state repositories. Thus, the reader's initial concern about the quality of the contents has greatly lessened with the concluding discussion of the preface.

Example 2

Another family history is totally without credits, footnotes, or recognition of any source, except in the acknowledgments, which consist of one page:

> I wish to here express my sincere thanks to my grandson Jaci Clark Sisson, for editing and for giving this book, which I have typed, a final typing. He has been a great help to his seventy-nine-year-old Granny. And my thanks to the following relatives, for the information they have given me on my ancestors: To my niece Lillian DeGroat, who had information that her mother-in-law, my eldest sister, had given her, and she passed it on to me; To Effie Fardel, my cousin of Stanhope, Iowa, on my mother's side; To Icel Williams, wife of my cousin Herschel Williams, Story City, Iowa; To Doris and Lowell Williams, Anaheim, California (Lowell is a second cousin on my father's side.) To Josephine and Jerry McMahan, Redondo Beach, California (Jerry is my sister Myrtle's son. They had information and pictures from the old family album.) (Sisson 1984, ii)

These acknowledgments are barely helpful. Detailed sources would have provided the researcher with a much better foundation. The author mostly expresses appreciation for family data that was shared. No indication is given of the types or quality of the records.

A review of the text indicates that some original sources were used. Names, dates, and places of immigration are noted; exact birth dates and places are mentioned, but without citing the sources. It appears that family records were used, although these are not mentioned in the narrative format of this family history. Because the book was published fairly recently, the author may be willing to furnish the necessary documentation if contacted.

Example 3

A family history of the Eldredge and other related families is a case where documentation was used but was not properly cited:

> Elisha Eldred (William) was born 1653 in Mass. and died in Eastham (Wellfleet) Oct. 14, 1739. He is buried in the old graveyard at the head of Duck Creek, where a stone marks the spot. His name on the gravestone is spelled Eldredg. William Lumpkin, the father-in-law of William Eldred, in his will dated July 23, 1668, names wife Tamesin, daughter Tamesin, wife of John Sunderling; and grandchildren, Wm. Gray, Elisha Eldred and Bethia Eldred. In 1693 Elisha Eldredg bought a tract of land in Harwich of Joseph Creek, an Indian. He afterwards sold to Isaac Atkins and removed to that part of Eastham which subsequently became the town of Wellfleet. Name of wife not known. His son Elisha

> Eldredge Jr. was active in church work and was opposed to the preaching of Mr. Oaks.
> Children of Number (4)
> Elisha Eldred (2) son of William Eldred (1) and
> 3 gen. 10 I Elisha Jr. b. about 1690.
> 3 " 11 II Bethia.
> ELDREDGE
> Elisha Eldredge, Jr,[3] (Elisha[2], William[1]) was born about 1690 and died Nov. 9, 1754 at Mansfield, Conn. He married Dorcas Mulford of Truro; she was born at Eastham Mch. 6, 1692/3 and died in Mansfield, Conn., about 1755. Her mother was Mary, dau. of Nathaniel Basset and granddaughter of Wm. Bassett, who came on Ship "Fortunr" [*sic*] in 1621. . . . (Lamont 1948, 6)

Interestingly, the title page, which shows 1948 as the year of publication, is faced with a picture and inscription reading, "Mr. and Mrs. George B. Lamont *on their Golden Wedding Anniversary,* March 29, 1949"; thus, the 1948 date, also given in the foreword, is questionable. Information in the text—such as exact dates and places, the name inscribed on the tombstone, and the name of the ship and the date of its arrival—all indicate that some research was conducted, but the sources are not cited in the text or as footnotes or endnotes. The information recorded in this family history needs to be documented.

One section of the history titled "Tiffany" begins with a brief citation of two sources of information: "'Tiffany Genealogy' by Nelson Otis Tiffany. Swansea Records . . ." (Lamont 1948, 89). This line indicates to the reader that some research was conducted in these two sources, but neither page numbers nor the exact title of the Swansea records are cited.

A different history of the Eldredge family includes much of the same data and suggests that the author of *Lamont-Eldredge Family Records* used the information from an earlier published account without giving credit:

> 2. Elisha[2] Eldred (William[1]), born in 1653, died in Eastham (Wellfleet) Oct. 14, 1739, and is buried in the old graveyard at the head of Duck Creek, where a stone marks the spot. His name on the gravestone is spelled *Eldredg.* William Lumpkin, the father-in-law of William Eldred, in his will dated 23 July, 1668, names wife Tamesin; daughter Tamesin, wife of John Sunderling; and grandchildren William Gray, Elisha Eldred, and Bethia Eldred. In 1693 Elisha Eldredg was in Harwich where he with Joseph Severance and Manoah Ellis, bought a tract of land of Joseph Crook, an Indian. He resided in the south part of the town in what is sometimes denominated the Doane neighborhood. He afterwards sold his interest in the above land to Isaac Atkins and removed to that part of Eastham which subsequently became the town of Wellfleet. It is not known who his wife was. His son Elisha Eldredge, Jr. was active in church work and was opposed to the preaching of Mr. Oakes.
>
> 3. Elisha[3] Eldredge (Elisha[2], William[1]), born about 1690, died in Mansfield, Ct., Nov. 9, 1754, married Dorcas, daughter of Thomas Mulford, of Truro. She was born in Eastham, March 6, 1692-93, and died in Mansfield, Ct., about 1755. Her mother was Mary, daughter of Nathaniel Basset and granddaughter of William Basset who came in the ship *Fortune* in 1621 (Eldredge 1896, 6).

A cursory review of these comparative portions from the two family histories shows a couple of spelling differences. In the first abstract, the Indian from whom Elisha Eldredg purchased a tract of land is listed as Joseph Creek; in the second, the Indian is shown as Joseph Crook. (In sixteenth-century handwriting, the *o* does look like a modern *e.*) The preacher's surname is spelled Oaks in the former and Oakes in the latter. The name of the ship *Fortune* is spelled *Fortunr* in the first, which appears to be a typographical error. Dorcas Mulford, wife of Elisha Eldredge, is listed in the second abstract as the daughter of Thomas Mulford of Truro. In the first abstract, Dorcas is shown as the daughter of Mary Bassett, but no mention of her father is given. In the second abstract, books and page numbers are not cited, but sources mentioned in the text include church records, wills, and land records. In both cases, the printed information should be verified with original records.

Example 4

A comparison of two or more published family histories often reveals additional information, as well as discrepancies and/or errors. Information is given on the same couple in two compilations: *An Elaborate History and Genealogy of the Ballous in America,* "carefully compiled and edited by Adin Ballou (1888)" and copyrighted by Ariel Ballou and Latimer W. Ballou, "proprietary publishers," and in Alexander Hamilton Hart's *The Hart Family As Far As Can Be Traced and Gathered* (1908). The Hart genealogy includes the following entry:

> 5-Lucia Adeline Hart, born Apr. 29, 1838, at Russell, Ohio. Married Albert Darius Ballou at Clifton, Wis. on Dec. 26, 1854. (Prents [*sic*] of Albert D. Ballou were of New England families, Darius Ballou and Abigail Bishop Ballou. He was born Nov. 10, at Monroe, Mass.) (Hart 1908, 11)

The Ballou family history gives the same details and includes considerably more information concerning Albert Darius Ballou, as is to be expected. It also provides a brief history of Albert's military service endeavors during the Civil War, but neither history tells that Lucia Adeline Hart and Albert Darius Ballou were divorced. In verifying the data with original sources, Albert's Civil War pension file was reviewed. The file includes the notation, "divorced in the court at Chicago, Ill. 1869, not married since." Both histories were printed more than two decades after the divorce, but neither mentioned this circumstance. The author of the Ballou history apparently did not mind reporting divorces, because the entry for Henry Martin Ballou states, "a divorce closed this union (Ballou 1888, 775)."

Yet a third family history includes other details for this couple. *The Nicholas Hart Genealogy* shows the following data:

> Lucia[8] Adolin [*sic*] Hart (Alexander H.[7], Lombard[6], Lombard[5], Richard[4], Richard[3], Richard[2], Nicholas[1]), born April 29, 1838, in Russell, Ohio, fifth child of Alexander H. and Mary, or Polly, (Eldredge) Hart; married at Clifton, now Hilbert, Wis., Dec. 26, 1854, Albert Darius Ballou, born in Monroe, Mass., Nov. 10, 1828, son of Darius Balou, born July 3, 1805, in

> Monroe, Mass., and his first wife, Abigail Bishop. This Abigail Bishop was a daughter of Joy and Abigail (Blakesley) Bishop.
>
> Mr. Ballou and wife resided at San Francisco, Cal., where he died March 20, 1899 (Hart 1903, 103).

This genealogy also fails to mention that Albert and Lucia were divorced. In fact, it not only excludes the divorce data, but it also includes a statement that suggests the couple remained together until his death in 1899. This third volume also erroneously states that Albert lived and died in California. These assertions are refuted by Albert's own statement of residence in his pension application and his final pension payment record, which show that he died 20 March 1899 in or near Topeka, Kansas (Ballou, "Civil War").

Example 5

Some family histories are created from a compilation of work done by several individuals. The introduction to *The Bebout Family in Flanders and North America* indicates that the published material was contributed by three researchers. The first section of the book is an article "Reprinted by permission from the New York Genealogical and Biographical Record April, 1935," titled "Chapter 1: The Bebout Family in Flanders," by William J. Hoffman. This portion of the manuscript is documented and includes research undertaken by Mr. Hoffman and "Mr. J. Goudswaard, a researcher of the Netherlands," who conducted the research in the town of Thielt. The text includes references as well as footnotes.

However, the use of the word *heir* in this first section could be misinterpreted. It is stated that Mayken Bibau "did not name any heirs." In this context, the word *heir* must denote descendants, for she left a will which mentions at least three heirs, including a cousin, *Jan Bybau filius Pieter haren cousijn,* another cousin, Maria Bibau, and Maria's husband, Pieter Beheyt (Flick 1943, 6–7). Mayken Bibau did not devise any property to her children; thus, it appears that she had none who survived.

The third section, written by the author, Alexander C. Flick, former state historian in Albany, New York, is also footnoted. It identifies his sources as court minutes, Van Rensselaer Bowier Manuscripts, two multi-volume histories of New York, Munsell's collections, the *New York Genealogical and Biographical Record,* church records, civil records, and will and probate records. This section contains a total of sixty-eight footnotes for just over six pages of text. No statements are given without supporting evidence. The fourth section, also written by A. C. Flick, includes nine pages of material that is not as well footnoted, but the text includes numerous citations. This section was also "reprinted by permission from the New York Genealogical and Biographical Record July, 1935." Footnotes show that original records were consulted, address questionable information, and detail conclusions. The concluding paragraph of this chapter also helps the reader evaluate the work:

> This preliminary study of the Bebout family in America down to the close of the American Revolution is, so far as known, the first serious attempt to reconstruct the history of the family. The results are in open conflict with some of the commonly accepted family traditions. No doubt there are errors in both the conjectures and in the interpretation of isolated facts. It is the hope of the writer that members of the family and interested genealogists will assist him to make the necessary corrections. Information on any phase of the family history will be welcomed.

NOTES

1. This number is based on a study of thirty-nine randomly selected American genealogies with indexes at the Family History Library. As partial support for this study, dividing the estimated 1.5 million entries in Rider's forty-eight-volume *American Genealogical Index* by the 750 sources used suggests an average of approximately two thousand names per published genealogy. Because later publications seem to be shorter, the smaller number is used here.
2. This figure was derived by adding the U.S. census counts for the 1920 census and each census thirty years earlier (1890, 1860, 1830, 1810), as well as census bureau estimates for 1630, 1670, 1690, 1720, 1740, and 1780. While the average American life span has almost always exceeded thirty years, this method accounts for adult immigrants and assures that the cumulative population is not underestimated.
3. Meredith B. Colket, Jr., was elected to the National Genealogy Hall of Fame (sponsored by the National Genealogical Society) in 1992.
4. My thanks to Wendy Elliott, who suggested many of the following questions.

REFERENCE LIST

Ballou, Adin, comp. and ed. 1888. *An Elaborate History and Genealogy of the Ballous in America*. Providence, R.I.: E. L. Freeman and Son, state printers.

Ballou, Albert D. "Civil War pension application papers." Certificate no. 662982.

Colket, Meredith B., Jr. 1968. "Creating a Worthwhile Family Genealogy." *National Genealogical Society Quarterly* 56 (4): 243–62 (December).

Converse, Charles Allen. 1905. *Some of the Ancestors and Descendants of Samuel Converse, Jr.* Boston: Eben Putnam.

Eldredge, Zoeth S. 1896. *Eldredge Genealogy. A Record of Some of the Descendants of William Eldredge of Yarmouth*. Boston.

Ferris, Mary Walton. 1931. *Dawes-Gates Ancestral Lines.* Milwaukee.

Filby, P. William. 1987. Preface in reprint edition of Frederick A. Virkus, *The Compendium of American Genealogy,* vol. 1. Baltimore: Genealogical Publishing Co.

Flick, Alexander C. 1943. *The Bebout Family in Flanders and North America*. Santa Rosa, Fla.: the author.

Gass, Frances, comp. 1964. *A Burnett Family of the South: Thomas Burnett, 1755–1780, of Virginia and North Carolina and His Descendants*. Washington, D.C.: National Publishing Co.

Greenwood, Val D. 1983. *The Researcher's Guide to American Genealogy.* Baltimore: Genealogical Publishing Co.

Hart, Alexander Hamilton. 1908. *The Hart Family as far as can be Traced and Gathered*. Los Angeles: n.p.

Hart, James Morrison, comp. 1903. *The Nicholas Hart Genealogy.* Pasadena, Calif.

Hatcher, Patricia Law. 1996. *Producing a Quality Family History*. Salt Lake City: Ancestry.

Kyvig, David E., and Myron A. Marty. 1978. *Your Family History: A Handbook for Research and Writing*. Arlington Heights, Ill.: AHM Publishing.

Lamont, Belle Eldredge, comp. 1948. *Lamont-Eldredge Family Records*. Albion, N.Y.: the author.

Mackenzie, George Norbury. 1907–20. *Colonial Families of the United States of America.* 7 vols. Reprint. Baltimore: Genealogical Publishing Co., 1966.

Munsell, Joel. 1900. *The American Genealogist, Being a Catalogue of Family Histories . . . Published in America, from 1771 to Date.* Reprint. Baltimore: Genealogical Publishing Co., 1971.

Roberts, Jayare. 1987. "Beyond the Begat Books." *Genealogical Journal* 16 (Spring-Summer).

Rubincam, Milton, ed. 1960. *Genealogical Research Methods and Sources.* Washington, D.C.: American Society of Genealogists.

Sisson, Lovey B. 1984. *The Last Leaf.* Los Angeles: Vantage Press.

Stratton, Eugene A. 1985. "The Evidence That Sir Richard de Braose Who Married Alice le Rus Was the Son of John and Margaret (Verch Llywelyn) de Braose." *Genealogist* 6 (1): 85–99 (Spring).

Totten, John R. 1921. "Some Genealogical Absurdities." *New York Genealogical and Biographical Record* (October): 295–301.

Virkus, Frederick A. 1942. *The Compendium of American Genealogy.* Vol 7. Reprint. Baltimore: Genealogical Publishing Co., 1987.

Whitmore, William H. 1875. *The American Genealogist: Being a Catalogue of Family Histories and Publications Containing Genealogical Information*. Albany: Joel Munsell.

Wright, Norman Edgar. 1974. *Building an American Pedigree: A Study in Genealogy*. Provo, Utah: Brigham Young University.

BIBLIOGRAPHY

Guides for Writing Genealogies

Barnes, Donald R., and Richard S. Lackey. *Write it Right: A Manual for Writing Family Histories and Genealogies.* Ocala, Fla.: Lyon Press, 1983.

Boyer, Carl, 3rd. *How to Publish and Market Your Family History.* 4th ed. Santa Clarita, Calif.: the author, 1993.

Colket, Meredith B., Jr. "Creating a Worthwhile Family Genealogy." *National Genealogical Society Quarterly* 56 (December 1968): 243–62.

Curran, Joan Ferris. *Numbering Your Genealogy: Sound and Simple Systems.* Arlington, Va.: National Genealogical Society, 1992.

Hatcher, Patricia Law. *Producing a Quality Family History.* Salt Lake City: Ancestry, 1996.

Mills, Elizabeth Shown. *Evidence! Citation and Analysis for the Family Historian.* Baltimore: Genealogical Publishing Co., 1997.

Phillimore, W. P. W. *How to Write the History of a Family: A Guide for the Genealogist.* London: Elliot Stock, 1887.

Worthy, Rita Binkley. *Write Your Family History.* 2nd ed., rev. Arlington, Va.: National Genealogical Society, 1992.

Nationwide Catalogs and Bibliographies

The American Genealogist, Being a Catalogue of Family Histories . . . Published in America, from 1771 to Date. 1900. Reprint. Baltimore: Genealogical Publishing Co., 1971.

Barrett, Ellen C. *A Catalogue of Printed and Manuscript Genealogies Issued in Separate Form to be Found in the Genealogy and Local History Division of the Los Angeles Public Library.* Los Angeles: Los Angeles Public Library, 1960. Supplement, 1965.

Bibliographic Guide to North American History. Boston: G. K. Hall, annual.

Biographical Books, 1876–1949 and *1950–1980.* New York: Bowker, 1980, 1983.

Daughters of the American Revolution. *Library Catalog.* Vols. 1, 3. Washington, D.C.: National Society, Daughters of the American Revolution, 1982, 1992.

Family History Library Catalog. Surname Section. Salt Lake City: Family History Library, annual.

Genealogies Cataloged by the Library of Congress Since 1986. Washington, D.C.: Catalog Distribution Services, 1991.

Glenn, Thomas. *A List of Some American Genealogies Which Have Been Printed in Book Form.* 1897. Reprint. Baltimore: Genealogical Publishing Co., 1969.

Hoffman, Marian. *Genealogical and Local History Books in Print.* 5th ed. 4 vols. Baltimore: Genealogical Publishing Co., 1996–97.

Kaminkow, Marion J. *A Complement to Genealogies in the Library of Congress: A Bibliography.* Baltimore: Magna Charta Book Co., 1981.

_____. *Genealogies in the Library of Congress: A Bibliography.* 2 vols. Baltimore: Magna Charta Book Co., 1972. Supplements 1977, 1986.

Kowallis, Gay P., and Laraine K. Ferguson. *The Genealogical Helper Index. . . .* Logan, Utah: Kowallis, 1983.

Meyerink, Kory L., comp. *Genealogical Publications: A List of 50,000 Sources from the Library of Congress.* CD-ROM. Salt Lake City: Ancestry, 1997.

National Genealogical Society Library Booklist. 5th ed. Arlington, Va.: National Genealogical Society, 1988.

National Union Catalog of Manuscript Collections (*NUCMC*). Washington, D.C.: Library of Congress, 1962–.

New York Public Library. *Dictionary Catalog of the Local History and Genealogy Division.* 18 vols. Boston: G. K. Hall, 1974.

Circulating Library Catalogs, Vol. 1: Genealogies. Boston: New England Historic Genealogical Society, 1992.

Schreiner-Yantis, Netti. *Genealogical and Local History Books in Print.* 4th ed. Springfield, Va.: Genealogical Books in Print, 1985–90. Supplements 1990, 1992.

Toedteberg, Emma, ed. *A Catalog of American Genealogies in the Long Island Historical Society.* 1935. Reprint. Baltimore: Genealogical Publishing Co., 1969.

UMI Guide to Family and Local Histories: A Microfiche Program. 3 vols. Ann Arbor, Mich.: University Microfilms International, 1990, 1993, 1995.

Nationwide Indexes and Analytical Catalogs

Catalogue of the Genealogical and Historical Library of the Colonial Dames of the State of New York. 1912. Reprint. Ann Arbor, Mich.: Gryphon Books, 1971.

Colket, Meredith B. *Founders of Early American Families, Emigrants from Europe 1607–1657.* Rev. ed. Cleveland, Ohio: Order of Founders and Patriots of America, 1985.

Crowther, George Rodney, 3rd. *Surname Index to Sixty-five Volumes of Colonial and Revolutionary Pedigrees.* Washington, D.C.: National Genealogical Society, 1964.

The Genealogical Index of the Newberry Library. 4 vols. Boston: G. K. Hall, 1960.

Greenlaw, William Prescott. *The Greenlaw Index of the New England Historic Genealogical Society.* 2 vols. Boston: G. K. Hall, 1979.

Index to American Genealogies and to Genealogical Material Contained in all Works Such as Town Histories, County Histories, Local Histories . . . and Kindred Works (Known as Munsell's Index). 1900. Reprint. Baltimore: Genealogical Publishing Co., 1967.

Index to Personal Names in the National Union Catalog of Manuscript Collections, 1959–1984. 2 vols. Alexandria, Va.: Chadwyck-Healey, 1988.

List of Titles of Genealogical Articles in American Periodicals and Kindred Works. Albany, N.Y.: Joel Munsell's Sons, 1899.

Old Surname Index File. 21 microfilm rolls. Salt Lake City: Genealogical Library, 1964.

Rider, Fremont, ed. *The American Genealogical-Biographical Index to American Genealogical, Biographical and Local History Materials.* Vols. 1–188+. Middletown, Conn.: Godfrey Memorial Library, 1952–. An earlier version was *The American Genealogical Index.* 48 vols., 1942–51.

The Sutro Library Family History Subject Catalog. 3rd ed. Sacramento: California State Library Foundation, 1990.

Torrey, Clarence A. *New England Marriages Prior to 1700.* Baltimore: Genealogical Publishing Co., 1985.

National Compendia and Dictionaries

Many published genealogies are available that trace American lines to European nobility. Such books could be considered genealogical dictionaries or compendia; however, they are not listed here. For such works, see chapter 20, "Medieval Genealogy."

American Ancestry: Giving the Name and Descent, in the Male Line, of Americans Whose Ancestors Settled in the United States Previous to the Declaration of Independence A.D. 1776. 12 vols. 1887–99. Reprint. Baltimore: Genealogical Publishing Co., 1968.

Burke's American Families with British Ancestry. Baltimore: Genealogical Publishing Co., 1977. Originally published in 1939 by Burke's Peerage in *A Genealogical and Heraldic Dictionary of the Landed Gentry of Great Britain and Ireland.*

Colonial and Revolutionary Lineages of America: A Collection of Genealogical Studies, Completely Documented, and Appropriately Illuminated, Bearing on Notable Early American Lines and Their Collateral Connections. 25 vols. West Palm Beach, Fla.: American Historical Co., 1939–68.

Lawrence, Ruth, ed. *Colonial Families of America.* 27 vols. New York: National Americana Society, 1928–48.

Mackenzie, George Norbury. *Colonial Families of the United States of America.* 7 vols. 1907–20. Reprint. Baltimore: Genealogical Publishing Co., 1966.

Virkus, Frederick A. *The Compendium of American Genealogy.* 7 vols. 1925–42. Reprint. Baltimore: Genealogical Publishing Co., 1987.

Periodical Indexes

Boyer, Carl, 3rd. *Donald Lines Jacobus's Index to Genealogical Periodicals.* Newhall, Calif.: Boyer Publications, 1983. This revision of Jacobus's *Index to Genealogical Periodicals* indexes most major periodicals published from 1870 to 1952.

Clegg, Michael B., and Curt B. Witcher. *Periodical Source Index (PERSI), 1845–1985.* 12+ vols. Fort Wayne, Ind.: Allen County Public Library Foundation, 1987–.

Genealogical Periodical Annual Index (GPAI). Bowie, Md.: Heritage Books, 1962–.

List of Titles of Genealogical Articles in American Periodicals and Kindred Works. Albany, N.Y.: Joel Munsell's Sons, 1899.

Regional Indexes

Crozier, William A. *A Key to Southern Pedigrees.* Southern Book Co., 1953.

Ireland, Norma Olin, and Winifred Irving. *Cutter Index: A Consolidated Index of Cutter's Nine Genealogy Series.* Fallbrook, Calif.: Ireland Indexing Service, n.d.

Swem, Earl Gregg. *Virginia Historical Index.* 2 vols. in 4. 1934–36. Reprint. Gloucester, Mass.: Peter Smith, 1965.

Regional Compendia and Dictionaries

Anderson, Robert Charles. *The Great Migration Begins: Immigrants to New England 1620–1633.* 3 vols. Boston: New England Historic Genealogical Society, 1995.

Armstrong, Zella, and Janie P. C. French. *Notable Southern Families.* 6 vols. 1918–33. Reprint. Baltimore: Genealogical Publishing Co., 1974.

Austin, John Osborne. *One Hundred and Sixty Allied Families.* 1893. Reprint. Baltimore: Genealogical Publishing Co., 1977.

Boddie, John Bennett. *Historical Southern Families.* 23 vols. Baltimore: Genealogical Publishing Co., 1957–80.

Burgess, Roy. *Early New Englanders and Kin.* Bowie, Md.: Heritage Books, 1992.

Cutter, William Richard. *New England Families: Genealogical and Memorial.* 4 vols. 1913. Reprinted and enl. New York: Lewis Historical Publishing Co., 1914.

Hardy, Stella Pickett. *Colonial Families of the Southern States of America.* 2nd ed. 1958. Reprint. Baltimore: Genealogical Publishing Co., 1968.

Savage, James. *A Genealogical Dictionary of the First Settlers of New England. . . .* 4 vols. 1860–62. Reprint. Baltimore: Genealogical Publishing Co., 1965.

Vaughn, Estelle R. *A Genealogical History of Seventeenth and Eighteenth Century Families of the Old South in America.* Lewes, Del.: the author, 1976.

Ethnic and Religious Groups: Bibliographies, Indexes, Compendia, and Dictionaries

Brecht, Samuel K. *The Genealogical Records of the Schwenkfelder Families.* New York: Rand McNally & Co., 1923.

Gingerich, Hugh F., and Rachel W. Kreider. *Amish and Amish Mennonite Genealogies.* Gordonville, Pa.: Pequea Publishers, 1986.

Heiss, Willard C. *Quaker Genealogies: A Preliminary List.* Indianapolis: the author, 1974.

_____, and Thomas D. Hamm. *Quaker Genealogies: A Selected List of Books.* Boston: New England Historic Genealogical Society, 1985.

Lareau, Paul J., and Elmer Courteau. *French-Canadian Families of the North Central States: A Genealogical Dictionary.* 8 vols. St. Paul, Minn.: Northwest Territory French and Canadian Heritage Institute, 1980.

Lart, Charles E. *Huguenot Pedigrees.* 1924–28. Reprint. Baltimore: Genealogical Publishing Co., 1973.

Schlegel, W. *Schlegel's German-American Families in the United States.* New York ed. 4 vols. New York: American Historical Society, 1916–26.

Stern, Malcom H. *First American Jewish Families: 600 Genealogies, 1654–1977.* Cincinnati: American Jewish Archives, 1978.

Zubatsky, David S., and Irwin M. Berent. *Source Book for Jewish Genealogy and Family Histories.* Teaneck, N.J.: Avotaynu, 1996.

Statewide Indexes and Bibliographies

The following are arranged alphabetically by state. Most states are not represented because such finding aids do not exist for them. Inquire at state historical societies or state libraries about manuscript or card indexes or listings of state family histories and genealogies.

Delaware (also see Maryland)

Virdin, Donald Odell. *Delaware Family Histories and Genealogies.* St. Michaels, Md.: Raymond B. Clark, Jr., 1984.

Georgia

Hehir, Donald M. *Georgia Families: A Bibliographic Listing.* Bowie, Md.: Heritage Books, 1993. References 1,100 surnames.

Kentucky

Hehir, Donald M. *Kentucky Families: A Bibliographic Listing.* Bowie, Md.: Heritage Books, 1993. One thousand five hundred references.

Maryland

Passano, Eleanor Phillips. *An Index to the Source Records of Maryland: Genealogical, Biographical, Historical.* 1940. Reprint. Baltimore: Genealogical Publishing Co., 1967.

Virdin, Donald Odell. *Maryland and Delaware Genealogies and Family Histories: A Bibliography of Books about Maryland and Delaware Families.* Bowie, Md.: Heritage Books, 1993. One thousand references.

Minnesota

Pope, Wiley R. *Minnesota Genealogical Index.* St. Paul: Minnesota Family Trees, 1984.

New Hampshire

New Hampshire Historical Society. *Card Index to Genealogies, Published and Manuscript.* 2 microfilm rolls. Concord: New Hampshire Historical Society, 1975.

New Jersey

Johnson, Maud E. "Genealogical Index to Books, Pamphlets, MSS, etc., in the New Jersey Historical Society Library." *Proceedings of the New Jersey Historical Society,* new series, 8 (2): 83–123 (April 1923).

Sinclair, Donald Arleigh. *New Jersey Family Index: A Guide to the Genealogical Sketches in New Jersey Collective Sources.* New Brunswick: Genealogical Society of New Jersey, 1991.

North and South Carolina

Hehir, Donald M. *Carolina Families: A Bibliography of Books about North and South Carolina Families.* Bowie, Md.: Heritage Books, 1994.

Ohio

Hehir, Donald M. *Ohio Families: A Bibliographic Listing of Books about Ohio Families.* Bowie, Md.: Heritage Books, 1993.

Oklahoma

Bivins, Willie Hardin, et al. *Southwest Oklahoma Keys.* Oklahoma City: Southwest Oklahoma Genealogical Society, 1982.

Pennsylvania

Genealogical Material Index: The Manuscript Card Catalog of the Historical and Genealogical Societies of Pennsylvania. 9 microfilm rolls. Salt Lake City: Genealogical Society of Utah, 1967.

Virdin, Donald Odell. *Pennsylvania Genealogies and Family Histories: A Bibliography of Books about Pennsylvania Families.* Bowie, Md: Heritage Books, 1992.

Rhode Island

Roberts, Gary Boyd. "Bibliography of Rhode Island Genealogies." In Ralph Crandall, ed., *Genealogical Research in New England.* Baltimore: Genealogical Publishing Co., 1984.

Virginia

Brown, Stuart E., Jr. *Virginia Genealogies: A Trial List of Printed Books and Pamphlets.* 2 vols. Berryville, Va.: Virginia Book Co., 1967, 1980.

Stewart, Robert Armistead. *Index to Printed Virginia Genealogies. . . .* 1930. Reprint. Baltimore: Genealogical Publishing Co., 1970.

Virdin, Donald O. *Virginia Families and Family Histories: A Bibliography of Books About Virginia Families.* Bowie, Md: Heritage Books, 1990. Three thousand titles.

Major Statewide Genealogical Dictionaries

Statewide genealogical dictionaries are available for approximately half of the states. This list is arranged alphabetically by state.

Alabama

Saunders, James E., and Elizabeth S. Blair. *Early Settlers of Alabama with Notes and Genealogies.* Reprint. Baltimore: Genealogical Publishing Co., 1969. There is a separate index by Lloyd F. Oliver, *Index to Colonel James Edmonds Saunders' Early Settlers of Alabama* (Tomball, Tex.: Genealogical Publications, 1978).

Alaska

MacLean, Edna A. *Genealogical Record of Barrow Families.* Barrow, Alaska: Naval Research Laboratory, 1971.

Milan, Fred, and Edna A. MacLean. *Genealogical Record of Point Hope, Wainwright, and Anaktuvuk Pass, Alaska/Eskimo Families.* N.p., n.d.

Arkansas

Clark, Mrs. Larry P. *Arkansas Pioneers and Allied Families.* Little Rock, Ark.: the author, 1976.

Colorado

Colorado Families: A Territorial Heritage. Denver: Colorado Genealogical Society, 1981.

Territorial Daughters of Colorado. *Pioneers of the Territory of Southern Colorado.* 4 vols. Monte Vista, Colo.: C.B.I. Offset Printers, 1980.

Connecticut

Cutter, William Richard, et al. *Genealogical and Family History of the State of Connecticut. . . .* 4 vols. New York: Lewis Historical Publishing Co., 1911. Indexed in Norma Olin Ireland and Winifred Irving's *Cutter Index: A Consolidated Index of Cutter's Nine Genealogy Series* (Fallbrook, Calif.: Ireland Indexing Service, n.d.).

Genealogies of Connecticut Families: From the New England Historical and Genealogical Register. 3 vols. Baltimore: Genealogical Publishing Co., 1983.

Goodwin, Nathaniel. *Genealogical Notes or Contributions to the Family History of Some of the First Settlers of Connecticut and Massachusetts.* 1856. Reprint. Baltimore: Genealogical Publishing Co., 1987.

Georgia

Austin, Jeannette Holland. *The Georgians: Genealogies of Pioneer Settlers.* Baltimore: Genealogical Publishing Co., 1984.

Gnann, Pearl R. *Georgia Salzburger and Allied Families.* Rev. ed. Savannah, Ga.: Mrs. C. LeBay and Georgia Genealogical Reprints, 1970.

Huxford, Folks. *Pioneers of Wiregrass Georgia. . . .* 7 vols. Homerville, Ga.: the author, 1951–75.

Hawaii

McKinzie, Edith Kawelohea. *Hawaiian Genealogies Extracted from Hawaiian Language Newspapers.* 2 vols. Honolulu: Brigham Young University—Hawaii, 1983, 1986.

Idaho

Gobble, John R. *Lineages of the Members (Past and Present), Idaho Society, Sons of the American Revolution, 1909 through 1961. . . .* Idaho Falls, Idaho: the author, 1962.

Kansas

The Forgotten Settlers of Kansas. Vol. 1. Topeka: Kansas Council of Genealogical Societies, 1983.

Kentucky

Cox, Mrs. Edgar L., and Thomas W. Westerfield. *Kentucky Family Records.* 8 vols. Owensboro, Ky.: West-Central Kentucky Family Research Association, 1970–82.

Fowler, Ila Earle. *Kentucky Pioneers and Their Descendants.* 1941–50. Reprint. Baltimore: Genealogical Publishing Co., 1967.

Genealogies of Kentucky Families: From the Filson Club History Quarterly. Baltimore: Genealogical Publishing Co., 1981.

Genealogies of Kentucky Families: From the Register of the Kentucky Historical Society. 2 vols. Baltimore: Genealogical Publishing Co., 1981.

Kozee, William Carlos. *Early Families of Eastern and Southeastern Kentucky, and Their Descendants.* Strasburg, Va.: Shenandoah Publishing House, 1961.

Louisiana

Arthur, Stanley, and George de Kernion. *Old Families of Louisiana.* New Orleans: Harmanson, 1931.

Maine

Little, George Thomas. *Genealogical and Family History of the State of Maine.* 4 vols. New York: Lewis Historical Publishing Co., 1909.

Noyes, Sybil, Charles Thornton Libby, and Walter Goodwin Davis. *Genealogical Dictionary of Maine and New Hampshire.* 1928–39. Reprint. Baltimore: Genealogical Publishing Co., 1983.

Maryland

Maryland Genealogies: A Consolidation of Articles from the Maryland Historical Magazine. 2 vols. Baltimore: Genealogical Publishing Co., 1980.

Massachusetts

Cutter, William Richard. *Genealogical and Personal Memoirs Relating to the Families of the State of Massachusetts.* 4 vols. New York: Lewis Historical Publishing Co., 1910.

Genealogies of Mayflower Families: From the New England Historical and Genealogical Register. 3 vols. Baltimore: Genealogical Publishing Co., 1985.

Mississippi

Johnson, Charles Owen, ed. *The Order of the First Families of Mississippi 1699–1817.* Ann Arbor, Mich.: Edwards Brothers, 1981.

Missouri

Bryan, William Smith, and Robert Rose. *A History of the Pioneer Families of Missouri. . . .* St. Louis, Mo.: Bryan, Brand & Co., 1876.

Hodges, Nadine, and Audrey L. Woodruff. *Missouri Pioneers: County and Genealogical Records.* 30 vols. Independence, Mo.: Woodruff, 1967–76.

Woodruff, Audrey L. *Missouri Miscellany: Statewide Missouri Genealogical Records.* 16 vols. Independence, Mo.: the author, 1976–83.

New Hampshire (also see Maine)

Stearn, Ezra S. *Genealogical and Family History of New Hampshire.* 4 vols. New York: Lewis Publishing Co., 1908.

New Jersey

Armstrong, William Clinton. *Pioneer Families of Northwestern New Jersey.* Lambertville, N.J.: Hunterdon House, 1979.

Chambers, Theodore F. *The Early Germans of New Jersey; Their History, Churches and Genealogies.* 1895. Reprint. Baltimore: Genealogical Publishing Co., 1982.

Cooley, Eli F., and William S. Cooley. *Genealogy of Early Settlers in Trenton and Ewing.* 1883. Reprint. Baltimore: Genealogical Publishing Co., 1976.

Howe, Paul S. *Mayflower Pilgrim Descendants in Cape May County, New Jersey.* 1921. Reprint. Baltimore: Genealogical Publishing Co., 1977.

Littell, John. *Family Records; or Genealogies of the First Settlers of the Passaic Valley (and Vicinity). . . .* 1851. Reprint. Baltimore: Genealogical Publishing Co., 1981.

Monnette, Orra Eugene. *First Settlers of Ye Plantations of Piscataway and Woodbridge Olde East New Jersey, 1664–1774.* 7 parts. Los Angeles: Leroy Carman Press, 1930–35. This material is of variable quality; use it with caution.

Stillwell, John E. *Historical and Genealogical Miscellany: Data Relating to the Settlement and Settlers of New York and New Jersey.* 5 vols. 1903–32. Reprint. Baltimore: Genealogical Publishing Co., 1970.

New York

Bergen, Teunis G. *Genealogies of the State of New York—Long Island Edition.* 3 vols. New York, 1915.

Bergen, Teunis G. *Register in Alphabetical Order, of the Early Settlers of Kings County, Long Island.* 1881. Reprint. New Orleans: Polyanthos, 1973.

Cutter, William Richard. *Genealogical and Family History of Central New York.* 3 vols. New York: Lewis Historical Publishing Co., 1912.

_____. *Genealogical and Family History of Northern New York.* 3 vols. New York: Lewis Historical Publishing Co., 1910.

_____. *Genealogical and Family History of Western New York.* 3 vols. New York: Lewis Historical Publishing Co., 1912.

Genealogies of Long Island Families, from the New York Genealogical and Biographical Record. 2 vols. Baltimore: Genealogical Publishing Co., 1987.

Jones, Henry Z, Jr. *The Palatine Families of New York 1709.* Universal City, Calif.: the author, 1985.

Pearson, Jonathan. *Contributions for the Genealogies of the Descendants of the First Settlers of the Patent and City of Schenectady, 1662–1800.* 1873. Reprint. Baltimore: Genealogical Publishing Co., 1982.

Pearson, Jonathan. *Contributions for the Genealogies of the First Settlers of the Ancient County of Albany, 1630–1800.* 1872. Reprint. Baltimore: Genealogical Publishing Co., 1984.

Reynolds, Cuyler. *Genealogical and Family History of Southern New York and Hudson River Valley.* 3 vols. New York: Lewis Historical Publishing Co., 1914.

_____. *Hudson-Mohawk Genealogical and Family Memoirs.* 4 vols. New York: Lewis Historical Publishing Co., 1911.

Seversmith, Herbert F. *Colonial Families of Long Island.* 5 vols. Washington, D.C., 1939–64.

Toler, Henry P. *New Harlem Register: A Genealogy of the Descendants of the 23 Original Patentees in the Town of New Harlem.* New York: New Harlem Pub. Co., 1903.

North Carolina

Hathaway, James R. B. *North Carolina Historical and Genealogical Register.* 3 vols. Edenton, N.C.: the author, 1900–03.

Smallwood, Marilu Burch. *Some Colonial and Revolutionary Families of North Carolina.* 3 vols. Washington, N.C.: the author, 1964.

Pennsylvania

Egle, William Henry, ed. *Notes and Queries: Historical, Biographical, and Genealogical, Relating Chiefly to Interior Pennsylvania.* 1894–1904. Reprint. Baltimore: Genealogical Publishing Co., 1971. This work is indexed in Eva Draegert Schory's *Everyname Index to Egle's Notes and Queries* (Decatur, Ill.: Decatur Genealogical Society, 1982).

Genealogies of Pennsylvania Families: Articles from the Pennsylvania Magazine of History and Biography. Baltimore: Genealogical Publishing Co., 1981.

Genealogies of Pennsylvania Families: From the Pennsylvania Genealogical Magazine. 3 vols. Baltimore: Genealogical Publishing Co., 1982.

Jordan, John W., et al., eds. *Colonial and Revolutionary Families of Pennsylvania.* 10 vols. New York: Lewis Publishing Co., 1911–61. Three volumes were reprinted by the Genealogical Publishing Co. of Baltimore in 1978.

Rhode Island

Austin, John Osborne. *The Genealogical Dictionary of Rhode Island: Comprising Three Generations of Settlers Who Came Before 1690. . . .* 1887. Reprint with additions and corrections. Baltimore: Genealogical Publishing Co., 1978.

Genealogies of Rhode Island Families: From the New England Historical and Genealogical Register. 2 vols. Baltimore: Genealogical Publishing Co., 1989.

Genealogies of Rhode Island Families: From Rhode Island Periodicals. 2 vols. Baltimore: Genealogical Publishing Co., 1983.

South Carolina

Allen, Penelope Johnson. *Leaves from the Family Tree.* Easley, S.C.: Southern Historical Press, 1982.

South Carolina Genealogies: Articles from the South Carolina Historical (and Genealogical) Magazine. 5 vols. Spartanburg, S.C.: Reprint Co., 1983.

Wooley, James E., ed. *A Collection of Upper South Carolina Genealogical and Family Records.* 3 vols. Easley, S.C.: Southern Historical Press, 1979–82.

Texas

Founders and Patriots of the Republic of Texas: Lineages of the Members of the Daughters of the Republic of Texas. 3 vols. Austin: Daughters of the Republic of Texas, 1963–85.

Utah

Esshom, Frank. *Pioneers and Prominent Men of Utah.* 1913. Reprint. Salt Lake City: Western Epics, 1966.

Virginia

du Bellet, Louise P. *Some Prominent Virginia Families.* 4 vols. in 2. 1907. Reprint. Baltimore: Genealogical Publishing Co., 1976.

Genealogies of Virginia Families: From Tyler's Quarterly Historical and Genealogical Magazine. 4 vols. Baltimore: Genealogical Publishing Co., 1981.

Genealogies of Virginia Families: From the Virginia Magazine of History and Biography. 5 vols. Baltimore: Genealogical Publishing Co., 1981.

Genealogies of Virginia Families: From the William and Mary College Quarterly. 5 vols. Baltimore: Genealogical Publishing Co., 1982.

Hayden, Horace Edwin. *Virginia Genealogies.* 1885. Reprint. Baltimore: Southern Book Co., 1959.

West Virginia

Butcher, Bernard Lee. *Genealogical and Personal History of the Upper Monongahela Valley, West Virginia. . . .* 3 vols. New York: Lewis Historical Publishing Co., 1912.

Wisconsin

History of the Great Kanawha Valley: With Family History and Biographical Sketches. 2 vols. Madison, Wis.: Brant, Fuller & Co., 1891.

Canadian Genealogical Dictionaries

Jette, Rene. *Dictionnaire genealogique des familles du Quebec.* Montreal: Les Presses de L'Universite de Montreal, 1983.

Tanguay, Cyprien. *Dictionnaire genealogique des familles canadiennes depuis la fondation de la colonie jusqu a nos jours.* 7 vols. 1871–90. New York: A.M.S. Press, 1969.

English Indexes

Barrow, Geoffrey B. *The Genealogist's Guide: An Index to Printed British Pedigrees and Family Histories, 1950–1975.* London: Research Publishing, 1977.

Marshall, George W. *The Genealogist's Guide.* 1903. Reprint. Baltimore: Genealogical Publishing Co., 1980.

Thomson, Theodore Radford. *A Catalogue of British Family Histories.* 2nd ed. London: Edward O. Beck, 1935.

Whitmore, John B. *A Genealogical Guide: An Index to British Pedigrees in Continuation of Marshall's Genealogists Guide.* London: Society of Genealogists, 1953.

COUNTY AND LOCAL HISTORIES OVERVIEW

Key Concepts in This Chapter

- Almost six thousand histories exist for U.S. counties—an average of almost two for each county.
- Publishing of county histories falls into five distinct time periods.
- Few county histories were published before the Civil War.
- Most county histories for southern states were published after World War I.
- The few national and regional indexes cover only a relatively small number of histories.
- The best indexes for county histories are statewide master subject indexes.
- Biographical information in county histories is usually quite accurate for recent generations.
- Clues about family members in county and local histories may not appear anywhere else.
- Hundreds of thousands of town histories are available.

Key Sources in This Chapter

- *A Bibliography of American County Histories*
- *Genealogical Publications: A List of 50,000 Sources from the Library of Congress*
- *Local Histories in the Library of Congress: A Bibliography*
- *America: History and Life*
- *American Biographical Index*
- *Index to Biographies in Local Histories in the Library of Congress*
- *Old Surname Index File*
- *Genealogical Index of the Newberry Library*

17

COUNTY AND LOCAL HISTORIES

Kory L. Meyerink

> It seems clear that he who would investigate the lives of the pioneers must find the most of his material between the covers of the quarto and folio county histories and nowhere else (Flagg 1915, i).

Published histories, especially those that focus on particular counties or towns, are vital aids for genealogists. While these, like other printed works, seldom provide primary information, Charles Flagg's 1915 assessment is still accurate. Histories often provide information about families that is not available in any original record or other compiled source. Information in histories can take the researcher well beyond the "bare bones" pedigree chart by supplying details about an ancestor's life and his geographical and chronological surroundings, helping the researcher transform the often-boring "genealogy" into an exciting and interesting "family history." Even if a published history does not mention an ancestor's name, it can be a valuable source for learning more about the events that influenced her life; it can also lead to other sources that do contain information about the ancestor.

Statewide histories can be useful, but their use is generally limited to helping the researcher understand the broader aspects of a state's history. This chapter focuses on county and local (usually meaning town) histories—how to use them and what might be found in them based on the eras in which they were published. It also addresses the incorrect use of these histories and suggests ways to evaluate the information found in them. While some of this discussion applies to statewide histories, the emphasis is on county and local histories, which are of greatest use to the researcher.

As with every record, the genealogist must be aware of the purpose for which a history was created; this allows the genealogist to better understand the information in the source. A key aspect of record evaluation is answering the question, Who created this source, when, and why? County and local histories are much like other genealogical sources in this respect: they were not created for the use of modern genealogists. Researchers use them, just as they use census or probate records, to learn more about individuals and their families; however, because county and local histories were not written for this purpose, the information which researchers seek may be lacking. Furthermore, many statements in these histories, both biographical and historical, would not meet current tests of accuracy or provability.

County and local histories were written to record the events of interest in a given locality. They typically have an upbeat or positive tone (no community wants to be portrayed in a negative light). An important fact is that in many (but not all) cases, they were written to be sold for a profit, so the subjects discussed are ones that most people were interested in; this accounts for the scandalous stories and recounting of major court cases, such as murder trials. It also explains why the people's home lives are not detailed. Some social history is always present in these books, but it is generic and may or may not apply to the researcher's family.

Of course, history is largely about people. Generally, the greater the population of a county, the more histories have been written about that county and its people. History also happens with the passage of time; it is difficult to write a history of a community that has existed for only a few years. These two factors explain why only nine states have county histories available for all of their counties.

Histories are very much like maps, offering researchers the varying details needed to make successful genealogical journeys. Statewide histories are comparable to statewide maps. As major points of interest, such as cities and turnpikes, are noted without detail on state maps, state histories give only the high points of states' histories. It is county and local histories that serve as the detailed maps that can show every street and many houses. Experienced genealogists use histories to provide both background and specific information about families and areas.

This chapter discusses county and local histories from a genealogical perspective. For a much more detailed treatment with an academic focus, serious researchers should consult David J. Russo's *Keepers of Our Past: Local History Writing in the United States, 1820s–1930s* (New York: Greenwood Press, 1988).

COUNTY HISTORIES

The county form of government in the United States has its origins in English history. However, over the course of more than 350 years, counties have evolved into uniquely American entities, having adopted some of the form and function of the New England town. Historically, only a small percentage of the population has lived in incorporated towns or cities. However, all Americans (except Alaskans—Alaska has no counties), both historically and currently, lived or live in a county. (In Louisiana, counties are called parishes, but they serve the same function and are considered as counties in this chapter.) Thus, the county has always been the most local social and governmental unit common to all Americans. (Towns, especially the New England towns, are discussed later.)

The life of a typical nineteenth-century American revolved first around his family and community and second around the county. It is no wonder, then, that as society progressed, a historical awakening happened in the counties. The publication of county histories paralleled the publication of genealogies (or family histories) as well as the rise of an industrialized society after the Civil War.

County histories should be a mainstay of initial research on any family. However, there are a variety of formats in such books, and the depth of coverage and accuracy of information in them is very uneven; therefore, obtaining a better understanding of county histories is vital to the genealogist. Unfortunately, it was very difficult until recently to make an accurate study of this topic because no comprehensive bibliography existed. That situation changed in 1985, when P. William Filby published *A Bibliography of American County Histories* (cited below).

Background Study of County History Publishing

Although Filby's bibliography is not complete and is at least thirteen years old, it stands as the definitive reference work for its topic. *American County Histories* provided most of the data for the detailed study of the numbers and distribution of county histories in this chapter. Supplemental information was gleaned from an analysis of many titles in Meyerink's *Genealogical Publications: A List of 50,000 Sources from the Library of Congress* (cited below). The results of the study were both expected and surprising. The graphs, tables, and many of the facts in this section are from this study. Some background information about both of these important bibliographies, as well as the study itself, will make the results more meaningful.

American County Histories. Filby's *A Bibliography of American County Histories* (Baltimore: Genealogical Publishing Co., 1985) is a state-by-state listing of more than 4,900 county histories published through 1984. The entries give complete bibliographic citations (author, title, publisher, date, and place of publication). They are not annotated, but the number of pages, when known, is given. Filby also identified approximately 660 reprints (with date, publisher, and place of each reprint) of these histories.

Filby's intention was to list only books that were truly histories, in whole or in part. Thus, books with titles such as *Biographies of Prominent Men . . .* or *Portrait and Biographical History of . . .* were omitted (see chapter 18, "Biographies," for these types of sources). Filby did not examine each book in person; rather, he relied heavily on secondary information, including the collections of the Library of Congress and the New York Public Library, as well as bibliographies for each state (see the chapter bibliography). In addition, he corresponded with at least one noted librarian in each state. Supplemental searches were made in book lists, reviews, and publishers' catalogs for recent titles (Filby 1985, ix–xii).

Alaska, Hawaii, and Puerto Rico are not included in *American County Histories*. Alaska has no counties, and the history of these three places is much different (and recent in some senses). Collective histories that treat a number of counties are included under the heading "Regional" at the beginning of each applicable state section. Where warranted, the counties in regional histories are cross-referenced in the state lists. When two to four counties are treated in one volume, the full citation is given under the county appearing first in the title. Other counties are cross-referenced to the first entry. Every type of county history is included, from the "mug books" (so-called because of the many portraits they contain) of the nineteenth and early twentieth centuries, to the histories of the 1940s inspired by the Work Projects Administration (WPA), to the recent bicentennial histories. Some histories were omitted if four or five other good ones existed. While short books of under one hundred pages were not deliberately omitted, some weeding was essential to identify true county histories. However, for many states, smaller publications "of less than fifty pages might be the only county [histories] available, and therefore these apparent lightweights have been included" (Filby 1985, xi). Some southern states are particularly well represented by master's theses done on various counties since the 1950s.

This study of county histories involved tabulating the number of histories listed for each state according to the year of first publication. Notations were made regarding the number of counties with at least one history listed, those with two histories listed, and those with three or more. Totals were calculated for each year and for five-year groups (1910 to 1914, 1915 to 1919, etc.) from 1850 through 1984. These tabulations were then totaled for each state and region and for the forty-eight continental states as a whole. This process yielded a fair picture of both the breadth and depth of coverage as well as the peak publishing times for each state.

Based on this information, the publishing of county histories seems to fall into five different eras whose dates fairly well match the experiences of many genealogists. Because the format and scope of histories have changed somewhat from one era to another, these eras provide a helpful framework with which to discuss the genealogical uses of county histories. Figure 17-1 illustrates the nationwide pattern.

Eight geographic regions were chosen for their similarity in settlement and migration patterns, as well as their geography and history. The publication pattern of county histories was much different from one region to another, as illustrated in figures 17-2 and 17-3. In terms of the number of histories produced, the eight regions are divided into four major and four minor regions; this is mostly a function of their populations and number of counties. The four major regions are:

Mid-Atlantic:	Delaware, New Jersey, New York, and Pennsylvania
Atlantic South:	Georgia, Kentucky, Maryland, North and South Carolina, Tennessee, Virginia, and West Virginia
Great Lakes:	Illinois, Indiana, Iowa, Michigan, Minnesota, Missouri, Ohio, and Wisconsin
Gulf South:	Alabama, Arkansas, Florida, Louisiana, Mississippi, and Texas

The four minor regions are:

New England:	Connecticut, Maine, Massachusetts, New Hampshire, Rhode Island, and Vermont
Plains states:	Kansas, Nebraska, North and South Dakota, and Oklahoma

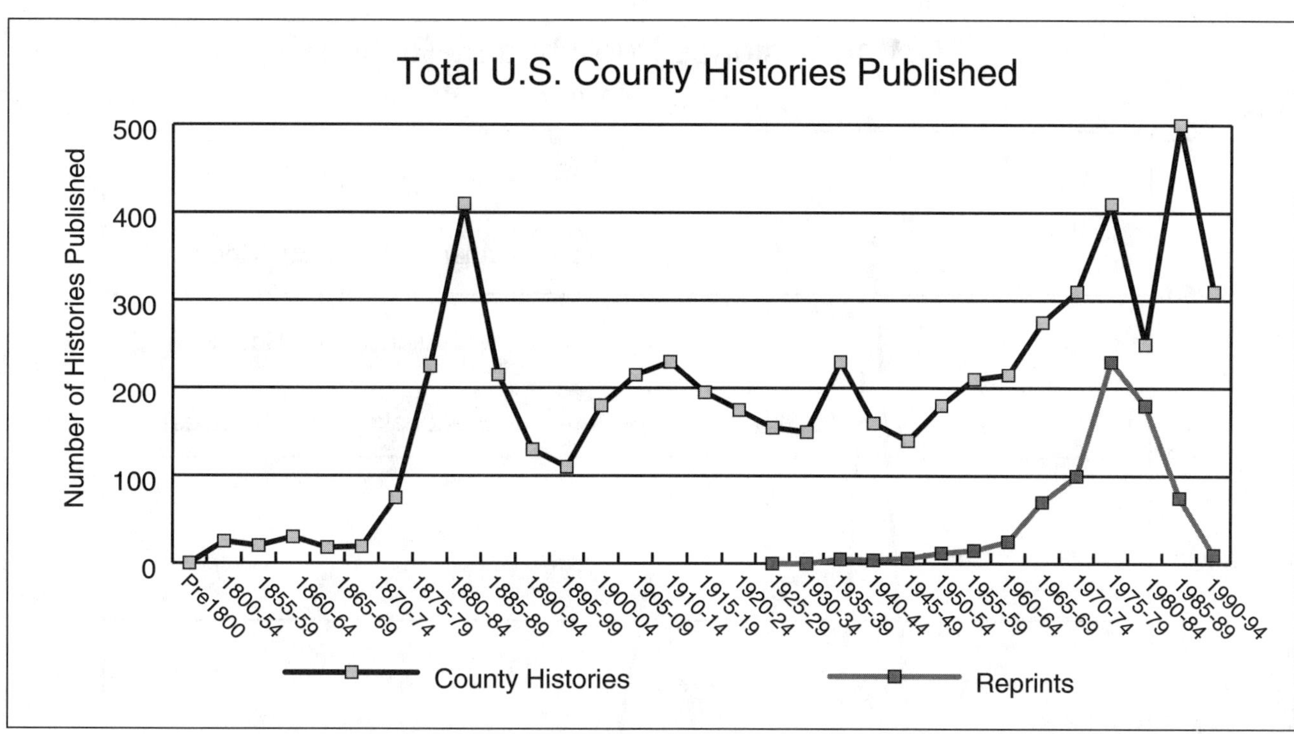

Figure 17-1. Total U.S. county histories published. (From Filby's *Bibliography of American County Histories* and Meyerink's *Genealogical Publications: A List of 50,000 Sources from the Library of Congress.*)

Mountain West:	Arizona, Colorado, Idaho, Montana, Nevada, New Mexico, Utah, and Wyoming
Pacific states:	California, Oregon, and Washington

Note that Alaska and Hawaii were not included in *American County Histories* because Alaska does not have counties and there are no county histories for Hawaii.

Genealogical Publications. *American County Histories* contains no histories published after December 1984, so an alternative source is needed to identify histories published after that date. The most comprehensive listing of recent county histories, and thousands of other sources, is Kory L. Meyerink, comp., *Genealogical Publications: A List of 50,000 Sources from the Library of Congress* (Salt Lake City: Ancestry, 1997). This electronic CD-ROM bibliography reproduces the complete Library of Congress catalog entries for selected books acquired by the library since 1969. Selection criteria for this bibliography included all English-language family histories, all books dealing with "genealogy," all books identified by the library as being county histories, and several other genealogically significant topics. The most recent books in *Genealogical Publications* are those that had been cataloged by the Library of Congress by October 1995. Because of its broad selection criteria, *Genealogical Publications* probably includes virtually every county history published from 1970 to early 1995. Some titles that were published in small quantities and not received by the Library of Congress (or had not yet been cataloged by mid-1995) do not appear in *Genealogical Publications*.

To cover the decade after *American County Histories*, the study examined county histories identified in *Genealogical Publications*. However, it was not possible to perfectly match Filby's definition of county histories when identifying and examining the more recent county histories extracted from Meyerink's compilation. While the study examined all of the titles in Filby's list, clearly only certain ones in Meyerink's list were comparable. Some of those selected may not have met Filby's more narrow criteria. Therefore, the quantity published and analysis of post-1984 county histories (which relies on titles selected from *Genealogical Publications*) can only be used to indicate recent trends. The study selected just over eight hundred county histories published from 1985 through 1995. Only fifteen histories carried a 1995 date, which is less than one-third the number of previous years and represents incomplete coverage due to the cutoff date. This was also the case in the analysis of *American County Histories*, where the twenty-two histories listed for 1984 represent about one-third the number of recent years; this number is also attributable to the cutoff date. Thus, the study shows artificial dips in the number of histories published in 1984 and 1995.

Summary of Findings. Only the Great Lakes region, where the major period of publication was in the 1880s and early 1900s, fits the classic pattern of county histories encountered by so many researchers. The Mid-Atlantic and Pacific states regions show some similarities but also significant differences. In several regions the major period of publication was the mid-twentieth century (Gulf and Atlantic South, the Plains states, and the Mountain West). The movement toward publishing histories, then, began in the 1870s in the Great Lakes and Mid-Atlantic regions and moved steadily south and west over the last one hundred years. The result has been a fairly constant stream of county histories. While there have been four peak periods, there has always been a constant base of activity below which publication numbers have not fallen. During any consecutive five-year period, beginning from 1875, at least 116 histories were published. On an annual basis, the fifteen histories published in

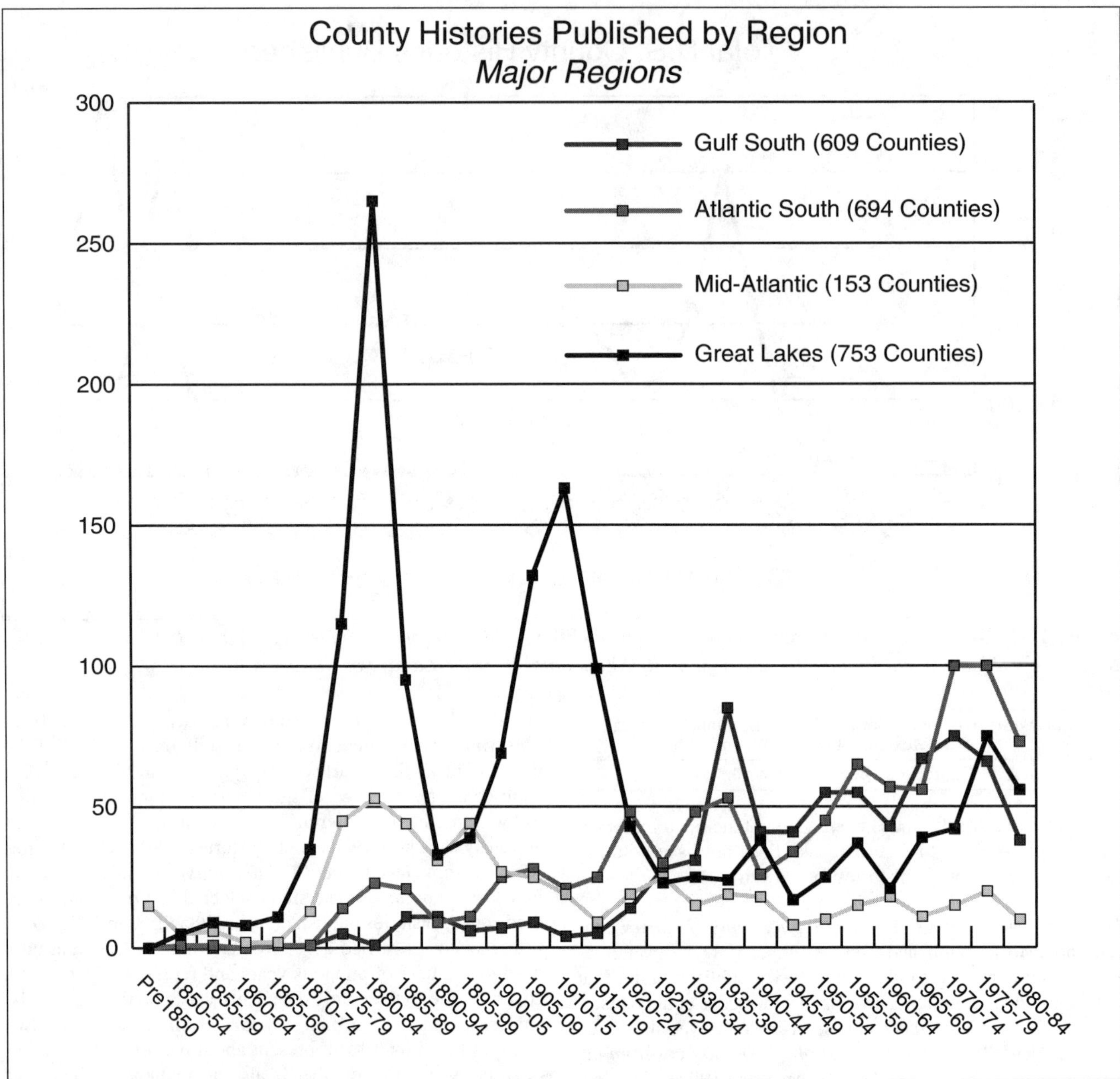

Figure 17-2. County histories published in major regions.

1873 represent the high mark to that date and only the second time more than eight were published (there had been thirteen in 1872). Since 1874 (with twenty-four histories), the last 120 years have seen at least eighteen histories published each year except 1944 and 1945 (when ten and eleven, respectively, were published).

Most genealogists labor under the assumption that virtually all county histories were published before 1920. Even Filby shared this view. He estimated the total, approximately five thousand, very well but suggested that "the number of county histories . . . has increased little since 1919" (1985, xi). Actually, of the approximately 4,929 histories in *American County Histories,* slightly more than half, 2,515, were published after 1929. This fact should spur the researcher to check more carefully for later histories, especially in the southern and western states.

Breadth of coverage (the number of counties in a state with at least one history) also seems to follow geographic patterns to some degree. Figure 17-4 illustrates the percentage of coverage (through 1984) for each state; the Northeast and Great Lakes states have the broadest coverage while the West has the thinnest coverage. Depth of coverage (number of counties with multiple histories by 1984) shows a similar pattern (table 17-1): New Jersey, New York, Ohio, and Pennsylvania have the greatest percentage of counties with three or more histories. Close behind are Colorado, Illinois, Indiana, Iowa, and West Virginia.

The focus of further discussion has to be on the content, format, qualities, and uses of these histories. The five eras into which they naturally seem to fall serve as reference points. These eras are as follows:

Early histories:	Everything published through 1869
Centennial:	1870 to 1899
New Century:	1900 to 1929

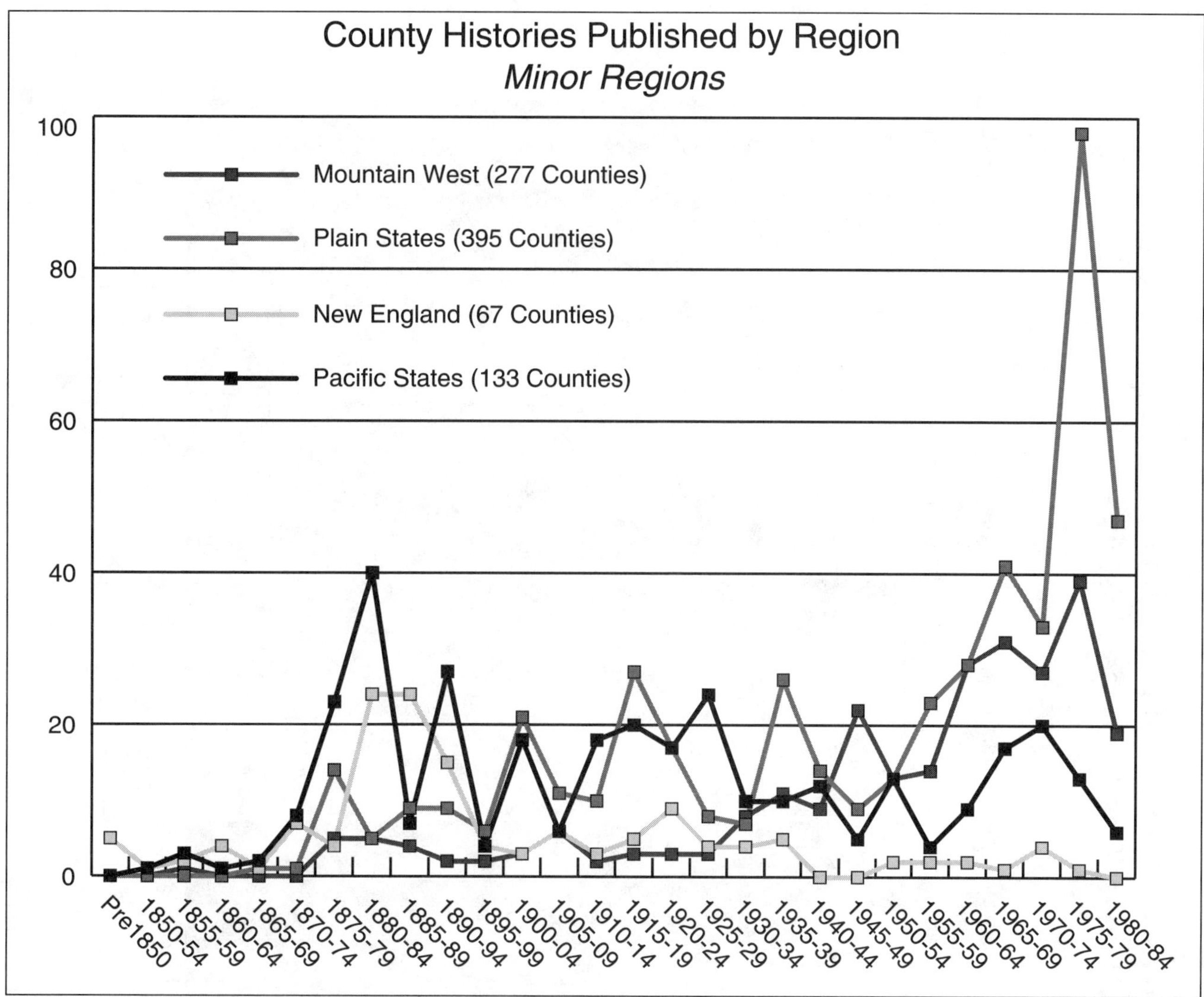

Figure 17-3. County histories published in minor regions.

World War II:	1930 to 1959
Modern:	Everything published in 1960 and later

Other writers have noticed the transformation in content and style of county histories over time. Diane Carothers identified four styles roughly corresponding to the five eras noted above, with the exception that she considered the centennial and New Century histories as the same style (1985, 26). These style names, and the dates, are the result of this writer's evaluation, as discussed throughout this chapter.

Although county histories have been grouped into five eras for this discussion and each era has several distinctions, these are broad generalities. Not every history follows the pattern discussed for its period; nor, of course, did authors and publishers completely change their styles at arbitrary times. Rather, county histories evolved. As publishers found what worked in one area, their methods were duplicated elsewhere; with that in mind, the changes in format, content, scope, and size are fascinating to trace.

Early Histories (Before 1870)

The publishing of county histories in the United States began with a slow but noble start. Before 1850, only twenty-two county histories were written, all of them for counties in the New England (five) and Mid-Atlantic (seventeen) regions. Over the next twenty years approximately seventy-four more such histories were published, with every region represented by at least one publication. Although the first county history in the Mountain West was published in 1858 and in the Plains states in 1868, the greatest interest was beginning to show in the Great Lakes region (thirty-four histories from 1850 to 1870). Actually, because of the great number of counties in that region (735), this number represents histories for less than 5 percent of its counties. In the New England and Mid-Atlantic regions, histories appeared for approximately 10 percent of the counties.

Few of these early histories were written with monetary gain as the primary factor. They were usually labors of love by longtime residents who saw that early settlers were dying and taking their communities' histories to their graves with them. Reading the preface to such an early work gives excellent insights about the author's purpose and methodology. This step is also important as the researcher evaluates the history.

In his 1851 *Annals and Recollections of Oneida (N.Y.) County,* Pomroy Jones commented that "if he could have foreseen the amount of labor with which he was about to tax him-

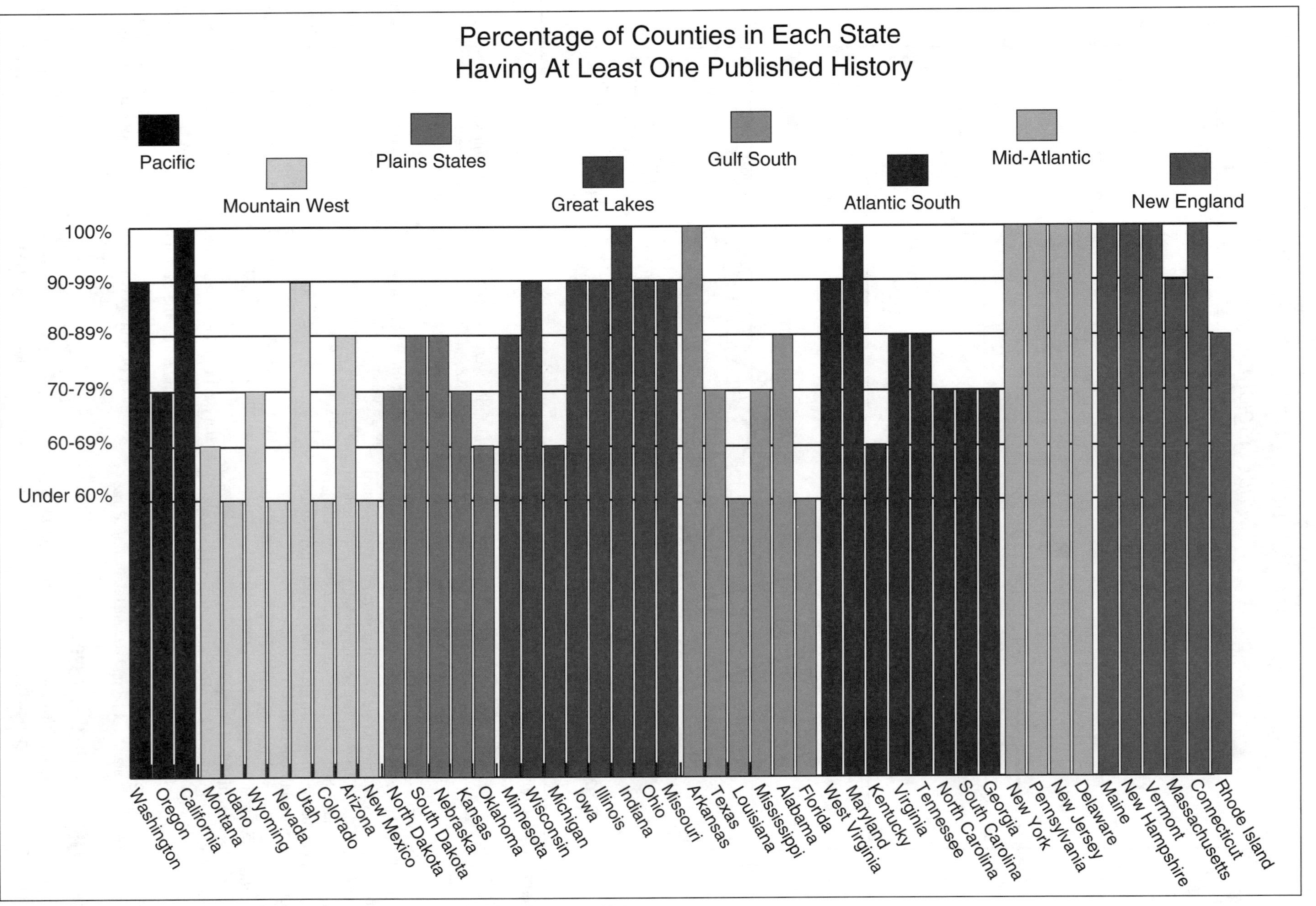

Figure 17-4. Percentage of counties in each state having at least one published history.

Table 17-1. United States County Histories (through 1984)

		Histories in State per Era:								*Counties with:*			
State	*State-hood*	*Pre-1870*	*1870–1899*	*1900–1929*	*1930–1959*	*1960–1984*	*Total Histories*	*Reprints*	*Total Counties*	*One or More*	*Two Only*	*Three or More*	*Peak Year(s)*
Alabama	1819	1	4	2	21	54	82	8	67	59	18	5	1976
Arizona	1912	0	2	2	0	17	21	0	14	12	4	2	1979
Arkansas	1836	0	7	6	23	30	66	10	75	75	26	12	1889, 1970s
California	1876	7	99	76	35	30	247	23	58	58	9	39	1875, 1883–
Colorado	1876	0	8	3	20	21	52	2	63	36	7	6	1939
Connecticut	1788	2	13	7	2	0	24	0	8	8	2	5	1880s
Delaware	1787	0	2	0	0	4	6	0	3	3	1	1	1976
Florida	1845	0	2	13	9	10	34	4	67	27	3	2	1927–1929
Georgia	1788	0	2	17	61	109	189	48	159	123	34	10	1933, 1976
Idaho	1890	0	3	4	13	14	34	4	44	25	11	2	1963
Illinois	1818	8	122	96	21	33	280	41	102	99	25	56	1878, 1883
Indiana	1846	5	109	89	26	27	256	66	91	91	24	58	1884, 1914
Iowa	1846	3	96	81	25	10	215	17	99	97	41	44	1979, 1915
Kansas	1861	1	22	38	21	56	138	16	105	83	30	15	1901, 1976
Kentucky	1792	0	17	19	37	39	112	21	120	73	28	9	1936, 1974
Louisiana	1812	0	2	2	17	32	53	3	64	34	11	3	1972
Maine	1820	1	10	6	5	5	27	0	16	15	5	3	1880
Maryland	1788	0	7	12	14	18	51	17	23	23	7	9	1881, 1956
Massachusetts	1788	4	23	12	5	1	45	2	14	13	0	10	1890, 1924
Michigan	1837	3	48	40	13	6	110	13	83	55	19	19	1880, 1906
Minnesota	1858	4	24	40	16	48	132	13	87	73	24	23	1916, 1976
Mississippi	1817	0	3	10	30	60	103	3	82	60	18	9	1968, 1976
Missouri	1821	0	55	34	14	31	134	21	114	104	33	29	1881, 1888, 1972
Montana	1889	0	0	5	4	33	42	0	56	38	8	1	1976
Nebraska	1864	0	15	34	28	50	127	8	93	82	26	18	1937, 1967
Nevada	1864	0	2	1	1	6	10	0	16	8	0	1	1964
New Hampshire	1788	1	9	2	1	1	14	4	10	10	2	3	1885
New Jersey	1787	2	25	24	16	12	79	6	21	21	1	19	1900, 1964
New Mexico	1912	0	1	2	5	19	27	0	32	17	3	3	1980
New York	1788	20	108	40	34	25	227	39	62	62	6	52	1878, 1897
North Carolina	1789	0	4	34	40	65	143	12	100	76	20	19	1949, 1983
North Dakota	1889	0	1	9	12	46	68	1	53	42	9	7	1976
Ohio	1803	5	91	100	34	43	273	58	88	86	15	66	1880, 1902, 1909
Oklahoma	1907	0	0	5	13	51	69	0	77	52	22	3	1976

State	*State -hood*	*Pre-1870*	*1870–1899*	*1900–1929*	*1930–1959*	*1960–1984*	*Total Histories*	*Reprints*	*Total Counties*	*Counties with: One or More*	*Two Only*	*Three or More*	*Peak Year(s)*
		Histories in State per Era:											
Oregon	1859	0	5	7	11	9	32	3	36	27	10	5	1902
Pennsylvania	1787	12	89	57	35	34	227	41	67	67	5	61	1883, 1887
Rhode Island	1790	0	3	0	0	0	3	0	5	4	0	0	1889
South Carolina	1788	1	5	13	12	29	60	15	46	34	6	7	1923, 1970
South Dakota	1889	0	6	9	17	45	77	3	67	56	21	13	1961, 1976
Tennessee	1796	1	20	17	33	37	108	36	95	79	28	17	1886, 1969
Texas	1845	2	16	34	205	119	376	25	254	201	57	52	1936, 1950–
Utah	1896	1	1	0	29	18	49	5	29	28	5	9	1947
Vermont	1791	5	20	3	0	1	29	0	14	14	4	8	1882
Virginia	1788	1	7	46	56	54	164	31	96	84	24	23	1907, 1938–
Washington	1889	0	3	20	6	27	56	6	39	38	12	10	1904, 1975
West Virginia	1863	0	17	27	20	30	94	20	55	53	19	23	1927, 1972
Wisconsin	1848	6	37	51	14	34	142	21	71	65	14	31	1881, 1976
Wyoming	1890	0	1	3	5	15	24	0	23	16	6	3	1976
Total U.S.		96	1,166	1,152	1,059	1,456	4,929	666	3,063	2,506	703	825	1882, 1976

self, possibly he might have quailed; but the pleasure in his research . . . entirely precluded the idea of an abandonment of his purpose" (1851, iii, iv). H. Banning Norton, author of the 1862 *History of Knox County, Ohio,* echoed this sentiment: "To write the history of my native county, and to rescue from oblivion the anecdotes and early incidents of its first settlers, has been with me a pleasant pastime" (1862, i). Norton's motivation was to preserve information for "those who may succeed us: I did not undertake it with expectation or purpose of gain" (1862, i). He even went so far as to point out that he then lived in Texas and did not intend to again live in Ohio and that, because he belonged to no political or religious organizations, he could represent all events and people fairly and correctly.

Sometimes, a history was commissioned by a group of interested persons or an organization within a county. The Berkshire Association of Congregational Ministers voted in 1826 to produce a history of its county. The association assigned different members to various tasks and expected the clergymen belonging to the association to write the histories of their own towns. The result became the second part of the 1829 *History of the County of Berkshire, Massachusetts.* As might be expected, the number of authors makes this history uneven, and the town histories section emphasizes the various churches' community involvement and facts and figures about the population. However, life at the time revolved around religion to a great extent, so this bias is less egregious than it would be in a more recent history.

Regardless of the reasons for which such early histories were written, their processes and contents were often similar. The typical author had a strong background in the history of the county, knew most of the leading citizens, was well established professionally, and was mature in years. A single author would almost certainly have had to be financially secure, because histories took time and money to produce. Pomroy Jones, for example, was a judge in the Oneida County court system. He was able to retire when a new state constitution changed the court structures. A native of Oneida county, he was around sixty years old when he wrote its history. Even with such a strong background, he laments being twenty-five years too late to make a "full and perfect notice of . . . the early settlement of the County" (Pomroy 1851, iv). Norton relied heavily on his memory and notes of conversations with "others, who have since deceased," which he collected "several years ago, when a resident of this place" (Norton 1862, ii).

While authors usually admit sole responsibility for the content and for the presentation of the incidents in their histories, it does not follow that each history is only one person's recollections. With a strong background in and knowledge of a county's history and people, the author usually interviewed numerous people to gather additional facts, resolve discrepancies, hear more stories, or get information about an event from an actual participant. Authors also went to the county and town record books to see who had been elected to various offices by how many votes, where the early town meetings were held, who were the first settlers, or when and why a town petitioned to be "set off" or independently incorporated. An author would read church records, old newspapers, and other early accounts of history, and then might go back and interview more people.

Authors also relied on the writings of others. A manuscript or previously published pamphlet about a town or an event in a county's history might have existed; writers often incorporated such works, in whole or in part. Speeches and booklets from earlier jubilee (fifty year) and centennial (one hundred year) celebrations were used by history authors as well.

Authors usually made little attempt to comment on the history or try to interpret it. Rather, they were content to record the what, when, where, and who of most events. The "how" aspect was also often overlooked, although that was easier to perceive when the factual statements were given. This process, however, led to a noncritical history. Because authors usually lived in the county and knew many of the people they wrote about, they portrayed persons and events in a positive light. If the person or event could not be portrayed positively, it often was overlooked. Certainly some negative events were recorded, such as natural calamities (bad winters, floods, droughts, etc.) and heinous crimes (the only murder or a bank robbery); however, this typically was because such events were too terrible to overlook and because there was an air of sensationalism about them.

Biographical sketches of individuals or families are rare in early histories. Eminent people, such as prominent first settlers, are usually discussed in depth, but even these longer treatments contain limited genealogical information; they may not name parents or children or even give the person's date or place of birth. However, a good researcher will read between the lines: How old was this person when he settled in the town, or when he died? Are his children mentioned elsewhere? Could other early settlers with the same surname be relatives? Even without clearly defined biographical sketches, histories contain valuable information about ancestors because they focus mostly on people, not just places or events. To find this information, an understanding of a history's arrangement is critical.

Many early histories have no table of contents, and none have adequate indexes. However, most follow a similar pattern. They usually have two parts (though the parts are seldom designated as such): general county information followed by town or township histories. The first part often begins by relating the geography and some early history of the state or, at least, an account of the first white people to visit the future county. This is followed by information on the first settlers, the creation of the county, and early churches and settlements (towns). The narrative proceeds chronologically, outlining major events in the history of the county—elections to county office, tax rates, resolutions to build schools, jails, courthouses, etc. Anecdotes from early settlers are often found in these chapters, and one or more chapters are usually devoted to the military service of the county's citizens (in colonial wars, the American Revolution, or the War of 1812, but not the Civil War, because most early histories were printed before it began).

The second part discusses the towns (in the East) or townships (in the Midwest) and their histories. Usually, one chapter is devoted to each town, the chapters being arranged alphabetically by town. Each chapter includes information similar to the county section but is focused on the town; the first settlers, marriages, churches, schools, etc., are all described. This part is where researchers often turn first for information about families; within these town histories lies a wealth of information (even if it is brief).

Usually the researcher knows where within the county an ancestor lived. Figure 17-5, from Norton's 1862 history of Knox County, Ohio, shows the brief information typically given about early settlers. However, the paragraph on James Blair opened the door to further research on the Blair family. James had been found in the 1850 census of Knox County, but nothing else was known of him. He was believed to have been the father of a younger James Blair, but proof, and the family's earlier residence, was needed. The tone of the paragraph suggests that James had recently died. The approximate death date (around 1860), residence, and status (former justice of the peace), all supplied by the history, enabled his will to be distinguished from those of other Blairs (a common name); it proved that he was the father of the younger James. The statement that he wrote poetry eventually led to a biographical work on Knox County writers (see figure 18-9 in chapter 18) that identified his birth place in Maryland and led back three more generations, including the finding in Maryland records that he had married a Waddle, a family also mentioned in the Knox history (and the subject of a small family history later found in a Knox County library)!

Another research problem was solved using the 1829 *A History of the County of Berkshire, Massachusetts* (Pittsfield, Mass.: Samuel W. Bush). The history of Peru (figure 17-6), written just fourteen years after Nathan Thompson's death (and while his son still lived in the town), notes that Peter, Daniel, and Nathan Thompson were "brothers, from the eastern part of this state." Nathan had been a "dead-end" ancestor—there were too many Nathan Thompsons born in Massachusetts to clearly identify him. However, knowing his brothers' names made it easy to identify all three of them in the *International Genealogical Index* (*IGI*) (see chapter 6, "Published Indexes"), which gave their parents' names; this led to locating the family in one of the dozen different Thompson family histories (genealogies), where additional information confirmed which Nathan was the correct ancestor. The key, however, had been the county history's identification of Nathan's brothers.

Because these histories are without indexes, researchers often overlook them or miss information in them; such was almost the case with the Blair and Thompson examples above. Thus, it is important to read every word in the town history sections for every town and neighboring towns where the ancestor lived—and do not overlook the first (general county) part. Browse each chapter thoroughly; look for related surnames, founding of churches of the ancestor's religion, and notices of marriages, births, and deaths; determine what year the family came to the county and read that period of the history line by line; note where other settlers came from.

Properly used, early histories can solve many research problems. Don't take everything that is written as fact, but use the information as a guide to further research. By and large, the information in such histories is reliable. For pre-1800 problems, these early references are sometimes the only ones available.

Centennial Histories (1870 to 1899)

The second era of county history publishing takes its name from the U.S. centennial, which occurred in 1876. As during the bicentennial, the various centennial celebrations throughout the country awakened a sense of history among the people: if the United States had a history, many felt, the county must also. Congress issued a joint resolution encouraging people to have historical sketches prepared and delivered during the "centennial anniversary of our national independence" (Russo 1988, 80). Further, the Centennial Commission "made a conscious effort to spur the writing of local history" (Hanna 1971, 294). During the thirty years from 1870 through 1899, at least 1,166 county histories were published—more than in any thirty-year period until the 1960s and 1970s. The success of these ventures has spawned similar publications for the last one hundred years.

In 1876, fifty-seven county histories were published. The number diminished very little during each of the following years,

KNOX COUNTY. 311

The most numerous families in this township are the McKees, Waddles, Halls and Blairs, descendants of early settlers, who cleared the way for the present.

Charles McKee emigrated from Ireland, with fourteen children, about 1808. Alexander McKee settled in this county in 1809; he resides on his old place on Big Jelloway, where was once an Indian camp; and when he first settled there, sixty-five Indians called at his hut, drank metheglin with him, and they had a jovial time all round.

The Halls, Sovernses, Pinkertons, Waddles, and Stewards have also been plenty in Brown. John Carghnan (pronounced Carnahan) was a wild Irishman of much note about 1826; he was a warm-hearted, impulsive creature; and "faith, an' he was a knowledgeable mon." Many anecdotes are quoted of him, which we have not room to produce.

Jacob Phifer from Strasburg, Germany, located in this township in 1818, when all was wild and new. He died Oct. 9, 1846, aged 89. He had served ten years a soldier in Europe, three years in the Revolutionary War, and three months in the war of 1812. The old soldier was the father of Freeman, John, James and Michael.

James Blair, our old friend, "God bless you," was one of the early stock. In 1816 he tended the old Shrimplin mill; moved to Brown in 1820, and has been one of its most prominent men, having served as justice long enough to entitle him to vote, and his decisions have been generally approved of by his fellow citizens. He has been engaged in

312 HISTORY OF

milling, farming, raising children, writing "poetry" and making himself generally useful. His memory will endure in Brown forever.

Zephaniah Wade, who commanded a company of Riflemen from Loudon co., Va., in 1777, moved to this county in October, 1816, with his son, Thomas. Zephaniah and his wife, Irene Longley, are both dead. J. J. Skillings has been one of the most active business men.

There have been a few small mills on Big Jelloway from its early settlement, but the want of water, during the year, has caused some of them to suspend. Emor Barret's grist mill was built about 1833, and is yet in operation. It is run by an overshot wheel 16 feet high. Thomas Wade has a saw mill 2½ miles above it run by an overshot wheel 30 feet high. A set of carding machines have also been run at this stand. The mills of James Blair, Ab. Whitney, and Joseph Hall have gone into dilapidation and decay.

Jacob Roof and his wife Polly, Jacob Darrow and Wm. Prior, Jacob Baugh, Daniel Worley and Richard Deakins, were old settlers.

SUCCESSIVE JUSTICES OF THE PEACE.

Samuel Barkhurst was the first, and Josias Ewing succeeded him in 1826.
1830. James McMillen; re-elected in 1833.
1831. James Blair; re-elected in 1834, '37, '40, '43, '46, '49.
1837. Thomas Wade; re-elected in 1840 and 1844.
1845. John W. Gurberson.
1846. Wm. Soverns; re-elected in 1850.
1850. Joseph Pinkley; re-elected in 1853 and 1857.
1852. Solomon C. Workman.
1854. John Hicks.
1856. J. W. Leonard; re-elected in 1859 and 1862.

Figure 17-5. From a history of Brown township in *A History of Knox County, Ohio, from 1779 to 1862 Inclusive.* This is an example of the information typically given about early settlers.

and in 1880 the number jumped to eighty-five published titles. The peak year was 1882, when ninety-eight histories were published—a number surpassed only during the bicentennial year of 1976. Publication then dropped off to an average of forty-three per year from 1885 to 1889 and twenty-seven per year in the early 1890s. In 1899, only eighteen county histories were published. Nevertheless, the flame had been ignited, and, except during World War II, at least eighteen county histories have been published every year since 1899.

Of the eight regions identified earlier, only the Gulf South and Mountain West seem to have been completely unaffected by this increase of publishing, though the Plains states and Atlantic South show only minor increases. These histories were not inexpensive. Hanna suggests that cost was a factor for the deep South, as those states were "impoverished for much of the period" and therefore have a "relatively small number of county histories" (1971, 295). In the other four regions, however, there was extensive publishing activity during the centennial period. In the New England and Mid-Atlantic regions, more histories were published than there were counties in those regions; for New England, with sixty-seven counties, there are seventy-eight histories from this era, while the 153 counties in the Mid-Atlantic region produced 229 histories! However, histories were not published for every county during these years (indeed, as late as 1984 three New England counties were without histories), but most were covered, several individual counties, obviously, having more than one history. The Great Lakes region produced 582 histories (for 735 counties), while the Pacific states, with only 133 counties, produced 109 county histories (mostly in California).

The centennial histories from these two regions are the county histories with which so many genealogists are familiar. They are also the ones that have been given the somewhat unfair appellation of "mug books" (because they typically contain many portraits)—unfair because it carries a negative connotation, especially among modern, scholarly researchers. While they do have significant shortcomings, centennial-era histories are valuable reference and research tools that contain information often available nowhere else. Understanding these sources is vital to the researcher.

Regional differences are minimal, so the sample histories discussed below were drawn from the Mid-Atlantic and Great Lakes regions because they produced the most histories. Interestingly, the approach pioneered in the early histories was useful when centennial histories were produced; however, the latter are generally much longer than their predecessors, providing much more information. These books are generally twice as large (in dimensions) and have twice the number of pages as the early histories; thus, approximately four times the amount of material was typically published in each. Because many used smaller type and a two-column format, that average could be five or six times the content of earlier publications.

Centennial histories are usually full size (ten inches high and eight inches wide)—*quarto* in library terms—and typically have eight hundred to one thousand or more pages. Dozens of individuals (sometimes more than one hundred) can be listed on each page. Further, each page contains references to between two and twelve families. Thus, each of these histories probably refers to between two thousand and four thousand families in each county (although many references are brief). The 1880 census figures show that many of these counties were not densely populated. In Pennsylvania, a more densely populated state, most rural counties had around forty thousand inhabitants. In Ohio, the figure is closer to thirty thousand; in Indiana, around twenty thousand; and in Iowa, closer to fifteen thousand Assuming about five persons per family at the time, these numbers suggest that most counties had between three thousand and eight thousand families—perhaps twice as many as recorded in an average history. Thus, it is possible that as many as half of the families in a county were noted in a history.

Considering that most researchers' nineteenth-century ancestry includes two to four families in each ancestral county, one can expect to find some information on one or more families in almost every county where ancestors lived in northern states in the 1800s. For example: one-quarter of this author's ancestors lived primarily in five counties in Pennsylvania, Ohio, and Iowa from 1830 to 1900; references to direct ancestors (not just siblings or cousins) have been found in histories from four of those counties. All were typical, middle-class farming families that did not achieve local greatness. Years of research into similar families in those localities indicates that these are typical, not abnormal, results.

A HISTORY

OF THE

TOWN OF PERU.

BY REV. JOSEPH M. BREWSTER.

THIS township included the greater part of Hinsdale until 1804. The whole was purchased at auction at Boston, June 2, 1762, for £1460. Nine townships were purchased at that time; among which this was denominated No. 2. It went into the hands of Oliver Partridge and Elisha Jones; and in honour of the former gentleman was called Partridgefield, from its incorporation in 1771, until 1806, when it received its present name. It is about 6 miles long and 4½ broad, embracing about 17,280 acres. Within these limits the settlement commenced about 1764. Between this time and 1768, Henry Badger from New Jersey, Nathaniel Stowell from Connecticut, Peter, Daniel and Nathan Thompson, brothers, from the eastern part of this State, in it, and Ebenezer Pierce not long after.

The town is bounded by Windsor on the north; by Cummington and Worthington in the county of Hampshire on the east; by Middlefield in the same county on the south, cornering on Washington on the south-west, and by Hinsdale on the west. Occupying the height of land on the Green mountain range, the climate is severe. The surface is uneven, and the soil in many places hard and stony. It is best adapted to grazing, though considerable quantities of rye, corn and oats are raised in favorable seasons. There is a limestone quarry, from which lime is made of the best quality. There are no large rivers or streams. The inhabitants are very generally farmers—industrious, temperate and

Figure 17-6. From *A History of the County of Berkshire, Massachusetts.*

What, then, can one expect to find in centennial county histories? As with early histories, they typically contain at least two major sections. The first is a discussion of general county history, and the second provides great detail about the various townships. Most also contain biographical sketches of county residents, which may be in a separate section or dispersed throughout the text. The key to using centennial histories lies in their tables of content (although a few, like their predecessors, do not have them). The tables of content are usually detailed and often function as partial indexes, listing some of the information by topic, such as illustrations, portraits, war records, and state laws.

The arrangement of centennial-era histories, as in early histories, progresses from early to modern times and broad areas to specific towns. Figures 17-7 and 17-8 show typical tables of contents from two Illinois histories. Note that the Winnebago County history listed in the table of contents shown in figure 17-7 includes more than two hundred pages of territorial and state history, arranged by topics, which are followed by town histories. The "Directory" is the biographical portion; it occupies the final 130 or so pages. The Knox County history shown in figure 17-8 also contains almost one hundred pages of state history, but its table of contents leads off with the county portion and is more detailed. Township histories comprise one chapter of the county portion, but another chapter is devoted to cities and towns. Biographical sketches make up a separate, final section.

Histories in other states followed a similar pattern, though the appearance of the tables of content may vary. Figure 17-9 is from a reprint of a Washington County, Ohio, history. Here again, the first one hundred pages focus on the history of the state. The rest of this lengthy book, however, focuses entirely on the county and its people. The townships section is longer than in the previous examples, and there is not a separate biographical section; rather, the biographies are dispersed throughout the history in appropriate places. They can be found in chapters on the bench and bar (lawyers), military chapters, and, most often, in the histories of the townships where the subjects resided. In this case, a separate listing, "Biographical," gives page numbers for each sketch.

Information on ancestors can be found throughout any such book, so one musn't stop with the table of contents. (An index, if available, can also be a starting point; indexes are discussed in greater detail later.) As noted before, be sure to read the township histories in their entirety for areas where ancestors lived. Also read applicable chapters that relate to what is known about the ancestor, such as occupation—whether he was a lawyer, doctor, elected official, or minister. (Unfortunately, a researcher usually does not know such information until she has found it in the history.) Browse through those chapters that contain many names, seeking ancestral surnames. Be sure to check for sections on societies, old settlers, pioneer life, religious societies, schools, and commercial ventures. In addition, there are two topics that require careful examination: military and biography.

CONTENTS.

HISTORICAL.

ILLUSTRATIONS.

LITHOGRAPHIC PORTRAITS.

WINNEBAGO COUNTY WAR RECORD.

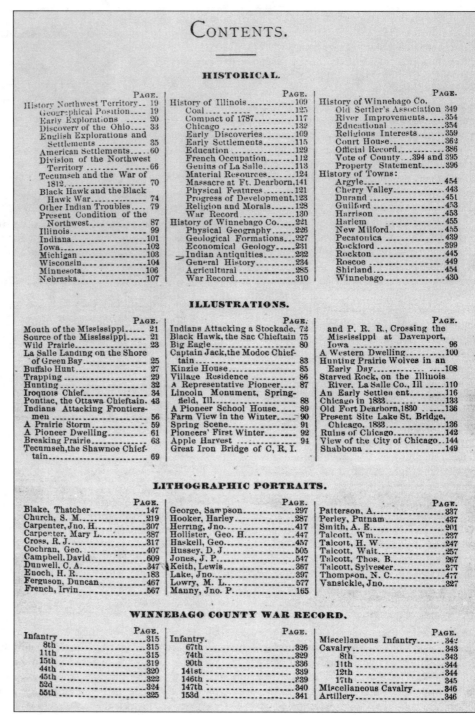

Figure 17-7. Contents pages from 1877 *History of Winnebago County, Illinois* (Chicago: Ottaway & Colbert).

Military Information. The Civil War had been over for less than twenty years when many centennial histories were published. These histories are overwhelmingly from the Northern, or Union, states, whose citizens were proud to have won the war and preserved the Union. Many soldiers from these counties had returned home and become leading citizens, and among the selling points for publishers were complete rosters of the counties' participation in the war, so the publishers worked very hard to compile accurate lists. One publisher wrote: "Our soldiers list is full and was very carefully compiled. Months of labor were bestowed upon this one item; and should there be a soldier whose name is not recorded here . . . investigation will show him credited to some other county. It was impossible to obtain the correct spelling of some of the names" (Chapman 1878, iv).

Lists were compiled from numerous sources, such as the War Department, state adjutant generals' records, and county draft and enlistment lists. The soldiers and their families often provided names and information also. Frequently, during the Civil War, entire military companies (or major portions of them) were recruited from each county; therefore, information is typically presented on a company-by-company basis. A brief history of each company is given, including where and when its members enlisted and for how long. The major battles and marches in which the company took part are also noted in a two- to three-paragraph sketch; this is usually followed by a listing of every county man in the unit, giving name, rank, and the result of enlistment (date of discharge, if killed, deserted,

vi CONTENTS.

DIRECTORY.

ABSTRACT OF ILLINOIS STATE LAWS.

MISCELLANEOUS.

Figure 17-7 (continued).

missing, promoted, etc.). The soldier's age or hometown might also be included.

For many of these companies there may be no published regimental history (see chapter 13, "Military Sources"), so a county history might contain the best available history for an ancestor's service. Of course, once an ancestor's service is established via a county history, the researcher will want to pursue other military records. Because such records are arranged by company and regiment, county histories can very helpful in locating them.

Almost every Northern family was touched by the Civil War. Even if a particular ancestor did not serve, he may well have had a brother who did. A close examination of the military service lists in a county history can lead to more information or discovery of a lost family member. If an every-name index is available for the history (they typically are included with reprints), check each entry for any surnames of interest; they may lead to clues about an ancestor in the text that are not apparent from the index entry. These lists can also be helpful for distinguishing among more than one soldier of the same name. For example, if the *Compiled Service Index* or the *Union Pension Index* lists many soldiers with the ancestor's name, a county history (if it is known what county the ancestor was from) may indicate which unit he served in. If the county is not known but several candidates have been gleaned from the above indexes, determine which counties the various companies were raised in (see chapter 13 for applicable references) and check the centennial-era histories for those counties. The clues therein should help identify which man is the ancestor.

Biographies. Most researchers turn to county histories because they contain biographical sketches; some hope to find multi-page sketches of middle-class ancestors that trace their lineage back several generations and name the European towns they or their ancestors came from. While researchers occasionally find such information, they are often disappointed. However, this disappointment stems from overexpectation. Important, helpful information can be found in a biography section, even if the ancestor is not listed.

Probably the most important fact to be aware of regarding biographical sketches is that most such sketches in centennial histories were paid for by their subjects. Furthermore, the subjects provided most of the information, often by answering a questionnaire. The actual writing of the sketch was usually done by the publisher's staff (Hanna 1971, 293). These facts yield both positive and less-positive results. Publishers wanted happy, satisfied subscribers, so virtually no negative information appears about the subjects (while positive adjectives are abundant). On the other hand, because the subject provided the information, it should be relatively free from error except for exaggeration and possible mistakes made during production of the book (which conceivably could result in a "lost" child, transposed date, or a wife's name being reversed). In other words, the raw facts—date and place of birth, relatives, employment, etc.—should be correct (Russo 1988, 150).

However, the researcher must be circumspect about biographical statements not based on the subject's personal knowledge, such as information about family members beyond grandparents, statements of descent from seventeenth-century ancestors, the revolutionary war service record of an ancestor, and similar information. This is not to say that such information is false, for it often is not. However, such statements usually reflect embellished family traditions and, sometimes, wishful thinking. Therefore, such information should serve only to guide further research.

The most prominent persons are seldom overlooked in the history portions of these works, but not all such persons chose to pay for inclusion via a biographical sketch. On the other hand, the same personal qualities that caused a person of that era to excel may have prompted him to have his family profiled in a county history. A man of lesser status might have seen the history as a way to raise his status in the local community, feeling that others who saw him featured prominently in such an impressive book would think better of him. This reasoning might be behind the fact that so many immigrants (especially Germans) are profiled in the county histories of Wisconsin, Minnesota, and Iowa. Hanna suggests how broad the coverage may be in these sections:

CONTENTS.

Figure 17-8. Contents pages from 1878 *History of Knox County, Illinois.*

> With the obvious limitation that few members of the working class are included, 'mug book' biographies cover a surprisingly large part of the social and economic spectrum. It should also be recognized that in rural and small-town America of the period when this literature flourished, the working class were a small minority. As might be expected, farmers and small businessmen predominate. The professions, especially law and medicine, are usually well represented; teachers and the clergy not quite so well. Almost all subjects are male heads of families, but an occasional spinster or widow is to be found (1971, 295–96).

Some sketches were paid for on a cents-per-word basis, and their length could be more a function of their subjects' means than their importance in the county (Carothers 1985, 31). Portraits, of course, cost extra. Most books were sold by subscription, and simply ordering a book could guarantee a

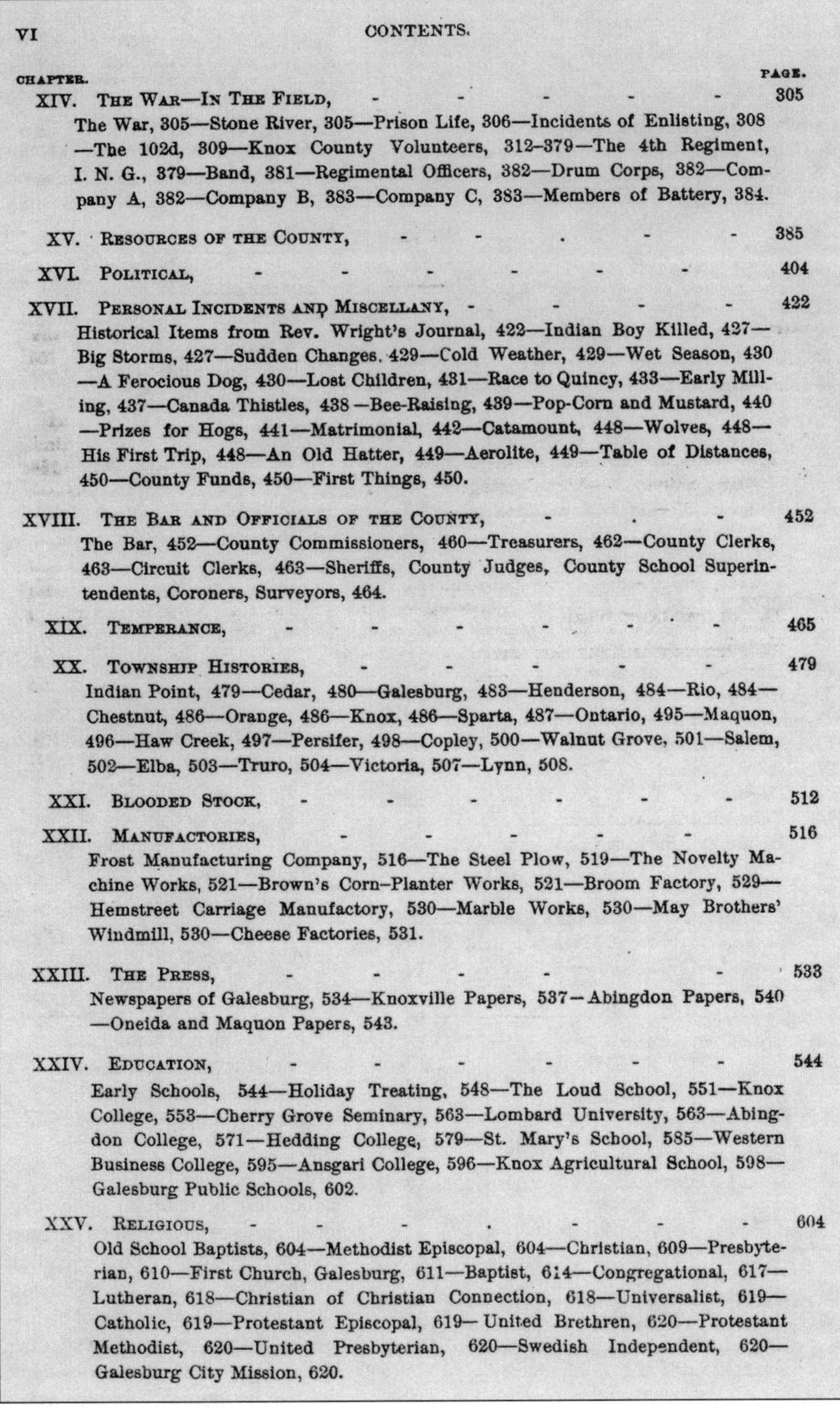

VI CONTENTS.

Figure 17-8 (continued).

and children are given, along with prior residences, military service, immigration, and accomplishments.

Some publishers were more generous about whom they included. Many a history of the centennial era includes a directory of the county's residents; usually these are labeled "Directory" rather than "Biography" in the table of contents (see figure 17-7). Typically, these lists were intended to include every adult male head of household in each township with his post office address; often, however, only landowners were included, as the lists were made from county recorders' records (deeds or land records). Figure 17-11, from a history of Winnebago County, Illinois, shows that biographical sketches were typically included in these directories. These sketches may have been paid for or may have been included in the subscription price. However, one should not assume that the one-line entries represent subscribers. This format is particularly common in Iowa, Illinois, and some Ohio histories (they are usually identified by their arrangement by township). Subscribers who did not pay an additional fee for a sketch are apparently those in bold type. The sketches are brief, but contain information similar to that noted above. In other histories more space was devoted to biographical sketches (especially in those in which the sketches were dispersed throughout the history). These sketches range from half a page to three or four pages (or more). Such lengthy biographies are likely to include more ancestral information about the subject, which, as discussed above, one should regard with circumspection.

Not every ancestor is the subject of such a sketch. However, in the absence of an every-name index, the researcher will miss important clues if she only searches the table of contents for a specific person. Every sketch names many other persons, including children and their spouses; therefore, one should read every sketch for anyone with a surname connected in any way to the ancestral family's—even if it is for the wife of a brother or husband of a sister. Even if an ancestor is not the subject of a sketch, a sketch about his brother, brother-in-law, or other relative will usually mention him and certainly other ancestors as well.

person's name in it; the sketch, however, was extra. The results of this policy often turned out like figure 17-10, from *History of Knox County, Illinois*. Here the publisher clearly states that "every subscriber . . . is given below, with personal sketches of many." Even these brief sketches are valuable. The birth date and place of the subject is usually given—including, sometimes, the town in a foreign country. Parents, wife,

CONTENTS. VII

Figure 17-8 (continued).

tant in a county's history, dead people and nonresidents didn't sell books—and they certainly didn't buy them). In such cases, one should focus on the history sections of the book or seek biographical sketches of family descendants who were still living in the county. (Even sketches of second or third cousins can be helpful if they include information about the common ancestor and her background. Perhaps an ancestor was a very early settler in a county. Many of his children, including the direct ancestor, might have moved to other states; yet, if some grandsons or a great-grandson was still in the county when the history was written, valuable information about the founding ancestor might be included in the history.)

Readers of biographical sketches in county histories should keep Charles Flagg's summary in mind:

> But after making all due allowance for the unsatisfactory character of these histories; nearly every sketch in them contains genealogical material and oftentimes an extended family record in several ancestral lines. Inadequate as may be the sketch of an emigrant ancestor, the descendants of the present generation are almost invariably located, thus furnishing clues for further investigation (1915, ii).

Annals. Another type of history became more popular during the centennial era but never rivaled the more common type described above; these are the local *annals*. In these histories the events and people of an area are discussed in chronological order. In fact, an annal can be considered the diary or journal of the area it covers. Such books seldom include sketches of paid subscribers but frequently include profiles of important or interesting people (even those who had been dead for years upon publication). Figure 17-12 is from an 1877 history that discusses interesting events from 1780, including the scalping of a local soldier. His descendants had long since moved west, but the information, which includes source notations, is historically interesting and was therefore included.

Annals often lack the narrative style usually associated with county histories. They typically present information in a

Biographical sketches almost always pertain to living people (unless they had recently died); therefore, the researcher should carefully note the publication date and be sure that the family he is researching indeed lived in that county at that time, or at least that the adult males did (because they are usually the subjects of the sketches). Histories from counties where a family formerly lived or where they were pioneers might include them but, if so, only in passing. (Unless they were very impor-

NEW INDEX and ADDENDA-ERRATA

CONTENTS.

HISTORICAL.

GENERAL HISTORY.

MARIETTA.

TOWNSHIPS AND VILLAGES.

BIOGRAPHICAL.

Figure 17-9. Contents page from 1881 *History of Washington County, Ohio* (reprint; Knightstown, Ind.: Bookmark, 1976).

BIOGRAPHICAL SKETCHES.

THE NAME AND POST-OFFICE ADDRESS OF EACH AND EVERY SUBSCRIBER FOR THE HISTORY OF KNOX COUNTY IS GIVEN BELOW, WITH PERSONAL SKETCHES OF MANY.

Adams, E. R., merchant, Galesburg.

Aldrich D. W., M. D., is a graduate of Bellevue Hospital Medical College, New York, 1874. He was born in Boone county, Ill., April 1, 1848; is the son of William Aldrich and Sarah (Bassett) Aldrich; was a student at Knox College, and in 1869–70 attended Rush Medical College at Chicago; was married Aug. 1, 1872, to Margarette McBride, and two children have been the fruits of the marriage; joined the United Baptist Church in 1877; has served as Supervisor and held the office of Coroner of Knox county. Republican in politics. His address is Gilson, where he is engaged in the practice of his profession.

Anderson, A. G., conductor, is the son of A. and Anna M. Anderson, of Sweden; was born in that country Oct. 26, 1844; came to America when twenty years of age; married Kate Lundquist Sept. 13, 1870; they have one child. Mr. A. is connected with the First Lutheran Church, Galesburg, where he resides. He is a Republican.

Anderson, Rev. Charles, President of Ansgari College, was born in Denmark, July 24, 1843; came to America with his parents in 1848; graduated at Illinois State University in 1863; in 1865 served as Chaplain of the 46th Wisconsin Infantry; in 1866–9 was pastor of the English Lutheran Church, Mt. Carroll, Ill.; 1869 to 1873 pastor of Second Lutheran Church, Galesburg; 1871–78 editor of *Zion's Banner;* 1873-75 Principal of the "Mission Institute," Keokuk, Ia.; 1875 to present time President of Ansgari College, Knoxville. He was married to Nettie A. Whipple; they have four children. Republican in politics.

Anderson, Miss Clara, residence, Galesburg.

Anderson, R. F., farmer; was born in Virginia Jan. 6, 1825; his parents were David and Mary Anderson, of Virginia. He attended school in a log school-house; came to Illinois in 1855; has been engaged in the mercantile business. Mr. Anderson was Alderman in 1873–4, and Mayor in 1875 of Yates City. He was married in 1847 to Miss Martha H. North, and they have had twelve children. He is connected with the M. E Church, and is independent in politics. Postoffice, Yates City.

Anderson, J. F., proprietor of Cornucopia restaurant, Main street, Galesburg.

Anderson, R. P., residence, Galesburg.

Anderson, J. W., merchant, Galesburg.

Anderson, Olof, son of Peter and Betsey (Nelson) Anderson, of Christianstad, Sweden; was born in Sweden; is a farmer by profession; removed to DeKalb county, Ill., in 1854, to Knox county, Ill., in 1856; was married to Hannah Ellison on the 13th of July, 1859. In political views he is a Republican. In 1854 he united with the Lutheran Church, and is a Trustee. He was shipwrecked off the coast of Newfoundland in 1857. All the passengers were lost but 5. P. O. Wataga.

Anderson, William F., merchant, born in Bedford county, Pa., May 17, 1835. His parents, John and Elizabeth Anderson, were natives of Penn. Was educated in the public schools of Penn.; removed to Warren co., Ill., thence to Knox county in September, 1858; was married to Sarah Cox, and they are the parents of four children; followed farming for some time; was a soldier in 102d Illinois Infantry; is a member of the United Brethren Church, of which he is Steward and Class Leader

Figure 17-10. Biographical sketches from 1878 *History of Knox County, Illinois* (Chicago: Blakely, Brown & March).

briefer style more similar to newspaper reporting. Indeed, annals were often written by newspaper reporters and were sometimes serialized in the local newspaper before being published. Where newspapers existed for the time period being covered, they were often used as sources by annals' compilers. Other sources for information in annals include town or county minutes, vital records from towns, churches, and cemeteries, and other official documents, such as tax lists and military documents.

Because they present information in a briefer style with less embellishment, annals are usually shorter than other histories of the centennial era. However, because much of the information in annals was taken directly from original records, and because they were frequently compiled by local historians or writers, they are often more reliable than other histories.

Most annals are highly structured and easy to identify as such (often including the word *annals* in the title), but this is not always the case. Figure 17-13 contains the same scalping story as did figure 17-12, but it is from a different informant in a different history; this particular history is also an annal, but it is more loosely formatted than the earlier example and does not carry *annals* as part of its title. The key consideration is that it is a chronological history that does not feature subscribers or focus as much on local townships as another history likely would.

Annals continued to be popular for preserving local history even after the centennial period. Some are even published today. Searching such histories is more difficult than others because their tables of contents are often brief and the information is not topically arranged. Using them, however, is worth the effort.

Evaluation. Researchers must also consider the way information was gathered or compiled for centennial histories and the motives behind their publication. The motives were usually less pure than those behind their earlier counterparts; a careful reading of the preface (if there is one) can answer many questions. Is an author acknowledged or was the work created by a publishing company whose office was in a major (not local) city? Some publishers established local offices through which subscriptions and some information passed, but most work was done at the company headquarters.

Publishers' prefaces always are positive and speak of the greatness of the county and helpfulness of the people. Reading between the lines, however, can aid the evaluation. One publisher wrote: "Without the aid and assistance of the survivors of the pioneers of 1834–1835 or of their immediate descendants, and numerous notes from their carefully written and well preserved diaries, our task would have been far more arduous and difficult" (*History of Winnebago* 1877, iii). This passage suggests that, beyond those interviews and early family records, research must have been conducted elsewhere—perhaps in town records or by interviewing more recent residents. The same source goes on to name seven persons "whose retentive memories" aided the compilation, including the editor of the newspaper. It is likely that the publisher advertised through the local newspaper and worked closely with its editor. While this person would have been very familiar with the area, one must wonder if nonsubscribers to the local paper were as well known to the editor as his subscribers. The county history also thanks the people of the county "for their liberal patronage," which, of course, indicates that this was a subscription-based history.

The editors of the 1878 *History of Knox County, Illinois* are even more explicit. In the preface they explain that they published twenty-five thousand copies of their promotional brochures, advertised in local newspapers, wrote hundreds of letters, and made hundreds of trips. They promise to print no more books than they have valid subscriptions for and admit that the biographical sketches are of their subscribers. The process of compilation is also outlined, including their search for "every important scrap of history." They claim to have read the public records page by page from their beginnings and also name several local notables who helped on the history and read the final work. Their list of acknowledgments includes three professors, virtually every county official, and "the various newspaper editors of the county." They had promised a book of 600 pages and delivered one of 750 pages (Chapman 1878, iv).

Publishers of centennial county histories were using the limited sources and means of their day. By and large, they tried to be fair and honest, but perhaps tended to be overly positive when presenting their histories. Most errors prove to be minor, such as inaccuracy by a year or two in citing the date of an event. Publishers were at the mercy of their informants, whose memories were not perfect and likely were colored by prejudice even more than the publishers were. Conflicting stories could not always be resolved; sometimes multiple versions are given. The modern researcher who is moderately skeptical and does not accept everything in such histories at face value will find them to be valuable tools for both genealogical and historical research.

NEW MILFORD TOWNSHIP. 555

NEW MILFORD.

ADAMS JOHN, pastor of M. E. Church; New Milford.

Agnew H. farm; Sec. 28; P. O. Kishwaukee.

Agnew Geo. farmer; P. O. Kishwaukee.

Agnew W. J. farm; S. 21; P.O. Kishwaukee.

Aiken Dan. farmer; Sec. 12; P. O. Rockford.

BALDRY WM. farmer; Sec. 12; P. O. New Milford.

BALDWIN BENJ. Farmer; Sec. 11; P.O. Rockford.

Banks R. farmer; Sec. 33; P.O. Kishwaukee.

Banks S. farm laborer; Sec. 33; P. O. Kishwaukee.

BARROSS R. M. Farmer; Sec. 31; P. O. New Milford; born near Rockford, July 17, 1853, his father being an early settler (1840); moved to California in fall of 1868; returned in 1871; married Orissa B. Evans, Sept. 1, 1874; born Oct. 18, 1854, in Rockford, Ill.; one child, Herbert H., born Jan. 1, 1876; owns 80 acres land, worth $30 per acre.

Bartlett J. R. farmer; Sec.22; P.O. Rockford.

Bauder F. M. lives with his father, P. G. Bauder; P.O. New Milford.

Bauder J. J. retired farmer; New Milford.

Bauder P. G. farm; S. 23; P.O. New Milford

Baxter C. M. farm; S. 30; P.O. New Milford.

Baxter G. W. farm; S.26; P.O. New Milford.

BAXTER MRS. JOHN, P. O. New Milford; born Dec. 29, 1806; married John Baxter in 1832; came to this Co. in Nov., 1843; has had eight children, Johanna, Lafayette, George, Levi H., Rosetta Ann, Francis Asbury, Chas. Merrit, Edgar H.; some of her children continue to reside in this Co., others have moved to other States.

Beale J. farmer; Sec. 23; P.O. New Milford.

BETTS E. B. South Bend Mill, situated at the mouth of Kill Buck creek; General Custom Grinding; making "New Process Flour" on all grists ground; P. O. New Milford; owns a half interest in the above mill, value $6,000; 2½ miles south of New Milford; Republican; Baptist; born in Jenner Tp., Somerset Co., Pa., Jan. 15, 1824; came to this State in 1846, and settled in Dupage Co., where he lived until 1855; came to Winnebago Co. in 1855, where he has since resided, except three years at Elgin; married Harriet Sterns, May 7, 1857, born in Bloomingdale, Dupage Co., Ill., Sept. 22, 1837; have four children; Mary Emma, born April 13, 1859; Fred. Grant, March 2, 1865; Lloyd F., March 29, 1868; Henry Sterns, Dec. 4, 1871.

Bordwell W. farm; S.31; P.O. New Milford.

Boyden C. A. carpenter; New Milford.

Brooks A. R. pastor First Wesleyan church; Kishwaukee.

BROWN SAM'L, (Deceased); came New Milford in 1836, and claimed the north ½ of Sec. 24, just north of the present village; married Angelina Hill, Sept. 8, 1839; she was born Dec. 17, 1815, in Sweden, Monroe Co., N. Y., and came to this State with her father, Henry Hill, Esq., in 1838, settling in Ogle Co.; has three children; Jonathan Eden, born Aug. 2, 1840, graduated at Lombard University, Galesburg, in 1860, believed to have been the first native graduate; Alice M., May 17, 1842; Sarah E., Feb. 24, 1848; Samuel Brown was born in Decatur, Otsego Co., N. Y., Oct. 11, 1809; died Aug. 2, 1866.

CARMICHAEL E. A. farmer; P.O. Kishwaukee.

CAMPBELL WM. H. Farmer; Sec. 22; P. O. New Milford; born in Cherry Valley, Otsego Co., N. Y., Sept. 6, 1832; came to this Co. March 10, 1857; married Mrs. M. A. Hall, May 2, 1859; she came to this Co. in 1840; born in Seneca, Ontario Co., N. Y., July 9, 1827; two children; Maud E., born April 11, 1860; Wm. H., Jr., March 10, 1871.

CAREY WALTER, Miller; P. O. New Milford; born at Stratford-on-Avon, England, March 10, 1846; settled in this State in 1852; learned his trade at Dixon, Ill., married Mary Wornick, Jan. 25, 1871; born Jan. 16, 1854; have three children, Wm. L., Josephine and Ruth; was a member of Co. D, 42d I. V. I.; wounded at Franklin, Tenn.; discharged Oct. 23, 1865.

Castle J. L. farm; S. 30; P. O. New Milford.

Clark C. C. farm; Sec. 25; P.O.New Milford.

Clark F. F. lives with his father, C. C.Clark.

Cline L. farmer; Sec. 12; P.O. New Milford.

CLOTHIER CYRUS, Farmer; Sec. 31; P. O. Kishwaukee; born in Oxford, Grenville Co., Ontario, May 13, 1833; came to this Co. with his father, Freeman Clothier, in the fall of 1838; lived here until he enlisted in the 74th I. V. I.; married Louisa Van Doren, Jan. 14, 1859; have four children; Wilford R., born July 22, 1860; Elmer, July 19, 1862; Adda M., May 8, 1866; Nellie M., April 3, 1870; is Constable at the present time; owns 88 acres, worth $3,500.

Clothier F. farm; Sec. 31; P.O. Kishwaukee.

Clothier G. laborer for Henry Agnew; P. O. Kishwaukee.

Clothier H. L. farm; S.32; P.O. Kishwaukee.

CLOTHIER LEWIS, Farmer; Sec. 32; P. O. Kishwaukee; Republican; Bap-

Figure 17-11. Township directory from 1877 *History of Winnebago County, Illinois* (Chicago: H. F. Kett & Co.).

New Century Histories (1900 to 1929)

County history publishing dropped off significantly in the late 1890s, but the dawning of the New Century revived interest in history. Some histories of this period even carried the New Century concept in their titles, such as *A Twentieth Century History of Marshall County, Indiana* (1908). Regardless of the reason, the next thirty years saw almost as many county histories published as had been published in the previous thirty years. Figure 17-1 shows that the publication of New Century histories was more widely distributed over the thirty years and was not just a function of one event, such as the U.S. centennial in the previous era. In any five-year period the average number published did not drop below thirty or rise above forty-eight. The New Century histories being published at this time reflect changes that were evolving in both style and format as well as the regions that were publishing local histories.

The Great Lakes region continued to dominate during this era with 528 histories published; most of these were actually the second or third histories written for particular counties. The second-busiest region was the Atlantic South. Its 175 histories more than doubled the total number published there before 1900. A big jump after 1920 also highlights a change in format and approach to county history. In the Mid-Atlantic region, which had been thoroughly covered earlier, 45 percent fewer total histories were published (124), while the Pacific states region remained fairly constant with 104 new histories. In both of these regions, as with the Great Lakes, many histories were the second or third for a county.

In the Plains states the number of histories was more than doubled: there were ninety-five new histories (patterned after their Great Lakes cousins). The Gulf South region (with sixty-seven) began waking up, especially during the last decade of the New Century era, mirroring the Atlantic South's lead. New England, as well covered as the Mid-Atlantic, dropped to thirty histories, while the Mountain West, with twenty, barely exceeded the number of its pre-1900 histories.

Friday, 14th July, Baltzer Klinesmith, who resided then on George Sholtz's land, lately owned by John Byler, on the second road south of Dreisbach's church leading to Jenkins' mills, and had a small clearing upon it, was killed. The versions of this story are quite numerous. The one in the "History of the West Branch," was furnished by George A. Snyder, Esquire, deceased. The dates I get from the widow's pension papers, and an old certificate, in which it is further stated that he was a private in Captain Joseph Green's company, Lieutenant John Cryder, in Colonel Kelly's battalion. My version is from one who often heard Mrs. Chambers tell it herself. She, with her father and sister, went out in the field to work. He, seeing some squirrels, sent Baltzer, junior, back for his gun. Meanwhile, the Indians came along and captured the old man and the two girls, Elizabeth and Catherine.

Just where the road winds around the hill, above Heimbach's blacksmith shop, on the road to New Berlin, they killed Klinesmith. Mrs. Dreisbach, the Judge's mother, pointed out the place. She helped carry his body down, and they buried it in the Dreisbach church-yard.

The Indians then made their way to the spring, north of New Berlin, where they left the girls in charge of an old man of their party, and went down Dry valley. After a little while it began to rain, and the Indian motioned the girls to gather brush to cover the flour bag. He laid down under a tree, with the tomahawk under his head. The girls, in passing with brush, worked it gradually from under him as he dozed. Elizabeth picked up the tomahawk, and made a motion to her sister to run. She then sank it into the old man's head. The old man yelled fearfully, and the girls ran. By this time the Indians were on their return, and heard the old man yell. They pursued the girls and fired on Catherine, just as she was springing over a fallen tree. The ball entered below the right shoulder-blade and came out at her side. She had the scars until her dying day, as large as a half dollar. She rolled herself under the tree, and the Indians passed over her, in pursuit of the

Figure 17-12. The Klinesmith family's encounter with local Native Americans described in the 1877 *Annals of Buffalo Valley, Pennsylvania* (reprint; New Orleans: Polyanthos, 1975).

This era was truly one of change, a fact often overlooked when researchers consider county histories. The stereotypical mug books faded away after 1920, giving rise to the belief that few new histories were written after that time. However, as mentioned earlier, more than half of the county histories identified by Filby were published after 1929, so the change that happened in this era is important—especially so in the two southern regions, which would soon dominate the production of histories. Many of the earlier comments about how data was gathered, and cautions to the researcher, apply to these histories as well and are not repeated here. The focus here is on the two types of histories published in this era. In the North a mature version of the centennial histories prevailed until about 1920. In the South, smaller, "semiprofessional" histories with a different approach from that in the North began to be produced. The major starting point for this newer type seems to have been around 1920.

Northern Style. The northern histories of the New Century era were similar to Centennial histories. They were printed on higher quality paper, and larger counties required two or more volumes to be well covered. However, they still were often produced by publishers (as opposed to dedicated authors), and they were generally sold by subscription. The biographical sections were much longer, occupying half or more of the pages (one or more volumes of multi-volume histories in large counties). Portraits were more plentiful; combined with the longer biographical sketches, the portraits seem to have earned these histories (more so than earlier histories) the appellation "vanity histories" or mug books.

The counties were now twenty to forty years older, so there was more history and more people to write about. The tendency for many counties in the North and West to produce second or third histories (when one had been done earlier) was very great. All but seven of the Mid-Atlantic states' counties have two or more histories; and, of the 670 Great Lakes counties with histories, 78 percent (521) have at least two histories. Of course, this abundance is helpful to researchers: the more histories that exist for a county, the more likely an ancestor is noted in one of them.

The typical large size of these newer histories implies that many required multiple authors. The preface of the 1911 *History of Manitowoc County, Wisconsin,* states that "credit, in a large measure, is due those who have contributed articles for

sister. Elizabeth, being active, reached Beatty's harvest field. The men ran to their rifles and pursued the Indians. When they came pretty near Catherine, one of the men, supposing an Indian in ambush, was about firing, when she pulled off her apron and waved it. They found her much weakened from loss of blood, but she soon recovered. Philip Pontius, still living, told me that the Indians were going to Beatty's, and George Rote, who was a lame man, but great on a halloo, frightened them back, by hallooing to an imaginary company to surround the black rebels. Klinesmith's widow drew a pension as late as 1819, at New Berlin. "Elizabeth married John Boal, moved to French creek, near Meadville first, and, in 1843, was still living in Ohio or Indiana, her husband, being one of those restless spirits, who fancy that the land is over-crowded, when the population exceeds one to every ten square miles, and she, from her courage and energy, being an excellent second to a man always exposed to the perils of frontier life."—*Manuscript of G. H. Snyder.*

Katy, as she was called, first married Daniel Campbell, a revolutionary soldier, and had, by him, two children, John, who died near Mifflinburg, and Ann, who married Robert Barber. They removed West, and are now both dead. Katy married next Robert Chambers, by whom she had one child, the first wife of John A. Vanvalzah, deceased. Notwithstanding her wound, she survived two husbands. My informant, William M. Vanvalzah, tells me that when a boy, many a night he heard her and old Captain Thompson talk over the events of their early life. Klinesmith's land, in Lewis township, was valued in 1810, Robert Chambers taking one portion, and Baltzer Klinesmith, junior, the other. Baltzer, junior, sold his land, some thirty years since, to Christian Mensch, and moved to a lot owned by his wife, near Hartleton, where he died, and is buried in the Laurelton grave-yard. His wife was a daughter of Melchior Smith, their children, David, Samuel, John Melchior, daughters Mary Ann and Margaret, who married Messrs. Stover, in Centre county. Catherine married —— Miller. Martin Trester, a few years after, found a rifle near the spring, supposed to belong to the old Indian.

Figure 17-12 (continued).

The biographical sections of these histories seem to have grown in importance; perhaps more people wanted to be included. Certainly publishers quickly learned that appeals to vanity sold more books, and they wanted the biographies to be correct, or at least to be approved by their subjects. The 1912 *History of Monroe County, Wisconsin,* states that "all the biographical sketches . . . were submitted to their respective subjects, or to the subscribers from whom the facts were obtained, for their approval or correction." Any corrections that were submitted were made and those never returned with corrections were published with "a small asterisk (*) . . . after the name of the subject" (Richards 1977, 5). This practice seems to have been fairly common and was noted in several other histories.

For all of the space the biographical section or volume occupied, it is often difficult to locate a person therein because these sections are seldom arranged by alphabet or by locality. This problem is compounded in the many histories that include no index or contents to the biographical section. Publishers evidently felt that readers would read these books as they would a novel, from start to finish, and not as a reference book. The only help in such cases is a separately published index, a reprint with a new index, or a lot of patience in browsing through some five hundred or more pages. Many histories do include a table of contents to the biographical sketches, but of course it will list only the subjects, not the many other persons also noted in the sketches. Also, many contents listings are not strictly alphabetical (for example, some only group subjects by the letter of the last initial). Some sketches are even listed in page number order; they require careful scanning.

Historical sections are handled much as they were in the earlier Centennial-era histories, with major subjects and/or townships being the topics of individual chapters. A review of the contents pages of several histories reveals certain similarities in their formats; this could be the result of a few publishers (such as Lewis and Goodspeeds, both in Chicago) dominating the field at this time.

This era also saw many more histories of large cities (Detroit, Chicago, Cleveland, etc.) published. These are not strictly county histories, so they are not part of the study made of Filby's *American County Histories;* nor do they do fit well in the "Local Histories" section of this chapter. Because the populations they served were usually greater than those of average counties, they could not focus on as many of the residents, but such histories do include lengthy biographical sections. Cities have no township subdivisions, so the history portions tend to take the chronological/subject approach rather than focusing on different localities (Russo 1988, 165).

World War I seems to mark the end of the northern (mug book) style of New Century histories. In the Great Lakes region, where they had been the most popular, only thirteen county histories were published in 1917—fewer than half the number of the previous year and the lowest number since 1901. From

this general history of the county" (Falge 1911–12, vol. 1, preface). Unfortunately, the contributors are seldom identified with their articles in such works. The 1914 *History of Buchanan County, Iowa,* expressed gratitude to those who wrote short sketches that the editors used. The editors of this volume also admit that an unnamed professional historian wrote the township histories (Church 1914, iii).

Prefaces continue to mention subscribers or "financial support," indicating that the works were not simply the altruistic endeavors of local historians. The sources of information, in addition to the unlabeled "contributions" noted above, are very similar to those used for Centennial-era histories: town record books, newspaper files, and interviews with elderly pioneers and their descendants. The Buchanan County history explains that "the difference in length of the various histories of societies, lodges, and churches . . . was not determined by their respective importance but by the accessibility of data" (Church 1914, iii). This would seem to be the case with most histories, so the researcher should not measure the relative importance of an ancestor or institution simply based on inclusion in a county history.

About this time a party of Indians assaulted the house of the Klinesmith family, which stood near the present site of New Berlin. The male members were at work in the field of a neighbor. The Indians plundered the house and carried away two of Klinesmith's daughters—one aged sixteen and the other fourteen. After securing their prisoners and booty the savages retired to a spring near by, where they halted. Not satisfied with the mischief they had done, they left the two girls in charge of the oldest Indian in the party, whilst the others started to the field for the purpose of murdering the men and securing their scalps. The old Indian lighted his pipe, and sat down at the foot of a tree to enjoy a smoke and at the same time watch the girls. In a short time rain began to fall, when Betsey, the eldest girl, intimated to the sentinel that she wished to cut a few branches from a tree to cover a small bag of flour that had been taken from her father's house. Little suspecting her real intention, the Indian permitted her to take one of the hatchets, or tomahawks, to do the cutting. She pretended to be very busily engaged at her work, and managed to get behind him, when she quickly, and with all her strength, buried the hatchet in his head! The main body finding the working party of white men too strong to attack, had started to return, and were near enough to hear the cry of the old Indian as he fell. The girls quickly fled, with the savages in pursuit, who fired on them. The younger girl, as she was in the act of springing over a fallen tree, was struck by a bullet, which entered below the shoulder blade and came out at the breast. She fell, but had presence of mind enough to roll under the log, which was raised a little from the ground. The Indians sprang over the log in pursuit of her sister without observing her. Betsey, being strong and active, gave them a lively chase, and the firing having alarmed the workmen, they came to her rescue. The Indians, fearing to cope with them, fled. The little girl was found under the fallen tree suffering from her wound and greatly terrified. Her wound, fortunately, was not dangerous, as the ball had passed through her body without touching any vital organ, and it soon healed. She grew to womanhood and married a man named Campbell. Becoming a widow, she married the second time, her husband's name being Chambers. The heroic Betsey also married, and with her husband removed to one of the Western States.

Figure 17-13. The Klinesmith family's encounter as described in the1889 *Otzinachson: A History of the West Branch Valley of the Susquehanna* (Williamsport, Pa.: Gazette and Bulletin Printing).

1919 to 1975, no more than thirteen were published in any given year in this region (except for nineteen in 1968), and in only ten of those years were ten or more published. Those that were published were less frequently of the mug book variety, for in the 1920s a new type of county history evolved.

Southern Style. The new type of history seems to have originated in the South. By the 1920s the South had healed, for the most part, from the ravages of the Civil War and Reconstruction. As southern pride grew, so did an interest in history.

Southern states are different demographically from northern ones; because county histories focus on people, those demographics account for important differences in southern histories. States in the South are generally smaller than those in the Great Lakes or Mountain West regions, yet they often have many more counties, resulting in much smaller counties; and the populations of the southern states are generally lower than those of the northern states. Furthermore, reflective of attitudes of the period, histories written from 1920 to the 1960s primarily focus on white families. Smaller counties, smaller populations, and white exclusivity meant that there were fewer subjects and, hence, less history to be written.

These factors may account for southern histories being produced later than northern histories. They also help explain the much shorter length of most southern histories. The great number of counties in southern states also explains why the breadth of coverage (number of counties with at least one history) is not as great in the South. Texas, as the largest state, would be expected to have the most counties, as it does (254); however, Georgia is twenty-first in size among the states, yet it is second in the number of counties (159). Kentucky ranks thirty-seventh in size and third in counties (120). Other southern states in the top ten in terms of number of counties include North Carolina (seventh, with one hundred), Virginia (ninth, with ninety-six), and Tennessee (tenth, with ninety-five).

Southern histories of the New Century era are reminiscent of the early (pre-1870) histories elsewhere. Most have only two hundred to four hundred pages, and most were written by local individuals who were interested in preserving their counties' history. Few were sold by subscription, and many of them lacked a great number of biographical sketches. Those sketches included are usually of truly notable persons in local history. Township histories are rare because local life did not focus on townships. However, many of these county histories include discussions of the towns or the major city and their history.

Material was gathered in a manner similar to earlier histories (except that there were generally no subscribers to appease and interview). Contributions from other authors were encouraged, and sometimes previous historical pamphlets or addresses were reprinted. These authors, like those of earlier histories, also had difficulty in clarifying facts, as "many of them [facts] were hard to find and get straight [and] some records are so vague, brief, and complicated, it is almost impossible to get the material desired." The same author "talked with many older people, received answers to questionnaires from others; was given help by county officials, librarians, etc." (Yowell 1926, 12). The 1920 *History of Edgecombe County, North Carolina,* used "a wide range of material, manuscript records, laws, newspapers, biographies, histories, and unwritten tradition" (Turner 1920, 9). Other authors credited general state histories from which they lifted information of local interest .

Virginia seems to have led the way with histories in the 1920s, and a pattern was set. These newer, shorter, more personal, and at times "folksy" histories usually contained interesting tidbits of local tales interspersed with historical events. During this decade, they began to replace the more formal, established histories of the North.

World War II Histories (1930 to 1959)

The county histories published from 1930 to 1959 are known as World War II histories because they flank that momentous event. During the actual war years there was a drop in publication to a low not seen since 1871, but this lull was brief (1944 to 1945) as Americans' attention turned to greater matters. Immediately after the war, histories rebounded, an average of thirty-eight being published every year in the 1950s. Despite the dip in the middle of this era, more than one thousand histories were printed—only 10 percent less than in each of the two previous eras. There are also similarities in the histories printed just before and just after the war that allow them to be grouped together. These similarities are found in format, content, and distribution.

The geographic trend that began in the 1920s continued into this era. Fifty-seven percent of World War II-era histories focused on counties in the two southern regions, the Gulf States taking the lead with 305; this represents an average of one history for every two counties. In the Atlantic South 270 new county histories were published, which is more than the total number printed before 1930. The other region to gain numbers at this time was the Mountain West. Its seventy-seven new histories represent almost a four-fold increase from the previous era. The Plains states region maintained its status with ninety-two new histories.

Publication dropped off in the regions that were, in a sense, saturated with previous histories. In the Great Lakes, only 163 works were published, while the Mid-Atlantic region produced eighty-five. The Pacific States dropped by half, to fifty-three, while New England produced only thirteen new histories.

The preponderance of southern histories is very important, for researchers often overlook the availability of county histories in southern states; it is in these states that more such sources are needed because fewer original sources are available for them. While southern histories are typically briefer from those of the North, they serve an important purpose. As noted earlier, the population of southern counties was significantly lower (on average) than in the northern counties; thus, despite the histories' brevity, the percentage of people noted in them may be almost as high.

Probably the greatest difference between the southern histories of this period and the northern mug books of a few decades earlier is that most southern histories were not subscription histories. Most were written by county natives who wanted to preserve their counties' history; the authors of some, especially in Georgia, were appointed by county officials. But they were local productions and there was no intent of making a profit. These factors explain why the breadth of coverage is so much less than in the North. Most southern states have histories for less than 80 percent of their counties, while in the North, most states have at least 95-percent coverage.

Where the writing of county histories has been dependent on native scholars, many counties will lack coverage. However, this lack is often compensated by the attitude of authors. A common feeling, expressed best by one author, was that his pages "were written as a 'labor of love'" (Tate 1935, 7). Add to this sentiment the encouragement offered by local and state governments, and one begins to understand the background of these southern histories. Georgia is an excellent example. In 1929, four years before the bicentennial of the state's founding, the state legislature passed a resolution requesting the judges of the superior courts to charge the county grand juries with finding suitable persons to prepare histories of their respective counties. This approach accounts for the large number of Georgia county histories published in the 1930s (thirty from 1930 to 1937). While other states may not have been as formal in their approach, the dozens of historical events and celebrations during these years encouraged local historians to take on the difficult task of compiling histories.

The authors were generally not professional historians but were usually middle-class people with historical interests and strong connections to their counties. The prefaces of this period are not unlike the prefaces quoted earlier. Information also was collected in much the same way: through interviews with older citizens; questionnaires to descendants of early families; previous talks, articles, or pamphlets on aspects of the county; local government record books; and old newspaper files. Sometimes several persons would write various sections for the chief author; as noted before, they were seldom identified directly with their contributions.

Format and content are not dissimilar from those of the larger northern histories. Most histories begin with the early settlement of the county and often include accounts about early Native Americans. General topics are then treated, such as the Civil War, county officials, churches, and schools. Brief histories of towns usually follow, and family sketches are last (figures 17-14 and 17-15). The family sketches are different from the biographical portions of the older northern histories (not only because they were not paid for by their subjects). They tend to focus on pioneer families and may cover two or three generations of a family in a folksy narrative. These accounts are often taken directly from family records or may have been written by the families themselves. Often just a few pages, these family sections account for 10 to 20 percent or more of a history; therefore, typically a smaller percentage of a county's families are noted than in northern histories. However, the body of the book may contain many lists of persons from military, town, county, census, church, and other records.

While this discussion has focused on southern histories of the World War II era, they were not the only ones published, nor were all histories of this era alike. Only 54 percent of the histories published in the era were from the two southern regions. Fifteen percent were published in the Great Lakes region, while the Mountain West and Plains states together produced 16 percent. These histories were not the mug book types of previous eras; they were locally produced histories created for reasons similar to the ones noted for southern histories. The approach in their creation may have been somewhat different but the end results were not.

The World War II-era period of histories seems to have been launched by the WPA's Historical Records Commission during the depression years of the 1930s. At that time the nation turned to its history to work through the Depression, both spiri-

• CONTENTS

Figure 17-14. Table of contents from 1935 *History of Pickens County* [Georgia] (reprint; Spartanburg, S.C.: Reprint Co., 1978) showing the "Family Accounts" as the last chapter.

tually and financially, in a sort of national catharsis. Each book was sponsored by an organization, such as a county history society, that worked with the WPA writers on the research and manuscripts (Carothers 1985, 33). However, the publishing of histories continued with increasing momentum long after the WPA was gone.

Another important type of history began primarily in the World War II era. With the newer, more scholarly treatment of history that resulted from the WPA projects, colleges and universities also directed their efforts to local history. County history was chosen as the subject of many theses and dissertations by graduate history students. For example, Filby's bibliography lists at least nineteen master's theses for Mississippi. Many of these are unpublished and consequently are not easy to access;[1] however, often they represent the only thorough histories produced for particular counties. (It was often the lack of a county history that encouraged a master's candidate to choose a county as a subject.) These histories differ from the good, but amateur histories of this period in that they usually focus more on events than people; the usual list of names or section on pioneer families may not be included. Nevertheless, if an unindexed, hard-to-locate thesis or dissertation is the only history of a county whose other records were destroyed or lost, it may prove well worth the effort to obtain a

CONTENTS

Figure 17-15. Table of contents from 1933 *History of Navarro* [Texas] (Dallas, Tex.: Southwest Press), showing "Pioneer Families" as the final chapter.

copy. See the bibliography at the end of this chapter for suggestions on finding and obtaining such works.

Modern Histories (1960 to the Present)

The period since 1960 has seen more county histories published than any other. The more than 1,450 histories published from 1960 through 1984 is at least 25 percent greater than in any other time period. The actual number published is probably even higher, as Filby undoubtedly missed some post-1980 histories in his bibliography because his method of compilation relied in part on older bibliographies. Consider also that these figures represent only twenty-five years of publishing; earlier eras have fallen into regular thirty-year intervals. An analysis of titles in *Genealogical Publications* for the period 1985 to 1994 suggests that more county histories were published in that decade than in any other ten-year period. The study, though perhaps with slightly looser selection criteria than Filby used for his bibliography, identified just over eight hundred histories: five hundred in the first five years and three hundred in the second five. Again, several histories published after 1990 were likely not counted because of the nature of the compilation.

This increased interest cannot be attributed to a single event, such as the U.S. bicentennial; increasingly more histories have been published since 1960. During the first half of the 1960s, an average of forty-three histories were published each year, while fifty-three per year were published during the second half. From 1970 to 1974 the yearly average climbed to sixty-three. The next five years included the bicentennial year of 1976, when 157 histories were published in just one year, sending the 1975-to-1979 average up to eighty-three per year. Discounting the 1976 figure, the average of the other four years of the late 1970s (1975, 1977 to 1979) is sixty-five, slightly better than in the early 1970s. The early 1980s figures are incomplete but show little decrease from these numbers. The total identified histories published during 1980 to 1983 average fifty-seven per year, with sixty-five known histories as late as 1983 alone. The 1985-to-1989 period averaged upwards of one hundred histories per year, with the numbers for 1990 to 1994 dropping back to approximately sixty per year.

Several factors seem to have helped sustain this pace. The "roots" phenomenon—the growing interest in genealogy that followed the appearance of Alex Haley's *Roots*—that accompanied the bicentennial contributed; so has the growing proliferation of county historical societies and local and state genealogical societies. Cheaper and faster means of printing have aided this growth, as has the trend of computer-aided desktop publishing with, or through, regional, local, and vanity publishers. Backing (or support) for these increased publications has come in large part from local societies, but the interest and technology had to exist first.

The growth seems to have been in two distinct types of history: the scholarly county history and what some researchers term the "scrapbook" history, the latter being much more common. Both are discussed in greater detail below, but first it is worth noting where these histories predominate. The southern and western states have published the greatest number of histories in this modern era. The Atlantic South has the most new histories with 627 for its nearly seven hundred counties. Two states, Georgia and North Carolina, combine for 45 percent of the pre-1985 total, while, during the last decade, Tennessee, Kentucky, and Virginia (in that order) account for 57 percent. The Gulf States are not far behind, having led the numbers in the previous era; their 428 histories average more than two for every three counties. Texas naturally leads with 44 percent of the histories, while Louisiana is at the low end with only 7 percent of the histories, and none since 1983.

The greatest surge of new histories, in terms of previous production and number of counties, comes from the Plains states, where 317 histories have been published in only five states. The distribution is fairly even, with Kansas and Nebraska leading. North Dakota trails, having published none since 1983. In the Mountain West, publications have almost tripled from the previous (World War II) era, with 214 new histories; one-fifth (20 percent) have been focused on Montana counties. The distribution is evenly spread throughout the rest of the region, with Colorado gaining, having published almost 40 percent of the new histories since 1985. The Great Lakes region actually has produced more than the Mountain West, with 398, an increase from the previous era. (However, this amount represents only approximately 70 percent of the number produced in each of the Great Lakes region's heyday periods, the Centennial and New Century eras.) The distribution is again fairly equal, Minnesota and Ohio each accounting for almost 20 percent of the total to take slim leads.

The remaining regions saw less activity until the late 1980s. In the Pacific states, the last decade more than equaled the first twenty-five years, with a total of 124 histories for 133 counties. California led the way with almost 48 percent of that total. The older Mid-Atlantic states had published just seventy-five histories by 1984, but then added fifty in the next decade; almost half of the total 125 histories pertain to Pennsylvania. New England, with only seventeen new histories, has averaged barely one for every four counties.

The county histories of the modern era vary in terms of form, content, direction, and scope more than those of any other era. However, most of the elements noted in earlier histories are found in all of the modern histories to some degree. This diversity reflects the diversity of the people and regions that lately have become active in writing, publishing, and promoting county histories. Some elements of the mug books of the Centennial and New Century eras are present, but two key elements are not. First, these are not subscription histories. Although most of the copies probably go to families included in a history's pages, such inclusion (in the family history section) is not dependent on prior purchase of a volume. As one history put it, "submission of these histories was strictly on a voluntary basis and open to all" (Norton 1983, 6). Second, these books are not the products of publishing companies like the earlier histories that were produced, edited, sold, and in every other way created by their publishers; rather, modern histories are almost all local efforts by a person or group of people backed (mostly with moral support) by a local historical society or other county group. (However, many of them are printed by subsidy publishers that specialize in local histories.)

The manner of collecting information for these histories is much as in earlier eras: Surveys of previously written histories (books, articles, pamphlets, etc.), early newspapers, county government records, and interviews with people were the sources. By the 1970s no pioneer settlers were living, but many families had stories (traditions or possibly only legends) which they shared with compilers or even just printed with minimal editing as they came from the families.

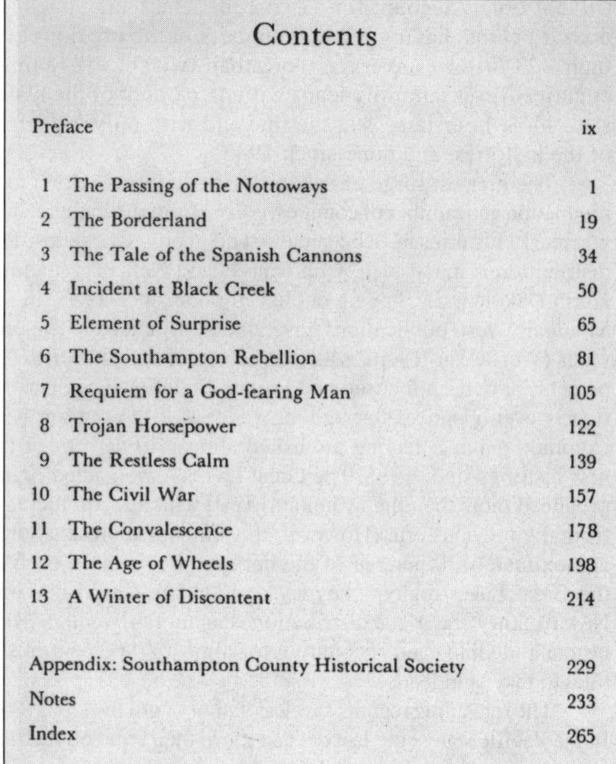

Contents

Figure 17-16. Table of contents from *Southampton County, Virginia* (Berryville, Va.: Virginia Book Co., 1978).

Content also covers many of the same topics as those of earlier eras: early settlement, lists of pioneers and local officials, churches, schools, military service, businesses, professionals, local towns, and local families. However, the quantity of text devoted to these topics varies widely, and some (often the local town histories) are absent altogether. Because the content depends greatly on what is supplied to the editor/compiler, coverage can be uneven. The section on local families may encompass more than 90 percent of the book or less than 10 percent, sometimes being so minimal that it is not a separate section but only some interspersed anecdotes.

It is possible to divide modern histories into two types based on the method of creation: scholarly histories and scrapbook histories.

Scholarly Histories. The *scholarly* or *semi-scholarly histories* comprise the first and apparently smaller group (perhaps 30 to 40 percent of the total). These are produced mostly in the two southern regions and follow the approach that has developed since the 1920s. They are usually the products of individuals or small groups of local writers who are well educated and versed in all or at least important aspects of their counties' history. Authors may receive support and encouragement from local historical societies or other groups but are generally independent of such groups. Such histories focus more on key events than on people. They may be short (two hundred to three hundred pages) or long (more than eight hundred pages) depending on their authors' devotion of time and effort. Most are well footnoted or source referenced and have few illustrations; biographical and family history sections tend to be brief or nonexistent. The contents pages in figures 17-16 and 17-17 illustrate these characteristics.

These scholarly histories follow the recent trends toward more objective, documented histories. Some contain a fair amount of material quoted from early records. The authors at times draw conclusions from studies in their field or advance new theories about why or how an event happened, rather than simply reporting old traditions. The emphasis on African Americans' contributions to history has improved significantly in histories published in this era, especially those after 1970. While these histories might seem to be less valuable to the average genealogist because of their limited discussion of people and families, they actually are very important. Some of these are the first real histories of particular counties, and they provide important background for understanding social structure (more important in southern states than in northern ones), migration and settlement patterns, and commercial centers.

The careful researcher approaches these histories with even more thoroughness than is required for Centennial histories. Do not stop at the indexes, for they are seldom complete and almost never are every-name indexes. Read every chapter dealing with any event, time period, lifestyle, occupation, etc., remotely related to an ancestor. Carefully follow the footnotes, for they will lead to other sources for research in the county which may have many names of interest. The insights gained will assist enormously in other searches.

Scrapbook Histories. The other, more prevalent, form of county history in the modern era is the *scrapbook history.* Typically these are produced by local historical societies and their members. They publish notices in local newspapers, send circulars, "twist the arms" of friends, and encourage county residents to contribute historical stories as well as family sketches. Photographs of places and families are used extensively. The books usually are printed in full-size (8 ½- by 11-inch) format and are bound with attractive covers.

The quality of the content in scrapbook histories varies. There is seldom much editorial direction; most groups publish almost everything submitted to them. The many illustrations, uneven reliability, and lack of editing make these very much county "scrapbooks." These characteristics should not be considered solely in a negative sense; it is often these very scraps of family history that can solve genealogical problems. Most of these histories devote more than half of their text to family sketches submitted by county residents. Usually there is no fee for the printing of a family sketch. To encourage brevity, some compilers charge (on a per-word basis) for text over a certain length (such as two hundred or five hundred words). Others try to edit submitted histories that are too long. These editors are local people who seldom attempt to retain important genealogical material; they simply shorten the narratives.

The family sketches (which are based heavily on family records and tradition, not research) are likely to contain genealogical information. Because most sketches were written in the last ten to twenty years, their writers (usually the family historian) are likely to be alive and would be glad to hear from a distant cousin working on the family ancestry. They will also have whatever documentation is available on the family (often more than was published) and may well be happy to share it. These family sketches usually trace a current family back to the first ancestor to settle in the county, so they are excellent tools

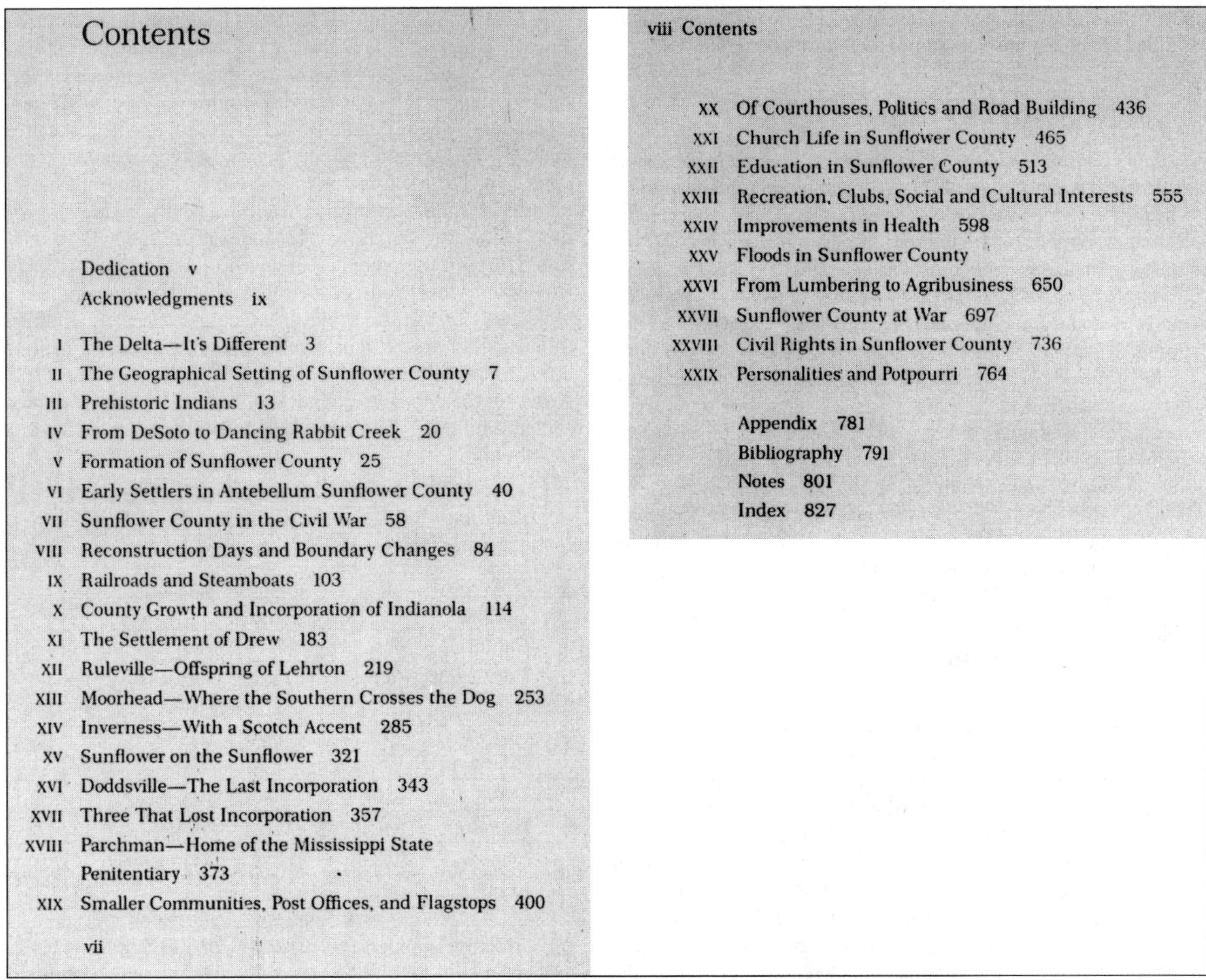

Contents

vii

viii Contents

Figure 17-17. Table of contents from *Fevers, Floods and Faith: A History of Sunflower County, Mississippi, 1844–1976* (Indianola, Miss., 1980).

for locating living relatives. Be sure to read every sketch for every person with any ancestral surname or with a name intermarried with the family. The writers of these sketches are usually named at the end of each sketch.

Some of the best examples of this type of county history are the County Heritage books published by North Carolina counties. These appear to have been encouraged by the state historical society, as their format and content are very similar and the printing and binding is virtually identical among them. The Rockingham County heritage book is representative of the others. It is slightly longer than many others, with 758 pages, including a good surname index (which only indexes the family histories section). The first 140 pages comprise the local history section (there is no table of contents) and include churches, towns, prominent persons, schools, military history, some chronological history, and many illustrations in no particular order. More than six hundred pages are left for the more than nine hundred family histories, which are arranged alphabetically. Illustrations are included here also, and many of the family histories have very brief source notes; all of them include the submitters'/writers' names. This book was published by the Rockingham County Historical Society; many of its members served as editors, indexers, etc. At least thirty such heritage books for North Carolina (almost one-third of the state's counties) have been published, beginning in 1980. Some North Carolina counties have recently published second volumes, suggesting that local response has been quite good. The publications of other states have not been as uniformly produced, but their contents are not dissimilar.

The lack of a table of contents in most scrapbook histories can be frustrating. Browse the local history section for information on churches, local towns and townships, fraternal societies, etc. Indexes are helpful but are not comprehensive (sometimes being only surname indexes), often covering only the family history section, not the local history. Furthermore, many family history sections are arranged alphabetically, and many indexes do not include the main entry for the surname; rather, they reference only the other places where the name appears. Sometimes the references are not page numbers but refer to the number assigned to the individual family history, and sometimes indexes are lacking altogether.

Like earlier county histories, scrapbook histories can be very helpful for research but must be carefully evaluated. Most information is unsubstantiated, but it is often correct. To overlook or quickly glance through such histories often results in missed clues and answers to research problems.

INDEXES AND REPRINTS

In the last several years, new tools have become available to help researchers access county histories—notably, indexes and reprints. These have made histories more accessible and help to locate information buried in the hundreds of pages of each history. The most useful, and perhaps most misunderstood, tool is the index.

There are at least as many kinds of indexes as there are kinds of county histories, and probably more. Two important things to remember are (1) that very few indexes—even those in the original book—are comprehensive (every name included) and (2) that almost every index has mistakes. For a full treatment of the uses and limitations of indexes in general, see chapter 6, "Published Indexes." However, some aspects of county history indexes are relevant for discussion here. Master indexes (which index several books) to county and local histories are available at the national, state, and local levels. In addition, many books contain their own indexes or have indexes that were published separately at later dates.

National and Regional Indexes

Many county and some local histories are indexed by sources that have no specific state focus; rather, they include sources from throughout the United States or from large regions of the country. Some of these indexes began as analytical library catalogs. Analytical catalogs differ from the standard catalogs found in libraries today in that they seek to create entries (usually index or catalog cards) for every significant section of a book or magazine—perhaps each chapter or article or every biographical sketch. Sometimes the criteria are more selective—including only notable persons, for example. The criteria vary from one index to another and sometimes even change during the course (many years) of creating an index. Therefore, the same source may be indexed in two or more indexes, but different elements (articles, sketches, information, etc.) may be indexed for each. However, in almost all cases, master national and statewide indexes of local histories *only index biographical sketches;* they do not index every name or even every significant mention of a person. The same limitation applies to the statewide sources discussed below.

Some of these national or multi-state indexes focus almost exclusively, or at least extensively, on county and local histories. None of these indexes comes close to indexing all of the thousands of local histories, but one should check them for the names being researched.

American Biographical Index (ABI). A useful collection that reproduces and indexes biographical sketches is Laureen Baillie, ed., *American Biographical Index* (*ABI*) (New York City: K. G. Saur, 1993), which indexes biographical sketches in 384 collective biographies. Many of the sources indexed are state, regional, or city histories, almost all of which were published before 1910. The six-volume index has 300,000 entries for approximately 280,000 persons. A 1,842-microfiche collection, *American Biographical Archive* (*ABA*), is also available; it reproduces the biographical sketches from the sources indexed. This set is explained in much more detail in chapter 18, "Biographies."

The Library of Congress Index to Biographies in State and Local Histories. This multi-state card file, available on thirty-one reels of microfilm, goes by various names, including *Index to Biographies in Local Histories in the Library of Congress* (Baltimore: Magna Charta Book Co., 1979). It includes approximately 170,000 names of persons whose biographical sketches appear in 340 local histories and collective biographies. The names in the index are arranged alphabetically, but it is not comprehensive. Most of the sources indexed are statewide publications; forty of them are also indexed in *ABI* (see above). Only fifty county-level sources are indexed, all but four of them for the states of California (eleven), Georgia (sixteen), Kentucky (nine) and Tennessee (ten). Twelve regional sources are included, covering parts of Arkansas (five), California (five), and Idaho (two). Of the 340 sources indexed, twenty-six states are represented only once. The remaining twenty-four states have this distribution:

Alabama	8	Louisiana	21
Alaska	3	Maryland	2
Arkansas	10	Mississippi	13
Arizona	6	Nevada	11
California	34	New York	2
Connecticut	3	North Carolina	10
Delaware	3	North Dakota	3
District of Columbia	3	Ohio	2
Georgia	36	Oklahoma	3
Hawaii	3	South Carolina	13
Idaho	12	Tennessee	32
Kentucky	50	Texas	27

Relatively extensive coverage for the South makes this tool especially helpful. An excellent review which points out some limitations is J. Carlyle Parker's "Book Reviews," *Genealogical Journal* 9 (March 1980): 39.

Genealogical Index of the Newberry Library. The four-volume *Genealogical Index of the Newberry Library* (Boston: G. K. Hall, 1960) is the old analytical catalog of the genealogical collection at the Newberry Library (Chicago). Between 1896 and 1916 the library's staff prepared index cards for references to families and individuals in the many genealogies and local histories then in the library's collection. While the *Genealogical Index* is not an every-name index to the approximately three thousand books cited, it is very complete, often referencing even single paragraphs about individuals or families.

The photocopies of cards comprise approximately 530,000 entries arranged alphabetically by surnames and variant spellings. Most surnames are subdivided by locality. General, nationwide references precede the locality entries. The entries in the index are very brief; careful study of an entry usually reveals the reference. Each entry includes only the author's name; a brief reference to the title of the book, such as the name of the town or county; the year of publication; and the page reference (or a notation to see the index of the work).

If an entry is difficult to understand, search the appropriate bibliography for the name of the author, town, or surname. Read the references in the catalog carefully for one that matches the brief information in the index. Because this index is so comprehensive, it is an excellent source for information on obscure families. In addition, its relatively heavy coverage of midwestern sources and early dates means that many of the Centennial and New Century histories of the Midwest are included. Because the index was discontinued in 1917, it includes no books published after that year. For additional information on this index, see chapter 16, "Family Histories and Genealogies."

Historical and Biographical Index. The *Historical and Biographical Index of North East, Mid East, Mid South, Mid West U.S.A., 1800 thru Early 1900* (Salt Lake City: Genealogical Society of Utah, 1989) was created by the Allen County Public Library (Fort Wayne, Indiana). Rather than a library catalog, it is an index to biographical sketches in county (and some local) histories and biographies. Available on thirty-three microfilm reels from the Family History Library of The Church of Jesus Christ of Latter-day Saints (LDS church) in Salt Lake City, it has approximately 180,000 references to sketches in books covering Massachusetts to Colorado. The total number of books indexed is not known, but most of the titles appear to cover Indiana and its neighbors: Michigan, Ohio, Illinois, and Kentucky. Other states in the Northeast, mid-East (that is, New Jersey), mid-South (Tennessee, West Virginia) and Midwest (Iowa, Wisconsin) are represented by some histories, thus making the rather lengthy name appropriate for this index. There appears to be no coverage for the far West or the deep South. Each entry gives full bibliographic information for the source and provides the page number of the individual reference.

While most of the books indexed were published in the 1800s, some date from the mid-twentieth century; thus, like the *Genealogical Index of the Newberry Library*, this index includes many Centennial and New Century histories. While there is some overlap between the two indexes, the *Historical and Biographical Index* seems to cover fewer sources in greater depth than does the *Genealogical Index of the Newberry Library.* There appears to be very little overlap of sources indexed with the *Library of Congress Index to Biographies in State and Local Histories* (discussed above).

Early Church Information File. The *Early Church Information File* (Salt Lake City: Genealogical Society of Utah, 1991) is an alphabetical card index on seventy-five rolls of microfilm was compiled by the staff of the Family History Library before 1989. It includes approximately 1.5 million entries from more than one thousand printed and original sources from the West and other areas of Mormon interest. While the emphasis is on members of the LDS church, almost anybody in the Intermountain West who lived before 1900 is likely to be in this index. In addition to local church, cemetery, and marriage records, many histories were indexed, including county, town, and congregational histories. Periodicals, personal diaries and journals, and collective biographies were indexed as well. Several other indexes have been incorporated into this file, thus adding to its value as a finding aid. The index cards usually give complete bibliographic information, including page numbers, so the researcher can find the source of the citation. It includes multiple entries for most persons. While many entries refer to biographical sketches, the indexers often cited any mention of an individual in a published work, thus indexing the sources in greater depth than usual.

Several significant genealogical indexes include county and local histories within their scope. The following indexes are more fully described in chapter 16, "Family Histories and Genealogies."

Greenlaw Index of the New England Historic Genealogical Society. William Prescott Greenlaw's two-volume *Greenlaw Index of the New England Historic Genealogical Society* (Boston: G. K. Hall, 1979) is an analytical card catalog that covers the collection of the New England Historic Genealogical Society. It complements the *Genealogical Index of the Newberry Library* very well because it includes books published between around 1900 and 1940; however, it is easier to use and more selective in its content. The index only references articles and sketches containing three or more generations, including local histories.

Old Surname Index File. Prior to 1964, the Library of the Genealogical Society of Utah (now the Family History Library) also kept an analytical surname catalog, now titled *Old Surname Index File,* twenty-one microfilm reels (Salt Lake City: Genealogical Society of Utah, 1976). Although the selection criteria were more restrictive than those for the *Genealogical Index of the Newberry Library,* this index provides 100,000 references to family, biographical, and genealogical information from worldwide (but mostly English-language) sources, including local histories. It is available at the Family History Library and through its branches (family history centers—see the introduction to *Printed Sources*).

Index to American Genealogies. *Index to American Genealogies and to Genealogical Material Contained in all Works Such as Town Histories, County Histories, Local Histories . . . and Kindred Works (Known as Munsell's Index)* (1900; reprint; Baltimore: Genealogical Publishing Co., 1967) represents one of the first attempts to index every printed genealogical reference. Despite its age, it has remained one of the most valuable tools for locating early genealogical information, including "town histories, county histories, local histories, historical society publications, biographies, historical periodicals, and kindred works." With the 1908 supplement, this index provides more than fifty-five thousand references to surnames from an estimated eight thousand different sources. It is not comprehensive but it does include the major occurrences of family information in the books cited.

Sutro Library Family History Subject Catalog. The Sutro branch of the California State Library is another major repository for local histories and compiled genealogies. The library's analytical family history card catalog is available as *The Sutro Library Family History Subject Catalog,* 3rd ed. (Sacramento: California State Library Foundation, 1990) on 182 microfiche; it includes 50,395 index cards. The entries in the catalog provide separate cards for every significant article or subject in a book. Many entries refer to the subjects of biographical sketches in local histories. In addition to those of western states, many eastern and midwestern histories have been indexed (especially Illinois).

Statewide Indexes

The most important type of index to consider is a relatively recent arrival: statewide indexes to county and local histories. Table 17-2 lists thirty such published indexes covering twenty-eight

Table 17-2. Published Statewide Indexes to County and Local Histories*

Title	*Author*	*Date*	*Format*	*No. of Entries or Persons*	*Sources*
Alaska People Index	Bradbury, C.	1986	2 vols.	20,000 names	24
Arizona (see Utah)	—	—	—	Not known	12 for Arizona
Arkansas Biographical Card File Index	History Commission	1994	53 microfilms	100,000	Not known
California Information File	State Library	1986	550 microfiche	1,400,000 entries	Not known
Index to Biographees in . . . Calif. Co. Hist.	Parker, J. C.	1979	Book	16,500/15,400	61
Colorado Portrait and Biography Index	Bromwell, H. E.	1935	2 microfilms	33,000 entries	170
[Florida] *Biographical Card Index*	St. Augustine Historical Society	1974	18 microfilms	Not known	Not known
Indiana Biographical Index	Geneal. Index. Ass.	1983	16 fiche	247,423 entries	537
Biographical Index to the County Hist. of Iowa	Morford, C.	1979	Book	40,540/40,000	131
Kansas Biographical Index	Smith, Patricia D.	1994	Book	35,500	20 (68 vols.)
Kentucky Index of Biograhical Sketches . . .	Cook, M. L.	1986	Book	22,500 entries	65
Maryland Biographical Sketch Index	Andrusko, S.M.	1983	Book	10,500/9250	33
Surname Guide to Massachusetts Town Histories	Longver, P. O.	1993	Book	56,000	128
Michigan Biography Index	Loomis, F.	1946, 73	4 microfilms	73,000 names	361
Minnesota Biographies, 1655–1912	Upham, W.	1912	Book	9,000 names	269
Nevada Biog. and Genealogical Sketch Index	Parker, J. C. and J. G.	1986	Book	7,230 entries	86
New Hampshire Notables Card File	N.H. Historical Society	1988	8 microfilms	32,000 entries	Not known
New Hampshire Genealogical Digest, 1623–1900	Towle, G. C.	1986	Book	6,660 names	7
New Jersey Biographical Index	Sinclair, D. A.	1993	Book	100,000 entries	237
New York State Library Surname Index	N.Y. State Library	1979	33 microfiche	65,000 entries	Hundreds
Ohio County History Surname Index	Ohio Historical Society	1936, 84	64 microfilms	450,000 entries	166
Oregon Biography Index (also see Washington)	Brandt and Guilford	1976	Book	17,250 names	47
Guide to Genealogical and Historical Research in Penn.	Hoenstine, F. G.	1978–90	3 books	100,000+ entries	3,038
Rhode Island Biograhical and Genealogical Sketch Index	Parker, J. C.	1991	Book	35,000/19,500	214
Dictionary of South Carolina Biography	Côté and Williams	1985	Book	13,300/10,099	52
Biographical Gazetteer of Texas	Morrison Books	1985–87	6 vols.	70,000/50,000	206
[Utah] *Mormons and Their Neighbors*	Wiggins, M. E.	1984	2 vols.	75,000 entries	194
Virginians and West Virginians, 1607–1870	Wardell, P. G.	1986–92	3 vols.	70,000 names	8
Timesaving Aid to Virginia-West Virginia Ancestors	Wardell, P. G.	1985–90	4 vols.	25,000 surnames	407
[Washington] *The Pacific Northwest: An Index*	Drazan, J. G.	1979	Book	1,700 entries (estimated)	83 for Washington
Subject Catalog . . . Library . . . Hist. Soc. of Wisconsin	State Historical Society	1971	23 vols.	45,000 entries	Not known

*The chapter bibliography contains full bibliographic citations for these indexes.

Table 17-3. Manuscript Statewide Indexes to County and Local Histories

Title	*Author/Owner*	*Format*	*Entries*	*Location**
Alabama Biography: An Index	Birmingham Public Library	Not known	22,500	Tutwiler Collection, 2100 Park Pl., Birmingham
Arkansas Biographical Index	University of Arkansas	Cards	7,500	Special Collections, Fayetteville
Connecticut Biography and Portrait Index	Kemp, Thomas J.	Manuscript	250,000	8401 Dell Rio Way No. 187, Tampa, Florida
[Delaware] "Genealogical Surname File"	State Archives	Files	120,000	Hall of Records, Dover
Florida Biography Index	State Library of Florida	Not known	25,000	R. A. Gray Bldg., Tallahassee
[Georgia] *Card Index to Biographical Sketches*	Atlanta Public Library	Cards	Not known	1 Margaret Mitchel Sq., Atlanta
[Hawaii] *Biographical File*	State Archives	Files	Not known	Iolani Palace, Honolulu
Idaho Biographical and Genealogical Sketch Index	Parker, J. C. and J. G.	Manuscript	24,600	2115 North Denair Ave., Turlock, California
Illinois Biographical Sketch	State Historical Library	Cards	135,000	Old State Capitol, Springfield
[Louisiana] *Index of Biographical Sketches*	New Orleans Public Library	Cards	Extensive	219 Loyola Ave., New Orleans
Maine Supplement to Munsell's Index	State Library	Cards	Not known	State House, Augusta
Surname Index to Maine Town Histories	Roderick, Dr. Thomas	Manuscript	14,000	4 Seely Rd, Bar Harbor
[Mississippi] *Biographical Index*	State Dept. Of Arch. and Hist.	Cards	200,000	P.O. Box 571, Jackson
Minnesota Biography Sketch Index	State Historical Society	Not known	100,000	690 Cedar St., St. Paul
Montana Biographical and Genealogical Sketch Index	Parker, J. C. and J. G.	Manuscript	42,000	2115 North Denair Ave., Turlock, California
[New Jersey] *Family Name Index*	State Library	Files	Not known	185 West. State St., Trenton
New York State Biog. . . . Geneal. . . . Index	Pohl, Gunther E.	Card	500,000	24 Waldon Pl., Great Neck
North Dakota Biography Index	State university library	Card	100,000	SU Station, P.O. Box 5599, Fargo
Rhode Island Index	Providence Public Library	Cards	Not known	150 Empire St., Providence
South Dakota Biographical and Genealogical Sketch Index	Parker, J. C. and J. G.	Manuscript	19,900	2115 North Denair Ave., Turlock, California
[Tennessee] *Biography Index*	State Library and Archives	Cards	Not known	403 Seventh Ave. North, Nashville
[Wisconsin] *Biography File*	State Historical Society	Cards	Not known	816 State St., Madison
Wyoming Biographical and Genealogical Sketch Index	Parker, J. C. and J. G.	Manuscript	8,600	2115 North Denair Ave., Turlock, California

* The information given in the "Location" column reflects address information not already given in another column.

states. Twenty-three major statewide unpublished indexes are listed in table 17-3. Between them, these tables identify indexes for forty-three states. For the states for which there is no index to local histories, begin by using the national and regional indexes described above. Each statewide index has a slightly different scope, but they have important similarities. The most important fact to remember is that none of them is an every-name index. The second important limitation is that they seldom index every available history for a state (Indiana is a notable exception).

Statewide indexes, both published and unpublished, are valiant efforts to give better access to county histories and to provide statewide finding aids for researchers. They have many of the same limitations (and others) as the indexes discussed above. The preface, introduction, or instructions are very important and must be read thoroughly; the limitations of each index should be carefully explained in such introductory sections. Some index only county histories (Kentucky, Iowa, Oregon); others may be only a few volumes of a projected but not yet complete set (Iowa, Texas, Virginia). Some index only surnames (New Hampshire, Pennsylvania), while others are limited to histories published before a certain date (California, Colorado, Minnesota). Some include local or town histories (especially those for New England), but the important consideration is the list of sources. Check it to determine whether the county of interest is included and which histories were indexed.

The actual number of sources indexed is not as important as the depth of coverage. Divide the number of names or index entries by the number of sources to determine the average number included from each indexed source. If most of the sources indexed have several hundred pages and the index averages only a few hundred names per source, it is obvious that some names were not included. The *Indiana Biographical Index* is a model index with almost a quarter of a million entries from 537 sources, but even it averages only 460 names per source. Of course, this average is higher than most. The *Ohio County History Surname*

Index may be the most thorough, with an average of 2,711 names per source; however, it indexes only 166 sources, while there were more than two hundred county histories for Ohio before the index's 1936 creation. Today Ohio has at least 298 county histories, not to mention local histories. The averages for Pennsylvania (thirty-three) and Virginia-West Virginia (sixty-one) seem very low, but they are surname indexes and only report the surname once for each volume (and many of Pennsylvania's 3,038 sources are not included in the surname index).

Published statewide indexes are a new phenomenon. Virtually all of the published indexes have appeared since 1977, and 60 percent have appeared since 1982; more are known to be in preparation (see table 17-3). Most research libraries purchase these books, so checking the local catalog will locate many. To learn about new statewide indexes, check with state historical societies and libraries. Their reference staffs should know if and where such indexes are available.

The indexes in table 17-3 are unpublished card, manuscript, or computer indexes that can be searched only in person or by correspondence. A small fee may be charged for a search, but it is well worth it for the breadth of coverage; do not hesitate to write or call the repository or indexer. There are probably many more unpublished indexes and historical/biographical collections in state and local libraries and archives. For most state collections there is some kind of index that includes the local sources within the state. Because most of these indexes only reference biographical sketches, see the discussion of statewide collections and indexes for biographical sources in chapter 18, "Biographies." It includes more detail about some of these indexes and other local collections.

Internal Indexes

Most histories published before 1920 included no index or a very brief and incomplete one. Often the names of the biographical subjects were printed as part of the contents page, but in a significant number of histories even this was not done. It is helpful if the biographical sketches were printed in alphabetical order, but every biographical sketch includes five to twenty or more other surnames that cannot be retrieved without an index. Even when an index appears in these books, it seldom includes every name. Usually only those names are included for which there is substantial material (often at least a paragraph) in the text. Lists of names, such as those of county officers, military servicemen, pastors, etc., are seldom included.

Many county histories have subject indexes (always incomplete) that do not even include the biographical section; this is particularly true when the biographical sketches are arranged alphabetically or when they are in the "directory" format, as was common in Centennial histories (1870 to 1899). The publishers reasoned that with the subjects (biographies) in alphabetical or geographical order, there was no need to index them. Be circumspect with such indexes.

Carefully evaluate the index. For a four hundred-page text, are citations included for pages in the three hundreds or only for those in the one hundreds and two hundreds? If not, this may suggest that the biographical sketches (usually the last section of the text) were not indexed at all. It is also wise to reverse the search process to evaluate the index. Find several names in the text with varying amounts of related information, and then determine how many appear in the index. A thorough test of this nature will quickly illustrate the scope of the index. An important but overlooked part of evaluation is to read the instructions or preface to the index. Often an introductory paragraph explains what type of information was and was not indexed. It will also mention if the numbers in the index are *not* page numbers; sometimes family, section, column, or other numbers are used instead of page numbers. If there is no information to the contrary, the numbers referred to are probably page numbers; however, if a person is not on the page cited, determine if other sections have the same page numbers or if other numbering sequences are used.

Separate Indexes

In recent years, indexes have been separately published for many pre-1920 county histories. These are more comprehensive than the original indexes (otherwise, there would be no need for them). Usually they are every-name indexes and include the given name and surname of every person listed in the book. However, these also must be carefully evaluated as outlined above. The indexer may have chosen not to index a lengthy list of names if it was already in alphabetical order (such as an early tax list printed in the history). Also, the index may only apply to one part of the book, such as the history or biography section. If two or more counties are treated in one book, the index may cover only one county. Usually, the coverage is explained in the preface or introduction to the index; read it completely and carefully.

Separate indexes are usually produced by local genealogical or historical societies in the counties to which the histories pertain. They are published in limited numbers because the demand is small and usually limited to local people and organizations (except for a few large genealogy libraries). Some are created by an individual or a group within the society. Presently, many are produced using computers. In fact, in the mid-1970s one company (the defunct Hamilton Computer Service) produced several such indexes for many major Pennsylvania county histories, as well as for some other areas. Such indexes seem to predominate in the Great Lakes region, where the mug books were so popular; however, they are also available for many counties in other states.

Locating separate indexes can be difficult; determining if one exists is almost as hard. Filby's *American County Histories* identifies many of them. If a research library has them, they are usually listed in the library catalog with or near the histories they index. Most state historical societies and libraries have the separate indexes that exist for counties in their states. They may also have bibliographies listing all relevant indexes that have been published. Of course, members of the local historical or genealogical society in the county to which the history pertains will know if an index is available. If research in a county for an ancestor is going to be more than cursory because of an ancestor's long-term residence there, a letter or telephone call to a local society or library is a good way to learn if such an index is available or in preparation. Perhaps no index has been published, but there is a card index at the local library. Concerted effort to find such indexes saves the time required to thoroughly read a five hundred- to six hundred-page history—but be sure to evaluate the index for comprehensiveness and reliability.

Multi-History Indexes

A similar type of index is the "multi-history" index for a locality. Generally these attempt to index all or several important histories for a city, county, or multi-county area. They usually include four to ten histories, and many are every-name indexes. Others are only "key-name" indexes, including only references to sources in which contain significant information about a person. (The more sources that are indexed, the less comprehensive an index can be because size becomes a limiting factor.) Multi-history indexes are rare but exist for areas such as Trenton, New Jersey, and South Bend, Indiana.

REPRINTS

Related to indexes are reprints of county histories. Although a few reprints were done in the nineteenth and early twentieth centuries, 98 percent of the more than 650 reprints have been done since 1950—90 percent since 1964. Reprinting steadily increased from an average of four per year in the early 1960s to eighteen per year in the early 1970s, to highs of ninety in 1979 and seventy-eight in 1980. Later figures are incomplete, but reprints seem to be on the decline; there were around ten per year in the early 1990s.

Reprinting seems to have been very regional to date. Two-thirds of all reprints are for two regions: the Great Lakes and the Atlantic South. Another 20 percent are for the Mid-Atlantic and the Gulf South. This distribution is logical because these regions have produced the most histories over the years, especially in earlier eras. Because more-recent histories are still available in research libraries, most reprints are of histories published before 1930. At least half of these reprints are from the Centennial and New Century eras. Certain states seem to have been more active than others; eight states have reprinted thirty-two or more histories: Indiana (seventy-five), Ohio (sixty-three), Georgia (fifty), Illinois (forty-eight), Pennsylvania (forty-seven), New York (forty-four), Tennessee (thirty-seven), and Virginia (thirty-two). These states, of course, are some of the most populous historically and are of the greatest interest to many researchers.

Reprints are a boon to researchers for two reasons: First, they make important sources (county histories) more available, allowing every research library in a state and several outside the state or region to purchase major sources of local history at a reasonable cost. Second, most reprints include every-name indexes, making the information in them easier to access. Indexes that were separately published earlier often are reprinted and bound with the history; the same cautions expressed earlier about indexes must be used with these: be sure to determine how comprehensive they are.

Sometimes only part of a history is reprinted because the original may have included two or more counties or a lengthy state history section; the reprint may eliminate other counties or the state history section and might even overlook the local history section, including only the biographical section. Be sure to read the preface to the reprint if one exists. Locating a reprint is much like locating any county or local history and is treated later in this chapter. Filby's *American County Histories* identifies most pre-1984 reprints.

LOCAL HISTORIES

Local histories generally focus on an area smaller than a county. Normally such histories are written about towns, political townships (not surveyors' townships), or cities. Sometimes two or more such divisions may be covered by one local history. (A history that treats several counties, such as those in a particular valley, becomes a regional or multi-county history.)

In New England and the Mid-Atlantic states (New York, Pennsylvania, and New Jersey), *towns* are the equivalent of *townships* in the midwestern and southern states. Commercial centers in an eastern town (whether incorporated or not) are usually called villages or, if large enough, cities. There may be several villages in a town (that is, township) but seldom more than one city. In the Midwest and the South the commercial centers of a township may be called towns, villages, or cities. Western states seldom use townships as governmental subdivisions, reserving them for land descriptions only; thus, local histories of the West invariably focus on a town, village, or city (that is, commercial centers). This discussion uses the terminology common to the locale being discussed; while this might seem confusing at first, the genealogist must become familiar with how different terms are used locally in order to understand the records.

Towns and townships are not large; therefore, such local histories focus on a relatively small group of people. In the Midwest, many political townships were established along surveyors' lines in keeping with the rectangular survey system common to public domain states. This system established the surveyor's township as a square parcel of land six miles on a side, totaling thirty-six square miles. Townships were further divided into thirty-six sections, each being one mile square. During the nineteenth century, the land in each section was usually owned by from four to ten families; thus, each township might have a rural population between 150 and 360 families. The commercial centers added appreciably to the population, but it is easy to see that, in the mid-to late 1800s, a midwestern township might have only around five hundred to eight hundred families or fewer at any given time; several of those families would have been closely related to each other.

In the eastern states (especially in the New England region), towns are seldom larger than their midwestern counterparts (townships). In Massachusetts and Connecticut the average town is less than twenty-five miles square. Only in areas of low population (mountains, state-owned land, etc.) are they appreciably larger than fifty square miles. Because local histories focus on smaller areas and smaller populations than do county histories, they cover a greater portion of the population, making them even more valuable, in many cases, than county histories. Smaller populations make local histories generally shorter than county histories, but they tend to be more detailed nonetheless (Russo 1988, 90–108).

Bibliographies

Unfortunately, no single comprehensive bibliography exists for all local (or town/township) histories, as one does for county histories (Filby's *American County Histories*); therefore, it is not possible to give detailed statistics and groupings for local histories as this chapter has done for county histories. The lack of such a nationwide local history bibliography is due to several factors. Primarily it is because there is no national organization to chair such an extensive and expensive project. Also, each person has a different idea of what a local history is. Should periodical articles be included and, if so, only scholarly ones or popular magazine articles as well? What about unpublished theses and dissertations? (Sometimes they are the only good histories available.) When is a work history and when is it genealogy? Can it be both?

In the 1980s, uniform bibliographies were completed for the six New England states—the first time such an effort had been made for an entire region. This project (the Committee for a New England Bibliography) also compiled two final volumes: an addenda or update to its previous state bibliographies and a general bibliography of the New England region (4,212 entries relevant to more than one state). The direct cost of this project was more than $850,000, not including volunteer time, donated/shared overhead, etc. The project took more than twenty years, and the first book (Massachusetts) appeared in 1976—thus the need for an update volume (with 11,742 new entries) that was published in 1989. The six states have yielded 57,375 separate bibliographic citations to works of history on the various states (Parks 1986, xvii). Naturally, not all of these entries were for local history citations, but for Connecticut, an average state, 77 percent of the nearly ten thousand entries are "for cities and towns," which is the bibliography's major arrangement. Further update volumes are planned.

While the above discussion illustrates both the scope and the problems of creating bibliographies of history for any given state, it must be noted that bibliographies of varying size, quality, and scope exist for almost every state. These are listed in the bibliography at the end of this chapter.

Local Histories in the Library of Congress. Edited by Marion J. Kaminkow, *Local Histories in the Library of Congress: A Bibliography* was published in five volumes (Baltimore: Magna Carta Book Co.) in 1975. This national bibliography is available in most research (academic and genealogy) and large public libraries. It is a good place to start, but it is far from complete. It includes almost seventy thousand local, county, and state history books for all fifty states. This number, however, is perhaps only one-fifth or less of all local histories written because it only includes books (not articles) deposited at the Library of Congress; this limits its coverage of locally produced history pamphlets printed in small numbers, as well as institutional and church histories. For Connecticut, for example, there are just over 1,300 entries in the Kaminkow set, while the Connecticut volume from the Committee for a New England Bibliography has 9,778 entries for the same state.

Value and Use

Local histories are very important and exist in great numbers, but they are often overlooked by genealogists simply because local research libraries do not list these records in their catalogs (this is true even of major research libraries, such as the Newberry Library, New York Public Library, and the Family History Library). It is important to seek these histories and search them. The final sections of this chapter discuss how to locate these histories.

Much of the discussion of county histories applies to local histories as well; their scope, authorship, reliability, and other characteristics are similar. Most local histories have been written by local community members who have some interest, background, or training in history. Many are not scholarly works, but this does not make them inaccurate. Authors usually researched their topics in old town meeting books, local newspapers, and diaries and other family records and interviewed the older local population. Local families are often the focal points of these histories; they may be treated in greater depth than in county histories. A key difference, however, is that few local histories were produced like the mug books of the 1880-to-1914 period; that is, few of them are subscription books created by a commercial publisher for profit. Rather, they are the products of countless hours of research and writing by a person devoted to his or her town or township.

With the exception of the lack of "subscription" publication, local histories, in their form and content, follow (to a degree) the form and content of the county histories being published in the same areas. The vast numbers of local histories published (perhaps 300,000) means that there is much greater variety in their structure and content than can be discussed here. It is not incorrect, however, to think of most of them as scaled-down versions of the basic county history types.

Like their "big brothers" (county histories), local histories are heavily focused on people and often include lists, such as early pioneers, taxpayers, those who served in the military, first marriages, and early censuses. A local history is usually presented chronologically with a state or county overview (very brief, if at all) at the beginning. Separate sections or chapters may be devoted to churches and religion, commerce, town meetings and votes, professionals, military events, court cases, etc. The first landowners or settlers are often prominent in the first chapters. Many local histories (but by no means all) include a biographical section, but this usually focuses on families (like southern county histories) rather than on individuals. Some later histories were sponsored or in part written by local groups or committees, but most are the product of a single person. Among the multitude of local histories, two distinct types possess enough similarities within each type and are different enough from the others to be discussed separately: the New England model and the modern local history booklet.

New England Model

Local history writing began to a great extent in New England in the mid-1800s. Many New England towns have provided us with unique local histories that have special interest to genealogists. Some, but not most, histories of New England towns include a lengthy and often fairly comprehensive genealogical section in which the lineages of most residents of the town are given, in family groups, back to the first person of that surname to settle in the town (Russo 1988, 51). These sections are formatted like the published genealogies of towns or families (see chapter 16), in which the first person of a surname is numbered 1 and his descendants each have a number and brief vital information, such as birth, marriage, and death dates. Such sections may replace or enhance the biographical sections of these books.

The sizes of such genealogy sections vary widely. Many New England local histories have five hundred to nine hundred or more pages. The genealogical section may be less than one-third or more than two-thirds of the book, but it always makes up a substantial portion. Generally only the earliest generations are treated; many only track the families down to the revolutionary war or early 1800s, even if the book was published one hundred years later. The information was compiled from many places, notably the town records; these sources were usually supplemented by family records or recourse to the published genealogies of those families (when they existed). Therefore, these sections are very much compiled sources with secondary information for which the genealogist should seek further proof. They seldom include source references or citations, and it is often impossible to locate the sources of statements in these genealogical sections; however, they often contain genealogical information available in no other source and have proved to be generally reliable. The authors were usually very competent local people who knew the families well. Local histories seldom include laudatory comments, nor do they trace the lineages back to prominent ancestors (such as a *Mayflower* passenger); thus, there is little cause or opportunity for including or perpetuating unfounded family traditions.

Because they only treat the family members who lived in the town, the genealogies may be very brief and cover only two generations of a family, or they may cover five or six generations (from the first settler to the publication date) on several pages. Figure 17-18, from the *History of Cornish, New Hampshire*, illustrates such a section.

Such genealogical sections appear in New England histories published at all dates, even very recently, but most seem to have been published between 1840 and 1910. They all represent only a part of a town's history; one must carefully review the history chapters as well. The history portion is arranged much like any other town history. The genealogical sections, however, seem to be almost exclusively in New England town histories; a very few can be found elsewhere (Russo 1988, 87, 94, 99). It must also be stressed that many New England histories lack genealogy sections for numerous reasons (too brief a history or previous publication of genealogical information among them); however, even those histories are valuable tools. Town histories with genealogical sections are available for about one-quarter of the older towns in New England; therefore, once an ancestor's town of residence has been established, these should be among the first sources consulted.

148 HISTORY OF CORNISH.

2. NEWELL J.[2] ELLIS (*Seneca*[1]) b. in Brandon, Vt., Sept. 5, 1840; m. first, Feb. 18, 1864, Sarah Medora Boardman of Cornish, dau. of Dr. Elijah and Martha Ann (Huggins) Boardman, b. June 21, 1844; d. Jan. 10, 1892; m. second, June 20, 1893, Adaline Hunt, dau. of Dr. Hunt of Bolton. Mr. Ellis enlisted in the 7th Vt. Regt. and served one year in the Civil War. (See Military.) Has since res. in Cornish. A farmer. He d. Aug. 10, 1905. Children, all by first marriage and b. in Cornish:

i. MARTHA E., b. April —, 1868; m. ——, Daniel Johnston of Mansfield, Mass., where they res. He is a manufacturer of hats.
ii. CHARLES B., b. March 9, 1872. Res. in Mansfield, Mass. A pressman in the hat business.
iii. MABEL M., b. Aug. 26, 1883; m. Aug. 23, 1902, Archie H. Deane, b. in Ia. Res. in Mansfield, Mass.

FAIRBANKS.

The Fairbanks are of English origin. The genealogist of the family has traced most of this numerous family to one parent stock, Jonathan Fairbanks, who was b. in the latter part of the 16th century and came to Boston in 1633. After three years he settled in Dedham, where he spent the remainder of his life. The house he then built is still standing, having been in the family ever since. The Mass. D. A. R. have recently kindly assumed its preservation, with all the ancient furniture and relics identified with its history.

1. ABEL FAIRBANKS of the sixth generation from Jonathan, b. in Plainfield, Conn., May 12, 1754; after living a few years in Brimfield, Mass., and Sharon, Vt., came to Cornish in 1788 or 1789 and spent about forty years of his life, and d. in Fairfield, Vt., March 27, 1842, aged 87. He was a farmer and carpenter, of steady and industrious habits and member of the Congregational Church. He had been a soldier in the Revolutionary War. He m. Sept. 25, 1777, Hannah Hobbs, dau. of Benjamin and Elizabeth (Flint) Hobbs. She d. April 9, 1840. Children:

i. CHESTER, b. March 11, 1778; d. Nov. 15, 1803.
ii. JOSEPH, b. April 19, 1779, in Brimfield, Mass. Came to Cornish with his father, living for a time there; rem. to Sheldon, Vt., where he m. June 11, 1804, Abigail Smith. Had seven children.
iii. BENJAMIN, b. March 9, 1781, in Brimfield, and d. in Fairfield, Vt., Feb. 28, 1856; m. Laura Fuller; had eight children.
iv. ABEL, b. Nov. 22, 1782; m. Betsey Rice; no children. Was a cooper by trade; d. in Fairfield, Vt., March 16, 1866.
2. v. RUFUS, b. June 18, 1785.
3. vi. HARVEY, b. Oct. 1, 1787.
vii. ZABAD, b. June 5, 1790, in Cornish. Was a graduate of Dartmouth College in class of 1810. Practiced medicine in Claremont many years; a railroad contractor, building the railroad from Schenectady to Ballston Spa. He was a man of commanding presence, of remarkable muscular development and also a man

Figure 17-18. Genealogy section from 1910 *History of the Town of Cornish, New Hampshire* (reprint; Spartanburg, S.C.: Reprint Co., 1975).

Modern Local History Booklets

Since the 1970s, and especially around the time of the bicentennial in 1976, many towns published small booklets about their history. Typically, these booklets were sponsored by town councils or local historical groups. They bear a slim resemblance to town histories published in earlier years and to various county histories. Of the different types of county histories, these town booklets most closely resemble the scrapbook histories of the modern era.

The typical modern local history booklet is a brief overview of the recent history of a town (usually a small town). Generally they are full size (8½ by 11 inches) with paper covers, between fifty and one hundred pages in length, and are perfect (staple) bound. Their pages often contain as many illustrations as text. They seldom contain biographical or family sections, but a very few key families may be noted as early settlers. Some of the topics usually included are churches, stores, early settlements, historic buildings, and major events. Interesting historical articles or stories from earlier town or county histories may appear as well. Figure 17-19 is an example from Lenora Koelbel's *Missoula the Way It Was, a Portrait of an Early Western Town* (Missoula, Mont.: Pictorial Histories Publishing Co., 1972).

Such publications may not be ideal for the family history researcher, but they cannot be dismissed because such a history

In 1889 Montana became a state which made it necessary for a new constitution to be written for Montana. Delegates to the constitutional convention met in Helena during July and August of 1889. As in any political venture, not everybody was pleased with the progress of the convention. *The Missoulian* wrote on July 17, 1889, that the convention seemed to be as busy as it could be doing nothing – "it adjourns regularly every day about breakfast time." The action taken by the convention in which Missoula had a part was in the decision of where the temporary state capital would be located until the question could be decided by the voters of the state in 1892. It was generally thought that Helena would remain the capital but when the question came up many of the Helena backers were away. Joe Marion, an early sheriff who lived in Frenchtown, proposed to the convention that Missoula be made the temporary capital. The delegates present voted forty-four to twenty-seven in favor of his proposal. At this point the remaining Helena backers called for a recess. According to the August 9th, 1923, edition of the *Kalispell Times,* the rest of the story goes as follows: William Muth, a Helena backer, was so sure his city would remain the capital that he went on a vacation to Yellowstone National Park. After he left, the Missoula backers were able to make Missoula the temporary capital. The Helena backers, after gaining the recess, quickly wired Mr. Muth who made a "wild night horseback ride forty-five miles to the railroad station where a special train was waiting for him." His return to Helena was followed by a successful effort to reconsider the Missoula vote. With Muth's vote the motion to reconsider Missoula as temporary state capital was passed by one vote. When the delegates voted a second time on the location of the temporary capital, Helena emerged the winner.

The Higgins Block with the Higgins bank on the corner of Main and Higgins was constructed in 1889 by C. P. Higgins. He wasn't able to see his project completed as he died before the buildings were finished. (Courtesy of F. F. Fowler and Ed Erlandson)

Figure 17-19. From Koelbel's *Missoula the Way It Was,* a modern local history booklet.

might be the only one ever printed for a particular town. It might note who settled the town and when, if records were destroyed, and other important facts. They also demonstrate that some people in the town are interested in history; correspondence with such persons often opens new doors. While the Stephenstown booklet noted above did not include the Spencer family, which had lived there, it led the researcher to the town historian's other records, including very helpful cemetery transcripts not available elsewhere.

Although some local history booklets focus more on events and things (autos, buildings, bridges, etc.) than on people, no history can completely ignore people, and one of those included may be the ancestor being sought. Such publications are seldom well indexed, but they are not too lengthy for a thorough reading, which will provide an introduction to local history. Some scholars refer to these as "scissors-and-tape" or "kitchen-table" publications, refusing even to call them histories. While these appellations may reflect the production process fairly accurately, a researcher should be more concerned with accessing the information, not with the format it appears in or the number of (or lack of) footnotes. Local history booklets can be hard to locate because they are too recent for many bibliographies and are printed in small numbers. Check with local historians or historical societies to learn if one exists for a town of interest. A state library should have copies of the histories published in that state.

It cannot be stressed too strongly that many forms of local history have been published over the last few years, and not all of them are of the modern local history booklet variety. These are described here because they are different from most others and because researchers need to be aware of their existence and their content.

Many other detailed and sometimes scholarly histories continue to be written about towns, townships, villages, and cities. They have many kinds of formats and approaches with varying types of content. It is not possible to classify, describe, or evaluate the many different towns and people they profile. Each one can contribute to the successful search for an inhabitant's background and ancestry.

Indexes

Local histories are not as well indexed as county histories, either on an individual or group basis. Most of the comments made about indexes in the county history section of this chapter are applicable here and need not be repeated. The statewide indexes listed in tables 17-2 and 17-3 include a few local histories. No statewide index can include every local history, so carefully read the introductions to these various indexes to fully understand the scope of each one; however, the unpublished card indexes (such as those for Connecticut, New Jersey, and New York) tend to include many local histories. Compare the number of sources indexed to the number of county histories published to determine if many local histories may have been included. Of the published statewide indexes, the most helpful for local histories seem to be those for Indiana, Michigan, Minnesota, Nevada, New Hampshire, Pennsylvania, and Utah; again, however, none is comprehensive.

Many older local histories, especially those of the New England model, have been partially indexed in some of the standard genealogical indexes. The following are described in greater detail in chapter 16, "Family Histories and Genealogies," but some brief comments are in order here. *Index to American Genealogies* (Munsell's index—cited earlier) includes surname references to hundreds of eastern (mostly New England) town histories published before 1908. Surnames are referenced in these histories when an article or genealogy about them is available in the book. The *Genealogical Index of the Newberry Library* (cited earlier) is similar but larger, and its focus is the Midwest. County histories are among the chief sources of its entries, but local histories are also included. Again, it is not an every-name index; rather, it includes only those families for which there are specific sketches. It does not include any books published after 1917.

The *Old Surname Index File* of the Family History Library (cited earlier) is a card index to numerous family and local history sources. Fremont Rider's *American Genealogical-Biographical Index,* vols. 1–188+ (Middletown, Conn.: Godfrey Memorial Library, 1952–) (see the discussion in chapter 16) focuses mostly on family histories but also includes some local histories (primarily New England). Its major benefit is that it is an every-name index.

Unfortunately, these statewide indexes and genealogical indexes include only a relatively few of the many thousands of local histories available to researchers. Because the individual books themselves are poorly indexed (if at all), one must be very careful in using them. The best way to use them successfully is to carefully search and evaluate each.

USING COUNTY AND LOCAL HISTORIES

With a clear understanding of how county and local histories were compiled, how the content varied, and what to expect in a history, one has only to use them correctly to enjoy much more success in research. To assist the researcher in using these histories, the rest of this chapter discusses the finding aids needed to learn if a history exists, where to locate the history once a title is known, and some general concepts about evaluating the information in a history.

Finding Aids

Numerous sources are available to help the researcher learn what county and local histories will be of interest for a particular family or locality. Three major sources were discussed earlier in this chapter: Filby's *Bibliography of American County Histories,* Kaminkow's *Local Histories in the Library of Congress,* and Meyerink's *Genealogical Publications*. The first two bibliographies are available in virtually every library, and all are excellent starting points. However, one must turn to more detailed sources to pursue comprehensive research.

After these major sources have been consulted, search local or state bibliographies and similar finding aids to learn what histories exist for a county or town. A bibliography is simply a list of books on a particular subject. It may be comprehensive or selective, limited to certain years, and, perhaps, annotated (meaning that a brief note follows the citation). Articles, dissertations, and theses may be included or excluded. The topic may be narrow (histories of the Wyoming Valley after 1900) or broad (U.S. local histories in the Library of Congress). For more information on the use and value of bibliographies, see chapter 5, "Bibliographies and Catalogs." The bibliography of this chapter includes a list of statewide bibliographies of histories.

Published catalogs from major research libraries as well as other sources are discussed in chapter 16, "Family Histories and Genealogies." Of particular value for local histories are the Family History Library's *Family History Library Catalog*™ and the eighteen-volume *Dictionary Catalog of the Local History and Genealogy Division* (of the New York Public Library), 18 vols. (Boston: G. K. Hall, 1974). Although the latter was published in 1974, annual updates are available from the same publisher as *Bibliographic Guide to North American History*. Recently published histories of particular interest to genealogists (including reprints of older histories) are often listed in *Genealogical and Local History Books in Print,* edited by Marian Hoffman, 5th ed. (Baltimore: Genealogical Publishing Co., 1996–97), which is updated every two to four years.

America: History and Life. An excellent source for publications since 1964 is *America: History and Life, a Guide to Periodical Literature* (Santa Barbara, Calif.: ABC-Clio, annual). This publication is recognized as the premier index and bibliography of periodical literature dealing with Canadian and U.S. history, including many genealogical journals. However, it is not just an index, nor is it limited to identifying periodical literature; rather, it seeks to abstract new books, dissertations, and major articles published about U.S. and Canadian history. Each volume includes approximately eight thousand abstracts and citations to articles in more than two thousand journals published worldwide. It also cites book reviews from more than one hundred major journals. These review citations make *America: History and Life* effectively a bibliography of new history books. Each quarterly issue arranges the periodical abstracts and the dissertation and review citations under all appropriate subject headings. A fifth issue is the annual index, which provides subject, author, title, and reviewer access to the entries published that year, making it the most comprehensive tool available for accessing current historical literature. *America: History and Life* is available at major academic research libraries in book and CD-ROM formats. It is also available online as part of CompuServe. The electronic formats identify 115,000 journal articles, seventy thousand reviews, and twenty-five thousand dissertations published since 1982.

Writings on American History. A comprehensive bibliography of history books published from 1902 to 1973, as well as selected articles, is *Writings on American History* (Washington, D.C.: Government Printing Office and American History Association, annual). Issued each year (except from 1904 to

1905 and 1941 to 1947), this bibliography originally identified all books and articles dealing with the history of the United States and British North America; beginning in 1936 it omitted Canadian and Latin American publications. Each volume is arranged by classification, with author, title, and subject indexes. The years 1962 to 1973 are published in two sets: four volumes covering articles and ten volumes covering books and monographs. Beginning in 1973 the series focused only on journal articles, and it ended with the 1989–90 volume. It is arranged by subject (including states). The lack of a detailed index means that careful searching is required, but this bibliography can be very helpful. An index for the early volumes is *Index to Writings on American History, 1902–1940* (Washington, D.C.: American History Association, 1956).

Bibliographer's Manual. Many local histories were published in the nineteenth century, especially in the northeastern states. The best listing of these works is Thomas L. Bradford's *Bibliographer's Manual of American History* (Philadelphia: Stan V. Henkels & Co., 1907). This source lists some six thousand state, county, and town histories published through 1903 and identifies virtually all local and state histories. Although mostly superseded by *Local Histories in the Library of Congress*, this five-volume set may still help to locate obscure titles not found in many libraries. It is especially helpful for early town histories, as no other applicable bibliography exists. The first four volumes are arranged alphabetically by author, while vol. 5 provides subject and locality access.

The best sources are statewide bibliographies of histories. They are more focused than national sources and typically include many items of strictly local interest that were produced in limited numbers. The chapter bibliography identifies at least one local history bibliography for most states (unfortunately, many are very dated or incomplete). When statewide sources are lacking, use regional, local, or national bibliographies. Brief bibliographies often appear at the ends of books and articles, so be sure to carefully go through those sections of other histories. Another excellent source to learn what county and local histories exist is the state library or historical society. Every state has one or both such institutions. By the very nature of their collections, they include most local histories for their state. Their staffs will also know of statewide bibliographies and updates to older bibliographies.

Locating Histories

After the existence of books and articles of interest has been determined, one must locate and obtain them. It can be as difficult to locate a history as it is to find information in it. However, several sources can lead to the locations of published histories.

Most people begin with the catalog at the local research library. It lists the histories available at that institution and available through its branches or any network that it may belong to. One can search under the name of the county or town in the subject catalog to see if the library has any books of interest; this can be a good way to begin because it allows one to access and search the book fairly quickly. However, the results of such a search can be incomplete because the researcher is relying on the book to have been cataloged completely so that it can be found by locality, and this may not be the case in many libraries. Books are cataloged most thoroughly and completely by what librarians call the *main entry,* which is usually the author, or, lacking an author, the work's title. Most researchers do not know the name of a local history's author, however, or the history's title, or even if a local history exists for a particular county or town, making it difficult to search by author or title.

While some histories will be found in a local research library, others will not. Several options are available for locating and using histories not in a local library. The first place to look is in other nearby research libraries, such as university or state libraries. If these libraries do not have the source, ask the local public library to try to obtain it through interlibrary loan. (Most public and academic libraries participate in interlibrary loan.) While genealogy (family history) books seldom circulate on interlibrary loan, most histories do. For more information on interlibrary loan, see the introduction to *Printed Sources*.

County and local histories can usually be found in the libraries of the area to which they pertain. Public libraries and local historical societies are good places to search for histories of their areas. State libraries (usually in the state capital) try to collect everything published about their states, so they are likely to have the most histories.

Most research libraries lack good collections of histories for areas outside their regions. Notable exceptions are the New York Public Library, the Library of Congress, the Allen County Public Library, the Newberry Library, and the Family History Library. Any of these might have an elusive history that cannot be found elsewhere. Often, a bibliography citing a history notes which libraries have it or indicates, in the introduction, where the histories can be found.

Rental libraries in some areas collect the histories of particular states or regions. For a fee, these libraries will mail a copy of any of their books. Local libraries and historical and genealogical societies usually are aware of rental libraries. A fine example is the Hoenstine Rental Library (Hollidaysburg, Pennsylvania), which has more than three thousand books on Pennsylvania families and histories. The New England Historic Genealogical Society (Boston) offers to its members a circulation library (by mail) of approximately twenty thousand titles. (Rental libraries are also discussed in the introduction to this book and are listed in appendix C.)

An excellent source for histories is the LDS Family History Library in Salt Lake City. Not only is its collection one of the largest, but most histories are available on microfilm through the library's more than 2,500 family history centers (branch libraries) located throughout the world. Most medium and large cities have LDS family history centers.

Microform Copies. More and more histories are being reproduced on microfilm and microfiche, making it possible for many other libraries to obtain copies. Researchers can also buy them at relatively low cost. Many titles are listed in *Guide to Microforms in Print* (Westport, Conn.: Microform Review, annual), which is available at most public libraries. Three major commercial firms specialize in microform copies of histories. Research Publications, 12 Lunar Drive, Woodbridge, CT 06525, has published nearly all pre-1907 county histories for California, Illinois, Indiana, Michigan, New York, Ohio, Pennsylvania, and Wisconsin. The Cox Library from Americana Unlimited (P.O. Box 50447, Tucson, AZ 85703) includes 1,979 titles (1,323 are county histories) on 615 reels of microfilm. Thirty-five states are represented in the collection; the Great Lakes and Mid-Atlantic regions are the most thoroughly represented.

The largest and most ambitious collection of microform histories is available from University Microfilms International (UMI), 300 North Zeeb Road, Ann Arbor, MI 48106. One of UMI's major sets is the Genealogy and Local History Series. This ongoing program assembles and preserves on microfiche documents of genealogical and historical value. Many research libraries have purchased all or part of this collection. Careful use of it will greatly aid research. These titles are reproduced and sold initially in sections, called parts, to academic libraries and other institutions. The titles are identified through a guide (booklet) to each part. After ten parts have been produced and distributed, UMI publishes a cumulative guide for those parts: the *UMI Guide to Family and Local Histories: A Microfiche Program,* 3 vols. (Ann Arbor, Mich.: University Microfilms International, 1990, 1993, 1995).

In 1990, the guide to the first ten parts included almost 3,400 local histories. In 1993, vol. 2 of the guide (to parts 11 through 20) added almost 2,800 histories. Vol. 3, issued in 1995, lists almost three thousand more local histories. Individual titles can be purchased through these guides. The three volumes list more than sixteen thousand titles, including 9,157 local history titles (coded LH). These are valuable local history sources; many of them are town or church histories (booklets) published fifty to one hundred or more years ago. Major county histories are also included. At this writing, coverage includes the Shenandoah Valley (especially North Carolina), Alabama, Connecticut, Georgia, Illinois, Indiana, Iowa, Kentucky, Maine, Massachusetts, Michigan, Mississippi, New Hampshire, New Jersey, New York, Ohio, Pennsylvania, Rhode Island, South Carolina, Vermont, and Wisconsin.

Each volume has separate geographic and name (mostly surname) indexes. If a research library has this collection, use the indexes (especially the geographic indexes) in the appropriate volumes to locate titles of interest. Once a particular book's title or author is known, search the appropriate indexes to determine if it is in the collection, then obtain that microfiche from the library's collection. The surname indexes also can be helpful for determining if a book has been published about a particular family.

UMI also has several other important research collections on microfilm, including almost every dissertation and thesis completed at U.S. universities and many nineteenth-century genealogies on microfilm.

A public librarian can suggest other ways to obtain these and other sources needed for research. Also see the introduction to this book for additional suggestions.

Evaluating Histories

This chapter has provided many suggestions for evaluating and locating county and local histories. Here a few additional comments are needed, and some previous comments bear repeating. First, keep in mind that most histories will not answer all questions, but a careful reading will always yield more information than will a brief check of the index.

Before searching for an ancestor's name in a history, the careful researcher thoroughly examines the book. Read the entire title page, including its back side. Look for a subtitle that describes the book. Determine the author and his or her qualifications. Degrees, memberships, and other distinctions will be listed below the author's name. (These should not be the only factors on which the author is judged, but they can be helpful.) Is the publisher familiar (Munsell, Lewis, etc.)? (Again, the publisher's name does not prove quality but it is part of the total evaluation.) Where was the work published? A local publisher may have paid more attention to local facts. A more-distant publisher suggests that the work is a mug book or scrapbook history. For recent books, look for Library of Congress catalog information. Lack of it suggests that the history is a locally produced volume of limited circulation. Some books indicate the number of copies printed; this is a clue about the size of the readership that the author/publisher had in mind. The publication or copyright date is essential. An ancestor who moved into the county after the book was published won't be in it, though the history may still be valuable for other relatives or background information.

Most important is to read every word of every introductory page, including the contents, preface, acknowledgments, foreword, introduction, prologue, and any other sections. These provide information about how the book was compiled, what the purpose in creating it was, who contributed, and what their qualifications were.

After getting acquainted with the book, turn to the table of contents. Choose a familiar subject (perhaps military history, a specific religious denomination or ethnic group, lawyers, etc.) and read that section. Evaluate how the author treats the topic. Is it evenhanded or one-sided (positive or negative)? This provides clues as to how other topics are handled. Realize, however, that the authors came "to praise Caesar, not to bury him" (to modify Shakespeare); they generally portray people and events in a positive manner. Be especially wary if a negative treatment is encountered.

When evaluating biographical sketches, remember that their subjects were usually the providers of the information contained in them. Therefore, sketches are usually quite accurate for the subject's immediate family, but the further back in time the information goes, the less likely it is to be correct. Always remember that biographical sketches are compiled works containing secondary information, which means that some editorial discretion has been used and some conclusions drawn from the original records; these may not be the same conclusions that another researcher would have made. Also, of course, they are printed works; typographical errors will exist. If all other records give an ancestor's middle initial as *W* and a historical sketch gives *M,* the initial probably was actually *W.*

Always search other available histories of an area, even after the information sought has been found; each work will include different subjects. Even if more than one book for a location is a subscription history, different subscribers will be included in each. Even if the same major events are related in two histories, there can be differences. Comparing such stories can reveal much about how histories were compiled and if they are biased. Indeed, as Archibald Hanna concludes,

> . . . the lowly "mug books" have their uses, and . . . much curious and rewarding information may be found therein. They are too big for bedside books, but I recommend an occasional hour of browsing on a drowsy afternoon (1971, 298).

NOTES

1. Virtually all U.S. theses and dissertations can be obtained in print or on microfilm from University Microfilms International, 300 North Zeeb Road, Ann Arbor, MI 48106.

REFERENCE LIST

Carothers, Diane Foxhill. 1985. "A Perspective View of County Histories." *Genealogical Journal* 14 (1) (Spring 1985).

Chapman, Charles. 1878. *History of Knox County, Illinois*. Chicago: Blakely, Brown and Marsh.

Church, Harry, and Katharyn Joella Chapell. 1914. *History of Buchanan County and Its People*. Chicago: S. J. Clarke Publishing Co.

Falge, Louis, ed. 1911–12. *History of Manitowoc County, Wisconsin*. 2 vols. Chicago: Goodspeed Historical Association. Reprint. Manitowoc, Wis.: Manitowoc County Genealogical Society, 1976–79.

Filby, P. William. 1985. *A Bibliography of American County Histories*. Baltimore: Genealogical Publishing Co.

Flagg, Charles A. 1915. *An Index of Pioneers from Massachusetts to the West, Especially the State of Michigan*. Salem, Mass.: Salem Press.

Hanna, Archibald, Jr. 1971. "Every Man his Own Biographer." *Proceedings of the American Antiquarian Society* 80 (2).

The History of Winnebago County, Illinois. 1877. Chicago: Kett and Co.

Jones, Pomroy. 1851. *Annals and Recollections of Oneida (N.Y.) County*. Rome, N.Y.: the author.

Norton, H. Banning. 1862. *A History of Knox County, Ohio*. Columbus, Ohio: R. Nevins.

Norton, Patty Virginia, and Layton R. Sutton. 1983. *Indian Territory and Carter County, Oklahoma, Pioneers. . . .* Dallas, Tex.: Taylor Publishing Co.

Parks, Roger, ed. 1986. *Connecticut: A Bibliography of Its History*. Hanover, N.H.: University Press of New England.

Richards, Randolph A., ed. 1977. *History of Monroe County, Wisconsin*. Chicago: C. F. Cooper & Co., 1912. Reprint. Evansville, Ind.: Unigraphic.

Russo, David J. 1988. *Keepers of Our Past: Local Historical Writing in the United States, 1820s–1930s*. Westport, Conn.: Greenwood Press.

Tate, Luke E. 1935. *History of Pickens County (Georgia)*. Atlanta: W. W. Brown.

Turner, J. Kelly, and J. L. Brigers, Jr. 1920. *History of Edgecombe County, North Carolina*. Raleigh, N.C.: Edwards & Broughton Co.

Yowell, Claude Lindsay. 1926. *A History of Madison County, Virginia*. Strasburg, Va.: Shenandoah Publishing.

BIBLIOGRAPHY

This bibliography contains most major national bibliographies for local histories. The state section includes one or two sources for all states except Alabama, the District of Columbia, Hawaii, Utah, and Wyoming (for which such bibliographies do not exist). Most of the state bibliographies listed are incomplete, but they are the best published to date. Others are broader than the field of history because specifically historical bibliographies are not available for those states. Many are dated, and additional efforts will be necessary to locate more recent titles.

National Bibliographies

America: History and Life, a Guide to Periodical Literature. Santa Barbara, Calif.: ABC-Clio, 1964–. Annual.

Bibliographic Guide to North American History. Boston: G. K. Hall, 1977–. Annual.

Bradford, Thomas Lindsley. *The Bibliographer's Manual of American History*. Philadelphia: Stan V. Henkels & Co., 1907.

Filby, P. William. *American and British Genealogy and Heraldry: A Selected List of Books*. 3rd ed. Boston: New England Historic Genealogical Society, 1983. Supplement, 1987.

_____. *A Bibliography of American County Histories*. Baltimore: Genealogical Publishing Co., 1985.

Hoffman, Marian. *Genealogical and Local History Books in Print*. 5th ed. 4 vols. Baltimore: Genealogical Publishing Co., 1996–97.

Kaminkow, Marion J. *Local Histories in the Library of Congress: A Bibliography*. 5 vols. Baltimore: Magna Charta Book Co., 1975.

Kuehl, Warren F. *Dissertations in History, 1970–1980*. Santa Barbara, Calif.: ABC Clio Information Services, 1980.

Meyerink, Kory L. *Genealogical Publications: A List of 50,000 Sources from the Library of Congress*. CD-ROM. Salt Lake City: Ancestry, 1997.

New York Public Library. *Dictionary Catalog of the Local History and Genealogy Division*. 18 vols. Boston: G. K. Hall, 1974.

Peterson, Clarence Stewart. *Consolidated Bibliography of County Histories in Fifty States in 1961*. 2nd ed. Baltimore: Genealogical Publishing Co., 1963.

UMI Guide to Family and Local Histories: A Microfiche Program. 3 vols. Ann Arbor, Mich.: University Microfilms International, 1990, 1993, 1995.

Writings on American History. Washington, D.C.: Government Printing Office and American Historical Association, 1903–72. Annual, 1903–40 and 1948–61. Includes books and periodical articles.

Writings on American History: A Subject Bibliography of Articles, 1962–1973. Millwood, N.Y.: Kraus-Thomson Organization Ltd., 1974–. Annual through 1990.

Writings on American History: A Subject Bibliography of Books and Monographs, 1962–73. White Plains, N.Y.: Kraus International Publishers, 1985. Also see the *Index to Writings on American History, 1902–1940* (Washington, D.C.: American Hist. Association, 1956).

Young, Arthur P. *Cities and Towns in American History: A Bibliography of Doctoral Dissertations*. Westport, Conn.: Greenwood Press, 1989.

State Bibliographies

For statewide histories, see the bibliography of chapter 18. (Many of the statewide biographical sources listed there are also state histories.)

Alaska

Ricks, Melvin Byron. *Melvin Ricks' Alaska Bibliography: An Introductory Guide to Alaskan Historical Literature*. Portland, Oreg.: Binforn & Mort for the Alaska Historical Commission, 1977.

Arizona

Powell, Donald M. *Arizona Gathering II: An Annotated Bibliography, 1950–69.* Tucson: University of Arizona Press, 1973.

Arkansas

Clark, Georgia H., and Bruce R. Parham. *Arkansas County and Local Histories: A Bibliography.* Fayetteville: Mullins Library of the University of Arkansas, 1976.

California

California Local History: A Bibliography and Union List of Library Holdings. 2nd ed. Stanford, Calif.: Stanford University Press, 1970. Supplement (covering 1961 to 1970), 1976.

Colorado

Wynar, Bohdan S., and Roberta J. Depp, eds. *Colorado Bibliography.* Littleton, Colo.: Libraries Unlimited, 1980.

Connecticut

Kemp, Thomas J. *Connecticut Researcher's Handbook.* Detroit: Gale Research Co., 1981.

Parks, Roger, ed. *Connecticut: A Bibliography of Its History.* Hanover, N.H.: University Press of New England, 1986.

Delaware

Hugh M. Morris Library, Reference Dept. *Bibliography of Delaware, 1960–1974.* Newark: University of Delaware, 1976.

Reed, Henry Clay, and Marion Bjhomason Reed, comps. *A Bibliography of Delaware through 1960.* Newark: University of Delaware Press for the Institute of Delaware History and Culture, 1966.

Florida

Bodziony, Gill Todd. *Genealogy and Local History: A Bibliography.* Rev. ed. Tallahassee: State Library of Florida, 1978.

Harris, Michael H., comp. *Florida History: A Bibliography.* Metuchen, N.J.: Scarecrow Press, 1972.

Georgia

Dorsey, James E. *Georgia Genealogy and Local History: A Bibliography.* Spartanburg, S.C.: Reprint Co., 1983.

Simpson, John Eddins. *Georgia History: A Bibliography.* Metuchen, N.J.: Scarecrow Press, 1976.

Idaho

Nelson, Milo G., and Charles A. Webbert. *Idaho Local History: A Bibliography With a Checklist of Library Holdings.* Moscow: University Press of Idaho, 1976.

Illinois

Wolf, Joseph C. *A Reference Guide for Genealogical and Historical Research in Illinois.* Detroit: Detroit Society for Genealogical Research, 1967.

Indiana

Harter, Stuart. *Indiana Genealogy and Local History Sources Index.* Fort Wayne, Ind.: the author, 1985.

Wendel, Carolynne L. *Aids for Genealogical Searching in Indiana: A Bibliography.* Rev. ed. Detroit: Detroit Society for Genealogical Research, 1970.

Iowa

Petersen, William John. *Iowa History Reference Guide.* Iowa City: State Historical Society of Iowa, 1952.

Kansas

Anderson, Lorene, and Alan W. Farley. "Bibliography of Town and County Histories of Kansas." *Kansas Historical Quarterly* 21 (Autumn 1955): 513–51.

Curtis, Mary B. "Bibliography of Kansas: The Formative Years." *Magazine of Bibliographies* 1 (2) (December 1972).

Kentucky

Coleman, John Winston. *A Bibliography of Kentucky History.* Lexington: University of Kentucky Press, 1949.

Inside Kentucky: Containing a Bibliography of Source Materials on Kentucky. Frankfort, Ky., 1974. From *Educational Bulletin of Kentucky* 42 (8).

Louisiana

Yoes, Henry E., 3rd, comp. *Bibliography of Louisiana Materials.* Hohnville, La., 1973.

Maine

Haskell, John D., Jr., ed. *Maine: A Bibliography of Its History.* Boston: G. K. Hall, 1977.

Maryland

Passano, Eleanor Phillips. *An Index of the Source Records of Maryland: Genealogical, Biographical, Historical.* Reprint. Baltimore: Genealogical Publishing Co., 1967, 363–478.

Massachusetts

Haskell, John D., Jr., ed. *Massachusetts: A Bibliography of Its History.* Hanover, N.H.: University Press of New England, 1983.

Michigan

Michigan Bureau of Library Services. *Michigan County Histories: A Bibliography.* Lansing: Michigan Department of Education, Bureau of Library Services, 1978.

Minnesota

Brook, Michael. *Reference Guide to Minnesota History.* St. Paul: Minnesota Historical Society, 1974.

Mississippi

Mississippi State Library Commission. *Mississippiana.* Vol. 1. Jackson: Mississippi State Library Commission, 1971.

Missouri

Luebbering, Patsy. *Publications Relating to Missouri Counties.* Jefferson City, Mo.: Records Management and Archives Service, 1980.

Montana

Richards, Dennis. *Montana's Genealogical and Local History Records.* Gale Genealogy and Local History Series, vol. 11. Detroit: Gale Research, 1981.

Nebraska

Nimo, Sylvia. *Nebraska Local History and Genealogy Reference Guide: A Bibliography of County Research Materials in Selected Repositories.* Papillion, Nebr.: the author, 1987.

Nevada

Paher, Stanley W. *Nevada: An Annotated Bibliography: Books and Pamphlets Relating to the History and Development of the Silver State.* Las Vegas: Nevada Publications, 1980.

New Hampshire

Haskell, John D., Jr., and T. D. Seymour Bassett, eds. *New Hampshire: A Bibliography of Its History.* Boston: G. K. Hall, 1979.

New Jersey

Burr, Nelson Rollin. *A Narrative and Descriptive Bibliography of New Jersey.* New Jersey Historical Series, vol. 21. Princeton, N.J.: Van Nostrand, 1964.

New Mexico

Swadesh, Frances Leon. *20,000 Years of History: A New Mexico Bibliography.* Santa Fe, N.M.: Sunstone Press, 1973.

New York

Nestler, Harold. *A Bibliography of New York State Communities: Counties, Towns, and Villages.* 3rd ed. Bowie, Md.: Heritage Books, 1990.

North Carolina

Stevenson, George. *North Carolina Local History: A Select Bibliography.* Raleigh, N.C.: State Department of Cultural Resources, 1975.

Thornton, Mary Lindsay. *A Bibliography of North Carolina, 1589–1956.* Westport, Conn.: Greenwood Press, 1973.

North Dakota

Rylance, Dan, and J. F. S. Smeall, comps. *Reference Guide to North Dakota History and North Dakota Literature.* Grand Forks: Chester Fritz Library of the University of North Dakota, 1979.

Ohio

Harter, Stuart. *Ohio Genealogy and Local History Sources Index.* Fort Wayne, Ind.: CompuGen Systems, 1986.

Oklahoma

Gibson, Arrell M. *Oklahoma: A Student's Guide to Localized History.* New York: Columbia University, 1965.

Oregon

Vaughn, Thomas. *A Bibliography of Pacific Northwest History.* Oregon Historical Society, n.d. Covers Oregon and Washington.

Pennsylvania

Hoenstine, Floyd G. *Guide to Genealogical and Historical Research in Pennsylvania.* Hollidaysburg, Pa.: the author, 1978. Supplements 1985, 1990.

Wall, Carol. *Supplement to Bibliography of Pennsylvania History.* Harrisburg: Pennsylvania Historical and Museum Commission, 1976.

Wilkinson, Norman B. *Bibliography of Pennsylvania History.* 2nd ed. Harrisburg: Pennsylvania Historical and Museum Commission, 1957.

Rhode Island

Parks, Roger, ed. *Rhode Island: A Bibliography of Its History.* Hanover, N.H.: University Press of New England, 1983.

South Carolina

Cote, Richard N. *Local and Family History in South Carolina: A Bibliography.* Easley, S.C.: Southern Historical Press, 1981.

Jones, Lewis P. *Books and Articles on South Carolina History.* 2nd ed. Columbia: University of South Carolina Press, 1991.

South Dakota

Alexander, Ruth A., et al., comps. *South Dakota: Changing, Changeless, 1889–1989* [*sic*]. Edited by Sue Laubersheimer. South Dakota Library Association, 1985.

Tennessee

Smith, Sam B., ed., and Luke H. Banker, comp. *Tennessee History: A Bibliography.* Knoxville: University of Tennessee Press, 1974.

Texas

Jenkins, John Holmes. *Cracker Barrel Chronicles: A Bibliography of Texas Town and County Histories.* Austin, Tex.: Pemberton Press, 1965.

Vermont

Bassett, T. D. Seymour, ed. *Vermont: A Bibliography of Its History.* Boston: G. K. Hall & Co., 1981.

Virginia

Virginia Local History: A Bibliography. Richmond: Virginia State Library, 1971. Supplement, 1976.

Washington (see Oregon)

West Virginia

Davis, Innis C. *A Bibliography of West Virginia.* Parts 1, 2. Charleston: West Virginia Department of Archives and History, 1939.

Forbes, Harold M. *West Virginia History: A Guide to Research.* Morgantown: West Virginia University Press, 1981.

Shetler, Charles. *Guide to the Study of West Virginia History.* Morgantown: West Virginia University Library, 1960.

Wisconsin

Gleason, Margaret. *Printed Resources for Genealogical Searching in Wisconsin: A Selective Bibliography.* Detroit: Detroit Society for Genealogical Research, 1964.

Schlinkert, Leroy. *Subject Bibliography of Wisconsin History.* Madison: State Historical Society of Wisconsin, 1947.

National Indexes

Baillie, Laureen, ed. *American Biographical Index.* 6 vols. New York City: K. G. Saur, 1993.

Index to Biographies in Local Histories in the Library of Congress. 31 microfilm reels. Baltimore: Magna Charta Book Co., 1979.

Old Surname Index File. 21 microfilm reels. Salt Lake City: Genealogical Society of Utah, 1976.

The Sutro Library Family History Subject Catalog. 3rd ed. Sacramento: California State Library Foundation, 1990.

Multi-State Indexes

The following multi-state and statewide indexes are usually the best places to start looking for biographical sketches in state and local sources. They are collective indexes to many titles within their areas or states. Virtually none are every-name indexes, and each has different rules for inclusion; however, all of them index the subjects of biographical sketches in histories and collective biographies.

Allen County Public Library. *Historical and Biographical Index of North East, Mid East, Mid South, Mid West U.S.A., 1800 Thru Early 1900.* 33 microfilm reels. Salt Lake City: Genealogical Society of Utah, 1989. Particularly good for Illinois, Indiana, Kansas, Kentucky, Ohio, Pennsylvania, and other areas in the central states.

Drazan, Joseph Gerald. *The Pacific Northwest: An Index to People and Places in Books.* Metuchen, N.J.: Scarecrow Press, 1979. 6,830 entries from 320 sources for Alaska, Idaho, Montanta, Oregon, Washington, and British Columbia and Yukon Territory in Canada.

Early Church Information File. 75 microfilm reels. Salt Lake City: Genealogical Society of Utah, 1991. Despite its LDS focus, provides excellent coverage for the Intermountain West: Arizona, Colorado, Idaho, Utah, and Wyoming.

Greenlaw, William Prescott. *The Greenlaw Index of the New England Historic Genealogical Society.* 2 vols. Boston: G. K. Hall, 1979. Includes books from all over the East, but best for Connecticut, Maine, Massachusetts, New Hampshire, Rhode Island, and Vermont.

Index to American Genealogies and to Genealogical Material Contained in all Works Such as Town Histories, County Histories, Local Histories . . . and Kindred Works (Known as Munsell's Index). 1900. Reprint. Baltimore: Genealogical Publishing Co., 1967. Particularly good for locating surnames in New England town histories.

Genealogical Index of the Newberry Library. 4 vols. Boston: G. K. Hall, 1960. Most references are for northern or midwestern sources.

The Sutro Library Family History Subject Catalog. 3rd ed. Sacramento: California State Library Foundation, 1990. Has some national coverage, but most families are from California and the West and from states from which settlers went to California.

Wiggins, Marvin E., comp. *Mormons and Their Neighbors.* 2 vols. Provo, Utah: Lee Library, Brigham Young University, 1984. Covers Utah, Idaho, Arizona, and Wyoming.

Statewide Indexes

The following list is arranged alphabetically by state and identifies the indexes noted in table 17-2. Additional manuscript indexes are noted in table 17-3 (because most index only biographical sketches, they are described in chapter 18).

Andrusko, Samuel M. *Maryland Biographical Sketch Index.* Silver Spring, Md.: the author, 1983.

Biographical Card Index [Florida]. 18 microfilm reels. St. Augustine, Fla.: St. Augustine Historical Society, 1974.

Bradbury, Connie, David A. Hales, and Nancy Lesh. *Alaska People Index.* Alaska Historical Commission Studies in History no. 203. 2 vols. Anchorage: Alaska Historical Commission, 1986.

Brandt, Patricia, and Nancy Guilford, eds. *Oregon Biography Index.* Oregon State University Bibliographic Series, no. 11. Corvallis: Oregon State University, 1976.

Bromwell, Henriette Elizabeth. *Colorado Portrait and Biography Index.* 4 vols. Denver, 1935.

California Information File. 550 microfiche. Bellevue, Wash.: Commercial Microfilm Service, 1986.

Cook, Michael Lewis. *Kentucky Index of Biographical Sketches in State, Regional, and County Histories.* Evansville, Ind.: Cook Publications, 1986.

Côté, Richard N., and Patricia H. Williams. *Dictionary of South Carolina Biography.* Vol. 1. Easley, S.C.: Southern Historical Press, 1985.

Hoenstine, Floyd G. *Guide to Genealogical and Historical Research in Pennsylvania.* Hollidaysburg, Pa.: the author, 1978. Supplements 1985, 1990.

Indiana Biographical Index. West Bountiful, Utah: Genealogical Indexing Associates, 1983.

Longver, Phyllis O., and Pauline J. Oesterlin. *A Surname Guide to Massachusetts Town Histories.* Bowie, Md: Heritage Books, 1993.

Loomis, Frances. *Michigan Biography Index.* 4 microfilm reels. Detroit: Detroit Public Library, 1946.

Ming, Virginia H., and William L. Ming. *Biographical Gazetteer of Texas.* 6 vols. Austin, Tex.: W. M. Morrison Books, 1985–87.

Morford, Charles. *Biographical Index to the County Histories of Iowa.* Vol. 1. Baltimore: Gateway Press, 1979. No further volumes as of 1997.

New Hampshire Notables Card File, 1600 to the Present. 8 microfilm reels. Salt Lake City: New Hampshire Historical Society, 1988.

New York State Library Surname Index. 33 microfiche. Albany: State Library of New York, 1979.

Ohio Historical Society. *Ohio County History Surname Index.* 64 microfilm reels. Columbus, Ohio, 1936, 1984.

Parker, J. Carlyle. *An Index to Biographies in 19th Century California County Histories.* Gale Genealogy and Local History Series, vol. 7. Detroit: Gale Research Co., 1979.

_____. *Rhode Island Biographical and Genealogical Sketch Index.* Turlock, Calif.: Marietta Publishing Co., 1991.

Parker, J. Carlyle, and Janet G. Parker. "Idaho Biographical and Genealogical Sketch Index." Turlock, Calif.: Marietta Publishing Co., in process.

_____. "Montana Biographical and Genealogical Sketch Index." Turlock, Calif.: Marietta Publishing Co., in process.

_____. *Nevada Biographical and Genealogical Sketch Index.* Turlock, Calif.: Marietta Publishing Co., 1986.

_____. "South Dakota Biographical and Genealogical Sketch Index." Turlock, Calif.: Marietta Publishing Co., in process.

_____. "Wyoming Biographical and Genealogical Sketch Index." Turlock, Calif.: Marietta Publishing Co., in process.

Sinclair, Donald A. *New Jersey Biographical Index, Covering Some 100,000 Biographies and Associated Portraits in 237 New Jersey . . . Collective Biographical Sources.* Baltimore: Genealogical Publishing Co., 1993.

Smith, Patricia D. *Kansas Biographical Index: State-Wide and Regional Histories.* Garden City, Kans.: the author, 1994.

Subject Catalog of the Library of the State Historical Society of Wisconsin. . . . 23 vols. Westport, Conn.: Greenwood Publishing Co., 1971.

Towle, Glenn C. *New Hampshire Genealogical Digest, 1623–1900.* Vol. 1. Bowie, Md.: Heritage Books, 1986.

True, Ransom B. *Biographical Dictionary of Early Virginia, 1607–1660.* 19 microfiche. Jamestown: Association for the Preservation of Virginia Antiquities, 1982. More than 100,000 entries refer to thirty thousand people who are mentioned in wills, deeds, court orders, published histories, and Virginia company records.

Upham, Warren, comp. *Minnesota Biographies, 1655–1912.* Collections of the Minnesota Historical Society, vol. 14. St. Paul: Minnesota Historical Society, 1912.

Wardell, Patrick G. *Timesaving Aid to Virginia-West Virginia Ancestors.* 4 vols. Athens, Ga.: Iberian Publishing Co., 1985–90.

_____. *Virginians and West Virginians, 1607–1870.* 3 vols. Bowie, Md.: Heritage Books, 1986–92.

BIOGRAPHIES OVERVIEW

Key Concepts in This Chapter

- Biographical sketches exist for from 5 to 7 million Americans.
- There are at least four thousand sources of biographical sketches.
- Book-length biographies are available for twenty-five thousand persons.
- Sources are available at four levels: national, state, local, and vocational.
- Many biographical sources are available at local public libraries.
- Statewide indexes of local sources are available for thirty-one states.
- Use statewide bibliographies to find county and local sources.

Key Sources in This Chapter

Bibliographies

- *Biographical Dictionaries and Related Works*
- *Biographical Books, 1876–1949* and *1950–1980*

Indexes

- *Biography and Genealogy Master Index*
- *Biography Index*

Dictionaries and Encyclopedias

- *Dictionary of American Biography*
- *National Cyclopedia of American Biography*
- *Who Was Who in America*

18

BIOGRAPHIES

Kory L. Meyerink

While a relevant published genealogy or a family history might be considered a great find by most genealogists, many would consider a biographical sketch of an ancestor to be almost as desirable. Such a recognition reflects the genealogist's desire to learn more about an ancestor than a name, date, or place. However, most researchers stop at the "wishful thinking" stage, not realizing the chances are good that a biographical sketch does exist for an ancestor or close relative.

Upwards of 5 to 7 million or more Americans have been the subjects of some form of collective biography.[1] Unfortunately, most researchers do not know how to locate these references because the vast majority of them are not among the "standard" genealogical sources, such as census, probate, land, and vital records. Most people are aware of the "who's who" books and the countywide collective biographies, such as *Portrait and Biographical Record of Kankakee County* (Illinois). However, after briefly searching a library's holdings for such books, many genealogists stop, thinking, I guess my ancestors were just plain old farmers.

However, there are approximately four thousand or more collective biographical sources for those 5 million or more Americans, each with hundreds of biographical sketches. In addition, book-length biographies have been published for upwards of twenty-five thousand persons, while published diaries and autobiographies account for approximately ten thousand more individuals. For obvious reasons, these biographies are fonts of valuable information. Regardless of how brief the sketch, it almost always gives the subject's name, birth date and birthplace, parents' names, residence, occupation, and spouse's name. Most give much more information, such as children's names, education, achievements, memberships in organizations, some personal life history, and other interesting facts.

The purpose of this chapter is to better acquaint researchers with these types of sources, including their typical coverage, where they can be found, and how to learn about them. There are two types of published biographical sources: *book-length biographies* are devoted to one person (although numerous relatives are included in great detail); and *collective biographies,* such as biographical encyclopedias, profile several persons (usually one hundred or more but sometimes only ten to twenty). Collective biographies cannot be as detailed as book-length biographies, but they include important and interesting information, and several pages may be devoted to each subject. The majority of this chapter focuses on collective biographies because many more persons are included in such sources, and because they are more difficult to locate and use.

Coverage in collective biographical works falls into four levels, around which this discussion is based: national, statewide, local, and vocational (which may have a national, statewide, or local focus). Much of the discussion in chapter 17, "County and Local Histories," about how local history books were compiled and how to evaluate them also applies to these sources. It is not repeated in depth here, but some concepts are briefly noted.

As with most published sources, biographies usually contain secondary information.[2] Such information is often correct; however, it has almost always been edited, then typeset and printed—stages where the original information may have been changed (deliberately or inadvertently). In addition, the original material may have been compiled from several other sources, not all of which were original documents. Often the subject of the biography or his immediate family provided most (if not all) of the information in a biography (even in many book-length biographies). While this degree of involvement suggests that the biography will contain accurate information, it also suggests *selective* information. In other words, usually only positive aspects of the subject's life and personality are discussed.

This chapter does not cover general reference sources, such as general-purpose encyclopedias, almanacs, and other standard references. Such sources often include helpful biographical material, but not as much as the sources discussed here. In addition, general reference sources usually include only the most notable persons. They serve as brief, easily accessible sources for an initial overview when research focuses on such notable persons.

To illustrate just how much these sources may pertain to a genealogist's ancestry, the examples in figures 18-2 through 18-13 have been carefully chosen. Each one pertains directly to the ancestry of this author's children, either as a direct ancestor, brother (and hence child) of a direct ancestor, or, in one case, a first cousin of an ancestor. Their ancestry is very typically American, with no "famous" ancestors, and mixes Dutch, German, Scotch Irish, and Scandinavian immigrants with colonial English and Dutch settlers in New York and New England.

NATIONAL BIOGRAPHICAL SOURCES

National biographical sources are very popular in North American libraries. They include as subjects persons who have achieved notoriety in some field, or among some group, on a national or multi-state level. Actors and politicians (and some who are both) are among those who come first to mind in this category, but they represent a surprisingly small percentage of the subjects. More than two and a half million people, most of them Americans, have been noted in more than two thousand volumes and editions of more than 675 collective biographical sources that treat Americans and others on a national level (*BGMI* 1992, 1). Most of these millions of people are certainly relatively unknown individuals, suggesting that many of the people profiled in national sources are not the very famous but simply those who have excelled in some area.

Since so many persons (and their families) are included in these sources, it is important to understand the scope and limitations of them. National sources can provide variable amounts of information on a subject. In fact, many of the persons included in one national source are also included in at least one other source. Differing information is usually included in different sources, so it is wise to locate as many as possible. The biographical information in these sources may comprise only a brief paragraph citing the subject's greatest accomplishments or awards, or it may be a multiple-page synopsis of the subject's life, including family background, philosophies, events that shaped his life, and other information. Often the biographical sketch averages one page and mostly includes factual information in a blend of the shorter or longer styles.

For the family historian, the greatest drawback to national sources is *not* the fact that usually only the most prominent persons are included in them; rather, the chief concern is that most subjects were born in the twentieth century. Naturally, everyone has fewer ancestors who lived in the twentieth century than in preceding periods, and genealogists usually are not researching twentieth-century ancestors because they already know about them from family sources. Table 18-1 shows that upwards of 80 percent of the subjects in national sources were born after 1900, while only between 1 and 4 percent were born before 1800. These numbers may be disappointing to the person researching colonial Virginia ancestors, but they are good news for the person who is trying to find living relatives.

If 80 percent of the almost 3 million Americans included in these sources were born after 1900, this amount represents more than 2 million persons—1 in fewer than 150 persons living today. Adult males account for approximately 90 percent of those entries, yet they account for only around 30 to 40 percent of the U.S. population (approximately 90 million). By this estimate, one in fifty adult males of the mid- to late twentieth century have been profiled in national sources. Since many modern extended families include well over fifty adult males, it is highly likely for most people that some relative is included in such a source; thus, they can help locate missing relatives. In addition, where the surname being researched is rare, they can help the researcher identify where families lived or determine how rare a name is. For example, the surname Meyerink is shared by only about sixty families in the United States. So far, research has uncovered only one Meyerink included in all national biographical sources (further confirming the estimate that one in fifty nuclear families—an adult male usually heads a nuclear family—is represented in these sources).

Table 18-1. Birth Dates of Subjects in *BGMI*

	Percentage of Subjects in:		
Birth Years	*Base Set*	*1985 Cumulation*	*1990 Cumulation*
Pre-1550	0.2	0.4	0
1500–99	1	1	0.3
1600–99	1	0.4	0.3
1700–99	2	1.3	0.7
1800–25	1	1.5	0.3
1826–50	4	2	1
1851–75	4	2	2
1876–99	9	8	4
1900–25	34	20	20
1926–50	27	46	46
Post-1950	1	3.5	6
No date given	16	12	20

Despite their focus on recent individuals, national sources can identify thousands of early ancestors as well. Averaging the birth date occurrences in table 18-1 shows that approximately 3 percent of the subjects in the *Biography and Genealogy Master Index* (discussed below under "Indexes") were born before 1800, while approximately 17 percent were born before 1900. Given the 2.6 million persons in this index, this still accounts for approximately 75,000 subjects born before 1800 and 440,000 subjects born before 1900. The other major index, *American Biographical Index* (discussed below under "Indexes"), has approximately 270,000 persons born before 1900 (figure 18-1). With relatively little duplication between these two indexes, national sources will identify biographical sketches for between half and three-quarters of a million historical individuals.

Bibliographies

Three major bibliographies identify virtually all of the collective biographies available at the national level. They also give good coverage to statewide and vocational sources. A discussion of their differences follows.

Biographical Dictionaries and Related Works. Robert Slocum's *Biographical Dictionaries and Related Works* (Detroit: Gale Research) appeared in its second edition in 1986. In two thick volumes it includes, according to its subtitle, "an international bibliography of more than 16,000 collective biographies, bio-bibliographies, selected genealogical works, bibliographies of biographies, biographical indexes, and selected portrait catalogs." The editor included thousands of foreign works as well as a comprehensive list of U.S. sources. The work is divided into countries and their subdivisions (states in the United States, provinces in Canada). In vol. 1, the U.S. section includes 67 bibliographies of biographies, 608 nationwide general compiled biographies, and 1,205 local (state, city, or regional) sources. In addition, vol. 2 includes more than eight thousand sources of vocational biographies arranged by vocation and usually subdivided geographically.

Since many of the titles listed are annually or irregularly issued series, many more thousands of sources are represented by the sixteen thousand titles. Each entry includes full bibliographic information and a brief annotation of one to five lines.

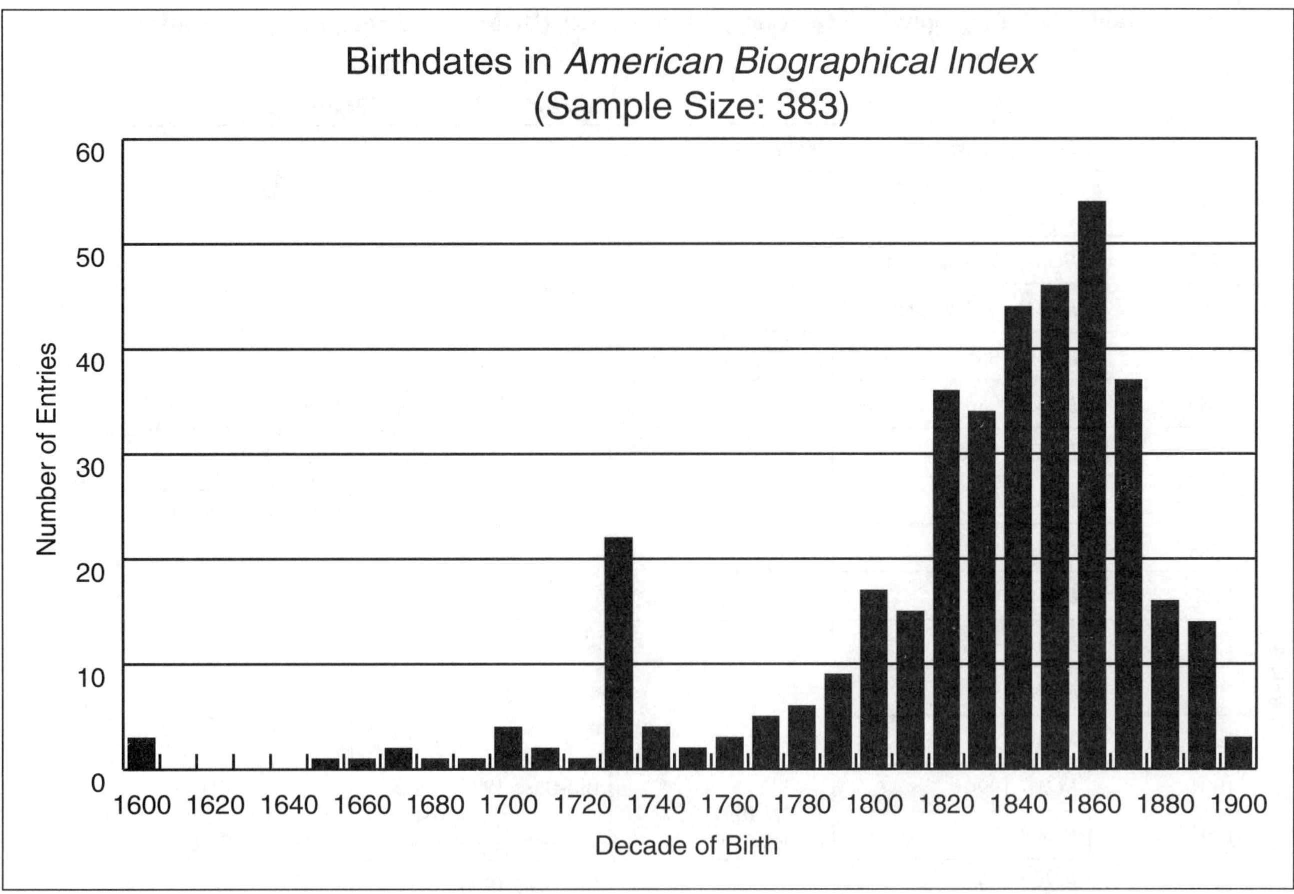

Figure 18-1. Birthdates in *American Biographical Index.*

Comprehensive author, title, and subject indexes combined with the topical index make it relatively easy to find the appropriate place to search for titles of interest. The editor has focused on biographical dictionaries, defining them as including brief biographical sketches of several persons and using the guideline of one hundred entries or more as a general cutoff point. In a few cases sources with fewer entries were included if the obscurity of the topic or area warranted it. Lengthy biographical studies of comparatively few persons are generally not included.

One other major omission is the "biographical dictionaries that dealt with . . . relatively limited geographical areas—especially towns, villages, and counties of the United States." On the other hand, the editor does include such works that deal with four or more counties or with significant cities (Slocum 1986, 8). Many major public and academic libraries have this source or at least the first edition (1967) with its two supplements (1972, 1978).

Biographical Sources. Another helpful reference is Diane J. Cimbala, Jennifer Cargill, and Brian Alley's *Biographical Sources: A Guide to Dictionaries and Reference Works* (Phoenix, Ariz.: Oryx Press). Also published in 1986, it describes far fewer books than Slocum's *Biographical Dictionaries and Related Works*, having only 689 entries. However, all sources in it are English-language works, and the vast majority are only about Americans. In addition, the annotations are much more complete, often describing the type of information in each sketch and the number of entries in each book. The editors considered shorter works as well, often listing sources with only fifteen to twenty entries. The books listed in *Biographical Sources* are found in most public libraries, whereas many in Slocum's bibliography are hard to find even in large academic research libraries. Its shorter list is obviously not comprehensive, but this fact and its focus on U.S. biographies makes it easier to find a reference listed in it. The editors' decision to include briefer works means that some listings will not be found in Slocum's bibliography. As with *Biographical Dictionaries and Related Works, Biographical Sources* does not list local (county and town) biographical collections, and its regional selection is much briefer than Slocum's.

ARBA Guide to Biographical Dictionaries. Yet another bibliography of collective biographies was published in 1986. The *ARBA Guide to Biographical Dictionaries,* edited by Bohdan S. Wynar (Littleton, Colo.: Libraries Unlimited, 1986), includes reprints of approximately five hundred reviews of biographical sources that appeared in *American Reference Books Annual* (*ARBA*) since 1969. It also includes approximately two hundred new entries yielding 718 titles, almost all of which were in print in 1986. It provides complete bibliographical descriptions and prices in addition to original reviews of the books. Like Slocum's work, it has a worldwide focus; however, it generally cites only books published since the 1960s. The text is divided into two parts: "Universal and National Biographies," in which the countries are arranged alphabetically (except the United States, which is first), and "Biographies in Professional Fields," which has twenty-one subject areas, such as applied arts, geography, history, social sciences, and sports. Indexes allow access by author/title or by subject. Like the other two bibliographies,

Table 18-2. Biography and Genealogy Master Index (BGMI)—Corresponding Formats

<table>
<tr><th>Year of Publication</th><th colspan="2">Print</th><th>Microfiche</th><th>Electronic</th></tr>
<tr><td>1980–81</td><td colspan="2">Biography and Genealogy Master Index, 2nd ed.</td><td rowspan="13"></td><td rowspan="13"><u>Online</u>
Entire database can be accessed through DIALOG File 287: Biography Master Index and GaleNet (both are updated annually)</td></tr>
<tr><td>1982</td><td>BGMI 1981–82 supplement</td><td rowspan="4">BGMI 1981–85 cumulation</td></tr>
<tr><td>1983</td><td>BGMI 1983 supplement</td></tr>
<tr><td>1984</td><td>BGMI 1984 supplement</td></tr>
<tr><td>1985</td><td>BGMI 1985</td></tr>
<tr><td>1986</td><td>BGMI 1986</td><td rowspan="5">BGMI 1986–90 cumulation</td></tr>
<tr><td>1987</td><td>BGMI 1987</td></tr>
<tr><td>1988</td><td>BGMI 1988</td></tr>
<tr><td>1989</td><td>BGMI 1989</td></tr>
<tr><td>1990</td><td>BGMI 1990</td></tr>
<tr><td>1991</td><td>BGMI 1991</td><td rowspan="5">BGMI 1991–95 cumulation</td></tr>
<tr><td>1992</td><td>BGMI 1992</td></tr>
<tr><td>1993</td><td>BGMI 1993</td></tr>
<tr><td>1994</td><td>BGMI 1994</td><td rowspan="2">Bio-Base 1995 master cumulation (supersedes all previous editions)</td><td rowspan="8"><u>CD-ROM</u>
Entire database is available as BGMI CD-ROM (updated annually)</td></tr>
<tr><td>1995</td><td>BGMI 1995</td></tr>
<tr><td>1996</td><td>BGMI 1996</td><td rowspan="5">BGMI 1996–2000 cumulation</td><td>Bio-Base 1996</td></tr>
<tr><td>1997</td><td>BGMI 1997</td><td>Bio-Base 1996–97</td></tr>
<tr><td>1998</td><td>BGMI 1998</td><td>Bio-Base 1996–98</td></tr>
<tr><td>1999</td><td>BGMI 1999</td><td>Bio-Base 1996–99</td></tr>
<tr><td>2000</td><td>BGMI 2000</td><td>Bio-Base 2000 master cumulation</td></tr>
</table>

ARBA Guide to Biographical Dictionaries contains very few local or regional sources.

Several specific sources for national biographies merit discussion. They include three major indexes, several biographical encyclopedias, smaller biographical dictionaries, and book biographies.

Indexes

There are several important indexes that provide good access to the biographical sketches in national-level sources.

Biography and Genealogy Master Index (BGMI). Any discussion of biographies, especially on a national level, must begin with Gale Research Company's (Detroit) major contribution to the field. Since the mid-1970s Gale has indexed a wide variety of biographical sources. Gale's initial efforts were published in various parts for different purposes and under different names. However, in 1980 that changed with the consolidation of several of Gale's biographical indexes into the second edition of *Biography and Genealogy Master Index* (*BGMI*). In eight volumes, *BGMI* provided index entries to more than 3 million biographical sketches in 350 different compiled biographies. Gale's indexing work has continued with annual supplements starting in 1982. New entries for 1985 were combined with those for 1982 to 1984 in a five-volume "1981–1985 Cumulation." Three volumes cumulate the indexes for 1986 to 1990, while three more cumulate 1991 to 1995. Annual supplements continue to be issued. This index is available in book, microfiche, and CD-ROM format and online (table 18-2).

Effective use of this helpful research tool requires a thorough understanding of its scope, content, and limitations. Because the book format of *BGMI* is the one found in most libraries, the following discussion focuses on the multi-volume book set. The various parts are referred to as the "base set" (eight volumes for 1980 to 1981), the "1985 cumulation" (for 1981 to 1985), the "1990 cumulation" (1986 to 1990), "1995 cumulation" (1991 to 1995), and the "supplements" (by year). The twenty volumes (through the 1998 supplement) index more than seven hundred biographical sources (in 2,100 volumes), most of which focus on North Americans. The indexes refer to more than 8.8 million entries in these sources. For many persons of worldwide fame there are dozens of entries. For example, in the base set alone there are seventy-one different references to Sir Winston Churchill. Other notable persons, with the number of entries for each in the base set, are:

Table 18-3. Analysis of BGMI Entries

	Number of Titles	*Number of Vols.*	*Number of Entries*	*Number of Individuals*	*Number of New Names*
Base Set	350	600	3,200,000	1,185,000	1,185,000
1985 Cumulation	215	465	2,250,000	1,184,000	722,000
1990 Cumulation	250	410	1,895,000	997,000	400,000
1995 Cumulation	240	400	2,200,000	1,050,000	500,000
1996–97 Supplements	70–90 each	120–140 each	App. 450,000	App. 375,000	App. 100,000
Totals	App. 700 unique	App. 1,900	10,500,000	Not applicable	App. 3 million

Benjamin Franklin	56
Richard Nixon	49
Thomas Jefferson	47
Abraham Lincoln	39
Shirley Temple	34
George Washington	33
John F. Kennedy	21
Daniel Boone	20
Albert Schweitzer	17

A careful study of approximately one thousand entries in the base set revealed that there were 2.7 different references (or entries) for the average subject. With 3.2 million entries in the base set, this suggests that just under 1.2 million different persons are included in those eight volumes.

The base set is larger than the rest and contains more retrospective entries; hence, the duplication figures for subsequent sets are somewhat lower. The subjects in the 1985 cumulation average 1.9 references each, meaning that the 2.25 million entries represent approximately 1.2 million different persons. The 1990 and 1995 cumulations also have approximately 1.9 entries per name. The annual supplements have a lower average—approximately 1.2 entries per name in each volume. The recent volumes generally are much more contemporary, with many subjects born in the 1940s, 1950s, and even the 1960s. Most genealogists seeking biographical sketches of ancestors will find the base set to be the most useful.

There is also substantial duplication of individuals between the base set and subsequent publications; many persons included in the cumulations or the annual supplements also were noted in earlier volumes. While multiple references are encouraging because more references to a person mean more information available to the researcher, they also result in each annual volume including fewer and fewer new names (those not indexed earlier in the series). In the 1985 cumulation, 61 percent of the names—approximately 722,000—were new to the series. In the 1990 cumulation, names new to the series (not previously indexed) accounted for approximately 40 percent of the 1 million individuals, for approximately 400,000 new names. In the 1995 cumulation, around 25 percent of the names are new to the series, adding approximately 500,000 persons. The annual supplements contain from 20 to 30 percent new names per volume, so each annual adds approximately 100,000 names not previously noted. Adding the unique name totals together shows that the 10 million entries through the 1997 supplement refer to approximately 3 million different people.

This analysis is summarized in table 18-3 and is corroborated by a study of the 1996 CD-ROM version of this database. The CD-ROM version states that more than 4 million individuals are indexed in *BGMI*. In actuality, this number is inflated because some individuals are represented by variable spellings of their names. A careful analysis of the entries on the CD-ROM showed that approximately 20 percent of the names are duplicates (differing only in variable spellings, missing middle initials, missing death dates, etc.). Subtracting 20 percent from the 4 million names in the database yields 3.2 million unique individuals.

Despite these duplications, or perhaps because of them, *BGMI* is the first place to look for biographical references. Since, usually, little is known about an ancestor, the researcher will not know how famous he may have been. Therefore, a search in *BGMI* may be surprising. The following discussion from *BGMI*'s introduction explains its content, scope, and editorial practices, and provides valuable suggestions for searching similar indexes.

> *BGMI* is a unique index that enables the user to determine which edition(s) of which publication to consult for biographical information. Almost as helpful, it also reveals if there is no listing for a given individual in the sources indexes. In cases where *BGMI* shows multiple listings for the same person, the user is able either to choose which source is the most convenient or to locate multiple sketches to compare and expand information furnished by a single listing.
>
> Biographical sources indexed in *BGMI* are of several different types: 1) biographical dictionaries, which supply information on a number of individuals in alphabetical order; 2) subject encyclopedias, which include some biographical entries; 3) volumes of literary criticism, which may contain only a limited amount of biographical information but give critical surveys of a writer's works; and 4) indexes, which do not provide immediate information but refer the user to a body of information elsewhere. *BGMI indexes only reference books containing multiple biographies; it does not index periodicals or books of biography about only one individual* (emphasis added).
>
> Sources indexed by *BGMI* cover both living and deceased persons from every field of activity and from all areas of the world. The sources are predominantly current, readily available, "standard" reference books (for example, the Marquis *Who's Who* series); however, *BGMI* also includes important retrospective sources and general subject sources that cover both contemporary and noncontemporary people.

Among the sources included in this index are general works, both current and retrospective, such as *Who's Who in America* and *Biography Index.* Also included are sources in special subject areas such as works on literature, fine and applied arts, business and music. Other subject areas covered in *BGMI* include dance, photography, law and politics, science, theater, medicine, and social science.

Although the majority of the sources indexed in *BGMI* cover the United States, this index also includes both current and retrospective titles covering individuals in foreign countries such as *The International Who's Who* and *The Dictionary of National Biography* [Great Britain].

Each citation gives the person's name followed by the years of birth and/or death as found in the source book. If a source has indicated that the dates may not be accurate, the questionable date(s) are followed by a question mark. If there is no year of birth, the death date is preceded by a lower case *d. The codes for the books indexed follow the dates* (emphasis added).

Walsh, William 1512?—1577 *DcNaB*
Sokoine, Edward d1985 *New YTBS 84*

References to names which are identical in spelling and dates have been consolidated under a single name and date entry, as in the example below for *Bernard Goodwin.* When a name appears in more than one edition or volume of an indexed work, the title code for the book is given only once and is followed by the various codes for the editions in which the name appears.

Goodwin, Bernard 1907— *IntMPA 81, -82, -84, WhoAm 80, -82, -84, WhoWor 82*

Another feature of *BGMI* is the portrait indicator. If the source has a portrait or picture of the person, this is indicated by the abbreviation *[port]* after the source code. Complete bibliographic citations to the titles indexed follow the introduction. All of the subjects, but only the subjects, in an indexed work are included in *BGMI.* Names of spouses, children, parents or other persons are not indexed.

Names appear in *BGMI* exactly as they are listed in the source books. No attempt has been made to determine whether names with closely similar spellings and dates refer to the same individual. Therefore, several listings for the same individual may sometimes be found:

Bellman, Richard 1920— *ConAu12NR*
Bellman, Richard 1920—1984 *ConAu112*
Bellman, Richard E 1920— *WhoAm 84*
Bellman, Richard Ernest 1920— *WhoFrS 84*

Despite the variations in the form of the name, it is probable that the same person is referred to in the above citations. Researchers will need to look under all possible listings for a name, especially in the cases of:

Names with prefixes or suffixes:

Angeles, Victoria DeLos
De Los Angeles, Victoria
Los Angeles, Victoria Dey

Pseudonyms, noms de plume, and stage names:
Clemens, Samuel Langhorne *and* **Twain,** Mark
Crosby, Bing *and* **Crosby,** Harry Lillis

Names which may be entered in the sources both under the full name and either initials or part of the name:

Eliot, T S *and* **Eliot,** Thomas Stearns
Welles, George Orson *and* **Welles,** Orson

With the source book code from *BGMI,* turn to the introductory pages of the index and look up the code. There will be a complete bibliographic citation for the source, often with a brief annotation. *BGMI* does not provide the page numbers for the sources it indexes. Most sources are arranged alphabetically, and those that aren't generally have individual indexes to locate the person referenced. Remember also that *BGMI* only indexes the subject of the biographical sketch. Other names, including spouses, children, parents, siblings, and earlier ancestors, are not indexed.

The CD-ROM version of *BGMI* allows for much faster and more convenient searching. The entire database is combined into one search, so multiple volumes do not have to be checked. Each entry includes the complete citation for the volume where the biography appears. In addition, a variety of unique searches can be made, such as for specific given names (including when a surname appears as a first or middle name) or persons with a specific birth year or range of birth years (such as all Winslows born before 1850). Searches can also be restricted to one or several specific titles included in the index. A Boolean search strategy (see chapter 5, "Bibliographies and Catalogs") can be used to combine search terms or to limit the search to one or several source titles. Libraries have the option of indicating which of the sources they hold.

Versions of *BGMI* can be found in many major academic and large public libraries. The database continues to be available in print form (as *Biography and Genealogy Master Index*), on microfiche (as *Bio-base*), on CD-ROM (as *Biography and Genealogy Master Index*) and online by subscription (as *Biography Master Index*) through vendors such as DIALOG (see http://www.krinfo.com) and Gale.net.

American Biographical Index and Archive. Next in importance to *BGMI* for biographical research is *American Biographical Index* (*ABI*), edited by Laureen Baillie (1993), and its companion set, *American Biographical Archive* (*ABA*) (1986–89), published by K. G. Saur of New York City. This set is an index *and* microfiche reprint of approximately 300,000 biographies from 368 sources (more than six hundred volumes) for local and national leaders in the United States and Canada. The sources used are primarily from the public domain and therefore were generally published before 1920. Therein lies the usefulness of this collection for family historians: the early cutoff date for publications means that virtually all of the persons included lived before 1900 (figure 18-1).

American Biographical Index is the six-volume book index to the *ABA*. It identifies every subject in the collection with their birth and death dates and occupation. The index citation also identifies which sources include the subject and cross-references the source to a complete bibliography; this makes the index useful for librarians and researchers who cannot purchase the microfiche set but may be able to find copies of the sources in a local library or through inter-library loan. The index also includes cross-references to other names of the subject (pseudonyms), such as Samuel Clemens for Mark Twain.

The 368 sources used for this collection were published between 1702 and 1956, but those dates are somewhat misleading. Fully 92 percent of the titles were published before 1920, and 55 percent were published before 1900. Relatively few were published in the early years of this range. Only three titles were published before 1800 and four more by 1820. Since 1820, most decades saw an increasing number of titles included, with, for example, twenty-five from the 1870s, thirty-seven from the 1880s, and sixty-seven from the 1890s. The largest number of titles—eighty-two, or 22 percent of the total—were published between 1900 and 1910. In fact, the thirty years from 1880 to 1909 saw 50 percent of the indexed titles published.

The selection of sources is quite broad, geographically and by scope. *ABA* and its companion index complement *BGMI* very well because many state and regional biographies were used, thus identifying thousands of obscure persons of limited importance. Approximately two-thirds of the sources are *not* indexed in *BGMI*. An analysis of the breadth of sources made by separating the scope of the titles into fourteen areas yields the following breakdown:[3]

Titles	*Scope of Titles Indexed*
48	National coverage
17	Multi-state coverage
92	Statewide coverage
26	Covers part of a state
7	City residents
68	Vocational (not religious or military)
27	Religious leaders
23	Military persons
4	University alumni
26	Canadians
16	Women
15	Blacks
8	Ethnic groups
6	American Indians

The breadth of coverage is further attested to by the small percentage of multiple entries for any individual. While nationally important persons are included, such as presidents and other politicians, inventors and scientists, businessmen and philanthropists, it appears that fewer than 10 percent of the individuals have more than one entry; therefore, approximately 280,000 distinct individuals are cited in the index. The geographic coverage is also very broad. Virtually every state is represented by at least one title—several by two or more. Thirty-four percent of the titles pertain to a state or smaller geographic area.

The microfiche reprint portion of *ABA* contains, on 1,842 microfiche, the complete biographical sketches from all 368 collective biographies cited in the index. The sketches, reproduced from the original books, are arranged in alphabetical order. In addition, when an individual is represented by several entries, each is given in its entirety, and they are arranged in the order of publication, allowing the researcher to find several sketches and compare them immediately. Inclusion of the actual sketches means that the user does not have to locate the books separately to find the biography; this is especially important because most of the titles are out of print, were printed in small quantities originally, and are very difficult to find in library collections. Even the Family History Library of The Church of Jesus Christ of Latter-day Saints (LDS church) lacks at least 25 percent of the titles. Around sixty major public, private, and academic libraries in the United States have purchased the entire collection.

K. G. Saur has also produced microfiche biographical archives for Great Britain, Germany, Italy, Scandinavia, and Spanish areas (including Portugal and Latin America). The indexes to these collections, including *ABI*, are available on CD-ROM from the same publisher as *World Biographical Index on CD-ROM*. Follow-ups that cover the first half of the twentieth century are available, including *American Biographical Archive*, series 2 (1996), which reproduces sketches from 127 sources on 734 microfiche.

Historical Indexes

Earlier efforts to provide comprehensive indexes (such as *BGMI* and *ABI*) produced sources that may still be found in larger biographical collections. Generally, these indexes have been considered "universal" biographical sources because they reference subjects of note from any country (although the emphasis has always been on North America, Great Britain, and Europe). Genealogist, who are typically more interested in historical persons than famous contemporary individuals, may find value in historical indexes because some of the sources they index are not included in either *BGMI* or *ABI*.

One of the earliest examples of an index to multiple biographical sources is Lawrence Barnett Phillips's *Dictionary of Biographical Reference*, 3rd ed. (Philadelphia: Gibbie, 1889; reprint; Detroit: Gale Research, 1982). With 100,000 entries from Europe and America, it indexes forty-two biographical dictionaries of the nineteenth century.

For early twentieth-century biographical dictionaries, see Albert Montefiore Hyamson's *A Dictionary of Universal Biography of All Ages and of All People*, 2nd ed. (New York: Dutton, 1951; reprint; Detroit: Gale Research, 1981), which provides more than 110,000 entries from twenty-three sources. Each entry includes the subject's nationality, profession, birth and death dates, and the source citation (however, most of the titles used were not completely indexed).

Also of value is Phyllis M. Riches's *An Analytical Bibliography of Universal Collected Biography: Comprising Books Published in the English Tongue in Great Britain and Ireland, America and the British Dominions* (London: Library Association, 1934; reprint; Detroit: Gale Research, 1980), which is claimed to index three thousand sources containing more than fifty-six thousand biographical sketches.

Periodical Indexes

While collective biographies are the major sources of biographical information, sketches about people also appear in other sources—notably in periodicals. Many of these biographical sketches have been indexed in *Biography Index*. This annual

Table 18-4. Major National Biographical Encyclopedias

Name of Set	*No. of Vols.*	*Publication Dates*	*Persons Included*	*No. of Names*	*Index*
American Biographical Archive	1,842 micro-fiche	1986–89	Cumulation of 368 biographical works published from 1702–1956 (mostly 1870–1920) covering North Americans at state and national levels	280,000	*ABI*
Appleton's Cyclopaedia of American Biography	6+1	1887–89, 1901	Prominent native and adopted citizens, early settlers (some living). Family members and genealogical information.	Approximately 19,000	*BGMI* base
Appleton's Cyclopaedia of Am. Biog., Supplement or: The Cyclopaedia of American Biography	6	1918–31	Similiar to above—mostly those famous since 1890.	Approximately 15,000	*BGMI* base
Dictionary of American Biography	20+ 8 supplements	1928–36, 1944–88	Deceased residents of U.S. who made significant contributions to American life or were of historical importance. Includes sources.	18,110	*BGMI*
Encyclopedia of American Biography (Old Series) or: American Biography: A New Cyclopedia	54	1916–33	Persons since Civil War with accomplishments in art, science, manufacturing, invention, commerce, religion, education, etc. Most living.	Approximately 60,000	No (series index to vol. 50)
Encyclopedia of American Biography (New Series)	40	1934–70	Continues the above series—mostly living persons. Lengthy sketches.	Approximately 13,300	*BGMI* 1985 cumulation
Herringshaw's National Library of American Biography	5	1909–14	Leaders of life and thought in the U.S. "Every name of eminence in the republic since its formation to the present time." Very brief.	35,000	ABI
National Cyclopedia of American Biography—Permanent Series	63	1898–1984	Those who made notable contributions to political, social, commercial, and industrial life, including genealogy. Deceased only.	Approximately 56,600	*BGMI* and 1–13 in *ABI*
National Cyclopedia of American Biography—Current Series	13	1938–84	Same as above but includes only living persons.	Approximately 11,600	No
Twentieth Century Biographical Dictionary of Notable Americans	10	1904	Authors, clergymen, editors, engineers, jurists, officials scientists, statesmen, and others making American history	Approximately 14,000	*BGMI* base
Who Was Who in America	11	1943–93	Deceased who were formerly in Who's Who in America. Sketches had been written and/or approved by subjects.	122,000	*BGMI*
Dictionary of Canadian Biography	12	1966–91	Notable Canadians who died by 1900. Scholarly articles, each approximately one page long. Sources included (arranged by death dates). Three later volumes in preparation (deaths 1901–30).	6,520	*BGMI*

Indexes: *ABI* (*American Biographical Index*); *BGMI* (*Biography and Genealogy Master Index*), including base set, 1985 and 1990 cumulated supplements, and annual supplements.

publication (since 1947) of the H. W. Wilson company (New York) is cumulated in book form at several-year intervals and is also available on CD-ROM.

The *Biography Index*'s arrangement is patterned after the same publisher's successful and popular *Reader's Guide to Periodical Literature.* It allows the user to locate biographies by subject or locality as well as by the person's name. Hundreds of periodicals and new books are reviewed each year, and biographical articles, chapters, and entire book-length biographies are noted in *Biography Index.* Like *BGMI,* the *Biography Index* leads to other sources, many of which are available in local public libraries or through interlibrary loan. The references are to articles published during the period covered by the index and so are usually about contemporary persons; however, many historical personalities also are treated in such articles. The articles and books that the *Biography Index* references are almost always longer and more detailed than the short descriptions found in collective biographies. Many are the products of research by their authors, and few were written by the subject. As products of research they may be more critical than otherwise and usually provide more sources of information, either in the text or in an accompanying bibliography. Such a source will provide the answers to practically any question that a genealogist might have. The *Biography Index* has been indexed in *BGMI,* so it is not necessary to search the individual indexes if *BGMI* is available. The indexed entries are found in the 1985 *BGMI* cumulation and subsequent volumes.

There are other sources for periodical articles on notable persons, including the standard periodical indexes, such as *Reader's Guide to Periodical Literature* and *Magazine Index* (however, most references in these indexes are also in *Biography Index*). They can be good beginning places if the local library does not have *BGMI* or the *Biography Index.*

An index to more obscure and generally more "scholarly" biographical articles is *People in History.* This two-volume 1988 index references articles and dissertations that cover a significant portion of a person's life. It was based on the database for *America: History and Life, a Guide to Periodical Literature* (Santa Barbara, Calif.: ABC-Clio, 1964–, annual) which abstracts all writings dealing with American history, including biography. It includes more than 7,600 citations from 737 journals (usually historical) on more than six thousand men and women in U.S. and Canadian history from colonial times to the present. All of the articles have been published since 1975. Since these articles and dissertations are generally in the field of history, a large percentage of the entries are for persons who lived before the twentieth century; therefore, *People in History* nicely complements the generally more recent subjects in *Biography Index.* Many local historians have written about more obscure persons in recent years, so a search in *People in History* may locate an ancestor. *People in History* is indexed in the 1990 cumulation of *BGMI,* making it easier to determine if there is an entry of interest before locating the source.

For more information on the use of periodicals and periodical indexes in genealogical research, see chapter 19, "Genealogical Periodicals."

Biographical Encyclopedias

Toward the end of the nineteenth century, several publishers determined that the United States needed a national biography similar to those in many European countries. The result was the creation of several multi-volume biographical encyclopedias, each with thousands of entries. Each encyclopedia had slightly different selection criteria, but the editors mainly sought prominent Americans who had contributed in one way or another to the history of the country. A few notable foreigners, such as the marquis de Lafayette, were included, but the subjects were usually presidents and governors, inventors, politicians, business leaders, statesmen, scientists, authors, philanthropists, and other generally "successful" persons—and almost all of them were men.

> **ARNOLD, Benedict,** governor of Rhode Island, b. in England, 21 Dec., 1615; d. 20 June, 1678. He lived for some time in Providence, and in 1637 was one of thirteen who signed a compact agreeing to subject themselves to any agreements made by a majority of the masters of families. In 1645 his knowledge of the native tongues gained him the office of messenger to negotiate with the Indians. and on one occasion they accused him of misrepresentation. In 1653 he moved to Newport, and in 1654 was elected assistant for that town. In 1657 he was one of the purchasers of the island of Conanicut. On 19 May, 1657, Roger Williams having retired from the presidency of the colony, Arnold was elected to the office, and he was again assistant in 1660. On 22 May, 1662, he was again elected president, and under the royal charter given in 1663 he was the first governor of the colony. To this office he was reëlected in May, 1664, and in 1669, 1677, and 1678. Gov. Arnold was instrumental in bringing about the reconciliation and union of the two colonies of Rhode Island and Providence plantations.

Figure 18-2. From *Appleton's Cyclopedia of American Biography*, vol. 1 (1887), page 93.

If the subject was living, he was usually invited to provide information for the article and sometimes even to write an initial draft. For deceased subjects, the editor usually employed a staff who researched the person's biography and prepared the entry. Some entries comprise a brief paragraph with the subject's birth and death information and a brief note of his accomplishments; however, many entries are a page or two in length and give much more information. Some editors included ancestors and/or children of the subject. Table 18-4 gives the key features of the major sets, including the number of persons profiled in each set.

Appleton's Cyclopedia. The first such set was *Appleton's Cyclopedia of American Biography* (New York: D. Appleton), which included both living and deceased Americans. For many subjects some ancestral information was given. Many entries are by family, leading off with a prominent head of a family and with other members (sons, daughters, nephews, cousins, etc.) profiled separately in the course of the article. Most articles are one to two columns long (one-half to one page) and are very informative about the subject's life. The alphabetically arranged entries often give some genealogical information about the subject's immediate family (figure 18-2).

First published in six volumes from 1887 to 1889, *Appleton's Cyclopedia* has been reprinted several times, most recently in 1968. A supplement was issued in 1901. From 1915 to 1931 a new, enlarged edition was printed in twelve volumes

Winslow

WINSLOW, EDWARD (Oct. 18, 1595–May 8, 1655), Pilgrim father, author, was born at Droitwich, Worcestershire, England, the son of Edward and Magdalene (Ollyver or Oliver) Winslow, people of some property and education. He himself received an excellent education (though not at a university) and had early social advantages enjoyed by none of the other Pilgrims. Apparently while traveling on the Continent in 1617 he came to know of John Robinson's Separatist congregation at Leyden and joined them, marrying Elizabeth Barker there on May 16, 1618. He earned his living as a printer, perhaps employed by William Brewster [*q.v.*], and despite his youth became an active member of the community. He sailed on the *Speedwell* in 1620, trans-shipping to the *Mayflower* when the former turned back. With him he took two servants, George Soule and Elias Story, and he purchased £60 stock in the venture. Three of his brothers later reached Plymouth.

Winslow aided in the first explorations and was one of the small band who landed at the site of Plymouth on Dec. 11/21, 1620. He was chosen envoy to greet Massasoit [*q.v.*] when that chief appeared at the settlement in the spring of 1621, and made the colonists' first treaty with the Indian. In July he was principal envoy to visit Massasoit at his home and in a later visit probably saved Massasoit's life. Next to Myles Standish Winslow was the Pilgrims' most important man in dealing with the Indians throughout his career in America. On May 12, 1621, his first wife having died in March, he married Susanna (Fuller) White, a widow—the first marriage at Plymouth. In 1622 he sent back to England by the *Fortune* four narratives of explorations and dealings with the Indians, and Gov. William Bradford [*q.v.*] sent a narrative of the voyage and the first year of the colony. The latter was retained by the captain of a French privateer which captured the *Fortune*, but Winslow's narratives reached London and were printed by George Morton [*q.v.*] in *A Relation or Iournall of the beginning and proceedings of the English Plantation setled at Plimoth in New England* (1622). They were thus the first accounts of these happenings to be published which had been written in America.

In the fall of 1623 he went to England, returning to Plymouth in March following, bringing "3. heifers and a bull, the first beginning of any catle of that kind in ye land" (Bradford, *post*, I, 353). Later in 1624 he became one of the five assistants, now appointed for the first time, and returned to England to negotiate with the merchants with whom the colonists had quar-

Winslow

reled before sailing in 1620. Here he published a narrative of the years 1621–23, *Good News from New England or a True Relation of Things Very Remarkable at the Plantation of Plymouth in New England . . . Written by E. W.* (1624). This, with the narratives previously mentioned, completes the only contemporary record of the first years, for Bradford's *History* seems not to have been begun before 1630. While in London, in a dramatic scene before the Merchant Adventurers, Winslow defended the Pilgrims with such success from accusations sent back to England by John Oldham [*q.v.*] and John Lyford that he was able to establish better relations, to borrow money, and to purchase supplies. His arrival at Plymouth in 1625 at the moment when Oldham was being beaten out of the colony is one of the dramatic scenes in Pilgrim history.

Winslow was one of the "undertakers" who in 1627 assumed the colony's debts in return for its trading privileges and he became the most active of their explorers and traders, setting up posts in Maine, on Cape Ann, on Buzzard's Bay, and later on the Connecticut River. This trade was in large measure the secret of Plymouth's commercial success. In 1629 Winslow superseded Isaac Allerton [*q.v.*] as the colony's agent, and in its interest made several further trips to England. He was largely instrumental in securing a grant of land in 1630 from the Council for New England and defended the colonists before the Privy Council in 1633 against the charges of Christopher Gardiner [*q.v.*], Ferdinando Gorges, and others. While he was attempting a similar mission for the Massachusetts colony in 1634, however, Archbishop Laud accused him of "teaching" in the Pilgrim church and of celebrating marriages, though a layman. These charges Winslow admitted, and he was in consequence thrown into prison for four months.

Always active in the administrative and judicial work of the colony, he was assistant nearly every year from 1624 to 1646, was governor in 1633, 1636, and 1644; aided in organizing the New England Confederation, and was Plymouth's representative. He played an important part in reorganizing colonial and local government in 1636 and in drafting the new code of laws, and resisted valiantly the encroachments of Massachusetts, Rhode Island, and Connecticut upon Plymouth's trading posts. In 1646 he was induced by Winthrop, much against the wishes of the Pilgrims, to return to England to defend the Massachusetts Bay Company against the charges of Samuel Gorton [*q.v.*]. When the latter published a tract stating his case (*Simplicities Defence against Seven-Headed Policy,*

Figure 18-3. From *Dictionary of American Biography,* vol. 20 (1936), pages 393–94.

Winslow

1646) Winslow replied with *Hypocrisie Unmasked by the True Relation of the Proceedings of the Governour and Company of the Massachusetts against Samuel Gorton* . . . (1646). To a tract written by John Child—*New-Englands Jonas* [Winslow?] *Cast up at London* (1647)—he retorted with *New Englands Salamander Discovered by an Irreligious and Scornfull Pamphlet* (1647). In 1649 he published *The Glorious Progress of the Gospel among the Indians in New England,* which led to the founding that year of the Society for the Propagation of the Gospel in New England, of which he was one of the incorporators.

These and other activities kept him occupied in England, and he never returned to Plymouth. In 1654 Cromwell appointed him chairman of a joint English and Dutch commission to assess damages for English vessels destroyed by the Dutch in neutral Denmark. At the end of that same year he was appointed chief of three commissioners, with Admirals Venables and Penn, to capture the Spanish West India colonies. Failing in this purpose, the fleet seized Jamaica, thus beginning the British possession of that island. On the return voyage Winslow died of fever, May 8, 1655, and was buried at sea with high honors. He was the first man to achieve success in England after receiving his training in affairs in America. He is the only Pilgrim of whom a portrait is known; his was painted in London in 1651.

[Winslow's own writings and William Bradford, *Hist. of Plymouth Plantation* (2 vols., 1912), ed. by W. C. Ford, are the chief authorities; Nathaniel Morton, *New-Englands Memoriall* (1669), was partly based on Winslow's papers, now lost; the best edition of Winslow's first narratives appears in *Mourt's Relation* (1865), ed. by H. M. Dexter; his *Good News from New England* is repr. in Alexander Young, *Chronicles of the Pilgrim Fathers* (1841), and with notes in Edward Arber, *The Story of the Pilgrim Fathers* (1897); *Hypocrisie Unmasked* was reprinted by the Club for Colonial Reprints, Providence, in 1916. Some letters of Winslow's are in Bradford's Letter Book, in *Mass. Hist. Soc. Colls.,* I ser. III (1794). See also R. G. Usher, *The Pilgrims and Their Hist.* (1918); J. A. Goodwin, *The Pilgrim Republic* (1888); D. P. and F. K. Holton, *Winslow Memorial* (2 vols., 1877–88); Thomas Birch, *A Coll. of the State Papers of John Thurloe* (1742), III, 249–52, 325; C. H. Firth and R. S. Rait, *Acts and Ordinances of the Interregnum* (3 vols., 1911); *Cal. of State Papers, Col. Ser., 1574–1600* (1860).] R. G. U.

under the title *The Cyclopedia of American Biography, Supplementary Edition.* The last six volumes, 1918 to 1931, have become known as *A Supplement to Appleton's Cyclopedia of American Genealogy,* primarily through Gale Research Company's 1976 reprint and Gale's *Biography and Genealogy Master Index.*

Dictionary of American Biography. The most scholarly and accepted biographical encyclopedia is the *Dictionary of American Biography* (*DAB*) (New York: C. Scribner), published in twenty volumes from 1928 to 1936. Eight supplements have been issued since 1944. No living persons are included in the dictionary; the eighth supplement (published in 1988), for example, covers persons who died between 1966 and 1970. The articles average one-half to one page in length; there are longer sketches for particularly well-known persons. The articles are written by a staff of scholars; each includes a note regarding the sources of the biographical material (figure 18-3). The subjects must have lived in the United States and made a significant contribution to American life. The *Dictionary of American Biography*'s restrictive selection criteria, professional staff, objective (non-laudatory) approach, and retrospective nature (subjects are profiled several years after death) make it the most popular multi-volume biographical set in use today. It is available in most libraries. The first twenty volumes are alphabetically arranged, as are each of the supplements. A complete index guide was published in 1981.

Encyclopedia of American Biography is the title on the spine of one of the largest biographical sets; however, the title page reads *American Biography: A New Cyclopedia* (New York: American Historical Society). It was published in fifty-four volumes from 1916 to 1933 and has become known as the Old Series due to a newer publication of forty volumes (1934 to 1970) under the title *Encyclopedia of American Biography (New Series).* Both were published by the American Historical Society. They focus on persons who were prominent, generally upper class, and who lived since the Civil War—hence, many were living at publication, especially of the Old Series. To some extent a vanity or "mug book" publication (see "County and Local Sources," below), it is very helpful nonetheless. The sketches in it tend to be longer, averaging two to four pages, and most were contributed by the subject or his family. They are devoted to preserving in accessible form the life records of people whose accomplishments received recognition in the arts, sciences, commerce, manufacturing, professions, religion, business, and society. Neither series is arranged in any understandable order, so the index is necessary.

The Old Series is *not* indexed in *BGMI,* but a separately published index to the first fifty volumes is available. The last four are individually indexed. The new series is indexed in *BGMI*'s 1985 cumulation and also in its own cumulative indexes in vols. 25, 35, and 40. These lengthy articles often include several generations of genealogies. The family names in those genealogical sections are included in the set's own indexes, but not in *BGMI.* A search of the indexes, therefore, may locate information on part of a lineage even if the subject is only distantly related to the researcher.

Herringshaw's National Library. For a briefer, "ready reference" source, Thomas William Herringshaw's *Herringshaw's National Library of American Biography* (Chicago: American

Publisher's Association) is useful. Published in five volumes from 1909 to 1914, it includes thirty-five thousand brief (one-paragraph) entries on "every name of eminence produced by this great republic since its formation to the present time." Its primary focus is on prominent persons of the nineteenth century, but it includes some colonial leaders. Although brief, most entries include a specific birth date and birthplace as well as the subject's occupation, achievements, and publications. Death information is provided for deceased individuals. It is arranged alphabetically and, while not indexed in *BGMI*, it is indexed in *ABI*.

National Cyclopedia. The two series of the *The National Cyclopedia of American Biography* (New York: James T. White) comprise the largest and longest running biographical encyclopedia published in the United States. It covers almost seventy thousand persons in the seventy-six volumes published from 1898 to its cessation in 1984. Its selection criteria are broader than those of the *Dictionary of American Biography,* but the articles are not usually as well written or researched. The articles were written by the office staff, often based on questionnaires or information provided by the family. Most articles are around one page in length, but many are longer. Many articles include a portrait of the subject; these are excluded from the *Dictionary ofAmerican Biography*. The editors focused on those who made notable contributions to U.S. life and who exemplify and perpetuate the progress and growth of the United States. Other biographical encyclopedias, notably the *Dictionary of American Biography,* provide much more interpretive biographical information, while the *National Cyclopedia* emphasizes information and is "generally reliable as to factual detail" (Yelton 1978, 5).

The Permanent Series (vols. 1 to 63) of the *National Cyclopedia* includes only deceased persons, while the Current Series (with volumes lettered *A* to *M*) includes only living persons. Many subjects of the earlier Current Series volumes (which began in 1930) were included in the later Permanent Series volumes after their deaths. The publisher's stated plan was to publish (in the Permanent Series) a final sketch of each subject in the Current Series after his or her death; however, this has not happened. Many never received their "final treatment"—especially those whose careers ended with less prominence than they found in early life (Yelton 1978, 18).

There is no particular arrangement between or within volumes (except that the earlier volumes grouped the subjects by vocation). When the series ceased publication in 1984, a vol. 63N was issued with both living and deceased subjects. A final edition of the index covering all volumes was also published—fortunately, for *BGMI* only indexes the Permanent Series (not the Current Series). Figure 18-4 is from the Current Series; though the subject (Lawrence Chamberlain) died in 1967, he never appeared in the Permanent Series. An advantage of using the index to the entire set is that it indicates which biographical articles have ancestral information and, in many cases, who the notable descendants of various immigrant ancestors are. Some topical entries are also in the index, such as those to cities or companies founded by the persons being profiled.

Twentieth Century Biographical Dictionary. The *Twentieth Century Biographical Dictionary of Notable Americans* (Boston: Biographical Society) was published in 1904 and reprinted in 1968 (ten volumes). It includes biographies of authors, administrators, military officers, editors, jurists, merchants, officials, philanthropists, scientists, statesmen, and others who have made U.S. history. It was first published from 1897 to 1903 as *The Cyclopedia ofAmerican Biographies* in seven volumes and again from 1900 to 1903 (also in seven volumes) as *Lamb's Biographical Dictionary of the United States.* The articles are somewhat shorter than those in similar works, seldom covering more than one page. The arrangement is alphabetical by the subject's name.

Who Was Who in America. *Who Was Who in America* (Chicago: Marquis, 1943–96) includes far more persons (approximately 127,000) in its twelve volumes than any other set, but the references are much shorter than those in the others (except for *Herringshaw's National Library*—see above), giving only brief vital information (dates of birth and death, spouse, and children) along with degrees, achievements, awards, positions, etc. (Compare figure 18-5 with figure 18-4; both profile the same person.) All entries are for deceased persons only; they were taken from the entries in the same publisher's *Who's Who in America* (see below) after the person's death. Thus, *Who Was Who* is a "cumulation" of the more than seventy years of *Who's Who* volumes. All of the subjects approved the information and the sketches before death (actually at the time of publication in *Who's Who in America*). Each of the eight numbered volumes is alphabetically arranged and includes persons who died during specific periods since 1897 through 1984 (for example, vol. 4 is for 1961 to 1968). A "Historical Volume" includes notable Americans who died between 1607 and 1896. The sketches in that volume were compiled by the publisher. A separately compiled comprehensive index is available and is included in *BGMI.*

Canadian Sources. Canadian research can also benefit greatly from similar sources. Slocum's *Biographical Dictionaries and Related Works* (see above under "National Biographical Sources—Bibliographies") lists more than 160 national and regional sources for Canada. In a research case on the Little family of early Massachusetts, the researcher learned that Otis Little's father and other relatives were prominent in the colony. Suspecting that their prominence gave Otis some advantages and notability, the researcher searched *BGMI.* A reference there led to the *Dictionary of Canadian Biography,* edited by George W. Brown, 12 vols. (Toronto: University ofToronto Press, 1966–91), which showed that Otis was one of Nova Scotia's first attorney generals; this explained his disappearance from Massachusetts records. Pursuing leads from the *Dictionary of Canadian Biography* led to other sources, and the researcher was eventually able to find documentation that proved that Otis was the father of Dr. William Little of Connecticut (no Connecticut source gave that information).

Biographical Dictionaries

Besides the large encyclopedia sets mentioned above, hundreds of other one- and two-volume sources profile notable Americans (usually in much briefer detail). Most of these focus on particular groups of individuals, such as educators or authors; they are discussed below under "Vocational Sources." Some, however, are national in scope and include Americans of all types.

Who's Who in America. The largest and most well known of this type of source is *Who's Who in America* (Chicago: Mar-

240 THE NATIONAL CYCLOPÆDIA

CHAMBERLAIN, Lawrence, investment banker and author, was born in New York city, Oct. 10, 1878, son of George Washington and Hattie Lawrence (Cummings) Chamberlain. His father was a physician. Mr. Chamberlain received his preparatory education at Phillips Academy, Andover, Mass., and was graduated B.A. at Yale University in 1902. After an additional year of study at the Yale graduate school as Porter fellow in English literature he received an M.A. degree in 1903. In 1904–05 he was in charge of the course of rhetoric at Dartmouth College. In 1906 he entered the bond business in the office of A. B. Leach & Co. in Boston. Three years later he removed to New York city and from 1910 to 1915 was with the bond department of the banking house of Kountze Bros. He then helped to organize and became a member of the New York stock exchange firm of Hemphill, White & Chamberlain. During 1919–25 he was in business for himself as president of

Lawrence Chamberlain and Co., Inc., originator of industrial security issues. Retiring from the investment banking business, he has since devoted his time and energies to social and economic research. During 1932–36 he was president and a director of Chamberlain Associates, Inc., a security research and fund management organization. After many years of service as a director of the Lord, Abbett group of investment companies: American Business Shares, Inc., Affiliated Fund, Inc., and Union Trusteed Funds, Inc., he has recently resigned to become investment consultant of these companies. He was formerly president of Mutual Investment Fund, Inc., and is at present (1946) a director; and also a director and member of the executive committee of Third Avenue Transit Corp., and a director of Westchester Street Transportation Co., Inc., and Surface Transportation Corp. of New York. Mr. Chamberlain has lectured on finance at the New York University school of commerce and on accounts and finance at the Wharton school of finance and commerce of the University of Pennsylvania, Yale, the Amos Tuck school of administration and finance of Dartmouth, Ohio State University and the American Institute of Banking, of which he is a regent. His published writings include "The Principles of Bond Investment" (1911 and several later editions), perhaps the most influential book in giving form and direction to the science of investment in the United States; "Work of the Bond House" (1912); "Investment and Speculation," with William W. Hay (1931), and many articles in financial newspapers and magazines. He was one of the founders of the Investment Bankers' Association of America, which he has long served as chairman of the education committee, vice president and member of the board of governors. In 1934 he was secretary of the organizing committee of the Institute of International Finance. He also assisted in raising funds to establish the Chamber of Commerce of the United States. He is a member of the Beta Theta Pi fraternity. In religion he is a Congregationalist. He has been married twice: (1) in Worcester, Mass., Dec. 30, 1901, to Berenice, daughter of Frederick B. Taylor, a lumber merchant, of Springfield, Mass.; (2) in Brooklyn, N.Y., Jan. 19, 1918, to Edna Owens, daughter of Reed Williams, an exporter, of Forest Hills, N.Y. By the first marriage he has one son, Lawrence; and by the second marriage three children: Walter, Virginia and Edwin Chamberlain.

Figure 18-4. Lawrence W. Chamberlain's biography in *The National Cyclopedia of American Biography,* vol. G (1946).

CHAMBERLAIN, W. Lawrence, banker, author; b. N.Y., Oct. 10, 1878; s. George Washington and Hattie L. (Cummings) C.; A.B., Yale, 1902, A.M., 1903; Porter fellowship in English lit. Yale, 1902-04; m. Berenice Taylor, 1902 (div. 1916); children—Lawrence Cummings, Virginia, Walter Case, Edwin Harvey; m. 2d, Edna Owens Williams, Jan. 19, 1918. In charge dept. rhetoric Dartmouth, 1904-05; entered bond bus., Boston, 1906, removed to N.Y., 1909; with Kountze Bros., 1910-15; mem. N.Y. Stock Exchange firm of Hemphill, White & Chamberlain, 1915-18; pres. Chamberlain Assos., Inc.; dir. Mut. Investment Fund, Inc, Westchester St. Transp. Co., Inc.; econ. cons. Am. Bus. Shares, Inc., Affiliated Fund, Inc., Union Trusteed Funds, Inc. Lectr. finance N.Y.U. Sch. Commerce, Accounts and Finance, U. Pa., Tuck Sch. Finance (Dartmouth), and Am. Inst. Bankers, N.Y. Regent Am. Inst. Banking; dir. Hedge Fund New Eng. Conglist. Mem. Beta Theta Pi. Author: The Principles of Bond Investment, 1911, 27; The Work of the Bond House, 1912; Investment and Speculation (with W. W. Hay), 1931. Died Dec. 18, 1961.

Figure 18-5. Chamberlain's biography in *Who Was Who in America,* vol. 4 (1961–68), page 164.

CHAMBERLAIN, Lawrence, banker, author; *b.* New York, Oct. 10, 1878; *s.* George Washington and Hattie L. (Cummings) C.; A.B., Yale, 1902, A.M., 1903; Porter fellowship in English lit., Yale Grad. Sch., 1902-4; *m.* Berenice Taylor, of Springfield, Mass., Jan. 3, 1902. In charge Dept. of Rhetoric, Dartmouth, 1904-5; entered bond business in Boston, 1906, removed to New York, 1909; with Kountze Bros., New York, 1910—; pres. The Bankers Book Co. Lecturer on finance, New York Univ. Sch. of Commerce, Accounts and Finance, U. of Pa., and Tuck Sch. of Finance, Dartmouth. Conglist. Mem. Beta Theta Pi. *Club:* Montclair Athletic. *Author:* The Principles of Bond Investment, 1911; The Work of the Bond House, 1912. Contbr. to financial mags. *Home:* 5 Hawthorne Place, Montclair, N. J. *Office:* 141 Broadway, New York.

CHAMBERLAIN, Lawrence, banker, author; b. New York, Oct. 10, 1878; s. George Washington and Hattie L. (Cummings) C.; A.B., Yale, 1902, A.M., 1903; Porter fellowship in English lit., Yale Grad. Sch., 1902-04; m. 2d, Edna Owens Williams, of London, Eng., Jan. 19, 1918; children—Lawrence Cummings, Virginia, Walter Case, Edwin Harvey. In charge dept. of rhetoric, Dartmouth, 1904-05; entered bond business in Boston, 1906, removed to New York, 1909; with Kountze Bros., 1910-15; mem. N.Y. Stock Exchange firm of Hemphill, White & Chamberlain, 1915-18; pres. Chamberlain Associates, Inc.; vice-president, secretary and director Mutual Investment Fund, Inc.; dir. American Business Shares, Incorporated, Union Trustees Funds, Inc., Affiliated Funds, Inc. Lecturer on finance, New York U. Sch. of Commerce, Accounts and Finance, U. of Pa., Tuck School Finance (Dartmouth), and Am. Inst. Bankers, N.Y. Trustee Am. Inst. of Banking; dir. Hedge Fund of New England. Conglist. Mem. Beta Theta Pi. Author: The Principles of Bond Investment, 1911, 27; The Work of the Bond House, 1912; Investment and Speculation (with W. W. Hay), 1931. Home: Greenwich, Conn.

Figure 18-6. Biographies of Lawrence Chamberlain from *Who's Who in America,* vol. 8 (1914–15), page 411 (top); and vol. 22 (1942–43), page 497 (bottom). The top entry is the first to appear for Chamberlain in *Who's Who in America;* the other is a later, mid-career entry.

quis). First published in 1899, it is now updated and reprinted in two volumes every two years. It includes only living persons who seem to be of greatest public interest. The subjects are invited to be included and to send information. Furthermore, each approves his sketch before publication. Those who choose not to participate are, by their own action, excluded. Most entries are repeated from one volume to the next, so they are not indexed in *BGMI.* After a person's death her entry appears in the next volume of *Who Was Who in America* (see above).

The entries are updated regularly, so the most recent volumes contain the most current information. For a historical perspective, search earlier volumes. Figure 18-6 contains two entries for the subject who appears in figure 18-5. One entry is the first entry to appear in *Who's Who in America* (1914); the other is a later, mid-career entry (1942). The entry in figure 18-5 is, of course, from after the subject's death and parallels entries from the volumes published shortly before his death.

Marquis also offers *Who's Who in the World;* four regional U.S. sources: *Who's Who in the East, Who's Who in the Midwest, Who's Who in the South and Southwest,* and *Who's Who in the West; Who's Who in American Women;* and two vocational volumes, *Who's Who in Law* and *Who's Who in Finance and Industry.* Each of these is periodically updated. To solve the access problems associated with nine separate volumes, the publisher recently began producing an annual *Who's Who in America Index* that indexes the most recent of each of the nine titles. The 1990 index referenced approximately 200,000 individuals in one or more of the *Who's Who* publications. Marquis has also combined its current *Who's Who* volumes on one CD-ROM with more than 750,000 entries as *The Complete Marquis Who's Who Plus.*

Historical Sources. Of greater interest to the genealogist are the numerous biographical dictionaries that were issued in the nineteenth and early twentieth centuries. One of the largest was Francis Samuel Drake's *Dictionary of American Biography* (1872; reprint; Detroit: Gale Research, 1974), with nearly ten thousand names. An earlier one was William Allen's *American Biographical Dictionary,* 3rd ed. (Boston: William Hyde and Co., 1857), which was an extensive revision of the 1809 and 1832 editions. Seven thousand deceased persons from the late eighteenth and early nineteenth centuries, most of whom are not in Allen's or Drake's works, are in Franklin Benjamin Hough's *American Biographical Notes* (Albany: Munsell, 1875; reprint; Harrison, N.Y.: Harbor Hill Books, 1974). Many of Hough's entries came from upstate New York newspapers.

Mitchell Harrison's *Prominent and Progressive Americans* (New York: New York Tribune) is a two-volume "encyclopedia of contemporaneous biography" from 1902–04. Everit Brown's *Dictionary of American Politics* (New York: A. L. Burt, published irregularly from 1888 to at least 1908) contains brief sketches of important American political leaders of the eighteenth and nineteenth centuries. Biographical sketches and pictures of more than one hundred "persons born abroad who came to the colonies in North America before the year 1701" are in Charles Knowles Bolton's *The Founders,* which was published in three volumes from 1919 to 1926 (Reprint; 3 vols. in 2; Baltimore: Genealogical Publishing Co., 1976). Unfortunately, Drake's appears to be the only one of these sources that is indexed in *BGMI;* however, one edition of each of these titles (except Bolton's) is included in *American Biographical Archive.*

Many volumes of biographies focus on the graduates of particular colleges and universities. Sometimes they contain only brief obituary notices, but often they contain detailed, researched biographical sketches of students who graduated one hundred to three hundred years ago. The best example of such a collection is *Sibley's Harvard Graduates,* 17 vols. (Boston: Massachusetts Historical Society and others, 1873–1974), whose seventeen volumes through 1974 profile each graduate from 1642 to 1721. Most prominent older eastern universities (Yale, Cornell, Princeton, Amherst, and others) have published similar works. They are listed in Slocum's *Biographical Dictionaries and Related Works* in the "General U.S." section; the colleges represented there are listed in table 18-5. Use the topical index in *Biographical Dictionaries and Related Works* to learn what alumni biography books were published for a particular college.

Table 18-5. College and University Alumni Biographies

College	*Alumnus Years*
Amherst	1822–1962
Bowdoin College	1794–1950
Brown University	1764–1904
Colby University	1822–1884
Columbia University	1867–1963
Dartmouth College	1771–1867
DePauw University	1837–1915
Gettysburg College	1832–1932
Harvard University	1642–1771
Kings College	1758–1776
Lafayette College	1826–1879
Middlebury College	1800–1853
Mount Holyoak College	1837–1937
Princeton University	1748–1794
Smith College	1871–1935
Swarthmore College	1862–1914
U.S. Naval Academy	1886–1900+
University of Pennsylvania	1878–1960
University of Michigan	1837–1921
University of North Carolina	Early–1924
Vassar College	Early–1938
Washington and Jefferson	1802–1902
Wesleyan University	1831–1931
West Point Academy	1802–1930
Williams College	1793–1875
Yale University	1701–1884

Obituaries. An obituary is often the only published biographical information about an ancestor. Some key obituary collections have been indexed. The *New York Times Obituaries Index,* 2 vols. (New York: New York Times, 1970, 1979), references most obituaries in that newspaper from 1858 to 1978. Almost every person of national prominence and many local persons are listed in this index. The deaths of almost twenty-five thousand notables between 1940 and 1979 are indexed in Felice D. Levy's *Obituaries on File,* 2 vols. (New York: Facts on File, 1979). Many other obituary indexes listed in Slocum's *Biographical Dictionaries* pertain to particular states or vocations. An excellent guide to obituary indexes, both published and manuscript files, is Betty M. Jarboe's *Obituaries: A Guide to Sources,* 2nd ed. (Boston: G. K. Hall, 1989).

Book-Length Biographies

At least twenty-five thousand Americans have been the subjects of book-length biographies or autobiographies. Admittedly, most of them are nationally prominent persons, such as presidents, statesmen, scientists, etc., but many were only of regional importance, such as leaders of small religious groups and state executives. Such persons are almost always included in compiled biographies, but just about any researcher would rather have a complete book about an ancestor than a two-page summary of her life.

None of the sources discussed so far identifies single-person biographies. If an ancestor or other relative was prominent enough, it is worthwhile to determine whether a book biography exists for that person. Many family stories claim that an ancestor was a close relative of some famous person. A book biography about that person will often prove (or disprove) such an assertion. In one case, a Bass family in Texas reported that an ancestor was said to have been the sister of the Texas outlaw Sam Bass. A trip to the local university library located two biographies of Sam Bass. One of them contained extensive information on Bass's relatives, showing that there was no connection to the sister; thus, research was able to proceed in positive directions and not down the wrong path. In another case, a successful hotelier needed to prove if and how he was related to a celebrity of the same name. A biography of the celebrity included seven generations of his surname line. It was easy to put the client's pedigree chart next to that of the celebrity to show that there was no connection.

Keep in mind that while most people have not been the subjects of book biographies, any person's near relative (cousin, brother, etc.) may have been. Governor Edward Winslow was a *Mayflower* passenger and prominent leader of Plymouth Colony. However, many persons descend from his much more obscure brother Kenelm. Edward's biography discusses his family in some depth and gives insight to the life and relatives of his brother as well. Also, if an ancestor was an alleged companion of a famous person ("he explored the West with Fremont"), a book biography of the famous person will likely prove or disprove the tradition. While this approach is more applicable to book biographies, it can be applied to a lesser degree to sketches in collective biographies.

An outstanding bibliography set that lists virtually every book biography published or distributed in the United States from 1876 to 1980 is the R. R. Bowker Company's *Biographical Books, 1876–1949* (1983) and *Biographical Books, 1950–1980* (1980). This set seeks to identify every U.S. book biography of the last century. Each volume has between thirty thousand and forty thousand entries for different books. Because many persons are the subjects of several biographies, the actual number of different persons referenced in the two volumes is approximately twenty-five thousand. These volumes include family histories (genealogies) with substantial biographical treatments of immigrants or common ancestors under that person's name. At the end of each volume are additional indexes by vocation, author, and title. A listing of biographical books *in print* is available for *Biographical Books, 1950–1980.* To learn about books published since 1980, consult *Biography Index* (described earlier).

Because the books are fully described (with complete cataloging information), they are easy to find in library catalogs. If not in a local library's collection, they will be available through interlibrary loan. The inclusion of genealogies makes it important to search this set for any colonial immigrant ancestor. If there is any hint that an ancestor is the subject of a book biography or may be related to someone who is, a search of *Biographical Books* may pay great dividends.

National sources are often under-used in research because most researchers feel that their ancestors were not very notable; however, millions of persons are noted in national sources. Take the time to consider and research the thousands of volumes available, especially because *BGMI* makes such an easy beginning.

Diaries and Autobiographies

A special form of biography is that written by the subject. While collective biographies often depend on information provided by or approved by the subject, self-written biographical material forms another class of biographies. Such personal accounts usually exist in one of three forms: diaries (including journals), autobiographies, and letters. Letters, while often including some biographical material, are not biographical in nature and are not discussed here. See chapter 15, "Documentary Collections," for a brief discussion of printed letter collections.

There are two significant differences between diaries and autobiographies: first, a diary is usually a periodic account (daily, weekly, monthly, or irregularly) of the events in the life of an individual; second, most diaries were not originally intended to be published. Indeed, they often contain the most personal and private of writings and are seldom published by the diarist; when it does occur, publication is usually after the death of the writer or at least several years after the events described in the diary. An autobiography, while written by the subject, is usually written retrospectively from a vantage point far removed from the events being described (with the exception of celebrity autobiographies, which are written to capitalize on the person's fame and usually are co- or ghostwritten). Often the writer is in the last stages of life, which may affect the accuracy of reported events. Also, autobiographies are generally written to be read by others. The writer may envision only a small audience (family and friends), but the scope of distribution does not affect the fact that the writer knew others would be reading about her life. Thus, objectivity is not a hallmark of autobiographies; often the author is seeking to explain or justify actions taken earlier in life. Even factual material can be considered suspect if it seems too laudatory.

The distinction between diary and journal is vague and varies according to the writer or editor. The term *journal* has become more popular recently and often signifies more substance or reflection by the author than a diary. However, a journal can also be a limited-term, regular account of observations of a particular event, such as a weather journal or a journal kept during scientific experiments. In addition, *journal* often refers to a published periodical, usually of academic/intellectual interest (as distinguished from a magazine). For these reasons, *diary* is the preferred term when discussing personal accounts that describe the various events in the life of an individual or family.

Published diaries are not as rare as one might think. To be sure, the odds that an ancestor's diary has been published are slim. In fact, most of our ancestors did not even keep a diary; however, some of them did, and more and more diaries are being published as scholars continue to seek primary information for social histories. Reflecting diaries' growing importance in the history field, the 1991 Pulitzer Prize for history went to Laurel Thatcher Ulrich for *A Midwife's Tale* (New York: Knopf, 1990), a biography based so heavily on a diary that it can almost be thought of as a published diary.

In the absence of an ancestor's diary, diaries of the ancestor's associates (spouse, children, other relatives, friends, neighbors, business colleagues, etc.) can provide crucial details for genealogical searches, and potentially more family history information than all other original genealogical records combined.

Finding published diaries can be problematical, at best. Most diaries are brief and seldom provide a book-length narrative when published. Consequently, many of them appear as articles in periodicals or as parts of other books, including local, social, or topical histories, individual biographies, historical novels, government reports, and other collected writings. A brief survey of the key bibliography, Laura Arksey, Nancy Pries, and Marcia Reed's *American Diaries: An Annotated Bibliography of Published American Diaries and Journals,* 2 vols. (Detroit: Gale Research, 1983, 1987), shows that published diaries appear in roughly equal numbers in full-length books, articles, and sections of books on broader topics. Most library catalogs do not identify articles in magazines or chapters of books, but *American Diaries* fully updates an older 1945 bibliography and identifies 6,046 published diaries covering the beginning of settlement in North America to 1980. The entries are well annotated and arranged by the earliest year of the diary (not the date of publication). The annotations identify the specific dates of the published portions of the diaries (many are only published in part) and briefly describe the content. Indexes to names, subjects, and geographic locations make it easy to find a published diary for a particular person, or diaries dealing with persons who lived in a specific place.

A significant collection of diaries (and some letters) is in Kenneth Holmes's ten-volume *Covered Wagon Women: Diaries and Letters from the Western Trails, 1840–1890* (Glendale, Calif., and Spokane, Wash.: Arthur H. Clark Co., 1981–91). This collection publishes rare and usually previously unpublished personal accounts of the travels and trials of women who crossed the American frontier between 1840 and 1890. For a comprehensive bibliography of personal accounts of traveling the American west, see Merrill J. Mattes's *Platte River Road Narratives* (Urbana: University of Illinois Press, 1988).

An *autobiography* presents a much different picture of the subject than can be found in virtually any other source. In an autobiography, the subject has a chance to tell the story "her way"; this, of course, can mean wide disparity among autobiographies in terms of writing quality, objectivity, and comprehensiveness. Most autobiographies are written late in the subject's life and in reality are "reminiscences." Bibliographer Merton Coulter warns about the reliability of such accounts:

> Time is of the very essence of reliability in reminiscences, but as few people feel in the reminiscent mood until many years have elapsed since the event, there is constant danger that a treacherous memory will produce distortion of past events. Yet where the writer checks his memory against established records, diaries, or other personal material, his narrative becomes much more reliable. Autobiographies are in

> these respects essentially the same as reminiscences and, therefore, have the same values and discounts (1948, xii).

However, despite these difficulties, an autobiography gives the researcher the opportunity to see its writer's public side. Despite the potential inaccuracies of autobiographies, they can be considered "original records" in that they are not themselves compiled from original records. Sometimes the author bases the autobiography on diaries or letters written earlier in life, and in that sense parts of an autobiography may be considered compiled. However, almost every autobiography contains substantial information about its subject that has never been recorded on any other document; in that sense autobiographies are original records (except for the editing done before publication). Despite their original nature, the information in an autobiography cannot always be considered "primary" because it was usually recorded long after the events took place. When the information deals with other persons besides the subject, it may be as much hearsay as information recorded in any other source. For these reasons, autobiographical information must be evaluated as carefully as any other biographical source.

Most autobiographies seem to have been published as books. Certainly an adult who feels the need to write an autobiography has enough information for a book-length text. Autobiographies that appear in periodical articles or as chapters or sections of longer books typically do not cover the subject's entire life; rather, they describe a limited portion of that life, such as a soldier's time in the military. There are at least eleven thousand autobiographies of Americans, and "more appear in print every week" (Briscoe 1982, ix). Some have been published in very small numbers (often in typescript), while others have appeared under the imprint of the biggest commercial publishers in North America. Unfortunately, very few libraries collect many autobiographies, except those of notable or famous persons. Those with small press runs can be very difficult to find. For these reasons, comprehensive bibliographies must be used as finding aids.

While many autobiographies can be found in Bowker's *Biographical Books* set (see "Book-Length Biographies," above), many have been printed in such small numbers that they have escaped the notice of bibliographers. Two comprehensive bibliographies are available to help the researcher find autobiographies. In 1962, Louis Kaplan published *A Bibliography of American Autobiographies* (Madison: University of Wisconsin Press, 1961). This annotated bibliography of 6,377 items includes many titles that appear to be typescripts held by various repositories. Kaplan limited his list to those works published before 1945 and further excluded autobiographies included in genealogical works, collective biographies, periodicals, and newspapers. He also identifies the repositories where any cited but unpublished manuscripts reside. Arranged alphabetically by author, Kaplan's *Bibliography* has a subject index that indicates occupation, historical events, and geographic locations.

Kaplan's guide was continued by Mary Louise Briscoe in *American Autobiography 1945–1980: A Bibliography* (Madison: University of Wisconsin Press, 1982). Briscoe has identified 5,008 works published by private and commercial presses. A few pre-1945 titles that were missed by Kaplan are included as well. Briscoe omitted the same class of books as did Kaplan (genealogies, collective biographies, etc.) as well as manuscript autobiographies. The arrangement is similar to Kaplan's work, with entries listed alphabetically by author and a subject index. Briscoe based her work on the entries in *Biography Index* (described above under "Historical Indexes—Periodical Indexes"), but personally examined each book to verify the citation and to write the very descriptive annotations. Briscoe's definition of autobiography is a bit broader than that given above; she includes memoirs, diaries, journals, and letter collections that are autobiographical (for example, the journals of Lewis and Clark) as well as nonfiction works that have substantial autobiographical sections. Indeed, some entries are duplicated in *American Diaries*, which was published five years later (although its compilers apparently did not use Briscoe's work while preparing their bibliography). Briscoe also includes some published collections of personal documents deemed autobiographical, such as selections of Abraham Lincoln's speeches and writings.

STATEWIDE SOURCES

Many people have achieved prominence on a statewide or regional level without being profiled in a national biography source—state legislators, local government officials, presidents of small companies, founders of towns or counties, and people who rendered other important service to a state or region. Many successful businessmen achieve local prominence. The information in statewide biographical sources tends to be similar to that found in national sources. Depending on the scope of the book, a sketch might be a brief paragraph or several pages in length.

Slocum's *Biographical Dictionaries and Related Works* (see above under "National Biographical Sources—Bibliographies") lists more than 1,200 sources for U.S. state and regional (four or more counties by Slocum's definition) biographies. If each of these averages only 400 names (and that seems a conservative guess), then at least half a million persons are profiled in these volumes. Only around one-tenth of these sources are included in *ABI,* from which approximately 100,000 of its entries come; this suggests that upwards of 1 million Americans could be profiled in statewide sources (and most of those persons do not appear in national sources). It is not practical to discuss specific titles here, but Slocum's bibliography is briefly annotated and can help to determine which sources may be the most helpful. The bibliography at the end of this chapter lists more than 140 of the largest or most accessible statewide sources (at least two are listed for each state).

Formats

Statewide biographical sources come in several formats. Some comprise one or more volumes devoted solely to biographical sketches, such as Alonzo Phelps's two-volume *Contemporary Biography of California's Representative Men* (San Francisco: A. L. Bancroft and Co., 1881). One of the largest such sets is the twenty-six-volume *Encyclopedia of Pennsylvania Biography* (New York: Lewis Historical Publishing Co., 1914–48), by John W. Jordan, et. al. Others may comprise the final two to four volumes of a multi-volume state history, such as Charles B. Galbreath's five-volume *History of Ohio* (Chicago: American Historical Society, 1925), in which the last three volumes contain biographical sketches. The scope and coverage in these two forms were similar from 1876 to 1925. Generally they included only those prominent persons who were living at the time the volumes were compiled. Deceased persons of major

CAHOON, REYNOLDS. Came to Utah 1848.
Married Thurza Stiles: Their children: Palaski; William F., m. Nancy M. Gibbs; Daniel; Andrew, m. Mary Carruth; m. Margaret Carruth; m. Jeannette Carruth; Mahonri. Family home Murray, Utah.

CAHOON, ANDREW (son of Reynolds Cahoon and Thurza Stiles). Came to Utah 1848.
Married Mary Carruth (daughter of William Carruth), who was born Oct. 1828. Their children: Joseph, m. Mary Ann McComie; Emma, m. Richard Winder; Louie, m. Lewis A. Copeland. Family home Murray, Utah.
Married Margaret Carruth (daughter of William Carruth), who was born March 25, 1832. Their children: Alonzo A., m. Mary Ann Erickson; John P., m. Elizabeth Gordon; Albert m. Mary Clark; Reynolds, m. Margaret Davis; Maria A., m. David O. Mackay; Daniel Farrington, m. Naoma Tripp; Lucy, m. Harvey C. Carlisle; Margaret Melissa d. infant. Family home Murray.
Married Jeannette Carruth (daughter of William Carruth), who was born 1825. Their children: Rachel, m. Samuel Wooley; Jane W., m. Harry Haines; James W., m. Ellen Proctor; Reuben, m. Melvina Morgan. Family home Murray.
Missionary to Scotland 1845-47; bishop of South Cottonwood ward fifteen years; served in Echo Canyon campaign. Surveyor; farmer. Died 1900 at Murray.

CAHOON, WILLIAM F. (son of Reynolds Cahoon and Thurza Stiles of Nauvoo, Ill.). Born Nov. 7, 1813 at Harpersfield, Ohio. Came to Utah Sept. 1848.
Married Nancy M. Gibbs Jan. 17, 1836, Kirtland, Ohio (parents lived at Kirtland). She was born July 27, 1818. Their children: Nancy E.; Lerona E., m. Myron B. Durfee; John F., m. Margaret Sharp; Ermina Sarah Prudence, m. John Osborn Angell; Thurza Viola, m. Albert Angell; William M., m. Martitia Smith; Daniel C.; Joseph M. b. March 2, 1853, m. Mary E. Ensign Oct. 1, 1876; Henry R., m. Anna Durfee; Stephen T., m. Anna Irons; Andrew C. Family home Salt Lake City, Utah.
High priest; missionary. Carpenter. Said to have pulled first curtain on the famous Salt Lake theatre stage. Died April 1897, Salt Lake City.

CAHOON, JOSEPH M. (son of William F. Cahoon and Nancy M. Gibbs). Born March 2, 1853, Salt Lake City.
Married Mary E. Ensign Oct. 1, 1876, Salt Lake City (daughter of Lewman Ensign and Mary A. Garn of Massachusetts and Ohio. Came to Utah 1847). She was born Sept. 23, 1859. Their children: Joseph H. b. July 22, 1877, m. Ceora D. Woody; Ashley E. b. Aug. 8, 1880; Eugene A. b. Oct. 14, 1882, m. Esther King; Ethel b. Jan. 28, 1885, m. Harlow Grove; Harold M. b. Jan. 21, 1889, m. Olive Shepard; Silvia D. b. Jan. 15, 1891; Margaret E. b. Jan. 13, 1894; Marian B. b. May 7, 1902. Railroad man.

Figure 18-7. An entry from a statewide biographical source, *Pioneers and Prominent Men of Utah* (Salt Lake City: Utah Pioneers Book Publishing Co., 1913), page 788.

stature, such as former governors, were often included as well, however. Figure 18-7 is an example of such a source.

Some statewide sources take the format of an encyclopedia, such as Jim Comstock's twenty-five-volume *West Virginia Heritage Encyclopedia* (Richwood, W.Va.: the author, 1976), in which historical topics, articles on towns and counties, and other information is arranged alphabetically and interfiled with biographical sketches. Brief outline sketches patterned after the successful who's who books comprise another format; Jo Conner's *Who's Who in Arizona* (Tucson, Ariz.: the author, 1913) is an example. This format has been more popular in recent decades and, as the name implies, usually includes only living persons. The encyclopedia format is best for locating persons who had died by the time the source was published.

Magazines and Journals

Periodicals form another type of statewide source for biographical information. Most states have a state historical society that publishes a scholarly journal (often published quarterly). Virtually every issue has one or more articles that are biographical in whole or in part. Usually these are lengthy, scholarly, well-researched efforts that devote several pages to part or all of the subject's life; they are always well documented. An excellent example of such a periodical is the *Pennsylvania Magazine of History and Biography.*

Finding biographical information in such sources is not always easy. Most periodical volumes are indexed, and many older journals have comprehensive indexes to their articles. If such an index does not exist for a periodical in the area of research, contact the society that publishes it, for it may have a card index. Two indexes described earlier that cover several journals (although not usually as thoroughly as other sources) are *Biography Index* (since 1946) and *People in History* (for articles after 1975). The best index for historical periodicals is *America: History and Life* (see chapter 17, "County and Local Histories"). For more information on periodicals see chapter 19, "Genealogical Periodicals."

After one determines which sources to search, it may be difficult to obtain copies because they are typically produced and distributed within the state to which they pertain. The discussion in chapter 17 about locating county and local histories applies here as well.

COUNTY AND LOCAL SOURCES

The previous discussion has focused on biographies of persons who were prominent enough to be noted at the national, state, or regional level. Unfortunately, most ancestors simply will not appear in such sources, but county and local biographical sources may include virtually anyone in a locality. While the most "successful" persons are usually the ones included, fame or preeminence was not a condition for inclusion. Furthermore, most of these sources focus on persons who lived in the nineteenth century, not on those who have become famous in the last thirty to fifty years. The number of county and local biographical sketches is unknown, but if each of Filby's five thousand county histories (see chapter 17) averages only two hundred biographies, they would total 1 million. This total would not include all the biographies in county biographies (discussed below) and local histories, which could easily add another million.

Many of the same sources discussed in chapter 17, "County and Local Histories," can be used to search for biographical information at the local level. County histories, for example, usually include a section with biographies of many county residents. Most of the discussion in chapter 17 about how these were compiled, how to use them, where they are located, and how to evaluate the information applies here as well and is not repeated. Many local biographical sources were compiled during the periods referred to in chapter 17 as the Centennial and New Century eras. The discussion of these periods and their county histories is especially applicable here.

County Biographies

Much of chapter 17 is based on a study of P. William Filby's *A Bibliography of American County Histories* (Baltimore: Genealogical Publishing Co., 1985). It is important to note, however, that Filby *did not* include in his bibliography those books that he judged to be solely biographical in nature. Hundreds of county histories were published at the end of the nineteenth century. They were often called "mug books" because they were devoted heavily to biographical sketches, often with pictures of the subjects. Filby points out the historical usefulness of such works in his preface and then suggests (page ix) that

> these works pose a problem for the bibliographer, however. Books beginning with titles such as 'Historical and Biographical . . .' can contain a history of the county and *consist in the main of biographies,* yet they are often the only history available. For this reason I have included them in this bibliography. On the other hand, books entitled *Biographies of Prominent Men . . . have been omitted,* as have those bearing such titles as *Portrait and Biographical Histories . . .*" (emphasis added).

Both Filby and Slocum omitted local collective biographies from their bibliographies, so it is difficult to get a true picture of the breadth and scope of such works. Many county and local biographical books are listed in the various statewide bibliographies at the end of chapter 17. Another source—perhaps the most helpful at present—is Clarence S. Peterson's *Consolidated Bibliography of County Histories in Fifty States in 1961,* 2nd ed. (Baltimore: Genealogical Publishing Co., 1963). Filby's bibliography is much more complete, but Peterson did not exclude county books that were "biography only."

A survey of around twenty common titles for "biography-only" county sources (such as *Portrait and Biographical Record of . . .*) in the *Family History Library Catalog*™ located approximately 150 titles covering approximately four hundred counties. Checking this list briefly against Peterson's work and some state bibliographies located several additional ones. The result of this brief survey is shown in "Counties Known to Have Collective Biographies" (following pages), which lists counties (by state) for which biography-only books are available that are *not* in Filby's bibliography. It is important to note that many books include two or more (sometimes up to nine) counties.

A brief analysis of "Counties Known to Have Collective Biographies" reveals some interesting facts. The states included in the table (those for which several county biographies were found) are primarily in the Northeast and the Midwest; this concentration parallels the proliferation of county histories during the Centennial and New Century eras. Clearly these books were part of that great publishing wave. This table represents only a sampling of localities for which collective biographies are available and should be only a starting point for research. The careful researcher will search library catalogs as well as local and state bibliographies for all areas of interest. Remember that most county histories also include biographical sketches.

Localities other than counties cannot be overlooked. Collective biographies featuring the citizens of many towns and cities are available. Slocum's bibliography does include biographical works for major cities, including Baltimore, Boston, Chicago, Cincinnati, Cleveland, Columbus, Davenport, Denver, Des Moines, Detroit, Houston, Indianapolis, Kansas City (Missouri), Los Angeles, Louisville, Milwaukee, New York City, Newark, Philadelphia, Pittsburgh, Rochester, St. Louis, Salt Lake City, San Francisco, Seattle, South Bend, Syracuse, Toledo, and Washington, D.C. A useful, if dated, source for city histories, many of which contain biographical sketches, is Thomas L. Bradford's *Bibliographer's Manual of American History,* 5 vols. (Philadelphia: Stan V. Henkels and Co., 1907–10; reprint; Detroit: Gale Research, 1968). For other cities, check the appropriate state catalogs and bibliographies.

The typical county biography book looks very much like the county histories published in the same time period. They are so similar, in fact, that many researchers fail to distinguish between them. The major difference, of course, is that county histories include lengthy sections on the history of the county (as much as 90 percent of the text). County biographies include no history; however, some include lengthy biographical sketches of very famous or important persons—usually U.S. presidents and the governors of the state where the county is situated. Such sketches, of course, made the books more valuable (at the time of publication) and easier to sell. (While the average farmer might not buy a book with his neighbor's biography in it, how could he turn it down if the presidents *and* his neighbor were in it?) In fact, the inclusion of famous persons was a major selling point for county biographies of the Centennial and New Century eras. Like the county histories of this era, many of them were subscription books, meaning that anybody could be included who chose to pay for the sketch and perhaps (but not necessarily always) to buy a copy. Imagine the thrill of seeing your name and biography (along with a portrait at extra cost) next to those of George Washington, Thomas Jefferson, and Abraham Lincoln!

Many of the immigrants living in the Midwest at the end of the nineteenth century were especially anxious to illustrate their success in such a manner; perhaps vanity, not success, was one of the chief motivations for inclusion. Their representation points out the fact that almost any family can be represented in a county or local biography. As with county histories, be sure to read the biographies for all persons whose surnames appear in the family at that time and place or who may have married a family member (figure 18-8).

Relatively few county biographies have had an every-name index published for them, and fewer still have been reprinted, so they differ from county histories in these regards. Although most have a table of contents, the names there represent only the persons being profiled (not their spouses, children, parents, etc.). The indexes listed in tables 17-2 and 17-3 (chapter 17) can be helpful for many states. Many of these indexes include county biographies but, again, these are not every-name indexes; they usually index only the subject. The larger ones, such as the Ohio, Indiana, and Michigan indexes, generally include all available county biographies. No county biographies (or histories) have yet been indexed in *BGMI.*

Regional Family History

Although most county biographies follow the standard mug book format of one- to three-page sketches, each focusing on one person's life history, another format was also popular: books with a family history or genealogical focus were popular in New England and New York. These tended to include all or most of the surnames of an area (county, valley, or multi-county, etc.) and included more genealogical and less biographical information. Portraits were also less common in this format. Most of

Counties Known to Have Collective Biographies

Each of the following counties is represented in at least one local collective biography (in addition to any county histories that may be available). To locate collective biographies for counties on this list, first check the *Family History Library Catalog*, then search statewide bibliographies for the state(s) of interest.

Connecticut
Fairfield
Hartford
Litchfield
Middlesex
New Haven
New London
Tolland
Windham

Illinois
Adams
Bond
Boone
Brown
Bureau
Calhoun
Carroll
Cass
Champaign
Christian
Clinton
Coles
Cook
De Kalb
De Witt
Du Page
Edgar
Effingham
Ford
Fulton
Grundy
Hancock
Hardin
Henderson
Henry
Iroquois
Jackson
Jasper
Jefferson
Jo Daviess
Johnson
Kane
Kankakee
Kendall
Knox
Lake
La Salle
Lee
Livingston
Logan
McDonough
McHenry
McLean
Macon
Macoupin
Madison
Marion
Marshall
Mason
Massac
Monroe
Montgomery
Morgan
Moultrie
Ogle
Peoria
Perry
Piatt
Pike
Pope
Putnam
Randolph
Richland
Rock Island
St. Clair
Sangamon
Schuyler
Scott
Shelby
Stark
Stephenson
Tazewell
Vermilion
Warren
Washington
Whiteside
Will
Winnebago
Woodford

Indiana
Bartholomew
Benton
Boone
Cass
Clinton
Delaware
Elkhart
Fountain
Grant
Greene
Hamilton
Hancock
Hendricks
Howard
Huntington
Jasper
Jay
Jefferson
Lake
La Porte
Madison
Marion
Miami
Montgomery
Newton
Parke
Porter
Pulaski
Randolph
St. Joseph
Starke
Tippicanoe
Tipton
Vanderburgh
Wabash
Warren

Iowa
Adams
Audobon
Benton
Boone
Buchanan
Calhoun
Cherokee
Clayton
Clinton
Crawford
Delaware
Des Moines
Dubugue
Fayette
Grundy
Hamilton
Henry
Ida
Iowa
Jackson
Jasper
Jefferson
Johnson
Jones
Keokuk
Lee
Linn
Louisa
Mahaska
Marshall
Montgomery
Muscatine
Page
Polk
Pottawattamie
Poweshiek
Sac
Scott
Shelby
Van Buren
Wapello
Washington
Wayne
Webster
Wright

Maine
Aroostock
Cumberland
Franklin
Hancock
Knox
Lincoln
Oxford
Piscataquis
Sagadahoc
Somerset
Waldo
Washington
York

Maryland
Baltimore
Cecil
Harford

Massachusetts
Barnstable
Berkshire
Essex
Franklin
Hampden
Hampshire
Middlesex
Norfolk
Plymouth
Suffolk
Worcester

Michigan
Allegan
Barry
Berrien
Branch
Calhoun
Cass
Clinton
Eaton
Genesee
Gratiot
Hillsdale
Huron
Ingham
Ionia
Jackson
Kalamazoo
Lapeer
Lenawee
Livingston
Mecosta
Midland
Montcalm
Muskegon
Newaygo
Oakland
Osceola
Ottawa
St. Joseph
Sanilac
Shiawassee
Tuscola
Van Buren
Washtenaw

Minnesota
McLeod
Meeker
Pope
Stevens
Winona

Missouri
Atchison
Buchanan
Carroll
Chariton
Clay
Clinton
Jackson
Johnson
Lafayette
Lincoln
Linn
Marion
Nodaway
Pettis
Pike
Ralls
Ray
St. Charles
Saline
Warren

Nebraska
Buffalo
Butler
Cass
Fillmore
Franklin
Gage
Harlan
Johnson
Kearney
Lancaster
Otoe
Pawanee
Phelps
Polk
Seward
York

New Hampshire
Belnap
Cheshire
Grafton
Hillsboro
Merrimack
Rockingham
Strafford
Sullivan

New Jersey
Burlington
Camden
Essex
Hunterdon
Middlesex
Monmouth
Morris
Somerset
Warren

New York
Albany
Broome
Cayuga
Chatauqua
Chemung
Chenango
Clinton
Columbia
Delaware
Dutchess
Erie
Essex
Fulton
Greene
Livingston
Madison
Monroe
Montgomery
New York
Niagra
Orange
Otsego
Queens

Rensselaer
Rockland
Saratoga
Schenectady
Schoharie
Schuyler
Seneca
Suffolk
Ulster
Washington
Wyoming

Ohio
Allen
Auglaize
Butler
Carroll
Clark
Cuyahoga
Defiance
Delaware
Fairfield
Fayette
Fulton
Greene
Guernsey
Hamilton
Hardin
Harrison
Henry
Holmes
Huron
Knox
Licking
Logan
Lorain
Lucas
Madison
Mahoning
Marion
Mercer
Miami
Morrow
Ottawa
Pickaway
Portage
Putnam
Richland
Sandusky
Scioto
Shelby
Stark
Summit
Tuscarawas
Van Wert
Wayne
Williams
Wood

Pennsylvania
Allegheny
Beaver
Bedford
Blair
Cambria
Carbon
Centre
Chester
Clarion
Clearfield
Clinton
Crawford
Cumberland
Dauphin
Fayette
Franklin
Huntingdon
Jefferson
Juniata
Lackawana
Lancaster
Lebanon
Lehigh
Mifflin
Monroe
Montgomery
Northampton
Perry
Pike
Schuylkill
Snyder
Somerset
Susquehanna
Union
Washington
Wayne
Wyoming

Vermont
Bennington
Essex
Rutland
Windsor

Wisconsin
Adams
Brown
Buffalo
Columbia
Dane
Dodge
Florence
Fond du Lac
Grant
Green
Green Lake
Iowa
Jefferson
Kenosha
La Crosse
Lafayette
Langlade
Lincoln
Marathon
Marinette
Marquette
Milwaukee
Oconto
Oneida
Outagamie
Portage
Racine
Rock
Sauk
Shawano
Sheboygan
Trempealeau
Vernon
Vilas
Walworth
Waukesha
Waupaca
Waushara
Winnebago
Waupaca
Wood

these were not subscription books; rather, they sought to record much of the genealogy of the area. In fact, a form of the word *genealogy* was often part of the title, such as *Hudson-Mohawk Genealogical and Family Memoirs,* from which the example in figure 18-9 is taken.

The information in these county and local sources must be treated with caution because the earlier generations of a family's lineage were often the product of inaccurate and incorrect research. While local biographies are, in the main, credible because the subject usually provided the information, information on earlier generations must always be suspect in any source if the subject did not have direct personal knowledge of them. This type of local or county biography must be treated with as much (or more) care as that given the evaluation of a compiled genealogy.

Another difference between county biographies and regional compendia makes the "genealogical" biographies (regional compendia) of greater interest to the researcher than local collective biographies: their emphasis on history. The typical county biography usually includes only persons who were living when it was published (most were published between 1875 and 1925), thus effectively limiting such sources to nineteenth-century research. The genealogical biographies, however, sometimes extend back more than two hundred years. They should be searched for any ancestor who lived at any time in the relevant location (but again, they should be carefully evaluated).

USING STATE AND LOCAL SOURCES

Two tasks face the researcher who is attempting to find and use biographical sketches in statewide sources. First, the researcher must learn in which of the hundreds of titles a person was profiled. While *American Biographical Index* (see above under "National Biographical Sources—Indexes") is a good place to start, virtually no county or local sources are included in that index, and fewer than one hundred statewide sources were used. The second task is to find a copy of the book or books being sought.

State, county, and local sources for collective biographies are indexed in the same works that index county and local histories. Indeed, often the collective, statewide indexes to local histories only index biographical sketches, not every name or every substantial mention of a person. Therefore, the discussion of indexes in chapter 17 and the indexes cited in tables 17-2 and 17-3 (chapter 17) are the best sources for state and local biographies as well. There are many more county and local sources than state sources, but most state collections and indexes include the local sources that exist for the state as well.

National and Multi-State Indexes

There are a few indexes with national or multi-state coverage that focus almost exclusively, or at least extensively, on county and local sources; their scope is simply broader than one state. None of these indexes comes close to indexing all of the thousands of local histories, but they are worthy of note and are briefly described here. For a full discussion of the first four indexes mentioned below and other useful indexes, see chapter 17.

Index to Biographies in Local Histories in the Library of Congress (Baltimore: Magna Carta Book Co., 1979) is a card index on thirty-one microfilm reels. It cites approximately 170,000 sketches in 340 histories. While all states are represented by at least one title, the southern states are better covered, with ten to fifty titles for most southern states. However, fewer than 20 percent of the titles indexed are county or multi-county (regional) sources; most of the sources indexed are state histories and state collective biographies.

The Allen County Public Library (Fort Wayne, Indiana) created *Historical and Biographical Index of North East, Mid East, Mid South, Mid West U.S.A., 1800 thru Early 1900* (Salt

WILLIAM GROVE, Jr., is one of the reliable and progressive farmers and representative men of Benner township, Centre county. Through his earnest, persistent labors his fine farm of 125 acres is in a high state of culture and improved with excellent buildings, which stand as monuments to his thrift and enterprise.

A native of Centre county, Mr. Grove was born in Gregg township, July 28, 1840, a son of John and Louisa (Klinesmith) Grove. The family has long been identified with the interests of this section of the State. The maternal grandfather of our subject was killed and scalped by the Indians, in the Penn's Valley massacre of 1776. The father was born in Middleburg, Snyder Co., Penn., of German lineage, and on coming to Centre county located in Harris township, where he followed farming throughout life.

In 1861 our subject wedded Miss Sarah Neese, a daughter of David and Sarah (Kerstetter) Neese, who are also of German descent. Her grandfather took up his residence in Penn's Valley in 1780. Seven children have been born to Mr. and Mrs. Grove, as follows: Emanuel H., who is married, and is living in College township, Centre county; Alice R., wife of Jacob Mayer, of Spring township, Centre county; Susan, wife of David Shearer, of Jefferson county, Penn.; William H., who is married and living in Penn township, Centre county, on his grandfather's old homestead; John F.; Emma V., wife of Warren Minnimire, of Bellefonte, Penn.; and Anna H., at home.

In his political affiliation, Mr. Grove is an inflexible adherent to the doctrines and principles of the Democratic party, but has no aspirations for popular preferment. He is a public-spirited, enterprising man, and takes an active interest in everything which seems to promise benefit to the community. He enjoys the esteem and confidence of his neighbors, is a consistent member of the Lutheran Church, and, fraternally, is connected with the Grange.

Figure 18-8. From *Commemorative Biographical Record of Central Pennsylvania Including the Counties of Centre, Clinton, Union and Snyder* (Chicago: J. H. Beers & Co., 1898), page 467.

Lake City: Genealogical Society of Utah, 1989). It is available on thirty-three microfilm reels from the Family History Library and includes approximately 180,000 cards with references to county histories and biographies from Massachusetts to Colorado. The heaviest representation in this index is for the Great Lakes states.

Another index with a Midwest emphasis is the *Genealogical Index of the Newberry Library,* 4 vols. (Boston: G. K. Hall, 1960). It is the old analytical card catalog of the Newberry Library in Chicago. These four large volumes include approximately 530,000 entries to books published before 1917. While many non-biographical sources are included, a significant number of county and local histories and biographies make up part of this index.

The *Early Church Information File* (Salt Lake City: Genealogical Society of Utah, 1991) is an alphabetical card index on seventy-five rolls of microfilm with approximately a million and a half entries from around one thousand sources about members of the LDS church and others who lived in the Intermountain West. Despite its LDS focus, almost anyone in the Intermountain West who lived before 1900 is likely to be in this index. It includes multiple entries for most persons.

Biofile Southwest is a computer-generated biographical dictionary of approximately twenty thousand persons who appear in the historical records of New Spain from the Spanish colonial period. Multiple indexes and source documentation make this a significant tool to use for early residents of the southwestern U.S. It is available at Documentary Relations Southwest, University of Arizona (Tucson).

Statewide Indexes and Collections

Tables 17-2 and 17-3 (chapter 17) list several statewide indexes to county and local histories. Most such indexes provide full bibliographic information for the sources indexed, and they often indicate where copies can be found.

For several states there are unique unpublished (usually card) indexes and significant biographical collections that can be found in unexpected places. The existence of a card index is a good indication that the library or archive that created it has a significant collection of biographical sources. The following discussion gives brief descriptions of manuscript collections, indexes, and special collections for thirty-five states and the District of Columbia. Because these sources are note published, they are not included in the chapter bibliography. Some of these remarks relate to indexes noted in table 17-3.

For the fourteen states not included below, begin searching at the state library or archive, then at university libraries and public libraries in large cities, any of which will usually have substantial local history and biography collections. The states not included below are Alaska, Delaware, Kansas, Maryland, Massachusetts, Nebraska, Nevada, New Mexico, North Carolina, Ohio, Oklahoma, Oregon, South Carolina, and West Virginia. Several, however, are represented by helpful indexes noted in table 17-2 and in the bibliography of this chapter. The following comments are arranged alphabetically by state within geographic regions.[4]

New England. For Connecticut, Thomas J. Kemp is creating the Connecticut Biography and Portrait Index, which currently has more than 250,000 entries. It can be searched for a nominal fee by writing to Kemp at 8401 Del Rio Way No. 187, Tampa, FL 33617. For Maine, many published biographies of state residents are available at the Maine Historical Society. Two separate indexes covering Maine town histories and periodicals are available from Dr. Thomas Roderick, 4 Seely Road, Bar Harbor, ME 04609.

The best collection of published biographies in New Hampshire is at the New Hampshire Historical Society, where the library also has the New Hampshire Notables Card File, an index to biographical references with approximately thirty-two thousand entries. This card file is also available on microfilm on eight microfilm reels from the Family History Library as *New Hampshire Notables Card File, 1600 to the Present* (Salt Lake City: New Hampshire Historical Society, 1988). The Rhode Island Historical Society has by far the largest collection of bio-

HUDSON AND MOHAWK VALLEYS 1751

Troy, Albany county, New York, August 1, 1873. He escaped the epidemic that carried off four of the brothers. He was an attendant at the private school of Miss Harris; later at Troy Academy and Albany Academy. He left school at the holiday recess, 1889, to go to work, starting as an apprentice in the cutting room of his father's factory the first Monday in January, 1890. He rose through successive grades to be a member of the William Barker Company. He is a member of the Troy Citizens Corps, Pafraet Dael Club, Colonial Club, Chamber of Commerce, Albany Academy Alumni Association, Island Golf Club, Lametide Fish and Game Club, Beck Literary Society, and others. He is secretary of the Society Sons of the Revolution, and greatly interested in the compiling and preservation of family records and genealogies. It is from his perfectly kept and arranged records that the material for this family line is obtained. He married, October 12, 1899, Florence Herring, born in Harrington Park, Bergen county, New Jersey, and educated at the Englewood and Paterson, New Jersey, high schools. Child: William, born in Troy, New York, March 25, 1908. Mr. Barker resides in Troy, New York.

("Mayflower" line of Mary E. Dayton, wife of William Barker).

The Dayton family of England can be traced to Robert de Deighton, and the year 1305. In America the family begins with Ralph Dayton and the year 1636. He was born in St. Martin-in-the-Fields, London, England, 1598; married there Agnes, daughter of Henry Pool, and by her had two sons, Robert and Samuel. After the death of his wife he emigrated to New England (Boston), where he arrived in 1636. In 1639 he was of New Haven, Connecticut, where he is mentioned at length in the early records, church and town. He was one of the original settlers at Easthampton, Long Island, where his deed to land is the earliest on record except perhaps the Indian deed. He was constable and a man of importance. He married (second) in New Haven it is believed, Dorothy Brewster, by whom he had a son, Brewster Dayton. He married (third) Mary, widow of John Haynes, in June, 1656. He died at Easthampton in 1658.

(II) Robert, eldest son of Ralph and his first wife, Agnes (Pool) Dayton, was born in London, England, in 1630, died at Easthampton, Long Island, April 16, 1712. He married, 1652, Elizabeth, daughter of John (2) and granddaughter of John (1) and Annie Woodruff, the first settlers. Children: Elizabeth, Samuel (see forward), Beriah.

(III) Samuel, eldest son of Robert and Elizabeth (Woodruff) Dayton, was born in Easthampton, Long Island, in 1665, died there January 30, 1746. He married Dorothy ———, who died March 22, 1750, aged eighty-six years. Children: Robert, Daniel, Joanna, Nathan, Jonathan, Samuel and Elizabeth.

(IV) Nathan, son of Samuel and Dorothy Dayton, was born at Easthampton, Long Island, 1702, died there October 3, 1763. He married, November 11, 1725, Amy Stratton, born 1698, died September 25, 1749. Children: Samuel, Nathan, Nathan, Amy, Elizabeth, Abraham, Joana, Abraham, Jonathan.

(V) Captain Nathan (2), son of Nathan (1) and Amy (Stratton) Dayton, was baptized at Easthampton, Long Island, 1728, died there 1773. He married, January 27, 1751, Phebe Mulford. Children: Nathan, Jonathan, Samuel, Elizabeth, Mary, Abraham, Elias, Joana, Amy and Phoebe.

(VI) Nathan (3), son of Nathan (2) and Phoebe (Mulford) Dayton, was born at Easthampton, Long Island, about 1754, died in Rensselaerville, Albany county, New York, October 26, 1842. He left Long Island about 1800 and settled in Albany county, where he died. He served in the revolutionary war, enlisting in March or April, 1776, as private in Captain John Davis's company, Colonel Henry B. Livingston's regiment, New York militia, served nine months. He drew a revolutionary pension, and the papers, still preserved, show his service. He was a farmer of Albany county, New York.

Nathan Dayton married Mehitable Hutchinson, and they were the parents of twelve children. He married (second) Ruth, widow of Nathan Crary, of Mystic, Connecticut. Children: Nathan, Abraham, Hannah, Phoebe, Elias, Maria, Henry, Lewis M., Helen, Samuel H., Eliza C.

(VII) Samuel H., son of Nathan (3) and Mehitable (Hutchinson) Dayton, was born in Easthampton, Long Island, where he was baptized 1790; he died in Troy, New York, July, 1864. He was a farmer of Albany county; later removed to near Troy, Rensselaer county, New York, where he died. He served in the war of 1812. He married, in 1812, Sarah Searles Crary, born in Groton, Connecticut, May 25, 1793, died in Troy, New York, March 6, 1846, daughter of Nathan and Ruth (Searles) Crary. Her widowed mother became the second wife of Nathan Dayton. Children of Samuel H. and Sarah S. (Crary) Dayton: Harriet, Nathan C., Clarice, Emma P., Edwin C., Jesse C., George C., Helen, Eliza C., Mary A. It is through

Figure 18-9. A page from a local family history, *Hudson-Mohawk Genealogical and Family Memoirs,* vol. 4 (New York: Lewis Historical Publishing Co., 1911), page 1751.

graphical material for that state, including the Rhode Island Index. The University of Vermont at Burlington has the largest and most complete collection of biographical materials.

Mid-Atlantic States. For New Jersey, the best collections of published biographies are at the state library, the state historical society, and Rutgers University. The state library has a Family Name Index that is a partial index to significant material in New Jersey genealogies, periodicals, histories, and biographies. Send a self-addressed, stamped envelope with a request for a limited search of this index. New York residents are indexed in a private card file in the possession of Gunther Pohl, 24 Walden Place, Great Neck, NY 11020, while the best collections of published biographies in New York are at the New York Public Library and New York State Library.

Numerous sources are available for Pennsylvania. The Pennsylvania Historical Society and the Genealogical Society of Pennsylvania in Philadelphia have the best collections of published biographies. Before World War II, the Federal Writers Project collected typed biographical sketches abstracted from local histories and various biographical encyclopedias. These are at the state archive as Pennsylvania Encyclopedia Biography Field Notes for American Guide Series. They have also been microfilmed on seventeen reels. The Index to Pennsylvania County Histories is a seventy-five thousand-card index to people of western Pennsylvania at the Carnegie Library of Pittsburgh. The staff will search for two or three specific names, but there is a fee if photocopies are requested.

Southern States. In Alabama, the Birmingham Public Library is compiling Alabama Biography: An Index to Biographical Sketches of Individual Alabamians, which has approximately 22,500 entries. For Arkansas, see the Arkansas Biographical Card File Index, 1819–1950, at the Arkansas History Commission (also available on fifty-three microfilm reels through the Family History Library). In addition, in 1889 and 1890 the Goodspeed Publishing Company published a series of regional biographical encyclopedias (eastern, northeast, southern, western Arkansas, etc.). Most have been reprinted, and separately published indexes are available (see Filby's *Bibliography of American County Histories,* discussed above under "County and Local Sources—County Biographies").

Many prominent people made their homes temporarily in Washington, D.C. A collection of published biographies for the District of Columbia is at the Library of Congress. For Florida, the St. Augustine Historical Society has prepared a Biographical Card Index and an alphabetical Biographical and Genealogical File. These were microfilmed and are available at the Family History Library. In addition, the State Library of Florida houses the Florida Biography Index, which has approximately twenty-five thousand entries.

The Georgia State Archives has a large collection of early twentieth-century biographical questionnaires. It is arranged alphabetically and is available on fifteen reels of microfilm. An extensive card index to Kentucky biographies is at the Special Collections and Archives of the Margaret I. King Library, University of Kentucky. The New Orleans Public Library has a card file to biographical references in published works.

The Mississippi State Department of Archives and History has a Biographical Index with approximately 200,000 entries from numerous sources, including state and local histories and biographical directories. For residents of Tennessee, consult the McLung Collection, which contains biographical material. It is found at the Lawson McGhee Library in Knoxville. In Texas, the Biographical Sketch File is an ongoing project based on the Texas Collection at Baylor University; it has been partially published in Virginia H. and William L. Ming's *Biographical Gazetteer of Texas,* 6 vols. (Austin, Tex.: W. M. Morrison Books, 1985–87). The S. Bassett French collection of "Biographical Sketches" is at the Virginia State Library.

Midwestern States. The Illinois State Archives has a massive card index to biographies found in local histories. A search of this index can be requested for one or two names. The archive also has a complete collection of the county biographical volumes of the *Historical Encyclopedia of Illinois.* Between 1900 and 1921, Munsell Publishing (Chicago) created unique volumes for many Illinois counties; each volume began with several hundred pages (identical in each volume) about the history of Illinois. Each volume was titled *Historical Encyclopedia of Illinois and History of* [____] *County* (or similar).

In Indiana, the Allen County Public Library has a major collection of biographical sources for the state as well as for most Midwest states. The Indiana State Library is currently adding to a card index of names found in "who's who"-style works, and the William H. English Collection at the state historical society contains photographs and biographical information about many territorial and nineteenth-century public officials. Each county in Indiana is also the subject of a separately published master index of biographical information in local histories. These volumes, generally titled [____] *County, Indiana: Index of Names of Persons and of Firms,* were begun in the 1930s by the Work Projects Administration and completed in the 1980s as the County History Indexing Project, Family History Section of the Indiana Historical Society. In typescript and published in limited numbers, the volumes typically index ten to twenty published sources for each county.

The Iowa Historical Society has a collection of typed biographies compiled by the Citizens Historical Association. Two other major collections of Iowa biographies are available at the state archive: the Biographical Data Collection consists of alphabetical personal history surveys, and the Biography Files are alphabetized folders of newspaper clippings and correspondence. In Michigan, the Burton Historical Collection at the Detroit Public Library, the Bentley Historical Library at the University of Michigan (Ann Arbor), and the Library of Michigan (Lansing) have extensive collections of biographical works.

The Minnesota Historical Society has the Minnesota Biography Sketch Index, which has more than 100,000 entries from a variety of sources, including early obituaries. In Missouri, the public libraries in St. Louis and Kansas City also have good collections, but there is no statewide biographical index or major manuscript collection. The Wisconsin State Historical Society houses an extensive Biography File created by the Historical Records Survey.

Western States. For Arizona, Carl Hayden has compiled a vast alphabetical collection of biographical information concerning early settlers. It is found at the Hayden Library of Arizona State University (Tempe) and on microfilm at the Family History Library. In California, the Daughters of the American Revolution (DAR) prepared a twenty-six-volume biographical collection between 1929 and 1962 of Records of the Families of California Pioneers. It is found at the DAR Library (Washington, D.C.)

and at the Family History Library. Each volume has an every-name index, and the Family History Library has an index to the principal persons in the collection that is available on microfilm.

The Colorado Historical Society has a biographical vertical file. It also has the Bromwell Index, which is a five-volume alphabetical listing of prominent people in Colorado up to 1933. The Hawaii State Archives has a biographical file to published and manuscript information. The North Dakota Biography Index is a card index with more than twenty-seven thousand cards and 100,000 entries indexing 460 titles published before 1981. It is available through the North Dakota Institute for Regional Studies at North Dakota State University (Fargo). The best collections of published biographies in South Dakota are at the South Dakota Office of History and at the University of South Dakota (Vermillion). However, there is no statewide biographical index or major manuscript collection.

For Utah, the Historical Department of the LDS church houses biographical sketches, manuscripts, photographs, and church records with personal data. Additional biographical material is available at the state historical society and the Family History Library. For Washington residents the Suzzallo Library at the University of Washington has the best collection of biographical materials. The best collection of published biographies in Wyoming is at the state archive. The American Heritage Center at the University of Wyoming also collects biographical works.

J. Carlyle and Janet Parker, publishers of biographical sketch index books for Nevada and Rhode Island (table 17-3), have compiled manuscript indexes to sketches for four other western states: Idaho, Montana, South Dakota, and Wyoming. Before publication they will search these indexes for a small fee. Contact Marietta Publishing Co., 2115 North Denair Avenue, Turlock, CA 95382.

VOCATIONAL SOURCES

Probably the most overlooked sources of biographical information are the thousands of biographical sketch books that focus on persons with a common vocation. *Vocation* is used very broadly here to include any group of persons with something in common: occupation, trade, sex, religion, ethnic background, hobby, or some other characteristic.

It is difficult to determine how many such works there are for the United States and Canada. Slocum's *Biographical Dictionaries and Related Works* (see above under "National Biographical Sources—Bibliographies") lists approximately 8,300 sources under "Biography by Vocation," but most of those are for foreign countries. Still, the section for the United States is usually the longest in any of the subdivisions with geographic arrangements. Most subdivisions include general (international) works followed by the biographical sources arranged by country. Thus, the United States has 15 percent of the geographic titles under "Education and Scholarship" and 27 percent under "Music." Of the vocational titles identified by geographic location, more than seven hundred pertain to the United States and one hundred to Canada. On the other hand, "Athletics and Games" are subdivided by sport (not country), and the United States is the focus of most of the 190 titles in that section.

It seems to be a safe estimate that more than one thousand of Slocum's "vocational" titles apply to North American residents—almost twice as many sources as those included for the national (United States) level. Furthermore, many of these sources are issued periodically (annually, every five years, etc.), accounting for several thousand total volumes. These volumes average between three hundred and one thousand or more entries, which would suggest another one-half to one million or more biographical sketches of Americans. Because these sketches are specific to various vocations, the duplication rate is bound to be much lower for these sources than for the national sources discussed earlier.

Slocum's work uses the following vocational divisions:

- Arts (including fine arts and painting, performing arts, and music)
- Athletics and games
- Education and scholarship
- Language and literature
- Law
- Library science
- Medicine
- Dentistry
- Philosophy (with psychology and occultism)
- Religion
- Science
- Social science
- Technology (applied science)

Other types of biographies that are not strictly occupational are generally included with the country, state, or vocation where they best fit. For example, most military biographical sources are listed under the country, while *Female Poets of America* is listed under poetry because there is no separate "female" category (although such books are numerous).

Vocational biographical sources come in various formats, but two seem to predominate: some treat relatively few persons in great depth, much like *The National Cyclopedia of American Biography.* Others take a brief approach, giving only the bare facts, like the *Who's Who in America* series.

Most of these sources focus on persons of the twentieth century; however, several volumes (usually at least one or two in each field) focus on historical figures. Thus, there are dozens of sources to search for an ancestor who is known to have accomplished much in a particular field. Some families have traditions which hold that a certain ancestor was the first person in history to do a certain thing or invented something or discovered something important. Researchers who are seeking proof of such traditions should consult vocational biographical sources.

Vocational biographies exist for every geographical level: town or city, county, state, and nation. If a vocational source exists for an ancestor's occupation for the county where the ancestor's entire life was lived, he will most likely be included. Statewide vocational sources often list everyone of a particular profession within the state. Books such as *The Silversmiths of Virginia from 1694 to 1850* provide a wealth of information on a few persons who worked in an obscure trade.

JAMES BLAIR, JR.

One of the pioneer poets of Knox County was James Blair, Jr. who was born in Blair's Valley, Washington County, Maryland, in 1790, of Scotch-Irish parentage. He was a typical Southern gentleman noted for his warm hospitality and congeniality. Throughout his life he was engaged in numerous activities—milling, farming, rearing children, and writing poetry. Having come to Ohio in the year 1808, he built the second grist mill in Knox County. Being a well-educated man, and having the confidence and esteem of his neighbors in Brown Township, he was chosen Justice of the Peace and served in that capacity for twenty-one years.

During his long life, James Blair, Jr. made contributions to Knox County literature by way of articles and poems which were published in the papers of that period. The most noted of his poems are, "Looking Backwards," "Turncoats," and "On the Banks of the Jelloway."

He died in 1863 at the age of seventy-three years, and was buried at Amity, Knox County, Ohio. In 1917, his grandson, Judge Park B. Blair of Mount Vernon, Ohio, moved, from the old Blair farm, an ancient stone millwheel once used in the old grist mill of his grandfather, over one hundred years ago, and having it properly inscribed, erected it as a monument or headstone at the grave of his grandfather, James Blair, Jr. in the Amity cemetery.

Figure 18-10. An example from a vocational source, Mary Quigley Elliott, comp., *Biographical Sketches of Knox County Writers* (Mount Vernon, Ohio, 1937), page 19.

(painter, musician, stage actor, or even architect), a biographical sketch of the person may be hidden in any of hundreds of books.

A dictionary of Dutch artists provided helpful clues in research on the birth of a Dutch immigrant to New York named Adam Dingman. He had come from the city of Harlem, where a painter of the same name had been born about the same time. The Harlem birth records included only two Adam Dingmans for the time period in question. The very brief sketch of the painter gave his birth date, so the researcher could eliminate his birth record and focus research on the other one, which eventually proved to be the immigrant's.

Another example illustrates an important use of any biographical source. Family traditions often ascribe greater importance to an ancestor then the person actually achieved, and sometimes an ancestor can be confused with another person of greater prominence who lived in the same place at the same time; a biographical source can distinguish the two. Ambrose Spenser lived in eastern New York around the same time as an early mayor of Albany by the same name. With the mayor's biography at hand, a researcher can check any reference to Ambrose Spencer to learn if it pertains to the mayor or to the much more obscure farmer.

A researcher was able to solve a research problem on the Haig family of Philadelphia with such sources. The family had a pottery shop in colonial Philadelphia. An obscure book based on a doctoral dissertation profiled all the persons in Philadelphia involved in pottery; it included important information about the Haig family, including the alleged town of origin in Scotland.

Be sure to search library catalogs and bibliographies under all governmental jurisdictions for books that may discuss persons in an ancestor's occupation. Note that Slocum's bibliography generally lists only vocational biographical sources at the national or international level.

Some fields of endeavor seem to have produced a substantial number of vocational biographies and deserve comment here.

Writers. Books about writers (authors, poets, etc.) seem to be the most numerous, due probably to public desire to learn about specific authors. *Biographical Sources* (see above under "National Biographical Sources—Bibliographies") lists more than one hundred different books about U.S. authors. Thirteen percent of the titles in Slocum's bibliography are devoted to "Language and Literature." Many of these feature historical writers who were of little notoriety. Many local and regional books are also available about writers. Figure 18-10 is from a county source, *Biographical Sketches of Knox County Writers.* This book includes only a brief article on James Blair, Jr., but it provided several important facts (notably, Blair's birthplace) that led to two earlier generations.

Art. The various art fields are also very well represented among vocational biographies. If an ancestor was an artist of any kind

Government Leaders. Politics and government provide notoriety to many people, and dozens of biographical books are available for this field. Here again there is a fair collection of historical coverage. Books are available profiling all persons who were presidential cabinet officers; congressmen; state, territorial, and colonial governors; Federal and state judges; big city mayors; and other officers. There is even a *Who Was Who in American Politics,* which includes four thousand political figures who lived before the 1970s. Some of these sources contain fairly detailed information about political figures from very early in America's history, as figure 18-11 illustrates.

Religion. Religious leaders have also been the subjects of many compiled biographies, among them a number of historical figures. Virtually every American colonial clergyman is briefly sketched in five related books by Frederick Lewis Weis (figure 18-12). Some religious biographical sources are nondenominational, but these generally only include the most prominent persons. Most religious sources focus on a particular denomination, usually at the state or national level (sometimes the city or county level). National biographical dictionaries and encyclopedias exist for the following denominations: (Dutch) Reformed Church, Southern Baptist, Presbyterian, Episcopal, Roman Catholic, Evangelical, Society of Friends (Quaker), Lutheran, Mennonite, Methodist, LDS (Mormon), Congregationalist, Seventh-Day Adventist, Unitarian, United Brethren in Christ, Church of the Brethren, and others. Generally these include ministers, some circuit preachers, lay leaders, and national council members. Many focus on persons of historical significance rather than contemporary members of the faith.

Professionals. The professions represent another common category for vocational biographies. Historically the two largest and most important professions have been law and medicine. Many national-level collective biographies exist for these fields, but of greater importance are the multitude of local sources of biographies. Books about the lawyers and judges of the area exist for most large cities and counties. Many with titles like *The Bench and Bar of*. . . were produced in the late nineteenth and early twentieth centuries. They are very much like the county mug books of that era except that they were often sponsored by local bar organizations. Doctors were also the subjects of many biographies. Books and articles with titles like *Medicine Men of* . . . abound for many areas of the nineteenth-century United States.

Teachers. Education is a field with tremendous recent growth in biographical sources. Slocum's work lists almost fifty U.S. sources for educational biographies, many of which are annuals; several others are listed under "Library Science." Very few of these are historical in nature, but a few have attempted to profile past educators. Faculty guides dating back up to one hundred years are available for some major universities. Most education sources, however, are of the brief "who's who" variety, as illustrated in figure 18-13.

Military. Some people devoted all or part of their lives to military careers. Dozens of military biographical sources are available, many of which are historical in nature. Any commissioned officer of the regular U.S. Army is profiled in at least one or more sources. Many volunteer officers are also included in some sources, although most focus primarily on career servicemen. One of the largest is *Who Was Who in American History: The Military* (Chicago: Marquis, 1974), which contains profiles of more than ten thousand deceased military leaders who lived as early as 1607. Other sources are available for the other branches of the service. If family tradition or military records indicate that an ancestor was an officer, don't overlook military biographies.

Rhode Island / 380

ARNOLD, Benedict, 1657-1660, 1662-1666, 1669-1672, 1677-1678

Born on December 21, 1615 at (or near) Leamington, Warwickshire, England, the son of William and Christian (Peak) Arnold. Brother of Elizabeth, Joanna and Stephen. Married on December 17, 1640 to Damaris Westcott; father of Benedict, Josiah, Oliver, Caleb, Godsgift, Freelove, Damaris, Penelope and another who died young.

Arrived in New England with his family in June 1635. With his father, became one of the first settlers of Providence in the late 1630's, and in 1651 moved to Newport. Served from 1654 to 1663 as a member of the General Court (Assembly) of Commissioners which, until the implementation of the Charter of 1663, acted as a legislative body for the colony; also served as an Assistant for Newport at various times between 1654 and 1661. Named President of the colony in the spring of 1657, filling that office until 1660, and again from 1662 to 1663. Became the first Governor of Rhode Island (after the Charter of 1663 was received in November of that year); served as governor, with two intervals, until his death in 1678.

Arnold's tenure as chief executive spanned over two decades of Rhode Island history. Perhaps this period's most significant political development was the granting of a royal charter to the colony in 1663, a charter which replaced the patent that had been issued by authority of Parliament during the English Civil Wars. Partly because of a confusion over jurisdiction which this charter had failed to resolve, Rhode Island and Connecticut were soon involved in a bitter quarrel over the Narragansett Country. In 1664 a royal commission arrived in the colony and, in an effort to settle the issue, proclaimed the Narragansett Country to be the "King's Province" and placed it temporarily under Rhode Island. Nevertheless, the dispute, which was further complicated by a group of proprietors who claimed to hold a mortgage on the territory, continued to be a fertile source of dissension throughout Arnold's administration. With the Narragansett question still unsettled, Arnold died in office on June 19, 1678.

Bibliography: Hamilton Bullock Tompkins, "Benedict Arnold, First Governor of Rhode Island," Newport Historical Society, *Bulletin*, no. 30 (October 1919), 1-18; Elisha Stephen Arnold, comp., *The Arnold Memorial: William Arnold of Providence and Pawtuxet, 1587-1675, and a Genealogy of His Descendants* (Rutland, Vt., 1935); Ethan L. Arnold, *An Arnold Family Record: 323 Years in America. A Record of Some of the Descendants of William Arnold and His Son, Governor Benedict Arnold of Rhode Island and His Grandson, Benedict Arnold, Junior, 1635 to 1958* [Elkhart, Ind., 1958].

Figure 18-11. An example from another vocational source, *Biographical Directory of American Colonial and Revolutionary Governors, 1607–1789* (Westport, Conn.: Meckler Books, 1980).

THOMAS CARTER, A.M., b. Hinderclay, Suffolk, Eng., bapt. July 3, 1608, son of James Carter; St. John's Coll., Camb., A. B., 1629/30; A.M., 1633; came to N. E., 1637; served as minister at Dedham and Watertown; Ord. Woburn, Nov. 22, 1642, as the first minister; sett. Woburn, 1642-1684; d. Woburn, Sept. 5, 1684.

Figure 18-12. An entry from Frederick Lewis Weis's *The Colonial Clergy and the Colonial Churches of New England* (Lancaster, Mass., 1936), page 50.

MEYERINK, K. GEORGE
St Joseph, Michigan; b: Nov 22, 1908; m: Harriet C.; c: Gale, Gretchen, Peter, Kory, Penny; p: Mr and Mrs Arthur P. Chamberlain; ed: Natl Radio Inst 1929-30; Cornell U 1930-32; Michigan State U 1960-; career: Lake Michigan College, Instr of Appliance Serv 1966-; Serv Associates, Owner 1961-66; Whirlpool Corp, Prod Serv Engr 1955-61; Natl Presto Industries, Chief Engr App Div 1952-55; Homelite Corp, Prod Engr, Elec Engr 1942-52; civic: IKEE; BSA, Coun Advancement Chm, Silver Beaver Award; Evans Sch Bd, Treas; honors: Author of Appliance Service Handbook 1973, Science and Mechanics, Numerous Articles on Service.

Figure 18-13. An entry from another vocational source, *1974 Outstanding Educators of America* (Washington, D.C.: Outstanding Educators of America, 1974), page 325.

Ethnic Sources. Biographical sources highlight the contributions of ethnic groups through sketches of their notable members. The largest collections of these works focus on Native Americans, African Americans, and Jews. However, many European ethnicities are represented in national or local sources, including Italians, Germans, Norwegians, Poles, Dutch, Swedes, Danes, Swiss, French, and most other nationalities. Search the subject index of Slocum's bibliography under the nationality or race of an ancestor to determine whether there is a biography of interest. Also consult the sources in chapter 4, "Ethnic Sources."

African Americans. Recently, more attention has been given the biographies of black Americans. Chadwyck-Healey has recently reprinted on microfiche four hundred biographical dictionaries with thirty thousand entries as *Black Biographical Dictionaries, 1790–1950* (Alexandria, Va., 1987–89). Much like *American Biographical Archive,* this collection assembles obscure biographical sources from the past so that researchers can compare several sketches about notable African Americans. The three-volume index, *Black Biography, 1790–1950: A Cumulative Index* (Alexandria, Va.: Chadwyck-Healey, 1991) is also a stand-alone research tool that provides, where known, the subject's name, date and place of birth, occupation, religion, existence of an illustration, and a reference number that leads to the book(s) among *Black Biographical Dictionaries, 1790–1950* that contain a biographical note. For more recent subjects, see *Who's Who Among Black Americans,* which, in its sixth edition (Detroit: Gale Research, 1990), profiles more than seventeen thousand men and women.

Women. The contributions of women have been seriously overlooked in the United States until recent years. Fortunately, their contributions are being acknowledged through numerous biographical sources focusing on women. Women are not totally absent from the sources discussed thus far, but they are not included proportionately as subjects. This oversight is primarily due to earlier U.S. society, which discouraged women from becoming leaders in any field (although some certainly did). While the best way to seek biographical information about most women is to search for their husbands, many sources now available focus on women. These books are national or local in scope; some mirror the biographical encyclopedias and dictionaries by including women in any field or of any accomplishment, while some focus on women in specific vocations (writers are popular). Two important collections include the three-volume *Notable American Women, 1607–1950: A Biographical Dictionary* (1971) and *Women in Particular: An Index to American Women* (1984), which indexes fifteen thousand women, mostly of the past, in fifty-four collective works. Norma Ireland has published *Index to Women of the World From Ancient to Modern Times* (1970) and a supplement (1988) which each include thirteen thousand to sixteen thousand citations of sketches in collective biographies.

Well over one hundred titles focusing on notable women exist. Slocum's *Biographical Dictionaries and Related Works* (see above under "National Biographical Sources—Bibliographies") files them with the country, state, or vocation which the subjects best fit. *Biographical Sources* (see above under "National Biographical Sources—Bibliographies") lists almost forty in a separate category. The best way to locate a female ancestor is to check both the "regular" sources that might apply and sources focusing solely on women.

LOCATING BIOGRAPHICAL WORKS

Most libraries have large biography collections because of the great public interest in many of the subjects. Unfortunately, many of these collections focus on modern biographies, although the larger biographical encyclopedias and dictionaries are available at most libraries. State and university libraries generally have the largest collections of national sources. For state and local sources the best libraries are those in the area represented by the biography—especially the libraries of county historical societies. Much of the discussion in chapter 17 about locating local or county histories applies here as well.

The bibliographies and indexes discussed in this chapter will help determine which biographies are of greatest interest. Also review the state bibliographies in chapter 17. A local librarian can help locate copies and obtain them through interlibrary loan, if necessary. Many publishers are reprinting some of these works in book (Gale Research), microfilm (Cox and Research Publications), microfiche (University Microfilms International, Ann Arbor, Michigan), and, most recently, in electronic format, either on CD-ROM or on the Internet (Ancestry, Salt Lake City). Researchers and libraries may be interested in purchasing specific titles to build their collections.

Since the 1970s, scholars have begun to pay more attention to collective biographies and have written articles describing their creation and uses. For more information on local biographical sources, see Archibald Hanna's "Every Man His Own Biographer," *Proceedings of the American Antiquarian Society* 80 (1970): 291–98. Donald C. Yelton's short but excellent set of four essays about collective biographies, *Brief American Lives: Four Studies in Collective Biography* (Metuchen, N.J.: Scarecrow Press, 1978), describes the selection process and anomalies of three of the most important biographical encyclopedias. For a librarian's perspective, see Jack A. Clarke's "Biographical Directories, the Fine Line Between Vanity and Pride," *RQ* (Fall 1982): 76, and the excellent discussion by William A. Katz in chapter 9, "Biographical Sources," of his *Introduction of Reference Work: Volume 1, Basic Information Sources* (New York: McGraw-Hill, 1974 [and later editions of this classic library reference aid]). For guidance in using the many online sources for biographical research, see Marydee Ojala, "The Never-Ending Search for People," *Online* (September-October 1994): 105–10. Dedicated researchers will study these and other writings to better understand biographical sources.

NOTES

1. Exact figures regarding the number of persons who have been the subjects of biographical sketches are hard to come by. This figure combines the numbers for the national (3 million), state (500,000), local (1 million to 2 million), and vocational (500,000 to 2 million) sketches discussed in this chapter. The discussion throughout this chapter will indicate how these figures were determined.
2. In cases where the subject provided the information, some of that information can be considered primary. See the discussion of genealogical information in the introduction to *Printed Sources*.
3. The totals for this breakdown are greater than the 368 sources used because some titles were counted in two categories.
4. Some of the sources in the following discussion were first discussed in J. Carlyle Parker's *Going to Salt Lake City to Do Family History Research*, 2nd ed. (Turlock, Calif.: Marietta Publishing Co., 1993), chapter 8, "Is There a Biographical Sketch about Your Ancestor?"

REFERENCE LIST

Briscoe, Mary Louise, ed. 1982. *American Autobiography, 1945–1980: A Bibliography*. Madison: University of Wisconsin Press.

Coulter, E. Merton. 1948. *Travels in the Confederate States: A Bibliography*. Norman: University of Oklahoma Press.

Slocum, Robert B., ed. 1986. *Biographical Dictionaries and Related Works*. 2 vols. Detroit: Gale Research.

Yelton, Donald C. 1978. *Brief American Lives: Four Studies in Collective Biography*. Metuchen, N.J.: Scarecrow Press.

BIBLIOGRAPHY

This bibliography lists many of the key sources that researchers may wish to refer to, including bibliographies, indexes, national biographical sources, and statewide sources.

National Biographical Indexes

Baillie, Laureen, ed. *American Biographical Index*. 6 vols. New York City: K. G. Saur, 1993.

Biography and Genealogy Master Index. 17+ vols. Edited by Miranda C. Herbert and Barbara McNeil. Detroit: Gale Research, 1980, 1985, 1990. Annual supplements.

Biography Index. New York: H. W. Wilson Co., 1947–. Annual.

Black Biography 1790–1950: A Cumulative Index. Alexandria, Va.: Chadwyck-Healey, 1991.

Bureau of Indian Affairs Library. *Biographical and Historical Index of American Indians and Persons Involved in Indian Affairs*. 8 vols. Boston: G. K. Hall, 1966.

Dargan, Marion. *Guide to American Biography, Part 1: 1607–1815* and *Part 2: 1815–1933*. Albuquerque: University of New Mexico Press, 1949, 1952.

Herman, Kali. *Women in Particular: An Index to American Women*. Phoenix: Orxy Press, 1984.

Hyamson, Albert Montefiore. *A Dictionary of Universal Biography of All Ages and of All People*. 1916. Reprint. Baltimore: Clearfield Co., 1995. 2nd ed. New York: Dutton, 1951. Reprint. Detroit: Gale Research Co., 1981.

Index to Biographies in Local Histories in the Library of Congress. 31 microfilm reels. Baltimore: Magna Charta Book Co., 1979.

Ireland, Norma Olin. *Index to Women of the World from Ancient to Modern Times*. Westwood, Mass.: F. W. Faxon Co., 1970.

______. *Index to Women of the World from Ancient to Modern Times. A Supplement*. Metuchen, N.J.: Scarecrow Press, 1988.

Kinnell, Susan K., ed. *People in History*. 2 vols. Santa Barbara, Calif.: ABC-Clio, 1988.

Kline, Jane, comp. *Biographical Sources for the United States*. Washington, D.C.: Library of Congress, General Reference and Bibliography Division, 1961.

Levy, Felice D. *Obituaries on File*. 2 vols. New York: Facts on File, 1979.

McMann, Evelyn de R. *Canadian Who's Who Index 1898–1984*. Toronto: University of Toronto Press, 1986.

New York Times Obituaries Index. 2 vols. New York: New York Times, 1970, 1979.

Old Surname Index File. 21 microfilm reels. Salt Lake City: Genealogical Society of Utah, 1976.

Phillips, Lawrence Barnett. *Dictionary of Biographical Reference*. 3rd ed. Philadelphia: Gibbie, 1889. Reprint. Detroit: Gale Research, 1982.

Riches, Phyllis M. *An Analytical Bibliography of Universal Collected Biography: Comprising Books Published in the English Tongue in Great Britain and Ireland, America and the British Dominions*. London: Library Association, 1934. Reprint. Detroit: Gale Research, 1980.

Who's Who in America Index. Wilmette, Ill.: Marquis Who's Who, 1975–. Annual.

National Bibliographies

ARBA Guide to Biographical Dictionaries. Edited by Bohdan S. Wynar. Littleton, Colo.: Libraries Unlimited, 1986.

Arksey, Laura, Nancy Pries, and Marcia Reed. *American Diaries: An Annotated Bibliography of Published American Diaries and Journals*. Vol. 1, 1492–1844; vol. 2, 1845–1980. Detroit: Gale Research, 1983, 1987.

Biographical Books, 1876–1949. New York: R. R. Bowker, 1983.

Biographical Books, 1950–1980. New York: R. R. Bowker, 1980.

Bradford, Thomas L. *Bibliographer's Manual of American History*. 5 vols. Philadelphia: Stan V. Henkels and Co., 1907–10. Reprint. Detroit: Gale Research, 1968.

Brignano, Russell. *Black Americans in Autobiography: An Annotated Bibliography of Autobiographies and Autobiographical Books Written Since the Civil War*. Durham, N.C.: Duke University Press, 1974.

Briscoe, Mary Louise, ed. *American Autobiography, 1945–1980: A Bibliography*. Madison: University of Wisconsin Press, 1982. Identifies five thousand privately and commercially published books.

Cimbala, Diane J., Jennifer Cargill, and Brian Alley. *Biographi-*

cal Sources: A Guide to Dictionaries and Reference Works. Phoenix, Ariz.: Oryx Press, 1986.

Filby, P. William. *A Bibliography of American County Histories*. Baltimore: Genealogical Publishing Co., 1985.

Jarboe, Betty M. *Obituaries: A Guide to Sources.* 2nd ed. Boston: G. K. Hall, 1989. Contains 3,547 entries for books, and some articles, that abstract, copy, or index obituaries, death records, and tombstones.

Kaplan, Louis. *A Bibliography of American Autobiographies.* Madison: University of Wisconsin Press, 1961. Contains 6,377 entries dated prior to 1946.

Mattes, Merrill J. *Platte River Road Narratives.* Urbana: University of Illinois Press, 1988. FHL 978 E63m. An excellent, evaluative bibliography, mostly including diaries and accounts; some letters. Includes published and private sources.

O'Neill, Edward H. *Biography by Americans, 1658–1936: A Subject Bibliography*. Philadelphia: University of Pennsylvania Press, 1939. Reprint. Boston: Gregg Press, 1972. Seven thousand references, including 707 collective works with indexes to individuals.

Peterson, Clarence S. *Consolidated Bibliography of County Histories in Fifty States in 1961.* 2nd ed. Baltimore: Genealogical Publishing Co., 1963.

Slocum, Robert B., ed. *Biographical Dictionaries and Related Works.* 2 vols. Detroit: Gale Research, 1986.

Sweeney, Patricia E. *Biographies of American Women: An Annotated Bibliography.* Santa Barbara, Calif.: ABC-Clio, 1990. Includes 1,391 book biographies on seven hundred women.

National Biographical Encyclopedias

The titles in the following list which are indexed in *American Biographical Index* are marked with an asterisk (*).

*The American Biographical Archive.** New York: K. G. Saur, 1986–89.

*Appleton's Cyclopedia of American Biography.** 6 vols. and supplement. Edited by James G. Wilson and John Fiske. New York: D. Appleton, 1887–9, 1901. Rev. ed., 1915.

Appleton's Cyclopedia of American Biography, Supplement, or: The Cyclopedia of American Biography. Edited by Charles Dick and James Holmans. 6 vols. New York: Press Association Compilers, 1918–31. These supplemental volumes to the 1915 revised edition are numbered 7 through 12.

Black Biographical Dictionaries, 1790–1950. Alexandria, Va.: Chadwyck-Healey, 1987–89.

Chamberlain, Joshua L. *Universities and Their Sons.** 5 vols. Boston: R. Herndon Co., 1898–1900.

*Contemporary American Biography.** 3 vols. New York: Atlantic Publishing and Engraving Co., 1895–1902.

Current Biography. New York: H. W. Wilson Co., 1940–. A monthly publication with annual cumulation. Provides biographical sketches of currently prominent persons throughout the world.

Dexeter, Franklin Bowditch. *Biographical Sketches of the Graduates of Yale College.* 6 vols. New York: Holt, 1885–1912.

Dictionary of American Biography. 20 vols. and 8 supplements. New York: C. Scribner, 1928–36, 1944–88.

Dictionary of Canadian Biography. Edited by George W. Brown. 12 vols. Toronto: University of Toronto Press, 1966–91.

Encyclopedia of American Biography (Old Series), or: American Biography: A New Cyclopedia. 54 vols. New York: American Historical Society, 1916–33.

Encyclopedia of American Biography (New Series). Edited by Winfield Scott Downs. 40 vols. New York: American Historical Society, 1934–70.

Herringshaw, Thomas William. *Herringshaw's National Library of American Biography.** 5 vols. Chicago: American Publisher's Association, 1909–14.

James, Edward T., ed. *Notable American Women, 1607–1950: A Biographical Dictionary.* 3 vols. Cambridge, Mass.: Belknap Press, Harvard University, 1971. Scholarly articles on 1,359 women, including source information.

*The National Cyclopedia of American Biography—Permanent Series.** 63 vols. New York: James T. White, 1892–84. Only vols. 1 through 13 are in *American Biographical Index.*

The National Cyclopedia of American Biography—Current Series. 13 vols. New York: James T. White, 1930–84.

Shipton, C. K., et al., eds. *Sibley's Harvard Graduates.* 17 vols. Boston: Massachusetts Historical Society and others, 1873–1974.

Sprague, William Buell. *Annals of the American Pulpit.** 9 vols. New York: R. Carter, 1857–69.

Thrapp, Dan L. *Encyclopedia of Frontier Biography*. Lincoln: University of Nebraska Press, 1988. Contains 4,500 entries.

Twentieth Century Biographical Dictionary of Notable Americans. Edited by John Howard Brown. 10 vols. Boston: Biographical Society, 1904. Reprint. Detroit: Gale Research, 1968. A "corrected edition of a work previously published under the titles: *The Cyclopedia of American Biography* (1897–1903) and *Lamb's Biographical Dictionary of the United States* (1900–1903)." It was apparently also published as *Biographical Dictionary of America* in 1906 by the same company.

Who Was Who in America. 12 vols. plus index. Chicago: Marquis, 1943–93.

American Biographical Dictionaries

The titles in the following list which are indexed in *American Biographical Index* are marked with an asterisk (*). Most of them are historical in nature.

Allen, William. *The American Biographical Dictionary.** 2nd ed. Boston: William Hyde and Co., 1832. Contains 1,800 entries. The first edition (with seven hundred entries), published in 1809, and the third edition (Boston: J. P. Jewett, 1857) are not indexed in *American Biographical Index.*

The American Slave: A Composite Autobiography. 19 vols. Supplement. Edited by George P. Rawick. 12 vols. Westport, Conn.: Greenwood Publishing Co., 1972, 1977. Slave narratives reprinted from typewritten records prepared in 1941.

American Women, 1935–1940. 2 vols. Detroit: Gale Research, 1981. Contains twelve thousand entries.

Belknap, Jeremy. *American Biography.** 3 vols. New York: Harper & Bros., 1843.

Biographical Cyclopedia of American Women. 2 vols. New York: Halvord Publishing Co., 1924–25. Reprint. Detroit: Gale Research, 1974.

Bolton, Charles Knowles. *The Founders.* 1919–26. Reprint (3 vols. in 2). Baltimore: Genealogical Publishing Co., 1976.

Brown, Everit. *A Dictionary of American Politics.** New York: A. L. Burt, irregular from 1888 to at least 1908. The 1892 edition is indexed in *American Biographical Index.*

Cirker, Hayward. *Dictionary of American Portraits.* New York: Dover Publications, 1967. Contains 4,045 portraits, early to the beginning of the twentieth century.

Drake, Francis Samuel. *Dictionary of American Biography.** 1872. Reprint. Detroit: Gale Research, 1974. Contains approximately ten thousand entries.

French, Benjamin Franklin. *Biographia Americana.* New York: D. Mallory, 1825. Contains 181 entries.

Green, Harry Clinton. *The Pioneer Mothers of America.* 3 vols. New York: G. P. Putnam, 1912.

Griswold, Rufus Wilmot. *The Biographical Annual: Containing Memoirs of Eminent Persons, Recently Deceased.* New York: Linen and Fennell, 1841.

Hafen, Leroy R., ed. *The Mountain Men and the Fur Trade of the Far West: Biographical Sketches of the Participants.* 10 vols. Glendale, Calif.: Arthur H. Clark Co., 1969–72.

Hall, Henry. *America's Successful Men of Affairs.* 2 vols. New York: New York Tribune, 1895–96.

Hanaford, Phebe Ann Coffin. *Daughters of America, or Women of the Century.* Boston: B. B. Russell, 1883.

Harrison, Mitchell C. *Prominent and Progressive Americans.** 2 vols. New York: New York Tribune, 1902–04.

Herringshaw, Thomas William. *Herringshaw's Encyclopedia of American Biography of the Nineteenth Century.* Chicago: American Publisher's Association, 1907.

Herringshaw's American Blue Book of Biography: Prominent Americans of [1912]. Chicago: American Publisher's Association, 1913–. Published almost annually through 1926 with slight title variations.

Hough, Franklin Benjamin. *American Biographical Notes: Being Short Notices of Deceased Persons, Chiefly Those Not Included in Allen's or Drake's Biographical Dictionary.** Albany: Munsell, 1875. Reprint. Harrison, N.Y.: Harbor Hill Books, 1974. Approximately 5,700 entries.

Jones, Abner Dumont. *The American Portrait Gallery.* New York: J. M. Emerson, 1855.

Kingston, John. *The New American Biographic Dictionary.* Baltimore: J. Kingston, 1810. Second edition published 1811 as *The New Pocket Biographical Dictionary.*

Lossing, Benson J. *Eminent Americans.** New York: Mason Brothers, 1857. The 1855 edition, under the title *Our Countrymen,* has 326 sketches of deceased Americans in 407 pages.

Men of America: A Biographical Dictionary of Contemporaries. Edited by John W. Leonard. New York: L. R. Hamersly, 1908. 2,188 pages. Second edition published 1910 as *Men and Women of America.*

Mothers of Achievement in American History, 1776–1976. Rutland, Vt.: C. E. Tuttle Co., 1976.

Preston, Wheeler. *American Biographies.* New York: Harper & Brothers, 1940. Reprint. Detroit: Gale Research Co., 1974. Contains approximately 5,700 entries.

Principal Women of America. London: Mitre Press, 1932. Contains 1,500 entries.

Rogers, Thomas J. *A New American Biographical Dictionary.* 4th ed. Philadelphia: S. F. Bradford, 1829. Third edition printed in Easton, Pennsylvania (1824).

Schubert, Frank N. *On the Trail of the Buffalo Soldier: Biographies of African Americans in the U.S. Army, 1866–1917.* Wilmington, Del.: Scholarly Resources, 1995. Documents eight thousand individuals.

Van Doren, Charles, ed. *Webster's American Biographies.* Springfield, Mass.: Merriam Co., 1979. Contains 3,082 entries.

Who Was Who in American History: The Military. Chicago: Marquis, 1974.

Who's Who Among Black Americans. 6th ed. Detroit: Gale Research, 1990. Contains seventeen thousand entries.

Who's Who in America. Chicago: Marquis, 1899–. Biennial. The 1992–93 edition includes 80,500 entries.

Willard, Frances E., and Mary A. Livermore. *A Woman of the Century: Fourteen Hundred-Seventy Biographical Sketches; Accompanied by Portraits of Leading American Women in All Walks of Life.* 2 vols. Buffalo, N.Y.: C. W. Moulton, 1893. Reprint. Detroit: Gale Research Co., 1967. Contains 1,470 entries.

Multi-State Biographical Indexes

The following multi-state and statewide indexes are usually the best sources to start searching for biographical sketches in state and local sources. These are collective indexes to many titles within their areas or states. Virtually none are every-name indexes, and each has different rules for inclusion. However, all of them index the subjects of biographical sketches in histories and collective biographies. The statewide indexes are arranged alphabetically by state.

Allen County Public Library. *Historical and Biographical Index of North East, Mid East, Mid South, Mid West U.S.A., 1800 thru Early 1900.* 33 microfilm reels. Salt Lake City: Genealogical Society of Utah, 1989.

Early Church Information File. 75 microfilm reels. Salt Lake City: Genealogical Society of Utah, 1991. Excellent coverage for the Intermountain West.

Drazan, Joseph Gerald. *The Pacific Northwest: An Index to People and Places in Books.* Metuchen, N.J.: Scarecrow Press, 1979. Contains 6,830 entries from 320 sources for Alaska, Idaho, Montana, Oregon, and Washington and British Columbia and Yukon Territory in Canada.

Genealogical Index of the Newberry Library. 4 vols. (also on 8 microfilm reels). Boston: G. K. Hall, 1960. Most references are for northern or midwestern sources.

Wiggins, Marvin E., comp. *Mormons and Their Neighbors.* 2 vols. Provo, Utah: Lee Library, Brigham Young University, 1984. Covers Utah, Idaho, Arizona, and Wyoming.

Statewide Published Biographical Indexes

This list is arranged alphabetically by state.

Bradbury, Connie, David A. Hales, and Nancy Lesh. *Alaska People Index*. Alaska Historical Commission Studies in History no. 203. 2 vols. Anchorage: Alaska Historical Commission, 1986.

California State Library. *California Information File*. 550 microfiche. Bellevue, Wash.: Commercial Microfilm Services, 1986.

Parker, J. Carlyle. *An Index to Biographies in 19th Century California County Histories*. Gale Genealogy and Local History Series, vol. 7. Detroit: Gale Research Co., 1979.

Bromwell, Henriette Elizabeth. *Colorado Portrait and Biography Index*. 4 vols. Denver, 1935.

Parker, J. Carlyle, and Janet G. Parker. *Idaho Biographical and Genealogical Sketch Index*. Turlock, Calif.: Marietta Publishing Co., in progress.

Indiana Biographical Index. Compiled by Jimmy B. Parker and Lyman De Platt. 16 microfiche. West Bountiful, Utah: Genealogical Indexing Associates, 1983.

Morford, Charles. *Biographical Index to the County Histories of Iowa*. Vol. 1. Baltimore: Gateway Press, 1979. No further volumes.

Cook, Michael Lewis. *Kentucky Index of Biographical Sketches in State, Regional, and County Histories*. Evansville, Ind.: Cook Publications, 1986.

Andrusko, Samuel M. *Maryland Biographical Sketch Index*. Silver Spring, Md.: the author, 1983.

Loomis, Frances. *Michigan Biography Index*. 4 microfilm reels. Detroit: Detroit Public Library, 1946. Woodbridge, Conn.: Research Publications, 1973.

Upham, Warren, comp. *Minnesota Biographies, 1655–1912*. Collections of the Minnesota Historical Society, vol. 14. St. Paul, Minn.: the society, 1912.

Parker, J. Carlyle, and Janet G. Parker. *Montana Biographical and Genealogical Sketch Index*. Turlock, Calif.: Marietta Publishing Co., in progress.

_____. *Nevada Biographical and Genealogical Sketch Index*. Turlock, Calif.: Marietta Publishing Co., 1986.

New Hampshire Notables Card File, 1600 to the Present. 8 microfilm reels. Salt Lake City: New Hampshire Historical Society, 1988.

Towle, Glenn C. *New Hampshire Genealogical Digest, 1623–1900*. Vol. 1. Bowie, Md.: Heritage Books, 1986.

Sinclair, Donald A. *New Jersey Biographical Index, Covering some 100,000 Biographies and Associated Portraits in 237 New Jersey . . . Collective Biographical Sources*. Baltimore: Genealogical Publishing Co., 1993.

Ohio Historical Society. *Ohio County History Surname Index*. 64 microfilm reels. Columbus, Ohio, 1984.

Brandt, Patricia, and Nancy Guilford, eds. *Oregon Biography Index*. Oregon State University Bibliographic Series, no. 11. Corvallis: Oregon State University, 1976.

Hoenstine, Floyd G. *Guide to Genealogical and Historical Research in Pennsylvania*. Hollidaysburg, Pa.: the author, 1978, 1985.

Parker, J. Carlyle. *Rhode Island Biographical and Genealogical Sketch Index*. Turlock, Calif.: Marietta Publishing Co., 1991.

Côté, Richard N., and Patricia H. Williams. *Dictionary of South Carolina Biography*. Vol. 1. Easley, S.C.: Southern Historical Press, 1985.

Parker, J. Carlyle, and Janet G. Parker. *South Dakota Biographical and Genealogical Sketch Index*. Turlock, Calif.: Marietta Publishing Co., in progress.

Ming, Virginia H., and William L. Ming. *Biographical Gazetteer of Texas*. 6 vols. Austin, Tex.: W. M. Morrison Books, 1985–87.

True, Ransom B. *Biographical Dictionary of Early Virginia, 1607–1660*. 19 microfiche. Jamestown, Va.: Association for the Preservation of Virginia Antiquities, 1982. More than 100,000 entries refer to thirty thousand people who are mentioned in wills, deeds, court orders, published histories, and Virginia company records.

Wardell, Patrick G. *Timesaving Aid to Virginia-West Virginia Ancestors*. 4 vols. Athens, Ga.: Iberian Publishing Co., 1985–90.

Subject Catalog of the Library of the State Historical Society of Wisconsin. . . . 23 vols. Westport, Conn.: Greenwood Publishing Co., 1971.

Parker, J. Carlyle, and Janet G. Parker. *Wyoming Biographical and Genealogical Sketch Index*. Turlock, Calif.: Marietta Publishing Co., in progress.

Statewide Biographies

The following is a selective list of statewide sources. Some statewide collective biographies have been indexed in national-level sources. The titles in the following list indexed in *American Biographical Index* are marked with an asterisk (*). Those indexed in *Index to Biographies in Local Histories in the Library of Congress* are marked with a dagger (†).

Alabama

Du Bose, Joel Campbel, ed. *Notable Men of Alabama*. 2 vols. Atlanta, Ga.: Southern Historical Association, 1904.

Garrett, William. *Reminiscences of Public Men in Alabama, for Thirty Years.*† Atlanta, Ga.: Plantation Publishing Co., 1872.

Owen, Thomas McAdory. *History of Alabama and Dictionary of Alabama Biography.**† 4 vols. 1921. Reprint. Spartanburg, S.C.: Reprint Co., 1978.

Alaska

Atwood, Evangeline, and Robert N. DeArmond. *Who's Who in Alaskan Politics: A Biographical Dictionary of Alaskan Political Personalities, 1884–1974*. Portland, Oreg.: Bindor and Mort, 1977.

Harrison, Edward S. *Nome and Seward Peninsula: History, Description, Biographies, and Stories*. Seattle: the author, 1905.

Arizona

A Historical and Biographical Record of the Territory of Arizona.† Chicago: McFarland & Poole, 1896.

American Biographical Encyclopedia, Volume 1: Arizona Edition. Phoenix: P. W. Pollock, 1967.

Conners, Jo. *Who's Who in Arizona. Volume 1.* Tucson, Ariz.: the author, 1913.

*Portrait and Biographical Record of Arizona. . . .**† Chicago: Chapman Publishing Co., 1901.

Arkansas

Hallum, John. *Biographical and Pictorial History of Arkansas.** 2 vols. Albany, N.Y.: Weed, Parsons & Co., 1887.

Shinn, Josiah H. *Pioneers and Makers of Arkansas.*† Genealogical and Historical Publishing Co., 1908.

Thomas, David Yancey, ed. *Arkansas and Its People: A History, 1541–1930.*† 4 vols. New York: American Historical Society, 1930. Vols. 3 and 4 are biographical.

California

Bancroft, Hubert Howe. *California Pioneer Register and Index 1542–1848: Including Inhabitants of California, 1769–1800 and List of Pioneers.* Baltimore: Regional Publishing Co., 1964.

Hunt, Rockwell Dennis, ed. *California and Californians.*† Chicago: Lewis Publishing Co., 1932.

Phelps, Alonzo. *Contemporary Biography of California's Representative Men. . . .* 2 vols. San Francisco: A. L. Bancroft and Co., 1881.

Colorado

Portrait and Biographical Record of the State of Colorado. . . . 2 vols. Chicago: Chapman Publishing Co., 1899.

Stone, Wilbur Fiske. *History of Colorado.* 6 vols. Chicago: S. J. Clarke Publishing Co., 1918–19. Vols. 2 through 6 are biographical.

Connecticut

Cutter, William Richard, ed. *Genealogy and Family History of the State of Connecticut.* 4 vols. New York: Lewis Historical Pub. Co., 1911.

Genealogical and Biographical Records of American Citizens: Connecticut. 26 vols. Hartford, Conn., 1929–49.

Hart, Samuel, et al. *Encyclopedia of Connecticut Biography, Genealogical-Memorial: Representative Citizens.* 11 vols. Boston: American Historical Society, ca. 1917–23.

Osborn, Norris Galpin, ed. *Men of Mark in Connecticut.** 5 vols. Hartford, Conn.: W. R. Goodspeed, 1906–10.

Delaware

Biographical and Genealogical History of the State of Delaware. 2 vols. Chambersburg, Pa.: J. M. Runk, 1899.

Historical and Biographical Encyclopedia of Delaware. Wilmington, Del.: Aldine Pub. and Engraving Co., 1883.

District of Columbia (also see Virginia)

American Biographical Directories, District of Columbia . . . 1908–1909. Washington, D.C.: Potomac Press, 1908.

U.S. Department of State. *Register of Officers and Agents, Civil, Military, and Naval, in the Service of the United States.* Washington, D.C.: Government Printing Office, 1816–. Annual.

Williamson, Stanley. *Who's Who in the Nation's Capital.* Washington, D.C.: Ransdell. Biennial.

Florida (also see Georgia)

Chapin, George M. *Florida, 1513–1913.** 2 vols. Chicago: S. J. Clarke Publishing Co., 1914.

Cutler, Harry Gardner. *History of Florida, Past and Present. . . .* 3 vols. Chicago and New York: Lewis Publishing Co., 1923. Vols. 2 and 3 are biographical.

Georgia

Biographical Souvenir of the States of Georgia and Florida.† Chicago: F. A. Battey and Co., 1889.

Coleman, Kenneth. *Dictionary of Georgia Biography.* Athens: University of Georgia Press, 1983.

Knight, Lucian Lamar. *A Standard History of Georgia and Georgians.**† 6 vols. Chicago: Lewis Publishing Co., 1917. Vols. 4 through 6 are biographical.

Northern, William J. *Men of Mark in Georgia. . . .**† 7 vols. 1907–12. Reprint. Spartanburg, S.C.: Reprint Co., 1975.

Hawaii

*History of Hawaii and its Builders.** Honolulu Star-Bulletin, 1925.

Siddall, John William, et al. *Men of Hawaii. . . .* 5 vols. Honolulu: Honolulu Star-Bulletin, 1917–35.

Idaho

Hawley, James H. *History of Idaho: The Gem of the Mountains.*† 4 vols. Chicago: S. J. Clarke Publishing Co., 1920. Vols. 2 through 4 are biographical.

An Illustrated History of the State of Idaho. . . .† 4 vols. in 2. Chicago: Lewis Publishing Co., 1899.

Illinois

*Encyclopedia of Biography of Illinois.** 3 vols. Chicago: Century Publishing and Engraving Co., 1892–1902.

The United States Biographical Dictionary and Portrait Gallery of Eminent and Self-Made Men: Illinois Volume.† 2 vols. Chicago and New York: American Biographical Publishing Co., 1883.

Indiana

*A Biographical History of Eminent and Self-Made Men of the State of Indiana. . . .**† 2 vols. Cincinnati, Ohio: Western Biographical Publishing Co., 1880.

Dunn, Jacob Piatt. *Indiana and Indianans.** 5 vols. Chicago and New York: American Historical Society, 1919. Vols. 3 through 5 are biographical. A separate every-name index was published in 1939.

Iowa

Gue, B. F., and Benjamin F. Shambaugh. *Biographies and Portraits of the Progressive Men of Iowa. . . .**† 2 vols. Des Moines, Iowa: Conaway and Shaw, 1899.

A Memorial and Biographical Record of Iowa. 2 vols. 1896. Reprint. Marceline, Mo.: Walsworth Publishing Co., 1978.

Kansas

A Biographical History of Central Kansas. 2 vols. New York: Lewis Publishing Co., 1902.

Kansas Pioneers. Topeka, Kans.: Topeka Genealogical Society, 1976.

The United States Biographical Dictionary: Kansas. . . .† Chicago and Kansas City, Mo.: S. Lewis and Co., 1879.

Kentucky

*The Biographical Encyclopedia of Kentucky. . . .** 1 vol. in 2. Cincinnati, Ohio: J. M. Armstrong, 1878.

Gresham, John M. *Biographical Encyclopedia of the Commonwealth of Kentucky. . . .* Chicago: the author, 1896.

Johnson, E. Polk. *A History of Kentucky and Kentuckians.*† Chicago: Lewis Publishing Co., 1912.

Westerfield, Thomas W., and Sam McDowell. *Kentucky Genealogy and Biography.* 6 vols. Owensboro, Ky.: Genealogical Reference, 1969–70. These are reprinted from the biographical sections of various editions of *Kentucky: A History of the State,* by W. H. Perrin, et al., published during the 1880s.

Louisiana

*Biographical and Historical Memoirs of Louisiana. . . .**† 2 vols. in 3. 1892. Reprint. Baton Rouge, La.: Claitor's Pub. Div., 1975.

Conrad, Glenn R. ed. *A Dictionary of Louisiana Biography.* Lafayette: Louisiana Historical Association, 1989.

Louisianians and Their State: A Historical and Biographical Text Book of Louisiana.† New Orleans: Louisiana Historical and Biographical Association, 1919.

Maine

Herndon, Richard, et al. *Men of Progress: Biographical Sketches and Portraits of Leaders in Business and Professional Life in and of the State of Maine.* Boston: New England Magazine, 1897.

*Representative Men of Maine.** Portland, Maine: Lakeside Press, 1983.

Maryland

Biographical Cyclopedia of Representative Men of Maryland and District of Columbia.† Baltimore: National Biographical Publishing Co., 1879.

Boyle, Esmeralda. *Biographical Sketches of Distinguished Marylanders.** Baltimore: Kelly, Piet & Co., 1877.

Spencer, Richard Henry. *Genealogical and Memorial Encyclopedia of the State of Maryland. . . .* 2 vols. New York: American Historical Society, 1919.

Steiner, Bernard C. *Men of Mark in Maryland. . . .** 4 vols. Washington, D.C.: Johnson-Wynne Co., 1907–12.

Massachusetts

Bacon, Samuel Atkins, ed. *Biographical History of Massachusetts.* 10 vols. Boston: Massachusetts Biographical Society, 1911–18.

*Biographical Cyclopedia of Massachusetts of the Nineteenth Century.** New York: Metropolitan Publishing & Engraving Co., 1879.

Michigan

*American Biographical History of Eminent and Self-Made Men: Michigan Volume.** Cincinnati, Ohio: Western Biographical Pub. Co., 1878.

Michigan: A Centennial History of the State and Its People. 5 vols. Chicago: Lewis Pub. Co., 1939. Vols. 3 through 5 are biographical.

Moore, Charles. *History of Michigan.** 4 vols. Chicago: Lewis Publishing Co., 1915.

Minnesota

Barnquist, Joseph Alfred Arner. *Minnesota and Its People.* 4 vols. Chicago: S. J. Clarke, 1924. Vols. 3 and 4 are biographical.

Castle, Henry Anson. *Minnesota: Its Story and Biography.* 3 vols. Chicago: Lewis Publishing Co., 1915. Vols. 2 and 3 are biographical.

Marquis, Albert Nelson. *The Book of Minnesotans: A Biographical Dictionary of Leading Living Men of the State of Minnesota.** Chicago: the author, 1907.

Upham, Warren, and Rose Barteau Dunlap. *Minnesota Biographies, 1655–1912.** Collections of the Minnesota Historical Society, vol. 14. St. Paul: Minnesota Historical Society, 1912.

Mississippi

*Biographical and Historical Memoirs of Mississippi.**† 2 vols. 1891. Reprint. Spartanburg, S.C.: Reprint Co., 1978.

Rand, Clayton. *Men of Spine in Mississippi.*† Gulfport, Miss.: Dixie Press, 1940.

Rowland, Dunbar. *History of Mississippi, the Heart of the South.* 4 vols. 1925. Reprint. Spartanburg, S.C.: Reprint Co., 1978. Volumes 3 and 4 are biographical.

_____. *Mississippi: Comprising Sketches of Counties . . . and Persons.** 2 vols. in 4. 1907. Reprint. Spartanburg, S.C.: Reprint Co., 1976. Vols. 3 and 4 are biographical.

Missouri

Bryan, William S. *A History of the Pioneer Families of Missouri.*† St. Louis, Mo.: Bryan, Brand and Co., 1876.

Conrad, Howard Louis. *Encyclopedia of the History of Missouri, a Compendium of History and Biography for Ready Reference.** 6 vols. New York: Southern History Co., 1901.

Van Nada, M. L. ed. *The Book of Missourians.* Chicago: T. J. Steele, 1906.

Montana

*Progressive Men of the State of Montana.**† 1 vol. in 2. Chicago: A. W. Bowen and Co., 1901.

Stout, Tom. *Montana, Its Story and Biography. . . .* 3 vols. Chicago: American Historical Society, 1921. An every-name index exists. Vols. 2 and 3 are biographical.

Nebraska

Baldwin, Sara Mullin, and Robert Morton Mullin. *Nebraskana: Biographical Sketches of Nebraska Men and Women of Achievement Who Have Been Awarded Life Membership in the Nebraskana Society.* Hebron, Nebr.: Baldwin Co., 1932.

Compendium of History, Reminiscence and Biography of Nebraska . . . . Chicago: Alden Publishing Co., 1912.

Sheldon, Addison Erwin. *Nebraska: The Land and the People.* 3 vols. Chicago: Lewis Publishing Co., 1931. Vols. 2 and 3 are biographical.

Nevada

Angel, Myron, ed. *History of Nevada: With Illustration and Biographical Sketches of Its Prominent Men and Pioneers.*† Oakland, Calif.: Thompson & West, 1881.

Scrugham, James G. *Nevada: A Narrative of the Conquest of a Frontier Land . . .*† 3 vols. Chicago: American Historical Society, 1935. Vols. 2 and 3 are biographical.

New Hampshire

Biographical Sketches of Representative Citizens of the State of New Hampshire. American Series of Popular Biographies, New Hampshire Edition. Boston: New England Historical Publishing Co., 1902.

Pillsbury, Hobart. *New Hampshire . . . a History.* 9 vols. New York: Lewis Historical Publishing Co., 1927–29. Vols. 5 through 9 are biographical.

New Jersey

Cyclopedia of New Jersey Biography: Memorial and Biographical. 5 vols. New York: American Historical Society, 1921–23.

Lee, Francis Bazley. *Genealogical and Memorial History of the State of New Jersey. . . .** 4 vols. New York: Lewis Historical Publishing Co., 1910.

Nelson, William. *Nelson's Biographical Cyclopedia of New Jersey.* 2 vols. New York: Eastern Historical Publishing Society, 1913.

Ogden, Mary Depue. *Memorial Cyclopedia of New Jersey.** 4 vols. Newark, N.J.: Memorial History Co., 1915–21.

New Mexico

Chavez, Fray Angelico. *Origins of New Mexico Families in the Spanish Colonial Period. . . .* 1954. Reprint. Albuquerque, N.M.: University of Albuquerque, 1973.

Coan, Charles F. *A History of New Mexico . . . Historical and Biographical.* 3 vols. Chicago: American Historical Society, 1925. Vols. 2 and 3 are biographical.

*An Illustrated History of New Mexico and Biographical Mention of Many of Its Pioneers and Prominent Citizens of Today. . . .**† Chicago: Lewis Publishing Co., 1895.

New York

Fitch, Charles Elliott. *Encyclopedia of Biography of New York. . . .* 4 vols. New York: American Historical Society, 1916.

Hamm, Margherita A. *Famous Families of New York.*† 2 vols. New York: G. P. Putnam's Sons, 1902.

*Men of Mark of New York . . . During the Last Decade of the 19th Century.** 2 vols. Buffalo, N.Y.: Geo. E. Matthews & Co., 1892.

The Men of New York. 2 vols. Buffalo: G. E. Matthews, 1898.

Leonard, John W. *Who's Who in New York City and State.** 3rd ed. New York: L. R. Hamersley and Co., 1907.

North Carolina (also see South Carolina)

Ashe, Samuel A. ed. *Biographical History of North Carolina from Colonial Times to the Present.**† 10 vols. Greensboro, N.C.: Charles L. Van Noopen, 1905–17.

Foote, William H. *Sketches of North Carolina: Historical and Biographical.*† New York: R. Carter, 1846.

North Carolina Biography.† Vols. 4–6, *History of North Carolina.* 6 vols. Chicago: Lewis Publishing Co., 1919.

Powell, William S. *Dictionary of North Carolina Biography.* Chapel Hill: University of North Carolina Press, 1979–. Vols. 1 through 4, completed through 1992, include surnames *A* to *O*.

North Dakota

Aberle, George P. *Pioneers and Their Sons. . . .* 2 vols. Bismarck, N.D.: Tumbleweed Press, 1966.

Compendium of History and Biography of North Dakota Containing a History of North Dakota. . . . Chicago: Geo. A. Ogle & Co., 1900.

Crawford, Lewis F., et al. *History of North Dakota and North Dakota Biography.*† 3 vols. Chicago and New York: American Historical Society, 1931. Volumes 2 and 3 are biographical.

Lounsberry, Clement Augustus. *North Dakota History and People, Outlines of American History.** 3 vols. Chicago: S. J. Clarke, 1917. Vols. 2, 3, and 4 are biographical.

Ohio

Brennan, Joseph F. *The Biographical Cyclopedia and Portrait Gallery with an Historical Sketch of the State of Ohio.** 6 vols. Cincinnati, Ohio: Western Biographical Publishing Co., 1883–95.

Galbreath, Charles B. *History of Ohio.* 5 vols. Chicago: American Historical Society, 1925. Vols. 3 and 5 contain biographies.

Hildereth, Samuel P. *Biographical and Historical Memoirs of the Early Pioneer Settlers of Ohio.**† Cincinnati: H. W. Derby & Co., 1852.

Oklahoma

O'Beirne, Harry F., and E. S. O'Beirne. *The Indian Territory: Its Chiefs, Legislators and Leading Men.* St. Louis: C. B. Woodward Co., 1892.

*Portrait and Biographical Record of Oklahoma. . . .** Chicago: Chapman Publishing Co., 1901.

Thoburn, Joseph Bradfield. *A Standard History of Oklahoma. . . .* 5 vols. Chicago: American Historical Society, 1916. Vols. 3 through 5 are biographical.

Oregon

Carey, Charles Henry. *History of Oregon.* 3 vols. Pioneer History Publishing Co., 1922. Vols. 2 and 3 are biographical.

Gaston, Joseph. *The Centennial History of Oregon, 1811–1912. . . .**† 4 vols. Chicago: S. J. Clarke Publishing Co., 1912. Vols. 2 through 4 are biographical.

Pennsylvania

Encyclopedia of Contemporary Biography of Pennsylvania. 3 vols. New York: Atlantic Publishing and Engraving Co., 1889–93.

Jordan, John W., et al. *Encyclopedia of Pennsylvania Biography.* 26 vols. New York: Lewis Historical Publishing Co., 1914–48. Index to vols. 1 through 20 published in 1932.

Robson, Charles, ed. *The Biographical Encyclopedia of Pennsylvania of the Nineteenth Century.**† Philadelphia: Galaxy, 1874.

Rhode Island

*Biographical Cyclopedia of Representative Men of Rhode Island.**† 2 vols. Providence, R.I.: National Biographical Publishing Co., 1881.

Representative Men and Old Families of Rhode Island: Genealogical and Historical Sketches of Prominent and Representative Citizens of Many of the Old Families. 3 vols. Chicago: J. H. Beers & Co., 1908.

South Carolina

Cyclopedia of Eminent and Representative Men of the Carolinas of the Nineteenth Century.† Madison, Wis.: Brant & Fuller, 1892.

Hemphill, J. C. *Men of Mark in South Carolina . . . A Collection of Biographies of Leading Men of the State.**† 4 vols. Washington, D.C.: Men of Mark Publishing Co., 1907–09.

Snowden, Yates, and H. G. Cutler. *History of South Carolina.*† 5 vols. Chicago: Lewis Publishing Co., 1920. Vols. 3 through 5 are biographical.

South Dakota

Kingsbury, George Washington. *History of Dakota Territory and South Dakota: Its History and Its People by George Martin*

Smith. 5 vols. Chicago: S. J. Clarke Co., 1915. Vols. 4 and 5 contain biographical sketches.

*Memorial and Biographical Record: An Illustrated Compendium of Biography Containing a Compendium of Local Biography.**† Chicago: G. A. Ogle Co., 1898.

Tennessee

Allison, John Roy V. *Notable Men of Tennessee: Personal and Genealogical with Portraits.* 2 vols. Atlanta, Ga.: Southern Historical Association, 1905.

Crutchfield, James A. *Timeless Tennesseans.* Huntsville, Ala.: Strode Publishers, 1984.

Hale, William T. and Dixon L. Merritt. *A History of Tennessee and Tennesseeans.**† 8 vols. Chicago: Lewis Publishing Co., 1913.

Moore, John Trotwood, and Austin P. Foster. *Tennessee, the Volunteer State, 1760–1923.*† 4 vols. Chicago: S. J. Clark Publishing Co., 1923. Vols. 2 through 4 are biographical.

Speer, William S. *Sketches of Prominent Tennesseans.*† Nashville, Tenn.: A. B. Tavel, 1888.

Texas

Bailey, Ernest Emory. *Texas Historical and Biographical Record with a Genealogical Study of Historical Family Records.* Austin: Texas Historical and Biographical Record, n.d.

Biographical Souvenir of the State of Texas. 1889. Reprint. Easley, S.C.: Southern Historical Press, 1978.

Chamblin, Thomas S., ed. *The Historical Encyclopedia of Texas.* 2 vols. Dallas: Texas Historical Institute, 1982.

Davis, Ellis Arthur, and Edwin H. Grobe. *The New Cyclopedia of Texas.*† 4 vols. Dallas: Texas Development Bureau, 1929.

De Cordova, Jacob. *Texas: Her Resources and Her Public Men.*† Philadelphia: E. Crozet, 1858.

Utah

Esshom, Frank. *Pioneers and Prominent Men of Utah.* 1913. Reprint. Salt Lake City: Western Epics, 1966.

Jenson, Andrew. *Latter-day Saint Biographical Encyclopedia.** 4 vols. Salt Lake City: Jenson History Co., 1901–36.

Portrait, Genealogical and Biographical Record of the State of Utah. Chicago: National Historical Board, 1902.

Vermont

Carleton, Hiram. *Genealogical and Family History of the State of Vermont.* 2 vols. New York: Lewis Publishing Co., 1903.

Dodge, Prentiss Cutler. *Encyclopedia, Vermont Biography.* Burlington, Vt.: Ullery Publishing Co., 1912.

Hemenway, Abbey Maria. *Vermont Historical Gazetteer: A Magazine Embracing a History of Each Town, Civil, Ecclesiastical, Biographical and Military.* 5 vols. Burlington, Vt.: A. M. Hemenway, 1868–91.

Ullery, Jacob G. *Men of Vermont.* Brattleboro, Vt.: Transcript Publishing Co., 1894.

Virginia

Brock, Robert Alonza. *Virginia and Virginians.*† 2 vols. Richmond, Va., and Toledo, Ohio: H. H. Hardesty, 1888.

*Eminent and Representative Men of Virginia and the District of Columbia of the Nineteenth Century.** Madison, Wis.: Brant & Fuller, 1893.

*Men of Mark in Virginia.** 5 vols. Washington, D.C.: Men of Mark Publishing Co., 1906–09.

Tyler, Lyon Gardiner. *Encyclopedia of Virginia Biography.** 5 vols. New York: Lewis Historical Publishing Co., 1915.

Wardell, Patrick G. *Virginians and West Virginians, 1607–1870.* 3 vols. Bowie, Md.: Heritage Books, 1986, 1988, 1992.

Washington

*Sketches of Washingtonians.** Seattle: W. C. Wolfe & Co., 1906.

Pollard, Lancaster. *A History of the State of Washington.*† 4 vols. New York: American Historical Society, 1937. Vols. 3 and 4 are biographical.

Washington, West of the Cascades. 3 vols. Chicago: S. J. Clarke, 1917. Vols. 2 and 3 are biographical.

Who's Who in Washington State: A Compilation of Biographical Sketches of Men and Women Prominent in the Affairs of Washington State. Seattle: H. Allen Publishing, 1927.

West Virginia (also see Virginia)

Atkinson, George Wesley. *Prominent Men of West Virginia.* Wheeling, W.Va.: W. L. Callin, 1890.

Callaham, James Morton. *History of West Virginia, Old and New.* 3 vols. Chicago: American Historical Society, 1923. Vols. 2 and 3 are biographical.

Comstock, Jim. *West Virginia Heritage Encyclopedia.* 25 vols. Richwood, W.Va.: the author, 1976. Primarily biographical and geographical sketches from other published sources.

_____. *Supplemental Series.* Vols. 1–8. Richwood, W.Va.: the author, 1974.

*Men of West Virginia.**† 2 vols. Chicago: Biographical Publishing Co., 1903.

Wisconsin

Dictionary of Wisconsin Biography. Madison, Wis.: State Historical Society, 1960.

Nelke, David I. *Columbia Biographical Dictionary and Portrait Gallery. . . .* Chicago: Lewis Publishing Co., 1895.

U.S. Biographical Dictionary and Portrait Gallery of Eminent and Self-Made Men. Chicago: American Biographical Publishing, 1877.

Usher, Ellis B. *Wisconsin: Its Story and Biography, 1848–1913.* 8 vols. Chicago: Lewis Publishing Co., 1914. Vols. 4 through 8 are biographical.

Wyoming

Bartlett, Ichabod S. *History of Wyoming.** 3 vols. Chicago: S. J. Clarke, 1918. Vols. 2 and 3 are biographical.

Beard, Frances B. *Wyoming from Territorial Days to the Present.* 3 vols. Chicago: American Historical Society, 1933. Vols. 2 and 3 are biographical.

*Progressive Men of the State of Wyoming.**† Chicago: A. W. Bowen & Co., 1903.

GENEALOGICAL PERIODICALS OVERVIEW

Key Concepts in This Chapter

- Upwards of six thousand periodicals have information for family historians.
- Genealogical periodicals are like small specialty libraries.
- Any kind of record may appear in periodicals.
- Locality periodicals are especially effective in abstracting local original records.
- Most periodicals are published by societies (especially genealogical and historical societies).
- Journals provide scholarly treatment for compiled genealogies.
- Topical periodicals cover ethnic and religious groups, as well as other special interests.
- Excellent indexes provide access to the vast majority of genealogical periodicals.
- Thousands of surname publications are published by associations and individuals.
- Hundreds of significant articles are available through reprint series.

Key Sources in This Chapter

- *New England Historical and Genealogical Register*
- *National Genealogical Society Quarterly*
- *American Genealogist*
- *Everton's Genealogical Helper*
- *Ancestry*
- *Genealogical Computing*
- *Bibliography of Genealogy and Local History Periodials with Union List of Major U.S. Collections*
- *Meyer's Directory of Genealogical Societies in the U.S.A. and Canada*
- *Genealogist's Address Book*
- *Periodical Source Index*
- *Genealogical Periodical Annual Index*
- *Donald Lines Jacobus's Index to Genealogical Periodicals*
- *Combined Retrospective Index to Journals in History, 1838–1974*
- *Genealogical Research Directory*

19

GENEALOGICAL PERIODICALS

Kory L. Meyerink

The wide variety of periodicals issued by genealogical and historical societies, as well as by private individuals and companies, represents one of the great untapped resources for family historians. The probable reason for their under-utilization is that most researchers do not know the broad scope of their content or the ease of access to these collections. A survey of twenty-eight genealogical "how-to" books reveals that very little attention has been paid to the periodical literature in the field.[1] Although genealogical magazines are mentioned in some manuals and textbooks, Kip Sperry's now-dated *Survey of American Genealogical Periodicals and Periodical Indexes,* Gale Genealogy and Local History Series, vol. 3 (Detroit: Gale Research, 1978) is the only in-depth study of their value and limitations.

Genealogical periodicals contain an abundance of information. There are articles on family genealogies, family histories, abstracts of wills and land records, church registers, Society of Friends (Quaker) meeting records, military and pension records, Loyalist records, oaths of allegiance, cemetery records and inscriptions,[2] passenger lists, immigration and naturalization records, census enumerations (Federal, state, and local), mortality schedules, journals and daybooks, discoveries of previously unknown source materials, the holdings of archives and of genealogical and historical societies, queries about families, tax and assessment lists, newspaper death notices, marriage notices, obituaries, marriage licenses and vital (birth and death) records, genealogical sources and repositories in foreign countries, origins of American colonial families, royal and noble pedigrees (real and alleged), ethnic studies (black, Jewish, Hispanic, and others), book reviews, news of family reunions, methods and pitfalls of research, corrections to previously published works, humor to be found in genealogy, studies in eugenics, and so on. In addition to journals and magazines with significant genealogical content, many genealogical societies publish newsletters which report the activities of members, the work being accomplished by other societies, and forthcoming meetings and conferences to be held in the United States, Canada, and abroad.

Hundreds of thousands of pages of genealogical information have been published in genealogical periodicals over the past 150 years, and most of that information is still useful for genealogists. Unfortunately, many researchers are unaware that periodicals comprise a remarkable source—that the answers to many of their "brick wall" problems are already in print. Jones, Eakle, and Christensen suggest that "This source is *largely untapped* by researchers who, blissfully unaware they exist, duplicate the research which is published in these volumes" (1972, 80). Clearly, with the explosive growth of genealogical periodicals in the last two decades (figure 19-1), it is time for a detailed discussion of this important source.

This chapter provides the necessary background for a researcher to effectively use periodicals. It discusses their historical development and describes their typical content. It also identifies the various types of periodicals, along with key titles for these types. A related source, the historical periodical, is also covered. There follows a discussion on locating periodicals and on indexes, for these can lead the researcher to many answers. The chapter bibliography includes every periodical cited in the chapter, as well as hundreds of other important periodicals.

The avid researcher seeking more information and a deeper understanding should refer to Sperry's *Survey of American Genealogical Periodicals and Periodical Indexes*. Although it lacks coverage of the important changes that have taken place since its publication in 1978, it remains an authoritative, if dated, source for information on genealogical periodicals.

DEVELOPMENT OF GENEALOGICAL PERIODICALS[3]

The oldest continuously published genealogical periodical in the United States—actually, as Tim Beard has pointed out, the oldest in the world (1977, 57)—is the *New England Historical and Genealogical Register,* the publication of the New England Historic Genealogical Society (101 Newbury Street, Boston, MA 02116). The society was founded in 1844, and the *Register* appeared in January 1847 under the editorship of the Reverend William Cogswell, D.D. For over a century and a half, the *Register* has set high standards in genealogical scholarship. The centennial history of the society notes that

> . . . the primary purpose of *The Register* was to provide a repertory of hitherto unpublished historical and genealogical material, important in itself, and essential to a good understanding of New England history in its broadest and most comprehensive sense. To be stressed at all times were the origins and ancestries of New England families (Hill 1945, 16–17).[4]

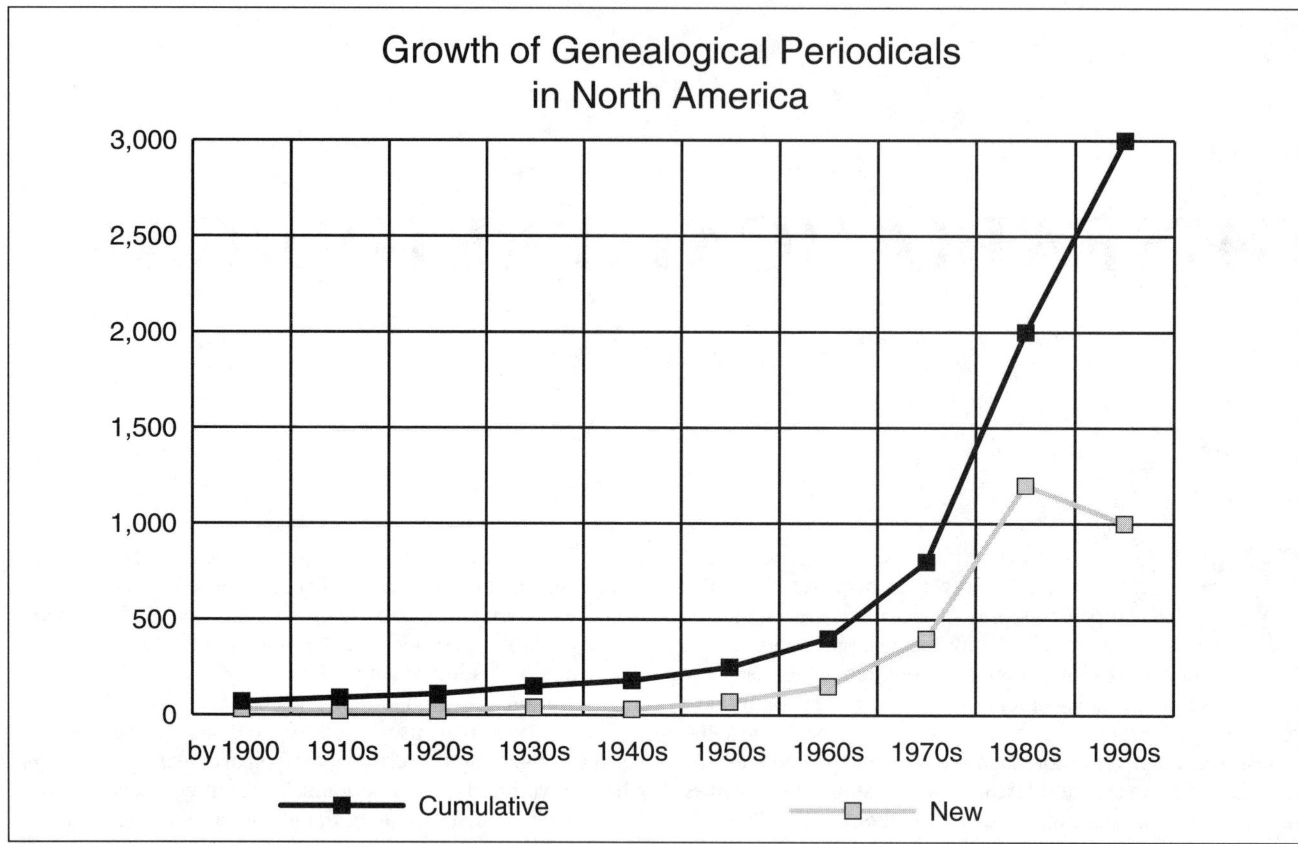

Figure 19-1. The growth of genealogical periodicals in North America.

In the early twentieth century, under the leadership of the late medievalist G. Andrews Moriarity, chairman of the Committee on English and Foreign Research, the *Register* published scholarly articles on the British and European noble and royal pedigrees of New England colonists and corrected many errors in previously published works. Some of the most eminent genealogists of the United States and England have contributed to the *Register's* pages.

The *Register* was joined in 1870 by the *New York Genealogical and Biographical Record,* issued by the New York Genealogical and Biographical Society (122 East Fifty-eighth Street, New York NY 10022). In addition to source materials and families of English extraction, early Dutch settlers of New York and New Jersey received attention in its pages. The society was fortunate to have among its members William J. Hoffman, a native of Rotterdam who was a naturalized American citizen. He took a keen interest in his compatriots who came to America in the seventeenth century, and in the 1930s and 1940s he published a series of well-documented articles in the *Record* titled "An Armory of American Families of Dutch Descent." He traced the families for a number of generations before their emigration to New Netherlands, correcting many errors in earlier published works and identifying families that had bona fide coats of arms.

In 1894, the Genealogical Society of Pennsylvania (1300 Locust Street, Philadelphia, PA 19107) began *Publications of the Genealogical Society of Pennsylvania,* which was renamed the *Pennsylvania Genealogical Magazine* in 1948. Philadelphia was the center of the Quaker colonies, so the periodical's pages abound with articles on Friends meeting records, as well as probate and administrative records, cemetery inscriptions, Bible records, church registers, and family genealogies. From 1979 to 1988, the magazine published a series of valuable articles by Helen Hutchison Woodroofe titled "A Genealogist's Guide to Pennsylvania Records." The series began with state-level records and continued with a county-by-county guide of "hidden sources" in the collections of the Genealogical Society of Pennsylvania. The series has since been republished as a book by the society.

A number of small genealogical periodicals (all defunct now) appeared in the last years of the nineteenth century and the first years of the twentieth century. One of the more important periodicals, the *Utah Genealogical and Historical Magazine,* published many helpful articles during the thirty years (1910 to 1940) of its existence. In 1912 it contained a series of articles titled "Lessons in Genealogy" that was later reprinted in book form; a completely revised edition was published in 1914. This series was probably the first effort to educate researchers in the techniques of genealogical research.

The National Genealogical Society (4527 Seventeenth Street North, Arlington, VA 22207), founded in Washington, D.C., in 1903, began the *National Genealogical Society Quarterly* in 1912. The *Quarterly* began modestly, with only twelve pages, and early issues contained some irrelevant articles, including one on Santa Claus and another on the family of Julius Caesar. When Dr. Gaius Marcus Brumbaugh became editor in 1917, the *Quarterly* began a new course. Its pages became a forum in which Brumbaugh and other societies and historians pressured the Federal authorities to create a national archive. In his early editorials, Brumbaugh pointed out that, due to apathy, carelessness, and fires, national historical treasures were gradually disappearing. His was among the first voices to call for the creation of a national archive, which finally opened its doors to researchers in 1934. The creation in 1960 of a board of contributing editors for the *Quarterly* assured a steady flow of articles of the highest quality. For a number of years the *Quarterly* has devoted attention to minorities—African Americans, Native Americans, and Hispanics.

In 1932, Donald Lines Jacobus began publication of the *American Genealogist* (now published by David L. Green, P.O. Box 398, Demorest, GA 30535) as successor to his *New Haven Genealogical Magazine.* From the beginning it maintained the highest requirements for scholarship, and the leading genealogists of the United States and England contributed well-documented articles. A series of articles on how to do genealogical research, many of them written by Jacobus himself, educated the beginner in methods, sources, and techniques of research. Jacobus was the true founder of the modern school of genealogical investigation. Under his successors, the late Dr. George E. McCracken, the late Robert M. and Ruth M. Sherman, and the present coeditors, Dr. David L. Greene, Robert Charles Anderson, and Marsha Hoffman Rising, it continues to hold the highest place among genealogical periodicals. The large number and wide variety of articles, which usually deal with colonial America, make it popular with experienced researchers who find new information for their own research in almost every issue. Indeed, the success of the *American Genealogist* has enabled it to be one of the few independent periodicals to survive its founding editor.

During the last half-century, and especially since the mid-1970s, genealogical societies and periodicals have proliferated tremendously, especially in the West. In some states, such as Ohio, Texas, and California, there are more than one hundred societies (many focusing on just one county). Most of these publish magazines or newsletters. Historical societies and family and surname associations have grown just as fast, and they also publish periodicals of interest to the family historian. In addition, a growing number of independent periodicals offer assistance to researchers. Figure 19-1 shows the growth of the genealogical periodicals, indicating that periodicals comprise one of the fastest-growing segments of the genealogical literature.

Today, genealogical periodicals are available for virtually every locality and topic, and they serve a growing number of subscribers at relatively low cost. However, because of that diversity, most periodicals have relatively small (but stable) circulations. Of the thousands of periodicals, only a few dozen have more than one thousand subscribers; this can make the smaller ones hard to find, because many libraries do not acquire those with limited areas of interest. Table 19-1 identifies many of the major periodicals, with their approximate circulation and subscription cost.

Defunct Periodicals

Hundreds of formerly existing periodicals are no longer published, and some of them will not be missed. There are a few, however, whose importance continues, even three-quarters of a century after their demise. These include *Tyler's Quarterly Historical and Genealogical Magazine, Notes and Queries: Historical and Genealogical Relating Chiefly to Interior Pennsylvania, "Old Northwest" Genealogical Quarterly,* the *Utah Genealogical and Historical Magazine,* and the *Jerseyman*. These and many others are found in genealogy libraries and other historical collections.

Table 19-1. Major Genealogical Periodicals (1997)

Annual Subscription Cost ($)	*Title*	*Approximate Circulation*
General Interest		
21	*Ancestry*	18,000
0	*The Family Tree*	60,000
21	*Everton's Genealogical Helper*	42,000
28	*Heritage Quest*	12,000
National and Regional		
11	*Forum* (FGS)	6,000
35	*Genealogical Journal* (Utah)	1,200
35	*NGS Quarterly*	13,500
25	*New York Genealogical and Biographical Record*	2,300
35	*New England Historical and Genealogical Register*	16,500
20	*American Genealogist*	1,700
50	*William and Mary Quarterly*	3,300
Major States, Cities, and Provinces		
20	*Ansearchin' News* (Tennessee)	2,100
29	*Connecticut Nutmegger*	4,500
15	*Detroit Society for Genealogical Research Magazine*	1,100
40	*Families* (Ontario)	6,000
15	*Genealogical Magazine of New Jersey*	950
20	*Hawkeye Heritage* (Iowa)	3,000
20	*Hoosier Genealogist* (Indiana)	7,500
20	*Illinois State Genealogical Society Quarterly*	3,000
25	*Kentucky Ancestry*	5,500
20	*Magazine of Virginia Genealogy*	2,000
25	*North Carolina Genealogical Society Journal*	2,300
10	*Pennsylvania Genealogical Magazine*	2,000
30	*Pennsylvania Magazine of History and Biography*	3,000
27	*Report* (Ohio)	6,500
15	*St. Louis Genealogical Society Quarterly*	2,400
20	*Virginia Genealogist*	1,200
Special Interest		
35	*Association of Professional Genealogists Quarterly*	600
24	*Avotaynu* (Jewish)	1,500
25	*Genealogical Computing*	5,500
18	*German Genealogical Society of America Bulletin*	3,000
19	*Palatine Immigrant*	2,400
25	*Pennsylvania Mennonite Heritage*	3,100

Periodicals cease publication for a number of reasons, chief among them being lack of readership. The second most common cause is waning interest or resources of the publisher; this is especially the case for the many "independent" periodicals—those that are published by dedicated individuals with no major organization supporting them. Sometimes the organization behind a periodical ceases to exist, and with it the publication. Sometimes the organization changes its focus and determines the periodical is no longer needed. Rising printing and postage costs also force some titles to end publication. In fact, almost every periodical stops production at some point in time. Currently, fewer than two dozen strictly genealogical periodicals that began before 1950 are still being published (Cappon 1964, 27). However, for every periodical that ceases publication, several more begin. Most are published "on a shoestring," and many do not last more than a few years, but they still publish important information of value to all family historians. Fortunately, the significant growth of new periodicals is directly connected to a similar growth in genealogical societies. These societies provide "homes" and support networks for these new periodicals.

Even older defunct periodicals have research value. Such a periodical might have printed the only published account of a family and the only preserved information from long-lost family records. Although complete sets of some older publications are rare, researchers still have access to the best articles. The significant articles in many of these defunct periodicals were reprinted in various series by Genealogical Publishing Company (Baltimore), as discussed below. The sources described in the section titled "Locating Genealogical Periodicals" will help to determine others of value.

CONTENTS OF PERIODICALS

A wide variety of materials are published in genealogical periodicals. A genealogical periodical can be thought of as a small genealogical library whose collection focuses on the locality or topic the periodical serves. Because accessing periodicals can be difficult, even for the most experienced researcher, it is useful to review the breadth of items that one can find in these sources; this should encourage more researchers to dig a bit deeper and try a bit harder to locate and search periodicals for their areas of interest. Jacobus defines the reasons for covering such a broad spectrum of information:

> Bearing in mind that the subscribers to any genealogical journal are interested in different surnames and in families of different localities, the chief need of such a journal is diversification, the treatment of as many surnames and localities as possible (1956, 7).

Copied Original Records: Transcripts and Abstracts

One of the greatest services that periodicals perform is to reproduce documents of genealogical interest in their pages; this makes the original records much easier to read and to search. In addition, it is likely that the periodical issue's index will identify many more names in the record than the original document's index.

Virtually all types of genealogical documents have been transcribed or abstracted in periodicals. *A transcription* is the word-for-word printing of an original document in which the original punctuation and spelling usually are left intact. An *abstract* is an abridged, or abbreviated, version of the record which omits repetitive or nonessential information. Abstracts vary greatly in quality, especially regarding the depth or quantity of information included. Some abstracts include only the names of the parties involved, dates of the events, and the amount of money involved. Others include all variable information (that which was not preprinted) in the records. Abstracts sometimes contain corrected, or modern, spellings, and punctuation is almost always changed in abstracts.

Transcriptions are much less common in periodicals than are abstracts. Transcribed records typically include Bible records, sextons' or cemetery records, censuses, church registers, passenger lists, obituaries, tax lists, and vital record registers (births, marriages, and deaths).

Many genealogical records have been, and continue to be, abstracted in genealogical periodicals. However, the records most commonly seen in abstract form are court, land, military, probate, and naturalization records, as well as minutes of church, town, and other organization meetings (see figure 19-2). Of course, any record, including those noted above as transcriptions, can be abstracted. Most of the chapters in part 3, "Printed Original Records," of *Printed Sources* deal with periodical publication of these respective record types.

Transcripts and abstracts are usually found in those periodicals that cover particular local areas, such as a city or county. Such periodicals are often published by local genealogical societies or private parties. Transcriptions and abstracts are usually published in installments, which can be frustrating to researchers because some of the larger sets of records can take many years to be completely published.

Compiled Records

Genealogies. Another major component of many genealogical periodicals is the compiled genealogy. Genealogies are often published in periodicals when researchers learn significant information about several generations of a family, but the number of people covered is too small for a book. Many researchers publish corrections or updates to earlier book genealogies in periodicals as well.

Genealogical periodicals are responsible for the development of the classic formats now used for published genealogies. During the first quarter-century of the *New England Historical and Genealogical Register*'s existence, the authors of family genealogies adopted a wide variety of arrangements for presenting their material. Finally, in the 1880s, out of desperation, the editors developed a standard method of showing descent (Colket 1968, 253). In it, the first ancestor of a family was assigned the Arabic numeral 1, and all of his children listed under him, along with his wife or wives, bore the Roman numerals i, ii, iii, iv, v, etc. The children who carried on the line were assigned consecutive Arabic numerals, and their children, when grouped under a married couple, bore Roman numerals, and so on. Known as the Register Style, this method has been adopted by a great many genealogical writers and periodical editors.

The *New York Genealogical and Biographical Record,* developed a variation of this style. Often called the Record or Modified Register System, many prefer it because all members of a family are assigned Arabic numerals. The children grouped under a married couple may or may not be given Roman numerals, but the consecutive Arabic numbers show how many members of the family a genealogist has located. The *National Genealogical Society Quarterly* has adopted a version of this style, and it is now more commonly called the NGSQ style.

These are the preferred styles used in periodicals for treating compiled genealogies. In fact, their use has become so widespread that many book-length genealogies use one of these variations. The ease of use of such systems has made the compiled genealogy one of the major types of content found in periodicals; they are especially prevalent in the more formal and established journals of national and regional significance, though local periodicals use these systems also. For a further discussion of these and other styles, see chapter 16, "Family Histories and Genealogies."

EARLY SETTLERS 231

Early Church Records

d—dismissed. D—died. w—wife. m—married.
W. C.—Western Country, any land west of their residence at the time

North Granville, N. Y., Church Records

Admitted in 1817.
Chamberlain, Richard and w, Lydia, d 1823.
Congdel, Mr. and Mrs.
Day, Meritta, d 1817 to Ruport.
Everts, Sally, d 1817.
Eldridge, Almira.
Fletcher, Salome, d 1821.
Goodrich, Mrs. Fear, d 1826 to Rochester.
Harvy, Ebenezer and w, Sarah, from Fort Ann.
Kingsbury, Jacket, Hannah.
Loomis, Aaron. Murry, Thirza.
Pier, Clarissa, d 1817.
Streeter, Mrs.
Admitted in 1818.
Goodman, Mrs. Triphosa Murrel from Bolton.
Admitted in 1819.
Beecher, Martha. Burdick, Stanton.
Griffith, Warren, d 1819 to Andoverborough.
Dillaway, Elizabeth H., w of Rev. Samuel from Boston, d 1833 to Poultney, Vt.
Nicholson, Spencer, 48y.
Parks, Widow, 52y. Rue, Mary, 24y.
Vaughan, Ashley, 18y.
Admitted in 1826.
Brown, Cynthia, 18y. Judd, Miss.
Jones, Comfort.
Parker, Eunice, 19y, d 1826.
Admitted in 1827.
Boynton, Roena, 20y.
Brown, Ann, 20y.
Chapin, Curtis, 18y, son of Adna.
Dutcher, Jane, 16y.
Gillette, Abraham D., 20y.
Gilbert, Mrs., 38y; Lois, 17y.
Judd, Harriet, 18y.
Potter, Joseph and w, Nancy, from Edinburgh.

Figure 19-2. Church records are among those most commonly seen in abstract form in genealogical periodicals. This example is from *Early Settlers of New York State: Their Ancestors and Descendants* 2 (6) (December 1935).

Compiled genealogies sometimes also refer to lines of ascent (going back in time) for particular individuals or couples. Many society-sponsored periodicals print members' ancestral charts (or pedigree charts) as well. These are printed directly from charts members send in or are recreated on standard forms used by the society. Unfortunately, such charts usually go back no further than five generations, which, for the average living genealogist, barely reaches the early 1800s; usually this is not far enough back to locate an ancestor common to other readers, so there is no opportunity for sharing research and results. In addition, while such charts are helpful in a note-keeping system, they allow too few generations per page on the printed page, leaving much "white space" which could otherwise carry important information.

One solution to this problem was pioneered more than forty years ago by Donald Lines Jacobus in the *American Genealogist.* Jacobus's solution, now known by its German name, *ahnentafel* (literally, "ancestor table"), was a line-by-line listing of a person and his or her ancestors (figure 19-3). The most recent person (the subject) is assigned number 1, his or her parents 2 and 3, grandparents 4, 5, 6, and 7, and so on. The father of each person in the table has a number twice that of the child; the mother's number is always one more than the father's. Thus, a page might have up to sixty-four lines on it representing six generations—two more generations and four times the number of ancestors than the usual four-generation (sixteen-name) ancestor (pedigree) chart. In whatever form compiled genealogies are printed in periodicals, it is their presence that is most important. Many research solutions can be found in such articles.

Another important purpose of compiled genealogical material is to instruct the readers, by way of example, how to conduct research. An excellent example of this approach is the *National Genealogical Society Quarterly,* which follows Jacobus's advice:

> . . . an article is truly instructive if it gives in minute detail the items dug out of court records, deeds, wills, and the often meagre vital or church records, and then shows how these fragments are pieced together into an organic pedigree, discussing the problems involved and explaining the reasons for the conclusions reached (1956, 6).

Biographical Material. Other compiled items found in some periodicals are brief biographies of individuals. These biographies often appear in local society publications as two- to five-page histories written by society members about notable pioneers or colorful ancestors they have researched. Sometimes a biographical sketch pertains to only part of an individual's life. Lengthy, scholarly biographies often appear in the journals of historical societies. For more information on finding biographies, see chapter 18, "Biographies."

Background Information

In general, methodological and historical articles are seldom lengthy or scholarly treatises laden with footnotes and advanced historical theories; rather, they often comprise only a few pages written in simple narrative style. For most readers of such articles, this treatment is sufficient. Of course, there is a place for more lengthy, scholarly articles when complicated topics are examined or new views of history are presented. Such articles are usually found in the periodicals of historical societies and in genealogical journals (see "Types of Periodicals—Journals" and "Types of Periodicals—Historical Periodicals," below).

Methodology. Some of the most important types of background articles found in genealogical periodicals are "how-to" articles.

ANCESTOR TABLES

LXIII. ANCESTOR TABLE, NEIL BAILEY REYNOLDS
Address: 123 Glen Ave., Scotia 2, N.Y.

—I
1. Neil Bailey Reynolds, 1903- , Scotia, N.Y.
—II
2. Kent Comstock Reynolds, 1874- , Ballston; Scotia, N.Y.
3. Eleanor May Cannell, 1872-1950, Halfmoon; Scotia, N.Y.
—III
4. Abram Reynolds, 1835-1910, Hebron, Washington Co.; Ballston.
5. Nancy Helen Comstock, 1837-1910.
6. William Henry Cannell, 1843-1935, Springfield, Mass.
7. Margaret Jane Teachout, 1847-1928.
—IV
8. Caleb Reynolds, 1811-1899, Pine Plains; Round Lake, N.Y.
9.* Jane Crozier, 1812-1848, Argyle, N.Y.
10. John Comstock, 1797-1854, Pittstown; Ballston, N.Y.
11. Ann Louisa Stitt, 1806-1845.
12. James H. Cannell, 1813-1882, Norfolk, England; Waterford, N.Y.
13. Hannah Base, 1816-1853.
14. James Teachout, 1797-1880, Halfmoon, N.Y.
15. Mary Bailey, 1810-1895.
—V
16. Abraham Reynolds, 1785-1853, Pine Plains & Greenwich, N.Y.
17. Maria Streever, 1787-1865.
18.*Alexander Crozier, - .
19.*
20. Theophilus Comstock, 1753-1829, Pittstown, N.Y.
21. Lucinda Comstock, 1758-1823.
22. John Stitt, 1782-1821, Pittstown, N.Y.
23. Nancy Agan, 1779-1821.
24.*John Cannell, - , Loddon, Norfolk, England.
25.*
26.*Benjamin Base, - , England; Waterford, N.Y.
27.*Sarah ——, 1793- , England; Waterford, N.Y.
28. John C. Teachout, 1771-1814, New Hackensack; Halfmoon, N.Y.
29. Hannah Swartwout, 1777-1860.
30. Henry Bailey, 1776-1846, Halfmoon; Jefferson Co., N.Y.
31. Eleanor Andrews, 1778-1853.
—VI
32.*Caleb Reynolds, c.1739- , Greenwich, Conn.; Pine Plains.
33.*Hannah (Sarah) Brown, - .
34.*John Adam Streever, 1760-1804, Dutchess & Washington Cos.,N.Y.
35.*Elizabeth ——, - .
36 to 39.*
40. Samuel Comstock, 1725-1817, New Milford, Conn.
41. Elizabeth Baldwin, 1725-1823.
42. John Comstock, 1719-1798, New Milford, Conn.
43. Deborah Welch, 1721-1787.
44.*James Stitt, -1817, Belfast, Ireland; Pittstown, N.Y.
45.*Amy Head, - .
46.*John Agan, 1747-1801, Pittstown, N.Y.
47.*Abiah ——, 1747-1802.
48 to 55.*

Figure 19-3. An ahnentafel from *American Genealogist* 33 (4) (October 1957), page 253.

Clear explanations from experienced researchers are very helpful to other researchers and aid in the general growth of genealogy, both as a hobby and as a profession. However, with periodical editors' perpetual need for articles, articles of dubious value often creep in. Sometimes editors reprint what they believe to be interesting articles from other periodicals or accept the written meanderings of lesser-trained researchers offering foolproof advice for successful research. The wide-ranging quality of methodology articles calls for an attitude of "reader beware."

Copied articles present particular problems. First among them is the issue of copyright. Simply noting that an article was previously printed in a certain periodical does not absolve an editor from seeking permission from the original publisher. Furthermore, the periodical from which an article was copied might not be the original publisher, and therefore might not have the right to grant permission to reprint. The copyright for most genealogical articles is held by the original author, not the organization or individual who published the article. Second, too often an editor shortens an article to meet space constraints, sometimes omitting key information in doing so. Third, information in an article might have been superseded, become out of date, or simply be wrong. An original author might know this and could potentially save an editor and the periodical from embarrassment, but can only do so if the editor seeks permission to reprint. A reprinted article that circulated a few years ago was based on incorrect information, claiming erroneously that comprehensive lists of passengers leaving England were stored in a certain maritime museum.

Their value ranges widely, from definitive discussions on topics of permanent importance to brief, weak, often erroneous comments on topics of little interest or on topics which have been thoroughly discussed many times before. Many such articles explain how to use particular sources or records. They may describe records or explain how particular researchers solved problems using particular records. Other methodology articles discuss the types of records available for specific localities (see "Repository Holdings," below). Difficult-to-use or unique sources are often featured in such articles.

Hints and Helps. Similar to methodology articles but providing less instruction are the numerous articles that provide factual material of value to the genealogist. Such material might be as simple as the definitions of obscure terms—causes of death or the names of outdated occupations, for example. It might also consist of a table indicating what Social Security numbers were issued in which states or on what dates a Federal census was taken. Included in this category are discussions of naming patterns, calendar changes, and illustrations of old handwriting. Although these "factual" pieces are sometimes intended as filler

Beyond Pedigrees: Organizing and Enhancing Your Work. By Beverly DeLong Whitaker. Salt Lake City: Ancestry, 1993. Paperback, 96 pp. $12.95.

Ancestry, a major publisher of genealogical instruction books, has added another to its growing list of books aimed at the beginner or relatively new hobbyist, and this title has much to offer. Generally this is a good overview of the many "practical" suggestions and helps that are not taught in the classic texts. Of course, those classics have generally focused on description of records and how to obtain them, whereas Whitaker has a different focus here.

The author's stated purpose is "to go 'beyond pedigrees,' searching for information which can help me visualize what life was like for my ancestors." While this is a noble goal, and should be the goal for all genealogists, she only partially succeeds. Along her path, however, are several useful suggestions that new and experienced researchers would do well to review. Whitaker advocates the creation of a personal "genealogical tool kit" to take on research trips and to use at the home office (or kitchen table or wherever else you work with your files and documents). Fortunately her description is not full of minutia, but a rather brief discussion of suggestions such as forms, bibliography of common sources, an expense record, maps, etc.

The many suggestions will help researchers become family historians, not just genealogists. This includes strong encouragement and ideas about organizing your materials and immersing yourself into your research by working it into vacations, belonging to genealogical societies, and using periodicals to their fullest, to name a few. She includes several useful (and not so useful) forms that are explicitly offered to the reader to modify or make as many copies as needed. Indeed the entire tone of the book is friendly and upbeat, reminding the reader that this is what has worked for her and maybe the reader will find them useful, but to pick and choose what you want.

The question format for the chapter titles is annoying. Titles such as "If I study geography, will I be a better genealogist?" seem almost self-evident and tend to "talk down" to the reader. A better title would be "How will studying geography make me a better genealogist." The same comments apply to the other seven chapters which cover topics such as appropriate procedures, filing your information, getting assistance, using photographs and memorabilia, and sharing what you learn.

The text is generally easy to read but at times the suggestions are too brief for the novice researcher; more detail would have been helpful. There are also several glaring omissions, such as Ancestral File in the chapter on sharing, and accredited genealogists in the section about hiring professional help. Such omissions should have been caught by the publisher's staff, especially since the publisher is in Salt Lake City! Computers, as a tool in organizing or managing data, are woefully overlooked. None of the dedicated genealogical programs are even hinted at. The reader gets the impression that the author does not use a computer, but threw in a couple of paragraphs "just in case."

The bibliography is eclectic in its coverage, and without annotations the reader cannot choose which texts will help the most. Exactly half of the 26 titles are from Ancestry, but this is not just the publisher's doing, for they do have a significant collection of introductory texts. Rather it hints at the author's inadequate exposure to genealogical texts.

All in all, this is a useful collection of genealogical management hints that many of us will eventually discover either by trial and error or by verbal exchange of ideas at our local genealogical society. The primary value of this book is to have many of them gathered together in one place. Although following her suggestions will perhaps not result in the "intimate ancestral portraits" she claims, you will learn more about them and their times, and likely become a better researcher in the process.

Kory L. Meyerink, AG

Figure 19-4. A book review from *Genealogical Journal* 22 (4) (1994), pages122 through 124.

by editors, they also provide important information that helps researchers make more sense of the records they use.

Historical Information. Related to methodology articles are those that give historical background about an era or area. No one researcher can know the history of every place where each ancestor lived, but an understanding of local and national history is crucial to successful research. Historical knowledge makes ancestors' lives more relevant by helping researchers appreciate what their ancestors' lives were like.

Geographical Information. In addition to historical materials, some periodicals provide geographic assistance as well. Popular local articles deal with forgotten places in a county or state, ghost towns, changes of town names, and how town names came to be. Editors sometimes reprint sections from old gazetteers or copy old maps showing earlier towns and boundaries.

Reviews and Notices of Books and Computer Software. Important and common content items in periodicals are reviews and notices of new book and computer software releases. Almost every society that publishes a periodical also has a growing book collection. Societies add to their collections through purchases and donations. To encourage donations, societies review and/or note the arrival of books. This practice gives publishers a bit of advertising, helps societies' collections grow, and helps readers learn about new books and software that might be of value to their research.

Book *notices* are simply bibliographical citations of new books. They indicate the author, title, publication information, and cost and often include an annotation describing the book (from a couple of lines to a paragraph or two). Book notices are sometimes called *acquisition lists.* Book *descriptions,* however, are becoming more popular. These go beyond book notices by adding one or two brief paragraphs describing the book, often taken from the preface, book jacket, introduction, or the publisher's promotional literature. Unfortunately, these are usually called (inaccurately) book reviews.

A true book review should give some evaluation of the book (figure 19-4). Because book descriptions are often called reviews, true evaluative reviews are now generally termed critical or analytical reviews. These terms do not necessarily indicate a negative appraisal of a book. Rather, they refer to the critical evaluation of a book's content.

There is an unfortunate trend in critical reviews to praise books that do not deserve praise. This trend may be due to an attitude held by many reviewers: that any genealogical publication should be welcomed with open arms because any published information is needed in this relatively small field. It may also result from reviewers' lack of knowledge about subject matter, or from a tendency to be kind to authors because, as with almost all genealogical publications, their books are labors of love which seldom produce profits. This tendency does a great disservice to genealogy (which may even be the reviewer's profession) and to fellow researchers. On the other hand, reviewers who do not point out the benefits of books also perform a disservice to readers. It is important to indicate benefits to the potential user, as well as problems. Most books have both strong and weak points.

Readers should pay strict attention to critical book reviews, where numerous errors in books are discussed and corrected. Many librarians read reviews to determine if their libraries should purchase particular books. Good reviewers ensure that their criticisms are fair and objective and can be supported

#1846 THARP, THRAP, THORP, TREMBLY: Asher Tharp, etc., wife Mary: Children Jacob, Joel, Asher, Josiah, Moses, Mary, Huldah (b. 1792 N. J.), Abagail and Abraham. Asher bought land in Muskingum County, Ohio, 1804, from Ebenezer Drake of Morris County, N. J. Asher d. Ohio 1826. Was he same as Asher Tharp m. Mary Trembly 1776 New Providence Presbyterian Church, N. J.? Was he the Asher Tharp of Morris County, serjeant, Western Battalion, Revolution? Who was Asher M. Thorp, admin. 1833, Essex County, N. J Frances and Indianna Thorp connected with estate? ADD: Mrs. R. B. Hunt, 8034 Ridge Drive Northeast, Seattle, Washington 98115

#1847 SHELDON, THARP: Who were parents of Thomas Sheldon b. N. J. 1789, who married Huldah Tharp, b. N. J. 1792, ? Oldest child Asher. Thomas Sheldon moved from Muskingum County, Ohio to Holmes County ca. 1830. See above Tharp Query. Sheldon children: Asher, Catherine, William Harriet, Mary (Polly), Phoebe?, Hester, Thomas Jefferson, Sarah, Martha, George W. and Susan. ADD: Mrs. R. B. Hunt, 8034 Ridge Drive, Northeast, Seattle, Washington 98115

#1848 TOMPKINS: Michael Tompkins bapt. 1615 d. Newark, N. J. 1670 m. Mary who d. 1699. Had son Samuel b. 1661, will probated 1757 Newark, N. J. Had daughter Esther. Whom did she marry? ADD: Mrs. H. T. Jeffery, 72 Maple Ave., Palmyra, N. Y. 14522

Figure 19-5. Queries from *New Jersey Genesis Quarterly* 16 (2) (January 1969).

by the proper evidence. The periodicals best known for the quality of their critical reviews include the *National Genealogical Society Quarterly, American Genealogist, New England Historical and Genealogical Register, New York Genealogical and Biographical Record, Genealogical Journal*, and the *Genealogist* (the last two are discussed below under "Major Genealogical Journals").

Society News and Events. Because most genealogical periodicals are published by societies, they serve an important need for information among societies' members. A society's periodical is a vehicle for dispersing news about the society. Society news includes lists of newly acquired books, minutes of meetings, elections of officers, profiles of members, announcements of special programs or speakers, agendas for upcoming meetings, announcements of new society publications, discussion of current issues (such as laws affecting access to genealogical records), and many other items.

Generally this type of information is of a current nature and has little long-term or archival value (unlike compiled genealogies or methodology articles). Librarians call such "newsy" articles *ephemeral* (meaning "non-permanent"). Very few indexes include them, and periodicals that are exclusively ephemeral are seldom cataloged by libraries. Rather, the issues from the most recent year or two are kept in the "vertical file," and older issues are discarded.

Many societies publish a regular newsletter in addition to a less-frequent, larger periodical (see "Types of Periodicals," below). Society news and events are usually published in the newsletter. Many state and most local societies, however, publish only one periodical and include society news in the first or last few pages.

Regardless of its limited genealogical value, society news is an important means for keeping societies' memberships informed. Well-rounded researchers briefly review such sections to keep in touch with the growth of a society and the field of genealogy. Even in older issues, such articles can help the researcher become familiar with the sponsoring society and thereby better understand and judge the accuracy of significant articles.

Genealogical News. In addition to informing members about what is happening in a society, many periodicals publish genealogical news as well. This news might concern pending vital records legislation in a state or the most recent records to be microfilmed by the National Archives. An editor might also include news from other organizations, such as information about major genealogical conferences. Frequently these news items are copied (reprinted) from other periodicals.

Many copied articles concern the impending destruction or closure of key record repositories; unfortunately, such articles are sometimes based on incomplete or faulty information. Rely on the major national, regional, and state periodicals to provide key news of major interest. Local periodicals are generally the best sources for local news and events that will be well known to their editors.

Finding Aids

Periodicals perform a great service when they help their readers access the variety of genealogical sources needed for research. Many periodicals publish a variety of finding aids that provide this service. These aids include queries, indexes, and lists of sources at local archives and libraries.

Queries. A great service that many periodicals provide is the inclusion of a query section. Queries are brief requests from individual subscribers for help in solving genealogical problems. If a problem concerns hard-to-find family information, the ancestor's name, date of birth or death, and place of residence are usually given. The requested information might be the name of a spouse, children, or, most often, parents. The address of the requestor is given to facilitate a response (figure 19-5).

Queries seldom contain significant genealogical material, but each refers to a source (the requesting individual) for more information. There is usually a small fee to place a query for those who are not subscribers or members of the society. Over time, some of the addresses given in queries become outdated as researchers move; however, the periodical publisher might know the researcher's current address (if the person has remained a subscriber).

The popularity of queries reflects two important aspects of genealogy. First, there is a willingness to share among genealogists. While many queries go unanswered, many others generate responses; otherwise, they would not be so popular. Second, queries remind researchers that others share some of the same ancestors. This knowledge should encourage participation in "ancestor-sharing" databases, which will help reduce the great amount of duplication that occurs in research.

Some periodical publishers allow only subscribers or society members to place queries. Many allow subscribers to place one query (or a set number) without charge; additional queries are charged a small fee. Other periodicals base the charge on the length of the query (number of words or lines), with the initial few lines or words free or at a reduced rate. Many periodicals allow nonsubscribers to publish queries for slightly higher fees. These publishers recognize that queries from outside their subscriber group serve their members, who sometimes find distant relatives with new information through them.

Most genealogical periodicals do not include true advertisements, so queries are among the few sources that allow their publishers to generate some of the money necessary to produce the periodical. Queries are regular features of many periodicals, most often appearing in state, local interest, and special interest periodicals and in a few journals and newsletters. The largest and most extensive query section in any periodical, with approximately seven thousand entries in every issue, is the "Roots Cellar," a feature of the most well known and circulated genealogical magazine, *Everton's Genealogical Helper* (described under "Types of Periodicals—General Interest," below). Some periodicals exist solely to publish queries; they are described under "Types of Periodicals—Query Magazines," below.

Indexes to Sources. Every genealogist soon learns that many, if not most, of the sources he or she wishes to search are not indexed. To fill this void, genealogical periodicals often publish indexes to the sources that exist for their localities. A periodical might index the local county's entries in a state census, court naturalization records, probate files, or an old county history, for example. These indexes might refer to the surnames only, or to the major parties (typically for probate or land records), or to every name in a record. Like transcripts and abstracts, indexes in periodicals often are published in several installments, depending on the length of the record being indexed.

The types of periodicals that most commonly publish source indexes include state, special interest, and local interest periodicals. Partial indexes, particularly of all the persons with a particular surname in a record, can often be found in surname periodicals.

Indexes to Periodicals. The contents of genealogical periodicals themselves can be difficult for researchers to access, so many periodicals include indexes to the material they have published. These usually take the form of annual indexes. The major journals publish an annual index as part of the last issue of the year or volume. Others publish them separately so as to not delay the last issue. Still others publish them within the next volume (year), frequently in the first issue. Surprising, however, is the large number of periodicals that do not publish indexes to their contents; typically these are the smaller periodicals, such as those issued by county genealogical societies.

Descriptions of Repository Holdings. Genealogical records are found in many different locations. No single library, archive, or repository has all the records necessary to successfully pursue any person's ancestry. The saying "the solution is where one finds it" serves to illustrate the importance of knowing as much as possible about the holdings of genealogical repositories.

Many periodicals meet this need by describing the records to be found in libraries, archives, and other repositories of interest to their readers. Such an article might be a one- or two-page listing of a few sources at the nearby public library, or it might be an ongoing series of installments exploring all or many of the records at a state archive. In any case, such articles serve to guide researchers to sources.

Many periodicals are published by societies that house (separately or in conjunction with a local library) growing collections of genealogical sources. Such sources are often published books. Each issue of the periodical usually includes a list of new books acquired by the society, which lets members know how the collection is growing and allows them to plan part of their next research trip to the local collection (see figure 19-6).

A host of other types of articles also appear less frequently in genealogical periodicals. These include articles noting the humor in genealogical situations and records (showing that genealogists are not always overly serious in their pursuits). Other articles discuss adoption research, medical aspects of genealogy, and state laws. Still others are success stories, comments on serendipitous findings, and any other genealogy-related items. All of these serve to "round out" the sometimes very traditional genealogist.

Jacobus, an experienced genealogical journal editor, reminds us that editors may have less discretion than they want as they compile a periodical:

> The readers should remember, however, that editors cannot always be choosers. Contributors submit articles on the subjects that interest them, and editors have to select what seems best and most reliable from such articles as are *available* (1956, 9).

TYPES OF PERIODICALS

Genealogical periodicals can be classified in several ways, including by type of publisher, frequency of issue, type of printing, number of pages, orientation (locality, group, or surname), and scope or content. Most of the following discussion defines seven different types based on their scope or content, but it is useful to briefly consider some other classifications.

A common division in some directories is by publisher. A genealogical periodical is either published by a society or it is an "independent periodical" published by a private party—usually an individual but sometimes a company. Both the best and weakest of periodicals are found in both of these categories.

The vast majority of current periodicals are published by societies of one kind or another. Upwards of two thousand are published by state and local genealogical societies, and a similar number by historical societies (figure 19-7). Other publishing societies include ethnic and religious groups, lineage societies, family or surname associations, and special interest societies. Society publications exist to serve their memberships and to publish material of interest to them. Most of the periodicals that have the largest circulations are published by societies; this is partly due to their longevity (societies often outlive individuals), sharing of work, greater visibility (societies are more "active" in genealogy than are individuals, so subscribers may feel that their membership gives them more than just a subscription), and often lower prices (higher circulation and more volunteer effort, along with some advertising, can help keep costs down). However, privately produced periodicals continue to flourish. Currently, approximately 10 percent of the geographically oriented periodicals are issued by private parties, as are most surname periodicals.

ACCESSION LIST

DONATIONS [Presented by the author or publisher unless otherwise noted]

BIOGRAPHY

Richard BARRETT'S journal. New York and Canada, 1816. Edited . . . by Thomas Brott and Philip Kelley. Winfield, KS: Wedgestone Pr., c. 1983. 128 p.

Nathan A. CUSHMAN. A rugged individualist. Memoirs by his sons . . . Text by Franklin P. Cole, editor. Portland, ME: Casco Prtg. Co., 1984. 161 p. [Richard Cushman]

Random reminiscences of men and events. By John D. ROCKEFELLER. Tarrytown, NY: Sleepy Hollow Pr. and Rockefeller Archive Center. 124 p. $12.95. [Kenn Stryker-Rodda]

The life of the Reverend Mr. George TROSS. Written by himself . . . Edited by A.W. Brink, Montreal: McGill-Queen's Univ. Pr., 1974. 140 p. [Donald W. Francis]

The works of Daniel WEBSTER. Vol. 1. 4th ed. Biographical memoir of the public life of Daniel Webster by Edward Everett. Boston: Little, Brown, 1853. 457 p. [Karen M. Bristoll]

GENEALOGY

A genealogical history of Henry ADAMS of Braintree, Mass. . . . Compiled and edited by Andrew N. Adams. Rutland, VT, Tuttle Co., 1898. 1238 p. [Harold Hazleton]

The AXFORDS of Oxford, New Jersey . . . Compiled by William Clinton Armstrong. [Reprint] Washington, NJ: Geneal. Researchers, 1984. 78 p. $5.00.

Account book for the farmer, 1876; Amos BARBER II (1838–1889). Compiled and edited by Addie L. Shields. Plattsburgh, NY, c. 1984. 76 p.

The BARNHART-BURGE genealogy and family history. Compiled . . . By Bernice Barnhart Salts and Walter Salts. West Lebanon, IN, 1979. ca. 85 p.

Of Mary BREWSTER. The identity of Mary, wife of Elder William Brewster of the Mayflower . . . By John G. Hunt. Bowling Green, Va., 1984. 39 p.

The CLEM genealogy supplement. Compiled by Walter Salts. West Lebanon, IN, 1982. [ca. 220 p.]

The search for a heritage. [COGSWELL FAMILY]. By Alan and Micky Cogswell. [N.p.], 1982. 355 p. [Gordon H. Tully].

CORBIN–WAITE–COOPER of Baltimore County and City. By Dorothy Cooper Knoff. Baltimore: Gateway Pr., 1983. 127 p. $17.00.

The COYER clan and the CARRIER connection. 2d. ed. By John Edward Armstrong. Madison, WI: Printed by Kramer Prtg., 1982. 178 p. $18.00.

Figure 19-6. List of new acquisitions from *New York Genealogical and Biographical Record* 115 (4) (October 1984).

The number of pages and yearly issues of periodicals vary widely. Some are issued once a year (annually), twice a year (semiannually), or three times each year. A few are issued every other month (bimonthly), but most are monthly (some newsletters) or, most commonly, quarterly (four times per year). Very few are issued weekly; those that have attempted weekly publication have usually changed to semimonthly, monthly, or less frequent publication. Few issues are less than twelve pages in length (except newsletters) or more than one hundred; most are between twenty and fifty pages. Most periodicals are either full size (8 ½ by 11 inches) or half size (*booklet* size) (5 ½ by 8 ½ inches).

Genealogical periodicals are usually oriented either to a geographic area (nation, state, region, county, or area), a topic (computers, *Mayflower* immigrants, Italian immigrants, etc.), or to a particular family or surname (and all its variations). Figure 19-8 shows these groupings. While this initial breakdown is a helpful one, there are too many variations in the geographically oriented periodicals for it to be meaningful. For this discussion, the scope and content are defined in seven classes of periodicals: journals, general interest, state and local interest, topical, query, newsletters, and surname.

Approximately three hundred independent periodicals exist (not counting surname and family publications) which are not sponsored by organizations or large commercial companies. These are labors of love, for their editors/publishers seldom make more than enough money to cover printing and mailing costs. They seldom have editorial staffs—perhaps just a few contributors who support the effort by writing articles and abstracting records. Most have fewer than four hundred subscribers. Some have been amazing long lived, lasting thirty years or more. Others come and go in just a few years as their editors' interest or drive wanes or as sufficient subscriptions fail to materialize.

Periodicals are printed by almost all methods available today. Many of the larger ones are typeset and printed by large presses. Most, however, are set in typescript (today this term indicates use of a computer word processor) and printed in small quantities (many have only a few hundred subscribers) on small local presses. Historically, many were printed by mimeograph after having been painstakingly typed.

Journals

Many important genealogical periodicals follow the *journal* style, which is a pattern established by scholarly publications in many unrelated fields. Such periodicals strive to print only the best, most accurate, and useful genealogical material. Their articles have the hallmarks of a scholarly outlook: in-depth treatment, careful and clear writing, notes (both source references and explanatory notes), information of lasting value, topics or discoveries that often are new to the field, and authors who are acknowledged experts in their fields.

Genealogical journals are typically published quarterly (some only two or three times a year). Their content consists almost exclusively of compiled genealogies, methodology, and book reviews and notices. Almost all of the major U.S. and Canadian genealogical periodicals are of this type (except for the general interest magazines described below). Many have a broad geographic focus, such as the entire United States or a multi-state region. Some statewide periodicals are also considered journals; by their nature, many of these have assumed regional importance. Many journals are among those periodicals that have been in existence for several decades. Many journals have evolved from smaller, less-important publications.

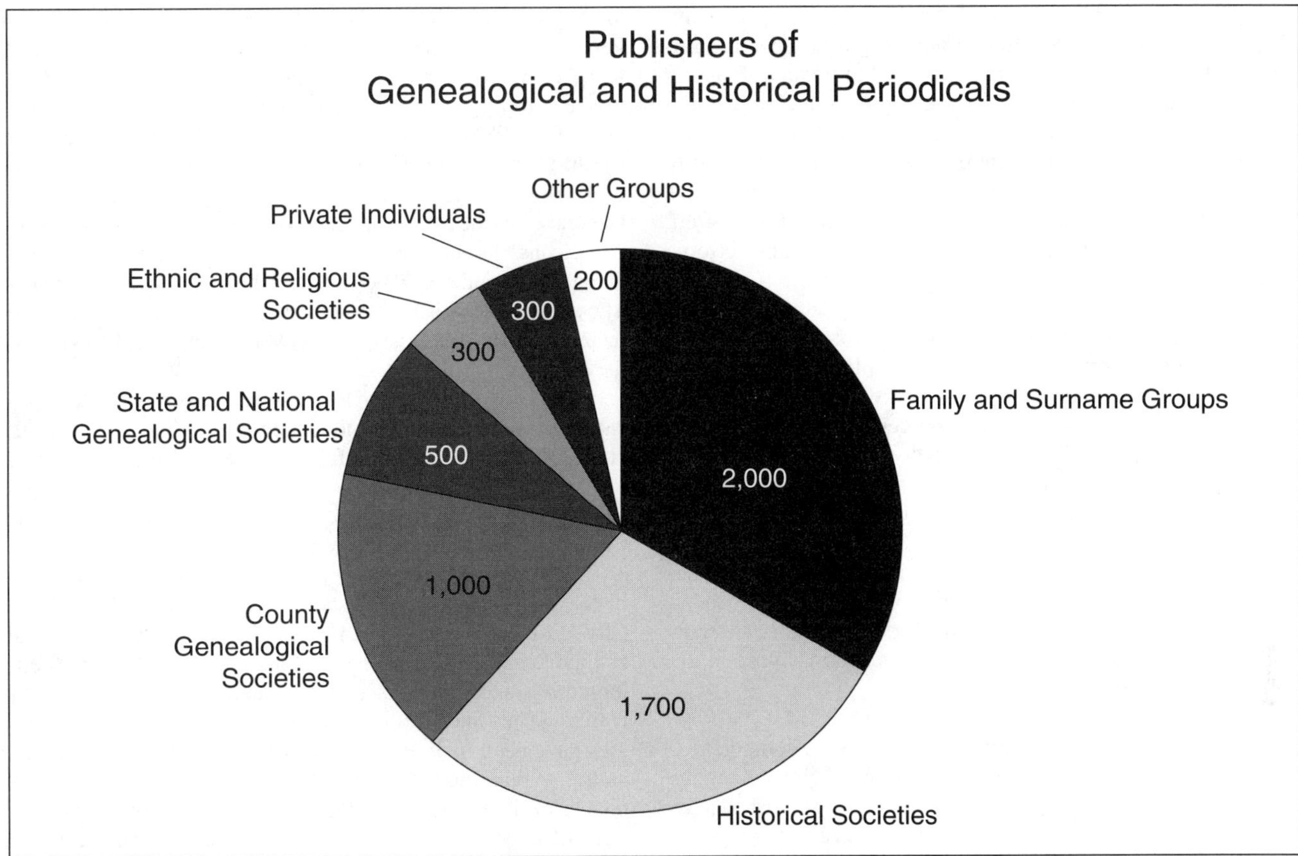

Figure 19-7. Organizations that publish genealogical and historical periodicals.

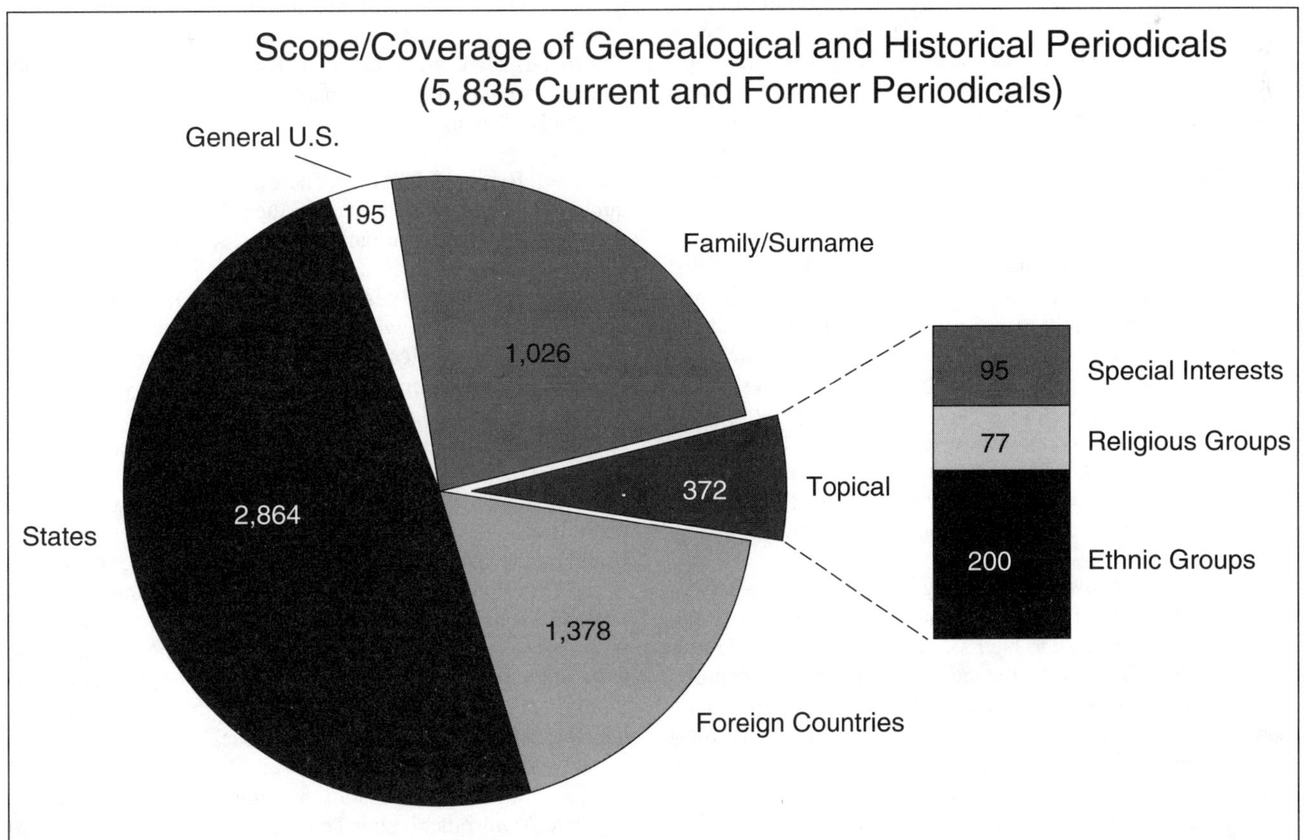

Figure 19-8. Scope/coverage of genealogical and historical periodicals (5,835 current and former periodicals).

The importance of major journals lies in their content. Articles on methodology and compiled genealogies are important to all genealogists and, as noted before, are of lasting value. There are many sources that do not warrant inclusion in any of the myriad how-to books available (including this one), and many families are too small to make publishing a family history of several hundred pages feasible. Journal articles are especially appropriate forums for such information. Often, book-length genealogies require updates and corrections. Jacobus suggests that

> . . . a serious journal should include from time to time articles of a critical nature which explore the inadequacy and unacceptable nature of data which has appeared in various printed sources. . . . A genealogical journal fails in its duty if it does not at times take issue with the fictions and misconceptions of the past which still clutter the field (1956, 8).

As does any compiled source, journal articles include secondary information, and some errors will be found in them. However, the care with which modern journal articles are written and edited eliminates many mistakes and makes them excellent sources for beginning research.

Major Genealogical Journals. Over the years, some genealogical periodicals have earned a reputation as being among the best in the field. Generally these are older, well-established journals that publish compiled genealogies as well as other types of articles. Two excellent articles by David L. Green, "Scholarly Genealogical Journals in America," *American Genealogist* 61 (July-October 1985): 116–20 and 63 (July 1988): 138–44, discuss important national and regional journals, including an evaluation of their strengths and weaknesses. Eugene A. Stratton continued the discussion in his chapter on "The Scholarly Journals" in *Applied Genealogy* (Salt Lake City: Ancestry, 1988). Sharon Carmack discussed the topic from a writer's perspective in "Genealogical Writer's Market," *Association of Professional Genealogists Quarterly* 8 (3): 61–63 (September 1993); 8 (4): 93–94 (December 1993; 9 (1): 15–17 (March 1994). These references are well worth reading.

It is important to delineate some of the key journals that serve as examples in the field and that publish some of the best genealogical scholarship to be found. The section above on the "Development of Genealogical Periodicals" mentioned five important journals: the *New England Historical and Genealogical Register,* the *New York Genealogical and Biographical Record,* the *Pennsylvania Genealogical Magazine,* the *National Genealogical Society Quarterly,* and the *American Genealogist.* In addition to these historically significant journals, each of which is at least sixty-five years old, some others are worthy of mention.

The *Genealogist* (published by the American Society of Genealogists, Twenty-five Rodeo Avenue 22, Sausalito, CA 94965) was begun in 1980 by Dr. Neil D. Thompson, FASG. He borrowed the title from one of the most revered (and long-defunct) English periodicals because he intended to maintain a certain standard of excellence. The *Genealogist* is indeed one of the most scholarly magazines in the United States. It accepts articles which may not be acceptable to other journals because of their length. In the volumes that have appeared to date, Thompson has published heavily documented articles dealing with families from many of the states, the West Indies, England, Scotland, Byzantium, Mexico, Persia, and India. He has also published two German ancestor tables of American families, one going back to the fifteenth century and the other to the thirteenth century. Beginning with vol. 2, no. 2 (Fall 1981), an ancestor table of King Charles II of England by Dr. Thompson and Col. Charles M. Hansen was published serially. In vols. 7 and 8 (1986–87), the king's lineage in all lines was traced to the fourteenth century. This series is important for Americans claiming royal pedigrees and yearning to belong to hereditary societies in which membership is based on such claims. The authors' work is built on the most reliable sources; they corrected errors in previously printed works and carefully evaluated the evidence.

It is difficult for such a time-intensive effort as the publication of a journal to be undertaken by one individual. In the early 1990s the *Genealogist* fell behind in its publication schedule, and in 1996 Thompson turned the journal over to the American Society of Genealogists, where it is currently edited by Charles M. Hansen and Glade Ion Harris.

The *Genealogical Journal* has been published quarterly by the Utah Genealogical Association (P.O. Box 1144, Salt Lake City, UT 84110) since 1972, maintaining a high degree of scholarship from its beginning. Its contents are international in scope, including discussions of source materials in all parts of the United States and Europe. Although some compiled genealogies have been included in it, most articles are instructional in nature, explaining sources (such as World War I draft records), historical situations (including fraud in genealogy), and collections of major repositories—including, but not limited to, the Family History Library of The Church of Jesus Christ of Latter-day Saints (LDS church) in Salt Lake City. Other articles have covered such diverse subjects as migrations, Indo-European languages, and Jewish surnames. Many of the journal's articles are by authors who work with the outstanding collections of the Family History Library, but the Utah Genealogical Association and its journal have no relationship to the library or to its sponsor, the LDS church.

State and Regional Journals. There are some periodicals whose quality is worthy of note, though their focus is only a specific state, group of states, or part of a state. Researcher are wise to search their pages early in the process of tracing families in areas covered by these periodicals. The *New York Genealogical and Biographical Record* was discussed above under "Development of Genealogical Periodicals." The *Detroit Society for Genealogical Research Magazine* (published by the Detroit Society for Genealogical Research, 5201 Woodward Avenue, Detroit, MI 48202) publishes material from Michigan and those states where many Michigan residents have ancestry, especially New York and other northeastern states. Its cumulative indexes make it an easy source to use. *Mayflower Descendant* (published by the General Society of Mayflower Descendants, P.O. Box 3297, Plymouth, MA 02361) began publishing again in 1985 after a hiatus of almost fifty years. Its focus on *Mayflower* families carries it into most northern states, although most of its material comes from Plymouth Colony and New England. The *Western Pennsylvania Genealogical Society Quarterly* (published by the Western Pennsylvania Genealogical Society, 4338 Bigelow Boulevard, Pittsburgh, PA 15213) is an example of a society journal that covers an otherwise overlooked part of a key state. Many other regional publications are listed in the chapter bibliography.

General Interest

A few periodicals have been intended to fill a perceived need to take genealogy to the masses; like *Time* or the *Saturday Evening Post,* they have tried to be very broad in their appeal. Historically, they have not been successful; however, with the growing popularity of genealogy and the increasing adoption of a traditional "magazine" approach by these periodicals, there is evidence that more of them are succeeding. Those that have flourished have served the hobbyist genealogist with simple how-to articles, queries, and advertisements. Using this approach, they have become some of the highest-circulating magazines in genealogy and are important sources of new information. They are also beginning to appear on newsstands and in the mass-market subscription services.

Three such magazines and a tabloid-style publication presently dominate the field; some others are also worth noting.

Genealogical Helper. *Everton's Genealogical Helper* was begun in 1947 and is issued bimonthly (six times a year) by The Everton Publishers (P.O. Box 368, Logan, UT 84323). This first and biggest of the magazines is "dedicated to helping more people find more genealogy." It is the largest genealogical periodical in terms of circulation and pages per year. Each issue has approximately three hundred pages, including surname, subject, and locality indexes for all of the issue's content (including advertisements). More than half of the *Helper* consists of display advertisements, mostly for genealogical books and services, and many of the regular departments, such as the "Bureau of Missing Ancestors" and the "Books Wanted" section, consist of paid advertisements (classified ads) as well. However, each issue also has three to five short feature articles, such as "The Consular Records from the Old Russian Consulates," "Organizing and Operating Family Associations," "Yes, You Can Write Your Family History," "If You Are a Genealogy Teacher," "Family Legends and the Search for Identity," and so on.

The magazine's regular features include "Relatively Speaking," a collection of unusual or amusing genealogical anecdotes, quips, quotations, or research stories; "The Question and Answer Box"; "The Computer Helper"; "Everton's Roots Cellar," a computerized listing of individuals others are researching; and many short columns. Of particular note is the "New on the Bookshelf" section, with brief descriptions (called book reviews in the *Helper*) of new books that have been sent to the publisher's corporate library (which is open to the public) in return for a mention in the magazine. Each issue describes upwards of 150 books, and the section is widely regarded as the most comprehensive listing available of new genealogical books. The *Helper* publishes annual directories in almost every issue; these cover locality periodicals (January-February), surname periodicals (March-April), genealogical libraries (May-June), genealogical societies (July-August), and professional genealogical researchers (September-October). Because the publisher relies on individuals to send information for these directories (and professional genealogists are charged for their entries), they are not comprehensive.

Each issue is printed on newsprint in black ink only. The inexpensive printing and the high percentage of promotional (advertising) material help keep the subscription fee quite low. Considering the wealth of its content, subscribing to the *Helper* is an excellent way for family history researchers to keep in touch with what is happening in the world of genealogy and family history research.

Ancestry. Published by Ancestry Incorporated, P.O. Box 476, Salt Lake City, UT 84110, *Ancestry* is a full-color, newsstand-quality magazine which grew out of the publisher's *Ancestry Newsletter* in 1994. Issued bimonthly, the magazine currently has sixty-eight pages. Each issue has several feature articles and major columns, such as "Research Cornerstones" and "Library and Archive Sources," many of them written by some of the United States' most prominent genealogists. The layout and design of the this magazine are of a much higher quality than the other general interest magazines discussed here, and it currently includes less advertising.

Heritage Quest. *Heritage Quest: The Genealogy Magazine* was begun in 1985. Six issues are published per year with a strong focus on how-to articles. Published by the American Genealogical Lending Library (AGLL) (P.O. Box 329, Bountiful, UT 84011), *Heritage Quest* is intended for the American hobbyist and includes numerous articles on research in the United States, as well as most major foreign countries. An average issue of approximately 150 pages includes around twenty-five major articles and a host of regular columns, including genealogical news and a calendar of upcoming genealogical events (figure 19-9). Many of *Heritage Quest*'s regular writers are well-known genealogists. Because there is much less advertising and promotional text in *Heritage Quest* than in the *Genealogical Helper*, *Heritage Quests*'s articles tend to be longer and contain more helpful information. Of particular interest are the lengthy "Question and Answer" articles in each issue for German, Irish, and other research. The magazine is printed in two colors on white, regular-quality paper and has more "eye appeal" and better layout than the *Helper*.

Family Tree. The *Family Tree,* from the Odom Genealogy Library (P.O. Box 1110, Moultrie, GA 31776), is a unique genealogical periodical. Published on newsprint in tabloid style, it is issued every two months at no cost to subscribers. Costs are covered by advertising and volunteer postage donations. This unique distribution method has made the *Family Tree* the most subscribed-to genealogical periodical in the few short years since its 1991 introduction. In addition to the advertisements that make up a large percentage of each issue's approximately sixty pages, there is a clear Scottish focus and an eclectic collection of genealogical news gleaned from many other periodicals. The chief purpose of the *Family Tree* is to promote the activities and growing collection of the Odom Library, which has become a major repository for Scottish sources and the records of dozens of Scottish clans. The *Family Tree* contains no feature articles and few regular columns; however, it is worthwhile to review the advertisements and the news, although some of it, as is often the case with copied articles, is of dubious value.

Other general interest magazines include:

American Genealogy Magazine. *American Genealogy Magazine* is published by a group of genealogists (Datatrace Systems, P.O. Box 1587, Stephenville, TX 76041) rather than a publishing company or library; hence, it has a lower profile than other general interest publications. Also issued bimonthly, it has a mix of articles similar to the major state publications (discussed below), including an emphasis on transcripts and abstracts of original records. It includes records from all North American locales. Some articles are lengthy and are continued in multiple issues. Also discussed in it are repositories and their

Figure 19-9. Table of contents from *Heritage Quest* (November-December 1996).

collections, computer genealogy, and other topics. Issues also include queries reprinted from the current issue of the *National Queries Forum* (see below under "Query Magazines").

Genealogy Bulletin. Begun in 1989 by William Dollarhide, the useful, bimonthly newsletter *Genealogy Bulletin* combines methodology articles with a computerized database of genealogical queries. It generally has fewer articles than other periodicals, but they are typically more in-depth; the queries are clearer and easier to sift through than many as well. The *Genealogy Bulletin* is published by AGLL (P.O. Box 329, Bountiful, UT 84011).

Family Chronicles. *Family Chronicles* was launched in 1996 by Moorshead Magazines (10 Gateway Boulevard, Suite 490, North York, Ontario, Canada M3C 3T4). Many of its articles are currently written by the company staff, who, at times, appear to lack experience in family history. Nevertheless, the publisher has created a credible, full-color magazine, in part through its experience in publishing other magazines, and appears poised to help *Family Chronicles* grow rapidly. The magazine focuses on the needs of North American genealogists with a mix of interesting articles. Each issue has around eight articles that include coverage of computer and general-interest topics, as well as tips, a calendar of events, and questions and answers. Often included as well is a section containing transcribed genealogical data from an obscure source.

State and Local

By far the majority of genealogical periodicals are society-sponsored periodicals that focus on the records and families of specific areas. Virtually every state and region of North America has a genealogical society that publishes a periodical. Some societies publish two periodicals: a "regular" periodical, such as a journal, and a newsletter. In addition, many cities and counties east of the Mississippi (especially in the Midwest) are home to genealogical societies and their periodicals. Those in the chapter bibliography, which cites approximately 250 such titles, represent a sampling of the major state and multi-county periodicals. There are more than 1,500 such periodicals in the United States alone, not to mention newsletters and historical society publications (discussed later).

Any of the content described above can be found in state and local publications, although there is a minimal amount of compiled genealogical material (genealogies, biographies, etc.). Local records and society news are the mainstays of these publications. Important records often are abstracted as ongoing series. State and local periodicals also include queries, book reviews and notices, and ancestor charts. In fact, they are so diverse that almost any type of article may be found in them. Serious genealogists read the periodicals for the states and counties where their ancestors lived (especially hard-to-find ancestors).

State and local periodicals of note because of their longevity and the consistent quality of their content include the *Connecticut Nutmegger, Families* (Ontario), *Illinois State Genealogical Society Quarterly, Hawkeye Heritage* (Iowa), *Hoosier Genealogist* (Indiana), *Filson Club Historical Quarterly* (Kentucky), *Maryland and Delaware Genealogist, Western Maryland Genealogy, Genealogical Magazine of New Jersey,* the *Report* (Ohio), and *Ohio: The Crossroad of Our Nation* (all cited in the chapter bibliography).

Many of the independent periodicals focus on research in particular localities. Some, such as the *Hoosier Journal of Ancestry, Kentucky Genealogist,* and *Virginia Genealogist,* deal with the records and families of entire states. Most provide data on parts of states, such as *Rowan County Register, Lancaster County Connections,* and *South Jersey Magazine* (all cited in the chapter bibliography).

Topical

Most topical periodicals focus on specific ethnic or religious groups, but there are also journals for colonial ancestry, computer genealogy, lineage societies, and other interests; these are valuable sources for methodology articles and background information for the topic of interest. While there are literally hundreds of such periodicals (figure 19-8), they can most easily be divided into those focusing on ethnic backgrounds and those serving other special interests.

Ethnic Background and Foreign Ancestry. Research into foreign ancestry and various ethnic groups often differs, in varying degrees, from American-British research. Different records, customs, migration and settlement patterns, and even languages need to be explained to researchers who were not raised in a particular ethnic culture. The growth of interest in ethnic research (see chapter 4, "Ethnic Sources") has been mirrored by a growing number of periodicals that focus on these areas. Today there are close to two hundred periodicals for ethnic genealogical research. As reflected by English-language periodicals, the areas of greatest interest seem to be (in descending order of number of publications) German, Jewish, French, African American, Irish, Hispanic, and Native American ancestry. Other periodicals exist for Acadian, Dutch, Italian, Polish, Swiss, and many other ethnic groups. Although not all of the periodicals covering each ethnic group can be discussed here, it is worthwhile to profile some prominent examples.

Avotaynu—The International Review of Jewish Genealogy (published by Avotaynu, P.O. Box 1134, Teaneck, NJ 07666) is an excellent example of an ethnic-oriented periodical. This quarterly publication has grown along with genealogical interest in its topic to the point where its publisher is now the largest publisher of Jewish genealogical material in the world. Each thirty-two-page issue explores issues and sources of value to Jewish genealogists, including profiles of repositories, research success stories, customs that affect research, questions and answers about research problems, and international news about Jewish records and their availability. Realizing that many readers are not steeped in Jewish traditions and customs, the articles define necessary terms and are easy to follow. *Avotaynu* has partly been the cause of the growth in Jewish genealogical research, not just a response to that growth.

German Genealogical Digest (published by Laraine Ferguson, 245 North Vine, Suite 106, Salt Lake City, UT 84103), begun by Larry Jensen in 1985 and currently edited by Laraine Ferguson, provides in-depth articles about a variety of German sources and research procedures. Articles include geographic tips, handwriting and language aids, border changes, types of sources to be found at various archives, and other useful material. This quarterly magazine, which also publishes queries, has a long list of qualified contributors who help maintain its quality.

The Irish at Home and Abroad (published by Dwight Radford and Kyle Betit, P.O. Box 521806, Salt Lake City, UT 84152) was begun in 1993. Its articles discuss the nature of Irish research and sources, detailing what records are available and where to find them. It also informs the reader about Irish customs, history, and geography.

Like the three titles described above, many ethnic and foreign-interest titles are independent periodicals, such as the *Canadian Genealogist, Die Pommerschen Leute* (focusing on Pomerania and Prussia), *Gaelic Gleanings,* and the *Swedish American Genealogist.* Others are published by societies serving specific interests, such as the *Palatine Immigrant, Afro-American Historical and Genealogical Society Journal* (Afro-American Historical and Genealogical Society), *de Halve Maen* (Holland Society of New York), and the *Eaglet* (Polish Genealogical Society of Michigan) (all cited in the chapter bibliography).

Special Interests. Many other periodicals serve a variety of special interests. These include religious groups, lineage societies, computer usage in genealogy, adoption, and military interests. Research sources and techniques vary for each of these interests. Special interest periodicals are often published by societies, so they contain significant amounts of society news as well. The content of many lineage society magazines deals mostly with the publishing societies. Some particularly useful examples are discussed here.

The *DAR Magazine* (published by the Daughters of the American Revolution, 1776 D St., Washington, DC 20006) is an excellent example of a lineage society publication. It has a large readership and represents an important segment of the genealogical field. Its content is primarily society news, but it also includes some important contributions, such as an ongoing list of revolutionary war soldiers' graves.

APG Quarterly (published by the Association of Professional Genealogists, P.O. Box 40393, Denver, CO 80204) is an example of an association newsletter that grew into a larger publication. Each thirty-two-page issue includes four or five feature articles exploring issues of interest to professional genealogists, including client relationships, preparing to teach genealogy, writing for publication, and becoming a professional researcher. News of the society is joined by regular departments that identify significant accomplishments of members, profile professional genealogists, respond to thought-provoking questions, review books, and give tips on running a small business. Nationally known contributors and professional editing have done much to improve not only the *Quarterly* but also the image of the Association of Professional Genealogists. That, after all, is part of the mission of any society-sponsored periodical.

Genealogical Computing (published by Ancestry Incorporated, P.O. Box 476, Salt Lake City, UT 84110) is the premiere magazine dealing with the increasingly important intersection of genealogy and computers. Currently issued four times a year, each forty-eight-page-plus issue includes articles about genealogy-related computer topics, such as finding data on the Internet, what resources are available for certain kinds of research, and interviews with software developers and other leaders in the field. Software and CD-ROM reviews provide excellent detail to help readers choose which products will help them in their research. Tips for using some of the most popular software programs help users become more efficient. Most issues also include a directory to such items as databases, current software, computer interest groups, and online services.

Mennonite Family History (published by J. Lamar and Lois Ann Mast, P.O. Box 171, Elverson, PA 19520) is an independent periodical begun in 1982 that focuses on Mennonite families and culture. Its articles discuss family traditions, records in both the United States and Europe, and the origins of U.S. families in the Old World.

Other examples of special interest publications include *Antique Week* (deals with antiques, genealogy, and history), the *Second Boat* (colonial immigration and genealogy), *Mayflower Descendant* (discussed earlier), and the *Loyalist Gazette* (from the United Empire Loyalists Association) (all cited in the chapter bibliography).

Query Magazines

A unique kind of genealogical periodical focuses almost exclusively on publishing queries. While some have been published since the 1960s, query magazines have become increasingly popular and specialized since the 1990s. Most of the nationwide query publications also include one to three brief methodology articles and perhaps some genealogical news, but the queries define the magazines. They are all subscription publications, but many of them will print one or more queries free for subscribers. Also of note are a growing number of topic- or state-specific query publications, usually issued at unspecified intervals. These have become known as "query booklets."

Genealogical Research Directory. The largest publication devoted strictly to queries, *Genealogical Research Directory* (U.S. distributor: Jan Jennings, 3324 Crail Way, Glendale, CA 91206) is actually an annual book (since 1981). Each issue contains approximately 100,000 new entries from all over the world. Edited by Keith A. Johnson and Malcolm R. Sainty, this source is found in most major genealogical libraries, although most of the purchasers are individual researchers. Any researcher may pay a small fee to list the individuals sought. Purchase of the book is not required for a listing. Its worldwide scope makes it especially useful for finding researchers in other countries who are interested in the same family as an American researcher. Back issues usually remain in print for several years. Similar books exist specifically for England, Germany, and some other countries.

Family Puzzlers. *Family Puzzlers* (published by Heritage Papers, P.O. Box 7776, Athens, GA 30604) is the longest-running query publication, having been published by Mary Bondurant Warren since 1964. It is a twenty-page weekly magazine that prints queries free of charge for its more than two thousand subscribers. Each issue also has a brief feature article, book reviews, and an index.

Lost and Found. *Lost and Found: National Genealogical Query Newsletter* (P.O. Box 207, Wathena, KS 66090) began in 1984 and is published by Ethel M. Weber six times per year. Subscribers to this thirty-two-page newsletter may submit unlimited queries, while nonsubscribers pay a small fee. In addition to its subscribers, it is distributed to more than one thousand genealogical societies in the United States, Canada, England, Ireland, and Germany.

National Queries Forum. The *National Queries Forum* (P.O. Box 593, Santa Cruz, CA 95061) began in 1990 and is published six times per year by Michael Cooley. This forty-page magazine is published as a small, newsprint booklet. It includes no articles—only queries, a surname index to the queries, and some display advertising. Each subscriber may have a short query printed at no charge. The magazine is also available on floppy diskette.

State and Topical Query Booklets. Several statewide and topical query magazines are published on an occasional basis by individuals. Typically these booklets are from twenty-five to thirty pages; they are published as sufficient queries are received (usually at least once per year). Typical titles include *Quaker Queries, Pennsylvania Queries, Maryland Connection Queries, Mid-Atlantic Queries and Reviews,* and *German Queries*. The queries are printed at no charge, but they must pertain to the state or topic of the specific publication. Many publishers also include book reviews for appropriate books. All of them appear to be independent publications compiled by individual researchers. The nature of these publications makes publishing information subject to change as the publishers move or cease publication. The best methods for locating them are to review the advertisements in *Everton's Genealogical Helper* and to check the periodical holdings of major genealogical libraries. On the facing page is a list of query publications for states and topics as of 1995–96.

Newsletters

The recent advent of cheaper printing costs has allowed many societies to publish two periodicals: a "regular" periodical, such as a journal, and a newsletter. Newsletters are typically much briefer than other periodicals, averaging five to twelve pages, and they are often issued more frequently (sometimes monthly). Their content is often of a transitory nature, and hence many libraries keep them in their vertical files. (A vertical file is a nonpermanent collection of materials having only short-term value.)

Query Publications for States and Topics

States		Regions	Topics
Alabama [12], [11]	Montana [1]	New England [4]	Civil War [6]
Alaska [1]	New Jersey [7]	Mid-Atlantic (Del., N.J., Md., Pa.) [4]	Dutch [11]
Arizona [1]	New Mexico [1]	New York, Connecticut, Rhode Island, Vermont [19]	German [9]
Colorado [1]	New York [5]	Northeast [14]	Gold Rush [1]
Georgia [8], [11]	North and South Carolina [4], [16]	Ohio-Indiana-Iowa [4]	Irish [4]
Hawaii [1]	North and South Dakota [6]	Oregon-Washington [18]	Italian [4]
Illinios [2], [11]	Ohio [4]	Pacific Northwest [10]	Military [3]
Indiana [4]	Oklahoma [15]	Southwest [14]	Oregon Trail [3]
Iowa [4]	Oregon [3]		Quaker [7]
Kansas [2]	Pennsylvania [4], [16]		Scandinavian [10]
Kentucky [7], [8], [13]	Rhode Island [9]		Scottish [17]
Maryland [11]	Tennessee [8], [16]		
Massachusetts [4]	Texas [1], [13]		
Minnesota [6]	Virginia [16]		
Mississippi [11]	Virginia and West Virginia [9]		
Missouri [3], [5]	Wisconsin [2]		
	Wyoming [1]		

Publishers' Addresses

[1] Frontier Genealogy Resources, Mary T. Howard, P.O. Box 22026, Milwaukie, OR 97269
[2] Marjory Cory-Hall, P.O. Box 305, Sultan, WA 98294
[3] Family Publications, Rose Caudle Terry, 5626 Sixtieth Dr. NE, Marysville, WA 98270
[4] Pioneer Publications, Shirley Penna-Oakes, P.O. Box 1179, Tum Tum, WA 99034
[5] Carolyn Wilson Weidner, 2206 West Borden Road, Spokane, WA 99204
[6] Beverly Dorfner, P.O. Box 3192, Arlington, WA 98223
[7] Ruby Simonson McNeill, North 4015 Magruerite Road, Spokane, WA 99212; or 323 Cedarcrest Court East, P.O. Box 779, Napavine, WA 98565
[8] E. Dale Smith, South 4204 Conklin, Spokane, WA 99203
[9] Bette Butcher Topp, West 1304, Cliffwood Court, Spokane, WA 99218
[10] Anne Long, Rt. 2, Box 671, Grangville, ID 83530
[11] MLH Research, MariLee Beatty Hagness, 3916 Bramble Road, Anniston, AL 36201
[12] Bell Enterprises, West 2418 Wellesley, Spokane, WA 99205
[13] Partin Publications, 230 Wedgewood, Nacogdoches, TX 75961
[14] Old Time Publications, North 3420 Donwood, Spokane, WA 99216
[15] Janet M. Damm, S.E. 310 Camino, Pullman, WA 99163
[16] Bever Publications, P.O. Box 3056, Wichita Falls, TX 76309
[17] Sims Publishing, P.O. Box 9576, Sacramento, CA, 95823
[18] Oregon-Washington Queries, P.O. Box 985, Okanogan, WA 98840
[19] Sleeper Queries, 94-1476 Lanikuhana Ave no. 543, Mililani, HI 96789
Note: Addresses are subject to change, and publishers may choose to cease publication of any booklet.

Newsletters usually include society news and events (announcements of conferences, etc.), queries, and book notices (not reviews). Information taken from other periodicals is often included as well; such information is usually of a methodological nature but is very brief—a paragraph or two at most. Newsletters are focused on their publishers' members/subscribers and not on others who may read them at a later time (such as a researcher in a library ten years after publication).

Some societies—typically smaller or newer societies of local interest—only publish newsletters; these publications occasionally include material of permanent value. As they grow, these societies sometimes begin publishing more substantial periodicals, either in addition to or evolving from an existing newsletter. Most of the largest societies publish newsletters, but three significant ones deserve discussion.

FGS Forum. The FGS *Forum* is the quarterly publication of the Federation of Genealogical Societies (P.O. Box 830220, Richardson, TX 75083-0220). It serves as the newsletter of the North American genealogical community. Each forty-page issue contains articles dealing with current genealogical events and activities. The "News in Brief" section features significant events in various states, while "State Reporting" identifies new publications and projects of the member societies. A "Records Access" column keeps readers aware of changing circumstances in different states. Other columns spotlight family associations, ethnic or international groups, and editing techniques. Fifteen to twenty book reviews discuss many of the major new genealogical books, and the "Calendar of Events" identifies conferences and seminars of more than local interest.

NGS Newsletter. The *NGS Newsletter* is published every other month by the National Genealogical Society (4527 Seventeenth Street North, Arlington, VA 22207). In addition to reporting the news and activities of the society, each issue includes a few brief articles about research procedures, several dozen detailed queries from members, and a lengthy list of "Library Acquisitions" from the society's library that acts as a condensed list of recent publications. The sections about news from members and member societies often identify new publications. In recent years, the National Genealogical Society has taken the lead in protecting genealogical consumers by combating companies that make spurious claims, and the *Newsletter* keeps the public updated on these activities. While each issue has around thirty pages, the newsletter also includes a sixteen-page insert, the *NGS/CIG Digest* (prepared by the society's Computer Interest Group), which has articles about computer applications in genealogy, as well as software reviews and other computer news.

NEXUS. *NEXUS,* the newsletter of the New England Historic Genealogical Society (101 Newbury Street, Boston, MA 02116), is important not only for its feature articles about methodology and sources, but also because it represents the oldest and largest society in the nation. It is published six times per year, and each issue contains around forty pages of articles discussing New England research. The regular features include a frequent column on "Notable Kin," dozens of queries, news about new publications for New England, and acquisitions of major new collections in the library. News of the society and its many sponsored events, as well as some advertising, rounds out each issue.

Family and Surname Periodicals

Many periodicals focus on one family or on a surname and its variants. Many family and surname periodicals are published by individuals interested in particular names; they are most closely related to the special interest periodicals described above. Others are published by family associations. Titles such as *Chamberlain Chain,* the *Frenchline,* and *Loomis Families of America* promise exciting finds for researchers interested in specific surnames. Some publications in this group focus on one family rather than on all individuals who share the surname. Such periodicals usually treat the ancestors and descendants of an ancestral couple.

Surname periodicals, regardless of how they are published, are intended to locate and publish information about people who share surnames of interest. While many are little more than newsletters, they are still significant research tools. Surname periodicals include all types of articles, from compiled genealogies and abstracts of original records to queries and indexes. Methodology articles are limited, as are book reviews and notices, unless they pertain to the surname of interest. Surname periodicals often reprint articles and excerpts from books, such as biographical sketches relating to the surname.

Surname periodicals are truly their publishers' labors of love. Typically, the fees charged for them are barely enough to cover printing and postage costs; their editors' time is seldom, if ever, compensated monetarily. These circumstances result in one of the more unfortunate characteristics of these periodicals: their relatively short life span. Most surname periodicals do not last more than five years, and very few continue beyond fifteen years. Often their editors/publishers run out of time or funds to pursue the venture, or they lose interest.

Virtually all of the longer-lasting surname periodicals are published by family or surname associations. These involve more people, helping to spread the effort required to produce them. Some such periodicals have been able to flourish for more than a quarter of a century.

For researchers, surname periodicals and their publishers can be a great help. Finding a periodical for a surname of interest is much like finding a published genealogy for the family. Most of the information will not be directly helpful, but it is likely that some will pertain to the family being researched. Most of the information is secondary in nature and should be proved further, but, in essence, such a periodical becomes a master index to dozens or hundreds of records and identifies where information on the particular surname can be found.

Unfortunately, the nature of family and surname periodicals makes them difficult to find. Few libraries subscribe to them, and their publishers do not advertise heavily in other periodicals. There is no single list of surname periodicals, but a review of the major finding aids for these periodicals suggests that there may be more than two thousand. Two sources discussed below under "Locating Genealogical Periodicals" are the best sources for finding these hidden treasures. Elizabeth Bentley's *Directory of Family Associations* and Michael Clegg's *Bibliography of Genealogy and Local History Periodicals with Union List of Major U.S. Collections* identify most of the current family and surname periodicals. For a shorter list, check the annual directory of family organizations in the March-April issue of *Everton's Genealogical Helper.*

Many of these periodicals are only published for a short time yet have significant content. Look for defunct family publications at the major genealogical libraries (the Family History Library, Library of Congress, Allen County Public Library in Fort Wayne, Indiana, and others). Some directories list addresses from years ago, though the editor may have moved and/or the publication ceased. For older periodicals, check J. Konrad's *Directory of Genealogical Periodicals,* 4th ed. (Munroe Falls, Ohio: Summit Publications, 1981), which listed 530 surname periodicals in 1981, and the Family Registry™ (a ceased query file that includes addresses of family organizations; it is available at most LDS family history centers). Finding relevant surname periodicals and subscribing to them (they are relatively inexpensive) is well worth the effort and cost.

Historical Periodicals

While the focus of this chapter is on genealogical periodicals, the several hundred historical periodicals also contain material that is very valuable for genealogists but is usually overlooked. Every state has at least one statewide historical association, and many counties also have historical societies. Every state and most county societies publish periodicals; most of them are similar in nature to the journals described above. They are well written, give sources, and they often explore areas and concepts not treated elsewhere. Jones, Eakle, and Christensen remind us that

> since the seventeenth century, [societies] have published journals, proceedings and transactions in which biographies, local and family histories, genealogical queries, extracts and transcriptions of original documents and record analyses of genealogical value have appeared (1972, 80).

Biography is a mainstay of such publications, making them of great interest to family historians, who are often researching the very subjects of these biographical articles. Local history is treated in depth in these periodicals as well. Local history can add great insight to research and, not infrequently, can help solve genealogical problems.

Many historical societies have existed for scores of years; some are more than one hundred years old and have been publishing journals since they were founded. Cumulative indexes are often available to make it easier to search their many publications. The chapter bibliography includes at least one major historical periodical for each state.

Historical societies are usually larger (in terms of membership) and better funded than genealogical societies. Many maintain research libraries; in fact, some historical societies sponsor or support local genealogical societies. The extra funding and membership enable these societies to generally produce products of higher quality than many genealogical societies. Their publications are usually published quarterly, like those of most genealogical societies, but each issue may include more than one hundred pages. Along with articles of historical interest, they usually contain book reviews (including reviews of genealogical books) and articles about research sources and methodology.

LOCATING GENEALOGICAL PERIODICALS

Because there is a wide variety of periodicals, both current and defunct, and because they are so widely distributed, no single source can list them all or indicate how useful any one will be. However, several tools published in the last few years will help researchers determine if a periodical of interest exists.

Bibliographies

Comprehensive bibliographies are usually the best sources for identifying periodicals because they are likely to contain remarks about the periodicals listed, and they often list defunct titles. However, they are not updated as frequently as the directories discussed later.

Bibliography of Genealogy and Local History Periodicals. *Bibliography of Genealogy and Local History Periodicals with Union List of Major U.S. Collections,* edited by Michael Clegg (Fort Wayne, Ind.: Allen County Public Library Foundation, 1990), is an excellent starting point for a search. This list was published in 1990 by the Allen County Public Library Foundation of Fort Wayne, Indiana, to complement its *Periodical Source Index* (described below under "Indexes"). This bibliography seeks to identify every English-language and French-Canadian periodical dealing with genealogy or history. With approximately 5,400 title listings, including many foreign titles, it is more comprehensive than any other bibliography.

The great size of Clegg's bibliography can be overwhelming. It includes current and defunct titles and usually has separate entries for the various titles that many periodicals have used. It lists virtually all locality periodicals, as well as many surname periodicals. The arrangement is strictly by title, although titles are sometimes hard to determine because many society publications are simply titled the *Journal* or *Newsletter* of the particular society. In such cases, the editors often included the name of the society as part of the title, but this practice was not followed consistently. A subject index aids the alphabetical arrangement. The subjects are usually state or country names, although topics and family names also appear. Thus, the subject index seldom identifies a specific county with a periodical, although the actual entry indicates the publisher, which is often a society.

The bibliography provides the name, years of publication, frequency, and publisher (with address for current titles) of each periodical (figure 19-10). International standard serial numbers (ISSN) and subscription prices appear (when available), but there is no description of the periodical, leaving the researcher to wonder whether the title is a major genealogical reference or a four-page newsletter with little substantive information. Titles that are part of the *Periodical Source Index* also have a four-letter identification code, such as TXCL (which stands for *Coryell Kin* of the the Coryell County [Texas] Genealogical Society). A significant part of each listing is a reference naming which of eleven major research libraries have copies of that periodical. In fact, the bibliography was largely created as a union list (as the full title indicates), with the eleven libraries contributing their lists of serials. This list helps the researcher know where the title can be found and can act as a measure of the periodical's importance.

Those periodicals that can be found in most or all of the listed libraries are clearly the major ones in the field; they will often be available at many other libraries as well. Titles available at only one or two libraries are quite rare and will be difficult to locate elsewhere; for those that are still being published, write to their publishers and inquire about repositories that have copies. Also ask about indexes to the periodical and (if the publisher will make a search) any search fees. The entry may indicate that the periodical is at the Allen County Public Library. If so, the staff there will copy articles for a small fee (see the discussion under "Indexes—*Periodical Source Index,*" below).

American Genealogical Periodicals. *American Genealogical Periodicals: A Bibliography with a Chronological Finding List,* edited by Lester J. Cappon (New York: New York Public Library, 1964), is an older, but still useful, bibliography. Cappon listed 155 titles, providing full bibliographic information for each, but omitted periodicals issued by patriotic societies or those devoted to particular families or surnames. While many were published by genealogical societies, Cappon found that nearly two-thirds were published by individual persons or partnerships as independent magazines. This, he suggests, is the reason why a great many ceased publication, most in less than five years. Of the 115 periodicals that began before 1950, only around twenty were still being published in 1962. Many others have ceased publication since then, such as the *Alabama Genealogical Register* (1959 to 1980). Even though many of the magazines listed are defunct, they are worth knowing about, for most published solid genealogical information about their particular areas or interests. The identification of these now-defunct titles is the greatest value of Cappon's thirty-two-page listing. Cappon, it should be noted, did not confine his list strictly to genealogical periodicals; he also included some historical magazines that contained genealogical material, such as the *Virginia Magazine of History and Biography,* published since 1893; the *Maine Historical Magazine,* issued from July 1885 to December 1894; and others. Note, however, that the number of genealogical periodicals has increased dramatically since 1964, so most peri-

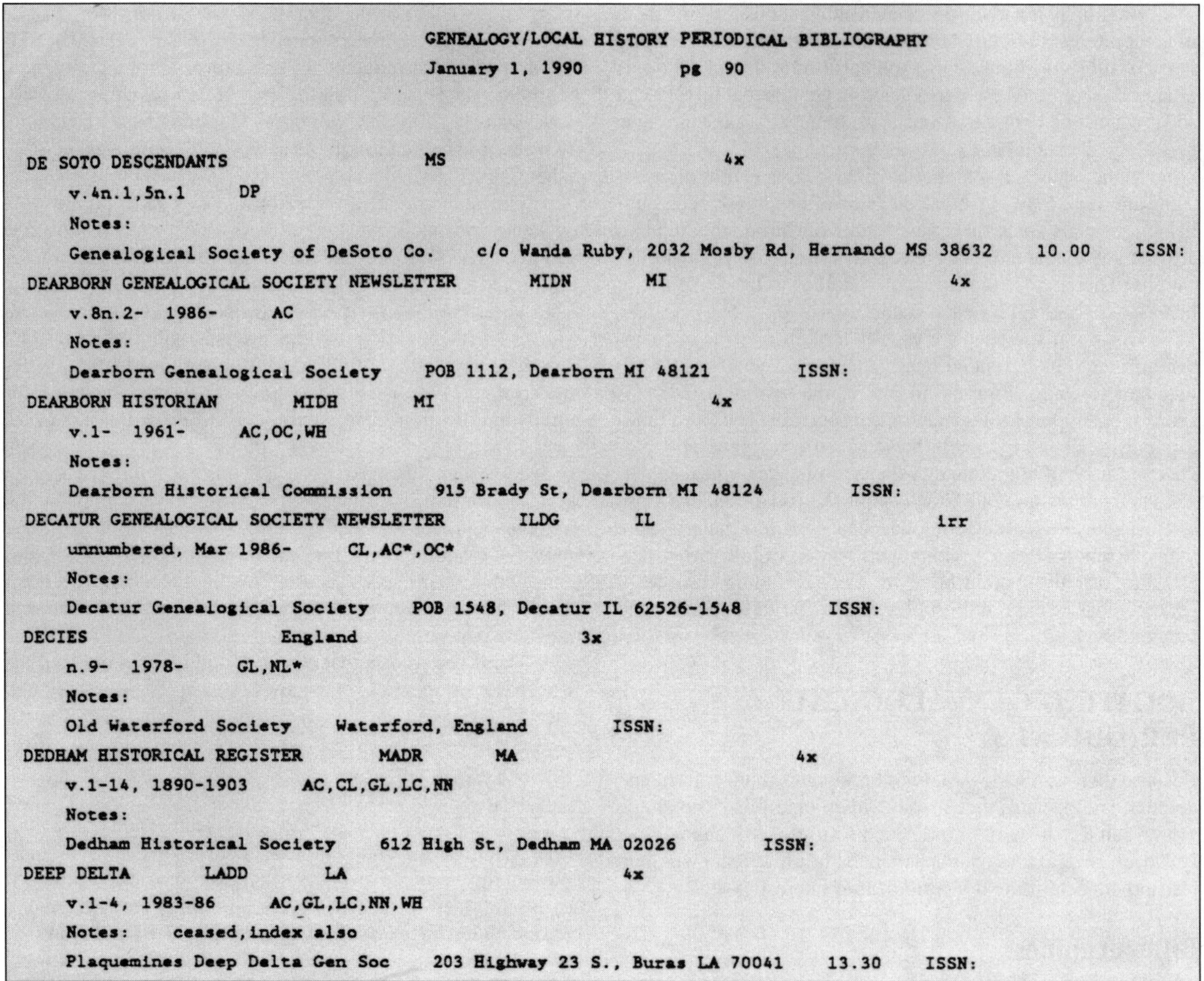
GENEALOGY/LOCAL HISTORY PERIODICAL BIBLIOGRAPHY
January 1, 1990 pg 90

DE SOTO DESCENDANTS MS 4x
v.4n.1,5n.1 DP
Notes:
Genealogical Society of DeSoto Co. c/o Wanda Ruby, 2032 Mosby Rd, Hernando MS 38632 10.00 ISSN:
DEARBORN GENEALOGICAL SOCIETY NEWSLETTER MIDN MI 4x
v.8n.2- 1986- AC
Notes:
Dearborn Genealogical Society POB 1112, Dearborn MI 48121 ISSN:
DEARBORN HISTORIAN MIDH MI 4x
v.1- 1961- AC,OC,WH
Notes:
Dearborn Historical Commission 915 Brady St, Dearborn MI 48124 ISSN:
DECATUR GENEALOGICAL SOCIETY NEWSLETTER ILDG IL irr
unnumbered, Mar 1986- CL,AC*,OC*
Notes:
Decatur Genealogical Society POB 1548, Decatur IL 62526-1548 ISSN:
DECIES England 3x
n.9- 1978- GL,NL*
Notes:
Old Waterford Society Waterford, England ISSN:
DEDHAM HISTORICAL REGISTER MADR MA 4x
v.1-14, 1890-1903 AC,CL,GL,LC,NN
Notes:
Dedham Historical Society 612 High St, Dedham MA 02026 ISSN:
DEEP DELTA LADD LA 4x
v.1-4, 1983-86 AC,GL,LC,NN,WH
Notes: ceased,index also
Plaquemines Deep Delta Gen Soc 203 Highway 23 S., Buras LA 70041 13.30 ISSN:

Figure 19-10. Entries from *Bibliography of Genealogy and Local History Periodicals with Union List of Major U.S. Collections.* The entries provide the name, years of publication, frequency, and publisher (with address for current titles) of each periodical.

odicals, especially surname, ethnic, and county publications, are not in this list. Nevertheless, it does provide quite comprehensive coverage of pre-1964 periodicals.

Historical Bibliographies. Historical journals are incompletely represented in the two previous bibliographies. In addition to the many specialized bibliographies and directories available at many academic libraries, two general lists of historical journals are significant. Eric H. Boehm, Barbara H. Pope, and Marie S. Ensign's *Historical Periodicals Directory,* 5 vols. (Santa Barbara, Calif.: ABC-Clio, 1981) lists U.S. and Canadian periodicals in vol. 1. More detailed information about English-language journals is in Janet Fyfe's *History Journals and Serials: An Analytical Guide* (Westport, Conn.: Greenwood Press, 1986).

Periodical Union Lists. A *union list* is a bibliography that also identifies which (of many, not all) libraries have copies of the sources listed. Two major union lists identify most American periodicals, including hundreds of genealogical publications. The *Union List of Serials in Libraries of the United States and Canada,* 3rd ed., 5 vols. (New York: H. W. Wilson Co., 1965), edited by Edna Brown Titus, identifies more than 156,000 pre-1950 periodicals and identifies which of nearly one thousand libraries had copies of each. For more recent periodicals, see *New Serials Titles: A Union List of Serials Commencing Publication after December 31, 1949* (Washington, D.C.: Library of Congress, 1953–). Subject indexes are available to help locate genealogical and historical titles among the thousands of entries; nevertheless, the sheer number of non-genealogical periodicals in these sources tends to obscure genealogical publications. Also, many of the smaller, recent titles are not listed in these sources.

Directories

While bibliographies greatly simplify the search for genealogical periodicals, directories are also necessary at times. Most genealogical periodicals are geographically focused and are published by local historical and genealogical societies. Such societies are identified in directories, but directories typically identify only current societies or publishers and their periodicals. Their scope may not be limited to genealogical societies

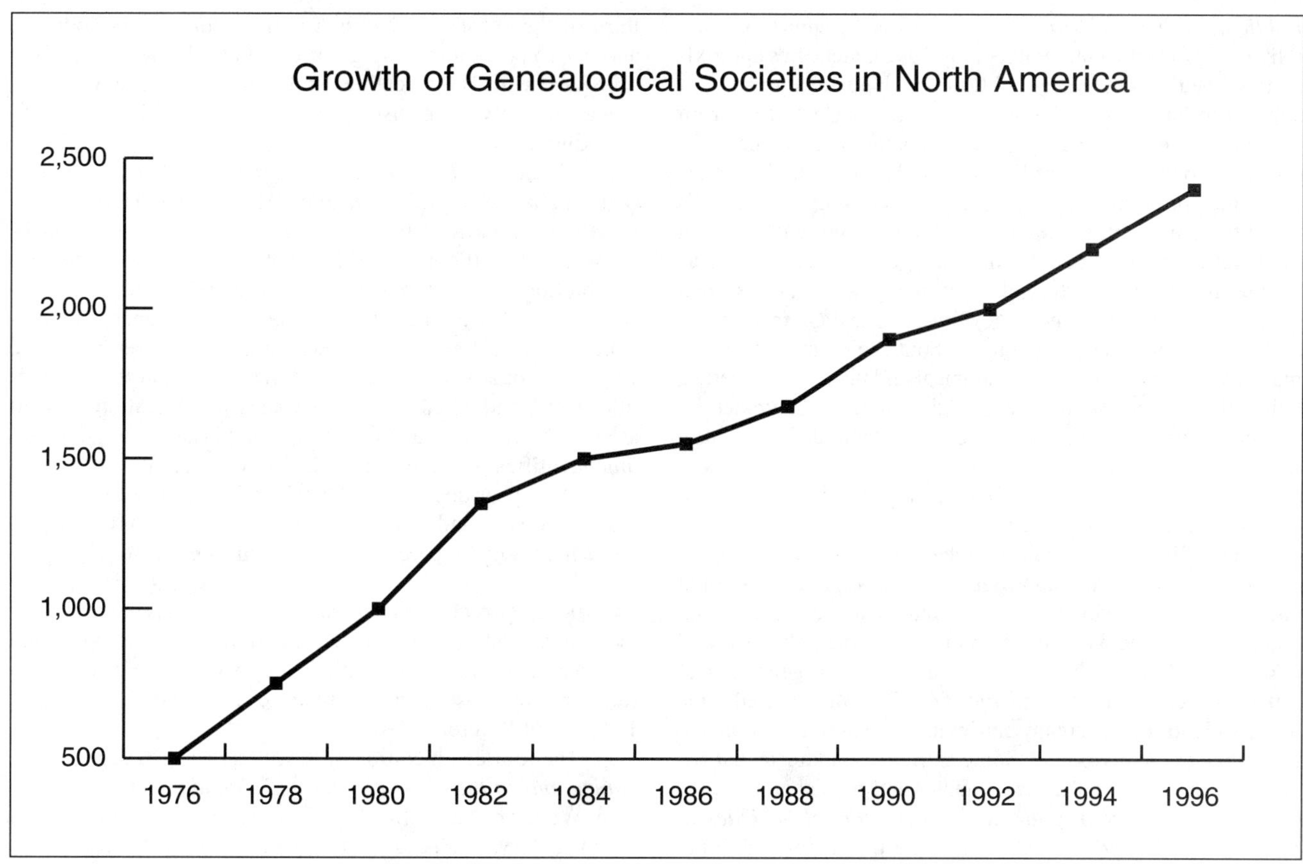

Figure 19-11. Growth of genealogical societies in North America. (Based on *Meyer's Directory of Genealogical Societies in the United States and Canada.*)

and periodicals, but they will provide current addresses. Three significant directories will help in locating periodicals of interest and their publishers. Some of these directories are updated every other year, so be sure to consult the most current edition; addresses, fees, and other information change frequently.

The Genealogist's Address Book. *The Genealogist's Address Book,* by Elizabeth Petty Bentley, 3rd ed. (Baltimore: Genealogical Publishing Co., 1995), is a wide-ranging list of addresses of value to genealogists, but it is limited to U.S. addresses. It includes government offices (except county offices), libraries, archives, ethnic and religious organizations, publishers, and other special resources, as well as historical and genealogical societies. Many of these organizations publish one or more periodicals, which are identified throughout the directory. Some of the organizations have minimal bearing on genealogical research, while others are exclusively focused on family history. *The Genealogist's Address Book* is divided into four parts—national, state, ethnic and religious, and special resources—each of which is further divided into appropriate groups. The general index lists the organizations and groups alphabetically. A separate "Index to Periodicals and Newsletters" lists approximately 4,100 U.S. publications alphabetically, identifying the publishers in parentheses.

Meyer's Directory of Genealogical Societies in the United States and Canada. *Meyer's Directory of Genealogical Societies in the U.S.A. and Canada: With an Appended List of Independent Genealogical Periodicals,* edited by Mary K. Meyer (Mt. Airy, Md.: the editor), identifies more than 2,200 current genealogical societies (most of which publish some type of periodical, if only a newsletter) and more than two hundred independent periodicals. It is published every two years (the eleventh edition appeared in 1996) and is divided into five sections: (1) Canadian societies, arranged alphabetically by province and thereunder alphabetically by society name; (2) U.S. societies, also alphabetical by state and thereunder by society name; (3) special-interest societies and periodicals, listed alphabetically by topic; (4) umbrella groups, such as state councils; and (5) independent periodicals. Some editions have addenda that list changes of address, late registration, and societies and publications received too late for placement under the proper heading in the main text. There is no index, so societies must be sought within each state, and the independent periodicals must be found by their titles.

The listing for each society may include the following information: name, address, telephone number, date founded, number of members, annual dues, library information (number of volumes and microfilms, hours and days of service, staff), titles of publications, and areas of interest. Unfortunately, most societies did not complete the registration forms provided, so up to 70 percent of the entries consist only of societies' names and addresses. Many of these apparently are newer societies. Indeed, Meyer's directory is an excellent indicator of the growth of genealogical societies and periodicals; its listings have grown fourfold in the twenty years of its existence (figure 19-11).

Directory of Genealogical and Historical Publications in the U.S. and Canada. *Directory of Genealogical and Historical*

Publications in the U.S. and Canada, edited by Dina C. Carson (Niwot, Colo.: Iron Gate Publishing, 1992), identifies approximately five thousand serial publications. Upon examination, it appears to have been compiled over a number of years from various sources, rather than by direct contact with the publishers. Some publications are listed more than once under different names or addresses. For example, *Nebraska Ancestree* is listed three times in succession, with a different address each time, yet each entry includes the state genealogical society as the publisher. The directory also lists many defunct titles, such as *Genealogy Digest, Genealogy America,* and *Genealogy Tomorrow*, but provides no notation about their status. The vast majority of publishers are genealogical and historical societies, although a number of family associations and most commercial publishers appear as well. Although the title describes this as a directory of publications, only serial publications (periodicals) are included; books and monographs are generally not listed (although a few seem to have crept in).

The directory is arranged alphabetically by title of publication. An index to the approximately 3,200 publishers listed cites the pages on which their publications are described. Each entry provides the name of the publication, the publisher, and the address. Some publications of only marginal genealogical interest appear, such as *Magazine of the Civil War.* The editor is usually identified, and many entries indicate the circulation and frequency of the periodical. Some entries also indicate that advertising is accepted. The same author and publisher also produced *Directory of Genealogical and Historical Societies in the U.S. and Canada* (1992); it may be useful for additional information on societies.

General Periodical Directories. Every possible source should be checked to locate a periodical of interest. There are several standard periodical sources in most public libraries; three major directories identify most periodicals, and each lists a significant number under the subject of genealogy. Each of the three is available in print, on CD-ROM, and online.

The Standard Periodical Directory (New York: Oxbridge Communications, annual) bills itself as "the largest authoritative guide to United States and Canadian periodicals." The 1997 (twentieth) edition includes approximately ninety thousand publications arranged under approximately 250 subject headings. The "Genealogy" subject heading lists 888 periodicals alphabetically by title, while 1,378 are listed under "History." Many of the 899 titles under the "Ethnic" heading also have significant genealogical value. Approximately 30 percent of the genealogy listings are for surname periodicals, while most of the rest focus on specific localities, such as counties. In addition to title, publisher, address, and telephone number, each entry provides a brief description, the frequency, circulation, subscription price, advertising rates, editor's name, and whether the publication includes book reviews (figure 19-12). This directory's chief limitation is its exclusive focus on North American periodicals.

Ulrich's International Periodicals Directory (New Providence, N.J.: R. R. Bowker, annual) lists more than 130,000 periodicals throughout the world under almost eight hundred different subject headings. The subject "Genealogy and Heraldry" generally identifies between nine hundred and one thousand titles alphabetically. The listing includes the title, starting year, frequency, subscription price, and address. Most also include circulation, editor's name, and a brief description. Almost one-third of the entries are North American surname periodicals; another 15 percent are foreign titles. Approximately half of the titles deal with U.S. localities and special interests. The periodicals in the various history subject headings are also worth checking.

The Serials Directory: An International Reference Book (Birmingham, Ala.: EBSCO, annual) lists 160,000 U.S. and international titles available from eighty-seven thousand publishers worldwide. It consists of five volumes; the first three contain bibliographic listings for titles arranged alphabetically by subject. Along with the title, cost, address, frequency, and publisher, the directory identifies which titles are peer reviewed, which accept advertising and book reviews, what their former titles were, and whether they have ceased publication, as well as size of circulation and date of the first issue. The index volume identifies periodicals by title. More than nine hundred periodicals appear under the "Genealogy" subject heading; most are for the U.S. and Canada, perhaps 30 percent having a surname focus and 20 percent dealing with foreign areas.

Additional Directories. Several other directories are useful for locating periodicals, primarily because most genealogical and historical periodicals are published by societies. For more information on most of these directories and others, see chapter 1, "General Reference."

The fourteenth edition of the *Directory of Historical Organizations in the United States and Canada,* edited by Mary Bray Wheeler (Nashville: American Association for State and Local History, 1990), identifies thousands of historical societies, museums, and other groups with interest in history. It also identifies the periodicals published by the organizations.

The third edition of Elizabeth Petty Bentley's *Directory of Family Associations* (Baltimore: Genealogical Publishing Co., 1996) identifies more than five thousand active groups and individuals collecting information on surnames or descendants of particular families. Many of these groups publish some kind of periodical, if only a newsletter, which the directory usually identifies.

Federation of Genealogical Societies [year] *Membership Directory* (Richardson, Tex.: Federation of Genealogical Societies) is an annual guide to most North American genealogical societies. It was first issued in 1995. Each member society of the Federation of Genealogical Societies (FGS) is invited to provide extensive information on its activities, including the books and periodicals it publishes. More than five hundred of the most active genealogical societies belong to the Federation of Genealogical Societies, and this directory provides extensive information on most of them.

The *Encyclopedia of Associations* (Detroit: Gale Research Co.) is an annual, multi-volume directory of thousands of nationwide organizations. While many of them are not concerned with genealogy, the encyclopedia includes genealogical, lineage, and hereditary associations and identifies their chief publications. Several supplemental volumes identify local associations as well.

Reprints

Because many valuable articles published in older periodicals are difficult to obtain (often only several hundred copies having been printed), reprints have become popular. The Genealogy and Local History series from University Microfilms Interna-

GENEALOGY

Reed, Read, Reid Roots Surname Booklets Family Publications, 5628 60th Dr NE, Marysville, WA 98270-9509; Title Tel # (360) 653-8394 Publ., Ed.-Rose Candle Terry; *CA* Bk. Revs. 1994 IR $10/copy **Subs.** Indv. $10 Can. $12 For. $12 **Adv.** 8½ x 11 Desktop 35pp. Report 1076-2957

Regional Archivist
See: HISTORY

Reid Family Newsletter & Data Reid Family Newsletter & Data, PO Box 488, Due West, SC 29639-0488 Publ.-Elizabeth Austin; Newsl.

Relatively Speaking Alberta Genealogical Society, Box 12015, Edmonton, AB T5J 3L2 Canada; Title Tel # (403) 455-7028 Ed.-Judy Bradley; Family history, research, queries, book reviews, articles of genealogical interest. *A* Bk. Revs. 1973 Q $4/copy **Subs.** Indv. $20 Inst. $22 Can. $20 **Circ.** 800 8½ x 11 Mimeo 44pp. Color-cov. Jour. 0701-8878

Report Ohio Genealogical Society, P.O Box 2625, Mansfield, OH 44906-0625; Title Tel # (419) 522-9077 Title Fax # (419) 522-0224 Ed.-Jean Nathan; Records of genealogical interest to researchers: Court records, Bible charts, family information, etc., concerning Ohio ancestors. *A* Bk. Revs. 1959 Q $6/copy **Subs.** Indv. $27 Can. $37 For. $37 **Circ.** 6,550 Subs. 6,550 **Adv.:** $120 5% ads 8½ x 11 Sheetfed 62pp. Color-cov. **Rent List** Jour.

Research News Family History World, PO Box 22045, Salt Lake City, UT 84122-0045; Title Tel # (801) 250-6717 Publ., Ed.-Arlene Eakle, Circ. Mgr.-JoAnn Jackson; Research tips, reviews, how-to suggestions, new source publication. *B* Bk. Revs. 1982 IR Ind/Abs/Online: GAPI $4/copy **Circ.** 10,000 **Adv.** 8½ x 11 Desktop 4pp. No Color Newsl.

Researcher Researcher, PO Box 206, Chillicothe, MO 64601-0206 Publ.-Elizabeth Ellsberry; Newsl.

Researcher, The Tacoma-Pierce County Genealogical Society, PO Box 1952, Tacoma, WA 98401-1952; Title Tel # (206) 572-6650 Ed.-Persis Shook; A quarterly reference for researchers of genealogy. Local records, Washington state records, U.S. regional records as well as how-to articles, queries, book reviews, membership data. *A* Bk. Revs. 1961 Q Ind/Abs/Online: GPAI, PERSI **Subs.** Indv. $14 Can. $20 **Circ.** 450 8½ x 11 Desktop 50pp. No Color Jour. 1051-8681

Researching Ouachita-Calhoun Counties AR O-C Genealogical Society, PO Box 2092, Camden, AR 71701-2092 *A* $6/copy **Subs.** Indv. $10 Newsl. 8756-9817

Reunions
See: FAMILY

Robbins Cousins Ashby Newsletter, 1013 Illinois St, Bicknell, IN 47512-3000; Title Tel # (812) 735-2530 Publ., Ed.-Carol Hulen; Clearinghouse for all Robbins family records, everywhere. Queries & ads free to subscribers. Bk. Revs. 1985 Q $3/copy **Subs.** Indv. $10 Mimeo Newsl.

Robert McKay Clan Newsletter Robert McKay Clan Newsletter, 5319 Manning Pl NW, Washington, DC 20016-5311; Title Tel # (202) 363-3663 Ed.-Wallace Shipp; News of family members, deaths, marriages, donations, changes of address, reunions. Historical articles, genealogy & resources. *A* Bk. Revs. 1965 A Free **Circ.** 221 8½ x 11 Offset 24pp. Color-2 Newsl. Available on: Microfilm

Robertson Report Name Game Enterprises, 4204 S Conklin St, Spokane, WA 99203-6235; Title Tel # (509) 747-4903 Includes misc info on all spellings, lineages, queries & every name index. Submission of lineages & queries is free. *C* Bk. Revs. 1984 IR $8/copy **Subs.** For. $9 Offset 35pp. Color-cov. Jour. Available on: Floppy disk 0898-5448

Rodziny Polish Genealogical Society, 984 N Milwaukee Ave, Chicago, IL 60622-4101 Ed. in Chief-William Hoffman; Information on Polish genealogy. *A* Ethnic Grp. Polish SA 8½ x 11 24pp. No Color Jour.

Rogers Research Data McNeill Enterprises, PO Box 779, Napavine, WA 98565-0779; Title Tel # (360) 262-3300 1993 $8/copy **Subs.** Indv. $8 **Circ.** 250 Index/Abstract 1086-8429

Rogue Digger Rogue Valley Genealogical Society, 133 S Central Ave, Medford, OR 97501-7221; Title Tel # (503) 770-5848 Publ., Ed.-Jean Maack; Genealogy, history, maps, vital records, family records and queries. *CA* Bk. Revs. 1966 Q $5/copy **Subs.** Indv. $20 Inst. $20 **Circ.** 350 **Adv.:** $25 1% ads 8½ x 11 Offset 40pp. Color-cov. Jour. 0048-8534

Root Digger Newsletter Solano County Genealogical Society, Inc., PO Box 2494, Fairfield, CA 94533-0249; Title Tel # (707) 446-6869 Ed.-Jennie Wright; Current events of Solano County Genealogical Society. Historical records of Solano county , such as church indexes, newspapers , vital records, etc. *A* 1981 M **Subs.** Indv. $13 **Circ.** 260 Subs. 180 8½ x 11 20pp. No Color Newsl.

Root Digger Quarterly Solano County Genealogical Society, Inc., PO Box 2494, Fairfield, CA 94533-0249; Title Tel # (707) 446-6869 Ed.-Jennie Wright; Information of interest to genealogists researching in U.S. & world as well as information about Solano County, California. *BAC* Bk. Revs. 1983 BM $3/copy **Subs.** Indv. $13 **Circ.** 260 Subs. 180 8½ x 11 12pp. No Color Jour.

Figure 19-12. From *The Standard Periodical Directory.* In addition to title, publisher, address, and telephone number, each entry provides a brief description, the frequency, circulation, subscription price, advertising rates, editor's name, and whether the publication includes book reviews.

tional (Ann Arbor, Michigan), described in chapters 16 and 17, includes microfiche copies of several early periodicals. The list includes both prominent and obscure titles, such as the *New York Genealogical and Biographical Record* (vols. 1 through 76), *"Old Northwest" Genealogical Quarterly* (all fifteen volumes), *Connecticut Quarterly* (all four volumes), and *Indiana Magazine of History* (first nine volumes). The series includes at least 132 different periodicals originating in areas from the East to the Midwest. It includes numerous historical society yearbooks and collections, surname magazines, and early town magazines.

Over the years, the Genealogical Publishing Company (Baltimore) has reprinted selected articles from dozens of major genealogical journals in one- to five-volume sets. The selected articles generally share a common theme, such as ship passenger lists, compiled genealogies, or transcribed source records (table 19-2). Examples include *Virginia Tax Records: From the Virginia Magazine of History and Biography,* the *William and Mary College Quarterly, Tyler's Quarterly,* and *Pennsylvania Vital Records: From the Pennsylvania Genealogical Magazine and the Pennsylvania Magazine of History and Biography.* Sometimes the entire run of the periodical is reprinted (especially if it only consists of a few volumes). The publisher adds an every-name index to the reprinted articles and, often, a significant preface that discusses the periodical and explains the selection criteria and related information. Many genealogical libraries purchase these reprint series, making the articles much easier to locate and use.

The advent of CD-ROMs in genealogical publishing has encouraged the electronic "reprinting" of many journals. Fore-

Table 19-2. Periodical Reprints by Genealogical Publishing Company

Title of Journal	*Scope of Selection*	*No. of Volumes*	*Year*
DAR Magazine	Source records	1	1975
Early Settlers of New York State	Entire periodical	2	1993
Filson Club Historical Quarterly	Kentucky families	1	1981
Filson Club Historical Quarterly	Records of Jefferson County	1	1988
Gateway to the West	Entire periodical	2	1989
Genealogical Magazine of New Jersey	New Jersey families	2	1996
Gentleman's Magazine	American vital records, 1731–1868	1	1987
Journal of the American Irish Historical Society	Irish settlers in America	2	1979
Maryland Historical Magazine	Maryland genealogies	2	1980
Maryland Historical Magazine	Maryland rent rolls	1	1976
Mayflower Descendant	Various *Mayflower* articles	1	1978
New England Historical and Genealogical Register	Rhode Island families	2	1989
New England Historical and Genealogical Register	Passengers to America	1	1977
New England Historical and Genealogical Register	English origins of families, 1st series	3	1984
New England Historical and Genealogical Register	English origins of families, 2nd series	3	1985
New England Historical and Genealogical Register	Connecticut families	3	1983
New England Historical and Genealogical Register	*Mayflower* families	3	1985
New England Historical and Genealogical Register	*Mayflower* source records	1	1986
New England Historical and Genealogical Register	Suffolk county wills	1	1984
New York Genealogical and Biographical Record	Immigrants to Middle Colonies	1	1992
New York Genealogical and Biographical Record	English origins of colonists	1	1991
New York Genealogical and Biographical Record	Data from colonial newspapers	1	1977
New York Genealogical and Biographical Record	Data from colonial N.Y. newspapers	1	1977
New York Genealogical and Biographical Record	Long Island families	2	1987
New York Genealogical and Biographical Record	Long Island source records	1	1987
New York Genealogical and Biographical Record	Rhode Island families	2	1989
North Carolina Historical and Genealogical Register	Entire periodical	3	1970
Ohio Genealogical Quarterly	Ohio source records	1	1986
"Old Northwest" Genealogical Quarterly	Ohio cemetery records	1	1984
"Old Northwest" Genealogical Quarterly	Ohio marriages	1	1980
Pennsylvania Folklife	Rhineland emigrants	1	1981
Pennsylvania Genealogical Magazine	Pennsylvania families	3	1982
Pennsylvania Genealogical Magazine; Pennsylvania Magazine of History and Biography	Pennsylvania vital records	3	1983
Pennsylvania German Society Proceedings and Addresses	Pennsylvania German church records	3	1983
Pennsylvania German Society Proceedings and Addresses	Indentures	1	1973
Pennsylvania German Folklore Society	German immigrants, 1709–86	1	1984
Pennsylvania Magazine of History and Biography	Pennsylvania families	1	1981
Pennsylvania Magazine of History and Biography	Ship passenger lists, 1641–1819	1	1975
Pennsylvania Magazine of History and Biography	Baptisms and burials, Christ Church	1	1982
Register of the Kentucky Historical Society	Early tax records	1	1984
Register of the Kentucky Historical Society	Kentucky marriage records	1	1983
Register of the Kentucky Historical Society	Kentucky families	2	1981
Rhode Island (various periodicals)	Rhode Island families	2	1983
Tyler's Quarterly Historical and Genealogical Magazine	Virginia families	4	1981
Virginia Magazine of History and Biography, William and Mary Quarterly, Tyler's Quarterly Historical and Genealogical Magazine	Virginia tax records	1	1983

Title of Journal	*Scope of Selection*	*No. of Volumes*	*Year*
Virginia Magazine of History and Biography, William and Mary Quarterly, Tyler's Quarterly Historical and Genealogical Magazine	Virginia will records	1	1982
Virginia Magazine of History and Biography, William and Mary Quarterly, Tyler's Quarterly Historical and Genealogical Magazine	Virginia land records	1	1982
Virginia Magazine of History and Biography, William and Mary Quarterly, Tyler's Quarterly Historical and Genealogical Magazine	Virginia military records	1	1983
Virginia Magazine of History and Biography, William and Mary Quarterly, Tyler's Quarterly Historical and Genealogical Magazine	Virginia vital records	1	1982
Virginia Magazine of History and Biography, William and Mary Quarterly, Tyler's Quarterly Historical and Genealogical Magazine	Virginia marriage records	1	1982
Virginia Magazine of History and Biography	Virginia families	5	1981
Virginia Magazine of History and Biography	Virginia gleanings in England (wills)	1	1980
William and Mary Quarterly	Virginia families	5	1982
Yearbook of the Pennsylvania German Folklore Society	Pennsylvania German immigrants, 1709–86	1	1984
Various periodicals	Ship passenger lists, etc.	2	1979

most among the recent releases is the *New England Historical and Genealogical Register* on CD-ROM from Brøderbund Software (Novato, California). The first 147 volumes are reproduced as graphic images on nine CD-ROMs. The every-name index is easily searchable, and the software can display an image of any page noted in the index. Another company, Search and Research, has released a CD-ROM reprint of the *Mayflower Descendant* that includes images of the original pages and electronic text that allows complete, every-word searches.

Bibliographies, directories, and reprints provide researchers with a starting point when searching for genealogical periodicals. They can be found in most large libraries. The chapter bibliography lists many other sources to consult. Kip Sperry's *Survey of American Genealogical Periodicals and Periodical Indexes* (cited earlier) lists some five hundred periodicals that were published in the 1970s. While some of these have ceased publication, many more have been started, and their total number appears to be at least 2,500 today (not including surname and historical periodicals). Figure19-1 was prepared from only a few sources (Cappon's *American Genealogical Periodicals*, *Genealogical Periodical Annual Index* [described below under "Indexes"], and the chapter bibliography), but it illustrates the tremendous growth of genealogical periodicals in recent years. It does not attempt to include all such periodicals.

It is also important not to overlook the catalog of the Family History Library in Salt Lake City. The microfiche *Family History Library Catalog*™ (available at more than 2,500 local LDS family history centers) lists more than 2,100 North American periodicals by locality, along with approximately five hundred British and five hundred European (including Scandinavian) periodicals. Surname periodicals (there were around 750 active ones in 1997), although not as thoroughly collected by the library, are found in the surname section of the catalog.

Contact local historical and genealogical societies and public libraries in the areas where ancestors lived; their staffs are often aware of more obscure, but not less important, local periodicals.

INDEXES

There is a wealth of material to be found in genealogical periodicals. The greatest difficulty in using periodicals is the problem of access: How does the researcher learn that an article of interest has been printed somewhere? The natural solution to this problem is the index. There are now sufficient indexes for genealogical periodicals so that the average researcher should, with some diligence, be able to find several articles of interest. However, using indexes to genealogical periodicals requires care; articles of value may remain undiscovered if an index is not used properly.

Over the years several indexes, most only partially effective, have appeared. Using them effectively, however, demands a clear understanding of their strengths and weaknesses. An earlier discussion of indexes to periodicals is Sperry's excellent *Survey of American Genealogical Periodicals and Periodical Indexes*. Unfortunately, due to its age, it does not discuss some significant indexes. Chapter 6 of this book, "Published Indexes," is also worthy of review.

The following discussion focuses on composite, or master, indexes, which treat several periodicals in one index. These are not every-name indexes; rather, they only index chief subjects of periodical articles. These subjects are usually family names or geographic locations. Some publishers have created every-name indexes for some or all of their periodicals' volumes. In the last few years, numerous periodicals have begun publishing annual (or even every-issue) indexes to every name. Cumulative every-name indexes (covering several years or volumes) are rare, and each covers only one periodical.

Today there are two annual indexes to genealogical periodicals, each of which aims to index the majority of genealogical periodicals appearing each year; given the ever-increasing number of such periodicals, this is becoming a mammoth task. The *Periodical Source Index* (described below), which first appeared in 1987, demands the attention of any responsible genealogical researcher, in part for its retrospective index. However, *PERSI* must be fully understood to be used effectively. Also, although it is somewhat superceded by *PERSI,* the researcher must understand the other annual index, the *Genealogical Periodical Annual Index* (described below), with thirty-one volumes through 1992.

These two indexes differ in content. Neither is an every-name index; rather, they are subject indexes: only the subject(s) of the articles are included. In genealogy, families and individuals are often the subjects of articles; thus, many citations are to given and family names. Each also indexes source articles for specific localities, which are the staple of local periodical publishing. The following discussion of their merits and limitations should help the researcher use both to the greatest benefit.

Periodical Source Index

The annual *Periodical Source Index* (Fort Wayne, Ind.: Allen County Public Library Foundation, 1987–), known as *PERSI* by the publisher and most users, is a project of the Genealogy Department of the Allen County Public Library (Fort Wayne, Indiana). This library has long had one of the best genealogical collections in the United States. The indexing project, made possible by a bequest to the library, was begun by Michael Clegg, who still oversees its production. Library staff and hired assistants prepare the index entries.

The index actually has two separate parts. The annual indexes comprise the first part; the first volume appeared in 1987, covering periodicals published during calendar year 1986, with a 1986 publication date. Annual volumes have been published since. The second part is a sixteen-volume retrospective index covering periodicals published from 1847 through 1985. It was published in four segments, each with four volumes. Supplemental retrospective volumes will be issued as material is located and indexed.

Scope. The goal of *PERSI* is to index all English-language and French-Canadian genealogical periodicals. The project indexes all periodicals of any genealogical value which the Allen County Public Library receives. These include major and minor genealogical periodicals, newsletters, and many state historical society publications. While the library encourages publishers to donate copies of their periodicals for indexing, not all cooperate. The library seeks periodicals which have not been donated and, if necessary, subscribes to them. This process makes *PERSI*'s coverage as comprehensive as possible. For the annual index volumes, *PERSI* includes all periodicals received in a calendar year (which may not match the date on the publication's masthead; many periodicals are published behind schedule). The exception was the 1986 (first) annual volume, which only included periodicals with a 1986 date. Periodicals with earlier dates were included in the retrospective part.

The list of sources indexed includes approximately 4,400 periodicals, but this is the total title list for the entire project, not for any one volume. The list includes a number of defunct titles that are indexed only in the retrospective part. Many periodicals have also changed names, and the various versions are listed separately. While it is not readily known how many titles are included in any particular annual *PERSI* volume, approximately 3,500 current titles are indexed in the 1996 volume, including many historical publications. Most foreign-language periodicals are not indexed, and the current indexing excludes surname and family-oriented periodicals as well. Also, while other indexes (described below) index a larger number of historical periodicals, *PERSI* includes many of the significant statewide scholarly history journals. For others, see *America: History and Life* (described below under "Indexes to History Periodicals").

PERSI is selective regarding what content is indexed for the various periodicals included. The staff seeks to index items which are deemed to be of permanent research value; therefore, they do not index society or genealogical news, membership lists, book reviews, queries, pedigree charts, or family group sheets which may have been printed.

The Allen County Public Library Foundation also publishes an excellent bibliography of periodicals: *Bibliography of Genealogy and Local History Periodicals with Union List of Major U.S. Collections* (described above under "Locating Genealogical Periodicals—Bibliographies"). It completely identifies the periodicals being indexed. It is a much more comprehensive listing of periodicals than *PERSI* because it includes titles not at the library, such as foreign titles found only at the Family History Library, as well as hundreds of family/surname publications.

Arrangement. *PERSI* has a column format, and each part (annual and retrospective) has five separate sections: U.S. places, Canadian places, foreign places, research methodology, and family records. Each part is arranged alphabetically by the place, surname, or type of record (research methodology section), followed by (in separate columns): the title of the article, journal abbreviation, volume number, issue number, month, and year (figure 19-13). In the three place sections, articles from common localities are further arranged under twenty-one different record types—cemetery, deed, military, tax, wills, etc. Articles that do not correspond to one of these types are listed as "other." In the U.S. places section, states are listed according to their two-letter postal abbreviations; thus, Iowa (IA) comes before Idaho (ID), Illinois (IL), and Indiana (IN), while Massachusetts (MA) comes before Maine (ME). The general U.S. section comes between Texas (TX) and Utah (UT). State listings are further arranged alphabetically by county; articles dealing with the entire state are listed before those for counties.

The journal abbreviation is always a four-letter code; the full names of the periodicals are listed in the appendix. The first two letters usually indicate the country or state which the publication covers. AM stands for America and CN for Canada, while postal codes are usually used for U.S. states. The second two letters usually represent the title of the periodical. The volume and number columns identify which issue of the publication the article appears in. Page numbers are not given. The month and year columns indicate the issue's date; the month column may include the season or quarter of the issue as well. Because the appendix lists only the names (and not the addresses) of the indexed periodicals, the *Bibliography of Genealogy and Local History Periodicals* (discussed above under "Locating Genealogical Periodicals—Bibliographies") must be consulted for more complete information, including names of publishers and their addresses.

To conserve space and to avoid duplicating information (such as the locality), *PERSI* often uses descriptive titles rather than the exact titles of the articles; because of this, and the lack of page numbers, the user must carefully check the periodical's table of contents, and, on occasion, leaf through the issue to find the article referred to in the index. Articles continued from one issue to another are listed separately and may not always carry the same title.

PERiodical Source Index
01/20/97 pg 99

STATE	COUNTY	RECORD TYPE	TITLE OF ARTICLE	JOURNAL	VOL	NUM	MON	YEAR
GA	Whitfield	Other	Prices at A.R. McDaniel's, 1933	GAWM	11	3	Jan	1992
GA	Whitfield	Other	T.M. Kirby-Lillie Blount marriage, 1872	GAWM	12	1	Jul	1992
GA	Whitfield	School	Dalton high school history	GAWM	14	4	Sum	1995
GA	Whitfield	School	Dalton schools in 1932	GAWM	10	2	Oct	1990
GA	Whitfield	School	Varnell school history	GAWM	15	2	Win	1996
GA	Whitfield	Tax	Tax receivers notice, 1919	GAWM	9	4	Apr	1990
GA	Wilkes	History	Robert Toombs house, Washington	AMUD	59	2	Feb	1996
GA	Wilkes	Military	Revolution/Militia, 1778	ALGA	5	5	Sep	1996
GA	Wilkes	Probate	Returns of administrations, 1810-17, B	FAPZ		1458	Sep	1996
GA	Wilkes	Vital Records	Marriages, 1791-1850 (sel.)	GASV	10	5	May	1996
GA	Wilkes	Vital Records	Marriages, 1791-1850, A-B	GASV			Mar	1996
GA	Wilkes	Vital Records	Marriages, 1791-1850, P-Z	GASV	10	7-8	Jul	1996
GA	Wilkes	Vital Records	Marriages, 1791-1850, index, C-H	GASV			Apr	1996
GA	Wilkinson	Other	Notes on Wilkinson co.	AMGO	10	5-6	Sep	1995
HI		Biography	Hawaiian lodge no. 21 of CA, Masons, 1859-80	HIKK			Apr	1996
HI		Biography	Historic Hawai'i honors preservationists, 1995	HIHH			Jun	1995
HI		Biography	New Englanders to Hawaii, E-L	AMUG	2	6	Nov	1993
HI		Biography	U.S. Consular despatches, 19th century	NGSQ	84	1	Mar	1996
HI		Church	Pan Pacific Federation in Young Buddhists, photo	AMWH	27	3	Aut	1996
HI		Court	Petition for Henry Sheldon, 1864	HIKK	5	6	Dec	1996
HI		History	Captian James Cook in Hawaiian Islands	PASQ			Nov	1996
HI		History	First to Hawaii-bird of paradise C-2, 1927	AMFB	18	4	Win	1995
HI		History	Hawaiian land titles and tenure, 1800s	HIJH	30			1996
HI		History	Honolulu culture and politics, 1890-1920	HIJH	30			1996
HI		History	Hula: genealogy in motion	AMHQ		63	May	1996
HI		History	Kauai as separate kingdom, 1810	HIJH	30			1996
HI		History	Land and soverignty history	AMAL	13	2	Sum	1996
HI		History	Marriage customs and laws in Hawaiian Kingdom	HIKK			Oct	1995

Figure 9-13. Entries from the *Periodical Source Index.*

PERSI has a separate methodology section which uses the twenty-one record type categories used in the locality sections as well as an "other" category. (Half or more of the articles are listed as "other.") In recent issues, the articles are sorted by key word within each record type. The methodology section only includes articles dealing with several states or no particular locality. Methodology articles dealing with specific countries, states, or counties are listed under those localities.

PERSI is available in book format at major genealogical libraries throughout North America. A microfiche version of the retrospective part and the first five annuals is available at North American LDS church family history centers (see the introduction to *Printed Sources*). In 1997, Ancestry published *PERSI* on CD-ROM for individual and institutional purchase. This version cumulates the four segments of the retrospective part, as well as all of the annual volumes to date, into one searchable source.

Genealogical Periodical Annual Index

Genealogical Periodical Annual Index (*GPAI*) was a privately compiled and printed index from its inception in 1962 (vol. 1) until it temporarily ceased after indexing the periodicals for 1969. Publication was restarted by Laird C. Towle of Heritage Books (1540-E Pointer Ridge Place, Bowie, MD 20716) with the index for 1974 (vol. 13). The volumes for 1970 to 1973 have not been published. Heritage Books has maintained this useful index since 1974. Each index covers the periodicals published and received during a year. As is common with efforts of its magnitude, *GPAI* sometimes lags a few years. As of late 1997, the most recent volume indexed 1992 periodicals. There is no retrospective cumulation.

Scope. *GPAI* is published for the genealogical community, and its publisher relies on the various periodical publishers to donate copies of their publications. The index has included a growing number of genealogical periodicals, beginning with seventy-eight in 1962 and now numbering approximately three hundred. Because *GPAI*'s focus has always been on the major genealogical periodicals, it does not include various historical publications. Furthermore, many small periodicals, especially those of small societies, have not participated. However, most key periodicals willingly donate issues for indexing.

The indexers aim to be comprehensive and include any material deemed to be of permanent value, such as published genealogies, Bible records, lineages, source transcripts, research methodology, and even reviews of genealogical books and computer software. In addition, *GPAI* indexes ancestor charts and family group records (sheets) under the major surnames. It does not index queries, news of societies, or other transient material, nor does it index reprinted material.

GPAI includes surname periodicals, but it simply identifies the periodical under the name of the subject family. In those entries, complete information about such periodicals is given:

LONGMIRE (continued)
Nancy Ann see William Edward BROWN
LOOK, surname periodical, Look...ing, Ruth Harrison Jones, 2816 Sloat Rd, Pebble Beach CA 93953
LOOMIS, Chester A f1825 NY, diary abstr of journey from NY to IL 1825 WCR 7:1:95
Elizabeth see Josias HULL
fam cem CT 1700s CTN 19:3:422
LOONEY, fam hist VA, bk rev BWG 15:2:155
LORCH, Wilhelm Georg Sr w Ana Maria ____, geneal, bk rev NFB 17:4:65
LORD, fam hist NJ, bk rev NYR 117:3:180
Stephen J b1827 w Martha Clay, GA, anc ch GGS 22:2:99
Theodore see Eliza Jane CARD
LORENTZEN, Hans Christian see Carolina HANSEN
LOSCH, Catherine see John Adam Joseph BINGENHEIMER
LOTHROP, John b1584 biog CTN 19:3:518

LOUISIANA (continued)
place name hist sketches KSL 7:1:7
successions 1840-1910 KSL 7:3:59
Calcasieu Parish, civil suits 1897-1910 KSL 7:4:83
Dequincy, Rigmaiden Cem KSL 9:4:88 10:1:16 10:2:44
hist sketch KSL 2:2:3
inquests 1910-1914 index KSL 8:3:68
Lake Charles, airplane accidents (fatal) at Gerstner Field 1917-1919 KSL 4:4:62
Lake Charles, census (vet) 1890 KSL 4:1:2
Lake Charles, Corporation Cem KSL 6:3:29
Lake Charles, Epis Ch of the Good Shepherd births & bapt 1880s-1900s KSL 2:3:6 2:4:10 KSL 3:2:5 3:3:14 3:4:10
Lake Charles, Epis Ch of the Good Shepherd deaths 1887-1914 KSL 6:1:13 6:3:35
Lake Charles, Epis Ch of the Good Shepherd marr 1887-1914

Figure 19-14. Entries from the *Genealogical Periodical Annual Index.*

Table 19-3. Common Title Abbreviations for Popular Genealogical Periodicals

Title of Periodical	*Traditional*	GPAI	PERSI
Pennsylvania Genealogical Magazine	*PGM*	*PA*	*PSGM*
Mayflower Descendant	*MD*	*TMD*	*MYFD*
The Genealogist	*TG*	*TG*	*GNYY*
New England Historical and Genealogical Register	*NEHGR*	*NER*	*NEHG*
American Genealogist	*TAG*	*AG*	*AMGN*
New York Genealogical and Biographical Record	*NYGBR*	*NYR*	*NYGB*
Genealogical Magazine of New Jersey	*GMNJ*	*GMN*	*NJGM*
Virginia Genealogist	*VG*	*VAG*	*VAGN*
Genealogical Journal	*GJ*	*GJ*	*UTGJ*
Everton's Genealogical Helper	*GH*	*GH*	*GNHR*
Heritage Quest	*HQ*	*HQ*	*AMHQ*
National Genealogical Society Quarterly	*NGSQ*	*NGS*	*NGSQ*
Detroit Society for Genealogical Research Magazine	*DSGRM*	*DM*	*DSGR*
APG Quarterly	*APGQ*	*APG*	*AMPG*
Genealogical Magazine of New Jersey	*GMNJ*	*GMN*	*NJGM*
North Carolina Genealogical Society Journal	*NCGSJ*	*NCJ*	*NCGJ*
Kentucky Historical Society Register	*KHSR*	*REG*	*KYHR*

name, editor, address, and, if applicable, the original ancestor(s) whom the periodical traces.

Arrangement. *GPAI* uses a paragraph format for its citations. The subject, state, or surname is given in uppercase letters, followed by more specific information, such as the title of the article, county or town, or given name and dates. The abbreviation of the source then follows, with the volume, issue number, and starting page number. All entries in *GPAI* are listed in one alphabetical sequence (figure 19-14). *GPAI* includes all citations to continued articles (within the issues indexed) in one index entry.

The index includes hundreds of citations under "Methodology" in the index; within this section, the citations are arranged by key word (sometimes by more than one key word). In addition, many other subjects are found throughout *GPAI,* such as "French-Canadian Genealogy," "Mennonite," and "Revolutionary War." Unfortunately, there is no thesaurus (subject list) for the user, who does not know which term to look under (such as heraldry, royalty, nobility, etc.) for information.

All of the indexed periodicals are listed in the front of the index according to their abbreviation codes. The list includes the complete address for each periodical's publisher and identifies which issues are included in that index. Note that the *GPAI* periodical abbreviations (codes) are different from the *PERSI* codes, and both are different from the traditional periodical abbreviations used in genealogical literature (table 19-3).

PERSI has eclipsed *GPAI* to a significant degree, but there are still some reasons to use *GPAI* in family history research. First, because of its thirty-year history and its inexpensive price, it is found in many genealogical libraries, including smaller ones whose budgets do not allow them to acquire *PERSI.* Second, *GPAI* provides page numbers for the articles cited, making them easier to find. Finally, the periodicals indexed in *GPAI* are more likely to be available at a wide number of research libraries; many of the periodicals indexed in *PERSI* have a very limited circulation and may be difficult to locate.

Despite the strengths and value of the two major current indexes, it is important to be aware of some earlier genealogical indexes. In addition, some other indexes exist which provide access to periodicals not covered by the standard genealogical indexes.

Table 19-4. Some Major Periodicals Included in Jacobus's *Index to Genealogical Periodicals*

		Volumes and Years Indexed		
Title Code	*Journal*	*Vol. 1 (1936)*	*Vol. 2 (1949)*	*Vol. 3 (1953)*
A1	*New England Historical and Genealogical Register*	51-85, 1897–1931	86-100, 1932–46	101-106, 1947–52
A2	*New York Genealogical and Biographical Record*	1-62, 1870–1931	63-77, 1932–46	78-83, 1947–52
B1	*Genealogical Magazine of New Jersey*	1-6, 1925–31	7-20, 1931–45	21-25, 1946–50
B2	*Nebraska and Midwest Genealogical Records*	1-9, 1923–31	10-18, 1932–43	
B3	*Connecticut Magazine*	1-12, 1895–1908		
B4	*The American Genealogist*	1-8, 1923–32	9-23, 1932–47	24-28, 1948–52
Dt	*Detroit Society for Genealogical Research Magazine*		2-10, 1938–47	10-16, 1947–52
E	*"Old Northwest" Genealogical Quarterly*	1-15, 1885–95		
J	*South Carolina Historical and Genealogical Magazine*	1-30, 1900–29	31-47, 1930–46	48-53, 1947–52
M	*National Genealogical Society Quarterly*	1-19, 1912–31	20-34, 1932–46	35-40, 1947–52
P	*Genealogical Society of Pennsylvania Publications* (later *Pennsylvania Genealogical Magazine*)	1-11, 1895–1931	11-1, 1932–45	15-19, 1947–52
Q1	*Pennsylvania Magazine of History and Biography*	1-54, 1877–1930	55-63, 1931–39	
U	*Utah Genealogical and Historical Magazine*	1-22, 1910–31	23-30, 1932–39	
V1	*Tyler's Quarterly*	1-12, 1919–31	13-28, 1931–47	29-32, 1947–51
V3	*Virginia Magazine of History and Biography*		40-53, 1932–46	55-60, 1947–52
X	*Maryland Genealogical Bulletin*	1-2, 1930–31	3-17, 1932–46	18-21, 1947–51
Y1	*Collections of the Essex Institute*	51-67, 1915–31	68-82, 1932–46	83-88, 1947–52
Z	*DAR Magazine*	1-64, 1892–1930 (in part)	68-82, 1932–46	

Jacobus's Indexes

From 1932 to 1953, Donald Lines Jacobus published his well-known *Index to Genealogical Periodicals* in three volumes (1932, 1948, and 1953). These were reprinted in 1973 and 1978 in one volume by the Genealogical Publishing Company. The indexes were divided into sections: name, place, family and Bible records, revolutionary war records, pensions, topic, and, in vol. 3, "My Own Index," a selective index of families in certain pedigree and ancestral books that treated New England or Long Island. Jacobus indexed more than sixty periodicals in vol. 1 and fewer in vols. 2 and 3, covering the years 1870 to 1952.

Jacobus's indexes were the first true indexes to genealogical periodicals. He included most major periodicals of the time period, including those that might be considered as only of historical interest today. However, he overlooked some periodicals of clearly local interest.

The *Index to Genealogical Periodicals* was also the first periodical index to assign a code to each periodical for use in the index entries. Thus, A1 stands for the *New England Historical and Genealogical Register* and is followed by the volume and page number of the article being cited. A version of this system has been used in most subsequent periodical indexes. The numerous sections in Jacobus's three volumes can be cumbersome to search, yielding eleven separate indexes. Table 19-4 shows the major periodicals Jacobus indexed, indicating which volumes in the periodicals are found in which of his indexes and giving his code for each periodical.

To consult so many indexes was rather bewildering if one wanted to find something quickly. Thirty years later Carl Boyer, 3rd, took the material from Jacobus's *Index to Genealogical Periodicals* and rearranged it in one volume with three sections: name, place, and topic. Published as *Donald Lines Jacobus's Index to Genealogical Periodicals,* rev. ed. (Newhall, Calif.: Boyer Publications, 1983), Boyer's revision is a complete reworking of Jacobus's indexes. Not only are they combined in one volume, but the typeface is larger and easier to read. In addition, Boyer used different periodical abbreviations, most of which are the standard abbreviations, making it easier for the user to determine the name of the periodical. Neither version provides every-name indexes; rather, like almost all such indexes, the approximately twenty thousand references refer only to the main subjects of the articles.

Indexes to History Periodicals

While the indexes described above are the most helpful for finding genealogical material in genealogical periodicals, numerous other indexes provide access to the often-untapped literature in historical journals. On a nationwide basis, *America: History and Life, a Guide to Periodical Literature* (Santa Barbara, Calif.: ABC-Clio, annual) is recognized as the premier index to periodical literature dealing with Canadian and U.S. history, including many genealogical journals. It began in 1964 and includes abstracts of the articles to help determine their usefulness in a specific context. It also indexes dissertations and book reviews, making it the most comprehensive tool for accessing current historical literature. *America: History and Life* is available at major academic research libraries in book and CD-ROM formats and is also available online through vendors like DIALOG (http://www.krinfo.com).

Writings on American History (Washington, D.C.: American Historical Association) is an annual bibliography of articles and books (until 1973) about American history dating from 1902 to 1990 (with a gap from 1941 to 1947), with a cumulative index from 1902 to 1940. For a fuller discussion of both of these indexes, see chapter 17, "County and Local Histories."

Combined Retrospective Index to Journals in History, 1838–1974 (CRIS/History), is part of a comprehensive effort to index earlier social science literature in three fields: sociology, political science, and history. Originally compiled by Carrollton Press (Washington, D.C.), it is now distributed by Research Publications (Woodbridge, Connecticut). The three indexes are collectively called the Combined Retrospective Index Sets—hence CRIS. Each of them is arranged first by subject, then by key word. Separate volumes provide an author index. The history index is international in scope, indexing more than 150,000 articles from the earliest issues through the 1974 volumes of 243 English-language periodicals. It is arranged by 342 subject categories in nine volumes. The subjects include various countries, with the major countries being subdivided into time periods and topics, such as religion or military. Of greatest interest to family historians are the countries and areas having the subdivision of "Biography and Genealogy." These include, among others, Africa, Canada, England and Wales, Europe, France, Ireland, Italy, Germany, Russia, Scotland, and the United States.

Vols. 1 through 4 cover "World History Subject Categories," while 5 through 9 cover U.S. categories. The "Biography and Genealogy" category for the U.S. consists of more than three hundred pages in vol. 6, with more than twenty-six thousand entries listing persons appearing in the titles of journal articles. (Presidents are treated separately in vol. 9.) The index is arranged in columns, with the key words (within each subject category) on the left, followed by the reference title, author, year, volume, journal code, and page (figure 19-15). The journal code is a three-digit number that refers to the list of history journals printed at the beginning of the index.

Worth noting is the fact that a check of eighty-six North American journals indexed in CRIS/History showed that only forty-six were also indexed in *PERSI*. Furthermore, eighteen were not even listed in *Bibliography of Genealogy and Local History Periodicals,* the companion to *PERSI*. Of titles dealing with foreign areas, *PERSI* indexes only a few, so the overlap is minimal. Thus, CRIS/History is an excellent source for articles dealing with individuals and families not in the standard genealogical periodicals. Unfortunately, articles about specific localities, such as towns and counties, are not easy to find in CRIS/History. States are listed alphabetically as subject categories in vol. 9, where some localities appear as keywords.

CRIS/History is not in most genealogical libraries, nor are the other history indexes discussed here. Seek them at major college and university libraries, especially those with significant history departments.

An often overlooked index is the *Bibliography of American Historical Societies: Annual Report of the American Historical Association for the Year 1905,* 2nd ed., rev. and enl. (1907; reprint; Detroit: Gale Research, 1966). At the time this bibliography was published (1905), most genealogical information was being published in historical periodicals issued by historical societies. The 1905 report contains a bibliography of all publications of U.S. historical associations and includes tables of contents for every issue. The two-volume report is well indexed; if a family name or geographic location appears in the title of an article, the index will lead the researcher to the publication and issue with that article.

Biographical information on many individuals is found in historical and other non-genealogical periodicals as well as in genealogical magazines. These are well indexed in *Biography Index* (discussed in chapter 18, "Biographies").

Waldenmaier's Indexes

After Jacobus's indexes, the next attempt to index genealogical articles was by Inez Waldenmaier, whose *Genealogical Newsletter and Research Aids* (Washington, D.C.: the compiler, 1955–63) and *Annual Index to Genealogical Periodicals and Family Histories* (published as part of the former) cover the years 1956 to 1962.

Probably the most overlooked general genealogical indexes, these indexes include more than eleven thousand entries for works published over an eight-year period. This set of indexes had a rather inauspicious beginning as part of the editor's *Genealogical Newsletter and Research Aids.* In fact, vol. 1 of the index does not refer to any genealogical periodicals at all. Waldenmaier began her index by listing newly published local (chiefly county) histories and published (compiled) genealogies of families. In 1956, the first volume included approximately 285 references to books published in 1955. Newly published books were included through all eight volumes. The second year, however, Waldenmaier expanded her index by including articles of a local history (including local records) or compiled genealogy nature published in eight major genealogical periodicals.

Waldenmaier's indexes were always published as part of her newsletter. They have separate alphabetical sequences for the county histories and the genealogies. Often they contain separate surname indexes to published Bible records. The county histories and records section is arranged alphabetically by state and county; the genealogy section is often only an alphabetical surname index (Waldenmaier only indexed these two major types of articles).

The number of periodicals Waldenmaier indexed climbed rather steadily (with a slight drop in vol. 6, 1960), from 22 in vol. 3 (1956–57) to 61 in vol. 7 to 111 in vol. 8, covering 1962 publications. After the first few volumes she began titling the index portion of her newsletter *Annual Index to Genealogical Periodicals and Family Histories.* Some libraries have bound the index pages of the newsletter under that title, while others kept it as part of the newsletter; search for it under both titles. It has never been reprinted and is fairly rare, so it is generally found only in larger libraries.

Parts of vol. 9 were published, but they appear to repeat many of the citations in vol. 8. Perhaps the appearance of the more thorough *GPAI* in 1963 contributed to this index's demise.

Other Indexes

Before the 1920s there were relatively few periodicals with genealogical information. Indexes to these periodicals generally also index many other types of literature, such as compiled genealogies and local histories. Most of these sources are discussed in greater detail elsewhere in this book—notably chapter 16, "Family Histories and Genealogies." The earliest indexes were published in the nineteenth century by Joel Munsell Publishers. That company published several editions of what is known as *Index to American Genealogies (and to Genealogical Material Contained in all Works Such as Town Histories, County Histories, Local Histories . . . and Kindred Works (Known as Munsell's Index)* (reprint; Baltimore: Genealogical Publishing Co., 1967), which culminated in a fifth edition published in 1900. The fifth edition's fifty-five thou-

UNITED STATES BIOGRAPHY AND GENEALOGY

Excludes Presidents (See Volume IX).

See Also Names Sorted as Keywords Under Subject Categories.

KEYWORD		REFERENCE TITLE	AUTHOR	YEAR	VOLUME	JOUR	PAGE
HERRICK	(CONT)	MYRON T HERRICK	EO RANDALL	1913	22	412	470
		ROBERT HERRICK & RACE QUEST	LM SIMMS JR	1971	39	398	34
HERRING		FISHER HERRING GARRARD COUNTY		1917	15	472	68
		JAMES HERRING SCHOOLMASTER 1810		1954	72	384	9
HERRMAN		AUGUSTINE HERRMAN	G COPE	1891	15	440	321
HERRON		GEN F J HERRON		1867	5	15	801
		GEORGE D HERRON		1914	2	394	733
		FRANCIS JAY HERRON	G CARLSON	1930	11	436	141
		GEORGE D HERRON	RT HANDY	1950	19	89	91
		PROFESSOR GEORGE D HERRON IOWA COLLEGE	HR DIETERICH	1964	37	15	401
		GEORGE D HERRON 1890 PROGRESVS	RM CRUNDEN	1973	42	15	81
HERSEY		•JOHN HERSEY & AM CONSCIENCE		1974	43	435	24
HERSHEY		BEN HERSHEY LUMBER BARON	JJ FISHBURN	1947	28	436	289
HERTZOG		JOSEPH HERTZOG EARLY PHILA MERCHANT		1940	14	46	65
HERZ		HENRI HERZ PHILA	HB HILL, ETAL	1958	25	439	58
HESS		JOHN W HESS		1931	4	544	47
HESSELIUS		GUSTAVUS HESSELIUS ORGAN BUILDER		1905	29	440	129
		HESSELIUS FAMILY 1737-1820		1926	21	353	277
HESSELTINE		WILLIAM BEST HESSELTINE		1964	47	591	170
HESTER		GEORGE KNIGHT HESTER	GK HESTER	1926	22	232	131
		ELIZABETH FULTON HESTER	EM BOSTIC	1928	6	76	449
HESTON		THOMAS HESTON	AM HESTON	1899	3	384	106
		•ZEBULON HESTON		1922	11	456	21
		•SMITH HESTON		1924	13	456	54
HETH		HENRY HETH	JL MORRISON JR	1962	8	77	5
		HENRY HETH	JL MORRISON JR	1962	8	77	300
		HARRY HETH HARD LUCK GEN CIVIL-WAR	WW HASSLER	1966	5	78	13
HEUSLER		BASIL HEUSLER		1943	20	231	62
HEUSTON		EDMOND TAYLOR HEUSTON	RL WILLIAMS	1945	23	76	416
HEWAT		ALEXANDER HEWAT	ED JOHNSON	1954	20	276	50
HEWES		JOHN PAUL JONES LETTER JOSEPH HEWES		1906	13	565	87
		HEWES ELIHU		1920	53	364	25
		JOSEPH HEWES	AJ MCCURRY	1963	40	389	455
HEWETT		EDGAR LEE HEWETT		1947	22	385	190
		EDGAR LEE HEWETT	RC EULER	1963	5	19	287
HEWIT		AUGUSTINE F HEWIT	JP MARSCHALL	1969	38	89	88

Figure 19-15. Entries from *Combined Retrospective Index to Journals in History, 1838–1974.*

sand entries include every reference in the earlier indexes, making it unnecessary to search earlier editions.

This surname index refers to articles about families published in more than twenty periodicals and newspapers as well as hundreds of local and family histories. A supplement published in 1908 covered publications since 1900. The fifth edition has been reprinted several times with the 1908 supplement included. As a surname index, *Index to American Genealogies* does not include articles oriented to localities, and only the major surname in each article is indexed. A companion volume identifies 1,400 articles about families (not localities) published before 1900: *List of Titles of Genealogical Articles in American Periodicals and Kindred Works* (Albany, N.Y.: Joel Munsell's Sons, 1899). A complementary work identifying published records by localities is Appleton Prentiss Clark Griffin's *Index of the Literature of American Local History in Collections Published in 1890–95* (Boston: Carl H. Heintzemann, 1896).

There are some other helpful indexes for earlier publications. Be sure to check the *Genealogical Index of the Newberry Library,* 4 vols. (Boston: G. K. Hall, 1960), which has more than half a million entries from pre-1918 works (described in chapter 16). *The Greenlaw Index of the New England Historic Genealogical Society,* 2 vols. (Boston: G. K. Hall, 1979), includes references to compiled genealogies in several significant periodicals covering the Northeast (also described in chapter 16). *Cumulated Magazine Subject Index, 1907–1949,* 2 vols. (Boston: G. K. Hall, 1964), indexes many important periodicals, including some significant defunct and ongoing genealogical titles. It is a cumulated edition of *Annual Magazine Subject Index,* and, although it is a general magazine index, many of its 253,000 entries are genealogical references.

Another national index of note is Kip Sperry's *Index to Genealogical Periodical Literature, 1960–1977* (Detroit: Gale Research, 1979). This index does not index surname articles, compiled genealogies, or local records and history; rather, it focuses on methodological articles that appeared in major genealogical journals during the period indicated in its title. This focus can be very helpful for information on how to use a specific source or the content of a record. Sperry's index provides access to a vast body of often untapped material of tremendous instructional value.

Statewide Indexes

A growing number of indexes are now available that index several periodicals for a single state. Their formats are usually similar to *GPAI, PERSI,* or Jacobus' indexes. They focus on articles about places and families of specific states and usually cover a handful of specific periodicals. Often they index periodicals in greater depth than do nationwide indexes, so they should be searched even if the same periodicals are included in other indexes. They are also cumulative—several years of issues are in one index. Presently such statewide indexes are available for Arizona, Connecticut, Georgia, Kentucky, Michigan, Minnesota, Missouri, Ohio, Texas, and Virginia. These are listed in the chapter bibliography.

Statewide biographical indexes are available for more than thirty states, and many of these include information from periodicals. They are discussed in detail in chapter 18, "Biographies."

CONCLUSION

Genealogical periodicals are too often overlooked by researchers. The increasing number of such sources publishing more and more compiled genealogies and original sources makes it important to learn how to find and use these "miniature libraries" of local and topical information. Fortunately, several new bibliographies, directories, and indexes make it easier than ever before to locate the ancestral information in these publications.

Instructional and reference articles are also common in genealogical periodicals. These will help any researcher learn about new sources, repositories, and techniques to make the search for family history more rewarding. All that remains is to take the time to consult these excellent sources.

NOTES

1. The books consulted were the American Society of Genealogists' *Genealogical Research: Methods and Sources,* vol. 1, rev. ed., edited by Milton Rubincam (Washington, D.C.: American Society of Genealogists, 1980); Val D. Greenwood's *Researcher's Guide to American Genealogy,* 2nd ed. (Baltimore: Genealogical Publishing Co., 1990); Archibald F. Bennett's *Guide for Genealogical Research* (Salt Lake City: Genealogical Society of The Church of Jesus Christ of Latter-day Saints, 1951); Bennett's *Finding Your Forefathers in America* (Salt Lake City: Bookcraft Co., 1957); Bennett's *Advanced Genealogical Research* (Salt Lake City: Bookcraft Co., 1959); E. Kay Kirkham's *The ABC's of Genealogical Research* (Salt Lake City: Deseret Book, 1955); Kirkham's *Simplified Genealogy for Americans* (Salt Lake City: Deseret Book, 1968); Laureen Richardson Jaussi and Gloria Duncan Chaston's *Fundamentals of Genealogical Research* (Salt Lake City: Deseret Book, 1972); Gilbert H. Doane and James B. Bell's *Searching for Your Ancestors: The How and Why of Genealogy,* 6th ed. (Minneapolis: University of Minnesota Press, 1992); F. Wilbur Helmbold's *Tracing Your Ancestry* (Birmingham, Ala.: Oxmoor House, 1976); Bill R. Linder's *How To Trace Your Family History* (New York: Everest House Publishers, 1978); Yaffa Draznin's *Family Historian's Handbook* (New York: Jove Publications, 1978); Harriet Stryker-Rodda's *How To Climb Your Family Tree: Genealogy for Beginners* (Philadelphia and New York: J. B. Lippincott Co., 1977); Noel C. Stevenson's *Genealogical Evidence: A Guide to Standards of Proof Relating to Pedigrees, Ancestry, Heirship and Family History* (Laguna Hills, Calif.: Argean Press, 1979); Ethel W. Williams's *Know Your Ancestors: A Guide for Genealogical Research* (Rutland, Vt.: Charles E. Tuttle Co., 1969); George Olin Zabriskie's *Climbing Your Family Tree Systematically* (Salt Lake City: Parliament Press, 1969); Timothy Field Beard, with Denise Demong, *How To Find Your Family Roots* (New York: McGraw-Hill Book Co., 1977); Norman E. Wright's *Preserving Your American Heritage* (Provo, Utah: Brigham Young University Press, 1981); Eugene A. Stratton's *Applied Genealogy* (Salt Lake City: Ancestry, 1988); Vincent L. Jones, Arlene H. Eakle, and Mildred H. Christensen's *Family History for Fun and Profit* (Salt Lake City: Genealogical Institute, 1972); George K. Schweitzer's *Handbook of Genealogical Sources* (Knoxville, Tenn.: the author, 1991); G. G. Vandagriff's *Voices in Your Blood* (Kansas City: Andrews and McMeel, 1993); Ira Wolfman's *Do People Grow on Family Trees?* (New York: Workman Publishing, 1991); Desmond Walls Allen and Carolyn Earle Billingsley's *Beginner's Guide to Family History Research,* rev. ed. (Bryant, Ark.: Research Associates, 1991); Ralph Crandall's *Shaking Your Family Tree* (Camden, Maine: Yankee Books, 1986); Emily Anne Croom's *Unpuzzling Your Past* (Cincinnati: Betterway Books, 1983); Emily Anne Croom's *Genealogist's Companion and Sourcebook* (Cincinnati: Betterway Books, 1994); and John and Carolyn Cosgriff's *Turbo Genealogy: An Introduction to Family History Research in the Information Age* (Salt Lake City: Ancestry, 1997).

   Most of these books do not discuss genealogical periodicals at all; most of those that do provide only one to three pages on the subject, sometimes including an all-too-short list of some periodicals. Two notable exceptions are Stratton's (1988) excellent chapter on the "Scholarly Journals" and Croom's (1994) introduction to academic journals and their indexes.

2. There is a distinction between cemetery records and inscriptions, although many people write about them as if they were the same. The tombstone inscriptions in a cemetery lot may not represent all of the people in a lot. It is always advisable to consult the record book in the cemetery office to get a complete list of persons buried in a lot.

3. Thanks to the late Milton Rubincam, who provided much of the original text for this section.

4. Although this work gives a rather glowing account of the *Register,* the noted genealogist H. Minot Pitman, in his article "The Progress of Genealogical Literature in America," *NGS Quarterly* 50 (6) (March 1962), points out that there was little improvement in it by 1861, and that its present importance did not begin until 1911. Another early periodical, the *New York Genealogical and Biographical Record,* was also slow in its development.

REFERENCE LIST

Beard, Timothy Field, with Denise Demong. 1977. *How To Find Your Family Roots.* New York: McGraw-Hill Book Co.

Cappon, Lester J. 1964. *American Genealogical Periodicals: A Bibliography with a Chronological Finding List.* New York: New York Public Library.

Colket, Meredith B., Jr. 1968. "Creating a Worthwhile Family Genealogy." *National Genealogical Society Quarterly* 56 (4): 243–62 (December).

Hill, William Carroll. 1945. *A Century of Genealogical Progress.* Boston: New England Historic Genealogical Society.

Jacobus, Donald Lines. 1956. "The Function of a Genealogical Periodical." *New England Historical and Genealogical Register* (January 1956).

Jones, Vincent L., Arlene H. Eakle, and Mildred H. Christensen. 1972. *Family History for Fun and Profit.* Salt Lake City: Genealogical Institute.

BIBLIOGRAPHY

Current periodicals cited in this bibliography include the most recent known address. Defunct periodicals include only the editor, city, and dates of publication.

Bibliographies, Directories, and Guides

Also see "Indexes," below.

Boehm, Eric H., Barbara H. Pope, and Marie S. Ensign. *Historical Periodicals Directory.* 5 vols. Santa Barbara, Calif.: ABC-Clio, 1981.

Cappon, Lester J. *American Genealogical Periodicals: A Bibliography with a Chronological Finding List.* New York: New York Public Library, 1964.

Carmack, Sharon DeBartolo. "Genealogical Writer's Market. *Association of Professional Genealogists Quarterly* 8 (3): 61–63 (September 1993); 8 (4): 93–94 (December 1993; 9 (1): 15–17 (March 1994).

Carson, Dina C., ed. *Directory of Genealogical and Historical Publications in the U.S. and Canada.* Niwot, Colo.: Iron Gate Publishing, 1992.

_____, ed. *Directory of Genealogical and Historical Societies in the U.S. and Canada.* Niwot, Colo.: Iron Gate Publishing, 1992.

Clegg, Michael Barren. *Bibliography of Genealogy and Local History Periodicals with Union List of Major U.S. Collections.* Fort Wayne, Ind.: Allen County Public Library Foundation, 1990.

"Directory of Locality Periodicals." *Everton's Genealogical Helper.* January-February (annual). Logan, Utah: Everton Publishers.

"Directory of Surname Periodicals." *Everton's Genealogical Helper.* March-April (annual). Logan, Utah: Everton Publishers.

Fyfe, Janet. *History Journals and Serials: An Analytical Guide.* Westport, Conn.: Greenwood Press, 1986.

Green, David L. "Scholarly Genealogical Journals in America, Parts One and Two." *American Genealogist* 61 (July-October 1985): 116–20; 63 (July 1988): 138–44.

Konrad, J. *A Directory of Genealogical Periodicals.* 4th ed. Munroe Falls, Ohio: Summit Publications, 1981.

Meyer, Mary K., ed. *Meyer's Directory of Genealogical Societies in the USA and Canada.* 11th ed. Mt. Airy, Md.: the editor, 1996.

New Serials Titles: A Union List of Serials Commencing Publication after December 31, 1949. Washington, D.C.: Library of Congress, 1953– , and supplements.

Directory of Historical Organizations in the United States and Canada. 14th ed. Nashville, Tenn.: American Association for State and Local History, 1990.

Sperry, Kip. *A Survey of American Genealogical Periodicals and Periodical Indexes.* Gale Genealogy and Local History Series, vol. 3. Detroit: Gale Research, 1978.

The Standard Periodical Directory. Annual. New York: Oxbridge Communications, 1978–.

Towle, Laird C. *Genealogical Periodicals: A Neglected Treasure.* Bowie, Md.: Heritage Books, 1982.

Townsend, Mrs. Charles D., and Donald Lines Jacobus. "Current Genealogical Periodicals." *American Genealogist* 38 (April 1962): 118–28; 39 (February 1963): 61–64.

Ulrich's International Periodicals Directory. Annual. New York: R. R. Bowker Co., 1932–.

Union List of Serials in Libraries of the United States and Canada. Edited by Edna Brown Titus. 3rd ed. 5 vols. New York: H. W. Wilson Co., 1965.

Surname Periodical Directories

Bentley, Elizabeth Petty. *Directory of Family Associations.* 3rd ed. Baltimore: Genealogical Publishing Co., 1996.

"Family Associations and Their Leaders." *Everton's Genealogical Helper.* March-April (annual). Logan, Utah: Everton Publishers.

"Family Periodical Publications." *Everton's Genealogical Helper.* March-April (annual). Logan, Utah: Everton Publishers.

Ganier, Merle. *Family Periodicals and Reunions.* Fort Worth, Tex.: the author, 1995.

Konrad, J., ed. *A Directory of "One Name" Family Periodicals.* Munroe Falls, Ohio: Summit Publications, 1983.

Maerz, C. M. *The Guide to Family Associations and Newsletters (Past and Present).* Bloomington, Minn.: the compiler, 1996.

McCay, Betty L., comp. *Family Surname Publications.* Indianapolis: Ye Olde Genealogie Shoppe, 1975.

Nationwide Indexes

America: History and Life, a Guide to Periodical Literature. Annual. Santa Barbara, Calif.: ABC-Clio, 1964–.

Biography Index. Annual. New York: H. W. Wilson, 1947– .

Boyer, Carl, 3rd. *Donald Lines Jacobus's Index to Genealogical Periodicals.* Rev. ed. Newhall, Calif.: Boyer Publications, 1983.

Combined Retrospective Index to Journals in History, 1838–1974. 11 vols. Washington, D.C.: Carrollton Press, 1977–78.

Cumulated Magazine Subject Index, 1907–1949. 2 vols. Boston: G. K. Hall, 1964.

Genealogical Periodical Annual Index (GPAI). Annual. Bowie, Md.: Heritage Books, 1962–. An annual index of more than 250 currently published periodicals.

The Greenlaw Index of the New England Historic Genealogical Society. 2 vols. Boston: G. K. Hall, 1979.

Griffin, Appleton Prentis Clark. *Bibliography of American Historical Societies: Annual Report of the American Historical Association for the Year 1905.* Vol. 2. 2nd ed., rev. and enl. 1907. Reprint. Detroit: Gale Research, 1966.

_____. *Index of the Literature of American Local History in Collections Published in 1890–95.* Boston: Carl H. Heintzemann, 1896.

Index to American Genealogies and to Genealogical Material Contained in all Works Such as Town Histories, County Histories, Local Histories . . . and Kindred Works (Known as Munsell's Index). 1900. Reprint. Baltimore: Genealogical Publishing Co., 1967.

Index to Writings on American History, 1902–1940. Washington, D.C.: American Historical Association, 1956.

List of Titles of Genealogical Articles in American Periodicals and Kindred Works. Albany, N.Y.: Joel Munsell's Sons, 1899.

Jacobus, Donald Lines. *Index to Genealogical Periodicals.* 3 vols. 1932, 1948, 1953. Reprint. 3 vols. in 1. Baltimore: Genealogical Publishing Co., 1973, 1978. Revised by Boyer; see above.

Periodical Source Index (PERSI). Annual. Fort Wayne, Ind.: Allen County Public Library Foundation, 1987–. This index includes a retrospective series for pre-1986 articles, as well as annual volumes since 1986.

Sperry, Kip. *Index to Genealogical Periodical Literature, 1960–1977*. Gale Genealogy and Local History Series, vol. 9. Detroit.: Gale Research, 1979.

Waldenmaier, Inez. *Annual Index to Genealogical Periodicals and Family Histories*. Published as part of *Genealogical Newsletter and Research Aids*. 9 vols. Washington, D.C.: the compiler, 1955–63.

Writings on American History. Annual. Washington, D.C.: American Historical Association, 1902–. Indexes books and periodical articles through 1973—periodicals only since 1973.

Statewide Indexes to Genealogical Periodicals

University of Arizona Library. *The Arizona Index: A Subject Index to Periodical Articles About the State*. 2 microfilms. Boston: G. K. Hall, 1978.

The *Connecticut Periodical Index* and a collection of more than two hundred periodicals are at the Pequot Library, 720 Pequot Avenue, Southport, CT 06490.

Bell, Carol Willsey. *Ohio Genealogical Periodical Index: A County Guide*. 4th ed. Youngstown, Ohio: the compiler, 1983.

Buckway, G. Eileen. *Index to Texas Periodicals*. Salt Lake City: Family History Library, 1987.

Finnell, Arthur Louis. *Minnesota Genealogical Periodical Index*. Marshall, Minn.: Finnell Richter and Association, 1980.

"Georgia Genealogy in [year]: A Bibliography." Appears regularly in *Georgia Genealogical Society Quarterly*.

Grover, Robert L. *Missouri Genealogical Periodical Index: A County Guide, 1960–1982*. Independence: Missouri Territory Pioneers, 1983.

Quigley, Maud. *Index to Family Names in Genealogical Periodicals*. Grand Rapids: Western Michigan Genealogical Society, 1981.

_____. *Index to Hard-to-Find Information in Genealogical Periodicals*. Grand Rapids: Western Michigan Genealogical Society, 1981.

_____. *Index to Michigan Research Found in Genealogical Periodicals*. Grand Rapids: Western Michigan Genealogical Society, 1979.

Swem, Earl Gregg. *Virginia Historical Index*. 2 vols. in 4. 1934–36. Reprint. Gloucester, Mass.: Peter Smith, 1965.

Trapp, Glenda K., and Michael L. Cook. *Kentucky Genealogical Index*. Evansville, Ind.: Cook Publications, 1985.

General Interest Magazines

American Genealogy Magazine. 1986–. Published by Datatrace Systems, P.O. Box 1587, Stephenville, Texas 76041.

Ancestry. 1994–. Published by Ancestry Incorporated, P.O. Box 476, Salt Lake City, UT 84110.

Everton's Genealogical Helper. 1947–. Published by The Everton Publishers, P.O. Box 368, Logan, UT 84323.

Family Chronicles. 1996–. Published by Moorshead Magazines, 10 Gateway Boulevard, Suite 490, North York, Ontario, Canada, M3C 3T4.

The Family Tree. 1991–. Published by the Odom Genealogy Library, P.O. Box 1110, Moultrie, GA 31776.

Genealogy Bulletin. 1989–. Published by AGLL, Inc., P.O. Box 329, Bountiful, UT 84011.

Heritage Quest: The Genealogy Magazine. 1985–. Published by AGLL, Inc., P.O. Box 329, Bountiful, Utah 84011.

Canadian Periodicals

The British Columbia Genealogist. 1971–. Published by the British Columbia Genealogical Society, P.O. Box 94731, Vancouver, British Columbia, Canada V67 2A8.

Canadian Genealogist. 1979–. Published by George and Elizabeth Hancocks, 172 King Henry's Boulevard, Aigincourt, Ontario, Canada M1T 2V6.

Families. 1961–. Published by the Ontario Genealogical Society, Box 66 Station Q, Toronto, Ontario, Canada M4T 2L7.

Generations. 1976–. Published by the Manitoba Genealogical Society, P.O. Box 2066, Winnipeg, Manitoba, Canada R3C 3R4.

Lost in Canada. 1975–94. Published by Joy Reisinger, 1020 Central Avenue, Sparta, WI 54656.

Nova Scotia Genealogist. 1983–. Published by the Genealogical Association of Nova Scotia, P.O. Box 641, Sta. M., Halifax, NS B3J 2T3.

Relatively Speaking. 1973–. Published by the Alberta Genealogical Society, P.O. Box 12019, Edmonton, Alberta, Canada T5J 3L2.

Saskatchewan Genealogical Society Bulletin. 1970–. Published by the Saskatchewan Genealogical Society, P.O. Box 1894, Regina, Saskatchewan, Canada S4P 3E1.

U.S. Periodicals

American Archivist. 1938–. Published by the Society of American Archivists, 600 South Federal, Suite 504, Chicago, IL 60605. Cumulative indexes for vols. 1–20 and 21–30.

The American Genealogist. 1932–. Published by David L. Green, P.O. Box 398, Demorest, GA 30535. Cumulative index for vols. 1–60.

Family Records Today. 1980–. Published by the American Family Records Association, 311 East Twelfth Street, Kansas City, MO 64106.

Forum. 1989–. Published by the Federation of Genealogical Societies, P.O. Box 830220, Richardson, TX 75083-0220.

Genealogical Journal. 1972–. Published by the Utah Genealogical Association, P.O. Box 1144, Salt Lake City, UT 84110.

The Genealogist. 1980–. Published by the American Society of Genealogists, Twenty-five Rodeo Avenue 22, Sausalito, CA 94965.

National Genealogical Society Quarterly. 1912–. Published by the National Genealogical Society, 4527 Seventeenth Street North, Arlington, VA 22207.

NGS Newsletter. 1975–. Published by the National Genealogical Society, 4527 Seventeenth Street North, Arlington, VA 22207.

Prologue: The Journal of the American National Archives. 1969–. Published by the National Archives Trust Fund Board, Washington, DC 20408.

Historical Book Review Sources

The following sources review hundreds of new historical publications each year.

American Historical Review. 1895–. Published by the American Historical Association, 400 A Street S.E., Washington, DC 20003.

Canadian Historical Review. 1920–. Published by University of Toronto Press, 5201 Dufferin Street, North York, Ontario M3H 5T8.

Journal of American History. 1907–. Published by the Organization of American Historians, 112 North Bryan Street, Bloomington, IN 47408.

Southwestern Historical Quarterly. 1897–. Published by the Texas State Historical Association, P.O. Box 8011, Austin, TX 78712.

Pacific Historical Review. 1932–. University of California Press, 2120 Berkeley Way No. 5812, Berkeley, CA 94720.

Reviews in American History. 1973–. Published by Johns Hopkins University Press, 2715 North Charles Street, Baltimore, MD 21218.

Query Magazines (Nationwide Coverage)

For the many statewide and topical query magazines, see table 19-2.

Family Puzzlers. 1964–. Published by Mary Bondurant Warren, Heritage Papers, P.O. Box 7776, Athens GA 30604.

Genealogical Queries Magazine. 1989–. Published by Robert J. Wilson, 169 Melody Lane, Tonawanda, NY 14150.

Genealogical Query Index. 1983–. Published by Taproot Publishers, P.O. Box 15153, Dallas, TX 75201.

Genealogical Research Directory. 1981–. Edited by Keith A. Johnson and Malcolm R. Sainty. U.S. distributor: Jan Jennings, 3324 Crail Way, Glendale, CA 91206.

Lost and Found: National Genealogical Query Newsletter. 1984–. Published by Ethel M. Weber, P.O. Box 207, Wathena, KS 66090.

The National Queries Forum. 1990–. Michael Cooley, P.O. Box 593, Santa Cruz, CA 95061. Since 1994 published as part of *American Genealogy Magazine*.

Query Quarterly. 1989–. P.O. Box 277, Ripley, OK 74062.

Southern Queries. 1990–. Edited by Steve Smith. P.O. Box 726, Durham, NC 27702-0726.

Topical Periodicals

Afro-American Historical and Genealogical Society Journal. 1980–. Published by the Afro-American Historical and Genealogical Society, P.O. Box 73086, Washington, DC 20056. Cumulative index for vols. 1–10.

APG Quarterly (formerly *APG Newsletter*). 1979–. Published by the Association of Professional Genealogists, P.O. Box 40393, Denver, CO 80204.

Antique Week. 1968–. Published by Mayhill Publications, P.O. Box 90, Knightstown, IN 46148.

Avotaynu—The International Review of Jewish Genealogy. 1985–. Published by Avotaynu, P.O. Box 1134, Teaneck, NJ 07666.

DAR Magazine. 1892–. Published by the Daughters of the American Revolution, 1776 D Street, Washington, DC 20006.

Die Pommerschen Leute. 1982–. Published by Myron Gruenwald, 1260 Westhaven Drive, Oshkosh, WI 54904.

The Eaglet. 1981–. Published by the Polish Genealogical Society of Michigan, Detroit Public Library, Burton Historical Collection, 5201 Woodward Avenue, Detroit, MI 48202.

Gaelic Gleanings. 1981–. Published by Peggy Magee, ed., P.O. Box 26507, Prescott, AZ 86312.

Genealogical Computing. 1981–. Published by Ancestry Incorporated, P.O. Box 476, Salt Lake City, UT 84110.

German Genealogical Digest. 1985–. Published by Laraine Ferguson, 245 North Vine, Suite 106, Salt Lake City, UT 84103.

Goin' West: A Record of Some Who Went West, 1830–1880. 1984–. Published by Richard Nelson, P.O. Box 4575, Oceanside, CA 92054.

Heritage Review (merged with *Der Stammbaum*). 1969–. Published by the Germans from Russia Heritage Society, 1008 East Central Avenue, Bismarck, ND 58501. Cumulative index, 1971–78.

The Irish at Home and Abroad. 1993–. Published by Dwight Radford and Kyle Betit, P.O. Box 521806, Salt Lake City, UT 84152.

Loyalist Gazette. 1963–. Published by the United Empire Loyalists Association, 23 Prince Arthur Avenue, Toronto, Ontario, Canada, M5R 1B2.

Mennonite Family History. 1982–. Published by J. Lemar and Lois Ann Mast, eds., P.O. Box 171, Elverson, PA 19520.

Overland Journal. 1983–. Published by the Oregon-California Trails Association, P.O. Box 1019, Independence, MO 64051.

The Palatine Immigrant. 1976–. Published by Palatines to America, Capitol University, P.O. Box 101, Columbus, OH 43209.

Polish Genealogical Society Newsletter. 1979–. Published by the Polish Genealogical Society of Chicago, 948 Milwaukee Avenue, Chicago, IL 60622.

Quaker Yeoman. 1974–. Published by James E. Bellarts, 2339 S.E. Brookwood Avenue No. 108, Hillsboro, OR 97123.

Swedish American Genealogist. 1978–. Published by Nils W. Olson, ed., P.O. Box 2186, Winter Park, FL 32790.

The Swiss Connection. 1992–. Published by Marilyn Wellauer, 2845 North Seventy-second Street, Milwaukee, WI 53210.

Regional Periodicals

Detroit Society for Genealogical Research Magazine. 1937–. Published by the Detroit Society for Genealogical Research, 5201 Woodward Avenue, Detroit, MI 48202. Cumulative indexes through vol. 30.

Eastern Genealogical PPQ. 1993–. Published by Kross Publications and Research, P.O. Box 9, Franklin Park, NJ 08823.

Mayflower Descendant. 1935–. Published by the General Society of Mayflower Descendants, P.O. Box 3297, Plymouth, MA 02361.

Midwest Genealogical Register. 1968–. Published by the Midwest Genealogical and Historical Society, P.O. Box 1121, Wichita, KS 67201.

Midwestern Heritage. 1973–. Published by Janlen Enterprises, 2236 South Seventy-seventh Street, West Allis, WI 53219. Covers Illinois, Iowa, Kansas, Missouri, Nebraska, and Wisconsin.

New England Historical and Genealogical Register. 1847–. Published by the New England Historic Genealogical Society, 101 Newbury Street, Boston, MA 02116. Every-name index to vols. 1–50, 51–147. First 147 volumes also available on CD-ROM.

New York Genealogical and Biographical Record. 1870–. Published by the New York Genealogical and Biographical Society, 122 East Fifty-eighth Street, New York, NY 10022.

NEXUS. 1984–. Published by the New England Historic Genealogical Society, 101 Newbury Street, Boston, MA 02116.

Oklahoma Genealogical Society Quarterly Four States Genealogist. 1963–. Published by the Indian Nations Press, 812 Mayo Building, Tulsa, OK 74103. Covers Arkansas, Kansas, Missouri, and Oklahoma.

"Old Northwest" Genealogical Quarterly. 1898–1912. Old Northwest Genealogical Society, Columbus, Ohio.

The Second Boat. 1980–. Published by Bachelor/Dormer, P.O. Box 398, Machias, ME 04654.

Southern Genealogists Exchange Quarterly. 1957–. Published by the Southern Genealogists Exchange Society, P.O. Box 2801, Jacksonville, FL 32203.

Tri-State Packet. 1977–. Published by the Tri-State Genealogical Society, c/o Willard Library, 21 First Avenue, Evanston, IN 47710. Covers Illinois, Kentucky, and Indiana.

Tylers Quarterly Historical and Genealogical Magazine. 1919–52. Published by Lyon G. Tyler, Richmond, Virginia.

State Periodicals

The following bibliography is not comprehensive; rather, it lists some of the major periodicals for each state. See "Bibliographies, Directories, and Guides," above, for sources to help locate other periodicals.

Alabama

Alabama Genealogical Register. 1959–68. Published by Elizabeth Thomas, ed., Pass Christian, Mississippi.

Alabama Genealogical Society Magazine. 1967–. Published by the Alabama Genealogical Society, AGS Depository/Samford University, 800 Lakeshore Drive, Birmingham, AL 35229.

Alabama Historical Quarterly. 1930–. Published by the Alabama State Department of Archives and History, 624 Washington Avenue, Montgomery, AL 36130. Cumulative index for vols. 1–40.

Deep South Genealogical Quarterly. 1962–. Published by the Mobile Genealogical Society, P.O. Box 6224, Mobile, AL 36604.

Pioneer Trails. 1959–. Published by the Birmingham Genealogical Society, P.O. Box 2432, Birmingham, AL 35201. Cumulative index to 1970.

Settlers of Northeast Alabama. 1962–. Published by the Northeast Alabama Genealogical Society, P.O. Box 674, Gadsen, AL 35902.

Tap Roots. 1964–. Published by the Genealogical Society of East Alabama, P.O. Drawer 1351, Auburn, AL 36830.

Valley Leaves. 1966–. Published by the Tennessee Valley Genealogical Society, P.O. Box 1568, Huntsville, AL 35807.

Alaska

North Star Nuggets. 1975–. Published by the Fairbanks Genealogical Society, c/o Betty Feakes, ed., 1552 Noble Street, Fairbanks, AK 99701.

Pathfinder: A Monthly Journal of the Pioneers of Alaska, 1919–1926. Ketchikan, Alaska, 1919–26.

Arizona

Copper State Bulletin (formerly *Southern Arizona Genealogical Society Bulletin*). 1965–. Published by the Arizona State Genealogical Society, P.O. Box 42075, Tucson, AZ 85733.

Journal of Arizona History (formerly *Arizoniana*). 1960–. Published by the Arizona Historical Society, 949 East Second Street, Tucson, AZ 85719.

Arkansas

Arkansas Family Historian. 1962–. Published by the Arkansas Genealogical Society, 4200 A Street, Little Rock, AR 72205.

Arkansas Historical Quarterly. 1942–. Published by the Arkansas Historical Association, Historical Department, University of Arkansas, Fayetteville, AR 72701. Cumulative index for vols. 1–35.

Backtracker. 1972–. Published by Northwest Arkansas Genealogical Society, P.O. Box K, Rogers, AR 72756.

Flashback. 1951–. Published by Washington County Historical Society, P.O. Box 357, Fayetteville, AR 72701.

Melting Pot Quarterly. 1978–. Published by the Melting Pot Genealogical Society, 400 Winans Avenue, Hot Springs, AR 71901.

California

Ash Tree Echo. 1966–. Published by the Fresno Genealogical Society, P.O. Box 1429, Fresno, CA 92516.

California History. 1922–. Published by the California Historical Society, 2090 Jackson Street, San Francisco, CA 94109. Cumulative indexes for vols. 1–40 and 41–54.

Leaves and Saplings. 1972–. Published by the San Diego Genealogical Society, 3030 Kellogg Street, San Diego, CA 92106.

Orange County Genealogical Society Quarterly. 1962–. Published by the Orange County Genealogical Society, P.O. Box 1587, Orange, CA 92668.

Santa Clara County Historical and Genealogical Society. Quarterly. 1964–. Published by the Santa Clara County Historical and Genealogical Society, City Library, 2635 Homestead Road, Santa Clara, CA 95051.

The Searcher. 1964–. Published by the Southern California Genealogical Society, 103 South Golden Mall, Burbank, CA 92406.

Valley Quarterly. 1962–. Published by the San Bernardino Valley Genealogical Society, P.O. Box 2505, San Bernardino, CA 92406.

Colorado

Boulder Genealogical Society Quarterly. 1968–. Published by the Boulder Genealogical Society, P.O. Box 3246, Boulder, CO 80307.

Colorado Genealogist. 1939–. Published by the Colorado Genealogical Society, P.O. Box 9671, Denver, CO 80209. Subject index for 1939–81.

Colorado Magazine. 1923–. Published by the Colorado Historical Society, Colorado Heritage Center, 1300 Broadway, Denver, CO 80203. Cumulative index for vols. 1–25, 26–37.

Pinon Whispers. 1980–. Published by the Southeastern Colorado Genealogical Society, P.O. Box 4086, Pueblo, CO 81003.

Connecticut

Connecticut Ancestry (formerly *Stamford Genealogical Society Bulletin*). 1958–. Published by the Connecticut Ancestry Society, P.O. Box 249, Stamford, CT 06904.

Connecticut History. 1967–. Published by the Center for Connecticut Studies, Eastern Connecticut State College, Willimantic, CT 06226.

Connecticut Maple Leaf. 1983–. Published by the French-Canadian Genealogical Society of Connecticut, P.O. Box 262, Rocky Hill, CT 06067.

Connecticut Nutmegger. 1968–. Published by the Connecticut Society of Genealogists, P.O. Box 435, 2906 Main Street, Glastonbury, CT 06033.

Connecticut Quarterly. 1895–98. Published by the Connecticut Magazine Co., Hartford, CT.

Delaware (also see Maryland)

Delaware Genealogical Society Journal. 1980–. Published by the Delaware Genealogical Society, 505 Market Street Mall, Wilmington, DE 19801.

Delaware History. 1946–. Published by the Historical Society of Delaware, 505 Market Street, Wilmington, DE 19801.

Florida

Ancestry. 1966–. Published by the Palm Beach County Genealogical Society, P.O. Box 1745, West Palm Beach, FL 33402.

Florida Genealogist. 1977–. Published by the Florida State Genealogical Society, P.O. Box 43010, Jacksonville, FL 32203.

Florida Historical Quarterly. 1908–. Published by the Florida Historical Society, University of South Florida Library, Tampa, FL 33620. Cumulative index to vols. 1–35 and 36–53.

Florida Genealogical Society Journal. 1961–. Published by the Florida Genealogical Society, P.O. Box 18624, Tampa, FL 33679.

South Florida Pioneers. 1974–. Published by Richard M. Livingston, P.O. Box 3749, North Fort Myers, FL 33918.

Georgia

Georgia Genealogical Magazine. 1961–. Published by Rev. Silas Emmett Lucas, Jr., P.O. Box 738, Easley, SC 29641. Cumulative index to 1972.

Georgia Genealogical Society Quarterly. 1964–. Published by the Georgia Genealogical Society, P.O. Box 38066, Atlanta, GA 30334.

Georgia Historical Quarterly. 1917–. Published by the Georgia Historical Society, 501 Whitaker Street, Savannah, GA 31401.

Georgia Pioneers. 1964–. Published by the Georgia Pioneers Genealogical Society, P.O. Box 1028, Albany, GA 31702.

Huxford Genealogical Society Quarterly. 1974–. Published by the Huxford Genealogical Society, P.O. Box 595, Homerville, GA 31634.

Northwest Georgia Historical and Genealogical Society Quarterly. 1976–. Published by the Northwest Georgia Historical and Genealogical Society, P.O. Box 5063, Rome, GA 30161.

Hawaii

Hawaiian Journal of History. 1967–. Published by the Hawaiian Historical Society, 560 Kawaiahao Street, Honolulu, HI 96813.

Idaho

Idaho Genealogical Society Quarterly. 1958–. Published by the Idaho Genealogical Society, 325 West State Street, Boise, ID 83702.

Idaho Yesterdays. 1957–. Published by the Idaho State Historical Society, 610 North Julia Davis Drive, Boise, ID 83702. Cumulative index to vols. 1–20.

Illinois

Central Illinois Genealogical Quarterly. 1965–. Published by the Decatur Genealogical Society, P.O. Box 2205, Decatur, IL 61526.

Chicago Genealogist. 1968–. Published by the Chicago Genealogical Society, P.O. Box 1160, Chicago, IL 60690. Queries are indexed to 1981.

Circuit Rider. 1969–. Published by the Sangamon County Genealogical Society, P.O. Box 1829, Springfield, IL 61705.

Illiana Genealogist. 1965–. Published by the Illiana Genealogical and Historical Society, P.O. Box 207, Danville, IL 61834.

Illinois State Genealogical Society Quarterly. 1969–. Published by the Illinois State Genealogical Society, P.O. Box 157, Lincoln, IL 61656.

Illinois State Historical Society Journal. 1908–. Published by the Illinois State Historical Society, Old State Capitol, Springfield, IL 62706. Cumulative index to vols. 1–25, 26–50, 51–60, 61–70.

Where the Trails Cross. 1970–. Published by the South Suburban Genealogical and Historical Society, P.O. Box 96, South Holland, IL 60473.

Indiana

Genealogy. 1973–87. Published by the Genealogy Section, Indiana Historical Society, 315 West Ohio Street, Indianapolis, IN 46202.

Hoosier Genealogist. 1961–. Published by the Family History and Genealogy Section of Indiana Historical Society, 315 West Ohio Street, Indianapolis, IN 46202.

Hoosier Journal of Ancestry. 1967–. Published by N. K. Sexton, P.O. Box 33, Little York, IN 47139. Index for 1971–79.

Indiana Genealogist. 1989–. Published by the Indiana Genealogical Society, P.O. Box 10507, Fort Wayne, IN 46852.

Indiana Magazine of History. 1905–. Published by the Indiana State Department of History, Bloomington, IN 47506. Cumulative index to vols. 1–25, 26–50, 51–75.

Iowa

Annals of Iowa. 1893–. Published by the Iowa State Historical Department, Division of Historical Museum and Archives, East 12th and Grand Avenue, Des Moines, IA 50319.

Cedar Tree. 1971–. Published by the Northeast Iowa Genealogical Society, 503 South Street, Waterloo, IA 50701.

Hawkeye Heritage. 1966–. Published by the Iowa Genealogical Society, P.O. Box 7735, Des Moines, IA 50322. Cumulative index to 1975.

The Wahkaw. 1981–. Published by the Woodbury County Genealogical Society, 3412 Old Lakesport Road, Sioux City, IA 51106.

Kansas

The Descender. 1968–. Published by the Montgomery County Genealogical Society, P.O. Box 444, Coffeyville, KS 67337.

Heritage Genealogical Society Quarterly. 1971–. Published by the Heritage Genealogical Society, P.O. Box 73, Neodesha, KS 66757.

Kansas History (formerly *Kansas Historical Quarterly*). 1931–. Published by the Kansas State Historical Society, 120 West Tenth Street, Topeka, KS 66757.

Kansas Kin. 1963–. Published by the Riley County Kansas Genealogical Society, 2005 Claflin, Manhattan, KS 66502.

The Pioneer. 1977–. Published by the Douglas County Genealogical Society, P.O. Box 3664, Lawrence, KS 66044.

The Treesearcher. 1959–. Published by the Kansas Genealogical Society, P.O. Box 103, Dodge City, KS 67801.

Kentucky

Bluegrass Roots. 1973–. Published by the Kentucky Genealogical Society, P.O. Box 153, Frankfort, KY 40524.

The Bulletin. 1968–. Published by the West-Central Kentucky Family Research Association, P.O. Box 1932, Owensboro, KY 42302.

East Kentuckian. 1965–. Published by Clayton Cox, P.O. Box 24202, Lexington, KY 40524.

Filson Club Historical Quarterly. 1926–. Published by the Filson Club, 118 East Breckenridge Street, Louisville, KY 40203.

Kentucky Ancestors. 1965–. Published by the Kentucky Historical Society, P.O. Box H, Frankfort, KY 40602.

Kentucky Genealogist. 1959–. Published by James R. Bentley, 201-B, 3621 Brownsboro Road, Louisville, KY 40207.

Kentucky Pioneer Genealogy and Records. 1979–. Published by McDowell Publications, Route 4, Box 314, Utica, KY 42376.

Register of the Kentucky Historical Society. 1903–. Published by the Kentucky Historical Society, P.O. Box H, Frankfort, KY 40602. Subject index for vols. 1–43.

Louisiana

L'Heritage. 1978–. Published by the St. Bernard Genealogical Society, P.O. Box 271, Chalmette, LA 70044.

Louisiana Genealogical Register. 1954–. Published by the Louisiana Genealogical and Historical Society, P.O. Box 335, Baton Rouge, LA 70821. Cumulative subject index to 1974.

Louisiana History. 1960–. Published by the Louisiana Historical Association, P.O. Box 44211, Baton Rouge, LA 70804.

New Orleans Genesis. 1962–. Published by the Genealogical Research Society of New Orleans, P.O. Box 51791, New Orleans, LA 70151.

Terrebonne Life Lines. 1981–. Published by the Terrebonne Genealogical Society, P.O. Box 295, Station 2, Houma, LA 70151.

Maine

Downeast Ancestry. 1977–. Published by the News-Journal, 60 Court Street, Machaias, ME 04654.

Maine Genealogical Inquirer. 1965–. Published by Mr. and Mrs. Michael J. Denis, P.O. Box 253, Oakland, ME 04963.

Maine Historical Magazine. 1885–94. Published by Joseph W. Porter, Bangor, Maine.

Maine Historical Society Quarterly. 1973–. Published by the Maine Historical Society, 485 Congress Street, Portland, ME 04010.

Maine Seine. 1979–. Published by the Maine Genealogical Society, P.O. Box 221, Farmington, ME 04938.

Maryland

Maryland and Delaware Genealogist. 1959–. Published by Raymond B. Clark, P.O. Box 352, St. Michaels, MD 21663.

Maryland Genealogical Society Bulletin. 1961–. Published by the Maryland Genealogical Society, 201 West Monument Street, Baltimore, MD 21201.

Maryland Historical and Genealogical Bulletin. 1930–50. Published by Roland F. Hayes, Jr., ed.

Maryland Historical Magazine. 1906–. Published by the Maryland Historical Society, 201 West Monument Street, Baltimore, MD 21201. Comprehensive card index at the Maryland State Archives for 1906–60.

Maryland Magazine of Genealogy. 1978–. Published by the Maryland Historical Society, 201 West Monument Street, Baltimore, MD 21201.

Western Maryland Genealogy. 1985–. Published by Donna Valley Russel, 709 East Main Street, Middletown, MD 21769.

Massachusetts

Berkshire Genealogist. 1978–. Published by the Berkshire Family History Association, P.O. Box 1437, Pittsfield, MA 01201.

Essex Antiquarian. 1897–1909. Published by the Essex Antiquarian, Salem, MA.

Massachusetts Historical Society, Proceedings. 1791–. Published by the Massachusetts Historical Society, 1154 Boylston Street, Boston, MA 02215. Cumulative index to vols. 1–20, 1–20 (second series), 41–60, 61–80.

MASSOG. 1977–. Published by the Massachusetts Society of Genealogists, P.O. Box 215, Ashland, MA 01721.

Michigan

Family Trails. 1967–. Published by the State Department of Education, Michigan State Library, Box 30007, Lansing, MI 48909.

Michigan Heritage. 1959–73. Published by the Kalamazoo Valley Genealogical Society, Kalamazoo, Michigan.

Michigan Historical Collections. 1877–1929. Published by the Michigan Historical Commission, Lansing, Michigan. Index to vols. 1–30.

Michigan History. 1917–. Published by the Michigan Department of State, Box 30029, Lansing, MI 48909. Cumulative index to vols. 1–25, 26–46, 47–57.

Michigana. 1955–. Published by the Western Michigan Genealogical Society, Grand Rapids Public Library, Sixty Library Plaza N.E., Grand Rapids, MI 49503.

Minnesota

Minnesota Genealogist. 1970–. Published by the Minnesota Genealogical Society, P.O. Box 16069, St. Paul, MN 55116. Cumulative index to 1979.

Minnesota History. 1915–. Published by the Minnesota Historical Society, 690 Cedar Street, St. Paul, MN 55101.

Northland Newsletter. 1968–. Published by the Range Genealogical Society, P.O. Box 726, Buhl, MN 55713.

Prairieland Register: Genealogical Records from Southwestern Minnesota. 1977–. Published by the Prairieland Genealogical Society, 703 North Sixth Street, Marshal, MN 56258.

Mississippi

Itawamba Settlers. 1981–. Published by the Itawamba Historic Society, P.O. Box 7, Mantachie, MS 38855.

Mississippi Coast Historical and Genealogical Society Quarterly. 1981–. Published by the Mississippi Coast Historical and Genealogical Society Quarterly, P.O. Box 513, Biloxi, MS 39533.

Mississippi Genealogical Exchange. 1955–. Published by the Mississippi Genealogical Exchange, P.O. Box 434, Forest, MS 39074.

Mississippi Genealogy and Local History. 1969–. Published by Irene S. Gillis, P.O. Box 9114, Shreveport, LA 71109.

Northeast Mississippi Historical and Genealogical Society Quarterly. 1980–. Published by the Northeast Mississippi Historical and Genealogical Society, P.O. Box 434, Tupelo, MS 38802.

Missouri

Kansas City Genealogist. 1960–. Published by the Heart of America Genealogical Society and Library, c/o Kansas City Public Library, 311 East Twelfth Street, Kansas City, MO 64106.

Missouri Historical Review. 1906–. Published by the State Historical Society of Missouri, Corner of Hitt and Lowry Streets, Columbia, MO 65201. Cumulative index to vols. 1–25 and 26–45.

Missouri Miscellany. 1973–84. 17 vols. Published by Mrs. Howard W. Woodruff, Independence, Missouri.

Missouri Pioneers: County and Genealogical Records. 1967–76. 30 vols. Published by Nadine Hodges and Mrs. Howard W. Woodruff, Independence, Missouri.

Missouri State Genealogical Association Journal. 1981–. Published by the Missouri State Genealogical Association, P.O. Box 833, Columbia, MO 65205.

Ozar' Kin. 1979–. Published by the Ozarks Genealogical Society, P.O. Box 3494 GS, Springfield, MO 65808.

Pioneer Times. 1975–. Published by the Mid-Missouri Genealogical Society, P.O. Box 715, Jefferson City, MO 65101.

St. Louis Genealogical Society Quarterly. 1968–. Published by the St. Louis Genealogical Society, 1695 South Brentwood Boulevard, St. Louis, MO 63144.

Montana

Central Montana Wagon Trails. 1979–. Published by the Lewiston Genealogical Society, 701 West Main, Lewiston, MT 59457.

Montana: The Magazine of Western History. 1951–. Published by the Montana Historical Society, 225 North Roberts, Helena, MT 59601.

Treasure State Lines. 1976–. Published by the Great Falls Genealogical Society, 1400 First Avenue North, Great Falls, MT 59401.

Trees and Trails. 1976–. Published by the Flathead Valley Genealogical Society, P.O. Box 584, Kalispell, MT 59901.

Tri-County Searcher. 1980–. Published by the Broken Mountain Genealogical Society, P.O. Box 261, Chester, MT 59522.

Nebraska

Nebraska Ancestree. 1978–. Published by the Nebraska State Genealogical Society, P.O. Box 756, Alliance, NE 69301.

Nebraska and Midwest Genealogical Record. 1923–44. Published by the Nebraska Genealogical Society, Lincoln, Nebraska.

Nebraska History. 1918–. Published by the Nebraska State Historical Society, 1500 R, Lincoln, NE 68508. Cumulative index to vols. 1–40.

Roots and Leaves. 1978–. Published by the Eastern Nebraska Genealogical Society, P.O. Box 541, Fremont, NE 68025.

Nevada

Chart and Quill. 1979–. Published by the Northeastern Nevada Genealogical Society, P.O. Box 1903, Elko, NV 89801.

Nevada Historical Society Quarterly. 1957–. Published by the Nevada Historical Society, 1555 East Flamingo, Suite 253, Las Vegas, NV 89109.

Nevada State Genealogical Society Newsletter. 1981–. Published by the Nevada State Genealogical Society, P.O. Box 20666, Reno, NV 89503.

New Hampshire

The Genealogist. 1975–. Published by the American-Canadian Genealogical Society, P.O. Box 668, Manchester, NH 03105.

Historical New Hampshire. 1944–. Published by the New Hampshire Historical Society, 30 Park Street, Concord, NH 03301. Cumulative index to vols. 1–25.

New Hampshire Genealogical Record. 1903–10. Published by the New Hampshire Genealogical Society.

New Hampshire Yesterday. 1982– . Published by Stephen D. Thomas, 64 Beacon Street, Concord, NH 03301.

New Jersey

Cape May County Magazine of History and Genealogy. 1931–. Published by Cape May County Historical and Genealogical Society, Route 9, Cape May Court House, NJ 08210.

Genealogical Magazine of New Jersey. 1925–. Published by the Genealogical Society of New Jersey, P.O. Box 1291, New Brunswick, NJ 08903. Cumulative indexes to 1975.

Historical and Genealogical Journal (with Yearbook). 1948–. Published by the Atlantic County Historical Society, 907 Shore Road, Somers Point, NJ 08244.

The Jerseyman. 1891–1905. Published by the Hunterdon County Historical Society, Fleming, New Jersey.

New Jersey Genesis. 1953–71. Published by Harold A. Sonn, later by Carl M. Williams. Cumulative index.

New Jersey History. 1845–. Published by the New Jersey Historical Society, 230 Broadway, Newark, NJ 07104. Cumulative index to vols. 1–36 (1846–1919) and 1920–31.

South Jersey Magazine. 1972–. Published by Shirley R. Bailey, P.O. Box 847, Millville, NJ 08332.

Vineland Historical Magazine. 1930–. Published by the Vineland Historical and Antiquarian Society, P.O. Box 35, Vineland, NJ 08360.

New Mexico

New Mexico Genealogist. 1962–. Published by the New Mexico Genealogical Society, P.O. Box 8734, Albuquerque, NM 87108.

New Mexico Historical Review. 1926–. Published by the University of New Mexico, 1013 Mesa Vista Hall, Albuquerque, NM 87131. Cumulative index to vols. 1–15, 16–30, 31–45.

New York

De Halve Maen. 1934–. Published by the Holland Society of New York, 122 East Fifty-eighth Street, New York, NY 10022. Cumulative index to 1977.

The Dutchess. 1973–. Published by the Dutchess County Genealogical Society, P.O. Box 708, Poughkeepsie, NY 12603.

New York Historical Society Quarterly. 1917–. Published by the New York Historical Society, 170 Central Park West, New York, NY 10024.

New York History. 1919–. Published by the New York State Historical Association, Lake Road, Cooperstown, NY 13326. Cumulative indexes every ten years.

Tree Talks. 1961–. Published by the Central New York Genealogical Society, P.O. Box 104, Colvin Station, Syracuse, NY 13205. The organization also publishes a query magazine, *Cousin Huntin'*. Some volumes are rearranged by counties (not date of publication).

Western New York Genealogical Society Journal. 1974–. Published by the Western New York Genealogical Society, P.O. Box 338, Hamburg, NY 14075.

Yesteryears. 1957–. Published by Malcolm O. Goodelle, 3 Seymour Street, Auburn, NY 13021.

North Carolina

Bulletin of the Genealogical Society of Old Tryon County. 1973–. Published by the Genealogical Society of Old Tryon County, P.O. Box 938, Forest City, NC 28043.

Carolina Genealogist. 1969–85. Published by Heritage Papers, Route 2, Box 65, Danielsville, GA 30633.

North Carolina Genealogical Society Journal. 1975–. Published by the North Carolina Genealogical Society, P.O. Box 1492, Raleigh, NC 27602.

North Carolina Genealogy (formerly *The North Carolinian*). 1955–. Published by W. P. Johnson, P.O. Box 1770, Raleigh, NC 27602.

North Carolina Historical Review. 1924–. Published by the North Carolina Division of Archives and History, 109 East Jones Street, Raleigh, NC 17611.

Quarterly Review. 1974–. Published by the Eastern North Carolina Genealogy Society, P.O. Box 395, New Bern, NC 28560.

Rowan County Register. 1986–. Published by Jo White Linn, P.O. Box 1948, Salisbury, NC 28145.

North Dakota

Dakota Homestead Historical Newsletter (formerly *Bismarck-Mandan Historical and Genealogical Society Quarterly*). 1972–. Published by the Bismarck-Mandan Historical and Genealogical Society, 2708 North 4th Street, Bismarck, ND 58501.

North Central North Dakota Genealogical Record. 1978–. Published by the Mouse River Loop Genealogical Society, P.O. Box 1391, Minot, ND 58702.

North Dakota History. 1926–. Published by the State Historical Society of North Dakota, North Dakota Heritage Center, Capitol Grounds, Bismark, ND 58505. Cumulative index to vols. 1906–80.

Ohio

Firelands Pioneer. 1858–. Published by the Firelands Historical Society, 4 Cass Avenue, Norwalk, OH 44857. Indexed for 1858–1937.

Gateway to the West. 1968–78. 11 vols. Published by Anita Short, Arcanum, Ohio.

Ohio: The Crossroad of Our Nation (formerly *Ohio Records and Pioneer Families*). 1960–. Published by the Ohio Genealogical Society, P.O. Box 2625, Mansfield, OH 44906.

Ohio History. 1887–. Published by the Ohio Historical Society, Ohio Historical Center, I-71 and Seventeenth Avenue, Columbus, OH 43211.

The Report. 1961–. Published by the Ohio Genealogical Society, P.O. Box 2625, Mansfield, OH 44906.

Oklahoma

Chronicles of Oklahoma. 1923–. Published by the Oklahoma Historical Society, Wiley Post Historical Building, Oklahoma City, OK 73105.

Oklahoma Genealogical Society Quarterly (formerly *The Bulletin*). 1961–. Published by the Oklahoma Genealogical Society, P.O. Box 12986, Oklahoma City, OK 73157.

Texarkana U.S.A. Genealogists Quarterly. 1974–. Published by the Texarkana U.S.A. Genealogical Society, P.O. Box 2323, Texarkana, TX 75504.

Tree Tracers. 1976–. Published by the Southwest Oklahoma Genealogical Society, P.O. Box 2882, Lawton, OK 73502.

Tulsa Annals. 1966–. Published by the Tulsa Genealogical Society, P.O. Box 585, Tulsa, OK 74101.

Oregon

Beaver Briefs. 1969–. Published by the Willamette Valley Genealogical Society, P.O. Box 2083, Salem, OR 97308.

The Bulletin. 1951–. Published by the Genealogical Forum of Portland, Oregon, 1410 S.W. Morrison, Portland, OR 97205.

Coos Genealogical Forum Bulletin. 1966–. Published by the Coos Genealogical Forum Library, P.O. Box 1067, North Bend, OR 97459.

Mt. Hood Trackers. 1959–. Published by the Mt. Hood Genealogical Forum, P.O. Box 703, Oregon City, OR 97045.

Oregon Genealogical Society Bulletin. 1962–. Published by the Oregon Genealogical Society, P.O. Box 1214, Eugene, OR 97440.

Oregon Historical Quarterly. 1900–. Published by the Oregon Historical Society, 1230 S.W. Park Avenue, Portland, OR 97205. Cumulative index to vols. 1–40 and 41–61.

Rogue Digger. 1966–. Published by the Rogue Valley Genealogical Society, P.O. Box 628, Ashland, OR 97520.

Pennsylvania

Keystone Kuzzins. 1972–. Published by the Erie Society for Genealogical Research, P.O. Box 1403, Erie, PA 16512. Cumulative index to 1981.

Lancaster County Connections. 1984–. Published by Gary T. Hawbaker, P.O. Box 207, Elizabethtown, PA 17033.

Notes and Queries: Historical and Genealogical Relating Chiefly to Interior Pennsylvania. 1894–1900. Published by Dr. William H. Egle, Harrisburg, Pennsylvania.

Now and Then. 1868–. Published by the Muncy Historical Society, 504 South Main, Muncy, PA 17756. Cumulative index to 1960.

Pennsylvania Genealogical Magazine. 1895–. Published by the Genealogical Society of Pennsylvania, 1300 Locust Street, Philadelphia, PA 19107.

Pennsylvania German Society Proceedings and Addresses. 1890–1966. 63 vols. Continued by *Publications of the Pennsylvania German Society.* 1968–. Published by the Pennsylvania German Society, P.O. Box 397, Birdsboro, PA 19508.

Pennsylvania Magazine of History and Biography. 1877–. Published by the Historical Society of Pennsylvania, 1300 Locust Street, Philadelphia, PA 19107. Cumulative index to vols. 1–75.

Pennsylvania Traveler-Post (formerly *Pennsylvania Ancestors and Their Descendants Today*). 1964–. Published by Richard Williams and Mildred Williams, P.O. Box 307, Danboro, PA 18916.

Western Pennsylvania Genealogical Society Quarterly. 1974–. Published by the Western Pennsylvania Genealogical Society, 4338 Bigelow Boulevard, Pittsburgh, PA 15213.

Western Pennsylvania Genealogical Society Journal and *Jots from the Point.* 1974–. Published by the Western Pennsylvania Genealogical Society, 4338 Bigelow Road, Pittsburgh, PA 15213.

Your Family Tree. 1948–. Published by Floyd G. Hoenstine, 414 Montgomery Street, P.O. Box 208, Hollidaysburgh, PA 16648.

Rhode Island

Rhode Island Genealogical Register. 1978–. Published by the Rhode Island Families Association, P.O. Box 585, East Princeton, MA 01517.

Rhode Island History. 1942– . Published by the Rhode Island Historical Society, 110 Benevolent Street, Providence, RI 02906.

Rhode Island Roots. 1973–. Published by the Rhode Island Genealogical Society, P.O. Box 7618, Warwick, RI 02887-7618.

South Carolina (also see North Carolina)

Carolina Herald. 1974–. Published by the South Carolina Genealogical Society, P.O. Box 16355, Greenville, SC 29606.

Names in South Carolina. 1954–. Published by the Department of English, University of South Carolina, Columbia, SC 29208.

South Carolina Historical Magazine (formerly *South Carolina Historical and Genealogical Magazine*). 1900–. Published by the South Carolina Historical Society, 100 Meeting Street, Charleston, SC 29401. Cumulative index to 1980.

South Carolina Magazine of Ancestral Research. 1973–. Published by Brent Holcomb, P.O. Box 21766, Columbia, SC 29221.

Transactions of the Huguenot Society of South Carolina. 1888–. Published by the Huguenot Society of South Carolina, 25 Chalmers Street, Charleston, SC 29401.

South Dakota (also see North Dakota)

Black Hills Nuggets. 1968–. Published by the Rapid City Society for Genealogical Research, P.O. Box 1495, Rapid City, SD 57709.

Pioneer Pathfinder. 1975–. Published by the Sioux Valley Genealogical Society, P.O. Box 655, Sioux Falls, SD 57101.

South Dakota Genealogical Society Quarterly. 1982–. Published by the South Dakota Genealogical Society, P.O. Box 873, Pierre, SD 57501.

South Dakota History. 1970–. Published by the South Dakota Historical Society, 800 Governors Drive, Pierre, SD 57501.

Tree Climber. 1983–. Published by the Aberbeen Area Genealogical Society, P.O. Box 494, Aberdeen, SD 57401.

Tennessee

Ansearchin' News. 1954–. Published by the Tennessee Genealogical Society, P.O. Box 12124, Memphis, TN 38112.

Family Findings. 1969–. Published by the Midwest Tennessee Genealogical Society, P.O. Box 3343, Jackson, TN 38303.

Pellissippian. 1980–. Published by the Pellissippian Genealogical and Historical Society, 118 Hicks, Clinton, TN 37716.

River Counties Quarterly. 1972–. Published by Jill Garrett, 610 Terrace, Columbia, TN 38401.

Tennessee Historical Quarterly. 1942–. Published by the Tennessee Historical Society, 403 Seventh Avenue North, Nashville, TN 37219. Cumulative index to vols. 1–25.

Texas

Footprints. 1968–. Published by the Fort Worth Genealogical Society, P.O. Box 9767, Fort Worth, TX 76107.

Heart of Texas Records (formerly *Central Texas Genealogical Society Bulletin*). 1958–. Published by the Central Texas Genealogical Society, 1717 Austin Avenue, Waco, TX 76701.

Our Heritage. 1959–. Published by the San Antonio Genealogical and Historical Society, P.O. Box 17461, San Antonio, TX 78217.

The Roadrunner. 1974–. Published by the Chaparral Genealogical Society, P.O. Box 606, Tomball, TX 77375.

Southwestern Historical Quarterly. 1897–. Published by the Texas State Historical Association, Sid Richardson Hall 2/306, University Station, Austin, TX 78712. Cumulative index to vols. 1–40, 41–60, 61–70, 71–80.

Stalkin' Kin. 1973–. Published by the San Angelo Genealogical and Historical Society, P.O. Box 3453, San Angelo, TX 76902.

Stirpes. 1961–. Published by the Texas State Genealogical Society, 2507 Tannehill, Houston, TX 77008.

Yellowed Pages. 1971–. Published by the Southeast Texas Genealogical and Historical Society, P.O. Box 3827, Beaumont, TX 77704.

Utah

Utah Genealogical and Historical Magazine. 1910–40. Published by the Genealogical Society of Utah.

Utah Historical Quarterly. 1928–. Published by the Utah State Historical Society, 300 Rio Grande, Salt Lake City, UT 84101.

Vermont

Branches and Twigs. 1972–. Published by the Genealogical Society of Vermont, Route 3, Box 986, Putney, VT 05346.

Vermont History. 1954–. Published by the Vermont Historical Society, Pavilion Building, 109 State Street, Montpelier, VT 05602.

Virginia

Magazine of Virginia Genealogy (formerly *Virginia Genealogical Society Quarterly Bulletin*). 1963–. Published by the Virginia Genealogical Society, P.O. Box 7469, Richmond, VA 23221.

The Southside Virginian. 1982–. Published by Lyndon H. Hart and J. Christian Kolbe, P.O. Box 3684, Richmond, VA 23235. Index for vols. 1–8 available.

Tidewater Virginia Families: A Quarterly Magazine of History and Genealogy. 1992–. Published by Virginia Lee Hutcheson Davis, P.O. Box 876, Urbanna, VA 23175.

Tyler's Quarterly Historical and Genealogical Magazine. 1919–52. Published by Mrs. Lyon G. Tyler, Richmond, Virginia.

Virginia Appalachian Notes. 1977–. Published by the Southwestern Virginia Genealogical Society, P.O. Box 12485, Roanoke, VA 24026.

The Virginia Genealogist. 1957–. Published by John Frederick Dorman, P.O. Box 4883, Washington, D.C. 20008. Cumulative index for vols. 1–20.

Virginia Magazine of History and Biography. 1893–. Published by the Virginia Historical Society, P.O. Box 7311, Richmond, VA 24026.

Virginia Tidewater Genealogy. 1970–. Published by the Tidewater Genealogical Society, P.O. Box 76, Hampton, VA 23669.

William and Mary Quarterly (formerly *William and Mary College Quarterly Historical Magazine*). 1892–. Published by the Institute of Early American History and Culture, P.O. Box 220, Williamsburg, VA 23187. Published in three series: first series (1892–1920), second series (1921–43), and third series (1944–present).

Washington

Appleland Bulletin. 1972–. Published by the Genealogical Society of North Central Washington, P.O. Box 613, Wenatchee, WA 98801.

The Bulletin. 1964–. Published by the Eastern Washington Genealogical Society Library, P.O. Box 1826, Spokane, WA 99120.

Bulletin of the Whatcom Genealogical Society. 1970–. Published by the Whatcom Genealogical Society, P.O. Box 1493, Bellingham, WA 98227.

The Researcher. 1969–. Published by the Tacoma Genealogical Society, P.O. Box 1952, Tacoma, WA 98401.

L.O.G.: Ledger of Genealogy. 1984–. Published by West Virginia Genealogical Society, P.O. Box 249, Elkview, WV 25071.

Trailbreakers. 1971–. Published by the Clark County Genealogical Society, P.O. Box 2728, Vancouver, WA 98668.

Yakima Valley Genealogical Society Bulletin. 1973–. Published by the Yakima Valley Genealogical Society, P.O. Box 445, Yakima, WA 98907.

West Virginia

Journal of the Kanawha Valley Genealogical Society. 1977–. Published by the Kanawha Valley Genealogical Society, P.O. Box 8765, South Charleston, WV 25303.

Tri-County Researcher. 1976–. Published by Mrs. Ethel Briggs, P.O. Box 157, New Martinsville, WV 26155.

West Augusta Historical and Genealogical Society Newsletter. 1974–. Published by the West Augusta Historical and Genealogical Society, 2515 Tenth Avenue, Parkersburg, WV 26101.

West Virginia History. 1939–. Published by the West Virginia Department of Culture and History, Cultural Center, Capitol Complex, Charleston, WV 25303.

Wisconsin

Badger History. 1947–. Published by the State Historical Society of Wisconsin, 816 State Street, Madison, WI 53706.

Genealogical Gems. 1982–. Published by the Fox Valley Genealogical Society, P.O. Box 1592, Appleton, WI 54913.

La Crosse Area Genealogical Quarterly. 1974–. Published by the La Crosse Area Genealogical Society, P.O. Box 1782, La Crosse, WI 54602.

M.C.G.S. Reporter. 1969–. Published by the Milwaukee County Genealogical Society, P.O. Box 27326, Milwaukee, WI 53227.

Wisconsin Magazine of History. 1917–. Published by the State Historical Society of Wisconsin, 816 State Street, Madison, WI 53706. Cumulative index to vols. 1–55.

Wisconsin State Genealogical Society Newsletter. 1954–. Published by the Wisconsin State Genealogical Society, 5049 La Crosse Lane, Madison, WI 53705. Cumulative index to 1963.

Wyoming

Annals of Wyoming. 1923–. Published by the Wyoming State Archives, Barrett Building, Cheyenne, WY 82002.

Bits and Pieces. 1965–. Published by M. E. Brown, P.O. Box 746, Newcastle, WY 84701.

Fremont County Nostalgia News. 1980–. Published by the Fremont County Genealogical Society, c/o Riverton Branch Library, 1330 West Park, Riverton, WY 82501.

Periodical Reprints from Genealogical Publishing Company

All published by Genealogical Publishing Company (Baltimore); year of publication as given.

American Vital Records from the Gentleman's Magazine, 1731–1868. 1987.

Baptisms and Burials from the Records of Christ Church, Philadelphia, 1709–1760, from the Pennsylvania Magazine of History and Biography. 1982.

Early Kentucky Tax Records: From the Register of the Kentucky Historical Society. 1984.

Early Kentucky Settlers: The Records of Jefferson County, Kentucky, from the Filson Club History Quarterly. 1988.

Early settlers of New York State: Their Ancestors and Descendants. 2 vols. 1993.

Emigrants to Pennsylvania, 1641–1819: A Consolidation of Ship Passenger Lists from the Pennsylvania Magazine of History and Biography. 1975.

English Origins of American Colonists: From the New York Genealogical and Biographical Record. 1991.

English Origins of New England Families: From the New England Historical and Genealogical Register, First Series. 3 vols. 1984.

English Origins of New England Families: From the New England Historical and Genealogical Register, Second Series. 3 vols. 1985.

Gateway to the West. 2 vols. 1989.

Genealogical Data from Colonial New York Newspapers: A Consolidation of Articles from the New York Genealogical and Biographical Record. 1977.

The Genealogical Department: Source Records from the DAR Magazine, 1947–1950. 1975.

Genealogical Data from Colonial New York Newspapers: A Consolidation of Articles from the New York Genealogical and Biographical Record. 1977.

Genealogies of Connecticut Families: From the New England Historical and Genealogical Register. 3 vols. 1983.

Genealogies of Kentucky Families: From the Filson Club History Quarterly. 1981.

Genealogies of Kentucky Families: From the Register of the Kentucky Historical Society. 2 vols. 1981.

Genealogies of Long Island Families from the New York Genealogical and Biographical Record. 2 vols. 1987.

Genealogies of Mayflower Families: From the New England Historical and Genealogical Register. 3 vols. 1985.

Genealogies of New Jersey Families from the Genealogical Magazine of New Jersey. 2 vols. 1996.

Genealogies of Pennsylvania families: From the Pennsylvania Genealogical Magazine. 3 vols. 1982.

Genealogies of Pennsylvania Families: From the Pennsylvania Magazine of History and Biography. 1981.

Genealogies of Rhode Island Families: From the New England Historical and Genealogical Register. 2 vols. 1989.

Genealogies of Rhode Island Families: From Rhode Island Periodicals. 2 vols. 1983.

Genealogies of Virginia Families: From the Virginia Magazine of History and Biography. 5 vols. 1981.

Genealogies of Virginia Families: From the William and Mary College Quarterly Historical Magazine. 5 vols. 1982.

Genealogies of Virginia Families: From Tyler's Quarterly Historical and Genealogical Magazine. 4 vols. 1981.

Immigrants to the Middle Colonies: A Consolidation of Ship Passenger Lists and Associated Data from the New York Genealogical and Biographical Record. 1978.

Irish Settlers in America: A Consolidation of Articles from the Journal of the American Irish Historical Society. 2 vols. 1979.

Kentucky Marriage Records: From the Register of the Kentucky Historical Society. 1983.

Long Island Source Records: From the New York Genealogical and Biographical Record. 1987.

Maryland Genealogies: A Consolidation of Articles from the Maryland Historical Magazine. 2 vols. 1980.

Maryland Rent Rolls: Baltimore and Anne Arundel Counties, 1700–1707, 1705–1724: A Consolidation of Articles from the Maryland Historical Magazine. 1976.

The Mayflower Reader: A Selection of Articles from the Mayflower Descendant. 1978.

New World Immigrants: A Consolidation of Ship Passenger Lists and Associated Data from Periodical Literature. 2 vols. 1979.

The North Carolina Historical and Genealogical Register. 3 vols. 1970–1971.

Ohio Marriages: Extracted from the "Old Northwest" Genealogical Quarterly. 1977.

Ohio Source Records from the Ohio Genealogical Quarterly. 1986.

Passengers to America: A Consolidation of Ship Passenger Lists from the New England Historical and Genealogical Register. 1977.

Pennsylvania German Church Records of Births, Baptisms, Marriages, Burials, etc.: From the Pennsylvania German Society Proceedings and Addresses. 3 vols. 1983.

Pennsylvania Vital Records: From the Pennsylvania Genealogical Magazine and the Pennsylvania Magazine of History and Biography. 3 vols. 1983.

Mayflower Source Records: Primary Data Concerning Southeastern Massachusetts, Cape Cod, and the Islands of Nantucket and Martha's Vineyard: From the New England Historical and Genealogical Register. 1986.

Pennsylvania German immigrants, 1709–1786: Lists Consolidated from Yearbooks of the Pennsylvania German Folklore Society. 1984.

Record of Indentures of Individuals Bound Out as Apprentices, Servants, etc., and of German and Other Redemptioners in the Office of the Mayor of the City of Philadelphia, October 3, 1771, to October 5, 1773 (From: Pennsylvania-German Society. Proceedings and Addresses). 1973.

Rhineland Emigrants: Lists of German Settlers in Colonial America (From Pennsylvania Folklife Magazine). 1981.

Suffolk County Wills: Abstracts of the Earliest Wills upon Record in the County of Suffolk, Massachusetts: From the New England Historical and Genealogical Register. 1984.

Virginia Land Records: From the Virginia Magazine of History and Biography, the William and Mary College Quarterly, and Tyler's Quarterly. 1982.

Virginia Marriage Records: From the Virginia Magazine of History and Biography, the William and Mary College Quarterly, and Tyler's Quarterly. 1982.

Virginia Military Records: From the Virginia Magazine of History and Biography, the William and Mary College Quarterly, and Tyler's Quarterly. 1983.

Virginia Tax Records: From the Virginia Magazine of History and Biography, the William and Mary College Quarterly, and Tyler's Quarterly: With an Index by Gary Parks. 1983.

Virginia Vital Records: From the Virginia Magazine of History and Biography, the William and Mary College Quarterly and Tyler's Quarterly. 1982.

Virginia Will Records: From the Virginia Magazine of History and Biography, the William and Mary College Quarterly, and Tyler's Quarterly. 1982.

Virginia Gleanings in England: Abstracts of 17th and 18th-century English Wills and Administrations Relating to Virginia and Virginians: A Consolidation of Articles from The Virginia Magazine of History and Biography. 1980.

MEDIEVAL GENEALOGY OVERVIEW

Key Concepts in This Chapter

- A wide variety of published material of varying quality is available for medieval research.
- Use published genealogies as clues; use original records to document lineages.
- It is worthwhile to learn some Latin, the language of the records.
- The noble and upper classes are well covered in printed literature.
- Land tenure regulations created numerous records of value.
- Documentation of government activties was recorded on various *rolls.*
- The record accounting for the estate after a tenant's death is an *inquisition post mortem.*
- Heralds recorded claims to coats of arms, often covering several generations of a family.

Key Sources in This Chapter

- *Ancestral Roots of Certain American Colonists Who Came to America before 1700*
- "Medieval Heritage: The Ancestry of Charles II of England" in the *Genealogist*
- *The Complete Peerage of England, Scotland, Ireland, Great Britain, and the United Kingdom; Extant, Extinct or Dormant*
- *Europäische Stammtafeln: Neue Folge*
- Manorial records
- Patent and close rolls
- Victoria county histories
- Inquisitions post mortem

20

MEDIEVAL GENEALOGY

Glade I. Nelson and John M. Kitzmiller, 2nd

There are two great misconceptions regarding genealogies from the pre-parish-register period. The first is that there are insufficient surviving records to adequately identify and link families. The second is that the only individuals who can be researched in the genealogical records of the medieval period are those of royal or noble ancestry.

In fact, there are great numbers of pre-parish-register (before the mid-1500s) genealogical records. It has generally been thought that these records are limited to coverage of upper class populations, but that is not correct. The original records do require specialized linguistic, paleographic (study of ancient handwriting), and socio-historic skills to effectively use them. Fortunately, there is a vast array of primary source translations and even more secondary sources dealing with medieval genealogy and heraldry. As might be expected, the quality of printed sources is variable.

Some works can be considered classics; they are superbly compiled and meet the highest standards of scholarship. Some, however, are based on the flimsiest of evidence. There is much regarding the medieval genealogies compiled in the 1800s and early 1900s that is distinctly inadequate, but this fact should not deter those who want to extend their pedigrees into the pre-parish-register era. Be aware of the pitfalls, how to avoid them, and how to build upon the material that is available.

Most initial medieval research is conducted in printed sources. It would be impossible, in this chapter, to give even a brief account of all of the printed sources available for the medieval time period, so only some of the most significant, useful, and more readily available records are discussed. Original records are often used in the construction of medieval lineages, but they are beyond the scope of this introductory discussion.

This chapter can only be an introduction to medieval genealogy sources. Following some general comments, truly secondary compilations—printed genealogies, periodicals and society publications, and university records—will be examined. The rest of the chapter introduces three major categories of printed records: the "rolls"; inquisitions post mortem; and heralds visitations of England. The last are secondary in the sense that they are abstracts, compilations, or translations of original sources. They are but representative of many additional records available for the medieval period.

BACKGROUND AND INSTRUCTIONAL MATERIALS

Surprisingly little material is available to instruct the novice researcher in the process of researching a medieval pedigree. Most of the available guides are introductory in nature and focus on specific sources, but not on methodology; this is unfortunate, because the methodology of medieval research differs significantly from the research methodology that most genealogists are familiar with. Most of the sources that modern genealogists are trained to use are not available for the medieval period. Different sources require different methodology and different skills to be applied to that methodology.

The single most important fact to recognize is that the medieval period records available today were not designed for family historians; nor were they designed to make lineage links easy to accomplish. These record sources all had specific purposes associated with a governing structure, and it is critical to research success to understand why the records were created, who used them, what they state or imply, and what their relative value is. The status of an ancestor located through these sources can be discerned by comparison with others in the same source.

The major record types that are useful in medieval research are those that deal with the ownership and transfer of land. Land tenure—how land is held (from the crown or other feudal superiors)—is an important facet of research. The reason is quite simple: a major source of revenue to the crown and all those in the feudal system was the taxation of land or services. The payment of taxes and the heirship and identification of following generations of taxpayers generated records. Lists of individuals who owned land and were taxed for land or services were maintained for centuries.

Perhaps the best way to learn the principles of medieval research is to carefully analyze some of the findings of earlier researchers in this field and to note how they used the available sources. A master of this type of research is J. Horace Round. His books, cited under "History Sources," below, comprise an excellent starting point. For examples of the present state of medieval research, see the *Genealogist* (Sausalito, Calif.: American Society of Genealogists). In addition, some books and selected chapters and articles by other noted scholars are available; read them to gain the necessary knowledge before venturing into the realm of medieval pedigree research.

Instructional Materials

Broughton, Bradford B. *Dictionary of Medieval Knighthood and Chivalry: Concepts and Terms.* New York: Greenwood Press, 1986. This helpful source explains many of the unique terms encountered in medieval records.

Coddington, John Insley. "Royal and Noble Genealogy." In *Genealogical Research: Methods and Sources.* Rev. ed. Vol. 1. Edited by Milton Rubincam. Washington, D.C.: American Society of Genealogists, 1980. Also see the brief chapter titled "English Feudal Genealogy," by G. Andrew Moriarity, in the same volume. These are "must-read" sources.

Gunderson, Robert C. "Connecting Your Pedigree into Royal, Noble, and Medieval Families." Series 445, *World Conference on Records: Preserving Our Heritage.* Salt Lake City: Corporation of the President of The Church of Jesus Christ of Latter-day Saints, 1980. Mainly concerned with compiled and/or secondary sources.

Humphrey-Smith, Cecil R. "An Introduction to English Medieval Genealogy." *Genealogical Journal* 3 (2): 35–45 (Summer 1974). Reprinted with a preface as "An Introduction to Medieval Genealogy, Part I" in *Family History* 9 (49/51): 3–15 (April 1975).

_____. *An Introduction to Medieval Genealogy: Part II, Bibliography and Glossary.* Northgate, Canterbury, Kent: the author, 1974.

Kitzmiller, John M., 2nd. *A Brief Introduction to Medieval Genealogy.* Salt Lake City: Manuscript Publishing Foundation, 1996.

Pine, Leslie G. *The Genealogist's Encyclopedia.* Reprint. 1969. New York: Collier, 1970. The first four chapters discuss ancient and medieval genealogies, with some methodological hints.

Reed, Paul C. "Medieval Families Identification Unit." In *The Library: A Guide to the LDS Family History Library.* Salt Lake City: Ancestry, 1988. Although focusing on the collection of the Family History Library of The Church of Jesus Christ of Latter-day Saints, this chapter is an excellent bibliography of sources, arranged by country. Many of the same sources are also noted throughout this chapter. Some of the annotations offer methodological advice.

Sheppard, Walter Lee. "Myths in British Genealogy." *National Genealogical Society Quarterly* 53 (September 1965): 163–68, 214–16.

Stratton, Eugene A. "Essay in Medieval English Land Tenure." Appendix B in the author's *Applied Genealogy.* Salt Lake City: Ancestry, 1988.

Wagner, Sir Anthony R. *Pedigree and Progress: Essays in the Genealogical Interpretation of History.* Chichester, Sussex: Phillimore, 1975.

_____. *English Genealogy.* 2nd ed. (enlarged). London: Oxford University Press, 1972.

UNDERSTANDING HISTORY

A complete understanding and appreciation of medieval genealogy or its sources is impossible without a solid background in the history of governance. Great historical and genealogical treatises are available to help. Of greatest value to the genealogist are works such as those produced by the venerable J. Horace Round (mentioned previously), whose high scholarship remains a standard for would-be genealogists.

History is constantly undergoing new interpretations. New publications are usually available in local public libraries and in university and college libraries.

History Sources

Clark, G. N., ed. *The Oxford History of England.* Various eds. Oxford: Clarendon Press. Vols. 1–8 cover through the reign of Elizabeth I.

Graves, Edgar B. *A Bibliography of English History: Based on the Sources and Literature of English History from the Earliest Time to About 1485 by Charles Gross.* Oxford: Clarendon Press, 1975.

Hussey, J. M., ed. *The Cambridge Medieval History.* 4 vols. London: Cambridge University Press, 1966.

Langer, William L., ed. *Encyclopedia of World History: Ancient, Medieval and Modern.* 5th ed. London: Harrap, 1972.

Martin, G. H., and Sylvia McIntyre. *A Bibliography of British and Irish Municipal History.* Vol. 1, *General Words.* Welwyn Garden City: Leicester University Press, 1972.

Paetow, Louis John. *A Guide to the Study of Medieval History.* Rev. ed. Reprint. Millwood, N.Y.: Kraus, 1980. Outdated, but still of value for material published before 1917.

Painter, Sidney. *A History of the Middle Ages: 284–1500 A.D.* New York: Knopf, 1953.

_____. *Studies in the History of the English Feudal Barony.* Baltimore: Johns Hopkins Press, 1943.

Powicke, F. Maurice, and E. B. Frye, ed. *Handbook of British Chronology.* 2nd ed. London: Royal Historical Society, 1961.

Round, J. (John) Horace. *Family Origins and Other Studies.* London: Constable, 1930. Reprint. Baltimore: Genealogical Publishing Co., 1970.

_____. *Feudal England: Historical Studies on the Eleventh and Twelfth Centuries.* London: S. Sonnenschein, 1895.

_____. *Geoffrey de Mandeville.* London: Longmans, Green, 1892.

_____. *Peerage and Pedigree: Studies in Peerage Law and Family History.* 2 vols. London: J. Nisbet, 1910. Reprint. Baltimore: Genealogical Publishing Co., 1970.

_____. *Studies in Peerage and Family History.* London: A. Constable, 1901.

Runciman, Steven. *A History of the Crusades.* 3 vols. London: Cambridge University Press, 1951–54.

Sheppard, Walter Lee, Jr. *Feudal Genealogy.* Washington, D.C.: National Genealogical Society, 1975.

Strayer, Joseph R., ed. *Dictionary of the Middle Ages.* 11+ vols. New York: Charles Scribner's Sons, 1982–.

LANGUAGE AND PALEOGRAPHY

Most original medieval documents are in Latin, legal Latin (a type of stylized shorthand), French, or early native idioms. Fortunately, scholars have translated many of these as they prepared secondary sources. Latin terms and phrases are frequently retained in them, however, so knowledge of the language of the records, particularly Latin, will enhance understanding of medieval records. Surprisingly, for many documents a rudimentary knowledge of terms and a fairly good understanding of Latin word endings will suffice to determine if the record is of interest and whether the ancestral surname is mentioned. Access to non-English-language dictionaries, particularly where terms are explained, is vital.

A second major hurdle to overcome, in some cases as difficult as reading a foreign language, is the paleography, or handwriting, of the document in question. There are several types of "hands," or handwriting styles, that can be quite difficult to read—especially some of the court hands. One of the major sources for examples is M. B. Parkes's *English Cursive Book Hands 1250–1500* (Oxford, England: Clarendon Press, 1969). For other sources see the bibliography below.

Another obstacle, actually a common occurrence in dealing with medieval persons, is multi-language identification. Prominent individuals were known by various names depending upon the language of the record describing them; some of the names might not be readily apparent as referring to the same person. For example, Charlemagne, Karl der Grossen, Charles the Great, and Carlos Magnus refer to the same person. While known to the descendants of the conquered Anglo-Saxon kingdom as "William," he was never known as such in life. He was born in France as Guillaume, married under that name, and died in France as Guillaume. There are also many contemporary records recording his name as Guglielmus.

The point to remember is that these names will be listed in an index alphabetically at a considerable distance from one another. Other given names are not easily recognized as relating to one person. A working knowledge of name variations in different languages is helpful when comparing printed genealogies from different cultures.

Language Sources

Chaplais, Pierre. *English Royal Documents: King John-Henry VI, 1199–1461*. Oxford: Clarendon Press, 1971.

Dawson, Giles E., and Laetitia Kennedy-Skipton. *Elizabethan Handwriting, 1500–1650*. London: Faber and Faber, 1966.

Gooder, Eileen A. *Latin for Local History: An Introduction.* London and New York: Longman, 1979.

Latham, R. E. *Revised Medieval Latin Word-Lists.* London: Oxford University Press, 1965. Gives the Latin term, its meaning, and the year that its use began.

Martin, Charles Trice, comp. *The Record Interpreter: A Collection of Abbreviations, Latin Words and Names Used in English Historical Manuscripts and Records.* 2nd ed. London: Stevens and Sons, 1949. An excellent listing of Latin legal terms and abbreviations.

Morris, Janet. *A Latin Glossary for Family and Local Historians.* Birmington, England: Federation of Family History Societies, 1989.

Parkes, M. B. *English Cursive Book Hands 1250–1500.* Oxford, England: Clarendon Press, 1969.

The Oxford English Dictionary. 12 vols. and supplements. Oxford, England: Clarendon Press, 1978. Good for multiple meanings of the same term.

Robinson, Mairi. *The Concise Scots Dictionary.* Aberdeen, Scotland: University Press, 1985.

Simpson, D. P. *Cassell's New Latin Dictionary.* New York: Funk and Wagnall's, 1968.

Wright, C. E. *English Vernacular Hands from the Twelfth to the Fifteenth Centuries.* Oxford, England: Clarendon Press, 1960.

PRINTED GENEALOGIES

There is a greater variety of scholarship, and hence accuracy and reliability, in printed genealogies than in any other category of medieval genealogical material. Use these records with extreme caution; give careful attention to sources used by authors. Experienced researchers learn to recognize compilers who were meticulous and therefore reliable. A healthy skepticism can help to avoid the temptation to accept information as fact simply because it has been printed.

The number of printed genealogies dealing with the medieval period is far too extensive to list any but the best ones, the most extensively used ones, and the ones most accessible through university libraries or larger public libraries. Whenever using printed genealogies, be sure to use the most recent editions. Medieval lineages change often as once-established lines are disproved or reestablished through different connections. New lineages are also being proved and documented at an increasing rate. Printed genealogies take many forms, some of which are:

- "Gateway" ancestors or lineages
- Descendants of a common ancestor or ancestors
- Ancestry of a particular (usually well known) person
- Territorial families (royalty, nobility, or landed gentry concerned with the devolution of a title, dignity, or honor)
- Knighthood and orders
- Family genealogies

One of the best examples of a gateway lineage publication is Frederick Lewis Weis's *Ancestral Roots of Certain American Colonists Who Came to America before 1700,* now in its seventh edition (Baltimore: Genealogical Publishing Co., 1992), with additions and corrections by Walter Lee Sheppard, Jr., and David Faris (earlier editions had a slightly different title). In this type of publication the ancestry of a person is presented in lineal form, from one generation to another, with information concentrating on the person through whom the descent is traced. This "gateway" usually is the genealogical connection between the United States and England or Europe. In this type of presentation, the objective often is to trace descent from a historically prominent person, such as Charlemagne, William the Conqueror, or Alfred the Great This volume is being supplanted by the ongoing work of David Faris in his *Plantagenet Ancestry of Seventeenth-Century Colonists* (Baltimore: Genealogical Publishing Co., 1996 [and future editions]).

Lineage publications without supporting documentation must be used with caution, but they should not be disregarded; always use the sources that are available, because it is far easier to discern the inaccuracies in an existing lineage than it is to create a lineage. Such a sources can be a good starting point. The following example from John S. Wurts's *Magna Charta* (Philadelphia: Brookfield Publishing Co., ca. 1946) is a case in point. This work contains the lineage of Oliver Manwaring, who immigrated to New London, Connecticut, and was baptized at Dawlish, Devon, England, 16 March 1633/34. No proof or evidence of any kind is given, yet Manwaring's father, Oliver Manwaring, is listed with his wife, Prudence Eshe, daughter of Henry Eshe, Gent (this happens to be a royal connection, or *gateway,* but is not so noted). Going back one more generation, the next Manwaring is another Oliver (with no information given), the son of George Manwaring of Exeter, England. Starting only with this information, the researcher was able to prove that not only was it correct, but that Oliver Manwaring married Margaret Tarbock, who was a co-heiress of the Tarbocks of Lancashire. This was evidenced in the coat of arms on Oliver Manwaring's gravestone in New London (his wife was Hannah Raymond), where Manwaring correctly quartered a differenced version of Manwaring with Tarbock or Tarbox. (*Quartered* refers to the dividing of a shield into four parts, or quarters. As one looks at the shield the quarters are numbered left to right (1, 2) at the top and then in the lower half (3, 4). The Mainwaring arms should therefore be in the first and fourth quarters, with the Tarbock's arms in the second and third quarters. *Differencing* is a technique used to show that the bearer of the arms was *not* the direct heir. An individual in this position could only use arms that were "different," although they could closely resemble the main family's coat of arms.)

Among the most ambitious projects in genealogical literature are attempts to trace the descendants from a common ancestor or couple. Because most descendancy lists grow in a geometrical progression, the descendants can number in the thousands after only a few generations. Some very good examples exist, despite the massive amounts of research involved; some of them are noted below under "Descendants of a Common Ancestor."

The reverse of the last category occurs when a genealogist attempts to record the entire ancestry of a person. In this category there are fewer good examples, possibly because medieval ancestry tends to become widely distributed geographically in only a few generations, with attendant linguistic and record-keeping variations complicating the work. The best example is a current project by Neil D. Thompson and Col. Charles M. Hansen, "Medieval Heritage: The Ancestry of Charles II of England," being serially published in the *Genealogist,* beginning with vol. 2, no. 2 (Fall 1987).

Territorial genealogies are most commonly used to describe families among royalty, the nobility, or the landed gentry. A territorial genealogy is generally a variable form of descendancy genealogy, usually on a smaller scale or with geographic limitations. Detlev Schwennicke's *Europäische Stammtafeln: Neue folge,* 11 vols. (Marburg, Germany: Verlag von J. A. Stargardt, 1978–) is an example, although it is certainly not on a small scale. It is a considerably improved and expanded treatise on the previous work of Isenburg (see below under "Territorial Families [Royalty, Nobility, Landed Gentry]"). Beginners interested in the families it records should consult it first.

Many such sources are the result of a primary interest in recording the descent of a title, which means that genealogical information is sometimes secondary in these works. Nonetheless, they can be valuable for completing biographical information and they can lead to further information in other records through the notes and evidence presented.

Works that are highly recommended because of superior scholarship, presentation, or scope are denoted below (and in other lists throughout this chapter) by an asterisk (*).

Gateway Ancestors (Single-Line Lineage)

Call, Michel L. *Royal Ancestors of Some American Families.* Salt Lake City: the author, 1989. Previous editions were not well researched or documented, but this compilation of pedigree charts does give some interesting documentation.

Faris, David. *Plantagenet Ancestry of Seventeenth-Century Colonists.* Baltimore: Genealogical Publishing Co., 1996.

von Redlich, Marcellus Donald Alexander. *Pedigrees of Some of the Emperor Charlemagne's Descendants.* 3 vols. Baltimore: Genealogical Publishing Co., 1974–78. Use with caution because of the lack of documentary sources.

*Roberts, Gary Boyd. *The Royal Descents of 500 Immigrants to the American Colonies or the United States Who Were Themselves Notable or Left Descendants Notable in American History.* Baltimore: Genealogical Publishing Co., 1993. For a review pointing out some shortcomings, see the *American Genealogist* 69 (2): 125 (April 1994).

_____. *Ancestors of American Presidents.* Santa Clarita, Calif.: Carl Boyer, 3rd, 1989.

*Weis, Frederick Lewis. *Ancestral Roots of Certain American Colonists Who Came to America before 1700.* With additions and corrections by Walter Lee Sheppard, Jr., and David Faris. 7th ed. Baltimore: Genealogical Publishing Co., 1992. Earlier editions were published under the title *Ancestral Roots of Sixty Colonists Who Came to New England Between 1623 and 1650.*

*_____, and Arthur Adams. *The Magna Charta Sureties, 1215.* 4th ed. Baltimore: Genealogical Publishing Co., 1991. Use only the current edition.

Descendants of a Common Ancestor

*Anselme de Saint Marie, (Pierre de Guibours). *Historie généalogique et chronologique de la maison royale de France.* 9 vols. 1726. Reprint. New York and London: Johnson Reprint Co., 1967. This monumental work by a meticulous Catholic father used many sources no longer extant. It covers widely scattered royal descendants of the Capetian kings, such as the kings of Portugal and Hungary.

Balzer, Oswald. *Genealogia Plastów.* Krakow, Poland: Academia umieje tnosci, 1895.

*Brunner, S. Otto. *Nachkommen Gorms des Alten: Konig von Danemark.* Copenhagen: Personal historik Institut, 1964. An amazingly complete sixteen-generation listing of descendants of King Gorm, who lived in the 900s.

*Brandenburg, Erich. *Die Nachkommen Karls des Grossen,* 1935. Reprint. Frankfurt am Main, Germany: Zentralstelle fur deutsche Personen und Familiengeschichte, 1964.

Burke's Guide to the Royal Family. London: Burke's Peerage, 1973.

*Dupont, Jacques, and Jacques Saillot. *Cahiers de Saint Louis.* 28 numbers. Angers, France: Jacques Dupont, 1976–8(?). This work ended with the death of Jacques Dupont. It traced all known descendants of Louis IX (king of France from 1226 to 1270), including many into the 1600s.

*Lane, Henry Murray. *The Royal Daughters of England and Their Representatives.* 2 vols. London: Constable and Co., 1910–11. A good treatise on a theme too often neglected in medieval, and modern, genealogies: the female lines.

Lanz, Johann. *Die Nachkommen Eduards III von England.* Wien, Austria, 1974.

Rosch, Siegfried. *Caroli Magna Progenies: Pars 1.* Neustadt an der Aisch: Verlag Degener, 1977.

Wertner, Mór. *Az Arpádok csaleadi törtenete.* Nagybecskerek, Yugoslavia: Pleitz Fer Pal, 1892. Genealogy of the House of Arpad to the fourteenth century.

Ancestry of a Given Person

Joannis, J. D. *Les Seize Quartiers Généalogiques de Capetiens.* 4 vols. Lyon, France: Sauvegarde Historique, 1958–65. See especially vol. 4, with corrections by Michel Dugast Rouille.

Moriarity, George Andrews. *The Plantagenet Ancestry of King Edward III and Queen Philippa.* Salt Lake City: Mormon Pioneer Genealogy Society, 1985. While Moriarity's work was perhaps the best of its time, several lineages are now suspect. Unfortunately, the book was printed from a handwritten manuscript, and some volumes have not been reproduced satisfactorily owing to variations in the manuscript.

Paget, Gerald. *The Lineage and Ancestry of H. R. H. Prince Charles, Prince of Wales.* 2 vols. Edinburgh and London: Charles Skilton Ltd., 1977. Only the earlier generations extend into the medieval period.

*Stromeyer, Manfred. *Merian-Ahnen: aus dreizehn jahrhunderten.* Vols. 1–5. Konstanz, Germany: Jan Thorbecke Verlag KG, 1963–64. Vols. 6–8. Limburgh an der Lahn, Germany: C. A. Starke-Verlag, 1966–67. While beginning with a non-noble person, the ancestral lines extend through several gateway ancestors to an extremely wide coverage of European ruling families. It has a thorough, although complicated, index.

Stuart, Roderick W. *Royalty for Commoners: The Complete Known Lineage of John of Gaunt, Son of Edward III, King of England and Queen Philippa.* 2nd ed. Bowie, Md.: Heritage Books, 1992. For a detailed review by Dr. David H. Kelly pointing out the strengths and weaknesses of this book, see the *American Genealogist* 69 (2): 110–18 (April 1994).

*Thompson, Neil D., and Col. Charles M. Hansen. "A Medieval Heritage: The Ancestry of Charles II, King of England." Begun in the *Genealogist* 2 (2) (Fall 1987). In progress.

Turton, W. H. (William Harry). *Plantagenet Ancestry: Being Tables Showing Over 7,000 of the Ancestors of Elizabeth (daughter of Edward IV, and wife of Henry VII) the Heiress of the Plantagenets.* London, 1928. Reprint. Baltimore: Genealogical Publishing Co., 1968. The tables are handwritten in an awkward, fan-shaped arrangement. Modern scholarship has disputed many of the linkages. It is particularly weak in the Iberian lines.

Territorial Families (Royalty, Nobility, Landed Gentry)

Altschul, Michael. *A Baronial Family in Medieval England: The Clares.* Baltimore: Johns Hopkins Press, 1965. A good example of effective use of medieval genealogical records.

Anderson, Marjorie O. *Kings and Kingship in Early Scotland.* Totowa, N.J.: Rowman and Littlefield, 1973.

Bartrum, Peter C. *Welsh Genealogies, A.D. 300–1400.* University of Wales Press, ca. 1980.

_____. *Welsh Genealogies 1400–1500.* 18 vols. Aberystwyth, Wales: National Library of Wales, 1983. While many people place confidence in Bartrum's work, there is,, unfortunately, very little source documentation.

Burke, John. *A genealogical and heraldic history of the commoners of Great Britain and Ireland enjoying territorial possessions or high official rank; but uninvested with heritable honors. Four volumes, contains coats of arms and genealogies.* London : Published for Henry Colburn by R. Bentley, 1834–38.

Burke, Sir John Bernard. *Burke's genealogical and heraldic history of landed gentry of Ireland.* Edited by L. G. Pine. London: Burke's Peerage, 1958.

Brydges, Sir Samuel Egerton. *Collin's Peerage of England: Genealogical, Biographical, and Historical.* 9 vols. London: T. Bensley, 1812.

de la Chesnaye-Desbois, François Alexandre Aubert. *Dictionnaire de la Noblesse, contenant les généalogies, l'histoire et la chronologie des familles nobles de la France.* 19 vols. Paris: Schlessinger Freres, 1863–77.

Chaix-d'Est-Ange, Gustave. *Dictionnaire des families francaises, anciennes ou notables à la fin du XIXe siecle.* 20 vols. Evereux, France: Herissey, 1903–29.

*Cokayne, George Edward. *The Complete Peerage of England, Scotland, Ireland, Great Britain, and the United Kingdom; Extant, Extinct, or Dormant.* 12 vols. in 13. London: St. Catherine Press, 1910–59. Revised by the Hon. Vicary Gibbs. Contains meticulous detail on the peers, including much material on the antecedents of peers. Contains very little material about the families of peers unless it was incidental to identifying the peer. This work must be consulted for any British peer and his family.

Debrett's Illustrated Peerage, and Title of Courtesy, of the United Kingdom of Great Britain and Ireland. London: Dean, 1869.

Dodd, Charles R. *The Peerage, Baronetage, and Knightage of Great Britain and Ireland.* London: Whittaker, 1840.

*Fernandez de Bethencourt, Francisco. *Historia Genealógica y Heráldica de la Monarquía Española: Casa Real y Grandes de Espana.* 9 vols. Madrid: Establecimento Tipográphico de Enrique Teodoro, 1889–1912. A solid work on the families covered.

Franklin, Alfred. *Les Rois et les Gouvernements de France: de Hugue Capet à l'anné 1906: avec mise à jour en 1978.* Paris: A. J. Picard, 1978.

Gadd, Ronald P. *The peerage of Ireland: with lists of all Irish peerages past and present.* London: Irish Peers Association, 1985.

Garnier, Ed[uard]. *Tableaux généalogique des souverains de la France et de ses grand feudataires.* 2 vols. Paris: Librarie A. Frank, 1863.

Gayo, Manoel Jose da Costa Felgueiras. *Nobiliario de Families de Portugal.* 33 vols. Braga, Portugal: Oficinas Graficas de Pax, 1938–42.

*Garcia Carraffa, Alberto, and Arthuro Garcia Carraffa. *Diccionario Heráldico y Genealógico de Appelidoes Españoles y Americanos.* 86 vols. Madrid, Spain: Neuva Impenta Radio, 1952–63. Regrettably, the major author died before this project was completed. Only surnames beginning with *A* through *Ur* were printed. While lacking in adequate source documentation, this monumental work gives more detail on most Iberian families than can usually be found elsewhere.

Genealogisches handbuch zur Schwiezer Geschichte. 3 vols. Zurich, Switzerland: Schulthess, 1900–43.

James, Francis G. *Lords of the Ascendancy: The Irish House of Lords and ItsMembers, 1600–1800.* Blackrock, Co. Dublin, Ireland: Irish Academic Press, 1995.

LeHete, Thierry. *Les Capetiens.* Paris: Editions Christian, 1987.

Hübner, Johann. *Genealogische Tabellen, nebst denen darzu gehörigan genealogischen Fragen: zur Erläuterung der politischen HIstorie.* Leipzig: Johan Friedrich Glieditschens seel. Sohn., 1737–44. Contains many hard-to-find families. The German tables are generally reliable; all others must be used with caution.

Isenburg, Wihelm Karl Prinz von. *Die Ahnen der Deutschen Kaiser, Konige und ihrer Gemahlinnen.* Görlitz, Germany: C. A. Starke, 1932.

_____. *Stammtafeln zur Geschichte der Europäischen Staaten.* 5 vols. Marburg, Germany: Verlag von J. A. Starrgardt, 1956–78. A good reference work when produced, it is completely updated and superseded by Schwennicke (see below).

Konigsfeldt, J. P. F. *Genealogisk-historiske tabeller over de Nordiske rigers kongeslaegter: Anden omarbeidede udgave.* Copenhagen: Den Danske Historieks Forening, 1865. Much of the early saga material is currently being challenged.

Lane-Poole, Stanley. *The Mohannedan Dynasties: Chronological and Genealogical Tables with Historical Introductions.* New York: Frederick Ungar Publishing Co., 1965.

*Litta, Pompeo. *Familigie Celebri Italiane.* 12 vols. Milan, Italy: Paolo Emilio Giusti, 1819–71. While this is the best work to date covering many Italian families, its coverage varies considerably from one family to another.

Lloyd, Howell A. *The Gentry of South-West Wales, 1540–1640.* Cardiff: University of Wales Press, 1968.

Lloyd, J.Y.W. *The History of the Princes, the Lords Marchers, and the Ancient Nobility of Powys Fadog.* 9 vols. London: T. Richards, 1882.

Lodge, John. *The Peerage of Ireland.* 4 vols. London: W. Johnson, 1754. Revised and enlarged by Mervyne Archdall. 7 vols. Dublin: J. Moore, 1972.

Nichols, Thomas. *Annals and Antiquities of the Counties and the County Families ofWales.* 2 vols. London: 1872. Reprint. Baltimore: Genealogical Publishing Co., 1991.

O'Hart, John. *The Irish and Anglo-Irish landed gentry.* Shannon, Ireland: University Press, 1969.

*Paul, Sir James Balfour. *The Scots Peerage.* 12 vols. Edinburgh, Scotland: David Douglas, 1904–14. Among the outstanding features of this work is that it treats all children of peers and is well documented.

Rouillé, Marcel Dugast. *Les Maisons Souverains de l'Autriche: Babenberg, Habsbourg (Habsbourg-d'Espagne), Habsbourg-Lorraine (Lorraine).* Paris: the author, 1967.

*Rudt-Collenberg, Count W. H. *The Rupenides, Hethumides and Lusignans: The Structure of the Armeo-Cilician Dynasties.* Paris: Imprimerie A. Pignie, 1963. A valuable publication by a highly respected medievalist.

Ruvigny and Raineval, Melville Amadeus Henry Douglas . . . 9th Marquis of. *The Jacobite Peerage: Baronetage, Knightage and Grants of Honour.* A facsimile of the original edition of 1904. London: Skilton, 1974.

*Schwennicke, Detlev. *Europäische Stammtafeln: Neue folge.* 11 vols. Marburg, Germany: Verlag von J. A. Stargardt, 1978– . A considerably enlarged treatise begun by Wilhelm Karl Prinz von Isenburg, whose work this supersedes. Considerable information on Mediterranean families is found in these volumes. They were lacking in Isenburg, whose expertise was in the German families.

Sirjean, Gaston. *Encyclopedie généalogique de maisons souveraines du monde.* Paris, 1959.

*De Sousa, Antonio Caetano. *Historia Genealogica da casa real Portuguesa.* 12 vols. 1735–57. Reprint. Coimbra, Portugal: Atlantida, 1946–55.

_____. *Provas [Proofs].* 6 vols. 1739–48. Reprint. Coimbra, Portugal: Atlantida, 1946–54. Contains many original documents. This is a detailed account of a royal family that kept good genealogical records from the thirteenth century.

Stokvis, A. M. H. J. *Manuel d'Histoire de Généalogie et de Chronologie de Tous les Etats du Globe.* 3 vols. 1888–93. Reprint. Leiden: B. M. Israel, 1966. Unfortunately, Stokvis almost always follows male lines only. Contains material on some hard-to-find families.

*Sturdza, Mihail-Dimitri. *Dictionnaire Historique et Généalogique des Grandes Families de Grece, d'Albanie et de Constantinople.* Paris: the author, 1983. This recent book contains much material of value.

Swartz, Erick. *Genealogia Gothica.* 2 vols. Stockholm, Sweden, 1930, 1937.

Wedgewood, Josiah C. *History of Parliament: Biographies of the Members of the Commons House 1439–1509.* London: H.M. Stationary Office, 1936. A truly amazing source that contains a very detailed biography of the individuals involved as well as many of their coats of arms. Usually includes parents, titles, residences, death, and heirs.

Wegener, Wilhelm. *Genealogische Tafeln zur Mitteleuropäischen Geschichte.* Göttingen, Germany: Heinz Reise Verlag, 1962–69.

Title Studies

Banks, T. C. *Baronia Anglica Concentrata, or a Concentrated Account of all the Baronies Commonly Called Baronies in Fee; Deriving Their Origin from Writ of Summons, and Not from any Specific Creation.* 2 vols. Ripon, England: William Harrison, 1843–44.

Burke, Sir John Bernard. *A Genealogical and Heraldic History of the Extinct and Dormant Baronetcies of England, Ireland, and Scotland.* 1841. Reprint. Baltimore: Genealogical Publishing Co., 1977.

*Clay, John William. *The Extinct and Dormant Peerages of the Northern Counties of England.* London: James Nisbet, 1913.

Frank, Karl Friedrich von. *Standeserhebungen und Gnadenatkte für das Deutsche Reich und die österreichischen Erblande bis 1806 sowie kaiserlich österreichische: bis 1823 mit einigen Nachträgen zum "Alt-österreichischen Adels-Lexikon" 1823–1918.* 5 vols. Senftenegg, Austria: the author, 1967–74. Contains nobility grants of the German Empire, including Austria.

Haydn, Joseph. *The Book of Dignities: Rolls of the Official Personages of the British Empire.* London: Longman, Brown, Green, and Longmans, 1851.

Karnbach, William Francis Marmion. *Gaelic Titles and Forms of Address: A Guide in the English Language.* Kansas City, Mo.: Irish Genealogical Foundation, 1990.

Sanders, Ivon John. *English Baronies: A Study of Their Origin and Descent, 1086–1327.* N.p., 1960.

Solly, Edward. *An index of hereditary English, Scottish, and Irish titles of honour.* Baltimore : Genealogical Publishing Co., 1968. Originally published as *Index Society,* vol. 5, London, 1880.

Knighthood and Orders

Beltz, George Frederick. *Memorials of the Most Noble Order of the Garter, from Its Foundations to the Present Time.* London: W. Pickering, 1841.

Burke, Sir John Bernard. *The Knightage of Great Britain and Ireland.* Rev. ed. London: Edward Shurton, 1842.

Galloway, Peter. *The most illustrious order of St. Patrick 1783–1983.* Chichester, Sussex, England: Phillimore, 1983.

Holmes, Grace. *The Order of the Garter: Its Knights and Stall Plates 1348 to 1984.* Windsor, England: St. George's Castle, 1984.

Shaw, William A. *The Knights of England: A Complete Record from the Earliest Time to the Present Day of the Knights of all Orders of Chivalry in England, Scotland, and Ireland and of Knights Bachelors.* 2 vols. London: Central Chancery of the Orders of Knighthood, 1906.

Family Genealogies Guides

There are some excellent finding aids to printed records to search for a given family. The following are especially valuable:

*Arnaud, Etienne. *Repertoire de Généalogies Française Imprimées.* 3 vols. Nancy, France: Berger-Levrault, 1978.

*Barrow, Geoffrey B. *The Genealogist's Guide: An Index to Printed British Pedigrees and Family Histories 1950–1975: Being a Supplement to G. W. Marshall's Genealogist's Guide and J. B. Whitmore's Genealogical Guide.* London: Research Publishing, 1977.

*Marshall, George W. *The Genealogist's Guide.* Reprint. Baltimore, 1980.

*Pryce, Frederick R. *A Guide to European Genealogies: Exclusive of the British Isles: With an Historical Survey of the Principal Genealogical Writers.* High Wycombe, U.K.: University Microfilms, [1965].

*Saffroy, Gaston. *Bibliographie Généalogique, Heráldique et Nobiliare de la France des Origines à Nos Jours, Imprimés et Manuscrits.* 4 vols. Paris: the author, 1968–79.

**Stammfolgen-Verzeichnisse für das genealogische Handbuck des Adels und das deutsche Geschlechterbuch.* Limburg an der Lahn, Germany: C. A. Starke, 1969.

*Whitmore, J. B. *A Genealogical Guide.* London: Walford Brothers, 1953.

PERIODICALS AND SOCIETY PUBLICATIONS

For well over one hundred years there have existed many scholarly society publications, periodicals, and journal series containing substantial material on royalty, nobility, medieval families, and medieval records. Genealogy owes much to these societies and publishers for preserving valuable medieval information. Much excellent medieval material is, unfortunately, hidden in relatively obscure periodicals; however, the search is worth the discovery of a valuable article or document. As with all secondary sources, the accuracy of the information depends entirely upon the contributor.

A very valuable tool for locating material in periodicals is E. L. C. Mullins's *Guide to the Historical and Archaeological Publications of Societies in England and Wales, 1901–1933* (London: Athlone Press, University of London, 1968). For the time period covered, it lists and indexes the titles and authors of books and articles in more than four hundred local and national societies in England.

Some of the publication titles listed below may seem misleading, but they do contain articles on medieval families or records. Many publications also contain material from the post-parish-register time period, and several also contain non-genealogical material. Some of the more esoteric publications are available only in major public, university, or research libraries; many are available through interlibrary loan. Among the best publications with a wide area of interest are the following.

British Isles

The Ancestor: A Quarterly Review of County and Family History, Heraldry and Antiquities. Edited by Oswald Barron. Quarterly. London. 12 vols., 1902–05. Separate indexes to vols. 1–4, 5–8, and 9–12.

Camden Society Publications. Annual. Royal Historical Society, London. 1838 to date. Now in its fourth series.

Collectanea Topographica and Genealogica. Annual. London. 8 vols., 1834–43.

The Genealogical Magazine: A Journal of Family History, Heraldry and Pedigrees. Annual. London. 7 vols., 1898–1904.

The Genealogical Quarterly. Quarterly. London. 41 vols., 1932–74. The founding editor was Henry de Laval Walker.

The Genealogist: A Quarterly Magazine of Genealogical, Antiquarian, Topographical, and Heraldic Research. Quarterly. London. 38 vols., 1877–1922. The founding editor was George W. Marshall.

The Genealogists' Magazine. Quarterly. Society of Genealogists, London. 1925 to date.

The Harleian Society Publications. Annual. The Harleian Society, London. 1869–1977, vols. 1–117. A new series began in 1979 and is currently in progress.

The Journal of the Royal Historical and Archaeological Association of Ireland. Annual. Royal Society of Antiquaries of Ireland, Dublin. 1859 to date. Various titles.

Miscellanea Heraldica et Genealogica. Annual. London. 5 series, various volumes, 1866–1937. The founding editor was Joseph Jackson Howard.

Scottish Studies. Semiannual. School of Scottish Studies, University of Edinburgh. Edinburgh. 1957 to date.

The Topographer and Genealogist. Annual. London. 3 vols., 1846–58. Sequel to *Collectanea Topographica et Genealogica.* Edited by John Gough Nichols.

Many learned societies focused on one or several adjacent counties in England have published medieval genealogical works. The high quality and volume of material is probably best represented in the Cheshire and Lancashire areas, where the following excellent publications are produced.

Lancashire and Cheshire Antiquarian Society Transactions. Annual. Lancashire and Cheshire Antiquarian Society, Ilkley. 1883 to date.

Publications of the Chetham Society. Annual. Chetham Society, Manchester. First series, 113 vols.; second series, 110 vols.; third series in progress with 39 vols. through 1994.

Publications of the Record Society of Lancashire and Cheshire. Annual. Record Society of Lancashire and Cheshire, Manchester. 1931 to date.

Transactions of the Historic Society of Lancashire and Cheshire. Annual. Historic Society of Lancashire and Cheshire, Liverpool. 1985 to date.

While all of the county and city periodicals and society publications cannot be listed here, the following deserve special recognition for quality and coverage of medieval records.

Antiquities of Shropshire. Annual. London. 12 vols., 1854–60. Edited by Rev. R. W. Eyton.

Collections for a History of Staffordshire. Annual. Staffordshire Record Society, London. 1880 to date. Begun by the William Salt Archaeological Society. Currently in its fourth series.

The Northern Genealogist. Quarterly. Birmingham. 6 vols., 1895–1903. Vols. 1–5 are indexed. Edited by A. Gibbons.

Publications of the Dugdale Society. Annual. Dugdale Society, Oxford. 1921 to date. Primarily covers Warwickshire.

Publications of the Lincoln Record Society. Annual. Lincoln Record Society, Exeter. 1911 to date.

The Publication of the Surtees Society. Annual. Surtees Society, Leamington Spa. 1835 to date. Covers primarily the northeast counties of England.

The Publications of the Thoresby Society. Annual. Thoresby Society, Leeds. 1891 to date.

Transactions of the Thoroton Society of Nottingham. Annual. Thoroton Society, Nottingham. 1898 to date.

Continental Europe

Adler: Zeitschrift für Genealogie und Heraldik. Quarterly. Heraldisch Genealogischen Gesselschaft "Adler," Vienna, Austria. 1881 to date. Primarily covers Austria. Various titles.

Armas y Troféus: revista de história, heráldica, genealogia e de arte. Annual. Intituto Portugês de Heraldica, Lisbon, Portugal. 11 vols., 1959–70. Primarily covers Portugal, but contains material from other parts of Europe.

Bibliothèque de l'Ecole des Chartes. Société de l'Ecole des Chartes. Geneva, Switzerland. 1839 to date. Superior publication of family genealogies of medieval France and surrounding areas.

Cahiers de Civilisation Médiévale, Xe–XIIe Siecles. Centre d'Etudes Superieures de Civilisation Médiévale, Poitiers, France. Various dates, 1958 to date.

Der Deutscher Herold: zeitschrift für Wappen, Siegel-und Familienkunde. Annual. "Herold," Berlin. 65 vols., 1870–1932. Covers Germanic areas.

Genealogisches Jahrbuch. Annual. Zentralstelle für Personen- und Familiengeschichte, Neustadt. 1961 to date. Primarily covers Germanic areas.

Göttinger Genealogisch-Heraldischen Gesellschaft. *Der Schlüssel: Gesamtinhalts-verzeichnisse mit Ortsquellennachweisen für genealogische, heraldische und historische Zeitschriftenreihen.* Göttingen, Germany: Heinz Reise Verlag, 1950–. A very useful index to German genealogical and heraldic periodicals.

Héraldique et Généalogie: revue national de généalogie, d'héraldique et de sigillographie. Quarterly. Centre Généalogique de Paris et de l'Union Féderale Regionale Parisienne des Associations Généalogiques d'Ile de France, Versailles, France. 1968 to present. Covers primarily France, but with some material from throughout Europe.

Der Herold: Vierteljahrsschrift für Heraldik, Genealogie und verwandte Wissenschaften. Quarterly. Heraldik, Genealogie und verwandte Wissenschaften zu Berlin, Berlin. 1939 to date.

Hidalguía: La Revista de Genealógia, nobleza y armas. Quarterly. Instituto Salazar y Castro, Madrid, Spain. 1953 to date. Primarily covers Spain.

Jaarboek van het centraal bureau voor genealogie. Annual. Centraal Bureau voor Genealogie, 'S-Gravenhage, Netherlands. 1947 to date. Primarily covers the Netherlands.

Mediaeval Studies. Annual. Pontifical Institute of Mediaeval Studies, Toronto, Canada. 1939 to date.

Moyen Agé: revue historique. Quarterly. Brussels, Belgium. 1888 to date.

Personhistorisk Tidskrift. Annual. Stockholm. 1898 to date. Primarily covers Sweden.

Rivista Araldica. Annual. Collegio Araldico, Rome. 1903 to date. Centers on Italy.

Speculum: A Journal of Medieval Studies. Quarterly. Medieval Academy of America, Cambridge, Massachusetts. 1926 to date.

Turul: A Magyar Heraldikai es Genealogical Tarsasag. Annual. Kiadja A Magyar Heraldikai es Genealogiai Tarsasag, Budapest. 64 vols., 1883–1950. Primarily covers Hungary.

Conferences

The Confederation Internationale de Genealogie et d'Heraldique has held twenty-two congresses between 1929 and 1995. The proceedings and papers presented at these conferences have been printed. Many deal with heraldic science, but many excellent treatises on medieval families are found within the volumes as well. The proceedings and papers presented between 1929 and 1982 are indexed in Hanns Jager-Sunstenau's *Index Generalis* (Limburg, Germany, 1984).

American Publications

The following American publications have presented excellent material on medieval families, among many other articles. Of particular interest are articles by Arthur Adams, John Insley Coddington, Dr. David H. Kelley, George Andrews Moriarity, William Adams Reitwiesner, Walter Lee Sheppard, and Eugene A. Stratton. The continuing ancestry of Charles II, King of England, by Neil D. Thompson and Col. Charles M. Hansen in the *Genealogist* is a good example of documentation using a variety of original and printed sources. Some of the articles in the *Augustan* border on the fabulous, but others are better documented.

The American Genealogist. Quarterly. Demorest, Georgia, 1932 to date.

The Augustan: An International Journal of History, Genealogy and Heraldry. Quarterly. Augustan Society, Torrance, California, 1957 to date.

The Genealogist. Semiannual. Association for the Promotion of Scholarship in Genealogy. New York City, 1980 to date. Nearly every article in the *Genealogist* is a good example of how to write and properly document genealogical material. Many deal with the medieval period.

National Genealogical Society Quarterly. Quarterly. National Genealogical Society, Arlington, Virginia, 1912 to date. Edited by Elizabeth Shown Mills and Gary Bernard Mills.

New England Historical and Genealogical Register. Quarterly. New England Historic Genealogical Society, Boston, 1847 to date.

The Virginia Genealogist. Quarterly. Washington, D.C., 1957 to date. Edited by John Frederick Dorman.

This discussion has included sources for both Great Britain and continental Europe. The sources discussed in the remainder of this chapter pertain in a greater measure to British families; some are unique to British families. Other sources for different parts of Europe are seldom published, and when published they are very difficult for American researchers to access. Therefore, the following discussion focuses on British sources.

UNIVERSITY RECORDS AND REGISTERS OF CLERGY

In the Middle Ages, universities and schools were ecclesiastical institutions. University registers, a collection of loosely grouped records, are available for Oxford from around 1350. Records of graduation are generally available from the fifteenth century, but they are not generally complete until the sixteenth century. Undergraduate matriculation records are available from 1544 at Cambridge and from 1564 at Oxford.

The records of the colleges within each university vary considerably in the information recorded and the dates on which they were begun. Almost all university records include registers, admission books, and some financial accounts. They frequently include annotations which give a proven or possible relationship to a specific family.

Extensive records exist for many of the various colleges. For example, the publications of the Oxford Historical Society almost exclusively concern Oxford University. The society's first series of 101 volumes ran from 1885 to 1936. The new series, begun in 1939, continues to the present. Consult university records if a family member may have been a clerk or minister in the Church of England. The following example is a profile of a colonial immigrant from an alumni publication.

> LOOTHROP, LATHROP or LOTHROPP, JOHN. B.A. from QUEENS', 1606; M.A. 1609. S. of Thomas, of Etton, Yorks. Bapt. there, dec. 20, 1584. Ord. deacon (Lincoln) Dec. 20, 1607; C. of Bennington, Herts. P.C. of Egerton, Kent, 1609, till 1622 or 1624; afterwards nonconformist. Succeeded Henry Jacob as pastor of the Independent Church at Southwark, London. Imprisoned for two years; released on bail; escaped and sailed for Boston, 1634. Minister at Scituate, Mass., 1634-9. Minister at Barnstaple, Mass., 1639-53. Author, *Queries respecting Baptism.* Died Nov. 8, 1653. (D.N.B.; J.G. Bartlett.) (Venn 1922-27, part 1, vol. 3, 104)

John Le Neve's single volume of *Fasti Ecclesiae Anglicanae* appeared in 1716. The term *fasti* denotes a register or list. In this case the author simply compiled a biographical list of English ecclesiastics. Le Neve's original intention was to revise and update an earlier publication which listed the bishops of England and Wales. However, additional records were placed at his disposal and he enlarged the scope of his work to include deans, prebendaries, and other principal dignitaries. His work was enlarged and corrected by Thomas Duffy Hardy in 1854. Since then new sources of information for this subject and time period have become available.

The information is generally organized by diocese and order of precedence among the dignitaries. It normally includes the man's name, degrees, dates of offices, and details of any particular function held. While not a full biography, *Fasti Ecclesiae Anglicanae* does include substantial family history material. Source references refer frequently to fuller accounts of the man's life.

Fasti Ecclesiae Scoticane deals primarily with the post-medieval period, but it is mentioned here because of its excellent content.

Selected University Records

Emden, Alfred Brotherston. *Biographical Register of the University of Oxford to A.D. 1500.* 3 vols. Oxford, England: Clarendon Press, 1957–59.

_____. *Biographical Register of the University of Oxford, to A.D. 1500–1540.* Oxford, England: Clarendon Press, 1974.

Foster, Joseph. *Alumni Oxonienses: The Members of the University of Oxford, 1500–1714, Their Parentage, Birthplace, and Year of Birth, With a Record of Their Degrees Being the Matriculation Register of the University.* 4 vols. Oxford, England: Parker, 1891–92.

Venn, John, and John Archiband Venn. *Alumni Cantabrigienses: A Biographical List of All Known Students, Graduates and Holders of Office at the University of Cambridge, From the Earliest Times to 1900. Part 1: From the Earliest Times to 1751.* 4 vols. Cambridge, England: Cambridge University Press, 1922–27.

Registers of Clergy

Boutflower, Douglas Samuel, ed. *Fasti Dunelmenses: A Record of the Beneficed Clergy of the Diocese of Durham to the Dissolution of the Monastic and Collegiate Churches.* Publications of the Surtees Society, vol. 139. Durham, England: Andrews, 1926.

Cotton, Charles Philip. *Fasti Ecclesiae Hibernicae: The Succession of the Prelates and Members of the Cathedral Bodies of Ireland.* Dublin, Ireland: Charles, 1878.

Dixon, William Henry. *Fasti Eboracenses: Lives of the Archbishops of York.* London: Green, Longman, and Roberts, 1863.

Greenway, Dianna E., comp. *Fasti Ecclesiae Anglicanae, 1066–1300: III—Diocese of Lincoln.* London: University of London, 1977.

_____. *Fasti Ecclesiae Anglicanae, 1066–1300: II—Monastic Cathedrals (Northern and Southern Provinces).* London: University of London, 1971.

_____. *Fasti Ecclesiae Anglicanae, 1066–1300: I—St. Paul's, London.* London: University of London, 1968.

Horn, Joyce M., comp. *Fasti Ecclesiae Anglicanae, 1300–1541: XII—Introduction, Errata and Index.* London: University of London, 1967.

_____. *Fasti Ecclesiae Anglicanae, 1541–1857: III—Canterbury, Rochester and Winchester Dioceses.* London: University of London, 1971.

_____. *Fasti Ecclesiae Anglicanae, 1300–1541: VII—Chicester Diocese.* London: University of London, 1964.

_____. *Fasti Ecclesiae Anglicanae, 1541–1857: II—Chicester Diocese.* London: University of London, 1971.

_____. *Fasti Ecclesiae Anglicanae, 1300–1541: IX—Diocese of Exeter.* London: University of London, 1965.

_____. *Fasti Ecclesiae Anglicanae, 1300–1541: II—Hereford Diocese.* London: University of London, 1962.

_____. *Fasti Ecclesiae Anglicanae, 1300–1541: III—Salisbury Diocese.* London: University of London, 1962.

_____. *Fasti Ecclesiae Anglicanae, 1541–1857: I—Salisbury Diocese.* London: University of London, 1986.

_____. *Fasti Ecclesiae Englicanae, 1300–1541: V—St. Paul's, London.* London: University of London, 1963.

_____. *Fasti Ecclesiae Anglicanae, 1541–1857: I—St. Paul's, London.* London: University of London, 1969.

Horn, Joyce M., and Derrick Sherwin Bailey, comps. *Fasti Ecclesiae Anglicanae, 1541–1857: V—Bath and Wells Diocese.* London: University of London, 1979.

_____, and David M. Smith, comps. *Fasti Ecclesiae Anglicanae, 1541–1857: IV—York Diocese.* London: University of London, 1975.

Jones, B., comp. *Fasti Ecclesiae Anglicanae, 1300–1541: VIII—Bath and Wells Diocese.* London: University of London, 1964.

_____. *Fasti Ecclesiae Anglicanae, 1300–1541: X—Coventry and Lichfield Diocese.* London: University of London, 1965.

_____. *Fasti Ecclesiae Anglicanae, 1300–1541: VI—Northern Provinces (York, Carlisle and Durham).* London: University of London, 1963.

_____. *Fasti Ecclesiae Anglicanae, XI—The Welsh Dioceses (Bangor, Llandaff, St. Asaph, St. Davids).* London: University of London, 1965.

Jones, William Henry. *Fasti Ecclesiae Sarisberiensis: Or A Calendar of the Bishops, Deans, Archdeacons and Members of the Cathedral Body at Salisbury.* Salisbury, England: Brown, 1879.

King, H. P. F., comp. *Fasti Ecclesiae Anglicanae, 1300–1541: I—Diocese of Lincoln.* London: University of London, 1962.

Lawlor, Hugh Jackson. *The Fasti of St. Pattricks', Dublin.* Dundalk, Ireland: W. Tempest, 1930.

Le Neve, John. *Fasti Ecclesiae Anglicanae: Canterbury, Rochester, and Winchester Diocese, 1541–1857.* 1715. Corrected and continued to 1854 by T. Duffus Hardy. 3 vols. N.p., 1854.

Ollard, S. L. (Sidney Leslie). *Fasti Wyndesorienses: The Deans and Canons of Windsor.* Windsor, [England]: Oxley and Son, 1950.

Scott, Hew. *Fasti Ecclesiae Scoticanae: The Succession of Ministers in the Church of Scotland from the Reformation.* 7 vols. Edinburgh, Scotland: Oliver and Boyd, 1915–28.

Watt, D. E. R. (Donald Elmslie Robertson). *Fasti Ecclesiae Scotiacanae medii aevi ad anum 1638.* Publications of the Scottish Record Society, New Series, vol. 1. Edinburgh, Scotland: Smith and Ritchie, 1969.

MANORS AND MANORIAL DOCUMENTS

Manorial documents, and an understanding of what they contain and why, are very important in tracing medieval ancestors. The following description of manor records and their documents is drawn from John M. Kitzmiller's *A Brief Introduction to Medieval Genealogy* (Salt Lake City: Manuscript Publishing Foundation, 1996). These documents mainly concern land tenure, or how land was held of a superior (an individual to whom allegiance was owed).

The Normans introduced to England a new type of land tenure based upon the feudal system. The basis of this system was that *all* land was held of or from the king or through his appointed agents. Tenants who held land directly from the king were termed *mesne* tenants. They usually were of the higher ranking nobility, such as earls, dukes, and some barons. Other terms that were used in the records more often than mesne were *tenant-in-chief* or *tenant-in-capite*.

Few tenants-in-chief actually made personal use of the lands (such as living upon them). Many of them owned large parts of shires (counties), so they would assign their rights in return for a payment—service, money, etc.; this was an extension of the feudal system. The feudal lords owed their tenants protection and justice.

Another category of tenant was the *demesne* tenant. Demesne tenants were those lords who actually held and used lands personally. For example, land where the king had a residence was the king's demesne land. Many demesne tenants, though, had several mesne lords above them. In this hierarchy of ownership, the demesne tenant held directly from his mesne lord. The demesne tenant owed protection and justice to *his* tenants and owed service to his mesne lord. In the lowest category among those holding land were the actual tenants of the manors.

Most of the tenants in the feudal system lived on manors. A manor usually consisted of the lord of the manor's home, his tenants' dwellings, and enough tillable acreage to support them all. The collective manors and lands of a single lord were termed an *honour.* (In later times, however, this term applied only to those who held directly from the king.)

A *caput* or *capite* was the main manor or personal residence of a tenant-in-chief. These lands and services could not be subdivided. A *moiety* was a share in a manor or manors other than a caput that could be subdivided. Originally they could only be divided in half, but later the term *moiety* meant a percentage of the income from the manor(s).

Three Types of Land Tenure

All land was directly held by freehold (free of the lord of the manor's will), copyhold (held by a copy of rights from the lord of the manor), or leasehold (leased from the lord of the manor). *Knight's service* or *knight's fee*—also known as *chivalry*—was the most important form of freehold land tenure. A lord who held land via knight's service was required to provide a certain number of knights at predetermined times each year. Usually, the knights served for forty days; they might have been used to guard the lord's castle or as his bodyguard. A knight service was a fully equipped knight and squire and their retinue.

Land could be held by one, two, six, or ten knight's fees (a barony was usually twenty fees). The knight's fees comprised the annual rent or payment required to hold the land. When no male heir to an estate occurred, fees could be divided equally among daughters; this could result in fractional fees, such as one-half, one-third, or one-eighth. Later, the knights' service was translated into monetary payments. What all of this means to a researcher is that an individual's status in the community is reflected in the amount of knight's fees he held. The larger the relative number, the more prominent he was (and thus easier to trace).

Another freehold land tenure was known as *Frank Almoign.* These lands were held by spiritual service to the king, usually by saying a predetermined number of prayers for his soul. This was not a very common form of land tenure, and in most cases it was used by religious houses (monasteries, convents, abbeys, etc.).

The third form of freehold tenure was *serjeantry.* This term means *service* in Latin, and it always referred to service to the king. *Grand serjeantries* were services that brought the provider into direct contact with the king, such as that of the king's marshal. Land held by serjeantry could not be divided.

The records of nobles differ somewhat from those who held only a few knight's fees. For those associated with baronies, there were certain requirements that generated records. To be acknowledged a baron, a person had to pay a baronial *relief* (tax); these are recorded in the Exchequer (Fine and Pipe Rolls). A baron paid a one hundred-pound relief for his own complete barony, and £33.6s.8d for fractions of other baronies that he inherited through the marriage of ancestors with heiresses. A baron held his barony as a tenant-in-chief via knight's service.

The succession to a barony occurred by a *writ of summons,* which was a legal summons from the king. There writs were usually applied only to direct male line inheritors. No *dignity* (title) could be divided, so, when daughters inherited the lands, the barony ended. If there was only an heiress (a single daughter), her husband was summoned under the title of her father. Another source for tracing landed families is through medieval borough records. Grants by these families or the receipt of fees from them were recorded in borough records.

The Manor Concept

A *manor* could consist of a single parish, township, or estate. An *estate* could consist of one or several manors, and a group of estates would comprise an *honour* or *fee*. The rights or privileges of the lord of the manor were many. The first right was that of Sac and Soc, a legal jurisdiction claimed by the lord; it entailed the right to hold a court and the right to receive profits and services from the manor. The second major right was that of *tenancy at sill,* where a tenure was granted by the lord; this was entirely in his control and disposal.

Manorial Land Tenure

Land tenure associated with a manor was either freehold, copyhold, or leasehold. *Freehold* tenure was not subject to the customs of the manor or the will of the lord of the manor. The conveyance of freehold property was without restriction. This type of tenure was usually conveyed by *livery of seisin* (the process by which the feudal heir took possession of his property and was taxed), which was recorded on a deed of conveyance. This conveyance was sometimes called an *indenture of feoffment,* and the purchaser had to pay an entry fee called a *relief.*

A freeholder could lease his land. A lease was usually for a term of one year. The "occupier" entered property via a deed of grant (release). The freeholder held an interest in this land (reversion); the reversion was a *hereditament* (hereditary) and could be conveyed without livery of seisin (payment of a fee).

Copyhold was the more common method of manorial land tenure. Originally this was a tenure dependent upon the lord's will and the customs of the manor. The conditions of the tenure demanded some type of service in return for the copyhold; these were later changed to monetary payments. A tenant's title was written on the manor court rolls, of which the tenant received a copy (copyhold). The conveyance of copyhold tenure required the tenant to surrender title to the lord of the manor. The new tenant was admitted on payment of a fine (which wasn't abolished until 1922). The mortgage of a copyhold was termed a *conditional surrender.*

Leasehold tenure was land held by a lease that was usually for a fixed number of years. It could be held by a specified number of *lives,* which was recorded in the lease. If one of the lives died, a new individual could be inserted.

Records of the Manor

There are three major groups of records associated with a manor: estreats, Court Baron records, and Court Leet records. *Estreats* are the recording of legal proceedings; they are found on the Manor Court Rolls. The example below is from the Manor of Caldicot and Newton in Glamorgan, Wales:

> The Court Baron or Hamilot Court of Thomas Stoughton Esquire and Jane his wife Lord and Lady . . . of the said Manor. . . .
>
> To this Court came Francis Morgan of Shepton Mallet in the Count of Somerset Gentleman devisee in the named in and by a Codicil annexed to the last Will and Testament of Jane Morgan late of Shepton Mallet aforesaid spinster deceased bearing date the fifth day of June one thousand seven hundred and ninety seven and prayed to be admitted Tenant to All that one Tenement one Barn one Stable one Garden one Orchard etc. . . .
>
> . . . the said Lord and Lady of the said Manor by the Steward aforesaid did grant him the said Francis Morgan seizen of the said premises by the Rod according to the Custom of the said Manor. . . .
>
> . . . Francis Morgan hath given to the Lord and Lady of the said Manor for a ffine for such his estate and entry in the premises the sum of Two shillings and sixpence and having done his ffealty is admitted Tenant thereof. . . ."

The Court Baron was a manorial court that enforced the customs of the manor. It was on the property of the lord of the manor and so was a private jurisdiction. There was usually a jury that originally consisted of at least two freeholders. The jurisdiction of the court and its associated records were concerned with *escheats* (the reverting of the land to the lord of the manor if there were no legal heirs), surrenders and transfers of land, dower administration, management of the land, and keeping track of the rights of the lord and the tenants.

Court Leet, in this context, can be considered a manorial court. Its jurisdiction was the extension of royal authority at the local level. This court and its records were concerned with minor offences and also with the maintenance of roads, bridges, etc. Every male above the age of twelve (or sixteen) was required to attend; the Court Leet met twice a year.

This court was responsible for the View of Frankpledge. *Frankpledge* is a Saxon term denoting the fact that each individual in a tithing (an early Saxon land designation) was responsible for the actions of all. The manor court rolls have lists of those accountable.

The actual record of the Court Leet is almost a standardized form. The roll starts with a list of freeholders, and then has the "list of the homage," who originally were freeholders but later were copyholders and leaseholders. The "list of the jury" comprised copyholders and leaseholders.

Locations of English Manor Records

The gathering of English manor records occurred at the national, county, and local levels. At the national level, the main collection is located at the Public Record Office (Ruskin Avenue, Kew, Richmond-upon-Thames, Surrey TW9 4DO), Chancery Lane (Public Record Office, Chancery Lane, London WC2 1LR), and at the British Library (Great Russell Street, London WC1B 3DG). Printed indexes exist for both collections, while the Royal Commission on Historical Manuscripts (Quality House, Quality Court, Chancery Lane, London WC2A 1HP) has a comprehensive list of surviving manorial records.

At the county level, some manor records (or copies) have been deposited in local county record offices. The County Record Office Guides (available from each county record office) have lists of these, many of which have been published. The local level is the most problematic. Some records are still in the possession of current landowners. Many of these have been identified by the Historical Manuscripts Commission.

A major source is the ongoing Victoria county histories; these contain detailed information about the manors within each county. The descent of the manor is footnoted and documented, and in many cases the coats of arms of the individuals involved are included. Not all counties are given the same coverage. Generally, if the set was published after the 1960s, manorial rolls are not included. Histories are available (except for Northumberland and Westmoreland); they are referenced by *The Victoria History of the County of* [county name]. This series is listed below:

County	*Volumes*	*County*	*Volumes*
Bedford	3	Lincoln	2
Berkshire	4	Middlesex	8
Buckingham	4	Norfolk	2
Cambridge and Isle of Ely	8	Northampton	4
Cornwall	1	Nottingham	2
Cumberland	2	Oxford	12
Derby	2	Rutland	2
Devon	1	Shropshire	11
Dorset	3	Somerset	5
Durham	3	Stafford	17 (not yet a complete set)
Essex	9	Suffolk	2
Gloucester	11	Surrey	4
Hampshire	4	Sussex	9
Hereford	4	Warwick	8
Hertford	4	Wiltshire	15
Huntington	4	Worcester	4
Kent	3	Yorkshire East Riding	6
Lancaster	8	Yorkshire—City of York	1
Leicester	5	Yorkshire North Riding	2

In addition, for London within the Bars, Westminster, and Southwark there is one volume.

Manorial and Related Sources

Bethell, D. *EnglishAncestry*. Strines, Staff., England: Melandra, n.d.

Boutell, Rev. C. *The Monumental Brasses of England*. Cambridge, England: Macmillan & Co., 1849.

Breresford, M. W., and H. P. R. Finberg. *English Medieval Boroughs: A Hand List*. Totowa, N.J.: Rowman & Littlefield, n.d.

Camp, A. J. *Wills and Their Whereabouts*. Bridge Place, England: Phillimore & Co., 1963.

Cox, J., and T. Padfield. *Tracing Your Ancestors in the Public Record Office*. 4th ed. London: H.M. Stationery Office, 1990.

Coulton, G. G. *Medieval Village, Manor, and Monastery*. New York: Harper & Row, 1960.

Denman, D. R. *Origins of Ownership*. London: George Allen & Unwin, n.d.

Ellis, Mary. *Using Manorial Records*. London: PRO Publications in association with the Royal Commission on Historical Manuscripts, 1994.

FitzHugh, T. *A Dictionary of Genealogy*. Totowa, N.J.: Barnes & Noble Books, 1985.

Genealogical Society of Utah. *A List of Known Manor Court Rolls Principally Deposited in the Public Record Office, London, the British Museum, London, County Record Offices, Lambeth Palace Library, London, the Bodleian Library, Oxford.* 2 vols. Typescript copy prepared by the Research Department of the Genealogical Society of Utah, 1965–68.

Gun, W. T. J. "The Succession to Baronies by Writ of Summons." *Genealogists' Magazine* 5 (1) (1929).

Hainsworth, D. R. *Stewards, Lords andPeople: The Estate Steward and His World in Later Stuart England.* Cambridge, England: Cambridge University Press, 1992.

Harvey, P. D. A. *Manorial Court Rolls.* London: Published by the Historical Association, ca. 1993.

_____. *Medieval Manorial Records.* [Yorkshire], England: Yorkshire Archaeological Society, 1983.

Hobson, T. F. *A Catalogue of Manorial Documents Preserved in the Muniment Room of New College, Oxford.* London: Manorial Society, [1929].

John, E. *Land Tenure in Early England.* Leicester, England: Leicester University Press, 1964.

Latham, R. E. *Revised Medieval Latin Word-List.* London: Oxford University Press, 1965.

List and Index Society. *Exchequer, Treasury of The Receipt: Ancient Deeds—Series A.* N.p., 1978.

Lists of Manor Court Rolls in Private Hands. London: Manorial Society, 1907–10.

Maitland, F. W. *Domesday Book and Beyond.* Cambridge, England: Cambridge University Press, 1897.

Milsom, S. F. C. *The Legal Framework of English Feudalism.* Cambridge, England: Cambridge University Press, n.d.

Molyneux-Child, J. W. *Evolution of the English manorial system.* Lewes, [England]: Book Guild, ca. 1987. Includes a glossary of Domesday book words and phrases and a glossary of words in manorial records.

Palgrave-Moore, Patrick T. R. *How To Locate and Use Manorial Records.* Norwich, Norfolk, England: Elvery Dowers Publications, ca. 1985.

Park, Peter B. *My Ancestors Were Manorial Tenants: How Can I Find Out More About Them?* London: Society of Genealogists, ca. 1990.

Property and Privilege in Medieval and Early Modern England and Wales: Cartularies and Other Registers. Harvester Microform, 1986.

Sanders, I. J. *English Baronies: A Study of Their Origin and Descent 1086–1327.* Oxford, England: Clarendon Press, 1960.

Sharpe, R. R. *Calendar of Letter-Books of the City of London.* London: John Edward Francis, 1950.

Stuart, Denis. *Manorial Records: An Introduction to Their Transcription and Translation.* Chichester, Sussex, England: Phillimore & Co., ca. 1992.

Thompson, E. Margaret. *A Descriptive Catalogue of Manorial Rolls Belonging to Sir H. F. Burke, F.S.A., Garter-King-of-Arms: With Notes and Extracts Illustrating Manorial Custom.* London: Manorial Society, 1922–23.

Webb, Sidney. *The Manor and the Borough.* London: Frank Cass, 1963.

THE ROLLS

During the medieval period there were three primary functions of the central government: the chancery (secretarial), the exchequer (financial), and the courts of law (judicial). All grew out of the king's household. Information documenting the activities and accounts of these functions was recorded on parchment sheets which were sewn together, end to end, and then rolled up—hence the term *roll.*

The extant exchequer rolls start in 1129–30 with the Great Rolls of the Exchequer, more commonly called the Pipe Rolls. They list the annual revenue accounts of the county sheriffs and other similar officials for all of the counties of England. Auditing sessions were performed at Easter and at Michaelmas (29 September). The records of the Pipe Rolls concern *subinfeudation,* the practice of subdividing a feudal estate by a vassal, who in turn became feudal lord over his own tenants. For much of the earlier medieval period the Pipe Rolls are the only records for many individuals, places, and transactions. They have great genealogical value because relationships described in acquiring and transferring land provide linkage proofs; however, their use is limited to those who can read medieval Latin.

The Pipe Roll Society, organized to preserve the information recorded on the Pipe Rolls, began publishing edited material in 1884 and is still continuing this invaluable series. The society has begun a new series of publications whose scope has been expanded to include other records, such as cathedral charters, cartularies, and lay subsidies.

The extant chancery records began in 1199 with the practice of copying all important letters onto rolls to preserve an official copy. There are several roll series, but among the ones most used by genealogists are the Patent Rolls (1201 to 1920) and the Close Rolls (1204 to 1903). The Patent Rolls refer to grants of office, honors, and privileges to individuals or corporations. Below is a sample patent roll from 4 and 5 Philip and Mary.

> 4 AND 5 PHILIP AND MARY.–Part XV.
> 1558.
> 26 June. Whereas by patent under the great seal of the Court of Augmentations. 24 Nov., 3 Edw. VI, were leased for 21 years to Thomas Phaier, gentleman, all lands (100 ac. land, 10 ac. meadow) commonly called 'lez demeanes' of the lordship of Kilgaran and the herbage of the forest (100 ac.) in Kilgaran, co. Pembroke, all which were sometimes in the tenure of William Vaughan, late steward of the said lordship, and were of the lands of the late duke of Bedford, at a yearly rent of 4l. 1s. 4d.; which patent Phaier has surrendered into the Exchequer with intent as follows; Lease to him for 40 years of the said lands and herbage, except great trees, woods, mines and quarries, at the yearly rent of 4l. 1s. 4d.
> [m. 4l.] Phaier is to keep the lands in repair and may have sufficient 'housebote,' etc.
> By K. and Q.

The Close Rolls were records of private transactions between the crown and one or two persons only. They concern a vast number of topics. Below is a sample close roll from 28 Henry VI.

> 28 HENRY VI.
> Feb. 28.
> Westminster. To the bailiffs and citizens of Canterbury for the time being. Order during the nonage of John Broke the son to pay to his next friend to whom the heritage may not descend 3l. 9s. 5d. a year and the arrears since his father's death; as upon the finding of an inquisition, taken before the escheator in Kent, that John Broke died seised of 3l. 9s. 5d. a year of the farm of the said city, namely 23s. 1 1/4d. at Easter and 46s. 3 1/4d. at Michaelmas, as his share of 30l. a year which King Edward III by letters patent granted to William son of John Cundy and to his heirs in recompense for the bailiwick of the town of Sandewich, that John Broke was his cousin and one of his heirs, namely brother of Robert son of Joan daughter of Robert son of Margaret

> one of the daughters and heirs of Constance one of his sisters and heirs, that John Broke is his son and next heir, and is of the age of half a year and more, and that the money is held in chief by fealty only for all services, by writ of 26 February last the king ordered the escheator to deliver the money to the keeping of the said next friend of the heir.
> *Et erat patens.*

Other minor records or rolls start with the Liber Feodorum (Book of Fees). Known as Liber Feodorum from its inception in 1198 until 1383, this series was also known as Testa de Nevill by 1383. It contains knight's fees and serjeanties from the reigns of Henry III and Edward I. The Liber Feodorum was based on the need for an aid or *scutage* for marriage of the eldest daughter of Edward I in 1302. This tax was "voluntary," so King Edward needed to determine knight's fees and their holders and serjeanties that might yield revenues to the crown. More than five hundred documents were transcribed into the current three-volume Book of Fees.

The Calender of the Fine Rolls derives its name from fines or payments recorded on rolls (or membranes) of vellum. These rolls contain fines for licences and pardons for: (1) land alienation and acquisition; (2) Commissions of Oyer and Terminer (courts that tried felonies); and (3) charters and confirmations of charters. The Letters Patent and Letters Close Rolls comprise the largest and most important class; they relate to matters of crown financial interest, direct and indirect.

Rotuli Curiae Regis, or the Curia Regis Rolls and Records, contain early pleas from a period when English common law was still evolving. The pleas had no prescribed form; they were rather narrative and informal. They cover the years 1196 to 1242, and were records of the court held before the king's justiciars or justices. A large quantity of business was transacted before the justiciars, despite the expense. Many of the cases tried were insignificant; suits were brought for very inconsiderable portions of land. The most interesting aspect of these rolls is that every appellant supported his complaint with his own personal testimony.

The Chancery Rolls cover from 1199 to 1937; in them are recorded royal grants of land, privileges, and titles. They also contain title deeds and a section termed the Supplementary Close Rolls; these were supplementary to the Close Rolls and Patent Rolls. These records range from licences for exportation of wool to *respites of assizes of novel disseisin* (essentially a letter of protection granted to individuals who personally served the sovereign; it exempted them from paying the aid [tax] because of their service). Below is an example:

> Respites of an Aid in favour of persons serving in Scotland 31-32 Edw.I
> Alnwick 13 May 1303
> John de Ferariis, who is setting out for the king in Scotland, has letters of respite of the aid in co. Somerset, Gloucester, and Berks

The second division of the Chancery Rolls was the Welsh Rolls—seven rolls covering the period 5-23 Edward I (meaning the fifth through the twenty-third years of Edward I's reign). Their contents include letters patent, letters close, charters, and other documents relating to this period. An example of this roll is from "Membrane 10d. - Welshmen for whom the king will provide":

> Meilir ab Gronok, footman. Has always behaved himself well to the king from the beginning of the war, as is testified by R. de Grey, David, and the justiciary, and provision shall be made outside the king's table for 40s. for his costs upon this occasion, of the king's gift
> Meilir ab Eynun, Kadegon ab Madok, footmen. Have a bailiwick from the king, and therefore nothing shall be done for them.

The third of the Chancery Rolls is the Scutage Rolls, four rolls that are very similar to the Supplementary Close Rolls.

The *Calendar of the Charter Rolls* begins in 1 King John and goes to 8 Henry VIII (from the first year of King John's reign to the eighth year of King Henry the Eighth's). Presently there is no reliable guide to the rolls prior to the reign of King John. The current series of publications provides a calendar in English of the Charter Rolls from Henry III to Henry VIII. Most of the information came from documents already in the Exchequer, which were later known as records of the King's Remembrancer. The contents of the original rolls were assignments of serjeanties, ecclesiastical fees seized due to the interdict of 1208–1213, returns of fees, extracts from eyre rolls, etc.

Feudal Aids is a very important source that ranges from 1284 to 1431. The contents of these records are inquisitions and assessments relating to feudal aids. These records show the succession of holders of land used to assess reliefs and other feudal dues. The Feet of Fines or Pedes Finium are judgements as to ownership of land and property. These usually were called for when parties wished to establish title in the absence of documents.

Deeds comprise another source, but they are not common for the medieval period. Most were recorded in Latin; they usually contain transfers of land and are mainly from the twelfth and thirteenth centuries.

Published Rolls

Galbraith, Vivian H. *An Introduction to the Use of the Public Records.* [London]: Oxford University Press, 1934.

Calendar of various Chancery Rolls; Supplementary Close Rolls, Welsh Rolls, Scutage Rolls. London: Her Majesty's Stationery Office, 1912. Reprint. Kraus-Thomson, 1976.

Calendarium Rotulorum Chartarum et Inquisitionum Ad Quod Damnum. London, 1803.

Calendar of the Close Rolls Preserved in the Public Record Office: Edward I. 5 vols. London: Her Majesty's Stationery Office, 1900–54. Reprint. Nendeln, Liechtenstein: Kraus-Thomson Organization, 1970. (*Edward II,* 4 vols.; *Edward III,* 14 vols.; *Richard II,* 6 vols.; *Henry IV,* 5 vols.; *Henry V,* 2 vols.; *Henry VI,* 5 vols.; *Edward IV, Edward V, and Richard III, 1461–1585,* 3 vols.)

Calendar of the Patent Rolls Preserved in the Public Record Office: Edward I. 4 vols. Her Britannic Majesty's Stationery Office, 1898–1970. Reprint. Nendeln, Liechtenstein: Kraus-Thomson Organization, 1971. (*Edward II,* 5 vols.; *Edward III,* 16 vols.; *Richard II,* 6 vols.; *Henry IV,* 4 vols.; *Henry V,* 2 vols ; *Henry VI,* 6 vols.; *Edward IV, Edward V, Richard III, 1476–1485; Edward VI,* 6 vols.; *Philip and Mary,* 2 vols.)

Close Rolls of the Reign of Henry III Preserved in the Public Record Office. 14 vols. [London]: Public Record Office, 1902–38. Reprint. Nendeln, Liechtenstein: Kraus-Thomson Organization, 1970.

Patent Rolls of the Reign of Henry III Preserved in the Public Record Office. 6 vols. London: Her Britannic Majesty's Stationery Office, 1901–13. Reprint. Nendeln, Liechtenstein: Kraus-Thomson Organization, 1970.

Testa de Nevill sive Liber Feodorum in Curia Scaccarii. London, 1807.

INQUISITIONS POST MORTEM

An inquiry taken after the death of a person holding real estate in England is called an *inquisition post mortem* (often abbreviated I.P.M. or Inq.p.m.). These comprise one of the most important record sources which have been preserved, and they cover a significant time period for which few other records showing genealogical linkages are extant.

According to English feudal law, all land belonged to the king and reverted to the crown upon the death of the tenant. In order to continue possession, the heir (eldest son) had to pay a relief and had to pay homage to his feudal superior. The primary purpose of the inquisition was to insure that the king's rights as chief overlord were enforced and that the revenue was collected. When the heir was a minor, the property was held by the feudal superior until the heir came of age and was able to pay homage. The heir became a ward of the feudal superior, and wardships were of significant monetary value to a king; the rights to them were carefully guarded.

Upon the death of a tenant-in-chief, a royal officer received a writ from the king ordering him to determine what lands the deceased had held, the rents or services by which they were held, and the name and age of the heir. Normally a jury met to complete the requirements of the writ and to submit a report. Separate inquests were held in each county in which the deceased held land. The usefulness of inquisitions post mortem is limited by the fact that, often, only the heir was mentioned (particularly in early inquests). In some cases spouses—living or deceased—and other relatives were indicated. When the deceased left only daughters, they shared equally in a division of his properties. Many genealogical relationships have been determined from the information preserved in these inquests.

Inquisition post mortem records exist from the reign of Henry III (1261 to 1272) until the beginning of the Commonwealth period in 1649. The value of such direct evidence collected at the time of death is of great value to genealogists. The primary information in these records can generally be relied upon; all secondary information contained in them must be evaluated, as in all other records, to determine its reliability.

The originals, or contemporary copies, are housed at the Public Record Office in London. There is increasing interest in printing abstracts of inquisitions post mortem, especially among local record societies. There are also numerous published calendars, lists, and indexes. The most significant group of printed inquisition post mortem records is the collection of those preserved in the Public Record Office, *Calendar of Inquisitions Post Mortem and Other Analogous Documents Preserved in the Public Record Office,* 1st ser., 14 vols. (London: Public Record Office, 1904–52. Reprint. Nendeln, Liechtenstein: Kraus-Thompson Organization, 1973); 2nd ser., 2 vols. (London: H. M. Stationery Office, 1898, 1915. Reprint. Nendeln, Liechtenstein: Kraus-Thompson Organization, 1973). These records are English-language abstracts; hence, they make available to the public thousands of inquisitions post mortem in a readily usable form.

Below is part of an early inquisition post mortem for Simon de Pateshulle, 24 Edward I (1296):

> 369. SIMON DE PATESHULLE alias DE PATESHYLLE.
> *Writ,* 2 Dec. 24 Edw. I.
> ESSEX. *Inq.* made at Bulmere, 26 Jan 24 Edw. I.
> Belchamp William (*in Bello Campo Willelmi*). 72a arable, 4 1/2a. meadow, 3a. pasture, 20a. wood, works, ploughings of 'gavelacre,' and 14s. 10d. assised rents, held of Robert de Ver, earl of Oxford, by service of 1/18 knight's fee, of the inheritance of Isabel his wife daughter and heir of John de Stengreve.
> John his son, aged 4, is his next heir.
> LINCOLN. *Inq.* Thursday after St. Lucy, 24 Edw. I.
> Fryseby. 36 bovates of land, whereof 12 used to be held in demesne and are put to farm (*ad altam firmam*) to the bondmen who hold the remainder, a plot (*placea*) of meadow, and a moiety of a water-mill, held of the inheritance of Isabel daughter of John de Steyngreve, sometime his wife, of Richard Folyot, as the gift of Jordan Foliot his father to Simon de Steyngreve, grandfather of the said Isabel, in free marriage with Beatrice his daughter.
> Heir unknown, because he was born in distant parts.

The following is a later inquisition post mortem for James Whitney, 15 Henry VII (1500).

> 261. JAMES WHITNEY, esquire.
> *Writ* 10 August, 15 Henry VII; *inquisition* 27 October, 16 Henry VII.
> He as seised of the under-mentioned manors of Whiteney, Boughrede and Pencombe and land, &c. in Home Lacy and Fnoggesashe, in fee, and being so seised enfeoffed James Baskervile, knight, Simon Milborne Walter Baskervile, James Scudamore, esquires, John Breynton, William Burghill, Richard Lynke, rector of the church of Staundon, and Simon Heryng, thereof; the said James Baskervile afterwards died, and the said Simon and the others survived him and were, and still are, seised thereof in fee.
> James Baskervile, knight, Robert Vaughan of Hergest, Walter Baskervile, John Godeman of Hereford, and Rowland Blakeston, were seised of the under-mentioned manor of Ocle Pichard, &c., in fee, and being so seised, by charter, 3 March, 7 Henry VII, enfeoffed the said James, by the name of James Whiteney son of Robert Whiteney, esquire, and Blanch wife of the said James, daughter of Simon Milborne, esquire, thereof, to them and the heirs of their bodies between them begotten; they were seised thereof accordingly in fee tail, and ha issue between them Robert Whiteney; and afterwards the said James died, and the said Blanch survived him and is seised of the said manor, &c. in fee tail by survivorship, by the form of the gift.
> He died the last day of June last. Robert Whiteney aged 6 and more, is son and heir of him and of the said Blanch of their bodies begotten.
> MARCHES OF WALES. Manor of Whiteney and the advowson of the church of St. Peter of Whiteney appurtenant to the said manor, worth 10l., held of

Edward, duke of Buckingham, as of the castle and honor of Huntyngdon, service unknown.
Manor of Boughrede, worth five marks, held of the king by socage, viz. by service of 3d. yearly, for all service.
HEREFORD. Manor of Pencombe, worth 10l. held of the lord Bergenny, as of his lordship of Ewias Harold, service unknown.
Four messuages, 120a. meadow, 40a. pasture, in Home Lacy and Fnoggesasshe (sic), those in Home Lacy, worth 46s. 8d., held of the deah and chapter of St. Ethelbert of Hereford, service unknown, and those in Fnoggesasshe (sic), worth 20s. held of Thomas ap Harry, as of the manor of Eton Tregos, service unknown.
Manor of Ocle Pichard, worth 10l., held of John, lord Ferrers, as of the castle and honor of Webley, service unknown.
A messuage, 100a. land, 20a. meadow, in Kyngescaple; a messuage, 20a. land in Baisham; a toft, 16a. land in Brokhampton; a messuage 18a. land in Howcaple, worth 4 marks, held of Thomas, earl of Ormond, as of the castle of Kilpek, service unknown.
C. Series II. vol. 14 (19.) E. Series II. File 409. (2.)

Sources for Inquisitions Post Mortem

Calendar of Inquisitions Post Mortem and Other Analogous Documents Preserved in the Public Record Office. 1st ser. 14 vols. London: Public Record Office, 1904–52. Reprint. Nendeln, Liechtenstein: Kraus-Thompson Organization, 1973. 2nd ser. 2 vols. London: H. M. Stationery Office, 1898, 1915. Reprint. Nendeln, Liechtenstein: Kraus-Thompson Organization, 1973.

Calendarium Inquisitionum Post Mortum sive Escaetarum. London, 1808.

Calendar of Inquisitions Miscellaneous (Chancery). London: H.M. Stationery Office, 1916. Reprint. Kraus-Thomson Organization, 1973.

Inquisitions and Assessments Relating to Feudal Aids. London: Her Majesty's Stationery Office, 1899.

HERALDS' VISITATIONS OF ENGLAND

During the early development of heraldry, most of the great nobles had their own heralds. In 1484 King Richard III of England formed his heralds into a corporation called the College of Arms (sometimes called the Heralds' College). The "officers" of arms are *kings of arms, heralds,* and *pursuivants.* The last term is from medieval French; it designates a follower or "junior" herald. The kings of arms were the *chief* heralds.

Beginning in 1530, the officers of arms were commissioned to visit the various counties of England and there to inspect all of the arms in use. The records made during these visits are commonly called *visitations.* They have been preserved as an extremely valuable genealogical, as well as heraldic, record. These inspections continued until 1686.

The earliest visitation pedigrees were recorded in the homes of the arms holders, known as *armigers.* In the 1560s this process was deemed too slow and cumbersome, so by 1566 county sheriffs were notifying armigers to appear before the visiting heralds, usually at inns of the larger towns in the counties, where the heralds lodged.

Visitation pedigrees provide excellent clues for further research, but they cannot be fully accepted without corroborating evidence. There has been considerable criticism of the accuracy of heralds' visitations, as in J. Horace Round's *Family Origins and Other Studies,* edited by William Page (London: Constable, 1930). Sir Anthony Richard Wagner, in *English Genealogy,* states that the visitations made under the royal commission of 1530 were generally free from fabrications. The 1560 and later visitations include pedigrees containing fabricated information and must therefore be examined more critically. Most heralds of that time were not skilled genealogists. Robert Glover began to lay foundations of critical genealogy in 1567 with his entrance into the College of Arms.

An analysis of the printed pedigree often gives clues as to the source of the information and its reliability. In figure 20-1, from Walter C. Metcalfe, ed., *The Visitations of Hertfordshire: Made by Robert Cooke, Esq., Clarencieux, in 1572, and Sir Robert St. George, Kt., Clarencieus, in 1634, with Hertfordshire Pedigrees from Harleian mss. 6147 and 1546,* Publications of the Harleian Society, vol. 22 (London, 1886), the informant was "Theophilus Elmer of Much Hadham, co. Hertf., Archdeacon of London." He provided information regarding his grandfather, his parents, and his siblings. Obviously, the closer the generations are to him and the closer the dates to the year 1634, the more likely they are to be accurate. (Pedigrees going back more than three generations are likely to be based upon tradition or family documents that may not be accurate.) Every piece of information in this pedigree can logically be attributed to the personal knowledge of Theophilus Elmer.

Most of the visitations have been printed; the most active publisher has been the Harleian Society of London. Many others, including a few duplications, have been printed by county historical societies and even by private individuals. The printed pedigrees are often compilations of two or more visitations; this practice allows errors to creep in as interpretations are made regarding the original information. To learn about medieval sources, a good practice technique is to assemble proof for a visitation pedigree from the sources already discussed in this chapter.

Following is a list of the years in which visitations were made in the various counties of England, although not all of these are available in print. A valuable reference that helps to access these visitations is Lance Jacob's *Printed Visitations Pedigrees of England* (Salt Lake City: Church of Jesus Christ of Latter-day Saints, 1981).

County	*Years*
Bedfordshire	1566, 1582, 1634, 1669
Berkshire	1532, 1566, 1623, 1664–66
Buckinghamshire	1566, 1574, 1634, 1669–74
Cambridgeshire	1575, 1619, 1684
Cheshire	1533, 1566–67, 1580, 1613, 1663
Cornwall	1530, 1573, 1620
Cumberland	1530, 1573, 1615, 1666
Derbyshire	1569, 1611, 1634, 1662–64
Devonshire	1531, 1564, 1572, 1620
Dorsetshire	1531, 1565, 1623, 1677
Durham	1530, 1575, 1615, 1666
Essex	1552, 1558, 1570, 1612, 1634, 1664–68
Gloucestershire	1531, 1569, 1582–83, 1623, 1682–83
Hampshire	1530, 1575, 1622–24, 1686

THE VISITATION OF HERTFORDSHIRE, 1634. 31

Brisco of Aldenham.

ARMS.—*Quarterly*—1 *and* 4, *Argent, three greyhounds courant in pale Sable;* 2, *Gules, a saltire engrailed Argent,* CROSTON; 3, *Per pale Argent and Sable, a fleur-de-lis counterchanged,* WHINNE; *a mullet on a crescent for difference.*
CREST.—*A greyhound courant Sable, holding in the mouth a hare proper.*

Proofe hath bene made.

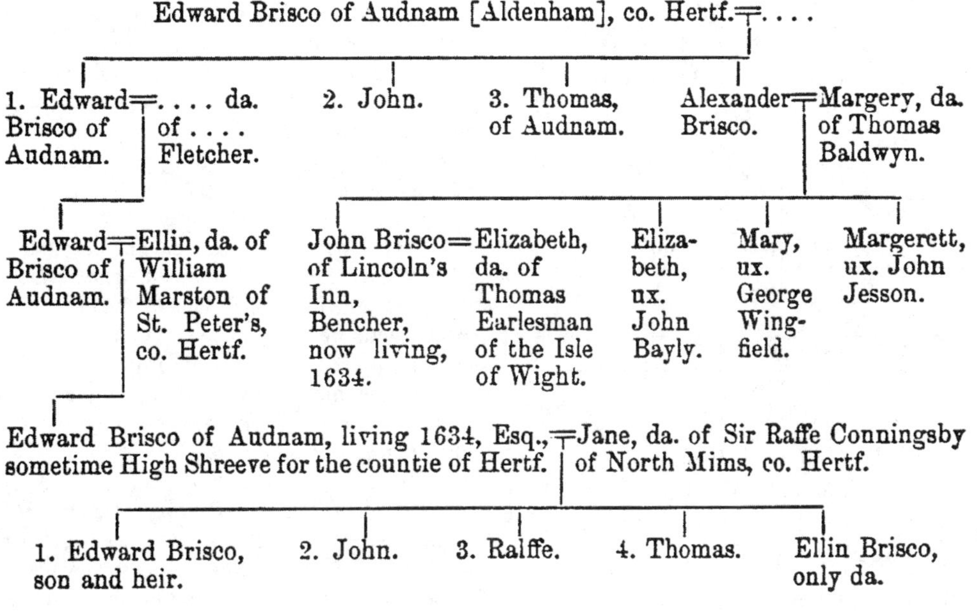

Edward Brisco of Audnam [Aldenham], co. Hertf.=. . . .

1. Edward=. . . . da. Brisco of Audnam. | of . . . . Fletcher. — 2. John. — 3. Thomas, of Audnam. — Alexander=Margery, da. Brisco. | of Thomas Baldwyn.

Edward=Ellin, da. of Brisco of Audnam. | William Marston of St. Peter's, co. Hertf.

John Brisco=Elizabeth, of Lincoln's Inn, Bencher, now living, 1634. | da. of Thomas Earlesman of the Isle of Wight. — Eliza-beth, ux. John Bayly. — Mary, ux. George Wing-field. — Margerett, ux. John Jesson.

Edward Brisco of Audnam, living 1634, Esq.,=Jane, da. of Sir Raffe Conningsby sometime High Shreeve for the countie of Hertf. | of North Mims, co. Hertf.

1. Edward Brisco, son and heir. — 2. John. — 3. Ralffe. — 4. Thomas. — Ellin Brisco, only da.

Brisco of St. Michael's.

The armes not proved, nor this descent allowed to be entred, Mr. Brisco doth promise to make good prooffe with the rest of his kinred in Michellmas Tearme, which he hath since done.

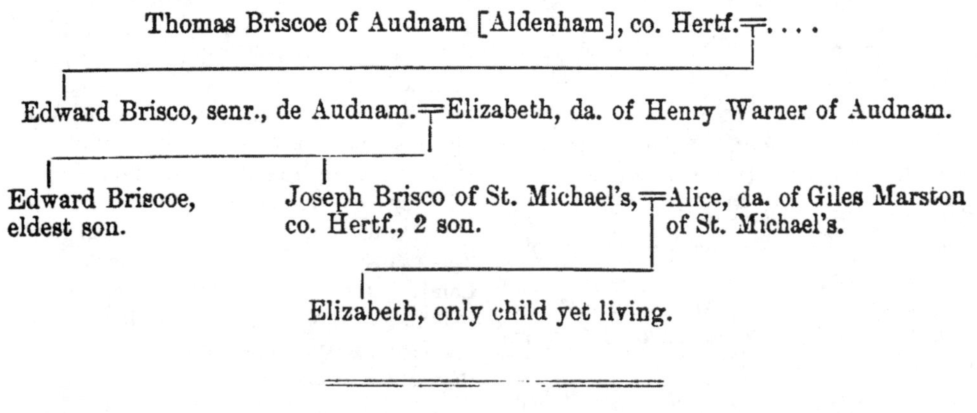

Thomas Briscoe of Audnam [Aldenham], co. Hertf.=. . . .

Edward Brisco, senr., de Audnam.=Elizabeth, da. of Henry Warner of Audnam.

Edward Briscoe, eldest son. — Joseph Brisco of St. Michael's,=Alice, da. of Giles Marston co. Hertf., 2 son. | of St. Michael's.

Elizabeth, only child yet living.

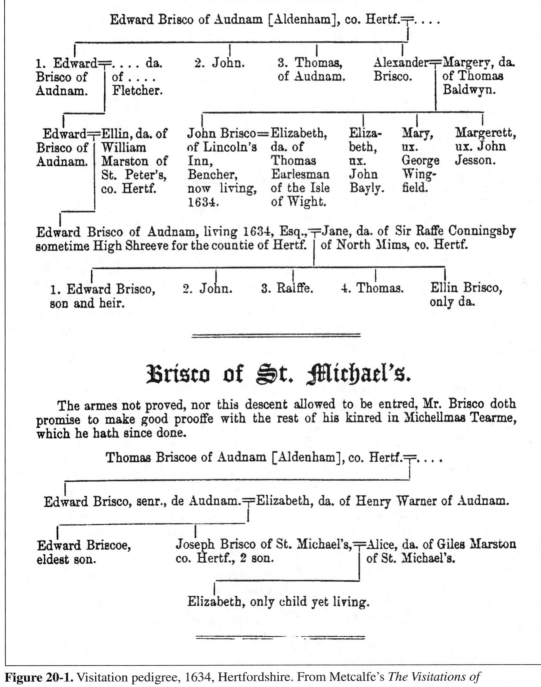

Figure 20-1. Visitation pedigree, 1634, Hertfordshire. From Metcalfe's *The Visitations of Hertfordshire.*

Herefordshire	1569, 1634, 1686
Hertfordshire	1572, 1634, 1669
Huntingdonshire	1564, 1613, 1686
Kent	1530, 1574, 1592–94, 1619, 1663
Lancashire	1533, 1567, 1613, 1664–65
Leicestershire	1563, 1619, 1682–83
Lincolnshire	1562–64, 1592, 1634, 1666
London	1568, 1633–35, 1664, 1687
Middlesex	1572, 1634, 1663
Monmouthshire	1683
Norfolk	1563, 1589, 1612, 1664–68
Northumberland	1564–66, 1618–19, 1681–82
Northamptonshire	1530–1575, 1615, 1666
Nottinghamshire	1530, 1569, 1575, 1614, 1662–64
Oxfordshire	1530, 1566, 1574, 1634, 1688
Rutlandshire	1618–19, 1681–82
Shropshire	1569, 1584, 1623, 1663
Somersetshire	1531, 1573, 1591, 1623, 1672
Staffordshire	1533, 1563, 1583, 1614, 1663–64
Suffolk	1561, 1577, 1612, 1664–68
Surrey	1530, 1572, 1623, 1662–68
Sussex	1530, 1574, 1633–34, 1662
Warwickshire	1563, 1619, 1682–83
Westmorland	1530, 1615, 1664
Wiltshire	1531, 1565, 1623, 1677
Worcestershire	1530, 1569, 1634, 1682
Yorkshire	1530, 1563–64, 1584–85, 1612, 1665–66

Heralds' Visitations Sources

Bridger, Charles. *An Index to Printed Pedigrees Contained in County and Local Histories, the Herald's Visitations, and in the More Important Genealogical Collections.* London: John Russell Smith, 1867. Reprint. Baltimore: Genealogical Publishing Co., 1969.

Chesshyre, Hubert, and Adrian Ailes. *Heralds of Today: A Biographical List of the Officers of the College of Arms.* Gerards Cross, England: Van Duren, 1986.

Dennys, Roger. *Heraldry and the Heralds.* London: Jonathan Cape, 1984.

Godfrey, Walter H., assisted by Sir Anthony Richard Wagner. *The College of Arms.* London: London Survey Committee, 1963.

Jacob, Lance. *Printed Visitations Pedigrees of England.* Salt Lake City: Church of Jesus Christ of Latter-day Saints, 1981.

Marshall, George W. *An Index to the Pedigrees Contained in the Printed Heralds' Visitations.* London: Robert Hardwicke, 1866.

Noble, Mark. *A History of the College of Arms: And the Lives of All the Kings, Heralds, and Pursuivants.* London: T. Egerton et al., 1805.

Round, John Horace. *Family Origins and Other Studies.* Edited by William Page. London: Constable, 1930.

Sims, R. (Richard). *An Index to the Pedigrees and Arms Contained in the Heralds' Visitations, and Other Genealogical Manuscripts in the British Museum.* London: John Russell Smith, 1849. Reprint. Baltimore: Genealogical Publishing Co., 1970.

Squibb, G. D. (George Drewry). *Visitation Pedigrees and the Genealogist.* Reprint. Canterbury, England: Phillimore, 1978.

Wagner, A. R. (Sir Anthony Richard). *Heralds of England.* London: Her Majesty's Stationery Office, 1967.

_____. *The Records and Collections of the College of Arms.* London: Burkes Peerage, 1952.

HERALDRY

"Heraldry is the science and art that deals with the use, display, and regulation of hereditary symbols employed to distinguish individuals, institutions, and corporations" (*New Encyclopædia Britannica* 1986, vol. 20, 565).

The practice of European heraldry has evolved from an obscure beginning in the twelfth century, or perhaps even earlier (see Beryl Platts's *Origin of Heraldry* [London: Proctor, 1980]). In western Europe, until the beginning of the sixteenth century, heraldry was primarily utilitarian. The need to identify opposing combatants in battle, when their faces were covered by helmets, resulted in warriors decorating their shields in patterns that were easily recognizable and definable and that eventually became hereditary. During the organized crusades in the Holy Land, the hot climate encouraged the wearing of a fabric covering over the chain mail armor worn by the crusaders. It became a common custom to repeat the shield pattern on this fabric or *surcoat.* From this practice arose the use of the English phrase *coat of arms.*

In many cases the choice of heraldic design was by whim, while in others there was a direct correlation with the bearer's name, residence, origin, or occupation. Not only did individuals or families use heraldic devices; they were also adopted by ecclesiastical families, towns and other political units, merchant companies, and eventually by almost any corporate body.

In many respects heraldry developed quite differently in the various corners of Europe. However, the basic rules covering coloration (or tintures) were fairly similar throughout western Europe. Two major classes of coloration—*metals* and *colours*—came into being. In the simplest form, the metals are gold and silver; the colours are red, blue, black, green, and purple, with the latter two only rarely used during this time. A third, scarcer, class is *furs,* of which the celebrated ermine used in the shield of Brittany is the most common. The common rule is that if the background of the shield is a metal, the designs placed on it, called *charges,* must be a color. And the reverse is true—metal on color, or color on metal. A fur can be placed on either metal or color, and either metal or color can be placed on a fur. However, there are many who delight in pointing out the not-infrequent exceptions to the rule.

At the time heraldry was developing in England, the upper classes using the practice spoke Norman French. The heraldic designs and devices were, therefore, described in that language. Even though English became the language of the country, the language of heraldry clung tenaciously to the French terms. In other parts of western Europe, heraldic descriptions have not maintained such a rigid adherence to ancient terminology.

Problems with the use of heraldic symbols, caused by marriage alliances, inheritance, and large numbers of offspring, arose early in the story of heraldry. Among the earliest solutions involving inheritance and alliances resulted in dividing the shield into two side-by-side parts (called *impaling*) or dividing the shield into four parts (called *quartering*). As some families made profitable marriage alliances and wished to display the heraldic symbols of each family, four parts became insufficient. The result, particularly in many of the Germanic areas, was shields with a myriad of divisions.

While the primary emphasis was on the shield and coat of arms, another aspect of heraldry developed in the use of a *crest.* Its origin was probably in early tournaments when knights would bind an object to their helmets with a wreath of twisted silk. Later, the *helm* (or helmet), depicting varying degrees of rank, was developed; *supporters* to uphold the shield became more common; and *mottos* were added. The entire assemblage is referred to as an *achievement;* for more important titles, the achievement can be very elaborate. As a general rule, the simpler the coat of arms, the older it is.

It became evident early in the development of heraldry that some form of control over the use of heraldic symbols was needed. During the fourteenth and fifteenth centuries this duty was gradually assigned to the heralds. They had been previously employed primarily as messengers and in conducting tournaments. Obviously, the term *heraldry* came directly from the heralds' title. Different countries found different solutions to deal with problems arising from younger sons using the "family" coat-of-arms. The most precise control of arms, and (according to most Scots) the most logical and systematic, is employed in Scotland.

The use of coats of arms has been associated with the landed classes from its inception. In the later medieval period it incorporated the concept of superiority. "To bear arms was the mark of a gentleman; therefore, to possess the desirable quality of gentility, a man needed to have armorial bearings" (*New Encyclopædia Britannica* 1986, vol. 20, 566). Modern genealogists overlook this very useful tool, perhaps disdaining with pride the need to understand a science which they feel advocates social superiority.

Despite what many are led to believe, basic heraldic principles can be learned quickly. With a few commonly used terms, most coats of arms can be understood. A good heraldic reference book can be relied upon to supply the more esoteric terms as the need arises. The following bibliography will be useful both for beginners or advanced researchers. The more basic publications can often be found in local public libraries, and almost all of the following can be obtained through interlibrary loan. Many are also available for purchase at local bookstores.

HERALDRY SOURCES

Basic Reference Works

Brooke-Little, J. P. (John Philip). *An Heraldic Alphabet.* New York: Arco, 1973.

Fox-Davies, Arthur Charles. *Heraldry Explained.* London: T. C. & E. C. Jack, 1906. Reprint. N.p., 1971.

Moncrieffe of that Ilk, Sir Iain. *Simple Heraldry.* Rev. ed. Edinburgh, Scotland: John Bartholomew, 1978.

Pine, Leslie Gilbert. *The Genealogist's Encyclopedia.* Reprint. New York: Weybright and Talley, 1977.

Planche, James Robinson. *The Pursuivant of Arms: Or, Heraldry Founded Upon Facts.* London: Chatto and Windus, 1873. Reprint. N.p., 1973.

Swinnerton, Iain. *Heraldry for Family Historians.* Birmingham, England: Federation of Family History Societies, 1995.

Wagner, Sir Anthony R. *Heraldry in England.* London: King Penguin Books, 1946. Reprint. N.p., 1953.

Wise, Terence. *Medieval Heraldry.* London: Osprey, 1980.

British Isles

Brault, Gerard J. *Early Blazon: Heraldic Terminology in the Twelfth and Thirteenth Centuries, with Special Reference to Arthurian Literature.* Oxford, England: Clarendon Press, 1972.

Brooke-Little, John Philip. *Boutell's Heraldry.* London and New York: Frederick Warne, 1978. First published in 1950, this book has had many editors and several editions.

Burke, Sir John Bernard. *The General Armory of England, Scotland, Ireland and Wales: Comprising a Registry of Armorial Bearings from the Earliest to the Present Time.* Reprint. Baltimore: Genealogical Publishing Co., 1976.

Dennys, Rodney. *Heraldry and the Heralds.* London: Jonathan Cape, 1982.

Dwynn, Lewys. *Heraldic Visitations of Wales.* 2 vols. Llandovery, Wales: William Rees, 1856.

Fox-Davies, Arthur Charles. *The Art of Heraldry: An Encyclopedia of Armory.* New York: Arno Press, 1976.

_____. *A Complete Guide to Heraldry.* 1909. Reprint. New York: Bonanza Books, 1985.

Franklyn, Julian. *Shield and Crest: An Account of the Art and Science of Heraldry.* 3rd ed. London: MacGibbon & Kee, 1971.

Gayre, Robert of Gayre and Nigg. *Heraldic Cadency: The Development of Differencing of Coats of Arms for Kinsmen and Other Purposes.* London: Faber and Faber, 1961.

_____. *The Nature of Arms: An Exposition of the Meaning and Significance of Heraldry with Special Reference to its Nobliary Aspects.* Edinburgh, Scotland: Oliver and Boyd, 1961.

Grenham, John. *Clans and families of Ireland: The heritage and heraldry of Irish clans and families.* Goldenbridge, Dublin, Ireland: Gill & Macmillan, 1993.

Gough, Henry, and James Parker. *A Glossary of Terms Used in Heraldry.* New ed. Detroit: Gale Research Co., 1966.

Humphrey-Smith, Cecil. *Anglo-Norman Armory.* Canterbury, England: Family History Northgate, 1973.

_____. *Anglo-Norman Armory Two: An Ordinary of Thirteenth-Century Armorials.* Canterbury, England: Institute of Heraldic and Genealogical Societies, 1984.

Innes, Sir Thomas. *Scots Heraldry.* 3rd ed. London: Johnston & Bacon, 1978.

Lynch-Robinson, Sir Christopher, and Adrian Lynch-Robinson. *Intelligible Heraldry: The Application of a Medieval System of Record and Identification to Modern Needs.* Reprint. Baltimore: Heraldic Book Co., 1967.

Milton, Roger. *Heralds and History.* London and Vancouver: David & Charles, 1978.

Nisbet, Alexander. *A system of heraldry, speculative and practical: with the true art of blazon according to the most approved heralds in Europe.* 2 vols. Edinburgh, Scotland: Printed for William Blackwood, Edinburgh. London: Rodwell and Martin, 1816.

Papworth, John Woody. *An Alphabetical Dictionary of Coats of Arms Belonging to Families in Great Britain and Ireland.* 1874. Reprint. Baltimore: Genealogical Publishing Co., 1977.

Phillimore, W. P. W. (William Phillimore Watts). *Heralds' College and Coats of Arms, Regarded From a Legal Aspect.* London: Phillimore & Co., 1904.

Pine, Leslie Gilbert. *American Origins.* Reprint. Baltimore: Genealogical Publishing Co., 1980.

_____. *The Genealogist's Encyclopedia.* Newton Abbott, England: David & Charles, 1969. See especially part 2, "Heraldry, Title, Peerage Law, and Orders of Chivalry."

_____. *Heraldry and Genealogy.* London: English Universities Press, 1974.

_____. *The Story of Heraldry.* Rutland, Vt.: C. E. Tuttle, 1967.

Platts, Beryl. *Origins of Heraldry.* London: Procter Press, 1980.

_____. *Scottish Hazard.* 2 vols. London: Procter Press, 1985. Discusses the movement of heraldry from the continent to Great Britain—especially into Scotland.

Siddons, Michael Powell. *The Development of Welsh Heraldry.* 3 vols. Aberystwyth: National Library of Wales, 1991–93. Without doubt the best source for Welsh heraldry. Vol. 1 discusses the development of Welsh heraldry; vol. 2 is a Welsh armorial (coats of arms listed by surname); and vol. 3 is an *ordinary* of Welsh arms (alphabetical by devices or charges of the arms themselves).

Wagner, Sir Anthony R. *Heralds and Ancestors.* London: Billing & Sons, 1978.

_____. *Historic Heraldry of Britain: An Illustrated Series of British Historical Arms, With Notes, Glossary, and an Introduction to Heraldry.* London: Phillimore, 1972.

Continental Europe

Arndt, Jürgen. *Wappenbilderordnung.* 2 vols. Neustadt an der Aisch: Bauer & Raspe, 1986, 1990. Handbook of German heraldic terminology with explanations in German.

Barczay, Oszkar. *A Heraldika Kezikonyve.* With supplements. Budapest, Hungary: Magy. Tud. Akademia, 1897.

Blanche, Pierre. *Dictionnaire et armorial des noms de famille de France.* Paris: Fayard, 1974. Dictionary of heraldry for French families.

Cadenas y Vicent, Vicente de. *Fundamentos de Héraldica: Ciencia del Blason.* Madrid, Spain: Hidalguia, 1975.

Fluvia, Armand de. *Diccionari General d'Heraldica: Glossari Angles, Castella, Frances, i Italia.* Barcelona, Spain: Edhasa, 1982.

Galbreath, Donald Lindsay. *Manuel de Blason.* Lausanne, Switzerland: Spes, 1977. Originally published in 1923.

Gevaert, Emile. *L'Héraldique: Son Esprit, Son Language et Ses Applications.* Brussels, Belgium: Bulletin des Metiers d'Art, n.d.

Hildebrandt, Adolf Matthias. *Wappenfibel, Handbuch der Heraldik.* Neustadt an der Aisch, [Germany]: Degener, 1967.

Leonhard, Walter. *Das grosse Buch der Wappenkunst: Entwicklung, Elemente, Bildmotive, Gestaltung.* Munich, Germany: Callwey, 1974.

Mandich, Donald R. *Russian heraldry and nobility.* Boynton Beach, Florida: Dramco, 1992.

Menendez Pidal de Navascues, Faustino. *Héraldica Medieval Española: La Casa Real de Leon y Castilla.* Vol. 1, *Madrid.* Hidalguia, 1982.

Neubecker, Ottfried. *Wappen-Bilder-Lexikon = Dictionnaire Heraldique = Encyclopedia of Heraldry.* Munich, Germany: Battenberg, 1974.

_____, and John Philip Brooke-Little. *Heraldry: Sources, Symbols, and Meaning.* London: Macdonald and Jane's, 1977.

Oswald, Gert. *Lexikon der Heraldik.* Mannheim, Germany, Vienna, Austria, and Zurich, Switzerland: Meyers Lexikonverlag, 1984.

North America

Beddoe, Alan B. *Canadian Heraldry.* Belleville, Ontario, Canada: Mika Publishing Co., 1981. A tremendous work on the use of heraldry in Canada, with many color plates of coats of arms of institutions and individuals.

Crozier, William A. *Crozier's General Armory: A Registry of American Families Entitled to Coat Armor.* Baltimore: Southern Book Co., 1957.

Zieber, Eugene. *Heraldry in America.* Baltimore Genealogical Publishing Co., 1977. Discusses the use of heraldry in America, especially as used on gravestones and bookplates.

Handbooks With Extensive Illustrations and Descriptions of Arms

Bergling, John Mauritz. *Heraldic Designs and Engravings: A Handbook and Dictionary of Heraldic Terms.* Rev. ed. Coral Gables, Fla.: V. C. Bergling, 1951.

Fairbairn, James. *Fairbairn's Book of Crests of the Families of Great Britain and Ireland.* 4th ed., rev. and enl., 1911. Reprint. Baltimore: Heraldic Book Co., 1968.

Jäger-Sunstenau, Hanns. *General-Index zu den Siebmacher'schen Wappenbüchern, 1605–1967.* Graz, Austria: Akademische Druck-u. Verlagsanstalt, 1984. General index to the Siebmacher heraldry books.

Louda, Jiri, and Michael Maclagan. *Heraldry of the Royal Families of Europe.* New York: Clarkson N. Potter, 1981. Excellent color artwork showing genealogies with descent and intermarriages.

Rietstap, Johannes Baptist. *Armorial General: Precede d'un dictionnaire des termes du blason.* 2 vols. Reprint. Baltimore: Genealogical Publishing Co., 1965.

Rolland, V. (Victor). *Armorial General Supplement.* 3 vols. Baltimore: Genealogical Publishing Co., 1965.

_____. *Illustrations to the Armorial General by J. B. Rietstap.* London: Heraldry Today, 1967.

Siebmacher, Johann. *J. Siebmacher's grosses und allgemeines Wappenbuch.* Nürnberg: Bauer & Raspe, 1857–1920. J. Siebmacher's armorial collection of German nobility.

Volborth, Carl Alexander von. *Heraldry: Customs, Rules, and Styles.* Poole, England: Blandford, 1981.

AN ILLUSTRATION

As a brief illustration of what can be accomplished using the sources discussed in this chapter, consider the following. The Ferrers family in England is a well-known medieval family represented by the Earls of Derby. However, there is another, unrelated, Ferrers family of the minor landed gentry that held land in the counties of Devon and Cornwall. Using the rolls, inquisitions, visitations, and local history, a chart of the lesser-known family was constructed (figure 20-2). These individuals were traced using the rolls as if they were a census. The identities of the holders of the various pieces of property were the major clues. In actuality, it was the property that was traceable.

This chart shows a six-generation connection from France to Devon, England. The family apparently did not come over with William the Conqueror, but arrived soon after. Sir Fulk FitzGilbert de Ferrers had female descendants whose lineages eventually appeared in New England. This is given as follows:

> Alice de Ferrers married Sir William Prouz, Lord of Gidley in Devon;
> Sir Richard Prouz was their son, and had;
> Thomasine Prouz, who married John Chudlegh;
> John Chudlegh, their son, married Jane Beauchamp;
> Sir James Chudleigh, their son, married Agnes/Joan Champernowne;
> James Chudleigh, their son, married Radigund _______;
> Petronell Chudleigh, their daughter, married Anthony Pollard;
> Joanne Pollard, their daughter, married Nicholas Ashe;
> Richard Esshe, their son, married Prudence Rudgley;
> Henry Eshe, their son, married Loveday Moyle;
> Prudence Esse or Eshe, their daughter, married Sir Oliver Mainwaring;
> Oliver Mainwaring, their son, came to Connecticut.

Although this kind of research is very time consuming, it is rewarding to assemble a proposed family from existing sources. With a bit of practice and with the information in this and other *Printed Sources* chapters, any researcher has the potential to do the same.

REFERENCE LIST

Venn, John, and John Archiband Venn. 1922–27. *Alumni Cantabrigienses: A Biographical List of All Known Students, Graduates and Holders of Office at the University of Cambridge, From the Earliest Times to 1900. Part 1: From the Earliest Times to 1751.* 4 vols. Cambridge: Cambridge University Press.

The New Encyclopædia Britannica. 1986. 15th ed. 32 vols. Chicago.

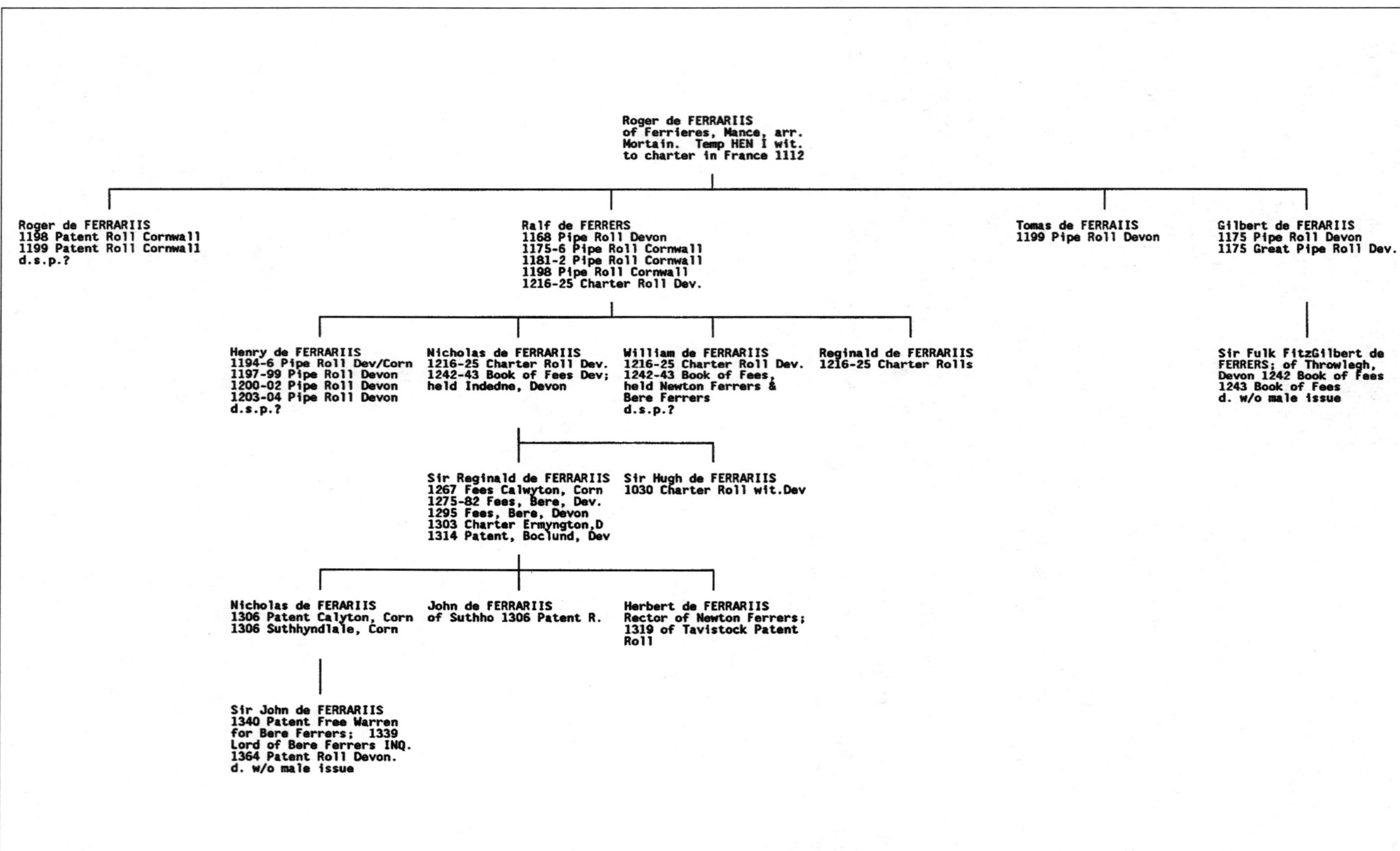

Figure 20-2. The Ferrers family of the minor landed gentry held land in the English counties of Devon and Cornwall. This chart was constructed using the rolls, inquisitions, visitations, and local history.

CONTRIBUTORS

Karen Clifford, AG, is president and CEO of Genealogy Research Associates (Monterey, California, and Salt Lake City, Utah) and is accredited in midwestern states research. She is an instructor in genealogy and computer courses at Hartnell College and Monterey Peninsula College as part of an Associate Degree Genealogy Program. Karen served as the director of the Monterey, California, Family History Center for eleven years and for sixteen years as a trainer for more than sixty-five volunteer staff members. She is currently serving as the vice president of the Federation of Genealogical Societies and as first vice president of the Utah Genealogical Association, and she was the founding president of the Monterey County Genealogy Society. She has authored three college genealogy textbooks and several family histories.

G. David Dilts, MLS, AG (German Research and LDS Records), has been employed at the Family History Library since 1975. He cataloged German, Austrian, Swiss, and Polish records from 1975 to 1980. He was a General and LDS Reference consultant from 1980 to 1987 and a senior LDS Reference consultant from 1987 to 1991. He has taught many computer classes at the library. David was the Family History Library's publications coordinator from 1991 from 1996 and is presently the senior U.S. Reference consultant. He was the chairman of Index Publishing from 1983 to 1989 and was responsible for the publication of thirty-two quality census indexes in three years. Since 1992 he has also been a genealogy instructor for the Brigham Young University Salt Lake Center. David has been the scoutmaster of Boy Scout Troop 39 since1988 and is the proud father of four scouts.

Richard W. Dougherty, AG, holds a Ph.D. in history from the University of Wisconsin-Madison. A Fulbright Scholar at the University of Bonn, Germany, his area of research specialization is tracing immigrant ancestors from Germany and central Europe. Accredited in German research by the Family History Library, he is also a member of the Concordia Historical Institute, the National Genealogical Society, the Utah Genealogical Association, and the Association of Professional Genealogists. He is the author of chapters on American, German, and central European collections in *The Library: A Guide to the LDS Family History Library* (Ancestry, 1988). Richard also contributed the chapter on church records in both editions of *The Source: A Guidebook of American Genealogy* (Ancestry, 1984 and 1997) and has written a number of journal articles and book reviews.

Wendy B. Elliott is a professor of history at California State University Fullerton and a nationally recognized genealogist with more than thirty years' experience. She developed and taught genealogy classes at local community colleges as well as a graduate-level course, "Genealogy for Librarians," for California State University San Jose's School of Library and Information Science. Wendy's article on the Jews of Boyle Heights—part of her dissertation—was published in the *Southern California Quarterly* Spring 1996. She coauthored and coedited *The Library: A Guide to the LDS Family History Library*, which received the American Library Association's "Reference Book of the Year" award in 1989. She contributed five chapters on the "Frontier South" for *Ancestry's Red Book: American State, County and Town Sources* (Ancestry, 1992). Wendy also has written numerous articles for national and local historical and genealogical publications. She currently serves on the Hall of Fame Committee for the National Genealogical Society and on the Awards and Records Preservation and Access committees for the Federation of Genealogical Societies (FGS). She has served on the board of directors for the Association of Professional Genealogists and the FGS and is a member of numerous genealogical and historical societies across the United States. In 1997 she was named a fellow of the Utah Genealogical Society.

Martha L. Henderson is department head of the Genealogy and Local History Department, Mid-Continent Public Library, Independence, Missouri, a position she has held since 1978. A graduate of the University of Missouri (BA in history), Martha also holds a master's degree in archival librarianship from the University of Denver. Active in local, state, and national genealogical societies, Martha is past president of the American Family Records Association. She is a past chair of the Genealogy Committee of the American Library Association and currently serves as chair-elect of that association's History Section. Martha is also the newsletter editor for the Missouri State Genealogical Association and is coeditor of *Genealogy from the Heartland,* a catalog of titles in the genealogy circulating collection of her library. She is active in her community, serving as chair of the Independence Tourism Advisory Board, and is a past president of the Independence West Rotary Club.

John M. Kitzmiller, 2nd, AG, is chairman and founder of The British Heritage Forum, a group of experienced professional genealogists specializing in all aspects of British research. John was elected a fellow of the Society of Genealogists (London) in 1993 (FSG); he is also a fellow of the Society of Antiquaries of Scotland (FSA [Scot]); fellow of the Royal Society of Antiquaries of Ireland (FSRAI [Ire]); accredited genealogist (England and Scotland); accredited heraldist, Heraldry Society of Canada and Heraldry Society of England (second-level certificates). He lectures internationally and has authored works on heraldry, military research, and British genealogy. John is also a genealogy instructor for various genealogical societies. He currently works as a user specialist for the LDS church's Family History Department.

Sandra Hargreaves Luebking is a professional genealogical and historical researcher. She has a BA degree in anthropology from the University of Illinois at Chicago and has completed graduate course work in history and communications at the University of Illinois at Springfield. She has been a lecturer at the Institute of Genealogy and Historical Research at Samford University since 1979. In 1990 she became the Course 1 coordinator. She is also the intermediate studies coordinator for the Genealogical Institute of Mid-America at the University of Illinois at Springfield; she has held that position since the establishment of the institute in 1994. She is the editor of *Forum,* the national quarterly magazine of the Federation of Genealogical Societies (FGS); *Carolyn Kuhn Royer: A Memoir;* and coeditor of *The Archives: A Guide to the National Archives Field Branches* (Ancestry, 1988). The last received a National Genealogical Society "Award for Excellence in Genealogical Methods and Sources." Her most recent publication is *The Source: A Guidebook of American Genealogy* (revised edition, 1997), coedited with Loretto D. Szucs for Ancestry. Recent honors are the David S. Vogels, Jr., Award (1992) for career contributions to the FGS; she was made a fellow of the Utah Genealogical Association (1993); and she received the Outstanding IGHR Alumni Award from Samford University (1995).

Kory L. Meyerink, MLS, AG, has been involved in nearly every aspect of genealogy and family history for the past twenty years. He began as a record searcher while attending Brigham Young University (BYU), Provo, Utah, where he received an associate's degree in Family and Local History and a BS degree in Psychology. He later received a master's degree in Library and Information Science. Two years in Germany gave him a fluency in the German language that has served him well in his professional research. He is accredited in four areas (Germany and the Midwest, eastern, and New England United States), specializing in tracing the origins of German and Dutch immigrants. He eventually joined the staff of the Family History Library as a reference consultant. Later, as the library's publication coordinator, he developed instructional and reference material for the thousands of family history centers supported by the library. He also served as the primary content consultant for PBS's *Ancestors* television series. In his recent work developing electronic products, Kory served as product manager for the *LDS Family History Suite* and also developed the largest genealogical gazetteer and largest genealogical bibliography available on CD-ROM.

As a teacher, Kory has spoken at many local, state, and national genealogical conferences throughout the United States and Canada, including those of the National Genealogical Society (NGS), Federation of Genealogical Societies (FGS), GENTECH, and, since 1991, the annual BYU Family History Conference. He also serves as an adjunct history faculty member for BYU's Salt Lake Center. As the founding director of the Salt Lake Institute of Genealogy, he developed one of the nation's largest such institutes. He has written extensively, including chapters in *The Library: A Guide to the LDS Family History Library,* both editions of *The Source: A Guidebook of American Genealogy,* and numerous articles and book reviews for the *Genealogical Journal, Association of Professional Genealogists Quarterly, Genealogical Computing, New York Genealogical and Biographical Record,* and the *Genealogist.* He is the author/presenter of *Doing Genealogy: Foundations for Successful Research,* an audio presentation with workbook.

Kory has served the genealogical community on national conference committees; as an officer of the Association of Professional Genealogists and the Utah Society, Sons of the American Revolution; and he is a member of the National Genealogical Society. Since 1996 he has been president of the Utah Genealogical Association. He currently conducts professional research in Salt Lake City, where he lives with his wife and the four of his five children still at home, where his e-mail address is Korym@msn.com.

Glade I. Nelson, AG, has been employed by the Family History Department of The Church of Jesus Christ of Latter-day Saints since 1978, where he is currently group manager of International Operations for the Family History Library. He was the Federation of Genealogical Societies' (FGS) treasurer from 1987 to 1990, president from 1991 to 1992, and immediate past president from 1993 to 1996; he received the FGS's George E. Williams Award in 1990 and the David F. Vogel Award in 1992. Glade was the Association of Professional Genealogists' (APG) treasurer from 1982 to 1983, president from 1984 to 1986, executive secretary from 1988 to 1991, and trustee from 1989 to 1990; and he received the APG's Graham T. Smallwood Jr. Award in 1987. He has lectured at national genealogical conferences in Australia, England, New Zealand, and throughout the United States. His articles have been published in the *American Genealogist,* the *Virginia Genealogist,* and the *Genealogical Journal.* Glade is a member of the Society of Australian Genealogists, the New England Historic Genealogical Society, the Utah Genealogical Association, International Society for British Genealogy and Family History, the Utah State Historical Society, and the Mormon History Association, and he is the national adjunct in the U.S. Mormon Battalion, Inc.

Carol Mehr Schiffman is president of Genealogy Unlimited, a mail-order genealogical supply company located in Orem, Utah. She taught numerous genealogical classes in Illinois for many years, volunteered at the Willmette Illinois Family History center for fifteen years, and has spoken at more than seventy genealogical workshops in the Midwest. Carol spoke at the National Genealogical Conference in 1985, family history seminars held at Brigham Young University in 1992 and 1993, at the German Genealogical Society of America Fall workshop in 1992, and the Salt Lake Institute of Genealogy in 1996. She has visited major map publishers in Germany and Austria, the U.S. Geological Survey Headquarters, and several major libraries in the United States. Carol wrote "The Map," a column in *Genealogy America.*

Benjamin Barnett Spratling, 3rd, is a graduate of Vanderbilt University School of Law, where he received a doctor of jurisprudence degree in 1971. He also received a master of laws (in taxation) degree from the University of Alabama Law School and a BS degree (economics) from Auburn University. He has been a member of the Alabama Bar since 1971 and practices law in Birmingham, Alabama, as a partner in the firm of Haskell Slaughter & Young. Ben is a member of the sections of Business Law, Taxation and Intellectual Property Law of the American Bar Association and is a former adjunct instructor of business law at the University of Alabama in Birmingham. Since 1992 he has been a faculty member at Samford University's Institute of Genealogy and Historical Research. Ben is past president of the Alabama Genealogical Society and is a present member of the Editorial Board of the *Alabama Genealogical Society Magazine*. He is also a state liaison for the Federation of Genealogical Societies' Records Preservation and Access Committee and a member of the National Genealogical Society and the Augusta Genealogical Society.

Kip Sperry, MLS, CG, AG, FASG, FNGS, FUGA, is an assistant professor of family history at Brigham Young University, Provo, Utah, and contributing editor for the *American Genealogist* and the *National Genealogical Society Quarterly*. Kip is a trustee, Board for Certification of Genealogists (Washington, D.C.) and the author of *Genealogical Research in Ohio* (Baltimore: Genealogical Publishing Co., 1997) and numerous other genealogical reference books and periodical articles. Kip served as the former editor of the *Genealogical Journal* and as a lecturer at many National Genealogical Society (NGS) annual conferences, Federation of Genealogical Societies (FGS) annual conferences, the Salt Lake Institute of Genealogy (1996, 1997), BYU annual genealogy and family history conferences, BYU conferences and workshops, and BYU campus education weeks. He has served as an NGS council member (1982 to 1992) and NGS national conference chairman (1984, 1985, 1991, and 1995). Biographical sketches appear in *Who's Who in the West,* 23rd edition, 1992-93; *Contemporary Authors, New Revision Series* (Gale Research), *Who's Who in Genealogy and Heraldry,* 2nd ed. (1990), and in other publications.

Loretto D. Szucs—"Lou"—holds a BS degree in history from Saint Joseph's College in Indiana and has been involved in genealogical research, teaching, lecturing, and publishing for more than twenty-five years. Previously employed as an archives specialist for the National Archives, she is currently vice-president of publishing for Ancestry Incorporated. She has served on the Illinois State Archives Advisory Board and on the governing boards of the Chicago Genealogical Society, the South Suburban Genealogical Society (Illinois), and the Illinois State Genealogical Society. Lou was the founding secretary for the Federation of Genealogical Societies (FGS) and has held various positions in that organization, including editor of the FGS *Forum*. She is the author of several publications, including *Chicago and Cook County Sources: A Genealogical and Historical Guide* (Ancestry, 1996). With Sandra Luebking, she coauthored *The Archives: A Guide to the National Archives Field Branches* (Ancestry, 1988). Honors Lou has received include a 1984 citation from the Archivists of the United States for her work to establish the volunteer program at the National Archives' Chicago regional branch; a 1987 National Genealogical Society (NGS) Award of Merit for *Chicago and Cook County Sources;* the 1990 David S. Vogels, Jr., Award for outstanding contributions to the FGS; the 1991 Award for Excellence in Genealogical Methods and Sources from the NGS; a 1992 Special Award from the Illinois Genealogical Society; and in 1995 she was named a fellow of the Utah Genealogical Association.

David T. Thackery has been curator of Local and Family History at the Newberry Library in Chicago since 1983, where he is responsible for collection development and reference services in genealogy. His writing has been published in a variety of genealogical publications, including *Ancestry* magazine. He has published a bibliography of Illinois county land ownership maps and atlases. David has written about various Civil War topics and is currently writing the history of a local regiment from his hometown in Ohio. He holds a bachelor's degree from Ohio's Wittenberg University and two master's degrees from the University of Chicago.

APPENDIX A

CD-ROMS FOR FAMILY HISTORIANS

Compiled by Alan E. Mann

CD-ROM (compact disc, read-only memory) publication is a popular new approach for publishing and disseminating information. Genealogical publishers are issuing an increasing number of CD-ROMs, and family historians are finding value in many other CD-ROMs that were not intended for genealogical research. CD-ROM technology allows publishers to produce and distribute vast amounts of information much less expensively. Often the data contained on a CD-ROM is so vast that it would occupy hundreds of volumes if published in book format.

Because so many new sources are being published each month, this appendix is a selective list indicating the major titles available as of early 1998. "Out of print" CDs and those with limited genealogical content are not listed. The list excludes most non-North American CDs, as well as personal, family, and other privately published CDs. This list's purposes are to consolidate many of the references made throughout the text of *Printed Sources,* to alert the reader to sources that are available, and to suggest (by its divisions) what sources to watch for in the future.

This directory identifies CD-ROM publication titles by category. Each title is followed by the publisher in parentheses. Publishers' addresses and telephone numbers follow the categorized list. A brief annotation follows those titles whose content may not be clear from the title. Price is not noted, but those over three hundred dollars (aimed at the institutional market) are marked with an asterisk (*). Further information and a full CD content description are usually available on the publisher's Web page. The Web page address (URL) is included with the contact information for each publisher at the end of this appendix.

GENERAL REFERENCE

Encyclopedias and Dictionaries

Compton's Interactive Encyclopedia (Compton)

Countries of the World Encyclopedia (Bureau)

Encarta (Microsoft)

Oxford English Dictionary (Oxford)*

General Bibliographies and Catalogs

Bibliographic Index (Wilson)*

Books in Print (Bowker)*

British National Bibliography on CD-ROM (Chadwyck)*

Global Books in Print (Bowker)*

Humanities Index, Humanities Abstracts, and *Humanities Full Text* (Wilson)*

Index to Legal Periodicals and Books (Wilson)*

Royal Historical Society British Bibliographies (Oxford)*

Ethnic Histories

African-American Biographical Database (Chadwyck)*

The African-American Newspapers: The Nineteenth Century (Scholarly)*

The Indian Question (GuildPress)

Historical Aids

America: History and Life (ABC-Clio)*

American History Explorer (Parsons)

Historical Abstracts on Disc (ABC-Clio)*

Historical Abstracts (ABC-Clio)*

ResourceLink series CDs:

- *18th Century American History* (ABC-Clio)*
- *19th Century American History* (ABC-Clio)*
- *20th Century American History* (ABC-Clio)*
- *Colonial American History* (ABC-Clio)*
- *American Government* (ABC-Clio)*

Total History (Bureau)

Various biographies and personal papers of American historical figures (H-bar); see their Web site

Telephone and Street Directories

DirectoryUSA (Parsons) U.S. residential telephone directory

PhoneDiskUSA (Digital) U.S. phone directories

Select Phone (ProCD) U.S. phone directories by region

Select Street Atlas (ProCD)

StreetAtlas USA and *AAA Map 'n' Go* (Parsons); one CD-ROM

StreetFinder Deluxe 1998 Edition (Rand)

TripMaker Deluxe 1998 Edition (Rand)

A-Info (TopWare); Austria telephone directory

B-Info (TopWare); Belgium telephone directory

CanadaPhone (ProCD); Canada telephone directory

D-Info Address und Telekommunikationsauskunft Deutschland (TopWare); Germany telephone directory

I-Info (TopWare); Italy telephone directory

NL-Info (TopWare); Netherlands telephone directory

UK-Info (TopWare); United Kingdom telephone directory

GENEALOGICAL REFERENCE

Archive Guides

ArchivesUSA (Chadwyck)*

Genealogy: Library of Congress (H-Bar); list of genealogy books and documents

National Inventory of Documentary Sources in the United Kingdom and Ireland (Chadwyck)*

National Inventory of Documentary Sources in the United States (Chadwyck)*

Maps and Gazetteers

American History Atlas (Parsons)

AniMap County Boundary Historical Atlas (Gold Bug)

The Digital Gazetteer of the U.S. (U.S. Geological Survey)

Early American Gazetteer: 1833; 1853 (GenRef)

Early New Hampshire Periodicals and 1874 Gazetteer (Heritage Books)

New Millennium World Atlas Deluxe Edition (Rand)

Omni Gazetteer (SilverPlatter)*

Instruction and Source Guides

Ancestry Genealogy Library (Ancestry); Library of Congress bibliographic database and twenty other reference works, miscellaneous vital record databases

Ancestry Reference Library, 1998 (Ancestry); includes eight general reference books

Encyclopedia of U.S. Counties (GenRef)

The Genealogist's All-in-One Address Book (Brøderbund), no. 115

Genealogy Set (H-Bar); partial Library of Congress catalog, archive and society address list, "how-to" guide

Handy Book for Genealogists (Everton)

Indexes, Genealogical Resources and Foster Library Catalogue (Lincoln) England

Vital Records Assistant (GenRef)

MAJOR INDEXES

FamilyArchives Census Indexes (Brøderbund); numerous indexes to U.S. census records

FamilyFinder Index (2 CDs) (Brøderbund); index to all genealogical CDs produced by Brøderbund.

Periodical Source Index (PERSI) on CD (Ancestry)

Genealogical Research Directory (Johnson)

ORIGINAL RECORDS ON CD-ROM

Census Records

1659 Census of County Cork, Ireland (Global Data)

1790 Census of South Carolina (Census View); complete, but without index

Census Microfilm Records: Virginia, 1850 (Brøderbund), no. 309

1850 Census of Arkansas (Census View); complete, but without index

1850 Census of South Carolina (Census View); complete, but without index

1850 Census of Texas (Census View); complete, but without index

Mortality Index: United States 1850-1880 (Brøderbund), no. 164

Irish of 1851 Census, Liverpool (Global Data)

African Americans in the 1870 Census (Brøderbund), no. 165; six states and four cities

Veterans' Schedules: U.S. Selected States, 1890 (Brøderbund), no. 131

U.S. Mortality Records for African American Slaves and Free Blacks (Global Data)

Pennsylvania 1870 Census Index (Heritage Quest); index only

Brøderbund Census Index series (note: indexes, not actual census records)

- *Census Index: Ohio 1880* (Brøderbund), no. 20
- *Census Index: Ontario, Canada 1871* (Brøderbund), no. 116
- *Census Index: Selected Counties of Ireland 1831, 1841* (County Londonderry, 1831; County Cavan, 1841) (Brøderbund), no. 197
- *Census Index: Massachusetts 1870* (Brøderbund), no. 284
- *Census Index: Western Pennsylvania 1870* (Brøderbund), no. 285
- *Census Index: Eastern Pennsylvania 1870* (Brøderbund), no. 286
- *Census Index: New York City 1870* (Brøderbund), no. 287
- *Census Index: Baltimore, Chicago, St. Louis 1870* (Brøderbund), no. 288
- *Census Index: North Carolina, South Carolina 1870* (Brøderbund), no. 289
- *Census Index: Virginia, West Virginia 1870* (Brøderbund), no. 290
- *Census Index: Georgia 1870* (Brøderbund), no. 291
- *Census Index: Colonial America 1634–1790* (Brøderbund), no. 310
- *Census Index: US Selected Counties 1790* (Brøderbund), no. 311

Census Index: US Selected Counties 1800 (Brøderbund), no. 312

Census Index: US Selected Counties 1810 (Brøderbund), no. 313

Census Index: US Selected Counties 1820 (Brøderbund), no. 314

Census Index: US Selected Counties 1830 (Brøderbund), no. 315

Census Index: US Selected Counties 1840 (Brøderbund), no. 316

Census Index: US Selected Counties 1850 (Brøderbund), no. 317

Census Index: US Selected States/Counties 1860 (Brøderbund) no. 318

Census Index: US Selected States/Counties 1870 (Brøderbund), no. 319

Census Index: US Selected States/Counties 1880 (Brøderbund), no. 320

Census Index: Idaho 1910 (Brøderbund), no. 335

Census View images of complete census without index—selected counties in selected census years: Alabama, Arkansas, Georgia, Illinois, Indiana, Kentucky, Missouri, North Carolina, Oklahoma, South Carolina, Tennessee, Texas, and Virginia (see Census View's Web site for details)

Church Records

Pennsylvania German Church Records, 1729–1870 (Brøderbund), no. 130

Church Records: Selected Areas of Pennsylvania 1600s–1800s (Brøderbund), no. 166

Church Records: Maryland and Delaware, 1600s–1800s (Brøderbund), no. 178

Land Records

Land Records: Alabama, Arkansas, Florida, Louisiana, Michigan, Ohio, Wisconsin 1790–1907 (Brøderbund), no. 255; same data as BLM CDs

General Land Office Records CD: Alabama (BLM)

General Land Office Records CD: Arkansas (BLM)

General Land Office Records CD: Florida (BLM)

General Land Office Records CD: Louisiana (BLM)

General Land Office Records CD: Michigan (BLM)

General Land Office Records CD: Minnesota (BLM)

General Land Office Records CD: Mississippi (BLM)

General Land Office Records CD: Ohio (BLM)

General Land Office Records CD: Wisconsin (BLM)

Other Records

Social Security Death Index: US 1937–1996 (Brøderbund), no. 110

Social Security Death Master File (GenRef)

New York Abstracts of Wills 1665–1801 (Heritage Books)

Irish Wills of Dublin 1400's to 1800's (Global Data)

Early Mississippi Records (Heritage Books) contains wills, graves, newspapers, histories

Inventaire des Greffes des Notaires du Regime Français (Quintin) Quebec notarial documents, first 25 volumes on one CD-ROM

Military Records

The Civil War CD-ROM (GuildPress); Army Official Record

Confederate Military History (GuildPress)

The Civil War: A Newspaper Perspective (Scholarly)*

Roll of Honor: Civil War Union Soldiers (Brøderbund), no. 351

Military Records: Confederate Soldiers, 1861–1865 (Brøderbund), no. 119; Confederate prisoners who died in the North

Veterans' Schedules: U.S. Selected States, 1890 (Brøderbund), no. 131

Selected New York Revolutionary War Records, 1775–1840 (Brøderbund), no. 132

Revolutionary Patriots: Maryland and Delaware, 1775–1783 (Brøderbund), no. 133

Massachusetts Civil War Soldiers and Sailors, 1861–1865 (Brøderbund), no. 134

Military Records: US Soldiers 1784–1811 (Brøderbund), no. 146

Revolutionary War Soldiers and Sailors, 1775–1782 (Brøderbund), no. 147

Sons of the American Revolution Revolutionary War Graves Register CD-ROM (Progeny)

Confederate Veteran Magazine 1984–1993 (Quintin)

Roster of the Confederate Soldiers of Georgia, 6 vols. (Quintin)

Index to the "OR" (Quintin/H-bar) Army Official Record

"I Was There," Eyewitness—Chickamauga, 1 vol. (Quintin)

Army Official Records on CD-ROM. (Broadfoot)*

U.S. Colored Troops In The Civil War (Broadfoot)

Civil War Originals Vol. 1 (Computer)

Numerous historical titles (H-bar); ask for a catalog or visit their Web site

Newspapers

The African-American Newspapers: The Nineteenth Century (Scholarly)*

The Civil War: A Newspaper Perspective (Scholarly)*

The Index to The Times, 1906–1980 on CD-ROM (Chadwyck)*

Obituaries on CD-ROM (Chadwyck)*; from British newspapers, 1985–present

Palmer's Index to The London Times, 1790–1905 on CD-ROM (Chadwyck)*

Pennsylvania Gazette (1728–1750) (Scholarly)*

Pennsylvania Newspaper Record: Delaware County, 1819–1879 (Scholarly)*

Vital Records and Cemeteries

Marriages Only

Maine Marriages 1892–1966 (Picton) includes all marriages all counties

U.S. Marriage Index, 1692–1850 (Heritage Quest)

FamilyArchives Marriage Records (Broderbund)

Marriage Index: Louisiana 1718–1925 (Brøderbund), no. 1

Marriage Index: Illinois, Indiana, Kentucky, Ohio, Tennessee 1720–1926 (Brøderbund), no. 2

Marriage Index: Alabama, Georgia, South Carolina 1641–1944 (Brøderbund), no. 3

Marriage Index: Maryland, North Carolina, Virginia 1624–1915 (Brøderbund), no. 4

Marriage Index: Arkansas, Mississippi, Missouri, Texas 1766–1981 (Brøderbund), no. 5

Marriage Index: Arkansas 1779–1992 (Brøderbund), no. 6

Marriage Index: Maryland 1655–1850 (Brøderbund), no. 224

Marriage Index: Arizona, California, Idaho, Nevada 1850–1951 (Brøderbund), no. 225

Marriage Index: Georgia 1754–1850 (Brøderbund), no. 226

Marriage Index: Selected States (Arkansas, California, Iowa, Louisiana, Minnesota, Missouri, Oregon, Texas) 1728–1850 (Brøderbund), no. 227

Marriage Index: Illinois, Indiana 1790–1850 (Brøderbund), no. 228

Marriage Index: Kentucky, North Carolina, Tennessee, Virginia, West Virginia 1728–1850 (Brøderbund), no. 229

Marriage Index: Massachusetts 1633–1850 (Brøderbund), no. 231

Marriage Index: Ohio 1789–1850 (Brøderbund), no. 400

Marriage Index: Selected Areas of New York 1639–1916 (Brøderbund), no. 401

Marriage Index: New York # 2 1740s–1880s (Brøderbund), no. 402

Marriage Index: U.S./International records 1340–1980 (Brøderbund), no. 403; Bill Yates collection of 700,000 (plus) marriages from thirty-two countries and fifty states

Central Pennsylvania Marriages: 1700's–1896 (Global Data); selected records only

NY, NJ, PA Marriages, 1725–1890 (Global Data); selected records only

Utah Marriages: 1850's–1992 (Global Data); three counties only

Births, Deaths, and/or Marriages

Territorial Vital Records 1800'2–1906 (Global Data) limited data AZ, CO, ID, UT, WY

California, Nevada, Oregon Births and Deaths 1753–1988 plus Clark Co. NV Marriages 1983–July 1996 (Global Data); selected records only

New York Birth and Death: 1809–1988 (Global Data); 2-CD set; selected records, all counties

Early Vital Records of Barnstable County (Cape Cod), Massachusetts (Search)

Early Vital Records of Plymouth County, Massachusetts (Search)

Early Vital Records of Suffolk County, Massachusetts (Search)

Birth Records: United States/Europe 900–1880 (Brøderbund), no. 17; from other Brøderbund CDs

Mayflower Vital Records, Deeds and Wills, 1600s–1900s (Brøderbund), no. 167

Pennsylvania Vital Records, 1700's–1800's (Brøderbund), no. 172; from Pennsylvania periodicals

Genealogies of Mayflower Families, 1500s–1800s (Brøderbund), no. 171

Early New Hampshire Periodicals and 1874 Gazetteer (Heritage Books)

Early Records of Hartford, CT (Heritage Books) 1644–1730, plus land and probate records

Virginia Vital Records #1, 1600s–1800s (Brøderbund), no. 174

Ohio Vital Records #1, 1790s–1870s (Brøderbund), no. 175

Ohio Vital Records #2, 1750s–1880s (Brøderbund), no. 177

Genealogical Records: The Ontario Register, 1780s–1870s (Brøderbund), no. 204

Royal Melbourne Institute of Technology, Australia Births, Marriages, and Deaths index series:

- *New South Wales Pioneer's Index: Pioneers Series (1788–1888)* (RMIT)
- *New South Wales Pioneer's Index: Federation Series (1888–1918)* (RMIT)
- *New South Wales Pioneer's Index: Between the Wars (1918–1945)* (RMIT)
- *Tasmanian Pioneer's Index: Federation Series* (1803–1899 (RMIT)
- *Victorian Pioneer's Index: Federation Series* (1937–1888) (RMIT)
- *Western Australian Pioneer's Index* (1841–1905) (RMIT)

Cemeteries

Ontario Cemetery Finding Aid v5.0 (GenRef)

Cemetery Records: Salt Lake City, 1848–1992 (Brøderbund), no. 168

COMPILED SOURCES

Biographies

Archives: Historical and Genealogical Records of West Central Ohio (Heritage Books)

Biography and Genealogy Master Index (Gale)*

Pioneer Heritage CD-ROM (Ancestry); Utah pioneer biographical data

Biographical CD-ROMs series:

- *American Cultural Leaders* (ABC-Clio)*
- *American Leaders: Profiles of Great Americans* (ABC-Clio)*
- *American Political Leaders* (ABC-Clio)*
- *American Social Leaders* (ABC-Clio)*
- *Current Leaders: Rulers of Nations in the 1990s* (ABC-Clio)*

Founding Leaders: Shapers of Modern Nations (ABC-Clio)*

Women Leaders: Rulers throughout History (ABC-Clio)*

Marquis' Who's Who (Gale)

Dictionary of National Biography (Oxford)* England

Italian Biographical Index (Saur)*

Spanish, Portuguese and Latin-American Biographical Index (Saur)*

World Biographical Index (Saur)*

African-American Biographical Database (Chadwyck)*

Cambridge Biographical Encyclopedia (Chadwyck)*

Biography Index (Wilson)*; index to biographies in periodicals

Wilson Current Biography (Wilson)*

Wilson Biographies (Wilson)*; includes *Wilson Current Biography*

Biographical Directory of the American Congress on CD-ROM (CQ)*

Women of the South in War Times (H-bar)

Woman's Work in the Civil War (H-bar)

Confederate Wizards of the Saddle (H-bar)

Various biographies and personal papers of American historical figures (H-bar); see H-bar's Web site

Family History Collections

Family History: New England Families #1 1600's–1800's (Brøderbund), no. 117

Family History: Virginia Genealogies #1, pre-1600 to 1900s (Brøderbund), no. 162

Virginia Genealogies #2, 1600s–1800s (Brøderbund), no. 186

Virginia Genealogies #3 (Brøderbund), no. 187

Family History: Pennsylvania Genealogies #1 (Brøderbund), no. 163

Genealogies of Long Island Families, 1600s–1800s (Brøderbund), no. 173

Connecticut Genealogies #1, 1600s–1800s (Brøderbund), no. 179

Rhode Island Genealogies #1, 1600s–1800s (Brøderbund), no. 180

New Jersey Genealogies #1, 1600s–1800s (Brøderbund), no. 182

Early Settlers of New York State, 1760–1942 (Brøderbund), no. 183

Kentucky Genealogies #1, 1700s–1800s (Brøderbund), no. 185

Immigration

Immigrants to the New World, 1600s–1800s (Brøderbund), no. 170

The Complete Book of Emigrants, 1607–1776 (Brøderbund), no. 350

English Origins of New England Families, 1500s–1800s (Brøderbund), no. 181

Mayflower Descendants (Search)

Lineage Databases

World Family Tree (Brøderbund); 16 CDs

Crystal Konnections (Kindred Konnections)

Founders and Patriots (Millisecond)

Pittsburg Family Forest (Millisecond)

Delaware Family Forest (Millisecond)

Nobility of the Roman Empire and Other European Nobility (GenQuest)

Family Pedigrees: Everton Publishers 1500–1990 (Brøderbund), no. 15

Family Pedigrees: UnitedAncestries 1500–1950 (Brøderbund), no. 100

Family Pedigrees: GENTECH95 and ARI 1500–1989 (Brøderbund), no. 108

Family History: 217 Genealogy Books (Brøderbund), no. 113; histories, genealogies, biographies from 217 books

Sons of the American Revolution Patriot Index (Progeny); patriots and descendants in pedigrees

In Search of Our Acadian Roots (CYR)

Local Histories (with genealogies)

Histories and Genealogies of Cumberland County, Maine (Heritage Books)

Histories and Genealogies of Essex Co., MA (Heritage Books)

A History of Newfoundland (Global Heritage)

The History of Queens County, (Nova Scotia) (Global Heritage)

History of the Counties of Argenteuil, Quebec and Prescott, Ontario (Global Heritage)

History of the County of Annapolis, (Nova Scotia) (Global Heritage)

History of the County of Yarmouth, (Nova Scotia) (Global Heritage)

Pioneer Life in the Bay of Quite, (Ontario) (Global Heritage)

Periodicals

New England Historical and Genealogical Register, 1847–1994 (Brøderbund)

The Mayflower Descendant with Other New England Town Records (Search)

Virginia Genealogist, Vols. 1–20 (Heritage Books)

Journal of Online Genealogy (Toolbox); 1996–1997 issues

Pennsylvania Vital Records, 1700's–1800's (Brøderbund), no. 172; from Pennsylvania periodicals

State Index: Upstate New York 1685–1910 (Brøderbund), no. 160; Valley Quarterlies

Other Compiled Sources

Historical and Genealogical Record of the First Settlers of Colchester County, (Nova Scotia) (Global Heritage)

Family History on Disc: Information Resources for Genealogists (RMIT); Australia

Canadian Genealogy Index, 1600s–1900s (Brøderbund), no. 118

GIS, Electronic Messages Vol. 1 (Brøderbund), no. 161

The New Jersey Biographical Index, 1800s (Brøderbund), no. 190

The Compendium of American Genealogy, 1600s–1800s (Brøderbund), no. 200

CD-ROM PUBLISHERS

ABC-Clio
130 Cremona Drive
Santa Barbara, CA 93117
Tel.: 805-968-1911
800-368-6868
Fax: 805-685-9685
E-mail: sales@abc-clio.com
http://www.abc-clio.com/

AGLL (see Heritage Quest)

Ancestry
266 West Center Street
Orem, UT 84059
Tel.: 800 262-3787
801-426-3500
Fax: 801-426-3501
E-mail: support@ancestry.com
http://www.ancestry.com/

R. R. Bowker
121 Chanlon Road
New Providence, NJ 07974
Tel.: 888-269-5372
800-323-3288
Fax: 908-665-3528
E-mail: info@bowker.com
http://www.Bowker.com/epcatalog/home/toc.html#CD-ROM

Broadfoot Publishing Co.
1907 Buena Vista Circle
Wilmington, North Carolina 28405
Tel.: 800-537-5243
910-686-4816
Fax: 910-686-4379
E-mail: bropubco@wilmington.net
http://broadfoot.wilmington.net/army_cd.html

Brøderbund Software
Banner Blue Division
39500 Stevenson Place, Suite 204
Fremont, CA 94539
Tel.: 800-315-0672
Fax: 415-382-4419 or (510) 794-9152
E-mail: sales@familytreemaker.com
http://www.familytreemaker.com/

Bureau of Electronic Publishing
141 New Road
Parsippany, NJ 07054
Tel.: 201-808-2700
800-828-4766
Fax: 201-808-2676
E-mail: 71261.3345@compuserve.com or JBT506A@prodigy.com or The Bureau@aol.com

Bureau of Land Management (BLM)—Eastern States
7450 Boston Boulevard
Springfield, VA 22153
Tel.: 703-440-1600
E-mail: records@es.blm.gov
http://www.access.gpo.gov/su_docs/sale/sale334.html

Census View
P.O. Box 39
Ripley, OK 74062
Tel.: 918-372-4624
E-mail: censusvu@galstar.com
http://www.galstar.com/~censusvu/

Chadwyck-Healey
1101 King Street
Alexandria, VA 22314
Tel.: 800-752-0515
703-683-4890
Fax: 703-683-7589
E-mail: sales@chadwyck.com
http://www.chadwyck.com/

Compton's New Media
2320 Camino Vida Roble
Carlsbad, CA 92009-1504
Tel.: 617-494-1200
800-284-2045
Fax: 617-577-9032
E-mail: cust_serv@learningco.com
http://www.comptons.com

Computer Archive Technology
P.O. Box 54
Boyds, MD 20841-0054
Tel.: 301-972-1355
Fax: 301-972-1355
E-mail: dmartincat@aol.com

CQ Staff Directories
185 Slaters Lane
Alexandria, VA 22314

Tel.: 703-739-0900
800-252-1722
Fax: 703-739-0234
E-mail: staffdir@staffdirectories.com

Yvon L. CYR
Village by the Arboretum
2 Ashcroft Court
Guelph, Ontario, Canada N1G 4X7
Tel.: 519-821-2222
Fax: 519-837-8292
E-mail: cajun@acadian.org
http://www.acadian.org/

Digital Directory Assistance
6931 Arlington Road, Suite 405
Bethesda, MD 20814
Tel.: 800-284-8353
617-639-2900
Fax: 402-331-6681
E-mail: sales@eriworld.com
http://www.phonedisc.com

Educational Resources
8910 West 62nd Terrace
Shawnne Mission, KS 66202
Tel.: 913-362-4600
Fax: 913-362-4637
E-mail: sales@eriworld.com
http://www.eriworld.com/

The Everton Publishers
P.O. Box 368
Logan, UT 84323-0368
Tel.: 800-443-6325
Fax: 801-752-0425
E-mail: order@everton.com
http://www.everton.com/cathbcd.html

FamilyArchives (see Broderbund)

FamilyTreeMaker (see Broderbund)

Gale Research
7625 Empire Drive
Florence, KY 41042
Tel.: 800-865-5840
313-961-6083
Fax: 800-414-5043
E-mail: gale-comment-output@list.gale.com
http://www.gale.com/

GenQuest
921 1/2 Woodbourne Avenue
Pittsburgh, PA 15226
Tel.: 412-341-1984
800-600-1415
E-mail: cs@genquest.com
http://www.genquest.com/bibliocd.html

GenRef
874 West 1400 North
Orem, UT 84057-2916
Tel.: 801-225-3256
E-mail: john@genref.com
http://www.genref.com/

Global Data
1623 West 3640 South
St. George, UT 84790
Tel.: 435-674-5980
801-485-4545
E-mail: globalcd@infowest.com
http://www.infowest.com/g/globalcd/genealogy.htm

Global Heritage Press
158 Laurier Avenue
Milton, Ontario Canada L9T 4S2
Tel.: 800-361-5168
905-875-2176
Fax: 905-875-1887
E-mail: email@globalgenealogy.com
http://www.globalgenealogy.com/cdbooks.htm

The Gold Bug
P.O. Box 588
Alamo, CA 94507
Tel.: 510-838-6277
E-mail: 70303.2363@compuserve.com
http://www.goldbug.com/

Guild Press of Indiana
435 Gradle Drive
Carmel, IN 46032
Tel.: 800-913-9563
317-848-6421
Fax: 317-848-6810
E-mail: info@guildpress.com
http://www.guildpress.com/

H-Bar Enterprises
1442 Davidson Loop
Oakman, AL 35579
Tel.: 800-432-7702
800-770-3250
205-622-2444
Fax: 205-622-3040
E-mail: hbar@oakman.tds.net or hbaral@aol.com
http://www.hbar.com/

Heritage Books
1540-E Pointer Ridge Place
Bowie, MD 20716

Tel.: 800-398-7709
Fax: 800-276-1760 or 301-390-7153
E-mail: heritagebooks@pipeline.com
http://www.heritagebooks.com/

Heritage Quest (a division of AGLL)
P.O. Box 329
Bountiful, UT 84011-0329
Tel.: 800-658-7755
Fax: 801-298-5468
E-mail: sales@heritagequest.com
http://www.heritagequest.com/

K. G. Saur Publishing
Ortlerstrasse 8; D-81373
München, Germany
Tel.: ++49 - (0)89 - 76902-0
Fax ++49 - (0)89 - 76902-150
E-mail: 100730.1341@compuserve.com
http://www.saur.de/home.htm

Keith Johnson and Malcolm Sainty
17 Mitchell Street
P.O. Box 795
North Sydney, New South Wales 2059
Australia
E-mail: grdxxx@ozemail.com.au
http://www.ozemail.com.au/~grdxxx/index.html

Kindred Konnections
P.O. Box 1882
Orem, UT 84059
Tel.: 800-288-6314
801-229-7967
E-mail: feedback@kindredkonnections.com
http://www.kindredkonnections.com/cd.html

Lincolnshire Archive Office
St. Rumbold Street
Lincoln, LN2 5AB
England
Tel.: 00 44 1522 526204
Fax.: 00 44 1522 530047
E-mail: archives@lincsdoc.demon.co.uk
http://www.demon.co.uk/lincs-archives/cd.htm

Microsoft
One Microsoft Way
Redmond, WA 98052-6399
Tel.: 206-882-8080
(800) 426-9400
Fax: 206-936-7329
http://www.microsoft.com/products/reference.htm

Millisecond Publishing Co. of Bethany Beach, Delaware
c/o Automated Research
1160 South State Street
Suite 220
Orem, Utah 84097-8237
Tel.: 888-473-6737
800-906-1776
E-mail: kristine@familyforest.com
http://www.familyforest.com/

Oxford University Press
2001 Evans Road
Cary, NC 27513
Tel.: 800-451-7556
800-445-9714
919-677-0977
Fax: 919-677-1303
E-mail: custserv@oup-usa.org
http://www1.oup.co.uk/E-P/

Parsons Technology
1700 Progress Drive
P.O. Box 100
Hiawatha, IA 52233
Tel.: 800-973-5111
319-395-9626
Fax: 319-395-0217
E-mail: webmaster@parsonstech.com
http://www.parsonstech.com/

Picton Press
P.O. Box 250
Rockport, ME 04856-0250
Tel.: 207-236-6565
Fax: 207-236-6713
E-mail: picton@midcoast.com
http://www.pictonpress.com/catalog/catalog.htm

Pro CD
5711 South 86th Circle
Omaha, NE 68127
Tel.: 800-992-3766
402-537-6180
Fax: 402-596-8997
E-mail: customer.service@procd.com
http://www.procd.com/

Progeny Publishing
Olympic Towers, Suite 200
300 Pearl Street
Buffalo, NY 14202
Tel.: 800-565-0018
Fax: 902-542-0562

E-mail: info@progeny2.com
http://www.progeny2.com/

RMIT Publishing
P.O. Box 12477
A'Beckett Street
Melbourne, Victoria 8006
Australia
Tel.: (03) 9349 4994
(03) 9341 3222
(03) 9341 3285
Fax: (03) 9349 4583
E-mail: tinaa@rmitpublishing.com.au
http://www.rmitpublishing.com.au/

Rand McNally
8255 North Central Park Avenue
Skokie, IL 60076
Tel.: 800-451-7266
847-329-6516
Fax: 847-673-6277
E-mail: consumeraffairs@randmcnally.com
http://www.randmcnally.com

Scholarly Resources (representing Accessible Archives)
104 Greenhill Avenue
Wilmington, DE 19805-1897
Tel.: 302-654-7713
800-772-8937
Fax: 302-654-3871
E-mail: zafiro@scholarly.com

Search and ReSearch Publishing
P.O. Box 436
Wheat Ridge, CO 80034
Tel.: 303-274-2411
Fax: 303-239-6525
E-mail: srpc@ix.netcom.com

SilverPlatter Information
100 River Ridge Drive,
Norwood, MA 02062-5043
Tel: 781-769-2599
Fax: 781-769-8763
E-mail: us_customerrelations@silverplatter.com
http://www.silverplatter.com/catalog.htm

Toolbox Internet Marketing Services
P.O. Box 76
Savoy, IL 61874
Tel.: 217-352-1309
E-mail: mhelm@tbox.com
http://www.onlinegenealogy.com/cdrom.htm

TopWare CD Service AG
Markircher Strasse 25
D-68229 Mannheim, Germany
Tel.: +49 2369 9167 20
Fax: +49 2369 9167 95
E-mail: KSSUPPORT@aol.com
http://www.topware.com/

U.S. Geological Survey
Attn: Roger Payne, GNIS Manager
523 National Center
Rushton, VA 20192
Tel.: 713-648-4544
800-USA-MAPS
E-mail: GNIS_Manager@usgs.gov
http://mapping.usgs.gov/www/gnis/

H. W. Wilson
950 University Avenue
Bronx, NY 10452-4224
Tel.: 800-367-6770
718-588-8400
Fax: 800-590-1617
E-mail: custserv@hwwilson.com
http://www.hwwilson.com/

APPENDIX B

MAJOR U.S. GENEALOGICAL LIBRARIES

This appendix identifies three types of genealogical libraries in the United States: major public and private libraries with significant genealogical collections, state libraries, and genealogical rental libraries. For additional addresses of other useful libraries, see *The Ancestry Family Historian's Address Book* (Salt Lake City: Ancestry, 1998), compiled by Juliana Szucs Smith, which contains the most extensive list of genealogical addresses, URLs, and e-mail addresses in print today.

LIBRARIES WITH NATIONAL OR REGIONAL COLLECTIONS

The following libraries have excellent collections that cover much more than just the state where they are located. These are often considered "destination" libraries—major collections around which entire trips may be planned. The list is arranged by region of the country. Within each region, libraries with the largest genealogical collections are listed first. An asterisk (*) indicates that the library is a private, not public, institution and therefore may have some usage restrictions or limited hours.

Eastern States

American Antiquarian Society*
185 Salisbury Street
Worcester, MA 01609-1634
Tel.: 508-755-5221

Godfrey Memorial Library*
134 Newfield Street
Middletown, CT 06457
Tel.: 860-346-4375
Fax: 860-347-9874
E-mail: godfrey@connix.com
http://www.godfrey.org

Historical Society of Pennsylvania
1300 Locust Street
Philadelphia, PA 19107
Tel.: 215-732-6201
Fax: 215-732-2680
E-mail: hsppr@aol.com
http://www.libertynet.ort/~pahist

New England Historic Genealogical Society Library*
99-101 Newbury Street
Boston, MA 02116-3007
Tel.: 616-536-5740
Fax: 617-536-7307
E-mail: nehgs@nehgs.org
http://www.nehgs.org

New York Genealogical and Biographical Society Library*
122 East Fifty-Eighth Street
New York, NY 10022-1939
Tel.: 212-755-8532
http://www.tnp.com/nycgenweb/NYG&BS.htm

New York Public Library
Local History and Genealogy Division
5th Avenue and 42nd Street
New York, NY 10016
Tel.: 212-340-0849
http://www.nypl.org

Southern States and Washington, D.C.

Dallas Public Library
Genealogy Section
1515 Young Street
Dallas, TX 75202
Tel.: 214-670-1400
Fax: 214-670-7839
http://central4.lib.ci.dallas.tx.us

Ellen Payne Odom Genealogical Library
204 Fifth Street, SE
P.O. Box 1110
Moultrie, GA 31776-1110

Tel.: 912-985-6540
Fax: 912-985-0936
E-mail: jenkinsm@mail.colquitt.public.lib.ga.us
http://www.firstct.com/fv/EPO.html

Houston Public Library
Clayton Library Center for Genealogical Research
5300 Caroline
Houston, TX 77004-6896
Tel.: 713-524-0101
http://sparc.hpl.lib.tx.us/hpl/clayton.html

L. W. Anderson Genealogical Library*
William Carey College, Hwy. 90
P.O. Box 1647
Gulfport, MS 39502
Tel.: 601-865-1554

Library of Congress
Local History and Genealogy Division
101 Independence Avenue, S.E.
Washington, D.C. 20540
Tel.: 202-287-5537
E-mail: lcweb@loc.gov
http://www.lcweb.loc.gov

National Genealogical Society Library*
4527 Seventeenth Avenue North
Arlington, VA 22207-2363
Tel.: 703-525-0050
Fax: 703-525-0052
E-mail: 76702.2417@compuserv.com
http://www.genealogy.org/~ngs

National Society, Daughters of the American Revolution Library*
1776 D Street, N.W.
Washington, D.C. 20006-5392
Tel.: 202-879-3229

National Society of the Sons of the American Revolution Library*
1000 South Fourth Street
Louisville, KY 40203
Tel.: 502-589-1776
Tel.: 505-589-1776
http://www.sar.org

University of Texas at Austin
The Center for American History
Sid Richardson Hall, Unit 2
Austin, TX 78713
Tel.: 512-495-4250
http://www.lib.utexas.edu

Midwestern States

Allen County Public Library
Reynolds Historical Genealogy Department
900 Webster Street
P.O. Box 2270
Fort Wayne, IN 46802
Tel.: 219-424-7241
http://www.acpl.lib.in.us

Detroit Public Library
Burton Historical Collection
5201 Woodward Avenue
Detroit, MI 48202
Tel.: 313-833-1480
Fax: 313-832-0877
E-mail: nvangor@cms.cc.wayne.edu
http://www.detroit.lib.mi.us

Mid-Continent Public Library
North Independence Branch
Genealogy and Local History Department
15616 East 24 Highway
Independence, MO 64050
Tel.: 816-252-0950
E-mail: ge@mcpl.lib.mo.us
http://www.mcpl.lib.mo.us/gen.htm

Minnesota Historical Society
345 Kellog Boulevard
St. Paul, MN 55102-1906
Tel.: 612-296-0332
http://www.mnhs.org

Newberry Library*
Local and Family History Section
Sixty West Walton Street
Chicago, IL 60610-3305
Tel.: 312-255-3512
E-mail: furmans@newberry.org
http://www.newberry.org

Public Library of Cincinnati and Hamilton County
800 Vine Street, Library Square
Cincinnati, OH 45202-2071
Tel.: 513-369-6905
Fax: 513-369-6067
E-mail: comments@plch.lib.oh.us
http://plch.lib.oh.us

St. Louis Public Library
History and Genealogy Department
1301 Olive Street
St. Louis, MO 63103
Tel.: 314-241-2288
Fax: 314-539-0393

E-mail: webmaster@slpl.lib.mo.us
http://www.slpl.lib.mo.us

State Historical Society of Wisconsin
Genealogy Section
816 State Street
Madison, WI 53706
Tel.: 608-264-6535
http://www.shsw.wisc.edu

Western Reserve Historical Society Library
Case Western Reserve University
10825 East Boulevard
Cleveland, OH 44106-1788
Tel.: 216-721-5722
http://www.cwru/edu

Western States

Brigham Young University
Harold B. Lee Library
Provo, UT 84602
Tel.: 801-378-6200
http://www.lib.byu.edu

Denver Public Library
Genealogy Division
Western History Collection
1357 Broadway
Denver, CO 80203-2165
Tel.: 303-571-2190

Family History Library*
Thirty-Five North West Temple Street
Salt Lake City, UT 84150
Tel.: 801-240-2331
http://www.lds.org/Family_History/How_Do_I_Begin.html

Family History Library*
Thirty-Five North West Temple Street
Salt Lake City, UT 84150
Tel.: 801-240-2331
http://www.lds.org/Family_History/How_Do_I_Begin.html

Los Angeles Public Library
History and Genealogy Department
630 West Fifth Street
Los Angeles, CA 90071
Tel.: 213-228-7400
Fax: 213-228-7409
E-mail: history@lapl.org
http://www.lapl.org/central/hihp.html

Ricks College
McKay Library
525 South Center
Rexburg, ID 83440
Tel.: 208-356-2377
http://www.ricks.edu

Seattle Public Library
Genealogy Section
1000 Fourth Avenue
Seattle, WA 98104
Tel.: 206-386-4625
http://www.spl.lib.wa.us/contents.html

STATE LIBRARIES

Every state has a state library or a related government department that functions as a state library—however, not every state library has a large collection of books about the state; some state libraries are only administrative offices that direct library services throughout the state. This list identifies the state library or similarly responsible department for every state, regardless of the nature of its collection. Even those without research collections can direct the researcher to the most useful libraries and collections in the state. State historical societies, which often have the best genealogical collection in a state, are not listed here unless they also serve as the state library. For a full list of state historical societies, see appendix C in *The Source: A Guidebook of American Genealogy,* rev. ed.

Alabama Department of Archives and History
624 Washington Avenue
Montgomery, Al 36130-3601
Tel.: 205-242-4435

Alaska State Library
State Office Building, Eighth Floor
Juneau, AK 99801
Tel.: 907-465-2921

Arizona Department of Library, Archives and Public Records
State Capitol
1700 West Washington
Phoenix, AZ 85007
Tel.: 602-542-3942

Arkansas State Library
Department of Education
1 Capitol Mall
Little Rock, AR 72201
Tel.: 501-682-1527

California State Library
California Section
914 Capitol Mall
P.O. Box 942837

Sacramento, CA 95814
Tel.: 916-654-0176

Colorado State Library
201 East Colfax Avenue
Denver, CO 80203
Tel.: 303-866-6728

Connecticut State Library
History and Genealogy Unit
231 Capitol Avenue
Hartford, CT 06106
Tel.: 203-566-3690

Delaware Division of Libraries
Department of Community Affairs
43 South Dupont Highway
Dover, DE 19901
Tel.: 302-736-4748

State Library of Florida
Florida Collection
Division of Library and Information Services
R.A. Gray Building, Second Floor
500 South Bronough Street
Tallahassee, FL 323990-0250
Tel.: 904-487-2073

Georgia Department of Archives and History
Office of Secretary of State
330 Capitol Avenue, S.E.
Atlanta, GA 30334
Tel.: 404-656-2350

Hawaii State Library
Hawaii and Pacific Section
478 South King Street
Honolulu, HI 96813
Tel.: 808-586-3535

Idaho State Historical Society
Genealogical Library
325 West State Street
Boise, ID 83702
Tel.: 208-334-2305

Illinois State Library
300 South Second Street
Springfield, IL 62701
Tel.: 217-782-5430

Indiana State Library
Indiana Division
140 North Senate Avenue
Indianapolis, IN 46204
Tel.: 317-232-3689

State Historical Society of Iowa
Library/Archives Bureau
600 East Locust, Capitol Complex
Des Moines, IA 50319
Tel.: 515-281-6200

Kansas State Library
Third Floor, Statehouse
Topeka, KS 66612
Tel.: 913-296-3296

Kentucky State Archives
Kentucky Department for Libraries and Archives
300 Coffee Tree Road
P.O. Box 537
Frankfort, KY 40602-0537
Tel.: 502-875-7000

State Library of Louisiana
760 North Third Street
P.O. Box 131
Baston Rouge, LA 70804-9125
Tel.: 504-922-1206

Maine State Library
State House Station, Number 64
Augusta, ME 04333
Tel.: 207-287-5600

Maryland State Archives
Hall of Records Building
350 Rowe Boulevard
Annapolis, MD 21401
Tel.: 410-974-3914

State Library of Massachusetts
George Fingold Library
341 State House
Beacon Street
Boston, MA 02133
Tel.: 617-727-2590

Library of Michigan
717 West Allegan Street
P.O. Box 30007
Lansing, MI 48909
Tel.: 517-373-1300

Minnesota Historical Society Research Center
345 Kellog Boulevard, West
Saint Paul, MN 55102-1906
Tel.: 612-296-2143

Mississippi Department of Archives and History
100 South State Street
P.O. Box 571
Jackson, MS 39205-0571
Tel.: 601-359-6850

Missouri State Library
301 West High Street
P.O. Box 387
Jefferson City, MO 65102
Tel.: 314-751-3615

Montana State Library
1515 East Sixth Avenue
Helena, MT 59620
Tel.: 406-444-3004

Nebraska State Historical Society
1500 R Street, Lincoln, NE 68508
P.O. Box 82554
Lincoln, NE 68501-2554
Tel.: 402-471-4771

Nevada State Library and Archives
Division of Archives and Records
100 Stewart Street
Carson City, NV 89710
Tel.: 702-687-5210

New Hampshire State Library
20 Park Street
Cconcord, NH 03301
Tel.: 603-271-2144

New Jersey State Library
Genealogy Section
185 West State Street
Trenton, NJ 08625-0520
Tel.: 609-292-6274

New Mexico State Library
Southwest Room
325 Don Gasper Avenue
Santa Fe, NM 87503
Tel.: 505-827-3805

New York State Library
Genealogy Section
Seventh Floor, Cultural Education Center
Empire State Plaza
Albany, NY 12230
Tel.: 518-474-5161

State Library of North Carolina
109 East Jones Street
Raleigh, NC 27601-2807
Tel.: 919-733-7222

North Dakota State Library
Liberty Memorial Building
Capitol Grounds
Bismarck, ND 58505
Tel.: 701-224-4622

State Library of Ohio
Genealogy Division
65 South Front Street
Columbus, OH 43266-0334
Tel.: 614-644-6966

Oklahoma Department of Libraries
200 N.E. Eighteenth Street
Oklahoma City, OK 73105-3298
Tel.: 405-521-2502

Oregon State Library
Winter and Court Streets, N.E.
Salem, OR 97310
Tel.: 503-378-4277

State Library of Pennsylvania
Forum Building
Walnut Street and Commonwealth Avenue
P.O. Box 1601
Harrisburg, PA 17105
Tel.: 717-787-4440

Rhode Island State Library
Office of the Secretary of State
337 Westminster Street
Providence, RI 02903
Tel.: 401-277-2353

South Carolina State Library
1500 Senate Street
P.O. Box 11469
Columbia, SC 29211
Tel.: 803-734-8666

South Dakota State Library
Memorial Building Branch
800 Governors drive
Pierre, SD 57501-2294
Tel.: 605-773-3131

Tennessee State Library and Archives
403 Seventh Avenue, North
Nashville, TN 37243-0312
Tel.: 615-741-2764

Texas State Library
1201 Brazos Street
P.O. Box 12927
Austin, TX 78711
Tel.: 512-463-5455

Utah State Library
2150 South 300 West
Salt Lake City, UT 84114
Tel.: 801-466-5888

Vermont Department of Libraries
Pavilion Office Building
109 State Street
Montpelier, VT 05609-0601
Tel.: 802-828-3268

Virginia State Library and Archives
Eleventh Street at Capitol Square
Richmond, VA 23219-3291
Tel.: 804-786-8929

Washington State Library
Washington/Northwest Collection
P.O. Box 9000
Olympia, WA 98504-0238
Tel.: 206-753-4024

West Virginia Division of Culture and History
The Cultural Center
1900 Kanawha Boulevard, East
Charleston, WV 25305-0300
Tel.: 304-558-0230

Wisconsin State Historical Society
816 State Street
Madison, WI 53706
Tel.: 608-264-6535

Wyoming State Library
Supreme Court and Library Building
3201 Capitol Avenue
Cheyne, WY 82002
Tel.: 307-777-7281

GENEALOGICAL RENTAL LIBRARIES

The following libraries circulate books (or microfilm) by mail for a fee. Contact them for a list of titles as well as costs and procedures for borrowing books. Most require membership for borrowing privileges.

Public Libraries and Genealogical Societies

AFRA Collection
Interlibrary Loan Dept.
Mid-Continent Public Library
15616 East 24 Highway
Independence, MO 64050
Tel.: 816-252-0950
Approximately three thousand circulating titles available via inter-library loan

AFRA Collection
(Bound periodicals, tapes, films)
Alexander Mitchell Public Library
Interlibrary Dept.
519 South Kline Street
Aberdeen, SD 57401
Tel.: 605-622-7097
Approximately six hundred titles available via Interlibrary loan.

Connecticut Historical Society
1 Elizabeth Street at Asylum Avenue
Hartford, CT 06105
Tel.: 203-236-5621
Sixteen thousand-volume circulating collection

NGS Library Loan Service
4527 Seventeenth Street, North
Arlington, VA 22207
Tel.: 703-525-0050

New England Historic and Genealogical Society
101 Newbury Street
Boston, MA 02116-3087
Tel.: 617-536-5740
Circulating collection of ten thousand volumes, including family histories

Private Companies and Collections

American Genealogical Lending Library
P.O. Box 244
Bountiful, UT 84010
Tel.: 801-298-5358
Around 250,000 titles on microfilm/microfiche

Genealogical Center Library
P.O. Box 71343
Atlanta, GA 30007-1343
Seven thousand books

Genealogy Unlimited
Rental Library & Supplies
Route 8, Box 702-J
Tucson, AZ 85748

Heritage Researchers Library
P.O. Box 836
Terre Haute, IN 47808

Hoenstine Rental Library
414 Montgomery Street
P.O. Box 208
Hollidaysburg, PA 16648
814-695-0632
More than three thousand books, most for Pennsylvania

Rent from Roberts
503 Locust St.
Mt. Vernon, IN 47620

Stagecoach Library for Genealogical Research
1840 South Wolcott Court
Denver, CO 80219
Tel.: 303-922-8856

APPENDIX C

GENEALOGICAL PUBLISHERS AND BOOKSELLERS

The following list of publishers and distributors is not comprehensive but represents most of the sources for new and reprinted published material. For additional addresses, see *The Genealogist's Address Book,* 3rd ed. (Baltimore: Genealogical Publishing Company, 1995), compiled by Elizabeth Petty Bentley.

When contacting publishers or booksellers, remember that toll-free lines (800 or 888 area codes) are generally for orders only. Also, limit your calls to normal business hours.

MAJOR GENEALOGY PUBLISHERS

The following publishers publish a wide variety of genealogical books covering areas throughout the United States; some also publish foreign research material.

Ancestry
P.O. Box 476
Salt Lake City, UT 84110
Tel.: 801-426-3500 or 800-262-3787
Fax: 801-426-3501
E-mail: support@ancestry.com
http://www.ancestry.com

Clearfield Co.
200 East Eager Street
Baltimore, MD 21202
Tel.: 410-625-9004

The Everton Publishers
P.O. Box 368
Logan, UT 84323-0368
Tel.: 435-752-6022 or 800-443-6325
Fax: 435-752-0425
E-mail: order@everton.com
http://www.everton.com

Genealogical Publishing Co.
1001 North Calvert Street
Baltimore, MD 21202-3897
Tel.: 410-837-8271 or 800-296-6687
Fax: 410-752-8492
http://www.genealogical.com

Heritage Books
1540-E Pointer Ridge Place
Bowie MD 20716
Tel.: 301-390-7709 or 800-398-7709
Fax: 800-276-1760 or 301-390-7153.
E-mail: heritagebooks@usa.pipeline.com
http://www.heritagebooks.com/

Heritage Quest
A division of AGLL
P.O. Box 329
Bountiful, UT 84011-0329
Tel.: 801-298-5446 or 801-298-5358; orders: 800-760-AGLL
Fax: 801-298-5468
E-mail: sales@agll.com or custserv@agll.com.
http://www.agll.com

National Archives Trust Fund
Dept. 510
P.O. Box 100793
Atlanta, GA 30384
Fax: 202-501-7170

Scholarly Resources
See below under "Library Reference Sources."

REGIONAL AND SPECIALTY PUBLISHERS

The following publishers specialize in books for a particular region or interest. Often the quality of their products is as good as or better than than that of some national publishers.

Ancestor Trails
5755 Cohasset Way
San Jose, CA 95123

Tel.: 408-227-1645
Fax: 408-226-7303
E-mail: ancestor@ancestor.com
http://www.ancestor.com

Arkansas Research
P.O. Box 303
Conway, AR 72033
Tel./Fax: 501-470-1120
E-mail: desmond@intellinet.com
http://biz.ipa.net/arkresearch

Avotaynu
P.O. Box 900
Teaneck, NJ 07666
Tel.: 201-837-8300
Fax: 201-387-2855
E-mail: info@avotaynu.com
http://www.avotaynu.com

Boyd Publishing Co.
P.O. Box 367
Milledgeville, GA 31061
Tel.: 912-452-4020; orders: 800-452-4035
http://www.hom.net/~gac

Broadfoot Publishing Co.
1907 Buena Vista Circle
Wilmington, NC 28405
Tel.: 910-686-4816; orders: 800-537-5243
Fax: 910-686-4379
E-mail: bropubco@wilmington.net
http://broadfoot.wilmington.net

Broken Arrow Publishing
4413 West Oakland
Broken Arrow, OK 74012-9123
E-mail: hoefling@ix.netcom.com
http://members.gnn.com/Hoefling/main1.htm

Byron Sistler and Associates
1712 Natchez Trace
P.O. Box 120934
Nashville, TN 37212
Tel.: 800-578-9475.
E-mail: sistler@nash.mindspring.com
http://www.mindspring.com/~sistler

Closson Press
1935 Sampson Drive
Apollo, PA 15613-9208
Tel.: 412-337-4482
Fax: 412-337-9484
E-mail: rclosson@nb.net
http://www.pacecc.com/closs97.htm

Cook Publications
3318 Wimberg Avenue
Evansville, IN 47720

Family Line Publications
Rear 63 E. Main St.
Westminster, MD 21157
Tel.: 410-876-6101 or 1-800-876-6103
E-mail: famline@cct.infi.net
http://pages.prodigy.com/Strawn/family.htm

G. K. Hall Co.
70 Lincoln Street
Boston, MA 02111
Tel.: 212-702-6789
Fax: 212-605-3036

Gale Research
A subsidary of International Thomson Publishing Inc.
835 Penobscot Building
645 Griswold St.
Detroit, MI 48226
Tel.: 313-961-2242 or 800-877-GALE
Fax: 800-414-5043 or 313-961-6083
E-mail: gale-comment-output@list.gale.com
http://www.gale.com

Genealogy Publishing Service
448 Ruby Mine Road
Franklin, NC 28734
Tel.: 704-524-7063

Greenwood Publishing Group
88 Post Road West
P.O. Box 5007
Westport, CT 06881-5007
Tel.: 203-226-3571, ext. 380
Fax: 203-222-1502
E-mail: nora@greenwood.com
http://www.greenwood.com

Heart of the Lakes Publishing
2989 Lodi Road
P.O. Box 299
Interlaken, NY 14847-0299
Tel.: 607-532-4997 or 800-782-9687

Heritage Papers
P.O. Box 7776
Athens, GA 30604-7776

Higginson Book Co.
See below under “Booksellers.”

Hunterdon House
38 Swan Street
Lambertville, NJ 08530
Tel.: 609-397-2523

Iberian Publishing Co.
548 Cedar Creek Drive
Athens, GA 30605-3408
Tel.: 404-546-6740 or 800-394-8634.
E-mail: iberian@iberian.com
http://www.iberian.com

Iron Gate Publishing
P.O. Box 999
Niwot, CO 80544

Kinseeker Publications
P.O. Box 184
Grawn, MI 49637
E-mail: vwilson577@aol.com
http://www.angelfire.com/biz/Kinseeker/index.html

Kinship
60 Cedar Heights Road
Rhinebeck, NY 12572
Tel.: 914-876-4592
E-mail: kelly@kinshipny.com
http://www.kinshipny.com

Library Reference Sources
ABC Clio Information
130 Cremona Drive
Santa Barbara, CA 93117
Tel.: 805-968-1911 or 800-368-6868
Fax: 1-805-685-9685
E-mail: sales@abc-clio.com
http://www.abc-clio.com

Marietta Publishing
2115 North Denair Avenue
Turlock, CA 95380
Tel.: 209-634-9473

Martin Genealogy Publications
4501 SW 62 Court
Miami, Florida 33155-5936
E-mail: pattimartin@juno.com
http://www.angelfire.com/biz/martingenealogypub

Mountain Press
P.O. Box 400
Signal Mountain, TN 37377-0400
Tel.: 615-886-6369

National Historical Publishing Co.
P.O. Box 539
Waynesboro, TN 38485-0539
Tel.: 615-722-5706; orders: 800-729-3885
Fax: 1-615-722-7293
E-mail: natlhist@aol.com
http://smtp.tbox.com/natlhist

Oldbuck Press
P.O. Box 1623
1025 Watkins Street
Conway, AR 72032
Tel./Fax: 800-884-8184

Oryx Press
P.O. Box 33889
Phoenix, AZ 85067-3889
Tel.: 800-279-6799
Fax: 800-279-4663
E-mail: info@oryxpress.com
http://www.oryxpress.com

Picton Press
P.O. Box 250
Rockport, ME 04856-0250
Tel.: 207-236-6565
Fax: 207-236-6713
E-mail: picton@midcoast.com
http://www.midcoast.com/~picton/catalog/catalog.htm

Pioneer Publishing
4315 Inwood Lane
Eugene, OR 97405

Precision Indexing
See Heritage Quest under "Major Genealogy Publishers," above.

The Reprint Co., Publishers
P.O. Box 5401
Spartanburg, SC 29304-5401
Tel.: 803-582-0732

Scarecrow Press
An imprint of University Press of America
52 Liberty Street, Box 4167
Metuchen, NJ 08840
E-mail: mslazak@scarecrowpress.com

Scholarly Resources
104 Greenhill Avenue
Wilmington, DE 19805
Tel.: 302-654-7713 or 800-772-8937
Fax: 302-654-3871

Southern Historical Press
P.O. Box 1267
Greenville, SC 29602-1267
Southern Historical Press
Tel.: 864-233-2346

Southwest Pennsylvania Genealogical Services
P.O. Box 253
Laughlintown, PA 15655
Tel.: 412-238-3176

TLC Genealogy
P.O. Box 403369
Miami Beach, FL 33140-1369
Tel.: 800-858-8558
Fax: 800-858-8558 (voice request first)
E-mail: info@tlc-gen.com or staff@tlc-gen.com
http://www.tlc-gen.com

MICROPUBLISHERS

AGLL
Heritage Quest
P.O. Box 329
593 West 100 North
Bountiful, Utah 84011-0329
Tel.: 801-298-5446 or 801-298-5358
Orders: 800- 658-7755
Fax: 801-298-5468
E-mail: sales@heritagequest.com
http://www.agll.com

Ancestor Publishers
6166 Janice Way
Arvada, CO 80004-5160
Tel.: 303-420-3460 or 800-373-0816
Fax: 303-425-9709
E-mail: ancestor@net1comm.com
http://www.firstct.com/fv/ancpub.html

Archive Publishing
57 Locust Street
P.O. Box 245
Oxford, MA 01540-0245
Tel.: 508-987-0881

Infotech Publications
P.O. Box 86
Bowling Green, MO 63334
Tel.: 314-669-5694
Fax: 314-669-5684

Research Publications
An imprint of Primary Source Media
12 Lunar Drive
Woodbridge, CT 06525
Tel.: 800-444-0799 or 203-397-2600
Fax: 203-397-3893
E-mail: sales@rpub.com
http://www.nelson.com/rpub

UMI
300 North Zeeb Road
P.O. Box 1346
Ann Arbor, MI 48106-1346
Tel.: 800-521-0600 or 734-761-4700
E-mail: info@umi.com
http://www.umi.com/hp/Support/BOD

ELECTRONIC PUBLISHERS

See appendix A.

PRIVATE (SELF) PUBLISHERS

These publishers generally publish only their own works. Many have a significant number of titles.

AKB Publishing
691 Weavertown Road
Myerstown, PA 17067

Carlberg Press
1782 Beacon Avenue
Anaheim, CA 92804-4515

Family History Educators
P.O. Box 510606
Salt Lake City, UT 84151-0606

Jensen Publications
P.O. Box 441
Pleasant Grove, UT 84062

Thode Translations
R.R.7, Box 306 Kern Road
Marietta, OH 45750-9437

Walswoth Publishing Co.
306 North Kansas Ave.
Marceline, MO 64658

SUBSIDY PUBLISHERS

These publishers will help publish a book for a fee.

Anundsen Publishing Co.
108 Washington Street
P.O. Box 230
Decorah, IA 52101
Tel.: 319-382-4295

The Bookmark
Mayhill Publications, Inc.
P.O. Box 90
Knightstown, IN 46148-9000
Tel.: 317-345-5133 or 800-876-5133

Curtis Media
530 Bedford Road, Suite 112
Bedford, TX 76022
Tel.: 817-285-7091 or 800-743-4388
Fax: 817-285-0176

E-mail: curmedia@aol.com
http://members.aol.com/curmedia/curtish/htm

Family History Publishers
845 South Main
Bountiful, UT 84010
Tel.: 801-295-7490

Gateway Press
1001 North Calvert St.
Baltimore, MD 21202-3897
Tel.: 410-837-8271 or 800-296-6687

Genealogy Publishing Service
573 Beasley Mine Road
Franklin, NC 28734
Tel.: 704-524-7063
E-mail: gpsbook@dnet.net
http://www.intertekweb.com/gpsbook

Heart of the Lakes Publishing
See under "Regional and Specialty Publishers," above.

Micro Dynamics Electronic Publishing
703 South State No. 9
Orem, UT 84058
Tel.: 888-327-6472
http://www.micro-dynamics.com

Penobscot Press
P.O. Box 250
Rockport, ME 04856-0250
Tel.: 207-236-6565
Fax: 207-236-6713
E-mail picton@midcoast.com
http://www.midcoast.com/~picton

Professional Press
P.O. Box 4371
Chapel Hill, NC 27515-4371
Tel.: 800-277-8960

The Reprint Co., Publishers
See under "Regional and Specialty Publishers," above.

Sloan Genealogy Publishing
5912 Maple
Mission, KS 66202
Tel.: 800-815-3954 or 913-722-5454
Fax: 913-722-5464

Taylor Publishing Co.
1550 West Mockingbird Lane
Dallas, TX 75235

Tennessee Valley Publishing
P.O. Box 52527
Knoxville, TN 37950-2527
Tel.: 800-762-7079

Windmill Publications
6628 Uebelback Road
Mt. Vernon, IN 47620
Tel.: 812-985-9214
E-mail: windmill@comsource.net
http://www.comsource.net/~windmill

BOOKSELLERS

While all publishers sell their own books, and some sell selected titles from other publishers, the following are those vendors that focus primarily on retail sales of books from other publishers. (Some publish occasionally, but their primary focus is on selling.)

Alice's Ancestral Nostalgia
P.O. Box 510092
Salt Lake City, UT 84151-0092
Tel.: 801-575-6510

Appleton Books and CDs
P.O. Box 241983
Charlotte, NC 28224-1983
Tel.: 800-777-3601 or 704-522-1062
Fax: 704-522-1079
E-mail: catalog.request@moobasi.com
http://www.moobasi.com

Barnette's Family Tree Book Co.
1217 Oakdale Street
Houston, Tx 77004
Tel.: 713-522-7444
http://www.neosoft.com/~seahorse/genealog.html

Blairs' Book Service
2503 Springpark Way
Richardson, TX 75082
Tel./Fax: 972-783-1008
E-mail: linda@glbco.com
http://www.glbco.com

Dee's Genealogy Service
17970 Anchor Drive
Jupiter, FL 33458

Dutch Family Heritage Society
2463 Ledgewood Drive
West Jordan, UT 84084-5738

Family Tree
109 Bull Street
LaGrange, GA 30241

Family Tree Bookshop
9-B Goldsborough Street
Easton, MD 21601
Tel.: 410-820-5252

Fax: 410-820-5254
E-mail: lkeddie@aol.com
http://pages.bluecrab.org/famtree

Frontier Press
P.O. Box 3715
Galveston, Texas 77552
Phone Orders: 800-772-7559
Fax: 409-740-0138
E-mail: kgfrontier@aol.com
http://www.doit.com/frontier

Genealogical and Historical Booksource
P.O. Box 6443
Boise, Idaho 83707
E-mail: books@micron.net
http://www.omegaweb.co.uk/books/books.html

Genealogical Services
(AIS census indexes)
P.O. Box 890
West Jordan, UT 84084-0890
Tel.: 801-280-1554
E-mail: info@genservices.com
sales@genservices.com
http://www.genservices.com/

Genealogy Booksellers, Ltd.
208 George Street
Fredericksburg, VA 22401
Tel.: 703-373-7114

Genealogy House
3148 Kentucky Avenue South
Minneapolis, MN 55426-3471
Tel.: 612-920-6990
Fax: 612-560-1290 or 612-927-7155

Genealogy Unlimited
P.O. Box 537
Orem, UT 84059-0537
Tel.: 801-763-7132; orders: 800-666-4363
Fax: 801-763-7185
E-mail: genun@itsnet.com
http://www.itsnet.com/~genun

Global Genealogical Supply
158 Laurier Avenue
Milton, Ontario
CANADA L9T 4S2
Tel.: 800-361-5168 (U.S. and Canada)
Outside Canada or the USA: 905-875-2176
E-mail: email@globalgenealogy.com
http://www.globalgenealogy.com

Harbor Hill Books
P.O. Box 407
Harrison, NY 10528

Hearthstone Bookshop
5735-A Telegraph Road
Alexandria, VA 22303
Tel.: 1-703-960-0086; orders: 888-960-3300
Fax: 1-703-960-0087
E-mail: info@hearthstonebooks.com
http://www.hearthstonebooks.com

Heritage Quest's Genealogy Resource Center
122 West South Temple
Salt Lake City, UT 84101

Higginson Books
148-AB Washington Street
P.O. Box 778
Salem, MA 01970
Tel.: 508-745-7170
Fax: 508-745-8025

Indiana Roots
2160 Mann Drive
Beech Grove, IN 46107-1653

Interlink Bookshop and Genealogical Services
3840A Cadboro Bay
Victoria, British Columbia
CANADA
Tel.: 250 477-2708

Michiana History Publications
P.O. Box 1537
South Bend, IN 46634

Nuthatch Grove
5144 North Academy Boulevard, Suite 302
Colorado Springs, CO 80918-4002

Ye Old Genealogie Shoppe
P.O. Box 39128
Indianapolis, IN 46239
Tel.: 317-862-3330 or 800-419-0200
Fax: 317-862-2599
http://www.yogs.com

Olde Springfield Shoppe
P.O. Box 171
10 West Main Street
Elverson, PA 19520-0171
Tel.: 610-286-0258
Fax: 610-286-6860

Origins
4327 Milton Avenue (Highway 26)
Janesville, WI 53546
Tel.: 608-757-2777

Park Genealogical Books
P.O. Box 130968
Roseville, MN 55113-0968
Tel.: 612-488-4416.
Fax: 612 \ 488-2653
E-mail: mbakeman@parkbooks.com
http://www.parkbooks.com

Pioneer Distributing
476 Ash Avenue
Decatur, IL 62526
E-mail: tnash74528@aol.com

Platte Valley Books
P.O. Box 271
Hastings, NE 68902-0271
Tel.: 402-461-4272
E-mail: vf51029@tcgcs.com
http://www.hht.com/bus/secure/platte~1.html

Root of It All
P.O. Box 404
Wildomar, CA 92595

Skeleton Closet
P.O. Box 91392
Louisville, KY 40291
Tel.: 502-239-0480

Storbeck's
15550 West Woodview Drive
P.O. Box 510062
New Berlin, WI 53151-0062
Tel.: 414-821-1280 or 800-360-3555
Fax: 414-780-4541
E-mail: Mary@storbecks.com
http://www.storbecks.com

Willow Bend Books
39475 Tollhouse Road
Route 1, Box 15A
Lovettsville, VA 22080
Fax: 540-822-5292
E-mail: willowbend@mediasoft.net
http://www.mediasoft.net/ScottC/

ANTIQUARIAN, USED, AND RARE BOOKS

ACETO Bookman
5721 Antietam Drive
Sarasota, FL 34321

The Avid Reader
462 West Franklin Street
Chapel Hill, Nc 27516
Tel.: 919-933-9585
Fax: 919-933-1599
E-mail: Avid@Avidreader.com.
http://www.avidreader.com

Jonathan Sheppard Books
P.O. Box 2020, Plaza Station
Albany, NY 12220

Robert Murphy, Bookseller
3113 Bunker Hill Road
Marietta, GA 30062
Tel.: 770-973-1523
Fax: 770-973-3291
E-mail: genie@avana.net
http://www.abebooks.com/home/MURPHYBOOKS

Roots and Branches
P.O. Box 8625
Mission Hills, CA. 91346
Tel.: 818-366-5496
http://members.aol.com/RebelSher1/index.html

Stacey's Book Search
5712 Sweetwater N.W.
Albuquerque, New Mexico 87120
E-mail: rmcclend@highfiber.com
http://www.highfiber.com/~rmcclend/Index.html

Tuttle Antiquarian Books
28 South Main Street
Rutland, VT 05701
Tel.: 802-773-8229
Fax: 802-773-1493
E-mail: tuttbook@interloc.com
http://www.rmharris.com/pub/rmharris/alldlrs/ne/05701tut.html

SOCIETIES THAT PUBLISH AND/OR SELL

American Family Records Association
Mo.Valley Rm 311 East Twelfth Street
Kansas, MO 64106

Association of Professional Genealogists
P.O. Box 40393
Denver, CO 80204-0393
E-mail: apg-editor@apgen.org
http://www.apgen.org

Federation of Genealogical Societies
P.O. Box 830220
Richardson, TX 75083-0220
Tel.: 972-907-9297
E-mail: fgs-office@fgs.org
http://www.fgs.org

National Genealogical Society
Special Publications
4527 Seventeenth Street North
Arlington, VA 22207
Tel.: 703-525-0050
Fax: 703-525-0052
E-mail: 76702.2417@compuserv.com
http://www.genealogy.org/~ngs

New England Historic Genealogical Society
101 Newbury Street
Boston, MA 02116
Tel.: 888-296-3447
Fax: 617-536-7307
E-mail: nehgs@nehgs.org
http://www.nehgs.org

INDEX

B

C

D

F

G

H

I

J

K

L

M

N

O

P

Q

R

S

W

Y

Z